the Next EXIT®

The Most Accurate Interstate Highway Service Guide Ever Printed™

the Next EXIT® will save time, money and frustration.

This tool will help you find services along the ***USA Interstate Highways*** *like nothing you have ever used.*

Restaurants • Gas Stations • Hotels • RV Camping • And Much More

PO Box 888
Garden City, UT 84028
www.theNextExit.com

the Next Exit® USER GUIDE

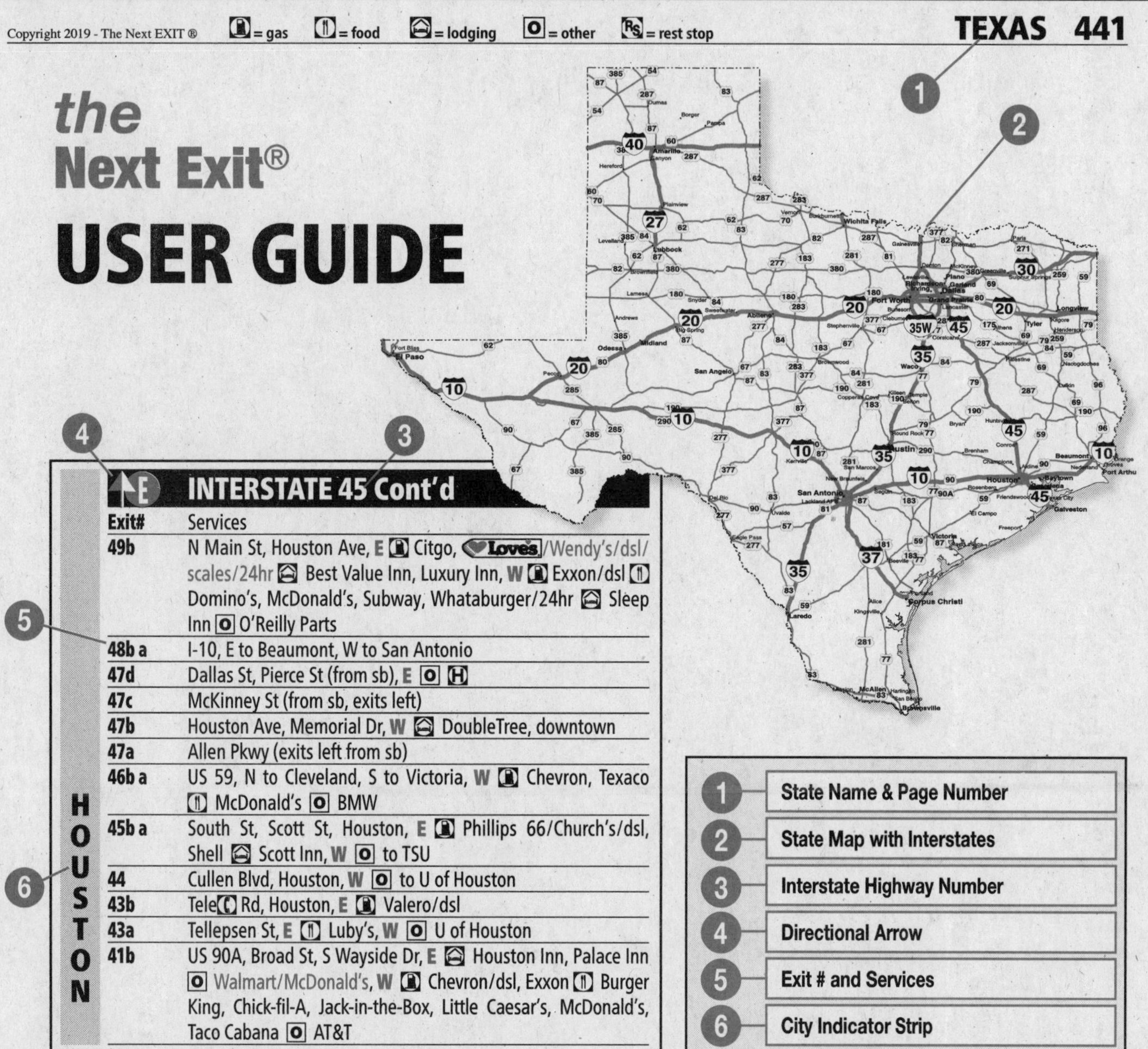

↑E INTERSTATE 45 Cont'd

Exit#	Services
49b	N Main St, Houston Ave, E Citgo, Loves/Wendy's/dsl/scales/24hr Best Value Inn, Luxury Inn, W Exxon/dsl Domino's, McDonald's, Subway, Whataburger/24hr Sleep Inn O'Reilly Parts
48b a	I-10, E to Beaumont, W to San Antonio
47d	Dallas St, Pierce St (from sb), E H
47c	McKinney St (from sb, exits left)
47b	Houston Ave, Memorial Dr, W DoubleTree, downtown
47a	Allen Pkwy (exits left from sb)
46b a	US 59, N to Cleveland, S to Victoria, W Chevron, Texaco McDonald's BMW
45b a	South St, Scott St, Houston, E Phillips 66/Church's/dsl, Shell Scott Inn, W to TSU
44	Cullen Blvd, Houston, W to U of Houston
43b	Tele Rd, Houston, E Valero/dsl
43a	Tellepsen St, E Luby's, W U of Houston
41b	US 90A, Broad St, S Wayside Dr, E Houston Inn, Palace Inn Walmart/McDonald's, W Chevron/dsl, Exxon Burger King, Chick-fil-A, Jack-in-the-Box, Little Caesar's, McDonald's, Taco Cabana AT&T

1. State Name & Page Number
2. State Map with Interstates
3. Interstate Highway Number
4. Directional Arrow
5. Exit # and Services
6. City Indicator Strip

Exit

Most states number exits by the nearest mile marker(mm). A few states use consecutive numbers, in which case mile markers are given in ( ). Mile markers are the little green vertical signs beside the interstate at one mile intervals which indicate distance from the southern or western border of a state. Odd numbered interstates run north/south, even numbered run east/west.

Services

Services are listed alphabetically by category **= gas** **= food** **= lodging** **= rest stop** **= other** services including camping.

"H" indicates an exit from which a hospital may be accessed, but it may not be close to the exit.

Services located away from the exit may be referred to by "access to," or "to" and a distance may be given.

A directional notation is also given, such as **N**, **S**, **E** or **W**

Directional Arrows

Follow exits DOWN the page if traveling from North to South or East to West, UP the page if traveling South to North or West to East.

Additional copies may be ordered by using the form supplied in the back of this book, or by visiting online at ***www.theNextExit.com***

the Next EXIT, inc. makes no warranty regarding the accuracy of the information contained in this publication. This information is subject to change without notice.

TABLE OF CONTENTS

Abbreviations & Symbols used in the Next EXIT ®

AFB ....Air Force Base
B&B ....Bed&Breakfast
Bfd............Battlefield
CNG..........Compressed Natural Gas
Ctr ....Center
Coll ....College
Cyn ....canyon
dsl.............diesel
$................Dollar
EVC ....Electric Vehicle Charger
LNG ....Liquid Natural Gas
Mem ....Memorial
Mkt ....Market
Mtn ....Mountain
mm ....mile marker
N ....north side of exit
S ....south side of exit
E ....east side of exit
W ....west side of exit

NM............National Monument
NHS ....Nat Hist Site
NWR ....Nat Wildlife Reserve
NF ....National Forest
H ....Hospital
✈ ....Airport
Picnic symbol ....Picnic Tables
NP.............National Park
NRA ....Nat Rec Area
pk ....park
pkwy ....parkway
rest. ....restaurant
nb ....northbound
sb ....southbound
eb ....eastbound
wb.............westbound
SP.............state park
SF ....state forest
Sprs..........springs

st ....street, state
sta ....station
TPK...........Turnpike
USPO ....Post Office
vet ....veterinarian
whse.........warehouse
@...............truckstop (full service)
red print....RV accessible
♿ ....Handicapped accessible
Telephone symbol ....Telephone
Gas symbol ....Gas
Food symbol ....Food
Lodging symbol ....Lodging
O ....Other
RS ....Rest Stop / Rest Area

More digital options are available at www.theNextExit.com

TABLE OF CONTENTS

All Expenses Paid

Mark Watson – Winter 2019

I always thought I would make it big someday, it was just a matter of time and place. When the end of the road seemed closer than the beginning, I began to fret about whether notoriety would wait and come posthumously, requiring me to enjoy it from the other side. Publishing nearly 30 editions of ***the Next EXIT*** certainly put my name into the public domain, but the multitudes that attend fame never showed up. "Do not worry," said my inner voice, "they are coming." And finally, they did, at least for my feet.

Last spring I received a probing text from my son asking if I was interested in driving with him from Utah to New York City. "I know you already travel a lot," he said, "but would you like to go on a cross-country excursion, stopping at popular attractions along the way to take and post photos?"

"Sure," I replied, "what's another five thousand miles among family? Count me in. Why are we doing this?"

"On account of the dogs," he explained. "Daisy and Penelope are going to be on television for K9 Sport Sack and I could fly them to the studio, but they don't like air travel and you do not make famous dogs fly when they would rather not, see?" He added that his young daughter, also TV bound, would be arriving with her entourage and we needed to be in NYC in time to retrieve her from the airport. Continuing, he assigned me the responsibilities of choosing our route, selecting the notable sites and ensuring that we made the scheduled pick up. His company would underwrite the cost of the trip and I needed only to be a serviceable assistant. All of it sounded like adventure to me, so I rose to the occasion. "Interstate 90," I typed, "when do we leave?" Then I went shopping for new shoes.

"As the father of nine I hauled many people and much material to the farthest corners of the country, but famous dogs, well that would be a different animal."

It took a good week for anticipation to dispatch the imps of second-thought, but I finally settled into the idea, all the time wondering how the doggy travel thing was done. As the father of nine I hauled many people and much material to the farthest corners of the country, but famous dogs, well that would be a different animal. Where would we put their kennels, in the back of the van or near the front seats so they could visit with us as we drive? Children will tell you when they need a rest stop, but what about a Chihuahua Mix or a Maybe Terrier? When you open the van doors, people step out, stretch and head to the facilities. Not so with dogs. They bolt from place to place, sniffing out multiple spots that suit only themselves. They argue with other canines regardless of their size and if you leash them, they simply drag you along. These were legitimate questions which needed answers, but the week's journey cleared things up. Famous dogs, it seems, do not ride in kennels, but in the lap of their master, no matter if he is the driver or the passenger. Woof!

Continued Next Page

We supplied ourselves with pet accessories and headed to Yellowstone. After parking, we placed the puppies into the sacks on our backs and wandered out to where Old Faithful waited, snapping pictures as we went. We were viewed like the opening act of a rock concert as the crowd kept one eye on us, the other on the geyser. When the eruption concluded, the cameras swung back to us while we returned to the van. It was as if no one had ever seen a dog in a knapsack before. This became the pattern everywhere we went over the next six days: sack up the pups, walk out to the attraction, take images and smile, wave at the adulation of the other sightseers. Once back inside the car, we posted the pics, rewarded the dogs and continued east.

Devil's Tower, Deadwood, Mount Rushmore, Wall Drug and the Badlands were all under fog the second day out, but this only elevated our spectacle to the main event. Wherever we went the folks seemed excited to see us. Improving weather made the Corn Palace, the Jolly Green Giant, and Mouse Haus Cheese Haus delightful stops, and by the end of day three we had fairly breezed through UW Madison, Brewers Stadium, and Wrigley Field. With Chicago behind us, this carload of football fans streaked toward South Bend.

Near the midpoint of that fourth day, in the shadow of Touchdown Jesus mistakes were made that proved nearly fatal to the objective of our journey. Who knew that famous dogs' stomachs don't tolerate sardines? We opened our second container of the delicious little fish only to realize that more than one serving was too many for our liking. There stood our best friends, looking hopefully up at us, wondering why something so aromatic was not being passed around. So, we shared. By the time we reached the Rock and Roll Hall of Fame and Browns Stadium, one of our group had begun to trot.

Things got worse the next day at Niagara Falls, and well before Cooperstown the girls had turned against ground travel, anything smelling remotely like sardines and us. Fortunately, we still had 36 hours to restore their health and confidence before the TV spot. Since we needed a little housecleaning, we stopped in Newburgh, washed the car and vacuumed most of the shedding from our rolling kennel. I considered bathing the dogs with the pressure washer but scrapped that idea in the interest of improving relations. Coasting into Times Square, we checked in and immediately started a search for Kaopectate.

Cement sidewalks, which are plentiful in NYC, can never replace grass for a pooch privy, but the medicine made things better. After a trip to La Guardia that gathered all our TV stars into one cluster, we toured the city despite a persistent rainstorm.

The next morning, broadcast headquarters welcomed us like celebrities. We were scanned for contraband, ushered into the green room and offered breakfast finger foods. Well-known personalities visited for the next hour asking questions and taking notes, as anticipation mounted. The famous dogs basked in the sunshine of their big moment while I sat quietly out of the limelight, smiling when appropriate but otherwise acting the wallflower whose only purpose was to ferry everyone to this place.

Then it happened.

In swept the show host and her staff, filming the Facebook feed, a less formal version of the TV spot. The smart phones panned the room, capturing the magic of two little dogs who were rescued from a dumpster and a fighting ring, forever changing their lives from despair to notability, and spawning a new industry in the process. The story was compelling, heartwarming and wildly successful as a marketing means, reaching many thousands of customers. And through it all, I looked in from the very edge of fame, with only my feet within camera range.

Our traveling dog show headed west before noon. It took us longer to get across the George Washington Bridge than New Jersey, but once Pennsylvania came into view the concrete ribbon of Interstate 80 beckoned us homeward, and we enthusiastically accepted the call. Within 48 hours, we had reached our terminus, untangled our baggage and broken up the group. Normalcy returned in the weeks that followed, and no credit card bills presented for payment. Gas, food, lodging and incidentals had all been paid by the famous dogs.

As the trip of the year fades into reflection, it naturally mingles with other similar journeys, but the singularity of this one is likely to persist. There will probably never be another quite like it. That's OK, because any time I need to relive the experience, I simply look down at my feet. I am still breaking in those new shoes. ❖

ALABAMA

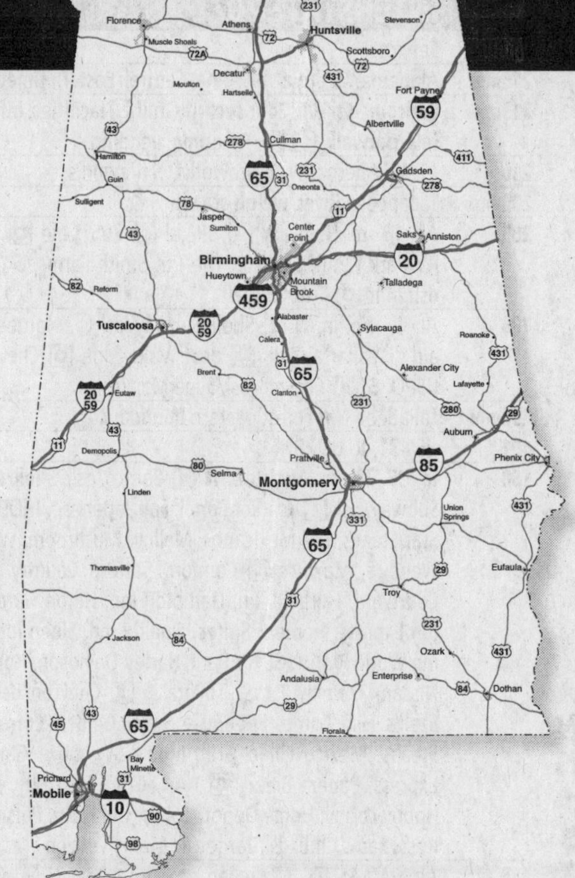

INTERSTATE 10

Exit#	Services
66.5mm	Alabama/Florida state line
66mm	**Welcome Ctr full [handicapped] facilities, litter barrels, petwalk, [phone], [picnic], vending**
53	rd 64, Wilcox Rd, **N** [gas] Marathon/Oasis/Chester's/Stuckey's/Subway/dsl/scales/24hr/@ [O] Riverside RV Park, Styx River Resort, **S** [gas] Chevron/dsl [O] Azalea Acres RV Park, fireworks, Hilltop RV Park (1.5 mi), Wilderness RV Park
49	Rd 68, Baldwin Beach Express, to Gulf Shores, Orange Beach, Gulf SP
44	AL 59, Loxley, **N** [gas] Loves/Arby's/dsl/scales/24hr [lodging] Bay Inn, **S** [gas] Chevron/dsl, Exxon/dsl, RaceWay/dsl [food] Burger King, Hardee's, McDonald's, Waffle House [lodging] Loxley Motel (3mi), WindChase Inn [O] to Gulf SP
38	AL 181, Malbis, **N** [food] CA Dreaming, Chick-fil-A, Cracker Barrel, Half Shell Oyster House, IHOP, Logan's Roadhouse, Marble Slab, McDonald's, Moe's SW Grill, Newk's Eatery, Olive Garden, Panera Bread, Pizza Hut, Poor Mexican, Ruby Tuesday, Sonic, Starbucks, Stix Asian, Taco Bell, Waffle House, Wendy's [lodging] Best Western, Comfort Inn, Holiday Inn Express, La Quinta [O] $Tree, Advance Parts, Barnes&Noble, Belk, Best Buy, Dillard's, GNC, Goodyear/auto, Michael's, Old Navy, Petsmart, Publix, Ross, Tuesday Morning, Verizon, Walgreens, World Mkt, **S** [gas] Chevron/dsl, Shell/LA Subs, Texaco/dsl [food] Burger King, Don Carlos, Firehouse Subs, Mellow Mushroom, Zaxby's [lodging] Malbis Motel (1mi), Woodspring Suites [O] AT&T, Honda, Hyundai, Lowe's, Nissan, Sam's Club/gas, Toyota, URGENT CARE, VW
35	US 90, US 98, **N** [gas] Marathon, Shell [food] Beef O'Brady's, China Fun [lodging] Courtyard, Fairfield Inn [O] Bass Pro Shops, JC Penney, Kohl's, Piggly Wiggly, Rite Aid, to Blakeley SP, USPO, **S** [gas] Exxon/dsl, Shell/dsl [food] Arby's, Bangkok Thai, Boudreaux's Cajun Grill, Burger King, Dickey's BBQ, Domino's, Dragon City Buffet, Dunkin Donuts, El Rancho Mexican, Firehouse Subs, Five Guys, Foosackly's Chicken Fingers, Hooters, IHOP, Jubilee Diner, Longhorn Steaks, Los Tacos, Maddio's, McDonald's, Mediterranean Sandwich, O'Charley's, Papa John's, Pizza Hut, S China Rest., Smoothie King, Starbucks, Subway, Taco Bell, Waffle House, Waffle House (2), Zaxby's [lodging] Comfort Suites, Eastern Shore Motel, Hampton Inn, Hilton Garden, Homewood Suites, Microtel [O] [H], $Tree, AT&T, Dick's, Fresh Mkt, GNC, Hobby Lobby, Home Depot, Office Depot, Petco, TJ Maxx
30	US 90/98, Battleship Pkwy, **N** [food] Blue Gill Rest., Ed's Seafood Shed, Oyster House, **S** [O] same as 27
27	US 90/98, Battleship Pkwy, Gov't St, **S** [food] Cafe Del Rio, Felix's Fish Camp, R&R Seafood, Ralph&Kacoo'sSeafood [lodging] Battleship Inn [O] to USS Alabama
26b	Water St, Mobile, downtown, **N** [lodging] Candlewood Suites, Hampton Inn, Holiday Inn, Quality Inn, Renaissance, to Visitors Ctr
26a	Canal St (from eb), same as 26b
25b	Virginia St, Mobile, **N** [gas] Shell/dsl
25a	Texas St (from wb, no return)
24	Broad St, to Duval St, Mobile, **N** [gas] Chevron/dsl
23	Michigan Ave, **N** [gas] Shell/dsl
22b a	AL 163, Dauphin Island Pkwy, **N** [gas] Citgo [O] Family$, **S** [gas] Exxon/Subway, Mobil/dsl [food] Checker's, Hart's Chicken, Kim's Palace, Waffle House [O] $General
20	I-65 N, to Montgomery
17	AL 193, Tillmans Corner, to Dauphin Island, **N** [gas] Chevron [food] Boiling Pot, Crazy Hibachi, Firehouse Subs, Five Guys, Golden Corral, IHOP, Ruby Tuesday, Zaxby's [O] [H], AT&T, auto repair, Lowe's, Office Depot, URGENT CARE, Verizon, Walmart/Subway
15b a	US 90, Tillmans Corner, to Mobile, **N** [gas] Chevron, Murphy USA/dsl, RaceWay/dsl [food] Arby's, Aztecas Mexican, Burger King, Checkers, Domino's, Godfather's, Hooters, KFC, King's Buffet, Little Caesar's, McDonald's, Papa John's, Popeye's, Russell's BBQ, Shrimp Basket, Subway, Taco Bell, Waffle House [lodging] Baymont Inn, Best Inn, Best Value Inn, Comfort Suites, Days Inn, EconoLodge, Hampton Inn, Holiday Inn, Holiday Inn Express, Home 2 Suites, InTown Suites, La Quinta, Motel 6, Quality Inn, Red Roof Inn, Rodeway Inn, Super 8 [O] $General, $Tree, AutoZone, BigLots, CarQuest, Family$, Firestone/auto, Mike's Transmissions, O'Reilly Parts, PepBoys, Rite Aid, vet, Walgreens, Winn-Dixie, **S** [gas] Chevron/Circle K, Exxon, RaceWay/dsl, Shell/dsl [food] Hardee's, Waffle House [O] Advance Parts, auto repair, B&R Campers, Johnnys RV Ctr, Peterbilt, tires, transmissions, USPO, vet
13	to Theodore, **N** [gas] Clark/dsl, Pilot/Wendy's/dsl/scales/24hr, Shell/Subway [food] Burger King, Church's, McDonald's, Waffle House [O] Advance Parts, auto repair, Family$, Greyhound Prk, Rite Aid, Rouse's Mkt, transmissions, Walmart Mkt/dsl, **S** [gas] Chevron/dsl [O] Bellingraf Gardens, I-10 Kamping, Paynes RV Park (4mi)
10	rd 39, Bayou La Batre, Dawes, **N** [food] Waffle House [O] Kenworth
4	AL 188 E, to Grand Bay, **N** [gas] Exxon, Shell/Subway, TA/Dunkin Donuts/Popeye's/Country Pride/dsl/scales/24hr/@ [food] Arby's, McDonald's, Sam's Super Burger, Waffle House [O] Bumper Parts, **S** [gas] Chevron [food] Hardee's [O] Trav-L-Kamp
1mm	**Welcome Ctr eb, full [handicapped] facilities, info, litter barrels, petwalk, [phone], [picnic], RV dump**
0mm	Alabama/Mississippi state line

MOBILE

THEODORE

AL

INTERSTATE 20

Exit #	Services
215mm	Alabama/Georgia state line, Central/Eastern time zone
213mm	**Welcome Ctr wb, 24hr security, full facilities, info, litter barrels, petwalk, , , RV dump, vending**
210	AL 49, Abernathy, **N** fireworks, **S** fireworks
209mm	Tallapoosa River, **weigh sta wb**
205	AL 46, to Heflin, **N** BP/dsl 205 Cafe Cane Creek RV Park (2mi), Exit 205 Tire Ctr, Smith Farms, **S** Chevron/dsl/24hr Truck Repair
199	AL 9, Heflin, **N** Shell/Subway/dsl Hardee's, McDonald's, Vallarta Grill Best Value Inn Chevrolet, Ford, USPO, **S** Chevron/dsl, SuperMart/dsl
198mm	Talladega Nat Forest eastern boundary
191	US 431, to US 78
188	to US 78, to Anniston, **N** Samco/dsl, Shell/dsl, Texaco/Subway/dsl Cracker Barrel, Fuji Japanese, IHOP, KFC, LoneStar Steaks, Los Mexicanos, Mellow Mushroom, Waffle House, Wendy's, Zaxby's Comfort Suites, Country Inn&Suites, Courtyard, Fairfield Inn, Hampton Inn, Hilton Garden, Holiday Inn Express, Home 2 Suites, Quality Inn, Sleep Inn Camping World RV Ctr, GS RV Park, Harley-Davidson, Honda, Lowe's, Nissan, O'Reilly Parts, Toyota, **S** Chevron/dsl Arby's, Ezell's Fish Camp, Firehouse Subs, Golden Corral, Longhorn Steaks, Mexico Lindo Grill, Moe's SW, Olive Garden, Panda Express, Panera Bread AAA, AT&T, Best Buy, Dick's, GNC, Hobby Lobby, Home Depot, Kohl's, Old Navy, Petsmart, Publix, Ross, Sams Club/dsl, Target, TJ Maxx, Verizon
185	AL 21, to Ft McClellan, to Anniston, **N** Chevron/dsl, GrubMart/dsl, Shell/dsl, Texaco Applebee's, Arby's, Bojangles, Burger King, Capt D's, China Luck, CiCi's Pizza, Hardee's, HoneyBaked Ham, Jack's Rest., Logan's Roadhouse, Los Mexicanos, McAlister's Deli, McDonald's, O'Charley's, Papa John's, Pizza Hut, Red Lobster, Red Pepper Grill, Shoney's, Sonic, Starbucks, Super Buffet, Taco Bell, Waffle House, Western Sizzlin Best Value Inn, Liberty Inn, Red Carpet Inn $General, Advance Parts, Aldi Foods, BooksAMillion, CVS Drug, Dillard's, Firestone/auto, Ford, JC Penney, Martin's Foods, Rite Aid, Sears/auto, **S** Chevron/dsl, Circle K/dsl/scales, Murphy USA/dsl, RaceWay, Valero/Subway/dsl Chick-fil-A, Jefferson's Rest, Outback Steaks, Waffle House, Wendy's Comfort Inn, EconoLodge, Key West Inn, Motel 6, Super 8 H, $Tree, Cobb Automotive, Walmart
179	AL 202, to US 78, to Munford, Coldwater, **N** Chevron/Subway/dsl China King, Jack's Rest. $General, Anniston Army Depot, Rite Aid, Winn Dixie, **S** Marathon/dsl
173	AL 5, Eastaboga, **S** Sunoco/cafe Mapco/Stuckey's to Speedway/Hall of Fame
168	AL 77, to Talladega, **N** Exxon/QV/Domino's, Marathon/KFC/Taco Bell, Pilot/dsl/scales/24hr Jack's Rest., Waffle House, **S** AOC/Burger King, Chevron/Subway/dsl, TA/Popeye's/dsl/scales/24hr McDonald's, MT Grill, Rana's Mexican Comfort Inn, Days Inn, Lincoln Inn Hall of Fame, to Speedway
165	Embry Cross Roads, **N** Hi-Tech/dsl, Pilot/Subway/dsl/scales/24hr Paradise Island RV Park, **S** 165 TP/Huddle House/dsl, I-20TrkStp/rest./dsl/scales/24hr Doghouse Grill McCaig Motel
164mm	Coosa River
162	US 78, Riverside, **N** Safe Harbor RV Park, **S** Chevron/dsl Best Value Inn/rest
158	US 231, Pell City, **N** Marathon/dsl, Murphy USA/dsl Arby's, Azteca Mexican, Buffalo Wild Wings, Chick-fil-A, City Mkt Grill, Cracker Barrel, Golden Rule BBQ, Hwy 55 Cafe, Jade E Chinese, Krystal, Wendy's, Zaxby's Comfort Suites, Hampton Inn, Holiday Inn Express H, $Tree, AT&T, City Tire, Home Depot, URGENT CARE, Walgreens, Walmart/Subway, **S** Shell/dsl, Texaco/dsl, Valero Akita Japanese, Burger King, Dunkin Donuts/Baskin Robbins, Hardee's, Jack's Rest., KFC, Little Caesar's, McDonald's, Pell City Steaks, Pizza Hut, Subway, Taco Bell, Waffle House Quality Inn $General, AutoZone, Chrysler/Dodge/Jeep, CVS Drug, Ford, O'Reilly Parts, Verizon
156	US 78 E, to Pell City, **S** Chevron/dsl, Shell/dsl
153	US 78, Chula Vista
152	Cook Springs
147	Brompton, **N** Sunoco, Valero TC/dsl/scales/24hr, **S** Loves/McDonald's/Subway/dsl/scales/24hr, Valero/dsl/deli
144	US 411, Leeds, **N** 76/dsl, RaceWay/dsl, Shell/Subway Arby's, Bojangles, Burger King, Cracker Barrel, Krystal, Logan's Roadhouse, Milo's Burgers, Pizza Hut, Ruby Tuesday, Waffle House, Wendy's, Zaxby's Best Western+, Comfort Inn, Super 8 $Tree, Publix, Verizon, **S** Chevron, RaceWay/dsl Capt D's, Chick-fil-A, El Cazador Mexican, Guadalajara Jalisco Mexican, Hardee's, KFC, Little Caesar's, McDonald's, Sakura Steaks, Taco Bell, Waffle House Days Inn $General, Advance Parts, AT&T, AutoZone, Lowe's, O'Reilly Parts, Walgreens, Walmart/Subway
140	US 78, Leeds, **N** Distinctive Outlets/famous brands, **S** Chevron, Marathon Subway Best Value Inn, Hampton Inn Bass Pro Shop
139mm	Cahaba River
136	I-459 S, to Montgomery, Tuscaloosa
135	US 78, Old Leeds Rd, **N** Shell/dsl B'ham Race Course
133	US 78, to Kilgore Memorial Dr, (wb return at 132), **N** Chevron, Exxon/Circle K/dsl Golden Rule BBQ, Hamburger Heaven, Jack's, Krystal, Waffle House Red Roof Inn, Siesta Motel same as 132, **S** Shell McDonald's Hampton Inn, Holiday Inn Express, Quality Inn Tire Engineers
132b a	US 78, Crestwood Blvd, **N** Chevron, Exxon/Circle K/dsl Golden Rule BBQ, Hamburger Heaven, Jack's, Krystal, Subway, Waffle House Red Roof Inn, Siesta Motel $General, Aamco, O'Reilly Parts, same as 133, **S** Chevron, Exxon, Marathon/dsl, Murphy Express/dsl, Shell, Texaco/dsl Arby's, Bojangles, Burger King, Capt D's, Chick-fil-A, Domino's, El Cazador Mexican, Honeybaked Ham, IHOP, KFC, King Buffet, Los Arcos Mexican, McDonald's, Milo's Burgers, New China Buffet, Olive Garden, Pancho's Mexican, Shrimp Basket, Starbucks, Taco Bell, Zaxby's Comfort Inn, Delux Inn, Garden Suites H, $Tree, Advance Parts, Aldi Foods, Burlington Coats, Firestone/auto, Home Depot, Office Depot, PepBoys, Ross, TJ Maxx, Tuesday Morning, URGENT CARE, Verizon, Walgreens, Walmart
130b	US 11, 1st Ave, **N** Chevron, Petro, Sunoco AutoZone, Family$, Piggly Wiggly, **S** Chevron/dsl McDonald's, Pacific Seafood Relax Inn, Sky Inn
130a	I-59 N, to Gadsden
I-59 S and I-20 W run together from B'ham to Meridian, MS	
129	Airport Blvd, **N** Ramada , **S** Mobil, Shell/dsl, Shell/dsl Hardee's, Kabob House Best Inn, Holiday Inn
128	AL 79, Tallapoosa St, **N** Circle K/Subway/dsl/scales, Shell/Wings/dsl
126b	31st St, **N** Shell/dsl, Texaco/dsl McDonald's Family$

ANNISTON · PELL CITY · LEEDS

 = gas = food = lodging = other = rest stop

INTERSTATE 20 Cont'd

Exit#	Services
BIRMINGHAM	
126a	US 31, US 280, 26th St, Carraway Blvd, **N** Church's, KFC, Rally's
125b	22nd St, **N** Subway Sheraton, Westin
125a	17th St, to downtown
124b a	I-65, S to Montgomery, N to Nashville
123	US 78, Arkadelphia Rd, **N** Chevron, Jet-Pep, Pilot/Wendy's/dsl/scales/24hr (0.5mi), Shell/dsl Popeye's Days Inn, **S** H, to Legion Field
121	Bush Blvd (from wb, no return), Ensley, **N** Exxon, Marathon
120	AL 269, 20th St, Ensley Ave, **N** Jet-Pep KFC Honda, **S** Chevron H, Toyota
119b	Ave I (from wb)
119a	Lloyd Noland Pwky, **N** Chevron/dsl, Sunoco/dsl Burger King, Fairfield Seafood, McDonald's, Subway, **S** Mobil, Texaco H
118	AL 56, Valley Rd, Fairfield, **S** Shell Papa John's Best Inn Advance Parts, Home Depot, URGENT CARE
115	Allison-Bonnett Memorial Dr, **N** Marathon/dsl, RaceWay/dsl, Shell/dsl Church's, Jack's, Los Reyes, Subway, Zaxby's Advance Parts, O'Reilly Parts, USPO
BESSEMER	
113	18th Ave, to Hueytown, **S** Chevron/dsl/24hr, Marathon McDonald's
112	18th St, 19th St, Bessemer, **N** RaceWay/dsl, Shell Jack's Rest. tire/repair, **S** Chevron, Sunoco/dsl KFC, Muffaletta's Italian, Rally's, Subway, Sykes BBQ Advance Parts, FMS Drug, Lowe's, NAPA, O'Reilly Parts, Walgreens
110	AL Adventure Pkwy, **N** Splash Adventure Funpark, **S** H
108	US 11, AL 5 N, Academy Dr, **N** Circle K Applebee's, Carnation Buffet, Catfish Cabin, Cracker Barrel, Waffle House Best Western, Comfort Inn, Country Inn&Suites, Fairfield Inn, Holiday Inn Express, Quality Inn, Wood Spring Suites Chevrolet, Chrysler/Dodge/Jeep, Nissan, **S** Chevron/Church's/dsl, Murphy USA/dsl, Shell Burger King, Domino's, Jade Garden, Little Caesar's, McDonald's, Milo's Burgers, Ruby Tuesday, Sonic, Wendy's, Zaxby's Economy Inn, Hampton Inn, Knights Inn, Motel 6 H, $Tree, BigLots, Ford, PepBoys, to civic ctr, Verizon, Walmart/Subway
106	I-459 N, to Montgomery
104	Rock Mt Lake, **S** FLYING J/Subway/dsl/LP/24hr
100	to Abernant, **N** Loves/McDonald's/Subway/dsl/scales/24hr, **S** Citgo, Exxon, Petro/Valero/Iron Skillet/Popeyes/dsl/scales/24hr/@ $General, Tannehill Ironworks Camping, Tannehill SP (3mi)
97	US 11 S, AL 5 S, to W Blocton, **S** Chevron/KFC/dsl, Citgo/dsl, Exxon/Subway/dsl Jack's Rest., La Tortilla Grill Cahaba River NWR
89	Mercedes Dr, **N** Greystone Inn, **S** Mercedes Auto Plant
86	Vance, to Brookwood, **N** Marathon/Huddle House/Subway/dsl, Shell/dsl/rest./24hr
85mm	**both lanes, full facilities, litter barrels, petwalk, , , RV dump, vending**
79	US 11, University Blvd, Coaling, **S** Chevron/dsl, Texaco/dsl
77	Cottondale, **N** Chevron/McDonald's, Pilot/Wendy's/dsl/scales/24hr, TA/BP/Taco Bell/dsl/scales/24hr/@ Arby's, Pizza Hut, Ruby Tuesday Hampton Inn, Microtel Blue Beacon, Harley Davidson, SpeedCo, USPO, **S** Chevrolet
76	US 11, E Tuscaloosa, Cottondale, **N** Chevron, Marathon, Shell/dsl Burger King, Cracker Barrel, Waffle House Centerstone Inn, Howard Johnson, Western Motel, Wingate Inn, Woodspring Suites Sunset 2 RV Park, transmissions, **S** Pilot/Subway/dsl/scales/24hr, Texaco/dsl Rodeway Inn

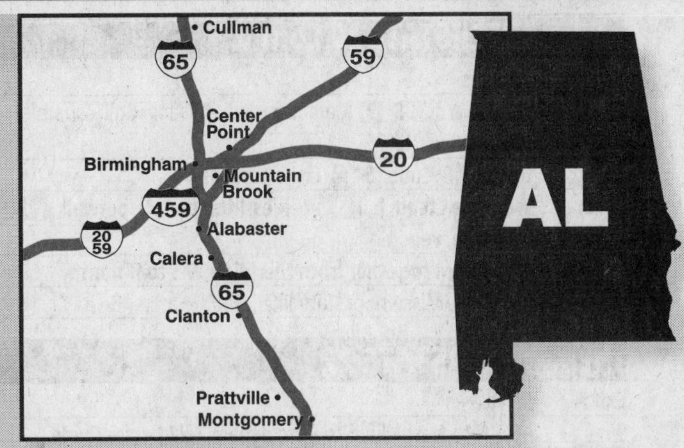

Exit#	Services
TUSCALOOSA	
73	US 82, McFarland Blvd, Tuscaloosa, **N** Chevron/dsl, Circle K, RaceWay, Shell Applebee's, Arby's, Buffalo Wild Wings, Burger King, Capt D's, Chick-fil-A, Chipotle, Five Guys, Full Moon BBQ, Jason's Deli, Krystal, Longhorn Steaks, Moe's SW Grill, O'Charley's, Olive Garden, Panera Bread, Popeye's, Red Lobster, Shrimp Basket, Starbucks, TCBY, Waffle House Best Value Inn, Best Western, Comfort Suites, Guest Lodge, Holiday Inn Express, Masters Inn H, $General, Aamco, Advance Parts, AT&T, Barnes&Noble, Belk, Best Buy, CVS Drug, Firestone/auto, Goodyear/auto, Home Depot, JC Penney, Michael's, OK Tire, Old Navy, PepBoys, Rite Aid, Ross, SteinMart, Target, Verizon, vet, **S** Jet-Pep/dsl, Marathon Buffet City, Checkers, Cheddar's, Chili's, Hardee's, KFC, Logan's Roadhouse, McDonald's, Papa John's, Pizza Hut, Sonic, Subway, Taco Bell, Taco Casa, Trey Yuen Cinese Ambassador Inn, Candlewood Suites, Country Inn&Suites, Days Inn, EconoLodge, La Quinta, Motel 6, Quality Inn, Ramada Inn, Super 8 $General, $Tree, Chrysler/Dodge/Jeep, NAPA, Office Depot, Rite Aid, Sam's Club/gas, TJ Maxx, U-Haul, Walmart/Subway
71b	I-359, Al 69 N, to Tuscaloosa, **N** H, to Stillman Coll, U of AL
71a	AL 69 S, to Moundville, **S** Chevron, Citgo/dsl, Mapco/Quiznos/dsl, Shell/dsl Arby's, Baumhower's Rest., Chick-fil-A, Costa BBQ, Hooters, IHOP, LoneStar Steaks, OutBack Steaks, Pizza Hut, Ryan's, Waffle House, Wendy's, Zaxby's Baymont Inn, Courtyard, Fairfield Inn, Hilton Garden Advance Parts, Goodyear/auto, Kia/Mazda/VW, Lowe's, O'Reilly Parts, PepBoys, to Mound SM, URGENT CARE
68	Northport-Tuscaloosa Western Bypass
64mm	Black Warrior River
62	Fosters, **N** Chevron/Subway/dsl $General, Foodland, USPO, vet
52	US 11, US 43, Knoxville, **N** Circle K/dsl
45	AL 37, Union, **S** Chevron/Subway/dsl, Texaco/dsl South Fork Rest Econolodge, Travel Inn Greene Co Greyhound Park
40	AL 14, Eutaw, **N** to Tom Bevill Lock/Dam, **S** Marathon H
39mm	**wb, full facilities, litter barrels, petwalk, , , RV dump, vending**
38mm	**eb, full facilities, litter barrels, petwalk, , , RV dump, vending**
32	Boligee, **N** Marathon/rest./dsl/24hr, **S** Chevron/Subway/dsl
27mm	Tenn-Tom Waterway, Tombigbee River
23	rd 20, Epes, to Gainesville
17	AL 28, Livingston, **S** Chevron/Subway/dsl, Exxon/L&B/dsl/24hr, Shell/dsl, Spirit Burger King, Diamond Jim's/Mrs Donna's, McDonald's, Pizza Hut Comfort Inn, Western Inn repair/24hr

AL

INTERSTATE 20 Cont'd

Exit#	Services
8	AL 17, York, S Marathon/New Orleans Grill/dsl/scales/@ Best Inn
1	to US 80 E, Cuba, S Citgo/rest./dsl
.5mm	**Welcome Ctr eb, full facilities, litter barrels, petwalk, , , RV dump, vending**
I-20 E and I-59 N run together from Meridian, MS to B'ham	
0mm	Alabama/Mississippi state line

INTERSTATE 22

Exit #	Services
96	I-65, N to Nashville, S to Birmingham, **I-22 begins/ends.**
93	rd 77
91	rd 105, to Brookside
89	rd 65, to Adamsville, Graysville
87	rd 112, to Graysville
85	US 78, Birmingham
81	rd 45, W Jefferson
78	rd 81, Dora, Sumiton, N TJ's/dsl
72	rd 61, Cordova
70	rd 22, Cordova, Parish
65	Bevill Ind Pkwy, Jasper, N Hampton Inn (3mi) H, to Walker Co Lake, S Loves/McDonald's/Subway/dsl/scales/24hr Cracker Barrel, Waffle House Sleep Inn Buick/Cadillac/Chevrolet/GMC
63	AlL 269, Jasper, Parish, N Chevron/deli/dsl
61	AL 69, Jasper, Tuscaloosa, N RJ's Deano's Hickory Pit
57	AL 118 E, Jasper, N Chevron, Shell/dsl The Barn Rest.
53	to AL 118
52	AL 118, Carbon Hill
46	rd 11, Carbon Hill, Nauvoo, S Chevron/dsl, Shell
39	AL 13, Natural Bridge, Eldridge
34	AL 233, Glen Allen, Natural Bridge
30	AL 129, Brilliant, Winfield, S Chevron/deli/dsl, Shell/deli/dsl Huddle House Hampton Inn
26	AL 44, Brilliant, Guin, S Holiday Inn H
22	rd 45
16	US 43, US 278, Hamilton, Guin, S Shell/deli/dsl
14	Hamilton, N Texaco/dsl Huddle House Days Inn (1mi), EconoLodge (1mi), Keywest Inn
11	AL 17, Hamilton, Sulligent, N Citgo/dsl H
7	Hamilton, Weston, N H
3	rd 33
0mm	Alabama/Mississippi State Line

INTERSTATE 59

Exit #	Services
241.5mm	Alabama/Georgia state line, Central/Eastern time zone
241mm	**Welcome Ctr sb, full facilities, litter barrels, petwalk, , , RV dump, vending**
239	to US 11, Sulphur Springs Rd, E camping
231	AL 40, AL 117, Hammondville, Valley Head, E camping (5mi), DeSoto SP, W Victory Fuel
224	49th St, to Ft Payne
222	US 11, to Ft Payne, **1 mi E** Delta Arby's, Hardee's, Jack's Rest., KFC, Krystal, Pizza Hut, SteviB's Pizza, Subway, Toke Thai Grill, Wingstop Quality Inn Chevrolet, Foodland/dsl, W Citgo/dsl, JetPep/dsl Waffle King

FT PAYNE

Exit #	Services
218	AL 35, Ft Payne, E Capt D's, Don Chico Mexican, DQ, Jack's, Jefferson's Burgers, McDonald's, New China, Papa John's, Sonic, Taco Bell, Western Sizzlin, Zaxby's $General, Advance Parts, Alabama Museum, AutoZone, BigLots, Buick/GMC, Chrysler/Dodge/Jeep, O'Reilly Parts, URGENT CARE, W Kangaroo/dsl, MapCo, Murphy USA/dsl, Victory Fuel Burger King, Chow King, Cracker Barrel, Hardee's, Huddle House, Los Arcos, Ruby Tuesday, Ryan's, Santa Fe Steaks, Subway, Waffle House Days Inn, EconoLodge, Hampton Inn, Holiday Inn Express H, $Tree, AT&T, Ford/Lincoln, GNC, Lowe's, Verizon, Walgreens, Walmart, Will's Creek RV Park
205	AL 68, Collinsville, E Delta Jack's Rest. Travelers Inn to Little River Canyon, Weiss Lake, W BP/dsl, MapCo
188	AL 211, to US 11, Gadsden, E Jet-Pep Noccalula Falls Camping, W Clean Fuels/dsl/E85

GADSDEN

Exit #	Services
183	US 431, US 278, Gadsden, E Jet-Pep/dsl, Shell, Texaco/dsl Magic Burger, Waffle House Days Inn, HomeLodge, Rodeway Inn st police, W Chevron, Exxon, Jet-Pep McDonald's, Pizza Hut, Subway, Taco Bell
182	I-759, to Gadsden
181	AL 77, Rainbow City, to Gadsden, E Petro/Popeye's/dsl/scales/24hr/@ Days Inn, W Kangaroo/dsl, Murphy Express/dsl Arby's, Bubba Rito's SW Grill, Cracker Barrel, Domino's, Hardee's, Los Arcos, Lucky Wok, McDonald's, Old Mexico Grille, Ray's BBQ, Ruby Tuesday, Subway, Waffle House, Wendy's Best Western, Comfort Suites, Fairfield Inn, Hampton Inn, Holiday Inn Express $General, $Tree, O'Reilly Parts, Verizon, Walmart/Papa John's
174	to Steele, E Loves/Subway/Chester's/dsl/scales/24hr, W etPep/dsl, Shell/rest/dsl
168mm	**sb, full facilities, litter barrels, petwalk, , , RV dump, vending**
166	US 231, Whitney, to Ashville, E BP, W Texaco/dsl Huddle House, Jack's Rest., Subway
165mm	**nb, full facilities, litter barrels, petwalk, , , RV dump, vending**
156	AL 23, to US 11, Springville, to St Clair Springs, W Murphy USA/dsl, Shell /dsl Azteca's Mexican, China Stix, Hardee's, Pizza Hut, Taco Bell, Waffle House $Tree, AT&T, Walmart/Subway
154	AL 174, Springville, to Odenville, E Exxon/dsl, W Chevron, Citgo, MapCo, Shell/dsl, Valero/Subway Choppin Block Rest., Jack's Rest., McDonald's, Sal's Rest., Smokin Grill BBQ vet
148	to US 11, Argo, E Shell Jack's, Subway
143	Mt Olive Church Rd, Deerfoot Pkwy, E Chevron/dsl/CNG, Shell/dsl (1mi) Munoz Mexican Publix (1mi)

TRUSSVILLE

Exit #	Services
141	to Trussville, Pinson, E Bama/dsl, Shell/Subway/dsl, Texaco/dsl Applebee's, Cracker Barrel, Guthrie's, LoneStar Steaks, McDonald's, Papa John's, Pizza Hut, Taco Bell, Waffle House, Wendy's Comfort Inn, Holiday Inn Express, Quality Inn Harley-Davidson, W BP, Chevron, Shell/dsl Arby's, Buffalo Wild Wings, Burger King, Chick-fil-A, Costa's Italian, DQ, East Buffet, Frontera Grill, Jack's, Konomi Japanese, Krystal, Little Caesars, Milo's Burgers, Moe's SW Grill, Momma Goldberg's Deli, Palace Asian, Paul's Hotdogs, Ruby Tuesday, Seafood&Chicken Box, Whataburger, Zaxby's $Tree, Ace Hardware, Advance Parts, Aldi Foods, AT&T, BigLots, CVS Drug, GNC, Kohl's, Marshalls, Office Depot, Petsmart, Sam's Club/gas, Verizon, vet, Walgreens, Walmart/Subway
137	I-459 S, to Montgomery, Tuscaloosa

INTERSTATE 59 Cont'd

Exit#	Services
134	to AL 75, Roebuck Pkwy, W Chevron, Marathon/Kangaroo, Murphy USA/dsl, Shell/dsl Arby's, Burger King, Chick-fil-A, China Buffet, Hardee's, Los Arcos, McDonald's, Milo's Burgers, Pizza Hut, Subway, Taco Bell, Waffle House Best Inn H, $Tree, Aldi Foods, AT&T, CVS Drug, GNC, Honda, NTB, O'Reilly Parts, Rite Aid, URGENT CARE, V Tires, Walgreens, Walmart/ Burger King
133	4th St, to US 11 (from nb), W Papa John's $General, same as 134, USPO
132	US 11 N, 1st Ave, E same as 131, W Chevron, Shell/dsl Krispy Kreme city park
131	Oporto-Madrid Blvd (from nb), E Chevron, Marathon/Subway Church's, Little Caesars, Rally's CVS Drug, Family$, O'Reilly Parts, same as 132, U-Haul
130	I-20, E to Atlanta, W to Tuscaloosa

I-59 S and I-20 W run together from B'ham to Mississippi. See Alabama Interstate 20, exits 129-1.

INTERSTATE 65

Exit #	Services
366mm	Alabama/Tennessee state line
365	AL 53, to Ardmore, E Budget Inn
364mm	**W Welcome Ctr sb, full facilities, info, litter barrels, petwalk, , RV dump, vending**
361	Elkmont, W BP/dsl Momma D's Rest. antiques, repair
354	US 31 S, to Athens, W Chevron/dsl Capt D's, Domino's, Jack's Rest., Little Caesar's, McDonald's, Pizza Hut, Rooster's Cafe, Subway Mark Motel H, $General, Advance Parts, city park, CVS Drug, HomeTown Mkt, Northgate RV Park, Walgreens
351	US 72, to Athens, Huntsville, E Exxon, RaceWay/dsl, Shell/Subway, Valero/dsl Buffalo Wild Wings, Burger King, Cracker Barrel, Dunkin Donuts, Jack's, Las Trejas Mexican, Lawler's BBQ, McDonald's/RV Parking, Taco Bell, Waffle House, Wendy's Econolodge, Hampton Inn, Quality Inn, Travel Inn $General, Publix, Russell Stover, Verizon, Verizon, vet, W Chevron/dsl, Citgo/dsl, Marathon, Murphy USA Applebee's, Arby's, Bojangle's, Burger King, Catfish Cabin, Chick-fil-A, DQ, Firehouse Subs, Hardee's, IHOP, KFC, Krystal, Logan's Roadhouse, Papa John's, Papa Murphy's, Pizza Hut, Popeye's, Ruby Tuesday, Shoney's, Sonic, Starbucks, Steak-Out, Subway, Zaxby's Best Western, Days Inn, Fairfield Inn, Holiday Inn Express, Sleep Inn, Super 8 H, $General, $Tree, Advance Parts, Aldi Foods, AT&T, Big Lots, Chevrolet, Chrysler/Dodge/Jeep, Ford, Goodyear/auto, Lowe's, O'Reilly Parts, Pepboys, SaveALot Foods, Staples, to Joe Wheeler SP, Tuesday Morning, Walmart
347	Brownsferry Rd, Huntsville, W Chevron Swan Creek RV Park
340b	I-565, to Huntsville, E to Alabama Space & Rocket Ctr
340a	AL 20, to Decatur, W Chevron/dsl Courtyard (7mi), Hampton Inn (7mi), Holiday Inn Express (7mi)
337mm	Tennessee River
334	AL 67, Priceville, to Decatur, E Marathon/dsl, RaceWay/dsl JW's Steaks Days Inn, Super 8 $General, Family$, Foodland, W Chevron/dsl, Mapco/dsl, Pilot/Subway/Wendy's/dsl/scales/24hr Burger King, DQ, Hardee's, Krystal, McDonald's, Pizza Hut, Taco Bell, Taste of China, Waffle House Comfort Inn H, Johnston RV Ctr, Publix

ATHENS

DECATUR

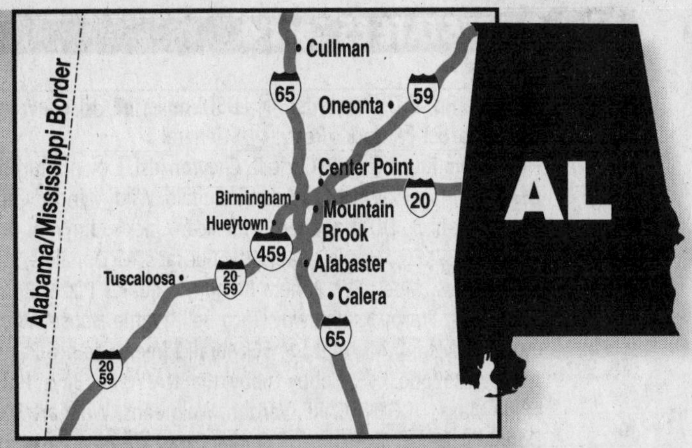

CULLMAN

Exit#	Services
328	AL 36, Hartselle, E Cracker Barrel, W Chevron/dsl, Cowboys/dsl, Jet-Pep/dsl, Ztrac Huddle House Red Roof Inn $General, vet
325	Thompson Rd, to Hartselle
322	AL 55, to US 31, to Falkville, Eva, E Marathon/Chester's/dsl, W Chevron, Loves/McDonald's/Subway/dsl/scales/24hr Log Cabin Rest. $General
318	US 31, to Lacon
310	AL 157, Cullman, West Point, E 76/dsl, Chevron/Popeye's, Conoco/Subway/dsl, Shell/dsl, Texaco/Wendy's/dsl Arby's, Bueno Vista Mexican, Burger King, Cracker Barrel, Denny's, KFC, Lawler's BBQ, Little Caesar's, Logan's Roadhouse, McDonald's, Panda Express, Ruby Tuesday, Taco Bell, Waffle House, Zaxby's Best Western, Comfort Suites, Hampton Inn, Holiday Inn Express, La Quinta, Quality Inn, Sleep Inn H, Buick/GMC, Ford/Lincoln, Verizon, Walmart, W Exxon/dsl, Marathon/dsl Best Value Inn
308	US 278, Cullman, E Days Inn Smith Farms, W Chevron $General, Chrysler/Dodge/Jeep, flea mkt
305	to Al 69
304	AL 69 N, Good Hope, to Cullman, E Exxon/dsl, Jet-Pep/dsl, Pilot/Wendy's/Dunkin Donuts/dsl/scales/24hts, Shell/dsl/scales Hardee's, Waffle House EconoLodge H, Good Hope Camping, Johnston RV Ctr, W Jet-Pep $General, to Smith Lake Camping
301mm	**E both lanes, full facilities, litter barrels, petwalk, , , RV dump, vending**
299	AL 69 S, to Jasper, E Jet-pep/dsl Millican RV Ctr, repair/tires, W Chevron/dsl, Petro/Burger King/Popeye's/Papa John'sdsl/scales/24hr, Shell/McDonald's/dsl Jack's Rest., Subway $General
291	AL 91, to Arkadelphia, E Jet-Pep/dsl Country View RV Park (1mi), W Shell/dsl/24hr 291 Roadhouse Rest.
291mm	Warrior River
289	to Blount Springs, W Citgo to Rickwood Caverns SP
287	US 31 N, to Blount Springs, E Jet-Pep/dsl
284	US 31 S, AL 160 E, Hayden, E Shamrock/dsl, Sunoco/dsl, Valero Travel Center/dsl Jack's URGENT CARE, W tires
282	AL 140, Warrior, E Chevron/Subway/dsl, Exxon/McDonald's, Shell/Dunkin Donuts/Little Caesars/dsl Hardee's, Pizza Hut, Taco Bell, W Marathon Huddle House
281	US 31, to Warrior
280	to US 31, to Warrior, E Chevron/dsl vet
279mm	Warrior River
275	to US 31, Morris

[gas] = gas [food] = food [lodging] = lodging [other] = other [RS] = rest stop

N INTERSTATE 65 Cont'd

Exit#	Services
272	Mt Olive Rd, E Shell/dsl LDS Temple, W Chevron/dsl, Citgo/dsl Jack's Rest. $General
271	Fieldstown Rd, E BP/Circle K, Chevron/dsl, Exxon, Murphy USA/dsl, RaceWay/dsl Arby's, Buffalo Wild Wings, Capt D's, Chick-fil-A, DQ, Habanero's Mexican, Jack's, Jim'n Nick's BBQ, Joel's, KFC, Kumo's Asian, Little Caesar's, McDonald's, Milo's Burgers, Moe's SW, Panera Bread, Pasquales Pizza, Pizza Hut, Sonic, Starbucks, Subway, Taco Bell, Waffle House, Wendy's, Zaxby's Microtel $General, $Tree, Advance Parts, AT&T, AutoZone, CVS, Hobby Lobby, Kia, NAPA, PepBoys, Publix, TJ Maxx, URGENT CARE, Verizon, Walgreens, Walmart/McDonald's, W Shell/dsl Cracker Barrel Best Western
267	Walkers Chapel Rd, to Fultondale, E BP/dsl, Jet-Pep, Murphy Express/dsl, Shell/Subway/dsl Applebee's, Arby's, Bojangles, Burger King, Casa Fiesta, Chick-fil-A, Chili's, Domino's, Firehouse Subs, Five Guys, Fullmoon BBQ, Hardee's, Jack's Rest., Logan's Roadhouse, McDonald's, O'Charley's, Outback Steaks, Shoney's, Stix Asian, Waffle House, Whataburger, Wintzell's Oyster House, Zaxby's Comfort Inn, Comfort Suites, Fairfield Inn, Hampton Inn, Holiday Inn Express, Home 2 Suites, La Quinta $General, AAA, Aldi Foods, AT&T, Best Buy, Books-A-Million, CVS Drug, GNC, JC Penney, Lowe's, O'Reilly Parts, Rite Aid, Ross, Target, URGENT CARE, USPO, Verizon, Volvo/Mack Trucks, Winn-Dixie, W Chevron/dsl
265b	US 31, Fultondale, E Chevron/dsl Days Inn, Econolodge
265a	I-22 W, to Memphis
264	41st Ave, W FLYING J/Denny's/dsl/LP/scales/24hr, LNG
263	33rd Ave, E Chevron/dsl, W Exxon
262b a	16th St, Finley Ave, E Chevron, Marathon/dsl, Sunoco/dsl Kenworth, W Chevron, Fuel City/dsl Capt D's, McDonald's, Popeye's
261b a	I-20/59, E to Gadsden, W to Tuscaloosa
260b a	6th Ave N, E Citgo, Shell, Texaco Mrs Winner's Tourway Inn Chevrolet, Chrysler/Dodge/Jeep, Hyundai, Nissan, Subaru, W Chevron/dsl Tire Pros, to Legion Field
259b a	University Blvd, 4th Ave, 5th Ave, E Chevron/dsl Capt D's, McDonald's, Ted's Cafeteria H, W Chevron/dsl Goodyear
258	Green Springs Ave, E Chevron, Shell, Sunoco/dsl Exotic Wings
256b a	Oxmoor Rd, E Exxon, Marathon, Mobil/dsl, Shell Acapulco Grill, Alfredo's Pizza, Burger King, Domino's, Firehouse Subs, Hunan Rest., KFC, McDonald's, Papa Murphy's, Paw Paw Patch, Popeyes, Purple Onion, San Miguel Mexican, Taco Bell, The Baskits, Zaxby's Howard Johnson $Tree, Aldi Foods, AutoZone, BigLots, Firestone/auto, Food World, Fred's, K-Mart, Midas, Office Depot, Omega Tire Pros, PepBoys, Publix, Tire Engineers, Tuesday Morning, URGENT CARE, Walgreens, Walmart Mkt, W Chevron, Texaco/dsl Hamburger Heaven, Hardee's, Jim'n Nick's BBQ, Waffle House Best Inn, Best Value Inn, Comfort Inn, EconoLodge, Motel 6, Quality Inn, Super 8 Batteries+, Valley Tire, vet
255	Lakeshore Dr, E BP/Circle K H, to Samford U, URGENT CARE, W Chevron, Shell Arby's, Chick-fil-A, Chili's, Costas BBQ, Hooters, IHOP, La Catrina Mexican, Landry's Seafood, McAlister's Deli, McDonald's, Milo's Burger, Moe's SW Grill, Mr Wang's, O'Charley's, Okinawa Grill, Outback Steaks, Starbucks, Subway, Taco Bell, Taco Casa, Wendy's Best Western, Candlewood Suites, Country Inn&Suites, Drury Inn, Extended Stay, Hampton Inn, Hilton Garden, Holiday Inn, La Quinta, Residence
255	Continued Inn, TownePlace Suites $Tree, AT&T, Goodyear/auto, Hobby Lobby, Lowe's, Sam's Club/gas, Verizon, Walmart/Subway
254	Alford Ave, Shades Crest Rd, E Chevron vet, W BP/dsl, Shell/dsl
252	US 31, Montgomery Hwy, E Chevron, Shell, Sunoco, Texaco/dsl Arby's, Backyard Burger, Bruster's, Capt D's, ChuckECheese's, Hardee's, Ichiban Japanese, Milo's Burger, Waffle House Baymont Inn, Days Inn H, Aamco, GMC, NAPA, PepBoys, Verizon, vet, Volvo, VW, W Exxon/dsl, Shell/dsl, Sunoco/dsl Burger King, Chick-fil-A, FishMkt Rest., Full Moon BBQ, Golden Rule BBQ, Habanero's Mexican, Krispy Kreme, Krystal, Mandarin House, McDonald's, Outback Steaks, Papa John's, Papa Murphy's, Purple Onion, Salvatore's Pizza, Starbucks, Subway, Waffle House EconoLodge $Tree, Acura, Advance Parts, AutoZone, Cadillac, Chevrolet, Chrysler/Dodge/Jeep, Firestone, Goodyear/auto, Honda, Hyundai, Mr Transmission, Nissan, Publix, Rite Aid, Staples, TJ Maxx, vet
250	I-459, to US 280
247	rd 17, Valleydale Rd, E BP/Circle K Hardee's, Jeffersons Wings Goodyear/auto, Lowe's, W Marathon, RaceWay/dsl, Shell/dsl Arby's, Backyard Burger, IHOP, Milo's Burgers, Papa John's, RagTime Café, Subway, Waffle House, Zapatas Mexican Homewood Suites, InTown Suites, La Quinta Publix, Rite Aid, vet, Walgreens
246	AL 119, Cahaba Valley Rd, E to Oak Mtn SP, W Chevron, Kangaroo/Subway/dsl/scales, Murphy USA/dsl, RaceWay/dsl, Shell/dsl 2 Pesos Mexican, Applebee's, Arby's, Burger King, Capt D's, Chick-fil-A, Cracker Barrel, DQ, Dunkin Donuts, Golden Corral, Hooters, Johnny Ray's BBQ, KFC, Krystal, Margarita Grill, McAlister's Deli, McDonald's, Pizza Hut, Purple Onion, Ruby Tuesday, Sonic, Taco Bell, TX Roadhouse, Waffle House, Wendy's, Whataburger Best Western, Comfort Suites, Fairfield Inn, Hampton Inn, Holiday Inn Express, Quality Inn, Ramada, Sleep Inn, Travelodge, ValuePlace H, $Tree, Advance Parts, AutoZone, Firestone/auto, Harley-Davidson, Kia, Mazda, NAPA, O'Reilly Parts, Verizon, Walmart
242	rd 52, Pelham, E Chevron/dsl, Exxon/dsl, Shell/dsl Johnny Ray's BBQ, Subway CVS Drug, Publix, W Shelby Motel (2mi) H, Good Sam Camping (1mi)
238	US 31, Alabaster, Saginaw, E Murphy USA/dsl Arby's, Buffalo Wild Wings, Chick-fil-A, DQ, Firehouse Subs, Full Moon BBQ, Habanero's Mexican, HoneyBaked Ham, Jim'n Nick's BBQ, Longhorn Steaks, McDonald's, Mizu Japanese, Moe's SW Grill, Momma Goldberg Deli, O'Charley's, Olive Garden, Panda House, Panera Bread, Ruby Tuesday, Starbucks, Steak'n Shake, Taco Bell Candlewood Suites $Tree, AT&T, Belk, Best Buy, Books-A-Million, Dick's, GNC, JC Penney, Lowe's, NTB, Old Navy, Petsmart, Ross, Target, TJ Maxx, URGENT CARE, Walmart/Subway, W Chevron/dsl, Shell/dsl Waffle House, Whataburger Shelby Motel H
234	Shelby County Airport, E BP/Subway/dsl, W Chevron/dsl, Shell/dsl Buick/GMC, Camping World RV Ctr
231	US 31, Saginaw, E GasBoy, Murphy USA/dsl, Shell/dsl Bojangles, Capt D's, Cracker Barrel, Ezell's Catfish Cabin, McDonald's, Milo's Burgers, Pizza Hut, Subway, Taco Bell, Waffle House, Zaxby's, Zopapan Mexican Hampton Inn, Quality Inn $Tree, AT&T, Burton RV Ctr, Publix, Rolling Hills RV Park, URGENT CARE, Verizon, Walmart/Subway
228	AL 25, to Calera, E Marathon/dsl, Shell/dsl Calera Inn, W Chevron/dsl Little Caesar's, Subway $General, Family$, to Brierfield Iron Works SP (15mi)

FULTONDALE · BIRMINGHAM · HOOVER · PELHAM

INTERSTATE 65 Cont'd

CLANTON

Exit#	Services
227mm	Buxahatchie Creek
219	Union Grove, Thorsby, E Chevron/dsl, Exxon/Subway/dsl Peach Queen Camping, W Shell/dsl Jack's Rest., Smokey Hollow Rest.
213mm	**both lanes, full facilities, litter barrels, petwalk, RV dump, vending**
212	AL 145, Clanton, E Chevron/dsl Nissan, Toyota, W Headco/dsl, Texaco/Subway H, Buick/Chevrolet/GMC, Chrysler/Dodge/Jeep, One Big Peach
208	Clanton, E Loves/Arby's/dsl/scales/24hr Higgins Ferry RV Park (8mi), W Exxon/dsl Shoney's Clanton Inn Dandy RV Park/Ctr, Heaton Pecans, KOA
205	US 31, AL 22, to Clanton, E Jet-Pep/dsl/E85, Shell/dsl, Texaco/dsl McDonald's, Waffle House, Whataburger Best Western, Days Inn, Holiday Inn Express, Scottish Inn Peach Park, to Confed Mem Park (9mi), **0-2 mi** W Chevron/dsl, Murphy USA/dsl, Shell/dsl Boomerang's Grill, Burger King, Capt D's, Jack's Rest., KFC, New China Buffet, Papa John's, Pizza Hut, San Marcos Mexican, Subway, Taco Bell, Wendy's, Zaxby's Key West Inn $General, $Tree, auto repair, Durbin Farms Mkt, Verizon, Walmart
200	to Verbena, E Texaco/dsl, W Sunoco
195	Worlds Largest Confederate Flag
186	US 31, Pine Level, E Confederate Mem Park (13mi), W Chevron/dsl, Exxon/dsl, Texaco/Subway/dsl Shann's Kitchen H
181	AL 14, to Prattville, E Chevron/dsl, Entec/dsl Jack's, W BP, Marathon/Kangaroo, QV, Shell/DQ/dsl Cracker Barrel, Los Toros, McDonald's, Ruby Tuesday, Subway, Waffle House, Wendy's EconoLodge, Hometowne Suites, La Quinta, Quality Inn, Super 8 H
179	US 82 W, Millbrook, E Chevron/dsl/24hr Country Inn&Suites, Key West Inn, Sleep Inn K&K RV Ctr/Park, **0-2 mi** W Liberty/dsl, Murphy Express/dsl, RaceWay/dsl, Shell/dsl Applebee's, Arby's, Beef'O'Brady's, Bruster's, Burger King, Capt. D's, Chappy's Deli, Chick-fil-A, Chipotle, CiCi's Pizza, City Buffet, El Patron, Five Guys, Hardee's, IHOP, Jim'n Nick's BBQ, KFC, Krystal, Las Casitas Mexican, Logan's Roadhouse, Longhorn Steaks, McAlister's Deli, McDonald's, Mellow Mushroom, Mexico Tipico, Moe's SW Grill, O'Charley's, Olive Garden, Outback Steaks, Panda Express, Popeyes, Ryan's, Shoney's, Sonic, Starbucks, Steak'n Shake, Subway, Waffle House, Zaxby's Courtyard, Days Inn, Hampton Inn, Holiday Inn Express, Howard Johnson, Rodeway Inn $General, $Tree, AT&T, AutoZone, Bass Pro Shops, Belk, Best Buy, BigLots, Books-A-Million, Chevrolet, CVS Drug, Firestone/auto, Ford, GNC, Hobby Lobby, Home Depot, JC Penney, Kohl's, Lowe's, Michael's, Office Depot, O'Reilly Parts, PepBoys, Petsmart, Publix, Ross, Target, TJ Maxx, URGENT CARE, Verizon, vet, Walmart
176	AL 143 N (from nb, no return), Millbrook, Coosada
173	AL 152, North Blvd, to US 231
172mm	Alabama River
172	Clay St, Herron St, E Embassy Suites, Hampton Inn, Renaissance Hotel, W Chevron/dsl
171	I-85 N, Day St
170	Fairview Ave, E Citgo/Subway, Sunoco/dsl Church's, McDonald's, Wing Master Advance Parts, AutoZone, CVS Drug, Family$, O'Reilly Parts, Piggly Wiggly, Rite Aid, W Family$
169	Edgemont Ave (from sb), E Liberty

MILLBROOK

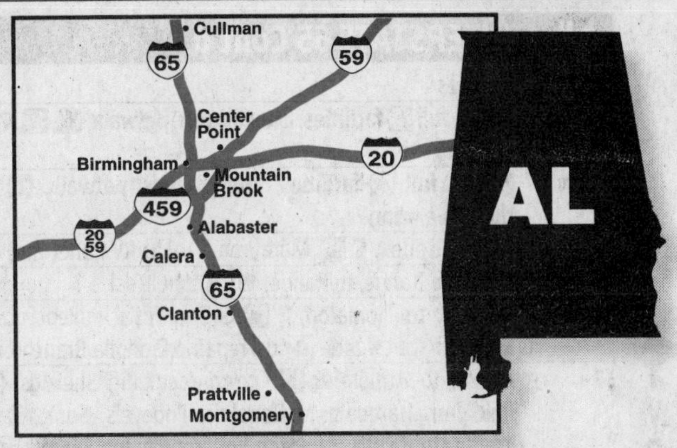

MONTGOMERY

Exit#	Services
168	US 80 E, US 82, South Blvd, E Circle K/dsl, Entec/dsl, TA/Marathon/Country Pride/dsl/24hr/@ Arby's, Burger King, Capt D's, KFC, McDonald's, Pizza Hut, Popeye's, Taco Bell, Waffle House Best Inn, Economy Inn H, The Woods RV Park, W Chevron/dsl, RaceWay/dsl, Shell/Subway/dsl DQ, Hardee's, Wendy's Candlelight Inn, KeyWest Inn, Super 8
167	US 80 W, to Selma
164	US 31, Hyundai Blvd, Hope Hull, E Liberty, Saveway/dsl/scales/24hr, Shell/dsl El Amigo Mexican auto repair, Montgomery Camping, W Chevron, Liberty/Subway, Marathon Burger King, Hardee's, McDonald's, Waffle House Comfort Suites, Fairfield Inn, Hampton Inn, Holiday Inn, Motel 6, Quality Inn auto repair
158	to US 31, Tyson, E Loves/Subway/Godfather's/Chester's/dsl/scales/24hr, Shell/DQ/Stuckey's Montgomery South RV Park, W FLYING J/Denny's/dsl/scales/24hr
151	AL 97, to Letohatchee, E Marathon/dsl, W Link
142	AL 185, to Ft Deposit, E Petro+/dsl Priester's Pecans, Subway auto parts, W Chevron
133mm	**both lanes, full facilities, litter barrels, petwalk, RV dump, vending**
130	AL10 E, AL 185, to Greenville, E Chevron/dsl, PaceCar/dsl, Shell Arby's, Capt D's, China Town, Hardee's, KFC, McDonald's, Old Mexico, Papa John's, Pizza Hut, Waffle House, Wendy's Days Inn, Quality Inn $General, $Tree, Advance Parts, CVS Drug, Fred's Store, O'Reilly Parts, Super Foods, to Sherling Lake Park, Walgreens, W Exxon/Subway/dsl, Mobil, Murphy USA/dsl, Texaco/dsl Bates Turkey Cafe, Burger King, Cracker Barrel, Krystal, Ruby Tuesday, Shoney's, Sonic, Taco Bell Baymont Inn, Best Western, Comfort Inn, Hampton Inn, Holiday Inn Express AT&T, Chevrolet, Verizon, Walmart/Subway
128	AL 10, to Greenville, E Shell/Smokehouse H, W Marathon
114	AL 106, to Georgiana, E Hank Williams Museum, W Chevron, Marathon auto repair
107	rd 7, to Garland
101	to Owassa, E Marathon/dsl, W Owassa/dsl dsl repair, Owassa RV Park
96	AL 83, to Evergreen, E Chevron, Shell Burger King, Hardee's, KFC/Taco Bell, McDonald's, Shoney's, Shrimp Basket, Subway, Waffle House, Wendy's, Zaxby's Sleep Inn H, Piggly Wiggly, vet, W Spirit/Subway/dsl EconoLodge, Evergreen Inn, Quality Inn
93	US 84, to Evergreen, E Liberty/dsl, W Loves/Arby's/dsl/scales/24hr, Shell/dsl

GREENVILLE

EVERGREEN

AL

INTERSTATE 65 Cont'd

ATMORE

Exit#	Services
89mm	**sb, full facilities, litter barrels, petwalk, , ,RV dump, vending**
85mm	**nb, full facilities, litter barrels, petwalk, , , RV dump, vending**
83	AL 6, to Lenox, E Marathon/dsl RV Park (4mi)
77	AL 41, to Range, to Range, W Shell/dsl
69	AL 113, to Flomaton, E Chevron/dsl, Jet-Pep/Subway/dsl, Shell/dsl/scales/24hr dsl repair, Magnolia Branch Camping
57	AL 21, to Atmore, E Chevron/dsl/24hr, Shell/dsl Fairfield Inn, Hardee's, McDonald's, Popeye's, Sonic, Taco Bell, Waffle House Hampton Inn, Holiday Inn Express Wind Creek Indian Gaming, W Shell/dsl to Kelley SP
54	Escambia Cty Rd 1, E Chevron/Subway/dsl to Creek Indian Res, W Shell/diner/dsl $General
45	to Perdido, W Chevron/dsl
37	AL 287, Gulf Shores Pkwy, to Bay Minette, E Marathon/dsl
34	to AL 59, to Bay Minette, Stockton
31	AL 225, to Stockton, E to Blakeley SP, W Shell/Subway/dsl Landing RV Park (2mi)
29mm	Tensaw River
28mm	Middle River
25mm	Mobile River
22	Creola, E River Delta RV Park (1mi)
19	US 43, to Satsuma, E Chevron/dsl/24hr, Pilot/Arby's/dsl/scales/24hr McDonald's, Waffle House La Quinta, W Chevron/dsl, Shell I-65 RV Park (1.5mi)
15	AL 41, E Chevron, Shell/Pizza Inn/DQ/dsl China Chef, Church's, Godfather's Pizza, Pizza Hut Family$, O'Reilly Parts, Rite Aid, Rouse's Mkt, Walgreens, W Circle K, Shell/Subway/dsl $General
13	AL 158, AL 213, to Saraland, E Murphy USA/dsl, Shell/dsl Goldberg's Deli, Krystal, Marble Slab, Rotolo's Pizza, Ruby Tuesday, Waffle House, Whataburger, Wintzell's Oyster House Comfort Suites, Country Inn Suites, Days Inn, EconoLodge, Microtel, Quality Inn, Red Lion Inn $Tree, AT&T, URGENT CARE, Walmart/McDonald's, W Exxon/Subway Cracker Barrel Baymont Inn, Fairfield Inn, Holiday Inn Express, TownePlace Suites to Chickasabogue Campground
10	W Lee St, E Kangaroo, Shell/Subway M Star Hotel
9	I-165 S, to I-10 E, to Mobile
8b a	US 45, to Prichard, E Chevron/Circle K/dsl, Texaco/dsl $General, Family$, tires/repair, W 1st Stop, Citgo, Energize/dsl, Loves/Subway/dsl/scales/24hr, Texaco/dsl, Valero/dsl Burger King, Domino's, Hardee's, McDonald's $General, Advance Parts, CVS Drug, Family$, O'Reilly Parts
5b	US 98, Moffett Rd, E Exxon/dsl, Texaco/dsl BJ's BBQ, Burger King, Church's, McDonald's, Sub King AutoZone, Family$, PepBoys, W Hardee's Super 8 auto repair
5a	Spring Hill Ave, E Burger King, Dreamland BBQ, McDonald's H, Mr Transmission, PepBoys, W Chevron/dsl, Shell/dsl Hibachi Express, Starbucks, Subway, Waffle House, Zaxby's Extended Stay America, Wingate Inn
4	Dauphin St, E BP/Circle K/dsl, Shell/dsl Checkers, Chick-fil-A, Cracker Barrel, Krystal, McDonald's, Taco Bell, Taco Bell, Waffle House, Wendy's Comfort Suites, Jameson Inn, Red Roof Inn, Rodeway Inn $General, Buick/GMC, Food-Champs, Lowe's, Mercedes, same as 3 & 5a, Walmart/McDonald's, W H

MOBILE

Exit#	Services
3	Airport Blvd, E Shell Burger King, Cane's, Logan's Roadhouse, Macaroni Grill, McDonald's, Morrison's Cafeteria, Santa Fe Grill, Starbucks, Waffle House, Wendy's Marriott H, $Tree, Acura, Belk, Best Buy, BigLots, Cadillac, Dillard's, Firestone/auto, Ford, Goodyear/auto, Harley-Davidson, Honda, Infiniti, Land Rover, Marshalls, Michaels, Nissan, Old Navy, Sam's Club/gas, Staples, Target, Verizon, W BudgetZone/dsl, Shell/dsl Arby's, Bamboo Japanese, Baumhowers, Boiling Pot, Burger King, Carrabba's, Cheddar's, China Doll, Chipotle, ChuckECheese, Denny's, Dunkin Donuts, Firehouse Subs, Goldberg's Deli, Honeybaked Ham, Hooters, IHOP, Jason's Deli, Lenny's Subs, Los Rancheros Mexican, Marble Slab, Melting Pot, Moe's SW Grill, Newk's Cafe, O'Charley's, Olive Garden, Osaka Japanese, Outback Steaks, Panda Express, Panera Bread, Popeye's, Red Lobster, Ruby Tuesday, Starbucks, Subway, Taco Bell, Waffle House Ashberry Suites, Baymont Inn, Best Value Inn, Comfort Inn, Courtyard, Drury Inn, EconoLodge, Fairfield Inn, Family Inn, Hampton Inn, Hilton Garden, Holiday Inn, Homewood Suites, InTowne Suites, La Quinta, Motel 6, Quality Inn, Residence Inn, Woodspring Suites $General, $Tree, AT&T, BooksAMillion, Fresh Mkt Foods, Home Depot, JoAnn Fabrics, Office Depot, PepBoys, Petsmart, Ross, SteinMart, TJ Maxx, to USAL, U-Haul, vet, Walgreens
1b a	US 90, Government Blvd, E Raceway/dsl, Shell/dsl Dickey's BBQ, Firehouse Subs, Five Guys, McAlister's Deli, Newk's Eatery, Panda Buffet, Starbucks, Steak'n Shake Home 2 Suites $Tree, AT&T, Audi/Porsche/VW, Best Buy, BMW, Chevrolet, Costco/gas, Dick's, Dodge, Family$, Field&Stream, Hobby Lobby, Kia, Lexus, Lincoln/Volvo, Mazda, Old Navy, Petco, Ross, Subaru, Toyota, Verizon, W Shell/dsl Waffle House
0mm	I-10, E to Pensacola, W to New Orleans, **I-65 begins/ends on I-10.**

INTERSTATE 85

LANETT

Exit #	Services
80mm	Alabama/Georgia state line, Chattahoochee River
79	US 29, to Lanett, E Murphy USA, Shell/Circle K Arby's, Burger King, Capt D's, Chuck's BBQ, DQ, Dunkin Donuts, KFC, Krystal, Little Caesar's, McDonald's, Pizza Hut, San Marcos Mexican, Subway, Taco Bell, Waffle House, Wendy's, Wing Stop H, $General, $Tree, Advance Parts, repair, Verizon, Walmart, W Exxon/QV, JetPep, RaceWay/dsl Domino's, Jin Japanese Steaks, Sonic EconoLodge AutoZone, CVS Drug, Kroger, O'Reilly Parts, to West Point Lake, vet
78.5mm	**Welcome Ctr sb, full facilities, litter barrels, petwalk, , , vending**
77	AL 208, to Huguley, E Jet Pep/Church's/dsl, Shell/Circle K/dsl Waffle House Quality Inn Chevrolet, Chrysler/Dodge/Ford/Lincoln, Ford, W Hampton Inn fireworks
76mm	Eastern/Central time zone
70	AL 388, to Cusseta, E BigCat/dsl, Sunoco/Louie's/dsl/scales/24hr/@, W fireworks
66	Andrews Rd, to US 29
64	US 29, to Opelika, E Sunoco/dsl, W Tiger/dsl
62	US 280/431, to Opelika, E Chevron/dsl, Eagle/dsl, Marathon/dsl, Shell/Circle K/Church's/dsl Burger King, Durango Mexican, McDonald's, Subway, Taco Bell, Wasabi Japanese, Wok'n Roll Rest. Days Inn, EconoLodge, Motel 6, Quality Inn, Red Carpet Inn, Red Roof Inn $General, W GrubMart, JetPep Capt. D's, Cracker Barrel, Sizzlin Steaks, Waffle House Comfort Inn, Magnuson Hotel Buick/Chevrolet/GMC, Chrysler/Dodge/Jeep, Ford, H&W Tire, Harley-Davidson, USA Stores/famous brands

AL

INTERSTATE 85 Cont'd

OPELIKA

AUBURN

MONTGOMERY

Exit #	Services
60	AL 51, AL 169, to Opelika, E RaceWay/dsl Hardee's $General, W auto repair
58	US 280 W, to Opelika, E Eagle/Guthrie's/dsl Freddy's, Wild Wing Cafe Hampton Inn, Holiday Inn Express, Home 2 Suites, La Quinta golf, W Chevron/Subway/dsl Arby's, Brick Oven Pizza, Buffalo Wild Wings, BurgerFi, Chick-fil-A, Chipotle, El Patron Mexican, Huddle House, Jersey Mike's, Jim Bob's, Logan's Roadhouse, Longhorn Steaks, Marble Slab, McDonald's, Moe's SW Grill, New Tokyo, Newk's Eatery, O'Charley's, Olive Garden, Pyro's Pizza, Sonic, Starbucks, Steak'n Shake, Taziki's, Waffle House, Which Wich?, Zaxby's Fairfield Inn, Microtel, Motel 6 , AT&T, Best Buy, Books-A-Million, Dick's, Hobby Lobby, Home Depot, Kohl's, Kroger/dsl, Lowe's, Office Depot, Old Navy, PetCo, Ross, Target, TJ Maxx, URGENT CARE, World Mkt
57	Bent Creek Rd, W Exxon, Mapco Baumhower's Victory Grille, Moe's Original BBQ, Shakey's Pizza, Venditori's Italian, Waffle House, Wendy's Hilton Garden, Sleep Inn Sam's Club/gas
51	US 29, to Auburn, E Chevron/dsl, Grub Mart Courtyard, Hampton Inn, Tru $General, Cadillac/Chevrolet, Leisure Time RV Park/Camping, Nissan, to Chewacla SP, Toyota, vet, W Chevron/Subway/dsl, Murphy USA Arby's, Burger King, Dunkin Donuts, El Dorado Mexican, Firehouse Subs, Jack's, Jim'n Nick's BBQ, KJ's Fish Camp, Krystal, Little Caesar's, McDonald's, Ozzio's Italian, Philly Connection, Pizza Hut, Ruby Tuesday, Shrimp Basket, Sonic, Taco Bell, Waffle House, Wendy's, Zaxby's Clarion, EconoLodge, Holiday Inn Express, Microtel, Pannie George's Kitchen, Quality Inn, Sleep Inn Advance Parts, Ford/Lincoln, Kia, tires/repair, to Auburn U, URGENT CARE, Walmart, Winn-Dixie
50	Cox Rd
44mm	**both lanes, 24hr security, full facilities, litter barrels, petwalk, , , RV dump, vending**
42	US 80, AL 186 E, Wire Rd, E dsl repair/tires, to Tuskegee NF, W Torch 85/rest./dsl/24hr
38	AL 81, to Tuskegee, E to Tuskegee NHS, Tuskegee University
32	AL 49 N, to Tuskegee, E Sunoco/dsl
26	AL 229 N, to Tallassee, E Chevron/Guthrie's/dsl
22	US 80, to Shorter, E Loves/McDonald's/Subway/dsl/scales/24hr, Petro/Valero/rest./dsl/scales/24hr Days Inn Wind Drift RV Park
16	Waugh, to Cecil, E Entec/Subway/dsl auto repair
15	AL 108 W, Pike Rd
11	US 80, AL 110, to Mitylene, to Mt Meigs, E Liberty/dsl, Murphy USA/dsl, Shell/Subway/dsl Anthony's Rest., Bojangle's, Bruster's, Burger King, Cracker Barrel, Jose's Grill, Krystal, McDonald's, Milo's, Taco Bell, Top China, Waffle House Candlewood Suites, Comfort Inn, Country Inn&Suites, Fairfield Inn, Holiday Inn Express, Sleep Inn Hobby Lobby, Home Depot, O'Reilly Parts, Walmart/Subway, W Chevron/dsl Microtel
9	AL 271, to AL 110, to Auburn U/Montgomery, E Arby's, BoneFish Grill, Buffalo Wild Wings, Chick-fil-A, Chili's, Chipotle Mexican, Del Taco, Firebirds Grill, Five Guys, Full Moon BBQ, Genghis Grill, Ixtapa Mexican, La Jolla Rest., Moe's SW Grill, Outback Steaks, Panera Bread, Pieology, Red Robin, Ruby Tuesday, Sonic, Starbucks, Taziki's Cafe, Twin Peaks, TX Roadhouse, Wendy's, Zoe's Kitchen Hampton Inn, Staybridge Suites, TownePlace Suites AT&T, Books-A-Million, Costco/gas, Dick's, Dillard's, EarthFare Foods, Firestone/auto,

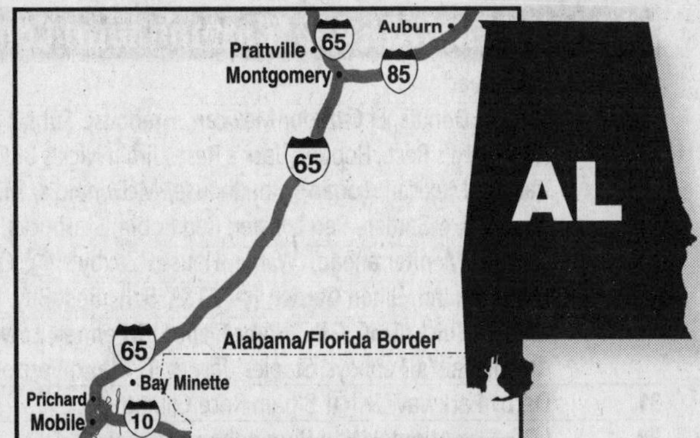

Exit #	Services
9	Continued Jo-Ann Fabrics, Kohl's, Michael's, Old Navy, Petsmart, Ross, Target, URGENT CARE, Verizon, vet, Whole Foods Mkt, World Mkt, W
6	US 80, US 231, AL 21, East Blvd, **0-2 mi** E Chevron, Exxon/dsl, RaceWay/dsl, Shell Arby's, Baumhowers Rest., Burger King, Carrabba's, Chick-fil-A, Gangnam Grill, Golden Corral, Hardee's, Jason's Deli, KFC, Longhorn Steaks, Los Cabos, Los Vaqueros Mexican, McDonald's, Ming's Garden, Olive Garden, Piccadilly Cafe, Popeyes, Rock Bottom Cafe, Schlotzsky's, Starbucks, Subway, Sushiyama, Taco Bell, Waffle House, Wendy's, Zaxby's Arlington Lodge, Best Inn, Comfort Inn, Country Inn&Suites, Courtyard, Extended Stay America, Home-Towne Suites, La Quinta, Quality Inn, Quality Roof Inn, Residence Inn, Sleep Inn, Springhill Suites, Wingate Inn, Woodspring Suites $General, $Tree, Acura, Best Buy, Books-A-Million, Family$, Ford/Lincoln, Fresh Mkt Foods, Home Depot, Honda, Hyundai, Lowe's, Office Depot, Pepboys, PetCo, Subaru, TJ Maxx, Tuesday Morning, UHaul, USPO, Walmart/McDonald's, Winn-Dixie, W Chevron, Liberty, Mapco/dsl, Shell Arby's, Capt D's, Hardee's, Hibachi Buffet, IHOP, Jan's Rest., Krispy Kreme, Krystal, McDonald's, Outback Steaks, Red Lobster, Saigon Bistro, Taco Bell, Waffle House Alabama Hotel, Baymont Inn, Comfort Suites, Drury Inn, Express Inn, Motel 6, Ramada Inn $General, Audi/VW, BMW, Buick/Cadillac/GMC, Chevrolet, Chrysler/Dodge/Jeep, Firestone/auto, Fred's Store, Infiniti, JC Penney, Kia, Lexus, Mercedes, Nissan, Sam's Club/gas, to Gunter AFB, Toyota, Volvo
4	Perry Hill Rd, E Chappy's Deli, Marco's Pizza Fresh Mkt, W Cannon/dsl, Chevron Hardee's, Subway Hilton Garden, Homewood Suites $General, Express Oil Change, Rite Aid, vet
3	Ann St, E Chevron Arby's, Bojangle's, Capt D's, Domino's, KFC, Krystal, McDonald's, Taco Bell, Waffle House, Wendy's, Zaxby's Red Roof Inn Pepboys, W Entec, Murphy USA/dsl, PaceCar, Ztec Burger King, Chick-fil-A, CiCi's Pizza, Hardee's, Popeye's Stay Lodge $Tree, AT&T, Office Depot, O'Reilly Parts, Ross, Verizon, Walmart/Subway
2	Forest Ave, E CVS Drug, W
1	Court St, Union St, downtown, E Marathon/dsl, W to Ala St U
0mm	**I-85 begins/ends on I-65, exit 171 in Montgomery**

INTERSTATE 459 (Birmingham)

Exit #	Services
33b a	I-59, N to Gadsden, S to Birmingham
32	US 11, Trussville, N Marathon/dsl, S BP/Wendy's, Chevron/dsl, RaceWay/dsl, Shell/dsl Arby's, Bojangles, Burger King, Cajun Steamer, Chili's, China Palace, Coldstone,

= gas = food = lodging = other = rest stop

AL AZ

INTERSTATE 459 (Birmingham) Cont'd

BIRMINGHAM

Exit	Services
32	Continued Dunkin Donuts, El Cazador Mexican, Firehouse Subs, Five Guys, Habanero's Rest., Hooters, Jack's Rest., Jim'n Nick's BBQ, KFC, La Bamba Mexican, Logan's Roadhouse, McDonald's, Mizu Japanese, Olive Garden, Red Lobster, Red Robin, Starbucks, Subway, Taziki's Mediterranean, Waffle House, Zaxby's Courtyard, Hampton Inn, Hilton Garden AT&T, Belk, Best Buy, Books-A-Million, Buick/GMC, GNC, Home Depot, JC Penney, Lowe's, Mazda, Michael's, Pepboys, Staples, Target, TJ Maxx, Verizon
31	Derby Parkway, N B'ham Race Course
29	I-20, E to Atlanta, W to Birmingham
27	Grants Mill Rd, N Hampton Inn Fiat, S Chevron/dsl Audi/Porsche, BMW, Chrysler/Dodge/Jeep, Land Rover, Lexus, Mini
23	Liberty Parkway, S Billy's Grill, DQ, Taziki's Greek Hilton Garden
19	US 280, Mt Brook, Childersburg, N Chevron/dsl CA Pizza Kitchen, Cheesecake Factory, Chuy's Mexican, Flemings Rest., Johnny Rockets, Lime Tex Mex, Macaroni Grill, Panera Bread, PF Chang's, Seasons Grille, Village Tavern, Which Wich?, Zoe's Kitchen AT&T, Barnes&Noble, Belk, Old Navy, Verizon, **0-3 mi** S BP/Circle K, Chevron, Marathon, Shell, Shell Arby's, Asian Rim, Black Pearl Asian, Buffalo Wild Wings, Burger King, Carrabba's, Chick-fil-A, Chili's, Chipotle Mexican, Cracker Barrel, Edgar's Rest., Full Moon BBQ, Jason's Deli, Jimmy John's, Kobe Japanese, Logan's Roadhouse, Longhorn Steaks, McDonald's, Milo's Burgers, Mooyah Burgers, Newk's Eatery, Pablo's, Papa John's, Pappadeaux, Pizza Hut, Schlotzsky's, Starbucks, Steak'n Shake, Subway, Superior Grill, Suriname 280, Taco Bell, Taziki's Greek, Tilted Kilt, Wendy's, Zaxby's Courtyard, Days Inn, Drury Inn, Extended Stay America, Hampton Inn, Hilton, Homewood Suites, Hyatt Place, La Quinta, Marriott, Quality Inn, Residence Inn, SpringHill Suites AT&T, Autozone, Best Buy, CVS Drug, Firestone/auto, Fresh Mkt Foods, Goodyear/auto, Home Depot, Kohl's, NTB, Staples, Target, vet, Walgreens, Winn-Dixie, World Mkt
17	Acton Rd, N Shell/dsl Krystal, McDonald's, S Comfort Inn

HOOVER

Exit	Services
15b a	I-65, N to Birmingham, S to Montgomery
13	US 31, Hoover, Pelham, N Exxon/dsl, Shell/dsl, Sunoco/dsl Burger King, Chick-fil-A, Fish Mkt Rest., Full Moon BBQ, Golden Rule BBQ, Habanero's, Krispy Kreme, Krystal, McDonald's, Outback Steaks, Papa John's, Purple Onion, Salvatori's Pizza, Starbucks, Subway Econolodge $Tree, Acura, AutoZone, Cadillac, Chevrolet, Firestone/auto, Goodyear/auto, Honda, Hyundai, Mr Transmission, Nissan, Publix, Rite Aid, Staples, TJ Maxx, vet, S Exxon, Jet-Pep, Shell/dsl Arby's, Bonefish Grill, CA Pizza Kitchen, Chick-fil-A, Chipotle Mexican, Firebird's Grill, Firehouse Subs, J Alexander's Rest., Jason's Deli, Jim'n Nicks BBQ, La Paz, McDonald's, Moe's BBQ, Moe's SW Grill, Newk's Eatery, Olive Garden, Panera Bread, Pizza Hut, Ruby Tuesday, Steak'n Shake, Stix Asian, Sumo Japanese, Taco Bell, Twin Peaks Rest., Wendy's Courtyard, Days Inn, Embassy Suites, Hampton Inn, Hyatt Place, Hyatt Regency/Wynfrey Hotel Barnes&Noble, Belk, Best Buy, Costco/gas, Dick's, GNC, Hancock Fabrics, Home Depot, Infiniti, JC Penney, Jo-Ann Fabrics, Macy's, Mercedes, Michael's, NTB, Office Depot, PepBoys, Petsmart, Ross, Sam's Club/gas, Tuesday Morning, Verizon, Walgreens, World Mkt
10	AL 150, Waverly, N Beef o Brady's, Frontera Mexican Grill, Jimmy John's, McDonald's, Starbucks $Tree, Kohl's, Marshall's, PetCo, Sprouts Mkt, Target, URGENT CARE, S Marathon/Kangaroo/dsl, Shell Hampton Inn, Hyatt Place Ford/Lincoln, Publix/deli, Toyota, Walgreens

BESSEMER

Exit	Services
6	AL 52, to Bessemer, N Shell/dsl, S Chevron/dsl, Jet-Pep, Texaco/Taco Bell Arby's, China Wok, Domino's, Fish Hook Rest., McDonald's, Pizza Hut, Railroad Cafe, Subway, Waffle House, Wendy's Sleep Inn $General, CVS Drug, RV Camping, Winn-Dixie
1	AL 18, Bessemer, N Exxon/dsl, Shell/dsl Burger King, Chick-fil-A, Firehouse Subs, Full Moon BBQ, Habanero's Mexican, Logan's Roadhouse, McAlister's Deli, Taco Bell AAA, AT&T, GNC, Michaels, Petsmart, Publix, Ross, Target, URGENT CARE, S Sunoco/dsl Bojangles, China King, McDonald's, San Antonio Grill, Subway, Zaxby's Advance Parts, CVS Drug, Meineke, Piggly Wiggly, to Tannehill SP, Verizon
0mm	**I-459 begins/ends on I-20/59, exit 106.**

ARIZONA

INTERSTATE 8

Exit #	Services
178b a	I-10, E to Tucson, W to Phoenix, **I-8 begins/ends on I-10, exit 199.**
174	Trekell Rd, to Casa Grande, **2-4 mi** N H, food, gas, lodging
172	Thornton Rd, to Casa Grande, **5-8 mi**, N gas food Francisco Grande Resort, Holiday Inn
171mm	Santa Cruz River
169	Bianco Rd
167	Montgomery Rd
163mm	Santa Rosa Wash
161	Stanfield Rd
151	AZ 84 E, Maricopa Rd, to Stanfield, S Vija Trkstp/dsl Saguaro RV Park
151mm	**litter barrels, picnic area wb,**
149mm	**litter barrels, picnic area eb,**
144	Vekol Rd
140	Freeman Rd

GILA BEND

Exit #	Services
119	Butterfield Trail, to AZ 85, I-10, Gila Bend, **3 mi**, N Shell/dsl/scales, Shell/Subway/dsl/scales/RV Park/24hr Little Italy, Subway America's Choice Inn, Best Western, Knights Inn, Space Age/rest, Yucca Motel $General, Augie's RV Park, Sanborn RV Resort
117mm	Sand Tank Wash
115	AZ 85, to Gila Bend, N Circle K, Loves/Taco Bell/dsl/scales/24hr, Texaco/dsl Burger King, Carl's Jr, Don Jose Mexican, McDonald's Best Western, El Coronado Motel, Yucca Motel H, Avila Bend Mkt, Family$, Goodyear/auto, NAPA
111	Citrus Valley Rd
106	Paloma Rd
102	Painted Rock Rd, N Painted Rock Petroglyph Site (11mi)
87	Aqua Caliente Rd, Sentinel Rd, Sentinel, Hyder, N Sentinel Gen Store/dsl RV Camping
85mm	**wb, full facilities, litter barrels, petwalk, , , vending**
84mm	**eb, full facilities, litter barrels, petwalk, , , vending**

AZ

INTERSTATE 8 Cont'd

Exit #	Services
78	Spot Rd
73	Aztec, S [other] Oasis RV Park/dump (4mi)
67	Dateland, S [gas] Texaco/Quiznos/dsl [other] Oasis RV Park/dump (2mi)
56mm	**[rest stop] both lanes, full [handicapped] facilities, litter barrels, petwalk, [phone], [picnic], vending**
54	Ave 52 E, Mohawk Valley
42	Ave 40 E, to Tacna, N [gas] Chevron/dsl [food] Jac's Whistlestop Cafe [lodging] Chaparral Motel [other] USPO, S [other] Copper Mtn RV Park
37	Ave 36 E, to Roll
30	Ave 29 E, Wellton, N [gas] Circle K/dsl [food] Geronimo Mexican [lodging] Desert Motel [other] NAPA, Tier Drop RV Park, USPO, S [gas] Chevron/dsl [food] Chen's Chinese, Dusty's Pizza & Wings, Fusion Deli, Jack-in-the-Box [lodging] Microtel
24mm	Ligurta Wash
23mm	Red Top Wash
22mm	**parking area/litter barrels both lanes**
21	Dome Valley, N [other] Ligurta Sta RV park, Yuma Proving Ground (16mi)
17mm	**insp sta eb**
15mm	Fortuna Wash
14	Foothills Blvd, N [other] Sundance RV Park, S [food] Domino's, Foothills Eatery, Mi Fajita [other] auto/RV care/lube ctr, Family$, Foothill Hardware, Foothills RV Park, Hank's IGA/dsl
12	Fortuna Rd, to US 95 N, N [gas] Chevron/dsl, FLYING J/Giant/dsl/scales/24hr [food] DayBreakers Cafe, Jack-in-the-Box, Las Palapas Tacos, McDonald's, Pizza Hut, Starbucks, Taco Bell [lodging] Comfort Inn, Courtesy Inn [other] Caravan RV Park, Oasis RV Park, Shangri La RV Park, S [gas] Shell/Burger King/dsl, SP/dsl [food] A&W/KFC, Applebee's, Daboyz Pizza, Denny's, DQ, Little Caesar's, Subway [lodging] Microtel [other] $General, 99c Store, Big O Tire, CVS Drug, Family$, Fry's Foods/dsl, GNC, O'Reilly Parts, URGENT CARE, USPO, Walgreens
9	32nd St, to Yuma, S [food] Del Taco, Panda Express [other] RV Parks, Verizon, Walmart/McDonald's
7	AZ 195, Araby Rd, N [gas] Circle K/dsl, S [gas] Chevron/Jack-in-the-Box/dsl, Circle K/dsl [other] RV Parks, RV World, to AZWU
3	AZ 280 S, Ave 3E, N [gas] Arby's [lodging] Candlewood Suites, Holiday Inn Express, S [gas] Love's/Chester's/Subway/dsl/scales/24hr [other] CarQuest, Harley-Davidson, to Marine Corp Air Sta
2	US 95, 16th St, Yuma, N [gas] Circle K [food] Ah-So Steaks, Buffalo Wild Wings, Burrito Grill, Chick-fil-A, Chili's, Chipotle Mexican, ChuckeCheese, Coldstone Creamery, Cracker Barrel, Del Taco, Denny's, Famous Dave's BBQ, Firehouse Subs, Five Guys, Hawaiian BBQ, In-N-Out, Jack-in-the-Box, Kneaders, Lin's Chinese, Logans Roadhouse, Mimi's Cafe, Olive Garden, Panda Express, Penny's Diner, Pita Pit, Red Lobster, Starbucks, Subway [lodging] Best Western, Days Inn, Fairfield Inn, Hampton Inn, Holiday Inn, Homewood Suites, La Fuente Inn, Motel 6, OakTree Inn, Shilo Inn, SpringHill Suites, TownePlace Suites, Wingate Inn [other] AT&T, Best Buy, Dillards, GNC, JC Penney, Jo-Ann Fabrics, Kohl's, Marshall's, Old Navy, PetsMart, Ross, Sam's Club/gas, Target, Verizon, S [gas] 76/dsl, Arco/dsl, Chevron/Blimpie/dsl, Shell [food] Applebee's, Burger King, Carl's Jr, Chretin's Mexican, Golden Corral, IHOP, Jack-in-the-Box, McDonald's, Subway, TX Roadhouse, Village Inn Pizza, Wendy's [lodging] Comfort Inn, Motel 6, Radisson, Super 8 [other] [H], BigLots, Family$, Home Depot, Staples

WELLTON

YUMA

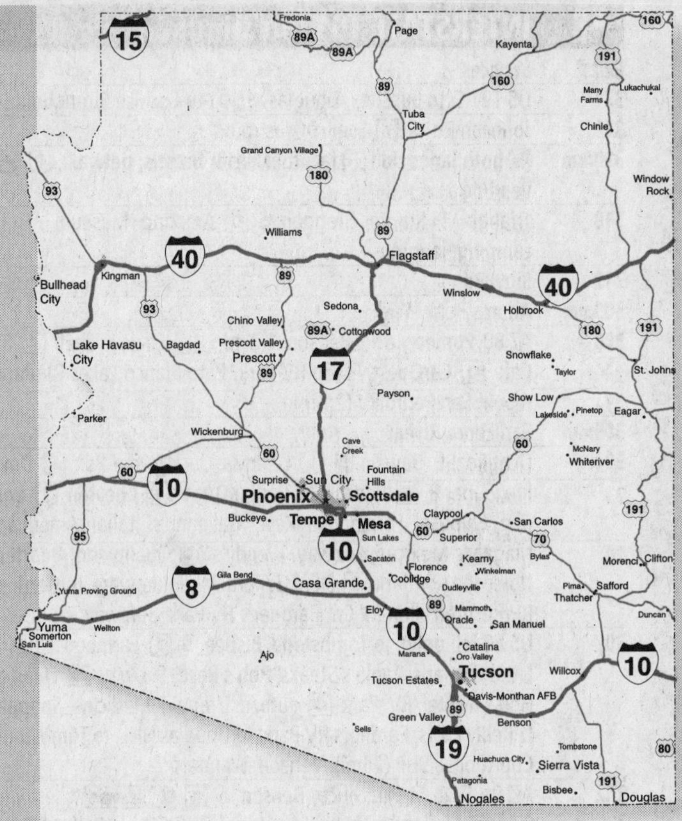

Exit #	Services
1.5mm	**weigh sta both lanes**
1	Redondo Ctr Dr, Giss Pkwy, Yuma, S on 4th Ave E [gas] Chevron, Circle K/dsl [food] Jack-in-the-Box, Yuma Landing Rest. [lodging] Best Western, Hilton Garden, N [other] to Yuma Terr Prison SP
0mm	Arizona/California state line, Colorado River, Mountain/Pacific time zone

INTERSTATE 10

Exit #	Services
391mm	Arizona/New Mexico state line
390	Cavot Rd
389mm	**[rest stop] both lanes, full [handicapped] facilities, litter barrels, petwalk, [phone], [picnic], vending**
383mm	**weigh sta eb, weigh/insp sta wb**
382	Portal Rd, San Simon
381mm	San Simon River
378	Lp 10, San Simon, N [gas] 4K Trkstp/Chevron/Noble Romans/Quiznos/dsl/scales/24hrs/@ [other] auto/dsl/RV repair
366	Lp 10, Bowie Rd, N [gas] Shell/Jerky/dsl, S [other] Alaskan RV park
362	Lp 10, Bowie Rd, N camping, gas, lodging, S to Ft Bowie NHS
355	US 191 N, to Safford
352	US 191 N, to Safford, same as 355
344	Lp 10, to Willcox, N [other] Lifestyle RV Park
340	AZ 186, to Rex Allen Dr, N [gas] TA/Shell/Popeye's/Subway/dsl/scales/24hr/@ [lodging] Holiday Inn Express, Super 8 [other] Apple Annie's Country Store, Magic Circle RV Park, RV/Truckwash, truck/auto repair, visitor info, S [gas] Chevron/dsl/24hr, Circle K, Texaco/dsl [food] Burger King, Carl's Jr, McDonald's, Pizza Hut [lodging] Days Inn, Quality Inn, Rodeway Inn [other] [H], $General, Ace Hardware, auto/tire/RV repair, AutoZone, Beall's, Family$, Grande Vista RV Park, KT's Mkt, Medicine Shoppe, Safeway, to Chiricahua NM, Verizon
336	AZ 186, Willcox, S [gas] Chevron/dsl/LP [lodging] Royal Western Lodge [other] Ft Willcox RV Park, Life Style RV Park

WILLCOX

E INTERSTATE 10 Cont'd

Exit #	Services
331	US 191 S, to Sunsites, Douglas, S to Cochise Stronghold
322	Johnson Rd, S Shell/DQ/dsl/gifts
320mm	**both lanes, full facilities, litter barrels, petwalk, , , vending**
318	Triangle T Rd, to Dragoon, S Amerind Museum (1mi), camping, lodging
312	Sibyl Rd
309mm	Adams Peak Wash
306	AZ 80, Pomerene Rd, Benson, **1-2 mi** S Circle K, Shell 86 Cafe CarQuest, El Rio RV Park, Pato Blanco Lakes RV Park, repair, San Pedro RV (2mi)
305mm	San Pedro River
304	Ocotillo St, Benson, N Denny's, Jack-in-the-Box Days Inn, Super 8 Benson RV Park, KOA, S Chevron Beijing Chinese, Farmhouse Rest, Galleano's Italian-American, Magaly's Mexican, Subway, Wendy's Quality Inn, Quarter-Horse Inn/RV Park H, $General, Ace Hardware, Butterfield RV Resort, Dillon RV Ctr, Pardner's RV Park, Safeway, Walmart
303	US 80 (eb only), to Tombstone, Bisbee, S Farmhouse Rest., Little Caesar's, Pablo's Steaks, Reb's Rest., Subway Quarter Horse Motel/RV Park auto/dsl/repair, Medicine Shoppe, O'Reilly Parts, Pardners RV Park, to Douglas NHL, to Tombstone Courthouse SHP (26mi), Verizon, Walmart
302	AZ 90 S, to Ft Huachuca, Benson, S Loves/Chester's/Subway/dsl/scales/24hr, Shell/dsl KFC/Taco Bell, McDonald's Comfort Inn, Motel 6 AZ Legends RV Resort, Cochise Terrace RV Park, Ft Huachuca NHS (25mi)
299	Skyline Rd
297	Mescal Rd, J-6 Ranch Rd, N Chevron/dsl
292	Empirita Rd
291	Marsh Station Rd
288mm	Cienega Creek
281	AZ 83 S, to Patagonia
279	Colossal Cave Rd, Wentworth Rd, N QuikMart/dsl AZ Pizza Co, DQ, Montgomery's Grill to Colossal Caves (7mi), USPO
275	Houghton Rd, N Panda Express Adventure Bound RV Resort, Discount Tire, to Saguaro NP (10mi), Walmart, S to fairgrounds (1mi)
273	Rita Rd, N Shell/Subway/dsl, S fairgrounds
270	Kolb Rd, S Bay RV Resort, Voyager RV Resort
269	Wilmot Rd, N Chevron/A&W/dsl Travel Inn, S Shell/pizza/subs/dsl
268	Craycroft Rd, N Circle K, Mr T/dsl/LP, Pilot/Subway/Taco Bell/dsl/lp/scales/24hr/@, TTT/rest/dsl/scales/24hr Crazy Horse RV Park, Freightliner, truck/RV wash, S dsl repair
267	Valencia Rd, N Shell/Jack-in-the-Box Pima Air&Space Museum, S Valero/dsl
265	Alvernon Way, N Davis-Monthan AFB
264b a	Palo Verde Rd, N Circle K/dsl Denny's, Shell/Wendy's/dsl, Waffle House Comfort Inn, Crossland Suites, Days Inn, Holiday Inn, Red Roof Inn Camping World RV Resort, Freedom RV Ctr, S Arby's, McDonald's Quality Inn, Studio 6 La Mesa RV Ctr, Lazy Days RV Ctr/Resort, Pedata RV Ctr
263b	Kino Pkwy N, N Shell/dsl Culver's, In-N-Out, Starbucks AT&T, Costco/gas, Verizon, Walmart/Subway
263a	Kino Pkwy S, N H, S Arco/dsl, Shamrock Burger King, KFC, Little Caesar's, Mandarin Buffet, Papa John's, Taco Bell $Tree, AutoZone, Family$, Food City, Fry's Foods, O'Reilly Parts, to Tucson Intn'l Airport, Walgreens
262	Benson Hwy, Park Ave, S Arco/dsl, Chevron/McDonald's/dsl, Circle K/dsl Carl's Jr. Best Value Inn, Motel 6, Rodeway Inn, Western Inn Mack/Volvo Trucks, USPO
261	6th/4th Ave, N GasCo Little Caesar's, Los Portales EconoLodge Discount Tire, Family$, Food City, USPO, S Circle K/dsl Church's, El Indio, Jack-in-the-Box, Panda Express, Silver Saddle Steaks, Whataburger Lazy 8 Motel Big O Tire, El Super Foods, Family$, Midas, O'Reilly Parts
260	I-19 S, to Nogales
259	22nd St, Starr Pass Blvd, N Circle K/dsl, S Kettle, Waffle House Clarion, Regal Inn, Silverbell Inn, Super 8, Travel Inn
258	Congress St, Broadway St, N Circle K Hotel Tuscan, S Carl's Jr Days Inn, Howard Johnson, Motel 6, River Park Inn, Travelodge
257a	St Mary's Rd, S Shell/dsl Burger King, Church's, Denny's, Eegee's Cafe, Furr's Cafeteria, Jack-in-the-Box, Little Caesar's, Whataburger Country Inn&Suites, Ramada Ltd. H, Family$, Food City, Pima Comm Coll
257	Speedway Blvd, N Best Western, EconoLodge H, U of AZ, Victory Motorcycles, S Arco/dsl museum, Old Town Tucson
256	Grant Rd, N Circle K auto/dsl repair, Burger King, Jack-in-the-Box, Sonic Walgreens, S Circle K, QT/dsl, Shell/dsl Arby's, Del Taco, Eegee's Cafe, IHOP, Waffle House Comfort Inn, Grant Inn, Hampton Inn, Holiday Inn Express, Super 8 Ace Hardware, Safeway, Walgreens
255	AZ 77 N, to Miracle Mile
254	Prince Rd, N Circle K, Valero/dsl $General, O'Reilly Parts, Walgreens, S golf, Kenworth, Prince of Tucson RV Park
252	El Camino del Cerro, Ruthrauff Rd, N Arco Ruthrauff RV Ctr, S Shell/Jack-in-the-Box/dsl
251	Sunset Rd
250	Orange Grove Rd, N Arco/dsl, Circle K/dsl Burger King, Culver's, Domino's, Firehouse Subs, Golden Corral, Little Caesar's, Subway, Tulioberto's, Wendy's Big O Tire, Costco/gas, diesel repair, Home Depot, Petsmart, South Forty RV Park, Sprouts Mkt, Staples, URGENT CARE, vet
248	Ina Rd, N Chevron/dsl, Circle K/dsl, Shell/dsl Bisbee Breakfast Club, Carl's Jr, ChickeNuevo, Chuy's Mesquite, DQ, Eegee's Cafe, Five Guys, Hooters, Jack-in-the-Box, Jade Garden, Losbetos Cafe, Lupita's Cafe, McDonald's, Miss Saigon, Molinitas Mexican, Papa John's, Peter Piper's Pizza, Pollo Loco, Starbucks, Subway, Taco Bell, Waffle House InTown Suites, Motel 6 $Tree, 99c Store, auto repair, AutoZone, BigLots, CarQuest, CVS Drug, Discount Tire, Firestone/auto, Fry's Foods/dsl, Goodyear/auto, Hancock Fabrics, Lowe's, Michael's, Midas, O'Reilly Parts, PepBoys, Target, U-Haul, Walgreens, Walmart Mkt, S Circle K Denny's, Starbucks Best Western, Red Roof Inn, Travelodge Ace Hardware, Freedom RV Ctr, Harley-Davidson
246	Cortaro Rd, N Circle K/Arby's/dsl, QT/dsl IHOP, Wendy's, S Shell/dsl Boston's Rest, Burger King, Chili's, Chopstix, Cracker Barrel, Eegee's Rest., In-N-Out, KFC/Taco Bell, Little Caesars, McDonald's, Nana's Mexican, Native New Yorker, New Town Asian, Panda Express, Starbucks, Subway, TX Roadhouse Comfort Inn, Days Inn, Holiday Inn Express, La Quinta, Super 8 access to RV camping, Ace Hardware, AT&T, Batteries+, GNC, Kohl's, O'Reilly Parts, USPO, Verizon, Walmart/McDonald's
244	Twin Peaks Rd, N Tucson Outlets/famous brands
242	Avra Valley Rd, S , RV camping, Saguaro NP (13mi)
240	Tangerine Rd, to Rillito, N A-A RV Park, S USPO

BENSON

TUCSON

INTERSTATE 10 Cont'd

Exit #	Services
236	Marana, S Chevron/dsl/LP, Circle K/dsl McDonald's, R&R Pizza auto repair, Family$, Sun RV Park
232	Pinal Air Park Rd, S Pinal Air Park (3mi)
228mm	to frontage rd, wb pulloff
226	Red Rock, S USPO
219	Picacho Peak Rd, N Shell/DQ, Shell/Subway/dsl, S Ostrich Ranch, Pichaco Peak RV Park, to Picacho Peak SP
212	Picacho (from wb), S KOA
211b	AZ 87 N, AZ 84 W, to Coolidge, S KOA
211a	Picacho (from eb), S KOA, state prison
208	Sunshine Blvd, to Eloy, N Pilot/Subway/DQ/dsl/scales/24hr dsl repair, S FLYING J/Denny's/dsl/scales/24hr Blue Beacon
203	Toltec Rd, to Eloy, N Chevron/McDonald's/playplace/24hr, Circle K/dsl Carl's Jr, El Caballito Mexican Best Value Inn, Super 8 Desert Valley RV Park, dsl/tire repair, S TA/A&W/Taco Bell/dsl/RV dump/24hr/@ Pizza Hut golf, truckwash
200	Sunland Gin Rd, Arizona City, N Petro/Iron Skillet/dsl/scales/24hr/@, Pride/Subway/dsl/24hr Burger King, Eva's Mexican Days Inn, Travelodge Blue Beacon, Eagle Truckwash, Las Colinas RV Park, S Loves/Arby's/Baskin-Robbins/dsl/24hr Golden 9 Rest Motel 6 Speedco Lube
199	I-8 W, to Yuma, San Diego
198	AZ 84, to Eloy, Casa Grande, N Robson Ranch Rest./golf (3mi)
194	AZ 287, Florence Blvd, to Casa Grande, N Tesla EVC Buffalo Wild Wings, Cactus Moon Grill, Cane's, Chick-fil-A, Culver's, In-N-Out, Krispy Kreme, Mimi's Cafe, Olive Garden, Rubio's, Subway Dillard's, GNC, JC Penney, Kohl's, Marshall's, Michael's, Petsmart, Ross, Staples, Sunscape RV Park (7mi), Target, Verizon, Walgreens, World Mkt, **0-2 mi** S 76/DQ, Arco/dsl, Chevron/Little Caesars/dsl, Circle K/gas Arby's, Burger King, Carl's Jr, Chili's, China Buffet, Chipotle Mexican, Church's, Coldstone, Cracker Barrel, Del Taco, Denny's, Eegee's, Filiberto's Mexican, Golden Corral, IHOP, Jack-in-the-Box, JB's, Jimmy John's, LJ Silver/Taco Bell, Macayo's Mexican, McDonald's, Panda Express, Papa John's, Papa Murphy's, Peter Piper Pizza, Sonic, Starbucks, Subway, T&M Italian, Wendy's Comfort Inn, Holiday Inn Express, Legacy Suites, Mainstay Suites, Quality Inn, Super 8 H, $Tree, 99cents Store, AT&T, AutoZone, Big Lots, Big O Tire, CVS Drug, Discount Tire, Encore Camping (2mi), Family$, Fiesta Grande RV Resort, Food City, Fry's Food/drug/dsl, Goodyear/auto, Home Depot, Jo-Ann Fabrics, Lowe's, U-Haul, URGENT CARE, Verizon, vet, Walgreens, Walmart/McDonald's
190	McCartney Rd, N to Central AZ Coll, S Circle K/dsl Barro's Pizza (3mi)
185	AZ 387, to Casa Grande, Casa Grande Ruins NM, S Eva's Mexican (6mi) Francisco Grande (6mi), Holiday Inn (6mi) Fry's Food/gas (6mi), hwy patrol, to Casa Grande Ruins NM, Val Vista RV camping (3mi)
183mm	**wb, full facilities, litter barrels, petwalk, vending**
181mm	**eb, full facilities, litter barrels, petwalk, vending**
175	AZ 587 N, Casa Blanca Rd, Chandler, Gilbert, S Chevron/dsl
173mm	Gila River
167	Riggs Rd, to Sun Lake, N Shell/dsl Akimel Smoke Shop
164	AZ 347 S, Queen Creek Rd, to Maricopa, N gas to Chandler Airport

CASA GRANDE

CHANDLER

Exit #	Services
162b a	Wild Horse Pass Rd, Sundust Rd, N Loves/Arby's/dsl/scales/24hr McDonald's Best Western+ MoTorCoach Resort, S Chevron/dsl Sheraton Resort, Wildhorse Pass Hotel/Casino Firebird Sports Park, Gila River Casino, Phoenix Outlets/famous brands
161	AZ 202 E, Pecos Rd
160	Chandler Blvd, to Chandler, N Chevron/dsl, Circle K, Circle K/dsl Can't Stop Smokin' BBQ, Denny's, Filiberto's Mexican, Marie's Rest., McDonald's, Rudy's BBQ, Sandella's Flatbread Cafe, Starbucks, Subway, US Egg Cafe, Wendy's, Whataburger Comfort Inn, Fairfield Inn, Hampton Inn, Hawthorn Suites, Homewood Suites, Motel 6, Quality Inn, Radisson, Super 8 $Tree, Aamco, ADS Auto Repair, CVS, Firestone/auto, Harley-Davidson, to Compadre Stadium, U-Haul, vet, Walmart Mkt, Williams AFBcar repair:ADS Auto Repair, S 7-11, Chevron/dsl, Circle K/dsl, Shell/dsl Bell Italian Pizza, Brazilian Bull Steaks, Carl's Jr, Cracker Barrel, Del Taco, Dunkin Donuts, Hong Kong Buffet, Jersey Mike's, Qdoba, Spinato's Pizzaria, Starbucks, Tukee's Grille, Waffle House, Wendy's Extended Stay America, Holiday Inn Express, InTown Suites, La Quinta H, AT&T, AutoZone, Discount Tire, Kohl's, URGENT CARE
159	Ray Rd, N Circle K, Shell Buca Italian, Carrabba's, Charleston's Rest., Chipotle Mexican, Fleming's Steaks, Frederico's Mexican, Genghis Grill, Habit Burger, In-N-Out, Jasons Deli, Jimmy John's, Longhorn Steaks, McDonald's, Nabers Rest., Outback Steaks, Paradise Cafe, Pei Wei Asian, Red Lobster, Roy's Hawaiian, Rumbi Grill, Sandbar Mexican, Starbucks, Subway, Tejas, Zoe's Kitchen Courtyard AJ's Fine Foods, Audi, BMW, Chevrolet, Ford, Home Depot, Lexus, Lowe's Whse, Mercedes, PetsMart, Sam's Club/gas, Verizon, S Circle K/dsl Barro's Pizza, Boston Mkt, Chick-Fil-A, Five Guys, Honeybaked Ham, IHOP/24hr, Jack-in-the-Box, Kneaders Cafe, Mellow Mushroom, Mimi's Café, Native Grill, Neo Tokyo, On-the-Border, Peter Piper Pizza, Pizza Hut, Rubio's, Subway, Uncle Bear's Grill, Vincent's Pizza, Wendy's Extended Stay America, Extended Stay America AT&T, auto repair, Barnes&Noble, Best Buy, Fresh&Easy Mkt, Hobby Lobby, JC Penney, Jo-Ann Fabrics, Marshall's, Michael's, PetCo, Ross, Sprouts Mkt, Target, Verizon
158	Warner Rd, N Circle K/dsl, QT Carl's Jr, Dunkin Donuts, Forefathers Cheesteaks, Port of Subs, Topical Smoothie Drury Inn Dick's, IKEA, S Circle K/dsl, Minute Mart/dsl AZ Sandwich Co., Burger King, ChuckeCheese, DQ, Hillside Spot Cafe, Macayo's Mexican, McDonald's, Nello's Pizza, Panda Garden, Ruffino's Italian, Taco Bell, Zipp's Grill Ace Hardware, Basha's Foods, Big O Tire, Goodyear/auto, vet

AZ

INTERSTATE 10 Cont'd

Exit #	Services
157	Elliot Rd, N Chevron/dsl, QT/dsl, Shell/Circle K/dsl Applebee's, Arby's, Burger King, Crackers Cafe, Crazy Buffet, Fuddrucker's, Jimmy John's, Kabab Palace, Kobe Japanese, McDonald's, Olive Garden, Oregano's Pizza Bistro, Panda Express, Red Robin Rest., Sonic, Starbucks, Subway, Taco Bell, Wendy's, YC Mongolian Grill Days Inn&Suites $Tree, Acura, Buick, Cadillac/GMC, Chrysler/Dodge/Jeep, Costco/gas, Discount Tire, Fiat, Honda, Hyundai, Kia, Mazda, Mini, NAPA, Nissan, PetsMart, Ross, Savers, Staples, Toyota, URGENT CARE, Volvo, Walmart, S Circle K/Dsl, Shell/Circle K/dsl Biscuits, Cactus Jack's, Niros Gyros, Original Burrito, Pacific Gardens Asian, Starbucks, Sub Factory, Subway Clarion, Sheraton auto repair, O'Reilly Parts, Safeway, vet, Walgreens
155	Baseline Rd, Guadalupe, N Circle K/dsl, Shell/Circle K/Popeye's/dsl Carl's Jr, ClaimJumper, Ell Pollo Loco, Joe's Crabshack, KFC, McDonald's, Poliberto's Tacos, Rainforest Cafe, Subway, Taco Bell, Waffle House, Wendy's Best Western, Candlewood Studios, Holiday Inn Express, InnSuites, Ramada, Residence Inn, SpringHill Suites, TownePlace Suites AutoZone, AZ Mills/Famous Brands, CVS Drug, Food City, Home Depot, Marshall's, Parts Authority, Ross, Walgreens, S 7-11, Arco/dsl, QT Aunt Chilada's Mexican, China Town, Denny's, Little Caesar's, Sonic, Subway Fry's Electronics, Fry's Foods, URGENT CARE
154	US 60 E, AZ 360, Superstition Frwy, to Mesa, N to Camping World (off Mesa Dr)
153b	Broadway Rd E, N Denny's Comfort Suites, Extended Stay America, La Quinta, Quality Inn, Red Roof Inn, Sheraton to Diablo Stadium, S Chevron/dsl, Shell/Circle K/Del Taco/24hr Goodcents Deli, Panda Express, Papa John's, Pizza Hut, Port of Subs, Taco Bell, Whataburger Country Inn & Suites, Homewood Suites Staples
153a	AZ 143 N, N Denny's Courtyard, Fairfield Inn, Hilton, Holiday Inn, La Quinta, Sleep Inn to Diablo Stadium, S same as 153b
152	40th St, N Shell/dsl U Phoenix, S Shell/Circle K Burger King, Quiznos
151mm	Salt River
151b a	28th St, 32nd St, University Ave, N Waffle House Drury Inn, Extended Stay America, Hilton Garden, Holiday Inn Express AZSU, U Phoenix, S Circle K/dsl, QT/dsl McDonald's
150b	24th St E (from wb), N Motel 6 Air Nat Guard, S Best Western/rest.
150a	I-17 N, to Flagstaff
149	Buckeye Rd, N Sky Harbor Airport
148	Washington St, Jefferson St, N Chevron/dsl, Shell, Tiemco/dsl Carl's Jr, McDonald's Motel 6, Sterling Hotel to Sky Harbor Airport, S Circle K H
147b a	AZ 51 N, AZ 202 E, to Squaw Peak Pkwy
146	16th St (from sb), N Shell/Circle K Filiberto's Mexican, S Circle K, Shamrock/dsl Church's, Jack-in-the-Box, Little Caesar's, Salsita's Mexican H, O'Reilly Parts, Ranch Mkt
145	7th St, N Chicos Tacos, McDonald's, Sonic, Starbucks, Subway, Taco Bell, Whataburger H, Safeway Foods, Walgreens, S Circle K, Shell, Sinclair/dsl Jimmy John's Holiday Inn Express, Hyatt, Sheraton, Springhill Suites to Chase Field
144	7th Ave, N Circle K Chipotle, Five Guys, Habit Burger, Jersey Mike's, NY Pizza, Peiwei Asian, Potbelly, Starbucks, Zoe's Kitchen, S Circle K central bus dist
143c	US 60, 19th Ave (from wb), downtown
143b a	I-17, N to Flagstaff, S to Phoenix
142	27th Ave (from eb, no return), N Comfort Inn
141	35th Ave, N Jack-in-the-Box, Rita's Mexican, S Shell/Circle K
140	43rd Ave, N 7-11, Circle K/dsl, Shell Filberto's Mexican, KFC, Little Caesar's, Pizza Hut, Salsita's Mexican, Subway Woodspring Suites AutoZone, Family$, Food City, Fry's Mercado/gas, Walgreens
139	51st Ave, N Chevron/dsl, Circle K Burger King, Domino's, El Pollo Loco, McDonald's, Sonic Best Value Inn, Budget Inn, Crossland Suites, Holiday Inn, InTown Suites, La Quinta, Motel 6, Red Roof Inn, Travelodge Food City, S QT/dsl/scales, Shell/dsl Carl's Jr, Filiberto's Mexican, IHOP, Port of Subs, Taco Bell Comfort Inn, Days Inn, Super 8, Travelers Inn
138	59th Ave, N Circle K, Valero Los Armandos Mexican, Papa John's, Subway 7-11, AutoZone, Family$, O'Reilly Parts, URGENT CARE, Walgreens, S Liberty/Chester's/dsl/24hr Waffle House Blue Beacon/scales
137	67th Ave, N Circle K/dsl, QT, Shell/dsl Church's, S FLYING J/Denny's/dsl/LP/24hr
136	75th Ave, N Chevron/dsl, Circle K A&W/LJ Silver, CiCi's Pizza, Coco's, Denny's, Hooters, IHOP, Lin's Buffet, Longhorn Steaks, McDonald's, Olive Garden, Pizza Hut/Taco Bell, Red Lobster, Starbucks, Subway, TX Roadhouse, Wendy's, Whataburger $Tree, AT&T, Big Lots, Big O Tire, Dillards, Home Depot, La Mesa RV Ctr, Lowe's, Ross, Target, Walmart, S Arco
135	83rd Ave, N Circle K, QT Burger King, Jack-in-the-Box, Waffle House Best Western, Premier Inn, Victory Inn K-Mart, Sam's Club/gas
134	91st Ave, Tolleson, N Circle K/dsl
133b	Lp 101 N
133a	99th Ave, N Chevron/dsl Cafe Rio, Cane's, Carrabba's, Chick-fil-A, China City, Chipotle Mexican, ClaimJumper, HoneyBaked Ham, Ichiban Rest., Island's Burgers, Jimmy John's, McDonald's, Native Grill, Panda Express, Paradise Cafe, Peter Piper Pizza, Pita Kitchen, Red Robin, Rumbi Grill, Smashburger, Starbucks, Subway, Taco Bell, Village Inn Courtyard Best Buy, Costco/gas, Discount Tire, GNC, Hobby Lobby, Marshall's, Old Navy, PetCo, Ross, URGENT CARE, Verizon, S Pilot/Subway/Wendy's/dsl/scales/24hr CarMax, Chevrolet
132	107th Ave, N Walgreens, S Camping World RV Ctr, Chrysler/Jeep, Dodge/Ram, Fiat, Honda, Hyundai, Kia, Mazda, Nissan, Toyota, VW
131	Avondale Blvd, to Cashion, N Circle K/dsl, S Culver's, Jack-in-the-Box, Panda Express, Ruby Tuesday Hilton Garden, Homewood Suites CVS Drug, to Phoenix Intnl Raceway
129	Dysart Rd, to Avondale, N Chevron/dsl, Shell/Circle K/dsl Buffalo Wild Wings, Chick-fil-A, ChuckECheese, Fiesta Mexican, In-N-Out, Jack-in-the-Box/24hr, Manuel's Mexican, Mimi's Cafe, Nakomo Japanese, NYPD Pizza, Ono Hawaiian BBQ, Panda Express, Peiwei Asian, Starbucks, Subway, Taco Bell, Tomo Japanese Holiday Inn Express $Tree, AT&T, AutoZone, Discount Tire, Fry's Foods, JC Penney, Jo-Ann Fabrics, Kohl's, Lowe's, PetsMart, Sprouts Mkt, Tuesday Morning, Verizon, vet, Walmart, S AZ Frybread, Black Bear Diner, Del Taco, Golden Corral, IHOP, KFC, McDonald's, Peter Piper Pizza, Subway, Waffle House, Whataburger Quality Inn,

PHOENIX

PHOENIX

INTERSTATE 10 Cont'd

129	Continued Super 8 Brakemasters, Food City, Home Depot, Pepboys, S&S Tire/repair, Sam's Club/gas, Walgreens
128	Litchfield Rd, N Circle K/dsl Applebee's, Black Angus Steaks, Caballero, Carl's Jr, Chili's, Chipotle Mexican, Cracker Barrel, Denny's, Five Guys, Freddy's Steakburger, Gus' NY Pizza, Hayashi Japanese, Jimmy John's, Macaroni Grill, Macavo's Mexican, McDonald's, Raul&Theresa's Mexican, Starbucks, Subway, Wendy's, Wildflower Bread Co. Hampton Inn, Holiday Inn Express, Residence Inn H, Barnes&Noble, Best Buy, Michael's, Ross, Target, to Luke AFB, URGENT CARE, Wigwam Resort/rest (3mi), S Circle K/dsl Arby's, Burger King, Eggs&More, Little Caesar's, Ramiro's Mexican, Rudy's BBQ, Schlotsky's Best Western, TownePlace Suites AutoZone, BigLots, Buick/GMC, Ford, O'Reilly Parts
127	Bullard Ave, N PF Chang's, Red Robin
126	PebbleCreek Pkwy, to Estrella Park, N Ah-So Steaks, Ariba Mexican, Barro's Pizza, Native Grill, Olive Garden, Paradise Cafe, Red Lobster, Rubio's, Taco Bell, TX Roadhouse $Tree, Cal Ranch, Firestone/auto, Old Navy, PetCo, Staples, TJ Maxx, Walgreens, S QT/dsl Augie's Grill, Austin's Rest., Burger Joint, Filiberto's Mexican, McDonald's, Panda Express, Pizza Hut, Senor Taco, Starbucks, Subway, Yan's Chinese Comfort Suites Ace Hardware, Fletcher Tire, Safeway Foods/dsl, Verizon, vet, Walgreens, Walmart
125	Sarival Ave, Cotton Lane (from wb)
125mm	Roosevelt Canal
124	AZ 303
123	Citrus Rd, to Cotton Ln, S Phoenix RV Park, Uhaul
122	Perryville Rd
121	Jackrabbit Trail, N Chevron/dsl, S Circle K/dsl CarQuest
120	Verrado Way, N Valero/dsl Culver's
117	Watson Rd, S Circle K/dsl Carl's Jr, Chipotle Mexican, Cracker Barrel, Denny's, Dunkin Donuts, El Pollo Loco, Federico's Mexican, Firehouse Subs, Jack-in-the-Box, KFC, Little Caesar's, McDonald's, Native NY Grill, Palermo's Pizza, Panda Express, Papa John's, Peter Piper Pizza, Subway, Taco Bell, Wendy's Holiday Inn Express $Tree, AT&T, AutoZone, Discount Tire, Fletcher's Tire, Fry's Foods/dsl, Lowe's, PetsMart, URGENT CARE, Verizon, vet, Walgreens, Walmart/McDonald's
114	Miller Rd, to Buckeye, S Chevron Travel Ctr/Sams Deli/grill/dsl/E85/LP/24hr, Loves/Chester's/Subway/dsl/scales/24hr, QT/dsl Burger King Days Inn Ford, Leaf Verde RV Park
112	AZ 85, to I-8, Gila Bend, S Subway (3mi)
109	Sun Valley Pkwy, Palo Verde Rd
104mm	Hassayampa River
103	339th Ave, S TA/Country Pride/Pizza Hut/Shell/Subway/Taco Bell/dsl/scales/LP/24hr/@ truckwash
98	Wintersburg Rd
97mm	Coyote Wash
95.5mm	Old Camp Wash
94	411th Ave, Tonopah, S Chevron/dsl, Mobil/dsl, Shell/Cafe Charro/Noble Roman's/Subway/dsl/LP/24hr Oscar's Place Cantina Saddle Mtn RV Park, tires/repair, USPO
86mm	**both lanes, full facilities, litter barrels, petwalk, vending**
81	Salome Rd, Harquahala Valley Rd
69	Ave 75E

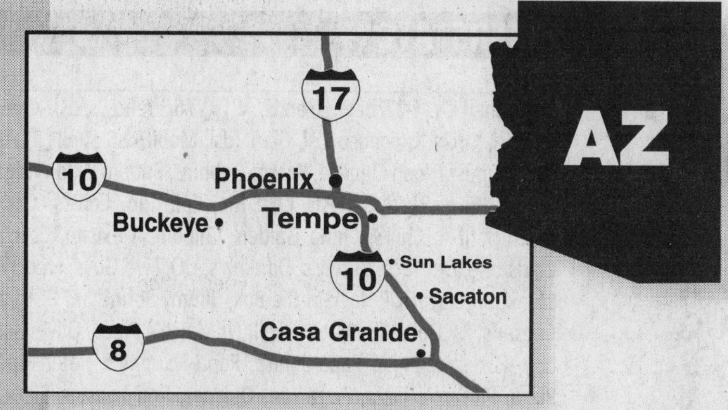

QUARTZSITE

53	Hovatter Rd
52mm	**both lanes, full facilities, litter barrels, petwalk, vending**
45	Vicksburg Rd, N Zip TC/Chevron/Subway/dsl/scales/LP/24hr, S Pride/Pizza Hut/dsl/scales/24hr Jobski's dsl Repair/towing, Kofa NWR, RV Park, tires
31	US 60 E, to Wickenburg, **12 mi** N camping, food
26	Gold Nugget Rd
19	Quartzsite, to US 95, Yuma, N Arco/dsl, Chevron/dsl, Shell/dsl Taco Mio Beall's, Family$, Roadrunner Foods, RV camping
18mm	Tyson Wash
17	US 95, AZ 95, Quartzsite, N Mobil/Burger King/LP/dsl, Pilot/DQ/Subway/dsl/scales/24hr Carl's Jr, McDonald's, Quartzsite Yacht Grill, Times 3 Rest. Stagecoach Motel/rest. $General, RV camping, tires/repair, S Loves/Chester's/Subway/dsl/24hr Super 8 Desert Gardens RV Park, Lifestyles RV Ctr
11	Dome Rock Rd
5	Tom Wells Rd, N Chevron/Subway/dsl/scales/24hr
4.5mm	**both lanes, full facilities, litter barrels, petwalk, vending**
3.5mm	**AZ Port of Entry, weigh sta**
1	Ehrenberg, to Parker, N 76/dsl, Texaco Family$, River Lagoon RV Resort, S FLYING J/Wendy's/dsl/LP/scales/lube/repair/tires/24hr Best Western
0mm	Arizona/California state line, Colorado River, mountain/pacific time zone

INTERSTATE 15

Exit #	Services
29.5mm	Arizona/Utah state line
27	Black Rock Rd
21mm	turnout sb
18	Cedar Pocket, S parking area, Virgin River Canyon RA/camping
16mm	**truck parking both lanes**
15mm	**truck parking nb**
14mm	**truck parking nb**
10mm	**truck parking nb**
9	Desert Springs
8.5mm	Virgin River
8	Littlefield, Beaver Dam, E RV park, **1 mi** W camping, food, gas/dsl, lodging
0mm	Arizona/Nevada state line, mountain/pacific time zone

AZ

INTERSTATE 17

FLAGSTAFF

Exit #	Services
341	McConnell Dr, **I-17 begins/ends**, N 76/Wendy's/dsl, Chevron/dsl, Circle K, Conoco/dsl, Giant/dsl, Mobil/dsl, Shell Arby's, August Moon Chinese, Baskin-Robbins, Buffalo Wild Wings, Burger King, Buster's Rest., Cafe Rio, Cafe Rio, Cane's, Carl's Jr, Chick-fil-A, Chili's, China Garden, Chipotle Mexican, Coco's, Coldstone, Del Taco, Denny's, Domino's, DQ, Five Guys, Freddy's Steakburgers, IHOP, Jack-in-the-Box, Jimmy John's, KFC, Little Caesar's, McDonald's, Native Grill, Ni Marco's Pizza, Olive Garden, Panda Express, Papa John's, Papa Murphy's, Peter Piper Pizza, Picazzo's Pizza, Pizza Hut, Quiznos, Red Lobster, Sizzler, Starbucks, Subway, Taco Bell Baymont Inn, Best Inn, Budget Inn, Canyon Inn, Comfort Inn, Courtyard, Days Inn, Drury Inn, EconoLodge, EconoLodge, Embassy Suites, GreenTree Inn, Hampton Inn, Hilton Garden, Knights Inn, La Quinta, Motel 6, Quality Inn, Sleep Inn, SpringHill Suites, Super 8 H, $Tree, AT&T, Barnes&Noble, Basha's Foods, Discount Tire, Jo-Ann Crafts, Kohl's, Michael's, O'Reilly Parts, Petsmart, Ross, Safeway, Sprouts Mkt, Staples, Target, Verizon, Walgreens, Walmart
340b a	I-40, E to Gallup, W to Kingman
339	Lake Mary Rd (from nb), Mormon Lake, E Circle K/dsl AZ Mtn Inn access to same as 341
337	AZ 89A S, to Sedona, Ft Tuthill RA, W camping
333	Kachina Blvd, Mountainaire Rd, E Mountainaire Rest. (1mi) Abineau B&B, W Shell/Subway/dsl county park
331	Kelly Canyon Rd
328	Newman Park Rd
326	Willard Springs Rd
322	Pinewood Rd, to Munds Park, E Shell/dsl, Woody's/ds Lone Pine Rest. golf, Motel in the Pines, W Chevron/dsl Munds RV Park
322mm	Munds Canyon
320	Schnebly Hill Rd
317	Fox Ranch Rd
316mm	Woods Canyon
315	Rocky Park Rd
313mm	scenic view sb, litter barrels
306	Stoneman Lake Rd
300mm	**runaway truck ramp sb**
298	AZ 179, to Sedona, Oak Creek Canyon, **7-15 mi** W Burger King, Cowboy Club Rest., Joey's Bistro Belrock Inn, Diamond Resort, Hilton, La Quinta, Radisson/cafe, Wildflower Inn Rancho Sedona RV Park
297mm	**both lanes, full facilities, litter barrels, petwalk, , , vending**
293mm	Dry Beaver Creek
293	Cornville Rd, McGuireville Rd, to Rimrock, E McGuireville Nikki's Grill, W 76/dsl, Conoco/Beaver Hollow/dsl El Patio Grill

CAMP VERDE

Exit #	Services
289	Middle Verde Rd, Camp Verde, E Chevron/dsl Sonic, The Gathering Rest. Cliff Castle Hotel/casino/rest. to Montezuma Castle NM, W Distant Drums RV Park
288mm	Verde River
287	AZ 260, to AZ 89A, Cottonwood, Payson, E Shell/Subway/dsl/RV dump/LP/24hr Burger King, Carl's Jr, Denny's, DQ, Gabriela's Mexican, Los Betos Mexican, McDonald's, Starbucks, Taco Bell Comfort Inn, Days Inn, Super 8 Territorial RV Park (1mi), Trails End RV Park, Zane Grane RV Park (9mi), W Chevron/Wendy's/dsl/24hr RV camping, to Jerome SP
285	Camp Verde, Gen Crook Tr, **3 mi** E Rio Verde Mexican Territorial Town Inn to Ft Verde SP, Trail End RV Park, Zane Gray RV Park (9mi)
281mm	safety pullout area nb
278	AZ 169, Cherry Rd, to Prescott
269mm	Ash Creek
268	Dugas Rd, Orme Rd
265.5mm	Agua Fria River
263b a	AZ 69 N, Cordes Jct Rd (262 from nb), to Prescott, E Chevron, Shell/Noble Roman's/Subway/dsl/LP/24hr Cafe Charo, McDonald's Cordes Jct Motel/RV Park Family$
259	Bloody Basin Rd, to Crown King, Horse Thief Basin RA
256	Badger Springs Rd
252	**Sunset Point, /scenic view both lanes, full facilities, , litter barrels, , vending**
248	Bumble Bee, W Horsethief Basin RA
244	Squaw Valley Rd, Black Canyon City, E Chilleen's on 17 BBQ/Steaks, W Shell Beni's Pizza Mountain Breeze Motel Bradshaw Mtn RV Resort (2mi), Family$
243.5mm	Agua Fria River
242	Rock Springs, Black Canyon City, E KOA (1mi), W 76/dsl, Shell Beni's Pizza, Rock Springs Cafe Bradshaw Mtn RV Resort, Mtn Breeze Motel Ron's Mkt
239.5mm	Little Squaw Creek
239mm	Moore's Gulch
236	Table Mesa Rd
232	New River, E RoadRunner Rest.
231.5mm	New River

ANTHEM

Exit #	Services
229	Anthem Way, Desert Hills Rd, E Circle K Hungry Howie's, McDonald's, Pizza Hut, Rosati's Pizza, Starbucks, Subway, Taco Bell, Wendy's CVS Drug, Safeway, URGENT CARE, W Chevron/dsl, Circle K/dsl Del Taco, Denny's, Fresca's Mexican, Subway Hampton Inn $Store, Anthem Outlets/famous brands/food court, Discount Tire, Harley-Davidson, Meineke, O'Reilly Parts, Tobias Auto, U-Haul, Walmart
227	Daisy Mtn Dr, E Circle K/dsl Cafe Provence, Domino's, Jack-in-the-Box, Roberto's Mexican, Starbucks, Streets of NY Deli, Streets of NY Deli, Subway CVS Drug, Fry's Foods, GNC, Verizon, vet
227mm	Dead Man Wash
225	Pioneer Rd, W Pioneer AZ Museum, Pioneer RV Park
223	AZ 74, Carefree Hwy, to Wickenburg, E Chevron AZool Grill, Chili's, Denny's, Good Egg Cafe, In-N-Out, McDonald's, Ray's Pizza, Starbucks, Subway, Taco Bell Albertson's/Osco, GNC, Home Depot, Kohl's, Staples, W Cibola Vista Camping (11mi)
222	Dove Valley
221	AZ 303, Senora Desert Dr
220	Dixileta (from nb)
219	Jomax Rd
218	Happy Valley Rd, E Circle K/dsl, Shell Applebee's, Bajio, Buffalo Wild Wings, Burger King, Carl's Jr, Chipotle Mexican, Coldstone, IHOP, Jack-in-the-Box, Jersey Mike's Subs, Joey's Hotdogs, Johnny Rocket's, L&L Hawaiian BBQ, Logan's Roadhouse, Mellow Mushroom Pizza, Olive Garden, Panda Express, Paradise Cafe, PF Chang's, Rays Pizza, Red Robin, Sauce Pizza, Shane's Ribshack, Smash Burger, Starbucks, Subway, TGIFriday's, Zupas Courtyard, Hampton Inn, Homewood Suites, Residence Inn $Tree, Barnes&Noble, Best Buy, Big O Tire, Dick's, Lowe's, Old Navy, O'Reilly Parts, PetCo, Ross, Staples, TJ Maxx, Verizon, vet, Walmart, World Mkt, W to Meg&DeLyle's

INTERSTATE 17 Cont'd

Exit #	Services
217	Pinnacle Peak Rd, E Drury Inn, Hilton Garden Phoenix RV Park
215a	Rose Garden Ln, same as 215b
215b	Deer Valley Rd, E Shell/Circle K Arby's, Armando's Mexican, Culvers, Dunkin Donuts, Jack-in-the-Box, McDonald's, Sonic, Subway, Taco Bell, Wendy's Little Dealer RV Ctr, W Arco/dsl, Circle K/dsl Cracker Barrel, Denny's, Times Square Italian, Waffle House Days Inn, Extended Stay America H, U-Haul
214c	AZ 101 loop
214b	Yorkshire Dr, W 7-11 Chick-fil-A, Chili's, Chipotle, In-N-Out, Jack-in-the-Box, Jimmy John's, Macaroni Grill, Pizza Hut, Wendy's Budget Suites H, AT&T, Costco/gas, Michael's, Petsmart, Ross, Target
214a	Union Hills Dr, E Circle K/dsl, Valero, W Arco/dsl Comfort Inn, Sleep Inn, Studio 6
212b a	Bell Rd, Scottsdale, to Sun City, E Chevron/dsl, Circle K, QT, Shell/dsl Big Apple Rest., Caramba Mexican, IHOP, Jack-in-the-Box, LJ Silver, Manuel's Mexican, McDonald's, Schlotzsky's, Shenanigan's Grill, Waffle House Fairfield Inn, Motel 6, Super 8 Big O Tire, Chevrolet, Chrysler/Jeep/Dodge, Discount Tire, Fiat, Ford, Honda, Hyundai, Kohl's, Lincoln, Mazda, Nissan, O'Reilly Parts, Sam's Club/gas, Toyota, U-Haul, Volvo, Walmart, W Applebee's, Denny's, Native New Yorker, US Egg Breakfast Red Roof Inn Fry's Foods/dsl
211	Greenway Rd, E Embassy Suites, La Quinta 7-11
210	Thunderbird Rd, E Circle K/dsl, Valero/dsl/LP Asian Cafe, Barro's Pizza, Hong Kong Chinese, Jack-in-the-Box, Macayo's Mexican, Pizza Hut/Taco Bell, Subway, Wendy's CVS Drug, Home Depot, Walgreens, W Jamba Juice, McDonald's, Port of Subs, Whataburger Travelodge Best Buy, Fry's Electronics, Lowe's
209	Cactus Rd, W 7-11, Chevron/dsl, QT/dsl China Harvest, Tuliaberto's Mexican Holiday Inn
208	Peoria Ave, E Fajita's, First Watch Cafe, Native Grill, Outback Steaks, Pappadeaux, Sweet Tomatoes Candlewood Suites, Comfort Suites, Crowne Plaza, Extended Stay America, Homewood Suites, Hyatt Place, W QT/dsl Black Angus, Buffalo Wild Wings, Burger King, Cane's, Chili's, Chipotle Mexican, Coldstone, Culvers, Fat Burger, Filiberto's Mexican, Hibachi Grill, Hooters, In-N-Out, Jason's Deli, Longhorn Steaks, Mi Pueblo, Mimi's Cafe, Mongolian BBQ, Old Country Buffet, Olive Garden, Peter Piper Pizza, Red Lobster, Sizzler, Souper Salad, Starbucks, Subway, TX Roadhouse, Wendy's Metro Plaza, Premier Inn $Tree, AT&T, Barnes&Noble, Dillard's, Discount Tire, Firestone/auto, Macy's, Michael's, PetCo, Petsmart, Ross, Staples, Tire Pros/repair, URGENT CARE, Verizon
208.5mm	Arizona Canal
207	Dunlap Ave, E Circle K, Shell/dsl Blimpie, Domino's, Fajitas, First Watch Cafe, Fuddrucker's, Jack-in-the-Box, Native Grill, Outback Steaks, Steaken Burger, Subway, Sweet Tomatoes, Wong's Comfort Suites, Courtyard, Mainstay Suites, Sheraton, SpringHill Suites, TownPlace Suites Aamco, CVS Drug, URGENT CARE, W Chevron/dsl Bobby-Q's Rest., Denny's, Schlotzsky's, Subway Woodspring Suites Midas, repair, U-Haul
206	Northern Ave, E Circle K/dsl, Shell/dsl Boston Mkt, Burger King, Del Taco, Denny's, Dunkin Donuts, El Pollo Loco, Gyros House, IHOP, Los Compadres, McDonald's, Papa John's, Pizza Hut, Starbucks, Subway, Uncle Tony's Pizza Best

SCOTTSDALE

PHOENIX

AZ

Exit #	Services
206	Continued Western Albertson's/Osco, AutoZone, Sprouts Mkt, URGENT CARE, Walgreens, W Arco, QT DQ Motel 6, Residence Inn, Super 8 $General, auto repair, vet
205	Glendale Ave, E 7-11, QT Pizza Patron, Subway Ace Hardware, Fry's Foods/dsl, repair, transmissions, vet, W Circle K/dsl Jack-in-the-Box, Lenny's Burger 7-11, O'Reilly Parts, to Luke AFB, Walgreens
204	Bethany Home Rd, E Arco, Chevron/dsl, Shell/Church's/dsl Carl's Jr, Dunkin Donuts, KFC, Mandarin Buffet, McDonald's, Papa Joe's, Pizza Hut/Taco Bell, Subway, Tulioberto's Mexican, Whataburger H, $Tree, BigLots, Costco/gas, JC Penney, Petsmart, Ross, Target, URGENT CARE, Walgreens, Walmart, W Shell, Valero Burger King, Familia Lorito, Great Dragon Knights Inn auto repair, Food City, Jiffy Lube, Savers
203	Camelback Rd, E Church's, Country Boy's Rest., Filiberto's Mexican, Little Caesars $General, Chrysler/Dodge/Jeep, Discount Tire, Family$, Hyundai, Kia, W Circle K/dsl, QT DQ, Jack-in-the-Box, McDonald's Quality Inn AutoZone, to Grand Canyon U, USPO
202	Indian School Rd, E Arco/dsl Domino's, Federico's Mexican, Pizza Hut, Subway Ace Hardware, CVS Drug, Food City, Little RV Ctr, W Shell, Sinclair/dsl, Valero/dsl Lenny's Burgers Motel 6, Travel Inn 7-11, Wide World of Maps
201	Thomas Rd, E Chevron/McDonald's/playplace Arby's, Denny's, Dunkin Donuts, Jack-in-the-Box, Starbucks Days Inn, La Quinta Circle K, W Carl's Jr, Subway NAPA
200b	McDowell Rd, Van Buren, E Purcell's Tire, W Knights Inn
200a	I-10, W to LA, E to Phoenix
199b	Jefferson St (from sb), Adams St (from nb), Van Buren St (from nb), E Circle K Jack-in-the-Box to st capitol, W Circle K/gas La Canasta Mexican Penny Pincher Parts, PepBoys
199a	Grant St
198	Buckeye Rd (from nb)
197	US 60, 19th Ave, Durango St, E Jack-in-the-Box, to St Capitol, Whataburger $General, AutoZone
196	7th St, Central Ave, W Shell/dsl
195b	7th St, Central Ave, E Circle K/dsl Jack-in-the-Box, McDonald's, Taco Bell EZ 8 Motel H, NAPA Care
195a	16th St (from sb, no EZ return), E Shell/Subway/dsl Burger King to Sky Harbor Airport
194	I-10 W, to AZ 151, to Sky Harbor Airport

I-17 begins/ends on I-10, exit 150a

PHOENIX

AZ

INTERSTATE 19

TUCSON

Exit #	Services
I-19 uses kilometers (km)	
101b a	I-10, E to El Paso, W to Phoenix. **I-19 begins/ends on I-10, exit 260.**
99	AZ 86, Ajo Way, **E** Circle K, Shell Eegee's Cafe, Hamburger Stand, Peter Piper Pizza, Pizza Hut, Subway, Taco Bell, Wienerschnitzel H, auto repair, Family$, Fry's Foods, GNC, Goodyear/auto, U-Haul, URGENT CARE, vet, Walgreens, **W** Circle K, QT/dsl, Shell/dsl Burger King, Church's, Domino's, Little Caesars, Losbetos Mexican, McDonald's $General, city park, Family$, Food City, Jiffy Lube, museum, to Old Tucson
98	Irvington Rd, **E** Arco/dsl Jimmy John's, TX Roadhouse AutoZone, Fry's Foods/drug/dsl, **W** Chevron, Circle K/dsl Buffalo Wild Wings, China Olive Buffet, Coldstone, Five Guys, McDonald's, Olive Garden, Panda Express, Peter Piper Pizza, Red Lobster, Starbucks, Subway $Tree, AT&T, Best Buy, Discount Tire, Family$, Food City, Home Depot, JC Penney, Marshall's, Michael's, Old Navy, Petsmart, Ross, Target, Verizon
95b a	Valencia Rd, **E** Circle K, Shell Chickenuevo, Church's, Donut Wheel, Eegee's Cafe, Jack-in-the-Box, Little Caesars, McDonald's, Peter Piper Pizza, Sonic, Subway, Whataburger, Yokohama Asian $General, $Tree, Aamco, AutoZone, Brake Masters, Family$, Food City, Jiffy Lube, O'Reilly Parts, to ✈, USPO, Walgreens, **W** Circle K/dsl Arby's, Burger King, Carl's Jr, Casa Valencia, Chili's, China Dragon, Denny's, DQ, El Taco Tote, Golden Corral, Grand Buffet, Hamburger Stand, Little Caesars, Papa John's, Papa Murphy's, Pizza Hut, Subway, Taco Bell, Wendy's 99c Store, Big O Tire, BigLots, CVS Drug, Lowe's, repair, transmissions, URGENT CARE, Walgreens, Walmart
92	San Xavier Rd, **W** to San Xavier Mission (2mi)
91.5km	Santa Cruz River
87	Papago Rd
80	Pima Mine Rd, **E** Agave Rest., Diamond Casino

GREEN VALLEY

Exit #	Services
75	Helmut Peak Rd, to Sahuarita, **E** Shell/dsl/e-85 Asian Sky Rest, Dunkin Donuts/Baskin Robbins, Mama's Hawaiian BBQ, McDonald's, Starbucks, Subway Fry's Foods/drug, USPO, vet
69	US 89 N, Duval Mine Rd., Green Valley, **E** 50's Diner, Carl's Jr., Denny's, Little Caesars, Panda House, Pizza Hut, Rigoberto's, Subway 99c Store, Ace Hardware, AutoZone, BigLots, Fletcher's Repair, Jo-Ann Fabrics, O'Reilly Parts, Petco, Ross, Verizon, Walgreens, Walmart/Subway, **W** Circle K Arby's, Burger King, Domino's, Jerry Bob's Rest., Manuel's Mexican, Papa Murphy's, Starbucks, Taco Bell Holiday Inn Express Big O Tire, Ford/Hyundai, Green Valley RV Resort, NAPA, Safeway/dsl, Titan Missile Museum, URGENT CARE, USPO, vet
65	Esperanza Blvd, to Green Valley, **E** Shell/repair/dsl, **W** AZ Family Rest., La Placita Mexican Best Western/rest, Comfort Inn Ace Hardware, Walgreens
63	Continental Rd, Green Valley, **E** Quail Creek Rest. (7mi) golf, San Ignacio Golf Club/rest., USPO, **W** Chevron/HotStuff Pizza KFC, McDonald's, Starbucks CVS Drug, Merle's Parts, repair/tires, Safeway, to Madera Cyn RA, TrueValue, Verizon, Walgreens
56	Canoa Rd, **W** San Ignacio Inn, Wyndham Resort
54km	**both lanes, full facilities, litter barrels, petwalk, vending**
48	Arivaca Rd, Amado, **2-3 mi E** Amado Inn DeAnza RV Resort (2mi), Mtn View RV Park, **W** Cow Palace Rest. Amado Mkt/gas, JJ's Auto Repair

AMADO

Exit #	Services
42	Agua Linda Rd, to Amado, **E** Mtn View RV Park
40	Chavez Siding Rd, Tubac, **E** Tubac Golf Resort
34	Tubac, **E** El Mercado Elvira's Cafe, Tubac Deli, Tubac Hamburgers, Tubac Jack's Rest., Tubac Pizza to Tubac Presidio SP, Tubac Golf Resort, Tubac Mkt, USPO
29	Carmen, Tumacacori, **E** to Tumacacori Nat Hist Park, food, gas, lodging
25	Palo Parado Rd
22	Pec Canyon Rd
17	Rio Rico Dr, Calabasas Rd, **W** Chevron/dsl/LP Hua Mei Chinese, Nickles Diner, Wood Oven Pizza Esplendor Resort IGA Foods, JC Auto Repair/Lube, USPO, vet
12	AZ 289, to Ruby Rd, **E** Pilot/Wendy's/dsl/scales/24hr, **W** to Pena Blanca Lake RA

NOGALES

Exit #	Services
8	AZ 82 (exits left from sb, no return), Nogales, **E** Circle K Mi Casa RV Park
4	AZ 189 S, Mariposa Rd, Nogales, **E** FasTrip/dsl Bella Mia Rest., China Buffet, Chuyitos Hotdogs, City Salads, DQ, Dragon Buffet, Exquisito Mexican, Gorilla Pizza, Jack-in-the-Box, KFC, Little Caesars, McDonald's, Panda Express, Panda Express, Pizza Pollis, Subway, Toscanos Mariposa Hotel, Motel 6 $General, $Tree, Ace Hardware, AutoZone, Buick/GMC, Chevrolet, Ford, GNC, Home Depot, JC Penney, Petsmart, Ross, Safeway, Walgreens, Walmart/McDonald's (N Grand Ave), **W** Circle K/dsl Carl's Jr, IHOP Best Western, Candlewood Suites, Holiday Inn Express Mexico Insurance
1b	Western Ave, Nogales
1a	International St
0km	**I-19 begins/ends in Nogales**, Arizona/Mexico Border, **1/2 mi N** Circle K, Jr's Fuel Depot/dsl, Shell Church's, Denny's, Jack-in-the-Box, McDonald's, Peter Piper Pizza, Pizza Hut, Subway AutoZone, CarQuest, Family$, Food City, museum, NAPA, O'Reilly Parts, PepBoys

INTERSTATE 40

Exit #	Services
359.5mm	Arizona/New Mexico state line
359	Grants Rd, to Lupton, **N Welcome Ctr/ both lanes, full facilities, litter barrels, petwalk,** Speedy's/dsl/rest./24hr Tee Pee Trading Post/rest., YellowHorse Indian Gifts
357	AZ 12 N, Lupton, to Window Rock, **N** USPO
354	Hawthorne Rd
351	Allentown Rd, **N** Chee's Indian Store, Indian City Gifts
348	St Anselm Rd, Houck, **N** Ft Courage Food/gifts
347.5mm	Black Creek
346	Pine Springs Rd
345mm	Box Canyon

CHAMBERS

Exit #	Services
344mm	Querino Wash
343	Querino Rd
341	Ortega Rd, Cedar Point, **N** Armco/gas/gifts
340.5mm	**insp/weigh sta both lanes**
339	US 191 S, to St Johns, **S** Conoco/dsl Family$, RV Park, USPO
333	US 191 N, Chambers, **N** to Hubbell Trading Post NHS, USPO, **S** Mobil/dsl Days Inn/rest.
330	McCarrell Rd
325	Navajo, **S** Shell/Subway/Navajo Trading Post/dsl/24hr
323mm	Crazy Creek
320	Pinta Rd
316mm	Dead River
311	Painted Desert, **N** Painted Desert/dsl Painted Desert, Petrified Forest NP

AZ

INTERSTATE 40 Cont'd

Exit #	Services
303	Adamana Rd, N Stewarts/gifts, S Painted Desert Indian Ctr
302.5mm	Big Lithodendron Wash
301mm	Little Lithodendron Wash
300	Goodwater
299mm	Twin Wash
294	Sun Valley Rd, N Root 66 RV camping, S Knife City
292	AZ 77 N, to Keams Canyon, N Conoco/Burger King/dsl/24hr dsl repair
289	Lp 40, Holbrook, N Chevron/dsl, Hatch's/dsl Denny's, Mesa Rest. Best Western, Days Inn, EconoLodge, Howard Johnson, Motel 6, Quality Inn, Sahara Inn, Travelodge Goodyear
	HOLBROOK
286	Navajo Blvd, Holbrook, N 76/dsl, Circle K, Maverik/dsl Aliberto's Mexican, Burger King, Carl's Jr, Hilltop Cafe, McDonald's, Taco Bell, Tom & Suzie's 66 Motel, Lexington Inn, Super 8 $General, KOA, OK RV Park, O'Reilly Parts, Econolodge, Taco Bell, S Chevron/dsl, Fuel Express/dsl, MiniMart/gas, Speedy Dsl DQ, Rte 66 Cafe Best Value, El Rancho Motel/rest., Knights Inn H, Dodge/Ford/Lincoln, museum, rockshops, Scotty & Son Repair, SW Transmissions, Little Caesars
285	US 180 E, AZ 77 S, Holbrook, **1 mi** S Giant/dsl Butterfield Steaks Economy Inn, Globetrotter Hotel, Wigwam Motel Best Hardware, Family$, **RS/ /litter barrels**, Safeway, to Petrified Forest NP
284mm	Leroux Wash
283	Perkins Valley Rd, Golf Course Rd, S TA/Shell/Popeyes/dsl/scales/24hr/@
280	Hunt Rd, Geronimo Rd, N Geronimo Trading Post
277	Lp 40, Joseph City, N Loves/Chester's/Subway/scales/dsl/24hr, S RV camping, to Cholla Lake CP
274	Lp 40, Joseph City, N food, gas, lodging, RV camping
269	Jackrabbit Rd, S Jackrabbit Trading Post
264	Hibbard Rd
257	AZ 87 N, to Second Mesa, N camping, to Homolovi Ruins SP, S trading post
256.5mm	Little Colorado River
	WINSLOW
255	Lp 40, Winslow, N Winslow Fuel/dsl Mi Pueblo Mexican Best Western+ Take-A-Rest RV Park, S FLYING J/Denny's/dsl/LNG/scales/RV Dump/24hr Sonic Chrysler/Dodge/Jeep, Nissan, RS
253	N Park Dr, Winslow, N Chevron, Maverik/dsl Capt Tony's Pizza, Pizza Hut $General, Ford, O'Reilly Parts, tires/lube, Walmart/Subway, AutoZone, Carl's Jr, S Alfonso's Mexican, LJ Silver/Taco Bell, McDonald's, Subway Motel 6, Quality Inn, Travelodge H, Family$, NAPA, Safeway, China Town
252	AZ 87 S, Winslow, S 76/dsl Entre Chinese EconoLodge, Rodeway Inn
245	AZ 99, Leupp Corner
239	Meteor City Rd, Red Gap Ranch Rd, S to Meteor Crater
235mm	**RS both lanes, full facilities, info, litter barrels, petwalk,**
233	Meteor Crater Rd, S Mobil/Meteor Crater RV Park/dump to Meteor Crater NL
230	Two Guns
229.5mm	Canyon Diablo
225	Buffalo Range Rd
219	Twin Arrows, N Twin Arrows Resort/Casino
218.5mm	Padre Canyon
211	Winona, N Shell/dsl/repair

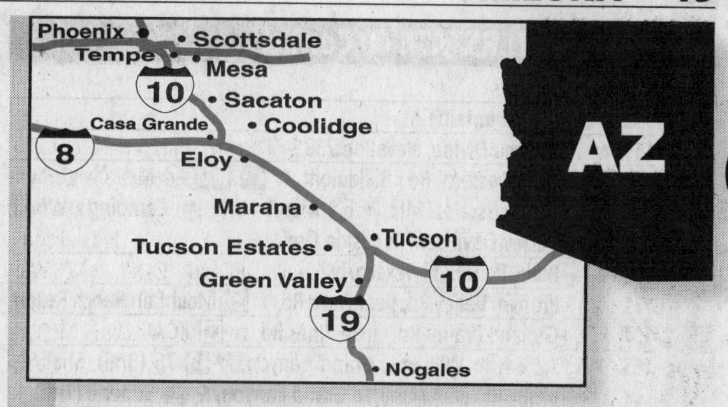

Exit #	Services
207	Cosnino Rd
204	to Walnut Canyon NM
201	US 89, Flagstaff, to Page, N 76/Express Stop/dsl, Chevron/dsl, Circle K/dsl, Maverik/dsl, Shell, VP/dsl Burger King, Del Taco, Denny's, Jack-in-the-Box, LJ Silver/Taco Bell, McDonald's, Pizza Hut, Sizzler, Village Inn, Wendy's Best Western, Country Inn Suites, Days Inn, Howard Johnson, Mtn View Inn, Super 8, Travelodge H, auto repair, Best Buy, Chrysler/Dodge/Jeep/Fiat, CVS Drug, Dillard's, Discount Tire, Evert's RV Center, Family$, Family$, Home Depot, Honda, JC Penney, KOA, Marshall's, Nissan/Subaru, Old Navy, O'Reilly Parts, Pepboys, PetCo, Safeway/dsl, Toyota, Tuesday Morning, VW, World Mkt, S Mobil/dsl, Shell/dsl Oregano's Pizza Fairfield Inn, Hampton Inn, Sonesta Suites, Wyndham Resort
	FLAGSTAFF
198	Butler Ave, Flagstaff, N Chevron, Conoco/dsl, Shell Burger King, Country Host Rest., Cracker Barrel, Culver's, Denny's, McDonald's, Outback Steaks, Sonic, Starbucks, Subway, Taco Bell, Texas Roadhouse Comfort Inn, Holiday Inn Express, Howard Johnson, La Quinta, Motel 6, Quality Inn, Ramada, Rodeway Inn, Super 8 AutoZone, NAPA, Sam's Club/gas, U-Haul, vet, Walgreens, Walmart, S Mobil, Sinclair/Little America/dsl/motel/@ Black Bart's Steaks/RV Park
197.5mm	Rio de Flag
195b	US 89A N, McConnell Dr, Flagstaff, N 76/Wendy's/dsl, Chevron, Chevron/dsl, Circle K, Conoco/dsl, Giant/dsl, Mobil/dsl, Shell Arby's, August Moon Chinese, Baskin-Robbins, Buffalo Wild Wings, Burger King, Buster's Rest., Cafe Rio, Cane's, Carl's Jr, Chick-fil-A, Chili's, China Garden, Chipotle Mexican, Coco's, Coldstone, Country Host Rest., Del Taco, Denny's, Domino's, DQ, Dunkin Donuts, Five Guys, Freddy's Steakburgers, IHOP, Jack-in-the-Box, Jimmy John's, Little Caesar's, McDonald's, Native Grill, Ni Marco's Pizza, Olive Garden, Panda Express, Papa John's, Papa Murphy's, Peter Piper Pizza, Picazzo's Pizza, Pizza Hut, Quiznos, Red Lobster, Sizzler, SmashBurger, Starbucks, Subway, Taco Bell Baymont Inn, Best Inn, Budget Inn, Canyon Inn, Comfort Inn, Courtyard, Days Inn, Drury Inn, EconoLodge, Embassy Suites, GreenTree Inn, Hampton Inn, Hilton Garden, Howard Johnson, Knights Inn, La Quinta, Motel 6, Quality Inn, Sleep Inn, SpringHill Suites, Super 8 H, $Tree, AT&T, Barnes&Noble, Basha's Foods, Discount Tire, GNC, Jo-Ann Crafts, Kohl's, Michael's, Natural Grocers, O'Reilly Parts, Petsmart, Ross, Safeway, Sprouts Mkt, Staples, Target, Verizon, Walgreens, Walmart
195a	I-17 S, AZ 89A S, to Phoenix
192	Flagstaff Ranch Rd
191	Lp 40, to Grand Canyon, Flagstaff, **5 mi** N Chevron, Maverik, Whistle Stop/dsl Galaxy Diner Best Value, Budget Host, Comfort Inn, Days Inn, EconoLodge, Radisson, Super 8, Travel Inn, Travelodge CarQuest, Chevrolet/Cadillac, Home Depot, Kia, Kit Carson RV Park, O'Reilly Parts, vet, Woody Mtn Camping

AZ

INTERSTATE 40 Cont'd

Exit #	Services
190	A-1 Mountain Rd
189.5mm	Arizona Divide, elevation 7335
185	Transwestern Rd, Bellemont, N Pilot/McDonald's/Subway/dsl/scales/24hr/@ Motel 6, S Camping World, Harley-Davidson/Roadside Grill
178	Parks Rd, N Texaco/dsl
171	Pittman Valley Rd, Deer Farm Rd, S Mountain Ranch Resort
167	Garland Prairie Rd, Circle Pines Rd, N KOA
165	AZ 64, to Williams, Grand Canyon, N 76 (8mi), Shell/dsl (4mi) KOA (4mi), to Grand Canyon, S Super 8 (1mi)
	WILLIAMS
163	Williams, N Chevron/dsl, Loves/Arby's/dsl/scales/24hr Quality Inn Canyon Gateway RV Park, S Circle K, Mobil/dsl, Mustang/dsl, Shell/dsl Jack-in-the-Box, KFC/Taco Bell, McDonald's, Old Town Rest., Pancho's Mexican, Pine Country Rest., Pizza Hut, Red Garter Rest, Rod's Steaks, Rte 66 Diner, Twisters Soda Fountain Canyon Motel/RV Park, EconoLodge, El Rancho Motel, Grand Canyon Railway Hotel, Howard Johnson, Knights Inn, Mountainside Motel, Ramada Inn, Rodeway Inn, Rodeway Inn, The Lodge Motel, Travelodge $General, same as 161, USPO
161	Lp 40, Golf Course Dr, Williams, N RV camping, 0-3 mi S Circle K, Conoco/dsl/LP, Shell Buffalo Pointe Inn, DQ, Jessica's Rest., Maria's Tacos AZ Motel, Best Value, Best Western, Budget Host, Canyon Country Inn, Comfort Inn, Days Inn, Grand Canyon Hotel, Highlander Motel, Motel 6, Westerner Motel H, Family$, Safeway, to Grand Canyon Railway
157	Devil Dog Rd
155.5mm	**litter barrels, safety pullout wb**
151	Welch Rd
149	Monte Carlo Rd, N dsl repair
148	County Line Rd
146	AZ 89, to Prescott, Ash Fork, N Mobil/dsl, Shell/dsl Lulu Belle's BBQ, Ranch House Cafe Ash Fork Inn Family$
144	Ash Fork, N Ash Fork Inn Grand Canyon RV Park, museum/info, USPO, S Chevron/Piccadilly's/dsl, Texaco/dsl/RV Park auto/RV repair
139	Crookton Rd, to Rte 66
	SELIGMAN
123	Lp 40, to Rte 66, to Grand Canyon Caverns, Seligman, N Chevron/A&W, Shell/dsl Copper Cart Cafe, Lilo's Rest., Pizza Joint, Snow Cap Burgers Canyon Lodge, Deluxe Inn, Stagecoach 66 Motel, Supai Motel KOA (1mi), repair, USPO, S Chevron/Subway/dsl, (same as 121)
121	Lp 40, to Rte 66, Seligman, N 76/dsl, Chevron/A&W Copper Cart Cafe, Lilo's Rest., Roadkill Cafe Canyon Lodge, Route 66 Motel/pizza, Supai Motel KOA (1mi), repair (same as 123), to Grand Canyon Caverns, USPO
109	Anvil Rock Rd
108mm	Markham Wash
103	Jolly Rd
96	Cross Mountain Rd
91	Fort Rock Rd
87	Willows Ranch Rd
86mm	Willow Creek
79	Silver Springs Rd
75.5mm	Big Sandy Wash
73.5mm	Peacock Wash
71	US 93 S, to Wickenburg, Phoenix
66	Blake Ranch Rd, N Petro/Iron Skillet/dsl/scales/24hr/@ Blake Ranch RV Park, SpeedCo Lube
60mm	Frees Wash
59	DW Ranch Rd, N Loves/Chester's/Subway/dsl/scales/24hr Hualapai Mtn Park (9mi), truckwash
57mm	Rattlesnake Wash
	KINGMAN
53	AZ 66, Andy Devine Ave, to Kingman, N FLYING J/Denny's/dsl/LP/scales/24hr, Chevron/dsl, Maverik/dsl, Terrible's/dsl, Texaco/dsl Arby's, Burger King, Denny's, Jack-in-the-Box, McDonald's, Pizza Hut, Taco Bell Days Inn, EconoLodge, Knights Inn, Motel 6, Super 8, Travelodge $General, Basha's Foods, Blue Beacon, dsl/tire repair, Freightliner, Goodyear, Harley-Davidson, KOA (1mi), S Mobil/dsl, Shell/dsl/repair ABC Chinese, JB's, Oyster's Mexican, Sonic Best Western, Comfort Inn, Days Inn, High Desert Inn, Holiday Inn Express, Magnuson, Rodeway Inn, Rte 66 Motel, SpringHill Suites Chrysler/Dodge/Jeep, Kia, NAPA, Sunrise RV Park, Uptown Drug
51	Stockton Hill Rd, Kingman, N Arco/dsl, Chevron, Circle K/dsl Carl's Jr, Chili's, Chipotle Mexican, Cracker Barrel, Del Taco, Domino's, Five Guys, Golden Corral, IHOP, In-N-Out, KFC, McDonald's, Panda Express, Papa John's, Papa Murphy, Plaza Bonita, Scotty's Rest., Sonic, Starbucks, Subway, Taco Bell Hampton Inn H, $General, $Tree, AutoZone, AZ RV Depot/repair, BigLots, BrakeMasters, Buick/Chevrolet, CVS Drug, Discount Tire, Ford/Lincoln, Home Depot, Honda, Hyundai, Oil Can Henry's, O'Reilly Parts, PetCo, Petsmart, Ross, Safeway/gas, Smith's Foods/dsl, Staples, Superior Tire, TrueValue, Verizon, vet, Walgreens, Walmart, S Circle K Kingman Co Steaks, Little Caesars, Paco's Mexican, Pizza Hut Home 2 Suites 99cent Store, CarQuest, Family$, JC Penney, Safeway/dsl, Sears
48	US 93 N, Beale St, Kingman, N 76/dsl, Chevron/dsl, Mobil/dsl, Shell/dsl, TA/Country Pride/Popeye's/dsl/scales/24hr @, Texaco/dsl, USA/Subway/dsl, Woody's Wendy's Budget Inn, Economy Inn, Tristate Inn 4A Tire/auto/RV repair, S Chevron/Quiznos/dsl Calico's Rest., Carl's Jr AZ Inn, Motel 6 city park, Ft Beale RV Park, Mohave Museum
46.5mm	Holy Moses Wash
44	AZ 66, Oatman Hwy, McConnico, to Rte 66, S Crazy Fred's/café/dsl Canyon West RV Camping (3mi), truckwash
40.5mm	Griffith Wash
37	Griffith Rd
35mm	Black Rock Wash
32mm	Walnut Creek
28	Old Trails Rd
26	Proving Ground Rd, S AZ Proving Grounds
25	Alamo Rd, to Yucca, N USPO
23mm	**both lanes, full facilities, litter barrels, petwalk, , , vending**
21mm	Flat Top Wash
20	Santa Fe Ranch Rd
18.5mm	Illavar Wash
15mm	Buck Mtn Wash
13.5mm	Franconia Wash
13	Franconia Rd
9	AZ 95 S, to Lake Havasu City, Parker, London Br, S Chevron/dsl, Loves/Carl's Jr/Subway/dsl/scales/24hr, Pilot/Wendy's/dsl/scales/24hr Havasu RV Park, Prospectors RV Resort
4mm	**weigh sta both lanes**
2	Needle Mtn Rd
1	Topock Rd, to Bullhead City, Oatman, N camping, food, gas, to Havasu NWR
0mm	Arizona/California state line, Colorado River, Mountain/Pacific time zone

ARKANSAS

INTERSTATE 30

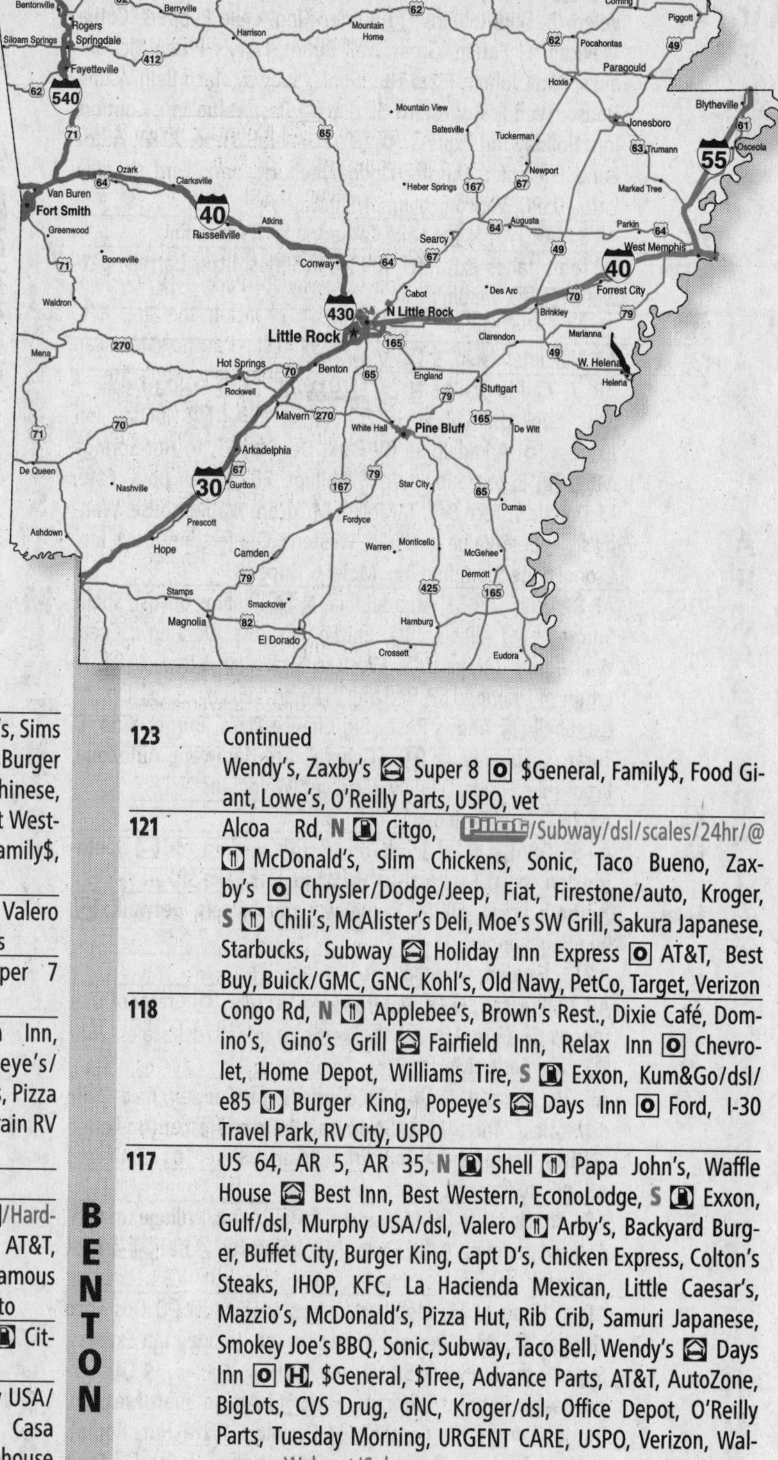

LITTLE ROCK

Exit #	Services
I-30 begins/ends on I-40, exit 153b.	
143b a	I-40, E to Memphis, W to Ft Smith
142	15th St, S Super Stop/dsl
141b	US 70, Broadway St, downtown, N Exxon, U.S. Fuel Burger King U-Haul, Verizon Arena, S Phillips 66, Valero/dsl KFC/LJ Silver, McDonald's, Popeye's, Taco Bell, Wendy's Family$
141mm	Arkansas River
141a	AR 10, Cantrell Rd, Markham St (from wb), W to downtown
140	9th St, 6th St, downtown, N Phillips 66, Shell Pizza Hut Holiday Inn USPO, S SuperStop Comfort Inn
139b	I-630, downtown
139a	AR 365, Roosevelt Rd, N Exxon Sim's BBQ AutoZone, S Shell Family$, Kroger
138b	I-530 S, US 167 S, US 65 S, to Pine Bluff
138a	I-440 E, to Memphis, S
135	W 65th St, N Exxon/dsl, Shell/dsl, Valero/dsl Budget Host, S Rodeway Inn
134	Scott Hamilton Dr, S Exxon/dsl Best Value Inn, Motel 6
133	Geyer Springs Rd, N Exxon, Hess, Mobil Church's, Sims BBQ, Subway, S Citgo, Phillips 66, Shell Arby's, Burger King, El Chico, KFC, Little Caesar's, McDonald's, Panda Chinese, Rally's, Sonic, Taco Bell, Waffle House, Wendy's Best Western, Comfort Inn, Quality Inn, Rest Inn CVS Drug, Family$, Goodyear/auto, Kroger/gas, Walgreens
132	US 70b, University Ave, N RaceWay/dsl, SuperStop, Valero Best Value Inn, S Kum&Go/dsl O'Reilly Parts
131	McDaniel Dr, N U-Haul, S Economy Inn, Super 7 Inn Firestone

MABELVALE

Exit #	Services
130	AR 338, Baseline Rd, Mabelvale, N Cimarron Inn, EconoLodge Harley-Davidson, S Shell/Popeye's/dsl Applebee's, China Buffet, Dixie Cafe, McDonald's, Pizza Hut, Sonic, Taco Bueno, Wendy's $Tree, Chevrolet, Crain RV Ctr, GNC, Home Depot, URGENT CARE, Walmart/Subway
129	I-430 N
128	Otter Creek Rd, Mabelvale West, N Loves/Hardee's/Subway/dsl/scales/24hr David's Burger AT&T, Bass Pro Shop, Cavender's, Little Rock Outlets/famous brands, S Exxon/dsl Super 8 Purcell Tire/auto
126	AR 111, County Line Rd, Alexander, N Shell/dsl, S Citgo/Subway Cherokee RV Park/dump (4mi)
123	AR 183, Reynolds Rd, to Bryant, Bauxite, N Murphy USA/dsl, Shell Arby's, Backyard Burgers, Burger King, Casa Mexicana, Cracker Barrel, Dickey's BBQ, Domino's, Firehouse Subs, Great Wall Buffet, IHOP, KFC, Papa John's, Pasta Jack's Italian, Pizza Hut, Ruby Tuesday, Subway, Ta Molly's, Taste of D-Light, Waffle House, Whole Hog Cafe Berkshire Inn, Best Value Inn, Comfort Inn, Hampton Inn, Holiday Inn Express, Hometown Hotel, La Quinta $Tree, AT&T, AutoZone, CVS Drug, Tire Pros, vet, Walgreens, Walmart/Subway, S Exxon/dsl, Kum&Go/dsl/e85, Mapco/dsl/e85, Valero/dsl Bryant Cafe, Chick-fil-A, Dunkin Donuts, Hardee's, Little Caesar's, Logan's Roadhouse, McDonald's, Mi Ranchito, Sonic, Taco Bell,

BENTON

Exit #	Services
123	Continued Wendy's, Zaxby's Super 8 $General, Family$, Food Giant, Lowe's, O'Reilly Parts, USPO, vet
121	Alcoa Rd, N Citgo, Pilot/Subway/dsl/scales/24hr/@ McDonald's, Slim Chickens, Sonic, Taco Bueno, Zaxby's Chrysler/Dodge/Jeep, Fiat, Firestone/auto, Kroger, S Chili's, McAlister's Deli, Moe's SW Grill, Sakura Japanese, Starbucks, Subway Holiday Inn Express AT&T, Best Buy, Buick/GMC, GNC, Kohl's, Old Navy, PetCo, Target, Verizon
118	Congo Rd, N Applebee's, Brown's Rest., Dixie Café, Domino's, Gino's Grill Fairfield Inn, Relax Inn Chevrolet, Home Depot, Williams Tire, S Exxon, Kum&Go/dsl/e85 Burger King, Popeye's Days Inn Ford, I-30 Travel Park, RV City, USPO
117	US 64, AR 5, AR 35, N Shell Papa John's, Waffle House Best Inn, Best Western, EconoLodge, S Exxon, Gulf/dsl, Murphy USA/dsl, Valero Arby's, Backyard Burger, Buffet City, Burger King, Capt D's, Chicken Express, Colton's Steaks, IHOP, KFC, La Hacienda Mexican, Little Caesar's, Mazzio's, McDonald's, Pizza Hut, Rib Crib, Samuri Japanese, Smokey Joe's BBQ, Sonic, Subway, Taco Bell, Wendy's Days Inn H, $General, $Tree, Advance Parts, AT&T, AutoZone, BigLots, CVS Drug, GNC, Kroger/dsl, Office Depot, O'Reilly Parts, Tuesday Morning, URGENT CARE, USPO, Verizon, Walgreens, Walmart/Subway
116	Sevier St, N Citgo/dsl, Exxon Troutt Motel, S Phillips 66 Capri Inn
114	US 67 S, Benton, S Valero/McDonald's/dsl Sonic $General
113mm	insp sta both lanes
111	US 70 W, Hot Springs, N Cloud 9 RV Park, to Hot Springs NP
106	Old Military Rd, N Alon/JJ's Rest./dsl/scales/@, S JB'S RV Park
99	US 270 E, Malvern, S H

INTERSTATE 30 Cont'd

MALVERN

Exit #	Services
98b a	US 270, Malvern, Hot Springs, N Valero/dsl Super 8, S Murphy USA/dsl, Phillips 66/dsl, Shell/dsl, Valero, Valero/Baskin-Robbins Burger King, Chile Peppers, Cotija Mexican, El Parian, Great Wall Buffet, Larry's Pizza, McDonald's, Papa John's, Pizza Hut, Sonic, Subway, Taco Bell, Waffle House, Wendy's, Western Sizzlin Best Value Inn, Comfort Inn, Holiday Inn Express H, $General, $Tree, AT&T, AutoZone, Chevrolet, Chrysler/Dodge/Jeep, city park, Ford, O'Reilly Parts, USPO, Verizon, Walmart/Subway
97	AR 84, AR 171, N Lake Catherine SP, RV camping
93mm	**(both lanes exit left), full facilities, litter barrels, petwalk, , , vending**
91	AR 84, Social Hill
83	AR 283, Friendship, S Valero/dsl
78	AR 7, Caddo Valley, N Pilot/PJ Fresh Deli/dsl/scales/24hr, Shell/dsl, Valero/dsl Cracker Barrel Holiday Inn Express Arkadelphia RV Park, De Gray SP, to Hot Springs NP, S Exxon/Subway/dsl, Phillips 66 Fat Boys Cafe, McDonald's, Taco Bell, TaMolly's Mexican, Waffle House, Wendy's Best Value Inn, Best Western, Comfort Inn, Days Inn, EconoLodge, Hampton Inn, Motel 6, Super 8
73	AR 8, AR 26, AR 51, Arkadelphia, N Phillips 66/dsl, Shell/Stuckey's Allen's BBQ, Chicken Express, Domino's, Great Wall Buffet, McDonald's, Western Sizzlin $Tree, AT&T, to Crater of Diamond SP, Verizon, Walmart/Subway, S Exxon/dsl, Shell Andy's Rest., Big Cheese Pizza, Burger King, El Torero's, Subway H, $General, Ace Hardware, AutoZone, Brookshire Foods, O'Reilly Parts, vet, Walgreens
69	AR 26 E, Gum Springs
63	AR 53, Gurdon, N South Fork Trkstp/Citgo/rest./dsl Southfork Inn, S Shell/dsl to White Oak Lake SP
56mm	**both lanes, full facilities, litter barrels, petwalk, , vending, vending**
54	AR 51, Gurdon, Okolona
46	AR 19, Prescott, N Valero/cafe/dsl/24hr Crater of Diamonds SP (31mi), S Love's/Hardee's/dsl/scales/24hr Casa Carlos Mexican
44	AR 24, Prescott, N TA/Country Pride/Subway/Taco Bell/dsl/scales/24hr/@, S Norman's 44 Trkstp/rest/dsl/scales/@ Best Value Inn to S Ark U, truckwash
36	AR 299, to Emmett
31	AR 29, Hope, N Shell/dsl Relax Inn, Village Inn/RV park st police, S Exxon/dsl, Valero/dsl KFC Best Value Inn H
30	AR 4, Hope, N Mobil/dsl, Murphy USA/dsl Dos Loco Gringos Best Western, Hampton Inn, Holiday Inn Express, Super 8 Millwood SP, Verizon, Walmart/Subway, S Exxon/Baskin-Robbins/Wendy's, Shell Amigo Juan Mexican, Burger King, Little Caesar's, McDonald's, Pizza Hut, Roma's Italian, Sonic, Subway, Taco Bell, Waffle House Days Inn H, $Tree, AT&T, AutoZone, Buick/Chevrolet/GMC, Bumper Parts, Ford, Fred's, Old Washington Hist SP, O'Reilly Parts, Super 1 Foods/gas, Walgreens
26mm	**weigh sta both lanes**
18	rd 355, Fulton, N Red River Trkstp/dsl
17mm	Red River
12	US 67 (from eb), Fulton
7mm	**Welcome Ctr eb, full facilities, info, litter barrels, petwalk, , , vending**
7	AR 108, Mandeville, N FLYING J/Denny's/dsl/LP/24hr Sunrise RV Park truckwash
3	I-49, N to Ft Smith, S to Shreveport
2	Four States Fair Pkwy, Texarkana, N RoadRunner/dsl, Shell/Circle K/dsl, S Camp I-30 Trkstp Ferguson Fairpark, Nick's RV Ctr
1	US 71, Jefferson Ave, Texarkana, N Copeland's Rest., Johnny Tamales Best Western, Comfort Suites, Hampton Inn, Holiday Inn, Holiday Inn Express KOA, S Country Host Inn
0mm	Arkansas/Texas state line

ARKADELPHIA

HOPE

INTERSTATE 40

WEST MEMPHIS

Exit #	Services
285mm	Arkansas/Tennessee state line, Mississippi River
284mm	**weigh sta wb**
281	AR 131, S to Mound City
280	Club Rd, Southland Dr, N Blu/dsl/LNG/24hr, Pilot/Wendy's/dsl, S FLYING J/Denny's/dsl/LP/24hr, Love's/Subway/dsl, Petro/Iron Skillet/dsl/24hr/@ KFC/Taco Bell, McDonald's Best Western, Deluxe Inn, Express Inn, Super 8 Blue Beacon, SpeedCo Lube
279b	I-55 S (from eb)
279a	Ingram Blvd, N Margaritas Mexican Days Inn, Homegate Inn, Knights Inn, Red Roof Inn Ford, Southland Racetrack, S Citgo/dsl, Phillips 66, Shell /dsl Cross Creek Rest., Waffle House Best Value Inn, Clarion, EconoLodge, Hampshire Inn, Motel 6, Ramada, Relax Inn
278	AR 77, 7th St, Missouri St, **N Welcome Ctr/ /full facilities, , litter barrels, petwalk,** Shell/dsl, **S on Missouri** Exxon, MapCo, Phillips 66/dsl, Shell Applebee's, Burger King, Cracker Barrel, Domino's, Krystal, Lenny's Subs, Little Caesar's, McDonald's, Papa John's, Pizza Hut, Popeye's, Shoney's, Subway, Taco Bell, Wendy's Comfort Suites, Extend Suites, Holiday Inn Express H, $Tree, Goodyear/auto, Kroger/dsl, Walgreens, Walmart
277	I-55 N, to Jonesboro
276	AR 77, Rich Rd, to Missouri St (from eb, same as 278), S Exxon, MapCo, Murphy Express/dsl, Phillips 66/dsl, Shell Applebee's, Burger King, Domino's, Fusion Buffet, Krystal, Lenny's Subs, Little Caesar's, McDonald's, Mi Pueblo Mexican, Papa John's, Pizza Hut, Popeye's, Shoney's, Subway, Taco Bell, Wendy's Extend Suites H, $Tree, AT&T, Family$, Goodyear/auto, Kroger/dsl, Walgreens, Walmart
275	AR 118, Airport Rd, S Shell/DQ/dsl Huddle House city park, URGENT CARE
274mm	**weigh sta eb, parking area wb**
271	AR 147, to Blue Lake, S Exxon/Chester's/dsl, Valero/dsl tires, to Horseshoe Lake
265	US 79, AR 218, to Hughes
260	AR 149, to Earle, N Citgo/Subway, TA/Country Pride/Burger King/Taco Bell/dsl/scales/24hr/@, Valero/dsl Relax Inn Shell Lake Camping, S Citgo dsl repair
256	AR 75, to Parkin, Parkin Archeological Park (12mi)
247	AR 38 E, to Widener
245mm	St Francis River
243mm	**wb, full facilities, litter barrels, petwalk, , , vending**
242	AR 284, Crowley's Ridge Rd, N H, to Village Creek SP
241b a	AR 1, Forrest City, N Citgo/DQ/dsl, Shell/Popeye's/dsl Don Jose Mexican, HoHo Chinese, Wendy's Best Value, Comfort Suites, Days Inn, Econolodge, Hampton Inn, Holiday Inn Express, Luxury Inn, Super 8 st police, S Citgo/dsl, Exxon/dsl, Murphy USA/dsl, Shell/dsl Burger King, Domino's,

FORREST CITY

INTERSTATE 40 Cont'd

241b a Continued
Dragon China, Iguanas Mexican, KFC, McDonald's, Ole Sawmill Cafe, Pizza Hut, Sonic, Subway, Taco Bell, Waffle House Quality Inn, Red Roof Inn $Tree, AT&T, Food Giant, Fred's, O'Reilly Parts, Save-A-Lot Foods, Verizon, Walgreens, Walmart

239 AR 1, to Wynne, Marianna

235mm eb, full facilities, litter barrels, petwalk, , vending

234mm L'Anguille River

233 AR 261, Palestine, N Loves/Chester's/Subway/dsl/scales/24hr Rest Inn, S Exxon/dsl

221 AR 78, Wheatley, N SweetPea/dsl/repair, S MapCo/Subway/dsl, Valero/Pitstop/diner/dsl

BRINKLEY

216 US 49, AR 17, Brinkley, N Citgo, Mobil/dsl Best Inn, Days Inn, EconoLodge, Super8/RV Park, Sure Stay dsl repair, KFC/Taco Bell, Los Piños Mexican, S Exxon/Baskin-Robbins/dsl, Shell, Victory/dsl Gene's BBQ, McDonald's, New China, Pizza Hut, Sonic, Subway, Waffle House Heritage Inn/RV Park $General, AT&T, Family$, Fred's, Kroger, O'Reilly Parts

205mm Cache River

202 AR 33, to Biscoe

200mm White River

199mm both lanes, full facilities, litter barrels, no , , vending

193 AR 11, to Hazen, N Exxon/Chester's/dsl Lower White River RV Park, S Citgo/dsl, Loves/Carl's Jr/dsl/scales/24hr El Amigo Mexican Super 8, Travel Inn

183 AR 13, Carlisle, S Citgo, Conoco/dsl, Exxon/Subway/dsl, Valero/dsl Nick's BBQ, Pizza 'N More, Sonic Days Inn $General

LONOKE

175 AR 31, Lonoke, N Phillips 66, Valero/dsl Burger King, Marachi Mexican, McDonald's, Waffle House Best Western, Days Inn, Economy Inn, Hampton Inn, Holiday Inn Express AT&T, Verizon, Walmart, S Shell/Subway KFC/Taco Bell, Pizza Hut, Sonic Perry's Motel $ Tree, $General, Goodyear/auto, O'Reilly Parts, vet

173 AR 89, Lonoke

169 AR 15, Remington Rd

165 Kerr Rd

161 AR 391, Galloway, N Loves/Chester's/subs/dsl/scales/24hr Camping World RV Ctr, S IA-80 TruckOMat/dsl/scales, LNG, Petro/Iron Skillet/dsl/scales/24hr/@, Pilot/Subway/Pizza Hut/dsl/scales/24hr Days Inn Blue Beacon, dsl repair, Freightliner, Southern Tire Mart, SpeedCo, Burger King

159 I-440 W, S

157 AR 161, to US 70, N Exxon/dsl, S Hess, Mobil/dsl, Shell/dsl, Valero/dsl Burger King, McDonald's, Sonic, Taco Bell Days Inn, EconoLodge, Quality Inn, Red Roof Inn, Rest Inn, Super 8 Family$

156 Springhill Dr, N Kum&Go/dsl, Mapco/dsl, Murphy USA/dsl Cracker Barrel Candlewood Suites, Fairfield Inn, Hilton Garden, Holiday Inn Express, Residence Inn, Walmart

155 US 67 N, US 167, to Jacksonville (exits left from eb), Little Rock AFB, **0-3 mi N on US 167/McCain Blvd** Murphy USA/dsl, Phillips 66/dsl, Shell, Valero/dsl Arby's, Bar Louie, BJ's Rest., Buffalo Wild Wings, Burger King, Cactus Jacks, Carino's Italian, Chick-fil-A, Chili's, ChuckECheese's, Chuy's TexMex, CiCi's Pizza, Corky's BBQ, David's Burgers, Dixie Cafe, El Porton Mexican, Firehouse Subs, Five Guys, Fox & Hound, Golden Corral, Hog Wild Cafe, Hooters, IHOP, Jason's Deli, Jimmy John's, Kanpai Japanese, McDonald's, Newk's Eatery, Old Chicago

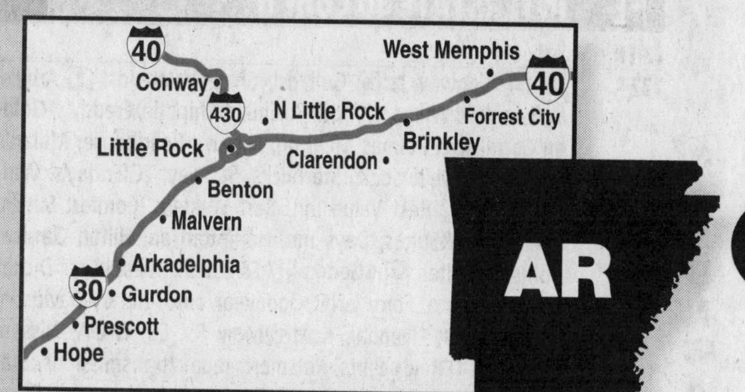

AR

LITTLE ROCK

155 Continued
Pizza, Olive Garden, On-the-Border, Outback Steaks, Panera Bread, Pizza Hut, Popeyes, Rally's, Red Lobster, Saddle Creek Grill, Sonic, Subway, Super King Buffet, Taco Bell, Taziki's Mediterranean, TGIFriday's, TX Roadhouse, US Pizza, Waffle House, Wendy's Candlewood Suites, Comfort Inn, Courtyard, Hampton Inn, Hilton Garden, Holiday Inn Express, La Quinta, Motel 6, Super 8 H, $Tree, Aamco, AT&T, Barnes&Noble, Best Buy, BigLots, Books-A-Million, Buick/GMC, Chevrolet, Chrysler/Dodge/Jeep, Dillard's, Firestone/auto, Ford, Home Depot, Honda, Hyundai, JC Penney, Jo-Ann, Kia, Kroger, Lincoln, Lowe's, Mazda, Michael's, Nissan, Office Depot, PepBoys, PetCo, Petsmart, Ross, Sam's Club/gas, Steinmart, Target, TJ Maxx, Toyota, URGENT CARE, Verizon, vet, VW, Walgreens, Walmart/Subway, Dick's, Freddy's, Hideaway Pizza, Saltgrass Steaks, Whole Hog Cafe

154 to Lakewood (from eb)

153b I-30 W, US 65 S, to Little Rock

153a AR 107 N, JFK Blvd, N Exxon, Mapco/dsl, Shell Schlotzsky's Best Value Inn vet, S Exxon Bogie's Grill Best Western+, Motel 6, Quality Inn, Red Roof Inn, Super Stay Inn H, USPO, Baymont Inn, Murphy Express/dsl, Taco Bueno

152 AR 365, AR 176, Camp Pike Rd, Levy, N Exxon, Shel Burger King, KFC, Little Caesar's, McDonald's, Mexico Chiquito, Pizza Hut, Señor Tequila, Sonic, Subway, Taco Bell, US Pizza, Waffle House $General, AutoZone, Family$, Kroger/gas, O'Reilly Parts, S Shell Chicken King H, Family$, Save a Lot

150 AR 176, Burns Park, Camp Robinson, S camping, info

148 AR 100, Crystal Hill Rd, N Shell, S Citgo/dsl, Exxon/dsl KOA

147 I-430 S, to Texarkana

142 AR 365, to Morgan, N Shamrock, Valero/dsl Razorback Inn Bumper Parts, Trails End RV Park, S Kum&Go/dsl, Shell/dsl KFC, McDonald's, Razorback Pizza, Smokeshack BBQ, Subway, Waffle House Best Value Inn, Holiday Inn Express, Quality Inn $General, Autozone

135 AR 365, AR 89, Mayflower, N Hess/dsl, S Exxon/dsl, Valero Sonic, Subway $General, Harp's Mkt

134mm **truck parking both lanes**

132 Baker-Wills Pkwy, S VP Fuel

129 US 65B, AR 286, Conway, N Sam's Club/dsl On the Border $Tree, AT&T, BAM!, Buick/GMC, Kia, Michael's, Petco, Ross, David's Burgers, Hideaway Pizza, Red Robin, Rita's Custard, Subway, S Exxon/dsl, MapCo/dsl Subway H, Chevrolet, Chrysler/Dodge/Jeep, Honda, st police, to Toad Suck SP, Toyota, Burge's Cafe, Meineke, URGENT CARE

AR

INTERSTATE 40 Cont'd

Exit #	Services
127	US 64, Conway, N Gulf/dsl, Shell, Valero/dsl Arby's, Buffalo Wild Wings, Chick-fil-A, Chili's, Chipotle, Freddy's, Golden Corral, Las Palmas Mexican, Logan's Roadhouse, Mulan's Buffet, Popeye's, Sonic, Starbucks, Subway, TGIFriday's, Waffle House Best Value Inn, Best Western, Comfort Suites, Country Inn&Suites, Days Inn, Hampton Inn, Hilton Garden, Home 2 Suites $General, AT&T, Belk, Best Buy, Dick's, Firestone/auto, Ford, GNC, Goodyear/auto, Harley-Davidson, Home Depot, Hyundai, Kohl's, Moix RV Ctr, NAPA, Nissan, Old Navy, O'Reilly Parts, Petsmart, repair/transmissions, Staples, Target, TJ Maxx, to Lester Flatt Park, Verizon, vet, Blaze Pizza, S RaceWay, Shell/dsl, Valero/dsl Burger King, Church's, Colton's Steaks, Dunkin Donuts/Baskin Robbins, Jimmy John's, LJ Silver, McDonald's, Rally's, Saigon Rest., Taco Bell, Tacos 4 Life, Taziki's Mediterranean, Wendy's, Whole Hog Cafe Kings Inn AutoZone, BigLots, Family$, Fred's Drugs, Hobby Lobby, Kroger/gas, tires, Walgreens, Captain Hook's, CVS
125	US 65, Conway, N Conoco/dsl, Exxon/Subway/dsl China Town, Cracker Barrel, El Acapulco Mexican, McDonald's, Mkt-Place Deli Quality Inn $Tree, JC Penney, Office Depot, Sears, S Citgo, CNG, Horton's, Mobil/dsl, Murphy USA/dsl Burger King, Cast Iron Skillet, CiCi's Pizza, David's Burgers, Dixie Cafe, Firehouse Subs, Fuji Steaks, IHOP, Los Potrillos Mexican, McAlister's Deli, Mexico Chiquito, New China, Outback Steaks, Panera Bread, Ruby Tuesday, Russo's Italian Kitchen, Sonic, Starbucks, Subway, Waffle House, Wendy's Candlewood Suites, Comfort Inn, Fairfield Inn, Holiday Inn Express, Howard Johnson, La Quinta, Microtel, Motel 6, Super 8 H, Advance Parts, AT&T, Lowe's, tires, Walmart
124	AR 25 N, to Conway, S Alon/Hess/dsl, Kum&Go/dsl DQ, KFC, Popeye's H, vet
120mm	Cadron River
117	to Menifee
112	AR 92, Plumerville, N Exxon/dsl, S Country Store/ds USPO
108	AR 9, Morrilton, N Ford/Lincoln, S Murphy USA, Shell/Pizza Pro/dsl, Valero Chop Stix, Colton's Steaks, Hardees, Mama DeLuca's Pizza, McDonald's, Ortega's Mexican, Pizza Hut, Sonic, Subway, Taco Bell, Waffle House, Wendy's Holiday Inn Express, Super 8 H, $General, Ace Hardware, AT&T, Chrysler/Dodge/Jeep, Kroger, NAPA, to Petit Jean SP (21mi), Verizon, vet, Walmart, AutoZone, Blue Diamond Cafe
107	AR 95, Morrilton, N Sunoco/dsl Best Value Inn I-40/107 RV Park, S Loves/Subway/dsl/24hr Morrilton Drive Inn, Yesterdays Rest. Days Inn Bumper Parts
101	Blackwell, N Blackwell TrkStp/Citgo/Domino's/diner/dsl/scales/24hr Utility Trailer Sales
94	AR 105, Atkins, N Exxon/Subway/dsl, VP/McDonald's/dsl El Parian Mexican, Sonic $General, S Casey's/dsl Cash Saver Foods
88	Pottsville, S $General, truck repair/wash
84	US 64, AR 331, Russellville, N FLYING J/Denny's/dsl/scales/LP/24hr, Shell/dsl Ivys Cove RV Retreat, S Phillips 66, Pilot/Subway/Wendy's/dsl/scales Chick-fil-A, CiCi's Pizza, Hardee's, McDonald's, Mulan's Buffet, Sonic, Waffle House Comfort Inn, Quality Inn H, $Tree, AT&T, Belk, Buick/Chevrolet/GMC, Chrysler/Dodge/Jeep, GNC, Hobby Lobby, Hyundai, JC Penney, K-Mart, Lowe's, Nissan, Petsmart, Ross, Staples, TJ Maxx, Toyota, USPO
83	AK 326, Weir Rd, S Phillips 66/dsl, Walmart Gas/dsl Buffalo Wild Wings, DQ, McAlisters Deli, Popeye's, Starbucks, Steak'n Shake, Subway, Sumo, Taco Bell, Taco John's Comfort Inn $General, AutoZone, Firestone/auto, Ford/Lincoln, Mazda, NAPA, O'Reilly Parts, Verizon, Walmart/McDonald's, Zaxby's, Chili's
81	AR 7, Russellville, N SuperStop/dsl CJ's Burgers Motel 6 $General, Outdoor RV Ctr/Park, Courtyard, S Exxon/dsl, Phillips 66/dsl, Shell Arby's, Burger King, Cagle's Mill Rest., Colton's Steaks, Cracker Barrel, Dixie Café, Firehouse Subs, IHOP, La Huerta Mexican, New China, Ruby Tuesday, Subway, Waffle House Best Value, Best Western, Clarion, Days Inn, Econolodge, Fairfield Inn, Hampton Inn, La Quinta, Super 8 RV camping, to Lake Dardanelle SP
80mm	Dardanelle Reservoir
78	US 64, Russellville, S Darrell's Mkt Fat Daddy's BBQ H, Mission RV Park, to Lake Dardanelle SP
74	AR 333, London
72mm	**wb, full facilities, litter barrels, petwalk, , , vending**
70mm	**overlook wb, litter barrels**
68mm	**eb, full facilities, litter barrels, petwalk, , , vending**
67	AR 315, Knoxville, S USPO
64	US 64, Clarksville, Lamar, S Valero/dsl Dad's Dream RV Park
58	AR 21, AR 103, Clarksville, N Casey's/dsl, Shell, Valero Emerald Dragon Chinese, KFC, La Chiquita Mexican, McDonald's, Pizza Hut, Subway, Taco Bell, Waffle House Best Western, Executive Inn, Quality Inn, Super 8 H, $General, Buick/Chevrolet, S Murphy USA/dsl Arby's, China Fun, Wendy's $Tree, AT&T, Chrysler/Dodge/Jeep, Ford, Walmart/Subway
57	AR 109, Clarksville, N Fuel Stop/dsl Sonic, Subway Family$, Harp's Mkt, S Shell/Steak'n Shake/dsl Truckwash, TrueValue
55	US 64, AR 109, Clarksville, N Hardee's, Kountry Kitchen Grille Hampton Inn, Holiday Inn Express, Sunset Inn, S Valero/AutoTruck/dsl st police
47	AR 164, Coal Hill
41	AR 186, Altus, N Swiss Family Rest., S Wiederkehr Rest. (4mi) winery (4mi)
37	AR 219, Ozark, S Loves/Subway/dsl/scales/24hr, Valero/McDonald's/dsl KFC/Taco Bell Best Value Inn H
36mm	**both lanes, full facilities, litter barrels, petwalk, , **
35	AR 23, Ozark, N Valero/Red Hog BBQ/dsl/scales Hillbilly Hideout Rest, 3 mi S Oxford Inn, Ozark Inn H, Aux Arc Park (5mi), to Mt Magazine SP (20 mi)
24	AR 215, Mulberry, S Vine Prairie Park
20	Dyer, N Short Stop/dsl, S Phillips 66/dsl, Shell/dsl Mill Creek Inn
13	US 71 N, to Fayetteville, N Shell, Sunoco/dsl Burger King, Catfish Hole, China Fun, Cracker Barrel, KFC, La Fiesta Mexican, Pizza Parlor, Subway, Taco Bell Quality Inn $General, Crabtree RV Ctr/Park, KOA (2mi), Lake Ft Smith SP, O'Reilly Parts, to U of AR, Bumper Parts, Hog Pizza, S Murphy USA/dsl, Valero/dsl, Workman's Braum's, Geno's Pizza, McDonald's, Pizza Hut, Sonic Days Inn AT&T, Coleman Drug, Harp's Foods, Shoppers Value Foods, Walgreens, Walmart, $Tree
12	I-49 N, to Fayetteville, N to Lake Ft Smith SP
9mm	**weigh sta both lanes**
7	I-540 S, US 71 S, to Ft Smith, Van Buren, S H

CONWAY

MORRILTON

RUSSELLVILLE

CLARKSVILLE

INTERSTATE 40 Cont'd

VAN BUREN

Exit #	Services
5	AR 59, Van Buren, N Citgo/dsl, Murphy USA/dsl, VP Fuels Arby's, Burger King, Chili's, Domino's, Firehouse Subs, Golden Wok, La Fiesta Mexican, Little Caesar's, McDonald's, Starbucks, Zaxby's Best Western, Hampton Inn $Tree, Advance Parts, AT&T, CVS Drug, Lowe's, NAPA, USPO, Verizon, Walmart/Subway, Aldi, Tropical Cafe, S Casey's/dsl, Shell/dsl Braum's, Geno's Pizza, KFC/Taco Bell, La Fresas Mexican, Sonic, Subway, Waffle House, Wendy's Holiday Inn Express, Sleep Inn, Super 8 $General, Grizzle Tire, Outdoor RV Park, Shoppers Value Foods, truckwash, vet, Walgreens, Colton's Steaks, Frank's Italian
3	Lee Creek Rd, N Shell/dsl Park Ridge Camping
2.5mm	**Welcome Ctr eb, full facilities, info, litter barrels, petwalk, vending**
1	to Ft Smith (from wb), Dora
0mm	Arkansas/Oklahoma state line

INTERSTATE 49 (Fayetteville)

BENTONVILLE

Exit #	Services
93	US 71B, Bentonville, **I-49 begins/ends on US 71 N.**
88	AR 72, Bentonville, Pea Ridge, E Casey's River Grille Courtyard, Simmon's Suites, W Kum&Go/dsl, Shell/dsl Smokin' Joe's Ribs Walmart Visitors Ctr
86	US 62, AR 102, Bentonville, Rogers, E TownePlace Suites Pea Ridge NMP, Sam's Club/gas, Walmart Mkt, W Shell/dsl Arby's, Dunkin Donuts, McDonald's, Sonic, Subway, Taco Bell ValuePlace
85	US 71B, AR 12, Bentonville, Rogers, E Conoco/dsl Abuelo's, Applebee's, Arby's, Atlanta Bread, Boar's Nest, Carino's Italian, Chick-fil-A, Chili's, Colton's Steaks, Copeland's Rest., Dixie Café, Freddy's Burgers, IHOP, Logan's Roadhouse, McDonald's, Napoli's Pizza, On-the-Border, Outback Steaks, Quiznos, Red Robin, Sonic, Starbucks Candlewood Suites, Country Inn&Suites, Fairfield Inn, Hampton Inn, Homewood Suites, Hyatt Place, Mainstay Suites, Residence Inn AT&T, Barnes&Noble, Beaver Lake SP, Belk, Firestone/auto, Jo-Ann, Kohl's, Lowe's, Marshalls, Office Depot, PetCo, Prairie Creek SP, Ross, Staples, Verizon, W Kum&Go/dsl, Murphy Express/dsl, Shell Azul Tequila Mexican, Billy Sims BBQ, Braum's, Buffalo Wild Wings, Chipotle, Cracker Barrel, Denny's, Firehouse Subs, HoneyBaked Ham, Jimmy John's, Joe's Italian, Jonny Brusco's Pizza, Krispy Kreme, Lenny's Subs, Lin's Garden, Mama Fu's Asian, McAlister's Deli, Panera Bread, Shogun Japanese, Smashburger, Starbucks, Subway, Taco Bueno, Taziki's Mediterranean Cafe, Village Inn, Waffle House, Whole Hog Cafe, Zaxby's Best Western, Comfort Suites, Days Inn, DoubleTree Hotel, EconoLodge, Hilton Garden, Holiday Inn Express, La Quinta, Microtel, Motel 6, Sheraton, SpringHill Suites, Super 8 H, BMW, Buick/GMC, Cadillac, Chevrolet, Christian Bros Auto, Chrysler/Dodge/Jeep, Honda, Hyundai, Kia, Mazda, Mercedes, Nissan, Toyota, URGENT CARE
83	AR 94 E, Pinnacle Hills Pkway, E Phillips 66 After 5 Grill, Bariola's Pizza, ChuckECheese's, Dickey's BBQ, Firehouse Subs, Five Guys, Genghis Grill, Jimmy John's, Maddio's Pizza, Mojitos Mexican, Olive Garden, Panda Express, Qdoba, Red Lobster, Slim Chickens, Starbucks, Steak'n Shake, Taco Bell H, Home Depot, Horse Shoe Bend Park, URGENT CARE, Walgreens, W Bonefish Grill, Carrabba's, Coldstone, Crabby's Seafood Grill, Grub's Grille, Mellow Mushroom, Ruth's

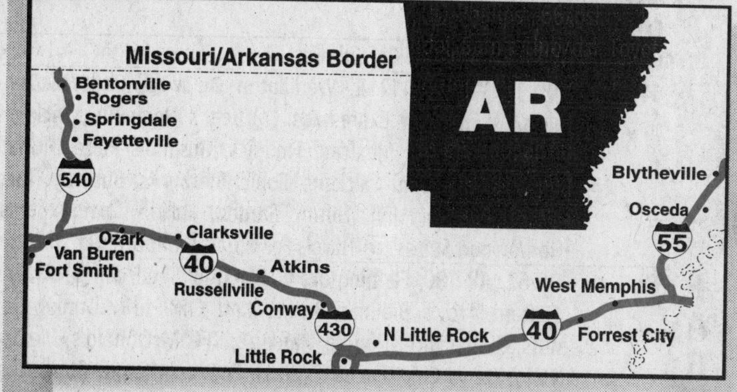

FAYETTEVILLE

Exit #	Services
83	Continued Chris Steaks, Subway, The Egg&I, Theo's, Tropical Smoothie ALoft, Embassy Suites, Holiday Inn, Staybridge Suites
82	Promenade Blvd, E Fish City Grill, Food Pavilion, Houlihan's, Longhorn Steaks, Mimi's Cafe, PF Chang's, Twin Peaks, TX Land&Cattle H, AT&T, Best Buy, Cabela's, Dillard's, Fresh Mkt, GNC, Gordman's, Hancock Fabrics, JC Penney, Old Navy, Petsmart, Target, TJMaxx, Verizon, W Chuy's Mexican, Deluxe Cafe, Pei Wei, Roma Italian Walmart Mkt/dsl
81	Pleasant Grove Rd, E Murphy USA/dsl Backyard Burger, Chick-fil-A, Golden Corral, Gusano's Pizzaria, McDonald's, Moe's SW, Papa Murphy's, Starbucks, Subway, Taco Bueno, Whataburger Burlington, Cavender's, Firestone/auto, Walgreens, Walmart, W Casey's/dsl
78	AR 264, Lowell, Cave Sprgs, Rogers, E Kum&Go/dsl, Shell/dsl Arby's, Dickey's BBQ, Domino's, DQ, KFC, LJ Silver, McDonald's, Sonic, Subway, Taco Bell $General, auto repair, Camping World RV Ctr, Super 8, W Kum&Go/dsl
76	Wagon Wheel Rd, E Shell/Subway/dsl to Hickory Creek Park
73	Elm Springs Rd, E Kum&Go/dsl, VP/dsl Eureka Pizza, Patrick's Burgers, Whataburger ValuePlace Chevrolet, Family$, W Shell/dsl, Walmart/dsl McDonald's, MJ Pizzaria, Panda Express Walmart
72mm	**weigh sta nb**
72	US 412, Springdale, Siloam Springs, E Citgo/dsl, Kum&Go/dsl, Phillips 66 Angus Jack's Burgers, Applebee's, Braum's, Denny's, Dickey's BBQ, Golden Dragon Buffet, Guadalajara Grill, Jimmy John's, Little Caesar's, McDonald's, Mkt Place Rest., Panda, Sonic, Subway, Sunset Grill, Taco Bell, Waffle House, Wendy's, Western Sizzlin Comfort Inn, DoubleTree Hotel, Extended Stay America, Fairfield Inn, Hampton Inn, Holiday Inn, La Quinta, Residence Inn, Royal Inn, Sleep Inn, Super 8 $General, AT&T, Big O Tire, Harp's Mkt, Kenworth/Volvo Trucks, Lowe's, Office Depot, O'Reilly Parts, URGENT CARE, Verizon, Walgreens, W Casey's/dsl, Murphy Express/dsl, Pilot/Burger King/dsl/scales/24hr Arby's, Buffalo Wild Wings, Cracker Barrel, Domino's, Flying Burrito, Jose's Mexican, McDonald's, Popeye's, Rib Crib, Subway, Taco Bueno, Tropical Smoothie Buick/GMC, Harp's Mkt/dsl, Hobby Lobby, NW RV Ctr
71mm	**weigh sta sb**
70	Don Tyson Pkwy, E Casey's/dsl, Walmart/dsl Walmart Mkt
69	Johnson Mill Blvd, Johnson, E Inn at the Mill Rest. Inn at the Mill, TownePlace Suites
67	US 71B, Fayetteville, E H
66	AR 112, Garland Ave, E Phillips 66/dsl, W Acura, Chevrolet, Fiat, Honda, Hyundai, Sam's Club/dsl, Toyota

= gas = food = lodging = other = rest stop

AR

INTERSTATE 49 (Fayetteville) Cont'd

FARMINGTON

Exit #	Services
65	Porter Rd, W Kia, Subaru
64	AR 16 W, AR 112 E, Wedington Dr, W Citgo/McDonald's/dsl, Murphy Express/dsl Boar's Nest BBQ, Dickey's BBQ, El Matador Mexican, Freddy's, Gusano's Pizza, Hunan Manor, IHOP, Slim Chickens, Sonic, Starbucks, Subway, Taco Bell Comfort Inn, Hilton Garden, Holiday Inn Express, Homewood Suites Harp's Food/gas, Walmart Mkt
62	US 62, AR 180, Farmington, E Citgo, Shell/dsl Andy's Custard, Arby's, Braum's, Burger King, Chick-fil-A, Dunkin Donuts, Ginger Rice&Noodle, Hardee's, KFC, McDonald's, Mexico Viejo, Ozzys Cafe, Panda Express, Popeye's, Sonic, Starbucks, Subway, Taco Bell, Taco Bueno, Thai Wok, Waffle House, Wendy's, Whataburger, Zaxby's Best Western, Candlewood Suites, EconoLodge Bumper Parts, W Murphy USA/dsl Denny's, Firehouse Subs, Lucy's Diner, Papa Murphy's, Pavilion Buffet, Ruby Tuesday Baymont Inn, Days Inn, Hampton Inn, Regency 7 Motel, Super 8, ValuePlace $Tree, Aldi Foods, AT&T, AutoZone, Lowe's, Verizon, Walgreens, Walmart/McDonald's
61	US 71, to Boston Mtn Scenic Lp, sb only
60	AR 112, AR 265, Razorback Rd, E Staybridge Suites Southgate RV Park, to U of AR
58	Greenland, W Phillips 66/McDonalds/dsl/scales/24hr Sonic
53	AR 170, West Fork, E Harp's/dsl Harp's Mkt, Winn Creek RV Resort (4mi), W to Devils Den SP
45	AR 74, Winslow, W to Devils Den SP
41mm	Bobby Hopper Tunnel
34	AR 282, to US 71, Chester, W USPO
29	AR 282, to US 71, Mountainburg, **1 mi E** $General, to Lake Ft Smith SP
24	AR 282, to US 71, Rudy, E Loves/Chester's/dsl/scales/24hr, Shell/dsl Red Hog BBQ Boston Mtns Scenic Lp, KOA
21	Collum Ln
20	to I-40 (from sb). **I-49 N begins/ends on I-40, exit 12.**

INTERSTATE 49 (Texarkana)

Exit #	Services
42	**I-49 (Texarkana) begins/ends on US 59.**
41	Sanderson Ln
37b a	I-30, E to Little Rock, W to Dallas
35	Arkansas Blvd, Four States Pkwy, E fairgrounds, W Brangus Steaks, Park Place Rest. $General
32	US 82, 19th St, 9th St, E Shell/dsl, Valero/dsl Subway, TA Molly's Mexican $General, CashSaver
31	AR 196, Genoa Rd
29b a	US 71, Texarkana, US 59, to Houston, W Shell/dsl
26	AR 237
24	Rd 10, Ferguson
18	N Fouke Rd
16	US 71, Fouke
6	Rd 197, Spruell Rd
4	US 71, Doddridge
0mm	Arkansas/Louisiana state line

INTERSTATE 55

BLYTHEVILLE

Exit #	Services
72mm	Arkansas/Missouri state line
72	State Line Rd, **weigh sta sb**
71	AR 150, Yarbro
68mm	**Welcome Ctr sb, full facilities, litter barrels, petwalk,**
67	AR 18, Blytheville, E Mobil/dsl, Murphy Express/dsl Burger King, Hardee's, Las Brisas Mexican, Waffle Inn, Zaxby's Best Value Inn, Days Inn/RV park Chrysler/Dodge/Jeep, Lowe's, Verizon, Walmart/Subway, W Citgo/dsl, Phillips 66/dsl, Shell El Puerto Mexican, GreatWall Chinese, Grecian Steaks, McDonald's, Olympia Steaks, Perkins, Pizza Hut, Pizza Inn, Sonic, Subway, Taco Bell, Wendy's Comfort Inn, Fairview Suites, Hampton Inn, Holiday Inn, Quality Inn, Super 8 H, AT&T, AutoZone, Bumper Parts, Family$, Ford/Nissan, Little Caesar's
63	US 61, to Blytheville, E Shearins RV Park (2mi), Loves/IHOP/Chester's/Godfather's/dsl/scales/24hr, W Citgo/McDonald's/dsl, Dodge's Store/dsl, Exxon/Baskin-Robbins/Chester's/Pizza Hut/dsl Deerfield Inn, Relax Inn H, truckwash
57	AR 148, Burdette, E NE AR Coll
53	AR 158, Victoria, Luxora
48	AR 140, to Osceola, E Shell/Baskin-Robbins/Chester's/dsl McDonald's (3mi), Pizza Inn (3mi), Sonic (3mi), Subway3 (mi) Days Inn, Deerfield Inn, EconoLodge H, Huddle House, Mamma Mia's
45mm	**truck parking nb, litter barrels**
44	AR 181, Keiser
41	AR 14, Marie, E to Hampson SP/museum
36	AR 181, to Wilson, Bassett
35mm	**truck parking sb, litter barrels**
34	AR 118, Joiner
23b a	US 63, AR 77, to Marked Tree, Jonesboro, ASU, E Citgo/chicken/pizza
21	AR 42, Turrell, W Valero/pizza/dsl/scales/24hr
17	AR 50, to Jericho
14	rd 4, to Jericho, E Citgo/dsl/scales/24hr, W Citgo/Stuckey's Chevrolet, KOA
10	US 64 W, Marion, E Citgo/Baskin-Robbins/Subway/scales, Shell/McDonald's KFC/Taco Bell, Sonic, Tops BBQ, Wendy's Comfort Inn, Hallmarc Inn $General, Family$, Mkt Place Foods, USPO, W Exxon/dsl, Shamrock Andrey Grill, Burger King, Colton's Steaks, Mi Pueblo, Tropical Cafe, Zaxby's Best Value Inn, Hampton Inn, Journey Inn AutoZone, to Parkin SP (23mi), Fairfield Inn
9mm	**truck parking nb, weigh sta sb**
8	I-40 W, to Little Rock
	I-55 and I-40 run together 3 mi. See I-40, exits 278-279b.
5	(279 a from I-40) Ingram Blvd, E **Welcome Ctr/ /full facilities, , litter barrels, petwalk** Margaritas Mexican Days Inn, Homegate Inn, Knights Inn, Red Roof Inn Ford, Southland Racetrack, W Citgo/dsl, Phillips/dsl, Shell/dsl Cross Creek Rest., Waffle House Best Value Inn, Clarion Inn, EconoLodge, Hampshire Inn, Motel 6, Ramada, Relax Inn
4	King Dr, Southland Dr, E FLYING J/Denny's/dsl/LP/scales/RV dump, LNG, Loves/Subway/dsl/scales/@, Petro Iron Skillet/rest./dsl/24hr/@, Pilot/Subway/Wendy's/dsl scales/24hr, Valero/dsl KFC/Taco Bell, McDonald's Best Western, Deluxe Inn, Express Inn, Super 8 Blue Beacon SpeedCo Lube, W Pancho's Mexican Sunset Inn
3b a	US 70, Broadway Blvd, AR 131, Mound City Rd (exits left from nb), W Budget Inn
2mm	**weigh sta nb**
1	Bridgeport Rd
0mm	Arkansas/Tennessee state line, Mississippi River

W MEMPHIS

AR

INTERSTATE 430 (Little Rock)

Exit #	Services
13b a	**I-40. I-430 begins/ends on I-40, exit 147.**
12	AR 100, Maumelle, W Kum&Go/dsl/e85 NAPA, O'Reilly Parts, vet
10mm	Arkansas River
9	AR 10, Cantrell Rd, W Maumelle Park, Pinnacle Mtn SP
8	Rodney Parham Rd, E Conoco/dsl, Kroger/dsl, Phillips 66/dsl, Shell Arby's, Baskin-Robbins, Dunkin Donuts, Firehouse Subs, McDonald's, Mt Fuji Japanese, Sonic, Starbucks, Subway, Taco Bell, Terri Lynn's BBQ, Tropical Smoothie Cafe, US Pizza La Quinta $General, AAA, Advance Parts, AutoZone, Drug Emporium, get, Kroger, TJ Maxx, Walgreens, W Exxon Burger King, Chili's, Dixie Cafe, Domino's, Franke's Café, Marco's Pizza, Olive Garden, Ponchito's Mexican, Shorty Small's Ribs, Starbucks, Wendy's Best Western Audi, Cadillac, Firestone/auto, GNC, vet, Volvo
6b	Kanis Rd, Markham St, to downtown, E Shell Burger King, Kroger, Red Lobster, Subway Candlewood Suites, Comfort Inn, Motel 6, SpringHill Suites Burlington Coats, Ross, W Exxon/dsl Applebee's, Bobby's Country Cookin', Butcher Shop Steaks, Cactus Jack's, Chi Rest., Church's, Denny's, Famous Dave's BBQ, IHOP, Jason's Deli, KFC, Khalil's Grill, Kobe Japanese, Lenny's Subs, Macaroni Grill, McAlister's Deli, McDonald's, Mexico Cafe, Mimi's Cafe, On-the-Border, Outback Steaks, PF Chang's, Pizza Hut, Popeye's, Purple Cow, Shotgun Dan's Pizza, Slim Chickens, Sonic, Starbucks, Taco Bell, Tokyo House, Twin Peaks, Waffle House, Wendy's, West End Steaks, Whole Foods Mkt Courtyard, Crowne Plaza, Embassy Suites, Extended Stay America, Holiday Inn, La Quinta, Ramada Ltd $Tree, AT&T, Barnes&Noble, Best Buy, Michael's, Office Depot, PetsMart, Sam's Club/gas, Verizon, Walmart
6a	I-630, E to Little Rock, E H
5	Kanis Rd, Shackleford Rd, E Arby's, BJ's Rest., ChuckE-Cheese, Copeland's Rest., Cracker Barrel, Longhorn Steaks, Panda Garden, Samurai Steaks, TX Roadhouse, Zangna Thai Comfort Suites, Home 2 Suites, La Quinta, Towneplace Suites AT&T, Gordman's, JC Penney, Jo-Ann, Verizon, Walmart/Subway, W Shell Dunkin Donuts, Krispy Kreme, Mooyah Burger, Panera Bread Extended Stay America, Hampton Inn, Hilton Garden, Residence Inn, Wingate Inn H, Lexus

LITTLE ROCK

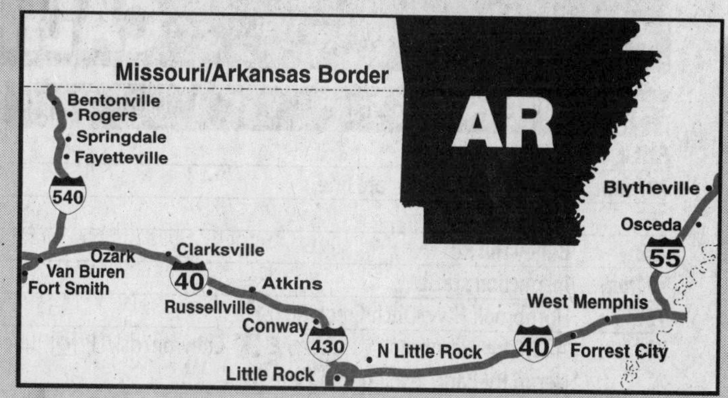

Exit #	Services
4	AR 300, Col Glenn Rd, E American Pie Pizza, Subway, Wendy's Holiday Inn Express, Woodspring Suites Toyota, W Valero/Burger King/dsl Sonic BMW, Chrysler/Dodge/Jeep, Ford, Honda, Hyundai, Infiniti, Jaguar, Land Rover, Mazda, Mercedes, Nissan, Subaru, VW
1	AR 5, Stagecoach Rd, W Mapco/dsl/e85, Phillips 66, Valero/Domino's Down Home Rest., Subway $General, CBI Tires, Walgreens
	I-430 begins/ends on I-30, exit 129.

INTERSTATE 440 (Little Rock)

Exit #	Services
11	**I-440 begins/ends on I-40, exit 159.**
10	US 70, W Peterbilt
8	Faulkner Lake Rd
7	US 165, to England, S Valero/dsl Agricultural Museum, Toltec Mounds SP, Willow Beach SP
6mm	Arkansas River
5	Fourche Dam Pike, LR Riverport, N Exxon/dsl, Shell/Subway McDonald's Travelodge Kenworth, S Phillips 66/dsl, Valero/dsl
4	Lindsey Rd
3	Bankhead Dr, N Comfort Inn LR Airport, S Valero Boston's Rest., Waffle House Days Inn, Holiday Inn, Holiday Inn Express
1	AR 365, Springer Blvd, S Little Rock Ntl Cemetery
0mm	**I-440 begins/ends on I-30, exit 138.**

NOTES

CALIFORNIA

INTERSTATE 5

Exit #	Services
797mm	California/Oregon state line
796	Hilt
793	Bailey Hill Rd
791mm	**inspection sta sb**
790	Hornbrook Hwy, Ditch Creek Rd
789	A28, to Hornbrook, Henley, **E** [gas] Chevron/dsl/LP [other] Blue Heron RV Park/rest., to Iron Gate RA
786	CA 96, Klamath River Hwy, **W** [RS] **both lanes, full [handicap] facilities, info, litter barrels, petwalk,** [phone], [picnic], to Klamath River RA
782mm	Anderson Summit, elevation 3067
780mm	vista point sb
779mm	Shasta River
776	Yreka, Montague, **E** [lodging] Holiday Inn Express [other] Yreka RV Park, **W** [gas] Mobil/dsl [food] Casa Ramos Mexican, J&D Diner, Puerto Vallarta [lodging] Mtn View Inn, Super 8 [other] Grocery Outlet
775	Miner St, Central Yreka, **W** [gas] 76/dsl, Chevron/dsl [food] Grandma's House, Poor George's, RoundTable Pizza, Subway [lodging] Best Western, Budget Inn, EconoLodge, Klamath Motel, Relax Inn, Rodeway Inn, Yreka Motel [other] [H], Ace Hardware, Baxter Parts, CarQuest, Dunn Automotive, museum, NAPA, Rite Aid, USPO
773	CA 3, to Ft Jones, Etna, **E** [other] Les Schwab, tires, Trailer Haven RV Park, **W** [gas] Shell/dsl, Valero/dsl [food] BlackBear Diner, Burger King, Carl's Jr, Jefferson's Roadhouse, KFC, McDonald's, Starbucks, Subway, Taco Bell [lodging] Baymont Inn, Comfort Inn, Motel 6 [other] [H], $Tree, AAA, AT&T, AutoZone, CHP, Ford, JC Penney, O'Reilly Parts, Raley's Foods, Verizon, Walmart
770	Shamrock Rd, Easy St, **W** [gas] Beacon/LP, Fuel 24/7/dsl [other] RV camping
766	A12, to Gazelle, Grenada, **E** [gas] Shell/dsl, **W** [gas] Chevron/dsl/24hr [other] RV camping
759	Louie Rd
753	Weed Airport Rd, [RS] **both lanes, full [handicap] facilities, litter barrels, petwalk,** [phone], [picnic]
751	Stewart Springs Rd, Edgewood, **E** [other] Lake Shasta RA/RV camp (2mi), **W** [other] RV camp (7mi)
748	to US 97, to Klamath Falls, Weed, **E** [gas] Chevron, Shell/dsl, Spirit/dsl [food] Ellie's Cafe, Pizza Factory, Subway [lodging] Hi-Lo Motel/rest., Motel 6, Summit Inn, Townhouse Motel [other] auto repair, golf, NAPA, Ray's Foods, RV camping
747	Central Weed, **E** [other] auto repair, same as 748, **W** Coll of Siskiyou
745	S Weed Blvd, **E** [gas] Chevron/dsl, Pilot/Subway/dsl/scales/24hr, Shell/dsl [food] Burger King, Dos Amigos Mexican, McDonald's/RV parking, Starbucks, Taco Bell [lodging] Comfort Inn, Quality Inn, Sis-Q Inn [other] Friendly RV Park, Grocery Outlet
743	Summit Dr, Truck Village Dr
742mm	Black Butte Summit, elevation 3912
741	Abrams Lake Rd, **W** [lodging] Abrams Lake RV Park
740	Mt Shasta City (from sb), **E** [gas] Pacific Pride/dsl/LP, Shell/dsl/CFN [lodging] Cold Creek Inn [other] KOA, repair, vet
738	Central Mt Shasta, **E** [gas] 76/dsl, Chevron/dsl, Shell/dsl/LP [food] BlackBear Diner, Burger King, KFC/Taco Bell, RoundTable Pizza, Subway [lodging] Best Western/Treehouse Rest., Mt Shasta Inn, Travel Inn [other] [H], Best Hardware, NAPA, O'Reilly Parts, Ray's Foods, Rite Aid, USPO, visitors info, **W** [lodging] Lake Siskiyou RV Park, Mt Shasta Resort/rest., Sisson Museum
737	Mt Shasta City (from nb), **E** [food] Casa Ramos, LaiLai Chinese, Lily's Rest., Piemont Italian, Wayside Grill [lodging] Alpine Lodge, Choice Inn, Evergreen Lodge, Swiss Holiday Lodge [other] McCloud RV Park, same as 738
736	CA 89, to McCloud, to Reno, **E** [lodging] Swiss Holiday Lodge
735mm	**weigh sta sb**
734	Mott Rd, to Dunsmuir
732	Dunsmuir Ave, Siskiyou Ave, **E** [food] Penny's Diner [lodging] Travelodge, **W** [gas] Chevron/dsl [lodging] Acorn Inn, Cedar Lodge
730	Central Dunsmuir, **E** [food] Burger Barn, Cornerstone Cafe, Dunsmuir Brewery Rest., Pizza Factory [lodging] Dunsmuir Inn, Hotel Dunsmuir/Rest [other] Dunsmuir Mkt, True Value, USPO, **W** [gas] Chevron/dsl/LP [food] Hitching Post, Wild Land Burgers [lodging] Cave Springs Motel [other] city park
729	Dunsmuir (from nb), **E** [gas] Manfredi's/deli/dsl [lodging] auto repair, Dunsmuir Lodge [other] to hist dist
728	Crag View Dr, Dunsmuir, Railroad Park Rd, **W** [other] Railroad Park Motel/RV Park
727	Crag View Dr (from nb), RV Camping
726	Soda Creek Rd, to Pacific Crest Trail
724	Castella, **W** [gas] Chevron/dsl [other] Castle Crags SP, RV camping, USPO
723mm	vista point nb
723	Sweetbrier Ave
721	Conant Rd
720	Flume Creek Rd
718	Sims Rd, **W** [other] RV camping
714	Gibson Rd
712	Pollard Flat, **E** [gas] Pollard Flat/dsl/LP [food] Pollard Flat Diner
710	Slate Creek Rd, La Moine
707	Delta Rd, Dog Creek Rd, to Vollmers
705mm	[RS] **sb, full [handicap] facilities, litter barrels,** [phone], [picnic]
704	Riverview Dr, **E** [food] Klondike Diner [lodging] Lakehead Lodge/RV Camping
702	Antlers Rd, Lakeshore Dr, to Lakehead, **E** [gas] Chevron/Subway/dsl [lodging] Antlers RV Park, Lakehead Camping, Neu Lodge Motel [other] auto repair, USPO, **W** [gas] Texaco/dsl [food] Allyson's Rest., Bass Hole Rest. [lodging] Lakeshore Mkt, Shasta Lake Motel/RV [other] Villa RV Park
698	Salt Creek Rd, Gilman Rd, **W** [lodging] Salt Creek Resort/RV Park [other] Trail In RV Park
695	Shasta Caverns Rd, to O'Brien
694mm	[RS] **nb, full [handicap] facilities, litter barrels, petwalk,** [phone], [picnic]
693	Packers Bay Rd (from sb)
692	Turntable Bay Rd
690	Bridge Bay Rd, **W** [food] Tail of a Whale Rest. [lodging] Bridge Bay Motel
689	Fawndale Rd, Wonderland Blvd, **E** [lodging] Fawndale Lodge, Fawndale Oaks RV Park, **W** [lodging] Wonderland RV Park
687	Wonderland Blvd, Mountain Gate, **E** [gas] Chevron/dsl/LP [food] La Fogata [other] Mountain Gate RV Park, Ranger Sta, **W** [gas] Shell/dsl/LP
685	CA 151, Shasta Dam Blvd, Project City, Central Valley, **W** [gas] 76/Circle K/dsl, Shell/Burger King/dsl/LP, Valero/dsl [food] McDonald's, Pizza Factory, Taco Shop [lodging] Shasta Dam Motel [other] NAPA, Rite Aid, Sentry Foods, USPO, vet
684	Pine Grove Ave, **W** [gas] Valero/dsl/LP
682	Oasis Rd, **E** [other] CA RV Ctr, Peterbilt, **W** [gas] Arco, Shell/Subway/dsl [other] CHP, Towtally RV Ctr, U-Haul

CA

INTERSTATE 5 Cont'd

Exit #	Services
681b	(from sb, no re-entry) CA 273, Market St, Johnson Rd, to Central Redding, **W** [other] [H]
681a	Twin View Blvd, **E** [gas] Chevron/dsl [lodging] Motel 6, Ramada Ltd [other] Harley-Davidson, **W** [gas] Pacific Pride/dsl [food] El Zarape [lodging] Best Western+, Comfort Suites, Fairfield Inn
680	CA 299E, **1/2 mi W** [gas] Arco, Chevron/dsl [food] A&W/KFC, Carl's Jr, Giant Burger, Little Caesar's, McDonald's, Papa Murphy's, Popeye's, RoundTable Pizza, Starbucks, Subway [other] AutoZone, O'Reilly Parts, Raley's Foods, Redding RV Camp, Redding RV Park, ShopKO, transmissions, Twin View RV Park, Walgreens

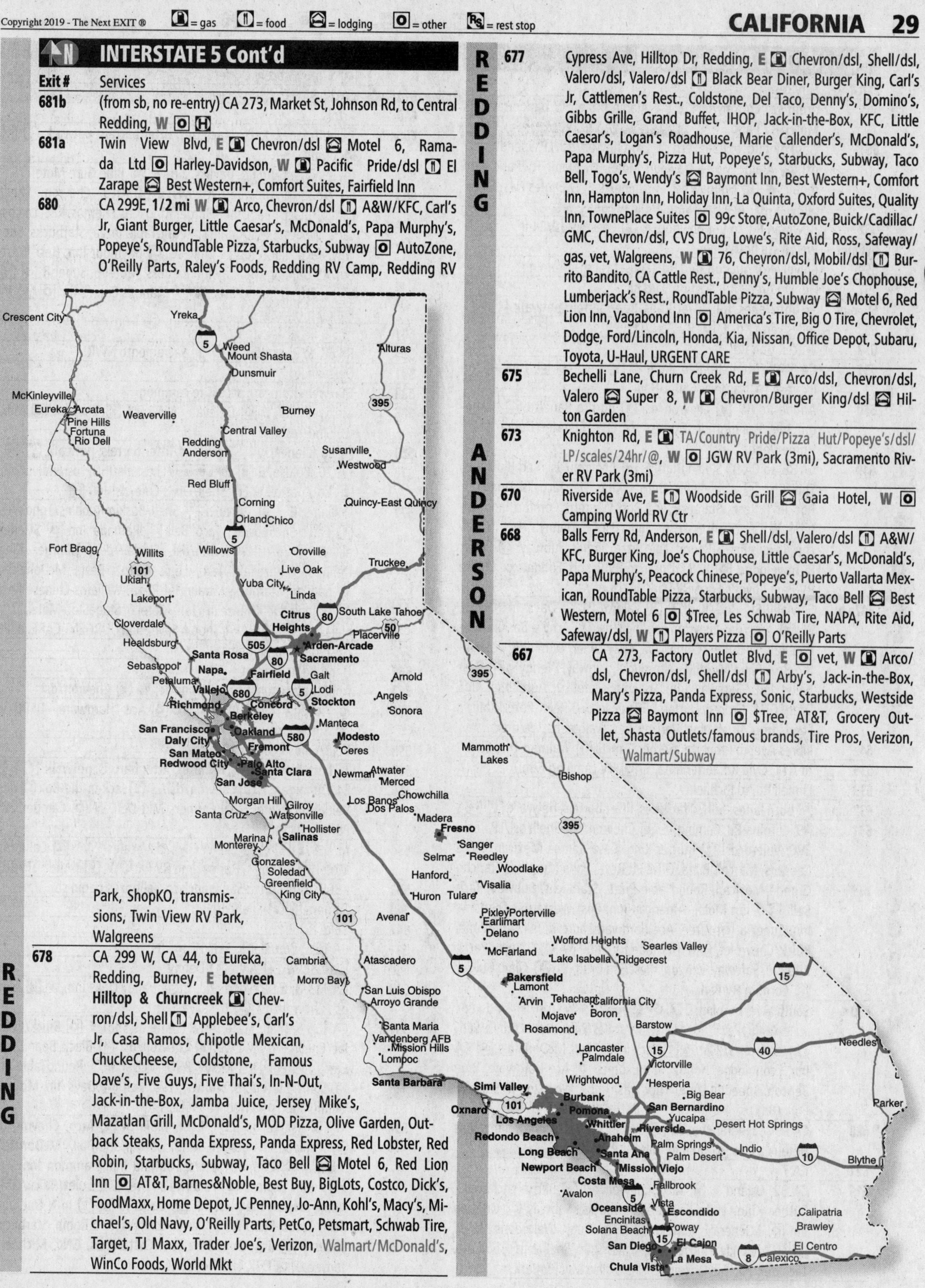

REDDING

Exit #	Services
678	CA 299 W, CA 44, to Eureka, Redding, Burney, **E between Hilltop & Churncreek** [gas] Chevron/dsl, Shell [food] Applebee's, Carl's Jr, Casa Ramos, Chipotle Mexican, ChuckeCheese, Coldstone, Famous Dave's, Five Guys, Five Thai's, In-N-Out, Jack-in-the-Box, Jamba Juice, Jersey Mike's, Mazatlan Grill, McDonald's, MOD Pizza, Olive Garden, Outback Steaks, Panda Express, Panda Express, Red Lobster, Red Robin, Starbucks, Subway, Taco Bell [lodging] Motel 6, Red Lion Inn [other] AT&T, Barnes&Noble, Best Buy, BigLots, Costco, Dick's, FoodMaxx, Home Depot, JC Penney, Jo-Ann, Kohl's, Macy's, Michael's, Old Navy, O'Reilly Parts, PetCo, Petsmart, Schwab Tire, Target, TJ Maxx, Trader Joe's, Verizon, Walmart/McDonald's, WinCo Foods, World Mkt
677	Cypress Ave, Hilltop Dr, Redding, **E** [gas] Chevron/dsl, Shell/dsl, Valero/dsl, Valero/dsl [food] Black Bear Diner, Burger King, Carl's Jr, Cattlemen's Rest., Coldstone, Del Taco, Denny's, Domino's, Gibbs Grille, Grand Buffet, IHOP, Jack-in-the-Box, KFC, Little Caesar's, Logan's Roadhouse, Marie Callender's, McDonald's, Papa Murphy's, Pizza Hut, Popeye's, Starbucks, Subway, Taco Bell, Togo's, Wendy's [lodging] Baymont Inn, Best Western+, Comfort Inn, Hampton Inn, Holiday Inn, La Quinta, Oxford Suites, Quality Inn, TownePlace Suites [other] 99c Store, AutoZone, Buick/Cadillac/GMC, Chevron/dsl, CVS Drug, Lowe's, Rite Aid, Ross, Safeway/gas, vet, Walgreens, **W** [gas] 76, Chevron/dsl, Mobil/dsl [food] Burrito Bandito, CA Cattle Rest., Denny's, Humble Joe's Chophouse, Lumberjack's Rest., RoundTable Pizza, Subway [lodging] Motel 6, Red Lion Inn, Vagabond Inn [other] America's Tire, Big O Tire, Chevrolet, Dodge, Ford/Lincoln, Honda, Kia, Nissan, Office Depot, Subaru, Toyota, U-Haul, URGENT CARE
675	Bechelli Lane, Churn Creek Rd, **E** [gas] Arco/dsl, Chevron/dsl, Valero [lodging] Super 8, **W** [gas] Chevron/Burger King/dsl [lodging] Hilton Garden

ANDERSON

Exit #	Services
673	Knighton Rd, **E** [gas] TA/Country Pride/Pizza Hut/Popeye's/dsl/LP/scales/24hr/@, **W** [other] JGW RV Park (3mi), Sacramento River RV Park (3mi)
670	Riverside Ave, **E** [food] Woodside Grill [lodging] Gaia Hotel, **W** [other] Camping World RV Ctr
668	Balls Ferry Rd, Anderson, **E** [gas] Shell/dsl, Valero/dsl [food] A&W/KFC, Burger King, Joe's Chophouse, Little Caesar's, McDonald's, Papa Murphy's, Peacock Chinese, Popeye's, Puerto Vallarta Mexican, RoundTable Pizza, Starbucks, Subway, Taco Bell [lodging] Best Western, Motel 6 [other] $Tree, Les Schwab Tire, NAPA, Rite Aid, Safeway/dsl, **W** [food] Players Pizza [other] O'Reilly Parts
667	CA 273, Factory Outlet Blvd, **E** [other] vet, **W** [gas] Arco/dsl, Chevron/dsl, Shell/dsl [food] Arby's, Jack-in-the-Box, Mary's Pizza, Panda Express, Sonic, Starbucks, Westside Pizza [lodging] Baymont Inn [other] $Tree, AT&T, Grocery Outlet, Shasta Outlets/famous brands, Tire Pros, Verizon, Walmart/Subway

CA

INTERSTATE 5 Cont'd

Exit #	Services
665	(from sb) Cottonwood, E Alamo Motel/RV park, Travelers Motel/RV Park
664	Gas Point Rd, to Balls Ferry, E Chevron/dsl/LP, Speedwaay/dsl Alamo Motel, Travelers Motel Alamo RV Park, auto repair, W Holiday/dsl, Sunshine/dsl Eagles Nest Pizza, Subway Ace Hardware, Holiday Foods, vet
662	Bowman Rd, to Cottonwood, E Chevron/dsl/24hr
660mm	**weigh sta both lanes**
659	Snively Rd, Auction Yard Rd, (Sunset Hills Dr from nb)
657	Hooker Creek Rd, Auction Yard Rd
656mm	**both lanes, full facilities, litter barrels, petwalk**
653	Jellys Ferry Rd, E RV Park/LP
652	Wilcox Golf Rd
651	CA 36W (from sb), Red Bluff, W Arco/dsl Holiday Inn Express same as 650, UHaul
RED BLUFF	
650	Adobe Rd, W Chevron/dsl Burrito Bandito Hampton Inn, Holiday Inn Express CHP, Chrysler/Dodge/Jeep, Home Depot
649	CA 36, to CA 99 S, Red Bluff, E Chevron/dsl, Red Bluff Gas, Shell/dsl Applebee's, Burger King, Del Taco, McDonald's, Rockin' R Rest., Starbucks Best Western, Comfort Inn, Motel 6, W Gas4Less/dsl, Mobil/dsl Denny's, Los Mariachis, Luigi's Pizza, RoundTable Pizza, Shari's, Subway Super 8, Travelodge AT&T, Durango RV Resort, Foodmaxx, O'Nite RV Park, River's Edge RV Park, Verizon, vet
647a b	S Main St, Red Bluff, E Valero/dsl Days In, W Arco/dsl, Chevron/dsl, Shell/dsl Arby's, Baskin-Robbins, China Buffet, China Doll, Cozy Diner, Domino's, Jack-in-the-Box, Papa Murphy's, Starbucks, Subway, Wendy's Best Value Inn, Gateway Inn, Triangle Motel AutoZone, CVS Drug, GNC, Grocery Outlet, I-5 Tire/auto, O'Reilly Parts, Raley's Food/drug, True Value, Verizon, vet, Walgreens, Walmart
642	Flores Ave, to Proberta, Gerber, **1 mi** E Walmart Dist Ctr
636	rd A11, Gyle Rd, to Tehama, E RV camping (7mi)
633	Finnell Rd, to Richfield
632mm	**both lanes, full facilities, litter barrels, petwalk**
CORNING	
631	A9, Corning Rd, Corning, E Chevron/dsl, Shell/dsl/LP, Tesla EVC, Valero/dsl Burger King, Casa Ramos Mexican, Little Caesar's, Marco's Pizza, Olive Pit Rest., Papa Murphy's, Rancho Grande Mexican, RoundTable Pizza, Starbucks, Subway, Taco Bell 7 Inn Motel, American Inn, Best Western+, Economy Inn, Super 8 $Tree, Ace Hardware, auto repair, AutoZone, Buick/Chevrolet, Ford, Heritage RV Park, NAPA, O'Reilly Parts, Rite Aid, Safeway, Verizon, West End Drug, W Giant Burger Corning RV Park
630	South Ave, Corning, E Loves/Denny's/dsl/LP/RV dump/scales/24hr, Petro/Iron Skillet/dsl/scales/24hr/@, TA/Arby's/Subway/dsl/scales/24hr/@ Jack-in-the-Box, McDonald's CA Inn, Econolodge, Holiday Inn Express Ace Hardware, Blue Beacon, SpeedCo Lube, truck wash/lube, Woodson Br SRA/RV Park (6mi)
628	CA 99W, Liberal Ave, W Chevron/dsl/24hr Rolling Hills Hotel/Casino Rolling Hills RV Park
621	CA 7
619	CA 32, Orland, E Arco, Chevron/dsl Berry Patch Rest., Burger King, Little Caesar's, Starbucks, Subway Orlanda Inn $General, AutoZone, CVS Drug, Walgreens, W Pilot/Wendy's/PJ Fresh/dsl/scales/24hr, Shell/dsl I-5 Cafe, Taco Bell Old Orchard RV Park, Parkway RV Park
618	CA 16, E Shell/dsl El Potrero Mexican Orland Inn $Tree, Grocery Outlet
614	CA 27
610	Artois
608mm	**both lanes, full facilities, litter barrels, petwalk, RV dump**
607	CA 39, Blue Gum Rd, Bayliss, **2 mi** E Blue Gum Motel
603	CA 162, to Oroville, Willows, E Arco, Chevron, Shell/dsl Black Bear Diner, Burger King, Casa Ramos, KFC, La Cascada Mexican, McDonald's, RoundTable Pizza, Starbucks, Subway, Taco Bell, Wong's Chinese Baymont Inn, Best Western/RV parking, Holiday Inn Express, Motel 6, Super 8 $Tree, CHP, O'Reilly Parts, W Nancy's Café/24hr RV Park (8mi), Walmart
601	rd 57, E Chevron/dsl/24hr
595	Rd 68, to Princeton, E to Sacramento NWR
591	Delevan Rd
588	Maxwell (from sb), access to camping
586	Maxwell Rd, E Delevan NWR, W Chevron Maxwell Inn/rest.
583	**both lanes, full facilities, litter barrels, petwalk**
WILLIAMS	
578	CA 20, Colusa, E Loves/Chester's/IHOP/dsl/scales/24hr hwy patrol, W Shell/Orv's Cafe/dsl
577	Williams, E Arco/dsl, Shell/Baskin-Robbins/Togo's/dsl Carl's Jr, Subway, Taco Bell Ramada Inn $General, W 76/dsl, Chevron/dsl, Sinclair/dsl Burger King, Denny's, Granzella's Rest., Louis Cairo's Rest., McDonald's/RV parking, Starbucks, Straw Hat Pizza, Williams Chinese Rest. Econolodge, Granzella's Inn, Motel 6, StageStop Motel, Travelers Inn NAPA, Shop'n Save Foods, URGENT CARE, USPO
575	Husted Rd, to Williams
569	Hahn Rd, to Grimes
567	frontage rd (from nb), to Arbuckle, W Chevron/dsl
566	to College City, Arbuckle, E Ace Hardware, USPO, W Sinclair/dsl $General
559	Yolo/Colusa County Line Rd
557mm	**both lanes, full facilities, litter barrels, petwalk**
556	E4, Dunnigan, E Chevron/dsl/LP Jack-in-the-Box Best Value Inn, Motel 6 Farmers Mkt Deli, W Camper's RV Park/golf (1mi)
554	rd 8, E Pilot/Wendy's/dsl/scales/24hr California Motel Denny's, HappyTime RV Park, W United TP/dsl
553	I-505 (from sb), to San Francisco, callboxes begin sb
548	Zamora, E Shell/dsl
WOODLAND	
542	Yolo
541	CA 16W, Woodland, **3 mi** W
540	West St, W Arco Denny's
538	CA 113 N, E St, Woodland, E Valley Oaks Inn, W CFN/dsl, Chevron/dsl Best Western
537	CA 113 S, Main St, to Davis (same as 536), E Buick/Cadillac/Chevrolet/GMC, W Chevron/dsl Black Bear Diner, Carl's Jr, Denny's, Dickey's BBQ, McDonald's, RoundTable Pizza, Sonic, Starbucks, Subway, Taco Bell Days Inn, Motel 6, Quality Inn $Tree, Food4Less
536	rd 102 (same as 537), **E on Main St** Arco, Chevron/dsl Applebee's, Burger King, Jack-in-the-Box, McDonald's, Subway Comfort Suites, Fairfield Inn, Hampton Inn, Holiday Inn Express America's Tire, Chevrolet/Buick/GMC, Home Depot, Walmart, W Circle K/dsl In-N-Out, Jimboy's Tacos, MOD Pizza, Panda Express, Red Robin, Starbucks, Subway Best Buy, Best Buy, Costco/gas, GNC, Michael's, Target, URGENT CARE, Verizon

INTERSTATE 5 Cont'd

SACRAMENTO

Exit #	Services
531	rd 22, W Sacramento
530mm	Sacramento River
529mm	sb, full facilities, litter barrels, petwalk
528	Airport Rd, E Arco
525b	CA 99, to CA 70, to Marysville, Yuba City
525a	Del Paso Rd, E Chevron A&W/KFC, BurgerIM, Chicken'n Waffles, Denny's, IHOP, In-N-Out, Jack-in-the-box, Jersey Mike's, Jimmy John's, Malabar Rest., Panda Express, Panera Bread, Papa Murphy's, Pizza Guys, Sizzler, Sizzler, Taco Bell Hampton Inn, Hilton Garden, Holiday Inn Express, Homewood Suites Rite Aid, Safeway Foods/dsl, W Subway Sheraton Four Points Walgreens
524	Arena Blvd, E Huckleberry's, Papa John's, Subway Sleep Train Arena, W Panda Garden, RoundTable Pizza, Starbucks Jimboy's Tacos Bel-Air Food/Drug/dsl
522	I-80, E to Reno, W to San Francisco
521b	W El Camino Ave (from nb, no return), West El Camino, W Shell/dsl Carl's Jr, Jack-in-the-Box, Jamba Juice, Starbucks, Subway, Togo's/Baskin-Robbins Courtyard, Hilton Garden, Residence Inn, SpringHill Suites
521a	Garden Hwy, W Courtyard
520	Richards Blvd, E Chevron/dsl Denny's, McDonald's Governor's Inn, Hawthorn Suites, W Arco, Shell Nena's Mexican Best Value Inn, Best Western, Comfort Suites, Days Inn, La Quinta, Motel 6 waterfront park
519b	J St, Old Sacramento, E Holiday Inn, Vagabond Inn, W Embassy Suites Railroad Museum
519a	Q St , downtown, Sacramento, W Embassy Suites, to st capitol
518	US 50, CA 99, Broadway, E services downtown
516	Sutterville Rd, E 76/dsl, Chevron/dsl La Bou Cafe, Macau Cafe Sprouts Mkt, Wm Land Park, zoo
515	Fruitridge Rd, Seamas Rd
514	43rd Ave, Riverside Blvd (from sb), E 76/repair
513	Florin Rd, E Arco, Chevron/dsl Rosalinda's Mexican, RoundTable Pizza $Tree, Bel Air Foods, CVS Drug, O'Reilly Parts, W Burger King, JimBoy's Tacos, L&L Hawaiian BBQ, Panda Garden, Shari's, Starbucks, Subway, Wings Stop Marshall's, Nugget Mkt, Rite Aid
512	CA 160, Pocket Rd, Meadowview Rd, to Freeport, E Chargepoint, Shell/dsl, Valero/dsl Baskin Robbins/Togo's, IHOP, KFC, McDonald's, Starbucks, Wendy's AT&T, Home Depot, Staples, vet, Walgreens
510	Cosumnes River Blvd
508	Laguna Blvd, E 76/Circle K/dsl/LP, Chevron/Taco Bell/dsl, Shell A&W/KFC, Starbucks, Subway, Wendy's Extended Stay America, Hampton Inn Jiffy Lube, Laguna Auto/RV Repair, U-Haul
506	Elk Grove Blvd, E Arco/dsl, Chevron/dsl, Shell Carl's Jr, Flaming Grill Burger, Pete's Grill, Wasabi Grill Holiday Inn Express
504	Hood Franklin Rd
498	Twin Cities Rd, to Walnut Grove
493	Walnut Grove Rd, Thornton, E CFN/dsl, Chevron/Subway/dsl
490	Peltier Rd
487	Turner Rd
485	CA 12, Lodi, E FLYING J/Denny's/Subway/dsl/scales/24hr, Arco, Chevron/dsl, Loves/Arby's/dsl/scales/24hr, Shell/dsl, Sinclair/Rocky's Rest./dsl/scales/24hr Burger King, Carl's Jr,

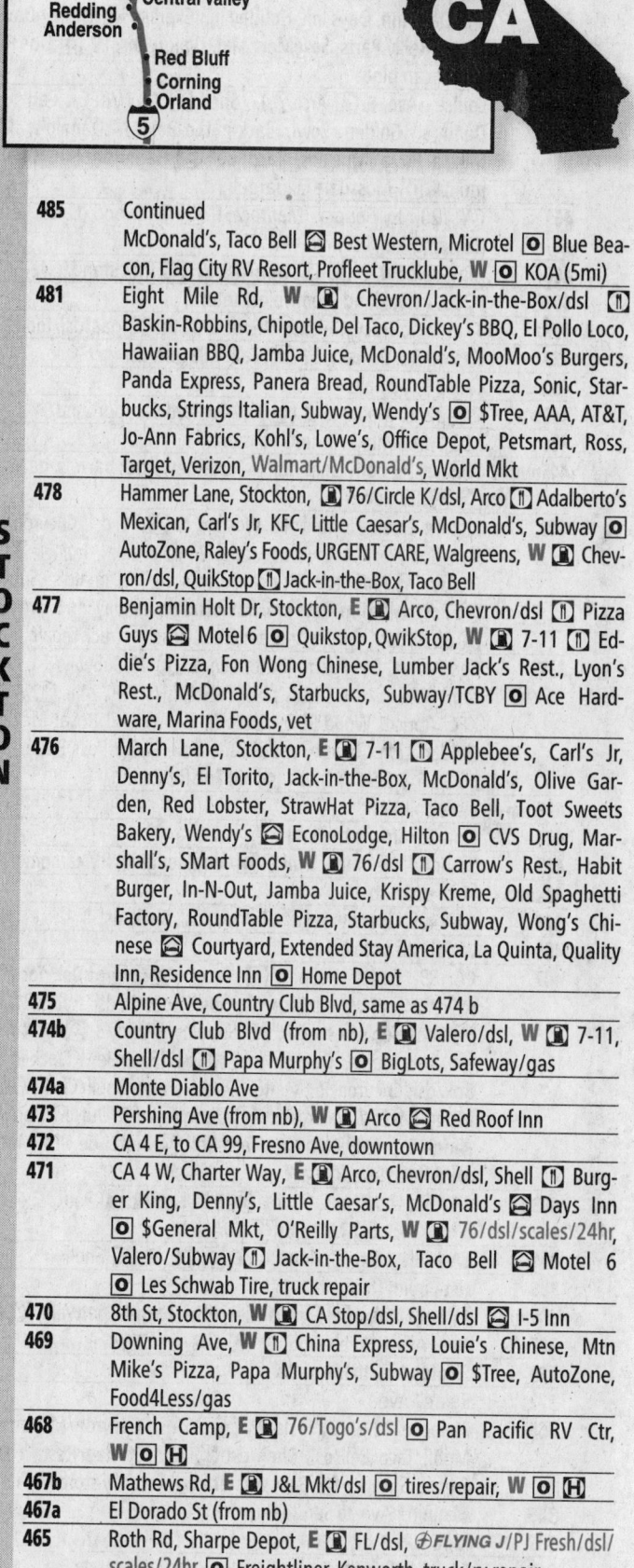

CA

STOCKTON

Exit #	Services
485	Continued McDonald's, Taco Bell Best Western, Microtel Blue Beacon, Flag City RV Resort, Profleet Trucklube, W KOA (5mi)
481	Eight Mile Rd, W Chevron/Jack-in-the-Box/dsl Baskin-Robbins, Chipotle, Del Taco, Dickey's BBQ, El Pollo Loco, Hawaiian BBQ, Jamba Juice, McDonald's, MooMoo's Burgers, Panda Express, Panera Bread, RoundTable Pizza, Sonic, Starbucks, Strings Italian, Subway, Wendy's $Tree, AAA, AT&T, Jo-Ann Fabrics, Kohl's, Lowe's, Office Depot, Petsmart, Ross, Target, Verizon, Walmart/McDonald's, World Mkt
478	Hammer Lane, Stockton, 76/Circle K/dsl, Arco Adalberto's Mexican, Carl's Jr, KFC, Little Caesar's, McDonald's, Subway AutoZone, Raley's Foods, URGENT CARE, Walgreens, W Chevron/dsl, QuikStop Jack-in-the-Box, Taco Bell
477	Benjamin Holt Dr, Stockton, E Arco, Chevron/dsl Pizza Guys Motel 6 Quikstop, QwikStop, W 7-11 Eddie's Pizza, Fon Wong Chinese, Lumber Jack's Rest., Lyon's Rest., McDonald's, Starbucks, Subway/TCBY Ace Hardware, Marina Foods, vet
476	March Lane, Stockton, E 7-11 Applebee's, Carl's Jr, Denny's, El Torito, Jack-in-the-Box, McDonald's, Olive Garden, Red Lobster, StrawHat Pizza, Taco Bell, Toot Sweets Bakery, Wendy's EconoLodge, Hilton CVS Drug, Marshall's, SMart Foods, W 76/dsl Carrow's Rest., Habit Burger, In-N-Out, Jamba Juice, Krispy Kreme, Old Spaghetti Factory, RoundTable Pizza, Starbucks, Subway, Wong's Chinese Courtyard, Extended Stay America, La Quinta, Quality Inn, Residence Inn Home Depot
475	Alpine Ave, Country Club Blvd, same as 474 b
474b	Country Club Blvd (from nb), E Valero/dsl, W 7-11, Shell/dsl Papa Murphy's BigLots, Safeway/gas
474a	Monte Diablo Ave
473	Pershing Ave (from nb), W Arco Red Roof Inn
472	CA 4 E, to CA 99, Fresno Ave, downtown
471	CA 4 W, Charter Way, E Arco, Chevron/dsl, Shell Burger King, Denny's, Little Caesar's, McDonald's Days Inn $General Mkt, O'Reilly Parts, W 76/dsl/scales/24hr, Valero/Subway Jack-in-the-Box, Taco Bell Motel 6 Les Schwab Tire, truck repair
470	8th St, Stockton, W CA Stop/dsl, Shell/dsl I-5 Inn
469	Downing Ave, W China Express, Louie's Chinese, Mtn Mike's Pizza, Papa Murphy's, Subway $Tree, AutoZone, Food4Less/gas
468	French Camp, E 76/Togo's/dsl Pan Pacific RV Ctr, W H
467b	Mathews Rd, E J&L Mkt/dsl tires/repair, W H
467a	El Dorado St (from nb)
465	Roth Rd, Sharpe Depot, E FL/dsl, FLYING J/PJ Fresh/dsl/scales/24hr Freightliner, Kenworth, truck/rv repair

INTERSTATE 5 Cont'd

Exit #	Services
463	Lathrop Rd, E Chevron/dsl/LP, Joe's Trkstp/Togo's/dsl/scales, TowerMart/dsl, Valero/dsl Baskin-Robbins, China Wok, CK Grill, Dickey's BBQ, Little Caesar's, Mi Kasa Japanese, Milan's Pizza, Papa Murphy's, Starbucks, Subway Comfort Inn, Days Inn, Days Inn, Holiday Inn Express Harley-Davidson, O'Reilly Parts, SaveMart Mkt, Walgreens, W Dos Reis CP, RV camping
462	Louise Ave, E Arco/dsl, Shell A&W/KFC, Carl's Jr, Denny's, Golden Bowl, Jack-in-the-Box, McDonald's, Mtn Mike's Pizza, Quiznos, Taco Bell Hampton Inn, Quality Inn, W Mossdale CP, Target
461	CA 120, to Sonora, Manteca, E Oakwood Lake Resort Camping, to Yosemite
460	Mossdale Rd, E Chevron/dsl, W fruit stand/cafe
458b	I-205, to Oakland (from sb, no return)
458a	11th St, to Tracy, Defense Depot, 2 mi W gas/dsl/food
457	Kasson Rd, to Tracy, W Valley Pacific/dsl
452	CA 33 S, Vernalis
449b a	CA 132, to Modesto, E The Orchard Campground
446	I-580 (from nb, exits left, no return)
445mm	**Westley both lanes, full facilities, litter barrels, petwalk, , , RV dump**
441	Ingram Creek, Howard Rd, Westley, E 76/dsl, Chevron/dsl, Joe's Trvl Plaza/Denny's/dsl/scales/24hr, Westley Triangle TruckStp/dsl Antojito's Mexican, Carl's Jr, McDonald's, Subway Best Value Inn, Days Inn, EconoLodge, Holiday Inn Express, W Shell/dsl fruits, Ingram Creek Rest. truck repair
434	Sperry Ave, Del Puerto, Patterson, E 76/Subway/dsl, Chevron, FLYING J/Wendy's/PJ Fresh/dsl/scales/24hr A&W/KFC, Apricot Wood BBQ, Carl's Jr, Denny's, El Rosal Mexican, Golden Lion Chinese, Jack-in-the-Box, Lamp Post Pizza, Starbucks Best Western Kit Fox RV Park
430mm	vista point nb
428	Fink Rd, Crow's Landing
423	Stuhr Rd, Newman, 5 mi E food, lodging, RV camping
422mm	vista point sb
418	CA 140E, Gustine, E Chevron/dsl, Shell/dsl
409	**weigh sta both lanes**
407	CA 33, Santa Nella, E Arco, Love's/Del Taco/dsl/scales/24hr, TA/Shell/Country Pride/Popeye's/dsl/scales/24hr/@ Andersen's Rest., Carl's Jr, Subway, Wendy's Best Western/Andersen's, Quality Inn, W 76/Circle K/Jack-in-the-Box/dsl, Chevron, Rotten Robbie/dsl/scales, Shell/Circle K/Jack-in-the-Box/dsl, Valero/dsl Denny's, In-N-Out, McDonald's, Panda Express, Starbucks, Taco Bell Hotel de Oro, Motel 6 Santa Nella RV Park
403b a	CA 152, Los Banos, 6 mi E H, 1 mi W Petro/Shell/diner/dsl/24hr Motel 6 KOA
391	CA 165N, Mercy Springs Rd, E H, W Shell
388	vista point (from nb)
386mm	**both lanes, full facilities, litter barrels, petwalk, ,**
385	Nees Ave, to Firebaugh, W Chevron/CFN/Subway/dsl/scales
379	Shields Ave, to Mendota
372	Russell Ave
368	Panoche Rd, E Tesla, W 76/dsl, Chevron/McDonald's, Mobil/Taco Bell/dsl, Shell/dsl Apricot Tree Rest., Fosters Freeze, Subway Best Western country store
365	Manning Ave, to San Joaquin
357	Kamm Ave
349	CA 33 N, Derrick Ave
337	CA 33 S, CA 145 N, to Coalinga
334	CA 198, to Lemoore, Huron, E Shell/Subway/dsl/24hr Harris Ranch Inn/rest., W 76, Chevron, Valero/Quiznos/dsl Burger King, Carl's Jr, Denny's, McDonald's, Oriental Express Chinese, Taco Bell Best Western, Motel 6, Travelodge H
325	Jayne Ave, to Coalinga, W Arco, Shell/Baja Fresh/dsl Sommerville RV Park/LP H
320mm	**both lanes, full facilities, litter barrels, petwalk, ,**
319	CA 269, Lassen Ave, to Avenal, W Hillcrest TP/76/Subway/dsl/scales/24hr
309	CA 41, Kettleman City, E 76/Subway/TCBY, CFN/dsl, Chevron/McDonald's, Mobil/Starbucks/dsl/24hr, Shell/Baja Fresh/dsl, Valero/dsl Carl's Jr, Denny's, In-N-Out, Jack-in-the-Box, Pizza Hut/Taco Bell Best Value Inn, Best Western Bravo Farms Mercantile
305	Utica Ave
288	Twisselman Rd
278	CA 46, Lost Hills, E Buford Star Mart/dsl/LP to Kern NWR, W 76/Quiznos, Chevron/dsl, Love's/Arby's/dsl/scales/24hr, Mobil/McDonald's/dsl/LP, Pilot/Wendy's/dsl/scales/24hr, Shell/Pizza Hut/Subway/Taco Bell/dsl, Valero/dsl Carl's Jr, Denny's, Jack-in-the-Box Days Inn, Motel 6 Lost Hills RV Park, Royal Truck Wash/lube
268	Lerdo Hwy, to Shafter
262	7th Standard Rd, Rowlee Rd, to Buttonwillow
259mm	**Buttonwillow both lanes, full facilities, litter barrels, petwalk, ,**
257	CA 58, to Bakersfield, Buttonwillow, E 76/Circle K/Quiznos/dsl, Arco/dsl, Chevron/dsl, Shell/dsl, Speedy Fuel/dsl/wash, TA/Mobil/Pizza Hut/Taco Bell/dsl/scales/24hr/@ Carl's Jr, Denny's, McDonald's, Starbucks, Subway, Tita's Mexican, Willow Ranch BBQ EconoLodge, Motel 6, Super 8 Castro's Tire/Truckwash, W Valero/dsl
253	Stockdale Hwy, E Chevron/Subway/dsl, Shell/dsl/24hr IHOP, Jack-in-the-Box Best Western, Vagabond Inn, W Tule Elk St Reserve
246	CA 43, to Taft, Maricopa, to Buena Vista RA
244	CA 119, to Pumpkin Center, E Mobil/dsl, W Chevron/dsl/LP
239	CA 223, Bear Mtn Blvd, to Arvin, E Bear Mtn RV Resort, W RV camping, to Buena Vista RA
234	Old River Rd
228	Copus Rd, E Murray Farms Mkt
225	CA 166, to Mettler, 2-3 mi E , /dsl
221	I-5 and CA 99 (from nb, exits left, no return)
219b a	Laval Rd, Wheeler Ridge, E Shell/dsl, TA/Shell/Popeye's/Subway/scales/@ Black Bear Diner, Burger King, Carl's Jr, Pieology, Pizza Hut, Starbucks, Taco Bell Microtel Blue Beacon, Tejon Outlets/famous brands, W Chevron/dsl, Mobil/dsl, Petro/Iron Skillet/Subway/dsl/scales/24hr/@ Baskin-Robbins, Chipotle Mexican, Del Taco, In-N-Out, Maurício's Mexican, McDonald's, Panda Express, Starbucks, Subway, Wendy's, Yogurtland Best Western
218	**truck weigh sta sb**
215	Grapevine, E Valero/dsl Denny's, Jack-in-the-Box, W Shell/ds Don Perico Grill Ramada Ltd
210	Ft Tejon Rd, W to Ft Tejon Hist SP, towing/repair
209mm	**brake check area nb**
207	Lebec Rd, W antiques, CHP, towing, USPO
206mm	**both lanes, full facilities, petwalk, , litter barrels, vending**

WESTLEY

SANTA NELLA

BUTTONWILLOW

FT TEJON

CA

INTERSTATE 5 Cont'd

Exit #	Services
205	Frazier Mtn Park Rd, **W** FLYING J/dsl/LP/24hr/@, Arco, Chevron/Subway/dsl/24hr, Shell/Quiznos/dsl/LP Jack-in-the-Box, Los Pinos Mexican Holiday Inn Express, Motel 6 auto repair/towing, NAPA Autocare, to Mt Pinos RA
204	elev 4144, Tejon Pass, **truck brake insp sb**
202	Gorman Rd, to Hungry Valley, **E** 76/dsl, Chevron/dsl/LP Carl's Jr, El Grullense, Ranch House Rest. EconoLodge, **W** Shell/dsl McDonald's auto repair
199	CA 138 E, Lancaster Rd, to Palmdale
198b a	Quail Lake Rd, CA 138 E (from nb)
195	Smokey Bear Rd, Pyramid Lake, **W** Pyramid Lake RV Park
191	Vista del Lago Rd, **W** visitors ctr
186mm	**brake inspection area sb**, motorist callboxes begin sb
183	Templin Hwy, **W** Ranger Sta, RV camping

CASTAIC

Exit #	Services
176b a	Lake Hughes Rd, Parker Rd, Castaic, **E** 7-11, Arco/dsl, Castaic Trkstp/dsl/24hr, Pilot/Wendy's/dsl/scales/24hr/@, Shell/dsl Baskin-Robbins, Cajun Chicken, Carl's Jr, Denny's, Domino's, El Pollo Loco, Fosters Freeze, Jersey Mike's, McDonald's, Mike's Diner, Panda Express, PapaZ Burger, Pizza Factory, Popeye's, Red Dot Pizza, Starbucks, Subway, Waba Grill, Wok's Chinese Castaic Inn, Days Inn, Rodeway Inn $Tree, Benny's Tire/repair, Castaic Lake RV Park, O'Reilly Parts, to Castaic Lake, vet, **W** 76/repair, Mobil Jack-in-the-Box, Taco Bell auto repair, Walgreens
173	Hasley Canyon Rd, **W** Pizza Hut, Subway Ralph's Foods
172	CA 126 W, to Ventura, **E** Courtyard, Embassy Suites
171mm	**weigh sta nb**
171	Rye Canyon Rd (from sb), **W** Chevron, Shell/dsl Del Taco, Jack-in-the-Box, Jimmy Dean's, Starbucks, Subway, Tommy's Burgers Six Flags
170	CA 126 E, Magic Mtn Pkwy, Saugus, **E** Azul Tequila Mexican, Denny's, Rustic Eatery, Sam's Grille, Shrimp Haus, Starbucks Best Western/rest., Holiday Inn Express, **W** Chevron/dsl El Torito, Marie Callender's, Red Lobster, Wendy's Hilton Garden Six Flags of CA

SANTA CLARITA

Exit #	Services
169	Valencia Blvd, **W** Fat Burger, Nick'n Willy's Pizza, Panda Express, Robeks, Starbucks, Subway Verizon
168	McBean Pkwy, **E** H, **W** Baskin-Robbins, Cabo Cabana, Chili's, ChuckeCheese, ClaimJumper, Jamba Juice, Jersey Mikes Subs, Macaroni Grill, Mamma Mia Italian, Mod Pizza, Pick up Stix, Starbucks, Subway, Urbane Cafe Michael's, Old Navy, Verizon, Vons Foods, WorldMkt
167	Lyons Ave, Pico Canyon Rd, **E** 76/Circle K/dsl, Chevron/dsl, Shell/dsl Burger King, Wendy's, **W** Arco, Shell/dsl Cabo Cabana, Carl's Jr, Chuy's, Coco's, Del Taco, Denny's, El Pollo Loco, Fortune Express Chinese, Golden Spoon, IHOP, In-N-Out, Jack-in-the-Box, Jersey Mike's, McDonald's, Outback Steaks, Spumoni Italian, Taco Bell, Wood Ranch BBQ, Yamato Japanese Comfort Suites, Extended Stay America, Fairfield Inn, Hampton Inn, La Quinta, Residence Inn AT&T, Camping World RV Ctr, GNC, Jiffy Lube, Marshall's, Old Navy, Petsmart, Ralph's Foods, Ross, Staples, SteinMart, Walmart/McDonald's

SYLMAR

Exit #	Services
166	Calgrove Blvd
162	CA 14 N, to Palmdale
161b	Balboa Blvd (from sb)
160a	I-210, to San Fernando, Pasadena
159	Roxford St, Sylmar, **E** Chevron/dsl, Mobil/dsl Denny's/24hr, McDonald's Good Nite Inn, Motel 6
158	I-405 S (from sb, no return)

Lemoore • Hanford • Huron • Avenal • 5 • Bakersfield • Frazier Park • Lebec • Lancaster • Palmdale • Santa Clarita • Santa Paula • Simi Valley • Oxnard • Thousand Oaks • 5 • Pasadena • Alhambra • Los Angeles • Downey • CA

Exit #	Services
157b a	SF Mission Blvd, Brand Blvd, **E** 76, Arco, Chevron/dsl, Mobil/dsl, Shell Carl's Jr, In-N-Out, Little Caesar's, New Asia, Pollo Gordo, Popeye's, Subway, Taco Bell, Winchell's H, Honda, Rite Aid, Vallarta Mkt
156b	CA 118
156a	Paxton St, Brand Ave (from nb), **E** G&M/dsl 7-11

ARLETA

Exit #	Services
155b	Van Nuys Blvd (no EZ nb return), **E** Arco Jack-in-the-Box, KFC/LJ Silver, McDonald's, Pizza Hut, Popeye's Discount Parts, USPO, **W** Domino's auto repair
155a	Terra Bella St (from nb), **E** USA
154	Osborne St, to Arleta, **E** Arco, Chevron/dsl AutoZone, BigLots, Food4Less, Ross, Target, **W** 76, Mobil/Burger King 7-11
153b	CA 170 (from sb), to Hollywood
152a	Sheldon St, **E** Big Jim's Rest. H, auto repair, Big O Parts
152	Lankershim Blvd, Tuxford, **E** Superfine/dsl/scales

SUN VALLEY

Exit #	Services
151	Penrose St
150b	Sunland Blvd, Sun Valley, **E** 76/dsl, Mobil Acapulco Rest., Carl's Jr, El Pollo Loco, Old Time Burger, Papa John's, Quiznos, Subway, Town Café, Yoshinoya Economy Inn $Tree, 7-11, Grocery Outlet, Sunland Produce, **W** Chevron/7-11, Shell McDonald's, Starbucks
150a	GlenOaks Blvd (from nb), **E** Arco/dsl Willows Motel
149	Hollywood Way, **W** Shell/dsl U-Haul
148	Buena Vista St, **E** Hampton Inn, **W** 76/dsl Jack-in-the-Box Quality Inn, Ramada Inn
147	Scott Rd, to Burbank, **E** Sevan/dsl, **W** HomeTown Buffet, Jamba Juice, Krispy Kreme, Olive Garden, Outback Steaks, Panda Express, Sharky's Mexican, Starbucks, Wendy's Courtyard, Extended Stay America Best Buy, Lowe's, Marshall's, Michael's, REI, Staples, Target, Verizon
146b	Burbank Blvd, **E** 76/repair Baskin-Robbins, Buffalo Wild Wings, CA Pizza Kitchen, Carl's Jr, Chevy's Mexican, Chipotle, ChuckECheese's, Corner Cafe, El Pollo Loco, Harry's Rest., Hooters, IHOP, In-N-Out, Islands Burger, Jersey Mike's, McDonald's, Pizza Hut, Popeye's, Robek's Juice, Shakey's Pizza, Starbucks, Starbucks, Subway, Taco Bell, Tommy's Burgers, Yoshinoya, Zankou Chicken Barnes&Noble, CVS Drug, IKEA, Macy's, Office Depot, Old Navy, Ralph's Foods, Ross, Sprouts Mkt, **W** McDonald's, Subway Costco/gas, Discount Tire, Walmart
146a	Olive Ave, Verdugo, **E** BJ's Rest., Black Angus Holiday Inn USPO, **W** H, 7-11, Chevrolet, Metro RV Ctr
145b	Alameda Ave, **E** Chevron Baskin-Robbins/Togo's, Habit Burger, Starbucks CarMax, CVS Drug, Home Depot, IKEA, Ralph's Foods, Trader Joes, Walgreens, **W** 76/dsl, Arco, Shell Burbank Inn U-Haul
145a	Western Ave, **W** Gene Autrey Museum
144b a	CA 134, Ventura Fwy, Glendale, Pasadena

CA

LOS ANGELES AREA

INTERSTATE 5 Cont'd

Exit #	Services
142	Colorado St
141a	Los Feliz Blvd, E H, W Griffith Park, zoo
140b	Glendale Blvd, E 76, Valero Dunkin Donuts, Starbucks, Subway, W Valero
140a	Fletcher Dr (from sb), W Arco, Chevron
139b a	CA 2, Glendale Fwy
138	Stadium Way, Figueroa St, E 76, Chevron, USA IHOP, McDonald's Home Depot, W to Dodger Stadium
137b a	CA 2, Glendale Fwy, W 76
136b	Broadway St (from sb), W 76
136a	Main St, E 76, Chevron/24hr Chinatown Express, Jack-in-the-Box, McDonald's H
135c	I-10 W (from nb), Mission Rd (from sb), E Jack-in-the-Box, McDonald's H, W 76/dsl
135b	Cesar Chavez Ave, W H
135a	4th St, Soto St, E Sinclair/dsl city park, W 76/dsl
134b	Ca 60 E (from sb), Soto St (from nb)
134a	CA 60 W, Santa Monica Fwy
133	Euclid Ave (from sb), Grand Vista (from nb), W Mobil
132	Calzona St, Indiana St, E Arco/dsl
131b	Indiana St (from nb), E Arco/dsl, Valero/dsl
131a	Olympic Blvd, E H, W Jack-in-the-Box, King Taco
130c b	I-710 (exits left from nb), to Long Beach, Eastern Ave, E McDonald's
130a	Triggs St (from sb), E outlet mall, W Denny's/24hr Destiny Inn
129	Atlantic Blvd N, Eastern Ave (from sb), E Carl's Jr, Chipotle, Panda Express, Starbucks, Subway Doubletree Hyundai, outlets/famous brands, W Denny's, Steven's Steaks
128b	Washington Blvd, Commerce, E Chevron/dsl/repair/24hr McDonald's Crowne Plaza Hotel/casino, Doubletree Costco/gas, outlets/famous brands, W Arco Del Taco, Subway
128a	Garfield Blvd, E Crown Plaza/casino Home Depot, Office Depot, W 76
126b	Slauson Ave, Montebello, E Shell/dsl, Valero/dsl Mollie's Burger, Ozzie's Diner, Starbucks Quality Inn, Travelodge, W Arco Denny's Motel 6, Ramada Inn
126a	Paramount Blvd, Downey, E Shell/Jack-in-the-Box/dsl
125	CA 19 S, Lakewood Blvd, Rosemead Blvd, E Arco, Mobil Arthurs Cafe, Sam's Burgers, Starbucks EconoLodge, Guesthouse Inn, W Chris&Pitt's BBQ, Golden Corral, McDonald's, Subway, Taco Bell, Toppings Pizza Ralph's Foods
124	I-605
123	Florence Ave, to Downey, E Mobil, W Honda, repair
122	Imperial Hwy, Pioneer Blvd, E Chevron Applebee's, Habit Burgers, IHOP, Jack-in-the-Box, Jimmy John's, McDonald's, Panda Express, Pizza Hut, Subway, Wendy's, Wood Grill Buffet O'Reilly Parts, Rite Aid, Target, USPO, W 7-11 Alberts Mexican, Denny's, Panda King, Pizza Hut, Rally's, Shakey's Pizza, Wienerschnitzel Imperial Inn, Keystone Motel, Motel 6 Toyota, Walmart
121	San Antonio Dr, to Norwalk Blvd, E IHOP, Jack-in-the-Box, McDonald's, Outback Steaks, Starbucks, Wood Grill Buffet Doubletree Inn Rite Aid, Target, W Shell auto repair
120b	Firestone Blvd (exits left from nb)
120a	Rosecrans Ave, E 76/7-11/dsl Casa Adelita, Jim's Burgers, KFC, Little Caesar's, Starbucks, Subway H, W Arco/24hr Guesthouse Inn El Monte RV Ctr

NORWALK

ANAHEIM

Exit #	Services
119	Carmenita Rd, Buena Park, E Arco Burger King Ford Trucks, Lowe's, W Galaxy Burgers Budget Inn, Dynasty Suites
118	Valley View Blvd, E Arco/dsl In-N-Out, Northwoods Inn, Starbucks, Subway, Wendy's Extended Stay America, Holiday Inn Select, Residence Inn, W Thompson's RV Ctr, to Camping World
117	Artesia Blvd, Knott Ave, E Chevron Extended Stay America CarMax, W Knotts Berry Farm, to Camping World RV Ctr
116	CA 39, Beach Blvd, E Chevron Travelodge BMW, Buick/GMC, CarMax, Chevrolet, Honda, Mercedes, Nissan, Tesla, Toyota, W Chevron Arby's, Black Angus, Denny's, Fuddruckers, KFC, Pizza Hut, Subway, Wendy's Hilton, Holiday Inn H, Stater Bros, Target, to Knotts Berry Farm, Verizon
115	Manchester (from nb), same as 116
114b	CA 91 E, Riverside Fwy, E to
114a	Magnolia Ave, Orangethorpe Ave, E Mobil/dsl Burger King, Burger Town, Taco Bell 7-11, Harley-Davidson
113c	CA 91 W (from nb)
113b a	Brookhurst St, LaPalma, E Chevron/dsl Subway, W Arco, Texaco/dsl Burger King, Carl's Jr, Starbucks Home Depot, Staples
112	Euclid St, E Arco Happy Dragon, IHOP, Marie Callender's, McDonald's, Rubio's, Starbucks, Subway, Taco Bell, Wendy's AAA, El Super, GNC, Old Navy, PetCo, Ross, TJ Maxx, Verizon, Walmart, W 76, Mobil Charley's Subs, Denny's, KFC/LJ Silver, Subway, Wok Experience Aldi Foods, Target, Verizon
111	Lincoln Ave, to Anaheim, E La Villa Mexican, Ruby's Diner, Starbucks vet
110b	Ball Rd (from sb), E 7-11, Chevron/dsl, Shell Burger King, Carolina's Italian, El Pollo Loco, KFC, McDonald's, Shakey's Pizza, Starbucks, Subway, Taco Bell Best Value Inn, Days Inn, Frontier Inn, Sheraton Anaheim RV, Traveler's World RV Park, W Arco/24hr, Shell/dsl Best Western, Budget Inn, Holiday Inn, Majestic Garden Hotel, Staybridge Suites, Super 8, Travelodge Disneyland, USPO
110a	Harbor Blvd, E Chevron, Shell Shakey's Pizza, Starbucks, Taco Bell Days Inn, Frontier, Ramada Anaheim Harbor RV Park, **0-2 mi** W Captain Kidd's, Coldstone, Dennys, IHOP, McDonald's, Mimi's Cafe, Mortons Steaks, Panera Bread, Tony Roma's Anaheim Resort, Best Western+, Camelot Inn, Candy Cane Inn, Castle Inn Suites, Clarion, Courtyard, Del Sol Inn, Fairfield Inn, Hampton Inn, Hilton Garden, Howard Johnson, Hyatt House, ParkVue Inn, Portofino Inn, Ramada Inn, Red Lion, Sheraton, Travelodge, Tropicana Inn multiple hotels & restaurants, same as 109, to Disneyland
109	Katella Ave, Disney Way, E Arco Baskin-Robbins, Carl's Jr, Denny's, McDonald's, Panda Express, Starbucks, Subway, To-go's TownePlace Suites Angels Stadium, W Chevron Bubba Gump Shrimp, CA Pizza Kitchen, Cheesecake Factory, McCormick&Schmick, PF Chang's, Roy Roy's, Subway Best Value Inn, Cambria, Comfort Inn, Desert Palms Suites, Extended Stay America, Hilton, Hotel Indigo, Hyatt House, Kings Inn, Little Boy Blue, Marriott, Peacock Suites, Ramada Inn, Residence Inn, Riviera Motel, SpringHill Suites, Staybridge Suites, Worldmark, Wyndham Garden 7-11, CVS, to Disneyland
107c	St Coll Blvd, City Drive, E Del Taco Embassy Suites, W Alo Hotel, Ayres Hotel, Doubletree Hotel

INTERSTATE 5 Cont'd

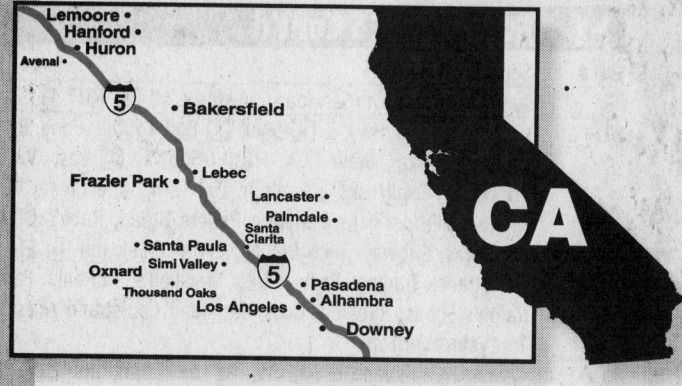

Exit #	Services
107b a	CA 57 N, Chapman Ave, E Burger King, Del Taco, Denny's, Jack-in-the-Box, Waba Grill Motel 6, W Chevron Krispy Kreme, Lucille's BBQ, Starbucks, Taco Bell, Wendy's Ayres Inn, DoubleTree H, Best Buy
106	CA 22 W (from nb), Garden Grove Fwy, Bristol St
105b	N Broadway, Main St, E 7-11 Baskin-Robbins, CA Pizza Kitchen, Carl's Jr, Chipotle, Corner Bakery Cafe, Habit Burgers, Jamba Juice, Olive Garden, Papa Johns, Polly's Café, Rubio's Grill, Starbucks, Subway, Taco Bell, Togo's Days Inn, Red Roof Inn H, Barnes&Noble, CVS Drug, JC Penney, Macy's, Staples, Verizon, W Golden West Motel, Travel Inn Bowers Museum
105a	17th St, E 76/dsl/24hr Hometown Buffet, IHOP, McDonald's Chevrolet, CVS Drug, same as 104b, Walgreens, W Chevron YumYum Donuts 7-11
104b	Santa Ana Blvd, Grand Ave, E Gavilan, Hometown Buffet, IHOP, KFC/LJ Silver, Marie Callender, McDonald's, Popeye's, Starbucks, Subway, Taco Bell, Taco Sinaloa, Waba Grill $Tree, AT&T, CVS Drug, O'Reilly Parts, Target, vet, Walgreens, W Kia
104a	(103c from nb), 4th St, 1st St, to CA 55 N, E Chevron, Shell, US Gas Del Taco
103b	CA 55 S, to Newport Beach
103a	CA 55 N (from nb), to Riverside
102	Newport Ave (from sb), E Arby's, Jack-in-the-Box, W Arco Carl's Jr, Domino's, Little Caesar's American Tire Depot
101b	Red Hill Ave, E Mobil/dsl, Shell/repair Del Taco, Denny's, Starbucks, Wendy's Key Inn BigLots, U-Haul, W Arco/24hr, Chevron/24hr, Valero Pizza Shack, Taco Bell 7-11, Stater Bros
101a	Tustin Ranch Rd, E McDonald's Acura, Buick/GMC, Cadillac, Chrysler/Dodge/Jeep, Costco, Ford/Lincoln, Hyundai, Infiniti, Lexus, Mazda, Nissan, Toyota
100	Jamboree Rd, E Shell Baja Fresh, BJ's Rest., Boston Mkt, Burger King, CA Pizza, Carl's Jr, Chick-fil-A, Corner Bakery, Daphne's Greek, DQ, El Pollo Loco, In-N-Out, Islands Burger, Lazy Dog Cafe, Macaroni Grill, Miguel's Mexican, Panda Express, Panera Bread, Pick-up Stix, Rubio's, Starbucks, Subway, Taco Bell, Taco Rosa AAA, AT&T, Barnes&Noble, Best Buy, Costco, Dick's, Home Depot, Lowe's, Old Navy, Petsmart, Ralph's Foods, REI, Rite Aid, Ross, Sprouts Mkt, Target, TJ Maxx, Verizon
99	Culver Dr, E Shell/24hr vet, W Buffalo Wild Wings, Domino's
97	Jeffrey Rd, E Arco Baskin-Robbins, Juice-it-Up, Starbucks, Subway Albertson's, Kohl's, W 76/dsl China Garden, Thai Cafe 99 Ranch Mkt, vet
96	Sand Canyon Ave, Old Towne, W 76/dsl Denny's, Jack-in-the-Box, Knowlwood Burgers La Quinta H
95	CA 133 (toll), Laguna Fwy, N to Riverside, S Laguna Beach
94b	Alton Pkwy, E Shell/Subway/dsl Carl's Jr, Starbucks Extended Stay America Costco/gas, Office Depot, Walmart, W Brio, CA Pizza, Capital Grill, Cheesecake Factory, Chipotle Mexican, Dave&Buster's, Johnny Rockets, Panda Express, PF Chang's, Pieology, Ruby's Diner, Starbucks, Wahoo's Fish Tacos, Wood Ranch, Yardhouse Rest. Doubletree Inn Barnes&Noble, Nordstrom, Old Navy, Target
94a	I-405 N (from nb)
92b	Bake Pkwy, W CarMax, Toyota, same as 92a

TUSTIN

IRVINE

Lemoore • Hanford • Huron • Avenal • 5 • Bakersfield Frazier Park • Lebec Lancaster • Palmdale • Santa Clarita • Santa Paula Simi Valley • Oxnard Thousand Oaks 5 • Pasadena • Alhambra Los Angeles • Downey CA

CA

Exit #	Services
92a	Lake Forest Dr, Laguna Hills, E Chevron/24hr, Shell/dsl Buffalo Wild Wings, Dickey's BBQ, IHOP, Jack-in-the-Box, McDonald's, Panera Bread, Peppino's Italian, RoundTable Pizza, Starbucks, Subway, Taco Bell, The Hat, Waba Grill, Which Wich? Best Western, Holiday Inn, Quality Inn America's Tire, AT&T, Chevrolet, Chrysler/Dodge/Jeep, Ford/Lincoln, Honda, Hyundai, Mazda, Nissan, Subaru, VW, W Chevron/24hr, Shell Carl's Jr, Coco's, Del Taco, McDonald's, Pizza 900, Subway Comfort Inn, Courtyard AZ Leather, Best Buy, BMW/Mini
91	El Toro Rd, E Chevron/dsl, USA Arby's, Asia Buffet, Baskin-Robbins, Cafe Rio, Chipotle Mexican, Corner Baker Cafe, Del Taco, Denny's, Dunkin Donuts, El Pollo Loco, Fuddrucker's, Habit Burger, Honeybaked Ham, Jack-in-the-Box, Jamba Juice, Jersey Mike's, Lucille's BBQ, Luna Grill, McDonald's, Mr Wok, Panda Express, PeiWei Asian, Sizzler, Subway, Tommy's Burgers 99c Store, AT&T, CVS Drug, Firestone/auto, Home Depot, Petsmart, Ralph's Foods, Ross, Staples, Verizon, W 76, Chevron/dsl BJ's Rest., CA Pizza Kitchen, Cane's, Chick-fil-A, El Torito, FarmerBoys, In-N-Out, King's Fishhouse, Ruby's Diner, Starbucks, Subway Laguna Hills Lodge H, CVS Drug, Firestone/auto, Just Tires, Marshall's, Trader Joe's, USPO, Walgreens
90	Alicia Pkwy, Mission Viejo, E Del Taco, Denny's, Five Guys, Subway $Tree, America's Tire, AT&T, CVS Drug, O'Reilly Parts, Target, W Chevron Carl's Jr, Little Caesar's, Stefano's, Togo's, Wendy's AAA, BigLots, Dick's, URGENT CARE, vet
89	La Paz Rd, Mission Viejo, E Arco/24hr, Shell Pizza Hut, Ralph's, Starbucks, Taco Bell, TK Burgers vet, W 76/dsl Cecilia's Grill, DQ, Dunkin Donuts, Flamingos Mexican, Hot Off the Grill, Jack-in-the-Box, Krispy Kreme, McDonald's, Outback Steaks, Starbucks, Villa Roma, Wienerschnitzel Hills Hotel 7-11, Best Buy, Jo-Ann Fabrics, Midas, PetCo, to Laguna Niguel Pk
88	Oso Pkwy, Pacific Park Dr, E 76/dsl/repair, Chevron/repair Carl's Jr, Starbucks, Subway Fairfield Inn golf
86	Crown Valley Pkwy, E 76, Arco, Chevron Buffalo Wild Wings, Cheesecake Factory, Chili's, Islands Grill, Ruby's Diner H, Macy's, vet, W Chevron/dsl Costco/gas
85b	Avery Pkwy, E Shell/dsl Broken Yolk, Coco's, Del Taco, Jack-in-the-Box, Jimmy John's, Mongolian BBQ, Papa John's, Starbucks, Subway Hampton Inn Acura, America's Tire/auto, Audi/Infiniti, Burlington, Jaguar/Land Rover, Lexus, Volvo, World Mkt, W Arco/dsl, Chevron A's Burgers, Carl's Jr, In-N-Out Best Value Laguna Inn American Tire Depot, Cadillac/GMC, Costco/gas, Hyundai, Mercedes
85a	CA 73 N (toll)

LAGUNA HILLS

MISSION VIEJO

[gas] = gas [food] = food [lodging] = lodging [other] = other [RS] = rest stop

CA

INTERSTATE 5 Cont'd

Exit #	Services
83	Junipero Serra Rd, to San Juan Capistrano, W 76/7-11, Shell
82	CA 74, Ortego Hwy, E Shell Bad to the Bone BBQ, Ballpark Pizza, Bravo CA Fresh, Subway Best Western, W Shell/dsl Carl's Jr, Del Taco, Jade China, KFC, Marie Callender's, McDonald's, Panera Bread, Ruby's Diner, Starbucks, Subway, Taco Bell Cedar Creek Inn $Tree, Capistrano Trading Post, GNC, Marshall's, O'Reilly Parts, Ralph's Foods, Rite Aid, Ross, San Juan Capistrano Mission, TrueValue, Verizon
81	Camino Capistrano, E VW, W on Capistrano Shell Baskin Robbins, Domino's, El Adobe Rest., Eng's Chinese, KFC, Pizza Hut, Ricardo's Mexican, Starbucks Residence Inn CHP, Chrysler/Dodge/Jeep, Ford, Goodyear/auto, Honda, Nissan, PetCo, Rite Aid, Ross, San Juan Capistrano SP (1mi), Toyota, Trader Joe's, Vons Foods
79	CA 1, Pacific Coast Hwy, Capistrano Bch, Capistrano, W Arco/24hr, Chevron/dsl, Costco/gas A's Burgers, Carl's Jr, Del Taco, Denny's, El Pollo Loco, Jack-in-the-Box, McDonald's, Subway Best Western, DoubleTree $Tree, Aamco, AutoZone, Petsmart, Ralph's Foods, Rite Aid, Staples, USPO, vet
78	Camino de Estrella, San Clemente, E 76/dsl China Well, Flame Broiler, Habit Burger, RoundTable Pizza, Rubio's, Starbucks, Subway, Wahoo's Fish Taco H, AAA, CVS Drug, Ralph's Foods, Stater Bros Foods, Trader Joe's, vet, W USA/dsl Las Golondrinas O'Reilly Parts, Sprouts Mkt, TJ Maxx
77	Ave Vista Hermosa
76	Ave Pico, E Mobil/Circle K Chipotle, Golden Spoon, Juice it Up, McDonald's, Panda Express, SmashBurger Albertson's/Sav-On, GNC, W Chevron Del Taco, Denny's/24hr, Pick-up-Stix, Pizza Hut, Stuft Pizza, Subway Holiday Inn Express 99c Store, Outlets/famous brands, Staples, tires/repair, Tuesday Morning, USPO, vet
75	Ave Palizada, Ave Presidio, W Valero Baskin-Robbins, Mr. Pete's Burgers, Sonny's Pizza, Starbucks, Subway, Taka-O Japanese Holiday Inn 7-11, AutoZone, CVS Drug, Rite Aid, TrueValue
74	El Camino Real, E Chevron/dsl Budget Lodge, San Clemente Inn, Tradewinds Motel same as 75, W 76/dsl Biggie's Burger, Subway, Taco Bell, Tommy's Rest. 7-11, O'Reilly Parts, Ralph's Foods
73	Ave Calafia, Ave Magdalena, E 76/dsl, Shell Jack-in-the-Box, Molly Bloom's Cafe, Pedro's Tacos, Sugar Shack Cafe Calafia Beach Motel, C-Vu Inn, Hampton Inn, LaVista Inn, San Clemente Motel, Travelodge 7-11, repair/tires, W to San Clemente SP
72	Cristianitios Ave, E Cafe Del Sol, Carl's Jr. Comfort Suites, San Clemente Surf Inn San Mateo RV Park/dump, W to San Clemente SP
71	Basilone Rd, W San Onofre St Beach
67mm	**weigh sta both lanes**
66mm	viewpoint sb
62	Las Pulgas Rd
59mm	**Aliso Creek [RS] both lanes, full [handicapped] facilities, litter barrels, petwalk, [phone], [picnic], RV dump, vending**
54c	Oceanside Harbor Dr, W Chevron, Mobil Del Taco, Denny's/24hr Days Inn, Harbor Inn, Holiday Inn to Camp Pendleton
54b	Hill St (from sb), to Oceanside, W Chevron, Mobil Denny's, In-N-Out Days Inn, Holiday Inn, Rodeway Inn
54a	CA 76 E, Coast Hwy
53	Mission Ave, Oceanside, E 7-11/dsl, Arco/24hr, Mobil/dsl Alberto's Mexican, Arby's, Armando's Tacos, Armando's Tacos, Burger King, Jack-in-the-Box, KFC, McDonald's, Starbucks Ramada, Travelodge Bussry's Automotive, CarQuest, El Super Mkt, W El Pollo Loco, Panda Express, Subway, Wendy's 99c Store, AutoZone, Walmart Mkt
52	Oceanside Blvd, E Arco Alberto's Mexican, IHOP, McDonald's, Pizza Hut, Starbucks, Subway, Taco Bell, Wienerschnitzel $Tree, CVS Drug, Frazier Farms Mkt, W GM/dsl Best Western
51c	Cassidy St (from sb)
51b	CA 78, Vista Way, Escondido, E Chevron/dsl, Shell Applebee's, Boston Mkt, Buffalo Wild Wings, Burger King, Carl's Jr, Cheesecake Factory, Chili's, Chipotle, ChuckECheese's, Dave&Buster's, Domino's, Islands Rest., Jersey Mike's, Macaroni Grill, McDonald's, Mimi's Café, Olive Garden, Outback Steaks, QuikWok, Red Lobster, Rubio's, Starbucks, Subway, TX Roadhouse $Tree, Best Buy, CVS Drug, Dick's, Firestone/auto, JC Penney, Macy's, Marshall's, Michael's, PetCo, Sprouts Mkt, Staples, Stater Bros Foods, Target, Tuesday Morning, Verizon, Vons Foods, Walmart, World Mkt, W Hunter Steaks
51a	Las Flores Dr
50	Elm Ave, Carlsbad Village Dr, E Shell Lotus Thai Bistro, W 7-11 Al's Cafe, Carl's Jr, Denny's/24hr, Jack-in-the-Box, KFC/Taco Bell, Mikko Japanese, Subway Extended Stay America, Motel 6 Albertson's, TrueValue
49	Tamarack Ave, E 76/dsl, Chevron Village Kitchen Days Inn Rite Aid, Vons Foods, W Arco Stag&Lion Grille
48	Cannon Rd, Car Country Carlsbad, E Acura, Buick/GMC/Cadillac, Chevrolet, Chrysler/Dodge/Jeep, Ford, Honda, Kia, Lexus, Lincoln, Mazda, Mercedes, VW, W West Mart West Steak&Seafood Hyatt House, West Inn
47	Carlsbad Blvd, Palomar Airport Rd, E 7-11, Chevron, Mobil/dsl BJ's Rest., Carl's Jr, Corner Bakery Cafe, Islands Burgers, Kings Fish House, Panda Express, PF Chang's, Ruby's Diner, SeaFire Rest., Starbucks, Strauss Brewery Rest., Subway Taco Bell Carlsbad by the Sea, Motel 6 AT&T, Carlsbad Ranch/Flower Fields, Chrysler/Dodge/Jeep, Costco/gas, Ford GNC, outlet mall, W Shell/dsl In-N-Out, McDonald's Miguel's Mexican, Pisco Rotisserie Hilton Garden S Carlsbad St Bch
45	Poinsettia Lane, W Shell/dsl Benihana, El Pollo Loco Jack-in-the-Box, Pick-Up Stix, Starbucks, Subway Holiday Inn Express, La Quinta, Motel 6, Ramada Ace Hardware Porsche/Volvo, Ralph's Foods, Rite Aid
44	La Costa Ave, E vista point, W Chevron/dsl
43	Leucadia Blvd, E Quality Inn, W Shell/service Starbucks
42b	Encinitas Blvd, E Chevron/dsl, Mobil, Valero Honey Baked Ham, In-N-Out, Oggi's Pizza CVS Drug, NAPA, Petco to Quail Botanical Gardens, vet, W Shell Denny's, Little Caesar's, Subway, Wendy's Best Western/rest., Days Inn
41a	Santa Fe Dr, to Encinitas, E Shell Carl's Jr, El Nopal to 7-11, W Domino's, Schooner Pizza H, Rite Aid vet, Vons Foods
40	Birmingham Dr, E Chevron, Valero El Pueblo Holiday Inn Express, W Arco
39mm	viewpoint sb
39	Manchester Ave, E to MiraCosta College

CAPISTRANO

SAN CLEMENTE

OCEANSIDE

CARLSBAD

ENCINITAS

 = gas = food = lodging = other = rest stop

INTERSTATE 5 Cont'd

LA JOLLA

Exit #	Services
37	Lomas Santa Fe Dr, Solana Bch, E Baskin-Robbins, Habit Burger, Jersey Mike's, Pizza Nova, Samurai Rest., Starbucks Vons Foods, We-R-Fabrics, W Mobil Carl's Jr, Jamba Juice, Panda Express, Panera Bread, Starbucks AT&T, CVS Drug, Discount Tire, GNC, Marshall's, Sprouts Mkt, Staples
36	Via de La Valle, Del Mar, E Chevron, Mobil Chipotle, Coffee Bean, McDonald's, Milton's Deli, Taste of Thai, Urban Pizza Albertson's/SavOn, Gelson's Mkt, PetCo, Verizon, Whole Foods Mkt, W Arco/24hr, Shell/dsl Denny's, FishMkt Rest., Red Tracton's Rest. Hilton racetrack
34	Del Mar Heights Rd, E Shell/dsl, W 7-11 Broken Yolk Cafe, Bushfire Kitchen, Jack-in-the-Box, Jersey Mike's, Starbucks AAA, CVS Drug, vet, Vons Foods
33	Carmel Mtn Rd, E Arco, Shell/repair Ruth's Chris, Taco Bell, Tio Leo's Mexican DoubleTree Hotel, Hampton Inn, Marriott, Residence Inn
32	CA 56 E, Carmel Valley Rd
31	I-805 (from sb)
30	Sorrento Valley Rd
29	Genesee Ave, E H
28b	La Jolla Village Dr, E Embassy Suites, Hyatt, Marriott H, to LDS Temple, W Mobil/dsl BJ's Rest., CA Pizza Kitchen, Chipotle Mexican, Dominos, Flame Broiler, Islands Burgers, Jamba Juice, Mrs Gooch's, RockBottom Café, Rubio's, Starbucks Sheraton AT&T, Best Buy, CVS Drug, Marshall's, PetsMart, Ralph's Foods, Ross, Trader Joe's, Verizon, Whole Foods Mkt
28a	Nobel Dr (from nb), E Hyatt LDS Temple, W same as 28b
27	Gilman Dr, La Jolla Colony Dr
26b	CA 52 E
26a	La Jolla Rd (from nb)
23b	CA 274, Balboa Ave, E Del Taco, Starbucks H, Costco/gas, W 7-11, 76/repair In-N-Out, McDonald's, Rubio's, Sonic, Wienerschnitzel Holiday Inn Express, La Quinta, Red Roof Inn, San Diego Motel Discount Tire, Ford, Mission Bay Pk, Nissan, Toyota
23a	Grand Ave, Garnet Ave, same as 23b
22	Clairemont Dr, Mission Bay Dr, E Shell, USA Best Western Chevrolet, VW, W to Sea World Dr

SAN DIEGO AREA

Exit #	Services
21	Sea World Dr, Tecolote Dr, E Shell Seaside Inn Aamco, Circle K, PetCo, W Hilton Old Town SP, Seaworld
20	I-8, W to Nimitz Blvd, E to El Centro, CA 209 S (from sb), to Rosecrans St
19	Old Town Ave, E Arco, Shell Courtyard, La Quinta
18b	Washington St, E Holiday Inn Express
18a	Pacific Hwy Viaduct, Kettner St
17b	India St, Front St, Sassafras St, E Mobil, W
17a	Hawthorn St, Front St, E H, W Mobil/dsl Motel 6, Sheraton
16b	6th Ave, downtown
16a	CA 163 N, 10th St, E H, AeroSpace Museum, W Shell Burger King, Del Taco, Jack-in-the-Box, McDonald's Days Inn, Downtown Lodge, El Cortez Motel, Holiday Inn, Marriott
15c b	CA 94 E (from nb), Pershing Dr, B St, W civic ctr
15a	CA 94 E, J St, Imperial Ave (from sb)
14b	Cesar Chavez Pkwy
14a	CA 75, to Coronado, **W toll rd to Coronado**
13b	National Ave SD, 28th St, E Jack-in-the-Box, Little Caesar's, Panda Express, Starbucks, Subway AutoZone,

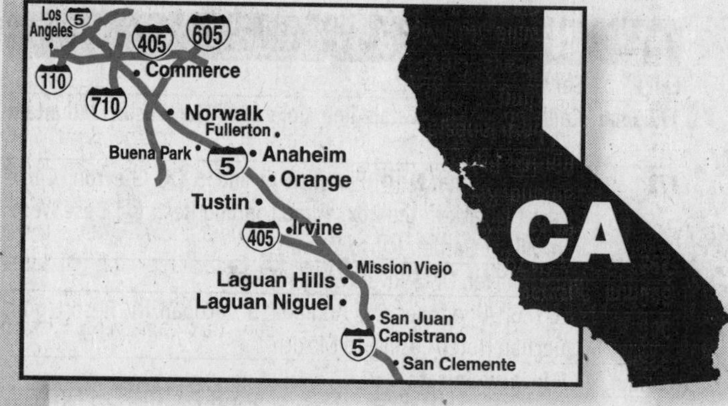

SAN DIEGO AREA

Exit #	Services
13b	Continued W Shell Burger King, Del Taco, El Pollo Loco, McDonald's
13a	CA 15 N, to Riverside
12	Main St, National City
11b	8th St, National City, E Arco Jack-in-the-Box Cassia Hotel, Howard Johnson, National City Inn, Ramada Inn, Rodeway Inn
11a	Harbor Dr, Civic Center Dr
10	Bay Marina, 24th St, Mile of Cars Way, E Chick-fil-A, Chipotle, Denny's, Freddy's, In-N-Out, Jersey Mike's, Starbucks, W Best Western+
9	CA 54 E
8b	E St, Chula Vista, E Arco, Black Angus, Denny's, Taco Bell Days Inn, Motel 6, W GoodNite Inn
8a	H St
7b	J St (from sb)
7a	L St, E 76, Shell/dsl China Vista Inn NAPA
6	Palomar St, E Arco Carl's Jr., DQ, HomeTown Buffet, IHOP, KFC, Little Caesar's, McDonald's, Panda Express, Starbucks, Subway Palomar Inn $Tree, 7-11, Costco/gas, Food4Less, Jack-in-the-Box, Michael's, Office Depot, Petco, Ross, Target, Walmart, Yoshinoya, W Valero
5b	Main St, to Imperial Beach, E Arco
5a	CA 75 (from sb), Palm Ave, to Imperial Beach, E Arco, USA Armando's Mexican, Papa John's, Starbucks 7-11, Discount Tire, Soto's Transmissions, W 7-11, 76, Arco, Shell Boll Weevil Diner, Burger King, Carl's Jr, Coldstone Creamery, IHOP, McDonald's, Rally's, Subway, Wienerschnitzel Prime Inn, Super 8 99c Store, AutoZone, CVS Drug, GNC, Home Depot, Von's Foods, Walmart

SAN YSIDRO

Exit #	Services
4	Coronado Ave (from sb), E Chevron/service, Shell/service Taco Bell EZ 8 Motel 7-11, W Arco, Hollister/dsl Denny's Motel 6 to Border Field SP
3	CA 905, Tocayo Ave, W 7-11
2	Dairy Mart Rd, E Arco/24hr Burger King, Carl's Jr, Coco's, KFC, McDonald's Best Western Pacifica RV Resort, W Quality Inn
1b	Via de San Ysidro, W Chevron, Mobil/dsl Denny's Knights/RV park, Motel 6, Travelodge
1a	I-805 N (from nb), Camino de la Plaza (from sb), E Burger King, Jack-in-the-Box, KFC, McDonald's, Subway Holiday Motel AutoZone, W Achiato Mexican, IHOP, Iron Wok, McDonald's, Starbucks, Sunrise Buffet $Tree, Baja Duty-Free, border parking, factory outlet, Marshall's, Old Navy, Ross, TJ Maxx

California state line, US/Mexico Border, customs, **I-5 begins/ends.**

YUMA

CA

INTERSTATE 8

Exit #	Services
172.5mm	California/Arizona state line, Colorado River, Pacific/Mountain time zone
172	4th Ave, Yuma, N Paradise Casino, S Chevron, Circle K/dsl Jack-in-the-Box, Yuma Landing Rest. Best Western, Hilton Garden to Yuma SP
170	Winterhaven Dr, S Rivers Edge RV Park
166	CA 186, Algodones Rd, Andrade, S Cocopah RV Resort/golf, Quechan Hotel/Casino, to Mexico
165mm	**CA Insp/weigh sta**
164	Sidewinder Rd, N st patrol, S Shell/LP/dsl Pilot Knob RV Park
159	CA 34, Ogilby Rd, to Blythe
156	Grays Well Rd, N Imperial Dunes RA
155mm	**both lanes (exits left), full facilities, litter barrels, petwalk,**
151	Gordons Well
146	Brock Research Ctr Rd
143	CA 98, to Calexico, Midway Well
131	CA 115, VanDerLinden Rd, to Holtville, **5 mi** N food, gas, lodging, RV camping
128	Bonds Corner Rd
125	CA 7 S, Orchard Rd, Holtville, **4 mi** N food, gas/dsl
120	Bowker Rd
118b a	CA 111, to Calexico, N Country Life RV Park
116	Dogwood Rd, S Arco/dsl Burger King, Carino's, Chili's, ChuckeCheese, Denny's, Famous Dave's BBQ, Fortune Garden, Jack-in-the-Box, Olive Garden, Sombrero Mexican, Starbucks, Subway Fairfield Inn, TownePlace Suites $Tree, 99c, Americas Tire, Best Buy, Dillard's, JC Penney, Kohl's, Macy's, Marshall's, Michael's, PetCo, Ross, Staples
115	CA 86, 4th St, El Centro, N 7-11/dsl, Arco/dsl, Chevron/dsl, FillCo/dsl, Shell/dsl Carl's Jr, Exotic Thai, Jack-in-the-Box, Las Palmitas Tacos, Lucky Chinese, McDonald's Holiday Inn Express, Motel 6 Family$, O'Reilly Parts, U-Haul, S 7-11/Subway, Mobil/dsl/scales IHOP, In-N-Out, Johnny's Burritos, Panda Express, Taco Bell Best Western, Comfort Inn, Rodeway Inn AutoZone, Buick/Chevrolet/GMC/Cadillac, Desert Trails RV Park, Home Depot, Honda, Hyundai, Lucky Foods
114	Imperial Ave, El Centro, N 7-11/dsl, Arco, Chevron/dsl, Chevron/dsl, USA/dsl Applebee's, Broken Yolk Cafe, Burger King, Carl's Jr, Carrow's, Church's, Coldstone, Del Taco, Denny's, Domino's, El Pollo Loco, Farmer Boys, Golden Corral, Jack-in-the-Box, Jack-in-the-Box, KFC, La Resaca, Little Caesar's, McDonald's, Mexicali Grill, Papa John's, Pizza Hut, Rally's, Sizzler, Sonic, Starbucks, Subway, Taco Bell, TasteeFreez Burgers, Wendy's Clarion, Crown Motel, Super 8, SuperStar Inn, Vacation Inn/RV Park, Value Inn H, $General Mkt, $Tree, 99c Store, Chrysler/Dodge/Jeep, Costco/gas, Discount Tire, Food4Less, Ford, Goodyear/auto, Jo-Ann, Lowe's, Nissan, O'Reilly Parts, PepBoys, Rite Aid, st patrol, Target, Toyota, Verizon, Von's Foods, Walgreens, Walmart
111	Forrester Rd, to Westmorland
108mm	**Sunbeam both lanes, full facilities, litter barrels, petwalk, , , RV dump**
107	Drew Rd, Seeley, N Sunbeam RV Park, to Sunbeam Lake, S Rio Bend RV Park
101	Dunaway Rd, Imperial Valley, N st prison, elev 0 ft
89	Imperial Hwy, CA 98, Ocotillo, N Red Feathers Mkt/Cafe, RV camping, USPO, S Chevron/dsl Desert Museum
87	CA 98 (from eb), to Calexico
81mm	**eb, runaway truck ramp**
80	Mountain Springs Rd
77	In-ko-pah Park Rd, N , towing
75mm	**brake insp area eb,**
73	Jacumba, S Chevron/dsl, Shell/Subway/dsl/24hr RV camping
65	CA 94, Boulevard, to Campo, S MtnTop/dsl Back Country Inn auto repair, to McCain Valley RA (7mi), USPO
63mm	elev 4140 ft, Tecate Divide
62mm	Crestwood Summit, elev 4190 ft
61	Crestwood Rd, Live Oak Springs, S Golden Acorn Trkstp/casino/dsl Live Oak Sprs Country Inn info
54	Kitchen Creek Rd, Cameron Station, S food, RV camping
51	rd 1, Buckman Spgs Rd, to Lake Morena, **both lanes, full facilities, litter barrels, petwalk, , , RV dump**, S , /dsl/LP, Lake Morena CP (7mi), Potrero CP (19mi), RV camping
48	**insp sta, wb**
47	rd 1, Sunrise Hwy, Laguna Summit, elev 4055 ft, to Laguna Mtn RA
45	Pine Valley, Julian, N Calvin's Rest., Frosty Burger, Major's Diner Pine Valley Inn city park, Mtn Mkt, Pine Valley/gas, to Cuyamaca Rancho SP, USPO, vet
44mm	Pine Valley Creek
42mm	elev 4000 ft
40	CA 79, Japatul Rd, Descanso, N Descanso Rest. to Cuyamaca Rancho SP
37mm	elev 3000 ft, vista point eb
36	E Willows, N Alpine Sprs RV Park, casino, Viejas Indian Res
33	W Willows Rd, to Alpine, N Alpine Sprs RV Park, casino, same as 36, Viejas Outlets/famous brands, S ranger sta
31mm	elev 2000 ft
30	Tavern Rd, to Alpine, N Chevron/dsl, Shell/dsl, S 76/Circle K American Grill, Carl's Jr, Greek Village Grill, La Carreta, Little Caesar's, Mananas Mexican, Mediterraneo Grill, Panda Machi Chinese, Subway Ayre's Lodge Ace Hardware, city park, CVS Drug, Farmers Mkt, Rite Aid
27	Dunbar Lane, Harbison Canyon, N Flinn Sprgs CP, RV camping
25mm	elev 1000 ft
24mm	
23	Lake Jennings Pk Rd, Lakeside, N Arco/Jack-in-the-Box/dsl/24hr, to Lake Jennings CP RV camping, S 7-11 Burger King, Karla's Mexican, Marechiaro's Pizza
22	Los Coches Rd, Lakeside, N 7-11, Eagle/dsl/LP, East County Gas Albert's Mexican, Giant Pizza, Laposta Mexican RV camping/dump, S Shell/dsl Denny's, Giant NY Pizza, McDonald's, Panda Express, Subway, Taco Bell Vons Foods, Walmart
20b	Greenfield Dr, to Crest, N Chevron/dsl, Sky Fuel/dsl Jack-in-the-Box, Marieta's Mexican, McDonald's, Panchos Tacos, Subway 7-11, 99c Store, Albertson's, auto repair, AutoZone, Ford, RV camping, st patrol, URGENT CARE, vet, S Mobil/dsl/LP
20a	E Main St (from wb, no EZ return), N Budget Inn Ford, repair, Vacationer RV Park, S Arco Cadillac
19	2nd St, CA 54, El Cajon, N 76/dsl, Arco, Chevron/dsl Marechio's Italian, Pancake House CVS Drug, Meineke, USPO, Vons Foods, Walgreens, S Gas Depot, Golden State/dsl, Shell Arby's, Baskin-Robbins, Burger King, Carl's Jr

EL CENTRO

EL CAJON

INTERSTATE 8 Cont'd

19	Continued Estrada's Mexican, IHOP, Jack-in-the-Box, KFC, Little Caesar's, McDonald's, Popeye's, Subway, Taco Bell, Taco Shop, Wings n Things Best Value Inn $Tree, 7-11, CarQuest, Firestone/auto, Jiffy Lube, PepBoys, PetCo, Sprouts Mkt, Walgreens, Walmart Mkt
18	Mollison Ave, El Cajon, N Chevron Denny's Best Western, Days Inn, S Arco, QuickTrip/dsl Los Garcia's EconoLodge
17c	Magnolia Ave, CA 67 (from wb), to Santee, N Arco Del Taco, El Pollo Loco, Jack-in-the-Box, Jersey Mike's, Panda Express, Starbucks AT&T, Food4Less, Target, S Shell/service New East Buffet, Panda Express, Perry's Cafe, Rubio's Motel 6, Super 8 Nudo's Drug, Ross
17b	CA 67 (from eb), same as 17 a&c
17a	Johnson Ave (from eb), N Applebee's, Boston Mkt, Burger King, Carl's Jr, Coco's, Five Guys, Hacienda Mexican, Jamba Juice, KFC, Little Caesar's, LJ Silver, McDonald's, New Century Buffet, On the Border, O's American Kitchen, Rubio's, Ruby's Diner, Subway $Tree, Best Buy, CVS Drug, Dick's, Goodyear/auto, Home Depot, Honda, JC Penney, Lexus, Macy's, Marshall's, Mazda, Office Depot, PetsMart, Subaru, Toyota, Walmart, S Aamco, KIA, vet
16	Main St, N Arco Denny's, Sombrero Mexican Relax Inn 7-11, S Chevron/dsl, Super Star brakes/transmissions, Nissan
15	El Cajon Blvd (from eb), N Quality Inn, S 76/dsl Wrangler BBQ BMW
14c	Severin Dr, Fuerte Dr (from wb), N USA/dsl Anthony's Fish Grotto, Charcoal House Rest., La Casa Blanca Holiday Inn Express, S Brigantine Seafood Rest.
14b a	CA 125, to CA 94
13b	Jackson Dr, Grossmont Blvd, N Chevron Arby's, BJ's Rest., Casa de Pico, Chili's, ChuckeCheese, ClaimJumper, Fuddrucker's, Olive Garden, Panera Bread, Red Lobster, Shakey's Pizza, Starbucks H, $Tree, Best Buy, CVS Drug, Macy's, O'Reilly Parts, Staples, Target, USPO, Verizon, vet, Walmart, World Mkt, S Honeybaked Ham, Jack-in-the-Box Discount Tire, Ford, Hyundai, Ross, Walmart Mkt
13a	Spring St (from eb), El Cajon Blvd (from wb), S El Pollo Loco, Starbucks, Subway Hitching Post 99c Store, AutoZone
12	Fletcher Pkwy, to La Mesa, N Shell/dsl Carl's Jr, Chipotle Mexican, McDonald's, Pick Up Stix Heritage Inn 7-11, Costco, S El Torito, Starbucks, Subway Motel 6 99c Store, Chevrolet, San Diego RV Resort
11	70th St, Lake Murray Blvd, N Shell/dsl Subway, S Shell/7-11/dsl Aiken's Deli, Denny's, Marie Callender's H, auto repair, URGENT CARE
10	College Ave, N Chevron/dsl Windmill Farms Mkt, S H, to SDSU
9	Waring Rd, N Days Inn, Rodeway Inn
8	Fairmount Ave (7 from eb), to Mission Gorge Rd, N 7-11, Mobil, Sky/dsl, USA/dsl Arby's, Black Angus, Carl's Jr, Chili's, Coco's, El Pollo Loco, Filippi's Pizza, Jack-in-the-Box, Jamba Juice, Jersey Mike's, McDonald's, Roberto's Tacos, Rubio's, Sombrero Mexican, Starbucks, Subway, Szechuan Chinese, Togo's, Wendy's Motel 6 H, AutoZone, CVS Drug, Discount Tire, Home Depot, Honda, Rite Aid, Toyota, Tuesday Morning, Vons Foods
7b a	I-15 N, CA 15 S, to 40th St

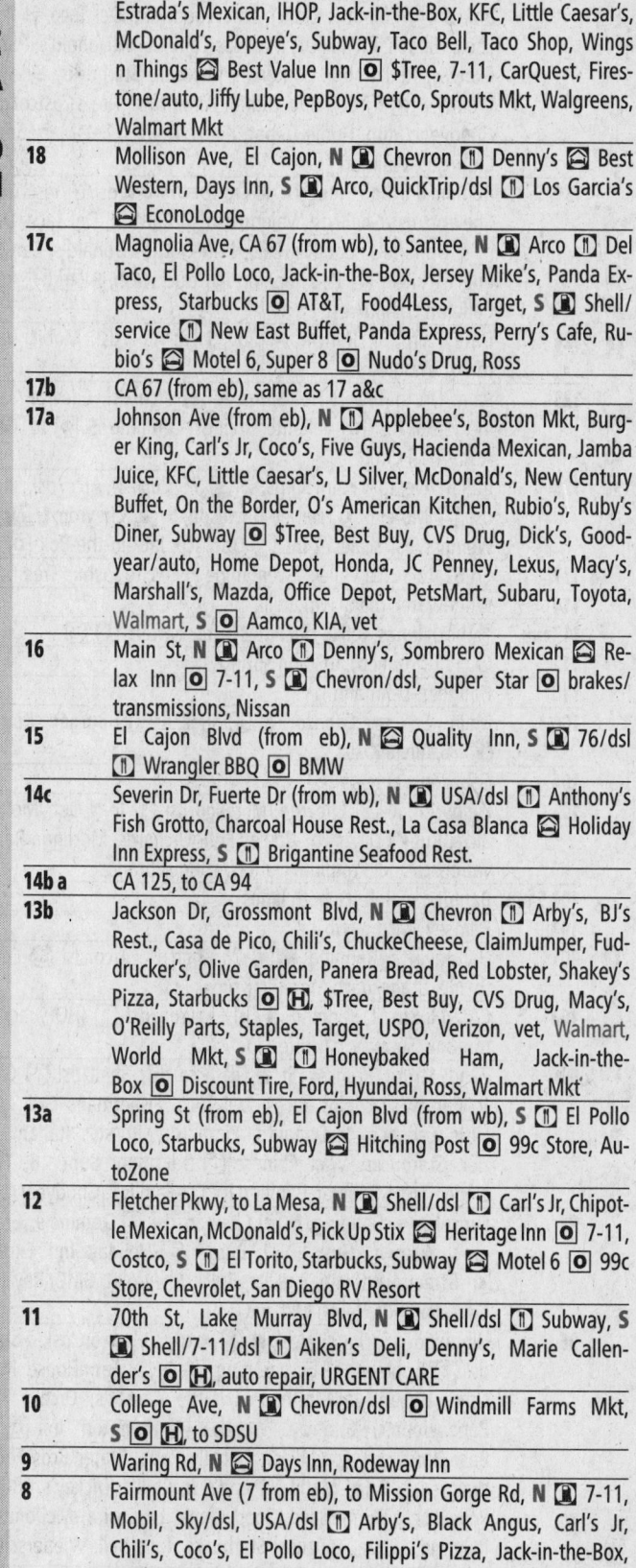

SAN DIEGO AREA

San Diego
5
Escondido
Lakeside
Pine Valley
El Centro
Holtville
Bard
El Cajon
8
Calexico
8
Fontana
Bonita
Yuma
Wellton
Tijuana
US/Mexico Border
Mexicali
CA

SAN DIEGO AREA

POINT LOMA

6b	I-805, N to LA, S to Chula Vista
6a	Texas St, Qualcomm Way, N Dave&Buster's, same as 5
5	Mission Ctr Rd, N Chevron Broken Yolk Cafe, Chipotle Mexican, Corner Cafe, El Pollo Loco, Fuddrucker's, Gordon Biersch Rest., Habit Burger, Hooters, In-N-Out, King's Fishouse, Lazy Dog Rest., Mimi's Cafe, On The Border, Outback Steaks, Panda Express, Peiwei Asian, Pick-Up Stix, Robek Juice, Rubio's, Sammy's Woodfired Pizza, Starbucks, Subway, Taco Bell, Tilted Kilt Marriott, Sheraton AT&T, Best Buy, Chevrolet, Lincoln, Marshall's, Michael's, Nordstrom Rack, Old Navy, Staples, Target, Trader Joe's, S Arco Benihana, Denny's, Fuji Japanese, Mission Valley Cafe, Wendy's Comfort Suites, Hilton, La Quinta, Sheraton Buick/GMC/Cadillac, Chrysler/Dodge/Jeep, Mazda
4c b	CA 163, Cabrillo Frwy, S to downtown, zoo
4a	Hotel Circle Dr (from eb), CA 163 (from wb)
3a	Hotel Circle, Taylor St, N Hunter Steaks Comfort Suites, Crowne Plaza, Handlery Hotel, Motel 6, Town&Country Motel golf, S Adam's Cafe, Albie's Rest., Ricky's Rest., Valley Kitchen Best Western, Candlewood Suites, Comfort Inn, Courtyard, Days Hotel, DoubleTree Inn, Extended Stay America, Hampton Inn, Howard Johnson, King's Inn/rest., Mission Valley Hotel, Residence Inn, Super 8, Travelodge, Vagabond Inn vet
2c	Morena Blvd (from wb)
2b	I-5, N to LA, S to San Diego
2a	Rosecrans St (from wb), CA 209, S Shell Chipotle Mexican, ChuckECheese, Del Taco, Denny's, In-N-Out, Panda Express, Starbucks, Subway Goodnite Inn, Hampton Inn Staples
1	W Mission Bay Blvd, Sports Arena Blvd (from wb), N to SeaWorld, S Arby's, Buffalo Wild Wings, Chick-fil-A, Chili's, Jack-in-the-Box, McDonald's, Phil's BBQ, Red Lobster, Wendy's Ramada Ltd, Wyndham Garden Dick's, Home Depot, Ralph's, Target, U-Haul, Von's
0mm	**I-8 begins/ends on Sunset Cliffs Blvd, 1/4 mi W** 76, Shell/repair Jack-in-the-Box, Kaiserhof Cafe, N Mission Bay Park

INTERSTATE 10

Exit #	Services
245mm	California/Arizona state line, Colorado River, pacific/mountain time zone
244mm	**inspection sta wb**
243	Riviera Dr, S The Cove RV Park
241	US 95, Intake Blvd, to Needles, Blythe, N Mobil/dsl, Shell/dsl Steaks'n Cakes Rest. Days Inn, M Star Motel, Relax Inn auto/RV repair/24hr, Burton's RV Park, S Hampton Inn McIntyre Park
240	7th St, N 76/dsl, EZ Mart China Garden Blue Line Motel, BudgetInn, KnightsInn, Motel6 $General, Albertson's,

CA

CA

INTERSTATE 10 Cont'd

BLYTHE

Exit	Services
240	Continued AutoZone, Ford, repair, Rite Aid, S [other] Buick/Chevrolet, Chrysler/Dodge/Jeep
239	Lovekin Blvd, Blythe, N [gas] Mobil/dsl, Shell/Quiznos [food] Carl's Jr, Del Taco, Domino's, Jack-in-the-Box, McDonald's, Popeye's, Rosita's Mexican, Sizzler, Starbucks [lodging] Best Western, Clarion, Emerald Inn, Red Roof Inn, Regency Inn, Willow Inn [other] [H], $Tree, Ace Hardware, Goodyear/auto, O'Reilly Parts, Verizon, S [gas] 24/Chester's/dsl, Chevron/dsl, Valero/Circle K, VP/dsl [food] Ampola Mexican, Burger King, Denny's, Pizza Studio, Subway, Taco Bell [lodging] Comfort Suites, Motel 6, Quality Inn, Super 8 [other] city park
236	CA 78, Neighbours Blvd, to Ripley, N [gas] Valero/dsl, S to Cibola NWR
232	Mesa Dr, N [gas] 76/dsl/rest./scales/24hr/@, Valero/dsl [other] Airport
231	**weigh sta wb**
222mm	Wileys Well Rd, N **[rest stop] both lanes, full [handicapped] facilities, litter barrels, petwalk, [phone], [picnic], S** to st prison
217	Ford Dry Lake Rd
201	Corn Springs Rd
192	CA 177, Rice Rd, to Lake Tamarisk, N [other] camping, USPO
189	Eagle Mtn Rd
182	Red Cloud Rd
177	Hayfield Rd
173	Chiriaco Summit, N [gas] Chevron/Foster's Freeze/dsl/24hr [food] Chiriaco Rest [other] Patton Museum, truck/tire repair
168	to Twentynine Palms, to Mecca, Joshua Tree NM
162	frontage rd
159mm	**Cactus City [rest stop] both lanes, full [handicapped] facilities, litter barrels, petwalk, [picnic]**
147mm	0 ft elevation
146	Dillon Rd, to CA 86, to CA 111 S, Coachella, N [gas] Chevron, Love's/Carl's Jr/dsl/24hr [food] Del Taco, S [gas] Chevron/Jack-in-the-Box, TA/Shell/Country Pride/Taco Bell/dsl/24hr/@ [other] Spotlight Casino, truckwash
145	CA 86 S (from eb)

INDIO

Exit	Services
144	CA 111 N, CA 86 S, Indio, N [lodging] Holiday Inn Express, Quality Inn [other] Classic RV Park, Fantasy Sprgs Casino/Hotel/Cafe
143	Jackson St, Indio, N [gas] Arco/dsl [food] IHOP, KFC, La Casita Mexican, McDonald's, Panda Express, Starbucks, Subway, Taco Bell [other] $Tree, AT&T, AutoZone, BigLots, CVS Drug, GNC, Home Depot, Marshall's, PetCo, Ramona Tire/auto, Ross, Target, Verizon, Walgreens, WinCo Foods, S [other] 7-11
142	Monroe St, Central Indio, N [other] RV camping, Walmart, S [gas] 76, Mobil, Shell/dsl/LP [food] Mexicali Cafe, Subway, Taco Jalisco [lodging] Best Value Inn [other] $General
139	Jefferson St, Indio Blvd, N [other] hwy patrol, Shadow Hills RV Resort
137	Washington St, Country Club Dr, to Indian Wells, N [gas] Arco, Chevron/dsl [food] Burger King, Coco's, Del Taco, Legends and Icons Grill, Mario's Italian, Papa John's, Popeye's, Starbucks, Winchell's [lodging] Comfort Suites, Motel 6 [other] 1000 Trails RV Park, Buick/GMC, Ford, Honda, McMahon's RV Ctr, Rite Aid, Stater Bros, Toyota, TrueValue, VW, Walgreens, S [gas] 76/Circle K, Mobil/Circle K [food] Carl's Jr, China Wok, Domino's, Goody's Cafe, La Casita Mexican, Lili's Chinese, Pizza Hut, Pronto Mexican, Quiznos, Subway, TJ's Mexican, ToGo's/Baskin-Robbins, Wendy's [other] Firestone/auto, Goodyear/auto
134	Cook St, to Indian Wells, S [gas] Arco, Mobil/Circle K/dsl [food] Applebees, Carl's Jr, Coldstone, Firehouse Grill, Goody's Cafe, Jack-in-the-Box, Pueblo Viejo Grill, Starbucks, Subway [lodging] Courtyard, Hampton Inn, Hilton/Homewood Suites, Residence Inn [other] vet

PALM SPRINGS

Exit	Services
131	Monterey Ave, Thousand Palms, N [gas] Arco [food] Jack-in-the-Box, S [food] Chipotle, Clark's Cafe/Food Mkt, Del Taco, El Pollo Loco, Hibachi City, IHOP, Maracas Cantina, McDonald's, Panda Express, Red Robin, Santana's Mexican, Starbucks, Subway, Wendy's [other] $Tree, 99c Store, America's Tire, Costco/gas, Goodyear/auto, Home Depot, Kohls, Lowe's, PetsMart, Sam's Club/gas, Walmart
130	Ramon Rd, Bob Hope Dr, N [gas] Flying J/dsl/LP/rest./24hr, Chevron/dsl, Shell/dsl, Valero/dsl [food] Carl's Jr, Del Taco, Denny's, Domino's, Goody's Cafe, In-N-Out, McDonald's, San Miguel Mexican [lodging] Red Roof Inn [other] truckwash, S [other] [H], Agua Caliente Casino/rest.
126	Date Palm Dr, Rancho Mirage, S [gas] Arco/dsl, Mobil, Valero [other] Walgreens
123	Palm Dr, to Desert Hot Sprgs, N [gas] Arco/dsl, Chevron/Jack-in-the-Box/dsl [other] Caliente Springs Camping, S [other] to Gene Autry Trail (3mi)
120	Indian Ave, to N Palm Sprgs, N [gas] 76/Circle K, Arco/dsl, Shell/dsl [lodging] Motel 6 [other] Harley-Davidson, S [gas] Chevron, Pilot/Wendy's/dsl/scales/24hr [food] Del Taco, Jack-in-the-Box [other] [H]
117	CA 62, to Yucca Valley, Twentynine Palms, to Joshua Tree NM
114	Whitewater, many windmills
113mm	**[rest stop] both lanes, full [handicapped] facilities, litter barrels, [phone], [picnic]**
112	CA 111 (from eb), to Palm Springs
110	Haugeen-Lehmann
106	Main St, to Cabazon, N [gas] Shell/dsl [food] Burger King, S [gas] 76/Circle K/dsl
104	Cabazon, same as 103
103	Fields Rd, N [gas] Chevron, Morongo/dsl [food] In-N-Out, McDonald's, Ruby's Diner [other] Hadley Fruit Orchards, Morongo Reservation/casino, Premium Outlets/famous brands
102.5mm	**Banning weigh sta both lanes**

BANNING

Exit	Services
102	Ramsey St (from wb)
101	Hargrave St, Banning, N [gas] 76/Church's, Arco/dsl [lodging] Country Inn, Stagecoach Motel [other] tires
100	CA 243, 8th St, Banning, N [gas] Chevron/dsl [food] IHOP, Jack-in-the-Box, Subway [other] Rite Aid
99	22nd St, to Ramsey St, N [gas] Arco/dsl, Shell/dsl [food] Carl's Jr, Carrow's, Chelos Tacos, Del Taco, Fishermans Grill, KFC, Little Caesar's, McDonald's, Pizza Hut, Russo's Italian, Sizzler, Starbucks, Wall Chinese [lodging] Days Inn, Super 8, Travelodge [other] $General, Banning RV Ctr, Family$, Goodyear/auto
98	Sunset Ave, Banning, N [gas] Chevron/dsl [food] Domino's, Gramma's Kitchen, Gus Jr #7 Burger [lodging] Holiday Inn Express [other] $Tree, AutoZone, BigLots, Buick/Chevrolet/GMC, Ray's RV Ctr, repair, Rio Ranch Mkt, vet
96	Highland Springs Ave, N [gas] Arco, Chevron/dsl, Shell/dsl [food] Applebee's, Burger King, Denny's, FarmHouse Rest., Guy's Italian, Jack-in-the-Box, Little Caesar's, Orchid Thai, Papa John's, Subway, Wendy's [lodging] Hampton Inn [other] [H], Best Hardware, Food4Less, O'Reilly Parts, Stater Bros Foods, Walgreens, S [gas] Mobil [food] Carl's Jr, Chili's, Dickey's BBQ, El Pollo Loco, FarmerBoys, Good China, La Casita, McDonald's, Palermo's Pizza, Quiznos, Starbucks, Taco Bell, Wienerschnitzel [other] $Tree, Albertson's, Best Buy, GNC, Home Depot, hwy patrol, Kohls, PetCo, Ramona Tire/auto, Rite Aid, Ross, Verizon, Walmart/Subway
95	Pennsylvania Ave (from wb), Beaumont, N [food] Country Jct Rest., Jasmine Thai, Marla's Rest. [lodging] Rodeway Inn [other] AutoZone, Meineke, Miller RV Ctr

INTERSTATE 10 Cont'd

BEAUMONT

Exit #	Services
94	CA 79, Beaumont, N 76/dsl, USA Baker's DriveThru, BMG Mexican, Casa Palacios, McDonald's, Popeye's, YumYum Donuts Best Value Inn, Best Western Family$, NAPA, O'Reilly Parts, S Arco/dsl, Shell/Circle K/dsl Del Taco, Denny's, Jack-in-the-Box, Subway RV camping, vet
93	CA 60 W, to Riverside
92	San Timoteo Canyon Rd, Oak Valley Pkwy, N Chevron/dsl Sand Trap Grill, Subway Holiday Inn Express golf, Rite Aid, S golf
91mm	**wb, full facilities, litter barrels, petwalk,**
90	Cherry Valley Blvd, N truck/tire repair
89	Singleton Rd (from wb), to Calimesa
88	Calimesa Blvd, N Arco/dsl, Chevron/dsl, Shell/dsl Best Wok, Burger King, Carl's Jr, Denny's, Isabella's Italian, McDonald's, NY Pizzaria, Subway, Taco Bell, Tang's Chinese Calimesa Inn Fresh&Easy Foods, Stater Bros Foods, Walgreens, S Big Boy, Jack-in-the-Box
87	County Line Rd, to Yucaipa, N FasTrip/dsl, Shell/dsl Baker's DriveThru, Del Taco Best Value $General, auto repair/tires, SavALot Foods, USPO, vet
86mm	**Wildwood eb, full facilities, litter barrels, petwalk,**
85	Live Oak Canyon Rd, Oak Glen
83	Yucaipa Blvd, N Arco/dsl, Chevron/dsl, Mobil Baker's DriveThru, Starbucks, S Subway
82	Wabash Ave (from wb)

REDLANDS

Exit #	Services
81	Redlands Blvd, Ford St, S 76
80	Cypress Ave, University St, N to U of Redlands, S H
79b a	CA 38, 6th St, Orange St, Redlands, N Chevron, USA Redlands Rest. Budget Inn, Stardust Motel Stater Bros Foods, S 76, Shell Chipotle Mexican, Corner Cafe, Domino's, Eureka Burger, Las Cuentes Mexican, Phoenicia Greek, Rubio's, Starbucks, Subway Firestone/auto, Office Depot, O'Reilly Parts, Sprouts Mkt, Trader Joe's, Verizon, Von's Foods
77c	(77b from wb) Tennessee St, N 7-11 Jack-in-the-Box, Shakey's Pizza Home Depot, Toyota, S Shell Arby's, Bakers DriveThru, Burger King, Carl's Jr, Coco's, El Burrito, El Pollo Loco, LJ Silver, Papa John's, Subway, Taco Bell Ayers Hotel, Comfort Suites, Dynasty Suites, Motel 6 American Tire Depot, Ford, USPO, vet
77b	(77c from wb) CA 210, to Highlands

SAN BERNARDINO

Exit #	Services
77a	Alabama St, N 76/Circle K/dsl Buffet Star, Cafe Rio, Chick-fil-A, Chili's, Coldstone Creamery, Denny's, Famous Dave's BBQ, Five Guys, Hawaiian BBQ, Jamba Juice, Jersey Mike's, Macaroni Grill, Magic Wok, Noodle 21 Asian, Red Robin, Starbucks, Subway, Tom's Charburgers Best Value Inn, Motel 7 West, Super 8 AT&T, Barnes&Noble, GNC, JC Penney, Jo-Ann Superstore, Kohl's, Marshall's, Michael's, PetCo, Target, U-Haul, Verizon, World Mkt, S Chevron, Shell Del Taco, IHOP, McDonald's, Nick's Burgers, Old Spaghetti Factory, Pizza Hut, Zabella's Mexican Country Inn&Suites, GoodNite Inn $Tree, 7-11, 99c Store, BigLots, Chevrolet, CVS Drug, Discount Tire, Goodyear/auto, K-Mart, Lowe's, Midas, Nissan, PepBoys, Ross, Tuesday Morning
76	California St, N Mill Creek Rest. funpark, museum, S Arco, Shell/LP/dsl Applebee's, Bravo Burger, Jack-in-the-Box, Jose's Mexican, Little Caesar's, Panda Express, Red Chili Szechuan, Subway, Wendy's, Wienerschnitzel AT&T, AutoZone, Food4Less, Just Tires, Mission RV Park, Walmart

CA

SAN BERNARDINO

Exit #	Services
75	Mountain View Ave, Loma Linda, N Valero/dsl, S Shell/Circle K/dsl Domino's, FarmerBoys Burgers, Lupe's Mexican, Subway
74	Tippecanoe Ave, Anderson St, N BJ's Rest., Chipotle Mexican, El Pollo Loco, Hawaiian BBQ, In-N-Out, Jack-in-the-Box, Jamba Juice, Panera Bread, Pick-Up Stix, Pollo Campero, Starbucks, Subway, Tasty Goody Fairfield Inn, Hampton Inn, Homewood Suites, Residence Inn Costco/gas, Sam's Club/gas, Staples, S 76/dsl Baker's DriveThru, Del Taco, HomeTown Buffet, KFC, Napoli Italian, Wienerschnitzel auto repair, Honda, Hyundai, to Loma Linda U
73b a	Waterman Ave, N 76, Shell/dsl Baja Fresh, Black Angus, Buffalo Wild Wings, Chili's, ChuckeCheese, ClaimJumper, Coco's, El Torito, Five Guys, IHOP, King Buffet, Lotus Garden Chinese, Mimi's Café, Olive Garden, Outback Steaks, Panda Express, Red Lobster, Sizzler, Souplantation, Subway, TGIFriday's, Togo's Best Western, Days Inn, Hilton Garden, La Quinta, Quality Inn, San Bernardino Hotel, Super 8 7-11, Best Buy, Home Depot, Office Depot, PetsMart, S Arco Burger King, Carl's Jr, Gus Jr Burger #8, McDonald's, Popeye's, Starbucks, Taco Bell Motel 6 Camping World RV Ctr, El Monte RV Ctr, repair
72	I-215, CA 91
71	Mt Vernon Ave, Sperry Ave, N 7-11, Trkstp/dsl/LP Alberto's Mexican Colony Inn, Colton Motel, Comfort Inn repair
70b	9th St, N Mobil Denny's, Domino's, McDonald's, P&G Burgers, Starbucks, Subway Holiday Inn Express NAPA, Stater Bros Foods, USPO
70a	Rancho Ave, N Del Taco, Jack-in-the-Box, KFC/Taco Bell, Wienerschnitzel
69	Pepper Dr, N Chevron Baker's DriveThru
68	Riverside Ave, to Rialto, N Chevron/dsl, I-10 Trkstp/dsl/scales, USA Burger King, Burger King, Coco's, El Pollo Loco, HomeTown Buffet, Jack-in-the-Box, McDonald's, Panda Express, Starbucks, Subway, Taco Joe's American Inn, Days Inn, ValleyView Inn dsl repair, Midas, Pepboys, Walmart, S Shell/Circle K/dsl
66	Cedar Ave, to Bloomington, N Arco, Valero/dsl Baker's DriveThru, Burger King, DQ, FarmerBoys Burgers, Subway, Taco Bell, S 7-11
64	Sierra Ave, to Fontana, N Arco, Mobil, Shell, Valero/dsl Arby's, Billy J's Rest., China Cook, China Panda, ChuckeCheese, Del Taco, Denny's, El Gallo Giro, Hawaiian BBQ, IHOP, In-N-Out, Jack-in-the-Box, KFC, Little Caesar's, McDonald's, Pancho Villa's, Papa John's, Pizza Hut/Taco Bell, Popeye's, Sizzler, Sub Shop, Subway, Wendy's, Wienerschnitzel, Yoshinoya Best Value Inn, EconoLodge, Motel 6, Valley Motel H, $Tree, AutoZone, BigLots, Cardenas Foods, CVS Drug,

CA

INTERSTATE 10 Cont'd

ONTARIO

64 Continued
Food4Less, GNC, Just Tires, PepBoys, Rite Aid, Stater Bros Foods, Verizon, **S** [gas] Chevron/dsl [food] Alvaro's Mexican, Brandon's Diner, China Buffet, Circle K, Del Taco, Los Jalapeños, Shakey's Pizza, Shrimp House, Subway, Tasty Goody [lodging] Hilton Garden [other] AutoZone, Ross, Target, TJ Maxx

63 Citrus Ave, **N** [gas] 76, Gasco [food] Baker's DriveThru, Subway [other] Ford, **S** [gas] 7-11/dsl, Arco/dsl

61 Cherry Ave, **N** [gas] Arco, Chevron, Fontana Trkstp/dsl/24hr, Valero/dsl [food] Carl's Jr, Del Taco, Jack-in-the-Box [other] Mack/Volvo, truck sales, **S** [gas] 3 Sisters Trkstp/dsl/@, 76/Circle K, North American Trkstp/dsl [food] Farmer Boy's Rest., La Chaquita [other] Peterbilt

59 Etiwanda Ave, Valley Blvd

58b a I-15, N to Barstow, S to San Diego

57 Milliken Ave, **N** [gas] 76/dsl, Arco/24hr, Chevron, Mobil/Cherony's/dsl, Shell [food] Applebee's, Baja Fresh, BJ's Rest., Burger King, Carl's Jr, Chevy's Mexican, Chick-fil-A, Chipotle, Dave&Buster's, Del Taco, Denny's, El Pollo Loco, Famous Dave's BBQ, Fat Burger, Fourth and Mill, Fuddrucker's, Hooters, IHOP, In-n-Out, Jack-in-the-Box, Jamba Juice, Jersey Mike's, KFC, Krispy Kreme, McDonald's, Mkt Broiler, New York Grill, Olive Garden, Outback Steaks, Panda Express, Panera Bread, Rain Forest Cafe, Ramona's Mexican, Red Lobster, Rubio's, Sonic, Starbucks, Subway, Taco Bell, Tokyo Wako, Wendy's, Wienerschnitzel [lodging] Ayre's Suites, Country Inn&Suites, Courtyard, Hampton Inn, Hilton Garden, Holiday Inn Express, Homewood Suites, Hyatt Place, TownePlace Suites [other] $Tree, America's Tire, Carmax, Costco/gas, Jo-Ann Fabrics, Kohl's, Marshall's, Ontario Mills Mall, Petsmart, Ross, Sam's Club/gas, Staples, Target, Verizon, **S** [gas] TA/Shell/Pizza Hut/Subway/Taco Bell/dsl/rest./24hr/@ [lodging] Rodeway Inn

56 Haven Ave, Rancho Cucamonga, **N** [gas] Mobil [food] Benihana, Black Angus, El Torito, Five Star Pizza, Hamburger Mary's [lodging] Aloft Hotel, Best Western, Extended Stay America, La Quinta, Ontario Airport Hotel, Ontario Grand Inn, **S** [food] Panda Chinese, TGIFriday's [lodging] Embassy Suites, Fairfield Inn

55b a Holt Blvd, to Archibald Ave, **N** [gas] Arco, Mobil/dsl [food] Baker's Drive-thru, Burgertown USA, Joey's Pizza, Starbucks, Subway, Weinerschnitzel

54 Vineyard Ave, **N** [gas] 76/Circle K [food] Carl's Jr, Del Taco, El Pollo Loco, Great China, Pizza Hut/Taco Bell, Popeye's, Rocky's Pizza, Subway [other] AutoZone, Rite Aid, Stater Bros Foods, **S** [gas] 76/dsl, Mobil, Quick Gas/dsl [food] Denny's, In-N-Out, Jack-in-the-Box, Marie Callenders, Porter's Steaks, Rossa's Italian, Spires Rest., Starbucks, Subway, Wendy's, Yoshinoya Japanese [lodging] Azure Suites, Best Western, Comfort Suites, DoubleTree Inn, Folk Inn, Holiday Inn, Motel 6, Ontario Airport Inn, Quality Inn, Ramada Inn, Red Roof Inn, Residence Inn, Sheraton [other] Buick/Cadillac/Chevrolet/GMC, to Airport, USPO

53 San Bernardino Ave, 4th St, to Ontario, **N** [gas] 7-11, Arco, Shell [food] Carl's Jr, Domino's, Golden Corral, Jack-in-the-Box [lodging] EconoLodge, Motel 6, **S** [gas] Arco/24hr, Chevron, Ontario Fuel/dsl [food] Denny's, Little Caesar's, McDonald's, Subway, YumYum Donuts [lodging] Days Inn, Travelodge [other] city park

51 CA 83, Euclid Ave, to Ontario, Upland, **N** [other] [H]

50 Mountain Ave, to Mt Baldy, **N** [gas] Chevron, Mobil/Circle K/dsl, Shell/dsl [food] Corky's Kitchen, Dunkin Donuts, El Torito, Hawaiian BBQ, HoneyBaked Ham, Panda Express, Subway, Wendy's [lodging] Super 8 [other] $Tree, AT&T, CVS Drug, GNC, Hobby Lobby, Home Depot, Michaels, Staples, **S** [gas] 76/dsl [food] Carl's Jr, Casa Jimenez, Chopstix, Coldstone, Juice it Up, Starbucks, Wingnuts [other] vet, Walmart/Subway

MONTCLAIR

49 Central Ave, to Montclair, **N** [food] Carl's Jr., Chipotle Mexican, El Pollo Loco, Gen Korean BBQ, John's Incredible Pizza, McDonald's, Panda Garden Buffet, Paradise Buffet, Pizza Hut, Rodrigo's Mexican, Starbucks, Subway, Taco Bell, Waba Grill [other] $Tree, 99c Store, America's Tire, AutoZone, Barnes&Noble, Best Buy, Firestone/auto, Giant RV Ctr, Harley-Davidson, JC Penney, Just Tires, Macy's, PepBoys, PetCo, Ross, same as 48, Target, vet, **S** [gas] Chevron, USA [food] Dickey's BBQ, Fulin Chinese, Jack-in-the-Box, Jersey Mike's, Starbucks, Subway, Tommy's Burgers, Wienerschnitzel [other] 7-11, Acura/Honda/Infiniti/Nissan, AT&T, Costco/gas, Stater Bros

48 Monte Vista, **N** [food] Acapulco Mexican, Applebee's, Black Angus, Chilis, Elephant Bar Rest., Olive Garden, Red Lobster [other] Macy's, Nordstrom's, same as 49, **S** [other] [H]

47 Indian Hill Blvd, to Claremont, **N** [gas] Shell/dsl [food] BC Cafe [lodging] Claremont Lodge, Knights Inn, **S** [gas] 76/dsl, Chevron/McDonald's [food] Carl's Jr, Chipotle, Denny's, In-N-Out, Norm's Rest., Popeye's, RoundTable Pizza, Starbucks, Subway [lodging] Motel 6 [other] Hyundai, Toyota, Verizon

46 Towne Ave, **N** [gas] 7-11, Chevron/dsl [food] Jack-in-the-Box

45b Garey Ave, to Pomona, **N** [gas] USA/dsl [other] [H], vet, **S** [gas] Chevron, Shell/dsl [food] Del Taco

45 White Ave, Garey Ave, to Pomona

44 (43 from eb) Dudley St, Fairplex Dr, **N** [gas] Arco/dsl [food] Coco Palm, Denny's [lodging] LemonTree Motel, **S** [gas] Chevron/24hr [food] Jack-in-the-Box, McDonald's, Starbucks [other] 7-11

42b CA 71 S (from eb), to Corona

42a to I-210, CA 57 S

41 Kellogg Dr, **S** [other] to Cal Poly Inst

40 Via Verde

38b Holt Ave, to Covina, **N** [food] Hamiltons Steaks [lodging] Vanllee Suites

38a Grand Ave, **N** [gas] 76, Arco/dsl [food] Denny's, Misky Misky Peruana [lodging] Best Western+ [other] 7-11

37b Barranca St, Grand Ave, **N** [gas] [food] BJ's Rest., Carl's Jr, Chili's, Chipotle Mexican, El Torito, Habit Burgers, Hawaiian BBQ, Hooters, Islands Rest., Marie Callender, Mariposa Mexican, Pacific Fish Grill, Starbucks, Waba Grill [lodging] Fairfield Inn, Hampton Inn, Holiday Inn [other] $Tree, Albertsons, CVS Drug, Dick's, Hobby Lobby, IKEA, Marshalls, Petsmart, Ross, Target, Verizon, **S** [food] In-N-Out, McDonald's [lodging] 5 Star Inn, Days Inn, same as 37a

COVINA

37a Citrus Ave, to Covina, **N** [gas] Chevron [food] Buffalo Wild Wings, Burger King, Del Taco, IHOP, Jack-in-the-Box, Jersey Mike's, Millie's Rest., Starbucks, Subway, TGIFriday's, Yum Yum Donuts [other] Acura, Albertsons, AT&T, Baja Ranch Foods, Buick/GMC, Chevrolet, CVS Drug, Kia, Marshall's, Nissan, Office Depot, VW, Walmart, **S** [gas] 76/7-11 [food] Classic Burger [other] Cadillac, same as 37b

36 CA 39, Azusa Ave, to Covina, **N** [gas] 76/dsl, Arco/24hr [food] Denny's, Green Field Brazillian, McDonald's, Norm's Rest., Papa John's, Subway [other] $Tree, American Tire Depot, BigLots, Chrysler/Dodge/Jeep, CVS Drug, Food4Less, Stater Bros, **S** [gas] Mobil, Shell/dsl [other] Audi, Ford, Honda, Mercedes, Toyota

35 Vincent Ave, Glendora Ave, **N** [gas] Chevron [other] auto repair, **S** [gas] [food] Blaze Pizza, Chipotle, Five Guys, Gen Korean BBQ, Jamba Juice, Lazy Dog Rest., Lucille's BBQ, Mikomi Japanese, Panera Bread, Pizza Hut, Red Robin, Starbucks, Subway, Weinerschnitzel [other] Best Buy, Firestone/auto, JC Penney, Macy's, Michael's, USPO, Verizon

34 Pacific Ave, **N** [gas] 76, **S** [gas] Shell [other] [H], Discount Tire, same as 35

INTERSTATE 10 Cont'd

EL MONTE

LOS ANGELES AREA

Exit #	Services
33	Puente Ave, N Chevron Denny's, Farmer Boy's, Guadalajara Grill, McDonald's, Panda Express, Sizzler, Starbucks Courtyard, Motel 6 AT&T, Home Depot, Verizon, Walmart, S Jack-in-the-Box Regency Inn Harley-Davidson
32b	Francisquito Ave, to La Puente, N Valero, S Carl's Jr, In-N-Out, Wienerschnitzel Grand Park Inn hwy patrol
32a	Baldwin Pk Blvd, N Chevron/McDonald's IHOP, Jack-in-the-Box, Papa Johns, Pizza Hut/Taco Bell, Starbucks, Subway, Wendy's, Yum Yum Donuts CVS Drug, Food4Less, Target, transmissions, S H
31c	(31b from wb) Frazier St, N 7-11
31b a	(31a from wb) I-605 N/S, to Long Beach
30	Garvey Ave, S Rte 66
29b	Valley Blvd, Peck Rd, N Chevron Baskin-Robbins, Burger King, Carl's Jr., Denny's, Jamba Juice, KFC, Papa Johns, Shakey's Pizza, Subway, Taco Bell, Yoshinoya Motel 6 Honda, Hyundai, Lexus, Nissan, Toyota, Walgreens, S McDonald's, Tommy's Burgers, Waba Grill
29a	S Peck Rd (from eb)
28	Santa Anita Ave, to El Monte, S 76/dsl 7-11, vet
27	Baldwin Avenue, Temple City Blvd, S Arco/24hr Denny's, same as 26b a
26b	CA 19, Rosemead Blvd, Pasadena, N Habit Burger, Chipotle, Coldstone, IHOP, Jamba Juice, Starbucks, Subway $Tree, GNC, Office Depot, Target, S Del Taco, Jack-in-the-Box, Starbucks
26a	Walnut Grove Ave
25b	San Gabriel Blvd, N Shell Carl's Jr, Popeye's, Taco Bell Budget Inn, S 7-11
25a	Del Mar Ave, to San Gabriel, N Mobil auto repair, S Shell/dsl, USA Travelodge
24	New Ave, to Monterey Park, N KFC, to Mission San Gabriel
23b	Garfield Ave, to Alhambra, S 76, Arco Grand Inn H, auto repair
23a	Atlantic Blvd, Monterey Park, N Pizza Hut, Popeye's, Starbucks H, S Courtyard, Monterey Park Inn Ralph's Foods
22	Fremont Ave, N H, S Papa Johns, Subway 7-11
21	I-710, Long Beach Fwy, Eastern Ave (from wb)
20b a	Eastern Ave, City Terrace Dr, S Chevron/service, Mobil Burger King, McDonald's
19c	Soto St (from wb), N Chevron/dsl H, city park, S 76, Mobil
19b	I-5 (from wb), US 101 S, N to Burbank, S to San Diego
19a	State St, N H
17	I-5 N
16b	I-5 S (from eb)
16a	Santa Fe Ave, San Mateo St, S 76/dsl, Mobil industrial area, Penske Trucks
15b	Alameda St, N 76/dsl Jack-in-the-Box, to downtown, S industrial area
15a	Central Ave, N Shell/repair, S Shell
14b	San Pedro Blvd, S industrial
14a	LA St, N conv ctr, S El Pollo Loco, McDonald's 99c Store, O'Reilly Parts, Rite Aid, URGENT CARE
13	I-110, Harbor Fwy
12	Hoover St, Vermont Ave, N Chevron Burger King, McDonald's, Subway AutoZone, CVS Drug, PepBoys, S 76, Chevron Jack-in-the-Box, Papa Johns, Yoshinoya Ralph's Foods

Los Angeles · El Monte · Covina · Clairemont · Pomona · Upland · South Fontana · Colton · San Bernardino · Redlands · Beaumont · 10 · 5 · 110 · 605 · 215 · CA

SANTA MONICA

Exit #	Services
11	Normandie Ave, Western Ave
10	Arlington Ave, N 76, Chevron
9	Crenshaw Blvd, N Mobil, S 76, Chevron El Pollo Loco, McDonald's, Subway, Taco Bell, Yoshinoya U-Haul
8	La Brea Ave, N Valero/dsl USPO, S Chevron AutoZone
7b	Washington Blvd, Fairfax Ave, S Mobil, same as 8
7a	La Cienega Blvd, Venice Ave (from wb), N Chevron/24hr, Mobil Carl's Jr., Del Taco Aamco, Firestone/auto, S Subway
6	Robertson Blvd, Culver City, N Chevron/dsl, Valero Domino's, Taco Bell EZ Lube, S Del Taco
5	National Blvd, N Papa John's, Starbucks, Subway, Taco+ Rite Aid, Von's Foods, S Arco
4	Overland Ave, S Mobil/dsl
3b a	I-405, N to Sacramento, S to Long Beach
2c b	Bundy Dr, N Chevron, Shell/dsl Taco Bell Cadillac/GMC, Staples
2a	Centinela Ave, to Santa Monica, N Taco Bell, S McDonald's, Trader Joe's Travelodge
1c	20th St (from wb), Cloverfield Blvd, 26th St (from wb), N 76/dsl, Chevron, Shell/repair H
1b	Lincoln Blvd, CA 1 S, N Denny's, McDonald's, Starbucks BrakeMasters, Toyota, Tuesday Morning, USPO, Vons Foods, S Chevron/dsl, Shell Dominos, Jack-in-the-Box, Subway Doubletree Suites 7-11, Firestone/auto, U-Haul
1a	4th, 5th, (from wb)
0	Santa Monica Blvd, to beaches, **I-10 begins/ends on CA 1.**

INTERSTATE 15

BAKER

Exit #	Services
298	California/Nevada state line, services in NV
291	Yates Well Rd
289	**weigh sta sb**
286	Nipton Rd, E Mojave Nat Preserve, to Searchlight
281	Bailey Rd
276mm	**brake check area for trucks, nb**
272	Cima Rd, E Shell/cafe/dsl/towing
270mm	**Valley Wells both lanes, full facilities, litter barrels, petwalk,**
265	Halloran Summit Rd
259	Halloran Springs Rd
248	to Baker (from sb), same as 246
246	CA 127, Kel-Baker Rd, Baker, to Death Valley, W Tesla EVC, 76/dsl, Arco, Chevron/Subway/Fatburger/Pizza Hut/dsl, Chevron/Taco Bell, Shell/DQ/dsl, Shell/Jack-in-the-Box/dsl, Valero, Valero/A&W/Pizza Hut/Subway/dsl Arby's, Burger King, Carl's Jr, Del Taco, Denny's, Mad Greek Café BunBoy Hotel, Santa Fe Motel Alien Fresh Jerky, Baker Mkt Foods, Country Store, repair, USPO, World's Tallest Thermometer

INTERSTATE 15 Cont'd

BARSTOW

Exit #	Services
245	to Baker (from nb), same as 246
239	Zzyzx Rd
233	Rasor Rd, E Shell/Rasor Sta/dsl/towing/24hr
230	Basin Rd
221	Afton Rd, to Dunn, W Mini Mkt
217mm	**both lanes, full facilities, litter barrels, petwalk,**
213	Field Rd
206	Harvard Rd, to Newberry Springs
198	Minneola Rd, W Cali Burger, Shell/dsl
197mm	**agricultural insp sta sb**
196	Yermo Rd, Yermo
194	Calico Rd, E Eddie World/dsl, Tesla EVC
191	Ghost Town Rd, E Arco/24hr, Mohsen Oil Trkstp/dsl/24hr Jack-in-the-Box, Peggy Sue's 50s Diner, Penny's Diner Baymont Inn, W Chevron/dsl, Shell/Subway/dsl/24hr Calico GhostTown (3mi), KOA
189	Ft Irwin Rd
186	CA 58 W, to Bakersfield
184	E Main, Barstow, Montera Rd (from eb), to I-40, E 76/dsl Grill It, McDonald's, Mega Tom's Burgers, Popeye's, Starbucks, Subway Arco, Best Western, Travelodge Walmart, W Chevron, Circle K, Mobil/dsl, USA/dsl Alberto's, Burger King, Carl's Jr, China Town Buffet, Del Taco, Denny's, Di Napoli's Italian, IHOP, Jack-in-the-Box, Jenny's Grill, Little Caesar's, LJ Silver, Wienerschnitzel Astrobudget Motel, Best Motel, Budget Inn, CA Inn, Days Inn, Desert Inn, EconoLodge, Economy Inn, Motel 6, Quality Inn/rest., Ramada Inn, Rodeway Inn, Super 8 $Tree, 99Cent Store, AutoZone, Family$, O'Reilly Parts, U-Haul/LP, URGENT CARE, Von's Foods
184a	I-40 E (from nb), **I-40 begins/ends**
183	CA 247, Barstow Rd, E Circle K, Valero/7-11/dsl Jimenez Mexican, Pizza Hut, Subway $General, Rite Aid, W Food4Less/dsl, Shell H, Food4Less, Marshall's, Mojave River Valley Museum, st patrol
181	L St, W Main, Barstow, W Arco/dsl, Chevron, USA Foster's Freeze Baymont Inn Firestone/auto, Home Depot, NAPA, tires/towing
179	CA 58, to Bakersfield
178	Lenwood, to Barstow, E FLYING J/Denny's/dsl/24hr, 76/dsl, Arco/dsl, Chevron, Shell/dsl, Valero Arby's, Big Boy, Burger King, Carl's Jr, Chili's, Chipotle Mexican, Del Taco, Denny's, El Pollo Loco, Fatburger, Habit Burger, IHOP, In-N-Out, Jack-in-the-Box, Jersey Mike's, Oggi's, Panda Express, Panera Bread, Starbucks, Subway, Tommy's Burgers Ayres Hotel, Comfort Suites, Hampton Inn, Holiday Inn Express Blue Beacon, Old Navy, Tanger Outlet/famous brands/food ct, W Loves/Chester's/Godfather's/dsl/scales/24hr/@, Pilot/Subway/dsl/scales/24hr, TA/Shell/Country Fare/Subway/dsl/scales/24hr/@ McDonald's Days Inn repair, truckwash, Zippy Lube
175	Outlet Ctr Dr, Sidewinder Rd
169	Hodge Rd
165	Wild Wash Rd
161	Dale Evans Pkwy, to Apple Valley
157	Stoddard Wells Rd, to Bell Mtn
154	Stoddard Wells Rd, to Bell Mtn, E Shady Oasis Camping/LP, W 76/dsl, Mobil Franky's Diner Motel 6, Queens Motel
153.5mm	Mojave River
153b	E St

VICTORVILLE

Exit #	Services
153a	CA 18 E, D St, to Apple Valley, E Arco H, repair, W Arco/Subway/dsl
151b	Mojave Dr, Victorville, E Mobil/dsl Rodeway Inn, W Valero/dsl Economy Inn, Sunset Inn
151a	La Paz Dr, Roy Rogers Dr, E Chevron, Shell/dsl Burger King, Carl's Jr, El Pollo Loco, HomeTown Buffet, IHOP, Jack-in-the-Box, McDonald's, Wendy's, Wienerschnitzel $General, $Tree, 99c Store, AutoZone, BigLots, Costco/gas, Fiat, Food-4Less, Goodyear/auto, Harley-Davidson, Pepboys, Rite Aid, Toyota, W Arco Carl's Jr, Dickey's BBQ, Domino's, Farmer Boys, Golden ChopStix, Hawaiian BBQ, In-N-Out, Panda Express, Papa John's, Starbucks, Subway Americas Tire, Buick/GMC, Chrysler/Dodge/Jeep, Home Depot, Honda, Kia, Nissan, Stater Bros, Verizon, Walgreens, WinCo Foods
150	CA 18 W, Palmdale Rd, Victorville, E Baker's Drive-Thru, Burger King, Denny's, KFC, Richie's Diner Greentree Inn, Red Roof Inn, W 76/dsl, Arco, Circle K Coco's, Del Taco, House of Joy, La Casita Mexican, McDonald's, Pizza Hut, Raul's Mexican, Starbucks, Subway, Taco Bell, Tom's Rest. Budget Inn, Days Inn, Holiday Inn H, $General, Aamco, AutoZone, CVS Drug, Ford, Hyundai, Kamper's Korner RV, Mazda, Target, Town&Country Tire, vet
148	LaMesaRd, NisqualiRd, E RedRoofInn, W Baskin-Robbins, Buffalo's, ChuckeCheese, Fatburger AT&T, Petsmart
147	Bear Valley Rd, to Lucerne Valley, **0-2 mi** E 76/Circle K/dsl, Arco, Chevron, Mobil Arby's, Baker's Drive-Thru, Burger King, Carl's Jr, Del Taco, Dragon Express, John's Pizza, KFC, Los Alazanes Mexican, Los Toritos, Marie Callender's, McDonald's, Panda Express, Red Robin, Starbucks, Steak'n Shake, Steer'n Stein, Tacos Mexico, Wienerschnitzel Best Value Inn, Comfort Suites, Day&Night Inn, EconoLodge, Extended Stay, Extended Studio Hotel, La Quinta, Travelodge Affordable RV Ctr, America's Tire, AutoZone, Firestone/auto, Home Depot, Michael's, O'Reilly Parts, Range RV, Rite Aid, Scandia Funpark, Tire Depot, Vallarta Foods, vet, Walmart/McDonald's/auto, W 76/Circle K, Arco, Chevron/dsl, Valero/dsl Applebee's, Archibald's Drive-Thru, Baja Fresh, Carino's, Chili's, Chipotle Mexican, Cracker Barrel, Del Taco, El Pollo Loco, El Tio Pepe Mexican, Farmer Boy's Rest., Freddy's Custard, Giuseppe's, Jack-in-the-Box, Little Caesar's, McDonald's, Mimi's Cafe, Olive Garden, Outback Steaks, Pancho Villa's, Red Lobster, RoadHouse Grill, Sonic, Starbucks, Subway, Tokyo Steaks, Wendy's Hawthorn Suites 99c Store, AAA, Barnes&Noble, Best Buy, CVS Drug, Dick's, Goodyear/auto, Hobby Lobby, JC Penney, Kohl's, Lowe's, Macy's, Rite Aid, Stater Bros., Verizon, Walgreens, Walmart

HESPERIA

Exit #	Services
143	Main St, to Hesperia, Phelan, E Chevron/dsl, Mobil/Alberto's, Shell/Popeye's/dsl Arby's, Burger King, Chipotle, Del Taco, Denny's, IHOP, In-N-Out, Jack-in-the-Box, Panda Express, Quiznos, Starbucks Courtyard, SpringHill Suites Walmart/Subway, W 76/dsl, Arco/dsl Baker's Drive-thru, FarmerBoys, Five Guys, Golden Corral, Subway, Waba Grill Holiday Inn Express, Motel 6 Desert Willow RV Park, GNC, Jo-Ann Fabrics, Marshall's, Ross, SuperTarget, URGENT CARE, Verizon
141	US 395, Joshua St, Adelanto, W Arco/dsl, Pilot/Wendy's/dsl/scales/24hr Outpost Café repair, RV supply ctr, truck/RV wash, Zippy Lube
140	Ranchero Rd
138	Oak Hill Rd, E Chevron/dsl Summit Inn Café, W Oak Hills RV Village/LP
137mm	**brake check sb**, Cajon Summit, elevation 4260

INTERSTATE 15 Cont'd

Exit #	Services
131	CA 138, to Palmdale, Silverwood Lake, E gas Chevron food McDonald's other Silverwood SRA, W gas 76/Circle K/Del Taco/LP, Shell/Subway/dsl/LP lodging Best Western
130mm	**weigh sta both lanes**, elevation 3000
129	Cleghorn Rd
124	Kenwood Ave
123	I-215 S, to San Bernardino, E gas Arco other to Glen Helen Park
122	Glen Helen Parkway
119	Sierra Ave, W gas Arco/dsl, Chevron/dsl, Shell/Del Taco/dsl, Valero/dsl food Jack-in-the-Box, McDonalds other to Lytle Creek RA
118	Duncan Canyon Rd
116	Summit Ave, E gas 7-11, Chevron food Chili's, Coldstone, Del Taco, El Ranchero, Five Guys, Hawaiian BBQ, Jack-in-the-Box, Juice It Up, Little Caesar's, Panera Bread, Quiznos, Roundtable Pizza, Starbucks, Subway, Taco Bell, Wendy's other $Tree, CVS Drug, GNC, Kohl's, Marshall's, Michael's, Petsmart, Ross, Staples, Stater Bros, Target, Verizon
115b a	CA 210, Highland Ave, E to Lake Arrowhead
113	Base Line Rd, E gas USA food Denny's, Jack-in-the-Box, Logans Roadhouse, Pizza Hut, Rosa Maria's, Starbucks lodging Comfort Inn
112	CA 66, Foothill Blvd, E gas Chevron food Asia Buffet, Claim-Jumper, Golden Spoon, In-N-Out, Panda Express, Subway, Taco Bell, Wienerschnitzel other $City, Food4Less, Jiffy Lube, Walmart, **1-2 mi** W gas 76/dsl, Chevron/dsl food Baker's, Buffalo Wild Wings, Carino's, Cheesecake Factory, Chick-fil-A, Chipotle Mexican, Del Taco, Denny's, El Pollo Loco, El Torito, Flemings Steaks, Islamadora Fish Co, Jack-in-the-Box, Joe's Crab Shack, Johnny Rockets, Kings Fishouse, Lucille's BBQ, Old Spagetti Factory, Paisano's Rest., PF Chang's, Popeyes, Red Robin, Richie's Diner, Shakey's Pizza, Starbucks, TGIFriday's, The Hat Grill, Wendy's lodging Sheraton 4 Points other AT&T, AutoZone, Bass Pro Shops, Best Buy, Fresh&Easy Mkt, Home Depot, JC Penney, Macy's, Office Depot, Sears Grand
110	4th St, E gas Arco/dsl food Baker's, Subway, W gas 76/dsl, Arco, Chevron/Alberto's Mexican/dsl, Shell/dsl food Applebee's, Arby's, Baja Fresh, Baskin-Robbins, BJ's Rest., Boston's, Burger King, Carl's Jr, Chevy's Mexican, Chick-fil-A, Chipotle, Chop Sticks, Coco's, Daphne's Greek, Del Taco, Denny's, El Pollo Loco, Famous Dave's BBQ, Fat Burger, Fuddruckers, Hooters, IHOP, In-N-Out, Jack-in-the-Box, Jamba Juice, Juice It Up, KFC, Krispy Kreme, Lazy Dog Cafe, McDonald's, Mkt Broiler, New City Buffet, NY Grill, Olive Garden, Outback Steaks, Panera Bread, Rain Forest Cafe, Red Brick Pizza, Red Lobster, Rubio's, Sonic, Starbucks, Subway, Tokyo Tokyo, Wendy's, Wienerschnitzel, Wing Place lodging Ayre's Suites, Country Inn&Suites, Courtyard, Hampton Inn, Hilton Garden, Holiday Inn Express, Homewood Suites, Hyatt Place, TownePlace Suites other $Tree, America's Tire, Costco/gas, JC Penney, Jo-Ann Fabrics, Kohl's, Marshall's, Ontario Mills Mall, Petsmart, Sam's Club/gas, Staples, Target, Tire Pros, Verizon
109b a	I-10, E to San Bernardino, W to LA
108	Jurupa St, E gas Chevron/dsl food Burger King, Del Taco, El Gran Burrito, Starbucks, Subway other Affordable RV, BMW, Chrysler/Dodge/Jeep, Family RV Ctr, Fiat, Honda, Hyundai, Lexus, Mazda, Mini, Nissan, Subaru, Toyota, Volvo, VW, W gas Arco food Carl's Jr other Ford, Kia, Scandia funpark
106	CA 60, E to Riverside, W to LA
105	Cantu-Galleano Ranch Rd
103	Limonite Ave, E food Asado Grill, Carl's Jr, Del Taco, Denny's, Five Guys, Hawaiian BBQ, Jamba Juice, Subway other Lowe's,

CUCAMONGA

ONTARIO

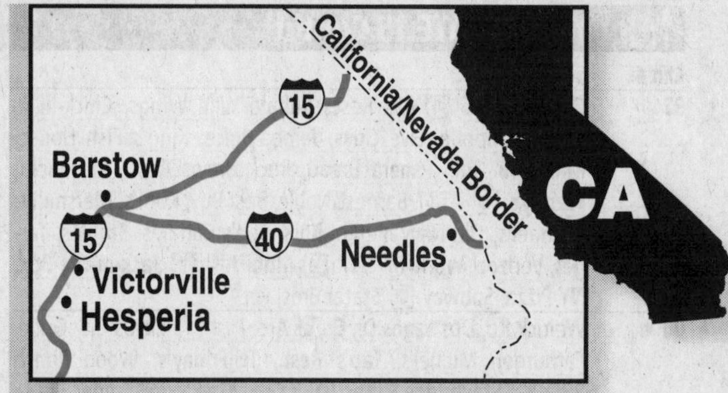

Exit #	Services
103	Continued Michael's, PetCo, Ross, W gas Chevron food Applebee's, Blaze Pizza, Buffalo Wild Wings, Carino's, Chipotle, Coldstone, Dickey's BBQ, Domino's, Farmer Boys, Habit Burger, Jersey Mike's, Juice it Up, Little Caesar's, McDonald's, On-the-Border, Pacific Fish Grill, Panda Express, Panera Bread, Pick Up Stix, Starbucks, Subway, Taco Bell, Tutti Frutti Yogurt, Wendy's other AT&T, Best Buy, GNC, Home Depot, Kohl's, Nestle Tollhouse, Petsmart, Ralph's Foods/gas, Staples, Target, TJ Maxx, Verizon, Vons Foods/gas, Walgreens
100	6th St, Norco Dr, Old Town Norco, E gas 76/dsl, Chevron food Jack-in-the-Box, McDonald's other Rite Aid, W gas Arco, Valero/dsl food Big Boy, Norco's Burgers, Starbucks, Wienerschnitzel lodging Fairfield Inn other Brake Masters, Jiffy Lube, USPO, vet
98	2nd St, W gas Mobil, Shell/dsl, Thrifty food Baja Fish Tacos, Burger Basket, Burger King, Carl's Jr, Del Taco, In-N-Out, Pancake House, Pizza Hut, Polly's Cafe, Subway other $Tree, 7-11, Ace Hardware, Chrysler/Dodge/Jeep, Ford, Norco Tires, Schwab Tire, Stater Bros
97	Yuma Dr, Hidden Valley Pkwy, E gas 7-11 food Chick-fil-A, Hot Dog Shoppe, Marco's Pizza, Shogun Japanese, Starbucks, Starbucks, Subway, Waba Grill other Kohl's, Stater Bros, W gas 76/dsl, Chevron, Shell/dsl food Alberto's Mexican, Burger City Grill, Carl's Jr, Chipotle, Denny's, Domino's, Fantastic Cafe, Five Guys, Hawaiian BBQ, Hickory Joe's BBQ, Jack-in-the-Box, Jamba Juice, Jersey Mike's, Jimmy John's, KFC, McDonald's, Miguel's Jr, Papa John's, Pieology, Popeye's, Rodrigo's Mexican, Rubio's, Taco Bell, Wahoos Fish Taco lodging Hampton Inn, Howard Johnson Express other America's Tire, AT&T, AutoZone, BigLots, GNC, Hobby Lobby, O'Reilly Parts, Staples, Target, URGENT CARE, Verizon, Walgreens, Walgreens, Winco
96b a	CA 91, to Riverside, beaches
95	Magnolia Ave, E gas Chevron/Jack-in-the-Box/dsl food Islands Burgers, Shamrock's Grill lodging Residence Inn other AAA, Lowe's, Office Depot, W gas Mobil/Circle K, Shell food Baskin-Robbins, Broken Yolk, Coco's, Jersey's Pizza, Little Caesar's, McDonald's, Sizzler, Subway, Waba Grill lodging Holiday Inn Express other $Tree, AT&T, CVS Drug, El Super Mkt, O'Reilly Parts, Sonic, Stater Bros Foods
93	Ontario Ave, to El Cerrito, E gas Shell/dsl food Sombrero Mexican, Starbucks other Mtn View Tire, vet, W gas 76/Circle K, Arco, Chevron food Chipotle, Chopstix, Del Taco, Denny's, El Pollo Loco, Hawaiian BBQ, In-N-Out, Jack-in-the-Box, Jersey Mike's, Juice It Up, KFC, Magic Wok, McDonald's, Miguel's Jr, Papa John's, Pieology, Porky's Pizza, Rubio's, SpringHill Suites, Subway, Taco Bell, Tommy's Burgers, Wienerschnitzel other Albertson's/Sav-On, America's Tire, AutoZone, CVS Drug, Home Depot, Sam's Club/gas, USPO, Walmart
92	El Cerrito Rd

NORCO

EL CERRITO

CA

INTERSTATE 15 Cont'd

Exit #	Services
91	Cajalco Rd, E [food] BJ's Rest., Buffalo Wild Wings, Chick-fil-A, Chili's, Chipotle, Five Guys, Jamba Juice, King's Fish House, Macaroni Grill, Panera Bread, Rock Brews Rest., Starbucks, Wendy's [other] AT&T, Barnes&Noble, Best Buy, Kohl's, Marshall's, Michael's, Old Navy, PetCo, Ross, See's Candies, Staples, Target, Verizon, World Mkt, W [gas] Mobil/dsl [food] Jack-in-the-Box, NY Pizza, Subway [other] Stater Bros, vet
90	Weirick Rd, Dos Lagos Dr, E [gas] Arco/dsl [food] Citrus City Grille, Fatburger, Miguel's, Tap's Rest., TGIFriday's, Wood Ranch BBQ [lodging] Staybridge Suites [other] 7 Oaks Gen Store, Trader Joe's
88	Temescal Cyn Rd, Glen Ivy, E [gas] Shell, W [gas] Arco/dsl [food] Carl's Jr, Tom's Farms/BBQ
85	Indian Truck Trail, W [food] Pizza Hut, Starbucks, Subway [other] CVS Drug, Von's Foods/dsl
81	Lake St
78	Nichols Rd, W [gas] Arco/dsl [other] Outlets/famous brands
77	CA 74, Central Ave, Lake Elsinore, E [gas] Arco, Chevron, Mobil/Circle K/dsl [food] Archibald's, Burger King, Chili's, Del Taco, Dickey's BBQ, Douglas Burgers, Golden Corral, Hawaiian BBQ, Juice It Up, Panda Express, Submarina, Taco Del Mar, Tom's ChiliBurgers, Wendy's [other] $Tree, AT&T, Costco/gas, Lowe's, Petsmart, Staples, Valvoline, W [food] El Pollo Loco, Farmer Boys, Golden Chop Stix, IHOP, McDonald's, Papa John's, Starbucks, Subway, Wienerschnitzel [other] 99c Store, Aldi Foods, Home Depot, Marshall's, PetCo, Target, Verizon, Walgreens
75	Main St, Lake Elsinore, W [gas] Main St Gas/dsl [other] 7-11, tires/repair
73	Railroad Cyn Rd, to Lake Elsinore, E [gas] 76/7-11, Shell/Circle K/dsl [food] Alberto's Mexican, Denny's, El Pollo Loco, In-N-Out, KFC, Peony Chinese, Starbucks [lodging] Holiday Inn Express [other] GNC, Jiffy Lube, O'Reilly Parts, URGENT CARE, Verizon, vet, Von's Foods, Walmart/McDonald's, W [gas] Arco, Chevron, Mobil/Circle K/dsl [food] Annie's Cafe, Cafe China, Carl's Jr, Del Taco, Don Jose's Mexican, King Kabob, McDonald's, Pizza Hut, Sizzler, Subway, Taco Bell, Vincenzo's [lodging] Best Western+, Quality Inn, Travel Inn [other] $Tree, 7-11, AutoZone, BigLots, Buick/GMC, Chevrolet, CVS Drug, Express Tire/auto, Firestone/auto, Ford, Stater Bros, vet, Walgreens
71	Bundy Cyn Rd, E [gas] Shell/Circle K, W [gas] Arco [food] Jack-in-the-Box
69	Baxter Rd
68	Clinton Keith Rd, E [gas] Chevron/dsl, USA [food] Denny's, Golden Spoon, Los Jilbetos Tacos, Los Reyes Grill, McDonald's, Panda Express, Starbucks, Subway [other] [H], Ace Hardware, Albertsons/Sav-on, W [gas] 7-11, Arco/dsl [food] Del Taco, Jack-in-the-Box, Stadium Pizza, Starbucks, Tresino's Italian, Yellow Basket Burgers [other] Baron's Mkt, Rite Aid, Stater Bros
65	California Oaks Rd, Kalmia St, E [gas] 76/Circle K/dsl, Chevron, Shell/7-11/dsl [food] Burger King, Carl's Jr, Chili's, Chipotle, DQ, Jade Chinese, Jamba Juice, Jersey's Pizza, Jimenez Mexican, KFC, Little Caesar's, McDonald's, Papa John's, Starbucks, Subway, Wings'N Things [lodging] Comfort Inn [other] $Tree, Albertson's/Sav-On, AutoZone, Express Tire, O'Reilly Parts, Rite Aid, Target, Tuesday Morning, vet, Walgreens, W [gas] Arco/dsl, Chevron [food] Applebee's, Chick-fil-A, Farmer Boys, Jack-in-the-Box, Juice it Up, Pick Up Stix, Sizzlin Steer, Taco Bell [other] America's Tire, Giant RV Ctr, Kohl's, Lowe's, Office Depot, PetCo
64	Murrieta Hot Springs Rd, to I-215, E [gas] 7-11, Shell/dsl [food] Buffalo Wild Wings, Carl's Jr, El Pollo Loco, Hungry Bull, Richie's Diner, Rubio's, Sizzler, Starbucks, Wendy's [other] Ralph's
64	Continued Foods, Rite Aid, Ross, Sam's Club/gas, Walgreens, W [gas] 7-11, Shell/Popeye's/dsl [food] Arby's, Chuy's, Coldstone, Denny's, IHOP, Jersey Mike's Subs, McDonald's, Panda Express, Starbucks, Subway, Tom's Burgers, Wienerschnitzel [other] 99c Store, AAA, American Tire Depot, AT&T, Best Buy, BigLots, CarMax, Home Depot, Petsmart, Staples, Walmart/McDonald's
63	I-215 N (from nb), to Riverside
62	French Valley Pkwy (from sb, no return), W [food] Los Cabos [other] BMW, O'Reilly Parts, VW
61	CA 79 N, Winchester Rd, E [gas] 76/dsl, Chevron [food] Baja Fresh, Baskin-Robbins/Togo's, BF Greek Rest., BJ's Rest., Burger King, CA Pizza Kitchen, Chick-fil-A, Chipotle Mexican, Coldstone, Corner Cafe, Del Taco, Dickey's BBQ, El Torito, Famous Dave's, Fatburger, Five Guys, Freebirds Burrito, Harry's Grill, Hometown Buffet, Islands Burgers, Jamba Juice, Lazy Dog Cafe, Lucille's BBQ, Macaroni Grill, McDonald's, Mimi's Cafe, Ming's, Olive Garden, Outback Steaks, Panda Express, Panera Bread, PF Chang's, Red Ginger Chinese, Red Lobster, Red Robin, Shakey's Pizza, Shogun Chinese, Souplantation, Starbucks, Subway, Taco Bell, TGIFriday's, Tilted Kilt, Wahoo's, Yellow Basket Hamburgers [other] $Tree, 99c Store, America's Tire, AT&T, AutoZone, Barnes&Noble, Costco/gas, CVS Drug, Express Tire, Express Tire, Food4Less, GNC, Hobby Lobby, Hyundai, JC Penney, Jo-Ann Fabrics, K-Mart, Lowe's, Macy's, Nissan, Office Depot, Old Navy, PepBoys, PetCo, Ramona Tire, Roots Mkt, See's Candies, TJ Maxx, Trader Joe's, Verizon, WinCo Foods, World Mkt, W [gas] Arco, Chevron/dsl [food] Arby's, Banzai Japanese, Chin's Gourmet Chinese, Del Taco, El Pollo Loco, Farmer Boys, In-N-Out, Jack-in-the-Box, Patsy's Country Kitchen, Serrano's Grill, Starbucks, Subway, Super China, Tacos El Gallo, Vail Ranch Steakhouse, Wendy's [lodging] Best Western, Extended Stay America, Fairfield Inn, Holiday Inn Express, La Quinta, Quality Inn [other] NAPA, Richardson's RV Ctr, st patrol, tires/repair, vet
59	Rancho California Rd, E [gas] Arco, Mobil/Circle K/dsl, Shell/dsl [food] Black Angus, Chili's, ClaimJumper, Del Taco, Golden Spoon, Jilberto's Mexican, Little Caesar's, Marie Callender's, Pat&Oscar's Rest., Peony Chinese, Pizza Hut, RoundTable Pizza, Rubio's, Starbucks, Subway, Times Square NY Pizza [lodging] Embassy Suites [other] BigLots, CVS Drug, Ford, Mazda, Michael's, Subaru, Target, URGENT CARE, Verizon, vet, Von's Foods, W [gas] 76/Circle K/dsl, Chevron [food] Alberto's Mexican, Denny's, McDonald's, Mr Kabob Grill, Penfold's Cafe, Rosa's Café, Starbucks, Vince's Spaghetti [lodging] Hampton Inn, Motel 6, Rancho California Inn, Rodeway Inn, SpringHill Suites [other] to Old Town Temecula, USPO
58	CA 79 S, to Indio, Temecula, E [gas] Mobil/Circle K/dsl, Valero/Circle K/dsl [food] Carl's Jr, Del Taco, Domino's, Domino's, Francesca's Italian, Golden Bowl Asian, In-N-Out, Los Jilberto's, Starbucks, Utopizza, Wing-n-Things [other] 7-11, Ace Hardware, America's Tire, CVS Drug, Valvoline, W [gas] Arco, Shell/dsl [food] Baskin-Robbins, Eldorado Mexican, Garage Rest., Hungry Howie's, Leinzo Charro Mexican, Wienerschnitzel [lodging] Ramada Inn [other] Express Tire, Harley-Davidson
55mm	**check sta nb**
54	Rainbow Valley Blvd, 2 mi E [gas] gas [food] food, W [other] CA Insp Sta
51	Mission Rd, to Fallbrook, W [other] [H]
46	CA 76, to Oceanside, Pala, E [other] RV camp, W [gas] Mobil/Circle K [food] McGrath's Grill [lodging] Quality Inn [other] Pala Meas Mkt
44mm	San Luis Rey River
43	Old Hwy 395

LAKE ELSINORE

MURRIETA

TEMECULA

INTERSTATE 15 Cont'd

ESCONDIDO

Exit #	Services
41	Gopher Canyon Rd, Old Castle Rd, **1 mi E** Welk Resort RV camping
37	Deer Springs Rd, Mountain Meadow Rd, **W** Arco
34	Centre City Pkwy (from sb)
33	El Norte Pkwy, **E** Arco, Shell/dsl Arby's, DQ, IHOP, Papa John's, Starbucks Best Western CVS Drug, Express Tire/auto repair, RV Resort, vet, Von's Foods, **W** 76/7-11/dsl, Circle K Jack-in-the-Box, Killer Pizza, Rita's Custard, Subway, Wendy's vet, Von's Foods
32	CA 78, to Oceanside
31	Valley Pkwy, **E** Arco Chili's, ChuckeCheese, Cocina del Charro, Firehouse Subs, McDonald's, Olive Garden, Panda Express, Rock'N Jenny's Subs, Thai Kitchen H, Barnes&Noble, Meineke, Michael's, PetCo, URGENT CARE, **W** Express Applebee's, Burger King, Carl's Jr, Chipotle Mexican, Coco's, Del Taco, El Pollo Loco, Five Guys, In-N-Out, Jamba Juice, Mike's BBQ, Panera Bread, Pick Up Stix, Port of Subs, Primo's Mexican, Soup Plantation, Starbucks, Subway, Wendy's Comfort Inn, Holiday Inn Express 7-11, Albertson's, AT&T, BigLots, CVS Drug, Dick's, GNC, Home Depot, Lexus, Ross, Staples, Target, TJ Maxx, Verizon, World Mkt
30	9th Ave, Auto Parkway, **E** Infiniti, Mercedes, **W** same as 31
29	Felicita Rd
28	Centre City Pkwy (from nb, no return), **E** Center City Café Escondido Lodge vet
27	Via Rancho Pkwy, to Escondido, **E** Chevron/dsl, Shell BJ's Rest., Cheesecake Factory, Macaroni Grill, On-the-Border, Panera Bread, Red Robin JC Penney, Macy's, Nordstrom, San Diego Animal Park, Target, **W** Shell/Quiznos/dsl McDonald's, Starbucks, Subway Verizon
26	W Bernardo Dr, to Highland Valley Rd, Palmerado Rd
24	Rancho Bernardo Rd, to Lake Poway, **E** Arco, Mobil/Circle K Chef Chin, Cojita's Taco, Pizza Hut, Soup Plantation, Starbucks, Stirfresh, Sub Marina, Subway Hilton Garden AT&T, Barons Mkt, GNC, Von's Foods, **W** 76/Circle K, Chevron/7-11 Elephant Bar Rest., Starbucks Holiday Inn Express, Radisson
23	Bernardo Ctr Dr, **E** Chevron Burger King, Carl's Jr, Coco's, Denny's, Hibachi Buffet, Jack-in-the-Box, Little Caesar's, McDonald's, Quiznos, Robeks Juice, RoundTable Pizza, Rubio's 7-11, CVS Drug, Express Tire/auto, Firestone/auto, vet
22	Camino del Norte
21	Carmel Mtn Rd, **E** Chevron, Shell/dsl Athens Greek, Baskin-Robbins, Boston Mkt, Broken Yolk Cafe, CA Pizza Kitchen, Carl's Jr, Chick-fil-A, China Fun, Chipotle Mexican, ClaimJumper, DQ Orange Julius, El Pollo Loco, Habit Burgers, In-N-Out, Islands Burgers, Jamba Juice, Little Tokyo, Marie Callender's, McDonald's, Olive Garden, O's American Kitchen, Panda Express, Panera Bread, Rubio's, Sombrero Mexican, Subway, Taco Bell, TGIFriday's, Wendy's, Which Wich? Residence Inn AT&T, Barnes&Noble, Best Buy, Costco/gas, GNC, Home Depot, Marshall's, Michael's, PetCo, Ralph's Foods, Rite Aid, Ross, Sears Outlet, See's Candies, Sprouts Mkt, Staples, TJ Maxx, Trader Joe's, USPO, Valvoline, Verizon, **W** Chevron Jack-in-the-Box, Starbucks 7-11, Albertson's, Big O Tire, Office Depot
19	CA 56 W, Ted Williams Pkwy
18	Rancho Penasquitos Blvd, Poway Rd, **E** Arco Alvero's Mexican, Papa John's AAA, **W** 76/dsl, Mobil/dsl IHOP, McDonald's, Mi Ranchito Mexican, MXN Cafe, NY

CARMEL MTN

CA

MIRA MESA

Exit #	Services
18	Continiued Pizza, Starbucks, Subway La Quinta 7-11
17	Mercy Rd, Scripps Poway Pkwy, **E** USA/dsl Chili's, Wendy's, Yanni's Grill Residence Inn, SpringHill Suites, **W** Chevron KFC, Que Pasa Mexican, Starbucks
16	Mira Mesa Blvd, to Lake Miramar, **E** Bruski Burgers, ChuckeCheese, Denny's, Filippi's Pizza, Filippi's Pizza, Gyu-Kaku Japanese, Lucio's Mexican, Nok Thai, Pizza Hut, Shozen BBQ Comfort Suites, Holiday Inn Express Trader Joe's, USPO, **W** Arco, Shell Applebee's, Arby's, Buca Italian, Coldstone, El Patron, In-N-Out, Islands Burgers, Jack-in-the-Box, Jamba Juice, Jersey Mike's Subs, McDonald's, Mimi's Café, MXN Mexican, On the Border, Panera Bread, Pick Up Stix, Popeye's, Rubio's, Starbucks, Subway, Wings n Things Albertson's/Sav-On, AutoZone, Barnes&Noble, Best Buy, BigLots, CVS Drug, Discount Tire, GNC, Home Depot, Old Navy, Ralph's Foods, Rite Aid, Ross, USPO, Verizon
15	Carroll Canyon Rd, to Miramar College, **E** Carl's Jr, Subway
14	Pomerado Rd, Miramar Rd, **W** Chevron/dsl, Mobil, Shell/dsl, USA/dsl Carl's Jr, Chin's Rest., IHOP, Rice King, Subway Best Western, Holiday Inn, Quality Inn Audi/Porsche, aviation museum, Land Rover, vet
13	Miramar Way, US Naval Air Station
12	CA 163 S (from sb), to San Diego
11	to CA 52
10	Clairemont Mesa Blvd, **W** Boll Weevil Rest., Carl's Jr, China Express, Giovanni's, Giovanni's Pizza, Jack-in-the-Box, Jersey Mike's, La Salsa, McDonald's, Panda Express, Primo's Mexican, Robeks, Rubio's, Spice House Cafe, Starbucks, Subway, Sunny Donuts, Taco Bell, Taco Bell, Togo's, Wendy's 7-11, vet
9	CA 274, Balboa Ave
8	Aero Dr, **W** Arco, Chevron/dsl Baskin-Robbins/Togo's, Jack-in-the-Box, McDonald's, Papa John's, Pick Up Stix, Rubio's, Sizzler, SmashBurger, Starbucks, Submarina, Subway, Taco Bell Holiday Inn $Tree, AT&T, Express Tire/auto, Fry's Electronics, Petsmart, Verizon, Von's Foods, Walmart/McDonald's
7b	Friars Rd W, **W** Coldstone, Dragon Chinese, IHOP, Islands Burgers, Luna Grill, McDonald's, Oggi's Pizza, Playa Grill, Starbucks, Subway Costco/gas, Lowe's, San Diego Stadium
7a	Friars Rd E
6b	I-8, E to El Centro, W to beaches
6a	Adams Ave, downtown
5b	El Cajon Blvd, **E** Pearson/dsl/E85/NG Subway Carquest, Ford, **W** Chevron/dsl, United Oil Church's Pep-Boys
5a	University Ave, **E** Chevron/dsl Burger King, Jack-in-the-Box
3	I-805, N to I-5, S to San Ysidro
2b	(2c from nb) CA 94 W, downtown

SAN DIEGO AREA

= gas = food = lodging = other = rest stop

CA

INTERSTATE 15 Cont'd

Exit #	Services
2a	Market St, E Costco/gas
1c	National Ave, Ocean View Blvd
1b	(from sb) I-5 S, to Chula Vista
1a	(from sb) I-5 N. **I-15 begins/ends on I-5.**

INTERSTATE 40

NEEDLES

Exit #	Services
155	California/Arizona state line, Colorado River, pacific/mountain time zone
153	Park Moabi Rd, to Rte 66, **N** boating, camping
149mm	insp both lanes
148	5 Mile Rd, to Topock, Rte 66 (from eb)
144	US 95 S, E Broadway, Needles, **N** Chevron/dsl/24hr, Mobil, Shell/dsl/LP Domino's 99cStore, Harris Repair/towing, Rite Aid, **S** Best Value Inn $Tree, Stout Tires/repair
142	J St, Needles, **N** J St Gas, Valero/dsl Jack-in-the-Box, McDonald's Rodeway Inn Big O Tire, NAPA, **S** Denny's Days Inn, Motel 6 H
141	W Broadway, River Rd, Needles, **N** River City Pizza Best Motel, Desert Mirage Inn, River Valley Motel, **S** Chevron/dsl, Mobil/dsl, Shell/DQ/dsl Carl's Jr, Panda Garden, River Cafe, Taco Bell, Wagon Wheel Rest. Best Western, Budget Inn, Knights Inn, Relax Inn, Rio Del Sol Inn auto/RV/tire/repair
139	River Rd Cutoff (from eb), **N** Desert View RV Park, KOA, Hist Rte 66, rec area
133	US 95 N, to Searchlight, to Rte 66
120	Water Rd
115	Mountain Springs Rd, elev 2770, High Springs Summit
107	Goffs Rd, Essex, **N** gas/dsl/food, Hist Rte 66
106mm	**both lanes, full facilities, litter barrels, petwalk,**
100	Essex Rd, Essex, **N** Mitchell Caverns, to Providence Mtn SP
78	Kelbaker Rd, to Amboy, E Mojave Nat Preserve, Kelso, **S** RV camping (14mi), Hist Rte 66
50	Ludlow, **N** 76/DQ, **S** Chevron/dsl Ludlow Cafe Ludlow Motel
33	Hector Rd, to Hist Rte 66
28mm	**both lanes, full facilities, litter barrels, petwalk,**
23	Ft Cady Rd, to Newberry Spgs, **N** Mobil/Circle K/dsk, **S** Newberry Mtn RV Park, Twins Lake RV Park (8mi)
18	Newberry Springs, **N** Valero/dsl, **S** Chevron/Subway/dsl/LP
12	Barstow-Daggett Airport, **N**
7	Daggett, **N** RV camping (2mi), to Calico Ghost Town
5	Nebo St (from eb), to Hist Rte 66
2	USMC Logistics Base, **N** Pennywise Inn
1	E Main St, Montara Rd, Barstow, **1 mi N** Chevron, Circle K, Circle K/dsl, Shell/dsl, Travelodge, USA/dsl, Valero Burger King, Carl's Jr, China Town Buffet, Del Taco, Denny's, Di Napoli's Italian, Grill It, Hollywood Subs, IHOP, Jack-in-the-Box, Jenny's Grill, Little Caesar's, LJ Silver, McDonald's, Panda Express, Popeye's, Starbucks, Taco Bell, Tom's Burgers, Wienerschnitzel Astrobudget Motel, Best Motel, Best Western, Budget Inn, CA Inn, Days Inn, Desert Inn, EconoLodge, Economy Inn, Motel 6, Quality Inn/rest., Ramada Inn, Rodeway Inn, Super 8 $Tree, 99Cent Store, AutoZone, Family$, O'Reilly Parts, U-Haul/LP, Von's Foods, **S** Arco Walmart/McDonald's/auto
0mm	**I-40 begins/ends on I-15 in Barstow.**

BARSTOW

INTERSTATE 80

TRUCKEE

Exit #	Services
208	California/Nevada state line
201	Farad
199	Floristan
194	Hirschdale Rd, **N** Stampede Dam, to Boca Dam, **S** RV Park
191	**(from wb), inspection sta, weigh sta**
190	Overland Trail
188	CA 89 N, CA 267, to N Shore Lake Tahoe, **N** Coachland RV Park, USFS, **S** same as 186
186	Central Truckee (no eb return), **S** 76/dsl, Beacon Burger Me, Casa Baeza Mexican, El Toro Bravo Mexican, Jax Truckee Diner, Marg's Taco Bistro, Wagon Train Café Hilltop Lodge, Truckee Hotel CA Welcome Ctr
185	CA 89 S, to N Lake Tahoe, **N** DQ, Golden Rotisserie, Panda Express, Port of Subs, RoundTable Pizza, Starbucks, Zano's Pizza H, 7-11, Ace Hardware, NAPA, New Moon Natural Foods, Rite Aid, Safeway Foods, URGENT CARE, Verizon, **S** Shell/dsl McDonald's, Pizzaria, Starbucks, Subway auto repair, CVS Drug, O'Reilly Parts, SaveMart Foods, to Squaw Valley
184	Donner Pass Rd, Truckee, **N** Shell/dsl La Bamba Mexican, Smokey's Kitchen Sunset Inn vet, **S** Chevron/dsl Taco Bell Truckee Donner Lodge chain service, RV camp/dump, to Donner SP
181mm	vista point both lanes
180	Donner Lake (from wb), **S** Donner Lake Village Resort
177mm	Donner Summit, elev 7239, **both lanes, full facilities, litter barrels, petwalk, , view area**
176	Castle Park, Boreal Ridge Rd, **S** Boreal Inn/rest. Pacific Crest Trailhead, skiing
174	Soda Springs, Norden, **S** Sugar Bowl/dsl Summit Rest. Donner Summit Lodge chain services
171	Kingvale, **S** Shell
168	Rainbow Rd, to Big Bend, **S** Rainbow Lodge/rest. RV camping
166	Big Bend (from eb)
165	Cisco Grove, **N** RV camp/dump, skiing, snowmobiling, **S** Chevron/dsl/24hr Subway chain services
164	Eagle Lakes Rd
161	CA 20 W, to Nevada City, Grass Valley
160	Yuba Gap, **S** boating, camping, , skiing, snowpark
158	Laing Rd, **S** Sierra Woods Lodge/café USPO
157mm	**brake check area, wb**
158a	Emigrant Gap (from eb), **S** Sierra Woods Lodge/café USPO
156	Nyack Rd, Emigrant Gap, **S** Shell/Burger King/dsl Nyack Café USPO
156mm	**brake check area**
155	Blue Canyon
150	Drum Forebay
148b	Baxter, **N** chainup services, food, RV camping
148a	Crystal Springs
146	Alta
145	Dutch Flat, **N** Monte Vista Rest., **S** 76/dsl chainup services, Dutch Flat RV Resort, hwy patrol
144	Gold Run (from wb), **N** chainup, food, gas/dsl,
143mm	**both lanes, full facilities, litter barrels, petwalk,**
143	Magra Rd, Gold Run, **N** chainup services
140	Magra Rd, Rollins Lake Rd, Secret Town Rd
139	Rollins Lake Road (from wb), RV camping

INTERSTATE 80 Cont'd

Exit #	Services
	COLFAX
135	CA 174, to Grass Valley, Colfax, N 76/dsl, Beacon/dsl McDonald's, Pizza Factory, Starbucks, Taco Bell, TJ's Roadhouse Colfax Motel $General, NAPA, Sierra Mkt Foods, S Chevron/dsl, Valero/dsl Shang Garden Chinese, Subway
133	Canyon Way, to Colfax, S Dine'n Dash Cafe Chevrolet, Plaza Tire
131	Cross Rd, to Weimar
130	W Paoli Lane, to Weimar, S Weimar Store/dsl
129	Heather Glen, elev 2000 ft
128	Applegate, N Valero/dsl/LP chainup services
125	Clipper Gap, Meadow Vista
124	Dry Creek Rd
123	Bell Rd
	AUBURN
122	Foresthill Rd, Ravine Rd, Auburn, N Marriott, S Awful Annie's Rest., Burger King, Ikeda's Cafe, Sizzler, Starbucks, Subway Best Western, Rodeway Inn same as 121
121	Lincolnway (from eb), Auburn, N Mobil, Mobil/dsl, Valero/dsl JimBoy's Tacos, Starbucks, Taco Bell, Wienerschnitzel Red Lion Inn, Foothills Motel, Motel 6, Super 8, S Arco, Auburn/dsl, Chevron/dsl, Gas&Shop, Shell/dsl Awful Annie's Rest., Black Bear Diner, Burger King, Burrito Shop, Carl's Jr, Hawaiian BBQ, Jack-in-the-Box, Joe Caribe Bistro, KFC, McDonald's, Pete's Grill, Sierra Grill, Sizzler, Starbucks, Subway Best Western, Rodeway Inn Ikeda's Cafe, Raley's Foods, Verizon
120	Russell Ave (from wb), same as 121, to Lincolnway from eb
119c	Elm Ave, Auburn, N 76/dsl, Shell/dsl Burger&Cream, Roundtable Pizza, Starbucks Holiday Inn CVS Drug, Grocery Outlet, Rite Aid, SaveMart Foods, Staples, Verizon
119b	CA 49, to Grass Valley, Auburn, N 76/dsl, Shell/dsl In-N-Out Holiday Inn RV Connection, Staples
119a	Maple St, Nevada St, Old Town Auburn, S Valero Cafe Delicias, Tio Pepe Mexican USPO
118	Ophir Rd (from wb)
116	CA 193, to Lincoln
115	Indian Hill Rd, Newcastle, N transmissions, USPO, S Mobil/dsl, Valero/dsl Denny's CHP
112	Penryn, N 76/dsl, Chevron/dsl Subway
110	Horseshoe Bar Rd, to Loomis, N Burger King, RoundTable Pizza, Starbucks, Taco Bell Raley's Food
109	Sierra College Blvd, N 7-11/dsl, Arco/dsl, Chevron/McDonald's/dsl Blast Pizza, Carl's Jr, Chipotle, Mooyah Burger, Noodles&Co, Panera Bread, Subway Camping World RV Ctr, GNC, Rocklin RV Ctr, Ross, Steinmart, Target, Tesla, Verizon, S Shell/dsl Dickey's BBQ, In-N-Out, Jimboy's Tacos, Mod Pizza, Panda Express, Starbucks, Wing Stop AT&T, Bass Pro Shop, Petsmart, TJ Maxx, Walmart
	ROCKLIN
108	Rocklin Rd, N Valero/dsl A&W/KFC, Adalberto's Mexican, Arby's, Baskin-Robbins, Denny's, Golden Dragon, Jack-in-the-Box, Jamba Juice, Koja Kitchen, Milo's, Papa Murphy's, RoundTable Pizza, Starbucks, Subway, Taco Bell Comfort Inn, Days Inn, SureStay Inn CVS Drug, GNC, Land Rover, Mercedes, Porsche, Safeway Foods, S Arco Little Caesar's Rocklin Park Hotel vet
106	CA 65, to Lincoln, Marysville, **1 mi N on Stanford Ranch Rd** 76, Arco, Shell Black Bear Diner, Carl's Jr, Cheesecake Factory, Chipotle, IHOP, Jack-in-the-Box, KFC, McDonald's, Olive Garden, On-the-Border, PF Changs, Ruth's Chris Steaks, TGIFriday Courtyard, Holiday Inn Express, Homewood Suites,

California/Nevada Border
15
Barstow
15
40
Needles
Victorville
Hesperia
CA

CA

Exit #	Services
	ROCKLIN
106	Continued Hyatt Place AutoZone, Barnes&Noble, Best Buy, Costco/dsl, JC Penney, Macy's, Marshall's, Michael's, Nordstrom's, Old Navy, Ross, Sprouts Mkt, Staples
105b	Taylor Rd, to Rocklin (from eb), N Cattlemen's Rest., S 76/Burger King/dsl, Chevron Islands Burgers, Subway, Tahoe Joe's Courtyard, Fairfield Inn, Hilton Garden, Holiday Inn Express, Larkspur Suites, Residence Inn H, funpark
105a	Atlantic St, Eureka Rd, S 76/7-11/dsl, Shell/Circle K Brookfield's Rest., Chicago Fire Rest., In-N-Out, Taco Bell, Wendy's H, Acura, America'sTire, Buick/GMC, Carmax, Chevrolet, Chrysler/Dodge/Jeep, Fiat, Ford, Home Depot, Honda, Hyundai, Infiniti, Kia, Lexus, Mazda, Nissan, Petsmart, Subaru, Target, Toyota, VW
103b a	Douglas Blvd, N 76/dsl, Arco/dsl, Chevron/7-11, Shell/dsl Burger King, Carolina's Mexican, Claim Jumper, McDonald's, Mongolian BBQ, Popeye's, Starbucks, Subway Best Western, Extended Stay America, Heritage Inn $Tree, Ace Hardware, Autozone, Big O Tire, BigLots, BrakeMasters, Goodyear, Grocery Outlet, Midas, O'Reilly Parts, Rite Aid, Trader Joe's, S Carl's Jr, Chevy's, Del Taco, Denny's, Jack-in-the-Box, Lorenzo's Mexican, Outback Steaks, Panera Bread, Rubio's, Sizzler, Subway Best Western, Hampton Inn H, Fry's Electronics, Hobby Lobby, Office Depot, Ross, Target
	CITRUS HEIGHTS
102	Riverside Ave, Auburn Blvd, to Roseville, N Arco/dsl, Chevron/dsl Starbucks auto repair, Meineke, S Chevron/7-11, Shell, Towne Mart Back 40 TX BBQ, Baskin-Robbins, CA Burgers, Jack-in-the-Box, Subway $General, auto repair, AutoZone, BMW Motorcycles, Camping World RV Ctr, NAPA, Schwab Tire
100	Antelope Rd, to Citrus Heights, N Carl's Jr, Extreme Hummus, Giant Pizza, McDonald's, Papa Murphy's, Popeye's, RoundTable Pizza, Subway, Taco Bell, Wendy's $Tree, 7-11, O'Reilly Parts, Raley's Foods, vet
100mm	**weigh sta both lanes**
98	Greenback Lane, Elkhorn Blvd, Orangedale, Citrus Heights, N Baskin Robbins, Carl's Jr, Little Caesar's, McDonald's, Pizza Hut, Starbucks, Subway, Taco Bell $General, CVS Drug, Safeway Foods
96	Madison Ave, N Chevron/dsl, Mobil/dsl Brookfield's Rest., Denny's, Jack-in-the-Box, Mongolian BBQ, Ninja Asian, Starbucks Motel 6, Super 8 funpark, to McClellan AFB, S Arco, Shell/dsl Burger King, Chick-fil-A, Chipotle Mexican, El Pollo Loco, IHOP, In-N-Out, Jack-in-the-Box, McDonald's, Panda Express, Starbucks, Subway, Wienerschnitzel Crowne Plaza, La Quinta 7-11, Acura, AT&T, Chevrolet, Firestone/auto, Ford, Office Depot, PepBoys, Schwab Tire, Target, Verizon, Volvo, Walgreens
95	CA 99 S

INTERSTATE 80 Cont'd

Exit #	Services
94b	Auburn Blvd
94a	Watt Ave, N ⛽ 76/dsl, Arco 🍴 Carl's Jr, Del Taco, Golden Corral, Jack-in-the-Box, KFC, McDonald's, Panda Express, Starbucks, Subway, Taco Bell 🛏 Best Value Inn ⊙ $Tree, Firestone/auto, McClellan AFB, Walmart, S ⛽ 76/dsl, Arco, Chevron, Shell 🍴 Denny's, Jimboy's Tacos, Quiznos, Starbucks, Wendy's 🛏 Red Roof Inn ⊙ AutoZone, Grocery Outlet
93	Longview Dr
92	Winters St
91	Raley Blvd, Marysville Blvd, to Rio Linda, N ⛽ Arco, Chevron/dsl, S ⊙ $General, Hooten Tires, USPO, Valley Tire, Viva Mkt
90	Norwood Ave, N ⛽ Arco/Jack-in-the-Box, Valero 🍴 Little Caesar's, McDonald's, RoundTable Pizza, Starbucks, Subway ⊙ Rite Aid, Viva Foods, Walgreens, S ⊙ $General
89	Northgate Blvd, Sacramento, N 🍴 Cilantro's Mexican, L&L Hawaiian BBQ, Subway ⊙ Fry's Electronics, S ⛽ Arco, Shell, Valero/Circle K 🍴 524 Mexican, Carl's Jr, Classic Burgers, El Pollo Loco, IHOP, KFC, LampPost Pizza, LJ Silver, McDonald's/playplace, Subway, Taco Bell 🛏 Econolodge, Extended Stay America ⊙ $Tree, Foodsco Foods, O'Reilly Parts, PepBoys, Schwab Tire
88	Truxel Rd, N ⛽ Chevron/McDonald's, Shell/dsl 🍴 Applebee's, BJ's Rest, Buffalo Wild Wings, Casa Ramos, Chili's, Chipotle Mexican, Del Taco, Firehouse Subs, Hooters, In-N-Out, Logan's Roadhouse, On the Border, Panda Express, Panera Bread, Rubio's, Sandwich Spot, Starbucks, Subway, Tokyo Steakhouse 🛏 Staybridge Suites ⊙ AT&T, Barnes&Noble, Best Buy, GNC, Home Depot, Michael's, Old Navy, Petsmart, Power Balance Pavilion, Ross, See's Candies, Staples, Target, TJ Maxx, Verizon, Walmart, World Mkt
86	I-5, N to Redding, S to Sacramento, to CA 99 N
85	W El Camino, N ⛽ 49er Trkstp/Silver Skillet/dsl/scales/24hr/@, Chevron/Subway/dsl/24hr 🍴 Black Bear Diner, Burger King 🛏 Fairfield Inn, Super 8, S ⛽ Arco
83	Reed Ave, N ⛽ Chevron/dsl 🍴 Jack-in-the-Box, Panda Express, Starbucks, Subway 🛏 Extended Stay America, Hampton Inn, Spring Hill Suites, S ⛽ Arco/24hr, Shell/McDonald's/dsl 🍴 Burger King, Chipotle, Five Guys, IHOP, In-N-Out, Taco Bell ⊙ America's Tire, Firestone/auto, GNC, Home Depot, IKEA, Petco, Ross, Walmart
82	US 50 E, W Sacramento
81	Enterprise Blvd, W Capitol Ave, W Sacramento, N ⛽ Arco/dsl, Chevron 🛏 Granada Inn, S ⛽ 7-11 🍴 Eppie's Diner, Starbucks, Subway ⊙ KOA
78	Rd 32A, E Chiles Rd, S ⊙ Fruit Stand
75	Mace Blvd, N ⛽ Arco ⊙ Target, TJ Maxx, to Mace Ranch, Verizon, S ⛽ Chevron/dsl, Gas&Shop/dsl, Sinclair/dsl, Valero/dsl 🍴 Cindy's Rest., Domino's, McDonald's, Starbucks, Subway, Taco Bell 🛏 Days Inn, Motel 6 ⊙ American River RV Ctr, Chevrolet, Chrysler/Dodge/Jeep, Honda, Kia, La Mesa RV Ctr, Nissan, Nugget Mkt Foods, Toyota
73	Olive Dr (from wb, no EZ return)
72b a	Richards Blvd, Davis, N ⛽ Shell 🍴 In-N-Out, Redrum Burger 🛏 University Park Inn ⊙ NAPA, S ⛽ Chevron/dsl 🍴 Applebee's, Carl's Jr, IHOP, KFC, Starbucks 🛏 Holiday Inn Express, La Quinta ⊙ Jiffy Lube, O'Reilly Parts
71	to UC Davis
70	CA 113 N, to Woodland, N ⊙ H
69	Kidwell Rd
67	Pedrick Rd, N ⛽ 76/LP, Chevron/dsl/24hr ⊙ produce
66b	Milk Farm Rd (from wb)
66a	CA 113 S, Currey Rd, to Dixon, S ⛽ Chevron/dsl, Shell/dsl, Valero/Popeye's/dsl 🍴 Cattlemen's Rest., Jack-in-the-Box, La Cocina, Papa Murphy's, Subway, Wendy's 🛏 Country Inn Suites ⊙ Schwab Tires, Walmart
64	Pitt School Rd, to Dixon, S ⛽ Chevron/24hr, Valero/24hr 🍴 Arby's, Asian Garden, Baskin Robbins, Burger King, Capital China, Denny's, IHOP, Little Caesar's, Maria's Mexican, Mary's Pizza, McDonald's, Pizza Guys, Solano Bakery, Starbucks, Subway, Taco Bell 🛏 Best Western, Motel 6 ⊙ Safeway/dsl
63	Dixon Ave, Midway Rd, N ⛽ Truck Stp/dsl, S ⛽ Arco/LP/lube, Chevron/dsl 🍴 Alheli's Drive Thru, Carl's Jr, Mr Taco 🛏 Super 8 ⊙ Dixon Fruit Mkt
60	Midway Rd, Lewis Rd, Elmyra, N ⊙ Produce Mkt, RV camping (3mi)
59	Meridian Rd, Weber Rd
57	Leisure Town Rd, N ⊙ H, Camping World, S ⛽ 76/McDonald's, Arco, Chevron/dsl, QuikStop 🍴 Black Oak Rest., Clay Oven Grill, Hideaway Grill, Jack-in-the-Box, King's Buffet, Popeye's, Starbucks, Subway, Taco Bell 🛏 Comfort Suites, Extended Stay America, Fairfield Inn, Holiday Inn Express, Motel 6, Quality Inn, Residence Inn ⊙ Buick/GMC, Chevrolet, Chrysler/Dodge/Jeep, Harley-Davidson, Home Depot, Honda, Kohl's, Mazda, Nissan, Toyota, VW
56	I-505 N, to Winters
55	Nut Tree Pkwy, Monte Vista Dr, Allison Dr, N ⛽ 7-11, 76/Circle K, Chevron 🍴 Boudin SF Sourdough, Buckhorn BBQ, Buffalo Wild Wings, Burger King, Chipotle, Denny's, El Pollo Loco, Fenton's Creamery, Firehouse Subs, Five Guys, Food Court, Habit Burger, Hawaiian BBQ, Hisui Japanese, IHOP, Jamba Juice, Krispy Kreme, McDonald's, Murillo's Mexican, Nations Burger, Noodles&Co, Panda Express, Panera Bread, Pelayo's Mexican, Pieology Pizza, Round Table Pizza, Rubio's, Starbucks, Subway, Taco Bell, Wendy's, Yen King Chinese 🛏 Best Value Inn, Best Western, Super 8 ⊙ America's Tire, Best Buy, Big O Tire, CVS Drug, Firestone/auto, Lowe's Whse, Michael's, Nugget Foods, Old Navy, Petsmart, See's Candies, U-Haul, Verizon, World Mkt, S ⛽ Arco/24hr, Chevron/24hr 🍴 Applebee's, BJ's Grill, Black Oak Rest., Carl's Jr, Chick-fil-A, Chili's, Coldstone Creamery, Dickey's BBQ, Favela's Mexican Grill, Freebirds Burrito, Grocery Outlet, Home Towne Buffet, In-N-Out, Jack-in-the-Box, Jamba Juice, Mel's Diner, Olive Garden, Popeye's, Red Robin, Starbucks, Starbucks, String's Italian, Subway, Tahoe Joe's Steaks, Togo's 🛏 Comfort Suites, Courtyard, Fairfield Inn, Holiday Inn Express, Motel 6, Residence Inn ⊙ H, GMC, GNC, Jo-Ann Fabrics, Marshall's, PetCo, Ross, Safeway, Sam's Club/dsl, Staples, Target, Vacaville Stores/famous brands, Walmart/McDonald's
54b	Mason St, Peabody Rd, N ⛽ Chevron/7-11, Conservative Fuel/dsl 🛏 Hampton Inn ⊙ CVS Drug, NAPA, O'Reilly Parts, Schwab Tire, S ⛽ Shell 🍴 Carl's Jr, Domino's, Starbucks, Subway ⊙ $Tree, 7-11, Costco/gas
54a	Davis St, N ⛽ Chevron/McDonald's 🍴 Outback Steaks 🛏 Hampton Inn, S 🍴 DQ, Sonic ⊙ repair, WinCo Foods
53	Merchant St, Alamo Dr, N ⛽ Chevron, Merchant/dsl, Shell/dsl 🍴 Baldo's Mexican, Baskin-Robbins, Black Bear Diner, RoundTable Pizza, Tony's Rest. 🛏 Alamo Inn ⊙ BigLots, S ⛽ 76/dsl 🍴 Jack-in-the-Box, KFC, McDonald's, Pizza Hut, Rita's Custard, Starbucks, Subway ⊙ Walmart Mkt
52	Cherry Glen Rd (from wb)
51b	Pena Adobe Rd, S 🛏 Ranch Hotel
51a	Lagoon Valley Rd, Cherry Glen

SACRAMENTO

DAVIS

VACAVILLE

CA

INTERSTATE 80 Cont'd

Exit #	Services
48	N Texas St, Fairfield, S gas Arco/24hr, Chevron/dsl, Shell food El Pollo Loco, Jim Boy's Tacos, McDonald's, Panda Express, Round-Table Pizza, Starbucks, Subway, Texas Roadhouse lodging Best Value Inn other CVS, Lowe's, Raley's Foods
47	Waterman Blvd, N food Dynasty Chinese, RoundTable Pizza, Starbucks, Subway other Chevrolet/Subaru, Safeway, to Austin's Place, S other museum, to Travis AFB
45	Travis Blvd, Fairfield, N gas Arco/24hr, Chevron food Baskin-Robbins, Burger King, Denny's, Domino's, Huckleberry's Cafe, In-N-Out, McDonald's, Peking Rest., Subway, Taco Bell, To-go's lodging Courtyard, Motel 6 other $Tree, CHP, Meineke, PetCo, Raley's Foods, S gas 76/dsl food Buffalo Wild Wings, Carino's Italian, Chevy's Mexican, Chick-fil-A, Chipotle Mexican, Coldstone, Five Guys, Fuddrucker's, HomeTown Buffet, Jamba Juice, Mimi's Café, Panda Express, Panera Bread, Pieology, Red Lobster, Red Robin, Rubio's, Starbucks, Subway, Wing Stop lodging Hilton Garden other H, AT&T, Barnes&Noble, Best Buy, Firestone/auto, JC Penney, Macy's, Michael's, Ross, Trader Joe's, Verizon
44	W Texas St, same as 45, Fairfield, N gas A&A/dsl, KwikServ/dsl food ChuckeCheese, Gordito's Mexican, Popeye's, Starbucks lodging Extended Stay America other Staples, S gas Valero/dsl food Baldo's Mexican, McDonald's, Paleyo's Mexican other 99c Store, Acura/Honda, CarMax, Chrysler/Jeep/Dodge, Ford/Lincoln, Home Depot, Hyundai, Infiniti, Mercedes, Nissan, O'Reilly Parts, Target, Toyota, VW, Walgreens
43	CA 12 E, Abernathy Rd, Suisun City, S other Budweiser Plant, Walmart
42mm	**weigh sta both lanes, (phone)**
41	Suisan Valley Rd, N lodging Homewood Suites, Staybridge Suites, S gas 7-11, 76, Chevron/dsl, Shell/dsl, Valero/dsl food Arby's, Burger King, Carl's Jr, Cenario's Pizza, Del Taco, Denny's, Green Bamboo, Jack-in-the-Box, Jersey Mike's, McDonald's, Starbucks, Straw Hat Pizza, Subway, Taco Bell, Wendy's lodging Best Western, Comfort Inn, Fairfield Inn, La Quinta, Motel 6, Travelodge other Fairfield RV Ctr, Scandia FunCtr, vet
40	I-680 (from wb)
39b	Green Valley Rd, I-680 (from eb), N food Happy Garden, Hawaiian BBQ, Hinata, Peloyas Mexican, RoundTable Pizza, Starbucks, Subway lodging Homewood Suites, Staybridge Suites other Costco/gas, CVS, Safeway, TJ Maxx, S gas Arco other Kia
39a	Red Top Rd, N gas Chevron food Jack-in-the-Box
36	American Canyon Rd
34mm	**(RS) wb, full (handicapped) facilities, info, litter barrels, petwalk, (phone), (picnic), vista parking**
33b a	CA 37, to San Rafael, Columbus Pkwy, N gas Chevron/dsl, Valero/dsl food Baskin-Robbins, Carl's Jr. lodging Best Western, Courtyard other funpark, S same as 32
32	Redwood St, to Vallejo, N gas Chevron food Denny's, Panda Garden lodging Best Value Inn, Motel 6 other H, S gas Shell, Valero food Applebee's, Black Angus, Black Bear Diner, Chevy's Mexican, Chick-fil-A, Chipotle, Coldstone, Habit Burger, IHOP, Jamba Juice, Jimmy John's, Little Caesar's, McDonald's, Mtn. Mike's Pizza, Olive Garden, Panda Express, Papa Murphy's, Red Lobster, Rubio's, Starbucks, Subway, Taco Bell, Wendy's, Wing Stop lodging Comfort Inn, Ramada Inn other $Tree, AT&T, AutoZone, Best Buy, Cadillac/Chevrolet, Chrysler/Dodge/Jeep, Costco/gas, CVS, Home Depot, Honda, Hyundai, Kohl's, Lowe's, Marshall's, Mazda, Michael's, PepBoys, PetCo, Ross, Safeway, Target, Toyota, Verizon, vet

FAIRFIELD

VALLEJO

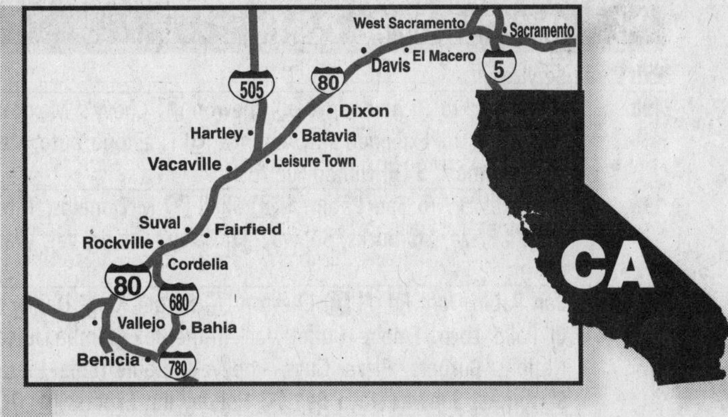

CA

Exit #	Services
31b	Tennessee St, to Vallejo, S gas Flyers, Valero/dsl food Jack-in-the-Box, Pizza Guys lodging Great Western Inn, Howard Johnson other Grocery Outlet, USPO
31a	Solano Ave, Springs Rd, N food Burger King, Church's, Subway, Szechuan, Taco Bell lodging Rodeway Inn, Super 8 other Mi Pueblo Mkt, Rite Aid, U-Haul, S gas Chevron, Grand Gas, Quik-Stop food DQ, McDonald's, Pizza Hut, Subway lodging Express Inn other Island Pacific Foods, O'Reilly Parts
30c	Georgia St, Central Vallejo, N gas Safeway/gas, S gas Chevron/Starbucks/dsl food McDonald's lodging California Motel
30b	Benicia Rd (from wb), S gas Chevron/dsl food McDonald's, Starbucks
30a	I-780, to Martinez
29b	Magazine St, Vallejo, N gas Gas&Shop/dsl food Starbucks, Subway lodging 7 Motel, Economy Inn, El Rancho other Tradewinds RV Park, S food McDonald's lodging Travel Inn other 7-11
29a	CA 29, Maritime Academy Dr, Vallejo, N gas 5 Star Gas, Chevron/dsl lodging Motel 6
28mm	**pay toll from eb, toll plaza**
27	Pomona Rd, Crockett, N food Dead Fish Seafood, vista point
26	Cummings Skyway, to CA 4 (from wb), to Martinez
24	Willow Ave, to Rodeo, N food Straw Hat Pizza, Subway other Safeway, USPO, S gas 76/dsl food Burger King, Mazatlan, Mtn Mike's Pizza, Starbucks, Willow Garden Chinese
23	CA 4, to Stockton, Hercules, N gas Shell food Extreme Pizza, Jack-in-the-Box, Starbucks, S food Dragon Terrace, McDonald's, RoundTable Pizza, Subway, Taco Bell other BigLots, Home Depot, Lucky Foods, Rite Aid
22	Pinole Valley Rd, S gas Arco/24hr, Chevron/dsl food Chipotle, Five Guys, Jack-in-the-Box, Jamba Juice, Krispy Kreme, Mod Pizza, Red Onion Rest., Subway other 7-11, Trader Joe's, Walgreens
21	Appian Way, N gas Pinole Express food China Delights, McDonald's, Pizza Hut other CVS, O'Reilly Parts, Safeway, S gas Valero/dsl food Burger King, Carl's Jr, ChuckECheese, Coldstone, Dickey's BBQ, Due Rose Italian, Hawaiian BBQ, HomeTown Buffet, In-N-Out, KFC, Mel'sOriginal Shakes, Mtn Mike's Pizza, Panda Express, Papa Murphy's, RoundTable Pizza, Sizzler, Starbucks, Subway, Taco Bell, Wendy's, Wing Stop lodging Days Inn, Motel 6 other $Tree, AT&T, AutoZone, Best Buy, Goodyear/auto, Grocery Outlet, K-Mart, Lucky Foods
20	Richmond Pkwy, to I-580 W, N gas Chevron/dsl food IHOP, McDonald's, Me&Ed's Pizza, Subway other 99c Store, Buick/GMC, Chrysler/Dodge/Jeep, Ford, Hyundai, Kia, Nissan, Ross, Toyota, VW, S gas Shell/dsl food Applebee's, Cheese Steak, In-N-Out, Mel's Original Shakes, Outback Steaks, Panda Express, Panera Bread, RoundTable Pizza other FoodMaxx, Michael's, O'Reilly Parts, Petsmart, Staples, Target, TJ Maxx

VALLEJO

RICHMOND

= gas = food = lodging = other = rest stop

CA

INTERSTATE 80 Cont'd

EL CERRITO BERKELEY

Exit #	Services
19b	Hilltop Dr, to Richmond, N Chevron Chevy's Mexican Courtyard, Extended Stay America Firestone/auto, Macy's, Walmart, S Hilltop Fuel/dsl
19a	El Portal Dr, to San Pablo, S Shell McDonalds, Mtn. Mike's Pizza, Starbucks, Subway Raley's Foods, vet, Walgreens
18	San Pablo Dam Rd, N Chevron Burger King, Denny's, El Pollo Loco, Empire Buffet, Jack-in-the-Box, Jamba Juice, Nations Burgers, Pizza Guys, Popeye's, RoundTable Pizza, Starbucks, Subway, Taco Bell Holiday Inn Express H, $Tree, AutoZone, Big Lots, FoodMaxx, Ross, Walgreens
17	Macdonald Ave (from eb), McBryde Ave (from wb), Richmond, N Arco/24hr Burger King, S Chevron/24hr Wendy's auto repair
16	San Pablo Ave, to Richmond, San Pablo, S Chevron KFC, LJ Silver, Subway, Wendy's
15	Cutting Blvd, Potrero St, to I-580 Br (from wb), to El Cerrito, N Arco Panda Express Target, S Valero/dsl Church's, Denny's, IHOP, Jack-in-the-Box, McDonald's, Starbucks, Trevino's Mexican $Tree, Home Depot, Honda, Safeway, Staples, Walgreens
14b	Carlson Blvd, El Cerrito, N KwikServ 40 Flags Motel, S Best Value Inn
14a	Central Ave, El Cerrito, S 76, Shell/dsl, Valero Burger King, Chipotle, KFC, Nations Burgers
13	to I-580 (from eb), Albany
12	Gilman St, to Berkeley, N Golden Gate Fields Racetrack, S Target
11	University Ave, to Berkeley, S Element/dsl, 76, Econo Gas La Quinta to UC Berkeley
10	CA 13, to Ashby Ave
9	Powell St, Emeryville, N Shell Chevy's Mexican Hilton Garden, S Black Bear Diner, Burger King, CA Pizza Kitchen, Denny's, Jamba Juice, PF Chang's, Starbucks, Togo's Courtyard, Hyatt House, Sheraton Barnes&Noble, Marshall's, Old Navy, Petco, Ross, Trader Joe's
8c b	Oakland, to I-880, I-580
8a	W Grand Ave, Maritime St
7mm	**toll plaza wb**
5mm	SF Bay
4a	Treasure Island (exits left)
2c b	Fremont St, Harrison St, Embarcadero (from wb)
2a	4th st (from eb), S Shell
1	9th st, Civic Ctr, downtown SF
1b a	**I-80 begins/ends on US 101 in SF.**

INTERSTATE 110 (Los Angeles)

LA AREA

Exit #	Services
21	**I-110 begins/ends on I-10.**
20c	Adams Blvd, E Chevron Audi, Chrysler/Dodge/Jeep, LA Convention Ctr., Mercedes, Nissan, Office Depot, VW
20b	37th St, Exposition Blvd, W Chevron/McDonald's Radisson Chevrolet
20a	MLK Blvd, Expo Park, W Chevron McDonald's, Subway
19b	Vernon Ave, E Mobil Tacos El Gavilan, W 76/24hr, Shell Burger King, Jack-in-the-Box, Tom's Burger Rite Aid, Ross
18b	Slauson Ave, E Mobil, W 76
18a	Gage Blvd, E Arco Church's, Hercules Burgers
17	Florence Ave, E Shell Jack-in-the-Box, W Chevron, Valero Burger King, Little Caesar's, McDonald's, Pizza Hut, Subway
16	Manchester Ave, E Arco El Pollo Loco, Little Caesar's, McDonald's, Subway, Winchell's AutoZone, W Church's, Jack-in-the-Box, Popeye's, Tam's Burgers
15	Century Blvd, E Arco, Shell/Subway/dsl Burger King, McDonald's, W 76/dsl
14b	Imperial Hwy, W Chevron/dsl Jack-in-the-Box, McDonald's
14a	I-105
13	El Segundo Blvd, E Taco Bell, W Shell
12	Rosecrans Ave, E Arco/24hr, Valero, W Chevron/McDonald's, Sinclair Jack-in-the-Box, KFC/LJ Silver, Pizza Hut, Popeye's, Subway, Yoshinoya 7-11, casino
11	Redondo Beach Blvd, E McDonald's, W Mobil FarmerBoys, Subway H, casino, Ross, Staples
10b a	CA 91, 190th St, W Arco Jack-in-the-Box, Krispy Kreme, McDonald's, Subway, Taco Bell Food4Less, Ranch Mkt, Sam's Club
9	I-405, San Diego Fwy
8	Torrance Blvd, Del Amo, E Burger King, Chile Verde, Starbucks, Waba Grill, W Mobil, Shell/Subway/dsl
7b	Carson St, E KFC Cali Inn vet, W Harbor Fuel, Shell Carl's Jr., FatBurger, In-N-Out, Jack-in-the-Box, Los Paisas Mexican, McDonalds, Pizza Hut, Starbucks, Subway, Wienerschnitzel H, Autozone, Bella Vida Drug, Numero Uno Mkt, O'Reilly Parts, Rite Aid
5	Sepulveda Blvd, E McDonald's, Starbucks Albertson's, Home Depot, Staples, Target, W Arco/24hr, Chevron, Mobil/dsl Burger King, Carl's Jr, McDonald's, Popeye's, Starbucks, Subway, Taco Bell Motel 6 $Tree, 99c Store, AT&T, Big Lots, Food4Less, Ross
4	CA 1, Pacific Coast Hwy, E Arco Jack-in-the-Box, Pizza Hut, Wienerschnitzel $Tree, W 76, Mobil, United/dsl Del Taco, Denny's, El Pollo Loco, Subway Best Western H, PepBoys, Rite Aid, transmissions
3b	Anaheim St, E Dunkin Donuts
3a	C St
1b	Channel St, W Arco, Chevron Big Nick's Pizza, Larry's Hamburgers 7-11, Home Depot, Target
1a	CA 47, Gaffey Ave
0mm	**I-110 begins/ends.**

INTERSTATE 205 (Tracy)

TRACY

Exit #	Services
12	**I-205 begins wb, ends eb, accesses I-5 nb.**
9	MacArthur Dr, Tracy, S Chevron/Jack-in-the-Box/Subway/dsl Tracy Outlet Ctr/famous brands
8	Tracy Blvd, Tracy, N 76/Mean Gene's Burger/dsl, Chevron, Shell/dsl Denny's Holiday Inn Express, Motel 6, S Arco Arby's, Burger King, In-N-Out, Lyon's Rest., McDonald's, Milano Pizza, Nations Burgers, Pizza Guys, Starbucks, Straw Hat Pizza, Subway, Wendy's Best Western, Microtel, Quality Inn H, CHP, CVS Drug, Mi Pueblo Mkt, O'Reilly Parts
6	Grant Line Rd, Antioch, N Chevron/dsl Applebee's, Buffalo Wild Wings, Burger King, Dickey's BBQ, Famous Dave's BBQ, Five Guys, Golden Corral, Hometown Buffet, IHOP, Jamba Juice, Olive Garden, Panda Express, Red Robin, RoundTable Pizza, Rubio's, Sonic, Squeeze Inn Burger, Starbucks, Strings Italian, Subway, Taco Bell, TX Roadhouse, Wienerschnitzel Extended

TRACY

INTERSTATE 205 (Tracy) Cont'd

6	Continued Stay America, Fairfield Inn, Hampton Inn America's Tire, AT&T, Barnes&Noble, Best Buy, Chevrolet, Chrysler/Dodge/Jeep, Costco/gas, Ford, Home Depot, Honda, Hyundai, JC Penney, Les Schwab Tire, Macy's, Marshall's, Michael's, Nissan, Petsmart, Ross, See's Candies, Staples, Target, Toyota, Verizon, VW, Walmart/McDonald's/auto, WinCo Foods, World Mkt, World Mkt, S 7-11, 76/Subway/dsl, Arco, Shell/dsl A&W/KFC, Black Bear Diner, Carl's Jr, Chili's, Hawaiian BBQ, Mtn Mike's Pizza, Popeye's Rite Aid
4	11th St (from eb), to Tracy, Defense Depot
2	Mtn House Pkwy, to I-580 E
0mm	**I-205 begins eb/ends wb, accesses I-580 wb.**

INTERSTATE 210 (Pasadena)

Exit #	Services
85a	**I-210 begins/ends on I-10, exit 77.**
84	San Bernardino Ave, W Habit Burger Hobby Lobby, Old Navy, Ross, TJ Maxx
83	W 5th St, Greenspot Rd, E Chevron/dsl Del Taco, Dickey's BBQ, In-N-Out, Subway, Waba Grill AT&T, Lowe's, Staples
82	Base Line Rd, E Arco, Valero Carl's Jr, KFC/Taco Bell, McDonald's, Subway, Wendy's Albertson's, CVS Drug, Walgreens, W 76/dsl Baker's, Popeye, Starbucks AutoZone, CVS Drug, Family$
81	CA 330 N, to Big Bear
79	Highland Ave, N Chevron/Subway, Shell/dsl Baker's, Coco's, IHOP, Taco Bell, Wienerschnitzel/Tastee Freez, S Del Taco, El Pollo Loco, KFC $Tree, 99c Store, O'Reilly Parts, Rite Aid, Target, Walmart Mkt
78	Del Rosa Ave, N 7-11, Shell Del Taco, S Circle K, Exxon, Valero Jack-in-the-Box, McDonald's CVS Drug, Stater Bros, Walgreens
76	Waterman Ave, S Mobil/7-11/dsl H
75	CA 259 (from wb), H St
74	I-215 N, to Barstow, S to San Bernardino
73	State St, University Pkwy, N American, USA $General
71	Riverside Ave, N Chevron Carl's Jr, Del Taco, Panda Paradise, Starbucks, Subway GNC, Ralph's Foods, Rite Aid, Verizon, Walgreens, S Arco Chipotle, In-N-Out, Jack-in-the-Box 7-11, URGENT CARE
70	Ayala Dr, S city park
68	Alder Ave, N Arco/Subway/dsl
67	Sierra Ave, N Applebee's, Boston's, Carl's Jr, Dickie's BBQ, El Pollo Loco, Jamba Juice, McDonald's, Mimi's Cafe, Panda Express, Papa Murphy's, Pizza Hut, Starbucks, Subway, Tio's Mexican, Waba Grill $Tree, Costco/gas, Jo-Ann, Lowe's Whse, Petco, Schwab Tire, Verizoncar repair:7-11, S Chevrolet, Honda, Nissan
66	Citrus Ave, N El Ranchero, FarmerBoys Rest., Jimmy John's, Juice It Up, Pick Up Stix, Popeye's, Red Brick Pizza, Taco Bell America's Tire, AutoZone, Home Depot, Ralph's Foods, Walgreens, S Arco/dsl
64	Cherry Ave
63	I-15 N to Barstow, S to San Diego
62	Day Creek Blvd, S Arco/dsl, Shell Chinese Food, Jack-in-the-Box, Starbucks, Subway, Wendy's Ralph's Foods
60	Milliken Ave, S Mobil/Circle K/dsl Subway, Taco Bell Albertsons, CVS Drug, vet

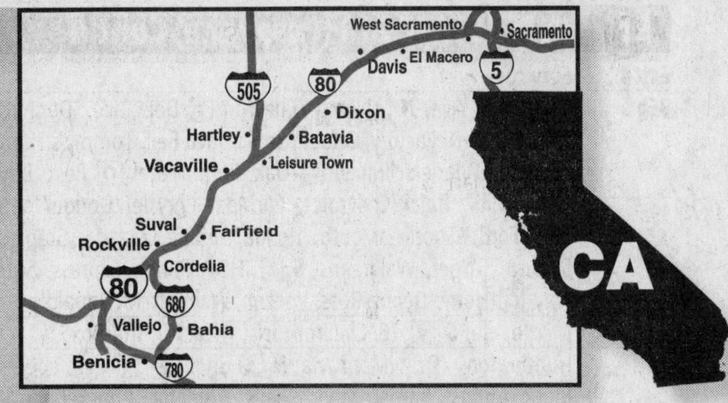

CA

SAN DIMAS

59	Haven Ave, N 7-11, 76, Mobil Corky's Kitchen, Del Taco, Domino's, Jack-in-the-Box, McDonald's, Subway, Tio's Mexican Trader Joe's, vet, Vons Foods, Walgreens
58	Archibald Ave, S Bamboo Garden, Barboni's Pizza, Carl's Jr Stater Bros, vet
57	Carnelion St, S Baskin-Robbins, Del Taco, El Ranchero Mexican, Juice It Up, Papa John's, Starbucks, Subway Rite Aid, Vons Foods, Walgreens
56	Campus Ave, N Arco/dsl, S Carl's Jr, Chick-fil-A, Chili's, Chipotle, El Pollo Loco, Golden Spoon Yogurt, Habit Burger, Hawaiian BBQ, Jersey Mike's, Magic Wok, Panera Bread, Pick Up Stix, Pieology Pizza, Qdoba Mexican, Starbucks, Subway, Which Wich? AT&T, Dick's, GNC, Goodyear/auto, Haggen Mkt, Home Depot, Kohl's, Office Depot, Petsmart, Target, TJ Maxx, Verizon
54	Mtn Ave, Mount Balde
52	Baseline Rd
50	Towne Ave
48	Fruit St, Via Verde, S Shell Chipotle, El Pollo Loco, In-N-Out, Jersey Mike's, Jimmy John's, McDonald's, Myabi Japanese, Panda Express, Panera Bread, Pizza Hut, Round Table Pizza, Rubio's Grill, Starbucks, Subway Kohl's, Marshall's, Staples, Target, U of LaVerne, vet
47	Foothill Blvd, LaVerne, N Mobil Mr D's, S 76/dsl IHOP, Jack-in-the-Box, Starbucks, The Grill House, Togo's GNC
46	San Dimas Ave, San Dimas, N San Dimas Canyon CP
45	CA 57 S
44	Lone Hill Ave, Santa Ana, N Panda Express, S Chevron Baja Fresh, Chili's, Chipotle, Coco's, Corner Bakery Cafe, In-N-Out, Olive Garden, Subway, Wendy's Barnes&Noble, Best Buy, Chevrolet, Chrysler/Dodge/Jeep, Costco/gas, Ford, Home Depot, Hyundai, Kohl's, Old Navy, Petsmart, Sam's Club/gas, Staples, Toyota, Verizon, Walmart/auto
43	Sunflower Ave
42	Grand Ave, to Glendora, N 76, Valero/dsl Carl's Jr, Denny's, El Pollo Loco H
41	Citrus Ave, to Covina
40	CA 39, Azusa Ave, N Arco/24hr, Chevron/dsl, Mobil/dsl, Shell/Del Taco Jack-in-the-Box Rodeway Inn, Super 8, S Chevron In-N-Out Best Value 7-11, Family$, Rite Aid
39	Vernon Ave (from wb), same as 38
38	Irwindale, N Arco, Shell/Subway/dsl Carl's Jr, FarmerBoys Rest., McDonald's, Taco Bell Costco/gas
36b	Mt Olive Dr, N Mobil/dsl Subway CVS, Fresh&Easy Mkt
36a	I-605 S

CA

INTERSTATE 210 (Pasadena) Cont'd

MONROVIA

PASADENA

Exit #	Services
35b a	Mountain Ave, N Arco, Chevron Del Taco, Denny's, Old Spaghetti Factory, Qdoba, Sonic, Taco Bell, Tommy's Hamburgers, Wienerschnitzel Oak Park Motel Best Buy, BMW/Mini, Buick/Chevrolet, CarMax, Chrysler/Dodge/Jeep, Fiat, Ford, Goodyear/auto, Honda, Infiniti, Mazda, Staples, Subaru, Target, Walgreens, S IHOP, Panda Express, Subway Home Depot, Ross, Verizon, Walmart/McDonald's
34	Myrtle Ave, S 76, Chevron/dsl Jack-in-the-Box
33	Huntington Dr, Monrovia, N Shell/dsl Applebee's, Black Angus, Burger King, Chili's, Chipotle, ChuckeCheese, Domenico's Italian, Domino's, Jack-in-the-Box, Jersey Mike's, Jimmy John's, LeRoy's Rest., McDonald's, Mimi's Cafe, Panda Express, Panera Bread, Papa Murphy's, Popeye's, RoundTable Pizza, Rubio's, Smashburger, Starbucks Courtyard Baja Ranch Foods, GNC, Kohl's, Marshall's, Pepboy's, Petsmart, Rite Aid, Sprouts Mkt, Trader Joe's, vet, Walgreens, S Baja Fresh, BJ's Grill, Capistrano's, Capital Seafood, ClaimJumper, Derby Rest., Golden Dragon, Olive Garden, Outback Steaks, Pieology, Red Lobster, Robeks Juice, Soup Plantation, Starbucks, Subway, Taisho Rest., Togo's, Tokyo Wako, Zen Buffet DoubleTree, Embassy Suites, Extended Stay America, Extended Stay America (2), Hampton Inn, Hilton Garden, OakTree Inn, Residence Inn, SpringHill Suites Verizon
32	Santa Anita Ave, Arcadia, N 76, Arco McDonald's, Pizza Hut, Subway Ralph's Foods, Rite Aid, Walgreens, S Chevron/dsl In-N-Out carwash, vet
31	Baldwin Ave, to Sierra Madre
30b a	Rosemead Blvd, N 76/dsl, Arco Baskin Robbins, ChuckeCheese, Corner Bakery Cafe, Del Taco, Habit Burger, Island Burger, Jamba Juice, Panda Express, Panera Bread, Pick Up Stix, Starbucks, Subway AT&T, CVS Drug, Marshall's, Ralph's Foods, Rite Aid, Toyota, Verizon, Whole Foods Mkt, S Coco's, Jack-in-the-Box Best Value Inn, Best Western Big O Tires, Sprouts Mkt, Staples, World Mkt
29b a	San Gabriel Blvd, Madre St, N Chipotle Mexican, El Torito, Pizza Rey, Starbucks, Togo's Best Buy, Dick's, Old Navy, Petsmart, Ross, S Subway Best Western, Holiday Inn Express, Hotel La Reve Buick/Chevrolet/GMC, Cadillac, Land Rover Staples, Target
28	Altadena Dr, Sierra Madre, S Chevron, Mobil Just Tires
27b	Allen
27a	Hill Ave
26	Lake Ave, N Mobil/Circle K/dsl AutoZone
25b	CA 134, to Ventura
25a	Del Mar Blvd, CA Blvd, CO Blvd (exits left from eb)
24	Mountain St
23	Lincoln Ave, S Lincoln Motel tire service
22b	Arroyo Blvd, N Jack-in-the-Box, S to Rose Bowl
22a	Berkshire Ave, Oak Grove Dr
21	Gould Ave, S Arco, Chevron McDonald's, RoundTable Pizza, Subway, Trader Joe's Firestone/auto, Just Tires, La Canada Automotive, Petco, Ralph's Foods
20	CA 2, Angeles Crest Hwy, S 76, Shell
19	CA 2, Glendale Fwy, S H
18	Ocean View Blvd, to Montrose
17b a	Pennsylvania Ave, La Crescenta Ave, La Crescenta, N 76, Shell/7-11, Valero Baja Fresh, Burger King, Domino's, Little Caesar's, Starbucks, Subway, Togo's, Wienerschnitzel Office Depot, O'Reilly Parts, Ralph's Foods, Rite Aid, Toyota, USPO, Verizon, vet, Vons Foods, Walgreens, S Gardenia Mkt/deli
16	Lowell Ave
14	La Tuna Cyn Rd
11	Sunland Blvd, Tujunga, N Chevron, Mobil/dsl, Shell Coco's, Jack-in-the-Box, Panda Express, Pizza Hut, Starbucks, Subway, Yum Yum Donuts 7-11, city park, O'Reilly Parts, Ralph's Foods, Rite Aid, Verizon
9	Wheatland Ave
8	Osborne St, Lakeview Terrace, N Ranch Side Cafe 7-11
6a	Paxton St
6b	CA 118
5	Maclay St, to San Fernando, S 76/dsl, Chevron El Pollo Loco, KFC, McDonald's, Quizno's, Subway, Taco Bell Home Depot, Office Depot
4	Hubbard St, N Chevron Denny's, Yum Yum Donuts 99c Store, AutoZone, Fresh&Easy, S Mobil/dsl, Shell El Caporal Mexican, Jack-in-the-Box, Shakey's Pizza, Starbucks, Subway USPO, Von's Foods
3	Polk St, S Arco, Chevron/dsl KFC H, 7-11
2	Roxford St, N Arco/dsl Fresh&Fast Mexican H, Jiffy Lube, S Travelodge
1c	Yarnell St
1b a	**I-210 begins/ends on I-5, exit 160.**

INTERSTATE 215 (Riverside)

SAN BERNARDINO

Exit #	Services
55	**I-215 begins/ends on I-15.**
54	Devore, E Arco/dsl, Shell, W Tony's Diner
50	Palm Ave, Kendall Dr, E 7-11, Arco Albertacos, Burger King, Mi Cocina Mexican, Starbucks, Subway, W Denny's
48	University Pkwy, E 76/Circle K, Chevron/dsl Alberto's, Baskin Robbins/Togo's, Carl's Jr, Del Taco, Domino's, IHOP, KFC, Little Caesar's, McDonald's, Papa John's, Starbucks, Subway, Wienerschnitzel AT&T, Jiffy Lube, Ralph's Foods, Staples, W Arco, Mobil/dsl/LP Don Martin Grill, Jack-in-the-Box, Taco Bell Days Inn, Motel 6 Verizon, Walmart/Subway
46c a	CA 210, Redlands, to Pasadena, E golf, W golf
46b	Highland Ave
45a	CA 210 E, Highlands
45	Baseline Rd, E 76, Arco
44a	CA 66 W, 5th St, E In-N-Out Best Value Inn, Country Inn, Golden Star Inn, Leisure Inn, Rodeway Inn
43	2nd St, Civic Ctr, E Chevron/dsl Del Taco, Honeybaked Ham, In-N-Out, McDonald's, Starbucks, Subway, Taco Bell Best Value Inn $Tree, Food4Less, Ford, Marshall's, Ross
42b	Mill St, E Carl's Jr, Jack-in-the-Box AutoZone, W Shell Yum-yum Donuts
42a	Inland Ctr Dr, E Chevron/dsl Carl's Jr, Jack-in-the-Box, Wienerschnitzel AutoZone, Macy's, O'Reilly Parts, Sears/auto, W Arco/dsl
41	Orange Show Rd, E 76/dsl, World Burger Mania, ChuckECheese, Jose's Mexican, Subway, Sundowners Rest., Viva Villa Grill Knights Inn, Orange Show Inn 7-11, 99c Store, BigLots, Chrysler/Dodge/Jeep, Firestone/auto, Kelly Tire, Target, W AT&T, Kia, Mitsubishi, Nissan, Subaru, Toyota, VW
40b a	I-10, E to Palm Springs, W to LA
39	Washington St, Mt Vernon Ave, E 5 Point/repair, 76/Circle K, Arco Baker's Drive-Thru, China Town, DQ, George's Burgers, Siquio's Mexican, Starbucks, Taco Joe's Colton Inn BigLots, Goodyear/auto, Jiffy Lube, W Buffet Star, Carl's Jr,

INTERSTATE 215 (Riverside) Cont'd

RIVERSIDE

39 Continued
Church's, Del Taco, Denny's, Graziano's Pizza, Jack-in-the-Box, McDonald's, Starbucks, Subway, Taco Patron Red Tile Inn 99c Store, GNC, multiple RV dealers, Ross, Walmart/auto

38 Barton Rd, E Arco, Shell/Circle K/dsl Miguel's Mexican, Quiznos AutoZone, Stater Bros., W Demetri's Burgers vet

37 La Cadena Dr, (Iowa Ave from sb), E Shell/dsl Jack-in-the-Box Holiday Inn Express

36 Center St, to Highgrove, E Chevron/Subway/dsl, W Valero/dsl

35 Columbia Ave, E Arco/dsl, W Circle K

34b a CA 91, CA 60, Main St, Riverside, to beach cities

33 Blaine St, 3rd St, E 76, Shell, Valero Baker's Drive-Thru, Jack-in-the-Box, Starbucks Stater Bros., Valvoline

32 University Ave, Riverside, W Mobil/dsl, Shell, Thrifty Canton Chinese, Carl's Jr, Coco's, Denny's, Domino's, Fatburger, Gus Jr, IHOP, Jack-in-the-Box, Jersey Mike's, Little Caesar's, Mandarin Chinese, Papa John's, Pizza Hut, Rubio's, Santana's Mexican, Shakey's Pizza, Starbucks, Subway, Taco Bell, Wienerschnitzel Comfort Inn, Courtyard, Motel 6 $Tree, AT&T, Food4Less, O'Reilly Parts, Rite Aid, USPO, Walgreens

31 MLK Blvd, El Cerrito

30b Central Ave, Watkins Dr

30a Fair Isle Dr, Box Springs, E Marjon RV Ctr, W 76/Circle K/Subway/dsl Jack-in-the-Box Ford, Nissan

29 CA 60 E, to Indio, E Arco, Shell/dsl Applebee's, Baffalo Wild Wings, Baker's Drive-Thru, BJ's Rest., Burger Boss, Carl's Jr, Chick-fil-A, Chili's, Chipotle Mexican, El Pollo Loco, Five Guys, Golden Chop Stix, Hawaiian BBQ, Home Town Buffet, Hooters, Jamba Juice, Jason's Deli, Jersey Mike's, John's Pizza, McDonald's, Miguel's Mexican, Mimi's Cafe, Olive Garden, Outback Steaks, Panda Express, Panera Bread, Portillo's Hot Dogs, Round Table Pizza, Rubio's, Starbucks, Subway, Waba Grill, Wendy's, Wienerschnitzel Ayres Hotel, Hampton Inn $Tree, 99c Store, Best Buy, Costco/gas, JC Penney, Jo-Ann Fabrics, Lowe's, Macy's, Marshall's, Michael's, Old Navy, PetCo, Petsmart, Ross, Staples, Target, TJ Maxx, Verizon, Walmart, WinCo Foods, World Mkt

28 Eucalyptus Ave, Eastridge Ave, E Bravo Burgers, Hooters Sam's Club/gas, Target, Walmart, same as 29

27b (27c from sb) Alessandro Blvd, E Arco/dsl auto repair, Big O Tire, W Chevron Farmer Boys

27a Cactus Ave to March ARB, E 76/Circle K/dsl, Chevron/dsl Carl's Jr, Gus Jr

25 Van Buren Blvd, E March Field Museum, W Riverside Nat Cem

23 Harley Knox Blvd

PERRIS

22 Ramona Expswy, E Arco, Chevron/dsl, Mobil/Circle K, Shell/Subway/dsl Farmer Boys, Harry's Cafe, McDonald's, Papa John's, Starbucks, Subway, Valentino's Pizza, W 76/Circle K/dsl/LP, Arco/dsl/scales/24hr Jack-in-the-Box

19 Nuevo Rd, E Arco, Chevron/dsl, Mobil/Circle K Baskin-Robbins, Burger King, Carl's Jr, China Palace, Del Taco, El Pollo Loco, IHOP, Jenny's Rest., McDonald's, Pizza Hut, Sizzler, Starbucks, Subway AutoZone, Food4Less, GNC, Rite Aid, Stater Bros Foods, Walmart

17 CA 74 W, 4th St, to Perris, Lake Elsinore, E Shell, W Chevron Del Taco, Denny's, Jack-in-the-Box, Jimenez Mexican, Little Caesar's, Popeye's Holiday Inn Express AutoZone, Chrysler/Dodge/Jeep/Kia

CA

MURRIETA

15 CA 74 E, Hemet, E Jack-in-the-Box Sun Leisure Motel

14 Ethanac Rd, E KFC/Taco Bell Richardson's RV, W 76/dsl, Circle K/dsl Carl's Jr, Del Taco, Ono Hawaiian BBQ, Starbucks, Subway Home Depot, Just Tires, Verizon, WinCo Foods

12 McCall Blvd, Sun City, E Valero/dsl Wendy's Best Value Inn, Motel 6 H, W Chevron/dsl, United Oil Coco's, Domino's, McDonald's, Papa Murphy's, Santana's Mexican, Subway $Tree, Rite Aid, Stater Bros, Von's Foods, Walgreens

10 Newport Rd, Quail Valley, E Shell/Del Taco/dsl Cathay Chinese, Jack-in-the-Box, Papa John's, Subway, Taco Bell $Tree, AutoZone, GNC, Ralph's Foods, Ross, vet, W Circle K/dsl Applebee's, Baskin-Robbins, BJ's Rest., Chipotle Mexican, In-N-Out, Miguel's Mexican, NY Pizza, Panda Express, Panera Bread, Red Robin, Starbucks, Subway, TX Roadhouse, Yellow Basket Cafe AT&T, Best Buy, CVS Drug, Kohl's, Lowe's, Michael's, Old Navy, PetCo, Staples, SuperTarget, TJ Maxx, URGENT CARE, Verizon, vet

7 Scott Rd, E 7-11, Arco/dsl Carl's Jr, Del Taco, Jack-in-the-Box, Submarina, Subway, Wood Rock Fire Pizza Albertson's/SavOn, Verizon, vet, Walgreens, W Marco's Pizza

4 Clinton Keith Rd, W Arco/dsl Del Taco, Jersey Mike's, Juice It Up, Starbucks, Subway Mtn View Tire, Target, URGENT CARE, Verizon, Walgreens

2 Los Alamos, E Shell Board'z Grill, Cojito's Mexican, In-N-Out, Miguel's Jr Mexican, Peony Chinese, Starbucks, Taco Bell USPO, W Mobil/Circle K/dsl ChuckeCheese, Jack-in-the-Box, McDonald's, Pizza Hut, Starbucks, Subway, TJ's Pizza CVS Drug, Stater Bros., vet

1 Murrieta Hot Springs, E 7-11, Shell/dsl Alberto's Mexican, Buffalo Wild Wings, Carl's Jr, El Pollo Loco, Habit Burger, Hungry Bull, Richie's Diner, Rubio's, Sizzler, Starbucks, Submarina, Wendy's $Tree, Dick's, Ralph's Foods, Rite Aid, Ross, Sam's Club/gas, Verizon, vet, Walgreens, W Richie's Diner, Starbucks

0mm I-215 begins/ends on I-15.

INTERSTATE 280 (Bay Area)

Exit #	Services
58	**4th St, I-280 begins/ends,** N Whole Foods Mkt, S Shell
57	7th St, to I-80, downtown
56	Mariposa St, downtown
55	Army St, Port of SF
54	US 101 S, Alemany Blvd, Mission St, E Shell
52	San Jose Ave, Bosworth St (from nb, no return)
51	Geneva Ave
50	CA 1, 19th Ave, W Chevron SFSU, to Bay Bridge

CA

INTERSTATE 280 (Bay Area) Cont'd

SAN FRANCISCO

Exit #	Services
49	Daly City, Daly City, E 76/dsl/LP, Flyers Toyota, Walgreens, W 76, Arco Carl's Jr, Domino's, IHOP, In-N-Out, Krispy Kreme, McDonald's, Val's Rest. Hampton Inn
47a	Serramonte Blvd, Daly City (from sb), same as 47b
47b	CA 1, Mission St (from nb), Pacifica, E Chipotle, Hawaiian BBQ, Popeye's, RoundTable Pizza, Sizzler, Starbucks H, $Tree, Chevrolet, Chrysler/Jeep/Dodge, Ford, Fresh Choice Foods, Hyundai, Lexus, Michael's, Nissan, Target, Verizon, VW/Subaru, W JC Penney, Target
46	Hickey Blvd, Colma, E Chevron/dsl, Shell/dsl, W Shell/dsl/24hr Boston Mkt, Celia's Rest., Habit Burger, Koi Palace, Max's Filipino, Moonstar, Outback Steaks, Panera Bread, Pieology 7-11, AT&T, CVS, Petsmart, Ross, Sprouts Mkt, Target
45	Avalon Dr (from sb), Westborough, W Arco/24hr, Valero/dsl Five Guys, McDonald's, Subway, Take One Pizza AT&T, Pacific Mkt, Safeway, Skyline Coll, Walgreens/24hr
44	(from nb), W same as 45
43b	I-380 E, to US 101, to SF Airport
43a	San Bruno Ave, Sneath Ave, E Au's Kitchen, Baskin-Robbins, Cafe Grillades, Carl's Jr, Extreme Pizza, Jamba Juice, Nueve Mexican, Pasta Pomodoro, Starbucks CVS, GNC, Mollie Stones Mkt, W 76, Chevron, Kwik Serv Shari's 7-11
42	Crystal Springs (from sb), E county park
41	CA 35 N, Skyline Blvd (from wb, no EZ return), to Pacifica, 1 mi W Chevron
40	Millbrae Ave, Millbrae, E Chevron
39	Trousdale Dr, to Burlingame, E H
36	Black Mtn Rd, Hayne Rd, W vista point, golf
36mm	**Crystal Springs wb, full facilities, litter barrels, petwalk, picnic table**
35	CA 35, CA 92W (from eb), to Half Moon Bay
34	Bunker Hill Dr
33	CA 92, to Half Moon Bay, San Mateo
32mm	vista point both lanes
29	Edgewood Rd, Canada Rd, to San Carlos, E H
27	Farm Hill Blvd, E Cañada Coll
25	CA 84, Woodside Rd, Redwood City, 1 mi W Chevron/dsl Buck's Rest., Firehouse Bistro Robert's Mkt, USPO
24	Sand Hill Rd, Menlo Park, 1 mi E Shell Starbucks CVS, Safeway
22	Alpine Rd, Portola Valley, E H, W Shell/autocare Amigos Grill, Lobster Shack Bianchi's Mkt
20	Page Mill Rd, to Palo Alto, E H, to Stanford U
16	El Monte Rd, Moody Rd
15	Magdalena Ave
13	Foothill Expswy, Grant Rd, E Chevron/24hr Red Pepper Grill, Starbucks, Subway Rite Aid, Trader Joe's, Verizon, W to Rancho San Antonio CP
12b a	CA 85, N to Mtn View, S to Gilroy
11	Saratoga, Cupertino, Sunnyvale, E Chevron/dsl Chipotle, Starbucks Cupertino Inn Goodyear/auto, Michael's, Rite Aid, Ross, Safeway, SteinMart, W 76, Chevron, Valero BJ's Rest., Outback Steaks, Starbucks, Willy's BBQ Aloft, Juniper Hotel Apple Computer HQ, Sprouts Mkt
10	Wolfe Rd, E Arco/24hr Mod Pizza, Panchero's, Starbucks Courtyard, Hilton Garden Ranch Mkt, W Alexander Steaks, Benihana, Vallco Dynasty Chinese FreshChoice Foods, JC Penney, Vallco Fashion Park

SAN JOSE

Exit #	Services
9	Lawrence Expswy, Stevens Creek Blvd (from eb), N El Pollo Loco, McDonald's, Panda Express, Starbucks AT&T, Marshall's, Nissan, Safeway, Verizon, S Rotten Robbie, Shell IHOP, Subway Woodcrest Hotel 7-11
7	Saratoga Ave, N Arco/24hr, Chevron/24hr Burger King, Happi House, Harry's Hofbrau, Lion Foods, McDonald's, Starbucks, Subway, Taco Bell, Togo's TownePlace Suites 7-11, Chevrolet, Ford, PepBoys, Walmart Mkt, S 76, Shell, Valero Applebee's, Lyon's Rest. Sheraton
5c	Winchester Blvd, Campbell Ave (from eb)
5b	CA 17 S, to Santa Cruz, I-880 N, to San Jose
5a	Leigh Ave, Bascom Ave
4	Meridian St (from eb), N Big Lots, FoodMaxx, Harley Davidson, S Chevron Subway 7-11
3b	Bird Ave, Race St, N Chevron
3a	CA 87, N Hilton, Marriott, Westin
2	7th St, to CA 82, N conv ctr
1	10th St, 11th St, N 7-11, to San Jose St U
0mm	**I-280 begins/ends on US 101.**

INTERSTATE 405 (Los Angeles)

LOS ANGELES AREA

Exit #	Services
73	**I-5, N to Sacramento, I-5, S to LA.**
72	Rinaldi St, Sepulveda, E Chevron/dsl Arby's, McDonald's, Presidente Mexican, Starbucks, Subway H, Nissan, Toyota, W Shell Best Value Inn
71	CA 118 W, Simi Valley
70	Devonshire St, Granada Hills, E 76, Arco, Sinclair/dsl Mandarin Island, Millie's Rest., Papa John's, Safari Room Rest, Starbucks, Subway Rite Aid, Verizon, Vons Foods
69	Nordhoff St, E Mobil/dsl China Wok, Coldstone, Del Taco, KFC, Panda Express, Pollo Campero, Starbucks, Subway Hillcrest Inn 7-11, Marshalls, Vallarta Foods, Walgreens, W 76/dsl, Arco Jack-in-the-Box, Pizza Hut
68	Roscoe Blvd, to Panorama City, E 76/dsl, Shell Burger King, Denny's, Horseless Carriage Rest., Jack-in-the-Box, Kountry Folks Rest., Little Caesar's, McDonald's, Panda Express, Taco Bell, Yoshinoya Holiday Inn Express 7-11, AutoZone, Ford, Jaguar/Volvo, Lincoln, U-Haul, W Chevron/dsl, Shell/dsl Tommy's Burgers Motel 6
66	Sherman Blvd, Reseda, E Chevron, Mobil/LP McDonald's, Starbucks Motel 6 H, BigLots, CVS Drug, Jon's Foods, W 76/dsl/24hr Taco Bell USPO
65	Victory Blvd, Van Nuys, E Carl's Jr, El Pollo Loco, Fatburger, Jack-in-the-Box, Subway, Wendy's H, Costco/gas, CVS Drug, El Monte RV Ctr, Office Depot, PepBoys, Staples, W Arco/24hr
64	Burbank Blvd, E Chevron, Shell Denny's, Zankou Chicken Best Western, Hampton Inn Target
63b	US 101, Ventura Fwy
63a	Ventura Blvd (from nb), E Mobil Cheesecake Factory, El Pollo Loco, PF Chang's Whole Foods Mkt, W Ameci Pizza, CA Chicken Cafe, Corner Bakery Cafe, IHOP, McDonald's Courtyard, Valley Inn
63a	Valley Vista Blvd (from sb)
61	Mulholland Dr, Skirvall Dr
59	Sepulveda Blvd, Getty Ctr Dr, W to Getty Ctr
57	Sunset Blvd, Morega Dr, E 76/dsl, Chevron/24hr to UCLA, W Luxe Hotel
56	Waterford St, Montana Ave (from nb)
55c b	Wilshire Blvd, E H, downtown

INTERSTATE 405 (Los Angeles) Cont'd

Exit #	Services
55a	CA 2, Santa Monica Blvd, E Chevron, Mobil, Mobil, Shell Coffee Bean, Del Taco, Fatburger, Jack-in-the-Box, Jamba Juice, Jin Jiang Chinese, Starbucks 7-11, LDS Temple, Porsche, Staples, Tesla, W 76, Chevron/dsl Subway Holiday Inn Express vet
54	Olympic Blvd, Peco Blvd, E Mobil Islands Burgers, Starbucks, Subway USPO, W Big Tomy's Rest. Best Buy, Marshall's, Michael's, Petsmart
53	I-10, Santa Monica Fwy
52	Venice Blvd, E Chevron/service, Shell/dsl Carl's Jr, Subway Ramada 7-11, **services W on Sepulveda** SP/dsl FatBurger
51	Culver Blvd, Washington Blvd, E Dear John's Café, Domino's, Taco Bell vet, W 76/repair, CIC Gas
50b	CA 90, Slauson Ave, to Marina del Rey, E Arco/24hr Del Taco, El Pollo Loco, HoneyBaked Ham, Shakey's Pizza, Winchell's $Tree, BigLots, Goodyear/auto, Just Tires, Office Depot, Old Navy
50a	Jefferson Blvd (from sb), E Coco's, Jack-in-the-Box PetsMart, Rite Aid, Target, W to LA Airport
49	Howard Hughes Pkwy, to Centinela Ave, E Chevron/dsl, Mobil/dsl BJ's Brewhouse, Five Guys, Lucille's BBQ, Qdoba, Sizzler, Subway Courtyard, Sheraton Best Buy, CVS Drug, Ford, Honda, JC Penney, Macy's, Marshall's, Target, Tesla, W Chevron Buffalo Wild Wings, Chick-fil-A, Chuy's Mexican, Dinah's Rest., Habuki Japanese, Islands Burgers, Starbucks Extended Stay America Howard Hughes Ctr, Nordstrom
48	La Tijera Blvd, E Mobil/sl Burger King, ChuckeCheese, El Pollo Loco, Jamba Juice, KFC, McDonald's, Starbucks, Subway, Taco Bell, TGIFriday's Best Western 99c Store, CVS Drug, Ralph's Foods, Ross, Vons Foods, W 76, Arco Wendy's USPO
47	CA 42, Manchester Ave, Inglewood, E 76/Circle K/dsl/24hr Carl's Jr, Subway Best Western, Economy Inn 7-11, W 76, Arco, Mobil/7-11, Shell Arby's, Burger King, Denny's, El Pollo Loco, Jack-in-the-Box, Subway Days Inn CarMax, Home Depot
46	Century Blvd, E El Pollo Loco, Hawaiian BBQ, Little Caesar's, Panda Express, Rally's Best Western, Motel 6, Quality Inn, Tivoli Hotel 7-11, W 76, Arco/24hr, Chevron/dsl, Shell Carl's Jr, Denny's, McDonald's, Taco Bell Crowne Plaza, Embassy Suites, Hilton, Holiday Inn, La Quinta, Marriott, Residence Inn, Travelodge, Westin Hotel to LAX
45	I-105, Imperial Hwy, E 76/dsl, Shell, Valero El Pollo Loco, Jack-in-the-Box, McDonald's, Starbucks Best Value Inn, Candlewood Suites, Hampton Inn, Holiday Inn Express
44	El Segundo Blvd, to El Segundo, E 76, Chevron/dsl, Thrifty Burger King, Cougars Burgers, Jack-in-the-Box, Subway El Segundo Inn transmissions, W Denny's Ramada Inn
43b a	Rosecrans Ave, to Manhattan Beach, E 76, Shell Denny's, El Pollo Loco, Pizza Hut, Starbucks, Subway, Waba Grill Best Buy, CVS Drug, Food4Less, Ford/Lincoln, Home Depot, Marshall's, Michael's, Ross, TJ Maxx, Verizon, Walmart Mkt, W Arco Blaze Pizza, Cafe Rio, Carl's Jr, Chipotle Mexican, Coffee Bean, Flemings Rest., Hawaiian BBQ, Houston's, Jamba Juice, Luigi's Rest., McDonald's, Robeks Juice, Sansai Japanese, Starbucks, Subway Ayres Hotel, Hyatt, SpringHill Suites, TownePlace Suites REI, AT&T, Barnes&Noble,

HAWTHORNE

TORRANCE

CARSON

Exit #	Services
43b a	Continued Costco/gas, CVS Drug, Office Depot, Old Navy, Porsche, Subaru, Trader Joe's, VW
42b	Inglewood Ave, E Arco, Shell Del Taco, Denny's, Domino's, In-N-Out, Panda Wok CVS Drug, Marshall's, PetCo, Vons Foods, Walmart Mkt, W Chevron/dsl, Chevron/dsl (2) Chile Verde Mexican, Subway 99c Store, repair
42a	CA 107, Hawthorne Blvd, E Chevron Carl's Jr, Jack-in-the-Box, McDonald's, Panda Express, Papa John's, Spires Rest., Starbucks, Wendy's, Wienerschnitzel Baymont Inn, Best Western, Days Inn 99c Store, CVS Drug, El Super Foods, O'Reilly Parts, PepBoys, vet, W Arco/24hr, USA/dsl Boston Mkt, Del Taco, Sizzler, Starbucks, Subway, Taco Bell, Yoshinoya AutoZone, Macy's, Nordstom, Walgreens
40b	Redondo Beach Blvd (no EZ sb return), Hermosa Beach, E 76, Arco/24hr ChuckeCheese, Jack-in-the-Box golf, W Coldstone, RoundTable Pizza, Starbucks $Tree, AutoZone, CVS Drug, Walgreens
40a	CA 91 E, Artesia Blvd, to Torrance, W Chevron Carl's Jr, Starbucks, YumYum Donuts
39	Crenshaw Blvd, to Torrance, E Arco/24hr, Shell Coffee Bean, El Pollo Loco, McDonald's USPO, W Shell/Subway/dsl Jiffy Lube
38b	Western Ave, to Torrance, E 76/dsl, Arco, Chevron Chipotle, Del Taco, Denny's, In-N-Out, Jersey Mike's, Local Place, Panda Express, Papa John's, Quiznos, Starbucks, Wendy's Dynasty Inn Albertson's/Sav-On, AT&T, GNC, Toyota, W Mobil Courtyard
38a	Normandie Ave, to Gardena, E Travelodge, W Shell/dsl Carl's Jr, Hong Kong Cafe, On + On Asian, Pizza Hut/Taco Bell, Quiznos, Starbucks, Subway, Wienerschnitzel Extended Stay America $Tree, AT&T, AutoZone, Office Depot, Walmart
37b	Vermont Ave (from sb), E Paradise Rest., W Holiday Inn
37a	I-110, Harbor Fwy
36	Main St (from nb)
36mm	**weigh sta both lanes**
35	Avalon Blvd, to Carson, E Chevron, Mobil Buffalo Wild Wings, Carson Buffet, Chili's, Chipotle, ChuckeCheese, Denny's, Five Guys, Jack-in-the-Box, Jamba Juice, Jersey Mike's, Jersey Mike's, McDonald's, Olive Garden, Panda Express, Panera Bread, Pieology, Pizza Hut, Shakey's Pizza, Sizzler, Smashburger, Starbucks, Subway, Tokyo Grill, Tony Roma, WingStop Motel 6 America's Tire, AT&T, Firestone/auto, IKEA, JC Penney, Just Tires, Old Navy, PepBoys, Target, Verizon, Walmart Mkt, W Arco, Mobil Carl's Jr, McDonald's Kia, O'Reilly Parts, Ralph's Foods, USPO

= gas = food = lodging = other = rest stop

CA

INTERSTATE 405 (Los Angeles) Cont'd

Exit #	Services
34	Carson St, to Carson, E EconoLodge, W 76/dsl, Mobil Carl's Jr, Jack-in-the-Box, Subway DoubleTree Inn
33b	Wilmington Ave, E Shell/dsl Carson Burgers, W Chevron/Jack-in-the-Box/dsl, Shell/Subway/dsl Del Taco, Spires Rest. Chevrolet/Hyundai, Honda, Nissan, Toyota
33a	Alameda St
32d	Santa Fe Ave (from nb), E SC Fuels, W 76, Chevron/24hr, Oasis/dsl Fantastic Burgers, Tom's Burgers
32c b	I-710, Long Beach Fwy
32a	Pacific Ave (from sb)
30b	Long Beach Blvd, E Arco/dsl Subway 7-11, W United H
30a	Atlantic Blvd, E Arby's, Carl's Jr, Denny's/24hr, El Torito, Jack-in-the-Box, Polly's Cafe CVS Drug, Staples, Target, vet, Walgreens, W Applebee's, Chipotle, In-N-Out, Starbucks H, $Tree, Home Depot, PetCo, Ross
29c	Orange Ave (from sb)
29b a	Cherry Ave, to Signal Hill, E Mobil/dsl Fantastic Burgers Ford, Lincoln, Mazda, W 76/dsl America's Tire, Best Buy, Buick/GMC, Cadillac, Chrysler/Dodge/Jeep, Costco/gas, Home Depot, Honda, Mercedes, Mini, Nissan
27	CA 19, Lakewood Blvd, E Marriott, W Chevron, Shell Spires Rest., Subway Extended Stay America, Holiday Inn, Residence Inn H, Goodyear/auto, Verizon
26b	Bellflower Blvd, E Burger King, Carl's Jr, Denny's, Jamba Juice, KFC, Papa John's, Starbucks, Subway, Togo's Ford, Lowe's, Verizon, W Chevron, Mobil/dsl Hof's Hut, IHOP, McDonald's, Pick-Up Stix, Pieology, Wendy's H, AT&T, BigLots, CVS Drug, Goodyear/auto, See's Candies, Target, TJ Maxx, Trader Joe's, USPO
26a	Woodruff Ave (from nb)
25	Palo Verde Ave, W Del Taco, Domino's, Starbucks, Subway, Taco Bell
24b	Studebaker Rd (from sb)
24a	I-605 N
23	CA 22 W, 7th St, to Long Beach
22	Seal Beach Blvd, Los Alamitos Blvd, E 76/dsl, Chevron/repair/24hr, Mobil/dsl Baja Fresh, CA Pizza Kitchen Daphne's Greek, Chick-fil-A, Chipotle, Hot Off the Grill, In-N-Out, Islands Burgers, Jamba Juice, Kobe Japanese, Macaroni Grill, Marie Callenders, Peiwei Asian, Pick-Up Stix, Rubio's, Spaghettini Grill, Starbucks, Subway Ayres Hotel AT&T, CVS Drug, GNC, Kohl's, Marshall's, Ralph's Foods, Sprouts Mkt, Staples, Target, Verizon, **1 mi** W 76/dsl, Chevron Carl's Jr, Del Taco, Denny's, Domino's Hampton Inn
21	CA 22 E, Garden Grove Fwy, Valley View St, E Dillon RV Ctr
19	Westminster Ave, to Springdale St, E 76/dsl, USA Café Westminster, Carl's Jr, Chipotle, In-N-Out, KFC, McDonald's, Pizza Hut, Popeye's Motel 6, Quality Inn $Tree, 7-11, Albertson's, America's Tire, AutoZone, BigLots, Home Depot, O'Reilly Parts, Rite Aid, Ross, W 76/dsl, Chevron/dsl/24hr Ranchito Mkt, Starbucks, Subway Best Western, Courtyard Inn
18	Bolsa Ave, Golden West St, W Mobil/dsl Del Taco, El Torito, Jack-in-the-Box, Outback Steaks, Rodrigo's Mexican, Starbucks, TGIFriday, Wendy's $Tree, CVS Drug, JC Penney, Jo-Ann Fabrics, Jons Foods, Macy's, Target
16	CA 39, Beach Blvd, to Huntington Bch, E Chevron Jack-in-the-Box, Subway Hotel 39 H, Infiniti, PepBoys, Toyota, U-Haul, W Mobil/service Arby's, BJ's Rest.,
16	Continued Buca Italian, Burger King, CA Pizza Kitchen, Cheesecake Factory, Chick-fil-A, Chipotle Mexican, Islands Burgers, Jack-in-the-Box, Macaroni Grill, Marie Callender's, McDonald's, Panera Bread, Starbucks, Subway Comfort Suites, SpringHill Suites AT&T, Barnes&Noble, Chrysler/Dodge/Jeep, Costco/gas, Firestone/auto, Kohl's, Old Navy, REI, See's Candies, Staples, Target, Verizon, Whole Foods Mkt
15b a	Magnolia St, Warner Ave, E Del Taco, Mel's Diner, Sizzler, W Chevron, Mobil/Circle K Magnolia Café, Quang Trang Rest., Starbucks, Tommy's Burgers, Winchell's Motel 6 7-11, Aldi Foods, CVS Drug, Tuesday Morning
14	Brookhurst St, Fountain Valley, E Arco/24hr, Chevron, Mobil, Shell Carl's Jr, Del Taco, KFC, Sabrosada Mexican, Taco Bell Ayres Inn, Courtyard, Residence Inn Sam's Club/gas, Thompson's RV Ctr, W Arco, Berri Bros/dsl, Shell/dsl, USA/dsl Applebee's, Black Angus, ClaimJumper, Coldstone, Corner Bakery Cafe, Dickey's BBQ, Dunkin Donuts, Islands Burgers, Jamba Juice, Jersey Mike's, Mandarin Chinese, Mimi's Cafe, Pick Up Stix, Rubio's, Starbucks, Subway, Wendy's H, Albertson's, Office Depot, Ralph's Foods, Rite Aid, TJ Maxx, Verizon, vet
12	Euclid Ave, E Tesla EVC Cancun Fresh, Coffee Bean, FlameBroiler, Jimmy John's, McDonald's, Panda Express, Souplantation, Starbucks, Subway, Taco Bell H, $Tree, Costco/gas, PetsMart, Ross, Tire Whse
11b	Harbor Blvd, to Costa Mesa, E Hooters La Quinta, W Arco, Chevron, Mobil Cane's, Chick-fil-A, Denny's, El Pollo Loco, Five Guys, Flame Broiler, IHOP, In-N-Out, Jack-in-the-Box, McDonald's, Panera Bread, Sonic, Starbucks, Subway, Taco Bell Motel 6, Super 8, Vagabond Inn Acura, AutoZone, CarMax, Chevrolet, Chrysler/Dodge/Jeep, Honda, Nissan, Rite Aid, Sprouts Mkt, Target, Vons Foods
11a	Fairview Rd, E Starbucks Best Buy, Marshall's, Old Navy, Verizon, W 76, Chevron, Shell Del Taco, Jack-in-the-Box, Round Table Pizza CVS Drug, O'Reilly Parts, Stater Bros
10	CA 73, to CA 55 S (from sb), Corona del Mar, Newport Beach
9b	Bristol St, E Chevron/dsl Antonello's Italian, Baskin-Robbins, Boudin SF Cafe, Buffalo Wild Wings, Capital Grill, Chick-fil-A, China Olive, Chipotle Mexican, ClaimJumper, Corner Bakery, In-N-Out, Jack-in-the-Box, Maggiano's Rest., McDonald's, Morton's Steaks, Pizza Hut, Red Robin, Starbucks, Subway, TGIFriday Marriott Suites, Westin Hotel $Tree, AT&T, BigLots, Bloomingdale's, CVS Drug, Firestone/auto, GNC, Macy's, Michael's, PetCo, Rite Aid, Staples, Trader Joe's, Vons Foods, W 76/Circle K/dsl, Chevron/dsl Del Taco, El Pollo Loco, Subway, Wahoo's Fish Taco Crowne Plaza, Hilton 7-11, PepBoys, vet
9a	CA 55, Costa Mesa Fwy, to Newport Bch, Riverside
8	MacArthur Blvd, E Chevron, Mobil/Subway Carl's Jr, Jersey Mike's, McCormick&Schmick's, McDonald's, Starbucks Embassy Suites, Homewood Suites, W Chevron El Torito, Gulliver's Ribs, IHOP Atrium Hotel, Hilton, to
7	Jamboree Rd, Irvine, E Shell Andrei's Rest., Del Taco, Soup Plantation Courtyard, Hotel Irvine, Hyatt, Residence Inn, W Houston's, Melting Pot, North Italia, Panini Cafe, Ruth's Chris Steaks, Starbucks, Subway, Wahoo's Fish Taco, Which Wich? Marriott Verizon
5	Culver Dr, W Alfie's Gas, Chevron/dsl Carl's Jr, Subway Ace Hardware, Rite Aid, Wholesome Choice Mkt
4	Jeffrey Rd, University Dr, E Chevron, Mobil/Circle K CA Pizza Kitchen, El Pollo Loco, Golden Spoon, I Can Korean BBQ,

COSTA MESA

IRVINE

INTERSTATE 405 (Los Angeles) Cont'd

4	Continued McDonald's, Mooyah Burgers, Olive's Branch, Pick-Up Stix, Pizza 90, Square One Pizza, Starbucks, Togo's H, CVS Drug, Gelson's Mkt, Ralph's Foods, Verizon, Walgreens, W Mobil/dsl Korean House, Subway vet, ZionMart
3	Sand Canyon Ave, E H, URGENT CARE, W Arco/dsl Johnny's NY Pizza, Sharkey's Mexican, Starbucks, Subway, Thai Bamboo, Thai Bamboo, Two Left Forks Albertson's, CVS Drug, vet
2	CA 133, to Laguna Beach, E Courtyard, DoubleTree Inn
1c	Irvine Center Dr, E Cheesecake Factory, Chipotle Mexican, Dave&Buster's, Panda Express, PF Chang's, Pieology, Wahoo's Fish Tacos Barnes&Noble, Macy's, Nordstrom, Target, W 7-11 Burger King, Puesto Mexican, Starbucks, Togo's Big O Tire, URGENT CARE, Whole Foods Mkt
1b	Bake Pkwy, W Carmax, Toyota
1a	Lake Forest
0mm	**I-405 begins/ends on I-5, exit 132.**

INTERSTATE 505 (Winters)

Exit #	Services
33	**I-5. I-505 begins/ends on I-5.**
31	CR 12A
28	CR 14, Zamora
24	CR 19
21	CA 16, to Esparto, Woodland, W Guy's Food/fuel La Plazita
17	CR 27
15	CR 29A
11	CA 128 W, Russell Blvd, W Arco/dsl, Chevron/24hr RoundTable Pizza, Subway, Taco Bell $General, Lorenzo's Mkt
10	Putah Creek Rd, no crossover...same as 11
6	Allendale Rd
3	Midway Rd, E RV camping
1c	Vaca Valley Pkwy, E H, W Vaca Valley TC/Chevron/Blimpie/dsl
1b	**I-80 E. I-505 begins/ends on I-80.**

INTERSTATE 580 (Bay Area)

Exit #	Services
79	**I-580 begins/ends, accesses I-5 sb.**
76b a	CA 132, Chrisman Rd, to Modesto, E 76/dsl RV camping (5mi)
72	Corral Hollow Rd
67	Patterson Pass Rd, E Subway, W Shell/7-11/dsl
65	I-205 (from eb), to Tracy
63	Grant Line Rd, to Byron
59	N Flynn Rd, S Brake Check Area, many wind-turbines, Altamont Pass, elev 1009
57	N Greenville Rd, Laughlin Rd, Altamont Pass Rd, to Livermore Lab, S 76/7-11/dsl Best Western, La Quinta Harley-Davidson
56mm	**weigh sta both lanes**
55	Vasco Rd, to Brentwood, N 7-11, Arco, Chevron/dsl, Gas&Shop/dsl, QuikStop/dsl A&W/KFC, Country Waffles, McDonald's, Wienerschnitzel/Tastee Freez Toyota, S 7-11, Valero/dsl Jack-in-the-Box, Taco Bell Quality Inn

LIVERMORE

54	CA 84, 1st St, Springtown Blvd, Livermore, N Chevron/dsl Zpizza DoubleTree, Motel 6, Springtown Inn 7-11, S 76, Chevron, Shell, Valero/Circle K Applebee's, Burger King, Chili's, Chipotle, IHOP, Jamba Juice, McDonald's, Panda Express, Panera Bread, Peking Chinese, Starbucks, Subway, Taco Bell, Togo's America's Tire, Big Lots, CVS Drug, GNC, Lowe's Whse, Petco, Ross, Safeway/gas, Target, TJ Maxx, vet
52	N Livermore Ave, S 7-11, Chevron Baja Fresh, Coldstone, Denica's Kitchen, In-N-Out, Jack-in-the-Box, Popeye's, Quizno's, String's Italian Hawthorn Suites AT&T, Home Depot, Honda, Kohl's, Schwab Tire, Subaru, USPO, Walmart/Subway
51	Portola Ave, Livermore (no EZ eb return), S Ford/Lincoln
50	Airway Blvd, Collier Canyon Rd, Livermore, N Chevron/dsl Wendy's Comfort Inn, Courtyard, Hampton Inn, Hilton Garden, Holiday Inn Express, Residence Inn Costco/gas, S Carl's Jr, Cattlemen's Rest., Cholula's, Starbucks, Subway Extended Stay America 7-11
48	El Charro Rd, O'Fallon Rd, N Chevron/dsl BJ's Rest., Fresh Pixx, Jersey Mike's, Panera Bread, Starbucks Dick's, Target, S Chrysler/Dodge/Jeep, SF Outlets/famous brands
47	Santa Rita Rd, Tassajara Rd, N Baja Fresh, Buffalo Wild Wings, Coco Cabana Buick/GMC, GNC, Kia, Lowe's, Safeway, S Shell McDonald's, Ozora Steaks, Pizza Guys, Subway $Tree, Acura, AutoZone, BMW/Mini, Chevrolet/Cadillac, CVS Drug, Goodyear/auto, Lexus, Ranch Mkt, Trader Joe's

PLEASANTON

46	Hacienda Dr, Pleasanton, N Shell Applebee's, Black Angus, Chipotle, Five Guys, Fuddruckers, Habit Burger, Lazy Dog Rest., Mimi's Cafe, On-the-Border, Papa John's, Quiznos, Starbucks, Urban Plates Hyatt Place Barnes&Noble, Best Buy, Old Navy, TJ Maxx, Toyota, Verizon, Whole Foods Mkt, S Red Robin, Subway H, Kohl's, Walmart/McDonald's
45	Hopyard Rd, Pleasanton, N 76, Chevron/dsl, Shell/dsl IHOP, Subway La Quinta America's Tire, El Monte RV Ctr, Fiat, Honda, Hyundai, Mazda, Nissan, Office Depot, O'Reilly Parts, U-Haul, VW, S Chevron/dsl, Shell/dsl Arby's, Black Bear Diner, Burger King, Chili's, Denny's, Faz Rest., In-N-Out, Nations Burgers, Specialty's Cafe Bakery, Starbucks, Taco Bell Best Western, Courtyard, Doubltree, Larkspur Landing, Motel 6, Sheraton Home Depot, Mercedes, Verizon
44b	I-680, N to San Ramon, S to San Jose
44a	Foothills Rd, San Ramon Rd, N 76/dsl, Chevron/dsl, Shell/dsl, Valero Baskin Robbins, Burger King, Casa Orozco, Chipotle Mexican, ChuckeCheese, Country Waffles, Elephant Bar Rest., Frankie Johnnie & Luigi's Too, Freebirds Burrito, Habit Burger, Hana Japan, Hooters, Korean BBQ,

CA

CA

INTERSTATE 580 (Bay Area) Cont'd

CASTRO VALLEY

44a Continued
McNamara's Steaks, Outback Steaks, Panda Express, Panera Bread, Popeye's, RoundTable Pizza, Starbucks, Subway, To-go's Holiday Inn $Tree, Big Lots, CVS Drug, Hobby Lobby, Jo-Ann, Marshall's, Michael's, O'Reilly Parts, PetCo, PetsMart, Ranch Mkt Foods, REI, Ross, Safeway/gas, Sprouts, Target, **S** Baja Fresh, CA Pizza Kitchen, Cheesecake Factory, PF Chang's Marriott, Residence Inn, Sheraton JC Penney, Macy's, Nordstrom, Sears

39 Eden Canyon Rd, Palomares Rd, **S** rodeo park

37 Center St, Crow Canyon Rd, **N** Dickey's BBQ, Panda Express, Subway GNC, Petco, Rite Aid, Safeway, **S** 76/dsl, Chevron/dsl, same as 35

35 Redwood Rd (from eb), Castro Valley, **N** 76/dsl, Chevron/dsl Burger King, Chipotle Mexican, KFC, McDonald's, Round Table Pizza, Starbucks, Taco Bell, Wendy's Comfort Suites, Holiday Inn Express CVS, Goodyear, Lucky Foods, Rite Aid, Safeway, Walgreens

34 I-238 W, to I-880, CA 238, **W off I-238** Jack-in-the Box 99c Store

33 164th Ave, Miramar Ave, **E** Chevron/dsl, National Fairmont Inn

32 150th Ave, Fairmont, **E** H, **W** 76/dsl, Mash/dsl, Shell Arby's, Burger King, Chili's, Denny's, Jamba Juice, Starbucks, Subway, Tito's Cafe $Tree, CVS, Goodyear, Kohl's, Lucky Foods, Michael's, Old Navy, Pepboys, Ross, Staples, Target

31 Grand Ave (from sb), Dutton Ave, **W** Valero Rite Aid

30 106th Ave, Foothill Blvd, MacArthur Blvd, **W** Arco

29 98th Ave, Golf Links Rd, **E** Shell Oakland Zoo, **W** 76/dsl, Valero

27b Keller Ave, Mtn Blvd, **E** repair

27a Edwards Ave (from sb, no EZ return), **E** US Naval Hospital

26b Seminary Rd, **E** Observatory/Planetarium, **W** Seminary

26a CA 13, Warren Fwy, to Berkeley (from eb)

25b a High St, to MacArthur Blvd, **E** Razzo's Pizza, Subway O'Reilly Parts, USPO, vet, **W** Valero Walgreens

24 35th Ave (no EZ sb return), **E** Chevron Taco Bell, **W** Energy, QuikStop

OAKLAND AREA

23 Coolidge Ave, Fruitvale, **E** Shell/dsl Little Caesar's, McDonald's, Subway CVS, Farmer Joe's

22 Park Blvd, **W** Arco H

21b Grand Ave, Lake Shore, **E** 76/24hr, Chevron/dsl Chipotle, KFC, Subway CVS, Trader Joe's, USPO, Walgreens

21a Harrison St, Oakland Ave, **E** Quikstop, **W** Honda

19d c CA 24 E, I-980 W, to Oakland

19b West St, San Pablo Ave, **E** Panera Bread Extended Stay America Best Buy, Home Depot, Michael's, Office Depot, Safeway, Target

19a I-80 W

18c Market St, to San Pablo Ave, downtown

18b Powell St, Emeryville, **E** Burger King, CA Pizza Kitchen, Denny's, Elephant Bar/Grill, Jamba Juice, PF Chang's, Starbucks, Togo's Courtyard, Sheraton, Woodfin Suites Barnes&Noble, Old Navy, Ross, Trader Joe's, **W** Shell Chevy's Mexican Hilton Garden

18a CA 13, Ashby Ave, Bay St, same as 18b

17 University Ave, Berkeley, **E** 76, University Gas La Quinta to UC Berkeley

16 Gilman St, **E** Golden Gate Fields Race Track, **W** Target

13 Albany St, Buchanan St (from eb)

12 Central Ave (from eb), El Cerrito, **E** Shell/dsl, Valero, **W** Costco/gas

11 Bayview Ave, Carlson Blvd

10b Regatta Blvd, **E** Golden Gate/dsl

10a S 23rd St, Marina Bay Pkwy, **E** Subway, **W** Artisan Kitchen CVS

9 Harbour Way, Cutting Blvd, **E** Arco, **W** Burger King

8 Canal Blvd, Garrard Blvd, **W** Chevron/dsl Days Inn, Marina Inn Suites

7b Castro St, to I-80 E, Point Richmond, downtown industrial

7a Western Drive (from wb), Point Molate

5mm Richmond-San Rafael Toll Bridge

2a Francis Drake Blvd, to US 101 S, **E** Extended Stay America BMW, Home Depot, Honda

1b Francisco Blvd, San Rafael, **E** 76, Beacon, Circle K Burger King, La Croissant Motel 6, Travelodge Mazda, tires, U-Haul, **W** Subway $Tree, Office Depot, to San Quentin, USPO

1a US 101 N to San Rafael, **I-580 begins/ends on US 101.**

INTERSTATE 605 (Los Angeles)

Exit # Services

27c Huntington Dr. **I-605 begins/ends.** Mobil/dsl Subway CVS Drug, Fresh&Easy Foods

27 I-210

26 Arrow Hwy, Live Oak, **E** Santa Fe Dam, **W** Irwindale Speedway

24 Lower Azusa Rd, LA St

23 Ramona Blvd, **E** Mobil Del Taco/24hr

22 I-10, E to San Bernardino, W to LA

21 Valley Blvd, to Industry, **E** 76, Chevron/Chester's/Subway/dsl Taco Nazo, Winchell's Donuts Valley Inn

19 CA 60, Pamona Fwy

18 Peck Rd, **E** Shell, **W** Ford Trucks

17 RoseHills Rd

16 Beverly Blvd

15 Whittier Blvd, **E** 76/dsl Carl's Jr, Taco Bell, YumYum Donuts GoodNite Inn 7-11, **W** Arco, Shell Pizza Hut, Shakey's Pizza, Starbucks, Subway, Tommy's Burgers Howard Johnson AutoZone, Rite Aid

14 Washington Blvd, to Pico Rivera, **E** Firestone/auto

13 Slauson Ave, **E** Arco, Mobil Denny's Motel 6 H

12 Telegraph Rd, to Santa Fe Springs, **E** 76, Chevron Del Taco, Jack-in-the-Box, Jersey Mike's, KFC, Subway, Yoshinoya, **W** Arco/dsl

12mm I-5

11 Florence Ave, to Downey, **E** Arco Honda

10 Firestone Blvd, **E** ChuckeCheese, KFC, McDonald's, Sam's Burgers, Starbucks, Subway, Waba Grill Best Western 99c Store, Audi/BMW/Porsche, Costco/gas, CVS Drug, Food4Less, Verizon, Walgreens, **W** Chevron/repair Starbucks Chrysler/Dodge/Jeep, Office Depot, Target

LA AREA

8 I-105, Imperial Hwy, **E** Chevron Domino's, KFC, LJ Silver, McDonald's, Taco Bell CVS Drug, Food4Less, **W** Arco

9 Rosecrans Ave, to Norwalk, **E** Chevron, Mobil Little Caesar's, McDonald's, Pizza Hut, Starbucks, Subway H, Walgreens, **W** Motel 6 7-11

7 Alondra Blvd, **E** 7-11, Chevron Frantone's Rest., In-N-Out, KFC, RC Burgers CVS Drug, Home Depot, Staples, **W** Shell Del Taco

6 CA 91

LA AREA

INTERSTATE 605 (Los Angeles) Cont'd

Exit #	Services
5	South St, E [food] Baja Fresh, BJ's Rest., Blaze Pizza, Buffalo Wild Wings, CA Pizza Kitchen, Carl's Jr, Cheesecake Factory, Chick-fil-A, Coco's, Coldstone, DQ, Five Guys, Four Seasons Buffet, Gen Korean BBQ, Jamba Juice, Lazy Dog Cafe, Lucille's BBQ, Olive Garden, Panda Express, Panera Bread, Panera Bread, Peking Wok, Starbucks [O] Aldi Foods, AT&T, Dick's, Firestone/auto, Macy's, Nordstrom's, Target, Verizon, W [gas] Shell/service, Valero [O] Acura, Buick/GMC, Chevrolet, Chrysler/Dodge/Jeep, Ford, Honda, Hyundai, Infiniti, Kia, Land Rover, Lexus, Mazda, Nissan, Toyota, VW
4	Del Amo Blvd, to Cerritos, E [food] Del Taco, Loft Hawaiian, Omega Burgers, Starbucks
3	Carson St, E [gas] [food] Little Caesar's, McDonald's, Popeye's, Starbucks, Subway, Wienerschnitzel [lodging] Lakewood Inn [O] 7-11, CVS Drug, Food4Less, O'Reilly Parts, W [gas] Chevron/Subway/dsl, Sam's Club Gas [food] Carl's Jr, Chick-fil-A, Del Taco, Denny's, El Pollo Loco, El Torito, In-N-Out, Island's Burgers, Jack-in-the-Box, Lucille's BBQ, Panda Express, Roadhouse Grill, Starbucks, SuperMex, TGIFriday's [O] America's Tire, Barnes&Noble, Lowe's, Michael's, Old Navy, Petsmart, Ross, Sam's Club, Verizon, Walmart/auto
1	Katella Ave, Willow St, E [gas] Shell [food] Madera's Steaks, McDonald's, Polly's Cafe, Starbucks [O] [H], CVS Drug, W Eldorado Regional Park
0mm	**I-605 begins/ends on I-405.**

CONCORD

INTERSTATE 680 (Bay Area)

Exit #	Services
71b a	I-80 E, to Sacramento, W to Oakland, **I-680 begins/ends on I-80.**
70	Green Valley Rd (from eb), Cordelia, W [O] Kia, N [gas] Arco [O] Costco/gas, CVS, Safeway
68	Gold Hill Rd, W [gas] Chevron/dsl
65	Marshview Rd
63	Parish Rd
61	Lake Herman Rd, E [gas] Texaco/Jack-in-the-Box/dsl, W [gas] Chevron/Carl's Jr/dsl/24hr, Gas City/dsl [O] vista point
60	Bayshore Rd, industrial park
58	I-780, to Benicia, **toll plaza**
56	Marina Vista, to Martinez
55mm	Martinez-Benicia Toll Br
54	Pacheco Blvd, Arthur Rd, Concord, W [gas] Chevron/dsl, Shell/dsl
53	CA 4 E to Pittsburg, W to Richmond, Pittsburg
52	CA 4 E, Concord, Pacheco, E [food] Blaze Pizza, Buffalo Wild Wings, Habit Burger, Hometown Buffet, Jimmy John's, Noodles&Co, Starbucks, Subway, Taco Bell [lodging] Clarion, Crowne Plaza [O] Ford/Lincoln, Home Depot, Hyundai, Infiniti/VW, Kia, Petco, Sam's Club, Seafood City Mkt, Toyota, Trader Joe's, USPO, W [gas] Grand Gas, Shell/24hr, Valero/dsl [food] A&W/KFC, Burger King, Denny's, In-N-Out, Lucille's BBQ, McDonald's, Round Table Pizza, Taco Bell, Wendy's [O] AutoZone, Firestone/auto, Harley Davidson, Nordstrom's, O'Reilly Parts, Pepboys, Ross, Safeway/dsl, Schwab Tire, Target
51	Willow Pass Rd, Taylor Blvd, E [food] Benihana Rest., Claim Jumper, Denny's, Elephant Bar Rest., Fuddruckers, Jamba Juice, Krispy Kreme, Lazy Dog Rest., Lin's Buffet, Panera Bread [lodging] Hilton [O] Hobby Lobby, Old Navy, REI, Willows Shopping Ctr, World Mkt, W [food] Baja Fresh, Red Robin, Tahoe Joe's Steaks [O] JC Penney, Macy's, See's Candies, URGENT CARE
50	CA 242 (from nb), to Concord

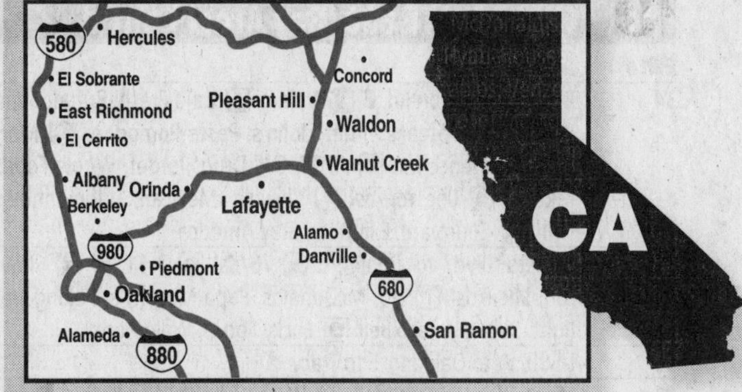

WALNUT CRK

Exit #	Services
49b	Monument Blvd, Gregory Lane (from sb), E [gas] 76/dsl [food] Country Waffles, Hawaiian BBQ, Panda Express, Pieology, Rubio's, Starbucks, Wing Stop [O] $Tree, AT&T, Dick's, Kohl's, Marshall's, W [gas] Chevron/dsl [food] Boston Mkt, Chipotle, Corner Bakery Cafe, Five Guys, Jack-in-the-Box, Jack's Rest., Jamba Juice, McDonald's, Mtn Mike's Pizza, Nations Burgers, Original Pancakes, Pizza Hut, Starbucks, Subway, Sweet Tomatoes, Taco Bell [lodging] Courtyard, Hyatt [O] Big O Tire, Grocery Outlet, Michael's, Rite Aid, Ross, Safeway Foods, Staples, Tuesday Morning
49a	Contra Costa Blvd (from nb)
48	Treat Blvd, Geary Rd, E [gas] Chevron [food] Back 40 BBQ, Heavenly Cafe, Starbucks, Subway [lodging] Embassy Suites, Extended Stay America [O] 7-11, Best Buy, Office Depot, W [gas] Chevron, Shell [food] Black Angus, Chick-fil-A, Freebirds Burrito, Habit Burger, IHOP, Jimmy John's, Starbucks, Wendy's, Yan's China Bistro [O] Volvo, Walgreens
47	N Main St, to Walnut Creek, E [gas] Chevron [food] Fuddrucker's, Jack-in-the-Box, Taco Bell [lodging] Marriott, Motel 6 [O] Cadillac, Chrysler/Dodge/Jeep, Honda, Jaguar, Land Rover, Mercedes, Nissan, Target, VW, W [gas] 76/7-11/dsl/24hr [food] Domino's [lodging] Holiday Inn Express [O] NAPA, Porsche, Subaru
46b	Ygnacio Valley Rd
46a	SR-24 W
45b	Olympic Blvd, Oakland
45a	S Main St, Walnut Creek, E [O] [H]
44	Rudgear (from nb)
43	Livorna Rd
42b a	Stone Valley Rd, Alamo, W [gas] Chevron/dsl, Shell/dsl [food] Alamo Grill, Don Jose's, Panera Bread, Papa Murphy's, Round Table Pizza, Starbucks, Subway, Taco Bell, Xenia's [O] CVS, Rite Aid, Safeway, USPO, vet
41	El Pintado Rd, Danville
40	El Cerro Blvd
39	Diablo Rd, Danville, E [gas] Chevron [food] China Gourmet, Taco Bell [O] Mt Diablo SP (12mi), W [gas] Valero
38	Sycamore Valley Rd, E [gas] Shell [food] Black Bear Diner, Esin, Maria Maria, Starbucks, Subway [lodging] Best Western, W [gas] 76/dsl, Valero/dsl [O] CVS, Lucky Foods
36	Crow Canyon Rd, San Ramon, E [gas] Shell/dsl [food] Baskin Robbins, Burger King, Carl's Jr, Cheese Steak Shop, Chili's, Dickey's BBQ, Habit Burger, Jamba Juice, On Fire Pizza, Panda Express, Panera Bread, Primavera Ristorante, Round Table Pizza, Ruggie's Rest., Starbucks, Starbucks (2), Subway, Zachary's Pizza [lodging] Extended Stay America [O] [H], Big O Tire, Costco, GNC, Marshall's, Office Depot, PetCo, Rite Aid, Sea's Candies, Sprouts, W [gas] 76, Chevron/dsl, Shell/autocare, Valero [food] Chipotle Mexican, Giuseppe's Italian, In-N-Out, McDonald's, Nation's Burger's, Subway, Taco Bell, Togo's [lodging] Hyatt House Hotel [O] 7-11, CVS Drug, Home Depot, Safeway, Staples, Verizon, vet

SAN RAMON

CA

INTERSTATE 680 (Bay Area) Cont'd

Exit #	Services
34	Bollinger Canyon Rd, E Valero Baja Fresh, Buffalo Wild Wings, Izzy's Steaks, Jimmy John's, Pasta Pomodoro Marriott, Residence Inn AT&T, CVS Drug, Target, Whole Foods Mkt, W Chevron/dsl Chevy's Mexican, Clementine's Grill Courtyard, Extended Stay America
31	Alcosta Blvd, to Dublin, E 76/dsl 7-11, W Chevron, Shell/dsl DQ, McDonalds, Papa Murphy's, Peking Delight, Subway, Taco Bell Lucky Foods, Walgreens
30	I-580, W to Oakland, E to Tracy
29	Stoneridge, Dublin, E DoubleTree, W Baja Fresh, Cheesecake Factory, PF Chang's, Taco Bell Sheraton JC Penney, Macy's, Nordstrom, Sears
26	Bernal Ave, Pleasanton, E Chevron/Jack-in-the-Box/dsl Dickey's BBQ, Habit Burger, Jamba Juice, Jersey Mike's, Lindo's Mexican, Panda Express, Round Table Pizza, Starbucks, Subway CVS, Safeway/dsl
25	Sunol Blvd, Pleasanton
21b a	CA 84, Calvaras Rd, Sunol, W to Dumbarton Bridge
20	Andrade Rd, Sheridan Rd (from sb), E Sunol Super Stp/dsl
19mm	**weigh sta nb**
19	Sheridan Rd (from nb)
18	Vargas Rd
16	CA 238, Mission Blvd, to Hayward, E Shell McDonald's, W H
15	Washington Blvd, Irvington Dist, E QuikStop
14	Durham Rd, to Auto Mall Pkwy, W 76/Subway/24hr, Jack-in-the-Box Fry's Electronics, Home Depot, Walmart
12	CA 262, Mission Blvd, to I-880, Warm Springs Dist, W 76, Valero Burger King, Carl's Jr, Denny's, Jack-in-the-Box, KFC, RoundTable Pizza, Subway, Taco Bell Extended Stay America, Motel 6 CVS, Ross, Safeway
10	Scott Creek Rd
9	Jacklin Rd, E Bonfare Mkt, W Shell/dsl
8	CA 237, Calaveras Blvd, Milpitas, E 76, Shell/repair King Wah, Round Table Pizza, Shabu House, Starbucks, Subway Executive Inn 7-11, Oceans SuperMkt, W Shell El Torito, Giorgio's Italian, IHOP, Jamba Juice, McDonald's, Mtn Mike's Pizza, Panda Express, Red Lobster, Starbucks, Subway Embassy Suites, Extended Stay America CVS, Safeway, Staples
6	Landess Ave, Montague Expswy, E 76, Arco, Chevron Burger King, Jack-in-the-Box, McDonald's, Starbucks, Subway, Taco Bell, Togo's Firestone/auto, Lucky Foods, Rite Aid, Target, vet, Walgreens
5	Capitol Ave, Hostetter Ave, E Shell Carl's Jr, Popeye's Lucky Foods, W 7-11
4	Berryessa Rd, E Arco/24hr, Shell/dsl Denny's, Lee's Sandwiches, McDonald's, Round Table Pizza, Starbucks, Taco Bell $Tree, AutoZone, CVS, Safeway
2b	McKee Rd, E 76, Chevron, Shell/dsl Burger King, Chipotle, HomeTown Buffet, Jamba Juice, Panda Express, Popeye's, Starbucks, Togo's, Wienerschnitzel, Wingstop $Tree, GNC, Grocery Outlet, Marshall's, Mi Pueblo Mkt, Ross, Target, Walgreens, W World Gas Baskin-Robbins, Lee's Sandwiches, McDonald's, RoundTable Pizza, Subway, Wendy's, Yum Yum Donuts H, Kohl's
2a	Alum Rock Ave, E Shell/dsl/24hr Jack-in-the-Box, Taco Bell, W Chevron, Valero Carl's Jr AutoZone
1d	Capitol Expswy
1c	King Rd, Jackson Ave (from nb), E L&D Gas, Shell El Pollo Loco, Jack-in-the-Box, Kings Burger, Starbucks, Subway, Tropicana Buffet AT&T, Target, Verizon, Walgreens
1b	US 101, to LA, SF
1a	(exits left from sb) **I-680 begins/ends on I-280.**

FREMONT

SAN JOSE

INTERSTATE 710 (LA)

Exit #	Services
23	**I-710 begins/ends on Valley Blvd.** E Arco
22b a	I-10
20c	Chavez Ave
20b	CA 60, Pamona Fwy, E King Taco, Monterey Hill Rest., W Shell AutoZone
20a	3rd St
19	Whittier Blvd, Olympic Blvd, W McDonald's
17b	Washington Blvd, Commerce, W Commerce Trkstp/dsl/rest.
17a	Bandini Blvd, Atlantic Blvd, industrial
15	Florence Ave, E Alfredo's Mexican, Applebee's, Coldstone, Dunkin Donuts, El Pollo Loco, IHOP, Jack-in-the-Box, KFC, Little Caesar's, McDonald's, Panda Express, Starbucks, Subway, Taco Bell Quality Inn $Tree, casino, Food4Less, Marshall's, Rite Aid, Ross, W Chevron
13	CA 42, Firestone Blvd, E Arco Burger King, Denny's, Golden Bowl, Hooters, McDonald's, Panda Express, Starbucks, Subway Guesthouse Inn El Super Foods, Ford, GNC, Sam's Club, Target
12b a	Imperial Hwy, E GM/dsl Carl's Jr., El Pollo Loco, Subway, W 76, Arco, Chevron/dsl Church's, KFC, McDonald's, Panda Express, Starbucks, Subway, Taco Bell, Wienerschnitzel, Winchell's AutoZone, El Super Mkt, Manny's Repair, Walgreens
11b a	I-105
10	Rosecrans Ave
9b a	Alondra Ave, E Chevron/dsl Jack-in-the-Box Home Depot
8b a	CA 91
7b a	Long Beach Blvd, E 76/dsl, Chevron, Mobil, Sinclair El Cortez Mexican, McDonald's, Sizzler CVS Drug, W Arco/24hr Jack-in-the-Box, Subway Luxury Inn
6	Del Amo Blvd
4	I-405, San Diego Freeway
3b a	Willow St, E Arco, Chevron/dsl Baskin-Robbins, Domino's, Pizza Hut, Wienerschnitzel Albertson's, Walgreens, W 76, Arco KFC, Popeye's AutoZone
2	CA 1, Pacific Coast Hwy, E 76/dsl, Arco/mart, Chevron, Mobil Hong Kong Express, KFC, McDonald's Best Western, La Mirage Inn, Travel Eagle Inn Ranch Mkt, W 76/service, PCH Trkstp/dsl, Shell/Carl's Jr/dsl Alberto's Mexican, Golden Star Rest., Jack-in-the-Box, McDonald's, Taco Bell, Tom's Burgers, Winchell's Hiland Motel, SeaBreeze Motel
1d	Anaheim St, W auto repair
1c	Ahjoreline Dr, Piers B, C, D, E, Pico Ave
1b	Pico Ave, Piers F-J, Queen Mary
1a	Harbor Scenic Dr, Piers S, T, Terminal Island, E Hilton

I-710 begins/ends in Long Beach.

LA AREA

INTERSTATE 780 (Vallejo)

Exit #	Services
7	**I-780 begins/ends on I-680.**
6	E 5th St, Benicia, N Fast&Easy, S 7-11, 76/dsl China Garden Holiday Inn Express Big O Tire, repair
5	E 2nd St, Central Benicia, N Valero/dsl Best Western, S Kimono Steaks, McDonald's, Nations Burger, Subway

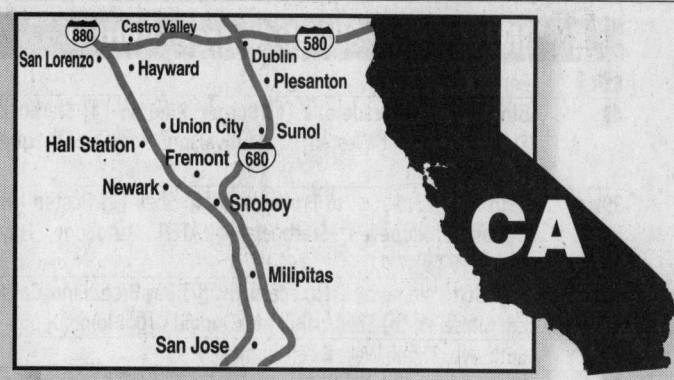

INTERSTATE 780 (Vallejo) Cont'd

BENICIA

Exit #	Services
4	Southampton Rd, Benicia, N Burger King, Ensenada Mexican, Huckleberry's, Jamba Juice, Panda Express, RoundTable Pizza, Starbucks, Subway $Tree, Ace Hardware, AT&T, Raley's Foods
3b	Military West
3a	Columbus Pkwy, N Chevron/dsl Burger King, McDonald's, Mtn Mike's Pizza, Napoli Pizza, Papa Murphy's, Starbucks, Subway CVS, Jiffy Lube, S to Benicia RA
1d	Glen Cove Pkwy, N Hwy Patrol, S Domino's, J's Garden, Subway GNC, Safeway
1c	Cedar St
1b a	**I-780 begins/ends on I-80.**

INTERSTATE 805 (San Diego)

SAN DIEGO AREA

Exit #	Services
28mm	I-5 (from nb), **I-805 begins/ends on I-5.**
27.5	CA 56 E (from nb)
27	Sorrento Valley Rd, Mira Mesa Blvd
26	Vista Sorrento Pkwy, E Mobil/dsl Chili's, Flame Broiler, Jamba Juice, McDonald's, Quizno's, Rubio's, Starbucks, Subway Country Inn, Courtyard, Extended Stay America, Holiday Inn Express, Hyatt House Staples
25b a	La Jolla Village Dr, Miramar Rd, **1 mi** E 76/dsl Discount Tire, Firestone, W Corner Cafe, Cozymel's Cantina, Donovan's Grill, Harry's Grill, PF Chang's, Seasons Fresh Grill Embassy Suites, Marriott H, Macy's, Nordstom's
24	Governor Dr
23	CA 52
22	Clairemont Mesa Blvd, E 7-11/dsl, Chevron/dsl, Mega/Subway/dsl, Shell Arby's, Burger King, Carl's Jr, Chipotle Mexican, Coco's, Godfather Rest., Jersey Mike's, McDonald's, Rubio's Grill, Souplantation, Starbucks, Subway, Tommy's Burgers Food4Less, Ford/Kia, Nissan, Ranch Mkt, Verizon, Walmart, W Gas Buga Korean BBQ, Subway Best Western, CA Suites, Motel 6
21	CA 274, Balboa Ave, E 7-11, 76, Arco/dsl, Chevron/dsl Applebee's, Islands Burger, Jack-in-the-Box CarMax, Chevrolet, Chrysler/Dodge/Jeep, Jaguar, VW
20	CA 163 N, to Escondido
20a	Mesa College Dr, Kearney Villa Rd, W H
18	Murray Ridge Rd, to Phyllis Place
17b	I-8, E to El Centro, W to beaches
16	El Cajon Blvd, E Arco, Ultra Pancho Villa Mkt, W Carl's Jr, Jack-in-the-Box, Rudford's Rest., Subway, Wendy's O'Reilly Parts
15	University Ave, E Chevron Subway, W 76/dsl, USA/dsl Starbucks CVS Drug, Fresh&Easy Mkt, Walgreens
14	CA 15 N, 40th St, to I-15
13b	Home Ave, MLK Ave
13a	CA 94
12b	Market St
12a	Imperial Ave, E Homeland Gas/dsl, United, W Asia Wok, Cojita's Taco, Domino's, KFC/LJ Silver, Sizzler, Subway 99c Store, Home Depot
11b	47th St
11a	43rd St, W Giant Pizza, Jack-in-the-Box, Subway AutoZone, CVS Drug, Northgate Mkt
10	Plaza Blvd, National City, E Chow King, McDonald's, Pizza Hut, Popeye's, Starbucks, Subway, Winchell's H, AutoZone,

CA

Exit #	Services
10	Continued Firestone/auto, Vallarta Foods, vet, Walgreens, Well's Drug, W USA Bistro City Chinese, Carl's Jr, Family House Rest., IHOP, Jubilee Chicken/burgers, Little Caesar's, Papa John's, Subway, Wings n Things Holiday Inn Express, Motel 6, Stardust Inn AT&T, Big Lots, CVS Drug, Discount Tire, Firestone/auto, Jo-Ann Fabrics, O'Reilly Parts, Walmart
9	Sweetwater Rd, E Applebee's, Outback Steaks Sweetwater Inn 7-11, JC Penney, Macy's, W Chevron/7-11/dsl Ben's Rest., Carl's Jr, Denny's, Hanaoka Japanese, Mike's NY Pizza, Pizza Hut, Pizza Hut, Starbucks, Subway, Taco Bell CVS Drug, Food4Less, Goodyear/auto, Staples
8	CA 54
7c	E St, Bonita Rd, E **on Bonita Plaza Rd** Applebee's, El Torito, Outback Steaks, Red Robin, Starbucks, Subway JC Penney, Macy's, Target, W Chevron/dsl, Circle K, Shell/dsl Burger King, Denny's, La Tequila Mexican Comfort Inn, La Quinta
7b a	H St, E Shell China China, Coldstone, Daphne's CA Greek, D'Lish Pizza, Honeybaked, Jack-in-the-Box, Robeks Juice, Subway, Taco Bell CVS Drug, Marshall's, Vons Foods, W Caffe Tazza
6	L St, Telegraph Canyon Rd, E Arco/dsl Little Caesar's, Mandarin Canyon, McDonald's, Starbucks, Subway H, Olympic Training Ctr, Rite Aid, vet, Von's Foods, W 76/Circle K/dsl, USA Canada Steakburger 7-11
4	Orange Ave, E Olympic Training Ctr
3	Main St, Otay Valley Rd, E Shell/dsl Panda Express, Souplantation Ford/Kia, Honda, Kohl's, Nissan, PetsMart, Staples, Toyota, W Circle K/dsl Best Western
2	Palm Ave, E Arco, Chevron Carl's Jr, Hometown Buffet, Starbucks, Subway, Taco Bell AT&T, Home Depot, Meineke, Tire Pros, USPO, Von's Foods, Walmart/McDonald's, W Chevron Golden House Chinese, KFC, Little Caesar's, McDonald's
1b	CA 905, E Brown Field Airport, Otay Mesa Border Crossing
1a	San Ysidro Blvd, E Shell/dsl, Valero Church's 99c Store, CVS Drug, Factory2U, O'Reilly Parts, W 76, Chevron, Mobil/dsl, Shell Denny's, McDonald's Motel 6
0	**I-805 begins/ends on I-5.**

INTERSTATE 880 (Bay Area)

Exit #	Services
46b a	I-80 W (exits left). I-80 E/580 W.
44	7th St, Grand Ave, downtown
42b a	Broadway St, E KFC, McDonald's Marriott, W Jack London Inn to Jack London Square
41a	Oak St, Lakeside Dr, downtown

= gas = food = lodging = other = rest stop

INTERSTATE 880 (Bay Area) Cont'd

OAKLAND AREA

Exit #	Services
40	5th Ave, Embarcadero, E Burger King, W Starbucks, Subway Best Western, Executive Inn, Homewood Suites, Motel 6
39b a	29th Ave, 23rd Ave, to Fruitvale, E Shell Boston Mkt, DonutStar, Popeye's, Starbucks AT&T, AutoZone, FoodMaxx, W 7-11
38	High St, to Alameda, E Mash/dsl Bay Breeze Inn, Coliseum Motel, W Shell/dsl McDonald's Home Depot
37	66th Ave, Zhone Way, E coliseum
36	Hegenberger Rd, E Arco/24hr, Shell/dsl Burger King, Chubby Freeze, Denny's, Jack-in-the-Box/24hr, McDonald's, Taco Bell Comfort Inn, Day's Hotel, La Quinta, Motel 6, Quality Inn Freightliner, GMC/Volvo, W 76/dsl, Chevron/Del Taco/dsl, Shell Black Bear Diner, Chipotle, Francesco's Rest., In-N-Out, Jamba Juice, Panda Express, Red Brick Pizza, Starbucks, Subway, Subway, Wing Stop Best Western, Courtyard, Econolodge, Hilton, Holiday Inn, Holiday Inn Express, Red Lion Harley-Davidson, Infiniti, Lexus, to Oakland Airport, Toyota
35	98th Ave, W
34	Davis St, W Shell/Burger King Hawaiian BBQ, Togo's $Tree, Costco/gas, Home Depot, Office Depot, See's Candy, Verizon, Walmart/McDonald's
33b a	Marina Blvd, E Chevron/dsl, Valero Jack-in-the-Box, La Salsa Mexican, Panda Express, Pieology, Starbucks, Taco Bell Chevrolet, Ford/Lincoln, Honda, Hyundai, Kia, Marshall's, Nissan, Nordstrom's, Volvo, W Flyers/dsl A&W/KFC, Denny's
32	Washington Ave (from nb), Lewelling Blvd (from sb), W 76/dsl, Arco, Chevron Jack-in-the-Box, McDonald's, Mtn Mike's Pizza, Papa Murphy's, Subway Nimitz Motel 99c Store, Big O Tire, CVS, Food Maxx, GNC, Jo-Ann, Safeway, same as 30, Walgreens/24hr
31	I-238 (from sb), to I-580, Castro Valley
30	Hesperian Blvd, E National In-N-Out, Starbucks, Taco Bell O'Reilly Parts, Walmart/Subway, Wheel Works, W 76, Arco, Chevron Black Angus, Peking Garden, Round Table Pizza Hilton Garden, Nimitz Inn 99c Store, CVS, Food Maxx, Lucky Foods, same as 32, USPO
29	A St, San Lorenzo, E 880/dsl/e85 McDonald's Best Western Costco, tires/repair, W 76/7-11/dsl, Valero/dsl Burger King, Chef Ming, Five Guys, Hawaiian BBQ, Jamba Juice, Pizza Hut, Rigatoni's Italian, Starbucks, Subway Days Inn, La Quinta, Rodeway Inn $Tree, Home Depot, Mi Pueblo Foods, Target
28	Winton Ave, W Chevron Applebee's, Buffalo Wild Wings, Coldstone, Elephant Grill, Famous Dave's BBQ, Hawaiian BBQ, Hometown Buffet, Olive Garden, Panda Express, Panera Bread, Sizzler, Subway Dick's, Firestone/auto, Goodyear/auto, JC Penney, Macy's, O'Reilly Parts, Ross, Verizon
27	CA 92, Jackson St, E 76/dsl, Valero Asian Wok, Hawaiian BBQ, Mtn Mike's Pizza, Nations Burgers, Papa John's, Popeye's, Round Table Pizza, Starbucks, Subway, Taco Bell 7-11, CVS, Grocery Outlet, Lucky Foods, Safeway, Walgreens, W San Mateo Br
26	Tennyson Rd, E 76, All Star dsl, Shell Jack-in-the-Box, KFC O'Reilly Parts, Walgreens, W H
25	Industrial Pkwy (from sb), E Golden Gate/dsl, Industrial/dsl Fuzhou Kitchen, Starbucks, Straw Hat Pizza, Subway, W Pheonix Lodge
24	Whipple Rd, Dyer St, E 76/dsl, Chevron/dsl/24hr Country Waffles, Denny's, Hawaiian BBQ, McDonald's, Panda Express, Starbucks, Subway, Taco Bell, Wing Stop Best Value Inn, Motel 6 FoodMaxx, Home Depot, PepBoys, Target, W Shell Andersen Baker a Cafe, Applebee's, Baskin-Robbins, Buckhorn Grill, Buffalo Wild Wings, Chevy's Mexican, Chili's, Chipotle, Coldstone, Fuddrucker's, IHOP, In-N-Out, Jamba Juice, Jollibee, Krispy Kreme, La Salsa Mexican, Mtn Mike's Pizza, Pasta Pormadora, Starbucks, Texas Roadhouse, TGIFriday, Togo's, Tomatina Italian Extended Stay America, Hampton Inn, Holiday Inn Express AT&T, Best Buy, GNC, Lowe's Whse, Lucky Foods, Michael's, PetCo, Tuesday Morning, Verizon, Walmart
23	Alvarado-Niles Rd, E Shell Crowne Plaza 7-11, W Shell Burger King Walmart, (same as 24)
22	Alvarado Blvd, Fremont Blvd, E Fortune Kitchen, Subway Motel 6 Lucky Foods
21	CA 84 W, Decoto Rd to Dumbarton Br, E 7-11 McDonald's Walgreens
19	CA 84 E, Thornton Ave, Newark, E U-Haul, W Chevron/dsl, Shell Carl's Jr, KFC, Mtn Mike's Pizza, My Cafe, Round Table Pizza, Subway, Taco Bell 7-11, BigLots, Home Depot
17	Mowry Ave, Fremont, E 76/Circle K, Chevron/dsl, QuikStop, Valero Applebee's, Chick-fil-A, Denny's, Olive Garden, Papa Murphy's, Starbucks, Subway Best Western, Extended Stay America, Residence Inn H, Lucky Foods, W Arby's, BJ's Rest., Bombay Garden, Jack-in-the-Box, Little Caesar's, McDonald's, Papa John's, Ray's Chinese, Ray's Crabshack, Red Robin, Subway, Taco Bell Chase Suites, Comfort Inn, EZ 8 Motel, Homewood Suites, Towneplace Suites Chrysler/Dodge/Jeep, Firestone/auto, Ford, JC Penney, Jiffy Lube, Lion Mkt, Macy's, Mazda, Target, VW
16	Stevenson Blvd, E Arco/dsl, Shell Jack-in-the-Box, Outback Steaks $Tree, W Chevron Carl's Jr, ChuckeCheese, Isla Filipino, Nijo Castle Japanese, Starbucks, Subway, World Gourmet Buffet Doubletree Fiat, Ford, Walmart
15	Auto Mall Pkwy, E Arco, Chevron/dsl, W Shell/dsl Applebee's, Asian Pearl, Bennigan's, Blaze Pizza, Buffalo Wild Wings, Chick-fil-A, Chipotle, ClaimJumper, Coldstone, Dickey's BBQ, Dog Haus, Firehouse Subs, Five Guys, Habit Burger, Hawaiian BBQ, In-N-Out, Jamba Juice, Krispy Kreme, MilkCow Cafe, Mkt Broiler, Panchero's, Panda Express, Panera Bread, PF Chang's, Rubio's, Starbucks, Subway, Wendy's, Which Wich?, Wing Stop Holiday Inn Express Acura, AT&T, BMW, Buick/GMC/Cadillac, Chevrolet, Costco/gas, Dick's, Honda, Jo-Ann Fabrics, Kia, Kohl's, Lexus, Lowe's Whse, Mercedes, Nissan, Nordstrom's, Old Navy, Target, TJ Maxx, Toyota, Verizon, Volvo
14mm	**weigh sta both lanes**
13	Fremont Blvd, Irving Dist, W Chevron/Subway McDonald's Extended Stay America, GoodNite Inn, La Quinta, Marriott
13a	Gateway Blvd (from nb), E Comfort Inn
12	Mission Blvd, E Burger King, Carl's Jr, Denny's, Jack-in-the-Box, KFC, Subway, Taco Bell Comfort Inn CVS, Safeway, to I-680, W Courtyard, Hampton Inn, Hyatt Place
10	Dixon Landing Rd, E McDonald's Residence Inn 7-11
8b	CA 237, Alviso Rd, Calaveras Rd, to McCarthy Rd, Milpitas, E 76/7-11/dsl, Arco Black Bear Diner, Burger King, Chili's, Denny's, King Egg Roll, Lee's Sandwiches, Milpitas Buffet Best Western, Chili Palace, Days Inn, Heritage Inn

FREMONT

SAN JOSE AREA

INTERSTATE 880 (Bay Area) Cont'd

8b Continued
7-11, BigLots, Grocery Outlet, O'Reilly Parts, Walgreens, W Applebee's, Black Angus, Happi House, In-N-Out, Macaroni Grill, McDonald's, On the Border, Starbucks, Subway, Taco Bell, Togo's Crowne Plaza, Extended Stay America, Hampton Inn, Hilton Garden, Larkspur Landing Hotel, Staybridge Suites $Tree, AT&T, Best Buy, Chevron, GNC, Michael's, Petsmart, RanchMkt Foods, Ross, Verizon, Walmart/McDonald's/auto

8a Great Mall Parkway, Tasman Dr, E Honda, Toyota

7 Montague Expswy, E Shell/dsl, Valero Carl's Jr, Jack-in-the-Box Quality Inn U-Haul, W Chevron/dsl Beverly Heritage Hotel, Sheraton

5 Brokaw Rd, E Lowe's Whse, W America's Tire, CHP, Ford Trucks, Fry's Electronics

4d Gish Rd (nb only), W auto/dsl repair/transmissions

4c b US 101, N to San Francisco, S to LA

4a 1st St, E Chevron/dsl, Shell/repair Subway, W Cathay Chinese, Denny's/24hr, Genji Japanese Caravelle Inn, Comfort Suites, Country Inn Suites, Days Inn, Extended Stay America, EZ 8 Motel, Holiday Inn, Residence Inn, Springhill Suites, Vagabond Inn, Wyndham Garden 7-11

3 Coleman St, E Valero/dsl, W Chevron/dsl Chipotle, In-N-Out, Mod Pizza, Smoking PIG BBQ, Starbucks, Which Wich? Lowe's, Staples

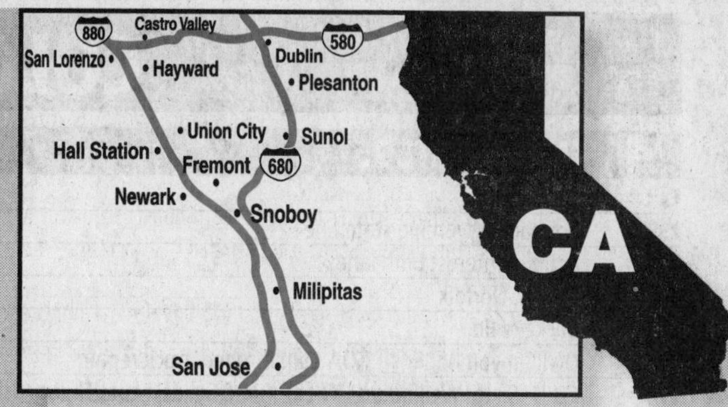

CA

2 CA 82, The Alameda, W Shell/repair Bill's Cafe, Round Table Pizza, Starbucks, Subway, Taco Bell Best Western, Santa Clara Inn, St. Francis Hotel, Sterling Motel, Valley Inn Safeway, Santa Clara U

1d Bascom Ave, to Santa Clara, W Rotten Robbie/dsl, Valero Burger King

1c Stevens Creek Blvd, San Carlos St, E Valero/dsl, Valley/dsl The Row Hotel H, W Arby's, CheeseCake Factory, Jack-in-the-Box, Yard House 7-11, Audi/VW, Best Buy, Chevrolet, CVS, Ford, Goodyear/auto, Kia, Lexus, Macy's, Nordstrom's, Old Navy, Safeway, Subaru

1b **I-280. I-880 begins/ends on I-280**

1a Ca 17 to Santa Cruz.

NOTES

COLORADO

INTERSTATE 25

Exit #	Services
299	Colorado/Wyoming state line
296	point of interest both lanes
293	to Carr, Norfolk
288	Buckeye Rd
281	Owl Canyon Rd, E KOA Campground, truck repair
278	CO 1 S, to Wellington, W Kum&Go/dsl, Loaf'N Jug/dsl, Shell/dsl Burger King, Domino's, McDonald's, Subway, Taco John's Days Inn Bella Mkt, Family$, USPO, vet
271	Mountain Vista Dr, W Budweiser Brewery
269b a	CO 14, to US 87, Ft Collins, E CF&G Cookhouse, McDonald's Best Value Inn, W Shell/dsl Denny's, Hacienda Real, Waffle House 9 Motel, Comfort Inn, Days Inn, EconoLodge, La Quinta, Motel 6, Red Lion Inn, Rodeway Inn, Super 8 to CO St U, vet
268	Prospect Rd, to Ft Collins, W H, **Welcome Ctr/ both lanes, full facilities, litter barrels, , petwalk**
267mm	**weigh sta both lanes**
266mm	E st patrol
265	Harmony Rd, Timnath, E Murphy USA/dsl Chick-fil-A, Freddy's, Starbucks, Taco Bell Costco/dsl, Schwab Tires, Walmart/Subway, **2-3 mi W** Shell/dsl Austin's Grill, BJ's Rest., Carrabba's, Chipotle, Famous Dave's, Firehouse Subs, Five Guys, HuHot, IHOP, Jersey Mike's, Macaroni Grill, McAlister's Deli, Old Chicago, Outback Steaks, Panera Bread, Papa John's, Qdoba, Red Robin, Rustic Oven, SmashBurger, Sprouts Mkt, Starbucks, Subway, Texas Roadhouse, Tom+Chee, Village Inn, Wahoo's, Which Wich? Cambria Suites, Comfort Suites, Courtyard, Hampton Inn, Hilton Garden, Holiday Inn Express, Homewood Suites, Residence Inn H, Kohl's, Lowe's, Office Depot, Safeway/gas, Sam's Club, Staples, Target, Verizon, Walgreens, World Mkt
262	CO 392 E, to Windsor, E 7-11/dsl, Shell/Subway/dsl Arby's, Pueblo Viejo, Taco John's AmericInn vet, W Powder River RV Ctr
259	Crossroads Blvd, E 7-11/dsl, Shell/dsl Boot Grill, Carl's Jr, Nordy's, Palomino Mexican, Perkins, Qdoba Mexican, Subway Candlewood Suites, Embassy Suites, Holiday Inn Express, Woodspring Suites, W Hooters BMW, Buick/GMC, CarMax, Chevrolet, Harley-Davidson, Hyundai, Mercedes, Mini, Subaru, to
257b a	US 34, to Loveland, E 7-11/dsl, Shell/dsl Bent Fork Grill, Biaggi Italian, BoneFish Grill, Culver's, East Coast Pizza, On-the-Border, PF Chang's, Qdoba, Red Robin, Rock Bottom Rest., Starbucks AT&T, Barnes&Noble, Best Buy, Dick's, GNC, Macy's, See's Candies, Verizon, W Conoco/dsl Buffalo Wild Wings, Carino's Italian, Chick-fil-A, Chili's, Chipotle Mexican, Cracker Barrel, IHOP, Jimmy John's, KFC/Taco Bell, LoneStar Steaks, McDonald's, Mimi's Cafe, Noodles&Co, Old Chicago, Panera Bread, Starbucks, Subway, Wendy's Best Western, Fairfield Inn, Hampton Inn, Residence Inn H, Jo-Ann Fabrics, Loveland Outlets/famous brands, Loveland RV Resort, Marshall's, museum, Old Navy, Petsmart, Ross, Sportsman's Whse, Staples, Target, to Rocky Mtn NP
255	CO 402 W, to Loveland
254	to CO 60 W, to Campion, E Johnson's Corner/Sinclair/café/dsl/scales/motel/24hr Budget Host RV retreat/service
252	CO 60 E, to Johnstown, Milliken, W Loaf'n Jug/Subway/dsl
250	CO 56 W, to Berthoud, W Loves/Subway/dsl/scales/24hr to Carter Lake
245	to Mead
243	CO 66, to Longmont, Platteville, E Conoco/dsl, Kum&Go/dsl, Shell/7-11 Rancheros Rest., Red Rooster Rest. Camping World/K&C RV Ctr, tires, vet, W to Estes Park, to Rocky Mtn NP
241mm	St Vrain River
240	CO 119, to Longmont, E Shell/7-11/dsl Burger King, Carl's Jr, Del Taco, Good Times Grill, Pizza Hut, Popeye's, Qdoba, Starbucks, Wendy's Best Western, Comfort Suites, Woodspring Suites Century RV Ctr, Home Depot, Kia, Lexus, Toyota, Transwest RV Ctr, W 7-11/Subway/dsl, Conoco/dsl/scales/24hr, Shell/Circle K/dsl Arby's, McDonald's, Pizza Hut/Taco Bell, Waffle House 1st Inn, Best Value Inn, Quality Inn, Super 8, Travelodge museum, to Barbour Ponds SP, truckwash, Valley Camper RV Ctr
235	CO 52, Dacono, E Kum&Go/dsl Ford, Infiniti, W Conoco/dsl/LP McDonald's, Pepper Jacks Grille, Starbucks, Subway Harley-Davidson, to Eldora Ski Area
232	to Erie, Dacono
229	CO 7, to Lafayette, Brighton, E Buffalo Wild Wings, Chick-fil-A, Chili's, Famous Dave's BBQ, Goodtimes Burgers, Gunther Toody's, La Fogata, Starbucks, Subway, Village Inn AT&T, Costco/gas, Dick's, Home Depot, Petsmart, Sears Grand
228	E-470 (**tollway**), to Limon
226	144th Ave, E Murphy Express/dsl Firehouse Subs, Freddy's Cabela's, Hobby Lobby, W HuHot Mongolian, Mimi's Cafe, Mooyah Burgers, Panera Bread, Red Robin, Rusty Bucket, Starbucks, Which Wich? H, $Tree, AT&T, JC Penney, Macy's, Marshall's, Old Navy, REI, Ross, Staples, Target, Verizon
225	136th Ave, W Valero/dsl Big Burrito, Carl's Jr, KFC/LJ Silver, Starbucks, Subway Advance Parts, Firestone/auto, Lowe's, URGENT CARE, Walmart/McDonald's
223	CO 128, 120th Ave, to Broomfield, E Conoco, Valero/dsl Applebee's, Bad Daddy's Burger Bar, Burger King, Café Rio, Chick-fil-A, Chipotle Mexican, Coldstone, Fazoli's, First Watch Cafe, Jimmy John's, Jim'N Nick's BBQ, Krispy Kreme, LoneStar Steaks, Longhorn Steaks, McDonald's, Olive Garden, Outback Steaks, Panda Express, Panera Bread, Smashburger, Sonic, Starbucks, Subway, Taziki's Cafe, Tequila's Mexican, TGIFriday's DoubleTree, EconoLodge, Hampton Inn, Holiday Inn Express, Ramada Inn $Tree, Albertson's, AT&T, Barnes&Noble, Big O Tire, Brakes+, CarQuest, Discount Tire, GNC, Meineke Michael's, O'Reilly Parts, PetCo, Sprouts Mkt, Target, Tires+ Verizon, vet, Walgreens, W Conoco/dsl, Shell/Circle K/Popeye's/dsl, Valero/dsl CB Potts Rest., Chili's, Cracker Barrel DQ, Hooters, Laguna's Mexican, Perkins, Qdoba, Starbucks, Subway, Village Inn Rest., Wendy's Comfort Suites, Cottonwood Suites, Extended Stay America, Fairfield Inn, La Quinta, Super 8
221	104th Ave, to Northglenn, E Conoco, Shell Buffalo Wild Wings, Burger King, CiCi's Pizza, Denny's, DQ, Firehouse Subs, Old Chicago, Qdoba, Subway, Texas Roadhouse H, GNC, Home Depot, King's Soopers, Tires+, Walgreens, W 7-11, Shell/Circle K/dsl Applebee's, Atlanta Bread, Blackeyed Pea, Cinzzetti's Italian, GoodTimes Burger, Gunther Toody's, McDonald's Seoul BBQ, Starbucks, Taco Bell, The Armadillo Best Buy

FT COLLINS · LOVELAND · LONGMONT · BROOMFIELD

INTERSTATE 25 Cont'd

THORNTON

221 Continued
Fiat, Firestone/auto, Ford, Goodyear/auto, Hyundai, Jo-Ann Fabrics, Lowe's, Marshalls, Office Depot, Petsmart, Ross, Sheplar's

220 Thornton Pkwy, E Golden Corral, Rico Pollo (H), AT&T, Hobby Lobby, Sam's Club/gas, Thornton Civic Ctr, Walmart/McDonald's, W Shell, Valero/dsl, Western/dsl Subway

219 84th Ave, to Federal Way, E Shell/dsl, Valero/dsl Arby's, McDonald's, Quiznos, Sonic, Starbucks, Subway, Taco Bell, Taco Star, Waffle House O'Reilly Parts, W Econogas, Valero/dsl Burger King, DQ, El Fogon, McDonald's, Popeye's, Santiago's Mexican, Village Inn Rest. Motel 6 (H), AutoZone, CarQuest, Discount Tire, Meineke, Save-A-Lot, vet

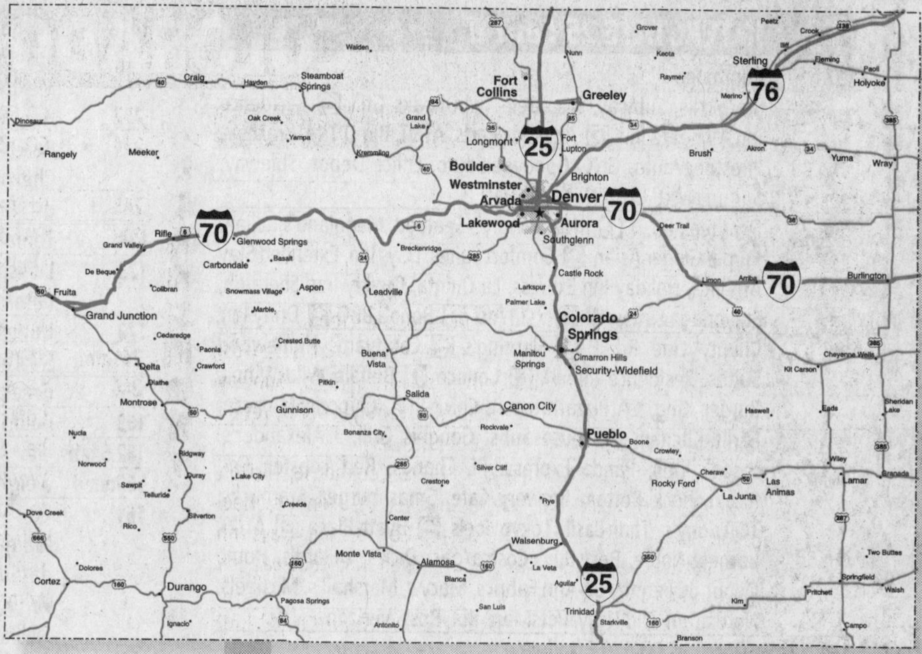

217 US 36 W (exits left from nb), to Boulder, W Ammco Subway Chevrolet, Toyota

216b a I-76 E, to I-270 E

215 58th Ave, E Burger King, McDonald's, Steak Escape, Subway, Wendy's Comfort Inn URGENT CARE, W Conoco/dsl, Shamrock/dsl Super 8 O'Reilly Parts

214c 48th Ave, E coliseum, W Village Inn Rest. Clarion, Quality Inn

214b a I-70, E to Limon, W to Grand Junction

213 Park Ave, W 38th Ave, 23rd St, downtown, E Conoco Domino's, McDonald's, Starbucks La Quinta, W Town&Country Motel

DENVER AREA

212c 20th St, downtown, Denver

212b a Speer Blvd, E museum, downtown, W Conoco/dsl, Shell/dsl Starbucks, Subway Hampton Inn, Ramada, Residence Inn, Super 8 AutoZone, Walgreens

211 23rd Ave, E funpark

210c CO 33 (from nb)

210b US 40 W, Colfax Ave, W Denny's, KFC Ramada Inn/rest. Mile High Stadium

210a US 40 E, Colfax Ave, E civic center, U-Haul, downtown

209c 8th Ave

209b 6th Ave W, US 6, W Shell/dsl

209a 6th Ave E, downtown, Denver

208 CO 26, Alameda Ave (from sb), E Shamrock/dsl Burger King, Denny's Home Depot, same as 207b, W Conoco/dsl

207b US 85 S, Santa Fe Dr, same as 208

207a Broadway, Lincoln St, E Griff's Burgers USPO

206b Washington St, Emerson St, E Whole Foods Mkt, W (H)

206a Downing St (from nb)

205b a University Blvd, W to U of Denver

204 CO 2, Colorado Blvd, E Conoco/dsl, Loaf'n Jug, Shamrock, Shell/Circle K Arby's, Black Eyed Pea, Chili's, Domino's, GoodTimes Grill, Hacienda Colorado, IHOP, Jimmy John's, McDonald's, Noodles&Co, Old Chicago Pizza, Pizza Hut, Qdoba, Smashburger, Starbucks, Subway, Taco Bell, Tokyo Joe's, Village Inn Rest., Wahoo's, Whole Foods Mkt Belcaro Motel, Courtyard, Fairfield Inn, Hampton Inn Barnes&Noble, Best Buy, Chevrolet, Home Depot, Mercedes/BMW, Petco, Ross, Safeway

204 Continued
Foods, Staples, vet, VW, Walgreens, W Conoco A&W/KFC, Dave&Buster's, McDonald's, Pei Wei, Perkins, Which Wich La Quinta Natural Grocers, Office Depot, USPO

203 Evans Ave, E Rockies Inn, W Cameron Motel Ford

202 Yale Ave, W BeauJo's CO Pizza, Chipotle Mexican GNC, King's Sooper, Michaels, Petsmart

201 US 285, CO 30, Hampden Ave, to Englewood, Aurora, E Conoco/Circle K/LP, Shamrock, Shell Chick-fil-A, Chipotle Mexican, Coldstone, Domino's, Firehouse Subs, Jimmy John's, McDonald's, Noodles&Co, NY Deli, Panera Bread, Qdoba, Smashburger, Starbucks, Subway, Wahoos Fish Taco, Zanitas Mexican Embassy Suites Discount Tire, King's Sooper/dsl, Omaha Steaks, Petco, Target, URGENT CARE, Verizon, vet, Walgreens, Whole Food Mkt, W Conoco/7-11 Burger King, Starbucks Safeway

200 I-225 N, to I-70

199 CO 88, Belleview Ave, to Littleton, E Baker St Grill, Chipotle Mexican, Cool River Cafe, Fiocchi's Pizzeria, Fornaio Rest., Garcia's Mexican, Great Northern Rest., Noodles&Co, Pancake House, Panera Bread, Qdoba, Starbucks, Wendy's, Which Wich? Hampton Inn, Hilton Garden, Hyatt Place, Marriott, W Conoco, Shamrock McDonald's, Pappadeaux Café, Pizza Hut/Taco Bell Extended Stay Am, Extended Stay America Lexus

198 Orchard Rd, E Del Frisco's Steaks Shepler's, W Shell/Circle K/dsl Subway DoubleTree vet

197 Arapahoe Blvd, E Conoco/dsl, Shell/Circle K/dsl A&W/KFC, Bros BBQ, Burger King, Chick-fil-A, Del Taco, Dickie's BBQ, Domino's, El Parral, El Tapatio Mexican, Gunther Toody's Rest., Hoong's Palace, McDonald's, Outback Steaks, Pat's Cheesesteak, Pizza Hut, Qdoba, Schlotsky's, Smashburger, Sonic, Starbucks, Subway, Volcano Chinese, Wendy's Best Western, Courtyard, Extended Stay America, Hawthorn Suites, Hyatt House, LaQuinta, Motel 6, Sleep Inn Chrysler/Jeep, Discount Tire, Ford, Home Depot, Honda, Hyundai, Kia, Lowe's Whse, Mazda, Nissan, Subaru, Target, Toyota, USPO, Walmart, W Phillips 66/dsl, Shell/dsl, Valero/dsl Arby's, Boston Mkt, CB & Potts, Chipotle Mexican, DQ, Elephant Bar Rest., Five Guys, Garbanzo Grill, Goodtimes, Jamba Juice, Jimmy John's, Macaroni Grill, McDonald's, Papa Murphy's, Qdoba, Red Robin,

DENVER AREA

INTERSTATE 25 Cont'd

197 Continued
Starbucks, Subway, Taco Bell, Twin Peaks Grill Residence Inn, Wingate Inn Advance Parts, AT&T, Big O Tire, Brakes+, Firestone/auto, GNC, Goodyear/auto, Office Depot, Safeway, Sprouts Mkt, URGENT CARE, vet

196 Dry Creek Rd, E IHOP, Landry's Seafood, Maggiano's Italian, Purple Ginger Asian Comfort Suites, Days Inn, Extended Stay America, Holiday Inn Express, La Quinta, Quality Inn, Sheraton, Staybridge Suites, W 7-11/dsl Bono's BBQ Drury Inn

195 County Line Rd, E Fleming's Courtyard, Homewood Suites, Residence Inn, W Conoco Buffalo Wild Wings, Burger King, CA Pizza Kitchen, Chick-fil-A, Chipotle Mexican, Earl's Kitchen, Firehouse Subs, Genghis Grill, J Alexander's, Jason's Deli, Panda Express, PF Changs, Red Lobster, Red Robin, Rock Bottom Brewery/Cafe, Smashburger, Starbucks, TGIFriday's, Thai Basil, Tokyo Joe's Hyatt Place AT&T, Barnes&Noble, Best Buy, Costco/gas, Dick's, Dillard's, Home Depot, JC Penney, Jo-Ann Fabrics, Macy's, Marshall's, Michaels, Nordstrom, Old Navy, PetsMart, REI, Ross, Verizon

194 CO 470 W, CO 470 E (**tollway**)

193 Lincoln Ave, to Parker, E 7-11/dsl, Conoco, Valero/dsl Carl's Jr, Hacienda Colorado, Starbucks, Subway Candlewood Suites, Hilton Garden, W Conoco/dsl Chili's, Chipotle Mexican, Firehouse Subs, Five Guys, Garbanzo Grill, Heidi's, KFC, McDonald's, Noodles&Co, Papa John's, Papa Murphy's, Pizza Hut/Taco Bell, Qdoba, Starbucks, Subway Hampton Inn, Marriott H, Discount Tire, GNC, Safeway, Sprouts Mkt, Target

192 Ridgegate Pkwy, W TownePlace Suites H, Cabela's

191 no services

190 Surrey Ridge, Surrey Ridge

188 Castle Pines Pkwy, W Conoco/dsl, Shell/Circle K/Taco Bell/dsl La Dolce Vita, Las Fajitas Mexican, Papa John's, Papa Murphy's, Starbucks, Subway, Wendy's Big O Tires, Discount Tire, King's Sooper/dsl, Safeway, URGENT CARE, vet, Wlagreens

CASTLE ROCK

187 Happy Canyon Rd, W **services 2 mi**

185 Castle Rock Pkwy, W Phillips 66/7-11 Del Taco Petco, Sam's Club/dsl, TJ Maxx, Verizon

184 Founders Pkwy, Meadows Pkwy, to Castle Rock, E Conoco/dsl, Shell/Circle K/dsl A&W/KFC, Applebee's, Baskin-Robbins, Chick-fil-A, Chipotle Mexican, Coldstone, Five Guys, Goodtimes Grill, Jimmy John's, Little Caesars, Noodles&Co, Outback Steaks, Panera Bread, Parry's Pizza, Qdoba, Red Robin, Sonic, Starbucks, Subway, Taco Bell, Wendy's $Tree, Advance Parts, AT&T, Brakes+, Discount Tire, Firestone/auto, GNC, Goodyear/auto, Grease Monkey, Home Depot, Just Brakes, King's Sooper, Kohl's, Michael's, Natural Grocers, Office Depot, O'Reilly Parts, Petsmart, Sprouts Mkt, Target, Verizon, vet, Walgreens, Walmart, W Loaf'n Jug/dsl Arby's, Blackeyed Pea, Cafe Rio, Chili's, Food Court, Freddy's Steakburger, IHOP, McDonald's, MOD Pizza, Popeye's, Potbelly, Rockyard Grill, Smashburger Best Western+, Comfort Suites, Days Inn, Hampton Inn, Holiday Inn Express Castle Rock Outlet/famous brands, King's Sooper/dsl, Lowe's, Midas, st patrol

182 CO 86, Castle Rock, Franktown, E 7-11/dsl, Conoco/dsl, Phillips 66/dsl Augustine Grill, B&B Cafe, Castle Cafe, El Meson Mexican Castle Pines Motel vet, W Shell/Circle K/dsl, Valero/dsl Burger King, Domino's, Guadalajara Mexican, Jack-in-the-Box, McDonald's, Old West BBQ, Santiago's Mexican, Village Inn, Waffle House, Wendy's Castle Inn, LaQuinta, Super 8 NAPA

LARKSPUR

181 CO 86, Wilcox St, Plum Creek Pkwy, Castle Rock, E Phillips 66, Valero/dsl, Western/dsl Blimpie, DQ, El Meson Mexican, Jimmy John's, Papa John's, Papa Murphy's, Pizza Hut, Quiznos, Starbucks, Stumpy's Pizzaria, Subway, Taco Bell Castle Rock Motel AutoZone, Big O Tire, Buick/Chevrolet/GMC, Chrysler/Dodge/Jeep, Ford, Midas, Safeway/dsl, Tuesday Morning, URGENT CARE, USPO, Walgreens

174 Tomah Rd, W Yogi Bear's Campground

173 Larkspur (from sb, no return), **3 mi** W Conoco/Larkspur Cafe/dsl/

172 Upper Lake Gulch Rd, Larkspur, **2 mi** W Conoco/dsl/ Larkspur Pizza Cafe, Spur Grill USPO

167 Greenland

163 County Line Rd

162.5mm elev 7352, Monument Hill

162mm **weigh sta both lanes**

161 CO 105, Woodmoor Dr, E Kum&Go/dsl, Sinclair 3 Margaritas Mexican, Jimmy John's, Papa John's Ramada/Sundance Mtn Lodge/rest. CO Hts RV Park (2mi), vet, W 7-11, Phillips 66/dsl Arby's, Domino's, La Casa Fiesta New Mexican, McDonald's, Rosie's Diner, Starbucks, Subway, Taco Bell, Village Inn Big O Tire, Natural Grocers, Safeway/dsl, USPO, Walgreens

158 Baptist Rd, E Murphy USA/dsl, Shell/Circle K/Popeye's/dsl/24hr Borriello Bros. Pizza, Carlos Miguel's, Chili's, Coldstone, Freddy's Steakburgers, McDonald's, Mexican Grill, Papa Murphy's, Qdoba, Subway, TX Roadhouse Fairfield Inn Advance Parts, AutoZone, Christian Bros. Auto, Discount Tire, GNC, Home Depot, Jiffy Lube, King's Sooper, Kohl's, Natural Grocers, O'Reilly Parts, Petsmart, Staples, URGENT CARE, Verizon, Walgreens, Walmart/Subway, W Pilot/Arby's/dsl/scales/24hr, Shamrock/dsl/scales

156b N Entrance to USAF Academy, E Loaf'n Jug/Subway/dsl Bourbon Bros Kitchen, C B & Potts Rest., Costa Vida, Jimmy John's, Kneaders Cafe, Wendy's AT&T, Bass Pro Shops, W visitors center

156a Gleneagle Dr, E mining museum

153 InterQuest Pkwy, E Kum&Go/dsl Cheddar's, CO Mtn Brewery/rest., Dickey's BBQ, Freddy's, Jersey Mike's, Starbucks, Taco Bell, Zoup! Drury Inn, Hampton Inn, Residence Inn

152 scenic overlook on sb

151 Briargate Pkwy, E 7-11 Biaggi's, CA Pizza Kitchen, Garbanzo Grill, Marco's Pizza, Panera Bread, PF Changs, Qdoba, Salsa Brava Mexican, Starbucks, Ted's MT Grill Hilton Garden, Homewood Suites AT&T, to Black Forest

150b a CO 83, Academy Blvd, E Shamrock/dsl, Shell/Circle K/dsl A&W, Amanda's Fonda, Applebee's, Baskin-Robbins, Buffalo Wild Wings, Burger King, Chick-fil-A, Chipotle Mexican, Coldstone, Cracker Barrel, Crave Burgers, Culver's, Del Taco, Denny's, Drifters Hamburgers, Egg&I Café, Elephant Bar Rest., Extreme Pizza, Famous Dave's, Firehouse Subs, Five Guys, HuHot Mongolian, IHOP, Jason's Deli, Jimmy John's, KFC, McDonald's, Mimi's Café, Noodles&Co, Olive Garden, Olive Garden, On-the-Border, Panera Bread, Pei Wei, Qdoba, Red Robin, Salt Grass Steaks, Schlotzsky's, Sonic, Starbucks, Steak'n Shake, Subway, Tokyo Joe's Grill, Wendy's Academy Hotel, Comfort Suites, Days Inn, Drury Inn, EconoLodge, Howard Johnson, Super 8 $Tree, Advance Parts, AT&T, Barnes&Noble, Best Buy, Chevrolet, Dick's, Dillard's, Firestone/auto, Ford, Hobby Lobby, Home Depot, Hyundai, JC Penney, Kia, King's Sooper, Macy's, Marshall's, Michael's, Midas, Natural Grocers, Old Navy, O'Reilly Parts, PepBoys, Petsmart, REI, Ross, Sam's Club/gas,

CO

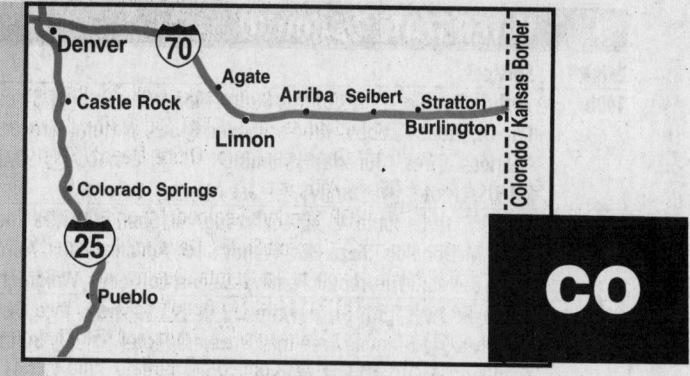

INTERSTATE 25 Cont'd

150b a Continued
to Peterson AFB, URGENT CARE, Verizon, VW, Walmart/Subway, Whole Foods Mkt, W S Entrance to USAF Academy

149 Woodmen Rd, E Carl's Jr, Carraba's Nissan, W Shell/Circle K/dsl Hooters, Old Chicago Pizza, Outback Steaks, TGIFriday's Comfort Inn, Embassy Suites, Fairfield Inn, Hampton Inn, Holiday Inn Express, Microtel, Staybridge Suites

148 Corporate Ctr Dr, Nevada Ave, E BJ's Rest., Bonefish Grill, Chipotle Mexican, Hacienda Colorado, Noodles&Co, Panera Bread, Pita Pit, Smashburger, Tokyo Joe's Grill, Which Wich? The Lodges BMW, Costco/gas, Harley-Davidson, Kohl's, Lowe's, Petco, SteinMart, Trader Joe's, W Shell/Circle K Crestwood Suites, Extended Stay America, Hyatt House, Marriott to Rodeo Hall of Fame

146 Garden of the Gods Rd, E Conoco/7-11, Shell/Circle K/dsl Carl's Jr, Caspian Cafe, Drifter's Burgers, McDonald's Best Value Inn, La Quinta Aamco, W Conoco/7-11, Exxon/dsl, Phillips 66/Circle K, Shamrock/dsl Applebee's, Arby's, Arceo's Mexican, Blackeyed Pea, Chick-fil-A, Freddy's Steakburgers, Jimmy John's, Mollica's Italian, Sonic, Souper Salad, Subway, Taco Bell, Taco Bueno, Village Inn, Wendy's Days Inn, Hyatt Place, Quality Inn, Super 8 $Tree, AutoZone, Discount Tire, to Garden of Gods, vet

145 CO 38 E, Fillmore St, E Conoco/7-11, Shamrock/dsl, Western/dsl Arby's, Burger King, Carl's Jr, DQ, Lucky Dragon, McDonald's, Subway, Taco Bell Budget Host H, Advance Parts, Walgreens, W Kum&Go/dsl Waffle House Best Western+, Motel 6, Super 8

144 Fontanero St

143 Uintah St, E 7-11 Uintah Fine Arts Ctr

142 Bijou St, Bus Dist, E The Antlers Hotel Firestone/auto, visitor info, W Denny's Clarion, Holiday Inn Express, Quality Inn

141 US 24 W, Cimarron St, to Manitou Springs, W Shell/7-11/dsl, Sinclair/dsl Arby's, Capt D's, La Casita Mexican, McDonald's, Popeye's, Sonic, TX Roadhouse Acura, Audi, AutoZone, Brakes+, Buick/GMC, Cadillac, Chevrolet, Chrysler/Dodge/Jeep, Discount Tire, Ford, Grease Monkey, Hobby Lobby, Hyundai, Infiniti, Kia, Land Rover/Jaguar, Lexus, Lincoln, Mazda, Meineke, Mercedes, NAPA, Office Depot, Porsche, Subaru, to Pikes Peak, Toyota, Volvo, VW, Walmart/McDonald's

140b US 85 S, Tejon St, E Peerless Tires, W Conoco/dsl access to same as 141

140a Nevada Ave, E Kum & Go/dsl Chateau Motel, Howard Johnson repair, W 7-11, Shamrock Arceo's Mexican, Burger King, China Kitchen, Chipotle Mexican, IHOP, KFC, McDonald's, Noodles&Co, On the Border, Panda Express, Panera Bread, Rancho Alegre Mexican, Red Robin, Schlotzsky's, Starbucks, Subway, Taco Bell, Taco Express, Wendy's Rodeway Inn, Sunsprings Motel, Travel Star Inn $Tree, access to auto dealers at 141, Big O Tire, Family$, Michael's, Midas, Natural Grocers, Office Depot, O'Reilly Parts, Petsmart, Ross, Safeway Foods, Tuesday Morning, Walgreens

139 US 24 E, to Lyman, Peterson AFB

138 CO 29, Circle Dr, E Conoco, Shell/Circle K/dsl McDonald's Days Inn, Hotel Elegante, Super 8 , Kohl's, URGENT CARE, zoo, W 7-11 Arby's, Buffalo Wild Wings, Burger King, Carl's Jr, Carrabba's, Chili's, ChuckeCheese, Culver's, Denny's, Fazoli's, Flatiron Grill, Macaroni Grill, Outback Steaks, Smoothie King, Subway, Village Inn Best Western,

COLORADO SPRINGS

138 Continued
Comfort Inn, Courtyard, DoubleTree Hotel, Fairfield Inn, Hampton Inn, La Quinta, Residence Inn AT&T, GNC, PetCo, Target

135 CO 83, Academy Blvd, E to , W Jersey Mike's, MOD Pizza, Qdoba, Starbucks Ft Carson, Sam's Club/dsl, to Cheyenne Mtn SP, Verizon, Walmart/Subway

132 CO 16, Wide Field Security, E Loves/Subway/dsl Camping World RV Ctr, KOA

128 to US 85 N, Fountain, Security, E 7-11, Loaf'n Jug/Subway/dsl Family$, USPO, W Tomahawk/Exxon/rest./dsl/24hr/@ Fountain Inn, Super 8 Freightliner

125 Ray Nixon Rd

123 no services

122 to Pikes Peak Meadows, W Pikes Peak Intn'l Raceway

119 Rancho Colorado Blvd, Midway

116 county line rd

115mm **nb, full facilities, litter barrels, petwalk,**

114 Young Hollow

112mm **sb, full facilities, litter barrels, petwalk,**

110 Pinon, W Maggie's Farm/dsl

108 Purcell Blvd, Bragdon, E racetrack, W KOA

106 Porter Draw

104 Eden, W Loves/Chester's/Subway/dsl/scales/24hr Peterbilt

102 Eagleridge Blvd, E Loaf'n Jug/dsl Burger King, Subway, TX Roadhouse Candlewood Suites, Holiday Inn Express Big O Tire, Home Depot, Sam's Club/gas, W Conoco/dsl Buffalo Wild Wings, Cactus Flower Mexican, Chili's, Cracker Barrel, IHOP, Mexican Grill, Starbucks, Village Inn, Wonderful Bistro Best Western, Comfort Inn, EconoLodge, Hampton Inn, La Quinta, Ramada, Wingate Inn Best Buy, Cavender's Boots, Dick's, frontage rds access 101, Harley-Davidson, Kohl's, Old Navy, PetCo

101 US 50 W, Pueblo, E Capt D's, Coldstone, Country Buffet, Denny's, Margaritas Mexican, Ruby Tuesday, Souper Salad Baymont Inn Barnes&Noble, CO Tire, Dillard's, JC Penney, Jo-Ann, Petsmart, Ross, Target, TJ Maxx, U-Haul, Verizon, Walmart/Subway, W Conoco/7-11, Loaf'n Jug/dsl, Shell/dsl, Valero/dsl Applebee's, Arby's, Arriba Mexican, Blackeyed Pea, Carl's Jr, China Rest., Chipotle Mexican, Country Kitchen, DJ's Steaks, Domino's, DQ, Fazoli's, Golden Corral, Jack-in-the-Box, Little Caesar's, Manhattan's Pizza, McAlister's Deli, McDonald's, Noodles&Co, Old Chicago, Olive Garden, Papa John's, Papa Murphy's, Pass Key Rest., Pizza Hut, Popeye's, Red Lobster, Starbucks, Subway, SW Grill, Taco Bell, Wendy's Clarion, Days Inn, Motel 6, Quality Inn, Rodeway Inn, Super 8 Aamco, Advance Parts, Albertson's, AT&T, AutoZone, Brakes+, Chevrolet, Chrysler/Dodge/Jeep, Discount Tire, EmergiCare, Ford/Lincoln, frontage rds access 102, Hyundai, Kia/Mazda, K-Mart, Lowe's, Midas, NAPA, Nissan, O'Reilly Parts, Staples, Subaru, Toyota, Verizon, vet, Walgreens

PUEBLO

CO

INTERSTATE 25 Cont'd

Exit #	Services
100b	29th St, Pueblo, E Country Buffet, Mongolian Grill $Tree, Car Dr, Hobby Lobby, King's Sooper Foods, Natural Grocers, Peerless Tires, Tuesday Morning, W Conoco Sonic USA Motel Family$, Grease Monkey, Safeway
100a	US 50 E, to La Junta, E Loaf'n Jug/dsl, Shell Little Caesar's, McDonald's, Pizza Hut, Wendy's Advance Parts, AutoZone, Belmont Tire/repair, Family$, Save-A-Lot Foods, Walgreens
99b a	Santa Fe Ave, 13th St, downtown, W Subway, Taco Bell, Wendy's Bramble Tree Inn, Travelers Motel H, Buick/Cadillac/GMC, CarQuest, Honda
98b	CO 96, 1st St, Union Ave Hist Dist, Pueblo, W Loaf'n Jug/dsl Carl's Jr Courtyard
98a	US 50E bus, to La Junta, W Sonic
97b	Abriendo Ave
97a	Central Ave, W Alta/dsl McDonald's $General
96	Indiana Ave, W H
95	Illinois Ave (from sb), W to dogtrack
94	CO 45 N, Pueblo Blvd, W Loaf'n Jug/dsl, Western/dsl Subway, Taco Bell Hampton Inn, Microtel Forts RV Park, to Lake Pueblo SP
91	Stem Beach
88	Burnt Mill Rd
87	Verde Rd
83	no services
77	Hatchet Ranch Rd, Cedarwood
74	CO 165 W, Colo City, E Shamrock/deli/dsl/24hr Obie's BBQ KOA, W **both lanes, full facilities, litter barrels, petwalk, , vending,** Sinclair/Subway/dsl Max's Place Days Inn/rest., 71 Graneros Rd
67	to Apache
64	Lascar Rd
60	Huerfano
59	Butte Rd
56	Redrock Rd
55	Airport Rd
52	CO 69 W, to Alamosa, Walsenburg, W Conoco/dsl, Loaf'n Jug/dsl (2mi), TA/Phillips 66/A&W/dsl Carl's Jr (2mi), George's Rest., KFC/Taco Bell, Subway (2mi) Best Western, Budget Host/RV Park Country Host RV Park, Dakota RV Park/camping, Family$ (2mi), San Luis Valley, to Great Sand Dunes NM
50	CO 10 E, to La Junta, W H
49	Lp 25, to US 160 W, Walsenburg, 1 mi W Loaf'n Jug/dsl Carl's Jr., Subway Lathrop SP, to Cuchara Ski Valley
42	Rouse Rd, to Pryor
41	Rugby Rd
34	Aguilar
30	Aguilar Rd, W Green Earth RV Park
27	Ludlow, W Ludlow Memorial
23	Hoehne Rd
18	El Moro Rd, W **both lanes, full facilities, litter barrels, petwalk,**
15	US 350 E, Goddard Ave, E Burger King, Pizza Hut Super 8 H, AutoZone, Big R Ranch Store, Family$, W Shell/dsl Frontier Motel/café
14	Commercial St, downtown, Trinidad, same as 13b
13b	Main St, Trinidad, E **CO Welcome Ctr** Exxon/dsl KFC/Taco Bell, McDonald's, Sonic Days Inn CarQuest, H, Safeway Foods/dsl, Trinidad Motor Inn, W Conoco/dsl Monument Lake, to Trinidad Lake
13a	Santa Fe Trail, Trinidad, E RV camping
11	Starkville, E Shell/Wendy's/dsl/24hr Tequila's Mexican Budget Host/RVPark, Holiday Inn, Rodeway Inn Summit RV Park, to Santa Fe Trail, weigh/check sta, W La Quinta, Quality Inn/rest Big O Tire, Grease Monkey, O'Reilly Parts, Walmart
8	Springcreek
6	Gallinas
2	Wootten
1mm	scenic area pulloff nb
0mm	Colorado/New Mexico state line, Raton Pass, elev 7834, **weigh sta sb**

WALSENBURG · TRINIDAD · BURLINGTON · LIMON

INTERSTATE 70

Exit #	Services
450mm	Colorado/Kansas state line
438	US 24, Rose Ave, Burlington, N Hi-Lo Motel, Sloan's Motel H, $General, Bomgaars, Buick/Cadillac/Chevrolet/GMC, CarQuest, Family$, Ford/Lincoln, NAPA, O'Reilly Parts, Outback RV Park, Safeway Foods, S Sinclair/Reynaldo's Mexican/dsl/24hr truck repair
437.5mm	**Welcome Ctr wb, full facilities, historical site, info, litter barrels, petwalk, ,**
437	US 385, Burlington, N Conoco/dsl, Phillips 66/dsl Arby's, Burger King, Dish Room, McDonald's, Pizza Hut, Subway Burlington Inn, Burlington Stay Inn, Chaparral Motel Quality Inn, Western Motel H, ShopKO, S Love's/Carl's Jr/dsl/scales/24hr/@ Best Western+, Fairfield Inn Woodspring Suites
429	Bethune
419	CO 57, Stratton, N Cenex/dsl, Conoco/dsl Dairy Treat Claremont Inn/café, Rodeway Inn Marshall Ash Village Camping, Trails End Camping
412	Vona, 1/2 mi N ,
405	CO 59, Seibert, N Shady Grove Camping/RV dump, S Conoco/dsl tire repair
395	Flagler, N Loaf'N Jug/dsl I-70 Diner, Subway Little England Motel Flagler SWA, G&B RV camping, NAPA S Cenex/dsl golf
383	Arriba, N DJ/café/dsl motel, S **both lanes full facilities, litter barrels, petwalk, , point of interest,** RV camping
376	Bovina
371	Genoa, N , , , point of interest, S H
363	US 24, US 40, US 287, to CO 71, to Hugo, Limon, **13 mi S** H
361	CO 71, Limon, N Ace Hardware, S Shell/Wendy's/dsl Sinclair/dsl Golden China, Pizza Hut 1st Inn Gold, Coyote Motel KOA, RV camping, st patrol
360.5mm	**weigh/check sta both lanes**
359	to US 24, to CO 71, Limon, N FLYING J/IHOP/dsl/scales LP/24hr dsl repair, RV camping, S Qwest/dsl, Sinclair/dsl TA/Phillips 66//Subway//Country Pride/dsl/scales/24hr/@ Arby's, McDonald's, Oscar's Grill, Taco Bell Baymont Inn, Comfort Inn, EconoLodge, Holiday Inn Express, Microtel, Quality Inn Super 8 Chrysler/Dodge/Jeep
354	no services
352	CO 86 W, to Kiowa
348	to Cedar Point
340	Agate, 1/4 mi S /dsl,
336	to Lowland
332mm	**wb, full facilities, info, litter barrels, petwalk, , vending**

INTERSTATE 70 Cont'd

Exit #	Services
328	to Deer Trail, N Phillips/dsl, S Shell/dsl USPO
325mm	East Bijou Creek
323.5mm	Middle Bijou Creek
322	to Peoria
316	US 36 E, Byers, N Sinclair/dsl Budget Host Thriftway Foods/Drug, S Tri Valley Country Burger Rest. USPO
310	Strasburg, N Conoco/dsl Coronas Mexican, KT's BBQ, Patio Cafe, Subway Country Gardens RV Camping (3mi), dsl/auto repair, KOA, NAPA, USPO, vet, Western Hardware
306	Kiowa, Bennett
305	Kiowa (from eb)
304	CO 79 N, Bennett, N Conoco/Hotstuff Pizza/dsl, Love's/McDonald's/dsl/scales/24hr Carl's Jr, China Kitchen, High Plains Diner, Starbucks, Subway, Taco Bell Family$, King Soopers Foods/dsl, O'Reilly Parts, USPO, S Ace Hardware
299	CO 36, Manila Rd, S Shamrock/dsl
295	Lp 70, Watkins, N Shell/Tomahawk/rest/dsl/24hr/@ Biscuit's Cafe, Lulu's Cafe Country Manor Motel USPO
292	CO 36, Airpark Rd
289	E-470 Tollway, 120th Ave, CO Springs
288	US 287, US 40, Lp 70, Colfax Ave (exits left from wb)
286	CO 32, Tower Rd, N Murphy Express/dsl Chick-fil-A, Chili's, Chipotle Mexican, Del Taco, DQ, Firehouse Subs, McAlister's Deli, Noodles&Co, Panda Express, Starbucks, Wendy's $Tree, AT&T, Best Buy, Brakes+, Discount Tire, GNC, Home Depot, Les Schwab Tire, Office Depot, O'Reilly Parts, PetCo, Verizon, Walmart/Subway
285	Airport Blvd, N Denver Int Airport, S FLYING J/Denny's/dsl/scales/24hr, Conoco/McDonald's/dsl Comfort Inn, Quality Inn Harley-Davidson
284	I-225 N (from eb)
283	Chambers Rd, N Conoco, Shell/Circle K/Popeye's A&W/KFC, Anthony's Pizza, Applebees, Chicago Grill, Jimmy John's, LJ Silver/Taco Bell, Outback Steaks, Pizza Hut, Qdoba, Sonic, Subway, Ted's MT Grill, Urban Sombrero, Wendy's, Zume Asian A Loft, Cambria Suites, Country Inn&Suites, Crowne Plaza, Econolodge, Hampton Inn, Hilton Garden, Homewood Suites, Hyatt Place, Marriott, Residence Inn, TownePlace Suites, Woolley's Suites Tires+, U-haul, S Shamrock Burger King, Jack-in-the-Box Crossland Suites, Woodspring Suites RV America, URGENT CARE
282	I-225 S, to Colorado Springs
281	Peoria St, N 7-11, Conoco/dsl, Shell/dsl Ajua Mexican, Burger King, Del Taco, Domino's, GoodTimes Burgers, McDonald's, Peoria Grill, Quizno's, Starbucks, Subway Holiday Inn Express, La Quinta, Rodeway Inn, Timbers Motel Big O Tire, Family$, S Phillips 66/dsl, Shamrock/dsl Bennett's BBQ, Denny's, Ho Mei Chinese, Taco Bell, Taco Mex Motel 6, Rodeway Inn, Star Hotel, Stay Inn auto/RV repair, Goodyear/auto
280	Havana St, N Embassy Suites
279b	Central Ave, N Drury Inn, Residence Inn
279	I-270 W, US 36 W (from wb), to Ft Collins, Boulder
278	CO 35, Quebec St, N Sapp Bros/Sinclair/Subway/dsl/@, TA/dsl/rest./24hr/@ Bar Louie, Coldstone, Del Taco, Islamorada Fish Co, Jim'n Nick's BBQ, La Sandia Cantina, Marco's Pizza, Olive Garden, Qdoba, Red Lobster, Red Robin, Starbucks, Subway, TGIFriday's, TX Roadhouse, Wahoo's, Which Wich? Best Inn, Comfort Inn, Staybridge Suites Bass Pro Shops, JC Penney, Macys, Old Navy, Super Target, S Walmart Gas Arby's,

DENVER AREA

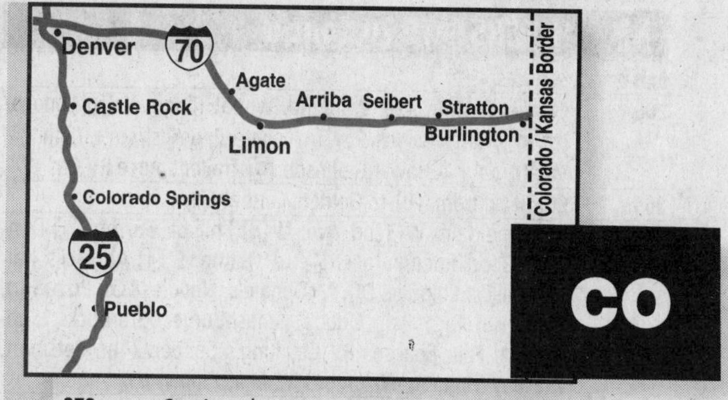

CO

Exit #	Services
278	Continued Buffalo Wild Wings, Country Buffet, Famous Dave's BBQ, IHOP, Jimmy John's, La Mariposa, McDonald's, Panda Express, Panera Bread, Papa John's, Smashburger, Sonic, Subway Best Western, Courtyard, DoubleTree Hilton, DoubleTree Hotel, Holiday Inn, Renaissance Inn, Super 8 AT&T, GNC, Home Depot, Office Depot, Petsmart, Ross, Sam's Club, Tires+, Walgreens, Walmart/Subway
277	to Dahlia St, Holly St, Monaco St, frontage rd
276b	US 6 E, US 85 N, CO 2, Colorado Blvd, S Conoco/Subway/dsl Carl's Jr, Domino's, KT'S BBQ, Starbucks
276a	Vasquez Ave, N Pilot/Wendy's/dsl/scales/24hr Western Inn Blue Beacon, Ford Trucks, Peterbilt, S 7-11 Burger King
275c	York St (from eb)
275b	CO 265, Brighton Blvd, Coliseum, N 7-11
275a	Washington St (from wb), N 7-11 Pizza Hut, S Conoco/dsl McDonald's
274b a	I-25, N to Cheyenne, S to Colorado Springs
273	Pecos St, N Conoco/7-11/dsl Family$, SavALot Foods, S 7-11 Quiznos Autocare
272	US 287, Federal Blvd, N Phillips 66/dsl, Sinclair Burger King, Goodtimes Burgers, Little Caesar's, McCoy's Rest., McDonald's, Pizza Hut, Rico Pollo, Subway, Taco Bell, Village Inn, Wendy's, Winchell's Motel 6 $Tree, 7-11, Advance Parts, Family$, tires, S Conoco/Mkt/dsl El Padrino Mexican, Popeye's, Starbucks Travelers Inn
271b	Lowell Blvd, Tennyson St (from wb)
271a	CO 95, S funpark
270	Sheridan Blvd, N Shell/dsl, S Murphy Express/dsl El Paraiso Mexican, Grammy's Pizza Family$, Firestone/auto, fun park, Schwab Tire, Walmart
269b	I-76 E (from eb), to Ft Morgan, Ft Collins
269a	CO 121, Wadsworth Blvd, N 7-11, Conoco, Shell/dsl Anthony's Pizza, Applebee's, BeauJo's, Bennet's BBQ, Chick-fil-A, Chipotle Mexican, Coldstone, Country Buffet, El Tapatio Mexican, Fazoli's, HuHot, IHOP, Jimmy John's, Kukoro Japanese, McDonald's/playplace, Red Robin, Ruby Tuesday, Smiling Moose Deli, Starbucks, Subway, Taco Bell, TX Roadhouse $Tree, Advance Parts, Big O Tire, city park, Costco/gas, Discount Tire, Home Depot, Lowe's, Petsmart, Sam's Club, Tires+, URGENT CARE
267	CO 391, Kipling St, Wheat Ridge, N Conoco, Shell/Carl's Jr/Circle K/dsl Burger King, Denny's, Einstein Bros, Jack-in-the-Box, Lil Nick's Pizza, Margarita's Mexican, Panda Express, Popeye's, Qdoba, Quiznos, Starbucks, Subway American Inn, Motel 6 7-11, AT&T, Cadillac/Chevrolet, GNC, NAPA, Natural Grocers, repair, Target, Verizon, vet, S Conoco/Mkt/dsl, Shell Taco Bell, Three Agaves Mexican, Village Inn, Winchell's Affordable Inn, Best Value Inn, Comfort Inn, Holiday Inn Express, Super 8 Ketelesen RV Ctr

WHEAT RIDGE

CO

INTERSTATE 70 Cont'd

LAKEWOOD

Exit #	Services
266	CO 72, W 44th Ave, Ward Rd, Wheat Ridge, **N** Conoco/dsl transmissions, **S** TA/Country Pride/dsl/scales/24hr/@, Valero/dsl Howard Johnson Trailer Source RV Ctr
265	CO 58 W (from wb), to Golden, Central City
264	Youngfield St, W 32nd Ave, **N** Phillips 66/mkt Denny's, GoodTimes Burgers La Quinta, **S** Abrusci's Italian, Chili's, Chipotle, DQ, McDonald's, Noodles&Co, Pizza Hut, Pizza Hut/Taco Bell, Qdoba, SmashBurger, Starbucks, Subway Four Seasons RV Ctr, King's Sooper/24hr, Petsmart, Tuesday Morning, Walgreens, Walmart/Subway
263	Denver West Blvd, **N** Marriott/rest., **S** Coldstone, Freddy's, Jamba Juice, Keg Steaks, Macaroni Grill, Mimi's Cafe, Noodles&Co, Olive Garden, Qdoba, Twin Peaks Barnes&Noble, Best Buy, Old Navy, same as 262, Whole Foods Mkt
262	US 40 E, W Colfax, Lakewood, **N** Sinclair/dsl El Señor Sol Mexican, Jack-in-the-Box, Lil' Ricci's Cafe, Subway Hampton Inn, Holiday Inn Express Buick/GMC, Camping World RV Ctr, Chrysler/Jeep, Dodge, Home Depot, Honda, Hyundai, Kohl's, PetCo, Staples, Subaru, transmissions, U-Haul, vet, **S** Shell/Circle K/dsl/LP Bonefish Grill, Cafe Rio, Carrabba's, Chick-fil-A, Chipotle Mexican, Five Guys, Garbanzo Grill, Jamba Juice, Jimmy John's, Mimi's Cafe, Mod Mkt Eatery, Native Foods Cafe, On-the-Border, Outback Steaks, Panera Bread, Pei Wei Asian, Pieology, Wendy's, Which Wich?, Yard House Courtyard, Days Inn/rest., Mtn View Inn, Residence Inn Chevrolet, Lexus, Marshall's, Old Navy, same as 263, Target, Toyota, Verizon, World Mkt
261	US 6 E (from eb), W 6th Ave, to Denver
260	CO 470, to Colo Springs
259	CO 26, Golden, **N** Shamrock/dsl Hampton Inn (2mi), Holiday Inn Express (2mi) Heritage Sq Funpark, **S** Music Hall, to Red Rocks SP
257mm	**runaway truck ramp eb**
256	Lookout Mtn, **N** to Buffalo Bill's Grave
254	Genesee, Lookout Mtn, **N** to Buffalo Bill's Grave, **S** Conoco/Genesee Store Chart House Rest., Guido's Pizza, Hideaway Cafe vet
253	Chief Hosa, **S** RV Camping,
252	(251 from eb), CO 74, Evergreen Pkwy, **S** Phillips 66 El Señor Sol, Illegal Burger, McDonald's, Qdoba, Starbucks Comfort Suites Big O Tire, Echo Mtn Ski Area, Home Depot, King Sooper (2mi), Walmart/Subway
248	(247 from eb), Beaver Brook, Floyd Hill, **S** antiques
244	US 6, to CO 119, to Golden, Central City , Eldora Ski Area
243	Hidden Valley, **N** Valero/dsl
242mm	tunnel
241b a	rd 314, Idaho Springs West, **N** Phillips 66/McDonald's/dsl, Shell/dsl, Sinclair, Western/dsl/e85 Carl's Jr, Cherry Blossom Chinese, Marion's Rest., Picci's Pizzaria, Smokin' Yards BBQ, Starbucks, Subway, Wildfire Rest. 6&40 Motel, Argo Inn, Columbine Inn, H&H Motel, Idaho Springs Hotel, JC Motel CarQuest, Safeway Foods/Drug, USPO
240	CO 103, Mt Evans, **N** Kum&Go/dsl, Shell/dsl, Sinclair/dsl 2 Bros Deli, Azteca Mexican, Beaujo's Pizza, Buffalo Rest., Jiggie's Cafe, Main St Rest., Tommy Knocker Grill, West Winds Cafe same as 241, vet, **S** to Mt Evans
239	Idaho Springs, **S** camping
238	Fall River Rd, to St Mary's Glacier
235	Dumont (from wb)
234	Downeyville, Dumont, **N** Sinclair/Subway/dsl Starbucks, Taco Bell ski rentals, **S** **weigh sta both lanes**

IDAHO SPRINGS

SILVERTHORNE

Exit #	Services
233	Lawson (from eb)
232	US 40 W, to Empire, **N** Rocky Mtn NP, to Berthoud Pass, Winterpark/Sol Vista ski areas
228	Georgetown, **S** Exxon/Subway/dsl, Shell/dsl, Valero/dsl Blue Sky Cafe, Mountain Buzz Cafe Best Value Inn, Chateau Chamonix Family$, visitors ctr
226.5mm	scenic overlook eb
226	Georgetown, Silver Plume Hist Dist, **N** repair
221	Bakerville
220mm	Arapahoe NF eastern boundary
219	**parking area (eb only)**
218	no services
216	US 6 W, Loveland Valley, Loveland Basin, ski areas
214mm	Eisenhower/Johnson Tunnel, elev 11013
213mm	**parking area eb**
205	US 6 E, CO 9 N, Dillon, Silverthorne, **N** 7-11, Kum&Go/dsl, Shell/7-11/dsl, Sinclair/dsl, Tesla EVC Cafe Toro, Chipotle Mexican, Dominos, Mint Cafe, Mtn Lyon Café, Murphy's Cafe, Old Chicago, Quiznos, Wendy's, Which Wich? 1st Interstate Inn, Days Inn, La Quinta, Luxury Suites, Quality Inn, Silver Inn AutoZone, Buick/Cadillac/Chevrolet/GMC, CarQuest, Chrysler/Dodge/Jeep, Ford, Lowe's, Murdoch's, Outlets/famous brands, Subaru, Target, TrueValue, **S** Conoco, Shell/dsl Arby's, Bamboo Garden, Blue Moon Deli, Burger King, Chimayo Burrito, Dam Brewery/Rest., DQ, Fiesta Mexican, Jimmy John's, McDonald's, Nick'n Willy's Pizza, Noodles&Co, Nozawa Japanese, Pizza Hut, Qdoba, Red Mtn Grill, Ruby Tuesday, SmashBurger, Smiling Moose Cafe, Starbucks, Subway, Sunshine Cafe Comfort Suites, Dillon Inn, Hampton Inn, Super 8 AT&T, City Mkt Foods/gas, GNC, Natural Grocers, Outlets/famous brands, Petco, Tuesday Morning, Verizon, vet, Walgreens
203.5mm	scenic overlook both lanes
203	CO 9 S, to Breckenridge, Frisco, **S** 7-11, Conoco/Wendy's/dsl, Shell/dsl, Valero/dsl Hacienda Real Mexican, KFC, Q4U BBQ, Rio Grande Mexican, Spinelli's Pizza/Subs, Sporting News Grill, Starbucks, Subway, Szechuan Chinese, Taco Bell Alpine Inn, Baymont Inn, Holiday Inn, Ramada Ltd, Summit Inn Big O Tire, Meadow Creek Tire/auto, NAPA, RV Resort (6mi), Safeway Foods, to Breckenridge Ski Area, Verizon, Walmart, Whole Foods Mkt
201	Main St, Frisco, **S** Loaf N' Jug Backcountry Brew Pub, Bagali's Italian, Blue Spruce Inn, Boatyard Pizzaria, Butterhorn Cafe, Frisco Emporium, Greco's Pastaria, Log Cabin Cafe, Lost Cajun Rest., Moosejaw Cafe, Rainbow Ct Rest. Frisco Lodge, Hotel Frisco, Snowshoe Motel museum/visitor info RV camping, to Breckenridge Ski Area, USPO
198	Officers Gulch, emergency callbox
196mm	scenic area (wb only)
195	CO 91 S, to Leadville, **1 mi S** Conoco/dsl Healthy Tomato Deli Copper Lodging to Copper Mtn Ski Resort
190	**S** **both lanes, full facilities, litter barrels,**
189mm	**parking area both lanes**, Vail Pass Summit, elev 10662 ft
180	Vail East Entrance, **services 3-4 mi S**
176	Vail, **S** ski info/lodging
173	Vail Ski Area, **N** Phillips 66, Shell/dsl Casa Mexico, May Palace, McDonald's, Old Forge Pizza, Qdoba, Subway, Westside Cafe Holiday Inn Ace Hardware, City Mkt Foods/deli Safeway Food/Drug, USPO, **S** Conoco/dsl/LP Marriott Streamside Hotel
171	US 6 W, US 24 E, to Minturn, Leadville, **N** Ski Cooper ski area, **2 mi S** Shell Magusto's Italian, Minturn Steak Minturn Inn RV Camping, USPO

FRISCO

VAIL

INTERSTATE 70 Cont'd (E)

Exit #	Services
169	Eaglevale, (from wb), no return
168	William J. Post Blvd, **S** [food] Castle Peak Grill [other] Home Depot, Verizon, Walmart/McDonald's
167	Avon, **N** [gas] Exxon/7-11/dsl, Shell [food] Northside Kitchen [other] vet, **S** [food] Boxcar Rest., Burger King, Domino's, Fiesta Jalisco Mexican, Gondola Pizza, Montana's Smokehouse, Pazzo's Pizza, Starbucks, Subway [lodging] Avon Ctr Lodge, Christie Lodge, Comfort Inn, Sheraton, Westin [other] City Mkt/drugs, GNC, ski info, to Beaver Creek/Arrowhead Ski, URGENT CARE, USPO, Walgreens
163	Edwards, **S** [rest stop] **both lanes, full** [handicap] **facilities, litter barrel,** [picnic], **RV dump** [gas] Conoco/dsl, Shell/Wendy's/dsl [food] Cafe Milano, Dive Cafe, East Asian, Fiestas Cafe, Gashouse Rest., Gore Range Brewery, Henry's Chinese, Main St Grill, Marble Slab Creamery, Marko's Pizza, Old Forge Pizza, Smiling Moose, Starbucks, Subway, Zino's Italian [lodging] Riverwalk Inn [other] AT&T, to Arrowhead Ski Area, USPO, Village Mkt
162mm	scenic area eb
159mm	Eagle River
157	CO 131 N, Wolcott, **N** to Steamboat Ski Area
147	Eagle, **N** [gas] Kum&Go/dsl [food] Burger King, Roberto's Italian, Starbucks [lodging] AmericInn, Comfort Inn, Holiday Inn Express [other] AT&T, City Mkt Foods, **S** [rest stop] **both lanes, full** [handicap] **facilities, info** [gas] Conoco/dsl, Shell/dsl, Sinclair/Subway/dsl [food] Eagle Diner, Gourmet China, Grand Ave Grill, Moe's Original BBQ, Pazzo's Pizzaria, Primavera Mexican, Taco Bell, Wendy's [lodging] Best Western, Eagle Lodge&Suites, Hawthorn Suites [other] AutoZone (3mi), Costco/dsl (3mi), USPO, vet
140	Gypsum, **S** [gas] Conoco, Kum&Go/dsl, Shell/dsl [food] Asian Fusion, Buffalo Grill, Gypsum Grill, Ridley's Mkt, Tu Casa Mexican [other] [airport], Family$, O'Reilly Parts, River Dance Resort camping, USPO
134mm	Colorado River
133	Dotsero, **N** [other] River Dance RV Camping (3mi)
129	Bair Ranch, **S** [rest stop] **both lanes, full** [handicap] **facilities, litter barrels, petwalk,** [picnic]
128.5mm	**parking area eb**
127mm	tunnel wb
125mm	tunnel
125	to Hanging Lake (no return eb)
123	Shoshone (no return eb)
122.5mm	exit to river (no return eb)
121	to Hanging Lake, Grizzly Creek, **S** [rest stop] **both lanes, full** [handicap] **facilities, litter barrels,** [picnic]
119	No Name, [rest stop] **both lanes, full** [handicap] **facilities), rafting, RV camping**
118mm	tunnel
116	CO 82 E, to Aspen, Glenwood Springs, **N** [gas] Kum&Go/dsl, Shell/dsl [food] Chomp's Rest., Fiesta Guadalajara, KFC, Qdoba, Subway, Tequilas Rest., Village Inn [lodging] Best Western, Glenwood Springs Inn, Hampton Inn, Holiday Inn Express, Hotel Colorado, Hotel Glenwood Springs, La Quinta, Silver Spruce Motel, Starlight Motel [other] Hot Springs Bath, Land Rover, **0-2 mi S** [gas] Conoco, Phillips 66/dsl, Shamrock/dsl, Shell, Sinclair [food] 19th St Diner, Chang Thai Cuisine, China Town, Domino's, Jimmy John's, McDonald's, Pizza Hut, Starbucks, Subway, Taco Bell, Taipei Japanese, Wendy's [lodging] Caravan Inn, Cedar Lodge, Frontier Lodge, Hotel Denver [other] [hospital], 7-11, Alpine Tire, AutoZone, B.Thornal DDS, Chrysler/Dodge/Jeep, City Mkt Foods, city park, Midas, NAPA, Office Depot, Rite Aid, Safeway Foods, to Ski Sunlight, USPO, Walmart

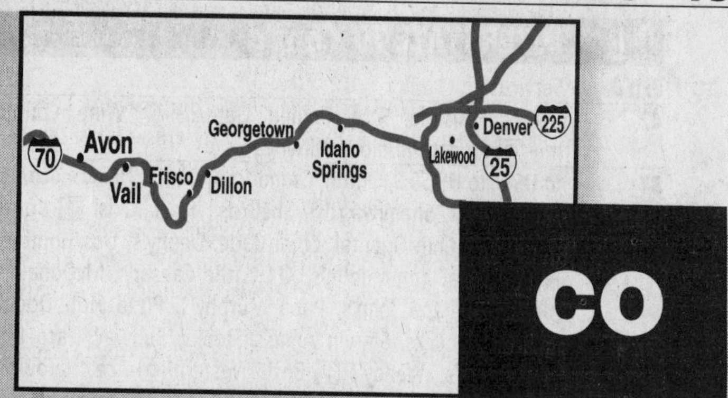

Exit #	Services
114	W Glenwood Springs, **N** [gas] 7-11, Exxon/Arby's/dsl, Shell/dsl [food] Culver's, Jilberito's Mexican, Rte 6 Grill House, Vicco's Charcoal Burger [lodging] Affordable Inn, Hanging Lake Inn, Ponderosa Motel, Red Mtn Inn, Rodeway Inn [other] Big O Tire, Carquest, Chevrolet, Discount Tire, Ford, Honda, O'Reilly Parts, Ross, Subaru, Toyota, Verizon, **S** [gas] Kum&Go/DQ/dsl [food] Chili's, Moe's SW Grill, Russo's Pizza, Starbucks, Zheng Asian [lodging] Courtyard, Glenwood Suites, Quality Inn, Residence Inn [other] AT&T, Audi/VW, Harley-Davidson, Lowe's, Natural Grocers, PetCo, Target, URGENT CARE, Verizon
111	South Canyon
109	Canyon Creek
108mm	**parking area both lanes**
105	New Castle, **N** [gas] Conoco/dsl, Kum&Go/dsl [food] Hong's Garden, McDonald's, New Castle Diner, Subway [lodging] Econolodge [other] City Mkt Foods/deli, Elk Creek Campground (4mi), **S** [other] Best Hardware
97	Silt, **N** [gas] Kum&Go/dsl, Sinclair/dsl, Tim's/dsl [food] Brickhouse Italian [lodging] Red River Inn [other] $General, to Harvey Gap SP, **S** [lodging] Holiday Inn Express [other] Heron's Nest RV Park, KOA
94	Garfield County Airport Rd
90	CO 13 N, Rifle, **N** [rest stop] **both lanes, full** [handicap] **facilities, litter barrels, NF Info,** [picnic], **RV dump** [gas] Conoco/dsl, Kum&Go/dsl, Phillips 66/dsl, Shell [food] Dickey's BBQ [lodging] Gateway Lodge [other] Rifle Gap SP (10mi), .USPO, **S** [gas] Kum&Go/dsl, Phillips 66/Subway/dsl [food] Burger King, Domino's, Little Caesar's, McDonald's/playplace, Rib City Grill, Sonic, Starbucks, Subway, Taco Bell [lodging] Comfort Inn, Hampton Inn, La Quinta, Rodeway Inn [other] [hospital], AutoZone, O'Reilly Parts, Verizon, Walmart/Subway
87	to CO 13, West Rifle
81	Rulison
75	Parachute, **N** [rest stop] **both lanes, full** [handicap] **facilities, info, litter barrels, petwalk,** [phone], [picnic], [gas] CNG, Shell/Wienerschnizel/dsl, Sinclair/dsl [food] El Tapatio Mexican, Hong's Garden Chinese, Outlaws Rest., Subway [lodging] Comfort Inn, Parachute Inn [other] NAPA, USPO, vet, **S** [gas] Phillips 66/Domino's/dsl, Shell/Wendy's/dsl [lodging] Candlewood Suites, Days Inn [other] Family$, RV Park (4mi)
72	US 6, W Parachute
63mm	Colorado River
62	De Beque, **N** [gas] Kum&Go/Subway/dsl
50mm	Colorado River, **parking area eb**, tunnel begins eastbound
49mm	Plateau Creek
49	CO 65 S, to CO 330 E, to Grand Mesa, Powderhorn Ski Area
47	Island Acres St RA, **N** [other] CO River SP, RV camping, **S** [gas] Exxon/rest./dsl
46	Cameo
44	Lp 70 W, to Palisade, **3 mi S** [other] food, gas, lodging
43.5mm	Colorado River

INTERSTATE 70 Cont'd

GRAND JCT · **FRUITA**

Exit #	Services
42	US 6, Palisade, **S** Golden Gate/dsl Wine Country Inn Fruitstand/store, wineries
37	to US 6, to US 50 S, Clifton, Grand Jct, **0-1 mi S** Conoco/dsl, Maverik/dsl, Shamrock/dsl, Shell/dsl, Sinclair/dsl Burger King, Chin Chin Oriental, China Jade, Denny's, Dos Hombres, Enzo's Pizza, Jimmy John's, KFC, Little Caesar's, McDonald's/playplace, Papa John's, Papa Murphy's, Pizza Hut, Qdoba, Sonic, Starbucks, Starvin Arvin's Steaks, Subway, Taco Bell, Taco John's, Wendy's Best Western Ace Hardware, AutoZone, City Mkt Food/dsl, Family$, GNC, Murdoch's Store, O'Reilly Parts, repair, RV Ranch, URGENT CARE, USPO, vet, Walgreens, Walmart/gas (2mi)
31	Horizon Dr, Grand Jct, **N** Shell/dsl Pantuso Mexican, Peppers Rest., Tepanyaki Rest., Village Inn, Wendy's Best Value Inn, Clarion, Comfort Inn, Courtyard, Econolodge, Grand Vista Hotel, Holiday Inn, La Quinta, Motel 6, Ramada Inn, Residence Inn Harley-Davidson, Zarlingo's Repair, **S** Exxon/Subway/dsl, Shell/dsl Applebee's, Aztecas, Burger King/playland, Denny's, Enzo's Pizza, Freddy's, Good Pastures Rest., Nick'n Willy's Pizza, Sang Garden, Starbucks, Taco Bell Days Inn, Doubletree Hotel, Mesa Inn, Quality Inn, Rodeway Inn, Super 8, Super 8, Travelodge H, CO NM, golf, Safeway Food/drug/gas, Shop'n Save, to Mesa St Coll, visitors ctr
28	Redlands Pkwy, 24 Rd, **N** Kenworth, **0-2 mi S** Candlewood Suites, Woodspring Suites city park, same as 26, Subaru, VW
26	US 6, US 50, Grand Jct, **N** Loves/Carl's Jr/dsl/scales/Lp/24hr, Pilot/PJ Fresh/dsl/scales/24hr Hyundai, Jct W RV Park, **0-4 mi S** TA/Conoco/A&W/dsl Boston's Grill, Buffalo Wild Wings, Burger King, Cafe Rio, Chick-fil-A, Chili's, Chipotle Mexican, ChuckeCheese, Citrolas Italian, Coldstone, Costa Vida, Del Taco, Famous Dave's BBQ, Genghis Grill, Golden Corral, Grand Buffet, Honeybaked Ham, IHOP, Jimmy John's, McDonald's/playplace, Mi Mexico, Noodles&Co, Olive Garden, Outback Steaks, Papa Murphys, Qdoba, Red Lobster, Red Robin, Schlotzky's, Sonic, Starbucks, Subway, Taco Bell, Tequila's, Wendy's, Which Wich? Holiday Inn Express, Red Roof Inn $Tree, AT&T, AutoZone, Barnes&Noble, Best Buy, Big O Tire, Buick/Chevrolet, Cabela's, Chrysler/Dodge/Jeep, City Mkt/dsl, Ford, Freightliner, Hobby Lobby, Home Depot, JC Penney, Kohl's, Lowe's, Michael's, Mobile City RV Park, Natural Grocers, Nissan, Office Depot, Old Navy, PetCo, Petsmart, Ross, Sam's Club/dsl, Scott RV Ctr, Sprouts Mkt, Target, TJ Maxx, Toyota, Verizon, Walmart/McDonald's
19	US 6, CO 340, Fruita, **N** Conoco/dsl Burger King, Munchie's Burgers/Pizza Balanced Rock Motel H, City Mkt Foods/deli/24hr, city park, NAPA, USPO, Walgreens, **S Welcome Ctr, full facilities, litter barrels, petwalk, RV dump** Exxon/Quiznos/dsl/24hr, LNG, Shell/Wendy's/dsl/24hr DQ, Dragon Treasure Chinese, El Tapatio Mexican, FeedLot Rest., Jimmy John's, McDonald's/playplace, Pablo's Pizza, Rib City Grill, Starbucks, Subway, Taco Bell Comfort Inn, La Quinta, Super 8 dinosaur museum, Monument RV Park, Peterbilt/Volvo, to CO NM, vet
17mm	Colorado River
15	CO 139 N, to Loma, Rangely, **N** /dsl, to Highline Lake SP
14.5mm	**weigh/check sta both lanes**
11	Mack, **2-3 mi N** , /dsl
2	Rabbit Valley, **N** to Trail Through Time
0mm	Colorado/Utah state line

INTERSTATE 76

STERLING · **FT MORGAN**

Exit #	Services
185mm	**I-76 begins/ends on NE I-80, exit 102.**
184mm	Colorado/Nebraska state line
180	US 385, Julesburg, **N Welcome Ctr/ both lanes, full facilities, info, RV dump, RV dump** Shell Subway Budget Host H, **S** Conoco/dsl
172	Ovid
165	CO 59, to Haxtun, Sedgewick, **N** Lucy's Cafe
155	Red Lion Rd
149	CO 55, to Fleming, Crook, **S** Sinclair/dsl/café
141	Proctor
134	Iliff
125	US 6, Sterling, **0-3 mi N** **both lanes full facilities, litter barrels, petwalk, vending, RV dump** Cenex/dsl, HR/dsl Arby's, Bamboo Garden, Burger King, Domino's, DQ, KFC/LJ Silver, Little Caesar's, McDonald's, Mi Ranchito, Old Town Bistro, Papa Murphy's, Pizza Hut, Sonic, Subway, Taco Bell, Taco John's, Village Inn, Wendy's 1st Interstate Inn, Best Western H, $Tree, AutoZone, Buick/Chevrolet, Chrysler/Dodge/Jeep, Family Food Mkt, Ford/Lincoln, Home Depot museum, N Sterling SP, NAPA, O'Reilly Parts, st patrol, USPO Verizon, vet, Walgreens, Walmart, **S** Reata/dsl Country Kitchen Comfort Inn, Ramada Inn, Super 8, Travele Inn RV Camping
115	CO 63, Atwood, **N** Sinclair/dsl H, **S** Steakhouse
102	Merino
95	Hillrose
92	to US 6 E, to US 34, CO 71 S
90b a	CO 71 N, to US 34, Brush, **N** Brush Trkstp/Shell/Subway dsl/24hr China Buffet, Pizza Hut, Wendy's Econolodge **S** Conoco/dsl McDonald's Microtel
89	Hospital Rd, **S** Loves/Carl's Jr/dsl/scales/24hr H golf
86	Dodd Bridge Rd
82	Barlow Rd, **N** Maverick's Grill Comfort Inn, Rodewa Inn Silver Spur Camping, **S** Reata/dsl/scales, USA dsl Burger King $Tree, Walmart/Subway
80	CO 52, Ft Morgan, **N** City Park, Golf, RV Camping, **S** Conoco/dsl, Maverik/dsl, Sinclair/dsl, Western/dsl Arby's, DC El Jacal Mexican, McDonald's, Sonic, Subway, Taco Bell, Tac John's, Wonderful House Chinese Central Motel, Hampto Inn, Sands Inn, Super 8 H, AutoZone, Family$, Toyota, Verizon, Walgreens
79	CO 144, to Weldona, (no wb return)
75	US 34 E, to Ft Morgan, **S** Shell/pizza/dsl Embe Rest. Clarion st patrol
74.5mm	**weigh sta both lanes**
73	Long Bridge Rd
66b	US 34 W (from wb), to Greeley
66a	CO 39, CO 52, to Goodrich, **N** Phillips 66/dsl RV Camping, to Jackson Lake SP, **S** **both lanes, full facilities, litter barrels, petwalk, vending** Sinclair/cafe/dsl/e-85
64	Wiggins
60	to CO 144 E, to Orchard
57	rd 91
49	Painter Rd (from wb)
48	to Roggen, **N** Conoco/dsl, **S** USPO
39	Keenesburg, **S** Shell/dsl Dos Hijos Mexican Kee Motel Family$, Tim's Car Clinic
34	Kersey Rd

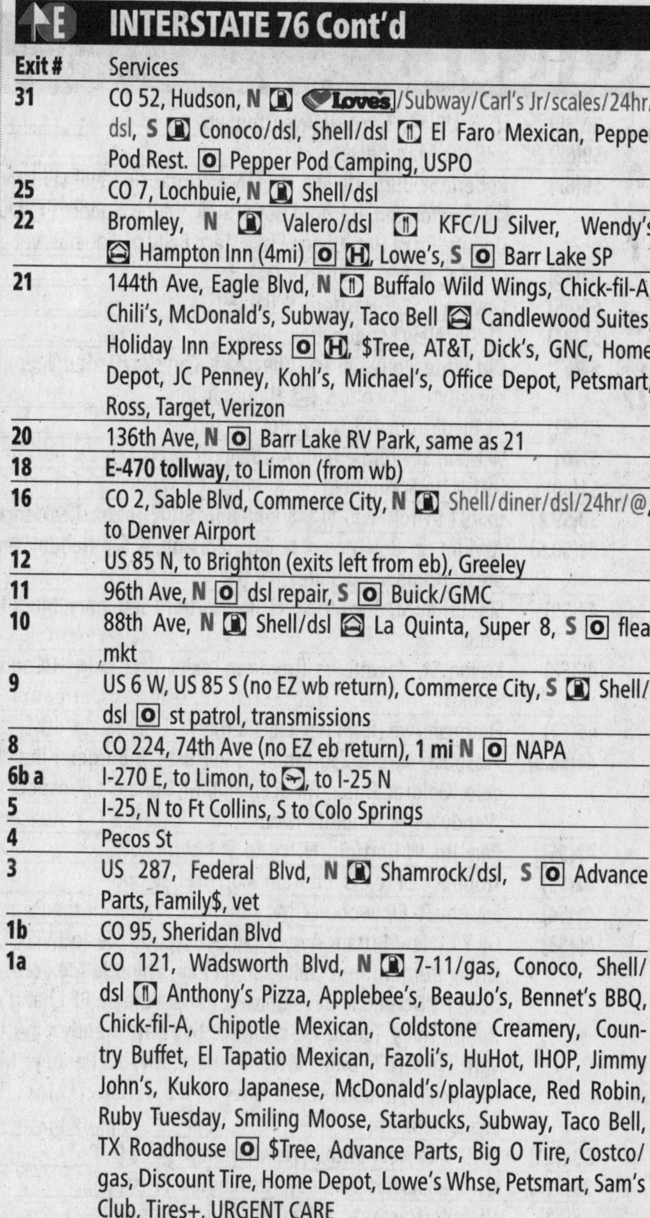

INTERSTATE 76 Cont'd

Exit #	Services
31	CO 52, Hudson, N Loves/Subway/Carl's Jr/scales/24hr/dsl, S Conoco/dsl, Shell/dsl El Faro Mexican, Pepper Pod Rest. Pepper Pod Camping, USPO
25	CO 7, Lochbuie, N Shell/dsl
22	Bromley, N Valero/dsl KFC/LJ Silver, Wendy's Hampton Inn (4mi) H, Lowe's, S Barr Lake SP
21	144th Ave, Eagle Blvd, N Buffalo Wild Wings, Chick-fil-A, Chili's, McDonald's, Subway, Taco Bell Candlewood Suites, Holiday Inn Express H, $Tree, AT&T, Dick's, GNC, Home Depot, JC Penney, Kohl's, Michael's, Office Depot, Petsmart, Ross, Target, Verizon
20	136th Ave, N Barr Lake RV Park, same as 21
18	**E-470 tollway**, to Limon (from wb)
16	CO 2, Sable Blvd, Commerce City, N Shell/diner/dsl/24hr/@, to Denver Airport
12	US 85 N, to Brighton (exits left from eb), Greeley
11	96th Ave, N dsl repair, S Buick/GMC
10	88th Ave, N Shell/dsl La Quinta, Super 8, S flea mkt
9	US 6 W, US 85 S (no EZ wb return), Commerce City, S Shell/dsl st patrol, transmissions
8	CO 224, 74th Ave (no EZ eb return), **1 mi N** NAPA
6b a	I-270 E, to Limon, to ✈, to I-25 N
5	I-25, N to Ft Collins, S to Colo Springs
4	Pecos St
3	US 287, Federal Blvd, N Shamrock/dsl, S Advance Parts, Family$, vet
1b	CO 95, Sheridan Blvd
1a	CO 121, Wadsworth Blvd, N 7-11/gas, Conoco, Shell/dsl Anthony's Pizza, Applebee's, BeauJo's, Bennet's BBQ, Chick-fil-A, Chipotle Mexican, Coldstone Creamery, Country Buffet, El Tapatio Mexican, Fazoli's, HuHot, IHOP, Jimmy John's, Kukoro Japanese, McDonald's/playplace, Red Robin, Ruby Tuesday, Smiling Moose, Starbucks, Subway, Taco Bell, TX Roadhouse $Tree, Advance Parts, Big O Tire, Costco/gas, Discount Tire, Home Depot, Lowe's Whse, Petsmart, Sam's Club, Tires+, URGENT CARE

I-76 begins/ends on I-70, exit 269b.

DENVER

INTERSTATE 225 (Denver)

Exit #	Services
12b a	I-70, W to Denver, E to Limon
10	US 40, US 287, Colfax Ave, E Conoco/dsl, Shell/dsl, Sinclair Burger King, Del Taco, Domino's, DQ, El Pelicano Seafood, KFC, McDonald's, Pizza Hut/Taco Bell, Popeye's, Starbucks, Subway, Village Inn, Wendy's 7-11, Aamco, Advance Parts, Chevrolet, Family$, King's Sooper/gas, NAPA, Walgreens, W Conoco/dsl, Shamrock/dsl Caribou Coffee, Chipotle Mexican, Noodles&Co, Panera Bread, Smashburger, Which Wich? SpringHill Suites H, U-Haul
9	Co 30, 6th Ave, E Conoco/dsl Denny's Travelodge, Woodspring Suites, W Shell/dsl H
8	Alameda Ave, E Valero/dsl Atlanta Bread, BJ's Rest., Chick-fil-A, Chili's, Coldstone, FatBurger, Jamba Juice, Jimmy John's, L&L BBQ, Macaroni Grill, Mimi's Cafe, Panda Express, Sabor Mexican, Starbucks, TGIFriday, Wingstop AT&T, Barnes&Noble, Dillards, Hobby Lobby, JC Penney, Macy's, Michael's, Petsmart, Ross, Super Target, W Conoco/dsl, Shell/Circle K $Tree
7	Mississippi Ave, Alameda Ave, E Arby's, Burger King, Chubby's Mexican, ChuckeCheese, CiCi's, Fazoli's, Guadalajara Mexican, McAlister's Deli, Schlotsky's, Sonic, Starbucks, Subway, Tokyo Joe's, Village Inn Best Western, Holiday Inn Express, La Quinta Best Buy, Burlington Coats, Home Depot, JoAnn Fabrics, Sam's Club/gas, Tires +, Verizon, Walmart, W IHOP, McDonald's, Mirage Rest., Senor Ric's, Waffle House 7-11, AutoZone, Pepboys
5	Iliff Ave, E 7-11 Ajuua Mexican, Applebee's, Boston Mkt, Carrabba's, Hibachi Japanese, Joe's Crabshack, Outback Steaks, Real de Minas Mexican, Rosie's Diner, Ruby Tuesday, Sweet Tomatoes, TX Roadhouse Comfort Inn, Crestwood Suites, Extended Stay America, Extended Stay America (2), Fairfield Inn, Motel 6, W Conoco Dragon Boat, Legends Grill, Subway DoubleTree 7-11
4	CO 83, Parker Rd, E Radisson Cherry Creek SP, W Shell/dsl Big Burrito, DQ, Little Caesar's, Popeye's, Starbucks, Subway, Taco Bell, Wendy's $Tree, 7-11, Firestone/auto, King Sooper/dsl
2b	Yosemite St
2	DTC Blvd, Tamarac St, W Conoco/7-11 Fel Fel Mediterranean, La Fogata Mexican, Sonic, South Garden Chinese, Subway $Tree, Goodyear/auto
1b a	**I-25. I-225 begins/ends on I-25, exit 200.**

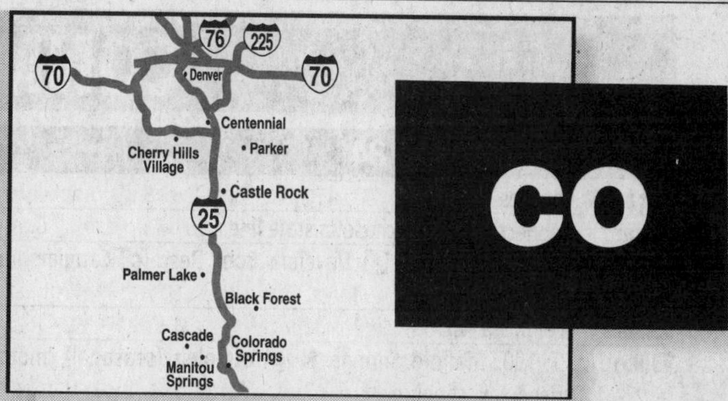

DENVER

CO

INTERSTATE 270 (Denver)

Exit #	Services
4	I-70
3	N TA/Burger King/Country Pride/Popeye's/Pizza Hut/dsl/24hr/@, S Sapp Bros/Sinclair/Subway/dsl/@
2b a	US 85, CO 2, Vasquez Ave, N Arby's, Carls Jr, Chipotle Mexican, Jack-in-the-Box, KFC/LJ Silver, McDonald's, Taco Bell, Wendy's TDS Tire, Walgreens, Walmart
1b	York St
1a	I-76 E, to Ft Morgan
1c	I-25 S, to Denver

NOTES

CONNECTICUT

CT

INTERSTATE 84

Exit #	Services
98mm	Connecticut/Massachusetts state line
74(97)	CT 171, Holland, S Traveler's Book Rest. Campers Inn RV Ctr, RV camping
95mm	weigh sta wb
73(95)	CT 190, Stafford Springs, N camping (seasonal), motor speedway, st police
72(93)	CT 89, Westford, N Ashford Motel, camping (seasonal)
71(88)	CT 320, Ruby Rd, S TA/Shell/Burger King/Country Pride/dsl/scales/24hr/@ Dunkin Donuts Rodeway Inn
70(86)	CT 32, Willington, N S Mobil/dsl, Sunoco/dsl RV Camping
85mm	both lanes, campers, full facilities, info, litter barrels, petwalk, vending
69(83)	CT 74, to US 44, Willington, S RV camping, st police
68(81)	CT 195, Tolland, N Gulf/dsl, Mobil Dunkin Donuts, Papa T's Rest., Subway NAPA, S Citgo Camille's Pizza AT&T, Big Y Foods, vet
67(77)	CT 31, Rockville, N Mobil, Shell/dsl Beni's Grill, Burger King, China Taste, Dunkin Donuts, McDonald's, Subway S Nathan Hale Mon
66(76)	Tunnel Rd, Vernon
65(75)	CT 30, Vernon Ctr, N Cumberland/dsl, Mobil/dsl, Shell Brick Oven Pizza, Buffet Palace, Burger King, Donuts Donuts, KFC, Oki Asian, Rein's Deli, Simply Thai, Vernon Diner Days Inn, Red Roof Inn Firestone/auto, K-Mart, Meineke, Stop&Shop/gas
64(74)	Vernon Ctr, N Sunoco 99 Rest., Angellino's Italian, Anthony's Pizza, D'angelo's, Denny's, Dunkin Donuts, Friendly's, McDonald's, Moe's SW, Rita's Custard, Starbucks, Taco Bell, Wood'n Tap Holiday Inn Express $Tree, AutoZone, CVS Drug, Goodyear/auto, PriceChopper, Staples, TJ Maxx, vet, S Motel 6 VW
63(72)	CT 30, CT 83, Manchester, S Windsor, N Azteca Mexican, Chipotle Mexican, Dunkin Donuts, HomeTown Buffet, IHOP, Longhorn Steaks, McDonald's, Outback Steaks, Panera Bread, Red Robin, Smashburger, Starbucks, Subway, TGIFriday's Courtyard, Residence Inn AT&T, Best Buy, Marshall's, PetCo, same as 62, Verizon, Walgreens, Walmart, S BP/dsl, Shell/dsl, Sunoco/dsl, Xtra Misaki Buffet, Tomato Joe's Baymont Inn, Best Value Inn, Extended Stay America, Motel 6 Big Y Mkt, Hyundai, Kohl's, Nissan, Subaru, Toyota, U-Haul
62(71)	Buckland St, N Mobil/Dunkin Donuts/dsl Artisanal Burger, Bertucci's, Bonefish Grill, Boston Mkt, Burton's Grill, Chili's, Dave&Buster's, Five Guys, Friendly's, Hooters, Maggie McFly's, Market Grill, Moe's SW Grill, Olive Garden, Panchero's, Panera Bread, Starbucks, Taco Bell, Ted's MT Grill Fairfield Inn, Hampton Inn $Tree, Barnes&Noble, BigLots, Dick's, Hobby Lobby, Home Depot, JC Penney, Jo-Ann Fabrics, LL Bean, Lowe's, Macy's, Michael's, Old Navy, PetsMart, same as 63, Target, Town Fair Tire, Verizon, S Shell/dsl Buffalo Wild Wings, Burger Fi, Carrabba's, ChuckeCheese, Dunkin Donuts, Golden Dragon, McDonald's, Sonic, Subway, TX Roadhouse, Wendy's BJ's Whse/gas, Firestone/auto, GNC, Honda, USPO
61(70)	I-291 W, to Windsor
60(69)	US 6, US 44, Burnside Ave (from eb)
59(68)	I-384 E, Manchester
58(67)	Roberts St, Burnside Ave, N Margaritas Grill, Nolita Ristorante Comfort Inn, Hartford Hotel, S Mobil, Sunoco Dunkin Donuts, Pizza Hut, Queen Pizza, Taco Bell Cabelas, vet
57(66)	CT 15 S, to I-91 S, Charter Oak Br
56(65)	Governor St, E Hartford, S
55(64)	CT 2 E, New London, downtown
54(63)	Old State House, N Chevrolet, Chrysler/Dodge/Jeep, Ford, Kia, Lexus, Lincoln, S Hampton Inn
53(62)	CT Blvd (from eb), S Holiday Inn
52(61)	W Main St (from eb), downtown
51(60)	I-91 N, to Springfield
50(59.8)	to I-91 S (from wb), N Radisson, S Hilton, Residence Inn
48(59.5)	Asylum St, downtown, N Radisson, S Holiday Inn Express, Homewood Suites
47(59)	Sigourney St, downtown, N Hartford Seminary, Mark Twain House
46(58)	Sisson St, downtown (from wb, exits left), N UConn Law School
45(57)	Flatbush Ave (from wb, exits left)
44(56.5)	Prospect Ave, N Mobil, Shell/dsl Burger King, D'angelo, Goldroc Diner, Hibachi Grill, McDonald's, Prospect Pizza, Wendy's ShopRite Foods
43(56)	Park Rd, W Hartford, N to St Joseph Coll
42(55)	Trout Brk Dr (exits left from wb), to Elmwood
41(54)	S Main St, Elmwood, N American School for the Deaf
40(53)	CT 71, New Britain Ave, S Sunoco/dsl, Tesla EVC Brio Grille, Burger King, Chili's, China Pan, Chipotle Mexican, D'angelo, McDonald's, Olive Garden, Panera Bread, PF Chang's, Red Robin, Ruby Tuesday, Starbucks, Subway, Wendy's Courtyard AT&T, Barnes&Noble, Best Buy, JC Penney, Macy's, Michael's, Nordstrom, Old Navy, PetCo, Target, TJ Maxx, Trader Joe's, Verizon
39a(52)	CT 9 S, to New Britain, Newington, S
39(51.5)	CT 4, (exits left from eb), Farmington, N
38(51)	US 6 W (from wb), Bristol, N same as 37
37(50)	Fienemann Rd, to US 6 W, N Shell Dunkin Donuts, Subway Hampton Inn, Marriott, S Noble/Dunkin Donuts/dsl Extended Stay America
36(49)	Slater Rd (exits left from eb), S
35(48)	CT 72, to CT 9 (exits left from both lanes), New Britain, S
34(47)	CT 372, Crooked St, N Gulf/dsl, Sunoco Applebee's, Friendly's, McDonald's, Starbucks, Taco Bell, Wendy's Fairfield Inn $Tree, AT&T, Big Y Mkt, Dick's, Ford/Lincoln, Kohl's, Lowe's, Marshall's, Old Navy, Petsmart, VW
33(46)	CT 72 W, to Bristol (exits left from eb)
32(45)	Ct 10, Queen St, Southington, N Cumberland Farms, Exxon, Shell/dsl Bertucci's, Buffalo Wild Wings, Burger King, Chili's, D'angelo, Denny's, Dunkin Donuts, Gobi Mongolian, IHOP, JD's Rest., KFC, Liberty Pizza, Luenhop, McDonald's, Moe's SW Grill, Noodles&Co, Outback Steaks, Puerto Vallarta, Smashburger, Starbucks, Subway, Taco Bell Motel 6 $Tree, 7-11, AutoZone, BJ's/gas, CVS Drug, GNC, Home Depot, Jo-Ann, O'Reilly Parts, PetCo, ShopRite Foods, Staples, TJ Maxx, TownFair Tire, Verizon, S Mobil, Speedway, Sunoco Aziagos Italian, Dunkin Donuts, El Sombrero, Friendly's, Nardelli's Cafe, Panera Bread, Pizza Hut, Rita's Custard, Subway, TD Homer's Grill, Wendy's, Wood'n Tap Grill Days Inn, Holiday Inn Express

VERNON CTR · WINDSOR · HARTFORD · SOUTHINGTON

INTERSTATE 84 Cont'd

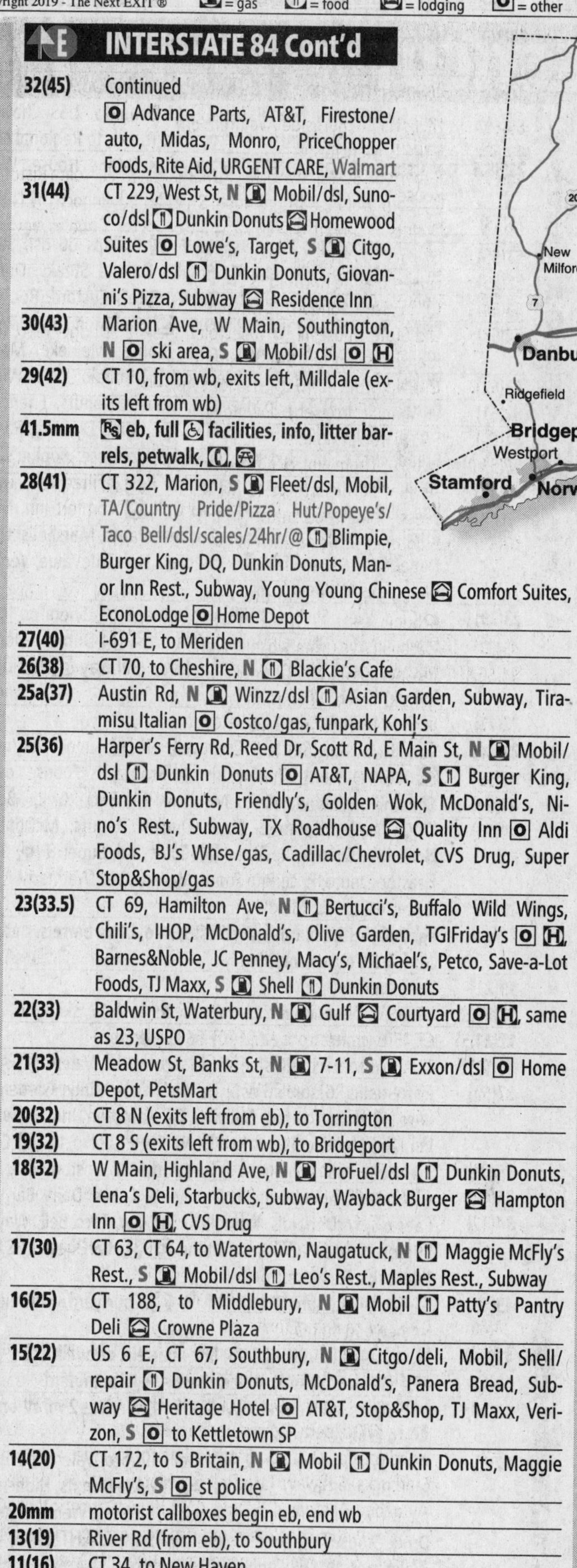

32(45) Continued [other] Advance Parts, AT&T, Firestone/auto, Midas, Monro, PriceChopper Foods, Rite Aid, URGENT CARE, Walmart

31(44) CT 229, West St, N [gas] Mobil/dsl, Sunoco/dsl [food] Dunkin Donuts [lodging] Homewood Suites [other] Lowe's, Target, S [gas] Citgo, Valero/dsl [food] Dunkin Donuts, Giovanni's Pizza, Subway [lodging] Residence Inn

30(43) Marion Ave, W Main, Southington, N [other] ski area, S [gas] Mobil/dsl [other] [H]

29(42) CT 10, from wb, exits left, Milldale (exits left from wb)

41.5mm [rest stop] eb, full [accessible] facilities, info, litter barrels, petwalk, [phone], [picnic]

28(41) CT 322, Marion, S [gas] Fleet/dsl, Mobil, TA/Country Pride/Pizza Hut/Popeye's/Taco Bell/dsl/scales/24hr/@ [food] Blimpie, Burger King, DQ, Dunkin Donuts, Manor Inn Rest., Subway, Young Young Chinese [lodging] Comfort Suites, EconoLodge [other] Home Depot

27(40) I-691 E, to Meriden

26(38) CT 70, to Cheshire, N [food] Blackie's Cafe

25a(37) Austin Rd, N [gas] Winzz/dsl [food] Asian Garden, Subway, Tiramisu Italian [other] Costco/gas, funpark, Kohl's

25(36) Harper's Ferry Rd, Reed Dr, Scott Rd, E Main St, N [gas] Mobil/dsl [food] Dunkin Donuts [other] AT&T, NAPA, S [food] Burger King, Dunkin Donuts, Friendly's, Golden Wok, McDonald's, Nino's Rest., Subway, TX Roadhouse [lodging] Quality Inn [other] Aldi Foods, BJ's Whse/gas, Cadillac/Chevrolet, CVS Drug, Super Stop&Shop/gas

23(33.5) CT 69, Hamilton Ave, N [food] Bertucci's, Buffalo Wild Wings, Chili's, IHOP, McDonald's, Olive Garden, TGIFriday's [other] [H], Barnes&Noble, JC Penney, Macy's, Michael's, Petco, Save-a-Lot Foods, TJ Maxx, S [gas] Shell [food] Dunkin Donuts

22(33) Baldwin St, Waterbury, N [gas] Gulf [lodging] Courtyard [other] [H], same as 23, USPO

21(33) Meadow St, Banks St, N [gas] 7-11, S [gas] Exxon/dsl [other] Home Depot, PetsMart

20(32) CT 8 N (exits left from eb), to Torrington

19(32) CT 8 S (exits left from wb), to Bridgeport

18(32) W Main, Highland Ave, N [gas] ProFuel/dsl [food] Dunkin Donuts, Lena's Deli, Starbucks, Subway, Wayback Burger [lodging] Hampton Inn [other] [H], CVS Drug

17(30) CT 63, CT 64, to Watertown, Naugatuck, N [food] Maggie McFly's Rest., S [gas] Mobil/dsl [food] Leo's Rest., Maples Rest., Subway

16(25) CT 188, to Middlebury, N [gas] Mobil [food] Patty's Pantry Deli [lodging] Crowne Plaza

15(22) US 6 E, CT 67, Southbury, N [gas] Citgo/deli, Mobil, Shell/repair [food] Dunkin Donuts, McDonald's, Panera Bread, Subway [lodging] Heritage Hotel [other] AT&T, Stop&Shop, TJ Maxx, Verizon, S [other] to Kettletown SP

14(20) CT 172, to S Britain, N [gas] Mobil [food] Dunkin Donuts, Maggie McFly's, S [other] st police

20mm motorist callboxes begin eb, end wb

13(19) River Rd (from eb), to Southbury

11(16) CT 34, to New Haven

10(15) US 6 W, Newtown, N [food] Fig's Rest., Foundry Kitchen, Subway, Villa Rest., S [gas] Citgo/dsl, Mobil/dsl [food] Blue Colony Diner, Pizza Palace, Starbucks

SOUTHBURY

9(11) CT 25, to Hawleyville, S [food] McGuire's Alehouse

8(8) Newtown Rd, N [gas] Global, Mobil/dsl [food] Applebee's, Outback Steaks [lodging] La Quinta [other] Best Buy, Harley-Davidson, Lowe's, Volvo, S [gas] Shell/dsl, Sunoco [food] 99 Rest., Black Angus, Boston Mkt, Burger King, Chili's, Denny's, Dunkin Donuts, Friendly's, Ichiro Steaks, Little Caesar's, McDonald's, Puerto Vallarta, Rizzuto's, Subway, Taco Bell [lodging] Best Western, Courtyard, Days Inn, Hampton Inn, Holiday Inn/rest., Microtel [other] $Tree, Aldi Foods, Goodyear/auto, Marshall's, Staples, Stop&Shop, Subaru, Target, Town Fair Tire, Verizon, Walmart

7(7) US 7N/202E, to Brookfield (exits left from eb), New Milford, 1 mi N on Federal Rd [gas] Mobil, Sunoco [food] Arby's, Chick-fil-A, Five Guys, KFC, McDonald's, Moe's SW, Panera Bread, Pizza Hut, Starbucks, Subway, Wendy's [other] AT&T, Bj's Whse/gas, Costco/gas, CVS Drug, Firestone/auto, Ford, GNC, Home Depot, Jo-Ann Fabrics, Kohl's, Michael's, Petco, ShopRite Foods, Stew Leonards, TJ Maxx, Town Fair Tire, Toyota, Verizon, Walgreens

6(6) CT 37 (from wb), New Fairfield, N [gas] Gulf [food] Burger King, Castello's Italian, Dunkin Donuts, Elmer's Diner, Grand Century Buffet, McDonald's, Moon Star Chinese [other] $Tree, CVS Drug, Rite Aid, S [gas] Shell [food] KFC

5(5) CT 37, CT 39, CT 53, Danbury, N [gas] Gulf/dsl, Shell [lodging] Best Value Inn, S [gas] Mobil [food] Dunkin Donuts, Taco Bell [other] [H], to Putnam SP

4(4) US 6 W/202 W, Lake Ave, N [gas] Exxon, Gulf/dsl, Shell/dsl [food] Dunkin Donuts, McDonald's [lodging] Ethan Allen Hotel, Maron Hotel, Super 8 [other] CVS Drug, Stop&Shop Foods, S [food] Chuck's Steaks [lodging] Residence Inn, to mall

3(3) US 7 S (exits left from wb), to Norwalk, S [gas] Mobil/Burger King/dsl [food] Agave Mexican, Brio Grille, Buffalo Wild Wings, Cheesecake Factory, Coldstone, Olive Garden, Panera Bread, Red Lobster [other] AT&T, Barnes&Noble, Dick's, JC Penney, LL Bean, Lord&Taylor, Macy's, Petco, Whole Foods Mkt

2b a(1) US 6, US 202, Mill Plain Rd, N [gas] Mobil/dsl [food] Chipotle, Rosy Tomorrows, Starbucks, Tuscanero's Pizza [lodging] Hilton Garden, Holiday Inn Express [other] Rite Aid, Staples, Trader Joe's, S **Welcome Ctr/weigh sta, full [accessible] facilities, info, [picnic], litter barrels, petwalk,** [lodging] SpringHill Suites [other] to Old Ridgebury

1(0) Saw Mill Rd, N [lodging] Hilton Garden, Holiday Inn Express, Maron Hotel

0mm Connecticut/New York state line

DANBURY

CT

CT

INTERSTATE 91

WINDSOR AREA

Exit #	Services
58mm	Connecticut/Massachusetts state line
49(57)	US 5, to Longmeadow, MA, **E** Pride/dsl, Valero Backyard Grille, McDonald's Holiday Inn Meineke, repair, **W** Sunoco/dsl Baco's Pizza, Cloverleaf Café, DQ, Dunkin Donuts, Pizza Palace $General, Chrysler/Dodge
48(56)	CT 220, Elm St (same as 47), **E** Mobil/dsl Arby's, Burger King, Denny's, Dunkin Donuts, Figaro, Friendly's, Jason's Seafood, McDonald's, Outback Steaks, Oyama Japanese, Panera Bread, Ruby Tuesday, TGIFriday's, Wendy's $Tree, AutoZone, Best Buy, Costco/gas, Dick's, Firestone/auto, Home Depot, Honda, Hyundai, Jo-Ann Fabrics, Kohl's, Nissan, Target, TownFair Tire, Toyota, USPO, VW
47(55)	CT 190, to Hazardville (same as 48), **E** 99 Rest., Acapulcos Mexican, Cheng's Garden, Chipotle, D'angelo, Domino's, Dunkin Donuts, Longhorn Steaks, McDonald's, Moe's SW Grill, Olive Garden, Pizza Hut, Plaza Azteca Mexican, Red Robin, Starbucks, Subway, Taco Bell Hampton Inn, Motel 6, Red Roof Inn H, Advance Parts, Aldi Foods, AT&T, Barnes&Noble, Big Y Foods, CVS Drug, Ford, Goodyear, Marshall's, Michael's, NAPA, Old Navy, PetCo, Petsmart, Rite Aid, ShopRite, Staples, Stop&Shop/gas, URGENT CARE, Verizon, Walgreens
46(53)	US 5, King St, to Enfield, **E** Mobil Astro's Rest., **W** Hacienda Del Sol Enfield Inn
45(51)	CT 140, Warehouse Point, **E** Shell Burger King, Chen's Chinese, Cracker Barrel, Dunkin Donuts, Friendly's, Jake's Burgers, Sofia's Rest., Subway Comfort Inn to Trolley Museum, **W** Sunoco/dsl Clarion Advance Parts
44(50)	US 5 S, to E Windsor, **E** Sunoco/dsl Dunkin Donuts, KFC, Sky Diner, Taco Bell, Wendy's Baymont Inn Walmart
49mm	Connecticut River
42(48)	CT 159, Windsor Locks, **E** Longview RV Ctr, **W** same as 41
41(47)	Center St (exits with 39), **W** Ad's Pizzaria HillPoint Hotel
40(46.5)	CT 20, **W** Old New-Gate Prison
39(46)	Kennedy Rd (exits with 41), Community Rd, **E** vet, **W** Shell/dsl Charkoon, Chili's $Tree, GNC, PetCo, Stop&Shop Foods, Target
38(45)	CT 75, to Poquonock, Windsor Area, **E** Mobil/dsl Buffalo Wild Wings, China Sea, Dunkin Donuts, Izote SW Grill, Pizzarama, Subway AT&T, PriceChopper Foods, to Ellsworth Homestead, **W** River City Grill Courtyard, Hilton Garden, Hyatt House Suites, Marriott
37(44)	CT 305, Bloomfield Ave, Windsor Ctr, **E** Mobil/dsl McDonald's, **W** Sunoco Residence Inn
36(43)	CT 178, Park Ave, to W Hartford
35b(41)	CT 218, to Bloomfield, to S Windsor, **E** food, gas/dsl
35a	I-291 E, to Manchester
34(40)	CT 159, Windsor Ave, **E** Shell/dsl, **W** Citgo/dsl Flamingo Inn, RanchHouse Rest. H
33(39)	Jennings Rd, Weston St, **E** Cadillac, Fiat, Jaguar, VW, **W** Mobil, Sunoco/dsl Burger King, Dunkin Donuts, McDonald's, Subway Super 8, Travel Inn CarMax, Honda, Hyundai, Infiniti, Mazda, Mercedes, Midas, Nissan, Subaru, Toyota
32b(38)	Trumbull St (exits left from nb), **W** Hilton, Radisson H, Goodyear, to downtown
32a	(exit 30 from sb), I-84 W
29b(37)	I-84 E, Hartford
29a(36.5)	US 5 N, CT 15 N (exits left from nb), **W** H, capitol, civic ctr, downtown

ROCKY HILL

Exit #	Services
28(36)	US 5, CT 15 S (from nb), **W** Citgo Burger King, Dunkin Donuts, Wendy's
27(35)	Brainerd Rd, Airport Rd, **E** Mobil/Dunkin Donuts/Subway/dsl, Shell/Dunkin Donuts/dsl McDonald's, USS Chowder Days Inn, Hartford Suites Ford Trucks, to Regional Mkt
26(33.5)	Marsh St, **E** CT MVD, **W** Silas Deane House, Webb House
25(33)	CT 3, Glastonbury, Wethersfield
24(32)	CT 99, Rocky Hill, Wethersfield, **E** Phillips 66/dsl, Sunoco Algarve Grill, Chuck's Steaks, Dakota Steaks, Dunkin Donuts, McDonald's, On-the-Border, Rita's Custard, Rockyhill Pizza, Saybrook Seafood, Subway Hampton Inn, Howard Johnson, Super 8 Aldi Foods, Kohl's, Meineke, Monro, **W** Mobil, Shell/dsl, Valero/dsl Buffalo Wild Wings, Burger King, D'Angelo, Denny's, Dunkin Donuts, Friendly's, Ginza Cuisine, HomeTown Buffet, KFC, Ming Dynasty, Panera Bread, Pizza Hut, Red Lobster, Sake Japanese, Sophia's Pizzaria, Starbucks, Subway, Tamarind Rest., Tilted Kilt, Townline Diner, Wendy's, Wood-n-Tap Grill Comfort Inn, Motel 6 $Tree, AT&T, CVS Drug, Goodyear/auto, Marshalls, Office Depot, Stop&Shop, TJMaxx, TownFair Tire, TrueValue, Verizon, Walgreens, Walmart/Subway
23(29)	to CT 3, West St, Rocky Hill, Vet Home, **E** Sheraton to Dinosaur SP, **W** Mobil, Valero/dsl Dunkin Donuts, Michelangeo's Pizza, Papa John's, Subway Residence Inn IGA Foods
22(27)	CT 9, to New Britain, Middletown
21(26)	CT 372, to Berlin, Cromwell, **E** Sunoco/dsl/repair Crowne Plaza, Quality Inn Krauszer's Foods, Lowe's, **W** Citgo/Subway/dsl, Mobil/dsl Baci Grill, Burger King, Chili's, Cromwell Diner, Dunkin Donuts, McDonald's, Nordelli's, Oyama Japanese Courtyard, Super 8 $Plus, Firestone/auto, Price Rite Foods, Verizon, vet, Walmart
20(23)	Country Club Rd, Middle St
22mm	**/weigh sta nb, full facilities, info, litter barrels, petwalk, , RV dump, vending**
19(21)	Baldwin Ave (from sb)
18(20.5)	I-691 W, to Marion, access to same as 16 & 17, ski area
17(20)	CT 15 N (from sb), to I-691, CT 66 E, Meriden
16(19)	CT 15, E Main St, **E** Gulf/dsl, Mobil/dsl, Valero American Steaks, Gianni's Rest., Huxley's Cafe, Kings Garden Chinese, Olympos Diner, Subway Hampton Inn, Hawthorn Inn, The Meridan Inn URGENT CARE, Volvo, **W** Getty/dsl, Gulf/repair, Shell/dsl Boston Mkt, Boston Mkt, Burger King, Dominos, Dunkin Donuts, KFC, Les' Dairy Bar, Little Caesar's, McDonald's, Nordelli's, Subway, Taco Bell, Wayback Burgers, Wendy's Comfort Inn H, CarQuest, CVS Drug, Hancock's Drug, Verizon, Walgreens

WALLINGFORD

Exit #	Services
15(16)	CT 68, to Durham, **E** golf, **W** Courtyard, Fairfield Inn, Homewood Suites
15mm	**sb, full facilities, info, litter barrels, petwalk,**
14(12)	CT 150 (no EZ return), Woodhouse Ave, Wallingford
13(10)	US 5 (exits left from nb), Wallingford, **services 2 mi W on US** to Wharton Brook SP
12(9)	US 5, Washington Ave, **E** Shell, Sunoco, Valero Bosto Mkt, Burger King, D'angelo's, DQ, Dunkin Donuts, Hibachi Buffet, McDonald's, Popeyes, Starbucks, Subway, Wendy's CV Drug, Stop&Shop Food, Town Fair Tire, URGENT CARE, USPC Walgreens, **W** Citgo, Gulf/dsl, Mobil Arby's, Athena Diner, Dunkin Donuts, Outback Steaks Best Western/Ha ry's Grill Advance Parts, BigY Foods/drug, vet
11(7)	CT 22 (from nb), North Haven, same as 12

INTERSTATE 91 Cont'd

NEW HAVEN

Exit #	Services
10(6)	CT 40, to Cheshire, Hamden
9(5)	Montowese Ave, W Berkshire/dsl, Sunoco Buffalo Wild Wings, Dunkin Donuts, Dynasty Chinese, Friendly's, Longhorn Steaks, McDonald's, Olive Garden, Panera Bread, Red Lobster, Ruby Tuesday, Subway, Wendy's $Tree, AT&T, Barnes&Noble, Best Buy, BigLots, BJ's Whse/gas, GNC, Home Depot, Michael's, Nissan/Jeep, PetCo, Petsmart, Target, TJMaxx, URGENT CARE, Verizon
8(4)	CT 17, CT 80, Middletown Ave, E 7-11, Citgo, Global/dsl, Mercury/dsl, Shell, Sunoco Burger King, Country House Rest., Dunkin Donuts, Exit 8 Diner, KFC, McDonald's, Taco Bell Days Inn Advance Parts, Aldi Foods, AutoZone, Lowe's, vet, Walgreens, Walmart/Subway
7(3)	Ferry St (from sb), Fair Haven, W Speedway/dsl NAPA
6(2.5)	Willow St (exits left from nb), Blatchley Ave, E repair
5(2)	US 5 (from nb), State St, Fair Haven
4(1.5)	State St (from sb), downtown
3(1)	Trumbull St, downtown, W Peabody Museum
2(.5)	Hamilton St, downtown, New Haven
1(.3)	CT 34W (from sb), New Haven, W H, downtown

I-91 begins/ends on I-95, exit 48.

INTERSTATE 95

MYSTIC

GROTON

Exit #	Services
94mm	Connecticut/Rhode Island state line
93(111)	CT 216, Clarks Falls, E Shell/dsl/repair Subway, to Burlingame SP, W Mobil/dsl, Pilot/Shell/Stuckey's/Roy Rogers/Sbarro's/dsl/scales/24hr Dunkin Donuts Budget Inn, Stardust Motel
92(107)	CT 2, CT 49 (no EZ nb return), **sb, full facilities**, Pawcatuck, E Shell Dunkin Donuts, McDonald's La Quinta H, Stop&Shop, W Cedar Park Suites FoxWoods (8mi), KOA
91(103)	CT 234, N Main St, to Stonington, E H
90(101)	CT 27, Mystic, E Shell/Domino's/Dunkin Donuts/dsl Boathouse Rest., Five Guys, Friendly's, Go Fish, McDonald's, Mystic Diner, Starbucks, Steak Loft EconoLodge, Hilton, Holiday Inn Express, Howard Johnson, Hyatt Place aquarium, Mystic Outlet Shops, W Mobil/Subway/dsl Antonio's Ristorante, Dunkin Donuts, Frank's Grille Days Inn, Hampton Inn, Quality Inn, Ramada Inn, Residence Inn Chevrolet, Chrysler/Dodge/Jeep, Ford, RV camping, TrueValue, VW
89mm	Mystic River, scenic overlook nb, scenic overlook
89(99)	CT 614, Mystic St, Allyn St, W camping (seasonal)
88(98)	CT 117, to Noank, E , W Octagon Steaks, Starbucks Marriott
87(97)	Sharp Hwy (exits left from sb), Groton, E Applebee's Hampton Inn , to Griswold SP
86(96)	rd 184 (exits left from nb), Groton, E 99 Rest., Applebee's Hampton Inn, Rodeway Inn Walgreens, W Cory's/dsl, Mobil/dsl, Shell/dsl, Speedway Bayou Smokehouse, Chinese Kitchen, Domino's, Dunkin Donuts, Flanagan's Diner, Groton Rest., Moe's SW, Panera Bread, Subway, Taco Bell Best Western, Groton Inn, Super 8 Advance Parts, GNC, Honda, Kia, Kohl's, Midas, Stop&Shop, to US Sub Base, Verizon
85(95)	US 1 N, Groton, downtown, E NAPA
84(94)	CT 32 (from sb), New London, downtown

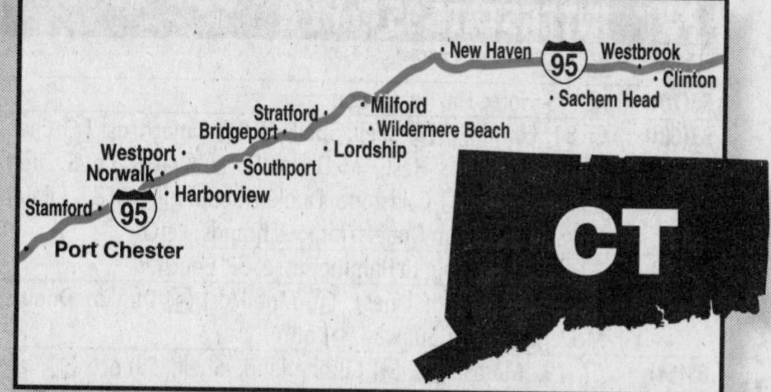

NEW LONDON

NIANTIC

Exit #	Services
83(92)	CT 32, New London, E to Long Island Ferry
82a(90.5)	frontage rd, New London, E Mobil/dsl TX Roadhouse AutoZone, Goodyear/auto, NSA Foods, same as 82, Staples, TownFair Tire, W Sunoco Chili's, Outback Steaks Clarion, SpringHill Suites Marshall's, Petsmart, same as 82, ShopRite Foods
82(90)	CT 85, to I-395 N, New London, W Mobil/Dunkin Donuts Buffalo Wild Wings, Coldstone, Jersey Mike's, Longhorn Steaks, Moe's SW, Olive Garden, Panera Bread, Ruby Tuesday, Smashburger, Starbucks, Subway BAM, Best Buy, Dick's, Home Depot, JC Penney, Macy's, Michael's, PetCo, Target, Verizon
90mm	**weigh sta both directions**
81(89.5)	Cross Road, W Rodeway Inn $Tree, BJ's Whse/gas, Lowe's, Walmart/McDonald's
80(89.3)	Oil Mill Rd (from sb), W Rodeway Inn
76(89)	I-395 N (from nb, exits left), to Norwich
75(88)	US 1, to Waterford
74(87)	rd 161, to Flanders, Niantic, E Citgo/dsl, Cory's/repair, Mobil Burger King, Country Gourmet, Dunkin Donuts, Illiano's Grill, Starbucks Best Value Inn, Days Inn, Motel 6, Sleep Inn Ford, Stop&Shop/gas, Tires+, Verizon, W Shell Five Guys, Flanders Seafood, Kings Garden Chinese, McDonald's, Osaka Japaneses, Shack Rest., Smokey O'Grady's BBQ, Subway, Yummy Yummy Pizza CVS Drug, IGA Foods, Rite Aid, TrueValue
74mm	**sb, full facilities, st police**
73(86)	Society Rd
72(84)	to Rocky Neck SP, **2 mi** E food, lodging, RV camping, to Rocky Neck SP
71(83)	4 Mile Rd, River Rd, to Rocky Neck SP, **1 mi** E camping (seasonal), beaches
70(80)	US 1, CT 156, Old Lyme, W Shell/dsl Dunkin Donuts, Morning Glory Cafe, Subway Old Lyme Inn/dining Big Y Foods, Griswold Museum, Rite Aid, USPO, vet
69(77)	US 1, CT 9 N, to Hartford, W Otter Cove Quality Inn
68(76.5)	US 1 S, Old Saybrook, E Mobil, Shell/dsl Cloud 9 Deli, Mystic Mkt Kitchen, W Buick/GMC, Chevrolet, Chrysler/Dodge/Jeep, Hyundai, Kia, Nissan, VW
67(76)	CT 154, Elm St (no EZ sb return), Old Saybrook, E Pasta Vita Itaian same as 68
66(75)	to US 1, Spencer Plain Rd, E Citgo/dsl Blue Crab Steaks, Brick Oven Pizza, Cuckoo's Nest Mexican, Dunkin Donuts, Five Guys, Sal's Pizza, Samurai Japanese, Wayback Burgers EconoLodge, Saybrook Motel, Super 8 Benny's Mkt, Big Y Mkt, Kohl's, NAPA, transmissions, URGENT CARE, vet
65(73)	rd 153, Westbrook, E Mobil/Dunkin Donuts, Valero Cafe Rotier, Cristy's Rest., Denny's, Subway Honda, H, Old Navy, Tanger Factory Stores/famous brands, Toyota, USPO, Walgreens

INTERSTATE 95 Cont'd

MADISON

Exit #	Services
64(70)	rd 145, Horse Hill Rd, Clinton
63(68)	CT 81, Clinton, E Shell, Shell/dsl/LP, Sunoco/dsl Chester's BBQ, Chips Rest., McDonald's, Subway CVS Drug, USPO, vet, W Coldstone, Dunkin Donuts AT&T, Clinton Crossing Premium Outlets/famous brands, PetCo
62(67)	E RV camping, to Hammonasset SP, beaches
66mm	**service area both lanes,** Mobil/dsl Dunkin Donuts, McDonald's (sb), Subway atm
61(64)	CT 79, Madison, E Cumberland, Shell, Sunoco Cafe Allegre, Starbucks, Subway CVS Drug, Stop&Shop, USPO, Verizon
61mm	East River
60(63.5)	Mungertown Rd (from sb, no return), E food, lodging
59(60)	rd 146, Goose Lane, Guilford, E Citgo, Mobil/24hr, Shell/DQ/dsl Avest Pizza, Dunkin Donuts, First Garden, Grand Apizza, McDonald's, Shoreline Diner, Wendy's, Whole Enchilada Comfort Inn, Tower Motel $Tree, Big Y Foods, NAPA, transmissions, Verizon, Walmart, W st police, URGENT CARE
58(59)	CT 77, Guilford, E on US 1 Dunkin Donuts, Gulf/dsl, Mobil, Wave/dsl, Xpress CVS Drug, to Henry Whitfield Museum, Walgreens, W st police
57(58)	US 1, Guilford, E Shell/Dunkin Donuts/dsl, W Fresh Mkt, Land Rover, Michael's
56(55)	rd 146, to Stony Creek, E Rodeway Inn, W Mobil, Shell/dsl, TA/Popeye's/Starbucks/Subway/dsl/scales/24hr/@ 56 Diner, Dunkin Donuts, USS Chowderpot Baymont Inn, Best Value Inn Freightliner, Stop&Shop Foods

BRANFORD

Exit #	Services
55(54)	US 1, E Branford/repair, Cumberland, Shell/dsl Carson's Rest., Hornet's Nest Deli, Lynn's Rest., Marco Pizzaria Days Inn, Holiday Inn Express, Motel 6 Ford, vet, Walgreens, W Gulf, Mobil/Dunkin Donuts/dsl Brother's Deli, Cafe Fiore, Chuck's Margarita Grill, Parthenon Diner, Su Casa Mexican
54(53)	Cedar St, Branford, E Mobil, Stop&Shop Gas Dragon East Chinese, Dunkin Donuts, La Luna Ristorante Kia, Staples, Subaru, W Krauszer's Foods, NAPA
52mm	**service area both lanes,** Mobil/dsl/24hr Dunkin Donuts, McDonald's (nb), Subway
52(50)	rd 100, North High St, E to Trolley Museum, W st police
51(49.5)	US 1, Easthaven, E Speedway/dsl, Sunoco, Valero/dsl Boston Mkt, Chili's, Dunkin Donuts Quality Inn $Tree, Chevrolet, Hobby Lobby, Lexus, TJ Maxx, W Dunkin Donuts, Wendy's AutoZone, CarMax, Home Depot, Hyundai
50(49)	Woodward Ave (from nb), E Shell Ft Nathan Hale, US Naval/Marine Reserve

NEW HAVEN

Exit #	Services
49(48.5)	Stiles St (from nb)
48(48)	I-91 N, to Hartford
47(47.5)	CT 34, New Haven, W Mobil/Dunkin Donuts/dsl Brazi's Italian, Greek Olive Diner La Quinta Ikea, Long Wharf Theater, same as 46
46(47)	Long Wharf Dr, Sargent Dr, E Lenny & Joe's Rest., W Mobil/Dunkin Donuts/dsl Brazi's Italian, Greek Olive Diner La Quinta Ikea, Long Wharf Theater
45(46.5)	CT 10 (from sb), Blvd, W Dunkin Donuts, McDonald's same as 44
44(46)	CT 10 (from nb), Kimberly Ave, E Super 8, W DQ, Dunkin Donuts, McDonald's, Popeyes same as 45
43(45)	CT 122, 1st Ave (no EZ return), West Haven, W 1st Fuel/dsl, Xtra H, NAPA, to U of New Haven, vet

CT

MILFORD

Exit #	Services
42(44)	CT 162, Saw Mill Rd, E Pizza Hut EconoLodge, W Shell American Steaks, Denny's, Dunkin Donuts, Starbucks, Subway, TX Roadhouse, Uncle Willie's BBQ Best Western, Hampton Inn Aldi Foods, Firestone/auto, Walmart/Subway
41(42)	Marsh Hill Rd, to Orange
41mm	**service area both lanes,** Mobil/dsl Dunkin Donuts, McDonald's, Subway
40(40)	Old Gate Lane, Woodmont Rd, E Citgo/dsl, Pilot/Wendy's/dsl/scales/24hr, Shell, Sunoco Cracker Barrel, Duchess Rest., Dunkin Donuts, Gipper's Rest., Popeyes, Titlted Kilt Hilton Garden, Holiday Inn Express, Mayflower Motel, Milford Inn Blue Beacon, Lowe's, Midas
39(39)	US 1, to Milford, E Cumberland Farms/dsl Athenian Diner, Chicago Grill, Dunkin Donuts, Friendly's, Hooters, Mama Teresa's Howard Johnson, Super 8 $Tree, CVS Drug, Firestone/auto, Mazda/Volvo, ShopRite Foods, URGENT CARE, vet, Walgreens, W on US 1 Mobil Boston Mkt, Boston Mkt, Buffalo Wild Wings, Burger King, Chili's, Chipotle Mexican, DiBella Subs, Domino's, Dunkin Donuts, Hometown Buffet, HoneyBaked Ham, McDonald's, Panera Bread, Sonic, Starbucks, Subway, Taco Bell, Villano's Rest. Acura, Advance Parts, AT&T, Barnes&Noble, BigLots, Chrysler/Dodge/Jeep, Costco/gas, Dick's, Jo-Ann Fabrics, Macy's, Marshall's, Michael's, Old Navy, PetCo, Rite Aid, Shop&Shop/gas, Staples, Target, Town-Fair Tire, Walmart/Subway, Whole Foods Mkt
38(38)	CT 15, Merritt Pkwy, Cross Pkwy
37(37.5)	High St (no ez nb return), E Gulf, Sunoco, USA Subway 7-11, Toyota, vet
36	Plains Rd, E Dunkin Donuts, Gusto Italian Hampton Inn Aldi Foods
35(37)	Bic Dr, School House Rd, E Citgo Wendy's Fairfield Inn AutoZone, Buick/GMC, Chevrolet, CVS Drug, Dennis' Parts, Ford/Lincoln, Honda, Kia, Land Rover, Nissan, Stop&Shop Foods/gas, Subaru, Walgreens, W Red Roof Inn, Residence Inn, SpringHill Suites
34(34)	US 1, Milford, E on US 1 Dunkin Donuts, McDonald's, Pizza Hut, Subway, Taco Bell Devon Motel $Tree, Hyundai Walgreens
33(33.5)	US 1 (from nb, no EZ return), CT 110, Ferry Blvd, E Shell/dsl Sunoco/dsl Danny's Drive-In, Lumi Rest., Riverview Bistro Subway $Tree, BJ's Whse, PetCo, Staples, W 99 Rest. McDonalds, Villa Pizza Home Depot, Marshall's, ShopRite Foods, Stop&Shop/dsl, USPO, Walmart/Subway
32(33)	W Broad St, Stratford, E Petra/Subway/dsl, W Gulf dsl Dunkin Donuts
31(32)	South Ave, Honeyspot Rd, E Gulf/Dunkin Donuts Honeyspot Motel, Quality Inn, W Citgo/dsl NAPA, Town Fair Tire
30(31.5)	Lordship Blvd, Surf Ave, E Gulf/dsl, Shell/dsl Dunkin Donuts Stratford Hotel URGENT CARE, W Massey dsl
29(31)	rd 130, Stratford Ave, Seaview Ave, W H
28(30)	CT 113, E Main St, Pembrook St
27(29.5)	Lafayette Blvd, downtown, W Dunkin Donuts H, Barnum Museum
27a(29)	CT 25, CT 8, to Waterbury
26(28)	Wordin Ave
25(27)	CT 130 (from sb, no EZ return), State St, Commerce Dr, Fairfield Ave, E Audi, Infiniti, Mercedes, Porsche, USPO, W McDonald's

INTERSTATE 95 Cont'd

Exit #	Services
24(26.5)	Black Rock Tpk, **E** [food] Blackrock Oyster Bar, Fairfield Pizza, Rio Bravo, Sweet Basil [lodging] Best Western [other] BJ's Whse/Subway, Lexus, Porsche, Staples, USPO, Verizon, **W** [gas] Gulf [other] Firestone/auto, Nissan
23(26)	US 1, Kings Hwy, **E** [gas] Sunoco/dsl [food] Chipotle, Five Guys [other] CVS Drug, Home Depot, Petco, Whole Foods Mkt
22(24)	Round Hill Rd, N Benson Rd
23.5mm	**service area both lanes,** [gas] Mobil/dsl [food] FoodCourt (sb), McDonald's
21(23)	Mill Plain Rd, **E** [gas] Citgo/dsl, Mobil/dsl [food] Avellino's Italian, DQ, Geronimo SW Grill, Kiraku Japanese, Rawley's Drive-In, Starbucks, Subway, Wilson's BBQ [other] Hemlock Hardware, Rite Aid
20(22)	Bronson Rd (from sb)
19(21)	US 1, Center St, **W** [gas] BP, Shell/dsl [food] Athena Diner, Baskin-Robbins/Dunkin Donuts, Panera Bread, Subway [lodging] Westport Inn [other] Balducci's Mkt, Honda, Stop&Shop, TownFair Tire, Walgreens
18(20)	to Westport, **E** [other] beaches, Sherwood Island SP, st police, **1 mi W on US 1** [gas] Gulf, Mobil [food] Angelina's Trattoria, Arby's, Bertucci's Italian, Fresh Mkt, McDonald's, Sakura Japanese, Sherwood Diner, Starbucks, Subway [other] Barnes&Noble, Toyota, URGENT CARE, Walgreens
17(18)	CT 33, rd 136, Westport
16(17)	E Norwalk, **E** [gas] Citgo, Gulf, Mobil/dsl, Shell/dsl [food] Baskin-Robbins/Dunkin Donuts, Eastside Café, Penny's Diner, Subway [other] Rite Aid
15(16)	US 7, to Danbury, Norwalk, **E** [gas] Shell [other] Walgreens, **W** [gas] Exxon, Sunoco
14(15)	US 1, CT Ave, S Norwalk, **E** [other] st police, **W** [gas] Shell/Dunkin Donuts [food] Burger King, Dunkin Donuts, Post Road Diner, Silver Star Diner, Subway, Wendy's [other] [H], Barnes&Noble, Best Buy, CVS Drug, Kohl's, Old Navy, Petsmart, same as 13, ShopRite Foods, Stop&Shop, TJ Maxx, TownFair Tire
13(13)	US 1 (no EZ return), Post Rd, Norwalk, **W** [gas] Mobil, Shell, Sunoco [food] American Steaks, Bertucci's, Chipotle Mexican, Darien Diner, Friendly's, KFC, McDonald's, Palmwich [lodging] DoubleTree Hotel [other] AT&T, Costco, Home Depot, Mini, same as 14, Staples, vet, Walmart
12.5mm	**service area nb,** [gas] Mobil/dsl [food] Dunkin Donuts, McDonald's, Subway
12(12)	rd 136, Tokeneke Rd (from nb, no return), **W** [food] deli
11(11)	US 1, Darien, **E** [gas] Exxon [lodging] Chuck's Steaks [other] Chevrolet, Nissan, repair, vet, **W** [gas] Gulf [food] Panera Bread [other] BMW, Whole Foods Mkt
10(10)	Noroton, **W** [gas] Shell, Standard [other] vet
9.5mm	**service area sb,** [gas] Mobil/dsl [food] McDonald's, Subway
9(9)	US 1, rd 106, Glenbrook, **E** [lodging] Best Value Inn, **W** [gas] Gulf [food] Dunkin Donuts, McDonald's, Subway [other] Advance Parts, Meineke
8(8)	Atlantic Ave, Elm St, **E** [gas] Sunoco, **W** [lodging] Marriott [other] [H]
7(7)	CT 137, Atlantic Ave, **W** [food] PF Chang's [lodging] Hampton Inn, Marriott [other] Barnes&Noble, same as 8, USPO
6(6)	Harvard Ave, West Ave, **E** [gas] Gulf [food] City Limits Diner, Starbucks [lodging] La Quinta [other] Advance Parts, Petsmart, Subaru, USPO, **W** [gas] Shell [lodging] Super 8 [other] [H]
5(5)	US 1, Riverside, Old Greenwich, **W** [gas] BP, Mobil, Shell [food] Boston Mkt, Corner Deli, Hunan Cafe, McDonald's, Starbucks, Taco Bell, Valbello Ristorante [lodging] Hyatt Regency [other] A&P Mkt, CVS Drug, GNC, Staples, USPO, Walgreens
4(4)	Indian Field Rd, Cos Cob, **W** [other] Bush-Holley House Museum
3(3)	Arch St, Greenwich, **E** [other] Bruce Museum, **W** [gas] Shell [other] [H], Lexus
2mm	**weigh sta nb**
2(1)	Delavan Ave, Byram
0mm	Connecticut/New York state line

NORWALK

GREENWICH

New Haven
95
Westbrook
Clinton
Sachem Head
Stratford
Milford
Bridgeport
Wildermere Beach
Lordship
Westport
Norwalk
Southport
Harborview
Stamford
95
Port Chester
CT

CT

INTERSTATE 395

Exit #	Services
55.5mm	Connecticut/Massachusetts state line
53(54)	E Thompson, to Wilsonville
50(50)	rd 200, N Grosvenor Dale, **W** [other] W Thompson Lake Camping (seasonal)
49(49)	to CT 12 (from nb, exits left), Grosvenor Dale, same as 99
47(47)	US 44, to E Putnam, **E** [food] Dunkin Donuts, Empire Buffet, McDonald's/playplace, Subway, Wendy's [other] $Tree, Advance Parts, CVS Drug, Giant Pizza, GNC, Stop&Shop/gas, **W** [gas] Mobil, Shell/dsl/repair [other] Walmart/Subway
46(46)	to CT 12, Putnam, **W** [lodging] King's Inn [other] [H]
45(45)	Kennedy Dr, to Putnam, **E** [other] Ford, **W** [other] [H]
43(43)	Ballouville, **W** [food] Gold Eagle Rest. [lodging] Comfort Inn
41(41)	CT 101, to Dayville, **E** [gas] Gulf, Shell/dsl [food] Burger King, China Garden, Dayville Mexican, Domino's, Dunkin Donuts, Subway, Yamoto Japanese, Zip's Diner [lodging] Budget Inn [other] $General, $Tree, Aldi Foods, Kohl's, Town Fair Tire, Walgreens, **W** [gas] Mobil/Taco Bell/dsl, Shell/dsl [food] 99 Rest., Dunkin Donuts, McDonald's, Mozzarella's Grill [other] AT&T, city park, GNC, Lowe's, Michael's, PetCo, Staples, Stop&Shop, Target, TJ Maxx, Verizon
38(39)	to S Killingly, **W** [food] Dunkin Donuts, Giant Pizza [other] st police
37(38)	US 6 W, to Danielson, to Quinebaug Valley Coll
35(36)	to US 6 E (from nb), to Providence
35mm	[rest stop] **both lanes, full [handicap] facilities,** [gas] Mobil/dsl [food] Dunkin Donuts, Subway
32(32)	CT 14, to Sterling, Central Village, **E** [gas] Cumberland, Gulf/repair [food] Billy's Pizza, Pizza Pizzaz [other] Rite Aid, RV camping, USPO, **W** [gas] Shell/Dunkin Donuts/dsl [food] Dunkin Donuts, Frank O's Pizza, Subway [lodging] Knights Inn [other] $General, transmissions
29(30)	CT 14A to Plainfield, **E** [other] RV camping (seasonal), **W** [gas] Mobil
28(28)	Lathrop Rd, to Plainfield, **E** [gas] Shell/Domino's/dsl [food] Dunkin Donuts, HongKong Star Chinese, Subway, Wendy's [lodging] La Quinta, Quality Inn [other] Big Y Foods, Ford, Hyundai/VW, Mazda, **W** [gas] Gulf, Sunoco/dsl [food] Bakers Dozen Cafe, McDonald's, Mr Z's Rest. [other] Advance Parts, CVS Drug
24(24)	rd 201, Hopeville, **E** [other] Hopeville Pond SP, RV camping
22(23)	CT 164, CT 138, to Pachaug, Preston, **E** [gas] Exxon/Petro Max/Dunkin Donuts/dsl [other] $Tree, RV camping, **W** [lodging] AmericInn

PUTNAM

PLAINFIELD

INTERSTATE 395 Cont'd

Exit #	Services
21(21)	CT 12, Jewett City, E [food] Chili's, Panera Bread, Ruby Tuesday [other] Aldi Foods, AT&T, Dick's, GNC, Home Depot, Kohl's, Lowe's, Michael's, PetCo, Target, Verizon, Walmart/Dunkin Donuts, W [gas] Gulf/dsl, Mobil/dsl, Shell/dsl [food] McDonald's [other] Val-U Foods, vet
19a(20)	CT 169 (from nb), Lisbon, W [other] RV camping
18(18)	rd 97, Taftville, E [gas] Gulf/dsl, W [gas] 7-11/dsl
14(14)	to CT 2 W, CT 32 N, Norwichtown, E [food] Friendly's [other] tires, W [gas] Global/Dunkin Donuts/dsl, Mobil/dsl, Shell/dsl [food] Illiano's Grill, Prime Rest., Subway, Yantic River Inn [lodging] Courtyard, Rosemont Suites [other] Ace Hardware
13b a(14)	CT 2 E, CT 32 S, Norwich, E [other] [H]
11(12)	CT 82, Norwich, E [gas] Mobil, Shell/dsl [food] 99 Rest., Burger King, Chinese Buffet, Dunkin Donuts, Five Guys, KFC/Taco Bell, Little Caesar's, McDonald's, Mr Pizza, Papa Gino's, Popeye's, Starbucks, Subway, Wendy's [other] $Tree, AT&T, Jo-Ann Fabrics, Rite Aid, ShopRite Foods, Staples, TJ Maxx, TownFair Tire, Verizon, W [lodging] Holiday Inn [other] Big Y Foods, Walmart
9a(10)	CT 2A E, to Ledyard, E [other] to Pequot Res
8.5mm	**service plaza sb,** [gas] Mobil/dsl [food] Dunkin Donuts, Subway [other] st police nb
6(6)	rd 163, to Uncasville, Montville, 1 mi E [gas] Mobil/dsl [food] Dunkin Donuts, Friendly Pizza, McDonald's, Subway [other] repair, Rite Aid
5(5)	CT 32 (from sb, exits left), to New London, RI Beaches
2(2)	CT 85, to I-95 N, Colchester, 1/2 mi E [gas] Dunkin Donuts, Shell/dsl [lodging] Oakdell Motel

I-95. I-395 begins/ends on I-95, exit 76.

NORWICHTOWN

CT

INTERSTATE 691

Exit #	Services
	I-691 begins/ends on I-91.
12(12)	Preston Ave
11(11)	I-91 N, to Hartford
10(11)	I-91 S, to New Haven, CT 15 S, W Cross Pkwy
9	Berlin Tpk
8(10)	US 5, Broad St, N [gas] HH Gas, Irving, Shell/dsl [food] Broad St Pizza, DQ
7(9)	downtown (no ez wb return), Meriden (from wb), S [gas] Citgo
6(8)	Lewis Ave (from wb, no EZ return), to CT 71, N [food] Ruby Tuesday [other] [H], Best Buy, Dick's, Macy's, Old Navy, Target, TJ Maxx, S [gas] 7-11 [food] Subway
5(7)	CT 71, to Chamberlain Hill (from eb, no EZ return), N [other] [H], Best Buy, Target, S [gas] 7-11/gas [food] Subway
4(4)	CT 322, W Main St (no re-entry from eb), N [gas] Sunoco [food] Dunkin Donuts, Hubbard Park Pizza [other] [H]
3mm	Quinnipiac River
3(1)	CT 10, to Cheshire, Southington, N [food] Sam's Clams Rest., Tony's Rest.
2(0)	I-84 E, to Hartford
1(0)	I-84 W, to Waterbury
	I-691 begins/ends on I-84.

NOTES

DELAWARE

INTERSTATE 95

Exit #	Services
23mm	Delaware/Pennsylvania state line, motorist callboxes for 23 miles sb
11(22)	to I-495 S, DE 92, Naamans Rd, E [other] $General, Burlington Coats, Goodyear/auto, Jo-Ann Fabrics, SaveALot, WaWa, W [gas] Shell/Circle K/dsl, WaWa/dsl [food] KFC/Taco Bell [lodging] Crowne Plaza [other] CVS Drug, Home Depot, Rite Aid
10(21)	Harvey Rd (no nb return)
9(19)	DE 3, to Marsh Rd, E [food] Dunkin Donuts [other] Rockwood Museum, st police, to Bellevue SP
8b a(17)	US 202, Concord Pike, to Wilmington, E [other] Home Depot, to Brandywine Park
7b a(16)	DE 52, Delaware Ave
6(15)	DE 4, MLK Blvd, E [food] Joe's Crabshack, McDonald's [other] AAA, Fresh Grocer Foods, Rite Aid, W [gas] Liberty [other] Family$
5c(12)	I-495 N, to Wilmington, to DE Mem Bridge
5b a(11)	DE 141, to US 202, to New Castle, Newport, E [lodging] Sheraton
4b a(8)	DE 1, DE 7, to Christiana, E [food] Bahama Breeze, Brio Tuscan Grille, CA Pizza Kitchen, Cheesecake Factory, Don Pablo, Foodcourt, JB Dawson's Rest., Panera Bread, Ted's MT Grill [other] Barnes&Noble, Cabela's, Costco, Dick's, JC Penney, Macy's, Michael's, Nordstrom, PetCo, Target, W [food] Applebee's, Dunkin Donuts, Firebird's Grill, Fuddrucker's, Jimmy John's, Marble Slab Creamery, Michael's Rest., Olive Garden, Red Lobster [lodging] Country Inn&Suites, Courtyard, Days Inn, Extended Stay America, Hampton Inn, Hilton, Quality Inn, Red Roof Inn [other] [H], AAA, Best Buy, casino/racetrack, Home Depot, Petsmart, TJ Maxx, Verizon
3b a(6)	DE 273, to Newark, Dover, E [gas] BP, Exxon/dsl [food] Bertucci's, Bob Evans, Boston Mkt, Ciao Pizza, Famous Dave's BBQ, Olive Grill Italian, Red Robin, Shell Hammer's Grille, Wendy's [lodging] Ramada Inn, Residence Inn, Sheraton, Staybridge Suites, TownePlace Suites [other] Acme Foods, Boscov's, Jo-Ann Fabrics, Old Navy, Staples, Walgreens, W [gas] Getty, Shell/dsl [food] Denny's, Dunkin Donuts [lodging] Comfort Inn, Holiday Inn Express, Motel 6 [other] 7-11
5mm	**service area both lanes (exits left from both lanes),** [gas] Sunoco/dsl [food] Baja Fresh, Burger King, Famiglia, Popeye's, Starbucks [other] info
1b a(3)	DE 896, to Newark, to U of DE, Middletown, W [gas] Exxon, Shell/dsl, Sunoco [food] Boston Mkt, China Garden, Dunkin Donuts, Friendly's, Jersey Mike's, Malin's Deli, Mario's Pizza, McDonald's, TGIFriday's [lodging] Baymont Inn, Candlewood Suites, Embassy Suites, Homewood Suites, Red Roof Inn, Rodeway Inn [other] DE Tire Ctr
1mm	**toll booth, st police**
0mm	Delaware/Maryland state line, motorist callboxes for 23 miles nb

NEWARK

INTERSTATE 295 (Wilmington)

Exit #	Services
15mm	Delaware/New Jersey state line, Delaware River, Delaware Memorial Bridge
14.5mm	**toll plaza**
14	DE 9, New Castle Ave, to Wilmington, E [gas] [food] Giovanni's Cafe [other] Advance Parts, CVS Drug, Family$, Firestone/auto, Harley-Davidson/rest., Rite Aid, Super G Foods, W [gas] Shell, Super/dsl [food] Dunkin Donuts, McDonald's [lodging] Best Night Inn, Budget Inn, SuperLodge
13	US 13, US 40, to New Castle, E [gas] BP, Shell/dsl, Speedway/dsl, Sunoco/dsl, WaWa [food] Applebee's, Arby's, Arner's Rest, Burger King, Checkers, DogHouse, Dove Diner, Dunkin Donuts, Hooters, IHOP, KFC, Krispy Kreme, Little Caesar's, McDonald's, Popeye's, Season's Pizza, Taco Bell, TGIFriday's, Wendy's [lodging] Quality Inn, Super 8 [other] $General, $Tree, Acura, AutoZone, Big Lots, BJ's Whse/gas, Chevrolet, Chrysler/Jeep/Dodge, Cottman Transmissions, Fiat, Ford, GNC, Home Depot, Hyundai, Lincoln, Mazda, Nissan, PepBoys, repair, Ross, Save-a-Lot, Staples, Toyota, URGENT CARE, Verizon, Walgreens, Walmart, W [gas] WaWa/dsl [food] Dunkin Donuts [lodging] Clarion, Fairfield Inn [other] Ford Trucks, Lowe's
12	I-495, US 202, N to Wilmington

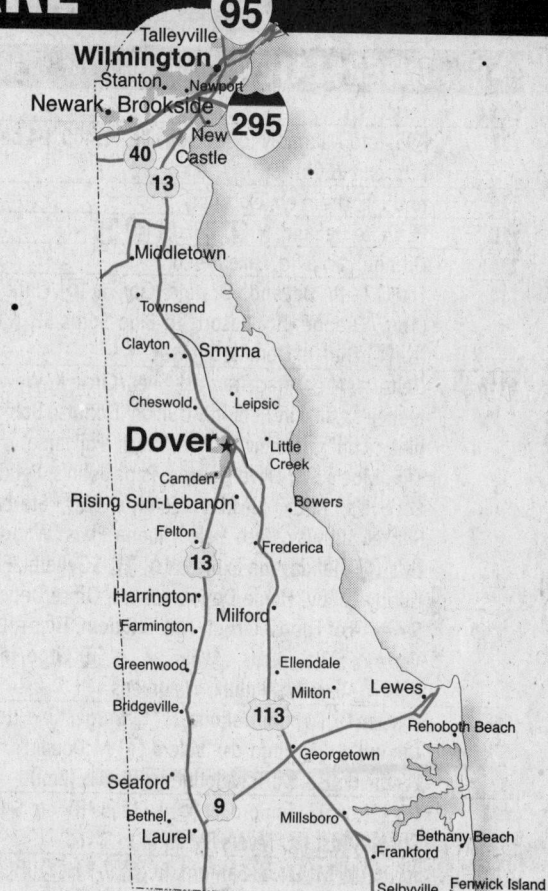

I-295 begins/ends on I-95.

WILMINGTON

INTERSTATE 495

Exit #	Services
11mm	**I-95 N. I-495 begins/ends on I-95.**
5(10)	US 13, Phila Pike, Claymont, W [gas] BP, Exxon/dsl, Sunoco/dsl, WaWa/dsl [food] Arby's, Boston Mkt, Burger King, Dunkin Donuts, McDonald's [lodging] Milan Motel [other] Aamco, Family$, Food Lion, USPO
4(5)	US 13, rd 3, Edgemoor Rd, to Fox Point Park
3(4)	12th St
2(3)	rd 9A, Terminal Ave, Port of Wilmington
1(1)	US 13, E [gas] WaWa/dsl [food] Dunkin Donuts [lodging] Clarion [other] Ford Trucks, Lowe's
0mm	**I-95 S. I-495 begins/ends on I-95.**

DE

= gas = food = lodging = other = rest stop

FLORIDA

INTERSTATE 4

Exit #	Services
132	I-95, S to Miami, N to Jacksonville, FL 400. **I-4 begins/ends on I-95, exit 260b.**
129	to US 92 (from eb, exits left)
118	FL 44, to DeLand, N BP/dsl H
116	Orange Camp Rd, Lake Helen
114	FL 472, to DeLand, Orange City, N Clark Campground (1mi), Orange City Resort, to Blue Sprgs SP, S RaceTrac/dsl Dunkin Donuts, Subway
111b a	Deltona, N RaceTrac/dsl, Shell/Circle K, Wawa/dsl Applebee's, Baskin-Robbins/Dunkin Donuts, Bob Evans, Chick-fil-A, Chili's, Denny's, Five Guys, Fujiyama, Jimmy John's, KFC, Moe's SW, Olive Garden, Papa John's, Perkins, Pizza Hut, Popeye's, Ruby Tuesday, Sonny's BBQ, Starbucks, Steak'n Shake, Subway, Taco Bell, Tijuana Flats, Woody's BBQ, Zaxby's Holiday Inn Express H, $General, Firestone/auto, Hobby Lobby, Home Depot, Lowe's, Office Depot, Publix/deli, Save-A-Lot Foods, Target, Tire Kingdom, Tires+, URGENT CARE, Verizon, Walgreens, Walmart, S Citgo/repair Wendy's Family$, Publix, Walgreens
108	Dirksen Dr, DeBary, Deltona, N Burger King, IHOP Hampton Inn, S Citgo/dsl, Valero McDonald's, Subway (2mi), Waffle House Travelodge Publix (2mi)
104	US 17, US 92, Sanford, N La Mesa RV Ctr, S Marathon/Subway/dsl Myers RV Ctr
101c	rd 46, to Mt Dora, Sanford, N 7-11 IHOP, Subway, Tijuana Flats Ace Hardware, Audi, Ford, vet, S 7-11, Chevron/dsl, Mobil, Murphy USA/dsl, RaceTrac/dsl, Shell/dsl Buffalo Wild Wings, Burger King, Carrabba's, Cheddar's, Chianti's Pizza, Chipotle, Cracker Barrel, Don Pablo, Dunkin Donuts, El Paso Mexican, Firehouse Subs, Habaneros, Honeybaked Ham, Hooters, Joe's Crabshack, LJ Silver/Taco Bell, Logan's Roadhouse, Longhorn Steaks, McDonald's, Mellow Mushroom, Olive Garden, Orlando Alehouse, Outback Steaks, Panda Express, Panera Bread, PDQ Grill, Pollo Tropical, Red Lobster, Red Robin, Rte 46 Smokehouse, Smokey Bones BBQ, Steak'n Shake, Subway, Wendy's Comfort Inn, SpringHill Suites H, $Tree, Aldi Foods, AT&T, Beall's, Best Buy, Big Lots, BJ's Whse/gas, Books-A-Million, Chrysler/Dodge/Jeep, CVS Drug, Dick's, Dillard's, GNC, Goodyear/auto, Harley-Davidson, JC Penney, Jo-Ann Fabrics, Macy's, Marshall's, Michael's, Old Navy, PetCo, Ross, Target, Tire Kingdom, Tuesday Morning, Tuffy Auto, URGENT CARE, Verizon, Walmart, World Mkt
101a b	rd 46a, FL 417 (**toll**), FL 46, Sanford, Heathrow, N Applebee's, Coldstone, Crisper's, Duffy's Grill, F&D Cafe, FishBones, Friendly Confines Grill, McDonald's, Moe's SW Grill, Papa Joe's Pizza, Ruth's Chris Steaks, Shula's 347 Grill, Subway, Terra Mia Pizza Hampton Inn, Marriott, Residence Inn, Westin Publix, URGENT CARE, Walgreens, S Giovanni's, Jersey Mike's, Marco's Pizza, Smokey Joe's BBQ 7-11, Acura, CarMax, CVS Drug, Honda, Infiniti, Kohl's, Mercedes, Publix, Sam's Club/gas, Toyota
98	Lake Mary Blvd, Heathrow, N Shell Casey's Grill, Luigino's Italian, Panera Bread, RW Blue Grill, Stonewood Grill, Subway Courtyard, Hyatt Place CVS Drug, Walgreens, Winn-Dixie, S 7-11, BP/24hr, Marathon/Kangaroo/dsl, Mobil/dsl Arby's, Baskin-Robbins/Dunkin Donuts, Bob Evans,
98	Continued Boston Mkt, Burger Fi, Burger King, Chick-fil-A, Chili's, China King, Chipotle Mexican, Chop Stix, Domino's, Dunkin Donuts, Firehouse Subs, Fred's Mkt, Jason's Deli, Jimmy John's, KFC, Longhorn Steaks, Marble Slab, McDonald's, Mikado Japanese, Noodles&Co, Panera Bread, Papa Joe's Pizza, Papa John's, Papa Murphy's, Starbucks, Steak'n Shake, Subway, Taco Bell, Tilted Kilt, Wendy's, Which Wich? Candlewood Suites, Extended Stay America, Hilton Garden, Homewood Suites, La Quinta Advance Parts, AT&T, Fresh Mkt, GNC, Goodyear/auto, Home Depot, Office Depot, Petsmart, Publix, Ross, Staples, Target, Tires+, TJ Maxx, USPO, Verizon, Walgreens
95mm	**both lanes, 24hr security, full facilities, litter barrels, petwalk, , , vending**
94	FL 434, to Winter Springs, Longwood, N 7-11, Chevron, Mobil/7-11/dsl Burger King, China Gate, FirstWatch Cafe, Imperial Dynasty, Jimmy John's, Kobe Japanese, Melting Pot Rest., Mykonos Greek, Panera Bread, Papa Joe's Pizza, Starbucks, Starbucks, Tijuana Flats, Wendy's CVS Drug, Publix, vet, S Bonefish Grill, Boston Mkt, Carmela's Rest., Pickle's NY, Smokehouse H
92	FL 436, Altamonte Springs, N 7-11, Chevron/dsl, Shell/Circle K/dsl Boston Mkt, Checkers, Chick-fil-A, Chipotle Mexican, ChuckeCheese, Cracker Barrel, Kobe Japanese, Little Caesar's, Longhorn Steaks, McDonald's, Olive Garden, Perkins, Pollo Tropical, Popeye's, Red Lobster, Sweet Tomatoes, Taco Bell, Twin Peaks, Waffle House, WingHouse Days Inn, Hampton Inn, Howard Johnson, Quality Inn, Ramada, Remington Inn, Residence Inn, SpringHill Suites Best Buy, CVS Drug, Family$, Firestone/auto, O'Reilly Parts, Tire Kingdom, U-Haul, URGENT CARE, Walgreens, S BP/Circle K, Chevron, Mobil/dsl, Speedway/dsl Bahama Breeze, Burger King, Chili's, Coldstone, Denny's, Duffy's Grill, Dunkin Donuts, Five Guys, Jason's Deli, Moe's SW Grill, Orlando Alehouse, Panda Express, Pei Wei, Starbucks, Steak'n Shake, Subway, Wendy's Embassy Suites, Extended Stay America, Hilton H, Advance Parts, Albertson's, AT&T, Barnes&Noble, CVS Drug, Dillard's, JC Penney, Marshall's, PetCo, Publix, Ross, Whole Foods Mkt
90b a	FL 414, Maitland Blvd, N 7-11 Applebee's, Chick-fil-A, Oak Grill, Wendy's Extended Stay America, Extended Stay America (2), Homewood Suites, Sheraton, S Maitland Art C
88	FL 423, Lee Rd, N 7-11 Christner's Rest., IHOP, Little Caesar's, LJ Silver/Taco Bell, McDonald's, Popeye's, Shell Rest., Wild Rice Buffet Europe Inn, InTown Suites, Motel 6, Quality Inn Advance Parts, Family$, Firestone/auto, Home Depot, O'Reilly Parts, VW, S Chevron/dsl, Sunoco Denny's Aamco, BMW
87	FL 426, Fairbanks Ave (no eb re-entry), N Speedway/Dunkin Donuts/dsl
86	Par St (from eb, no re-entry), S Shell/Circle K
85	Princeton St, S 7-11 Wendy's Comfort Suites
84	FL 50, Colonial Dr, Ivanhoe Blvd, N Crowne Plaza
83b	US 17, US 92, FL 50, Amelia St (from eb), N Crowne Plaza
83a	FL 526 (from eb), Robinson St
83	South St (from wb), downtown
82c	Anderson St E, Church St Sta Hist Dist, downtown
82b	Gore Ave (from wb), S H, downtown
82a	FL 408 (**toll**), to FL 526
81b c	Kaley Ave, S Mobil H

DELTONA

HEATHROW

ALTAMONTE SPGS

FL

INTERSTATE 4 Cont'd

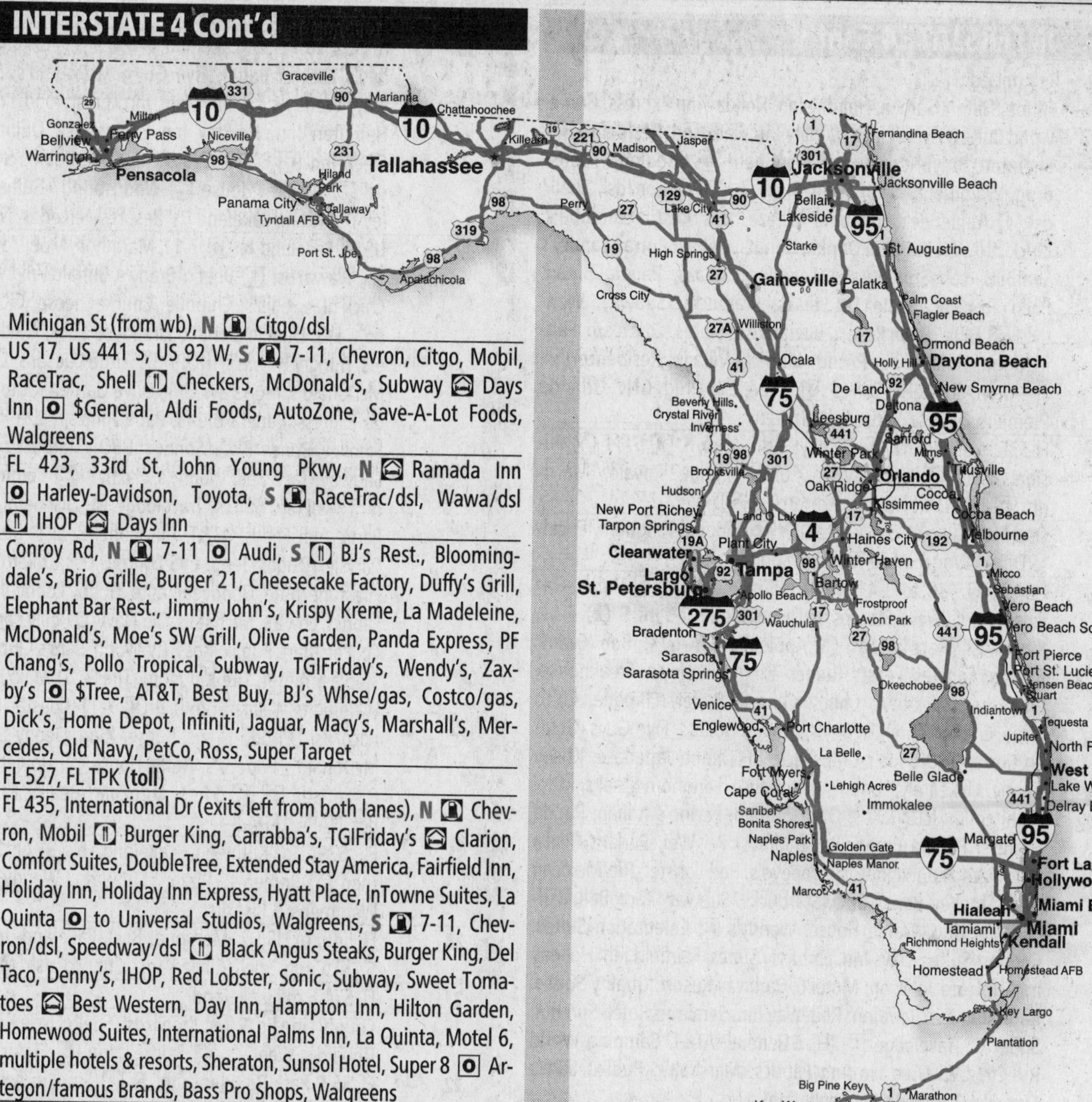

ORLANDO

81a Michigan St (from wb), N Citgo/dsl

80b a US 17, US 441 S, US 92 W, S 7-11, Chevron, Citgo, Mobil, RaceTrac, Shell Checkers, McDonald's, Subway Days Inn $General, Aldi Foods, AutoZone, Save-A-Lot Foods, Walgreens

79 FL 423, 33rd St, John Young Pkwy, N Ramada Inn Harley-Davidson, Toyota, S RaceTrac/dsl, Wawa/dsl IHOP Days Inn

78 Conroy Rd, N 7-11 Audi, S BJ's Rest., Bloomingdale's, Brio Grille, Burger 21, Cheesecake Factory, Duffy's Grill, Elephant Bar Rest., Jimmy John's, Krispy Kreme, La Madeleine, McDonald's, Moe's SW Grill, Olive Garden, Panda Express, PF Chang's, Pollo Tropical, Subway, TGIFriday's, Wendy's, Zaxby's $Tree, AT&T, Best Buy, BJ's Whse/gas, Costco/gas, Dick's, Home Depot, Infiniti, Jaguar, Macy's, Marshall's, Mercedes, Old Navy, PetCo, Ross, Super Target

77 FL 527, FL TPK (**toll**)

75b a FL 435, International Dr (exits left from both lanes), N Chevron, Mobil Burger King, Carrabba's, TGIFriday's Clarion, Comfort Suites, DoubleTree, Extended Stay America, Fairfield Inn, Holiday Inn, Holiday Inn Express, Hyatt Place, InTowne Suites, La Quinta to Universal Studios, Walgreens, S 7-11, Chevron/dsl, Speedway/dsl Black Angus Steaks, Burger King, Del Taco, Denny's, IHOP, Red Lobster, Sonic, Subway, Sweet Tomatoes Best Western, Day Inn, Hampton Inn, Hilton Garden, Homewood Suites, International Palms Inn, La Quinta, Motel 6, multiple hotels & resorts, Sheraton, Sunsol Hotel, Super 8 Artegon/famous Brands, Bass Pro Shops, Walgreens

74b N Universal Studios (from wb)

74a FL 482, Sand Lake Rd, N 7-11, Chevron Chick-fil-A, Dunkin a Donuts, Fresca Italian, McDonald's, O'Charley's, Pei Wei, Wendy's, Zoe's Kitchen Drury Inn H, $Tree, GNC, Michael's, Publix, Tire Kingdom, Walgreens, Walmart/McDonald's, Whole Food Mkt, S BP/Circle K/dsl, Shell/Circle K/dsl Bahama Breeze, BJ's Rest., Boston Lobster, Brickhouse Grill, Buffalo Wild Wings, Burger King, Capital Grille, Carrabba's, Charley's Steaks, Checkers, Chili's, China Jade, ChuckECheese, Chuy's Mexican, CiCi's Pizza, Coldstone, Dave&Buster's, Del Frisco's, Denny's, Domino's, Don Pablo's, Fish Bones Rest., Friendly's, Golden Corral, Hooters, IHOP, Joe's Crabshack, Kobe Japanese, Longhorn Steaks, Maggiano's, McDonald's, Miller's Alehouse, Ming Court, Olive Garden, Outback Steaks, Panda Express, Perkins, Pizza Hut, Ponderosa, Popeye's, Red Robin, Senor Frogs, Subway, TGIFriday's, Tommy Bahama's, Tony Roma, Twin Peaks, Uno, Vito's Chophouse, Yardhouse Avanti Resort, Best Western, Castle Hotel, Comfort Inn, Courtyard, Crowne Plaza, EconoLodge, Embassy Suites, Extended Stay America, Fairfield Inn, Hampton Inn, Hampton Inn (2), Holiday Inn Express, Homewood Suites, Hyatt Place, Hyatt Regency, La Quinta, La Quinta (2), Ramada Inn, Residence Inn, Rosen Suites, Sonesta Suites, Springhill Suites, Wyndham Resort Harley-Davidson, Ripley's Believe-it-or-not!, Walgreens

ORLANDO

72 FL 528 E (**toll**, no eb re-entry), to Cape Canaveral, N USPO, S Hilton to ✈

71 Central FL Pkwy (from eb no re-entry), S 7-11/dsl, Chevron, Wawa/dsl Bonefish Grill, Buffalo Wild Wings, KFC, McDonald's, Mellow Mushroom, Panera Bread, Starbucks, Taco Bell, TGIFridays, Wendy's Fairfield Inn, Hampton Inn, Hilton Garden, Renaissance Resort, Residence Inn, Springhill Suites, to SeaWorld CVS, Publix, Walgreens

68 FL 535, Lake Buena Vista, N 7-11, Mobil/dsl, Shell/Circle K/dsl AleHouse, Black Angus Steaks, Black Fire Brazilian Steaks, Buffalo Wild Wings, Burger King, Chevy's Mexican, Chili's, China Buffet, CiCi's Pizza, Denny's, Domino's, Dragon Super Buffet, Dunkin Donuts, El Patron, Firehouse Subs, Flipper's Pizzaria, Fuddrucker's, Giordano's, Hooters, IHOP, Jamba Juice, Joe's Crabshack, Johnnie's Rest., Kobe Japanese, Macaroni Grill, McDonald's, Noodles&Co, Olive Garden, Papa John's, Perkins, Pizza Hut, Qdoba, Red Lobster, Seadog Brewing, Shoney's, Sofrito Latin Cafe, Steak'n Shake, Subway, Sweet Tomatoes, Taco Bell, TGIFriday's, The Knife Argentinian Steaks, Tom+Chee, Uno, Waffle House B Resort, Clarion, Comfort Inn, Courtyard, Delta Orlando, DoubleTree, Embassy Suites, Extended Stay America, Fairfield Inn, Hampton Inn, Hawthorn Suites,

FL

INTERSTATE 4 Cont'd

ORLANDO

68 Continued
Hilton, Hilton Garden, Holiday Inn, Holiday Inn Express, Homewood Suites, Hyatt Place, Quality Inn, Radisson, Residence Inn, Sheraton, StayBridge Suites, Wyndham Gooding's Foods/drug, Walgreens, Winn Dixie, **S** 7-11, Chevron/dsl, Shell/dsl Applebee's, Bahama Breeze, BJ's Rest., Carrabba's, Chick-fil-A, CiCi's Pizza, Dunkin Donuts, Golden Corral, Landry's Seafood, LoneStar Steaks, Longhorn Steaks, Panera Bread, Pollo Tropical, Santa Fe Steaks, Starbucks, Subway, Wendy's Blue Heron Resort, Buena Vista Suites, Courtyard, Fairfield Inn, Holiday Inn Resort, Marriott Village, Residence Inn, Sheraton, SpringHill Suites $Tree, CVS Drug, GNC, Orlando Premium Outlets, Verizon, Walgreens

67 Fl 536, to Epcot, **N** DisneyWorld, **1 mi**, **S** 7-11 Fusion Rest. Buena Vista Suites, Caribe Royale, Marriott CVS Drug, multiple resorts, to

65 Osceola Pkwy, to FL 417 (**toll**), **N** Animal Kingdom, Epcot, to DisneyWorld, Wide World of Sports

64b a US 192, FL 536, to FL 417 (**toll**), to Kissimmee, **N** Harley-Davidson, Hollywood Studios, to DisneyWorld, **0-3 mi**, **S** 7-11, Mobil/dsl, RaceTrac/dsl Applebee's, Arby's, Bob Evans, Boston Lobster Feast, Burger King, Charley's Steakhouse, Checkers, Chick-fil-A, Chili's, Chinese Buffet, Chipotle, CiCi's Pizza, Cracker Barrel, Denny's, Dunkin Donuts, Five Guys, Golden Corral, IHOP, Joe's Crabshack, KFC, Kobe Japanese, Krispy Kreme, Little Italy, Logan's Roadhouse, Longhorn Steaks, Macaroni Grill, McDonald's, Olive Garden, Pacino's Italian, Panda Express, Panera Bread, Papa John's, Pei Wei, Perkins, Pizza Hut, Pizza Hut, Ponderosa, Popeye's, Red Lobster, Rio Mexican Grill, Smokey Bones BBQ, Starbucks, Subway, Taco Bell, TGIFriday's, Uno, Waffle House, Wendy's Celebration Suites, Comfort Suites, Days Inn, Embassy Suites, Fairfield Inn, Holiday Inn, Howard Johnson, Motel 6, Parkway Resort, Quality Suites, Radisson, Red Roof Inn, Rodeway Inn, Seralago Hotel, Sun Inn, Super 8, Travelodge H, $General, AT&T, Camping World RV Ctr, CVS Drug, Jo-Ann Fabrics, Marshall's, Publix, Sam's Club/dsl, Target, USPO, Walgreens

62 FL 417 (**toll**, from eb), World Dr, Celebration, **N** to Disney-World, **S** to

60 Fl 429 N (**toll**), Apopka

58 FL 532, to Kissimmee, **N** 7-11, BP/Circle K/dsl Chili's, China One, Dunkin Donuts, McDonald's, Pizzaria, Subway, Wendy's Championship Gate Resort Publix, Walgreens, **S** Reunion Resort (2mi)

55 US 27, to Haines City, **N** 7-11, Chevron/dsl, Loves/Arby's/dsl/scales/24hr, Sunoco/dsl Burger King, Cracker Barrel, Denny's, McDonald's, Waffle House, Wendy's Comfort Inn, Hampton Inn, Holiday Inn Express, Quality Inn FL Camp Inn (5mi), Ford, **S** 7-11, Marathon/dsl, RaceTrac/dsl, Wawa/dsl Bob Evans, CiCi's Pizza, Davenport's Ale House, Grand China, Perkins, Popeye's, Sake Steaks, Subway, Taco Bell Days Inn, Ramada Inn H, $Tree, AT&T, Best Buy, Books-A-Million, Deer Creek RV Resort, Dick's, Family$, GNC, JC Penney, KOA, Michael's, Petsmart, Ross, Staples, Target, Theme World RV Park, to Cypress Gardens, tourist info

48 rd 557, to Winter Haven, Lake Alfred, **S** Marathon/dsl

46mm **both lanes, 24hr security, full facilities, litter barrels, petwalk, , vending**

44 FL 559, to Auburndale, **S** Loves/Arby's/dsl/scales/24hr, Shell/Subway/dsl/scales/24hr

41 FL 570 W **toll**, Auburndale, Lakeland

LAKELAND

38 FL 33, to Lakeland, Polk City

33 rd 582, to FL 33, Lakeland, **N** 7-11, Exxon/dsl Applebee's, Cracker Barrel, Five Guys, McDonald's, Starbucks, Subway, Wendy's Baymont Inn, Crestwood Suites, Days Inn, Hampton Inn, Holiday Inn Express, La Quinta, Quality Inn, Sleep Inn BMW, CVS Drug, GNC, Publix, **S** Marathon/dsl Waffle House Woodspring Suites H, Harley-Davidson, Lakeland RV Resort, Mercedes, Nissan

32 US 98, Lakeland, **N** 7-11, Marathon, Mobil/dsl, Murphy USA/dsl, Wawa/dsl Beef o' Brady's, Buffalo Wild Wings, Checkers, Chick-fil-A, Chili's, Chipotle, ChuckeCheese, CiCi's Pizza, Domino's, DQ, Dunkin Donuts, Firehouse Subs, Golden Corral, Hooters, Hungry Howie's, IHOP, KFC, Little Caesar's, Longhorn Steaks, McDonald's, Moe's SW Grill, Olive Garden, Outback Steaks, Panda Express, Panera Bread, Papa John's, Pizza Hut, Red Lobster, Smokey Bones BBQ, Sonny's BBQ, Starbucks, Steak'n Shake, Subway, Taco Bell, Wendy's, Zaxby's Comfort Inn, La Quinta, TownPlace Suites, Travelodge $General, $Tree, Advance Parts, Aldi Foods, AT&T, AutoZone, Beall's, Best Buy, Big Lots, Chrysler/Dodge/Jeep, CVS Drug, Dick's, Dillard's, Discount Tire, Firestone/auto, Goodyear/auto, Hobby Lobby, JC Penney, JoAnn Fabrics, Lowe's, Michael's, Old Navy, O'Reilly Parts, PepBoys, PetCo, Petsmart, Publix, Ross, RV World, Sam's Club/gas, Save a Lot, Staples, Target, Tire Kingdom, Tires+, TJ Maxx, Toyota, Verizon, Walgreens, Walmart (2mi), **S** 7-11, Coastal, RaceTrac/dsl, Sunoco/dsl Bob Evans, Burger King, Denny's, Dunkin Donuts, McDonald's, Popeye's, Waffle House Howard Johnson, Motel 6, Ramada H, $Tree, AutoZone, Beall's, Family$, Home Depot, NAPA, U-Haul

31 FL 539, to Kathleen, Lakeland, **N** Circle K/dsl, Marathon Romeo's Pizza, Subway, Wendy's Publix/dsl Walgreens, **S** hist dist

28 FL 546, to US 92, Memorial Blvd, Lakeland (from eb re-entry) **S** Citgo, Shell/Circle K/dsl, Sunoco/dsl Hardee's

27 FL 570 E **toll**, Lakeland

25 County Line Rd, **S** Mobil/dsl, Shell/Circle K/Subway McDonald's, Wendy's Fairfield Inn FL Air Museum

22 FL 553, Park Rd, Plant City, **N** Smokin Aces BBQ Chevrolet, **S** Shell/Circle K/Subway Arby's, Burger King Denny's, Popeye's Comfort Inn, Holiday Inn Express

21 FL 39, Alexander St, to Zephyrhills, Plant City, **S on FL 39** BP dsl, Mobil/dsl Knights Inn, Red Rose Inn/rest.

19 FL 566, to Thonotosassa, **N** Marathon/dsl, **S** RaceTrac dsl, Wawa/dsl Applebee's, BuddyFreddy's Rest., Burger King, Carrabba's, Lin's Chinese, Little Caesar's, McDonald's, Mi Casa, OutBack Steaks, Pizza Hut/Taco Bell, Sonny's BBQ, Starbucks, Subway, Waffle House Hampton Inn H, $General, AT&T, GNC, Publix, Walgreens

MANGO

17 Branch Forbes Rd, **N** Citgo/dsl, Marathon/dsl Dinosaur World, **S** BP, Citgo/dsl, Shell/Circle K/Subway/dsl Advance Parts, AutoZone

14 McIntosh Rd, **N** BP/dsl Camping World RV Ctr, Windward RV Park (2mi), **S** 7-11/dsl, Marathon/dsl, Race Way/dsl, Speedway/dsl Burger King, McDonald's/playplace East Tampa RV Park, General RV Ctr, Tampa RV Ctr

12mm **weigh sta both lanes**

10 rd 579, Mango, Thonotosassa, **N** FLYING J/Denny's/dsl/LP/scales/24hr, Sunoco, TA/Arby's/Popeye's/dsl/scales/24hr/ Bob Evans, Cracker Barrel Country Inn&Suites, Hampton Inn Ford/Lincoln, Hillsboro River SP, Lazy Day's RV Ctr Resort, **S** Shell/Circle K/dsl Hardee's, Subway, Wendy's Masters Inn

FL

INTERSTATE 4 Cont'd

TAMPA

Exit #	Services
9	I-75, N to Ocala, S to Naples
7	US 92W, to US 301, Hillsborough Ave, N Mobil/dsl, Mobil/rest./dsl/scales/24hr, Wawa/dsl Waffle House Hard Rock Hotel/casino, S BP, Speedway/Dunkin Donuts/dsl, Wawa/dsl Five Guys, WingHouse Comfort Suites, Holiday Inn Express, La Quinta, Red Roof Inn FL Expo Fair
6	Orient Rd (from eb)
5	FL 574, MLK Blvd, N McDonald's truck/rv wash, S BP, Mobil, Sunoco/Subway Wendy's Fairfield Inn Kenworth
3	US 41, 50th St, Columbus Dr (exits left from eb), N Chevron/dsl, Shell/Subway/dsl Days Inn, Quality Inn $General, to Busch Gardens, S Marathon/dsl, Sunoco/Circle K/dsl Burger King, Checkers, Church's, KFC, McDonald's, Salem's Subs, Subway, Taco Bell Rodeway Inn Advance Parts, Family$, Save-A-Lot, URGENT CARE
1	FL 585, 22nd, 21st St, Port of Tampa, S Sunoco Burger King, McDonald's museum

I-4 begins/ends on I-275, exit 45b.

INTERSTATE 10

JACKSONVILLE

Exit #	Services
363mm	**I-10 begins/ends on I-95, exit 351b.**
362	Stockton St, to Riverside, S BP, Gate H
361	US 17 S (from wb)
360	FL 129, McDuff Ave, S Sunoco Popeye's
359	Luna St, to Lenox Ave (from wb)
358	FL 111, Cassat Ave, N Shell/Subway/dsl, Sunoco/Godfather's/Quiznos/dsl Burger King, McDonald's, Popeye's AutoZone, S BP/dsl, RaceWay/dsl Baskin-Robbins/Dunkin Donuts, Domino's, Krispy Kreme, Pizza Hut, Royal Buffet, Taco Bell, Wendy's Advance Parts, Discount Tire, Lowe's, Walgreens
357	FL 103, Lane Ave, N CNG, Speedway/dsl Andy's Sandwiches Knights Inn, Stars Rest Inn, S BP, Shell/dsl Applebee's, Bono's BBQ, Cross Creek Steaks, Hardee's, KFC, Lee's Dragon, McDonald's Diamond Inn, Sleep Inn CVS Drug, Firestone/auto, Home Depot, Office Depot, PepBoys
356	I-295, N to Savannah, S to St Augustine
355	Marietta, N Flash, S Speedway/Dunkin Donuts/dsl Domino's
354	Hammond Blvd
351	FL 115, Chaffee Rd, to Cecil Fields, N Kangaroo/dsl $General, Campers RV Ctr, S Shell/Subway/dsl, Valero Cracker Barrel, King Wok, McDonald's, Mr Chubby's Wings, Perard's Italian, Subway, Wendy's Best Western, Fairfield Inn, Hampton Inn, Holiday Inn Express Family$, Winn-Dixie
350	FL 23, Cecil Commerce Ctr Pkwy
343	US 301, to Starke, Baldwin, S Pilot/Subway/dsl/scales/24hr, TA/Shell/Arby's/dsl/scales/24hr/@, Valero Burger King, McDonald's, Waffle House Red Roof Inn
336	FL 228, to Maxville, Macclenny, N Murphy USA/dsl Starbucks H, fireworks, GNC, Walmart/Subway
335	FL 121, to Lake Butler, Macclenny, N Mobil, Shell/dsl China Dragon, Crystal River Seafood, Domino's, Firehouse Subs, Hardee's, KFC, Krystal, McDonald's, Pier 6, Pizza Hut, Subway, Taco Bell, Waffle House, Wendy's, Woody's BBQ, Zaxby's Motel 6 H, $General, $Tree, Advance Parts,

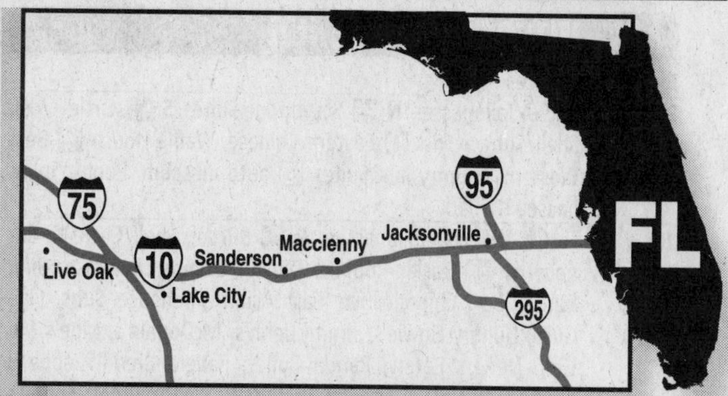

LAKE CITY LIVE OAK

Exit #	Services
335	Continued AutoZone, Save-A-Lot Foods, USPO, Verizon, vet, Walgreens, Winn-Dixie, S Exxon/dsl, RaceWay/dsl Burger King, China Buffet, San Jose Mexican EconoLodge, Travelodge
333	rd 125, Glen Saint Mary, N Citgo/dsl/e85
327	rd 229, to Raiford, Sanderson
324	US 90, to Olustee, Sanderson, S Mobil/dsl, Osceola NF, to Olustee Bfd
318mm	**both lanes, 24hr security, full facilities, litter barrels, petwalk, , vending**
303	US 441, Lake City, N Chevron/dsl Lake City Camping (1mi), Lake City RV Resort, S Shell/dsl, Sunoco/dsl Huddle House Days Inn H
301	US 41, to Lake City, N Marathon/Busy Bee/dsl to Stephen Foster Ctr, S H
296b a	I-75, N to Valdosta, S to Tampa
294mm	**both lanes, 24hr security, full facilities, litter barrels, petwalk, , vending**
292	rd 137, to Wellborn
283	US 129, to Live Oak, N Busy Bee/Burger King/Dunkin Donuts/dsl/24hr, to Boys Ranch, S BP, Chevron/dsl, Exxon/dsl, Murphy USA/dsl, Shell/dsl China Buffet, Hungry Howie's, Krystal, McDonald's, Subway, Taco Bell, Waffle House, Wendy's, Zaxby's EconoLodge, Holiday Inn Express, Quality Inn H, $Tree, GNC, Lowe's, Verizon, Walmart
275	US 90, Live Oak, N to Suwannee River SP, S H
271mm	**truck insp sta both lanes**
269mm	Suwannee River
265mm	**both lanes, 24hr security, full facilities, litter barrels, petwalk, , vending**
264mm	**weigh sta both lanes**
262	rd 255, Lee, N to Suwannee River SP, S Jimmy's/Chevron/Red Onion Grill/dsl/scales/24hr/@, Loves/Arby's/dsl/scales/24hr
258	FL 53, N Chevron/McDonald's/dsl, Mobil/DQ/Subway/Wendy's/dsl/scales/24hr Denny's, Waffle House Best Western, Days Inn, Super 8 H, S Deerwood Inn Jellystone Camping, Madison Camping
251	FL 14, to Madison, N Mobil/Arby's/24hr H
241	US 221, Greenville, N Mobil/DQ
234mm	**both lanes, 24hr security, full facilities, litter barrels, petwalk, ,**
233	rd 257, Aucilla, N Shell/dsl
225	US 19, to Monticello, N Camper's World Camping, S Chevron/McDonald's/dsl, Mobil/Arby's/dsl, Sunoco/dsl Days Inn, Super 8 A Stones Throw RV Park, KOA
217	FL 59, Lloyd, S BP/rest/dsl/scales/24hr, Shell/Subway/dsl EconoLodge

FL

INTERSTATE 10 Cont'd

Exit #	Services
209b a	US 90, Tallahassee, N Staybridge Suites, S Circle K/dsl, Shell/Subway/dsl Eastern Chinese, Waffle House Best Western, Country Inn&Suites auto museum, Publix, Tallahassee RV Park
203	FL 61, US 319, Tallahassee, N BP/dsl, Shell/Circle K, Sunoco/dsl Baskin-Robbins/Dunkin Donuts, Bonefish Grill, Burger Bar, Chipotle, Far East Asian, Firehouse Subs, Five Guys, Hungry Howie's, Jimmy John's, McDonald's, Moe's SW Grill, Newk's Eatery, Panda Buffet, Panera Bread, Pepper's Cantina, Popeye's, Shogun Japanese, Smashburger, Sonny's BBQ, Starbucks, Subway, Taco Bell, Trader Joe's, Waffle House, Wendy's, Which Wich? $Tree, AT&T, Books-A-Million, CVS Drug, Discount Tire, Fresh Mkt Foods, GNC, Hobby Lobby, Petco, Publix, SteinMart, SuperLube, TJ Maxx, Walgreens, Walmart (3mi), S Citgo, Marathon/dsl Carrabba's, Chick-fil-A, McDonald's, Osaka Japanese, Outback Steaks, Steak'n Shake, Subway, Ted's MT Grill, TGIFriday's, TX Roadhouse, Village Inn, Zaxby's Courtyard, Extended Stay America, Hampton Inn, Hilton Garden, Holiday Inn Express, Mainstay Suites, Residence Inn H, Advance Parts, Goodyear/auto, Home Depot, Infiniti, Office Depot, O'Reilly Parts, Petsmart, U-Haul, URGENT CARE
199	US 27, Tallahassee, N Chevron/dsl, Kangaroo/dsl, McKenzie/dsl Burger King, Domino's, McDonald's, Papa John's, Pizza Hut, Starbucks, Subway, Taco Bell, Waffle House Baymont Inn, Baymont Inn, Best Western, Country Inn&Suites, Fairfield Inn, Holiday Inn, Microtel, Quality Inn $General, Ace Hardware, Advance Parts, AutoZone, Big Oak RV Park (2mi), CVS Drug, Family$, USPO, vet, Walgreens, Walmart, Winn-Dixie, S Chevron/dsl, Shell, Shell/Circle K Arby's, Boston Mkt, Chick-fil-A, China Buffet, ChuckECheese, Cracker Barrel, Crystal River Seafood, Denny's, DQ, Dunkin Donuts, El Jalisco, Firehouse Subs, Golden Corral, Guthrie's, Hardee's, Hooters, IHOP, Kacey's Rest, Krispy Kreme, Little Caesar's, Longhorn Steaks, McDonald's, Melting Pot, Papa John's, Red Lobster, Sonic, Sonny's BBQ, Starbucks, Subway, Wendy's, Whataburger, Zaxby's EconoLodge, Howard Johnson, La Quinta, Motel 6, Red Roof Inn, Rodeway Inn, Suburban Hotel, Travelodge, Wingate Advance Parts, AT&T, AutoZone, Barnes&Noble, Belk, city park, CVS Drug, PepBoys, Publix, Ross, Staples, Sun Tire, Tuffy Auto, U-Haul, Verizon, vet, Walgreens
196	FL 263, Tallahassee, S Chevron/dsl, Inland/dsl, Murphy USA/dsl, Shell/dsl, Stop'n Save Gas Applebee's, DQ, Dunkin Donuts, Firehouse Subs, KFC, McDonald's, Sonic, Steak'n Shake, Subway, Taco Bell, Waffle House, Wendy's, Zaxby's Sleep Inn $Tree, Advance Parts, AutoZone, Chrysler/Dodge/Jeep, Harley-Davidson, Home Depot, Hyundai, Lowe's, Mazda, Office Depot, Toyota, Verizon, Walgreens, Walmart
194mm	**both lanes, 24hr security, full facilities, litter barrels, petwalk, vending**
192	US 90, to Tallahassee, Quincy, N FLYING J/Denny's/dsl/LP/scales/24hr, BP Comfort Inn, Howard Johnson Camping World RV Ctr (2mi), S Pilot/Subway/dsl/scales/24hr Waffle House Best Western
181	FL 267, Quincy, 1 mi N Murphy USA/dsl Domino's, Mayflower Chinese H, Walmart, S BP/dsl, Citgo/ds Hampton Inn, Holiday Inn Express, Parkway Inn, to Lake Talquin SF
174	FL 12, to Greensboro, N Marathon/dsl, Shell/Burger King/dsl
166	rd 270A, Chattahoochee, N to Lake Seminole, S Shell/dsl to Torreya SP, Triple C RV Park (1mi)
161mm	**both lanes, 24hr security, full facilities, litter barrels, petwalk, vending**
160mm	Apalachicola River, central/eastern time zone
158	rd 286, Sneads, N Lake Seminole, to Three Rivers SP
155mm	**weigh sta both lanes**
152	FL 69, to Grand Ridge, Blountstown, N Exxon/dsl, Marathon/dsl
142	FL 71, to Marianna, Oakdale, N Murphy USA/dsl, Pilot/Arby's/dsl/scales/24hr Beef'O'Brady's, Burger King, Firehouse Subs, Hong Kong Chinese, Pizza Hut, PoFolks, Ruby Tuesday, San Marco's Mexican, Sonny's BBQ, Waffle House Comfort Inn, Days Inn, Econolodge, Fairfield Inn, Marianna Inn, Microtel, Quality Inn, Super 8 H, $Tree, AT&T, Lowe's, to FL Caverns SP (8mi), Verizon, Walmart/Subway, S Chevron/dsl, TA/Pizza Hut/Popeye's/Taco Bell/dsl/scales/24hr/@ Dickey's BBQ, DQ, McDonald's Best Value Inn Dove Rest RV Park
136	FL 276, to Marianna, N to FL Caverns SP (8mi)
133mm	**both lanes, 24hr security, full facilities, litter barrels, petwalk**
130	US 231, Cottondale, N Chevron, Sunoco/dsl Hardee's, Subway, S Loves/Chester's/McDonald's/dsl/scales/24hr/@
120	FL 77, to Panama City, Chipley, N Exxon/Burger King/Stuckey's, Marathon/dsl, Murphy USA/dsl, Shell/dsl Angel's Buffet, Arby's, Cancun Mexican, Dunkin Donuts, Hardee's, Hungry Howie's, JinJin Chinese, KFC, McDonald's, Pizza Hut, Sonic, Subway, Waffle House, Wendy's Comfort Inn, Days Inn/rest., Executive Inn, Quality Inn, Super 8 H, $General, $Tree, Advance Parts, Brickyard Mkt, NAPA, O'Reilly Parts, Verizon, Walmart, S Falling Water SP
112	FL 79, Bonifay, N Chevron, Shell/dsl, Tom Thumb/dsl Burger King, Cancun Mexican, Castaway Cafe, Hardee's, Hungry Howie, McDonald's, Pizza Hut, Subway, Waffle House Bonifay Inn, Holiday Inn Express, Tivoli Inn H, FL Springs RV Camping, Fred's, S Panama City Beach
104	rd 279, Caryville
96	FL 81, Ponce de Leon, N $General, to Ponce de Leon SRA, Vortex Spring Camping (5mi), S **both lanes, 24hr security, full facilities, litter barrels, petwalk** Shell/dsl, Sunoco, Sunoco/Subway/dsl Ponce de Leon Motel
85	US 331, De Funiak Springs, N Murphy USA/dsl, Sunoco/dsl Arby's, Beef O'Brady's, Burger King, Hungry Howie's, McLain's Steaks, Pizza Hut, Sonic, Subway, Taco Bell, Waffle House Econolodge, Regency Inn, Sundown Inn, Super 8 $General, $Tree, AT&T, Buick/Chevrolet, Lowe's, Verizon, Walgreens, Walmart, winery, Winn-Dixie, S Sunoco, Sunoco/dsl, Sunoco/dsl KFC, McDonald's, Whataburger Best Western H
70	FL 285, to Ft Walton Bch, Eglin AFB, N Loves/McDonald's/Subway/dsl/scales24hr, RaceWay/dsl Sleep Inn I-10 Truck Ctr, S Econolodge Dixie RV Ctr
60mm	**both lanes, 24hr security, full facilities, litter barrels, petwalk, vending**
56	FL 85, Crestview, Eglin AFB, N BP/dsl, Mobil/Chester's/dsl Applebee's, Beef O'Brady's, Burger King, Capt D's, China 1, Dunkin Donuts, Firehouse Subs, Golden Asian, Hungry Howie's, Hunon Chinese, Krystal, Lenny's Subs, McDonald's, Mia's Italian, Panera Bread, Papa Murphy's, Ryan's, Sonic, Starbucks, Taco Bell Country Inn&Suites, EconoLodge H, $General,

FL

TALLAHASSEE

QUINCY

CHIPLEY

INTERSTATE 10 Cont'd

CRESTVIEW

56 Continued
Advance Parts, AT&T, AutoZone, BigLots, GNC, Lowe's, Publix, Staples, URGENT CARE, Verizon, Walgreens, Walmart, **S** Exxon/dsl, Tom Thumb/dsl Arby's, Cracker Barrel, Hardee's, Hooters, LaRumba Mexican, Waffle House, Wendy's, Whataburger, Zaxby's Baymont Inn, Best Value Inn, Comfort Inn, Holiday Inn Express, Quality Inn, Super 8 Buick/GMC, Chevrolet, Chrysler/Dodge/Jeep, Ford, Stay Suites

45 rd 189, to US 90, Holt, **N** Marathon (1mi) Eagle's Landing RV Park, to Blackwater River SP, **S** River's Edge RV Park (1mi)

31 FL 87, to Ft Walton Beach, Milton, **N** Exxon/dsl Waffle House Holiday Inn Express Blackwater River SP, KOA, **S** BP, Shell/dsl Blackwater Inn, Milton Inn

31mm **both lanes, 24hr security, full facilities, litter barrels, petwalk, ,**

28 rd 89, Milton, **N**

27mm Blackwater River

26 rd 191, Bagdad, Milton, **N** Shell/Circle K/dsl , $General, **S** Chevron/DQ/Stuckey's Pelican Palms RV Park

22 N FL 281, Avalon Blvd, **N** RaceWay/dsl, Tom Thumb McDonald's, **S** Shell/Circle K/Subway/dsl Waffle House Red Roof Inn Avalon Landing RV Park (3mi)

18mm Escambia Bay

17 US 90, Pensacola, **N** Marathon/dsl, **S** Exxon/DQ Quality Inn/rest.

PENSACOLA

13 FL 291, to US 90, Pensacola, **N** Exxon, Shell/dsl Arby's, Capt D's, Denny's, La Hacienda Mexican, McDonald's, Santino's Cafe, Subway, Taco Bell, Waffle House Comfort Inn, Days Inn, Holiday Inn, La Quinta , $Tree, CVS Drug, Ross, U-Haul, Walgreens, **S** Cheddar's, ChuckECheese, Dickey's BBQ, Egg&I Cafe, Fazoli's, HoneyBaked Ham, Jimmy John's, Moe's SW, O'Charley's, Shrimp Basket Rest, TX Roadhouse, Waffle House, Wendy's, Whataburger Baymont Inn, Best Value Inn, Courtyard, Econolodge, Extended Stay America, Fairfield Inn, Hampton Inn, Mainstay Suites, Red Roof Inn, Springhill Suites, Super 6 Inn, TownePlace Suites $General, Big Lots, Books-A-Million, Firestone/auto, GNC, Hobby Lobby, JC Penney, Jo-Ann Fabrics, Mr Transmission, PepBoys, Petsmart, TJ Maxx, Tuesday Morning, U-Haul, Verizon

12 I-110, to Pensacola, Hist Dist, Islands Nat Seashore

10b a US 29, Pensacola, **N** Kangaroo/dsl/scales, Murphy USA/dsl Church's, Hardee's, Ryan's, Sonic $Tree, Advance Parts, AT&T, AutoZone, Carpenter's RV Ctr, GNC, Office Depot, O'Reilly Parts, Tires+, Walmart, **0-2 mi**, **S** RaceWay/dsl, Shell/Circle K, Tom Thumb 3D Burgers, Capt D's, IHOP, McDonald's, Pizza Hut, Smokey's BBQ, Subway, Waffle House, Wendy's, Whataburger Best Value Inn, Executive Inn, Key West Inn, Luxury Suites, Magnuson Hotel, Motel 6, Pensacola Inn $General, Buick/Cadillac/GMC, Chevrolet, Chrysler/Dodge/Jeep, Ford, funpark, Harley-Davidson, Honda, Hyundai, Kia, Lincoln, Mazda, NAPA Autocare, Nissan, Subaru, Toyota

7b a Fl 297, Pine Forest Rd, **N** Chevron Beef'O'Brady's, Starbucks, Wendy's Best Western, Garden Inn, Quality Inn, Woodspring Suites Publix, transmissions, Walmart Mkt, **S** Raceway/dsl, Shell, Tom Thumb Burger King, Cracker Barrel, Hardee's, McDonald's, Ruby Tuesday, Sonny's BBQ, Subway, Waffle House, Wayne's Diner Country Inn&Suites, Days Inn, Econolodge, Hampton Inn, Holiday Inn Express, Red Roof Inn Big Lagoon SRA (12mi)

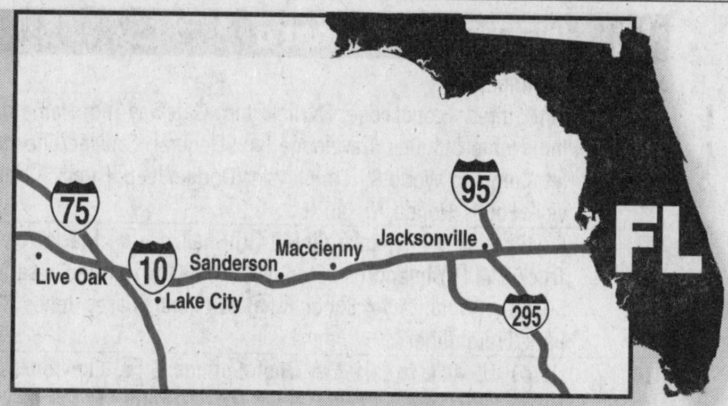

5 US 90 A, **N** Shell/Circle K, Shell/dsl Beef'O Brady's, Hot Head Burrito, Jersey Mike's, Ollie's Grill, Papa Murphy's, Starbucks, Wendy's AT&T, Publix/gas, Verizon, Walgreens, **S** Leisure Lakes Camping

4mm **Welcome Ctr eb, 24hr security, full facilities, info, litter barrels, petwalk, , , vending, wi-fi**

3mm **weigh sta both lanes**

1mm **inspection sta eb**

0mm Florida/Alabama state line, Perdido River

INTERSTATE 75

FL

Exit #	Services
471mm	Florida/Georgia state line
469mm	**Welcome Ctr sb, full facilities, info, litter barrels, petwalk, , , vending**
467	FL 143, Jennings, **W** Marathon/dsl N Florida Inn fireworks, Jennings Camping
460	FL 6, Jasper, **E** Indian River Fruit/gas, Marathon/Burger King/dsl, Marathon/Huddle House/dsl Budget Inn, **W** Pilot/Subway/dsl/scales/24hr, Shell/dsl, Sunoco/dsl American Inn Suwanee River SP
451	US 129, Jasper, Live Oak, **E** Loves/Arby's/dsl/scales/24hr, Mobil/DQ/Subway/dsl, **W** Marathon/Wendy's/dsl Suwanee Music Park (4mi), to FL Boys Ranch
448mm	**weigh sta both lanes**
446mm	insp sta both lanes
443mm	Historic Suwanee River
439	to FL 136, White Springs, Live Oak, **E** Gate/dsl/e-85, Shell/dsl McDonald's Suwanee RV Camping (4mi), to S Foster Ctr, **W** Best Value Inn
435	I-10, E to Jacksonville, W to Tallahassee
427	US 90, to Live Oak, Lake City, **E** Chevron/dsl, Exxon, Gas'n Go, Murphy USA/dsl, Shell/dsl Applebee's, Arby's, Buffalo Wild Wings, Burger King, Cedar River Seafood, Chef's Brazilian Steaks, Chick-fil-A, CiCi's, Cracker Barrel, Domino's, DQ, Dunkin Donuts, El Potro, Elliano's Coffee, Firehouse Subs, Gondolier Italian, Hardee's, IHOP, Krystal, Longhorn Steaks, McDonald's, Moe's SW Grill, Neapolitan Pizza, Ole Times Buffet, Olive Garden, Panda Express, Panera Bread, Papa John's, Pizza Hut, Red Lobster, Ruby Tuesday, Sonny's BBQ, Starbucks, Steak'n Shake, Subway, Taco Bell, TX Roadhouse, Waffle House, Wendy's, Zaxby's Best Inn, Cypress Inn, Days Inn, Driftwood Inn, Holiday Inn, Quality Inn, Ramada Ltd, Rodeway Inn , $Tree, Advance Parts, AT&T, AutoZone, Belk, BigLots, CVS Drug, Discount Tire, Ford/Lincoln, Home Depot, Inn&Out RV Park, JC Penney, Kia, Lowe's, Michael's, Petsmart, Publix, Tire Kingdom, TireMart, TJ Maxx, Toyota, Verizon, Walgreens, Walmart, **W** Chevron/dsl, Marathon/Subway, Shell/dsl, Sunoco Bob Evans, China One, Waffle House Best Value Inn, Comfort Suites, Country

LAKE CITY

INTERSTATE 75 Cont'd

LAKE CITY

427 Continued
Inn&Suites, EconoLodge, Fairfield Inn, Gateway Inn, Hampton Inn, Home 2 Suites, Travelodge $General, Cadillac/Chevrolet, Camping World RV Ctr, Chrysler/Dodge/Jeep, Family$, Harvey's Foods, Honda, Nissan

423 FL 47, to Ft White, Lake City, E Shell/dsl Mack/Volvo Trucks, W Inland/dsl, Stop-N-Go/USPO Little Caesar's, Subway, Wendy's Super 8 $General, Casey Jones RV Park, Freightliner

414 US 41, US 441, to Lake City, High Springs, E Chevron/dsl, Exxon, Pitstop Traveler's Inn $General, W Marathon/dsl, Shell/Wendy's/dsl Country Skillet, Subway antiques, to O'Leno SP (5 mi)

413mm **both lanes, 24hr security, full facilities, litter barrels, petwalk, vending**

409mm Santa Fe River

404 rd 236, to High Springs, E Chevron/fruits/gifts, Citgo/dsl, Marathon, W High Springs Camping

399 US 441, to High Sprs, Alachua, E BP, Kangaroo Domino's, El Toro, McDonald's, Mi Apa Latin Cafe, Moe's SW Grill, NY Pizza, Pizza Hut, Sonny's BBQ, Subway, Taco Bell, Waffle House EconoLodge, Quality Inn $General, Advance Parts, AT&T, AutoZone, CVS Drug, Family$, Hitchcock's Foods, Lowe's, Traveler's Campground (1mi), Verizon, vet, Walgreens, W Exxon/Kangeroo, Kangaroo/Wendy's, Mobil/Dunkin Donuts/dsl, RaceWay/dsl Hungry Howie's, Zaxby's Best Value Inn, Royal Inn Publix

GAINESVILLE

390 FL 222, to Gainesville, E Circle K/Subway/dsl, Marathon/McDonald's/dsl, Valero/dsl Burger King, Chan's Chinese, Pomodoro Cafe, Sonny's BBQ, Wendy's Publix, Walgreens, W Shell/DQ/Dunkin Donuts/dsl Wahoo Grill Best Western Harley-Davidson, vet

387 FL 26, to Newberry, Gainesville, E Chevron/dsl, Shell/dsl, Sunoco BJ's Rest., Bono's BBQ, Boston Mkt, Buffalo Wild Wings, Burger King, Dunkin Donuts, FoodCourt, HoneyBaked Ham, Jason's Deli, McAlister's Deli, McDonald's, Ocean Buffet, Panda Express, Panera Bread, Perkins, Red Lobster, Red Robin, Ruby Tuesday, Starbucks, Subway, Wendy's La Quinta H, AT&T, Belk, Books-A-Million, Dillard's, Hobby Lobby, JC Penney, Office Depot, PetCo, to UF, Verizon, W BP, Chevron/dsl, Exxon/dsl, Marathon/dsl Applebee's, Hardee's, Krystal, Moe's SW Grill, Napolatanos Rest., Peppers Mexican, Pizza Hut, Taco Bell, Waffle House Baymont Inn, Best Value Inn, Days Inn, EconoLodge, TownePlace Suites $Tree, Advance Parts, Goodyear/auto, Home Depot, K-Mart, PepBoys, Publix, tires/repair, TJ Maxx, vet, Walgreens

384 FL 24, to Archer, Gainesville, E Exxon/dsl, Shell, Valero/dsl Arby's, Asian Wok, Blaze Pizza, BoneFish Grill, Burger King, BurgerFi, Carrabba's, Chick-fil-A, Chili's, Chipotle Mexican, Chuy's Mexican, CiCi's Pizza, Coldstone, Domino's, DQ, Firehouse Subs, Five Guys, Gainesville Alehouse, Hungry Howie's, KFC, McAlister's Deli, McDonald's, Moe's SW Grill, Olive Garden, Outback Steaks, Panda Express, Panera Bread, Panera Bread, Papa John's, Pizza Hut, Pollo Tropical, Sonny's BBQ, Starbucks, Steak'n Shake, Subway, Taco Bell, TGIFriday's, Tijuana Flats, TX Roadhouse, Waffle House, Wendy's, Wing House, Zaxby's, Zoe's Kitchen Comfort Inn, Courtyard, Extended Stay America, Hampton Inn, Hilton Garden, Homewood Suites, Motel 6, Red Roof Inn, Residence Inn, Sleep Inn, SpringHill Suites, Super 8, The Lodge $Tree, AT&T, AutoZone, Best Buy, CVS Drug, Discount Tire, Firestone/auto, GNC, Jo-Ann, Kohl's,

384 Continued
Lowe's, Michael's, Old Navy, Petsmart, Publix, Publix, Ross, Target, Trader Joe's, Tuesday Morning, Verizon, Walgreens, Walmart, W Marathon/dsl Cracker Barrel Country Inn&Suites, Holiday Inn Express to Bear Museum

382 FL 121, to Williston, Gainesville, E Marathon/dsl, Mobil/dsl First Wok, Little Caesar's, McDonald's, Subway Publix, USPO, W Chevron/dsl, Circle K/dsl, Shell/dsl 43rd St Deli Quality Inn, Rodeway Inn, Woodspring Suites Fred Bear Museum

381mm **both lanes, 24hr security, full (handiacpped) facilities, litter barrels, petwalk, vending**

374 rd 234, Micanopy, E BP, Chevron/dsl antiques, to Paynes Prairie SP, W Micanopy Inn repair

368 rd 318, Orange Lake, E Jim's/BBQ, Petro/BP/Iron Skillet/dsl/scales/24hr/@ Wendy's Grand Lake RV Park (3mi), W Ocala N RV Camping

OCALA

358 FL 326, E Marathon/McDonald's/dsl, Pilot/Arby's/dsl/scales/24hr, Pilot/Wendy's/dsl/scales/24hr, Sunoco/FL Citrus Ctr/dsl auto/truck repair, Freightliner, W Love's/Chester's/Subway/dsl/scales/24hr, Shell/Circle K/dsl DQ

354 US 27, to Silver Springs, Ocala, E Marathon/dsl, RaceTrac/dsl Burger King, Rascal's BBQ Golden Palms Inn, W BP/dsl, Chevron/dsl, Shell/dsl Blanca's Cafe, China Taste, CiCi's, Darrell's Diner, McDonald's, Pizza Hut, Roma Italian, Subway Budget Host, Comfort Suites, Days Inn, Howard Johnson, Motel 6 $General, $Tree, AT&T, Family$, GNC, Nelson's Trailers, Oaktree Village Camping, Publix, Walgreens, Winn-Dixie

352 FL 40, to Silver Springs, Ocala, E Chevron/dsl, Mobil/Circle K/dsl, RaceTrac/dsl, Sunoco/dsl, Valero/dsl Dunkin Donuts, McDonald's, Subway, Taco Bell, Waffle House, Wendy's, Zaxby's Days Inn/café, Motor Inn/RV Family$, to Silver River SP (8mi), W Shell/dsl Burger King, Denny's, Waffle House Red Roof Inn, Super 8 Holiday Trav-L Park

350 FL 200, to Hernando, Ocala, **0-2 mi**, E BP/dsl, Citgo/dsl, Texaco/dsl Applebee's, Arby's, Black Bear Smokehouse, Bob Evans, Boston Mkt, Burger King, Carrabba's, Checkers, Chick-fil-A, Chili's, Chipotle, ChuckECheese, Cody's Roadhouse, Coldstone, Crisper's, Domino's, El Toreo Mexican, Firehouse Subs, Five Guys, Freddy's, Golden Corral, Hardee's, Hungry Howie's, Jersey Mike's, Jimmy John's, Krystal, Lee's Chicken, Logan's Roadhouse, Maddio's Pizza, McDonald's, Moe's SW Grill, Ocean Buffet, Olive Garden, Outback Steaks, Panda Express, Panera Bread, Papa John's, Papa Murphy's, PDQ Grill, Pizza Hut, Red Lobster, Ruby Tuesday, Smoothie King, Sonic, Sonny's BBQ, Starbucks, Stevie B's Pizza, Subway, Taco Bell, Wendy's, Yummy House, Zaxby's Country Inn&Suites, Hilton, La Quinta, Quality Inn H, $Tree, Acura, Advance Parts, Aldi Foods, Belk, Best Buy, Chevrolet, CVS Drug, Discount Tire, Goodyear/auto, Hobby Lobby, Home Depot, Honda, Hyundai, JC Penney, Jo-Ann Fabrics, Kia, Lowe's, Macy's, Mazda, Michael's, Nissan, Office Depot, O'Reilly Parts, PepBoys, Petsmart, Ross, Staples, Target, Tire Kingdom, TJ Maxx, Toyota, Tuesday Morning, Tuffy Auto, URGENT CARE, Verizon, Walgreens, Walmart, W Marathon, RaceTrac/dsl, Tesla EVC, Valero/Kangaroo Bonefish Grill, Burger King, Cracker Barrel, Crazy Cucumber, Dunkin Donuts, Edo Japanese, Gator's Dockside, KFC, Las Margaritas, McAlister's Deli, McDonald's, Mimi's Cafe, Panera Bread, Starbucks, Steak'n Shake, Tijuana Flats, Waffle House, Yamato Japanese Best Western, Courtyard, Fairfield Inn, Hampton Inn, Holiday Inn, Homewood Suites, Residence Inn,

INTERSTATE 75 Cont'd

INVERNESS

350 Continued
AT&T, Barnes&Noble, BMW, Buick/GMC, Cadillac, Dick's, Dillard's, Kohl's, Ocala RV Park, Old Navy, PetCo, Porsche, Sam's Club/gas, Tires+, Verizon, vet, VW, Walgreens

346mm **both lanes, 24hr security, full facilities, litter barrels, petwalk, , vending**

341 rd 484, to Belleview, E Exxon/dsl, Marathon/fruit, RaceTrac/dsl, Shell/dsl Baskin-Robbins/Dunkin Donuts, Cracker Barrel, KFC/Taco Bell, Sonny's BBQ, Zaxby's Microtel, Sleep Inn drag racing museum, FL Citrus Ctr, W Pilot/DQ/Wendy's/dsl/scales/24hr McDonald's, Subway, Waffle House Hampton Inn Ocala Sun RV Resort, outlets

338mm **weigh sta both lanes**

329 FL 44, to Inverness, Wildwood, E Marathon/dsl, Pilot/Steak'n Shake/dsl/scales/24hr, Sunoco Burger King, McDonald's, Waffle House, Wendy's FL Citrus Ctr, KOA, W Citgo/dsl/repair/24hr, Pilot/dsl/scales/24hr, TA/BP/Pizza Hut/Popeye's/Subway/dsl/scales/24hr/@ IHOP, KFC Budget Inn, Days Inn, Motel 6 truck repair, truckwash

328 FL TPK (from sb), to Orlando

321 rd 470, to Sumterville, Lake Panasoffkee, E Spirit/deli/dsl/scales/24hr Coleman Correctional, W Chevron/Circle K/dsl, Mobil/Hardee's/Subway/dsl Countryside RV Park, KOA

314 FL 48, to Bushnell, E Citgo, Murphy USA/dsl, Shell/Circle K/Subway Hong Kong Chinese, KFC/Taco Bell, Little Caesar's, McDonald's, Wendy's Bushnell Inn $Tree, AutoZone, BlueBerry Hill RV Camp, Red Oaks Camp (1mi), to Dade Bfd HS, Verizon, vet, Walmart, W Loves/Arby's/dsl/scales/24hr, Sunoco/dsl Beef'O'Brady's, Sonny's BBQ Microtel Flagship RV Ctr

309 rd 476, to Webster, E Breezy Oaks RV Park (1mi), Sumter Oaks RV Park (1mi)

307mm **both lanes, 24hr security, coffee, full facilities, litter barrels, petwalk, , vending**

DADE CITY

301 US 98, FL 50, to Dade City, E RaceTrac/dsl Beef'O'Brady's, Cracker Barrel, Dunkin Donuts, McDonald's, Monticello's Pizzaria, Subway, Taco Bell, Waffle House, Wendy's Days Inn, Holiday Inn Express $General, Advance Parts, Winn-Dixie, W Burger King Hampton Inn, Microtel, Quality Inn H

293 rd 41, to Dade City, E Citgo (2mi) to Sertoma Youth Ranch, W Travelers Rest Resort RV Park (3mi)

285 FL 52, to Dade City, New Port Richey, E Flying J/Denny's/dsl/LP/scales/24hr H, Blue Beacon

279 FL 54, to Land O' Lakes, Zephyrhills, E Speedway/Dunkin Donuts/dsl Applebee's, Burger King, Chili's, China Wok, City Grill, Gonna China, Las Vallartas, Papa's John's, Pizza Hut/Taco Bell, Sonny's BBQ, Subway, Waffle House, Wendy's Ace Hardware, Advance Parts, Beall's, Fiat, Ford, Happy Days RV Camping (9mi), Kia, Leasure Days RV Park (7mi), Nissan, Publix, Ralph's RV Camping (7mi), to Hillsborough River SP (18mi), Toyota, Walgreens, Walmart, W 7-11, Marathon, Mobil/Dunkin Donuts, Shell/Circle K/dsl Beef'O'Brady's, ChuckeCheese, Cody's Roadhouse, Cracker Barrel, DQ, Hardee's, Hungry Howie's, Marco's Pizza, McDonald's, Outback Steaks, Winghouse Best Western, EconoLodge, Rodeway Inn, Sleep Inn $General, $Tree, Advance Parts, Best Buy, Chevrolet, CVS Drug, Dick's, GNC, Goodyear/auto, Honda, Hyundai, Mazda, Michael's, Old Navy, Petsmart, Quail Run RV Camping, Ross, Tire Kingdom, TJ Maxx, Tuffy Auto, URGENT CARE, Verizon, Winn Dixie

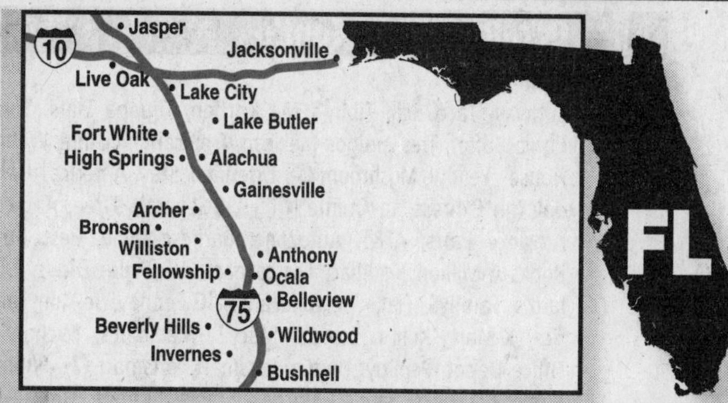

TAMPA

277mm **both lanes, 24hr security, full facilities, litter barrels, petwalk, , vending**

275 FL 56, Land O Lakes, Tarpon Springs, E BP/Dunkin Donuts/dsl, Gate/dsl, RaceTrac/dsl Buffalo Wild Wings, TX Roadhouse Hampton Inn, Holiday Inn Express Mercedes, Mini, Publix (2mi), vet, W Shell/dsl Abuelo's, Culver's Tampa Outlets/famous brands, Walgreens

274 I-275 (from sb), to Tampa, St Petersburg

270 rd 581, Bruce B Downs Blvd, E 7-11, Mobil, Shell/Circle K/Taco Bell/dsl, Speedway/dsl Baskin-Robbins/Dunkin Donuts, Boston Mkt, Chick-fil-A, Chili's, Chipotle, Coldstone, DQ, Glory Days Grill, Jimmy John's, Kobe Japanese, Kobe Japanese, Liang's Asian Bistro, McDonald's, Moe's SW Grill, Panera Bread, Papa John's, Pizza Hut, Ruby Tuesday, Senor T's, Starbucks, Steak'n Shake, Subway, TGIFriday's, Tijuana Flats, Wendy's Holiday Inn Express, La Quinta AT&T, Best Buy, CVS Drug, GNC, Home Depot, Kauffman Tire, Michael's, Publix, Tires+, Verizon, vet, Walgreens, Walmart/Subway, W 7-11 McDonald's, Olive Garden, Red Lobster, Stonewood Grill SpringHill Suites $Tree, BJ's Whse/Subway/gas, CVS Drug, Jo-Ann Fabrics, Lowe's, Petsmart, Ross, Staples, USPO

266 rd 582A, Fletcher Ave, W Shell/Circle K/dsl Baskin-Robbins/Dunkin Donuts, Bob Evans, Lenny's Subs, Starbucks, Wendy's Courtyard, Extended Stay America, Fairfield Inn, Hampton Inn, Hilton Garden, Holiday Inn Express, Residence Inn, Sleep Inn, Sleep Inn H

265 FL 582, Fowler Ave, Temple Terrace, E flea mkt, Happy Traveler RV Park, W Marathon, Sunoco, Value/dsl IHOP, Marco's Pizza Ramada Inn to Busch Gardens, to USF

261 I-4, W to Tampa, E to Orlando

260b a FL 574, to Mango, Tampa, E Citgo/dsl, Mobil, Shell/Circle K/Subway Baskin-Robbins/Dunkin Donuts, China Wok, Domino's, Waffle House Walgreens, Winn Dixie, W Citgo, Mobil Quality Inn, Residence Inn, Sheraton, Staybridge Suites Family$

257 FL 60, Brandon, E Mobil (2), Mobil/dsl, Shell/Circle K, Tesla EVC, WaWa/dsl Bahama Breeze, Boston Mkt, Brandon Ale House, Buffalo Wild Wings, Checkers, Cheddar's, Cheescake Factory, Chick-fil-A, Chili's, Chipotle, ChuckECheese, Corner Bakery Cafe, Denny's, Dunkin Donuts, Firehouse Subs, Firehouse Subs, Five Guys, Ford's Garage, Honeybaked Ham, Hungry Howie's, Jimmy John's, KFC, Kobe Japanese, Krispy Kreme, Little Caesar's, LJ Silver, Longhorn Steaks, Macaroni Grill, McDonald's, McDonald's (2), Mission BBQ, Moe's SW Grill, Olive Garden, Outback Steaks, Panda Express, Panera Bread, Papa John's, Popeye's, Portillo's, Qdoba, Red Lobster, Smokey Bones BBQ, Smoothie King, Starbucks, Steak'n Shake, Steak'n Shake,

FL

INTERSTATE 75 Cont'd

BRANDON

257 Continued
Subway, Taco Bell, Tibby's NO Kitchen, Tijuana Flats, Tops China Buffet, Tres Amigos Mexican, Tropical Smoothie, Waffle House, Yellow Mushroom [lodging] Extended Stay America, Holiday Inn Express, La Quinta [other] [H], $General, $Tree, Aamco, Advance Parts, AT&T, AutoZone, Barnes&Noble, Best Buy, Books-A-Million, Cadillac, Costco/gas, CVS Drug, Dick's, Dillard's, Family$, Fiat, Firestone/auto, JC Penney, Jo-Ann Fabrics, K-Mart, Kohl's, Lowe's, Macy's, Marshall's, Michael's, Office Depot, PepBoys, PetCo, Petsmart, Petsmart (2), Publix, Publix (2), Ross, Sam's Club/gas, Staples, Target, Tires+, TJ Maxx, Verizon, Walgreens, Walmart, **W** [gas] Citgo/dsl, Marathon, Shell [food] Bob Evans, Burger King, Hooters, McDonald's, Sonny's BBQ, Subway, Sweet Tomatoes, Wendy's [lodging] Clarion, Comfort Suites, Country Inn&Suites, Courtyard, Embassy Suites, Fairfield Inn, Homewood Suites, La Quinta, Motel 6, Red Roof Inn, SpringHill Suites [other] Bass Pro Shops, Buick/GMC, Chevrolet, Chrysler/Dodge/Jeep, Ford, Harley-Davidson, Home Depot, Honda, Hyundai, Kia, Mazda, Nissan, Office Depot, Toyota, VW

256 FL 618 W (**toll**), to Tampa

254 US 301, Riverview, **E** [gas] Thornton's/dsl, WaWa/dsl [food] Panda Express, Steak'n Shake [other] CVS Drug, Firestone/auto, Home Depot, Target, **W** [gas] 7-11/dsl [food] China 1, Crazy Cafe, Dunkin Donuts, McDonald's, Pizza Hut, Smokin' Pig BBQ, Starbucks, Subway [lodging] Hilton Garden [other] GNC, Publix

250 Gibsonton Dr, Riverview, **E** [gas] 7-11/dsl, RaceWay/dsl, Victory Lane/dsl, WaWa/dsl [food] Beef'O'Brady's, Burger King, DQ, Hungry Howie's, Jola Pizza, Little Caesar's, McDonald's, New China, Pizza Hut, Ruby Tuesday, Subway, Taco Bell, Wendy's [other] $Tree, Alafia River RV Resort, Beall's, CVS Drug, Family$, Hidden River RV Resort (4mi), Lowe's, Save-a-Lot, USPO, Walgreens, **W** [gas] Murphy USA/dsl [other] Walmart/McDonald's

246 rd 672, Big Bend Rd, Apollo Bch, **E** [gas] 7-11, Speedway/dsl, Thornton's/dsl [food] Applebee's, Beef'O'Brady's, Buffalo Wild Wings, Burger King, China Taste, DQ, East Coast Pizza, Firehouse Subs, First Watch Cafe, Little Caesar's, McDonald's, Mi Casa, Panera Bread, Papa John's, PDQ Cafe, Pita's, Pizza Hut, Popeye's, Qdoba, Sakura Japanese, Sonic, Starbucks, Subway, Taco Bell, Tijuana Flats, Village Inn, Wendy's [other] $General, $Tree, Ace Hardware, Advance Parts, AT&T, AutoZone, Beall's, Dunkin Donuts, Firestone/auto, GNC, Goodyear/auto, [H], Kauffman Tire, Marshall's, Publix, Sam's Club/gas, Tire Choice, Tuffy Auto, URGENT CARE, Verizon, vet, Walgreens, Walmart Mkt, WaWa/dsl, Winn Dixie, **W** [gas] Shell/Circle K/Dunkin Donuts/dsl

240b a FL 674, Sun City Ctr, Ruskin, **E** [gas] Shell [food] Beef'O'Brady's, Bob Evans, BubbaQue's BBQ, Burger King, Checkers, China Star, Denny's, Dunkin Donuts, Hungry Howie's, Little Caesar's, Pizza Hut, Popeye's, Sonny's BBQ, Subway, Taco Bell, Wendy's [lodging] Comfort Inn [other] [H], AT&T, Beall's, GNC, Home Depot, to Little Manatee River SP, Verizon, **W** [gas] Circle K/dsl, Marathon/dsl, RaceTrac/dsl [food] China Wok, KFC, McDonald's [lodging] Ruskin Inn [other] $General, auto repair, BigLots, NAPA, SunLake RV Resort (1mi)

237mm [rest stop] **both lanes, 24hr security, full [handicapped] facilities, litter barrels, petwalk, [phone], [picnic], vending**

229 rd 683, Moccasin Wallow Rd, to Parrish, **E** [other] Little Manatee Sprs SRA (10mi), **W** [other] Circle K, Fiesta Grove RV Park (3mi), Frog Creek RV Park (3mi), Terra Ceia RV Village (2mi), Winterset RV Park (3mi)

228 I-275 N, to St Petersburg

BRADENTON

224 US 301, to Bradenton, Ellenton, **E** [gas] Mobil, Shell/Circle K/dsl [food] Applebee's, Checkers, Chili's, Dunkin Donuts, Hungry Howie's, King's Wok, McDonald's, Peach's Rest., Ruby Tuesday, Subway, Taco Bell, Wendy's, Winghouse, Woody's River Grill [lodging] Hampton Inn, Sleep Inn [other] $General, $Tree, Ace Hardware, Beall's, Ellenton Outlets/famous brands, GNC, K-Mart, TJ Maxx, USPO, Walgreens, **W** [gas] Pilot/dsl [food] Anna Maria's, Waffle House [lodging] Red Roof Inn, Super 8

223 Manatee River

220b a FL 64, to Zolfo Springs, Bradenton, **E** [other] Lake Manatee SRA, **W** [gas] Citgo/dsl, Marathon/dsl, RaceTrac/dsl, Shell/Circle K/dsl [food] Burger King, Cracker Barrel, Dunkin Donuts, IHOP, KFC, LJ Silver, McDonald's, Sonny's BBQ, Starbucks, Subway, Waffle House, Wendy's [lodging] Best Value Inn, Best Western+, Days Inn, Motel 6, Quality Inn, Sunrise Inn [other] [H], Encore RV Resort (1mi), Gerzeny's RV Ctr, Harley-Davidson, Toyota, Walmart

217b a FL 70, to Arcadia, **E** [gas] Speedway/dsl [food] Burger King, Culver's, Hungry Howie's, Jersey Mike's, Menchie's, PDQ Cafe, TX Roadhouse, Wasabi Foods [lodging] Holiday Inn Express [other] GNC, Tire Choice/auto, Walmart/Subway, **W** [gas] 7-11/dsl, Marathon, Dunkin Donuts/dsl, RaceTrac/dsl, Shell/Circle K [food] Applebee's, Bob Evans, Bogey's Rest., Boneyard BBQ, Chick-fil-A, DQ, Freddy's, Gecko's Grill, Jimmy John's, LJ Silver/Taco Bell, McDonald's, Papa John's, Rice Bowl, Starbucks, Subway [lodging] Country Inn&Suites [other] $Tree, Beall's, CVS Drug, Lowe's, Pleasant Lake RV Resort, Publix, Tire Kingdom, Tires+, Tuffy Auto, Verizon

SARASOTA

213 University Parkway, to Sarasota, **E** [gas] Mobil/Subway/dsl [food] Alamo Steaks, Broken Egg Cafe, Chili's, First Watch Cafe, Little Greek, Pizza Hut [lodging] Fairfield Inn, Holiday Inn, Hyatt Place [other] [H], GNC, Publix, URGENT CARE, Walgreens, **W** [gas] WaWa/dsl [food] Apollonian Mediterranean, Blaze Pizza, BoneFish Grill, Brio, Buffalo Wild Wings, BurgerFi, Capital Grille, Carrabba's, Cheesecake Factory, Chicken Kitchen, Chipotle Mexican, Daily Eats, Five Guys, Jason's Deli, Jersey Mike's Subs, Jimmy John's, Kumo Japanese, Moe's SW Grill, Newk's Eatery, Panera Bread, Pei Wei, Ruby Tuesday, Seasons Rest., Selmon Rest., Starbucks, Stonewood Grill, Subway, Sweet Tomatoes, Tijuana Flats, Tom+Chee, Valentino's, Wendy's, Zoe's Kitchen [lodging] Homewood Suites, Courtyard, Hampton Inn [other] $Tree, AT&T, Best Buy, BJ's Whse/gas, CVS Drug, Dillard's, Fresh Mkt Foods, Home Depot, Jo-Ann Fabrics, Kohl's, Macy's, Marshall's, Michael's, Old Navy, PetCo, Ross, Staples, SteinMart, Target, TJ Maxx, to Ringling Museum, Verizon, vet, Whole Foods Mkt

210 FL 780, Fruitville Rd, Sarasota, **E** [other] Sun-N-Fun RV Park (1mi), **W** [gas] Marathon/dsl, Mobil/7-11/dsl, RaceTrac/dsl, Shell/dsl [food] Applebee's, Bob Evans, Burger King, Checkers, Chick-fil-A, Chipotle, Culver's, Daruma Japanese, Dunkin Donuts, Firehouse Subs, Five Guys, Gecko's Grill, Gonzalez Asian, Jersey Mike's, Jets Pizza, Longhorn Steaks, McDonald's, Perkins, Ping's Chinese, Pollo Tropical, Rodizio Grill, Starbucks, Subway, Super Buffet, Taco Bell [lodging] Homewood Suites (2mi), La Quinta, Mainstay Suites, Sleep Inn [other] $Tree, Advance Parts, AT&T, CVS Drug, GNC, Lowe's, Office Depot, Publix, Sam's Club, Target, Tire Kingdom, Winn-Dixie

207 FL 758, Sarasota, **E** [gas] RaceTrac/dsl, **W** [gas] BP/Subway/dsl, Marathon/Dunkin Donuts/Subway [food] Arby's, Chili's, Domino's, First Watch Cafe, Jimmy John's, Joey D's Eatery, McDonald's, Panera Bread, Pizza Hut, Sarasota Alehouse, Starbucks, Steak'n Shake, Taco Bell [lodging] Hampton Inn [other] [H], Beall's, Home Depot, Publix, to Selby Botanical Gardens (8mi), Verizon, vet, Walgreens, Walmart

FL

INTERSTATE 75 Cont'd

Exit #	Services
205	FL 72, to Arcadia, Sarasota, E Myakka River SP (9mi), W 7-11/dsl, Marathon/Jimmy John's/dsl, Mobil/7-11/dsl, Shell/Circle K Applebee's, Burger King, Chick-fil-A, Dunkin Donuts, Gecko's Grill, McDonald's, Starbucks, Subway, Waffle House, Wendy's Days Inn, Holiday Inn Express, Quality Inn Acura, Audi, Beall's, BMW, CVS Drug, Infiniti, Jaguar, Land Rover, Lexus, Mercedes/Smart, O'Reilly Parts, Publix, Tire Kingdom, Turtle Beach Camping (8mi), USPO, vet, Walgreens, Walmart Mkt, Windward Isle RV Park
200	FL 681 S (from sb), to Venice, Osprey, Gulf Bchs
195	Laurel Rd, Nokomis, E Shell/USPO/dsl Subway, W Encore RV Park (2mi), Scherer SP (6mi)
193	Jaracanda Blvd, Venice, W RaceTrac/dsl, Shell, Speedway/dsl, WaWa/dsl BrewBurgers, China Taste, Cracker Barrel, Culver's, Dunkin Donuts, McDonald's, Ping's Chinese, Tomatillo's Best Western+, Fairfield Inn, Holiday Inn Express CVS Drug, Publix, Verizon
191	rd 777, Venice Rd, to Englewood, W Encore RV Park (3mi), KOA (6mi), to Myakka SF (9mi)
182	rd 771, Sumter Blvd, to North Port
179	rd 779, Toledo Blade Blvd, North Port, W Mobil/Subway/dsl, Shell//dsl Burger King Publix
170	rd 769, to Arcadia, Port Charlotte, E 7-11/dsl, Murphy USA/dsl, RaceTrac/dsl Applebee's, Culver's Hampton Inn, Holiday Inn Express Lettuce Lake Camping (7mi), Riverside Camping (5mi), Walmart, W Mobil/Circle K/DQ/dsl, Shell/Circle K/Dunkin Donuts, Speedway/dsl Burger King, Cracker Barrel, Domino's, DQ, Golden China, Jets Pizza, McDonald's, Papa John's, Pizza Hut, Starbucks, Subway, Taco Bell, Top China, Waffle House, Wendy's Country Inn&Suites, La Quinta, Sleep Inn H, $General, $Tree, Ace Hardware, Advance Parts, Beall's, CVS Drug, Publix, vet, Walgreens, Winn-Dixie
167	rd 776, Port Charlotte
164	US 17, Punta Gorda, Arcadia, E 7-11/dsl, RaceWay/dsl, Shell/Circle K/dsl King House Chinese, RV camping, Subway, vet $General, Winn-Dixie, W Fisherman's Village Rest. (2mi) H
161	rd 768, Punta Gorda, W Marathon/DQ, Murphy USA/dsl, Pilot/Arby's/dsl/scales/24hr, Shell/dsl Burger King, McDonald's, Pizza Hut, Subway, Waffle House, Wendy's Best Value Inn, Holiday Inn Express, Knights Inn Encore RV Park (2mi), Walmart
160mm	**weigh sta both lanes**
158	rd 762, Tropical Gulf Acres, Tuckers Grade, E Babcock-Wells Wildlife Mgt Area
143	FL 78, to Cape Coral, N Ft Myers, E Marathon/dsl Seminole Camping (1mi), Up River Camping, W Loves/Subway/Wendy's/dsl/scales/24hr Encore RV Camping
141	FL 80, Palm Bch Blvd, Ft Myers, E Marathon, Sunoco/dsl Cracker Barrel, Waffle House Comfort Inn, Woodspring Suites, W Gulf, Mobil, Speedway/Dunkin Donuts/dsl Domino's, Hardee's, KFC, Papa John's, Popeye's, Subway, Taco Bell $General, BigLots, CVS Drug, Family$, North Trail RV Ctr, Save-A-Lot, USPO, vet
139	Luckett Rd, Ft Myers, E Camping World RV Service/supplies, Cypress Woods RV Resort, W Pilot/Subway/dsl/scales/24hr/@
138	FL 82, to Lehigh Acres, Ft Myers, E 7-11/dsl Hyatt Place, W Mobil/dsl, RaceTrac/dsl, Sunoco/dsl Peterbilt

VENICE — PUNTA GORDA — FT MYERS

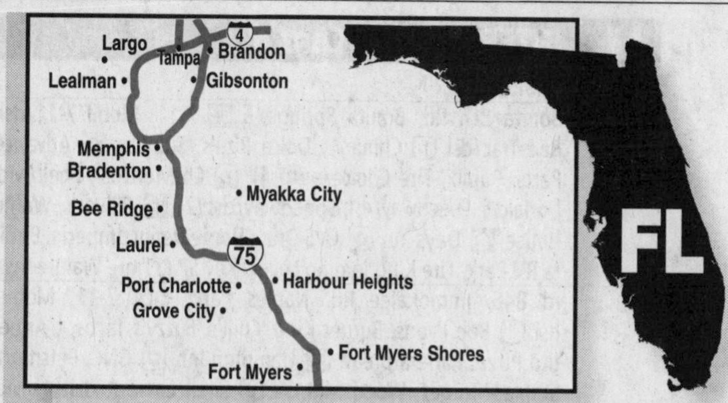

Exit #	Services
136	FL 884, Colonial Blvd, Ft Myers, E 7-11/dsl Bajio, Bella Mozzarella, Buffalo Wild Wings, Domino's, Firehouse Subs, Five Guys, McAlister's Deli, Moe's SW, Pizza Hut, Starbucks, Subway Candlewood Suites, Holiday Inn Express GNC, Home Depot, PetCo, Ross, Staples, Target, Winn Dixie, W 7-11/dsl, Marathon/dsl, Murphy USA/dsl, RaceTrac/dsl, Shell/Circle K/dsl Applebee's, Bellacino's, Bob Evans, Burger King, Chick-fil-A, Chili's, China King, Chipotle, Culver's, Dickey's BBQ, Dunkin Donuts, First Watch Cafe, Golden Corral, LJ Silver/Taco Bell, McDonald's, Panda Express, Pollo Tropical, Steak'n Shake, Subway, Tijuana Flats, Tropical Cafe, TX Roadhouse Woodspring Suites H, $Tree, AT&T, Beall's, BJ's Whse/gas, Hobby Lobby, Kohl's, Lowe's, Petsmart, Publix, Tire Choice/auto, Verizon, Walmart/McDonald's
131	rd 876, Daniels Pkwy, to Cape Coral, E **both lanes, 24hr security, full facilities, vending, litter barrels, petwalk,** RaceTrac/dsl, Shell/Subway/dsl Cracker Barrel, Fat Katz Comfort Inn, Dsys Inn, Sheraton Audi, CVS Drug, Harley Davidson, Porsche W 7-11, RaceTrac/dsl, Shell/Circle K/dsl, Speedway/Dunkin Donuts/dsl Arby's, Beef'O'Brady's, Burger King, Denny's, DQ, La Grotia, McDonald's, New China, Papa John's, Sports Page Grill, Starbucks, Subway, Taco Bell, Two Meatballs Italian, Waffle House, Wendy's Baymont Inn, Best Western, Hampton Inn, La Quinta, Quality Inn, SpringHill Suites, Travelodge H, AT&T, CVS Drug, Publix, Tire Choice/auto, Tuffy Auto, Walgreens
128	Alico Rd, San Carlos Park, E 7-11 Arby's, Aurelio's Pizza, BJ's Rest., BurgerFi, Carrabba's, Cheddar's, Chick-fil-A, Chili's, Chipotle, Connor's Steaks, Culver's, Famous Dave's BBQ, First Watch Cafe, Jason's Deli, Jimmy John's, Longhorn Steaks, McDonald's, Miller's Alehouse, Moe's SW Grill, Olive Garden, Outback Steaks, Panera Bread, PDQ Cafe, Pei Wei, PF Chang's, Pincher's Crabshack, Pita Pit, Pollo Tropical, Red Robin, Rita's, Starbucks, Subway, Taco Bell, Tijuana Flats, Twin Peaks, Zaxby's Courtyard, Drury Inn, Hilton Garden, Holiday Inn, Homewood Suites, Residence Inn $Tree, AT&T, Bass Pro Shop/Islamorada Fish Co, Belk, Best Buy, Costco/gas, Dick's, GNC, JC Penney, Jo-Ann Fabrics, Marshall's, PetCo, Ross, Staples, Target, Verizon, W 7-11/dsl, Marathon/Dunkin Donuts/dsl, RaceTrac/dsl Family$
123	rd 850, Corkscrew Rd, Estero, E Marathon/7-11/dsl, Shell/Dunkin Donuts/dsl Beef'O'Brady's, China Gourmet, Duffy's Grill, Dunkin Donuts, Ford's Garage, Marsala's Italian, McDonald's, Naples Flat Bread, Perkins, Subway, Wasabi Steaks CVS Drug, GNC, Johnson Tire/auto, Miramar Outlet/famous brands, Publix, W 7-11, Mobil/dsl, Speedway/Dunkin Donuts/dsl Applebee's, Arby's, Culver's, Rib City, Ruby Tuesday Embassy Suites, Hampton Inn Chevrolet, Koreshan SHS (2mi), Lowe's, Tire Choice/auto, Woodsmoke RV Park (4mi)

FT MYERS — CAPE CORAL — ESTERO

FL

= gas = food = lodging = other = rest stop

NAPLES

MIAMI

FL

INTERSTATE 75 Cont'd

Exit #	Services
116	Bonita Bch Rd, Bonita Springs, E 7-11, Mobil/7-11/dsl, RaceTrac/dsl China A, Dolce Rita's, Subway Advance Parts, Publix, Tire Choice/auto, W Chevron/dsl, Shell/McDonald's, Speedway/dsl, Speedway/dsl (2) Culver's, Waffle House Days Inn CVS Drug, Home Depot, Imperial Bonita RV Park, Tire Kingdom, to Lovers Key SP (11mi), Walgreens
111	rd 846, Immokalee Rd, Naples Park, E 7-11, Mobil/dsl Bob Evans, Burger King, Chili's, Fuzzy's Tacos, L'Appetito Pizza, Panera Bread Hampton Inn GNC, Petsmart, Staples, Target, World Mkt, W Shell/Circle K/dsl McDonald's, Skillets, Subway H, Publix, to Delnor-Wiggins SP, Verizon, Walmart
107	rd 896, Pinebridge Rd, Naples, E BP/McDonald's/dsl China Garden, Giovanni Ristorante, Subway, Tropical Smoothie H, Publix, vet, Walgreens, W RaceTrac/dsl, Shell/Circle K/dsl Burger King, Five Guys, Hooters, IHOP, Napoli Pizza, Perkins, Senor Tequilas, Sophia's Rest., Starbucks, Waffle House Best Western, Hawthorn Suites, Spinnaker Inn Harley-Davidson, Johnson Tire/auto, Nissan, URGENT CARE, vet
105	rd 886, to Golden Gate Pkwy, Golden Gate, E Subway CVS Drug, W to , zoo
101	rd 951, to FL 84, to Naples, E Shell/Subway/dsl Fairfield Inn, SpringHill Suites, Woodspring Suites H, W Marathon/Subway/dsl, Mobil/Subway/dsl, Shell/dsl Chili's, China Dragon, Cracker Barrel, Dunkin Donuts, McDonald's, Taco Bell, Waffle House Comfort Inn, Holiday Inn Express, La Quinta, Super 8 $Tree, AT&T, Club Naples RV Resort, KOA (7mi), vet, Walmart
100mm	toll plaza eb
80	FL 29, to Everglade City, Immokalee, W Big Cypress NR, Everglades NP, Smallwoods Store
71mm	Big Cypress Nat Preserve, hiking, no security
63mm	**W both lanes, 24hr security, full facilities, litter barrels, petwalk, , , vending**
49	rd 833, Snake Rd, Big Cypress Indian Reservation, E Miccosukee Service Plaza/deli/dsl museum, swamp safari
41mm	**rec area eb, litter barrels,**
38mm	**rec area wb, litter barrels,**
35mm	**W /rec area both lanes, 24hr security, full facilities, litter barrels, petwalk, , , vending**
32mm	**rec area both lanes, litter barrels,**
25mm	motorist callboxes begin/end, **toll plaza wb**
23	US 27, FL 25, Miami, South Bay
22	FL 84 W, NW 196th, Glades Pkwy, W Publix, same as 21
21	FL 84 W (from nb), Indian Trace, W Exxon/dsl, Shell Las Rikuras, McDonald's, Papa John's, Spain's Cuisine CVS Drug
19	I-595 E, FL 869 **(toll)**, Sawgrass Expswy
15	Royal Palm Blvd, Weston, Bonaventure, W Chevron, Mobil BurgerFi, Carolina Ale House, Flanigan's Rest, La Granja, Los Verdes, Lucille's Cafe, Moon Thai, Offerdahl's Grill, Pollo Tropical, Subway, Wendy's Comfort Suites, Courtyard, Residence Inn H, Meineke, Tires+, USPO, VW
13b a	Griffin Rd, E Shell/dsl, Usave/dsl Burger King, Donato's Rest., DQ, Outback Steaks, Waffle House Goodyear/auto, LDS Temple, Porsche, Publix, vet, W 7-11/dsl, Tom Thumb/dsl Anthony's Pizza, Aprezo 2 Venezuelan, Bone Fish Grill, Chick-fil-A, Chili's, Chipotle, Coldstone, Domino's, Dunkin Donuts, HoneyBaked Ham, Jimmy John's, McDonald's, Panera Bread, Pei Wei, Pizza Heaven, Starbucks, Weston Diner AT&T, Fiat, Home Depot, Honda, Hyundai, Nissan/Volvo, Office Depot, Publix, Toyota, vet, Walgreens
11b a	Sheridan St, E Chevron Cracker Barrel, Wendy's Hampton Inn, Holiday Inn Express Audi, BMW, H (3mi), Piccolo Park, W Shell/dsl China One, Coldstone, Little Caesar's, McDonald's, Original Pancake House, Piola Pizza, Romeus Cuban, Starbucks, Subway, TGIFriday's Firestone/auto, Lowe's, Publix, URGENT CARE, Verizon, vet, Walgreens
9b a	FL 820, Pine Blvd, Hollywood Blvd, E Marathon, Shell BJ's Rest., Boston Mkt, Brimstone Woodfire Grill, Brio Italian, Cheesecake Factory, Chick-fil-A, Chili's, First Watch Cafe, Fuddrucker's, Habit Burger, Havana 1957, HoneyBaked Ham, Jason's Deli, La Granja, Lime Mexican Grill, McDonald's, Sal's Italian, Sergio's Grill, Starbucks, Subway, The Pub, Tijuana Flats, Twin Peaks, Village Tavern, Wendys H, Barnes&Noble, BJ's Whse/gas, Chrysler/Dodge/Jeep, Dick's, Mercedes, Old Navy, Petsmart, Publix, Trader Joe's, USPO, Verizon, Walgreens, Walmart, W Chevron/dsl, Marathon/dsl, Mobil Burger King, BurgerFi, Chipotle Mexican, Corner Bakery Cafe, Dickey's BBQ, Firehouse Subs, KFC/Taco Bell, La Granja, Las Vegas Cuban, Marco's Pizza, Mazda Mediterranean, Panda Express, Sal's Italian, SmashBurger, Starbucks, Sweet Tomatoes, Wasabi, Wendy's, Wingstop $Tree, Acura, Advance Parts, AT&T, AutoZone, Costco/gas, CVS Drug, GNC, Lexus, Petco, Publix, Ross, Sedano's Foods, Subaru, Tires+, TJ Maxx, Tuesday Morning, vet, Walgreens, Whole Foods Mkt
7b a	Miramar Pkwy, E Chevron Baskin-Robbins/Dunkin Donuts, Blue Ginger Rest., Jimmy John's, La Carreta, McDonald's Papa John's, Pollo Tropical, Sal's Italian, Starbucks, Subway, Tijuana Flats, Wendy's Courtyard, Hilton Garden, Residence Inn, Wingate Inn $Tree, Publix, USPO, vet, Walgreens W Mobil, Shell Anthony's Pizza, Benihana, Chick fil-A, Chili's, Chipotle, Coldstone, Jersey Mike's, McDonald's Orient Chef, Panera Bread, Primo's Pizza, Starbucks, Subway TX Roadhouse H, city park, CVS Drug, GNC, Home Depot Marshall's, Ross, SuperTarget, Verizon, Winn-Dixie
5	to FL 821 (from sb), FL TPK **(toll)**
4	FL 860, NW 186th, Miami Gardens Dr, E Chevron Mobil Carrabba's, Dunkin Donuts, McDonald's, Sub way AT&T, CVS Drug, GNC, Publix/deli, Sedanos Foods, ve
2	NW 138th, Graham Dairy Rd, W Mobil, Shell/dsl China Casa, China Wok, IHOP, Latin Cuban Cafe, Little Caesar's, Mc Donald's, Pollo Tropical, Starbucks, Subway, Wendy's $General, Aldi Foods, AT&T, GNC, Publix, Ross, vet, Walgreens
1b a	**I-75 begins/ends on FL 826, Palmetto Expswy,** multiple services on FL 826.

INTERSTATE 95

Exit #	Services
382mm	Florida/Georgia state line, St Marys River
381mm	**inspection sta both lanes**
380	US 17, to Yulee, Kingsland, E Osprey RV Park, W Shell/d
378mm	**Welcome Ctr sb, 24hr security, full facilities, litter barrel petwalk, , , vending**
376mm	**weigh sta both lanes**
373	FL 200, FL A1A, to Yulee, Callahan, Fernandina Bch, E Flash Krystal, Marathon/dsl, RaceWay/dsl Burger King, DQ, KF McDonald's, Wendy's Best Western, Comfort Inn, Holida Inn Express to Ft Clinch SP (16mi), W BP/Subway/ds Flash/dsl
366	Pecan Park Rd, E Loves/Chester's/Subway/dsl/scale 24hr, W Flea&Farmer's Mkt, Pecan Park RV Camping
363b a	Duval Rd, E Mobil/7-11/dsl Arby's, BJ's Rest., Blaz Pizza, Boston's, Buffalo Wild Wings, Buffalo's Philly, Carrabba'

INTERSTATE 95 Cont'd

JACKSONVILLE

363b a Continue
Chick-fil-A, Chili's, Chipotle, Coldstone, Cracker Barrel, Firehouse Subs, Five Guys, Green Papaya, Hardee's, Jimmy John's, Logan's Roadhouse, McDonald's, Mellow Mushroom Pizza, Moe's SW Grill, Newk's Eatery, Olive Garden, Outback Steaks, Panda Express, Panera Bread, Pollo Tropical, Red Lobster, Starbucks, Sticky Fingers, Subway, Taco Bell, Wasabi, Wendy's A Loft $Tree, AT&T, AutoZone, Best Buy, Dick's, Discount Tire, GNC, Goodyear/auto, Hobby Lobby, Lowe's, Marshall's, Michael's, Old Navy, Petsmart, Ross, Tire Kingdom, URGENT CARE, Verizon, Walgreens, Walmart/Subway, **W** BP/dsl, Flash/dsl, Sunoco/Subway, Valero/dsl Denny's, Longhorn Steaks, Millhouse Steaks, Ruby Tuesday, Waffle House, Zaxby's Airport Inn, Best Airport Inn, Comfort Suites, Courtyard, Crowne Plaza, Days Inn, Econolodge, Fairfield Inn, Hampton Inn, Hilton Garden, Holiday Inn Express, Hyatt Place, Jacksonville Plaza Hotel, Microtel, Red Roof Inn, Residence Inn, SpringHill Suites, Travelodge , Gore's RV Ctr

362b a I-295 S, FL 9A, to Blount Island, Jacksonville

360 FL 104, Dunn Ave, Busch Dr, **E** Gate/dsl Hardee's, Waffle House Woodspring Suites NAPA, Sam's Club/gas, USPO, **W** BP/dsl, Chevron/dsl, Marathon/dsl, Shell/dsl, Sunoco, Valero Arby's, Burger King, Capt D's, Chan's Chinese, Checker's, China Buffet, CiCi's, Country Cabin Rest., Dunkin Donuts, Firehouse Subs, KFC, Krystal, Little Caesar's, McDonald's, New China, Papa Murphy's, Pizza Hut, Popeye's, Sonny's BBQ, Starbucks, Subway, Taco Bell, Wendy's Knights Inn, Motel 6, River City Inn $Tree, Aamco, Advance Parts, Camping World RV Ctr, CVS Drug, Family$, PepBoys, Publix, Tires+, Walgreens

358b a FL 105, Broward Rd, Heckscher Dr, **E** zoo, **W** BP/dsl

357mm Trout River

357 FL 111, Edgewood Ave, **W** BP/dsl, Texaco/dsl

356b a Fl 115, FL 117, Lem Turner Rd, Norwood Ave, **E** Hardee's, **W** BP/dsl, RaceWay/dsl, Shell, Speedway/Dunkin Donuts Burger King, Checker's, Golden EggRoll, Ho-Ho Chinese, Krystal, Popeye's, Subway, Taco Bell Advance Parts, King Tires, Save-A-Lot, Walgreens

355 Golfair Blvd, **E** Shell, **W** Chevron/dsl, RaceWay/dsl

354b a US 1, 20th St, to Jacksonville, to AmTrak, MLK Pkwy

353d FL 114, to 8th St, **E** McDonald's H, Walgreens

353c US 23 N, Kings Rd, downtown

353b US 90A, Union St, Sports Complex, downtown

353a Church St, Myrtle Ave, Forsythe St, downtown

352d I-10 W, Stockton St (from sb), Lake City

352c Monroe St (from nb), downtown

352b a Myrtle Ave (from nb), downtown

351d Stockton St, **W** H, downtown

351c Margaret St, downtown

351b I-10 W, to Tallahassee

351a Park St, College St, H, to downtown

351mm St Johns River

350b FL 13, San Marco Blvd, **E** H

350a Prudential Dr, Main St, Riverside Ave (from nb), to downtown, **E** Extended Stay America, Hampton Inn, **W** Panera Bread Hilton Garden, Homewood Suites

349 US 90 E (from sb), to beaches, **W** Shell/dsl Scottish Inn, downtown

348 US 1 S (from sb), Philips Hwy, **W** Scottish Inn, Super 8

347 US 1A, FL 126, Emerson St, **E** Chevron/dsl, Shell Hot Wok Advance Parts, Family$, O'Reilly Parts, **W** BP/dsl, Gate, Gate/dsl, Speedway/dsl Dunkin Donuts, McDonald's,

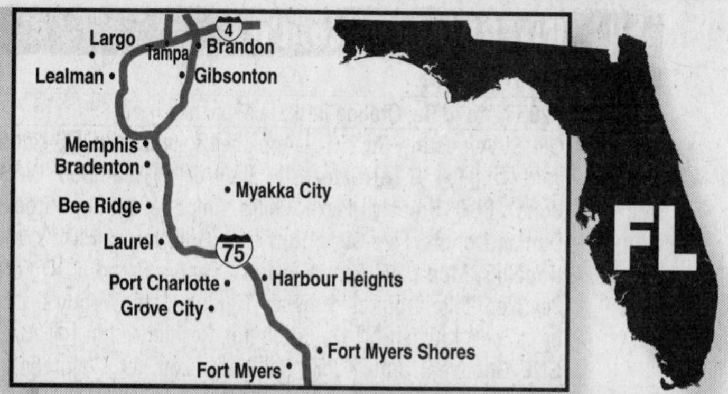

JACKSONVILLE

347 Continued
Taco Bell Emerson Inn Chevrolet, Goodyear/auto

346b a FL 109, University Blvd, **E** BP, Shell, Speedway/dsl, Sunoco/dsl Baldino's Subs, Capt D's, Checkers, DQ, Firehouse Subs, Happy Garden Chinese, Hungry Howie's, Korean BBQ, Krystal, Pizza Hut, Subway, Ying's Chinese, Zaxby's H, Ace Hardware, CVS Drug, Family$, Fresh Fields Mkt, Meineke, NAPA, Sun Tire, Tires+, Tires+, Winn-Dixie, **W** BP/dsl, RaceTrac/dsl Baskin-Robbins/Dunkin Donuts, Burger King, Famous Amos, KFC, Krispy Kreme, McDonald's, Papa John's, Sonny's BBQ, Taco Bell, Wendy's, Whataburger Days Inn, Econolodge, Super 8 $Tree, auto repair, AutoZone, Family$, TJ Maxx, U-Haul

345 FL 109, University Blvd (from nb), **E** Gate/dsl/24hr, Mobil/Subway/dsl, Speedway/dsl Bono's BBQ, Parisian Sandwich, Vino's Pizza H

344 FL 202, Butler Blvd, **E** Gate/dsl Dave&Buster's Best Western, Candlewood Suites, Country Inn Suites, Extended Stay America, Holiday Inn Express, Marriott, Radisson H, USPO, **W** BP/dsl, Shell, Texaco/dsl Applebee's, Baskin-Robbins/Dunkin Donuts, Chick-fil-A, Cracker Barrel, Jimmy John's, McDonald's, Sonic, Starbucks, Waffle House, Wendy's, Whataburger/24hr, Zaxby's Baymont Inn, Courtyard, Extended Stay America, Extended Stay America (2), Fairfield Inn, Hampton Inn, Hometown Inn, La Quinta, Red Roof Inn, TownePlace Suites

341 FL 152, Baymeadows Rd, **E** BP/dsl, Gate/dsl, Shell/dsl Arby's, Chili's, Four Rivers Smokehouse, Hardee's, Jimmy John's, Krystal, Panda Express, Subway Comfort Suites, Embassy Suites, Extended Stay America, Ramada Inn Advance Parts, Autozone, Publix, Tires+, Walgreens, **W** Mobil/Kangaroo, Shell Al's Pizza, Denny's, Dunkin Donuts, Firehouse Subs, Gator's Dockside, IHOP, Jersey Mike's, KFC, Larry's Subs, Little Caesar's, McDonald's, Pagoda Chinese, Red Lobster, Taco Bell, Waffle House, Wendy's, Woody's BBQ Best Inn, Days Inn, Hawthorn Suites, InTown Suites, Knights Inn, La Quinta, Motel 6, Quality Inn, Residence Inn, Sheraton, Suburban Inn $Tree, AT&T, BJ's Whse/gas, CVS Drug, Discount Tire, Harley-Davidson, Lowe's, Office Depot, Pepboys, Verizon

340 FL 115, Southside Blvd (from nb)on FL 115, **E** Marathon/Kangaroo Five Guys, Fusion Buffet, Longhorn Steaks, Newk's Eatery Aldi, AT&T, Home Depot, Michael's, Petsmart, same as 339, Target

339 US 1, Philips Hwy, **E** BP/Circle K/dsl, Exxon/Kangaroo/dsl, RaceTrac/dsl Arby's, Bono's BBQ, Buca Italian, Buffalo Wild Wings, Burger King, Chick-fil-A, Coldstone, Latitude 360 Grille, McDonald's, Mikado, Moe's SW Grill, Olive Garden, Ruby Tuesday, Starbucks, Taco Bell $Tree, Belk, Best Buy, Chevrolet, Dillard's, Ford, JC Penney, Mazda, Nissan, Tire Kingdom, Toyota, vet, Volvo, Walmart, **W** BP/dsl Benito's Italian, Salsa's Mexican, Steak&Shake, Subway

INTERSTATE 95 Cont'd

Exit #	Services
337	I-295 N, to rd 9a, Orange Park, Jax Beaches
335	Old St Augustine Rd, E [food] Applebee's, Starbucks [lodging] Courtyard [other] [H], W [gas] Gate/dsl, Shell/dsl [food] Bamboo Wok, Bono's BBQ, Brooklyn Pizza, Chili's, Chipotle, Daruma Steaks, Dunkin Donuts, Five Guys, Hurricane Grill, Jersey Mike's, McDonald's, Moe's SW, Panda Express, Panera Bread, PDQ Cafe, Pei Wei, Pollo Tropical, Subway, Tijuana Flats, Wendy's, Zaxby's, Zoe's Kitchen [lodging] Hampton Inn, Residence Inn [other] AT&T, GNC, Goodyear/auto, Kohl's, Publix, Verizon, vet, Walgreens
333	FL 9b, to US 1, I-295, N Jacksonville Beaches
331mm	**[Rs] both lanes, 24hr security, full [handicapped] facilities, litter barrels, petwalk, [phone], [picnic], vending**
329	rd 210, Green Cove Springs, Ponte Vedra Beach, E [gas] Pilot/McDonald's/dsl/scales/24hr, Sunoco/fruit, TA/Mobil/Subway/dsl/scales/24hr/@ [food] Waffle House, W [gas] Circle K/dsl, Mobil/Subway/dsl/USPO, Shell/dsl [food] Burger King, China Wok, Domino's, Dunkin Donuts, Firehouse Subs, Jenk's Pizza, Los Portales, Papa John's, Starbucks, Tropical Smoothie, Yummy Asian [other] AT&T, CVS Drug, fireworks, Goodyear/auto, vet, Winn-Dixie
323	International Golf Pkwy, E [gas] BP/dsl/USPO, Shell/Subway/dsl [lodging] St Augustine Suites, W [food] Cino's Pizza, King Wok, Village Grill/Subs [lodging] Renaissance Resort [other] vet, World Golf Village
318	FL 16, Green Cove Sprgs, St Augustine, E [gas] Chevron/DQ/dsl, Gate/dsl/fruit, Mobil/Kangaroo/dsl, Shell/dsl [food] Burger King, Dunkin Donuts, Krystal, McDonald's, NY Diner, Starbucks, Subway [lodging] Comfort Inn, Courtyard, Fairfield Inn, Holiday Inn Express, La Quinta, Quality Inn, St Augustine Motel [other] Cadillac, Camping World RV Ctr, Ford/Lincoln, Gore's RV Ctr, St Augustine Outlets/Famous Brands, W [gas] Exxon, RaceTrac/dsl [food] Cracker Barrel, Denny's, Giovanni's Italian, IHOP, KFC, Lemongrass Asian, Ruby Tuesday, Sonny's BBQ, Taco Bell, Wendy's [lodging] Best Western, Days Inn, Hampton Inn, Howard Johnson, Scottish Inn, Super 8, Wingate Inn [other] Discount Tire, funpark, St Augustine Outlets
311	FL 207, St Augustine, E [gas] BP/Subway/dsl, RaceTrac/dsl [food] Burger King, Dunkin Donuts [other] [H], flea mkt, Indian Forest RV Park (2mi), KOA (7mi), St Johns RV Park, to Anastasia SP, W [lodging] Quality Inn
305	FL 206, to Hastings, Crescent Beach, E [gas] FLYING J/Denny's/Subway/dsl/LP/scales/24hr [other] to Ft Matanzas NM, truck repair, W [other] truck repair
302mm	**[Rs] both lanes, 24hr security, full [handicapped] facilities, litter barrels, petwalk, [phone], [picnic], vending**
298	US 1, to St Augustine, E [gas] BP/dsl, Indian River Fruit, Marathon [other] to Faver-Dykes SP, W [gas] Mobil/DQ/dsl, Sunoco/dsl
293	Matanzas Woods Pky
289	to FL A1A (**toll** br), to Palm Coast, E [gas] Exxon, Mobil/7-11, RaceTrac/dsl, Shell [food] Anthony's Pizza, China Express, Cracker Barrel, Denny's, Dunkin Donuts, Grand China, Hungry Howie's, KFC, McDonald's, Metro Diner, Salsa's Mexican, Starbucks, Wendy's [lodging] Best Western, Fairfield Inn, Microtel, Red Roof Inn [other] Beall's, CVS Drug, Publix, Staples, Walgreens, W [gas] Citgo, Exxon, Exxon/Kangaroo/dsl, Kangaroo/dsl, Shell/dsl [food] Baskin-Robbins/Dunkin Donuts, Bob Evans, Bruster's, Carrabba's, Chick-fil-A, China King, China One, Golden Corral, Houligan's, Joe's NY Pizza, McDonald's, Nathan's Cafe, Outback Steaks, Ruby Tuesday, Sakura Japanese, Sonny's BBQ, Steak'n Shake, Subway, Taco Bell, Wendy's, Zaxby's [lodging] Days Inn
289	Continued [other] $General, $Tree, Advance Parts, AutoZone, Beall's, Belk, CVS Drug, Ford, GNC, Home Depot, Kohl's, Lowe's, Publix, Tire Kingdom, Tuffy Auto, USPO, Verizon, Walgreens, Walmart, Winn-Dixie
286mm	**weigh sta both lanes**
284	FL 100, to Bunnell, Flagler Beach, E [gas] Mobil/dsl, Shell/dsl [food] Burger King, Domino's, Joe's Pizza, McDonald's, Oriental Garden, Subway, Woody's BBQ [lodging] Hampton Inn, Holiday Inn Express [other] Ace Hardware, Winn-Dixie, W [gas] Interstate 100 [food] McDonald's, Panda Express, Pizza Hut, Subway [lodging] Hilton Garden [other] [H], $Tree, AT&T, Chevrolet, Chrysler/Dodge/Jeep, Dunkin Donuts, Michael's, Olive Garden, Panera Bread, Petsmart, Ross, Target, TJ Maxx, Verizon
278	Old Dixie Hwy, E [gas] 7-11 [food] King Chinese, Mezzaluna Pizza [other] Bulow RV Park (3mi), Publix, to Tomoka SP, vet, W [gas] BP/dsl [other] Holiday Travel Park, vet
273	US 1, E [gas] Mobil, RaceTrac/dsl [food] McDonald's, Waffle House [lodging] La Quinta, Motel 6 [other] fruit/fireworks, Giant Rec RV Ctr, W [gas] Exxon/Burger King, Loves/Arby's/dsl/scales/24hr [food] Daytona Pig Stand BBQ, DQ, Houligan's [lodging] Days Inn, Econolodge, Howard Johnson, Scottish Inn, Super 8 [other] Encore RV Park, Harley-Davidson
268	FL 40, Ormond Beach, E [gas] Speedway/dsl, Sunoco/dsl, Valero/dsl [food] Agave Cantina, Applebee's, Boston Mkt, Chick-fil-A, Chili's, Chipotle, Denny's, Dustin's BBQ, Houligan's, Jersey Mike's, Mama Mia's Pizza, Panera Bread, Papa John's, Pie Five, Red Bowl, Starbucks, Steak'n Shake, Subway, Taco Bell, Takeya Steaks, Wendy's, Wok&Roll [lodging] Sleep Inn [other] [H], $General, $Tree, Beall's, Discount Tire, GNC, Love Whole Foods, Lowe's, Petco, Publix, Ross, Tire Kingdom, to Tomoka SP, USPO, vet, Walmart, W [gas] 7-11, BP/Dunkin Donuts, Citgo/dsl, RaceTrac/dsl, Texaco [food] Cantina Mezcal, Cracker Barrel, Little Italy, McDonald's [lodging] Baymont Inn, Hampton Inn [other] Walgreens
265	LPGA Blvd, Holly Hill, Daytona Beach, E [gas] 7-11, Shell/Circle K/Dunkin Donuts/dsl [food] Vince Carter Rest., Wendy's [other] CVS Drug, Tanger Outlets/famous brands, W [lodging] Holiday Inn [other] BMW, Chrysler/Dodge/Jeep, Fiat, Ford, Infiniti, Lincoln, Mazda, Mercedes, Mini, Nissan, VW
261b a	US 92, to DeLand, Daytona Bch, E [gas] 7-11, Citgo/dsl, RaceWay/dsl, Speedway/Dunkin Donuts/dsl, Sunoco/dsl [food] Applebee's, Asian Grill, Bahama Breeze, Bahama Breeze, BJ's Rest., Bob Evans, Buffalo Wild Wings, Burger King, Burger King, Burger King, Carrabba's, Checkers, Cheddar's, Cheddar's, Chick-fil-A, Chili's, Chipotle Mexican, Cracker Barrel, Daytona Ale House, Firehouse Subs, Five Guys, Honeybaked Ham, Honeybaked Ham, Hooters, IHOP, Jersey Mike's Subs, Jimmy John's, Krystal, Krystal, Longhorn Steaks, McDonald's, Olive Garden, Outback Steaks, Panda Express, Panda Express, Panera Bread, Red Lobster, Ruby Tuesday, Smoke Shack BBQ, Starbucks, Starbucks, Subway, Taco Bell, Tijuana Flats, Waffle House, Wendy's, Winghouse [lodging] Best Western, Best Western, Courtyard, Courtyard, Extended Stay America, Extended Stay America, Hampton Inn, Hilton Garden, Holiday Inn Express, Homewood Suites, La Quinta, Quality Inn, Residence Inn [other] [H], $Tree, AT&T, Barnes&Noble, Bass Pro Shops, Beall's, Best Buy, BigLots, Books-A-Million, Dick's, Dillard's, Firestone/auto, Hobby Lobby, Home Depot, JC Penney, Jo-Ann Fabrics, Macy's, Michael's, Old Navy, PepBoys, Petsmart, Staples, SteinMart, Target, TJMaxx, to Daytona Racetrack, Tuesday Morning, Verizon, World Mkt, W [gas] BP/dsl, RaceTrack/dsl [food] McDonald's [lodging] Days Inn, Motel 6 [other] flea mkt, KOA

ST AUGUSTINE · PALM COAST · ORMOND BEACH · DAYTONA

FL

INTERSTATE 95 Cont'd

Exit #	Services
260b a	I-4, to Orlando, FL 400 E, to S Daytona, E RaceTrac/dsl/e85, Shell/Circle K/dsl
256	FL 421, to Port Orange, E BP, Murphy USA/dsl, Shell/dsl, WaWa/dsl Applebee's, Bob Evans, Boston Mkt, Burger King, Chicken Salad Chick, Chick-fil-A, Chili's, Chipotle, Culver's, Daily Grind Burgers, Denny's, Domino's, Dustin's BBQ, Golden Corral, Houligan's, KFC, McDonald's, Mellow Mushroom, Moe's SW, Monterrey Grill, Panera Bread, Papa John's, Pollo Tropical, Red Bowl Asian, Smoothie King, Sonny's BBQ, Starbucks, Stonewood Grill, TGIFriday's, Tijuana Flats Country Inn&-Suites, La Quinta BigLots, BJ's/gas, CVS Drug, Daytona Beach RV Park, Home Depot, Lowe's, Save-a-Lot, Super Target, Tuffy Auto, Verizon, vet, Walgreens, Walmart, W 7-11/dsl, Marathon/dsl China Chef, ChuckECheese, Coldstone, Five Guys, Luigi's Pizzaria, Malibu Beach Grill, McDonald's, Olive Garden, Panda Express, Popeye's, Red Robin, Subway, Takara Steaks, TX Roadhouse, Waffle House, Wendy's $Tree, AT&T, Belk, Firestone/auto, GNC, Kohl's, Love Whole Foods, Marshall's, Michael's, PetCo, Publix, Walgreens
249b a	FL 44, to De Land, New Smyrna Beach, E New Smyrna RV Camp (3mi), W Chevron/dsl McDonald's Walmart/Subway
244	FL 442, to Edgewater, E Marathon/dsl truck repair
231	rd 5A, Scottsmoor, E BP/Stuckey's/dsl Crystal Lake RV Park
227mm	**sb, 24hr security, full facilities, litter barrels, petwalk, vending**
225mm	**nb, 24hr security, full facilities, litter barrels, petwalk, vending**
223	FL 46, Mims, E McDonald's, W BP, Chevron/dsl $General, KOA/LP, Seasons RV Park
220	FL 406, Titusville, E BP/dsl, Shell/Hungry Howie's/dsl Beef O'Brady's, First Wok, Kelsey's Pizza, McDonald's, Subway, Valentino's Rest., Wendy's Executive Garden Inn H, $General, $Tree, Advance Parts, GNC, O'Reilly Parts, Publix, Tires+, to Canaveral Nat Seashore, Walgreens
215	FL 50, to Orlando, Titusville, E BP/KFC/dsl, Chevron/Subway/dsl, Exxon/Circle K, Murphy USA/dsl, Shell/Dunkin Donuts/dsl Burger King, Denny's, Durango Steaks, McDonald's, Panda Express, Sonny's BBQ, Starbucks, Taco Bell, Waffle House, Wendy's Best Western, Ramada Inn Aldi Foods, AT&T, Ford, GNC, Home Depot, Lowe's, Marshall's, Pepboys, PetCo, Staples, Target, Tire Kingdom, to Kennedy Space Ctr, Walmart, W Cracker Barrel, IHOP Days Inn, Fairfield Inn, Hampton Inn, Holiday Inn, Quality Inn Christmas RV Park (8mi), Great Outdoors RV/golf Resort
212	FL 407, to FL 528 **toll** (no re-entry sb)
208	Port St John
205	FL 528 (**toll** 528), to Cape Canaveral & Cape Port AFS, City Point
202	FL 524, Cocoa, E FLYING J/Wendy's/dsl/scales/24hr, Shell/dsl Museum of History & Science, W BP/dsl Days Inn
201	FL 520, to Cocoa Bch, Cocoa, E BP/dsl, Exxon/Circle K, Pilot/Subway/dsl/scales/24hr IHOP, Waffle House Best Western, Budget Inn H, fireworks, Sams Club/gas, W Chevron/dsl, Shell/Burger King, Sunoco/dsl McDonald's Holiday Inn Express Camping World RV Ctr
195	FL 519, Fiske Blvd, E 7-11, Mobil/dsl Baci Pizza, Ruby Tuesday Swiss Inn H, Discount Tire, Lowe's, Space Coast RV Park

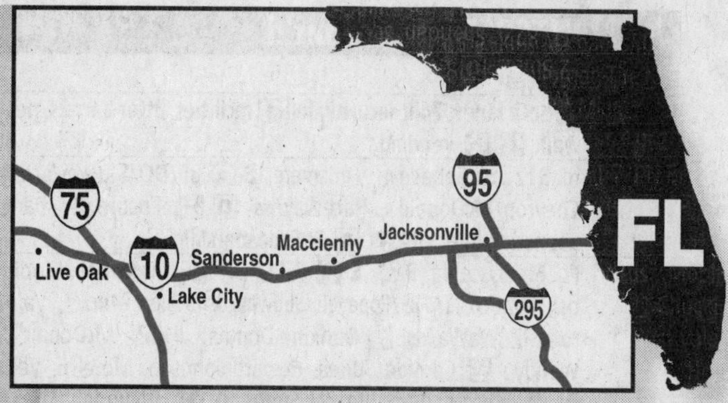

Exit #	Services
191	rd 509, to Satellite Beach, Viera, E 7-11, BP, Speedway/dsl, Sunoco/dsl Bob Evans, Carrabba's, Chick-fil-A, Domino's, DQ, Firehouse Subs, Jimmy John's, McDonald's, Papa John's, Perkins, Pizza Hut/Taco Bell, Sonny's BBQ, Subway, Uno Grill, Wendy's Hampton Inn, Holiday Inn AT&T, CVS Drug, Publix, Tires+, to Patrick AFB, Tuffy Auto, URGENT CARE, Walgreens, zoo, W Murphy USA/dsl, Shell/dsl Asian Wok, Bonefish Grill, Buffalo Wild Wings, Burger King, Chili's, Chipotle, Coldstone, Cracker Barrel, Five Guys, Longhorn Steaks, Melting Pot, Moe's SW Grill, Outback Steaks, Panera Bread, Pizza Gallery, Pollo Tropical, Starbucks, Steak'nShake, Subway, Tijuana Flats, Which Wich? La Quinta H, $Tree, AT&T, Belk, Books-A-Million, GNC, Hobby Lobby, Kohl's, Lexus, Michael's, Office Depot, Old Navy, PetCo, Petsmart, Ross, SuperTarget, Tire Kingdom, TJ Maxx, Verizon, Walmart/McDonald's, World Mkt
188	FL 404, Patrick AFB, Satellite Beach
183	FL 518, Melbourne, Indian Harbour Beach, E 7-11, BP/dsl, Marathon/Dunkin Donuts, RaceTrac/dsl, WaWa/dsl H, art museum, AT&T, W Flea Mkt
180	US 192, to Melbourne, E BP/dsl, Cumberland/dsl, Mobil/dsl, RaceTrac/dsl, Shell/Circle K, Sunoco/dsl ChuckECheese, Denny's, Dunkin Donuts, Waffle House Best Value Inn, Budget Inn, Days Inn, Fairfield Inn, Hampton Inn, Holiday Inn Express, La Quinta, Melbourne Suites, Woodspring Suites H, Ace Hardware, fireworks, Lowe's, Sam's Club/gas, Subaru, Volvo
176	rd 516, to Palm Bay, E 7-11, BP/Circle K/dsl, Murphy USA/dsl, Pro Energy, RaceTrac/dsl Baskin Robbins/Dunkin Donuts, Chick-fil-A, Cracker Barrel, Denny's, Golden Corral, Popeye's, Starbucks, Tijuana Flats Hampton Inn, Quality Inn Aldi Foods, Bass Pro Shops, BJ's Whse/gas, GNC, Harley-Davidson, Office Depot, Verizon, Walgreens, Walmart, W 7-11, Mobil/dsl, Shell Buffalo Wild Wings, Burger King, Firehouse Subs, Five Guys, Long Doggers, Longhorn Steaks, McDonald's, Michelli's Pizzeria, Moe's SW Grill, Panda Express, Panera Bread, Pollo Tropical, Subway, Wendy's $Tree, AT&T, CVS Drug, Discount Tire, Giant RV Ctr, Kohl's, Marshall's, Michael's, PetCo, Publix, Ross, Target, URGENT CARE, vet, Walgreens
173	FL 514, to Palm Bay, E RaceTrac/dsl, Shell, Sunoco/dsl Holiday Inn Express H, Firestone/auto, Ford, truck/RV repair, W Mobil/dsl, Speedway, Sunoco/dsl Arby's, Burger King, Chick-fil-A, IHOP, Japanese Buffet, McDonald's/playplace, Panda Express, Sonic, Sonny's BBQ, Subway, Taco Bell, TX Roadhouse, Waffle House, Wendy's Comfort Suites, Motel 6 $General, Advance Parts, CVS Drug, Gatto's Tire/auto, Home Depot, Lowe's, Publix, Tire Kingdom, URGENT CARE, USPO, Verizon, Walgreens, Walmart

PORT ORANGE · TITUSVILLE · MELBOURNE · PALM BAY · FL

INTERSTATE 95 Cont'd

OKEECHOBEE

Exit #	Services
168mm	**[RS] both lanes, 24hr security, full [handicap] facilities, litter barrels, petwalk, [phone], [picnic], vending**
156	rd 512, to Sebastian, Fellsmere, **E** [gas] BP/DQ/Stuckey's/dsl, Chevron/McDonald's, RaceWay/dsl [other] [H], Encore RV Park, Sebastian Inlet SRA, **W** [other] St Sebastian SP
147	FL 60, Osceola Blvd, **E** [gas] 7-11, BP/dsl, Citgo/dsl, Mobil/dsl, Sunoco, TA/BP/Popeye's/Subway/dsl/scales/24hr/@, Valero/dsl, WaWa/dsl [food] Dunkin Donuts, IHOP, McDonald's, Wendy's [lodging] Comfort Suites, Howard Johnson, Motel 6, Vero Beach Resort, Vero Beach Suites [other] [H], Hyundai, USPO, vet, **W** [gas] Shell/dsl [food] Cracker Barrel, McDonald's, Steak'n Shake [lodging] Country Inn&Suites, Hampton Inn, Holiday Inn Express [other] Vero Beach Outlets/famous brands
138	FL 614, Indrio Rd, **3 mi**, **E** [other] Oceanographic Institute
133mm	**[RS] both lanes, 24hr security, full [handicap] facilities, litter barrels, petwalk, [phone], [picnic], vending**
131b a	FL 68, Orange Ave, **E** [other] [H], to Ft Pierce SP, **W** [gas] FLYING J/Denny's/Subway/dsl/LP/scales/24hr, Loves/Hardee's/dsl/scales/24hr [other] Blue Beacon
129	FL 70, to Okeechobee, **E** [gas] Citgo, Murphy USA, RaceTrac/dsl, Shell, Sunoco/dsl [food] Applebee's, Cowboys BBQ, Golden Corral, Sonic, Waffle House [other] [H], $General, $Tree, Advance Parts, AT&T, Firestone/auto, Home Depot, URGENT CARE, Walgreens, Walmart/Subway, **W** [gas] Citgo, Loves/Arby's/dsl/24hr/@, Marathon/scales/dsl, Mobil/Dunkin Donuts/Subway, Pilot/McDonald's/dsl/scales/24hr [food] Burger King, Cracker Barrel, Golden Bear Rest., KFC, La Granja, LJ Silver, McDonald's, Red Lobster, Steak'n Shake, Subway, Waffle House, Wendy's [lodging] Best Value Inn, Comfort Suites, Days Inn, Fairfield Inn, Hampton Inn, Holiday Inn Express, La Quinta, Motel 6, Quality Inn, Rodeway Inn, Sleep Inn [other] to FL TPK, Treasure Coast RV Park
126	rd 712, Midway Rd, **E** [gas] Marathon/Subway/dsl
121	St Lucie West Blvd, **E** [gas] 7-11, Mobil/Dunkin Donuts, Murphy USA/dsl, Shell/Subway/dsl [food] Arby's, Bob Evans, Burger King, Carrabba's, Cheddar's, Chili's, Chipotle Mexican, First Watch, Five Guys, Frank&Al's Pizza, Friendly's, Hokkaido, Jersey Mike's, Jimmy John's, KFC, Little Caesar's, McDonald's, Moe's SW Grill, Outback Steaks, Panda Express, Panera Bread, Pollo Tropical, Ruby Tuesday, Starbucks, Subway, Taco Bell, TGIFriday's, Tijuana Flats, Wendy's [lodging] Hampton Inn, Holiday Inn Express, Residence Inn, SpringHill Suites, TownePlace Suites [other] $Tree, AT&T, Beall's, CVS Drug, GNC, Outdoor Resorts Camping (2mi), PetCo, Publix/deli, Ross, Staples, SteinMart, Tire Kingdom, Tires+, URGENT CARE, USPO, Verizon, Walgreens, Walmart, **W** [gas] Chevron/dsl [lodging] Hilton Garden, MainStay Suites, Sheraton Resort, Sleep Inn [other] PGA Village
120	Crosstown Pkwy
118	Gatlin Blvd, to Port St Lucie, **E** [gas] BP/dsl, Chevron/Dunkin Donuts/Subway/dsl, Mobil/Dunkin Donuts, RaceTrac, Sunoco/e85 [food] McDonald's, Taco Bell, Wendy's [other] AutoZone, Bass Pro Shops, Home Depot, Sam's Club/gas, Tire Kingdom, Tires+, vet, Walgreens, Walmart, **W** [gas] WaWa/dsl [food] Culver's, Longhorn Steaks, McDonald's, Olive Garden, Panda Express, Panera Bread, Recovery Grill, Subway, Tropical Smoothie [lodging] Homewood Suites [other] [H], AT&T, GNC, Michael's, Old Navy, Petsmart, Publix, Target, TJ Maxx
114	Becker Rd
112mm	**weigh sta sb**
110	FL 714, to Martin Hwy, Palm City, **E** [other] [H]
106mm	**[RS] both lanes, 24hr security, full [handicap] facilities, litter barrels, petwalk, [phone], [picnic], vending**
102	Rd 713, High Meadow Ave, Palm City
101	FL 76, to Stuart, Indiantown, **E** [gas] Chevron/dsl, RaceTrac/dsl, Sunoco/dsl [food] Popeye's, Baskin-Robbins/Dunkin Donuts, Cracker Barrel, La Forchetta Pizza, McDonald's, Wendy's [lodging] Courtyard, Holiday Inn Express [other] [H], city park, Publix, Walgreens, **W** [gas] Marathon/DQ/dsl, Mobil/dsl
96	rd 708, to Hobe Sound, **E** [other] Dickinson SP (11mi), RV camping
92mm	**weigh sta nb**
87b a	FL 706, to Okeechobee, Jupiter, **E** [gas] Citgo, Mobil/dsl, Shell/dsl, Sunoco [food] Cheeseburgers&More, Chipotle, Domino's, Duffy's Rest., Dunkin Donuts, First Watch Cafe, Five Guys, Giuseppe's, Hurricane Grill, IHOP, Jersey Mike's Subs, KFC, McDonald's, Panera Bread, Park Ave Grill, Pollo Tropical, Rancho Chico, Starbucks, Subway, Taco Bell, Tijuana Flats, Tomato Pie, Vinny's Pizza, YumYum [lodging] Comfort Inn, Fairfield Inn [other] [H], Advance Parts, AT&T, BMW, GNC, Home Depot, PepBoys, Petsmart, Publix, Tire Kingdom, to Dickinson SP, URGENT CARE, vet, Walgreens, Walmart, Winn-Dixie, **W** [gas] Sunoco [other] CVS Drug, to FL TPK
83	Donald Ross Rd, **E** [gas] Marathon/Subway, Shell/deli [food] McDonald's [lodging] Hampton Inn (3mi), Holiday Inn Express (3mi), Homewood Suites [other] [H], AT&T, CVS Drug, Publix, stadium, Walgreens
79c	FL 809 S (from sb), Military Tr, **W** same services as 79b, to FL TPK
79a b	FL 786, PGA Blvd, **E** [gas] Shell/dsl [food] Chili's, Moe's SW, Yardhouse Rest. [lodging] Hilton Garden, Marriott [other] [H], Best Buy, Michael's, PetCo, Publix, Whole Foods Mkt, **W** [gas] Shell/dsl [food] Blaze Pizza, Bonefish Grill, Chipotle Mexican, J Alexanders, Outback Steaks, Panera Bread, Starbucks, Three Forks Rest. [lodging] DoubleTree Hotel, Embassy Suites [other] CVS Drug, Publix
77	Northlake Blvd, to W Palm Bch, **E** [gas] Shell/dsl, Speedway [food] Applebee's, Arby's, Burger King, Checkers, Chick-fil-A, Giovanni's Rest., Habit Burger, Jersey Mike's, Jimmy John's, La Granja, McDonald's, Miami Subs, Panera Bread, Pollo Tropical, Starbucks, Taco Bell [other] [H], $Tree, AT&T, Buick/Chevrolet/GMC, Chrysler/Dodge/Jeep, Costco, CVS Drug, Ford, Ford, Hobby Lobby, Home Depot, Hyundai, Jo-Ann, Kia, Lowe's, PepBoys, Ross, Staples, Target, vet, VW, Walgreens, **W** [gas] Chevron, Mobil/dsl, Shell, Sunoco/dsl [food] Duffy's Grill, Dunkin Donuts, Original Pancakes, Papa John's, Pizza Hut, Subway, Wendy's [lodging] Inn of America [other] Advance Parts, CVS Drug, Publix, Tires+, vet, Winn-Dixie
76	FL 708, Blue Heron Blvd, **E** [gas] Marathon/dsl, Shell/dsl, WaWa/dsl [food] Wendy's [lodging] Travelodge [other] Honda, Nissan, **W** [gas] 7-11/dsl, Chevron/dsl, Cumberland Farms, Marathon/Subway/dsl, RaceTrac/dsl [food] Burger King, Denny's, McDonald's [lodging] Super 8
74	FL 702, 45th St, **E** [gas] 7-11/dsl [food] Burger King, IHOP [lodging] Days Inn [other] [H], Cadillac, URGENT CARE, Walgreens, **W** [gas] RaceTrac/dsl [food] Cracker Barrel, McDonald's, Pollo Tropical, Subway, Taco Bell, Wendy's [lodging] Courtyard, Extended Stay America, Holiday Inn Express, Homewood Suites, Red Roof Inn, Residence Inn, SpringHill Suites [other] FoodTown, Harley-Davidson, Sams Club/gas, Walmart
71	Lake Blvd, Palm Beach, **E** [gas] Marathon/Dunkin Donuts/dsl [food] BJ's Rest., McDonald's, Pei Wei, Red Robin, Starbucks [lodging] Best Western, Hawthorn Suites [other] [H], Best Buy, Home Depot, Old Navy, Petsmart, Ross, Target, TJ Maxx, Whole Foods Mkt, **W** [gas] Texaco/dsl, Valero [food] Chick-fil-A, Chipotle

W PALM BEACH

FL

PALM BEACH

INTERSTATE 95 Cont'd

71 Continued
Mexican, Dunkin Donuts, Hooters, Raindancer Steaks, Red Lobster, Sweet Tomatoes, Tijuana Flats, Twin Peaks La Quinta, Ramada URGENT CARE, vet, Walgreens

70b a FL 704, Okeechobee Blvd, E Ruth's Chris Steaks Hilton, Marriott, W BP/dsl, Chevron/dsl, Mobil/dsl, Shell, Speedway, Valero/dsl Arby's, Burger King, Checkers, ChuckECheese, Denny's, Firehouse Grill, IHOP, McDonald's, PDQ Cafe, Pizza Hut, Pollo Tropical, Starbucks, Subway, Taco Bell $Tree, Advance Parts, Aldi Foods, AT&T, Audi/Porsche, BMW/Mini, Chevrolet, Firestone/auto, GNC, Hyundai, Mercedes, Michael's, Office Depot, Staples, Verizon, VW

69b W to

69a Belvedere Rd, W BP, Shell, WaWa/dsl Burger King, IHOP, Wendy's Courtyard, DoubleTree, Embassy Suites, Hampton Inn, Hilton Garden, Holiday Inn/rest., Stay Inn, Studio 6

68 US 98, Southern Blvd, E Coastal, W Palm Gas Subway CVS Drug, Publix, W Hilton

66 Forest Hill Blvd, W Chevron/dsl, Sunoco Dunkin Donuts Advance Parts

64 10th Ave N, W Citgo, Marathon/Circle K/dsl, Mobil/dsl, Murphy USA/dsl Chili's, Dunkin Donuts, Flanigan's Grill, Taco Bell, Wendy's Woodspring Suites CVS Drug, Ford, President Foods, Ross, Tires+, Walgreens, Walmart/Subway

63 6th Ave S, W H

61 FL 812, Lantana Rd, E Shell Domino's, Dunkin Donuts, KFC, Little Caesar's, McDonald's, Riggins Crabhouse, Subway Motel 6 $General, 7-11, Ace Hardware, AutoZone, CVS Drug, Publix, W H, Costco/gas

60 Hypoluxo Rd, E Chevron/dsl, Mobil/dsl, RaceTrac/dsl, Shell/dsl Popeye's, Subway, Taco Bell, Wendy's Comfort Inn, Holiday Inn Express, Super 8 Family$, NAPA, Tire Kingdom, Tire Pros, Tires+, Winn-Dixie, W Valero/dsl Anchor Inn Rest. Advance Parts

59 Gateway Blvd, W Mobil/7-11/dsl Bonefish Grill, Boynton Alehouse, BurgerFi, Carrabba's, Chili's, Egg&I Cafe, Firehouse Subs, Golden Phoenix Chinese, McDonald's, PizzaRox, Starbucks, Subway, Tropical Smoothie Hampton Inn, TownePlace Suites $Tree, AT&T, CarMax, CVS Drug, Kohl's, Publix, Ross, Tuesday Morning, vet

57 FL804, Boynton Bch Blvd, E Marathon/dsl KFC Boynton Beach Inn H, USPO, W BP, Chevron/dsl, Mobil, Shell Applebee's, Burger King, Checkers, Chick-Fil-A, Dunkin Donuts, Golden Corral, KFC, La Brasa, Little Caesar's, Olive Garden, Sonic, Starbucks, Steak'n Shake, Subway, TGIFriday's, Tijuana Flats, TX Roadhouse, Wendy's $Tree, 7-11, Barnes&Noble, BJ's Whse/gas, CVS Drug, Dick's, GNC, Office Depot, Old Navy, PetCo, Petsmart, Publix, SteinMart, TJ Maxx, USPO, vet, Walgreens, Walmart

56 Woolbright Rd, E Shell McDonald's, Panera Bread, Smashburger, Subway, Tijuana Flats, Wendy's H, 7-11, GNC, Jo-Ann Fabrics, Publix, vet, Walgreens, W Marathon/McDonald's, RaceTrac/dsl Burger King, Cracker Barrel, Dunkin Donuts Advance Parts, Home Depot, Lowe's, Staples, Walgreens

52b a FL 806, Atlantic Ave, W Chevron/dsl, Shell/dsl Dunkin Donuts, Sandwich Man, Silver Wok, Subway H, Tires+, transmissions, Verizon, vet, Walgreens

51 rd 782, Linton Blvd, E Shell Arby's, Chick-fil-A, Chipotle Mexican, DQ, Duffy's Grill, Five Guys, KFC, McDonald's, Outback Steaks, Pollo Tropical, Starbucks, Steak'n Shake, Subway, Taco Bell,

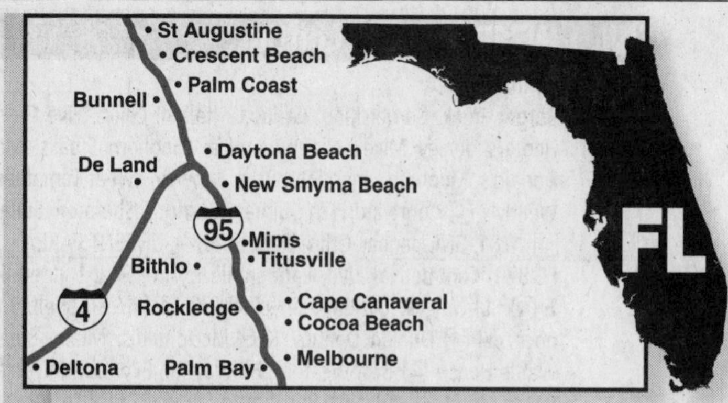

51 Continued
Tijuana Flats, Wendy's $Tree, AT&T, Chevrolet, Ford, Home Depot, Marshall's, Mercedes, Michael's, Petsmart, Publix, Ross, Target, Tire Kingdom, TJ Maxx, W Shell Dunkin Donuts, Little Caesar's H, AutoZone, URGENT CARE

50 Congress Ave, W Mobil Hilton Garden, Residence Inn Costco/gas

48b a FL 794, Yamato Rd, E Mobil Panera Bread CVS Drug, W BP/dsl, Mobil Blue Fin, Dunkin Donuts, Jersey Mike's Subs, Jimmy John's, McDonald's, Miller's Alehouse, Sal's Italian, Starbucks, The Grille, Wendy's Embassy Suites, Hampton Inn, Ramada, SpringHill Suites, TownePlace Suites

FL

45 FL 808, Glades Rd, E Mobil/dsl J Alexander's Rest., Jamba Juice, PF Chang's Fairfield Inn Barnes&Noble, CVS Drug, Whole Foods Mkt, W Marathon Brewzzi Cafe, Brio Italian Grill, CA Pizza Kitchen, Capital Grille, Cheesecake Factory, Chili's, Chipotle Mexican, Farmer's Table, Hooters, Houston's Rest., Madison's Grill, Maggiano's Italian, Moe's SW Grill, Morton Steaks, Season's Rest., Starbucks Courtyard, Marriott, Renaissance, Wyndham Garden Publix

44 Palmetto Park Rd, E Valero/dsl Denny's, Dunkin Donuts, Subway, Taco Bell, Tomasso's Pizza Publix, USPO

42b a FL 810, Hillsboro Blvd, E Marathon, Shell/dsl Dunkin Donuts, Hook Fish&Chicken, McDonald's, Popeye's, Wendy's Doubletree, Hampton Inn, La Quinta Advance Parts, W Chevron/dsl, Mobil/dsl, WaWa/dsl Checkers, Dunkin Donuts, Subway La Quinta CVS Drug, Home Depot, Walgreens

41 FL 869 (toll), SW 10th, to I-75, E Mobil/7-11 Cracker Barrel, Pizza Express Extended Stay America, Woodspring Suites, W Best Western+, Quality Suites

POMPANO BEACH

39 FL 834, Sample Rd, E Marathon/dsl, Shell/dsl, Speedway/dsl Taco Bell H, $General, AutoZone, Save-A-Lot, U-Haul, W Chevron, Citgo/dsl, Mobil, Mobil/dsl, Solo/dsl, Sunoco/dsl, WaWa/dsl Burger King, Checkers, IHOP, La Granja, McDonald's, Miami Subs, Subway CarMax, Costco/gas, CVS Drug, Family$, Seabra Foods, vet

38b a Copans Rd, E Marathon/7-11 McDonald's Land Rover, Mercedes, PepBoys, Porche/Audi, W Chevron, Mobil/dsl Home Depot, NAPA

36b a FL 814, Atlantic Blvd, to Pompano Beach, E RaceTrac/dsl KFC/Pizza Hut/Taco Bell, Miami Subs, **1 mi** W Marathon, Mobil/dsl, Murphy USA/dsl Baskin-Robbins/Dunkin Donuts, Burger King, Golden Corral, KFC/LJ Silver, McDonald's, Pollo Tropical, Subway, Wendy's $Tree, Chevrolet/Mazda, CVS Drug, to FL TPK, USPO, Walmart/Subway

33b a Cypress Creek Rd, E Marathon, Speedway Duffy's Diner, Subway Extended Stay America, Hampton Inn, Westin Hotel 7-11, W Shell/repair Arby's, Blaze Pizza,

FL

FT LAUDERDALE

INTERSTATE 95 Cont'd

33b a Continued
Burger Freak, Burger King, Carlucci's Italian, Chili's, Five Guys, Hooters, Jersey Mike's, Jimmy John's, Longhorn Steaks, McDonald's, Moonlite Diner, Starbucks, Subway, Sweet Tomatoes, Wendy's [lodging] Courtyard, La Quinta, Marriott, Sheraton Suites [other] AT&T, GNC, Jaguar, Office Depot, Tires+, URGENT CARE

32 FL 870, Commercial Blvd, Lauderdale by the Sea, Lauderhill, **E** [food] Subway, **W** [gas] Chevron, Circle K, Mobil/dsl, Shell, Sunoco/dsl [food] Dunkin Donuts, KFC, McDonald's, Miami Subs, Waffle House [lodging] Best Western, Holiday Inn Express, Universal Palms Motel [other] Advance Parts, auto repair, BJ's Whse/gas

31b a FL 816, Oakland Park Blvd, **E** [gas] 7-11, Chevron, Mobil/dsl [food] Burger King, Denny's, Dunkin Donuts, Little Caesar's, McDonald's, Miami Subs, Subway, Wendy's [other] Lowe's, Publix, Walgreens, **W** [gas] Chevron/dsl, Exxon, RaceTrac/dsl, Shell, Valero [food] Baskin-Robbins/Dunkin Donuts, Burger King, Checkers, KFC, Subway [lodging] Days Inn [other] $General, Home Depot, Toyota, USPO, Walgreens

29b a FL 838, Sunrise Blvd, **E** [gas] Marathon/dsl, Mobil/dsl, Shell, Sunoco/dsl/e85 [food] Burger King, Miami Subs, Popeye's [other] Advance Parts, auto repair/tires, AutoZone, Family$, to Birch SP, **W** [gas] BP, Exxon/dsl, Marathon, Shell, Valero [food] China Bowl, Church's, Dunkin Donuts, KFC, McDonald's, Snapper's Fish&Chicken, Subway [other] [H], Family$

27 FL 842, Broward Blvd, Ft Lauderdale, **E** [other] [H]

26 I-595 (from sb), FL 736 (from nb), Davie Blvd, **E** [other] to [airport]

25 FL 84, **E** [gas] 7-11, Marathon, Marathon/dsl, RaceTrac/dsl, Sunoco/dsl, Texaco [food] Dunkin Donuts, Li'l Red's BBQ, McDonald's, Ruby Chinese, Subway, Wendy's [lodging] Best Western, Candlewood Suites, Hampton Inn, Holiday Inn Express, Motel 6, Sky Motel [other] $Tree, BigLots, Firestone/auto, U-Haul, Walgreens, Winn-Dixie, **W** [lodging] Ramada Inn, Red Carpet Inn, Rodeway Inn

24 I-595 (from nb), to I-75, **E** [other] to [airport]

23 FL 818, Griffin Rd, **E** [lodging] Ft Lauderdale Hotel, **W** [gas] Mobil [food] Dunkin Donuts, Subway, Wendy's [lodging] Courtyard, Fairfield Inn, Homewood Suites, Residence Inn [other] Bass Pro Shops, Publix

22 FL 848, Stirling Rd, Cooper City, **E** [gas] Mobil/Dunkin Donuts/dsl [food] AleHouse Grill, Burger King, Chipotle Mexican, Dave&Buster's, Firehouse Subs, McDonald's, Moonlite Diner, Red Lobster, Sal's Italian, Subway, Sweet Tomatoes, Taco Bell, TGIFriday's, Wendy's, Yum Berry Yogurt [lodging] Hampton Inn, Hilton Garden, Hyatt House, Hyatt Place, La Quinta, Quality Inn, SpringHill Suites [other] Advance Parts, BJ's Whse, GNC, Home Depot, K-Mart, Marshall's, Michael's, Old Navy, Petsmart, Ross, to Lloyd SP, Verizon, **W** [food] Las Vegas Cuban, Subway [lodging] Best Western, Cambria Suites, Comfort Suites, Home 2 Suites [other] CVS Drug, PepBoys, Tire Kingdom, vet, Walgreens

21 FL 822, Sheridan St, **E** [gas] Chevron/dsl, Cumberland Farms/gas, Marathon/Dunkin Donuts/dsl [food] Domino's, **W** [gas] Shell [food] Denny's, McDonald's [lodging] Days Inn, Holiday Inn

HOLLYWOOD

20 FL 820, Hollywood Blvd, **E** [gas] Shell [food] IHOP, Miami Subs [lodging] Hollywood Gateway Inn [other] Goodyear/auto, U-Haul, vet, **W** [gas] Chevron/dsl, Marathon [food] Boston Mkt, Burgers&Shakes, China Hollywood, Coldstone, McDonald's, Offerdahl's Grill, Starbucks, Subway, Taco Bell, Waffle Works, Wendy's [other] [H], Publix, Target, Walgreens

19 FL 824, Pembroke Rd, **E** [gas] Orion/dsl, Shell [other] Family$, **W** [gas] Mobil/dsl

18 FL 858, Hallandale Bch Blvd, **E** [gas] 7-11, Exxon, Shell [food] Baskin-Robbins/Dunkin Donuts, Burger King, Denny's, IHOP, KFC, La Granja, Little Caesar's, McDonald's, Miami Subs,

18 Continued
Pollo Tropical, Subway, Taco Bell, Wendy's, Won Ton Garden [lodging] Best Western+ [other] Family$, Goodyear/auto, Tire Kingdom, vet, Walgreens, Winn-Dixie, **W** [gas] Mobil/dsl, RaceTrac/dsl [other] [H], Advance Parts

16 Ives Dairy Rd, **E** [other] [H], **W** [gas] Marathon/7-11 [food] Subway

14 FL 860, Miami Gardens Dr, N Miami Beach, **E** [other] [H], Oleta River SRA, **W** [gas] Shell/dsl, Valero/dsl

12c US 441, FL 826, FL TPK, FL 9, **E** [gas] 7-11, Chevron, Exxon/dsl, Marathon/dsl, Marathon/dsl, Speedway, Valero/dsl [food] Baskin-Robbins/Dunkin Donuts, Burger King, La Granja, McDonald's, Starbucks, Subway, Taco Bell/Pizza Hut, Wendy's [lodging] Rodeway Inn [other] [H], PepBoys, Toyota

12b US 441 (from nb), same as 12c

12a FL 868 (from nb), FL TPK N

11 NW 151st (from nb), **W** [gas] Sunoco/dsl [food] McDonald's [other] Advance Parts, Winn-Dixie

10b FL 916, NW 135th, Opa-Locka Blvd, **W** [gas] Chevron, Mobil/dsl [food] Checkers, Pizza Hut, Subway

10a NW 125th, N Miami, Bal Harbour, **W** [gas] Shell [food] Burger King, Wendy's [other] $General

9 NW 119th (from nb), **W** [gas] 7-11/dsl, Marathon/McDonald's [food] KFC, Pollo Tropical, Popeye's [other] Advance Parts, AutoZone, CVS Drug, Family$, Walgreens, Winn-Dixie

8b FL 932, NW 103rd, **E** [gas] Chevron, Shell [other] 7-11, **W** [gas] Sunoco, Sunshine/dsl [food] $General, Baskin-Robbins/Dunkin Donuts, Bravo Foods

8a NW 95th, **E** [gas] Chevron, **W** [gas] 7-11/dsl, CR/dsl, Mobil/dsl [food] McDonald's [other] [H], Advance Parts, Walgreens

7 FL 934, NW 81st, NW 79th, **E** [gas] Chevron/dsl, Valero/dsl, **W** [gas] Sunoco [food] Checkers

6b NW 69th (from sb)

6a FL 944, NW 62nd, NW 54th, **W** [food] China Town, McDonald's, Subway [other] Family$, Presidente Mkt, Walgreens

4b a I-195 E, FL 112 W (**toll**), Miami Beach, **E** downtown, **W** [other] [airport]

MIAMI

3b NW 8th St (from sb)

3a FL 836 W (**toll**) (exits left from nb), **W** [other] [H], to [airport]

2d I-395 E (exits left from sb), to Miami Beach

2c NW 8th, NW 14th (from sb), Miami Ave, **E** [other] Port of Miami

2b NW 2nd (from nb), downtown Miami

2a US 1 (exits left from sb), Biscayne Blvd, downtown Miami

1b US 41, SW 7th, SW 8th, Brickell Ave, **E** [gas] Chevron, Citgo [food] Burger King, Graziano's, McDonald's, Pepper's Mexican Grill, Subway, Wendy's [lodging] Extended Stay America, Hampton Inn [other] CVS Drug, GNC, Publix, **W** [gas] Shell [food] Papa John's

1a SW 25th (from sb), downtown, to Rickenbacker Causeway, **E** [other] to Baggs SRA

0mm **I-95 begins/ends on US 1. 1 mi S [gas] Mobil**

INTERSTATE 275 (Tampa)

Exit # Services

59mm **I-275 begins/ends on I-75, exit 274.**

53 Bearss Ave, **E** [gas] Citgo/dsl, Wawa/dsl [food] Culver's [other] Carmax, Walmart, **W** [gas] BP, Chevron/dsl, Marathon/Dunkin Donuts, RaceTrac/dsl, Shell/dsl [food] Burger King, IHOP, McDonald's, Popeye's, Subway [lodging] Vista Inn [other] Aldi Foods, BigLots, CVS Drug, GNC, Ross

52 Fletcher Ave, **E** [gas] Citgo/dsl, Marathon, Mobil/dsl, RaceTrac/dsl, Speedway, Sunoco, Wawa/dsl [food] Arby's, Bruno's Pizza, Church's, DQ, Krystal, McDonald's, Popeye's [lodging] Days Inn [other] [H], Aldi Foods, Family$, to USF, Toyota, Walmart, **W** [gas] Citgo, Marathon, Mobil [lodging] Super 8 [other] Cadillac, Family$, Jaguar, Save-A-Lot

INTERSTATE 275 (Tampa) Cont'd

TAMPA

Exit #	Services
51	FL 582, Fowler Ave, E Citgo/dsl, Marathon/dsl, Mobil/dsl, Shell/Circle K A&W/LJ Silver, Burger King, Chili's, Chipotle Mexican, Denny's, Firehouse Subs, Five Guys, Jason's Deli, Jimmy John's, KFC, Longhorn Steaks, McDonald's, Panda Express, Pizza Hut, Shell Rest., Sonic, Starbucks, Steak'n Shake, Subway, Taco Bell, TGIFriday's, Waffle House, Wendy's Clarion, Embassy Suites, Holiday Inn, Hyatt Place, La Quinta, Wingate Inn $General, $Tree, Advance Parts, AT&T, CVS Drug, O'Reilly Parts, Verizon, Walgreens, Winn Dixie, W Rodeway Inn Audi, BMW, Chevrolet, NAPA, Porsche, VW
50	FL 580, Busch Blvd, E Citgo, Marathon Burger King, McDonald's, Olive Garden, Popeye's, Red Lobster, Subway, Taco Bell Hampton Inn, Holiday Inn Express, La Quinta, Red Roof Inn $General, Advance Parts, AutoZone, Busch Gardens, Family$, Walgreens, W Burger King $Tree, Advance Parts, CVS Drug, Family$, Firestone/auto, Home Depot, Walmart Mkt
49	Bird Ave (from nb), E Family$, W Checkers, KFC, Krispy Kreme, McDonald's, Subway, Wendy's $General, K-Mart, Save-A-Lot
48	Sligh Ave, E Marathon, Sunoco USPO, W zoo
47b a	US 92, to US 41 S, Hillsborough Ave, E Marathon, Mobil/dsl, Shell/Circle K Burger King, Checkers, McDonald's, Popeye's, Subway, Taco Bell, Wendy's Advance Parts, Ross, vet, Walgreens, Walmart, W BP, Shell/Circle K Papa John's, Starbucks Dutch Motel
46b	FL 574, MLK Blvd, E Advance Parts, Walgreens, Winn Dixie, W Chevron/dsl McDonald's H
46a	Floribraska Ave (from sb, no return)
45b	I-4 E, to Orlando, I-75
45a	Jefferson St, downtown E
44	Ashley Dr, Tampa St, downtown W
42	Howard Ave, Armenia Ave, W Marathon/dsl Popeye's
41c	Himes Ave (from sb), W RJ Stadium
41b a	US 92, Dale Mabry Blvd, E Marathon, Marathon (2), Mobil/dsl, Shell/Circle K, Wawa/dsl Brickhouse Grill, Burger King, Carrabba's, Chick-Fil-A, Crispers, Don Pan Cuban, Donatello Italian, Grill 116, IHOP, J.Alexanders Rest, Jersey Mike's Subs, Little Caesar's, Pei Wei, Pizza Hut, Ruby Tuesday, Shells Rest., Starbucks, Subway, Village Inn Best Western, Courtyard, Quality Inn, Tahitian Inn/cafe AT&T, Barnes&Noble, CVS Drug, Office Depot, Publix, Tire Kingdom, to MacDill AFB, Trader Joe's, Verizon, W Marathon/Dunkin Donuts Burger King, Chili's, China 1, Chipotle, Denny's, Jimmy John's, Joe's Pizza, McDonald's, Moe's SW Grill, Sonic, Starbucks, Subway, Sweet Tomatoes, Wendy's Fairfield Inn, Hilton, Howard Johnson, Residence Inn Best Buy, Chrysler/Dodge/Jeep, Family$, Home Depot, Honda, Petsmart, Staples, Target, to RJ Stadium, Walmart, Whole Foods Mkt, Winn Dixie
40b	Lois Ave, W Marathon/dsl Charley's Rest. Double-Tree Hotel, Sheraton
40a	FL 587, Westshore Blvd, E BP, Chevron/dsl, Citgo/Subway Burger King, Chipotle Mexican, Gogo's Greek, Jimmy John's, Maggiano's Rest., McDonald's, Panera Bread, PF Chang's, Season's Grill, Starbucks, Taco Bell, Waffle House Crowne Plaza, Embassy Suites Firestone, JC Penney, Macy's, Old Navy, PetCo, Walgreens, W Shell/Subway Blue Water Grill Hampton Inn, Holiday Inn, Marriott, Ramada Inn, SpringHill Suites
39b a	FL 60 W, W to

95
Fort Pierce
River Park
Okeechobee
Palm City
Hobe Sound
Canal Point
Jupiter
Palm Beach
Wellington
Delray Beach
Boca Raton
Coral Springs
Pompano Beach
75
Davie
Fort Lauderdale
FL

ST PETERSBURG

Exit #	Services
32	Fl 687 S, 4th St N, to US 92 (no sb re-entry)
31b a	9th St N, MLK St N (exits left from sb), info
30	FL 686, Roosevelt Blvd, **0-2mi W** Rally Bascom's Chophouse, Burger King, Chil-fil-A, Cracker Barrel, Mamma Mia's, McDonald's, Starbucks, Subway, Taco Bell, Wendy's Comfort Inn, Courtyard, Extended Stay America, Fairfield Inn, Hampton Inn, Holiday Inn, La Quinta, Marriott, Quality Inn, Red Roof Inn, Sleep Inn, SpringHill Suites, Super 8 CVS Drug, Publix
28	FL 694 W, Gandy Blvd, Indian Shores, **0-2mi W** Citgo, Murphy USA/dsl, Speedway/dsl, WaWa/dsl Applebee's, BJ's Brewhouse, Bob Evans, Buffalo Wild Wings, Burger King, Cheddar's, Chick-fil-A, Chili's, Chipotle, Coldstone, Dunkin Donuts, Firehouse Subs, Five Guys, IHOP, McDonald's, Moe's SW, Panda Express, Panera Bread, Pizza Hut/Taco Bell, Pollo Tropical, Sonny's BBQ, Starbucks, Subway, Wendy's La Quinta $Tree, Bentley, BMW, Cadillac, GNC, Home Depot, Honda, Marshall's, Michael's, Office Depot, PetCo, Publix, Rolls Royce, Target, U-Haul, Walgreens, Walmart
26b a	54th Ave N, E Cracker Barrel Comfort Inn, Holiday Inn Express, W RaceTrac/dsl Waffle House Knights Inn H, Harley-Davidson, NAPA
25	38th Ave N, to beaches, W Citgo/dsl, Wawa/dsl Burger King, Hardee's Subaru, VW, Walgreens
24	22nd Ave N, W Citgo/dsl, RaceTrac/dsl, Wawa/dsl Dunkin Donuts, Little Caesar's Advance Parts, Home Depot, Lowe's
23b	FL 595, 5th Ave N, E H
23a	I-375, E The Pier, Waterfront, downtown
22	I-175 E, Tropicana Field, E H
21	28th St S, downtown
20	31st Ave (from nb), downtown
19	22nd Ave S, Gulfport, W Chevron, Citgo, Shell/dsl Church's, KFC Family$
18	26th Ave S (from nb)
17	FL 682 W, 54th Ave S, Pinellas Bayway, **W services on US 19 (34th St)** 7-11, Sunoco/dsl Beef'O'Brady's, Bob Evans, Burger King, China Wok, Domino's, Dunkin Donuts, IHOP, McDonald's, Papa John's, Pizza Hut, Portofino Italian, Subway, Taco Bell, Wendy's Bayway Inn, Crystal Inn $Tree, AT&T, Beall's, CVS Drug, GNC, Publix, St Pete Beach, to Ft DeSoto Pk, vet, Walmart/McDonald's
16	Pinellas Point Dr, Skyway Lane, to Maximo Park, E Magnuson Resort, W marina
16mm	**toll plaza sb**
13mm	N Skyway Fishing Pier, **W both lanes, full facilities, litter barrels, petwalk, , , vending**
10mm	Tampa Bay

FL

INTERSTATE 275 (Tampa) Cont'd

Exit #	Services
7mm	S Skyway Fishing Pier, **E** **both lanes, full facilities, litter barrels, petwalk, , , vending**
6mm	**toll plaza nb**
5	US 19, Palmetto, Bradenton
2	US 41, (last nb exit before **toll**), Palmetto, Bradenton, **E** Circle K, Fiesta Grove RV Resort, Frog Creek Campground, Terra Ceia Village Campground, Winterset RV Resort, **W** Shell/DQ/Subway/dsl
0mm	**I-275 begins/ends on I-75, exit 228.**

INTERSTATE 295 (Jacksonville)

Exit #	Services
61b a	**I-295 begins/ends on I-95, exit 337.**
60	US 1, Philips Hwy, **E** RaceTrac/dsl Buick/GMC, Honda, Toyota, VW, **W** BP/dsl Chevrolet, Ford, Mazda, Nissan, Tire Kingdom, Volvo
58	FL 9b (from sb)
56	FL 152, Baymeadows Rd, **E** Gate/dsl McDonald's Holiday Inn Chrysler/Dodge/Jeep, Fiat, **W** Shell Carrabba's, China Wok, Hurricane Grill, Outback Steaks, Sticky Fingers, Tequila's Mexican, Tony D's Pizza, Wendy's Hampton Inn Publix, SteinMart, URGENT CARE, Walgreens, Winn Dixie
54	Gate Pkwy, **W** Melting Pot, Otaki Japanese Steaks
53	FL 202, Butler Blvd, **1 mi W on Gate Pkwy** Shell/dsl Arby's, Bahama Breeze, BJ's Rest, Bono's BBQ, Brio Grille, Burger-Fi, Cantina Laredo, Capital Grill, Cheesecake Factory, Chick-fil-A, Chipotle Mexican, Cooper's Hawk, J Alexander's, Maggiano's Italian, McDonald's, Mimi's Cafe, Moxie Kitchen, Ovinte, Panda Express, Panera Bread, Pei Wei, PF Chang's, Pollo Tropical, Seasons Rest, Ted's MT Grill, Wasabi, Wendy's, Zaxby's, Zoe's Kitchen Sheraton $Tree, AT&T, Barnes&Noble, Best Buy, Costco, CVS Drug, Dick's, Dillard's, Jo-Ann, Nordstrom, Old Navy, Petsmart, REI, Ross, Staples, Target, Verizon
52	U of NF Dr, Town Center Pkwy, same as 53
51	US 90, Beach Blvd, **E** Burger King, Dunkin Donuts, Jimmy John's, **W** Shell Arby's, Checkers, McDonald's, Pizza Hut, Sonic, Taco Bell InTown Suites $Tree, Advance Parts, Sam's Club/gas, USPO, vet, Walgreens, Winn-Dixie
49	St John's Bluff Rd (from nb), **E** BP, Shell Papa John's Holiday Inn Express, InTown Suites $Tree, Nissan, O'Reilly Parts
48	FL 10, to Atlantic Blvd
47	Monument Rd, **E** Marathon/Kangaroo/dsl Domino's, Hong Kong Chinese, Mudville Grille vet, **W** Gate/dsl Ruby Tuesday Courtyard, Hampton Inn Walmart/McDonald's
46	FL 116 E, Wonderwood Connector, Merrill Rd, **E** Candlewood Suites, **W** Woodspring Suites
44mm	St John's River
41	FL 105, Heckscher Dr, Zoo Pkwy, **E** Gate/dsl, **W** Valero/Kangaroo/dsl Wendy's Holiday Inn Express zoo
40	Alta Dr, **E** Molly Brown's Grill, Viva Mexican
37	Pulaski Rd, **E** Marathon/Kangaroo/dsl
36	US 17, Main St, **E** Kangaroo/dsl DQ, McDonald's Winn-Dixie, **W** Subway
35b a	I-95, S to Jacksonville, N to Savannah
33	Duval Rd, **W**
32	FL 115, Lem Turner Rd, **E** 7-11/dsl Burger King, China Wok, McDonald's (1mi), Subway, Waffle House, Wendy's $Tree, Home Depot, Walmart/McDonald's, **W** Flamingo Lake RV Resort, Lakeside Cabins/RV Park
30	FL 104, Dunn Ave, **E** 7-11/dsl, Gate/dsl, Shell (1mi), Valero (1mi) McDonald's (1mi), **W** Big Tree RV Park
28b a	US 1, US 23, to Callahan, Jacksonville, **E** Kangaroo/dsl, **W** auto repair, BP/DQ/dsl, RaceTrak/dsl Wendy's, **S** Valero/Kangaroo/Subway/dsl
25	Pritchard Rd, **W** Kangaroo/Subway/deli/dsl/24hr
22	Commonwealth Ave, **E** BP/dsl Burger King, Hardee's, Waffle House, Zaxby's Quality Inn dogtrack, **W** Wendy's Comfort Suites, Country Inn&Suites
21b a	I-10, W to Tallahassee, E to Jacksonville
19	FL 228, Normandy Blvd, **E** BP/dsl, Murphy USA/dsl Burger King, Capt D's, El Potro, Firehouse Subs, Golden Corral, Hot Wok, McDonald's, Panda Express, Papa John's, Sonic, Waffle House, Wendy's $Tree, AT&T, CVS Drug, Save-A-Lot, Walgreens, Walmart, **W** BP, RaceTrac/dsl, Shell/dsl, Speedway/dsl Famous Amos, Golden China, Hardee's, KFC, Larry's Subs, McDonald's, Pizza Hut, Popeye's, Sam's Seafood Rest., Whataburger Advance Parts, CVS Drug, Family$, Publix, Walgreens, Winn-Dixie
17	FL 208, Wilson Blvd, **E** 7-11/dsl, BP/Subway/dsl, Speedway/Dunkin Donuts/dsl China Wok, Hardee's $General, Advance Parts, FL RV Ctr, Walmart Mkt, **W** Kangaroo
16	FL 134, 103rd St, Cecil Field, **E** BP/dsl, Gate/dsl, Murphy Express/dsl, RaceTrac/dsl, Speedway Applebee's, Capt D's, Firehouse Subs, Krispy Kreme, Krystal, Papa John's, Pizza Hut, Popeye's, Sonic, Wendy's, Ying's Chinese Hospitality Inn $General, $Tree, Advance Parts, AT&T, CVS Drug, GNC, Goodyear/auto, NAPA, Save-A-Lot Foods, Tires+, U-Haul, URGENT CARE, Walmart/McDonald's, **W** BP/dsl, Exxon/dsl, Shell Burger King, DQ, Dunkin Donuts, IHOP, KFC, Little Caesar's, McDonald's, Subway, Taco Bell, Waffle House Aamco, AutoZone, Family$, Goodyear/auto, O'Reilly Parts, Publix, Sun Tires, vet, Walgreens
12	FL 21, Blanding Blvd, **E** BP, RaceTrac/dsl, Speedway/Dunkin Donuts/dsl, Texaco Burger King, Dunkin Donuts, Larry's Subs, McDonald's, Pizza Hut, Subway $General, Acura, Audi, Best Buy, BMW, Buick/GMC, Cadillac, CarMax, Chrysler/Dodge/Jeep, CVS Drug, Fiat, Ford, Honda, Hyundai, Infiniti, Lexus, Lincoln, Mazda, Mercedes/Smart, Nissan, Office Depot, Subaru, U-Haul, USPO, VW, Walgreens, **W** BP, Carrabba's, Marathon/Kangaroo/dsl, Shell Applebee's, Arby's, Buffalo Wild Wings, Burger King, Chick-fil-A, Chili's, China Buffet, Chipotle Mexican, ChuckeCheese, Denny's, Dick's Wings, Firehouse Subs, Five Guys, HoneyBaked Ham, Hooters, KFC, Krystal, Kyodai Steaks, Longhorn Steaks, Mission BBQ, Olive Garden, Orange Park Ale House, Outback Steaks, Panda Express, Panera Bread, Papa John's, Red Lobster, Ruby Tuesday, Starbucks, Steak'n Shake, Sweet Tomatoes, Taco Bell, Ted's MT Grill, TGIFriday's, Thai Garden, Wendy's Country Inn Suites, La Quinta, Motel 6, Quality Inn, Red Roof Inn, Super 8 H, $Tree, AT&T, Belk, Books-A-Million, Dick's, Dillard's, Discount Tire, Firestone/auto, Goodyear/auto, Home Depot, JC Penney, Jo-Ann Fabrics, Michael's, O'Reilly Parts, PepBoys, Petsmart, Publix, Sam's Club/gas, Tires+, TJMaxx, Toyota, Verizon, Walgreens, Walmart/dsl
10	US 17, FL 15, Roosevelt Blvd, Orange Park, **E** Best Western, **W** BP/dsl, Chevron/dsl, RaceTrac/dsl, Speedwayd-sl Aron's Pizza, Cracker Barrel, Dunkin Donuts, Four Rivers

JACKSONVILLE

FL

INTERSTATE 295 (Jacksonville) Cont'd

10 Continued
Smokehouse, Krystal, McDonald's, Subway, Waffle House, Wendy's [lodging] Courtyard, Days Inn, Fairfield Inn, Hampton Inn, Hilton Garden, Holiday Inn, Rodeway Inn [O] [H], $Tree, CVS Drug, General RV Ctr, Harley-Davidson, Sun Tire, vet, Winn-Dixie

7mm St Johns River, Buckman Br

5b a FL 13, San Jose Blvd, **E** [gas] Speedway/dsl, Valero/DQ/dsl [food] Arby's, Bob Evans, Bono's BBQ, Carrabba's, Chick-fil-A, Crystal River Seafood, Dickey's BBQ, Domino's, Famous Amos, Firehouse Subs, Five Guys, HoneyBaked Ham, Krystal, McDonald's, Outback Steaks, Popeye's, Red Elephant Pizza, Smoothie King, Starbucks, Steak'n Shake, The Loop Pizza, Village Inn, Which Wich?, Zaxby's [lodging] La Quinta, Ramada Inn [O] Aamco, Advance Parts, BigLots, CVS Drug, Firestone/auto, Office Depot, PepBoys, Publix, Save-A-Lot, Sun Tire, Target, Tire Kingdom, Tires+, URGENT CARE, Verizon, Whole Foods Mkt, **W** [gas] BP,

5b a Continued
Citgo, Shell [food] Al's Pizza, Bonefish Grill, Bruster's, Chili's, Chipotle Mexican, Dunkin Donuts, Golden Corral, Hardee's, Jimmy John's, Krispy Kreme, Mama Fu's, Mandarin Ale House, McDonald's, Moe's SW Grill, Newk's Eatery, Osaka Grill, Panera Bread, Papa John's, Papa Murphy's, Pizza Hut, Pollo Tropical, Starbucks, Subway, Taco Bell, Tree Steakhouse [O] $Tree, Advance Parts, AT&T, AutoZone, Barnes&Noble, Goodyear/auto, Marshall's, Michael's, NAPA, PetCo, Publix, Staples, SteinMart, Tire Kingdom, TJ Maxx, U-Haul, vet, Walgreens, Walmart, Winn-Dixie, World Mkt

3 Old St Augustine Rd, **E** [gas] BP/dsl, Shell/dsl [food] Burger King, Little Caesar's, Little China, McDonald's, Pizza Hut, Salento Steaks, St Mary's Seafood, Taco Bell, Wendy's [lodging] Holiday Inn Express [O] $General, $Tree, CVS Drug, GNC, Hobby Lobby, Publix/deli, Winn-Dixie, **W** [gas] Gate/dsl, Marathon/Kangaroo/dsl [food] Firehouse Subs, KFC, Rosy's Mexican, Subway, Vino's Pizza [O] Lowe's, vet, Walgreens

NOTES

FL

GEORGIA

INTERSTATE 16

Exit #	Services
167b a	W Broad, Montgomery St, Savannah, **0-1 mi N** [gas] Chevron, Enmark, Parker's [lodging] Best Western, Courtyard, DoubleTree, Fairfield Inn, Hampton Inn, Hilton Garden, Holiday Inn, Quality Inn, Residence Inn, Springhill Suites, **S** [food] Burger King, Popeye's, Wendy's [other] **I-16 begins/ends in Savannah.**
166	US 17, Gwinnet St, Savannah, Savannah Visitors Ctr
165	GA 204, 37th St (from eb), to Ft Pulaski NM, Savannah College
164b a	I-516, US 80, US 17, GA 21
162	Chatham Pkwy, **S** [gas] Shell/dsl [food] Kan Pai Japanese, Larry's Subs, Nicky's Pizza, Sunrise Rest. [other] Chrysler/Dodge/Jeep, Kia, Lexus, Subaru, Toyota
160	GA 307, Dean Forest Rd, **N** [gas] Pilot/Subway/dsl/scales, Shell/dsl [food] Ronnie's Rest., Waffle House
157b a	I-95, S to Jacksonville, N to Florence
155	Pooler Pkwy, **N** [gas] Murphy USA/dsl [food] Jalapeno's Mexican, Papa John's, Subway, Wasabi Fusion [other] Lowe's, to Airport, Verizon, **S** [gas] BP/dsl
152	GA 17, to Bloomingdale
148	Old River Rd, to US 80
144mm	**weigh sta both lanes**
143	US 280, to US 80, **S** [gas] El Cheapo/dsl, Gas'n Go/Subway/dsl
137	GA 119, to Pembroke, Ft Stewart
132	Ash Branch Church Rd
127	GA 67, to Pembroke, Ft Stewart, **N** [gas] BP/dsl, Shell/dsl [food] Bay South Rest., Gator Rest. [other] antiques
116	US 25/301, to Statesboro, **N** [gas] Chevron/rest/dsl/scales/24hr [food] Magnolia Springs SP (45 mi), to GA S U, **S** [lodging] Patriot Inn
111	Pulaski-Excelsior Rd, **S** [gas] Citgo/Grady's Grill/dsl [other] Beaver Run RV Park, tires/repair
104	GA 22, GA 121, Metter, **N** [gas] BP/dsl/scales/24hr, Exxon, Parker's/dsl, Shell/dsl [food] Bevrick's Grille, Burger King, Chinese Buffet, DQ, El Mariachi, Jomax BBQ, KFC/Taco Bell, McDonald's, Papa Buck's BBQ, Pizza Hut, Pond House Grill, Shogun, Subway, Waffle House, Zaxby's [lodging] American Inn, Days Inn, Econo Inn, Garden Inn [other] [H], Chevrolet, info, O'Reilly Parts, Rite Aid, to Smith SP, **S** [gas] Marathon/dsl, Phillips 66/dsl [other] Ford
101mm	Canoochee River
98	GA 57, to Stillmore, **S** [gas] BP/dsl/24hr, Chevron/dsl [other] to Altahama SP
90	US 1, to Swainsboro, **N** [gas] Gasco/Subway/dsl, Marathon/dsl
88mm	Ohoopee River
84	GA 297, to Vidalia, **N** [other] truck sales
78	US 221, GA 56, to Swainsboro
71	GA 15, GA 78, to Soperton, **N** [gas] Chevron/dsl
67	GA 29, to Soperton, **S** [gas] Chevron/dsl, Marathon/dsl [food] Huddle House
58	GA 199, Old River Rd, East Dublin
56mm	Oconee River
54	GA 19, to Dublin, **S** [gas] Chevron/dsl/24hr
51	US 441, US 319, to Dublin, **N** [gas] BP/Stuckey's/Subway/dsl, Flash/gas, Neighbor's/dsl, Pilot/dsl/scales/24hr [food] Arby's, Burger King, KFC, King's Inn/rest., McDonald's, Ruby Tuesday, Sanchez Border Grill, Taco Bell, Waffle House, Wendy's [lodging] Baymont Inn, Best Western, Days Inn, Holiday Inn Express, Quality Inn, Relax Inn, Super 8 [other] [H], $General, Chrysler/Dodge/Jeep, Steve's RV, **S** [gas] Chevron/dsl [food] Cracker Barrel, Longhorn Steaks, Zaxby's [lodging] Hampton Inn, La Quinta [other] Pinetucky Camping (2mi), to Little Ocmulgee SP, visitor ctr
49	GA 257, to Dublin, Dexter, **N** [gas] Chevron/dsl [other] [H], **S** [gas] Loves/Chester's/Subway/dsl/scales/24hr
46mm	**[RS] wb, full [♿] facilities, litter barrels, petwalk, [phone], [picnic], RV dump, vending**
44mm	**[RS] eb, full [♿] facilities, litter barrels, petwalk, [phone], [picnic], RV dump, vending**
42	GA 338, to Dudley
39	GA 26, to Cochran, Montrose
32	GA 112, Allentown, **S** [gas] Chevron/dsl
27	GA 358, to Danville
24	GA 96, to Jeffersonville, **N** [gas] Marathon/dsl, **S** [gas] Exxon/Huddle House/dsl/24hr [lodging] Suburban Inn [other] museum, to Robins AFB
18	Bullard Rd, to Jeffersonville, Bullard
12	Sgoda Rd, Huber, **N** [gas] Marathon/dsl
6	US 23, US 129A, East Blvd, Ocmulgee, **N** [gas] Shell/Circle K/DQ, Texaco/dsl [food] McDonald's, Waffle House [other] GA Forestry Ctr, to [airport], **S** [gas] Chevron/Huddle House/dsl/scales/24hr, Friendly Gus [food] Subway
2	US 80, GA 87, MLK Jr Blvd, **N** [lodging] Marriott [other] [H], conv ctr, Ocmulgee NM, **S** [gas] Marathon/dsl [other] to Hist Dist
1b	GA 22, to US 129, GA 49, 2nd St (from wb), **S** [other] [H]
1a	US 23, Gray Hwy (from eb), **N** [gas] Citgo, Flash/dsl, QuikServe, Valero [food] Arby's, Burger King, Chen's Wok, DQ, El Sombrero Mexican, Fincher's BBQ, Hardee's, Hong Kong Express, Krispy Kreme, Krystal, Little Caesar's, McDonald's, Papa John's, Subway, Taco Bell, Wendy's [other] [H], Attaway Tire, CVS Drug, Family$, Kroger, O'Reilly Parts, U-Haul, Walgreens, **S** [gas] Jumbo's, Sunoco/dsl [food] Burger King, Checker's, Krystal, Pizza Hut, Waffle House, Zaxby's
0mm	I-75, S to Valdosta, N to Atlanta. **I-16 begins/ends on I-75, exit 165 in Macon.**

City labels in margins: METTER, DUBLIN, OCMULGEE, MACON, AUGUSTA; GA

INTERSTATE 20

Exit #	Services
202mm	Georgia/South Carolina state line, Savannah River
201mm	**Welcome Ctr wb, full [♿] facilities, litter barrels, petwalk, [phone], [picnic], vending**
200	GA 104, Riverwatch Pkwy, Augusta, **N** [gas] Pilot/Wendy's/dsl/scales/24hr [food] Waffle House [lodging] Baymont Inn, Candlewood Suites, Comfort Suites, Ecco Suites, Microtel, Quality Inn, Sleep Inn, Woodspring Suites [other] Freightliner, **S** [other] Cabela's, Costco/gas
199	GA 28, Washington Rd, Augusta, **0-3 mi N** [gas] BP, RaceWay, Shell/Circle K, Sprint [food] Applebee's, Baskin-Robbins/Dunkin Donuts, Burger King, CA Dreaming, Capt D's, Checkers, Chick-fil-A, Denny's, Domino's, DQ, Fujiyama Japanese, Krystal, Longhorn Steaks, McDonald's, Mi Rancho Mexican, Piccadilly, Pizza Hut, Rhinehart's Seafood, Starbucks, Steakout, Veracruz Mexican, Waffle House, Wife Saver Rest, Wild Wing Cafe [lodging] Clarion, Courtyard, Econolodge, Hampton Inn, Hilton Garden, Holiday Inn Express, Homewood Suites, La Quinta, Masters Inn, Scottish Inn, Sheraton, Sunset Inn, Super 8, Travelodge [other] $Tree, AutoZone, Buick/GMC, Chevrolet, Chrysler/Dodge/Jeep, Hyundai, Infiniti, Lexus, Mercedes, NAPA, Nissan, Toyota, Tuesday Morning,

INTERSTATE 20 Cont'd

199 Continued
S BP, Circle K/dsl, Shell/Circle K/dsl Arby's, BoneFish Grill, Carrabba's, Crazy Turk's Pizza, Five Guys, HoneyBaked Ham, Hooters, Krispy Kreme, McDonald's, Moe's SW Grill, New Peking, Olive Garden, Outback Steaks, Red Lobster, Roadrunner Cafe, Shangri La, Straw Hat Pizza, Subway, Taco Bell, T-Bonz Steaks, Teresa's Mexican, TGIFriday's, Thai Jong Rest., TX Roadhouse, Vallarta Mexican, Waffle House, Wendy's, Zaxby's Best Western, Country Inn&Suites, Knights Inn, Magnolia Inn, Motel 6, Parkway Inn, Staybridge Suites, Westbank Inn $Tree, AT&T, CVS Drug, Firestone/auto, Fresh Mkt Foods, Goodyear/auto, Kroger/dsl, Midas, PepBoys, Publix, SteinMart, Tire Kingdom, Verizon, Walgreens, Whole Food Mkt

196b GA 232 W, N Enmark, Murphy Express/dsl Checkers, Golden Corral, Krystal, Salsa's Grill, Stevi B's Pizza Baymont Inn, Travel Inn Aldi Foods, Discount Tire, GNC, Home Depot, Lowe's, NTB, O'Reilly Parts, Sam's Club/dsl, URGENT CARE, Walgreens, Walmart, Sprouts Mkt

196a I-520, Bobby Jones Fwy, S Atlanta Bread Co, Buffalo Wild Wings, Carolina Alehouse, Chick-fil-A, Chili's, Dunkin Donuts, Genghis Grill, Logan's Roadhouse, Macaroni Grill, McDonald's, O'Charley's, Panera Bread, Starbucks, Sticky Fingers, Subway, Waffle House DoubleTree Hotel H, Best Buy, Hobby Lobby, Michael's, Office Depot, Old Navy, Petsmart, Rite Aid, Staples, Target, Tires+, to , Verizon, vet

195 Wheeler Rd, N Sprint Barnyard Burgers Hyatt Place CarMax, S Shell/Circle K/Blimpie Guiseppe's Pizza, Sonic Days Inn H, BP/dsl, Harley-Davidson, Rite Aid, URGENT CARE

194 GA 383, Belair Rd, to Evans, N Shell/Circle K/dsl, Sprint Bojangles, Burger King, Hungry Howie's, Popeye's, Sun Kwong Chinese, Taco Bell, Waffle House, Wendy's GA Inn Family$, Food Lion, Fun Park, S BP/DQ/dsl, Fuel Express, Pilot/Subway/dsl/scales/24hr Cookout, Cracker Barrel, McDonald"s, Steak'n Shake, Waffle House Augusta Inn, Best Suites, Best Value Inn, Best Western, Comfort Inn, Hampton Inn, Hawthorn Suites, Holiday Inn, Howard Johnson, Quality Inn, Red Roof Inn, Super 8, Wingate Inn Goodyear/auto, Kenworth

190 GA 388, to Grovetown, N TPS/dsl/scales/24hr Waffle House, S Murphy Express/dsl Applebee's, Arby's, Chick-fil-A, Culver's, Jersey Mike's, Mi Rancho Home 2 Suites AT&T, Verizon, Walmart

189mm **weigh sta both lanes**

183 US 221, to Harlem, Appling, N Cushman RV Ctr, S Exxon/dsl to Laurel&Hardy Museum

182mm **both lanes, full facilities, litter barrels, petwalk, , , RV dump, vending**

175 GA 150, N Chevron/rest/dsl/24hr Express Inn to Mistletoe SP

172 US 78, GA 17, Thomson, N Loves/Chester's/Subway/dsl/scales/24hr Waffle House Chrysler/Dodge/Jeep, S Circle K/dsl, Citgo/DQ/dsl, M&A/dsl, Marathon/dsl, RaceWay/dsl Arby's, Bojangles, Burger King, Checkers, Chick-fil-A, Domino's, Habaneros Mexican, Kiosco Mexican, Krystal, LJ Silver, Lucky Chinese, McDonald's, MingWah Chinese, Pizza Hut, Popeye's, Ryan's, Taco Bell, Waffle House, Wendy's, Zaxby's Comfort Inn, EconoLodge, Hampton Inn, Rodeway Inn, White Columns Inn H, $General, Advance Parts, AutoZone, Bi-Lo, Family$, O'Reilly Parts, URGENT CARE, Verizon, Walgreens

THOMSON

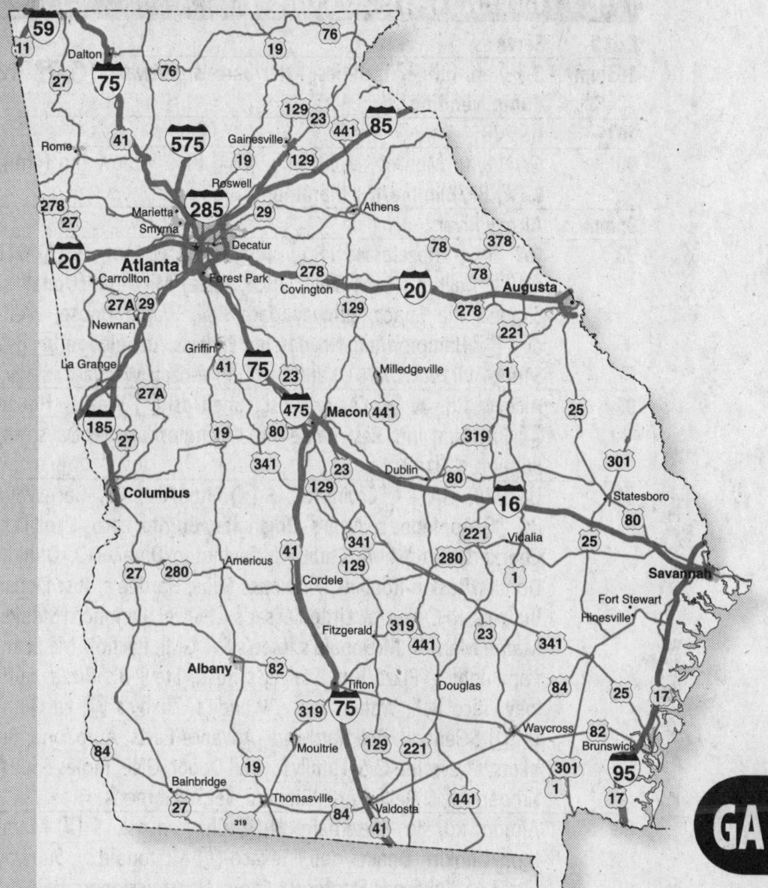

GA

169 Thomson

165 GA 80, Camak

160 E Cadley Rd, Norwood

154 US 278, GA 12, Barnett

148 GA 22, Crawfordville, N to Stephens SP

138 GA 77, GA 15, Siloam, N FLYING J/Denny's/dsl/LP/scales/24hr, S Chevron/dsl

130 GA 44, Greensboro, N BP/dsl, Valero/Subway DQ, McDonald's, Pizza Hut, Waffle House, Wendy's, Zaxby's Holiday Lodge, Quality Inn $General, Buick/Chevrolet, Greensboro Tire/repair, S Chevron/dsl H, Home Depot/gas

121 to Lake Oconee, Buckhead, S Chevron/dsl Museum of Art (3mi)

114 US 441, US 129, to Madison, N Chevron/Subway/dsl, Citgo/dsl, Pilot/Huddle House/dsl/scales/24hr, RaceWay/dsl Arby's, Burger King, Chick-fil-A, Cracker Barrel, Hong Kong Buffet, KFC, Krystal, McDonald's, Pachos Mexican, Pizza Hut, Steak'n Shake, Taco Bell, Waffle House, Wendy's, Zaxby's Comfort Inn, Hampton Inn, Quality Inn H, $General, $Tree, Advance Parts, AutoZone, Ingles Foods/gas, Lowe's, O'Reilly Parts, Rite Aid, Verizon, Walmart, S Flash/dsl, Shell, TA/BP/Country Pride/Popeye's/dsl/scales/24hr/@ Waffle House Deerfield Inn, Holiday Inn Express, Super 8, Wingate Inn Country Boys RV Park (1mi), truckwash/service

113 GA 83, Madison, N BP/dsl H, st patrol, S Exxon/dsl

108mm **N wb, full facilities, litter barrels, petwalk, , , RV dump, vending**

105 Rutledge, Newborn, N Valero/pizza/dsl Hard Labor Creek SP

MADISON

INTERSTATE 20 Cont'd

Exit #	Services
103mm	S rest stop eb, full facilities, litter barrels, petwalk, phone, picnic, RV dump, vending
101	US 278
98	GA 11, to Monroe, Monticello, N lodging Blue Willow Inn (4mi), S gas BP/Blimpie/dsl, Marathon
95mm	Alcovy River
93	GA 142, Hazelbrand Rd, N other Home Depot, S gas QT/dsl food Bullrito's Cafe, Chili's, IHOP, Jersey Mike's, McDonald's, Shane's Rib Shack, Subway, Taco Bell, Waffle House, Wendy's lodging Hampton Inn, Holiday Inn Express, Travelodge other H, $Tree, Aldi Foods, AT&T, Kauffman Tire, Verizon, Walmart/Subway
92	Alcovy Rd, N gas Chevron/dsl, Shell/dsl food Waffle House lodging Baymont Inn, Best Value Inn, Covington Lodge, Days Inn, Super 8, S other H
90	US 278, GA 81, Covington, S gas Citgo/dsl, QT, RaceWay/dsl food Applebee's, Arby's, Bojangles, Burrito Loco, Capt D's, Checkers, Chick-fil-A, Church's, Covington Diner, DQ, Dunkin Donuts/Baskin-Robbins, Firehouse Subs, Hardee's, Just Dogs/Burgers, KFC, Krystal, Little Caesar's, LJ Silver, Longhorn Steaks, Mama Maria's, McDonald's, Moe's SW Grill, Pacho's Mexican, Papa John's, Pizza Hut, Stalvey's Rest., Stevi B's Pizza, Subway, Taco Bell, Waffle House, Wendy's, Zaxby's lodging La Quinta other $General, Ace Hardware, Advance Parts, AutoZone, BigLots, Chevrolet, CVS, Family$, Food Depot, GNC, Ingles Foods, Kroger/dsl, O'Reilly Parts, Rite Aid, vet, Walgreens
88	Almon Rd, to Porterdale, N gas Chevron/dsl, S gas Marathon/Dunkin Donuts/deli, Texaco food McDonald's, Subway (2mi) other Riverside Estates RV Camp, transmissions/repair
84	GA 162, Salem Rd, to Pace, N gas BJ's Whse/gas, Marathon/dsl other Chrysler/Dodge/Jeep, S gas Citgo, QT, RaceWay/dsl, Shell/dsl food Baskin-Robbins, Burger King, Dunkin Donuts, Hardee's, KFC, Los Bravos Mexican, McDonald's, Quiznos, Subway, Taco Bell, Waffle House, Wendy's other Advance Parts, Family$, Food Depot, Ingles/gas, Olympic Auto, O'Reilly Parts, PepBoys, Rite Aid
82	GA 138, GA 20, Conyers, N gas BP/dsl, QT food Applebee's, Bruster's, Chili's, ChuckECheese, Coldstone, Cracker Barrel, Don Tello's, Golden Corral, IHOP, O'Charley's, Outback Steaks, Red Lobster, Sonic, Subway lodging Country Inn&Suites, Days Inn, Hampton Inn, Holiday Inn Express, Jameson Inn, La Quinta other AT&T, Belk, Chevrolet/Buick/GMC, Courtyard, Ford, Harley-Davidson, Home Depot, Jo-Ann, Kohl's, Michael's, Office Depot, Old Navy, Petsmart, Staples, Tires+, TJ Maxx, U-Haul, Walmart, S gas Chevron, Shell/dsl food Blimpie, Burger King, Capt D's, Checkers, Chick-fil-A, CiCi's Pizza, Dunkin Donuts/Baskin-Robbins, Firehouse Subs, Folk's Rest., Frontera Mexican, Grand Buffet, HoneyBaked Ham, Hooters, Jim'n Nick's BBQ, KFC, Krystal, Little Caesar's, Mandarin Garden, McDonald's, Mellow Mushroom, Milano Cafe, Moe's SW Grill, Panda Express, Panera Bread, Piccadilly Cafe, Popeye's, Ruby Tuesday, Silver Dragon, Sonny's BBQ, Starbucks, Subway, Taco Bell, Waffle House lodging Microtel other $General, $Tree, Aldi Foods, BigLots, Discount Tire, Firestone/auto, GNC, Goodyear/auto, Hobby Lobby, Honda, Hyundai, Kauffman Tire, Kroger/gas, NTB, PepBoys, Publix, Ross, Target, USPO, Verizon, Walgreens
80	West Ave, Conyers, N gas Shell/dsl, Valero/dsl food Domino's, DQ, Subway, Waffle House lodging Best Value Inn, Motel 6 other Conyers Drug, Family$, Meineke, Piggly Wiggly, S gas QT/dsl, Texaco/dsl food Fish House, Longhorn Steaks, McDonald's lodging Comfort Inn other Nissan, vet
79mm	parking area eb
78	Sigman Rd, N gas Shell/dsl, Texaco food Waffle House
75	US 278, GA 124, Turner Hill Rd, N gas BP/dsl, Citgo/dsl, S food Applebee's, Arizona's, Bruster's, Buffalo Wild Wings, Chicken&Waffles, Chick-fil-A, Chili's, Don Tello's Mexican, Firehouse Subs, Grand China, IHOP, Kampai's Steaks, McDonald's, Olive Garden, Panera Bread, Smokey Bones BBQ, Steak n'Shake, Steak'n Shake, Subway, Taco Bell, TGIFriday, Zaxby's lodging Comfort Inn, Comfort Suites, Fairfield Inn, Hilton Garden, Holiday Inn Express, Hyatt Place other $Tree, AT&T, Big Lots, Dillard's, JC Penney, Kia, Kohl's, Macy's, Marshalls, PetCo, Rite Aid, Ross, Staples, Target, Tires+, Toyota, Verizon, Walmart
74	Evans Mill Rd, GA 124, Lithonia, N gas BP/Circle K, Chevron, Shell food Capt D's, McDonald's, Pizza Hut, SoulFood Rest., Subway, Wendy's other Advance Parts, CVS Drug, O'Reilly Parts, S gas Citgo/dsl food Da-Bomb Wings/Seafood, DQ, Dudley's Rest., Krystal, Waffle House lodging Microtel other $General
71	Hillandale Dr, Farrington Rd, Panola Rd, N gas QT/dsl, Shell/dsl food Burger King, Checkers, KFC, McDonald's, Rib Tips, Waffle House, Wings&Philly lodging Budgetel, Quality Inn, Super 8 other Family$, S gas BP/dsl, Citgo, Murphy USA/dsl, Shell/dsl food Dunkin Donuts, IHOP, Marco's Pizza, New China, Popeye's, Ruby Tuesday, Subway, Taco Bell/LJ Silver, Town Wings, Wendy's lodging Red Roof Inn other Lowe's, Publix, Tires+, Verizon, Walgreens, Walmart/McDonald's
68	Wesley Chapel Rd, Snapfinger Rd, N food Capt D's, Checkers, Chick-fil-A, China Cafeteria, Church's, Dunkin Donuts, KFC, Little Caesar's, New China, Subway, Taco Bell, Waffle House lodging Economy Inn other $General, DJ's Repair, Home Depot, Kroger, NTB, S gas Chevron/dsl, Mobil, QT, Shell/dsl food Dragon Chinese, JJ's Fish& Chicken, McDonald's, Popeye's lodging Super Inn other Family$, USPO
67b a	I-285, S to Macon, N to Greenville
66	Columbia Dr (from eb, no return), N gas Chevron
65	GA 155, Candler Rd, to Decatur, N gas Chevron, Citgo, Marathon/dsl food Pizza Hut, Popeye's, Red Lobster, Wendy's lodging Best Value Inn other CVS Drug, U-Haul, S gas BP, Chevron, Shell/dsl, Texaco food Baskin-Robbins/Dunkin Donuts, Burger King, Checkers, Church's, DQ, KFC, McDonald's, Subway, Taco Bell, Waffle King lodging Country Hearth Inn other BigLots, Firestone/auto, Macy's
63	Gresham Rd, N gas Chevron, Citgo/dsl food American Deli other Walmart/Subway, S gas Citgo, Marathon, Shell, Texaco/dsl food Church's
62	Flat Shoals Rd (from eb, no return)
61b	GA 260, Glenwood Ave, N gas Chevron, Texaco/dsl
61a	Maynard Terrace (from eb, no return)
60b a	US 23, Moreland Ave, N gas Texaco, Valero lodging Atlanta Motel other Advance Parts, S gas Citgo/dsl, Shell food Checkers, Krystal, LJ Silver, McDonald's, Wendy's
59b	Memorial Dr, Glenwood Ave (from eb)
59a	Cyclorama, N gas Chevron/Blimpie/dsl other MLK Site, S gas BP/Subway other Confederate Ave Complex, CVS
58b	Hill St (from wb, no return), N gas Shell food Mrs. Winners
58a	Capitol St (from wb, no return), N to GA Dome, S Capital Inn, downtown
57	I-75/85
56b	Windsor St (from eb)
56a	US 19, US 29, McDaniel St (eb only), N gas Chevron/dsl
55b	Lee St (from wb), Ft McPherson, S gas Exxon, Shell food Church's, Popeye's, Taco Bell, West Inn Food Court other $Family, Maxway, Sav-A-Lot
55a	Lowery Blvd, S gas Exxon/dsl, Shell food Church's, Popeye's, Taco Bell, West Inn Food Court other Family$, Maxway, Sav-A-Lot

COVINGTON · CONYERS · LITHONIA · ATLANTA AREA · GA

ATLANTA AREA

INTERSTATE 20 Cont'd

Exit #	Services
54	Langhorn St (from wb), to Cascade Rd
53	MLK Dr, to GA 139, N [gas] Chevron, Shell/dsl, S [gas] Texaco/dsl [other] auto repair
52b a	GA 280, Holmes Dr, High Tower Rd, S [gas] Chevron [food] Hong Kong Chinese, McDonald's, Wendy's [other] AutoZone, CVS Drug, Family$
51b a	I-285, S to Montgomery, N to Chattanooga
49	GA 70, Fulton Ind Blvd, N [gas] Citgo/dsl, Shamrock/dsl [food] Wendy's [lodging] Budgetel, Days Inn [other] [airport], S [gas] BP/dsl, Chevron/dsl, Texaco/dsl, Valero [food] Grand Buffet, McDonald's, Waffle House [lodging] Fairview Inn, Red Roof Inn [other] U-Haul
48mm	Chattahoochee River
47	Six Flags Pkwy (from wb), N [gas] [lodging] EconoLodge, S [lodging] Knights Inn, Sleep Inn, Wingate Inn [other] Six Flags Funpark
46b a	Riverside Parkway, N [gas] Citgo/Church's, Marathon, QT/dsl [food] Hong Kong Buffet, Waffle House [lodging] Super 8 [other] Family$, S [gas] Texaco [food] Wendy's [lodging] Knights Inn, Sleep Inn, Wingate Inn [other] Six Flags Funpark
44	GA 6, Thornton Rd, to Lithia Springs, N [gas] BP, QT, RaceTrac/dsl, Shell/dsl, Valero [food] Applebee's, BBQ House, Bojangles, Burger King, Chick-fil-A, Church's, Domino's, Firehouse Subs, Golden Dragon Chinese, Hardee's, IHOP, KFC, Krystal, McDonald's, Olive Tree Rest., Popeye's, Ruby Tuesday, Shoney's, Sonic, Subway, Taco Bell, Waffle House, Wendy's, Zaxby's [lodging] Budget Inn, Holiday Inn Express, InTowne Suites, Quality Inn [other] $General, AT&T, Atlanta West Camping (2mi), Autozone, Carmax, Chevrolet, Ford, Harley Davidson, Home Depot, Honda, Hyundai, Kroger/gas, Midas, Nissan, Office Depot, Tires+, Verizon, vet, VW, Walgreens, S [gas] Shell [food] Bei Jin China, Cracker Barrel, Fiesta Mexican [lodging] Candlewood Suites, Country Inn&Suites, Courtyard, Fairfield Inn, Hampton Inn, Hilton Garden, Motel 6, SpringHill Suites [other] Chrysler/Dodge/Jeep, Kia, to Sweetwater Creek SP, Toyota, Walmart
42mm	**weigh sta eb**
41	Lee Rd, to Lithia Springs, N [gas] Marathon/dsl
37	GA 92, to Douglasville, N [gas] RaceTrac/dsl, Shell/dsl [food] Blimpie, Checker's, Chick-fil-A, Church's, DQ, Kenny's Rest., Krystal, Longhorn Steaks, Martin's Rest., McDonald's, Pizza Hut, Popeye's, Subway, Taco Bell, Waffle House, Wendy's [lodging] Best Value Inn, Comfort Inn, Days Inn, EconoLodge, Quality Inn, Ramada Ltd, Royal Inn [other] [H], AutoZone, CVS Drug, Family$, Kroger/dsl, NAPA, O'Reilly Parts, Tires+, Walgreens, S [gas] Chevron/dsl, QT, Texaco/dsl [food] Domino's, Waffle House [other] $General, Aamco, Advance Parts, Ingles Foods
36	Chapel Hill Rd, N [other] [H], S [gas] QT, Shell/dsl [food] Arby's, Carrabba's, China Garden, Coldstone, Daruma, Five Guys, Joe's Crabshack, Johnny's Subs, Logan's Roadhouse, McDonald's, O'Charley's, Olive Garden, Outback Steaks, Panda Express, Provino's Italian, Shane's Rib Shack, Starbucks, Subway, TX Roadhouse, Waffle House [lodging] Hampton Inn [other] $Tree, Aldi Foods, Belk, BigLots, Dillard's, Discount Tire, Firestone/auto, Hobby Lobby, JC Penney, Kohl's, Macy's, Marshall's, Michael's, Old Navy, Petsmart, Rite Aid, Ross, Target, Verizon
34	GA 5, to Douglasville, N [gas] RaceTrac/dsl, Texaco/dsl [food] Atlantic Grill, Cracker Barrel, Stevie B's Pizza, Waffle House, Williamson Bros BBQ, Zaxby's [lodging] Holiday Inn Express, La Quinta, Sleep Inn [other] $Tree, Kauffman Tires, Sam's Club, URGENT CARE, Walmart, S [gas] Chevron/dsl, Circle K, Shell/dsl [food] Applebee's, Bruster's, Buffalo Wild Wings, Burger King, Chick-fil-A, ChuckECheese, DQ, Dunkin Donuts, El Tio Mexican, Fiesta Mexican,

DOUGLASVILLE

Kennesaw • 75 • Roswell • Duluth • Marietta • Dunwoody • 285 • 85 • Smyrna • North Atlanta • Tucker • Douglasville • 20 • 285 • Atlanta • Redan • 285 • 85 • 20 • Chapel Hill • Cliftondale • Forest Park • Conyers • Palmetto • 85 • Jonesboro • Stockbridge • 75 • GA

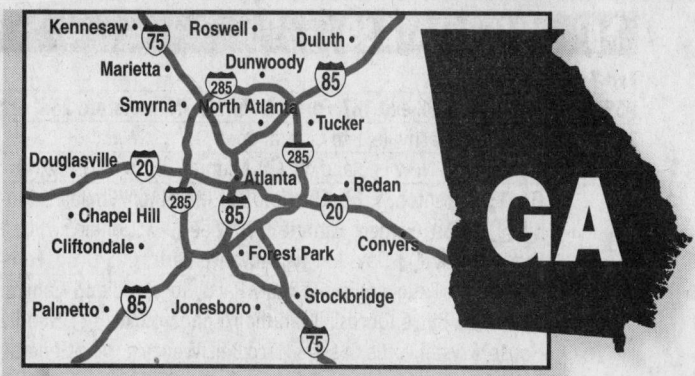

Exit #	Services
34	Continued Folk's Rest., Golden Corral, HoneyBaked Ham, IHOP, KFC, King Buffet, Krystal, La Salsa, LJ Silver, McDonald's, Moe's SW Grill, Monterrey Mexican, Papa John's, Pizza Buffet, Popeyes, Quiznos, Red Lobster, Seabreeze Seafood, S'more BBQ, Sonic, Steak'n Shake, Subway, Taco Bell, Taco Mac, Waffle House, Wasabi Japanese, Wendy's [lodging] InTown Suites [other] Advance Parts, AT&T, Batteries+, Best Buy, Goodyear/auto, Home Depot, Jo-Ann Crafts, Kroger/dsl, Lowe's, Meineke, NTB, Office Depot, O'Reilly Parts, PepBoys, Publix, Tuesday Morning, U-Haul, vet, Walgreens
30	Post Rd, S [gas] Shell/dsl
26	Liberty Rd, Villa Rica, N [gas] Shell/dsl, Swifty/dsl [food] China Wok, Johnny's Pizza, McDonald's, Mex-Grill, Olive Tree Rest., Subway, Sumo Japanese, Waffle House [other] [H], $General, Publix, vet, Walgreens, S [gas] Chevron, Pilot/Subway/dsl/scales/24hr [lodging] American Inn
24	GA 101, GA 61, Villa Rica, N [gas] BP/dsl, RaceTrac/dsl, Shell/dsl [food] Arby's, Chick-fil-A, Hardee's, KFC/Taco Bell, Krystal, Lin's Garden Chinese, McDonald's, Pizza Hut, Romero's Italian, Sonic, Stix Grill, Subway, Waffle House, Wendy's [lodging] Comfort Inn, Days Inn, EconoLodge, Super 8 [other] [H], Advance Parts, AT&T, AutoZone, CVS Drug, Ingles Foods, Rite Aid, Walgreens, S [gas] QT, Shell/dsl [food] Bojangles, Burger King, Capt D's, Domino's, El Ranchito Mexican, O'Charley's, Papa John's, Waffle House, Zaxby's [other] $Tree, Chevrolet, GNC, Home Depot, to W GA Coll, URGENT CARE, Verizon, Walmart/Subway
21mm	Little Tallapoosa River
19	GA 113, Temple, N [gas] FLYING J/dsl/scales/24hr, Pilot/Subway/Wendy's/dsl/scales/24hr/@ [food] El Tapatio's, Fortune Star Chinese, Hardee's, McDonald's, Temple Pizza, Waffle House [other] Ingles Foods/gas
15mm	**weigh sta wb**
11	US 27, Bremen, Bowdon, N [gas] Chevron/dsl, Marathon/dsl, Murphy USA/dsl, Valero/Domino's/dsl [food] Arby's, Capt D's, Checker's, Chopsticks Chinese, Cracker Barrel, Jack's, Juanito's, KFC/Taco Bell, Little Caesar's, McDonald's, Papa John's, Subway, Waffle House, Wendy's, Zaxby's [lodging] Hampton Inn, Holiday Inn Express, Microtel, Motel 6, Quality Inn [other] [H], $General, Advance Parts, Ford, Ingles Foods/gas, URGENT CARE, Verizon, Walmart/McDonald's, S [gas] BP/dsl, Circle K/dsl [food] John Tanner SP
9	Waco Rd, N [gas] Loves/Chesters/Subway/dsl/scales/24hr [other] Jellystone RV Park (2mi)
5	GA 100, Tallapoosa, N [gas] Exxon/dsl, Robinson's/dsl/24hr [food] Waffle House [other] Big Oak RV park, S [gas] Newborn TrkStp/rest/dsl/24hr/@, Pilot/KFC/Taco Bell/dsl/scales/24hr, Robinson/Subway [food] DQ, GA Diner [lodging] Super 8 [other] to John Tanner SP, truck repair/wash
1mm	**Welcome Ctr eb, full [handicapped] facilities, litter barrels, petwalk, [phone], [picnic], vending**
0mm	Georgia/Alabama state line, Eastern/Central time zone

VILLA RICA

BREMEN

= gas = food = lodging = other = rest stop

INTERSTATE 59

Exit #	Services
I-59 begins/ends on I-24, exit 167. For I-24, turn to TN Interstate 24.	
20mm	I-24, W to Nashville, E to Chattanooga
TRENTON	
17	Slygo Rd, to New England, W Midnite/dsl KOA (2mi)
11	GA 136, Trenton, E Chevron/dsl, Marathon/Circle K, Mobil Asian Garden, Guthrie's, Hardee's, McDonald's, Pizza Hut, Subway Days Inn Advance Parts, CVS Drug, Family$, Fred's Drug, Ingles, O'Reilly Parts, to Cloudland Canyon SP, W BP, Citgo/dsl, Marathon/Kangaroo/dsl Huddle House, Krystal, Little Caesars, Taco Bell, Wendy's $General, Food City, Food Outlet
4	Rising Fawn, E Citgo, W BP/dsl, Pilot/Subway/dsl/scales/24hr camping
0mm	Georgia/Alabama state line, eastern/central time zone

INTERSTATE 75

Exit #	Services
355mm	Georgia/Tennessee state line
354mm	Chickamauga Creek
353	GA 146, Rossville, E Marathon Cloud Springs Lodge, W BP/Subway/dsl, Shell/dsl Cabela's, Costco/gas
352mm	**Welcome Ctr sb, full facilities, info, litter barrels, petwalk, vending**
350	GA 2, Bfd Pkwy, to Ft Oglethorpe, E Chevron/dsl/24hr, Mobil/Kangaroo/dsl Hampton Inn, Hometown Inn, W RaceTrac/dsl Subway H, KOA, to Chickamauga NP
348	GA 151, Ringgold, E BP/Kangaroo/dsl, Mapco Cracker Barrel, Hardee's, KFC, Los Maguey Mexican, McDonald's, Pizza Hut, Sonic, Subway, Taco Bell, Waffle House Holiday Inn Express, Super 8 $General, Advance Parts, AutoZone, Chevrolet, Chrysler/Dodge/Jeep, CVS Drug, Ingles, vet, Walgreens, W Exxon/dsl Domino's, Guthries, Krystal, New China, Wendy's Ace Hardware, Family$, Food Lion, Northgate RV Ctr, Peterbilt, truck repair
345	US 41, US 76, Ringgold, E BP, W Cochran's TP/rest./dsl/scales/24hr/@, Kangaroo/Subway/dsl/scales/24hr, Shell Waffle House
343mm	**weigh sta both lanes**
341	GA 201, to Varnell, Tunnel Hill, W BP/Mapco, Chevron carpet outlets
DALTON	
336	US 41, US 76, Dalton, Rocky Face, E Mapco, Murphy USA/dsl, RaceTrac/dsl Checkers, Waffle House H, Ford/Lincoln, Home Depot, Kohl's, PetCo, Verizon, Walmart/Subway, W BP/dsl, Exxon Los Pablos, Tijuana Mexican, Wendy's Baymont Inn, carpet outlets, Econolodge, Guest Inn, Motel 6, Staylodge
333	GA 52, Dalton, E BP/dsl, Exxon/dsl, RaceTrac/dsl Applebee's, Bruster's, Burger King, Capt D's, Chick-fil-A, CiCi's Pizza, Cracker Barrel, DQ, El Patron Mexican, Five Guys, Fuji Japanese, IHOP, Jersey Mike's Subs, KFC, Las Palmas Mexican, LJ Silver, Longhorn Steaks, McDonald's, O'Charley's, Outback Steaks, Panda Express, Panera Bread, Pizza Hut, Schlotzsky's, Shoney's, Sonic, Starbucks, Steak'n Shake, Subway, Taco Bell, Tony's Italian, Waffle House Days Inn, Hampton Inn, Red Roof Inn $Tree, AT&T, BigLots, Chevrolet, Chrysler/Dodge/Jeep, Harley-Davidson, Kroger/dsl, TJ Maxx, Tuesday Morning, Walgreens, W Bojangle's, Chili's, Red Lobster, Zaxby's Comfort Inn, Country Inn Suites, Courtyard, Holiday Inn, Holiday Inn Express, Howard Johnson, La Quinta, Quality Inn, Super 8 NW GA Trade/Conv Ctr
328	GA 3, to US 41, E BP/Circle K/dsl, Pilot/Arby's/dsl/scales/24hr Waffle House, Wendy's Best Value Inn, W carpet outlets
326	Carbondale Rd, E LNG, Pilot/McDonald's/Subway/dsl/scales, W BP
RESACA	
320	GA 136, to Lafayette, Resaca, E Flying J/Denny's/dsl/LP/24hr truck repair/parts
319mm	**sb, full facilities, litter barrels, Oostanaula River, petwalk, vending**
318	US 41, Resaca, E Pilot/DQ/Wendy's/scales/dsl/24hr Hardee's Rodeway Inn, W Pure, Shell/dsl Chuckwagon Rest. Best Inn, Budget Inn, Duffy's Motel, Executive Inn
317	GA 225, to Chatsworth, E New Echota HS, Vann House HS, W Marathon (1mi) Express Inn
CALHOUN	
315	GA 156, Redbud Rd, to Calhoun, E Subway, Waffle House Food Lion, KOA (2mi), W BP/dsl Arby's, Shoney's Ramada H, Rite Aid, URGENT CARE
312	GA 53, to Calhoun, E Shell/dsl Applebee's, Cracker Barrel, Longhorn Steaks, Wendy's Country Inn&Suites, Days Inn, Fairfield Inn, La Quinta Calhoun Outlets/famous brands, W BP/Arby's, Chevron/dsl/24hr, Marathon/Kangaroo, Murphy USA, RaceTrac/dsl Bojangles, Burger King, Capt D's, Checkers, Chick-fil-A, China Palace, Church's, DQ, Dunkin Donuts, Eastern Buffet, El Nopal Mexican, Gondolier Pizza, Hibachi Buffet, Huddle House, IHOP, KFC, Krystal, Little Caesar's, LJ Silver, McDonald's, Pizza Hut, Popeyes, Ruby Tuesday, Starbucks, Subway, Taco Bell, Tokyo Steaks, Waffle House, Zaxby's Baymont Inn, Holiday Inn Express, Motel 6, Scottish Inn, Super 8 $General, Advance Parts, AT&T, AutoZone, GNC, Goodyear/auto, Home Depot, Ingles, Kroger/dsl, NAPA, Office Depot, Verizon, vet, Walmart
ADAIRSVILLE	
308mm	**nb, full facilities, litter barrels, petwalk, vending**
306	GA 140, Adairsville, E Click/dsl, Patty's Tkstp/rest./dsl, QT/dsl/scales/24hrs, Valero/dsl Cracker Barrel, Wendy's Hampton Inn truck repair, W Adairsville TP/dsl/scales, BP/dsl, Chevron/dsl, Exxon/dsl Burger King, Hardee's, McDonald's, Subway, Taco Bell, Waffle House, Zaxby's Magnuson Hotel, Quality Inn, Ramada Ltd Advance Parts, AT&T, AutoZone, Family$, Food Lion, Harvest Moon RV Park
296	Cassville-White Rd, E Pilot/McDonald's/Subway/dsl/scales, TA/BP/Burger King/Pizza Hut/Popeye's/Taco Bell/dsl/scales/24hr/@, Texaco/dsl Cartersville North Inn truckwash, W Chevron, Citgo/dsl, Marathon/dsl Country Hearth Inn KOA
293	US 411, to White, E Sunoco/dsl, Texaco/dsl Quality Inn, W Chevron/dsl, Marathon AJ's Cafe, Waffle House Clarion Harley-Davidson, mineral museum, RV camping, st patrol
290	GA 20, to Rome, E Chevron/dsl, Circle K/dsl, Exxon/Subway/dsl Arby's, McDonald's, Wendy's Best Value Inn, Best Western, Country Inn Suites, EconoLodge, Motel 6, Red Roof Inn, Super 8, W BP/dsl, Murphy USA (1.5mi), Shell/dsl Cracker Barrel, Shoney's, Waffle House, Zaxby's Days Inn, Hampton Inn H, $Tree, Lowe's, Rite Aid, RV camping (7mi), Walmart/McDonald's
288	GA 113, Cartersville, 0-2 mi W Exxon/Subway/dsl, Kangaroo/dsl Applebee's, Bojangles, Bruster's, Burger King, Chick-Fil-A, Chili's, CiCi's, Gondolier Pizza, IHOP, KFC, Krystal, Larry's Subs, Longhorn Steaks, Los Reyes Mexican, McDonald's, McDonald's, Ming Moon, Moe's SW Grill, Papa John's, Red Lobster, Starbucks, Steak'n Shake, Subway, Taco Bell, Waffle House, Wendy's Fairfield Inn, Hilton Garden, Knights Inn

GA

INTERSTATE 75 Cont'd

288 Continued
O $General, $Tree, AT&T, Belk, Big Lots, Chrysler/Dodge/Jeep, GNC, Goodyear/auto, Hobby Lobby, Honda, Kohl's, Kroger/dsl, O'Reilly Parts, Publix, Staples, Target, TJ Maxx, to Etowah Indian Mounds (6mi), USPO, Verizon

286mm Etowah River

285 Emerson, **E** gas Sunoco lodging Red Top Mtn Lodge O to Red Top Mtn SP, **W** O to Allatoona Dam

283 Allatoona Rd, Emerson, **E** gas camping (2mi), **W** gas Loves /McDonald's/Subway/dsl/scales/24hr food Chick-fil-A, Wendy's lodging Hampton Inn, Sleep Inn, **S** lodging MainStay Suites

280mm Allatoona Lake

ACWORTH

278 Glade Rd, to Acworth, **E** gas Exxon/dsl, Shell lodging Best Value O McKinney Camping (3mi), to Glade Marina, **W** gas Marathon/dsl, RaceTrac/dsl food Bojangles, KFC, Krystal, Papa John's, Pizza Hut, Subway, Taco Bell, Waffle House lodging Best Inn O AutoZone, Ingles/cafe, O'Reilly Parts, Rite Aid

277 GA 92, Acworth, **E** gas BP/Dunkin Donuts/dsl, RaceTrac/dsl food Hardee's, Waffle House lodging Days Inn, Holiday Inn Express, La Quinta O Cabela's, **W** gas Chevron/dsl, Shell/DQ/dsl food Bamboo Garden, China Chef, Domino's, La Bamba Mexican, McDonald's, Sonic, Subway, Waffle House, Wendy's, Zaxby's lodging Best Western, Econolodge, Quality Inn, Super 8 O $General, Advance Parts, CVS Drug, Family$, Goodyear/auto, Publix, Walgreens

273 Wade Green Rd, **E** gas BP/dsl, RaceTrac/dsl food Arby's, Burger King, Dunkin Donuts, Firehouse Subs, Happy Panda, Las Palmas Mexican, Marco's Pizza, McDonald's, Papa John's, Sam's Eatery, Subway, Taco Bell, Waffle House lodging Magnuson Motel, Sleep Inn O BigLots, GNC, Goodyear/auto, O'Reilly Parts, Publix, Rite Aid, Tires+, **W** gas Shell, Texaco/dsl food BBQ Street, Donny's Rest., Johnny's Pizza/Subs, Mandarin Cafe, Starbucks, Wendy's, Wing Zone O $Tree, Home Depot, Kauffman Tire, Kroger/gas, Verizon, Walgreens

271 Chastain Rd, to I-575 N, **E** gas Chevron food CA Dreaming, Chick-Fil-A, Cookout, Cracker Barrel, Del Taco, Dunkin Donuts/Baskin Robbins, Firehouse Subs, Five Guys, Los Reyes, Maddio's Pizza, O'Charley's, Panda Express, Panera Bread, Ruth's Chris Steaks, Starbucks, Taco Mac, Tin Lizzy Cantina, Zaxby's lodging Best Western, Comfort Suites, Embassy Suites, Fairfield Inn, Residence Inn, **W** gas Shell/dsl, Swifty Save Gas/Blimpie food Arby's, Jimmy John's, Mellow Mushroom, Taco Bell, Waffle House, Wendy's lodging Baymont Inn, SpringHill Suites, Sun Suites O museum

MARIETTA

269 to US 41, to Marietta, **E** gas Shell/dsl food Applebee's, Fuddrucker's, Fujihana, Honey Baked Ham, Jimmy John's, Longhorn Steaks, McDonald's, Olive Garden, Penang Asian, Provino's, Red Lobster, Shogun Japanese, Smashburger, Smoothie King, Starbucks, Subway, Twin Peaks lodging Comfort Inn, Holiday Inn Express, La Quinta, Red Roof Inn O Belk, Firestone/auto, Home Depot, JC Penney, Macy's, Marshall's, Midas, Pepboys, TJ Maxx, Verizon, **W** gas BP/dsl, Exxon food Bahama Breeze, Burger King, Carrabbas, Chick-fil-A, Chili's, Chipotle, ChuckeCheese, Chuy's Mexican, Coldstone, Copelands Grill, Golden Corral, Jason's Deli, Joe's Crabshack, Melting Pot, On-the-Border, Outback Steaks, Panera Bread, Pollo Tropical, Rafferty's, Starbucks, Steak'n Shake, Sweet Tomato, Ted's MT Steaks, TGIFriday, Tilted Kilt, Willy's Mexican lodging Courtyard, Day's Inn, Hampton Inn, Hilton Garden, Homewood Suites, Quality Inn, Wingate Inn O Best Buy, Buick/GMC, CarMax, Chevrolet, Costco/gas, Dick's, Ford/Lincoln, Hobby Lobby, Jo-Ann Fabrics, Kia/Toyota, Michaels, Nissan, NTB, Old Navy, PetsMart, REI, Subaru, Target, to Kennesaw Mtn NP, VW

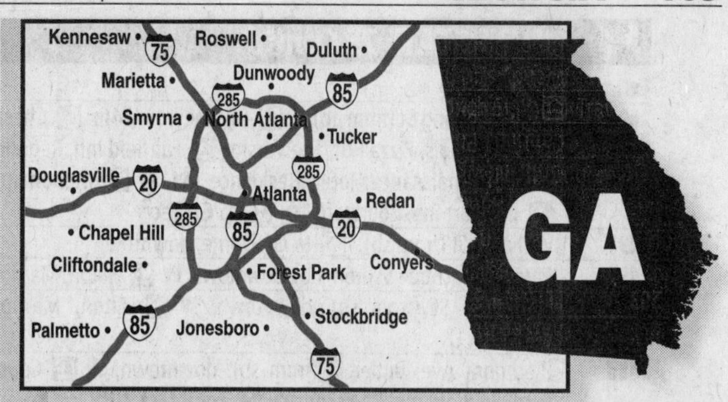

MARIETTA

268 I-575 N, GA 5 N, to Canton

267b a GA 5 N, to US 41, Marietta

265 GA120, N Marietta Pkwy, **W** gas Chevron/dsl, Shell/dsl lodging Days Inn O Advance Parts, Family$, Office Depot, O'Reilly Parts

263 GA 120, to Roswell, **E** gas Chevron, QT, Shell, **W** gas Exxon/dsl, QT food Applebee's, China Kitchen, DQ, Hardee's, Haveli Rest., Piccadilly's, Subway, Tasty China lodging Econolodge, Hampton Inn, Ltd Suites, Radisson, Super 8 O U-Haul, Verizon

261 GA 280, Delk Rd, to Dobbins AFB, **E** gas Exxon/dsl, RaceTrac/dsl, Shell, Shell/Subway/dsl food China Wok, Cosmopolitan Cafeteria, Hardee's, KFC/Taco Bell, Little Caesar's, Marco's Pizza, McDonald's, Ruby Tuesday, Waffle House lodging Courtyard, Drury Inn, Howard Johnson, Motel 6, Ramada, **W** gas BP, Chevron/dsl food Cracker Barrel, Dave&Busters lodging Baymont Inn, Days Inn, Holiday Inn Express, Marietta Hotel, Quality Inn

SMYRNA

260 Windy Hill Rd, to Smyrna, **E** gas BP/dsl food Boston Mkt, Frontera Mex, Fuddrucker's, Houston's Rest., Jersey Mike's Subs, NY Pizza, Pappadeaux Seafood, Pappasito's Cantina, Rose&Crown, Schlotzsky's, Subway lodging Best Value Inn, Country Hearth Inn, Extended Stay America, Hilton Garden, Hyatt, Marriott O CVS Drug, USPO, **W** gas Chevron, Conoco, Gulf/dsl, Shell food Arby's, Chick-fil-A, McDonald's, Panda Express, Popeye's, Starbucks, Subway, Waffle House, Wendy's lodging Comfort Inn, Country Inn&Suites, Courtyard, Days Inn, DoubleTree, Masters Inn, Red Roof Inn, Sky Suites O H, Target

259b a I-285, W to Birmingham, E to Greenville, Montgomery

258 Cumberland Pkwy, **E** lodging Hyatt House, **W** food Chick-fil-A, Chipotle Mexican, Copelands Rest, Firehouse Subs, Hooters, Longhorn Steaks, Moe's SW Grill, Shane's Ribshack, Subway lodging Homewood Suites O Krogers

257mm Chattahoochee River

256 to US 41, Northside Pkwy

ATLANTA

255 US 41, W Paces Ferry Rd, **E** gas Chevron, Shell/dsl food Blue Ridge Grill, Caribou Coffee, Chick-fil-A, Flying Biscuit Cafe, Houston's Rest., McDonald's/playplace, OK Café, Pero's Pizza, Smoothie King, Starbucks, Steak'n Shake, Taco Bell, Willy's Mexicana O H, Ace Hardware, CVS Drug, Publix, **W** gas Exxon

254 Moores Mill Rd

252b Howell Mill Rd, **E** gas Shell/auto food Chick-fil-A, Chipotle, Domino's, Jersey Mike's, McDonald's, Willy's Grill O Goodyear/auto, Publix, Rite Aid, USPO, **W** gas Shell food Arby's, Chin Chin Chinese, La Parrilla Mexican, Piccadilly, Starbucks, Subway, Taco Bell, Waffle House, Wendy's O Ace Hardware, Firestone/auto, GNC, Kroger, NTB, Office Depot, Petsmart, Ross, TJ Maxx, Verizon, Walmart

252a US 41, Northside Dr, **E** O H, **W** gas Shell food Little Zio's lodging InTown Suites

251 I-85 N, to Greenville

250 Techwood Dr (from sb), 10th St, 14th St, **E** lodging Travelodge

GA

INTERSTATE 75 Cont'd

Exit #	Services
249d	10th St, Spring St (from nb), E BP, Chevron/24hr Checker's, Domino's, Pizza Hut, The Varsity Fairfield Inn, Regency Suites, Renaissance Hotel, Residence Inn, W McDonald's Comfort Inn, Courtyard H, to GA Tech
249c	Williams St (from sb), to GA Dome, downtown
249b	Pine St, Peachtree St (from nb), downtown, W Hilton, Marriott
249a	Courtland St (from sb), downtown, W Hilton, Marriott GA St U
248d	Piedmont Ave, Butler St (from sb), downtown, W Courtyard, Fairfield Inn, Radisson H, Ford, MLK NHS
248c	GA 10 E, Intn'l Blvd, downtown, W Hilton, Holiday Inn, Marriott Marquis, Radisson
248b	Edgewood Ave (from nb), W H, downtown, hotels
248a	MLK Dr (from sb), W st capitol, to Underground Atlanta
247	I-20, E to Augusta, W to Birmingham
246	Georgia Ave, Fulton St, E Comfort Inn, Country Inn& Suites, Holiday Inn stadium, W KFC GSU, to Coliseum
245	Ormond St, Abernathy Blvd, E Comfort Inn, Country Inn& Suites stadium, W st capitol
244	University Ave, E Chevron, Exxon NAPA, W Mrs Winner's
243	GA 166, Lakewood Fwy, to East Point
242	I-85 S, to
241	Cleveland Ave, E BP, Chevron/Subway/dsl Checkers, Church's, McDonald's Advance Parts, W Citgo/dsl, ExpressZone, Marathon Ameican Deli, Burger King, Krystal, Papa John's American Inn $Tree, AutoZone, Big Lots, CVS Drug, Family$, Kroger, Walgreens
239	US 19, US 41, E Chevron/dsl Waffle House USPO, W Texaco Chick-fil-A, IHOP, McDonald's, Wendy's Best Western to
238b a	I-285 around Atlanta
237a	GA 85 S (from sb)
237	GA 331, Forest Parkway, E BP, Chevron/dsl, Shell/McDonald's, SunPetro/dsl Burger King, Mr Taco, Subway, Waffle House Econolodge Farmer's Mkt, W BP, Exxon/Subway/dsl Quizno's Atlanta Inn, Ramada Ltd Lee Tires/repair
235	US 19, US 41, GA 3, Jonesboro, E Chevron/dsl, Circle K/Subway/dsl, Texaco/dsl Super 8, Travelodge, W Chevron/dsl, Citgo, Texaco/dsl Applebee's, Burger King, Checkers, ChuckeCheese, Dunkin Donuts, Hibachi Grill, Hooters, Little Caesar's, McDonald's, Popeye's, Red Lobster, Waffle House, Zaxby's Amercan Inn, Econolodge, Motel 6 H, $General, $Tree, Little Giant Farmers Mkt, Office Depot, O'Reilly Parts
233	GA 54, Morrow, E BP/dsl, Citgo, Gulf Cookout, Cracker Barrel, IHOP, Krystal, Taco Bell, Waffle House, Wendy's Best Western, Comfort Suites, Days Inn, Drury Inn, Red Roof Inn Walmart, W Chevron/dsl, Exxon/dsl, QT/dsl China Café, Golden Buddha, KFC, Lenny's Subs, Olive Garden, Subway, Three$ Cafe, Waffle House, Wendy's Hampton Inn, Quality Inn Acura, Buick/GMC/Mazda, Burlington Coats, Cadillac, Costco/gas, Fiat, Harley-Davidson, Kia, Macy's, Nissan, Sam's Club/gas, TJ Maxx, Toyota
231	Mt Zion Blvd, E Chrysler/Dodge/Jeep, Ford/Lincoln, Honda, W BP/Circle K/Subway/dsl, Chevron, Texaco/dsl Arby's, Atlanta Bread, Bruster's, Burger King, Carrabba's, Chili's, China King, Chipotle, City Cafe Diner, Joe's Crabshack, Longhorn Steaks, McDonald's, Moe's SW Grill, Mo-Jo's Wings, Panda Express, Papa John's, Pizza Hut, Skyboxx Rest.,
231	Continued Steak'n Shake, Taco Bell, TGIFriday, Truett's Rest., Waffle House, Wendy's, Wok Asian, Zaxby's Best Value Inn, Country Inn&Suites, Extended Stay America, Sun Suites AT&T, Barnes & Noble, Best Buy, Home Depot, NTB, Petsmart, Publix, Ross, Verizon
228	GA 54, GA 138, Jonesboro, E Raceway/dsl Applebee's, Broadway Diner, Chick-fil-A, Frontera Mexican, Golden Corral, Honeybaked Ham, IHOP, Krystal, Marco's Pizza, O'Charley's, Piccadilly's, Stevi B's Pizza, Subway, Taco Mac, Tokyo Seafood, Waffle House, Wing Nuts Comfort Inn, Day's Inn, Express Inn, Hampton Inn, Holiday Inn, La Quinta, Red Roof Inn H, Kroger/dsl, Lowes Whse, Office Depot, Tires+, URGENT CARE, Verizon, W Marathon, Mobil, Raceway/Wendy's/dsl Dragon Garden Chinese, McDonald's, Ranchero's Mexican Fairfield Inn CarMax, CVS Drug, Kohl's
227	I-675 N, to I-285 E (from nb)
224	Hudson Bridge Rd, E Shell/dsl, Texaco/dsl Chick-fil-A, China Wok, DQ, Italian Oven, Johnny's NY Pizza, KFC, La Hacienda, Outback Steaks, Pueblo Mio, Serafino Itlian, Starbucks, Sticky Cactus Mexican, Subway, Waffle House, Wendy's Quality Inn H, Kauffman Tire, Publix, Rite Aid, Walgreens, W Murphy USA/dsl, QT Arby's, China Cafe, Firehouse Subs, McDonald's, Mellow Mushroom, Taco Bell, Zaxby's Super 8 $Tree, AT&T, AutoZone, Discount Tire, GNC, Verizon, Walmart
222	Jodeco Rd, E Citgo, Shell, Texaco Hardee's, W Fifteenth St Pizza Atlanta So. RV Camping
221	Jonesboro Rd, E QT/dsl, Shell/dsl Kauffman Tire, Kroger/gas (2mi), W American Deli, Arby's, Burger King, Cheddar's, Chili's, Firehouse Subs, Golden Corral, Hong Kong Cafe, Hooters, La Parrilla, Logan's Roadhouse, Longhorn Steaks, Marble Slab Creamery, McDonald's, Mike's Burger, O'Charley's, Olive Garden, Red Lobster, Rocky's Pizza, Starbucks, Subway, Truett's Grill, Wendy's, Wild Wing Cafe, Yuki Hibachi Courtyard, Fairfield Inn, Home 2 Suites AT&T, AutoZone, Belk, Best Buy, Books-A-Million, Dick's, Home Depot, Marshall's, Michael's, Old Navy, PetsMart, Ross, Sam's Club/gas, Staples, Target, Verizon
218	GA 20, GA 81, McDonough, E BP/dsl, Murphy USA/dsl, QT, Texaco American Deli, Applebee's, Arby's, Burger King, China King, China Star, Cracker Barrel, DQ, IHOP, KFC, Maritza&-Frank's Rest., McDonald's, Mesquite Mexican, Moe's SW Grill, Montego Bay Cafe, OB's BBQ, Pizza Hut, Popeye's, Ruby Tuesday, Sakura Hibachi, South Side Diner, Taco Bell, Three $ Cafe, Waffle House, Zaxby's Baymont Inn, Best Western, Economy Inn, Howard Johnson, Super 8 $General, $Tree, Aamco, Discount Tire, Goodyear, Lowe's Whse, Office Depot, Rite Aid, URGENT CARE, Walmart, W RaceTrac/dsl, Shell Chick-fil-A, Dunkin Donuts, El Agade Mexican, Firehouse Subs, Folks Rest., Freddy's, Hardee's, Ichiban Express, Jimmy John's, Starbucks, Subway, Waffle House Comfort Suites, Econolodge, Fair Bridge Inn, Hampton Inn, Hilton Garden, Holiday Inn Express, Motel 6 Advance Parts, AT&T, Hobby Lobby, Honda, JC Penney, Kia, Kohl's, NTB, TJ Maxx, Toyota, Verizon
216	GA 155, McDonough, Blacksville, E Shell/dsl, Sunoco Honk Kong Express, Sonic Best Value, Day's Inn, Rodeway Inn Chevrolet/Buick/GMC, Ford, GMC, Hyundai, Tire South, W BP, Chevron, Citgo/dsl/24hr, Exxon/dsl, QT Bass BBQ, Da Vinci's Pizza, El Jimador, Graffiti's Oizza, Krystal, Kuma Japanese, Steve's Cafe, Subway, Waffle House Country Inn&Suites, Quality Inn, Sleep Inn

ATLANTA

MORROW

JONESBORO

MCDONOUGH

GA

INTERSTATE 75 Cont'd

Exit #	Services
212	to US 23, Locust Grove, E BP/McDonald's/dsl, Chevron/Burger King, Marathon/Quizno's, Murphy USA/dsl, QT/dsl, Shell/dsl American Deli, Capt D's, Denny's, Hamburger Mike's, IHOP, KFC/Taco Bell, Koji Japanese, Little Caesar's, Pizza Hut, San Diego Mexican, Shane's Ribshack, Subway, Sunrise China, Waffle House, Wendy's, Zaxby's Executive Inn, La Quinta, Ramada, Red Roof Inn $Tree, Advance Parts, AT&T, Ingles/gas, NapaCare, Tanger Outlet/famous brands, Verizon, Walmart, W Exxon/dsl, Shell/DQ/dsl Subway Comfort Suites, Scottish Inn, Sundown Lodge, Super 8 Bumper Parts
205	GA 16, to Griffin, Jackson, E BP, W Chevron/Subway/dsl Hogfather's BBQ Forest Glen RV Park
201	GA 36, to Jackson, Barnesville, E Loves/McDonald's/dsl/grill/scales/24hr, Pilot/DQ/Wendy's/dsl/scales/24hr/@, TA/Subway/Taco Bell/dsl/scales/24hr/@ Blue Beacon, W FLYING J/Denny's/dsl/LP/24hr, BP/dsl Waffle House Speedco Lube, truckwash
198	Highfalls Rd, E Exxon (1mi) High Falls BBQ High Falls Lodge High Falls SP, HighFalls RV Park (1mi)
193	Johnstonville Rd, W Marathon/dsl
190mm	**weigh sta both lanes**
188	GA 42, E Shell Budget Inn, Hill Top Garden Inn RV camping, to Indian Springs SP
187	GA 83, Forsyth, E Econolodge, Regency Inn KOA, W Citgo/dsl, Exxon/Circle K, Marathon, Shell, Valero/dsl Burger King, Capt D's, DQ, Hardee's, McDonald's, Subway, Taco Bell, Waffle House, Wendy's Day's Inn $Tree, Advance Parts, Family$, Freshway Foods, O'Reilly Parts, Verizon, Walmart/dsl
186	Tift College Dr, Juliette Rd, Forsyth, E Jarrell Plantation HS (18mi), KOA, W BP/dsl, Chevron/dsl, Marathon Waffle House Holiday Inn Express, Motel 6, Super 8 H, CVS Drug, Ingles/Deli
185	GA 18, E L&D RV Park (2mi), W Exxon/Circle K, Shell/dsl Shoney's Comfort Inn Ford, st patrol
181	Rumble Rd, to Smarr, E BP/dsl
179mm	**RS sb, full facilities, litter barrels, petwalk, vending**
177	I-475 S around Macon (from sb)
175	Pate Rd, Bolingbroke (from nb, no re-entry)
172	Bass Rd, E McDonald's, Zaxby's Bass Pro Shop, W Citgo/dsl, Flash/DQ/dsl Chick-fil-A, Genghis Grill, Homewood Suites, Magarita's Mexican, Mellow Mushroom, Natalia's Rest., Subway, Taco Bell, Zheng's Wok Microtel, Woodspring Suites CVS, Publix, to Museum of Arts&Sciences
171	US 23, to GA 87, Riverside Dr, E BP, Marathon/dsl Barbarito's Cantina, Bonefish Grill, Buca Italian, Chili's, Firehouse Subs, GA Bob's BBQ, Jersey Mike's, La Parrilla, TX Roadhouse, Wild Wing Cafe SpringHill Suites Acura, AT&T, Barnes & Noble, Belk, BMW, Dick's, Dillard's, GNC, Hobby Lobby, Jo-Ann, Mercedes, Petsmart, Subaru, Verizon, Volvo, W Lexus, Toyota
169	to US 23, Arkwright Dr, E Shell/Circle K/24hr Carraba's, Logan's Roadhouse, Outback Steaks, Waffle House, Wager's Grill Candlewood Suites, Comfort Inn, Country Inn & Suites, Courtyard, Fairfield Inn, Hampton Inn, Holiday Inn, Home 2 Suites, La Quinta, Red Roof Inn, Residence Inn, Sleep Inn Buick/Cadillac/GMC, W Chevron/dsl, Marathon/dsl Arby's, Buffalo Wild Wings, Burger King, Cheddar's, Chick-fil-A, Chipotle, Cracker Barrel, Dunkin Donuts, Five Guys,

FORSYTH

MACON

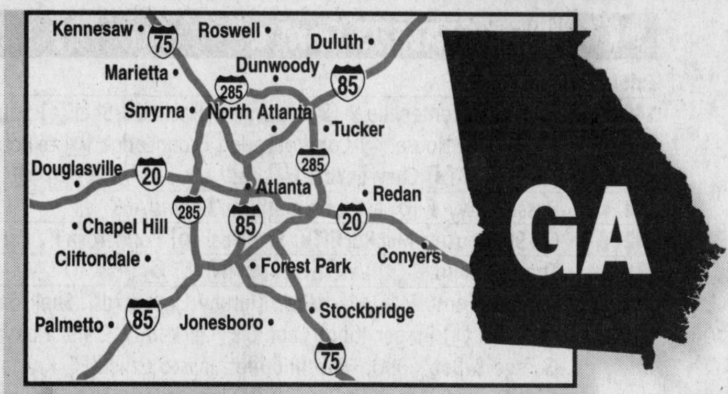

Exit #	Services
169	Continued Guitarras Mexican, Hooters, IHOP, Joy's Buffet, KFC, Krystal, Little Caesar's, Longhorn Steaks, Mandarin Chinese, McDonald's, Panda Express, Panera Bread, Papa John's, Starbucks, Steak'n Shake, Steve B's Pizza, Subway, Taco Bell, Waffle House, Wendy's Baymont Inn, Budgetel, Days Inn, Extended Stay America, Quality Inn, Rodeway Inn, Travelodge, Wingate Inn H, $General, $Tree, Ace Hardware, Chrysler/Jeep/Dodge, GNC, Goodyear/auto, Hyundai, Kia, Kroger/dsl, Mazda, O'Reilly Parts, Publix, Tuesday Morning
167	GA 247, Pierce Ave, E United Inn, W Exxon, Fastrip/dsl, Shell/Circle K/dsl, Shell/dsl Applebee's, Loco's Grill, Marco's Pizza, Metropolis Mediterranean, S&S Cafeteria, Shogun Japanese, SteakOut, Waffle House Best Western/rest., Holiday Inn Express, Howard Johnson, Magnuson Hotel, Palmtree Extended Stay Firestone/auto, Rite Aid
165	I-16 E, to Savannah
164	US 41, GA 19, Forsyth Ave, Macon, E Sid's Rest. H, hist dist, W Citgo/dsl museum
163	GA 74 W, Mercer U Dr, E Hilton Garden to Mercer U, W Citgo
162	US 80, GA 22, Eisenhower Pkwy, W Citgo/dsl, Lo-lo Gas, Sunoco/dsl Burger King, Capt D's, Checker's, Krispy Kreme, Krystal, McDonald's, Mrs Winners, Overtyme Grill, Subway, Wendy's InTown Suites $Tree, O'Reilly Parts, PepBoys, Save-A-Lot Foods, Walgreens
160	US 41, GA 247, Pio Nono Ave, E Flash/dsl, RaceWay/Dunkin Donuts/dsl Waffle House, W BP, Enmark/dsl Arby's, DQ, KFC, McDonald's, Subway, Waffle House $General, Advance Parts, Family$, O'Reilly Parts, Piggly Wiggly, Raffield Tire, Roses
156	I-475 N around Macon (from nb)
155	Hartley Br Rd, E Shell/KFC/dsl Domino's, Subway, Waffle House, Wendy's Kroger/dsl, Verizon, W Citgo/dsl, Flash/DQ/dsl McDonald's, Zaxby's Best Value Inn Advance Parts, CVS Drug
153	Sardis Church Rd, E Citgo/dsl
149	GA 49, Byron, E Chevron/dsl, Shell/dsl Burger King, Casa Mexico, Denny's, GA Bob's BBQ, Krystal, Marco's Pizza, McDonald's, Pizza Hut, Subway, Waffle House, Wendy's, Zaxby's Best Western, Comfort Suites, Holiday Inn Express, Super 8 Campers Inn RV Ctr, Mid-State RV Ctr, Peach Stores/famous brands, W Citgo/dsl/24hr, Flash/dsl, Marathon/dsl, RaceWay/dsl, Texaco/dsl DQ, Hardee's, Hudson's BBQ, Waffle House Budget Inn, Days Inn, EconoLodge, Quality Inn $General, Advance Parts, Bumper Parts, Camping World RV Ctr, Chevrolet, Ford, Interstate RV Ctr/park, O'Reilly Parts, Verizon

MACON

GA

INTERSTATE 75 Cont'd

Exit #	Services
146	GA 247, to Centerville, E Exxon/dsl, Flash/dsl, Shell Subway, Waffle House Comfort Lodge, EconoLodge to Robins AFB, W Chevron/dsl, Pilot/Arby's/dsl/24hr
144	Russel Pkwy, E aviation museum, Robins AFB
142	GA 96, Housers Mill Rd, E Shell/dsl Ponderosa RV Park
138	Thompson Rd, E Valero/dsl, W
136	US 341, Perry, E Flash/dsl, Murphy Express/dsl, Shell/Circle K/dsl Burger King, Capt D's, Chick-fil-A, China House, George & Bob's BBQ, Hibachi Buffet, Jalisco Grill, KFC, Krystal, Little Caesar's, Longhorn Steaks, McDonald's, Pizza Hut, Red Lobster, Sonny's BBQ, Steamers Seafood, Subway, Taco Bell, Waffle House, Wendy's, Zaxby's Great Inn, Hampton Inn, Howard Johnson, Jameson Inn, Motel 6, Rodeway Inn, Super 8 , $General, $Tree, Ace Hardware, Advance Parts, Boland's RV Park, GNC, Kroger/dsl, NAPA, Verizon, Walmart, W Shell/Circle K/dsl Applebee's, Grill Master BBQ Days Inn, EconoLodge, Hardee's, Holiday Inn Express, Knights Inn, Passport Inn, Quality Inn, Ramada Inn Crossroads Travel Oark
135	US 41, GA 127, Perry, E Chevron/dsl, Flash/dsl, Flash/dsl (2), Shell, Texaco/dsl Cracker Barrel, DQ, Subway, Waffle House Best Western, Budget Inn, Comfort Inn, Relax Inn, Travelodge Chrysler/Dodge/Jeep, GA Nat Fair, Kia, W Fair Harbor RV Park, st patrol
134	South Perry Pkwy, W Microtel Buick/Chevrolet/GMC, Ford
127	GA 26, Henderson, E Twin Oaks Camping, W Shell/dsl
122	GA 230, Unadilla, E Chevron/dsl Chevrolet/Ford
121	US 41, Unadilla, E Borum/repair, Flash/DQ/dsl Subway Scottish Inn $General, Family$, Firestone, Piggly Wiggly, Southern Trails RV Resort, USPO, W Citgo/rest./dsl/scales/24hr
118mm	**sb, full facilities, litter barrels, petwalk, , RV dump, vending**
117	to US 41, Pinehurst, W GasnGo/Subway/dsl
112	GA 27, Vienna
109	GA 215, Vienna, E Pilot/McDonalds/dsl/scales/24hr, W Shell/dsl, Sunoco Popeye's Executive Inn $General Mkt, Cotton Museum
108mm	**nb, full facilities, litter barrels, petwalk, , RV dump, vending**
104	Farmers Mkt Rd, Cordele
102	GA 257, Cordele, E Sunoco/dsl, W Smoothie's BBQ
101	US 280, GA 90, Cordele, E BP/dsl, Pilot/Arby's/dsl/scales/24hr, Shell Denny's, Golden Corral, Waffle House Fairfield Inn, Holiday Inn Express, Motel 6, Ramada Inn Ford, st patrol, W Flash/dsl, Gas'n Go, Sunoco, VP/Subway Burger King, Capt D's, Chick-fil-A, Cracker Barrel, DQ, Hachi Japanese Grill, Hardee's, KFC, Krystal, Little Caesar's, Los Compadres, McDonald's, New China, Pizza Hut, Sonic, Subway, Taco Bell, TJ's Rest, Wendy's, Zaxby's Ashburn Inn, Athens 8 Motel, Baymont Inn, Best Western, EconoLodge, Hampton Inn, Quality Inn, Travelodge $General, $Tree, Advance Parts, AT&T, AutoZone, Belk, Harvey's Foods, Home Depot, J Carter HS, Kauffman Tire, O'Reilly Parts, Save-A-Lot, to Veterans Mem SP, Verizon, Walgreens, Walmart
99	GA 300, GA/FL Pkwy, E Marathon/DQ/dsl, W Waffle House Comfort Inn to Chehaw SP
97	to GA 33, Wenona, E Cordele RV Park, dsl repair, W KOA, truckwash
92	Arabi, E Shell/Plantation House, W Southern Gates RV Park
85mm	**nb, full facilities, litter barrels, petwalk, , vending**
84	GA 159, Ashburn, W Chevron/DQ/Blimpie/dsl/24hr Ashburn Inn/RV Park
82	GA 107, GA 112, Ashburn, W BP, Shell, Sunoco/dsl Carroll's Sausage & Country Store/RV Park, KFC, McDonald's, Pizza Hut, Shoney's, Subway, Waffle House, Zaxby's Best Western, Days Inn, Super 8 $General, Auto Value Parts, Buick/Chevrolet/GMC, Fred's, O'Reilly Parts, Piggly Wiggly, Rite Aid, to Chehaw SP
80	Bussey Rd, Sycamore, E Marathon/dsl, Valero, W Allen's Tires
78	GA 32, Sycamore, E to Jefferson Davis Mem Pk (14mi)
76mm	**sb, full facilities, litter barrels, petwalk, , vending**
75	Inaha Rd
71	Willis Still Rd, Sunsweet, W Citgo/dsl
69	Chula-Brookfield Rd, E Sunoco/dsl Economy Inn
66	Brighton Rd
64	US 41, Tifton, E BP/dsl Waffle House , $General, Harvey's Foods, W Shell
63b	8th St, Tifton, E Flash/dsl/e-85 Firehouse Subs, Los Compadres Jo-Ann, Publix, TJ Maxx, W Pit Stop BBQ GA Museum of Agriculture
63a	2nd St, Tifton, E BP/dsl, Marathon Arby's, Asahi Xpress, Barberito's, Checker's, El Metate, JoJo's Rest., KFC, Krystal, McDonald's, Pizza Hut, Ranchero's Grill, Red Lobster, Subway, Taco Bell, Waffle House EconoLodge, Super 8 $General, $Tree, Big Lots, W Bob's/dsl El Cazadore Mexican Motel 6, Quality Inn
62	US 82, to US 319, Tifton, E BP, Flash/dsl Applebee's, Bojangles, Charles Seafood, Chili's, Cracker Barrel, DQ, Golden Corral, Hardee's, King Buffet, Logan's Roadhouse, Ole Times Buffet, Sonic, Tokyo Japanese, Waffle House, Zaxby's Comfort Inn, Country Inn&Suites, Fairfield Inn, Hampton Inn, Holiday Inn Express, Microtel $Tree, Advance Parts, AutoZone, BigLots, Family$, Ford/Lincoln, NAPA, O'Reilly Parts, Pecan Outlet, Save-A-Lot, Staples, W EZ Mart, Flash/dsl, Murphy USA/dsl, RaceWay/dsl, Shell/dsl Burger King, Capt D's, Chick-fil-A, Dick's Wings, HogBones BBQ, Little Caesar's, Longhorn Steaks, McDonald's, Oishi Japanese, Olive Garden, Pizza Hut, Ruby Tuesday, Starbucks, Subway, Waffle House, Wendy's Days Inn, Hilton Garden, Scottish Inn $General, AT&T, Chevrolet, Chrysler/Dodge/Jeep, Hobby Lobby, Honda, Lowe's, Toyota, URGENT CARE, Verizon, Walmart/Subway
61	Omega Rd, E Nissan, W Shell/Waffle King/pizza/dsl/24hr Howard Johnson Harley-Davidson, Pines RV Park
60	Central Ave, Tifton, E Chevron Dragon 1 Chinese, W Pilot/Steak'n Shake/Subway/dsl/scales/24hr Blue Beacon, KOA
59	Southwell Blvd, to US 41, Tifton, E Loves/Hardee's/dsl/24hr
55	to Eldorado, Omega, E Shell/Magnolia Plantation/dsl
49	Kinard Br Rd, Lenox, E Dixie/dsl Extended Stay, W BP/dsl/24hr repair
47mm	**both lanes, full facilities, litter barrels, petwalk, , vending**
45	Barneyville Rd, E Economy Inn
41	Rountree Br Rd, E Citgo, W to Reed Bingham SP
39	GA 37, Adel, Moultrie, E Citgo/dsl, Dixie Gas, McDonald's Quick Gas DQ, Hardee's, Subway, Waffle House Scottish Inn, Super 8 , $General, Ace Hardware, Advance Parts Family$, Harvey's Foods, O'Reilly Parts, Piggly Wiggly, Rite Aid W BP, Citgo/dsl/scales, Shell Burger King, Capt D's

PERRY

CORDELE

ASHBURN

TIFTON

GA

INTERSTATE 75 Cont'd

ADEL

39	Continued China Buffet, IHOP, Taco Bell, Wendy's, Western Sizzlin Days Inn, Hampton Inn to Reed Bingham SP, Verizon, Walmart
37	Adel, E Liberty/dsl GMC
32	Old Coffee Rd, Cecil, E Citgo/dsl Stagecoach Inn, W Chevron/dsl Cecil Bay RV Park
29	US 41 N, GA 122, Hahira, Sheriff's Boys Ranch, E Harvey's Mkt, Huddle House, Slice Pizza NAPA, vet, W Big Foot TC/cafe/dsl/24hr, Citgo/dsl Hahira Inn
23mm	**weigh sta both lanes**
22	US 41 S, to Valdosta, E BP, Subway/dsl Waffle House Best Western H, Buick/Chevrolet/GMC, Mazda, W Citgo/dsl Burger King, DQ Howard Johnson Valdosta Oaks RV Park

VALDOSTA

18	GA 133, Valdosta, E Citgo/dsl, Exxon, Flash, Mobil Applebee's, Arby's, Atl. Bread Co, Beijing Cafe, Bruster's, Buffalo Wild Wings, Burger King, Chick-fil-A, Chili's, Chow Town, Ci-Ci's Pizza, Cracker Barrel, Crystal River Seafood, Denny's, Dick's Wings, El Potro Mexican, El Toreo, Fazoli's, Five Guys, Honeybaked Ham, Hooters, KFC, Krystal, Little Caesar's, Longhorn Steaks, Marble Slab, McDonald's, Ole Times Country Buffet, Olive Garden, Outback Steaks, Panda Express, Red Lobster, Shane's Ribshack, Sonny's BBQ, Starbucks, Steak'n Shake, Subway, Taco Bell, TX Roadhouse, Waffle House, Wendy's, Zaxby's Baymont Inn, Comfort Suites, Country Inn&Suites, Courtyard, Drury Inn, Hilton Garden, Holiday Inn Express, InTown Suites, Jolly Inn, La Quinta, Motel 6, Quality Inn, Rodeway Inn $Tree, AT&T, Belk, Best Buy, Books-A-Million, Family$, Goodyear/auto, Hobby Lobby, Home Depot, JC Penney, Kohl's, Lowe's, Michael's, Office Depot, Old Navy, Petsmart, Publix, Ross, Target, TJ Maxx, URGENT CARE, Verizon, Walgreens, W BP/dsl, RaceWay/dsl, Shell Days Inn, EconoLodge, Sleep Inn, Super 8 RiverPark Camping, Toyota
16	US 84, US 221, GA 94, Valdosta, E BP/dsl, Citgo/DQ/dsl, Murphy Express/dsl, Pure/dsl, Shell/dsl, Sunoco Aligatou Japanese, Bojangles, Bubba Jax Crab Shack, Burger King, Cheddar's, IHOP, McDonald's, Pizza Hut, Smokin' Pig BBQ, Sonic, Waffle House, Wendy's Best Value Inn, Comfort Inn, Days Inn, Fairfield Inn, Hampton Inn, Holiday Inn, Motel 6, Quality Inn, Super 8 Sam's Club/gas, to Okefenokee SP, Walmart/Subway, W Shell/dsl/24hr Austin's Steaks Briarwood Inn, Kinderlou Inn
13	Old Clyattville Rd, Valdosta, W Wild Adventures Park
11	GA 31, Valdosta, E LNG, Pilot/Dunkin Donuts/dsl/scales/24hr, Pilot/Subway/dsl/24hr/@ Waffle House Travelers Inn truckwash, W Quick Gas $General
5	GA 376, to Lake Park, E Citgo, Flash Foods/Stuckey's/dsl, RaceWay/dsl, Shell Chick-fil-A, Cowboys Grill, Domino's, Farmhouse Rest., Krystal, Lin's Garden Chinese, Rodeo Mexican, Subway, Taco Bell, Waffle House, Zaxby's Motel 6, Quality Inn $Tree, antiques, Eagles Roost Camping, Family$, Fred's, Horizon RV Ctr, USPO, Winn-Dixie, W Exxon/dsl, Shell/dsl Cracker Barrel, McDonald's, Pizza Hut, Wendy's Best Value Inn, Days Inn, Hampton Inn, Travelodge Camping World RV Ctr, GS Camping
3mm	**Welcome Ctr nb, full facilities, litter barrels, petwalk, vending**
2	Lake Park, Bellville, E TA/BP/Arby's/dsl/scales/24hr/@ SpeedCo, W FLYING J/Denny's/Subway/dsl/LP/scales/24hr lube/tires/wash
0mm	Georgia/Florida state line

Stockbridge
Jonesboro
75
McDonough
Greenwood
Luella
Locust Grove
Walker Mill
High Falls
Unionville
Box Ankle
Higgins Mill
Forsyth
Smarr
75
Arkwright
Lizella
Macon
Groveland Park
16
GA

INTERSTATE 85

LAVONIA

Exit #	Services
179mm	Georgia/South Carolina state line, Tugaloo River, Lake Hartwell
177	GA 77 S, to Hartwell, E BP/gifts/dsl Dad's Grill to Hart SP, W Tugaloo SP
176mm	**Welcome Ctr sb, full facilities, info, litter barrels, petwalk, vending**
173	GA 17, to Lavonia, E Raceway/dsl Bojangles, La Cabana Mexican, McDonald's, Subway, Taco Bell, Waffle House Magnuson Hotel $General, Lavonia Foods, Rite Aid, W Chevron/dsl, Exxon/dsl Burger King, DQ, Hardee's, J Peters Grill, Pizza Hut, Shoney's, Zaxby's Hampton Inn, Holiday Inn Express, Super 8 Chrysler/Dodge/Jeep, Ford, to Tugaloo SP
171mm	**weigh sta nb**
169mm	**weigh sta sb**
166	GA 106, to Carnesville, Toccoa, E Exxon/dsl, Pilot/Dunkin Donuts/DQ/Wendy's/dsl/scales/24hr Subway, W Echo Trkstp/Chevron/Echo Rest./dsl/scales/24hr
164	GA 320, to Carnesville, E Chevron/dsl/24hr
160	GA 51, to Homer, E Maathon/Subway/dsl/24hr Sterling RV Ctr, to Russell SP, Ty Cobb Museum, Victoria Bryant SP, W FLYING J/dsl/24hr, Petro/BP/Iron Skillet/dsl/scales/24hr/@ Blue Beacon
154	GA 63, Martin Br Rd

COMMERCE

149	US 441, GA 15, to Commerce, Homer, E Murphy USA, QT/dsl, TA/Shell/Country Pride/dsl/scales/24hr/@ Bojangles, Capt D's, El Azteca, Grand Buffet, Koji Japanese, Krispy Kreme, Longhorn Steaks, Outback Steaks, Papa John's, Sonny's BBQ, Taco Bell, Waffle House, Zaxby's Days Inn, Hampton Inn, Red Roof Inn, Scottish Inn H, $General, $Tree, AT&T, Chrysler/Dodge/Jeep, Funopolis, GNC, O'Reilly Parts, URGENT CARE, Walmart/Subway, W BP/Krystal/dsl, RaceTrac/dsl, Valero/dsl Applebee's, Arby's, Burger King, Chick-fil-A, Cracker Barrel, DQ, Five Guys, Hawg Wild BBQ, La Hacienda, McDonald's, Pizza Hut, Ruby Tuesday, Ryan's, Sonic, Starbucks, Subway, Wendy's Best Inn, Best Western, Comfort Suites, Fairfield Inn, Holiday Inn Express, Howard Johnson, Motel 6, Quality Inn, Super 8, Travelodge Home Depot, Pritchett Tires, Tanger Outlet/famous brands, Verizon
147	GA 98, to Commerce, E Citgo/dsl, Loves/Dunkin Donuts/dsl/24hr H, W Gulf
140	GA 82, Dry Pond Rd, E Freightliner, W RV & Truck Repair
137	US 129, GA 11 to Jefferson, E RaceTrac/dsl Arby's, Bojangles, El Jinete Mexican, KFC/Taco Bell, McDonald's, Waffle House, Zaxby's Quality Inn museum, W QT/dsl/scales/24hr Burger King, Waffle House, Wendy's flea mkt

GA

[gas] = gas [food] = food [lodging] = lodging [other] = other [rest stop] = rest stop

JEFFERSON

INTERSTATE 85 Cont'd

Exit #	Services
129	GA 53, to Braselton, E Chevron/dsl, Shell/Golden Pantry/dsl La Hacienda Mexican, Waffle House Best Western USPO, W Pilot/McDonald's/dsl/scales/24hr Cracker Barrel, Domino's, El Centinela, Stonewall's BBQ, Subway, Tea Garden Chinese, Wendy's, Zaxby's
126	GA 211, to Chestnut Mtn, E Circle K/Burger King/dsl, Shell/dsl Subway, Waffle House Country Inn&Suites, W BP/dsl Chateau Elan Winery/rest., China Garden, Papa John's Holiday Inn Express Publix, vet
120	to GA 124, Hamilton Mill Rd, E BP, QT/dsl Arby's, Buffalo's Café, Burger King, Caprese Rest., Firehouse Subs, Five Guys, McDonald's, Moe's SW Grill, Riverside Pizza, Starbucks, Subway, Wendy's, Zaxby's Aldi Foods, auto repair, Home Depot, Kohl's, Publix/Deli, RV World of GA (1mi), vet, W Chevron, Murphy USA/dsl, Shell/dsl Barbarito's, Chick-fil-A, Chili's, El Molcajate, Hardee's, Italy's Pizza, Little Caesar's, Taco Bell $Tree, AT&T, CVS Drug, O'Reilly Parts, Tires+, USPO, Verizon, Walmart/Subway
115	GA 20, to Buford Dam, E Waffle House Pepboys, W Arby's, Atlanta Bread, Bonefish Grill, Bruster's, Burger 21, Burger King, Cheesecake Factory, Chick-fil-A, Chili's, Chipotle, ChuckeCheese, East Coast Wings, Einstein's Bagels, Firehouse Subs, Genghis Grill, Honeybaked Ham, Kani House, Krispy Kreme, Longhorn Steaks, Macaroni Grill, Maddio's Pizza, McDonald's, Mimi's Cafe, Moe's SW Grill, O'Charley's, Olive Garden, On-the-Border, Panda Express, Panera Bread, PF Chang's, Provino's Italian, Red Lobster, Shogun Japanese, Sonny's BBQ, Starbucks, Steak n' Shake, Subway, Taco Mac, Ted's MT Grill, TGIFriday's, Tilted Kilt, Waffle House, Wendy's, Which Wich? Country Inn&Suites, Courtyard, Hampton Inn, SpringHill Suites, Wingate Inn $Tree, AT&T, Barnes&Noble, Belk, Best Buy, Buick/GMC, Costco/gas, Dick's, Dillard's, Discount Tire, Fiat, Firestone/auto, Honda, Hyundai, JC Penney, Lowe's, Macy's, Mall of GA, Marshall's, Mazda, Michael's, Nissan, Nordstrom Rack, PetCo, Petsmart, REI, Ross, Sam's Club/gas, Staples, SteinMart, Target, TJ Maxx, to Lake Lanier Islands, Toyota, Tuesday Morning, Verizon, Von Maur, VW, Walmart
113	I-985 N (from nb), to Gainesville
111	GA 317, to Suwanee, E BP/dsl, Valero/dsl Applebee's, Arby's, Checker's, Chick-fil-A, Cracker Barrel, Dunkin Donuts, Orient Garden, Outback Steaks, Philly Connection, Pizza Hut, Pizza Hut/Taco Bell, Schlotsky's, Subway, Waffle House, Wendy's Comfort Suites, Courtyard, Fairfield Inn, Motel 6, Quality Inn, Sun Suites CVS Drug, GNC, O'Reilly Parts, W Chevron/dsl, Murphy USA/dsl, QT/dsl, Raceway/dsl, Shell Dunkin Donuts, Greek Island, HoneyBaked Ham, IHOP, Jimmy John's, KFC, McDonald's, Moe's SW Grill, Sonic, Subway, Taco Mac Red Roof Inn, Super 8 $Tree, Advance Parts, AT&T, Lowe's, Office Depot, Walmart
109	Old Peachtree Rd, E McAlister's, McDonald's, Mi Casa Mexican Hampton Inn, Homewood Suites Bass Pro Shops, Publix, W Arena Tavern, Carrabba's, Chick-fil-A, China Delight, Firehouse Subs, Five Guys, Jim&Nicks BBQ, Starbucks, Subway, Tilted Kilt, Waffle House Hilton Garden, Holiday Inn, Residence Inn Home Depot
108	Sugarloaf Pkwy (from nb), E Hampton Inn, Homewood Suites, W Carrabba's, Chick-fil-A, Tin Lizzy Cantina Hilton Garden, Holiday Inn Gwinnett Civic Ctr
107	GA120,toGA316E,Athens,E Shell BurgerKing,Carino's, Dave&Busters, Dunkin Donuts, Subway, Zaxby's Bass Pro

SUWANEE

DULUTH

ATLANTA AREA

Exit #	Services
107	Continued Shops, Books-a-Million, Burlington Coats, Discount Tire, Rite Aid, Ross, Saks 5th Ave, Suburban Tire, W BP/dsl, Chevron Bojangles, China Gate, McDonald's, Subway, Waffle House La Quinta, Suburban Lodge
106	Boggs Rd (from sb, no return), Duluth, W QT/dsl/24hr Mercedes
104	Pleasant Hill Rd, E Chevron/e85, QT/dsl, Shell/dsl, Valero/dsl Bahama Breeze, Burger King, Chick-fil-A, Costas Nayaritas, Don Pedro Mexican, East Pearl, Fung Mei Chinese, GA Diner, Golden House, Joe's Crabshack, McDonald's, Popeye's, Schlotsky's, Stevie B's Pizza, Subway, Super Buffet, TGIFriday's, Waffle House, Wendy's Best Western, Candlewood Suites, Comfort Suites, Fairfield Inn, Hampton Inn Suites, Holiday Inn Express, Residence Inn, Sonesta $General, $Tree, Advance Parts, Best Buy, Family$, Home Depot, Publix, URGENT CARE, Walgreens, W BP/Dunkin Donuts/dsl, Chevron/dsl, Valero/dsl Applebee's, Arby's, Barnacle's, Bruster's, Burger King, Checker's, Chili's, Chipotle Mexican, Hooters, IHOP, Jimmy John's, KFC, Krispy Kreme, McDonald's, Melting Pot, Olive Garden, On the Border, Panda Express, Red Lobster, Starbucks, Steak'n Shake, Subway, Taco Bell, Wendy's Courtyard, Extended Stay America, Hyatt Place, Jameson Inn, Quality Inn, Wingate Inn, Wyndham Garden AT&T, Audi, Batteries+, Belk, BMW, Buick/GMC, Firestone/auto, Ford, Fry's Electronics, Goodyear/auto, Honda, Hyundai, Infiniti, JC Penney, Jo-Ann Fabrics, Kia, Macy's, Marshall's, Nissan, PetCo, Rite Aid, Staples, Subaru, TJ Maxx, Toyota, Verizon
103	Steve Reynolds Blvd (from nb, no return), W QT/dsl, Shell Dave&Buster's, Waffle House InTown Suites $Tree, Big Lots, Costco/gas, Kohl's, Petsmart, same as 104, Sam's Club
102	GA 378, Beaver Ruin Rd, E QT, Shell/dsl, Valero/dsl Subway, W Citgo
101	Lilburn Rd, E QT, Shell/dsl Blimpie, Bruster's, Burger King, Domino's, Hong Kong Buffet, Jimmy John's, KFC, Krystal, McDonald's/playplace, Starbucks, Taco Bell, Waffle House Guesthouse Inn, InTown Suites, Super 8 Jones RV Park, W Chevron, Marathon/dsl, QT Arby's, China Panda, El Taco Veloz, Papa John's, Pizza Plaza, Subway, Waffle House, Wendy's Knights Inn, Red Roof Inn CarMax, Chrysler/Dodge/Jeep, Lowe's
99	GA 140, Jimmy Carter Blvd, E Shell/dsl Checker's, Chick-fil-A, Cracker Barrel, Denny's, Dunkin Donuts, McDonald's, Papa John's, Pizza Hut/Taco Bell, Pollo Campero, Subway Congress Suites, Courtyard, Horizon Inn, La Quinta, Motel 6, Rite4Us Inn Advance Parts, Aldi Foods, Family$, U-Haul, Walgreens, W Chevron/dsl, QT/dsl, Valero/dsl Hibachi Grill, Hong Kong Buffet, Pappadeaux Steak/seafood, Sonic, Waffle House, Wendy's Country Inn&Suites, Days Inn, Microtel, Rodeway Inn AutoZone, CarQuest, NTB, O'Reilly Parts, PepBoys
96	Pleasantdale Rd, Northcrest Rd, E Burger King, Pleasantdale Chinese, W Exxon/dsl, QT/dsl Subway Atlanta Lodge
95	I-285
94	Chamblee-Tucker Rd, E Chevron/Subway/dsl, Shell/dsl to Mercer U, W QT/dsl DQ, Waffle House Motel 6, Super 8
93	Shallowford Rd, to Doraville, E Shell Hop Shing Chinese, Marco's Pizza, Subway Publix, U-Haul, W Shell/dsl Quality Inn

GA

INTERSTATE 85 Cont'd

Exit #	Services
91	US 23, GA 155, Clairmont Rd, E [gas] Chevron/dsl, QT/dsl [food] IHOP, Mo's Pizza, Popeye's [other] repair, URGENT CARE, W [gas] [food] McDonald's, Waffle House [lodging] Extended Stay America, Holiday Inn Express, Marriott [other] NTB, Sam's Club/dsl
89	GA 42, N Druid Hills, E [gas] Chevron/Subway/dsl, QT, Shell/dsl [food] Arby's, Boston Mkt, Burger King, Chick-fil-A, El Torero, Fortune Cookie, Grub Burger, Jersey Mike's, McDonald's, Moe's SW Grill, Newk's Eatery, Panera Bread, Penn Sta Subs, Piccadilly's, Starbucks, Taco Bell, Tin Roof Cantina, Willy's Mexicana, Zoe's Kitchen [lodging] Courtyard [other] $Tree, Firestone/auto, GNC, Target, Walgreens, W [gas] Chevron/dsl, Exxon/dsl, Shell [food] HoneyBaked Ham, Krystal, McDonald's, Waffle House [lodging] DoubleTree, Hampton Inn, Red Roof Inn [other] CVS Drug, Just Brakes
88	Lenox Rd, GA 400 N, Cheshire Br Rd (from sb), E [gas] Valero/dsl [food] McDonald's [lodging] La Quinta
87	GA 400 N (from nb)
86	GA 13 S, Peachtree St, E [gas] BP, Chevron [food] Papa John's, Wendy's [lodging] Intown Inn [other] Sprouts Mkt, vet
85	I-75 N, to Marietta, Chattanooga
84	Techwood Dr, 14th St, E [gas] BP, Shell [food] CheeseSteaks, La Bamba Mexican, Thai Cuisine, VVV Ristorante Italiano [lodging] Best Western, Hampton Inn, Marriott, Sheraton, Travelodge [other] Woodruff Arts Ctr, W [food] Blimpie [lodging] Courtyard, Knights Inn [other] CVS Drug, Dillard's, Office Depot, to Georgia Tech
77	I-75 S
76	Cleveland Ave, E [gas] Citgo/dsl [food] Burger King, Papa John's [other] [H], $Tree, AutoZone, BigLots, CVS Drug, Family$, Kroger, Walgreens, W [gas] Shell/dsl, Texaco/dsl [food] Chick-fil-A, Church's [other] CVS, O'Reilly Parts
75	Sylvan Rd, E [gas] Shell/dsl
74	Loop Rd, [other] Aviation Commercial Center
73b a	Virginia Ave, E [gas] Citgo/dsl [food] Jimmy John's, Jonny's Pizza, Landmark Diner, Malone's Grill, McDonald's, Pizza Hut, Ruby Tuesday, Schlotsky's, Spondivit's Rest., Waffle House, Wendy's, Willy's Mexican [lodging] Courtyard, Drury Inn, Hilton, Motel 6, Renaissance Hotel, Residence Inn, W [gas] Chevron/Subway, Shell [food] Arby's, BBQ Kitchen, Blimpie, Giovanna's Italian, Happy Buddha Chinese, KFC, La Fiesta Mexican, Waffle House [lodging] Country Inn&Suites, Crowne Plaza, DoubleTree, EconoLodge, Fairfield Inn, Hampton Inn, Hilton Garden, Holiday Inn, Homewood Suites, Hyatt Place, Palms Hotel, Staybridge Inn, Wellesley Inn
72	Camp Creek Pkwy
71	Riverdale Rd, Atlanta Airport, E [food] Ruby Tuesday [lodging] Courtyard, Fairfield Inn, Hampton Inn, Holiday Inn, Hyatt Place, La Quinta, Microtel, Sheraton/grill, Sleep Inn, Super 8, W [lodging] Days Inn, Embassy Suites, Hilton Garden, Holiday Inn Express, Marriott, Westin Hotel
70	I-85 (from sb)
69	GA 14, GA 279, E [gas] Chevron/dsl, Citgo, Exxon/dsl, Valero [food] Blimpie, Bojangles, Burger King, Checker's, China Cafe, Church's, Cozumel, KFC, Krystal, McDonald's, Piccadilly Cafeteria, Subway, Taco Bell, Waffle House, Wendy's [lodging] Comfort Inn, Days Inn, Quality Inn, Super 8, Travelodge, Windsor Atl Hotel [other] AutoZone, Family$, U-Haul, URGENT CARE, W [gas] Chevron/dsl, Texaco [food] Waffle House [lodging] EconoLodge
68	I-285 Atlanta Perimeter (from nb)
66	Flat Shoals Rd, W [gas] BP, Chevron/dsl/24hr, Shell/Blimpie [food] King's Rest., Waffle House [lodging] Motel 6

ATLANTA AREA

Kennesaw • 75 • Roswell • Duluth • Marietta • Dunwoody 285 85 Smyrna • North Atlanta • Tucker 285 Douglasville 20 • Atlanta • Redan 285 85 20 • Chapel Hill Cliftondale • • Forest Park Conyers Palmetto • 85 Jonesboro • • Stockbridge 75 GA

Exit #	Services
64	GA 138, to Union City, E [gas] BP/dsl, RaceTrac/dsl [food] Waffle House [lodging] EconoLodge, Western Inn [other] BMW/Mini, Chevrolet, Chrysler/Dodge/Jeep, CVS Drug, Ford/Lincoln, Honda, Infiniti, Kia/Nissan, Lexus, Toyota, VW, W [gas] Chevron/dsl, QT, Shell/dsl [food] Arby's, Burger King, Capt D's, China Garden, China King, Corner Cafe, Dunkin Donuts, IHOP, KFC, Krystal, McDonald's, Papa John's, Pizza Hut, Sonic, Southern Grill, Subway, Taco Bell, Wendy's, Zaxby's [lodging] Best Western, Comfort Inn, Country Hearth Inn, Garden Inn, La Quinta, Magnuson Hotel, Microtel [other] $Tree, Advance Parts, AT&T, BigLots, Firestone/auto, Kroger/dsl, NTB, O'Reilly Parts, PepBoys, vet, Walgreens, Walmart/Subway
61	GA 74, to Fairburn, E [gas] BP/Huddle House/dsl/scales/24hr, QT/dsl, RaceWay/dsl, Shell [food] Bojangle's, Chick-fil-A, Cracker Barrel, Dunkin Donuts, Hardee's, Krystal, Marco's Pizza, McDonald's, Starbucks, Taco Bell, Waffle House, Wendy's, Zaxby's [lodging] Best Western+, Country Inn&Suites, Fairfield Inn, Hampton Inn, Holiday Inn Express, Wingate Inn [other] Fairburn Tires, vet, W [gas] Chevron/dsl, Sun Petro/dsl [lodging] Efficiency Motel
56	Collinsworth Rd, W [gas] Marathon/dsl, Shell [food] Frank's Rest. [other] South Oaks Camping
51	GA 154, to Sharpsburg, E [gas] Marathon/dsl, Texaco/Subway/dsl [food] Hardee's, W [gas] Chevron/dsl, Shell/Circle K/dsl [food] Waffle House
47	GA 34, to Newnan, E [gas] BP, Chevron/dsl, Marathon/Subway/dsl, QT, Shell/dsl [food] Applebee's, Arby's, Asian Chef, Capt D's, Chin Chin, Dunkin Donuts, Fried Tomato Buffet, Hooters, La Hacienda, Longhorn Steaks, Marco's Pizza, Moe's SW Grill, Panda Express, Red Lobster, Ruby Tuesday, Sprayberry's BBQ, Steak'n Shake, Stevi B's Pizza, TX Roadhouse, Waffle House, Wendy's [lodging] Country Inn&Suites, Hampton Inn, Quality Inn, Springhill Suites [other] [H], Aldi Foods, GNC, Goodyear/auto, Hobby Lobby, Home Depot, Jo-Ann, Kauffman Tire, Kohl's, Lowe's, Petsmart, Ross, Walmart/McDonald's, W [gas] RaceTrac/dsl [food] Burger King, Checkers, Chick-fil-A, Coldstone, Cracker Barrel, Firehouse Subs, Five Guys, Goldberg's Deli, Golden Corral, HoneyBaked Ham, IHOP, Jimmy John's, KFC, Krystal, La Parrilla Mexican, Newk's Cafe, O'Charley's, Olive Garden, Panera Bread, Red Robin, Rockback Pizza, Shane's BBQ, Shoney's, Starbucks, Taco Bell, Taco Mac, Thai Heaven, Tokyo Japanese, Yogli Mogli, Zaxby's [lodging] Best Western, Comfort Inn, La Quinta, Motel 6, Newnan Inn [other] $General, $Tree, AT&T, Barnes&Noble, Belk, Best Buy, BigLots, BJ's Whse/gas, Buick/Cadillac/GMC, Chevrolet, Dick's, Dillards, Ford/Lincoln, Hyundai, JC Penney, Michael's, Office Depot, Old Navy, Publix, Target, Tires+, TJ Maxx, Toyota, Verizon, vet, Walgreens
44	Poplar Rd, E [other] [H]

FAIRBURN

NEWNAN

INTERSTATE 85 Cont'd

LAGRANGE

Exit #	Services
41	US 27/29, Newnan, E Pilot/Subway/Wendy's/dsl/scales/24hr Little White House NHS, Roosevelt SP, W BP/dsl Huddle House, McDonald's, Waffle House Best Value Inn, Economy Inn, Falcon Inn, Super 8 $General, repair
35	US 29, to Grantville, W BP/dsl, Marathon/dsl
28	GA 54, GA 100, to Hogansville, E Valero/dsl, W Chevron/dsl, Loves/Arby's/dsl/scales/24hr, Shell/dsl Int-nat'l Cafe, McDonald's, Nachos Mexican, Roger's BBQ, Subway, Waffle House, Wendy's Garden Inn, Woodstream Inn Ingles
23mm	Beech Creek
22mm	**weigh sta both lanes**
21	I-185 S, to Columbus
18	GA 109, to Mountville, E Marathon/Domino's Rodeway Inn, Wingate Inn Little White House HS, to FDR SP, W BP/dsl, Exxon/Circle K/dsl, Mobil/dsl, RaceTrac/dsl, Shell/dsl, Valero Applebee's, Banzai Japanese, Burger King, Chick-fil-A, Cracker Barrel, Firehouse Subs, IHOP, Juanito's Mexican, Longhorn Steaks, Los Nopales, McDonald's, Mi Casa Mexican, Moe's SW Grill, Starbucks, Subway, Waffle House, Wendy's, Zaxby's Baymont Inn, Comfort Inn, Holiday Inn Express, La Quinta, Lafayette Garden Inn, Quality Inn, Super 8 AT&T, Belk, Chrysler/Dodge/Jeep, Ford/Lincoln, Hobby Lobby, Home Depot, Honda, Hyundai, JC Penney, TJ Maxx, Verizon
14	US 27, to La Grange, W Exxon, Marathon, Shell/Summit/dsl Waffle House Hampton Inn
13	GA 219, to La Grange, E Exxon/Shirley's Kitchen/dsl/scales/24hr Waffle House Sunrise Inn, W Pilot/Subway/dsl/scales/24hr, Shell/dsl Arbys, McDonald's H
10mm	Long Cane Creek
6	Kia Blvd, W Kia Plant
2	GA 18, to West Point, E Chevron/dsl, Shell/Summit/dsl Best Value, W Subway (1.5) camping, to West Point Lake
.5mm	**Welcome Ctr nb, full facilities, litter barrels, petwalk, , , vending**
0mm	Georgia/Alabama state line, Chattahoochee River

GA

INTERSTATE 95

SAVANNAH

Exit #	Services
113mm	Georgia/South Carolina state line, Savannah River
111mm	**Welcome Ctr/weigh sta sb, full facilities, info, litter barrels, petwalk, , , vending**
109	GA 21, to Savannah, Pt Wentworth, Rincon, E Enmark/dsl, Pilot/McDonald's/Subway/dsl/scales/24hr Waffle House Best Western, Country Inn&Suites, Hampton Inn, Mulberry Grove Inn Frieghtliner, W Flash/dsl, Murphy Express/dsl, Shell/Circle K/Blimpie/dsl Bojangles, Dunkin Donuts, El Ranchito, Happy Wok, Island Grill, Port Side Seafood, Sweet Tea Grill, Wendy's, Zaxby's Comfort Suites, Days Inn, Holiday Inn Express, Palm Extended Stay, Quality Inn, Savannah Inn, Sleep Inn, Super 8 CVS Drug, Family$, Food Lion, Whispering Pines RV Park (3mi)
107mm	Augustine Creek
106	Jimmy DeLoach Pkwy
104	Savannah Airport, E BP, Shell/Wendy's/dsl Sam Sneed's Grill, Waffle House, Waffle House Candlewood Suites, Comfort Suites, Country Inn&Suites, DoubleTree, Fairfield Inn, Hampton Inn, Hilton Garden, Holiday Inn Express,

SAVANNAH

Exit #	Services
104	Continued Hyatt Place, SpringHill Suites, Staybridge Suites, TownePlace Suites, Wingate Inn to , W Murphy USA, Parkers/dsl, Shell/Subway Applebee's, Arby's, Buffalo Wild Wings, Cheddar's, Chick-fil-A, Chili's, Chipotle, CookOut, DQ, Fatz Cafe, Firehouse Subs, Five Guys, Hilliard's Rest., IHOP, Jalapeños, Jersey Mike's, Jimmy John's, Krystal, Little Caesar's, Logan's Roadhouse, Longhorn Steaks, McAlister's Deli, McDonald's, Mellow Mushroom, Moe's SW, Olive Garden, Panda Express, Panera Bread, Ruby Tuesday, Shane's Rib Shack, Sonic, Starbucks, Steak'n Shake, TX Roadhouse, Wild Wing Cafe, Zaxby's Embassy Suites, Holiday Inn, Red Roof Inn, Residence Inn AT&T, Chevrolet, Dick's, GNC, Goodyear, Hobby Lobby, Home Depot, Michael's, Petsmart, Publix, Ross, Sam's Club/gas, Savannah Tire, Tanger Outlets/famous brands, TJ Maxx, URGENT CARE, Verizon, Walmart/McDonald's
102	US 80, to Garden City, E El Cheapos/Baldinos Subs, Enmarket/dsl, Flash/dsl Bojangles, Cracker Barrel, Dickey's BBQ, Guerrero Mexican, Hiranos Steaks, Jersey Style Subs, KFC, Krystal, Larry's Subs, Los Bravos Mexican, McDonald's, Peking Chinese, Spanky's, Subway, Taco Bell, Waffle House Best Western, Microtel, Motel 6, Quality Inn, Travelodge Camping World RV Ctr, Family$, Food Lion, museum, to Ft Pulaski NM, W Gate/dsl, Marathon, Shell Burger King, Domino's, El Potro Mexican, Hardee's, Italian Pizza, Pizza Hut, Wendy's, Western Sizzlin EconoLodge, Holiday Inn, La Quinta, Magnolia Inn, Ramada, Sleep Inn $General
99b a	I-16, W to Macon, E to Savannah
94	GA 204, to Savannah, Pembroke, E 76/dsl/e85, BP/dsl, Exxon, Murphy USA/dsl (2mi), Shell/dsl Applebee's, Cracker Barrel, Denny's, Hardee's, Houlihan's, IHOP, McDonald's, Perkins, Ruby Tuesday, Sonic Baymont Inn, Best Inn, Best Western, Clarion, Comfort Suites, Country Inn Suites, Days Inn, EconoLodge, Fairfield Inn, Hampton Inn, Holiday Inn, Holiday Inn Express, Howard Johnson, La Quinta, Quality Inn, Red Roof Inn, San's Boutique Hotel, Scottish Inn, Sleep Inn, SpringHill Suites, Super 8, Travelodge H, Factory Stores/Famous Brands, GNC, Walmart (2mi), W Chevron/dsl, Sunoco Hooters, Shellhouse Rest, Subway, Waffle House Motel 6, Rodeway Inn Harley-Davidson, Indian Motorcycles, Savannah Oaks RV Park (2mi)
91mm	Ogeechee River
90	GA 144, Old Clyde Rd, to Ft Stewart, Richmond Hill SP, E Exxon/dsl, Parkers DQ, Jalapeno's, Pizza Hut, Subway, Zaxby's AT&T, Kroger/deli/dsl, URGENT CARE, Verizon, W Loves/McDonald's/dsl/scales/24hr, Marathon/dsl Gore's RV Ctr
87	US 17, to Coastal Hwy, Richmond Hill, E BP/Subway, Chevron/dsl, RaceWay/dsl China 1, Denny's, Domino's, Fuji Japanese, Molly McPherson's Grill, Papa Murphy's, Smokin' Pig BBQ, Southern Image Rest., Steamer's Rest., Waffle House Days Inn, Motel 6, Royal Inn, Scottish Inn, Travelodge Food Lion, URGENT CARE, W McDonald's, Shell/dsl, Sunoco/dsl, TA/BP/Pizza Hut/Popeye's/dsl/scales/24hr/@ Arby's, KFC/Taco Bell, Waffle House, Wendy's Best Western+, EconoLodge, Fairfield Inn, Hampton Inn, Holiday Inn Express, Quality Inn, Super 8 KOA
85mm	Elbow Swamp
80mm	Jerico River
76	US 84, GA 38, to Midway, Sunbury, E hist sites, W Gulf/McDonald's/dsl, Parker's/dsl, Shell/dsl/scales Huddle House, Smokin' Pig BBQ H

INTERSTATE 95 Cont'd

Exit #	Services
67	US 17, Coastal Hwy, to S Newport, E [gas] BP/Subway/dsl, Citgo/dsl, El Cheapo, Shell/McDonald's [food] Jones BBQ [other] Harris Neck NWR, W [gas] Texaco
58	GA 99, GA 57, Townsend Rd, Eulonia, E [gas] BP/dsl, Citgo [other] $General, USPO, W [gas] Exxon/dsl, Shell/Stuckey's/dsl, Snappy [food] Huddle House [lodging] Motel 6 [other] Lake Harmony RV Park, McIntosh Lake RV Park
55mm	**weigh sta both lanes**
49	GA 251, to Darien, E [gas] Mobil/dsl [food] DQ, McDonald's, Waffle House [other] Ford, Inland Harbor RV Park, W [gas] BP/dsl/scales, Parker's [food] Burger King, KFC/Taco Bell, Ruby Tuesday, Wendy's [lodging] Days Inn, Econolodge, Hampton Inn, Quality Inn, Super 8
47mm	Darien River
46.5mm	Butler River
46mm	Champney River
45mm	Altamaha River
42	GA 99, E to Hofwyl Plantation HS
41mm	**[RS] sb, full [handicapped] facilities, info, litter barrels, petwalk, [phone], [picnic], vending**
38	US 17, GA 25, N Golden Isles Pkwy, Brunswick, E [gas] RaceTrac/dsl [food] McDonald's, Millhouse Steaks [lodging] Comfort Suites, Country Inn&Suites, Embassy Suites (2mi), Fairfield Inn, Holiday Inn, Microtel [other] [H], Nissan, W [gas] Flash, Marathon/dsl, Parker's, Shell/dsl [food] China Town, Denny's, Huddle House, Subway, Toucan's, Waffle House [lodging] Best Western+, Courtyard, EconoLodge, Guest Cottage Motel, Hampton Inn, Quality Inn, Sleep Inn [other] $General, Family$, Harley-Davidson, Toyota, Winn Dixie
36b a	US 25, US 341, to Jesup, Brunswick, E [gas] Chevron/Subway/dsl, Exxon/dsl, RaceWay/dsl [food] Burger King, Cracker Barrel, IHOP, KFC, Krystal, McDonald's, Pizza Hut, Starbucks, Taco Bell, Waffle House, Wendy's [lodging] Days Inn, Jameson Inn, La Quinta, Motel 6, Red Roof Inn, Tropical Inn [other] Jack's Tires, W [gas] Parker's/dsl, Shell/dsl [food] Capt Joe's Seafood, China Buffet, Huddle House, Larry's Subs, Sonny's BBQ, Waffle House [lodging] Clarion, Comfort Inn, Economy Inn, Magnuson Inn, Ramada Inn, Stay Express, Super 8 [other] $General, Advance Parts, AutoZone, CVS Drug, Family$, Fred's, URGENT CARE, Winn-Dixie
33mm	Turtle River
30mm	S Brunswick River
29	US 17, US 82, GA 520, S GA Pkwy, Brunswick, E [gas] Exxon/dsl, Flash, Loves/Godfather's/Subway/Chester's/dsl/scales/24hr, Mobil/dsl [food] Bubba Jack's Crab Shack, Huddle House, Krystal, McDonald's, Zaxby's [lodging] Comfort Suites [other] Blue Beacon, SpeedCo, W [gas] FLYING J/Denny's/dsl/LP/scales/24hr, Shell/Dunkin Donuts/dsl, TA/BP/Burger King/Starbucks/Subway/dsl/24hr [food] Domino's, Larry's Subs, Waffle House, Zachry's Rest [lodging] EconoLodge, Motel 6, Super 8 [other] $General, Family$, Golden Isles Camping, TA Truck Service, Winn Dixie
27.5mm	Little Satilla River
26	Dover Bluff Rd, E [gas] Mobil/Stuckey's/dsl
22	Horse Stamp Church Rd
21mm	White Oak Creek
19mm	Canoe Swamp
15mm	Satilla River
14	GA 25, to Woodbine, W [food] Chevron/Sunshine/rest/dsl/scales/24hr [lodging] Stardust Motel (3mi)
7	Harrietts Bluff Rd, E [gas] Flash/dsl, Shell/Subway, W [gas] BP/dsl [other] Walkabout Camping/RV Park

BRUNSWICK

ST MARYS

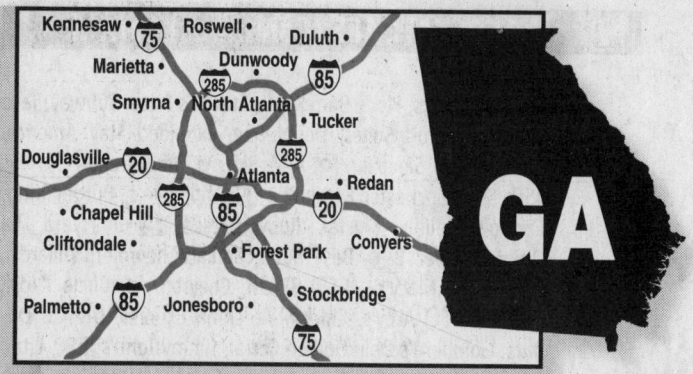

Exit #	Services
6.5mm	Crooked River
6	Laurel Island Pkwy, E [gas] Gtrac Express/dsl, Shell/Chester's/dsl
3	GA 40, Kingsland, to St Marys, E [gas] Chevron, El Cheapo/dsl, Flash/dsl, Mobil, Murphy USA/dsl, Shell/Subway, Sunoco [food] Angelo's Italian, Applebee's, Burger King, Capt D's, Chick-fil-A, DQ, Dunkin Donuts, Firehouse Subs, KFC, Little Caesar's, Longhorn Steaks, McDonald's, OPS Kitchen, Papa John's, Ruby Tuesday, Sonny's BBQ, Taco Bell, Waffle House, Wendy's, Zaxby's [lodging] Best Western, Comfort Suites, Country Inn&Suites, Days Inn, Fairfield Inn, Hawthorn Suites, Magnolia Inn, Microtel, Motel 6, Quality Inn, Red Roof Inn, Rodeway Inn, Sleep Inn [other] [H], $Tree, Buick/Chevrolet, Chrysler/Dodge/Jeep, CVS Drug, Ford, GNC, Lowe's, NAPA, Publix, Tire Kingdom, to Crooked River SP, to Submarine Base, URGENT CARE, Verizon, Walgreens, Walmart, Winn-Dixie, W **Welcome Ctr/info** [gas] Flash/dsl, Petro/Popeye's/dsl/scales/24hr/@, RaceWay/dsl, Shell/dsl [food] Cracker Barrel, Denny's, Domino's, IHOP, Millhouse Steaks, Waffle House [lodging] Baymont Inn, EconoLodge, Hampton Inn, La Quinta, Springfield Suites, Travelers Inn [other] Ace Hardware, Advance Parts, Fred's, Kiki RV Park
1	St Marys Rd, to Cumberland Is Nat Seashore, E **Welcome Ctr nb, full [handicapped] facilities, [phone], vending, [picnic], litter barrels, petwalk,** [gas] Pilot/Subway/PJ Fresh/dsl/scales/24hr, Shell/dsl W [gas] BP/dsl, Chevron/dsl, Pilot/Dunkin Donuts/Wendy's/dsl/scales/24hr [food] Little Pearl's Bistro [other] Country Oaks RV Park, KOA
0mm	Georgia/Florida state line, St Marys River

INTERSTATE 185 (Columbus)

Exit #	Services
48	**I-85. I-185 begins/ends on I-85.**
46	Big Springs Rd, E [gas] Shell/dsl, W [other] tires
42	US 27, Pine Mountain, E [gas] Marathon/dsl, Summit/dsl [food] Waffle House [other] Little White House HS, Pine Mtn Camping, to Callaway Gardens
34	GA 18, to West Point, E [other] to Callaway Gardens
30	Hopewell Church Rd, Whitesville, W [gas] Shell/dsl [other] $General
25	GA 116, to Hamilton, W [other] RV camping
19	GA 315, Mulberry Grove, W [gas] Chevron/dsl/24hr
14	Smith Rd
12	Williams Rd, W [gas] Chevron, Summit/dsl [lodging] Country Inn&Suites, Microtel [other] **Welcome Ctr/rest rooms**
10	US 80, GA 22, to Phenix City, W [other] Springer Opera House
8	Airport Thruway, E [food] Bojangles, Great Wall [other] $Tree, GNC, Home Depot, Walmart/Subway, W [gas] Marathon/dsl, Shell [food] Applebee's, Baskin Robbins, Ben's Chophouse, Blue Iguana Grill, Burger King, Cafe Le Rue, Capt D's, Country Road Buffet, Fuddruckers, Hardee's, Houlihan's, IHOP, McDonald's, Mikata Japanese,

GA

[gas icon] = gas [food icon] = food [lodging icon] = lodging [other icon] = other [RS] = rest stop Copyright 2019 - The Next EXIT ®

COLUMBUS

INTERSTATE 185 (Columbus) Cont'd

8 Continued
Outback Steaks, Pickle Barrel Cafe, Stevi B's Pizza, Subway, Taco Bell [lodging] Comfort Suites, DoubleTree, Extended Stay America, Hampton Inn, Sleep Inn [other] AAA, BigLots, Office Depot

7 45th St, Manchester Expswy, **E** [food] Applebee's, Burger King, Carino's Italian, Krystal, Ruby Tuesday [lodging] Courtyard, La Quinta, Super 8 [other] Best Buy, Cadillac/Chevrolet, Dillard's, JC Penney, Macy's, **W** [gas] BP/dsl, Chevron/dsl, Circle K/dsl, Marathon [food] Arby's, Chick-fil-A, China Express, Dunkin Donuts, Goldberg's Deli, Golden Corral, Jimmy John's, KFC, Little Caesar's, Logan's Roadhouse, Lucky China, McDonald's, Pizza Hut, Ryan's, Shogun Japanese, Sonic, Starbucks, SteakOut, Subway, Waffle House [lodging] Fairfield Inn, Holiday Inn, TownePlace Suites [other] [H], $General, Advance Parts, Big T Tire/repair, Civil War Naval Museum, Midas, Mr Transmission

6 GA 22, Macon Rd, **E** [gas] Chevron/dsl, Circle K/dsl [food] Bruster's, Burger King, DQ, Little Caesar's, Taco Bell, Waffle House [lodging] Best Western, Comfort Inn, Days Inn [other] $General, Rite Aid, U-Haul, vet, Walgreens, **W** [gas] Chevron/dsl, Shell/dsl [food] American Deli, Capt D's, ChuckeCheese, Cici's, Country's BBQ, Denny's, DunkinDonuts/Baskin Robbins, Firehouse Subs, Jimmy John's, Longhorn Steaks, McDonald's, Subway, Zaxby's [lodging] Efficiency Lodge, La Quinta [other] AT&T, CVS Drug, Fred's, GNC, Goodyear/auto, Publix, TJ Maxx, Tuesday Morning, Verizon

4 Buena Vista Rd, **E** [gas] BP, Circle K, Solo [food] Burger King, Capt D's, Checkers, Church's, Krystal, McDonald's, Papa John's, Pizza Hut, Subway, Taco Bell, Waffle House, Zaxby's [other] $Tree, AutoZone, Family$, Firestone/auto, Goodyear/auto, O'Reilly Parts, Rainbow Foods, repair, USPO, vet, Walgreens, Walmart, Winn-Dixie, **W** [gas] Marathon

3 St Marys Rd, **E** [food] Domino's [lodging] Microtel [other] Family$, **W** [gas] FuelTech/dsl, Shell/dsl [food] Hardee's, Shark Seafood/Chicken [other] $General, Ace Hardware, Piggly Wiggly

1b a US 27, US 280, Victory Dr, **0-3 mi W** [gas] Chevron/dsl, Circle K, Liberty, RaceWay/dsl [food] Burger King, Capt D's, Checkers, Krystal, McDonald's, Papa John's, Sonic, Subway, Taco Bell, Waffle House, Wendy's [lodging] Candlewood Suites, Columbus Inn, EconoLodge, Holiday Inn Express, Motel 6, Suburban Lodge [other] $General, Advance Parts, AutoZone, CVS Drug, Family$, O'Reilly Parts, Piggly Wiggly, Verizon

0mm I-185 begins/ends on Victory Dr

INTERSTATE 285 (Atlanta)

ATLANTA AREA

Exit # Services

62 GA 279, S Fulton Hwy, Old Nat Hwy, **N** [gas] Chevron/dsl, Texaco [food] Waffle House [lodging] Econolodge, **S** [gas] Chevron, Citgo, Exxon, Shell, Valero [food] American Deli, Blimpie, Bojangles, Burger King, Checker's, China Cafeteria, Church's, Cozumel Mexican, KFC, Krystal, McDonald's, Piccadilly Cafeteria, Subway, Taco Bell, Waffle House, Wendy's [lodging] Baymont Inn, Day's Inn, Quality Inn, Super 8, Travelodge, Windsor Atl Hotel [other] AutoZone, Family$, Midas, O'Reilly Parts, U-Haul

61 I-85, N to Atlanta, S to Montgomery

60 GA 139, Riverdale Rd, **N** [lodging] Fairfield Inn (2mi), Microtel (2mi), Wingate Inn (2mi), **S** [gas] QT/dsl, Shell/dsl, Valero/dsl [food] Checkers, Church's, McDonald's, Papa John's, Waffle House [lodging] Best Western, Day's Inn, Quality Hotel [other] $General, Advance Parts, Family$

59 Clark Howell Hwy, **N** [other] air cargo

58 I-75, N to Atlanta, S to Macon (from eb), to US 19, US 41, to Hapeville, **S** [gas] BP/dsl, Citgo/dsl, Exxon/dsl [food] American Deli, Jimmy John's, Subway, Tijuana Joe's, Waffle House, Wendy's [lodging] Home Lodge Motel

55 GA 54, Jonesboro Rd, **N** [lodging] Super 8, **S** [gas] BP/dsl, Citgo/dsl, Shell/dsl, Texaco/dsl [food] DaiLai Vietnamese, McDonald's [other] Family$, Home Depot, repair

53 US 23, Moreland Ave, to Ft Gillem, **N** [gas] BP/dsl, Citgo/dsl, **S** [gas] Chevron/dsl, Citgo [food] Wendy's [lodging] EconoLodge [other] USPO

52 I-675, S to Macon

51 Bouldercrest Rd, **N** [gas] BP, Pilot/Wendy's/dsl/24hr [food] Checkers, Domino's, Hardee's, KFC, WK Wings [other] Family$, Wayfield Foods, **S** [gas] Exxon/dsl, Shell/Blimpie/dsl, Texaco/dsl

48 GA 155, Flat Shoals Rd, Candler Rd, **N** [gas] BP, Chevron, Citgo/dsl, Shell/dsl, Texaco/dsl [food] Burger King, Checkers, Church's, DQ, Dunkin Donuts/BR, KFC, McDonald's, Taco Bell, Waffle King, WK Wings [lodging] Gulf American Inn [other] BigLots, Macy's, **S** [gas] Citgo, QT, Texaco/dsl [food] Burger King, China One, Sonic, Subway [other] Family$

46b a I-20, E to Augusta, W to Atlanta

44 GA 260, Glenwood Rd, **E** [gas] Sunoco/dsl [lodging] EconoLodge, **W** [gas] Exxon/dsl, Texaco/dsl, Valero/dsl

43 US 278, Covington Hwy, **E** [gas] Chevron/Subway, Texaco/dsl [food] Waffle House [other] U-Haul, **W** [gas] Mystik/dsl, QT, RaceTrac/dsl, Texaco/dsl [food] HoneyBaked Ham, Wendy's [lodging] Best Inn [other] Advance Parts, Family$

42 (from nb), [other] Marta Station

41 GA 10, Memorial Dr, Avondale Estates, **E** [gas] Citgo, Mystik [food] Applebee's, Baskin-Robbins/Dunkin Donuts, Burger King, Church's, Domino's, IHOP, Pancake House, Pizza Hut, Subway, Taco Bell, Waffle House, Wendy's [lodging] Best Value Inn, Budgetel, United Suites [other] $Tree, Advance Parts, Atl Tires, AutoZone, Family$, Firestone/auto, GNC, Office Depo, Ross, transmissions, U-Haul, USPO, Walgreens

40 Church St, to Clarkston, **E** [gas] Chevron, Marathon/dsl, Texaco [other] auto repair, **W** [other] [H]

39b a US 78, to Athens, Decatu

38 US 29, Lawrenceville Hwy, **E** [gas] Citgo, QT/dsl, RaceTrac/dsl [food] Bojangle's, Waffle House [lodging] Best Value Inn, Knights Inn [other] [H], **W** [gas] Citgo/dsl [food] Bruster's [lodging] Masters Inn, Motel 6 [other] AutoZone, CVS Drug

37 GA 236, to LaVista, Tucker, **E** [gas] Chevron/dsl, Exxon [food] Checkers, Folks Rest., Hudson Grille, IHOP, O'Charley's, Piccadilly's, Pollo Tropical, Waffle House [lodging] Comfort Suites, Days Inn [other] DeKalb Tire/auto, Firestone/auto, Target, **W** [gas] BP/Domino's, Chevron, Shell/dsl [food] Blue Ribbon Grill, Capt D's, Chick-fil-A, Chipotle, Coco Cabana Cuban, Dunkin Donuts, Eduardo's Mexican, HoneyBaked Ham, Jason's Deli, Kacey's Rest., Kobe Steaks, Lucky Key Chinese, Maddio's Pizza, Marlow's Tavern, McDonald's, Mellow Mushroom, Moe's SW, Monterrey Mexican, Panda Express, Panera Bread, Pizza Hut, Popeye's, Red Lobster, Starbucks, Subway [lodging] Courtyard, DoubleTree, Holiday Inn, Quality Inn [other] $Tree, Aldi Foods, AT&T, Best Buy, Goodyear/auto, JC Penney, Kohl's, Kroger, Michael's, Office Depot, Petsmart, Publix, TJ Maxx, Verizon

36 Northlake Pkwy (from sb, no return)

34 Chamblee-Tucker Rd, **E** [gas] Texaco/dsl [food] $3 Cafe, China Star, Galaxy Diner, Hunan Inn, Jersey Mike's Subs, KFC/Taco Bell, Moe's SW Grill, Wendy's [other] Advance Parts, Goodyear/auto, Kroger, Rite Aid, USPO, **W** [gas] Citgo, Shell [food] McDonald's, Subway [other] BigLots, vet

33b a I-85, N to Greenville, S to Atlanta

GA

INTERSTATE 285 (Atlanta) Cont'd

Exit #	Services
32	US 23, Buford Hwy, to Doraville, E BP/dsl Baldino's Subs, Bojangle's, Burger King/playland, Checkers, Chick-fil-A, McDonald's, Waffle House, White Windmill Café, Zaxby's Advance Parts, Firestone/auto, Marshalls, PepBoys, W Citgo, QT/dsl McDonald's, Monterrey Mexican, Subway, Waffle House Clarion $Tree, Aamco, Meineke
31b a	GA 141, Peachtree Ind, to Chamblee, W Arby's, Baskin-Robbins/Dunkin Donuts, Chick-fil-A, IHOP, McDonald's, Pizza Hut, Subway, Wendy's Acura, Advance Parts, AT&T, Audi, Brandsmart, Buick/GMC, Chevrolet, Chrysler/Dodge/Jeep, CVS Drug, Firestone/auto, Ford, Honda, Hyundai, Infiniti, Kia, Lexus, Mazda, Mini, Nissan, Office Depot, Porsche, Toyota, VW, Walgreens
30	Chamblee-Dunwoody Rd, N Shallowford Rd, to N Peachtree Rd, N BP/dsl, BP/Dunkin Donuts, Shell, Texaco/dsl Bagel&-Co. Deli, Burger King, Marco's Pizza, McDonald's, Starbucks, Subway, Takorea, Waffle House Kroger, Tuesday Morning, S Exxon/dsl, Mobil, Shell, Texaco/dsl, Valero La Botana Mexican, Mad Italian Rest., Papa John's, Taco Bell, Wendy's, Wild Ginger Thai Residence Inn
29	Ashford-Dunwoody Rd, N Exxon/Subway Brio Tuscan, Broken Egg, CA Pizza Kitchen, Capital Grille, Cheesecake Factory, Chick-fil-A, Chili's, Corner Bakery&Cafe, Fogo de Chao, J. Alexander's, Jason's Deli, Maddio's Pizza, Maggiano's Little Italy, McCormick&Schmick's, McDonald's, McKendrick Steaks, Memphis BBQ, Newk's Eatery, Olive Garden, PF Chang's, Popeye's, Schlotzsky's, Seasons 32 Grill, Starbucks, Wild Wing Cafe Crowne Plaza, Hampton Inn Barnes&Noble, Best Buy, Dillard's, Hobby Lobby, Macy's, Marshalls, Nordstrom, Old Navy, USPO, Walmart, S Hilton Garden
28	Peachtree-Dunwoody Rd (no EZ return wb), N Arby's, Chuy's Mexican, Domino's, Five Guys, Panera Bread, Subway, Uncle Julio's Mexican, Willy's Mexican Comfort Suites, Courtyard, Extended Stay America, Extended Stay America (2), Fairfield Inn, Hampton Inn, Hilton Suites, Holiday Inn Express, La Quinta, Marriott, Microtel, Residence Inn, Sheraton, Westin Costco/gas, GNC, Home Depot, Publix, Rite Aid, Ross, Target, TJ Maxx, S H
27	US 19 N, GA 400, 2 mi N LDS Temple
26	Glenridge Dr (from eb), Johnson Ferry Rd
25	US 19 S, Roswell Rd, Sandy Springs, N BP, Shell/dsl, Shell/dsl Andres Mexican, Bobbys Burgers, Boston Mkt, Burger King, Chick-fil-A, Chipotle Mexican, Domino's, Dunkin Donuts, Egg Harbor Café, El Azteca Mexican, Firehouse Subs, Five Guys, Hudson Grille, IHOP, Jimmy John's, Longhorn Steaks, Maya Steaks, McDonald's, Mellow Mushroom, Moe's SW Grill, Pizza Hut, Roasters, Starbucks, Steak'n Shake, Subway, Taco Bell, Waffle House, Wendy's, Willy's Mexican, Zaxby's Comfort Inn $Tree, Aldi Foods, AT&T, CVS Drug, DeKalb Tire, Lowe's, Marshalls, Mr Tire, NAPA AutoCare, Office Depot, PepBoys, PetCo, Publix, Target, Toyota, Trader Joe's, Tuesday Morning, URGENT CARE, Verizon, Walgreens, Whole Foods Mkt, S Chevron/dsl, Citgo, Shell Barberitos, El Taco Veloz, Five Seasons Rest., Marlow's Tavern, Panda Express, Starbucks, Taco Mac Publix, Staples, Target, URGENT CARE
24	Riverside Dr
22	New Northside Dr, to Powers Ferry Rd, N Shell/Subway/dsl Extended Stay America, S BP, Chevron/dsl McDonald's, Ray's Rest., Rio Bravo, Subway, Waffle House Wyndham CVS Drug, Publix, vet

ATLANTA AREA

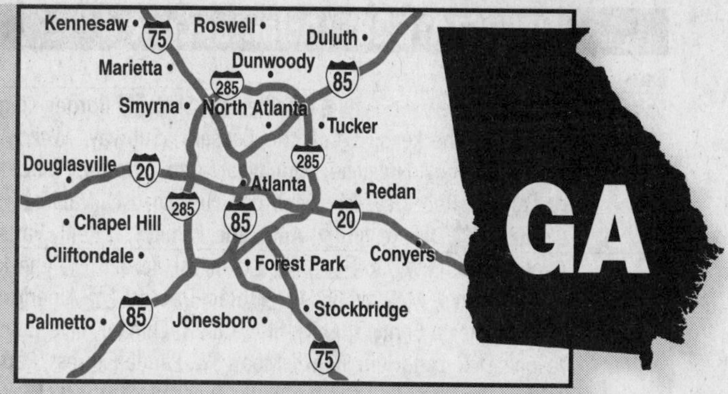

Exit #	Services
21	(from wb), N Chevron Harry's Pizza, Homestead Village Extended Stay America BMW/Mini
20	I-75, N to Chattanooga, S to Atlanta (from wb), to US 41 N
19	US 41, Cobb Pkwy, to Dobbins AFB, N BP/dsl, Marathon, QT Applebee's, Bruster's, Burger King, Carrabba's, Chucke-Cheese, Del Taco, Dunkin Donuts, IHOP, Jade Palace, KFC, McDonald's, Olive Garden, Panda Express, Papa John's, Red Lobster, Scalini's Italian, Subway, Taco Bell, Thompson Bros BBQ, Waffle House, Wendy's, Zaxby's DoubleTree, Extended Stay America, Hampton Inn, Holiday Inn Express, Hyatt, Residence Inn, Wingate Inn $Tree, Aldi Foods, Best Buy, Braves Stadium, Cadillac, Chevrolet, Discount Tire, Honda, Hyundai, Kia, Lexus, Marshall's, Michael's, NTB, Office Depot, PetsMart, Ross, Target, Verizon, Walgreens, S Buffalo Wild Wings, Cheesecake Factory, Chick-fil-A, Chipotle Mexican, Corner Bakery Cafe, Firehouse Subs, Hooters, Jason's Deli, Longhorn Steaks, Maggiano's Italian, PF Chang's, Pizza Hut, Pollo Tropical, Schlotsky's, Stoney River Steaks, Subway, Tilted Kilt, Zoe's Kitchen Courtyard, Hampton Inn, Homewood Suites, Renaissance, Sheraton Suites AT&T, Barnes&Noble, Costco/gas, Macy's, Old Navy, USPO
18	Paces Ferry Rd, to Vinings, N Panera Bread Fairfield Inn, La Quinta, S QT/24hr Chick-fil-A, Starbucks, Subway, Willy's Grill Extended Stay America Goodyear/auto, Home Depot, Publix, Verizon
16	S Atlanta Rd, to Smyrna, N Five Guys, Waffle House Days Inn H, S Chevron/Subway/dsl, Shell/dsl Jersey Mike's Kroger
15	GA 280, S Cobb Dr, E Araamda U-Haul, W BP/dsl, Mobil, RaceTrac/dsl, Shell Arby's, Chick-fil-A, China Cafe, Dunkin Donuts, IHOP, Jimmy John's, Krystal, McDonald's, Subway, Taco Bell, Zaxby's Baymont Inn, Comfort Inn, Country Inn Suites, Knight's Inn, Sun Suites
14mm	Chattahoochee River
13	Bolton Rd (from nb)
12	US 78, US 278, Bankhead Hwy, E Petro/Iron Skillet/dsl/scales/24hr/@, Shell/dsl/24hr, Valero/dsl Burger King Blue Beacon, W BP, Texaco
10b a	I-20, W to Birmingham, E to Atlanta (exits left from nb), W to Six Flags
9	GA 139, MLK Dr, to Adamsville, E Quikmart, Shell Family$, O'Reilly Parts, Wayfield Foods, W Chevron, Shell, Texaco/dsl Checker's, Church's, KFC/Taco Bell, McDonald's $General, Family$
7	Cascade Rd, E Exxon/dsl Papa John's Kroger, W BP/dsl, Shell/dsl Applebee's, China Express, KFC, Little Caesar's, McDonald's, Pizza Hut, Starbucks, Subway, Wendy's GNC, Home Depot, Publix, Tires+, Walgreens, Walmart

ATLANTA AREA

GA

INTERSTATE 285 (Atlanta) Cont'd

Exit #	Services
5b a	GA 166, Lakewood Fwy, E [gas] Chevron, Shell [food] Burger King, Capt D's, Checker's, KFC, Little Caesar's, Subway, Wendy's [other] CVS Drug, Firestone, Goodyear/auto, Kroger, Macy's, W [gas] BP, RaceWay/dsl, Shell/dsl, Texaco/dsl, Valero [food] Church's [lodging] Deluxe Inn [other] AutoZone, Family$, O'Reilly Parts
2	Camp Creek Pkwy, to [airport], E [gas] Exxon/dsl, Texaco [food] Checker's, Church's, McDonald's, W [gas] RaceTrac/dsl [food] American Deli, Bruster's, Carino's, Chick-fil-A, Chili's, China 1, Five Guys, Jason's Deli, LongHorn Steaks, Moe's SW, Panda Express, Papa John's, Popeyes, Red Lobster, Ruby Tuesday, Starbucks, Taco Bell, TGIFriday, Wendys, Zaxby's [lodging] Courtyard, Hampton Inn, Holiday Inn Express [other] $Tree, AT&T, Barnes&Noble, BJ's Whse/gas, Lowes Whse, Marshall's, Old Navy, PetsMart, Publix, Ross, Staples, Target, TJ Maxx, Verizon, Walgreens
1	Washington Rd, E [gas] Texaco/dsl, W [gas] Chevron/dsl

INTERSTATE 475 (Macon)

MACON

Exit #	Services
16mm	**I-475 begins/ends on I-75, exit 177.**
15	US 41, Bolingbroke, **1 mi** E [gas] Exxon/dsl/LP, Marathon/dsl
9	Zebulon Rd, E [gas] Marathon/dsl, Shell/Circle K/24hr [food] Applebee's, Buffalo's Café, Chick-fil-A, Johnny's NY Pizz, Krystal, Macon Pizza Co, Margarita's Mexican, McAlister's Deli, McDonald's, Moe's SW, NU Way Wieners, Papa John's, Pizza Hut, Sonic, Subway, Taco Bell, Taki Japanese, Tutti Frutti, Waffle House, Wendy's [lodging] Baymont Inn, Comfort Suites, Fairfield Inn, Sleep Inn [other] [H], Goodyear/auto, Kohl's, Kroger/dsl, Lowe's, URGENT CARE, USPO, Verizon, Walgreens, Walmart/Subway, W [gas] Marathon/dsl, Sunoco/dsl [food] Marco's Pizza, Polly's Cafe, Zaxby's [other] Advance Parts, CVS Drug
8mm	**[rest stop] nb, full [handicapped] facilities, litter barrels, petwalk, [phone], [picnic], vending**
5	GA 74, Macon, E [gas] RaceWay/dsl [food] Waffle House [other] Harley-Davidson, to Mercer U, W [gas] Flash/Subway/dsl, Texaco/Church's/dsl [food] Capt D's [lodging] A1 Economy [other] $General, Tires+, to Lake Tobesofkee, vet
3	US 80, Macon, **0-2 mi** E [gas] Marathon/dsl, Murphy USA/dsl, RaceWay, Shell/Circle K/Subway [food] Aldi Foods, Applebee's, Burger King, Chick-fil-A, China Buffet, Cracker Barrel, DQ, Firehouse Subs, Golden Corral, JL's BBQ, Margarita's Mexican, McAlister's Deli, McDonald's, Papa John's, S&S Cafeteria, Silver Bay Seafood, Smokin' Pig BBQ, Taco Bell, Waffle House, Zaxby's [lodging] Best Inn, Best Western, Bridgeview Inn, Comfort Suites, Days Inn, Discovery Inn, EconoLodge, Hampton Inn, Holiday Inn Express, La Quinta, Motel 6, Quality Inn, Ramada Inn, Red Roof Inn, Super 8, Woodspring Suites [other] $Tree, AT&T, Best Buy, BigLots, CVS Drug, Dick's, Discount Tire, Firestone/auto, GNC, Home Depot, Honda, Kroger/gas, Lowe's, Macy's, Marshall's, Michael's, Nissan, Office Depot, Old Navy, Petsmart, Ross, Sam's Club/gas, Staples, Target, Verizon, vet, VW, Walmart/Subway, W [gas] Shell/Circle K, Sunoco/dsl [food] Burger King [lodging] Best Value Inn, Windsor Economy Inn
1	Hartley Bridge Rd, same as I-75 exit 156
0mm	**I-475 begins/ends on I-75, exit 156.**

INTERSTATE 575

CANTON

Exit #	Services
30mm	**I-575 begins/ends on GA 5/515.**
27	GA 5, Howell Br, to Ball Ground
24	Airport Dr
20	GA 5, to Canton, E [gas] [food] Bojangles, Buffalo's Cafe, Casey's Rest., Chick-fil-A, Dos Margaritas Mexican, Jin's Buffet, Stevi B's Pizza, Waffle Wouse, Wendy's [lodging] Econolodge, Homestead Inn, Motel 6 [other] AT&T, Chevrolet, Chrysler/Dodge/Jeep, GNC, Toyota, Verizon, Walmart, W [gas] RaceTrac/dsl, Shell/Subway, Texaco/dsl [food] Applebee's, Arby's, Cracker Barrel, Five Guys, Honeybaked Ham, Longhorn Steaks, McDonald's, O'Charley's, Okinawa Steaks, Outback Steaks, Panda Express, Provino's, Red Lobster, Seven Tequilas Mexican, Starbucks, Zaxby's [lodging] Best Western, Hampton Inn, Holiday Inn Express [other] [H], Belk, Home Depot, Michaels, Publix, Ross
19	GA 20 E, Canton, E [food] Bobby's Burgers, Chick-fil-A, Chipotle, IHOP, Jimmy John's, La Parrilla Mexican, Maddio's Pizza, McDonald's, Olive Garden, Starbucks, Subway, Taco Mac, Waffle House, Which Wich?, Zaxby's [other] Best Buy, BooksAMillion, Dick's, Goodyear/auto, Kohl's, Lowe's, NTB, Petsmart, Target, TJ Maxx
17	GA 140, to Roswell (from sb), Canton
16	GA 20, GA 140, W [gas] Citgo, RaceTrac/dsl [food] Burger King, KFC, Mandarin House, Papa John's, Subway, Taco Bell, Waffle House [other] $General, Advance Parts, Rite Aid
14	Holly Springs, E [gas] Texaco/dsl [food] Domino's, Ichiban Buffet, Las Palmas Mexican, Pizza Hut [lodging] Pinecrest Motel [other] vet, Walmart/Subway, W [gas] Chevron, Shell/dsl [food] Dunkin Donuts, Golden China, McDonald's, Subway, Taste of Italy, Viva Mexico, Wendy's, Zaxby's [other] Autozone, Family$, Kauffman Tire, Kroger/dsl, Publix, Verizon, Walgreens
11	Sixes Rd, E [gas] Chevron/dsl, QT [food] Shane's Ribshack, Zaxby's [other] Home Depot, Verizon
9	Ridgewalk Pkwy, E [food] Applebee's, Chick-fil-A, Five Guys, McDonald's, Panda Express [other] outlets/famous brands
8	Towne Lake Pkwy, to Woodstock, E [gas] Shell/dsl [food] Subway, Waffle House [other] Ford, W [gas] Phillips 66, QT [food] Chili's, Longhorn Steaks [other] Tuesday Morning, Walgreens

WOODSTOCK

Exit #	Services
7	GA 92, Woodstock, E [gas] Chevron, QT [food] Arby's, Bubba Q's Rest., Burger King, Capt D's, Checker's, Chick-fil-A, Chin Chin, Del Taco, DQ, Dunkin Donuts, Firehouse Subs, Folk's Kitchen, Honeybaked Ham, Maddio's Pizza, McDonald's, Moe's SW Grill, O'Charley's, Resturante Mexico, Ruby Tuesday, Starbucks, Stevi B's Pizza, Subway, Taco Bell, Waffle House [lodging] Comfort Suites, Hampton Inn, InTown Suite [other] Camping World, Firestone/auto, Goodyear/auto, W [gas] Texaco/dsl [food] Hacienda Vieja Mexican, IHOP, Jimmy John's, Schlotzky's, Steak'n Shake, Taco Mac [lodging] Microtel [other] AT&T, Atlanta Bread, Big Lots, BJ's Whse/gas, Discount Tire, GNC, Home Depot, Honda, Kohl's, Lowe's Whse, Old Navy, Petsmart, Target, Verizon
4	Bells Ferry Rd, W [gas] QT, RaceTrac/dsl, Shell/dsl [food] Arby's, Burger King, Dunkin Donuts, Pizza Hut, Ralph's Grill, Subway, Waffle House [other] Pepboys, Publix, Walgreens
3	Chastain Rd, to I-75 N, W [gas] Chevron [food] CA Dreaming, Cookout, Cracker Barrel, Del Taco, Firehouse Subs, Five Guys, Los Reyes, Maddio's Pizza, Marlow's Tavern, O'Charley's, Panda Express, Papa's Cuban, Ruth's Chris Steks, Starbucks, Taco Mac [lodging] Best Western, Comfort Suites, Embassy Suites, Fairfield Inn, Residence Inn, Springhill Suites [other] to Kennesaw St Coll
1	Barrett Pkwy, to I-75 N, US 41, E [gas] Murphy USA/dsl, QT [food] Bobby's Burgers, Buffalo Wild Wings, Burger King, Moe's SW Grill, Pacific Grill, Starbucks, Stevi B's Pizza, Texas Roadhouse, Twisted Kitchen, Waffle House, Wendy's, Zaxby's [other] $Tree, AT&T, Barnes&Noble, CVS Drug, Kauffman Tire, Petco, Publix, Ross, SteinMart, Tuesday Morning, Walmart/Subway, W [gas] Shell/dsl [food] Applebee's, Fuddrucker's, Fujihana

INTERSTATE 575 Cont'd

STOCKBRIDGE

1	Continued Honeybaked Ham, Jimmy John's, Longhorn Steaks, McDonald's, Olive Garden, Provino's Italian, Red Lobster, Shogun Japanese, Smashburger, Starbucks, Subway, Twin Peaks Comfort Inn, Holiday Inn Express, La Quinta, Red Roof Inn Belk, Firestone/auto, Home Depot, Marshall's, Midas, Pepboys, TJ Maxx, Verizon
0mm	**I-575 begins/ends on I-75, exit 268.**

INTERSTATE 675

Exit #	Services
10mm	I-285 W, to Atlanta Airport, E to Augusta. **I-675 begins/ends on I-285, exit 52.**
7	Anvil Block Rd, Ft Gillem, **E** Chevron/dsl Waffle House, Wendy's $Tree, Walmart/Subway, **W** Exxon/dsl
5	Forest Pkwy, **E** Texaco/dsl, **W** BP/dsl, QT/dsl/scales, Texaco/dsl McDonald's, Waffle House
2	US 23, GA 42, **E** BP, Texaco, Valero/Subway/dsl El Granero Mexican, **W** Chevron/dsl, Citgo Waffle House Family$, Food Depot, GoodTime/auto, Rite Aid, USPO
1	GA 138, to I-75 N, Stockbridge, **E** Citgo/dsl, Exxon/dsl, Murphy USA/dsl, QT, Sunoco/dsl Burger King, Capt D's, Checker's, Church's Chicken, DQ, Dunkin Donuts, Golden Corral, Hibachi Buffet, KFC, Krispy Kreme, Little Caesar's, McDonald's, Olympia Pizza, Papa John's, Popeye's, Taco Bell, Waffle House, Wendy's, Zaxby's Best Value, Econolodge, Knights Inn, Magnolia Inn, Quality Inn, Sleep Inn, Stay Inn, Stockbridge Inn $General, $Tree, Advance Parts, Aldi Foods, BigLots, CVS Drug, Goodyear/auto, NAPA, Pepboys, Walmart, **W** Raceway/dsl Applebee's, Broadway Diner, Chick-fil-A, Frontera Mexican, Honeybaked Ham, IHOP, Krystal, O'Charley's, Piccadilly's, Subway, Taco Mac, Tokyo Seafood, Waffle House Comfort Inn, Day's Inn, Express Inn, Hampton Inn, Holiday Inn, La Quinta, Red Roof Inn Kroger/dsl, Lowes Whse, Office Depot, Tires+, URGENT CARE, Verizon
0mm	**I-675 begins/ends on I-75, exit 227.**

INTERSTATE 985 (Gainesville)

GAINESVILLE

Exit #	Services
24.5	**I-985 begins/ends on US 23, 25mm.**
24	to US 129 N, GA 369 W, Gainesville, **N** QT/dsl McDonald's, Papa John's, Taco Bell H, Autozone, Kroger/dsl, **S** BP/dsl, Chevron/dsl Double B Burger, Rabbittown Cafe, Subway
22	GA 11, Gainesville, **N** QT/dsl, Shell/dsl Burger King, **S** Chevron/dsl, Shell/dsl Waffle House Motel 6 $General
20	GA 60, GA 53, Gainesville, **N** RaceTrac/dsl, **S** Kangaroo/Subway/dsl Waffle House
17	GA 13, Gainesville
16	GA 53, Oakwood, **N** Arby's, Burger King, Capt D's, DQ, Dunkin Donuts, El Sombrero Mexican, Firehouse Subs, Hardee's, KFC, McDonald's, Napoli's Pizza, Pizza Hut, Steak'n Shake, Taco Bell, Waffle House, Zaxby's Best Western, Jameson Inn $Tree, Aldi Foods, Camping World RV Ctr, Chrysler/Dodge/Jeep, Sam's Club/dsl, Walmart/Subway, **S** QT/dsl Buffalo's Cafe, Chick-Fil-A, Krystal, La Parilla Mexican, Sonic, Sonny's BBQ, Subway, Waffle House, Wendy's Quality Inn Ace Hardware, AutoZone, Kauffman Tire, O'Reilly Parts, Publix, Slack Parts, Toyota, Walgreens
12	Spout Springs Rd, Flowery Branch, **N** Exxon/dsl, **S** Chevron/dsl, Marathon/Subway/dsl Burger&Shake, Chick-fil-A, Chili's, China Garden, CrossRoads Grill, Domino's, El Sombrero Mexican, Firehouse Subs, Little Caesar's, Napoli's Pizza, Shane's Ribshack, Shogun Japanese Hampton Inn AT&T, GNC, Home Depot, Kohl's, Petsmart, Publix, Rite Aid, Ross, Target, TJ Maxx, Verizon, Walgreens
8	GA 347, Friendship Rd, Lake Lanier, **N** Chevron/dsl, QT/dsl, Shell/dsl Blimpie, Burger King, Cracker Barrel, McDonald's, Mykonos Cafe, Shoney's, Subway, Vinny's NY Grill, Waffle House, Wendy's, Zaxby's Holiday Inn Express $General, Advance parts, Family$, O'Reilly Parts, Publix, URGENT CARE, Verizon, vet, **S** Camper City RV Ctr, Harley Davidson
4	US 23 S, GA 20, Buford, **N** QT, Shell/dsl Arby's, Bojangles, Burger King, Capt D's, Golden Buddah, Golden Corral, Hardee's, IHOP, KFC, McDonald's, Pizza Hut, Subway, Taco Bell, Waffle House, Wendy's, Zaxby's Best Value Inn, Holiday Inn Express Ace Hardware, Chrysler/Dodge/Jeep, Hobby Lobby, Home Depot, Kia, NAPA Autocare, NTB, O'Reilly Parts, **S** Chevron/dsl, Exxon/dsl, Mtn Express/dsl Asia Buffet, Sonny's BBQ, Stevi B's Pizza, Viva Mexico $Tree, Firestone/auto, Honda, Kauffman Tire, Lowes Whse, Walmart
0mm	**I-985 begins/ends on I-85.**

GA

NOTES

IDAHO

INTERSTATE 15

Exit#	Services
196mm	Idaho/Montana state line, Monida Pass, continental divide, elev 6870
190	Humphrey
184	Stoddard Creek Area, E [O] Historical Site, RV camping, W [O] Stoddard Creek Camping
180	Spencer, E [F] Opal Country Café/gas [O] High Country Opal Store, W [F] Spencer Grill/RV Park
172	no service
167	ID 22, Dubois, E [RS] **both lanes, full [H] facilities, litter barrels, petwalk, [C], picnic table,** [G] Phillips 66/dsl [O] city park, USPO, W [O] Nez Pearce Tr, to Craters NM
150	Hamer, E [O] Ron's Tire, USPO, W [O] Camus NWR
143	ID 33, ID 28, to Mud Lake, Rexburg, W [O] Sacajawea Hist Bywy, **weigh sta both lanes**
142mm	hist site, roadside parking
135	ID 48, Roberts, E [G] Exxon/cafe/dsl/LP [O] city park
128	Osgood Area, E [G] Osgood/dsl [O] camping (6mi)
119	US 20 E, to Rexburg, Idaho Fallson Lindsay, E [G] Sinclair/dsl [F] Denny's, Jaker's Steaks, Outback Steaks, Sandpiper Rest. [L] Best Western+, Fairbridge Inn, Hampton Inn, Hilton Garden, LeRitz Hotel, Motel 6, Quality Inn, Safari Inn, Shilo Inn/rest., Super 8, Tru Hilton [O] LDS Temple, same as 118, Snake River RV Park/camping, W [G] Sinclair/dsl
118	US 20, Broadway St, Idaho Falls, E [G] Phillips 66/dsl, Walmart/dsl [F] Applebee's, Arctic Circle, Buffalo Wild Wings, Carl's Jr, Cedric's Rest., Chili's, Culver's, Domino's, Famous Dave's BBQ, Jimmy John's, MacKenzie River Grill, Olive Garden, Panda Express, Shari's Rest., Smitty's Pancakes, Starbucks, Wendy's [L] Candlewood Suites, Fairfield Inn, Hampton Inn, Hilton Garden, Residence Inn, SpringHill Suites [O] [H], Candy Jct, Ford, Harley-Davidson, LDS Temple, same as 119, tires, URGENT CARE, Verizon, Walmart/Subway, W [G] Exxon/dsl, Phillips 66/dsl, Sinclair/McDonald's [F] Arby's, Burger King, Fiesta Ole, Five Buck Pizza, Hong Kong Rest., Jack-in-the-Box, Los Adalaberto's Mexican, O'Brady's, Papa Murphy's, Pizza Hut, Subway [L] Comfort Inn, Motel 6, Motel West [O] Albertsons, AutoZone, Camping World RV Ctr, O'Reilly Parts, Walgreens
116	US 26, Sunnyside Rd, Ammon, Jackson, E [O] [H], BMW, Chevrolet, Honda, Sunnyside Acres RV Park, Toyota, VW, W [G] Exxon/diesel [F] DoubleDown Grill [L] Sleep Inn
113	US 26, to Idaho Falls, Jackson, E [G] Blu LNG/dsl, Chevron/Burger King/dsl, FLYING J/Subway/dsl/24hr/@, Loves/McDonald's/dsl/scales/24hr [F] Subway [O] [H], Jack's Tires, Peterbilt
108	Shelley, Firth Area, **1 mi** E [O] RV Park/dump
101mm	[RS] **both lanes, full [H] facilities, geological site, litter barrels, petwalk, [C], [P]**
98	Rose-Firth Area
94.5mm	Snake River
93	US 26, ID 39, Blackfoot, E [G] Chevron/Jimmy John's/dsl, Maverik/dsl, Sinclair/Stinker/dsl [F] Arby's, Burger King, Domino's, Homestead Rest., Hong Kong Garden, Little Caesar's, McDonald's, Papa Murphy's, Pizza Hut, Roberto's Mexican, Subway, Taco Bell, Taco Time, Wendy's [L] Best Western, Super 8 [O] $Tree, AutoZone, Bealls, Chrysler/Dodge/Ford/Jeep, city park,
93	Continued Kesler's Foods, O'Reilly Parts, Point S Auto, Ridley's Mkt, Schwab Tire, URGENT CARE, Verizon, Walgreens, Walmart/Subway, W [G] Sinclair/A&W/dsl [O] Riverside Boot/saddleshop (4mi)
90.5mm	Blackfoot River
89	US 91, S Blackfoot, W [G] Sinclair/Sage Cafe/dsl
80	Ft Hall, W [G] Phillips 66/rest./dsl/casino [L] Shoshone Bannock Hotel/casino
72	I-86 W, to Twin Falls
71	Pocatello Creek Rd, Pocatello, E [G] Chevron/Burger King/dsl, Phillips 66/dsl, Shell/dsl [F] Applebee's, Jack-in-the Box, Perkins, Sandpiper Rest., Subway [L] Best Western, Clarion, La Quinta, Quality Inn, Red Lion Inn, Super 8 [O] KOA (1mi), **0-2 mi** W [G] Exxon, Maverik/dsl [F] Arby's, Bamboo Garden, Butter Burr's Lickety Split, Butter Burr's Rest., Café Rio, Carl's Jr, Changs Garden Chinese, Coldstone, El Caporal, Golden Corral, Jamba Juice, KFC, Mandarin House, McDonald's, Papa Murphy's, Ridley's Mkt, Senor Iguana's Mexican, Sizzler, Sonic, Starbucks, Subway, Taco Bell, Taco Time, Thai Kitchen, Wendy's, Winger's [O] $Tree, Advance Parts, AutoZone, BigLots, Buick/GMC, Chevrolet, Fred Meyer/dsl, Harley-Davidson, Hyundai, O'Reilly Parts, Subaru, Tuesday Morning, Walgreens, WinCo Foods
69	Clark St, Pocatello, E [G] Chevron/cafe/dsl, Maverik/dsl, Sinclair/Arctic Circle/dsl [F] Jakers Grill [L] Hampton Inn, Holiday Inn Express, TownePlace Suites [O] [H], W [O] museum, to ID St U
67	US 30/91, 5th St, Pocatello, E [G] Exxon/dsl, **1-2 mi** W [G] Chevron/dsl, Shell/dsl [F] Elmer's Dining, Goody's Deli, Jimmy John's, McDonald's, Pizza Hut, Subway, Taco Bell [L] Rodeway Inn, Thunderbird Motel [O] [H], city park, info, museum, Old Fort Hall, RV dump
63	Portneuf Area, W [O] RV camp/dump, to Mink Creek RA
59mm	**weigh sta both lanes**
58	Inkom (from sb), **1/2 mi** W [G] Sinclair/café/dsl [O] Bisharat' Mkt, Pebble Creek Ski Area, repair, USPO
57	Inkom (from nb), same as 58
47	US 30, to Lava Hot Springs, McCammon, E [G] FLYING J/dsl scales/LP/RV dump/24hr, Chevron/A&W/Taco Time/dsl [F] Subway [O] Lava Hot Springs RA, McCammon RV Park, to KOA
44	Lp 15, Jenson Rd, McCammon, Eaccess to food
40	Arimo, E [O] USPO
36	US 91, Virginia
31	ID 40, to Downey, Preston, E [G] Shell/Flags West/café/dsl/motel/24hr/@ [O] Downata Hot Springs RV camping (6mi)
25mm	[RS] **sb, full [H] facilities, litter barrels, petwalk, [C], [P]**
24.5mm	Malad Summit, elevation 5574
22	to Devil Creek Reservoir, E RV camping
17	ID 36, to Weston, to Preston
13	ID 38, Malad City, W [G] Chevron/Burger King, Chevron/dsl Phillips 66/café/dsl [F] Me&Lou's Rest., Pines Rest., Sperow BBQ, Subway [L] Village Inn Motel [O] [H], 3R's Tire, Family pioneer museum, repair, RV dump
7mm	**Welcome Ctr nb, full [H] facilities, info, litter barrels, petwalk, [C], [P], vending**
3	to Samaria, Woodruff
0mm	Idaho/Utah state line

DUBOIS

IDAHO FALLS

BLACKFOOT

POCATELLO

ID

INTERSTATE 84

Exit#	Services
275mm	Idaho/Utah state line
270mm	both lanes, full facilities, geological site, litter barrels, petwalk
263	Juniper Rd
257mm	Sweetzer Summit, elev 5530
254	Sweetzer Rd
245	Sublett Rd, to Malta, N Sublett/dsl/café
237	Idahome Rd
234mm	Raft River
229mm	/weigh sta both lanes, full facilities, litter barrels, petwalk
228	ID 81, Yale Rd, to Declo
222	I-86, US 30, E to Pocatello
216	ID 77, ID 25, to Declo, N Phillips 66/Food Court/dsl, to Walcott SP, Village of Trees RV Park, S Sinclair/Pit Stop Grill/dsl
215mm	Snake River
211	ID 24, Heyburn, Burley, N Sinclair/A&W/café/dsl Wayside Cafe Tops Motel Country RV Village/park, S Loves/Carl's Jr./dsl/scales/24hr Riverside RV Park, truck repair, truck wash
208	ID 27, Burley, N Phillips 66/dsl Conner's Cafe Super 8 Kenworth, S Chevron/Subway/dsl/24hr, Maverik/dsl, Shell/dsl, Sinclair/dsl Aguila's Mexican, Arby's, Burger King, Denny's, El Caporal, Guadalajara Mexican, Jack-in-the-Box, KFC, Little Caesar's, McDonald's, Morey's Steaks, Perkins, Taco Bell, Wendy's Best Western+, Budget Motel, Fairfield Inn $Tree, Beall's, Buick/GMC, Cal Ranch Store, CarQuest, Chrysler/Dodge/Jeep, Commercial Tire, NAPA, O'Reilly Parts, to Snake River RA, URGENT CARE, Verizon, Walmart
201	ID 25, Kasota Rd, to Paul, N Kasota RV Park
194	ID 25, to Hazelton
188	Valley Rd, to Eden
182	ID 50, to Kimberly, Twin Falls, N Sinclair/dsl Gary's RV Ctr/park/dump, S Shell/Blimpie/Taco Time/dsl/scales/24hr/@ Garden of Eden Cafe Amber Inn auto/truck/rv repair, to Shoshone Falls scenic attraction
173	US 93, Twin Falls, N FLYING J/dsl/LP/24hr/@, Phillips 66/dsl Subway Comfort Inn, Red Lion Inn Blue Beacon, Freightliner, KOA (1mi), to Sun Valley, 5 mi S Chevron/Subway/dsl, Maverik/dsl, Phillips 66/dsl, Shell/dsl, Sinclair, Walmart Fuel/dsl Applebee's, Arby's, Arctic Circle, Baskin-Robbins, Blaze Pizza, Buffalo Wild Wings, Burger King, Cafe Rio, Carino's, Chick-fil-A, Chili's, Coldstone, Costa Vida, Culver's, Denny's, Dickey's BBQ, DQ, Five Guys, Golden Corral, Habit Burger, Idaho Joe's, IHOP, IHOP, Jack-in-the-Box, Jakers Grill, Jamba Juice, Jimmy John's, KFC, La Fiesta, Mandarin Chinese, McDonald's, Noodles&Co, Outback Steaks, Panda Express, Papa John's, Papa Murphy's, Perkins, Pizza Hut, River Rock Grill, Shari's, Sizzler, Sonic, Starbucks, Subway, Taco Bell, Tomato's Italian, Wendy's, Wok In Grill Best Western, Fairfield Inn, Hampton Inn, Hilton Garden, Holiday Inn Express, La Quinta, Motel 6, Quality Inn, Red Lion, Super 8 $Tree, AT&T, AutoZone, Barnes&Noble, Best Buy, Buick/GMC, Chevrolet, Chrysler/Dodge/Jeep, Coll of S ID, Commercial Tire, Costco/gas, Dick's, Ford/Lincoln, Fred Meyer/dsl, Home Depot, Honda, Hyundai, JC Penney, Jo-Ann Fabrics, LDS Temple, Les Schwab Tire, Lowe's, Mazda/VW, Michael's, Nissan, Old Navy, O'Reilly Parts, Petco, Petsmart, Point S Automotive, Ross, ShopKO,

BURLEY

TWIN FALLS

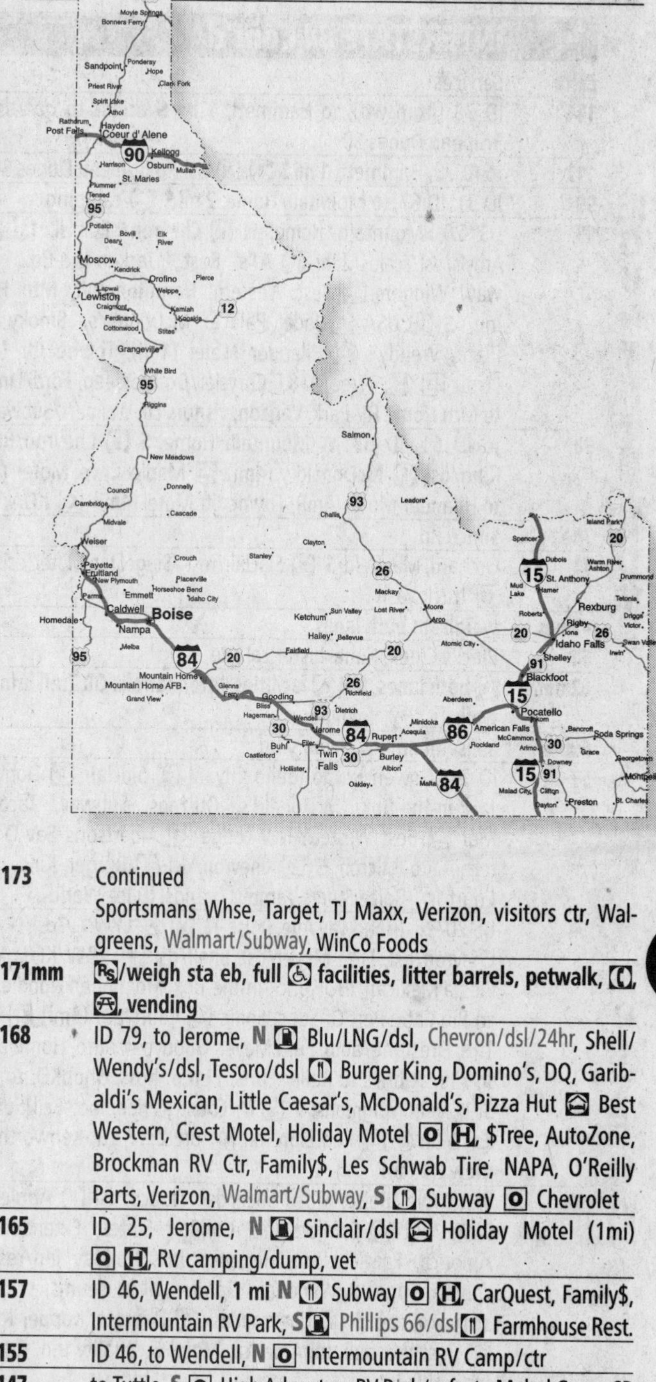

ID

Exit#	Services
173	Continued Sportsmans Whse, Target, TJ Maxx, Verizon, visitors ctr, Walgreens, Walmart/Subway, WinCo Foods
171mm	/weigh sta eb, full facilities, litter barrels, petwalk, vending
168	ID 79, to Jerome, N Blu/LNG/dsl, Chevron/dsl/24hr, Shell/Wendy's/dsl, Tesoro/dsl Burger King, Domino's, DQ, Garibaldi's Mexican, Little Caesar's, McDonald's, Pizza Hut Best Western, Crest Motel, Holiday Motel $Tree, AutoZone, Brockman RV Ctr, Family$, Les Schwab Tire, NAPA, O'Reilly Parts, Verizon, Walmart/Subway, S Subway Chevrolet
165	ID 25, Jerome, N Sinclair/dsl Holiday Motel (1mi) RV camping/dump, vet
157	ID 46, Wendell, 1 mi N Subway CarQuest, Family$, Intermountain RV Park, S Phillips 66/dsl Farmhouse Rest.
155	ID 46, to Wendell, N Intermountain RV Camp/ctr
147	to Tuttle, S High Adventure RV Park/cafe, to Malad Gorge SP
146mm	Malad River
141	US 26, to US 30, Gooding, N S Phillips 66/café/dsl, Sinclair/dsl Amber Inn, Hagerman Inn (9mi) Hagerman RV Village (8mi)
137	Lp 84, to US 30, to Pioneer Road, Bliss, 2 mi S Sinclair/Stinker/dsl/24hr camping
133mm	both lanes, full facilities, info, litter barrels, petwalk
129	King Hill
128mm	Snake River
125	Paradise Valley
122mm	Snake River
121	Glenns Ferry, 1 mi S Sinclair/dsl, Veltex/dsl Hansen Motel/cafe, Redford Motel Carmela Winery/rest., Family$, fudge factory, NAPA, tires, to 3 Island SP, Trails Break RV camp/dump
120	Glenns Ferry (from eb), same as 121

INTERSTATE 84 Cont'd

Exit#	Services
114	ID 78 (from wb), to Hammett, **1 mi S** access to gas/dsl, to Bruneau Dunes SP
112	to ID 78, Hammett, **1 mi S** [food], [gas]/dsl, to Bruneau Dunes SP
99	ID 51, ID 67, to Mountain Home, **2 mi S** [lodging] camping
95	US 20, Mountain Home, **N** [gas] Chevron/KFC/dsl, Pilot/Arby's/dsl/scales/24hr [food] AJ's Rest., Jack-in-the-Box, Subway, Wingers [lodging] Best Western, Hampton Inn, Mtn Home Inn, **S** [gas] USA [food] Jade Palace, McDonald's, Smoky Mtn Pizza, Wendy's [lodging] Hilander Motel (1mi), Towne Ctr Motel (1mi) [other] [H], $Tree, AT&T, Chrysler/Dodge/Jeep, Ford/Lincoln, to Mtn Home RV Park, Verizon, visitors ctr, Walmart/Subway
90	to ID 51, ID 67, W Mountain Home, **S** [gas] Chevron/Burger King/dsl [food] McDonald's (4mi) [lodging] Maple Cove Motel (4mi), to Hilander Motel (4mi), Towne Ctr Motel (4mi) [other] KOA
74	Simco Rd
71	Orchard, Mayfield, **S** [gas] Sinclair/rest./StageStop Motel/dsl/24hr [other] truckwash
66mm	**weigh sta both lanes**
64	Blacks Creek, Kuna, historical site
62mm	**[RS] both lanes, full [handicap] facilities, litter barrels, OR Trail info, petwalk, [phone], [picnic], vending**
59b a	S Eisenman Rd, Memory Rd
57	ID 21, Gowen Rd, to Idaho City, **N** [gas] Sinclair [food] Domino's, Jack-in-the-Box, McDonald's, Quiznos, Subway, Taco Del Mar [lodging] Best Western/NW Lodge [other] Albertsons/Sav-On, Peterbilt, to Micron, **S** [gas] Chevron/dsl [food] Burger King, FoodCourt [other] Boise Stores/famous brands, ID Ice World
54	US 20/26, Broadway Ave, Boise, **N** [gas] FLYING J/dsl/LP/24hr, Chevron/dsl, Fred Meyer/dsl, Shell/dsl [food] A&W/KFC, Arby's, Fiesta Mexican, IHOP, Jack-in-the-Box, Mongolian Noodles, Pizza Pie Cafe, Port Of Subs, Sonic [lodging] Courtyard (3mi) [other] Big O Tire, Firestone/auto, Fred Meyer, Goodyear/auto, Home Depot, Jo-Ann Fabrics, O'Reilly Parts, PetCo, Ross, ShopKO, to Boise St U, vet, Walgreens, **S** [gas] TA/Country Pride/Taco Bell/Subway/dsl/24hr/@ [lodging] Red Lion Inn [other] Bretz RV Ctr, Kenworth, Mtn View RV Park
53	Vista Ave, Boise, **N** [gas] Shell/dsl, Texaco/dsl [food] Applebee's, Pizza Hut [lodging] Comfort Inn, Comfort Suites, Extended Stay America, Fairfield Inn, Hampton Inn, Holiday Inn/rest., La Quinta, Super 8, Wyndham Garden [other] museums, st capitol, st police, zoo, **S** [gas] Chevron/dsl [food] Denny's, Kopper Kitchen [lodging] Best Western, InnAmerica, Motel 6, Quality Inn, Rodeway Inn [other] [airport]
52	Orchard St, Boise, **N** [gas] Maverik/dsl, Shell/dsl [food] Subway [other] BMW Motorcycles, Fiat, GMC
50b a	Cole Rd, Overland Rd, **N** [gas] Chevron/dsl, Shell, Sinclair [food] Cancun Mexican, Cobby's Sandwiches, Eddie's Rest., McDonald's, Outback Steaks, Pizza Hut, Subway, Taco Bell, Taco Time [other] Grocery Outlet, LDS Temple, transmissions, **S** [gas] Phillips 66/dsl, Shell/dsl [food] A&W/KFC, Black Bear Diner, Burger King, Carino's, Carl's Jr, Chapala Mexican, Chuck-a-Rama, Cracker Barrel, Del Taco, Goodwood BBQ, Jimmy John's, Lucky Palace Chinese, McGrath's FishHouse, Nato's Mexican, On the Border, Panda Express, Papa John's, Sonic, Starbucks, Tucano's Brazilian Grill, Twin Peaks [lodging] Hampton Inn, Hilton Garden, Homewood Suites, Howard Johnson's, Oxford Suites [other] Commercial Tire, Costco/gas, Dillon RV Ctr, Discount Tire, Einstein Oilery, Les Schwab Tire, Lowe's, Meineke, USPO, Verizon, vet, Walmart/McDonald's
49	I-184 (exits left from eb), to W Boise, **N** [other] [H]
46	ID 55, Eagle, **N** [gas] Chevron/McDonald's/dsl [food] Buffalo Wild Wings, Del Taco, Ling&Louie's, Los Beto's, Mi Casa, Smash Burger, Starbucks, Subway [lodging] Hampton Inn, Holiday Inn Express, La Quinta [other] [H], **S** [gas] Chevron/dsl [food] Beef'O'Brady's, Chicago Connection, Dickey's BBQ, Dutch Bros Coffee, Happy Teriyaki, Jack-in-the-Box, Jimmy John's, Joy Garden, Panda Garden, Pita Pit, Qdoba, Rudy's Grill, Sakana Japanese, Subway, Taco Bell, TCBY, The Griddle [lodging] Candlewood Suites, Courtyard, TownePlace Suites, Tru [other] AAA, Harley-Davidson, Indian Motorcycles, URGENT CARE, vet
44	ID 69, Meridian, **N** [gas] Chevron/dsl, Maverik/dsl, Sinclair [food] 50's Cafe, A&W/KFC, China Wok, DQ, Jimmy John's, McDonald's, Panda Express, Pizza Hut, Shari's, Starbucks, Subway, Taco Bell, Taco Time, Wendy's [lodging] Best Western+, Motel 6 [other] AT&T, Home Depot, Johnny's Autocare, Les Schwab Tire, Sierra Trading Post, Verizon, WinCo Foods, **S** [gas] Shell/dsl [food] Starbucks, Carl's Jr, JB's, Papa John's [lodging] Mr Sandman Inn [other] Camping World RV Ctr, Ford, Lowe's, O'Reilly Parts, Walgreens, Walmart, waterpark
42	Ten Mile Rd
38	Garrity Blvd, Nampa, **N** [gas] Chevron/dsl, Walmart Gas/dsl [food] Dutch Bros Coffee, Jack-in-the-Box, Los Betos, Port of Subs, Sonic [lodging] Hampton Inn, Home 2 Suites [other] Buick/GMC, Cadillac/Chevrolet, Chrysler/Dodge/Jeep, Ford, Hyundai, Infiniti, Kia, Nissan, Toyota, Walmart/Subway, **S** [gas] Phillips 66/dsl, Shell/dsl [food] Fiesta Guadalajara, Jimmy John's, McDonald's, Panda Express, Papa Murphy's, Pizza Hut, Popeye's, Starbucks, Subway, Taco Bell, Wendy's [lodging] Holiday Inn Express [other] [H], Freddy's, Garrity RV Park, JC Penney, Verizon, War Hawk Museum, Winco Foods
36	Franklin Blvd, Nampa, **N** [gas] Blu/LNG/dsl, Maverik/dsl [food] Jack-in-the-Box [lodging] Shilo Inn/rest., **S** [gas] Chevron/dsl, Shell/Subway/dsl/RV dump/scales/4hr [lodging] Sleep Inn [other] [H], Bretz RV Ctr, Freightliner, Honda, Mason Cr RV Park
35	ID 55, Nampa, **S** [gas] Maverik/dsl, Shell/dsl [food] Denny's [lodging] Nampa Inn, Rodeway Inn, Super 8
33b a	ID 55 S, Midland Blvd, Marcine, **N** [food] Blaze Pizza, Chick-fil-A, Cracker Barrel, Dickey's BBQ, Habit Burger, McDonald's, Olive Garden, Panera Bread, Qdoba Mexican, Sonic, Subway, TGIFriday's, Winger's [lodging] Fairfield Inn, Holiday Inn [other] AT&T, Best Buy, Costco/gas, Dick's, Discount Tire, Gordmans, Hobby Lobby, [H], Kohl's, Michael's, Old Navy, PetCo, Petsmart, Sportsmans Whse, Target, TJ Maxx, Verizon, World Mkt, **S** [gas] Shell/dsl [food] Applebee's, Arby's, Baskin-Robbins, Blimpie, Buffalo Wild Wings, Carl's Jr, Chipotle, Coldstone, Costa Vida, DQ, Golden Corral, IHOP, Jack-in-the-Box, Jade Garden, Jalapeno's Grill, Jimmy John's, Mongolian BBQ, Outback Steaks, Papa Murphy's, Pizza Hut, Red Robin, Shari's Rest, Smashburger, Smokey Mtn Grill, Starbucks, Subway, Taco Bell, TX Roadhouse, Wendy's, Zupas Kitchen [other] $Tree, Home Depot, Jo-Ann Fabrics, Lowe's, Nampa Tire, NAPA, Point S Automotive, Ross, Savers, Shopko, Staples, U-Haul, Verizon, Verizon (2), vet, Walgreens, WinCo Foods
29	US 20/26, Franklin Rd, Caldwell, **N** [gas] FLYING J/Denny's/dsl/LP/scales/24hr [other] Ambassador RV camping, RV dump, **S** [gas] Sage/Sinclair/cafe/dsl/24hr [food] Burger King, Dutch Bros [lodging] Best Western+, La Quinta
28	10th Ave, Caldwell, **N** [gas] Maverik/dsl [other] city park, U-Haul, **S** [gas] Chevron/dsl, Shell/dsl [food] Carl's Jr, Fiesta Mexican, Jack-in-the-Box, Mr V's Rest., Pizza Hut, Subway, Wendy's [other] [H], AutoZone, Point S Automotive, Walgreens
27	ID 19, to Wilder, **1 mi S** [gas] Chevron/dsl [other] visitor info
26.5mm	Boise River

MOUNTAIN HOME · BOISE · EAGLE · NAMPA · CALDWELL · ID

INTERSTATE 84 Cont'd

Exit#	Services
26	US 20/26, to Notus, N Caldwell Campground, S Sinclair/dsl RV Resort
25	ID 44, Middleton, N Sinclair/dsl 44 Burgers/shakes, S Insp sta eb
17	Sand Hollow, N Sinclair/Sand Hollow Café/dsl Country Corners RV Park
13	Black Canyon Jct, S Sinclair/rest./motel/dsl/scales/24hr
9	US 30, to New Plymouth
3	US 95, Fruitland, N Chevron/A&W/dsl Neat Retreat RV Park (5mi), to Hell's Cyn RA (26mi)
1mm	**Welcome Ctr eb, full facilities, info, litter barrels, petwalk,**
0mm	Idaho/Oregon state line, Snake River

INTERSTATE 86

POCATELLO

Exit#	Services
63b a	I-15, N to Butte, S to SLC. **I-86 begins/ends on I-15, exit 72.**
61	US 91, Yellowstone Ave, Pocatello, N Exxon, Maverik/dsl, Shell/dsl Arby's, Arctic Circle, Burger King, Chapala Mexican, Domino's, Five Mile Café, Jack-in-the-Box, Lei's BBQ, Papa Murphy's, Subway, Tres Hermanos, Wendy's Motel 6, Travelodge $Tree, AutoZone, Bargain Tire, Crossroads RV Ctr, Family$, O'Reilly Parts, Smith's Foods/dsl, vet, S Exxon/dsl, Phillips 66/dsl Buffalo Wild Wings, Chili's, Costa Vida, Denny's, Firehouse Subs, Five Guys, Freddy's, Great Wall, IHOP, Jimmy John's, MacKenzie River Grill, McDonald's, Noodles&Co, Panda Express, Panera Bread, Pizza Hut, Pizza Pie Café, Popeye's, Red Lobster, Red Robin, Starbucks, TX Roadhouse AT&T, Cal Ranch Store, Chrysler/Dodge/Jeep, Costco/gas, Dick's, Discount Tire, Ford/Lincoln, Hobby Lobby, Home Depot, Honda, JC Penney, Jo-Ann Fabrics, Kia, Lowe's, NAPA, Nissan, PetCo, Petsmart, Ross, Schwab Tire, ShopKo, TJ Maxx, Toyota, Verizon, Walgreens, Walmart
58.5mm	Portneuf River
58	US 30, W Pocatello, N Batise Springs RV Park/dump (1mi-seasonal)
56	N Pocatello Reg Airport, S Sinclair/dsl/24hr
52	Arbon Valley, S Phillips 66/Bannock Peak/dsl casino
51mm	Bannock Creek
49	Rainbow Rd
44	Seagull Bay
40	ID 39, American Falls, N Sinclair/dsl (1mi), Texaco Pizza Hut, Subway, Tres Hermanos Mexican American Motel auto repair, Family$ (1mi), Jiffy Lube, NAPA, Schwab Tire, to Am Falls RA, Willow Bay RV Park/dump, S Hillview Motel
36	ID 37, to Rockland, American Falls, 2 mi N Shell/dsl Falls Motel , 2 mi S Indian Springs RV Resort
33	Neeley Area
31mm	**wb, full facilities, hist site, litter barrel, petwalk, picnic table, vending**
28	N Register Rock Hist Site, RV camping/dump, to Massacre Rock SP
21	Coldwater Area
19mm	**eb, full facilities, hist site, litter barrel, petwalk, picnic table, vending**
15	Raft River Area
1	I-84 E, to Ogden. **I-86 begins/ends on I-84, exit 222.**

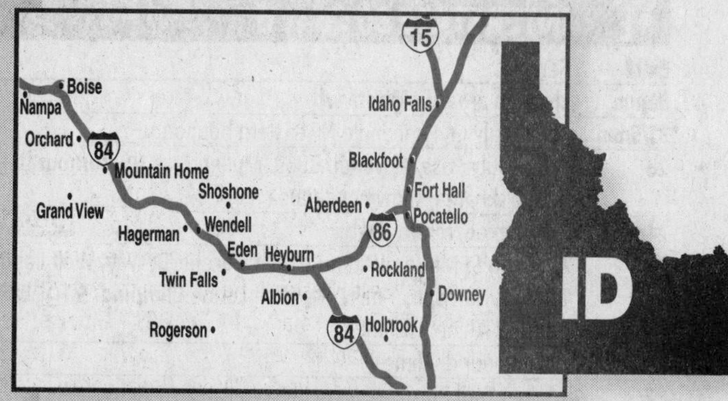

INTERSTATE 90

WALLACE KELLOGG

Exit#	Services
74mm	Idaho/Montana state line, Pacific/Central time zone, Lookout Pass elev 4680
73mm	scenic area/hist site wb
72mm	scenic area/hist site eb
71mm	**runaway truck ramp wb**
70mm	**runaway truck ramp wb**
69	Lp 90, Mullan, N Sinclair/dsl Mullan Trail grocery/RV Park, museum, USPO
68	Lp 90 (from eb), Mullan, same as 69
67	Morning District, Morning District
66	Gold Creek (from eb)
65	Compressor District
64	Golconda District
62	ID 4, Wallace, S Conoco Pizza Factory, Smokehouse Rest. Brooks Hotel, Stardust Motel Harvest Foods, museum, Wallace RV Park
61	Lp 90, Wallace, S Conoco/dsl Pizza Factory, Smokehouse Rest., Trailside Cafe Brooks Hotel/rest., Wallace Inn auto repair, info ctr, same as 62
60	Lp 90, Silverton, S RV camping
57	Lp 90, Osburn, S 76/dsl Blue Anchor RV Park, Stein's Foods, USPO
54	Big Creek, N hist site
51	Lp 90, Division St, Kellogg, N Conoco/dsl Trail Motel , Bender Drug, Buick/Cadillac/Chevrolet/GMC, Chrysler/Dodge/Jeep, Schwab Tire, Stein's Foods, vet, S Moose Creek Grill USPO
50	Hill St (from eb), Kellogg, N Humdinger Drive-In Trail Motel Ace Hardware, Benzer Drug, NAPA, Stein's Foods, tires, S Conoco/dsl museum, Silver Mtn Ski/summer resort/rec area, Yoke's Foods
49	Bunker Ave, N Conoco/dsl McDonald's, Sam's Drive-In, Subway Silverhorn Motel/rest. , S Noah's Canteen, Silver Mtn Rest. Fairbridge Inn, Morning Star Lodge city park, museum, RV dump, Silver Mtn RA
48	Smelterville, S Dave Smith Tire, O'Reilly Parts, USPO, Walmart
45	Pinehurst, S Chevron/dsl/repair, Conoco/dsl By-the-way Camping, Harvest Foods, TrueValue, USPO
43	Kingston, N Conoco/dsl, S Exxon/dsl/rv dump, USPO
40	Cataldo, N Timbers Roadhouse, USPO, S RV Park
39.5mm	Coeur d' Alene River
39	Cataldo Mission, S Nat Hist Landmark, Old Mission SP
34	ID 3, to St Maries, Rose Lake, S Conoco/dsl, Rose Lake/dsl Rose Lake Cafe White Pines Scenic Rte
33	**chain removal eb**

ID

INTERSTATE 90 Cont'd

COUER d' ALENE

Exit#	Services
32mm	**chainup area/weigh sta wb**
31.5mm	4th of July Cr, Panhandle NF eastern boundary
28	4th of July Pass, elevation 3069, Mullen Tree HS, turnout both lanes, ski area, snowmobile area
24mm	**chainup eb, removal wb**
22	ID 97, to St Maries, L Coeur d' Alene Scenic ByWay, Wolf Lodge District, Harrison, **1 mi N** Wolf Lodge Camping, **S** Lake Coeur d'Alene RV Park
20.5mm	Lake Coeur d' Alene
17	Mullan Trail Rd
15	Lp 90, Sherman Ave, Coeur d' Alene, **N** forest info, Lake Coeur D' Alene RA/HS, **S** Chevron, Exxon/dsl, Mobil/dsl/LP Jimmy's Cafe, Michael D's Eatery, Moontime Cafe, O'Shay's Rest., Roger's Burgers, Zip's Rest. Baymont Inn, BudgetSaver Motel, El Rancho Motel, Flaming Motel, Holiday Motel, Japan House Suites, State Motel, Two Lakes Motel auto repair, Harvest Foods, tourist info
14	15th St, Coeur d' Alene, **S** TAJ Mart Jordon's Grocery
13	4th St, Coeur d' Alene, **N** A&D/dsl Atilano's Mexican, Baskin Robbins, Carl's Jr, Davis Donuts, Denny's, DQ, IHOP, Jimmy John's, Little Caesar's, Original Mongolian BBQ, Panda Express, Starbucks, Subway, Taco Time, Wendy's Ramada Inn AutoZone, BigLots, Costco/gas, NAPA, same as 12, Schwab Tire, Verizon, **S** Exxon/dsl Thai Bamboo Maserati/Alfa Romeo
12	US 95, to Sandpoint, Moscow, **N** Exxon/dsl, Holiday/dsl, Mobil/dsl, Walmart/dsl Applebee's, Arby's, Buffalo Wild Wings, Cafe Rio, Chili's, China Town, Del Taco, Elmer's, Golden Corral, JB's Rest., Jimmy John's, MacKenzie River Pizza, McDonald's, Olive Garden, Panda Express, Panera Bread, Pizza Hut, Red Lobster, Taco Bell, Tomato St., TX Roadhouse Best Western+, Comfort Suites, Fairbridge Inn, Motel 6, Quality Inn, Super 8 $Tree, Advance Parts, Albertson's, AT&T, Best Buy, Blue Dog RV, Buick/GMC, Cadillac, Combs RV, Discount Tire, Ford/Subaru, Fred Meyer/dsl, Grocery Outlet, Home Depot, JC Penney, Jo-Ann Fabrics, Kia, Kohl's, Michael's, Natural Grocers, O'Reilly Parts, PetCo, Ross, Safeway/dsl, Super 1 Foods, Target, TireRama, TJ Maxx, Toyota, Tuesday Morning, U-Haul, URGENT CARE, Verizon, Walgreens, Walmart/Subway, **S** Conoco/dsl, Mobil Asian Twist, Jack-in-the-Box, Jamba Juice, Papa Murphy's, Qdoba Mexican, Shari's, Starbucks La Quinta H, Albertson's, AT&T, GNC, Rite Aid, same as 13, ShopKO/drugs, Staples
11	Northwest Blvd, **N** Conoco/dsl Cracker Barrel, Firehouse Subs, Jack-in-the-Box, MOD Pizza, Subway, Sweet Burrito, Thai Express Lowe's, WinCo Foods, **S** Exxon/dsl, SpeeDee Anthony's, Azteca Mexican, Bullman's Woodfired Pizza, Coldstone, Ipanema Brazilian, Martino Tuscan, McDonald's, Outback Steaks, Red Robin, SF Sourdough, Starbucks Days Inn, Hampton Inn, Holiday Inn Express, Springhill Suites, Staybridge Suites H, Honda, Riverwalk RV Park, Verizon
8.5mm	**Welcome Ctr/weigh sta eb, RS both lanes, full facilities, info, litter barrels, petwalk,**
7	ID 41, to Rathdrum, Spirit Lake, **N** 76/dsl Burger King, Del Taco, Domino's, NY Pizza, Papa Murphy's, Pita Pit, Popeye's, Sonic, Starbucks, Subway, Wendy's $Tree, AT&T, auto repair, Chevrolet, Chrysler/Dodge/Jeep, Couer d'Alene RV Park, Hyundai, Nissan, VW, Walmart/Subway, **S** Chevron/dsl, Coleman/dsl A&W/KFC, Capone's Grill, DQ Quality Inn Robins RV Ctr, truck repair, Verizon, vet
6	Seltice Way, **N** 7-11 La Cabana Mexican, Paul Bunyan Burgers, Pizza Hut NAPA, Super 1 Foods, Walgreens, **S** 76/dsl/LP Denny's, Dueling Irons Cafe, Fuki Japanese, Little Caesar's, McDonald's, Old European Cafe, Rancho Viejo Mexican, Taco Bell, Timbers Rest. Ace Hardware, O'Reilly Parts, TireRama, USPO, vet, Yoke's Foods
5	Lp 90, Spokane St, Treaty Rock HS, **N** 76/dsl, Exxon/dsl Corner Cafe, Golden Dragon, Hunter's Rest., Papa John's, Rob's Seafood/burgers, Subway, WhiteHouse Grill AutoZone, Blue Dog RV Ctr, Meineke, Perfection Tire/repair, Schwab Tire, **S** Handy Mart/Pacific Pride/dsl Red Lion Inn visitors ctr
2	Pleasant View Rd, **N** FLYING J/Conoco/Subway/dsl/LP/scales/24hr, Exxon/dsl, Love's/Carl's Jr/dsl/scales/24hr McDonald's, Toro Viejo Mexican Sure Stay Inn+ RV/truckwash, Suntree RV Park, **S** Exxon/dsl Zip's Drive-in Riverbend Inn, Sleep Inn dogtrack
1	Beck Rd, **N** Panda Express Cabela's, Walmart/Subway, **S** greyhound track
0mm	Idaho/Washington state line

INTERSTATE 184 (Boise)

BOISE

Exit#	Services
6mm	**I-184 begins/ends on 13th St**, downtown, Shell Bonefish Grill, Chandler's Steaks, Five Guys, PF Chang's Hampton Inn, Safari Inn, The Grove Office Depot, USPO
5	River St (from eb), **W** Chevron McDonald's Red Lion
4.5mm	Boise River
3	Fairview Ave, to US 20/26 E, **W** Joe's Crabshack, Tepanyaki Japanese Boise Inn, Cottonwood Suites, Riverside Hotel Commercial Tire
2	Curtis Rd, to Garden City, **E** Shell H
1b a	Cole Rd, Franklin Rd, **E** Chevron/Subway/dsl Acura, Chrysler/Dodge/Jeep, Honda, Jaguar, Land Rover, Mercedes, Volvo, **W** Chevron/dsl, Sinclair/dsl Applebee's, Cafe Ole, Cafe Rio, Carl's Jr, Cheesecake Factory, Chick-fil-A, Chili's, Chipotle, Dave&Buster's, Fujiyama Japanese, Golden Corral, IHOP, Jalapeno's, McDonald's, Noodles&Co, Old Chicago Pizza, Olive Garden, Port of Subs, Quiznos, Red Lobster, Red Robin, Rumbi Island Grill, Shari's, Sizzler, Smash Burger, Starbucks, Wendy's Candlewood Suites, La Quinta, Residence Inn AT&T, AT&T, Audi/VW, Best Buy, Cabela's, Dick's, Dillard's, JC Penney, Kohl's, Macy's, Michael's, Old Navy, PetCo, Petsmart, REI, Ross, Target, TJ Maxx, Tuesday Morning, Verizon
0mm	**I-184 begins/ends on I-84, exit 49.**

NOTES

ILLINOIS

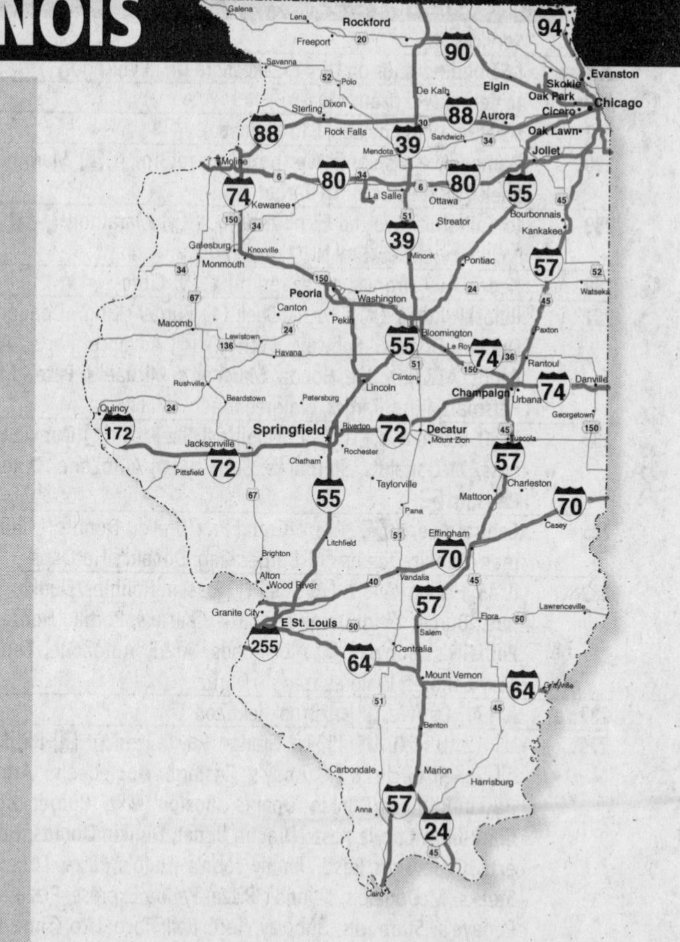

INTERSTATE 24

Exit #	Services
38mm	Illinois/Kentucky state line, Ohio River
37	US 45, Metropolis, N [RS] **both lanes, full [handicap] facilities, info, litter barrels, petwalk, [picnic], vending**, S [gas] BP/Quiznos/dsl [food] China House, McDonald's, Pizza Hut, Sonic [lodging] Best Value Inn, Holiday Inn Express, Metropolis Inn, Motel 6, Super 8 [other] [H], $General, Buick/Chrysler/Dodge/GMC/Jeep, camping, Chevrolet, Ft Massac SP, O'Reilly Parts, Plaza Tire, to Riverboat Casino
27	to New Columbia, Big Bay
16	IL 146, Vienna, N [other] Gambit Golf, S [gas] BP/dsl, Citgo/dsl, FastStop [food] DQ, Jumbo Grill, McDonald's, Subway, Vienna Diner [lodging] Limited Inn [other] vet
14	US 45, Vienna, S [other] camping
7	to Goreville, Tunnel Hill, N [other] winery (7mi), S [other] camping, to Ferne Clyffe SP
1	I-57, N to Chicago, S to Memphis. **I-24 begins/ends on I-57, exit 44.**

INTERSTATE 39

ROCKFORD

Exit #	Services
122.5	**I-39 and I-90 run together into Wisconsin. See Illinois Interstate 90, exits 15mm-1.**
122b a	US 20 E, Harrison Ave, to Belvidere (last nb exit before toll rd), W [gas] Fas Fuel/Subway/dsl, Mobil, Tesla EVC [food] Arby's, Bergner's, Burger King, DQ, Granite City Rest., Lung Fung, Rosati's, Rosati's Pizza, Sonic, Taco Bell, TGIFriday's [other] Barnes&Noble, BMW, Buick/Chevrolet/GMC, Collier RV Ctr, Goodyear/auto, Harley-Davidson, JC Penney, Macy's, Menards, Schnuck's Foods/gas, Tires+, vet, VW, Walgreens
119	US 20 W, Alpine Rd, to Rockford
116.5mm	Kishwaukee River
115	Baxter Rd, E [gas] Shell/Subway/dsl/scales/24hr/@
111	IL 72, to Monroe Center, E [gas] BP/Sunrise Family Rest./dsl/24hr, Marathon (1mi)
104	IL 64, to Oregon, Sycamore, W [food] Grubsteakers Rest/truck parking (2mi)
99	IL 38, to De Kalb, Rochelle, 0-2 mi W [gas] Murphy USA/dsl, Murphy USA/dsl, Petro/Iron Skillet/dsl/scales/RV Dump/@, Phillips 66/Circle K/dsl, Road Ranger/Pilot/Subway/dsl/scales/24hr, Shell/dsl [food] Arby's, Butterfly Rest, China Wok, Culver's, Dunkin Donuts, Jimmy John's, Little Caesar's, McDonald's, New China, Pizza Hut, Subway, Taco Bell, Wendy's [lodging] Comfort Inn, Country Hearth Inn, Holiday Inn Express, Super 8 [other] [H], $General, $Tree, Blue Beacon, GNC, O'Reilly Parts, Sullivan's Foods, Verizon, Walgreens, Walmart
97b a	I-88 **tollway**, to Moline, Rock Island, Chicago
93	Steward
87	US 30, to Sterling, Rock Falls, E [other] to Shabbona Lake SP, W [other] Yogi Bear Camping (16mi)
84.5mm	[RS] **both lanes, full [handicap] facilities, litter barrels, petwalk, [phone], [picnic], playground, vending**
82	Paw Paw, **3 mi** E [gas] Casey's (3mi), W many wind turbines
72	US 34, to Mendota, Earlville, W [gas] BP/Cindy's/dsl/scales/24hr, Road Ranger/Pilot/Subway/dsl/scales/24hr [food] KFC/Taco Bell, McDonald's [lodging] Quality Inn, Super 8/truck parking [other] [H]
67.5mm	Little Vermilion River
66	US 52, Troy Grove, E [other] KOA (6mi)

OGLESBY

Exit #	Services
62.5mm	Tomahawk Creek
59b a	I-80, E to Chicago, W to Des Moines
57	US 6, to Peru, La Salle, **1-2 mi** W [gas] Casey's [lodging] Daniel's Motel [other] city park
56mm	Illinois River, Abraham Lincoln Mem Bridge
54	Oglesby, E [gas] BP/dsl, Casey's, Phillips 66/dsl, Shell [food] Burger King, Delaney's Rest., KFC/Taco Bell, McDonald's, Root Beer Stand, Subway [lodging] Best Western, Days Inn [other] Starved Rock SP, W [gas] Loves/Hardee's/dsl/scales/24hr
52	IL 251, to La Salle, Peru
51	IL 71, to Hennepin, Oglesby
48	Tonica, E [gas] Casey's [other] city park
41	IL 18, to Streator, Henry
35	IL 17, to Wenona, Lacon, E [gas] BP/dsl, Casey's (2mi), Shell/Burger King/dsl/RV dump [food] Subway [lodging] Best Value Inn/truck parking
27	to Minonk, E [gas] Casey's (2mi), Pilot/Road Ranger/Subway/Woody's Rest./dsl/24hr [lodging] Motel 6 [other] NAPA
22	IL 116, to Peoria, Benson
14	US 24, to El Paso, Peoria, E [gas] BP/Subway/dsl/24hr, Casey's/dsl, Freedom/dsl [food] DQ, Hardee's, McDonald's, Woody's Family Rest. [lodging] Days Inn [other] Buick/Chevrolet/GMC, city park, Ford, IGA Foods, USPO, W [food] Monical's Pizza [lodging] Super 8 [other] $General, Hickory Hill Camping (4mi), PROMPT CARE
9mm	Mackinaw River
8	IL 251, Lake Bloomington Rd, E [other] Lake Bloomington, W [other] Evergreen Lake, to Comlara Park
5	Hudson, **1 mi** E [gas] Casey's/dsl
2	US 51 bus, Bloomington, Normal
0mm	**I-39 begins/ends on I-55, exit 164.**

INTERSTATE 55

CHICAGO AREA

Exit #	Services
295mm	**I-55 begins/ends on US 41**, Lakeshore Dr, in Chicago.
293a	to Cermak Rd (from nb)
292	I-90/94, W to Chicago, E to Indiana
290	Damen Ave, Ashland Ave (no EZ nb return), E Marathon, Shell Starbucks Target
289	to California Ave (no EZ nb return), E Marathon, Pilot/Road Ranger/Subway/dsl, Thornton's/dsl
288	Kedzie Ave, (from sb no ez return), E Citgo
287	Pulaski Rd, E BP/dsl, Shell Burger King, Domino's, Dunkin Donuts, Subway, Wendy's Advance Parts, Aldi Foods, AT&T, Dodge, Honda, Marshall's, Michael's, Pete's Mkt, Petsmart, Ross, Target, Walgreens
286	IL 50, Cicero Ave, E BP, Mobil/dsl, Shell/dsl Dunkin Donuts, McDonald's, Starbucks, Subway AutoZone, O'Reilly Parts, to
285	Central Ave, E BP/dsl, Grand Prix/Dunkin Donuts, Minuteman/Dunkin Donuts Burger King, Donald's HotDogs
283	IL 43, Harlem Ave, E Shell Baskin-Robbins/Dunkin Donuts, Burger King, Domino's, Little Caesar's, Portillo HotDogs, Potbelly's, Subway Aldi Foods, AT&T, AutoZone, Fannie May Candies, Walgreens
282b a	IL 171, 1st Ave, W Brookfield Zoo
279b	US 12, US 20, US 45, La Grange Rd, **0-2 mi** W BP, Mobil, Shell/Circle K Andy's Custard, Applebee's, Arby's, Baskin-Robbins/Dunkin Donuts, Boston Mkt, Burger King, Chick-fil-A, Cocula Rest., Dragon Buffet, Dunkin Donuts, Hooters, JC Georges Rest., Jimmy John's, Ledo's Pizza, LoneStar Steaks, McDonald's, Nonno's Pizza, Panda Express, Pizza Hut, Popeye's, Starbucks, Subway, Taco Bell, Taco Tico, Time Out Grill, TX Roadhouse, Via Bella, Wendy's, White Castle Best Western+, Holiday Inn $Tree, Aldi Foods, Best Buy, Buick/Cadillac/GMC, Chevrolet, Chrysler/Dodge/Jeep, Discount Tire, Firestone/auto, Ford, GNC, Harley Davidson, Home Depot, Honda, Jo-Ann Fabrics, Kohl's, Mazda, Menards, NAPA, Nissan, NTB, O'Reilly Parts, PepBoys, PetCo, Petsmart, Sam's Club/gas, Subaru, Target, Toyota, Verizon, VW, Walmart
279a	La Grange Rd, **to I-294 toll**, S to Indiana
277b	**I-294 toll** (from nb), S to Indiana
277a	**I-294 toll**, N to Wisconsin
276c	Joliet Rd (from nb)
276b a	County Line Rd, E Capri Rest., China King, Ciazza's Grill, Cooper's Hawk, Eddie Merlot's, Patti's Sunrise Cafe, Starbucks, Subway, Topaz Rest. Extended Stay America, Marriott, Quality Inn Tuesday Morning, W SpringHill Suites
274	IL 83, Kingery Rd, E Shell, W BP/dsl, Mobil/dsl, Shell Bakers Square, Buffalo Wild Wings, Chick-fil-A, Chipotle Mexican, Denny's, Dunkin Donuts, Jamba Juice, Jimmy John's, MOD Pizza, Panera Bread, Papa John's, Patio BBQ, Portillo's HotDogs, Potbelly's Rest., Starbucks, Wendy's Econolodge, Holiday Inn, La Quinta, Red Roof Inn Ford/KIA, GNC, Marshall's, Marshall's, Michael's, Staples, Target, Verizon
273b a	Cass Ave, W Shell Al Chile Mexican, Chuck's Rest., Rosati's Pizza, Uncle Mao's Chinese
271b a	Lemont Rd, E Extended Stay America, W Shell
269	**I-355 toll**, to W Suburbs
268	(from sb only), Joliet, same as 267
267	IL 53, Bolingbrook, E 55 Trkstp/rest./dsl/scales/24hr/@, BP/dsl McDonald's Ramada Ltd, Super 8 Chevrolet, W Shell/Circle K, Speedway/dsl Burger King, Cheddar's,

BOLINGBROOK

IL

JOLIET

Exit #	Services
267	Continued Denny's, Dunkin Donuts, El Burrito Loco, Family Square Rest., Golden Chopsticks, Golden Corral, McDonald's, Popeye's, Starbucks, Subway, Wendy's, White Castle Hampton Inn, Hilton Garden, Holiday Inn, Quality Inn, Residence Inn, SpringHill Suites $Tree, Aldi Foods, Fiesta Mkt, NAPA, Tony's Mkt, U-Haul, Walgreens, Walmart
266mm	**weigh sta both lanes**
263	Weber Rd, E 7-11, BP/dsl, Speedway/Dunkin Donuts/dsl/e85 Burger King, Burrito's, Culver's, Doc Watson's Smokehouse, KFC, Little China, McDonald's, Michael's Pizza, Popeye's, Subway, Todake Steaks, White Castle Days Inn, Holiday Inn Express Ace Hardware, BB Rest., Discount Tire, GNC, Reba's Automotive, Walgreens, W Mobil/Jimmy John's/dsl, Shell/Circle K Arby's, Cracker Barrel, Wendy's Comfort Inn, Country Inn&Suites, Extended Stay America, Woodspring Suites
261	IL 126 (from sb), to Plainfield
257	US 30, to Joliet, Aurora, E Shell/Circle K Anthony's Rest. Applebee's, Baskin-Robbins/Dunkin Donuts, Burger King, Chipotle, ChuckeCheese, Denny's, Diamand's Rest., Five Guys, Fresh Thyme Mkt, Hooters, LoneStar Steaks, McDonald's, Outback Steaks, Panera Bread, Red Lobster, Steak'n Shake, Subway, Taco Bell, TGIFriday's, TX Roadhouse, Wendy's Best Western+ Comfort Inn, Fairfield Inn, Hampton Inn, Home 2 Suites, Motel 6, Super 8 $Tree, Aldi Foods, AT&T, AutoZone, Barnes&Noble, Best Buy, Dick's, Discount Tire, Firestone/auto, Home Depot, Honda, JC Penney, Jo-Ann Fabrics, Macy's, Michael's, NTB, Old Navy, Petsmart, Ross, Target, Verizon, W Mobil, dsl Blue's BBQ, Luigi's Pizza Chevrolet, Ford
253b a	US 52, Jefferson St, Joliet, E Citgo/dsl, Mobil/dsl, Shell Joe's Rest., McDonald's Best Western, Econolodge, Elk's Motel, La Quinta, Wingate Inn H, Ford, Freedom Automotive, Freightliner, Harley-Davidson, Rick's RV Ctr, W BP dsl, Shell Burger King, Casa Maya, DQ, Rosati's Pizza, Starbucks, Subway 7-11, Chrysler/Dodge/Jeep, Jewel-Osco, vet
251	IL 59 (from nb), to Shorewood, access to same as 253 W
250b a	I-80, W to Iowa, E to Toledo
248	US 6, Joliet, E Pilot/Dunkin Donuts/Subway/dsl/24hr Speedway/dsl Taco Burrito King, W BP/McDonald's Thornton's/dsl/scales
247	Bluff Rd
245mm	Des Plaines River
244	Arsenal Rd, E Exxon/Mobil Refinery
241	to Wilmington
241mm	Kankakee River
240	Lorenzo Rd, E BP/dsl, W Mobil/pizza/dsl/scales/24hr Petro/Shell/Iron Skillet/dsl/scales/24hr/@ Knights Inn
238	IL 129 S, to Wilmington (from nb), Braidwood
236	IL 113, Coal City, E EZ Living RV Ctr, Fossil Rock Camping W Casey's, Shell/DQ/dsl KFC/Taco Bell, Little Caesar's Los 3 Burritos, WhistleStop Cafe
233	Reed Rd, E Marathon/dsl Jones-sez BBQ
227	IL 53, Gardner, E Casey's Gardner Rest., Subway $General, truck/tire repair, W BP/dsl
220	IL 47, Dwight, E BP/Burger King/dsl, Loves/Hardee's dsl/scales/24hr, Marathon/Circle K/dsl/24hr Arby's, Dwight Chinese, Dwight Pizza, McDonald's, Pete's Rest., Subway Classic Motel, Super 8
217	IL 17, Dwight, E Casey's, Shell/Circle K/dsl/24hr DQ, R 66 Rest. Ace Hardware, CVS Drug, Family$, NAPA, ShopK
213mm	Mazon River
209	Odell, E USPO

INTERSTATE 55 Cont'd

Exit #	Services
201	IL 23, Pontiac, 0-3 mi E DQ, La Mex 4H RV Camp (seasonal) RV Ctr, Pontiac RV Ctr, W truck repair
198mm	Vermilion River
197	IL 116, Pontiac, E BP/dsl, Shell/dsl, Thornton's/dsl Arby's, Baby Bull's Rest., Burger King, Cafe Fontana, Dunkin Donuts, KFC, LJ Silver, McDonald's, Monical's Pizza, Pizza Hut, Subway, Taco Bell, Wendy's Best Western, Hampton Inn, Quality Inn, Super 8 $General, $Tree, Advance Parts, Aldi Foods, AT&T, AutoZone, Big R Store, Buick/Chevrolet/Cadillac/GMC, Chrysler/Dodge/Jeep/Lincoln, Firestone/auto, Lincoln, Verizon, Walgreens, Walmart/Subway, W Mobil/dsl H
193mm	**both lanes, full facilities, litter barrels, petwalk, , , vending**
187	US 24, Chenoa, E Casey's/dsl, Phillips 66/McDonald's/dsl, Shell/Subway/dsl Best Value Inn, Chenoa Family Rest.
179mm	Des Plaines River
178	Lexington, E BP/McDonalds/dsl, Freedom/dsl Subway $General, W Chevrolet
178mm	Mackinaw River
171	Towanda, E FastStop/dsl
167	Lp 55 S Veterans Pkwy, to Normal, 0-3 mi E BP/Circle K, Marathon/Circle K/dsl Alexander's Steaks, Applebee's, Bandana's BBQ, Biaggi's Ristorante, Bob Evans, Burger King, Carlos O'Kelly's, Chick-fil-A, Chili's, Chipotle Mexican, ChuckeCheese, Coldstone, Destihl Rest., DQ, Fazoli's, Fiesta Ranchera Mexican, FlatTop Grill, Hardee's, IHOP, Jason's Deli, Jimmy John's, Jimmy John's (2), Krispy Kreme, Logan's Roadhouse, Lonestar Steaks, McDonald's, Monical's Pizza, Noodles&Co, Olive Garden, Outback Steaks, Panda Express, Panera Bread, Papa John's, Pizza Hut, Pizza Ranch, Popeye's, Portillo's, Potbelly, Qdoba Mexican, Red Lobster, Red Robin, Schlotzsky's, Smashburger, Sonic, Starbucks, Steak'n Shake, Subway, Taco Bell, Tony Roma's, Wendy's, Wild Berries Rest. Baymont Inn, Candlewood Suites, Chateau, Comfort Suites, Courtyard, Hampton Inn, Holiday Inn Express, Motel 6, Quality Inn, Super 8 H, $Tree, Advance Parts, Aldi Foods, AT&T, AutoZone, Barnes&Noble, Best Buy, CVS Drug, Dick's, Fresh Mkt, GNC, Goodyear/auto, Gordman's, Hobby Lobby, Home Depot, Honda, Hyundai, HyVee, Jewel-Osco, Jo-Ann Fabrics, Kohl's, Kroger/dsl, Lowe's, Meijer/dsl, Meineke, Menards, Michael's, Midas, Office Depot, Old Navy, O'Reilly Parts, PetCo, Sam's Club/gas, Schnuck's Foods, Target, TJ Maxx, to , Tuesday Morning, Tuffy, Verizon, Von Maur, Walgreens, Walmart/Subway
165b a	US 51 bus, to Bloomington, E BP/Circle K, Mobil/Arby's/dsl, Qik-n-EZ, Shell/Burger King/dsl Denny's, Dunkin Donuts, McDonald's, Moe's SW Grill, Rosati's Pizza, Smoothie King, Starbucks, Steak'n Shake, Subway, Uncle Tom's Pancakes, Wendy's Baymont Inn, Motel 6, Radisson, Super 8 H, $General, $Tree, Discount Tire, Schnuck's Foods, to Ill St U, Verizon, Walgreens, W dsl repair
164	I-39, US 51, N to Peru
163	I-74 W, to Peoria
160b a	US 150, IL 9, Market St, Bloomington, E BP/Circle K, Freedom/dsl, Pilot/Wendy's/dsl/scales/24hr, Shell/repair, TA/Country Pride/dsl/scales/24hr/@ Arby's, Cracker Barrel, Culver's, KFC, McDonald's, Popeye's, Subway, Taco Bell Days Inn, EconoLodge, Hawthorn Suites, Quality Inn, Quality Suites, Red Roof Inn H, Advance Parts, Blue Beacon, Family$, Peterbilt, W Marathon/Circle K/dsl, Murphy USA/dsl Bob Evans, Fiesta Ranchera Mexican, Steak'n Shake/24hr Comfort Suites, Country Inn&Suites, Fairfield Inn, Hampton Inn, Holiday Inn Express, Ramada Ltd Aldi Foods, Farm&Fleet, Walmart

PONTIAC

NORMAL

BLOOMINGTON

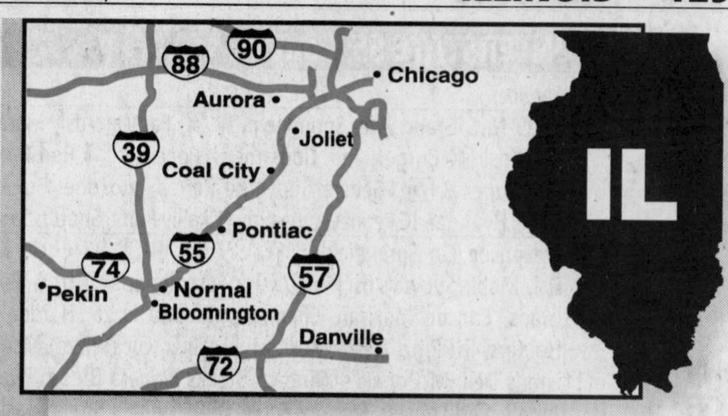

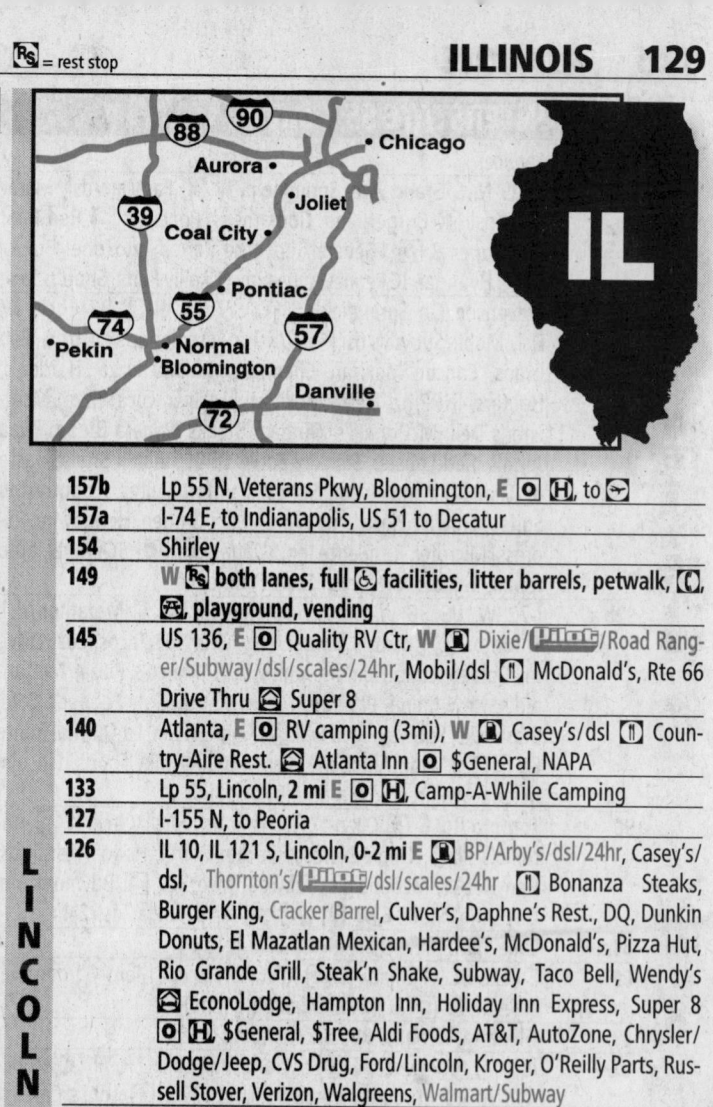

Exit #	Services
157b	Lp 55 N, Veterans Pkwy, Bloomington, E H, to
157a	I-74 E, to Indianapolis, US 51 to Decatur
154	Shirley
149	**W both lanes, full facilities, litter barrels, petwalk, , , playground, vending**
145	US 136, E Quality RV Ctr, W Dixie/Pilot/Road Ranger/Subway/dsl/scales/24hr, Mobil/dsl McDonald's, Rte 66 Drive Thru Super 8
140	Atlanta, E RV camping (3mi), W Casey's/dsl Country-Aire Rest. Atlanta Inn $General, NAPA
133	Lp 55, Lincoln, 2 mi E H, Camp-A-While Camping
127	I-155 N, to Peoria
126	IL 10, IL 121 S, Lincoln, 0-2 mi E BP/Arby's/dsl/24hr, Casey's/dsl, Thornton's/Pilot/dsl/scales/24hr Bonanza Steaks, Burger King, Cracker Barrel, Culver's, Daphne's Rest., DQ, Dunkin Donuts, El Mazatlan Mexican, Hardee's, McDonald's, Pizza Hut, Rio Grande Grill, Steak'n Shake, Subway, Taco Bell, Wendy's EconoLodge, Hampton Inn, Holiday Inn Express, Super 8 H, $General, $Tree, Aldi Foods, AT&T, AutoZone, Chrysler/Dodge/Jeep, CVS Drug, Ford/Lincoln, Kroger, O'Reilly Parts, Russell Stover, Verizon, Walgreens, Walmart/Subway
123	Lp 55, to Lincoln, E H
119	Broadwell
115	Elkhart
109	IL 123, Williamsville, E Casey's Subway, W Loves/McDonalds/dsl/scales/24hr Huddle House New Salem SHS
107mm	**weigh sta sb**
105	Lp 55, to Sherman, W Casey's Cancun Mexican, China King, Fairlane Diner, Fire&Ale Grill, Ricco's Pizza, Sam's Too Pizza, Subway Conv Ctr, County Mkt Foods, hist sites, Military Museum, repair, Riverside Park Campground, Verizon, vet, Walgreens
103mm	**sb, full facilities, litter barrels, petwalk, , , vending**
102mm	Sangamon River
102mm	**nb, full facilities, litter barrels, petwalk, , , vending**
100b	IL 54, Sangamon Ave, Springfield, W BP/Circle K, Marathon/Circle K, Murphy USA/dsl, Shell/dsl Arby's, Buffalo Wild Wings, Burger King, Culver's, DQ, Hickory River BBQ, Jimmy John's, McDonald's, Panda Express, Parkway Cafe, Penn Sta Subs, Sonic, Steak'n Shake, Taco Bell, Thai Basil, Wendy's, Wings Etc, Xochimilco Mexican, Yummy House Northfield Suites, Ramada , Aldi Foods, AT&T, GNC, Harley-Davidson, Lowe's, Menards, to Vet Mem, Verizon, Walmart/Subway
100a	Il 54, E to Clinton, E Road Ranger/Pilot/Subway/dsl/scales/24hr Kenworth/Ryder/Volvo, truckwash
98b	I-72, IL 97, Springfield, W BP/Circle K, Casey's, Shell/dsl Chesapeake Seafood House, Freddy's Steakburger, Hardee's, Mario's Pizza, McDonald's, Starbucks, Subway Best Western, Lincoln's Lodge H, city park, Ford Trucks, to Capitol Complex, Walgreens
98a	I-72 E, US 36 E, to Decatur

LINCOLN

INTERSTATE 55 Cont'd

SPRINGFIELD

Exit #	Services
96b a	IL 29 N, S Grand Ave, Springfield, W FasMart/dsl, Marathon/dsl Burger King, Godfather's, Popeye's Red Roof Inn, Super 8 $General, Advance Parts, AutoZone, Buick/GMC, Hyundai, JC Penney, museum, O'Reilly Parts, Shop'n Save
94	Stevenson Dr, Springfield, E KOA (7mi), W BP/Circle K/Dsl, Mobil/Subway/dsl, Shell/dsl Applebee's, Arby's, Bob Evans, Cancun Mexican, Cheddar's, Gallina Pizza, Hardee's, Hooters, IHOP, La Fiesta Mexican, LJ Silver, Luca Pizza, McAlister's Deli, McDonald's, Outback Steaks, Panera Bread, Papa John's, Red Lobster, Smokey Bones BBQ, Steak'n Shake, Taste of Thai Candlewood Suites, Comfort Suites, Country Inn Suites, Crowne Plaza, Drury Inn, Hilton Garden, Holiday Inn Express, Microtel, Residence Inn, Wingate Inn $General, auto repair, BigLots, CVS Drug, GNC, Walgreens
92b a	I-72 W, US 36 W, 6th St, Springfield, W Marathon/dsl, Thornton's Arby's, Burger King, Chadito's Tacos, Cozy Drive In, Golden Corral, Jimmy John's, KFC, Marco's Pizza, McDonald's, New China, Pizza Hut, Pizza Ranch, Sgt. Pepper's Cafe, Starbucks, Subway, Taco Bell Comfort Inn, La Quinta, Route 66 H, Aldi, AutoZone, CarX, County Mkt Foods, Lincoln, Mazda, Walgreens, Walmart/McDonald's
90	Toronto Rd, E Qik-n-EZ/Wendy's/dsl, Shell/Circle K Antonio's Pizza, China Express, Cracker Barrel, Head West Subs, Hen House, McDonald's, Subway, Taco Bell Baymont Inn, Day's Inn, Motel 6, W Pilot/Road Ranger/dsl/24hr
89mm	Lake Springfield
88	E Lake Dr, Chatham, E KOA, to Lincoln Mem Garden/Nature Ctr, W JJ RV Park/camping (2mi)
83	Glenarm, W JJ RV Park/camping (4mi)
82	IL 104, to Pawnee, E to Sangchris Lake SP, W Mobil/Auburn Trvl Ctr/Subway/scales/dsl/rest/24hr Toni's Cafe antiques/crafts
80	Hist 66, Divernon, W antiques
72	Farmersville, W Phillips 66/Subway/dsl/24hr, Shell
65mm	**both lanes, full facilities, litter barrels, petwalk, playground, vending**
63	IL 48, IL 127, to Raymond
60	IL 108, to Carlinville, E Kamper Kampanion RV Park, W Shell/dsl/LP/café Magnuson Grand Hotel/cafe antiques, to Blackburn Coll
56mm	**weigh sta nb**
52	IL 16, Hist 66, Litchfield, E BP, Casey's, Faststop/deli/dsl/scales, Murphy USA/dsl, Phillips 66/Jack-in-the-Box/dsl, Shell A&W/LJ Silver, Arby's, Ariston Café, Burger King, China Town, Denny's, DQ, El Rancherito Mexican, Huddle House, Jimmy John's, Jubelt's Rest., KFC, Maverick Steaks, McDonald's, Pizza Hut, Ruby Tuesday, Subway, Taco Bell, Wendy's Best Value Inn, Hampton Inn, Holiday Inn Express, Quality Inn, Super 8 H, $General, $Tree, Aldi Foods, AT&T, Buick/Cadillac/Chevrolet/GMC, Ford, Goodyear/auto, IGA Foods, NAPA, O'Reilly Parts, Rte 66 Museum, Verizon, vet, Walgreens, Walmart/Subway, W st police
44	IL 138, to Benld, Mt Olive, E Crossroads Diner, Rte 138 Cafe Mother Jones Mon
41	to Staunton, E Country Classic Cars, W Casey's DQ Super 8 H, $General, Chrysler/Dodge/Jeep
37	Livingston, New Douglas, W Shell/dsl Gasperoni's Café Country Inn/cafe AutoCare, IGA Foods, USPO
33	IL 4, to Staunton, Worden
30	IL140, Hamel, E Loves/McDonald's/Subway/dsl/scales/24hr Innkeeper Motel, W Shell Weezy's Grill

LITCHFIELD

COLLINSVILLE

Exit #	Services
28mm	**both lanes, full facilities, litter barrels, petwalk, vending**
23	IL 143, Edwardsville, E Phillips 66/dsl
20b	I-270 W, to Kansas City
20a	I-70 E, to Indianapolis
I-55 S and I-70 W run together 18 mi.	
18	IL 162, to Troy, E Casey's/dsl, Phillips 66/Circle K/dsl, Pilot/Arby's/dsl/scales/24hr, TA/BP/Country Pride/dsl/scales/24hr/@, ZX Alfonzo's Pizza, Burger King, China King, Domino's, DQ, Dunkin Donuts, El Potro Mexican, Jack-in-the-Box, Little Caesar's, McDonald's/playplace, Pizza Hut, Subway H, $General, Ace Hardware, O'Reilly Parts, Schuette's Mkt, Speedco, truckwash, USPO, vet, Walgreens, W Cracker Barrel, Fire'n Smoke Kitchen, Joe's Pizza, Taco Bell Best Western, Holiday Inn Express, Motel 6, Red Roof Inn, Super 8 Freightliner, Verizon
17	US 40 E, to Troy, to St Jacob
15b a	IL 159, Maryville, Collinsville, 0-2 mi E Phillips 66/Circle K/dsl, VP/dsl, Zx Gas Asia Garden, Carisillo's Mexican, KFC, McDonald's, Sonic, Subway $General, Advance Parts, Aldi Foods, AutoZone, CVS Drug, Ford/Lincoln, O'Reilly Parts, vet, Walgreens, W Loyalty Inn
14mm	**weigh sta sb**
11	IL 157, Collinsville, E Casey's A&W/LJ Silver, Denny's, Golden Corral, Little Caesar's, McDonald's, Penn Sta Subs, Qdoba Mexican, St Louis Bread Co, Starbucks, Waffle House, Wendy's Best Value Inn AT&T, Dobbs Tire, Gateway RV Ctr, GNC, Home Depot, Midas, Verizon, Walgreens, Walmart/Subway, W Motomart/dsl/24hr Applebee's, Arby's, Bandana's BBQ, Bob Evans, Burger King, Colton's Steaks, Culver's, DQ, Jimmy John's, Pizza Hut, Porter's Steaks, Ruby Tuesday, Steak'n Shake, White Castle/24hr, Zapata's Mexican Comfort Inn, Days Inn, DoubleTree Inn, Drury Inn, Fairfield Inn, Hampton Inn, La Quinta, Super 8 Buick/GMC, st police
10	I-255, S to Memphis, N to I-270
9	Black Lane (from nb, no return), E Fairmount RaceTrack
6	IL 111, Great River Rd, Fairmont City, E Exxon Relax Inn, Royal Budget Inn auto repair, W Horseshoe SP
4b a	IL 203, Granite City, E BP/dsl Western Inn, W Pilot/Subway/Taco Bell/dsl/scales/24hr/@ Gateway In Raceway
3c	Exchange Ave
3b	I-70 W, to KC
3a	I-64 E, IL 3 N, St Clair Ave
2b	3rd St
2a	M L King Bridge, to downtown E St Louis
1	IL 3, to Sauget (from sb)
I-55 N and I-70 E run together 18 mi.	
0mm	Illinois/Missouri state line, Mississippi River

INTERSTATE 57

Exit #	Services
358mm	I-94 E to Indiana, **I-57 begins/ends on I-94, exit 63 in Chicago.**
357	IL 1, Halsted St, E auto repair, W Shell/Dunkin Donuts, Supersave McDonald's, Shark's, Subway Walgreen
355	111th St, Monterey Ave, W BP, Citgo
354	119th St, W Citgo/Dunkin Donuts Chili's, Panda Express, Subway $Tree, AT&T, GNC, Jewel-Osco, Marshall's, PetCo, Target
353	127th St, Burr Oak Ave, E Citgo, GoLo, Shell Burger King, Dillinger's Drive-In, Dunkin Donuts, McDonald's, Wendy's M Hotel, Magnuson, Plaza Inn Ace Hardware

IL

INTERSTATE 57 Cont'd

CHICAGO

Exit	Services
353	Continued Advance Parts, Family$, Walgreens, W [gas] BP, Citgo/dsl [other] [H], JJ Fish&Chicken
352mm	Calumet Sag Channel
350	IL 83, 147th St, Sibley Blvd, E [gas] Marathon/dsl [food] Checker's, Domino's, Harold's Chicken, McDonald's, Subway [other] $General, Aldi Foods, Family$, O'Reilly Parts, W [other] USPO
348	US 6, 159th St, E [gas] BP/dsl, Clark, Marathon/dsl [food] Baskin-Robbins/Dunkin Donuts, Burger King, McDonald's, Popeye's, Subway, Taco Bell, White Castle [other] $Tree, AutoZone, U-Haul, Walgreens, W [gas] Gas Depot/dsl, Mobil/dsl
346	167th St, Cicero Ave, to IL 50, E [gas] BP, Shell/dsl [food] Applebee's, Baskin-Robbins/Dunkin Donuts, Harold's Chicken, Kenny's Ribs, McDonald's, Panda Express, Pizza Hut, Shark's Fish&Chicken, Sonic, Wendy's [lodging] Best Western [other] AT&T, GNC, Walmart/Subway, W [gas] Shell [other] 7-11
345b a	I-80, W to Iowa, E to Indiana, to I-294 N toll to Wisconsin
342	Vollmer Rd, E [gas] Shell/Circle K/dsl [other] [H]
340b a	US 30, Lincoln Hwy, Matteson, E [gas] BP, Marathon/dsl [food] A&W/LJ Silver, Afusion Asian, Bar Louie, Bocce's Grill, Burger King, Chipotle, ChuckeCheese, Culver's, Dusties Buffet, Five Guys, Fuddrucker's, Giordano's, Harold's Chicken, Hibachi Grill, IHOP, Jimmy John's, KFC, McDonald's, Olive Garden, Panda Express, Panera Bread, Pepe's, Perros Bros Gyros, Pizza Hut, Red Lobster, Rosati's, Shark's, Starbucks, Subway, Wendy's, White Castle, Wing Stop/Dunkin Donuts [lodging] Country Inn&Suites, Hampton Inn, Holiday Inn, La Quinta, Quality Inn [other] $Tree, Aldi Foods, AT&T, Chrysler/Dodge/Jeep, Discount Tire, Firestone/auto, GNC, Home Depot, JC Penney, Marshall's, Menards, NTB, PepBoys, Petsmart, Ross, Target, USPO, Verizon, Walgreens, W [other] Buick/Cadillac/GMC, Ford/Lincoln, Honda, Hyundai, Kia, Nissan, Toyota, Walgreens
339	Sauk Trail, to Richton Park, E [gas] BP/dsl, Marathon/dsl [food] Domino's, McDonald's, Uncle John's BBQ/Ribs [other] Family$, Walgreens, W [other] Walmart/dsl
337	Stuenkel Rd
335	Monee, E [gas] BP/Dunkin Donuts/Subway/dsl, Petro/Iron Skillet/dsl/e-85/scales/24hr/@, Pilot/McDonald's/dsl/scales/24hr [food] Burger King, Culver's, KFC/Taco Bell, Lucky Burrito, Schoops Rest. [lodging] Best Value, Country Host Motel, Red Roof Inn, Super 8 [other] AdvanceParts, Blue Beacon
332mm	**Prairie View Rest Area both lanes, full [handicapped] facilities, info, litter barrels, petwalk, [phone], [picnic], vending**
330mm	**weigh sta both lanes**
327	to Peotone, E [gas] Casey's, Shell/Circle K [food] McDonald's/RV parking
322	Manteno, E [gas] BP/McDonald's/dsl, Casey's/dsl, Phillips 66/Subway [food] DQ, Jimmy John's, KFC/Pizza Hut/Taco Bell, Monical's Pizza, Pizza Hut, Wendy's [lodging] Country Inn&Suites, Howard Johnson [other] Harley-Davidson, vet, W [gas] BP/Dunkin Donuts/Dallas
320	E. 6000N Rd
315	IL 50, Bradley, E [gas] EVC, F&F, Shell/Circle K/Burger King [food] Buffalo Wild Wings, Cracker Barrel, McDonald's, Noodles&Co, Olive Garden, Panera Bread, Red Lobster, Starbuck's, Taco Bell, TGIFriday's, Tucci's Rest., White Castle [lodging] Comfort Inn, Fairfield Inn, Holiday Inn Express, Magnuson [other] Aldi, AT&T, Barnes&Noble, Best Buy, Chrysler/Dodge/Jeep, Dick's, Discount Tire, JC Penney, Kohl's, Marshall's, Michael's, PetCo, Petsmart, Ross, Staples, Target, Verizon, Walmart/Subway, W [gas] BP/dsl, Phillips 66/CircleK/dsl, Shell/Circle K/dsl, Speedway/dsl [food] Applebee's, Arby's, Bakers Square, Coyote

MATTESON

BRADLEY

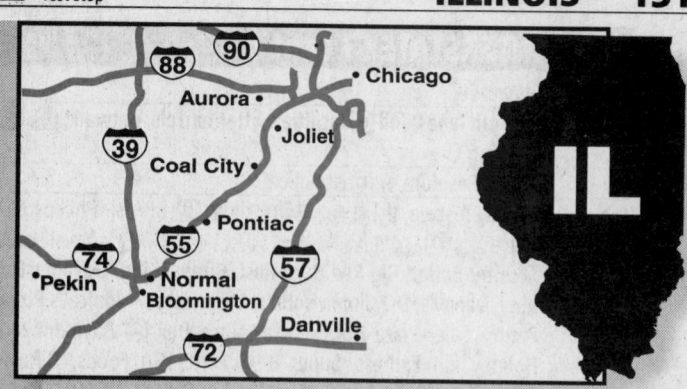

KANKAKEE

Exit	Services
315	Continued Canyon, Denny's, El Cortez Mexican, IHOP, LJ Silver, Mancino's Pizza, McDonald's, Oberweis Ice Cream, Panda Express, Steak'n Shake, Subway, Texas Roadhouse, Wendy's [lodging] Quality Inn, Rte. 50 Motel, Super 8 [other] $Tree, AT&T, Bradley RV Ctr, Buick/GMC, Chevrolet, Hobby Lobby, Honda, Hyundai, Jo-Ann Fabrics, Kia, Lowe's, Menards, Nissan, O'Reilly, to Kankakee River SP, URGENT CARE, Verizon, vet
312	IL 17, Kankakee, W [gas] BP/dsl, Marathon/dsl, Shell/Circle K [food] McDonald's, PoorBoy Rest. [other] [H], $ General, Advance Parts, Family$
310.5mm	Kankakee River
308	US 45, US 52, to Kankakee, E [gas] Loves/Arby's/dsl/scales/24hr [other] KOA (3mi), W [gas] Gas Depot, Murphy USA, Speedway/Dunkin Donuts/Subway/dsl [food] El Mexicano, KFC/Taco Bell [lodging] Fairview Motel, Hilton Garden [other] $Tree, [RV dump] Aldi Foods, Walmart/Subway
302	Chebanse, W [other] truck repair
297	Clifton, W [gas] Phillips 66/Circle K/DQ/dsl [other] $General
293	IL 116, Ashkum, E [gas] BP/Subway/dsl [other] tires, W [food] Loft Rest. [other] st police
283	US 24, IL 54, Gilman, E [gas] K&H Trkstp/BP/dsl/scales/24hr/@, Mobil/dsl, Pilot/Denny's/dsl/scales/24hr [food] Burger King, DQ, McDonald's, Monical's Pizza, Red Door Rest. [lodging] Motel 6, Super 8, W [gas] BP/Subway/dsl
280	IL 54, Onarga, E [gas] Casey's, Phillips 66 [other] USPO, W [other] Lake Arrowhead RV camping
272	to Roberts, Buckley
268.5mm	**[rest stop] both lanes, full [handicapped] facilities, litter barrels, petwalk, [phone], [picnic], vending**
261	IL 9, Paxton, 0-1 mi E [gas] Casey's, Phillips 66/dsl [food] Hardee's, Monical's Pizza, Pizza Hut, Subway [other] Buick/Cadillac/Chevrolet/GMC, IGA Foods, TrueValue, USPO, W [gas] Phillips/dsl [food] Country Garden Rest. [lodging] Paxton Inn
250	US 136, Rantoul, 0-1 mi E [gas] BP/Circle K, Casey's/dsl, Mobil/Circle K/dsl [food] Arby's, Burger King, Dunkin' Donuts, Hardee's, McDonald's, Monical's Pizza, Papa John's, Red Wheel Rest., Subway, Taco Bell [lodging] Days Inn, Heritage Inn, Holiday Inn Express, Super 8 [other] $General, Chrysler/Dodge/Jeep, Ford, NAPA, to Chanute AFB, vet, Walgreens, Walmart
240	Market St, E [gas] Road Ranger/Pilot/McDonald's/dsl/scales [other] Kenworth/Volvo, truck/tire repair, W [other] D&W Lake Camping/RV Park
238	Olympian Dr, to Champaign, W [gas] Mobil/Circle K/dsl [food] DQ [lodging] Microtel [other] RV/dsl repair
237b a	I-74, W to Peoria, E to Urbana
235b	I-72 W, to Decatur
235a	University Ave, to Champaign, E [other] [H], U of Ill
232	Curtis Rd
229	to Savoy, Monticello, E [gas] Marathon/dsl

RANTOUL

IL

= gas = food = lodging = other = rest stop

INTERSTATE 57 Cont'd

Exit #	Services
221.5mm	**both lanes, full facilities, litter barrels, petwalk, vending**
220	US 45, Pesotum, E st police
212	US 36, Tuscola, E FuelMart/dsl, W BP/dsl, Phillips 66/Circle K, Pilot/Road Ranger/dsl/scales/24hr Amish Land Country Buffet, Big Red Barn Rest, Burger King, Daylight Donuts, Denny's, DQ, Jimmy John's, McDonald's, Monical's Pizza, Pantry Cafe, Pizza Hut, Subway, Taco Bell Baymont Inn, Holiday Inn Express, Super 8 Ford, IGA Foods, O'Reilly Parts, ShopKO, Tuscola Outlets/Famous Brands, Verizon
203	IL 133, Arcola, E Best Western, W Phillips 66/Subway/dsl, Sunrise/dsl DQ, El Toro Mexican, Hen House, McDonalds, Monical's Pizza Arcola Inn, Comfort Inn $General, city park, NAPA, Rockome Gardens (5mi), vet
192	CtyRd 1000 N, Rd 18
	MATTOON
190b a	IL 16, to Mattoon, E BP/dsl H, Fox Ridge SP, to E IL U, W Huck's, Murphy USA/dsl, Phillips 66/Subway/dsl A&W/LJ Silver, Alamo Steaks, Arby's, Buffalo Wild Wings, Cracker Barrel, Denny's, Domino's, Don Sol Mexican, DQ, El Vaquero Mexican, Freddy's, Japanese Steaks, Jimmy John's, Jumbo Buffet, KFC, Lee's Chicken, McDonald's/playplace, McHugh's, Pizza Hut, QQ Buffet, Stadium Grill, Steak'n Shake, Taco Bell, Wendy's Baymont Inn, Comfort Suites, Hampton Inn, Holiday Inn Express, Suite Dreams, Super 8 $General, $Tree, Aldi Foods, BigLots, CVS Drug, Home Depot, JC Penney, Joann, Petsmart, Staples, Verizon, Walgreens, Walmart/Subway
184	US 45, IL 121, to Mattoon, E Phillips 66/Subway/dsl, W McDonald's Motel 6, Quality Inn to Lake Shelbyville
177	US 45, Neoga, E FuelMart/Subway/dsl/e-85 NAPA, W Casey's/dsl (1mi) $General
166.5mm	**both lanes, full facilities, litter barrels, petwalk, vending**
163	I-70 E, to Indianapolis
	I-57 S and I-70 W run together 6 mi.
	EFFINGHAM
162	US 45, Effingham, E Motomart Harley-Davidson, W Pilot/McDonald's/dsl/scales/24hr Subway Camp Lakewood (2mi), truck repair
160	IL 33, IL 32, Effingham, E Domino's, Jimmy John's, McAlister's Deli, Papa John's, Pizza Hut Best Western, Fairfield Inn, Quality Inn H, $General, Aldi Foods, AutoZone, Save-a-Lot, Verizon, vet, W FLYING J/Denny's/dsl/LP/scales/24hr, Murphy USA/dsl, Phillips 66/dsl, TA/Popeye's/dsl/@ Arby's, Buffalo Wild Wings, Burger King, Chili's, Chipotle, Cracker Barrel, Denny's, El Rancherito Mexican, Fujiyama Steaks, KFC, LJ Silver, McDonald's, Panda Express, Panera Bread, Starbucks, Steak'n Shake, Taco Bell, TGIFriday's, Wendy's Country Inn&Suites, Days Inn, Hampton Inn, Holiday Inn, La Quinta, Super 8 $Tree, AT&T, Blue Beacon, Camp Lakewood RV Park, Ford/Lincoln, Hodgson Mill Mercantile, Kohl's, Menards, Peterbilt, SpeedCo, Verizon, Walmart/Subway
159	US 40, Effingham, E Phillips 66/dsl, Speedway/Speedy's Cafe/dsl/24hr China Buffet, Culver's, Hardee's, Little Caesar's, Niemerg's Rest, Subway Abe Lincoln Motel, Best Value Inn, Comfort Suites, EconoLodge, Lexington Inn Honda, O'Reilly Parts, tires/repair, Walgreens, W Petro/Iron Skillet/dsl/24hr/@ Baymont Inn Blue Beacon, Freightliner
	I-57 N and I-70 E run together 6 mi.
157	I-70 W, to St Louis
151	Watson, 5 mi E Percival Springs RV Park
150mm	Little Wabash River
145	Edgewood, E Phillips 66/dsl city park
135	IL 185, Farina, E Shell/Subway/dsl $General, Ford
127	to Kinmundy, Patoka
	SALEM
116	US 50, Salem, E Huck's/dsl, Motomart, Shell/Circle K/dsl Burger King, Domino's, Hardee's, La Cocina Mexican, LJ Silver, McDonald's, Pizza Hut, Pizza Man, Subway, Taco Bell, Village Garden, Wendy's Holiday Inn Express H, AutoZone, Chrysler/Dodge/Jeep, CVS Drug, GMC, NAPA, O'Reilly Parts, Save-A-Lot, to Forbes SP, USPO, W Murphy USA/dsl, Phillips 66/dsl Applebee's, Arby's, Denny's, El Rancherito, KFC Guesthouse Inn, Salem Inn, Super 8 $Tree, AT&T, Buick/Chevrolet, Carlisle Lake (23mi), Ford, Salem Tires, Walmart
114mm	**both lanes, full facilities, litter barrels, petwalk, playground, vending**
109	IL 161, to Centralia, W Biggie's General Store/cafe/dsl
103	Dix, E Phillips 66/dsl Red Carpet Inn
96	I-64 W, to St Louis
	MT VERNON
95	IL 15, Mt Vernon, E Hucks, Phillips 66/Circle K/dsl Agave Mexican, Asian Buffet, Bandana's BBQ, Domino's, El Rancherito Mexican, Fazoli's, Hardee's, Hardee's, KFC, Little Caesar's, LJ Silver, McAlister's Deli, McDonald's, Moe's SW Grill, Panda Express, Panera Bread, Papa John's, Pizza Hut, Starbucks, Steak'n Shake, Subway, Taco Bell, Waffle Co, Wendy's Best Inn, Best Value Inn, Comfort Suites, Drury Inn, Motel 6, Super 8 H, Aldi Foods, AT&T, AutoZone, Big Lots, Chevrolet/Cadillac, Chrysler/Dodge/Jeep, CVS Drug, Ford/Lincoln, Harley-Davidson, Hobby Lobby, JC Penney, Kroger/dsl, Midas, O'Reilly Parts, Prompt Care, Ross, Verizon, Walgreens, W FLYING J/Hucks/Country Cookin/dsl/scales/24hr, Pilot/Denny's/dsl/scales/24hr, Shell/Circle K/dsl, TA/Country Pride/Popeye's/dsl/24hr/@, Tesla EVC Applebee's, Arby's, Bob Evans, Buffalo Wild Wings, Burger King, Chili's, Cracker Barrel, Double Overtime Grill, Jimmy John's, LoneStar Steaks, McDonald's, Ryan's, Sonic, Subway Days Inn, Doubletree, Fairfield Inn, Hampton Inn, Holiday Inn Express, Quality Inn $Tree, Archway RV Park, Buick/GMC, Freightliner, Kohl's, Lowe's, NAPA, Staples, Toyota, truckwash, Verizon, Walmart
94	Veteran's Memorial Dr, E H, W Menards
92	I-64 E, to Louisville
83	Ina, E Love's/McDonald's/dsl/scales Uncle Joe's BBQ tire/trailer repair, W to Rend Lake Coll
79mm	**sb, full facilities, info, litter barrels, petwalk, playground, vending**
77	IL 154, to Whittington, E Shell/dsl Lake Cove Resor[t] Whittington Woods RV Park, W Birdies Grille Sea[sons] at Rend Lake Lodge/rest. golf, to Rend Lake, Wayn[e] Fitzgerrell SP
74mm	**nb, full facilities, litter barrels, petwalk, playground, vending**
	BENTON
71	IL 14, Benton, E Phillips 66/dsl Arby's, Hardee's, KFC/Taco Bell, Pizza Hut Econolodge, Gray Plaza Mote[l], Magnuson Hotel H, AutoZone, CVS Drug, KOA (1.5mi), O'Reilly Parts, Plaza Tire, W Murphy USA/dsl, Phillips 66/dsl Applebee's, Burger King, McDonald's, Subway $Tree, AT&T, to Rend Lake, Verizon, Walmart
65	IL 149, W Frankfort, E Gas-4-Less, Phillips 66/Circle K/dsl, ROC/dsl China Star, Dixie Cream Deli, Don Luna Mexican, Hardee's, La Fiesta Mexican, LJ Silver, Mike's Drive-In, Miranda's Rest., Sonic, Subway Gray Plaza Motel CVS Drug, MadPricer Foods, NAPA, W Casey's/dsl McDonald's, Pizza Hut Best Value Inn $General, $Tree, AT&T, Buick/Chevrolet/GMC, Chrysler/Dodge/Jeep, Kroger, VF Factory Stores

IL

INTERSTATE 57 Cont'd

MARION

Exit #	Services
59	to Herrin, Johnston City, E Citgo/dsl/e85, ZX/dsl DQ, McDonald's, Subway $General, Bandy Drug, camping (2mi), NAPA, W H, camping (4mi)
54b a	IL 13, Marion, E Phillips 66/dsl Arby's, Fazoli's, Hardee's, KFC, La Fiesta Mexican, Little Caesar's, LJ Silver, Papa John's, Pizza Hut, Subway, Tequila's Mexican, Wendy's EconoLodge $General, Advance Parts, Aldi Foods, AutoZone, Ford/Hyundai/Lincoln, Kroger/gas, Plaza Tire, Sav-A-Lot Foods, USPO, Walgreens, W Huck's/dsl, Phillips 66/dsl, Pilot/Subway/dsl/scales/24h 17th St Grill, Applebee's, Asian Bistro, Backyard Burger, Bob Evans, Buffalo Wild Wings, Burger King, Culver's, Hong Kong BBQ, IHOP, Jimmy John's, Krispy Kreme, Logan's Roadhouse, Mackie's Pizza, McAlister's Deli, McDonald's, O'Charley's, Panera Bread, Red Lobster, Ryan's, Sonic, Steak'n Shake, Taco Bell, Wok'n Roll Buffet Best Inn, Comfort Inn, Country Inn&Suites, Drury Inn, Fairfield Inn, Hampton Inn, Holiday Inn Express, Super 8 H, $Tree, AT&T, Buick/Chevrolet/GMC, Chrysler/Dodge/Jeep, Dillard's, Harley-Davidson, Home Depot, Honda, Menards, Mercedes, Nissan, Sam's Club/gas, Subaru, Target, Toyota, Verizon, Walmart/Subway
53	Main St, Marion, E Casey's/dsl DQ Motel Marion H, Marion Camping/RV Park, NAPA, W Motomart Cracker Barrel, HideOut Steaks Best Western, Comfort Suites, Quality Inn
47mm	**weigh sta both lanes**
45	IL 148, 1 mi E King Tut's Food/dsl Lake Tree Inn camping, dsl repair, vet
44	I-24 E to Nashville
40	Goreville Rd, E camping, Ferne Clyffe SP, scenic overlook
36	Lick Creek Rd, W vineyards
32mm	**Trail of Tears Rest Area both lanes, full facilities, info, litter barrels, petwalk, playground, vending**
30	IL 146, Anna, Vienna, W Fast Stop/dsl H, auto/RV repair
25	US 51 N (from nb, exits left), to Carbondale
24	Dongola Rd, W BP/dsl Subway $General
18	Ullin Rd, W Fast Stop/dsl EEE BBQ Best Value Inn Chevrolet, st police
8	Mounds Rd, to Mound City, E Huckleberry's Rest. K&K AutoTruck/dsl/repair
1	IL 3, to US 51, Cairo, E Quality Inn $General, camping, Mound City Nat Cem (4mi), W camping
0mm	Illinois/Missouri state line, Mississippi River

INTERSTATE 64

Exit #	Services
131.5mm	Illinois/Indiana state line, Wabash River
131mm	**Skeeter Mtn Welcome Ctr wb, full facilities, litter barrels, petwalk, vending**
130	IL 1, to Grayville, N Casey's (2mi), Pilot/Road Ranger/dsl/scales/24hr Guadalajara Mexican, Subway Super 8, Windsor Oaks Inn/rest. Beall Woods SP (10mi)
124mm	Little Wabash River
117	Burnt Prairie, S CountryMark/dsl ChuckWagon Charlie's Café antiques
110	US 45, Mill Shoals
100	IL 242, to Wayne City, N Citgo/dsl
89	to Belle Rive, Bluford
86mm	**wb, full facilities, litter barrels, petwalk, vending**

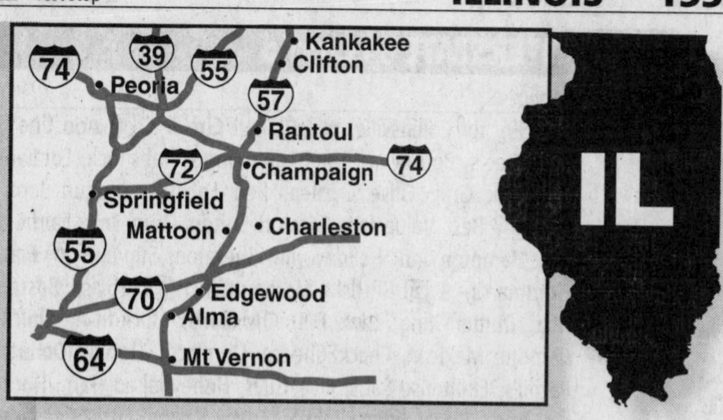

O'FALLON

Exit #	Services
82.5mm	**eb, full facilities, litter barrels, petwalk, vending**
80	IL 37, to Mt Vernon, 2 mi N Hucks/dsl/24hr, Phillips 66/Circle K/Burger King/dsl $General
78	I-57, S to Memphis, N to Chicago
	I-64 and I-57 run together 5 mi. See I-57, exits 95-94.
73	I-57, N to Chicago, S to Memphis
69	Woodlawn
61	US 51, to Centralia, Richview
50	IL 127, to Nashville, N to Carlyle Lake, S Citgo/rest/E-85/dsl, Little Nashville/Conoco/rest/dsl/scales/24hr, Shell/dsl McDonald's Best Western H
41	IL 177, Okawville, S Pilot/Road Ranger/dsl/24hr Burger King, DQ, Subway Original Springs Motel, Super 8 $General, truck repair, USPO
37mm	Kaskaskia River
34	to Albers, 3 mi N Casey's
27	IL 161, New Baden, N Casey's/dsl, Shell/dsl China King, Four Corners Pizza, Good Ol Days Rest., McDonald's, Subway $General, Chevrolet, S Loves/Hardee's/dsl/scales/24hr
25mm	**both lanes, full facilities, info, litter barrels, petwalk, vending**
23	IL 4, to Mascoutah, N Mobil/dsl, Phillips 66/Huddle House/dsl/RV dump Best Western+, S
21	Rieder Rd
19b a	US 50, IL 158, N Motomart/dsl Amore Italian, Subway Super 8 H, S to Scott AFB
18mm	**weigh sta eb**
16	to O'Fallon, Shiloh, N Bella Milano, Sonic, The Egg & I Hilton Garden CVS Drug, Harley-Davidson, URGENT CARE, S Motomart/dsl 54th St. Grille, Applebee's, Arby's, Aroy Thai, Buffalo Wild Wings, China King, Coldstone, Cracker Barrel, Freddy's, Golden Corral, Jersey Mike's, Jimmy John's, La Casa Mexicana, Little Caesar's, McAlister's Deli, McDonald's, Noodles&Co, Qdoba, Ravanelli's Rest., St. Louis Bread Co., Starbucks, Subway, TX Roadhouse, White Castle Drury Inn, Holiday Inn Express AT&T, Dierbergs Foods, Dobb's Tire, Menard's, Michael's, Target, vet, World Mkt
14	O'Fallon, N Motomart, Phillips 66/Circle K, Shell/dsl IHOP, Japanese Garden, Steak'n Shake, Subway Country Inn&Suites, Extended Stay America, La Quinta, Sleep Inn, Suburban Inn Cadillac, Chevrolet, Ford, O'Reilly Parts, S Chevy's Mexican, Culver's, Hardee's, Jack-in-the-Box, KFC, La Parrilla Mexican, McDonald's, O'Charley's, Panda Express, Papa Murphy's, Sake Grill, Schiappa's Pizza, Syberg's Rest., Taco Bell Candlewood Suites, Days Inn, Quality Inn Aldi Foods, BMW, Home Depot, Honda, Hyundai, Kia, Mazda, Nissan, Petsmart, Sam's Club/gas, Toyota, VW, Walmart

INTERSTATE 64 Cont'd

COLLINSVILLE

Exit #	Services
12	IL 159, to Collinsville, N Shell/Circle K Agostino's, Applebee's, Bob Evans, Houlihan's, Joe's Crabshack, Lotawata Creek Grill, Olive Garden, Red Lobster, Shogun Japanese Best Value Inn, Comfort Suites, Drury Inn, Fairfield Inn, Hampton Inn, Holiday Inn, Sheraton, Super 8 Fiat, Gordman's, S BP/dsl, Motomart/dsl Arby's, Boston Mkt, Burger King, Capt D's, Cheddar's, Chick-fil-A, Chili's, Chipotle Mexican, ChuckECheese, Domino's, Dunkin Donuts, Fazoli's, Firehouse Subs, Five Guys, Honeybaked Ham, Hooters, Imo's Pizza, Jimmy John's, Krispy Kreme, Little Caesar's, LJ Silver, Longhorn Steaks, McAlister's Deli, McDonald's, Popeye's, Red Robin, Ruby Tuesday, Smokey Bones BBQ, St. Louis Bread, Steak'n Shake, Subway, Taco Bell, Wasabi, Wendy's, White Castle $General, $Tree, Aamco, Advance Parts, AT&T, Barnes&Noble, Best Buy, BigLots, Burlington Coats, CarX, Dick's, Dillard's, Dobb's Tire, Firestone/auto, Hobby Lobby, JC Penney, Jo-Ann Fabrics, Kohl's, Lowe's, Macy's, Marshall's, Meineke, Midas, NTB, Old Navy, O'Reilly Parts, PetCo, Ross, Russell Stover, Schnuck's Foods, TJ Maxx, Tuesday Morning, Verizon, vet, Walgreens
9	IL 157, to Caseyville, N Gulf/Subway, Huck's/dsl Hardee's Western Inn, S Cracker Barrel, Domino's, DQ, McDonald's, Taco Bell Best Inn, Motel 6, Quality Inn, Rodeway Inn
7	I-255, S to Memphis, N to Chicago
6	IL 111, Kingshighway, N BP, Mobil Church's, Ray's Rest.
5	25th St
4	15th St, Baugh
3	I-55 N, I-70 E, IL 3 N, to St Clair Ave, to stockyards
2b a	3rd St, S gas
1	IL 3 S, 13th St, E St Louis, N Casino Queen
0mm	Illinois/Missouri state line, Mississippi River

IL

INTERSTATE 70

Exit #	Services
156mm	Illinois/Indiana state line
154	US 40 W
151mm	weigh sta wb
149mm	wb, full facilities, info, litter barrels, petwalk, , , vending
147	IL 1, Marshall, N Pilot/Road Ranger/Church's/dsl/scales/24hr Crossroads Rest., S Casey's (1mi), DQ, Marathon/Arby's/dsl, Phillips 66/dsl Burger King, Los Tres Caminos, McDonald's, Pizza Hut, Sam's Steaks, Subway, Wendy's Lincoln Suites, Relax Inn, Super 8 antiques, Ford, Lincoln Trail SP, Walmart
136	to Martinsville, S Phillips 66/dsl/24hr
134.5mm	N Fork Embarras River
129	IL 49, Casey, N KOA (seasonal), RV service, S Casey's, DQ, Marathon/Circle K/dsl, Phillips 66/dsl Hacienda Mexican, McDonald's, Pizza Hut, Subway Days Inn $General, IGA Foods
119	IL 130, Greenup, S Casey's/dsl, Loves/Chester's/IHOP/dsl/scales/24hr, Phillips 66/dsl Backyard BBQ, DQ, Subway Budget Host, Greenup Motel $General, hist sites, NAPA
105	Montrose, N Spring Creek Camping (1mi), S BP/dsl, Phillips/dsl Fairview Inn
98	I-57, N to Chicago.

I-70 and I-57 run together 6 mi. See I-57, exits 159-162.

VANDALIA

Exit #	Services
92	I-57, S to Mt Vernon
91mm	Little Wabash River
87mm	**both lanes, full facilities, info, litter barrels, petwalk, , , playground, RV dump, vending**
82	IL 128, Altamont, N Casey's/dsl, Phillips 66/Subway/dsl/24hr Dairy Bar, Joe's Pizza/pasta, McDonald's Altamont Motel, Cobblestone Inn $General, city park, S Relax Inn
76	US 40, St Elmo, N Casey's Waldorf Motel Timberline Camping (2mi)
71mm	weigh sta eb
68	US 40, Brownstown, N Okaw Valley Kamping, S truck repair
63.5mm	Kaskaskia River
63	US 51, Vandalia, N Chuck Wagon Cafe, LJ Silver Best Value Inn, S Casey's, Phillips 66, Phillips 66/Burger King/24hr Arby's, China Gate, DQ, McDonald's, Pizza Hut, Rancho Nuevo Mexican, Sonic, Subway, Wendy's Economy Inn, Jay's Inn H, Aldi Foods, city park, County Mkt Foods, hist site
61	US 40, Vandalia, N Fast Stop/Denny's/dsl/scales/24hr, S Murphy USA/dsl China King, Embers Pizza, Huddle House, KFC/Taco Bell, Ponderosa Holiday Inn Express, Ramada $Tree, AT&T, AutoZone, Verizon, Walmart
52	US 40, Mulberry Grove, N Casey's/dsl Timber Trail Camp-In (2mi), S Cedar Brook Camping (1mi)
45	IL 127, Greenville, N Love/Subway/dsl/scales/24hr, Shell/dsl Chang's Buffet, Domino's, Huddle House, KFC/Taco Bell, Los Amigos, Lu-Bob's Rest., McDonald's EconoLodge, Red Carpet Inn, Super 8 H, S Comfort Inn American Farm Heritage Museum, RV Service, to Carlyle Lake
41	US 40 E, to Greenville
36	US 40 E, Pocahontas, S BP/dsl, Phillips 66/dsl Funderburk's Grill Lighthouse Lodge, Powhatan Motel/rest., Tahoe Motel truck/tire repair
30	US 40, IL 143, to Highland, S Shell/dsl/wifi Blue Springs Café H, Tomahawk RV Park (7mi)
26.5mm	**Silver Lake both lanes, full facilities, litter barrels, petwalk, , , vending**
24	IL 143, Marine, 4 mi S H
21	IL 4, Troy
15b a	I-55, N to Chicago, S to St Louis, I-270 W to Kansas City.

I-70 and I-55 run together 18 mi. See I-55, exits 1-18.

Exit #	Services
19mm	motorist callboxes begin wb every 1/2mile
0mm	Illinois/Missouri state line, Mississippi River

INTERSTATE 72

URBANA

Exit #	Services
183mm	**1 mi E on University** Gas Depot, Thornton's/dsl Arby's, Burger King, Garcia's Pizza, Ichiban Buffet, Jimmy John's KFC, La Bamba Mexican, McDonald's, Monical's Pizza, Original Pancakes, Papa John's, Pizza Hut, Sonic, Subway, Taco Bell TX Roadhouse, Za's Italian $General, Advance Parts, AutoZone, Big Lots, County Mkt Foods, CVS Drug, O'Reilly Parts Schnuck's Foods/e85, Walgreens
182b a	I-57, N to Chicago, S to Memphis, to I-74
176	IL 47, to Mahomet
172	IL 10, Lodge, Seymour
169	White Heath Rd
166	IL 105 W, Market St, N H, Ford, S Mobil/Subway/d[illegible] Red Wheel Rest. Best Western, Foster Inn city park railway museum
165mm	Sangamon River

INTERSTATE 72 Cont'd

Exit #	Services
164	Bridge St, 1 mi S Mobil/Circle K/dsl China Star, DQ, Hardee's, McDonald's, Monical's Pizza, Pizza Hut, Subway $General, Buick/Chevrolet, Chrysler/Dodge/Jeep, USPO
156	IL 48, to Weldon, Cisco, N Friends Creek Camping (may-oct) (3mi)
153mm	both lanes, full facilities, litter barrels, petwalk, , , vending
152mm	Friends Creek
150	Argenta
144	IL 48, Oreana, S Pilot/McDonald's/Subway/dsl/scales/24hr Sleep Inn , Chrysler/Dodge/Jeep, Honda, Hyundai, Pressley RV Ctr (3mi)
141b a	US 51, Decatur, N Shell/Circle K Applebee's, Buffalo Wild Wings, Cheddar's, Cracker Barrel, HomeTown Buffet, McDonald's, O'Charley's, Pizza Hut, Red Lobster, Steak'n Shake, Subway, Taco Bell, TX Roadhouse Baymont Inn, Country Inn&Suites, Fairfield Inn, Hampton Inn, Homewood Suites, Quality Inn, Ramada Ltd, Residence Inn $Tree, AT&T, Bergner's, Best Buy, Buick/Cadillac/GMC, Harley-Davidson, Hobby Lobby, Kohl's, Lowe's, Menards, Petsmart, Ross, Verizon, Von Maur, S Arby's, Burger King, El Rodeo Mexican, Fuji Japanese, La Fondita, Monical's Pizza, Olive Garden, Panera Bread, Papa Murphy's, Starbucks , Jo-Ann Fabrics, Sam's Club, Target, Verizon, Walgreens, Walmart/Subway
138	IL 121, Decatur, S
133b a	US 36 E, US 51, Decatur, S Phillips 66/Subway/dsl Best Value Inn, Decatur Hotel/rest.
128	Niantic
122	to Mt Auburn, Illiopolis, N FastStop/dsl
114	Buffalo, Mechanicsburg, 2 mi S Gas Depot/dsl USPO
108	Riverton, Dawson
107mm	Sangamon River
104	Camp Butler, 2 mi N McDonald's, Starbucks, Subway Best Rest Inn, Best Western, Lincoln Inn, Park View Motel golf
103b a	I-55, N to Chicago, S to St Louis, IL 97, to Springfield.

I-72 and I-55 run together 6 mi. See I-55, exits 92-98.

Exit #	Services
97b a	6th St, I-55 S, Loop 55 N (from eb), 6th St, I-55 S, N Road Ranger Golden Corral, McDonald's, Pizza Ranch Comfort Inn, La Quinta, Rte 66 Aldi Foods, Lincoln, Mazda, Walmart
96	MacArthur Blvd, N Tesla EVC Engrained Brewing Co Scheels
93	IL 4, Springfield, N Hucks, Thorntons/dsl Applebee's, Arby's, Bakers Square, Burger King, Chili's, Chipotle Mexican, Cooper's Hawk Rest., Denny's, Five Guys, Ginger Asian, Jersey Mike's, Jimmy John's, Longhorn Steaks, Los Agaves Mexican, Los Rancheros Mexican, McDonald's, Noodles&Co, Olive Garden, Panda Express, Panera Bread, Penn Sta Subs, Popeye's, Qdoba, Red Robin, Sonic, Starbucks, Subway, Taco Bell, TGIFriday's, TX Roadhouse, Wasabi Japanese, Wendy's Courtyard, Fairfield Inn, Quality Inn, Sleep Inn Aldi Foods, AT&T, Barnes&Noble, Bergner's, Best Buy, County Mkt Foods, Dick's, Discount Tire, Gordman's, Hobby Lobby, Jo-Ann Fabrics, Kohl's, Lowe's, Macy's, Michael's, Office Depot, Old Navy, PetCo, Petsmart, Ross, Sam's Club/gas, Staples, Target, TJ Maxx, Verizon, Walgreens, Walmart, S Meijer/dsl/E85 Bob Evans, Monical's Pizza, O'Charley's, Steak'n Shake Hampton Inn, Staybridge Suites Cadillac, Chevrolet, Chrysler/Jeep, Fiat, Ford, Honda, Menards

DECATUR

SPRINGFIELD

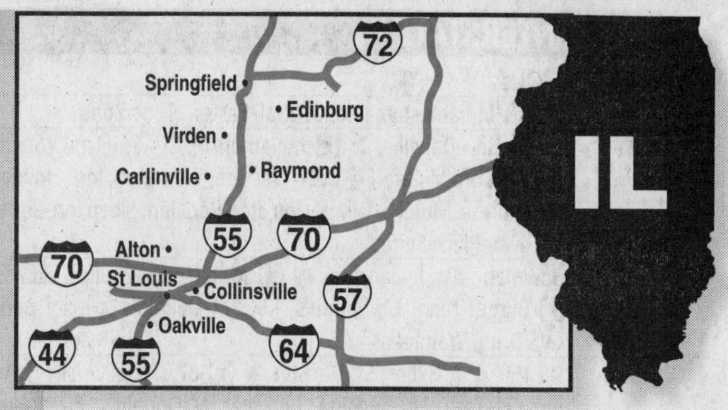

Exit #	Services
91	Wabash Ave, to Springfield, N Qik-n- EZ/dsl Bella Milano, Buffalo Wild Wings, Culver's, Firehouse Subs, IHOP, McDonald's, Mimosa Thai, Papa Frank's Italian Audi/VW, Dodge/Ram, Kia/Subaru, Nissan, Toyota, S Colmans RV Ctr
82	New Berlin, S Pilot/Road Ranger/Subway/dsl $General
76	IL 123, to Ashland, Alexander
68	to IL 104, to Jacksonville, 2 mi N BP/Circle K, Casey's/dsl
64	US 67, to Jacksonville, 2 mi N BP/Circle K/dsl, Casey's, FastStop/dsl, Loves/IHOP/dsl/scales/24hr, Qik-n-EZ/Subway/dsl KFC, Little Caesar's, McDonald's Baymont Inn, Comfort Inn, Holiday Inn Express , $General, CVS Drug, Family$, Hopper RV Ctr, Walgreens
60	to US 67 N, to Jacksonville, 6 mi N on IL 104 , food, gas, lodging
52	to IL 106, Winchester, N golf, 2 mi S food, gas, lodging
46	IL 100, to Bluffs
42mm	Illinois River
35	US 54, IL 107, to Pittsfield, Griggsville, 4 mi N food, gas, lodging, S , Jellystone Camping (6mi), st police
31	to Pittsfield, New Salem, 5 mi S , Jellystone Camping, food, gas, lodging
20	IL 106, Barry, S FastStop/dsl/24hr, Shell/dsl Subway, Wendy's Ice House Inn
10	IL 96, to Payson, Hull
4a	I-172, N to Quincy
1	IL 106, to Hull
0mm	Illinois/Missouri state line, Mississippi River.

Exits 157 & 156 are in Missouri.

Exit #	Services
157	to Hannibal, MO 179, S Ayerco, BP, Phillips 66, Shell/dsl Mark Twain Dinette, Subway Best Value Inn, Best Way Inn, Best Western, Hotel Mark Twain auto repair, visitor info
156	US 61, New London, Palmyra. **I-72 begins/ends in Hannibal, MO on US 61.** N BP, Casey's/dsl, Conoco/dsl, Murphy USA/dsl Burger King, Country Kitchen, Domino's, Gabriella's Mexican, Golden Corral, Hardee's, LJ Silver, McDonald's, Mi Mexico, Pizza Hut, Royal Garden, Rustic Oak Grill, Sonic, Subway, Taco Bell $General, $Tree, Aldi Foods, BigLots, Ford, JC Penney, Lowe's, Walmart, 0-2 mi S Ayerco, Shell/dsl Cassano's Subs, China King, DQ, Gran Rio Mexican, Hardee's, Jimmy John's, KFC, Logue's Rest, Wendy's Days Inn, EconoLodge, Hannibal Inn, Holiday Inn Express, Motel 6, Super 8 $General, AT&T, AutoZone, Buick/Chevrolet, Chrysler/Dodge/Jeep, County Mkt Foods, CVS Drug, O'Reilly Parts, Walgreens

IL

= gas = food = lodging = other = rest stop

INTERSTATE 74

Exit #	Services
221mm	Illinois/Indiana state line, Central/Eastern Time Zone
	DANVILLE
220	Lynch Rd, Danville, N Marathon/dsl/scales (1mi), Shell/dsl Border Cafe Best Western, Hampton Inn, Holiday Inn Express, Motel 6, Quality Inn, Red Roof Inn, Sleep Inn, Super 8, TownePlace Suites
216	Bowman Ave, Danville, N Mobil/dsl, Phillips 66/dsl Burger King, Godfather's, KFC, McDonald's city park, CVS Drug, Walgreens
215b a	US 150, IL 1, Gilbert St, Danville, N BP/Circle K/dsl Arby's, El Toro, La Potosina, LJ Silver, McDonald's, Pizza Hut, Steak'n Shake, Subway, Taco Bell Best Western, Days Inn H, Aldi Foods, BigLots, S Casey's/dsl, Marathon/Circle K/dsl, Marathon/dsl Burger King, Green Jade Chinese, Mike's Grill, Monical's Pizza, Rich's Rest. $General, $Tree, AutoZone, Big R, Buick/Chevrolet/GMC, County Mkt, Family$, Forest Glen Preserve Camping (11mi), Toyota
214	G St, Tilton
210	US 150, MLK Dr, 2 mi N Marathon Little Nugget Steaks H, to Kickapoo SP
206	Oakwood, N Loves/Hardee's/dsl/scales/24hr, S Casey's (1mi), Phillips 66/Subway/dsl/scales, Pilot/PJ Fresh/dsl/scales/24hr McDonald's $General
200	IL 49 N, to Rankin
197	IL 49 S, Ogden, S Phillips 66/Godfather's/dsl Rich's Rest. city park
192	St Joseph, S Casey's, Shell/dsl DQ, Monical's Pizza, Subway antiques
185	IL 130, University Ave
	CHAMPAIGN
184	US 45, Cunningham Ave, Urbana, N F&F Hyundai, Kia, Mazda, Toyota, VW, S Marathon/Circle K/Subway/dsl, Shell/dsl Arby's, Cracker Barrel, Hickory River BBQ, McDonald's, Steak'n Shake, Toro Loco, Wendy's Eastland Suites, Motel 6 $General, auto repair, vet
183	Lincoln Ave, Urbana, S Circle K/dsl, Marathon/Circle K/dsl Urbana Garden Rest. Comfort Suites, Holiday Inn Express, Knights Inn, Ramada Inn, Sleep Inn, Wyndham Garden H, Harley-Davidson, to U of IL
182	Neil St (same as 181), Champaign, N Alexander's Steaks, Bob Evans, Buca Italian, Food Court, McDonald's, Old Chicago, Olive Garden, Panera Bread, Taco Bell, TGIFriday's, Za's Italian Baymont Inn, La Quinta, Quality Inn, Red Roof Inn, Super 8 Barnes&Noble, Bergner's, Cadillac/Chevrolet, Chrysler/Dodge/Jeep, Dick's, Field&Stream, Gordman's, Hobby Lobby, Kohl's, Macy's, Mercedes/Volvo, Office Depot, Sears Hometown, TJ Maxx, Tuesday Morning, Verizon, S Mobil/Circle K
181	Prospect Ave (same as 182), Champaign, N Murphy USA/dsl Applebee's, Best Wok, Blaze Pizza, Buffalo Wild Wings, Burger King, Chili's, Chipotle, Culver's, Denny's, Denny's, Fazoli's, Firehouse Subs, Five Guys, HuHot Mongolian, Longhorn Steaks, O'Charley's, Oishi Asian, Outback Steaks, Panda Express, Penn Sta Subs, Portillo's, Red Lobster, Ruby Tuesday, Starbucks, Steak'n Shake, Subway, Super Niro's Gyros, Super Niro's Gyros, Wendy's Candlewood Suites, Country Inn&Suites, Courtyard, Drury Inn, Extended Stay America, Fairfield Inn, Quality Inn, Residence Inn, Residence Inn, Wingate Inn, Woodspring Suites $Tree, Advance Parts, Aldi Foods, AT&T, Best Buy, Ford/Lincoln, Ford/Lincoln, Jo-Ann, Jo-Ann, Lowe's, Meijer/dsl, Menards, Michael's, Nissan, Nissan, Petsmart, Sam's Club/gas, Staples, Target, Tires+, Verizon, Walmart/Subway,
181	Continued S Marathon/Circle K, Mobil/Jimmy John's, Phillips 66/dsl, Shell/dsl Arby's, Dos Reales Mexican, Dunkin Donut LJ Silver, McDonald's, Popeye's Best Value Inn, Days In $General, CarX, Home Depot, NAPA, Tire Barn, Walgreens
179b a	I-57, N to Chicago, S to Memphis
174	Lake of the Woods Rd, Prairieview Rd, N BP, Casey's, Mobi Circle K/dsl $General, auto repair, Lake of the Woods SP, T Cup RV Park, S Marathon/Subway/dsl McDonald's
172	IL 47, Mahomet, N R&S RV Sales, S Exxon/Domino's dsl, Mobil/dsl Arby's, Azteca, DQ, El Toro Mexican, He House Rest., Los Zerapes, Monical's Pizza, Peking House, Sub way, The Wok Heritage Inn Ace Hardware, CVS Dru IGA Foods, NAPA, Walgreens
166	Mansfield, S Phillips 66/dsl Mansfield Gen. Store/Rest
159	IL 54, Farmer City, S Casey's/dsl, Huck's/Godfather's/d Imo's Cafe, Subway Budget Motel, Days Inn $General, NAPA, to Clinton Lake RA, USPO
156mm	**both lanes, full facilities, litter larrels, petwalk, playground, vending**
152	US 136, to Heyworth
149	Le Roy, N Casey's/dsl, Loves/Arby's/dsl/scales/24 Jack's Cafe, McDonald's, Roma Pizza, Subway Holiday Inn Express $General, IGA Foods, NAPA, to Morain View SP, TrueValue, S Shell/Woody's Rest./dsl/scales/24 Days Inn camping, Clinton Lake
	BLOOMINGTON
142	Downs, N Mobil/Pizza/Subs/dsl/24hr USPO
135	US 51, Bloomington, N Huck's/dsl, Mobil/Circle K/d McDonald's, Pizza Hut $General, S BP/dsl
134b[157]	N H, to airport, Veterans Pkwy, to Bloomington
134a	I-55, N to Chicago, S to St Louis, I-74 E
	I-74 and I-55 run together 6 mi. See I-55, exits 157b-160b a.
127[163]	I-55, N to Chicago, S to St Louis, I-74 W to Peoria
125	US 150, to Bloomington, Mitsubishi Motorway
123mm	**weigh sta wb**
122mm	**weigh sta eb**
120	Carlock, N BP/dsl/repair Carlock Rest., S Kan Komfort Camping (Apr-Oct)
114.5mm	**both lanes, full facilities, litter barrels, petwalk, vending**
113.5mm	Mackinaw River
112	IL 117, Goodfield, N Shell/Subway/dsl Busy Corner Res Eureka Coll, Jellystone Camping (1mi), Reagan Home, Timberline RA, USPO
102b a	Morton, N Mobil/Arby's/dsl/scales/24hr Baskin Robins/Dunkin Donuts, Burger King, Cracker Barrel, Culver's, Steak Shake, Taco Bell Baymont Inn, Best Value Inn, Days In Holiday Inn Express, Park Inn, Quality Inn Chrysler/Dodge Jeep, Farm&Fleet, Freightliner, Walmart/Subway, S B Circle K, Casey's/dsl, Marathon/Circle K, Subway Chi Dragon, Domino's, Great Harvest Bread Co, Jimmy John's, Fiesta, Lin's Buffet, McDonald's, Monical's Pizza, Pizza Hut, Pizza Ranch $Tree, Buick/GMC, CVS Drug, Ford, Kroger/d O'Reilly Parts, Verizon
101	I-155 S, to Lincoln
99	I-474 W, airport
98	Pinecrest Dr
96	95c (from eb), US 150, IL 8, E Washington St, E Peoria, N Fa Stop/dsl Subway, Super Gyros Super 8 O'Reilly Pa
95b	(from eb) IL 116, to Metamora
95a	N Main St, Peoria, N Shell/dsl Burger King Hampton Inn, Paradice Hotel/Casino, S BP/Circle K A&W/

INTERSTATE 74 Cont'd

Exit	Services
95a	Continued Silver, Bob Evans, Chick-fil-A, Chipotle Mexican, Firehouse Pizza, Hardee's, IHOP, Jason's Deli, Jersey Mike's, Jimmy John's, Johnny's Italian Steaks, McDonald's, Moe's SW, Noodles&Co, Panda Express, Panda Express, Papa Murphy's, Pizza Hut, Popeye's, Potbelly, Red Robin, Subway, Taco Bell, Tequilas Grill, Wendy's Best Value Inn, Best Western+, Fairfield Inn, Holiday Inn $Tree, Advance Parts, Aldi Foods, AT&T, Costco/gas, CVS Drug, GNC, Goodyear/auto, Gordman's, Kohl's, Kroger, Ross, Target, Verizon, Walgreens
94	IL 40, RiverFront Dr, S Hucks/Godfather's/dsl Arby's, Buffalo Wild Wings, Chili's, Culver's, Granite City Grill, Logan's Roadhouse, Lorena's Mexican, Panera Bread, Papa John's, Qdoba Mexican, Shogun, Slim Chickens, Steak'n Shake, TX Roadhouse, Uncle Buck's Grill Embassy Suites, Holiday Inn Express Bass Pro Shop, Lowe's, PetsMart, Verizon, Walmart/Subway
93.5mm	Illinois River
93b	US 24, IL 29, Peoria, **N** BP, **S** Mark Twain Hotel civic ctr
93a	Jefferson St, Peoria, **N** BP, **S** Two 25 Grill Mark Twain Hotel, Marriott, Sheraton to civic ctr
92b	Glendale Ave, Peoria, **S** H, downtown
92a	IL 40 N, Knoxville Ave, Peoria, **S** Sheraton H
91	University St, Peoria
90	Gale Ave, Peoria, **S** Marathon to Bradley U, $General
89	US 150, War Memorial Dr, Peoria, **N on War Memorial** BP/Circle K, Marathon/dsl Burger King, Dunkin Donuts, Golden Corral, IHOP, McDonald's, Papa Murphy's, Perkins, Popeye's, Steak'n Shake, Wendy's Baymont Inn, Comfort Suites, Courtyard, EconoLodge, Extended Stay America, Quality Inn, Red Roof Inn, Residence Inn, Super 8 Aldi Foods, AT&T, AutoZone, Barnes&Noble, Best Buy, Chevrolet/Cadillac, Hobby Lobby, Lowe's, Midas, NAPA, PetsMart, Target, Tires+, U-Haul, vet, Walgreens, Walmart/Subway
88	to US 150, War Memorial Dr, **N** Shell Arby's, Avanti's Rest., Baskin Robins/Dunkin Donuts, Biaggi's, Chick-fil-A, Chipotle, ChuckECheese, Firehouse Subs, Five Guys, Panda Express, Panera Bread, Portillo's, Red Lobster, Sonic Motel 6, SpringHill Suites $Tree, JC Penney, Michael's, Ross, Verizon, Walgreens
87b a	I-474 E, IL 6, N to Chillicothe, **S**
82	Edwards Rd, Kickapoo, **N** Mobil/dsl/service, Shell/Subway/dsl Jubilee Café to Jubilee Coll SP, **S** USPO, Wildlife Prairie SP
75	Brimfield, Oak Hill, **N** Casey's/dsl
71	to IL 78, to Canton, Elmwood
62mm	**both lanes, full facilities, litter barrels, petwalk, vending**
61.5mm	Spoon River
54	US 150, IL 97, Lewistown, **N** TravL Park Camping (1mi), **S** Mobil/dsl (2mi) Alfano's Pizza (2mi)
51	Knoxville, **S** BP/dsl, Loves/Subway/Chester's/dsl/scales/24hr, Phillips 66/Charley's Subs/dsl/scales Hardee's, McDonald's Best Value Inn
48b a	E Galesburg, Galesburg, **N** Best Western Harley-Davidson, **S** BP/Circle K/dsl, HyVee/dsl, Phillps 66/Beck's/dsl DQ, Hardee's, Jalisco Mexican, KFC, Marco's Pizza, McDonald's, Pizza Hut, Subway, Taco Bell Baymont Inn, Holiday Inn Express Family$, HyVee Foods, Lincoln-Douglas Debates, Sav-A-Lot Foods, to Sandburg Birthplace, Walgreens
46b a	US 34, to Monmouth, **N** Nichol's dsl Service, **1 mi S** Buffalo Wild Wings, Crazy Buffet, Mi Casa Mexican, Pizza Ranch

PEORIA

GALESBURG

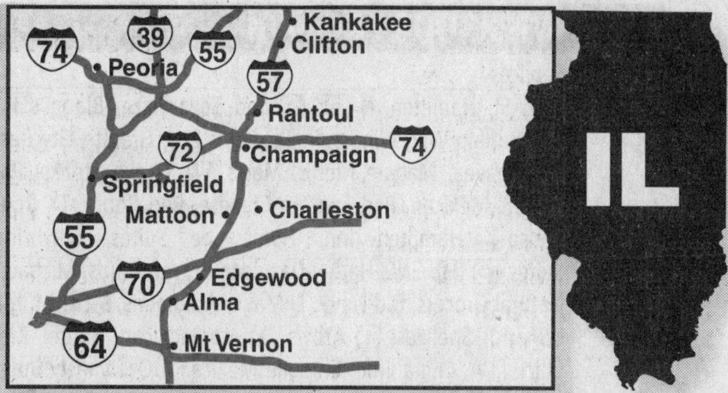

Exit	Services
46b a	Continued H, Aldi Foods, AT&T, Kohl's, Menards, Toyota, Verizon, vet, Walmart/Subway
32	IL 17, Woodhull, **N** BP/dsl, Shell/dsl Subway $General, **S** Pilot/dsl/scales/24hr Shady Lakes Camping (8mi)
30mm	**wb, full facilities, litter barrels, petwalk, playground, RV dump, vending**
28mm	**eb, full facilities, litter barrels, petwalk, playground, RV dump, vending**
24	IL 81, Andover, **N** Casey's (2mi) camping
14mm	I-80, E to Chicago, I-80/I-280 W to Des Moines
8mm	**weigh sta wb**
6mm	**weigh sta eb**
5b	US 6, Moline, **S** Shell/dsl Bare Bones BBQ, McDonald's, MT Jack's Best Inn, Country Inn&Suites, Hampton Inn, Holiday Inn Express, La Quinta, Motel 6, Quality Inn
5a	I-280 W, US 6 W, to Des Moines
4b a	IL 5, John Deere Rd, Moline, **N** BP/7-11, Phillips 66, Shell/dsl Applebee's, Burger King, Chipotle Mexican, Culver's, Hungy Hobo, Osaka Buffet, Panera Bread, Ryan's, Starbucks, Steak'n Shake, Subway, Wendy's Residence Inn $Tree, Cadillac, Farm&Fleet, Honda, Hyundai, Lowe's, Menard's, Staples, Subaru, Tires+, Toyota, Volvo, Walmart/Subway, **S** BP/7-11 A&W/LJ Silver, Arby's, Buffalo Wild Wings, China Cafe, Denny's, KFC, Los Agaves, McDonald's, New Mandarin Chinese, Qdoba Mexican, Taco Bell Best Western, Comfort Inn, Fairfield Inn, Motel 6 $General, Best Buy, Buick/GMC, Chevrolet, Chrysler/Dodge/Jeep, Dillards, Firestone/auto, Ford/Lincoln, Goodyear/auto, Gordman's, JC Penney, Mazda, Nissan, PetCo, Von Maur, Walgreens, Younkers
3	23rd Ave, Moline, **N** Economy Inn
2	7th Ave, Moline, **S** QuikStop La Casa Mexican riverfront, to civic ctr, USPO
1	3rd Ave (from eb), Moline, **S** QuickStop Stoney Creek Inn
0mm	Illinois/Iowa state line, Mississippi River.
Exits 4-1 are in Iowa.	
4	US 67, Grant St, State St, Bettendorf, **N** BP/dsl Hardee's, McDonald's, Subway Waterfront Conv Ctr CarQuest, **S** Village Inn Rest. City Ctr Motel $General
3	Middle Rd, Locust St, Bettendorf, **S** BP/dsl China Taste, Grinders Rest., Jimmy John's, McDonald's, Pizza Ranch, Red Ginger Asian, Starbucks, Subway Hilton Garden H, AT&T, Burlington Coats, Hobby Lobby, Home Depot, Marshall's, Schuck's Foods, Verizon, Walgreens
2	US 6 W, Spruce Hills Dr, Bettendorf, **N** BP/dsl, Phillips 66 Domino's, Old Chicago Pizza Courtyard, EconoLodge, Ramada Inn, Super 8, The Lodge Hotel/rest. U-Haul, **S** Hyvee Gas Applebee's, KFC, Panera Bread, Red Lobster AmericInn, Days Inn, Holiday Inn, La Quinta Buick/GMC, Gordman's, Kohl's, Lowe's, PetCo, Sam's Club/gas, st patrol

MOLINE

BETTENDORF

INTERSTATE 74 Cont'd

Exit #	Services
1	53rd St, Hamilton, N [gas] [food] Bad Boyz Pizza, Biaggi's Italian, Buffalo Wild Wings, Chili's, Coldstone, Granite City Rest., Los Agaves, Maggie Moo's, Moe's SW, Osaka Steaks, Panchero's Mexican, Red Lantern Chinese, Red Robin, TX Roadhouse [lodging] Hampton Inn, Homewood Suites, Staybridge Suites [other] [H], GNC, Harley-Davidson, HyVee Foods, Michael's, Natural Grocers, Old Navy, TJ Maxx, Walgreens, S [gas] Murphy USA/dsl, Shell/dsl [food] Arby's, Azteca Mexican, Burger King, Chick-fil-A, China Cafe, Chipotle Mexican, DQ, Dynasty Buffet, Golden Corral, HuHot, Hungry Hobo, IHOP, La Rancherita, Noodles&Co., PepperJax Grill, Quiznos, Sonic, Starbucks, Steak'n Shake, Subway, Taco Bell, Village Inn Rest., Wendy's [lodging] Sleep Inn [other] $Tree, Aldi Foods, AT&T, Best Buy, Costco/dsl, Dick's, Discount Tire, Field&Stream, Meineke, PetsMart, Staples, Target, Verizon, Walmart

I-74 begins/ends on I-80, exit 298. Exits 1-4 are in Iowa.

INTERSTATE 80

Exit #	Services
163mm	Illinois/Indiana state line
161	US 6, IL 83, Torrence Ave, N [gas] [food] Burger King, Chili's, Culver's, Dixie Kitchen, Hooters, IHOP, Kenny's Ribs, Liang's Garden, New China Buffet, Oberweiss, Olive Garden, Subway, Wendy's [lodging] Comfort Suites, Extended Stay America, Holiday Inn Express, Howard Johnson Express, Red Roof Inn, Sleep Inn [other] $General, $Tree, Aldi Foods, Best Buy, CarX, Chrysler/Jeep/Dodge, Fannie May Candies, Firestone/auto, Home Depot, Honda, JustTires, PepBoys, Ultra Foods, S [gas] Allstar, Marathon, Mobil [food] Burger King, China Chef, DQ, Dunkin Donuts, Golden Crown, Johnny K's Cafe, McDonald's, Round the Clock, Subway [other] AT&T, Auto Clinic, Chevrolet, O'Reilly Parts, Saab, SunRise Foods, vet, Walgreens, Walmart/Subway
160b	I-94 W, to Chicago, **tollway begins wb, ends eb**
160a	IL 394 S, to Danville
159mm	**Oasis,** [gas] Mobil/dsl [food] McDonald's, Panda Express, Starbucks, Subway
157	IL 1, Halsted St, N [gas] Citgo/dsl, Marathon/dsl [food] Burger King [lodging] Chicago Southland Hotel, Clarion, Comfort Inn, Comfort Suites, EconoLodge, Regency Inn, S [gas] Citgo, Delta Sonic, Shell, Speedway [food] Applebee's, Arby's, Athens Gyros, Boston Mkt, Burger King, Chili's, Dunkin Donuts, Fannie May Candies, KFC, McDonald's, Panda Express, Pizza Hut, Popeye's, Starbucks, Subway, Taco Bell, Washington Square Rest., Wendy's, White Castle [lodging] Homewood Hotel, Super 8 [other] $Tree, Aldi Foods, AT&T, Best Buy, Chevrolet, Discount Tire, Fanny May Candies, Firestone/auto, Goodyear/auto, Home Depot, Jewel-Osco, Jo-Ann Fabrics, Kohl's, Menards, PepBoys, PetCo, Target, TJ Maxx, Walgreens
156	Dixie Hwy (from eb, no return), S [gas] Mobil [food] Leona's Rest. [other] golf
155	I-294 N, Tri-State Tollway, **toll plaza**
154	Kedzie Ave (from eb, no return), N [gas] Speedway, S [other] [H]
151b a	I-57 (exits left from both directions), N to Chicago, S to Memphis
148b a	IL 43, Harlem Ave, N [gas] Speedway/dsl [food] Buffalo Wild Wings, Burger King, Cracker Barrel, Culver's, Egg&I Grill, Hamada of Japan, Joyyee Asian, Pop's Italian Beef, Side Street Tavern, Submarina, Tin Fish Grill, Wendy's [lodging] Comfort Suites, Fairfield Inn, Hampton Inn, Holiday Inn, La Quinta, Sleep Inn, Wingate Inn [other] AT&T, Tinley Park Convention Center, Verizon,
148b a	Continued S [food] Arby's, Panera Bread, Subway, Taco Bell, TGIFriday's [other] ampitheater, Best Buy, Carmax, Dick's, GNC, Kohl's, Michael's, Old Navy, PetsMart, Ross, SuperTarget, TJ Maxx
147.5mm	**weigh sta wb**
145b a	US 45, 96th Ave, N [food] Arby's, Arrenello's Pizza, Baskin-Robbins, Dunkin Donuts, Egg&I, Tokyo Steaks, TX Roadhouse [lodging] Country Inn&Suites, Hilton Garden [other] Harley-Davidson, vet, **0-2** S [gas] BP, Shell/Circle K/dsl/24hr [food] Beggar's Pizza, Chipotle, Denny's, Doc's Smokehouse, Dominos, DQ, Legends, Mind Ribs, Mobil, Rising Sun Chinese, Starbucks, Stoney Pt Grill, Subway, Wendy's, White Castle [lodging] Super 8 [other] Firestone/auto repair, vet
143mm	**weigh sta eb**
140	SW Hwy, **I-355 N Tollway**, US 6 S
137	US 30, New Lenox, N [food] Williamson's Rest., S [gas] Shell/Circle K/dsl, Speedway/dsl [food] Al's Hotdogs, Beggar's Pizza, Buffalo Wild Wings, Burger King, KFC, McDonald's/playplace, Paisano's Pizza, Subway, Taco Bell [other] Ace Hardware, Goodyear auto, Jewel-Osco/dsl, vet, Walgreens
134	Briggs St, N [gas] Speedway, S [gas] Mobil/dsl, Shell/dsl [other] Lube, Martin Camping
133	Richards St
132b a	US 52, IL 53, Chicago St
131.5mm	Des Plaines River
131	US 6, Meadow Ave, N [other] to Riverboat Casino
130b a	IL 7, Larkin Ave, N [gas] Delta Sonic/dsl, Marathon/24hr, Mobil, CircleK/dsl, Shell, Speedway [food] Baskin-Robbins/Dunkin Donuts, Bob Evans, Boston Mkt, Burger King, Checkers, Culver's, DQ, JJ Fish&Chicken, KFC, Little Caesar's, McDonald's, Steak'n Shake, Subway, Taco Bell, Wendy's, White Castle [lodging] Budget Inn, Clarion, Motel 6, Quality Inn, Red Roof Inn, Rodeway Inn [other] [H], 7-11, AT&T, auto repair, Cadillac/Chevrolet, Discount Tire, Goodyear/auto, Meineke, Pepboys, Sam's Club/gas, to U of St Francis, S [gas] Mobil/dsl
127	Houbolt Rd, to Joliet, N [gas] 7-11, BP/deli [food] Burger King, China Kitchen, Cracker Barrel, Dunkin Donuts, Heros Sports Grill, Jimmy John's, JimmyK's, McDonald's, Subway [lodging] Candlewood Suites, Comfort Inn, Fairfield Inn, Hampton Inn, Holiday Inn & Suites, TownePlace Suites [other] Riverboat Casino
126b a	I-55, N to Chicago, S to St Louis
125.5mm	Du Page River
122	Minooka, N [gas] Citgo/dsl, S [gas] BP, Pilot/Arby's/scales/dsl/24hr [food] 2-Fers Pizza, Baskin-Robbins/Dunkin Donuts, KFC, McDonald's/playplace, Rosati's Pizza, Subway, Taco Bell, Wendy's [lodging] Hampton Inn, TownePlace Suites [other] $General, 7-11
119mm	[RS] **wb, full [handicap] facilities, litter barrels, petwalk, [phone], [picnic], playground, vending**
117mm	[RS] **eb, full [handicap] facilities, litter barrels, petwalk, [phone], [picnic], playground, vending**
116	Brisbin Rd
112	IL 47, Morris, N [gas] Pilot/Subway/dsl/scales/24hr, Pilot/Subway/dsl/scales/24hrs, TA/BP/RPlace/scales/dsl/24hr/@ Bellacino's, Chili's, IHOP [lodging] Comfort Inn, Days Inn, Holiday Express, Quality Inn [other] $General, Menards, URGENT CARE S [gas] BP/dsl, Mobil/dsl, Shell, Spirit [food] Buffalo Wild Wings, Burger King, Culver's, DQ, Dunkin Donuts, Hong Kong Chinese, KFC/LJ Silver, Little Caesar's, Maria's Ristorante, McDonald's, Morris Diner, Pizza Hut, Rosati's Pizza, Subway, Taco Bell, Wendy's [lodging] Park Motel, Sherwood Oaks Motel, Super 8 [other] $Tree, Aldi Foods, AT&T, AutoZone, Big R Store, Buick/Cadillac, Chevrolet, Chrysler/Dodge/Jeep, Fisher Parts, Ford, GMC, GM

IL

CHICAGO AREA

MORRIS

INTERSTATE 80 Cont'd

112	Continued Jewel-Osco, to Stratton SP, transmissions/repair, Verizon, Walgreens, Walmart/Subway
105	to Seneca
97	to Marseilles, S Shell/dsl Four Star Camping (5mi), Glenwood Camping (4mi), to Illini SP
93	IL 71, Ottawa, N Pilot/Road Ranger/Subway/dsl/scales/24hr, Shell/rest./dsl, S Hank's Farm Rest., New Chiam H
92.5mm	Fox River
90	IL 23, Ottawa, N BP/Subway Arby's, Cracker Barrel, Taco Bell Hampton Inn, Holiday Inn Express AT&T, F&F, Honda, Toyota, Walmart/McDonald's, S BP/dsl/LP, Thornton's/dsl Culver's, Dunkin Donuts, Hardee's, KFC/LJ Silver, Papa Murphy's, Sunfield Rest. EconoLodge, Fairfield Inn, Super 8, Surrey Motel H, $Tree, Aldi Foods, Ford/Lincoln/Kia, Harley-Davidson, Kroger, O'Reilly Parts, USPO
81	IL 178, Utica, N Love's/McDonald's/Subway/dsl/scales/24hr Hickory Hollow Camping, KOA (2mi), S Shell/Jimmy Johns/dsl Starved Rock Inn repair, to Starved Rock SP, visitor info
79b a	I-39, US 51, N to Rockford, S to Bloomington
77.5mm	Little Vermilion River
77	IL 351, La Salle, S FLYING J/Denny's/dsl/scales/24hr UpTown Grill (3mi) Daniels Motel (1mi) st police
75	IL 251, Peru, N BP, Shell/rest./dsl/24hr 4Star Rest., Arby's, McDonald's, Olive Garden, Starbucks, Taco Bell Holiday Inn Express, Quality Inn, Super 8 Kohl's, Petsmart, Walmart/Dunkin Donuts/Subway, S BP, Shell Applebee's, Buffalo Wild Wings, Burger King, Culver's, DQ, IHOP, Jalepeno's Mexican, Jimmy John's, Master Buffet, McDonald's, Mi Margarita, Papa John's, Pizza Hut, Red Lobster, Steak'n Shake, Subway, Wendy's Fairfield Inn, Hampton Inn, La Quinta H, $Tree, Advance Parts, Aldi Foods, AT&T, AutoZone, BigLots, Buick/GMC, Chevrolet/Mercedes, Chrysler/Dodge/Jeep, CVS Drug, Ford/Hyundai/Lincoln, Goodyear/auto, Hobby Lobby, Home Depot, HyVee Food/dsl, Jo-Ann Fabrics, Marshall's, Menards, Mercedes, Midas, NAPA, Nissan, O'Reilly Parts, Staples, Target, Verizon, Walgreens
73	Plank Rd, N Sapp Bros/Subway/dsl/scales/@ Barney's Lake Camping, Kenworth/Volvo, Big Apple Rest., Speedway/Speedway Cafe/dsl
70	IL 89, to Ladd, N Casey's, S BP (3mi), Shell (3mi) Spring Valley Motel H, golf
61	I-180, to Hennepin
56	IL 26, Princeton, N Road Ranger/Pilot/scales/dsl/@ Super 8, S BP/Beck's/dsl, Shell/dsl Big Apple Rest., Burger King, Coffee Cup Rest., Culver's, KFC, McDonald's, Subway, Wendy's AmericInn, Days Inn, EconoLodge H, $General, antiques, AutoZone, Buick/Cadillac/Chevrolet, O'Reilly Parts, Pennzoil, Sullivan's Food/gas/E-85, vet, Walmart
51mm	**RS both lanes, full facilities, litter barrels, petwalk, playground, RV dump, vending**
45	IL 40, N antiques, to Ronald Reagan Birthplace (21mi), S Hennepin Canal SP
44mm	Hennepin Canal
33	IL 78, to Kewanee, Annawan, N Shabbona RV Ctr/Camp (3mi), S Cenex/dsl, FS/dsl/E-85, Shell/Subway/dsl Best Western to Johnson-Sauk Tr SP
27	to US 6, Atkinson, N Casey's (1mi)
19	IL 82, Geneseo, N BP/dsl, Casey's/dsl Culver's, DQ, Happy Joe's Pizza, Hardee's, McDonald's, New China, Pizza Hut,

OTTAWA

PERU

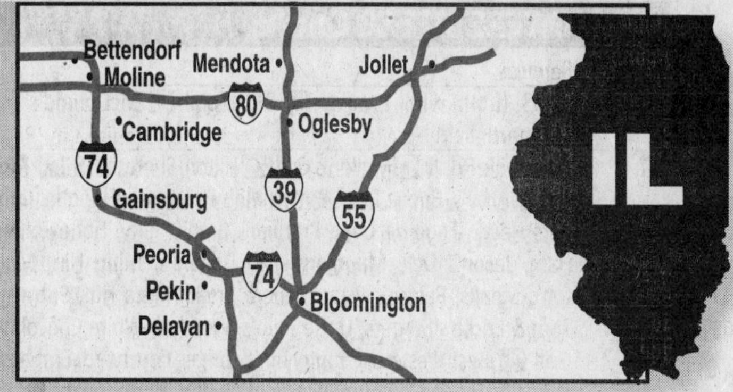

GENESEO

19	Continued Subway, Sweet Pea's Grill Best Western H, $General, Ford, SaveALot Foods, Verizon, Walgreens, Walmart, S Los Ranchitos Mexican
10	I-74, I-280, W to Moline, E to Peoria
9	US 6, to Geneseo, N Lavender Crest Winery/Cafe, S Niabi Zoo
7	Colona, N Shell/dsl Country Fixins Rest.
5mm	Rock River
4a	IL 5, IL 92, W to Silvis, S Lundeen's Camping, st police
4b	I-88, IL 92, E to Rock Falls
2mm	**weigh sta both lanes**
1.5mm	**Welcome Ctr eb, full facilities, info, litter barrels, petwalk, scenic overlook**
1	IL 84, 20th St, Great River Rd, E Moline, N BP/dsl Bros Rest. camping, The Great River Rd, **3 mi S** camping
0mm	Illinois/Iowa state line, Mississippi River

INTERSTATE 88

OAKBROOK

Exit #	Services
139.5mm	**I-88 begins/ends on I-290.**
139	I-294, S to Indiana, N to Milwaukee
138mm	**toll plaza**
137	IL 83 N, Cermak Rd, N Cheesecake Factory, Clubhouse Rest., Ditka's Rest., McDonald's Marriott Barnes&Noble, Lord&Taylor, Macy's, Nieman-Marcus
136	IL 83 S, Midwest Rd (from eb), N Shell/Circle K Chipotle Mexican, Denny's, Devon Steaks, Giordano's Rest., Jamba Juice, Jimmy John's, McDonalds, Noodles&Co, Redstone Grill, Starbucks, Subway, Twin Peaks, Which Wich? Courtyard, Holiday Inn, La Quinta, Staybridge AT&T, Big Lots, Costco/gas, Home Depot, Nordstrom's, Old Navy, REI, TJ Maxx, Walgreens, World Mkt
134	Highland Ave (no EZ wb return), N Barbokoa, Benihana, Brick House, Brio Grille, Buca Italian, Burger King, Capital Grille, Chama Guacha Brazilian, Champps Grill, Chick-fil-A, Chipotle, Claimjumper Rest., Fuddruckers, Harry Caray's, Honey-Jam Cafe, Hooters, Kona Grill, Kyoto, McCormick & Schmick's, Melting Pot, Miller's Rest., Noodles&Co, Olive Garden, Olive Therapy Pizza, Panera Bread, PF Chang's, Portillo's Hotdogs, Potbelly, Red Lobster, Rockbottom Brewery, Ruby Tuesday, Starbucks, Starbucks, Subway, TGIFriday's, Tom&Eddie's Burgers, Uncle Julio's Comfort Inn, Embassy Suites, Extended Stay America, Holiday Inn Express, Hyatt Place, Marriott, Red Roof Inn, Westin Hotel H, $Tree, Best Buy, Dick's, Home Depot, JC Penney, Kohl's, Marshall's, Michael's, Petsmart, Ross, Target, Tuesday Morning, Verizon, Vonmaur, S Parkers Ocean Grill
132	I-355 N (from wb)
131	I-355 S (from eb)

IL

= gas = food = lodging = other = rest stop

INTERSTATE 88 Cont'd

NAPERVILLE

Exit #	Services
130	IL 53 (from wb), 1 mi N BP, Mobil McDonald's Walmart
127	Naperville Rd, N Mullen's Grill Hilton, Sheraton, S Mobil Arby's, Buona Beef, Butterfield's Pancakes, Chipotle, Coopers Hawk, Fogo de Chao Brazilian, Granite City, HoneyBaked Ham, Jason's Deli, Maggiano's, McDonald's, Ming Hin, Morton's Steaks, Paisan's Pizza, Panera Bread, Pizza Hut, Subway, Tom & Eddie's Burgers, Uncle Julio's, Wendy's, White Chocolate Grill Best Western, Country Inn & Suites, Courtyard, Embassy Suites, Extended Stay America, Fairfield Inn, Hampton Inn, Marriott, Motel 6, Regency Inn $Tree, CVS, Staples, Subaru
125	Winfield Rd, N BP, Mobil Hyatt House, Hyatt Place, Resedence Inn H, Walgreens, S Buffalo Wild Wings, CA Pizza Kitchen, Chipotle Mexican, Corner Bakery Cafe, Eddie Merlot, Masala, McDonald's, Potbelly, Red Robin, Rockbottom Brewery, Starbucks, Twin Peaks, Zoup Hilton Garden, Springhill Suites SuperTarget
123	IL 59, N Speedway/dsl CarMax, S BP/Domino's, Delta Sonic, Speedway Baskin Robbins/Dunkin Donuts, Cracker Barrel, Firehouse Subs, Jimmy John's, McDonald's, Oberweis, Starbucks, Subway, TX Roadhouse, Wendy's Extended Stay America, Fairfield Inn, Red Roof Inn, Sleep Inn, Towneplace Suites $Tree, 7-11, CVS Drug
119	Farnsworth Ave, N BP, Shell, Thornton's/dislike Chipotle, McDonald's, Noodles&Co, Panera Bread, Papa Bear Rest., Quizno's, Sonic, Starbucks Fox Valley Inn, Motel 6 Advance Parts, AT&T, Firestone/auto, GNC, Premium Outlets/Famous Brands, Verizon, Walgreens, Walmart/Subway, S Marathon, Moble, Shell, Speedway Baskin-Robbins/Dunkin Donuts, Goody's, Little Caesar's, McDonald's, Mike&Denise's Pizza, Subway, Taco Bell $General, 7-11, AutoZone, Family$, Walgreens
118mm	toll plaza
117	IL 31, IL 56, to Aurora, Batavia, N BP/dsl A&W 7-11, S Mobil, Speedway/dsl, Thornton's/dsl Baskin-Robbins/Dunkin Donuts, Burger King, Culver's, Denny's, McDonald's, Nikarry's, Popeye's, Subway, Taco Bell, Wendy's, White Castle Baymont Inn H, $General, $Tree, Ace Hardware, Advance Parts, AutoZone, Cermak Foods, Family$, Firestone, GNC, O'Reilly Parts, Ross, U-Haul, Walgreens
115	Orchard Rd, N Dunkin Donuts, McDonald's, Subway $Tree, Best Buy, Chrysler/Dodge/Jeep, Ford/Lincoln, Hyundai, JC Penney, Kia, Michaels, Nissan, PetCo, Subaru, Target, Verizon, Woodman's/dsl, 0-2 mi S 7-11 Arby's, Buffalo Wild Wings, Chili's, Chipotle, IHOP, Jimmy John's, Panera Bread, Papa Saverio's, Pizza Hut, Starbucks, Wendy's Candlewood Suites, Hampton Inn, Holiday Inn AT&T, CVS Drug, Discount Tire, Home Depot, Office Depot
114	IL 56W, to US 30 (from wb, no EZ return), to Sugar Grove
109	IL 47 (from eb), Elburn
94	Peace Rd, to IL 38, N H
93mm	**Dekalb Oasis/24hr both lanes,** Mobil/dsl McDonald's, Panda Express, Starbucks, Subway
92	IL 38, IL 23, Annie Glidden Rd, to DeKalb, 2-3 mi N BP, Road Ranger/dsl, Shell Baskin-Robbins, Burger King, Chipotle Mexican, Culver's, Dunkin Donuts, Fatty's, Happy Wok Chinese, IHOP, Jct Rest., Jersey Mike's, McDonald's, Miki MOto, Molly's Eatery, Panda Express, Papa John's, Pizza Hut, Pizza Pros, Pizza Villa, Potbelly, Starbucks, Subway, Taco Bell, Tom&Jerry's, Topper's Pizza Baymont Inn, Hampton Inn, Red Roof Inn, Super 8 CVS, Ford, Illini Tire, Schnuck's Food/Drug, to N IL U, Walgreens

DEKALB

IL

DIXON

Exit #	Services
86mm	toll plaza
78	I-39, US 51, S to Bloomington, N to Rockford
76	IL 251, Rochelle, N BP/dsl, Casey's, Shell H, For tires/repair
56mm	toll plaza
54	IL 26, Dixon, N Murphy USA/dsl, Pilot/Road Range dsl/24hrs Hardee's, Las Palmas, Panda Chinese, Pizz Hut Comfort Inn, Super 8 H, $Tree, Aldi, GNC, to Joh Deere HS, to Ronald Reagan Birthplace, to St Parks, URGEN CARE, Verizon, Walmart
44	US 30 (last free exit eb), N Leisure lake RV Ctr (2mi), foo gas, lodging
41	IL 40, to Sterling, Rock Falls, 1-2 mi N Mobil/d Shell American Grill, Arby's, Arthur's Deli, Burger Kin Candlelight Rest., Culver's, Gazi's Rest., Hardee's, Jimm John's, McDonald's/playplace, Perna's Pizza, Pizza Hut, Re Apple Rest., Subway Country Inn&Suites, Days Inn, Holida Inn Express, Super 8 H, $General, AutoZone, Harley-Da vidson, O'Reilly Parts, Sav-a-Lot, Verizon, Walgreens, Walmar
36	to US 30, Rock Falls, Sterling
26	IL 78, to Prophetstown, Morrison, N to Morrison-Rockwood S
18	to Albany, Erie
10	to Port Byron, Hillsdale, S Phillips 66/dsl, Shell/Subwa scales/dsl/24hr
6	IL 92 E, to Joslin, N Jammerz Roadhouse (2mi), S Su set Lake Camping (1mi)
2	Former IL 2
1b a	I-80, W to Des Moines, E to Chicago
0mm	IL 5, IL 92, W to Silvis. Lundeen's Camping, to Quad City Down **I-88 begins/ends on I-80, exit 4b.**

E MOLINE

INTERSTATE 90

CHICAGO AREA

Exit #	Services
0mm	Illinois/Indiana state line, **Chicago Skyway Toll Rd begins/en**
1mm	US 12, US 20, 106th St, Indianapolis Blvd, N Mobil Burger King, Starbucks, Taco Bell Aldi Foods, AutoZone, casino, Jewel-Osco, S Citgo Beggars Pizz McDonald's auto repair
2.5mm	Skyway Oasis McDonald's **toll plaza**
3mm	87th St (from wb)
4mm	79th St, services on 79th St and Stoney Island Ave
5.5mm	73rd St (from wb)
6mm	State St (from wb), S Citgo
7mm	I-94 N (mile markers decrease to IN state line)
I-90 E and I-94 E run together. See I-94 exits 43b - 59a.	
84	I-94 W, Lawrence Ave, N BP/dsl
83b a	Foster Ave (from wb), N Elly's Pancakes, Subway Advance Parts, Firestone/auto, Walgreens
82c	Austin Ave, to Foster Ave
82b	Byrn-Mawr (from wb)
82a	Nagle Ave
81b	Sayre Ave (from wb)
81a	IL 43, Harlem Ave, S Gas Depot, Shell Dunkin Donut Popeye's, Sally's Pancakes, Wendy's $Tree, AutoZone
80	Canfield Rd (from wb), N Walgreens
79b a	IL 171 S, Cumberland Ave (from wb), N 7-11, Mobil A Burgers, Dunkin Donuts/Baskin Robbins, Hooters, McDonald' Nancy's Pizza, Outback Steaks Marriott, SpringHill Suite Westin Hotel Hampton Inn, Mariano's Mkt, S Bar Lo ie's, Starbucks Holiday Inn, Hyatt, Renaissance
78	I-294, I-190 W, N Mobil McDonald's Hampton In Westin, S Hyatt to O'Hare Airport

CHICAGO AREA

INTERSTATE 90 Cont'd

Exit #	Services
76	IL 72, Lee St (from wb), **N** [food] Buona, Chili's, Chipotle, Culver's, IHOP, Jimmy John's, Longhorn Steaks, Panda Express, Steak'n Shake, Subway [lodging] Extended Stay America, Radisson, Residence Inn [other] Target, **S** [food] McDonald's [lodging] Best Western, Holiday Inn Express, Holiday Inn Select, Sheraton Gateway
73	Elmhurst Rd (from wb), **S** [gas] Shell [food] Burger King, McDonald's, Subway, White Castle [lodging] Best Western, Days Inn, In-Towne Suites, La Quinta, Motel 6, Super 8, Wyndham Garden
70	Arlington Hts Rd, **S** [gas] Mobil, Shell [food] Subway [lodging] Sheraton [other] Chevrolet, **N on Algonquin** [gas] BP/dsl, Shell/dsl [food] Arby's, Buona Beef, Chef Ping, Chipotle Mexican, Coopers Hawk, Denny's, Five Guys, Honey Baked Ham, Jimmy Johns, McDonald's, Noodles&Co, Panda Express, Panera Bread, Pie Five, Potbelly's, Steak'n Shake [lodging] Comfort Inn, Courtyard, DoubleTree, Holiday Inn Express, Red Roof Inn, Wingate Inn [other] AT&T, GNC, Lowe's Whse, Meijer/dsl, NTB, Staples, vet, Walmart
68	I-290, IL 53, **N on Algonquin** [lodging] Embassy Suites, Holiday Inn, Holiday Inn Express, Renaissance Inn, **1 mi S on Golf Rd** [food] CA Pizza Kitchen, Cheesecake Factory, Chevy's Mexican, Hooters, Joe's Crabshack, Longhorn Steaks, Maggiano's, Olive Garden, Panera Bread, Qdoba, Red Robin, Starbucks, Subway, TGI Friday's, Uno [lodging] Extended Stay America, Hyatt, Residence Inn [other] AT&T, Costco/gas, Firestone/auto, JC Penney, Lord&Taylor, Macy's, Marshall's, Michael's, Nordstrom, Old Navy, Petsmart, Trader Joe's
65	Roselle Rd (from wb, no return), **N** [other] Medieval Times Funpark, **S** [gas] Mobil [food] Boston Mkt, Chipotle Mexican, Denny's, Fox-&Hound, Jimmy John's, KFC, McDonald's, Melting Pot, Outback Steaks, Panda Express, Papa John's, Subway, Taco Bell, Wendy's [lodging] Country Inn&Suites, Extended Stay America, Extended Stay America (2), Holiday Inn Express, Radisson [other] 7-11, Buick/GMC, Carmax, Chrysler/Dodge/Jeep, Fiat, Firestone/auto, Jewel-Osco, Mazda, Office Depot, O'Reilly Parts, PetCo, TJ Maxx, Walgreens
62	Barrington Rd (from wb), **N** [food] Apple Villa Pancake House, Gino's East, Hunan Beijing, Jersey's Grill, Jimmy John's, Lucky Monk [lodging] Hilton Garden [other] vet, **S** [gas] BP, Mobil/dsl [food] Buona Beef, Burger King, Chili's, Domino's, IHOP, Macaroni Grill, McDonald's, Moretti's, Starbucks, Steak'n Shake, Subway, Sweet Caroline's [lodging] Hampton Inn, Hawthorn Suites, Hyatt Place, La Quinta, Quality Inn, Red Roof Inn [other] U-Haul
59	IL 59, **N** [food] Buffalo Wild Wings, Chipotle Mexican, Claim Jumper Rest., Cooper's Hawk Rest., Culver's, Dunkin Donuts, Firehouse Subs, Jersey Mike's, Jimmy John's, Moe's SW Grill, Noodles&Co, Panda Express, Panera Bread, Potbelly, Red Robin, Rookie's Grill, Ruth's Chris Steaks, Starbucks, Subway, Which Wich? [lodging] Marriott [other] Cabela's, CVS Drug, Duluth Trading, GNC, Petsmart, Ross, Target, TJ Maxx, Verizon, World Mkt
58	Beverly Rd (from wb)
56	IL 25, **N** [lodging] Lexington Inn, **S** [gas] BP/dsl, Shell/dsl, Speedway/dsl [food] Arby's, Baker Hill Pancakes, Subway, Wendy's [other] Advance Parts, city park, NAPA AutoCare
54b a	IL 31, **N** [gas] BP, Thornton's [food] Alexander's Rest., Baskin-Robbins/Dunkin Donuts [lodging] Courtyard, Hampton Inn, Holiday Inn, Quality Inn, Super 8, TownePlace Suites
53.5mm	**Elgin Toll Plaza,** [phone]
52	Randall Rd, **N** [gas] Shell [food] Big Sammy's Hot Dogs, Burnt Toast, Cafe Roma, DQ, Jimmy John's, Jimmy's Charhouse, Mr Wok, Panera Bread, Rookies Grill, Starbucks, Village Pizza

SCHAUMBURG

ELGIN

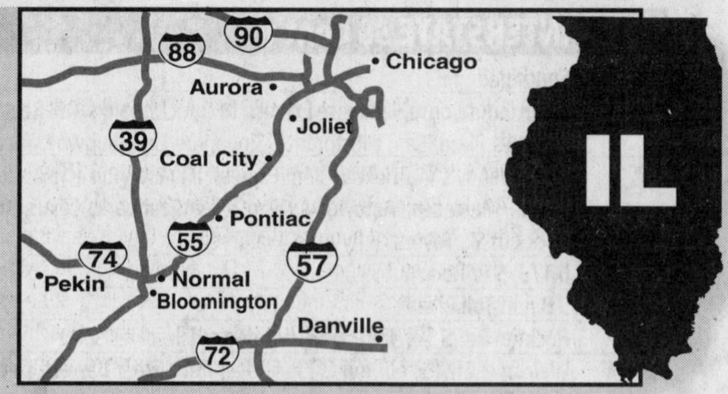

Exit #	Services
52	Continued [lodging] Comfort Suites, Country Inn&Suites [other] Honda, VW, **S** [gas] 7-11 [lodging] Candlewood Suites [other] [H], Subaru
46	IL 47, to Woodstock, **N** [other] Ford, General RV Ctr, Huntley Outlets/famous brands
42	US 20, Marengo, **N** [gas] Citgo/Mexican Grill/dsl/scales/24hr, Pilot/Road Ranger/Subway/dsl/scales/24hr, Speedway/Speedy's Cafe/dsl/24hr, TA/BP/Country Pride/Burger King/Popeye's/dsl/scales/24hr/@ [food] McDonald's, Wendy's [lodging] Super 8 [other] access to services at exit 46 (6mi), Ford, Huntley Outlets, to museums
38mm	**Marengo Toll Plaza (from eb)**
25	Genoa Rd, to Belvidere, **N** [gas] Murphy USA/dsl [food] Applebee's, Rosati's Pizza, Starbucks, Subway [other] Verizon, Walmart/Dunkin Donuts
24mm	**Belvidere Oasis both lanes,** [gas] Mobil/7-11/dsl/24hr [food] Food Court, McDonald's, Panda Express, Sbarro, Starbucks, Subway [other] [phone]
20	Irene Rd
18mm	Kishwaukee River
17mm	I-39 S, US 20, US 51, to Rockford, **S** funpark
15	US 20, State St, **N** [gas] Mobil/dsl, Phillips 66/Subway/dsl [food] Cracker Barrel [lodging] Baymont Inn, Clocktower Resort, Days Inn, **0-2 mi S** [gas] FasFuel/dsl, Mobil/dsl [food] Applebee's, Buffalo Wild Wings, Burger King, Chick-fil-A, Chili's, Chipotle Mexican, City Buffet, Coldstone, Culver's, Denny's, Dos Reales, Fiesta Cancun, Five Guys, Gerry's Pizza, Giovanni's Rest., Hoffman House Rest., Hooters, IHOP, Jason's Deli, Jersey Mike's, Jimmy John's, KFC/LJ Silver, Lino's Italian, LoneStar Steaks, Longhorn Steaks, Machine Shed Rest, McDonald's, Noodles&-Co, Old Chicago Grill, Olive Garden, Outback Steaks, Panda Express, Panera Bread, Panino's Drive-Thru, Perkins, Pizza Hut/Taco Bell, PotBelly, Red Lobster, Red Robin, Ruby Tuesday, Starbucks, Steak'n Shake, Stone Eagle Tavern, Subway, ThunderBay Grille, TX Roadhouse, Wendy's [lodging] Candlewood Suites, Comfort Inn, Courtyard, Extended Stay America, Fairfield Inn, Hampton Inn, Hilton Garden, Holiday Inn, Motel 6, Quality Suites, Radisson, Red Roof Inn, Residence Inn, Sleep Inn, Staybridge Suites, Super 8 [other] [H], $Tree, Advance Parts, Aldi Foods, AT&T, Best Buy, BigLots, Burlington Coats, Cadillac, Chrysler/Dodge/Jeep, Dick's, Discount Tire, GNC, Gordman's, Hobby Lobby, Home Depot, Hyundai, JoAnn Fabrics, Kohl's, Lowe's, Marshall's, Mazda, Michael's, Nissan, Old Navy, Old Time Pottery, PetCo, Petsmart, Ross, Sam's Club/gas, Schnuck's Foods, Subaru, Target, Tuesday Morning, Valli Foods, Verizon, Walgreens, Walmart/McDonald's
12	E Riverside Blvd, Loves Park, **0-2 mi S** [gas] BP, Mobil/dsl, Phillips 66/dsl, Road Ranger/Pilot/Subway/dsl, Shell/dsl [food] 2nd Cousin's Grill, Arby's, BeefARoo, Ciaobella, Culver's, DQ, Greenfire

ROCKFORD

IL

INTERSTATE 90 Cont'd

12	Continued Rest., India House, Japanese Express, KFC, McDonald's, RBI Rest., Rosatti's Pizza, Sam's Ristorante, Singapore Grill, Subway, Taco Bell, Wendy's Holiday Inn Express, Quality Inn Audi/Honda/Mercedes, Autowerks, Farm&Fleet, funpark, Lexus, to Rock Cut SP, Toyota, Tuffy Auto, Walgreens
8	Il 173, **S** to Rock Cut SP
3.5mm	**S Beloit Toll Plaza**
3	Rockton Rd, **S** Loves/Hardee's/dsl/scales/24hr
1.5mm	**Welcome Ctr/ eb, full facilities, info, litter barrels, petwalk, , , playground, RV dump**
1	US 51 N, IL 75 W, S Beloit, **N** Road Ranger/McDonald's/dsl, **S** FLYING J/Denny's/dsl/scales/24hr, Road Ranger/Pilot/Subway/dsl/E85/scales/24hr Best Western, Tollway Inn Finnegan's RV Ctr
0mm	Illinois/Wisconsin state line

INTERSTATE 94

Exit #	Services
77mm	Illinois/Indiana state line
I-94 and I-80 run together 3 mi. See I-80, exit 161.	
74[160]b	I-80/I-294 W
74a	IL 394 S, to Danville
73b a	US 6,159th St, **N** Loves/Hardee's/dsl/scales/24hr, Mobil Applebee's, Buffalo Wild Wings, Continental Rest., Denny's, Outback Steaks, Panda Express, Sonic, Starbucks, Taco Bell, Tilly's, White Castle BigLots, Cadillac, Goodyear Commercial Tire, Hyundai, JC Penney, Kia, Lincoln, Macy's, Marshall's, Nissan, PetCo, Ross, Sam's Club, Toyota, USPO, vet, **S** BP, Marathon Checkers, Harold's Chicken, Little Caesar's, McDonald's, Papa John's, Popeye's, Shark's, Subway Holland Inn Aldi Foods, Family$, Jewel-Osco, O'Reilly Parts, Stanfa Tire/repair
71b a	Sibley Blvd, **N** BP/dsl, Citgo, Mobil/dsl McDonald's, Nick's Gyros, Popeye's, Shark's, Subway Baymont Inn $Tree, Family$, Pete's Mkt, **S** Circle K/Checkers/dsl, Marathon/dsl, Shell Baskin-Robbins/Dunkin Donuts, Burger King, KFC, Taco Bell, Wendy's, White Castle Best Motel $General, Advance Parts, AutoZone, Family$, Food-4Less/gas, Menards, Walgreens
70b a	Dolton
69	Beaubien Woods (from eb), Beaubien Woods Forest Preserve
68b a	130th St
66b	115th St, **S** McDonald's
66a	111th Ave, **S** Citgo/dsl, Shell H, $Tree, Firestone/auto, Ross, Walmart
65	103rd Ave, Stony Island Ave
63	I-57 S (exits left from wb)
62	Wentworth Ave (from eb), **N** Citgo Burger King, KFC, **S** McDonald's
61b	87th St, **N** BP, Shell/dsl Burger King, McDonald's, **S** Starbucks, Subway $Tree, AutoZone, Burlington Coats, Food4Less, Home Depot, Jewel-Osco, Marshall's, O'Reilly Parts, Staples, Verizon
61a	83rd St (from eb), **N** Shell Subway st police
60c	79th St, **N** Mobil, Shell Walgreens, **S** Falcon Church's, Subway
60b	76th St, **N** BP, Mobil, Shell Walgreens, **S** KFC, Popeye's
60a	75th St (from eb), **N** BP, Shell Aldi Foods, **S** KFC, Popeye's
59c	71st St, **N** BP, **S** McDonald's
59a	I-90 E, to Indiana Toll Rd
58b	63rd St (from eb), **N** BP, **S** Mobil
58a	I-94 divides into local and express, 59th St, **S** Mobil
57b	Garfield Blvd, **N** Checker's Family$, Walgreens, Citgo, Mobil, Shell/24hr Wendy's
57a	51st St
56b	47th St (from eb)
56a	43rd St, **S** BP/Subway/dsl, Citgo/dsl
55b	Pershing Rd
55a	35th St, **S** to New Comiskey Park
54	31st St
53c	I-55, Stevenson Pkwy, N to downtown, Lakeshore Dr
53b	I-55, Stevenson Pkwy, S to St Louis
52c	18th St (from eb), **N** Whole Foods
52b	Roosevelt Rd, Taylor St (from wb), **N** Citgo Chipotle Best Buy, Home Depot, Walgreens, Whole Foods Mkt
52a	Taylor St, Roosevelt Rd (from eb), **N** Citgo
51h-i	I-290 W, to W Suburbs
51g	E Jackson Blvd, downtown
51f	W Adams St, downtown
51e	Monroe St (from eb), downtown, **S** Crowne Plaza Walgreens, Whole Foods
51d	Madison St (from eb), **S** Crowne Plaza Walgreen Whole Foods, downtown
51c	E Washington Blvd, downtown
51b	W Randolph St, downtown
51a	Lake St (from wb)
50b	E Ohio St, **S** Marathon, downtown
50a	Ogden Ave
49b a	Augusta Blvd, Division St, **N** Acura, Lexus, Mercede **S** BP, Shell
48b	IL 64, North Ave, **N** BP, **S** Mercedes
48a	Armitage Ave, **N** Best Buy, Kohl's, Lexus, **S** She Jaguar, Land Rover, Volvo
47c b	Damen Ave, **N** car/vanwash
47a	Western Ave, Fullerton Ave, **N** Mobil Burger Kin Dunkin Donuts, Popeye's, Starbucks, Subway Costco/ga Home Depot, Jo-Ann Fabrics, Pepboys, Petsmart, Staples, Target, **S** Marathon
46b a	Diversey Ave, California Ave, **S** IHOP/24hr, Popeye's Walgreens
45c	Belmont Ave
45b	Kimball Ave, **N** Marathon/dsl CVS Drug, Home Depo **S** Shell Dunkin Donuts, Subway Aldi Foods, Best Buy, Walgreens
45a	Addison St
44b	Pulaski Ave, Irving Park Rd, **N** Mobil/Subway, Shell/dsl
44a	IL 19, Keeler Ave, Irving Park Rd, **N** Mobil/Subway, Shell dsl to Wrigley Field
43c	Montrose Ave
43b	I-90 W
43a	Wilson Ave
42	W Foster Ave (from wb), **S** Marathon/service, Mob Subway
41mm	Chicago River, N Branch
41c	IL 50 S, to Cicero, to I-90 W
41b a	US 14, Peterson Ave, **N** Whole Foods Mkt
39b a	Touhy Ave, **N** BP/dsl, Shell/Circle K Cassidy Tire, Toyota, **S** BP, Citgo, Mobil, Shell Bar Louie's, Baskin-Robbins/Dunkin Donuts, Brickhouse Rest., Buffalo Wild Wing Burger King, Chili's, Chipotle Mexican, ChuckeCheese, Corn

CHICAGO AREA

INTERSTATE 94 Cont'd

39b a	Continued Bakery Cafe, Jersey Mike's, Jimmy John's, McDonald's, Noodles&Co, Outback Steaks, Panda Express, Penn Sta Subs, Red Robin, Sander's Rest., Shallot's Bistro, Starbucks, Subway, Tilted Kilt Holiday Inn Barnes&Noble, Best Buy, Dick's, Fresh Farms Mkt, GNC, Jewel-Osco, Michael's, Nissan, PepBoys, Petsmart, Ross, Tuesday Morning, vet, Walgreens, Walmart
37b a	IL 58, Dempster St, **N** Shell Panda Express, Subway, **S** BP/dsl, Shell Pizza Hut Midas
35	Old Orchard Rd, **N** BP, Shell Bloomingdale's, Buffalo Wild Wings, CA Pizza Kitchen, CheeseCake Factory, McCormick&Schmick's Rest H, Lord&Taylor, Macy's, Nissan, Nordstrom's, **S** Ruby Tuesday Extended Stay America, Hampton Inn, Residence Inn
34c b	E Lake Ave, **N** BP/dsl Corner Bakery Cafe, Five Guys, Panda Express, Starbucks, Subway Fresh Mkt Foods, GNC, Walgreens, **S** Shell DQ, Jimmy John's, Starbucks auto repair
34a	US 41 S, Skokie Rd (from eb)
33b a	Willow Rd, **S** Shell Dunkin Donuts, Starbucks Mariano's Mkt, USPO, Walgreens
31	E Tower Rd, **S** BMW, Carmax, Infiniti, Land Rover, Mercedes, Toyota, vet, Volvo
30b a	Dundee Rd (from wb, no EZ return), **S** Citgo/dsl Barnaby's Rest., Chipotle, Morton's Steaks, Noodles&Co, Panera Bread, Potbelly, Roti Mediterranean, Ruth's Chris Steaks, Starbucks Renaissance Mariano's Mkt
29	US 41, to Waukegan, to Tri-state tollway
28	IL 43, Waukegan Rd (from eb), **N** BP, Shell Dunkin Donuts/Baskin Robbins, Mod Pizza, Noodles&Co, Starbucks Courtyard, Embassy Suites, Red Roof Inn Hobby Lobby, Home Depot, Jewel-Osco, Just Tires
25	I-294 S, Lake-Cook Rd (from sb), **E** Embassy Suites, Hyatt, **W** J Alexander's Rest.
24	Deerfield Rd (from nb), **W** Mobil Marriott Suites
21	IL 22, Half Day Rd, **E** Leaf Cafe La Quinta, **W** Homewood Suites
19	IL 60, Town Line Rd, **E** H, **W** Hilton Garden, Residence Inn Costco/gas
18mm	**Lake Forest Oasis both lanes,** Mobil/7-11/dsl KFC/Taco Bell, McDonald's, Panda Express, Starbucks, Subway info
16mm	IL 176, Rockland Rd (no nb re-entry), **E** Harley-Davidson, to Lamb's Farm
14mm	IL 137, Buckley Rd, **E** Chicago Med School, to VA H
11mm	IL 120 E, Belvidere Rd (no nb re-entry), **E** H
10mm	IL 21, Milwaukee Ave (from eb, no eb re-entry), **E** H, Six Flags
8mm	IL 132, Grand Ave, **E** Speedway/dsl Baskin-Robbins/Dunkin Donuts, Burger King, ChuckeCheese, Cracker Barrel, Cravings Red Hots, Culver's, Golden Corral, Ichibahn, IHOP, Jimmy John's, Joe's Crabshack, KFC/LJ Silver, Mama K's Zpizza, McDonald's, Oberweiss, Old Chicago Red Hots, Olive Garden, Outback Steaks, Rosati's Pizza, Starbucks, Subway Baymont Inn, Country Inn&Suites, Extended Stay America, Hampton Inn, Key Lime Cove Resort, La Quinta, Super 8 Six Flags Park, **0-2 mi W** Shell/Circle K Bakers Square, Boston Mkt, Buffalo Wild Wings, Chili's, Chipotle Mexican, Denny's, Five Guys, Giordano's Pizza, Jersey Mike's Subs, Jimano's Pizza, LoneStar Steaks, McDonald's, Noodles&Co, Panda Express, Panera Bread, Penn Sta Subs, Pizza Hut, Portillo's, Potbelly's, Red Lobster, Red Robin, Ruby Tuesday, Starbucks, Steak'n Shake,

GURNEE

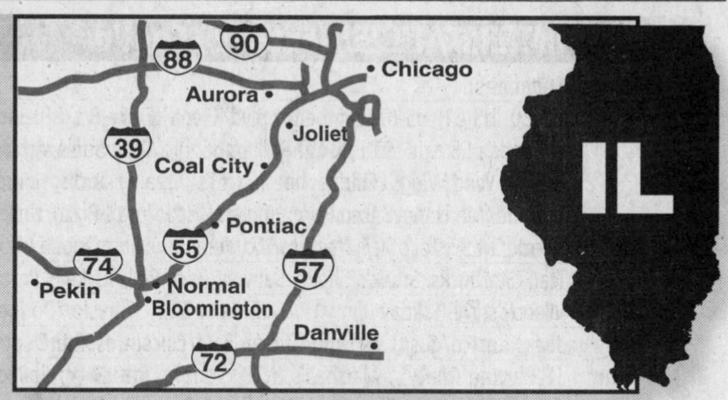

8mm	Continued Taco Bell, TGIFriday's, Uno Grill, Wendy's, White Castle Comfort Inn, Fairfield Inn, Holiday Inn $Tree, AT&T, AutoZone, Bass Pro Shops, Best Buy, Buick/GMC, Chrysler/Dodge/Jeep, Goodyear, Gurnee Mills Outlet Mall/famous brands, Home Depot, Honda, Hyundai, Jewel-Osco, Kohl's, Macy's, Mariano's Mkt, Marshall's, Menards, Michael's, Old Navy, Petsmart, Ross, Sam's Club, Target, TJ Maxx, Tuesday Morning, Verizon, VW, Walgreens, Walmart
5mm	**Waukegan toll plaza**
2	IL 173 (from nb, no return), Rosecrans Ave, **E** to IL Beach SP
1b	US 41 S, to Waukegan (from sb)
1a	Russell Rd, **E** I-94 RV Ctr, **W** Citgo/dsl/scales, TA/Country Pride/dsl/scales/24hr/@ Peterbilt
0mm	Illinois/Wisconsin state line

INTERSTATE 255 (St Louis)

Exit #	Services
I-255 begins/ends on I-270, exit 7.	
30	I-270, W to Kansas City, E to Indianapolis
29	IL 162, to Glen Carbon, to Pontoon Beach, Granite City
26	Horseshoe Lake Rd, **E** st police
25b a	I-55/I-70, W to St Louis, E to Chicago, Indianapolis
24	Collinsville Rd, **E** Jack-in-the-Box Shop'n Save, **W** Fairmount Racetrack
20	I-64, US 50, W to St Louis, E to Louisville. **Services 1 mi E off I-64, exit 9.**
19	State St, E St Louis, **E** Western Inn, **W** Holten SP
17b a	IL 15, E St Louis, to Belleville, Centreville, **E** FLYING J/Denny's/dsl/scales/24hr, **W** Phillips 66 auto repair
15	Mousette Lane, **E** H, **W** Peterbilt
13	IL 157, to Cahokia, **E** Phillips 66, **W** BP, MotoMart Capt D's, China Express, Classic K Burgers, Domino's, Hardee's, KFC, Little Caesar's, McDonald's, Pizza Hut, Rally's, Subway, Taco Bell, White Castle Comfort Inn $General, $Tree, Advance Parts, Aldi Foods, AutoZone, Dobb's Tires, Family$, Schnuck's, Shop'n Save Foods, Walgreens, Walmart
10	IL 3 N, to Cahokia, E St Louis, **W** Fuelmart/Subway/dsl
9	to Dupo, **W** Hucks
6	IL 3 S, to Columbia (exits left from sb), **E** Phillips 66, Shell/dsl/24hr Hampton Inn (2mi) Chevrolet
4mm	Missouri/Illinois state line, Mississippi River
3	Koch Rd
2	MO 231, Telegraph Rd, **N** Conoco, Shell/Circle K Great Wall, Little Caesar's, McDonald's, Pizza Hut/Taco Bell, Steak'n Shake, Waffle House Advance Parts, AT&T, Jefferson Barracks Nat Cem, Petco, SaveALot, Walmart/Subway, **S** Phillips 66/dsl, QT, Shell/Circle K/dsl China Wok, DQ, Dunkin Donuts Verizon

IL

INTERSTATE 255 (St Louis) Cont'd

Exit #	Services
1d c	US 50, US 61, US 67, Lindbergh Blvd, Lemay Ferry Rd, accesses same as I-55 exit 197 E, **N** Phillips 66 Applebee's, Arby's, Buffalo Wild Wings, ChuckeCheese, CiCi's Pizza, Dillard's, Hometown Buffet, HoneyBaked Ham, Hooters, IHOP, Imo's Pizza, Krispy Kreme, McAlister's Deli, Noodles&Co, Penn Sta Subs, Qdoba Mexican, Starbucks, Steak'n Shake, Subway, Taco Bell, Tucker's Place, Wendy's Holiday Inn AT&T, Best Buy, Chrysler/Dodge/Jeep, Costco/gas, CVS Drug, Dick's, Ford/Lincoln, Home Depot, JC Penney, Macy's, Marshall's, NTB, Verizon, vet, **S** Phillips 66 Jack-in-the-Box, Jimmy John's, McDonald's, Rich & Charlie's Italian, White Castle $General, $Tree, BigLots, Firestone, Old Navy, Petsmart, Sam's Club/gas, Walgreens
1b a	I-55 S to Memphis, N to St Louis.
I-255 begins/ends on I-55, exit 196.	

INTERSTATE 270

See Missouri Interstate 270 (St Louis)

INTERSTATE 294 (Chicago)

CHICAGO AREA

Exit #	Services
I-294 begins/ends on I-94, exit 71.	
I-294 & I-80 run together 5 mi. See I-80, exits 155-160.	
5mm	I-80 W, access to I-57
5.5mm	167th St, **toll booth,**
6mm	US 6, 159th St, **E** Citgo, Exxon/dsl, Marathon, Mobil/dsl, Shell/dsl $Tree, AutoZone, Family$, **W** BP/dsl Baskin-Robbins/Dunkin Donuts, Burger King, McDonald's, Popeye's, Subway, Taco Bell, White Castle Chicago Inn&Suites $Tree, AutoZone, U-Haul, Walgreens
11mm	Cal Sag Channel
12mm	IL 50, Cicero Ave, **E** BP, Shell/dsl Dunkin Donuts, Subway, White Castle Home Depot, O'Reilly Parts, **W** BP, Shell/dsl Applebee's, Boston Mkt, Chipotle, Culver's, IHOP, Lone Star Steaks, Panda Express, Pizza Hut, Popeye's, Portillo's Dogs, Potbelly, Starbucks, Subway Baymont Inn, Days Inn, DoubleTree, Holiday Inn Express AT&T, Best Buy, GNC, JoAnn, Kohl's, NTB, PepBoys, Petsmart, Ross, Target, TJ Maxx, Ultra Foods, Walgreens, Walmart/Subway
18mm	US 12/20, 95th St, **E** Marathon Buffalo Wild Wings, Chick-fil-A, Starbucks, TX Corral H, CarMax, Discount Tire, Mazda, **W** 7-11, BP, Shell, Speedway/dsl Arby's, Baskin-Robbins, Burger King, Denny's, Dunkin Donuts, Jimmy John's, Les Bros Rest., McDonald's, Papa John's, Prime Time Rest., Subway, Taco Bell, The Pit Ribhouse, Wendy's Motel 6 $Tree, AutoZone, Jewel-Osco, Walgreens
20mm	**toll booth,**
22mm	75th St, Willow Springs Rd
23mm	I-55, Wolf Rd, to Hawthorne Park
25mm	**Hinsdale Oasis both lanes,** Mobil/7-11/dsl KFC/Taco Bell, McDonald's, McDonald's, Panda Express, Sbarro, Subway
28mm	US 34, Ogden Ave, **E** zoo, **W** BP, Shell/deli Dunkin Donuts, McDonald's, Starbucks H, Ferrari/Maserati, Firestone/auto, LandRover, Whole Foods Mkt
28.5mm	Cermak Rd (from sb, no return)
29mm	**I-88 tollway**
30mm	**toll booth,**
31mm	IL 38, Roosevelt Rd (no EZ nb return), **E** Shell/dsl Hillside Manor Motel vet
32mm	I-290 W, to Rockford (from nb)
34mm	I-290 (from sb), to Rockford
38mm	**O'Hare Oasis both lanes,** Mobil/7-11/dsl KFC, McDonald's, Panda Express, Sbarro, Starbucks, Subway, Taco Bell, TCBY
39mm	IL 19 W (from sb), Irving Park Rd, **E** Citgo, Marathon/dsl, Shell/dsl Dunkin Donuts, McDonald's, Starbucks, Subway, Wendy's Comfort Suites 7-11, Aldi Foods, Walgreens, **W** BP/Subway/desk Mirage Rest. Candlewood Suites, Hampton Inn, Sheraton
40mm	I-190 W, **E** Mobil Basil's Kitchen, McDonald's, Starbucks Courtyard, Doubletree, Embassy Suites, Hampton Inn, Hilton, Hilton Garden, Holiday Inn, Hyatt, Hyatt Regency, Marriott, Rosemont Suites, Westin
41mm	**toll booth,**
42mm	Touhy Ave, **W** Mobil/service Tiffany's Rest. Comfort Inn, Radisson
43mm	Des Plaines River
44mm	Dempster St (from nb, no return), **E** Wendy's H, CVS Drug, **W** Dunkin Donuts, Subway
46mm	IL 58, Golf Rd, **E** Mobil/Dunkin Donuts/dsl, Shell/Subway/dsl Omega Rest. Wyndham CVS Drug, Golf Mill Mall, Meijer, Meineke, Target, **W** H
49mm	Willow Rd, **W** BP/Subway/dsl Chipotle, Jimmy John's, McDonald's, Pie Five Pizza, Starbucks, TGIFriday's Best Western, Country Inn Suites, Courtyard, Motel 6 CVS Drug, Mariano's Mkt
53mm	Lake Cook Rd (no nb re-entry), **E** Embassy Suites, Hyatt, **W** J Alexander's
I-294 begins/ends on I-94.	

INTERSTATE 355 (Illinois)

Exit #	Services
31mm	**I-355 begins/end on I-290 .**
30	US 20, W Lake St, **E** Marathon, Mobil/dsl Baskin-Robbins/Dunkin Donuts, Burger King, Chipotle, Culver's, Famous Dave's BBQ, Firehouse Subs, IHOP, Jimmy John's, La Hacienda Mexican, Panda Express, Panera Bread, Ristorante de Marco's, Starbucks Hampton Inn Midas, Sam's Club/gas, Verizon, Walmart/Subway, **W** Shell Dave&Buster's, Venuti's Rest
29	Army Trail Rd, **E** Mobil/dsl, Shell/dsl Serino's Deli, **W** BP/dsl, Mobil/dsl Hilton Garden
27	IL 64, E North Ave, **E** BP/Subway/dsl, Burger King, Comfort Suites, Fairfield Inn, McDonald's, Shell/Circle K, Thornton's/dsl Jimmy John's, **W** Speedway/dsl Ramada Art's RV Ctr, Suburban Tire/auto
24	Roosevelt, **E** Mobil Dunkin Donuts, Subway Crowne Plaza Cadillac, Mariano's Mkt, Toyota, **W** Jimmy John's NAPA, Pete's Mkt
22	IL 56, Butterfield Rd, **E** Arby's, Brick House Rest., Burger King, Chama Gaucha Brazilian, Chipotle Mexican, Fuddrucker's, Hooters, Melting Pot, Olive Garden, Panera Bread, Portillo's, Red Lobster, Ruby Tuesday, Starbucks, Subway, Zoup! Comfort Inn, Extended Stay America, Holiday Inn Express, Marriott, Red Roof Inn $Tree, Best Buy, Kohl's, Michael's, Petsmart, Ross, Verizon, **W** Carlucci Italian DoubleTree Suites 7-11, Home Depot
20mm	I-88 E/I-355 run together
19	US 34, Ogden Ave, **E** Shell Culver's, Jimmy John's, McDonald's InTown Suites AT&T, Buick/GMC, Chrysler/Dodge/Jeep, Ford, **W** Baskin-Robbins/Dunkin Donuts Extended Stay America Chevrolet, Speedway/dsl, vet
18	Maple Ave, **1 mi W** BP, Mobil, Shell/Circle K KFC/Taco Bell, McDonald's Jewel Osco, Walgreens

INTERSTATE 355 (Illinois) Cont'd

Exit #	Services
16	63rd St, Hobson Rd, **E** [gas] Mobil/dsl, Thornton's/McDonald's/dsl [food] Steven's Rest, Subway [other] AutoZone, Familia Fresh Mkt, GNC, Target, Walgreens
15	W 75th St, **E** [gas] Mobil [food] Arby's, Bakers Square Rest [other] Hobby Lobby, Home Depot, Sam's Club/gas, **W** [gas] Marathon [food] Dunkin-Donuts, El Burro Loco, McDonald's, Pizza Italiano [other] Jewel-Osco
14	87th St, Baughton Rd, **E** [gas] BP, Shell [food] Al's Pizza, Dunkin-Donuts, McDonald's, Oberweiss, Subway, Wendy's [other] Costco/gas, CVS Drug, **W** [gas] Mobil [food] Bar Louie, Buffalo Wild Wings, Famous Dave's BBQ, Five Guys, IHOP, Jimmy John's, Longhorn Steaks, Panda Express, Panera Bread, Potbelly, Starbucks, Ted's MT Grill [lodging] ALoft [other] AT&T, Barnes&Noble, Bass Pro Shops, Discount Tire, IKEA, Macy's, Meijer/gas, Verizon, Walgreens
12	I-55
8	127th St, **E** [food] Burger King, Jimmy John's, KFC, McDonald's, Starbucks, Subway, Taco Bell [other] Aldi Foods, AT&T, Firestone/auto, Jewel-Osco, Jiffy Lube, Pepper's Autocare, USPO, Verizon, Walgreens
6	IL 171, Archer Ave, 143rd St, **E** [other] Kohl's, Target, vet
4	159th Ave, IL 7, Orland Park, Homer Glen, **E** [gas] Citgo/dsl, **W** [H] URGENT CARE
3mm	**toll booth both directions**
1	US 6, **E** [gas] Rte 6 Food'n Fuel/Dunkin Donuts/dsl, **W** [other] [H]
0mm	I-80 E, W, **I-355 begins/ends on I-80 exit 140.**

PEORIA

INTERSTATE 474 (Peoria)

Exit #	Services
15	I-74, E to Bloomington, W to Peoria
9	IL 29, E Peoria, to Pekin, **N** [gas] Shell/Arby's/dsl, Thornton's [food] DQ, Driftwood Pizza, Taco John's [other] $General, Riverboat Casino (6mi), **S** [gas] BP/Subway/dsl, Casey's [food] Denny's, Domino's, Lian Wang, McDonald's, Rosati's Pizza [other] Chrysler/Dodge/Jeep, Toyota
8mm	Illinois River
6b a	US 24, Adams St, Bartonville, **S** [gas] BP/dsl, Mobil/dsl [food] Hardee's, KFC, McDonald's, Tyroni's Café
5	Airport Rd, **S** [gas] Mobil/e85/dsl [other] [airport]
3a	to IL 116, Farmington, **S** [other] Wildlife Prairie Park
0b a	I-74, W to Moline, E to Peoria.
I-474 begins/ends on I-74, exit 87.	

INDIANA

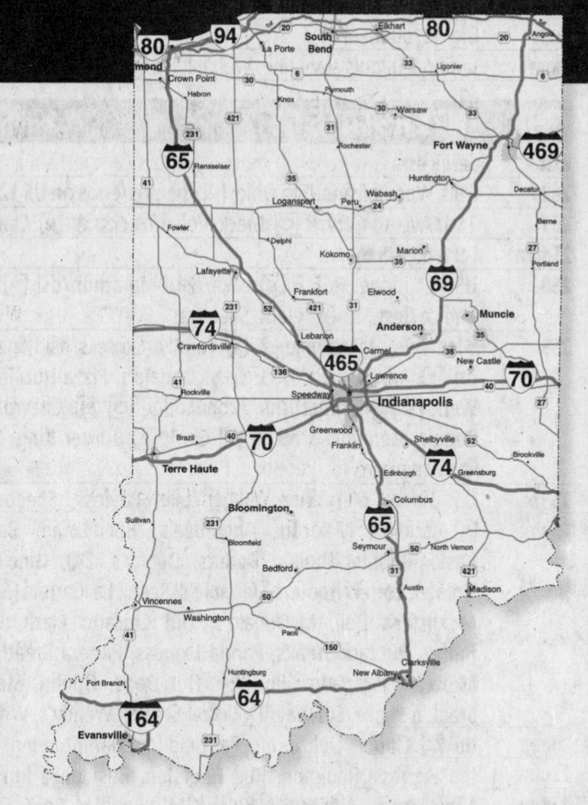

INTERSTATE 64

Exit #	Services
124mm	Indiana/Kentucky state line, Ohio River
123	IN 62 E, New Albany, **N** [gas] Marathon/dsl, Shell/Circle K [food] DQ [other] [H], Family$, Firestone/auto, Save-A-Lot, **S** [gas] Shell/Circle K, Valero [food] Daisy's Cafeteria, Subway, Waffle House [lodging] Best Western, Holiday Inn Express
121	I-265 E, to I-65 (exits left from eb), **N** access to [H]
119	US 150 W, to Greenville, **N** [gas] Marathon [food] Bean St Cafe, Bearno's Buffet, Beef O'Brady's, Chillburger, China Cafe, Domino's, DQ, El Nopal, McDonald's, Papa John's, Sam's Family Rest., Subway, Taco Bell, Tumbleweed SW Grill [other] AutoZone, JayC Foods, Rite Aid, URGENT CARE, Walgreens
118	IN 62, IN 64W, to Georgetown, **N** [gas] Marathon/dsl/24hr, Shell/Circle K [food] Korner Kitchen, McDonald's [lodging] Red Roof Inn [other] CashSaver Foods, Mr. Hardware, **S** [gas] Marathon/dsl
115mm	**Welcome Ctr wb, full [handicapped] facilities, litter barrels, [phone], [picnic], vending**
113	to Lanesville
105	IN 135, to Corydon, **N** [gas] Marathon/dsl, Shell [food] Big Boy [lodging] Comfort Inn, **S** [gas] 5 Star, BP/dsl [food] Alberto's Italian, Arby's, Beef O'Brady's, Burger King, Cracker Barrel, Culver's, Domino's, DQ, El Nopal Mexican, Hong Kong Buffet, Jimmy John's, KFC, Lee's Chicken, LJ Silver, McDonald's, O'Charley's, Papa John's, Papa Murphy's, Pizza Hut, Ryan's, Subway, Taco Bell, Waffle House, Wendy's, White Castle [lodging] Baymont Inn, Hampton Inn, Holiday Inn Express, Super 8 [other] [H], $Tree, Advance Parts, AT&T, AutoZone, Big O Tire, Buick/Chevrolet, Chrysler/Dodge/Jeep, CVS Drug, Family$, Ford, Verizon, Walgreens, Walmart/Subway
100mm	Blue River
97mm	**parking area both lanes**
92	IN 66, Carefree, **N** [other] Marengo Caves, **S** [gas] Marathon/dsl/rest./24hr, Pilot/Subway/dsl/scales/24hr [food] Big Dadd's Rest., Country Style Rest. [lodging] Red Carpet Inn [other] Carefree Truckwash, Harrison Crawford SF, repair, to Wyandotte Caves
88mm	Hoosier Nat Forest eastern boundary
86	IN 37, to Sulphur, **N** to Patoka Lake, **S** food, gas, scenic route
79	IN 37, to Tell City, St Croix, **S** [gas] Marathon/Subshop/pizza/dsl [other] to Hoosier NF, to OH River Br
76mm	Anderson River
72	IN 145, to Birdseye, **N** [other] to Patoka Lake, **S** [other] St Meinrad Coll, winery (2mi), gas
63	IN 162, to Ferdinand, **N** [gas] Sunoco/dsl [food] China Garden, McDonald's, Subway, Taco Bell, Wendy's [lodging] Comfort Inn, Red Roof Inn [other] CVS Drug, Ferdinand SF, **S** [other] Lake Rudolph RV Camping (8mi)

CORYDON

INTERSTATE 64 Cont'd

Exit #	Services
58mm	**both lanes, full facilities, info, litter barrels, vending**
57	US 231, to Dale, Huntingburg, N, S Chuckles/dsl Denny's, Wendy's Baymont Inn, Motel 6 Lincoln Boyhood Home, Lincoln SP
54	IN 161, to Holland,Tennyson
39	IN 61, Lynnville, N Marathon Monterrey Mexican USPO
32mm	N Wabash & Erie Canal
29b a	I-69 N, IN 57 N&S, to Evansville
25b a	US 41, to Evansville, N FLYING J/Denny's/dsl/scales/24hr, Loves/Wendy's/dsl/24hr, Pilot/Subway/Taco Bell/dsl/24hr Baymont Inn Blue Beacon, truck repair/lube, S Marathon/dsl Arby's, Denny's, McDonald's, Stoll's Amish Rest. Holiday Inn Express, Quality Inn, Red Roof Inn, Super 8 st police, to U S IN
18	IN 65, to Cynthiana, S Motomart/dsl/24hr
12	IN 165, Poseyville, S CountryMark/Subway/dsl Red Wagon Rest. NAPA, New Harmonie Hist Area/SP
7mm	**Black River Welcome Ctr eb, full facilities, litter barrels, petwalk,**
5mm	Black River
4	IN 69 S, New Harmony, Griffin, **1 mi N** USPO, **S** Harmony St Park
2mm	Big Bayou River
0mm	Indiana/Illinois state line, Wabash River

INTERSTATE 65

Exit #	Services
262	I-90, W to Chicago, E to Ohio, **I-65 begins/ends on US 12, US 20.**
261	15th Ave, to Gary, E Mack/Volvo Trucks, W Clark
259b a	I-94/80, US 6W
258	US 6, Ridge Rd, E Luke/dsl, Marathon/dsl Diner's Choice Rest., W Clark, Save Gas
255	61st Ave, Merrillville, E Family Express/dsl, Speedway/dsl Arby's, Cracker Barrel, McDonald's, Pizza Hut/Taco Bell, Wendy's Comfort Inn, EconoLodge H, Chevrolet, I-65 Repair, Menards, **1 mi W** Clark Burger King, Subway Walgreens
253b	US 30 W, Merrillville, W Luke, Payless, Speedway/dsl Abuelo's Mexican, Applebee's, Bar Louie, Barnelli's, Baskin-Robbins/Dunkin Donuts, Denny's, DQ, Gino's Rest., Golden Corral, Hooters, Johnnie's Rest., La Carreta Mexican, McAlister's Deli, McDonald's, Old Chicago Pizza, Oriental Buffet, Outback Steaks, Panda Express, Panera Bread, Pepe's Mexican, Pizza Hut, Portillo's Hot Dogs, Qdoba, Starbucks, Steak'n Shake, Subway, TX Corral Steaks, Wendy's, White Castle Clarion, Deluxe Inn, Fairfield Inn, Hampton Inn, Holiday Inn Express, Radisson, Red Roof Inn, Residence Inn H, $Tree, Acura, Aldi Foods, Buick/GMC, Cadillac, CarX, Chrysler/Dodge/Jeep, CVS Drug, Discount Tire, Fanny May Candies, Ford/Lincoln, Hyundai, Mazda, Meijer/dsl, Midas, NTB, Old Time Pottery, Staples, Subaru, U-Haul, Verizon, Walgreens
253a	US 30 E, E BP/Luke/dsl, Speedway/dsl Bakers Square, BC Osaka, Bob Evans, Buffalo Wild Wings, Chick-fil-A, Chili's, Chipotle Mexican, ChuckeCheese, Culver's, Firehouse Subs, IHOP, Jimmy John's, Joe's Crabshack, KFC/LJ Silver, Longhorn Steaks, McDonald's, Olive Garden, Popeye's, Potbelly, Red Lobster, Red Robin, Sheffield's Rest., Starbucks, Starbucks (2), Taco Bell, TGIFriday's, Wendy's Best Value Inn, Best Western, Candlewood Suites, Comfort Suites, Country Inn&Suites, Extended
253a	Continued Stay America, Hilton Garden, La Quinta, Motel 6, Quality Inn Staybridge Suites, Super 8 AT&T, Audi/VW, AutoZone, Best Buy, BigLots, Carmax, Costco/gas, Dick's, Firestone/auto, Hobby Lobby, Home Depot, Honda, JC Penney, Jo-Ann, Kia, Kohl's, Lowe's, Macy's, Michael's, Nissan, Office Depot, Old Navy, Pet Co, Petsmart, Ross, Sam's Club/gas, Target, Tire Barn, TJ Maxx, Toyota, Tuesday Morning, vet, Walmart/McDonald's
249	109th Ave, W Speedway/dsl China Garden, Dunkin Donuts, Golden Apple Rest., Jimmy John's, La Quesadilla, Rosati's Pizza $Tree, Aldi, GNC, Verizon, Walgreens
247	US 231, Crown Point, E Korean/Vietnam Vet Mem, W Family Express H
241mm	**weigh sta sb**
240	IN 2, Lowell, E FLYING J/Denny's/dsl/24hr/@, Pilot/Wendy's/ dsl/scales/24hr Arby's, McDonald's, Subway Comfort Inn, Super 8 truck repair, truck wash, W st police
234mm	Kankakee River
231mm	**both lanes, full facilities, info, litter barrels, petwalk, vending**
230	IN 10, Roselawn, E Loves/Arby's/dsl/scales/24hr, TA BP/Country Pride/dsl/scales/24hr/@, W Citgo/Subway, Family Express/e85 China Wok, J&J Pizza, Sycamore Drive-In $General, CVS Drug, Fagen Drug, Lake Holiday Camping, Oak Lake Camping, SaveALot, TrueValue
220	IN 14, Winamac, W BP/Subway/dsl, CNG Fair Oaks Farms Store
215	IN 114, Rensselaer, E Family Express/dsl/e85/24hr Arby's, DQ, KFC, McDonald's, Taco Bell Baymont Inn, Comfort Suites, Interstate Motel H, W Marathon/Trail Tree Rest./dsl/24hr Burger King Economy Inn fireworks, tires/repair/towing/24hr
212mm	Iroquois River
205	US 231, Remington, E Crazy D/dsl H, to St Joseph's Co
201	US 24/231, Remington, E Caboose Lake RV Camping, W Family Express/dsl, Petro/Shell/Iron Skillet/dsl/scales/24hr/@, Pilot/Subway/dsl/scales/24hr KFC, McDonald's Sunset Inn, Super 8
196mm	**both lanes, full facilities, info, litter barrels, petwalk, vending**
193	US 231, to Chalmers, E Marathon/DQ
188	IN 18, to Brookston, Fowler, many windmills
178	IN 43, W Lafayette, E Phillips 66/Subway/dsl, Speedway Taco Bell McDonald's, Wendy's EconoLodge museum, st police, to Tippecanoe Bfd, W to Purdue U
176mm	Wabash River
175	IN 25, Lafayette, E BP/dsl, Family Express/dsl/e85 W H
172	IN 26, Lafayette, E Cracker Barrel, DQ, El Rodeo, Fox's Pizza Starbucks, Steak'n Shake, Subway, White Castle Baymont Inn, Candlewood Suites, Comfort Inn, Comfort Suites, Days Inn, La Quinta, Motel 6, TownePlace Suites Meijer/dsl e85, visitor's ctr, W Luke/dsl, Mobil/Circle K/dsl, Speedway/dsl Arby's, Bob Evans, Burger King, Camille's Cafe Cheddar's, Chick-fil-A, Chili's, Chipotle, ChuckeCheese, Coldstone, Culver's, Denny's, Don Pablo, Fazoli's, Firehouse Subs Golden Corral, Grindstone Charlie's, HuHot, IHOP, Jets Pizza Jimmy John's, KFC, Logan's Roadhouse, Longhorn Steaks McAlister's Deli, McDonald's, Moe's SW Grill, Mtn Jack's, Noodles&Co, Olive Garden, Outback Steaks, Pizza Hut, Red Lobster, Sonic, Spageddie's, Starbucks, Steak'n Shake, Subway, Taco Bell, TGIFriday's Courtyard, Doubletree, Eco Lodge

IN

MERRILLVILLE

LAFAYETTE

INTERSTATE 65 Cont'd

172 Continued
Fairfield Inn, Hampton Inn, Holiday Inn Express, Homewood Suites, Knights Inn, Quality Inn, Red Roof Inn, Residence Inn, Super 8 [other] [H], $General, $Tree, Aamco, Chevrolet, CVS Drug, Discount Tire, Fresh Thyme Mkt, Gordman's, Harley Davidson, Hobby Lobby, Home Depot, Hyundai, Lowe's, Nissan, Office Depot, Sam's Club/gas, Target, TJ Maxx, to Purdue U, Toyota, USPO, Verizon, vet, Walgreens, Walmart/Subway

168 IN 38, IN 25 S, Dayton, E [gas] BP/Subway, CNG, Phillips 66/Circle K/dsl

158 IN 28, to Frankfort, E [gas] BP/Subway/dsl [other] Mack/Volvo, 2 mi W [lodging] Lincoln Lodge Motel

150mm [RS] sb, full [handicapped] facilities, info, litter barrels, petwalk, [phone], [picnic], vending

148mm [RS] nb, full [handicapped] facilities, info, litter barrels, petwalk, [phone], [picnic], vending

146 IN 47, Thorntown, W [other] camping

141 US 52 W (exits left from sb), Lafayette Ave, E [other] [H]

LEBANON

140 IN 32, Lebanon, E [gas] BP/repair, Marathon/dsl [food] Denny's, Depot Rest., McDonald's, Stats Grill, White Castle [lodging] Quality Inn [other] [H], AutoZone, Goodyear/auto, Menards, O'Reilly Parts, Pomp's Tires, W [gas] McClure/dsl/e85, Shell [food] Arby's, Flapjacks Pancakes, KFC, Steak'n Shake, Subway, Taco Bell [lodging] Best Value Inn, EconoLodge, Holiday Inn Express, Motel 6 [other] truckwash

139 IN 39, Lebanon, E [gas] Speedway/dsl [food] Penn Sta Subs, Starbucks, Wendy's, W [gas] FLYING J/Huddle House/dsl/LP/scales/24hr [other] Donaldson's Chocolates

138 to US 52, Lebanon, E [gas] BP/dsl

133 IN 267, Whitestown, W [gas] Love's/McDonald's/Subway/dsl/scales/24hr

130 IN 334, Zionsville, E [gas] Marathon/Starbucks/dsl, Shell/Circle K/Subway/dsl [food] Buffalo Wild Wings, Burger King, Cracker Barrel, El Rodeo Mexican, Flapjacks Pancakes, Fox's Pizza, Gandolfo's Deli, McDonald's, Pie Five, Taco Bell, Which Wich? [other] [H], AT&T, CVS Drug, Lowe's, Meijer/dsl, Verizon, vet, W [gas] TA/BP/Popeye's/dsl/scales/24hr/@

129 I-865 E, to I-465 E, US 52 E (from sb)

126mm Fishback Creek

124 71st St, 1 mi E [gas] [food] Starbucks, Steak'n Shake [lodging] Candlewood Suites, Courtyard, Hampton Inn, Hilton Garden, Holiday Inn Express, Residence Inn, Wingate Inn, W [other] Eagle Creek Park

123 I-465 S, S [other] to [airport]

121 Lafayette Rd, E [gas] Speedway (2), Speedway/dsl [lodging] Quality Inn, W [gas] Shell/Circle K [food] Applebee's, Arby's, Church's, Fazoli's, La Bamba Burritos, Wendy's [lodging] Executive Inn [other] [H], $Tree, Aldi Foods, AT&T, Batteries+Bulbs, Best Buy, Discount Tire, Family$, GNC, Hyundai, Kia, Mazda, Nissan, PepBoys, same as 119, SaveALot, Tire Barn, Toyota, vet, Walmart/Subway

119 38th St (no nb return), Dodge, W [gas] Phillips 66, Speedway/dsl [food] KFC, McDonald's, Papa John's, Pizza Hut, Red Lobster, Taco Bell [other] Advance Parts, Aldi Foods, Best Buy, Chevrolet, Hyundai, Meijer/dsl, same as 121, Tires+

117.5mm White River

117 MLK St (from sb), W [gas] Marathon/dsl

116 29th St, 30th St (from nb), W [other] Marian Coll

115 21st St, E [gas] Shell/Circle K [other] [H], W [other] museums, zoo

114 MLK St, West St, downtown

113 US 31, IN 37, Meridian St, to downtown, E [other] [H]

112a I-70 E, to Columbus

111 Market St, Michigan St, Ohio St, E [food] Hardee's [other] museum, W [other] City Market

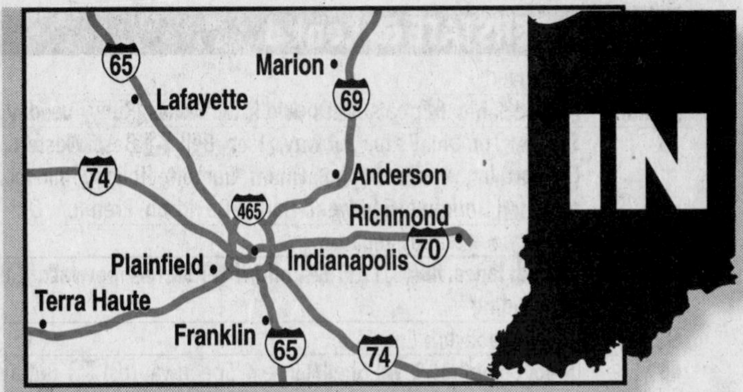

INDIANAPOLIS AREA

110b I-70 W, to St Louis

110a Prospect St, Morris St, East St

109 Raymond St, E [other] [H], W [gas] BP, Speedway/dsl [food] Little Caesar's, White Castle [other] CVS Drug, Family$, Safeway

107 Keystone Ave, E [gas] Phillips 66 [lodging] Best Value Inn [other] [H], W [gas] Phillips 66/dsl, Speedway/dsl, Valero [food] Big Kahuna Pizza, Burger King, Denny's, DQ, McDonald's, Subway, Wendy's [lodging] Comfort Inn [other] $General, U of Indianapolis, Walmart Mkt

106 I-465 and I-74

103 Southport Rd, E [gas] BP/McDonald's, Shell/Circle K [food] Arby's, Chicago Grill, Chick-fil-A, Hardee's, Hotbox Pizza, Jersey Mike's, Jimmy John's, Longhorn Steaks, Mr Wok, Noble Roman's, O'Charley's, Panda Express, Panera Bread, Penn Sta Subs, Pizza Hut, Qdoba, Rally's [other] Aldi Foods, AT&T, Firestone/auto, Harley-Davidson, Home Depot, Kohl's, Meijer/dsl/e85, Menards, Staples, Target, W [gas] Marathon/Circle K, Phillips 66, Speedway/dsl [food] Bob Evans, Burger King, Carrabba's, Cheeseburger Paradise, Cracker Barrel, KFC, McDonald's, Scotty's Brewhouse, Stacked Pickle, Starbucks, Steak'n Shake, Subway, TX Roadhouse, Waffle House, Wendy's [lodging] Baymont Inn, Best Western, Comfort Suites, Country Inn&Suites, Courtyard, Fairfield Inn, Hampton Inn, Motel 6, Super 8 [other] [H]

101 CountyLine Rd, E [food] Candlewood Suites, W [gas] Murphy USA/dsl, Shell/Circle K/dsl [food] Buffalo Wild Wings, Cheddar's, El Meson Mexican, Fireside Rest., Lindo Mexico, Pasquale's Pizza, Popeye's, Primanti Bros, Sonic, Taco Bell, Tokyo Buffet, Zaxby's [lodging] Hilton Garden, Holiday Inn Express, Woodspring Suites [other] [H], Costco/dsl, Kroger/dsl, Verizon, Walmart/Subway

GREENWOOD

99 Greenwood, E [gas] Road Ranger/Pilot/Subway/dsl/scales/24hr, W [gas] Marathon, Shell/Circle K, Sunoco [food] Arby's, Byrd's Cafeteria, China Wok, Denny's, Main St Grille, McDonald's, Puerto Vallarta, Starbucks, Subway, Taco Bell, Waffle House, White Castle [lodging] InTown Suites, La Quinta, Red Carpet Inn, Red Roof Inn [other] [H], Camping World RV Ctr, Sam's Club, vet

97 Worthsville Rd, W [gas] Circle K/dsl

95 Whiteland, E [gas] FLYING J/Denny's/scales/dsl/LP/RV dump/24hr [other] Blue Beacon, SpeedCo, tires, W [gas] Love's/Arby's/dsl/scales/24hr, Pilot/McDonald's/dsl/scales/24hr/@

90 IN 44, Franklin, W [gas] Marathon/Subway/dsl, Shell/Circle K [food] Burger King, McDonald's/RV Parking, Waffle House [lodging] Baymont Inn, Motel 6, Quality Inn [other] [H], golf

85mm Sugar Creek

82mm Big Blue River

80 IN 252, to Flat Rock, Edinburgh, W [gas] Marathon/dsl, Shell/dsl

76b a US 31, Taylorsville, E [gas] Shell/Circle K/dsl, Speedway/dsl [food] A&W/KFC, Burger King, El Toreo Mexican, Waffle House [lodging] Red Roof Inn [other] [H], $ General, Toyota, W [gas] Marathon, Ricker's/dsl, Thornton's/café/dsl [food] Applebee's, Arby's, Cracker Barrel,

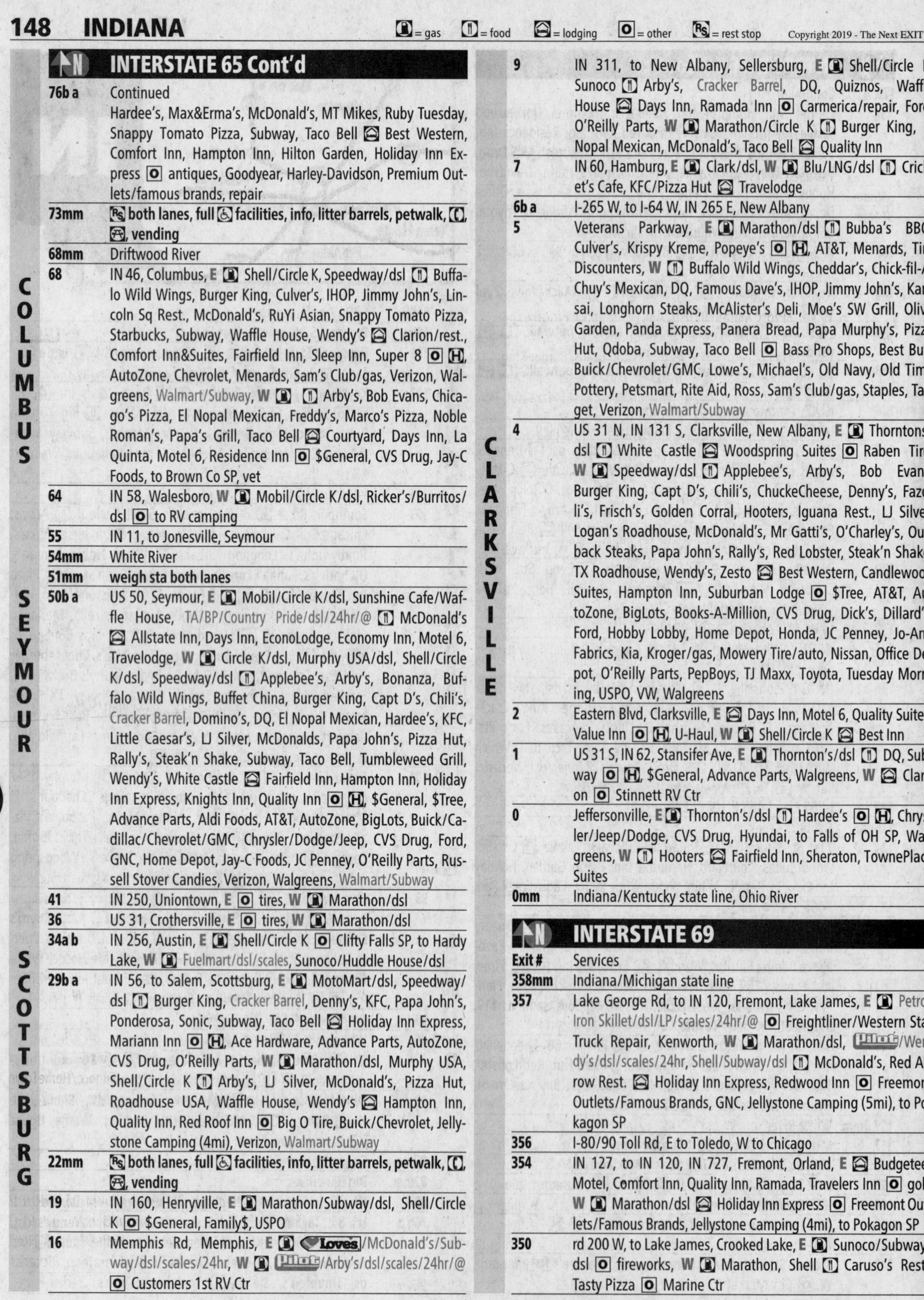

INTERSTATE 65 Cont'd

Exit	Services
76b a	Continued Hardee's, Max&Erma's, McDonald's, MT Mikes, Ruby Tuesday, Snappy Tomato Pizza, Subway, Taco Bell Best Western, Comfort Inn, Hampton Inn, Hilton Garden, Holiday Inn Express antiques, Goodyear, Harley-Davidson, Premium Outlets/famous brands, repair
73mm	**both lanes, full facilities, info, litter barrels, petwalk, , vending**
68mm	Driftwood River

COLUMBUS

Exit	Services
68	IN 46, Columbus, **E** Shell/Circle K, Speedway/dsl Buffalo Wild Wings, Burger King, Culver's, IHOP, Jimmy John's, Lincoln Sq Rest., McDonald's, RuYi Asian, Snappy Tomato Pizza, Starbucks, Subway, Waffle House, Wendy's Clarion/rest., Comfort Inn&Suites, Fairfield Inn, Sleep Inn, Super 8 H, AutoZone, Chevrolet, Menards, Sam's Club/gas, Verizon, Walgreens, Walmart/Subway, **W** Arby's, Bob Evans, Chicago's Pizza, El Nopal Mexican, Freddy's, Marco's Pizza, Noble Roman's, Papa's Grill, Taco Bell Courtyard, Days Inn, La Quinta, Motel 6, Residence Inn $General, CVS Drug, Jay-C Foods, to Brown Co SP, vet
64	IN 58, Walesboro, **W** Mobil/Circle K/dsl, Ricker's/Burritos/dsl to RV camping
55	IN 11, to Jonesville, Seymour
54mm	White River
51mm	**weigh sta both lanes**

SEYMOUR

Exit	Services
50b a	US 50, Seymour, **E** Mobil/Circle K/dsl, Sunshine Cafe/Waffle House, TA/BP/Country Pride/dsl/24hr/@ McDonald's Allstate Inn, Days Inn, EconoLodge, Economy Inn, Motel 6, Travelodge, **W** Circle K/dsl, Murphy USA/dsl, Shell/Circle K/dsl, Speedway/dsl Applebee's, Arby's, Bonanza, Buffalo Wild Wings, Buffet China, Burger King, Capt D's, Chili's, Cracker Barrel, Domino's, DQ, El Nopal Mexican, Hardee's, KFC, Little Caesar's, LJ Silver, McDonalds, Papa John's, Pizza Hut, Rally's, Steak'n Shake, Subway, Taco Bell, Tumbleweed Grill, Wendy's, White Castle Fairfield Inn, Hampton Inn, Holiday Inn Express, Knights Inn, Quality Inn H, $General, $Tree, Advance Parts, Aldi Foods, AT&T, AutoZone, BigLots, Buick/Cadillac/Chevrolet/GMC, Chrysler/Dodge/Jeep, CVS Drug, Ford, GNC, Home Depot, Jay-C Foods, JC Penney, O'Reilly Parts, Russell Stover Candies, Verizon, Walgreens, Walmart/Subway
41	IN 250, Uniontown, **E** tires, **W** Marathon/dsl
36	US 31, Crothersville, **E** tires, **W** Marathon/dsl
34a b	IN 256, Austin, **E** Shell/Circle K Clifty Falls SP, to Hardy Lake, **W** Fuelmart/dsl/scales, Sunoco/Huddle House/dsl

SCOTTSBURG

Exit	Services
29b a	IN 56, to Salem, Scottsburg, **E** MotoMart/dsl, Speedway/dsl Burger King, Cracker Barrel, Denny's, KFC, Papa John's, Ponderosa, Sonic, Subway, Taco Bell Holiday Inn Express, Mariann Inn H, Ace Hardware, Advance Parts, AutoZone, CVS Drug, O'Reilly Parts, **W** Marathon/dsl, Murphy USA, Shell/Circle K Arby's, LJ Silver, McDonald's, Pizza Hut, Roadhouse USA, Waffle House, Wendy's Hampton Inn, Quality Inn, Red Roof Inn Big O Tire, Buick/Chevrolet, Jellystone Camping (4mi), Verizon, Walmart/Subway
22mm	**both lanes, full facilities, info, litter barrels, petwalk, , vending**
19	IN 160, Henryville, **E** Marathon/Subway/dsl, Shell/Circle K $General, Family$, USPO
16	Memphis Rd, Memphis, **E** Loves/McDonald's/Subway/dsl/scales/24hr, **W** Pilot/Arby's/dsl/scales/24hr/@ Customers 1st RV Ctr
9	IN 311, to New Albany, Sellersburg, **E** Shell/Circle K Sunoco Arby's, Cracker Barrel, DQ, Quiznos, Waffle House Days Inn, Ramada Inn Carmerica/repair, Ford O'Reilly Parts, **W** Marathon/Circle K Burger King, E Nopal Mexican, McDonald's, Taco Bell Quality Inn
7	IN 60, Hamburg, **E** Clark/dsl, **W** Blu/LNG/dsl Cricket's Cafe, KFC/Pizza Hut Travelodge
6b a	I-265 W, to I-64 W, IN 265 E, New Albany

CLARKSVILLE

Exit	Services
5	Veterans Parkway, **E** Marathon/dsl Bubba's BBQ Culver's, Krispy Kreme, Popeye's H, AT&T, Menards, Tire Discounters, **W** Buffalo Wild Wings, Cheddar's, Chick-fil-A, Chuy's Mexican, DQ, Famous Dave's, IHOP, Jimmy John's, Kansai, Longhorn Steaks, McAlister's Deli, Moe's SW Grill, Olive Garden, Panda Express, Panera Bread, Papa Murphy's, Pizza Hut, Qdoba, Subway, Taco Bell Bass Pro Shops, Best Buy, Buick/Chevrolet/GMC, Lowe's, Michael's, Old Navy, Old Time Pottery, Petsmart, Rite Aid, Ross, Sam's Club/gas, Staples, Target, Verizon, Walmart/Subway
4	US 31 N, IN 131 S, Clarksville, New Albany, **E** Thorntons/dsl White Castle Woodspring Suites Raben Tire **W** Speedway/dsl Applebee's, Arby's, Bob Evans, Burger King, Capt D's, Chili's, ChuckeCheese, Denny's, Fazoli's, Frisch's, Golden Corral, Hooters, Iguana Rest., LJ Silver Logan's Roadhouse, McDonald's, Mr Gatti's, O'Charley's, Outback Steaks, Papa John's, Rally's, Red Lobster, Steak'n Shake TX Roadhouse, Wendy's, Zesto Best Western, Candlewood Suites, Hampton Inn, Suburban Lodge $Tree, AT&T, AutoZone, BigLots, Books-A-Million, CVS Drug, Dick's, Dillard's, Ford, Hobby Lobby, Home Depot, Honda, JC Penney, Jo-Ann Fabrics, Kia, Kroger/gas, Mowery Tire/auto, Nissan, Office Depot, O'Reilly Parts, PepBoys, TJ Maxx, Toyota, Tuesday Morning, USPO, VW, Walgreens
2	Eastern Blvd, Clarksville, **E** Days Inn, Motel 6, Quality Suites, Value Inn H, U-Haul, **W** Shell/Circle K Best Inn
1	US 31 S, IN 62, Stansifer Ave, **E** Thornton's/dsl DQ, Subway H, $General, Advance Parts, Walgreens, **W** Clarion Stinnett RV Ctr
0	Jeffersonville, **E** Thornton's/dsl Hardee's H, Chrysler/Jeep/Dodge, CVS Drug, Hyundai, to Falls of OH SP, Walgreens, **W** Hooters Fairfield Inn, Sheraton, TownePlace Suites
0mm	Indiana/Kentucky state line, Ohio River

INTERSTATE 69

Exit #	Services
358mm	Indiana/Michigan state line
357	Lake George Rd, to IN 120, Fremont, Lake James, **E** Petro/Iron Skillet/dsl/LP/scales/24hr/@ Freightliner/Western Star Truck Repair, Kenworth, **W** Marathon/dsl, Pilot/Wendy's/dsl/scales/24hr, Shell/Subway/dsl McDonald's, Red Arrow Rest. Holiday Inn Express, Redwood Inn Freemont Outlets/Famous Brands, GNC, Jellystone Camping (5mi), to Pokagon SP
356	I-80/90 Toll Rd, E to Toledo, W to Chicago
354	IN 127, to IN 120, IN 727, Fremont, Orland, **E** Budgeteer Motel, Comfort Inn, Quality Inn, Ramada, Travelers Inn golf, **W** Marathon/dsl Holiday Inn Express Freemont Outlets/Famous Brands, Jellystone Camping (4mi), to Pokagon SP
350	rd 200 W, to Lake James, Crooked Lake, **E** Sunoco/Subway/dsl fireworks, **W** Marathon, Shell Caruso's Rest., Tasty Pizza Marine Ctr

INTERSTATE 69 Cont'd

Exit #	Services
348	US 20, to Angola, Lagrange, E Marathon/Subway/dsl, Speedway/Taco Bell/dsl McDonald's Happy Acres Camping (1mi), University Inn (2mi) H, W Loves/ Hardee's/dsl/scales/24hr Circle B RV Prk (2mi)
345mm	Pigeon Creek
344mm	sb, full facilities, info, litter barrels, petwalk, vending
340	IN 4, to Hamilton, Ashley, Hudson, 1 mi W Marathon/Subway/dsl
334	US 6, to Waterloo, Kendallville, E Subway $General, W BP/dsl, Marathon/dsl/24hr Maria's Pancakes
329	IN 8, to Garrett, Auburn, E BP, Lassus, Speedway/dsl, Speedway/dsl (2) Applebee's, Arby's, Bob Evans, Burger King, DQ, Hungry Howie's, Jimmy John's, KFC, Little Caesar's, McDonald's, Papa John's, Peking Buffet, Penguin Point Rest., Pizza Hut, Ponderosa, Richard's Rest., Starbucks, Steak'n Shake, Subway, Taco Bell, Wendy's Comfort Suites, Days Inn, Holiday Inn Express, La Quinta, Quality Inn, Super 8 H, $General, $Tree, Ace Hardware, Advance Parts, AT&T, AutoZone, Buick/Chevrolet/ RV Ctr, Chrysler/Dodge/Jeep, CVS Drug, Ford, GNC, Kroger/ dsl, Walmart/Subway, W Marathon/dsl Buffalo Wild Wings, Cebolla's Mexican, Cracker Barrel, Paradise Buffet, Subway Hampton Inn Home Depot, Verizon
326	rd 11A, to Garrett, Auburn, E Auction Park, W Fireside Camping
324	nb, full facilities, info, litter barrels, vending
317	Union Chapel Rd, E H
316	IN 1 N, Dupont Rd, E Lassus/Elmo's/dsl, Phillips 66/Burger King Arby's, Culver's, Taco Bell Comfort Suites, Hampton Inn H, W Speedway/dsl Bagger Dave's Burgers, Bob Evans, Cozy Nook Cafe, Domino's, Jimmy John's, Mancino's Grinders, McDonald's, Panera Bread, Pine Valley Grill, Starbucks, Trolley Grill Baymont Inn, La Quinta
315	I-469, US 30 E, W Woodspring Suites
312b a	Coldwater Rd, E BP/dsl, Marathon, Sunoco Agaves Mexican, Arby's, Chili's, Cork'N Cleaver, Firehouse Subs, Fortune Buffet, Hall's Factory Rest., Hunan Chinese, IHOP, Jimmy John's, Koto Japanese, Mister Coney, Papa John's, Rally's, Red Lobster, Red River Steaks, Steak'n Shake, Subway, Taco Bell, Wendy's Hotel Ft Wayne, Hyatt Place $Tree, Dick's, Hobby Lobby, Hyundai, JoAnn Fabrics, O'Reilly Parts, PetCo, Tuesday Morning, Tuffy Auto, U-Haul, Walmart/Subway, W Marathon Salsa Grille
311b a	US 27 S, IN 3 N, E Shell/dsl, Sunoco/dsl Arby's, Cheddar's, ChuckECheese's, DQ, Fazoli's, Golden Corral, Hall's Rest., Longhorn Steaks, McDonald's, Olive Garden, Starbucks, TGIFriday's, Tim Horton's Candlewood Suites, Hawthorn Suites, TownePlace Suites Aldi Foods, Barnes&Noble, Chevrolet, Chrysler/Dodge/Jeep, Costco/gas, Discount Tire, Fiat, Ford/ Lincoln, Honda, Infiniti, JC Penney, Macy's, Nissan, Subaru, Toyota, Verizon, W BP/dsl, Lassus/Elmo's Pizza/dsl, Marathon/dsl Applebee's, Burger King, Chipotle, Cracker Barrel, Culver's, Hardee's, IHOP, Logan's Roadhouse, McDonald's, Panda Express, Sapporo Japanese, Starbucks, Subway, Taco Bell, TX Roadhouse Best Value Inn, Best Western, Comfort Inn, Days Inn, EconoLodge, Extended Stay America, Fairfield Inn, Guesthouse Motel, Hampton Inn, Quality Inn, Super 8 Belle Tire, CVS Drug, Home Depot, Lowe's, Meijer/dsl/E85, Sam's Club/gas, VW

AUBURN

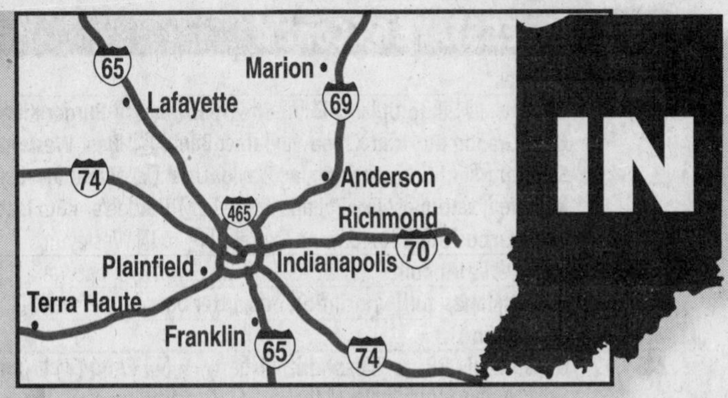

FT WAYNE

Exit #	Services
309b a	US 33, Goshen Rd, Ft Wayne, E Phillips 66/dsl, Pilot/ dsl/scales/24hr, Shell Liberty Diner, McDonald's Country Hearth Inn, Knights Inn, Motel 6, Red Roof Inn, Travel Inn H, auto/dsl repair, Blue Beacon, NAPA
305b a	IN 14 W, Ft Wayne, E Lassus, Murphy USA, Shell/Subway/ dsl, Speedway/dsl/LP Arby's, Biaggi's, Burger King, Chick-fil-A, Chipotle Mexican, Coldstone, Domino's, Eddy Merlot Rest., Firehouse Subs, Flat Top Grill, Great Wall Buffet, Logan's Roadhouse, McAlister's Deli, Noodles&Co., O'Charley's, Panda Express, Panera Bread, Penn Sta Subs, Qdoba, Smokey Bones BBQ, Starbucks, Steak'n Shake, Subway, Taco Bell, Tilted Kilt Eatery, Tuscano's, Wendy's Klopfenstein Suites H, $General, $Tree, Acura, Advance Parts, Audi/Porsche, Barnes&Noble, Best Buy, BigLots, BMW, Buick/GMC, Cadillac, Chevrolet, Chrysler/Dodge/Jeep, Dick's, Ford/Lincoln, Gordman's, Harley-Davidson, Kia, Kohl's, Lexus, Lowe's, Marshall's, Mazda, Meijer/dsl, Menards, Michael's, NAPA, Old Navy, Patriot Tire/auto, Petsmart, Staples, Target, to St Francis U, Toyota, Tuesday Morning, Verizon, vet, Volvo, Walmart/Subway
302	US 24, to Jefferson Blvd, Ft Wayne, E Subway (1mi), Taco Bell (1mi) Extended Stay America, Hampton Inn, Residence Inn H, IN Wesleyan Ft Wayne, W Lassus, Marathon/ dsl Applebee's, Arby's, Bob Evans, Buffalo Wild Wings, Coventry Tavern Rest., McDonald's, Naked Chopstix, Outback Steaks, Pizza Hut, Salsa Grille, Sara's Rest., Starbucks, Wendy's, Zesto Drive-In Best Western, Comfort Suites, Hilton Garden, Holiday Inn Express, Homewood Suites, Staybridge Suites Kroger/dsl, Meineke, st police, Walgreens
299	Lower Huntington Rd, E to
296b a	I-469, US 24 E, US 33 S, E to
286	US 224, to Huntington, Markle, E Marathon/dsl, Phillips 66/Subway/dsl, Sunoco/dsl Daily Diner, DQ, Vinatelli's Econolodge, Motel 6 H, repair/tires, W Roush Lake, to Huntington Reservoir
280mm	weigh sta sb/parking area nb
278	IN 5, to Warren, Huntington, E Phillips 66/dsl Huggy Bear Motel, W Marathon/Subway/dsl, Sunoco/HomeTown Diner/dsl/scales/24hr McDonald's, Ugalde's Rest. Arlington Inn, Comfort Inn H, fireworks, RV camping, to Salamonie Reservoir
276mm	Salamonie River
273	IN 218, to Warren
264	IN 18, to Marion, Montpelier, E Loves/McDonalds/dsl/ scales/24hr, W BP/Subway/dsl, FLYING J/Wendy's/dsl/ scales/24hr Arby's Best Value Inn H, Harley-Davidson, Ram
260mm	Walnut Creek

IN

INTERSTATE 69 Cont'd

Exit #	Services
259	US 35 N, IN 22, to Upland, E Shell/Subway Burger King, Casa Grande Mexican, China 1, Cracker Barrel Best Western, Super 8 Mar-Brook Camping, Taylor U, W Marathon/dsl, McClure Trkstp/dsl/24hr, Phillips 66/dsl Hardee's, KFC/Taco Bell, Starbucks Holiday Inn Express to IN Wesleyan
255	IN 26, to Fairmount
250mm	**both lanes, full facilities, info, litter barrels, pet walk, , vending**
245	US 35 S, IN 28, to Alexandria, Albany, E Petro/Shell/Iron Skillet/Subway/dsl/scales/24hr/@ RV Camping
241	IN 332, to Muncie, Frankton, E BP/Subway/dsl H, to Ball St U
234	IN 67, to IN 32, Chesterfield, Daleville, E Pilot/Subway/dsl/scales/24hr, Shell Arby's, Pizza Hut, Smokehouse BBQ, Taco Bell, Waffle House, White Castle Budget Inn H, W McClure/dsl/E85, Pilot/Denny's/dsl/scales/24hr, Speedway/dsl 3rd Generation Pizza, McDonald's, Subway, Wendy's Travel Inn Timberline Valley Camping (3mi)
226	IN 9, IN 109, to Anderson, E A&W/KFC, Culver's, Golden Corral, MT Mike's Fairfield Inn, Hampton Inn, Holiday Inn Express, Quality Inn, Red Roof Inn Meijer/dsl, Menards, visitors ctr, W BP, Marathon/dsl, Speedway/dsl Applebee's, Arby's, Bob Evans, Buffalo Wild Wings, Burger King, Cracker Barrel, Fazoli's, IHOP, Jimmy John's, LoneStar Steaks, McDonald's, Olive Garden, Panda Express, Panera Bread, Papa Murphy's, Payless Mkt/dsl, Penn Sta Subs, Perkins, Pizza Hut, Ponderosa, Popeye's, Qdoba, Red Lobster, Riviera Maya, Ruby Tuesday, Starbucks, Steak'n Shake, Subway, Supreme Buffet, Taco Bell, Waffle House, Wendy's, White Castle Best Value Inn, Best Western, Comfort Inn, Days Inn, Motel 6, Super 8 H, $Tree, AT&T, Big Lots, Cadillac/Chevrolet, Chrysler/Dodge/Jeep, GNC, Hobby Lobby, Honda, Kohl's, Marshall's, Nissan, O'Reilly Parts, Petsmart, Tire Barn, to Anderson U, to Mounds SP, Toyota, Verizon, vet, Walmart/Subway
222	IN 9, IN 67, to Anderson, W Speedway/dsl Skyline Chili H
219	IN 38, Pendleton, E Marathon Burger King, McDonald's, Subway, W Pine Lakes Camping
214	IN 13, to Lapel, E BP/dsl, Loves/McDonald's/dsl/scales24hr Waffle House, W Pilot/Subway/dsl/scales/24hr camping
210	IN 238, to Noblesville, Fortville, E BP/dsl Arby's, Culver's, DQ, Starbucks, Subway, Taco Bell, Wendy's, Which Wich? H, W EVC, Shell/dsl Aspen Grill, Chick-fil-A, Chuy's, Coldstone, Famous Dave's, Five Guys, Houlihan's, McAlister's Deli, McDonald's, Mo's Cafe, Olive Garden, Panda Express, Paradise Cafe, Perkins, Primanti Bros, Qdoba, Red Robin, Stone Creek Rest., Tuscano's Cambria Suites, Holiday Inn Express $Tree, AT&T, Cabela's, CVS Drug, Dick's, Earth Fare Foods, Firestone/auto, GNC, JC Penney, Old Navy, Sleepy Bear Camping, Steinmart, Verizon
205	IN 37 N, 116th St, to Noblesville, Fishers, E Bent Cafe Asian, Penn Sta Subs, Sunrise Cafe Fresh Mkt, Kroger, URGENT CARE, W Shell/Circle K, Speedway Brixx Pizzaria, Coldstone, Five Guys, Handel's Ice Cream, Happy Dragon, Jet's Pizza, Marco's Pizza, McAlister's Deli, McDonald's, Moe's SW Grill, O'Charley's, Original Pancakes, Qdoba, Riviera Mexican, Starbucks, Steak'n Shake, Subway, Verde Mexican, Wendy's, Wild Ginger Asian Hampton Inn AT&T, CVS Drug, Firestone/auto, Target, URGENT CARE
203	96th St, E Marathon/dsl, Marathon/dsl (2), Murphy USA/dsl, Shell/Circle K Applebee's, Blimpie, Bubba's Rest., Cracker Barrel, Donato's Pizza, Dunkin Donuts, Gandolfo's Deli, IHOP, Jersey Mike's, Jimmy John's, McDonald's, Noodles&Co., Panera Bread, Qdoba, Rita's, Ruby Tuesday, Sahm's Grill, Slimm's Pizza, Smoothie King, Starbucks, Steak'n Shake, Subway, Tijuana Flats, Wendy's AmericInn, Baymont Inn, Hilton Garden, Holiday Inn Express, Studio 6 $Tree, AT&T, Fry's, GNC, Kohl's, Marsh Mkt, Meijer/dsl, PepBoys, PetCo, Staples, Tuesday Morning, Verizon, Walmart, W Marathon/dsl Arby's, Bob Evans, Burger King, Culver's, DJ's Hotdogs, Izakya Japanese, Journey Rest., La Cabana, Panda Express, Peterson's Steaks/seafood, Quiznos, Starbucks, Taco Bell, Wolfie's Grill Comfort Suites, Residence Inn, SpringHill Suites, Staybridge Suites Aldi Foods, Home Depot, Menards, NAPA, Sam's Club/gas, vet
201	82nd St, Castleton, E Shell Boston Mkt, Burger King, Golden Corral, Jet's Pizza, O'Charley's, Red Robin Drury Inn, Extended Stay America, Red Roof Inn, Super 8 H, CVS Drug, Lowe's, vet, Walgreens, W Speedway/dsl Applebee's, Arby's, Burger King, Castleton Grill, Charleston's Rest., Denny's, Domino's, Fazoli's, Firehouse Subs, Formosa Buffet, Hooters, Houlihan's, Jimmy John's, Joe's Grille, KFC, LJ Silver, Longhorn Steaks, Los Cabos Mexican, McAlister's Deli, McDonald's, Olive Garden, Pizza Hut, Popeye's, Rally's, Red Lobster, Skyline Chili, Starbucks, Subway, Taco Bell, Thai Orchid, Twin Peaks, Wendy's Candlewood Suites, Days Inn, Hampton Inn, Motel 6, Suburban Suites Aamco, Advance Parts, AutoZone, Best Buy, CarX, Dick's, Discount Tire, Firestone/auto, fireworks, Goodyear/auto, JC Penney, Macy's, Midas, O'Reilly Parts, Tire Barn, Verizon
200mm	I-465 around Indianapolis. **I-69 begins/ends on I-465, exit 37, at Indianapolis.**

ANDERSON

INDIANAPOLIS AREA

INTERSTATE 70

Exit #	Services
156.5mm	Indiana/Ohio state line, **weigh sta**
156b a	US 40 E, Richmond, N Petro/BP/Iron Skillet/dsl/24hr/@ Fairfield Inn Blue Beacon, S Murphy USA/dsl, Shell/dsl, Speedway/dsl, Sunoco A&W/LJ Silver, Applebee's, Arby's, Big Boy, Buffalo Wild Wings, Buffalo Wings&Rings, Burger King, Chili's, Chipotle Mexican, Cracker Barrel, El Rodeo Mexican, Fazoli's, Galo's Italian, Golden Corral, IHOP, Jade House Chinese, Jimmy John's, KFC, McAlister's Deli, McDonald's, MCL Cafeteria, O'Charley's, Olive Garden, Papa Murphy's, Pizza Hut, Rally's, Red Lobster, Starbucks, Steak'n Shake, Subway, Taco Bell, TX Roadhouse, Yamato Japanese Best Western, Days Inn, EconoLodge, Hampton Inn, Holiday Inn, Motel 6, Quality Inn $General, $Tree, Advance Parts, Aldi Foods, AT&T, Best Buy, Big Lots, Buick/GMC, Chevrolet, Chrysler/Dodge/Jeep, Dick's, Dillard's, Firestone/auto, Ford, Hobby Lobby, JC Penney, Jo-Ann Fabrics, Kohl's, Kroger/dsl, Lowe's, Menards, O'Reilly Parts, Save-A-Lot Foods, Tires+, TJ Maxx, Toyota/Nissan, U-Haul, Verizon, Walgreens, Walmart/Subway
153	IN 227, to Whitewater, Richmond, **2 mi N** Grandpa's Farm RV Park (seasonal), KOA
151b a	US 27, to Chester, Richmond, N Fricker's Rest. Honda, KOA, S Shell Bob Evans, Burger Time, Carver's Rest., El Bronco Mexican, Hardee's, McDonald's, Subway, Taco Bell, Wendy's Comfort Inn, Red Roof Inn H, CVS Drug, Harley-Davidson, Meijer/dsl/E85

RICHMOND

INTERSTATE 70 Cont'd

Exit #	Services
149b a	US 35, IN 38, to Muncie, N Loves/Hardee's/dsl/scales/24hr, S Shell/dsl Camping World RV Ctr
148mm	**weigh sta wb**
145	Centerville, N Marathon/DQ/Godfather's/dsl Super 8 Goodyear/truck repair, S Warm Glow Candles/cafe
145mm	Nolands Fork Creek
144mm	**wb, full facilities, info, litter barrels, petwalk, , , vending**
141mm	Greens Fork River
137	IN 1, to Hagerstown, Connersville, N Amish Cheese, S BP/Arby's/dsl/24hr, Shell/Burger King, Speedway/dsl/e85 McDonald's
131	Wilbur Wright Rd, New Lisbon, S Shell/Pizza Hut/Taco Bell/dsl/scales/24hr/@ New Lisbon RV park
126mm	Flatrock River
123	IN 3, to New Castle, Spiceland, N All American Inn (3mi), Holiday Inn Express (3mi) H, S FLYING J/Denny's/Subway/dsl/LP/scales/24hr, Mr Fuel/rest./dsl/scales/24hr Montgomery's Steaks tires/repair
117mm	Big Blue River
115	IN 109, to Knightstown, Wilkinson, N Loves/McDonald's/Subway/dsl/scales/24hr, Speedway/rest./dsl/scales/24hr Burger King Jellystone Camping
107mm	**both lanes, full facilities, litter barrels, petwalk, , , vending**
104	IN 9, Greenfield, Maxwell, N Speedway/dsl, S Circle K/dsl, Murphy USA/dsl, Shell/Circle K, Speedway/dsl Applebee's, Arby's, Bamboo Garden, Bob Evans, Buffalo Wild Wings, Burger King, Chicago's Pizza, China Inn, Cracker Barrel, Culver's, Firehouse Subs, Hardee's, Jimmy John's, KFC, Little Caesar's, McDonald's, Mi Casa Mexican, MT Mike's Steaks, O'Charley's, Papa John's, Papa Murphy's, Penn Sta Subs, Pizza Hut, Ponderosa, Popeye's, Qdoba, Starbucks, Steak'n Shake, Subway, Taco Bell, Waffle House, Wasabi, Wendy's, White Castle Comfort Inn, Country Inn&Suites, Fairfield Inn, Greenfield Inn, Hampton Inn, Holiday Inn Express, Quality Inn, Super 8 H, $General, $Tree, Advance Parts, Aldi Foods, AutoZone, Big Lots, CVS Drug, GNC, Home Depot, Kohl's, Kroger/dsl, Petsmart, Verizon, Walgreens, Walmart
96	Mt Comfort Rd, N Pilot/Pizza Hut/dsl/scales/24hr, Speedway/Subway/dsl Burger King, Wendy's, S Shell/Circle K McDonald's KOA (seasonal), Mt Comfort RV Ctr
91	Post Rd, to Ft Harrison, N Mobil/Circle K Cracker Barrel, Denny's, Outback Steaks, Steak'n Shake, Wendy's InTown Suites, La Quinta Lowe's, st police, S Admiral, BP/dsl, Shell/dsl, Speedway Hardee's, Jack-in-the-Box, KFC/Taco Bell, Little Caesar's, Waffle House Country Hearth Inn, Days Inn CVS Drug, Family$, Home Depot
90	I-465 (from wb)
89	Shadeland Ave, I-465 (from eb), N Marathon/dsl Bob Evans Baymont Inn, Comfort Inn, Holiday Inn Express, Welcome Inn Toyota, U-Haul, S Admiral/dsl, Circle K, Exxon/dsl, Marathon, Speedway/dsl Arby's, Burger King, Damon's, Domino's, Four Seasons Diner, Jimmy John's, Lincoln Sq Rest., McDonald's, Papa John's, Penn Sta Subs, Rally's, Red Lobster, Starbucks, Subway, Taco Bell, TX Roadhouse, Wendy's Always Inn, Best Value Inn, Candlewood Suites, Delta Hotel, Express Inn, Fairfield Inn, Marriott, Quality Inn $General, CarX, Chevrolet, Chrysler/Dodge/Jeep, CVS Drug, Honda, Kia, Kroger/gas, Mazda, Nissan

GREENFIELD

INDIANAPOLIS AREA

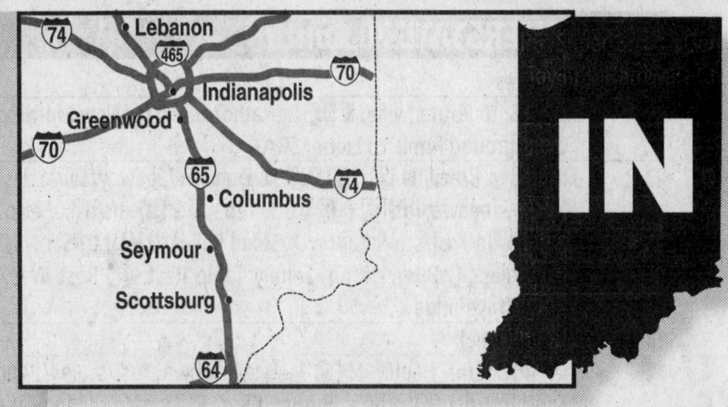

Exit #	Services
87	Emerson Ave, N BP/McDonald's, Speedway/dsl, S Shell H
85b a	Rural St, Keystone Ave, N Shell Church's fairgrounds, S Shell/dsl
83b(112)	I-65 N, to Chicago
83a(111)	Michigan St, Market St, S Hardee's, downtown
80(110a)	I-65 S, to Louisville
79b	Illinois St, McCarty St, downtown
79a	West St, N Speedway/dsl Holiday Inn, Holiday Inn Express, Hyatt, JW Marriott, Staybridge Suites H, Govt Ctr, Lucas Oil Stadium, zoo
78	Harding St, to downtown, S Marathon/Subway Wendy's
77	Holt Rd, N Phillips 66/dsl Rally's, Steak'n Shake, S Speedway/Speedy's Cafe/dsl McDonald's
75	Airport Expswy, to Raymond St (no EZ wb return), N Marathon/dsl, Speedway/dsl Indy's Rest., Jimmy John's, Library Rest., Subway, Waffle House Candlewood Suites, Courtyard, Extended Stay America, Fairfield Inn, Hyatt Place, La Quinta, Ramada, Red Roof Inn, Residence Inn, Super 8, Wyndham NAPA, to
73b a	I-465 N/S, I-74 E/W
69	(only from eb) to I-74 E, to I-465 S
68	Six Points Rd, N , S Mobil/dsl Burger Theory, Subway Hampton Inn, Hilton Garden, Holiday Inn, Home 2 Suites
66	IN 267, to Plainfield, Mooresville, N Blu/dsl, BP, Shell/Circle K, Speedway/dsl, Thornton's/dsl Arby's, Bob Evans, Burger King, Coachman Rest., Cracker Barrel, Golden Corral, McDonald's, Narita Japanese, Nonna's Italian, Steak'n Shake, Subway, Taco Bell, Waffle House, White Castle Baymont Inn, Best Western+, Budget Inn, Comfort Inn, Days Inn, Embassy Suites, Hampton Inn, Holiday Inn Express, Homewood Suites, Indianapolis Airport Suites, La Quinta, Quality Inn, Staybridge Suites, Super 8, Wingate Inn, Woodspring Suites Buick/GMC, Chateau Thomas Winery, Harley-Davidson
65mm	**both lanes, full facilities, info, litter barrels, petwalk, , , vending**
59	IN 39, to Belleville, N Loves/McDonald's/Subway/dsl/scales/24hr, S TA/Country Pride/dsl/scales/24hr/@, truckwash
51	rd 1100W, S Koger's/Sunoco/dsl/rest./24hr repair/towing/24hr
41	US 231, to Greencastle, Cloverdale, S BP/dsl, Casey's (2mi), Marathon/dsl/scales/24hr Arby's, Chicago's Pizza, El Cantarito, McDonald's, Subway, Taco Bell Days Inn, EconoLodge, Holiday Inn Express, Motel 6, Super 8 $General, Family$, Jordan's Carcare, NAPA, Taylor's Hardware, to Lieber SRA, Value Mkt Foods

INTERSTATE 70 Cont'd

Exit #	Services
37	IN 243, to Putnamville, S Marathon/dsl Misty Morning Campground (4mi), to Lieber SRA
23	IN 59, to Brazil, N Pilot/McDonald's/Subway/dsl/scales/24hr, Speedway/dsl H, truck repair, S BP/dsl, Petro/Iron Skillet/dsl/scales/24hr/@, Road Ranger/Pilot/Subway/dsl/scales Burger King, Family Table Rest. Best Western+, Travelodge
15mm	Honey Creek
11	IN 46, Terre Haute, N Pilot/Subway/dsl/scales/24hr, Thornton/dsl Arby's, Burger King, McDonald's, Monical's Pizza, Real Hacienda, Sonic, Taco Bell Holiday Inn Express, Home 2 Suites $Tree, Aldi Foods, GNC, Meijer/dsl, Verizon, Walmart, S KOA
7	US 41, US 150, Terre Haute, N Casey's/dsl, Marathon/dsl, Sunoco/dsl, Thornton's/dsl Applebee's, Bandana's BBQ, Bob Evans, Coyote's Mexican Hacienda, Cracker Barrel, Dunkin Donuts, East Star Buffet, Fazoli's, IHOP, Moe's SW Grill, NewDay Cafe, Pizza Hut, Real Hacienda Mexican, Starbucks, Steak'n Shake, Tokyo Japanese, TX Roadhouse Comfort Suites, Days Inn, Drury Inn, Fairfield Inn, La Quinta, PearTree Inn, Super 8 AT&T, AutoZone, Chrysler/Jeep, O'Reilly Parts, URGENT CARE, S Speedway/dsl, Thornton's/dsl Arby's, Baskin-Robbins, Buffalo Wild Wings, Burger King, Cheddar's, Chick-fil-A, Chili's, Denny's, DQ, Five Guys, Fuddrucker's, Golden Corral, Hardee's, Jimmy John's, KFC, LJ Silver, Longhorn Steaks, Los Tres Caminos, McDonald's, Monical's Pizza, Olive Garden, Outback Steaks, Panda Express, Panda Garden, Panera Bread, Papa John's, Penn Sta Subs, Popeye's, Qdoba, Rally's, Red Lobster, Ruby Tuesday, Starbucks, Subway, Taco Bell, TGIFriday's, Wendy's, White Castle Hampton Inn, Holiday Inn, Motel 6, SpringHill Suites H, $Tree, Aldi Foods, AT&T, Best Buy, Big O Tire, BigLots, BooksAMillion, Buick/Cadillac/GMC, Burlington Coats, Chevrolet, Dodge, Ford, Fresh Thyme Mkt, Goodyear/auto, Harley-Davidson, Hobby Lobby, Hyundai, JC Penney, Jo-Ann Fabrics, Kohl's, Kroger/dsl, Lowe's, NAPA, Nissan, Old Navy, Petsmart, Ross, Sam's Club/gas, Staples, Tire Barn, TJ Maxx, Verizon, Walgreens, Walmart
5.5mm	Wabash River
3	Darwin Rd, W Terre Haute, N to St Mary of-the-Woods Coll
1.5mm	**Welcome Ctr eb, full facilities, info, litter barrels, petwalk, vending**
1	US 40 E (from eb, exits left), to Terre Haute, W Terre Haute
.5mm	**weigh sta eb**
0mm	Indiana/Illinois state line

TERRE HAUTE

INTERSTATE 74

Exit #	Services
171.5mm	Indiana/Ohio state line
171mm	**weigh sta wb**
169	US 52 W, to Brookville, S Chevrolet
168.5mm	Whitewater River
164	IN 1, St Leon, N Shell/Subway/dsl, Sunoco/Pizza/dsl, S BP/Blimpie/dsl Skyline Chili
156	IN 101, to Sunman, Milan, S BP/dsl KOA (2mi)
152mm	**both lanes, full facilities, litter barrels, petwalk, vending**
149	IN229,toOldenburg,Batesville,N Marathon,Shell/dsl China Buffet, McDonald's, Pizza Hut, Pizza King, Subway, Toros Mexican, Wendy's Hampton Inn $General, Advance Parts,
149	Continued Kroger/dsl, ShopKo, URGENT CARE, Verizon, S A[...]by's, DQ, KFC/Taco Bell, La Rosa's Pizza, Skyline Chili, Steak'[...] Shake Quality Inn H, CVS Drug, O'Reilly Parts
143	to IN 46, New Point, N Petro/Iron Skillet/Subway/ds[...] scales/24hr/@, S Hwy 46 Inn
134b a	IN 3, to Rushville, Greensburg, S BP/dsl, Marathon/DQ[...] Subway, Speedway/dsl A&W, Arby's, Big Boy, Buffal[...] Wings&Rings, Burger King, Chili's, El Chile Poblano, El Repa[...]ro Mexican, Great Wall Buffet, Jimmy John's, KFC/LJ Silve[...] Lincoln St Grill, Little Caesar's, McDonald's, Papa John's, Pizz[...] Hut, Taco Bell, Waffle House, Wendy's Baymont Inn, Holiday Inn Express, Quality Inn $General, $Tree, Aldi Food[...] AT&T, AutoZone, Buick/Chevrolet, Chrysler/Dodge/Jeep, CV[...] Drug, Ford, GNC, O'Reilly Parts, TrueValue, Verizon, Walgreen[...] Walmart/Subway
132	US 421, to Greensburg, S BP/dsl, CNG Hampton In[...] Holiday Inn Express (2mi)
130mm	Clifty Creek
123	Saint Paul, S Love's/McDonald's/Subway/dsl/scales/24hr repair
119	IN 244 E, to Milroy
116	IN 44, to Shelbyville, Rushville, N Marathon/Circle K/ds[...] S BP/dsl, Country Mark/dsl, Marathon, Murphy USA/ds[...] Sunoco/dsl Agustin's Mexican, Applebee's, Arby's, Bellac[...]no's, Bob Evans, Buffalo Wild Wings, Burger King, China Wok[...] Cholula Mexican, Denny's, Domino's, DQ, Dunkin Donuts, Fazoli's, Jimmy John's, KFC, King Buffet, McDonald's, Papa John's[...] Penn Sta Subs, Pizza Hut, Rally's, Starbucks, Subway, Taco Bel[...] Wendy's, White Castle Quality Inn H, $General, $Tree[...] Ace Hardware, Advance Parts, Aldi Foods, AT&T, AutoZone, Bi[...]gLots, Chevrolet, Ford, GNC, Kroger/dsl, Midas, O'Reilly Parts[...] Verizon, Walgreens, Walmart/Subway
115mm	Little Blue River
113mm	Big Blue River
113	IN 9, to Shelbyville, N Speedway/dsl Cracker Barrel, T[...] Corral, Wendy's, S Shell, Shell/Circle K/Subway/dsl McDonald's, Waffle House Comfort Inn, EconoLodge, Hampton Inn, Holiday Inn Express, Super 8 H
109	Fairland Rd, N Pilot/McDonald's/dsl/scales/24hr Indiana Downs/casino, S Brownie's Marine
103	London Rd, to Boggstown
102mm	Big Sugar Creek
101	Pleasant View Rd, N Country Mark/dsl/repair
99	Acton Rd
96	Post Rd, N Marathon/Subway/dsl/24hr McDonald's, [...] Shell/Circle K/dsl Taco Bell, Wendy's Chevrolet
94b a	I-465/I-74 W, I-465 N, US 421 N.

I-74 and I-465 run together 21 miles. See I-495, exits 2-16, and 52-53.

Exit #	Services
73b	I-465 N, access to same services as 16a on I-465
73a	I-465 S, I-74 E
71mm	Eagle Creek
68	Ronald Reagan Pkwy, N H
66	IN 267, Brownsburg, N Citgo/dsl, Shell/Circle K Applebee's, Asia Wok, Buffalo Wild Wings, Dunkin Donuts[...] Papa's Pizzaria, Starbucks, Steak'n Shake, Subway, Tequil[...] Mexican Hampton Inn, Quality Inn Big O Tire, Midas[...] S BP/dsl, Speedway/dsl Arby's, Bob Evans, Burge[...] King, China's Best, Elegance Rest., Firehouse Subs, Five Guys[...] HoWah, IHOP, Jimmy John's, KFC, Little Caesar's, McAlister'[...] Deli, McDonald's, Mediterranean Pizza, Papa Murphy's, Pen[...] Sta Subs, Qdoba, Starbucks, Taco Bell, The Toros Mexican[...]

GREENSBURG

SHELBYVILLE

BROWNSBURG

IN

INTERSTATE 74 Cont'd

66 Continued
Wendy's, White Castle Comfort Suites, Super 8 AT&T, Firestone/auto, Ford, GNC, Kohl's, Kroger/gas, Lowe's, O'Reilly Parts, USPO, Verizon, Walmart/Subway

61 to Pittsboro, **S** Loves/Godfather's/Subway/dsl/scales/24hr

58 IN 39, to Lebanon, Lizton, **S** Sunoco/dsl/e85 $General

57mm **both lanes, full facilities, litter barrels, petwalk, , vending**

52 IN 75, to Advance, Jamestown, **2 mi S** camping, food, gas

39 IN 32, to Crawfordsville, **S** Pilot/Subway/dsl/scales/24hr

34 US 231, to Linden, **S** Marathon/dsl, McClure/dsl, Mobil/Circle K, Speedway, Sunoco/dsl Cracker Barrel, McDonald's, Subway Best Western+, Comfort Inn, Hampton Inn, Holiday Inn Express, Knights Inn, Motel 6, Rodeway Inn, Super 8 H, KOA (1mi), Sugar Creek Campground (4mi)

25 IN 25, to Wingate, Waynetown

15 US 41, to Attica, Veedersburg, **1 mi S** Casey's/dsl, Marathon/dsl, Valero/Subway Apple Tree Diner camping, Family$, to Turkey Run SP

8 Covington, **N** Marathon/dsl, Valero/dsl Benjamin's, Overpass Pizza fireworks

7mm Wabash River

4 IN 63, to Newport, **N** Pilot/Arby's/dsl/scales/24hr Beefhouse Rest.

1mm **Welcome Ctr eb, full facilities, info, litter barrels, petwalk, , , vending**

0mm Indiana/Illinois state line, Eastern/Central Time Zone

INTERSTATE 80/90

Exit # Services

157mm Indiana/Ohio state line

153mm **toll plaza, litter barrels**

144 I-69, US 27, Angola, Ft Wayne, **N** Petro/Iron Skillet/dsl/scales/24hr/@, Pilot/Wendy's/dsl/scales, Shell/Subway/dsl McDonald's, Red Arrow Rest. Redwood Inn Freightliner/Western Star/truck repair, services on IN 120, **S** Marathon/dsl Comfort Inn, Holiday Inn Express, Quality Inn, Travelers Inn Freemont Outlet Shops/famous brands, GNC, golf/rest, Jellystone Camping (5mi), to Pokagon SP

131.5mm Fawn River

126mm **Ernie Pyle TP both lanes,** Sunoco/dsl RV dump, Popeye's, Starbucks

121 IN 9, to Lagrange, Howe, **2 mi N** Marathon, Murphy USA/dsl, Speedway/dsl Applebee's, Buffalo Wild Wings, Burger King, Culver's, Fiesta Mexican, Golden Buddha, Hot'n Now, KFC, King Dragon, Little Caesar's, McDonald's, Pizza Hut, Subway, Taco Bell, Wendy's American Inn, Best Western+, Hampton Inn, Regency Inn, Travel Inn $Tree, AT&T, CarQuest, Family$, Ford, GNC, H (4mi), Kroger, Meijer/dsl, Rite Aid, Walgreens, Walmart/Subway, **S** Marathon/dsl Holiday Inn Express, Super 8 H (8mi)

120mm Fawn River

108mm **trucks only both lanes**

107 US 131, IN 13, to Middlebury, Constantine, **0-3 mi N** Marathon/dsl, Speedway/dsl Country Table Rest., McDonald's Patchwork Quilt Inn, Plaza Motel $General, **1 mi S** BP/Blimpie/dsl Yup's DairyLand McKenzie House B&B Eby's Pines RV Park, KOA (apr-nov)

101 IN 15, to Goshen, Bristol, **0-2 mi S** Mobil/7-11, Speedway/dsl Subway Eby's Pines Camping (3mi), USPO

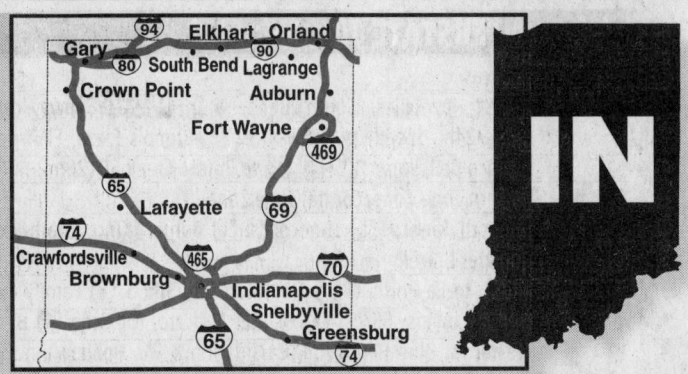

Gary, Elkhart, Orland, South Bend, Lagrange, Crown Point, Auburn, Fort Wayne, Lafayette, Crawfordsville, Brownburg, Indianapolis, Shelbyville, Greensburg — 94, 90, 80, 469, 65, 69, 74, 465, 70 — IN

ELKHART

96 Rd 1, E Elkhart, **2 mi S** BP/dsl, Marathon, Mobil/7-11 Arby's, China Star, DQ, McDonald's, Subway, Taco Bell Ace Hardware, RV/MH Hall of Fame

92 IN 19, to Elkhart, **N** Marathon, Mobil/7-11/dsl, Phillips 66/Subway/dsl Applebee's, Cracker Barrel, Perkins, Steak'n Shake Best Western, Candlewood Suites, Comfort Suites, Country Inn&Suites, Diplomat Motel, EconoLodge, Fairfield Inn, Fairway Inn, Hampton Inn, Hilton Garden, Holiday Inn Express, Microtel, Quality Inn, Sleep Inn, Staybridge Suites, Turnpike Motel $General, Aldi Foods, CVS Drug, Elkhart Campground (1mi), Martin's Foods, Tiara RV Ctr, transmissions, Walgreens, **0-2mi S** Exxon, Marathon/dsl, Speedway/dsl Arby's, Buffalo Wild Wings, Burger King, Callahan's, Chubby Trout, Culver's, DQ, Dunkin Donuts, El Camino Real, Jets Pizza, Jimmy John's, KFC, King Wha Chinese, LJ Silver, Matterhorn Rest., McDonald's, Noodles&Co, North Garden Buffet, Olive Garden, Panda Express, Papa John's, Penn Sta Subs, Pizza Hut, Qdoba, Red Lobster, Subway, Taco Bell, TX Roadhouse, Wendy's, Wings Etc. Baymont Inn, Budget Inn, Daylite Inn, Garden Inn, Red Roof Inn, Super 8 H, $Tree, Advance Parts, AT&T, AutoZone, Belle Tire, CarQuest, Family$, Honda, Indian Motorcycles, Lowe's, Menards, O'Reilly Parts, Petsmart, Ross, Verizon, Walmart/Subway

MISHAWAKA

91mm Christiana Creek

90mm **Schricker TP both directions,** Sunoco/7-11/dsl Starbucks RV Dump, Z Mkt

83 to Mishawaka, **N** BP/dsl, Phillips 66/dsl, Phillips 66/Subway/dsl Applebee's, Bar Louie, Five Guys, Granite City Grill, Olive Garden, Starbucks, Subway, Wendy's Best Western, Country Inn&Suites, Fairfield Inn, Hampton Inn, Holiday Inn Express, Super 8 Barnes&Noble, Best Buy, Costco/dsl, CVS Drug, JC Penney, KOA (mar-nov), Macy's, Martin's Foods/gas, Menards, Michael's, Ross, Target, Verizon, Walgreens, **S** H

SOUTH BEND

77 US 33, US 31B, IN 933, South Bend, **2 mi N on frtge rd** Admiral, Mobil/dsl, Murphy USA/dsl Applebee's, Arby's, Burger King, DQ, Dunkin Donuts, Eleni's Rest., Fazoli's, Hacienda Mexican, Jimmy John's, Jimmy John's, KFC, Little Caesar's, Marco's Pizza, McDonald's, McDonald's, Papa John's, Pizza Hut, Ponderosa, Sonic, Starbucks, Steak'n Shake, Subway Comfort Suites, Hampton Inn, Motel 6, Staybridge Suites, Suburban Lodge, Waterford Lodge $Tree, Aldi Foods, AutoZone, BMW/Mazda, Meijer/dsl/24hr, NAPA, O'Reilly Parts, TrueValue, vet, Walgreens, Walmart/Subway, **S** Marathon, Phillips 66/Subway/dsl American Pancake House, Bob Evans, HoPing House Chinese, King Gyros, Perkins, Pizza King, Taco Bell, Wendy's Best Value Inn, Econolodge, Hilton Garden, Holiday Inn Express, Microtel, Quality Inn, St Marys Inn H, CarX, to Notre Dame

76mm St Joseph River

IN

INTERSTATE 80/90 Cont'd

Exit #	Services
72	US 31, to Niles, South Bend, N Pilot/Subway/dsl/scales/24hr, Speedway/Subway/dsl Bruno's Pizza, El Arriero, Taco Bell, Super 8, S to Potato Creek SP (20mi)
62mm	Eastern Time Zone/Central Time Zone
56mm	**TP both lanes,** Sunoco/dsl Burger King, Starbucks litter barrel
49	IN 39, to La Porte, N Hampton Inn, **3mi S** Family Express, Phillips 66/dsl DQ, El Bracero Mexican Best Western+, Blue Heron Inn, Cassidy Inn & RV, Holiday Inn Express, Travelodge
39	US 421, to Michigan City, Westville, S Purdue U North Cent
38mm	**trucks only both lanes, litter barrels**
31	IN 49, to Chesterton, Valparaiso, N Family Express/dsl, Phillips 66, Speedway/dsl AJ's Pizza, Bob Evans, Clock Rest., Culver's Hilton Garden CVS Drug, Sand Creek RV Park (3mi, Apr-Oct), Strack&Van Til Mkt, Tire Pros, to IN Dunes Nat Lakeshore, S Hampton Inn (8mi), Super 8 (8mi)
24mm	**toll plaza**
23	Portage, Port of Indiana, **0-2 mi N** Marathon, Shell Denny's, Mark's Grill $Inn, Baymont Inn, Best Western, Country Inn&Suites, Days Inn, Quality Inn, Super 8, S BP, Speedway/dsl Burger King, CiCi's Pizza, DQ, Dunkin Donuts, El Contarito Mexican, Jimmy John's, KFC, Little Caesar's, McDonald's, Rosewood Rest., Starbucks, Subway, Wendy's Ace Hardware, Advance Parts, AutoZone, Family$, GNC, O'Reilly Parts, Town&Country Mkt, USPO, Verizon, Walgreens
22mm	**TP both lanes,** Sunoco/dsl Ladson Grill
21mm	**I-90 and I-80 run together eb, separate wb. I-80 runs with I-94 wb. For I-80 exits 1 through 15, see Indiana Interstate 94.**
21	I-94 E to Detroit, I-80/94 W, US 6, IN 51, Lake Station, S FLYING J/Denny's/dsl/scales/24hr/@, Mr Fuel/dsl/scales/24hr, Pilot/Road Ranger/Subway/dsl/scales, TA/BP/Popeye's/dsl/scales/24hr/@ Blue Beacon, Blue Beacon
17	I-65 S, US 12, US 20, Dunes Hwy, to Indianapolis
14b	IN 53, to Gary, Broadway, S Citgo
14a	Grant St, to Gary, S H
10	IN 912, Cline Ave, to Gary, N casino
5	US 41, Calumet Ave, to Hammond, S Nice'n Easy, Race-Co, Speedway/dsl Arby's, Aurelio's Pizza, Dunkin Donuts, Johnel's Rest., KFC, McDonald's, Subway, Taco Bell, White Castle Quality Inn, Ramada Inn, Super 8 Aldi Foods, AutoZone, Murray's Parts, Walgreens
3	IN 912, Cline Ave, to Hammond, N to Gary Reg Airport, S BP
1.5mm	**toll plaza**
1mm	US 12, US 20, 106th St, Indianapolis Blvd, N Citgo, Mobil, Shell/dsl casino, S Burger King, KFC, McDonald's Aldi Foods, auto repair, Jewel-Osco
0mm	Indiana/Illinois state line

PORTAGE

IN

INTERSTATE 94

Exit #	Services
46mm	Indiana/Michigan state line
43mm	**Welcome Ctr wb, full facilities, info, litter barrels, petwalk, vending**
40b a	US 20, US 35, to Michigan City, N McDonald's (3mi) H, S Speedway/dsl
34b a	US 421, to Michigan City, N BP/dsl, Family Express/e-85, Speedway/dsl, Speedway/White Castle/dsl Arby's, Baskin-Robbins/Dunkin Donuts, Buffalo Wild Wings, Burger King, Chili Crawford's Eatery, Culver's, Denny's, El Bracero Mexican, Fies Cantina, Hibachi Buffet, IHOP, Jimmy John's, KFC, LJ Silver, McDonald's, Olive Garden, Panda Express, Panera Bread, Pizza Hut/Taco Bell, Red Lobster, Ryan's, Schoop's Rest., Sophia's Pancakes, Starbucks, Steak'n Shake, Subway, TX Corral, Wendy's ABC Mote Baymont Inn, Clarion, Comfort Inn, Country Inn&Suites, Hampto Inn, Knights Inn, Microtel, Red Roof Inn, Super 8, Travel Inn $General, $Tree, Advance Parts, Aldi Foods, AT&T, AutoZon Big R, BigLots, Family$, Fannie May Candies, Ford/Lincoln, GN Hobby Lobby, JC Penney, Jo-Ann Fabrics, Kohl's, Lowe's, Meije dsl, Menards, Midas, Petsmart, Ross, Save-a-Lot, TJ Maxx, Verizon, Walgreens, Walmart/Subway, S Speedway/Subway/dsl scales/24hr Buick/Chevrolet/GMC, Harley-Davidson
29mm	**weigh sta both lanes**
26b a	IN 49, Chesterton, N to IN Dunes SP, S BP/White Castle, Speedway/dsl A&W/KFC, Applebee's, Arby's, Burger King, DQ, Dunkin Donuts, El Salto Mexican, Gelsosomo's Pizza, Happy Wok, Jimmy John's, Lemon Tree Grill, Little Caesar' LJ Silver, McDonald's, Papa John's, Pizza Hut, Subway, Taco Bell, Tao Chen's, Third Coast Cafe, Wendy's Best Western, EconoLodge, Hilton Garden (3mi), Lakeside Inn, Quality Inn H, Advance Parts, AutoZone, Jewel-Osco, Sand Camping (5mi), to Valparaiso, Verizon, Walgreens
22b a	US 20, Burns Harbor, N Shell/Subway/dsl/scales/LP, TA/BP Country Pride/Pizza Hut/Popeye's/Taco Bell/dsl/scales/24hr/ Comfort Inn fireworks, S Luke/dsl, Pilot/McDonald's/Subway/dsl/scales/24hr Camp-Land RV Ctr, Chevrolet, fireworks, Ford, Kia, Nissan, repair, Toyota
19	IN 249, to Port of IN, Portage, N Family Express dsl/e-85 Corner Bistro, DQ, Longhorn Steaks, McDonald' Quaker Steak&Lube, Starbucks, Subway Affordable Suite Country Inn&Suites Bass Pro Shops, S Marathon/ds Shell/Luke Denny's, Shenanigans Grill Best Wester Days Inn, Dollar Inn, Hampton Inn, Super 8, Travel Inn
16	access to I-80/90 **toll** road E, I-90 **toll** road W, IN 51N, Ripley S same as 15b&a
I-94/I-80 run together wb.	
15b	US 6W, IN 51, N FLYING J/Denny's/dsl/scales/24hr/@ MrFuel/dsl/scales/24hr, TA/BP/Popeye's/Subway/dsl/scales/24hr/ Ponderosa, Wing Wah Blue Beacon, Blue Beacon
15a	US 6E, IN 51S, to US 20, S BP/Luke, GoLo, Road Ranger/Pilot/Subway/dsl/scales/24hr Burger King, DQ, Silver, Papa John's, Ruben's Café, Wendy's Ace Hardware Walgreens
13	Central Ave (from eb)
12b	I-65 N, to Gary and **toll** road
12a	I-65 S (from wb), to Indianapolis
11	I-65 S (from eb)
10b a	IN 53, Broadway, N 23rd St Gas, Clark JJ Fish S GoLo DQ, Rally's
9	Grant St, N Clark $Tree, Advance Parts, County Mk Foods/gas, Family$, Walgreens, S Citgo, Loves/Denny's/dsl/scales/LP/24hr/@, Petro/Iron Skillet/Pizza Hut/dsl scales/24hr, Speedway/dsl Burger King, Church's, Dunkin Donuts, McDonald's, Subway $Tree, Aldi Foods, AutoZone Fagen Drug, Firestone/auto, Midas
6	Burr St, N Pilot/Subway/dsl/scales/24hr/@, TA/Country Pride/Pizza Hut/Taco Bell/dsl/scales/24hr/@ J&J Fish Chicken, Philly Steaks, Rico's Pizza SpeedCo, S GoLo Mr Fuel/dsl/24hr

MI CITY

CHESTERTON

GARY AREA

INTERSTATE 94 Cont'd

Exit #	Services
5	IN 912, Cline Ave, S BP, Speedway/dsl Arby's, Culver's, DQ, Jedi's Garden Rest., KFC, McDonald's, Pizza Hut, Popeye's, Subway, Taco Bell, Wendy's, White Castle Best Western, Hometowne Lodge, Motel 6 $Tree, Family$, Fannie May Candies
3	Kennedy Ave, N GoLo, Speedway Burger King, Domino's, Dunkin Donuts/Baskin Robbins, McDonald's repair, Walgreens, S Sixers Buffalo Wild Wings, Cracker Barrel, Squigi's Pizza, Subway, Wendy's Courtyard, Fairfield Inn, Hampton Inn, Residence Inn **IN Welcome Ctr**, USPO
2	US 41S, IN 152N, Indianapolis Blvd, N GoLo, Luke, SavAStop Dunkin Donuts, House Of Pizza, Papa John's, Pepe's Mexican, Petros Rest., Pizza Hut, Popeye's, Rally's, Schoop's Burgers, Stuffed Pepper, Subway, Taco Bell, Wally's Gyros, Wendy's, Wheel Rest. CarX, Chevrolet, Family$, Goodyear, Midas, vet, S Pilot/dsl/scales/24hr JJ Fish, Starbucks, White Castle Comfort Inn Aldi Foods, Cabela's, Walmart/Subway
1	US 41N, Calumet Ave, N Speedway/dsl Barton's Pizza, Baskin-Robbins/Dunkin Donuts, Subway Walgreens, S BP, CT Fuel, GoLo, Marathon Arby's, Baskin-Robbins/Dunkin Donuts, Boston Mkt, Burger King, Canton House Chinese, Chipotle, Edwardo's Pizza, El Salto Mexican, Firehouse Subs, Five Guys, Fortune House, Munster Gyros, Panera Bread, Pizza Hut, Subway, Taco Bell, Wendy's $Tree, AT&T, Jewel-Osco, Staples, Target, URGENT CARE, Verizon, vet
0mm	**Indiana/Illinois state line**

INDIANAPOLIS AREA

INTERSTATE 465 (Indianapolis)

Exit #	Services
	I-465 loops around Indianapolis. Exit numbers begin/end on I-65, exit 106.
53b a	I-65 N to Indianapolis, S to Louisville
52	Emerson Ave, N BP/dsl, Marathon, Shell/Circle K, Speedway/dsl Burger King, Domino's, El Mariachi, KFC, LJ Silver, Subway, Taco Bell, Waffle House Motel 6 H, $General, S Murphy USA/dsl, Speedway/dsl Arby's, Bamboo House, China Buffet, DJ's Hotdogs, DQ, Egg Roll, El Puerto Mexican, Fazoli's, Firehouse Subs, Fujiyama, Hardee's, Jets Pizza, Jimmy John's, Little Caesar's, McDonald's, Papa John's, Papa Murphy's, Pizza Hut, Ponderosa, Rally's, Starbucks, Steak'n Shake, Subway, Taco Bell, Wendy's, White Castle Holiday Inn Express, La Quinta, Red Roof Inn, Super 8 $Tree, Advance Parts, AT&T, AutoZone, CarX, GNC, Goodyear/auto, Kroger/dsl, Lowe's Whse, Meineke, O'Reilly Parts, Verizon, vet, Walgreens, Walmart/Subway
	I-74 W and I-465 S run together around S Indianapolis 21 miles.
49	I-74 E, US 421 S
48	Shadeland Ave (from nb)
47	US 52 E, Brookville Rd, E Marathon, Speedway/dsl Bugsy's Grill, Burger King, McDonald's, Subway, Taco Bell Baymont Inn CVS Drug, Family$, vet
46	US 40, Washington St, E Marathon, Phillips 66, Shell/dsl, Speedway/dsl Arby's, Blueberry Hill Pancakes, Church's, LJ Silver, Olive Garden, Skyline Chili, Steak'n Shake, Yen Ching Chinese $General, Advance Parts, AutoZone, Ford, Meineke, O'Reilly Parts, W Thornton's/dsl Applebee's, Bob Evans, Fazoli's, McDonald's, Subway Comfort Stay Buick/GMC, Hyundai, PepBoys

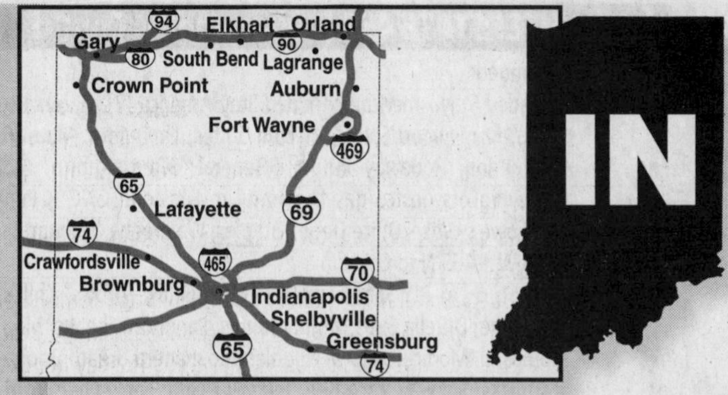

Exit #	Services
44b	I-70 E, to Columbus
44a	I-70 W, to Indianapolis
42	US 36, IN 67 N, Pendleton Pike, E Cafe Heidelberg, Chile Verde, Hardee's, Papa's Rest., Popeye's, Skillet Rest., Wendy's $General, $Tree, Menards, Save-A-Lot Foods, U-Haul, W GetGo/dsl, Speedway/dsl, Thornton's/dsl Arby's, Domino's, Dunkin Donuts, KFC, LJ Silver, Los Rancheros, McDonald's, Rally's, Subway, Taco Bell, Waffle House, White Castle H, Advance Parts, Aldi Foods, CVS Drug, Family$, Meineke, Menards, O'Reilly Parts
40	56th St, Shadeland Ave, E Marathon, to Ft Harrison SP
37b a	I-69, N to Ft Wayne, IN 37, E H, W services on frontage rds
35	Allisonville Rd, N Bravo Italian, Buca Italian, Buffalo Wild Wings, Dave&Buster's, Hardee's, MCL Cafeteria, Melting Pot, On-the-Border, Outback Steaks Courtyard Costco/gas, Firestone/auto, JC Penney, Jo-Ann Fabrics, Macy's, REI, Van Maur, S Shell, Speedway/dsl Chipotle, ChuckeCheese, Five Guys, Noodles&Co, Panera Bread, Papa John's, Pie Five, Qdoba, White Castle Quality Inn $Tree, Michael's, Petsmart, Ross, TJ Maxx, Trader Joe's
33	IN 431, Keystone Ave, N BP/McDonald's, Marathon/dsl Bob Evans, Coopers Hawk, Steak'n Shake Acura, BMW/Mini, Chevrolet, Fiat, Ford, Harley-Davidson, Honda, Hyundai, Infiniti, Kia, Mercedes, Nissan, Porsche, Subaru, Toyota, S Benihana, Champp's, Cheesecake Factory, Chipotle, Fleming's Steaks, LePeep Rest., Maggiano's, McAlister's Deli, PF Chang's, Pizza Hut, Ruth Chris Steaks, Seasons 52, Starbucks, Sullivan's Steaks, TGIFriday's Hyatt Place, Marriott, Sheraton Kohl's, Nordstrom's
31	US 31, Meridian St, N Comfort Inn, Courtyard, Holiday Inn H, S Marathon/DQ/dsl, Shell/Circle K/dsl Another Broken Egg Cafe, Arby's, Firebirds Grill, Granite City, McAlister's Deli, McDonald's, Paradise Cafe Bakery, Starbucks Drury Inn
27	US 421 N, Michigan Rd, N Marathon, Speedway/dsl Applebee's, Burger King, DQ, HoneyBaked Ham, Jimmy John's, KFC/Taco Bell, McDonald's, Olive Garden, Outback Steaks, Red Robin, Subway, Wendy's Holiday Inn Express, Red Roof Inn AutoZone, Best Buy, Buick/GMC, Chevrolet, Chrysler/Dodge/Jeep, Home Depot, Kohl's, Marshall's, PetCo, Target, Walgreens, S Citgo/dsl, Marathon, Shell/Circle K Arby's, Blaze Pizza, Burger King, Chick-fil-A, Chipotle Mexican, CiCi's, Cracker Barrel, Denny's, El Meson Mexican, Famous Dave's, Five Guys, Hardee's, Jack-in-the-Box, McAlister's Deli, McDonald's, Noodles&Co, Panda Express, Panera Bread, Papa Murphy's, Pizza Hut, Popeye's, Qdoba, Rally's, Ruby Tuesday, Steak'n Shake, Subway, Taco Bell, Tilted Kilt, TX Roadhouse, Wendy's, White Castle, Yen Ching Chinese, Zaxby's Best Western, Comfort Inn, Days Inn, Drury Inn, Embassy Suites,

INTERSTATE 465 (Indianapolis) Cont'd

27	Continued Extended Stay America, Extended Stay America (2), Gatehouse Suites, Homewood Suites, InTown Suites, La Quinta, Motel 6, Quality Inn, Rodeway Inn $General, $Tree, Aamco, Aldi Foods, BigLots, Costco/gas, Discount Tire, Firestone, GNC, JC Penney, Lowe's Whse, Office Depot, Staples, Walgreens, Walmart
25	I-865 W, I-465 N to Chicago
23	86th St, E BP, Speedway/dsl Abuelo's, Arby's, Chili's, Coldstone, DiBella Subs, Jimmy John's, Longhorn Steaks, Macaroni Grill, Monical's Pizza, Noodles&Co, Panera Bread, Qdoba, Starbucks, Subway, Taco Bell, Ted's MT Grill, Tom+Chee, Traders Mill Grill, Wendy's Extended Stay America, Fairfield Inn, InTown Suites H, AT&T, Big-O Tires, BooksAMillion, Dick's, Michael's, Old Navy, Petsmart
21	71st St, E BP/dsl Chef Mike's, Hardee's, McDonald's, Steak'n Shake, Subway Candlewood Suites, Clarion Inn, Courtyard, Hampton Inn, Holiday Inn Express, TownePlace Suites, W Gatsby's, Hotbox Pizza, Jimmy John's, LePeep, Starbucks Hilton Garden, Residence Inn, Wingate Inn
20	I-65, N to Chicago, S to Indianapolis
19	56th St (from nb), E Marathon, Speedway/dsl
17	38th St, E BP, Marathon/dsl, Shell/Circle K, Speedway DQ, El Maguey Mexican, Golden Corral, Jack-in-the-Box, Little Caesar's, Red Lobster, Steak'n Shake, Subway, White Castle $General, $Tree, AutoZone, Chevrolet, CVS Drug, Family$, Home Depot, Meijer, O'Reilly Parts, W Arby's, Burger King, Chili's, Cracker Barrel, IHOP, Jersey Mike's, McDonald's, Taco Bell, TGIFriday's Baymont Inn Target
I-74 W and I-465 S run together around S Indianapolis 21 miles.	
16b	I-74 W, to Peoria
16a	US 136, to Speedway, E Circle K, Shell/Circle K, Thornton's/dsl Applebee's, Arby's, Buffalo Wild Wings, Burger King, Chicago's Pizza, Chipotle, Denny's, El Rodeo, Firehouse Subs, Grindstone Charley's, Hardee's, Jimmy John's, KFC, LJ Silver, McDonald's, Papa Murphy's, Pizza Hut, Starbucks, Subway, Taco Bell, White Castle $Inn, Courtyard $General, $Tree, Advance Parts, AT&T, Big Lots, CarX, CVS Drug, Firestone/auto, GNC, Goodyear/auto, Kohl's, Kroger/dsl, PetCo, TJ Maxx, Tuesday Morning, Verizon, W BP/dsl Clarion
14b a	10th St, E Peking Chinese, Penn Sta, Pizza Hut, Wendy's H, Lowe's Whse, Walmart Mkt, W Shell/Circle K, Speedway/dsl Arby's, Fazoli's, Flapjacks, Marco's Pizza, McDonald's, Rally's, Starbucks, Taco Bell CVS Drug, Walgreens
13b a	US 36, Rockville Rd, E Mobil Kazablanka Grill Holiday Inn Express, Microtel, Motel 6, Wingate Inn Sam's Club, W Speedway/dsl Bob Evans Best Western
12b a	US 40 E, Washington St, E BP/dsl Burger King, China Inn, Church's, Fazoli's, McDonald's, Papa John's, Pizza Hut, Taco Bell, Wendy's, White Castle $General, $Tree, $Tree, Ace Hardware, Advance Parts, AutoZone, CVS Drug, Family$, Kroger/gas, O'Reilly Parts, Speedway Parts, U-Haul, vet, W Circle K/dsl, Phillips 66/dsl, Thornton's/dsl Arby's, Hardee's, Jimmy John's, LJ Silver, McDonald's, Steak'n Shake, Subway Regal 8 Inn $General, CarX, Goodyear/auto, Save-A-Lot Foods
11b a	Sam Jones Expwy, E Marathon/dsl, Speedway/dsl Indy's Rest., Jimmy John's, Library Rest., Subway, Waffle House Candlewood Suites, Courtyard, Extended Stay America, Fairfield Inn, Hyatt Place, La Quinta, Quality Inn, Ramada Inn, Residence Inn, Super 8, Wyndham, W Crowne Plaza, Radisson
9b a	I-70, E to Indianapolis, W to Terre Haute
8	IN 67 S, Kentucky Ave, E Phillips 66/dsl H, W B McDonald's/dsl, Shell/Subway/dsl, Speedway/dsl Burg King, Culver's, Denny's, KFC, Rally's Country Inn&Suit Walmart Mkt
7	Mann Rd (from wb), E H
4	IN 37 S, Harding St, N Mr Fuel/dsl/scales, Pilot/Subway dsl/scales/24hr Omelette Shoppe Best Inn, Quali Inn H, Blue Beacon, S FLYING J/Arby's/PJ Fresh/ds LP/scales/24hr/@, Marathon Hardee's, McDonald's, Ta Bell, Waffle House, White Castle Knight's Inn Freigh liner, SpeedCo, TruckoMat/scales
2b a	US 31, IN 37, N BP/dsl, Marathon/Dunkin Donuts/d Arby's, China Garden, CiCi's, Domino's, El Azabache, Gol en Wok, KFC, King Gyros, Little Caesar's, LJ Silver, MCL Caf teria, Penn Sta Subs, Pizza Hut, Qdoba, Steak'n Shake, Whi Castle $General, $Tree, Advance Parts, Aldi Foods, AT& AutoZone, CarQuest, Family$, Firestone/auto, GNC, Kroge gas, Marshall's, Meineke, Midas, Save-A-Lot, U-Haul, S B dsl, Speedway/dsl 8 Lucky Buffet, Bob Evans, El Jalapeñ McDonald's, Red Lobster, Subway, Taco Bell, Wendy's Con fort Inn, Holiday Inn Express, Indy Lodge, Super 8, Travel In CVS Drug, Walgreens
53b a	I-65 N to Indianapolis, S to Louisville

I-465 loops around Indianapolis. Exit numbers begin/end on I-65, exit 10

INTERSTATE 469 (Ft Wayne)

Exit #	Services
31c b a	I-69, US 27 S, Auburn Road. **I-469 begins/ends.**
29mm	St Joseph River
29b a	Maplecrest Rd, W Lassus/DQ/Subway/dsl, Marathon/dsl
25	IN 37, to Ft Wayne, W Murphy USA/dsl Agaves Me ican, Antonio's Pizza, Applebee's, Bob Evans, Buffalo Wi Wings, Cracker Barrel, DQ, Steak'n Shake, Subway, Wendy' Wings Etc, Zianos Italian AT&T, Discount Tire, Kohl's, Ma shall's, Meijer/dsl, Menards, Michael's, Office Depot, Petsmar Verizon, Walgreens, Walmart/McDonald's
21	US 24 E
19b a	US 30 E, to Ft Wayne, E FLYING J/Huddle House/Subway dsl/LP/scales/24hr, Sunoco/Taco Bell/dsl Freightliner, Mack Volvo, Peterbilt, truck/tire repair, W Marathon Garno Italian, Golden Gate Chinese, Mancino's Grinders, Richard Rest., Zesto Drive-In Holiday Inn Express $General
17	Minnich Rd
15	Tillman Rd
13	Marion Center Rd
11	US 27, US 33 S, to Decatur, Ft Wayne, E Shell/Subway/dsl
10.5mm	St Marys River
9	Winchester Rd
6	IN 1, to Bluffton, Ft Wayne, W to
2	Indianapolis Rd, W to
1	Lafayette Ctr Rd

NOTES

IOWA

INTERSTATE 29

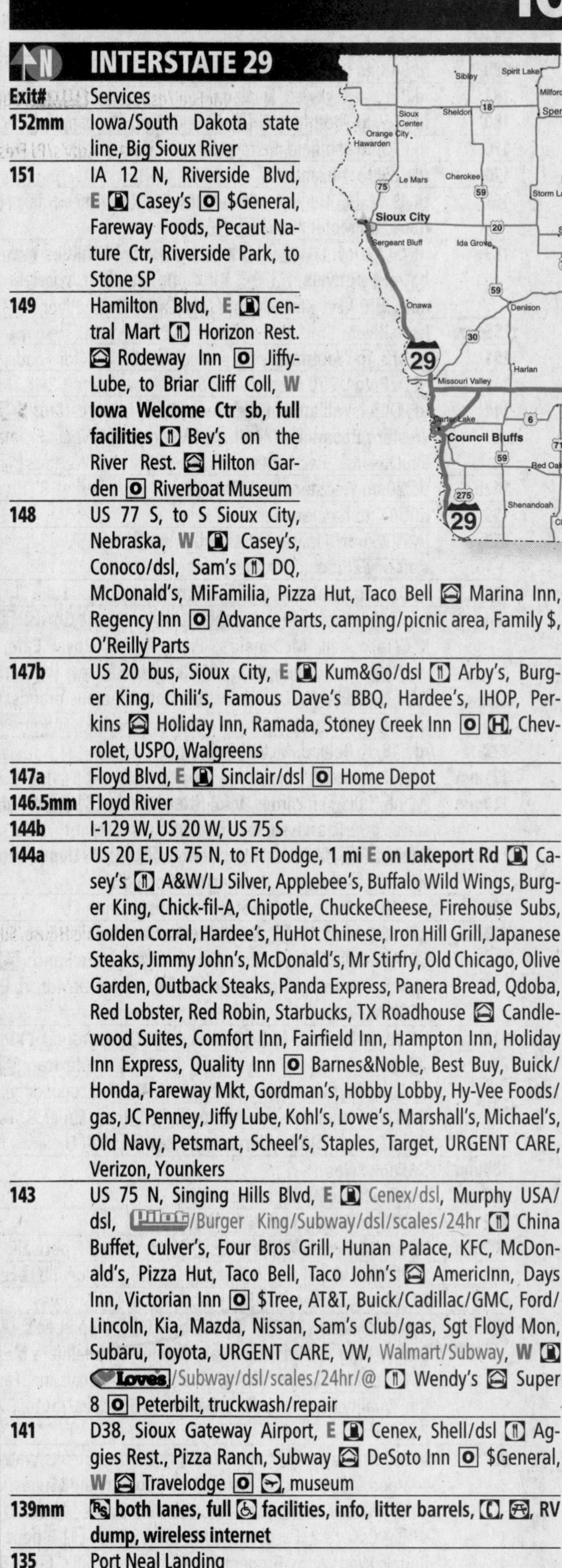

Exit#	Services
152mm	Iowa/South Dakota state line, Big Sioux River
151	IA 12 N, Riverside Blvd, **E** [gas] Casey's [other] $General, Fareway Foods, Pecaut Nature Ctr, Riverside Park, to Stone SP
149	Hamilton Blvd, **E** [gas] Central Mart [food] Horizon Rest. [lodging] Rodeway Inn [other] Jiffy-Lube, to Briar Cliff Coll, **W** **Iowa Welcome Ctr sb, full facilities** [food] Bev's on the River Rest. [lodging] Hilton Garden [other] Riverboat Museum
148	US 77 S, to S Sioux City, Nebraska, **W** [gas] Casey's, Conoco/dsl, Sam's [food] DQ, McDonald's, MiFamilia, Pizza Hut, Taco Bell [lodging] Marina Inn, Regency Inn [other] Advance Parts, camping/picnic area, Family $, O'Reilly Parts
147b	US 20 bus, Sioux City, **E** [gas] Kum&Go/dsl [food] Arby's, Burger King, Chili's, Famous Dave's BBQ, Hardee's, IHOP, Perkins [lodging] Holiday Inn, Ramada, Stoney Creek Inn [other] [H], Chevrolet, USPO, Walgreens
147a	Floyd Blvd, **E** [gas] Sinclair/dsl [other] Home Depot
146.5mm	Floyd River
144b	I-129 W, US 20 W, US 75 S
144a	US 20 E, US 75 N, to Ft Dodge, **1 mi E on Lakeport Rd** [gas] Casey's [food] A&W/LJ Silver, Applebee's, Buffalo Wild Wings, Burger King, Chick-fil-A, Chipotle, ChuckeCheese, Firehouse Subs, Golden Corral, Hardee's, HuHot Chinese, Iron Hill Grill, Japanese Steaks, Jimmy John's, McDonald's, Mr Stirfry, Old Chicago, Olive Garden, Outback Steaks, Panda Express, Panera Bread, Qdoba, Red Lobster, Red Robin, Starbucks, TX Roadhouse [lodging] Candlewood Suites, Comfort Inn, Fairfield Inn, Hampton Inn, Holiday Inn Express, Quality Inn [other] Barnes&Noble, Best Buy, Buick/Honda, Fareway Mkt, Gordman's, Hobby Lobby, Hy-Vee Foods/gas, JC Penney, Jiffy Lube, Kohl's, Lowe's, Marshall's, Michael's, Old Navy, Petsmart, Scheel's, Staples, Target, URGENT CARE, Verizon, Younkers
143	US 75 N, Singing Hills Blvd, **E** [gas] Cenex/dsl, Murphy USA/dsl, Pilot/Burger King/Subway/dsl/scales/24hr [food] China Buffet, Culver's, Four Bros Grill, Hunan Palace, KFC, McDonald's, Pizza Hut, Taco Bell, Taco John's [lodging] AmericInn, Days Inn, Victorian Inn [other] $Tree, AT&T, Buick/Cadillac/GMC, Ford/Lincoln, Kia, Mazda, Nissan, Sam's Club/gas, Sgt Floyd Mon, Subaru, Toyota, URGENT CARE, VW, Walmart/Subway, **W** [gas] Loves/Subway/dsl/scales/24hr/@ [food] Wendy's [lodging] Super 8 [other] Peterbilt, truckwash/repair
141	D38, Sioux Gateway Airport, **E** [gas] Cenex, Shell/dsl [food] Aggies Rest., Pizza Ranch, Subway [lodging] DeSoto Inn [other] $General, **W** [lodging] Travelodge [other] [airport], museum
139mm	**[Rs] both lanes, full [handicap] facilities, info, litter barrels, [phone], [picnic], RV dump, wireless internet**
135	Port Neal Landing

SIOUX CITY

Exit#	Services
134	Salix, **W** [other] camping
132mm	**weigh sta sb, [Rs] parking only nb, [picnic], litter barrels**
127	IA 141, Sloan, **E** [gas] Casey's/dsl, Kum&Go/Subway/dsl [lodging] Homestead Inn, WinnaVegas Inn [other] RV Park, **W** [gas] Pony Express (3mi) [other] to Winnebago Indian Res/hotel/casino (3mi)
120	to Whiting, **W** [other] camping
112	IA 175, Onawa, **E** [gas] Cenex/dsl, Conoco/Subway/dsl [food] DQ, McDonald's, Michael's Rest. [lodging] Super 8 [other] [H], NAPA, On-Ur-Wa RV Park, repair, ShopKo, **2 mi W** [other] Keel Boat Exhibit, KOA, Lewis&Clark SP
110mm	**[Rs] both lanes, full [handicap] facilities, info, litter barrels, petwalk, [phone], [picnic], RV dump, wireless internet**
105	E60, Blencoe
96mm	Little Sioux River
95	F 20, Little Sioux, **E** [gas] gas [other] Loess Hills SF (9mi), **W** [other] Woodland RV Park
92mm	Soldier River
91.5mm	[Rs] both lanes, parking only, litter barrels
89	IA 127, Mondamin, **1 mi E** [gas] Jiffy Mart/dsl
82	F50, Modale, **1 mi W** [gas] Heartland/dsl
79mm	**[Rs] both lanes, full [handicap] facilities, info, litter barrels, [phone], [picnic], RV dump, wireless internet**
75	US 30, Missouri Valley, **E Iowa Welcome Ctr (5mi)** [gas] Shell/dsl/24hr [food] Arby's, McDonald's, Penny's Diner, Subway [lodging] Oaktree Inn [other] [H] (2mi), to Steamboat Exhibit, **W** [gas] Cenex/dsl, PetroMart/dsl [food] Burger King, Taco John's, The Edge Rest. [lodging] Best Value Inn, DeSoto Inn, Rath Inn [other] Buick/Chevrolet
72.5mm	Boyer River
72	IA 362, Loveland, **E** [gas] Desoto/dsl, **W** [other] to Wilson Island SP (6mi)
71	I-680 E, to Des Moines
I-29 S & I-680 W run together 10 mi.	
66	Honey Creek **W** [other] RV Camping
61b	I-680 W, to N Omaha, **W** Mormon Trail Ctr
I-29 N & I-680 E run together 10 mi	
61a	IA 988, to Crescent, **E** [gas] Casey's/dsl
56	IA 192 S (sb only, exits left), Council Bluffs, **E** [other] [H], URGENT CARE, Walmart

MO VALLEY

IA

COUNCIL BLUFFS

INTERSTATE 29 Cont'd

Exit#	Services
55	N 25th, Council Bluffs, E Cenex/dsl, Sinclair URGENT CARE (1mi), Walmart/Subway (1mi)
54b	N 35th St (from nb), Council Bluffs
54a	G Ave (from sb), Council Bluffs
53b	I-480 W, US 6, to Omaha (exits left from nb)
53a	9th Ave, S 37th Ave, Council Bluffs, E Phillips 66, Shell Days Inn, W Harrah's Hotel/Casino
52	Nebraska Ave, E Phillips 66/dsl Hooters, Quaker Steak, Ruby Tuesday Comfort Suites, Holiday Inn Express, Microtel, SpringHill Suites, Woodspring Suites Bass Pro Shops, W AmeriStar Hotel/casino, Hampton Inn, Holiday Inn
51	I-80 W, to Omaha
I-29 and I-80 run together 3 miles. See Iowa I-80, exits 1b-3.	
48	I-80 E (from nb), to Des Moines, E H
47	US 275, IA 92, Lake Manawa, E Iowa School for the Deaf, W Buffalo Wild Wings, Famous Dave's, Firehouse Subs, Freddy's, Longhorn Steaks, Olive Garden, Panda Express, Panera Bread, Pepperjax Grill, Pizza Ranch, Qdoba, Starbucks $Tree, AT&T, Dick's, Hobby Lobby, Kohl's, Petsmart, Target, TJ Maxx, Verizon
42	IA 370, to Bellevue, W K&B Saddlery, to Offutt AFB, truck parts
38mm	**both lanes, full facilities, info, litter barrels, petwalk, RV dump, wireless internet**
35	US 34 E, to Glenwood, E McDonalds (4mi) Western Inn (4mi) RV Park, W BP/rest/dsl, Loves/Subway/dsl/scales/24hr Bluff View Motel Harley-Davidson
32	US 34 W, Pacific Jct, to Plattsmouth
24	L31, to Tabor, Bartlett
20	IA 145, Thurman
15	J26, Percival, **1-2 mi E** gas/dsl
11.5mm	**weigh sta nb**
10	IA 2, to Nebraska City, Sidney, E to Waubonsie SP (5mi), W Cenex/Godfathers/dsl/E85, Pilot/Subway/dsl/scales/24hr, Sapp Bros/Apple Barrel Rest/dsl/scales/24hr Wendy's Motel 6, Super 8 antiques, dsl/tire repair, IA Info, Lewis&Clark Ctr (3mi), to Arbor Lodge SP, Victorian Acres RV Park (3mi)
1	IA 333, Hamburg, **1 mi E** Casey's/dsl Blue Moon Grill Hamburg Inn H, NAPA, Stoner Soda Fountain
0mm	Iowa/Missouri state line

CLEAR LAKE

INTERSTATE 35

Exit#	Services
219mm	Iowa/Minnesota state line
214	rd 105, to Northwood, Lake Mills, E Royal Motel (7mi), W **Welcome Ctr both lanes, full facilities, litter barrels, petwalk, RV dump, vending, wireless internet** BP/Burger King/dsl, Kum&Go/dsl Country Inn&Suites, Holiday Inn Express casino
212mm	**weigh sta sb, nb, litter barrels**
208	rd A38, to Joice, Kensett, windmills
203	IA 9, to Manly, Forest City, W to Pilot Knob SP
202mm	Winnebago River
197	rd B20, **8 mi E** Lime Creek Nature Ctr
196mm	**both lanes, litter barrels, parking only**
194	US 18, to Mason City, Clear Lake, E Kwik Star/dsl/24hr Chevrolet, Freightliner, H (8mi), W Casey's/dsl, Kum&Go/dsl, Pilot/Subway/dsl/scales Arby's, Bennigan's, Culver's, DQ, KFC/Taco Bell, McDonald's, Perkins, Wendy's AmericInn, Best Western, Best Western, Microtel Ford
193	rd B35, to Mason City, Emery, E Kum&Go/Taco John's/dsl/e85 Super 8 truckwash, W Seven Stars Rest. to Clear Lake SP
190	US 18, rd 27 E, to Mason City
188	rd B43, to Burchinal
182	rd B60, to Rockwell, Swaledale
180	rd B65, to Thornton, W Cenex (2mi) camping
176	rd C13, to Sheffield, Belmond
170	rd C25, to Alexander
165	IA 3, E Dudley's Corner/Rest./dsl AmericInn (9mi), Hampton Motel (9mi) H (7mi)
159	rd C47, Dows, W **both lanes, full facilities info, litter barrels, petwalk, RV dump, vending, wireless internet** BP/Arby's/Godfather's/dsl/24hr
155mm	Iowa River
151	rd R75, to Woolstock
147	rd D20, to US 20 E
144	rd D25, Williams, E Boondocks Trkstp/cafe/dsl Best Western, Boondocks Motel RV camping, W FLYING J Subway/dsl/scales/24hr
142b a	US 20, to Webster City, Ft Dodge
139	rd D41, to Kamrar
133	IA 175, to Jewell, Ellsworth, W Kum&Go/Subway/dsl, Loves/rest./dsl/scales/24hr
128	rd D65, to Stanhope, Randall, **5 mi W** Little Wall Lake Pk
124	rd 115, Story City, W Casey's, Kum&Go/dsl DQ, KFC/Taco Bell, McDonald's, Pizza Ranch, Royal Cafe, Subway Comfort Inn, Super 8, Viking Motel/rest antiques, Ford, Goodlife RV Ctr, VF Factory Stores/famous brands, Whispering Oaks Camping
123	rd E18, to Roland, McCallsburg
121mm	prairie area sb
120mm	**nb, full facilities, info, litter barrels, RV dump scenic prairie area sb, vending, wireless internet**
119mm	**sb, full facilities, litter barrels, RV dump, vending, wireless internet**
116	rd E29, to Story, **2 mi W** Story Co Conservation Ctr
113	13th St, Ames, W Kum&Go/Burger King/dsl/E-85, Phillips 66/Arby's Burger King, Jimmy John's, Pizza Ranch Holiday Inn Express, Quality Inn H, Harley-Davidson, ISU, to USDA Vet Labs
111b a	US 30, to Nevada, Ames, E Twin Acres Campground (11mi), W Kum&Go/DQ/Subway/dsl El Azteca Mexican AmericInn, Baymont Inn, Country Inn&Suites, EconoLodge, Fairfield Inn, Hampton Inn, Microtel, Red Roof, Super 8, Towne Place Suites Chrysler/Dodge/Jeep, to IA St U
109mm	S Skunk River
106mm	**weigh sta sb, nb, no restrooms**
102	IA 210, to Slater, **3 mi W** Subway
100mm	**both lanes, full facilities, litter barrels, petwalk**
96	to Elkhart, W to Big Creek SP (11mi), Saylorville Lake
94	NE 36th St, Ankeny, W Kum&Go/dsl Subway
92	1st St, Ankeny, W Kum&Go, QT Applebee's, Arby's, Burger King, Cazador Mexican, Fazoli's, Guadalajara Mexican, KFC, Subway, Tokyo Steaks, Village Inn Days Inn, Fairfield Inn, Quality Inn, Ramada, Super 8 Goodyear/auto, O'Reilly Parts, Tires+
90	IA 160, Ankeny, E Casey's/dsl Outback Steaks, Waterfront Seafood AmericInn, Comfort Inn, Country Inn&Suites, Courtyard, Holiday Inn Express, Homewood Suites Buick/GMC, W Casey's 2, Casey's/dsl, MurphyUSA/dsl B-bops Rest, Buffalo Wild Wings, Burger King, Chick-fil-A, Chili's, China Buffet

AMES

ANKENY

IA

INTERSTATE 35 Cont'd

90	Continued Chipotle, Culver's, Fuzzy's Tacos, HuHot Chinese, IHOP, Jimmy John's, Los Charro, Maid Rite, Marble Slab, McDonald's, Noodles&Co, Okoboji, Old Chicago, Olive Garden, Panchero's Mexican, Panda Express, Panera Bread, Pepperjax, Perkins, Starbucks, Subway, Taco Bell, Tasty Tacos, Wendy's AT&T, Best Buy, Big O Tires, Chevrolet, Chrysler/Dodge/Jeep, Duluth Trading, Ford, GNC, Home Depot, Jo-Ann Fabrics, Kohl's, Menards, Michael's, Petsmart, Staples, Target, TJ Maxx, to Saylorville Lake (5mi), Tuesday Morning, Tuffy Auto, Verizon, Walgreens, Walmart/Subway
89	Corporate Woods Dr, E Hampton Inn, W Woodspring Suites F&F/dsl, Sam's Club/dsl
87b a	I-235, I-35 and I-80
I-35 and I-80 run together 14 mi around NW Des Moines. See I-80, exits 124-136.	
72c	(124 from I-80) University Ave, **See I-80, exit 124.**
72b	I-80 W
72a	I-235 E, to Des Moines
70	Civic Pkwy, Mills, E Kum&Go/McDonald's Fire Creek Grill, Legend's Grill, Quiznos, Starbucks Hy-Vee Foods/gas, Verizon, vet, Walgreens, W Casey's/dsl Applebee's, Bar Louie, BoneFish Grill, Bravo Italiana, Buffalo Wild Wings, Caribou Coffee, Cheesecake Factory, Chick-fil-A, Draught House 50, Fleming's Rest., Fuddruckers, Iron Wok, Jimmy John's, Joe's Crabshack, Johnny's Italian Steaks, Joseph's Steaks, Monterrey Mexican, Noodles&Co, On-the-Border, Panda Express, Panera Bread, PF Chang's, Red Robin, Tasty Tacos, Wellman's Grill Courtyard, Drury Inn, Hilton Garden, Holiday Inn, Residence Inn H, $Tree, Aldi Foods, Barnes&Noble, Best Buy, Costco/gas, Dick's, Dillards, Firestone/auto, Kohl's, Lowe's, Old Navy, PetCo, Scheel's Sports, Target, TJ Maxx, Trader Joe's, Verizon, Walmart, Younkers
69b a	Grand Ave, W Des Moines
68.5mm	Racoon River
68	IA 5, 7 mi E to ✈, to Walnut Woods SP
65	G14, to Norwalk, Cumming, W John Wayne Birthplace (14mi), Madison Co Museum (14mi)
61mm	North River
56	IA 92, to Indianola, Winterset, W Good Life RV Ctr
56mm	Middle River
53mm	**nb, litter barrels, no restrooms**
52	G50, St Charles, St Marys, W Casey's/dsl John Wayne Birthplace (14mi), museum (14mi)
51mm	**sb, litter barrels, no restrooms**
47	rd G64, to Truro, W Kum&Go (4mi)
45.5mm	South River
43	rd 207, New Virginia, E Kum&Go/Subway/dsl
36	rd 152, to US 69, 3 mi E Blue Haven Motel, Evergreen Inn, W st patrol
34	Clay St, Osceola, W Pilot/Subway/dsl/scales/24hr Lakeside Casino Resort/camping
33	US 34, Osceola, E Casey's/dsl/scales McDonald's, Pizza Hut, Subway Best Value Inn, Quality Inn, Super 8 H, Ford, Goodyear, Hy-Vee Foods, O'Reilly Parts, W BP/Arby's/dsl KFC/Taco Bell AmericInn Harley-Davidson, Walmart
32mm	**both lanes, full facilities, litter barrels, petwalk, RV dump, vending, wireless internet**
31mm	**parking area sb, weigh sta nb**
29	rd H45

DES MOINES

OSCEOLA

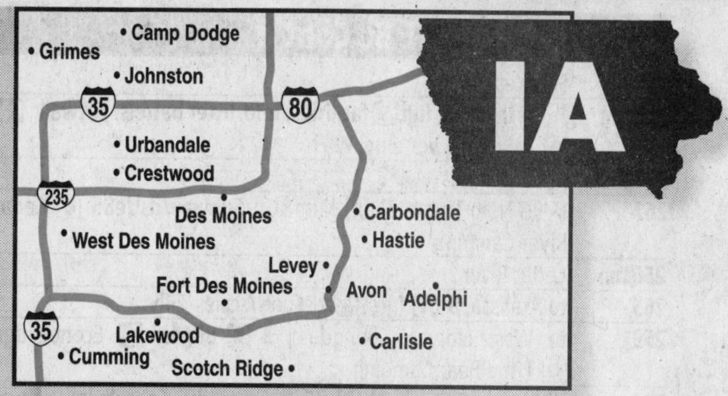

22	rd J14, Van Wert
18	rd J20, to Grand River
12	rd 2, Decatur City, Leon, 5 mi E Shell/dsl Little River Motel (5mi) H
7.5mm	Grand River
7mm	**both lanes, full facilities, info, litter barrels, petwalk, RV dump, vending, wireless internet**
4	US 69, to Davis City, Lamoni, E to 9 Eagles SP (10mi), W IA **Welcome Ctr** Casey's (2mi), Kum&Go/dsl/e85 Maid-Rite Cafe, Pizza Hut (2mi), QC Rest., Subway (2mi) Chief Lamoni Motel, Super 8 auto/truck repair
0mm	Iowa/Missouri state line

INTERSTATE 80

Exit#	Services
307mm	Iowa/Illinois state line, Mississippi River
306	US 67, to Le Claire, N BP/A&W (2mi), Shell/dsl Bierstube Grill, Hungry Hobo, McDonald's, Pizza Hut, Steventon's Rest., Subway Comfort Inn, Holiday Inn Express, Super 8 Buffalo Bill Museum, Slagles Foods, S BP (2mi)
301	Middle Rd, to Bettendorf
300mm	**both lanes, full facilities, litter barrels, petwalk, RV dump, vending, WiFi**
298	I-74 E, to Peoria, S st patrol, to H
295b a	US 61, Brady St, to Davenport, N BP/dsl Fiat, to Scott CP, **0-2 mi** S BP, KwikStar/dsl, Shell Burger King, Cracker Barrel, Happy Joe's Pizza, Hardee's, Hooters, Los Agaves Mexican, McDonald's, Mo Brady's Steaks, Olive Garden, Papa John's, ThunderBay Grille, Village Inn Rest. Baymont Inn, Best Western+, Casa Loma Suites, Clarion, Country Inn&Suites, Motel 6, Quad City Inn, Quality Inn, Residence Inn, Super 8, Travelodge, Wickliffe Inn $General, AutoZone, CarQuest, Firestone/auto, Honda, Hyundai, JC Penney, Lexus, Menards, Nissan, Tires+, Toyota, US Adventures RV Ctr, vet, Von Maur, VW
292	IA 130 W, Northwest Blvd, N FLYING J/Denny's/dsl/LP/scales/24hr, Loves/Arby's/dsl/scales/24hr Comfort Inn Farm&Fleet, Interstate RV Park (1mi), Peterbilt, truckwash, S BP/McDonald's/dsl, Shell Machine Shed Rest. Days Inn Freightliner
290	I-280 E, to Rock Island
284	Y40, to Walcott, N Pilot/Arby's/dsl/24hr/scales, TA/IA 80/BP/DQ/Pizza Hut/Taco Bell/Wendy's/dsl/scales/24hr/@ Checkered Flag Grille, Gramma's Rest. Comfort Inn Blue Beacon, IA 80 Trucking Museum, IA 80 Truck-o-Mat, SpeedCo Lube, tires, S Pilot/Subway/dsl/24hr McDonald's Days Inn Cheyenne Camping Ctr, Walcott CP
280	Y30, to Stockton, New Liberty
277	Durant, 2 mi S Casey's/dsl, Fifth St Petro/dsl Subway
271	US 6 W, IA 38 S, to Wilton

DAVENPORT

IA

E INTERSTATE 80 Cont'd

IOWA CITY

Exit#	Services
270mm	**Rs both lanes, full facilities, info, litter barrels, petwalk, RV dump, vending, WiFi**
268mm	parking areas
267	IA 38 N, to Tipton, N Kum&Go/Subway/dsl/e85 Cedar River Camping
266mm	Cedar River
265	to Atalissa, S Pilot/dsl only/scales/24hr
259	to West Liberty, Springdale, S BP/dsl EconoLodge Little Bear Camping
254	X30, West Branch, N BP/Quiznos/dsl, Casey's Hoover NHS, Jack&Jill Foods, USPO, S Kum&Go Casa Tequila Mexican, McDonald's Days Inn Chrysler/Dodge/Jeep
249	Herbert Hoover Hwy, N winery (2mi), S Wildwood Smokehouse golf
246	IA 1, Dodge St, N BP/Subway/dsl Jimmy John's, Jonsy's Clarion URGENT CARE, S Sinclair Bob's Pizza Travelodge
244	Dubuque St, Iowa City, N Coralville Lake, S H, museum, to Old Capitol
242	to Coralville, N Twelve 01 Kitchen Hampton Inn, Radisson, S BP, Kum&Go/dsl 30 Hop Cafe, Applebee's, Arby's, Back Pocket Brewing, Bandana's BBQ, Burger King, Casa Azul, DQ, Dunkin Donuts, Edge Water Grill, Hardee's, IA Riverpower Rest., McDonald's, Milio's Sandwiches, Mondo's Cafe, Monica's Rest., Old Chicago Grill, Panera Bread, Papa John's, Peking Buffet, Perkins, Sparti's Gyros, Subway, Taco John's, Wig&Pen Rest. Baymont Inn, Best Western, Big Ten Inn, Comfort Inn, Heartland Inn, Homewood Suites, IA Lodge, Marriott, Quality Inn, Super 7, Super 8 H, auto repair, vet, Von Maur, Walgreens
240	IA 965, to US 6, Coralville, N Liberty, N BP, Casey's/dsl Buffalo Wild Wings, Cheddar's, Culver's, Jimmy John's, La Cava Mexican, McDonald's, Steak'n Shake, TX Roadhouse, Village Inn, Wendy's AmericInn, Country Inn&Suites, Suburban Lodge Colony Country Camping (3mi), Costco/gas, Gordman's, Harley-Davidson, Kohl's, Michael's, PetCo, TJ Maxx, URGENT CARE, Walgreens, Walmart/Subway, S Casey's/dsl Caribou Coffee, Chili's, Coldstone, Food Court, Huhot Mongolian, IHOP, Jimmy John's, Longhorn Steaks, Mellow Mushroom, Noodles&Co, Olive Garden, Panchero's Mexican, Papa Murphy's, Pizza Hut, Red Lobster, Starbucks, Taste of China, Which Wich? Comfort Suites, Holiday Inn Express, Residence Inn Ace Hardware, Advance Parts, Barnes&Noble, Best Buy, Dillard's, Discount Tire, Hobby Lobby, HyVee Foods/dsl, JC Penney, Lowe's, Old Navy, Scheel's Sports, Target, Tires+, U-Haul, Verizon, Younkers
239b	I-380 N, US 218 N, to Cedar Rapids
239a	US 218 S
237	Tiffin, N Kum&Go/Subway/dsl Jon's Rest (1mi) (seasonal), S Sun& Fun RV Ctr
236mm	**Rs both lanes, full facilities, litter barrels, petwalk, RV dump, vending, wireless internet**
230	W38, to Oxford, N Sleepy Hollow Camping, S Kalona Village Museum (15mi)
225	US 151 N, W21 S, N Heritage Inn, to Amana Colonies, S Casey's 7 Villages Rest., MaidRite Cafe Motel 6, Ramada
220	IA 149 S, V77 N, to Williamsburg, N BP, Casey's/Landmark Rest./dsl Arby's, McDonald's, Subway Cozy House Inn, Crest Motel, Super 8 factory outlets/famous brands, GNC, Old Navy, S Days Inn $General, Williamsburg Tire/auto
216	to Marengo, N Kum&Go/Subway/dsl H (8mi)
211	to Ladora, Millersburg, S Lake IA Park (5mi)
208mm	**Rs both lanes, full facilities, litter barrels, petwalk, RV dump, vending, wireless internet**
205	to Victor
201	IA 21, to Deep River, N Pilot/Subway/dsl/scales/24hr Pleasant Stay Inn, S KwikStar/Denny's/dsl/scales/24hr/@, truck repair
197	to Brooklyn, N TA/Country Pride/Dunkin Donuts/dsl/scales/24hr/@
191	US 63, to Montezuma, S to Diamond Lake SP (9mi)
182	IA 146, to Grinnell, 0-2 mi N Casey's, Kum&Go/Subway/dsl/24hr Casa Margaritas, Grinnell Steakhouse, KFC/Taco Bell, McDonald's, Pizza Ranch Best Western, Comfort Inn, Country Inn, Quality Inn, Super 8 $General, Ace Hardware, Buick/Chevrolet/GMC, Chrysler/Dodge/Jeep, H (4mi), HyVee Foods, O'Reilly Parts, Verizon, vet, Walmart
180mm	**Rs both lanes, full facilities, litter barrels, petwalk, playground, RV dump (eb) wireless internet, vending, weather info**
179	IA 124, to Oakland Acres, Lynnville
175mm	N Skunk River
173	IA 224, Kellogg, N Phillips 66/Best Burger/dsl/24hr Kellogg RV Park, Rock Creek SP (9mi), S Pella Museum
168	SE Beltline Dr, to Newton, 1 mi N Casey's/dsl, Murphy USA/dsl Arby's, Taco John's $Tree, KOA (seasonal), Walmart, S Loves/Chester's/McDonald's/dsl/scales, Valero/dsl AmericInn, Boulders Inn Iowa Speedway
164	US 6, IA 14, Newton, N Casey's/dsl, Phillips 66/Subway/dsl Culver's, KFC/Taco Bell, MT Mikes, Okoboji Grill, Perkins, Pizza Ranch Days Inn, EconoLodge, Quality Inn, Super 8 H, museum, S Best Value Inn Cadillac/Chevrolet, Chrysler/Jeep/Dodge, Ford/Lincoln, to Lake Red Rock
159	F48, to Jasper, Baxter
155	IA 117, Colfax, N BP/McDonald's/dsl Subway Colfax Inn, Microtel truck repair, S Casey's, Kum&Go/pizza/dsl/e85/24hr
153mm	S Skunk River
151	**weigh sta wb**
149	Mitchellville
148mm	**Rs both lanes, full facilities, litter barrels, petwalk, RV dump, vending, wireless internet**
143	Altoona, Bondurant, S Casey's/dsl, Kum&Go/dsl Hampton Inn, Holiday Inn Express RV One Ctr
142b a	US 65, Hubble Ave, Des Moines, S BP, FLYING J/Max's Diner/dsl/scales/24hr/@, Git'n Go Bianchi Boys Pizza, Big Steer Rest., Burger King, Culver's, Jethro's BBQ, KFC/Taco Bell, McDonald's/playplace, Perkins, Pizza Hut, Subway, Taco John's Adventureland Inn, Best Western+, Comfort Inn, Motel 6, My Place, Quality Inn Adventureland Funpark, Blue Beacon, camping, casino, Freightliner, Peterbilt
141	US 6 W, US 65 S, Pleasant Hill, Des Moines, S Uncle Buck's Grill Bass Pro Shops
137b a	I-35 N, I-235 S, to Des Moines

I-80 W and I-35 S run together 14 mi.

Exit#	Services
136	US 69, E 14th St, Camp Sunnyside, N BP/dsl, Casey's Bonanza Steaks, MT Mikes Budget Inn, Motel 6, Quality Inn, Rodeway Inn Allied Tire, antiques, Volvo, 0-1 mi S Casey's/dsl, QT/Burger King/dsl/scales/24hr, Star Gas Arby's, Fazoli's, Hardee's, KFC, McDonald's, Papa Murphy's, Pueblo Viejo Mexican, Subway, Taco Bell, Taco John's, Village Inn, Wendy's Baymont Inn, Travelodge $General, Advance Parts,

NEWTON

IA

INTERSTATE 80 Cont'd

136 Continued
Aldi Foods, AutoZone, CarX, Family$, O'Reilly Parts, Tires+, TruckLube, USPO

135 IA 415, 2nd Ave, Polk City, **N** Kum&Go/dsl Smokey D's BBQ antiques, Harley-Davidson, Ryder Trucks, **S** Git'n Go, QT, Shop&Save Earl's Tire, NAPA, st patrol

133mm Des Moines River

131 IA 28 S, NW 58th St, **N** Casey's, QT Bandit Burrito, Chopsticks, DQ, El Mariachi Mexican, Greenbriar Rest., Jimmy John's, Pagliai's Pizza, Panera Bread, Sonic, Subway, VanDee's Icecream/Sandwiches AmericInn Ace Hardware, Acura, Audi/VW, Goodyear/auto, Hy-Vee Food/dsl, USPO, vet, **S** BP/dsl/LP/24hr, Casey's, QT Applebee's, Arby's, Bamboo Buffet, Bennigan's, Buffalo Wild Wings, Burger King, Carlos O'Kelly's, Chipotle Mexican, Cici's Pizza, Dunkin Donuts, Famous Dave's BBQ, Fazoli's, Hardee's, IHOP, Jimmy John's, KFC, McDonald's, Noodles&Co, Old Chicago, Panda Express, Perfect Taco, Perkins, Pita Pit, Popeye's, Starbucks, Subway, Taco John's, Wendy's Days Inn, EconoLodge, Holiday Inn, Quality Inn, Ramada/Rest., Super 8 $Tree, Advance Parts, AT&T, Big Lots, BigLots, CarX, Chevrolet, Dahl's Food/Fuel, Firestone/auto, Ford, Goodyear/auto, Hobby Lobby, Kia, Kohl's, NAPA, Nissan, Office Depot, Old Navy, PriceChopper, Staples, Target, Toyota, URGENT CARE, Verizon, vet, Younkers

129 NW 86th St, Camp Dodge, **N** Kum&Go Burger King, Legends Grill, McDonald's, Okoboji Grill, Panchero's Mexican, Planet Sub, Starbucks, TX Roadhouse, Village Inn Hilton Garden, Stoney Creek Inn, TownePlace Suites Dahl's Foods, Verizon, **S** Casey's, Kum&Go/dsl Arby's, B-Bops Burgers, Culver's, Friedrich's Coffee, Overtime Grill, Papa Murphy's, Pizza Ranch, Ruby Tuesday, Subway, Viva La Bamba Fairfield Inn, Hampton Inn, Holiday Inn Express, Microtel Walgreens

128 NW 100th St

127 IA 141 W, Grimes, **N** **BP/dsl**, QT/dsl MaidRite Cafe, McCoy's Grill, Subway to Saylorville Lake, Toyota, **S** Kum&Go/dsl/e85 McDonald's, Quiznos Firestone/auto, Home Depot, Target

126 Douglas Ave, Urbandale, **E** Casey's/dsl EconoLodge, Extended Stay America Chevrolet, **W** Kum&Go/dsl, **Pilot/Subway/dsl/scales/24hr/@** Mama Lacona's

125 US 6, Hickman Rd, **E** IA Machine Shed Rest., Starbucks, Subway Clive Hotel, Hotel Renovo, Sleep Inn CarMax, Fiat, Honda, Hyundai, to Living History Farms, **W** Kum&Go/dsl, **Loves/Denny's/dsl/scales/LP/24hr** Chrysler/Dodge/Jeep, Menards

124 (72c from I-35 nb), University Ave, **E** Git'n Go/dsl Applebee's, Bakers Square, Chili's, Chuck-fil-A, Huhot Mongolian, Jason's Deli, KFC, Little Caesars, McDonald's, Mi Mexico, Mi Mexico, Outback Steaks, Qdoba Mexican, RockBottom Rest./brewery, Starbucks, TCBY, Twin Peaks, Wobbly Boots BBQ Courtyard, Days Inn, Sheraton, Sterling Suites, Super 8, Wildwood Lodge AT&T, Barnes&Noble, Best Buy, Home Depot, Kohl's, Lowe's, Marshall's, Office Depot, Petsmart, Target, Verizon, Whole Foods Mkt, World Mkt, **W** Kum&Go/Burger King, QT Biaggi's Rest, Caribou Coffee, **Cracker Barrel**, El Rodeo Mexican, Jersey Mike's, Other Place Grill, Panera Bread, Red Rossa Pizza, Wendy's, Z'Marik's Cafe Best Western, Country Inn&Suites, La Quinta H, Granite City Food, Walgreens

I-80 E and I-35 N run together 14 mi.

123b a I-80/I-35 N, I-35 S to Kansas City, I-235 to Des Moines

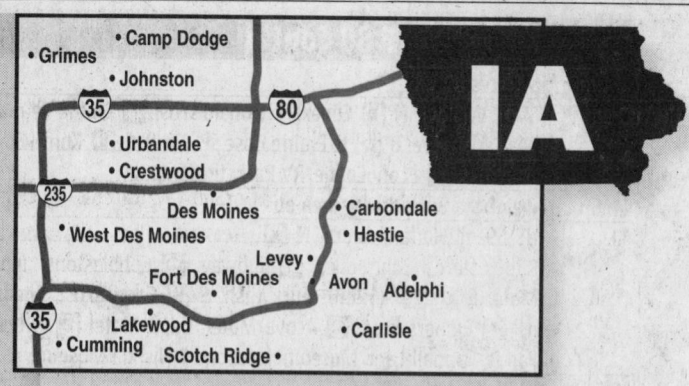

DES MOINES

Camp Dodge
Grimes
Johnston
35
80
IA
Urbandale
Crestwood
235
Des Moines
Carbondale
Hastie
West Des Moines
Levey
Fort Des Moines
Avon
Adelphi
35
Lakewood
Carlisle
Cumming
Scotch Ridge

122 (from eb) 60th St, W Des Moines, **N** H, same as 121

121 74th St, W Des Moines, **N** Biaggi's Rest., Panera Bread, Red Rossa Pizza Hampton Inn, Staybridge Suites H, Granite City Foods, HyVee Food/gas, Walgreens, **S** Kum&Go/Subway Arby's, Burger King, Culver's, McDonald's, Perkins, Quiznos, Taco John's Candlewood Suites, Fairfield Inn, Marriott, Motel 6, SpringHill Suites, vet

118 Grand Prairie Pky, **N** Kum&Go/dsl

117 R22, Booneville, Waukee, **N** Kum&Go/dsl/e85 Organic Farm Rest. Timberline Camping (2mi), **S** Rube's Steaks, Waveland Rest. (2mi)

115mm **weigh sta eb**

113 R16, Van Meter, **1 mi S** Casey's Veteran's Cemetary

112mm N Racoon River

111mm Middle Racoon River

110 US 169, to Adel, DeSoto, **N** camping (6mi), **S** Casey's/dsl, Kum&Go/dsl/e85 Countryside Inn, Edgetowner Motel $General, John Wayne Birthplace (14mi), USPO

106 F90, P58, **N** KOA (apr-oct)

104 P57, Earlham, **S** Casey's (1mi)

100 US 6, to Redfield, Dexter, **N** Casey's (2mi) Drew's Chocolate (2mi)

97 P48, to Dexter, **N** camping, Casey's (2mi)

93 P28, Stuart, **N** Casey's/dsl/scales, Kum&Go/dsl/e85 Burger King, McDonald's/playplace, Subway AmericInn, Best Value Inn $General, Chevrolet, city park, Hometown Foods, **S** Phillips 66/dsl Country Kitchen Economy Inn NAPA

88 P20, Menlo

86 IA 25, to Greenfield, Guthrie Ctr, **N** to Spring Brook SP, **S** Hospital (13mi)

85mm Middle River

83 N77, Casey, **1 mi N** Kum&Go camping

80.5mm **both lanes, full facilities, litter barrels, petwalk, RV dump, vending, wireless internet**

76 IA 925, N54, Adair, **N** Casey's/dsl, Kum&Go/Subway/dsl Chuck Wagon Rest. Adair Budget Inn, Super 8 camping, city park

75 G30, to Adair

70 IA 148 S, Anita, **S** to Lake Anita SP (6mi)

64 N28, to Wiota

61mm E Nishnabotna River

60 US 6, US 71, to Atlantic, Lorah, **S** Conoco/dsl/24hr Sunset Inn

57 N16, to Atlantic, **N** Nelsen RV Ctr, **S** H (7mi)

54 IA 173, to Elk Horn, **6 mi N** Tivoli Inn **Welcome Ctr/wifi**, Windmill Museum

51 M56, to Marne

IA

INTERSTATE 80 Cont'd

Exit#	Services
46	M47, Walnut, N Cenex/McDonald's/dsl Emma Jean's Rest. Super 8 to Prairie Rose SP (8mi), S Kum&Go/ pizza/dsl EconoLodge/RV Park, tires/repair
44mm	**weigh sta wb/parking area eb**
40	US 59, to Harlan, Avoca, N FLYING J/Taco John's/Maid-Rite Cafe/dsl/24hr/scales Subway Cobblestone Inn, Motel 6 H (12mi), truckwash, S Casey's/dsl, Shell/ dsl Embers Rest. Acova Motel, Capri Motel Avoca Foods, Farmall-Land Museum (seasonal), Nishna Museum
39.5mm	W Nishnabotna River
34	M16, Shelby, N BP/rest./dsl/e85, Shell/Cornstalk Cafe/ dsl DQ, Godfather's Shelby Country Inn/RV Park, S Loves/McDonald's/Chester's/dsl/scales/24hr
32mm	**Rs both lanes, parking only**
29	L66, to Minden, S Casey's/dsl Midtown Motel (2mi) winery (4mi)
27	I-680 W, to N Omaha
23	IA 244, L55, Neola, S Kum&Go/dsl/e85 camping, to Arrowhead Park
20mm	**Welcome Ctr eb/Rs wb, full facilities, litter barrels, petwalk, RV dump, vending, Wireless Internet**
17	G30, Underwood, N Cenex/Subway/dsl/24hr Underwood Motel truck/tire repair
8	US 6, Council Bluffs, N Casey's/dsl (1mi) $General, H (3mi), S st patrol
5	Madison Ave, Council Bluffs, N BP/dsl Burger King, FoodCourt, Great Wall Chinese, KFC, McDonald's, Papa Murphy's, Starbucks, Subway AmericInn HyVee Foods/ drug, Verizon, Walgreens, S Phillips 66 DQ, Village Inn Rest. Western Inn Family Fare Mkt
4	I-29 S, to Kansas City
3	IA 192 N, Council Bluffs, N to Hist Dodge House, S Casey's/ dsl, Shell/dsl, TA/Valero/Country Pride/dsl/scales/24hr/@ Applebee's, Beijing Rest., Burger King, Cracker Barrel, Dickey's BBQ, DQ, Fazoli's, Golden Corral, Hardee's, Huhot Mongolian, Jimmy John's, La Mesa Mexican, LJ Silver, McDonald's, Perkins, Red Lobster, Subway, Taco Bell Days Inn, Fairfield Inn, Motel 6, Red Roof Inn Advance Parts, Aldi Foods, Best Buy, Buick/ GMC, Cadillac/Chevrolet, Chrysler/Dodge/Jeep, Ford, Freightliner, Gordman's, Home Depot, Hyundai/Subaru, Kia, Menards, Nissan, Outdoor Recreation RV, Sam's Club/gas, truck/dsl repair, U-Haul, Walmart/Subway
1b	S 24th St, Council Bluffs, N BP, Casey's, Pilot/Arby's/ scales/dsl/24hr, Sapp Bros/Burger King/dsl Famous Dave's BBQ, Hooters, Quaker Steak&Lube, Ruby Tuesday, Uncle Buck's American Inn, Best Western, Country Inn&Suites, Hilton Garden, Holiday Inn Express, Microtel, SpringHill Suites, Super 8 Bass Pro Shop, Blue Beacon, Camping World RV Ctr, casino, Horseshoe RV Park, Peterbilt, SpeedCo, S **Welcome Ctr, full facilities** Culver's, TX Roadhouse JC Penney, PetCo, ShopKO
1a	I-29 N, to Sioux City
0mm	Iowa/Nebraska state line, Missouri River

COUNCIL BLUFFS

IA

INTERSTATE 235 (Des Moines)

Exit#	Services
15	I-80, E to Davenport
12	US 6, E Euclid Ave, E Casey's Burger King, Dragon House Chinese, Papa John's, Perkins, Tasty Tacos $Tree, HyVee Foods/drug, Walgreens, W QT/dsl Midas, NAPA
11	Guthrie Ave, W Kum&Go/dsl CarQuest
10b a	IA 163 W, E University Ave, Easton Dr
9	US 65/69, E 14th, E 15th, N Subway Walgreens, S McDonald's, Quiznos, Tasty Tacos H, st capitol, URGENT CARE, zoo
8b	E 6th St, Penn Ave (from wb), N H
8a	3rd St, 5th Ave, N Holiday Inn H, S Embassy Suites, Marriott, Quality Inn Conv Ctr
7	Keo Way
6	MLK Blvd/31st St, N Drake U, S Governor's Mansion
5b	42nd St, Science & Art Ctr, N Git'n Go Papa John's Drake Automotive
5a	56th St (from wb), N golf
4	IA 28, 63rd St, to Windsor Heights, S Historic Valley Jct, zoo
3	8th St, W Des Moines, N Kum&Go B-Bop's Café, Burger King, Papa Murphy's, Starbucks HyVee Foods, PetCo, Sam's Club/gas, Walmart/Subway, S BP, Kum&Go/dsl/ e85 Dunkin Donuts, Jimmy John's, Lemon Grass Thai, Tacos Andreas Days Inn
2	22nd St, 24th St, W Des Moines, N BP, Casey's/dsl, Kum&Go/ dsl, QT/dsl Arby's, ChuckeCheese, Culver's, Famous Dave's BBQ, Hardee's, Hibachi Buffet, Jethro's BBQ, McDonald's, Smash-Burger, Taco Bell, Village Inn $Tree, CarX, Firestone/auto, Gordman's, Meineke, Michael's, Midas, Walgreens
1b	Valley West Dr, W Des Moines, N BP/dsl Chipotle Mexican, Cozy Cafe, Hamilton's Rest., Hurricane Grill, Jimmy John's, La Hacienda, Noodles&Co, Olive Garden, Panda Express, Panera Bread, Red Lobster, Subway Valley West Inn AT&T, Best Buy, Home Depot, HyVee Foods, JC Penney, Marshall's, Target, Von Maur, Whole Foods Mkt, Younker's

I-235 begins/ends on I-80, exit 123.

DES MOINES

INTERSTATE 280 (Davenport)

Exit#	Services
18b a	I-74, US 6, Moline, S Shell/dsl Bare Bones BBQ, McDonald's, MT Jack's Best Inn, Country Inn&Suites, Hampton Inn, Holiday Inn Express, La Quinta, Motel 6, Quality Inn
15	Airport Rd, Milan, **1 mi** N Hardee's, MaidRite Café, McDonald's, Subway auto repair, Buick/Chevrolet, Firestone
11b a	IL 92, to Andalusia, Rock Island, S Jumer's Hotel/casino/ rest. KOA Camping
9.5mm	Iowa/Illinois state line, Mississippi River
8	rd 22, Rockingham Rd, to Buffalo
6	US 61, W River Dr, to Muscatine, W camping
4	Locust St, rd F65, 160th St, E H, St Ambrose U, to Palmer Coll, W Shell/Subway/dsl
1	US 6 E, IA 927, Kimberly Rd, to Walcott, **3 mi** E Murphy USA/dsl Applebee's, Culver's, Harlan's Rest., Steak'n Shake, Subway, Wendy's Discount Tire, GNC, Walmart

I-280 begins/ends on I-80, exit 290.

INTERSTATE 380 (Cedar Rapids)

Exit#	Services
73mm	**I-380 begins/ends on US 218, 73mm in Waterloo.** E BP/dsl, W Clark Pizza Hut
72	San Marnan Dr, W Casey's, Kwik Star/Dallas/e85 A&W/ LJ Silver, Applebee's, Burger King, Carlos O'Kelly's, Chick-fil-A, DQ, Freddie's, Hardee's, IHOP, Jimmy John's, Little Ceasar's, Lone Star, Longhorn Steaks, McDonald's, Noodles&Co, Olive Garden, Panchero's, Panda Express, Panera Bread, Red Lobster, Starbucks, Subway, Taco Bell, Taco John's, Tokyo Bay, Wendy's Baymont Inn, Candlewoods Suites, Comfort Inn, Country Inn&Suites, Days Inn, Fairfield Inn, Hampton Inn, Holiday Inn Express, Motel 6, Super 8 Advance Parts, Aldi Foods, AT&T, Barnes & Noble,

WATERLOO

INTERSTATE 380 (Cedar Rapids) Cont'd

72 Continued
Best Buy, Chevrolet, Chrysler/Dodge/Jeep, CVS Drug, Dick's, Dillards, Ford, Gordman's, Hobby Lobby, Home Depot, HyVee Foods, Jo-Ann Fabrics, KIA, Menards, PetCo, PetsMart, Staples, Target, Tires+, TJ Maxx, Verizon, Walmart

71 I-380, US 20, IA 27, Cedar Rapids, Cedar Falls, Dubuque, **W** on US 18 Isle Hotel/Casino

70 River Forest Rd

68 Elk Run Heights, Evansdale Dr, **E** FLYING J/Denny's/dsl/scales/24hr, Pilot/RR/Junie's/Subway/dsl/scales/24hr/@ Arby's, McDonald's Days Inn Freightliner, Paine's RV Ctr, truckwash/repair

66 Gilbertville, Raymond

65 US 20 E, Dubuque

62 rd d-38, Gilbertville

55 rd v-65, Jesup, La Port, **W** Hickory Hills Park, McFarlane Park

54mm **weigh sta sb**

51mm **weigh sta nb**

49 rd d-48, Brandon, **1 mi W** food, gas

43 IA 150, Independence, Vinton, **E** Casey's/dsl Urbana Inn Suites truckwash

41 Urbana, **E** Lazy Acres RV Park, **W** Casey's/dsl $General

35 rd w-36, Center Point, **E** BP, Casey's, Sinclair/McDonald's/Subway/dsl/scales/24hr $General, Chrysler/Dodge/Jeep/Ford, **W** Pleasant Creek SRA (5mi)

28 rd e-34, Robins, Toddville, **E** BP/dsl, **W** Wickiup Outdoor Learning Ctr (5mi)

25 Boyson Rd, Hiawatha, **E** Casey's Culver's Buick/GMC/Cadillac, Ketelsen RV Ctr, Kia, Nissan, Subaru, **W** Toyota/Mazda

24 IA 100, Blairs Ferry Rd, **E** KwikShop/dsl Buffalo Wild Wings, Domino's, Hardee's, KFC, Las Glorias Mexican, McDonald's, Scott Family Rest., Wendy's Comfort Inn, Country Inn&Suites, Days Inn, Residence Inn Advance Parts, Chrysler/Dodge/Jeep, CVS Drug, Honda, O'Reilly Parts, Target, **W** Fas Fuel Adelitas Mexican, Arby's, Burger King, Dunkin' Donuts, Freddy's, Pizza Hut, Starbucks, Subway, Taco Bell Aldi Foods, AutoZone, GNC, Lowe's, Sam's Club/gas, Walmart

CEDAR RAPIDS

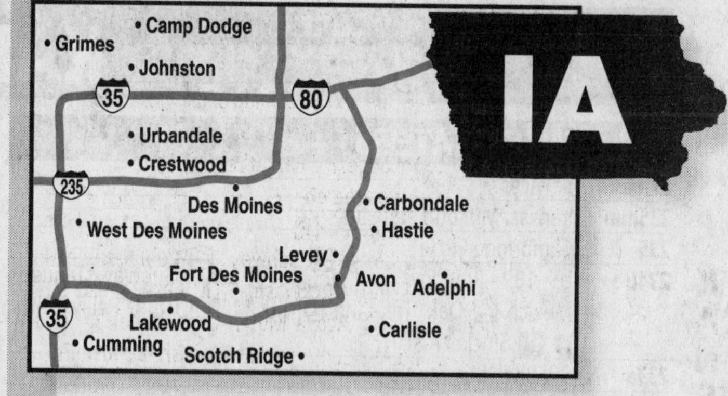

22 Glass Rd, 32nd St, **E** KwikShop/dsl Papa Johns

21 H St, Cedar Rapids, downtown

20b 7th St E, Cedar Rapids, **E** H, downtown

20a US 151 Bus., **E** DoubleTree

19b 1st Ave W, **W** NAPA

18 Wilson Ave, museums

17 33rd ave SW, Hawkeye Downs, **W** Casey's, Casey's/dsl (2) Burger King, Cancun, McDonald's, Taco Bell, Wendy's Clarion, Econolodge, Economy Inn, Fairfield Inn, Hampton Inn, Holiday Inn Express, Hometown Inn, Motel 6, Quality Inn, Red Roof Inn, Residence Inn, Super 8, Super 8

16 US 30 W, US 151 S, US 218 N, Tama

13 Ely, **E** Pilot/Arby's/dsl/scales/24hr, **W** Casey's/A&W/dsl, Casey's/dsl/scales, Kwik Star/dsl/e85 McDonald's, Subway AmericInn, Country Inn&Suites

12mm **both lanes, littler barrels, petwalk, RV Dump, vending, wireless internet**

10 rd f-12, Shueyville, Swisher, **E** BP/dsl Lake Mcbride SP, **W** Amana Colonies

8mm Iowa River

4 rd f-28, North Liberty, **E** Casey's/Blimpie, Kum&Go/dsl/e85 Sleep Inn Colony Country RV Park (5mi)

0b a I-80 E to Iowa City, W to Des Moines, **I-380 begins/ends on I-80.**

IA

NOTES

KANSAS

INTERSTATE 35

KANSAS CITY AREA

Exit#	Services
235mm	Kansas/Missouri state line
235	Cambridge Circle
234b a	US 169, Rainbow Blvd, E Sonic, Subway, Taqueria Mexico Oak Tree Inn KU MED CTR, O'Reilly Parts, W Sinclair/dsl
233a	SW Blvd, Mission Rd
233b	37th Ave (from sb)
232b	US 69 N, E Phillips 66/dsl, QT Burger King, China Star, Cici's, McDonald's, Subway, Taco Bell Aldi Foods, Lowe's, Price Chopper, Walgreens, Walmart
232a	Lamar Ave, E Wood Spring Suites
231b a	I-635 (exits left from sb)
230	Antioch Rd (from sb)
229	Johnson Dr, E QT/dsl Chili's, China Garden, Jack-in-the-Box, Jimmy John's, McDonald's, Starbucks, Subway, Taco Bell AT&T, Dick's, GNC, Hen House Mkt, Hobby Lobby, Home Depot, IKEA, Marshall's, Old Navy, Petsmart, Verizon, Walgreens, W Cenex/dsl
228b	US 56 E, US 69, Shawnee Mission Pkwy, E Shell Caribou Coffee, Denny's, Krispy Kreme Drury Inn, Extended Stay America, Super 8 BMW/Mini, W A&W, Arby's, LJ Silver, McAlister's Deli, Panera Bread, Pizza Hut, Subway AutoZone, Discount Tire, Famil$, Firestone/auto, Ford, Goodyear/auto, Jo-Ann Fabrics, O'Reilly Parts, Russell Stover, Walgreens
228a	67th St, E Quality Inn CarMax, W Phillips 66/dsl Hyundai, Infiniti, Jaguar, Land Rover, Lexus, Maserati, Mercedes, Porsche Smart, Toyota
227	75th St, E McDonald's Extended Stay America H, Acura, Audi, Walmart, W QT/dsl Domino's, Sonic, Starbucks, Subway, Taco Bell, Wendy's Hampton Inn Hyundai, URGENT CARE
225b	US 69 S (from sb), Overland Pkwy
225a	87th St, E Green Mill Rest, Wendy's Holiday Inn, W Phillips 66/dsl Dunkin Donuts, Taco Bell, Zarda BBQ
224	95th St, E Applebee's, BD Mongolian BBQ, Burger King, Cheddar's, Chick-fil-A, Chipotle Mexican, Five Guys, Houlihan's, Jimmy John's, KFC, McDonald's, Noodles&Co, On-the-Border, Outback Steaks, Panda Express, Pie Five, Subway, Taco Bell, Winstead's Cafe, Zoe's Kitchen Crossland Suites, Crowne Plaza, La Quinta, Motel 6, Quality Inn, Super 8 H, Advance Parts, Barnes&Noble, Best Buy, Dillard's, Firestone/auto, Hobby Lobby, JC Penney, Kohl's, Macy's, Nordstrom, Office Depot, PetCo, Ross, Sam's Club/gas, Target, Verizon, W Phillips 66 Mi Ranchito Costco/gas, O'Reilly Parts, U-Haul
222b a	I-435 W & E
220	119th St, E Conoco/7-11, Phillips 66, Phillips 66/dsl A&W, Buffalo Wild Wings, Burger King, Chick-fil-A, Chipotle Mexican, Chuy's, Coldstone, Cracker Barrel, Firehouse Subs, Five Guys, Five Guys, Freddy's, Granite City Cafe, Hira's Steak, IHOP, Jimmy John's, KC Joe's BBQ, KC Super Buffet, LJ Silver, Master Wok, McDonald's, Mr Gyros Greek, Noodles&-Co, Old Chicago, Olive Garden, Panda Express, Panera Bread, Papa Murphy's, Pei Wei, Penn Sta Subs, Pie Five, Planet Sub, Popeye's, Red Lobster, Schlotzsky's, Smashburger, Starbucks, Steak'n Shake, Subway, Taco Bell, Twin Peaks, TX Roadhouse, Wendy's, Zaxby's, Zoe's Kitchen Fairfield Inn, Hampton Inn,
220	Continued Hilton Garden, Holiday Inn Express, Residence Inn, Wood Spring Suites AT&T, Best Buy, Chrysler/Dodge/Jeep, Dick's, Fiat, GNC, Goodyear/auto, Home Depot, Honda, Marshall's, Michael's, Natural Grocers, NTB, Old Navy, Petsmart, Ross, Target, U-Haul, Verizon, Whole Foods Mkt, W Houlihan's, Jason's Deli, Longhorn Steaks, Starbucks Bass Pro Shops
218	135th, Santa Fe St, Olathe, E Phillips 66/dsl Applebee's, Burger King, Chapala Mexican, China Buffet, Church's, McDonald's, Other Place Grill, Papa John's, Perkins, Pizza St, Sheridan's Custard, Subway, Taco Bell $General, $Tree, Ace Hardware, Aldi Foods, AutoZone, BigLots, Discount Foods, Ford/Lincoln, GNC, Hobby Lobby, Kohl's, Midas, Office Depot, vet, W Domino's, KFC, McDonald's, Subway, Taco Bell, Waffle House Rodeway Inn Aamco, Advance Parts, Buick/GMC, Chevrolet, Harley-Davidson, Hyundai, Kia, Meineke, Nissan, O'Reilly Parts, Subaru, Toyota, VW
217	Old Hwy 56 (from sb), same as 215
215	US 169 S, KS 7, Olathe, E Phillips 66/dsl, QT/dsl Chipotle Mexican, IHOP, Jimmy John's, MOD Pizza, Panera Bread, Red Robin Candlewood Suites, Quality Inn Aldi Foods, Discount Tire, GNC, Home Depot, Jiffy Lube, NTB, Target, W Phillips 66/dsl/scales/24hr 54th St Grill, Chili's, McDonald's, Taco Bell, Wendy's Best Western, Days Inn, Econolodge, La Quinta, Motel 6 H, Burlington Coats, Mazda
214	Lone Elm Rd, 159th St
213mm	**weigh sta both lanes**
210	US 56 W, Gardner, W Phillips 66/dsl, QT/dsl Arby's, Burger King, KFC, McDonald's, Perkins, Pizza Hut, Sonic, Subway, Taco Bell, Waffle House Super 8 AutoZone, Price Chopper, Walgreens, Walmart
207	US 56 E, Gardner Rd, E Olathe RV Ctr, W Phillips 66/dsl, Phillips 66/dsl (2)
205	Homestead Lane
202	Edgerton
198	KS 33, to Wellsville, W food, gas
193	Tennessee Rd, Baldwin
188	US 59 N, to Lawrence
187	KS 68, Ottawa, W Phillips 66/dsl Central RV Ctr, Midwest RV Ctr
185	15th St, Ottawa
183	US 59, Ottawa, E Loves/Hardee's/dsl/scales/24hr, W BP, Ottawa/dsl, Phillips 66/dsl Applebee's, Burger King, Freddy's, McDonald's, Nagoya Japanese, Old 56 Rest., Pizza Hut, Sirloin Stockade, Taco Bell, Wendy's Best Western, Comfort Inn, Days Inn, EconoLodge, Super 8 H, $General, $Tree, Advance Parts, Ford, Walmart
182b a	US 50, Eisenhower Rd, Ottawa
176	Homewood, W RV camping
175mm	**RS both lanes, full facilities, litter barrels, petwalk, RV dump, vending, wireless internet**
170	KS 273, Williamsburg, W Gas&Food
162	KS 31 S, Waverly
160	KS 31 N, Melvern
155	US 75, Burlington, Melvern Lake, E Conoco/Subway/dsl, TA/Shell/Wendy's/dsl/scales/24hr/@ Wyatt Earp Inn dsl repair
148	KS 131, Lebo, E Casey's, Cenex/dsl Universal Inn $General, W to Melvern Lake
141	KS 130, Neosho Rapids, E NWR (8mi)

OLATHE

OTTAWA

KS

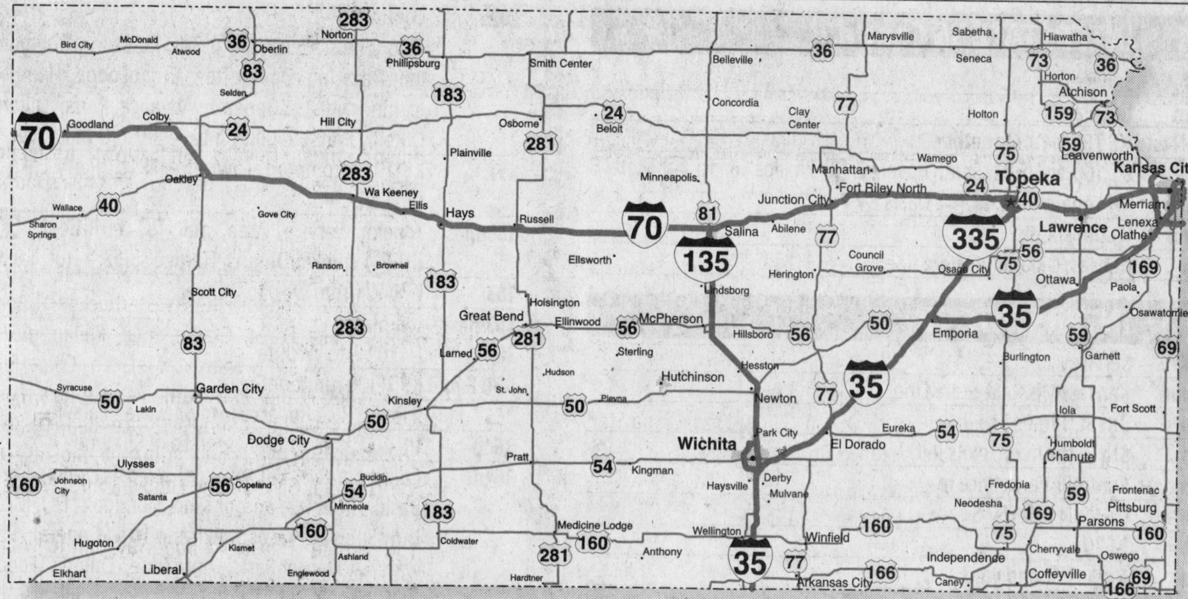

INTERSTATE 35 Cont'd

EMPORIA

Exit#	Services
138	County Rd U
135	County Rd R1, W Dieker RV Ctr, RV camping/
133	US 50 W, 6th Ave, Emporia, **1-3 mi** E Casey's Budget Host
131	KS 57, KS 99, Burlingame Rd, E Phillips 66/Circle K/dsl Goodcents Subs, Hardee's Dillon's Food, repair, Tire Pros
130	KS 99, Merchant St, E Phillips 66/dsl Subway CVS Drug, Emporia SU, Lyon Co Museum
128	Industrial Rd, E Arby's, Bruff's Steaks, Burger King, China Buffet, Gambino's Pizza, Ichiban Japanese, Spangles, Subway EconoLodge, Knights Inn, Motel 6 H, $General, Aldi Foods, AT&T, JC Penney, Walgreens, W Phillips 66/WhichWich?/dsl Applebee's, Braum's, Domino's, IHOP, KFC, McDonald's, MT Mike's Steaks, Pizza Hut, Pizza Ranch, Planet Sub, Starbucks, Taco Bell Candlewood Suites, Comfort Inn, Hampton Inn, Holiday Inn Express, La Quinta, Quality Inn $Tree, Staples, Verizon, Walmart/Subway
127c	KS Tpk, I-335 N, to Topeka
127b a	US 50, KS 57, Newton, E FLYING J/Huddle House/dsl/LP/scales/24hr, Casey's/dsl Arby's, China Buffet, Papa John's Best Inn, Best Western/rest., Days Inn, Rodeway Inn, Super 8 Buick/Chevrolet, Chrysler/Dodge/Jeep, dsl repair, Ford/Lincoln, Kenworth, NAPA, Nissan, PriceChopper Foods, Tires4Less, Toyota, W Emporia RV Park
127mm	I-35 and I-335 KS Tpk, I-35 S and KS tpk S run together, **toll plaza**

I-35 S and KS Tpk S run together.

Exit#	Services
125mm	Cottonwood River
111	Cattle Pens
97.5mm	**Matfield Green Service Area (both lanes exit left),** Phillips 66/dsl Hardee's/Dunkin Donuts
92	KS 177, Cassoday, E Fuel'n Service,
76	US 77, El Dorado N, **3 mi** E Casey's, Phillips 66/dsl Pizza Hut, Taco Bell Stardust Motel $General, Ace Hardware, city park, Dillon's Foods/dsl, El Dorado SP, Walgreens
71	KS 254, KS 196, El Dorado, E Casey's/dsl, Phillips 66/dsl, QT/dsl Arbys, Braum's, Burger King, Domino's, Freddy's, Gambino's Pizza, Hog Wild BBQ, Jimmy's Egg, KFC, LJ Silver, McDonald's, Pizza Hut, Sonic, Spangles, Subway Days Inn,

WICHITA

Exit#	Services
71	Continued Holiday Inn Express, Motel 6, Red Coach Inn, Sunset Inn, Super 8 H, $General, AutoZone, Buick/Cadillac, Bumper Parts, Deer Grove RV Park, KS Oil Museum, O'Reilly Parts, Verizon, Walmart
65mm	**Towanda Service Area (both lanes exit left),** Phillips 66/dsl Hardee's/Dunkin Donuts
62mm	Whitewater River
57	21st St, Andover, W golf,
53	KS 96, Wichita
50	US 54, Kellogg Ave, E **on Kellogg Ave** Beijing Bistro, Burger King, Golden Corral, IHOP, McDonald's, Panda Express, Subway, Taco Bell $Tree, Acura, AT&T, CarMax, Costco/dsl, Infiniti, Lincoln, Lowe's, Mazda, Michael's, Nissan, Petsmart, Subaru, Verizon, VW, Walmart/Subway, W **on Kellogg Ave** BJ's Rest., Bubba's Rest., Carlos Kelly's, Chipotle Mexican, Denny's, Firehouse Subs, Green Mill Rest., LJ Silver, Logan's Roadhouse, Longhorn Steaks, Noodles&Co, Old Chicago Pizza, Red Lobster Best Western, Comfort Inn, Days Inn, Extended Stay America, Fairfield Inn, Hampton Inn, Hawthorn Suites, Holiday Inn, La Quinta, Marriott, Motel 6, Super 8 AT&T, Bosley Tires, Cadillac/Chevrolet, CarQuest, Chrysler/Dodge/Jeep, Dillard's, Fiat, Firestone/auto, Ford, Honda, JC Penney, Ross, TJ Maxx, Toyota, USPO, Von Maur
45	KS 15, Wichita, E Spirit Aero Systems
44.5mm	Arkansas River
42	47th St, I-135, to I-235, Wichita, W QT/dsl Applebee's, Arby's, Braum's, Burger King, Carlos O'Kelly's, Domino's, Godfather's, Goodcents Subs, Heritage Rest., Hog Wild BBQ, IHOP, KFC, Little Caesar's, LJ Silver, McDonald's, New China, Pizza Hut, Spangles Rest., Subway, Taco Bell Best Western, Days Inn, Holiday Inn Express, Quality Inn, Springfield Inn, Super 8, Woodspring Suites $General, $Tree, Air Capital RV Park, Dillon's Foods/dsl, O'Reilly Parts, Verizon
39	US 81, Haysville, W JumpStart Sonic, Subway Express Inn, Sleep Inn
33	KS 53, Mulvane, E Mulvane Hist Museum, W Hampton Inn, Kansas Star Casino/Hotel Wyldewood Winery
26mm	**Belle Plaine Service Area (both lanes exit left),** Phillips 66/dsl McDonald's
19	US 160, Wellington, **3 mi** W KFC, McDonald's, Penny's Diner OakTree Inn KOA

KS

INTERSTATE 35 Cont'd

Exit#	Services
17mm	**toll plaza**
I-35 N and KS TPK N run together.	
4	US 166, to US 81, South Haven, E ⛽ Phillips 66/dsl 🏨 Motel 6 [O] repair/tires, W [O] Oasis RV Park
1.5mm	**weigh sta nb**
0mm	Kansas/Oklahoma state line

INTERSTATE 70

Exit#	Services
424mm	Kansas/Missouri State Line
423b	3rd St, James St
423a	5th St (from eb, exits left)
422d c	Central Ave, service rd
422b a	US 69 N, US 169 S
421b	I-670
421a	S [O] railroad yard
420b a	US 69 S, 18th St Expswy, N ⛽ Cenex/dsl, Sinclair/Subway/dsl 🍴 China Town, Jack-in-the-Box, Tapatio Mexican [O] GNC, SunFresh Foods
419	38th St, Park Dr, access to 10 motels
418b	I-635 N (eb only)
418a	I-635 S
417	57th St
415a	KS 32 E (from eb)
415b	to US 24 W, State Ave, Kansas Cityon US 24, N 🍴 Papa John's, Taco Bell 🏨 Gables Motel [O] Lowe's
414mm	**parking area both lanes, vehicle insp sta wb**
414	78th Ston, **N on US 24** ⛽ Phillips 66, QT/dsl 🍴 Arby's, Burger King, Capt D's, Domino's, Hardee's, KFC, Krispy Kreme, Lucky Chinese, McDonald's, Papa John's, Papa Murphy's, Sonic, Subway, Taco Bell, Wendy's 🏨 Days Inn [O] [H], $Tree, Advance Parts, BigLots, Buick/GMC, CVS Drug, Firestone/auto, Marshall's, O'Reilly Parts, Petsmart, PriceChopper Foods, SavALot, Tires+, Walgreens, XPress/auto/tire, S ⛽ 🏨 American Motel, Comfort Inn
411b	I-435 N, [O] to KCI Airport, access to Woodlands Racetrack
411a	I-435 S
410	110th St, N 🏨 Chateau Avalon, Great Wolf Lodge [O] Cabela's, KS Speedway
225mm	**I-70 W and KS TPK W run together.**
224	KS 7, to US 73 (last free exit wb before KS TPK), Bonner Springs, Leavenworth, N ⛽ Phillips 66/7-11/dsl, QT/dsl 🍴 El Potro Mexican, KFC/Taco Bell, Waffle House 🏨 Holiday Inn Express, Super 8 [O] museum, S ⛽ 🍴 Arby's, Burger King, Goodcents Subs, Lin's Chinese, McDonald's, Papa Murphy's, Pizza Hut, Taco John's [O] $Tree, Ace Hardware, AutoZone, Cottonwood RV Camp, Nachbar Automotive, PriceChopper Foods, Walgreens, Walmart/Subway
217mm	**toll booth**
212	Eudora, Tonganoxie
209mm	**Lawrence Service Area (both lanes exit left) full facilities,** ⛽ Phillips 66/dsl 🍴 McDonald's
204	US 24, US 59, to E Lawrence, S ⛽ Cenex/dsl, Phillips 66/Subway 🍴 Burger King 🏨 Motel 6, SpringHill Suites (1mi) [O] $General, O'Reilly Parts
203mm	Kansas River
202	US 59 S, to W Lawrence, **S on US 40** ⛽ Conoco, Phillips 66/dsl, Zarco/dsl 🍴 Burger King, Domino's, Dunkin Donuts, Jimmy John's, Kobe Japanese, McDonald's, Sonic, Subway, Taco Bell,
202	Continued Taco John's, Wendy's 🏨 Best Value Inn, Baymont Inn, Comfort Inn, Days Inn, DoubleTree, EconoLodge, Hampton Inn, Quality Inn [O] [H], $General, Advance Parts, Dillon's Foods/gas, O'Reilly Parts, to Clinton Lake SP, to U of KS, vet, Walgreens
197	KS 10, Lecompton, Lawrence, N [O] Perry Lake SP, S [O] Clinton Lake SP
188mm	**Topeka Service Area, full ♿ facilities,** ⛽ Phillips 66/dsl 🍴 Dunkin Donuts, Hardee's, Pizza Hut, Taco Bell
183	I-70 W (from wb), to Denver
367mm	**toll plaza**
366	I-470 W, to Wichita
I-70 E and KS TPK E run together	
365	21st St, Rice Rd, access to Shawnee Lake RA
364b	US 40 E, Carnahan Ave, to Lake Shawnee
364a	California Ave, **0-1 mi S** ⛽ BP/dsl, Phillips 66/dsl 🍴 Arby's, Baskin-Robbins, Burger King, Domino's, DQ, McDonald's, Pizza Hut, Subway, Tacos Mexicano [O] $General, $Tree, Ace Hardware, Advance Parts, AutoZone, Dillon's Food/gas, O'Reilly Parts, repair, vet, Walgreens, Walmart/Subway
363	Adams St, S ⛽ Phillips 66/dsl
362c	10th Ave (from wb), N 🏨 Ramada Inn, S [O] st capitol
362b a	to 8th Ave, N 🏨 Ramada, S [O] to St Capitol, downtown
361b	3rd St, Monroe St
361a	1st Ave, S Ryder
359	MacVicar Ave, S [O] [H], Kenworth
358b a	Gage Blvd
357b a	Fairlawn Rd, 6th Ave, S ⛽ Phillips 66, Valero/dsl 🏨 Best Western, Motel 6 [O] $General, NAPACare, vet
356b a	Wanamaker Rd, N 🍴 Red Robin 🏨 Hyatt Place [O] KS Museum of History, S ⛽ BP, Murphy Express/dsl, Phillips 66/dsl 🍴 Applebee's, Arby's, Buffalo Wild Wings, Burger King, Chick-fil-A, Chili's, Chipotle Mexican, ChuckECheese, CiCi's Pizza, Coldstone, Cracker Barrel, Denny's, Five Guys, Freddy's Steakburgers, Golden Corral, Hardee's, Hooters, HuHot Chinese, IHOP, Jason's Deli, Jersey Mike's Subs, Jimmy John's, Jose Pepper's, Longhorn Steaks, McAlister's, McDonald's, Noodles&Co, Old Chicago, Olive Garden, On-the-Border, Panda Express, Panera Bread, Papa John's, Perkins, Pie Five Pizza, Pizza Hut, Qdoba, Red Lobster, Sonic, Spangles, Starbucks, Steak'n Shake, Taco Bell, Taco John's, TX Roadhouse, Wendy's 🏨 Baymont Inn, Candlewood Suites, Clubhouse Inn, Comfort Suites, Country Inn&Suites, Courtyard, Days Inn, Econolodge, Fairfield Inn, Hampton Inn, Hilton Garden, Holiday Inn Express, Homewood Suites, Quality Inn, Relax Inn, Residence Inn, Sleep Inn, Super 8, Woodspring Suites [O] $Tree, AAA, Aldi Foods, AT&T, AutoZone, Barnes&Noble, Best Buy, Dick's, Dillard's, Goodyear/auto, Hobby Lobby, Home Depot, JC Penney, Jo-Ann, Kohl's, Lowe's, Menards, Michael's, Natural Grocers, Old Navy, PetCo, Sam's Club/gas, Target, TJ Maxx, Tuesday Morning, URGENT CARE, Verizon, Walmart/Subway
355	I-470 E, US 75 S, to VA MED CTR, Topeka, **1 mi S** same as 356, air museum
353	KS 4 W, to Auburn Rd
351	frontage rd (from eb), Mission Creek
350	Valencia Rd
347	West Union Rd
346	Carlson Rd, to Rossville, Willard
343	Ranch Rd
342	Keene-Eskridge Rd, access to Lake Wabaunsee
341	KS 30, Maple Hill, S ⛽ 24-7/Subway/café/dsl/RV dump
338	Vera Rd, S ⛽ Valero/Baskin-Robbins/dsl

KANSAS CITY · BONNER SPGS · LAWRENCE · LAWRENCE · TOPEKA

KS

INTERSTATE 70 Cont'd

Exit#	Services
336mm	(exits left from both lanes), full facilities, litter barrels, petwalk, RV parking, wireless internet
335	Snokomo Rd, Paxico, Skyline Mill Creek Scenic Drive
333	KS 138, Paxico, N Mill Creek RV Park, winery
332	Spring Creek Rd
330	KS 185, to McFarland
329mm	weigh sta both lanes
328	KS 99, to Alma, S Wabaunsee Co Museum
324	Wabaunsee Rd, N Grandma Horners Store&Factory
322	Tallgrass Rd
318	frontage rd
316	Deep Creek Rd
313	KS 177, to Manhattan, 8 mi N Phillips 66 Chili's, IHOP, Longhorn Steaks, McAlister's Deli, McDonald's, Olive Garden, Sonic, Taco Bell, TX Roadhouse, Wendy's Best Western, Candlewood Suites, Comfort Inn, Fairfield Inn, Hampton Inn, Hilton Garden, Motel 6, Quality Inn, Super 8 Aldi Foods, JC Penney, to KSU, Walmart/Subway
311	Moritz Rd
310mm	both lanes, full facilities, litter barrels, petwalk, RV dump
307	McDowell Creek Rd, scenic river rd to Manhattan
304	Humboldt Creek Rd
303	KS 18 E, to Ogden, Manhattan, N to KSU
301	Marshall Field, N Cavalry Museum, Custer's House, KS Terr Capitol, to Ft Riley
300	US 40, KS 57, Council Grove, S hist church
299	Flinthills Blvd, to Jct City, Ft Riley, N Cenex/dsl Stacy's Rest. EconoLodge, Grandview Plaza Inn, Great Western Inn
298	Chestnut St, to Jct City, Ft Riley, N Shell/dsl/24hr Arby's, Cracker Barrel, Family Buffet, Freddy's Steakburgers, JC's BBQ, La Fiesta, Pizza Hut, Qdoba, Starbucks, Taco Bell, Tokyo Steaks Best Western, Candlewood Suites, Comfort Inn, Courtyard, Quality Inn $General, $Tree, CVS Drug, Verizon, Walmart/Subway
296	US 40, Washington St, Junction City, N Casey's, Cenex/dsl, Phillips 66, Shell/dsl IHOP, McDonald's, Munson's Prime, Peking Chinese, Sonic, Subway Budget Host/RV park, Express Inn, Hampton Inn, Jct City Inn, Super 8, Woodspring Suites Cadillac/Chevrolet, Haas Tire, Harley-Davidson, vet
295	US 77, KS 18 W, Marysville, to Milford Lake, N Sapp Bros/A&W/dsl/24hr Motel 6 H, Ford/Lincoln/Kia/Chrysler/Dodge/Jeep, RV Ctr, S Owls Nest Camping, truckwash
290	Milford Lake Rd
286	KS 206, Chapman, S Casey's/dsl, Cenex/dsl $General, Chapman Creek RV Park, KS Auto Racing Museum
281	KS 43, to Enterprise, N Phillips 66/dsl 4 Seasons RV Ctr/Park
277	Jeep Rd
275	KS 15, to Clay Ctr, Abilene, N Brookville Hotel/rest., Holiday Inn Express, S 24-7/Arby's/dsl, KwikShop, Sips Burger King, M&R Grill, McDonald's, Pizza Hut, Sonic, Subway Budget Inn, Super 8 H, $General, Auburn Drug, AutoZone, Buick/Cadillac/Chevrolet, CountryMart Foods, O'Reilly Parts, ShopKO, to Eisenhower Museum
272	Fair Rd, to Talmage, S Loves/Hardee's/dsl/scales/24hr Russell Stover Candies
266	KS 221, Solomon
265mm	both lanes, full facilities, litter barrels, petwalk, RV dump, vending

JCT CITY

ABILENE

Exit#	Services
264mm	Solomon River
260	Niles Rd, New Cambria
253mm	Saline River
253	Ohio St, N RV park, S FLYING J/Huddle House/dsl/LP/scales/24hr, LNG H, Harley-Davidson, Kenworth
252	KS 143, 9th St, Salina, N 24-7/Subway/dsl/24hr, Petro/Shell/Starbucks/Popeye's/dsl/24hr/@ IHOP, Iron Skillet, McDonald's Days Inn, Holiday Inn Express, La Quinta, Motel 6, Red Carpet, Rodeway Inn, Super 8 Blue Beacon, dsl repair, Freightliner, KOA, S Pilot/dsl/scales/24hr/@ Comfort Inn, EconoLodge
250b a	I-135, US 81, N to Concordia, S to Wichita
249	Halstead Rd, to Trenton
244	Hedville, S Phillips 66/dsl Rolling Hills Park (2mi)
238	to Brookville, Glendale, Tescott
233	290th Rd, Juniata
225	KS 156, to Ellsworth, S D&S/dsl Ft Harker Museum, Ft Larned HS
224mm	both lanes, full facilities, litter barrels, petwalk, RV dump
221	KS 14 N, to Lincoln
219	KS 14 S, to Ellsworth, S Conoco/dsl
216	to Vesper
209	to Sylvan Grove
206	KS 232, Wilson, N Travel Shoppe/rest. Wilson Lake (6mi), S RV camping
199	Dorrance, N to Wilson Lake, S Agco/dsl/food
193	Bunker Hill Rd, N Conoco/Sunmart/pizza/dsl/24hr, to Wilson Lake WA
189	US 40 bus, Pioneer Rd, Russell
187mm	parking area both lanes, litter barrels
184	US 281, Russell, N 24-7/dsl, Cenex/Fossil Sta./dsl A&W, McDonald's, Meridy's Rest., Pizza Hut, Sonic, Subway Days Inn, Fossil Creek Hotel, Quality Inn, Russell's Inn H, $General, Bumper Parts, CarQuest, Fossil Creek RV Park, JJJ RV Park, Klema Mkt, Shopko, st patrol
180	Balta Rd, to Russell
175	Gorham, 1 mi N Co-Op/dsl
172	Walker Ave
168	KS 255, to Victoria, S 255 Diner/dsl to Cathedral of the Plains
163	Toulon Ave
161	Commerce Parkway, S Volvo/Mack Trucks
159	US 183, Hays, N Cenex/Taco Grande/dsl, EVC, Qwest/dsl Applebee's, IHOP, Old Chicago, Pasta Jay's, Sims BBQ, Wendy's Best Western+, Comfort Inn, Fairfield Inn, Hampton Inn, Holiday Inn Express, Sleep Inn, TownePlace Suites AT&T, Chrysler/Dodge/Jeep, Ford/Lincoln, Harley-Davidson, Home Depot, Tesla EVC, Toyota, Verizon,

SALINA

RUSSELL

HAYS

INTERSTATE 70 Cont'd

Exit	Services
HAYS	
159	Continued Walmart/Subway, **S** 24-7/dsl, Love's, Phillips 66/dsl, Phillips 66/dsl/24hr, Sinclair/dsl A&W/LJ Silver, Arby's, Burger King, China Garden, Domino's, Freddy's, Jimmy John's, KFC, Lucky Buffet, McDonald's, Pheasant Run Pancakes, Pizza Hut, Qdoba, Sonic, Starbucks, Subway, Taco Bell, Taco Grande, Thirsty's Grill, Vernie's Hamburger House, Wendy's, Whiskey Creek Grill Baymont Inn, Days Inn, EconoLodge, Ft Hays Inn, Quality Inn, Rodeway Inn, Super 8 H, $Tree, Ace Hardware, Advance Parts, Chevrolet, Dillon's Foods/gas, Hobby Lobby, JC Penney, O'Reilly Parts, Tires 4 Less, Verizon, Walgreens
157	US 183 S byp, to Hays, **N** Peterbilt, **S** museum, st patrol, to Ft Hays St U, tourist info
ELLIS	
153	Yocemento Ave
145	KS 247 S, Ellis, **S** Casey's, Love's/DQ/Subway/dsl/scales/24hr Cancun Mexican Days Inn Railroad Museum, RV camping, to Chrysler Museum, USPO
140	Riga Rd
135	KS 147, Ogallah, **N** Frontier Selfserve/dsl, **S** to Cedar Bluff SP (13mi)
132mm	**both lanes, full facilities, litter barrels, petwalk, RV dump**
WAKEENEY	
128	US 283 N, WaKeeney, **N** Super 8
127	US 283 S, WaKeeney, **N** Jake & Chet's Cafe, Pizza Hut, Tropical Mexican Best Western+, KS Kountry Inn $General, **S** 24-7/McDonald's/dsl/24hr, Conoco/Subway/dsl EconoLodge antiques, auto repair, KOA
120	Voda Rd
115	KS 198 N, Banner Rd, Collyer
107	KS 212, Castle Rock Rd, Quinter, **N** Sinclair/dsl First Inn/rest. H, $General, Cobblestone Inn, **S** Conoco/dsl/24hr DQ, Pizza Sta
99	KS 211, Park, **1 mi N** Sinclair/dsl
97mm	**both lanes, full facilities, litter barrels, petwalk, RV dump, vending**
95	KS 23 N, to Hoxie
93	KS 23, Grainfield, **N** Sinclair/dsl
85	KS 216, Grinnell
79	Campus Rd
76	US 40, to Oakley, **S** TA/Shell/Buckhorn Rest./Subway/dsl/e-85/scales/24hr/@ Rodeway Inn, Sleep Inn H, Blue Beacon, Fick Museum
70	US 83, to Oakley, **N** Free Breakfast Inn, **S** Cenex/dsl Colonial Steaks H, antiques, Fick Museum, High-Plains RV Park
62	rd K, Mingo, **S** gas/dsl/
COLBY	
54	Country Club Dr, Colby, **N** LNG, Pilot/Subway/dsl/scales/24hr Hampton Inn H, truck/dsl repair
53	KS 25, Colby, **N** 24-7/Subway/dsl Arby's, Burger King, China Buffet, Jimmy John's, McDonald's, MT Mike's Steaks, Pizza Hut, Sonic, Subway, Taco John's Days Inn, Holiday Inn Express, Motel 6, Quality Inn, Sleep Inn, Super 8 H, $General, Dillon's Foods/dsl, dsl repair, Ford/Lincoln, Haas Tire, O'Reilly Parts, Prairie Museum, Quilt Cabin, RV park/antiques, visitors ctr, Walmart, **S** Petro/Phillips 66/scales/dsl/@ City Limits Grill, Qdoba, Quiznos, Starbucks, Village Inn American Inn, Comfort Inn Chrysler/Dodge/Jeep, truck repair
48.5mm	**both lanes, full facilities, litter barrels, petwalk, , , RV park/dump, vending**
45	US 24 E, Levant
36	KS 184, Brewster, **N** Fuel Depot/dsl
35.5mm	Mountain/Central time zone
GOODLAND	
27	KS 253, Edson
19	US 24, Goodland, **N** Pizza Hut $General, High Plains Museum, KOA, NAPA
17	US 24, KS 27, Goodland, **N** Cenex/dsl, Conoco, Phillips 66/dsl DQ, McDonald's, Reynaldo's Mexican, Sonic, Subway, Taco John's Best Value Inn, Comfort Inn, Econolodge, Motel 6, Super 8 H, CarQuest/Firestone, Chevrolet/GMC, Ford, Walmart, **S** 24-7/dsl/scales Steak'n Shake Holiday Inn Express Mid-America Camping, Tesla EVP
12	rd 14, Caruso
9	rd 11, Ruleton
7.5mm	**Welcome Ctr eb/ wb, full facilities, info, litter barrels, petwalk, , , RV dump, vending, wireless internet**
1	KS 267, Kanorado, **N** food, gas
.5mm	**weigh sta eb**
0mm	Kansas/Colorado State Line

INTERSTATE 135 (Wichita)

Exit#	Services
95b a	**I-70, E to KS City, W to Denver, US 81 N. I-135 begins/ends on I-70, exit 250.**
SALINA	
93	KS 140, State St, Salina, **E** art ctr, museum
92	Crawford St, **E** 24-7/dsl, KwikShop, Shell, Sinclair Arby's, Braum's, Cotijas Mexican, Great Wall Chinese, Gutierrez Mexican, Hickory Hut BBQ, Jim's Chicken, KFC, La Casita, La Hacienda, McDonald's, Russell's Rest., Spangles, Subway, Taco Bell, Western Sizzlin Ambassador Hotel, AmericInn, Baymont Inn, Days Inn, Econolodge, Value Inn&Suites $General, $Tree, Advance Parts, Dillon's Foods, Kansas Land Tires, NAPA, O'Reilly Parts, Walgreens, **W** Phillips 66/dsl Quality Inn
90	Magnolia Rd, **E** Casey's, Phillips 66/dsl Buffalo Wild Wings, Burger King, Carlos O'Kelly's, Chick-fil-A, Chili's, Coyote Canyon Café, Domino's, Freddy's Burgers, Goodcents Subs, Hog Wild BBQ, Hong Kong Buffet, IHOP, Jalisco Mexican, Longhorn Steaks, Marco's Pizza, McDonald's, Papa Murphy's, Qdoba, Schlotzsky's, Sonic, Spangles, Starbucks, Subway, Taco Bell Best Value Inn, Candlewood Suites $General, $Tree, Aldi Foods, AT&T, AutoZone, BigLots, Cadillac/Chevrolet, Dick's, Dillard's, Dillon's Foods/dsl, Hobby Lobby, Honda, JC Penney, Jo-Ann Fabrics, Kohl's, Marshall's, Old Navy, O'Reilly Parts, PetCo, Ross, Subaru, Toyota, Verizon, **W** Cenex/dsl Menard's
89	Schilling Rd, **E** KwikShop/dsl Applebee's, Daimaru Steaks, Five Guys, Olive Garden, Pizza Hut, Red Lobster, Rib Crib BBQ, Taco John's, Tucson's Steaks, Wendy's Country Inn&Suites, Courtyard, Hampton Inn, Hilton Garden, Holiday Inn Lowe's, Sam's Club/gas, Target, URGENT CARE Walmart/Subway, **W** Casey's Best Western, Comfort Suites, Super 8
88	Water Well Rd, **E** Sleep Inn Chrysler/Dodge/Jeep, Ford Nissan
86	KS 104, Mentor, Smolan
82	KS 4, Falun Rd, Assaria, **E** RV Camping
78	KS 4 W, Lindsborg, **W** to Sandz Gallery/Museum
72	Lindsborg, **4 mi E** Maxwell WR, McPherson St Fishing Lake **W** H, camping, food, gas, lodging, museum
68mm	**(both lanes exit left), full facilities, litter barrels petwalk , , RV dump**
65	Pawnee Rd

KS

INTERSTATE 135 (Wichita) Cont'd

MCPHERSON

Exit#	Services
62	Mohawk Rd
60	US 56, McPherson, Marion, E Loves/Hardee's/dsl/LP/scales/24hr, W 24/7/Burger King/dsl, Phillips 66/dsl Applebee's, Arby's, Braum's, Freddy's Burgers, Golden Dragon Chinese, KFC/LJ Silver, La Fiesta Mexican, McDonald's, MT Mike's, Perkins, Pizza Hut, Subway, Taco Bell, Taco John's, Woodie's BBQ Best Western, Days Inn, EconoLodge, Fairfield Inn, Hampton Inn, Holiday Inn Express, Knights Inn H, AutoZone, Buick/Cadillac/GMC, Chrysler/Dodge/Jeep, Ford, Walgreens, Walmart
58	US 81, KS 61, to Hutchinson, McPherson
54	18th Ave, Comanche Rd, Elyria
48	KS 260 E, Moundridge, 2 mi W gas
46	KS 260 W, Moundridge, 2 mi W truck repair, food, gas

NEWTON

Exit#	Services
40	Lincoln Blvd, Hesston, E Panda Kitchen AmericInn Cottonwood Grove RV Camping, W Casey's/dsl/24hr El Cerrito Grill, Lincoln Perk Coffee, Pizza Hut, Sonic, Subway Best Value Inn city park
34	KS 15, N Newton, to Abilene, KS 15, E RV camping, W Papa John's (1mi), Subway (1mi), Taco Bell (1mi) Kauffman Museum
33	US 50 E, to Peabody (from nb)
31	1st St, Broadway St, E LoneStar/dsl, Newell TC/dsl/@ Applebee's, CJ's Rest., KFC Days Inn, Holiday Inn Express, Newton Inn Cadillac/Chevrolet, Chrysler/Dodge/Jeep, Ford/Lincoln, W Braum's, MT Mike's Comfort Inn, Red Coach Inn
30	US 50 W, KS 15 (exits left from nb), to Hutchinson, Newton, W KwikShop/dsl Arby's, Panda Kitchen, Papa Murphy's, Pizza Hut, Sonic, Subway H, $Tree, AutoZone, Buick/GMC, Dillon's Foods, R Tires, Verizon, Walmart
28	SE 36th St, W Phillips 66/dsl Burger King Chisholm Trail Outlets/famous brands
25	KS 196, to Whitewater, El Dorado
23mm	**both lanes, full facilities, litter barrels, petwalk, RV dump, vending**
22	125th St
19	101st St, W RV camping
17	85th St, Valley Ctr
16	77th St, E Motel 6 Wichita Greyhound Park
14	61st St, E QT/dsl Applebee's, Chopstix, Cracker Barrel, Pizza Hut, Spangles Rest., Subway, Taco Bell, Wendy's Red Roof Inn Chevrolet, W Phillips 66/dsl KFC, McDonald's Quality Inn, Super 8 Goodyear/auto

WICHITA

Exit#	Services
13	53rd St, E Freightliner, Harley-Davidson, Volvo/Mack Trucks, W Phillips 66/dsl Arby's, Country Kitchen Best Western, Days Inn
11b	I-235 W, KS 96, to Hutchinson
11a	KS 254, to El Dorado
10b	29th St, Hydraulic Ave
10a	KS 96 E
9	21st St, E Valero Sonic $General, Wichita St U
8	13th St, E $General, W Pig In Pig Out BBQ
7b	8th St, 9th St, Central Ave., E School of Medicine
7a	downtown
6b	1st St, 2nd St, downtown
5b	US 54, US 400, Kellogg Ave, E QT/dsl
5a	Lincoln St, E DQ, W QT/dsl
4	Harry St, 1 mi E Arby's, Bionic Burger, Burger King, Denny's, Hardee's, Jimmy's Egg, LA Fried Chicken, Little Caesar's, McDonald's, NuWay Drive-Thru, Poblano Mexican, Shanghai Chinese, Spangles Rest., Subway, Taco Bell, Wendy's H, BigLots, CVS Drug, Firestone/auto, Goodyear/auto, W BD-C/dsl
3	Pawnee Ave, E Family$, O'Reilly Parts, W Jump-start/dsl Burger King, Pizza Hut, Spangles $General, AutoZone
2	Hydraulic Ave, E KwikShop, W McDonald's, Subway
2mm	Arkansas River
1c	I-235 N, 2 mi W Hilton
1b a	US 81 S, 47th St, E QT/dsl Days Inn, Holiday Inn Express, Quality Inn, Super 8, W Applebee's, Arby's, Braum's, Burger King, Carlos O'Kelly's, Domino's, Godfather's, Goodcents Subs, Heritage Rest., Hog Wild BBQ, IHOP, KFC, Little Caesar's, LJ Silver, McDonald's, New China, Pizza Hut, Spangles Rest., Subway, Taco Bell Best Western, Springfield Inn, Woodspring Suites $General, $Tree, Air Capital RV Park, Dillon's Foods/dsl, O'Reilly Parts, Verizon

I-135 begins/ends on I-35, exit 42.

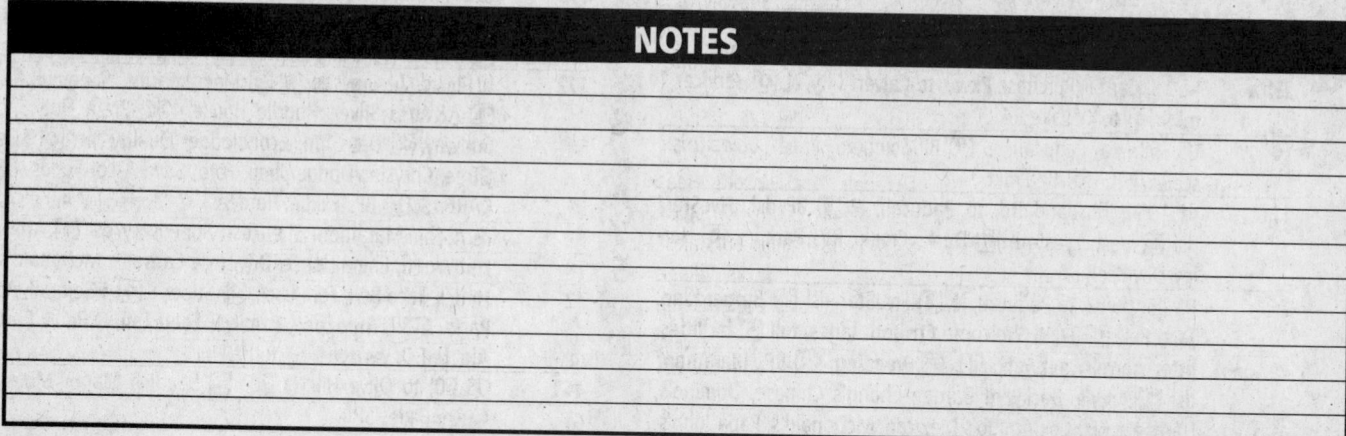

NOTES

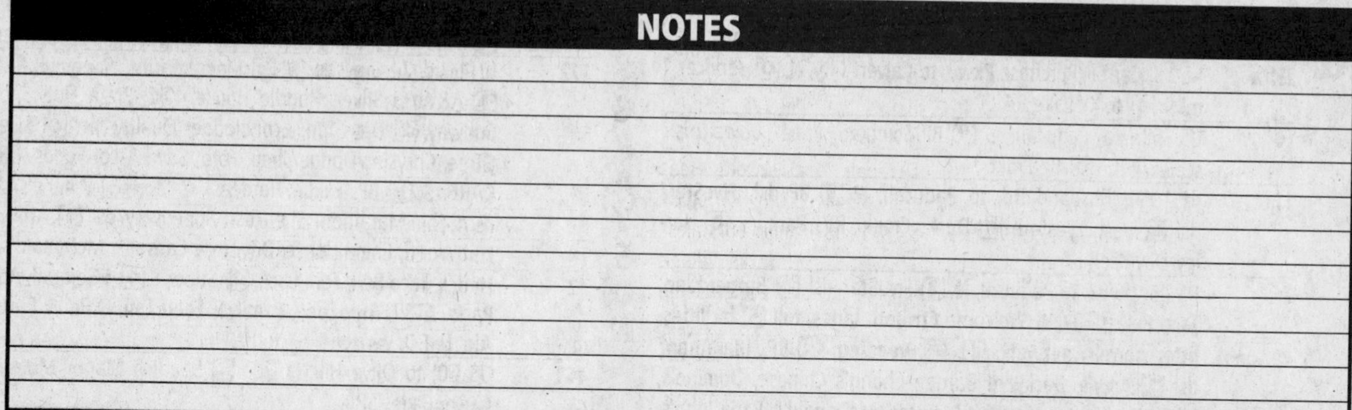

KENTUCKY

INTERSTATE 24

Exit#	Services
93.5mm	Kentucky/Tennessee state line
93mm	**Welcome Ctr wb, full facilities, litter barrels, petwalk, , vending**
91.5mm	Big West Fork Red River
89	KY 115, to Oak Grove, N to Jeff Davis Mon St HS, S Pilot/McDonald's/dsl/scales/24hr, Shell/Subway/dsl truck repair
86	US 41A, to Ft Campbell, Pennyrile Pkwy, Hopkinsville, N Marathon/Chester's/dsl/scales/24hr, S FLYING J/Denny's/dsl/LP/scales/24hr, Exxon/dsl, Pilot/Subway/Wendy's/dsl/scales/24hr McDonald's, Waffle House Candlewood Suites, Comfort Suites, Days Inn, Holiday Inn Express, Quality Inn, Sleep Inn H, truck wash
81	Pennyrile Pky N, to Hopkinsville
79mm	Little River
73	KY 117, to Gracey, Newstead
65	US 68, KY 80, to Cadiz, S BP/dsl, Marathon/dsl, Shell/dsl Cracker Barrel, KFC, McDonald's, Subway, Taco Bell, Wendy's Econolodge, Knights Inn, Super 7 Inn, Super 8 H, Chevrolet, golf, to NRA
56	KY 139, to Cadiz, Princeton, S Marathon/dsl KOA (9mi), NRA
47mm	Lake Barkley
45	KY 293, to Princeton, Saratoga, S Marathon/dsl Mineral Mound SP, RV Camping, to KY St Penitentiary
42	I-69 N, to W KY Pkwy, Elizabethtown
40	US 62, US 641, Kuttawa, Eddyville, N Regency Inn (2mi), Relax Inn camping, Mineral Mound SP, S BP/Wendy's/dsl/24hr, Exxon, Pilot/Huck's/Quiznos/dsl/scales/24hr Huddle House, SW Grill Days Inn, Hampton Inn camping, KY Lake Rec Areas, to Lake Barkley
36mm	**weigh sta both lanes,**
34mm	Cumberland River
31	KY 453, to Grand Rivers, Smithland, N BP/dsl Patti's Inn, S Exxon/dsl Miss Scarlett's Best Value Inn, Green Turtle Resort (3mi), Lighthouse Landing Resort Exit 31 RV Park, NRA
29mm	Tennessee River
27	US 62, to KY Dam, Calvert City, N BP/dsl, Marathon/dsl Cracker Barrel, DQ, KFC, McDonald's, Waffle House Days Inn, KY Dam Motel, Super 8 Cypress Lakes Camp, Freightliner, KOA, vet, S Loves/Arby's/dsl/scales/24hr Subway Econolodge truck repair
25b a	I-69 S, Carroll/Purchase Pkwy, to Calvert City, N services 1 mi S to KY Lake RA
16	US 68, to Paducah, S BP/Southern Pride/Subway/dsl/scales/24hr flea mkt
11	rd 1954, Husband Rd, to Paducah, N BP/dsl, FiveStar/dsl Best Western Duck Creek RV Park, S Harley-Davidson
7	US 45, US 62, to Paducah, N FiveStar/dsl Burger King, Taco Bell H, S **Welcome Ctr both lanes, full facilities, litter barrels, petwalk, , , vending,** BP, Marathon/dsl Arby's, Backyard Burger, Chong's Chinese, Domino's, Hardee's, KFC, Los Amigo's Mexican, McDonald's, Papa John's,

PADUCAH

Exit#	Services
7	Continued Popeye's, Sonic, Subway, Waffle House, Wendy's Travelers Inn AT&T, Banks Mkt/gas, CVS Drug, Family$, O'Reilly Parts, Plaza Tires, Verizon
4	US 60, to Paducah, N Applebee's, Bob Evans, Burger King, McDonald's, O'Charley's, Outback Steaks, Rafferty's Auburn Place, Candlewood Suites, Courtyard, Days Inn, Drury Inn, Fairfield Inn, Hampton Inn, Holiday Inn Express, Homewood Suites, La Quinta, Residence Inn, Westowne Inn Toyota, S BP, Murphy USA/dsl Arby's, Backyard Burger, Buffalo Wild Wings, Capt D's, Chick-fil-A, Chong's Chinese, ChuckeCheese, Coldstone, Cracker Barrel, Domino's, Fazoli's, Firehouse Subs, Gondolier Italian, Hananoki Hibachi, Hardee's, IHOP, Logan's Roadhouse, Los Amigos, Los Garcia's, McAlister's Deli, Olive Garden, Panchero's, Panera Bread, Penn Sta. Subs, Pizza Hut, Red Lobster, Sonic, Steak'n Shake, Taco Bell, Taco John's, Tokyo Hibachi, TX Roadhouse, Wendy's Comfort Suites, Country Inn&Suites, Drury Suites, Motel 6, PearTree Inn, Super 8, Thrifty Inn $General, $Tree, AAA, Advance Parts, Aldi Foods, AT&T, Best Buy, Books-A-Million, Dick's, Dillard's, Goodyear/auto, Hobby Lobby, Home Depot, JC Penney, Kohl's, Lowe's, Michael's, Office Depot, Old Navy, Petsmart, Plaza Tire, Sam's Club/gas, TJ Maxx, Tuesday Morning, Verizon, Walmart, Five Guys, Jimmy John's, Qdoba, Starbucks
3	KY 305, to Paducah, N Shell/dsl, Superway/dsl Best Value Inn, Comfort Inn/rest., Red Roof Inn, S Cheers/Noble Romans/dsl/e85, Pilot/Subway/dsl/scales/24hr Waffle Hut, Yu's Kitchen Baymont Inn Fern Lake Camping
0mm	Kentucky/Illinois state line, Ohio River

INTERSTATE 64

Exit#	Services
192mm	Kentucky/West Virginia state line, Big Sandy River
191	US 23, to Ashland, 1-2 mi N Exxon, Marathon/Subway/dsl, Speedway/dsl Arby's, Little Caesar's, McDonald's, Waffle House, Wendy's Ramada Ltd H, IGA Foods, Rite Aid, USPO
185	KY 180, Cannonsburg, 0-3 mi N Exxon/dsl, Marathon/dsl, Shell/McDonald's/USPO, Superquik Arby's, Bob Evans, Burger King, DQ, Gatti's Pizza, Hermanos Nunez Mexican, KFC, Subway, Taco Bell, Waffle House, Wendy's Days Inn, Fairfield Inn, Hampton Inn, Holiday Inn Express $Tree, H, Walmart/Subway, S FLYING J/Denny's/dsl/LP/scales/24hr
181	181 US 60, to Princess, N BP/dsl, S Marathon/dsl
179	rd 67, Industrial Pkwy, N KOA/@
174mm	**eb, full facilities, litter barrels, petwalk, , , vending**
173mm	**wb, full facilities, litter barrels, petwalk, , , vending**
172	rd 1, rd 7, Grayson, N Marathon/dsl, Superquik/dsl/24hr A&W/LJ Silver, Huddle House, KFC, Pizza Hut, Shoney's Subway Days Inn, Econolodge, Quality Inn $General $Tree, Chrysler/Dodge/Jeep, Ford, Save-A-Lot Foods, URGENT CARE, S BP, Exxon/Hardees, Loves/Wendy's/scales/dsl/24hr, Marathon, Shell/dsl, Speedway/dsl Arby's, Biscuit World, China House, DQ, Little Caesar's, McDonald's, Papa John's, Taco Bell, Toro Loco Super 8 $General, Advance Parts, AT&T, AutoZone, Family$, Food Fair, O'Reilly Parts, Rite Aid, USPO, Verizon
161	US 60, to Olive Hill, N Spanish Manor Motel to Carter Caves SP

GRAYSON

KY

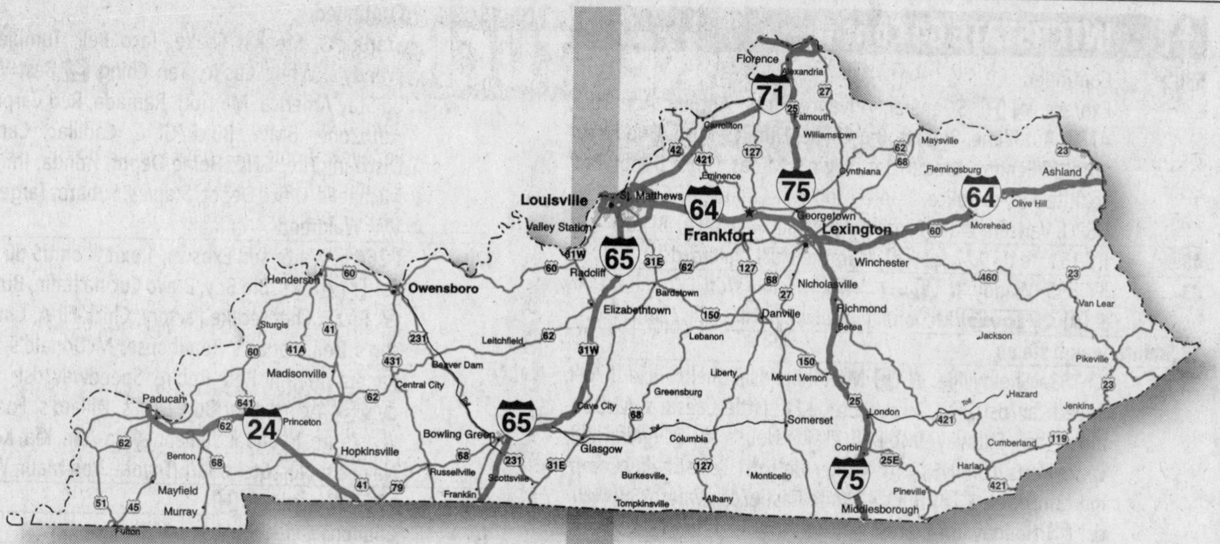

INTERSTATE 64 Cont'd

MOREHEAD

Exit#	Services
156	rd 2, to KY 59, to Olive Hill, S BP
148mm	**weigh sta wb**
141mm	**both lanes, full facilities, litter barrels, petwalk, vending**
137	KY 32, to Morehead, N BP/dsl, Speedway/dsl DQ, Huddle House AT&T, Big Lots, Kroger/dsl, Lowe's, Walmart/Subway, S BP/McDonald's/dsl/24hr, Marathon/dsl China Star, Cracker Barrel, Domino's, Don Señor, Hardee's, Lee's Chicken, Reno's Roadhouse Best Western, Days Inn, Hampton Inn, Motel 6, Red Roof Inn H, $General, Ace Hardware, auto repair, AutoZone, st police
133	rd 801, to Sharkey, Farmers, N Shell/dsl Chrysler/Dodge/Jeep/Ford, S BP/Subway/dsl Comfort Inn Outpost RV Park (4mi)
123	US 60, to Salt Lick, Owingsville
121	KY 36, to Owingsville, N BP/dsl, Exxon/dsl, Valero/dsl DQ, McDonald's, Subway $General, Family$, S Save-a-Lot Foods
113	US 60, to Mt Sterling, N Shell/dsl, S Pilot/McDonald's/Subway/dsl/scales/24hr
110	US 460, KY 11, Mt Sterling, N Shell/Krystal/Subway/dsl, Valero/dsl Cattleman's Roadhouse, Cracker Barrel Comfort Inn, Ramada Ltd, S BP/dsl, Exxon, Marathon, Marathon/dsl, Murphy Express/dsl, Speedway/dsl Applebee's, Arby's, Asian Buffet, Bojangle's, Burger King, Capt D's, City King Buffet, Don Señor, El Camino Real, Hardee's, KFC, Lee's Chicken, Little Caesar's, LJ Silver, Los Rodeos, McDonald's, Pizza Hut, Subway, Taco Bell, Waffle House, Wendy's Budget Inn, Days Inn H, $Tree, Advance Parts, Advance Parts, AT&T, AutoZone, Chevrolet, Chrysler/Dodge/Jeep, CVS Drug, Family$, Ford, JC Penney, Kroger, Lowe's, O'Reilly Parts, Verizon, Walmart/Subway
101	US 60
98.5mm	**eb, full facilities, litter barrels, petwalk, vending**
98	KY 402 (from eb), S Natural Bridge Resort SP
96b a	KY 627, to Winchester, Paris, N 96 Truck Plaza/dsl/rest./scales, BP/dsl, S Baymont Inn, Hampton Inn, Red Roof Inn Buick/Chevrolet/GMC

WINCHESTER

Exit#	Services
94	KY 1958, Van Meter Rd, Winchester, N Marathon/dsl/24hr, Shell/scales/dsl Comfort Inn, Value Stay Inn, S BP/dsl, Marathon/dsl, Murphy Express/dsl, Shell/dsl, Speedway/dsl Applebee's, Arby's, Big Boy, Bojangle's, Burger King, Capt D's, Dickey's BBQ, Domino's, Don Senor, DQ, El Camino Real, Fazoli's, Golden Corral, Great Wall Chinese, Hardee's, Jade Garden Chinese, Jimmy John's, KFC, Little Caesar's, McDonald's, Papa John's, Pizza Hut, Puerta Grande, Rally's, Sakura Express, Sir Pizza, Sonic, Starbucks, Subway, Taco Bell, Taste Of China, Waffle House, Wendy's Holiday Inn Express H, $Tree, Advance Parts, AT&T, auto repair, AutoZone, Chrysler/Dodge/Jeep, Kroger/dsl, Lowe's, Office Depot, O'Reilly Parts, Rite Aid, Tire Discounters, to Ft Boonesborough Camping, Verizon, Walgreens, Walmart/Subway
87	KY 859, Blue Grass Sta
81	I-75 S, to Knoxville
	I-64 and I-75 run together 7 mi. See I-75, exits 113-115.
75	I-75 N, to Cincinnati, access to KY Horse Park
69	US 62 E, to Georgetown, N antiques (6mi), to Georgetown Coll., S Equus Run Vineyards (2mi)
65	US 421, Midway, S BP/dsl, Shell/dsl McDonald's, Subway
60mm	**both lanes, full facilities, litter barrels, petwalk, vending**

FRANKFORT

Exit#	Services
58	US 60, Frankfort, N BP/dsl, Five Star/dsl, Shell/dsl, Speedway/dsl Arby's, Buffalo Wild Wings, Capt. D's, Cattleman's Roadhouse, DQ, KFC, McDonald's, Miguel's Mexican, Starbucks, Subway, Taco Bell, Waffle House, Wendy's, White Castle, Zaxby's Best Western, Bluegrass Inn, Fairfield Inn $General, $Tree, Buick/Chevrolet/GMC, Chrysler/Dodge/Jeep, Dick's, ElkHorn Camping (5mi), Ford/Lincoln, GNC, Honda, Kohl's, Kroger/gas, KYSU, Michael's, Nissan, TireDiscounters, TJMaxx, to KY St Capitol, to Viet Vets Mem, Toyota, Walgreens, S Cracker Barrel, Logan's Roadhouse
55mm	Kentucky River
53b a	US 127, Frankfort, N Marathon, Speedway/dsl, Speedway/dsl Applebee's, Arby's, Baskin-Robbins, Beef O'Brady's, Big Boy, Burger King, Capt D's, Carino's Italian, Chili's, China Buffet, CookOut, DQ, Fazoli's, Ginza Japanese, Hardee's, KFC, Longhorn Steaks, McDonald's, My Guadalajara, O'Charley's, Panera Bread, Penn Sta Subs, Qdoba Mexican, Sonic, Starbucks, Staxx BBQ, Steak'n Shake, Subway, Taco Bell, Tacos n More, Wendy's Best Value Inn, Days Inn, Hampton Inn, Holiday Inn

KY

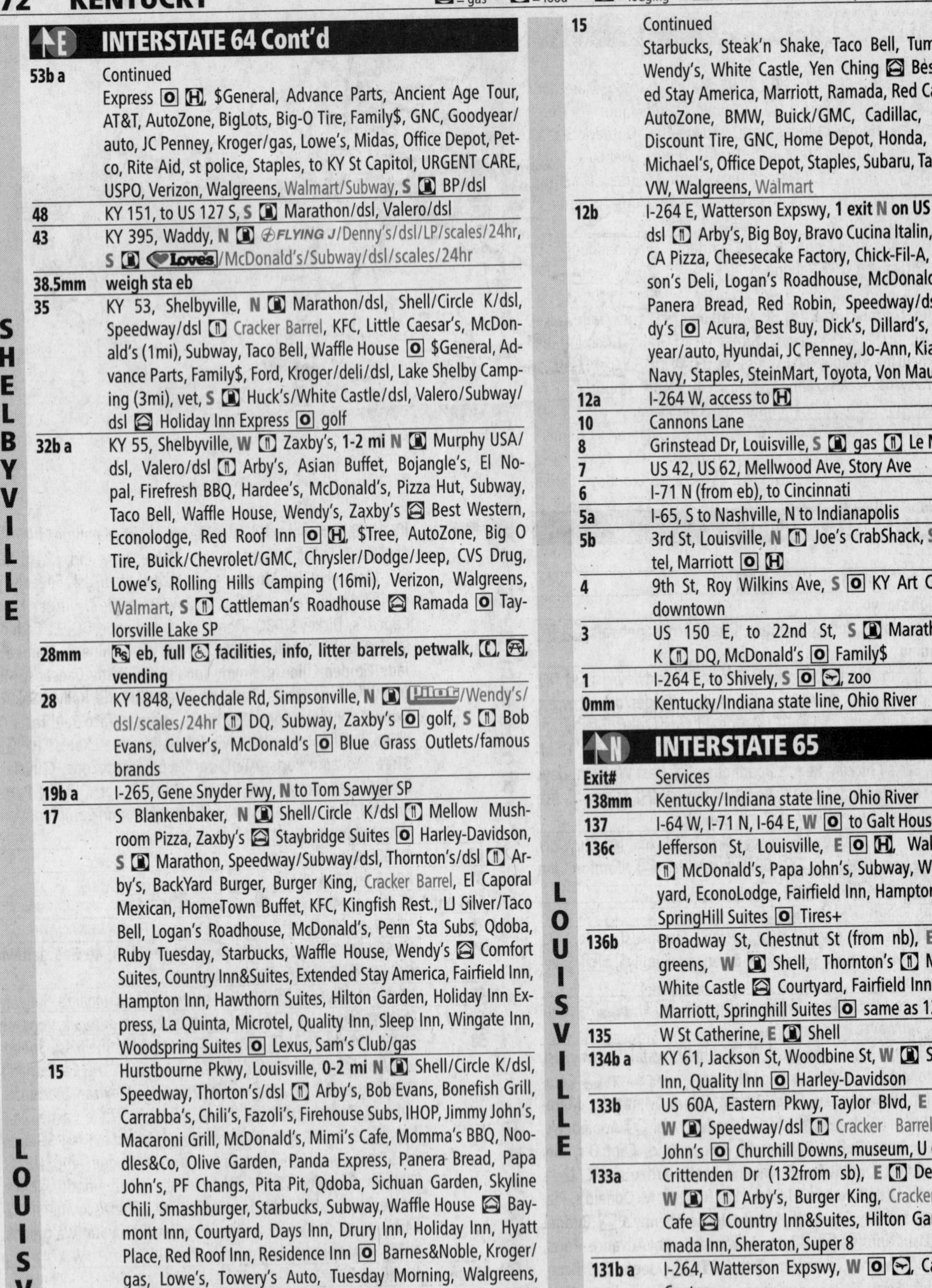

INTERSTATE 64 Cont'd

SHELBYVILLE

53b a Continued
Express [o] [H], $General, Advance Parts, Ancient Age Tour, AT&T, AutoZone, BigLots, Big-O Tire, Family$, GNC, Goodyear/auto, JC Penney, Kroger/gas, Lowe's, Midas, Office Depot, Petco, Rite Aid, st police, Staples, to KY St Capitol, URGENT CARE, USPO, Verizon, Walgreens, Walmart/Subway, **S** [gas] BP/dsl

48 KY 151, to US 127 S, **S** [gas] Marathon/dsl, Valero/dsl

43 KY 395, Waddy, **N** [gas] FLYING J/Denny's/dsl/LP/scales/24hr, **S** [gas] Loves/McDonald's/Subway/dsl/scales/24hr

38.5mm **weigh sta eb**

35 KY 53, Shelbyville, **N** [gas] Marathon/dsl, Shell/Circle K/dsl, Speedway/dsl [food] Cracker Barrel, KFC, Little Caesar's, McDonald's (1mi), Subway, Taco Bell, Waffle House [o] $General, Advance Parts, Family$, Ford, Kroger/deli/dsl, Lake Shelby Camping (3mi), vet, **S** [gas] Huck's/White Castle/dsl, Valero/Subway/dsl [lodging] Holiday Inn Express [o] golf

32b a KY 55, Shelbyville, **W** [food] Zaxby's, **1-2 mi N** [gas] Murphy USA/dsl, Valero/dsl [food] Arby's, Asian Buffet, Bojangle's, El Nopal, Firefresh BBQ, Hardee's, McDonald's, Pizza Hut, Subway, Taco Bell, Waffle House, Wendy's, Zaxby's [lodging] Best Western, Econolodge, Red Roof Inn [o] [H], $Tree, AutoZone, Big O Tire, Buick/Chevrolet/GMC, Chrysler/Dodge/Jeep, CVS Drug, Lowe's, Rolling Hills Camping (16mi), Verizon, Walgreens, Walmart, **S** [food] Cattleman's Roadhouse [lodging] Ramada [o] Taylorsville Lake SP

28mm [rest stop] **eb, full [handicapped] facilities, info, litter barrels, petwalk, [phone], [picnic], vending**

28 KY 1848, Veechdale Rd, Simpsonville, **N** [gas] Pilot/Wendy's/dsl/scales/24hr [food] DQ, Subway, Zaxby's [o] golf, **S** [food] Bob Evans, Culver's, McDonald's [o] Blue Grass Outlets/famous brands

LOUISVILLE

19b a I-265, Gene Snyder Fwy, **N** to Tom Sawyer SP

17 S Blankenbaker, **N** [gas] Shell/Circle K/dsl [food] Mellow Mushroom Pizza, Zaxby's [lodging] Staybridge Suites [o] Harley-Davidson, **S** [gas] Marathon, Speedway/Subway/dsl, Thornton's/dsl [food] Arby's, BackYard Burger, Burger King, Cracker Barrel, El Caporal Mexican, HomeTown Buffet, KFC, Kingfish Rest., LJ Silver/Taco Bell, Logan's Roadhouse, McDonald's, Penn Sta Subs, Qdoba, Ruby Tuesday, Starbucks, Waffle House, Wendy's [lodging] Comfort Suites, Country Inn&Suites, Extended Stay America, Fairfield Inn, Hampton Inn, Hawthorn Suites, Hilton Garden, Holiday Inn Express, La Quinta, Microtel, Quality Inn, Sleep Inn, Wingate Inn, Woodspring Suites [o] Lexus, Sam's Club/gas

15 Hurstbourne Pkwy, Louisville, **0-2 mi N** [gas] Shell/Circle K/dsl, Speedway, Thorton's/dsl [food] Arby's, Bob Evans, Bonefish Grill, Carrabba's, Chili's, Fazoli's, Firehouse Subs, IHOP, Jimmy John's, Macaroni Grill, McDonald's, Mimi's Cafe, Momma's BBQ, Noodles&Co, Olive Garden, Panda Express, Panera Bread, Papa John's, PF Changs, Pita Pit, Qdoba, Sichuan Garden, Skyline Chili, Smashburger, Starbucks, Subway, Waffle House [lodging] Baymont Inn, Courtyard, Days Inn, Drury Inn, Holiday Inn, Hyatt Place, Red Roof Inn, Residence Inn [o] Barnes&Noble, Kroger/gas, Lowe's, Towery's Auto, Tuesday Morning, Walgreens, **S** [food] Applebee's, BoomBozz Pizza, Buca Italian, Buffalo Wild Wing, Burger King, Cattleman's Roadhouse, Chick-fil-A, Chucke-Cheese, Coldstone, DQ, El Marlin Seafood, El Torazo Mexican, Famous Daves, Happy China, Home Run Burgers, J Gumbo's Cajun, Jason's Deli, Jumbo Buffet, Kansai Japanese, Longhorn Steaks, McAlister's Deli, McDonald's, Melting Pot, Moe's SW Grill, O'Charley's, Old Chicago, Panera Bread, Penn Sta. Subs, Pizza Hut, Qdoba, Shogun Japanese, Smokey Bones BBQ,

15 Continued
Starbucks, Steak'n Shake, Taco Bell, Tumbleweed SW Grill, Wendy's, White Castle, Yen Ching [lodging] Best Western, Extended Stay America, Marriott, Ramada, Red Carpet Inn [o] $Tree, AutoZone, BMW, Buick/GMC, Cadillac, Carmax, Chevrolet, Discount Tire, GNC, Home Depot, Honda, Infiniti, Kroger/gas, Michael's, Office Depot, Staples, Subaru, Target, Verizon, Volvo, VW, Walgreens, Walmart

12b I-264 E, Watterson Expswy, **1 exit N on US 60** [gas] Thornton's/dsl [food] Arby's, Big Boy, Bravo Cucina Italin, Buffalo Wild Wings, CA Pizza, Cheesecake Factory, Chick-Fil-A, Chuy's Mexican, Jason's Deli, Logan's Roadhouse, McDonald's, Outback Steaks, Panera Bread, Red Robin, Speedway/dsl, Taco Bell, Wendy's [o] Acura, Best Buy, Dick's, Dillard's, Ford/Lincoln, Goodyear/auto, Hyundai, JC Penney, Jo-Ann, Kia, Kohl's, Macy's, Old Navy, Staples, SteinMart, Toyota, Von Maur, Whole Foods Mkt

12a I-264 W, access to [H]

10 Cannons Lane

8 Grinstead Dr, Louisville, **S** [gas] gas [food] Le Moo

7 US 42, US 62, Mellwood Ave, Story Ave

6 I-71 N (from eb), to Cincinnati

5a I-65, S to Nashville, N to Indianapolis

5b 3rd St, Louisville, **N** [food] Joe's CrabShack, **S** [lodging] Galt House Hotel, Marriott [o] [H]

4 9th St, Roy Wilkins Ave, **S** [o] KY Art Ctr, science museum, downtown

3 US 150 E, to 22nd St, **S** [gas] Marathon/dsl, Shell/Circle K [food] DQ, McDonald's [o] Family$

1 I-264 E, to Shively, **S** [o] [airport], zoo

0mm Kentucky/Indiana state line, Ohio River

INTERSTATE 65

LOUISVILLE

Exit#	Services
138mm	Kentucky/Indiana state line, Ohio River
137	I-64 W, I-71 N, I-64 E, **W** [o] to Galt House, downtown
136c	Jefferson St, Louisville, **E** [o] [H], Walgreens, **W** [gas] Shell [food] McDonald's, Papa John's, Subway, White Castle [lodging] Courtyard, EconoLodge, Fairfield Inn, Hampton Inn, Hyatt, Marriott, SpringHill Suites [o] Tires+
136b	Broadway St, Chestnut St (from nb), **E** [o] [H], NAPA, Walgreens, **W** [gas] Shell, Thornton's [food] McDonald's, Subway, White Castle [lodging] Courtyard, Fairfield Inn, Hampton Inn, Hyatt, Marriott, Springhill Suites [o] same as 136c, Tires+
135	W St Catherine, **E** [gas] Shell
134b a	KY 61, Jackson St, Woodbine St, **W** [gas] Shell/Circle K [lodging] Days Inn, Quality Inn [o] Harley-Davidson
133b	US 60A, Eastern Pkwy, Taylor Blvd, **E** [food] Denny's, Subway **W** [gas] Speedway/dsl [food] Cracker Barrel, McDonald's, Papa John's [o] Churchill Downs, museum, U of Louisville
133a	Crittenden Dr (132from sb), **E** [food] Denny's, same as 133 **W** [gas] [food] Arby's, Burger King, Cracker Barrel, Hall of Fame Cafe [lodging] Country Inn&Suites, Hilton Garden, Holiday Inn, Ramada Inn, Sheraton, Super 8
131b a	I-264, Watterson Expswy, **W** [o] [airport], Cardinal Stadium, Exp Center
130	KY 61, Preston Hwy, **E on Ky 61** [gas] Shell/Circle K, Speedway dsl, Thornton's [food] Bob Evans, Domino's, Fazoli's, Little Caesar's, McDonald's, Papa John's, Popeye's, Rally's, Slabhouse BBQ, Subway, Waffle House, Wendy's [lodging] EconoLodge, Red Roof Inn, Super 8 [o] $General, $Tree, Aamco, AutoZone, Big O Tire, BigLots, Chevrolet/Kia, Dodge, Ford, GNC, O'Reilly Parts Sav-A-Lot Foods, Tires+, U-Haul

KY

INTERSTATE 65 Cont'd

Exit#	Services
128	KY 1631, Fern Valley Rd, E BP, Mapco/dsl/e85, Marathon/Circle K, Thornton's/dsl Big Boy, Dunkin Donuts, El Nopal Mexican, Hardee's, Indi's Rest., McDonald's, Outback Steaks, Shoney's, Subway, Taco Bell, Waffle House, Wendy's, White Castle, Zaxby's Baymont Inn, Comfort Suites, Days Inn, Holiday Inn, InTown Suites Sam's Club/gas, Walgreens, W UPS Depot
127	KY 1065, outer loop, E Cheddar's, TX Roadhouse, W McDonald's/RV Parking
125b a	I-265 E, KY 841, Gene Snyder Fwy
121	KY 1526, Brooks Rd, E BP, Marathon Burger King, Cracker Barrel, McDonald's, Subway, Tumbleweed Grill Comfort Inn, Fairfield Inn, Holiday Inn Express H, W BP/dsl, Pilot/Subway/dsl/scales/24hr Taco Bell, Waffle House Baymont Inn, EconoLodge, Hampton Inn, Quality Inn
117	KY 44, Shepherdsville, E BP/dsl, Valero Denny's Best Western/rest., Garden Inn KOA (2mi), vet, W Marathon, Speedway/dsl Arby's, Big Boy, Cattlemans Roadhouse, China Buffet, Domino's, DQ, El Nopal, El Tarasco, Fazoli's, KFC, Little Caesar's, LJ Silver, McDonald's/playplace, Mr Gatti's, Papa John's, Penn Sta Subs, Quiznos, Sonic, Starbucks, Subway, Taco Bell, Waffle House, Wendy's, White Castle Country Inn&Suites, Motel 6, Sleep Inn, Super 8 $General, Advance Parts, AT&T, AutoZone, BigLots, Family$, Kroger/dsl, Lowe's, NAPA, O'Reilly Parts, Rite Aid, SaveALot, Towery Tire/auto, Walgreens, Walmart/dsl
116.5mm	Salt River
116	KY 480, to KY 61, E Loves/Chester's/Subway/dsl/scales/24hr, Valero/dsl House of Quilts, W Marathon/dsl Grandma's RV Park/flea mkt
114mm	**sb, full facilities, litter barrels, petwalk, , , vending**
112	KY 245, Clermont, E Valero/dsl Bernheim Forest, Jim Beam Outpost, to My Old Kentucky Home SP (15mi)
105	KY 61, Lebanon Jct, W Pilot/McDonald's/Subway/dsl/scales/24hr/@, Speedway/dsl
102	KY 313, to KY 434, Radcliff, W to Patton Museum
94	US 62, Elizabethtown, E BP/dsl, Marathon/dsl Denny's, Waffle House, White Castle Days Inn, Quality Inn, Super 8 $General, W BP/dsl, Speedway/dsl Arby's, Burger King, Chalupa's Mexican, Cracker Barrel, Gatti's Pizza, HoneyBaked Ham, KFC/Taco Bell, McDonald's, Papa John's, Pizza Hut, Ruby Tuesday, Ryan's, Shoney's, Subway, TX Outlaw Steaks, TX Roadhouse, Wendy's Baymont Inn, Comfort Suites, Fairfield Inn, Hampton Inn, Holiday Inn Express, La Quinta, Motel 6, Ramada Inn, Wingfield Inn H, $General, Advance Parts, AutoZone, Crossroads Camping, Kroger/gas, Skagg's RV Ctr, st police, USPO, visitors ctr, Walgreens
93	to Bardstown, to BG Pky, E Maker's Mark Distillery (27mi), to My Old KY Home SP (25mi)
91	US 31 W, KY 61, WK Pkwy, Elizabethtown, E Marathon/dsl LJ Silver, Subway Best Value Inn, Royal Inn $General, to Lincoln B'Place, W Doug's/dsl, Marathon H
90mm	**weigh sta sb only**
86	KY 222, Glendale, E Pilot/McDonalds/dsl/scales/24hr Glendale Camping, trk repair, W Petro/Dunkin Donuts/dsl/scales/24hr/@ Glendale Economy Inn Blue Beacon
83mm	Nolin River
81	KY 84, Sonora, E Pilot/Subway/dsl/scales/24hr to Lincoln B'Place, W Five Star/dsl

ELIZABETHTOWN

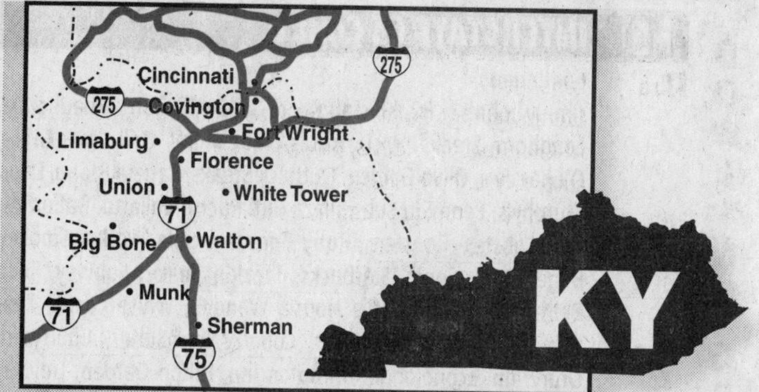

Exit#	Services
76	KY 224, Upton, E Marathon/dsl, W to Nolin Lake
75mm	eastern/central time zone
71	KY 728, Bonnieville
65	US 31 W, Munfordville, E BP/Subway/dsl, FiveStar/dsl DQ, El Mazatlan, King Buffet, McDonald's, Pizza Hut, Sonic Super 8 $General, Advance Parts, Fred's Store, IGA Foods, Save-A-Lot, W Marathon/dsl, Shell Bucky Bee's BBQ, to Nolin Lake
61mm	**both lanes, full facilities, Green River, info, litter barrels, petwalk, , , vending**
58	KY 218, Horse Cave, E Loves/McDonald's/dsl/scales/24hr/@ H, W Hampton Inn, Quality Inn KOA, to Mammoth Cave NP
53	KY 70, KY 90, Cave City, E BP/dsl, Gulf/dsl/repair, Shell/Subway/Sonic/dsl A&W/LJ Silver, Cracker Barrel, El Mazatlan, KFC, McDonald's, Pizza Hut, Wendy's Baymont Inn, Comfort Inn, Days Inn/rest., Motel 6, Red Roof Inn, Sleep Inn, Super 8 H, $General, Barren River Lake SP (24mi), Olde General Store, W Watermill Rest. Jellystone Camping, Mammoth Cave NP, Onyx Cave
48	KY 255, Park City, E Shell/Subway/dsl $General, Park Mammoth Resort, W Diamond Caverns Resort, to Mammoth Cave NP
43	Nun/Cumberland Pky, E to Barren River Lake SP
38	KY 101, Smiths Grove, W Exxon/dsl/scales, Marathon/Subway/dsl, Shell/Schlotsky's/dsl Bestway Pizza, McDonald's, Miss Betty's Diner, Wendy's Bryce Inn $General, auto repair, city park, IGA Foods
36	US 68, KY 80, Oakland, (no nb return)
31	to Bristol Rd
28	rd 446, to US 31 W, Bowling Green, W Huck's/dsl, Shell/dsl Hardee's, Jerry's Rest., McDonald's, Wendy's Best Value Inn, Country Hearth Inn, Super 8, Value Lodge H, Corvette Museum/cafe, to WKYU
26	KY 234, Bowling Green, W Shell/dsl Subway H, IGA Foods
22	US 231, Bowling Green, E Exxon/dsl, Marathon/Godfather's, Shell, Shell/dsl Cracker Barrel, Culver's, Domino's, El Maguey, El Mazatlan, Hardee's, Motor City Grill, Ryan's, Sonic, Waffle House, Zaxby's Baymont Inn, Best Western, Days Inn, Greenwood Hotel, HomeTowne Suites, Jameson Inn, La Quinta, Microtel, Quality Inn, Ramada Inn, Sleep Inn, Super 8 $General, Camping World, Harley-Davidson, URGENT CARE, USPO, W Marathon/dsl, Speedway/dsl Applebee's, Arby's, Beijing Chinese, Bob Evans, Bojangles, Bruster's, Buffalo Wild Wings, Burger King, Capt D's, Chick-fil-A, Chipotle, ChuckeCheese, Chuy's Mexican, Corner Bakery Cafe, Double-Dog's Chowhouse, Fazoli's, Firehouse Subs, Five Guys, Freddy's, Gondolier Italian, Honeybaked Ham, IHOP, Jersey Mike's,

INTERSTATE 65 Cont'd

BOWLING GREEN

Exit#	Services
22	Continued Jimmy John's, KFC, Krystal, Kyoto Steaks, Logan's Roadhouse, Longhorn Steaks, McDonald's, Moe's SW Grill, MT Grille, O'Charley's, Olive Garden, Outback Steaks, Panera Bread, Papa Murphy's, Penn Sta Subs, Pizza Hut, Puerto Vallarta, Rafferty's, Red Lobster, Roosters, Ruby Tuesday, Saladworks, Smokey Bones BBQ, Sonic, Starbucks, Steak'n Shake, Subway, Taco Bell, Toots Rest., Waffle House, Wendy's, White Castle, Zaxby's Candlewood Suites, Country Inn&Suites, Courtyard, Drury Inn, Econolodge, Hampton Inn, Hilton Garden, Holiday Inn, Holiday Inn Express, Home 2 Suites, Motel 6, Red Roof Inn H, $General, $Tree, Advance Parts, AT&T, AutoZone, Barnes&Noble, Best Buy, BMW/Mercedes, Buick/GMC/Cadillac, Cabela's, Chevrolet, Chrysler/Dodge/Jeep, CVS Drug, Dick's, Dillard's, Ford/Lincoln, Goodyear/auto, Hobby Lobby, Home Depot, Honda, Hyundai, JC Penney, Kia, KOA, Kohl's, Kroger/gas, Lowe's, Meijer, Michael's, Nissan, Old Navy, PetCo, Petsmart, Sam's Club/gas, Staples, Target, TJ Maxx, Toyota, Tuesday Morning, U-Haul, URGENT CARE, Walgreens, Walmart/McDonald's
20	WH Natcher Toll Rd, to Bowling Green, access to W KY U, W st police
6	KY 100, Franklin, E Shell/dsl/24hr truckwash, W Pilot/Subway/dsl/scales/24hr, Pilot/Wendy's/dsl/scales/24hr El Potrero Comfort Inn, Days Inn, Knights Inn H, Bluegrass RV Park, SpeedCo, TA Truck Service, truck&tires/repair, truckwash, Volvo Trucks
4mm	**weigh sta nb**
2	US 31 W, to Franklin, E FLYING J/Denny's/dsl/LP/scales/24hr, Keystop/Marathon/Burger King/dsl/24hr, W BP/dsl Cracker Barrel, Franklin Steakhouse, McDonald's, Oasis SW Grill, Solazteca, Waffle House Baymont Inn, EconoLodge, Hampton Inn, Holiday Inn Express, Quality Inn, Super 8 H, antiques
1mm	**Welcome Ctr nb, full facilities, litter barrels, petwalk, vending**
0mm	Kentucky/Tennessee state line

FRANKLIN

INTERSTATE 71

Exit#	Services
100	Kentucky/Ohio state line, Ohio River
I-71 and I-75 run together 19 miles. See I-75, exits 175-192.	
77[173]	I-75 S, to Lexington
75mm	**weigh sta sb**
72	KY 14, to Verona, E BP/dsl, Marathon/dsl Oak Creek Camping (5mi)
62	US 127, to Glencoe, E 62 TrkPlaza/rest./dsl, W Valero/dsl/rest. 127 Motel
57	KY 35, to Sparta, E Marathon/dsl Eagle Valley Camping (10mi), Sparta RV Park (3mi), W BP/dsl Ramada KY Speedway
55	KY 1039, W Loves/McDonald's/Subway/dsl/scales/24hr casino, KY Speedway
44	KY 227, to Indian Hills, W Marathon/dsl, Marathon/dsl, Murphy USA/dsl, Valero/dsl Arby's, Burger King, El Nopal, Hometown Pizza, KFC, McDonald's, Mi Viejo Mexican, New China, Subway, Taco Bell, Waffle House Hampton Inn, Holiday Inn Express, Quality Inn, Red Roof Inn, Super 8 H, $General, $Tree, AutoZone, Chevrolet, Ford, Gen. Butler SP, Kroger/dsl, Save-a-Lot Foods, URGENT CARE, Verizon, Walmart
43.5mm	Kentucky River
43	KY 389, to KY 55, English
34	US 421, New Castle, Campbellsburg, W Marathon/dsl, Valero/Subway/dsl st police
28	KY 153, KY 146, to US 42, Pendleton, E Pilot/Subway/dsl/scales/24hr/@, Valero/dsl, W Pilot/McDonald's/scales/dsl/24hr truck repair
22	KY 53, La Grange, E Murphy USA/dsl, Speedway/Rally's/dsl, Valero/dsl Applebee's, Beef O'Brady's, Burger King, Jumbo Buffet, Papa John's, Papa Murphy's, Subway, Waffle House, Wendy's Best Western-Ashbury, Comfort Inn H, $General, AT&T, Big-O Tire, GNC, Kroger/gas, Towery's Tire/auto, Verizon, Walgreens, Walmart/Subway, W Marathon/dsl Arby's, Cracker Barrel, Domino's, DQ, El Nopal, Hometown Pizza, KFC, LJ Silver, McDonald's, Taco Bell Quality Suites, Super 8 $Tree, Advance Parts, Buick/Chevrolet/GMC, Lee Tires, NAPA, Rite Aid, USPO, vet
18	KY 393, Buckner, W Marathon/dsl Subway Ford
17	KY 146, Buckner, W Thornton's/dsl/24hr USPO
14	KY 329, Crestwood, Pewee Valley, Brownsboro, E BP/dsl DQ, Hometown Pizza, McDonald's, Sonic, Starbucks, Subway
13mm	**Rs both lanes, full facilities, litter barrels, petwalk, vending**
9b a	I-265, KY 841, Gene Snyder Fwy, E Drury Inn, Hilton Garden Cabela's, Costco/gas, H, to Sawyer SP
5	I-264, Watterson Expswy (exits left from sb), E to Sawyer SP
2	Zorn Ave, E VA H, W Shell/dsl, Valero El Nopal Mexican, KingFish Rest. Ramada Inn WaterTower Art Museum
1b	I-65, S to Nashville, N to Indianapolis

LOUISVILLE

INTERSTATE 75

COVINGTON

Exit#	Services
193mm	Kentucky/Ohio state line, Ohio River
192	5th St (from nb), Covington, E BP/dsl, Shell/Circle K, Speedway/dsl Big Boy, Burger King, GoldStar Chili, McDonald's, Popeyes, Riverfront Pizza, Skyline Chili, Subway, Taco Bell, Waffle House, Wendy's, White Castle Courtyard, Extended Stay America, Holiday Inn, Radisson Lexus, Riverboat Casino W Hampton Inn
191	12th St, Covington, E H, museum, same as 192
189	KY 1072, Kyles Lane, W BP/dsl, Shell/dsl Big Boy Skyline Chili, Substation II Subs Rodeway Inn same a 188, Walgreens
188	US 25, US 42, Dixie Hwy, E Marathon Starbucks, Subway GNC, Kroger/dsl, Tuesday Morning, W Rodeway Inn Mercedes, same as 189
186	KY 371, Buttermilk Pike, Covington, E BP/dsl, Marathon/DQ/dsl Graeter's Ice Cream, Oriental Wok, Papa John's Montgomery Inn, Super 8, W BP, Speedway dsl, Sunoco/dsl Arby's, Baskin-Robbins/Dunkin Donuts Bonefish Grill, Burger King, Cancun Mexican, Chipotle Mexican Domino's, Empire Buffet, Firehouse Subs, GoldStar Chili, Jimmy John's, La Rosa's Pizza, Marco's Pizza, McDonald's, Miyako Steaks, Outback Steaks, Skyline Chili, Subway, Sweet Bas Thai $Tree, Field & Stream, Home Depot, Petco, Remk Foods, Staples, Verizon, Walgreens
185	I-275 E and W, W to airport
184	KY 236, Donaldson Rd, to Erlanger, E BP, Erlanger/Dunki Donuts Double Dragon Oriental, W Racers/Subway dsl, Speedway/dsl Peecox Grill, Waffle House Count

INTERSTATE 75 Cont'd

184 Continued
Hearth Inn, EconoLodge, Red Roof Inn, Wingate Inn [O] Goodyear/auto

182 KY 1017, Turfway Rd, E [gas] BP/dsl, Shell/dsl [food] Bamboo Garden, Big Boy, China City, Lee's Chicken, McDonald's, Papa John's, Subway, Taco Bell [lodging] Baymont Inn, Courtyard, Days Inn, Woodspring Suites [O] BigLots, CVS Drug, Family$, Office Depot, Remke Foods, USPO, W [food] Applebee's, Chick-fil-A, Chili's, CiCi's Pizza, Cracker Barrel, Famous Dave's BBQ, Firebowl Grill, Longhorn Steaks, Noodles&Co., O'Charley's, Potbelly, Rafferty's, Skyline Chili, Steak'n Shake, Subway, Wendy's [lodging] Comfort Inn, Extended Stay America, Hampton Inn, Hilton, Hyatt Place, La Quinta, SpringHill Suites [O] [H], Best Buy, Dick's, Home Depot, Jo-Ann, Kohl's, Lowe's, Meijer, Michael's, Petsmart, Sam's Club, Target, Turfway Park Racing

FLORENCE

181 KY 18, Florence, E [gas] Speedway/dsl, TA/Valero/Pizza Hut/Popeye's/Subway/dsl/24hr/@ [food] Kiwha Korean, Waffle House [lodging] Best Value Inn, Best Western, Heritage Inn [O] Chevrolet, W [gas] BP/dsl, Marathon/dsl, Speedway/dsl [food] Buffalo Wild Wings, Cheddar's, Chipotle Mexican, Chuy's Mexican, City BBQ, Currito Burrito, El Rio Grande, Fazoli's, Firehouse Subs, Fuji Steaks, Hooters, IHOP, Jersey Mike's, La Rosa's, Laughing Noodle, Logan's Roadhouse, Miyoshi Japanese, Panda Express, Panera Bread, Red Robin [lodging] Homewood Suites, Stay Lodge [O] AT&T, Buick/GMC, Chrysler/Jeep/Dodge, Ford, Honda, Hyundai, Mazda, Nissan, Tire Discounters, Toyota, URGENT CARE, Verizon, VW, Walmart/Subway

180a Mall Rd (from sb), W [food] Asian Buffet, BJ's Rest., Buca Italian, ChuckeCheese, GoldStar Chili, HoneyBaked Ham, Jimmy John's, Olive Garden, Pizza Hut, Qdoba, Skyline Chili, Smokey Bones BBQ, Starbucks, Subway, Taco Bell, Which Wich? [O] $General, $Tree, AT&T, Barnes&Noble, Harley Davidson, Hobby Lobby, JC Penney, Kroger/dsl, Macy's, Old Navy, same as 180, Staples, TJ Maxx, Tuesday Morning

180 US 42, US 127, Florence, Union, E [gas] BP/dsl, Speedway/dsl [food] Big Boy, Bob Evans, Capt D's, Chipotle Mexican, El Nopal Mexican, Mai Thai, McDonald's, Penn Sta Subs, Rally's, Red Lobster, Subway, Wendy's [lodging] Holiday Inn, Howard Johnson, Knights Inn, Motel 6, Quality Inn, Super 8 [O] Cadillac, funpark, Subaru, W [gas] Marathon/dsl, Murphy USA/dsl, Speedway/dsl [food] Arby's, Chick-fil-a, Dave&Buster's, KFC, Little Caesar's, LJ Silver, outback, Ponderosa, Waffle House, White Castle [lodging] Magnuson Hotel, Travelodge [O] CarX, Costco/dsl, Midas, O'Reilly Parts, PepBoys, Tire Discounters, Tires+, Walgreens

178 KY 536, Mt Zion Rd, E [gas] Marathon/Rally's/dsl, Speedway/dsl, Sunoco/Subway/dsl [food] Buffalo Bob's, Chopsticks, GoldStar Chili, Hot Head Burritos, Jersey Mike's Subs, La Fuentes Mexican, La Rosa's Pizza, Mad Mike's Burgers, Sonic, Steak'n Shake, Taco Bell [O] AutoZone, Goodyear/auto, Kroger

177mm **Welcome Ctr sb/[RS] nb, full [handicap] facilities, litter barrels, [phone], [picnic], RV dump, vending**

175 KY 338, Richwood, E [gas] Pilot/Subway/dsl/24hr, TA/BP/Country Pride/Taco Bell/dsl/24hr/@ [food] Arby's, Burger King, White Castle [lodging] Richwood Inn, W [gas] BP/dsl, Pilot/Subway/dsl/scales/24hr, Shell/dsl [food] GoldStar Chili, Gourmet Cafe, Hong Kong Cafe, McDonald's, Papa Dino's Pizza, Penn Sta Subs, Skyline Chili, Snappy Tomato Pizza, Waffle House, Wendy's [lodging] EconoLodge, Holiday Inn Express [O] to Big Bone Lick SP

173 I-71 S, to Louisville

171 KY 14, KY 16, to Verona, Walton, E [gas] BP/dsl, Marathon/DQ/dsl [food] China Moon, El Toro Mexican, McDonald's, Pizza Hut, Starbucks, Subway, Waffle House [O] AT&T, AutoZone, Kohl's, Kroger/dsl, Tire Discounters, URGENT CARE, Walton Drug, W [gas] FLYING J/Denny's/dsl/scales/24hr [O] Blue Beacon, Delightful Days RV Ctr, Oak Creek Camping (1mi), to Big Bone Lick SP, vet

168mm **weigh sta/rest haven sb**

166 KY 491, Crittenden, E [gas] BP/dsl, Sunoco/dsl [food] McDonald's [O] Chrysler/Dodge/Jeep, Cincinnati S Camping (2mi), W [gas] Marathon/dsl, Shell/Gold Star Chili [food] China Castle, Subway, Wendy's [O] $General, Grant Co Drugs

159 KY 22, to Owenton, Dry Ridge, E [gas] BP, Shell/dsl, Speedway/dsl [food] Arby's, Burger King, Happy Dragon Chinese, KFC/Taco Bell, La Rosa's, LJ Silver, McDonald's, Pizza Hut, Skyline Chili, Subway, Waffle House, Wendy's [lodging] Microtel, Red Roof Inn [O] [H], $General, Buick/Chevrolet, O'Reilly Parts, Verizon, Walmart, W [gas] Marathon/dsl, Speedway/dsl [food] Beavis Cafe/Bakery, Big Boy, Cracker Barrel [lodging] Hampton Inn, Quality Inn [O] Camper Village, Dry Ridge TowneCtr, Sav-A-Lot, Tire Discounters, Toyota

156 Barnes Rd, E [O] [H]

154 KY 36, Williamstown, E [gas] Marathon/dsl, Shell/dsl [O] [H], to Kincaid Lake SP, W [gas] Sunoco/dsl [food] El Jalisco Mexican [lodging] Best Value Inn, Sunrise Inn

144 KY 330, to Owenton, Corinth, E [gas] Noble's Trk Plaza/rest./dsl, Sunoco/dsl, W [gas] [food] North Star Cafe [lodging] North Star Inn

136 KY 32, to Sadieville, E [gas] Loves/Hardee's/dsl/scales/24hr

130.5mm **weigh sta nb**

129 rd 620, Cherry Blossom Wy, E [gas] Pilot/Wendy's/dsl/scales/24hr/@ [food] Waffle House [lodging] Days Inn, Motel 6, W [gas] Pilot/McDonald's/dsl/scales/24hr, Shell [O] Whispering Hills RV Park (3mi)

127mm **[RS] both lanes, full [handicap] facilities, litter barrels, petwalk, [phone], [picnic], vending**

GEORGETOWN

126 US 62, to US 460, Georgetown, E [gas] Marathon/dsl, Murphy USA/dsl [food] Applebee's, Asian Royal Buffet, Big Boy, Buffalo Wild Wings, Gold Star Chili, Jimmy John's, McDonald's, O'Charley's, Papa John's, Penn Sta Subs, Pepe's Mexican, Qdoba, Starbucks, Steak'n Shake, Subway [lodging] Holiday Inn Express [O] AT&T, Kohl's, Lowe's, Tire Discounters, URGENT CARE, Verizon, Walmart/Subway, W [gas] Marathon, Shell/Subway, Speedway/dsl [food] Cane's, Chick-fil-A, Cracker Barrel, Culver's, Fazoli's, KFC, Panera Bread, Ruby Tuesday, Waffle House [lodging] Baymont Inn, Best Western, Comfort Suites, Country Inn&Suites, Fairfield Inn, Hampton Inn, Hilton Garden, Microtel, Super 8 [O] [H], Buick/Chevrolet, Chrysler/Dodge/Jeep, same as 125, to Georgetown Coll

KY

INTERSTATE 75 Cont'd

GEORGETOWN

Exit#	Services
125	US 460 (from nb), Georgetown, E BP, Shell FatKats Pizza Knights Inn, W Swifty/dsl, Valero/dsl Arby's, DQ, Little Caesar's, LJ Silver, Taco Bell, Wendy's Winner's Circle Motel $Tree, Advance Parts, BigLots, Camping World, Midas, Outlets/Famous Brands, same as 126
120	rd 1973, to Ironworks Pike, KY Horse Park, E KY Horse Park Camping, W BP/dsl, Shell/dsl H
118	I-64 W, to Frankfort, Louisville
115	rd 922, Lexington, E Shell/Subway/dsl Cracker Barrel, McDonald's, Waffle House Best Western Global, Fairfield Inn, La Quinta, Sheraton SaddleHorse Museum (4mi), W Marathon/dsl Cortland's Kitchen, Denny's, Happy Dragon Chinese Clarion, Embassy Suites, Marriott/rest. museum
113	US 27, US 68, to Paris, Lexington, E BP/dsl, Speedway/dsl Waffle House Ramada Inn, W Marathon/dsl, Shell, Shell/dsl Arby's, Burger King, Capt D's, Donato's Pizza, DQ, Fazoli's, Golden Corral, Hardee's, Horseshoes Grill, Little Caesar's, McDonald's, Penn Sta Subs, Rally's, Subway, Taco Bell, Wendy's, Zaxby's Catalina Motel, Days Inn, Red Roof Inn Advance Parts, AutoZone, Bluegrass RV Ctr, Chevrolet, CVS Drug, Northside RV Ctr, O'Reilly Parts, Rupp Arena, to UK, Walmart
111	I-64 E, to Huntington, WV
110	US 60, Lexington, W Murphy USA/dsl, Shell/dsl, Speedway/dsl, Thorntons/dsl A&W Cafe, Arby's, Bob Evans, Calistoga Cafe, Cane's Chicken, Cracker Barrel, FirstWatch Cafe, McDonald's, Smashing Tomato, Starbucks, Tom+Chee Rest., Waffle House, Wendy's Baymont Inn, Comfort Inn, Country Inn&Suites, Guesthouse Inn, Hampton Inn, Holiday Inn Express, Howard Johnson, Microtel, Motel 6, Quality Inn, Super 8 H, Hobby Lobby, Lowe's, Rite Aid, Walmart/Subway
108	Man O War Blvd, E Shell Freddy's Cabela's, Costco/gas, Rite Aid, W Marathon/dsl, Meijer/dsl, Shell/KFC/Pizza Hut/Wendy's/dsl Applebee's, Arby's, Asuka Grill, Backyard Burger, BD Mongolian Grill, Big Boy, Blaze Pizza, BoneFish Grill, Carino's, Carrabba's, Cheddar's, Chick-fil-A, Chipotle Mexican, Coldstone, Culver's, Fazoli's, GoldStar Chili, IChing Asian, Logan's Roadhouse, Malone's, McDonald's, Old Chicago, Outback Steaks, Qdoba, Rafferty's, Red Lobster, Saul Good Rest., Starbucks, Steak'n Shake, Subway, Taco Bell, Ted's MT Grill, TGIFriday's, Waffle House Courtyard, Hilton Garden, Homewood Suites, Hyatt Place, Residence Inn, Sleep Inn, TownePlace Suites H, AT&T, Audi, Barnes&Noble, Best Buy, BigLots, Dick's, GNC, Gordmans, Harley-Davidson, Kohl's, Marshall's, Michael's, Old Navy, Petsmart, Ross, Staples, Target, Tire Discounters, Verizon, Walgreens
104	KY 418, Lexington, E BP/dsl, Shell/McDonald's Clarion, Comfort Inn, Days Inn, EconoLodge, La Quinta, W BP/dsl, Speedway/dsl Wendy's H
99	US 25 N, US 421 N, Clays Ferry
98mm	Kentucky River
97	US 25 S, US 421 S, Clay's Ferry
95	rd 627, to Boonesborough, Winchester, E BP/dsl, Loves/Arby's/dsl/scales/24hr camping, Ft Boonesborough SP, W Shell/Subway/dsl
90	US 25, US 421, Richmond, E Shell Cracker Barrel La Quinta, Red Roof Inn, Relax Inn, Super 7, W BP, Gulf/dsl, Marathon, Shell, Valero Big Boy, DQ, Hanger's Rest., Hardee's, McDonald's, Pizza Hut, Subway, Taco Bell, Waffle House, Wendy's Days Inn, Super 8 $General, vet
87	rd 876, Richmond, E BP/dsl, Marathon/dsl, Shell/dsl, Speedway/dsl A&W/LJ Silver, Arby's, Casa Fiesta Mexican, CookOut, Domino's, Fazoli's, Fong's Chinese, Hardee's, Hooters, King Buffet, Lee's Chicken, Little Caesar's, McAlister's Deli, McDonald's, Papa John's, Qdoba, Rally's, Subway, Taco Bell, Waffle House, Wendy's Best Western, Country Hearth Inn, Quality Quarters Inn H, $General, Aamco, Ace Hardware, AT&T, BigLots, Goodyear/auto, Rite Aid, to EKU, vet, W Marathon/Circle K, Shell/dsl Bob Evans, Buffalo Wild Wings, Burger King, Cane's, Chick-fil-A, Culver's, Firehouse Subs, Golden Corral, IHOP, Koto Japanese, Logan's Roadhouse, Olive Garden, Panera Bread, Ryan's, Starbucks, Steak'n Shake, Subway Comfort Suites, Hampton Inn, Holiday Inn Express, Quality Inn, TownePlace Suites Belk, Dick's, GNC, JC Penney, Meijer/dsl, Michaels, Petsmart, Tire Discounters, TJ Maxx, Verizon
83	to US 25, rd 2872, Duncannon Ln, Richmond, E Bluegrass Army Depot
77	rd 595, Berea, E H, KY Artisan Ctr/Cafe/Travelers Ctr, to Berea Coll, W Shell/dsl, Valero/Subway/dsl Smokehouse Grill Motel 6, Quality Inn, Red Roof Inn $General
76	KY 21, Berea, E BP, Marathon/Circle K, Shell/Burger King, Speedway/dsl A&W/LJ Silver, Arby's, Cracker Barrel, Dinner Bell Rest., Gold Star Chili, Hong Kong Buffet, Mario's Pizza, McDonald's, Old Town Amish Rest., Papa John's, Pizza Hut, Subway, Taco Bell, Wendy's, Wings Etc, Yamato Japanese Best Value Inn, Holiday Motel, Knights Inn H, $General, $Tree, URGENT CARE, Walmart, W 76 Fuel/dsl, BP/dsl, Marathon/dsl Lee's Chicken EconoLodge, Fairfield Inn, Holiday Inn Express Oh! Kentucky Camping, tires, Walnut Meadow RV Park
62	US 25, to KY 461, Renfro Valley, E Derby City/rest./dsl, Shell Hardee's, Little Caesar's Baymont Inn KOA (2mi), Renfro Valley RV Park/rest, W BP, Marathon/dsl, Marathon/Wendy's/dsl, Shell Arby's, El Dorado Mexican, Godfather's/Subway, KFC, Limestone Grill, McDonald's, Taco Bell Days Inn, EconoLodge H, Lake Cumberland, Rite Aid, to Big South Fork NRA
59	US 25, to Livingston, Mt Vernon, E Shell, TravelCtr/dsl El Cazador Mexican, Pizza Hut Kastle Inn, W Mtn View Inn
51mm	Rockcastle River
49	KY 909, to US 25, Livingston, E Camp Wildcat Bfd, W 49er/dsl/24hr RV Park, truck/tire repair
41	rd 80, to Somerset, London, E Speedway/dsl Arby's, Azteca Mexican, Burger King, Gondolier Italian, KFC, McDonald's, Subway, White Castle Days Inn, EconoLodge, Quality Inn, Red Roof Inn, Super 8 H, $General, Advance Parts, AutoZone, CVS Drug, Kroger/deli, Parsley's Tire/repair, st police, W BP/Home Cooker/dsl/24hr, Marathon/McDonald's, Shell/pizza, Sunoco/dsl, Valero/dsl Buffalo Wings&Rings, Cheddar's, Cracker Barrel, LJ Silver, Old Town Grill, Shiloh Roadhouse, Smokin' Barrel BBQ, Subway, Taco Bell, Waffle House, Wendy's Budget Host, Fairfield Inn, Hampton Inn Dog Patch Ctr
38	rd 192, to Rogers Pkwy, London, E BP/dsl, Marathon, Murphy USA/dsl, Shell/Mama's Subs/dsl, Speedway/dsl Big Boy, Burger King, Capt D's, Dino's Italian, Domino's, DQ Dunkin Donuts/Baskin Robins, El Dorado Mexican, Fazoli's Golden Corral, Great Wall Chinese, Hardee's, Huddle House Krystal, McDonald's, Penn Sta Subs, Pizza Hut, Starbucks Steak'n Shake, Subway, Sun Buffet, Taco Bell Baymont Inn

Side labels: GEORGETOWN (exits 125–115), LEXINGTON (113–104), RICHMOND (87), BEREA (77–62), LONDON (41–38)

KY

INTERSTATE 75 Cont'd

38 Continued
Comfort Suites, Country Inn&Suites, Holiday Inn Express, Microtel O $Tree, Advance Parts, AT&T, camping, E Kentucky RV Ctr, Ford/Lincoln, Kroger/dsl, Lowe's, NAPA, Nissan, Office Depot, Peterbilt, Rogers Pkwy to Manchester/Hazard, to Levi Jackson SP, USPO, Verizon, Walgreens, Walmart/Subway, W O H, to Laurel River Lake RA

34mm **truck haven, weigh sta both lanes**

30.5mm Laurel River

29 US 25, US 25E, Corbin, E Marathon, Murphy USA, Pilot/McDonald's/Subway/dsl/scales/24hr, Spur Oil David's Steaks, DQ, Huddle House, Mi Jalisco Mexican, Taco Bell Super 8 O Aldi Foods, AutoZone, Blue Beacon, Lowe's, to Cumberland Gap NP, Walmart/Subway, W BP/Krystal/dsl, Loves/Hardee's/dsl/scales/24hr/@, Marathon, Shell/dsl Cracker Barrel, Sonny's BBQ Baymont Inn, Fairfield Inn, Hampton Inn, Knights Inn, Quality Suites O KOA, tires/repair, to Laurel River Lake RA

CORBIN

25 US 25W, Corbin, E Speedway/dsl Applebee's, Arby's, Bojangle's, Burger King, Cayenne SW Grill, CB's Grill, Dino's Italian, McDonald's, Taco Bell, Wendy's EconoLodge, Holiday Inn Express, Landmark Inn, Red Roof Inn O H, auto repair/tires, W Shell El Dorado Mexican, Subway, Waffle House Best Western O to Cumberland Falls SP

15 US 25W, to Williamsburg, Goldbug, W Shell, Xpress/dsl O Cumberland Falls SP

14.5mm Cumberland River

11 KY 92, Williamsburg, E BP/dsl, Shell Arby's, El Dorado Mexican, Hardee's, KFC, Little Caesar's, McDonald's, Pizza Hut, Subway, Taco Bell Budget Inn, Cumberland Inn, Super 8 O $General, Advance Parts, AutoZone, Family$, museum, Save-A-Lot, Windham Drug, W Pilot/Wendy's/dsl/scales/24hr, Shell Burger King, DQ, Huddle House, Krystal, LJ Silver Hampton Inn O $Tree, to Big South Fork NRA, Walmart

1.5mm **Welcome Ctr nb, full facilities, litter barrels, petwalk, vending**

0mm Kentucky/Tennessee state line

INTERSTATE 275 (Cincinnati)

Exit# Services

84 I-71, I-75, N to Cincinnati, S to Lexington, Louisville

83 US 25, US 42, US 127, S Shell/Circle K/dsl, Thornton's/dsl Abuelo's Mexican, Buffalo Wings&Rings, Carrabba's, Chipotle, Coldstone, Dewey's Pizza, Donato's Pizza, First Watch Cafe, Five Guys, Gold Star Chili, Jimmy John's, KFC, Max&Erma's, McAlister's Deli, McDonald's, Moe's SW Grill, Panera Bread, Starbucks, Subway, Taco Bell, The Pub, Wendy's O $Tree, CarX, Dillard's, GNC, Verizon, Walgreens

82 rd 1303, Turkeyfoot Rd, S TGIFriday's O H

80 KY 17, Independence, N Speedway/dsl, United/dsl Arby's, Big Boy, Bob Evans, Buffalo Wild Wings, Burger King, El Ranchero Mexican, Golden Corral, Hot Head Burrito, Penn Sta Subs, Snappy Tomato Pizza, Subway, Taco Bell, TX Roadhouse, Wendy's, White Castle O AT&T, Petco, TireDiscounters, Verizon, Walmart/Subway, S Thornton's/dsl McDonald's, Waffle House

79 KY 16, Taylor Mill Rd, N BP, Marathon, Speedway/dsl Domino's, Goldstar Chili, McDonald's, Peking Chinese, Subway, Wendy's O $General, $Tree, Big Lots, Burlington Coats, CVS Drug, Kroger/gas, URGENT CARE, Walgreens,

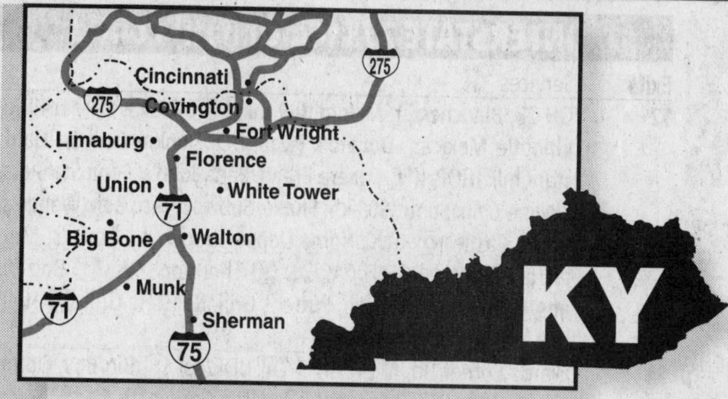

79 Continued
S BP/dsl El Jinete Mexican, Graeter's Rest., KFC/Taco Bell, La Rosa's Pizza, Marco's Pizza, McDonald's, Original Wok, Skyline Chili, Subway O Remke's Mkt, Verizon, vet

77 KY 9, Maysville, Wilder, N Hampton Inn, S Speedway/dsl, Thorntons/dsl, UDF/dsl DQ, Goldstar Chili, McDonald's, Mellow Mushroom Pizza, Subway, Waffle House Country Inn Suites

76 Three Mile Rd

74a Alexandria, (exits left from sb), to US 27

74b I-471 N, Newport, Cincinnati, N O H

73mm OH/KY state line, OH River

72 US 52 W, Kellogg Ave, S Marathon (2mi) O Coney Island Funpark

71 US 52 E, New Richmond

69 5 Mile Rd, W BP/dsl Big Boy, Carrabba's, Firehouse Subs, IHOP, La Rosa's Mexican, McDonald's, Moe's SW Grill, Outback, TGIFriday's O H, CVS, Kroger/gas, TireDiscounters

65 OH 125, Beechmont Ave, Amelia, E Shell, Speedway, UDF/dsl Hibachi Grill, Los Cazadores, Red Lobster, Ron's Chinese, Tender Towne, Wendy's Beechmont Motel O CarX, Family$, Ford, Lowe's, Tires+, Walgreens, W BP, Marathon, Speedway/dsl Big Boy, Bob Evans, Burger King, Butterbee's Grille, Chick-fil-A, Chipotle Mexican, McDonald's, Olive Garden, Peking Chinese, Skyline Chili, Smashburger, Starbucks, Waffle House, White Castle Best Western, Days Inn, Red Roof Inn O $Tree, Aldi Foods, AT&T, Audi, AutoZone, BigLots, Goodyear/auto, Home Depot, Honda, Kroger, O'Reilly Parts, Staples, Sumerel Tire/repair, Target, TireDiscounters, TJ Maxx, Toyota, Tuesday Morning, Verizon

63b a OH 32, Batavia, Newtown, E UDF Applebee's, Big Boy, Bob Evans, Burger King, Chick-fil-A, China Buffet, Chipotle, ChuckECheese, City BBQ, Firehouse Subs, Five Guys, Fuji Steaks, Golden Corral, Hwy 55 Cafe, Jimmy John's, KFC, LaRosa's Pizza, LJ Silver, Logan's Roadhouse, Longhorn Steaks, McDonalds, O'Charley's, Panera Bread, Penn Sta Subs, Pizza Hut, Popeye's, Skyline Chili, Skyline Chili, Sonic, Starbucks, Steak'n Shake, Taco Bell, Wendy's, White Castle Comfort Inn, Fairfield Inn, Hampton Inn, Holiday Inn O $Tree, Advance Parts, Aldi Foods, AT&T, Best Buy, Dick's, Dillard's, Firestone/auto, Hobby Lobby, JC Penney, Jo-Ann Fabrics, Jungle Jim's Mkt, Kohl's, Kroger/dsl, Marshall's, Meijer/dsl, PepBoys, Petsmart, Sam's Club/gas, URGENT CARE, Walmart/Subway, W Marathon, Speedway/dsl, Sunoco Gold Star Chili, Gramma's Pizza O Kroger, Midas

59 OH 452, US 50, Milford Pkwy, Hillsboro, S UDF/dsl Buffalo Wild Wings, Cracker Barrel, Dos Amigos, Goldstar Chili, Mint Bistro, Quaker Steak&Lube, Red Robin, Roney's Rest., Ruby Tuesday, Subway, TX Roadhouse, Wendy's Homewood Suites O Office Depot, Petsmart, Target, Verizon, Walmart

INTERSTATE 275 (Cincinnati) Cont'd

Exit#	Services
57	OH 28, Blanchester, Milford, **0-1 mi** N Arby's, Burger King, Chipotle Mexican, Donato's Pizza, DQ, Dunkin Donuts, Goldstar Chili, IHOP, KFC, Panera Bread, Papa John's, Penn Sta Subs, Skyline Chili, Sonic, Steak'n Shake, Subway, Taco Bell, Wendy's, White Castle GNC, Home Depot, Kroger/dsl, Lowe's, Meijer/dsl, Petco, URGENT CARE, S Thornton's/dsl Bob Evans, Cazadore's Mexican, Putter's Grill, Roosters Grill Holiday Inn Express Goodyear/auto, vet
54	Wards Corner Rd, N BP, S UDF/dsl Big Boy, Dominos, Goldstar Chili, Subway Hilton Garden
53mm	Little Miami River
52	Loveland, Indian Hill, N Marathon/Circle K/dsl, Shell, Speedway/dsl Arby's, Burger King, Penn Sta Subs, Pizza Hut, Skyline Chili, Starbucks, Subway, Taco Bell, Wendy's CVS Drug, Indian Motorcycles, URGENT CARE, Verizon, vet, Walgreens
50	US 22, OH 3, Montgomery, N Shell Buffalo Wild Wings, Chili's, deSha's Tavern, Dewey's Pizza, Donato's Puzza, DQ, Johnny Chan's, Melting Pot, Panera Bread, Starbucks, Subway, Taco Casa, Which Wich? Acura, AT&T, Fresh Thyme Mkt, GNC, Hyundai, Kroger/dsl, TJ Maxx, S BP/dsl, Shell/Subway/Dunkin Donuts El Jinete, Goldstar Chili, McDonald's, Merlot's Rest., Skyline Chili, Wendy's H
49	I-71 N to Columbus, S to Cincinnati
47	Reed Hartman Hwy, Blue Ash, S Chipotle, Jersey Mike's, Jimmy John's, Kanpai Japanese, Ruby Tuesday, Smashburger, Starbucks, Tropical Cafe DoubleTree, Hyatt Place, Quality Inn, Residence Inn
46	US 42, Mason, N Chipotle, KFC, Marie's Scrambler, Max&Erma's, McDonald's, Skyline Chili, Taco Bell, Wendy's, White Castle Holiday Inn, Motel 6, ValuePlace Advance Parts, CVS Drug, Goodyear/auto, Kroger/dsl, Walgreens, S Marathon/dsl, Shell, Speedway/dsl, UDF/dsl Arby's, El Rancho Grande, Waffle House Days Inn Midas, Mr Transmission, Tire Discounters
44	Mosteller Rd, N Subway, S Homewood Suites
43b a	I-75, N to Dayton, S to Cincinnati
42	OH 747, Springdale, Glendale, N Sunoco, Thorntons $General, Staples, S Shell/dsl BJ's Brewhouse, Blue Agave Mexican, Chick-fil-A, Chipotle, Firehouse Subs, La Rosa's Pizza, McDonald's, Noodles&Co, Panera Bread, Steak'n Shake, TGIFriday's BigLots, Chevrolet, Chrysler/Dodge/Jeep, Dillard's, Hancock Fabrics, Hobby Lobby, Lowe's, Macy's, Michael's, Office Depot, Petsmart, TJ Maxx, Verizon
41	OH 4, Springdale Pkwy, N Shell, Speedway/dsl, Sunoco/dsl Burger King, Hooters, Olive Garden, Pappadeaux, Rib City, Skyline Chili, SmoQ Rest., Wendy's La Quinta, S BP, UDF/dsl Beef'O'Brady's, DJ's Tavern, DQ, Goldstar Chili, Outback Steaks, Penn Sta Subs, Subway, White Castle Extended Stay America, Howard Johnson, Super 8 CVS Drug, Family$, O'Reilly Parts
39	Winton Rd, Winton Woods, N Asian Buffet, Chipotle, Golden Corral, IHOP, McDonald's, Old Spaghetti Factory, Panera Bread, Red Lobster, Steak'n Shake Comfort Suites, Hampton Inn Bass Pro Shops, CarMax, Home Depot, Kohl's, Meijer/dsl, Tire Discounters, S Marathon/dsl, Shell/dsl, UDF/dsl Big Boy, Cancun Mexican, China Garden, Cracker Barrel, Izzy's Cafe, Jade House Chinese, Jax Tavern, KFC, La Fiesta Mexican, Papa John's, Penn Sta Subs, Popeye's, Skyline Chili, Starbucks, Subway, Taco Bell, Wendy's Quality Inn, SpringHill Suites $Tree, AAA, Aldi Foods, AutoZone, Kroger/gas, Tires+, vet, Walmart
36	US 127, Hamilton, Mt Healthy, N Marathon/Circle K/dsl, Speedway Wendy's CVS Drug, S Shell/dsl, Sunoco, UDF Big Boy, China Island, La Rosa's Pizza, Little Caesars, McDonald's, Rally's, Subway, Taco Bell Advance Parts, Family$, O'Reilly Parts
33	US 27, US 126, Colerain Ave, N Speedway/dsl Burger King, Skyline Chili, Steak'n Shake, Wendy's Dick's, Jo-Ann, Lowe's, Petsmart, TireDiscounters, Walmart/Subway, S Shell Applebee's, Arby's, Big Boy, Bob Evans, Buffalo Wild Wings, Burger King, Cheddar's, Chipotle, Five Guys, Honeybaked Ham, IHOP, KFC, La Piñata Mexican, La Rosa's Pizza, LJ Silver, Logan's Roadhouse, Longhorn Steaks, McDonald's, Olive Garden, Outback Steaks, Panera Bread, Pizza Hut, Popeye's, Potbelly, Qdoba, Red Lobster, Starbucks, Taco Bell, TGIFriday's, White Castle Aldi Foods, AT&T, Best Buy, GNC, Hobby Lobby, JC Penney, Kroger, Macy's, Marshalls, Meijer/dsl, Michael's, Old Navy, Sumerel Tire/auto, Tires+, Tuesday Morning, URGENT CARE, Verizon, Walgreens
31	Ronald Reagan Hwy, Blue Rock Rd
28	I-74, US 52, E to Cincinnati, W to Indianapolis
25	I-74, E to Cincinnati, W to Indianapolis
21	Kilby Rd, Indian Springs Camping (3mi)
18mm	Ohio/Indiana State Line
16	US 50, Greendale, Lawrenceburg, W Ameristop/dsl, Shell/Circle K/Subway, Sinclair/dsl Buffalo Wings&Rings, Burger King, KFC, La Rosa's Pizza, Maverick's Grill, McDonald's, Taco Bell, Waffle House, White Castle Baymont Inn, Holiday Inn Express, Quality Inn, Riverside Inn casino, Chevrolet, Chrysler/Dodge/Jeep, Ford, TireDiscounters, Walgreens
14mm	Kentucky/Indiana state line, Ohio River
11	Petersburg
8b a	KY 237, Hebron, N Marathon/DQ/dsl, UDF/dsl Agave Mexican, Arby's, China Wok, Hebron Grille, Jets Pizza, Jimmy John's, Longnecks Grill, Papa John's, Penn Sta Subs, Pizza Hut, Strong's Pizza, Wendy's Remke's Mkt, URGENT CARE, S Speedway/Subway/dsl Burger King, Goldstar Chili, Skyline Chili, Sonic, Waffle House
4a b	KY 212, KY 20, N Shell/dsl Comfort Suites, Country Inn&Suites, Hampton Inn, Marriott, S DoubleTree (2mi) H, ✈
2	Mineola Pike, N Mobil/Rally's/Subway/dsl Holiday Inn, Quality Inn, S Shell/dsl Hot Head Burrito, Subway Courtyard Inn, Residence Inn

NOTES

KY

LOUISIANA

INTERSTATE 10

Exit#	Services
274mm	Louisiana/Mississippi state line, Pearl River
272mm	West Pearl River
270mm	Welcome Ctr wb, full facilities, info, litter barrels, petwalk, RV dump
267b	I-12 W, to Baton Rouge
267a	I-59 N, to Meridian
266	US 190, Slidell, N RaceTrac/dsl, Shell/dsl, TA/Country Pride/dsl/scales/24hr/@, Valero/dsl Arby's, Baskin-Robbins, Cane's Rest., Carreta's Mexican, Chesterfield Grill, Chick-fil-A, Copeland's Rest., Golden Dragon Chinese, KFC, Los Tres Amigos, McDonald's, NOLA Southern Grill, Panda Express, Retro Grill, Rotolo's Pizza, Shoney's, Sonic, Subway, Taco Bell, Wendy's, Zydecos Rest. Best Value Inn, Best Western, Deluxe Motel, Motel 6 H, CVS Drug, Firestone/auto, Freightliner, GNC, Harley-Davidson, Hobby Lobby, Office Depot, O'Reilly Parts, PepBoys, Petco, Rouse's Mkt, U-Haul, Walgreens, S Chevron/Subway/dsl, Murphy USA/dsl, RaceTrac/dsl Applebee's, Big Easy Diner, Cracker Barrel, Fuji Yama Hibachi, Hooters, McAlister's Deli, Outback Steaks, Ruby Tuesday, Sonic, Starbucks, TX Roadhouse, Waffle House Days Inn, La Quinta, Value Inn, Wingate Inn H, $General, $Tree, AT&T, CVS, Home Depot, Lowe's, repair/transmissions, Rite Aid, vet, Walmart/Subway
265	US 190, Fremaux Ave, N Shell/Purple Cow/dsl Cheddar's, Felipe's Mexican, Longhorn Steaks, Panera Bread, Starbucks Best Buy, Dick's, Kohl's, Michaels, Petsmart, TJ Maxx, Verizon
263	LA 433, Slidell, N Exxon/Circle K/dsl, Shell/dsl, Valero Oishii Buffet, Waffle House Hampton Inn, Super 8 repair, S Kangaroo/Subway/scales/dsl, Valero/dsl McDonald's, Taco Bell, Wendy's Holiday Inn Buick/GMC, Chevrolet/Cadillac, Chrysler/Dodge/Jeep, Ford, Honda, Hyundai, Kia, Mazda, Nissan, NO East RV Park (1mi), Pinecrest RV Park, Toyota
261	Oak Harbor Blvd, Eden Isles, N Exxon/Circle K/dsl Waffle House Sleep Inn, S Shell/Subway/dsl Bayou Country Store
255mm	Lake Pontchartrain
254	US 11, to Northshore, Irish Bayou, S Texaco/dsl
251	Bayou Sauvage NWR, S swamp tours
248	Michoud Blvd
246b a	I-510 S, LA 47 N, S to Chalmette, N to Little Woods
245	Bullard Ave, N Chevron/dsl, Shell/dsl Southern Smoque Diner, Waffle House Comfort Suites, Holiday Inn Express Family$, Honda, S Chevron/dsl, Shell Burger King, IHOP, KFC/Taco Bell, McDonald's, Papa John's, Super Cajun Seafood Baymont Inn, Motel 6 Chrysler/Dodge/Jeep, Home Depot, Nissan, PepBoys, Rite Aid, Tire Kingdom, Toyota, Walgreens, Walmart
244	Read Blvd, N Shell/dsl McDonald's Walgreens, S EZ Stop/dsl Popeye's, Subway, Waffle House, Wendy's Clarion, Days Inn, Knights Inn H, CVS, Lowe's, SaveALot Foods
242	Crowder Blvd, N Chevron, S Crowder Ctr, Exxon/dsl Subway Quality Inn Walgreens
241	Morrison Rd, N Big E-Z/dsl, FuelXpress/dsl
240b a	US 90 E, Chef Hwy, Downman Rd, N Shell/dsl Super 8 Chevrolet, U-Haul, USPO, S Chevron/dsl, DZ/dsl Delta Tires
239b a	Louisa St, Almonaster Blvd, N Big Easy TP/rest./dsl, Chevron/dsl, Exxon/dsl, FuelZone/dsl Burger King, Church's, McDonald's, Min Moon Chinese, Popeyes, Rally's, Subway, Taco Bell, Waffle House, Wendy's EconoLodge, Motel 6 $General, Family$, Goodyear/auto, Walgreens, Walmart, Winn-Dixie, S Day&Night/dsl
238b	I-610 W (from wb)
237	Elysian Fields Ave, N Mardi Gras Trkstp/Subway/dsl Lowe's
236c	St. Bernard Ave
236b	LA 39, N Claiborne Ave
236a	Esplanade Ave, downtown
235a	Orleans Ave, to Vieux Carre, French Qtr, S Chevron/dsl Clarion, Marriott, Sheraton
235b	Poydras St, N H, S to Superdome, downtown
234a	US 90A, Claiborne Ave, to Westbank, S Superdome
232	US 61, Airline Hwy, Tulane Ave, N Burger King, S Exxon, Shell McDonald's, Popeye's, Rallys, Subway, Wendy's Costco/gas, CVS, Family$, Firestone/auto, Pepboys, to Xavier U, USPO, vet
231b	Florida Blvd, WestEnd
231a	Metairie Rd
230	I-610 E (from eb), to Slidell

SLIDELL

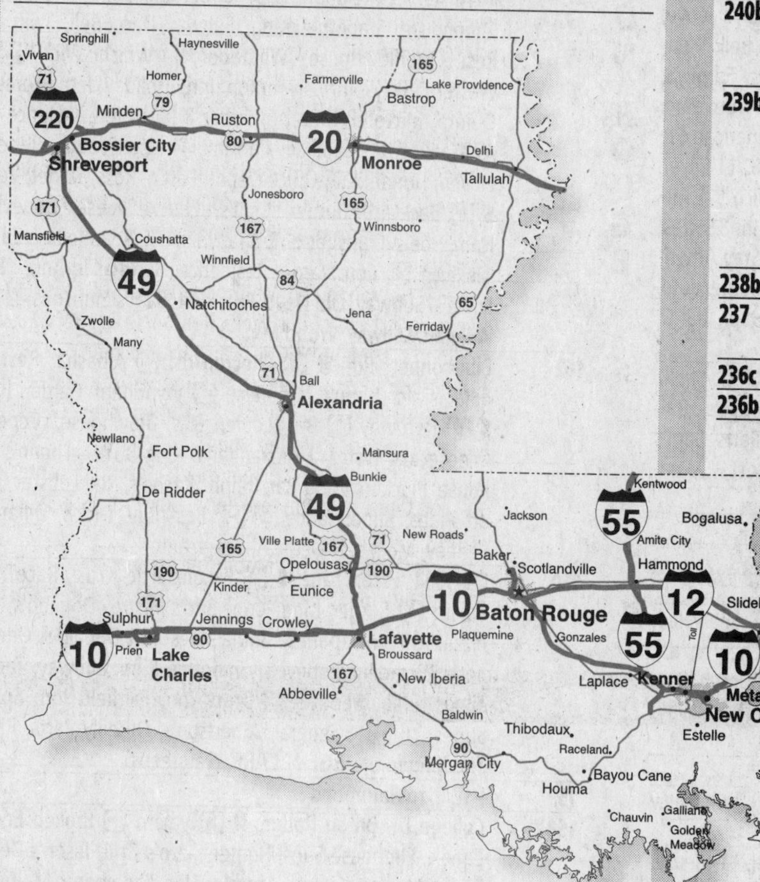

LA

INTERSTATE 10 Cont'd

NEW ORLEANS AREA

Exit#	Services
229	Bonnabel Blvd
228	Causeway Blvd, N [gas] Exxon/dsl, Shell/dsl [food] Buffalo Wild Wings, Cheesecake Factory, Cucina Italiana, Outback Steaks, PF Chang's, Red Lobster, Ruth's Chris Steaks, TGIFriday's [lodging] Best Western, Hampton Inn, Ramada [other] Dick's, Dillard's, JC Penney, Macy's, Whole Foods Mkt, S [gas] DZ, Exxon/Circle K [food] IHOP, Little Tokyo [lodging] Courtyard, Days Inn, Extended Stay America, Holiday Inn, La Quinta, Residence Inn, Sheraton
226	Clearview Pkwy, Huey Long Br, N [gas] Chevron/dsl, Exxon/Circle K/dsl [food] Cafe Dumonde, Cane's, Chili's, Copeland's Cheesecake Bistro, Corky's BBQ, Don's Seafood Hut, Hooters, Houston's Rest., Izzo's Burrito, Jimmy John's, Popeye's, Romano Italian, Starbucks, Taco Bell, Taco Tico, Zea Rotisserie [lodging] Sleep Inn [other] Target, Tire Kingdom, Walgreens, S [gas] Chevron, Danny&Clyde [food] Beijing Chinese, Burger King, Piccadilly, Smoothie King, Subway [lodging] Sun Suites, Super 8 [other] [H], AT&T, Buick/GMC, Firestone/auto
225	Veterans Blvd, N [gas] Chevron, DZ/dsl, Shell [food] Bonefish, Burger King, Coyote Blues, Denny's, Hooters, McDonald's, Panera Bread, Pei Wei [lodging] La Quinta [other] CVS Drug, Honda, Hyundai, Rite Aid, Rouses Mkt, URGENT CARE, S [gas] Shell/dsl [food] Burger King, Casa Garcia, ChuckeCheese, Little Caesars, Louisiana Purchase Kitchen, New Orleans Burgers, O'Henry's, Popeye's, Starbucks, Subway, Tiffin Pancakes, Wendy's [lodging] Evergreen Inn, Sheraton [other] $General, Acura, Best Buy, BigLots, BMW, Chevrolet, GNC, Home Depot, Jo-Ann Fabrics, Kia, Lexus, Michaels, Nissan, Office Depot, PepBoys, Petsmart, TJ Maxx, Verizon, vet, VW, Walgreens, Walmart
224	Power Blvd (from wb)
223b a	LA 49, Williams Blvd, N [gas] DZ/dsl, Exxon/dsl, Shell/dsl [food] Cafe Dumonde, Cane's Chicken, Fisherman's Cove, IHOP, Papa's Pizza, Popeye's, Rally's, Subway, Taco Bell, Wendy's [lodging] Fairfield Inn [other] $Tree, AutoZone, Dillards, Family$, Ford, Office Depot, PetCo, Save-a-Lot Foods, Target, TrueValue, Walmart Mkt, S [gas] Exxon/Circle K/dsl, Shell [food] American Pie Diner, Brick Oven, Don Jose's Grill, Dot's Diner, KFC/LJ Silver, McDonald's, Pollo Campero, Sonic, Subway, Taco Tico [lodging] Airport Inn, Comfort Suites, Contempra Inn, Country Inn&Suites, Crowne Plaza, DoubleTree, EconoLodge, Extended Stay America, La Quinta [other] $General, CVS Drug, Family$, Firestone/auto, Goodyear/auto, NAPA, Tire Kingdom, Toyota, U-Haul, USPO, Winn-Dixie
221	Loyola Dr, N [gas] Chevron, Circle K, Exxon/Circle K/dsl, Shell/dsl [food] Church's, Little Caesar's, McDonald's, Popeye's, Rally's, Subway, Taco Bell, VooDoo BBQ [other] Advance Parts, Sam's Club/gas, S [gas] Citgo/dsl, DZ [food] Michelle's Rest., Wendy's [lodging] Sleep Inn [other] $General, [airport], Family$
220	I-310 S, to Houma
214mm	Lake Pontchartrain
210	I-55N (from wb)
209	I-55 N, US 51, to Jackson, LaPlace, Hammond, N [gas] Shell/Huddle House/casino/dsl [lodging] Suburban Lodge, S [gas] Chevron/dsl, Circle K/dsl, Pilot/Subway/dsl/24hr/scales [food] Burger King, McDonald's, Waffle House, Wendy's [lodging] Best Western, Days Inn, Hampton Inn, Holiday Inn Express, Quality Inn
207mm	**weigh sta both lanes**
206	LA 3188 S, La Place, S [gas] Citgo/dsl, Shell/dsl [other] [H], Chrysler/Dodge/Jeep, Ford, Goodyear/auto
194	LA 641 S, to Gramercy, **4-6 mi** S [gas] Chevron, Shell, Taylors/dsl [food] Golden Grove Rest, McDonald's, Popeye's [other] [H], plantations

GONZALES

Exit#	Services
187	US 61, N to Sorrento, S to Gramercy
182	LA 22, Sorrento, N [gas] Shell/Popeye's/dsl, Texaco/dsl, S [gas] **Chevron/Subway/dsl/scales/24hr, SJ/dsl** [food] McDonald's, Waffle House [other] tourist info
179	LA 44, Gonzales, **1 mi** N [gas] Exxon/Popingo's Cafe/dsl, Murphy USA/dsl [food] Alabasha Cafe, Subway [other] $General, Buick/GMC, Fred's Store, Walgreens
177	LA 30, Gonzales, N [gas] Cracker Barrel/dsl, Shell/dsl [food] Burger King, El Paso Mexican, Jack-in-the-Box, McDonald's, Outback Steaks, Taco Bell, Taco Bell, Waffle House [lodging] Best Inn, Best Western, Budget Inn, Clarion, Highland Inn, Western Inn [other] [H], Home Depot, S [gas] Chevron/dsl, RaceTrac/dsl, Shell/dsl [food] Chili's, **Cracker Barrel**, Don's Seafood Hut, KFC, Logan's Roadhouse, Popeye's, Sonic, Starbucks, Subway, Tang Buffet, Wendy's [lodging] Comfort Suites, Hampton Inn, Holiday Inn Express, La Quinta, SpringHill Suites, Supreme Inn, TownePlace Suites [other] Cabela's, Tanger/famous brands, Vesta RV Park
173	LA 73, to Geismar, Prairieville, N [gas] Shell/dsl [other] vet, S [gas] Chevron/dsl, Exxon/dsl, Mobil/McDonald's/dsl, RaveTrac/dsl, Sunoco/dsl [food] Athenos Cafe, Burger King, DeAngelo's Pizza, Griffin Grill, Hot Wok, Las Palmas Mexican, Papa Murphy's, Pizza Hut, Popeye's, Smoothie King, Sonic, Subway [other] Family$, Harvest Foods, repair, Twin Lakes RV Park (1mi), Walgreens

BATON ROUGE

Exit#	Services
166	LA 42, LA 427, Highland Rd, Perkins Rd, N [gas] Chevron/Church's/dsl, Exxon/Circle K/dsl [food] Las Palmas Mexican, Popeye's, Ruffino's Italian, Sonic, Starbucks, Waffle House [other] Alexander's Mkt, funpark, Goodyear/auto, Home Depot, Tire Pros, S [gas] Shell/BBQ/dsl, Texaco/dsl [food] Subway
163	Siegen Lane, N [gas] Chevron, RaceTrac/dsl, Shell/Circle K/dsl [food] Arby's, Burger King, Cane's, CC's Coffee, Chee Burger, Chick-fil-A, China 1, CiCi's Pizza, Hooters, IHOP, Jason's Deli, McAlister's, McDonald's, Olive Garden, PoBoy Express, Ribs Chophouse, Smoothie King, Subway, Taco Bell, Twin Peaks Rest., Waffle House, Whataburger, Which Wich? [lodging] Best Western, Days Inn, Hampton Inn, Holiday Inn Express, La Quinta, Microtel, Motel 6, Super 8 [other] $Tree, Advance Parts, AT&T, BigLots, Cadillac, CarMax, Firestone/auto, Harley-Davidson, Honda, Kia, Office Depot, PetCo, Ross, Target, Verizon, S [food] Backyard Burger, Chili's, ChuckeCheese, Honeybaked Ham, Joe's Crabshack, Teppanyaki, TX Roadhouse, Zapata's Mexican [lodging] Courtyard, Residence Inn [other] Jo-Ann, Kohl's, Lowe's/Subway, Old Navy, Petsmart, Sam's Club/gas, TJ Maxx, **Walmart/Subway**, World Mkt
162	Bluebonnet Rd, N [gas] Chevron/dsl [food] Albasha Rest., Cadillac Cafe, Kabuki Japanese [lodging] Wyndham Garden [other] vet, S [gas] Raceway [food] Bar Louie, BJ's Brewhouse, Copeland's Cheesecake Bistro, J Alexander's, King Buffet, Logan's Roadhouse, Pluckers Wing Bar, Ralph&Kacoo's, Red Lobster [lodging] Hyatt Place, Renaissance [other] [H], Best Buy, Dick's, Dillard's, JC Penney, Macy's, Mall of LA, Sears/auto
160	LA 3064, Essen Lane, S [gas] Exxon/Circle K/dsl, RaceTrac/dsl, Valero [food] Burger King, Copeland's Bistro, Domino's, Gatti's Pizza, Ichiban Japanese, India's Rest., McDonald's, Omi Japanese, Piccadilly, Popeye's, Smoothie King, Subway, Taco Bell, Times Grill, Wendy's [lodging] Drury Inn, Fairfield Inn, Springhill Suites [other] [H], $General, Albertson's, O'Reilly Parts, Rite Aid, Tire Kingdom, URGENT CARE, Walgreens
159	I-12 E, to Hammond
158	College Dr, Baton Rouge, N [gas] Valero [food] Broken Egg Cafe, Cane's, Firehouse Subs, Hooters, Izzo's Grill, Jason's Deli, Koto Rest., Mansurs Rest., Marble Slab Creamery, Melting Pot

LA

INTERSTATE 10 Cont'd

BATON ROUGE

158 Continued
On-the-Border, Pelican House Rest., Subway, Sullivan's Rest., Waffle House, Wendy's Best Western, Chase Suites, Extended Stay America, Homewood Suites, Marriott H, Barnes&Noble, Meineke, Midas, **S** Chevron, Exxon/ dsl, Shell/Circle K Chick-fil-A, Chili's, Gino's Rest., IHOP, Jingdu Japanese, Marina's Mexican, McDonald's, Panda Express, Ruth's Chris Steaks, Sporting News Grill, Starbucks, Station Grill, Subway, Taco Bell, Tio Javi's Mexican Comfort Inn, Comfort Suites, Crowne Plaza, DoubleTree, Embassy Suites, Hampton Inn, Holiday Inn $Tree, Albertson's/Sav-On, AutoZone, Hobby Lobby, Office Depot, USPO, Verizon, Walgreens, Walmart/Subway

157b Acadian Thwy, **N** Chevron/dsl, Shell/Circle K Mestizo Grill, Rib's Rest. La Quinta, Radisson H, **S** Shell/Circle K/dsl Acme Oyster House, Coyote Blues Mexican, Galatoire's Bistro, Juban's Rest., Outback Steaks, Pei Wei Courtyard AT&T, PetCo, Trader Joe's, Tuesday Morning

157a Perkins Rd (from eb), same as 157b

156b Dalrymple Dr, **S** to LSU

156a Washington St

155c Louise St (from wb)

155b I-110 N, to Baton Rouge bus dist, **N**

155a LA 30, Nicholson Dr, Baton Rouge, **N** Belle Hotel, **S** Shell/Circle K/dsl to LSU

154mm Mississippi River

153 LA 1, Port Allen, **N** Chevron, Shell/Circle K/dsl Church's, Pizza Hut AutoZone, Family$, Kenworth, NAPA, O'Reilly Parts, repair, Walgreens, **S** Chevron, LA 1S TP/Exxon/Casino/dsl/scales/24hr, RaceTrac/dsl Burger King, Domino's, Hardee's, Smoothie King, Waffle House Magnuson Hotel $General, $Tree, AT&T, Verizon, Walmart/Subway

151 LA 415, to US 190, **N** Cash's Trk Plaza/dsl/scales/casino, Chevron/dsl, Emerald Plaza Trkstp/Champs Chicken/dsl, Exxon/dsl, Nino's/dsl/casino, Shell/Blimpie/dsl Bergeron's Cajun, Burger King, KFC/Taco Bell, McDonald's, Popeye's, Subway, Waffle House Best Western, Comfort Suites, Hampton Inn, Holiday Inn Express, Quality Inn, West Inn $General, **S** Valero/dsl/24hr, Loves/Arby's/dsl/scales/24hr Audubon Inn, Motel 6, Super 8 truck repair

139 LA 77, Grosse Tete, **N** Shell/Subway/dsl Big Heads BBQ Chevrolet, **S** Tiger/Country Store/dsl/rest./@

135 LA 3000, to Ramah

127 LA 975, to Whiskey Bay

126.5mm Pilot Channel of Whiskey Bay

122mm Atchafalaya River

121 Butte La Rose, **N Visitors ctr/ both lanes, full facilities, litter barrels, petwalk, , tourist info, vending, S** Lazy Cajun Grill (2mi) Frenchman's Wilderness Camground (.5mi)

115 LA 347, to Cecilia, Henderson, **N** Exxon/dsl/24hr, Shamrock/dsl, Texaco/dsl Chicken on the Bayou, Landry's Seafood Holiday Inn Express casinos, **S** Chevron/dsl, Exxon/Subway/dsl, Shell/McDonald's/dsl, Texaco/dsl, Valero/dsl Popeye's, Waffle House

109 LA 328, to Breaux Bridge, **N** Shell/dsl, Texaco/Quiznos/dsl/casino Microtel, **S** Conoco/dsl, Exxon/Domino's/dsl, Murphy USA/dsl, Pilot/Arby's/dsl/scales/24hr, Valero/Popeye's/dsl Burger King, City Buffet, Crazy Bout Cajun, Hacienda Real, McDonald's, Pizza Hut, Sonic, Taco Bell, Waffle House, Wendy's, Zapote Mexican, Zeus Best Value Inn,

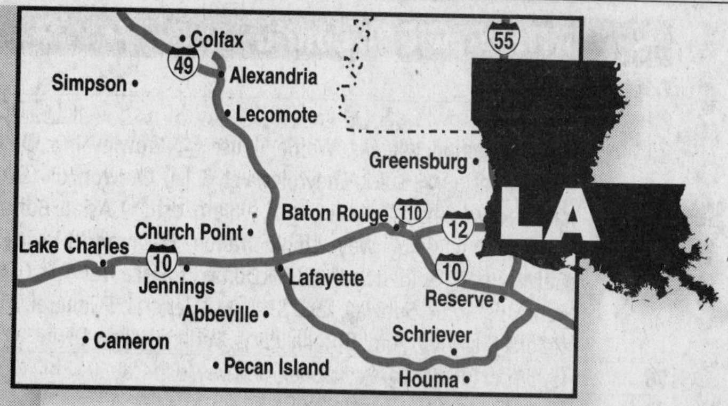

109 Continued
Super 8 $General, $Tree, AT&T, AutoZone, Chevrolet, Chrysler/Dodge/Jeep, city park, Family$, Ford/Lincoln, O'Reilly Parts, Pioneer RV Park, USPO, Verizon, Walgreens, Walmart/Subway, Winn-Dixie

108mm weigh sta both lanes

LAFAYETTE

104 Louisiana Ave, **S** Chick-fil-A, McDonald's, Subway, Taco Bell AT&T, GNC, JC Penney, Office Depot, PetCo, Ross, Target, Verizon

103b I-49 N, to Opelousas

103a US 167 S, to Lafayette, **S** Chevron/dsl, Murphy USA/dsl, RaceTrac/dsl, Shell/dsl, Valero Checkers, McDonald's, Pizza Hut, Popeye's, Subway, Taco Bell, Waffle House, Wendy's Baymont Inn, Best Value Inn, Best Western, Comfort Inn, EconoLodge, Fairfield Inn, Holiday Inn, Howard Johnson, La Quinta, Ramada, Super 8, TravelHost Inn H, $Tree, CVS Drug, Home Depot, repair, Super 1 Foods/gas, transmissions, Walmart/Subway

101 LA 182, to Lafayette, **N** Chevron/McDonald's, Shell/Subway/dsl, TA/Country Pride/dsl/scales/24hr/@ Burger King, Waffle House, Whataburger Red Roof Inn, **S** Exxon, RaceTrac/dsl, Shell/dsl, Shell/dsl, Texaco Cracker Barrel, Popeyes Days Inn, Drury Inn, Hilton Garden (2mi), Motel 6, Peartree Inn H, $General, Advance Parts, Family$, Kia, O'Reilly Parts

100 Ambassador Caffery Pkwy, **N** Exxon/Subway/dsl Gauthier's RV Ctr, Peterbilt, Ryder Trucks, **S** Chevron/dsl, RaceTrac/dsl, Shell/dsl Burger King, McDonald's, Pizza Hut/Taco Bell, Sonic, Waffle House, Wendy's Ambassador Inn, Hampton Inn, Microtel, Sleep Inn H, Southern Tire Mart

97 LA 93, to Scott, **S** Chevron/McDonald's, Shell/Church's/dsl Billy's Cracklings, Fezzo's Seafood, Huddle House, Popeye's, Rochetto's Pizza Comfort Inn, Holiday Inn Express, Howard Johnson Harley-Davidson, KOA

92 LA 95, to Duson, **N** Exxon/dsl/casino/RV dump/scales/24hr, Loves/Chester's/Wendy's/dsl/scales/24hr, **S** Chevron/dsl, Roady's/cafe/dsl/casino, Shell/Subway/dsl/casino Super 8 Frog City RV Park

87 LA 35, to Rayne, **N** Chevron/dsl, Shell/Subway/casino/dsl Burger King, Chef Roy's Rest., McDonald's Days Inn $General, RV camping, **S** Citgo/dsl, Frog City/Exxon/Cajun Rest./dsl, Shop Rite, Texaco/dsl, Valero/dsl Candyland Ice Cream, DQ, Gabe's Café, Great Wall Chinese, Pizza Hut, Popeye's, Sonic Best Western Advance Parts, Family$, O'Reilly Parts, Walgreens, Winn-Dixie

82 LA 1111, to E Crowley, **S** Chevron/dsl, Murphy USA Chili's, Wendy's H, $Tree, AT&T, GNC, Lowe's, Walgreens, Walmart/Subway

INTERSTATE 10 Cont'd

Exit#	Services
	CROWLEY
80	LA 13, to Crowley, N (gas) Conoco/Exit 80/dsl/rest./24hr (food) DQ, Fezzo's Seafood/steaks, Waffle House (lodging) Crowley Inn, Days Inn, Motel 6 (other) Buick/Chevrolet, vet, S (gas) Chevron/dsl, Exxon, Raceway/dsl, Tobacco+/gas, Valero/dsl (food) Asian Buffet, Burger King, Cajun Way, China Dragon, El Dorado Mexican, Gatti's Pizza, Golden Seafood, McDonald's, Pizza Hut, PJ's Grill, Popeye's, Sonic, Subway, Taco Bell (other) $General, $General, AutoZone, Family$, Ford, O'Reilly Parts, Verizon, Winn-Dixie
76	LA 91, to Iota, S (gas) Petro/Shell/Subway/dsl/scales/24hr
72	Egan, N (other) Cajun Haven RV Park
	JENNINGS
65	LA 97, to Jennings, S (gas) Shell/dsl/casino (lodging) Howard Johnson
64	LA 26, to Jennings, N (food) Los Tres Potrillos (other) LA Oil & Gas Park, RV Park, S (gas) Exxon/dsl, EZ Mart, Jennings Trvl Ctr/dsl/casino, Murphy USA/dsl, Valero/dsl (food) Burger King, Gatti's Pizza, General Wok Chinese, La Rumba Mexican, McDonald's, Pizza Hut, Popeye's, Shoney's, Sonic, Subway, Taco Bell, Waffle House, Wendy's (lodging) Days Inn, Hampton Inn, Motel 6 (other) (H), $General, $Tree, AT&T, AutoZone, Buick/GMC, Chrysler/Dodge/Jeep, Fred's Store, O'Reilly Parts, Verizon, Walgreens, Walmart/Subway
59	LA 395, to Roanoke, N (gas) Peto's TrvlCtr/Chevron/dsl/scales/24hr
54	LA 99, Welsh, S (gas) Citgo, Exxon/dsl/24hr, Valero (food) DQ, Subway
48	LA 101, Lacassine, S (gas) Exxon
44	US 165, to Alexandria, N (other) Quiet Oaks RV Park (10mi), S (food) Rabideaux's Cajun
43	LA 383, to Iowa, N (gas) Loves/Hardee's/dsl/scales/24hr, Pilot/Arby's/PJ Fresh/dsl/scales/24hr (food) Burger King (lodging) Howard Johnson Express, La Quinta (other) United RV Ctr, S (gas) Citgo/dsl, Shell/McDonald's/dsl, Valero (food) Boudreaux's Cajun, Sonic, Subway (other) $General, I-10 Outlet/famous brands, RV park
	LAKE CHARLES
36	LA 397, to Creole, Cameron, N (other) Jean Lafitte RV Park (2mi), S (gas) Cash Magic/grill/dsl/RV Dump, Chevron/dsl (lodging) Red Roof Inn (other) casino, Country Oaks RV Park
34	I-210 W, to Lake Charles
33	US 171 N, N (gas) Chevron/dsl, Conoco/dsl, Exxon/dsl, RaceWay/dsl/E85, Shell/dsl (food) Burger King, Church's, Subway, Taco Bell (lodging) Best Value, Best Western, Comfort Suites, Lake Charles Inn, Richmond Suites (other) $General, AutoZone, Family$, O'Reilly Parts, to Sam Houston Jones SP, S (lodging) EconoLodge, Holiday Inn Express, Motel 6
32	Opelousas St, N (gas) Exxon, S (lodging) EconoLodge, Holiday Inn Express, Motel 6
31b	US 90 E, Shattuck St, to LA 14, N (gas) Chevron/dsl/casino, S (gas) Valero/dsl
31a	US 90 bus, Enterprise Blvd, S (food) Popeye's
30b	downtown
30a	LA 385, N Lakeshore Dr, Ryan St, N (gas) Exxon (food) Steamboat Bill's Rest., Waffle House (lodging) Days Inn, Oasis Inn, S (food) Wendy's (lodging) Quality Suites
29	LA 385 (from eb), same as 30a
28mm	Calcasieu Bayou, Lake Charles
27	LA 378, to Westlake, N (gas) Chevron/dsl, Conoco/dsl, Shell/dsl, Valero (food) Burger King, El Tapatia Mexican, McDonald's, Popeye's, RoundTop Burger, Sonic, Subway (other) $General, Bumper Parts, Family$, Fred's, MarketBasket, O'Reilly Parts, to Sam Houston Jones SP (6mi), S (lodging) Inn at the Isle (other) Riverboat Casinos
26	US 90 W, Southern Rd, Columbia, N (gas) Exxon/dsl
25	I-210 E, to Lake Charles
	SULPHUR
23	LA 108, to Sulphur, N (gas) Chevron, Circle K, Exxon/dsl, Murphy USA, Shell (food) Burger King, Cane's, Chili's, China Wok, Hollier's Cajun Diner, Japanese Steaks, McDonald's, Popeye's, Subway, Taco Bell, Wendy's (lodging) Quality Inn (other) $General, $Tree, AT&T, Bumper Parts, Lowe's, Verizon, Walgreens, Walmart/Subway, S (gas) Chevron/Jack-in-the-Box/dsl, Citgo/Cash Magic/dsl, Sulphur Trkstp/Shell/Subway/dsl/casino (food) Cracker Barrel, Waffle House (lodging) Best Western+, Comfort Suites, Crossland Suites, Days Inn, Holiday Inn Express, Studio 6, Super 8 (other) Southern Tire Mart
21	LA 3077, Arizona St, N (gas) Conoco/dsl, Shell (food) Boiling Point Cajun, China Taste, Papa John's, Starbucks (other) (H), $General, AT&T, Chevrolet, CVS Drug, Ford, GNC, Kroger/gas, NAPA, Walgreens, S (gas) Chevron/dsl, Valero/dsl/casino (other) Hidden Ponds RV Park
20	LA 27, to Sulphur, N (gas) Chevron/dsl, Circle K, Conoco/dsl, Gulf, Valero/dsl (food) Burger King, Casa Ole Mexican, Checkers, Gatti's Pizza, Hollier's Cajun, Hong Kong Chinese, Joe's Pizza/pasta, Johnny T's Grill, La Rumba Mexican, LeBleu's Landing Cajun, Little Caesar's, McDonald's, Pitt Grill Cajun, Popeye's, Subway, Taco Bell, Wendy's (lodging) Best Value, Hampton Inn, Motel 6 (other) (H), Brookshire Bros/gas, Family$, Firestone/auto, Goodyear/auto, Jiffy Lube, S (gas) Conoco/dsl, Shell/dsl (food) Navroskey's Burgers, Pizza Hut, Sonic, Waffle House (lodging) Baymont Inn, Candlewood Suites, Fairfield Inn, Holiday Inn, La Quinta, Super Inn, Wingate Inn (other) casino, Stine, to Creole Nature Trail
8	LA 108, Vinton, N (gas) Chevron/dsl, Exxon/dsl (food) Cajun Cowboy's Rest. (other) V RV Park
7	LA 3063, Vinton, N (gas) FuelStop/dsl (food) Burger King, Sonic, Subway (other) $General, casino, S (gas) Loves/Arby's/dsl/scales/24hr
4	US 90, LA 109, Toomey, N (gas) Cash Magic/dsl/grill/casino, Chevron/dsl/casino, Shell/dsl (other) truck repair, S (gas) Conoco/dsl, Exxon/dsl, Valero/dsl/rest. (food) Subway (lodging) Best Western (other) casinos, RV Park
2.5mm	**weigh sta wb lanes**
1.5mm	**Welcome Ctr eb, full (handicapped) facilities, litter barrels, petwalk, (phone), (picnic)**
1	(from wb), Sabine River Turnaround
0mm	Louisiana/Texas state line, Sabine River

INTERSTATE 12

Exit#	Services
85c	I-10 E, to Biloxi. **I-12 begins/ends on I-10, exit 267.**
85b	I-59 N, to Hattiesburg
85a	I-10 W, to New Orleans
83	US 11, to Slidell, N (gas) Circle K/dsl, Exxon/dsl (food) Burger King, McDonald's, Sonic, Waffle House, S (gas) RaceTrak/dsl, Shell, Subway/dsl (other) (H)
80	Airport Dr, North Shore Blvd, N (gas) Circle K/Krystal dsl (food) Dickey's BBQ, IHOP, PJ's Coffee, Sonic (lodging) Comfort Inn (other) AT&T, Petsmart, Ross, Target, S (gas) Chevron, Shell dsl (food) Burger King, Chili's, ChuckECheese's, Domino's, McDonald's, Olive Garden, Starbucks, Subway, Taco Bell, Waffle House, Wendy's, Zea Grill (lodging) Candlewood Suites, Holiday Inn Express, Homewood Suites, La Quinta (other) $Tree, Burlington, Dillard's, Goodyear/auto, Home Depot, Jo-Ann, Marshall's, Sam's Club/gas, Walgreens, Walmart
74	LA 434, to Lacombe, N (gas) Chevron/Subway/dsl (other) (H), Steve RV Ctr, S (other) Big Branch Marsh NWR
68	LA 1088, to Mandeville

INTERSTATE 12 Cont'd

COVINGTON

Exit#	Services
65	LA 59, to Mandeville, **N** Chevron/dsl, Exxon/Danny&Clyde's/cafe/dsl, Shell/dsl Fat Spoon Cafe, Popeye's, Smoothie King, Sonic, Subway, Waffle House Comfort Suites, **S** Kangaroo/Arby's/dsl, Valero/Domino's/dsl El Rancho Mexican, Liu's Wok, McDonald's, PJ's Coffee, Quiznos camping, to Fontainebleau SP, vet, Winn-Dixie
63b a	US 190, Covington, Mandeville, **N** Chevron/dsl, Exxon, RaceTrac, Shell/Circle K Acme Oyster House, Applebee's, Burger King, Cane's, Chick-fil-A, Copeland's Grill, Dakota Rest., Don's Seafood, Dunkin Donuts, Four Seasons Chinese, HoneyBaked Ham, IHOP, Jimmy John's, Johnny's Pizza, La Carreta, Lee's Hamburgers, McAlister's Deli, Mellow Mushroom Cafe, North Shore Empress Asian, Osaka Japanese, Outback Steaks, Papi's Fajita Factory, Piccadilly, Sonic, Starbucks, Subway, Thai Chili, Waffle House, Wendy's, Zea Rotisserie Best Western, Clarion, Comfort Inn, Country Inn&Suites, Courtyard, Hampton Inn, Hilton Garden, Holiday Inn, Homewood Suites, Residence Inn, Staybridge Suites, Super 8 Ace Hardware, AT&T, AutoZone, Chevrolet, Chrysler/Dodge/Jeep, CVS Drug, Firestone/auto, GNC, Home Depot, Honda, Hyundai, Lowe's, Nissan, Office Depot, Petsmart, Rouse's Mkt, Subaru, Toyota, Verizon, Walmart/McDonald's, **S** H, st police, to New Orleans via **toll** causeway
60	Pinnacle Pkwy, to Covington, same as 59
59	LA 21, to Covington, Madisonville, **N** Chevron/dsl, Kangaroo, Shell/dsl Buffalo Wild Wings, Cafe Du Monde, Carreta's Grill, Chili's, Cracker Barrel, Firehouse Subs, Five Guys, Golden Wok, Isabella's Pizza, Italian Pie, Izzo's Burrito, Jimmy John's, McDonald's, Olive Garden, Panda Buffet, Panera Bread, PJ's Coffee, Safa Mediterranean, Sake Steaks, Seafood Grill, Smoothie King, Steak'n Shake, Subway, TX Roadhouse La Quinta H, $Tree, AT&T, AutoZone, CVS Drug, Hobby Lobby, Kohl's, Petco, URGENT CARE, Walgreens, Winn-Dixie, **S** Valero/Domino's Chick-fil-A, ChuckECheese's, Dickey's BBQ, Habaneros Mexican, Longhorn Steaks, Pardo's Grill, Taco Bell, Wendy's, Which Wich?, Zoe's Kitchen Holiday Inn Express Belk, Best Buy, Fairview Riverside SP, GNC, JC Penney, Marshall's, Michael's, Ross, Sam's Club/dsl, Target, Verizon, World Mkt
57	LA 1077, to Goodbee, Madisonville, **S** QuickWay/PoBoys/dsl Best Wok, Pizza Hut, PJ's Coffee, Subway to Fairview Riverside SP, vet
47	LA 445, to Robert, **1-3 mi N** Jellystone Camping, to Global Wildlife Ctr, **S** Chevron/dsl
42	LA 3158, to Airport, **N** Chevron/Quiznos/dsl/24hr, Texaco/dsl McDonald's, Popeye's Friendly Inn, **S** Shell/Subway/dsl H, Berryland RV Ctr
40	US 51, to Hammond, **N** RaceTrac/dsl, Shell/Circle K Burger King, Cane's, Chick-fil-A, China Garden, Church's, Coldstone, Don's Seafood, East of Italy, IHOP, Jimmy John's, McDonald's, Nagoya Rest., Olive Garden, Ryan's, Santa Fe Steaks, Shane's Rib Shack, Smoothie King, Sonic, Subway, Taco Bell, Wendy's, Which Wich? Best Western, Courtyard, Holiday Inn, Quality Inn AT&T, Best Buy, Books-A-Million, Dillard's, GNC, Harley-Davidson, JC Penney, Rite Aid, Target, TJ Maxx, U-Haul, Verizon, Walgreens, **S** Petro/Mobil/Subway/dsl/scales/24hr/@, Pilot/Arby's/dsl/scales/24hr, Shell/dsl Waffle House Colonial Inn, Days Inn, La Quinta H, $General, Blue Beacon, SpeedCo
38b a	I-55, N to Jackson, S to New Orleans
37mm	**weigh sta both lanes**

HAMMOND

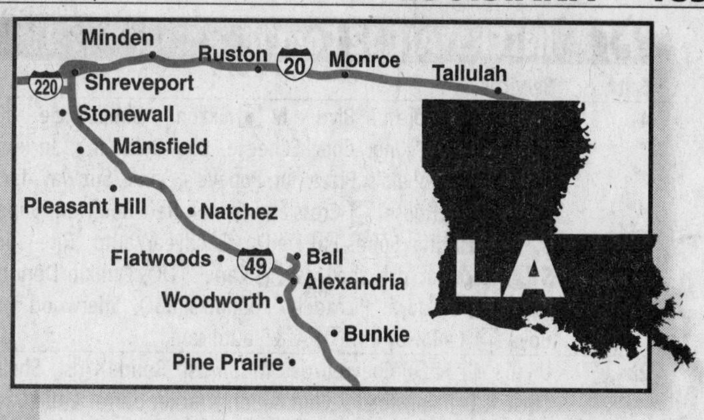

Exit#	Services
35	Pumpkin Ctr, Baptist, **N** Texaco/dsl $General, Dixie Camping World RV Service/Supplies, Punkin RV Park (2mi), **S** Chevron/Bayou Boyz/Subway/dsl
32	LA 43, to Albany, **N** Chevron/Subway/dsl, Exxon/dsl, Shell/Big River/dsl McDonald's, **S** to Tickfaw SP (11mi), tourist info
29	LA 441, to Holden, **N** Sunoco/dsl Berryland Campers
22	LA 63, to Frost, Livingston, **N** Chevron/dsl, Marathon/dsl Pizza Hut, Subway, Wayne's BBQ Carters Foods, Family$, Thrift Town Drug, USPO, **S** Lakeside RV Park (1mi)
19	to Satsuma, Colyell, **N** Exxon/dsl Subway
15	LA 447, to Walker, **N** Murphy Express/dsl, Shell/Subway/dsl, Texaco/dsl Burger King, China Wok, Domino's, Foochow Buffet, Jack-in-the-Box, McDonald's, Papa John's, Papa Murphy's, Pizza Hut, Popeye's, Quiznos, Sherwood PoBoy's, Sombrero Mexican, Sonic, Taco Bell, Waffle House, Wendy's La Quinta $General, $Tree, AT&T, AutoZone, NAPA, O'Reilly Parts, Verizon, Walgreens, Walmart/Subway, Winn-Dixie, **S** Chevron/dsl/24hr H
12	LA 1036, Juban Rd, **N** Marble Slab, Moe's SW Belk, Kohl's, Michael's, Old Navy, Petsmart, Ross, Rouse's Mkt, TJ Maxx, Verizon, **S** Shell/dsl
10	LA 3002, to Denham Springs, **N** Chevron, Exxon, RaceTrac/dsl, Shell/Circle K/dsl Arby's, Baskin-Robbins, Burger King, Cactus Café, Cane's, Chili's, Church's, Domino's, Don's Seafood, Gatti's Pizza, IHOP, McDonald's, Papa John's, Papi's Fajita, Pizza Hut, Popeye's, Ron's Seafood, Ryan's, Sonic, Starbucks, Subway, Taco Bell, Waffle House, Wendy's Best Value Inn, Candlewood Suites, Carom Inn, Comfort Suites, Hampton Inn, Motel 6 $General, $Tree, Advance Parts, Albertsons, AT&T, AutoZone, CVS Drug, Home Depot, Meineke, NTB, Office Depot, O'Reilly Parts, PetCo, Rite Aid, Tire Pros, Walgreens, Walmart/Subway, **S** Pilot/Subway/dsl/scales/24hr, Shell Cafe Phoenicia, El Rancho Mexican, Hardee's, Hooters, Islamorada Fish Co, Longhorn Steaks, Piccadilly, Rotolo's Pizza, VooDoo BBQ Days Inn, Highland Inn Bass Pro Shops, Cavender's, Chrysler/Dodge/Jeep, Ford, KOA, Sam's Club/dsl, Walgreens
8.5mm	Amite River
7	O'Neal Lane, **N** Mobil, RaceTrac/dsl La Quinta, Quality Inn Hobby Lobby, Toyota, **S** Murphy USA/dsl, RaceTrac/dsl, Shell, Texaco/Subway/dsl China King, Hardee's, Las Palmas Mexican, Little Caesar's, LoneStar Steaks, McDonald's, Popeye's, Rice Bowl, Sonic, Taco Bell, Waffle House, Wendy's H, $Tree, AutoZone, O'Reilly Parts, Walgreens, Walmart/Subway
6	Millerville Rd, **N** Chevron/dsl Chick-fil-A, Chili's Best Buy, Lowe's, Office Depot, Petsmart, Super Target, **S** Texaco/dsl Rotolo's Pizza, Subway Ace Hardware

INTERSTATE 12 Cont'd

BATON ROUGE

Exit#	Services
4	Sherwood Forest Blvd, N [gas] Exxon, Shell/Circle K/dsl [food] Burger King, ChuckECheese, Egg Roll King, Jack-in-the-Box, McDonald's, Pizza Hut, Popeye's, Sonic, Subway, Taco Bell, Waffle House [lodging] Crossland Suites, Red Roof Inn, Super 8, Woodspring Suites [other] Fred's, Goodyear/auto, Rite Aid, S [gas] RaceTrac/dsl, Shell/dsl [food] Cane's, DQ, Dunkin Donuts, Hardee's, Nagoya, Piccadilly, Podnuh's BBQ, Sherwood Po-Boys [lodging] Calloway Inn [other] AT&T, auto care
2b	US 61 N, N [gas] Chevron/dsl, Mobil/dsl, Rende's/dsl, Shell/Circle K [food] Applebee's, Chinese Inn, Cracker Barrel, Little Caesar's, McDonald's, Taco Bell [lodging] Days Inn, Holiday Inn, Knights Inn, Magnuson Hotel, Microtel, Motel 6, Sleep Inn [other] $Tree, Albertsons/gas, Burlington Coats, Dodge/Ram, GNC, Marshall's, Michael's, Nissan, PepBoys, SteinMart, Toyota, Walgreens, Walmart Mkt
2a	US 61 S, S [gas] Circle K, Exxon/Circle K/dsl [food] Burger King, China 1, Fernando's Mexican, Isabella's Pizza, Jimmy John's, McDonald's, Subway, Waffle House [other] $Tree, Costco/gas, Home Depot, Hyundai, Volvo
1b	LA 1068, to LA 73, Essen Lane, N [gas] Shell/Circle K/dsl [food] Cane's, China Wok, McDonald's, VooDoo BBQ [other] Family$, Le Blanc's Mkt, S [other] [H]
1a	I-10 (from wb). **I-12 begins/ends on I-10, exit 159 in Baton Rouge**

INTERSTATE 20

Exit#	Services
189mm	Louisiana/Mississippi state line, Mississippi River
187mm	**weigh sta both lanes**
186	US 80, Delta, S [gas] Chevron/Subway/dsl/24hr
184mm	**[rest stop] wb, full [handicapped] facilities, litter barrels, petwalk, [phone], [picnic], RV dump**
182	LA 602, Mound
173	LA 602, Richmond
171	US 65, Tallulah, N [gas] Chevron/Subway/dsl, Shell/dsl [food] Chopsticks Buffet, McDonald's, Wendy's [lodging] Days Inn, Super 8 [other] [H], S [gas] Exxon/dsl/scales, Loves/Arby's/dsl/scales/24hr, TA/Country Pride/dsl/scales/24hr/@, Texaco [food] Red Top Grill
164mm	Tensas River
157	LA 577, Waverly, N [gas] Waverly Trkstp/rest./dsl/24hr, S [gas] Chevron/Hunt Bros Pizza/dsl/24hr, Shell/rest./dsl/24hr [other] Casino, to Tensas River NWR
155mm	Bayou Macon
153	LA 17, Delhi, N [gas] Chevron/Subway, Texaco/dsl [food] Boomers, Burger King, Pizza Hut, Sonic [other] [H], $General, AT&T, Brookshire's Foods, Family$, Fred's, USPO, S [gas] Valero/dsl [lodging] Best Western, Executive Inn
148	LA 609, Dunn
145	LA 183, rd 202, Holly Ridge
141	LA 583, Bee Bayou Rd
138	US 425, Rayville, N [gas] Bud's, Pilot/Wendy's/dsl/scales/24hr [food] Fox's Pizza, McDonald's, Sonic [lodging] Days Inn [other] [H], $General, $Tree, AutoZone, Brookshire's Foods, Buick/Chevrolet, Family$, repair, Verizon, Walmart, S [gas] Chevron/Subway/dsl/24hr, Exxon/Circle K/Quiznos/dsl, RaceWay/dsl [food] Big John's Rest., Popeye's, Waffle House [lodging] Super 8
135mm	Boeuf River
132	LA 133, Start, N [gas] Exxon/dsl
128mm	Lafourche Bayou
124	LA 594, Millhaven, N [gas] Shell/dsl [other] st police, to Sage Wildlife Area
120	Garrett Rd, Pecanland Mall Dr, N [gas] Chevron/dsl [food] Applebee's, ChuckECheese, Copeland's Rest., Fiesta Linda, IHOP, Longhorn Steaks, McAlister's, O'Charleys, Olive Garden, Red Lobster, Ronin Habachi, Sonic [lodging] Courtyard, Residence Inn, TownePlace Suites [other] $Tree, AT&T, Belk, Best Buy, Dick's, Dillard's, Firestone/auto, Home Depot, JC Penney, Kohl's, Michael's, Old Navy, PetCo, Petsmart, Ross, Stein Mart, Target, TJ Maxx, S [gas] Shell/dsl [lodging] Best Western, Days Inn, Hampton Inn [other] Harley-Davidson, Hope's Campers, Lowe's, Ouachita RV Park, Pecanland RV Park, Sam's Club/gas
118b a	US 165, N [gas] Valero/dsl [lodging] Clarion, Motel 6, Stratford House Inn [other] Hyundai, Kia, Nissan, to NE LA U, S [gas] Chevron, Conoco/dsl, Exxon, Now Save/dsl, Shell/Circle K [food] Burger King, Capt D's, Church's, KFC, McDonald's, Popeye's, Sonic, Subway, Taco Bell, Wendy's [lodging] Comfort Suites, Hampton Inn, Motel 6, Super 8
117b	LA 594, Texas Ave, N [gas] Now Save/deli/dsl
117a	Hall St, Monroe, N [other] [H], Civic Ctr
116b	US 165 bus, LA 15, Jackson St, N [other] [H]
116a	5th St, Monroe
115	LA 34, Mill St, N [gas] Chevron
114	LA 617, Thomas Rd, N [gas] Murphy USA, RaceWay/dsl [food] Burger King, Cane's, Capt D's, Cheddar's, Chick-fil-A, El Chico, El Chile Verde, Five Guys, Grandy's, Hibachi Grill, IHOP, KFC, McAlister's Deli, McDonald's, Podnuh's BBQ, Popeye's, Subway, Taco Bell, Waffle House, Wendy's [lodging] Best Value Inn, Super 8, Wingate Inn [other] [H], AT&T, BigLots, Hobby Lobby, Office Depot, Rite Aid, Walgreens, Walmart/McDonald's, S [gas] Chevron, Exxon/Circle K/Subway/dsl [food] Buffalo Wild Wings, Chili's, Cracker Barrel, El Sombrero, Four Bros Rest., Genghis Grill, Hooters, Logan's Roadhouse, Outback Steaks, Peking Chinese, Pizza Hut, Ronin Hibachi, Sonic, TX Roadhouse, Waffle House [lodging] Best Western, Comfort Inn, La Quinta, Motel 6, Quality Inn, Red Roof Inn
113	Downing Pines Rd, S [lodging] Fairfield Inn, Hampton Inn, Hilton Garden, Holiday Inn Express, Home 2 Suites [other] Chrysler/Dodge/Jeep, Hyundai
112	Well Rd, N [gas] Conoco, Now Save/dsl, Shell/Circle K/dsl, Texaco/dsl [food] Burger King, DQ, McDonald's, Sam's Eatery, San Francisco TexMex, Sonic, Subway, Taco Bell, Waffle House, Zaxby's [other] Advance Parts, CVS Drug, Mac's Fresh Mkt, vet, Walgreens, Walmart Mkt/dsl, S [gas] Pilot/Subway/Wendy's/dsl/scales/24hr [other] Pavilion RV Park
108	LA 546, to US 80, Cheniere, N [gas] Shell/dsl, Smart/dsl
107	Camp Rd, rd 25, Cheniere
103	US 80, Calhoun, N [gas] Chevron, USA/dsl/24hr [food] Johnny's Pizza (1mi) [lodging] Avant Motel
101	LA 151, to Calhoun, S [gas] Chevron/Huddle House/Subway/dsl, Exxon [food] Sonic [other] 101 RV Park
97mm	**[rest stop] wb, full [handicapped] facilities, litter barrels, petwalk, [phone], [picnic], RV dump**
95mm	**[rest stop] eb, full [handicapped] facilities, litter barrels, petwalk, [phone], [picnic], RV dump**
93	LA 145, Choudrant, S [gas] Choudrant [other] camping, Jimmie Davis SP (28mi)
86	LA 33, Ruston, N [gas] Murphy USA, RaceWay/dsl, Shell/Circle K/Quiznos/dsl, Texaco/dsl [food] Arby's, Cane's Chicken, Cheeburger Cheeburger, Chili's, El Jarrito Mexican, Hot Rod BBQ, Huddle House, Log Cabin Grill, Logan's Roadhouse, Portico Grill, Ronin Hibachi, Ryan's, Sonic, Taco Bell, Whataburger, Buffet [lodging] Comfort Inn, Days Inn, Home 2 Suites [other] $Tree, AT&T, Buick/GMC, Cadillac/Chevrolet, Chrysler/Dodge/Jeep

INTERSTATE 20 Cont'd

RUSTON

86 Continued
Ford/Lincoln, Fred's, GNC, Lowe's, Toyota, vet, Walmart/Subway, S [gas] Spirit/dsl [lodging] Best Western, Fairfield Inn, Holiday Inn Express

85 US 167, Ruston, N [gas] Chevron/Subway, Exxon, Shell/Circle K [food] Applebee's, Burger King, Capt D's, Little Caesar's, McDonald's, Peking Chinese, Wendy's [lodging] Courtyard, Hampton Inn, Relax Inn [other] $General, Office Depot, Super 1 Foods, TrueValue, Walgreens, S [gas] Texaco, Valero/dsl [food] Pizza Hut [lodging] Best Value Inn, Sleep Inn [other] [H], Advance Parts, Verizon

84 LA 544, Ruston, S [gas] Chevron/dsl, Exxon [food] Domino's, Johnny's Pizza, Pizza Inn, Smoothie King, Starbucks, Subway, Waffle House [lodging] Super 8

81 LA 149, Grambling, S [gas] Chevron/Church's/dsl, Exxon [other] to Grambling St U

78 LA 563, Industry, S [gas] Texaco/dsl

77 LA 507, Simsboro

69 LA 151, Arcadia, N [gas] Chevron/dsl, Mobil/Burger King/dsl [food] La Fogata Mexican, S [gas] Exxon/dsl, Gulf/dsl, Shell/Church's/dsl [food] El Jarrito Mexican, McDonald's, Sonic, Subway [lodging] Days Inn [other] [H], $General, Brookshire Foods, Bumper Parts, Factory Stores/famous brands, Fred's, tires/repair

67 LA 9, Arcadia, N [other] to Lake Claiborne SP, S [gas] Shell/dsl/repair

61 LA 154, Gibsland, N [other] to Lake Claibourne SP

55 US 80, Ada, Taylor

52 LA 532, to US 80, Dubberly, N [gas] Exxon/dsl, Texaco/CJ's Diner/dsl

MINDEN

49 LA 531, Minden, N [gas] Loves/Arby's/dsl/scales/24hr, Murphy USA (3mi), Quick Draw TrkStp/Shell/dsl/rest./24hr, QuickDraw/Subway/dsl [food] KFC (3mi), Pizza Hut (3mi), Taco Bell (3mi) [other] Walmart (3mi), S [other] truck/tire repair

47 US 371 S, LA 159 N, Minden, N [gas] Chevron/dsl, Exxon/dsl, Valero/dsl [food] Beanie&Bubba's Grill [lodging] Best Western, Exacta Inn/rest., Holiday Inn Express, Southern Inn [other] [H], Ford, S [other] camping, to Lake Bistineau SP

44 US 371 N, Cotton Valley, N [gas] Exxon/Huddle House/dsl [food] Crawfish Hole #2, Nicky's Cantina, Sonic [lodging] Minden Motel (2mi) [other] Cinnamon Creek RV/camping, Family$, Lakeside RV Camping

38 Goodwill Rd, S [gas] Gulf/Rainbow Diner/dsl/24hr [other] Ammo Plant, truck/trailer repair

33 LA 157, Fillmore, S [gas] Exxon, Pilot/Arby's/dsl/scales/24hr [food] Pizza Hut, Waffle House [other] $General, Family$, Fred's, Lake Bistineau SP, USPO

26 I-220, Shreveport, 1 mi N [gas] RaceWay/dsl [lodging] Comfort Suites, Holiday Inn, Springhill Suites [other] Casino

23 Industrial Dr, N [gas] Exxon/dsl, Shell/Circle K, Valero/dsl [food] McDonald's, Popeye's, Sue's Country Kitchen, Taco Bell, Wendy's [lodging] Ramada Inn [other] O'Reilly Parts, RV Repair, st police, S [gas] Mobil/dsl [lodging] EconoLodge [other] Peterbilt, Southern RV Ctr

22 Airline Dr, N [gas] Citgo/dsl, Mobil/McDonald's/dsl, Shell/Circle K, Valero/dsl [food] Applebee's, Arby's, Burger King, Chili's, China Flag, DQ, Five Guys, Gatti's Pizza, IHOP, Johnny's Pizza, Logan's Roadhouse, Notini's Italian, Popeye's, Red Lobster, Shogun Steaks, Sonic, Starbucks, Subway, Taco Bell, TX Street Steaks, Waffle House [lodging] Country Hearth Inn, Crossland Suites, Rodeway Inn, Super 8 [other] [H], Albertsons, BigLots, Books-A-Million, CVS Drug, Dillard's, Firestone/auto, JC Penney, Meineke, Michael's, Office Depot, PepBoys, Tuesday Morning, Verizon, Walgreens,

SHREVEPORT

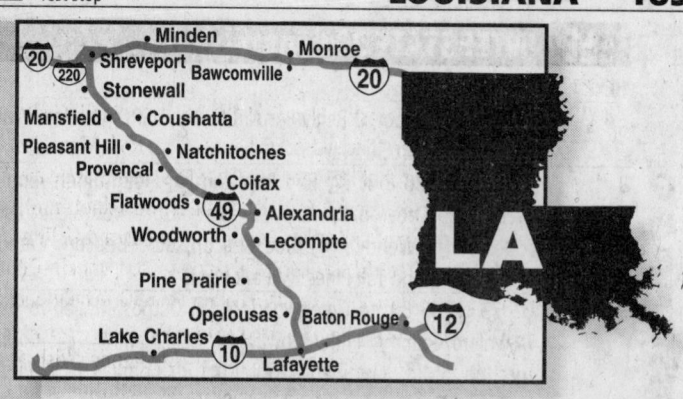

22 Continued
S [gas] Exxon/dsl, Gulf/dsl [food] Beard's Catfish/seafood, Capt John's, Church's, Griff's Burgers, Outback Steaks [lodging] Microtel, Quality Inn, Red Carpet Inn [other] AutoZone, Fred's, Super1 Foods, to Barksdale AFB

21 LA 72, to US 71 S, Old Minden Rd, N [gas] Shell/Circle K/dsl, Valero [food] DAQ's Grill, Denny's, Johnny's Pizza, McDonald's, Pancho's Mexican, Podnah's BBQ, Posado's Mexican, Ralph&Kacoo's, Subway, TX Roadhouse, Whataburger [lodging] Best Value Inn, Hampton Inn, Hilton Garden, Homewood Suites, La Quinta, MainStay Suites, TownePlace Suites [other] $General, Bayou RV Ctr, O'Reilly Parts, USPO, VW, S [gas] RaceWay [food] Waffle House, Wendy's [lodging] Days Inn, Motel 6, Woodspring Suites

20c to US 71 S, to Barksdale Blvd

20b LA 3, Benton Rd, same as 21

20a Hamilton Rd, Isle of Capri Blvd, N [gas] Circle K [lodging] Quality Inn, Wingate Inn, S [gas] Exxon [lodging] Bossier Inn, Travelodge [other] casino

19b Traffic St, Shreveport, N [lodging] Courtyard [other] Bass Pro Shop, casino, Chevrolet, S [other] casino, downtown

19a US 71 N, LA 1 N, Spring St, Shreveport, N [lodging] Chateau Suites, Hilton, Shreveport Hotel

18b-d Fairfield Ave (from wb), S [other] [H], downtown Shreveport

18a Line Ave, Common St (from eb), S [other] [H], downtown

17b I-49 S, to Alexandria

17a Lakeshore Dr, Linwood Ave

16b US 79/80, Greenwood Rd, N [other] [H], S [gas] Citgo/dsl [food] El Chico [lodging] Travelodge

16a US 171, Hearne Ave, N [gas] Shell/dsl [food] Subway [other] [H], vet, S [gas] Raceway/dsl [food] KFC, Wendy's [lodging] Cajun Inn

14 Jewella Ave, Shreveport, N [gas] Clark/dsl, Phillips 66/dsl, Valero [food] Burger King, Church's, McDonald's, Popeye's, Sonic, Subway, Whataburger [other] AutoZone, County Mkt Foods, Family$, O'Reilly Parts, Rite Aid, Super 1 Foods, Walgreens

13 Monkhouse Dr, Shreveport, N [food] Bro's Cafe [lodging] Best Western, Days Inn, Residence Inn, Super 8, Value Inn, S [gas] Citgo/dsl, Exxon/Subway/dsl, Valero/dsl [food] Waffle House [lodging] Baymont Inn, Hampton Inn, Holiday Inn Express, Merryton Inn, Moonrider Inn, Motel 6, Quality Inn, Regency Inn [other] to [airport]

11 I-220 E, LA 3132 E, to I-49 S

10 Pines Rd, N [gas] Chevron/dsl [food] DQ, Johnny's Pizza, Pizza Hut, Popeye's, Sam's Eatery, Subway [other] Meineke, S [gas] Circle K, Exxon/dsl, Murphy USA/dsl, Shell/Circle K/Quiznos/dsl [food] Burger King, CiCi's Pizza, Cracker Barrel, Domino's, Dragon Chinese, Great Wall Chinese, IHOP, KFC, McDonald's, Nicky's Mexican, Papa John's, Sonic, Taco Bell, Waffle House, Wendy's, Whataburger [lodging] Comfort Suites, Courtyard, Fairfield Inn, Hilton Garden, Holiday Inn, Homewood Suites, La Quinta, Sleep Inn, Woodspring Suites [other] $Tree, CVS Drug, Family$,

INTERSTATE 20 Cont'd

GREENWOOD

10	Continued GNC, Home Depot, O'Reilly Parts, Rite Aid, USPO, Verizon, Walgreens, Walmart/Subway
8	US 80, LA 526 E, N Red Roof Inn Freightliner, repair, tires, S Chevron/dsl, Citgo/dsl, Petro/Shell/Iron Skillet/dsl/scales/@ Wendy's Blue Beacon, Blue Beacon, Camper's RV Ctr/park, Tall Pines RV Park (1mi)
5	US 79 N, US 80, to Greenwood, N Outpost Travel Ctr/dsl, TA/Valero/Country Pride/Subway/dsl/scales/24hr/@ Country Inn, Mid Continent Motel RV park, S Pizza Hut $General, Southern Living RV Park
3	US 79 S, LA 169, Mooringsport, N Gator's RV Park (4mi), S FLYING J/Denny's/dsl/LP/scales/24hr, Loves/Arby's/dsl/scales/24hr Sonic SpeedCo
2mm	**Welcome Ctr eb, full facilities, litter barrels, petwalk, RV dump**
1mm	**weigh sta both lanes**
0mm	Louisiana/Texas state line

INTERSTATE 49

SHREVEPORT

Exit#	Services
246.5mm	Louisiana/Arkansas state line
245	LA 168, Ida, Rodessa
241	Rd 16, Mira Myrtis Rd, to Mira
237	LA 2, Plain Dealing, Hosston
234	US 71, Gilliam, Hosston
231	LA 170, Gilliam, Vivian, W H
228	LA 530, Belcher, Oil City
223	LA 169, Mooringsport
221	LA 173, Dixie, Blanchard
215	LA 1, N Market St **(I-49 begins/ends)**, E Dickey's BBQ Family$, vet
	I-49 begins/ends in Shreveport on I-20, exit 17.
206	I-20, E to Monroe, W to Dallas
205	King's Hwy, E Cane's, McDonald's, Piccadilly's, Taco Bell Dillard's, W Valero/dsl Burger King, LJ Silver, Subway Sleep Inn H
203	Hollywood Ave, Pierremont Rd, W Chevron/dsl
202	LA 511, E 70th St, E RaceWay/dsl, W Circle K SC Chicken $General, Family$
201	LA 3132, to Dallas, Texarkana
199	LA 526, Bert Kouns Loop, E Chevron/Arby's/dsl/24hr, Exxon/Circle K Burger King, KFC, Taco Bell, Wendy's Comfort Inn Home Depot, W RaceWay/dsl, Shell/dsl McDonald's, Sonic, Starbucks, Subway, Waffle House Brookshire Foods, Verizon
196	Southern Loop
196mm	Bayou Pierre
191	LA 16, LA 3276, to Stonewall, W Chevrolet/Buick
186	LA 175, to Frierson, Kingston, E Trailerhood RV Park (3mi), W Relay Sta./rest./casino/dsl/scales Heart of Haynesville RV Park (7mi)
177	LA 509, to Carmel, E Texaco/Eagles Trkstp/casino/dsl/rest., W Hwy 509 RV Park (4mi)
172	US 84, to Grand Bayou, Mansfield, W Civil War Site, New Rockdale RV Park (4mi)
169	Asseff Rd
162	US 371, LA 177, to Evelyn, Pleasant Hill

NATCHITOCHES

155	LA 174, to Ajax, Lake End, W Country Livin' RV Pk, Cowboys/dsl
148	LA 485, Powhatan, Allen
142	LA 547, Posey Rd
138	LA 6, to Natchitoches, E French Mkt/cafe/dsl, RaceWay/dsl Cane's (5mi), IHOP, Popeye's, Wendy's Best Western, Comfort Suites, Days Inn, Fairfield Inn, Holiday Inn Express H, Walmart (5mi), W Chevron/dsl/24hr, Exxon, Texaco/dsl Burger King, El Patio Nexican, Huddle House, McDonald's, Subway EconoLodge, Hampton Inn, Quality Inn Nakatosh RV Park, to Kisatchie NF
132	LA 478, rd 620
127	LA 120, to Cypress, Flora, E Exxon/dsl to Cane River Plantations
119	LA 119, to Derry, Cloutierville, E to Cane River Plantations
113	LA 490, to Chopin, E Express Mart TrkStp/dsl
107	to Lena, E USPO
103	LA 8 W, to Flatwoods, E Shell/dsl, W RV camping, to Cotile Lake
99	LA 8, LA 1200, to Boyce, Colfax, **6 mi** W Cotile Lake RV Camping
98	LA 1 (from nb), to Boyce
94	rd 23, to Rapides Sta Rd, E Rapides/dsl, W **LA Welcome Ctr, full facilities, litter barrels, petwalk, vending,** Loves/Arby's/dsl/scales/24hr Alexandria RV Park (2mi), I-49 RV Ctr

ALEXANDRIA

90	LA 498, Air Base Rd, W Chevron/dsl/CNG/24hr, Exxon/Subway/dsl, Shell/dsl, Texaco/Eddie's BBQ/dsl Burger King, Cracker Barrel, McDonald's Comfort Suites, Hampton Inn, La Quinta, Rodeway Inn, Super 8 Cabana RV Park
86	US 71, US 165, MacArthur Dr, **0-2 mi** W Chevron, Conoco/dsl, Exxon/dsl, Mobil/dsl, Shell/Circle K/dsl, Texaco/dsl, Valero/dsl Applebee's, Burger King, Cajun Landing Rest., Cane's, Chick-fil-A, Church's, CiCi's Pizza, Dominos, DQ, Eddie's BBQ, El Paso Mexican, El Reparo Mexican, Golden Corral, Little Caesar's, McDonald's, Outlaw's BBQ, Piccadilly, Popeye's, Schlotzsky's, Sonic, Subway, Taco Bell, Taco Bueno, TX Roadhouse Alexandria Inn, Best Value Inn, Best Western, Candlewood Suites, Comfort Inn, EconoLodge, Guesthouse Inn, Holiday Inn Express, Magnuson Inn, Motel 6, Quality Inn, Ramada Ltd, Super 8, Woodspring Suites $General, $Tree, Advance Parts, AutoZone, BigLots, Buick/GMC, Family$, Kia, Kroger/gas, NAPA, O'Reilly Parts, Petco, Rite Aid, Staples, Super 1 Foods, Tuesday Morning
85b	Monroe St, Medical Ctr Dr (from nb), E H
85a	LA 1, 10th St, MLK Dr, downtown
84	US 167 N, LA 28, LA 1, Pineville Expswy (no EZ nb return)
83	Broadway Ave, E Conoco, Valero $General, **1 mi** W Murphy USA/dsl Checker's, Little Caesar's, Sonic, Wendy's $Tree, AutoZone, Harley-Davidson, Walmart
81	US 71 N, LA 3250, Sugarhouse Rd, MacArthur Dr (from sb), W same as 80 and 83
80	US 71 S, US 167, MacArthur Dr, Alexandria, **0-3 mi** W Chevron/dsl, Exxon/dsl, Shell Buffalo Wild Wings, Burger King, Capt D's, Carino's Italian, Chili's, Copeland's Rest., IHOP, KFC, Logan's Roadhouse, McDonald's, Outback Steaks, Pizza Hut, Popeye's, Sonic, Subway, Taco Bell Courtyard $General, Albertsons, Best Buy, Dillard's, Family$, Ford/Lincoln, Hyundai, JC Penney, Marshall's, Mazda, Michael's, Old Navy, Petsmart, Sam's Club/gas, U-Haul
73	LA 3265, rd 22, to Woodworth, W Chevron/dsl/24hr LA Conf Ctr, RV camping, to Indian Creek RA

INTERSTATE 49 Cont'd

Exit#	Services
66	LA 112, to Lecompte, E Chevron/dsl/24hr Burger King, W Exxon/dsl museum (10mi)
61	US 167, to Meeker, E to Loyd Hall Plantation (3mi), Turkey Creek
56	LA 181, Cheneyville
53	LA 115, to Bunkie, E Sammy's/Chevron/dsl/casino/24hr Howard Johnson
46	LA 106, to St Landry, W to Chicot SP
40	LA 29, to Ville Platte, E Pilot/PJ Fresh/Subway/dsl/scales/24hr
35mm	E rec area both lanes, full facilities, litter barrels, petwalk, , RV dump, vending
27	LA 10, to Lebeau
25	LA 103, to Washington, Port Barre, W Citgo, Mobil Family$
23	US 167 N, LA 744, to Ville Platte, E Chevron/Subway/Stuckey's/dsl/scales/casino, Valero/dsl/casino, W Exxon/dsl/casino visitors ctr
19b a	US 190, to Opelousas, E Evangeline Downs Racetrack, W Chevron/dsl, Exxon/dsl, RaceTrac/dsl, Valero H, CVS Drug, Lowe's, USPO
18	LA 31, to Cresswell Lane, E Murphy USA/dsl Casa Ole's, Little Caesar's, Sombreros, Waffle House Comfort Inn, Holiday Inn $Tree, Chrysler/Dodge/Jeep, Ford/Lincoln, URGENT CARE, Verizon, Walmart/Subway, W Chevron/dsl, Shell, Valero/dsl Burger King, Cane's, Cresswell Lane, Domino's, Gatti's Pizza, Hacienda Mexican, McDonald's, Peking Buffet, Pizza Hut, Subway, Taco Bell, Wendy's Days Inn, Super 8 AT&T, Buick/GMC, Danny's Tires, Family$, Nissan, Piggly Wiggly, repair, Save-A-Lot, Walgreens
17	Judson Walsh Dr, E Texaco/dsl, Valero/dsl
15	LA 3233, Harry Guilbeau Rd, W Regency Inn H, Courvelle RV Ctr, Toyota
11	LA 93, to Grand Coteau, Sunset, E Chevron, Citgo/rest./dsl/24hr, Exxon/Popeye's/dsl, Valero/dsl Beau Chere Rest., McDonald's Primeaux RV Ctr, vet, W Subway $General, Family$, Janise's Foods
7	LA 182, W Primeaux RV Ctr
4	LA 726, Carencro, E Popeye's, Rotolo's Pizza, Taco Bell GNC, Super 1 Foods/gas, URGENT CARE, W Chevron/dsl, Texaco/dsl Burger King, King Wok, McDonald's Economy Inn $General, Champagne's Mkt, Family$, Fred's, USPO
2	LA 98, Gloria Switch Rd, E Chevron/deli/dsl Chili's, IHOP, Prejean's Rest., Wendy's Lowe's, W Shell/Church's/dsl Domino's, Great Wall Buffet, Picante Mexican, Subway
1c	Pont Des Mouton Rd, E Exxon/dsl/LP, Texaco/dsl, Valero/dsl Buffalo Wild Wings, Burger King Motel 6, Plantation Inn CVS, Walgreens, W Firestone/auto, Ford
0b a	I-10, W to Lake Charles, E to Baton Rouge, **US 167 S** Chevron/dsl, Murphy USA/dsl, RaceTrac/dsl, Shell, Shell/dsl, Valero Checker's, McDonald's, Pizza Hut, Popeye's, Subway, Taco Bell, Waffle House, Wendy's Baymont Inn, Best Value Inn, Best Western, Comfort Inn, EconoLodge, Fairfield Inn, Holiday Inn, Howard Johnson, La Quinta, Ramada, Super 8, Travel Host Inn H, $Tree, Home Depot, repair, Super 1 Foods/gas, transmissions, Walmart/Subway

I-49 begins/ends on I-10, exit 103.

OPELOUSAS

CARENCRO

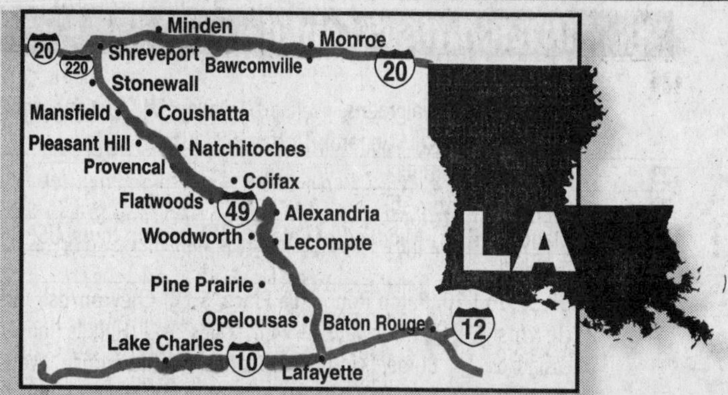

INTERSTATE 55

Exit#	Services
66mm	Louisiana/Mississippi state line
65mm	**Welcome Ctr sb, full facilities, litter barrels, petwalk, , , tourist info**
64mm	**weigh sta nb**
61	LA 38, Kentwood, E Chevron/dsl/24hr, Texaco Jam Chicken, Popeye's, Sonic $General, AutoZone, Family$, Fred's, IGA Foods, Super$, W Kangaroo/dsl, Kangaroo/dsl (2)
58.5mm	**weigh sta sb**
57	LA 440, Tangipahoa, E to Camp Moore Confederate Site
53	LA 10, to Greensburg, Fluker, W H
50	LA 1048, Roseland, E Chevron/dsl Subway (1mi)
46	LA 16, Amite, E Exxon/dsl, Murphy USA/dsl, RaceTrac/dsl Burger King, Master Chef, McDonald's, Mike's Catfish, Panda Garden, Popeye's, Smoothie King, Sonic, Subway, Taco Bell, Waffle House, Wendy's, Yamato Japanese Comfort Inn H, $Tree, AutoZone, Fred's, O'Reilly Parts, to Bogue Chitto SP, Verizon, Walgreens, Walmart/Subway, Winn-Dixie, W Colonial Inn, Holiday Inn Express Buick/Chevrolet/GMC
40	LA 40, Independence, E Best Stop H, W Indian Cr Camping (2mi)
36	LA 442, Tickfaw, E Chevron/dsl/24hr to Global Wildlife Ctr (15mi), W Exxon/dsl
32	LA 3234, Wardline Rd, E Chevron, Kangaroo/dsl, Texaco Burger King, McDonald's, Popeye's, Sarita Grill, Sonic, Subway, Taco Bell, Wendy's Lexington Inn Tony's Tire
31	US 190, Hammond, E Chevron/dsl/scales/24hr, Exxon/dsl, Murphy USA/dsl, RaceTrac/dsl Applebee's, Baskin-Robbins, Buffalo Wild Wings, Burger King, Cane's, Chili's, CiCi's Pizza, Cracker Barrel, Firehouse Subs, Hi-Ho 1 BBQ, McDonald's, Pizza Hut, Sonic, Starbucks, Taco Bell, Voodoo BBQ, Waffle House, Wendy's Comfort Inn, Hampton Inn, Super 8, Western Inn, Woodspring Suites H, $General, $Tree, Advance Parts, AT&T, AutoZone, Chrysler/Dodge/Jeep, CVS Drug, Family$, Hobby Lobby, LeBlanc's Foods Lowe's, Lowe's, Office Depot, Ross, Sav-A-Lot Foods, Tuesday Morning, URGENT CARE, Walgreens, Walmart/Subway, Winn-Dixie
29b a	I-12, W to Baton Rouge, E to Slidell
28	US 51 N, Hammond, E Exxon, RaceTrac/dsl, Valero/dsl Don's Seafood/Steaks, Great Wall Chinese Best Value Inn, Red Roof Inn H, Buick/GMC, dsl repair, Mitchell RV Ctr, Toyota
26	LA 22, to Springfield, Ponchatoula, E Chevron/dsl, Exxon/dsl, Murphy Express/dsl, RaceTrac/dsl/e85, Shell/dsl Burger King, China King, Hi-Ho BBQ, McDonald's/playplace, Papa John's, Pizza Hut, Popeye's, Smoothie King, Sonic, Subway, Taco Bell, Waffle House, Wendy's Microtel AutoZone, Bohning's Foods, CVS Drug, Family$, Ford, O'Reilly Parts,

AMITE

HAMMOND

LA

INTERSTATE 55 Cont'd

26 Continued
Rouse's Mkt, Walgreens, Walmart/Subway, **W** Kangaroo/Domino's/dsl $General, Tickfaw SP (13mi)

23 US 51, Ponchatoula

22 frontage rd (from sb)

15 Manchac, **E** Middendorf Café , swamp tours, USPO

7 Ruddock

1 US 51, to I-10, Baton Rouge, La Place, **S** Chevron/dsl, Circle K/dsl, Pilot/Subway/dsl/24hr/scales, Shell/Huddle House/casino/dsl Burger King, McDonald's, Waffle House, Wendy's Best Western, Days Inn, Hampton Inn, Holiday Inn Express, Quality Inn, Suburban Lodge

I-55 begins/ends on I-10, exit 209.

INTERSTATE 59

Exit# Services

11 Louisiana/Mississippi state line, Pearl River Turnaround, to Bogue Chitto NWR

5b Honey Island Swamp

5a LA 3081, Pearl River, **E** Riverside TrvlCtr/dsl

3 US 11 S, LA 1090, Pearl River, **0-1 mi W** Chevron/dsl, Interstate Fuels/dsl, Shell/Subway/dsl, Texaco McDonald's, Sonic, Waffle House Microtel AutoZone, Family$, Jubilee Foods/drug, NAPA

1.5mm **Welcome Ctr sb, full facilities, info, litter barrels, petwalk, , , RV dump**

1c b I-10, E to Bay St Louis, W to New Orleans

1a I-12 W, to Hammond. **I-59 begins/ends on I-10/I-12.**

INTERSTATE 210 (Lake Charles)

Exit# Services

12 **I-210 begins/ends on I-10, exit 34.**

11 US 90, Broad St, Fruge St, **E** Exxon/dsl, Shell/dsl, **W** Best Value Inn

10 Legion St, **E** Shell/dsl Luke's RV Ctr, **W** Kia, Nissan

8 LA 14, Gerstner Mem Dr, **N** Citgo/dsl Chili's, IHOP Hobby Lobby, **S** Murphy USA/dsl, Valero ChuckECheese, Kyoto, Logan's Roadhouse, Outback, Panda Buffet, Sonic, Taco Bell, Wendy's Quality Inn, Woodspring Suites $Tree, AT&T, Chrysler/Jeep/Dodge, GMC, Home Depot, Lowe's, Old Navy, Toyota, VW, Walmart

7b Enterprise Blvd, LA Blvd, **N** Conoco/dsl, Exxon/dsl Sonic, Subway Best Western, Super 8 $General, AutoZone, O'Reilly Parts, **S** Shell/dsl Chevrolet/Cadillac, Ford, Honda, Hyundai

6a LA 385, Ryan St, **N** Burger King, McDonald's, Popeye's, Tony's Pizza Comfort Inn Aamco, **S** Church's, CiCi's, Gatti's Pizza, Jason's Deli $General, Firestone/auto, Goodyear/auto, Tuesday Morning

5 Lake St, **N** McAlister's Deli, Wendy's Best Value Inn , AT&T, Best Buy, Dick's, Dillard's, Kohl's, Petco, Verizon

4 LA 1138, Nelson Rd, **N** Buffalo Wild Wings, Jo Jo's Chinese, Mongolian Grill, O'Charley's, Olive Garden, Sonic, Subway Candlewood Suites, Courtyard, Hampton Inn, La Quinta, Residence Inn, Springhill Suites, Wingate Inn Marshall's, Ross, Sam's Club/gas, Target, **S** Murphy USA/dsl, Tobacco+ Chick-fil-A, Panera Bread, Starbucks, TX Roadhouse Walmart/Subway

3 Golden Nugget Blvd, Prien Lake Rd, **N** casino/hotel

1b a **I-210 begins/ends on I-10, exit 25.**

SHREVEPORT

LA

INTERSTATE 220 (Shreveport)

Exit# Services

I-220 begins/ends on I-20, exit 26.

17b I-20, W to Shreveport, E to Monroe

17a US 79, US 80, **N** RaceWay/dsl, Shell/Circle K Taco Bell, Waffle House Comfort Suites, Holiday Inn, SpringHill Suites Racetrack/casino, **S** Chevron/Huddle House/dsl Silver Star Smokehouse

15 Shed Rd

13 Swan Lake Rd

12 LA 3105, Airline Dr, **N** Baskin-Robbins, Chick-fil-A, Dickey's BBQ, Firehouse Subs, Izzo's Burrito, McAlister's Deli, Newk's Eatery, Olive Garden, Papa Murphy's, Santa Fe Steaks, Starbucks, Subway, TaMolly's , AT&T, Belk, Best Buy, GNC, Old Navy, Petsmart, Ross, Sam's Club/gas, Target, Verizon, Walgreens, **S** Exxon/dsl, Murphy USA/dsl, Valero/dsl Applebee's, Burger King, Cane's, Capt D's, China Flag, McDonald's, Nicky's Rest., Panda Express, Ruby Tuesday, Ryan's, Smashburger, Sonic, Taco Bell, Trejo's Mexican, Wendy's Hampton Inn $Tree, Gateway Tire, Hobby Lobby, Home Depot, Kroger/dsl, Lowe's, vet, Walmart

11 LA 3, Bossier City, **N** RaceWay/dsl , Buick/GMC, Ford, Harley-Davidson, Lexus, RV Park, Subaru, Suzuki, Toyota **S** Valero/dsl Chrysler/Dodge/Jeep, Nissan

7b a US 71, LA 1, Shreveport, **N** Exxon/dsl, Shell/dsl Checkers, Domino's, Johnny's Pizza, Papa John's, Pizza Hut, Sonic, Subway, Waffle House, Whataburger/24hr Brookshire Foods/gas, Family$, Walgreens, **S** RaceWay/dsl, Shell, Valero/dsl Burger King, Carl's Jr, Church's, KFC, McDonald's, Podnah's BBQ, Popeye's, Taco Bell, Wendy's Royal Inn Advance Parts, AutoZone, County Mkt Foods, CVS Drug, Family$, O'Reilly Parts, repair/transmissions, Rite Aid, U-Haul

6 I-49 N

5 LA 173, Blanchard Rd, **N** Citgo/dsl

2 Lakeshore Dr

1a Jefferson Paige Rd, **S** Days Inn, Hampton Inn, Merryton Inn, Ramada Inn, Residence Inn, Super 8, Value Inn

1b c I-20, E to Shreveport, W to Dallas. **I-220 begins/ends on I-20, exit 11.**

INTERSTATE 610 (New Orleans)

Exit# Services

I-610 begins/ends on I-10.

4 Franklin Ave (from eb)

3 Elysian fields, **S** B Express, Shell Burger King, McDonald's, Waffle House , Lowe's

2b US 90, N Broad St, New Orleans St (from wb)

2c Paris Ave (from wb, no return), **S** Jimmy's, Shell/24hr Popeye's

2a St Bernard Ave (from eb), to LSU School of Dentistry, auto race track

1a Canal Blvd

1b I-10, to New Orleans

I-610 begins/ends on I-10.

MAINE

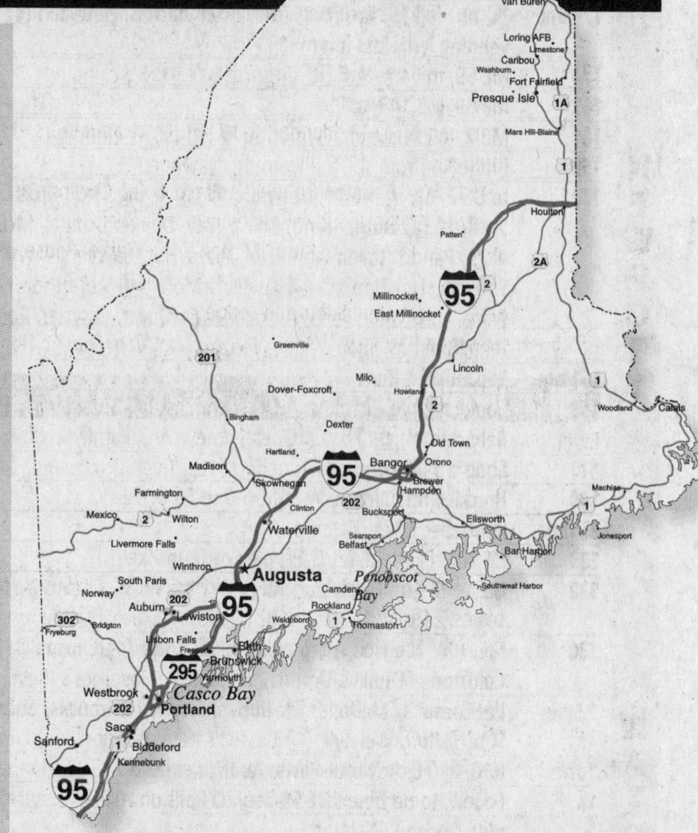

INTERSTATE 95

Exit#	Services
305mm	US/Canada border, Maine state line, US Customs. **I-95 begins/ends.**
305	US 2, to Houlton, **E** DFA Duty Free Shop, Houlton Airport
303mm	Meduxnekeag River
302	US 1, Houlton, **E** Irving/Circle K/dsl/24hr Amato's, Burger King, McDonald's, Pizza Hut, Tang's Chinese IGA Foods, Mardens, O'Reilly Parts/VIP Service, Rite Aid, **W** **both lanes, full facilities, litter barrels, petwalk,** , Citgo/Subway/dsl, Irving/Circle K/dsl/scales/@, Shell/Dunkin Donuts/dsl Tim Hortons/Coldstone Ivey's Motel, Shiretown Motel Arrowstook SP, Family$, Ford, Shop'n Save, Toyota, Walmart
301mm	B Stream
291	US 2, to Smyrna, **E** Brookside Motel/rest.
286	Oakfield Rd, to ME 11, Eagle Lake, Ashland, **W** Irving/Circle K/dsl, Valero/dsl A Place To Eat USPO
277mm	Mattawamkeag River, W Branch
276	ME 159, Island Falls, **E** Dysarts Fuel, Porter's/rest. Bishop's Mkt, USPO, **W** RV camping, to Baxter SP (N entrance)
264	to ME 11, Sherman, **E** Shell/dsl/LP/rest., **W** Irving/Circle K/dsl Katahdin Valley Motel to Baxter SP (N entrance)
259	Benedicta (from nb, no re-entry)
252mm	scenic view Mt Katahdin, nb
247mm	Salmon Stream
244	ME 157, to Medway, E Millinocket, **W** Irving/Circle K/dsl The Bridge Rest. Gateway Inn , city park, Pine Grove Camping (4mi), to Baxter SP (S entrance), USPO, vet
244mm	Penobscot River
243mm	**both lanes, full facilities, litter barrels, petwalk,**
227	to US 2, ME 6, Lincoln, **4 mi E** , RV camping,
219mm	Piscataquis River
217	ME 6, Howland, **E** Irving/95 Diner/dsl 95er Towing/repair, camping, LP
201mm	Birch Stream
199	ME 16 (no nb re-entry), to LaGrange
197	ME 43, to Old Town, **E** /dsl
196mm	Pushaw Stream
193	Stillwater Ave, to Old Town, **E** Citgo/dsl, Gulf/Subway/dsl, Irving/Circle K/dsl Burger King, China Garden, Dunkin Donuts, Governor's Rest., McDonald's, Tim Horton, Wendy's Black Bear Inn $Tree, IGA Foods, O'Reilly Parts/VIP Service
191	Kelly Rd, to Orono, **2-3 mi E** camping, food, gas, lodging
187	Hogan Rd, Bangor Mall Blvd, to Bangor, **E** Citgo Denny's Courtyard, Hampton Inn, Hilton Garden, TownePlace Suites Audi/VW, Buick/GMC, Cadillac/Chevrolet, Chrysler/Dodge/Jeep, Firestone/auto, Ford, Honda, Hyundai, Mazda, Mercedes, Nissan, Sam's Club/gas, Subaru, Volvo, **W** Citgo/dsl, Irving/Circle K/dsl Applebee's, Arby's, Buffalo Wild Wings, Bugaboo Creek Café, Burger King, Chicago Grill, Chili's, Dunkin Donuts, Five Guys, Green Tea Japanese, Happy China, KFC, Kobe Japanese, Las Palapas, Longhorn Steaks, McDonald's, Miguel's Mexican, Olive Garden, Papa Johns, Pizza Hut, Quiznos, Ruby Tuesday, Starbucks, Subway, TX Roadhouse, Wendy's Bangor Motel, Comfort Inn, Country Inn, Quality Inn $Tree, Advance Parts, AT&T, Best Buy, BigLots, BooksAMillion,
187	Continued Dick's, Goodyear/auto, Hannaford Foods, Harley-Davidson, Hobby Lobby, Home Depot, JC Penney, Jo-Ann Fabrics, Kia, Kohl's, LL Bean, Lowe's, Old Navy, O'Reilly Parts/VIP Service, PetCo, Petsmart, Staples, Target, Town Fair Tire, URGENT CARE, Verizon, Walmart
186	Stillwater Ave, same as 187
185	ME 15, to Broadway, Bangor, **E** Irving/Circle K/dsl Tri-City Pizza , **W** Citgo Amato's, BoBo Chinese, China Light, Coldstone/Tim Hortons, Governor's Rest., KFC, McDonald's, Moe's BBQ, Pizza Hut, Subway, Taco Bell CarQuest, Family$, Hannaford Foods, Rite Aid, TJ Maxx, Walgreens
184	ME 222, Union St, to Ohio St, Bangor, **E** Citgo, Irving Rite Aid, **W** Citgo, Gulf, Shell/dsl Burger King, Capt Nick's Rest., Dunkin Donuts, McDonald's, Nicky's Rest., Wendy's Sheraton $Tree, Hannaford Foods, Marshall's, Midas, RV Camping, to
183	US 2, ME 2, Hammond St, Bangor, **E** Citgo, Shell Angelo's Pizza, Papa Gambino's Pizza, Whoopie Pie Cafe Corner Store, Fairmont Mkt, NAPA, TrueValue, **W**
182b	US 2, ME 100 W, **W** Irving/Subway/dsl, Shell/dsl Dunkin Donuts, Ground Round, Tim Hortons Days Inn, EconoLodge, Fairfield Inn, Holiday Inn, Howard Johnson, Motel 6, Ramada Inn, Super 8, Travelodge O'Reilly Parts/VIP Service, RV camping, Tire Whse
182a	I-395, to US 2, US 1A, Bangor, downtown
180	Cold Brook Rd, to Hampden, **E** Citgo Angler's Rest. (1mi), **W** Citgo/dsl/24hr/@, Dysarts Fleet Fuel/dsl Best Western dsl repair, Mack, Volvo
178mm	**sb, full facilities, info, litter barrels, petwalk,** , **vending, wireless internet**
177mm	Soudabscook Stream

= gas = food = lodging = other = rest stop

INTERSTATE 95 Cont'd

Exit#	Services
176mm	**nb, full facilities, info, litter barrels, petwalk, , vending, wireless internet**
174	ME 69, to Carmel, **E** Citgo/dsl, **W** RV camping
167	ME 69, ME 143, to Etna
161	ME 7, to E Newport, Plymouth, **W** LP, RV camping
159	Ridge Rd (from sb), to Plymouth, Newport
157	**NEWPORT** — to US 2, ME 7, ME 11, Newport, **W** Irving/Circle K/dsl/24hr, Shell/dsl Burger King, China Way, Dunkin Donuts, McDonald's, Pando Italian American, Pizza Hut, Sawyers Dairy Bar, Subway, Tim Hortons Lovley's Motel Aubuchon Hardware, Auto Value Parts, AutoZone, CarQuest, Chrysler/Dodge/Jeep, Rite Aid, Shop'n Save, Verizon, Walmart/Dunkin Donuts
151mm	Sebasticook River
150	Somerset Ave, Pittsfield, **E** Irving/dsl Subway Pittsfield Motel H, CarQuest, Chevrolet, Family$, Rite Aid, Shop'n Save Foods
138	Hinckley Rd, Clinton, **W** 95 One-Stop/dsl
134mm	Kennebec River
133	US 201, Fairfield, **E** Purple Cow Pancakes
132	ME 139, Fairfield, **W** Irving/Circle K/Subway/dsl/scales/24hr
130	**WATERVILLE** — ME 104, Main St, Waterville, **E** Citgo Cappza's Pizza, Coldstone, Dunkin Donuts, Friendly's, Governor's Rest., Little Caesar's, McDonald's, Ruby Tuesday, Starbucks, Subway, Tim Horton, Wendy's Best Western, Comfort Inn, Fireside Inn H, Advance Parts, Audi/Mazda/VW, GNC, Hannaford Foods, Home Depot, JC Penney, O'Reilly Parts/VIP Service, Staples, Verizon, Walmart
129mm	Messalonskee Stream
127	ME 11, ME 137, Waterville, Oakland, **E** Irving/dsl/24hr, Xpress/dsl Applebee's, Burger King, DQ, Dunkin Donuts, KFC/Taco Bell, McDonald's, Pad Thai, Papa John's, Pizza Hut, Sam's Italian, Subway, Super Buffet, Weathervane Seafood Budget Host, EconoLodge, Hampton Inn H, AutoZone, Buick/Chevrolet, Chrysler/Dodge/Jeep, CVS Drug, Hannaford Foods, Jo-Ann Fabrics, Marden's, Shaw's Foods/Osco Drug, Tire Whse, TJ Maxx, Toyota, Verizon, **W** Shell/dsl Aubuchon Hardware, CarQuest, Ford/Lincoln
120	Lyons Rd, Sidney
117mm	**weigh sta both lanes**
113	ME 3, Augusta, Belfast
112	**AUGUSTA** — ME 27, ME 8, ME 11, Augusta, **E** Citgo Denny's, DQ, Dunkin Donuts, Longhorn Steaks, Olive Garden, Panera Bread, Red Robin, Rooster's, Ruby Tuesday, Sam's Italian, Subway Best Western Barnes&Noble, Dick's, GNC, Home Depot, Kohl's, Michaels, Old Navy, Sam's Club, TownFair Tire, Verizon, Walmart, **W** Irving/Circle K/dsl/24hr 99 Rest., Great Wall Chinese, KFC/Taco Bell, Wendy's Comfort Inn, Fairfield Inn Advance Parts
109	US 202, ME 11, ME 17, ME 100, Augusta, **E** Citgo/Dunkin Donuts/dsl, Irving/Circle K/dsl Amato's Rest., Applebee's, Arby's, Burger King, China King, Damon's Italian, Domino's, DQ, Friendly's, KFC, Little Caesar's, McDonald's, Pizza Hut, Subway, Tim Horton, Wendy's Senator Inn $Tree, Best Buy, BigLots, Family$, Lowe's, O'Reilly Parts/VIP Service, Petsmart, Shaw's Foods/Osco Drug, Staples, Target, U-Haul, USPO, vet, Walgreens, **W** Valero Margarita's Mexican, TX Roadhouse Hampton Inn, Motel 6, Quality Inn, Super 8 CarQuest, Chrysler/Dodge, Hannaford Foods, Honda, Hyundai, Jeep, Kia, Nissan, PetCo, Subaru, TJ Maxx, Toyota
103	to I-295 S (from sb), ME 9, ME 126, to Gardiner, **service plaza,** Citgo Burger King, Hersheys, Quiznos, Starbucks ZMkt
102	to I-295 S (from nb), rd 9, rd 106, **service plaza,** Citgo Burger King, Hersheys, Quiznos, Starbucks ZMkt
100mm	**toll plaza**
86	to ME 9, Sabattus
84mm	Sabattus Creek
80	**LEWISTON** — ME 196, Lewiston, **W on ME 196** Coast Fuels, Gendron's/dsl, Mobil, Shell/dsl, Sunoco, XPress/dsl Burger King, Cathay Hut Chinese, D'Angelo, Dunkin Donuts, Governor's Rest., KFC/Taco Bell, McDonald's, Papa John's, Pepper&Spice Thai, Sam's Italian, Subway Advance Parts, Motel 6, Ramada Inn, Super 8 H, $Tree, Family$, NAPA, Rite Aid, Staples, USPO
78mm	Androscoggin River
75	US 202, rd 4, rd 100, to Auburn, **E** Irving/Circle K/dsl, Mobil/Subway/dsl Danny Boy's Rest., Dunkin Donuts, Peking Chinese Fireside Inn RV Camping, **W** H
71mm	Royal River
66mm	**toll plaza**
63	US 202, rd 115, rd 4, to ME 26, Gray, **E** Citgo, Gulf, Mobil, Sunoco China Gray, Dunkin Donuts, Goody's Pizza, McDonald's, Subway $Tree, Ace Hardware, Family$, NAPA, Shop'n Save Mkt
59mm	**service plaza both lanes,** Citgo/dsl Chicago Pizza Starbucks atm
55mm	Piscataqua River
53	to ME 26, ME100 W, N Portland, **E** Irving/Circle K/Subway/dsl Dunkin Donuts, Maddens Grill H, Hannaford Foods
52	to I-295, US 1, Freeport
48	ME 25, to Portland, **E** Citgo Applebee's, Asian Bistro, Full Belly Deli, Little Caesar's, Subway Portland Inn $Tree, BigLots, BJ's Whse/gas, Chevrolet, CVS Drug, Fiat, Jo-Ann Fabrics, Lowe's, Sullivan Tire, vet, **W** Gulf, Irving/Circle K/dsl Amato's Rest., Burger King, Chipotle, Denny's, Dunkin Donuts, Egg&I Cafe, KFC/Taco Bell, McDonald's, Panera Bread, Pizza Hut, Ruby Tuesday, Seasons Grille, Wendy's Fireside Inn, Howard Johnson, Motel 6, Super 8, Travelodge Advance Parts, AT&T, CarQuest, Chrysler/Dodge/Jeep, Ford, GNC, Harley-Davidson, Home Depot, Hyundai, Kohl's, Lexus/Toyota, Lincoln, Midas, NAPA, O'Reilly Parts/VIP Service, Shaw's Foods/Osco Drug, Sullivan Tire, Tire Whse, vet
47	to ME 25, Rand Rd
47mm	Stroudwater River
46	to ME 22, Congress St, same as 45
45	**PORTLAND** — to US 1, Maine Mall Rd, S Portland, **E** Citgo/dsl, Sunoco/dsl Bugaboo Creek Steaks, Burger King, Chili's, Chipotle Mexican, Cracker Barrel, Dunkin Donuts, Five Guys, Food Court, Friendly's, Great Wall Chinese, Hokkaido Japanese, HomeTown Buffet, IHOP, Imperial China, Jimmy the Greek Rest., Longhorn Steaks, Macaroni Grill, McDonald's, Newick's Lobster House, Olive Garden, On the Border, Panera Bread, Pizza Hut, Qdoba, Ruby Tuesday, Sebago Brewing Rest., Starbucks, Tim Horton/Coldstone, UNO Pizzaria, Weathervane Seafood, Wendy's Comfort Inn, Courtyard, Days Inn, DoubleTree, EconoLodge, Fairfield Inn, Hampton Inn, Homewood Suites $Tree, Best Buy, BonTon, BooksAMillion, Dick's, Hannaford Foods, Honda, JC Penney, Macy's, Michael's, Nissan, Old Navy, PetCo, Staples, TJ Maxx, TownFair Tire, Verizon, **W** Applebee's, Starbucks Holiday Inn Express, Marriott Target

ME

INTERSTATE 95 Cont'd

Exit#	Services
44	I-295 N (from nb), to S Portland, Scarborough, **1 mi E on ME 114** Cumberland Chia Sen Chinese, KFC/Taco Bell, Little Caesars, Red Robin, Shogun Japanese, Subway, TX Roadhouse Homewood Suites, Residence Inn, TownePlace Suites H, AT&T, Lowe's, NAPA, O'Reilly/VIP Parts/service, Sam's Club/gas, Shaw's Foods/Osco Drug, Walmart/Dunkin Donuts
42mm	Nonesuch River
42	to US 1, E Famous Dave's, Portland Pie Cabela's, Scarborough Downs Racetrack (seasonal)
36	I-195 E, to Saco, Old Orchard Beach, E Hampton Inn KOA, Paradise Park Resort RV
35mm	E Ramada Inn/Saco Hotel Conference Ctr
33mm	Saco River
32	ME 111, to Biddeford, E Irving/Circle K/Subway/dsl Amato's Sandwiches, Dunkin Donuts, Ruby Tuesday, Wendy's Best Value Inn, Holiday Inn Express H, AAA, AutoZone, O'Reilly/VIP Parts/Service, Osco Drug, Shaw's Foods, Walmart, W Cumberland/dsl Applebees, Casa Fiesta Mexican, Kobe Japanese, Longhorn Steaks, Olive Garden, Panera Bread GNC, Home Depot, Kohl's, MarketBasket Foods, Michaels, Petsmart, Staples, Target, TJ Maxx, TownFair Tire, Verizon
25mm	Kennebunk River
25	ME 35, Kennebunk Beach, E Turnpike Motel
24mm	**service plaza both lanes,** Citgo/dsl Burger King, Hersheys, Popeye's, Starbucks atm, Z Mkt
19.5mm	Merriland River
19	ME 9, ME 109, to Wells, Sanford, W to Sanford RA
7mm	Maine Tpk begins/ends, **toll booth**
7	ME 91, to US 1, The Yorks, E Gulf, Irving/Circle K/dsl, Mobil/dsl, Shell China Bistro, Norma's Rest., Ruby's Grill, Wild Willy's Burgers, York 54 Cafe Best Western, Microtel, York Corner Inn H, Ford, Hannaford Foods, NAPA, Rite Aid, TrueValue, vet, **last exit before toll rd nb**
5.5mm	**weigh sta nb**
5mm	York River
4mm	**weigh sta sb**
3mm	**Welcome Ctr nb, full facilities, info, litter barrels, petwalk,** , **vending,** wireless,
2	(2 & 3 from nb), US 1, to Kittery, **E on US 1** 7-11/dsl, Irving/Circle K/dsl/scales Burger King, DQ, McDonald's, Robert's Maine Grill, Starbucks, Subway, Sunrise Grill, Tasty Thai, Weathervane Seafood Rest. Blue Roof Motel, Days Inn, Northeaster Hotel, Ramada Inn Outlets/Famous Brands, vet
1	ME 103 (from nb, no re-entry), to Kittery
0mm	Maine/New Hampshire state line, Piscataqua River

BIDDEFORD

INTERSTATE 295

Exit#	Services
	I-295 begins/ends on I-95 exit 103.
51	ME 9, ME 126, to Gardiner, Litchfield, **toll plaza, W service plaza,** Citgo Burger King, Hersheys, Quiznos, Starbucks ZMkt
49	US 201, to Gardiner
43	ME 197, to Richmond, E Irving/Quincey's Deli/dsl Dunkin Donuts, Subway, W KOA (5mi)
37	ME 125, Bowdoinham
31b a	ME 196, to Lisbon, Topsham, E Gibbs/dsl, Irving/Circle K/Dunkin Donuts/Subway 99 Rest., Arby's, Fairground Cafe, Firehouse Subs, Little Caesars, McDonald's, Panera Bread, Romeo's Pizza, Ruby Tuesday, Starbucks, Tim Horton's, Wendy's $Tree, AT&T, Best Buy, Dick's, Hannaford Foods, Home Depot, Jo-Ann Fabrics, Meineke, Nissan, O'Reilly Parts/VIP Service, PetCo, Rite Aid, Target, Tire Whse, Town Fair Tire, Toyota, Verizon, W Xpress Stop/dsl
30mm	Androscoggin River
28	US 1, Bath, **1 mi E on US 1** Cumberland/dsl, Irving/dsl, Mobil/dsl, Shell Amato's, Dunkin Donuts, McDonald's, Subway Best Value Inn, Comfort Inn, Fairfield Inn, Knights Inn, Travelers Inn H, Chevrolet/Mazda, Chrysler/Dodge/Jeep, Ford
24	to Freeport (from nb), **services 1 mi E on US 1**
22	ME 125, to Pownal, **1 mi E on US 1** Irving/Circle K Azure Cafe, Corsican Rest., Jameson Rest., Linda Bean's ME Kitchen, McDonald's, Sam's Italian, Starbucks, Subway, Tuscan Bistro Harraseeket Inn, Hilton Garden CVS Drug, LL Bean, outlets/famous brands, USPO, W to Bradbury Mtn SP
20	Desert Rd, Freeport, E Irving/Circle K Antonia's Pizza, Buck's BBQ, Dunkin Donuts, Thai Garden Rest. Comfort Suites, Econolodge, Hampton Inn, Holiday Inn Express, Super 8 RV camping, Shaw's Foods
17	US 1, Yarmouth, E **both lanes, full facilities, info** Day's Takeout, Muddy Rudder Rest. Best Western Delorme Mapping, Ford, W Citgo/dsl, Cumberland/dsl McDonald's, Pat's Pizza Ace Hardware, Hannaford Foods, O'Reilly Parts/VIP Service, Tire Whse
15	US 1, to Cumberland, Yarmouth, W Irving/dsl, Mobil 233 Grill, Chopstick Asian, Romeo's Pizza, Subway AT&T, Rite Aid
11	to I-95, ME Tpk (from sb)
10	US 1, to Falmouth, E Citgo/dsl, Irving/dsl Dunkin Donuts, Foreside Rest., House of Pizza, Leavitt & Sons Deli, McDonald's, Orchid Thai, Ricetta's Pizza, Starbucks, Subway, Wendy's Falmouth Inn Ace Hardware, Audi/VW, Goodyear/auto, Mazda, Rite Aid, Shaw's Foods, Staples, vet, Walmart
9mm	Presumpscot River
9	US 1 S, ME 26, to Baxter Blvd
8	ME 26 S, Washington Ave, E U-Haul
7	US 1A, Franklin St, E Miss Portland Diner AAA Car Care, AT&T, CarQuest, NAPA, Trader Joe's, Verizon, Walgreens, Whole Foods Mkt
6b a	US 1, Forest Ave, E Citgo H, Firestone/auto, USPO, W Mobil/dsl Burger King, Leonardo's Pizza, Pizza Hut, Stavro's Pizza, Subway CVS Drug, Hannaford Foods, U of SME, Walgreens
5b a	ME 22, Congress St, E Amato's Rest., D'Angelos, Denny's, Dunkin Donuts, Lang's Chinese, McDonald's, Subway La Quinta H, Sullivan Tire, W Gulf/Dunkin Donuts, Mobil/dsl Anania's Italian Clarion
3mm	Fore River
4	US 1 S, to Main St, to S Portland, **services E on US 1**
3	ME 9, to Westbrook St, no sb return, W Citgo/dsl, Irving/Circle K/dsl Buffalo Wild Wings, El Rodeo Mexican, Olive Garden, Seadog Brew Co., Subway, Wild Willy's Burger Chevrolet, Home Depot, Marshalls
2	to US 1 S, S Portland, E 7-11, Irving/Circle K/dsl, Mobil Dunkin Donuts Howard Johnson, Super 8, Best Western, Knights Inn, **services E on US 1**
1	to I-95, to US 1, **multiple services E on US 1**, same as 2
	I-295 begins/ends on I-95, exit 44.

FREEPORT

PORTLAND

ME

MARYLAND

INTERSTATE 68

Exit#	Services
82c	I-70 W, to Breezewood. **I-68 begins/ends on I-70, exit 1.**
82b	I-70 E, US 40 E, to Hagerstown
82a	US 522, Hancock, S [gas] Mobil/dsl, Sheetz/dsl [food] Hardee's, Park'n Dine, Pizza Hut, Subway [lodging] Hancock Motel, Super 8 [other] $General, Chevrolet, Happy Hills Camping, NAPA, Save-A-Lot Foods
77	US 40, MD 144, Woodmont Rd, S [other] RV camping
75mm	**runaway truck ramp eb**
74mm	**Sideling Hill [RS]/exhibit both lanes, full [handicap] facilities, vending,** 1269 ft (seasonal)
74	US 40, Mountain Rd (no return from eb)
73mm	Sideling Hill Creek
72	US 40, High Germany Rd, Swain Rd, S [gas] Citgo/dsl [food] Oak Barrel Cafe
68	Orleans Rd, N [gas] Exxon/dsl
67mm	Town Hill, elevation 940 ft, Town Hill
64	MV Smith Rd, S [other] scenic overlook, elevation 1040 ft, to Green Ridge SF HQ
62	US 40, 15 Mile Creek Rd, N [other] Billmeyer Wildlife Mgt Area
58.7mm	Polish Mtn, elevation 1246 ft
57mm	Town Creek
56mm	Flintstone Creek
56	MD 144, National Pike, Flintstone, S [gas] Billie's Gas&-Grub [lodging] Seven C's Lodge [other] USPO
52	MD 144, Pleasant Valley Rd (from eb), National Pike
50	Pleasant Valley Rd, N [gas] Tesla EVC [food] Lakeside Grill, Signature's Grill [lodging] Rocky Gap Lodge/golf/rest. [other] to Rocky Gap SP
47	US 220 N, MD 144, Dehaven Rd (from wb), Old National Pike, Bedford, S [gas] Loves/Arby's/dsl/scales/24hr [lodging] Sleep Inn
46	US 220 N, Dehaven Rd, Baltimore Pike, Naves Crossroads, N [gas] Sheetz/dsl [lodging] Cumberland Motel [other] $General, Advance Parts, S [gas] Loves/Arby's/dsl/scales/24hr [food] Puccini's Rest. [lodging] Sleep Inn
45	Hillcrest Dr, S [gas] Sunoco/dsl
44	US 40A, Baltimore Ave, Willow Brook Rd, to Allegany Comm Coll, N [lodging] Hampton Inn, S [other] [H], to Allegany Comm Coll
43d	Maryland Ave, N [lodging] Ramada [other] USPO, S [gas] Gulf/7-11/Subway [food] Chick-fil-A, Papa John's [other] [H], AT&T, AutoZone, Martin's Foods/gas
43c	downtown, same as 43b
43mm	Youghiogheny River
43b	MD 51, Industrial Blvd, N [food] McDonald's, Subway [lodging] Ramada [other] Family$, SaveALot Foods, S [gas] Sunoco/dsl [food] Roy Rogers, Taco Bell, Wendy's [lodging] Fairfield Inn
43a	to WV 28A, Beall St, Industrial Blvd, to Cumberland, Johnson St, N [gas] Sheetz
42	US 220 S, Greene St, Ridgedale
41	Seton Dr (from wb, no directory turn)
41mm	Haystack Mtn, elev 1240 ft
40	US 220 S, to US 40A, Vocke Rd, La Vale, N [gas] BP/dsl, Sheetz/dsl, Tesla EVC [food] Arby's, Asian Garden, Bob Evans, Burger King, Cracker Barrel, D'Atri Rest., Denny's, DQ, KFC, LJ Silver, McDonald's, New Orient, Pizza Hut, Rio Grande Mexican, Rita's Custard, Ruby Tuesday, Subway, TX Grill, Wendy's [lodging] Best Western, Comfort Inn, Holiday Inn Express, Super 8 [other] $General, Advance Parts, AT&T, AutoZone, CVS Drug, Harley-Davidson,
40	Continued Jo-Ann Fabrics, Lowe's, Mr Tire, NAPA, st police, Staples, URGENT CARE, S [food] Applebee's, Buffalo Wild Wings, Chick-fil-A, Wasabi Japanese [lodging] Motel 6 [other] $Tree, Aldi Foods, JC Penney, Kohl's, Martin's Foods/gas, Petsmart, Walmart/McDonald's
39	US 40A (from wb), same as 40
34	MD 36, to Westernport, Frostburg, N [gas] Sheetz/dsl, Valero/dsl [food] Burger King, Fox's Pizza, Mario's Italian, McDonald's, Pizza Hut, Subway [lodging] Hampton Inn, Quality Inn [other] [H], $General, Rite Aid, Save-A-Lot, Weis Mkt, S [other] to Dans Mtn SP
33	Midlothian Rd, to Frostburg, N [other] [H], S [other] to Dans Mt SP
31mm	**weigh sta eb**
30mm	Big Savage Mtn, elevation 2800 ft
29	MD 546, Finzel, N [food] Hen House Rest. (2mi) [other] Mason-Dixon Camping (4mi/seasonal), S [food] Savage River Lodge/rest. (4mi)
25.8mm	eastern continental divide, elevation 2610 ft
24	Lower New Germany Rd, to US 40A, S [other] to New Germany SP, to Savage River SF
23mm	Meadow Mtn, elevation 2780 ft
22	US 219 N, to Meyersdale, N [gas] Pilot/Arby's/dsl/scales/24hr, Sunoco/dsl [food] Burger King, IHOP, Little Caesar's, Penn Alps Rest., Subway [other] $General, Ford, Hilltop Fruit Mkt, NAPA, Rite Aid, Shop'n Save, TrueValue, S [gas] Valero/dsl [lodging] Comfort Inn [other] New Germany SP, Savage River SF
20mm	Casselman River
19	MD 495, to US 40A, Grantsville, N [gas] Exxon/Subway/dsl, Sunoco/dsl [lodging] Casselman Motel/rest. [other] Medicine Shoppe, USPO
15mm	Mt Negro, elevation 2740 ft
14mm	Keyser's Ridge, elevation 2880 ft
14b a	US 219, US 40 W, Oakland, N [gas] 7-11/dsl, Liberty/Ridge/rest/dsl [food] McDonald's, repair
6mm	**Welcome Ctr eb, full [handicap] facilities, info, litter barrels, petwalk, [phone], [picnic], vending**
4.5mm	Bear Creek
4	MD 42, Friendsville, N [gas] Exxon/dsl, Liberty/dsl [lodging] Youghiogheny Valley Motel [other] S&S Mkt, USPO, S [lodging] Sunset Inn [other] to Deep Creek Lake SP
0mm	Maryland/West Virginia state line

INTERSTATE 70

Exit#	Services
	I-70 begins/ends in Baltimore at Cooks Lane.
94	Security Blvd N, S [gas] Shell
91b a	I-695
87b a	US 29 (exits left from wb)to MD 99, Columbia, **2 mi** S on US 40 [gas] BP/dsl, Exxon/dsl, Gulf, Shell/dsl, Sunoco [food] Arby's, Baskin-Robbins/Dunkin Donuts, Boston Mkt, Burger King, Checkers, Domino's, Jimmy John's, McDonald's, Papa John's, Pizza Hut, Qdoba, Starbucks, Subway [other] 7-11, Acura, Advance Parts, Cadillac/Chevrolet, Carmax, CVS Drug, Giant Foods, Goodyear/auto, H Mart Foods, Home Depot, Honda, Infiniti, Kia, Mars Foods, Midas, Mr Tire, Nissan, Rite Aid, Safeway Foods, Verizon, Walgreens, Walmart
83	US 40, Marriottsville (no EZ wb return), **2 mi** S [lodging] Turf Valley Hotel/Country Club/rest.
82	US 40 E (from eb), same as 83
80	MD 32, Sykesville, N [other] golf, S [gas] High's/dsl [food] Subway, Tony's Pizzeria

INTERSTATE 70 Cont'd

FREDERICK

Exit#	Services
79mm	**weigh/insp sta wb,**
76	MD 97, Olney, **S** High's/dsl Subway
73	MD 94, Woodbine, **N** High's/dsl Baskin Robbins, China Yee, Dunkin Donuts, Harvest Chicken, McDonald's, Pizza Hut, Subway $Tree, Food Lion, Ramblin Pines RV Park (6mi), Verizon, **S** BP/dsl, Citgo Town Grill
68	MD 27, Mt Airy, **N** 7-11, Liberty/dsl Arby's, Baskin-Robbns/Dunkin Donuts, Burger King, Chipotle, Chong Yet Yin Chinese, Domino's, Five Guys, J&P Pizza, Jersey Mike' Subs, KFC/Taco Bell, Ledo's Pizza, McDonald's, Papa John's, Pizza Hut, Rita's Custard, Starbucks, Subway Ace Hardware, Advance Parts, AT&T, Food Lion, GNC, Goodyear, Mr Tire, Rite Aid, Safeway, Verizon, Walmart, **S** Exxon/dsl, Shell/dsl Budget Inn
66mm	**truckers parking area eb**
64mm	**weigh/insp sta eb**
62	MD 75, Libertytown, **N** Falcon Fuels, High's/dsl Asian Bistro, Baskin Robbins, Burger King, Domino's, Dunkin Donuts, McDonald's, Morgan's Grill CVS Drug, Food Lion, New Market Hist Dist
59	MD 144
57mm	Monocacy River
56	MD 144, **N** BP, Sheetz Beijing, Burger King, JR's Pizza, McDonald's, Roy Rogers, Taco Bell, Wendy's to Hist Dist, **S** Chesaco RV Ctr
55	South St, **1 mi N** BP, Sheetz/dsl same as 56
54	Market St, to I-270, **N** Costco/gas Super 8, **S** 7-11, Sheetz/dsl, Shell/dsl, SouStates/dsl, Valero/dsl, Wawa/dsl Applebee's, Arby's, BJ's Rest., Burger King, Checker's, Chick-fil-A, ChuckeCheese, Cracker Barrel, Golden Corral, KFC/Taco Bell, Longhorn Steaks, McDonald's, Olive Garden, Panera Bread, Papa John's, Peking Gourmet, Popeye's, Red Robin, Ruby Tuesday, Sonic, Subway, Waffle House Clarion, Country Inn Suites, Courtyard, Days Inn, EconoLodge, Extended Stay America, Fairfield Inn, Hampton Inn, Hilton Garden, Residence Inn, Sleep Inn $Tree, AAA, Aamco, Audi, Barnes&Noble, Best Buy, Buick/GMC, Chrysler/Dodge/Jeep, Dick's, Home Depot, Honda, Hyundai, JC Penney, Kia, Kohl's, Lincoln, Lowe's, Macy's, Michael's, Mr Tire, Nissan, Petsmart, Ross, Sam's Club/dsl, Staples, Target, Tires+, TJMaxx, Toyota, Volvo, Walmart
53b a	I-270 S, US 15 N, US 40 W, to Frederick
52b a	US 15 S, US 340 W, Leesburg
49	US 40A, Braddock Heights, **N on US 40** Carroll/dsl, Citgo/dsl, Exxon/dsl, GetGo, Shell/dsl, Sunoco, WaWa/dsl Arby's, Bob Evans, Boston Mkt, Burger King, Casa Rico Mexican, Chipotle, Denny's, Domino's, Dunkin Donuts, Famous Dave's BBQ, Flaming Grill, HoneyBaked Ham, KFC, Los Trios, McDonald's, Mtn View Diner, Outback Steaks, Pizza Hut, Popeye's, Red Horse Rest., Red Lobster, Roy Rogers, Starbucks, Subway, Taco Bell, Wendy's Comfort Inn, Motel 6 H, $General, 7-11, Aldi Foods, AT&T, AutoZone, Boscov's, CVS Drug, $Tree, Giant Eagle Foods, Home Depot, Meineke, Mr Tire, NTB, PepBoys, PetCo,

HAGERSTOWN

Exit#	Services
49	Continued Subaru, Verizon, Weis Foods, **S** camping, to Washington Mon SP
48	US 40 E, US 340 (from eb, no return), **1 mi N** same as 49
42	MD 17, Myersville, **N** Exxon, Sunoco/dsl Burger King, McDonald's, Old Town Diner Greenbrier SP (4mi), to Gambrill SP (6mi), **S** Crown/dsl Subway
39mm	**both lanes, full facilities, litter barrels, petwalk, , , vending**
35	MD 66, to Boonsboro, **S** Sheetz/dsl (1mi) camping, to Greenbrier SP
32b a	US 40, Hagerstown, **0-3 mi N** 7-11/dsl, BP, Exxon/dsl, Sheetz/dsl, Sunoco Baskin-Robbins/Dunkin Donuts, Bob Evans, Burger King, Cancun Cantina, Checkers, Coldstone, Denny's, DQ, El Ranchero Mexican, Family Diner, Five Guys, Jimmy John's, KFC, Ledo's Pizza, Little Caesar's, McDonald's, Papa John's, Pizza Hut, Popeye's, Sonic, Subway, Supreme Buffet, Taco Bell, TX Roadhouse, Wendy's Baymont Inn, Comfort Suites, Days Inn, Garden Plaza Hotel, Hampton Inn, Quality Inn, Super 8 H, $General, $Tree, Advance Parts, Aldi Foods, AT&T, AutoZone, Cadillac/Chevrolet, Chrysler/Dodge/Jeep, CVS Drug, Family$, Martin's Foods, Mercedes, Midas, Mr Tire, Nissan, Tires+, Toyota, URGENT CARE, Walgreens, Weis Foods, **S** Buick/GMC, Honda, Kia, Subaru/Mazda/VW
29b a	MD 65, to Sharpsburg, **N** EVgo EVC, Exxon/Subway/dsl, Sheetz/dsl, Tesla EVC FoodCourt, Longhorn Steaks H, Prime Outlets/famous brands, **S** EVC, Liberty/7-11/dsl Burger King, Cracker Barrel, McDonald's, Waffle House, Wendy's Sleep Inn Jellystone Camping, st police, to Antietam Bfd, Walmart
28	MD 632, Hagerstown
26	I-81, N to Harrisburg, S to Martinsburg
24	MD 63, Huyett, **N** Pilot/Subway/dsl/24hr, Sheetz/dsl (2mi), **S** Red Roof Inn C&O Canal, KOA (2mi)
18	MD 68 E, Clear Spring, **N** BP/dsl, Liberty Al's Grill, McDonald's Holiday Inn Express, Sleep Inn, **S** Exxon/dsl Wendy Hill Café
12	MD 56, Indian Springs, **S** Exxon/dsl Ft Frederick SP
9	US 40 E (from eb, exits left), Indian Springs
5	MD 615 (no immediate wb return), **N** Log Cabin Rest. (2mi)
3	MD 144, Hancock (exits left from wb), **S** ACT/Exxon/dsl, Liberty/rest./dsl/24hr Hardee's, Park'n Dine Hilltop Inn Blue Goose Mkt

MD

INTERSTATE 70 Cont'd

Exit#	Services
1b	US 522 (exits left from both lanes), Hancock, S Mobil/dsl, Sheetz/dsl Hardee's, Park'n Dine, Pizza Hut, Subway Hancock Motel, Super 8 $General, Chevrolet, Happy Hills Camp, NAPA, Save-A-Lot Foods
1a	I-68 W, US 40, W to Cumberland
0mm	Maryland/Pennsylvania state line, Mason-Dixon Line

INTERSTATE 81

HAGERSTOWN

Exit#	Services
12mm	Maryland/Pennsylvania state line
10b a	Showalter Rd, E
9	Maugans Ave, E BP, Sheetz/dsl, Shell/Domino's/dsl Fox's Pizza, Hometown Diner, McDonald's, Papa Murphy's, Pizza Hut, Pollo Loco, Quiznos, Subway, Taco Bell, Waffle House Hampton Inn $General, AutoZone, CVS Drug, Food Lion, Martin's Foods/gas, Meineke, vet, Walgreens, W Burger King, Dunkin Donuts Microtel Kenworth, Volvo
7b a	MD 58, Hagerstown, same as 6
6b a	US 40, Hagerstown, E Shell H, W Arby's, Chipotle Mexican, Five Guys, IHOP, Jersey Mike's Subs, KFC, McDonald's, Number One Chinese, Panera Bread, Ryan's, Starbucks, Subway, TGIFriday's, Uno Pizza, Wendy's $Tree, AT&T, Best Buy, Dick's, GNC, Home Depot, Marshall's, Petsmart, Walmart
5b a	Halfway Blvd, E AC&T/dsl Bob Evans, Boston Mkt, Boston Mkt, Buffalo Wild Wings, Burger King, Chick-fil-A, ChuckECheese's, CiCi's Pizza, Cinco de Mayo, Coldstone, El Ranchero Mexican, Fireside Rest., Golden Corral, Hard Times Cafe, Jimmy John's, McDonald's, Nikko Japanese, Noodles&Co, Olive Garden, Outback Steaks, Papa John's, Pizza Hut, Popeye's, Red Lobster, Red Robin, Roy Rogers, Ruby Tuesday, Sakura Steaks, Starbucks, Taco Bell, Tilted Kilt, Wendy's Country Inn&Suites, Courtyard, Holiday Inn Express, Homewood Suites, Motel 6, Ramada, SpringHill Suites $Tree, BigLots, BonTon, CVS Drug, Firestone/auto, Ford, Hobby Lobby, Hyundai, JC Penney, Kohl's, Lowe's, Martin's Foods/gas, Michael's, PetCo, Ross, Sam's Club/gas, Staples, Target, W Exxon/dsl/scales/24hr, Pilot/McDonald's/Subway/dsl/scales/24hr Super 8 Freightliner
4	I-70, E to Frederick, W to Hancock, to I-68
2	US 11, Williamsport, E AC&T/dsl, W Exxon/dsl, Sunoco/dsl China 88, McDonald's, Subway, Waffle House Red Roof Inn auto repair, KOA (4mi)
1	MD 63, MD 68, Williamsport, E Bowman/dsl Jellystone, to Antietam Bfd, W Citgo $General, KOA, NAPA
0mm	Maryland/West Virginia state line, Potomac River

INTERSTATE 83

BALTIMORE

Exit#	Services
38mm	Maryland/Pennsylvania state line, Mason-Dixon Line
37	to Freeland (from sb)
36	MD 439, Bel Air, W Filler-Up Maryland Line Inn Grill Holiday Travel Park (5mi), Merry Meadows Camping (5mi)
35mm	**weigh/insp sta sb**
33	MD 45, Parkton, E USPO
31	Middletown Rd, to Parkton, E golf
27	MD 137, Mt Carmel, Hereford, E Exxon/dsl Michael's Pizza, Monkton Grill, Subway 7-11, Graul's Foods, Hereford Drug, Mt Carmel Drug, USPO, vet
24	Belfast Rd, to Butler, Sparks
20	Shawan Rd, Hunt Valley, E Exxon/dsl, Mobil Burger King, CA Pizza, Carrabba's, Chick-fil-A, Chipotle Mexican, Coal Fire Cafe, Joe's Crabshack, McDonald's, Noodles&Co, Outback Steaks, Panera Bread, Pei Wei, Sakura Hibachi, Subway Courtyard, Embassy Suites, Holiday Inn Express, Hunt Valley Inn, Residence Inn Burlington Coats, Dick's, Giant Foods, Goodyear/auto, Marshall's, Verizon, vet, Wegman's Foods
18	Warren Rd (from nb, no return), Cockeysville, **services E on York Rd**
17	Padonia Rd, Deereco Rd, E 7-11, BP/dsl, Gulf/dsl, Marathon/dsl Applebee's, Bob Evans, Chili's, Macaroni Grill, Wendy's Extended Stay America, Hampton Inn, Holiday Inn Audi/VW, Chevrolet, Goodyear/auto, Lowe's Whse, Mars Mkt, Mr Tire, Porsche, Rite Aid, Sam's Club, Subaru, Target, USPO, **services E on York Rd**
16b a	Timonium Rd, E Sunoco/dsl Baja Fresh, Firehouse Subs, Little Caesar's, McDonald's N Baltimore Plaza Hotel, Red Roof Inn Infiniti/Nissan, Petsmart, REI, Rite Aid, ShopRite Foods, **services E on York Rd**
14	I-695 N
13	I-695 S, Falls Rd, E H, W st police
12	Ruxton Rd (from nb, no return)
10b a	Northern Parkway, E Exxon, Shell, W H
9b a	Cold Spring Lane
8	MD 25 N (from nb), Falls Rd
7b a	28th St, E H, W Baltimore Zoo
6	US 1, US 40T, North Ave, downtown
5	MD Ave (from sb), downtown
3	Chase St, Gilford St, downtown
2	Pleasant St (from sb), downtown
1	Fayette St, downtown Baltimore, **I-83 begins/ends.**

INTERSTATE 95

Exit#	Services
110mm	Maryland/Delaware state line
109b a	MD 279, to Elkton, Newark, E CF/dsl, FLYING J/Golden Corral/dsl/scales/24hr/@ Cracker Barrel, KFC/Taco Bell, McDonald's, Waffle House Days Inn, Elkton Lodge, Hampton Inn, Knights Inn, La Quinta, Motel 6 H, Blue Beacon, W 7-11, TA/Country Pride/dsl/24hr/@, WaWa/dsl Holiday Inn Express to U of DE
100	MD 272, to North East, Rising Sun, E FLYING J/Denny's/dsl/LP/24hr, Sunoco/dsl Burger King, Dunkin Donuts, Frank's Pizza, Little Caesar's, McDonald's, Waffle House, Wendy's Comfort Inn, Holiday Inn Express $General, $Tree, Advance Parts, AT&T, auto repair, Food Lion, Lowe's, PetCo, st police, to Elk Neck SP, Verizon, Walgreens, Walmart/Subway, W High's/dsl Hunan Wok, Pizza Hut Best Western zoo
96mm	**Chesapeake House service area (exits left from both lanes)** Sunoco/dsl Burger King, Peets Coffee, Pizza Hut, Popeye's, Wendy's
93	MD 275, to Rising Sun, US 222, to Perryville, E Exxon/dsl, Pilot/Subway/dsl/scales/24hr Denny's Days Inn H
92mm	**weigh sta/toll booth**
91.5mm	Susquehanna River
89	MD 155, to Havre de Grace **(last nb exit before toll), 1-3 mi** E Burger King, Chesapeake Grill, Dunkin Donuts, MacGregor's Rest., McDonald's, Waffle House Super 8, Van Divers B&B H, W to Susquehanna SP

MD

INTERSTATE 95 Cont'd

ABERDEEN

Exit#	Services
85	MD 22, to Aberdeen, E 7-11, Crown/dsl, Royal Farms/dsl, Shell/dsl Applebee's, Baskin-Robbins/Dunkin Donuts, Bob Evans, Burger King, Chap's Pit Beef, Chick-fil-A, IHOP, KFC, La Tolteca Mexican, Little Caesar's, McDonald's, Olive Tree Italian, Panera Bread, Papa John's, Rita's Custard, Subway, Taco Bell, Wendy's Comfort Inn, Days Inn, Hampton Inn, Hilton Garden, Holiday Inn Express, La Quinta, Red Roof Inn, Super 8, Travelodge $General, $Tree, Firestone/auto, GNC, Home Depot, Rite Aid, ShopRite Foods, Target, Verizon, Walgreens, W Courtyard, Residence Inn
81mm	**MD House service area (exits left from both lanes)** Sunoco/dsl Dunkin Donuts, Jerry's, Phillips Seafood, Starbucks, Wendy's
80	MD 543, to Riverside, Churchville, E 7-11, BP/Burger King, Shell/dsl, Sunoco Arby's, China Moon, Cracker Barrel, Lee's Asian Bistro, McDonald's, Pizza Hut, Riverside Grille, Riverside Pizzeria, Ruby Tuesday, Subway, Waffle House Candlewood Suites, Country Inn&Suites, Extended Stay America, Homewood Suites, SpringHill Suites, Wingate Inn Bar Harbor RV Park (4mi), Rite Aid, ShopRite Foods
77b a	MD 24, to Edgewood, Bel Air, E Exxon/dsl, Royal Farms/dsl, Sunoco/dsl Denny's, My 3 Sons Rest., Subway, Waffle House Comfort Inn, Hampton Inn, Holiday Inn Express, La Quinta, Motel 6, Ramada, Red Roof Inn, Sleep Inn Old Navy, W Exxon/dsl, WaWa/dsl Boston's, Chick-fil-A, Dickey's BBQ, KFC/Taco Bell, McDonald's, Panda Express, Panera Bread, Starbucks H, $Tree, BJ's Whse, GNC, JC Penney, Lowe's, Petsmart, Target, Walmart/Subway, Wegman's Foods
74	MD 152, Fallston, Joppatowne, E CF/dsl, Exxon/dsl, WaWa/dsl Friendly's, Subway Super 8 Toyota (1mi), W Royal Farms/dsl
70mm	Big Gunpowder Falls
67b a	MD 43, to White Marsh Blvd, US 1, US 40, E BP/dsl Applebee's, Chick-fil-A, Chipotle, Five Guys, Jimmy John's, Ledo Pizza, McDonald's, Noodles&Co, Panda Express, Panera Bread, Pie Five, Qdoba, Starbucks, Subway, Zoe's Kitchen Home 2 Suites Best Buy, Carmax, Chevrolet, Dick's, Lowe's, Michael's, on White Marsh Blvd, Petco, Target, TJ Maxx, W 7-11, Exxon/dsl All About Burger, Bertucci's, Buffalo Wild Wings, Burger King, Chili's, China Wok, Coldstone, Don Pablo, Kobe Japanese, McDonald's, Olive Garden, PF Chang's, Red Brick Sta., Red Lobster, Red Robin, Starbucks, Taco Bell, TGIFriday's, Tilted Kilt, TX Roadhouse, Wendy's Fairfield Inn, Hampton Inn, Hilton Garden, Residence Inn, Woodspring Suites AT&T, Barnes&Noble, Giant Foods, IKEA, JC Penney, Macy's, Mr Tire, Old Navy, Staples, to Gunpowder SP, USPO, Verizon
64b a	I-695 (exits left), E to Essex, W to Towson
62	to I-895 (from sb)

BALTIMORE

Exit#	Services
61	US 40, Pulaski Hwy, E BP, Shell/dsl McDonald's
60	Moravia Rd
59	Eastern Ave, W BP/dsl, Exxon, Royal Farms/dsl, WaWa Broadway Diner, McDonald's, Subway, Wendy's H, Home Depot, Shoppers Foods
58	Dundalk Ave, (from nb), E Citgo
57	O'Donnell St, Boston St, E TA/Buckhorn/Country Pride/Subway/dsl/scales/motel/@ McDonald's Best Western
56	Keith Ave
56mm	McHenry Tunnel, **toll plaza** (north side of tunnel)
55	Key Hwy, to Ft McHenry NM, **last nb exit before toll**

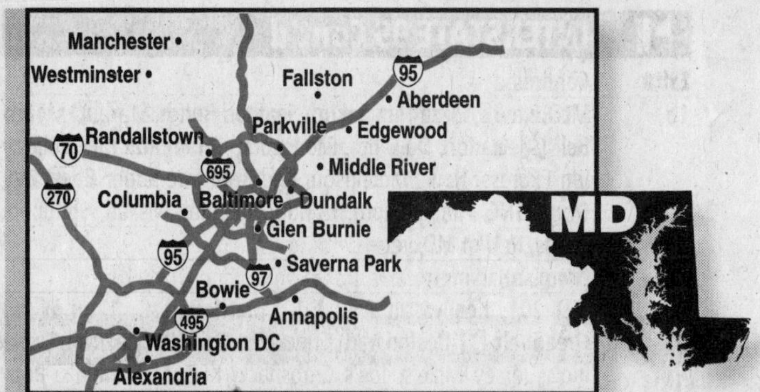

COLUMBIA

Exit#	Services
54	MD 2 S, to Hanover St, W H, Harris Teeter, downtown
53	I-395 N, to MLK, W Oriole Park, downtown
52	Russell St N, W H
51	Washington Blvd
50.5mm	**inspection sta nb**
50	Caton Ave, E Marathon/dsl, Shell/dsl, US/dsl Caton House, Loafers Grill, McDonald's Motel 6 7-11, Aldi Foods, auto repair, Midas, Toyota, W H
49b a	I-695, E to Key Bridge, Glen Burnie, W to Towson, to I-70, to I-83
47b a	I-195, to MD 166, to BWI Airport, to Baltimore
46	I-895, to Harbor Tunnel Thruway
43b a	MD 100, to Glen Burnie, **1 mi E on US 1** Exxon/Wendy's/dsl, Xtra Best Western
41b a	MD 175, to Columbia, E BP/dsl, Exxon/dsl, Shell/dsl, TA/Country Pride/Subway/dsl/scales/24hr/@ Arby's, Burger King, Frank's Diner, IHOP, McDonald's, Panda Express, Starbucks Comfort Suites, Holiday Inn, La Quinta, Red Roof Inn, Sleep Inn, Super 8 $Tree, Advance Parts, Mom's Organic Mkt, W Exxon Bob Evans, Fat Burger, Houlihan's, Jersey Mike's, McDonald's, Mimi's Cafe, Olive Garden, On the Border, TGIFriday's Extended Stay America, Homewood Suites H, Best Buy, Costco/gas, CVS Drug, Lowe's, Loyola U, Office Depot, Royal Farms, to Johns Hopkins U, Trader Joe's
38b a	MD 32, to Ft Meade, **2 mi E on US 1** BP/dsl, Exxon/Wendy's/dsl, Royal Farms, Shell/dsl Burger King, Dunkin Donuts, McDonald's, Subway, Taco Bell Comfort Inn, Extended Stay America H, to BWI Airport
37mm	**Welcome Ctr both lanes, full facilities, info, litter barrels, petwalk, , , RV Dump, vending**
35b a	MD 216, to Laurel, E Exxon, Shell/dsl McDonald's, Subway Weis Food/drug
34mm	Patuxent River
33b a	MD 198, to Laurel, E Exxon H, W Exxon/Blimpie/dsl, Shell Outback Steaks Holiday Inn
31	MD 200 (toll), to I-270
29	MD 212, to Beltsville, E Cherry Hill RV Resort, W Exxon/Blimpie/dsl Baskin-Robbins, Danny's Subs, KFC, McDonald's, Taco Bell, The Villa Rest., TJ's Rest., Wendy's Comfort Inn, Sheraton CVS Drug, Giant Foods
27	I-495 S around Washington
25b a	US 1, Baltimore Ave, to Laurel, College Park, E 7-11, BP/dsl, Exxon/dsl, Shell, Sunoco, Wawa/dsl Arby's, Buffalo Wild Wings, Burger King, Chipotle, Domino's, Dunkin Donuts, McDonald's, Moose Creek Steaks, Panera Bread, Papa John's, Pizza Hut/Taco Bell, Potbelly's, Starbucks, Subway, Wendy's Holiday Inn Advance Parts, Aldi Foods, AutoZone, Cherry Hill RV Resort, Costco/gas, CVS Drug, IKEA, PetCo, Rite Aid, URGENT CARE, US Agri Library, Verizon, W BP/24hr, Exxon, Shell, Xtra Azteca, Burger King, College Park Diner, Denny's, Dunkin Donuts, Hard Times Cafe, IHOP, Mamma Lucia,

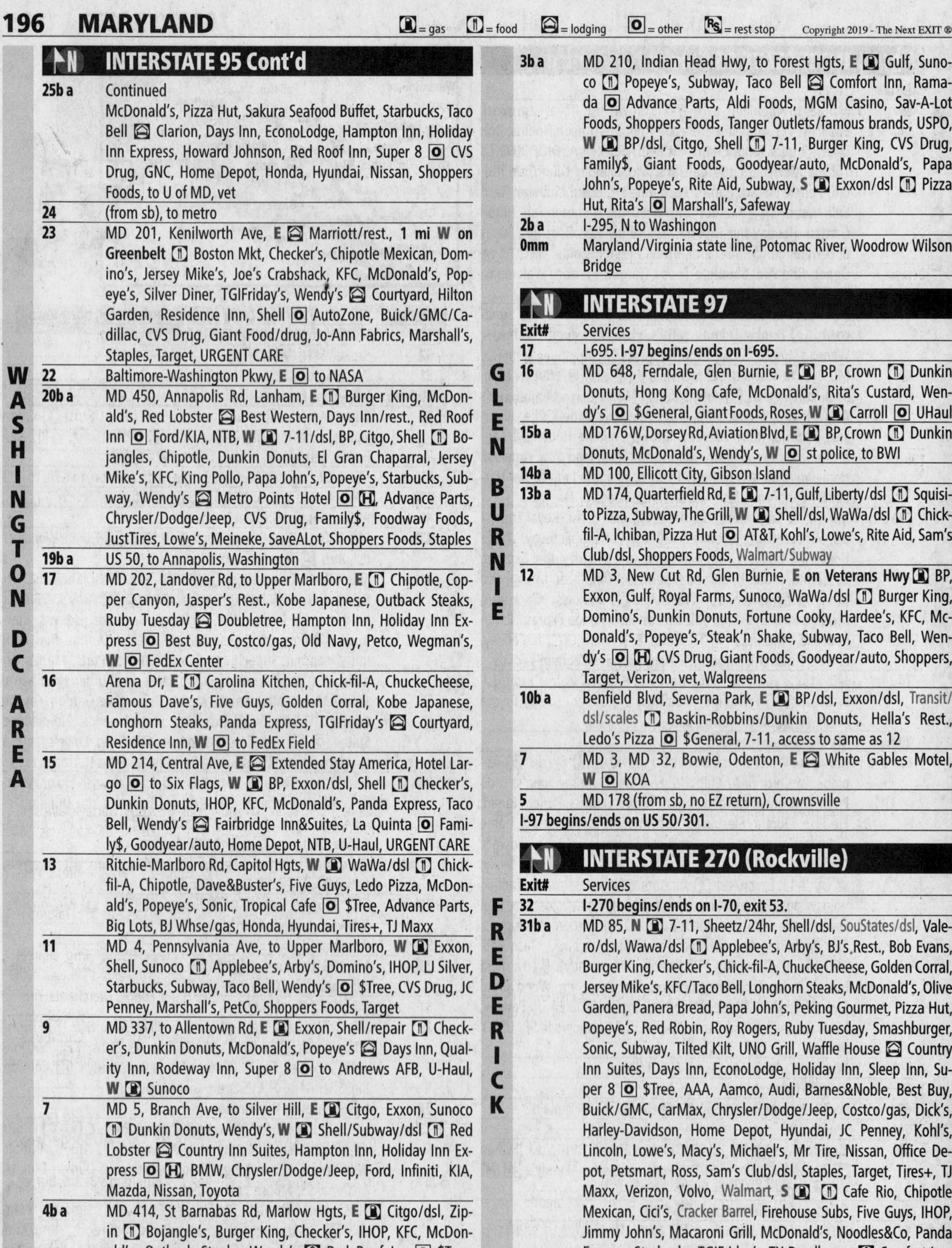

INTERSTATE 95 Cont'd

WASHINGTON DC AREA

Exit#	Services
25b a	Continued McDonald's, Pizza Hut, Sakura Seafood Buffet, Starbucks, Taco Bell Clarion, Days Inn, EconoLodge, Hampton Inn, Holiday Inn Express, Howard Johnson, Red Roof Inn, Super 8 CVS Drug, GNC, Home Depot, Honda, Hyundai, Nissan, Shoppers Foods, to U of MD, vet
24	(from sb), to metro
23	MD 201, Kenilworth Ave, **E** Marriott/rest., **1 mi W on Greenbelt** Boston Mkt, Checker's, Chipotle Mexican, Domino's, Jersey Mike's, Joe's Crabshack, KFC, McDonald's, Popeye's, Silver Diner, TGIFriday's, Wendy's Courtyard, Hilton Garden, Residence Inn, Shell AutoZone, Buick/GMC/Cadillac, CVS Drug, Giant Food/drug, Jo-Ann Fabrics, Marshall's, Staples, Target, URGENT CARE
22	Baltimore-Washington Pkwy, **E** to NASA
20b a	MD 450, Annapolis Rd, Lanham, **E** Burger King, McDonald's, Red Lobster Best Western, Days Inn/rest., Red Roof Inn Ford/KIA, NTB, **W** 7-11/dsl, BP, Citgo, Shell Bojangles, Chipotle, Dunkin Donuts, El Gran Chaparral, Jersey Mike's, KFC, King Pollo, Papa John's, Popeye's, Starbucks, Subway, Wendy's Metro Points Hotel H, Advance Parts, Chrysler/Dodge/Jeep, CVS Drug, Family$, Foodway Foods, JustTires, Lowe's, Meineke, SaveALot, Shoppers Foods, Staples
19b a	US 50, to Annapolis, Washington
17	MD 202, Landover Rd, to Upper Marlboro, **E** Chipotle, Copper Canyon, Jasper's Rest., Kobe Japanese, Outback Steaks, Ruby Tuesday Doubletree, Hampton Inn, Holiday Inn Express Best Buy, Costco/gas, Old Navy, Petco, Wegman's, **W** FedEx Center
16	Arena Dr, **E** Carolina Kitchen, Chick-fil-A, ChuckeCheese, Famous Dave's, Five Guys, Golden Corral, Kobe Japanese, Longhorn Steaks, Panda Express, TGIFriday's Courtyard, Residence Inn, **W** to FedEx Field
15	MD 214, Central Ave, **E** Extended Stay America, Hotel Largo to Six Flags, **W** BP, Exxon/dsl, Shell Checker's, Dunkin Donuts, IHOP, KFC, McDonald's, Panda Express, Taco Bell, Wendy's Fairbridge Inn&Suites, La Quinta Family$, Goodyear/auto, Home Depot, NTB, U-Haul, URGENT CARE
13	Ritchie-Marlboro Rd, Capitol Hgts, **W** WaWa/dsl Chick-fil-A, Chipotle, Dave&Buster's, Five Guys, Ledo Pizza, McDonald's, Popeye's, Sonic, Tropical Cafe $Tree, Advance Parts, Big Lots, BJ Whse/gas, Honda, Hyundai, Tires+, TJ Maxx
11	MD 4, Pennsylvania Ave, to Upper Marlboro, **W** Exxon, Shell, Sunoco Applebee's, Arby's, Domino's, IHOP, LJ Silver, Starbucks, Subway, Taco Bell, Wendy's $Tree, CVS Drug, JC Penney, Marshall's, PetCo, Shoppers Foods, Target
9	MD 337, to Allentown Rd, **E** Exxon, Shell/repair Checker's, Dunkin Donuts, McDonald's, Popeye's Days Inn, Quality Inn, Rodeway Inn, Super 8 to Andrews AFB, U-Haul, **W** Sunoco
7	MD 5, Branch Ave, to Silver Hill, **E** Citgo, Exxon, Sunoco Dunkin Donuts, Wendy's, **W** Shell/Subway/dsl Red Lobster Country Inn Suites, Hampton Inn, Holiday Inn Express H, BMW, Chrysler/Dodge/Jeep, Ford, Infiniti, KIA, Mazda, Nissan, Toyota
4b a	MD 414, St Barnabas Rd, Marlow Hgts, **E** Citgo/dsl, Zip-in Bojangle's, Burger King, Checker's, IHOP, KFC, McDonald's, Outback Steaks, Wendy's Red Roof Inn $Tree, CVS Drug, GNC, Home Depot, Petsmart, Ross, Safeway Foods, Staples, **W** Exxon/7-11/dsl, Shell/autocare China Best, McDonald's, Subway Family$
3b a	MD 210, Indian Head Hwy, to Forest Hgts, **E** Gulf, Sunoco Popeye's, Subway, Taco Bell Comfort Inn, Ramada Advance Parts, Aldi Foods, MGM Casino, Sav-A-Lot Foods, Shoppers Foods, Tanger Outlets/famous brands, USPO, **W** BP/dsl, Citgo, Shell 7-11, Burger King, CVS Drug, Family$, Giant Foods, Goodyear/auto, McDonald's, Papa John's, Popeye's, Rite Aid, Subway, **S** Exxon/dsl Pizza Hut, Rita's Marshall's, Safeway
2b a	I-295, N to Washingon
0mm	Maryland/Virginia state line, Potomac River, Woodrow Wilson Bridge

INTERSTATE 97

GLEN BURNIE

Exit#	Services
17	**I-695. I-97 begins/ends on I-695.**
16	MD 648, Ferndale, Glen Burnie, **E** BP, Crown Dunkin Donuts, Hong Kong Cafe, McDonald's, Rita's Custard, Wendy's $General, Giant Foods, Roses, **W** Carroll UHaul
15b a	MD 176 W, Dorsey Rd, Aviation Blvd, **E** BP, Crown Dunkin Donuts, McDonald's, Wendy's, **W** st police, to BWI
14b a	MD 100, Ellicott City, Gibson Island
13b a	MD 174, Quarterfield Rd, **E** 7-11, Gulf, Liberty/dsl Squisito Pizza, Subway, The Grill, **W** Shell/dsl, WaWa/dsl Chick-fil-A, Ichiban, Pizza Hut AT&T, Kohl's, Lowe's, Rite Aid, Sam's Club/dsl, Shoppers Foods, Walmart/Subway
12	MD 3, New Cut Rd, Glen Burnie, **E on Veterans Hwy** BP, Exxon, Gulf, Royal Farms, Sunoco, WaWa/dsl Burger King, Domino's, Dunkin Donuts, Fortune Cooky, Hardee's, KFC, McDonald's, Popeye's, Steak'n Shake, Subway, Taco Bell, Wendy's H, CVS Drug, Giant Foods, Goodyear/auto, Shoppers, Target, Verizon, vet, Walgreens
10b a	Benfield Blvd, Severna Park, **E** BP/dsl, Exxon/dsl, Transit/dsl/scales Baskin-Robbins/Dunkin Donuts, Hella's Rest., Ledo's Pizza $General, 7-11, access to same as 12
7	MD 3, MD 32, Bowie, Odenton, **E** White Gables Motel, **W** KOA
5	MD 178 (from sb, no EZ return), Crownsville

I-97 begins/ends on US 50/301.

INTERSTATE 270 (Rockville)

FREDERICK

Exit#	Services
32	**I-270 begins/ends on I-70, exit 53.**
31b a	MD 85, **N** 7-11, Sheetz/24hr, Shell/dsl, SouStates/dsl, Valero/dsl, Wawa/dsl Applebee's, Arby's, BJ's Rest., Bob Evans, Burger King, Checker's, Chick-fil-A, ChuckeCheese, Golden Corral, Jersey Mike's, KFC/Taco Bell, Longhorn Steaks, McDonald's, Olive Garden, Panera Bread, Papa John's, Peking Gourmet, Pizza Hut, Popeye's, Red Robin, Roy Rogers, Ruby Tuesday, Smashburger, Sonic, Subway, Tilted Kilt, UNO Grill, Waffle House Country Inn Suites, Days Inn, EconoLodge, Holiday Inn, Sleep Inn, Super 8 $Tree, AAA, Aamco, Audi, Barnes&Noble, Best Buy, Buick/GMC, CarMax, Chrysler/Dodge/Jeep, Costco/gas, Dick's, Harley-Davidson, Home Depot, Hyundai, JC Penney, Kohl's, Lincoln, Lowe's, Macy's, Michael's, Mr Tire, Nissan, Office Depot, Petsmart, Ross, Sam's Club/dsl, Staples, Target, Tires+, TJ Maxx, Verizon, Volvo, Walmart, **S** Cafe Rio, Chipotle Mexican, Cici's, Cracker Barrel, Firehouse Subs, Five Guys, IHOP, Jimmy John's, Macaroni Grill, McDonald's, Noodles&Co, Panda Express, Starbucks, TGIFriday's, TX Roadhouse Comfort Inn, Courtyard, Extended Stay America, Fairfield Inn, Hampton Inn, Hilton Garden, Homewood Suites, MainStay Suites, Residence Inn, TownePlace Suites Honda, Toyota

INTERSTATE 270 (Rockville) Cont'd

Exit#	Services
30mm	Monocacy River
28mm	scenic view wb, no rest rooms
26	MD 80, Urbana, N [gas] 7-11, Exxon, Royal Farms/dsl, Shell/dsl [food] Black Hog BBQ, Buffalo Wild Wings, Burger King, China Taste, Dunkin Donuts, Jimmy John's, Ledo's Pizza, McDonald's, Waffle House [other] Advance Parts, CVS Drug
22	MD 109, to Barnesville, Hyattstown, N [gas] Carroll/dsl [food] Denise Deli, Dunkin Donuts, Laurienzo Cafe [other] Food+
21mm	**weigh/insp sta both lanes**
18	MD 121, to Clarksburg, Boyds, N Little Bennett Pk, S [other] Clarksburg Outlets/famous brands, Blackhill Pk
16	MD 27, Father Hurley Blvd, to Damascus, N [gas] Exxon, Free State/dsl, Sunoco, Washington Express [food] Applebee's, Bob Evans, Jersey Mike's Subs, McDonald's, Starbucks [lodging] Extended Stay America [other] AT&T, Best Buy, Giant Foods, GNC, Home Depot, Kohl's, Michael's, PepBoys, Petsmart, Target, TJ Maxx, Verizon, Walmart
15b a	MD 118, to MD 355, N [lodging] Holiday Inn Express, S [gas] 7-11, BP/dsl, Exxon/Circle K, Sunoco/dsl [food] Baja Fresh, Burger King, Carrabba's, Chick-fil-A, Chipotle, Domino's, Firehouse Subs, Five Guys, Greene Turtle, IHOP, Longhorn Steaks, McDonald's, Panda Express, Panera Bread, Pizza Hut, Red Robin, Ruby Tuesday, Senor Tequilas, Starbucks, Taco Bell, Wendy's, Zoe's Kitchen [lodging] Extended Stay America, Fairfield Inn [other] Giant Foods, Honda, Mercedes/Smart Car, Nissan, Petco, Rite Aid, Safeway Foods
13b a	Middlebrook Rd (from wb)
11	MD 124, Quince Orchard Rd, N [gas] Exxon, Exxon [food] Boston Mkt, ChuckeCheese, Ichiban Rest., KFC, McDonald's, Panera Bread, Popeye's, Subway [lodging] Hampton Inn, Hilton, Holiday Inn, Homewood Suites, TownePlace Suites [other] Aamco, Acura, AT&T, Costco, CVS Drugs, Ford, Hyundai/Subaru, JC Penney, Lincoln, Lord&Taylor, Macy's, Mazda, Mini, Ross, Sam's Club, Toyota, Verizon, VW/Kia, S [gas] Shell/dsl [food] Buffalo Wild Wings, Dunkin Donuts, Jerry's Subs, Jimmy John's, McDonald's, Starbucks [lodging] Motel 6 [other] Advance Parts, Aldi Foods, Chevrolet, Chrysler/Dodge/Jeep, Fiat, Giant Foods, JoAnn Fabrics, Rite Aid, Seneca Creek SP, Staples
10	MD 117, Clopper Rd (from wb), same as 11
9b a	I-370, to Gaithersburg, Sam Eig Hwyon Washington Blvd, S [food] Copper Canyon Grill, Corner Cafe Bakery, Joe's Crabshack, Pizza Hut, Uncle Julio's [lodging] Courtyard [other] Barnes&Noble, Dick's, Kohl's, Target
8	Shady Grove Rd, N [gas] Shell/dsl [food] Burger King, Five Guys, Red Lobster, Subway [lodging] Red Roof Inn, Sheraton [other] 7-11, Best Buy, Home Depot, Office Depot, vet, S [food] Thatsamore [lodging] Courtyard, Marriott, Radisson, Residence Inn, Sleep Inn, SpringHill Suites [other] H
6b a	MD 28, W Montgomery Ave, S [gas] Shell [lodging] Best Western
5b a	MD 189, Falls Rd
4b a	Montrose Rd, S [food] Elevation Burger, Starbucks, Zoe's Kitchen [other] Harris Teeter, Walgreens
2	I-270/I-270 spur diverges eb, converges wb
1b a	MD 187, Old Georgetown Rd, S [gas] Exxon [food] Chipotle, Not Your Joe's, Subway [other] H, Balducci's Foods, Giant Foods, Verizon
1	(I-270 spur)Democracy Blvd, E [lodging] Marriott, W [gas] Exxon/dsl, Shell/dsl [other] Macy's, Nordstrom

I-270 begins/ends on I-495, exit 35.

GAITHERSBURG

ROCKVILLE

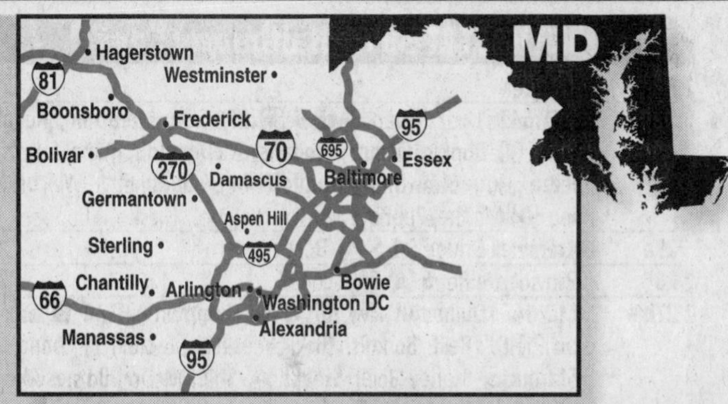

INTERSTATE 495 (DC)

See Virginia Interstate 495 (DC)

INTERSTATE 695 (Baltimore)

Exit#	Services
48mm	Patapsco River, Francis Scott Key Br
44	Broening Ave (from nb)
43	MD 157, **toll plaza**
42	MD 151 S, Sparrows Point (last exit before **toll** sb), E [gas] Citgo/dsl [other] North Point SP
41	MD 20, Cove Rd, W [gas] Royal Farms/dsl, WaWa [food] Burger King, McDonald's
40	MD 150, MD 151, North Point Blvd, (nb only)
39	Merritt Blvd, W [gas] [food] Burger King, Dunkin Donuts, McDonald's, Rita's [other] $Tree, Aldi Foods, Ford, Giant Foods, Honda, Hyundai, JC Penney, Mazda, Mr Tire, Walmart
38b a	MD 150, Eastern Blvd, to Baltimore, E [gas] Royal Farms, W [food] Applebee's, Arby's, Checker's, Chick-fil-A, Dunkin Donuts, Hibachi Buffet, Hip Hop Fish&Chicken [other] $Tree, AT&T, JC Penney, Kia/Nissan, Staples
36	MD 702 S (exits left from sb), Essex
35	US 40, N [gas] Sunoco, WaWa/dsl [food] Arby's, Chipotle Mexican, DQ, Dunkin Donuts, IHOP, Longhorn Steaks, Panda Express, Panera Bread, Sonic [other] Aldi Foods, Best Buy, Harley-Davidson, Home Depot, Mr Tire, NTB, Office Depot, PetCo, same as 34, Sam's Club/gas, U-Haul, Walmart
34	MD 7, Philadelphia Rd, N [food] McDonald's, Panda Express, Popeye's [lodging] La Quinta [other] H, $General, $Tree, Giant Foods, Goodyear/auto, Marshall's, S [gas] Exxon/dsl [other] same as 35, Walgreens
33b a	I-95, N to Philadelphia, S to Baltimore
32b a	US 1, Bel Air, N [gas] Exxon [food] Bob Evans, Burger King, Dunkin Donuts, Golden Corral, IHOP, McDonald's, Peking House, Taco Bell [other] $Tree, 7-11, BJ's Whse, Giant Foods, Merchants Tire/auto, Mr Tire/auto, Nissan, Toyota, Verizon, vet, Walmart, S [gas] Shell [food] Baskin-Robbins/Dunkin Donuts, Carrabba's, Papa John's, Rita's Custard, Subway, Szechuan Taste [other] 7-11, Goodyear/auto, Verizon
31c	MD 43 E (from eb, exits left)
31b a	MD 147, Harford Rd, N [gas] 7-11/dsl, BP, CF/dsl, CF/dsl (2), Sunoco [food] Dunkin Donuts, Wendy's [other] Chrysler/Dodge/Jeep, CVS Drug, Honda, VW, Walgreens, Weis Foods
30b a	MD 41, Perring Pkwy, N [gas] Shell [food] Bateman's Bistro, Burger King, Checker's, Chick-fil-A, Denny's, Dunkin Donuts, Five Guys, Hibachi Buffet, KFC, McDonald's, Popeye's, Rita's Custard, Starbucks, Subway, Taco Bell [other] $Tree, Advance Parts, Chevrolet, Ford/Lincoln, Goodyear/auto, Home Depot, Jo-Ann Fabrics, NTB, Office Depot, Ross, Safeway Foods, Shoppers Foods, Tuesday Morning, Verizon

= gas = food = lodging = other = rest stop

INTERSTATE 695 (Baltimore) Cont'd

Exit#	Services
29b	MD 542, Loch Raven Blvd, S BP, Gulf, Marathon, Royal Frms Dunkin Donuts, Hooters, McDonald's, Papa John's, Pizza Hut, Subway Comfort Inn, Days Inn, Welcome Inn Mr Tire, PepBoys
29a	Cromwell Bridge Rd, S Best Western
28	Providence Rd, S Sunoco
27b a	MD 146, Dulaney Valley Rd, N Hampton NHS, S Exxon BJ's Rest., Bonefish Grill, Cheesecake Factory, PF Chang's, Starbucks, Stoney River Steaks Sheraton Barnes&Noble, Fresh Mkt, Macy's, Trader Joe's
26b a	MD 45, York Rd, Towson, N BP, Citgo, Exxon/dsl, Oceanic, Sunoco/dsl Dunkin Donuts, Ocean Pride Rest., Pizza Hut, Subway Best Buy, Firestone/auto, Kia, Mazda, Mr Tire, NTB, Petco, Rite Aid, S Exxon, Shell Burger King, Five Guys, McDonald's, Towson Diner CVS Drug, Goodyear/auto, Honda, Hyundai, Lexus, Safeway Foods, Verizon, vet, Walgreens
25	MD 139, Charles St, S H
24	I-83 N, to York
23b	MD 25, Falls Rd, Baltimore, N Exxon/Circle K/dsl
23a	I-83 S, MD 25 N, Baltimore
22	Greenspring Ave
21	MD 129, to Stevenson Rd, Park Hghts Rd
20	MD 140, Reisterstown Rd, Pikesville, N Exxon/7-11/dsl Chipotle Mexican, Starbucks AT&T, Barnes&Noble, Trader Joe's, S BP/dsl, Shell/dsl, Sunoco/Subway McDonald's, Olive Branch Italian Doubletree, Ramada Inn Target, vet
19	I-795, NW Expswy
18b a	MD 26, Randallstown, Lochearn, E Shell/dsl, Sunoco/dsl Baskin-Robbins/Dunkin Donuts, KFC, Popeye's, Subway $General, Family$, W BP, Exxon/dsl, Shell/dsl Burger King, Dunkin Donuts, McDonald's, Sonic, Subway, Taco Bell H, 7-11, Firestone/auto, Giant Foods, Shoppers Foods, vet, Walgreens
17	MD 122, Security Blvd, E BP/repair, Shell City View Grill, Dunkin Donuts, Little Caesar's, McDonald's, Subway, Taco Bell Days Inn, Knights Inn, Motel 6 Chevrolet, Family$, Nissan, PriceRite Foods, Rite Aid, W Carroll/dsl, Exxon/dsl Burger King, Chipotle, Five Guys, McDonald's, Panera Bread, Popeye's, Rita's Custard Hampton Inn, Quality Inn Ford, Macy's, Old Navy, Rite Aid, Weis Foods
16b a	I-70, E to Baltimore, W to Frederick
15b a	US 40, Ellicott City, Baltimore, E Burger King, Checker's, Chick-fil-A, ChuckECheese's, KFC, McDonald's, Panda Express, Quiznos, Shirley's Diner, Subway Holiday Inn Express,
15b a	Continued Quality Inn $Tree, BigLots, CVS Drug, Dodge, Firestone auto, Lowe's, Marshall's, Mr Tire, Rite Aid, Ross, Safewa Foods/gas, Sam's Club/gas, Shoppers Foods, U-Haul, Wal greens, W BP/dsl, Exxon/dsl, Shell, Shell Applebee's Bob Evans, McDonald's, Popeye's, Starbucks, Starbucks, Subway, Taco Bell, TT Diner Ramada $Tree, Aamco, Ald Foods, Chrysler/Jeep, Firestone/auto, Giant Foods, Goodyear auto, Home Depot, Hyundai, NTB, Office Depot, Office Depot, PepBoys, Petsmart, Staples, Toyota, Verizon, Walgreens Walmart/McDonald's
14	Edmondson Ave, E Grilled Cheese&Co Royal Farms W Carroll Papa John's
13	MD 144, Frederick Rd, Catonsville, W BP, Gas+, Gul Baskin-Robbins/Dunkin Donuts, McDonald's, Subwa 7-11
12c b	MD 372 E, Wilkens, E H
11b a	I-95, N to Baltimore, S to Washington
10	US 1, Washington Blvd (from wb only), E Royal Farms dsl, WaWa 3 Bros Pizza, Chick-fil-A, Dunkin Donuts, IHOP Quiznos, Wendy's Beltway Motel/rest. Home Depot Office Depot, PetCo, Walmart, W Burger King
9	Hollins Ferry Rd, Lansdowne, E Carroll/Circle K/Subway Sunoco/7-11/dsl Victor's Deli Royal Farms
8	MD 168, Nursery Rd, N Exxon, Shell Hardee's, KFC McDonald's, Taco Bell, Wendy's Motel 6, S BP, Carroll dsl Dunkin Donuts, G&M Rest., Happy Garden Chinese, Rita's Custard, Seasons Pizza
7b a	MD 295, N to Baltimore, S BWI Airport
6b a	Camp Mead Rd (from eb)
5	MD 648, Ferndale, N Exxon/7-11/dsl, Shell/dsl Checker's, Dunkin Donuts Best Western, Comfort Inn NAPA, Hot Wok
4b a	I-97 S, to Annapolis
3b a	MD 2, Brooklyn Park, S Exxon, Royal Farms/dsl, Shell dsl Bob Evans, BoneFish Grill, Checker's, Chick-fil-A ChuckECheese's, Coldstone, Denny's, Five Guys, Golden Corral, Hibachi Buffet, HipHop Fish&Chicken, Ledo Pizza, McDonald's, Moe's SW, Noodles&Co, Panera Bread, Pappas Rest., Pi Five, Pizza Hut, Qdoba, Starbucks, Subway, Taco Bell, Wendy's Days Inn, Extended Stay America, Hampton Inn, La Quinta $Tree, Advance Parts, Aldi Foods, AT&T, AutoZone Best Buy, BigLots, Buick/GMC, Dick's, Hyundai, Just Tires Lowe's, Office Depot, PetCo, Salvo Parts, ShopRite Foods, Subaru, Target, Tuesday Morning, Verizon, Walgreens, Walmart
2	MD 10, Glen Burnie, S McDonald's Costco/gas, Home Depot, Petsmart
1	MD 174, Hawkins Point Rd, S Citgo/deli/dsl

NOTES

MASSACHUSETTS

INTERSTATE 84

STURBRIDGE

Exit#	Services
4(11)	I-84 begins/ends on I-90, Exit 9.
3b a(9)	US 20, Sturbridge, 0-2 mi N Citgo, Cumberland Farms Admiral O'Brien's, Bentley Rest., Burger King, Dunkin Donuts, Empire Village, Friendly's, McDonald's, Sturbridge Seafood, Subway, Village Pizza EconoLodge, Express Inn, Hampton Inn, Holiday Inn Express, Old Sturbridge Lodges, Sturbridge Host Hotel, Super 8 USPO, 0-2 mi S NE TrkStp/dsl, S&S, Shell/Dunkin Donuts/Subway Applebee's, Cracker Barrel, Uno Pizzaria, Wendy's Comfort Inn Marshall's, Michael's, Petco, Staples, Stop&Shop, Verizon, vet, Walmart/Subway
2(5)	MA 131, to Old Sturbridge Village, Sturbridge, 2 mi S Publick House, RV camping
4mm	picnic area wb, litter barrels
1(3)	Mashapaug Rd, to Southbridge, S Mobil/dsl, Pilot/deli/dsl/scales/24hr/@ Days Inn H
2mm	weigh sta both lanes
.5mm	eb
0mm	Massachusetts/Connecticut state line

INTERSTATE 90

BOSTON AREA

Exit#	Services
140mm	I-90 begins/ends near Logan Airport.
25	to I-93, to downtown Boston
24	to I-93, to downtown Boston
22(134)	Presidential Ctr, downtown
20(132)	MA 28, Alston, Brighton, Cambridge, N Courtyard, Doubletree Inn H, S Mobil
131mm	toll plaza
18(130)	MA Ave (from eb), N IHOP, McDonald's Day's Inn
17(128)	Centre St, Newton, N Bertucci's, Starbucks Crowne Plaza Honda, Nissan, Walgreens
16(125)	MA 16, W Newton, N Blue Ribbon BBQ CVS Drug, S Shell/repair
15(124)	I-95, N Speedway Marriott
123mm	toll plaza
14(122)	MA 30, Weston
117mm	Natick Travel Plaza eb, Gulf/dsl Dunkin Donuts, McDonald's info
13(116)	MA 30, Natick, S Cumberland, Mobil, Shell Boston Mkt, Burger King, Dunkin Donuts, Five Guys, Lotus Flower Chinese, McDonald's, Panera Bread, Papa Gino's, Stop&Shop Magnuson,
13(116)	Continued Red Roof Inn Best Buy, BJ's Whse, Home Depot, Kia, Kohl's, Lowe's, Macy's, Marshall's, REI, Target, TJ Maxx, USPO, Walmart
114mm	Framingham Travel Plaza wb, Gulf/dsl Boston Mkt, McDonald's info
12(111)	MA 9, Framington, N BP, Speedway Acapulco Mexican, Dunkin Donuts, Wendy's Motel 6, Sheraton, S Samba West Toyota
11a(106)	I-495, N to NH, S to Cape Cod
105mm	Westborough Travel Plaza wb, Gulf/dsl Boston Mkt, D'angelo, Dunkin Donuts, Papagino's gifts
11(96)	MA 122, to Millbury, N UMA Med Ctr
10a(95)	MA 146
94mm	Blackstone River
10(90)	I-395 S, to Auburn, I-290 N, Worcester, N Outback, Papa Gino's Comfort Inn, La Quinta, S Shell, Shell/repair/24hr Applebee's, D'angelo, Dunkin Donuts, Friendly's, Wendy's Fairfield Inn, Hampton Inn, Holiday Inn Express CVS Drug, Hyundai, Park'n Shop, TJ Maxx
84mm	Charlton Travel Plaza wb, Gulf/dsl McDonald's, info
80mm	Charlton Travel Plaza eb, Gulf/dsl McDonald's info, st police
79mm	toll plaza
9(78)	I-84, to Hartford, NYC, Sturbridge, access to H
67mm	Quaboag River
8(62)	MA 32, to US 20, Palmer, S on MA 32 Pride, Shell/dsl, Speedway Domino's, Jenny Chan's Chinese, McDonald's, Subway, Wendy's H, Big Y Foods, Chevrolet, CVS Drug, repair/transmissions, Rite Aid
58mm	Chicopee River
56mm	Ludlow Travel Plaza wb, Gulf/dsl Boston Mkt, D'angelo
55mm	Ludlow Travel Plaza eb, Gulf/dsl McDonald's,

INTERSTATE 90 Cont'd

Exit#	Services
7(54)	MA 21, to Ludlow, N Gulf, Pride/dsl, Sunoco, Verizon Burger King, Dunkin Donuts, Friendly's, Joy's Pizza, McDonald's, Starbucks, Subway Ace Hardware, Big Y Foods, CVS Drug, Jo-Ann Fabrics, S Shell/dsl Dominos, Taco Bell Holiday Inn Express
6(51)	I-291, to Springfield, Hartford CT, N Pride/50's Diner/Subway/dsl Dr Deegan's Steaks, Dunkin Donuts, McDonald's, Po's Chinese Motel 6 H, Basketball Hall of Fame, to Bradley Int Airport
5(49)	MA 33, to Chicopee, Westover AFB, N 99 Rest., Applebee's, Arby's, Buffalo Wild Wings, Chick-fil-A, Chipotle Mexican, Denny's, Dunkin Donuts, Friendly's, Little Caesar's, McDonald's, Panera Bread, PapaGino's, Popeye's, Royal Buffet, Starbucks, Subway, Wendy's Days Inn, Hampton Inn, Quality Inn, Residence Inn $Tree, Aldi Foods, Big Y Foods, BJ's Whse/gas, Chrysler/Dodge/Jeep, Home Depot, Honda, Marshall's, Marshall's, Monro, Nissan, Petsmart, Staples, Staples, Stop&Shop/gas, TownFair Tire, U-Haul, Verizon, Walmart/Subway, S Pride/Dunkin Donuts/Subway/dsl Buick/GMC
46mm	Connecticut River
4(46)	I-91, US 5, to Holyoke, W Springfield, N on US 5 Shell Dunkin Donuts Welcome Inn, S on US 5 Pride/dsl Donut Dip, Five Guys, Hooters, On the Border, Outback Steaks, Subway Hampton Inn, Red Roof Inn, Residence Inn, Springfield Inn, Super 8 BMW, Honda/Lexus/Toyota
41mm	st police wb
3(40)	US 202, to Westfield, N Mobil Alessio's Pizza, S Citgo/Subway/dsl, Shell/dsl Dunkin Donuts, Friendly's, McDonald's, Wendy's Holiday Inn Express, Quality Inn H, repair, vet
36mm	Westfield River
35.5mm	**runaway truck ramp eb**
29mm	**Blandford/Ludlow TP both lanes,** Gulf/dsl McDonald's info, vending
20mm	highest point on MA Tpk, 1724 ft
14.5mm	Appalachian Trail
2(11)	US 20, to Lee, Pittsfield, N Citgo, Shell/dsl, Sunoco Athena's Rest., Dunkin Donuts, Friendly's, McDonald's, Subway Morgan House/rest., Pilgrim Inn, Sunset Motel, Super 8 PriceChopper Foods, Rite Aid, True Value, S Big Y/dsl Orient Taste, Simply Grillicious, Subway, Villa Pizza Big Y Foods, Lee Outlets/famous brands
10.5mm	Hoosatonic River
8mm	**Lee Travel Plaza both lanes,** Gulf/dsl McDonald's atm, info, vending
4mm	**toll booth,**
1(2)	MA 41 (from wb, no return), to MA 102, W Stockbridge, the Berkshires, N Pleasant Valley Motel to Bousquet Ski Area
0mm	Massachusetts/New York state line

PITTSFIELD

INTERSTATE 91

Exit#	Services
55mm	Massachusetts/Vermont state line, call boxes
54mm	**parking area both lanes,**
28(51)	US 5, MA 10, Bernardston, E Fox Inn, W Sunoco Antonio's II Ristorante, Four-leaf Clover Rest., Hillside Organic Pizza Country Corner Store, RV camping, USPO
27(45)	MA 2 E (exits left from sb), Greenfield, E on US 5 Gulf, Speedway/Dunkin Donuts, Stop&Shop, Sunoco/dsl Burger King,
27(45)	Continued Denny's Pantry, Domino's, Dunkin Donuts, Goodies Rest., McDonald's, Subway H, $General, Aubuchon Hardware, AutoZone, Bond Parts, Chrysler/Dodge/Jeep, Honda, Walgreens
26(43)	MA 2 W, MA 2A E, Greenfield, E Planet/dsl, Shell/dsl Applebee's, Athens Pizza, China Gourmet, D'Angelo, Dunkin Donuts Quality Inn H, Chevrolet, Ford/Lincoln, Toyota, W Irving/Circle K, Valero 99 Rest., Asian Buffet, Friendly's, KFC/Pizza Hut/Taco Bell, McDonald's, Subway Days Inn, Hampton Inn $Tree, Big Y Foods, BJ's Whse, Family$, Home Depot, Staples, to Mohawk Tr, Verizon
39mm	Deerfield River
37mm	**weigh sta both lanes**
25(36)	MA 116 (from sb), S Deerfield, camping, hist dist, same as 24
24(35)	US 5, MA 10, MA 116, Deerfield (no EZ return), E Irving/Circle K/Dunkin Donuts/Subway/dsl Red Roof Inn Final Markdown, vet, Yankee Candle Co, W Roady's Trkstp/diner/dsl/24hr 24hr Diner
34.5mm	**parking area both lanes**
23(34)	US 5 (from sb), E Tom's Hot Dog Orchard Trailers, Rainbow Motel/camping
22(30)	US 5, MA 10 (from nb), N Hatfield, W Diamond RV Ctr
21(28)	US 5, MA 10, Hatfield, W Sunoco/dsl Subway Scottish Inn st police
20(26)	US 5, MA 9, MA 10 (from sb), Northampton, W Pride/Dunkin Donuts/dsl, Speedway/dsl Burger King, D'angelo's, KFC, McDonald's, PapaGino's Italian, Taco Bell H, AutoZone, Big Y Food/Drug, BigLots, Chevrolet, CVS Drug, Firestone/auto, Ford, Goodyear/auto, Honda, Hyundai, Kia, NAPA, Staples, Stop&Shop/gas, TownFair Tire, Toyota, U-Haul, Verizon, VW, Walgreens, Walmart/Subway
19(25)	MA 9, to Amherst, Northampton, 0-2 mi E Gulf, Phillips 66/Dunkin Donuts, Shell/dsl Primo Pizza Hampton Inn H, Nissan, to Elwell SP, vet
18(22)	US 5, Northampton, E Page's Loft Rest. Clarion, Country Inn&Suites (5mi), W Shell/Dunkin Donuts Fairfield Inn, Quality Inn to Smith Coll
18mm	scenic area both lanes
17b a(16)	MA 141, S Hadley, E Mobil/dsl, Shell/dsl Dunkin Donuts, Real China, Subway Days Inn Meineke, Rite Aid, Walgreens, W to Mt Tom Ski Area
16(14)	US 202, Holyoke, W Soldier's Home
15(12)	to US 5, Ingleside, E Shell/Dunkin Donuts Chicago Grill, Cracker Barrel, JP's Rest., Red Robin Howard Johnson H, Barnes&Noble, Best Buy, CVS Drug, Hobby Lobby, JC Penney, Macy's, Old Navy, PetCo, Target, TJ Maxx
14(11)	to US 5, to I-90 (Mass Tpk), E to Boston, W to Albany, E H
13b a(9)	US 5 N, W Springfield, E Pride/dsl Backyard Grill, Donut Dip, Five Guys, Hooters, On-the-Border, Outback Steaks, Shallot Thai, Subway Knights Inn, Red Roof Inn, Residence Inn, Springfield Inn, Super 8 BMW, Lexus/Toyota, W Mobil/dsl, Pride/dsl 99 Rest., Arby's, Bertucci's, Burger King, Cal's Grill, Carrabba's, Chili's, D'angelo's, Friendly's, IHOP, KFC, Longhorn Steaks, McDonald's, Nippon Grill, Olive Garden, Panera Bread, Pizza Hut, Tokyo Cuisine Bel Air Inn, Candlewood Suites, Clarion, Days Inn, EconoLodge, Hampton Inn, Quality Inn, Red Carpet Inn, Travelodge $Tree, Aldi Foods, AT&T, Chrysler/Dodge/Jeep, Costco, CVS Drug, Dick's, Fiat, GNC, Home Depot, Honda, Kohl's, Mazda, Michael's, Nissan, Staples, Stop&Shop, Subaru, TownFair Tire, Verizon
12(8.5)	I-391 N, to Chicopee
11(8)	Birnie Ave (from sb), E Mobil H

GREENFIELD

NORTHAMPTON

SPRINGFIELD

INTERSTATE 91 Cont'd

Exit#	Services
10(7.5)	Main St (from nb), Springfield, E [gas] Mobil
9(7)	US 20 W, MA 20A E (from nb), E [food] McDonald's, W [gas] Pride/Subway/dsl
8(6.5)	I-291, US 20 E, to I-90, E downtown
7(6)	Columbus Ave (from sb), E [gas] Pride/Subway/dsl [lodging] Marriott, Sheraton, W [other] to Basketball Hall of Fame
6(5.5)	Springfield Ctr, E [gas] Pride/Dunkin Donuts/Subway/dsl [food] Starbucks, W [food] Coldstone, Plan B Burger [other] Basketball Hall of Fame
5(5)	Broad St, E [gas] Mobil/dsl [lodging] Hampton Inn [other] Hyundai, W [gas] Sunoco/dsl [food] Chicago Grill, Subway [lodging] Hilton Garden [other] Buick/GMC, same as 4
4(4.5)	MA 83, Broad St, Main St, E [gas] Mobil/dsl [food] Antonio's Grinders [other] Hyundai, W [gas] Sunoco/dsl [food] Chicago Grill, Subway [lodging] Buick/GMC, Chevrolet, Hilton Garden, same as 5
3(4)	US 5 N, to MA 57, Columbus Ave, W Springfield, E [gas] Sunoco [food] Antonio's Pizza, W [other] Chevrolet
2(3.5)	MA 83 S (from nb), to E Longmeadow, E [food] Friendly's
1(3)	US 5 S (from sb)
0mm	Massachusetts/Connecticut state line, callboxes begin/end

INTERSTATE 93

METHUEN

Exit#	Services
47mm	Massachusetts/New Hampshire state line, callboxes begin/end
48(46)	MA 213 E, to Methuen, E [other] [H]
47(45)	Pelham St, Methuen, E [gas] Sunoco [food] Dunkin Donuts, Heavenly Donuts, McDonald's, Outback Steaks, W [gas] BP, Irving/Circle K/Subway/dsl [food] Fireside Rest., NE Seafood [lodging] Day's Hotel/rest. [other] Chrysler/Dodge/Jeep
46(44)	MA 110, MA 113, to Lawrence, E [gas] BP/repair, Mobil, Shell [food] Burger King, Dunkin Donuts, KFC/Taco Bell, McDonald's, PapaGino's, Pizza Hut [other] [H], $Tree, MktBasket Foods, Rite Aid, W [gas] Citgo, Super [food] Dunkin Donuts, Irish Cottage Rest., Jules Rest., Riverside Pizza, Royal Roast Beef [lodging] Passport Inn
45(43)	Andover St, River Rd, to Lawrence, E [lodging] Courtyard, Homewood Suites, Wyndham, W [gas] Mobil/Dunkin Donuts [food] Chateu Italian, Chili's [lodging] La Quinta, Residence Inn, SpringHill Suites [other] vet
44b a(40)	I-495, to Lowell, Lawrence, E [other] [H]
43(39)	MA 133, N Tewksbury, E [gas] Mobil/Dunkin Donuts, W [food] 99 Rest.
42(38)	Dascomb Rd, East St, Tewksbury, W [gas] Citgo/dsl [food] Dunkin Donuts, Luna Rossa Italian, Subway [other] 7-11
41(35)	MA 125, Andover, [other] st police
40(34)	MA 62, Wilmington
39(33)	Concord St, E [food] Dunkin Donuts, Subway [other] Shriners Auditorium, URGENT CARE
38(31)	MA 129, Reading, W [gas] Mobil/Dunkin Donuts/Subway/dsl [food] Burger King, Pacific Grove Chinese, Red Heat Tavern
37c(30)	Commerce Way, Atlantic Ave, W [food] Chipotle Mexican, Firehouse Subs, Starbucks [lodging] Red Roof Inn, Residence Inn [other] Pet-Co, Petsmart, Target, Verizon
37b a(29)	I-95, S to Waltham, N to Peabody
36(28)	Montvale Ave, E [gas] Mobil/Circle K [food] Deli Works, Dunkin Donuts [lodging] Courtyard, W [gas] BP, Gulf, Speedway/dsl [food] Bickford's Grille, Dunkin Donuts, McDonald's, O'Conner's Rest., Polcari's Italian, Wendy's [lodging] Best Western, Comfort Inn [other] [H]
35(27)	Winchester Highlands, Melrose, E [other] [H] (no EZ return to sb)

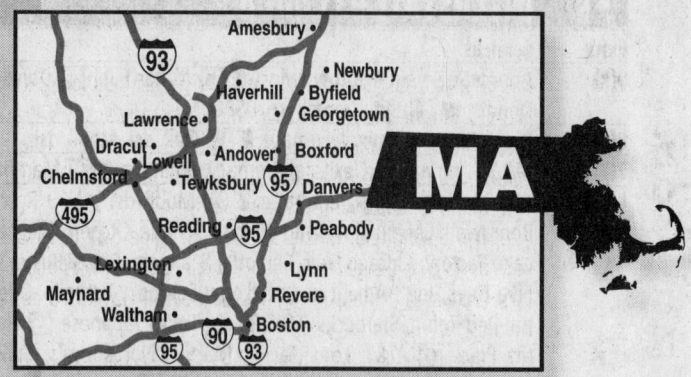

BOSTON AREA

Exit#	Services
34(26)	MA 28 N (from nb, no EZ return), Stoneham, E [gas] Mobil/dsl [food] Friendly's, W [other] [H]
33(25)	MA 28, Fellsway West, Winchester, W [other] [H]
32(23)	MA 60, Salem Ave, Medford Square, W [lodging] Hyatt Place [other] [H], to Tufts U
31(22)	MA 16 E, to Revere (no EZ return sb), W [gas] Fred's Gas, Mobil/dsl, Mr. C's/dsl [food] Avellino's Italian, Burger King, Dunkin Donuts, Pizza Hut [other] AutoZone, Chrysler/Dodge/Jeep, Kia, Nissan
30(21)	MA 28, MA 38, Mystic Ave, Somerville, W [gas] Mr. C's/dsl [food] Burger King [other] AutoZone, VW
29(20)	MA 28 (from nb), Somerville, E [food] 99 Rest., Dunkin Donuts [lodging] La Quinta [other] Home Depot, Staples, TJ Maxx, W [gas] Gulf, Speedway [food] Dunkin Donuts [other] same as 30, Stop&Shop
28(19)	Sullivans Square, Charles Town, downtown
27	US 1 N (from nb)
26(18.5)	MA 28 N, Storrow Dr, North Sta, downtown
25	Haymarket Sq, [other] Gov't Center
24(18)	Callahan Tunnel, E [other] [airport]
23(17.5)	High St, Congress St, W [lodging] Marriott
22(17)	Atlantic Ave, Northern Ave, South Sta, [other] Boston World Trade Ctr
21(16.5)	Kneeland St, ChinaTown
20(16)	I-90 W, to Mass Tpk
19(15.5)	Albany St (from sb), W [other] [H]
18(15)	Mass Ave, to Roxbury, W [other] [H]
17(14.5)	E Berkeley (from nb)
16(14)	S Hampton St, Andrew Square, W [food] Applebee's, Olive Garden, Panera Bread [lodging] Courtyard, Holiday Inn Express [other] Best Buy, Home Depot, Marshall's, Old Navy, Stop&Shop/gas, Target, TJ Maxx
15(13)	Columbia Rd, Everett Square, E [lodging] DoubleTree [other] JFK Library, to UMA, W [gas] Gulf, Speedway
14(12.5)	Morissey Blvd (from nb no return), E [other] JFK Library, W [gas] Shell
13(12)	Freeport St, to Dorchester, (from nb), W [gas] 7-11, Citgo [food] Boston Mkt, Deadwood Cafe, Freeport Tavern, Ruritan Pizza [lodging] Comfort Inn, Ramada [other] CVS Drug, Lambert's Mkt, Stop&Shop, Toyota
12(11.5)	MA 3A S (from sb, no EZ return), Quincy, E [gas] Express, repair [lodging] Best Western, W [gas] Gulf/Dunkin Donuts, Speedway/dsl [food] PapaGino's [other] AutoZone, CVS Drug, Staples, Verizon, Walgreens
11b a(11)	to MA 203, Granite Ave, Ashmont
10(10)	Squantum Ave (from sb), Milton, W [other] [H]

[gas] = gas [food] = food [lodging] = lodging [other] = other [Rs] = rest stop

INTERSTATE 93 Cont'd

BOSTON AREA

Exit#	Services
9(9)	Adams St, Bryant Ave, to N Quincy, E Milton Fuel Dunkin Donuts, W Shell/repair USPO
8(8)	Brook Pkwy, to Quincy, Furnace, E Gulf/dsl, Mobil/dsl
7(7)	MA 3 S, to Cape Cod (exits left from sb), Braintree, E Marriott
6(6)	MA 37, to Holbrook, Braintree, E Mobil/dsl 99 Rest., Boardwalk Café, Buffalo Wild Wings, CA Pizza Kitchen, Cheesecake Factory, Chicago Grill, Chipotle, D'angelo, Dave&Buster's, Five Guys, Joe's American Grill, Legal Seafood, Potbelly, Qdoba, Red Robin, Starbucks, TGIFriday's, Tokyo Japanese Hyatt Place AT&T, Lord&Taylor, Macy's, Nordstrom's, Sullivan Tire/auto, Target, URGENT CARE, W Citgo Ascari Café Candlewood Suites, Extended Stay America, Hampton Inn, Holiday Inn Express Barnes&Noble, Ford, VW
5b a(4)	MA 28 S, to Randolph, Milton, E Citgo, Mobil/dsl, Shell/dsl Domino's, Dunkin Donuts, La Scala, Lombardo's, Randolph Cafe, Wong's Chinese Comfort Inn AT&T
4(3)	MA 24 S (exits left from sb), to Brockton
3(2)	MA 138 N, to Ponkapoag Trail, Houghtons Pond
2b a(1)	MA 138 S, to Stoughton, Milton, E golf, W BlueHill/dsl, Mobil/dsl, Shell/dsl Blue Hills Grill, Dunkin Donuts Homewood Suites
1(0)	I-95 N, S to Providence. **I-93 begins/ends on I-95, exit 12.**

INTERSTATE 95

AMESBURY

Exit#	Services
89.5mm	**Welcome Ctr/[Rs] sb, full [handicapped] facilities, litter barrels, [picnic], Massachusetts/New Hampshire state line**
60(89)	MA 286, to Salisbury, beaches, E Mobil/dsl Cosmos Rest., Dunkin Donuts, Lena's Seafood Rest. Black Bear Camping (seasonal)
59(88)	I-495 S (from sb)
58b a(87)	rd 110, to I-495 S, to Amesbury, Salisbury, E Sunoco/Dunkin Donuts/Subway/dsl China Buffet, Niko's Place, Sylvan St Grille, Winner's Circle Rest. Ford, U-Haul, vet, W Irving Gas/Circle K, Mobil, Sunoco/dsl Acapulco's Mexican, Burger King, Dunkin Donuts, Friendly's, McDonald's, PapaGino's Fairfield Inn AT&T, Chevrolet, Stop&Shop, Verizon
57(85)	MA 113, to W Newbury, E Mobil/dsl, Shell/dsl/repair, Sunoco China One, D'angelo, Dunkin Donuts, Dunkin Donuts, Giuseppe's Italian, Hana Japan, McDonald's, Panera Bread, PapaGino's, Sal's Pizza, Wendy's [H], 7-11, GNC, Marshall's, Midas, MktBasket Foods, Rite Aid, Shaw's Foods, Verizon, Walgreens
56(83)	Scotland Rd, to Newbury, E st police
55(82)	Central St, to Byfield, E Gen Store Eatery, Parker River Grille, W Prime/dsl/repair
54b a(78)	MA 133, E to Rowley, W to Groveland, E vet
77mm	**weigh sta both lanes**
53b a(76)	MA 97, S to Topsfield, N to Georgetown
52(74)	Topsfield Rd, to Topsfield, Boxford
51(72)	Endicott Rd, to Topsfield, Middleton
50(71)	US 1, to MA 62, Topsfield, E Gulf/dsl, Mobil/dsl Honda, W S&S Supino's Rest., Timothy's Rest., TX Roadhouse DoubleTree, Knights Inn CVS Drug, st police, Staples, Stop&Shop
49(70)	MA 62 (from nb), Danvers, Middleton, W same as 50
48(69)	Hobart St (from sb), W Calitri's Italian Comfort Inn, Extended Stay America, Motel 6 Home Depot

PEABODY

Exit#	Services
47b a(68)	MA 114, to Middleton, Peabody, E Gulf/Dunkin Donuts, Sunoco Dunkin Donuts, Honey Dew Donuts, McDonald's, Olive Garden, Outback Steaks, PapaGino's, Pizza Hut, Subway Audi, Chevrolet, Chrysler/Dodge/Jeep, Infiniti, Lexus, Lowe's, NTB, Petsmart, Porsche, Subaru, TJ Maxx, Toyota, Trader Joe's, Verizon, vet, VW, Walmart, **W on US 1** Speedway/dsl Chili's, Hardcover Rest., TGIFriday's Motel 6, Residence Inn, TownePlace Suites Costco/gas, Home Depot, LandRover, Meineke, NAPA
46(67)	to US 1, W Best, Global, Gulf/dsl, Sunoco/dsl Dunkin Donuts, Honey Dew Donuts auto repair
45(66)	MA 128 N, to Peabody
44b a(65)	US 1 N, MA 129, E [H], W 7-11, Shell, Sunoco Bertucci's, Bros Kouzina Rest., Carrabba's, Dunkin Donuts, Marco's Italian, Santarpio's Pizza, Sonic, Wendy's Hampton Inn, Holiday Inn, Homewood Suites, Plaza Motel, SpringHill Suites
43(61)	Walnut St, Lynnfield, E to Saugus Iron Works NHS (3mi), W Sheraton golf
42(62)	Salem St, Montrose, E Irving/Circle K/Subway, Sunoco Dunkin Donuts, W Sheraton
41(60)	Main St, Lynnfield Ctr, E Shell
40(59)	MA 129, Wakefield Ctr, N Reading, E Bellino's Italian, Honey Dew Donuts city park, vet, W Gulf Dunkin Donuts, Mandarin Chinese Chevrolet, Mazda, REI

READING

Exit#	Services
39(58)	North Ave, Reading, E Clarion city park, Subaru, Volvo, W Shell/dsl Bertucci's, Chili's, Fuddrucker's, Longhorn Steaks, Macaroni Grill, Oye's Rest., Starbucks [H], Home Depot, Honda, Mkt Basket Foods, Staples, Stop&Shop Foods, URGENT CARE, Verizon
38b a(57)	MA 28, to Reading, E Gulf/repair, Mobil, Speedway/dsl 99 Rest., Burger King, Burger King, D'Angelo's/PapaGino's, Dunkin Donuts, Dunkin Donuts, Five Guys, Subway, Uno Fresco Cafe Advance Parts, AutoZone, CVS Drug, Ford, GNC, Marshall's, Michaels, Stop&Shop/gas, Walgreens, W Eleven Variety, Mobil/dsl, Shell, Sunoco Anthony's Roastbeef, Burger King, Calariso's Farm Stand, Domino's, Dunkin Donuts, Harrow's Chicken Pies, McDonald's, Sam's Bistro, Starbucks Meineke
37b a(56)	I-93, N to Manchester, S to Boston
36(55)	Washington St, to Winchester, E Dunkin Donuts, Fresh City, Sal's Pizza, Starbucks, Subway Hilton Hogan's Tires, Jaguar, Nissan, Staples, Toyota, W Sunoco 99 Rest., Bertucci's, Chicago Grill, China Pearl, d'Angelo, Dunkin Donuts, Joe's Grill, On the Border, Panera Bread, Papa Gino's Qdoba, Sarku Japan Courtyard, Fairfield Inn, Holiday Inn Express, Red Roof Inn $Tree, AT&T, CVS Drug, Kohl's Lowe's, Mkt Basket Foods, NTB, TJ Maxx, Town Fair Tire, USPO
35(54)	MA 38, to Woburn, E Scoreboard Grill Crowne Plaza [H], W Mobil/dsl Applebee's, Dunkin Donuts Sichuan Garden Extended Stay America city park, CVS Drug, Stop&Shop Foods
34(53)	Winn St, Woburn
33b a(52)	US 3 S, MA 3A N, to Winchester, E Bickford's Grille, Bonefish Grill, Café Escadrille, Capital Grille, ChuckeCheese, Coldstone, Dunkin Donuts, Panera Bread, Papa Razzi, Potbelly Seasons Grill, Starbucks, Subway Hyatt House CVS Drug, Honda, LL Bean, Marshall's, Michael's, Roche Bros Mkt W Prime, Speedway Chopps Grill Marriott [H] Audi/Porsche, Kia, Mercedes, repair
32b a(51)	US 3 N, MA 2A S, to Lowell, E Mobil/dsl, Shell Burger King, Burton's Grill, Chateau Italian, d'Angelo, Dunkin Donuts

INTERSTATE 95 Cont'd

LEXINGTON

32b a(51) Continued
Five Guys, McDonald's, Subway Hilton Garden, Sonesta Suites Best Buy, Jo-Ann, Midas, Mkt Basket Foods, Nordstrom, Old Navy, PetCo, Trader Joe's, Verizon, **W** Border Cafe, Buffalo Wild Wings, Cheesecake Factory, Chicago Grill, Chili's, Chipotle, Del Frisco's Grill, Legal Seafoods, Macaroni Grill, Noodles&Co, Qdoba, Wendy's Candlewood Suites, Extended Stay America AT&T, Barnes&Noble, Kohl's, Lord&Taylor, Macy's, Nordstrom, Staples, URGENT CARE

31b a(48) MA 4, MA 225, Lexington, **E** Gulf, Mobil/dsl/repair Alexander's Pizza, Qdoba, Starbucks Stop&Shop, Walgreens, **W** Gulf, Shell d'Angelo, Dunkin Donuts, Great Wall, Margarita's, McDonald's, Papa Gino's Bedford Plaza Hotel, Quality Inn Stop&Shop, TJ Maxx, vet

30b a(47) MA 2A, Lexington, **E** Sunoco/Dunkin Donuts/dsl, **W** ALoft, Element Hotel H, Hanscom AFB, to MinuteMan NP

46.5mm **travel plaza nb,** Gulf/dsl/CNG Honey Dew Donuts, McDonald's gifts

29b a(46) MA 2 W, Cambridge

28b a(45) Trapelo Rd, Belmont, **E** Gulf/dsl, Mobil/dsl Boston Mkt, Burger King, Dunkin Donuts, Friendly's, McDonald's, Panera Bread, Papa Gino's, Starbucks, Subway city park, Shaw's Foods/Osco Drugs

27b a(44) Totten Pond Rd, Waltham, **E** Shell Bonefish Grill, Copper House, Dunkin Donuts, Naked Fish Rest., Osteria Posto Best Western, Courtyard, Extended Stay America, Hilton Garden, Holiday Inn Express, Home Suites, Hyatt, Westin Hotel, **W** Bertucci's Rest., Green Papaya Thai Embassy Suites/The Grill AT&T, Costco, Home Depot, D'Angelo

26(43) US 20, to MA 117, to Waltham, **E** Sunoco/dsl, **W** Mobil/dsl Chicago Grill, Dunkin Donuts NTB, vet

25(42) I-90, MA Tpk

24(41) MA 30, Newton, Wayland, **E** Speedway Marriott/rest.

23(40) Recreation Rd (from nb), to MA Tpk

22b a(39) Grove St, **E** Hotel Indigo golf

NEWTON

38.5mm **travel plaza sb,** Gulf/dsl HoneyDew Donuts, McDonald's gifts

21b a(38) MA 16, Newton, Wellesley, **E** H, **W** Sunoco Dunkin Donuts, North End Pizza, Papa Razzi, Starbucks CVS Drug

20b a(36) MA 9, Brookline, Framingham

19(35) Highland Ave, Newton, Needham, **E** Speedway Acapulco's, Chipotle Mexican, D'Angelo, Five Guys, Fresh City, Mandarin Cuisine, Mighty Subs, Panera Bread, Papa Gino's, Petsmart, Starbucks Residence Inn, Sheraton/rest. AAA, CVS Drug, Marshall's, Michael's, PetCo, Staples, TJ Maxx, **W** Three Squares Rest. Chevrolet, Ford

18(34) Great Plain Ave, W Roxbury

33.5mm **parking area sb, litter barrels,**

17(33) MA 135, Needham, Wellesley

32mm **truck turnout sb**

DEDHAM

16b a(31) MA 109, High St, Dedham, **W** Mobil/dsl

15b a(29) US 1, MA 128, **0-2 mi E** Gulf Chili's, Joe's Grill, Legal Seafood, Panera Bread, PapaGino's, PF Chang's, Qdoba, Subway, Summer Shack, TGI Friday's, Victory Grille, Yard House Rest. Fairfield Inn, Holiday Inn, Residence Inn AT&T, AutoZone, Best Buy, BJ's Whse, Costco/gas, CVS Drug, EVC, LL Bean, Monro/service, PepBoys, PetCo, Staples, Star Foods, Tesla, Verizon, vet, Walgreens, Whole Foods Mkt, **0-2 mi W** Irving/dsl, Shell/dsl Burger King, Dunkin Donuts, Jade Chinese, McDonald's Budget Inn AAA, AT&T, Audi/Porsche,

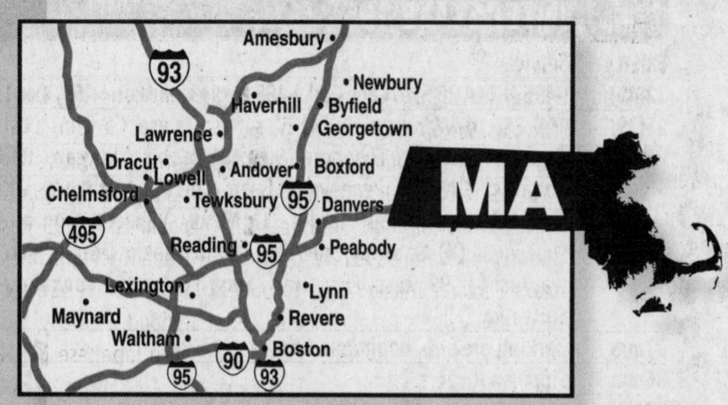

15b a(29) Continued
Buick/GMC, Chevrolet, Chrysler/Dodge/Jeep, Fiat, Honda, Kia, Mercedes, Toyota

14(28) East St, Canton St, **E** Hilton

27mm **sb, full facilities, litter barrels,**

13(26.5) University Ave

12(26) I-93 N, to Braintree, Boston, motorist callboxes end nb

11b a(23) Neponset St, to Canton, **E** Citgo/repair, Sunoco/dsl Dunkin Donuts, **2 mi W on US 1** Gulf/dsl, Sunoco Jake&Joe's Hampton Inn, The Chateau H, Chevrolet, Ferrari, Ford, Honda, Hyundai, Maserati, Nissan, Toyota, Volvo

22.5mm Neponset River

10(20) Coney St (from sb, no EZ return), to US 1, Sharon, Walpole, **1 mi W on US 1** Mobil 99 Rest., Bertucci's, British Beer Co, Chili's, Chipotle Mexican, Dunkin Donuts, Five Guys, Friendly's, IHOP, McDonald's, Outback Steaks, Panda Express, Panera Bread, PapaGino's, Starbucks, Subway, Taco Bell, TX Roadhouse Courtyard, Holiday Inn Express, Residence Inn, Sheraton Acura, Advance Parts, Barnes&Noble, CarMax, Home Depot, Jo-Ann, Kohl's, Old Navy, O'Reilly Parts, PetCo, Petsmart, Staples, Stop&Shop, TownFair Tire, VW, Walgreens

9(19) US 1, to MA 27, Walpole, **W** Gulf, Mobil/dsl, Stop$Shop Gas Applebee's, Dunkin Donuts, Starbucks Best Western, EconoLodge BigY Foods/drug, Lexus, same as 10, Stop&Shop, Walmart

8(16) S Main St, Sharon, **E** Dunkin Donuts Rite Aid, Shaw's Foods

7b a(13) MA 140, to Mansfield, **E** 99 Rest., Jake'nJoe's Grille Comfort Inn, Courtyard, Holiday Inn, Red Roof Inn, Residence Inn Stop&Shop/gas, **W** Shell/HoneyDew Donuts/dsl Dunkin Donuts, PapaGino's $Tree, AT&T

6b a(12) I-495, S to Cape Cod, N to NH

ATTLEBORO

10mm **Welcome Ctr/ nb, full facilities, info, litter barrels, petwalk,**

9mm **truck parking area sb**

5(7) MA 152, Attleboro, **E** H, **W** Gulf/dsl Barett's Alehouse, Wendy's Shaw's Foods/Osco Drug

4(6) I-295 S, to Woonsocket

3(4) MA 123, to Attleboro, **E** Shell/dsl Dunkin Donuts H, zoo

2.5mm **parking area/weigh sta both lanes, litter barrels, no restrooms**

2b a(1) US 1A, Newport Ave, Attleboro, **E** Mobil/dsl McDonald's, Olive Garden Home Depot, Market Basket Foods, Verizon, **W** Grampy's Kia

1(.5) US 1 (from sb), **E** Attleboro Inn Rite Aid, Volvo, **W** Speedway/dsl

0mm Massachusetts/Rhode Island state line

INTERSTATE 195

Exit #	Services
22(41)	I-495 N, MA 25 S, to Cape Cod. **I-195 begins/ends on I-495, exit 1.**
21(39)	MA 28, to Wareham, N BB's Rest., Casa Cancun, Cosi, Gourmet Garden, Longhorn Steaks, Qdoba Mexican, Red Robin GNC, JC Penney, LL Bean, Lowe's, Michael's, Old Navy, PetCo, Staples, Target, TJ Maxx, Verizon, Walmart/Subway, S Gateway Star/dsl, Mobil/Dunkin Donuts/Subway/dsl 99 Rest., Five Guys, Saga Fusion TownPlace Suites H
37mm	**parking area eb, boatramp, info**
36mm	Sippican River
20(35)	MA 105, to Marion, S RV camping (seasonal)
19b a(31)	to Mattapoisett, S Mobil Nick's Pizza, Ying Dynasty USPO
18(26)	MA 240 S, to Fairhaven, **1 mi** S 7-11 99 Rest., Burger King, China Cafe, Dunkin Donuts, Frontera Grill, Jake's Diner, McDonald's, PapaGino's, Pasta House, Riccardi's Italian, Subway, Taco Bell, Wendy's Hampton Inn $Tree, AutoZone, Brahmin Handbags, Buick/GMC, GNC, Marshall's, Mazda, Staples, Stop&Shop/gas, Sullivan Tire, TownFair Tire, Walgreens, Walmart
25.5mm	Acushnet River
17(24)	Coggeshall St, (from wb only), New Bedford, N 7-11/gas, Petro/dsl, Sunoco Dunkin Donuts, HoneyDew Donuts, Little Caesar's, McDonald's, Papa John's, Subway, Taco Bell GNC, Market Basket Foods, same as 16, URGENT CARE, Verizon
16(23)	Washburn St (from eb), N Sunoco McDonald's, Papa John's
15(22)	MA 18 S, New Bedford, S Mutual hist dist, to downtown, Whaling Museum
14(21)	Penniman St (from eb), New Bedford, downtown
13b a(20)	MA 140, N , S Sunoco Dunkin Donuts H, Buttonwood Park/zoo, CVS Drug, Shaw's Foods, Walgreens
12b a(19)	N Dartmouth, S Mobil/dsl, Mobil/Subway/dsl, Speedway 99 Rest., Applebee's, Azuma Asian, Buffalo Wild Wings, Burger King, Chipotle, ChuckeCheese, Coldstone, Dunkin Donuts, Five Guys, Friendly's, IHOP, Jimmy's Pizza, McDonald's, Olive Garden, Panera Bread, PapaGino's, Peking Garden, Ruby Tuesday, Subway, Taco Bell, TGIFriday's, Tropical Smoothie, TX Roadhouse, Wendy's Residence Inn $Tree, AT&T, Barnes&Noble, Best Buy, BJ's Whse/gas, Chevrolet, Dick's, Firestone/auto, Home Depot, JC Penney, Jo-Ann, Kia, Kohl's, Lowe's, Macy's, Michael's, Nissan, Old Navy, PetCo, st police, Stop&Shop/gas, Target, TJ Maxx, TownFair Tire, Toyota, USPO, Walgreens, Walmart
11b a(17)	Reed Rd, to Dartmouth, S Shell Dunkin Donuts
10(16)	MA 88 S, to US 6, Westport, S Cumberland CVS Drug, same as 9
9(15.5)	MA 24 N (from nb), Stanford Rd, Westport, S Rte 6 Gas, Supreme, Valero Dunkin Donuts, Galley Grill Hampton Inn White's Hospitality
8b	MA 24 N, (exits left from eb)
8a(15)	MA 24 S, Fall River, Westport
7(14)	MA 81 S, Plymouth Ave, Fall River, N Speedway 99 Rest., Boston Mkt, Burger King, D'angelo, Dunkin Donuts, HoneyDew Donuts, KFC, Subway, Wendy's H, CVS Drug, Hyundai, S Gulf, Shell Applebee's, McDonald's Stop&Shop, Sullivan Tire, Walgreens
6(13.5)	Pleasant St, Fall River, downtown
5(13)	MA 79, MA 138, to Taunton, S 7-11, Speedway/dsl Dunkin Donuts
12mm	Assonet Bay
4b a(10)	MA 103, to Swansea, Somerset, N Wilbur's Rogers Rest. repair, vet, S Shell Jillian's Grill Riverview Inn
3(8)	US 6, to MA 118, Swansea, Rehoboth, N Mobil/Dunkin Donuts, Speedway, Swansea/dsl Five Guys, Friendly's, McDonald's, Ruby Tuesday, Subway, Thai Taste, Wendy's $Tree, AT&T, BigLots, Firestone/auto, Jo-Ann Fabrics, Macy's, Marshall's, Petsmart, Price Rite Foods, Target, Verizon, Walmart/Subway, S Gulf Anthony's Seafood, Umi Japanese Holiday Inn Express, Swansea Motel Kia, NAPA, USPO
5.5mm	**parking area wb**
2(5)	MA 136, to Newport, S Mobil/24hr, Shell/24hr Dunkin Donuts, McDonald's, Subway CVS Drug, Toyota
3mm	**weigh sta eb**
1(1)	MA 114A, to Seekonk, N Crossroads/Subway/dsl, Exxon, Shell/dsl 99 Rest., Dunkin Donuts, HoneyDew Donuts, Newport Creamery Motel 6 vet, S Mobil/24hr, Speedway/dsl, Stop&Shop Gas/repair 1149 Rest., Applebee's, BigLots, Burger King, Chili's, Chipotle, Coldstone, D'Angelo, Dunkin Donuts, Five Guys, Friendly's, Hichigo Ichie Japanese, IHOP, Joe's Kitchen, Longhorn Steaks, McDonald's, Moe's SW, Outback Steaks, Panera Bread, PapaGino's, Plaza Azteca, Starbucks, Subway, Taco Bell, TGIFriday's, Wendy's Best Western, Clarion, Comfort Inn, Extended Stay America, Hampton Inn, Knights Inn, Mary's Motel $Tree, Acura, Advance Parts, AT&T, Best Buy, BigLots, BJ's/gas, Bob's Stores, Dick's, Firestone/auto, GNC, Hobby Lobby, Home Depot, Kohl's, Lowe's, Michael's, PepBoys, Petco, Sam's Club, Staples, Stop&Shop Foods, Target, TJMaxx, TownFair Tire, Verizon, Walmart
0mm	Massachusetts/Rhode Island state line. **Exits 8-1 are in RI.**
8(5)	US 1A N, Pawtucket, S Mobil/dsl Subway CVS Drug
7(4)	US 6 E, CT 114 S, to Barrington, Seekonk
6(3)	Broadway Ave, N Monro
5(2.5)	RI 103 E, Warren Ave
4(2)	US 44 E, RI 103 E, Taunton Ave, Warren Ave
3(1.5)	Gano St, S Wyndham Garden
2(1)	US 44 W, Wickenden St, India Pt, downtown, N Shell/dsl, S Wyndham Garden
1(.5)	Providence, downtown

I-195 begins/ends on I-95, exit 20 in Providence, RI. Exits 1-8 are in RI.

FALL RIVER · SEEKONK · PROVIDENCE

INTERSTATE 290

Exit#	Services
26b a(20)	I-495. **I-290 begins/ends on I-495, exit 25.**
25b a(17)	Solomon Pond Mall Rd, to Berlin, N EVC Bertucci's, Olive Garden, TGIFriday's Quality Inn, Residence Inn Best Buy, JC Penney, Macy's, mall/foodcourt, Old Navy, Target, S Guiseppe's Grille
24(15)	Church St, Northborough
23b a(13)	MA 140, Boylston, N Gulf/Dunkin Donuts/dsl, Shell/dsl
22(11)	Main St, Worchester, N Dunkin Donuts
21(10)	Plantation St (from eb), N Dunkin Donuts, same as 20
20(8)	MA 70, Lincoln St, Burncoat St, N Gulf/Subway/dsl, Shell/dsl Crown Chicken, Denny's, Dunkin Donuts, Five Guys, KFC, Kyoto, McDonald's, PapaGino's/D'Angelo, Plaza Azteca, Ruby Tuesday, Subway, Taco Bell, TX Roadhouse, Wendy's Quality Inn $Tree, Aldi Foods, AT&T, AutoZone, Barnes&Noble, CVS Drug, Dick's, Kohl's, Lowe's, Staples, Stop&Shop, Target, URGENT CARE, USPO, Walgreens

INTERSTATE 290 Cont'd

WORCESTER

Exit#	Services
19(7)	I-190 N, MA 12
18	MA 9, Framington, Ware, N Worcester Airport, S
16	Central St, Worcester, N 99 Rest., Starbucks Hilton Garden, Holiday Inn Express USPO
14	MA 122, Barre, Worcester, downtown
13	MA 122A, Vernon St, Worcester, downtown
12	MA 146 S, to Millbury
11	Southbridge St, College Square, W Culpepper's Cafe, N Shell/dsl Golden House Chinese, Wendy's Family$
10	MA 12 N (from wb), Hope Ave
9	Auburn St, to Auburn, E Shell Arby's, Auburn Town Pizza, Dunkin Donuts, McDonald's, Outback, PapaGino's, Starbucks, Subway, Yong Shing Comfort Inn, Holiday Inn Express (1mi), La Quinta Acura, AutoZone, Firestone/auto, Macy's, Midas, Petco, Shaw's Foods, Staples, TownFair Tire, USPO
8	MA 12 S (from sb), Webster, W Shell Holiday Inn Express
7	I-90, E to Boston, W to Springfield. **I-290 begins/ends on I-90.**

INTERSTATE 395

OXFORD

Exit#	Services
12.5	**I-395 begins/ends on I-290, exit 10.**
7(12)	to I-90 (MA Tpk), MA 12, E Holiday Inn Express, W Shell Bentley Cafe same as 6b
6b a(11)	US 20, E Cumberland Frank&Nancy's Cafe, Major League Roast Beef NAPA, Saab/VW, truck tires/repair, W Shell Applebee's, Chuck's Steakhouse, D'angelo, Dunkin Donuts, Friendly's, Wendy's Fairfield Inn, Hampton Inn BJ's Whse/dsl, Buick/Cadillac/GMC, Chevrolet, Ford, Home Depot, Hyundai, Nissan, TJ Maxx
5(8)	Depot Rd, N Oxford
4b a(6)	Sutton Ave, to Oxford, E Shell/Dunkin Donuts/dsl $Tree, Home Depot, MktBasket Foods, W Mobil/dsl Dunkin Donuts, McDonald's, NE Pizza, Subway Cahill's Tire/repair, Cumberland Farms, CVS Drug
3(4)	Cudworth Rd, to N Webster, S Oxford
2(3)	MA 16, to Webster, E RV Camping, Subaru, W BP/repair, Gulf, Sunoco Burger King, D'angelo, Dunkin Donuts, Empire Wok, Friendly's, HoneyDew Donuts, KFC/Taco Bell, Little Caesar's, McDonald's, Mexicali Grill, Panera Bread, PapaGino's, Wendy's $Tree, Advance Parts, AutoZone, CVS Drug, Ford, O'Reilly Parts, PriceChopper Foods, Rite Aid, Verizon, Walgreens
1(1)	MA 193, to Webster, E , W Mobil/dsl Golden Greek Rest., Wind Tiki Chinese Goodyear/auto
0mm	**Massachusetts/Connecticut state line**

INTERSTATE 495

Exit#	Services
119	**I-495 begins/ends on I-95, exit 59.**
55(119)	MA 110 (from nb, no return), to I-95 S, E Irving/Circle K, Mobil, Sunoco/dsl Acapulco Mexican, Burger King, Dunkin Donuts, Friendly's, McDonald's, PapaGino's Fairfield Inn AT&T, Chevrolet, Stop&Shop, Verizon, W Gulf CVS, NAPA
54(118)	MA 150, to Amesbury, W RV camping
53(115)	Broad St, Merrimac, W Citgo/repair Dunkin Donuts
114mm	**parking area sb (6AM-8PM), litter barrels, , restrooms**
52(111)	MA 110, to Haverhill, E Seafood Etc , W Racing Mart Biggart Ice Cream, Dunkin Donuts

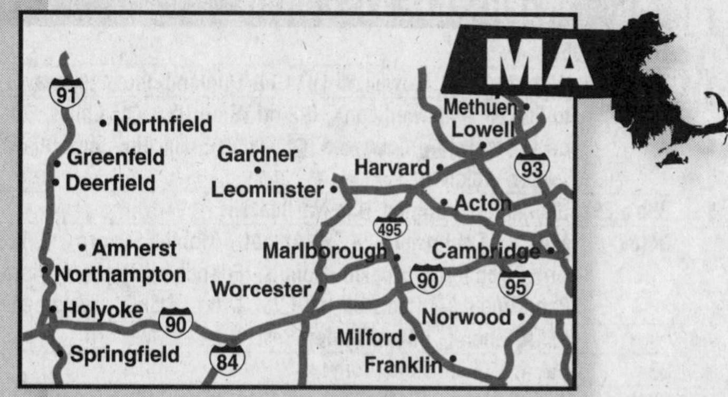

HAVERHILL

Exit#	Services
110mm	**parking area nb, litter barrels,**
51(109)	MA 125, to Haverhill, E Gulf Bros Pizza, China King, Dunkin Donuts , Family$, W Mobil/dsl Applebee's, Burger King, Dunkin Donuts, Friendly's, Li's Asian, Longhorn Steaks, Lucky Corner Chinese, McDonald's, Mr Mikes Grill, Starbucks, Taco Bell, Tuscan House Pizza, Wendy's Monro Service
50(107)	MA 97, to Haverhill, W Ford, Target
49(106)	MA 110, to Haverhill, E Gulf, Sunoco 99 Rest., Athens Pizza, Dunkin Donuts, McDonald's, Oriental Garden, PapaGino's Best Western, Hampton Inn Buick/Chevrolet/GMC, Chrysler/Dodge/Jeep, CVS Drug, Marshall's, MktBasket Foods, Walgreens
105.8mm	Merrimac River
48(105.5)	MA 125, to Bradford, E BJ's Whse/gas
47(105)	MA 213, to Methuen, 1-2 mi W Burger King, Chucke-Cheese, Friendly's, Joe's Crabshack, McDonald's, New Tokyo, Olive Garden, OrangeLeaf, Santana Rae's Mexican, Starbucks, TGIFriday's, Wendy's , Home Depot, Marshalls, MktBasket Foods, Old Navy, Stop&Shop, Target, The Mann Orchards/Bakery, Walmart/Subway
46(104)	MA 110, E Giovanni's Deli, Pleasant Valley Gas, Sunoco, W
45(103)	Marston St, to Lawrence, W Chevrolet, Honda, Kia, Nissan, VW
44(102)	Merrimac St, to Lawrence
43(101)	Mass Ave
42(100)	MA 114, E Gulf, Mobil, Wave Bertucci's, Boll Wood Grill, Boston Mkt, Burger King, Burtons Grill, Chipotle Mexican, Dunkin Donuts, Friendly's, Lee Chin Chinese, Panera Bread Holiday Inn Express Ace Hardware, CVS Drug, Kohl's, MktBasket Foods, PetCo, Staples, TJ Maxx, Walgreens, W Denny's, Dunkin Donuts, KFC, Little Caesar's, Pizza Hut/Taco Bell, Subway, Wendy's , Advance Parts, Family$, Marshall's, Monroe Service, O'Reilly Parts/VIP Service, vet
41(99)	MA 28, to Andover, E Dunkin Donuts Cadillac/Chevrolet
40b a(98)	I-93, N to Methuen, S to Boston
39(94)	MA 133, to Dracut, E Speedway Longhorn Steaks, McDonald's Extended Stay America, W Mobil/Circle K/dsl Cracker Barrel, Wendy's Fairfield Inn, Holiday Inn/rest., Residence Inn

LOWELL

Exit#	Services
38(93)	MA 38, to Lowell, E Petroil/dsl 99 Rest., Applebee's, Burger King, Dunkin Donuts, IHOP, Jade East, Waffle House Motel 6 Hogan Tire/auto, Home Depot, Honda, TownFair Tire, Toyota, URGENT CARE, Walmart, W Citgo, Mobil, Sunoco, USA/dsl Dunkin Donuts, Jillie's Rest., McDonald's, Milan Pizza, Wendy's Buick/GMC, Chevrolet, Chrysler/Dodge/Jeep, CVS Drug, Hannaford Foods, Kmart, Marshall's, Mazda, MktBasket Foods

INTERSTATE 495 Cont'd

LOWELL

Exit#	Services
37(91)	Woburn St, to S Lowell, W Gulf/Dunkin Donuts/Subway
35c(90)	to Lowell SP, Lowell ConX, 0-2 mi W on US 3 Chili's, Outback Steaks Courtyard Kia/VW, Lincoln, Shop&Save, Target, Walgreens
35b a(89)	US 3, S to Burlington, N to Nashua, NH
34(88)	MA 4, Chelmsford, E Ampet, Mobil, Sunoco 110 Grill, Domino's, Dunkin Donuts, Friendly's, Jimmy's Pizza, PapaGino's Radisson CVS Drug, USPO, Walgreens, W Shell Moonstone's Rest. Best Western
33	MA 4, N Chelmsford (from nb)
87mm	both lanes (8AM-8PM), full facilities, litter barrels, , vending
32(83)	Boston Rd, to MA 225, E Cumberland Farms, Gulf, Mobil British Beer Co, Burton's Grill, Chili's, Chipotle, D'angelo, Dunkin Donuts, Evviva Cucina, Five Guys, McDonald's, Panera Bread, PapaGino's, Starbucks, Subway Hampton Inn, Residence Inn H, CVS Drug, GNC, Jo-Ann Fabrics, Marshall's, MktBasket Foods, Petco, Rite Aid, to Nashoba Valley Ski Area, Verizon, vet, Walgreens, Whole Foods Mkt
31(80)	MA 119, to Groton, E Gulf, Mobil/dsl, Shell Dunkin Donuts, Littleton Subs, Subway, Yangtze River Chinese Aubuchon Hardware, CVS Drug, Donelan's Foods, Toyota, Verizon, vet
30(78)	MA 110, to Littleton, 1 mi E Shell CVS Drug, USPO vet, W Mobil/Dunkin Donuts vet H
29b a(77)	MA 2, to Leominster, E to Walden Pond St Reserve
28(75)	MA 111, to Boxborough, Harvard, E Gulf/Dunkin Donuts Holiday Inn
27(70)	MA 117, to Bolton, E Mobil/dsl Subway, W vet
26(68)	MA 62, to Berlin, E Gulf/Dunkin Donuts 110 Grill Holiday Inn Express H, BJ's Whse/gas, Cabela's, GNC, Lowe's, Market Basket, Michael's, Petsmart, TJ Maxx, Verizon, W Mobil/dsl
66mm	Assabet River
25b(64)	I-290, to Worchester
25a	to MA 85, Marlborough, 1 mi E Gulf, Mobil/dsl 99 Rest., Applebee's, Burger King, Checkerboards Rest., Dunkin Donuts, HoneyDew Donuts, KFC/Taco Bell, PapaGino's $Tree, AutoZone, Chevrolet, CVS Drug, Hannaford Foods, Hogan Tire/auto, PetCo, Stop&Shop/gas, Verizon, Walgreens, Walmart
24b a(63)	US 20, to Northboro, Marlborough, E Mobil/dsl Allora Rest., D'angelo, Dunkin Donuts, Lake Williams Pizza Holiday Inn, W Gulf, Shell 99 Rest., Boston Mkt, China Taste, Chipotle Mexican, Five Guys, Japan 1, Jersey Mike's, Longhorn Steaks, McDonald's/playplace, Panera Bread, PapaGino's, Starbucks, Subway, Wendy's Best Western, Courtyard, Embassy Suites, Extended Stay America, Hampton Inn $Tree, GNC, Hannaford Foods, Sullivan Tire/auto, URGENT CARE, vet
23c(60)	Simrano Dr, Marlborough
23b a(59)	MA 9, to Shrewsbury, Framingham, E Cumberland/Dunkin Donuts, Gulf Wendy's Red Roof Inn Cadillac, Volvo, 0-2 mi W Mobil/dsl, Shell Bertucci's, Burger King, Chateau Rest., Chipotle Mexican, D'angelo, Dunkin Donuts, Harry's Rest., Mandarin, McDonald's, Ruby Tuesday, Starbucks, Subway Courtyard, Doubletree Inn, Extended Stay America, Extended Stay America (2), Extended Stay America (3), Hampton Inn, Residence Inn H, Buick/GMC, CarMax, Chrysler/Dodge/Jeep, Marshall's, Staples, Stop&Shop, VW
22(58)	I-90, MA TPK, E to Boston, W to Albany

MARLBORO

MILFORD

Exit#	Services
21b a(54)	MA 135, to Hopkinton, Upton, E Cumberland, Mobil/Dunkin Donuts 110 Grill, Dynasty Chinese, Hiller's Pizza, Starbucks Verizon
20(50)	MA 85, to Milford, W Gulf/dsl/LP, Mobil/dsl 99 Rest., Pizza 85/deli, TGIFriday's, Wendy's Courtyard, Fairfield Inn, Holiday Inn Express, Quality Inn H, Best Buy, Lowe's, PetCo, Staples, Stop&Shop, Target, TJ Maxx, Toyota
19(48)	MA 109, to Milford, W Mobil/Circle K/dsl, Shell Alamo Mexican, Applebee's, Bugaboo Cr Steaks, Burger King, D'angelo, Dunkin Donuts, Five Guys, Friendly's, KFC, McDonald's/playplace, Panera Bread, PapaGino's, Subway Doubletree, La Quinta $General, $Tree, AutoZone, CVS Drug, Hannaford Foods, Jo-Ann Fabrics, Kohl's, Rite Aid, TownFair Tire
18(46)	MA 126, to Bellingham, E Chili's, McDonald's, Moe's SW Barnes&Noble, Michael's, MktBasket Foods, Old Navy, Staples, Verizon, Walmart/Subway, Whole Foods Mkt, W Mobil, Speedway/dsl, Sunoco/dsl Chicago Grill, DQ, Dunkin Donuts, Outback Steaks Home Depot, Petsmart
17(44)	MA 140, to Franklin, Bellingham, E Mobil/dsl, Shell/dsl, Tedeschi British Beer Co, Burger King, Chipotle, Dunkin Donuts, Firehouse Subs, Five Guys, HoneyDew Donuts, Longhorn Steaks, Noodles&Co, Panera Bread, PapaGino's, Pepper Terrace Thai, Starbucks, Subway, Taco Bell, Wendy's AT&T, AutoZone, Buick/GMC, CVS Drug, GNC, Marshall's, Stop&Shop, URGENT CARE, W Stop&Shop Gas 99 Rest., Hichigo Ichie Hibachi, Incontro Rest. Residence Inn BJ's Whse/Subway/gas
16(42)	King St, to Franklin, E Tedeschi Dunkin Donuts, Joe's Grill, King St Cafe, Spruce Pond Creamery Hampton Inn, W Hawthorn Inn
15(39)	MA 1A, to Plainville, Wrentham, E Shell Assisi Pizza, W Mobil/dsl Chicago Grill, Cracker Barrel, Dunkin Donuts, Friendly's, Ruby Tuesday Premium Outlets/famous brands
14b a(37)	US 1, to N Attleboro, E Shell/dsl Luciano's Rest. Arbor Motel Bass Pro Shops (4mi), W Mobil Chili's Dunkin Donuts, Panera Bread, The Tavern Holiday Inn Express casino, Lowe's, Macdonald's RV Ctr, NTB, Stop&Shop Target, TJ Maxx, vet
13(32)	I-95, N to Boston, S to Providence, access to H
12(30)	MA 140, to Mansfield, E Asian Grill, Bertucci's Italian, Buffalo Wild Wings, Chipotle Mexican, Coldstone, Dunkin Donuts Longhorn Steaks, Papa Gino's, Qdoba Mexican, Sake Japanese TGIFriday's AT&T, Best Buy, Firestone/auto, GNC, Home Depot, Kohl's, LL Bean, Michael's, PetCo, Shaw's Foods, Staples Verizon
11(29)	MA 140 S (from sb), 1 mi W Cumberland, Mobil Best Sandwich, Dunkin Donuts, Fiesta Mexican, Mandarin Chinese, McDonald's $Tree, Roche Bros Mkt
10(26)	MA 123, to Norton, E Dunkin Donuts QuickStop, W H
9(24)	Bay St, to Taunton, E Chateau Rest., W Dunkin Donuts Jaybo Cafe, Ruby Tuesday, Wendy's Extended Stay America, Holiday Inn $Tree, BJ's Whse, Tadeschi Foods, Watson Pond SP
8(22)	MA 138, to Raynham, E Mobil/dsl, Speedway/dsl Christopher's Pizza, HoneyDew Donuts, W AARC/dsl/repair Gulf/dsl, Stop'n Go/dsl Brothers Pizza, Cape Cod Cafe, China Garden, D'angelo, Dunkin Donuts, HoneyDew Donuts, Lucky Corner Chinese, McDonald's H, Ace Hardware, Mkt Basket Foods, USPO, Walmart

INTERSTATE 495 Cont'd

Exit#	Services
7b a(19)	MA 24, to Fall River, Boston, 1/2 mi E Mobil/dsl Burger King
18mm	**weigh sta both lanes**
17mm	Taunton River
6(15)	US 44, to Middleboro, **E** Super/dsl Burger King, Dunkin Donuts, Friendly's, PapaGino's, Subway, **W** Irving/Circle K/ Dunkin Donuts/dsl Fairfield Inn, Holiday Inn Express
5(14)	MA 18, to Lakeville, **E** Shell, Super/dsl D'Angelo, Dave's Diner, Harry's Grille, Lorenzo's Rest, PapaGino's, Persy's Place Cafe CVS Drug, Kelly's Tire, Trucchi's Mkt, **W** Massasoit SP, RV camping (seasonal)
4(12)	MA 105, to Middleboro, **E** Cumberland/dsl, PetroMax, Sunoco Best Pizza, China Sails, DQ, Dunkin Donuts, McDonald's Days Inn AutoZone, Rite Aid
11mm	**parking area eb**
10mm	**parking area both lanes**
3(8)	MA 28, to Rock Village, S Middleboro, **E** GeKo/dsl repair, **W** Mobil/Dunkin Donuts/Subway/dsl
2(3)	MA 58, W Wareham, **E** Mobil/dsl (2mi) to Myles Standish SF, **W** 7-11 RV camping
2mm	Weweantic River

I-495 begins/ends on I-195, MA 25 S.

NOTES

MICHIGAN

INTERSTATE 69

Exit#	Services
273mm	**Welcome Ctr/ eb, full facilities, litter barrels, petwalk**
199	Lp 69 (from eb, no return), to Port Huron, **0-2 mi S on Lp 69** Mobil/dsl, Speedway Arby's, Burger King, Jimmy John's, KFC, Little Caesar's, McDonalds, Subway, Taco Bell, Tim Horton's, Wendy's $General, Advance Parts, AutoZone, Kroger/gas, repair, Sam's Club/gas, to Port Huron, USPO

I-69 E and I-94 E run together into Port Huron. See I-94, exits 274-275mm.

Exit#	Services
198	I-94, to Detroit and Canada
196	Wadhams Rd, **N** BP/Wendy's, Marathon, Speedy Q/ dsl Hungry Howie's, McDonald's, Peking Kitchen, Subway, Taco Bell KOA (1mi), Vinckier Foods, Wadham's Drugs, **S** Pilot/Subway/dsl/scales/24hr golf
194	Taylor Rd, **N** Goodells CP, RV camping
189	Wales Center Rd, to Goodells, **S** golf
184	MI 19, to Emmett, **N** Citgo/dsl/scales/24hr repair, USPO, **S** Marathon/dsl/24hr
180	Riley Center Rd, **N** KOA
176	Capac Rd, **N** BP/McDonald's/dsl/scales, Loves/Chester's/dsl/scales/24hr Subway (2mi)
174mm	**wb, full facilities, litter barrels, petwalk, , vending**
168	MI 53, Imlay City, **N** BP/dsl, Speedway/dsl Big Boy, Burger King, DQ, Hungry Howie's, John's Country Kitchen, Little Caesar's, Lucky's Steaks, McDonald's, New China, Taco Bell, Wah Wong Chinese, Wendy's/Tim Horton Days Inn, M53 Motel, Super 8 AutoZone, Chevrolet, Chrysler/Dodge/ Jeep, Ford, GNC, Kroger/dsl, NAPA, O'Reilly Parts, Sav-On Drug, ShopKO, Verizon
163	Lake Pleasant Rd, to Attica
160mm	**eb, full facilities, litter barrels, petwalk, , vending**
159	Wilder Rd
158mm	Flint River

LAPEER

Exit#	Services
155	MI 24, Lapeer, **1 mi N** Speedy Q/dsl, Sunoco/dsl Apple Tree Rest., Applebee's, Arby's, Blind Fish Rest., Brian's Rest., Buffalo Wild Wings, Burger King, Checkers, DQ, Jet's Pizza, Jimmy John's, KFC, Leo's Coney Island, Little Caesar's, Mancino's, McDonald's, Nick's Grill, Sonic, Starbucks, Subway, Taco Bell, Tim Horton, Wah Wong Chinese, Wendy's Best Western, Holiday Inn Express H, $Tree, AT&T, AutoZone, Belle Tire, Home Depot, Kohl's, Kroger/gas, Meijer/dsl, Midas, Office Depot, O'Reilly Parts, Rite Aid, st police, URGENT CARE, Verizon, vet, Walgreens, **S** Mobil/dsl Chrysler/Dodge/Jeep, Harley Davidson
153	Lake Nepessing Rd, **S** camping, golf, to Thumb Correctional
149	Elba Rd, **N** Torzewski CP, **S** Country Mkt, RV/truck repair
145	MI 15, Davison, **N** Marathon, Shell/dsl, Speedway/dsl Apollo Rest., Applebee's, Arby's, Big Boy, Big John's Rest., Burger King, Chee Kong Chinese, Flag City Diner, Hungry Howie's, Italia Gardens, Jimmy John's, KFC, Little Caesar's, Lucky's Steaks, McDonald's, Pizza Hut, Senor Lucky, Subway, Taco Bell, Tim Horton, Tropical Smoothie Best Western AutoValue Parts, Buick/GMC, Davison Automotive, GNC, Rite Aid, Valley Tire, Verizon, Walgreens, YaYa Chicken, **S** Mobil/ dsl Sicilian Pizza vet
143	Irish Rd, **N** Speedway/dsl Menard's, **S** Shell/McDonald's/24hr Meijer/dsl/e-85

FLINT

Exit#	Services
141	Belsay Rd, Flint, **N** Marathon/Wendy's/dsl/24hr, Mobil Halo Burger, McDonald's, Subway, Taco Bell Walmart/ Subway/auto, **S** Sunoco/A&W/LJ Silver/dsl O'Malley's Grill
139	Center Rd, Flint, **N** Speedway/dsl Applebee's, Domino's, El Cozumel Mexican, Empire Wok, Halo Burger, Old Country Buffet, Olympic Grill, Quiznos, Starbucks, Subway, Tim Horton Aldi Foods, AT&T, Big Lots, Discount Tire, Home Depot, JC Penney, Jo-Ann Fabrics, Staples, **0-2 mi S** Bob Evans,

MI

INTERSTATE 69 Cont'd

139 Continued
China 1, Coney Island, DQ, Hungry Howie's, McDonald's, Red Baron Rest., Subway, Walli's Rest. Super 8 $Tree, Belle Tire, Meijer/dsl, Target, TJ Maxx, Verizon

138 MI 54, Dort Hwy, **N** BP/dsl, Speedway/dsl, Sunoco/dsl Big John's Rest., KFC, Little Caesar's, Tom's Coney Island, YaYa's Chicken H, $General, KanRock Tires, Rite Aid, Save-a-Lot, Walgreens, **0-2 mi S** Admiral, Marathon, Sunoco Arby's, Big John Steak, Burger King, Church's, Empress of China, KFC, McDonald's, Subway, Taco Bell Travel Inn $General, Advance Parts, AutoZone, Express Tire/auto, Family$, O'Reilly Parts, Rite Aid, Tuffy Auto, U-Haul, Walgreens

137 I-475, UAW Fwy, to Detroit, Saginaw

136 Saginaw St, Flint, **N** Sunoco/dsl H, U MI at Flint

135 Hammerberg Rd, industrial area

133b a I-75, S to Detroit, N to Saginaw, US 23 S to Ann Arbor

131 MI 121, to Bristol Rd, **1/2 mi N on Miller Rd** Bar Louie, BD Mongolian BBQ, Buffalo Wild Wing, Casa Real, Chili's, ChuckeCheese, Famous Dave's BBQ, Fortune Buffet, Golden Corral, Golden Moon Chinese, Halo Burger, Hooters, Leo's Coney Island, LJ Silver, Logan's Roadhouse, Olive Garden, Osaka Buffet, Outback Steaks, Panera Bread, Red Robin, Subway, Taco Bell, Telly's Coney Island, TX Roadhouse, Valley Diner $Tree, AT&T, Barnes&Noble, Belle Tire, Best Buy, BigLots, Discount Tire, Hobby Lobby, JC Penney, Jo-Ann Fabrics, Kohl's, Macy's, Michael's, Old Navy, PetCo, Petsmart, Target, TJ Maxx, USPO, Valley Tire, Verizon

129 Miller Rd, **S** Arby's, Burger King, McDonald's, Subway, Taco Bell, Wendy's Kroger/gas

128 Morrish Rd, **N** Meijer/dsl/e85, **S** Admiral, Mobil/dsl

126mm **eb, full facilities, info, litter barrels, petwalk,**

123 MI 13, to Saginaw, Lennon, **N** Speedway/dsl USPO

118 MI 71, to Corunna, Durand, **N** Durand Automotive, **S** Shell/dsl, Valero China House, Hungry Howie's, McDonald's, Subway, Wendy's Quality Inn Ace Hardware, CarQuest, Chevrolet, Family$, golf, Rite Aid

115mm Shiawassee River

113 Bancroft, **S** BP/dsl (1.5mi) RV camping

105 MI 52, to Owosso, Perry, **S** Citgo/Subway/dsl, Exxon/7-11, Mobil/dsl, Sunoco/dsl/scales/24hr Burger King, Cafe Sports, China Garden, Hungry Howie's, McDonald's, Taco Bell Heb's Inn Family$, IGA Foods, Rite Aid, RV camping, truck repair (1mi), USPO

101mm **wb, full facilities, litter barrels, petwalk,**

98.5mm Vermilion River

98 Woodbury Rd, to Laingsburg, Shaftsburg

94 Lp 69, Marsh Rd, to E Lansing, Okemos, **S** Admiral/dsl, Speedway/dsl McDonald's Gillette RV Ctr, Meijer/Subway/dsl/e85, Monticello's Mkt

92 Webster Rd, Bath

89 US 127 S, to E Lansing

87 Old US 27, to Clare, Lansing, **N** Marathon, Speedway/dsl Arby's, Bob Evans, Burger King, China Gourmet, Flap-Jack Rest., Little Ceasars, Mancino's, McDonald's, Subway, Tim Horton Sleep Inn Annie Rae RV Ctr, Chevrolet, Meijer/dsl, Verizon, vet, **S** Speedway/dsl American Inn GNC

85 DeWitt Rd, to DeWitt

84 Airport Rd

91 I-96 (from sb), W to Grand Rapids, Grand River Ave, Frances Rd, **W** FLYING J/Denny's/dsl/24hr

LANSING

93b a MI 43, Lp 69, Saginaw Hwy, to Grand Ledge, **0-2 mi N** Shell, Speedway/dsl Applebee's, Buffalo Wild Wings, Burger King, Carrabba's, Cheddar's, Chipotle, Denny's, Fazoli's, Finley's Grill, Frank's Grill, Hibachi Grill, Honeybaked Ham, Houlihan's, Logan's Roadhouse, Longhorn Steaks, McDonald's, Outback Steaks, Panera Bread, Qdoba, Red Robin, Subway Comfort Inn, Fairfield Inn, Hampton Inn, Motel 6, Quality Inn, Ramada Inn, Red Roof Inn, Residence Inn H, $Tree, Aldi, AT&T, Barnes&Noble, Best Buy, BigLots, Chrysler/Dodge/Jeep, Hobby Lobby, JC Penney, Kohl's, Kroger/dsl, Meijer/dsl/24hr, Target, TJ Maxx, vet, Walgreens, Younkers, **S** BP/Dunkin Donuts, QD, Sunoco/McDonald's Arby's, Biggby Coffee, Bob Evans, Cancun Mexican, Cracker Barrel, Culver's, Steak'n Shake SpringHill Suites Belle Tire, Buick/GMC, Discount Tire, Lowe's, Mazda/Volvo, Menards, Michael's, PetsMart, Staples, Walmart/Subway

95 I-496, to Lansing

72 I-96, E to Detroit, W to Grand Rapids

70 Lansing Rd

68mm **nb, full facilities, litter barrels, petwalk, , vending**

66 MI 100, to Grand Ledge, Potterville, **W** BP/dsl, Shell/Subway/dsl Charlie's Grill, McDonald's, to Fox Co Park

61 Lansing Rd, **E** Murphy USA/dsl Applebee's Comfort Inn $Tree, AutoZone, Buick/Chevrolet/GMC, Verizon, Walmart/Subway, **W** QD, Speedway/dsl Arby's, Big Boy, Biggby Coffee, Burger King, Jersey Subs, Jet's Pizza, KFC, Little Caesar's, McDonald's, Pizza Hut, Rally's, Taco Bell, Tasty Twist, Top Chinese, Wendy's H, Ace Hardware, Advance Parts, Charlotte Tires, Family$, Ford, NAPA, O'Reilly Parts, vet

60 MI 50, Charlotte, **E** Holiday Inn Express Meijer/dsl, URGENT CARE, **W** Admiral Best Value Inn H

57 Lp 69, Cochran Rd, to Charlotte, **E** RV camping

51 Ainger Rd, **1 mi E** gas food RV camping

48 MI 78, to Bellevue, Olivet, **1 mi E** Marathon/Subway/dsl to Olivet Coll

MARSHALL

42 N Drive N, Turkeyville Rd, **W** Cornwell's Rest. (1mi)

41mm **sb, full facilities, litter barrels, petwalk,**

38 I-94, E to Detroit, W to Chicago

36 Michigan Ave, to Marshall, **E** Admiral, Citgo/dsl/E85, Shell/Subway/dsl Applebee's, Arby's, Biggby Coffee, Little Caesar's, McDonald's, Pizza Hut, Speedy Chick, Taco Bell, Wendy's, Yin Hai Chinese Comfort Inn $General, $Tree, Ace Hardware, AT&T, AutoZone, Chevrolet, Family Fare Mkt/gas, NAPA, O'Reilly Parts, Rite Aid, Save-A-Lot, Tuffy Auto, Verizon, **W** Arbor Inn H, Chrysler/Dodge/Jeep

32 F Drive S, **E** Shell/dsl Moonraker Rest. (3mi) RV Camping

25 MI 60, to Three Rivers, Jackson, **E** BP/dsl, Sunoco/dsl, TA/Shell/Country Pride/dsl/scales/24hr/@ McDonald's, Subway $General, Auto Value Parts, auto/truck repair, RV camping

COLDWATER

23 Tekonsha, **W** access to RV camping

16 Jonesville Rd, **W** Waffle Farm Camping (2mi)

13 US 12, to Quincy, Coldwater, **E** Speedway/dsl Applebee's, Biggby Coffee, Bob Evans, Buffalo Wild Wings, Grand Buffet Hampton Inn, Holiday Inn Express, Red Roof Inn $Tree, Aldi Foods, AT&T, AutoZone, Belle Tire, BigLots, Buick/Chevrolet/GMC, GNC, Haylett RV Ctr, Home Depot, Meijer/dsl, Verizon, Walmart/Subway, Younkers, **W** Citgo/dsl, Speedway/dsl Arby's, Big Boy, Burger King, Coldwater Garden Rest., Culver's, Dickey's BBQ, Jimmy John's, KFC, Little Caesar's, McDonald's, Pizza Hut, Ponderosa, Subway, Taco Bell, Wendy's Best Western, Comfort Inn H, auto repair, Ford/Lincoln, O'Reilly Parts, Rite Aid, st police, Walgreens

INTERSTATE 69 Cont'd

Exit#	Services
10	Lp 69, Fenn Rd, to Coldwater, **W** [other] Harbor Cove RV Park (4mi)
8mm	**weigh sta nb**
6mm	**Welcome Ctr nb, full [handicap] facilities, litter barrels, petwalk, [phone], [picnic], vending**
3	Copeland Rd, Kinderhook, **W** [gas] BP/dsl [food] camping
0mm	**Michigan/Indiana state line**

INTERSTATE 75

SAULT STE MARIE

Exit#	Services
395mm	US/Canada Border, Michigan state line, **I-75 begins/ends at toll bridge to Canada.**
394	Easterday Ave, **E** [gas] Krist/dsl [food] McDonald's [lodging] Holiday Inn Express, Ramada Inn (2mi) [other] [H], to Lake Superior St U, **W Welcome Ctr/[RS], info,** [gas] Admiral/dsl, Holiday/dsl/currency exchange
392	3 Mile Rd, Sault Ste Marie, **E** [gas] Admiral/dsl, BP/dsl, Holiday/dsl, Marathon/dsl, Shell/dsl [food] Applebee's, Arby's, Buffalo Wild Wings, Burger King, Country Kitchen, Domino's, DQ, Great Wall Chinese, Indo China Garden, Jimmy John's, Little Caesar's, McDonald's, Pizza Hut, Studebaker's Rest., Subway, Taco Bell, Wendy's [lodging] Best Value Inn, Best Western, Comfort Inn, Days Inn, Hampton Inn, Park Inn, Plaza Motel, Quality Inn, Skyline Motel, Super 8 [other] [H], $Tree, Advance Parts, AT&T, AutoZone, BigLots, Buick/Chevrolet/GMC, Family Fare Mkt, Family$, Goodyear/auto, Jo-Ann Fabrics, Kohl's, NAPA, Save-a-Lot, Soo Locks Boat Tours, st police, TJ Maxx, Verizon, Walgreens, Walmart/Subway
389mm	**[RS] nb, full [handicap] facilities, info, litter barrels, petwalk, [phone], [picnic]**
386	MI 28, **E** [other] Clear Lake Camping (5mi), **W** [other] to Brimley SP
379	Gaines Hwy, **E** Clear Lake Camping, to Barbeau Area
378	MI 80, Kinross, **E** [gas] BP/dsl [food] Frank&Jim's Diner [other] [airport], golf, RV Camping, to Kinross Correctional
373	MI 48, Rudyard, **2 mi W** [gas] gas/dsl [food] food [lodging] lodging
359	MI 134, to Drummond Island, **W** [other] National Forest Camping
352	MI 123, to Moran, Newberry
348	H63, to Sault Reservation, St Ignace, **0-2 mi E** [food] Jose's Cantina [lodging] Bavarian Haus, Bayview Motel, Bear Cove Inn, Best Value Inn, Birchwood Motel, Cedars Motel, Comfort Inn, Evergreen Motel, Great Lakes Motel, Holiday Inn Express, Kewadin Inn, NorthernAire Motel, Pines Motel, Quality Inn [other] [H], [airport], casino, Castle Rock Camping, st police, to Mackinac Trail, **W** [other] Castle Rock Gifts
346mm	**[RS]/scenic turnout sb, full [handicap] facilities, litter barrels, petwalk, [picnic]**
345	Portage St (from sb), St Ignace
344b	US 2 W, **W** [gas] BP/dsl, Holiday/dsl, Shell/dsl [food] Big Boy, Burger King, Clyde's Drive-In, McDonald's, Subway, Suzy's Pasties [lodging] 4 Star Motel, Quality Inn, Sunset Motel, Super 8 [other] Ford, golf, Lakeshore RV Park
344a	Lp 75, St Ignace, **0-2 mi E** [gas] Shell [food] BC Pizza, Bentley's Cafe, Galley Rest., Mackinac Grille, Marina Rest., Northern Lights Rest. [lodging] Aurora Borealis Motel, Boardwalk Inn, Cedar Hill Lodge, Colonial House, Moran Bay Motel, Normandy Motel, Thunderbird Motel, Village Inn/rest., Voyager Motel [other] [H], $General, Ace Hardware, Bay Drug, Family Fare Mkt, Family$, NAPA, public marina, st police, Straits SP, to Island Ferrys, True-Value, USPO, Cedar Hill Lodge, Cedar Hill Lodge

MACKINAW CITY

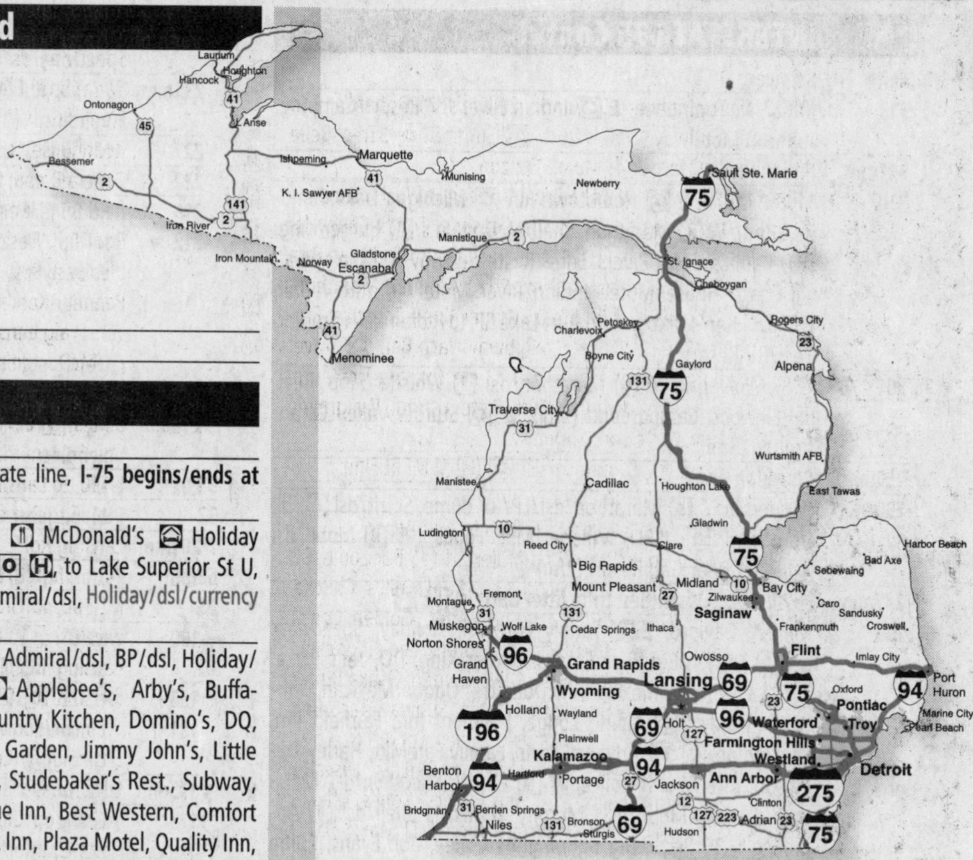

Exit#	Services
343mm	**E Welcome Ctr nb, full [handicap] facilities, litter barrels, [phone], [picnic], W museum, toll booth to toll bridge**
341mm	**toll bridge**, Lake Huron, Lake Michigan
339	US 23, Jamet St, **E** [food] Audie's Rest. [lodging] Days Inn, Knights Inn, LightHouse View Motel, Parkside Motel, Riviera Motel, Super 8, **W** [gas] Shell [food] Darrow's Rest., Mackinaw Cookie Co [lodging] Holiday Inn Express, Vindel Motel [other] Wilderness SP
338	US 23 (from sb), **E** [gas] Marathon/dsl [food] BC Pizza, Burger King, DQ, KFC, Mama Mia's Pizza, Pancake Chef, Subway, Wienerlicious [lodging] Baymont Inn, Court Plaza Hotel [other] Mackinaw Mkt, Mackinaw Outfitters, same as 337, USPO, **W** [lodging] Holiday Inn Express
337	MI 108 (from nb, no EZ return), Nicolet St, Mackinaw City, **E Welcome Ctr/[RS],** [gas] Citgo/dsl/LP [food] Blue Water Grill, Embers Rest., Lighthouse Rest., Mackinaw Pastie&Cookie Co., Starbucks [lodging] Bayside Inn, Beach House Cottages, Beach-Comber Motel, Bell's Melody Motel, Best Value Inn, Best Western, Bridge Vista Beach Motel, Bridgeview Motel, Budget Inn, Capri Motel, Clarion, Clearwater Lakeshore Motel, Comfort Inn, Crown Choice Inn, Days Inn, EconoLodge, Fairview Inn, Great Lakes Inn, Hamilton Inn, Mackinaw Inn, North Winds Motel, Quality Inn, Rainbow Motel, Ramada Ltd, Sundown Motel, Sunrise Beach Motel, Super 8, Thunderbird Inn, Waterfront Inn [other] Harley-Davidson, Old Mill Creek SP, Tee Pee Camping, to Island Ferrys, **W** [other] KOA, Wilderness SP
336	US 31 S (from sb), to Petoskey
328mm	**[RS] sb, full [handicap] facilities, info, litter barrels, petwalk, [phone], [picnic]**
326	C66, to Cheboygan, **E** [gas] gas/dsl [other] [H], Sea Shell City/gifts, st police
322	C64, to Cheboygan, **E** [other] [H], [airport], LP, st police
317mm	**[RS]/scenic turnout nb, full [handicap] facilities, info, litter barrels, petwalk, [phone], [picnic]**

MI

INTERSTATE 75 Cont'd

Exit#	Services
313	MI 27 N, Topinabee, E Indian River RV Resort/Camping, Johnson Motel
311mm	Indian River
310	MI 33, MI 68, E Hometown Inn Michigan Oaks Camping (3mi), W Marathon, Shell/McDonald's Burger King, DQ, Paula's Cafe, Rivers Edge Rest., Subway, Wilson's Rest. Coach House Motel, Indian River Motel auto repair, Family$, Ken's Mkt/gas, to Burt Lake SP, to Indian River Trading Post/RV Resort
301	C58, Wolverine, E Marathon/dsl Whistle Stop Rest. Elkwood Campground (5mi), W Sturgin Valley Campground (3mi)
297mm	Sturgeon River
290	Vanderbilt, E Marathon/dsl/LP/RV dump, Spirit/dsl Elk Horn Grill USPO, Village Mkt Foods, W Mobil/dsl Black Bear Golf Resort (2mi)
287mm	sb, full facilities, info, litter barrels,
282	MI 32, Gaylord, E Family Fare/dsl, Holiday, Speedway/dsl Arby's, Big Buck Steaks, Burger King, DQ, Jet's Pizza, KFC, La Senorita Mexican, McDonald's, Qdoba Mexican, Subway, Wendy's Alpine Lodge, Baymont Inn, Fairfield Inn, Quality Inn H, Advance Parts, Family FareMkt, Harley-Davidson, Rite Aid, st police, W BP/dsl, Marathon/dsl, Marathon/dsl (2), Mobil/dsl, Murphy USA/dsl, Shell/dsl Applebee's, BC Pizza, Big Boy, Biggby Coffee, Bob Evans, China Buffet, Coldstone/Tim Horton, Culver's, El Rancho Mexican, Jimmy John's, Little Caesar's, Mancino's Pizza, Panera Bread, Ponderosa, Ruby Tuesday, Starbucks, Taco Bell Hampton Inn, Holiday Inn Express $Tree, Aldi Foods, AT&T, BigLots, Chrysler/Dodge/Jeep, GNC, Hobby Lobby, Home Depot, Kenworth, Lowe's, Northern MI RV Ctr, Save-A-Lot Foods, Verizon, Walgreens, Walmart/Subway
279mm	45th Parallel halfway between the equator and north pole
279	Old US 27, Gaylord, E Marathon/Subway/dsl, Mobil/dsl, Shell Burger King, Mama Leone's Best Value Inn Ace Hardware, Buick/GMC, Chevrolet, Ford/Lincoln, st police, transmissions, W Bennethum's Rest., Stampede Saloon KOA (3mi)
277mm	nb, full facilities, info, litter barrels, petwalk,
270	Waters, E Marathon/dsl Hilltop Rest., W BP/dsl, Waters Inn Freeway North RV Ctr, to Otsego Lake SP, USPO
264	Lewiston, Frederic, W access to food camping
262mm	sb, full facilities, litter barrels, petwalk,
259	MI 93, E Hartwick Pines SP
256	(from sb), to MI 72, Grayling, access to same as 254
254	MI 72 (exits left from nb, no return), Grayling, 1 mi W Admiral/dsl, Marathon/dsl, Shell, Speedway/dsl Big Boy, Burger King, DQ, Keg'O'Nails, Little Caesar's, McDonald's, Pizza Hut, Subway, Taco Bell, Wendy's Days Inn, Ramada H, $General, 7-11, Ace Hardware, AT&T, Auto Value Parts, Family Fare Mkt, Family$, Ford, NAPA, O'Reilly Parts, Rite Aid, Save-A-Lot Foods, Verizon, Walgreens
251mm	nb, full facilities, info, litter barrels, petwalk, vending
251	4 Mile Rd, E Jellystone RV Park (5mi), W Marathon/Arby's/dsl/scales/RV Dump/24hr Super 8
249	US 127 S (from sb), to Clare
244	MI 18, Roscommon, 3 mi E Mobil/dsl, Shell/dsl McDonald's, W Valero/dsl Higgins Lake SP, KOA (1mi)
239	MI 18, Roscommon, S Higgins Lake SP, 3 mi E Marathon McDonald's/dsl camping, W camping, Higgins Lake S
235mm	sb, full facilities, info, litter barrels, petwalk, vending
227	MI 55 W, rd F97, to Houghton Lake, 5 mi W food
222	Old 76, to St Helen, 2-4 mi E food lodging camping
215	MI 55 E, West Branch, E Shell/dsl H
212	MI 55, West Branch, E Mobil/dsl, Murphy USA/dsl, Shell Subway/dsl Applebee's, Arby's, Big Boy, Burger King, KFC Lumberjack Rest., McDonald's, Ponderosa, Rally's, Taco Bell Tim Hortons, Wendy's Quality Inn, Super 8 H, Home Depot, st police, Walmart/Subway, West Branch Outlets/famous brands, W Marathon/dsl
210mm	nb, full facilities, info, litter barrels, petwalk, vending
202	MI 33, to Rose City, Alger, E Marathon/Narski's Mkt/jerky Mobil/jerky outlet/dsl, Shell/Subway/dsl camping
201mm	sb, full facilities, litter barrels, petwalk, , vending
195	Sterling Rd, to Sterling, 6 mi E gas Riverview Campin (seasonal)
190	MI 61, to Standish, E H, Standish Correctional, W Marathon, Mobil/jerky/dsl
188	US 23, to Standish, 2-3 mi E gas food camping
181	Pinconning Rd, E Shell/McDonald's/dsl Cheesehouse Diner Pinconning Inn (2mi), W BP/pizza/dsl/24hr
175mm	nb, full facilities, litter barrels, petwalk, , vendin
173	Linwood Rd, to Linwood, E Mobil/dsl/jerky Arby (2mi)
171mm	Kawkawlin River
168	Beaver Rd, to Willard, E to Bay City SRA, W Mobil/jerk
166mm	Kawkawlin River
164	to MI 13, Wilder Rd, to Kawkawlin, E Cracker Barre Lucky Steaks, Ponderosa, Uno AmericInn, Holiday Inn Express KanRock Tire, Meijer/dsl, Menards
162b a	US 10, MI 25, to Midland
160	MI 84, Delta, E Mobil/Subway, Shell/dsl, W Speedway/dsl Berger's Rest., Burger King, KFC/Taco Bell, McDonald's Econolodge RV World Super Ctr, to Saginaw Valley SU
158mm	sb, full facilities, litter barrels, petwalk, , vendin
155	I-675 S, to downtown Saginaw, 4 mi W Outback Steak Hampton Inn
154	to Zilwaukee
153mm	Saginaw River
153	MI 13 E Bay City Rd, Saginaw
151	MI 81, to Reese, Caro, E BP/McDonald's/dsl Vol Trucks, W FLYING J/Wendy's/dsl/LP/24hr
150	I-675 N, to downtown Saginaw, 6 mi W Outback Steak Hampton Inn
149b a	MI 46, Holland Ave, to Saginaw, W BP, Speedway/dsl Arby's, Big John's Steaks, Burger King, McDonald Popeye's, Subway, Taco Bell Motel 6 H, Advance Parts, Save-A-Lot Foods, USPO
144b a	Bridgeport, E Speedway/dsl Jellystone Camping (9mi) W Mobil/dsl/e-85, TA/Country Pride/dsl/scales/24hr/ Arby's, Big Boy, Cracker Barrel, Hungry Howie's, McDonald's, Subway, Taco Bell, Wendy's Baymont Inn, Knight Inn $General, Family$, Kroger/gas, Rite Aid, st police, US
143mm	Cass River
138mm	pull off both lanes
136	MI 54, MI 83, Birch Run, E Mobil/dsl/24hr Halo Burg KFC, Subway Best Value Inn, Best Western, Comfort In

GAYLORD

GRAYLING

SAGINAW

INTERSTATE 75 Cont'd

136 Continued
Hampton Inn, Holiday Inn Express [O] CarQuest, General RV Ctr, Mejier/dsl/E-85, Totten Tires, **W** [gas] BP, Citgo/7-11, Marathon [food] A&W, Applebee's, Arby's, Bagger Dave's Burgers, Bob Evans, Buffalo Wild Wings, Culver's, DQ, Leo's Coney Island, Little Caesar's, McDonald's, Sonic, Starbucks, Taco Bell, Tony's Rest., Uno, Victor&Merek's Pizza, Wendy's [lodging] Country Inn&-Suites [O] Birch Run Outlet/famous brands, Buick/Chevrolet, Family$, GNC, Old Navy, USPO

131 MI 57, to Montrose, **E** [gas] BP, Marathon [food] Arby's, Big John's Steaks, Burger King, DQ, KFC, McDonald's, Oriental Express, Subway, Taco Bell, Tim Hortons, Twins Pizza, Wendy's [O] AutoZone, Chevrolet, Chrysler/Dodge/Jeep, KanRock Tire, Tradewinds RV Ctr, vet, **W** [gas] Mobil/Rally's/dsl, Murphy USA/dsl [food] Applebee's, Big Boy, Lucky Steaks, Tropical Smoothie Cafe [O] $Tree, auto repair, Menards, Verizon, Walmart/Subway

129mm **[RS] both lanes, full [handicapped] facilities, litter barrels, petwalk, [phone], [picnic], vending**

126 to Mt Morris, **E** [gas] B&B/Halo Burger/dsl/scales/24hr, **W** [gas] BP/dsl

125 I-475 S, UAW Fwy, to Flint

122 Pierson Rd, to Flint, **E** [gas] BP/dsl, Marathon/dsl [food] McDonald's, Papa's Coney's, Subway [O] Family$, O'Reilly Parts, Tuffy Auto, **W** [gas] Citgo/dsl, ClicMart/dsl [food] Applebee's, Arby's, Bob Evans, Burger King, Cracker Barrel, Domino's, Halo Burger, LJ Silver, Red Lobster, Taco Bell, Tim Hortons, YaYa Chicken [lodging] Baymont Inn, Great Western Inn [O] $General, $Tree, Aldi Foods, AT&T, Belle Tire, Discount Tire, Home Depot

118 MI 21, Corunna Rd, **E** [gas] BP [food] Badawest Lebanese, Big John's Steaks, Burger King, Church's, Hungry Howie's, Little Caesar's, Taco Bell, Wing Fong Chinese, YaYa Chicken [O] [H], Advance Parts, Family$, Kroger/gas, Rite Aid, **W** [gas] BP/dsl, Marathon/Wendy's, Mobil, Speedway/dsl, Valero [food] A&W/KFC, Burger King, Mega Diner, Rally's, Tim Horton, White Castle [lodging] Economy Motel [O] $General, Aldi Foods, AutoZone, Buick, Chevrolet, GMC, Home Depot, KanRock Tire, Kroger/gas, O'Reilly Parts, Rite Aid, Sam's Club/gas, st police, Verizon, Walgreens, Walmart

117b Miller Rd, to Flint, **E** [gas] Speedway/dsl [food] Applebee's, Arby's, Classic Diner, Cottage Inn Pizza, Domino's, Fuddrucker's, McDonald's, Popeye's, Qdoba, Sonic, Subway, West Side Diner [lodging] Motel 6, Quality Inn, Rodeway Inn [O] Harley Davidson, Tuffy Auto, **W** [gas] Admiral, Marathon [food] Bar Louie, BD's Mongolian BBQ, Bob Evans, Casa Real, Chili's, ChuckeCheese, Famous Dave's BBQ, Golden Corral, Halo Burger, HoneyBaked Ham, Hooters, Italia Garden, Logan's Roadhouse, Olive Garden, Osaka Buffet, Outback Steaks, Pizza Hut, Red Robin, Salvatori's Ristorante, Starbucks, Subway, Taco Bell, Telly's Coney Island, TX Roadhouse, Valley Diner [lodging] Red Roof Inn, Super 8 [O] AT&T, Barnes&Noble, Best Buy, Big Lots, Dale's Foods, Discount Tire, Hobby Lobby, JC Penney, Jo-Ann Fabrics, Macy's, Michael's, Office Depot, Old Navy, PetCo, Petsmart, Target, U-Haul, Valley Tire, Verizon, vet

FLINT

117a I-69, E to Lansing, W to Port Huron

116 MI 121, Bristol Rd, **E** [gas] Mobil, Speedway/dsl [food] Capitol Coney Island, KFC, McDonald's [O] Advance Parts, AutoZone, **W** [gas] Marathon/dsl [O] [airport]

115 US 23 (from sb), **W on Hill Rd** [gas] Citgo, Mobil [food] Arby's, Jimmy John's, McDonald's, Redwood Steaks, Subway, Taco Bell, Tim Hortons [lodging] Best Western, Courtyard, Hampton Inn, Holiday Inn, Residence Inn [O] $Tree, Meijer/dsl

111 I-475 N (from nb), UAW Fwy, to Flint

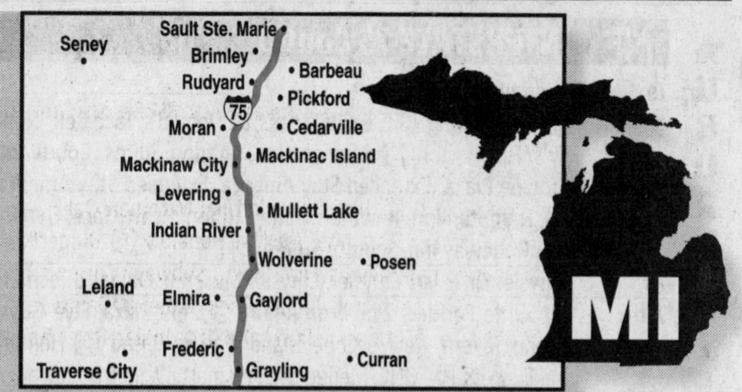

109 MI 54, Dort Hwy (no EZ return to sb)

108 Holly Rd, to Grand Blanc, **E** [gas] Sunoco/dsl [food] Bagger Dave's Burgers, Big Apple Bagels, Buffalo Wild Wings, Culver's, Halo Burger, Taco Bell [lodging] Comfort Inn, Holiday Inn Express [O] BMW/Mercedes/Toyota, Nissan, URGENT CARE, **W** [gas] BP/McDonald's/dsl [food] Arby's [O] [H]

106 Dixie Hwy (exits left from sb, no nb return), Saginaw Rd, to Grand Blanc

101 Grange Hall Rd, Ortonville, **E** [gas] Shell/dsl [O] Groveland Oaks Camping, Holly RA, KOA, **W** [gas] Shell/dsl [O] to Seven Lakes SP

98 E Holly Rd, **E** [gas] Mobil/Tubby's/dsl [O] Ford, golf

96mm **[RS] nb, full [handicapped] facilities, info, litter barrels, petwalk, [phone], [picnic], vending**

95mm **[RS] sb, full [handicapped] facilities, info, litter barrels, petwalk, [phone], [picnic], vending**

93 US 24, Dixie Hwy, Waterford, **E** [gas] BP/dsl [food] McDonald's [O] Chrysler/Dodge/Jeep, Kroger/gas (2mi), **1-3 mi W** [food] Wendy's [O] CVS Drug, GNC, Office Depot, to Pontiac Lake RA, Walgreens

91 MI 15, Davison, Clarkston, **E** [gas] Sunoco/dsl, **W** [gas] BP/dsl [food] Andiamo Italian [O] URGENT CARE

89 Sashabaw Rd, **E** [gas] Mobil/dsl [food] Culver's, Ruby Tuesday, Taco Bell, Tropical Smoothie Cafe [O] county park, **W** [gas] BP, Citgo [food] Chicken Shack, Dunkin Donuts, E Ocean Chinese, Guido's Pizza, Hong Kong Chinese, Hungry Howie's, Jimmy John's, Leo's Coney Island, Little Caesar's, McDonald's, Sagano Japanese, Starbucks, Subway, Tim Horton, Wendy's [O] $Tree, AT&T, CVS Drug, Kroger/dsl, vet

86mm **weigh sta sb**

84b a Baldwin Ave, **E** [gas] BP/dsl [food] Arby's, Big Boy, Chipotle, Joe's Crabshack, Longhorn Steaks, Panera Bread, Potbelly, Starbucks, Taco Bell, Wendy's [O] $Tree, Best Buy, Costco/gas, Discount Tire, Kohl's, Michael's, Nordstrom Rack, Old Navy, PetCo, Staples, **W** [gas] Mobil [food] Bar Louie, Chili's, Five Guys, Jimmy John's, Kerry's Coney Island, McDonald's, On-the-Border, Oriental Forest Buffet, Qdoba Mexican, Rainforest Cafe, Starbucks, Steak'n Shake, Subway [lodging] TownePlace Suites [O] AT&T, Bass Pro Shops, Batteries+Bulbs, Great Lakes Crossing Outlet/famous brands, Hampton Inn, Holiday Inn Express, Marshall's, TJ Maxx, USPO, Verizon, Vitamin Shoppe

83b a Joslyn Rd, **E** [food] Applebee's, Biggby Coffee, Checkers, Logan's Roadhouse, Olive Garden, Subway [O] Belle Tire, Home Depot, Jo-Ann Fabrics, Meijer/dsl, Sam's Club/gas, Target, **W** [gas] BP

81 MI 24, Pontiac (no EZ return), **E** [O] The Palace Arena, to Bald Mtn RA

79 University Dr, **E** [gas] BP [food] BD Mongolian, Domino's, Jimmy John's, Rio Wraps, Spargo Coney Island, Subway, Taste of Thailand [lodging] Extended Stay America, **W** [gas] Mobil, Speedway/dsl

MI

AUBURN HILLS TROY

INTERSTATE 75 Cont'd

79 Continued
Burger King, KFC, Lelli's Steaks, McDonald's, Taco Bell, Wendy's/Tim Horton Baymont Inn, Comfort Suites, Courtyard, Crowne Plaza, Extended Stay America, Extended Stay America (2), Hampton Inn, Hawthorn Suites, Hilton, Hyatt Place, Quality Inn, Rodeway Inn, Sonesta Suites

78 Chrysler Dr, E Chrysler, Chrysler Museum, Oakland Tech Ctr

77b a MI 59, to Pontiac, **2 mi E on Adams** 112 Pizza, Five Guys, Grand Tavern, Kerry's Cone Island, Panera Bread Holiday Inn Express GNC, Meijer/dsl, Petsmart, Walmart/Subway

75 Square Lake Rd (exits left from nb), to Pontiac, W , St Mary's Coll

74 Adams Rd

72 Crooks Rd, to Troy, W Cedar Grill, Jimmy John's, Kerby's Coney Island, Loccino Italian, Papa Romano's Pizza, Red Robin, Starbucks Embassy Suites

69 Big Beaver Rd, E Champp's Grill, Kona Grill, Shula's Steaks, TGIFriday's Drury Inn, Marriott, W BP Benihana, Bonefish Grill, Capital Grille, Carrabba's, Chipotle Mexican, Granite City Rest, J Alexander's, Jersey Mike's, Jimmy John's, Kruse&Muer, Maggiano's Italian, McCormick&Schmick's, Melting Pot Rest., Morton's Steaks, Noodles&Co, Papa Romano's Pizza, PF Chang's, Potbelly, Ruth's Chris Steaks, Starbucks Hampton Inn, Hilton Garden, Somerset Inn Macy's, Neiman Marcus, Nordstrom, Verizon

67 Rochester Rd, to Stevenson Hwy, E BP, Shell/dsl, Sunoco 2Booli Mediterranean, Bahama Breeze, Burger King, Detroit Burger Bar, Dickey's BBQ, Domino's, El Charro, Hills Grille, Hooters, Hungry Howies, Jimmy John's, McDonald's, Ntl Coney Island, Orchid Cafe, Panera Bread, Papa John's, PeiWei, Picano's Italian, Qdoba, Sakura Japanese, Subway, Taco Bell, Tim Hortons, Troy Deli, Wendy's Discount Tire, Fresh Thyme Mkt, Nordstrom Rack, Office Depot, Petsmart, REI, Tuesday Morning, Uncle Ed's Oil Shoppe, vet, W BP Courtyard, Quality Inn, Red Roof Inn tires/repair

65b a 14 Mile Rd, Madison Heights, E Mobil/dsl, Shell/dsl Azteca Mexican, Bob Evans, Burger King, Chili's, Chipotle, ChuckeCheese, Coldstone, Jersey Mike's, Jimmy John's, Krispy Kreme, Logan's Roadhouse, McDonald's, Panchero's, Panera Bread, Pizza Hut, Pizza Papalis, Red Robin, Sonic, Steak'n Shake, Taco Bell, Wendy's Motel 6, Red Roof Inn $Tree, AT&T, Barnes&Noble, Belle Tire, Best Buy, BigLots, CVS Drug, Dick's, Field & Stream, Firestone/auto, Ford, JC Penney, Jo-Ann Fabrics, Kohl's, Macy's, Michael's, Target, TJ Maxx, Verizon, W Mobil Applebee's, Dolly's Pizza, McDonald's, NY Coney Island, Outback Steaks, Twin Peaks Baymont Inn, Courtyard, Days Inn, EconoLodge, Extended Stay America, Fairfield Inn, Hampton Inn, Holiday Inn Express, Residence Inn, TownPlace Suites Costco/gas, Value Ctr Foods

63 12 Mile Rd, E Marathon/dsl Culver's, Green Lantern Rest., McDonald's, Penn Sta Subs, Red Lobster, Sero's Rest., Starbucks, Tim Hortons, TX Roadhouse Home Depot, Lowe's, Midas, Sam's Club/gas, Uncle Ed's Oil, USPO, vet, W Marathon, Speedway Col's Rest. Chevrolet, Costco/gas

62 11 Mile Rd, E Mobil, Synergy/dsl Biggby Coffee, Boodles Rest., Happy's Pizza, Jets Pizza, Telway Burgers 7-11, Advance Parts, CVS Drug, Key's Auto Care, repair/tires, Save-a-Lot, Walgreens, W BP, Marathon/dsl, Mobil KFC, Taco Bell, Tim Hortons, Tubby's Subs Belle Tire, vet

61 I-696 E, to Port Huron, W to Lansing, to Hazel Park Raceway

DETROIT AREA

60 9 Mile Rd, John R St, E Checkers, China 1 Buffet, DQ, Hardee's, McDonald's, Subway, Tim Hortons CVS Drug, Family$, Kroger/gas, O'Reilly Parts, USPO, W Exxon, Marathon, Mobil Tubby's Subs, Wendy's Hasting's Parts, repair

59 MI 102, 8 Mile Rd

58 7 Mile Rd, W BP/dsl

57 McNichols Rd, E Mobil/dsl LA Coney Island

56b a Davison Fwy

55 Holbrook Ave, Caniff St, E Mobil/dsl, W Grandy's Coney Island

54 E Grand Blvd, Clay Ave, W BP/dsl

53b I-94, Ford Fwy, to Port Huron, Chicago

53a Warren Ave, E Mobil, W BP

52 Mack Ave, E Shell/dsl McDonald's

51c I-375 to civic center, tunnel to Canada, downtown

51b MI 3 (exits left from nb), Gratiot Ave, downtown

50 Grand River Ave, downtown

49b MI 10, Lodge Fwy, downtown

49a Rosa Parks Blvd, E Firestone, Tiger Stadium, W Mobil/dsl

48 **I-96 begins/ends**

47b Porter St, E bridge to Canada, DutyFree/24hr, **MI Welcome Ctr**

47a MI 3, Clark Ave, E BP/Subway/dsl, W Marathon

46 Livernois Ave, to Hist Ft Wayne, E Marathon Universal Coney Island

45 Fort St, Springwells Ave, E BP/dsl, W Mobil McDonald's

44 Deerborn St (from nb)

43b a MI 85, Fort St, to Schaefer Hwy, E Shell/dsl, W Marathon Refinery to River Rouge Ford Plant

42 Outer Dr, E Marathon/dsl Happy's Pizza, W BP/dsl Family$, truck tires

41 MI 39, Southfield Rd, to Lincoln Park, E A&W, Tim Hortons, White Castle Aldi Foods, O'Reilly Parts, Walgreens, W Citgo/Tim Hortons, Mobil Burger King, Checker's, Hungry Howie, LJ Silver, McDonald's, Pizza Hut, Starbucks, Taco Bell, Wendy's Red Roof Inn AT&T, Belle Tire, GNC, Kroger/gas, Walgreens

40 Dix Hwy, E AAA/A&W/dsl, Marathon/dsl, Sunoco, Welcome Baskin-Robbins/Dunkin Donuts, Cathay House, Toma's Coney Island 7-11, CVS Drug, Meijer, repair, URGENT CARE, W Fuel Depot, Marathon Big Boy, Burger King, Checker's, DQ, LJ Silver, McDonald's, Pizza Hut, Starbucks, Taco Bell, Wendy's AT&T, auto repair, Belle Tire, Family$, Kroger/gas, Verizon, Walgreens

37 Allen Rd, North Line Rd, to Wyandotte, E BP/dsl, Shell/Tim Hortons Hampton Inn, Holiday Inn , Sam's Club/gas W Citgo/dsl, Sunoco Arby's, Burger King, Mallie's Grill McDonald's, Wendy's Comfort Suites, La Quinta, Motel 6

36 Eureka Rd, E Speedway, Sunoco Bob Evans, Denny's Golden Corral, Tim Hortons Super 8 vet, W Big Boy, Culver's, Famous Dave's, HoneyBaked Ham, Hooters, Jimmy John's, Leo's Coney Island, Little Daddy's Grill, McDonald's Panera Bread, Penn Sta Subs, Pizza Papalis, Primanti Bros, Qdoba, Starbucks, Subway, TX Roadhouse, Wendy's Red Roo Inn AT&T, Belle Tire, Best Buy, Big Lots, Dick's, Discoun Tire, Hobby Lobby, Home Depot, JC Penney, Jo-Ann, Kohl's Macy's, Meijer/dsl, Petsmart, Target, Verizon, Walgreens

35 US 24, Telegraph Rd, (from nb, exits left)

34b Sibley Rd, Riverview, W Sunoco/Baskin-Robbins/Dunki Donuts/Subway General RV Ctr

34a to US 24 (from sb), Telegraph Rd

MI

INTERSTATE 75 Cont'd

Exit#	Services
32	West Rd, to Trenton, Woodhaven, E FLYING J/Detroiter/IHOP/dsl/LP/scales/24hr/@, Speedway/dsl Applebee's, Bagger Dave's Burgers, Baskin-Robbins/Dunkin Donuts, Blue Margarita Mexican, Bob Evans, Buffalo Wild Wings, Chipotle, Christoff's Rest., Coldstone, Firehouse Subs, Five Guys, Jersey Subs, MOD Pizza, Olga's Kitchen, Panda Express, Panera Bread, Pizza Hut, Starbucks, Steak'n Shake, Stevi B's, Subway, Taco Bell, Tim Hortons, Wendy's, White Castle Aldi Foods, Belle Tire, Chevrolet, Chrysler/Dodge/Jeep, Discount Tire, Firestone/auto, Ford, GNC, Home Depot, Kohl's, Lowe's, Marshall's, Meijer/dsl, Michael's, Office Depot, O'Reilly Parts, Petsmart, Target, URGENT CARE, Verizon, Walmart, W BP/Tim Hortons, Citgo, Shell/Hardee's/dsl Andy's Pizza, Domino's, DQ, Jimmy John's, Little Caesar's, McDonald's, Sparta Coney Island, Subway Best Western/rest., Holiday Inn Express, Westwood Inn H, $Tree, AT&T, CVS Drug, Kroger/dsl, SavOn Drug, Walgreens
29	Gilbralter Rd, to Flat Rock, Lake Erie Metropark, E Citgo/dsl McDonald's, Peking Chinese, Sammy's Pizza, Subway, Wendy's H, GNC, Kroger/gas, W Marathon/Burger King/dsl Sleep Inn Ford
28	rd 85 (from nb), Fort St, E H
27	N Huron River Dr, to Rockwood, E Mobil/7-11/dsl Benito's Pizza, Marco's Pizza, Subway $General, Rite Aid, SaveALot, USPO, W Speedway/dsl Rockwoods Rest.
26	S Huron River Dr, to S Rockwood, E Sunoco/dsl Dixie Cafe, Drift Inn USPO
21	Newport Rd, to Newport, E BP/Subway/dsl, W Marathon/Burger King/dsl/24hr
20	I-275 N, to Flint
18	Nadeau Rd, E Loves/Subway/dsl/scales/24hr, W Pilot/Taco Bell/dsl/scales/24hr H
15	MI 50, Dixie Hwy, to Monroe, E Citgo Burger King, Red Lobster, Subway Best Value Inn, Days Inn, Hampton Inn, Holiday Inn Express to Sterling SP, W Pilot/Subway/dsl/scales/24hr, TA/BP/Country Pride/Pizza Hut/Popeye's/Tim Hortons/dsl/scales/24hr/@ Cracker Barrel, Denny's, El Maguey, IHOP, McDonald's, Taco Bell, Wendy's Quality Inn H, to Viet Vet Mem
14	Elm Ave, to Monroe
13	Front St, Monroe
11	La Plaisance Rd, to Bolles Harbor, W Marathon/Taco Bell/dsl, Speedway/dsl McDonald's Econolodge, Harbor Town RV Resort
10mm	**Welcome Ctr nb, full services, info, litter barrels, petwalk, vending**
9	S Otter Creek Rd, to La Salle, W antiques
7mm	**weigh sta both lanes**
6	Luna Pier, E Sunoco/Subway/dsl/scales Beef Jerky Unltd., Ganders Rest. Super 8 USPO
5	to Erie, Temperance
2	Summit St (no nb re-entry)
0mm	Michigan/Ohio state line

MONROE

INTERSTATE 94

Exit#	Services
275mm	**I-69/I-94 begin/end on MI 25,** N Pinegrove Ave in Port Huron BP, Shell/dsl, Speedway/dsl Arby's, McDonald's, Tim Horton, Wendy's Days Inn, Quality Inn Family$, Honda, Rite Aid, **tollbridge to Canada**

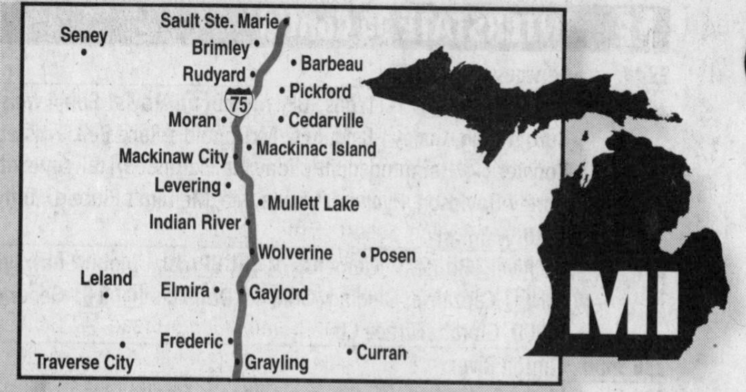

PORT HURON

Exit#	Services
274.5mm	Black River
274	Water St, Port Huron, N Cracker Barrel Best Western Lake Port SP, Port Huron RV Park, S SpeedyQ/dsl Bob Evans Comfort Inn, Fairfield Inn, Hampton Inn, Holiday Inn Express Menard's, O'Reilly Parts
273mm	**Welcome Ctr/ wb, full facilities, litter barrels, petwalk**
271	**I-69 E and I-94 E run together eb,** Lp I-69, **0-2 mi S on Lp 69** Mobil/dsl, Speedway Arby's, Burger King, Jimmy John's, KFC, Little Caesar's, McDonalds, Subway, Taco Bell, Tim Horton's, Wendy's $General, Advance Parts, AutoZone, Kroger/gas, repair, Sam's Club/gas, to Port Huron, USPO
269	Dove St, Range Rd, N Speedway/dsl Theo's Rest. Baymont Inn
266	Gratiot Rd, Marysville, **0-2 mi S** BP, Marathon/dsl/scales/24hr, Speedway/dsl Arby's, Big Boy, Burger King, China Lite, Dairy Boy, Daliono's, Four Star Grille, Hungry Howie's, Jets Pizza, Jimmy John's, KFC, Little Caesars, McDonald's, Mr Pita, Pelican Café, Seros Rest., Subway, Taco Bell, Tim Horton Super 8 H, $General, $Tree, AutoZone, CarQuest, CVS Drug, Meijer/dsl, O'Reilly Parts, Rite Aid, Verizon, vet, Wally's Foods
262	Wadhams Rd, N camping, S Mobil/dsl
257	St Clair, Richmond, N Sunoco/dsl, S BP/dsl st police
255mm	**eb, full facilities, info, litter barrels, petwalk,**
251mm	**wb, full facilities, info, litter barrels, petwalk,**
248	26 Mile Rd, to Marine City, N McDonald's (2mi), S 7-11/gas, Speedy Q (1mi) Asian Garden, My Place Cafe, Subway, Taco Bell, Tim Horton Mejier/dsl
247mm	Salt River
247	MI 19 (no eb return), New Haven
243	MI 29, MI 3, Utica, New Baltimore, N BP, Marathon/dsl, Sunoco/dsl Applebee's, Arby's, Buffalo Wild Wings, Burger King, Chophouse, Coldstone, Coney Island, Dimitri's Rest., Dolly's Pizza, Eagles Grill, Father&Son Pizzaria, Happy's Pizza, Jersey Mike's, Little Caesars, McDonald's, Noodles&Co, Panera Bread, Qdoba, Ruby Tuesday, Starbucks, Stevie B's Pizza, Tim Horton, TX Roadhouse, Wendy's, White Castle Chesterfield Motel $Tree, AutoZone, Belle Tire, Best Buy, Big Lots, Dick's, Discount Tire, GNC, Hobby Lobby, Home Depot, JC Penney, Jo-Ann Fabrics, Kohl's, Lowe's, Meijer/Subway/dsl, Michael's, NAPA, Old Navy, O'Reilly Parts, PetCo, PetsMart, Rite Aid, Staples, Target, TJ Maxx, URGENT CARE, Verizon, Walgreens, S Marathon/dsl/24hr, Speedway/dsl/24hr Big Boy, Buscemi's Pizza, Checkers, Taco Bell LodgeKeeper
241	21 Mile Rd, Selfridge, N Exxon/dsl/e85, Speedway/dsl China King, Hungry Howie's, Jets Pizza, Jimmy John's Advance Parts, AT&T, CVS Drug, same as 240, Verizon, vet

MI

INTERSTATE 94 Cont'd

DETROIT AREA

Exit#	Services
240	to MI 59, N 7-11/gas, BP, Mobil Arby's, Bob Evans, Burger King, Coney Island, KFC, McDonald's, Taco Bell, Twisted Rooster Hampton Inn, Holiday Inn Express $Tree, Ford, Harley-Davidson, Hyundai/Mazda, Kia, Menard's, Subaru, Tuffy Auto, Walmart
237	N River Rd, Mt Clemens, N BP/dsl, Mobil/Subway/dsl Captain's Landing Grill, McDonald's H, General RV Ctr, Gibraltar Trade Ctr
236.5mm	Clinton River
236	Metro Parkway, S Big Apple Bagels, Empire Chinese, Little Caesars, McDonald's, Subway H, CVS Drug, GNC, Kroger, URGENT CARE, Verizon
235	Shook Rd (from wb)
234b a	Harper Rd, 15 Mile Rd, N BP/McDonald's, Marathon/dsl, SpeedyQ, Sunoco/dsl Domino's, Gina's Cafe, Tim Horton's Family$, vet, S Shell China Moon, Subway, Travis Rest., Winners Grill URGENT CARE
232	Little Mack Ave (from wb only), N Citgo, Marathon, Mobil, Shell, Sunoco Coldstone, Denny's, Hooters, Longhorn Steaks, McDonald's, Pizza Hut, Red Robin Hampton Inn, Holiday Inn Express, Red Roof Inn, Relax Inn, Super 8, Victory Inn Advance Parts, Aldi Foods, Belle Tire, Discount Tire, Firestone, O'Reilly Parts, Sam's Club/gas, Staples, Target, Tuesday Morning, S Speedway/dsl Cracker Barrel, Culver's, IHOP Baymont Inn Home Depot, Jo-Ann Fabrics, Meijer/dsl/24hr, PetsMart, same as 231
231	(from eb), MI 3, Gratiot Ave, N Exxon/dsl, Marathon Applebee's, Arby's, Bob Evans, Burger King, Chili's, Chipotle, ChuckeCheese, Del Taco, Denny's, Famous Dave's BBQ, Logan's Roadhouse, Longhorn Steaks, Marco's Italian, McDonald's, National Coney Island, Panera Bread, PetCo, Pizza Hut, Potbelly, Qdoba, Ruby Tuesday, Starbucks, Subway, Tim Horton, TX Roadhouse Days Inn, Extended Stay America, Hampton Inn, Microtel Belle Tire, Best Buy, Dick's, Discount Tire, Firestone/auto, Honda/Acura, Kia, Kohl's, Kroger, Michael's, Nissan, Sam's Club/gas, Staples
230	12 Mile Rd, N Mobil/dsl, Sunoco/dsl BD's Mongolian, Jimmy John's, Outback Steaks, Starbucks, Taco Bell $Tree, AT&T, CVS Drug, Marshall's, Verizon, Walmart/Subway, S Marathon
229	I-696 W, Reuther Fwy, to 11 Mile Rd, S Shell/dsl, Speedway/dsl 7-11
228	10 Mile Rd, N 7-11, BP Baskin-Robbins, Donna's Rest., Eastwind Chinese, Friendly Rest., Jet's Pizza, Little Italy Pizza, Sugarbush Rest. Save Mor Drugs, URGENT CARE
227	9 Mile Rd, N Metro, Speedway/dsl, Sunoco DQ, McDonald's, Milestone Grill, Popeye's, Subway, Taco Bell, Tim Horton's, Wendy's $Tree, Aldi Foods, CVS Drug, Family$, Fresh Choice Foods, Office Depot, TrueValue, vet, S Mobil/dsl, Mobil/dsl Shore Pointe Motel Cadillac, Mercedes
225	MI 102, Vernier Rd, 8 Mile Rd, S BP/Subway, Mobil, Sunoco/dsl Coney Island, KFC, Taco Bell, Wendy's Kroger, Walgreens
224b	Allard Ave, Eastwood Ave
224a	Moross Rd, S Shell H, Family Foods
223	Cadieux Rd, S BP/Subway, Mobil, Shell/dsl, Sunoco Checkers, McDonald's, Papa's Pizza, Popeye's, Tubby's Subs, Wendy's, White Castle Family$, Rite Aid
222b	Harper Ave (from eb), S Hastings Auto
222a	Chalmers Ave, Outer Dr, N BP/Subway/dsl, Clark Coney Island, KFC, Little Caesars Family$
220b	Conner Ave, N BP, Sunoco
220a	French Rd, S Citgo
219	MI 3, Gratiot Ave, N Clark, Marathon/Subway Coney Island, McDonald's Family$, Farmer John's Foods, USPO, S Citgo Burger King
218	MI 53, Van Dyke Ave, N BP, Mobil/dsl
217b	Mt Elliott Ave, S Citgo, Mobil/dsl Royal BBQ
217a	E Grand Blvd, Chene St, S Marathon
216b	Russell St (from eb), to downtown
216a	I-75, Chrysler Fwy, to tunnel to Canada
215c	MI 1, Woodward Ave, John R St
215b	MI 10 N, Lodge Fwy
215a	MI 10 S, tunnel to Canada, downtown
214b	Trumbull Ave, to Ford Hospital
214a	(from wb)Grand River Ave
213b	I-96 W to Lansing, E to Canada, bridge to Canada, to Tiger Stadium
213a	W Grand (exits left from eb)
212b	Warren Ave (from eb)
212a	Livernois Ave, S Marathon/Subway/dsl, Sunoco/dsl
211b	Cecil Ave (from wb), Central Ave
211a	Lonyo Rd, S Sunoco Ford
210	US 12, Michigan Ave, Wyoming Ave, N Mobil/dsl, S BP/dsl, Sunoco/dsl Checkers
209	Rotunda Dr (from wb)
208	Greenfield Rd, Schaefer Rd, N Mobil/dsl Wendy's/Tim Horton 7-11, S River Rouge Ford Plant
207mm	Rouge River
206	Oakwood Blvd, Melvindale, N Marathon, Shell Applebee's, Biggby Coffee, Carino's, Chili's, Coldstone, Coney Island Five Guys, Jimmy John's, Little Caesar's, Longhorn Steaks, Olga's Kitchen, On-the-Border, Panda Express, Panera Bread, Potbelly Qdoba, Starbucks, Subway, Taco Bell AAA, Barnes&Noble Best Buy, GNC, Greenfield Village Museum, Home Depot, Jo Ann Fabrics, Lowe's, Meijer, Michael's, Old Navy, PetCo, Staples, Target, TJ Maxx, USPO, Verizon, S BP/dsl Burge King, Hungry Howie's, McDonald's, Sabina's, Subway, Tim Horton's Best Western, Holiday Inn Express $General $Tree, 7-11, CVS Drug, O'Reilly Parts, Rite Aid
205mm	Largest Uniroyal Tire in the World
204b a	MI 39, Southfield Fwy, Pelham Rd, N Marathon/dsl, Mobi Valero/dsl 7-11, to Greenfield Village, S Exxon/dsl Marathon/dsl, Marathon/dsl Walgreens
202b a	US 24, Telegraph Rd, N Citgo, Shell, Sunoco Burge King, Checkers, Dunkin Donuts, KFC, McDonald's, Pizza Hut Ram's Horn Rest., Subway, Taco Bell, Wendy's Advanc Parts, Aldi Foods, Rite Aid, Walgreens, **0-2 mi** S BP, Citgo dsl, Marathon/dsl, Valero/dsl Arby's, Big Boy, Burger King Dunkin Donuts, Hungry Howie's, Jimmy John's, KFC, Leon' Rest., Leo's Coney Island, Little Caesar's, LJ Silver, Marina' Pizza, McDonald's, New Hong Kong, Pancho's Mexican, Pizz Hut, Popeye's, Subway, Super China, Taco Bell, Teppanyaki, Tin Horton's/Coldstone, Wendy's Comfort Inn $Tree, AT&T AutoZone, Family$, Firestone/auto, Home Depot, Rite Aid, s police, U-Haul, Verizon, vet, Walgreens, Walmart/Burger King
200	Ecorse Rd, (no ez eb return), to Taylor, N Marathon/Subway dsl/scales Tim Horton's, S Citgo/dsl, Rich
199	Middle Belt Rd, S BP/dsl Checkers, McDonald's, Wendy's Days Inn, Knights Inn, Quality Inn

DETROIT AREA

MI

INTERSTATE 94 Cont'd

Exit#	Services
198	Merriman Rd, N Citgo/dsl, Marathon, Speedway/Speedy Cafe/dsl Big Boy, Bob Evans, Capitol Bistro, Fortune Chinese, Leonardo's Italian, McDonald's, Merriman St Grill, Sporting News Grill, Subway, Toarmina's Pizza Baymont Inn, Best Value Inn, Clarion, Comfort Inn, Courtyard, Embassy Suites, Extended Stay America, Fairfield Inn, Hampton Inn, Hilton Garden, Holiday Inn, Holiday Inn Express, Howard Johnson, La Quinta, Magnuson Hotel, Marriott, Red Lion Inn, Rodeway Inn, Sheraton, Sheraton Four Points, SpringHill Suites, Wyndham Garden Hotel, S Wayne Co Airport
197	Vining Rd
196	Wayne Rd, Romulus, N Shell/dsl Little Caesar's, McDonald's, Taco Bell $General, S Mobil/dsl Burger King, Subway
194b a	I-275, N to Flint, S to Toledo
192	Haggerty Rd, N BP/Tubby's/dsl, Mobil/dsl, S Lower Huron Metro Park
190	Belleville Rd, to Belleville, N BP/Quizno's/dsl, Marathon Applebee's, Arby's, Asian Garden, Coney Island, Cracker Barrel, Culver's, Happy's Pizza, Hungry Howie's, McDonald's, Taco Bell, Tim Horton, Twisted Rooster, Wendy's Hampton Inn, Holiday Inn Express, Red Roof Inn $Tree, AT&T, AutoZone, Belle Tire, Camping World RV Ctr, CVS Drug, Firestone/auto, Ford, Meijer/dsl, National RV Ctr, O'Reilly Parts, Verizon, Walgreens, Walmart, S Shell Burger King, China City, Dos Pesos Mexican, Mike's Kitchen, Subway Comfort Inn, Super 8 URGENT CARE, USPO
189mm	**wb, full facilities, info, litter barrels, petwalk, , , vending**
187	Rawsonville Rd, N Freightliner, S Mobil/dsl, Speedway/dsl Burger King, Denny's, KFC, Little Caesars, McDonald's, Pearl River Chinese, Pizza Hut, Taco Bell, Tim Horton, Wendy's $General, $Tree, Detroit Greenfield RV Park, GNC, K-Mart
185	US 12, Michigan Ave (from eb, exits left, no return), to frontage rds,
184mm	Ford Lake
183	US 12, Huron St, Ypsilanti, N Citgo/dsl H, to E MI U, S a Shell Buffalo Wild Wings, Coney Island, Jet's Pizza, McDonald's, Tim Horton's Marriott Kroger/dsl, st police
181b a	US 12 W, Michigan Ave, Ypsilanti, N Speedway/dsl Coney Island, Dunkin Donuts, Hong Kong Chinese, Roundtree Grill, Taco Bell, Tim Horton/Wendy's H, Aamco, BigLots, GNC, Walmart/Subway, **0-2 mi** S Citgo/Subway/dsl, Mobil/Circle K, Sunoco/dsl Harvest Moon Cafe, McDonald's Sam's Club/gas
180b a	US 23, to Toledo, Flint
177	State St, N BP, Mobil Bravo Italiana, Buffalo Wild Wings, Burger King, CA Pizza, Chipotle, Graham's Steaks, Los Amigos, Macaroni Grill, Max&Erma's, Mediterrano Rest, Olive Garden, Panda Express, PF Chang's, Red Robin, Wendy's Comfort Inn, Courtyard, Extended Stay America, Extended Stay America, Fairfield Inn, Hampton Inn, Hilton Garden, Holiday Inn, Holiday Inn Express, Kensington Court Inn, Red Roof Inn, Residence Inn, Sheraton, TownePlace Suites Firestone/auto, Honda, JC Penney, Macy's, Porsche, to UMI, URGENT CARE, Von Maur, VW, World Mkt, S Citgo/Subway/dsl, Speedway/dsl Coney Island, McDonald's, Taco Bell, Tim Horton's Motel 6 Belle Tire, Costco/gas, U-Haul

ANN ARBOR

Exit#	Services
175	Ann Arbor-Saline Rd, N Shell/Tim Horton's Applebee's, Bagger Dave's, Bella Italia, Dibella Subs, Moe's SW Grill, Old Carolina BBQ, Panera Bread, Subway, Tony Sacco's Pizza Candlewood Suites REI, to UMI Stadium, vet, Whole Foods Mkt, S ChuckECheese's, Five Guys, Joe's Crabshack, McDonald's, Outback Steaks, Panchero's, Subway, TGIFriday's AT&T, Best Buy, BigLots, Dick's, Jo-Ann Fabrics, Kohl's, Meijer/dsl/e-85, Petsmart, Target
172	Jackson Ave, to Ann Arbor, S Marathon Weber's Rest. Hampton Inn, Wyndham Garden Chevrolet/Cadillac, Ford, Hyundai, Mini, Nissan, Subaru, Toyota, N on Stadium Ave Marathon, Shell/dsl Burger King, Jersey Mike's, McDonald's, Noodles&Co, Quarter Rest., Subway, Taco Bell, Zingerman's Roadhouse H, $Tree, CVS, Goodyear/auto, Kroger, Midas, O'Reilly Parts, Plum Mkt, Rite Aid, Staples, TJ Maxx, Verizon, Walgreens
171	MI 14 (from eb, exits left), Ann Arbor, to Flint by U.S. 23
169	Zeeb Rd, N BP/dsl Big Boy, Grand Traverse Pies Co, McDonald's, Metzger's Rest. Holiday Inn Express, S Citgo/dsl Arby's, Biggby Coffee, Burger King, Creekside Grill, Culver's, Domino's, Panera Bread, Pizza Hut, Subway, Taco Bell, Wendy's, Westside Grill CVS Drug, Discount Tire, Lowe's, Meijer/dsl, Menard's, vet
167	Baker Rd, Dexter, N Pilot/Subway/scales/dsl/24hr, S Pilot/Arby's/dsl/scales/24hr, TA/BP/Popeye's/dsl/scales/24hr/@ McDonald's Blue Beacon
162	Jackson Rd, Fletcher Rd, S BP/Subway/dsl/24hr Stiver's Rest.
161mm	**eb, full facilities, litter barrels, petwalk, , , vending**
159	MI 52, Chelsea, N Shell/dsl, Speedway/dsl, Sunoco/dsl Big Boy, Biggby Coffee, Chelsea Grill, China Garden, Chinese Tonite, Jimmy John's, KFC/Taco Bell, McDonald's, Subway, Uptown Coney Island, Wendy's Comfort Inn, Holiday Inn Express H, $Tree, Ace Hardware, AutoZone, Buick/Chevrolet, Chrysler/Dodge/Jeep, Country Mkt Foods/drug, CVS Drug, Travel Land RV Ctr, USPO, Verizon, S Buick/Chevrolet
157	Jackson Rd, Pierce Rd, N Gerald Eddy Geology Ctr
156	Kalmbach Rd, N to Waterloo RA
153	Clear Lake Rd, N Marathon/dsl
151.5mm	**weigh sta both lanes**
150	to Grass Lake, S Mobil/Dunkin Donuts/Subway/dsl
150mm	**wb, full facilities, litter barrels, petwalk, , , vending**
147	Race Rd, N camping, to Waterloo RA, S lodging Holiday RV Camp
145	Sargent Rd, S BP McDonald's, Wendy's Colonial Inn
144	Lp 94 (from wb), to Jackson
142	US 127 S, to Hudson, **1 mi** S Meijer/dsl, Speedway/dsl Arby's, Bob Evans, KFC, McDonald's, Taco Bell, Wendy's $General, $Tree, Advance Parts, Kroger, Rite Aid, to MI Speedway, Verizon, Walgreens

INTERSTATE 94 Cont'd

JACKSON

Exit#	Services
141	Elm Rd, N Travelodge Chevrolet, Chrysler/Dodge/Jeep, Ford/Lincoln, Honda, Nissan, S H
139	MI 106, Cooper St, to Jackson, N st police/prison, S Citgo/Subway H, Meefhof Tire
138	US 127 N, MI 50, to Lansing, Jackson, N Red Lobster, Yen King Chinese Baymont Inn, Comfort Inn, Fairfield Inn, Hampton Inn, Super 8 vet, S Admiral, BP/dsl, Shell/dsl Arby's, Big Boy, Bob Evans, Burger King, Dunkin Donuts, Fazoli's, KFC, LJ Silver, Los Tres Amigos, McDonald's, Old Country Buffet, Outback Steaks, Panda Express, Panera Bread, Papa John's, Qdoba, Rally's, Starbucks, Subway, Wendy's Best Value Inn $Tree, Advance Parts, Aldi Foods, AT&T, AutoZone, Belle Tire, Best Buy, BigLots, Discount Tire, Family$, Home Depot, JoAnn Fabrics, Kohl's, Kroger/gas, Lowe's, Michael's, Midas, O'Reilly Parts, Petsmart, Target, TJ Maxx, URGENT CARE, Verizon, Walgreens
137	Airport Rd, N Marathon/dsl, Shell/Taco Bell Burger King, Denny's, McDonald's, Steak'n Shake, Subway, Wendy's Holiday Inn 7-11, Meijer/dsl, S BP/dsl Cracker Barrel, Culver's, LoneStar Steaks, Olive Garden Holiday Inn Express Sam's Club/gas, Save-A-Lot Foods
136	Lp 94, MI 60, to Jackson
135mm	**eb, full facilities, litter barrels, petwalk, vending**
133	Dearing Rd, Spring Arbor, S to Spring Arbor U
130	Parma
128	Michigan Ave, N BP/Burger King/scales/dsl/24hr RV camping
127	Concord Rd, N wineries
124	MI 99, to Eaton Rapids
121	28 Mile Rd, to Albion, N Mobil/Subway/dsl Arby's Days Inn, S AllStar/dsl, BP/dsl, Speedway/dsl Frosty Dan's, KFC, La Casa Mexican, Maria's Garden Rest., McDonald's, Pizza Hut Super 9 Inn H, $General, Albion Tire/auto, AutoZone, Buick/Chevrolet, Family Fare Foods, Family$, Ford, O'Reilly Parts
119	MI 199, 26 Mile Rd
115	22.5 Mile Rd, N Citgo/115 Rest./dsl/24hr
113mm	**wb, full facilities, litter barrels, petwalk, vending**
112	Partello Rd, S Loves/Hardee's/scales/dsl/24hr Schuler's Rest.
110	Old US 27, Marshall, N Shell/Country Kitchen/Subway/dsl/24hr, S Citgo/dsl Denny's, Pizza Hut (2mi), Schuler's Rest. (2mi) Hampton Inn, Holiday Inn Express H, sheriff
108	I-69, US 27, N to Lansing, S to Ft Wayne
104	11 Mile Rd, Michigan Ave, N Pilot/McDonald's/dsl/scales/24hr, TA/Country Pride/dsl/scales/24hr/@, S Citgo/Subway/dsl/e-85 Quality Inn/rest. casino
102mm	Kalamazoo River
100	rd 294, Beadle Lake Rd, N Moonraker Rest., S Citgo/dsl/repair Binder Park Zoo
98b	I-194 N, to Battle Creek
98a	MI 66, to Sturgis, S Citgo/Tim Horton/dsl Chili's, Los Aztecas, McDonald's, Ruby Tuesday, Schlotzsky's, Starbucks, Steak'n Shake Courtyard, Holiday Inn AT&T, Best Buy, Discount Tire, Kohl's, Lowe's, Meijer/dsl, Menards, Michael's, PetCo, same as 97, Sam's Club/gas, Staples, TJ Maxx, Verizon, Walgreens, Walmart/Subway
97	Capital Ave, to Battle Creek, N BP, Marathon Arby's, LoneStar Steaks, Lux Cafe, McDonald's, Old China, Red Lobster

MARSHALL

KALAMAZOO

Exit#	Services
97	Continued Comfort Inn, Knights Inn, S Citgo/Subway, Shell/dsl Applebee's, Bob Evans, Buffalo Wild Wings, Burger King, Canton Buffet, Cracker Barrel, Culver's, Denny's, Don Pablo, Fazoli's, Jimmy John's, La Cocina, Old Country Buffet, Panera Bread, Pizza Hut, Taco Bell, Wendy's Baymont Inn, Best Value Inn, Best Western, Fairfield Inn, Hampton Inn, Red Roof Inn, Rodeway Inn, Travelodge $Tree, AAA, Barnes&Noble, Belle Tire, BigLots, Firestone/auto, Harley Davidson, Hobby Lobby, Jo-Ann Fabrics, Target, Uncle Ed's Oil Shoppe, URGENT CARE, vet
96mm	**eb, full facilities, litter barrels, petwalk, vending**
95	Helmer Rd, 2 mi N Citgo/dsl Arby's, Big Boy Meijer/dsl/e-85, st police
92	Lp 94, rd 37, to Battle Creek, Springfield, N Citgo/Arlene's Trkstp/dsl/rest./24hr, Shell RV camping, to Ft Custer RA
88	Climax, N Galesburg Speedway
85	35th St, Galesburg, N Shell/dsl McDonald's, Subway Galesburg Speedway, River Oaks CP, to Ft Custer RA, S Colebrook CP, RV camping, Scott's Mill CP, Winery Tours
85mm	**wb, full facilities, litter barrels, petwalk, vending**
81	Lp 94 (from wb), to Kalamazoo
80	Cork St, Sprinkle Rd, to Kalamazoo, N Marathon/dsl, Speedway/dsl Arby's, Bennucci's Grill, Burger King, Crew Rest., Denny's, Godfather's, Taco Bell Baymont Inn, Clarion, Holiday Inn Express, Red Roof Inn, Sheraton Monro, vet, S BP/dsl, Speedway/dsl McDonald's, Michelle's Rest., Nob Hill Grill, Subway, Wendy's Candlewood Suites, EconoLodge, Motel 6, Quality Inn
78	Portage Rd, Kilgore Rd, N Mobil/Circle K China Hut, Summer Thyme Cafe AmericInn H, repair, S Marathon/dsl, Shell, Speedway Angelo's Italian, Biggby Coffee, Bravo Rest., Brewster's, Café Meli, CJ's Lubritorium, McDonald's, Pizza King, Subway, Taco Bell, Theo&Stacy's Rest. Country Inn&Suites, Days Inn, Hampton Inn AutoValue Parts, Fields Fabrics
76	Westnedge Ave, N Admiral, Meijer/dsl, Speedway/dsl Burger King, Grand Traverse Pie Co, Hibachi Buffet, Hooters, IHOP, Lee's Chicken, McDonald's, Old Chicago Grill, Outback Steaks, Papa John's, Papa Murphy's, Pizza Hut, Qdoba, Riviera Mayo, Root Beer Stand, Steak'n Shake, Subway, Taco Bell, Theo&Stacy's Rest. Courtyard, Homewood Suites $Tree, Advance Parts, BigLots, Discount Tire, Earth Fare, Family$, Firestone/auto, Goodyear/auto, Lowe's, Meijer, Midas, Office Depot, Walgreens, S Shell Antique Kitchen Rest., Applebee's, Biggby Coffee, Bilbo's Pizza, Bob Evans, Brann's Steaks, Burger King, Carrabba's, Chili's, ChuckECheese's, Coldstone, Culver's, Five Guys, HoneyBaked Ham, Jimmy John's, KFC, Little Caesars, LJ Silver, Logan's Roadhouse, Los Amigos Mexican, McDonald's, Moe's SW Grill, Noodles&Co, Olive Garden, Panchero's Mexican, Panera Bread, Penn Sta Subs, Pizza Hut, Qdoba Mexican, Red Lobster, Red Robin, Schlotzsky's, Subway, Taco Bell, Tim Horton, TX Roadhouse, Wendy's, Zoup! Holiday Motel $Tree, Aldi Foods, AT&T, AutoZone, Barnes&Noble, Belle Tire, Best Buy, Buick/Cadillac/GMC, Dick's, Fannie May Candies, Firestone/auto, Harding's Foods, Hobby Lobby, Home Depot, JC Penney, JoAnn Fabrics, Kohl's, Macy's, Menard's, Michael's, Monro, Old Navy, O'Reilly Parts, PepBoys, Petco, Sam's Club/gas, Target, TJMaxx, Tuesday Morning, Tuffy Auto, Uncle Ed's Oil Shoppe, URGENT CARE, Verizon, Walgreens, World Mkt
75	Oakland Dr
74b a	US 131, to Kalamazoo, N Kalamazoo Coll, to W MI U

INTERSTATE 94 Cont'd

Exit#	Services
72	9th St, Oshtemo, N Citgo/dsl, Speedway/dsl Arby's, Culver's, McDonald's, Taco Bell, Wendy's Hampton Inn, S Cracker Barrel Fairfield Inn, Microtel, Towne Place Suites
66	Mattawan, N Citgo/dsl, Speedway/Subway/dsl/scales/24hr Mancino's Italian Family$, Freightliner, R&S RV Service, Rossman Auto/repair, vet, S Shell/dsl Pizza Hut, Subway USPO, Wagoner's Foods
60	MI 40, Paw Paw, N Citgo, Speedway/dsl Arby's, Burger King, Chicken Coop, Copper Grille, McDonald's, Pizza Hut, Red's Root Beer, Subway, Subway, Taco Bell, Wendy's Comfort Inn, EconoLodge, Travelodge H, Advance Parts, AT&T, Buick/Chevrolet/GMC, Chrysler/Dodge/Jeep, Family Fare Foods, Ford, O'Reilly Parts, St Julian Winery, Walgreens, S Walmart/Subway
56	MI 51, to Decatur, N st police, S Citgo/dsl, Marathon/dsl
52	Lawrence
46	Hartford, N Shell/dsl McDonald's, Panel Room Rest., Subway, S fruit stand
42mm	**wb, full facilities, litter barrels, petwalk, , , vending**
41	MI 140, to Niles, Watervliet, N Citgo, Marathon/dsl, Shell/dsl Burger King, Chicken Coop, Frosty Boy, Mill Creek Charlie's Rest., Subway, Taco Bell Fairfield Inn H, KOA (Apr-Oct) (7mi)
39	Millburg, Coloma, Deer Forest, 0-1 mi N BP/dsl, Shell/dsl, Speedway/dsl, Wesco/dsl DQ, El Asadero Mexican, Friendly Grill, McDonald's, Subway Family$, Krenek RV Ctr, S fruit mkt, Jollay Mkt, wine tasting
34	I-196 N, US 31 N, to Holland, Grand Rapids
33	Lp I-94, to Benton Harbor, 2-4 mi N , sheriff's dept
30	Napier Ave, Benton Harbor, N Pilot/Wendy's/dsl/LP/24hr/@, Shell/dsl Knights Inn H, Blue Beacon
29	Pipestone Rd, Benton Harbor, N Applebee's, Asian Grill, Burger King, Cravings Bistro, El Rodeo Mexican, IHOP, Mancino's Pizza, McDonald's, Sophia's Pancake House, Steak'n Shake, Subway, Super Buffet, TX Corral Best Western, Days Inn, Hilton Garden, Motel 6, Red Roof Inn Aldi Foods, Best Buy, Big Lots, Chrysler/Dodge/Jeep, Home Depot, JC Penney, Jo-Ann Fabrics, Lowe's, Meijer/dsl, NAPA Autocare, Staples, Walmart/Subway, S BP/dsl Bob Evans Comfort Suites, Holiday Inn Express
28	US 31 S, MI 139 N, Scottdale Rd, to Niles, N Citgo/dsl, Marathon/dsl Burger King, Chicken Coop, Country Kitchen, DQ, Henry's Burgers, KFC, Little Caesars, Pizza Hut, Sonic, Subway, Taco Bell, Wendy's Best Value Inn, Rodeway Inn H, $Tree, AutoZone, Belle Tire, Chevrolet/Buick/GMC, Family$, Kohl's, M&W Tire, Michael's, Midas, NAPA, O'Reilly Parts, Petsmart, radiators/repair/transmissions, Rite Aid, Save-A-Lot, Target, TJ Maxx, U-Haul, vet, Walgreens
27mm	St Joseph River
27	MI 63, Niles Ave, to St Joseph, N Citgo Nye's Apple Barn, S Tesla 45 Five Guys, Moe's SW Grill, Panera Bread Goodyear
23	Red Arrow Hwy, Stevensville, N Admiral, Marathon/dsl, Shell/dsl Big Boy, Burger King, Chicago Grill, Cracker Barrel, Culver's, DQ, LJ Silver, McDonald's, Papa John's, Rio's Mexican, Subway Baymont Inn, Candlewood Suites, Comfort Suites, Super 8 Honda, Walgreens, S Five O'Clock Grill Hampton Inn Meijer/dsl/e85
22	John Beers Rd, Stevensville, N Chalet on the Lake to Grand Mere SP, S Marathon/dsl

BENTON HARBOR

Exit#	Services
16	Bridgman, N BP/Quiznos/dsl camping, to Warren Dunes SP, S Citgo Lydia's Rest., McDonald's, Olympus Rest., Pizza Hut, Roma Pizza, Subway Bridgman Inn auto repair, Chevrolet, Chrysler/Dodge/Jeep, Ford/Mazda, st police, vet
12	Sawyer, N Marathon/deli/dsl/scales/24hr truck wash, S TA/Burger King/Popeye's/Taco Bell/scales/dsl/24hr/@ Fitzgerald's Grill, Greenbush Brewing Super 8 USPO
6	Lakeside, Union Pier, N Round Barn Winery, St Julian Winery, S RV camping
4b a	US 12, to Three Oaks, New Buffalo, N Pizza Hut, Redamak's Hamburgers, Roma Pizza st police
2.5mm	**weigh sta both lanes**
1	MI 239, to Grand Beach, New Buffalo, 0-2 mi N Shell/Quiznos/dsl Brewster's Italian, Casey's Grille, Jimmy's Grill, McDonald's, Nancy's, Rosie's Rest., Stray Dog Grill, Subway Baymont Inn, Comfort Inn, Fairfield Inn, Holiday Inn Express, Super Inn $General, S Plaza1/dsl/scales/24hr Wendy's casino
.5mm	**Welcome Ctr eb, full facilities, info, litter barrels, petwalk, , , vending**
0mm	Michigan/Indiana state line

INTERSTATE 96

Exit#	Services
	I-96 begins/ends on I-75, exit 48 in Detroit.
191	I-75, N to Flint, S to Toledo, US 12, to MLK Blvd, to Michigan Ave
190b	Warren Ave, N BP/dsl
190a	I-94 E to Port Huron
189	W Grand Blvd, Tireman Rd, N BP/dsl, Mobil
188b	Joy Rd, N Church's
188a	Livernois, N Mobil, Shell/Subway Burger King, KFC, McDonald's, Wendy's
187	Grand River Ave (from eb)
186b	Davison Ave, I-96 local and I-96 express divide, no exits from express
186a	Wyoming Ave
185	Schaefer Hwy, to Grand River Ave, N Mobil, Shamrock Coney Island, McDonald's CVS Drug, S Sunoco/dsl
184	Greenfield Rd
183	MI 39, Southfield Fwy, exit from expswy and local
182	Evergreen Rd
180	Outer Dr, N BP/dsl/lube
180mm	I-96 local/express unite/divide
179	US 24, Telegraph Rd, N BP, Marathon/dsl Arby's, Baskin-Robbins/Dunkin Donuts, China King, Little Caesar's,

DETROIT AREA

MI

DETROIT AREA

INTERSTATE 96 Cont'd

179 Continued
McDonald's, Tim Horton's, White Castle [other] AutoZone, Chevrolet, Family$, Family$, OReilly Parts, URGENT CARE, S [gas] Marathon/dsl, Shell/dsl

178 Beech Daly Rd, N [gas] gas

177 Inkster Rd, N [gas] BP/Tim Horton [food] Subway [lodging] Best Value Inn [other] $General, 7-11, URGENT CARE

176 Middlebelt Rd, N [food] Bob Evans, IHOP, Olive Garden [lodging] Comfort Inn, 0-1 mi S [food] Applebee's, Biggby Coffee, Chili's, Culver's, Del Taco, Five Guys, Jimmy John's, Leo's Coney Island, Logan's Roadhouse, McDonald's, MOD Pizza, Noodles&Co, Outback, Panera Bread, Pizza Hut, Potbelly, Qdoba, Red Lobster, Starbucks [lodging] Crossland Suites [other] $Tree, AT&T, BigLots, Costco/gas, Dick's, Firestone/auto, GNC, Home Depot, Jo-Ann Fabrics, Marshall's, Meijer, Menard's, Michael's, Office Depot, Petsmart, Target, URGENT CARE, Verizon, Walgreens, Walmart

175 Merriman Rd, N [gas] Mobil/dsl, Speedway/dsl, S [gas] Exxon/dsl [food] Blimpie, Prime Grill

174 Farmington Rd, N [gas] Mobil/dsl, Sunoco [food] Looney Baker, S [gas] BP [food] KFC

173b Levan Rd, N [other] [H], to Madonna U

173a Newburgh Rd

I-275 and I-96 run together 9 miles.

170 6 Mile Rd, N [food] Bar Louie, Big Boy, Buffalo Wild Wings, Jimmy John's, Panera Bread, Qdoba, Red Robin [lodging] Best Western, Courtyard, Holiday Inn, Marriott [other] [H], Ace Hardware, Busch's Foods, GNC, O'Reilly Parts, Rite Aid, URGENT CARE, Verizon, Walgreens, S [gas] Marathon, Mobil [food] Applebee's, Brann's Steaks, Bravo Italian, Buca Italian, Charlie's Grille, Claddagh Rest., Fleming's, Food on Wood Grill, Jimmy John's, McDonald's, Mitchell's Fish Mkt, Noodles&Co, Panchero's, Papa Vino's, PF Chang, Potbelly, Subway, Tahini Grill, Tim Horton, Wendy's, Zoe's Pancakes [lodging] Fairfield Inn, Residence Inn, TownePlace Suites [other] Barnes&Noble, CVS, Kroger, Office Depot, Petsmart, REI

169b a 7 Mile Rd, N [food] Dave&Buster's, Doc's Grill, Little Daddy's [lodging] Embassy Suites, S [food] Andiamo's Cafe, Bahama Breeze Rest., Burger Fi, Champp's Rest., Chipotle, Gaucho Brazilian, Granite City Grill, J Alexander's Rest., Macaroni Grill, Mod Pizza, Rusty Bucket Rest., Tom Chee [lodging] Hyatt Place [other] Home Depot

167 8 Mile Rd, to Northville, S [gas] BP/dsl, Speedway/dsl [food] Aubree's Pizza, Benihana, Big Boy, Chili's, Five Guys, Kerry's Koney Island, McDonald's, On-the-Border, Panera Bread, Qdoba, Starbucks, Taco Bell, TGIFriday's, Zoup! [lodging] Extended Stay America, Hampton Inn, Holiday Inn Express, Quality Inn, Sheraton [other] Best Buy, Costco/gas, Dick's, Firestone/auto, Kohl's, Meijer/dsl, Target, to Maybury SP, Trader Joe's, Verizon

165 I-696, I-275, MI 5, Grand River Ave.

I-275 and I-96 run together 9 miles.

163 I-696 (from eb)

162 Novi Rd, to Walled Lake, Novi, N [gas] BP [food] Bar Louie, Black Rock Rest., Buddy's Pizzaria, Buffalo Wild Wings, CA Pizza, Carrabba's, Cheesecake Factory, ChuckECheese's, Coldstone, Denny's, Max&Erma's, McDonald's, Novi Chophouse, Red Lobster, Subway, Tilted Kilt Eatery [lodging] Crowne Plaza, Hilton Garden, Renaissance, Residence Inn [other] BigLots, Dick's, JC Penney, JoAnn Fabrics, Kohl's, Lord&Taylor, Macy's, Marshalls, Michael's, Midas, Nordstrom, Old Navy, S [gas] Mobil/dsl, Sunoco/dsl [food] Athenian Coney Island, Bagger Dave's Burgers, BD Mongolian BBQ, Big Salad, Biggby Coffee, Blaze Pizza, Bonefish Grill, Boston Mkt, Famous Dave's, Honeybaked Express, IHOP, Kim's Chinese, Maisano's Italian, Olive Garden, Panera Bread,

162 Continued
Pei Wei, Potbelly, Qdoba, Red Robin, Rojo Mexican, Steve&Rocky's, TGIFriday's, Tony Sacco Pizza, Wasabi, Wendy's [lodging] Courtyard, DoubleTree, Towne Place Suites [other] [H], Advance Parts, AT&T, Belle Tire, Better Health Foods, Chevrolet, Discount Tire, Firestone/auto, Hobby Lobby, Kia, NAPA, O'Reilly Parts, TJ Maxx, URGENT CARE, Verizon, Walmart

160 Beck Rd, 12 Mile Rd, S [gas] Shell/Tim Horton [food] Applebee's, China King, Guido's Pizza, Halo Burger, La Herraduro Mexican, Lee's Coney Island, Olga's Kitchen, Outback Steaks, Subway, Zoup! [lodging] Hyatt Place, Staybridge Suites [other] [H], GNC, Home Depot, Kroger, Staples, to Maybury SP

159 Wixom Rd, Walled Lake, N [gas] Marathon/dsl, Sunoco/dsl [food] Culver's, Leon's Rest., Papa Romano's Pizza, Quiznos, Wendy's [lodging] Holiday Inn Express [other] General RV Ctr, Meineke, Menard's, to Proud Lake RA, S [gas] Mobil/dsl, Shell, Valero/dsl [food] A&W/KFC, Arby's, Baskin-Robbins/Dunkin Donuts, Biggby Coffee, Burger King, Don's Diner, Jimmy John's, La Roca Mexican, McDonald's, Red Olive Rest., Stinger's Grill, Taco Bell [lodging] Comfort Suites [other] AutoZone, Lincoln, Meijer/dsl, Sam's Club/gas, Target

155b a to Milford, New Hudson, N [other] Camp Dearborn (5mi), Ford, to Lyon Oaks CP, S [gas] Sunoco [food] Applebee's, Arby's, Biggby Coffee, Jet's Pizza, Kensington Grill, Leo's Coney Island, McDonald's, Starbucks, Subway [other] AAA, AT&T, Belle Tire, Chevrolet, Discount Tire, Hyundai, Lowe's, URGENT CARE, Verizon, Walmart

153 Kent Lake Rd, N [other] Kensington Metropark, S [gas] BP/d [lodging] Country Meadows Inn (3mi)

151 Kensington Rd, N [other] Kensington Metropark, S [food] food [lodging] lodging [other] Island Lake RA

150 Pleasant Valley Rd (no return wb)

148b a US 23, N to Flint, S to Ann Arbor

147 Spencer Rd, N [gas] Mobil/dsl [food] Cherry's Cafe [other] st police, S [food] Bagger Dave's Burgers (2mi) [other] to Brighton St RA

145 Grand River Ave, to Brighton, N [gas] BP, Shell/dsl [food] Arby's, Baskin-Robbins/Dunkin Donuts, Cracker Barrel, Outback Steaks, Pizza Hut [lodging] Courtyard [other] [H], $General, Buick/GMC, Ford, Honda, Mazda, URGENT CARE, vet, S [gas] Marathon, Subway [food] Big Boy, Border Cantina, Burger King, Chili's, Firehouse Subs, Gourmet Garden, Halo Burger, IHOP, Jimmy John's, Leo's Coney Island, Lil Chef, McDonald's, Olga's Kitchen, Panera Bread, Pi's Asian, Red Robin, Starbucks, Taco Bell, Tim Horton, Wendy's [lodging] Holiday Inn Express, Homewood Suites [other] $Tree, AAA, Advance Parts, Aldi Foods, AT&T, Belle Tire, Best Buy, Bob's Tire, CVS Drug, Home Depot, JoAnn Fabrics, Marshall's, Meijer/dsl/E85, Michael's, O'Reilly Parts, Petsmart, Staples, Target, to Brighton Ski Area, USPO, Verizon, Verizon, Walgreens

141 Lp 96 (from wb, return at 140), to Howell, 0-2 mi N [gas] BP/dsl, Shell/Tim Horton/dsl, Speedway, Sunoco/dsl [food] Applebee's, Arby's, Asian Fusian Buffet, Aubree's Pizzaria, Biggby Coffee, Bluefin Steaks, Bob Evans, Buffalo Wild Wings, Jimmy John's, KFC, Leo's Coney Island, Little Caesars, Los Tres Amigos, McDonald's, Qdoba, Subway, Taco Bell, Wendy's, White Castle [other] $Tree, AT&T, Belle Tire, Big Lots, Chevrolet, Discount Tire, GNC, Home Depot, Kohl's, Lowe's, Meijer, O'Reilly Parts, TJ Maxx, URGENT CARE, Walmart

140 S Latson Rd, same as 141

137 D19, to Pinckney, Howell, N [gas] Mobil/dsl, Shell, Speedway/dsl, Sunoco/Baskin-Robbins/Dunkin Donuts/dsl [food] All Star Coney Island, Bock Brewing Co, Hog Wild BBQ, Joanna's ToGo, Wendy's [lodging] Kensington Inn [other] [H], Parts+, Spartan Tire, True Value, USPO, vet, S [food] Wooly Bully's Rest. [lodging] Howell Inn

INTERSTATE 96 Cont'd

Exit#	Services
135mm	**eb, full facilities, litter barrels, petwalk, , vending**
133	MI 59, Highland Rd, N Marathon/McDonald's/dsl Arby's, Leo's Coney Island Baymont, Holiday Inn Express Tanger Outlets/famous brands
129	Fowlerville Rd, Fowlerville, N Marathon/dsl, Shell/dsl, Sunoco/dsl A&W/KFC, Great Lakes Rest., McDonald's, Pizza Hut/Taco Bell, Wendy's Magnuson Hotel Chevrolet, O'Reilly Parts, Walmart, S Mobil/dsl Subway Chysler/Dodge/Jeep, Ford
126mm	**weigh sta both lanes**
122	MI 43, MI 52, Webberville, N Mobil/dsl/24hr McDonald's Sinclair Grill (2mi)
117	to Dansville, Williamston, N Marathon/Jersey's Giant Subs/dsl Spag's Grill (3mi), S Sunoco/dsl
111mm	**wb, full facilities, litter barrels, petwalk, , vending**
110	Okemos, Mason, N Marathon/dsl, Shell/Jimmy John's/dsl, Sunoco/Dunkin Donuts Applebee's, Arby's, Backyard BBQ, Big John's Steaks, Biggby Coffee, Coldstone/Tim Horton, Cracker Barrel, Culver's, Frank's Press Box Grille, Gilbert&Blake's, Grand Traverse Pie Co., Leaf Salad Bar, Little Caesars, McDonald's, Ozzy Mediterranean, Panchero's Mexican, Starbucks, Stillwater Grill, Subway, Taco Bell Comfort Inn, Fairfield Inn, Hampton Inn, Holiday Inn Express, Staybridge Suites 7-11, BMW/Porsche, Mercedes, to stadium, Verizon
106b a	I-496, US 127, to Jackson, Lansing, N St Police
104	Lp 96, Cedar St, to Holt, Lansing, N Admiral, Speedway/dsl Applebee's, Arby's, Asia's Finest, Big John's, Biggby Coffee, Blimpie, Bob Evans, Boston Mkt, Burger King, China King, Domino's, Fazoli's, Finley's Rest., Happy's Pizza, Hooters, Jet's Pizza, KFC, Los Tres Amigos, Mikado Grill, Panda Gourmet, Pizza Hut, Steak'n Shake, Taco Bell, TX Roadhouse, Wendy's, Zeus Coney Island Best Value Inn, Magnuson Hotel, Super 8 H, $Tree, Aldi Foods, AT&T, auto repair, Belle Tire, Cadillac, Chevrolet, Chrysler/Dodge/Jeep, Discount Tire, Family$, GNC, Hyundai, Kia, Lexus, Meijer/dsl, Menards, Target, Toyota, Tuffy Auto, vet, S Speedway/dsl Aldaco's Taco Bar, Burger King, Champion's Grill, China East Buffet, Dairy Dan, Famous Dave's BBQ, Flapjack Rest., Hungry Howie's, McDonald's, Subway, Tim Horton/Coldstone Causeway Bay Hotel Advance Parts, AutoZone, Budget Tire, CVS Drug, Family$, Kroger/gas, Lowe's, NAPA, Rite Aid, URGENT CARE, Verizon
101	MI 99, MLK Blvd, to Eaton Rapids, **0-3 mi** N QD Arby's, Tim Horton Kroger/gas, Meijer/dsl, S Speedway/Subway/dsl Coach's Grill, McDonald's, Wendy's
98b a	Lansing Rd, to Lansing, N Arby's, Wendy's Comfort Inn, Holiday Inn Express Harley-Davidson, S st police
97	I-69, US 27 S, S to Ft Wayne, N to Lansing
95	I-496, to Lansing
93b a	MI 43, Lp 69, Saginaw Hwy, to Grand Ledge, **0-2 mi** N Shell, Speedway/dsl Applebee's, Buffalo Wild Wings, Burger King, Carrabba's, Cheddar's, Chipotle, Denny's, Fazoli's, Finley's Grill, Frank's Grill, Hibachi Grill, Honeybaked Ham, Houlihan's, Logan's Roadhouse, Longhorn Steaks, McDonald's, Outback Steaks, Panera Bread, Qdoba, Red Robin, Subway Comfort Inn, Fairfield Inn, Hampton Inn, Motel 6, Quality Inn, Ramada Inn, Red Roof Inn, Residence Inn H, $Tree, Aldi, AT&T, Barnes&Noble, Best Buy, BigLots, Chrysler/Dodge/Jeep, Hobby Lobby, JC Penney, Kohl's, Kroger/dsl, Macy's, Meijer/dsl/24hr, Target, TJ Maxx, vet, Walgreens, Younkers, S

LANSING

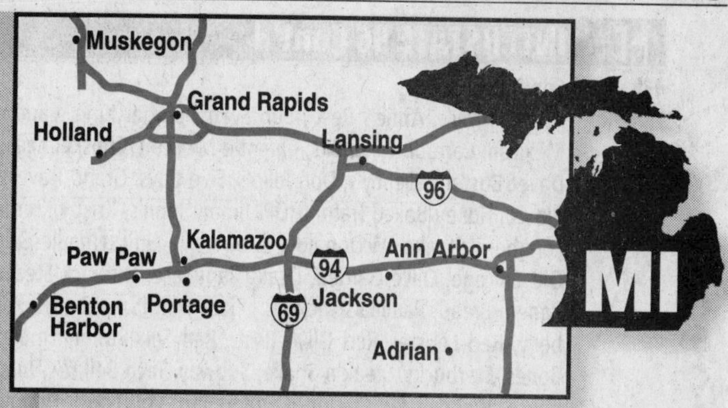

Exit#	Services
93b a	Continued BP/Dunkin Donuts, QD, Sunoco/McDonald's Arby's, Biggby Coffee, Bob Evans, Cancun Mexican, Cracker Barrel, Culver's, Steak'n Shake SpringHill Suites Belle Tire, Buick/GMC, Discount Tire, Lowe's, Mazda/Volvo, Menards, Michael's, Petsmart, Staples, Walmart/Subway
92mm	Grand River
91	I-69 N (from wb), US 27 N, to Flint
90	Grand River Ave, to (from wb), S FLYING J/Denny's/dsl/24hr
89	I-69 N, US 27 N (from eb), to Flint
87mm	**eb, full facilities, litter barrels, petwalk, , vending**
86	MI 100, Wright Rd, to Grand Ledge, S Mobil/McDonald's/dsl, Speedway/Subway/24hr
84	to Eagle, Westphalia
79mm	**wb, full facilities, info, litter barrels, petwalk, , vending**
77	Lp 96, Grand River Ave, Portland, N BP/dsl, Shell/Subway, Speedway/dsl Arby's, Biggby Coffee, Burger King, Little Caesar's, McDonald's, New China Buffet, Red Tomato Pizza American Heritage Inn CarQuest, Family$, Rite Aid, Tom's Foods, Verizon, S Tom's/dsl Wendy's
76	Kent St, Portland
76mm	Grand River
73	to Lyons-Muir, Grand River Ave
69mm	**weigh sta both lanes**
67	MI 66, to Ionia, Battle Creek, N Pilot/Subway/dsl/scales/24hr Corner Landing Grill Midway Motel, Super 8 H, Alice Springs RV Park (3mi), Lakeside Camping, Meijer/dsl (4mi), st police, Walmart (4mi)
64	to Lake Odessa, Saranac, N Ionia St RA, S I-96 Speedway
63mm	**eb, full facilities, litter barrels, petwalk, , vending**
59	Clarksville
52	MI 50, to Lowell, N Mobil/Subway/dsl fairgrounds, S Marathon/Noble Roman's/dsl (2mi)
46mm	Thornapple River
46	rd 6, to rd 37
44	36 St, S
43b a	MI 11, 28th St, Cascade, N Bagger Dave's, Biggby Coffee, Brann's Steaks, Cascades Grill, Culver's, Dunkin Donuts/Baskin Robbins, Firehouse Subs, Georgio's Pizza, Jet's Pizza, Jimmy John's, Macaroni Grill, New Beginnings Rest., Pal's Diner, Panera Bread, Pit Stop BBQ, Pizza Hut, Qdoba, Subway, Sundance Grill, Tim Horton's, Wendy's Baymont Inn, Best Western, Country Inn&Suites, Crowne Plaza, EconoLodge, Holiday Inn Express Ace Hardware, AT&T, Audi/Porsche/Subaru, Fresh Mkt, GNC, Meijer/dsl, Mercedes/Volvo/VW, Subaru, Verizon, Walmart, **0-3 mi** S Citgo, Shell, Speedway/dsl Applebee's,

MI

INTERSTATE 96 Cont'd

CASCADE

43b a Continued
Arby's, Arby's, Arnie's Rest., Bob Evans, Burger King, Cantina Mexican, Carrabba's, Chili's, Chipotle Mexican, ChuckeCheese, Dave&Buster's, Denny's, Don Julio's, Five Guys, Grand Traverse Pie Co, Honey Baked Ham, IHOP, Jimmy John's, Krispy Kreme, Longhorn Steaks, McDonald's, Moe's SW Grill, Noodles&Co, Old Chicago, Olive Garden, Osaka Japanese, Outback Steaks, Panera Bread, Paulina's Mexican, Pizza Hut, Pizza Ranch, Potbelly, Red Lobster, Red Olive Rest., Red Sun Buffet, Smokey Bones, Starbucks, Steak'n Shake, Subway, Taco Bell, TX Roadhouse, Wendy's [lodging] Clarion, Comfort Inn, Courtyard, DoubleTree, Drury Inn, Extended Stay America, Fairfield Inn, Hampton Inn, Hawthorn Suites, Homewood Suites, Motel 6, Ramada, Red Roof Inn, Residence Inn, SpringHill Suites, Wyndham Garden [other] $General, $Tree, Aldi Foods, Belle Tire, Best Buy, Big Lots, CarQuest, Costco/gas, Dick's, Ford/Mazda, Hobby Lobby, Home Depot, Honda, Hyundai/Kia, Jo-Ann Fabrics, Lowe's, Michael's, Monro Auto, Nissan, Office Depot, Old Navy, Petsmart, Sam's Club/gas, Staples, Target, TJ Maxx, Tuesday Morning, U-Haul, World Mkt

40b a Cascade Rd, N [gas] BP/dsl, Forrest Hills Fuel [food] Biggby Coffee, China Garden, Forrest Hills Rest., Great Harvest, Jets Pizza, Little Bangkok, Little Caesar's, Manna a Cafe, Subway [other] vet, Walgreens, S [gas] Shell/dsl, Speedway/dsl [food] Bonefish Grill, Jimmy John's, Zoup! [other] [H], Keystone Drug

39 MI 21 (from eb), to Flint

38 E Beltline Ave, to MI 21, MI 37, MI 44, N [gas] BP [food] Applebee's, Fuji Yama Japanese, Gus's Original, Red Hot Inn Rest., Wendy's [other] Meijer/dsl, RV camping, URGENT CARE, Verizon, S [food] Gravity Grille [lodging] Country Inn&Suites [other] [H]

37 I-196 (from wb, exits left), Gerald Ford Fwy, to Grand Rapids

36 Leonard St, 2 mi S [food] Arby's, Jimmy John's, McDonald's [other] sheriff's dept

33 Plainfield Ave, MI 44 Connector, N [gas] Citgo/dsl, Speedway/dsl [food] Arby's, Biggby Coffee, Charlie's Grille, Cheers Grill, Dunkin Donuts, Fred's Italian, Golden Dragon, Jimmy John's, KFC, Little Caesar's, McDonald's, Pizza Hut, Rice Wok, Russ' Rest., Subway, Taco Bell, Tim Horton's, Tokyo Roadhouse, Wendy's [lodging] Knights Inn, Lazy T Motel [other] $Tree, AAA, AutoZone, Belle Tire, BigLots, Chevrolet, Chrysler/Jeep, CVS, Discount Tire, Dodge, Firestone/auto, Ford, Goodyear/auto, Kia, Lowe's, Meijer/dsl, Midas, NAPA, Nissan/VW, O'Reilly Parts, Toyota, U-Haul, vet, Walgreens, S [gas] BP [food] Denny's

31mm Grand River

31b a US 131, N to Cadillac, S to Kalamazoo, 1 mi N [gas] Speedway/Subway/dsl [food] McDonald's

GRAND RAPIDS

30b a Alpine Ave, Grand Rapids, N [gas] BP/dsl, Marathon/dsl, Mobil [food] Applebee's, Buffalo Wild Wings, Checkers, ChuckeCheese, Cinco de Mayo, Coldstone, Culver's, El Burrito Mexican, Empire Buffet, Firehouse Subs, First Wok, Five Guys, Golden Corral, Hibachi Grill, IHOP, Jimmy John's, Little Caesar's, Logan's Roadhouse, McDonald's, Olive Garden, Outback Steaks, Panera Bread, Qdoba, Russ' Rest., Sonic, Starbucks, Steak'n Shake, Subway, Taco Bell, TGIFriday's, Three Happiness Chinese [lodging] Hampton Inn, Holiday Inn Express, SpringHill Suites [other] $Tree, Aldi Foods, AT&T, AutoZone, Belle Tire, Best Buy, CarQuest, Discount Tire, Ford, GNC, Hobby Lobby, Jo-Ann, Kohl's, Marshall's, Menards, Michael's, NAPA, PepBoys, PetCo, Sam's Club/gas, Target, TJ Maxx, Verizon, Walgreens, Walmart, S [gas] Admiral/dsl, Speedway/dsl [food] Arby's, Burger King, Fazoli's, KFC, LJ Silver, McDonald's, Papa John's, Pizza Hut,

GRAND RAPIDS

30b a Continued
Wendy's [lodging] Best Value Inn [other] Goodyear/auto, Home Depot, Meijer/dsl, Midas, O'Reilly Parts, U-Haul, URGENT CARE

28 Walker Ave, S [gas] Meijer/dsl/24hr [food] Bob Evans, McDonald's [lodging] Baymont Inn, Quality Inn

26 Fruit Ridge Ave, N [gas] Citgo/dsl, S [gas] Citgo/deli/dsl

25mm **[Rs] eb, full [handicapped] facilities, litter barrels, petwalk, [phone], [picnic]**

25 8th Ave, 4Mile Rd (from wb), S [gas] Marathon/dsl [lodging] Wayside Motel

24 8th Ave, 4Mile Rd (from eb), S [gas] Marathon/dsl [lodging] Wayside Motel

23 Marne, N [other] tires, S [food] Depot Café, Rinaldi's Café [other] Ernie's Mkt, fairgrounds/raceway, USPO

19 Lamont, Coopersville, N [food] food, S [other] LP

16 B-35, Eastmanville, N [gas] Citgo/Subway/dsl, Shell/Burger King/dsl, Speedway/dsl/24hr [food] #1 Chinese, Arby's, Hungry Howie's, Little Caesar's, McDonald's, New Beginnings Rest, Taco Bell [lodging] Rodeway Inn [other] Buick/Chevrolet, Family Fare Foods, Family$, Fun 'N Sun RV Ctr, Rite Aid, vet, S [gas] Pacific Pride/dsl [other] RV camping

10 B-31 (exits left from eb), Nunica, N [food] Turk's Rest S [other] Conestoga RV camping, golf course/rest.

9 MI 104 (from wb, exits left), to Grand Haven, Spring Lake S [gas] Marathon/dsl [other] to Grand Haven SP

8mm **[Rs] wb, full [handicapped] facilities, litter barrels, petwalk, [phone], [picnic], vending**

5 Fruitport (from wb, no return)

4 Airline Rd, S [gas] Speedway/dsl, Wesco/dsl [food] Burger Crest Diner, Dairy Bar, McDonald's, Subway, Village Inn [other] $General, auto/tire repair, Grover Drug, Orchard Mkt Foods, to P Hoffmaster SP, USPO, Water Park (5mi)

1c Hile Rd (from eb), S [food] Arby's, Asian Buffet, Bob Evans, Brann's Grille, Buffalo Wild Wings, Burger King, ChuckeCheese, Five Guys, Golden Corral, Grand Traverse Pie Co, Kazumi Steak, KFC/Taco Bell, Logan's Roadhouse, McDonald's, Olive Garden, Qdoba, Red Lobster, Red Robin, Starbucks, Subway, TX Roadhouse [lodging] Baymont Inn, Fairfield Inn, Hampton Inn [other] $Tree, AT&T, Barnes&Noble, Belle Tire, Best Buy, Dick's, Gordman's, Hobby Lobby, JC Penney, Jo-Ann Fabrics, Kohl's, Meijer/dsl, Menards, Old Navy, PetCo, Target, TJ Maxx, Verizon, VW/Audi, Nissan/Subaru/Toyota, Younkers

1b a US 31, to Ludington, Grand Haven, **2 mi N on Sherman Blvd** [food] Applebee's, Arby's, Fazoli's, Los Amigos, McDonald's, Panera Bread, Pizza Ranch, Red Wok, Subway, Wendy's [lodging] Airline Motel, Alpine Motel, Bel-aire Motel, Comfort Inn/rest. [other] [H], $Tree, All Seasons RV Ctr, Big Lots, GNC, Lowe's, Marathon/dsl, Norton Automotive, Petsmart, Sam's Club/gas, Staples, Walmart, S same as 1c

I-96 begins/ends on US 31 at Muskegon.

INTERSTATE 196 (Grand Rapids)

Exit#	Services
81mm	**I-196 begins/ends on I-96, 37mm in E Grand Rapids.**
79	Fuller Ave, N [other] sheriff, S [gas] Shell/dsl, Speedway/dsl [food] Biggby Coffee, Bill's Rest., Checkers, Elbow Room, KFC, Subway, Taco Bell, Wendy's [other] [H], Ace Hardware, Family$, Verizon, Walgreens
78	College Ave, S [gas] Mobil/Circle K [food] McDonald's, Omelet Shop [other] [H], Ford Museum
77c	Ottawa Ave, S [other] Gerald R Ford Museum, downtown
77b a	US 131, S to Kalamazoo, N to Cadillac
76	MI 45 E, Lane Ave, S [other] Gerald R Ford Museum, John Ball Park&Zoo

MI

INTERSTATE 196 (Grand Rapids) Cont'd

GRAND RAPIDS

Exit#	Services
75	MI 45 W, Lake Michigan Dr, N [other] to Grand Valley St U
74mm	Grand River
73	Market Ave, N [other] to Vanandel Arena
72	Lp 196, Chicago Dr E (from eb)
70	MI 11 (exits left from wb), Grandville, Walker, S [gas] BP/dsl, Shell [lodging] Days Inn [other] USPO, vet
69c	Baldwin St (from wb)
69b a	Chicago Dr, N [gas] Speedway [food] Biggby Coffee, Culver's, Domino's, Fazoli's, KFC, McDonald's, Peppino's Pizza, Subway, Taco Bell [other] $Tree, Advance a Parts, Aldi Foods, AutoZone, Meijer/dsl, O'Reilly Parts, USPO, Walgreens, S [gas] Admiral, Speedway/dsl [food] Adobe Mexican, Arby's, Brann's a Steaks, Little Caesar's, Rainbow Grill, Russ' Rest., Wings&More [lodging] Grand Village Inn, Holiday Inn Express [other] NAPA
67	44th St, N [gas] Mobil/dsl [food] Burger King, Cracker Barrel, Panera Bread, Steak'n Shake [lodging] Comfort Suites [other] Honda, Walmart/Subway, 0-2 mi S [food] Applebee's, Bagger Dave's, Big Boy, Carrabba's, Famous Dave's, Great Harvest Bread Co, IHOP, Jimmy John's, Kobe Japanese, Logan's Roadhouse, Noodles&Co, Olive Garden, On the Border, Qdoba, Red Lobster, Red Robin, Starbucks, Subway, TGIFriday's, Tropical Smoothie, TX Roadhouse, Uccello's Ristorante, Wendy's [lodging] Residence Inn [other] $Tree, Barnes&Noble, Best Buy, Chrysler/Dodge/Jeep, Costco/gas, Dick's, Discount Tire, Family Fare Foods, Fiat, Gordman's, Hobby Lobby, Home Depot, JC Penney, Kohl's, Lowe's, Macy's, Marshall's, Meijer/zeal, Michael's, Old Navy, Petsmart, Verizon, World Mkt, Younkers
64	MI 6 E, to Lansing (exits left from wb)
62	32nd Ave, to Hudsonville, N [gas] BP/dsl, Citgo/dsl [food] Arby's, Biggby Coffee, Burger King, Hudsonville Grille, Little Caesar's, McDonald's [lodging] Quality Inn [other] camping, Chevrolet, S [gas] Mobil/Subway/dsl/24hr [food] Rainbow Grill [lodging] Travelodge [other] Harley-Davidson, Harvest Foods
58mm	**[RS] eb, full [handicapped] facilities, litter barrels, petwalk, [phone], [picnic], vending**
55	Byron Rd, Zeeland, N [gas] Citgo/7-11 [food] Blimpie, McDonald's [other] [H], to Holland SP
52	16th St, Adams St, **2 mi** N [gas] Speedway/dsl [food] Burger King, Jimmy John's, Papa Murphy's, Pizza Ranch, Wendy's [other] [H], Meijer/dsl/e-85, S [gas] Loves/Hardee's/dsl/scales/24hr, Mobil/Subway/dsl
49	MI 40, to Allegan, N [gas] BP/McDonald's/dsl [lodging] Residence Inn, S [gas] Tulip City/Marathon/Subway/dsl/scales/24hr [food] Rock Island Rest. [other] truck repair, truck wash
44	US 31 N (from eb), to Holland, **3-5 mi** N [lodging] Country Inn [other] [H], food, gas
43mm	**[RS] wb, full [handicapped] facilities, info, litter barrels, petwalk, [phone], [picnic], vending**
41	rd A-2, Douglas, Saugatuck, N [gas] BP/dsl, Marathon/dsl, Shell/Subway/dsl [food] Burger King, Dairy Dayz, Spectators Grill [lodging] Best Western (1mi), Timberline Motel (3mi) [other] $General, NAPA, to Saugatuck SP, S [food] Belvedere Inn Rest. [other] Red Barn Gifts
38mm	Kalamazoo River
36	rd A-2, Ganges, N [gas] Shell [food] Christo's Rest., Pizza Mambo, Saugatuck Brewing Co, Zing Rest. [lodging] AmericInn, Blue Star Motel
34	MI 89, to Fennville, N [other] to West Side CP, S [gas] Shell [other] Cranes Pie Pantry (4mi, Lyons Farm Mkt, Winery Tours (seasonal)
30	rd A-2, Glenn, Ganges, N [other] to Westside CP (4mi)
28mm	**[RS] eb, full [handicapped] facilities, litter barrels, petwalk, [phone], [picnic], vending**
26	109th Ave, to Pullman, N [other] Dutch Farm Mkt

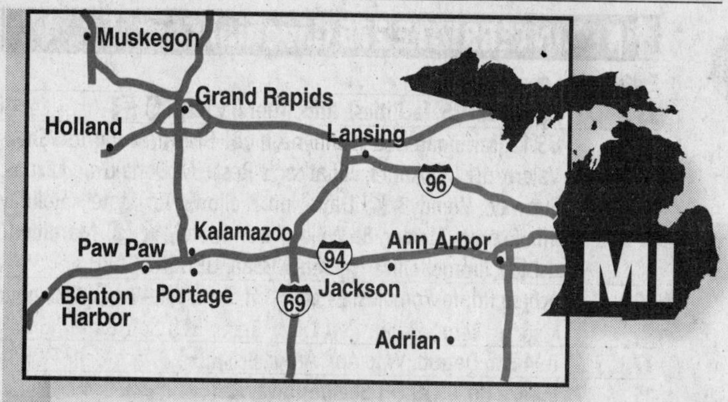

Exit#	Services
22	N Shore Dr, N [other] Cousin's RV Camping/rest., to Kal Haven Trail SP
20	rd A-2, Phoenix Rd, N [gas] BP/dsl, Marathon/dsl [food] Arby's, China Buffet, Taco Bell [other] [H], $Tree, AutoZone, Meijer/dsl, st police, Walgreens, S [gas] Murphy USA/dsl, Shell/dsl [food] Big Boy, McDonald's, Sherman's Dairybar, Wendy's [lodging] Baymont Inn, Comfort Suites, Hampton Inn, Holiday Inn Express [other] $General, Aldi Foods, Menards, Walmart
18	MI 140, MI 43, to Watervliet, **0-2 mi** N [gas] Shell/dsl, Sunoco/dsl [food] Burger King, Hungry Howie's, Little Caesar's, McDonald's, Pizza Hut [lodging] Great Lakes Inn, LakeBluff Motel [other] [H], auto repair, AutoValue Parts, Buick/Cadillac/GMC, Chevrolet, Chrysler/Dodge/Jeep, Ford/Lincoln, st police, Village Mkt Foods, **7 mi** S [other] KOA (Apr-Oct)
13	to Covert, N [other] RV camping, to Van Buren SP
7	MI 63, to Benton Harbor, N [food] DiMaggio's Pizza [other] RV camping
4	to Coloma, Riverside, S [gas] Shell/dsl [other] KOA (Apr-Oct)
2mm	Paw Paw River
1	Red Arrow Hwy, N [other] SW Michigan Airport
0mm	I-94, E to Detroit, W to Chicago

I-196 begins/ends on I-94, exit 34 at Benton Harbor.

INTERSTATE 275 (Livonia)

LIVONIA

Exit#	Services
	I-275 and I-96 run together 9 miles. See I-96, exits 165-170.
29	I-96 E, to Detroit, MI 14 W, to Ann Arbor
28	Ann Arbor Rd, Plymouth, E [gas] BP/Dunkin Donuts, Mobil, Shell/dsl [food] Denny's, Little Caesars, McDonald's [lodging] Red Roof Inn [other] $Tree, Verizon, vet, W [food] Burger King, Firehouse Subs, Grand Traverse Pie Co., Lee's Coney Island [lodging] Comfort Inn [other] Cadillac, CVS Drug, Lincoln, URGENT CARE, vet
25	MI 153, Ford Rd, Garden City, E [food] Hayden's Grill, Logan's Roadhouse, Parthenon Coney Island, Starbucks [other] Home Depot, Sam's Club, Walmart, W [gas] BP, Speedway, Valero/dsl [food] Applebee's, Basement Burger Bar, BD Mongolian BBQ, Black Rock Grill, Bob Evans, Boston Mkt, Bowery Grill, Buffalo Wild Wings, Burger King, Carrabba's, Carvel Ice Cream, Chili's, ChuckeCheese, Dunkin Donuts/Baskin-Robbins, Five Guys, JerseyMike's, Jimmy John's, KFC, Little Caesar's, McDonald's, Mexican Fiesta, Olga's Kitchen, Outback Steaks, Panera Bread, Pizza Hut, Potbelly, Subway, Taco Bell, TGIFriday's, Tilted Kilt, Tim Hortons/Coldstone, Wendy's, Wendy's, White Castle/Church's [lodging] Comfort Suites, Extended Stay America, Fairfield Inn, Hampton Inn, La Quinta [other] Advance Parts, Aldi Foods, Discount Tire, Firestone/auto, GNC, Hobby Lobby, IKEA, JC Penney, Jo-Ann, Kohl's, Lowe's, Marshall's, Meijer/dsl, Michael's, Midas, PetCo, Richardson's Drug, Target, Tuesday Morning, URGENT CARE, Verizon, vet, Walgreens

INTERSTATE 275 (Livonia) Cont'd

Exit#	Services
23	nb, full facilities), info, litter barrels,
22	US 12, Michigan Ave, to Wayne, E BP/dsl, Mobil/dsl, Shell, Valero/dsl Arby's, Jonathan's Rest., McDonald's, Quiznos, Subway, Wendy's Days Inn, Fellows Cr Motel, Holiday Inn Express, Super 8, Willo Acres Motel, W Marathon/dsl Jimmy John's Kia, Nissan, URGENT CARE
20	Ecorse Rd, to Romulus, E 7-11, Shell/dsl, W BP/Burger King/scales/dsl/24hr
17	I-94 E to Detroit, W to Ann Arbor, E
15	Eureka Rd, E , Shell/Subway/dsl
13	Sibley Rd, New Boston, W Mobil/Subway/dsl to Lower Huron Metro Park
11	S Huron Rd, W Sunoco/Burger King/dsl Iron Mike's Rest.
8	Will Carleton Rd, to Flat Rock
5	Carleton, South Rockwood, W Speedway/dsl, Sunoco/Subway/dsl $General, USPO
4mm	sb, full facilities, litter barrels,
2	US 24, to Telegraph Rd, W BP/dsl, Marathon/Subway/dsl $General
0mm	I-275 begins/ends on I-75, exit 20.

INTERSTATE 475 (Flint)

FLINT

Exit#	Services
17mm	I-475 begins/ends on I-75, exit 125.
15	Clio Rd, W BP Chevrolet
13	Saginaw St, E BP McDonald's, Taco Bell Advanced Parts, Family$, Kroger/gas, O'Reilly Parts, W Marathon Burger King, Little Caesar's
11	Carpenter Rd
10	Pierson Rd
9	rd 54, Dort Hwy, Stewart Ave, E BP/dsl McDonald's
8mm	Flint River
8b	Davison Rd, Hamilton Ave
8a	Longway Blvd, W Holiday Inn Express H, farmers mkt, USPO
7	rd 21, Court St, downtown Flint
6	I-69, W to Lansing, E to Port Huron
5	Atherton Rd (from sb), E Mobil/dsl
4	Hemphill Rd, Bristol Rd, E Speedway/dsl Rally's, Subway Rite Aid, W Speedway/dsl Little Caesar's, Tim Horton/Wendy's Family$, Kroger/dsl, vet
2	Hill Rd, E Speedway Applebee's, Bob Evans Wingate Inn vet, W Mobil/Tim Horton, Speedway/dsl Arby's, Burger King, Burger St Grill, Little Caesar's, McDonald's, Wendy's Rite Aid
	I-475 begins/ends on I-75, exit 111.

INTERSTATE 696 (Detroit)

DETROIT

Exit#	Services
	I-696 begins/ends on I-94.
28	I-94 E to Port Huron, W to Detroit, 11 Mile Rd, E 7-11, BP/dsl, Shell/dsl
27	MI 3, Gratiot Ave, N BP, Marathon, Valero Checkers, Firehouse Subs, McDonald's, National Coney Island, Tubby's Subs Costco/gas, S Marathon, Mobil/McDonald's/dsl, Shell Biggby Coffee, DQ, KFC, Subway, Taco Bell, Tim Horton's, White Castle Belle Tire, Chrysler/Dodge/Jeep, Family$, GNC, Goodyear/auto, Kroger/gas, Rite Aid, Sav-A-Lot Foods, TJ Maxx
26	MI 97, Groesbeck Ave, Roseville, N BP/dsl, S Omega Grill
24	Hoover Rd, Schoenherr Rd, N BP Burger King, KFC, S BP/dsl, Mobil/7-11 Boston Mkt, Del Taco, Doc's Rest., DQ, Little Caesar's, Red Lobster, Subway, Taco Bell, Tim Horton, Wendy's Holiday Inn Express $Tree, Advance Parts, CVS Drug, GNC, Home Depot, Kroger, Marshall's
23	MI 53, Van Dyke Ave, N BP, Marathon, Mobil/dsl Applebee's, Arby's, Baskin-Robbins/Dunkin Donuts, Juliano's Rest., McDonald's, Subway $General, Cadillac, Chrysler/Dodge/Jeep, Toyota, Walmart, S Luca's Coney Island Chevrolet/Buick/GMC, Discount Tire, Ford, Rite Aid, USPO, vet
22	Mound Rd, N BP/Burger King, Mobil/dsl
20	Ryan Rd, Dequindre Rd, N 7-11, Shell, Sunoco Ponderosa Knights Inn, Red Roof Inn auto repair, BigLots, vet, S Bob Evans, Church's, LA Coney Island, McDonald's Best Inn, Victory Suites transmissions
19	Couzens St, 10 Mile Rd, S Hazel Park Racetrack
18	I-75 N to Flint, S to Detroit
17	Campbell Ave, Hilton Ave, Bermuda, Mohawk, S Marathon/dsl
16	MI 1, Woodward Ave, Main St, N zoo, S Sunoco
14	Coolidge Rd, 10 Mile Rd, S Speedway Hungry Howie's, Jade Palace Chinese, Little Caesar's, Sahara Grill, Subway CVS Drug, Family$, URGENT CARE
13	Greenfield Rd, N Marathon, Mobil Church's, L George Coney Island, McDonald's, Ponderosa, Popeye's, Subway, White Castle $Tree, Aldi Foods, Family$, Save a Lot Foods, Sol's Automotive, URGENT CARE, S Shell, Sunoco Baskin-Robbins/Dunkin Donuts, Front Page Deli, Pita Cafe, Starbucks Rite Aid
12	MI 39, Southfield Rd, 11 Mile Rd, N Discount Tire, S Shell Happy's Pizza AT&T, Verizon
11	Evergreen Rd, S Mobil, Speedway/dsl Benito's Pizza, China Gourmet, Chipotle, Coldstone/Tim Horton's, Fuddrucker's, Jimmy John's, Potbelly, Qdoba, Subway, TGIFriday's Hawthorn Suites, Holiday Inn Express
10	US 24, Telegraph Rd, N Marathon, Mobil, Sunoco Biggby Coffee, Burger Joint, Chipotle, DiBella Subs, Fat Burger, Five Guys, Jimmy John's, Mezzanine Mediterranian, Noodles&Co, Panera Bread, Popeye's, Potbelly, Qdoba, Starbucks, Wendy's Baymont Inn, Embassy Suites, Extended Stay America, Red Roof Inn, Springhill Suites AT&T, Belle Tire, Best Buy, Buick/GMC, Chevrolet, Chrysler/Dodge/Jeep, Ford, Honda, Hyundai, Kia, Lexus, Lincoln, Lowe's, Meijer/dsl, Michael's, Mini, Nissan, Office Depot, Petsmart, Subaru, Verizon, S Mobil/7-11, Sunoco Kerry's Koney Island, Tim Horton's Candlewood Suites, Courtyard, Holiday Inn Express, Marriott, Quality Inn AutoZone, Family$
8	MI 10, Lodge Fwy
7	American Dr (from eb), N Embassy Suites, S Extended Stay America, Hilton Garden
5	Orchard Lake Rd, Farmington Hills, N Marathon, Mobil/dsl, Valero Arby's, Burger King, Camelia's Mexican, Coney Island, Hong Hua Chinese, Jet's Pizza, Jimmy John's, Kabuki Japanese, Marie's Scrambler, Ruby Tuesday, Starbucks, Subway, Wendy's Comfort Inn, Courtyard, Extended Stay America, Fairfield Inn CVS, Discount Tire, Holocaust Museum, Petco, to St Mary's Coll, Verizon
1	(from wb), I-96 W, I-275 S, to MI 5, Grand River Ave

MINNESOTA

MN

INTERSTATE 35

DULUTH

Exit#	Services
260mm	**I-35 begins/ends on MN 61 in Duluth.**
259	MN 61, London Rd, to Two Harbors, North Shore, W BP/dsl, Holiday/dsl, Holiday/dsl (2), ICO/dsl Blackwoods Grill, Dunn Bros Coffee, KFC, McDonald's, Perkins, Subway, Taco John's, Wendy's Days Inn, Esdgewater Inn
258	21st Ave E (from nb), to U of MN at Duluth, same as 259
256b	Mesaba Ave, Superior St, E ICO/DQ Bellisio's, Caribou Coffee, Famous Dave's BBQ, Grandma's Grill, Greenmill Rest., Grizzly's, Little Angie's Cantina, Old Chicago, Red Lobster, Smokehouse Rest., Subway, Timberlodge Steaks Canal Park Lodge, Comfort Suites, Hampton Inn, Inn at Lake Superior, Suites Hotel, W Holiday Inn, Radisson, Sheraton
256a	Michigan St, E waterfront, W H, downtown
255a	US 53 N (exits left from nb), W Mobil Kia, downtown
255b	I-535 spur, to Wisconsin
254	27th Ave W, W Holiday/Burger King/dsl, KwikTrip/dsl Duluth Grill, Little Caesar's, Subway Motel 6 USPO
253b	40th Ave W, W Holiday/dsl/CNG Perkins Comfort Inn, Super 8
253a	US 2 E, US 53, to Wisconsin
252	Central Ave, W Duluth, W Holiday/dsl, Mobil/Charley's/dsl China King Buffet, Domino's, Jimmy John's, KFC, McDonald's, Pizza Hut, Subway, Taco John's $Tree, Advance Parts, CVS Drug, Menards, O'Reilly Parts, Super 1 Foods, USPO, Walgreens
251b	MN 23 S, Grand Ave
251a	Cody St, E Allyndale Motel zoo
250	US 2 W (from sb), to Grand Rapids, **1/2 mi** W Holiday/dsl, Mobil/dsl/LP Blackwoods Grill AmericInn
249	Boundary Ave, Skyline Pkwy, E Holiday/dsl McDonald's Best Western to ski area, to Spirit Mtn RA, W **both lanes, full facilities, info, litter barrels, , , vending** Exxon/Subway/dsl Blackwoods Grill AmericInn, Best Value Inn Mack/Volvo
246	rd 13, Midway Rd, Nopeming, W Armor/dsl Dry Dock Rest.
245	rd 61, E Buffalo House Rest./camping
242	rd 1, Esko, Thomson, E Mobil
239.5mm	St Louis River
239	MN 45, to Cloquet, Scanlon, E Jay Cooke SP, KOA (May-Oct) (3mi), W Holiday, KwikTrip/dsl/e85 Trapper Pete's Steaks Golden Gate Motel H, Coates RV Ctr, dsl repair
237	MN 33, Cloquet, **1 mi** W Lemon Tree/dsl, Mobil, Murphy USA/dsl Applebee's, Arby's, DQ, Erbert&Gerberts, Little Caesar's, McDonald's, Papa Murphy's, Perkins, Pizza Hut, South Gate Pizza, Subway, Taco John's/Steak Escape, Wendy's AmericInn, Super 8 H, $Tree, AT&T, AutoZone,

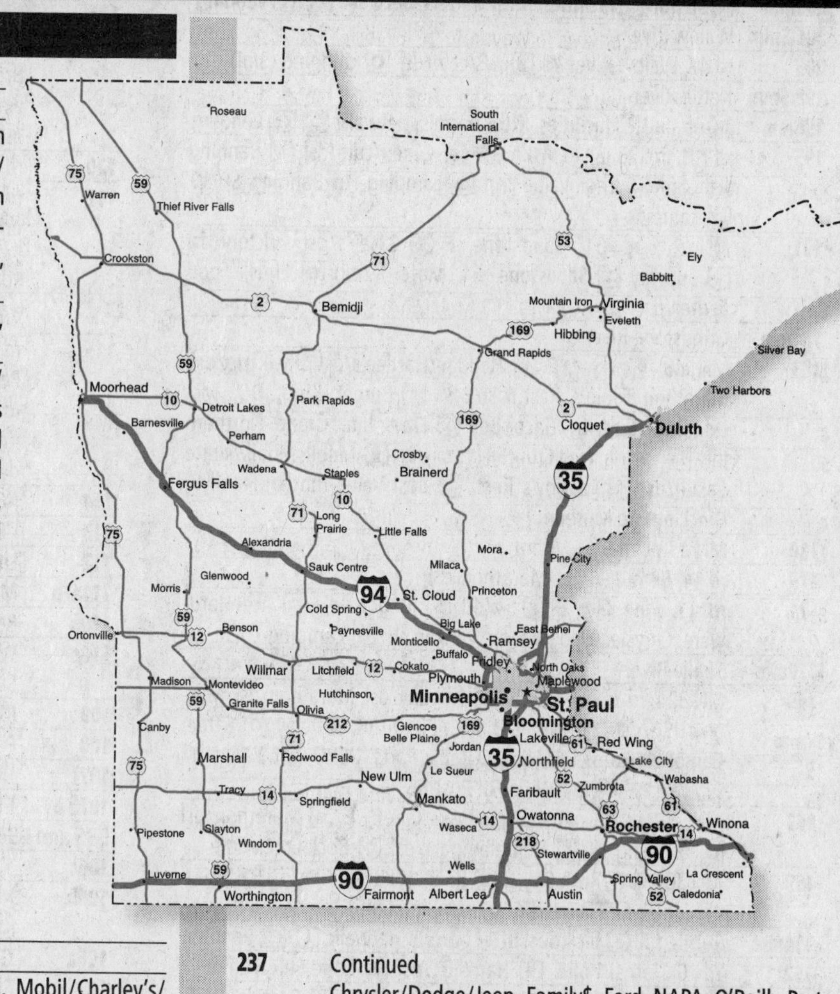

Exit#	Services
237	Continued Chrysler/Dodge/Jeep, Family$, Ford, NAPA, O'Reilly Parts, Super 1 Foods, Verizon, Walgreens, Walmart/Subway
236mm	**weigh sta both lanes**
235	MN 210, to Cromwell, Carlton, E BP/rest./dsl, ICO/dsl/24hr Spirits Rest. AmericInn, Royal Pines Motel to Jay Cooke SP, W Black Bear Casino/Hotel/rest.
235mm	Big Otter Creek
233mm	Little Otter Creek
227	rd 4, Mahtowa, E camping, W TJ's Country Store/gas (2 mi)
226mm	**nb, full facilities, litter barrels, petwalk, , , vending**
220	rd 6, Barnum, E Bear Lake Camping, W Mobil/café/dsl/24hr Lazy Bear Rest. Northwoods Motel Munger Tr
219mm	Moose Horn River
218mm	Moose Horn River
216	MN 27 (from sb, no EZ return), Moose Lake, **1-2 mi** W Cenex/dsl, Holiday/dsl Art's Café, DQ, Lazy Moose Grille Days Inn (4mi), Moose Lake Motel H, 1918 Museum, Ace Hardware, AutoValue Parts, Mkt Place Foods, O'Reilly Parts, to Munger Trail
214	rd 73, E camping, Moose Lake SP (2mi), W KwikTrip/dsl/e85/scales, Mobil/dsl McDonald's, Subway Days Inn, Moose Lake Motel H, Munger Trail, Red Fox Camping
209	rd 46, Sturgeon Lake, E Mobil/dsl Doc's Cafe Sturgeon Lake, W Ernie's Rest. (seasonal) Sturgeon Lake Motel camping (3mi)

MN

INTERSTATE 35 Cont'd

Exit#	Services
209mm	RS sb, full facilities, litter barrels, petwalk, phone, picnic, vending
206.5mm	Willow River
205	rd 43, Willow River, W gas BP/cafe/dsl other camping (2mi)
198.5mm	Kettle River
198mm	RS nb, full facilities, litter barrels, petwalk, phone, picnic, vending
195	rd 18, rd 23 E, to Askov, E gas Cenex/cafe/dsl food Banning Jct Cafe lodging Best Value Inn other camping, to Banning SP, W other camping
191	MN 23, rd 61, Sandstone, E gas Casey's/dsl, Victory/dsl food Subway lodging Sandstone 61 Motel (2mi) other Chris' Food Center/dsl
184mm	Grindstone River
183	MN 48, Hinckley, E gas Holiday/Hardee's/dsl, KwikTrip/dsl, Marathon/Tobie's Rest./dsl/E-85 food Burger King, DQ, McDonald's, Subway, Taco Bell lodging Days Inn, Grand Northern Inn other casino, to St Croix SP (15mi), W gas Mobil, Mobil/White Castle/dsl food Cassidy's Rest. lodging Best Value Inn other Family$, Hinckley Fire Museum
180	MN 23 W, rd 61, to Mora
175	rd 14, Beroun, E gas Marathon/dsl
171	rd 11, Pine City, E gas SA/dsl food McDonald's other Ace Hardware, Chrysler/Dodge/Jeep, Verizon, W other camping
170mm	Snake River
169	MN 324, rd 7, Pine City, E gas Holiday/dsl, Marathon/dsl, Murphy USA/dsl food A&W, DQ, KFC, Pizza Hut, Subway other $Tree, Campbell Auto/tire, Ford, O'Reilly Parts, USPO, vet, Walmart/Subway, W other to NW Co Fur Post HS
165	MN 70, to Grantsburg, Rock Creek, E gas Marathon/dsl other camping, W gas Heidelbergers/dsl food Rock Creek Cafe
159	MN 361, rd 1, Rush City, E gas Holiday/Burger King/dsl other $General, Rush City Foods, W other camping (2mi)
154mm	RS nb, full facilities, litter barrels, petwalk, phone, picnic, vending
152	rd 10, Harris, 1 mi E gas Harris 61/dsl food Kaffe Stuga Caffe
147	MN 95, to Cambridge, North Branch, E gas Casey's, Holiday/dsl food China Taste, Domino's, DQ, McDonald's, Oak Inn Rest., Perkins, Subway, Taco Bell lodging AmericInn, Budget Host other Family$, Fisk Tire, NAPA, O'Reilly Parts, to Wild River SP (14mi), vet, W gas Holiday/dsl/e85 food Burger King, Denny's, Dickey's BBQ, Don Lulu Mexican, Papa Murphy's other Chevrolet, County Mkt Foods, Ford, North Branch Outlets/famous brands, ShopKo, USPO, Verizon
143	rd 17, W gas Tesoro/dsl
139	rd 19, Stacy, E gas Gas+ food Rustic Inn Rest., Stacy Grill, Subway other city park, W gas KwikTrip/dsl/e85 other A-1 Tires
135	US 61 S, rd 22, Wyoming, E gas Casey's, Sinclair/dsl food DQ, Linwood Pizza, Subway, Tasty Asia other H, CarQuest, IGA Foods, WY Drug, W gas Shell/dsl food McDonald's, Village Inn Rest. other camping (10mi), golf, vet
132	US 8 (from nb), to Taylors Falls
131	rd 2, Forest Lake, E gas BP, Holiday/dsl, SA/dsl food Applebee's, Arby's, Burger King, Culver's, Joy Garden, KFC, McDonald's, Papa John's, Perkins, Quack's Cafe, Subway, Taco Bell, White Castle lodging AmericInn other Aldi Foods, AutoZone, O'Reilly Parts, RV/Auto repair, Target, Tires+, Verizon, Walgreens, Walmart/Subway, W gas Holiday/dsl food Famous Dave's BBQ, Jimmy John's, Papa Murphy's, Starbucks, Taco John's, Wendy's lodging Country Inn&Suites other AT&T, Buick/GMC, Cadillac/Chevrolet, Chrysler/Dodge/Jeep, Cub Foods, GNC, Home Depot, Jiffy Lube, Menards
131mm	RS sb, full facilities, litter barrels, petwalk, phone, picnic, vending
129	MN 97, rd 23, E gas Kwik Trip/dsl/e85 other camping (6mi), W gas Holiday/dsl other camping (1mi), Coates RV Ctr
128mm	weigh sta both lanes
127	I-35W, S to Minneapolis. See I-35W.
123	rd 14, Centerville, E gas Kwik Trip food Blue Heron Grill, Dunn Bros Coffee, McDonald's, Papa Murphy's other Festival Foods, vet, White Bear RV Ctr, W gas Mobil, Shell/Circle K food DQ, Fiesta Cancun, WiseGuys Pizza other auto repair
120	rd J (from nb, no return)
117	rd 96, E gas SA/dsl food Burger King, Carbone's Pizza lodging AmericInn other Goodyear/auto, NAPA, W gas Holiday food $5 Pizza, Applebee's, Arby's, Caribou Coffee, Culver's, McDonald's, Noodles&Co, Punch Pizza, Subway, Zen Asia other AutoZone, Cub Foods, Tires+, USPO, Walgreens
115	rd E, E gas BP/repair, SA/dsl food Jimmy John's, Jimmy's Rest., Perkins, Savoy Pizza lodging Country Inn&Suites, Fairfield Inn, Holiday Inn Express other URGENT CARE, W food Chipotle Mexican, KFC, Mad Jack's Cafe, Panera Bread, Papa Murphy's, Wendy's other $Tree, AT&T, Fresh Thyme Mkt, GNC, Target, Walmart
114	I-694 E (exits left from sb)
113	I-694 W
112	Little Canada Rd, E gas BP, W food Porterhouse Rest.
111a/b	MN 36 E, to Stillwater/MN 36 W, to Minneapolis
110b	Roselawn Ave
110a	Wheelock Pkwy, E gas BP, Gulf food May's Deli, Roadside Pizza, Subway
109	Maryland Ave, E gas SA/dsl, W food Wendy's other K-Mart
108	Pennsylvania Ave, downtown
107c	University Ave, E gas SA/dsl, W other H, to st capitol, downtown
107b a	I-94, W to Minneapolis, E to St Paul.
I-35 and I-94 run together.	
106c	11th St (from nb), Marion St, downtown
106b	Kellogg Blvd (from nb), E food Eagle St Grill lodging Holiday Inn other H, downtown
106a	Grand Ave, E other H
105	St Clair Ave
104c	Victoria St, Jefferson Ave
104b	Ayd Mill Rd (from nb)
104a	Randolph Ave
103b	MN 5, W 7th St, E food Burger King, W gas SA/dsl other Midas, USPO
103a	Shepard Rd (from nb)
102mm	Mississippi River
102	MN 13, Sibley Hwy, W gas BP, Holiday/Subway
101b a	MN 110 W, E gas BP/dsl food Caribou Coffee, McDonald's, Subway, Teresa's Mexican, Tommy Chicago's Pizza other Verizon, Walgreens, W gas SA/dsl/e85
99b a	I-494 W/I-494 E
98	Lone Oak Rd, E lodging Extended Stay America, Microtel other Sam's Club/gas, URGENT CARE, USPO, W gas Shell food Farmer Grandson's Eatery lodging Hampton Inn, Sonesta Suites
97b	Yankee Doodle Rd, E food Applebee's, Arby's, Buffalo Wild Wings, Burger King, Chipotle, Coldstone, Culver's, Domino's, DQ, Genghis Grill, Houlihan's, Jake's Grille, Jersey Mike's, Jimmy John's, KFC, Noodles&Co, Old Chicago Pizza, Panda Express, Panera Bread, Papa John's, Papa Murphy's, Perkins, Pizza Man, Potbelly, Qdoba, Smashburger, Taco Bell other $Tree, AT&T, Barnes&Noble, Best Buy, BigLots, GNC, Home Depot, Kohl's, Lunds&Byerly's Mkt, Michael's, Old Navy, O'Reilly Parts, Petsmart, TJ Maxx, Verizon, Walgreens, Walmart/Subway, W gas BP/dsl, SA/dsl food El Loro Mexican, Granite City, Starbucks, Subway lodging Best Western, Extended Stay America other Hobby Lobby, HyVee Foods, Marshall's, NAPA

HINCKLEY · FOREST LAKE · ST PAUL

MN

INTERSTATE 35 Cont'd

Exit#	Services
97a	Pilot Knob Rd, E [gas] Holiday, SA [food] Chili's, McDonald's, Wendy's [lodging] SpringHill Suites, TownePlace Suites [other] Discount Tire, Excel Repair, Firestone/auto, Kohl's, Tires+, Walmart/Subway, W [gas] BP/dsl, SA/dsl [food] Starbucks [lodging] Best Western, Holiday Inn Express, same as 97b
94	rd 30, Diffley Rd, to Eagan, E [gas] Holiday/dsl [food] Andiamo Italian [other] CVS Drug, Kowalski's Mkt/Starbucks, URGENT CARE, W [gas] Sinclair/dsl [other] Goodyear/auto
93	rd 32, Cliff Rd, E [gas] Holiday/dsl [food] Bonfire Grill, Sarpino's Pizza, Subway [other] Ace Hardware, W [gas] Holiday/dsl [food] Burger King, Caribou Coffee, Casper's Rest., Chipotle Mexican, Dolittle's Grill, DQ, Green Mill Rest., Hong Wong Chinese, Jimmy John's, Leeann Chin's, Noodles&Co, Papa John's, Papa Murphy's, Pizza Hut, Starbucks, Taco Bell, Wendy's, Which Wich? [lodging] Hilton Garden, Quality Inn, Staybridge Suites [other] $Tree, Cub Foods, O'Reilly Parts, Target, USPO, Walgreens
92	MN 77, Cedar Ave, E [other] Zoo, 1 mi W access to Cliff Rd services
90	rd 11, E [gas] KwikTrip [food] Pizza Man, Subway [other] Valley Natural Foods, vet, W [gas] SA/dsl
88b	rd 42, Crystal Lake Rd, E [food] Chianti Grill [other] Lund's&Byerly's Mkt, Petsmart, W [gas] BP, Holiday/dsl, SA/dsl, Shell [food] Applebee's, Arby's, Buca Italian, Burger Jones, Burger Jones, Burger King, Cam Ranh Bay, Chick-fil-A, Chili's, Chipotle Mexican, ChuckECheese, HoneyBaked Ham, IHOP, Jimmy John's, KFC, LeeAnn Chin, Little Caesar's, McDonald's, Noodles&Co, Old Country Buffet, Olive Garden, Outback Steaks, Panera Bread, Papa John's, Papa Murphy's, Pizza Hut, Porter Creek Grill, Red Lobster, Roasted Pear, Royal Buffet, Shogun Japanese, Smashburger, Starbucks, Taco Bell, TGIFriday's, Wendy's [lodging] AmericInn, Best Western, Fairfield Inn, Hampton Inn, InTown Suites [other] [H], $Tree, Ace Hardware, Advance Parts, AT&T, Barnes&Noble, Best Buy, Costco/gas, Cub Foods, Dick's, Discount Tire, Home Depot, JC Penney, Kohl's, Macy's, Michael's, Old Navy, PetCo, Target, Tires+, Tuesday Morning, Verizon, VW, Walgreens
88a	I-35W (from nb), N to Minneapolis. **See I-35W.**
87	Crystal Lake Rd (from nb), W [gas] Kwik Trip/dsl [other] Honda/Nissan, Hyundai, Mazda, Toyota
86	rd 46, E [gas] KwikTrip/dsl, SA/dsl [food] KFC, Starbucks [other] Harley-Davidson, W [food] McDonald's [other] auto repair, O'Reilly Parts
85	MN 50, E [gas] F&F/dsl, SA/dsl [food] Caribou Coffee, Culver's, Domino's, DQ, Eddie Cheng, Gerbert's Sandwiches, Green Mill Rest., Jimmy John's, Lakeville Chinese, Little Caesar's, Starbucks, Subway, Taco Bell, Wendy's [lodging] Quality Inn [other] $Tree, Advance Parts, Cub Foods, CVS Drug, GNC, Goodyear/auto, NTB, O'Reilly Parts, Verizon, Walgreens, W [gas] Holiday/dsl [food] Cracker Barrel, Perkins, Pizza Ranch [lodging] Baymont Inn
84	185th St W, Orchard Trail, E [gas] SA/dsl [food] Applebee's, Buffalo Wild Wings, Caribou Coffee, Quiznos, SawaJapan [other] Marshall's, Target
81	rd 70, Lakeville, E [gas] Holiday/dsl [food] Baldy's BBQ, McDonald's, Min Garden, Subway [lodging] Holiday Inn/rest., Motel 6, W [gas] SA/dsl [food] Harry's Cafe [lodging] Candlewood Suites [other] Walmart/Subway
76	rd 2, Elko, W [food] Endzone Grill [other] Elko Speedway
76mm	[RS] sb, full [handicap] facilities, litter barrels, petwalk, [phone], [picnic], vending
69	MN 19, to Northfield, New Prague, 7 mi E [gas] KwikTrip [food] Applebee's, Big Steer Rest., Caribou Coffee, McDonald's, Quarterback Rest., Subway, Taco Bell [lodging] AmericInn, College City Motel,

FARIBAULT

OWATONNA

St Paul
35
MN
Mankato
Fairbault
Owatonna
Worthington
Fairmont
Bancroft
90
90
Jackson
Albert Lea
Austin

Exit#	Services
69	Continued Country Inn&Suites, Super 8 [other] [H], Carleton Coll, St Olaf Coll, W [gas] FLYING J/Subway/dsl/scales/24hr
68mm	[RS] nb, full [handicap] facilities, litter barrels, petwalk, [phone], [picnic], vending
66	rd 1, to Dundas, 1 mi W [food] Boonie's Grill
59	MN 21, Faribault, 0-2 mi E [gas] KwikTrip, SA/Family Diner/dsl/scales/24hr [food] A&W, Arby's, Burger King, DQ, Hardee's, Joe's Cafe, KFC, Pizza Hut, Taco Bell, Taco John's [lodging] Best Value Inn, Days Inn, Grandstay [other] Aldi Foods, Buick/Chevrolet/GMC, Chrysler/Dodge/Jeep, O'Reilly Parts, repair, Satakah St Trail, vet, W [other] Harley-Davidson, 0-2 mi S [other] Ford/Lincoln
56	MN 60, Faribault, E [gas] KwikTrip [food] A&W, Arby's, Asian Buffet, Burger King, Jimmy John's, KFC, Little Caesar's, McDonald's, Perkins, Subway, Taco John's [other] [H], $Tree, Aldi Foods, AutoValue Parts, AutoZone, Buick/Chevrolet/GMC, Chrysler/Dodge/Jeep, Family$, Goodyear/auto, Hy-Vee Foods/dsl, JoAnn, O'Reilly Parts, Petsmart, TrueValue, Verizon, Walmart/Subway, W [food] Country Kitchen, DQ [lodging] Regency Inn [other] Sakatah Lake SP, same as 59
55	rd 48, (from nb, no return), 1 mi E [gas] KwikTrip, Mobil/dsl, SA/dsl [food] A&W, Arby's, Broaster Rest., Burger King, DQ, El Tequila Mexican, KFC, Southern China Cafe, Subway, Taco John's
48	rd 12, rd 23, Medford, E [gas] Casey's/dsl, W [food] McDonald's [other] Outlet Mall/famous brands
45	rd 9, Clinton Falls, W [gas] KwikTrip/dsl/scales [food] Caribou Coffee, Famous Dave's BBQ, Sportsman's Grille, Subway, TimberLodge Steaks, Wendy's [lodging] Comfort Inn, Holiday Inn [other] Buick/Chevrolet/Cadillac, Cabela's Sporting Goods, Russell-Stover Candies
43	rd 34, 26th St, Owatonna, E [other] Noble RV Ctr, W [other] [H]
42b a	US 14 W, rd 45, to Waseca, Owatonna, E [food] Hardee's, Kernel Rest. [lodging] Valu Stay Inn [other] AutoZone, CashWise Foods, Chrysler/Dodge/Jeep, Ford/Lincoln, O'Reilly Parts, repair, vet, W [gas] KwikTrip/dsl [food] Buffalo Wild Wings, Culver's, Don Juan Cantina, East Wind Buffet, McDonald's, Olivia's Rest., Panda Express, Perkins [lodging] Best Budget Inn, Super 8 [other] $Tree, Aldi, GNC, Kohl's, Lowe's, Verizon, Walmart/Subway
41	Bridge St, Owatonna, E [gas] Holiday/dsl [food] Applebee's, Arby's, Asian Kitchen, Burger King, DQ, Jimmy John's, KFC, Papa Murphy's, Red&Green Burrito, Starbucks, Subway, Taco Bell [lodging] Baymont Inn, Country Inn&Suites [other] Verizon, W [gas] F&F/dsl [lodging] Microtel [other] Target
40	US 14 E, US 218, Owatonna, 1 mi E on rd 45 [food] Godfather's, Little Caesar's, Taco John's [lodging] Oakdale Motel [other] Hy-Vee Foods/dsl, vet, Walgreens, WholesaleTire
38mm	Turtle Creek
35mm	[RS] both lanes, full [handicap] facilities, litter barrels, petwalk, [phone], [picnic], vending
34.5mm	Straight River

= gas = food = lodging = other = rest stop

INTERSTATE 35 Cont'd

ALBERT LEA

Exit#	Services
32	rd 4, Hope, 1/2 mi E Hope Oak Knoll Camping, 1 mi W gas food
26	MN 30, to Blooming Prairie, Ellendale, E Cenex/pizza/dsl, W Casey's/dsl/scales
22	rd 35, to Hartland, Geneva, 1 mi E food
18	MN 251, to Hollandale, Clarks Grove, W BP/dsl/LP
17mm	**weigh sta both lanes**
13b a	I-90, W to Sioux Falls, E to Austin, W H
12	US 65 S (from sb), Lp 35, Albert Lea, same as 11
11	rd 46, Albert Lea, E Loves/Wendy's/dsl/scales/24hr, Petro/Iron Skillet/McDonald's/Pizza Hut/dsl/scales/24hr/@ Comfort Inn, Holiday Inn Express dsl repair, KOA (may-oct/6mi), to Myre-Big Island SP, W Casey's, KwikTrip Burger King, Casa Zamora Mexican, GreenMill Rest., KFC, Perkins, Subway, Taco John's, Taco King, Trumble's Rest., Wok'n Roll Best Value Inn, Country Inn&Suites, Countryside Inn, Heritage Hotel, Motel 6 H, $Tree, Advance Parts, AutoValue Parts, AutoZone, Buick/GMC, CarQuest, Chrysler/Dodge/Jeep, Ford, Home Depot, Honda, Lincoln, NAPA, Nissan/VW, O'Reilly Parts, Volvo Trucks, Walmart/Subway
9mm	Albert Lea Lake
8	US 65, Lp 35, Albert Lea, 2 mi W Freeborn City Co-op/dsl DQ, Hardee's
5	rd 13, to Glenville, Twin Lakes, 3 mi W camping
2	rd 5
1mm	**Welcome Ctr nb, full facilities, litter barrels, petwalk, , , vending**
0mm	Minnesota/Iowa state line

INTERSTATE 35 West

MINNEAPOLIS

Exit#	Services
41mm	**I-35W begins/ends on I-35, exit 127.**
36	rd 23, E Holiday/dsl, W Minnoco/dsl Caribou Coffee, Don Julio, DQ, McDonald's, Subway, Tasty Asia Hampton Inn AT&T, Discount Tire, Kohl's, Super Target, Verizon
33	rd 17, Lexington Ave, E F&F/dsl, Holiday/dsl Burger King, Walmart/Subway Aldi Foods, W Applebee's, Arby's, Bonfire Rest., Caribou Coffee, Green Mill Rest., Taco Bell, Wendy's, Zantigo's Mexican Cub Foods, GNC, Home Depot, Michael's, Walgreens
32	95th Ave NE, to Lexington, Circle Pines, W Nat Sports Ctr
31b a	Lake Dr, E Shell/Circle K/dsl Quizno's, Red Ginger Asian Country Inn&Suites
30	US 10 W, MN 118, to MN 65
29	rd I, W Cenex/dsl
28c b	rd 10, rd H, W McDonald's, Mermaid Café, Taco Bell AmericInn, Days Inn
28a	MN 96, E Holiday/dsl, W Homewood Suites
27b a	I-694 E and W
26	rd E2, W Exxon/Circle K/dsl Jimmy John's, Limu Coffee USPO
25b	MN 88, to Roseville (no EZ return to sb), same as 25a
25a	rd D (from nb), E BP/dsl Courtyard, Fairfield Inn, Residence Inn, W Marathon/dsl, SA/dsl, Shell Barley John's, Caribou Coffee, Jake's Café, McDonald's, New Hong Kong, Perkins/24hr, Sarpino's Italian, Subway
24	rd C, E Burger King, India Palace Rest., Joe Senser's Rest. Hampton Inn, Home 2 Suites, Key Inn, Motel 6, Radisson USPO, Walmart, W Holiday Inn Express Buick/GMC, Chevrolet, Chrysler/Dodge/Jeep, Norm's Tires
23b	Cleveland Ave, MN 36
23a	MN 280, Industrial Blvd (from sb)
22	MN 280, Industrial Blvd (from nb), E Ramada Plaza
21b a	Broadway St, Stinson Blvd, E Ford/Isuzu Trucks, W Baja Sol, Burger King, Caribou Coffee, Leeann Chin, McDonald's, Taco Bell Cub Foods, GNC, Home Depot, Target
19	E Hennepin (from nb)
18	US 52, 4th St SE, University Ave, to U of MN
17c	11th St, Washington Ave, E Courtyard, W Mobil H, US Bank Stadium
17b	I-94 W (from sb)
17a	MN 55, Hiawatha
16b a	I-94 (from nb), E to St Paul, W to St Cloud, to MN 65
15	31st St (from nb), Lake St, E McDonald's, Taco Bell H, AutoZone
14	35th St, 36th St
13	46th St
13mm	Minnehaha Creek
12b	Diamond Lake Rd
12a	60th St (from sb), W Mobil Cub Foods
11b	MN 62 E, to , to
11a	Lyndale Ave (from sb)
10b	MN 62 W, 58th St
10a	rd 53, 66th St, E SA
9c	76th St (from sb)
9b a	I-494, MN 5, to , to
8	82nd St, E BMW, W Applebee's, Caribou Coffee, Jimmy John's, Panda Express, Red Lobster, Sonic, Starbucks, Subway Timberlodge Steaks, Wendy's Embassy Suites Chevrolet, Chrysler/Dodge/Jeep, GNC, Infiniti, Kia, Kohl's, TJ Maxx Verizon, Walgreens
7b	90th St
7a	94th St, E Goodyear/auto, W Holiday Inn
6	rd 1, 98th St, E Applebee's, Bakers Square, Domino's, Jimmy John's, Leeann Chin, McDonald's, Starbucks, Subway, Wendy's, White Castle Bloomington Drug, Festival Foods, Ford URGENT CARE, Walgreens, W SA/dsl
5	106th St
5mm	Minnesota River
4b	113th St, Black Dog Rd
4a	Cliff Rd, E Dodge, Subaru, Walmart
3b a	MN 13, Shakopee, Canterbury Downs, W Perkins
2	Burnsville Pkwy, E Carbone's Pizza, W Holida Clive's Roadhouse, Denny's, Gourmet Chinese, Perkin Best Value Inn, LivInn, Norwood Inn, Prime Rate Mote auto repair, vet
1	rd 42 (from sb), Crystal Lake Rd, E Shell Arby's, Burge King, Chianti Grill, HoneyBaked Ham, McDonald's, Old Countr Buffet, Roasted Pear, Taco Bell AmericInn, Best Wester Fairfield Inn, Hampton Inn H, Home Depot, Lunds&Bye ly's Mkt, PetsMart, W Holiday/dsl, SA/dsl Applebee' Buca Italian, Burger Jones, Burger King, Cam Ranh Bay, Chick-fil-A, Chili's, Chipotle, ChuckECheese, IHOP, Jimmy John's, KF LeAnn Chin, Little Caesar's, Noodles&Co, Olive Garden, Outback Steaks, Panera Bread, Papa John's, Papa Murphy's, Pizz Hut, Porter Creek Grill, Red Lobster, Royal Buffet, Shogun Jap anese, Smashburger, Starbucks, TGIFriday's, Wendy's I Town Suites $Tree, Ace Hardware, Advance Parts, AT& Barnes&Noble, Best Buy, Costco/gas, Cub Foods, Dick's, Di count Tire, JC Penney, Kohl's, Macy's, Michael's, Old Navy, Pe Co, Target, Tires+, Tuesday Morning, Verizon, VW, Walgreens

I-35W begins/ends on I-35, exit 88a.

MN

INTERSTATE 90

Exit#	Services
278mm	Minnesota/Wisconsin state line, Mississippi River
276	US 14, US 61, to MN 16, La Crescent, **N Welcome Ctr wb, full facilities, info, litter barrels, petwalk, , , vending,** S Kwik Trip (1mi)
273b a	Dresbach
271	Dakota
270	US 14, US 61, to Winona (from wb), N to OL Kipp SP/camping
267	rd 12, Nodine, N Great River Bluffs SP, S Kwik Trip/Hearty Platter Rest./dsl/e-85/scales/24hr/@
261mm	**weigh sta both lanes**
258	MN 76, to Houston, Ridgeway, Witoka, N gas, S camping
252	MN 43 N, to Winona, 7 mi N Taco Bell Express Inn, Holiday Inn Express, Plaza Hotel, Quality Inn , S vet
249	MN 43 S, to Rushford, N Peterbilt Trucks/repair
244mm	**eb, full facilities, litter barrels, petwalk, , , vending**
242	rd 29, Lewiston
233	MN 74, to Chatfield, St Charles, N Kwik Trip/LP/24hr (2mi) A&W (2mi), Subway (2mi) Whitewater SP, S BP/Amish Ovens Rest./dsl/RV dump/LP
229	rd 10, Dover
224	MN 42, rd 7, Eyota, N KwikTrip/dsl/e85 (3mi) Country Cafe (3mi)
222mm	**wb, full facilities, litter barrels, petwalk, , , vending**
218	US 52, to Rochester, S BP/dsl KOA (Mar-Oct) (1mi)
209b a	US 63, MN 30, to Rochester, Stewartville, **8-10 mi N** Clarion, EconoLodge, Hampton Inn, Super 8, **1 mi S** KwikTrip/dsl DQ, Pizza Ranch, Subway Best Inn Family$, Verizon
205	rd 6
202mm	**eb, full facilities, litter barrels, petwalk, , , vending**
193	MN 16, Dexter, N BP/Oasis Rest./dsl, S Windmill Motel
189	rd 13, to Elkton
187	rd 20, S Jellystone Camping
183	MN 56, to Rose Creek, Brownsdale, S Freeborn County Co-op/dsl/LP
181	28th St NE
180b a	US 218, 21st St NE, to Austin, Oakland Place, S Shell Rodeway Inn
179	11th Dr NE, to Austin, N KwikTrip/dsl/24hr
178b	6th St NE, to Austin, S Spam Museum
178a	4th St NW, N Culver's, Jimmy John's, Perkins, Torge's Grille AmericInn, Days Inn, Holiday Inn Buick/Chevrolet/GMC, vet, S KwikTrip/dsl Burger King, Hardee's, Subway
177	US 218 N, to Owatonna, Austin, Mapleview, N Applebee's, Arby's, China Star, El Patron Mexican, KFC, King Buffet, Pizza Hut, Pizza Ranch, Wendy's $Tree, Aldi Foods, AT&T, AutoZone, Hy-Vee Foods/gas, JoAnn Fabrics, O'Reilly Parts, ShopKO, Verizon, Walmart/Subway, Younkers, S Sinclair/McDonald's/dsl Super 8
175	MN 105, rd 46, to Oakland Rd, N Econolodge, S BP/dsl, Shell/dsl Chrysler/Dodge/Jeep, Ford/Lincoln, vet
171mm	**wb, full facilities, litter barrels, petwalk, , **
166	rd 46, Oakland Rd, N KOA/LP
163	rd 26, Hayward, S Freeborn County Co-op/dsl McDonald's (4mi), Pizza Hut (4mi), Trails Rest. (4mi) Holiday Inn Express (4mi) KOA, Myre-Big Island SP
161.5mm	**eb, full facilities, petwalk, , litter barrels**

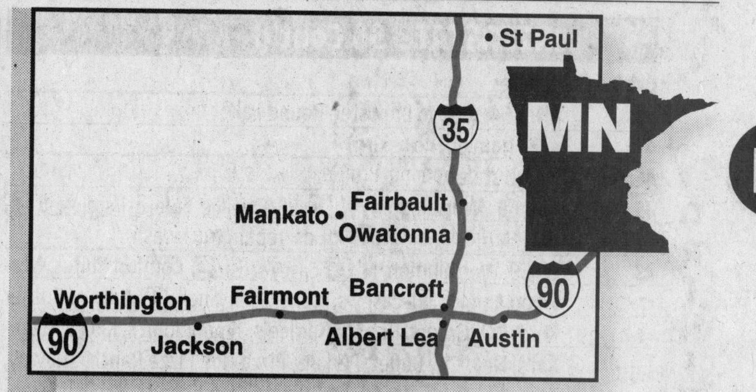

ALBERT LEA

Exit#	Services
159b a	I-35, N to Twin Cities, S to Des Moines
157	rd 22, Albert Lea, N Kenworth, S HyVee/dsl Applebee's, Arby's, Caribou Coffee, DQ, KwikTrip/dsl, McDonald's, Pizza Ranch, Plaza Morina Mexican AmericInn, Best Western+ Ace Hardware, Chevrolet, Harley-Davidson, Herberger's, Hy-Vee Foods, ShopKO, Verizon
154	MN 13, to US 69, to Manchester, Albert Lea, N SA/dsl, 3 mi S Best Value Inn
146	MN 109, to Wells, Alden, S Cenex/dsl/rest., Freeborn Co-Op Gas/dsl/E-85 truck/dsl repair
138	MN 22, to Wells, Keister, N Casey's (6mi)
134	MN 253, rd 21, to Bricelyn, MN Lake
128	MN 254, rd 17, Frost, Easton
119	US 169, to Winnebago, Blue Earth, S Blue Earth/dsl, Shell/dsl Country Kitchen, DQ, McDonald's, Pizza Hut, Subway AmericInn, Super 8 $General, Jolly Green Giant, Bomgaars
119mm	**both lanes, full facilities, litter barrels, petwalk, , , playground**
113	rd 1, Guckeen
107	MN 262, rd 53, to East Chain, Granada, S camping (May-Oct) (1mi), gas/dsl

FAIRMONT

Exit#	Services
102	MN 15, to Madelia, Fairmont, N Verizon, Walmart/Subway, **0-2 mi S** BP, Cenex/dsl, SA/dsl/24hr Arby's, Bean Town a Grill, Burger King, China Buffet, DQ, Green Mill Rest., Hardee's, McDonald's, Perkins, Pizza Ranch, Ranch Family Rest., Subway Budget Inn, Hampton Inn, Holiday Inn, Quality Inn, Super 8 $Tree, Ace Hardware, Advance Parts, auto repair, Chevrolet, Chrysler/Dodge/Jeep, Fareway Foods, Ford, Freightliner, Goodyear/auto, Hy-Vee Foods, NAPA, O'Reilly Parts, ShopKO, USPO, Walgreens
99	rd 39, Fairmont
93	MN 263, rd 27, Welcome, 1/2 mi S Casey's/dsl camping
87	MN 4, Sherburn, N Fox Lake Camping (3mi), S Casey's/dsl, Kum&Go/Subway/dsl/E-85
80	rd 29, Alpha
73	US 71, Jackson, N SA/dsl Burger King EconoLodge, Super 8 KOA, to Kilen Woods SP, S BP/DQ, Casey's/dsl Embers Rest., Pizza Ranch, Subway AmericInn, Earth Inn, Prairie Winds Motel Ace Hardware, Buick/Chevrolet, Chrysler/Dodge/Jeep, city park, Family$, Sunshine Foods, to Spirit Lake
72.5mm	W Fork Des Moines River
72mm	**wb, full facilities, litter barrels, petwalk, , , vending**
69mm	**eb, full facilities, litter barrels, petwalk, , , vending**
64	MN 86, Lakefield, N gas/dsl food camping, to Kilen SP (12mi)
57	rd 9, to Heron Lake, Spafford

= gas = food = lodging = other = rest stop

MN

INTERSTATE 90 Cont'd

Exit#	Services
50	MN 264, rd 1, to Brewster, Round Lake
47	rd 3 (from eb, no return)
46mm	**weigh sta eb**
45	MN 60, Worthington, N BP/Blueline Cafe/dsl/scales, S Holiday/dsl/scales/24hr dsl repair, truckwash
43	US 59, Worthington, N Casey's/dsl Comfort Suites, Norwood Inn, S Casey's, Cenex/dsl, Shell Arby's, Burger King, DQ, Ground Round, Hardee's, Jimmy John's, KFC, McDonald's, New City Buffet, Perkins, Pizza Hut, Pizza Ranch, Subway, Taco John's AmericInn, Holiday Inn Express H, $General, Ace Hardware, CarQuest, Chevrolet, Fareway Foods, Ford, Hy-Vee Foods/dsl, NAPA, O'Reilly Parts, ShopKO, Verizon, Walgreens, Walmart/Subway
42	MN 266, rd 25, to Reading, S Days Inn, Super 8
33	rd 13, to Wilmont, Rushmore
26	MN 91, Adrian, S Cenex/dsl, Kum&Go/Subway/dsl/E-85/24hr Countryside Steaks $General, Adrian Camping, city park
25mm	**wb, full facilities, litter barrels, petwalk,**
24mm	**eb, full facilities, litter barrels, petwalk,**
18	rd 3, Kanaranzi, Magnolia, N camping
12	US 75, Luverne, N BP/dsl/E-85, Casey's/dsl, Holiday/Subway/dsl McDonald's, Papa's Place Rest., Taco John's, Tasty Drive-In Cozy Rest Motel (1mi), GrandStay Hotel, Quality Inn H, $General, Buick/Cadillac/Chevrolet/GMC, Chrysler/Dodge/Jeep, Ford, Lewis Drugs, Pipestone NM, Sturdevant's Parts, to Blue Mounds SP, S Blue Stem Rest. Super 8 ShopKO
5	rd 6, Beaver Creek, N Local/dsl
3	rd 4 (from eb), Beaver Creek
1	MN 23, rd 17, to Jasper, N access to gas/dsl, to Pipestone NM
0mm	**Welcome Ctr eb, full facilities, info, litter barrels,** Minnesota/South Dakota state line

WORTHINGTON

INTERSTATE 94

Exit#	Services
259mm	Minnesota/Wisconsin state line, St Croix River
258	MN 95 N, to Stillwater, Hastings, Lakeland, N Bungalow Rest.
257mm	**Welcome Ctr wb, full facilities, litter barrels, petwalk, , vending, weigh sta wb**
253	MN 95 S, rd 15, Manning Ave, N StoneRidge Golf, S ski area, to Afton Alps SP
251	rd 19, Keats Ave, Woodbury Dr, S KwikTrip, SA/dsl Applebee's, Arby's, Burger King, Caribou Coffee, Chili's, Chipotle Mexican, ChuckECheese, Culver's, Dino's Rest., Dunn Bros Coffee, Fiesta Brava, Jersey Mike's, Lakes Grill, LeeAnn Chin, Little Chopstix, McDonald's, Noodles&Co, Papa Murphy's, Quiznos, Ray J's Grill, SmashBurger, Starbucks, Subway, Which Wich? Extended Stay America, Holiday Inn Express $Tree, AT&T, Discount Tire, Hobby Lobby, Michael's, Sam's Club/gas, Staples, Target, Trader Joe's, Verizon, Walmart/Subway, Woodbury Lakes Outlets/famous brands
250	rd 13, Radio Dr, Inwood Ave, N Buffalo Wild Wings, Caribou Coffee, Five Guys, Machine Shed Rest., Milio's Rest., Olive Garden, Red Lobster Hilton Garden, Holiday Inn Best Buy, S Holiday/e85 Domino's, DUC Vietnamese, Firehouse Subs, Jamba Juice, Little Caesar's, Pei Wei, Piada Italian, Pie Five, Potbelly, Qdoba, Starbucks, Taco Bell, Tamarack Rest.,

ST PAUL

Exit#	Services
250	Continued Wendy's, Wild Bill's Grill, Zupas Residence Inn Ald Foods, BigLots, Cabela's, Cub Foods, CVS Drug, Dick's, Fanni May, GNC, Gordman's, Heppner's Auto Ctr, Home Depot, J Penney, Jo-Ann, LandsEnd Inlet, Old Navy, Petsmart, Tires+ Verizon, vet
249	I-694 N & I-494 S
247	MN 120, Century Ave, N Denny's LivInn Harley-Davidson, S SA/dsl GreenMill Rest. Country Inn/rest. CarQuest, Chevrolet
246c b	McKnight Ave, N 3M, S Holiday Inn
246a	Ruth St (from eb, no return), N Culver's, Domino' Hoho Chinese, Jimmy John's, Leeann Chin $Tree, Cu Foods, Firestone/auto, GNC, TJ Maxx
245	White Bear Ave, N SA/dsl Subway Motel Walgreens, S Arby's, Davanni's Pizza/subs, Lo Ocampo, McDonald's, Papa John's, Popeye's, Sonic, Taco Be Wendy's Aldi Foods, Family$, NAPA, O'Reilly Parts, Targe
244	US 10 E, US 61 S, S Mounds/Kellogg
243	US 61, Mounds Blvd, S River Centre
242d	US 52 S, MN 3, 6th St, (exits left from wb), N Holida dsl Subway
242c	7th St, S SA
242b a	I-35E N, US 10 W, I-35E S (from eb)
241c	I-35E S (from wb)
241b	10th St, 5th St, to downtown
241a	12th St, Marion St, Kellogg Blvd, N Best Western+, S Paul's Cathedral
240	Dale Ave
239b a	Lexington Pkwy, Hamline Ave, N BP, SA DQ, Hardee Leeann Chin, Noodles&Co, Popeye's, White Castle $Tre Aldi, AutoZone, Cub Foods, Discount Tire, Herberger's, O'Rei Parts, Target, TJ Maxx, Verizon, S H
238	MN 51, Snelling Ave, N Culver's, Little Caesar's, McDo ald's, Peking Garden, Perkins CVS Drug, Family$, GN Rainbow Foods, same as 239, Walgreens, Walmart/Subw S Tires+
237	Cretin Ave, Vandalia Ave, to downtown
236	MN 280, University Ave, to downtown
235b	Huron Blvd
235mm	Mississippi River
235a	Riverside Ave, 25th Ave, N Fina Starbucks, S P kins, Taco Bell
234c	Cedar Ave, downtown
234b a	MN 55, Hiawatha Ave, 5th St, N Courtyard to downto
233b	I-35W N, I-35W S (exits left from wb)
233a	11th St (from wb), N downtown
231b	Hennepin Ave, Lyndale Ave, to downtown
231a	I-394, US 12 W, to downtown
230	US 52, MN 55, 4th St, 7th St, Olson Hwy, N US Bank Sta um, S H, Int Mkt Square
229	W Broadway, Washington Ave, N EZ Stop/dsl, Holid dsl Broadway Pizza, S Winner Burger King, Li Caesar's, McDonald's, Subway, Taco Bell, Wendy's $T AutoZone, Cub Foods, Family$, Walgreens
228	Dowling Ave N
226	53rd Ave N, 49th Ave N
225	I-694 E, MN 252 N, to Minneapolis

I-94 and I-494 run together. See I-494/694, exits 28-34.

Exit#	Services
216	I-94 W and I-494
215	rd 109, Weaver Lake Rd, N SA/dsl, Shell Angeno's, by's, Broadway Pizza, Burger King, Caribou Coffee, Chin Y

MINNEAPOLIS

MN

INTERSTATE 94 Cont'd

Exit	Services
215	Continued ChuckECheese's, Domino's, DQ, El Rodeo Mexican, Famous Dave's BBQ, Frankie's Pizza, Golden Corral, Great Harvest Bread Co., Jimmy John's, McDonald's, Papa John's, Papa Murphy's, Rita's, Starbucks, Subway, Taco Bell, Wendy's AT&T, Barnes&Noble, Cub Foods, GNC, Goodyear/auto, JC Penney, Kohl's, Lund&Byerly's Foods, Michael's, Midas, Old Navy, PetCo, same as 28, Tires+, USPO, Verizon, Walgreens, **S** Applebee's
214mm	**eb, full facilities, litter barrels,**
213	rd 30, 95th Ave N, Maple Grove, **N** SA/dsl Chipotle Mexican, Subway Cambria Suites Aldi Foods, GNC, Home Depot, Target, **S** Holiday/dsl Caribou Coffee, Culver's, Jersey Mike's, Jets Pizza, Leeann Chin, McDonald's, Starbucks, Teresa's Mexican, Which Wich?, White Castle $Tree, AT&T, BigLots, Discount Tire, Firestone/auto, Goodyear/auto, Hobby Lobby, KOA (2mi) (Apr-Oct), Menards, Sam's Club/gas, Verizon, Walgreens, Walmart/Subway
212	101st Ave (from eb)
207	MN 101, to Elk River, Rogers, **N** Holiday/dsl, SA/dsl, TA/Country Pride/dsl/scales/24hr/@ Applebee's, Arby's, Burger King, China Kitchen, Chipotle, Culver's, Davanni's Pizza, Denny's, Dickey's BBQ, Domino's, DQ, Hardee's, Jimmy John's, Maynard's, McDonald's, Noodles&Co, Papa Murphy's, Starbucks, Subway, Taco Bell, Wendy's Hampton Inn, Holiday Inn Express, Super 8 $Tree, AT&T, Cabela's, Camping World, Cub Foods, Discount Tire, GNC, Kohl's, NAPA, NTB, O'Reilly Parts, Target, Tires+, Verizon, vet, Walgreens, **S** BP/Circle K/dsl, Holiday BoBo Asian, Guadalajara Mexican, Minne's Diner AmeriInn Chevrolet, CVS Drug, TrueValue, URGENT CARE, USPO
205.5mm	Crow River
205	MN 241, rd 36, St Michael, **S** KwikTrip/dsl, SA/dsl
202	rd 37, Albertville, **N** Shell/dsl Emma Krumbee's Rest., **S** BP/dsl, SA/dsl, same as 201
201	rd 19 (from eb), Albertville, St Michael, **N** Andy's Pizza, Burger King, Five Guys, Hana Steaks, Michael B's Grill, Subway Country Inn&Suites Albertville Outlets/famous brands, Old Navy, **S** Casey's, Mobil/Circle K Caribou Coffee, China Dragon, Culver's, Little Caesar's, Papa Murphy's, Space Aliens Grill, Subway, Taco Bell Ace Hardware, auto repair, Coburn's/dsl, Goodyear/auto, Verizon
194	rd 18, rd 39, Monticello, **N** KwikTrip/dsl Caribou Coffee, Little Caesar's AT&T, GNC, Home Depot, Marshall's, Petsmart, Target, Verizon
193	MN 25, to Buffalo, Monticello, Big Lake, **N** Holiday/dsl Burger King, Caribou Coffee, KFC, Papa Murphy's, Perkins, Quiznos, Rancho Grande Mexican, Taco Bell AmericInn AutoValue Parts, Cub Foods, USPO, Walgreens, **S** Holiday/dsl, SA/dsl Applebee's, Arby's, Buffalo Wild Wings, China Buffet, Culver's, DQ, Jimmy John's, McDonald's, Pizza Ranch, Subway, Taco John's Best Western, Days Inn, Super 8 $Tree, Aldi Foods, AutoZone, Buick/GMC, Chevrolet, Goodyear/auto, Lake Maria SP, NAPA, O'Reilly Parts, Verizon, Walmart/Subway
187mm	**eb, full facilities, litter barrels, petwalk, , vending**
183	rd 8, to Silver Creek, Hasty, Maple Lake, **S** SA/rest./dsl/scales/24hr/@ camping, to Lake Maria SP
178	MN 24, to Annandale, Clearwater, **N** Holiday/Petro/dsl/scales/24hr/@ Burger King, DQ, Kettle, Subway, Taco Gringo Best Value Inn Clearwater Hardware, Coburn's Foods/gas, Parts City, repair, USPO, **S** A-J Acres RV Camping (Apr-Oct), Recreation Outdoor RV Ctr

MONTICELLO

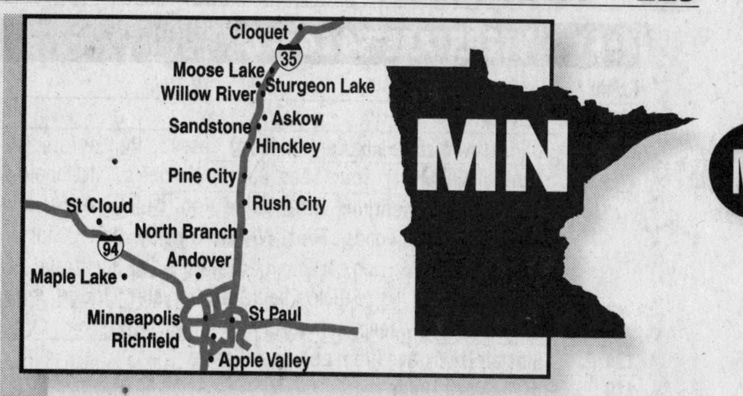

Exit	Services
178mm	**wb, full facilities, litter barrels, petwalk, , , vending**
173	Opportunity Dr
171	rd 7, rd 75, St Augusta, **N** Pilot/dsl/scales/24hr, Shell/Burger King/dsl McDonald's, RJ's Grill, Subway AmericInn, Holiday Inn Express, Travelodge Goodyear/auto, **S** Freightliner, Pleasureland RV Ctr
167b a	MN 15, to St Cloud, Kimball, 4 mi **N** Holiday, SA/dsl Applebee's, Arby's, Bonanza, Boulder Taphouse, Buffalo Wild Wings, Burger King, Caribou Coffee, Chick-fil-A, Chipotle, ChuckECheese's, Coldstone, Famous Dave's BBQ, Five Guys, Granite City Grill, Grizzly's Grill, IHOP, La Casita Mexican, Leeann Chin, McDonald's, Noodles&Co, Old Chicago Pizza, Olive Garden, Panda Express, Perkins, Pizza Ranch, Red Lobster, Red Robin, Sammy's Pizza, Starbucks, Subway, Taco Bell, Taco John's, TX Roadhouse, Wendy's, White Castle Country Inn&Suites, Days Inn, Fairfield Inn, Hampton Inn, Holiday Inn, Homewood Suites, Quality Inn, Super 8 AT&T, Barnes&Noble, Best Buy, CashWise Foods, Dick's, Fresh Thyme Mkt, Hobby Lobby, Home Depot, JC Penney, Jo-Ann Fabrics, Kohl's, Macy's, Michael's, Office Depot, Old Navy, Petsmart, Sam's Club, Save-A-Lot, Scheel's Sports, ShopKo, Subaru, Target, Walgreens, Walmart
164	MN 23, to St Cloud, Rockville, 4-6 mi **N** KwikTrip/dsl, SA/dsl Culver's, IHOP, KFC, Subway, Wendy's Astaria Inn $Tree, Discount Tire, Grande Depot Gourmet Foods, Honda, Hyundai, Kia, Menards, Petsmart, same as 167, Toyota
162.5mm	Sauk River
160	rd 2, to Cold Spring, St Joseph, **N** Coll of St Benedict
158	rd 75 (from eb exits left), to St Cloud, 3 mi **N** same as 160
156	rd 159, St Joseph, **S** St Johns U
153	rd 9, Avon, **N** Casey's/dsl, Tesoro/McDonald's/dsl Subway Budget Host city park, USPO, **S** El Rancho Manana Camping (10mi)
152mm	**both lanes, full facilities, litter barrels, petwalk, , , vending**
147	MN 238, rd 10, Albany, **N** Holiday/dsl, Shell/Godfather's/dsl A&W/Subway, DQ, Hillcrest Rest. Baymont Inn CVS Drug, golf, **S** Chrysler/Dodge/Jeep, NAPA, vet
140	rd 11, Freeport, **N** Cenex/dsl, Sinclair/dsl Ackie's Pioneer Rest., Charlie's Café auto repair, vet
137	MN 237, rd 65, New Munich
137mm	Sauk River
135	rd 13, Melrose, **N** Sinclair/dsl/repair, Victory/Subway/dsl Burger King, Cornerstone Buffet $General, **S** Casey's/dsl DQ, El Portal Mexican Super 8 TrueValue, vet
132.5mm	Sauk River
131	MN 4, to Paynesville, Meire Grove

ST CLOUD

MN

INTERSTATE 94 Cont'd

Exit#	Services
128mm	Sauk River
127	US 71, MN 28, Sauk Centre, N [gas] Casey's, Holiday/dsl, Trillium CNG [food] DQ, Four Seas Buffet, Hardee's, McDonald's, Subway [lodging] AmericInn, Best Value Inn [other] [H], Ace Hardware, Coborn's Foods, Ford, NAPA, O'Reilly Parts, Sinclair Lewis Home, Verizon, Walmart/Subway, S [gas] Shell/café/dsl/scales/24hr/@ [other] Buick/Chevrolet/Chrysler/Dodge/Jeep, Chrysler/Dodge/Jeep, Kenworth
124	Sinclair Lewis Ave (from eb), Sauk Centre
119	rd 46, West Union
114	MN 27, rd 3, to Westport, Osakis, **3 mi** N [gas] gas [food] A&W, Subway [lodging] lodging
105mm	**[RS] wb, full [handicap] facilities, litter barrels, petwalk, [phone], [picnic], vending**
103	*(ALEXANDRIA)* MN 29, to Glenwood, Alexandria, N [gas] F&F/dsl, Holiday/dsl, Simonson/dsl [food] Arby's, Burger King, Caribou Coffee, China Buffet, Culver's, Dolittle's Grill, Great Hunan, Hardee's, Jimmy John's, KFC, McDonald's, Perkins, Qdoba, Subway, Taco Bell, TN Roadhouse, Wendy's [lodging] AmericInn, Best Western, Days Inn, Hampton Inn, Super 8 [other] [H], $Tree, Aldi Foods, AT&T, AutoZone, Cadillac/Chevrolet/Mazda, Cub Foods, Goodyear/auto, Harley-Davidson, Herberger's, Jo-Ann Fabrics, Mazda, Menards, Target, Verizon, Walmart/Subway, S [gas] Holiday/dsl [lodging] Country Inn&Suites, Holiday Inn [other] Alexandria RV Ctr, Buick/GMC
100	MN 27, N [gas] Pilot/Subway/dsl/scales/24hr/@ [lodging] Best Inn/Alexandria RV Park (2mi) [other] [H], S [other] camping
100mm	Lake Latoka
99mm	**[RS] eb, full [handicap] facilities, litter barrels, petwalk, [phone], [picnic], vending**
97	MN 114, rd 40, to Lowry, Garfield
90	rd 7, Brandon, S camping, ski area
82	MN 79, rd 41, to Erdahl, Evansville, **2 mi** N [gas] BP/dsl [other] [H], S [other] camping
77	MN 78, rd 10, to Barrett, Ashby, N [gas] gas/dsl [other] camping, S [other] camping
69mm	**[RS] wb, full [handicap] facilities, litter barrels, petwalk, [phone], [picnic], vending**
67	rd 35, Dalton, N [other] camping, S [other] camping
61	*(FERGUS FALLS)* US 59 S, rd 82, to Elbow Lake, N [gas] Tesoro/café/dsl/LP/24hr [other] [H], camping (4mi), S [other] camping
57	MN 210 E, rd 25, Fergus Falls, N [other] [H]
55	rd 1, to Wendell, Fergus Falls, N [other] antiques
54	MN 210 W, Lincoln Ave, Fergus Falls, N [gas] Cenex/dsl, F&F/dsl, Tesoro/dsl [food] Applebee's, Arby's, Burger King, Family Diner, Hardee's, Hunan Spring Buffet, McDonald's, Papa Murphy's, Perkins, Pizza Hut, Pizza Ranch, Subway, Thrifty White Drug [lodging] AmericInn, Best Value Inn, Best Western, Comfort Inn, Motel 7, Super 8 [other] [H], $Tree, Aldi Foods, AT&T, Chrysler/Dodge/Jeep, Ford/Lincoln, GMC, Herberger's, Home Depot, Kenworth, museum, NAPA, O'Reilly Parts, SunMart Foods/dsl, Target, Tires+, Toyota, USPO, S [food] Mabel Murphy's Rest. [other] Walmart
50	rd 88, rd 52, to US 59, to Fergus Falls, Elizabeth, [other] camping
38	rd 88, Rothsay, S [gas] Tesoro/cafe/dsl/24hr [food] Powerhouse Grill [lodging] Comfort Zone Inn [other] tires
32	MN 108, rd 30,to Pelican Rapids, Lawndale, **19 mi** N [other] Maplewood SP
24	MN 34, Barnesville, N [food] Renee's Drive-in, **1 mi** S [gas] Cenex/dsl, Tesoro/dsl [food] DQ, Subway [other] $General, city park, Wagner Park Camping (May-Oct)
22	MN 9, Barnesville, **1 mi** S [gas] Cenex/dsl, Tesoro/dsl [food] DQ, Subway [other] $General
15	rd 10, Downer
8mm	Buffalo River
6	MN 336, rd 11, to US 10, Dilworth, N [other] to Buffalo River SP
5mm	**Red River weigh sta eb**
2b	*(MOORHEAD)* 34th St, Moorhead, **2 mi** N [gas] Casey's/dsl, Holiday/dsl/e-85, Tesoro [food] Arby's, Fry'n Pan, Hardee's, McDonald's, Perkins, Pizza Ranch, Subway [lodging] Travelodge [other] [H], $Tree, CVS Drug, Menards, Target, Tires+, Walmart/Subway
2a	no service
1mm	**Welcome Ctr eb, full [handicap] facilities, info, litter barrels, [phone], [picnic], vending**
1b	20th St, Moorhead (from eb, no return)
1a	US 75, Moorhead, N [gas] Cenex/dsl [food] Burger King, Crave Burger Co., Jimmy John's, Little Caesar's, Noodles&Co, Papa Murphy's, Qdoba, Starbucks, Village Inn [lodging] Courtyard [other] Family Fare Foods, Verizon, S [gas] Casey's, Holiday/dsl [food] Panchero's Mexican, Sarpino's Pizza, Snapdragon Asian, Speak Easy Rest., Subway [lodging] Days Inn, Grand Inn, Microtel, Super 8 [other] CVS Drug, Hornbacher's Mkt, Subaru, vet, Walgreens
0mm	Minnesota/North Dakota state line, Red River

INTERSTATE 494/694

Exit#	Services
I-494/I-694 loops around Minneapolis/St Paul.	
71	rd 31, Pilot Knob Rd, N [lodging] Courtyard, Fairfield Inn, S [lodging] Holiday Inn
70	I-35E, N to St Paul, S to Albert Lea
69	MN 149, MN 55, Dodd Rd, S [food] Caribou Coffee, Jimmy John's, McDonald's, Subway [lodging] Country Inn&Suites
67	MN 3, Roberts St, **1 mi** N [gas] BP, Holiday [food] Applebee's, Arby's, Baker's Square, Burger King, Chick-fil-A, Chipotle Mexican, Culver's, Jimmy John's, KFC, Noodles&Co, Panda Express, Panera Bread, Papa Murphy's, Taco Bell, White Castle [other] $Tree, Aamco, Aldi Foods, AT&T, Best Buy, Buick/GMC, Chevrolet, Cub Foods, Discount Tire, Ford, Home Depot, Honda, Hyundai, Kia, Lincoln, Lowe's, Mazda, NAPA, Nissan, NTB, O'Reilly Parts, Pep Boys, Petco, Target, Toyota, VW, Wagreens, Walmart
66	US 52, S [gas] [food] Applebee's, B-52 Burger, Outback Steaks [lodging] AmericInn, Holiday Inn Express, Microtel
65	7th Ave, 5th Ave
64b a	MN 56, Concord St, N [gas] KwikTrip/dsl/scales [food] Burger King, Subway [lodging] Clarion [other] Goodyear, Peterbilt, Stockmens/dsl, S [gas] Holiday/dsl [other] Chrysler/Jeep/Dodge, Parts+
63mm	Mississippi River
63c	Maxwell Ave
63b a	US 10, US 61, to St Paul, Hastings, S [gas] BP, SA [food] Burger King, Subway [lodging] Boyd's Motel [other] NAPA
60	Lake Rd, E [gas] SA/dsl [food] Carbone's Pizza, Milio's Sandwiches, W [other] [H]
59	Valley Creek Rd, E [gas] BP/repair, SA/dsl/LP [food] Applebee's, Chipotle Mexican, Coldstone, DQ, Jersey Mike's, Jimmy John's, Noodles&Co, Panda Express, Papa Murphy's, Perkins, Potbelly, Red's Savoy Pizza, Starbucks, Yang's Chinese [lodging] Key Inn [other] $Tree, Barnes&Noble, GNC, Kohl's, Lunds&Byerly's Mkt, Marshall's, PetCo, Target, URGENT CARE, USPO, Walgreens, W [gas] Shell [food] Bonfire Rest., Burger King, Keys Cafe, McDonald's, Sole Mio Italian, Subway [lodging] Hampton Inn [other] [H], Ace Hardware, Goodyear
58c	Tamarack Rd, E [food] Tavern Grill, Woodbury Cafe [lodging] La Quinta, Sheraton
58b a	I-94, E to Madison, W to St Paul. **I-494 S begins/ends, I-694 begins/ends.**

MN

INTERSTATE 494/694 Cont'd

Exit#	Services
57	rd 10, 10th St N, **E** SA/dsl IHOP, Pizza Man, Sgt Peppers Grill, Wild Boar Grill Best Western, **W** Holiday/dsl Burger King, Caribou Coffee, Hardee's, Hunan Buffet, KFC, Papa Murphy's, Starbucks $Tree, Cub Foods, HyVee/dsl
55	MN 5, **E** SA/dsl McDonald's Target, **W** Holiday/dsl, KwikTrip/dsl Subway Menards, st patrol
52b a	MN 36, N St Paul, to Stillwater, **W** F&F/dsl Burger King, Caribou Coffee, DQ
51	MN 120, **E** BP, SA/dsl Dulano's Pizza, Jethro's, Tacos Fresh, **W** The Corner/gas vet
50	White Bear Ave, **N** SA/dsl Cub Foods, Sam's Club/gas, **S** Acapulco, Arby's, Bakers Square, Buffalo Wild Wings, Caribou Coffee, Chili's, Chipotle, Denny's, Great Moon Buffet, IHOP, Jake's Grill, Jimmy John's, McDonald's, Noodles&Co, Olive Garden, Osaka, Outback Steaks, Perkins/24hr, Pizza Hut, Pizza Ranch, Popeye's, Red Lobster, Taco Bell, TGI Friday, Wendy's Emerald Inn Aamco, Barnes&Noble, Best Buy, Firestone/auto, Hobby Lobby, JC Penney, Jo-Ann Fabrics, Kohl's, Macy's, Marshall's, Michael's, Tires+, Verizon, Walgreens
48	US 61, **N** KwikTrip/dsl Acura, Chrysler/Dodge/Jeep, Ford, Honda, Hyundai, Kia, Lincoln, Subaru, **S** Chili's, Jake's Grill, McDonald's, Olive Garden, Subway H, Audi/Porsche, CarMax, Costco/gas, Lexus, Mercedes, Nissan, Toyota, Venburg Tire, Volvo
47	I-35E, N to Duluth
46	I-35E, US 10, S to St Paul
45	rd 49, Rice St, **N** Gas+, Mobil/dsl Subway, Taco Bell, **S** Burger King, Caribou Coffee
43b	Victoria St
43a	Lexington Ave, **N** Greenmill Rest., Red Robin Best Western+, Hilton Garden, **S** Exxon/Circle K/dsl Arby's, Cane's, Caribou Coffee, Chipotle, Davanni's Pizza, Five Guys, Jimmy John's, Leeann Chin, Noodles&Co, Papa John's, Papa Murphy's, Perkins, Potbelly, Starbucks, Subway, Wendy's Quality Inn AT&T, Cub Foods, GNC, Target, Trader Joe's
42b	US 10 W (from wb), to Anoka
42a	MN 51, Snelling Ave, **1 mi S** Shell/dsl Flaherty's Grill, Lindey's Steaks, McDonald's Country Inn&Suites vet
41b a	I-35W, S to Minneapolis, N to Duluth
40	Long Lake Rd, 10th St NW
39	Silver Lake Rd, **N** Acapulco Mexican, McDonald's, Subway Ford, U-Haul
38b a	MN 65, Central Ave, **N** Holiday/dsl Subway, **S** A&W/KFC, Applebee's, Asia Rest., Big Marina Deli, Chipotle, Domino's, Embers Rest., Flameburger Rest., Jimmy John's, La Casita Mexican, Leeann Chin, Little Caesar's, McDonald's, Papa John's, Pizza Hut, Sonic, Starbucks, Subway, Taco Bell, Wendy's LivInn Hotel $General, Advance Parts, Aldi Foods, AT&T, AutoZone, Discount Tire, Menards, Noodles&Co, PetCo, Target, Tires+, vet, Walgreens
37	rd 47, University Ave, **N** Holiday, SA/dsl Burger King, McDonald's, Panchero's, Papa Murphy's Pizza, Zantigo's Rest. Cub Foods, CVS Drug, Duluth Trading, Home Depot, NTB, **S** Bona Bros/repair, Shell
36	E River Rd
35mm	**I-494 W begins/ends, I-694 E begins/ends.**
35c	MN 252, **N** Holiday, SA
35b a	I-94 E to Minneapolis

MINNEAPOLIS

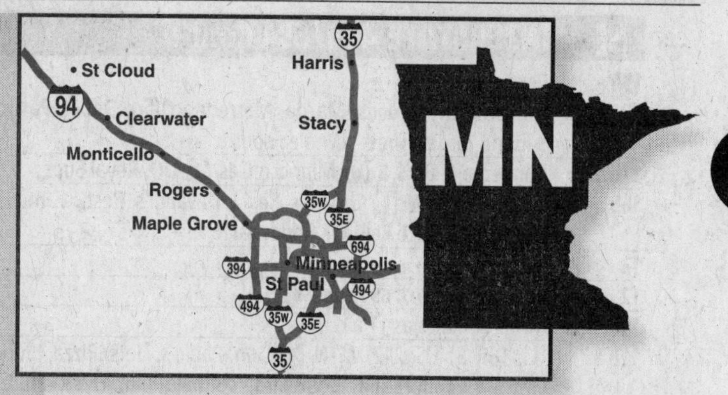

Exit#	Services
34	to MN 100, Shingle Creek Pkwy, **N** Denny's Best Western, Country Inn&Suites, Doubletree, Extended Stay America, Motel 6, Norwood Inn, Quality Inn, Super 8, **S** Ocean Buffet, Panera Bread, Rose Garden Embassy Suites AT&T, Target, Tires+, Walmart
33	rd 152, Brooklyn Blvd, **N** SA/dsl Culver's, Slim's Café, Subway Buick/GMC, Chevrolet, Honda, Toyota, USPO, VW, **S** AutoZone, Family$, Sun Foods, Walgreens
31	rd 81, Lakeland Ave, **N** SA/dsl Chipotle Mexican, Wagner's Drive-In, Wendy's CarMax, Target, U-Haul, **S** Northstar Inn
30	Boone Ave, **N** La Quinta, Marriott, **S** Home Depot
29b a	US 169, to Hopkins, Osseo
28	rd 61, Hemlock Lane, **N on Elm Creek** Arby's, Benihana, Biaggi's Italian, Buca Italian, Chick-fil-A, Chipotle Mexican, Coldstone, Dave&Buster's, Dickey's BBQ, Firehouse Subs, Five Guys, Freddy's, Granite City Rest., Leeann Chin, Malone's Grill, Mongo's Grill, Noodles&Co, Olive Garden, Panda Express, Panera Bread, Patrick's Cafe, PF Chang's, Pittsburgh Blue, Potbelly's, Red Lobster, Redstone Grill, Starbucks, Subway, TGI-Friday's, Wild Bill's Café, Zupas Courtyard, Hampton Inn, Holiday Inn, Staybridge Suites $Tree, Best Buy, Costco/gas, Dick's, Jo-Ann Fabrics, Lowe's, Marshalls, Petsmart, REI, Trader Joe's, Verizon, Whole Foods Mkt, World Mkt, **S** Perkins Asteria Suites
27	I-94 W to St Cloud, I-94/694 E to Minneapolis
26	rd 10, Bass Lake Rd, **E** Freedom Caribou Coffee, Culver's, McDonald's, Subway Extended Stay America vet, **W** BP, Holiday/dsl Jimmy John's, Pancake House, Pizza Hut, Rusty Taco, Solos Pizza Hilton Garden auto repair, CVS Drug
23	rd 9, Rockford Rd, **E** Holiday Chili's, Domino's, Five Guys, Sunshine Factory Grill AT&T, GNC, Kohl's, O'Reilly Parts, PetsMart, Target, TJ Maxx, Walgreens, **W** BP, Freedom/dsl DQ, LeAnn Chin, Subway, Toppers Pizza, Caribou Coffee
22	MN 55, **E** Holiday/dsl Broadway Pizza, Caribou Coffee, Green Mill Rest., Jimmy John's, McDonald's, Red Robin, Solos Pizza, Starbucks, Subway Crowne Plaza, Ramada, Red Roof Inn, Residence Inn, **W** Holiday/dsl Arby's, Burger King, Davanni's Rest., Firehouse Subs, Jake's Rest., Perkins, Wendy's Comfort Inn, Days Inn Goodyear/auto, Tires+
21	rd 6, **E** KwikTrip Discount Tire, Home Depot
20	Carlson Pkwy, **E** Holiday/dsl Pizza Hut, Subway, **W** Grizzy's Grill Country Inn&Suites
19b a	I-394 E, US 12 W, to Minneapolis, **1/2 mi W** BP, Holiday Chipotle, KFC, McDonald's BMW, Chevrolet, Goodyear/auto, Lexus, Nissan, **1 mi E off of I-394** Wendy's Barnes&Noble, Best Buy, Ford, JC Penney, Jo-Ann Fabrics,

MINNEAPOLIS

INTERSTATE 494/694 Cont'd

19b a Continued
Lunds&Byerly's Foods, Mazda, Mercedes, Office Depot, Petco, Subaru, Target, Tires+, Whole Foods

17b a Minnetonka Blvd, **E** Minnoco Gas DQ, Royal Subs

16b a MN 7, 1 mi **W** Christo's Rest., Davanni's Rest., Famous Dave's BBQ, Taco Bell Goodyear

13 MN 62, rd 62

12 Valleyview Rd, rd 39 (from sb)

11c MN 5 W, same as 11 a b

11b a US 169 S, US 212 W, **N** Don Pablo's, Jets Pizza, Subway Comfort Inn, Courtyard, Fairfield Inn, Hyatt Place, Residence Inn vet, **S** BP, Holiday Caribou Coffee, Champp's, Davanni's Rest., Jake's Grill, Leeann Chin, McDonald's, Old Chicago, Osaka Japanese, Panera Bread, Papa John's, Popeye's, Qdoba, Redstone Rest., Starbucks, Wildfire Steaks Extended Stay America, SpringHill Suites, TownePlace Suites $Tree, Barnes&Noble, Best Buy, Costco/gas, Cub Foods, Discount Tire, JC Penney, Office Depot, Petco, Target, Walgreens, Walmart

10 US 169 N, to rd 18

8 rd 28 (from wb, no return), E Bush Lake Rd, same as 7 a b

7b a MN 100, rd 34, Normandale Blvd, **N** Shell/dsl Burger King, Chili's, DQ, Jimmy John's, Starbucks, Subway, TGIFridays Days Inn, Doubletree, Sheraton, **S** Holiday/dsl El Loro Country Inn&Suites, Crowne Plaza, Hampton Inn, Hilton Garden, La Quinta, Staybridge Inn

6b rd 17, France Ave, **N** Mobil Fuddrucker's, Perkins Holiday Inn Express, Park Plaza Hotel, Residence Inn H, Marshall's, Michael's, Staples, Trader Joe's, World Mkt, **S** Denny's, Joe Senser's Grill, Olive Garden AmericInn, Hilton Buick/GMC, Hyundai, Mercedes, Toyota

6a Penn Ave (no EZ eb return), **S** Applebee's, Caribou Coffee, Jimmy John's, McDonald's, Red Robin, Starbucks, Subway, Which Wich? Embassy Suites, Home 2 Suites AT&T, Chevrolet, Chrysler/Jeep/Dodge, Fresh Thyme Mkt, Herberger's, Hobby Lobby, Kohl's, Target, TJ Maxx, Walgreens

5b a I-35W, S to Albert Lea, N to Minneapolis

4b Lyndale Ave, **N** BP, SA Boston Mkt, Chipotle Mexican, DQ, Eddie Cheng's, Noodles&Co, Papa John's, Potbelly, Sarpino's Pizza, Starbucks, Subway Candlewood Suites, Sheraton Best Buy, Honda, Lands End, PetsMart, **S** Extended Stay America Acura/Subaru, Lincoln, REI

4a MN 52, Nicollet Ave, **N** SA/dsl Taco Bell Menards, **S** Holiday/dsl Culver's, McDonald's La Quinta, Super 8 Home Depot, Sam's Club

3 Portland Ave, 12th Ave (from eb), **N** Arby's, Khan's BBQ AmericInn, **S** $Tree, Denny's, Jimmy John's, Outback Steaks, Pizza Hut, Subway Comfort Inn, Microtel, Quality Inn, Residence Inn Walgreens, Walmart/Subway

2c b MN 77, **N** Motel 6, **S** Outback Steaks Comfort Inn, Courtyard, Fairfield Inn, Hampton Inn, Hilton Garden, JW Marriott, Marriott, Northwood Inn, Radisson, Residence Inn, SpringHill Suites, TownePlace Suites IKEA, Macy's, Mall of America, Nordstrom's

2a 24th Ave, same as 2c b

1b 34th Ave, Nat Cemetary, **N** Holiday/dsl, **S** Crowne Plaza, Embassy Suites, Hilton, Hyatt Place, Hyatt Regency

1a MN 5 E, **N**

0mm Minnesota River. **I-494/I-694 loops around Minneapolis/St Paul.**

MISSISSIPPI

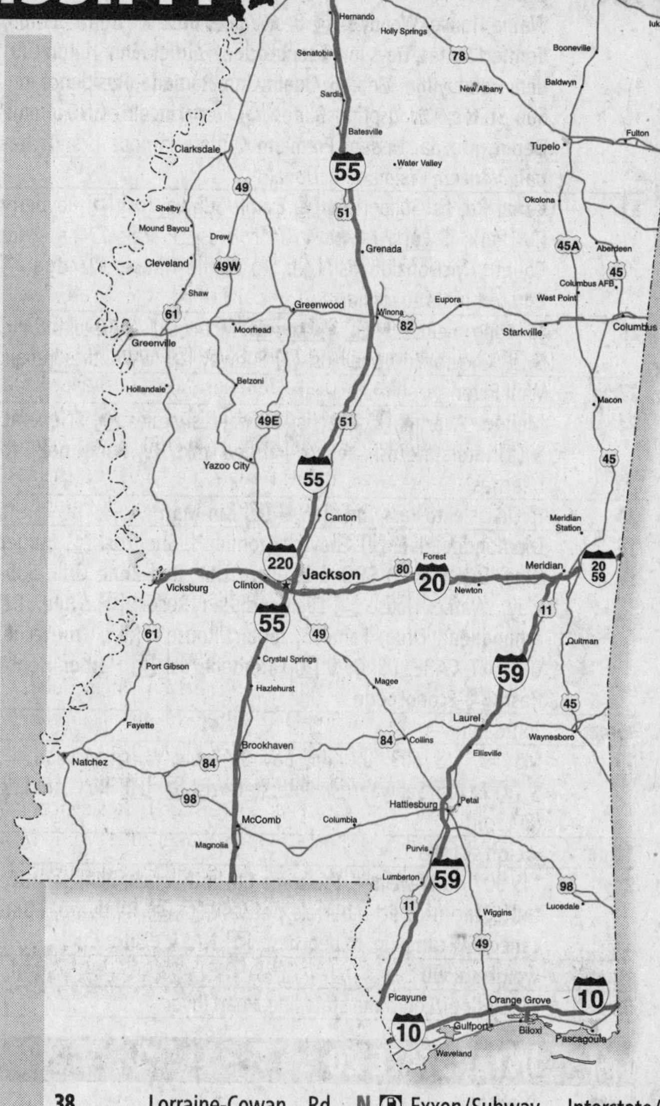

MS

INTERSTATE 10

MOSS POINT

Exit#	Services
77mm	Mississippi/Alabama state line, **weigh sta wb**
75	Franklin Creek Rd
75mm	**S Welcome Ctr wb, full facilities, litter barrels, petwalk, , , RV dump, weigh sta eb**
74mm	Escatawpa River
69	MS 63, to E Moss Point, **N** Raceway/dsl, Shell/Circle K/ Domino's/dsl/24hr Waffle House Best Value, Deluxe Inn, La Quinta, **S** Chevron/dsl/24hr, Exxon/Subway/dsl, Pilot/Moe's SW/dsl/scales/24hr, Shell Burger King, Cracker Barrel, Hardee's, KFC, McDonald's, Pizza Hut, Ruby Tuesday, San Miguel Mexican, Taco Bell, Waffle House, Wendy's Best Western, Comfort Inn, Days Inn, Hampton Inn, Holiday Inn Express, Quality Inn, Shular Inn H, Toyota
68	MS 613, to Moss Point, Pascagoula, **N** Chevron/dsl, Texaco/dsl Coco Loco Mexican, Tugus' Rest. Super 8, **S** Marathon/dsl H, Pelican Landing Conf Ctr
64mm	Pascagoula River
63.5mm	**both lanes, 24hr security, full facilities, litter barrels, petwalk, , , RV dump**
61	to Gautier, **N** MS Nat Golf Course, **1-3 mi S** Marathon/ dsl Hardee's, KFC, McDonald's, Pizza Hut, Sonic, Wendy's Best Western, Suburban Lodge Sandhill Crane WR, Shephard Camping
57	MS 57, to Vancleave, **N** Chevron/dsl/24hr Shed BBQ Journey's End Camping, tires/repair, **S** Exxon
50	MS 609 S, Ocean Springs, **N** Shell/Circle K/Domino's/ dsl Waffle House Best Western+, Country Inn&Suites, Motel 6, Quality Inn, Ramada Ltd, Red Roof Inn, Super 8 Martin Lake Camping (1mi), tires/repair, **S** Chevron/ McDonald's, Circle K/Subway/dsl, Marathon/dsl Denny's, El Rancho Mexican, Waffle House, Wendy's Comfort Suites, Days Inn, Hampton Inn, Holiday Inn Express, Quality Inn $General, Family$, Nat Seashore
46b a	I-110, MS 15 N, to Biloxi, **N** Chevron/dsl Beef O'Brady's, Beijing Chinese, Buffalo Wild Wings, Chick-fil-A, Chili's, Dickey's BBQ, Five Guys, IHOP, Logan's Roadhouse, Moe's SW Grill, Newk's Cafe, Olive Garden, Osaka Japanese, Outback Steaks, Panda Palace, Papa John's, Red Lobster, Ruby Tuesday, Salsarita 's, Samurai, Sonic, Starbucks, Subway, Waffle House, Wendy's, Whataburger, Which Wich? Courtyard, Home2 Suites, Regency Inn, Wingate Inn AT&T, Best Buy, CVS, Dick's, GNC, Kohl's, Lowe's, Marshall's, Mercedes, Michaels, NTB, Office Depot, Petsmart, Ross, Target, URGENT CARE, Verizon, vet, VW, Walgreens, Walmart, **S** H, BMW, Buick/GMC, to beaches
44	Cedar Lake Rd, to Biloxi, **N** Loves/Subway/dsl/ scales/24hr Chevrolet, **S** Circle K/dsl, Shell/dsl Applebee's, El Rey Mexican, El Saltillo, KFC/LJ Silver, McDonald's, Pop's Pizza, Sonic, Subway, Taco Bell, Waffle House La Quinta H, $General, Biloxi Nat Cem, Cedar Lake Drug, Harley-Davidson, Home Depot, O'Reilly Parts, to Jeff Davis Shrine (Beauvoir), vet
41	MS 67 N, to Woolmarket, **N** Chevron/dsl, Texaco/dsl golf (6mi), **S** Camping World, Freightliner, Mazalea RV Prk, Parkers Landing RV Prk, Southern Tire Mart
39.5mm	Biloxi River

BILOXI

GULFPORT

Exit#	Services
38	Lorraine-Cowan Rd, **N** Exxon/Subway, Interstate/dsl, Shell/Circle K/dsl Capt Al's Cafe, Domino's, McDonald's, Sonic Toyota, **S** Baywood RV Park (3mi), Foxes RV Park (8mi), to beaches
34b a	US 49, to Gulfport, **N** Circle K/dsl, Exxon, Shell/Circle K/ dsl Buffalo Wild Wings, Burger King, Cane's Chicken, Chick-fil-A, Chili's, ChuckeCheese, Cracker Barrel, Dickey's BBQ, Domino's, Firehouse Subs, Five Guys, Golden Corral, Hardee's, KFC, Krystal, Little Caesar's, Logan's Roadhouse, Longhorn Steaks, Marble Slab, McDonald's, Newk's Cafe, O'Charley's, O'Neal's PoBoy, Panda Palace, Papa John's, Pepper's Deli, Pizza Hut, Popeye's, Sicily's Italian Buffet, Sonic, Starbucks, Subway, Taco Bell, Taco Sombrero, TGIFriday's, TX Roadhouse, Waffle House, Wendy's, Whataburger Hampton Inn, Home 2 Suites, Sleep Inn H, $Tree, Advance Parts, AT&T, Barnes&Noble, Belk, Best Buy, Buick/Cadillac/Chevrolet, CVS Drug, Foley's RV Ctr, Food Giant/gas, Fred's Store, Goodyear/auto, Hobby Lobby, Honda, Michael's, NTB, Office Depot, Old Navy, Petsmart, Rite Aid, Ross, Sam's Club/dsl, TJ Maxx, URGENT CARE, USPO, Walgreens, Winn-Dixie, **S** Circle K/dsl, Murphy USA, RaceWay/ dsl, Shell/dsl Applebee's, Arby's, Burger King, Dynasty Buffet, Food Court, Hibachi Express, Hooters, IHOP, KFC/LJ Silver, Krispy Kreme, Los Tres Amigos, McAlister's Deli, McDonald's, Morelia's Mexican, Shrimp Basket, Sonic, Taco Bell, Tres Amigos,

INTERSTATE 10 Cont'd

GULFPORT

34b a Continued
Waffle House, Wendy's Best Value, Best Western, Clarion, Comfort Suites, Days Inn, EconoLodge, Fairfield Inn, Hilton Garden, Holiday Inn, Motel 6, Quality Inn, Ramada, Residence Inn, Sun Suites, Woodspring Suites Ford/Lincoln, GNC, Home Depot, Mazda, Nissan, Premium Outlets/famous brands, repair, Verizon, Walmart/McDonald's

31 Canal Rd, to Gulfport, N Exxon/Subway/dsl Bayberry RV Park, S FLYING J/Denny's/dsl/LP/scales/24hr, Pure Country/McDonald's/dsl/24hr Waffle House, Wendy's Comfort Inn, Legacy Inn

28 to Long Beach, N Loves/McDonald's/dsl/scales/24hr, S Chevron/dsl, Shell/dsl Subway NAPA, tires/repair

27mm Wolf River

24 Menge Ave, N Chevron/Subway/dsl/scales $General, S Interstate/dsl, Texaco flea mkt/RV Park, golf, to beaches

20 to De Lisle, to Pass Christian, N Kin-Mart

16 Diamondhead, N Chevron/Domino's, Shell/dsl Burger King, DQ, Fire Pit BBQ Grill, Pizza Hut, Red Zone Grill, Subway, Waffle House Diamondhead Resort $Tree, Diamondhead Drug, Family$, repair, Rouse's Mkt, TrueValue, URGENT CARE, USPO, S Giterdone/dsl Harbor House Rest. EconoLodge

15mm Jourdan River

13 MS 43, MS 603, to Kiln, Bay St Louis, N McLeod SP, S Exxon/Subway/dsl, Interstate/dsl H, RV Camping (8-13mi)

10mm **weigh sta eb**

2 MS 607, to Waveland, **Welcome Ctr both lanes, 24hr security, full facilities, litter barrels, petwalk, RV dump,** S Buccaneer SP, camping, to beaches, NASA Visitor Ctr

1mm **weigh sta wb**

0mm Mississippi/Louisiana state line, Pearl River

INTERSTATE 20

Exit# Services

172mm Mississippi/Alabama state line. **I-20 W and I-59 S run together to Meridian.**

170mm **weigh sta both lanes**

169 US 11, US 80, Kewanee, S Kewanee Trkstp/BBQ/dsl Simmons-Wright Gen Store

165 to US 11, Toomsuba, N Dee's/dsl, Sunoco/Subway, S Loves/Arby's/dsl/scales/24hr KOA (2mi)

164mm **Welcome Ctr wb, 24hr security, full facilities, litter barrels, petwalk, RV dump, vending, wi-fi**

160 to Russell, N TA/Country Pride/dsl/scales/24hr/@ Nanabe RV Camping (1mi), S Shell/dsl KOA (4mi)

157b a US 45, to Macon, Quitman

156 Jimmie Rodgers Pkwy

MERIDIAN

154b a MS 19 S, MS 39 N, Meridian, N MapleLeaf/dsl, Shell, Texaco/dsl Applebee's, Buffalo Wild Wings, Cracker Barrel, IHOP, Logan's Roadhouse, Penn's Rest, Waffle House, Western Sizzlin Days Inn, Drury Inn, Fairfield Inn, Hampton Inn, Hilton Garden, Holiday Inn, Home 2 Suites, Relax Inn, Rodeway Inn, Sleep Inn, Super 8, Super Inn, Western Motel auto repair, Back Country RV Ctr, Chrysler/Dodge/Jeep/Kia, U-Haul, S Chevron/dsl, Texaco/dsl Chick-fil-A, Chili's, CiCi's, Dickey's BBQ, Honey Baked Ham, McAlister's Deli, McDonald's, O'Charley's, Olive Garden, Outback Steaks, Popeye's,

154b a Continued
Red Lobster, Ryan's, Taco Bell Baymont Inn, Comfort Inn, Country Inn&Suites, Microtel $Tree, AT&T, Belk, Best Buy, Books-A-Million, Dillard's, Harley-Davidson, Jo-Ann Fabrics, PetCo, Ross, Sam's Club/gas, TJ Maxx, Tuesday Morning

153 MS 145 S, 22nd Ave, Meridian, N Shell, Xpress Lane Arby's, Bumper's Drive-In, Burger King, Capt D's, China Buffet, Hardee's, KFC, McDonald's, Pizza Hut, Subway, Wendy's H, $General, CarQuest, Cash Saver Foods, Ford/Nissan, Fred's, Goodyear/auto, S Exxon/dsl, Murphy USA/dsl, Texaco/dsl, Valero/dsl A&W/LJ Silver, Checkerboard Kitchen, El Norte Mexican, Waffle House Astro Motel, Budget 8 Motel, EconoLodge, Extended Suites, Hamilton Inn, Holiday Inn Express, La Quinta, Motel 6, Sleep Inn Chevrolet, Lowe's, Office Depot, Verizon, Walmart/McDonald's

MERIDIAN

152 29th Ave, 31st Ave, Meridian, N Chevron/dsl Ramada Ltd, S Royal Inn

151 James Chaney Dr, N tires, S Pilot/Subway/dsl/scales/24hr stockyards

150 US 11 S, MS 19 N, Meridian, N Exxon/dsl, Queen City Trkstp/dsl/rest./@ McDonald's, Waffle House Okatibbee Lake, RV camping, S Chevron/Stuckey's/Subway/dsl, Shell/dsl Peterbilt

130[149] I-59 S, to Hattiesburg. **I-20 E and I-59 N run together.**

129 US 80 W, Lost Gap, S Spaceway/Grill King/dsl/RV Dump/24hr

121 Chunky

119mm Chunky River

115 MS 503, Hickory

NEWTON

109 MS 15, Newton, N Shell/Jct Deli/dsl/24hr Los Parrilleros Thrifty Inn H, lube/repair, S Chevron/dsl Newton Jct/dsl, Texaco/dsl Cooks BBQ, Hardee's, KFC, Taco Bell, McDonald's, Panda Buffet, Pizza Hut, Sonic, Subway Zack's Steaks Days Inn $General, Advance Parts, AT&T AutoZone, Fred's, Piggly Wiggly, Walmart/Subway

100 US 80, Lake, Lawrence, N Marathon/rest/dsl

96 Lake, S Loves/Chester's/Subway/dsl/scales/24hr

95mm Bienville NF, eastern boundary, Bienville Nat Forest, Bienville Nat Forest

90mm **eb, 24hr security, full facilities, litter barrels, petwalk, RV dump**

FOREST

88 MS 35, Forest, N Murphy USA/dsl, Shell, Texaco/Chester's/dsl, Valero/dsl KFC, Las Parrillas Mexican, McDonald's, Popeye's, Taco Bell, Waffle House, Wendy's, Zhen's Garden Best Value Inn, Days Inn, EconoLodge, Holiday Inn Express H, $Tree, AT&T, O'Reilly Parts, Walgreens, Walmart/Subway, S Chevron/dsl/24hr Penn's Rest.

80 MS 481, Morton, S RV Camping

77 MS 13, Morton, N Exxon/McDonald's/dsl, Texaco dsl H, Green Tree RV Park (4mi), to Roosevelt SP, S Shell/Subway/dsl

76mm Bienville NF, western boundary

75mm **wb, 24hr security, full facilities, litter barrels, petwalk, RV dump**

68 MS 43, Pelahatchie, N Chevron/Subway/dsl, Texaco/rest./dsl/24hr Jellystone Camping, S Marathon/dsl

59 US 80, E Brandon, 2 mi S Shell/dsl

56 US 80, Brandon, N Shell/dsl El Potrillo Mexican, Krystal, Sonny's BBQ, Taco Bell Microtel AT&T, AutoZone, O'Reilly Parts, USPO, Verizon, S BP, Chevron, Exxon, Mac's Gas, Texaco/dsl DQ, Penn's Rest., Sonic, Waffle House, Wendy's Best Value Inn, Red Roof Inn Auto+, to Ross Barnett Reservoir, vet

INTERSTATE 20 Cont'd

Exit#	Services
	BRANDON
54	Crossgates Blvd, W Brandon, **N** [gas] Circle K/dsl, Exxon, Murphy USA [food] Abner's Chicken, Applebee's, Burger King, Chick-fil-A, China Buffet, Fernando's Fajita Factory, KFC, Little Caesar's, Mazzio's, McAlister's Deli, McDonald's, Newk's Rest, Papa John's, Pizza Hut, Popeye's, Subway, Waffle House [other] [H], $Tree, BigLots, Buick/GMC, Chevrolet, CVS Drug, Ford/Lincoln, Fred's, GNC, Kroger/dsl, Nissan, Office Depot, Piggly Wiggly, Scotty's Tire/repair, Toyota, Tuesday Morning, Walgreens, Walmart/Subway, **S** [gas] Circle K/dsl, Exxon/dsl, Mobil/Domino's/dsl [food] Steak Escape, Wendy's [lodging] La Quinta [other] Home Depot, Honda, Tire Pros
	PEARL
52	MS 475, **N** [gas] Exxon/Subway/dsl, RaceWay/dsl, Texaco/dsl [food] Waffle House [lodging] Quality Inn, Ramada, Sleep Inn, Super 8 [other] Peterbilt, to Jackson Airport
48	MS 468, Pearl, **N** [gas] Exxon/dsl, Shell/dsl, Texaco [food] Arby's, Baskin Robbins, Bumpers Drive-In, Cracker Barrel, Domino's, DQ, Dunkin Donuts, Jose's Rest., KFC, Kobe Japanese, Logan's Roadhouse, LoneStar Steaks, Los Parrilleros, McAlister's Deli, McDonald's, Mikado, Mikado Japanese, Moss Creek Fishouse, O'Charley's, Popeye's, Ruby Tuesday, Ryan's, Ryan's, Sonic, Subway, Waffle House, Wendy's [lodging] Baymont Inn, Best Western, Comfort Inn, Courtyard, Days Inn, Fairfield Inn, Hampton Inn, Hilton Garden, Holiday Inn Express, Motel 6 [other] AT&T, CarCare, **S** [gas] Exxon/dsl, Mobil/dsl [lodging] Candlewood Suites, Country Inn&Suites, La Quinta [other] $General, Family$
	JACKSON
47b a	US 49 S, Flowood, **N** [gas] FLYING J/Denny's/dsl/LP/RV dump/24hr, Loves/Subway/dsl/scales/24hr [food] Western Sizzlin [lodging] Airport Inn, Holiday Inn [other] Bass Pro Shop, MS Outlets/famous brands, Sam's Club/dsl, SpeedCo, **2-3 mi S** [gas] RaceWay/dsl [food] Waffle House [other] Freightliner, Kenworth, tires
46	I-55 N, to Memphis
45b	US 51, State St, to downtown
45a	Gallatin St, to downtown, **N** [gas] BP/dsl, Petro/Iron Skillet/dsl/scales/24hr/@, Shell [other] Blue Beacon, tires/truck repair, vet, **S** [gas] Pilot/McDonald's/dsl/scales/24hr [lodging] Hilltop Inn [other] Nissan
44	I-55 S (exits left from wb), to New Orleans
43b a	Terry Rd, **N** [gas] Exxon/dsl, Jasco [other] Apache RV Ctr
42b a	Ellis Ave, Belvidere, **N** [gas] BP, Citgo/dsl, Shell [food] Capt D's, Church's, McDonald's, Pizza Hut, Popeye's, Sonny's BBQ, Wendy's [lodging] Best Inn, Metro Inn, Scottish Inn, Super 8 [other] $Tree, Advance Parts, AutoZone, CarQuest, Family$, Firestone/auto, O'Reilly Parts, Sav-a-Lot Foods, transmissions, U-Haul, zoo, **S** [gas] Citgo/dsl, Exxon/dsl [food] DQ
41	I-220 N, US 49 N, to Jackson
40b a	MS 18 W, Robinson Rd, **N** [gas] Exxon/dsl, Jasco/dsl, Shell/dsl [food] Arby's, Krystal, Mazzio's, Piccadilly, Popeye's [other] $General, AT&T, Office Depot, USPO, **S** [gas] Chevron, Citgo/dsl, Murphy USA, RaceWay/dsl, Shell/Church's/dsl [food] Chan's Garden, IHOP, McDonald's, Subway, Waffle House, Wendy's [lodging] Quality Inn [other] [H], $Tree, GNC, Lowe's, Walmart/Subway
	CLINTON
36	Springridge Rd, Clinton, **N** [gas] Chevron/Burger King, Citgo/dsl, Murphy USA/dsl, Shell [food] Capt D's, Chick-fil-A, China Buffet, Chopstick Buffet, DQ, El Sombrero, Hungry Howie's, KFC, Kroger/dsl, Little Ceasar's, Mazzio's, McAlister's, McDonald's, Newk's Cafe, Smoothie King, Sonic, Starbucks, Subway, Taco Bell, Waffle House, Wendy's, Zaxby's [lodging] Comfort Inn, Days Inn, Fairfield Inn [other] $Tree, Advance Parts, AT&T, BigLots, CVS Drug, Family$, Fred's, Home Depot, Kroger/gas, O'Reilly Parts, Verizon, Walgreens, Walmart (2mi), **S** [gas] Exxon/Baskin-Robbins/

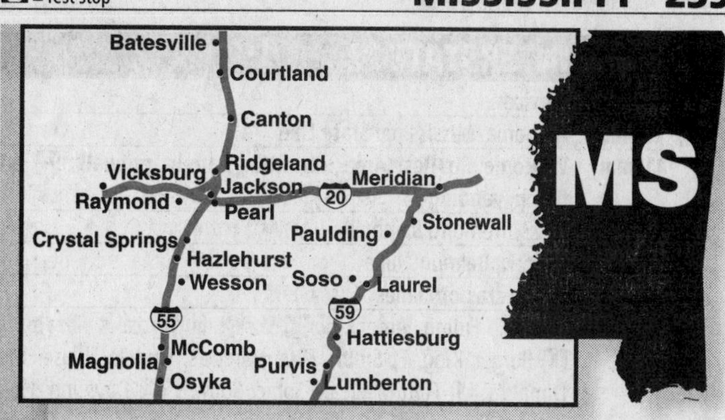

MS

Exit#	Services
36	Continued Quiznos/dsl, Valero/dsl [food] Applebee's, Bonsai, Froghead Grill, Pizza Hut, Popeye's, Salsa's Mexican, Shoney's [lodging] Best Western, Econolodge, Hampton Inn, Holiday Inn Express, Quality Inn, Super 8 [other] $General, Davis Tire, Springridge RV Park, vet
35	US 80 E, Clinton, **N** [gas] Chevron, Circle K/dsl, Shell/dsl [other] vet
34	Natchez Trace Pkwy
31	Norrell Rd
27	Bolton, **S** [gas] Chevron/dsl
19	MS 22, Edwards, Flora, **N** [other] Askew's Landing Camping (2mi), **S** [gas] Exxon/dsl, Shell/dsl [lodging] Relax Inn
17mm	Big Black River
15	Flowers
11	Bovina, **N** [gas] Exxon/Subway/dsl/24hr [other] RV camping
10mm	**weigh sta wb**
8mm	**weigh sta eb**
6.5mm	**parking area eb**
	VICKSBURG
5b a	US 61, MS 27 S, **N** [gas] Exxon/dsl, Shell/dsl [food] Sonic, **S** same as 4a
4b a	Clay St, **N** [gas] Shell [lodging] Hampton Inn, Motel 6, Super 8, Vicksburg Inn [other] [H], RV Park, to Vicksburg NP, **S** [gas] Shell/dsl, Texaco [food] Baskin Robbins, Bumper's Drive-In, China Buffet, Cracker Barrel, Little Caesar's, McAlister's deli, Pizza Inn, Rowdy's Rest., Subway, Waffle House, Wendy's [lodging] Beechwood Inn/rest., Comfort Suites, Courtyard, Econolodge, Holiday Inn Express, La Quinta, Quality Inn, Scottish Inn [other] $General, Outlet Mall/famous brands/deli, same as 5
3	Indiana Ave, **N** [gas] Shell/Subway/dsl [food] China King, McDonald's, Papa John's, Waffle House [lodging] Best Western, Deluxe Inn [other] Chevrolet, Chrysler/Dodge/Jeep, Corner Mkt Foods, Ford/Lincoln, Honda, Mazda, Nissan, Rite Aid, Toyota, **S** [gas] Shell/dsl [food] Goldie's BBQ, Heavenly Ham, KFC [lodging] Best Inn [other] Buick/Cadillac/GMC, Family$
1c	Halls Ferry Rd, **N** [gas] Exxon/dsl [food] Burger King, Sonic [lodging] Travel Inn [other] [H], CVS Drug, Durst Drugs, **S** [gas] Shell/dsl [food] Asian Kitchen, Capt D's, Chick-fil-A, DQ, El Sombrero Mexican, Garfield's Rest., Goldie's Express, Little Caesar's, Newk's Eatery, Pizza Hut, Popeye's, Shoney's, Subway, Taco Bell, Taco Casa, Wendy's, Whataburger [lodging] Candlewood Suites, Holiday Inn, Howard Johnson, Ramada Inn, Rodeway Inn [other] $General, Advance Parts, AT&T, Belk, BigLots, Dillard's, Fred's, Hobby Lobby, Home Depot, Kroger/dsl, TJ Maxx, USPO, Walgreens
1b	US 61 S, **S** [gas] Murphy Express/dsl, Shell/Domino's/dsl [food] McDonald's, Panda Buffet, Waffle House [other] $Tree, same as 1c, Verizon, Walmart/Subway
1a	Washington St, Vicksburg, **N Welcome Ctr both lanes, full [handicapped] facilities,** [phone] [gas] Shell/dsl [lodging] AmeriStar Hotel/Casino/RV Park, **S** [food] Waffle House [lodging] Best Value Inn, Days Inn
0mm	Mississippi/Louisiana state line, Mississippi River

MS

INTERSTATE 22

Exit#	Services
118mm	Alabama/Mississippi State Line
115mm	**Welcome Ctr/Rest Area wb, litter barrels, petwalk, [RV], RV dump, vending**
113	rd 23, Tremont, Smithville
108	rd 25 N, Belmont, Iuka
106mm	**weigh sta both lanes**
104	rd 25 S, Fulton, Amory, N [gas] Shell/cafe/dsl/scales, Texaco/dsl [food] Burger King, Ft Smith BBQ, Hardee's, Huddle House, McDonald's, Mi Toro Mexican, Sonic, Subway [lodging] Days Inn, Holiday Inn Express [other] $General, AutoZone, Brown's Auto Repair, Food Giant/dsl, Fred's, O'Reilly Parts, RV camping, Whitten HS, S [gas] Murphy USA/dsl [food] Peking Palace [other] AT&T, KFC, Los Compadres Mexican, Pizza Hut, URGENT CARE, Walmart, Wendy's
104mm	Tombigbee River/Tenn-Tom Waterway
101	rd 178, rd 363, Peppertown, Mantachie, N [gas] Marathon, S [gas] Dorsey Fuel/dsl (2mi)
97	Fawn Grove Rd
94	rd 371, Mantachie, Mooreville, N [gas] Woodchuck's/pizza/dsl
90	Auburn Rd, N [gas] Chevron/dsl
87	Veterans Blvd, N [gas] Shell/Chix Rest/dsl [food] Huddle House [lodging] Wingate Inn [other] E. Presley Campground/Park, S [other] Tombigbee SP
86	US 45 N, Tupelo, to Corinth, **1 exit** N [gas] Shell/dsl, Texaco, Valero [food] Abner's Rest., Applebee's, Baskin Robbins, Buffalo Wild Wings, Burger King, Capt D's, Chick-fil-A, Chili's, ChuckeCheese, Cracker Barrel, Crossroads Rib Shack, D'Casa Grill, Dickey's BBQ, Five Guys, IHOP, Kyoto Japanese, Lenny's Subs, Logan's Roadhouse, Longhorn Steaks, Margaritas Mexican, McDonald's, Mt Fuji Japanese, New China Buffet, Newk's Eatery, O'Charley's, Olive Garden, Pizza Hut, Pizza Pro, Red Lobster, Ryan's, Sake Japanese, Sonic, Subway, Taco Bell, Thai Garden, Waffle House, Wendy's [lodging] Best Inn, Best Western, Econolodge, Fairfield Inn, Hampton Inn [other] $Tree, AT&T, AutoZone, Barnes&Noble, Belk, Best Buy, CarMax, Dick's, Ford/Lincoln, Hobby Lobby, Home Depot, Hyundai, JC Penney, Jo-Ann, Kohl's, Kroger/gas, Lowe's, Mazda, Midas, NAPA, Nissan, Old Navy, Petsmart, Ross, Sam's Club/gas, Staples, TJ Maxx, Toyota, Tuesday Morning, URGENT CARE, Verizon, Walgreens, Walmart
85	Natchez Trace Pkwy
82	Barnes Crossing Rd, Coley Rd
81	rd 178, McCullough Blvd, N [gas] Loves/McDonald's/dsl/scales/24hr [lodging] Best Value Inn, S [gas] Exxon/dsl, Shell/dsl [food] Old Venice Pizza, Sonic [lodging] Super 8 [other] $General, USPO
76	rd 9 S, Sherman, Pontotoc, N [gas] Wild Bill's/dsl [other] Sherman RV Ctr
73	rd 9 N, to Magnolia Way, Blue Springs
64	rd 15, rd 30 E, Pontotoc, Ripley, N [gas] Eagle/dsl, S [gas] Circle K/dsl, Pilot/Arby's/scales/dsl/24hr
63	New Albany, N [gas] Dee's Oil/dsl [other] Buick/Chevrolet/GMC, Ford
62mm	Tallahatchie River
61	rd 30 W, W New Albany, N [gas] Dee's [food] China Buffet, Cracker Barrel, McAlister's Deli, McDonald's, Pizza Hut, Subway, Waffle House, Wendy's [lodging] Hampton Inn [other] [H], Rite Aid, Walgreens, S [gas] Exxon, Murphy USA/dsl, Shell [food] Burger King, Capt D's, Domino's, El Agave Mexican, Huddle House, KFC, Mi Pueblo Mexican, Taco Bell, Zaxby's [lodging] Comfort Inn, Economy Inn, Hallmarc Inn, Holiday Inn Express [other] $Tree, AT&T, Lowe's, to U of MS, Verizon, Walmart
60	Glenfield, to Oxford, N [gas] Pure [lodging] Budget Inn [other] Tire Pros, S [other] to U of MS
55	Myrtle
48	rd 178, Hickory Flat, S [gas] Exxon/Trkstp/rest/dsl/24hr
41	rd 346, Potts Camp, S [gas] Flicks/dsl [other] $General, NAPA
41mm	Tippah River
37	Lake Center, N [other] Chewalla Lake/RV camping
30	rd 7, rd 4, Holly Springs, Oxford, N [gas] Exxon, Shell/Chester's/BBQ [food] Burger King, Domino's, El Nopalito, Huddle House, KFC, Little Caesar's, McDonalds, Panda Buffet, Pizza Hut, Popeye's, Sonic, Subway, Taco Bell, Wendy's [lodging] Magnolia Inn [other] $General, AT&T, AutoZone, Liddy's Drug, O'Reilly Parts, Save-a-Lot, Wall Doxey SP/RV camping, S [gas] Shell/dsl [lodging] Days Inn, Quality Inn [other] Walmart
26	W Holly Springs
21	Red Banks, N [gas] Dee's Oil/dsl, Texaco/dsl
18	Victoria, E Byhalia, N [gas] Marathon/dsl, S [gas] Victoria/dsl
14	rd 309, Byhalia, N [gas] BP/dsl, Shell/dsl [lodging] Best Value Inn [other] Autozone, Fred's
12	I-269, MS 304
10	W Byhalia, N [gas] Marathon/dsl
6	Bethel Rd, Hacks Crossroad, N [gas] FLYING J/Subway//dsl/scales/LP/RV dump/24hr, BP, Exxon/Baskin Robbins/dsl [food] JR's Grill, Rancho Grande, Tops BBQ [lodging] Best Western+, Super 8 [other] truck repair, S [other] [H]
4	rd 305, Olive Branch, Independence, N [gas] BP/dsl, Shell/Circle K, Valero/Huddle House [food] DQ, Old Style BBQ, Pizza Hut [lodging] Holiday Inn Express [other] $General, Piggly Wiggly, USPO, S [gas] Exxon/dsl [other] CVS Drug
3.5mm	**weigh sta both lanes**
2	rd 302, Olive Branch, N [gas] Murphy Express/dsl [food] Abbay's Rest., Baskin-Robbins, Buffalo Wild Wings, Chick-fil-A, Chili's, Colton's Steaks, IHOP, Krystal, Lenny's Subs, McAlisters Deli, Mis Pueblos Mexican, O'Charley's, Starbucks, Wendy's [lodging] Candlewood Suites, Comfort Suites [other] $Tree, Ford, Home Depot, Lowe's, Verizon, Walmart/Subway, Hilton Garden, S [gas] Chevron/dsl, Shell/Circle K [food] Applebees, Backyard Burger, Burger King, Casa Mexicana, Honeybaked Ham, Hunan Chinese, McDonald's, Panera Bread, Papa John's, Steak Escape, Subway, Taco Bell, Waffle House, Zaxby's [lodging] Comfort Inn, Hampton Inn, Home 2 Suites [other] AutoZone, CVS Drug, GNC, Goodyear/auto, Kroger/dsl, Petco
1	Craft Rd, N [lodging] Candlewood Suites [other] Camping World RV Ctr, Chevrolet, Hyundai
0mm	Mississippi/Tennessee state line, **I-22 begins/ends. US 78 continues wb.**

CORINTH

OLIVE BRANCH

INTERSTATE 55

Exit#	Services
291.5mm	Mississippi/Tennessee state line
291	State Line Rd, Southaven, E [gas] Exxon, RaceWay/dsl, Shell/dsl [food] Interstate BBQ, Little Caesar's, Subway, Tops BBQ, Waffle House [lodging] Days Inn, Quality Inn, Southern Inn, Super 8 [other] Family$, Firestone/auto, Goodyear/auto, Kroger/dsl, Southaven RV Park, Walgreens, W [gas] Exxon, Valero [food] Capt D's, Checker's, Dale's Rest., El Patron Mexican, Lucky China, Sonic, Taco Bell, Wendy's [other] BigLots, Fred's, Mainstreet Automotive, Rite Aid, tires, USPO, Walgreens
289	MS 302, to US 51, Horn Lake, E [gas] BP/Circle K, Shell/Circle K [food] Abbays Rest., Backyard Burger, Baskin-Robbins, Buffalo Wild Wings, Burger King, Chick-fil-A, Chili's, Dunkin Donuts, Fazoli's, Firehouse Subs, Five Guys, Five Guys, Fox&Hound, Huey's Rest., IHOP, Jimmy John's, Jimmy John's, Krystal, Kublai Khan, Lenny's Subs, Logan's Roadhouse, Longhorn Steaks

SOUTHAVEN

INTERSTATE 55 Cont'd

289 Continued
McDonald's, Mi Pueblo, Nagoya Japanese, Naru Japanese, Newk's Eatery, O'Charley's, Olive Garden, On-the-Border, Outback Steaks, Red Lobster, Sonic, Starbucks, Steak'n Shake, Subway, Swanky's Tacos, Swanky's Tacos, TGIFriday's, Wendy's, Wing Stop, Wing Stop Candlewood Suites, Candlewood Suites, Comfort Suites, Courtyard, Fairfield Inn, Hampton Inn, Hilton Garden, Holiday Inn, Holiday Inn Express, Holiday Inn Express, Home2Suites, Homewood Suites, Residence Inn H, $Tree, Advance Parts, Aldi Foods, AT&T, Best Buy, Books-A-Million, Buick/GMC, Chevrolet, Chrysler/Dodge/Jeep, CVS Drug, Dillard's, Discount Tire, Discount Tire, Ford, GNC, Gordman's, JC Penney, Jo-Ann Fabrics, Lowe's, Marshall's, Nissan, Office Depot, Old Navy, PetCo, Sam's Club/gas, Tuesday Morning, URGENT CARE, Verizon, Walmart/Subway, **W** BP/Circle K, Phillips 66/dsl, Shell/Circle K/dsl Applebee's, Arby's, ChuckECheese's, Country Home Buffet, Cracker Barrel, Grand Buffet, Hardee's, Hardee's, Hooters, KFC, McDonald's, Memphis BBQ, Papa John's, Pizza Hut, Popeye's, Starbucks, Starbucks, Taco Bell, TX Roadhouse, Waffle House, Wendy's, Zaxby's Best Value Inn, Best Value Inn, Best Western, Comfort Inn, Drury Inn, EconoLodge, La Quinta, Motel 6, Sleep Inn CVS Drug, Family$, Gateway Tires/repair, Home Depot, Kroger, Meineke, Save-a-Lot Foods, Target, Walgreens

287 Church Rd, **E** Citgo/dsl Area 50 Grill, Domino's AutoZone, Tanger Outlets/famous brands, **W** Citgo/dsl, Mapco/dsl/deli, Shell/Circle K/dsl Boiling Point Seafood, Casa Mexicana, Dixie Queen, McDonald's, Sonic, Subway, Taco Bell, Three Guys Pizza, Waffle House Homegate Inn, Magnolia Inn El Daze RV Camping (1mi), Family$, Fred's, Harley-Davidson, Jellystone Camping, Southaven RV Ctr, Walgreens

285mm **weigh sta both lanes**

284 to US 51, Nesbit Rd, **W** Shell Happy Daze Dairybar USPO

283 I-69, MS 304, Tunica

280 MS 304, US 51, Hernando, **E** Exxon, Murphy USA/dsl Arby's, Buon Cibo, Capt D's, Domino's, Fins Grill, Guadalajara Mexican, KFC, Royal Buffet, Sonic, Steak Escape, Taco Bell, Zaxby's Days Inn, Hampton Inn $Tree, AT&T, GNC, Ultimate Tires/repair, URGENT CARE, Walgreens, Walmart/Subway, **W** Mobil, Shell/Circle K/dsl Brick Oven Rest., Coleman's BBQ, Lenny's Subs, Little Caesar's, McDonald's, Mi Pueblo, Mr Chen's, Papa John's, Pizza Hut, Subway, Taco Felix, Waffle House, Wendy's Super 8 AutoZone, Bryant Repair, Desoto Museum, Fred's, Kroger/gas, NAPA, to Arkabutla Lake, USPO, vet

279mm **Welcome Ctr sb, 24hr security, full facilities, litter barrels, petwalk, , , RV dump**

276mm **nb, 24hr security, full facilities, litter barrels, petwalk, , , RV dump**

273mm Coldwater River

271 MS 306, Coldwater, **W** Shell/dsl Subway Lake Arkabutla, Memphis S RV Park

265 MS 4, Senatobia, **W** Marathon/dsl, Pilot/Huddle House/dsl/scales/24hr, Shell/dsl Applebee's, Coleman's BBQ, Domino's, Hardee's, KFC, McDonald's, New China Buffet, Pizza Hut, Popeye's, Rio Lindo Mexican, Sonic, Subway, Taco Bell, Waffle House, Wendy's, Zaxby's Best Value Inn, Magnolia Inn H, CarQuest, Fred's, Kaye Mkt, USPO

263 rd 740, S Senatobia

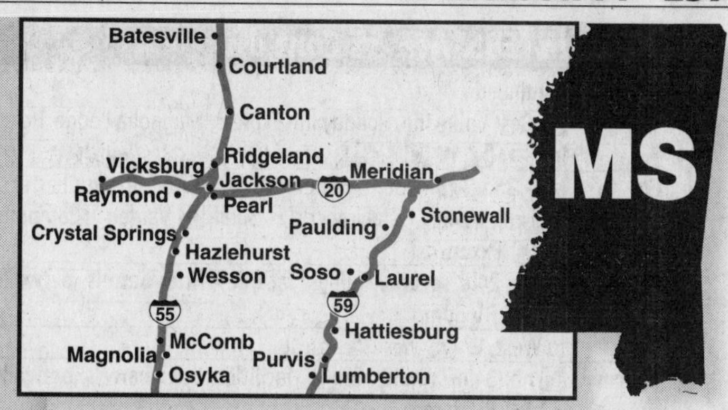

MS

BATESVILLE

257 MS 310, Como, **E** N Sardis Lake, **W** Citgo/dsl Windy City Grille (1mi) $General

252 MS 315, Sardis, **E** Chevron/dsl, Local/dsl McDonald's Lake Inn, Rodeway Inn NAPA, repair, RV camping, Sardis Dam, to Kyle SP, **W** BP/Subway/dsl, Shell/dsl Sonic $General, Fred's

246 MS 35, N Batesville, **E** to Sardis Lake, **W** Loves/McDonald's/Subway/dsl/scales/24hr, Shell/dsl

243b a MS 6, to Batesville, **E** Marathon/dsl, Mobil/dsl, Murphy USA/dsl, RaceWay/dsl Backyard Burger, Chili's, Mi Pueblo Mexican, Zaxby's Comfort Suites, Home 2 Suites H, $Tree, Lowe's, to Sardis Lake, to U of MS, Walmart/Subway, **W** BP, Exxon/dsl, Phillips 66/dsl, Shell/dsl Burger King, Burn's BBQ, Cafe Ole, Capt D's, Cracker Barrel, Domino's, Hardee's, Huddle House, KFC, Little Caesar's, McDonald's, New China, Pizza Hut, Popeye's, Sonic, Subway, Taco Bell, Waffle House, Wendy's, Yamato Hibachi Best Value Inn, Days Inn, EconoLodge, Hampton Inn, Holiday Inn $General, AT&T, AutoZone, Factory Stores/famous brands, Family$, Fred's, Kroger/dsl, O'Reilly Parts, Piggly Wiggly, Save-a-Lot, URGENT CARE, USPO, Walgreens

240mm **both lanes, 24hr security, full facilities, litter barrels, petwalk, , , RV dump**

237 to US 51, Courtland, **E** Pure/dsl, **W** $General

233 to Enid Dam, **E** RV camping, to Enid Lake

227 MS 32, Oakland, **E** to Cossar SP, **W** Sayle/Baskin Robbins/dsl, Shell/dsl Country Catfish $General

220 MS 330, Tillatoba, **E** Conoco/rest./dsl/@

211 MS 7 N, to Coffeeville, **E** Frog Hollow RV Park, **W** Exxon/Aunt M's/dsl, Marathon/dsl

208 Papermill Rd, **E** Monroe's/Chester's/dsl/scales Grenada Airport

GRENADA

206 MS 8, MS 7 S, to Grenada, **E** Exxon/dsl, Shell/dsl, Sprint Applebee's, China Buffet, Church's, Great Wall Chinese, Jake&Rip's Catfish, La Cabana Mexican, Little Caesar's, McAlister's Deli, McDonald's, No Way Jose, Pizza Hut, Pizza Inn, Shoney's, Simply Southern Cafe, Subway, Taco Bell, Wendy's Baymont Inn, Best Value Inn, EconoLodge, Grenada Inn, Hampton Inn, Holiday Inn Express, Knights Inn, Relax Inn, Rodeway Inn H, $General, $Tree, Advance Parts, AT&T, AutoZone, Chevrolet, CVS Drug, GNC, O'Reilly Parts, SaveALot, to Grenada Lake/RV camping, Walmart/McDonald's, **W** Exxon/Huddle House, Sayle/Baskin Robbins/dsl Waffle House Comfort Inn, Hilltop Inn Ford/Lincoln, Nissan, Toyota

199 Troutt Rd, S Grenada, **E** to camp McCain

195 MS 404, Duck Hill, **E** to Camp McCain, **W** Conoco/dsl

185 US 82, Winona, **E** Exxon, Shell/Kangaroo/Little Caesar's/dsl HuddleHouse, KFC, McDonald's, Sonic, Subway, Waffle House

MS

INTERSTATE 55 Cont'd

185 Continued
Best Value Inn, Holiday Inn Express, Magnolia Lodge, Relax Inn H, W Pilot/Taco Bell/dsl/scales/24hr/@

174 MS 35, MS 430, Vaiden, E 35-55 Trkstp/Chester's/dsl/scales/24hr, Chevron/dsl, Shell Vaiden Camping, W Exxon/dsl

173mm sb, 24hr security, full facilities, litter barrels, petwalk, RV dump

164 to West, W West Trkstp/dsl

163mm nb, 24hr security, full facilities, litter barrels, petwalk, RV dump

156 MS 12, Durant, E Shell/Chester's/dsl Subway Durant Motel/rest. (3mi), Oak Tree Inn, W H (7mi)

150 E Holmes Co SP, RV camping

146 MS 14, Goodman, W to Little Red Schoolhouse

144 MS 17, to Pickens, W Marathon/Baskin-Robbins/dsl/24hr to Little Red Schoolhouse

139 MS 432, to Pickens

133 Vaughan

128mm Big Black River

124 MS 16, to N Canton

CANTON

119 MS 22, to MS 16 E, Canton, E Exxon, Kangaroo/Subway/dsl, Marathon/dsl, Shell/Domino's, Valero/dsl El Sombrero Mexican, McDonald's, Pizza Hut, Popeye's, Sonic, Waffle House, Wendy's Best Value Inn, Best Western, Econolodge, Hampton Inn, Holiday Inn Express, La Quinta, Relax Inn, Super 8 H, $General Mkt, Family$, Nissan, O'Reilly Parts, to Ross Barnett Reservoir, W Chevron/KFC/dsl, Citgo, Love's/Arby's/dsl/scales/24hr/@, Texaco/Penn's/dsl Bumpers Drive-In, Two Rivers Steaks Walmart

118a b Nissan Parkway, E to Nissan

114a b Sowell Rd

112 US 51, Gluckstadt, E Exxon/Krystal/dsl Sonic Super 8 Goodyear/auto, W Shelk/Pizza Hut/dsl Camper Corral RV Ctr, vet

MADISON

108 MS 463, Madison, E Kangaroo/Mobil/dsl, Shell/dsl Applebee's, Backyard Burger, Burger King, Chick-Fil-A, Chili's, Corner Bakery Café, Dickey's BBQ, El Potrillo, Jimmy John's, La Guadalupe Mexican, Little Caesar's, Longhorn Steaks, Subway $Tree, AT&T, Best Buy, Dick's, GNC, Lowe's, Michael's, Office Depot, PetCo, SteinMart, Walmart, W Exxon/KFC/dsl BoneFish Grill, KFC, Nagoya Japanese, Papito's Grill, Pizza Inn, Schlotsky's, Subway, Tay's BBQ, Wendy's Hilton Garden CVS Drug, Home Depot, Kroger, Walgreens

107 Colony Park Blvd, Madison Ave, E Sam's Club/dsl

105c b Old Agency Rd, E Chevron/dsl Home2Suites Honda, Hyundai, W Biaggi's Ristorante, Five Guys, Panera Bread, PF Changs, Ruth's Chris Steaks, Smoothie King, Starbucks Hyatt Place Barnes&Noble, Fresh Mkt Foods, GNC

105a Natchez Trace Pkwy

104 I-220, to W Jackson

103 County Line Rd, E Chevron, Exxon/dsl, Murphy Express/dsl Bop's Custard, Bulldog Grill, Burgers&Blues Cafe, Cane's, Chick-fil-A, ChuckECheese's, Drago's Rest., Fortune Chinese, Grand China, HoneyBaked Ham, Jason's Deli, KFC, King Buffet, Krispy Kreme, Papito's Grill, Pizza Hut, Popeye's, Taco Bell, Wendy's, Whataburger, Zaxby's Cabot Lodge, Courtyard, Days Inn, EconoLodge, Extended Stay America, Hilton, Quality Inn, Red Roof Inn, Staybridge Suites $Tree, Acura, Belk, BigLots, Cadillac, Dillard's, JC Penney, Lowe's, Marshall's, Old Navy, Ross, TJ Maxx, to Barnett Reservoir, Tuesday Morning,

103 Continued
Verizon, Walmart, W Logan's Roadhouse, Nagoya Japanese, Olive Garden, Red Lobster, Subway Drury Inn, Holiday Inn Express, Motel 6 Home Depot, Jo-Ann Fabrics, Petsmart, Target, Upton Tire

102b Beasley Rd, Adkins Blvd, E Sunoco Cracker Barrel, Outback Steaks, Twin Peaks Rest. Super 8 Chevrolet, Ford, Nissan, Toyota, W Shell/dsl, Texaco/dsl Baskin-Robbins, Burger King, Chili's, Fuddrucker's, IHOP, Luby's, McDonald's, Waffle House Baymont Inn, Comfort Inn, Extended Stay America, Fairfield Inn, Howard Johnson, InTown Suites, La Quinta CarMax, Chrysler/Dodge/Jeep, frontage rds access 102a, Mercedes, Save-A-Lot Foods

102a Briarwood, E Rodeway Inn Buick/GMC, W Capt D's, Popeye's Clarion Chrysler/Dodge/Jeep, Porsche

100 North Side Dr W, E Chevron, Marathon/dsl, Sprint Burger King, Char Rest., McAlister's Deli, Papa John's, Piccadilly's, Pizza Hut, Starbucks, Subway, Wendy's Extended Stay America $Tree, Audi, Books-A-Million, CVS Drug, Firestone/auto, Goodyear/auto, Jaguar/LandRover, Kroger/dsl, Office Depot, SteinMart, Verizon, vet, VW, Walgreens, Whole Foods Mkt, W Exxon/dsl, FastLane, Shell Domino's, Hooters, Waffle House Select Motel, USA Inn

JACKSON

99 Meadowbrook Rd, Northside Dr E (from nb), E Newk's Eatery

98c b MS 25 N, Lakeland Dr, E Shell/dsl Parkside Inn LaFleur's Bluff SP, museum, W H,

98a Woodrow Wilson Dr (exits left from nb), downtown

96c Fortification St, E Studio 6 Suites, W H, Bellhaven College

96b High St, Jackson, E BMW, Chevrolet, Infiniti, Lexus W Exxon/Subway/dsl, Valero/Kangaroo/dsl Arby's Chimneyville Cafe, Domino's, Popeye's, Taco Bell, Waffle House Wendy's, Whataburger Best Value Inn, Best Western, Comfort Inn, Hampton Inn, Holiday Inn Express, Red Roof Inn, Regency Hotel H, fairgrounds, Honda, museum, st capitol Subaru/Volvo

96a Pearl St (from nb), Jackson, W access to same as 96b, downtown

94 (46 from nb), I-20 E, to Meridian, US 49 S

45b[I-20] US 51, State St, N Marathon, Petro/Iron Skillet/dsl scales/24hr, Shell, S Pilot/McDonald's/dsl/scales/24hr to downtown

45a Gallatin St (from sb), W Blue Beacon, N Marathon, Petro/Iron Skillet/dsl/scales/24hr, Shell, S Pilot/McDonald's dsl Nissan

92c (44 from sb), I-20 W, to Vicksburg, US 49 N

92b US 51 N, State St, Gallatin St

92a McDowell Rd, 1 mi E Petro/Iron Skillet/dsl/scales/24hr Pilot/McDonald's/dsl, W Citgo/dsl, Exxon, Marathon dsl, Shell McDonald's, Waffle House Family$, Food Depot, Fred's, Rite Aid, Roses

90b Daniel Lake Blvd (from sb), W Shell Harley-Davidson

90a Savanna St, E transmissions, W Gas Caney Creek RV Ctr

88 Elton Rd, W Exxon/dsl, Shell/Subway/dsl Camping World RV Ctr

85 Byram, E Blue Sky/dsl, Hungry Jack's/dsl Daddio's BBQ Krystal, Mexican Grill Comfort Inn, ValuePlace Swinging Bridge RV Park, W Byram/dsl, Chevron/dsl, Exxon/dsl Mobil/Kangaroo/dsl Backyard Burger, Burger King, Capt D's, Domino's, KFC, Mazzio's, McAlister's Deli, McDonald's, New China, Newk's Eatery, Papa John's, Pizza Hut, Popeye's, Sonic Subway, Taco Bell, Waffle House, Wendy's Best Value Inn

INTERSTATE 55 Cont'd

Exit	Services
85	Continued Holiday Inn Express $General, AutoZone, Family$, Mkt Place Foods, NAPA, O'Reilly Parts, Tire Depot, Walgreens, Walmart/Subway
81	Wynndale Rd, E repair, W Chevron/dsl/24hr
78	Terry, E Citgo/dsl, Texaco/Subway/dsl Buick/Chevrolet/GMC (1mi), Fred's, USPO, W Quick Trip $General
72	MS 27, Crystal Springs, E Exxon/Subway/dsl, Phillips 66/dsl Louise's Pit BBQ, McDonald's, Popeye's Ford
68	to US 51, S Crystal Springs, E gas/dsl Red Barn Produce, vet
65	to US 51, Gallman, E Stuckey's/dsl
61	MS 28, Hazlehurst, E Exxon/Circle K/Subway/dsl, Murphy Express/dsl, Phillips 66/dsl Burger King, KFC/Taco Bell, Los Parrilleros, McDonald's, Pizza Hut, Sonic, Waffle House, Wendy's Best Value Inn, Rodeway Inn, Western Inn H, $General, $Tree, Advance Parts, AT&T, Family$, Fred's, Piggly Wiggly, SaveALot, Verizon, Walgreens, Walmart
59	to S Hazlehurst
56	to Martinsville
54mm	**both lanes, 24hr security, full facilities, litter barrels, petwalk, , , RV dump, vending**
51	to Wesson, E Lake Lincoln SP, W Texaco/Country Jct Trkstp/dsl/rest.
48	Mt Zion Rd, to Wesson
42	to US 51, N Brookhaven, E Exxon/Subway, Shell/Gridiron Grill/dsl/scales/24hr H, W Super 8
40	to MS 550, Brookhaven, E Blue Sky, Exxon/Subway, Marathon/Domino's/dsl, Murphy USA/dsl, Shell/dsl Bowie BBQ, Burger King, China Buffet, Cracker Barrel, DQ, El Dorado Mexican, Hudgey's Rest., KFC, Krystal, Little Caesar's, Little Tokyo, Los Parrilleros, McDonald's, Mitchell's Steaks, Pizza Hut, Popeye's, Sonic, Taco Bell, Waffle House, Wards Burgers, Wendy's Best Value Inn, Comfort Inn, Hampton Inn, Holiday Inn Express, Lincoln Inn, Rodeway Inn, Spanish Inn H, $General, $Tree, AT&T, AutoZone, Buick/Cadillac/Chevrolet/GMC, CarQuest, Family$, Ford/Lincoln, Fred's, Gene's Tires, GNC, Honda, Nissan, O'Reilly Parts, Rite Aid, Save-A-Lot Foods, Toyota, Walgreens, Walmart/Subway, W IHOP Home Depot
38	US 84, S Brookhaven, W Chevron/dsl/24hr
30	Bogue Chitto, Norfield, E Shell/BogueChitto/dsl
24	Johnston Station, E to Lake Dixie Springs
20b a	US 98 W, to Natchez, Summit, E Marathon/dsl, Shell/dsl, Stop'n Shop/dsl, W Exxon/Subway/dsl, ShawnMart/dsl
18	MS 570, Smithdale Rd, N McComb, E Marathon, Murphy USA/dsl Burger King, McDonald's, Piccadilly's, Ruby Tuesday Holiday Inn Express H, AT&T, Belk, Hobby Lobby, JC Penney, Kia, Lowe's, Walgreens, Walmart/Subway, W Chevron/Mr Whiskers/dsl Applebee's, Arby's, El Dorado Mexican, Santa Fe Steaks Comfort Inn, Deerfield Inn, Hampton Inn Ford/Lincoln
17	Delaware Ave, McComb, E Blue Sky, Chevron/dsl, Exxon/Penn's Rest., Marathon/Subway/dsl, Pump&Savor Burger King, Domino's, Golden Corral, Kyoto Steaks, Little Caesar's, Pizza Hut, Popeye's, Smoothie King, Sonic, Taco Bell, Tortillo Soup, Waffle House, Wendy's Best Western, Quality Inn H, $General, AutoZone, Chrysler/Dodge/Jeep, CVS Drug, Family$, Fred's, Kroger, McComb Mkt, Office Depot, O'Reilly Parts, Rite Aid, Verizon, W Days Inn
15b a	US 98 E, MS 48 W, McComb, 1 mi E Citgo/dsl, Exxon/Subway, Presley QuikStop/dsl, Pump&Savor, Shell Church's, KFC

BROOKHAVEN

MCCOMB

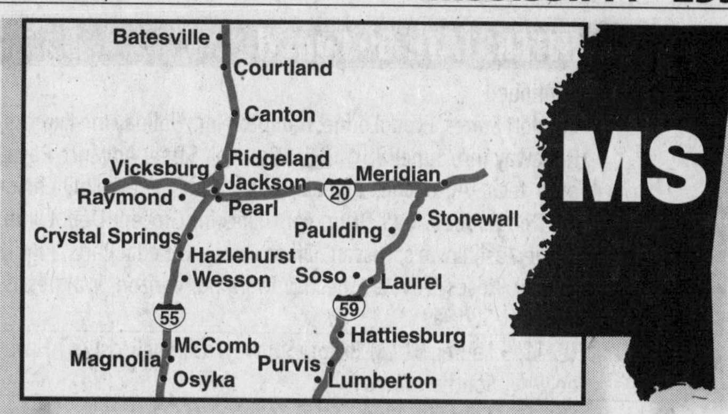

Exit	Services
15b a	Continued Camellian Motel $General, $Tree, Advance Parts, Family$, tires, vet, $Tree, W Marathon/dsl
13	Fernwood Rd, E truck repair, W Loves/Chester's/McDonald's/dsl/scales/24hr/@ golf, to Percy Quin SP
10	MS 48, Magnolia, 1 mi E Exxon/Subway/dsl, Marathon, Shell/dsl RV camping, Marathon
8	MS 568, Magnolia
4	Chatawa
3mm	**Welcome Ctr nb, 24hr security, full facilities, litter barrels, petwalk, , , RV dump**
2mm	**weigh sta nb**
1	MS 584, Osyka, Gillsburg
0mm	Mississippi/Louisiana state line

INTERSTATE 59

Exit#	Services
172mm	Mississippi/Alabama state line
I-59 S and I-20 W run together to Meridian. See I-20, exits 170mm-150.	
142	to US 11, Savoy, W to Dunns Falls
137	to N Enterprise, to Stonewall
134	MS 513, S Enterprise, E FastStop
126	MS 18, to Rose Hill, Pachuta, E BB/dsl, Pachuta TP/dsl
118	to Vossburg, Paulding
113	MS 528, to Heidelberg, E Chevron/dsl/24hr, Exxon/Subway/dsl, Shell Ward's Burgers
109mm	**litter barrels, no restrooms, parking area sb**
106mm	**litter barrels, no restrooms, parking area nb**
104	Sandersville
99	US 11, E Sleepy Hollow RV Park (1mi)
97	US 84 E, E Exxon/Huddle House/dsl/scales, Kangaroo/Subway/dsl Hardee's, Ward's Burgers, W Shell KFC, Vic's Rest.
96b	MS 15 S, Cook Ave
96a	Masonite Rd, 4th Ave
95d	(from nb)
95c	Beacon St, Laurel, W Burger King, Church's, McDonald's, Panda Chinese, Popeye's TownHouse Motel $General, Family$, Firestone/auto, Grocery Depot, H, JC Penney, museum of art, NAPA, USPO, Winn-Dixie
95b a	US 84 W, MS 15 N, 16th Ave, Laurel, 0-2 mi W Alliance/dsl, Chevron, Exxon/dsl, Murphy Express/dsl, Pure, Shell Applebee's, Arby's, Buffalo Wild Wings, Buffet City, Buffet Palace, Burger King, Cane's, Capt D's, Checkers, China Town, China Wok, Dickey's BBQ, Domino's, DQ, Eatza Pizza, Hardee's, IHOP, KFC, Laredo Grill, Little Caesar's, McDonald's, Mi Casita, Panda Express, Papa John's, Pizza Hut, Popeye's, Shipley's Donuts, Shoney's, Sonic, Subway, Sweet Peppers Deli, Taco Bell, Tokyo Grill, Waffle House, Ward's Burgers, Wendy's Best Western,

LAUREL

INTERSTATE 59 Cont'd

LAUREL

95b a Continued
Comfort Suites, EconoLodge, Hampton Inn, Holiday Inn Express, Rodeway Inn, Super 8 [O] [H], $General, $Tree, Advance Parts, auto tech, AutoZone, BigLots, Buick/GMC, Chevrolet, Chrysler/Dodge/Jeep, CVS Drug, Ford/Lincoln, Grocery Depot, Kia, Kroger/dsl, Lowe's, Nissan, Office Depot, O'Reilly Parts, Piggly Wiggly, Roses, Toyota, Tuesday Morning, Verizon, Walgreens, Walmart/Subway

93 US 11, S Laurel, W [gas] Exxon/Subway/dsl, Shell/dsl [food] Hardee's [O] Southern Tires

90 US 11, Ellisville Blvd, E [gas] Texaco/dsl [food] Huddle House, W [gas] Valero/dsl

88 MS 588, MS 29, Ellisville, E [gas] Chevron/dsl/24hr, Fast Mkt/dsl, Keith's/dsl [food] Domino's, KFC, Little Caesar's, McDonald's, Pizza Hut, Sonic, Subway, Ward's Burgers [O] $General, AutoZone, CashSaver, Ellisville Drug, Family$, NAPA, O'Reilly Parts, W [gas] Shell/dsl [lodging] Best Western

85 MS 590, to Ellisville

80 to US 11, Moselle, E [gas] Chevron/dsl/24hr

78 Sanford Rd

76 W [O] to Hattiesburg-Laurel Reg Airport

73 Monroe Rd, to Monroe

69 MS 42 E, Gandy Pkwy, to Petal, Eatonville

HATTIESBURG

67b a US 49, Hattiesburg, E [gas] Clark's/dsl, Exxon, Shell, Texaco, Valero/Kangaroo/dsl/scales [food] Arby's, Burger King, Cracker Barrel, DQ, Krystal, McDonald's, Waffle House [lodging] Budget Inn, Clarion, EconoLodge, Executive Inn, Motel 6, Quality Inn, Red Carpet Inn, Sleep Inn, Sunset Inn, Super 8 [O] $General, Hattiesburg Cycles, W [gas] Chevron, MapleLeaf/dsl, Pure/dsl, Shell/Subway, Stuckey's Express/dsl, Texaco [food] Sonic, Waffle House, Ward's Burgers, Wendy's [lodging] Candlewood Suites, Holiday Inn, Northgate Inn [O] URGENT CARE

65b a US 98 W, Hardy St, Hattiesburg, E [gas] JR Mart, Shell/dsl [food] Applebee's, Baskin Robbins, Bop's Custard, Buffalo Wild Wings, Cane's, Checkers, Chinese Express, CiCi's Pizza, Domino's, Ed's Burger Joint, Firehouse Subs, IHOP, Izzo's Pizza, Jimmy John's, Kobe Japanese, Lenny's Subs, Little Caesar's, McDonald's, Papa John's, Pizza Hut, Purple Parrot Cafe, Qdoba, Smoothie King, Starbucks, Subway, Tabella Italian, Taco Bell, Ward's Burgers [lodging] Courtyard, Days Inn, Fairfield Inn, La Quinta, Residence Inn, Super 8, TownePlace Suites, Western Motel [O] Corner Mkt Foods, CVS Drug, Goodyear/auto, Home Depot, [H], to USM, URGENT CARE, Verizon, vet, Walgreens, W [gas] Exxon/Domino's, Kangaroo, Shell/Jimmy John's/dsl, Texaco [food] Arby's, Burger King, Cheddar's, Chesterfield's Rest., Chick-fil-A, Chili's, China Buffet, ChuckECheese's, Dickey's BBQ, FireHouse Subs, Five Guys, Gatti Town Pizza, Georgia Blue Rest., Golden Corral, Grand China, Hardee's, HoneyBaked Ham, Hooters, Krispy Kreme, Logan's Roadhouse, Longhorn Steaks, Marble Slab, McAlister's Deli, McDonald's, Newk's Eatery, O'Charley's, Olive Garden, Outback Steaks, Panda Express, Papa Murphy's, Pepper's Deli, Pizza Hut, Plaid Rhino Burger, Popeye's, Red Lobster, Super King Asian, Taco Bell, TGIFriday's, Waffle House, Ward's Burgers, Wendy's, Yamato Japan, Zaxby's [lodging] Baymont Inn, Best Western, Comfort Suites, Hampton Inn, Hilton Garden, Home 2 Suites, Microtel, Ramada Inn, Sun Suites [O] [H], $Tree, Aamco, Advance Parts, AT&T, AutoZone, Belk, Best Buy, BigLots, Books-A-Million, Dick's, Dillard's, Firestone/auto, Goodyear/auto, Great Wall Buffet, Hobby Lobby, JC Penney, Kohl's, Lowe's, Michael's, Nissan, Office Depot, Old Navy, PetCo, Petsmart, Ross, Sam's Club/gas, SteinMart, Target, TJ Maxx, Tuesday Morning, Verizon, Walgreens, Walmart, Winn-Dixie

60 US 11, S Hattiesburg, E [gas] Shell/dsl, W [gas] Kangaroo/Subway/dsl/24hr, Texaco, Valero/dsl [food] Huddle House [O] Freightliner, Peterbilt

59 US 98 E, to US 49, Lucedale, MS Gulf Coast

56mm parking area both lanes, litter barrels, no restrooms

51 rd 589, to Purvis, W [gas] Chevron/dsl/24hr, Pinebelt Oil/dsl, Shell/dsl (2mi) [food] McDonald's (2mi), Pizza Hut (2mi), to Little Black Cr Water Park

48mm Little Black Creek

41 MS 13, to Lumberton, W [O] $General, to Little Black Cr Water Park

35 Hillsdale Rd, E [gas] Pitstop/dsl [lodging] to Kings Arrow Ranch, to Lake Hillside Resort

32mm Wolf River

29 rd 26, to Poplarville, W [gas] Loves/Arby's/dsl/scales/24hr, Pure/dsl [O] NAPA, tires/repair

27 MS 53, to Poplarville, Necaise, W [gas] Chevron/dsl [food] McDonald's [O] RV Camping (2mi)

19 to US 11, Millard

15 to McNeill, W [gas] McNeill Trkstop/rest./dsl

10 to US 11, Carriere, E [gas] Texaco/Huddle House/dsl [O] Clearwater RV Camp (5mi)

PICAYUNE

6 MS 43 N, N Picayune, E [food] Mi Sol Mexican, Paul's Pastries W [gas] Chevron/dsl [food] McDonald's, Sonic, Subway, Waffle House [lodging] Super 8 [O] [H], $General, Claiborne Hill Mkt, CVS Drug, Family$, Walgreens, Winn-Dixie

4 MS 43 S, to Picayune, E [gas] Murphy USA/dsl, RaceTrac/dsl [food] McDonald's, Rio Grande Mexican, Ryan's [O] $Tree AT&T, Buick/Cadillac/Chevrolet/GMC, Chrysler/Dodge/Jeep GNC, Home Depot, Nissan, Verizon, Walgreens, Walmart W [gas] Chevron/dsl, Exxon/dsl, Shell/dsl [food] Applebee's, Burger King, Domino's, Don's Seafood, Hardee's, IHOP, Little Caesar's, New Buffet City, Papa John's, Pizza Hut, Popeye's, Subway, Taco Bell, Tokyo Grill, Waffle House, Wendy's [lodging] Days Inn, EconoLodge, Heritage Inn, Holiday Inn Express [O] [H] $General, Advance Parts, AutoZone, Family$, Firestone/auto Ford/Lincoln, Fred's, O'Reilly Parts, Paw Paw's RV Ctr, Rite Aid URGENT CARE, Winn-Dixie

3mm Welcome Ctr nb, full [handicapped] facilities, litter barrels, petwalk, [phone], [picnic] RV dump, vending

1.5mm weigh sta both lanes

1 US 11, MS 607, E [O] NASA, W [gas] Chevron/dsl [food] Subway

0mm Mississippi/Louisiana state line, Pearl River

INTERSTATE 220 (Jackson)

Exit# Services

11mm I-220 begins/ends on I-55, exit 104.

9 Hanging Moss Rd, County Line Rd, E [gas] Marathon/dsl

8 Watkins Dr, E [gas] Exxon/Subway, Shell/Chester's/dsl

5b a US 49 N, Evers Blvd, to Yazoo City, E [gas] Citgo [food] KFC, Sonic [lodging] Star Motel [O] $General, Family$, Food Depot/gas W [gas] Exxon/Burger King, Forty Nine TS/Subway/dsl, Shell Baskin Robbin/dsl [O] $General

3 Industrial Dr

2b a Clinton Blvd, Capitol St, E [O] to Jackson Zoo, W [gas] RaceWay, Shell [food] McDonald's, Popeye's, Sonic [O] Family$

1b a US 80, E [gas] Citgo/dsl, Shell [food] Capt D's, Country Fisherman, DQ, KFC, McDonald's, Pizza Hut, Popeye's, Taco Bell, Wendy's [lodging] Best Inn, Scottish Inn [O] AutoZone, Firestone/auto, Mr Transmission, UHaul, W [gas] Citgo/dsl, Exxon/dsl [food] Arby's, Krystal [O] $General

0mm I-220 begins/ends on I-20, exit 41.

MISSOURI

MO

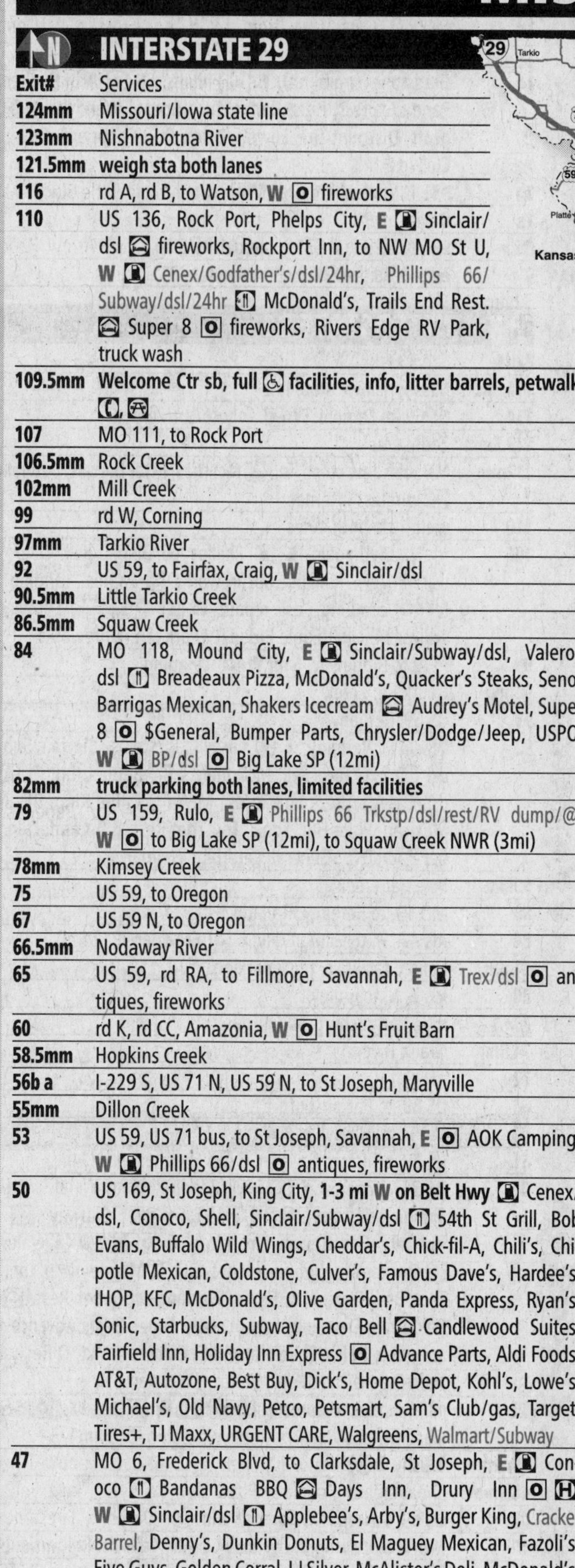

INTERSTATE 29

Exit#	Services
124mm	Missouri/Iowa state line
123mm	Nishnabotna River
121.5mm	**weigh sta both lanes**
116	rd A, rd B, to Watson, W fireworks
110	US 136, Rock Port, Phelps City, E Sinclair/dsl fireworks, Rockport Inn, to NW MO St U, W Cenex/Godfather's/dsl/24hr, Phillips 66/Subway/dsl/24hr McDonald's, Trails End Rest. Super 8 fireworks, Rivers Edge RV Park, truck wash
109.5mm	**Welcome Ctr sb, full facilities, info, litter barrels, petwalk,**
107	MO 111, to Rock Port
106.5mm	Rock Creek
102mm	Mill Creek
99	rd W, Corning
97mm	Tarkio River
92	US 59, to Fairfax, Craig, W Sinclair/dsl
90.5mm	Little Tarkio Creek
86.5mm	Squaw Creek
84	MO 118, Mound City, E Sinclair/Subway/dsl, Valero/dsl Breadeaux Pizza, McDonald's, Quacker's Steaks, Senor Barrigas Mexican, Shakers Icecream Audrey's Motel, Super 8 $General, Bumper Parts, Chrysler/Dodge/Jeep, USPO, W BP/dsl Big Lake SP (12mi)
82mm	**truck parking both lanes, limited facilities**
79	US 159, Rulo, E Phillips 66 Trkstp/dsl/rest/RV dump/@, W to Big Lake SP (12mi), to Squaw Creek NWR (3mi)
78mm	Kimsey Creek
75	US 59, to Oregon
67	US 59 N, to Oregon
66.5mm	Nodaway River
65	US 59, rd RA, to Fillmore, Savannah, E Trex/dsl antiques, fireworks
60	rd K, rd CC, Amazonia, W Hunt's Fruit Barn
58.5mm	Hopkins Creek
56b a	I-229 S, US 71 N, US 59 N, to St Joseph, Maryville
55mm	Dillon Creek
53	US 59, US 71 bus, to St Joseph, Savannah, E AOK Camping, W Phillips 66/dsl antiques, fireworks
50	US 169, St Joseph, King City, **1-3 mi W on Belt Hwy** Cenex/dsl, Conoco, Shell, Sinclair/Subway/dsl 54th St Grill, Bob Evans, Buffalo Wild Wings, Cheddar's, Chick-fil-A, Chili's, Chipotle Mexican, Coldstone, Culver's, Famous Dave's, Hardee's, IHOP, KFC, McDonald's, Olive Garden, Panda Express, Ryan's, Sonic, Starbucks, Subway, Taco Bell Candlewood Suites, Fairfield Inn, Holiday Inn Express Advance Parts, Aldi Foods, AT&T, Autozone, Best Buy, Dick's, Home Depot, Kohl's, Lowe's, Michael's, Old Navy, Petco, Petsmart, Sam's Club/gas, Target, Tires+, TJ Maxx, URGENT CARE, Walgreens, Walmart/Subway
47	MO 6, Frederick Blvd, to Clarksdale, St Joseph, E Conoco Bandanas BBQ Days Inn, Drury Inn H, W Sinclair/dsl Applebee's, Arby's, Burger King, Cracker Barrel, Denny's, Dunkin Donuts, El Maguey Mexican, Fazoli's, Five Guys, Golden Corral, LJ Silver, McAlister's Deli, McDonald's, New China Super Buffet, Pancheros, Panera Bread, Papa John's,

ST JOSEPH

Exit#	Services
47	Continued Papa Murphy's, Perkins, Pizza Hut, Red Lobster, Rib Crib BBQ, Sonic, Starbucks, Subway, Taco Bell, TX Roadhouse, Wendy's, Whiskey Creek Steaks Best Value Inn, Hampton Inn, Motel 6, Quality Suites, Ramada, Stoney Creek Inn $General, Apple Mkt Foods, BigLots, Buick/GMC, Chevrolet, CVS Drug, Dillard's, Firestone/auto, Ford/Lincoln, Hobby Lobby, Honda, HyVee Foods/dsl, JC Penney, Jo-Ann Fabrics, Nissan, Office Depot, Taco John's, Toyota, U-Haul, Verizon, vet, Walgreens
46b a	US 36, to Cameron, St Joseph, E to MWSU, **1 mi W on US 169** BP/dsl, FP/dsl, Murphy USA/dsl, Roadstar/dsl, Sinclair/dsl Burger King, Jimmy John's, Pizza Hut, Taco John's, Wendy's $General, Ace Hardware, AT&T, CVS, KIA, Klein RV Ctr, O'Reilly Parts, Walgreens, Walmart/Subway
44	US 169, to Gower, St Joseph, E Loves/Arby's/dsl/scales/24hr, Phillips 66 Nelly's Mexican, Subway Guesthouse Inn dsl repair, W Murphy USA/dsl, Shell/dsl/24hr DQ, El Maguey, Goodcents Subs, McDonald's, San Jose Steaks, Sonic, Taco Bell, Waffle House $Tree, Apple Mkt Foods, Chrysler/Dodge/Jeep, Harley-Davidson, Hyundai, Menards, Walmart/Subway
43	I-229 N, to St Joseph
39.5mm	Pigeon Creek
35	rd DD, Faucett, W Farris Trkstp/dsl/motel/rest/24hr/@
33.5mm	Bee Creek
30	rd Z, rd H, Dearborn, New Market, E Trex/Subway/dsl/24hr
29.5mm	Bee Creek
27mm	**both lanes, full facilities, litter barrels, petwalk, vending**
25	rd E, rd U, to Camden Point, E Trex/dsl
24mm	**weigh sta nb/truck parking sb**
20	MO 92, MO 273, to Atchison, Leavenworth, W antiques, to Weston Bend SP

ST JOSEPH

= gas = food = lodging = other = rest stop

MO

INTERSTATE 29 Cont'd

Exit#	Services
	PLATTE CITY
19.5mm	Platte River
19	rd HH, Platte City (sb returns at 18), W Casey's, Platte-Clay Fuel/dsl DQ, Maria's Mexican, Pizza Hut, Red Dragon Chinese, Roxanne's Cafe Quality Inn, Travelodge $General, Airport RV Park, CarQuest, O'Reilly Parts, same as 18, USPO
18	MO 92, Platte City, E Basswood RV Park (5mi), W Phillips 66/Jimmy John's, QT/dsl Arby's, Burger King, China Wok, Culver's, DQ, El Maguey, GoodCents Subs, McDonald's, Pizza Hut/Taco Bell, Pizza Shoppe, Sonic, Subway, Waffle House, Wendy's Ramada, Super 8 Buick/Chevrolet, Chrysler/Dodge/Jeep, CVS Drug, Ford, Goodyear/auto, PriceChopper Foods, same as 19, TrueValue, Verizon, Walgreens
17	I-435 S, to Topeka
15	Mexico City Ave, W Marriott
14	I-435 E (from sb), to St Louis
13	to I-435 E, E Extended Stay America, Fairfield Inn, Holiday Inn, Microtel, Plaza Hotel, Quality Suites, Sheraton, Super 8, W Marriott KCI Airport
	KANSAS CITY
12	NW 112th St, E BP, Conoco/dsl Best Western, Candlewood Suites, Comfort Inn, Days Inn, Extended Stay America, Hampton Inn, Hilton, W EconoLodge
10	Tiffany Springs Pkwy, E Phillips 66/dsl Beaches Cantina, SmokeBox BBQ Embassy Suites, Holiday Inn Express, Homewood Suites, Residence Inn, W Cracker Barrel, Ruby Tuesday, Waffle House, Wendy's Chase Suites, Courtyard, Drury Inn, Extended Stay America, Hyatt Place, Sleep Inn Buick/GMC, Harley-Davidson, Honda, Lexus, Nissan, Toyota
9b a	MO 152, to Liberty, Topeka
8	MO 9, rd T, NW Barry Rd, E Phillips 66/dsl Applebee's, Big Biscuit, Burger King, Chick-fil-A, Chili's, China Wok, Chipotle Mexican, ChuckeCheese, Dickey's BBQ, Five Guys, Golden Corral, Honeybaked Cafe, Hong's Buffet, Hooters, Houlihan's, Jason's Deli, Kato Japanese, On the Border, Panchero's, Panda Express, Panera Bread, Papa Murphy's, Rally House, Sheridan's Custard, Starbucks, Subway, Taco Bell, Wendy's, Winstead's Rest. H, $Tree, AutoZone, Best Buy, Ford, Hobby Lobby, Home Depot, HyVee/dsl, JC Penney, Lowe's, NTB, Petsmart, Ross, Target, Verizon, vet, Walmart, W Phillips 66/dsl, QT/dsl 54th St Grill, A&W/LJSilver, Abuelo's, Arby's, Bar Louie, BoLings Chinese, Bravo Italian, Buffalo Wild Wings, Granite City, Hardee's, Hereford House, Jimmy John's, McDonald's, Minsky's Pizza, Noodles&Co, Outback Steaks, Rainbow Oriental, Smokehouse BBQ, Sonic, Stone Canyon Pizza, Taco Bueno La Quinta, Motel 6, Super 8 AT&T, Barnes&Noble, CVS Drug, Dick's, Dillard's, Marshall's, Michael's, Old Navy, Staples, Tires+, Verizon
6	NW 72nd St, Platte Woods, E Sinclair/dsl vet, W Phillips 66 Iron Wok, Papa John's, Tasty Thai K-Mart
5	MO 45 N, NW 64th St, W Shell/dsl Bonefish Grill, Caribou Coffee, Chamas Brazilian Grill, Culver's, Goodcents Subs, IHOP, Luna Azteca, McDonald's, Papa Murphy's, Quiznos, Saki Asian, Starbucks, Subway, Taco Bell $General, CVS Drug, GNC, Hen House Mkt, HyVee, Sprouts Mkt, Tuesday Morning, vet
4	NW 56th St (from nb), W Phillips 66
3c	rd A (from sb), Riverside, W QT/dsl Corner Café, Sonic Rverside Automotive, USPO
3b	I-635 S
3a	Waukomis Dr, rd AA (from nb)
2b	US 169 S (from sb), to KC
2a	US 169 N (from nb), to Smithville
1e	US 69, Vivion Rd, E Phillips66/dsl Steak'n Shake Cadillac/Chevrolet, Fiat, Home Depot, Lincoln, Subaru
1d	MO 283 S, Oak Tfwy (from sb), W BP/dsl McDonald's, Subway CVS, O'Reilly Parts
1c	Gladstone (from nb), E Phillips 66 Arby's, Freddy's, Panda Express, Pizza Ranch, Taco Bueno, Wendy's H, BigLots, Discount Tire, Lowe's, Petco, PriceChopper Foods, Sam's Club/dsl
1b	I-35 N (from sb), to Des Moines
1a	Davidson Rd
8mm	I-35 N. I-29 and I-35 run together 6 mi.
0	exits 3-8a., See Missouri Interstate 35

INTERSTATE 35

Exit#	Services
114mm	Missouri/Iowa state line
114	US 69, to Lamoni, W Conoco/dsl/24hr
113.5mm	Zadie Creek
112mm	**MO welcome ctr sb, full facilities, litter barrels, petwalk, , wireless internet**
110	**weigh sta both lanes**
106	rd N, Blythedale, E Phillips 66/Dinner Bell Cafe/motel/dsl/24hr/@, Phillips 66/fireworks Eagles Landing Motel camping, dsl repair, W Loves/Subway/dsl/scales/24hr Eagle Ridge RV Park (2mi), fireworks
99	rd A, to Ridgeway, 5 mi W camping
94mm	E Fork Big Creek
	BETHANY
93	US 69, Bethany
92	US 136, Bethany, E Casey's/dsl/scales, Sinclair/Subway/dsl KFC/Taco Bell, McDonald's Budget Inn, W BP/dsl, Casey's/dsl, Kum&Go/dsl, MFA China King, DQ, Nopal Mexican, Pizza Hut, Sonic, TootToot Rest. Comfort Inn, Super 8 H, $General, Peterbilt, Walmart
90mm	Pole Cat Creek
88	MO 13, to Bethany, Gallatin
84	rds AA, H, to Gilman City, E Crowder SP (24mi)
81mm	limited facilities, truck parking
80	rds B, N, to Coffey
78	rd C, Pattonsburg, W gas/dsl
74.5mm	Grand River
72	rd DD
68	US 69, to Pattonsburg
64	MO 6, to Maysville, Gallatin
61	US 69, Winston, Gallatin, E Shell/rest./dsl/24hr
	CAMERON
54	US 36, Cameron, E Shell/Baskin-Robbins/Wendy's/dsl/24hr, Sinclair/dsl/scales/24hr McDonald's, Subway Comfort Inn, Guesthouse Inn, Motel 6 H, W Valero/dsl Burger King, Chinese Chef, DQ, El Maguey Mexican, KFC/Taco Bell, Pizza Hut, Sonic, Washington Street Rest. Best Value Inn, Days Inn, EconoLodge, Super 8 Advance Parts, antiques, Buick/Chevrolet/GMC, Cameron Mkt, O'Reilly Parts, Twin Creeks Tire, USPO, Verizon, Walmart
52	rd BB, Lp 35, to Cameron, E H, W Casey's $General, same as 54
49mm	Brushy Creek
48.5mm	Shoal Creek
48	US 69, Cameron, E to Wallace SP (2mi)
40	MO 116, Lathrop, E Trex/Country Cafe/dsl antiques
34.5mm	**both lanes, full facilities, litter barrels, petwalk, , vending**

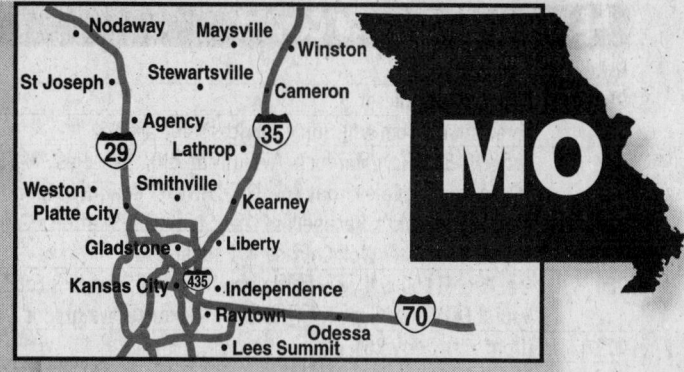

INTERSTATE 35 Cont'd

KEARNEY

Exit#	Services
33	rd PP, Holt, E auto repair, W BP/dsl, Conoco/dsl American Eagle Inn $General
30mm	Holt Creek
26	MO 92, Kearney, E Casey's/dsl, Phillips 66/dsl, QT/dsl China Wok, Jimmy John's, McDonald's, Papa Murphy's, Pizza Hut, Sonic Comfort Inn, Super 8 CVS Drug, Price Chopper, to Watkins Mill SP, True Value, Verizon, W Pilot/Taco Bell/dsl/scales/24hr Arby's, Burger King, Hunan Garden Chinese, JJ's Homestead Rest., Pizza Shoppe, Stables Grill, Subway EconoLodge, Quality Inn Goodyear/auto, O'Reilly Parts, to Smithville Lake
22mm	**parking area sb, weigh sta nb**
20	US 69, MO 33, to Excelsior Springs, E H
17	MO 291, rd A, **1 mi** E BP, QT/dsl A&W, CiCi's, Dickey's BBQ, Firehouse Subs, Hardee's, LJ Silver, McDonald's, Minsky's Pizza, Papa John's, Papa Murphy's, Perkins, Sonic, Subway, Taco Bell $General, Chevrolet, Days Inn, Firestone/auto, KC Auto, Liberty RV Ctr, O'Reilly Parts, same as 16, Walgreens, W Phillips 66/dsl, QT DQ, Masabi Japanese, McDonald's, Nicky's Pizza, Sonic, Subway, Zaxby's Sleep Inn, Woodspring Suites Price Chopper Foods, to KCI Airport, URGENT CARE, Walgreens
16	MO 152, Liberty, E EVC, Phillips 66 Baskin-Robbins, Chick-fil-A, CiCi's Pizza, Culver's, Domino's, Five Guys, IHOP, Jimmy John's, Margarita's, MOD Pizza, Olive Garden, Perkins, Pizza Hut, Pizza Ranch, Planet Sub, Red Robin, Starbucks, TX Roadhouse, Wendy's Days Inn, Super 8 H, Advance Parts, AutoZone, Chevrolet, CVS Drug, Dick's, Discount Tire, Firestone/auto, Gordman's, Hy-Vee/gas, Lowe's, Ross, URGENT CARE, Walgreens, W Murphy USA/dsl, Phillips 66/dsl 54th St Grill, Applebee's, Arby's, Buffalo Wild Wings, Burger King, Cheddar's, Chili's, Chipotle Mexican, Corner Cafe, Cracker Barrel, Fanner's Grill, Freddy's Burgers, Jose Peppers, Joy Wok, KFC, LongHorn Steaks, McDonald's, Noodles&Co, Old Chicago Pizza, Panda Express, Panera Bread, PepperJax Grill, Qdoba, Steak'n Shake, Subway, Taco Bell, Ted's Cafe Escondido, Waffle House Comfort Suites, Fairfield Inn, Hampton Inn, Holiday Inn Express Aldi Foods, AT&T, Best Buy, Christian Bros Auto, Ford, Home Depot, JC Penney, Jiffy Lube, Kohl's, Michael's, NAPA, NTB, Office Depot, Petsmart, Sam's Club/dsl, Sprouts Mkt, Target, TJ Maxx, Tuesday Morning, URGENT CARE, Verizon, Walmart/Subway
14	US 69 (exits left from sb), Liberty Dr, to Glenaire, Pleasant Valley, E Phillips 66, Sinclair/dsl, W QT/dsl/scales/24hr
13	US 69 (from nb), to Pleasant Valley, E Phillips 66, Sinclair/dsl, W QT/dsl/scales/24hr
12b a	I-435, to St Louis
11	US 69 N, Vivion Rd, E BP/dsl, Phillips 66/dsl Church's, McDonald's, W QT/dsl Sonic, Stroud's Rest., Subway CVS Drug, O'Reilly Parts, USPO, vet
10	N Brighton Ave (from nb), W QT/dsl Church's, Sonic CVS Drug
9	MO 269 S, Chouteau Trfwy, E Phillips 66 IHOP, McDonald's, Ming Garden, Papa Murphy's, Subway, Wing Stop Festival Foods, GNC, Harrah's Casino/rest., Target, W Wendy's (1mi)
8c	MO 1, Antioch Rd, E 7-11 Domino's Best Western auto repair, W Phillips 66, QT Dickey's BBQ, Waffle House AT&T, Walgreens
8b	I-29 N, US 71 N, KCI

LIBERTY

Nodaway Maysville Winston St Joseph Stewartsville Cameron Agency 29 35 Lathrop Weston Smithville Platte City Kearney Gladstone Liberty Kansas City 435 Independence Raytown 70 Odessa Lees Summit MO

I-35 S and I-29 S run together 6 mi.

KANSAS CITY

Exit#	Services
8a	Parvin Rd, E BP/dsl, Shell/dsl Subway O'Reilly Parts
6b a	Armour Rd, E Phillips 66/dsl Arby's, Burger King, Denny's, McDonald's, Quiznos, Subway EconoLodge, La Quinta H, repair, to Riverboat Casino, W Flash/dsl, Phillips 66, QT DQ, Jimmy John's, Lucky Dragon Chinese, Pizza Hut, Subway, Taco Bell, Wendy's American Inn, Holiday Inn Express URGENT CARE, USPO
5b	16th Ave, industrial district
5a	Levee Rd, Bedford St, industrial district
4.5mm	Missouri River
4b	Front St, E Isle of Capri Riverboat Casino/rest.
4a	US 24 E, Independence Ave
3	I-70 E, US 71 S, to St Louis
2g	I-35 N and I-29 N run together 6 mi
2e	Oak St, Grand-Walnut St, E Phillips 66 Marriott
2d	Main-Delaware, Wyandotte St, downtown
2a	I-70 W, to Topeka
2y	US 169, Broadway, to downtown
2w	12th St, Kemper Arena, to downtown
2v	14th St, to downtown
2u	I-70 E, to Broadway, E Denny's
1e	US 69, Vivion Rd, E Phillips66/dsl
1d	20th St (from sb), E Phillips 66
1c	27th St, SW Blvd, W Pennway (from nb), E Phillips 66 H
1a	SW Trafficway (from sb)
0mm	Missouri/Kansas state line

INTERSTATE 44

ST LOUIS

Exit#	Services
293mm	**I-44 begins/ends on I-70, exit 249 in St Louis.**
290a	I-55 S, to Memphis
290c	Gravois Ave (from wb), 12th St, S Jack-in-the-Box
290b	18th St (from eb), downtown
289	Jefferson Ave, St Louis, N Phillips 66 Subway Holiday Inn Express, Residence Inn Family$, SaveALot, S Conoco Lee's Chicken, McDonald's Family$
288	Grand Blvd, St Louis, N Water Tower Inn H, vet, S Jack-in-the-Box, Qdoba, St Louis Bread, Starbucks, Subway Family$
287b a	Kingshighway, Vandeventer Ave, St Louis, N BP, QT/dsl H, Jiffy Lube, U-Haul, S Chevrolet, to MO Botanical Garden, Walgreens
286	Hampton Ave, St Louis, N BP, Mobil, Phillips 66, Shell/Circle K Courtesy Diner, Denny's, Jack-in-the-Box, McDonald's, Steak'n Shake, Subway, Taco Bell zoo, S Shell/Circle K/dsl Bartolino's Rest., Hardee's, Wendy's Drury Inn, Holiday Inn, Red Roof Inn museums
285	SW Ave (from wb, no EZ return)

[gas] = gas [food] = food [lodging] = lodging [other] = other [RS] = rest stop

INTERSTATE 44 Cont'd

Exit#	Services
284b a	Arsenal St, Jamieson St
283	Shrewsbury (from wb), some services same as 282
282	Laclede Sta Rd, Murdock Ave (from eb), St Louis, N [gas] [food] Boardwalk Cafe, Front Row Grill, Hwy 61 Roadhouse, Imo's Pizza, McDonald's, Racanelli's Pizza, Starbucks, Stratton's Cafe, Subway, Webster Wok Chinese [other] Subaru, vet
280	Elm Ave, St Louis, N [gas] [food] Jamba Juice [other] Schnuck's Foods, 1 mi S [gas] Shell/Circle K [food] Steak'n Shake [other] Walgreens
279	(from wb), Berry Rd
278	Big Bend Rd, St Louis, N [food] Culver's, Hardee's [other] [H], Sam's Club/gas, URGENT CARE, S [gas] Mobil/dsl, QT
277b	US 67, US 61, US 50, Lindbergh Blvd, N [food] Arby's, Buffalo Wild Wings, Chili's, Chipotle Mexican, Dunkin Donuts, Jason's Deli, O'Charley's, Sonic, Steak&Rice Chinese, TX Roadhouse, White Castle [lodging] Best Western [other] [H], $Tree, AT&T, Harley-Davidson, Hobby Lobby, Lowe's Whse, Office Depot, PetCo, Target, TJ Maxx, Verizon, Walmart, S [gas] Phillips 66/dsl, Shell/Circle K/dsl [food] Burger King, Chick-fil-A, Denny's, Five Guys, Fuddrucker's, Helen Fitzgerald's Grill, IHOP, Lion's Choice, Longhorn Steaks, Panda Express, Ruby Tuesday, St Louis Bread, Steak'n Shake, Subway [lodging] Days Inn/rest., EconoLodge, Hampton Inn, Holiday Inn [other] Dobb's Auto/Tire, GNC, Home Depot, Marshall's, Old Navy, Petsmart, Ross, Stein Mart
277a	MO 366 E, Watson Rd, access to same as 277b S
276b a	I-270, N to Chicago, S Memphis
275	N Highway Dr (from wb), Soccer Pk Rd, N [gas] Pilot/Road Ranger/rest/dsl
274a b	Bowles Ave, N [gas] Road Ranger/Pilot/Subway/dsl, S [gas] Phillips 66/dsl, QT/dsl, ZX/dsl [food] Bandana's BBQ, Cracker Barrel, Denny's, Jack-in-the-Box, Krispy Kreme, McDonald's, White Castle [lodging] Drury Inn, Fairfield Inn, Holiday Inn Express, Motel 6, PearTree Inn, Stratford Inn, Super 8, TownePlace Inn
272	MO 141, Fenton, Valley Park, N [gas] Motomart, S [gas] Phillips 66/dsl [food] Bob Evans, Burger King, Hardee's, Jimmy John's, McDonald's, Ruby Tuesday, Starbucks, Steak'n Shake, Subway, Sugarfire BBQ, Taco Bell [lodging] Drury Inn, Hampton Inn [other] Save-A-Lot Foods
269	Antire Rd, Beaumont
266	Lewis Rd, N [other] golf, Rte 66 SP
266mm	Meramec River
265	Williams Rd (from eb)
264	MO 109, rd W, Eureka, N [gas] Phillips 66/dsl [food] Arby's, Burger King, Culver's, Domino's, Jimmy John's, Little Caesar's, McDonald's, Pizza Hut, Poor Richard's, Smokers BBQ, St Louis Bread, Taco Bell, White Castle [other] AT&T, Byerly RV Ctr, O'Reilly Parts, Schnuck's Foods, to Babler SP, Valvoline, S [gas] QT/dsl [other] Walgreens
261	Lp 44, to Allenton, N [gas] Motomart/McDonald's/dsl [food] China King, Denny's, Imo's Pizza, Lion's Choice, Steak'n Shake, Subway [lodging] Best Inn, Holiday Inn, Super 8 [other] $Tree, AutoZone, GNC, Jellystone RV Camping, same as 264, to Six Flags, Walmart, S [gas] Shell/Circle K/dsl [other] KOA
257	(256 from eb) Lp 44, Pacific, N [gas] Phillips 66, Pilot/Subway/dsl/scales/24hr [lodging] Comfort Inn [other] fireworks, S [gas] BP/dsl, Mobil/dsl, Motomart [food] El Agave Mexican, Hardee's, KFC, McDonald's, New China, Pizza Hut, Taco Bell [lodging] Quality Inn [other] $General, Chrysler/Dodge/Jeep, CVS Drug, O'Reilly Parts, Queen's Foods, SaveALot, st police
253	MO 100 E, to Gray Summit, S [gas] Phillips 66/dsl [lodging] Travelodge [other] CarQuest, fireworks, Shaw Nature Preserve
251	MO 100 W, to Washington, N [gas] BP/dsl, Mr Fuel/dsl/scales, Phillips 66/Burger King/dsl [other] $General, antiques, [H] (11mi)
247	US 50 W, rd AT, rd O, to Union, N [other] Harley-Davidson, Pin Oak Creek RV Park, S [other] to Robertsville SP
247mm	Bourbeuse River
242	rd AH, to Hist Rte 66
240	MO 47, St Clair, N [gas] Phillips 66/Taco Bell/dsl [food] Burger King [other] tire/auto, S [gas] Mobil/dsl [food] Domino's, McDonald's, Subway [lodging] Budget Lodge, Super 8 [other] $General, Country Mart Foods, NAPA, Save-A-Lot Foods, USPO
239	MO 30, rds AB, WW, St Clair, N [other] repair, S [gas] Phillips 66/dsl
238mm	**weigh sta both lanes**
235mm	**[RS] both lanes (both lanes exit left), full [handicapped] facilities, litter barrels, petwalk, [phone], [picnic], vending**
230	rds W, Stanton, S [gas] Amstar/fireworks [other] KOA, Meramec Caverns Camping (3mi), USPO
226	MO 185 S, Sullivan, N [gas] Flying J/Denny's/dsl/LP/scales/24hr [other] vet, S [gas] Phillips 66/Burger King [food] Applebee's, Arby's, China Buffet, DQ, Imo's Pizza, KFC, McDonald's, Steak'n Shake, Subway, Taco Bell [other] $General, $Tree, Aldi Foods, AutoZone, Lowe's, O'Reilly Parts, same as 225, to Meramec SP, Verizon, Walmart
225	MO 185 N, rd D, Sullivan, N [gas] Mobil, Phillips 66/dsl [food] Domino's, Du Kum Inn Rest [lodging] Baymont Inn, Best Value Inn, Family Inn, Super 8 [other] Chevrolet/Buick/GMC, Chrysler/Dodge/Jeep, Ford, S [gas] BP/Fas-Trip/dsl/café, ZX [food] Cracker Barrel, El Nopal Mexican, Jack-in-the-Box, Lion's Choice, Pizza Hut [lodging] Comfort Inn [other] [H], AT&T, city park, same as 226
218	rds N, C, J, Bourbon, N [gas] ZX/dsl [lodging] Budget Inn, S [gas] Mobil/dsl [food] Planet Sub, Subway [other] $General, Blue Sprgs Camping (6mi), Bourbon RV Ctr, Riverview Ranch Camping (8mi), Town&Country Mkt
214	rd H, Leasburg, N [gas] Mobil/dsl, S [food] Skippy's Rte 66 Rest. [other] to Onandaga Cave SP (7mi)
210	rd UU, N [other] Meremac Valley Resort, S [food] MO Hick BBQ (2mi) [other] winery
208	MO 19, Cuba, N [gas] Midwest/Phillips 66/Dotty's Rest./dsl/scales/24hr/@ [food] Country Kitchen, Huddle House, Pizza Hut [lodging] EconoLodge, Super 8 [other] antiques, Blue Beacon, S [gas] Casey's, Mobil [food] East Sun Chinese, Hardee's, Jack-in-the-Box, McDonald's, Sonic, Subway [lodging] Chateau Inn [other] $General, Mace Foods, O'Reilly Parts, to Ozark Nat Scenic Riverways, Walmart
203	rds F, ZZ, N [other] Ladybug RV Park, S [other] Rosatti Winery (2mi)
195	MO 8, MO 68, St James, Maramec Sprg Park, N [gas] BP/Circle K/dsl, Mobil/dsl [food] China King, McDonald's, Pizza Hut, Sonic, Subway [lodging] Economy Inn, Greenstay Inn [other] $General, Ford, O'Reilly Parts, Ray's Tires, to Maremac Winery, tours ctr, S [gas] Delano/dsl, Phillips 66/dsl [food] Burger King [lodging] Finn's Motel [other] CountryMart Foods
189	rd V, Industrial Park Dr, Hypoint, N [gas] Loves/McDonald's/Subway/dsl/scales/24hr, S [other] Mule Trading Post
186	US 63, MO 72, Rolla, N [gas] Sinclair [food] Steak'n Shake [lodging] Drury Inn, Hampton Inn, Sooter Inn [other] Big O Tire, Kia, Kohl's, Lowe's, Nissan, Plaza Tire, S [gas] Mobil/dsl, Phillips 66 [food] Buffalo Wild Wings, Colton's Steaks, Donut King, Koi Chinese, Lee's Chicken, Panera Bread [lodging] Budget Motel [other] [H]
185	rd E, to Rolla, N [other] hwy patrol, S [gas] Delano [food] Arby's, DQ, Gordoz Steaks, Hardee's, Huddle House, Jimmy John's, Kyoto Japanese, LJ Silver, Papa John's, Subway, Taco Bell, Wendy's [other] [H], CVS Drug, Ford, Kroger, UMO at Rolla

SULLIVAN

CUBA

ROLLA

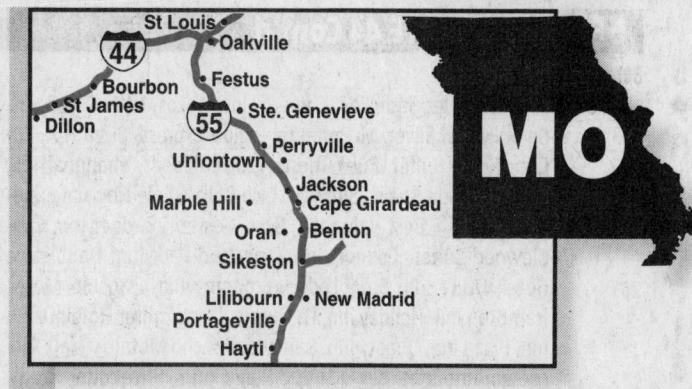

INTERSTATE 44 Cont'd

Exit#	Services
184	US 63 S, to Rolla, N [lodging] Comfort Suites, Holiday Inn Express, S [gas] Delano, MotoMart, Route 66 [food] Arby's, Bandana's BBQ, Burger King, Denny's, Little Caesars, LJ Silver, Los Cazadores, Lucky House Chinese, Maid-Rite, McDonald's, Penelope's Rest., Pizza Hut, Pizza Inn, Sirloin Stockade, Waffle House, Wendy's [lodging] Baymont Inn, Best Way Inn, Best Western, Days Inn, EconoLodge, Quality Inn, Sunset Inn, Super 8 [other] [H], Buick/Cadillac/GMC, Chevrolet, city park, CVS Drug, Kroger
179	rds T, C, to Doolittle, Newburg, S [gas] Phillips 66/dsl [food] Cookin' From Scratch Rest. [other] $General
178mm	**restrooms, truck parking both lanes**
176	Sugar Tree Rd, S [lodging] Vernelle's Motel [other] Arlington River Resort Camping (2mi)
172	rd D, Jerome, N [other] camping
169	rd J
166	to Big Piney
164mm	Big Piney River
163	MO 28, to Dixon, N [gas] Pilot/Road Ranger/Chesters/Subway/dsl/scales/24hr, S [gas] Phillips 66/dsl [food] Country Café, Sweetwater BBQ [lodging] Best Western, Country Hearth Inn, Days Inn [other] RV Park, Uranus Fudge a Factory
161b a	rd Y, to Ft Leonard Wood, N [gas] Mobil/dsl, Shell/dsl [food] Aussie Jack's, Cracker Barrel, Denny's, Domino's, Mama Mia Diner, Ocean Buffet, Papa Murphy's, Pizza Hut, Rte 66 Diner, Ruby Tuesday, Wendy's [lodging] Baymont Inn, Best Value Inn, Candlewood Suites, Comfort Inn, Fairfield Inn, Hampton Inn, Howard Johnson, Mainstay Suites, Red Roof Inn [other] AT&T, Kwik Kar, Lowe's, Toyota, visitors ctr, Walmart/Subway, S [gas] Cenex/dsl, Kum&Go/dsl [food] Arby's, Buffalo Wild Wings, Cantina Bravo, Colton's Steaks, Culver's, Hardee's, Little Caesar's, McDonald's, Panera Bread, Papa John's, Subway, Taco Bell, Waffle House [lodging] Budget Inn, EconoLodge, Holiday Inn Express, Liberty Lodge, Motel 6, Quality Inn, ZLoft Hotel [other] $General, $Tree, AutoZone, Chrysler/Dodge/Jeep, Family$, Ford/Lincoln, Mazda, NAPA, O'Reilly Parts, Verizon
159	Lp 44, to Waynesville, St Robert, N [gas] Road Star/dsl [food] DQ, Sonic [lodging] All Star Motel, Super 8 [other] auto repair, O'Reilly Parts, S [gas] Cenex/dsl [food] Don Jose [lodging] Alliance Inn [other] Big O Tire, Cadillac/GMC
158mm	Roubidoux Creek
156	rd H, Waynesville, N [gas] BP, Express Stop/dsl/E-85, Kum&Go/dsl [food] McDonald's, Subway [other] $General, Chevrolet, Price Cutter+
153	MO 17, to Buckhorn, N [lodging] Ft Wood Inn, S [gas] Shell/dsl [other] Glen Oaks RV Park
150	MO 7, rd P to Richland, S [food] Roadhouse Steaks
145	MO 133, rd AB, to Richland, N [gas] Sinclair/Oasis/cafe/dsl/24hr, S [other] camping
143mm	Gasconade River
140	rd N, to Stoutland, S [gas] Cenex/pizza/dsl
139mm	Bear Creek
135	rd F, Sleeper
130	rd MM, N [gas] Casey's /dsl, Conoco/dsl [food] Angie's Place [lodging] EconoLodge, Munger Moss Inn, S [gas] Kum&Go [other] [H]
129	MO 5, MO 32, MO 64, to Hartville, Lebanon, N [food] Applebee's, Arby's, Bamboo Garden, Bandana's BBQ, Burger King, DQ, Elm St Eatery, KFC, Little Caesars, LJ Silver, McDonald's, Papa Murphy's, Sonic, Steak'n Shake, Subway, Taco Bell, Wendy's [other] Aldi Foods, AT&T, AutoZone, Chevrolet, Ford, O'Reilly Parts, repair, Rte 66 Museum, Smitty's Foods, to Bennett Sprgs SP,

Exit#	Services
129	Continued to Lake of the Ozarks, Verizon, Walgreens, Walnut Bowl Factory, S [gas] Conoco/dsl, Phillips 66/dsl [food] Capt D's, Domino's, Hardee's, La Tolteca, Pizza Hut, T's Steaks [other] [H], $Tree, Lowe's, O'Reilly Parts, Sawyer Tire/auto, Walmart/Subway
127	Lp 44, Lebanon, N [gas] B&D/J Diner/dsl/scales/24hr, Phillips 66/dsl [food] Dowd's Catfish&BBQ, El Sombrero Mexican, Great Wall Chinese, Subway, Waffle House [lodging] Best Value Inn, Days Inn, Hampton Inn, Holiday Inn Express, Midwest Inn, Rte 66 Motel, Super 8 [other] $General, Chrysler/Dodge/Jeep, Cutlery/Walnut Bowl Outlet, Firestone/auto, S [gas] Conoco/McDonald's/dsl [food] Dickey's BBQ [other] Buick/Cadillac/GMC, Harley-Davidson, Russell Stover
123	County Rd, S [other] antiques, Happy Trails RV Ctr, Happy Trails RV Park
118	rds C, A, Phillipsburg, S [gas] Phillips 66 [other] Redmond's Gifts, tourist info
113	rds J, Y, Conway, N [gas] Conoco/dsl [food] Rockin Chair Café [lodging] Budget Inn [other] to Den of Metal Arts, S [gas] Sinclair/dsl [other] $General, SummerFresh Foods, USPO
111mm	**[RS] both lanes, full [handicapped] facilities, litter barrels, petwalk, [phone], [picnic], playground, vending**
108mm	Bowen Creek
107	Sparkle Brooke Rd, Sampson Rd
106mm	Niangua River
100	MO 38, rd W, Marshfield, N [gas] Murphy USA/dsl, Phillips 66 [other] $Tree, auto repair, Chevrolet, Chrysler/Dodge/Jeep, Ford, Walmart/Subway, S [gas] Casey's/dsl, Conoco/dsl, Phillips 66/dsl [food] DQ, El Charro, Golden China, Grillos Cafe, KFC/Rib Crib, McDonald's, Pizza Hut, Sonic, Subway, Taco Bell [lodging] Holiday Inn Express [other] $General, AutoZone, O'Reilly Parts, RV Express RV Park, Verizon, Walgreens
96	rd B, Northview, N Paradise RV Park (2mi)
89mm	**weigh sta both lanes**
88	MO 125, to Fair Grove, Strafford, N [gas] Love's/Hardee's/dsl/scales/rv dump/24hr, TA/Subway/Taco Bell/dsl/scales/24hr/@ [food] McDonald's [other] Camping World RV Ctr, truckwash, S [gas] Breaktime/dsl, Kum&Go [food] Fox's Pizza, Pizza Hut [lodging] Super 8 [other] $General, Strafford RV Park
84	MO 744, S [other] Peterbilt
82b a	US 65, to Branson, Fedalia, S [gas] Kum&Go/dsl, Phillips 66/dsl [food] Waffle House [other] Bull Shoals Lake, Kenworth, st patrol, to Table Rock Lake
80b a	rd H to Pleasant Hope, Springfield, N [gas] Conoco/rest./dsl/24hr, Kum&Go/dsl, Sinclair [food] Waffle House [lodging] Days Inn, Microtel, Super 8 [other] $General, S [gas] Casey's, Kum&Go/dsl, Phillips 66/Circle K/dsl, Shell [food] Andy's Custard, Applebee's, Bob Evans, Braum's, Buckingham BBQ, Cracker Barrel, Culver's, El Maguey Mexican, Fazoli's, Hardee's, Hong Kong Inn, Houlihan's,

SPRINGFIELD

INTERSTATE 44 Cont'd

80b a	Continued
	Ichiban Buffet, Jade East Chinese, Jose Locos, Little Tokyo, Little Tokyo, LJ Silver, McDonald's, Panda Express, Pizza Hut, Rib Crib, Royal Buffet, Ruby Tuesday, Schlotzsky's, Shanghai Inn, Sonic, Steak'n Shake, Subway, Taco Bell, Whole Hog Cafe, Ziggies Cafe Best Value Inn, Best Western, Budget Inn, Candlewood Suites, Comfort Inn, Dogwood Park Inn, Doubletree Hotel, Drury Inn, EconoLodge, Economy Inn, Flagship Motel, Hampton Inn, Holiday Inn, La Quinta, Lamplighter Hotel, Ozark Inn, Plaza Inn, Quality Inn, Ramada, Rancho Motel H, Aldi Foods, AutoZone, Big O Tire, O'Reilly Parts, PriceCutter Foods, Tire Express, U-Haul, Walmart/Subway
77	MO 13, KS Expswy, N Kum&Go/dsl/e-85 Lowe's, S Casey's/dsl, Phillips 66/dsl Arby's, Braum's, Buffalo Wild Wings, Chuckwagon BBQ, El Charro, Five Guys, Golden Corral, Goodcents, IHOP, Jimmy John's, McAlister's Deli, McDonald's, Moe's SW Grill, New China, Panera Bread, Papa John's, Papa Murphy's, Pizza Inn, Subway, Taco Bell, Waffle House $Tree, AT&T, BigLots, Drug Mart, GNC, Goodyear/auto, Hobby Lobby, PriceCutter Foods, Staples, Verizon, Walgreens, Walmart
75	US 160 W byp, to Willard, Stockton Lake, S Kum&Go/dsl Wendy's Courtyard, La Quinta
72	MO 266, to Chesnut Expwy, 1-2 mi S Casey's, Cenex, Kum&Go/dsl Alli's Rest., Arby's, China Wok, Hardee's, KFC, LJ Silver, McDonald's, Plaza Mexico, Sonic, Subway, Taco Bell, Taco Bueno, Waffle House Best Budget Inn, Best Western, Redwood Motel $General, AutoZone, city park, PriceCutter Foods
70	rds MM, B, N fireworks, S KOA (1mi), Wilson's Creek Nat Bfd (5mi)
69	to US 60, Springfield
67	rds N, T, Bois D' Arc, to Republic, S Conoco/dsl AmericInn (5mi) art glass
66mm	Pond Creek
64.6mm	Dry Branch
64.5mm	Pickerel Creek
61	rds K, PP, N Cenex/Hoods/dsl/scales/LP/24hr, Phillips 66 Hood I-44 Motel
58	MO 96, rds O, Z, to Carthage, Halltown, S Shell/dsl truck repair
57	to rd PP (from wb)
56.5mm	Turnback Creek
56mm	Goose Creek
52.5mm	**truck parking both lanes**
49	MO 174E, rd CCW, Chesapeake
46	MO 39, MO 265, Mt Vernon, Aurora, N Casey's/dsl, Gulf/dsl, Kum&Go/dsl, TA/Conoco/46Diner/dsl/scales/24hr/@ Bamboo Garden Chinese, El Azteca Mexican, KFC/LJ Silver, Mazzio's, McDonald's, Pizza Hut, Sonic, Subway, Taco Bell Best Western, USA Inn $General, Family$, O'Reilly Parts, PriceCutter Foods, True Value, S Conoco/dsl Best Value Inn to Table Rock Lake
44	rd H, to Monett, Mt Vernon, N Subway (1mi) Mid-America Dental/Hearing, Walmart
43.5mm	Spring River
38	MO 97, to Stotts City, Pierce City, N gas/dsl/repair/tires, S U of MO SW Ctr (4mi)
33	MO 97 S, to Pierce City, S Hungry House Cafe
29	rd U, to La Russell, Sarcoxie, N antiques, Beagle Bay RV Camping, OzarkLand Gifts, S Casey's (1mi), Kum&Go/Subway/dsl antiques
29mm	Center Creek
26	MO 37, to Reeds, Sarcoxie, N Bill's Truck/trailer repair
22	rd 100 N, N Colaw RV Ctr, S Consignment RV Sales
21mm	Jones Creek
18b a	I-49 N, US 71 N, MO 59 S, to Carthage, Neosho, N Coachlight RV Ctr/Camping
15	MO 66 W, Lp 44 (from wb), Joplin, N Tara Motel
15mm	Grove Creek
14mm	Turkey Creek
13	Prigmore Ave
11b a	I-49 S, US 71 S, MO 249 N, to Neosho, Ft Smith, S FLYING J Denny's/dsl/LP/scales/24hr/@, Goodyear Tires/repair, Speedco Blue Beacon, Kenworth
8b a	US 71, to Neosho, Joplin, N Conoco/dsl, Kum&Go/dsl, Phillips 66/dsl Andy's Custard, Applebee's, Arby's, Billy Sims BBQ, Bob Evans, Braum's, Buffalo Wild Wings, Carino's Italian, Casa Montez Mexican, Cheddar's, Chick-fil-A, Chipotle, ChuckeCheese, CiCi's, Denny's, Domino's, El Vallarta Mexican, Firehouse Subs, Five Guys, Freddy's, Garfield's, Golden Corral, Golden Dragon, Hardee's, HuHot, IHOP, Jim Bob's Steaks, Jimmy John's, Jimmy's Egg, King Palace, Logan's Roadhouse, Longhorn Steaks, McAlister's, McDonald's, Noodle&Grill, Ocean Rest., Olive Garden, Outback Steaks, Panda Express, Pitcher's Grill, Pizza Hut, Popeye's, Qdoba, Red Hot&Blue Grill, Red Lobster, Rib Crib, Ruby Tuesday, Schlotzsky's, Sonic, Starbucks, Steak'n Shake, Subway, Taco Bell, TX Roadhouse, Waffle House, Wasab Steaks, Wendy's Baymont Inn, Best Western, Candlewood Suites, Comfort Inn, Days Inn, Drury Inn, Fairfield Inn, Hampton Inn, Hilton Garden, Homewood Suites, Joplin Hotel, La Quinta, Motel 6, Quality Inn, Residence Inn, Sunrise Inn, Super 8 $Tree, Aldi Foods, AT&T, AutoZone, Best Buy, Books-A-Million, Chrysler/Dodge/Jeep, Discount Tire, Firestone/auto, Food4Less, Ford/Lincoln, Freightliner, Goodyear/auto, Hobby Lobby, Home Depot, Honda, Hyundai, JC Penney, Jo-Ann Fabrics, Kia, Kohl's, Lowe's, Macy's, Mercedes, Michael's, Nissan, Office Depot, O'Reilly Parts, Petsmart, Ross, Sam's Club/gas, Target, TJ Maxx, Toyota, Verizon, Walgreens, Walmart/Subway S Casey's Cracker Barrel, Fazoli's Microtel, TownePlace Suites vet, Wheelen RV Ctr
6	MO 86, MO 43 N, to Racine, Joplin, N Phillips 66 Moe's SW Grill, Schlotzsky's CVS Drug, Walgreens, S H, Harley-Davidson
5.5mm	Shoal Creek
4	MO 43 to Seneca, N Loves/Hardee's/dsl/scales/24hr S Conoco/Subway/dsl, Petro/Iron Skillet/Pizza Hut/Taco Bell/dsl/scales/24hr/@, Pilot/Wendy's/dsl/scales/24hr McDonald's Sleep Inn $General, fireworks, IA 80 Truckomat, KOA
3mm	**weigh sta both lanes**
2mm	**Welcome Ctr eb, litter barrels, full facilities, restrooms, vending; truck parking wb**
1	US 400, US 166W, to Baxter Springs, KS, N Downstream/dsl Downstream Casino/RV Park, Downstream RV Park S Sandstone Gardens
0mm	Missouri/Oklahoma state line

JOPLIN

INTERSTATE 49

Exit#	Services
184	I-435, I-470.
I-49 begins/ends, continues N as US 71.	
182	Red Bridge Rd, Longview Rd, E Phillips 66/dsl McDonald's auto repair, W 7-11, BP/dsl Woodspring Suites

INTERSTATE 49 Cont'd

Exit#	Services
181	Blue Ridge Blvd, E Shell/dsl Church's Best Value Inn NAPA, U-Haul, W Applebee's, Arby's, Goodcents Subs, IHOP, KFC, Papa John's, Pizza Hut, Wendy's $Tree, Advance Parts, AutoZone, Burlington Coats, CVS, GNC, Price Chopper, Tires+, TrueValue
180	(from sb), same as 181 w, W Jerry's Auto Repair
179	Main St, E Conoco Burger King, Capestre Mexican, Capt D's, Little Caesar's, Popeye's, Providence Pizzeria $General, Firestone/auto, Holiday Inn Express, to Longview Lake CP, W Phillips 66/dsl Taco Bell, TJ's Cafe, Waffle House transmissions, USPO, Walgreens
178	140th St, W Phillips 66/dsl
177	MO 150, E QT/dsl, Shell/dsl Sonic, Subway Harley Davidson
176	155th St, to Belton, W Conoco Domino's
175	rd Y, 163rd St, Belton, E Hampton Inn, W Conoco/dsl, QT/dsl Pizza Hut, Taco Bueno H, AutoZone, CVS, Menards, O'Reilly Parts, Price Chopper
174	MO 58, Belton, E QT, Shell/dsl Burger King, Church's, Golden Corral, KFC, Papa John's, Pizza Hut, Ryan's, Steak'n Shake, Taco Bell, Waffle House, Wendy's Comfort Inn Advance Parts, AT&T, Chrysler/Dodge/Jeep, Firestone/auto, H, Lowe's, NTB, Sam's Club/dsl, Walmart/Subway, W A&W/LJ Silver, Applebee's, Arby's, Bob Evans, Buffalo Wild Wings, Chipotle, IHOP, Jimmy John's, Jose Pepper's, Little Caesar's, Longhorn Steaks, McDonald's, New China, Papa Murphy's, Pepper Jax Cafe, Ruby Tuesday, Starbucks, Subway EconoLodge $Tree, Aldi Foods, Discount Tire, Express Auto Service, GNC, Home Depot, HyVee/dsl, Jo-Ann, Kohl's, Petsmart, Target, Verizon, Walgreens
172	N Cass Pkwy
167	MO C, J, Peculiar, E Casey's, FLYING J/Denny's/dsl/Lp/scales/24hr Subway Peculiar RV Park, W Sonic CountryMart/dsl, USPO
160	MO 291 N, Harrisonville, E Casey's/dsl, Murphy USA, QT/dsl Applebee's, Arby's, Baskin Robbins, Bonsai Grill, Branding Iron BBQ, Capt D's, El Mezcal Mexican, Hardee's, KFC, McDonald's, Subway, Sunrise Chinese, Taco Bell, Wendy's Caravan Motel, Harrisonville Inn $Tree, GNC, H, vet, Walmart, W Ford, Best Value Inn
159	MO 2 W, 7 N, Mechanic St, Harrisonville, E BP, Phillips 66/dsl Burger King, China Wok, DQ, Jimmy John's, Papa Murphy's, Pizza Hut, Starbucks Advance Parts, AT&T, CVS, DLS Tire/auto, Price Chopper, Verizon, vet, Walgreens
158	MO 2 E, Commercial Blvd, Harrisonville, E Conoco/dsl, Phillips 66 Best Burrito Comfort Inn Russell Stover, Sutherland's
157mm	**weigh sta both lanes**
157	MO 7 S, to Clinton, E W BP/dsl, Phillips 66 Slumber Inn
153	307th St
148mm	S Grand River
147	MO A, B, Archie, Drexel, W Conoco/dsl, Phillips 66 Mama's Kitchen
144	MO E, AA, Crescent Hill
141	MO 18, Adrian, to Clinton, W Casey's/dsl, Phillips 66/dsl Old 71 Cafe $General, NAPA
136	rds D, F, Passaic, to Butler, W McBee's Bratwurst/BBQ
131	MO 52 W, Butler, Amoret, E Conoco McDonald's, Pizza Hut, Sonic, Subway, TacoBell DaysInn, Super8 $General,

BELTON

HARRISONVILLE

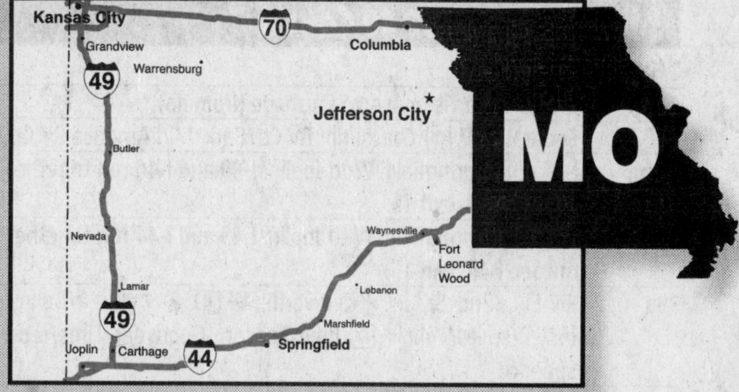

MO

Exit#	Services
131	Continued Chrysler/Dodge/Jeep/Ford, CountryMart, H, Walmart, W El Charro
130	US 71 Bus (from nb), to Butler
129	MO 52 E, Appleton City
120	rds B, A, Rich Hill, to Osceola, W Phillips 66/dsl Swope's Drive In $General, Food Fair Mkt/drug
116	Rd TT, to Panama
112	Horton, W Farm Mkt
110	Rd D, Stotesbury
107	Rd M, Compton Jct
103	Highland Ave, to Nevada, W Breakfast Cafe $General, Buick/Chevrolet/GMC, Osage Prairie RV Park
102b	49 Bus, W same as 103
102a	US 54, Nevada, to El Dorado Springs, W MFA/dsl/e85 54 Cafe, Rodeo Grill Centennial Park, Highly Tires
101	Rd K, Nevada, to Camp Clark, E Conoco/dsl, W Hot Spot/dsl, Murphy USA/dsl, Pilot/dsl/scales/24hr Burger King, Buzz's BBQ, Chinese Chef, Pizza Hut, Sonic, Subway Best Value Inn, Country Inn&Suites, Holiday Inn Express, Nevada Inn, Super 8 AutoZone, Chrysler/Dodge/Jeep/Ford, Verizon, Walmart/Subway, Wilson Tire
95	Rd E, Milo
91	Rds DD, BB, to Bellamy
88	Rds B, N, Sheldon, Bronaugh, E to Stockton Lake (33 mi)
83	Rds C, V, Irwin
80	Rds EE, DD
77	US 160, Lamar, Mindenmines, E Phillips 66, Sinclair/dsl/scales/24hr Bamboo House, KFC/Taco Bell, McDonald's, Pizza Hut, Sonic, Subway, Taco Palace Blue Top Inn, Super 8 $General, Blue Top Quiltshop, Family$, O'Reilly Parts, truck/trailer/tire repair, truckwash, W Conoco/Roady's/dsl, Murphy USA/dsl DQ H, Lamar Truck/tire, Walmart
74	30th Rd
70	MO 126, Golden City, Pittsburg
66	Rds K, H, Jasper, W Conoco/dsl, Judy's Trkstp/Cafe/dsl $General
63	Rds N, M
56	Garrison Ave (from sb), to Carthage, E Best Inn (2 mi)
55	Civil War Rd, to Carthage
53	MO 571 S, MO 96, MO 171 N, Central Ave, Carthage, E Casey's/dsl, Phillips 66/dsl Arby's, Boomer's BBQ, Burger King, LJ Silver, McDonald's, Sirloin Stockade, Sonic, Subway EconoLodge $General, Price Cutter
51	Fairview Ave, to Carthage
50	Rd HH, Fir Rd, E Murphy USA, Phillips 66/McDonald's/dsl Big Ben's BBQ, Hardee's, Iggy's Diner, Little Caesar's, Shakes Custard, Taco Bell, Wendy's Best Western, Super 8 $General, $Tree, Aldi Foods, Chrysler/Dodge/Jeep, Ford, Lowe's, Walgreens, Walmart/Subway, W H

NEVADA

CARTHAGE

MO

INTERSTATE 49 Cont'd

Exit#	Services
49	MO 571, Garrison Ave, to Carthage (from nb)
47	Cedar Rd, W [other] Coachlight RV Ctr/Park, Mid America RV Ctr
46mm	I-44, E to Springfield, W to Joplin. **I-49 and I-44 run together 7 mi. See I-44, exit 15.**
39b	I-44, E to Springfield, W to Joplin. **I-49 and I-44 run together 7 mi. See I-44, exit 15.**
39a	Rd FF, 32nd St, E [other] Kenworth, W [gas] FLYING J/Denny's/dsl/LP/scales/24hr/@ [other] Blue Beacon, Goodyear Tires/repair, Speedco
35	Rd V, Diamond, E [other] G Washington Carver NM
33	MO 175, Gateway Dr, W [gas] Phillips 66/dsl/deli [other] Shoal Creek RV Park
30	Iris Rd
27	MO 86, to Neosho, Racine, E [gas] Love's/McDonald's/Subway/dsl/scales/24hr, Phillips 66/dsl
24	US 60, to Neosho, Seneca, E [gas] Kum&Go/dsl/e85, Murphy USA [food] Burger King, Denny's, El Charro, KFC, LJ Silver, Taco Bell [lodging] Best Western, Super 8 [other] $Tree, Lowe's, Verizon, Walmart, W [other] Whispering Woods RV Park (12 mi)
20	Rd AA
17	Rds C, B, to Goodman, E [other] truck repair
16	MO 59 (from sb), Kelley Springs
10	MO 76, to Anderson, W [gas] Conoco/Subway/dsl [lodging] EconoLodge
7	Rd EE, to Pineville, Lanagan
5	Rd H, to Pineville.

I-49 begins/ends, US 71 continues S, W [other] Bib Elk Camping (1 mi)

INTERSTATE 55

ST LOUIS

Exit#	Services
209mm	Missouri/Illinois state line at St. Louis, Mississippi River
209b	to I-70 W to Kansas City
209a	W [other] Busch Stadium, to Arch
208	Park Ave, 7th St, W [gas] [food] Rally's, Taco Bell, White Castle [lodging] Hilton
207c b	I-44W, Truman Pkwy, to Tulsa
207a	Gravois St (from nb), E [gas] Midwest Petroleum, W [food] A-1 Chinese Wok, Jack-in-the-Box
206c	Arsenal St, E [other] Anheuser-Busch Tour Ctr, W [gas] Shell/dsl
206b	Broadway (from nb), Broadway (from nb)
206a	Potomac St (from nb)
205	Gasconade, W [other] [H]
204	Broadway, E [gas] Phillips 66, W [gas] Conoco/dsl [food] Hardee's, McDonald's, Subway [other] Family$, O'Reilly Parts, Walgreens
203	Bates St, Virginia Ave, W [gas] [other] 7-11
202c	Loughborough Ave, W [food] Burger King, China King, Little Caesar's, Qdoba, St Louis Bread Co, Starbucks [other] AutoZone, Firestone/auto, Lowe's Whse, Schnuck's Foods
202b	Germania (from sb)
202a	Carondelet (from nb)
201b	Weber Rd
201a	Bayless Ave, E [gas] [food] McDonald's, W [gas] 7-11/gas, Mobil/dsl [food] DQ, Jack-in-the-Box, Subway, Taco Bell [other] auto repair
200	Union Rd (from sb)
199	Reavis Barracks Rd, E [gas] Shell/Circle K [food] STL BBQ
197	US 50, US 61, US 67, Lindbergh Blvd, E [gas] Phillips 66 [food] Applebee's, Arby's, Buffalo Wild Wings, ChuckeCheese, CiCi's, Dillard's, Hometown Buffet, HoneyBaked Ham, Hooters, IHOP, Imo's Pizza, KFC, Krispy Kreme, McAlister's, Noodles&Co, Penn Sta Subs, Qdoba, Starbucks, Steak'n Shake, Subway, Taco Bell, Tucker's Place,
197	Continued Wendy's [lodging] Holiday Inn [other] AT&T, Best Buy, Chrysler/Dodge/Jeep, CVS Drug, Dick's, Dobbs Tire, Ford/Lincoln, Home Depot, JC Penney, Jo-Ann Fabrics, Macy's, Marshall's, NTB, Verizon, vet, W [gas] QT/dsl [food] Bob Evans, Culvers, Denny's, Golden Corral, O'Charley's, Panda Express, Pasta House [lodging] Best Value Inn [other] Aldi Foods, AT&T, CarMax, Chevrolet, Costco/gas, Honda, Hyundai, Kia, Mazda, Nissan, Target, VW
196b	I-270 W, to Kansas City
196a	I-255 E, to Chicago
195	Butler Hill Rd, E [gas] Phillips 66 [lodging] Hampton Inn [other] Advance Parts, Walgreens, Holiday Inn Express, Popeye's, W [gas] Phillips 66 [food] Burger King, Hardee's, Subway, Taco Bell, Waffle House [other] Schnuck's Foods, tires/repair
193	Meramec Bottom Rd, E [gas] QT/dsl [food] Cracker Barrel [lodging] Best Western [other] Midwest RV Ctr
191	MO 141, Arnold, E [gas] [food] 54th St Grill, Applebee's, Arby's, Bandana's BBQ, Capt D's, Chick-fil-A, China King, Denny's, Dunkin Donuts/Baskin Robbins, Fazoli's, Five Guys, Jack-in-the-Box, Jimmy John's, Las Fuentes, Lee's Chicken, Lion's Choice, LJ Silver, McDonald's, Panda Express, Papa John's, Rally's, Starbucks, Steak'n Shake, Super China Buffet, Taco Bell, Terrazza Grill, Wendy's [lodging] Drury Inn, Pear Tree Inn [other] Aldi Foods, AT&T, CVS Drug, Dobbs Tire, Gordman's, Hobby Lobby, Kohl's, NAPA, O'Reilly Parts, PetCo, Shop'n Save Foods, vet, Walgreens, Walmart/Subway, W [gas] Phillips 66/Circle K/dsl [food] Chili's, First Wok, Pasta House, Penn Sta Subs, Qdoba, St Louis Bread, Sunny St Cafe, TX Roadhouse [lodging] Woodspring Suites [other] $Tree, Dierberg's Foods, GNC, Lowe's, Office Depot, Petsmart, Ross, Verizon
190	Richardson Rd, E [gas] BP/McDonald's, Hucks, Phillips 66/dsl, Shell/Circle K/dsl [food] Culver's, Domino's, DQ, Pizza Hut, Ponderosa, Taco Bell, White Castle [other] $Tree, Advance Parts, Auto Tire, Firestone, Save-A-Lot Foods, URGENT CARE, W [gas] Phillips 66/dsl, Shell/Circle K/dsl [food] Burger King, Front Row Grill, Happy Wok, Imo's Pizza, McDonald's/playplace, Mr. Goodcents Subs, Ruby Tuesday, Waffle House [lodging] Quality Inn [other] 7-11, Aamco, AutoZone, GNC, Home Depot, Plaza Tire, Schnuck's Foods, Target, Walgreens
186	Imperial, Kimmswick, E [gas] Mobil, Shell/Circle K [food] Big Carl's BBQ, Blue Owl (1mi) [other] auto repair, W [gas] Phillips 66/Jack-in-the-Box/dsl [food] China Wok, Domino's, Ginono's Grill, Papa John's, Scottie's Grill, Subway [other] to Mastodon SP, USPO
185	rd M, Barnhart, Antonia, W [gas] Phillips 66, Phillips 66/dsl [other] Karsch's Mkt, USPO, Walgreens
180	rd Z, to Hillsboro, Pevely, E [gas] Mobil/dsl [food] Burger King, Domino's, Main St BBQ, Pizza Hut, Subway, Taco Bell [other] $General, Queens Foods, W [gas] Mr Fuel/dsl, Phillips 66/McDonald's/dsl/scales [lodging] Super 8 [other] auto repair, rv camping
178	Herculaneum, E [gas] QT/Wendy's/dsl/scales, Shell/Circle K [food] Cracker Barrel, DQ, Jack-in-the-Box, La Pachanga Mexican, Subway [other] Toyota, Little Caesar's, W [other] Buick/GMC, Cadillac/Chevrolet, Ford, vet
175	rd A, Festus, E [gas] Mobil, Murphy USA/dsl, Phillips 66/dsl [food] Arby's, Bob Evans, Burger King, Capt D's, China 1, Fazoli's, Hibachi Grill, Imo's Pizza, Jack-in-the-Box, McDonald's/playplace, Oriental Buffet, Panda Express, Papa John's, Sonic, St. Louis Bread Co, Steak'n Shake, Subway, Taco Bell, White Castle [lodging] La Quinta, Quality Inn [other] $Tree, Advance Parts, Aldi Foods, AT&T, AutoZone, CVS Drug, Dobbs Tire, GNC, Home Depot, Plaza Tire, Schnuck's Foods/gas, URGENT CARE, Walgreens, Walmart, Verizon, W [gas] Phillips 66/7-11/dsl, Phillips

INTERSTATE 55 Cont'd

Exit	Services
175	Continued 66/Domino's/dsl Hardee's, Jimmy John's, Ruby Tuesday, Waffle House, Whittaker's Pizza Comfort Inn, Holiday Inn Express Chrysler/Dodge/Jeep, Lowe's
174b a	US 67, Lp 55, Festus, Crystal City, E Phillips 66/dsl H
170	US 61, W BP/dsl/LP Gators Grill
165	rd TT (from sb)
162	rds DD, OO
160mm	**nb/weigh sta sb, full facilities, litter barrels, petwalk, , vending**
157	rd Y, Bloomsdale, E Phillips 66/Subway, W Loves/ Chester's/McDonald's/dsl/scales/24hr
154	rd O, to St Genevieve
150	MO 32, rds B, A, to St Genevieve, E DQ H, Hist Site (6mi), W Phillips 66/dsl Hawn SP (11mi)
143	rds J, M, N, Ozora, W Exxon/Subway/dsl/scales/24hr Econolodge truckwash
PERRYVILLE	
141	rd Z, St Mary
135	rd M, Brewer
129	MO 51, to Perryville, E MotoMart/McDonald's/dsl Burger King, KFC, Ponderosa, Taco Bell H, Ford, W Rhodes/IMO's/dsl China Buffet, Five Star Chinese, Subway Comfort Inn, Days Inn, Super 8 AT&T, Buick/Chevrolet, Chrysler/Dodge/Jeep, Walmart, Holiday Inn
123	rd B, Biehle, W Rhodes/dsl
119mm	Apple Creek
117	rd KK, to Appleton
111	rd E, Oak Ridge
110mm	**sb/full facilities, truck parking nb**
105	US 61, Fruitland, E Casey's, Phillips 66/dsl, Rhodes/dsl $General, Purcell Tires/repair, Trail of Tears SP (11mi), W D-Mart/dsl Bavarian Halle, DQ, Pizza Inn Drury Inn
CAPE GIRARDEAU	
102	LaSalle Ave, E Main St
99	US 61, MO 34, to Jackson, E RV camping, W Delmonico's Steaks Comfort Suites Hill Top RV, McDowell South RV Ctr
96	rd K, to Cape Girardeau, E Phillips 66/dsl Applebee's, Buffalo Wild Wings, Burger King, Chick-fil-A, China Town, CiCi's Pizza, Cracker Barrel, Daddy's Cheesecake, Denny's, Dexter BBQ, DQ, El Acapulco, Firehouse Subs, Golden Corral, Great Wall Chinese, Honey Baked Ham, IHOP, Logan's Roadhouse, O'Charley's, Olive Garden, Panera Bread, Papa Murphy's, Popeye's, Qdoba, Red Lobster, Ruby Tuesday, Starbucks, Steak'n Shake, Subway, Taco Bell, TX Roadhouse, Wendy's Auburn Place, Drury Lodge/rest., Hampton Inn, Holiday Inn Express, PearTree Inn H, AT&T, Barnes&Noble, Best Buy, BigLots, CVS Drug, Hobby Lobby, JC Penney, Macy's, Old Navy, Schnuck's Foods, to SEMSU, Verizon, W Shell McDonald's/playplace, Outback Steaks, Penn Sta Subs, White Castle Drury Suites, Quality Inn $Tree, Chrysler/Dodge/Jeep, Honda, Hyundai, Kohl's, Lowe's, Mazda, Nissan, PetCo, Plaza Tire, Sam's Club, Staples, Target, TJ Maxx, Toyota, Walmart/Subway
95	MO 74 E, E Mercato/dsl Candlewood Suites URGENT CARE, W Menard's
93a b	MO 74 W, Cape Girardeau
91	rd AB, to Cape Girardeau, E Rhodes/IMO's/dsl Staxx Diner Harley-Davidson, tire repair, vet, W , Capetown RV Ctr
89	US 61, rds K, M, Scott City, E Rhodes Burger King, Ice Cream Corner, Las Brisas Mexican, Pizza Hut, Pizza Pro, Subway $General, Bob's Foods, Medicap Drug, NAPA, Plaza Tire/auto

MO

Exit	Services
87	MO PP
80	MO 77, Benton, E Express/dsl, W Exxon/McDonald's/ dsl/fireworks Subway antiques, winery (8mi)
MINER	
69	rd HH, to Sikeston, Miner, E Peterbilt, W H, golf
67	US 60, US 62, Miner, E Breaktime/dsl Best Value Inn, Best Western+, Motel 6 Hinton RV Park, **0-2 mi W** Conoco, Hucks, Jasper's Gas, Mobil, QuickCheck Bo's BBQ, Buffalo Wild Wings, Burger King, Dexter BBQ, El Tapatio Mexican, Lambert's Rest., Little Caesar's, McDonald's, Papa Murphy's, Pizza Hut, Pizza Inn, Ruby Tuesday, Sergio's Mexican, Sonic, Subway, Taco John's, Wendy's Comfort Inn, Country Hearth Inn, Drury Inn, PearTree Inn, Super 8 H, $General, AutoZone, Buick/Chevrolet, Cadillac/GMC, CVS Drug, Family$, Food Giant, Food Giant, Raben Tires, Sikeston Outlets/famous brands, Walgreens
66b	US 60 W, to Poplar Bluff, **3 mi W on US 61/62** Breaktime/E-85 A&W/LJ Silver, Applebee's, Arby's, China Buffet, Colton's Steaks, DQ, El Bracero Mexican, Hardee's, La Ruleta Mexican, McDonald's, Sonic, Taco Bell Days Inn, Holiday Inn Express $Tree, Aldi Foods, AT&T, Chrysler/Dodge/Jeep, Ford/Lincoln, GNC, JC Penney, Lowe's, O'Reilly Parts, Walmart/Subway, Hampton Inn, Loves/Dunkin Donuts/dsl/scales/24hr, Watami, Zaxby's
66a	I-57 E, to Chicago, US 60 W
59mm	St Johns Bayou
58	MO 80, Matthews, E TA/Taco Bell/dsl/scales/24hr/@ to Big Oak Tree SP (24mi), truck repair, W FLYING J/Denny's/dsl/LP/RV dump/scales/24hr, LNG, Loves/Chester's/Subway/dsl/scales/24hr repair
52	rd P, Kewanee, E Mobil/BJ Trvl Ctr/BBQ/dsl
49	US 61, US 62, New Madrid, E Hunter-Dawson HS (3mi)
44	US 61, US 62, Lp 55, New Madrid, E Higgerson School Hust Site
42mm	**sb/full facilities, truck parking nb**
40	rd EE, St Jude Rd, Marston, E Pilot/Subway/dsl/scales/24hr Hunter Lodge, W MFA Travelodge
32	US 61, MO 162, Portageville, W Casey's, Phillips 66/dsl China King, McDonald's, Sonic, Subway $General
27	rds K, A, BB, to Wardell, E RV camping (2mi), W Delta Research Ctr
20mm	**nb, full facilities, litter barrels, petwalk, , picnic table, vending**
HAYTI	
19	MO 84, Hayti, E Double Nickel/dsl, Pilot/Arby's/dsl/scales/24hr, Shell KFC/Taco Bell, McDonald's, Pizza Hut Quality Inn, Regency Motel Lady Luck Casino/camping, Burger King, W Exxon/Hayti Trvl Ctr/Subway/dsl, Phillips/dsl, R&P/dsl Apple Barrel, Chubby's BBQ, Los Portales, Patty Ann's BBQ Drury Inn H, $General, CarQuest, Fred's Store, Hay's Foods, repair, USPO

= gas = food = lodging = other = rest stop

MO

N INTERSTATE 55 Cont'd

Exit#	Services
17b a	I-155 E, US 412, to TN
14	rds J, H, U, to Caruthersville, Braggadocio
10mm	**weigh sta nb**
8	US 61, MO 164, Steele, **E** truck repair, **W** Shell/Subway/dsl/scales Deerfield Inn
4	rd E, to Holland, Cooter
3mm	**truck parking both lanes**
1	US 61, rd O, Holland, **W** Shell/dsl/24hr
0mm	Missouri/Arkansas state line

N INTERSTATE 57

Exit#	Services
22mm	Missouri/Illinois state line, Mississippi River
18.5mm	**weigh sta both lanes**
12	US 62, MO 77, Charleston, **E** FLYING J/Huddle House/dsl/scales/24hr Eagle Inn JSH Towing/repair, **W** Casey's/dsl Las Brisas Mexican Super 8 vet, Waffle&Pancake House
10	MO 105, Charleston, **E** Exxon/Boomland/dsl McDonald's, Wally's Eatery Boomland RV Park, **W** Casey's China Buffet, Pizza Hut, Subway Quality Inn city park, CountryMart Foods, Plaza Tire
4	rd B, Bertrand
1b a	I-55, N to St Louis, S to Memphis.

I-57 begins/ends on I-55, exit 66.

E INTERSTATE 64

ST LOUIS

Exit#	Services
41mm	Missouri/Illinois state line, Mississippi River
40b a	Broadway St, to Stadium, to the Arch, **N** Hilton, Sheraton, stadium, **S** Dobb's Tire
40c	(from wb), I-44 W, I-55 S
39c	11th St (exits left), downtown
39b	14th St, **N** Sheraton, **S** BP, downtown
39a	21st St, Market St (from wb), **N** Drury Inn, Hampton Inn
38d	Chestnut at 20th St, **N** Drury Inn, Hampton Inn
38c	Jefferson Ave, St Louis Union Sta, **N** Joplin House, **S** Residence Inn
38a	Forest Park Blvd (from wb), **N** Shell
37b a	Market St, Bernard St, Grand Blvd, **N** Shell Del Taco Adam's Mark Hotel, Courtyard, Drury Inn, Hampton Inn, Hyatt, Marriott
36d	Vandeventer Ave, Chouteau Ave
36b a	Kingshighway, **N** H, **S** BP
34d c	Hampton Ave, Forest Park, **N** museums, zoo, **S** BP, Mobil, Phillips 66 Courtesy Diner, Hardee's, Imo's Pizza, Jack-in-the-Box, Smokin' Al's BBQ, Steak'n Shake, Subway, Taco Bell Hampton Inn
34a	Oakland Ave, **N** Del Taco, Subway H
33d	McCausland Ave, **N** Del Taco
33c	Bellevue Ave, **N** H
33b	Big Bend Blvd
32b a	Eager Rd, Hanley Rd, **S** Shell Chick-fil-A, Chipotle, Lion's Choice, McDonald's, Panda Express, Subway Best Buy, Dierberg's Foods, Home Depot, Petco, Petsmart, REI, Target, Trader Joe's, Whole Foods Mkt
31b a	I-170 N, **N** Burger King, CA Pizza Kitchen, Cheesecake Factory, Five Guys, IHOP, Maggiano's, PF Chang's, St Louis Bread Homewood Suites CVS Drug, Dillard's, Macy's,

CHESTERFIELD

Exit#	Services
31b a	Continued Nordstrom, Verizon, **S** Bonefish Grill, Chick-fil-A, Subway Dierberg's Foods, Drury Inn, Michael's, Target
30	McKnight Rd
28b	Clayton Rd (from wb)
28a	US 67, US 61, Lindbergh Blvd, **N** Honda, **S** Bricktops, Brio Grill, Fleming's Rest., Schneithouse Rest., St Louis Bread, Starbucks, Tim Hortons Hilton Shnuck's Foods
27	Spoede Rd
26	rd JJ, Ballas Rd, **N** H, **S** H
25	I-270, N to Chicago, S to Memphis
24	Mason Rd, **N** Courtyard, Marriott hwy patrol, LDS Temple
23	Maryville Centre Dr (from wb), **N** Courtyard, Marriott
22	MO 141, **N** H, **S** Five Guys, Hot Wok
21	Timberlake Manor Pkwy
20	Chesterfield Pkwy (from wb), same as 19b a
19b a	MO 340, Chesterfield Pkwy, Olive Blvd, **N** BP, Shell Charlie Gitto's, Sheridan's Custard, Taco Bell DoubleTree Hotel, Hampton Inn, Homewood Suites, Residence Inn, SpringHill Suites Dobb's Tire, Schnucks Foods, USPO, Walgreens, **S** Mobil California Pizza Kitchen, Cheesecake Factory, Chili's, Edgewild Rest., PF Chang's, Twin Peaks Drury Plaza Hotel, Hyatt Place Dillard's
17	Boones Crossing, Long Rd, Chesterfield Airport Rd, **N** Prestige Outlets/famous brands, **S** Mobil 54th St Grill, Bar Louie, Brickhouse Tavern, Buffalo Wild Wings, Cane's, Chick-fil-A, Culver's, East Coast Pizza, Fox&Hound, Hardee's, IHOP, Jason's Deli, Kaldi's Coffee, Lion's Choice, Longhorn Steaks, McDonald's, Mimi's Cafe, Old Spaghetti Factory, Olive Garden, Original Pancakes, Panda Express, Pie Five, Qdoba Mexican, Red Lobster, Red Robin, SmokeHouse Rest., Sonic, St Louis Bread, St Louis Bread, Steak'n Shake, Subway, Syberg's Cafe, Taco Bell, Wendy's Courtyard, Hampton Inn, Hilton Garden $Tree, Aldi Foods, AutoTire Care, AutoZone, Best Buy, Dick's, Dobb's Tire, Firestone/auto, Ford, GNC, Gordman's, Home Depot, Lowe's, Michael's, Old Navy, Petsmart, Ross, Sam's Club, Target, Verizon, Walgreens, Walmart, WorldMkt
16	Long Rd (from wb)
14	Chesterfield Airport Rd (from eb), **S** BP/dsl, Phillips 66/dsl Comfort Inn Premium Outlets/famous brands
13mm	Missouri River
11	Research Park Ctr Dr, **S** Wingate Inn
10	MO 94 (from wb), **N** Mercedes
9	rd k, O'Fallon, **N** Mobil, QT/dsl Arby's, Cracker Barrel, Culver's, Denny's, Las Margaritas, McDonald's, Starbucks, Subway, Walnut Grill, Wendy's Holiday Inn Express, Residence Inn, Sleep Inn, Staybridge Suites Chevrolet, Honda, H Walgreens
6	rd DD, Wing Haven Blvd, **N** Phillips 66 Bristol Seafood Hunan King, Massa's Italian, Outback Steaks, Subway Hilton Garden vet
4	rd N, **N** Phillips 66 Qdoba Mexican, Red Robin JC Penney, Petco, Shop'n Save, Target, **S** Murphy USA/dsl Phillips 66 Arby's, El Maguay, Jack-in-the-Box, McDonald's, Sonic, St. Louis Bread Co., Starbucks, Steak'n Shake, Subway Taco Bell, Wendy's, White Castle $Tree, Aldi Foods, AutoZone, Dobb's Tire, Firestone/auto, GNC, Lowe's, Walmart
2	Lake St. Louis Blvd, **N** Hucks/dsl BC's Rest., Max&Erma's Old Navy, Schnuck's Foods, Von Maur, Walgreens
1	Prospect Rd
0mm	I-70 E to St Louis, W to Kansas City

INTERSTATE 70

ST LOUIS

Exit#	Services
251.5mm	Missouri/Illinois state line, Mississippi River
251a	I-55 S, to Memphis, to I-44, to downtown/no return
249b	Tucker Blvd, downtown St Louis, S Mobil/dsl
249a	I-44 W, I-55 S
248b	St Louis Ave, Branch St
248a	Salisbury St, McKinley Br, S BP, Phillips 66
247	Grand Ave, N BP, Phillips 66/Subway/dsl Western Inn
246b	Adelaide Ave
246a	N Broadway, O'Fallon Park, N Loves/McDonald's/Subway/dsl/scales/24hr, Mobil/dsl Freightliner, truck tires
245b	W Florissant
245a	Shreve Ave, S BP
244b	Kingshighway, S Burger King, McDonald's, Subway Walgreens
244a	Bircher Blvd, Union Blvd, N BP/dsl, Mobil/dsl
243b	(243c from eb) Bircher Blvd
243a	Riverview Blvd
243	Goodfellow Blvd, N BP, Conoco/dsl
242b a	Jennings Sta Rd, S Western Inn
241b	Lucas-Hunt Rd, N Shell/Circle K, 3/4 mi S Church's, Lee's Chicken, McDonald's Walgreens
241a	Bermuda Rd, S H
240b a	Florissant Rd, N BP/McDonald's Family$, Schnuck's Foods
239	N Hanley Rd, N Hilton Garden, S BP
238c b	I-170 N, I-170 S, no return
238a	N Lambert-St Louis Airport, S Renaissance Hotel
237	Natural Bridge Rd (from eb), S Phillips 66, Shell Church's, Jack-in-the-Box, Rally's, Steak'n Shake, Waffle House Ramada Inn, Renaissance, Travelodge
236	Lambert-St Louis Airport, S BP/dsl Bandana's BBQ, Golden Pancake, Lombardo's Café Rafferty's Rest., Subway Best Value Inn, Drury Inn, Econolodge, Hampton Inn, Hilton, Holiday Inn, Holiday Inn Express, Marriott, Peartree Inn, Quality Inn
235c	Cypress Rd, rd B W, N to
235b a	US 67, Lindbergh Blvd, N Airport Plaza Hotel, S Lion's Choice Rest., TGIFriday's Crowne Plaza, Embassy Suites, Extended Stay America Menard's
234	MO 180, St Charles Rock Rd, N BP, Phillips 66/dsl A&W/LJ Silver, Applebee's, Arby's, Chimi's Mexican, Chipotle, Fazoli's, HomeTown Buffet, Imo's Pizza, Jack-in-the-Box, Jimmy John's, LoneStar Steaks, McDonald's, New China Buffet, Pizza Hut, Ponderosa, Red Lobster, St Louis Bread, Subway, Taco Bell, Wendy's, White Castle, Ya Hala Mediterranean H, $Tree, Aldi Foods, AT&T, AutoZone, Best Buy, CVS Drug, Hobby Lobby, Kohl's, Meineke, NTB, Office Depot, Petsmart, Save-A-Lot Foods, Target, Verizon, Walgreens, Walmart/Burger King, S IHOP, Lion's Choice Chrysler/Dodge/Jeep, Home Depot, Schnuck's, Shamel Tires/repair, Walgreens
232	I-270, N to Chicago, S to Memphis
231b a	Earth City Expwy, N Motomart, Phillips 66/Jack-in-the-Box/dsl Malone's Grill, McDonald's Candlewood Suites, Courtyard, Extended Stay America, Holiday Inn, Residence Inn, SpringHill Suites, S Mobil Burger King, Dave&Buster's, Subway Holiday Inn Express, Homewood Suites, La Quinta Hollywood Casino/Hotel, Riverport Ampitheatre
230mm	Missouri River
229b a	5th St, St Charles, N BP, Mobil/dsl, Motomart/dsl Bellacino's Italian, Buffalo Wild Wings, China House Buffet, Denny's, Dunkin Donuts, Firehouse Subs, Jack-in-the-Box, Lee's Chicken, Little Tokyo, McDonald's, Qdoba, Starbucks, TX Roadhouse, Waffle House Best Value Inn, Best Western, Comfort Suites Aldi Foods, Ameristar Casino, Bass Pro Shops, Gordman's, Walgreens, S QT/dsl Bar Louie, Cracker Barrel, Five Guys, Tuscanos Brazilian Drury Suites, Embassy Suites, Fairfield Inn
228	MO 94, to Weldon Springs, St Charles, N Mobil/dsl, QT/dsl Arby's, DQ, Imo's Pizza, Papa John's, Steak'n Shake Advance Parts, AutoZone, CVS Drug, GNC, NAPA, Schnuck's, Valvoline, S Mobil/dsl, QT Chinese Express, ChuckECheese, Fazoli's, Gingham's Rest., Grappa Grill, Jimmy John's, McAlister's Deli, Outback Steaks, Pizza Hut, Tilted Kilt Intown Suites $General, access to 227, Dobb's Tire
227	Zumbehl Rd, N Phillips 66/dsl, ZX Culpepper's Grill Super 8 Ford, Lowe's, Sav-A-Lot Foods, S BP, Hucks/dsl Applebee's, Big Woody's BBQ, Bob Evans, Capt D's, El Mariachi Mexican, Fratelli's Ristorante, Golden Corral, Hardee's, Hoho Chinese, Jack-in-the-Box, McDonald's, Papa Murphy's, Penn Sta Subs, Shogun, Smashburger, St Louis Bread, Subway, Taco Bell Red Roof Inn, TownePlace Suites $Tree, access to 228, Dierberg's Foods, GNC, Jiffy Lube, Michael's, NTB, Petco, Petsmart, Sam's Club/gas, Schnuck's Foods, URGENT CARE, vet, Walgreens, Walmart
225	Truman Rd, to Cave Springs, N Phillips 66/dsl Hampton Inn, Rodeway Inn Buick/GMC, Cadillac, Harley Davidson, Indian Motorcycles, Mazda, Subaru, U-Haul, VW, S Conoco, QT Bandanas BBQ, Burger King, Chimi's Mexican, Culver's, Denny's, Hibachi Grill, Hooters, IHOP, Jack-in-the-Box, KFC, Lion's Choice Rest., LJ Silver, Longhorn Steaks, Los Chavez Mexican, McDonald's, O'Charley's, Pasta House, Red Lobster, Steak'n Shake, Subway, Taco Bell, Thai Kitchen, Wendy's, White Castle Country Inn&Suites, Courtyard H, Advance Parts, AT&T, Batteries+Bulbs, Chrysler/Dodge/Jeep, Firestone, Hobby Lobby, Home Depot, Kia, Office Depot, Shop'n Save, Target, TJ Maxx, URGENT CARE, Verizon
224	MO 370 E
222	Mid-Rivers Mall Dr, rd C, St Peters, N QT/dsl/24hr Burger King CarMax, Chevrolet, Honda, Lincoln, Toyota, S Mobil/dsl Arby's, Bob Evans, Buffalo Wild Wings, Chili's, China Wok, Domino's, Fazoli's, HoneyBaked Ham, Joe's Crabshack, Max & Erma's, McDonald's/playplace, Olive Garden, Planet Sub, Qdoba, Red Robin, Ruby Tuesday, St Louis Bread, Steak'n Shake, Subway, Taco Bell, Wendy's Drury Inn, Extended Stay America Aldi Foods, Barnes&Noble, Best Buy, BigLots, Costco/gas, Dick's, Dillard's, Hyundai/Nissan/VW, JC Penney, Jo-Ann Fabrics, Kia, Macy's, Marshall's, NTB, Verizon

ST PETERS

= gas = food = lodging = other = rest stop

INTERSTATE 70 Cont'd

Exit#	Services
220	MO 79, to Elsberry, N Cherokee Lakes Camping (7mi), S 7-11/gas, BP, Phillips 66/dsl El Mezon, Gettemeier's Rest., Jack-in-the-Box, McDonald's/playplace, Pirrone's Pizzaria, Sonic, Subway Days Inn Dierberg's Foods, O'Reilly Parts, Walgreens
219	T R Hughes Blvd, S Comfort Inn
217	rds K, M, O'Fallon, N Hucks/dsl Baskin-Robbins, Burger King, Jack-in-the-Box, Piggy's BBQ, Pizza Hut/Taco Bell, Rally's, Sonic, Waffle House Firestone, Jiffy Lube, O'Reilly Parts, S Mobil/dsl, Phillips 66/dsl, QT Applebee's, Arby's, Bob Evans, Cappuccino's, Domino's, Fazoli's, Golden Corral, Jimmy John's, KFC, Lion's Choice Rest., McDonald's/playplace, Pantera's Pizza, Papa John's, Pizza Hut, Red Robin, St Louis Bread, Stefanina's Pizza, Subway, TX Roadhouse, Wendy's Advance Parts, Aldi Foods, Auto Tire, AutoZone, CVS Drug, GNC, Home Depot, Lowe's, Meineke, Midas, Schnuck's Foods, Shop'n Save Foods, Verizon, Walgreens, Walmart
216	Bryan Rd, N Super 8 Ford, Peterbilt, St Louis RV Ctr, S Conoco, Phillips 66/Jack-in-the-Box/dsl, QT DQ, Little Caesar's, Mr. Goodcents, Wendy's
214	Lake St Louis, N Phillips 66/McDonald's/dsl, S Phillips 66/dsl, Shell/Circle K Denny's, Hardee's Best Value Inn H
212	rd A, N Economy Inn Camping World, S Mobil Pizzamenti's Cafe Regency Plaza Hotel Chrysler/Dodge/Jeep
210b a	I-64, US 40 E, US 61 N, S H
209	rd Z, Church St, New Melle, N DQ, S Phillips 66/dsl Stone Summit Steaks Hampton Inn
208	Pearce Blvd, Wentzville Pkwy, Wentzville, N Mobil/dsl, QT/dsl 54th St Grill, 88 China, Applebee's, Arby's, Bob Evans, Buffalo Wild Wings, Chick-fil-A, China Buffet, Culver's, Domino's, El Maguey, Fritz's Custard, Hardee's, Jack-in-the-Box, Jimmy John's, KFC, Lion's Choice, Little Caesar's, McDonald's, Olive Garden, Panda Express, Papa John's, Penn Sta., Pizza Hut, Pizza Pro, Ruby Tuesday, St Louis Bread, Starbucks, Steak'n Shake, Subway, Sunny St Cafe, Taco Bell, Waffle House, Wendy's, White Castle Fairfield Inn H, $General, AT&T, AutoZone, Chevrolet, Dick's, Dierberg's Foods, Dobb's Tire, GNC, Home Depot, Kohl's, Lowe's, Michael's, NAPA, O'Reilly Parts, Petsmart, Ross, Sam's Club/dsl, Save-A-Lot, Schnuck's Food, Target, URGENT CARE, Verizon, Walgreens, Walmart, S BP/dsl Bandana's BBQ, Chimi's FreshMex, IHOP, TX Roadhouse Super 8 Hyundai, Thomas RV Ctr
204mm	**weigh sta both lanes**
203	rds W, T, Foristell, N Mr Fuel/dsl/scales, TA/BP/Pizza Hut/Popeye's/Taco Bell/dsl/scales/24hr/@ Quality Inn, S Phillips 66/McDonald's/dsl dsl repair
200	rds J, H, F (from wb), Wright City, N Phillips 66/dsl Ruiz Castillo's Mexican (1mi) $General, S Subway Super 7 Inn
199	rd J, H, F, Wright City, N Shell/McDonald's/dsl $General, S Super 7 Inn Volvo Trucks
198mm	**both lanes, full facilities, litter barrels, petwalk,**
193	MO 47, Warrenton, N Fast Lane/DQ/dsl, Mobil/dsl 1st Wok, Applebee's, Burger King, China House, Dominos, DQ, El Jimador Mexican, Jack-in-the-Box, Little Caesar's, McDonald's, Pizza Hut, Subway, Waffle House, Wendy's Best Value Inn, Holiday Inn Express, Super 8 Aldi Foods, AT&T, Moser's Foods, Walmart, S BP/dsl, Conoco/dsl, Phillips 66/dsl
193	Continued Denny's, Imo's Pizza, Papa John's, Taco Bell Baymont Inn AutoZone, CarQuest, Chevrolet, NAPA, O'Reilly Parts, Walgreens
188	rds A, B, to Truxton, S FLYING J/Denny's/dsl/LP/RV Dump/scales/24hr Motel 6
183	rds E, NN, Y, Jonesburg, 1 mi N Jonesburg Gardens Camping, S Phillips 66/Chester's/dsl USPO
179	rd F, High Hill, S Colonial Inn, Motel 70
175	MO 19, New Florence, N BP/dsl, Shell/dsl/24hr Dad's Jct Cafe, McDonald's Best Inn, Best Value Inn, Days Inn auto repair, Stone Hill Winery/gifts (15mi)
170	MO 161, rd J, Danville, N Red's/dsl Kan-Do RV Park, to Graham Cave SP, S Lazy Day RV Park
169.5mm	**truck parking**
168mm	Loutre River
167mm	**truck parking eb**
161	rds D, YY, Williamsburg, N Cranes/mkt Marlene's Rest. USPO
155	rds A, Z, to Calwood, N antiques
148	US 54, Kingdom City, N BP/dsl, Phillips 66/Burger King/dsl Taco Bell MO Tourism Ctr, to Mark Twain Lake, S Fast Lane/DQ/dsl, Gulf/Gasper's/Arby's/dsl/scales/@, Petro/Mobil/Iron Skillet/dsl/scales/24hr/@, Phillips 66/Subway/dsl/scales/24hr Denny's, McDonald's Days Inn, Holiday Inn Express, Motel 6, Quality Inn, Super 8 Ozarkland Gifts, Wheeler's Truckwash
144	rds M, HH, to Hatton, S fireworks
137	rds DD, J, to Millersburg, Stephens, S Ranch House BBQ antiques, Freightliner, to Little Dixie WA (4mi)
133	rd Z, to Centralia, N Camping World RV Ctr
131	Lake of the Woods Rd, N BP, Phillips 66/Subway/dsl Buckingham BBQ, George's Rest, Sonic Super 8 Harley-Davidson, S Conoco/dsl Jimmy John's Holiday Inn
128a	US 63, to Jefferson City, Columbia, N CNG, Mobil/dsl, QT Bandanas BBQ, Bob Evans, Burger King, China Garden, Cracker Barrel, Golden Corral, Hooters, KFC, McDonald's, Pizza Hut, Ruby Tuesday, Steak'n Shake, Taco Bell, Wendy's, White Castle Best Western+, Fairfield Inn, Hampton Inn, Hilton Garden, Red Roof Inn, Residence Inn, SpringHill Suites, Super 8 Bass Pro Shop, Home Depot, Menard's, Pine Grove RV Park, S BreakTime/dsl Applebee's, Baskin-Robbins, Chili's, Chipotle Mexican, CiCi's, Culver's, El Maguey, Firehouse Subs, Five Guys, Freddy's, Good Cents Subs, Houlihan's, IHOP, Kobe Japanese, Little Caesar's, Longhorn Steaks, Panda Express, Panera Bread, Sonic, Starbucks, Subway, TGIFriday's Country Inn&Suites, Drury Plaza, Motel 6, Quality Inn, Ramada, Staybridge Suites, Suburban Inn, Wingate Inn H, $Tree, HyVee Foods, Lowe's/Subway, Patricia's Foods, Sam's Club, Staples, Verizon, Walmart/McDonald's
128	Lp 70 (from wb), Columbia, N Shell Hardee's Honda, S Eastwood Motel H, Big O Tire, NAPA, same as 128a
127	MO 763, to Moberly, Columbia, N Waffle House Budget Host Chrysler/Dodge/Jeep, Fiat, Hyundai, Mazda, Toyota, transmissions, VW, S Phillips 66/dsl Super 7 Motel
126	MO 163, Providence Rd, Columbia, N Phillips 66/dsl Country Kitchen Quality Inn, Red Roof Inn CarQuest, McKnight Tire, same as 127, S BreakTime/dsl Burger King, Carlito's Mexican, Church's, DQ, LJ Silver, McDonald's, Pizza Hut, Subway, Taco Bell H, AutoZone, Buick/Cadillac/Chevrolet/GMC, Nissan, O'Reilly Parts

O'FALLON · WENTZVILLE · WARRENTON · COLUMBIA

MO

 [gas icon] = gas [food icon] = food [lodging icon] = lodging [other icon] = other [RS icon] = rest stop

E INTERSTATE 70 Cont'd

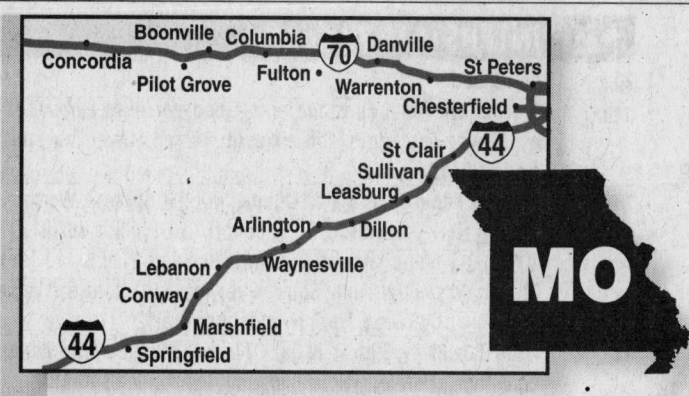

Exit#	Services
125	Lp 70, West Blvd, Columbia, N Comfort Suites, S Phillips 66/dsl Agave Mexican, Cheddar's, Domino's, Fazoli's, Imo's Pizza, JJ's Cafe, Olive Garden, Teppanyaki Grill Days Inn Aldi Foods, BMW, Firestone/auto, Kia, Mercedes, Mosers Foods, same as 124, Subaru, U-Haul, vet
124	MO 740, rd E, Stadium Blvd, Columbia, N Extended Stay America, S BreakTime, Phillips 66/dsl Applebee's, ChuckECheese, Denny's, Five Guys, Hardee's, Jazz Kitchen, KFC, Lee's Chicken, McDonald's, Pancheros, Panera Bread, Pizza Hut, Red Lobster, Ruby Tuesday, Smokehouse BBQ, Sports Zone Grill, Steak'n Shake, Subway, Taco Bell, TX Roadhouse, Wendy's Best Value Inn, Drury Inn, Holiday Inn, La Quinta, Royal Inn $Tree, AT&T, Barnes&Noble, Best Buy, Dick's, Dillard's, Ford, Hobby Lobby, JC Penney, Marshalls, Michael's, Natural Grocers, Old Navy, O'Reilly Parts, PetCo, Petsmart, same as 125, Target, to U of MO, URGENT CARE, Verizon
122mm	Perche Creek
121	US 40, rd UU, Midway, N Midway/dsl/rest., Phillips 66 Budget Inn tires/repair, S golf
117	rds J, O, to Huntsdale, Harrisburg
115	rd BB N, Rocheport, N to Katy Tr SP, winery
114.5mm	Missouri River
111	MO 98, MO 179, to Wooldridge, Overton, S Cenex/dsl/repair RV Park
106	MO 87, Bingham Rd, to Boonville, S Cenex/dsl
104mm	**RS both lanes, full facilities, litter barrels, petwalk, vending**
103	rd B, Main St, Boonville, N Breaktime, Casey's/dsl, Murphy USA/dsl China One Buffet, La Hacienda Mexican, McDonald's, Pizza Hut, Sonic, Subway, Taco Bell Days Inn, Super 8 H, NAPA, RV Express Camping, to Katy Tr SP, Walmart/Subway, S Cenex/dsl Rte B Cafe QT Inn Buick/Chevrolet/GMC
101	US 40, MO 5, to Boonville, N Pilot/Wendy's/dsl/24hr Arby's Comfort Inn, Holiday Inn Express, Isle of Capri Hotel (3mi) Buick/Cadillac/Chevrolet/GMC, Ford, Russell Stover Candies, S Loves/Hardee's/scales/dsl/24hr to Lake of the Ozarks
98	MO 41, MO 135, Lamine, N tires, to Arrow Rock HS (13mi), S Conoco/Ma's Kettle/dsl, Settlers/dsl repair
93mm	Lamine River
89	rd K, to Arrow Rock, N to Arrow Rock HS
84	rd J, N truck repair, Valero/DQ/Stuckey's
78b a	US 65, to Marshall, N Conoco/dsl fireworks, RV Park
77mm	Blackwater River
74	rd YY, N Cenex/Betty's/cafe/dsl/repair/24hr Welcome Motel
71	rds EE, K, to Houstonia
66	MO 127, Sweet Springs, N H, S BreakTime/dsl, Casey's/dsl Brownsville Sta Rest. Night Inn, Super 8 $General, Bumper Parts
65.5mm	Davis Creek
62	rds VV, Y, Emma
58	MO 23, Concordia, N TA/Country Pride/Subway/dsl/scales/24hr/@ El Patron, McDonald's $General, Bratchers Mkt, truck/RV wash, S Breaktime/dsl, Casey's/dsl, Cenex/dsl Dempsey's BBQ, Pizza Hut Best Value Inn, Budget Inn, Days Inn Bumper Parts
57.5mm	**RS both lanes, full facilities, litter barrels, petwalk, vending**

BOONEVILLE

CONCORDIA

Boonville, Columbia, 70, Danville, Concordia, Pilot Grove, Fulton, Warrenton, St Peters, Chesterfield, St Clair, 44, Sullivan, Leasburg, Arlington, Dillon, Lebanon, Waynesville, Conway, Marshfield, 44, Springfield, MO

MO

Exit#	Services
52	rd T, Aullville
49	MO 13, to Higginsville, N Casey's/dsl, Pilot/McDonald's/Subway/dsl/scales/24hr Sure Stay Inn to Confederate Mem, S Super 8 Great Escape RV Park
45	rd H, to Mayview
43mm	**weigh sta both lanes**
41	rds O, M, to Lexington, Mayview
38	MO 131 (from wb), Odessa, S BP/dsl, Phillips 66/dsl, Shell McDonald's, Pizza Hut, Sonic, Subway, Taco John's, Thompson's Country Kitchen $General Mkt, $Tree, O'Reilly Parts, same as 37
37	MO 131, Odessa, N Country Gardens RV Park/dump, S BP/dsl, Phillips 66/dsl, Shell El Camino Real, McDonald's, Pizza Hut, Sonic, Subway, Taco John's, Thompson's Country Kitchen Parkside Inn $General Mkt, $Tree, fireworks, NAPA, O'Reilly Parts, same as 38, Sunrise Mkt
35mm	**truck parking both lanes**
31	rds D, Z, to Bates City, Napoleon, N Bates City RV Camping, S Valero/dsl Bates City BBQ fireworks
29.5mm	Horse Shoe Creek
28	rd H, rd F, Oak Grove, N TA/Country Pride/Popeye's/dsl/scales/24hr/@ Oak Grove Inn Blue Beacon, KOA, S Casey's, Petro/BP/Iron Skillet/DQ/Wendy's/scales/dsl/@, QT/dsl China Buffet, Hardee's, KFC/Taco Bell, McDonald's, Pizza Hut, PJ's Rest., Subway, Waffle House EconoLodge Cash Saver Foods, Lake Paradise RV/Camping (9mi), O'Reilly Parts, SpeedCo Lube, Walgreens, Walmart
24	US 40, rds AA, BB, to Buckner, N Casey's/dsl Papa Murphy's Best Value Inn, Comfort Inn LifeStyle RV Ctr, Price Chopper, vet, S Conoco/Subway/dsl/scales/24hr McDonald's, Sonic Advance Parts, Trailside RV Park/Ctr
21	Adams Dairy Pkwy, N Camping World RV Ctr (1mi), S Murphy USA/dsl, Phillips 66/Burger King/dsl Arby's, Cane's, Chick-fil-A, Chipotle Mexican, Five Guys, Jersey Mike's, Olive Garden, Panda Express, Panera Bread, Pepper Jax Grill, Planet Sub, Sonic, Subway, Taco Bell, TX Roadhouse Courtyard AT&T, GNC, Gordman's, Home Depot, Kohl's, Michael's, NTB, PetCo, Ross, Target, TJ Maxx, Verizon, Walmart
20	MO 7, Blue Springs, N Phillips 66/dsl, QT/dsl Backyard Burger, Bob Evans, China 1, Custard's, Dunkin Donuts, Goodcents Subs, Minsky's Pizza, Papa Murphy's, Rancho Grande, Sonic, Subway Best Value Inn, Days Inn, Econolodge, Rodeway Inn $General, Ace Hardware, CVS Drug, NAPA, O'Reilly Parts, PriceChopper Foods, Walgreens, Walmart Mkt, S BP/dsl, QT, Valero/dsl Applebee's, Big Biscuit, Denny's, Firehouse Subs, Jack-in-the-Box, Jimmy John's, KFC, LJ Silver, McDonald's, Original Pizza, Starbucks, Subway, Taco Bell, Taco Bueno, Wendy's, Winsteads Cafe, Zarda's BBQ Hampton Inn, Quality Inn H, Advance Parts, Aldi Foods, AutoZone,

ODESSA

BLUE SPGS

INTERSTATE 70 Cont'd

20	Continued BigLots, Chevrolet, Firestone/auto, Goodyear/auto, Hobby Lobby, Hy-Vee Foods/gas, Office Depot, Russell Stover, transmissions, URGENT CARE
18	Woods Chapel Rd, N La Quinta, Motel 6, Super 8, Welcome Inn Harley-Davidson, S Conoco/dsl, Phillips 66/dsl, QT, QT (2) China Kitchen, KFC/Taco Bell, Las Playas Mexican, McDonald's, Pizza Hut, Sonic, Subway, Taco John's, Waffle House CVS Drug, Ford, Hyundai, same as 20
17	Little Blue Pkwy, 39th St, N QT/dsl Buffalo Wild Wings, Coldstone, Hereford House, Jimmy John's, Joe's Crabshack, On the Border, Saints Grill, Sonic, Twin Peaks Hilton Garden H, Menard's, World Mkt, S Arby's, BD Mongolian, Carrabba's, Chipotle Mexican, Corner Cafe, Culver's, Golden Corral, Hooters, IHOP, Kobe Steaks, McDonald's, Outback Steaks, Panera Bread, Pie Five, Qdoba, Red Robin, Subway Comfort Suites, Drury Inn, Holiday Inn Express, My Place Candlewood Suites, Carmax, Costco/gas, Lowe's
16mm	Little Blue River
15b	MO 291 N, Independence, **1 exit N on 39th St** Phillips 66, QT 54th St Grill, Applebee's, Burger King, Chick-fil-A, Chili's, ChuckECheese, Famous Dave's, Fazoli's, Logan's Roadhouse, Longhorn Steaks, McDonald's, Noodles&Co, Perkins, Smokehouse BBQ, Starbucks, Taco Bell, Zio's Italian Fairfield Inn, Residence Inn, Staybridge Suites H, AT&T, AutoZone, Barnes&Noble, Best Buy, Dick's, Dillard's, JC Penney, Jo-Ann, Kohl's, Macy's, Marshalls, NTB, Petsmart, Ross, Sam's Club/gas, Target, Walmart
15a	I-470 S, MO 291 S, to Lee's Summit, same as 14
14	Lee's Summit Rd, **1 mi N** Longhorn Steaks, S Tesla EVC Cheddar's, Cracker Barrel, Los Cabos, Old Chicago, Pizza Ranch, Slim Chickens Stoney Creek Hotel Bass Pro Shops, Duluth Trading, Hobby Lobby, Home Depot
12	Noland Rd, Independence, N Conoco/dsl, QT, Shell China Town, Denny's, Domino's, Hardee's, Mr Goodcents, Pizza St, Sheridan's Custard, Sonic, Subway Best Western, Super 8 $General, Advance Parts, Buick/GMC/Cadillac, Chevrolet, Chrysler/Jeep, CVS Drug, Firestone/auto, Ford, Office Depot, to Truman Library, TrueValue, Walgreens, Walmart Mkt, S Phillips 66/Kicks Arby's, Bandana's BBQ, Baskin Robbins, Burger King, HoneyBaked Ham, KFC/Taco Bell, Krispy Kreme, Ma Ma Garden, McDonald's, Olive Garden, Pizza Hut, Quiznos, Red Lobster, Ruby Tuesday, Steak'n Shake, Wendy's American Inn, Best Value Inn, Days Inn, Quality Inn, Red Roof Inn $Tree, BigLots, GNC, Gordman's, HyVee Foods/gas, Old Time Pottery, Petco, PriceChopper Mkt, Tires+, U-Haul
11	US 40, Blue Ridge Blvd, Independence, N A&W/LJ Silver, La Fuentes, Rosie's Cafe, Sonic, Subway, V's Italian, S 7-11, BP, Murphy USA/dsl, Sinclair Applebee's, Big Boy Burgers, Chipotle Mexican, Church's, East Buffet, Firehouse Subs, IHOP, McDonald's, Papa John's, Samurai Chef, Starbucks Family$, GNC, Lowe's, O'Reilly Parts, Verizon, vet, Walmart/Subway
10	Sterling Ave (from eb), same as 11
9	Blue Ridge Cutoff (from wb), N Denny's Adams Mark, Drury Inn, Woodspring Suites, S BP, Phillips 66/Subway Taco Bell Sheraton Sports Complex
8b a	I-435, N to Des Moines, S to Wichita
7b	Manchester Trafficway
7mm	Blue River
7a	US 40 E, 31st St
6	Van Brunt Blvd, N Conoco/7-11, Phillips 66/dsl, S McDonald's VA H
5c	Jackson Ave (from wb)
5b	31st St (from eb)
5a	27th St (from eb)
4c	23rd Ave
4b	18th St
4a	Benton Blvd (from eb), Truman Rd, N Super Stop/Wendy's/dsl Subway Advance Parts, Save-A-Lot Foods
3c	Prospect Ave, N Church's, S McDonald's
3b	Brooklyn Ave (from eb), N Church's, S Shell/dsl McDonald's
3a	Paseo St, S BP/dsl tires
2m	US 71 S, downtown
2l	I-670, to I-35 S
2j	11th St, downtown
2g	I-29/35 N, US 71 N, to Des Moines
2h	US 24 E, downtown
2e	MO 9 N, Oak St, S Phillips 66 Marriott
2d	Main St, downtown
2c	US 169 N, Broadway, S Phillips 66 Marriott
2b	Beardsley Rd
2a	I-35 S, to Wichita
0mm	Missouri/Kansas state line, Kansas River

INDEPENDENCE

KANSAS CITY

INTERSTATE 270 (St Louis)

Exit#	Services
15b a	I-55 N to Chicago, S to St Louis. **I-270 begins/ends in Illinois on I-55/I-70, exit 20.**
12	IL 159, to Collinsville, **1 mi N** QT/dsl, ZX/dsl Applebee's, Denny's, DQ, Hardee's, IHOP, Jack-in-the-Box, Jimmy John's, KFC, Little Caesar's, Papa John's, Subway Aldi Foods, AT&T, Chrysler/Dodge/Jeep, Home Depot, Lowe's, PetsMart, Sam's Club/dsl, Walgreens, Walmart, S H
9	IL 157, to Collinsville, N Comfort Inn, S BP/dsl Hampton Inn
7	I-255, to I-55 S to Memphis
6b a	IL 111, N FLYING J/Denny's/dsl/scales/24hr Hen House Rest. Motel 6 Blue Beacon/scales, Speedco, truck/trailer repair, S Mobil/dsl Denny's, McDonald's/playplace, Taco Bell Best Western+, Days Inn, Fairfield Inn, La Quinta, Super 8 to Pontoon Beach
4	IL 203, Old Alton Rd, to Granite City
3b a	IL 3, N Riverboat Casino, S Phillips 66 Hardee's, Waffle House Budget Motel, EconoLodge, Economy Inn, Sun Motel KOA, MGM Camping
2mm	Chain of Rocks Canal
0mm	Illinois/Missouri state line, Mississippi River
34	Riverview Dr, to St Louis, N **Welcome Ctr/ both lanes, full facilities, info, litter barrels,** Moto Mart/Subway,
33	Lilac Ave, N USPO, S Phillips 66/Jack-in-the-Box/dsl, QT/dsl/scales/24hr Hardee's
32	Bellefontaine Rd, N Shell/Circle K China King, McDonald's, Pizza Hut, Steak'n Shake Budget Inn Advance Parts, Family$, Firestone/auto, Schnuck's Foods, S White Castle Aldi Foods
31b a	MO 367, N BP, QT/dsl Jack-in-the-Box, Little Caesar's, McDonalds, Subway, Taco Bell H, $General, CVS Drug, Family$, Shop'n Save Foods, U-Haul, Walgreens
30b a	Hall's Ferry Rd, rd AC, N Conoco/dsl, QT/dsl, Shell/dsl Applebee's, Capt. D's, White Castle Knights Inn Ford/Lincoln, Kia, S BP/dsl, Conoco, Phillips 66 China Wok

ST LOUIS

INTERSTATE 270 (St Louis) Cont'd

30b a Continued
Church's, Cracker Barrel, IHOP, Steak'n Shake, Subway AutoZone, Home Depot, Meineke, O'Reilly Parts, Shop'n Save Foods

29 W Florissant Rd, N China Moon, Jack-in-the-Box, Lion's Choice, Pasta House $General, Aldi Foods, Dobb's Tire/auto, Family$, Firestone, GNC, Ross, S Phillips 66/dsl, QT/dsl Arby's, Burger King, Domino's, Hibachi Grill, Krispy Kreme, Little Caesar's, McDonald's, Starbucks $General, $Tree, AT&T, NTB, Sam's Club/gas, Walmart

28 Elizabeth Ave, Washington St, N Phillips 66/dsl Jack-in-the-Box, Subway, Taco Bell Chevrolet, Schnuck's Foods, Walgreens

27 New Florissant Rd, rd N, N Shell/Circle K CVS Drug

26b Graham Rd, N Hanley, N Phillips 66/7-11/dsl Arby's, LJ Silver, Starbucks Quality Inn, Red Roof Inn H, $Tree, S McDonald's Days Inn $General

26a I-170 S

25b a US 67, Lindbergh Blvd, N BP, Phillips 66, QT/dsl Bandana's BBQ, Burger King, Church's, Domino's, Five Guys, IHOP, Imo's Pizza, Jack-in-the-Box, Jimmy John's, McDonald's, Papa John's, Pizza Hut, Pueblo Nuevo Mexican, Starbucks, Subway, Taco Bell, Waffle House, Wendy's Comfort Inn, Holiday Inn Express, InTown Suites, La Quinta $General, AutoZone, Dierberg's Deli, Family$, Firestone/auto, Ford, GNC, Hyundai, NAPA, Nissan, O'Reilly Parts, Sav-a-Lot Foods, Schnuck's Foods, Toyota, Walgreens, S Jimmy John's Budget Inn, Crossland Suites Honda, USPO, VW

23 McDonnell Blvd, E Denny's, Quiznos Motel 6, W Mobil/dsl, QT/dsl Arby's, Jack-in-the-Box, Lion's Choice, McDonald's, Steak'n Shake, Subway, Taco Bell Buick/GMC

22b a MO 370 W, to MO Bottom Rd

20c MO 180, St Charles Rock Rd, E BP, Phillips 66/dsl A&W/LJ Silver, Applebees, Arby's, Chick-fil-A, Chimi's Mexican, Chipotle, Fazoli's, Hometown Buffet, Imo's Pizza, Jack-in-the-Box, Jimmy John's, Lonestar Steaks, McDonald's, New China Buffet, Pizza Hut, Qdoba, Red Lobster, St. Louis Bread, Subway, Taco Bell, Wendy's, White Castle, Ya Hala Mediterranean H, $Tree, Aldi Foods, AT&T, AutoZone, Best Buy, CVS Drug, Hobby Lobby, Kohl's, Meineke, NTB, Office Depot, Petsmart, Save-a-Lot, Target, Verizon, Walgreens, Walmart/Burger, W Bob Evans, Olive Garden, Waffle House Best Value Inn, Motel 6, Super 8

20b a I-70, E to St Louis, W to Kansas City

17 Dorsett Rd, E Bandana's BBQ, Papa John's, Syberg's Grill, Waffle House Drury Inn, Hampton Inn, Homewood Suites, W Mobil, Phillips 66/dsl, Shell Arby's, Denny's, Firehouse Subs, McDonald's, MOD Pizza, Steak'n Shake, Subway Motel 6 GNC, Schnuck's Mkt, Walgreens

16b a Page Ave, rd D, MO 364 W, E BP, QT, Shell/Circle K/dsl Hardee's, Hooters, McDonald's, Spazio Café, Starbucks Comfort Inn, Courtyard, Days Inn, DoubleTree, Extended Stay America, Extended Stay America (2), Extended Stay America (3), Fairfield Inn, Hawthorn Suites, La Quinta, Red Roof Inn, Residence Inn, Sheraton, Sonesta Suites

14 MO 340, Olive Blvd, E Phillips 66/dsl Applebee's, Bristol Cafe, Five Guys, Granite City, Lion's Choice Rest., McDonald's, Pasta House, Pei Wei, Pieology, Potbelly, Qdoba, Starbucks, Subway Courtyard, Drury Inn Aldi Foods, AT&T, BMW/Audi/Infiniti, Chevrolet, CVS Drug, Dierberg's Mkt, Land Rover/Jaguar, Lexus, Mercedes, Verizon, W Coldstone,

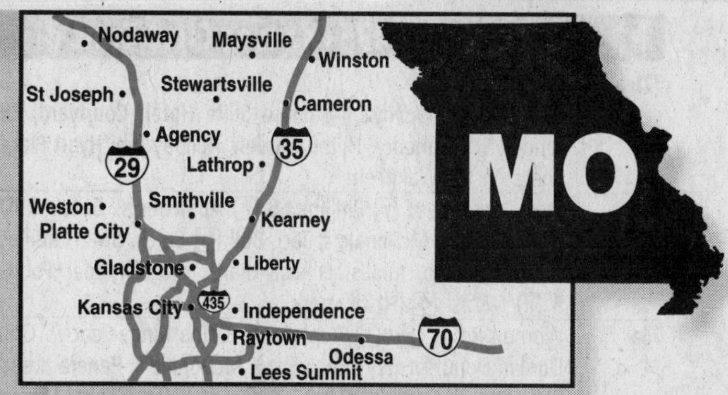

MO

14 Continued
IMO's Pizza, Jet's Pizza, La Salsa, Subway, TGIFriday's H, Dierberg's Foods, Kohl's, Schnuck's Mkt, vet, Walgreens

13 rd AB, Ladue Rd

12b a I-64, US 40, US 61, E to St Louis, W to Wentzville, E H

9 MO 100, Manchester Rd, E Bravo, Cane's, Chick-fil-A, Elephant Bar, Five Guys, Imo's Pizza, Jimmy John's, McAlister's Deli, McCormick&Schmick, McDonald's, Qdoba, Subway Barnes&Noble, Dick's, Macy's, Nordstrom, Schnuck's, W Shell Red Robin

8 Dougherty Ferry Rd, **2 mi** S Citgo/7-11, Mobil McDonald's H

7 Big Ben Rd, N H

5b a I-44, US 50, MO 366, E to St Louis, W to Tulsa

3 MO 30, Gravois Rd, N BP, Phillips 66 Bandana BBQ, Olive Garden, Outback Steaks Ford

2 MO 21, Tesson Ferry Rd, N Baskin Robbins, Jimmy John's, Joey B's, Panda Chinese, Pizza Hut, Shogun Japanese Acura, AutoZone, Buick/GMC, Dobb's Auto, O'Reilly Parts, Toyota, N **on Lindbergh** Mobil 54th St Grill, Burger King, Church's, Jack-in-the-Box, Olive Garden, Outback Steaks, Quizno's, Red Lobster, Subway, Taco Bell, TGIFriday's, Waffle House, White Castle Honda, Schnuck's Foods, Shop'n Save, Walgreens, S Shell/Circle K/dsl Chevy's Mexican, Little Caesar's Dierberg's Foods

1b a I-55 N to St Louis, S to Memphis

KANSAS CITY

INTERSTATE 435 (Kansas City)

Exit# Services

83 I-35, N to KS City, S to Wichita

82 Quivira Rd, Overland Park, N Burger King, Cheddar's, Chick-fil-A, KFC, Mimi's Cafe, Outback Steaks, Sonic, Taco Bell H, AT&T, Dillard's, JC Penney, Macy's, Nordstrom's, Target, S Boston Mkt, Domino's, McDonald's, Subway, Taco Bell, Wendy's Extended Stay America CVS Drug, Hen House Mkt

81 US 69 S, to Ft Scott

80 Antioch Rd

79 Metcalf Ave, N Conoco/7-11, Phillips 66/dsl/repair Buffalo Wild Wings, Carrabba's, Chartroose Caboose, ChuckECheese, D'Bronx Pizza, Denny's, Fox&Hound, Hardee's, Hooters, Jack-in-the-Box, Jose Pepper's, Krispy Kreme, Subway Comfort Inn, Days Inn, Embassy Suites, Extended Stay America, Hampton Inn, Homewood Suites, La Quinta, Motel 6, Overland Park Place Hotel, Super 8 H, AAA, Office Depot, vet, Walmart Mkt, S Applebee's, McDonald's, Panera Bread Drury Inn, Marriott, PearTree Inn

77b a Nall Ave, Roe Ave, N Brobeck's BBQ, Freddy's, Sonic, Winstead's Grill Best Value Inn USPO, S Corner

INTERSTATE 435 (Kansas City) Cont'd

77b a Continued
Bakery Cafe, Wendy's Chase Suite Hotel, Courtyard, Extended Stay America, Hilton Garden, Holiday Inn, Hyatt Place, Sheraton Walgreens

75b State Line Rd, N Phillips 66 Applebee's, Gate's BBQ, Jimmy John's, McDonald's, Taco Bell Buick/GMC/Cadillac, Goodyear/auto, Midas, O'Reilly Parts, PriceChopper Foods, S QT/dsl H, city park

75a Wornall Rd, N Applebee's, China King, Coach's Grill, Dunkin Donuts, Fuzzy's Taco Shop, McDonald's, Panera Bread, Pizza Hut, Subway Acura, Audi, Chevrolet, Honda, Nissan, Price Chopper, Toyota, VW

74 Holmes Rd, N Phillips 66/dsl Subway, Thai House, S Courtyard, Extended Stay America

73 103rd St (from wb)

71b a I-470/US 50 E, I-49/US 71S

70 Bannister Rd, E Phillips 66 Wendy's Walgreens, W Taco Bell Firestone/auto, Home Depot

69 87th St., E Conoco/dsl, QT McDonald's Capital Inn Advance Parts, W Days Inn

67 Gregory Blvd (same as 66a b), W Nature Ctr, zoo

66 MO 350 E, 63rd st

65 Eastwood Tfwy, W Conoco Church's, McDonald's, Peachtree Rest.

63c Raytown Rd, Stadium Dr (nb only), E to Sports Complex

63b a I-70, W to KC, E to St Louis

61 MO 78, 2 mi E Church's

60 MO 12 E, Truman Rd, 12th St, E Phillips 66/dsl, W QT

59 US 24, Independence Ave, E to Truman Library, W Hardee's CarQuest

57 Front St, E FLYING J/Conoco/rest/dsl/scales/24hr Blue Beacon, Kenworth, W Phillips 66/dsl, QT, Sinclair/dsl Denny's, McDonald's, Smugglers Rest., Subway, Waffle House Howard Johnson Plaza, Quality Inn URGENT CARE

56mm Missouri River

55b a MO 210, E Phillips 66/dsl, Pilot/PJ Fresh/dsl/scales/24hr Subway Ameristar Hotel/Casino, Motel 6 Ford/Volvo/GMC/Mercedes Trucks, Riverboat Casino

54 48th St, Parvin Rd, E Funpark, W All Star Grill, Taco Bell, Waffle House, Wendy's Candlewood Suites, Comfort Inn, Crossland Suites, Days Inn, Fairfield Inn, Hampton Inn, Holiday Inn, Super 8

52a US 69, E Phillips 66/dsl, W McDonald's, Pizza Hut, Subway $General, Walgreens

52b I-35, S to KC

51 Shoal Creek Dr, W LDS Temple

49b a MO 152 E, to I-35 N, Liberty, 2 mi E 54th St Grill, Applebee's, Bob Evans, Buffalo Wild Wings, Cracker Barrel, Longhorn Steaks, Steak'n Shake Best Western, Comfort Inn, Fairfield Inn, Hampton Inn, Holiday Inn Express, Super 8

47 NE 96th St

46 NE 108th St

45 MO 291, NE Cookingham Ave, E to I-35 N

42 N Woodland Ave

41b a US 169, Smithville, 4 mi N Kum&Go Burger King, McDonald's, Sonic Super 8

40 NW Cookingham

37 NW Skyview Ave, rd C, N Cenex (1mi), S golf (3mi)

36 to I-29 S, to KCI Airport, N Cenex, S Extended Stay America, Fairfield Inn, Holiday Inn, Marriott, Microtel, Plaza Hotel, Quality Suites, Sheraton, Super 8

31 I-29 N, to St Joseph, S to KC, Prairie Creek

29 rd D, NW 120th St

24 MO 152, rd N, NW Berry Rd

22 MO 45, Weston, Parkville, E The Station/DiBella's Pizza/dsl

20mm Missouri/Kansas state line, Missouri River

18 KS 5 N, Wolcott Dr, E to Wyandotte Co Lake Park

16 Donohoo Rd

15b a Leavenworth Rd, E Conoco/Subway/dsl Comfort Suites Woodlands Racetrack

14b a Parallel Pkwy, E Honda, Toyota, W Phillips 66/7-11/Subway/dsl Applebee's, Arby's, Bob Evans, Bryant's BBQ, Carino's Italian, Chick-fil-A, Chili's, Chipotle Mexican, Chuisano's Brick Oven, Culver's, Danny's Grill, Dave&Buster's, Five Guys, Fuddrucker's, Granite City Rest, Hooters, IHOP, Jack-in-the-Box, Jose Pepper's Grill, Longhorn Sreaks, McDonald's, Olive Garden, Panda Express, Panera Bread, Pizza Hut, Red Lobster, Sheridan's Custard, Sonic, Starbucks, Stix Asian, Taco Bell, Taco Bueno, Wendy's Candlewood Suites, Country Inn&Suites, Holiday Inn Express, Residence Inn AT&T, JC Penney, Kohl's, NTB, Old Navy, Sam's Club/dsl, Target, TJ Maxx, Verizon, Walmart

13b a US 24, US 40, State Ave, E Frontier Steaks water park, W Casa Agave, Famous Dave's BBQ, Lonestar Steaks Best Western, Chateau Avalon, Great Wolf Lodge, Hampton Inn Cabela's, KS Race Track, Russell Stovers

12b a I-70, KS Tpk, to Topeka, St Louis

11 Kansas Ave

9 KS 32, KS City, Bonner Springs, W Phillips 66/dsl

8b Woodend Rd, E Peterbilt, W Shell/Subway/dsl/scales

8.8mm Kansas River

8a Holliday Dr, to Lake Quivira

6c Johnson Dr

6b a Shawnee Mission Pkwy, E Chili's, Grand Wok, IHOP, McDonald's, Pizza Hut, Subway Aldi Foods, GNC, Home Depot, Kohl's, Lowe's, Michael's, NTB, Petsmart, Target, Walmart/Subway

5 Midland Dr, Shawnee Mission Park, E Conoco, Phillips 66/7-11/Subway/dsl Barley's Brewhaus, Chen's Kitchen, Eggtc Jose Pepper's Grill, Minsky's Pizza, Paula&Bill's Ristorante Wendy's Hampton Inn, W Hereford House Courtyard, Holiday Inn Express

3 87th Ave, E BP, Phillips 66/dsl Freddy's, McDonald's, Panera Bread, Papa John's, Papa Murphy's, Sonic, Taco Bell Ace Hardware, Aldi Foods, Sprouts Mkt, Walgreens, W Gambino's Pizza, Grand St Cafe, Hen House Mkt, Subway Hyatt Place

2 95th St

1b KS 10, to Lawrence

1a Lackman Rd, N Phillips 66/dsl Suburban Lodge

0mm **I-435 begins/ends on I-35.**

NOTES

MONTANA

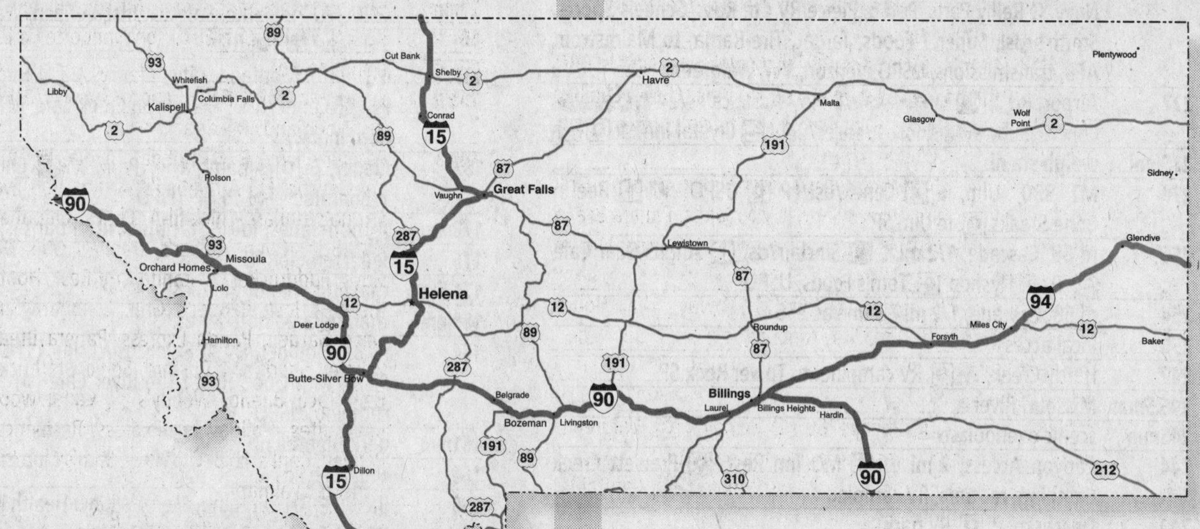

INTERSTATE 15

Exit#	Services
398mm	Montana/US/Canada Border, Sweetgrass
397	Sweetgrass, W **both lanes, full facilities, litter barrels, petwalk,** Gastrak Glocca Morra Motel/cafe Duty Free
394	ranch access
389	MT 552, Sunburst, W CFN/dsl Sunburst Mercantile, Sunburst RV Park, USPO
385	Swayze Rd
379	MT 215, MT 343, to Kevin, Oilmont, W Four Corners Café
373	Potter Rd
369	Bronken Rd
366.5mm	**weigh sta sb**
364	Shelby, E Lewis&Clark RV Park, W
363	US 2, Shelby, to Cut Bank, Shelby, **0-1 mi** E Cenex, Pilot/Exxon/Country Skillet/dsl/scales/24hr, Sinclair/dsl Dash Drive-In, Dixie Inn Steaks, Kowloon Chinese, Pizza Hut, Subway, The Griddle Comfort Inn, Crossroads Inn, Glacier Motel/RV Park, O'Haire Motel H, Albertsons, CarQuest, city park, Mark's Tire, Parts+, Shelby RV Park, TrueValue, USPO, visitor info, W Best Western ShopKo, to Glacier NP
361mm	**parking area nb**
358	Marias Valley Rd, to Golf Course Rd, E camping
357mm	Marias River
352	Bullhead Rd
348	rd 44, to Valier, W Lake Frances RA (15mi)
345	MT 366, Ledger Rd, E to Tiber Dam (42mi)
339	Conrad, E **/weigh sta both lanes, full facilities, litter barrels, petwalk,** W Calumet/dsl, Cenex/dsl, Conoco/dsl, Exxon/Subway/dsl A&W/Chester's, Home Cafe, Main Drive-In Northgate Motel, Super 8 H, Buick/Chevrolet/GMC, CarQuest, Conrad Tire/repair, Ford, IGA Foods, museum, Olson's Drug, Pondera RV Park, TrueValue, USPO, vet, Village Drug, Westco RV Ctr
335	Midway Rd, Conrad, **4 mi** W gas food lodging H, RV camping
328	MT 365, Brady, W Mtn View Co-op/dsl city park, USPO
321	Collins Rd
319mm	**both lanes, full facilities, litter barrels, petwalk,** **Teton River**
313	MT 221, MT 379, Dutton, W Cenex/dsl The Drive-In city park, USPO
302	MT 431, Power
297	Gordon
290	US 89 N, rd 200 W, to Choteau, W Conoco/dsl, Sinclair/dsl/LP/RV dump USPO
288mm	**parking area both lanes**
286	Manchester, W livestock auction, same as 290 (2mi)
282	US 87 N (from sb), NW bypass, **2-3 mi** E Conoco/dsl, Holiday/dsl Arby's, Buffalo Wild Wings, Burger King, Little Caesar's, McDonald's, New Peking, Subway, Taco Bell, Taco John's Days Inn $Tree, Ace Hardware, Albertsons/Osco, O'Reilly Parts, Sam's Club/gas, ShopKo, Staples, Tire-Rama, TJ Maxx, Walgreens, Walmart
280	US 87 N, Central Ave W, Great Falls, E Loaf 'N Jug/dsl A&W/KFC, Ford's Drive-In, Lippi's Kitchen, Papa John's Alberta Inn, Central Motel, Days Inn (3mi), Staybridge Suites city park, to Giant Sprgs SP, U-Haul/LP, vet, Whalen Tire
280mm	Sun River
278	US 89 S, rd 200 E, 10th Ave, Great Falls, E Calumet/dsl, Cenex/dsl, Conoco/dsl, Exxon/dsl, Holiday/Subway/dsl, Sinclair/dsl, Town Pump/dsl 4B's Rest., Applebee's, Arby's, Baskin-Robbins, Beef'O'Brady's, Best Wok, Boston's Pizza, Burger King, Café Rio, Chili's, Classic 50s Diner/casino, Coldstone, DQ, Fuddrucker's, Golden Corral, Hardee's, Jaker's Rest., JB's Rest., Jimmy John's, Little Caesar's, MacKenzie River Pizza, McDonald's, Ming's Chinese, Noodle Express, Papa John's, Papa Murphy's, Pita Pit, Pizza Hut, Sonic, Starbucks, Subway, Taco Bell, Taco Del Mar, Taco John's, Taco Treat, Wendy's, Wheat MT, ZPizza Best Western, Comfort Inn, Comfort Inn (2), Extended Stay America, Fairfield Inn, Hampton Inn, Hilton Garden, Holiday Inn, Holiday Inn Express, La Quinta, Motel 6, Super 8, Western Motel H, $Tree, Ace Hardware, Albertsons/Osco, AT&T, AT&T, AutoZone, Barnes&Noble, Big O Tire, BigLots, Cadillac/Chevrolet/Toyota, CarQuest, Chrysler/Dodge/Jeep, CVS Drug, Dick's RV Park, Firestone/auto, Ford, Gardner's RV Ctr, Harley-Davidson, Herberger's, Home Depot, Honda, JC Penney,

SHELBY

CONRAD

GREAT FALLS

MT

INTERSTATE 15 Cont'd

Exit	Services
278	Continued Jo-Ann Fabrics, KOA, Michael's, Midas, NAPA, Nissan, Old Navy, O'Reilly Parts, PetCo, Pierce RV Ctr, Ross, Scheels Sports, Smith's/dsl, Super 1 Foods, Target, Tire-Rama, to Malmstrom AFB, transmissions, USPO, Verizon, VW, Walgreens
277	Airport Rd, E FLYING J/Denny's/dsl/scales/24hr, Pilot/Conoco/Subway/casino/dsl/scales/24hr Crystal Inn, W
275mm	**weigh sta nb**
270	MT 330, Ulm, E Cenex/dsl/LP USPO, W Beef'n Bone Steaks to Ulm SP
256	rd 68, Cascade, **1/2 mi** E Sinclair/dsl Angus Bear Cafe Trout Flyshop Tom's Foods, USPO
254	rd 68, Cascade, **1/2 mi** E same as 256
250	local access
247	Hardy Creek, W RV camping, to Tower Rock SP
246.5mm	Missouri River
245mm	scenic overlook sb
244	Canyon Access, **2 mi** W MO Inn Rest. Prewett Creek Camping, rec area, RV camping
240	Dearborn, E RV park
239mm	**both lanes, full facilities, litter barrels, petwalk,**
238mm	Stickney Creek
236mm	Missouri River
234	Craig, E Izaak's Cafe, Trout Shop Café/lodge Flyshop boating, camping, rec area
228	US 287 N, to Augusta, Choteau
226	MT 434, Wolf Creek, E Exxon/dsl Oasis Café Wolf Creek Angler camping, to Holter Lake, W Frenchman&Me Café USPO
222mm	**parking area both lanes**
219	Spring Creek, Recreation Rd (from nb), Spring Creek, boating, camping
218mm	Little Prickly Pear Creek
216	Sieben
209	E to Gates of the Mtns RA
202mm	**weigh sta sb**
200	MT 279, MT 453, Lincoln Rd, W Sinclair/Bob's Mkt/dsl GrubStake Rest. Lincoln Rd RV Park, to ski area
194	Custer Ave, E Conoco/dsl Chili's, Hardee's, IHOP, Nagoya Japanese, Qdoba Comfort Suites, Residence Inn Costco/gas, GNC, Hobby Lobby, Home Depot, Staples, Super 1 Foods, TJ Maxx, W Cenex/dsl, Conoco/dsl, Exxon/dsl Applebee's, Arby's, Buffalo Wild Wings, Burger King, DQ, Jade Garden, Mackenzie River Pizza, McDonald's, Panda Express, Papa Murphy's, Pizza Hut, Quiznos, Steve's Cafe, Subway, Taco Bell, Taco Del Mar Holiday Inn Express $Tree, Albertson's, AT&T, AutoZone, CVS Drug, Helena RV Park (5mi), Jo-Ann, Lowe's, Macy's, Murdoch's, Natural Grocers, PetCo, Petsmart, Ross, ShopKo, Target, Verizon
193	Cedar St, Helena, E , W Conoco/dsl, Conoco/dsl, Exxon/dsl Godfather's, Little Caesar's, Perkins, Steffano's Pizza, Subway, Taco John's Quality Inn, Wingate Inn Ace Hardware, Chevrolet/Buick/GMC, O'Reilly Parts, Tire Rama, USPO, vet
192b a	US 12, US 287, Helena, Townsend, E Cenex, Conoco/dsl Burger King, Pizza Hut Hampton Inn Big Lots, Chrysler/Dodge/Jeep, D&D RV Ctr, Ford/Lincoln, Honda, Nissan, Schwab Tire, st patrol, Toyota, Walmart/Subway, W Exxon/dsl, Holiday, Sinclair/dsl DQ, Jimmy John's, L&D Chinese, McDonald's, Overland Express Rest., Papa John's, Papa Murphy's, Rte 12 Diner, Starbucks, Steve's Cafe, Taco John's, Taco Treat,

HELENA

Exit	Services
192b a	Continued Village Inn Pizza, Wendy's Baymont Inn, Days Inn, Fairfield Inn, Howard Johnson, Jorgenson's Inn, La Quinta, Motel 6, Radisson, Shilo Inn, Super 8 H, Albertson's, CVS Drug, GNC, J&J Tire/auto, Safeway/dsl, Verizon, Walgreens
190	S Helena, W H
187	MT 518, Montana City, Clancy, E Hugo's Pizza/casino, W Cenex/dsl Jackson Creek Cafe, MT City Grill Elkhorn Inn
182	Clancy, E Alhambra RV Park, W Chubby's Grill, Legal Tender Rest. to NF, USPO
178mm	**both lanes, full facilities, litter barrels, petwalk,**
176	Jefferson City, NF access
174.5mm	**chain up area both lanes**
168mm	**chainup area both lanes**
164	rd 69, Boulder, E Exxon/dsl/casino Elkhorn Cafe, Joe's Pizza, Mtn Good Rest., The River Café auto repair, RC RV camping, USPO
161mm	**parking area nb**
160	High Ore Rd
156	Basin, E camping, Merry Widow Health Mine/RV camping, W Basin Cr Pottery, USPO
154mm	Boulder River
151	to Boulder River Rd, Bernice, W camping, picnic area
148mm	**chainup area both lanes**
143.5mm	**chainup area both lanes**
138	Elk Park, W Sheepshead Picnic Area, wildlife viewing
134	Woodville
133mm	continental divide, elev 6368, continental divide
130.5mm	scenic overlook sb
129	I-90 E, to Billings
I-15 S and I-90 W run together 8 mi	
127	Harrison Ave, Butte, E Cenex/dsl, ConocoPhillips/dsl, Exxon/dsl, Exxon/dsl (2), Sinclair/dsl A&W/KFC, Arby's, Asia Buffet, Buffalo Wild Wings, Burger King, MacKenzie River Pizza, McDonald's, MT Club Rest., Perkins, Pizza Hut, Pizza Ranch, Silver Bow Pizza, Starbucks, Subway, Taco Bell, Three Amigos, Wendy's Best Western, Comfort Inn, Hampton Inn, Super 8 $Tree, American Car Care, Buick/Chevrolet/GMC, CarQuest, casinos, Chrysler/Dodge/Jeep, Ford, Hart's RV Ctr, Herberger's, Honda, Jo-Ann Fabrics, Kia, Murdoch's, NAPA, Petco, Rocky Mtn RV Ctr, Staples, Subaru, Toyota, Verizon, vet, Walmart/Subway, W Cenex/dsl, Conoco/dsl Derby Steaks, Domino's, DQ, El Taco Mexican, Hanging 5 Rest., Hardee's, John's Rest., Papa John's, Papa Murphy's, Quiznos, Royse's Burgers, Taco John's Days Inn, Fairfield Inn, Holiday Inn Express, La Quinta, Quality Inn Ace Hardware, AutoZone, Lisac's Tires, O'Reilly Parts, Safeway, Walgreens
126	Montana St, Butte, E Conoco/dsl, Exxon/dsl, W Chef's Garden Italian Eddy's Motel H, Safeway, Schwab Tire
124	I-115 (from eb), to Butte City Ctr
123mm	**weigh sta sb**
122	Rocker, E Pilot/Conoco/McDonald's/Subway/dsl/scales/24hr Econolodge casino, **weight sta nb**, W FLYING J Exxon/rest./dsl/LP/24hr Best Value Inn 2 Bar Lazy-H RV Camping
I-15 N and I-90 E run together 8 mi.	
121	I-90 W, to Missoula
119	Silver Bow, W Port of MT Transportation Hub
116	Buxton
112mm	Continental Divide, elevation 5879
111	Feely

BUTTE

INTERSTATE 15 Cont'd

Exit#	Services
109mm	**rest stop/weigh sta both lanes, full facilities, litter barrels, petwalk, phone, picnic**
102	rd 43, to Wisdom, Divide, W other rv camping (2mi), to Big Hole Nat Bfd (62mi)
99	Moose Creek Rd
93	Melrose, W food Hitchin Post Rest., Melrose Café/grill/dsl lodging Great Waters Inn (5mi), Pioneer Mtn Cabins other Sportsman Motel/RV Park, Sunrise Flyshop, USPO
85.5mm	Big Hole River
85	Glen, E other Willis Sta RV camping (3mi)
74	Apex, Birch Creek
64mm	Beaverhead River
63	Lp 15, rd 41, Dillon, Twin Bridges, E gas Cenex/dsl/LP/RV Dump, Exxon/dsl, Phillips 66/dsl food 4B's Rest., Lions Den, McDonald's, Pizza Hut, Subway lodging Best Western/rest., Fairbridge Inn, Motel 6, Quality Inn, Sundowner Motel, Super 8 other H, auto repair/tires, Buick/Chevrolet, CarQuest, city park, Family$, KOA, Les Schwab Tire, Murdoch's, museum, NAPA, O'Reilly Parts, Safeway/dsl, W MT U
62	Lp 15, Dillon, E food DQ, Sparky's Rest., Taco John's lodging Flyshop Inn other H, KOA, Southside RV Park, to W MT U, Van's/IGA Foods
60mm	Beaverhead River
59	MT 278, to Jackson, W other Bannack SP, Countryside RV Park/LP
56	Barretts, E other RV camping, W gas Sinclair/RV Park/dsl
55mm	**parking area sb, litter barrels**
52	Grasshopper Creek
51	Dalys (from sb, no return)
50mm	Beaverhead River
46mm	Beaverhead River
45mm	Beaverhead River
44	MT 324, E food Buffalo Lodge other Armstead RV Park, W other Clark Cyn Reservoir/RA, RV camping
38.5mm	Red Rock River
37	Red Rock
34mm	**parking area both lanes, litter barrels, restrooms**
29	Kidd
23	Dell, E gas Cenex/dsl food Yesterdays Calf-a other USPO
16.5mm	**weigh sta both lanes**
15	Lima, E rest stop both lanes, facilities, litter barrels, petwalk, gas Exxon/dsl, Tesla EVC food Jan's Café lodging Mtn View Motel/RV Park other ambulance, Big Sky Tire/auto, Ralph's Tire, USPO
9	Snowline
0	Monida, E other to Red Rock Lakes
0mm	Montana/Idaho state line, Monida Pass, elevation 6870

DILLON

INTERSTATE 90

Exit#	Services
554.5mm	Montana/Wyoming state line
549	Aberdeen
544	Wyola
530	MT 463, Lodge Grass, **1 mi S** gas gas/dsl food food lodging lodging
517.5mm	Little Bighorn River
514	Garryowen, N gas Conoco/Subway other Custer Bfd Museum, S other 7th Ranch RV camp (3mi)
511.5mm	Little Bighorn River
510	US 212 E, N gas Conoco/café/dsl/gifts other casino, casino, H, to Little Bighorn Bfd

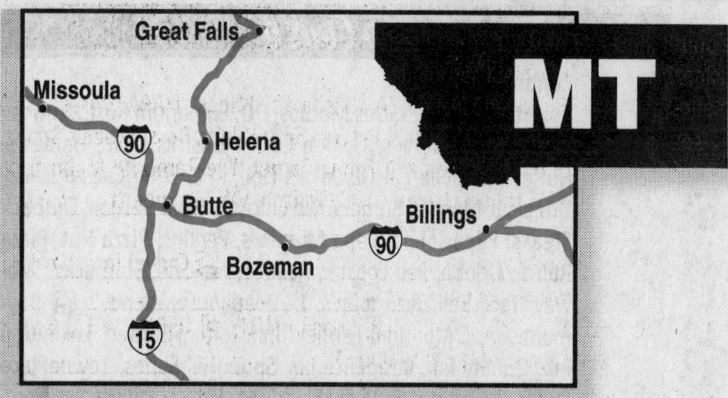

Exit#	Services
509.5mm	**weigh sta, both lanes exit left**
509.3mm	Little Bighorn River
509	Crow Agency, N gas Conoco, S other to Bighorn Canyon NRA
503	Dunmore
498mm	Bighorn River
497	MT 384, 3rd St, Hardin, N other fireworks, S lodging Western Motel other H, Bighorn Cty Museum
495	MT 47, City Ctr, Hardin, N gas Cenex/dsl, Loves/Hardee's/dsl/scales/24hr food Golden Bridge Chinese other KOA, S gas Cenex/dsl, Exxon/dsl, FLYING J/Conoco/Subway/dsl/LP/24hr food DQ, McDonald's, Pizza Hut, Taco John's lodging Rodeway Inn, Super 8, Western Motel other H, Chevrolet, Grand View Camping/RV Park, Sunset Village RV Park
484	Toluca
478	Fly Creek Rd
477mm	**rest stop both lanes, full facilities, litter barrels, petwalk, phone, picnic**
469	Arrow Creek Rd
462	Pryor Creek Rd
456	I-94 E, to Bismarck, ND
455	Johnson Lane, N gas Pilot/Conoco/McDonald's/dsl/scales/24hr, S gas FLYING J/dsl/LP/scales/24hr, Exxon/A&W/dsl food Burger King, Domino's, DQ, Jin's Chinese, Subway lodging Holiday Inn Express other Bretz RV Ctr, Verizon, Whalen Tire
452	US 87 N, City Ctr, Billings, **2-4 mi N on US 87** gas Conoco/Arby's/dsl/LP food Applebee's, Arby's, Burger King, Domino's, DQ, Fuddrucker's, Godfather's, Golden Phoenix, Jimmy John's, MacKenzie River Pizza, McDonald's, Panda Express, Papa John's, Papa Murphy's, Pizza Hut, Sonic, Starbucks, Subway, Taco Bell, Taco John's, Wendy's lodging Boothill Inn, Country Inn&Suites, Heights Motel other Ace Hardware, Albertsons/Osco, American Spirit RV Ctr, AT&T, AutoZone, BigLots, CarQuest, Cenex/dsl, CVS Drug, GNC, Holiday/dsl, Metra Rv Ctr, O'Reilly Parts, Petsmart, Target, Tire Rama, U-Haul, Verizon, vet, Walgreens, Walmart, S gas Cenex/dsl other RV Camping
451.5mm	Yellowstone River
450	MT 3, 27th St, Billings, N gas Conoco/dsl food Blondy's Cafe, Pizza Hut lodging Doubletree, Vegas Motel other H, CarQuest, city park, USPO, visitor ctr, S other KOA, Yellowstone River Camping
447	S Billings Blvd, N gas Conoco/Subway/dsl, Holiday/dsl food 4B's Rest., Burger King, DQ, Fiddlers Green Grill, McDonald's, Popeye's, Taco Bell lodging Best Western/Kelly, Comfort Suites, Days Inn, Extended Stay America, Hampton Inn, Ledgestone Hotel, My Place, Sleep Inn, Super 8 other Cabela's Sporting Goods, NAPA, Sam's Club/dsl, S other Freightliner, Kenworth, KOA (2mi), Yellowstone River Campground
446	King Ave, Billings, N gas Conoco/dsl, Conoco/dsl, Holiday/dsl, Phillips 66/dsl food Applebee's, Arby's, Asian Sea Grill, Bruno's Italian, Buffalo Wild Wings, Burger King, Cactus Creek Steaks, Café Rio, Carino's Italian, ChuckECheese's, City Brew Coffee,

HARDIN

BILLINGS

MT

INTERSTATE 90 Cont'd

BILLINGS

446 Continued Coldstone, Denny's, Dos Machos, DQ, Emporium Rest., Famous Dave's, Fuddrucker's, Golden Corral, Gusicks Rest., Hardee's, HuHot Mongolian, IHOP, Jake's Grill, KFC, Little Caesar's, McDonald's, MooYah Burgers, Old Chicago, Olive Garden, Outback Steaks, Papa John's, Papa Murphy's, Perkins, Pizza Hut, Pizza Ranch, Qdoba, Red Lobster, Rendezvous Grill, Starbucks, Subway, Taco Bell, Taco John's, TX Roadhouse, Wendy's [lodging] Baymont Inn, C'Mon Inn, Fairfield Inn, Hilton Garden, Lexington Inn, Quality Inn, Residence Inn, SpringHill Suites, TownePlace Suites, Western Executive Inn [other] $Tree, Albertsons/Osco, AT&T, AutoZone, Barnes&Noble, Best Buy, Chevrolet, Chrysler/Dodge/Jeep, Costco/gas, Dillards, Ford, Hobby Lobby, Home Depot, JC Penney, JoAnn Fabrics, Kia, Lisac's Tire, Lowe's, Mercedes, Michael's, Natural Grocers, Nissan, Office Depot, Old Navy, O'Reilly Parts, Petsmart, Ross, ShopKo, Subaru, USPO, Verizon, vet, Walmart/Subway, World Mkt, S [gas] Conoco/dsl [food] Cracker Barrel, Emporium Rest. [lodging] EconoLodge, Howard Johnson, Kelly Inn, La Quinta, Motel 6, Motel 6 (2), Radisson, Red Lion Inn [other] Volvo/Mack Trucks

443 Zoo Dr, to Shiloh Rd, N [gas] Holiday/dsl [food] Five Guys, MT Rib/Chophouse [lodging] Bighorn Resort/waterpark, Hampton Inn, Holiday Inn Express, Homewood Suites [other] Honda, Hyundai/Volvo/Buick, Pierce RV Ctr, zoo, S [other] Harley-Davidson, vet

439mm weigh sta both lanes

437 E Laurel, S [gas] TA/Sinclair/cafe/dsl/scales/casino/motel/RV Park/24hr

434 US 212, US 310, to Red Lodge, Laurel, N [gas] Cenex/dsl, Conoco/dsl, Exxon/dsl [food] Beartooth Grill, City Brew Coffee, Gauica's Mexican, Hardee's, McDonald's, Pizza Hut, Subway, Taco Bell, Taco John's [lodging] Best Western, Locomotive Inn [other] Ace Hardware, AutoZone, Chevrolet, CVS Drug, Ford, IGA Foods, O'Reilly Parts, Rapid Tire, Verizon, Walmart/Subway, S [other] Riverside Park/RV Camping, to Yellowstone NP

433 Lp 90 (from eb), same as 434

426 Park City, S [gas] Cenex/café/dsl/24hr, KwikStop [food] The Other Cafe [other] USPO

419mm [Rs] both lanes, full [handicap] facilities, litter barrels, petwalk, [phone], [picnic]

408 rd 78, Columbus, N [other] Mtn Range RV Park, S [gas] Conoco, Pilot/Exxon/dsl/24hr [food] Bearstone Cafe, McDonald's, Subway [lodging] Big Sky Motel, Super 8 [other] casino, city park, Family$, [H], IGA Foods, tires/repair, to Yellowstone

400 Springtime Rd

398mm Yellowstone River

396 ranch access

392 Reed Point, N [gas] Sure Stop/dsl [other] Old West RV Park, USPO

384 Bridger Creek Rd

381mm [Rs] both lanes, full [handicap] facilities, litter barrels, petwalk, [phone], [picnic]

377 Greycliff, S [other] KOA, Prairie Dog Town SP

370 US 191, Big Timber, 1 mi N [gas] Sinclair/dsl [lodging] Grand Hotel, Lazy J Motel [other] [H], Spring Creek RV Ranch (4mi), USPO, vet

369mm Boulder River

367 US 191 N, Big Timber, N [gas] Conoco/dsl, Exxon/dsl [food] Country Skillet [lodging] River Valley Inn, Super 8 [other] CarQuest, Family$, historic site/visitor info, Spring Creek Camping (3mi)

362 De Hart

354 MT 563, Springdale

352 ranch access

350 East End access

343 Mission Creek Rd, N [other] Ft Parker HS

340 US 89 N, to White Sulphur Sprgs, S [other] [airport]

LIVINGSTON

337 Lp 90, to Livingston, **2 mi** N [other] services in Livingston

333mm Yellowstone River

333 US 89 S, Livingston, N [food] Clark's Rest., DQ, Mark's In&Out, Pizza Hut, Taco John's [lodging] Budget Host, Livingston Inn, Quality Inn, Rodeway Inn, Yellowstone Pioneer Lodge [other] [H], Ace Hardware, Chrysler/Dodge/Jeep, ShopKo, Town&Country Foods, True Value Hardware, Verizon, Western Drug, S [gas] Cenex/dsl, Conoco/dsl, Exxon/dsl [food] Arby's, McDonald's, Rosa's Pizza, Subway [lodging] Comfort Inn, Super 8 [other] Albertsons/Osco, KOA (10mi), Osen's RV Park/Lp, to Yellowstone, URGENT CARE, vet

330 Lp 90, Livingston, **1 mi** N [gas] Cenex/Yellowstone Trkstp/dsl/rest./24hr

326.5mm chainup/chain removal area both lanes

324 ranch access

323mm chainup/chain removal area wb

322mm Bridger Mountain Range

321mm turnouts/hist marker both lanes

319 Jackson Creek Rd

319mm chainup area both lanes

316 Trail Creek Rd

313 Bear Canyon Rd, S [other] Bear Canyon Camping.

BOZEMAN

309 US 191 S, Main St, Bozeman, N [other] Subaru, Sunrise RV Park, S [gas] Cenex/dsl, Conoco/dsl, Exxon/dsl [food] MT Ale-Works [lodging] Ranch House Motel, Western Heritage Inn [other] [H], East Main Foods, repair, Tire Rama, to Yellowstone

306 MT 205, N 7th, to US 191, Bozeman, N [gas] Cenex [food] McDonald's, Panda Buffet [lodging] Fairfield Inn, La Quinta, Microtel, Motel 6, Ramada, Rodeway Inn, Super 8 [other] Murdoch's, ski area, Whalen Tire, S [gas] Conoco/Arby's/dsl, Exxon [food] Applebee's, Bar-3 BBQ, Dominos, DQ, Famous Dave's BBQ, Papa John's, Santa Fe Red's Cafe, Taco John's, Village Inn Pizza [lodging] Best Western, Bozeman Inn, Comfort Inn, Days Inn, Hampton Inn, Holiday Inn, Homewood Suites, Royal 7 Inn [other] Big O Tire, Firestone/auto, Museum of the Rockies, U-Haul, Verizon, Walmart/McDonald's

305 MT412, N 19th Ave, N [gas] Exxon [lodging] Mountainview Inn, **0-2 mi** S **[Rs], full [handicap] facilities, petwalk, [picnic]/litter barrels,** [gas] Conoco/dsl [food] A&W/KFC, Buffalo Wild Wings, Carino's Italian, City Brew Coffee, Clarks Fork Rest., Corner Bakery Cafe, Five Guys, IHOP, Jimmy John's, Mongolian BBQ, Noodles&Co, Old Chicago Pizza, Olive Garden, Outback Steaks, Papa Murphy's, Starbucks, Subway, Wasabi Grill, Wendy's [lodging] C'mon Inn, Comfort Suites, Country Inn Suites, Hilton Garden, Holiday Inn Express, My Place Extended Stay, Residence Inn, Spring-Hill Suites [other] AT&T, Costco/gas, Ford/Lincoln/RV Ctr, Home Depot, Lowe's, Michael's, Office Depot, Petsmart, REI, Ross, Smith's Foods/dsl, Staples, Target, TJMaxx, USPO, Verizon, vet, World MKT

BELGRADE

299 Airway Blvd, N [other] [airport]

298 MT 291, rd 85, Belgrade, N [gas] Cenex/dsl, Exxon/Subway/dsl [food] Burger King, DQ, McDonald's, Papa Murphy's, Pizza Hut, Rosa's Pizza, Starbucks, Taco Bell, Taco Time [lodging] Holiday Inn Express [other] Albertson's/Osco, NAPA, Town&Country Foods, Verizon, Whalen Tire, S [gas] FLYING J/Conoco/dsl/scales/LP, Pilot/Conoco/dsl/scales/24hr [food] Fiesta Mexicana [lodging] La Quinta, Quality Inn, Super 8 [other] Freightliner, Harley-Davidson, repair, Tire Factory, to Yellowstone NP, TrueValue

292.5mm Gallatin River

288 MT 288, MT 346, Manhattan, N [gas] Conoco/Subway/dsl [other] RV camping

283 Logan, S [other] Madison Buffalo Jump SP (7mi)

INTERSTATE 90 Cont'd

Exit#	Services
279mm	Madison River
278	MT 205, rd 2, Three Forks, Trident, N Missouri Headwaters SP, **1 mi** S Conoco/dsl Iron Horse Cafe Broken Spur Motel, Lewis&Clark Motel, Sacajawea Hotel CarQuest, golf
277.5mm	Jefferson River
274	US 287, to Helena, Ennis, N Conoco/dsl Wheat MT Bakery/deli Ft 3 Forks Motel/RV Park dsl repair, to Canyon Ferry SP, S Pilot/Exxon/Subway/dsl/scales/24hr Camp 3 Forks, Lewis&Clark Caverns SP, to Yellowstone NP
267	Milligan Canyon Rd
261.5mm	**chain-up area**
257mm	Boulder River
256	MT 359, Cardwell, S Cenex/dsl/RV Park Lewis&Clark Caverns SP, RV camping, to Yellowstone NP
249	rd 55, to rd 69, Whitehall, S Exxon/dsl A&W/KFC, Subway Rodeway Inn casino, Cliff's Tire/auto, to Virginia City NHS
241	Pipestone
240.5mm	**chainup/chain removal area both lanes**
238.5mm	**runaway ramp eb**
237.5mm	pulloff eb
235mm	**truck parking both lanes, litter barrels, restrooms**
233	Continental Divide, elev 6393, Homestake
230mm	**chain-up area both lanes**
228	MT 375, Continental Dr, S Conoco/dsl Harley-Davidson, Three Bears Foods
227	I-15 N, to Helena, Great Falls
I-90 and I-15 run together 8 mi. See Montana I-15, exits 122-127.	
123mm	**weight sta wb**
219	I-15 S, to Dillon, Idaho Falls
216	Ramsay
211	MT 441, Gregson, **3-5 mi** S Fairmont RV Park (Apr-Oct), food, lodging
210.5mm	**parking area wb**, Pintlar Scenic route info
208	rd 1, Pintler Scenic Loop, Georgetown Lake RA, Opportunity, Anaconda, S **both lanes, full facilities, gas, litter barrels, lodging, petwalk,** , , H, RV camp/dump, ski area
201	Warm Springs, S MT ST H
197	MT 273, Galen, S to MT ST H
195	Racetrack
187	Lp 90, Deer Lodge (no wb return), **2 mi** S Travelodge H, KOA (seasonal), Old MT Prison/auto museum, same as 184, Valley Foods
184	Deer Lodge, **0-1 mi** S Conoco/dsl/casino, Exxon/dsl/casino, Sinclair/Subway/dsl 4B's Rest., A&W, McDonald's, Pizza Hut Travelodge, Western Big Sky Inn H, city park, Family$, Grant-Kohrs Ranch NHS, Indian Creek Camping, KOA, Safeway/deli, Schwab Tire, USPO
179	Beck Hill Rd
175	US 12 E, Garrison, N hist site, RiverFront RV Park
175mm	Little Blackfoot River
174	US 12 E (from eb), S same as 175
170	Phosphate
166	Gold Creek, S Camp Mak-A-Dream, USPO
162	Jens
154	to MT 1 (from wb), Drummond, S Cenex/dsl, Conoco/dsl Parker's Rest., Wagon Wheel Café Drummond Motel, Sky Motel, Wagon Wheel Motel city park, Front St Mkt, Georgetown Lake RA, Pintler Scenic Lp
153	MT 1 (from eb), S same as 154

BUTTE

DEER LODGE

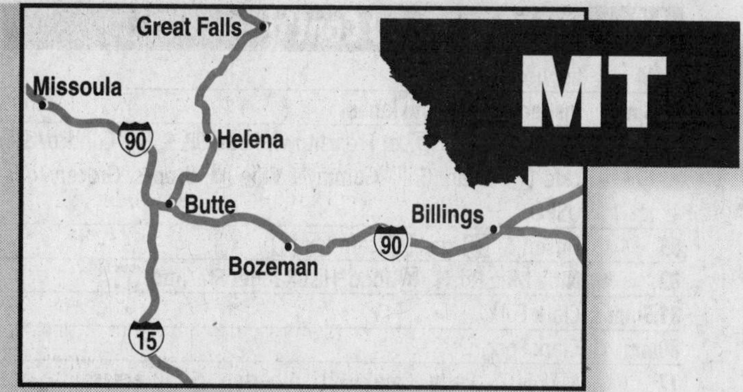

Exit#	Services
150.5mm	**weigh sta both lanes**
143mm	**both lanes, full facilities, litter barrels, petwalk,** ,
138	Bearmouth Area, N Chalet Bearmouth Camp/rest.
130	Beavertail Rd, S to Beavertail Hill SP
128mm	**parking area both lanes, litter barrels/restrooms**
126	Rock Creek Rd, S rec area
120	Clinton, N Conoco/dsl Poor Henry's Café (1mi W on frtg rd) Clinton Market, S USPO
113	Turah, S Turah RV Park/gas
109.5mm	Clark Fork
109mm	Blackfoot River
109	MT 200 E, Bonner, N Pilot/Exxon/Arby's/Subway/dsl/scales/casino/LP/24hr River City Grill hist site, USPO
108.5mm	Clark Fork
107	E Missoula, N Ole's/Conoco/dsl, Sinclair Reno Cafe Aspen Motel dsl repair
105	US 12 W, Missoula, S Cenex/dsl, Conoco/dsl, Sinclair/dsl Burger King, Five Guys, McDonald's, Pizza Hut, Qdoba, Subway, Taco Bell Campus Inn, Comfort Inn, DoubleTree, Motel 6, Thunderbird Motel Ace Hardware, Albertson's, Kingfisher Flyshop, O'Reilly Parts, U of MT, Verizon
104	Orange St, Missoula, S Conoco/dsl Pagoda Chinese, Taco John's Mtn Valley Inn, Red Lion Inn H, TireRama, to City Ctr
101	US 93 S, Reserve St, N Conoco/dsl Cracker Barrel, MacKenzie River Pizza, Starbucks Best Western+, C'Mon Inn, Motel 6, My Place ski area, **0-2 mi** S Cenex/dsl/LP, Conoco/dsl, Exxon/Subway/dsl Arby's, Buffalo Wild Wings, Burger King, Cafe Rio, Chipotle, Coldstone, Domino's, DQ, Famous Dave's BBQ, Freddy's, Fuddrucker's, HoagiVille, IHOP, Jimmy John's, Little Caesar's, McDonald's, MOD Pizza, MT Club Rest./casino, Old Chicago, Outback Steaks, Panda Express, Perkins, Pizza Hut, Popeye's, Quiznos, Rowdy's Cabin Rest., Stone Of Accord, Taco Bell, Taco Time/TCBY, Wendy's Courtyard, EconoLodge, Hampton Inn, Hilton Garden, Holiday Inn Express, La Quinta, Quality Inn, Ruby's Inn/rest., Staybridge Suites, Super 8, TownePlace Suites, Travelers Inn Albertson's, AT&T, Barnes&Noble, Best Buy, Bretz RV/Marine, Chevrolet/Cadillac, Costco/gas, dsl repair, Firestone/auto, GNC, Home Depot, Lowe's, Michael's, Old Navy, Petsmart, REI, Ross, Staples, Target, TJ Maxx, Verizon, VW, Walgreens, Walmart/Subway
99	Airway Blvd, S Mobil/dsl/24hr, Sinclair/dsl Stone Creek Lodge, Wingate Inn , Chrysler/Dodge/Jeep, Harley-Davidson, Kia
96	US 93 N, MT 200W, Kalispell, N Conoco/rest./dsl/scales/24hr/@, FLYING J/Exxon/McDonald's/dsl/scales/24hr WheatMT/deli Days Inn/rest. Jellystone RV Park (1mi), Jim&Mary's RV Park (1mi), Peterbilt, to Flathead Lake&Glacier NP, S Sinclair/dsl, TA/Sinclair/Country Pride/dsl/scales/24hr Tamarack Inn Kenworth

MISSOULA

MT

INTERSTATE 90 Cont'd

Exit#	Services
92.5mm	**inspection sta both lanes**
89	Frenchtown, N to Frenchtown Pond SP, S Conoco/dsl/café Alcan Grill, Gammy's Cafe Broncs Grocery/gas, USPO
85	Huson, S gas cafe
82	Nine Mile Rd, N food, Hist Ranger Sta/info,
81.5mm	Clark Fork
80mm	Clark Fork
77	MT 507, Petty Creek Rd, Alberton, S access to gas food lodging
75	Alberton, N Cenex/dsl USPO, S River Edge Rest. casino, motel, RV camp
73mm	**parking area wb, litter barrels**
72mm	**parking area eb, litter barrels**
70	Cyr
70mm	Clark Fork
66	Fish Creek Rd
66mm	Clark Fork
61	Tarkio
59mm	Clark Fork
58mm	**both lanes, full facilities, litter barrels, NF camping (seasonal), petwalk, ,**
55	Lozeau, Quartz
53.5mm	Clark Fork
49mm	Clark Fork
47	MT 257, Superior, N Conoco/dsl, Energy Partners/LP Durango's Rest./gas Big Sky Motel, Hilltop Motel , Family Foods, Mineral Drug, NAPA, USPO, S Pilot/Exxon/dsl/casino/24hr
45mm	Clark Fork
43	Dry Creek Rd, N NP camping (seasonal)
37	Sloway Area
34mm	Clark Fork
33	MT 135, St Regis, N Conoco/rest/dsl/gifts, Exxon, Sinclair Frosty Drive-In, Huck's Grill, Jasper's Rest., OK Café/casino Little River Motel, St Regis Motel, Super 8 antiques, city park, Nugget Camground, St Regis Campground (seasonal), to Glacier NP, USPO
30	Two Mile Rd, S fishing access
29mm	fishing access wb
26	Ward Creek Rd (from eb)
25	Drexel
22	Camels Hump Rd, Henderson, N antiques (1mi), camping (seasonal)
18	DeBorgia, N O'aces Rest. Black Diamond Guest Ranch, USPO
16	Haugan, N Exxon/dsl/24hr 50000 Silver $/motel/rest./casino/RV park
15mm	**weigh sta both lanes, exits left from both lanes**
10	Saltese, N Mangold's Motel
10mm	St Regis River
5	Taft Area, access to Hiawatha Trail
4.5mm	**both lanes, chainup/removal, full facilities, litter barrels, petwalk,**
0	Lookout Pass, access to Lookout Pass ski area/lodge, info
0mm	Montana/Idaho state line, Central/Pacific time zone, Lookout Pass elev 4680

INTERSTATE 94

Exit#	Services
250mm	Montana/North Dakota state line
248	Carlyle Rd
242	MT 7 (from wb), Wibaux, S **both lanes, full facilities, litter barrels, ,** Amsler's/dsl, Cenex/dsl/service Tastee Hut Beaver Creek Inn,
241	MT 261 (from eb), to MT 7, Wibaux, S same as 242
240mm	**weigh sta both lanes**
236	ranch access
231	Hodges Rd
224	Griffith Creek, frontage road
222.5mm	Griffith Creek
215	MT 335, Glendive, City Ctr, N Cenex/dsl C's Family Café, Penny's Diner Astoria Suites, Comfort Inn, Days Inn, Holiday Inn Express, Oak Tree Inn, Super 8 Glendive Camping (apr-oct), museum, Running's Hardware, S Exxon/dsl, Holiday/dsl Subway El Centro Motel, Glendive Inn, La Quinta , to Makoshika SP, Verizon
215mm	Yellowstone River
213	MT 16, to Sidney, Glendive, N Town Pump/dsl/scales st patrol, S Cenex/dsl, Sinclair/dsl Pizza Hut Riverside Inn Albertson's/Osco, Ford, NAPA, Reynolds Mkt
211	MT 200S (from wb, no EZ return), to Circle
210	Lp 94, to rd 200 S, W Glendive, S Cenex/dsl, Exxon/dsl Buick/Chevrolet, I-94 RV Park, Makoshika SP, Tire Rama
206	Pleasant View Rd
204	Whoopup Creek Rd
198	Cracker Box Rd
192	Bad Route Rd, S **/weigh sta both lanes, camping, full facilities, litter barrels, petwalk, , , weather info**
187mm	Yellowstone River
185	MT 340, Fallon, S café
184mm	O'Fallon Creek
176	MT 253, Terry, N Cenex/dsl, Four Corners/dsl Dizzy Diner Kempton Hotel , museum, Terry RV Oasis
170mm	Powder River
169	Powder River Rd
159	Diamond Ring
148	Valley Access
141	US 12 E, Miles City, N RV Camping
138	rd 59, Miles City, N Cenex/dsl, Conoco/dsl, Pilot/Exxon/dsl/24hr 4B's Rest., Arby's, Black Iron Grill, Boardwalk Rest., City Brew Coffee, DQ, Gallagher's Rest., Little Caesar's McDonald's, Mexico Lindo, MT Rib&Chophouse, Pizza Hut, Subway, Taco John's, Wendy's Best Western, EconoLodge, Motel 6, Sleep Inn , $Tree, Ace Hardware, Albertsons/Osco Buick/Chevrolet, casinos, Murdoch's, O'Reilly Parts, Verizon Walmart, S Cenex/dsl New Hunan Chinese Comfort Inn, Guesthouse Inn, MC Hotel, Super 8
137mm	Tongue River
135	Lp 94, Miles City, N KOA (Apr-Oct)
128	local access
126	Moon Creek Rd
117	Hathaway
114mm	**eb, full facilities, litter barrels, petwalk, ,**
113mm	**wb, full facilities, litter barrels, overlook, petwalk, ,**
106	Butte Creek Rd, to Rosebud, N food
103	MT 446, MT 447, Rosebud Creek Rd, N food
98.5mm	**weigh sta both lanes**

GLENDIVE

MILES CITY

FORSYTH

INTERSTATE 94 Cont'd

Exit#	Services
95	Forsyth, N [gas] Exxon/dsl, Forsyth Watering Hole [food] DQ [lodging] Sundowner Inn [other] [H], Ford, NAPA, to Rosebud RA, Van's/IGA, vet, S [other] Wagon Wheel Camping
93	US 12 W, Forsyth, N [gas] Exxon/dsl, Forsyth Watering Hole [food] Fitzgerald's Rest., Top That Eatery [lodging] Rails Inn, Restwel Inn, WestWind Motel [other] [H]
87	rd 39, to Colstrip
82	Reservation Creek Rd
72	MT 384, Sarpy Creek Rd
67	Hysham, 1-2 mi N [gas] gas [food] food [other] [phone]
65mm	[Rs] both lanes, full [handicap] facilities, litter barrels, petwalk, [phone], [vending]
63	ranch access
53	Bighorn, access to [phone]
52mm	Bighorn River
49	MT 47, to Hardin, Custer, S [food] Ft Custer Café [other] camping, to Little Bighorn Bfd
47	Custer, S [gas] Cenex/Custer Sta/dsl [food] Jct City Saloon/café [other] USPO
41.5mm	[Rs] wb, full [handicap] facilities, litter barrels, petwalk, [phone], [vending]
38mm	[Rs] eb, full [handicap] facilities, litter barrels, petwalk, [phone], [vending]
36	frontage rd, Waco
23	Pompeys Pillar, N [other] Pompeys Pillar Nat Landmark
14	Ballentine, Worden, S [food] Long Branch Café/casino
6	MT 522, Huntley, N [food] Pryor Creek Café/casino, S [food] golf
0mm	I-90, E to Sheridan, W to Billings, I-94 begins/ends on I-90, exit 456.

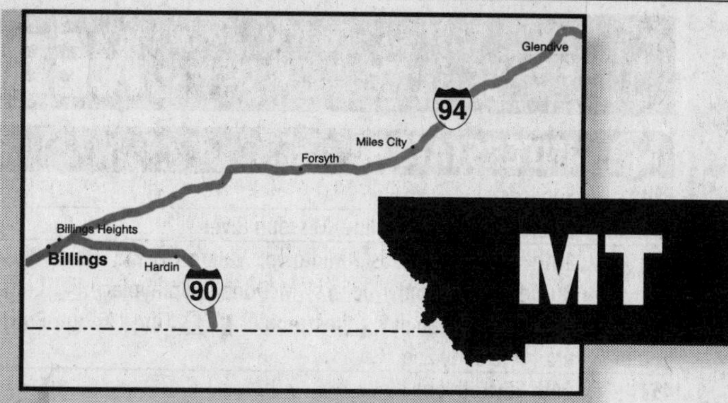

MT

NOTES

NEBRASKA

NE

INTERSTATE 80

OMAHA

Exit#	Services
455mm	Nebraska/Iowa state line, Missouri River
454	13th St, N [gas] BP/dsl, Midtown, Valero [food] Big Horn BBQ, Burger King, Jimmy John's, McDonald's/playplace [lodging] Comfort Inn [other] Family$, tires/repair, S [food] King Kong Burgers [other] Doorly Zoo
453	24th St (from eb)
452b	I-480 N, US 75 N, N [other] Eppley Airfield
452a	US 75 S
451	42nd St, N [gas] BP/dsl [other] [H], S [gas] Phillips 66 [food] Burger King, McDonald's, Taco Bell [other] Pitstop Lube
450	60th St, N [gas] Phillips 66 [other] NAPA, to U of NE Omaha, S [gas] Casey'/dsl [other] transmissions
449	72nd St, to Ralston, N [gas] BP, QT [food] Burger King, Spezia Italian [lodging] Baymont Inn, Best Value Inn, Comfort Inn, DoubleTree, Quality Inn, Ramada, Super 8 [other] [H], Walmart, S [gas] Cenex/dsl [food] Anthony's Steaks
448	84th St, N [gas] BP/dsl [food] Arby's, Crane Coffee, Denny's, Farmhouse Café, Great Wall Chinese, Husker Hounds, La Casa, Little Caesar's, McDonald's, Pizza Ranch, Subway, Taco Bell [lodging] Motel 6 [other] Ace Hardware, Advance Parts, CVS Drug, Jensen's Tire/auto, Mangelson's Crafts, ShopKO, USPO, S [gas] Kum&Go/dsl/e85, QT, Shell/dsl [food] Wendy's [other] Chevrolet, Kia
446	I-680 N, to Boystown
445	US 275, NE 92, I thru L St, N [gas] Casey's/dsl [food] Buffalo Wings&Rings, Cheddar's, Famous Dave's BBQ, Hardee's, Jason's Deli, Noodles&Co, Pita Pit, Qdoba, SmashBurger, Starbucks, Wendy's [lodging] Carol Hotel [other] Book-A-Million, Buick/GMC, Home Depot, Michael's, Nelsen's RV Ctr, PetCo, Sam's Club/gas, Super Target, Verizon, Walmart, S [gas] BP, QT/dsl [food] Arby's, Brew Burgers, Burger King, Dunkin Donuts, Godfather's Pizza, Hog Wild BBQ, Hunan Garden, Jimmy' Egg Cafe, Jimmy John's, LJ Silver, McDonald's, Runza, Subway, Taco Bell, Valentino's, Village Inn [lodging] Best Western, La Quinta, Motel 6, Super 8, Victorian Inn, Victorian Inn, Westmont Inn [other] Bag'n Save Foods, Family$, Jensen Automotive, O'Reilly Parts, URGENT CARE
444	Q St, N [gas] Casey's/dsl
442	126th St, Harrison St, N [other] Chrysler/Dodge/Jeep, Toyota, VW, S [gas] Phillips 66/dsl [food] Amigo's Mexican, Burger King, Coldstone, Dunkin Donuts, Houston's, Jimmy John's, Pizza West, Runza, Sonic, Summer Kitchen [lodging] Comfort Suites, Courtyard, Embassy Suites, Hampton Inn, My Place, Woodspring Suites [other] Cabela's, Costco/gas
440	NE 50, to Springfield, N [gas] BP/dsl/e85, Phillips 66/dsl, Sapp Bros/Subway/dsl/24hr/@ [food] Azteca Mexican, Cracker Barrel, Hardee's, McDonald's [lodging] Countryside Suites, EconoLodge, Hometown Lodge, Motel 6, Quality Inn, Red Carpet Inn [other] Ford, tires, S [gas] BP, to Platte River SP [other] [H]
439	439 NE 370, to Gretna, N [gas] Kum&Go/dsl [food] Arby's, Taco John's [lodging] Holiday Inn Express [other] Walmart/Subway, S [other] [H], museum, Volvo Trucks
432	US 6, NE 31, to Gretna, N [gas] Pump&Pantry/dsl/24hr [food] McDonald's, Subway [lodging] Super 8 [other] KOA, Nebraska X-ing/famous brands, S [gas] FLYING J/Denny's/dsl/LP/24hr [other] to Schramm SP
431mm	[RS] wb, full [handicap] facilities, info, litter barrels, petwalk, [phone], [picnic]
427mm	Platte River

LINCOLN

Exit#	Services
426	NE 66, to Southbend, N [other] museum, rv camping, to Mahoney SP
425.5	[RS] eb, full [handicap] facilities, litter barrels, petwalk, [phone], [picnic], vending
420	NE 63, Greenwood, N [gas] Cenex/cafe/dsl/scales/24hr [other] Pine Grove RV Park, S [gas] Shell/dsl [other] antiques, to Platte River SP, WWII Museum
416mm	weigh sta both lanes
409	US 6, to E Lincoln, Waverly, N [gas] Casey's (2mi) [food] McDonald's (2mi), Subway (2mi), S [other] [H]
405	US 77 N, 56th St, Lincoln, S [gas] Phillips 66 [other] [H], antiques, Freightliner, Peterbilt, truck service/wash/tires
403	27th St, Lincoln, 0-3 mi S [gas] Mobil, Phillips 66/Subway/dsl, Phillips 66/Wendy's/dsl, Shell [food] Amigos Mexican, Applebee's, Arby's, Asian Buffet, Burger King, Cane's, Carlos O'Kelly's, China Inn, CiCi's Pizza, Cracker Barrel, Culver's, daVinci's Italian, Dickey's BBQ, DQ, Fazoli's, Golden Corral, IHOP, Jimmy John's, King Kong Burger, Mazatlan Mexican, McDonald's, Papa John's, Papa Murphy's, Pizza Hut, Popeye's/Taco Inn, Ruby Tuesday, Runza, Schlotzsky's, Sonic, Taco Bell, Taco John's, Village Inn [lodging] AmericInn, Best Western+, Country Inn&Suites, Countryside Suites, Fairfield Inn, Hampton Inn, Holiday Inn Express, La Quinta, Microtel, Motel 6, Quality Inn, Red Roof Inn, Sleep Inn, Staybridge Suites, Super 8, TownePlace Suites, Woodspring Suites [other] $Tree, AutoZone, BMW, Buick/Chevrolet/GMC, Chrysler/Dodge/Jeep, Ford/Lincoln, GNC, Gordman's, Haas Tire, Home Depot, HyVee Foods, Lexus, Menards, Mercedes, Petsmart, Sam's Club/dsl, ShopKO, Super Saver Foods, to U NE, Toyota, URGENT CARE, Verizon, Walmart/McDonald's
401b	US 34 W, S [other] RV camping
401a	I-180, US 34 E, to 9th St, Lincoln
399	NW 12th St, Lincoln, N [gas] Gulf/FatDogs/dsl, Phillips 66/dsl [food] Baskin-Robbins, Big Ten Subs, McDonald's [lodging] Best Value Inn, Comfort Inn, Country Inn Suites, Fairfield Inn, Hampton Inn, Holiday Inn Express, Horizon Inn, Luxury Inn, Quality Inn, Rodeway Inn, Sunset Inn, Travelodge [other] to [airport], S [gas] Casey's/dsl [food] Subway [lodging] EconoLodge
397	US 77 S, to Beatrice
396	US 6, West O St (from eb), S [lodging] Rodeway Inn, Super 8
395	US 6, NW 48th St, S [gas] Phillips 66/dsl, Shoemaker's/Shell/dsl/scales/@ [lodging] Cobbler Inn [other] Harley-Davidson, truck repair
388	NE 103, to Crete, Pleasant Dale
382	US 6, Milford, S [gas] Phillips 66/dsl
381mm	[RS] eb, full [handicap] facilities, litter barrels, petwalk, [phone], [picnic], vending
379	NE 15, to Seward, 2-3 mi N [food] McDonald's [lodging] Sunset Inn [other] [H], antiques, Buick/Chevrolet/GMC, Ford, S [gas] Shell/dsl
375mm	truck parking (wb)
373	80G, Goehner, N [gas] gas
369	80E, Beaver Crossing, 3 mi S [other] [H], food, RV camping
366	80F, to Utica
360	93B, to Waco, N [gas] Phillips 66/Waco Rest/dsl/24hr, S [lodging] Double Nickel Camping
355mm	[RS] wb, full [handicap] facilities, info, litter barrels, petwalk, [phone], [picnic] vending
353	US 81, to York, N [gas] Conoco/dsl, Pump-N-Pantry/e85, Sapp Bros/Sinclair/Subway/scales/dsl, Shell/dsl [food] Arby's, Burger King, China Buffet, Dickey's BBQ, DQ, Golden Gate Chinese, KFC/Taco Bell, La Carreta Mexican, McDonald's, Runza, Starbucks, Taco John's, The Kitchen, Wendy's [lodging] Best Value Inn, Comfort Inn, Days Inn, Hampton Inn, Holiday Inn Express

YORK

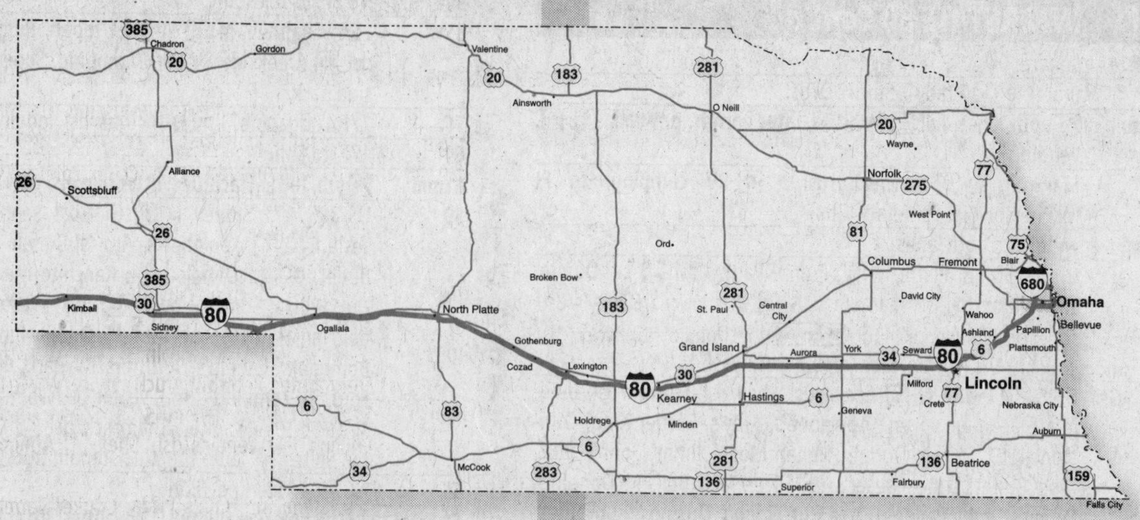

NE

AURORA

INTERSTATE 80 Cont'd

353 Continued
New Victorian Inn, Super 8, Yorkshire Motel, Buick/GMC, Chevrolet, Elms RV Park, Ford, RV Camp, Walmart/Subway, **S** Petro/Phillips 66/Iron Skillet/Pizza Hut/dsl/24hr/@, Shell/Huddle House/dsl Applebee's Best Western+, Motel 6 Blue Beacon, Freightliner, tires/wash/lube

351mm **eb, full facilities, info, litter barrels, petwalk, vending**

348 93E, to Bradshaw

342 93A, Henderson, **N** Prairie Oasis Camping, **S** Henderson Trkstp/dsl Subway Sun Motel

338 41D, to Hampton

332 NE 14, Aurora, 2-3 mi **N** Casey's McDonald's, Pizza Hut, Subway Budget Host, Ford, to Plainsman Museum, **S** Loves/Arby's/dsl/scales/24hr

324 41B, to Giltner

318 NE 2, to Grand Island, **S** KOA (seasonal)

317mm **wb, full facilities, info, litter barrels, petwalk, vending**

315mm **eb, full facilities, info, litter barrels, petwalk, vending**

314mm **Platte River**

314 Locust Street, to Grand Island, **4-6 mi N** food, gas, lodging

312 US 34/281, to Grand Island, **N** Bosselman/Pilot/Little Caesar's/Subway/scales/dsl/24hr, Fat Dogs Thunder Road Grill Motel 6, USA Inn, Mormon Island RA, to Stuhr Pioneer Museum, **S** Phillips 66/Arby's/dsl Days Inn, Quality Inn/Riverfront Grille Hastings Museum (15mi), Peterbilt

305 40C, to Alda, **N** Sinclair/dsl, TA/Country Pride/dsl/scales/24hr/@, **S** **Crane Meadows Nature Ctr/**

300 NE 11, Wood River, **N** to Cheyenne SRA, **S** Pilot/Subway/dsl/scales/24hr motel/RV park

291 10D, Shelton, **N** War Axe SRA

285 10C, Gibbon, **N** Petro Oasis/dsl RV camping, Windmill SP, **S** Country Inn

279 NE 10, to Minden, **N** Conoco/dsl, **S** Pioneer Village Camping (13mi)

275 NE 10, Kearney, **N** Archway Mon

275mm The Great Platte River Road Archway Monument

272 NE 44, Kearney, **N** Casey's, Casey's/dsl, Cenex/Subway/dsl, Pump&Pantry/dsl, Shell/dsl Amigo's, Angus Burger,

KEARNEY

272 Continued
Arby's, Burger King, Coppermill Steaks, DQ, Egg&I, El Limon, El Maguey, Firehouse Subs, Freddy's, Gourmet House Japanese, Hunan's Rest., King's Buffet, LJ Silver, McDonald's, Moe's SW, Old Chicago Rest, Perkins, Pizza Hut, Red Lobster, Ruby Tuesday, Runza, Taco Bell, Taco John's, USA Steaks, Wendy's, Whiskey Creek AmericInn, Candlewood Suites, Comfort Inn, Country Inn&Suites, Days Inn, EconoLodge, Fairfield Inn, Hampton Inn, Holiday Inn, Howard Johnson, La Quinta, Microtel, Midtown Western Inn, Motel 6, New Victorian Inn, Quality Inn, Ramada Inn, Rodeway Inn, Super 8, Western Inn South, Wingate Inn, $General, Apache Camper Ctr, Boogaart's Foods, Buick/Cadillac, Chevrolet, Chrysler/Dodge/Jeep, Kearney RV Park/camping, Museum of NE Art, to Archway Mon, U NE Kearney, Verizon, Walmart (3mi), **S** Qwest/dsl Skeeter's BBQ Best Western+, Holiday Inn Express

271mm **wb, full facilities, info, litter barrels, petwalk,**

269mm **eb, full facilities, info, litter barrels, petwalk,**

263 Rd 10 b, Odessa, **N** Sapp Bros./Apple Barrel Rest./dsl UP Wayside

257 US 183, Elm Creek, **N** Pilot/Subway/dsl/scales/24hr Rodeway Inn Antique Car Museum, Sunny Meadows Camping, **S** Nebraska Prairie Museum (9mi)

248 Overton, **N** Jay Bros/dsl

LEXINGTON

237 US 283, Lexington, **N** Casey's, Cenex/dsl, Gulf/dsl, Phillips 66/dsl Arby's, Baskin-Robbins, Burger King, Delight Donuts, DQ, Hong Kong Buffet, Little Caesar's, McDonald's, Pizza Hut, San Pedro Mexican, Sonic, Wendy's Comfort Inn, Days Inn, Econolodge, Holiday Inn Express, Minute Man Motel, $General, $Tree, Advance Parts, Buick/Chevrolet, Military Vehicle Museum, O'Reilly Parts, Plum Creek Foods, Verizon, Walmart/Subway, **S** Sinclair/dsl/@ Kirk's Café Super 8 to Johnson Lake RA (6mi)

231 Darr Rd

227mm **both lanes, full facilities, info, litter barrels, petwalk, vending**

222 NE 21, Cozad, **N** Casey's/dsl, Cenex/dsl Burger King, DQ, Panda Buffet, Pizza Hut, Runza, Subway Knights Inn, Rodeway Inn, $General, Firestone/auto, museum

211 NE 47, Gothenburg, **N** Cenex/dsl, Cenex/dsl/24hr Lasso Espresso, McDonald's, Mi Ranchito Mexican, NE Grill, Pizza Hut, Runza Comfort Suites, Howard Johnson, Travel Inn, Buick/Chevrolet, Carquest, Pony Express Sta Museum (1mi), ShopKO, **S** Blue Heron Camping/Gas

= gas = food = lodging = other = rest stop

NE

INTERSTATE 80 Cont'd

N PLATTE

Exit#	Services
199	Brady, N Brady 1 Stop/DQ/dsl
194mm	**both lanes, full facilities, litter barrels, petwalk, , , vending**
190	Maxwell, N Ranchland/dsl, S RV camping, to Ft McPherson Nat Cemetary (2mi)
181mm	**weigh sta both lanes**
179	to US 30, N Platte, N Pump&Pantry/dsl La Quinta, Tru Hilton RV camping, S FLYING J/Denny's/dsl/scales/LP/RV dump/24hr, Loves/McDonald's/Subway/dsl/scales/24hr tire/lube/repair, truckwash
177	US 83, N Platte, N Cenex/dsl, Shell/dsl, Sinclair/dsl, U-Fillem Amigo's Rest., Applebee's, Arby's, Burger King, Coldstone, DQ, Dunkin Donuts, Hunan Moon, Jimmy John's, KFC, King Buffet, Little Caesar's, LJ Silver/Taco Bell, McDonald's, Penny's Diner, Perkins, Pizza Hut, Qdoba, Quiznos, Ruby Tuesday, Runza, San Pedro Mexican, Sonic, Starbucks, Subway, Wendy's, Whiskey Creek Steaks Blue Spruce Motel, Fairfield Inn, Hampton Inn, Howard Johnson, Knights Inn, Motel 6, Oak Tree Inn, Quality Inn H, $General, $Tree, Advance Parts, Goodyear/auto, Harley-Davidson, Herberger's, Holiday RV Park, museum, Staples, SunMart Foods, Tire Pros, to Buffalo Bill's Ranch, Verizon, visitor ctr, Walgreens, Walmart/Subway, S Cenex, Gulf/Taco Bell/dsl/24hr, U-Fillem/Subway/dsl/RV dump Taco John's Best Western+, Comfort Inn, Days Inn, Holiday Inn Express, Super 8 Chevrolet/Cadillac, Chrysler/Dodge/Jeep, dsl repair, Ford/Lincoln, Hobby Lobby, Honda, Menards, Nissan, Seevers Tire/auto, to Lake Maloney RA, Toyota, vet, veterans memorial/info
164	56C, Hershey, N Shell/Western Cafe/dsl/24hr/@ KJ's Ranch Store
160mm	**both lanes, full facilities, info, litter barrels, petwalk, ,**
158	NE 25, Sutherland, N Park Motel (1mi) RV camping, S Sinclair/Godfather's Pizza/dsl RV camping
149mm	Central/Mountain time zone
145	51C, Paxton, N Shell/dsl/24hr Days Inn RV camping
133	51B, Roscoe
132mm	**wb, full facilities, info, litter barrels, petwalk, ,**
126	US 26, NE 61, Ogallala, N Casey's/dsl, Cenex/dsl, Kwik Stop, Sapp Bros/Shell/dsl/24hr, Watering Hole/dsl, Western/dsl Arby's, Front Street Cafe, Golden Village Chinese, Margarita's, McDonald's, Peking Chinese, Pizza Hut, Runza, Spur Steaks, Valentino's Days Inn, Lonesome Dove Lodge, Quality Inn, Travelodge H, $General, Bomgaars, Buick/Chevrolet/GMC, Chrysler/Dodge/Jeep, Firestone/auto, Ford/Lincoln, NAPA, O'Reilly Parts, SunMart Foods, to Lake McConaughy, U-Save Drug, Verizon, S Gulf/Subway/dsl, TA/Country Pride/dsl/scales/24hr/@ DQ, Mi Ranchito Mexican, Royal Buffet, Wendy's Holiday Inn Express, Rodeway Inn, Super 8 Ace Hardware, Countryview Camping, ShopKO, Sleepy Sunflower RV Park, truck repair, Walmart/dsl
124mm	**eb, full facilities, info, litter barrels, petwalk, ,**
117	51A, Brule, N Happy Jack's/dsl Riverside RV camping
107	25B, Big Springs, N Big Springs/dsl, FLYING J/Grandma Max's/Subway/dsl/scales/24hr/@ Sam Bass' Steaks Motel 6 truckwash, S McGreer's Camping
102	I-76 S, to Denver
102mm	S Platte River
101	US 138, to Julesburg, S truck parking
99mm	scenic turnout eb

OGALLALA

SIDNEY

Exit#	Services
95	NE 27, to Julesburg
85	25A, Chappell, N FVC/dsl/repair, Pump&Pantrydsl, Shell/dsl Creekside RV Park/Camping, Super Foods, USPO, wayside park
76	17F, Lodgepole, 1 mi N gas/dsl, lodging
69	17E, to Sunol
61mm	**wb, full facilities, litter barrels, petwalk, , , vending**
59	US 385, 17J, Sidney, N Gulf/dsl, Sapp Bros/Shell/dsl/24hr, Tesla EVC Applebee's, Arby's, Buffalo Point Rest., China 1 Buffet, DQ, McDonald's, Mi Ranchito Mexican, Perkins, Pizza Hut, Runza, Sonic, Subway Best Western+, Days Inn, Fairfield Inn, Hampton Inn, Motel 6, Quality Inn auto/dsl repair, Bomgaars, Cabela's Outfitters/RV Park, Chrysler/Dodge/Jeep, Ford, RV camping (2mi), visitor ctr, Walmart, S Loves/IHOP/dsl/scales/24hr, Shamrock/dsl Comfort Inn, Country Inn Suites auto tire/truck repair, truckwash
55	NE 19, to Sterling, Sidney
51.5mm	**/hist marker eb, full facilities, litter barrels, petwalk, , , vending**
48	to Brownson
38	rd 17 b, Potter, N FVC/dsl/LP repair
29	53A, Dix, 1/2 mi N food, gas
22	53E, Kimball, 1-2 mi N Kwik Stop, Vince's/dsl Pizza Hut, Subway Days Inn, Motel Kimball, Sleep4Less Motel city park, Kimball RV Park (seasonal), Main St Mkt, NAPA
20	NE 71, Kimball, 0-2 mi N Conoco/dsl, FVC/dsl, Kwik Stop, Vince's/dsl O'Henry's Diner, Pizza Hut, Subway 1st Interstate Inn, Days Inn, Motel Kimball, Sleep4Less Motel, Super 8 city park, Kimball RV Park (seasonal), Main St Mkt, NAPA ShopKO
8	53C, to Bushnell
1	53B, Pine Bluffs, 1 mi N RV camping
0mm	Nebraska/Wyoming state line

KIMBALL

INTERSTATE 680 (Omaha)

Exit#	Services
I-680 begins/ends on I-80, exit 27.	
29b a	I-80, W to Omaha, E to Des Moines.
28	IA 191, to Neola, Persia
21	L34, Beebeetown
19mm	**wb, full facilities, info, litter barrels, petwalk, ,**
16mm	**eb, full facilities, info, litter barrels, petwalk, ,**
15mm	scenic overlook
71	I-29 N, to Sioux City
66	Honey Creek
3b a	(61 b a from wb) I-29, S to Council Bluffs, IA 988, to Crescent E Casey's/dsl to ski area
1	County Rd
14mm	Nebraska/Iowa state line, Missouri River, Mormon Bridge
13	US 75 S, 30th St, Florence, E Shell/dsl Enzo's, Zesto Diner HyVee Drug, LDS Temple, Mormon Trail Ctr, W Florence/dsl
12	US 75 N, 48th St, E Cenex/dsl Burger King (2mi), Taco Bell (2mi)
9	72nd St, 1-2 mi E Kwikshop Burger King, Golden Corral, Jimmy John's, KFC, Panda Express, Taco Bell, Village Inn H, Big Lots, Marshall's, Petsmart, Target, Walgreens W Cunningham Lake RA
6	NE 133, Irvington, E BP, MurphyUSA/dsl Burger King, Jimmy John's $Tree, Verizon, Walmart/Subway/drugs/24hr W Legend's Grill, Villagio Pizzeria, Zesto Cafe Fairfield Inn, Holiday Inn Express

OMAHA

INTERSTATE 680 (Omaha)

Exit#	Services
5	Fort St, W KwikShop, QT Dunkin Donuts CVS Drug, HyVee Foods, Walgreens
4	NE 64, Maple St, E BP, W Kum&Go/dsl, Megasaver Burger King, China 1, Godfather's Pizza, Jimmy John's, La Mesa Mexican, McDonald's, Pizza Hut, Runza, Subway, Taco Bell, Taco John's Comfort Suites, La Quinta $General, Family Fare, O'Reilly Parts, vet
3	US 6, Dodge St, E Cheesecake Factory, Granite City Rest., JC Mandarin Chinese, Panera Bread, PF Chang's AmericInn, Marriott AAA, Audi/VW, BMW, Dick's, Hyundai, Jaguar/ Land Rover, JC Penney, Mazda, Mini, Subaru, Von Maur, Whole Foods Mkt, Younkers, W Phillips 66 Burger King, Chick-fil-A, China Buffet, Cilantro's, DQ, Jimmy John's, McDonald's, Starbucks, Subway, Which Wich? Best Western, Hampton Inn, Sheraton, Super 8, TownPlace Suites Cadillac, Chevrolet, Costco/gas, Discount Tire, Menard's
2	Pacific St, E Conoco Subway, W BP

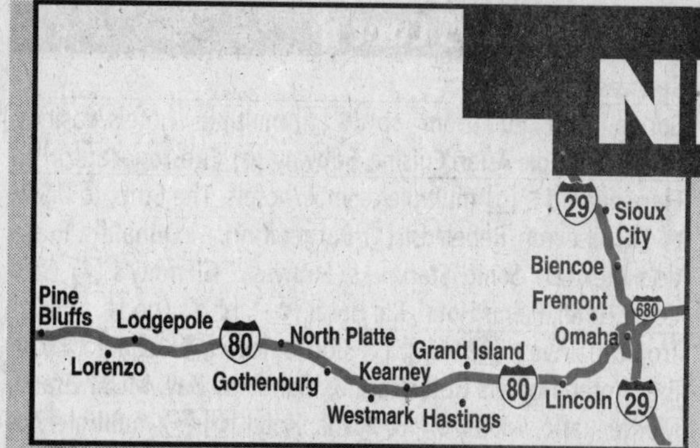

Exit#	Services
1	NE 38, W Center Rd, E Cenex/dsl Don Carmelo's, Don&-Millie's Rest., Subway, W Phillips 66 Arby's, Burger King, Dickey's BBQ, IHOP, Krispy Kreme, McAlister's Deli, Ozark BBQ, Starbucks, Subway, Taco Bell, Wendy's $Tree, Baker's Foods/dsl, Office Depot, TJ Maxx, Tuesday Morning
0mm	I-680 begins/ends on I-80, exit 446.

NE

NV

NEVADA

INTERSTATE 15

MESQUITE

Exit#	Services
123mm	Nevada/Arizona state line, Pacific/Mountain time zone
122	Lp 15, Mesquite E **NV Welcome Ctr both lanes, full facilities, petwalk,** Arco, Maverik/dsl, Shell/DQ/dsl Alberto's Mexican, Cafe Rio, Canton Chinese, Cucina Italiano, Dominos, Golden West Rest./casino, Jack-in-the-Box, KFC, Los Lupes, Panda Garden, Peggy Sue's Cafe, Taco Bell Best Western, Rising Star $General, Ace Hardware, AutoZone, Big O Tire, CarQuest, city park, Smith's/Subway/dsl, Sun Resort RV Park, USPO, Walgreens W 76/dsl/LP/RV park McDonald's, Starbucks Eureka Motel/casino, Virgin River Hotel/casino
120	Lp 15, Mesquite, Bunkerville E Shell/dsl, Sinclair/dsl, Terrible's McDonald's Casablanca Resort/casino/RV Park, Oasis Resort RV Park USPO, W Chevron/dsl Del Taco, Popeye's, Roberto's Tacos Holiday Inn Express H, $Tree, Ford/RV Ctr, Verizon, Walmart/Subway
118	Lower Flat Top Dr
112	NV 170, Riverside, Bunkerville
110mm	**truck parking both lanes, litter barrels**
100	to Carp, Elgin
96mm	**truck parking both lanes, litter barrels**
93	NV 169, to Logandale, Overton E Chevron (3mi) Lake Mead NRA, Lost City Museum
91	NV 168, Glendale W Arco/dsl Muddy River Rest. USPO
90.5mm	Muddy River
90	NV 168 (from nb), Glendale, Moapa W gas Moapa Indian Reservation, USPO
88	Hidden Valley
88mm	**parking area both lanes, litter barrels**
84	Byron
80	Ute
75	Valley of Fire SP, Lake Mead NRA E Chevron/dsl/24hr casino, fireworks
64	US 93 N, Great Basin Hwy, to Ely, Great Basin NP W Loves/Subway/Godfather's/dsl/scales/24hr
60mm	**livestock check sta sb**
58	NV 604, Las Vegas Blvd, to Apex, Nellis AFB
54	Speedway Blvd, Hollywood Blvd E Petro/Sinclair/dsl/scales/24hr/@ Race Day Cafe Las Vegas Speedway, W Speedee Mart/dsl
52	rd 215 W
50	Lamb Ave, **1-2 mi** E Comfort Inn Hitchin Post RV Park
48	Craig Rd E Arco, Pilot/KFC/Pizza Hut/dsl/scales/24hr, Shell, Sinclair/Subway/dsl Burger King, Jack-in-the-Box, Taco Bell, Zapata's Cantina Comfort Inn 7-11, Firestone/auto, Freightliner, to Nellis AFB, W 7-11 Cane's, Cannery Grill, Carl's Jr, Chipotle Mexican, Del Taco, Famous Dave's BBQ, Five Guys, In-N-Out, Jamba Juice, Marble Slab, Mulligan's, Panda Express, Sonic, Starbucks, Subway Best Western, Hampton Inn, Springhill Suites Batteries&Bulbs, Lowe's, Sam's Club/gas
46	Cheyenne Ave E CiCi's Pizza, Marianna's Mkt, Panda Express, Subway, Taco Bell $Tree, 7-11, NAPA, vet, W 7-11, Valero/Mortons/Subway/dsl/LP24hr Denny's, McDonald's, Tacos El Gordo Sunrise Inn Aamco, Blue Beacon, dsl repair, Kenworth, SpeedCo, tires
45	Lake Mead Blvd E Chevron, Rebel/dsl Arby's, Burger King, Jack-in-the-Box, McDonald's 7-11, PepBoys, W Arco/dsl
44	Washington Ave (from sb) E casinos
43	D St (from nb), same as 44
42b a	I-515 to LV, US 95 N to Reno, US 93 S to Phoenix
41b a	NV 159, Charleston Blvd E 7-11, Arco/dsl Cheesecake Factory, Chipotle Premium Outlets/famous brands, Walgreens, W Chevron, Rebel/dsl Carl's Jr, Del Taco, Jimmy John's, McDonald's, Starbucks, Wendy's H, CVS Drug, Smith's Foods
40	Sahara Ave E Artisan Hotel multiple casinos/hotels, The Strip, W 7-11, Arco/dsl, Chevron, Rebel/dsl, Shell Carl's Jr, Chipotle Mexican, DQ, El Pollo Loco, In-N-Out, KFC, Landry's Seafood, Los Tacos, Macaroni Grill, McDonald's, Panda Express, PDQ Cafe, Pizza Hut, Shilla BBQ, Starbucks, Subway, TGIFriday's, Wendy's Palace Sta. Hotel/Casino $Tree, AT&T, casinos, CVS Drug, Mariana's Mkt, Office Depot, Ross, TJ Maxx

LAS VEGAS

INTERSTATE 15 Cont'd

Exit#	Services
39	Spring Mtn Rd (from sb) E multiple hotels/casinos, W Multiple Asian Cuisine, Subway Firestone/auto
38b a	Flamingo Rd E multiple casinos/hotels, The Strip, to UNLV, W Chevron, Rebel/dsl Burger King, McDonald's, Ricardo's Mexican, Sonic, Starbucks, Subway, TGIFriday's Gold Coast Hotel, Palms Hotel, Rio Hotel Smith's Foods
37	Tropicana Ave E Rebel Coco's Rest. Bellagio, Excalíber Hotel, Hooters Hotel/casino, Mandalay Bay, MGM Grand, Monte Carlo, Motel 6, Tropicana Hotel multiple hotels/casinos, W Rebel/dsl, Shell/Subway, Standard, Texaco Burger King, Cane's, Dennys, In-N-Out, Jack-in-the-Box, McDonald's, Wendy's Budget Suites, Days Inn, Hampton Inn, La Quinta, Motel 6, Orleans Hotel, Siegel Suites
36	Russell Rd E multiple hotels/casinos, to W Chevron/Herbst/dsl Courtyard, Fairfield Inn, Holiday Inn Express, Residence Inn, Staybridge Suites
34	to I-215 E, Las Vegas Blvd, to The Strip E McCarran Airport
33	NV 160, to Blue Diamond, Death Valley E 7-11, Chevron/dsl, Rebel/dsl Bootlegger Bistro, Buffalo Wild Wings, Burger King, Cane's, Chili's, Chipotle Mexican, Denny's, Dickey's BBQ, Dunkin Donuts, Five Guys, Hawaiian BBQ, IHOP, Jersey Mikes, McDonald's, NY Pizza, Outback Steaks, Panda Express, Popeyes, Smashburger, Starbucks, Subway, Wienerschnitzel Baymont Inn, Budget Suites, Caribe Resort, Hilton Garden CVS Drug, factory outlet/famous brands, Oasis RV Resort, Smith's Foods, W Chevron/dsl, Shell, TA/Burger King/Subway/TacoTime/dsl/LP/scales/24hr/@ Cafe Rio, Carl's Jr, Chipotle, Del Taco, Domino's, Famous Dave's BBQ, In-N-Out, Jack-in-the-Box, McDonald's, Panda Express, Papa Murphy's, Subway Silverton Lodge/Casino AT&T, $Tree, 99c Store, Albertson's, Bass ProShops, BigLots, Discount Tire, GNC, Kohl's, Meineke, Office Depot, PetCo, Ross, Target, Verizon, Walgreens, WorldMkt
31	Silverado Ranch Blvd E Steak'n Shake South Point Hotel/Casino
30	W Cactus Ave W Chevron/dsl
27	NV 146, to Henderson, Lake Mead, Hoover Dam, **0-2 mi** E Arco, Chevron/dsl, Shell Burger King, Jack-in-the-Box, Starbucks, Subway Best Western, Hampton Inn Camping World, casino, W vet
25	NV 161, Sloan, **1 mi** E Camping World
24mm	**bus/truck check sta nb**
12	NV 161, to Goodsprings, Jean E Shell/dsl Denny's Gold Strike Casino/hotel, NV Correctional, NV HP, skydiving, USPO, W Chevron/dsl/24hr
1	Primm E Chevron/Subway/dsl, Texaco/dsl Carl's Jr, Dennys, KFC, Mad Greek Cafe, McDonald's, Panda Express, Starbucks, Taco Bell Buffalo Bill's Resort/casino, factory outlets, Primm Valley Resort/casino, W FLYING J/Subway/Qdoba/DQ/dsl/scales Whiskey Pete's Hotel/casino
0mm	Nevada/California state line

LAS VEGAS · JEAN

INTERSTATE 80

Exit#	Services
411mm	Nevada/Utah state line
410	US 93A, to Ely, W Wendover S **NV Welcome Ctr/info, full facilities,** Chevron/dsl, Pilot/Arby's/dsl/scales/24hr, Shell/Taco Time/dsl Burger King, McDonald's, Pizza Hut, Subway Knights Inn, Motel 6, Nugget Hotel/casino, Peppermill Hotel/casino/RV parking, Rainbow Hotel/casino, Red Garter Hotel/casino Best Hardware, city park, KOA, Smith's Foods/dsl,
407	Ola, W Wendover
405mm	Pacific/Mountain time zone
398	to Pilot Peak
390mm	Silverzone Pass, elevation 5940
387	to Shafter
378	NV 233, to Montello, Oasis
376	to Pequop
373mm	Pequop Summit, elev 6967, **both lanes, litter barrels, rest rooms**
365	to Independence Valley N prison camp
360	to Moor
354mm	**parking area eb**
352b a	US 93, Great Basin Hwy, E Wells N Chevron/dsl/LP, Conoco/dsl, Petro/Dunkin Donuts/dsl/café/casino Bella's Diner, Burger King/Subway Motel 6, Rest Inn Motel, Sharon Motel, Super 8 Crossroads RV Park, repair, Tire Factory, S FLYING J/dsl/scales/LP/casino/RV Dump/24hr, LNG, Loves/McDonalds/dsl/scales/24hr Hampton Inn Great Basin NP
351	W Wells N Wells/dsl/LP Family$, Mtn Shadows RV Park, Roy's Foods, USPO, Well's Hardware, S Angel Lake RV Park, to Angel Lake RA
348	to Beverly Hills N RV camping
343	to Welcome, Starr Valley N food Welcome RV Park
333	Deeth, Starr Valley
328	to River Ranch
321	NV 229, Halleck, Ruby Valley
318mm	N Fork Humboldt River
317	to Elburz
314	to Ryndon, Devils Gate N Sinclair/cafe/dsl, S RV camping
312mm	**check sta both lanes**
310	to Osino, **4 mi** S Valley View RV Park
303	E Elko N Flyers/CFN/dsl, Sinclair/Arctic Circle/dsl/24hr Wingers Holiday Inn Express, Home 2 Suites, Ledgestone Hotel, TownePlace Suites, S Chevron/dsl, Conoco/dsl, Maverik/dsl, Sinclair/dsl Blue Moon Rest., Burger King, Chef Cheng's Chinese, Domino's, DQ, Garibaldi's Mexican, McDonald's/playplace, Monkey Sun Chinese, Pizza Barn, Pizza Hut, Quiznos, Subway, Taco Time, Toki Ona Diner, Wendy's Best Value Inn, Best Western, Budget Inn, Comfort Inn, Days Inn, High Desert Inn, Hilton Garden, Holiday Motel, Motel 6, Quality Inn, Red Lion Inn/casino, Sheraton Four Points, Super 8, Travelodge H, Albertson's, AT&T, Big O Tires, Buick/Cadillac/Chevrolet/GMC, Cal Ranch Store, city park, Double Dice RV Park, Ford, Gold Country RV Park, Goodyear/auto, Iron Horse RV Park, JC Penney, Kenworth, NE NV Museum, Valley View RV Park
301	NV 225, Elko N Maverik/dsl 9 Beans/Burrito, Arby's, Burger King, Denny's, Greatwall Chinese, Jack-in-the-Box, Jimmy John's, Mattie's Grill, McDonald's/playplace, Papa Murphy's, Port of Subs, RoundTable Pizza Baymont Inn, Shilo Inn Suites AT&T, GNC, Home Depot, JoAnn Fabric, Marshall's, Petco, Raley's Foods, Ross, Verizon, Walmart/Subway, S Shell, Shell/dsl Costa Vida, Dos Amigos, KFC, Little Caesar's, Sergio's Mexican, Starbucks, Subway, Taco Bell American Inn, Centre Motel, Economy Inn, Elko Inn, Esquire Inn, Hampton Inn, Manor Inn, Midtown Motel, Rodeway Inn, Scottish Inn, Stampede Motel, Stockmen's Hotel/casino

WENDOVER · WELLS · ELKO · NV

INTERSTATE 80 Cont'd

301 Continued
Thunderbird Motel [other] [H], Advance Parts, [airport], AutoZone, Cimarron West RV Park, CVS Drug, Family$, O'Reilly Parts, Smith's Foods/dsl, transmission, Verizon

298 W Elko

292 to Hunter **N** [other] CA Trail Interpretive Ctr

285mm Humboldt River, tunnel

CARLIN

282 NV 221, E Carlin **N** [other] prison area

280 NV 766, Carlin **N** [food] Pizza Factory [other] Desert Gold RV Park, dsl repair, **S** [gas] Chevron/dsl, Pilot/Subway/dsl/scales/24hr [food] Chin's Cafe, Rigobertos Mexican, State Café/casino [lodging] Carlin Inn, Cavalier Motel [other] Ace Hardware, Family$, tires, USPO

279 NV 278 (from eb), to W Carlin, **1 mi S** [gas] Flyers/dsl

271 to Palisade

270mm Emigrant Summit, elevation 6114, **truck parking both lanes, litter barrels**

268 to Emigrant

261 NV 306, to Beowawe, Crescent Valley

259mm **[rest stop] both lanes, full [handicapped] facilities, litter barrels, petwalk, [picnic]**

257mm Humboldt River

254 to Dunphy

244 to Argenta

BATTLE MTN

233 NV 304, to Battle Mountain **N** [gas] Conoco/dsl [food] Mama's Pizza/deli [lodging] Royal Inn [other] [H], Ace Hardware, FoodTown

231 NV 305, Battle Mountain, **1 mi N** [gas] FLYING J/76/Blimpie/dsl/casino/24hr, Chevron/dsl, Maverik/dsl [food] El Aguila Real, Hide-a-way Steaks, McDonald's, Ming Dynasty, Owl Rest., Pizza Factory, Port of Subs [lodging] Big Chief Motel, Nevada Hotel, Owl Motel, Super 8 [other] [H], city park, Family$, Mills Drug, NAPA, NAPA Care, Tire Factory, USPO

229 NV 304, W Battle Mountain **N** [gas] FLYING J/76/dsl/casino/scales/24hr, Shell/dsl [food] Colt Rest./casino [lodging] Big Chief Motel, Rodeway Inn [other] Colt RV camping, NAPA Care, Tire Factory

222 to Mote

216 Valmy **N** [gas] Chevron/USPO/dsl, **S** **[rest stop] both lanes, full [handicapped] facilities, litter barrels, petwalk, [phone], [picnic], RV dump**

212 to Stonehouse

205 to Pumpernickel Valley

203 to Iron Point

200 Golconda Summit, elevation 5159, [other] **truck parking both lanes**, litter barrels

194 Golconda **N** [other] USPO

187 to Button Point **N** **[rest stop] both lanes, full [handicapped] facilities, litter barrels, petwalk, [phone], [picnic], RV dump**

WINNEMUCCA

180 NV 794, E Winnemucca Blvd

178 NV 289, Winnemucca Blvd, Winnemucca **S** [gas] Chevron/dsl, Maverik/dsl [food] Rte 66 Grill, Sonoma Grill [lodging] Budget Inn, Candlewood Suites, Cozy Motel, Frontier Motel, Valu Motel [other] [H], Advance Parts, carwash

176 US 95 N, Winnemucca **N** [gas] PacificPride/dsl, **S** [gas] FLYING J/dsl/LP/RV dump/24hr, Chevron/dsl/24hr, Conoco/dsl, G Gas, Kwik Serv/dsl [food] Burger King, China Garden, Dos Amigos Mexican, Dotty's, Griddle Rest., Jack-in-the-Box, KFC/LJ Silver, Little Caesar's, McDonald's/playplace, Pig BBQ, Pizza Hut, Port of Subs, RoundTable Pizza, Sid's Rest., Subway, Taco Bell, Taco Time [lodging] Best Western, Country Hearth Inn, Economy Inn, Holiday Inn Express, Holiday Motel, Model T Motel/casino/RVPark, Motel 6, Park Hotel, Pyrenees Motel, Quality Inn, Regency Inn, Santa Fe Inn, Scott Motel, Scottish Inn, Super 8, Winnemucca Inn/casino, Winner Hotel/casino [other] [H], auto/truck repair,

176 Continued
AutoZone, Ford, O'Reilly Parts, Ridley's Foods, RV camping, Schwab Tire, Verizon, Walmart/Subway

173 W Winnemucca **N** [gas] Pilot/Subway/dsl/scales/24hr, **S** [other] [airport]

168 to Rose Creek **S** [other] prison area

158 to Cosgrave **S** **[rest stop] both lanes, full [handicapped] facilities, litter barrels, petwalk, [phone], [picnic]**

151 Mill City **N** [gas] TA/Subway/Taco Bell/Fork/dsl/casino/24hr/@

149 NV 400, Mill City, **1 mi N** [gas] TA/Subway/Taco Bell/Fork/dsl/24hr/@, **S** [other] Star Point Gen. Store/RV camping

145 Imlay **S** [other] Star Peak RV Park

138 Humboldt

129 Rye Patch Dam **N** [other] to Rye Patch SRA, **S** [gas] Chevron/Rye Patch Trkstp/dsl

119 to Rochester, Oreana

112 to Coal Canyon **S** [other] to correctional ctr

LOVELOCK

107 E Lovelock (from wb), same as 106

106 Main St, Lovelock **N** [gas] Chevron/dsl/LP, PJ's Gas/subs/dsl [food] Black Rock Grill, Cowpoke Cafe, McDonald's, Pizza Factory [lodging] Cadillac Inn, Covered Wagon Motel, Punch Inn/casino, Royal Inn, Super 10 Motel [other] [H], auto care, city park/playground/restrooms, Family$, Lazy K Camping, Safeway Foods, USPO, **S** [gas] Conoco/Port of Subs/dsl24hr

105 W Lovelock (from eb) **N** [gas] Shop'n Go/dsl, Valero/dsl [food] La Casita Mexican [lodging] Lovelock Inn [other] [H], Brookwood RV Park, museum, NAPA, same as 106

93 to Toulon **S** [other] [airport]

83 US 95 S, to Fallon **S** **[rest stop] both lanes, full [handicapped] facilities, litter barrels, [phone], [picnic]**

78 to Jessup

65 to Hot Springs, Nightingale

50 NV Pacific Pkwy, Fernley

NV

 [gas] = gas [food] = food [lodging] = lodging [other] = other [rest stop] = rest stop

INTERSTATE 80 Cont'd

FERNLEY

Exit#	Services
48	US 50A, US 95A, to Fallon, E Fernley N [gas] FLYING J/Denny's/dsl/scales/Lp/24hr, S [gas] Chevron/dsl, Shell/dsl [food] Burger King, Dotty's Grill, Jack-in-the-Box, KFC, Louie's China, McDonald's, Moto Japanese, Papa Murphy's, Pizza Factory, Pizza Hut, Port of Subs, Silverado Rest./casino, Starbucks, Taco Bell [lodging] Best Western, Super 8 [other] $Tree, AutoZone, Chrysler/Dodge/Jeep, Lowe's, O'Reilly Parts, Raley's Mkt, tires, to Great Basin NP, URGENT CARE, USPO, Verizon, Walgreens, Walmart/Subway
46	US 95A, W Fernley N [gas] Loves/Arby's/dsl/scales/24hr, S [gas] Pilot/DQ/Wendy's/dsl/scales/24hr [lodging] Comfort Suites [other] Blue Beacon, SpeedCo
45mm	Truckee River
43	to Pyramid Lake, Wadsworth N [gas] Pyramid Lake/dsl/RV camping
42mm	**check sta eb, [rest stop] wb, full [handicapped] facilities, litter barrels, petwalk, [phone], [vending], wireless internet**
40	Painted Rock
38	Orchard
36	Derby Dam
32	USA Pkwy, Tracy, Clark Station S [gas] Golden Gate/Port of Subs/dsl/scales [food] Philly's, Subway [lodging] Studio 6
28	NV 655, Waltham Way, Patrick
27mm	scenic view eb
25mm	**check sta wb**
23	Mustang S [gas] Chevron/dsl/24hr
22	Lockwood

SPARKS

Exit#	Services
21	Vista Blvd, Greg St, Sparks N [gas] Chevron/McDonald's, Qwik-Stop [food] Del Taco [lodging] Fairfield Inn, Woodspring Suites [other] [H], S [gas] Petro/Iron Skillet/dsl/24hr/@ [lodging] Super 8 [other] Peterbilt, truckwash
20	Sparks Blvd, Sparks N [gas] 7-11, Shell/dsl [food] BJ's Rest., Buffalo Wild Wings, Burrito Bandito, Carl's Jr, Chick-fil-A, Chipotle, Fuddruckers, Jersey Mike's, Jimmy John's, Olive Garden, Outback Steaks, Panda Express, Papa John's, Popeye's, Starbucks, Subway, Taco Bell [lodging] Hampton Inn, Residence Inn [other] AT&T, Best Buy, Discount Tire, GNC, Lowe's, Old Navy, Petco, Scheel's Sports, Schwab Tire, Target, Tires+, TJ Maxx, Verizon, water funpark, S [gas] Petro/Iron Skillet/dsl/scales/24hr/@ [lodging] Super 8 [other] Freightliner
19	E McCarran Blvd, Sparks N [gas] Arco, Chevron/dsl, Sinclair/dsl, TA/Fuddrucker's/dsl/scales/@ [food] Applebee's, Baskin-Robbins, BJ's BBQ, Black Bear Diner, Burger King, Cane's, China King, Domino's, El Pollo Loco, Jack-in-the-Box, KFC, Little Caesar's, McDonald's, Pizza Hut, Pizza+, Port Of Subs, Sizzler, Taco Bell, Wendy's, Wienerschnitzel [lodging] Aloha Inn, Sunrise Motel, Windsor Inn [other] $Tree, 99c Store, AutoZone, BigLots, CVS Drug, Family$, Foodmaxx Foods, O'Reilly Parts, Ross, Victorian RV Park, S [food] Denny's, Super Burrito [lodging] Holiday Inn [other] NAPA
18	NV 445, Pyramid Way, Sparks N [gas] 7-11 [food] In-N-Out [lodging] Bourbon Square Casino, Nugget Courtyard, S [lodging] Nugget Hotel/casino
17	Rock Blvd, Nugget Ave, Sparks N [gas] Arco, Chevron, V/dsl [lodging] Safari Motel, Victorian Inn, Wagon Train Motel [other] casinos, O'Reilly Parts, S [lodging] Nugget Hotel/casino

RENO

Exit#	Services
16	B St, E 4th St, Victorian Ave N [gas] Arco [food] Jack's Cafe [lodging] Motel 6 [other] Rail City Casino, S [gas] Chevron/repair
15	I-580 S, US 395, to Carson City, Susanville, 0-1 mi S [lodging] Best Western, Holiday Inn Express, Hyatt Place, La Quinta [other] [airport], Costco/gas, Grand Sierra Resort, USPO, Walmart/McDonald's
14	Wells Ave, Reno N [lodging] Motel 6, S [gas] Chevron/dsl [food] Denny's [lodging] America's Best Inn, Days Inn, Ramada Inn [other] auto repair, Goodyear, Tire Pros
13	US 395, Virginia St, Reno N [gas] Shell/dsl [food] Taco Shop, S [other] [H], Circus Circus, to downtown hotels/casinos, to UNVReno, Walgreens
12	Keystone Ave, Reno N [gas] Arco [food] Pizza Hut, Starbucks [lodging] Gateway Inn, Motel 6 [other] 7-11, CVS Drug, Raley's Foods, S [gas] Chevron/dsl [food] Burger King, Jack-in-the-Box, KFC, Little Caesar's, McDonald's, Port of Subs, Round Table Pizza, Taco Bell, Wendy's [other] casinos, Keystone RV Park, Meineke, NAPA, O'Reilly Parts, SaveMart/drug
10	McCarran Blvd, Reno N [gas] 7-11/dsl, Arco [food] Applebee's Asian Wok, Baskin-Robbins, Bully's Grill, Burger King, Carl's Jr, Chili's, Chipotle, Del Taco, El Pollo Loco, Hawaiian BBQ, IHOP, Jack-in-the-Box, KFC, Little Caesar's, McDonald's, Papa Murphy's, Pizza+, Popeyes, Qdoba Mexican, RoundTable Pizza, Silver Chop Chinese, Starbucks, Subway, Taco Bell, Tacos el Rey [other] $Tree, AT&T, AutoZone, Big O Tires, Discount Tire, Kohl's, O'Reilly Parts, Petsmart, Ross, Safeway/dsl, SaveMart Foods, Staples, Tires+, Walgreens, Walmart/McDonald's, S [gas] 7-11 [other] Home Depot, URGENT CARE, vet
9	Robb Dr N [gas] Chevron/dsl, Maverik/dsl [food] Bully's Grill, Burger Me, Casa Grande, China Kitchen, Dickey's BBQ, Domino's, Jimmy John's, Moxie's Cafe, Port Of Subs, Starbucks, Subway [lodging] Hampton Inn [other] CVS Drug, Raley's Foods/dsl, URGENT CARE
8	W 4th St (from eb), Robb Dr, Reno S [other] RV camping
7	Mogul
6.5mm	**truck parking**/hist marker/scenic view both lanes
5	to E Verdi (from wb no return) N [food] Maria's Mexican
4.5mm	scenic view eb
4	Garson Rd, Boomtown N [gas] Chevron/Boomtown Hotel/dsl/casino [food] Mel's Rest. [other] Cabela's, KOA/RV dump
3.5mm	**check sta eb**
3	Verdi (from wb)
2.5mm	Truckee River
2	Lp 80, to Verdi N [gas] Sinclair/dsl/24hr [food] Jack-in-the-Box [lodging] Gold Ranch RV Resort/casino
0mm	Nevada/California state line

NV

NOTES

NEW HAMPSHIRE

INTERSTATE 89

LEBANON

Exit#	Services
61mm	New Hampshire/Vermont state line, Connecticut River
20(60)	NH 12A, W Lebanon, E [gas] Sunoco [food] 99 Rest., Chili's, Dunkin Donuts, KFC/Taco Bell, Lui Lui Pizza, Subway [other] GNC, Hannaford Foods, Jo-Ann Fabrics, LL Bean, Rite Aid, Shaw's Foods, TJ Maxx, Town Fair Tire, USPO, W [food] 7 Barrel Rest., Applebee's, Burger King, D'angelo's, Denny's, Five Guys, Friendly's, Koto Japanese, McDonald's, Moe's SW Grill, Panera Bread, Pizza Hut, Weathervane Seafood, Wendy's [lodging] Baymont Inn, Fireside Inn [other] $Tree, AT&T, Best Buy, BJ's Whse, BooksAMillion, CVS Drug, Home Depot, JC Penney, Kohl's, Midas, PriceChopper Foods, Staples, Verizon, Walgreens, Walmart
19(58)	US 4, NH 10, W Lebanon, E [gas] Gulf/dsl, Shell [food] China Station [other] AutoZone, Family$, Ford, Harley-Davidson, Honda, Pricechopper Foods, W [gas] Maplewoods/dsl, Sunoco/repair [other] Bond Parts
57mm	**Welcome Ctr/[RS]/weigh sta sb, full [handicapped] facilities, litter barrels, petwalk, [phone], [picnic], vending, weigh sta nb**
18(56)	NH 120, Lebanon, E [gas] Citgo/dsl/scales [lodging] Courtyard (3mi), Days Inn, Residence Inn (2mi) [other] [H], Cadillac/Chevrolet, Chrysler/Dodge/Jeep, Freightliner, Nissan, to Dartmouth Coll, Volvo/VW, Wilson Tire/repair, W [gas] Mobil/Subway/dsl, Shell [other] U-Haul
17(54)	US 4, to NH 4A, Enfield, E [other] RV Camping, vet
16(52)	Eastman Hill Rd, E [gas] Gulf/Subway/dsl, W [gas] Mobil/Dunkin Donuts/dsl [other] Whaleback Ski Area
15(50)	Montcalm
14(47)	NH 10 (from sb), N Grantham
13(43)	NH 10, Grantham, E [gas] Irving/Gen Store/dsl, W [gas] Irving/Circle K [food] Dunkin Donuts, Pizza Chef [other] repair, vet
40mm	**[RS] nb, full [handicapped] facilities, info, litter barrels, petwalk, [phone], picnic table, vending**
12A(37)	Georges Mills, W [other] food, lodging, [phone], RV camping, to Sunapee SP
12(34)	NH 11 W, New London, 2 mi E [gas] Irving/dsl [food] McKenna Rest. [lodging] Maple Hill Country Inn, New London Inn [other] [H]
11(31)	NH 11 E, King Hill Rd, New London, 2-3 mi E [food] Hole in the Fence Cafe [lodging] Fairway Motel, New London Inn, ski area
10(27)	to NH 114, Sutton, E [other] to Winslow SP, 1 mi W [lodging] lodging [other] to Wadleigh SB
26mm	**[RS] sb, full [handicapped] facilities, info, litter barrels, petwalk, [phone], [picnic], vending**
9(19)	NH 103, Warner, E [gas] Irving/Circle K/Dunkin Donuts/dsl, Shell/Subway/pizza [food] McDonald's [other] Aubuchon Hardware, Mkt-Basket Foods, Rollins SP, W [other] ski area, to Sunapee SP
8(17)	NH 103 (from nb, no EZ return), Warner, 1 mi W [gas] [food] [other] museum, to Rollins SP
15mm	Warner River
7(14)	NH 103, Davisville, E [other] camping, W [other] Pleasant Lake Camping
12mm	Contoocook River
6(10)	NH 127, Contoocook, E [gas] Sunoco [food] Country Fair Cafe [other] vet, W [other] Elm Brook Park, Sandy Beach Camping (3mi)
5(8)	US 202 W, NH 9 (exits left from nb), Hopkinton, W [other] food, RV camping (seasonal)
4(7)	NH 103, Hopkinton (from nb, no EZ return), E [gas] gas [other] Horse-Shoe Tavern
3(4)	Stickney Hill Rd (from nb)
2(2)	NH 13, Clinton St, Concord, E [other] [H], W [other] NH Audubon Ctr

WARNER

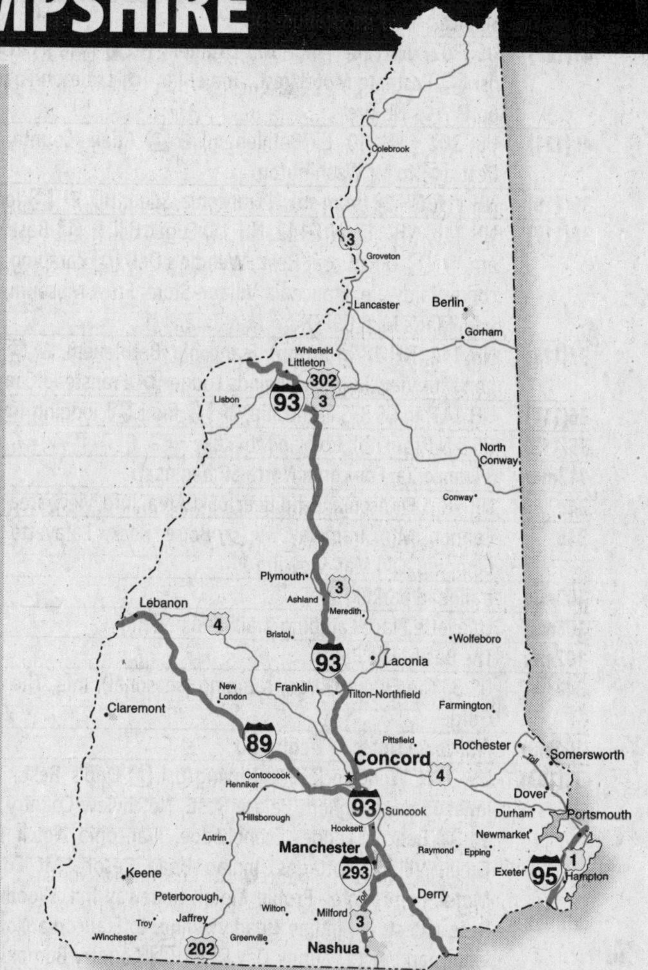

Exit#	Services
1(1)	Logging Hill Rd, Bow, E [gas] Mobil [food] Chen Yang Li Chinese [lodging] Hampton Inn
0mm	I-93 N to Concord, S to Manchester, **I-89 begins/ends on I-93, 36mm.**

INTERSTATE 93

Exit#	Services
2(11)	I-91, N to St Johnsbury, S to White River Jct. **I-93 begins/ends on I-91, exit 19.**
1(8)	VT18, to US2, to St Johnsbury, 2mi E [gas] gas [food] food [lodging] camping, lodging
1mm	**Welcome Ctr nb, full [handicapped] facilities, info, litter barrels, petwalk, [phone], [picnic], vending, WiFi**
131mm	Vermont/New Hampshire state line, Connecticut River, **exits 1-2 are in VT.**
44(130)	NH 18, NH 135, **W Welcome Ctr (8am-8pm)/scenic vista both lanes, full [handicapped] facilities, info, litter barrels, petwalk, [phone], [picnic]**
43(125)	NH 135 (from sb), to NH 18, Littleton, 1-2 mi W [other] [H], same as 42
42(124)	US 302 E, NH 10 N, Littleton, E [gas] Citgo/Quiznos, Gulf, Irving, Sunoco [food] Burger King, Deluxe Pizza, Dunkin Donuts, Littleton Diner, Pizza Hut, Subway [lodging] Beal House, Littleton Motel [other] Bond Parts, Family$, Rite Aid, USPO, Walgreens, W [gas] Mobil [food] 99 Rest., Applebee's, Asian Garden, McDonald's [lodging] Hampton Inn [other] $Tree, Aubuchan Hardware, Buick/Chevrolet, Chrysler/Dodge/Jeep, Home Depot, KOA (5mi), Lowe's, O'Reilly Parts/VIP Service, Shaw's Foods/Osco Drug, Staples, Tire Whse, TJ Maxx, Verizon, Walmart/Dunkin Donuts

LITTLETON

NH

INTERSTATE 93 Cont'd

Exit#	Services
41(122)	US 302, NH 18, NH 116, Littleton, E Irving/Circle K/dsl Eastgate Motel/rest., Travel Inn Littleton Food Co-op, W NE Tire
40(121)	US 302, NH 10 E, Bethlehem, E Adair Country Inn/Rest. to Mt Washington
39(119)	NH 116, NH 18 (from sb), N Franconia, Sugar Hill, W lodging
38(117)	NH 116, NH 117, NH 142, NH 18, Sugar Hill, E Best Western, W DutchTreat Rest., Wendle's Deli camping, Franconia Hardware, Franconia Village Store, Frost Museum, gifts, info, Mac's Mkt, USPO
37(115)	NH 142, NH 18 (from nb), Franconia, Bethlehem, W Cannon Mtn View Motel, Hillwinds Lodge Franstead Camping
36(114)	NH 141, to US 3, S Franconia, W food lodging golf
35(113)	US 3 N (from nb), to Twin Mtn Lake
112mm	S Franconia, Franconia Notch SP begins sb
34c	NH 18, S Franconia, Echo Beach Ski Area, info, view area
34b	Cannon Mtn Tramway, W Boise Rock, Lafayette Place Camping, Old Man Viewing
109mm	trailhead parking
108mm	Lafayette Place Camping, trailhead parking
107mm	The Basin, The Basin
34a	US 3, The Flume Gorge, camping (seasonal), info, The Flume Gorge
104mm	Franconia Notch SP begins nb
33(103)	US 3, N Woodstock, E Irving/dsl Dad's Rest., Fresolones Pizza, Longhorn Palace Rest., Notchview Country Kitchen Beacon Lodge, EconoLodge, Franconia Notch Motel, Green Village Cottages, Indian Head Resort, Mt Coolidge Motel, Pemi Motel, Profile Motel, Rodeway Inn, Woodward's Resort/Rest. Indian Head viewing, to Franconia Notch SP, waterpark, W Sunny Day Diner Country Bumpkin Cottages/Camping, Cozy Cabins, Mt Liberty Cabins, White Mtn Motel/Cottages Arnold's NAPACare, Clark's Trading Post, Cold Springs Camping, Tim's Repair, vet
32(101)	NH 112, Loon Mtn Rd, N Woodstock, E Irving, Mobil, Tedeschi/dsl 3 Cultures Deli, Black Mtn Burger, Cafe Nacho's, Cheng Garden Chinese, Common Man Rest., Dunkin Donuts, Elvio's Pizza, Flapjack's Pancakes, GH Pizza, Gordi's Fish&Steaks, Gypsy Cafe, McDonald's, Subway, White Mtn Bagel Deli Comfort Inn, Kancamagu's Lodge, Lincoln Sta. Lodge, Nordic Inn, South Mtn Resort Aubuchan Hardware, Family$, NAPA, PriceChopper Foods, Rite Aid, USPO, W Citgo Lafayette Dinner Train, Landmark II Rest., Peg's Café, Truant's Rest., Woodstock Inn Rest. Alpine Lodge, Autumn Breeze Motel, Carriage Motel, Cascade Lodge candy/fudge/gifts, USPO
31(97)	to NH 175, Tripoli Rd, E RV camping (seasonal), W KOA (2mi)
30(95)	US 3, Woodstock, E Lanterns End Grill, Tony's Rest. Jack-O-Lantern Inn/rest. golf, W camping (seasonal)
29(89)	US 3, Thornton, E Pemi River RV Park/LP, W Gilcrest Motel
28(87)	NH 49, Campton, E Gulf, Mobil Dunkin Donuts, Exit 28 Pizza Handy Man Hardware, RV camping, to ski area, USPO, W Irving/dsl Sunset Grill Branch Brook Camping, Chesley's Glory Sta., Mtn Vista RV Park, repair
27(84)	Blair Rd, Beebe River, E Country Cow Rest. Days Inn, Red Sleigh Condos
26(83)	US 3, NH 25, NH 3A, Tenney Mtn Hwy, W Common Man Inn, EconoLodge, Pilgrim Inn H
25(81)	NH 175 (from nb), Plymouth, W Citgo/dsl, Irving/Circle K/dsl Downtown Pizza, Fracher's Diner, HongKong Garden, House of Pizza, Lucky Dog Grill, Subway, Thai Smile H, Chase St Mkt, Plymouth State U, USPO
24(76)	US 3, NH 25, Ashland, E Gulf, Irving/Circle K/dsl, Mobil Ashland Pizza, Burger King, Common Man Diner, Dot's Bistro, Dunkin Dounts, Lucky Dragon Chinese, Village Grill Comfort Inn Bob's Mkt, Jellystone RV Camp (4mi), repair, USPO
23(71)	NH 104, NH 132, to Mt Washington Valley, New Hampton, E Irving/Circle K/dsl, Mobil/dsl Dunkin Donuts, Rossi Italian, Subway Clearwater Campground, info, Jellystone, USPO, W Homestead Rest. (2mi) RV Park (2mi), ski area
22(62)	NH 127, Sanbornton, **1-5 mi** W H, food, gas/dsl,
61mm	**sb, full facilities, info, litter barrels, petwalk, , , vending**
20(57)	US 3, NH 11, NH 132, NH 140, Tilton, E Irving/Circle K/dsl/24hr, Shell/Subway/dsl 99 Rest., Applebees, Burger King, Dunkin Donuts, Green Ginger Chinese, KFC, McDonald's, Starbucks, Thai Cuisine, Tilt'n Diner, UNO, UpperCrust Pizza, Wendy's Hampton Inn, Holiday Inn Express, Super 8 BJ's Whse/gas, Home Depot, Old Navy, O'Reilly Parts/VIP Service, Staples, Subaru, Tanger Outlet/famous brands, Walgreens, W Chili's, Pizza Hut Chrysler/Dodge/Jeep, Ford, Kohl's, Lowe's, MktBasket Foods, Nissan, USPO, VW, Walmart/Subway
56mm	Winnipesaukee River
19(55)	NH 132 (from nb no ez return), Franklin, W Gulf Ciao Italian H, antiques, NH Vet Home
51mm	**nb, full facilities, info, litter barrels, petwalk, , , vending**
18(49)	to NH 132, Canterbury, E Gulf to Shaker Village HS
17(46)	US 4 W, to US 3, NH 132, Boscawen, **4 mi** W gas
16(41)	NH 132, E Concord, E Mobil/dsl Quality Cash Mkt
15W(40)	US 202 W, to US 3, N Main St, Concord, W Citgo, Cumberland/Dunkin Donuts, Speedway Domino's, Friendly's Courtyard/café
15E	I-393 E, US 4 E, to Portsmouth
14(39)	NH 9, Loudon Rd, Concord, E Shell/dsl 99 Rest., Applebee's, Arnie's Place, Boloco Burritos, Buffalo Wild Wings, Burger King, Chicago Grill, D'angelo's, Dunkin Donuts, El Rodeo Mexican, Five Guys, Friendly's, KFC, LJ Silver/Taco Bell, Longhorn Steaks, McDonald's, Moritomo Japanese, Newick Lobster House, Olive Garden, Panera Bread, PapaGino's, Pizza Hut, Red Apple Buffet, Ruby Tuesday, Starbucks, Sunshine Oriental, TGIFriday's, Wendy's, Windmill Rest., Wok Inn $Tree, 7-11, AAA, Ace Hardware, Advance Parts, AutoZone, Best Buy, BonTon, BooksAMillion, city park, CVS, Dick's, GNC, Hannaford Foods, Home Depot, Irving/Circle K/Subway/dsl, JC Penney, L Bean, Lowe's, Meineke, Michael's, Midas, Mkt Basket Foods, Mobil, PetCo, Petsmart, Rite Aid, Sam's Club/gas, Shaw Foods/24hr, Shaw's Foods/Osco Drug, Shell/dsl, Staples, Sunoco/dsl, Target, TJ Maxx, TownFair Tire, URGENT CARE, USPO, Verizon, Walgreens, Walmart, W Citgo, Cumberland, Speedway Domino's, Gas Lighter Rest., Nonni's Rest., Siam Orchid, Tea Garden Rest. Holiday Inn hist sites, Jo-Ann, Marshall's, MktBasket, museum, to state offices, vet
13(38)	to US 3, Manchester St, Concord, E Cumberland, Sunoco/dsl, deli Beefside Rest., Brookside Pizza, Cityside Grille, Dunkin Donuts, Ichiban Japanese, Kaylen's Pizza, Red Blazer Rest., Veno's Italian Buick/GMC, Cadillac/Chevrolet, Chrysler/Dodge/Jeep, Harley-Davidson, Kia, Nissan, O'Reilly Parts/VIP Service

INTERSTATE 93 Cont'd

MANCHESTER

Exit	Services
13(38)	Continued Outdoor RV Ctr Subaru, Subaru, Tire Whse, Volvo, W Mobil/dsl, Speedway/dsl Burger King, Common Man Diner, D'angelo's, Dunkin Donuts, KFC, McDonald's Best Western, Comfort Inn, Fairfield Inn, Residence Inn H, Aubuchon Hardware, CVS Drug, Firestone, Goodyear/auto
12N(37)	NH 3A N, S Main, E Gulf, Irving/Subway/dsl/24hr Dunkin Donuts Days Inn Ford, Honda, Hyundai, Mazda, Toyota, W H
12S	NH 3A S, Bow Junction
36mm	I-89 N to Lebanon, toll road begins/ends
31mm	**both lanes, full facilities, info, vending**
11(28)	NH 3A, to Hooksett, 4 mi E Pilot/dsl/rest., toll plaza
28mm	I-293, Everett Tpk
10(27)	NH 3A, Hooksett, E Irving/Circle K/dsl Dunkin Donuts, Subway, Wendy's BJ's Whse, Home Depot, Kohl's, Petco, Target, W Irving/Circle K/Dunkin Donuts/dsl, Mr Gas Bass Pro Shop, MktBasket Foods, Walmart/Subway
26mm	Merrimac River
9N S(24)	US 3, NH 28, Manchester, E Irving/Dunkin Donuts/Circle K/dsl Fairfield Inn, W Manchester/dsl, Sunoco/dsl Burger King, Cheng Du Chinese, D'Angelo's, Happy Garden Chinese, La Carreta Mexican, Lusia's Italian, Mr Mac's Cafe, PapaGino's, Puritan Rest., Shorty's Mexican, Subway, Villaggio Ristorante H, Chrysler/Dodge/Jeep, city park, Hannaford Foods, Kia, Lincoln, O'Reilly Parts/VIP Service, U-Haul
8(23)	to NH 28a, Wellington Rd, W Currier Gallery, VA H
7(22)	NH 101 E, to Portsmouth, Seacoast
6(21)	Hanover St, Candia Rd, Manchester, E Dunkin Donuts, Wendy's vet, W Mobil/dsl, Shell Dunkin Donuts, McDonald's, Subway H, GNC, Goodyear/auto, Hannaford Foods
19mm	I-293 W, to Manchester (from nb), to
5(15)	NH 28, to N Londonderry, E Irving/Dunkin Donuts/dsl, Sunoco/dsl Poor Boy's Diner, W Shell/dsl Subway Sleep Inn

DERRY

Exit	Services
4(12)	NH 102, Derry, E Mobil/dsl, Mutual, Shell/dsl, Sunoco/dsl, Super Burger King, Cracker Barrel, Derry Rest., Juliano's Pizza, Poorboys Drive-In, Subway H, Advance Parts, R. Frost Farm, W 7-11, Global, Gulf/dsl/repair, Speedway 99 Rest., Dunkin Donuts, Ginger Garden, KFC/Taco Bell, McDonald's, PapaGino's, Wendy's, Whippersnappers Rest. AT&T, Ford, GNC, Hannaford Foods, Home Depot, Mkt Basket Foods, O'Reilly Parts/VIP Service, Shaw's Foods, Staples, TJ Maxx, USPO, Verizon
7mm	**weigh sta both lanes**
3(6)	NH 111, Windham, E Mobil/McDonald's House of Pizza, Windham Rest. URGENT CARE, vet, W B&H Capri Pizza, Dunkin Donuts, Klemm's Bakery, TJ's Roast Beef, Windham Deli Castleton Conference Ctr, CVS Drug, Osco Drug, Shaw's Foods, USPO

SALEM

Exit	Services
2(3)	to NH 38, NH 97, Salem, E Tuscan Kitchen Red Roof Inn, W A&A Rest., Blackwater Grill, Dunkin Donuts, Margarita's Cafe Holiday Inn, La Quinta URGENT CARE
1(2)	NH 28, Salem, E BP/dsl, Citgo/dsl, Gulf 99 Rest., Bickfords, Burger King, Chili's, Denny's, Grand China, LJ Silver, McDonald's, PapaGino's, Taco Bell, T-Bones Park View Inn AT&T, Barnes&Noble, Best Buy, Home Depot, JC Penney, Kohl's, Lord&Taylor, Macy's, Marshall's, Meineke, Michael's, MktBasket Foods, NTB, PetCo, Petsmart, racetrack, Shaw's Foods, Staples, Target, TJ Maxx, TownFair Tire, vet, Walgreens

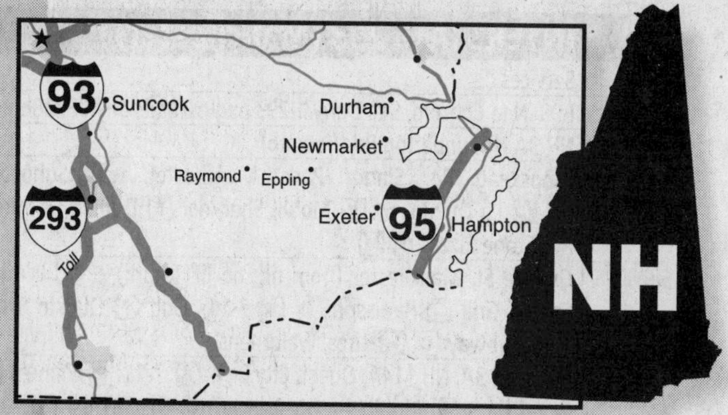

Exit	Services
1mm	**Welcome Ctr nb, full facilities, info, litter barrels, petwalk, vending**
0mm	New Hampshire/Massachusetts state line

INTERSTATE 95

PORTSMOUTH

Exit#	Services
17mm	New Hampshire/Maine state line, Piscataqua River
7(16)	Market St, Portsmouth, Port Authority, E Residence Inn, **0-2 mi** W BP, Mobil Applebee's, D'Angelo, Dunkin Donuts, Panera Bread, Qdoba, Ruby Tuesday, Starbucks, Wendy's Courtyard, Hampton Inn, Homewood Suites $Tree, BJ's Whse/gas, Marshall's, MktBasket Foods, PepBoys, PetCo, Rite Aid, Shaw's Foods, TJ Maxx, Verizon, vet, waterfront hist sites
6(15)	Woodbury Ave (from nb), Portsmouth, E Best Inn, W same as 7
5(14)	US 1, US 4, NH 16, The Circle, Portsmouth, E Gulf, Shell/dsl Roudabout Diner Anchorage Inn, Best Inn, Best Western, Fairfield Inn, Holiday Inn, Port Inn H, Buick/Cadillac/GMC, Chevrolet, U-Haul, W Chipotle, Longhorn Steaks, McDonald's Hampton Inn, Motel 6, Residence Inn Barnes&Noble, Best Buy, Dick's, Ford/Lincoln, Home Depot, Kohl's, Mazda, Michael's, Nissan, Old Navy, Staples, Sullivan Tire, Trader Joe's
4(13.5)	US 4 (exits left from nb), to White Mtns, Spaulding TPK, E H, W to Pease Int Trade Port
3a(13)	NH 33, Greenland
3b(12)	NH 33, to Portsmouth, E H, **0-2 mi** W Sunoco/dsl, TA/Country Pride/dsl/scales/24hr/@ Dunkin Donuts, McDonald's Lowe's, Mercedes, Target, VW
6.5mm	**toll plaza**
2(6)	NH 101, to Hampton, E H
4mm	Taylor River

SEABROOK

Exit#	Services
1(1)	NH 107, to Seabrook, **toll** rd begins/ends, E BP, Irving/Circle K/dsl, Monster Energy, Prime, Richdale, Sunoco/Subway/dsl, Xtra 99 Rest., Applebees, Chili's, Dunkin Donuts, Five Guys, HoneyDew Donuts, KFC/Taco Bell, McDonald's, PapaGino's, Pizza Hut, Sal's Pizza, Starbucks, Wendy's Hampshire Inn, Holiday Inn Express $Tree, Advance Parts, AutoZone, CVS Drug, Dick's, GNC, Home Depot, Jo-Ann Fabrics, Kohl's, Lowe's, Meineke, MktBasket Foods, NTB, Petsmart, Staples, Sullivan Tire, TJ Maxx, to Seacoast RA, TownFair Tire, Verizon, Walmart, W Citgo McGrath's Dining Seabrook Inn NAPA
.5mm	**Welcome Ctr nb, full facilities, litter barrels, petwalk, vending**
0mm	New Hampshire/Massachusetts state line

= gas = food = lodging = other = rest stop

INTERSTATE 293 (Manchester)

MANCHESTER

Exit#	Services
8(9)	I-93, N to Concord, S to Derry. **I-293 begins/ends on I-93, 28mm.**
7(6.5)	NH 3A N, Dunbarton Rd (from nb)
6(6)	Amoskeag Rd, Singer Park, Manchester, **E** Sunoco/dsl La Quinta, **W** Mobil, Shell/dsl Dunkin Donuts, Hot Stone Pizza H
5(5)	Granite St, Manchester (from nb, no EZ return), **E** World Sports Grill Radisson, **W** 7-11, Gulf Dunkin Donuts, Subway H, tires, Walgreens
4(4)	US 3, NH 3A, NH 114A, Queen City Br, **E** 7-11 Elliott H, **W on US 3** Mobil/dsl, Speedway/dsl, Z1 Gas/dsl Applebee's, Burger King, Chen's Garden, D'angelo's, DQ, Dunkin Donuts, Ipswich Clambake, KC's Rib Shack, KFC, Little Caesars, McDonald's, Panera Bread, Subway, Taco Bell, T-Bones, Wendy's Comfort Inn, EconoLodge Family$, Hannaford Foods, Subaru
3(3)	NH 101, **0-2 mi W** on US 3 Dunkin Donuts, IHOP Carrabba's, Chipotle, Fresh Mkt, Outback Steaks, Panera Bread, Starbucks Country Inn& Suites, Hampton Inn CVS Drug, Kohl's, Lexus, Lowe's, Macy's, Marshalls, Mini, O'Reilly Parts/VIP Service, Rite Aid, Staples, Target, URGENT CARE, vet
2.5mm	Merrimac River
2(2)	NH 3A, Brown Ave, **S** Mobil/dsl, Shell/Subway/dsl Airport Diner, Dunkin Donuts, McDonald's Holiday Inn, Super 8 Manchester Airport
1(1)	NH 28, S Willow Rd, **N** Mobil/dsl, Sunoco/dsl Boston Mkt, Burger King, Cactus Jack's, Chipotle Mexican, Coldstone, D'angelo's, Dunkin Donuts, Five Guys, Friendly's, McDonald's, Panera Bread, Papa John's, PapaGino's, Pizza Hut, Sal's Pizza, Starbucks, Subway, Taco Bell, Wendy's, Yee Dynasty Chinese Fairfield Inn, Holiday Inn Express, Sheraton H, $Tree, AT&T, AutoZone, Batteries+Bulbs, Buick/GMC, Chevrolet, CVS Drug, Hannaford Foods, Harley-Davidson, Home Depot, Mazda, Mercedes, Michael's, PepBoys, PetCo, Petsmart, Sam's Club, Sullivan Tire/repair, TJ Maxx, TownFair Tire, U-Haul, URGENT CARE, Verizon, vet, VW, Walmart, **S** Shell 99 Rest., Bertucci's, ChuckeCheese, D'angelo's, FoodCourt, Great Buffet, La Carreta, Longhorn Steaks, Masa Japanese Steaks, Olive Garden, Red Robin, TGIFriday's, TX Roadhouse Courtyard, TownePlace Suites Barnes&Noble, Best Buy, BMW, CarMax, Ford, Hobby Lobby, Honda, Hyundai, JC Penney, LL Bean, Macy's, Nissan, NTB, Old Navy, Staples, Toyota
0mm	I-93, N to Concord, S to Derry. **I-293 begins/ends on I-93.**

NH

NJ

NEW JERSEY

INTERSTATE 78

NEWARK

Exit#	Services
58b a	US 1N, US 9N, NJ Tpk
57	US 1S, US 9S, **N** Doubletree, Ramada Inn, **S** Courtyard, Fairfield Inn, SpringHill Suites to Newark Airport
56	Clinton Ave (exits left from eb)
55	Irvington (from wb), **N** Speedway/dsl Burger King, Wendy's, White Castle H, AutoZone
54	Hillside, Irvington (from eb), **N** Speedway/dsl Burger King, Wendy's, White Castle H, AutoZone
52	Garden State Pkwy
50b a	Millburn (from wb), **N** BP, Exxon, Lukoil Manny's Wieners Best Buy, Firestone/auto, Ford/Lincoln, Home Depot Superstore, Target, USPO, Whole Foods Mkt
49b a	NJ 124 (from eb), to Maplewood, same as 50b a
48	to NJ 24, to I-287 N, (exits left from eb), Springfield
48mm	I-78 eb divides into express & local
45	NJ 527 (from eb), Glenside Ave, Summit
44	(from eb), to Berkeley Heights, New Providence
43	to New Providence, Berkeley Heights
41	to Berkeley Heights, Scotch Plains
40	NJ 531, The Plainfields, **S** Valero H
36	NJ 651, to Warrenville, Basking Ridge, **N** Exxon Dunkin Donuts A&P, **S** Exxon
33	NJ 525, to Martinsville, Bernardsville, **N** 3West Rest., LingLing Chinese, Starbucks Courtyard, Hotel Indigo, Somerset Hills Inn USGA Golf Museum, **S** Exxon/7-11 Panera Bread Goodyear/auto, Verizon
32mm	scenic overlook wb
29	I-287, to US 202, US 206, I-80, to Morristown, Somerville, **S** H
26	NJ 523 spur, to North Branch, Lamington

CLINTON

Exit#	Services
24	NJ 523, to NJ 517, to Oldwick, Whitehouse, **2-3 mi S** Exxon/dsl, Gulf/dsl Readington Diner, Starbucks, Subway Kings Mkt, Rite Aid
20b a	NJ 639 (from wb), to Cokesbury, Lebanon, **S** Exxon, Shell dsl, Sunoco Cutting Board Deli, Dunkin Donuts, Janina Bistro, Kirsten's Italian Courtyard to Round Valley RA, vet
18	US 22 E, Annandale, Lebanon, **N** same as 17, **S** H, Honda
17	NJ 31 S, Clinton, **N** Exxon, Speedway, Valero/dsl Baskin-Robbins/Dunkin Donuts, Blimpie, Country Griddle, Finnigal's, McDonald's STS Tire/auto, to Voorhees SP
16	NJ 31 N (from eb), Clinton, **N** same as 17
15	NJ 173 E, to Pittstown, Clinton, **N** Express/repair, Shell/dsl Subway Holiday Inn museum, **S** Cracker Barrel Frank's Italian, Hunan Wok, Quiznos Hampton Inn H GNC, ShopRite Foods, TJMaxx, Verizon, Walmart/Dunkin Donuts
13	NJ 173 W (from wb), **N** Clinton Sta Diner, same as 12
12	NJ 173, to Jutland, Norton, **N** Clinton/dsl, Exxon/Dunkin Donuts/dsl, Pilot/Subway/dsl/scales/24hr Grand Colonial Rest. to Spruce Run RA, vet, **S** Shell Bagelsmith Deli
11	NJ 173, West Portal, Pattenburg, **N** Mobil, Shell/pizza dsl Chalet Rest., Landslide Rest. Jugtown Camping, police
8mm	**both lanes, litter barrels, no restrooms,**
7	NJ 173, to Bloomsbury, West Portal, **N** RV camping **S** Citgo/deli, Pilot/Subway/dsl/scales/24hr, TA/Burger King/Country Pride/dsl/scales/24hr/@
6mm	**weigh sta both lanes**
6	Warren Glen, Asbury (from eb)
4	Warren Glen, Stewartsville (from wb)
3	US 22, NJ 173, to Phillipsburg, **0-2 mi N** BP/dsl, Mobil/Subway/dsl, Penn Jersey Trkstp/dsl/scales/24hr, Speedway/dsl, U dsl, Wawa Applebee's, Burger King, Chick-fil-A, Dunkin Donuts, Frank's Trattoria, Friendly's, Key City Diner, McDonald

INTERSTATE 78 Cont'd

3	Continued Panera Bread, Perkins, Pizza Hut, Quaker Steak, Ruby Tuesday, Taco Bell, Teppanyaki, White Castle Best Value H, $Tree, Advance Parts, AutoZone, Best Buy, BonTon, Hobby Lobby, Home Depot, Honda, Kohl's, Lowe's, Marshall's, Meineke, Michael's, PetCo, ShopRite Foods, Staples, Stop&Shop, Target, Walmart/Subway, **S** Hyundai
0mm	New Jersey/Pennsylvania state line, Delaware River

INTERSTATE 80

Exit#	Services
I-80 begins/ends on I-95, exit 69.	
68	Leonia, Teaneck, **N** Marriott H
68b a	I-95, N to New York, S to Philadelphia, to US 46
67	to Bogota (from eb)
66	Hudson St, to Hackensack
65	Green St, S Hackensack
64b a	NJ 17 S, to US 46 E, Newark, Paramus, **S** BP/dsl Crow's Nest Rest. Hilton Stop&Shop
63	NJ 17 N, **N** BP, Exxon/dsl, Mobil/dsl, Shell/dsl, Sunoco, Wawa/dsl Burger King, Five Guys, Longhorn Steaks, Outback Steaks H, Acura, BMW, Harley-Davidson, Home Depot
62b a	GS Pkwy, to Saddle Brook, **N** Dunkin Donuts Holiday Inn, Marriott, **S** Crowne Plaza
61	NJ 507, to Garfield, Elmwood Park, **N** Marcal Paper Co
60	NJ 20, N to Hawthorne, **N** H, Lowe's, Michelin/Cooper Tires, Pepboys
59	Market St (from wb), to Paterson
58b a	Madison Ave, to Paterson, Clifton, **S** H
57c	Main St (from wb), to Paterson
57b a	NJ 19 S, to Clifton, downtown Paterson
56b a	Squirrelwood Rd, to Paterson, **S** Lukoil/Dunkin Donuts
55b a	Union Blvd (from wb, no EZ return), Totowa, **N** Shell/dsl, **S** Holiday Inn Cadillac
54	Minnisink Rd, to Paterson, **S** Dunkin Donuts Home Depot, mall
53	US 46 E, to NJ 3 (no eb return), to Wayne, Cliffton, **0-2 mi S** Exxon Applebee's, Bahama Breeze, Brio Tuscan Grill, CA Pizza, Chipotle, IHOP, Olive Garden, Ruby Tuesday, Sonic, TGIFriday's Bloomingdale's, Costco/gas, Hobby Lobby, JC Penney, Lord&Taylor, Macy's, Nissan, Office Depot, Old Navy
52	US 46, the Caldwells
48	to Montville (from wb), Pine Brook
47b	US 46 W, to Montclair, **N** Sunoco Five Guys, Longhorn Steaks, Wendy's Holiday Inn ShopRite Foods
47a	I-280 E, to The Oranges, Newark
45	to US 46, Lake Hiawatha, Whippany, **0-2 mi N on US 46** BP/dsl, Gulf/dsl, Sunoco/dsl Applebee's, Buffalo Wild Wings, Burger King, Eccola Rest., Empire Diner, Five Guys, Franco's Pizza, IHOP, Jasper Chinese, KFC, Longhorn Steaks, McDonald's, Moe's SW Grill, Outback Steaks, Pure Rest., Quin Dynasty, Sakura Japanese, Smashburger, Subway, Taco Bell, Wendy's Budget Inn, Holiday Inn/rest., Howard Johnson, Ramada Ltd, Red Roof Inn $Tree, Firestone, Home Depot, Michael's, PepBoys, PetCo, ShopRjte Foods, Staples, Verizon, Walgreens
43b a	I-287, to US 46, Boonton, Morristown
42b a	US 202, US 46, to Morris Plains, Parsippany, **0-1 mi N on US 46** 76/Dunkin Donuts/dsl, Exxon Fuddrucker's, McDonald's, TGIFriday's, Wendy's Courtyard, Days Inn, Fairfield Inn, Hampton Inn Marshall's, same as 39, Subaru

PATERSON

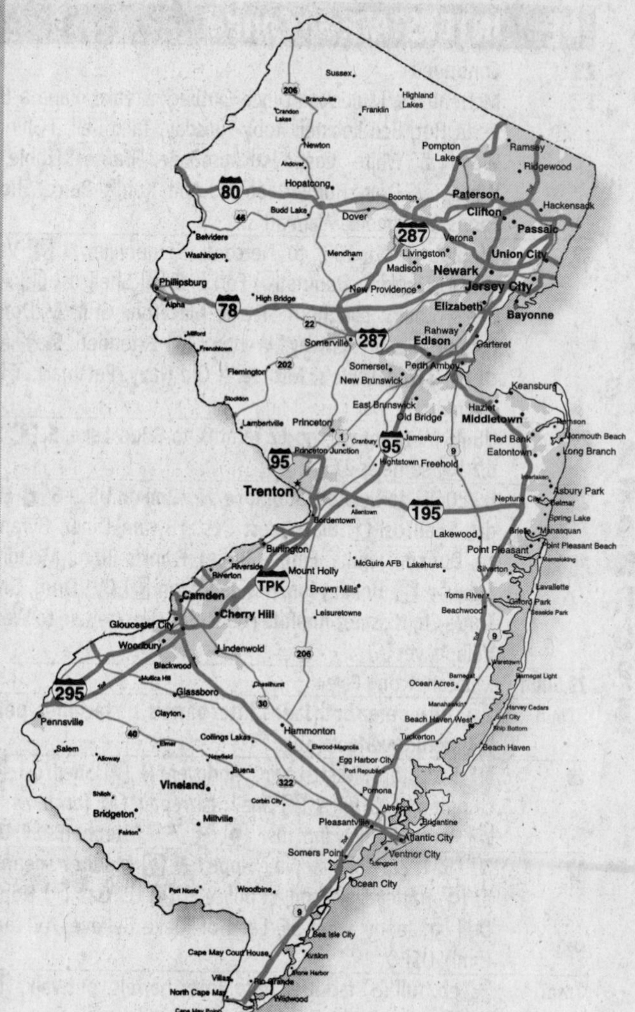

39	(38 from eb), US 46 E, to NJ 53, Denville, **0-2 mi N on US 46** Citgo/dsl, Enrite Gas, Exxon, Speedway/Dunkin Donuts, Sunoco Burger King, Casa Bella Italian, Charlie Brown's Steaks, Dunkin Donuts, Moe's SW Grill, Paul's Diner, Wendy's H, Chevrolet, Verizon, Walgreens, **S** Delta
37	NJ 513, to Hibernia, Rockaway, **N** Exxon/dsl, Shell Barn Rest., Dunkin Donuts, Hibernia Diner Hampton Inn, Rockaway Hotel, **S** H
35b a	to Dover, Mount Hope, **S** Exxon Buffalo Wild Wings, Chipotle, Coldstone, Dunkin Donuts, La Salsa Mexican, Olive Garden, Quiznos, Red Robin, Tiff's Burger Hilton Garden, Homewood Suites H, Best Buy, JC Penney, Lord&Taylor, Macy's, Michael's, Verizon
34b a	NJ 15, to Sparta, Wharton, **N** Exxon/dsl Fortune Buffet Rite Aid, **S** Dunkin Donuts, Good 5 Chinese, Panera Bread, Qdoba, Starbucks, Townsquare Diner H, $Tree, Big Lots, Costco/gas, Dick's, Home Depot, Petsmart, ShopRite Foods, Target, Walmart
32mm	**truck wb**
30	Howard Blvd, to Mt Arlington, **N** Exxon/dsl Blossom Asian, Cracker Barrel, Davy's Hotdogs, Dunkin Donuts, Frank's Pizza, Wingman Courtyard, Holiday Inn Express Quick-Chek Foods
28	US 46, to NJ 10, to Ledgewood, Lake Hopatcong, **1-2 mi S on US 46, NJ 10** Delta Gas, Speedway/dsl, Sunoco/dsl Boston Mkt, Domino's, Dunkin Donuts, Fuddruckers, KFC/LJ Silver,

NJ

 = gas = food = lodging = other = rest stop

INTERSTATE 80 Cont'd

28 Continued
McDonald's, Muldoons Diner, Outback Steaks, Panera Bread, Pizza Hut, Red Lobster, Ruby Tuesday, Taco Bell, TGIFriday's, Wendy's, White Castle AutoZone, Barnes&Noble, BJ's Whse, CVS Drug, Home Depot, Jo-Ann, Kohl's, Petco, ShopRite Foods, Walgreens, Walmart

27 US 206 S, NJ 182, to Netcong, Somerville, **N** Valero/dsl Dunkin Donuts Ford, **S** Shell/dsl Applebee's, Chili's, Longhorn Steaks, Macaroni Grill, McDonald's, Panera Bread, Subway, Wendy's Extended Stay America $Tree, Lowe's, Michael's, Old Navy, Petsmart, TJMaxx, Walmart

26 US 46 W (from wb, no EZ return), to Budd Lake, **S** Shell/dsl same as 27

25 US 206 N, to Newton, Stanhope, **N 1-2mi on US 206** Exxon/dsl, Shell/dsl Blackforest Rest., Byram Diner, Byram Pizza, Dunkin Donuts, Empire Buffet, Frank's Pizza, McDonald's, Subway Holiday Inn, Residence Inn CVS Drug, GNC, Int Trade Ctr, Nissan, ShopRite Foods, STS tires/repair, to Waterloo Village, vet

STANHOPE

23.5mm Musconetcong River

21mm **picnic area both lanes, litter barrels, no facilities, petwalk, scenic overlook (eb)**

19 NJ 517, to Hackettstown, Andover, **N** Shell/dsl RV camping, **1-2 mi S** Shell/dsl/repair Terranova Pizza Panther Valley Inn/rest. H, 7-11, Stephen's SP, USPO

12 NJ 521, to Blairstown, Hope, **N** Mediterranean Diner Harley-Davidson, st police, **S** US Gas Hope Mkt Deli Jenny Jump SF, Land of Make Believe, RV camping (5mi), USPO

7mm **eb, full facilities, info, litter barrels, petwalk, vending**

6mm scenic overlook wb, no trailers

4c to NJ 94 N (from eb), to Blairstown

4b to US 46 E, to Buttzville

4a NJ 94, to US 46 E, to Portland, Columbia, **N** TA/Pizza Hut/Taco Bell/dsl/scales/24hr/@ McDonald's RV camping, **S** USPO

3.5mm Hainesburg Rd (from wb), accesses services at 4

2 **weigh sta eb**

1mm Worthington SF

1 to Millbrook (from wb), **N** Worthington SF

0mm New Jersey/Pennsylvania state line, Delaware River

INTERSTATE 95

Exit#	Services
124mm	New Jersey/New York state line, Hudson River, Geo Washington Br
123mm	Palisades Pkwy (from sb)
73	NJ 67, Lemoine Ave, **W** Sunoco Five Guys, McDonald's A&P Mkt, GNC, Verizon, Walgreens
72 (122)	US 1, US 9, US 46, Ft Lee, **E** Doubletree, **W** Sunoco McDonald's
71 (121)	Broad Ave, Leonia, Englewood, **E** Lukoil, **W** Speedway Holiday Inn
70 (120)	to NJ 93, Leonia, Teaneck, **W** Marriott
69 (119)	I-80 W (from sb), to Paterson
68 (118)	US 46, Challenger Blvd, Ridgefield Park, **E** Exxon Lan Garden Chinese Day's Inn, Hampton Inn, Hilton Garden
117	**I-95 and NJ Turnpike run together sb**

NJ

NEW JERSEY TURNPIKE

Exit#	Services
I-95 & NJ Tpk run together sb.	
18 (117)	US 46 E, Ft Lee, Hackensack, **last exit before toll sb.**
17 (116)	Lincoln Tunnel
115mm	**Vince Lombardi Service Plaza nb, W** Sunoco/dsl Burger King, Nathan's, Popeye's
114mm	**toll plaza,**
16W (113)	NJ 3, Secaucus, Rutherford, **E** Shell, Speedway Hilton, **W** Extended Stay America Meadowlands
112mm	**Alexander Hamilton Service Area sb,** Sunoco/dsl Roy Rogers gifts
16E (112)	NJ 3, Secaucus, **E** Lincoln Tunnel
15W (109)	I-280, Newark, The Oranges
15E (107)	US 1, US 9, Newark, Jersey City, **E** Lincoln Tunnel
14c	Holland Tunnel
14b	Jersey City
14a	Bayonne
14 (105)	I-78 W, US 1, US 9, **2 mi W** Courtyard, Fairfield Inn, Spring-Hill Suites
102mm	**Halsey Service Area,** Sunoco/dsl Roy Rogers, other services in Elizabeth
13a (102)	Elizabeth, **E** Country Inn Suites, Courtyard, Embassy Suites, Extended Stay America, Residence Inn, **W** McDonald's Crowne Plaza, Days Inn, Hampton Inn, Hilton, Rennaisance, services on US1/US9
13 (100)	I-278, to Verrazano Narrows Bridge
12 (96)	Carteret, Rahway, **E** McDonald's Holiday Inn CVS Drug, Walgreens, **W** Executive Suites
93mm	**Cleveland Service Area nb, T Edison Service Area sb,** Burger King, Dunkin Donuts, Popeye's, Roy Rogers, Sbarro's, Starbucks, Starbucks
11 (91)	US 9, Garden State Pkwy, to Woodbridge, **E** McDonald's Hampton Inn $Tree, Home Depot, Walmart, **W** Speedway/dsl Residence Inn, The Forge Inn
10 (88)	I-287, NJ 514, to Perth Amboy, **E** Speedway/dsl Courtyard, Edison Hotel
9 (83)	US 1, NJ 18, to New Brunswick, E Brunswick, **E** Gulf, Mobil/dsl, Speedway/dsl Bone Fish Grill, Boston Mkt, Burger King, Carrabba's, Dunkin Donuts, Grand Buffet, Hooters, Jersey Mike's, KFC, McDonald's, Perkins, Popeye's, Starbucks Days Hotel, Motel 6 $Tree, AT&T, Best Buy, Dick's, Kohl's, Lowe's, Petsmart, ShopRite Foods, TJ Maxx, Walmart/Subway, **W** Exxon Famous Dave's, Houlihan's, On the Border Hilton, Holiday Inn Express
79mm	**Kilmer Service Area nb, Kilmer Service Area,** Burger King, Cookies and Creamery, Sbarro, Starbucks Sunoco/dsl
8a (74)	to Jamesburg, Cranbury, **W** Courtyard, Crowne Plaza
72mm	**Pitcher Service Area,** Sunoco/dsl Cinnabon, Dick Clark AB Grill, Nathan's, Roy Rogers, Starbucks
8 (67)	NJ 33, NJ 571, Highstown, **E** Petro/dsl, Shell/Dunkin Donuts/dsl, Speedway/dsl Prestige Diner Days Inn, Hampton Inn, Holiday Inn CVS Drug, vet, **W** Quality Inn, Townhouse Motel
7a (60)	I-195 W to Trenton, E to Neptune
59mm	**Richard Stockton Service Area sb,** Sunoco/dsl, Burger King, Nathan's, Pizza Hut, Quiznos, Roy Rogers, Starbucks, TCBY, **Woodrow Wilson Service Area nb,** Sunoco
7 (54)	US 206, to Bordentown, to Ft Dix, McGuire AFB, to I-295, Trenton, **W** AmeriGas, Delta/dsl, Exxon, Gulf, Love's/Wendy's/dsl/scales/24hr, Petro/Iron Skillet/dsl/scales/24hr/@, Sunoco, Valero/dsl Denny's, Dunkin Donuts, McDonald's

NEW JERSEY TURNPIKE

NEW JERSEY TURNPIKE Cont'd

7 (54) Continued
Best Western, Comfort Inn, Days Inn, Hampton Inn, Ramada Inn WaWa

6 (51) I-95 S, I-276, to PA Tpk. **I-95 & NJ Tpk merge nb, divide sb.**

5 (44) to Mount Holly, Willingboro, **E** AJ's Gas/dsl Applebee's, Charlie Brown's Steaks, Cracker Barrel, McDonald's, Recovery Grill Best Western, Hampton Inn, Hilton Garden, Quality Inn vet, **W** BP, Exxon/dsl, Valero/dsl Burger King, China House, Dunkin Donuts, IHOP, TGIFriday's Courtyard, Holiday Inn Express $Tree, AT&T, Dick's, Home Depot, Kohl's, Motel 6, Target

39mm **James Fenimore Cooper Service Area nb,** Sunoco/dsl Burger King, Cinnabon, Popeye's, Roy Rogers, TCBY gifts

4 (34) NJ 73, to Philadelphia, Camden, **E** US Gas, WaWa/dsl Applebee's, Chili's, Cracker Barrel, Dunkin Donuts, Kazumi, McDonald's, On-the-Border, Sage Rest., TGIFriday's, Wendy's Candlewood Suites, Comfort Inn, Extended Stay America, Hampton Inn, Hilton Garden, Holiday Inn Express, Hyatt House, Hyatt Place, Knights Inn, La Quinta, Rodeway Inn, Staybridge Suites, Wyndham Hotel BMW, Cadillac, Lexus, Mini, Toyota, Verizon, Whole Foods Mkt, **W** Lukoil Bob Evans, Miller's Alehouse, Starbucks aLoft, Courtyard, Fairfield Inn, Hotel ML, Red Roof Inn, Super 8, Westin

30mm **Walt Whitman Service Area sb, Walt Whitman Service Area,** Sunoco Cinnabon, Nathan's, Roy Rogers, TCBY gifts

3 (26) NJ 168, Atlantic City Expwy, Walt Whitman Br, Camden, Woodbury, **E** Pioneer, WaWa/dsl Antonietta's, Luigi's Pizza, Pat's Pizza, Phily Diner, Rita's Custard Days Inn, La Quinta Advance Parts, CVS Drug, Toyota, Walgreens, **W** Riggins, Shell/dsl, Valero/dsl Burger King, Club Diner, Dunkin Donuts, Vero Pizzaria, Wendy's Bellmawr Motel, EconoLodge, Howard Johnson, Red Roof Inn, Super 8

2 (13) US 322, to Swedesboro, **W** Shell/Dunkin Donuts/dsl

5mm **Barton Service Area sb, Fenwick Service Area nb,** Sunoco/dsl Burger King, Nathan's, Pizza Hut, Starbucks, TCBY

1 (1.2) Deepwater, **W** Gulf, Pilot/Subway/dsl/scales/24hr Comfort Inn, Friendship Motor Inn, Holiday Inn Express, Red Carpet Inn

1mm **toll road begins/ends**

2 (I-295) **I-295 N divides from toll road, I-295 S converges with toll road.**

1 (I-295) NJ 49, to Pennsville, **E** WaWa/dsl Applebee's, Burger King, Cracker Barrel, Dunkin Donuts, KFC/Taco Bell, McDonald's Hampton Inn, Super 8 Peterbilt, **W** Coastal Seaview Motel

0mm New Jersey/Delaware state line, Delaware River, Delaware Memorial Bridge

INTERSTATE 195

Exit# Services

36 Garden State Parkway N. **I-195 begins/ends on GS Pkwy, exit 98.**

35b a NJ 34, to Brielle, GS Pkwy S., Pt Pleasant, **0-2 mi S** Exxon/dsl, Getty/dsl, Lukoil/dsl Legends Japanese

31b a NJ 547, NJ 524, to Farmingdale, **N** to Allaire SP

28b a US 9, to Freehold, Lakewood, **N** LukOil/7-11/dsl, WaWa/dsl Ivy League Grill, Lino's Pizza, Stewart's Drive-In At 9 Motel, **S** Exxon, Gulf, LukOil, QuickChek/dsl, WaWa Applebee's, Arby's, Baskin-Robbins/Dunkin Donuts, Boston Mkt, Chick-fil-A, China Moon, Chipotle, Dunkin Donuts, Five Guys, IHOP, Jersey Mike's Subs, Longhorn Steaks, Luigi's Pizza, McDonald's, Panera Bread, Pizza Hut, Ruby Tuesday,

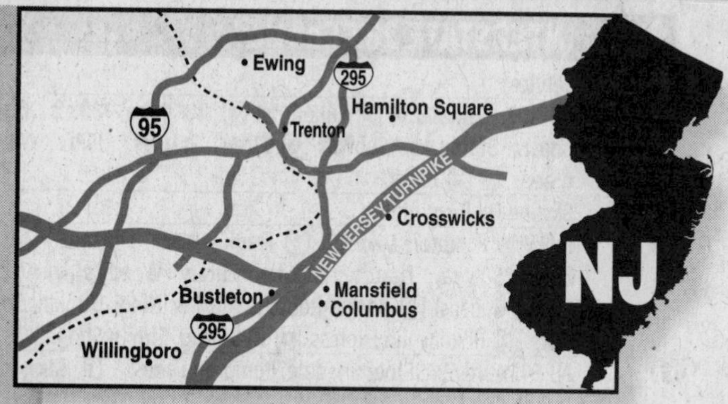

28b a Continued
Sonic, Starbucks, Subway, Taco Bell $Tree, Advance Parts, AT&T, Barnes&Noble, Best Buy, BJ's/dsl, CVS Drug, GNC, Hobby Lobby, Kohl's, Lowe's, Michael's, PepBoys, PetCo, Petsmart, repair, ShopRite Foods, Staples, Stop&Shop, Target, TJ Maxx, USPO, Verizon, vet, Walgreens, Walmart/McDonald's

22 to Jackson Mills, Georgia, **N** to Turkey Swamp Park, **2 mi S** McDonald's ShopRite Foods

21 NJ 526, NJ 527, to Jackson, Siloam

16 NJ 537, to Freehold, **N** Citgo/dsl, Sunoco FoodCourt, GianMarco's Pizza H, Jackson Outlets/famous brands, **S** WaWa/dsl Burger King, Chicken Holiday, Dunkin Donuts, KFC/LJ Silver, McDonald's, McGinns Pizzaria, Rio Grande Mexican, Tommy's Rest. Six Flags

11 NJ 524, Imlaystown, **N** to Horse Park of NJ

8 NJ 539, Hightstown, Allentown, **S** Shell (1mi), Valero/repair Sam's Deli vet

7 NJ 526, Robbinsville, Allentown, **N** Hampton Inn, **1 mi S** La Piazza Ristorante

6 NJ Tpk, N to NY, S to DE Memorial Br

5b a US 130, **N** Delta/dsl/repair, Valero/dsl Domino's, Dunkin Donuts, Rusert's Deli, ShrimpKing Rest., Taco Bell Homewood Suites AAA, vet, **S** GS Fuel/dsl, WaWa/dsl Chick-fil-A, Chili's, China Grill, Cracker Barrel, DQ, Jersey Mike's Subs, Longhorn Steaks, McDonald's, Outback Steaks, Panchero's, Panera Bread, Red Robin, Ruby Tuesday, Subway, TGIFriday's, Wendy's Hilton Garden, Residence Inn $Tree, AT&T, Barnes&Noble, BJ's Whse, GNC, Harry's Army Navy, Home Depot, Honda, Kohl's, Lowe's, Michael's, Old Navy, Petsmart, Ross, ShopRite Foods, Staples, to state aquarium, USPO, Verizon, Walmart

3b a Hamilton Square, Yardville, **N** H

2 US 206 S, S Broad St, Yardville, **S** BP, Shell/dsl Subway $Tree, 7-11, CVS Drug, Rite Aid

1b a US 206 (eb only), **N** Circle Deli, Taco Bell Advance Parts, Midas, **S** Papa John's ShopRite Foods

0mm **I-295, I-195 begins/ends.**

INTERSTATE 287

Exit# Services

68mm New Jersey/New York state line

66 NJ 17 S, Mahwah, **1-3 mi E** Gulf, Liberty/dsl, Mobil/dsl, Pilot/dsl, Sunoco/dsl, Valero/Subway/dsl Boston Mkt, Burger King, Dunkin Donuts, McDonald's Comfort Suites, Courtyard, Doubletree, Hampton Inn, Homewood Suites, Sheraton, Super 8 Buick/GMC, Cadillac, Chrysler/Dodge/Jeep, Home Depot, Honda, Hyundai

59 NJ 208 S, Franklin Lakes

= gas = food = lodging = other = rest stop

INTERSTATE 287 Cont'd

Exit#	Services
58	US 202, Oakland, E Lukoil/dsl Jr's Pizza, Mike's Doghouse, Starbucks, Subway $Tree, Staples, USPO, Walgreens, W Exxon
57	Skyline Dr, Ringwood
55	NJ 511, Pompton Lakes, E Frank's Pizza, Quizno's, Starbucks, Subway, Thatcher McGhee Eatery, Wendy's A&P, W Gulf/dsl Baskin-Robbins, Burger King, Dunkin Donuts Holiday Inn Express CVS Drug, Stop'n Shop
53	NJ 511A, rd 694, Bloomingdale, Pompton Lakes, E Sunoco, Valero Blimpie USPO
52b a	NJ 23, Riverdale, Wayne, Butler, **0-3 mi** E Delta, Gulf, Lukoil, Speedway/dsl, Valero/dsl 23 Buffet, Moe's SW Grill, Pompton Queen Diner, Stefano's Pizza H, GNC, Honda, Pepboys, Stop&Shop, TJ Maxx, Toyota, VW, W Lukoil, Lukoil Applebees, Chili's, Dunkin Donuts, Mangia Pizza, NJ Buffet, Subway, Wendy's Best Buy, BJ's Whse, Harley-Davidson, Home Depot, Jo-Ann, Lowes Whse, Staples, Target, Walmart
47	US 202, Montville, Lincoln Park, E Exxon Harrigan's Rest., Montville Inn Rest.
45	Myrtle Ave, Boonton, W Shell/dsl, Speedway Dunkin Donuts, McDonald's, Subway A&P Mkt, Buick/Chevrolet, Walgreens
43	Intervale Rd, to Mountain Lakes, E Valero/dsl, W Dodge
42	US 46, US 202 (from sb only), W 76/Dunkin Donuts/dsl, Exxon Fuddrucker's, McDonald's, TGIFriday's, Wendy's Courtyard, Day's Inn, Embassy Suites, Fairfield Inn, Hampton Inn Marshall's, Subaru, USPO
41b a	I-80, E to New York, W to Delaware Water Gap
40	NJ 511, Parsippany Rd, to Whippany, W BP, Shell/dsl, Woroco Gas Frank&Son Pizza, Subway, Wok's Chinese Embassy Suites (1mi) vet
39b a	NJ 10, Dover, Whippany, E Exxon, Shell Brookside Diner, Dunkin Donuts, Jersey Mike's, Melting Pot, Pancake House, Scallopini Rest., Whippany Diner CVS Drug, Farmtastic Mkt, Tuesday Morning, W Liberty/dsl, Lukoil, Raceway Atlanta Bread, Dunkin Donuts, Panchero's Mexican, Smashburger, Subway, Wendy's EconoLodge, Hilton, Hyatt House, Marriott Barnes&Noble, Buick/GMC, GNC, Harley Davidson, Kohl's, Stop'n Shop, Verizon
37	NJ 24 E, Springfield
36b a	rd 510, Morris Ave, Lafayette
35	NJ 124, South St, Madison Ave, Morristown, E Friendly's Richie's Country Store, vet, W Best Western H, Rite Aid, Walgreens
33	Harter Rd
33mm	E **truck nb, full facilities, litter barrels, petwalk, , vending**
30b a	to US 202, N Maple Ave, Basking Ridge, E Dolce Resort, W Gulf, Lukoil GrainHouse Rest., Vine Rest. Olde Mill Inn/rest.
26b a	rd 525 S, Mt Airy Rd, Liberty Corner, **3 mi** E Exxon Courtyard, Somerset Hotel
22b a	US 202, US 206, Pluckemin, Bedminster, E Exxon, Exxon/dsl Burger King, Coldstone, Dunkin Donuts, Golden Palace, Panchero's, Rocco's Pizza, Starbucks, Subway CVS Drug, Fresh Mkt, King's Foods, URGENT CARE, Verizon
21b a	I-78, E to NY, W to PA
17	US 206 (from sb), Bridgewater, W Exxon, Speedway Buffalo Wild Wings, CA Pizza, Cheesecake Factory, Chipotle Mexican,

BRIDGEWATER

Exit#	Services
17	Continued Dunkin Donuts, KFC, La Catena Ristorante, Maggiano's Italian, McCormick&Schmick's, McDonald's, TGIFriday, Wendy's Marriott Best Buy, Bloomingdale's, Lord&Taylor, Macy's
14b a	US 22, to US 202/206, E Speedway/dsl Chevrolet/Lexus, W Sunoco/dsl, Valero/dsl Houlihan's, Red Lobster Day's Inn Acura, Chrysler/Dodge/Jeep, Fiat, Ford, Infiniti, Kia, Mercedes, Nissan, Volvo
13b a	NJ 28, Bound Brook, E 76/dsl, BP/dsl 25 Burgers Burger King, Dunkin Donuts, Frank's Pizza, Girasole Rest. Little Caesar's 7-11, AT&T, AutoZone, QuickChek Mkt ShopRite Foods, Walgreens, W Applebees, ChuckeCheese McDonald's, Panchero's Hilton Garden H, 7-11, Costco, Home Depot, Marshall's, Michael's, Old Navy, PepBoys PetsMart, Target
12	Weston Canal Rd, Manville, E ShopRite (3mi), USPO W Soho Grill La Quinta
10	NJ 527, Easton Ave, New Brunswick, E Hotel Somerset W Exxon Dunkin Donuts, Lo Duca Pizza, Ruby Tuesday, Subway Candlewood Suites, Comfort Inn, Courtyard Doubletree, EconoLodge, Extended Stay America, Fairfield Inn Holiday Inn, Homewood Suites, Madison Suites, Residence Inn Sonesta Suites H, Garden State Exhibit Ctr
9	NJ 514, River Rd, W Gulf Embassy Suites, Radisson
8.5mm	**weigh sta nb**
8	Possumtown Rd, Highland Park
7	S Randolphville Rd, Piscataway, E Lukoil/dsl
6	Washington Ave, Piscataway, E Shell/7-11/dsl Popeye's, W Applebees, Chand Palace, Gourmet Oizza Healthy Garden, Longhorn Steaks, Olive Garden, Panera Bread Piscataway Pizza, Starbucks, Subway, TGIFriday's, Thai Basil 99c Depot, Aldi Foods, GNC, Lowes Whse, PetCo, same as 5, ShopRite Foods, Walmart/McDonald's
5	NJ 529, Stelton Rd, Dunellen, E BP/dsl, Gulf/dsl, Lukoil dsl Enzo's Pizza, KFC Ramada Ltd. Advance Parts Goodyear/auto, Home Depot, Meineke, Stop'n Shop, STS Tire auto, W Exxon, Gulf 365 Bistro, Brickhouse Rest., Burger King, Chipotle, Corner Cafe, Dunkin Donuts, Five Guys, Fontainbleu Diner, Friendly's, Gabrieles Grill, Gianni Pizza, IHOP Joe's Crabshack, Panda Express, Pizza Hut, Red Lobster, Red Robin, Ruby Tuesday, Taco Bell, Villa Pizza, Wendy's, White Castle Best Western, Hampton Inn, Holiday Inn, Motel 6 $Tree, Burlington Coats, Dick's, Hobby Lobby, Kohl's, Marshall's, NAPA, Pep Boys, Staples, Target, Verizon, Walgreens
4	Durham Ave (from nb, no EZ return), S Plainfield, E F One/dsl Subway H, Firestone/auto
3	New Durham Rd (from sb), E Shell, W Dunkin Donuts Red Onion Chinese Fairfield Inn, Red Roof Inn Walgreens
2b a	NJ 27, Metuchen, New Brunswick, E Brownstone Gr W BP, Lukoil Dunkin Donuts, Little Caesar's Costco/gas, Petsmart, USPO, Walmart/Subway
1b a	US 1, N Exxon/dsl, Raceway/dsl, Shell Benihana Champp's, Cheesecake Factory, Dunkin Donuts, Famous Dave's BBQ, Houlihan's, IHOP, Macaroni Grill, McDonald's, Menlo Park Diner, Panera Bread, Seasons Grill, Sonic, Uno, White Castle Barnes&Noble, Firestone/auto, Goodyear/auto, Macy's Midas, Nordstrom's, Target, S Shell/7-11/dsl Applebees, Boston Mkt, ChuckeCheese, McDonald's Comfort Inn Quality Inn $Tree, BJ's Whse, Home Depot, Infiniti, Land Rover/Jaguar/Porche, Mercedes, Office Depot, PepBoys, PetSmart Sam's Club/gas, Staples, Stop&Shop Foods, Volvo
0mm	**I-287 begins/ends on NJ 440, I-95, NJ Tpk.**

PISCATAWAY

NJ

INTERSTATE 295

Exit#	Services
77mm	New Jersey/Delaware state line, Delaware River, Delaware Memorial Bridge
76	1 NJ 29, to Trenton, **2 mi W** st police museum
75	NJ 579, to Harbourton, **E** LukOil (1mi) Dunkin Donuts, Red Star Pizza 7-11, **W** BP
73b a	Scotch Rd, **E** Courtyard, **W** H
72b a	NJ 31, to Ewing, Pennington, **E** Citgo/repair, Exxon/repair, LukOil/Dunkin Donuts/dsl SpringHill Suites Robbins Drug, **W** Exxon, LukOil/Blimpie/dsl Mizuki Asian, Starbucks ShopRite Foods, Stop&Shop Foods
71b a	Federal City Rd (sb only)
69b a	US 206, **W** LukOil/dsl Fox's Pizza, Starbucks
68b a	NJ 583, NJ 546, to Princeton Pike
67b a	US 1, to Trenton, New Brunswick, **E** Shell, WaWa/McDonald's/dsl Michael's Diner Howard Johnson, Sleepy Hollow Motel Acura, **0-3 mi W** LukOil/dsl Applebee's, Bahama Breeze, Big Fish Bistro, Bonefish Grill, Brick House Tavern, Brio Grille, Buffalo Wild Wings, Cheesecake Factory, Chipotle, ChuckECheese's, Corner Bakery Cafe, Dunkin Donuts, Firehouse Subs, Hooters, Houlihan's, Jersey Mike's, Joe's Crabshack, Olive Garden, On-the-Border, Outback Steaks, Panera Bread, Pei Wei, PF Chang's, Red Lobster, Seasons 32, Smashburger, Starbucks, Subway, TGIFriday's, Wendy's Clarion, Comfort Inn, Extended Stay America, Hyatt Place, Hyatt Regency, Red Roof Inn, Residence Inn $Tree, AT&T, Barnes&Noble, Best Buy, Buick/Cadillac/GMC, Chevrolet, Dick's, Firestone/auto, Hobby Lobby, Home Depot, JC Penney, Jo-Ann Fabrics, Kohl's, Lord&Taylor, Lowe's, Macy's, malls, Marshall's, Michael's, Mini, NTB, Old Navy, PepBoys, PetCo, Petsmart, REI, Ross, ShopRite Foods, Staples, Target, TJ Maxx, Trader Joe's, Verizon, Walmart, Wegman's Foods, Whole Foods Mkt
65b a	Sloan Ave, **E** Exxon Burger King, DeLorenzo's Pizza, Dunkin Donuts, Five Guys, New China Buffet, Subway, Taco Bell, Uno Grill Goodyear/auto, Risoldi's Mkt
64	NJ 535 N (from sb), to NJ 33 E, same as 63
63b a	NJ 33 W, rd 535, Mercerville, Trenton, **E on rd 33** Lukoil, Speedway/dsl, Valero Applebee's, Lucky Star Buffet, McDonald's, Pizza Hut, Popeye's, Stewart's Rootbeer, Subway, Vincent's Pizza Ace Hardware, auto repair, CVS Drug, Ford/Subaru, Rite Aid, USPO, **W** Exxon Dunkin Donuts, White Horse Diner Advance Parts, Family$, transmissions, Walgreens, Walmart, WaWa
62	Olden Ave N (from sb, no return), **W** Delta, Exxon
61b a	Arena Dr, White Horse Ave, **W** 7-11
60b a	I-195, to I-95, W to Trenton, E to Neptune
58mm	scenic overlook both lanes
57b a	US 130, to US 206, **E** Amera, Valero Denny's, Dunkin Donuts, McDonald's, Rosario's Pizza Best Western, Days Inn, Ramada Inn Aldi, **W** Starbucks Candlewood Suites Acme Foods, st police, Verizon
56	to US 206 S (from nb, no return), to NJ Tpk, Ft Dix, McGuire AFB, **E** Loves/Wendy's/dsl/scales/24hr, Petro/Iron Skillet/dsl/scales/24hr/@ Days Inn, Hampton Inn Blue Beacon, same as 57, **W** Candlewood Suites st police
52b a	rd 656, to Columbus, Florence, **3 mi E** Loves/Wendy's/dsl/scales/24hr, Petro/Iron Skillet/dsl/scales/24hr/@
47b a	NJ 541, to Mount Holly, NJ Tpk, Burlington, **E** BP, Exxon/dsl, Valero/dsl Applebee's, Burger King, China House, Cracker Barrel, Dunkin Donuts, IHOP, Recovery Grill, TGIFriday's

TRENTON

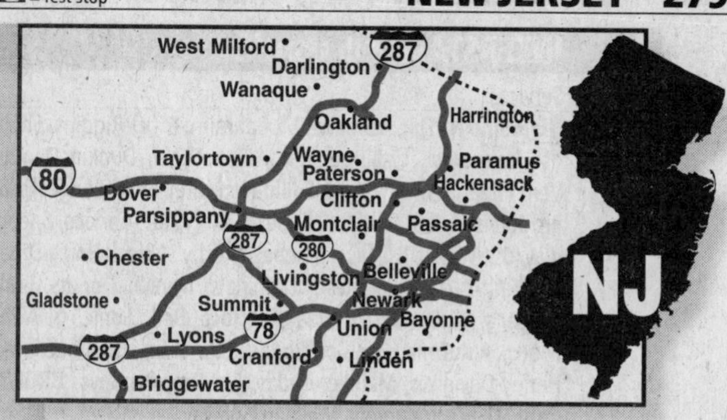

Exit#	Services
47b a	Continued Best Western, Courtyard, Hampton Inn, Hilton Garden, Holiday Inn Express, Motel 6, Quality Inn $Tree, AT&T, Dick's, Home Depot, Kohl's, Target, **W** BP, Citgo/dsl, Gulf/dsl, WaWa/dsl Checker's, Chick-fil-A, Dunkin Donuts, Kum Fong, Subway, Villa Pizza, Wendy's H, AutoZone, Marshall's, ShopRite, Walmart/Subway
45b a	to Mt Holly, Willingboro, **W** LukOil/dsl H, auto repair
43b a	rd 636, to Rancocas Woods, Delran, **W** Exxon Carlucci's Rest.
40b a	NJ 38, to Mount Holly, Moorestown, **E** Ruby Tuesday Residence Inn, **W** Amera/dsl, WaWa/dsl Anthony's Pizza, Arby's, Chick-fil-A, Chipotle, Dunkin Donuts, Jimmy John's, Naf Naf Grill, Panera Bread, Qdoba, Starbucks, Subway, TGIFriday's, Wendy's SpringHill Suites H, Costco/gas, GNC, Jo-Ann Fabrics, Petsmart, Target, TJ Maxx, UHaul, Wegman's Foods
36b a	NJ 73, to NJ Tpk, Tacony Br, Berlin, **E** LukOil/dsl Bob Evans, Miller's Alehouse, Starbucks aLoft, Courtyard, EconoLodge, Fairfield Inn, Hotel ML, Red Roof Inn, Super 8, TownePlace Suites, Westin, **W** Citgo, Shell, WaWa/dsl Bertucci's, Boscov's, Boston Mkt, Buffalo Wild Wings, Burger King, Chick-fil-A, Chipotle Mexican, Corner Cafe, Don Pablo, Dunkin Donuts, Five Guys, Friendly's, Jersey Mike's, Old Town Buffet, Panera Bread, Pei Wei, Perkins, PJ Whelahin's, Popeye's, The Melting Pot, Uno Grill, Wendy's Crossland Suites, Homewood Suites, Motel 6, Quality Inn $Tree, Acura, Advance Parts, AT&T, AutoZone, Barnes&Noble, Best Buy, Dick's, Fiat, Ford/Lincoln, Home Depot, Infiniti, Lord&Taylor, Lowe's, Marshall's, Michael's, Mr Tire, Old Navy, PepBoys, PepBoys, Petsmart, Ross, ShopRite Foods, Staples
34b a	NJ 70, to Camden, Cherry Hill, **E** BP, Exxon, WaWa Burger King, Dunkin Donuts, PJ Whelihans, Rock Hill Rest., Stacy's Korean BBQ Extended Stay America, Residence Inn Mavis Tire, Tires+, **W** Jersey Gas, LukOil, US Gas Dunkin Donuts, Famous Dave's BBQ, Han Dynasty, McDonald's, Norma's Rest., Ponzio's Rest, Qdoba, Rita's, Salad Works, Seasons Pizza, Starbucks Woodspring Suites H, $Tree, AT&T, CVS Drug, Goodyear/auto, Mom's Mkt, Rite Aid, vet, WaWa, Whole Foods Mkt
32	NJ 561, to Haddonfield, Voorhees, **E** LukOil/dsl Herman's Deli, Hunan Wok, Tucchi's Pizza, Vito's Pizza H, $Tree, Trio Tire, USPO, **W** Pioneer/dsl Burger King, Dunkin Donuts, Subway, Tutti Toscani 7-11, Ford
31	Woodcrest Station
30	Warwick Rd (from sb)
29b a	US 30, to Berlin, Collingswood, **E** Astro/dsl, Citgo/dsl, Valero/dsl, WaWa/dsl Arby's, Church's, Dunkin Donuts, McDonald's, Popeye's, Wendy's, Wild Wing Cafe AutoZone, Home Depot, Lowe's, Petsmart, ShopRite

CHERRY HILL

NJ

INTERSTATE 295 Cont'd

Exit#	Services
28	NJ 168, to NJ Tpk, Belmawr, Mt Ephraim, **E** Riggins, Shell/dsl, Valero/dsl Burger King, Club Diner, Dunkin Donuts, Vero Pizzaria, Wendy's Bellmawr Motel, EconoLodge, Howard Johnson, Red Roof Inn, Super 8, **W** BP, Conoco, Speedway/dsl, WaWa/dsl Applebee's, Arby's, Black Horse Diner, Chick-fil-A, Da Vinci'sRest., Domino's, Dunkin Donuts, Little Caesar's, McDonald's, Pizza Hut/Taco Bell, Sonic Acme Foods, AutoZone, Chrysler/Dodge, CVS Drug, Firestone/auto, Harley-Davidson, Meinke, Midas, Mr Tire, PepBoys, URGENT CARE, USPO, Walgreens, Walmart/Subway
26	I-76, NJ 42, to I-676 (exits left from sb), Walt Whitman Bridge, Walt Whitman Bridge
25b a	NJ 47, to Westville, Deptford
24b a	NJ 45, NJ 551 (no EZ sb return), to Westville, **E** H, AutoZone, **W** Chevrolet, Family$
23	US 130 N, to National Park
22	NJ 644, to Red Bank, Woodbury, **E** Citgo Dunkin Donuts, **1 mi W** Crown Point Trkstp/dsl/@
21	NJ 44 S, Paulsboro, Woodbury, **W** WaWa, Wendy's Westwood Motor Lodge
20	NJ 44, rd 643, to National Park, Thorofare, **E** Best Western, **W** Red Bank Inn
19	to NJ 44, rd 656, Mantua
18b a	rd 667, to rd 678, Clarksboro, Mt Royal, **E** Exxon/dsl, TA/Shell/Country Pride/dsl/scales/@ Dragon Nest Chinese, Dunkin Donuts, McDonald's RV camping, **W** Valero, WaWa/dsl
17	rd 680, to Mickleton, Gibbstown, **W** Burger King, Domino's, Dunkin Donuts, Mr Bee's Deli $General, Advance Parts, Family$, GNC, Rite Aid, ShopRite Foods
16b	rd 551, to Gibbstown, Mickleton
16a	rd 653, to Paulsboro, Swedesboro
15	rd 607, to Gibbstown
14	rd 684, to Repaupo
13	US 130 S, US 322 W, to Bridgeport (from sb, no return)
11	US 322 E, to Mullica Hill
10	Ctr Square Rd, to Swedesboro, **E** Citgo/dsl, WaWa/d Applebee's, Ciconte's Pizza, Dunkin Donuts, McDonald' Wendy's Hampton Inn, Holiday Inn, TownePlace Suite Acme Foods/Sav-On, Firestone/auto, Rite Aid, URGEN CARE, Verizon, **W** Camping World RV Supplies/service
7	to Auburn, Pedricktown
4	NJ 48, Woodstown, Penns Grove
3mm	**weigh sta nb**
2mm	**nb, full facilities, info, litter barrels, picnic table, dump, vending**
2c	to US 130 (from sb), Deepwater, **E** same as 2b, **W** FLYING J/Denny's/dsl/scales/LP/24hr, Sunoco/Dunkin Donut dsl/scales/24hr
2b	US 40 E, to NJ Tpk, **E** Gulf, Pilot/Subway/dsl/scale 24hr Comfort Inn, Friendship Motor Inn, Holiday Inn E press, Red Carpet Inn, **W** same as 2c
2a	to Delaware Bridge, US 40 W (from nb)
1c	NJ 551 S, Hook Rd, to Salem, **E** White Oaks Motel
1b	US 130 N (from nb), Penns Grove
1a	NJ 49 E, to Pennsville, Salem, **E** WaWa/dsl Applebee Burger King, Cracker Barrel, Dunkin Donuts, KFC/Taco Bell, M Donald's Hampton Inn, Super 8 Peterbilt, **W** Coas al/dsl Seaview Motel
0mm	New Jersey/Pennsylvania state line, Delaware River

NJ

NM

NEW MEXICO

INTERSTATE 10

LAS CRUCES

Exit#	Services
164.5mm	New Mexico/Texas state line
164mm	**Welcome Ctr wb, full facilities, litter barrels, petwalk,**
162	NM 404, Anthony, **S** Alon/dsl Family$, RV camping
160mm	**weigh sta wb**
155	NM 227 W, to Vado, **N** Western Sky's RV Park, **S** Chevron/El Viajero/dsl/scales/24hr, NTS/dsl/scales/24hr/@ $General, El Camino Real HS
151	Mesquite
144	I-25 N, to Las Cruces
142	Rd 188, Rd 101, Valley Dr, Las Cruces, **N** Chevron/dsl Chilito's Mexican, Dick's Cafe, IHOP, Whataburger Best Western, EconoLodge, Holiday Inn Express, Motel 6, Quality Inn, Ramada Inn, Super 8, Teakwood Inn H, auto/RV repair/tires, Cadillac/Chevrolet, Dalmont's RV Camping, Ford/Lincoln, Honda, Hyundai, Mazda, Nissan, NMSU, vet, **S** Alon/dsl USPO
140	NM 28, to Mesilla, Las Cruces, **N** Alon/dsl Applebee's, Blake's Lotaburger, BurgerTime, Cracker Barrel, Domino's, Golden Corral, K-Bob's, McDonald's, Murry Express, Starbucks, Subway Best Value Inn, Days Inn, Drury Inn, Hampton Inn, La Quinta, SpringHill Suites Buick/GMC, Kia, Toyota, VW, Walmart/McDonald's, **S** LunaRossa Pizza Comfort Inn Harley-Davidson, Holiday World RV Ctr, Siesta RV Park, United RV Ctr
139	NM 292, Amador Ave, Motel Blvd, Las Cruces, **N** Pilot Subway/dsl/scales/24hr, TA/Burger King/Pizza Hut/Taco Be dsl/24hr/scales/@, **S** PitStop Café Coachlight Inn/ Park NAPACare
138mm	Rio Grande River
135.5mm	**eb, full facilities, litter barrels, petwalk, , scenic vie**
135	US 70 E, to W Las Cruces, Alamogordo, **1 mi N** KOA
132	**N** fairgrounds, to , **S** Love's/Subway/dsl/scale 24hr
127	Corralitos Rd, **N** Exxon Bowlin's Trading Post, to fa grounds
120.5mm	**insp sta wb**
116	NM 549
111mm	**parking area wb, litter barrels**
102	Akela, **N** Exxon/dsl/gifts
85	East Motel Dr, Deming, **S** Chevron/dsl, Conoco/ Hampton Inn, Holiday Inn Express, La Quinta, Motel Quality Inn Buick/Cadillac/Chevrolet/GMC, Chrysl Dodge/Jeep, Dreamcatcher RV Park
82b	Railroad Blvd, Deming, **N** Chevron/dsl, **S** Conoc dsl DQ, Golden Star Chinese, IHOP, KFC, Little Caesa Ranchers Grill, Wendy's Days Inn, Grand Motel $Ge eral, $Tree, AutoZone, Big O Tire, Deming Visitors Ctr, Ford/L coln, Little Vinyard RV Park, NAPA, O'Reilly Parts, Roadrun RV Park, st police, Sunrise RV Park, to Rock Hound SP, Veriz Wagon Wheel RV Park, Walmart/Subway

 = gas = food = lodging = other = rest stop

INTERSTATE 10 Cont'd

DEMING

Exit#	Services
82a	US 180, NM 26, NM 11, Deming, N Chevron/dsl Blake's Lotaburger, S Exxon, Phillips 66 Burger King, China Rest., Denny's, Domino's, KFC, Palma's Italian, Pizza Hut, Rancher's Grill, Si Senor Butterfield Stage Motel H, Budget Tire, CarQuest, museum, Rockhound SP, to Pancho Villa SP, Walgreens
81	NM 11, W Motel Dr, Deming, S CNG, Shamrock/dsl Benji's Rest, El Camino Real, McDonald's, Sonic, Subway, Taco Bell Best Western, Comfort Inn, Deming Motel, Executive Motel, Super 8, Western Motel H, 81 Palms RV Park, city park, Hitchin Post RV Park, Rock Hound SP, to Pancho Villa SP
68	NM 418, S Petro/Iron Skillet/Starbucks/dsl/scales/24hr tires/repair
62	Gage, S Butterfield Station/Exxon/DQ/dsl
61mm	**wb, full facilities, litter barrels, petwalk, vending**
55	Quincy
53mm	**eb, full facilities, litter barrels, petwalk, vending**
51.5mm	Continental Divide, elev 4585
49	NM 146 S, to Hachita, Antelope Wells
42	Separ, S Bowlin's Continental Divide Trading Post/Gifts
34	NM 113 S, Muir, Playas
29	no service
24	US 70, E Motel Dr, Lordsburg, N FLYING J/Denny's/dsl/LP/scales/RV Dump/24hr, Pilot/Arby's/dsl/scales/24hr American Motel Horseman RV Park
23.5mm	**weigh sta both lanes**
22	NM 494, Main St, Lordsburg, N McDonald's Comfort Inn, Hampton Inn $General, Family$, NAPA, Saucedo's Foods, USPO, S Valero/dsl Kranberry's Rest. EconoLodge, Motel 10, Motel 6, Plaza Inn KOA
20b a	W Motel Dr, Lordsburg, N Loves/Godfather's Pizza/Subway/scales/dsl Days Inn, S Chevron/dsl/24hr, Visitors Ctr/full facilities info
15	to Gary
11	NM 338 S, to Animas
5	NM 80 S, to Road Forks, S dsl/tire repair, fireworks
3	Steins
0mm	New Mexico/Arizona state line

LORDSBURG

INTERSTATE 25

RATON

Exit#	Services
460.5mm	New Mexico/Colorado state line
460	Raton Pass Summit, elev 7834, **weigh sta sb**, E Cedar Rail Campground
454	2nd St, Lp 25, Raton, 2 mi W Crossroads Budget Host H, CarQuest, Ford
452	NM 72 E, Raton, E to Sugarite Canyon SP, W Conoco
451	US 64 E, US 87 E, Raton, E 87 Express/dsl, Chevron/dsl, CR/dsl/24hr Subway Summerlan RV Park, to Capulin Volcano NM, W Conoco/dsl, CR/dsl, Loaf'n Jug/dsl, Phillips 66 Arby's, Denny's, Domino's, DQ, K-Bob's, McDonald's, Sand's Rest., Sonic Best Value Inn, Best Western, Microtel, Oasis Motel/rest, Quality Inn, Robin Hood Motel, Rodeway Inn, Super 8, Texan Motel, Travelodge, Village Inn Motel H, $General, Ace Hardware, AutoZone, Family$, KOA, O'Reilly Parts, Super Save Foods, Visitor's Ctr/info
450	Lp 25, Raton, W Holiday Inn Express, Oasis Motel/rest. H, AutoZone, KOA, vet

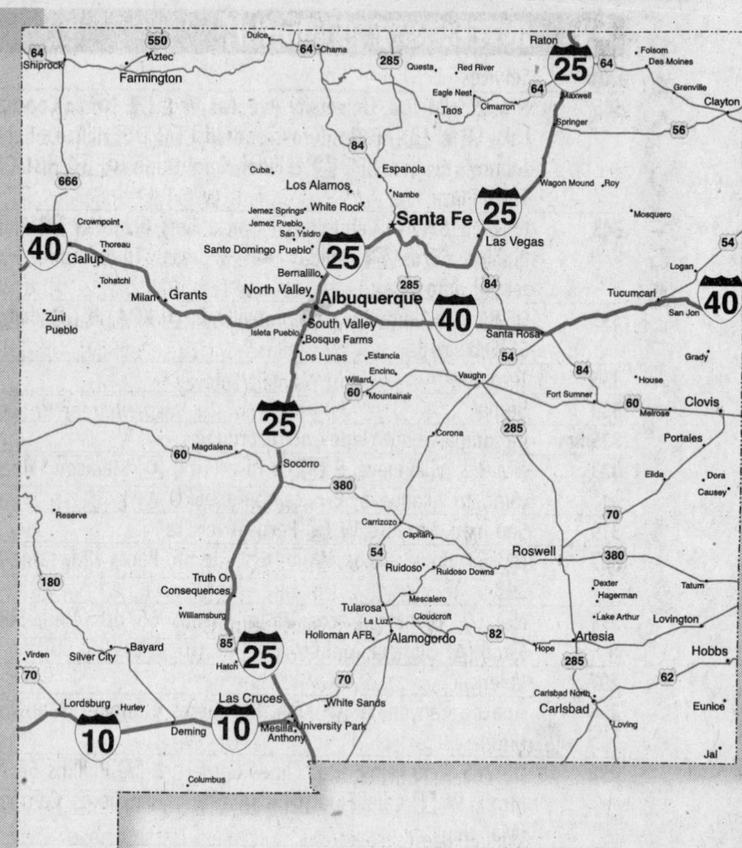

Exit#	Services
446	US 64 W, to Cimarron, Taos, 4 mi W camping, NRA Whittington Ctr
440mm	Canadian River
435	Tinaja
434.5mm	**both lanes, full facilities, litter barrels, petwalk, weather info**
426	NM 505, Maxwell, W Maxwell Station/dsl to Maxwell Lakes, USPO
419	NM 58, to Cimarron, E Chevron/Russell's/Subway/dsl/scales/24hr/@
414	US 56, Springer, 1 mi E Conoco/dsl, Crossroads/dsl Minnie's Dairy Delite Broken Arrow Motel, Oasis Motel Old Santa Fe Trail RV Park
412	US 56 E, US 412 E, NM 21, NM 468, Springer, 1 mi E Alon Brown Hotel/cafe CarQuest, Family$, Springer Foods, USPO
404	NM 569, Colmor, Charette Lakes
393	Levy
387	NM 120, to Roy, Wagon Mound, E Conoco/dsl, Phillips 66/dsl
376mm	**sb, full facilities, litter barrels, petwalk, RV camp**
374mm	**nb, full facilities, litter barrels, petwalk, RV camp**
366	NM 97, NM 161, Watrous, Valmora, W Ft Union NM, Santa Fe Trail
364	NM 97, NM 161, Watrous, Valmora
361	no service
360mm	**parking area both lanes**
356	Onava, Onava
352	E RV camping
347	to NM 518, Las Vegas, 0-2 mi W Loves/Chester's/dsl/scales/24hr, Phillips 66/Burger King, Pino/dsl/rest. Arby's, Hillcrest Rest., KFC, Little Moon Chinese, McDonald's, Sonic, Taco Bell, Wendy's Best Western, Budget Inn, Comfort Inn, Days Inn, Palamino Inn, Regal Motel, Super 8 H, Storrie Lake SP

NM

LAS VEGAS

INTERSTATE 25 Cont'd

Exit#	Services
345	NM 65, NM 104, University Ave, Las Vegas, E [O] to Conchas Lake SP, W [gas] Allsups, Crossroads/dsl [food] DQ, Hillcrest Rest., Johnny's Kitchen, KFC [lodging] El Fidel, Knights Inn [O] [H], Hist. Old Town Plaza
343	to NM 518 N, Las Vegas, E [O] Garcia Tires, **0-2 mi** W [gas] Alon, Phillips 66/dsl [lodging] Holiday Inn Express, Thunderbird Motel [O] auto repair
339	US 84 S, to Santa Rosa, Romeroville, E [O] KOA, W [gas] Phillips 66/Subway/dsl
335	Tecolote
330	Bernal
325mm	**parking area both lanes, no rest rooms**
323	NM 3 S, Villanueva, E [food] La Risa (1mi) [O] Madison Winery (6mi), to Villanueva SP/rv camping, USPO
319	San Juan, San Jose, W [gas] Pecos River Sta.
307	NM 63, Rowe, Pecos, W [O] Hist Rte 66, Pecos NM, same as 299
299	NM 50, Glorieta, Pecos, W [gas] Phillips 66 dsl (4mi), Shell (3mi) [O] Glorieta Conf Ctr
297	Valencia
294	Apache Canyon, W [O] KOA, Rancheros Camping (Mar-Nov) (3mi)
290	US 285 S, to Lamy, S to Clines Corners, E [gas] Phillips 66/dsl (1mi), W [food] Cafe Fina [O] KOA (3mi), Rancheros Camping (Mar-Nov)
284	NM 466, Old Pecos Trail, Santa Fe, W [food] Harry's Roadhouse, Pecos Trail Inn/Cafe [O] [H], museums
282	US 84, US 285, St Francis Dr, W [gas] Conoco/Wendy's/dsl, Mobil/dsl [food] Church's
278	NM 14, Cerrillos Rd, Santa Fe, E [O] RV Ctr, **0-4 mi** W [gas] Giant/dsl, Murphy Express/dsl, Phillips 66/dsl, Shell [food] Adelita's Mexican, Applebee's, Arby's, Blue Corn Cafe, Buffalo Wild Wings, Bumble Bee's Baja Grill, Burger King, Denny's, Domino's, Flying Tortilla, IHOP, KFC, Little Caesars, LJ Silver, Lotaburger, LuLu's Chinese, McDonald's, Olive Garden, Outback Steaks, Panda Express, Panera Bread, Papa Murphy's, Pizza Hut, Ranch House Steaks, Red Lobster, Schlotzsky's, Sonic, Starbucks, Taco Bell, Tortilla Flats [lodging] Best Western, Comfort Inn, Comfort Suites, Courtyard, Days Inn, Doubletree, EconoLodge, Fairfield Inn, Hampton Inn, Holiday Inn Express, Hyatt Place, La Quinta, Motel 6, Quality Inn, Santa Fe Inn, Super 8, Tranquilla Inn [O] AAA, Albertson's, AT&T, Best Buy, BigLots, BMW, Buick/GMC, Cadillac/Chevrolet, Chrysler/Dodge/Jeep, CVS Drug, Dillard's, Discount Tire, Firestone/auto, Ford/Lincoln, Harley-Davidson, Home Depot, Honda, JC Penney, Jo-Ann Fabrics, Kohl's, Land Rover, Lexus, Los Campos RV Park, Lowe's, Mazda, Mecedes/Smart, Meineke, Michaels, Natural Grocers, Peerless Tire, Penske, PepBoys, Petsmart, Ross, Sam's Club/gas, Santa Fe Outlets/famous brands, Sprouts Mkt, Staples, Subaru/VW, Target, TJ Maxx, Tuesday Morning, Verizon, Volvo, Walgreens, Walmart
276b a	NM 599, to NM 14, to Madrid, E [gas] Phillips 66/Allsup's [O] Santa Fe Skies RV Park, **4 mi** W [gas] Shell [O] Sunrise Springs
271	CR 50F, La Cienega
269mm	**[RS] nb, full [handicap] facilities, litter barrels, petwalk, [phone], [picnic]**
267	Waldo Canyon Rd, [O] insp sta., access to nb [RS]
264	NM 16, Pueblo, W [O] to Cochiti Lake RA
263mm	Galisteo River
259	NM 22, to Santo Domingo Pueblo, W [gas] Phillips 66/cafe/dsl [O] to Cochiti Lake RA (11mi)
257	Budaghers, W [O] Mormon Battalion Mon
252	San Felipe Pueblo, E [gas] San Felipe TC/dsl [food] San Felipe Casino/rest.
248	Rte 66, Algodones
242	US 550, NM 44 W, NM 165 E, to Farmington, Aztec, **0-2 m** W [gas] Chevron/dsl, Conoco/dsl, M&M/Burger King/dsl, Phillips 66/dsl, Valero/dsl [food] Denny's, Guang Dong Chinese, IHOP, KFC, Lotaburger, McDonald's, Pizza Hut, Sonic, Starbucks, Subway, Taco Bell, Twisters, Wendy's [lodging] Days Inn, Holiday Inn Express, Motel 6, Super 8 [O] $General, AutoZone, Casino, Home Depot, KOA, O'Reilly Parts, to Coronado SP, Walgreens, Walmart
240	NM 473, to Bernalillo, W [gas] Conoco/dsl [food] Abuelita's Mexican, Range Café [O] KOA, to Coronado SP, USPO, vet
234	NM 556, Tramway Rd, E [gas] Valero/Subway/dsl [O] casino, W [gas] Phillips 66/dsl
233	Alameda Blvd, E [gas] Chevron [food] Burger King [lodging] Comfort Suites, Motel 6, Staybridge Suites [O] Audi/Porsche, Lincoln, Meineke, Mercedes, Toyota, Volvo, W [gas] Phillips 66/Circle K/dsl [food] Carl's Jr [lodging] Best Value, Holiday Inn Express [O] Balloon Fiesta Park, CarMax
232	Paseo del Norte, Paseo del Norte, E [food] Chick-fil-A, China Luck, Chipotle Mexican, Five Guys, Freddy's Steakburgers, Jason's Deli, Jimmy John's, McDonald's, Panda Express, Panera Bread, Starbucks, Subway, Tomato Cafe, Wendy's [lodging] Howard Johnson [O] Aloha RV Ctr, AutoZone, Discount Tire, Kohl's, Lowe's, Office Depot, Target, Verizon, Walgreens, W [gas] Shell/Circle K [food] Arby's [lodging] Courtyard, Marriott
231	San Antonio Ave, E [gas] Alon/7-11 [food] Cracker Barrel, Denny's, Lotaburger [lodging] Comfort Suites, Hilton Garden, Homewood Suites, La Quinta, Quality Inn [O] [H], USPO, W [lodging] Baymont Inn, Crossland Suites, LaQuinta [O] Mazda, VW
230	San Mateo Blvd, Osuna Rd, Albuquerque, E [gas] Chevron, Circle K, Giant/dsl, Phillips 66/Circle K, Shell [food] Applebee's, Arby's, Azuma Grill, Bob's Burgers, Burger King, Chick-fil-A, Chili's, Cici's Pizza, Firehouse Subs, Furrs Buffet, Golden Corral, Hayashi, Hooters, Jack-in-the-Box, KFC, LJ Silver, McDonald's, Olive Garden, Papa John's, Pizza Hut/Taco Bell, Popeyes, Schlotzsky's, Sonic, Souper Salad, Starbucks, Subway, SweetTomatoes, Taco Bueno, Taco Cabana, Teriyaki Chicken, TX Roadhouse, Village Inn, Wendy's, Wienerschnitzel [lodging] Nativo Lodge [O] $Tree, Albertson's, AT&T, AutoZone, Brake Masters, Cadillac, CVS Drug, Fiat, Firestone, Firestone/auto, GNC, Just Brakes, Midas, NAPA, O'Reilly Parts, Peerless Tire, PepBoys, PetCo, Ross, Sprouts Mkt, Subaru, Tuesday Morning, U-Haul, Walgreens, W [gas] Circle K/dsl, Valero/dsl [food] McDonald's, Quiznos, Weck's Breakfast/lunch, Whataburger [lodging] Studio 6 [O] BMW/Mini
229	Jefferson St, E [food] ClaimJumper, Outback Steaks [lodging] Holiday Inn [O] same as 230, W [food] Boston's Pizza, Chama River Rest., Cheddar's, Chile Rio, Coldstone, Dickey's BBQ, Fox&Hound, Fuddrucker's, Genghis Grill, Mimi's Café, Nick&Jimmy's Grill, Papadeaux, Pars Cuisine, PF Chang's, Plum Cafe Asian, Red Robin, Subway, Twin Peaks Rest., TX Land&Cattle Steaks [lodging] Drury Inn, Hampton Inn, Hampton Inn, Residence Inn, TownePlace Suites [O] Lexus
228	Montgomery Blvd, E [gas] Alon/7-11/dsl, Chevron/dsl, Conoco/dsl [food] Fiestas Cantina, Lotaburger [lodging] Best Western [O] Discount Tire, W [gas] Shell/Circle K [food] Arby's, Carl's Jr, IHOP, McDonald's, Panda Express, Starbucks, Wendy's [lodging] InTown Suite [O] Acura, Costco/gas, Ford, Home Depot, Infiniti, Office Depot, Petsmart, REI, Sam's Club/gas, Sportsman's Whse
227b	Comanche Rd, Griegos Rd, E [O] UPS Depot

SANTA FE

ALBUQUERQUE

NM

INTERSTATE 25 Cont'd

ALBUQUERQUE

Exit#	Services
227a	Candelaria Rd, Albuquerque, E Circle K/dsl, Pump'n'Save/dsl, Shell, TA/Valero/Country Pride/dsl/scales/24hr/@ Applebee's, Little Anita's, Mesa Grill, Range Cafe, Subway, Village Inn Candlewood Suites, Crowne Plaza, Days Inn, Elegante Hotel, Fairfield Inn, Holiday Inn Express, La Quinta, Motel 1, Motel 76, Quality Inn, Rodeway Inn, Super 8, Travelodge Kenworth, W Chevron/dsl Ambassador Inn, Rodeway Inn Penske
226b a	I-40, E to Amarillo, W to Flagstaff
225	Lomas Blvd, E Phillips 66 Plaza Inn/rest. Chevrolet, W FillUp, Shell/Circle K/McDonald's Burger King, Carl's Jr, Starbucks Embassy Suites H
224	Lead Ave, Coal Ave, Grand Ave, Central Ave, E Alon/7-11 66 Diner Crossroads Motel H, W M&M Best Value Inn, EconoLodge, Hotel Parq Central, Knights Inn
223	Chavez Ave, E Motel 6 sports arena
222b a	Gibson Blvd, E Phillips 66/dsl Applebee's, Buffalo Wild Wings, Burger King, Dion's Pizza, Fuddrucker's, IHOP, Subway, Village Inn, Waffle House AmericInn, Best Western, Comfort Inn, Country Inn&Suites, Courtyard, Days Inn, Extended Stay America, Fairfield Inn, Hawthorn Suites, Hilton Garden, Holiday Inn Express, La Quinta, Quality Suites, Ramada Inn, Residence Inn, Sleep Inn, TownePlace Suites H, Kirtland AFB, museum, vet, W Alon/7-11/dsl Church's, Lotaburger
221	Sunport, E Holiday Inn, Homewood Suites, Hyatt Place, Staybridge Suites , USPO
220	Rio Bravo Blvd, Mountain View, E golf, **1-2 mi** W Shell/dsl, Valero/dsl Bob's Burgers, Burger King, Church's, KFC/Taco Bell, McDonald's, Pizza Hut, Subway Albertsons/Sav-On, Family$, O'Reilly Parts, vet, Walgreens
215	NM 47, E Isleta One Stop/dsl, Phillips 66/Subway/dsl casino, golf, st police, to Isleta Lakes RA/RV Camping
214mm	Rio Grande
213	NM 314, Isleta Blvd, W Chevron/Subway/dsl $General, vet
209	NM 45, to Isleta Pueblo
203	NM 6, to Los Lunas, E Chevron/dsl, Murphy USA/dsl, Shell/Circle K/Wendy's/dsl/24hr, Valero/dsl Applebee's, Benny's Burger, Del Taco, Denny's, Sonic, Starbucks Days Inn, Los Lunas Inn AutoZone, Big O Tire, Chevrolet, Chrysler/Dodge/Jeep, Ford, Home Depot, Lowe's, URGENT CARE, Walgreens, W Phillips 66/Subway/dsl Carl's Jr, Chili's, Coldstone, KFC, Mariscos Altamar, Panda Express Western Skies Inn Buick/GMC, Discount Tire, Verizon, Walmart/McDonald's
195	Lp 25, Los Chavez, **1 mi** E Roadrunner/grill/dsl Pizza Hut/Taco Bell Walmart/Subway
191	NM 548, Belen, E Conoco/dsl, Loves/Arby's/dsl/scales/24hr McDonald's, Pizza Hut Super 8 $General, USPO, Walgreens, W Rio Grande Diner Holiday Inn Express, RV park
190	Lp 25, Belen, **1-2 mi** E Conoco/dsl, Phillips 66 A&W/LJ Silver, McDonald's, Pizza Hut Super 8 $General, Affordable Tire/repair, AutoZone, USPO, Walgreens
175	US 60, Bernardo, E Salinas NM, W Kiva RV Park
174mm	Rio Puerco
169	E La Joya St Game Refuge Sevilleta NWR
167mm	**both lanes, full facilities, litter barrels, petwalk, , vending**
166mm	Rio Salado

BELEN

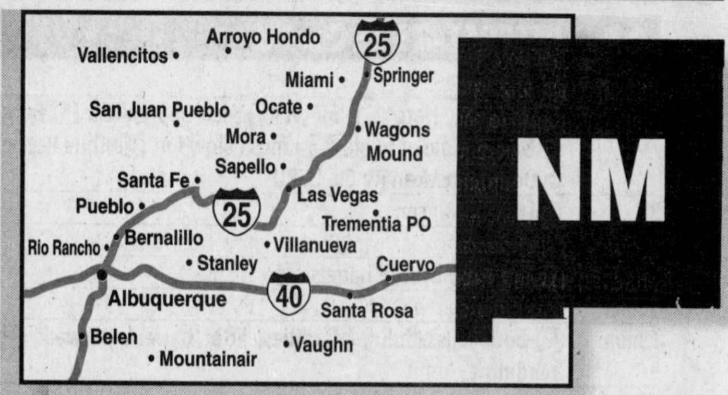

SOCORRO

Exit#	Services
165mm	**weigh sta/parking area both lanes**
163	San Acacia
156	Lemitar, W Phillips 66/dsl/24hr
152	Escondida, W to st police
150	US 60 W, Socorro, W Chevron/dsl, Exxon/dsl, Phillips 66/dsl, Valero/dsl Bodega Burger Co, Burger King, China Best, Denny's, Domino's, K-Bob's, Little Caesar's, Lotaburger, McDonald's, Pizza Hut, Socorro Springs Rest., Sofia's Kitchen, Sonic, Subway Best Value, Best Western, Comfort Inn, Days Inn, EconoLodge, Economy Inn, Holiday Inn Express, Sands Motel, Super 8 $General, Ace Hardware, AutoZone, Brooks Foods, CarQuest, Family$, Ford, NAPA, Smith's Foods, to NM Tech, Verizon, vet, Walmart
147	US 60 W, Socorro, W Chevron/dsl, Conoco/dsl/LP, Pump-N-Save/dsl, Shell/Circle K/dsl Arby's Rodeway Inn H, repair/transmissions, Socorro RV Park, to
139	US 380 E, to San Antonio, E to Bosque Del Apache NWR
124	to San Marcial, E Ft Craig, to Bosque del Apache NWR
115	NM 107, E Truck Plaza/dsl/rest./24hr to Camino Real Heritage Ctr
114mm	**both lanes, full facilities, litter barrels, petwalk, , RV parking, vending**
107mm	Nogal Canyon
100	Red Rock
92	Mitchell Point
90mm	La Canada Alamosa, La Canada Alamosa
89	NM 181, to Cuchillo, to Monticello, RV Park (4mi)
83	NM 52, NM 181, to Cuchillo, **3 mi** E Ivory Tusk Inn& Tavern Elephant Butte Inn/rest. Elephant Lake Butte SP, RV Park
82mm	**insp sta nb**
79	Lp 25, to Truth or Consequences, E Chevron/dsl, Circle K, Shell/dsl Blakes's Lotaburger, Denny's, K-Bob's, La Cocina Mexican, Los Arcos Steaks, McDonald's, Pizza Hut, Sonic, Subway Ace Lodge, Comfort Inn, Desert View Motel, Holiday Inn Express, Hot Springs Inn, Motel 6, Oasis Motel H, $General, AutoZone, O'Reilly Parts, to Elephant Butte SP, USPO, Verizon, Walmart
76	(75 from nb) Lp 25, to Williamsburg, E Conoco/dsl, FillUp/dsl, Phillips 66/dsl, Shell/dsl Maria's Mexican Rio Grande Motel Alco, auto/tire repair, Buick/Chevrolet/GMC, Cielo Vista RV Park, city park, Rio Grande RV Park, RJ RV Park, Shady Corner RV Park
71	Las Palomas
63	NM 152, to Hillsboro, Caballo, E Lakeview RV Park/dsl/LP
59	rd 187, Arrey, Derry, E to Caballo-Percha SPs
58mm	Rio Grande
51	rd 546, to Arrey, Garfield, Derry

T OR C

NM

INTERSTATE 25 Cont'd

Exit#	Services
41	NM 26 W, Hatch, 1 mi W Alon/Subway/dsl Burgers&More, Sparky's Cafe Kings Pillow Inn Chile Pepper Outlets, Franciscan RV Ctr, USPO
35	NM 140 W, Rincon
32	Upham
27mm	scenic view nb, litter barrels,
26mm	**insp sta nb**
23mm	**both lanes, full facilities, litter barrels, petwalk, vending**
19	Radium Springs, W Family$, Fort Selden St Mon, Leasburg SP, RV camping, USPO
9	Dona Ana, W Chucky's/dsl, Circle K/dsl Chachi's Mexican, Jake's Cafe $General, Family$, RV camping, USPO
6	US 70, to Alamogordo, Las Cruces, E Alon/dsl, Shell Domino's, IHOP, Outback Steaks, Papa Johns, Peter Piper Pizza, Pizzaria Uno, Red Brick Pizza, Ruby Tuesday, Starbucks, Subway Fairfield Inn, Holiday Inn Express, Motel 6, Staybridge Suites, Towneplace Suites H, AT&T, Sam's Club/gas, USPO, vet, W Alon/dsl, Chevron, Shell/dsl, Valero/dsl Burger King, BurgerTime, China Express, Domino's, DQ, Dunkin Donuts, KFC, Little Caesar's, Lotaburger, McDonald's, Sonic, Spanish Kitchen, Subway, Taco Bell, Whataburger/24hr, Wienerschnitzel $General, $Tree, Albertson's, AutoZone, CVS Drug, Family$, Kohl's, Lowe's, O'Reilly Parts, Verizon, vet, Walgreens
3	Lohman Ave, Las Cruces, E Alon/dsl, Shell Applebee's, Buffalo Wild Wings, Burger King, Cattle Baron Steaks, Chili's, ChuckeCheese, Dumkin Donuts, Empire Buffet, Farley's Grill, Fidencio's Mexican, Five Guys, Genghis Grill, Golden Corral, Hooters, Jack-in-the-Box, Jason's Deli, KFC, McAlister's Deli, Olive Garden, Pecan Grill, Red Lobster, Sonic, Starbucks, Village Inn, Whataburger Hotel Encanto Albertsons, AutoZone, Barnes&Noble, Dick's, Dillard's, Discount Tire, Home Depot, JC Penney, Marshalls, PetCo, Ross, Target, W Giant/dsl, Valero/dsl Arby's, Carl's Jr, Corner Bakery Cafe, McDonald's, Papa Murphy's, Quiznos, Subway, Taco Bell, TX Roadhouse, Wendy's Hampton Inn AT&T, Best Buy, Big Lots, Brake Masters, Hobby Lobby, NAPA, Old Navy, PepBoys, Petsmart, Staples, URGENT CARE, Verizon, vet, Walgreens, Walmart
1	University Ave, Las Cruces, E AlonSubway/dsl Hilton Garden H, golf, museum, st police, W Giant/dsl Dublin's Cafe, Lorenzo's Italian, McDonald's, Schlotsky's Comfort Suites, Sleep Inn, ValuePlace $Tree, Jo-Ann Fabrics, NMSU, Tuesday Morning
0mm	**I-25 begins/ends on I-10, exit 144 at Las Cruces.**

NM

LAS CRUCES

INTERSTATE 40

Exit#	Services
373.5mm	New Mexico/Texas state line, Mountain/Central time zone
373mm	**Welcome Ctr wb, full facilities, litter barrels, petwalk,**
369	NM 93 S, NM 392 N, Endee, N Chevron/Russell's Truck&Travel/Subway/dsl/scales/24hr
361	Bard
358mm	**weigh sta both lanes**
356	NM 469, San Jon, N Phillips 66/Dhillon//cafe/dsl repair, to Ute Lake SP, S Valero/dsl San Jon Motel city park, USPO
343	no service
339	NM 278, N
335	Lp 40, E Tucumcari Blvd, Tucumcari, N Conoco/dsl Bes Value, EconoLodge, Motel 6, Quality Inn, Rodeway Inn, Supe 8 to Conchas Lake SP, S KOA
333	US 54 E, Tucumcari, 0-1 mi N FLYING J/Phillips 66/dsl/LP scales/24hr, Loves/Arbys/Chester's/Godfather's/dsl/scale Fairfield Inn city park, Mtn Rd RV Park, truck repai truckwash
332	NM 209, NM 104, 1st St, Tucumcari, 0-2 mi N Shell/Circle K/Subway/dsl, Valero/Allsups/dsl Blake's Lotaburger, K-Bob's, McDonald's, Pizza Hut, Sonic, Taco Bell Best Western, Days Inn, Desert Inn, Holiday Inn Express, La Quinta H, $General, Ace Hardware, Dinosaur Museum, Family$, Lowe's Foods, st police, to Conchas Lake SP
331	Camino del Coronado, Tucumcari
329	US 54, US 66 E, W Tucumcari Ave
321	Palomas
311	Montoya
302mm	**both lanes, full facilities, litter barrels, petwalk, RV dump**
300	NM 129, Newkirk, N Rte 66/dsl to Conchas Lake S USPO
291	to Rte 66, Cuervo, N Cuervo Gas/repair
284	no service
277	US 84 S, to Ft Sumner, N Phillips 66/dsl, Pilot/Subway/dsl/scales/24hr Annie's Rest., DQ, Silver Moc Café Best Western, Budget Inn, Comfort Inn, Hampton Inn, Holiday Inn Express, Motel 6, Quality Inn NAPACare, S Loves/Carl's Jr/dsl/24hr, TA/Shell/Subway/dsl/24hr/@ truck/tire repair
275	US 54 W, Santa Rosa, N Chevron/dsl, Valero/Allsup's McDonald's, Rte 66 Rest., Santa Fe Grill Days Inn Econolodge, La Quinta, Rodeway Inn Santa Rosa Campin st police, S Shell/Circle K/dsl Joseph's Grill Lalon Motel/RV Park, Rodeway Inn, Sun'n Sand Motel/rest., Super Tower Motel H, $General, CarQuest, city park, Family NAPA, USPO
273.5mm	Pecos River
273	US 54 S, Santa Rosa, N Santa Rosa Lake SP, S Phillips 66/dsl Best Value Inn NAPACare, to Carlsbad Cavern NP
267	Colonias, N Sinclair/dsl
263	San Ignacio
256	US 84 N, NM 219, to Las Vegas
252	no service
251.5mm	**both lanes, full facilities, litter barrels, petwalk, RV dump**
243	Milagro, N Phillips 66/dsl
239	no service
234	N Exxon/Flying C/DQ/dsl/gifts
230	NM 3, to Encino, N to Villanueva SP
226	no service
220mm	**parking area both lanes, litter barrels**
218b a	US 285, Clines Corners, N Conoco/dsl/24hr, Phillips 6 dsl Clines Corners Rest., Subway, S to Carlsbad Caverns NP
208	Wagon Wheel
207mm	**both lanes, full facilities, litter barrels, petwalk,**
203	no service
197	to Rte 66, Moriarty, S Lisa's TC/dsl/rest./@ auto/RV repair, Glider Museum, same as 194

TUCUMCARI

SANTA ROSA

INTERSTATE 40 Cont'd

MORIARTY

Exit#	Services
196	NM 41, Howard Cavasos Blvd, N Pilot/Subway/dsl/scales/24hr, S Lisa's TC/dsl, Phillips 66/Circle K/dsl Blakes Lotaburger Quality Inn, Sunset Motel auto repair, city park, Family$, to Salinas NM (35mi), USPO
194	NM 41, Moriarty, S Alon/7-11/dsl, Conoco/dsl, TA/Shell/Burger King/Country Pride/Pizza Hut/dsl/24hr/scales/@ Arby's, Chili Hills Mexican, El Comedor Mexican, KFC/Taco Bell, Subway Best Value Inn, Best Western, Motel 6, Ponderosa Motel, Super 8 $General, Chevrolet/GMC, Moriarty Foods, RV Ctr, URGENT CARE
187	NM 344, Edgewood, N Conoco/DQ/dsl Denny's Walmart/McDonald's, S Phillips 66/dsl Chili Hills Mexican, China Chef, Domino's, McDonald's, Pizza Barn, Sonic, Subway Comfort Inn $Tree, auto/rv repair, AutoZone, Ford, O'Reilly Parts, Rte 66 RV Park, RV Camping, Smith's Foods/dsl, USPO, Walgreens
181	NM 217, Sedillo, S Route 66/dsl
178	Zuzax, S Zuzax/dsl/repair Hidden Valley RV Park, Leisure Mtn RV Park
175	NM 337, NM 14, Tijeras, N to Cibola NF, Turquoise Trail RV Park, S Subway USPO

ALBUQUERQUE

Exit#	Services
170	Carnuel
167	Central Ave, to Tramway Blvd, S Alon/7-11, Alon/7-11/dsl, Phillips 66/Circle K/dsl Blakes Lotaburger, Happy Garden, KFC, McDonald's, Starbucks, Subway, Taco Bell, Waffle House Budget Host, Deluxe Inn, EconoLodge, Motel 6, Quality Inn, Rodeway Inn, Suburban Lodge, Woodspring Suites $Tree, Rocky Mtn RV/marine, Smith's/gas, Sprouts Mkt, to Kirtland AFB, Valvoline
166	Juan Tabo Blvd, N Phillips 66/Circle K, Texaco/dsl AA Buffet, Dominos, McDonald's, Olive Garden, Peter Piper Pizza, Pizza Hut, Starbucks, Subway, Taco Bell, Twisters Diner, Village Inn Rest., Weck's Rest., Wendy's Guest Gate Inn, Super 8 $General, Albertson's, Discount Tire, Family$, Hobby Lobby, Midas, Sav-On Drug, Tuesday Morning, vet, S Sonic, Wienerschnitzel $General, Chisholm Trail RV Ctr, Holiday RV Ctr, KOA/LP, Myer's RV Ctr, repair
165	Eubank Blvd, N Chevron, Phillips 66/Circle K Applebee's, Owl Cafe, Panda Express, Sadie's Rest., Sonic Days Inn, Econolodge, Holiday Inn Express, Ramada $Tree, Best Buy, CarQuest, city park, PetCo, Target, S Circle K/dsl, Conoco/dsl Bob's Burgers, Boston Mkt, Burger King, Chick-fil-A, Chili's, Church's, Del Taco, Freddy's, IHOP, Jack-in-the-Box, Starbucks, Subway, Taco Bell, Taco Cabana, Twister's Burritos, Wendy's AutoZone, Costco/gas, Home Depot, O'Reilly Parts, Peerless Tires, Petsmart, repair, Ross, Sam's Club/gas, Toyota, Walgreens, Walmart/McDonald's
164	Lomas Blvd, Wyoming Blvd, N Circle K/dsl, Phillips 66/dsl Black Angus, Chick-fil-A, Dickey's BBQ, Dominos, Furr's Buffet, Krispy Kreme, Subway, Wendy's H, $Tree, NAPA, vet, Walgreens, Walmart, S Chrysler/Dodge/Jeep, Ford, Harley-Davidson, Honda, Hyundai, Kirtland AFB, Mazda, Subaru, transmissions, VW
162b a	Louisiana Blvd, N BJ's Rest., Blaze Pizza, Bravo Italian, Buca Italian, CA Pizza Kitchen, Cheesecake Factory, Chili's, Chipotle, Dave & Buster's, Elephant Bar Rest., Firehouse Subs, Five Guys, Fuddrucker's, Garduno's Mexican, Genghis Grill, Jasons Deli, La Madeleine, LePeep, Longhorn Steaks, Macaroni Grill, McAlister's Deli, Melting Pot, Ojos Locos, Panera Bread, Red Robin, Ruth's Chris, Seasons Grill 52, Starbucks,

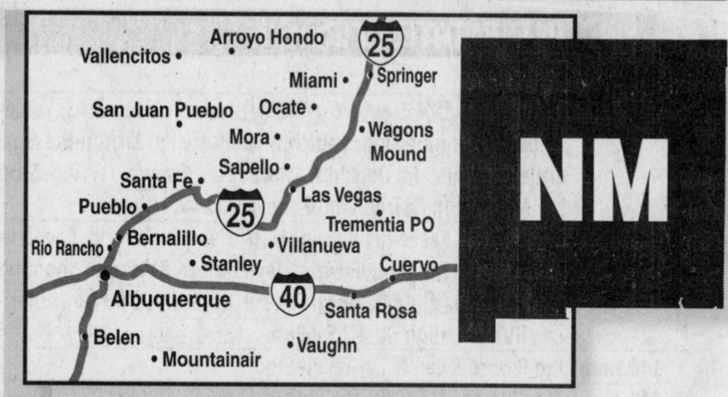

ALBUQUERQUE

Exit#	Services
162b a	Continued Subway Hilton Garden, Homewood Suites, Hyatt Place, Marriott, Sheraton AT&T, Barnes&Noble, Big O Tire, Dick's, Dillard's, Firestone/auto, JC Penney, Kohl's, Macy's, Petsmart, Target, TJ Maxx, Trader Joe's, Verizon, S Shell Burger King atomic museum
161b a	San Mateo Blvd, Albuquerque, N Giant/dsl, Shell Bob's Burgers, Denny's, Domino's, KFC, Pizza Hut, Starbucks, Subway, Taco Bell San Mateo Inn $Tree, Office Depot, Old Navy, Walmart Mkt, S Chevron/dsl Starbucks
160	Carlisle Blvd, Albuquerque, N Circle K/gas, Murphy Express/dsl, Shell, USA Applebee's, Blakes Lotaburger, China Wok, Jack-in-the-Box, Little Anita's, McDonald's, Papa Murphy's, Range Cafe, Rudy's BBQ, Sonic, Subway, Twisters Grill, Village Inn Rest., Whataburger Best Value Inn, Candlewood Suites, Crowne Plaza, Days Inn, EconoLodge, Elegante Hotel, Fairfield Inn, Hampton Inn, Holiday Inn Express, La Quinta, Motel 6, Quality Inn, Residence Inn, Suburban Motel, Super 8, Wyndham AutoZone, Firestone/auto, Walgreens, Walmart, S Chevron/dsl, Circle K Burger King Home 2 Suites H, Whole Foods Mkt
159b c	I-25, S to Las Cruces, N to Santa Fe
158	6th St, 8th St, 12th St, Albuquerque, N Loves/Subway/dsl $ General, U-Haul, S Chevron/dsl Comfort Inn
157b	12th St (from eb), N Four Winds/Burrito Co/dsl Laguna Burgers, McDonald's, Starbucks Holiday Inn Express Lowe's, Walgreens
157a	Rio Grande Blvd, Albuquerque, N Chevron Range Cafe, S Shell Ben Michaels, Blakes Lotaburger, Burger King, Little Anita's, Starbucks Best Western+/grill, Hotel Albuquerque repair
156mm	Rio Grande River
155	Coors Rd, Albuquerque, N Circle K, Mobil, Valero/dsl Applebee's, Arby's, Baskin-Robbins, Burger King, Chili's, Chipotle, Cracker Barrel, Golden Corral, IHOP, Krispy Kreme, McDonald's, Mimmo's Pizza, Panda Express, Panera Bread, Papa Murphy's, Sonic, Starbucks, Subway, Taco Cabana, Twisters Burritos, Wendy's, Wienerschnitzel, Wing Stop $Tree, AutoZone, Brake Masters, Family$, Firestone, GNC, Home Depot, Jiffy Lube, Verizon, Walgreens, Walmart/Subway, S Chevron/dsl, Phillips 66/Circle K/dsl, Shell, Valero Altamar Mexican, Blakes Lotaburger, Buffalo Wild Wings, China Buffet, Del Taco, Denny's, Dion's, Freddy's, McDonald's, Papa John's, Pizza Hut/Taco Bell, Subway, Twisters Burritos Days Inn, EconoLodge, Hampton Inn, La Quinta, Motel 6, Motel 76, Quality Inn, Rodeway Inn, Super 8 BigLots, Discount Tire, O'Reilly Parts
154	Unser Blvd, N Valero, Walmart/dsl McDonald's, Starbucks, Taco Bell GNC, to Petroglyph NM, Verizon, Walmart Mkt

NM

= gas = food = lodging = other = rest stop

INTERSTATE 40 Cont'd

Exit#	Services
153	98th St, S FLYING J/Denny's/dsl/LP/24hr, LNG, Valero-dsl Burger King, Church's, Godfather's, Jack-in-the-Box, Little Caesars, McDonald's, Starbucks, Subway, Wing Stop Microtel $Tree, AutoZone, truckwash/tire/lube
149	Central Ave, Paseo del Volcan, N Camping World, Enchanted Trails RV Camping, Freightliner, LaMesa RV Ctr, to Shooting Range SP, S Loves/Carl's Jr/dsl/scales 24hr American RV Park, High Desert RV Park
140.5mm	Rio Puerco River, N 66 Pit Stop
140	Rio Puerco, N 66 Pit Stop/dsl, S Rte 66 TC/DQ/Road Runner Cafe/hotel/casino/dsl/@
131	Canoncito
126	NM 6, to Los Lunas
120mm	Rio San Jose, Rio San Jose
117	Mesita
114	NM 124, Laguna, 1/2 mi N 66 Pit Stop/dsl
113.5mm	scenic view both lanes, litter barrels
108	Casa Blanca, Paraje, S Rte 66 TC/DQ/dsl/24hr casino, Dancing Eagle Mkt, RV park
104	Cubero, Budville
102	Sky City Rd, Acomita, N Sky City/McDonald's/hotel/casino/dsl Huwak'a Rest. casino, RV Park/laundry, S **both lanes, full facilities, litter barrels, petwalk,**
100	San Fidel
96	McCartys
89	NM 117, to Quemado, N Sky City/Subway/dsl/gifts, S El Malpais NM
85	NM 122, NM 547, Grants, N Alon/dsl, Phillips 66/dsl, Shell/dsl Asian Buffet, Blakes Lotaburger, Canton Cafe, Denny's, Pizza Hut, Subway, Taco Bell Best Western, Days Inn, Holiday Inn Express, Motel 6, Quality Inn, Sands Motel, Super 8, SureStay $Tree, AutoZone, Delta Tire, O'Reilly Parts, repair/transmissions/towing, Walgreens, Walmart, S Lavaland RV Park
81b a	NM 53 S, Grants, N Phillips 66/dsl Domino's, KFC, McDonald's, Sonic Ford, NAPA, USPO, S Blue Spruce RV Park, El Malpais NM, KOA/Cibola Sands RV Park
79	NM 122, NM 605, Milan, N Chevron/dsl, Loves/Chester's/Subway/dsl/scales/24hr DQ Crossroads Motel $ General, Bar-S RV Park, S Petro/Iron Skillet/dsl/scales/24hr/@ dsl repair, Speedco Lube
72	Bluewater Village, N Exxon/DQ/dsl
63	NM 412, Prewitt, S to Bluewater Lake SP (7mi)
53	NM 371, NM 612, Thoreau, N Giant/Blimpie/dsl Family$, NAPA, USPO
47	Continental Divide, elevation 7275, N Phillips 66 Continental Divide Trdg Post, towing/repair, S USPO
44	Coolidge
39	Refinery, N FLYING J/Subway/Dennys/dsl/scales/24hr/@
36	Iyanbito
33	NM 400, McGaffey, Ft Wingate, N museum, RV camping, to Red Rock SP
26	E 66th Ave, E Gallup, N Shell/Subway/dsl Denny's Comfort Suites, Holiday Inn Express, La Quinta, Sleep Inn, TownePlace Suites museum, Red Rock Camping, st police, to Red Rock SP, on Rte 66, S Conoco/dsl, Giant/dsl, Pronto Express, Shell/Ortega Gifts Blakes Lotaburger, Burger King, KFC, McDonald's, Sonic, Wendy's Days Inn, Fairfield Inn, Hacienda Motel, Roadrunner Motel $General, Family $, Verizon
22	Montoya Blvd, Gallup, N **both lanes, full facilities, info, S on Rte 66** Duke City/dsl, Gas Up, Giant/dsl, Phillips 66 Big Cheese Pizza, Church's, Domino's, DQ, Earl's Rest., Hong Kong Buffet, LJ Silver, Papa John's, Pizza Hut, Subway, Taco Bell Blue Spruce Motel, El Capitan Motel, El Rancho Motel/rest. Albertson's, O'Reilly Parts, Shop'n Save, Walgreens
20	US 491, to Shiprock, Gallup, N Alon/dsl, Giant/dsl Applebee's, Arby's, Big Cheese Pizza, Blakes Lotaburger, Burger King, CA Chinese, Carl's Jr., Church's, Cracker Barrel, Del Taco, Denny's, DQ, Freddy's, Golden Corral, KFC, King Dragon Chinese, Little Caesars, McDonald's, Panda Express, Pizza Hut, Sizzler, Sonic, Subway, Super Buffet, Taco Bell, Wendy's Comfort Inn, Hampton Inn, Hilton Garden, Quality Inn, SpringHill Suites $Tree, AT&T, AutoZone, Beall's, Big Lots, CarQuest, Chrysler/Dodge/Jeep, Family$, Hobby Lobby, Home Depot, JC Penney, Nissan, O'Reilly Parts, PepBoys, Safeway, Verizon, Walmart/McDonald's, on Rte 66, S Phillips 66/dsl Badlands Grill, Blakes Lotaburger, Don Diego's, El Charrito, El Sombrero Mexican, Garcia's Rest., McDonald's, Rte 66 Diner, Sonic Best Value Inn, Days Inn, Golden Desert Motel, Knights Inn, Rodeway Inn, Royal Holiday Motel, Super 8 Ford, Lincoln, Tire Factory
16	NM 118, W Gallup, Mentmore, N Loves/Chester's/Subway/dsl/24hr, Navajo/dsl/24hr, TA/Country Pride/dsl/scales/24hr/@, USave Trkstp/dsl Ace Truck/dsl Service, Blue Beacon, NKS Truck Repair, S Conoco/dsl, Shell/dsl, Valero/Allsup's Taco Bell, Virgie's Mexican Budget Inn, EconoLodge, Hampton Inn, Knights Inn, Microtel, Motel 6, Red Roof Inn, Travelodge Family $, USA RV Park
12mm	**inspection/weigh sta eb**
8	to Manuelito
3mm	**Welcome Ctr eb, full facilities, litter barrels, petwalk,**
0mm	New Mexico/Arizona state line

GRANTS

GALLUP

NM

NOTES

NEW YORK

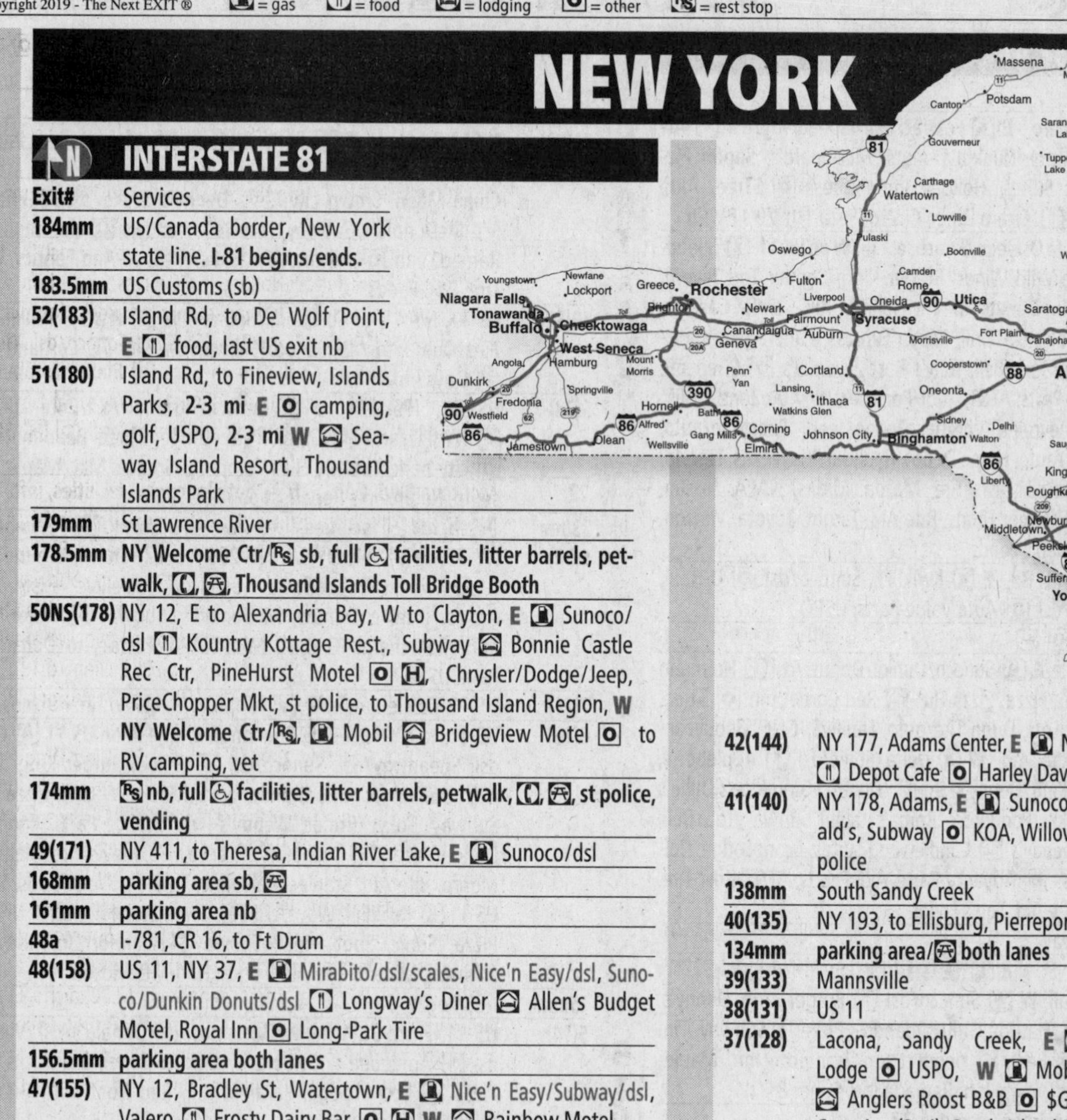

INTERSTATE 81

Exit#	Services
184mm	US/Canada border, New York state line. **I-81 begins/ends.**
183.5mm	US Customs (sb)
52(183)	Island Rd, to De Wolf Point, E food, last US exit nb
51(180)	Island Rd, to Fineview, Islands Parks, 2-3 mi E camping, golf, USPO, 2-3 mi W Seaway Island Resort, Thousand Islands Park
179mm	St Lawrence River
178.5mm	**NY Welcome Ctr/ sb, full facilities, litter barrels, petwalk, , , Thousand Islands Toll Bridge Booth**
50NS(178)	NY 12, E to Alexandria Bay, W to Clayton, E Sunoco/dsl Kountry Kottage Rest., Subway Bonnie Castle Rec Ctr, PineHurst Motel , Chrysler/Dodge/Jeep, PriceChopper Mkt, st police, to Thousand Island Region, W NY Welcome Ctr/ , Mobil Bridgeview Motel to RV camping, vet
174mm	**nb, full facilities, litter barrels, petwalk, , , st police, vending**
49(171)	NY 411, to Theresa, Indian River Lake, E Sunoco/dsl
168mm	**parking area sb,**
161mm	**parking area nb**
48a	I-781, CR 16, to Ft Drum
48(158)	US 11, NY 37, E Mirabito/dsl/scales, Nice'n Easy/dsl, Sunoco/Dunkin Donuts/dsl Longway's Diner Allen's Budget Motel, Royal Inn Long-Park Tire
156.5mm	**parking area both lanes**
47(155)	NY 12, Bradley St, Watertown, E Nice'n Easy/Subway/dsl, Valero Frosty Dairy Bar , W Rainbow Motel
154.5mm	Black River
46(154)	NY 12F, Coffeen St, Watertown, E Mobil/Dunkin Donuts/dsl Cracker Barrel, Shorty's Diner Home Depot, URGENT CARE, W Nice'n Easy/dsl
45(152)	NY 3, to Arsenal St, Watertown, E Mobil/Tim Horton/dsl, Sunoco Apollo Rest., Applebee's, Arby's, Buffalo Wild Wings, Burger King, Chipotle Mexican, CiCi's Pizza, Coldstone, Daily Buffet, Denny's, Dunkin Donuts, Five Guys, Friendly's, Japanese Steaks, Jreck Subs, KFC, McDonald's, Moe's SW Grill, Ponderosa, Riccardo's, Ruby Tuesday, Sonic, Starbucks, Taco Bell, Tilted Kilt Comfort Inn, EconoLodge, Fairfield Inn, Hampton Inn, Hilton Garden, Holiday Inn Express, Quality Inn $General, $Tree, Advance Parts, Aldi Foods, AT&T, AutoZone, BigLots, Jo-Ann Fabrics, Kost Tire, Mavis Discount Tire, Midas, Monro, PriceChopper Foods/24hr, Staples, TJ Maxx, USPO, Walgreens, W Fastrac Bob Evans, Olive Garden, Panera Bread, Pizza Hut, Red Lobster, Subway, TGIFriday's, TX Roadhouse Ramada Inn Best Buy, BonTon, Burlington Coats, Dick's, GNC, Hannaford Foods, JC Penney, Kohl's, Lowe's, Michael's, Old Navy, PetCo, Sam's Club, Target, to Sackets Harbor, Verizon, Walmart/Dunkin Donuts
149mm	**parking area nb,**
44(148)	NY 232, to Watertown Ctr, 3 mi E
147mm	**sb, full facilities, litter barrels, petwalk, , , vending**
43(146)	US 11, to Kellogg Hill
42(144)	NY 177, Adams Center, E Nice'n Easy/Mama Mia's Pizza/dsl Depot Cafe Harley Davidson, Tugger's Camping (12mi)
41(140)	NY 178, Adams, E Sunoco/dsl Dunkin Donuts, McDonald's, Subway KOA, Willows on the Lake RV Park, W st police
138mm	South Sandy Creek
40(135)	NY 193, to Ellisburg, Pierrepont Manor
134mm	**parking area/ both lanes**
39(133)	Mannsville
38(131)	US 11
37(128)	Lacona, Sandy Creek, E Two Bros Pizza Harris Lodge USPO, W Mobil/dsl Sandy Creek Diner Anglers Roost B&B $General, CarQuest, Colonial Court Camping (3mi), Sandy Island Beach SP, Tops/dsl
36(121)	NY 13, Pulaski, E Byrne Dairy/dsl, Valero Ponderosa Knights Inn Chevrolet, Ford, W KwikFill/dsl, Mobil/dsl, Nice'n Easy/Subway/dsl, Valero/dsl Arby's, Burger King, Dunkin Donuts, Eddy's Place, Jreck Subs, McDonald's, Paulanjo's Pizza, River House Rest., Stefano's Rest. 1880 House B&B, Super 8 Advance Parts, Aldi Foods, camping, Family$, fish hatchery, Kinney Drug, Mavis Tire, NAPA, Rite Aid, to Selkirk Shores SP, Top's Foods, URGENT CARE, Verizon
35(118)	to US 11, Tinker Tavern Rd, E Streamside RV Park
34(115)	NY 104, to Mexico, E Mobil/Maple View Rest./dsl/scales, W Feeder Creek Lodge (5mi) J&J (4mi), Jellystone Camping (9mi)
33(111)	NY 69, Parish, E Sunoco/dsl/24hr Grist Mill Rest. E Coast Resort (4mi) $General, Up Country RV Park (8mi), W Gulf, Mirabito/Dunkin Donuts/dsl Passarella Pizza USPO
32(103)	NY 49, to Central Square, E Mirabito/dsl, Sunoco/Subway/dsl Good Golly's Rest. Murphy's Automotive, W Fastrac/gas Burger King, Dunkin Donuts, McDonald's $Tree, Advance Parts, Ford, NAPA, Rite Aid, st police, URGENT CARE, Verizon, Walmart/Subway
31(99)	to US 11, Brewerton, E Oneida Shores Camping, W Mirabito/Tim Hortons/dsl, Nice'n Easy/dsl Dunkin Donuts, Lin Li's Chinese, Little Caesar's, McDonald's, Subway Days Inn $General, AT&T, Kinney Drugs, USPO, vet

WATERTOWN

PULASKI

NY

= gas = food = lodging = other = rest stop

INTERSTATE 81 Cont'd

Exit#	Services
30(96)	NY 31, to Cicero, E Fastrac/dsl, Speedway/dsl Arby's, Cracker Barrel, Dunkin Donuts, McDonald's, Sapori Pizza Comfort Suites, Holiday Inn Express $Tree, Aldi, W Kwikfill Cicero Diner, Cicero Pizza 70's RV Ctr
29(93)	I-481 S, NY 481, to Oswego, Syracuse, **1 mi W on US 11** Speedway Buffalo Wild Wings, Burger King, Copper Top Tavern, Denny's, Dunkin Donuts, Jimmy John's, KFC, Little Caesars, McDonald's, Moe's SW Grill, Panda Express, Panera Bread, Pizza Hut, Subway, Taco Bell, Tully's Rest., Wendy's $General, $Tree, Advance Parts, AT&T, Audi/Porsche/VW, AutoZone, BMW, Buick/GMC, Chevrolet, Chrysler/Dodge/Jeep, Firestone/auto, GNC, Goodyear/auto, Home Depot, Hyundai, Kia, Lexus, Lincoln, Lowe's, Marshall's, Mavis Tire, Mazda, Midas, NAPA, Nissan, PepBoys, PriceChopper Foods, Rite Aid, Target, Toyota, Verizon, Walmart, Wegman's Foods
28(91)	N Syracuse, Taft Rd, E KwikFill, Sunoco/dsl U-Haul, W Sunoco/dsl Auto Value Parts, USPO
27(90)	N Syracuse, E
26(89)	US 11, Mattydale, E Sunoco/Dunkin Donuts/dsl Hofmann Rest., Paladino's Pizza, Pizza Hut Red Carpet Inn $Tree, auto repair, BigLots, Dunn Tire/auto, Family$, GNC, Goodyear/auto, PetCo, Rite Aid, W Delta Sonic/dsl Applebee's, Arby's, Burger King, Denny's, Dunkin Donuts, Gino&Joe's, Julie's Diner, McDonald's, Ponderosa, Roma's Italian, Subway, Taco Bell, Tim Hortons, Wendy's Candlewood Suites, EconoLodge, Holiday Inn Express Advance Parts, Aldi Foods, AT&T, Kost Tire, Monro Auto, Rite Aid, Top's Foods
25a(88)	I-90, NY Thruway
25(87.5)	7th North St, E Pilot/McDonald's/dsl/scales/24hr NAPA, repair, W Sunoco/dsl Burger King, Denny's, Dunkin Donuts, Flatiron Grill, Iamondo's Pizzeria, Subway, Tim Hortons, Tully's Rest. Comfort Inn, Hampton Inn, Maplewood Inn/cafe, Quality Inn, Ramada Inn, Super 8
24(86)	NY 370 W, to Liverpool, same as 23
23(86)	NY 370 E, Hiawatha Blvd, E Stella's Diner, Wendy's Family$, W Speedway Cheesecake Factory, Dave&Busters, Panera Bread, PF Chang's Best Buy, Bon Ton, Dick's, JC Penney, Lord&Taylor, Macy's, TJ Maxx
22(85)	NY 298, Court St
21(84.5)	Spencer St, Catawba St (from sb), industrial area
20(84)	I-690 W (from sb), Franklin St, West St
19(84)	I-690 E, Clinton St, Salina St, to E Syracuse
18(84)	Harrison St, Adams St, E Crowne Plaza H, Civic Ctr, to Syracuse U
17(82)	Brighton Ave, S Salina St, W KwikFill, Valero/Chicken Basket
16a(81)	I-481 N, to DeWitt
16(78)	US 11, to Nedrow, Onondaga Nation, 1-2 mi W Valero McDonald's, Pizza Hut $General, Aldi
15(73)	US 20, La Fayette, E Sunoco/dsl La Fayette Inn, Old Tymes Rest. $General, NAPA, st police, USPO, vet, W McDonald's
71mm	**, truck insp sta both lanes**
14(67)	NY 80, Tully, E Nice'n Easy/deli/dsl A Pizza More, Tasty China Best Western $General, Chevrolet, Kinney Drug, USPO, W Burger King
13(63)	NY 281, Preble, E Mirabito/Dunkin Donuts/Subway/dsl to Song Mtn Ski Resort
60mm	**/truck insp nb, full facilities, litter barrels, petwalk, , vending**

SYRACUSE

CORTLAND

Exit#	Services
12(53)	US 11, NY 281, to Homer, W KwikFill, Sunoco/dsl, Valero Fabió's Italian, Little Italy H, $General, st police, to Fillmore Glen SP
11(52)	NY 13, Cortland, E Perkins Comfort Inn, Holiday Inn Express, Quality Inn, W Mobil/Dunkin Donuts/dsl Arby's, China Moon, Crown City Rest., Denny's, Dickey's BBQ, Friendly's, McDonald's, Subway, Taco Bell, Wendy's Hampton Inn, Ramada Inn Advance Parts, Family$, Jo-Ann Fabrics, Kost Tire, P&C Foods
10(50)	US 11, NY 41, to Cortland, McGraw, W Pitstop/Dunkin Donuts/Quesaritos/dsl, Sunoco/Subway/dsl/24hr Cortland Motel, Days Inn
9(38)	US 11, NY 221, W Sunoco/XtraMart/dsl/24hr, Valero NY Pizzaria Greek Peak Lodge, Three Bear Inn/rest. city park, Country Hills Camping, Gregg's Mkt, Maple Museum, Robinson's Repair, st police, USPO
33mm	**sb, full facilities, litter barrels, petwalk, , , vending**
8(30)	NY 79, to US 11, NY 26, NY 206 (no EZ return), Whitney Pt, E Kwikfill, Speedway, Sunoco Aiello's Ristorante, Arby's, Dunkin Donuts, McDonald's, Subway Hotel Griffin $General, Gregg's Mkt, NAPA, Parts+, to Dorchester Park, USPO
7(21)	US 11, Castle Creek, W Mirabito/Subway/Tim Hortons/dsl
6(16)	US 11, to NY 12, I-88E, Chenango Bridge, **E on US 11** Gulf/dsl, Speedway/dsl, Sunoco/dsl Arby's, Burger King, Denny's, Dunkin Donuts, Grande Pizza, Moe's SW Grill, Pizza Hut, Subway, Tokyo Buffet, Wendy's Advance Parts, Chrysler/Dodge/Jeep, CVS Drug, Kost Tire, Lowe's, Mavis Tire, Meineke, Monro, Rite Aid, Staples, Valvoline, Verizon, Weis Foods, **W on US 11** KwikFill, Wave/dsl China Star, Friendly's, Nirchi's Pizza, Sonic, Spot Diner, Subway Comfort Inn, Howard Johnson, Motel 6 Aldi Foods, Harley Davidson
15mm	I-88 begins eb
5(14)	US 11, Front St, **1 mi W** Sunoco/McDonald's/dsl, Valero/dsl Applebee's, Coldstone, Cracker Barrel, Starbucks, TLC Pizza EconoLodge, Fairfield Inn, Red Roof Inn Cutler Botanical Garden
4(13)	NY 17, Binghamton
3(12)	Broad Ave, Binghamton, W Valero KFC CVS Drug Weis Foods
3(10)	Industrial Park, same as 2
2(8)	US 11, NY 17, **1-2 mi W** Gulf/dsl, Loves/Wendy's/dsl/scales/24hr, TA/Country Pride/dsl/scales/24hr/@ Burger King, McDonald's, Subway, Taco Bell Del Motel
1(4)	US 11, NY 7, Kirkwood, **1-2 mi W** Conklin, Mirabito/dsl Hallo Berlin Rest. Kirkwood Motel
2mm	**Welcome ctr nb, full facilities, litter barrels, petwalk, , , vending**
1mm	**truck insp sta nb**
0mm	New York/Pennsylvania state line

BINGHAMTON

INTERSTATE 84

Exit#	Services
71.5mm	New York/Connecticut state line
21(69)	US 6, US 202, NY 121 (from wb), N Salem, same as 20
20N(67.5)	NY 22, Palling, N Mobil, Shell/dsl, Valero Dunkin Donuts, Portofinos Cadillac/Chevrolet, Ford, Honda, Subaru
20S	I-684, to NYC
19(65)	NY 312, Carmel, N st police, S Applebee's, Dunkin Donuts, Eveready Diner, Gaetano's Deli H, DeCicco's Mkt, Home Depot, Kohl's, Marshall's, Michael's, Verizon
18(62)	NY 311, Lake Carmel, S La Famiglia

INTERSTATE 84 Cont'd

Exit#	Services
17(59)	Ludingtonville Rd, S Speedway/dsl, Sunoco/dsl Cutillo's Rest., Dunkin Donuts, Gappy's Pizza, Lou's Rest.
56mm	elevation 965 ft
55mm	**Rs both lanes, full facilities, litter barrels, petwalk, vending**
16(53)	Taconic Parkway, N to Albany, S to New York
15(51)	Lime Kiln NY, **3 mi N** Mobil Dunkin Donuts Arbor Ridge Inn
13(46)	US 9, to Poughkeepsie, **N** Mobil/deli, Mobil/dsl, Shell/Dunkin Donuts/dsl A&W/KFC, Boston Mkt, Coldstone, Cracker Barrel, Fishkill Grill, Five Guys, Panera Bread, Red Line Diner, Ruby Tuesday, Starbucks, Subway, Taco Bell, Wendy's Courtyard, Extended Stay America, Extended Stay America, Hampton Inn, Hawthorn Inn, Hilton Garden, Holiday Inn Express, Hyatt House, Magnuson Hotel, Ramada Inn AT&T, Sam's Club, Verizon, Walmart, **S** Speedway/dsl Maya Cafe, McDonald's Home Depot
12(45)	NY 52 E, Fishkill, **N** Valero/dsl Green Garden, Sal's Pizza CVS Drug, USPO, **S** Mobil, Sunoco/dsl 84 Diner, Hometown Deli Quality Inn
11(42)	NY 9D, to Wappingers Falls, **1 mi N** Gulf/dsl, Mobil/dsl
41mm	**toll booth**
40mm	Hudson River
10(39)	US 9W, NY 32, to Newburgh, **N** Citgo/dsl, Sunoco Alexis Diner, Andiamo Rest., Burger King, Dunkin Donuts, Green Garden Chinese, KFC, McDonald's, New China, Papa John's, Pizza Hut, Planet Pizza, Subway $Tree, Advance Parts, BigLots, Family$, Firestone/auto, Monro, PriceChopper Foods, Rite Aid, Shop Rite Foods, Verizon, Walgreens, **S** Citgo/dsl, Shell/dsl, Sunoco H
8(37)	NY 52, to Walden, **N** 76/dsl
7b(36)	NY 300, Newburgh, **N** Mobil Daddy's Grill, DQ, Dunkin Donuts, Leo's Pizzaria, McDonald's, Newburgh Buffet, Perkins, Taco Bell, Wendy's $Tree, AT&T, AutoZone, BonTon, Marshall's, Mavis Tire, Midas, Office Depot, Stop&Shop Foods, **S** Speedway/dsl, Sunoco/dsl Applebee's, Burger King, Chili's, China City, Cosimos Ristorante, Denny's, Five Guys, IHOP, Ikaros Diner, Longhorn Steaks, Neptune Diner, Panera Bread, Pizza Mia, Sonic, Starbucks, Steak'n Stein, Subway, TGIFriday's, Union Sq Rest., Yobo Asian Days Inn, Hampton Inn, Howard Johnson, Ramada Inn, Super 8 $General, Adam's Farm Mkt, Aldi Foods, Barnes&Noble, Buick/GMC, Cadillac/Chevrolet, Chrysler/Dodge/Jeep, Ford/Lincoln, Home Depot, Honda, Kohl's, Lowe's, Meineke, Michael's, Nissan, Orange County Choppers/cafe, PetsMart, Target, Verizon, Walmart
7a(35)	I-87, NY Thruway, Albany, to NYC
6(34)	NY 17K, to Newburgh, **N** Mobil/dsl, Pilot/Arby's/dsl/scales/24hr Airport Diner Sheraton, **S** Shell/Dunkin Donuts/dsl Courtyard, Days Inn, Hampton Inn, Howard Johnson
5a(33)	NY 747, International Blvd, **S** Homewood Suites to Stewart Airport
5(29)	NY 208, Maybrook, **N** Mobil/dsl, Sunoco/dsl Burger King, Dunkin Donuts, McDonald's Holiday Inn Express CarQuest, Rite Aid, ShopRite Foods, Verizon, Walgreens, Winding Hills Camping, **S** Speedway/dsl, TA/Valero/Country Pride/Pizza Hut/dsl/scales/24hr/@ Prima's Deli, Renee's Deli, Subway Super 8 Advance Parts, auto/truck repair, Blue Beacon, st police
24mm	**Rs wb, full facilities, litter barrels, petwalk, vending**

NEWBURGH

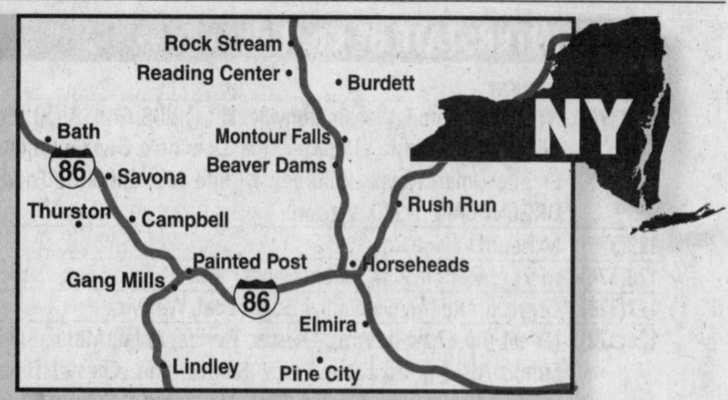

MIDDLETOWN

Exit#	Services
4(19)	NY 17, Middletown, **N** Mobil/24hr Americana Diner, Applebee's, Baskin-Robbins/Dunkin Donuts, Boston Mkt, Buffalo Wild Wings, Burger King, Chipotle, ChuckeCheese, Cosimo's Italian, Denny's, Five Guys, Friendly's, Fuji Japanese, Golden Corral, Hardee's, KFC, McDonald's, Olive Garden, Panera Bread, Papa John's, Perkins, Pizza Hut, Popeye's, Red Lobster, Ruby Tuesday, Sonic, Starbucks, Subway, Taco Bell, TX Roadhouse, Wendy's, Youyou Japanese Home 2 Suites, Howard Johnson, Middletown Motel, Super 8 $Tree, Aldi Foods, AT&T, AutoZone, Best Buy, Big Lots, CVS Drug, Dick's, Firestone/auto, GNC, Hannaford Foods, Hobby Lobby, Home Depot, Honda, JC Penney, Jo-Ann Fabrics, Kohl's, Lowe's, Macy's, Marshall's, Mavis Tire/auto, Michael's, Old Navy, PetCo, PetsMart, PriceChopper Foods, Rite Aid, Sam's Club/dsl, ShopRite/gas, Staples, Target, Tire Discount, TJ Maxx, U-Haul, Verizon, Walmart/Subway, **S** Chili's, El Bandido Mexican, Outback Steaks, Soho Grill, TGIFriday Courtyard, Hampton Inn, Holiday Inn, Microtel H, Midas, st police
17mm	**Rs eb, full facilities, litter barrels, petwalk, vending**
3(15)	US 6, to Middletown, **N** Citgo/dsl, Mobil, QuickChek/dsl, Shell, Sunoco Bro Bruno's Pizza, DQ, Dunkin Donuts, Hibachi Buffet, IHOP, McDonald's, Peking Chinese, Rita's Custard, Subway, Taco Bell, Wendy's Sleep Inn $General, Acura, Advance Parts, AutoZone, Buick/Chevrolet, Family$, Lexus, Mavis Discount Tire, Mazda, Meineke, Rite Aid, ShopRite Foods, Subaru, Verizon, VW, **S** Citgo/dsl, Geo/Dunkin Donuts/dsl Days Inn, Global Budget Inn Kia, Nissan, Toyota
2(5)	Mountain Rd, **S** Firehouse Deli
4mm	1272 ft eb, elevation 1254 ft wb
3mm	**parking area both lanes**
1(1)	US 6, NY 23, Port Jervis, **N** Arlene'n Tom's Diner, Baskin-Robbins/Dunkin Donuts H, Ford, **S** BP/dsl/LP, Citgo/dsl, Gulf/dsl, Pilot/Subway/dsl, Shell/dsl, Valero/dsl DQ, McDonald's, Village Pizza Days Inn $Tree, GNC, ShopRite Foods, TJ Maxx
0mm	New York/Pennsylvania state line, Delaware River

INTERSTATE 86

Exit#	Services
I-86 begins/ends on I-87, exit 16, toll booth	
131(379)	NY 17, **N** Applebee's Outlets/famous brands, **S** Gulf/dsl Chili's, Dunkin Donuts, KFC, Outback Steaks, Panera Bread, TGIFriday's, Uno Grill, Wendy's Days Inn, Hampton Inn $Tree, Best Buy, BJ's Whse, BMW, GNC, Home Depot, Kohl's, Michael's, Old Navy, Petsmart, Staples, Target, TJMaxx, Verizon, Walmart/Subway
130a(378)	US 6, Bear Mtn, to West Point (from eb, no return)

NY

INTERSTATE 86 Cont'd

Exit#	Services
130(377)	NY 208, Monroe, Washingtonville, N 208 Grill, S Mobil/dsl, Sunoco/dsl Burger King, Domino's, Dunkin Donuts, Empire Diner, Wayback Burger Rite Aid, ShopRite Foods, URGENT CARE, USPO, Verizon
129(375)	Museum Village Rd
128(374)	rd 51 (only from wb), Oxford Depot
127(373)	Greycourt Rd (from wb only), Sugar Loaf, Warwick
126(372)	NY 94 (no EZ wb return), Chester, Florida, N Mobil, Shell, Sunoco/dsl Bro Bruno Pizza, Burger King, Chester Diner, Dunkin Donuts, Lobster Pier Rest, McDonald's, Subway, Taco Bell, Wendy's Holiday Inn Express CVS Drug, GNC, Goodyear/auto, Rite Aid, ShopRite Foods, USPO, Verizon, S Lowe's
125(369)	NY 17M E, South St
124(368)	NY 17A, NY 207, N Gulf/Subway/dsl, Mobil/dsl, QuickChek/dsl Burger King, Dunkin Donuts, Friendly's, Goshen Diner, Pizza Hut CVS Drug, Verizon, S Comfort Inn Chrysler/Dodge/Jeep, Hyundai, URGENT CARE
123	US 6, NY 17M (wb only), Port Jervis
122a(367)	Fletcher St, Goshen
122(364)	rd 67, E Main St, Crystal Run Rd, N Chili's, Outback Steaks, Soho Grill, TGIFriday's Courtyard, Hampton Inn, Holiday Inn, Microtel URGENT CARE, S El Bandido Rest. H
121(363)	I-84, E to Newburgh, W to Port Jervis
120(363)	NY 211, N Mobil Buffalo Wild Wings, Cosimo's Ristorante, Fuji Japanese, Olive Garden, Perkins Home 2 Suites, Howard Johnson, Middletown Motel, Super 8 Best Buy, Dick's, Hannaford's Foods, Honda, JC Penney, Lowe's, Macy's, Mavis Discount Tire, Old Navy, PetCo, Sam's Club/dsl, ShopRite/gas, Target, S Americana Diner, Applebee's, Boston Mkt, Burger King, Chipotle, ChuckECheese, Denny's, Dunkin Donuts, Five Guys, Franco Di Roma Italian, Friendly's, Golden Corral, Hardee's, KFC, McDonald's, Panera Bread, Papa John's, Pizza Hut, Popeye's, Red Lobster, Ruby Tuesday, Sonic, Starbucks, Subway, Taco Bell, TX Roadhouse, Wendy's, YouYou Chinese $General, $Tree, Aldi Foods, AT&T, AutoZone, BigLots, Firestone/auto, GNC, Hobby Lobby, Home Depot, JoAnn, Kohl's, Marshall's, Michael's, Midas, Old Navy, Petsmart, PriceChopper, Rite Aid, ShopRite/gas, Staples, Tire Discount Ctr, TJMaxx, U-Haul, Verizon, Walmart/Subway
119(360)	NY 302, Circleville, to Pine Bush, Pine Bush, S Citgo/dsl, Valero/Dunkin Donuts/dsl Subway
118a(358)	NY 17M, Fair Oaks
118(358)	Fair Oaks, Circleville, N Economy Inn, S Citgo/dsl, Mobil/dsl
116(355)	NY 17K, Bloomingburg, N Mtn View Rest., S Citgo/dsl Quickway Diner
115	Burlingame Rd
114	Wurtsboro, Highview (from wb)
113(350)	US 209, Wurtsboro, Ellenville, N Mobil/dsl, Stewarts/gas Danny's Steaks Days Inn G-Mart Foods, S Giovanni's Café (2mi)
112(347)	Masten Lake, Yankee Lake, N Days Inn, S Yankee Lake
111(344)	(eb only), Wolf Lake, S Citgo/dsl
110(343)	Lake Louise Marie
109(342)	Rock Hill, Woodridge, N Citgo/dsl BHR Rest., Dutch's Cafe, Pizza Rock, RockHill Diner Sullivan Ramada Ace Hardware, auto repair, Hilltop Farms Camping (6mi), Super Mkt Trading Post, USPO, S Mobil/dsl Dragon Garden Chinese
108(341)	Bridgeville, same as 109
107(340)	Thompsonville, S Chevrolet, Chrysler/Dodge/Jeep, Toyota
106(339)	East Broadway, E. Broadway, N Ford/Lincoln, S Mobil/dsl Super 8 (2 mi) GMC Trucks, Hyundai, Toyota
105(337)	NY 42, Monticello, N Mobil/dsl, Valero Blue Horizon Diner, Bro Bruno's Pizza, Burger King, China City, Dunkin Donuts, Giovanni's Rest, KFC, McDonald's, Subway AutoZone, Home Depot, museum, ShopRite Foods, Staples, Walmart/McDonald's, S Citgo/dsl, Sunoco/dsl Miss Monticello Diner, Nugget Rest., Pizza Hut, Stewart's, Wendy's EconoLodge, Heritage Inn, Super 8 Advance Parts, Family$, NAPA, Rite Aid
104(336)	NY 17B, Raceway, Monticello, S Citgo/dsl, Mobil/Subway/dsl Albella Rest., Colosseo Rest., Tilly's Diner Best Western, Raceway Motel, Travel Inn AT&T, Swinging Bridge Camp
103	Rapp Rd (wb only)
102(332)	Harris, N H
101(327)	Ferndale, Swan Lake, S Mobil/dsl Swan Lake Camping (5mi)
100(327)	NY 52 E, Liberty, N Citgo/dsl, Sam's, Sunoco Burger King, Dunkin Donuts, Last Licks Cafe, Liberty Diner, McDonald's, Piccolo Italian, Pizza Hut, Subway, Taco Bell Days Inn, Knights Inn $Tree, Ace Hardware, Advance Parts, Rite Aid, ShopRite Foods, USPO, S Lincoln Motel Buick/Cadillac, Chrysler/Dodge/Jeep, Ford/Lincoln, NAPA, Swan Lake Camping (5mi)
100a	NY 52 W (no wb return), Liberty, S st police
99(325)	NY 52 W, to NY 55, Liberty, S Sunoco Catskill Motel
98(321)	Cooley, Parksville, N Mobil/dsl
97(319)	Morsston
96(316)	Livingston Manor, S Citgo, Sunoco Robinhood Diner Covered Bridge Camping, Mongaup Pond Camping, Peck Mkt, to Covered Bridge, USPO
313mm	**eb, full facilities, litter barrels, petwalk, , , vending, truck insp. sta (eb)**
94(311)	NY 206, Roscoe, Lew Beach, N Mobil/dsl, Sunoco/dsl Raimondo's Diner, Roscoe Diner Creekside B&B, Reynolds House Motel, Rockland House Motel, Roscoe Motel Beaverkill St Camping (8mi), Catskill Grocers, st police, USPO, S Mobil/dsl Tennanah Lake Motel
93(305)	to Cooks Falls (from wb)
92(303)	Horton, Cooks Falls, Colchester, S Sunoco/dsl Riverside Café/lodge Russell Brook Camping
90(297)	NY 30, East Branch, Downsville, N Sunoco Beaver-Del Camping, Oxbow Camping, Peaceful Valley Camping, S Branch Motel
295mm	**wb, full facilities, litter barrels, petwalk, , , vending**
89(293)	Fishs Eddy
87a(288)	NY 268 (from wb, no ez-return), same as 87
87(284)	NY 97, to NY 268, to NY 191, Hancock, Cadosia, S Mirabito/Subway/dsl, Sunoco, Valero McDonald's, New China Capra Inn, Hancock House Hotel Family$, NAPA, Rite Aid, Tops Foods
276mm	**parking area wb**
84(274)	Deposit, N Mirabito/dsl BC Pizza, New Moon Cafe, Pines Rest., Wendy's Deposit Motel, Laurel Bank Motel Family$, st police
83(272)	Deposit, Oquaga Lake
82(270)	NY 41, McClure, Sanford, N Cornerstone Cafe auto repair, Kellystone Park, S Scott's Family Resort Guestward Camping (3mi), Oquaga Creek SP
265mm	**parking area eb, litter barrels,**

MIDDLETOWN

NY

INTERSTATE 86 Cont'd

Exit#	Services
81(263)	E Bosket Rd
80(261)	Damascus, N Mirabito/dsl auto repair, Forest Hill Lake Park Camping (3mi)
79(259)	NY 79, Windsor, N Sunoco/dsl China Star, Maria's Pizza, Subway Big M Mkt, USPO, S Marian's Pizza/Subs Lakeside Camping (8mi)
78(256)	Dunbar Rd, Occanum
77(254)	W Windsor, N Sunoco/dsl McDonald's $General
76(251)	Haskins Rd, to Foley Rd
75(250)	I-81 S, to PA (exits left from wb)
I-86/I-81 run together 4 miles	
3	Colesville Rd (from eb), S Loves/Wendy's/dsl/scales/24hr, Mirabito/Dunkin Donuts/dsl, TA/Country Pride/dsl/scales/24hr Subway
I-86/I-81 run together 4 miles.	
3	Broad Ave (from wb, no return)
4NS	NY 7, **I-86/I-81 run together 4 miles.**
72(244)	I-81 N, US 11, Front St, Clinton St, (no wb re-entry), S Aamco
71(242)	Airport Rd, Johnson City, S Mirabito Microtel Walmart
70(241)	NY 201, Johnson City, N Mirabito, Speedway/dsl Arby's, Dunkin Donuts, Food&Fire BBQ, Friendly's, Great China, Ground Round, McDonald's, Papa John's, Pizza Hut, Ruby Tuesday, Taco Bell Best Western, Hampton Inn, La Quinta, Red Roof Inn $Tree, Bon-Ton, JC Penney, Mavis Tire, Mr Tire, PetCo, Wegman's Foods, S Home Depot
69(239)	NY 17C
238mm	Susquehanna River
68(237)	NY 17C, Old Vestal Rd, (from eb, no re-entry)
67(236)	NY 26, NY 434, Vestal, Endicott, **S on NY 434** Mirabito/dsl, Mirabito/dsl (2), Speedway/dsl, Stop'N Gas A&W/LJ Silver, Applebee's, Arby's, Burger King, CA Grill, Chili's, ChuckE-Cheese, Dunkin Donuts, IHOP, Jimmy John's, KFC, McDonald's, Moe's SW Grill, Olive Garden, Outback Steaks, Panera Bread, Pudgie's Pizza, Red Lobster, Red Robin, Starbucks, Subway, Taco Bell, TGIFriday's, Uno Grill, Wendy's Candlewood Suites, Comfort Suites, Courtyard, Hampton Inn, Holiday Inn Express, Homewood Suites, Parkway Motel $Tree, Aldi Foods, AT&T, Barnes&Noble, Best Buy, BigLots, CVS Drug, Dick's, Ford/Lincoln, Jo-Ann Fabrics, Kohl's, Lowe's, Mavis Tire, Meineke, Michael's, Mr Tire, Nissan, Old Navy, Petsmart, Price Rite Foods, Rite Aid, Sam's Club, Staples, Target, TJ Maxx, U-Haul, URGENT CARE, USPO, Verizon, vet, Volvo, VW, Walmart/Dunkin Donuts, Wies Foods
66(231)	NY 434, Apalachin, S KwikFill, Sunoco Big Dipper Drive-In, Blue Dolphin Diner, Dunkin Donuts, McDonald's, Perkins, Subway Comfort Inn, Quality Inn
65(225)	NY 17C, NY 434, Owego, N Sunoco A&W/KFC, Arby's, McDonald's, Panda Wok, Pizza Hut, Subway, Wendy's Hampton Inn, Holiday Inn Express, Red Roof Inn/rest. $General, Buick/GMC, Hickories Park Camping, Mr Tire, Top's Foods, Verizon, S st police
64(223)	NY 96, Owego, N Dunkin Donuts AutoZone, CVS Drug, Rite Aid, USPO, S Mobil/dsl
222mm	**wb, full facilities, litter barrels, petwalk, picnic tables, vending**
63(218)	Lounsberry, S Valero/rest./dsl/24hr
62(214)	NY 282, Nichols, S Citgo/pizza/dsl Hampton Inn Jim's RV Ctr, Tioga Downs Race Track (2mi)
212mm	**eb, full facilities, litter barrels, petwalk, , vending**

WINDSOR

VESTAL

OWEGO

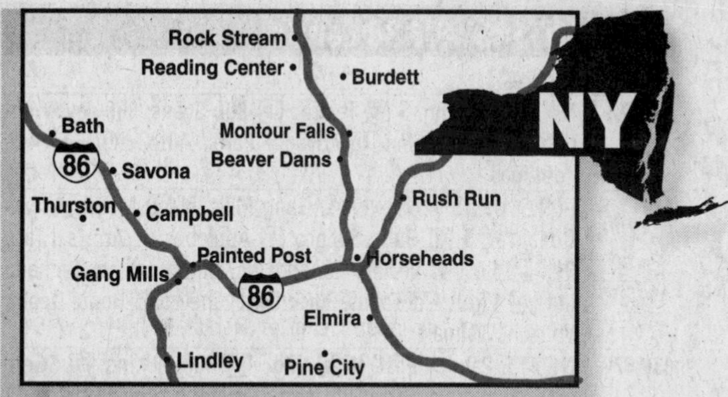

Exit#	Services
208mm	Susquehanna River
61(206)	NY 34, PA 199, Waverly, Sayre, N $General, Goodyear/gas, S Gulf, Sunoco/dsl Best Western/rest. Chrysler/Dodge/Jeep, Joe's RV Ctr, Nissan, Subaru
60(204)	US 220, to Sayre, Waverly, N O'brien's Inn, S Citgo/dsl, Mirabito/Dunkin Donuts/dsl Wendy's (3mi) Candlewood Suites, Comfort Inn, Hampton Inn Advance Parts, Aldi Foods, Rite Aid, Top's Foods, Toyota
59a(202)	Wilawana, S Sunoco/Subway/dsl
59(200)	NY 427, Chemung, N Dandy/dsl
58a(197)	to CR 60, Lowman
57(195)	rd 2, Lowman, Wellsburg, N Gardner Hill Campsites (4mi), USPO
56(190)	Jerusalem Hill, N Hilltop Rest., S Citgo/dsl, Sunoco/Dandy Pizza/Subway/dsl Dunkin Donuts, McDonalds Coachman Motel (3mi), Holiday Inn, Mark Twain Motel (3mi) H
54(186)	NY 13, to Ithaca
53(185)	Horseheads, S Sunoco/dsl Burger King, Domino's, Dunkin Donuts, Guiseppe's Pizza, Lin Buffet, McDonald's, Rico's Pizza, Subway, Wendy's Red Carpet Inn, Travelodge Advance Parts, Family$, Rite Aid
52b(184)	NY 14, to Watkins Glen, N Friendly's Holiday Inn Express, Knights Inn, S Denny's
52a(183)	Commerce Ctr, S Buffalo Wild Wings, Cracker Barrel, Red Robin, TX Roadhouse Fairfield Inn Aldi Foods, AT&T, Dick's, Jo-Ann Fabrics, Kohl's, Mavis Discount Tire, Petsmart, Walmart/McDonald's
51a(182)	Chambers Rd, N Sunoco/Subway/dsl Bon Ton, Chili's, Dunkin Donuts, McDonald's, Olive Garden, Outback Steaks, Red Lobster, Ruby Tuesday Candlewood Suites, Country Inn&Suites, Courtyard, Hampton Inn, Hilton Garden Firestone/auto, JC Penney, Nissan, S Applebee's, Charley's Subs, Five Guys, Moe's SW, Mt Fuji Japanese, Old Country Buffet, Panera Bread, Popeye's, Taco Bell, TGIFridays, Wendy's EconoLodge $Tree, Barnes&Noble, Best Buy, Buick/GMC/Cadillac, Field&Stream, Hobby Lobby, Honda, Hyundai, Lowe's, Michael's, Mr Tire, Old Navy, PetCo, Sam's Club, Staples, Subaru, Target, TJ Maxx, Top's Foods, Toyota, URGENT CARE, Verizon
50(180)	Kahler Rd, N to Airport
49(178)	Olcott Rd, Canal St, Big Flats, N , antiques, S Sunoco Picnic Pizza USPO
48(171)	NY 352, E Corning, N Citgo Budget Inn, Gate House Motel H
47(174)	NY 352, Gibson, E Corning, N Budget Inn, Gate House Motel
46(171)	NY 414, to Watkins Glen, Corning, N Ferenbaugh Camping (5mi), KOA (14mi), Watkins Glen Camping, S Sunoco Pizza Hut Comfort Inn, Radisson, Staybridge Suites Corning Glass Museum

ELMIRA

CORNING

NY

INTERSTATE 86 Cont'd

	Exit#	Services
CORNING	45(170)	NY 352, Corning, S Fastrac Bob Evans, Subway, Wendy's Fairfield Inn Advance Parts, AutoZone, Rite Aid, Tops/gas
	44a	I-99 S, US 15 S, NY 417 W, Gang Mills, N Mobil McDonald's, S Gulf, Sunoco Applebee's, Arby's, Taco Bell Best Value Inn, Corning Inn, Hampton Inn, Ramada Inn $Tree, Aldi Foods, Buick/GMC, Chevrolet, Home Depot, Verizon, Walmart
	43(167)	NY 415, Painted Post, N Citgo Burger King $General, AutoValue Parts, Big Lots, Firestone/auto, S 7-11 Denny's, Dunkin Donuts Hampton Inn, Holiday Inn Express
	167mm	**litter barrels, parking area wb**
	42(165)	Coopers Plains, N st police
	41(161)	rd 333, Campbell, N Sunoco/Subway/dsl Camp Bell Camping (1mi), S antiques, Cardinal Campsites (6mi)
	160mm	**eb, full facilities, litter barrels, petwalk, , , vending**
	40(156)	NY 226, Savona, N Select/dsl $General
BATH	39(153)	NY 415, Bath, N Chat-a-Whyle Rest. (3mi) National Hotel, S Jellystone (2mi)
	38(150)	NY 54, to Hammondsport, Bath, N Exxon/dsl, KwikFill Arby's, Burger King, Dunkin Donuts, Ling Ling Chinese, McDonald's/playplace, Pizza Hut, Rico's Pizza, Subway, Taco Bell Budget Inn, Days Inn, Microtel, Super 8 $General, Advance Parts, AT&T, Campers Haven Camping, Family$, Hickory Hill Camping (3mi), museum, Rite Aid, SaveALot, st police, to Keuka Lake, Top's Foods/gas, Verizon, Walgreens
	147mm	**wb, full facilities, litter barrels, petwalk, , , vending**
	37(146)	NY 53, to Prattsburg, Kanona, S Pilot/Subway/dsl/scales/24hr/@, Sunoco/Smokey's/dsl/scales st police, USPO, Wilkin's RV Ctr (1mi)
	36(145)	I-390 N, NY 15, to Rochester
HORNELL	35(138)	Howard, S to Lake Demmon RA
	34(130)	NY 36, Hornell, Arkport, 0-2 mi S KwikFill, Mobil/dsl Applebee's, Country Kitchen, Dunkin Donuts, McDonald's, Pizza Hut, Subway Days Inn, EconoLodge, Sunshine Motel $General, $Tree, Advance Parts, Aldi Foods, AutoZone, Chrysler/Dodge/Jeep, Ford, GNC, Lowe's, Verizon, Walmart/Subway, Wegman's Foods
	125mm	scenic overlook eb
	33(124)	NY 21, to Alfred, Almond, Andover, S 7-11/dsl Kanakadea Camping, Lake Lodge Camping (8mi), USPO
	117mm	2080 ft wb, elev 2110 ft eb, highest elevation on I-86
	32(116)	W Almond
	31(108)	Angelica, N Valero/dsl American House Inn
	30(104)	NY 19, Belmont, Wellsville, N Letchworth SP (27mi), S H, st police
	101mm	**eb, full facilities, litter barrels, petwalk, , , vending**
	29(99)	NY 275, to Bolivar, Friendship, S Miller&Brandes Gas, Mobil/Subway/dsl
	28(92)	NY 305, Cuba, N Moonwink's Rest. EconoLodge $General, Maple Lane RV Park, S Sunoco/dsl, Valero/dsl Charlie's Chicken Pizza, McDonald's, Subway H, Cuba Cheese Shop, Cuba Drug, Family$, Giant Foods
OLEAN	27(84)	NY 16, NY 446, Hinsdale, N food, S gas lodging
	26(79)	NY 16, Olean, S 7-11 Burger King, Pizza Hut, Subway, Wendy's Holiday Inn Express H
	25(77)	Buffalo St, Olean, S Citgo/dsl H, **2 mi S on NY 417** Applebee's, Burger King, Coldstone/Tim Hortons, Domino's, Friendly's, Little Caesar's, McDonald's, Perkins, Ponderosa,
	25(77)	Continued Subway Best Western, Fairfield Inn, Microtel $Tree, Advance Parts, Aldi Foods, AT&T, BJ's Whse/gas, GNC, Home Depot, Jo-Ann Fabrics, KwikFill, Old Navy, St Bonaventure U, Staples, Tops Foods/gas, Verizon, Walmart/Subway
	24(74)	NY 417, Allegany, **1 mi S** Mobil/7-11/dsl to St Bonaventure U
	73mm	**wb, full facilities, litter barrels, petwalk,**
	23(68)	US 219 S, N Allegany Jct./Subway/dsl, Sassy's Trkstp/dsl
	66mm	Allegheny River
SALAMANCA	21(61)	US 219 N, Salamanca
	20(58)	NY 417, NY 353, Salamanca, N Allegany Gas, Antone's Gas, Nafco Quickstop/Burger King/24hr, Seneca OneStop/dsl/24hr, VIP Gas Burger King, Little Caesar's, McDonald's Holiday Inn Express, Hotel Westgate AutoZone, Rail Museum, Seneca-Iroquis Museum, S casino
	19(54)	S Allegany SP, Red House Area
	18(51)	NY 280, S Allegany SP, Quaker Run Area
	17(48)	NY 394, Steamburg, S Seneca, WW/dsl
	16(41)	W Main St, Randolph, N Mobil/7-11/dsl R&M Rest. RV camping
	40mm	**parking area,**
	15(39)	School House Rd
	39mm	**parking area,**
	14(36)	US 62, Kennedy, **1 mi N** Keystone Gas Office Pizza/Subs, S RV camping
	32mm	Cassadaga Creek
JAMESTOWN	13(31)	NY 394, Falconer, S Keystone, Mobil/dsl Burger King Budget Inn, Red Roof Inn CVS Drug, Harley-Davidson
	12(28)	NY 60, Jamestown, N KwikFill/dsl st police, S Mobil/McDonald's/dsl Bob Evans Comfort Inn, Hampton Inn, Holiday Inn Express H
	11(25)	to NY 430, Jamestown, S gas/dsl food lodging
	22mm	**Welcome ctr/ eb, full facilities, litter barrels, petwalk, , vending**
	10(21)	NY 430 W, Bemus Point
	9(20)	NY 430 E (no EZ eb return), N Mobil/dsl Bemus Point Rest.
	19mm	Chautauqua Lake
	8(18)	NY 394, Mayville, N Keystone/dsl RV camping, USPO
	7(15)	Panama
	6(9)	NY 76, Sherman, N Keystone Gas Main Street Diner, Murdock's Rest. $General, city park, NAPA, Sherman Drug, USPO
	4(1)	NY 430, Findley Lake, N 86 Express Rest. Holiday Inn Express, S Blue Heron Inn, Peek'n Peak Conference Ctr to Peek'n Peak Ski Area
	0mm	New York/Pennsylvania state line. **Exits 3-1 are in PA.**
	3	PA 89, North East, Wattsburg, N gas food
	1b a	I-90, W to Erie, E to Buffalo.

I-86 begins/ends on I-90, exit 37.

INTERSTATE 87

Exit#	Services
176mm	US/Canada Border, NY state line, **I-87 begins/ends.**
43(175)	US 9, Champlain, E Duty Free America, W Peterbilt Trkstp/deli/dsl/scales/24hr/@ repair
42(174)	US 11 S, to Rouse's Point, Champlain, E Irving/dsl, Sunoco/Subway China Buffet, J-reck Subs, Pizza+ Ace Hardware, Chevrolet (3mi), Kinney Drug, PriceChopper, Rite Aid, USPO, W Mobil/dsl, Valero/dsl Dunkin Donuts, McDonald's, Papa John's
41(167)	NY 191, Chazy, E st police, W Miner Museum

INTERSTATE 87 Cont'd

Exit#	Services
162mm	**[RS] both lanes, full [handicap] facilities, info, litter barrels, petwalk, [phone], [picnic]**
40(160)	NY 456, Beekmantown, **E** [gas] Mobil/dsl [food] Conroy's Organics [lodging] Pt Auroche Lodge, Stonehelm Motel/café, **W** [other] Twin Ells Camping
39(158)	NY 314, Moffitt Rd, Plattsburgh Bay, **E** [gas] Mobil/dsl, Stewarts [food] A&W, Dunkin Donuts, Gino's Pizza, Gus' Rest [lodging] Rip van Winkle Motel, Super 8 [other] Plattsburgh RV Park, to VT Ferry, **W** [other] Shady Oaks Camping, to Adirondacks
38(154)	NY 22, NY 374, to Plattsburgh, **E** [gas] Mobil/dsl [food] Subway [other] Kinney Drug
37(153)	NY 3, Plattsburgh, **E** [gas] Stewarts, Sunoco [food] #1 Chinese, Buffalo Wild Wings, Burger King, China Buffet, Chipotle, Domino's, Dunkin Donuts, Five Guys, Guiseppe's Pizza, Jade Buffet, KFC, Koto Japanese, McDonald's, Michigans+ Rest., Panera Bread, Perkins, Pizza Hut, Starbucks, Subway, Taco Bell, TX Roadhouse, Wendy's [lodging] Comfort Inn, Holiday Inn [other] [H], Aldi Foods, BigLots, Buick/GMC, Family$, Ford, GNC, Kinney Drug, Michael's, Petsmart, Rite Aid, Sam's Club, Staples, TJ Maxx, TrueValue, Verizon, vet, Walgreens, Walmart, **W** [gas] Mobil, Shell, Sunoco/Jreck Subs [food] 99 Rest., Anthony's Rest., Applebee's, Butcher Block Rest., Dickey's BBQ, Dunkin Donuts, Friendly's, Ground Round, PriceChopper, Subway, Uno [lodging] Best Value Inn, Best Western, Days Inn, EconoLodge, Hampton Inn, La Quinta, Microtel [other] $Tree, Advance Parts, AT&T, AutoZone, Best Buy, Dick's, Harley-Davidson, Honda, JC Penney, Kinney Drug, Lowe's, Midas, Prays Mkt, Target, vet
151mm	Saranac River
36(150)	NY 22, Plattsburgh AFB, **E** [gas] Mobil/dsl [other] st police, U-Haul, **W** [gas] Shell/Dunkin Donuts/dsl
146mm	**[RS] nb, full [handicap] facilities, litter barrels, [phone] petwalk, [picnic], truck insp sta both lanes**
35(144)	NY 442, to Port Kent, Peru, **2-8 mi E** [other] Iroquois/Ausable Pines Camping, to VT Ferry, **W** [gas] Mobil/Dunkin Donuts/Subway/dsl, Mobil/repair [food] Livingood's Rest., McDonald's, Pasquale's Rest. [other] Aubuchon Hardware, Tops Foods, USPO, vet
143mm	emergency [phone] at 2 mi intervals begin sb/end nb
34(137)	NY 9 N, Ausable Forks, **E** [gas] Sunoco/dsl [food] Mac's Drive-in, Pleasant Corner Rest. [other] vet, **W** [other] Ausable River RV Camping, auto repair, Prays Mkt
136mm	[other] Ausable River
33(135)	US 9, NY 22, to Willsboro, **E** [gas] gas/dsl [food] food [lodging] lodging [other] RV camping, to Essex Ferry
125mm	N Boquet River
32(124)	Lewis, **E** [other] RV Camping, **W** [gas] Lukoil/dsl, Pierce's/dsl [food] Trkstp Diner [other] RV Camping, st police
123mm	**[RS] nb, [RS] sb, full [handicap] facilities, info, no restrooms, petwalk, [phone], [picnic]**
120mm	Boquet River
31(117)	NY 9 N, to Elizabethtown, Westport, **E** [gas] Mobil [lodging] HillTop Motel [other] RV camp/dump, **W** [other] [H], st police, vet
111mm	**[RS] nb, full [handicap] facilities, litter barrels, petwalk, [phone], [picnic], vending**
30(104)	US 9, NY 73, Keene Valley
99mm	**[RS] both lanes, full [handicap] facilities, litter barrels, petwalk, [phone], [picnic], trk insp sta**
29(94)	N Hudson, **E** [other] Jellystone Camping, USPO, **W** [other] Blue Ridge Falls Camping
28(88)	NY 74 E, to Ticonderoga, Schroon Lake, **E** [gas] Mt Severance Country Store, Sunoco/dsl [lodging] Maple Leaf Motel, Schroon Lake B&B [other] RV camp/dump, services on US 9, st police
27(81)	US 9 (from nb, no EZ return), Schroon Lake, **E** [gas] to gas/dsl [food] food [lodging] lodging

PLATTSBURGH

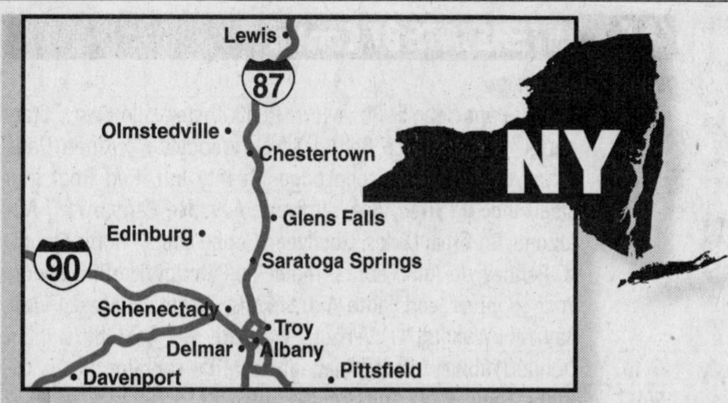

Exit#	Services
26(78)	US 9 (from sb, no EZ return), Pottersville, Schroon Lake, **E** [food] Cafe Adirondack, Family Deli [lodging] Lee's Corner Motel [other] RV Camping, **W** [gas] Valero/dsl [food] Black Bear Diner [other] USPO
25(73)	NY 8, Chestertown, **E** [gas] Crossroads Country Store [food] Suzie Q's Rest. [other] Country Haven Camping, **W** [gas] Mobil/dsl
24(67)	Bolton Landing, **E** [other] RV camping
67mm	Schroon River
66mm	**parking area sbs, [picnic]**
64mm	**parking area nbs, [picnic]**
23(58)	to US 9, Diamond Point, Warrensburg, **W** [gas] Citgo/dsl, Cumberland, Mobil/Dunkin Donuts/e85, Stewarts [food] Dragon Lee Chinese, Geroge Henry's Rest., McDonald's, Subway [lodging] Super 8 [other] Central Adirondack Tr, Family$, Ford, PriceChopper Foods, Riverview Camping, Schroon River Camping (3mi), ski area, Tops Foods
22(54)	US 9, NY 9 N, to Diamond Pt, Lake George, **E on US 9** [food] Big Smoke BBQ, Gino&Tony's, Guiseppe's Pizza, Mario's Italian, Monte Cristo's, Moose Tooth Grill [lodging] 7 Dwarfs Motel, Admiral Motel, Balsam Motel, Barberry Ct, Best Value Inn, Blue Moon Motel, Brookside Motel, EconoLodge, Georgian Lakeside Resort, Georgian Motel, Heritage Motel, Lake Crest Inn, Lake George Inn, Lake Haven Motel, Lake Motel, Marine Village Resort, Motel Montreal, Nordick's Motel, Oasis Motel, O'Sullivan's Motel, Park Lane Motel, Sundowner Motel, Surfside Motel [other] multiple services, PriceChopper Foods, same as 21, **W parking area both lanes**
21(53)	NY 9 N, Lake Geo, Ft Wm Henry, **E on US 9** [gas] Stewarts, Sunoco/dsl, Valero [food] A&W, Adirondack Brewery, Barnsider BBQ, Blacksmith Rest., Dining Room, DJ's Cafe, Gaslight Grill, Jasper's Steaks, Lobster Pot, Mama Riso's Italian, McDonald's, Mezzaluna's, Pizza Hut [lodging] Best Western, Ft William Henry Inn, Hampton Inn, Holiday Inn Resort, Lake View Inn, Lincoln Log Motel, Motel 6, Quality Inn, Rodeway Inn, Super 8, Tiki Hotel, Travelodge, Villager Motel, Windsor Hotel, Wingate Inn [other] city park, Harley-Davidson, King Phillip Camping, Lake George Camping, multiple services, Rite Aid, same as 22, USPO, waterpark, **W** [gas] Mobil/dsl/LP [lodging] Kathy's Cottages
51mm	**W** [other] Adirondack Park
20(49)	NY 149, to Ft Ann, **E** [gas] Mobil/Dunkin Donuts/dsl, Sunoco/dsl [food] Blue Moose Rest., Frank's Pizza, Johnny Rocket's, Logjam Rest., Olde Post Grille, Subway [lodging] Clarion, Comfort Suites, French Mtn Inn, Great Escape Lodge, Mohican Motel [other] 6 Flags Funpark, Factory Outlets/famous brands, Ledgeview RV Park (3mi), st police, waterpark
19(47)	NY 254, Glens Falls, **E** [gas] Mobil/dsl, Speedway, Sunoco [food] 99 Rest., Ambrosia Diner, Burger King, Chicago Grill, Dickey's BBQ, Dunkin Donuts, Five Guys, Friendly's, Giavano's Pizza, Golden Corral, KFC, Liberty Pizza, McDonald's, Moe's SW Grill, Mr B's Rest., Old China Buffet, Olive Garden, Outback Steaks, Panera

LAKE GEORGE

NY

INTERSTATE 87 Cont'd

GLENS FALLS

19(47) Continued
Bread, Papa John's, Pizza Hut, Red Lobster, Silo Rest., Starbucks, Subway, Taco Bell/LJ Silver, Wendy's Alpen Haus Motel, Budget Inn, EconoLodge, Quality Inn, Red Roof Inn, Sleep Inn $Tree, Ace Hardware, Advance Parts, AT&T, AutoZone, Bon Ton, Dick's, Goodyear, Hobby Lobby, Home Depot, JC Penney, Jo-Ann Fabrics, Meineke, Petco, Price Rite Foods, PriceChopper Foods, Rite Aid, Staples, Target, TJ Maxx, Tuesday Morning, USPO, Verizon, Walmart, **W** Mobil/Dunkin Donuts/Subway/dsl Ramada/rest. st police

18(45) Glens Falls, **E** Gulf/Subway/e-85/dsl, Speedway/dsl, Sunoco/dsl Carl R's Café, Dunkin Donuts, Pizza Hut, Steve's Place Rest. Days Inn H, CVS Drug, Hannaford Foods, Toyota, U-Haul, Walgreens, **W** Stewarts McDonald's, Taco Bell Super 8

43mm **both lanes, full facilities, litter barrels, petwalk, vending**

42mm Hudson River

17(40) US 9, S Glen Falls, **E** Citgo/dsl, Gulf, Speedway/Blimpie/Dunkin Donuts, Sunoco/dsl, Valero/Subway/dsl Dunkin Donuts, Fitzgerald's Steaks Budget Inn, Landmark Motel (1mi) Adirondack RV Camp, auto/truck repair/transmissions, Suzuki, vet, **W** Moreau Lake SP

16(36) Ballard Rd, Wilton, **E** Coldbrook Campsites, golf, **W** Mobil, Stewart's, Sunoco/Scotty's Rest./dsl/scales/24hr Mt View Acres Motel Alpin Haus RV Ctr

SARATOGA SPRINGS

15(30) NY 50, NY 29, Saratoga Springs, **E** Speedway/dsl, Sunoco 99 Rest., Applebee's, Burger King, Chicago Grill, Chipotle Mexican, Denny's, Dunkin Donuts, Five Guys, Friendly's, Golden Corral, KFC/Taco Bell, McDonald's, Moe's SW Grill, Osaka, Panera Bread, Subway, Sunny Wok, TGIFriday's Comfort Inn AT&T, Barnes&Noble, Best Buy, BJ's Whse, BonTon, Dick's, Ford, GNC, Hannaford Foods, Healthy Living Mkt, Home Depot, JC Penney, Kohl's, Lowe's, Mazda, Old Navy, Petsmart, PriceChopper Foods, Rite Aid, Staples, Subaru, Target, TJ Maxx, Toyota, Walgreens, Walmart, **W** Residence Inn H

14(28) NY 9P, Schuylerville, **2 mi W** Hampton Inn, Holiday Inn H, museum, racetrack

13(25) US 9, Saratoga Springs, **E** Bentley's Rest., DeLucia's Deli, Saratoga Pizza Place Budget Inn, Locust Grove Motel Ballston Spa SP, Nissan, **W** Mobil/Dunkin Donuts/dsl, Stewarts Finish Line Rest., Hibachi Grill, Jack Dillon's Rest., PJ's BBQ Best Western, Hilton Garden (4mi), Roosevelt Inn/rest., Top Hill Hotel Saratoga SP, vet

12(21) NY 67, Malta, **E** Getty/dsl, Sunoco/dsl Bentley's Rest., Dunkin Donuts, KFC/Taco Bell, Malta Diner, McDonald's, Starbucks, Subway Fairfield Inn AT&T, CVS Drug, GNC, PriceChopper Foods, Saratoga NHP, st police, Stewart's, Verizon, **W** Hyatt Place URGENT CARE

11(18) Round Lake Rd, Round Lake, **W** Gulf/dsl, Sunoco/dsl Mulligan's Rest. Hannaford Foods, Rite Aid, Stewarts

10(16) Ushers Rd, **E** Speedway/Dunkin Donuts/dsl, Xtra/dsl Ferretti's Rest. auto repair, **W** Stewarts

14mm **nb, full facilities, info, litter barrels, petwalk, vending**

9(13) NY 146, Clifton Park, **E** Speedway/Dunkin Donuts/dsl, USA Burger King, Caputo's Pizza, Chili's, Cracker Barrel, Delmonico's Steaks, Giffy's BBQ, Harborhouse Fish Fry, Mr Subb, Peddler's Grill, Pizza Hut, Red Robin, Snyder's Rest., Subway, Wheatfields Bistro Comfort Suites, Holiday Inn Express,

9(13) Continued
Residence Inn Advance Parts, Aldi Foods, BigLots, Goodyear/auto, Home Depot, Kohl's, Lowe's, Michael's, Midas, Petco, Rite Aid, Target, vet, **W** Mobil, Sunoco/dsl 5 Guys Burgers, 99 Rest., Bellini's Italian, Brick House Pizza, Buffalo Wild Wings, Chipotle Mexican, Dickey's BBQ, Dunkin Donuts, East Palace, East Wok, Friendly's, IHOP, La Fiesta, McDonald's, Moe's SW Grill, Olive Garden, Outback Steaks, Panera Bread, Pasta Pane, Ruby Tuesday, Salad Creations, Shane's Rib Shack, Starbucks, Subway, Taco Bell, TGIFriday's, Wendy's Best Western, Hampton Inn, Hilton Garden $Tree, AT&T, Chevrolet, CVS Drug, Firestone/auto, GNC, Hannaford Foods, JC Penney, Jo-Ann Fabrics, Marshall's, Petsmart, PriceChopper Foods, st police, Staples, Verizon, Walgreens

8a(12) Grooms Rd, to Waterford

8(10) Crescent, Vischer Ferry, **E** Speedway/Blimpie/Godfather's/dsl McDonald's USPO, **W** Gulf/NY Pizza/dsl, Sunoco Dunkin Donuts, Pancho's Mexican, Tufanos Pizza Ace Hardware, CVS Drug, Stewarts

8mm Mohawk River

7(7) NY 7, Troy, **E on US 9 N** Speedway/dsl Century House, Mr Subb Clarion, Comfort Inn, Days Inn, Holiday Inn Express, Sycamore Motel $General, Acura, Ford, Infiniti, Lexus, Nissan, Rite Aid, Volvo, **E on US 9 S** Sunoco Dunkin Donuts, McDonald's, Red Robin, Subway Hobby Lobby, Marshall's

6(6) NY 2, to US 9, Schenectady, **E** Mobil, Speedway Applebee's, Boston Mkt, Chicago Grill, ChuckeCheese, Circle Diner, Firehouse Subs, Joe's Crabshack, Mr Subb, Panera Bread, Rafferty's, Red Robin, Sake Japanese, Starbucks, Wendy's Cocca's Inn, La Quinta, Travelodge $Tree, CVS Drug, GNC, Hannaford Foods, Home Depot, Lowe's, Mavis Discount Tire, Michael's, Mkt Bistro, Petsmart, same as 7, Sam's Club, Staples, Toyota, VW, Walmart, **W** Mobil/dsl, Stewart's Carraba's, Chipotle Mexican, Denny's, DiBella's Subs, Dunkin Donuts, Kings Buffet, Ruby Tuesday, Subway Microtel, Quality Inn, Super 8 Goodyear/auto, Target, TJ Maxx, Verizon

5(5) NY 155 E, Latham, **E** DeeDee's Rest., Philly's Grill USPO

4(4) NY 155 W, Wolf Rd, **E on Wolf Rd** Mobil/Subway, Speedway/dsl, Sunoco 99 Rest., Arby's, Buffalo Wagon, Burger King, Capital Buffet, Chipotle Mexican, CiCi's Pizza, Denny's, Dunkin Donuts, Macaroni Grill, Maxie's Grill, McDonald's, Moe's SW Grill, Olive Garden, Outback Steaks, Pizza Hut, Red Lobster, Reel Seafood Co, Samurai, Starbucks, Subway, Ted's Fishfry, TX Roadhouse, Wolf Rd Diner, Wolf Rd Diner, Wolfs 1-11 Best Western, Courtyard, Hampton Inn, Holiday Inn, Homewood Suites, Marriott, Red Roof Inn, Staybridge Suites Chevrolet, CVS Drug, Firestone/auto, Hannfords Foods, Trader Joe's, **W** Bluestone Bistro, Koto Japanese Desmond Hotel, Hotel Indigo to Heritage Park

ALBANY

2(2) NY 5, Central Ave, **E on Wolf Rd** Mobil/dsl, Sunoco Bonefish Grill, Bucca Italian, Cheesecake Factory, Chili's, Delma's Diner, Five Guys, Honeybaked Ham, Hooters, IHOP, Panera Bread, PF Chang's, Starbucks, Taco Bell, Wendy's Cocca's Inn, Comfort Inn, Scottish Inn, SpringHill Suites, Travelodge Barnes&Noble, BJ's Whse/gas, Goodyear/auto, Jo-Ann Fabrics, Kost Tire, LL Bean, Lowe's, Macy's, Marshall's, PetCo, Staples, Target, Whole Foods Mkt, **W** Gulf/dsl, Mobil, USA/dsl Delmonico's Steaks, Domino's, Dunkin Donuts, La Fiesta Mexican, McDonald's, Moe's SW Grill, Smokey Bones BBQ, Subway, Truman's Grill, Wendy's Days Inn, EconoLodge, Howard Johnson, Motel 6, Quality Inn, Super 8

NY

INTERSTATE 87 Cont'd

2(2) Continued
Advance Parts, AT&T, Buick/GMC, Cadillac, Krause's Candy, Midas, PepBoys, ShopRite/gas, Subaru, Verizon, Walgreens

1W(1) NY State Thruway (from sb), I-87 S to NYC, I-90 W to Buffalo

1E(1) I-90 E (from sb), to Albany, Boston

1S(1) to US 20, Western Ave, **E on US 20** Getty 99 Rest., Burger King, Chipotle Mexican, Coldstone, Creo, Dunkin Donuts, Five Guys, Starbucks, TGIFriday's Best Western, CVS Drug, Days Inn, Hampton Inn AT&T, USPO, Verizon, vet, **W on US 20** Mobil, USA Capital City Diner, Dunkin Donuts, Hana Grill, Ichiban Japanese, McDonald's Adirondack Tires, PriceChopper Foods

1N(1) I-87 N (from nb), to Plattsburgh

149 I-87 N to Montreal, NY State Thruway goes west to Buffalo (I-90), S to NYC (I-87)

24(148) I-90 and I-87 N

23(142) I-787, to Albany, US 9 W, **E on US 9 W** Cumberland Farms/Dunkin Donuts/dsl, Sunoco/dsl Comfort Inn to Knickerbocker Arena, transmissions, **W** Stewarts Days Inn

139mm **parking area sb, litter barrels,**

22(135) NY 396, to Selkirk

21a(134) I-90 E, to MA Tpk, Boston

127mm **New Baltimore Travel Plaza both lanes,** Mobil/dsl Famous Famiglia, Quiznos, Roy Rogers, Starbucks, TCBY atm, info, wi-fi

21b(124) US 9 W, NY 81, to Coxsackie, **W** Sunoco/dsl, Trvl Plaza/Citgo/rest./dsl/scales/24hr McDonald's Best Western, Budget Inn, Holiday Inn Express, Red Carpet Inn $Tree, Boat'n RV Whse, repair, vet

21(114) NY 23, Catskill, **E** Mobil, Sunoco/dsl Catskill Motel/rest. (2mi), Pelokes Motel (2mi) Home Depot, to Rip van Winkle Br, transmissions, visitors ctr, **W** Anthony's Banquet Hall Astoria Motel, Rip Van Winkle Motel to Hunter Mtn/Windham Ski Areas

103mm **Malden Service Area nb,** Mobil/dsl Carvel Ice Cream, Hotdogs, McDonald's atm, **parking area sb,**

20(102) NY 32, to Saugerties, **E** Mobil/dsl, Stewarts, Sunoco Dunkin Donuts, Giordano's Pizza, McDonald's, Pizza Star, Starway Café, Subway Advance Parts, Big Lots, Chrysler/Dodge/Jeep, CVS Drug, Family$, PriceChopper Foods, Verizon, **W** Speedway/Blimpie/Dunkin Donuts/dsl, Sunoco/dsl Land&Sea Grill, Saugerties Diner Comfort Inn, Howard Johnson/rest. Blue Mtn Campground (5mi), Brookside Campground (10mi), KOA (2mi), Rip Van Winkle Campground (3mi), to Catskills

99mm **parking area nb, litter barrels,**

96mm **Ulster Travel Plaza sb,** Sunoco/dsl Nathan's, Pizza Hut, Roy Rogers, Starbucks, TCBY atm, , wi-fi

19(91) NY 28, Rhinecliff Br, Kingston, **E** QuickChek/dsl Blimpie, Olympic Diner, Picnic Pizza, Stadium Diner Garden Plaza Hotel, Super 8 access to I-587 E, Advance Parts, CVS Drug, Hannaford Foods, Kia, Walgreens, **W** NY Pizza, Roudigan's Steaks Motel 19, Quality Inn, Rodeway Inn, SuperLodge access to US 209, Camping World RV Ctr, Ford, Nissan

18(76) NY 299, to Poughkeepsie, New Paltz, **E** Mobil, Shell/dsl College Diner 87 Motel, EconoLodge, Rodeway Inn Lowe's, to Mid-Hudson Br, **W** Sunoco Burger King, Dunkin Donuts, Gabaletos Seafood, McDonald's, Pasquale's Pizza, Plaza Diner, Rino's Pizza, Rococo's Pizza, Subway Best Value Inn Advance Parts, AT&T, KOA (10mi), Midas, Rite Aid, ShopRite Foods, Stop'n Shop, Verizon, vet

NEWBURGH

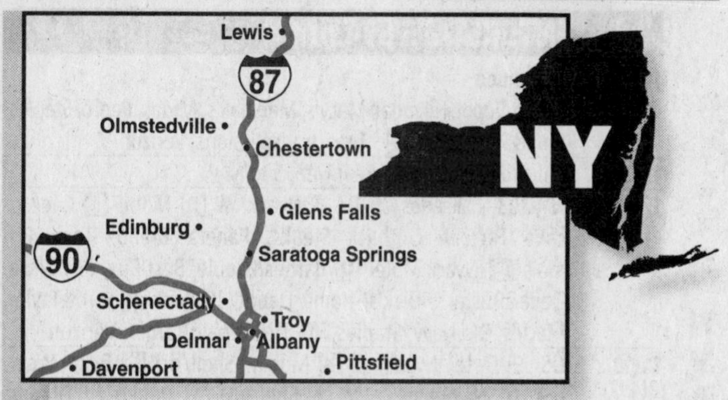

66mm **Modena service area sb,** Sunoco/dsl Carvel's Ice Cream, Chicago Grill, McDonald's, Moe's SW Grill atm, UPS, wi-fi

65mm **Plattekill Travel Plaza nb,** Sunoco/dsl Nathan's, Roy Rogers, Starbucks atm, info, wi-fi

17(60) I-84, NY 17K, to Newburgh, **E on NY 300 N** Mobil Daddy's Grill, DQ, Dunkin Donuts, Joe's Deli, McDonald's, Newburgh Buffet, Perkins, Taco Bell, Wendy's $Tree, AT&T, AutoZone, BonTon, Marshall's, Mavis Tire, Midas, Office Depot, Stop&Shop, **E on NY 300 S** Speedway/dsl, Sunoco/dsl Applebee's, Burger King, Chili's, China City, Cosimos Ristorante, Denny's, Five Guys, IHOP, Ikaros Diner, Longhorn Steaks, Neptune Diner, Panera Bread, Pizza Mia, Sonic, Starbucks, Steak&Stein, Subway, TGIFriday's, Union Sq Rest., Yobo Asian Days Inn, Howard Johnson, Ramada Inn, Super 8 $General, Adam's Food Mkt, Aldi Foods, Barnes&Noble, Buick/GMC, Cadillac/Chevrolet, Chrysler/Dodge/Jeep, Ford/Lincoln, Home Depot, Honda, Kohl's, Lowe's, Meineke, Michael's, Nissan, Petsmart, Target, Verizon, Walmart/McDonald's, Hampton Inn

16(45) US 6, NY 17, to West Point, Harriman, **W** Gulf/dsl Applebee's, Chicago Grill, Chili's, Dunkin Donuts, KFC, Outback Steaks, Panera Bread, TGIFriday's, Wendy's Days Inn, Hampton Inn $Tree, Best Buy, BJ's Whse, BMW, GNC, Home Depot, Kohl's, Michaels, Old Navy, Petsmart, st police, Staples, Target, TJ Maxx, Verizon, Walmart/Subway, Woodbury Outlet/famous brands

34mm **Ramapo Service Area sb,** Sunoco/dsl Carvel, McDonald's, Uno Pizza atm, wi-fi

33mm **Sloatsburg Travel Plaza nb,** Sunoco/dsl Burger King, Dunkin Donuts, Quiznos, Sbarro's atm, gifts, info

15a(31) NY 17 N, NY 59, Sloatsburg

15(30) I-287 S, NY 17 S, to NJ. **I-87 S & I-287 E run together.**

14b(27) Airmont Rd, Montebello, **E** Crowne Plaza, **W on NY9** Gulf/Dunkin Donuts/dsl Airmont Diner, Applebee's, Bagel Boys Cafe, Bella Vita Pizza, Friendly's, Pasta Cucina, Starbucks, Sutter's Mill Rest. Howard Johnson H, ShopRite Foods, Tall Man Tires, Walgreens, Walmart

14a(23) Garden State Pkwy, to NJ, Chestnut Ridge

14(22) NY 59, Spring Valley, Nanuet, **E** Citgo/dsl, Shell/dsl, Valero/dsl Burger King, Deliziosa Pizza, Domino's, IHOP, McDonald's, Planet Wings, Subway Fairfield Inn BMW, CarQuest, GNC, Maserati/Ferrari, Michael's, Target, TJ Maxx, Verizon, **W** Citgo, Gulf Baskin-Robbins/Dunkin Donuts, Bonefish, ChuckeCheese, Corner Bakery Cafe, Dunkin Donuts, Franko's Pizza, KFC/Taco Bell, Nanuet Diner, Panera Bread, Red Lobster, Smashburger, Starbucks, White Castle Days Inn, Hampton Inn, Hilton Garden $Tree, AT&T, Barnes&Noble, Fairway Mkt,

NY

INTERSTATE 87 Cont'd

Exit	Services
14(22)	Continued Home Depot, Hyundai, Macy's, Marshall's, Midas, PetCo, Staples, Stop&Shop Foods, STS Tires, transmissions, Verizon
13(20)	Palisades Pkwy, N to Bear Mtn, S to NJ
12(19)	NY 303, Palisades Ctr Dr, W Nyack, W [gas] Mobil [food] Cheesecake Factory, Outback Steaks, Panera Bread, Tony Roma's [lodging] Nyack Motel [other] Barnes&Noble, Best Buy, BJ's Whse, Dave&Buster's, Dick's, Home Depot, JC Penney, Lord&Taylor, Macy's, Old Navy, Staples, STS Tire/repair, Target, Verizon
11(18)	US 9W, to Nyack, E [gas] Mobil, Shell/dsl [lodging] Best Western [other] Walgreens, W [gas] Shell/dsl [food] Dunkin Donuts, McDonald's [lodging] Super 8 [other] H, J&L Repair/tire, Midas, Old World Food Mkt, VW
10(17)	Nyack (from nb), same as 11
14mm	Hudson River, Tappan Zee Br
13mm	**toll plaza**
9(12)	to US 9, to Tarrytown, E [gas] Shell, Speedway/dsl [other] CVS Drug, W [gas] Mobil [food] El Dorado West Diner [lodging] DoubleTree Hotel [other] Honda, Mavis Tire
8(11)	I-287 E, to Saw Mill Pkwy, White Plains, E [lodging] Hampton Inn, Marriott
7a(10)	Saw Mill River Pkwy S, to Saw Mill River SP, [other] Taconic SP
7(8)	NY 9A (from nb), Ardsley, W [lodging] Ardsley Acres Motel [other] H
6mm	**Ardsley Travel Plaza nb,** [gas] Sunoco/dsl [food] Burger King, Popeye's [other] vending
5.5mm	**toll plaza,** [phone]
6ba (5)	Stew Leonard Dr, to Ridge Hill, W [other] Costco, Home Depot, Stew Leonard's Farmfresh Foods
6(4.5)	Tuckahoe Dr, Yonkers, E [gas] Getty/repair [food] Marcellino's Pizza, McDonald's, Subway [lodging] Tuckahoe Motel [other] ShopRite Foods/drug, W [gas] Gulf, Mobil/dsl [food] Domino's, Dunkin Donuts, Kim Wei Chinese [lodging] Ramada Inn, Royal Regency Hotel
5(4.3)	NY 100 N (from nb), Central Park Ave, White Plains
4(4)	Cross Country Pkwy, Mile Sq Rd, E [other] Ford/Lincoln/Subaru, Macy's, Marshall's, TJ Maxx, W [gas] BP, Shell/dsl, Shell/Dunkin Donuts/dsl [food] Burger King [other] Chevrolet, Mavis Tire
3(3)	Mile Square Rd, E [other] GNC, Stop&Shop, Thriftway Drug, W [gas] BP, Citgo
2(2)	Yonkers Ave (from nb), Westchester Fair, E [gas] Mobil [other] Yonkers Speedway
1(1)	Hall Place, McLean Ave, E [food] Dunkin Donuts [other] A&P Foods/Subway
0mm	New York St Thruway and I-87 N run together to Albany
14(11)	McLean Ave, E [gas] A&P/dsl [food] Dunkin Donuts, Subway
13(10)	E 233rd, NE Tollway, [other] service plaza both lanes/Gulf/Dunkin Donuts
12(9.5)	Hudson Pkwy (from nb), Sawmill Pkwy
11(9)	Van Cortlandt Pk S
10(8.5)	W 230th St (from sb), W 240th (from nb), W [gas] Getty [food] Dunkin Donuts [other] H, Marshall's, Target
9(8)	W Fordham Rd, E [gas] BP/dsl [food] Dallas BBQ [other] H
8(7)	W 179th (from nb), W [other] Roberto Clemente SP
7(6)	I-95, US 1, S to Trenton, NJ, N to New Haven, CT
6(5)	E 153rd t, River Ave, Stadium Rd, E [other] Yankee Stadium
5(5)	E 161st, Macombs Dam Br, (exit 4 from nb), E [other] AT&T, Best Buy, Michael's, Target, Yankee Stadium
3(3)	E 138th St, Madison Ave Br, E [gas] BP/dsl
2(2)	Willis Ave, 3rd Ave Br, E [gas] Mobil/dsl, W [food] McDonald's
1(1)	Brook Ave, Hunts Point, E [gas] BP, Speedway
0mm	**I-87 begins/ends on I-278.**

NYACK · NYC AREA

INTERSTATE 88

Exit#	Services
25a	**I-90/NY Thruway. I-88 begins/ends on I-90, exit 25a.**
117mm	**toll booth** (to enter or exit NY Thruway)
25(116)	NY 7, to Rotterdam, Schenectady, **3 mi S** [gas] Gulf, Pilot/Dunkin Donuts/Subway/dsl/scales/24hr [food] Burger King, McDonald's, Peppino's Pizza, Top's Diner, Wagon Train BBQ [lodging] L&M Motel, Quality Inn [other] Frosty Acres Camping
24(112)	US 20, NY 7, to Duanesburg, N [gas] Stewart's, Valero/dsl [food] Dunkin Donuts [other] st police, S [food] Duanesburg Diner [other] USPO
23(101)	NY 30, to Schoharie, Central Bridge, N [gas] Apple Food/dsl [lodging] Holiday Motel [other] Hideaway Camping (2mi), Locust Park Camping, S [gas] Mobil/Subway/dsl [food] Apple Barrel Cafe, Dunkin Donuts [lodging] Hyland House B&B (2mi), Wedgewood B&B (2mi)
22(95)	NY 7, NY 145, to Cobleskill, Middleburgh, **2-5 mi N** [gas] Speedway/dsl, Stewart's/dsl, Sunoco [food] Dunkin Donuts, Pizza Hut, Subway [lodging] Colonial CT Motel, Holiday Motel, Super 8 [other] H, $General, $Tree, Advance Parts, AT&T, Buick/Chevrolet/GMC, Chrysler/Dodge/Jeep, Howe Caverns Camping, PriceChopper Foods, to Howe Caverns, Walmart/McDonld's, S [other] st police, Twin Oaks Camping (5mi)
21(90)	NY 7, NY 10, to Cobleskill, Warnerville, **2-3 mi N** [gas] Mobil/dsl, Speedway/dsl, Stewart's/dsl [food] Arby's, Burger King, Dairy Deli, KFC/Taco Bell, McDonald's, Pizza Hut, Subway [other] H, $General, Ace Hardware, AutoZone, CVS Drug, Mavis Tire, NAPA, PriceChopper Foods, SavaLot, TrueValue, Walmart/McDonald's
20(87)	NY 7, NY 10, to Richmondville, S [gas] Mobil/dsl, Sunoco/dsl [food] Reinhardt's Deli, Sub Express [lodging] Red Carpet Inn [other] USPO
79mm	[Rs] **wb, full [handicapped] facilities, litter barrels, petwalk, [phone], [picnic], vending**
19(76)	to NY 7, Worcester, N [gas] Stewart's, Sunoco/dsl
73mm	[Rs] **eb, full facilities, [picnic], litter barrels**
18(71)	to Schenevus, N [gas] Mirabito/dsl [food] Schenevus Rest.
17(61)	NY 7, to NY 28 N, Colliersville, Cooperstown, **2 mi N** [gas] Sunoco [lodging] Best Western (14mi), Red Carpet Inn [other] to Baseball Hall of Fame
16(59)	NY 7, to Emmons, N [food] Arby's, Brooks BBQ, Farmhouse Rest., Morey's Rest., Pizza Hut [lodging] Amber Life Motel, Rainbow Inn [other] PriceChopper Foods, Rite Aid
15	NY 28, NY 23, Oneonta, N [gas] Speedway [food] Dunkin Donuts, Friendly's, KFC [lodging] Townhouse Inn [other] H, Advance Parts, to Soccer Hall of Fame, USPO, S [gas] Mirabito/dsl, Speedway/dsl [food] Applebee's, Asian Temptations, Buffalo Wild Wings, Burger King, Denny's, McDonald's, Moe's SW, Mt Fuji Japanese, Panera Bread, Quiznos, Subway, Taco Bell, Wendy's [lodging] Budget Inn, Christopher's Lodge/rest., Courtyard, Holiday Inn, Sun Lodge, Super 8 [other] $Tree, Aldi Foods, AT&T, BJ's Whse/gas, Dick's, Ford, Hannaford Foods, Home Depot, JC Penney, Lowe's, Mr Tire, Petco, TJ Maxx, Verizon, Walmart
14(55)	Main St (from eb), Oneonta, N [gas] Stewart's, Sunoco [food] Alfresco's Italian [other] CarQuest
13(53)	NY 205, **1-2 mi N** [gas] Mirabito, Speedway, Valero/dsl [food] DQ, Dunkin Donuts, McDonald's [lodging] Celtic Motel, Hampton Inn, Motel 88 [other] Buick/Cadillac/Chevrolet/GMC, Family$, Gilbert Lake SP (11mi), Honda, Jellystone Park Camping, Kia, NAPA, Nissan, Rite Aid, st police, Subaru, to Susquehanna Tr
12(47)	NY 7, to Otego, S [gas] Mirabito/Subway/Tim Hortons/dsl/24hr
42	[Rs] **wb, facilities, tables, litter barrels**
11(40)	NY 357, to Unadilla, Delhi, S [other] KOA
39mm	[Rs] **eb, full [handicapped] facilities, litter barrels, petwalk, [phone], [picnic], vending**

COBLESKILL · ONEONTA

NY

INTERSTATE 88 Cont'd

Exit#	Services
10(38)	NY 7, to Unadilla, **2 mi N** KwikFill, Mirabito Country Motel (4mi) Great American Foods, st police, USPO
9(33)	NY 8, to Sidney, **N** Citgo/dsl, Sunoco China Buffet, Little Caesar's, McDonald's, Pizza Hut, Subway Algonkin Motel, Country Motel, Super 8 H, $General, Advance Parts, PriceChopper Foods, Tall Pines Camping, USPO
8(29)	NY 206, to Bainbridge, **N** Citgo/dsl, Sunoco Bob's Family Diner, Dunkin Donuts Algonkin Motel, Susquehanna Motel Auto Parts+, Chevrolet/GMC, Family$, Riverside RV Park, USPO, **S** to Oquage Creek Park
7(22)	NY 41, to Afton, **1-2 mi N** Mobil, Sunoco/dsl RiverClub Rest., Vincent's Rest. Afton Golf/rest., Kellystone Park, Smith-Hale HS
6(16)	NY 79, to NY 7, Harpursville, Ninevah, **S** Mirabito/Subway/dsl Gramma's Country Cafe Family$, to Nathanial Cole Park
5(12)	Martin Hill Rd, to Belden, **N** Gulf Trstp/dsl Belden Manor Camping
4(8)	NY 7, to Sanitaria Springs, **S** Speedway/dsl
3(4)	NY 369, Port Crane, **N** to Chenango Valley SP, **S** Fastrac/dsl, KwikFill
2(2)	NY 12a W, to Chenango Bridge, **N** Mirabito/Tim Horton's USPO
1(1)	NY 7 W (no wb return), to Binghamton
0mm	I-81, N to Syracuse, S to Binghamton. **I-88 begins/ends on I-81.**

INTERSTATE 90

Exit#	Services
0mm	New York/Massachusetts state line
(B23)	NY 22, to Austerlitz, New Lebanon, W Stockbridge, **N** Citgo/dsl/scales/24hr, Loves/Dunkin Donuts/Subway/dsl/scales/24hr, **S** Sunoco/dsl Berkshire Travel Lodge Woodland Hills Camp (3mi)
(B17)	**toll plaza,**
(B15)	NY 295, Taconic Pkwy, **1-2 mi S** gas
(B7)	US 9, NY Thruway W, to I-87, **toll booth**
12(20)	US 9, to Hudson, **N** Pilot/Subway/dsl/scales/24hr, **0-3 mi S** to Van Buren NHS
18.5mm	**/weigh sta wb, full facilities, litter barrels, petwalk, , vending**
11(15)	US 9, US 20, E Greenbush, Nassau, **N** Speedway/dsl, Sunoco/dsl Dunkin Donuts st police, **S** Stewart's Mercato's Pizza, My Place Host Field Inn, Knights Inn Rite Aid, USPO, vet
10(10)	Miller Rd, to E Greenbush, **S** Mobil/dsl Dunkin Donuts Comfort Inn
9(9)	US 4, to Rensselaer, Troy, **N** Mobil/dsl Applebee's, Domino's, Dunkin Donuts, Five Guys, McDonald's, Moe's SW, OffShore Pier Rest., Panera Bread, Starbucks, Subway, Taco Bell, The Sports Grill Holiday Inn Express, Residence Inn $Tree, AT&T, CVS Drug, Home Depot, Mavis Tire/auto, PetsMart, Staples, Target, Walmart, **S** Mobil/dsl, Stewart's Cracker Barrel, Denny's, Dunkin Donuts Hampton Inn Fairfield Inn
8(8)	NY 43, Defreestville
7(7)	Washington Ave (from eb), Rensselaer
6.5mm	Hudson River
6a	I-787, to Albany
6(4.5)	US 9, Northern Blvd, to Loudonville, **N** Stewart's Mr Subb, NY Pizza Red Carpet Inn H

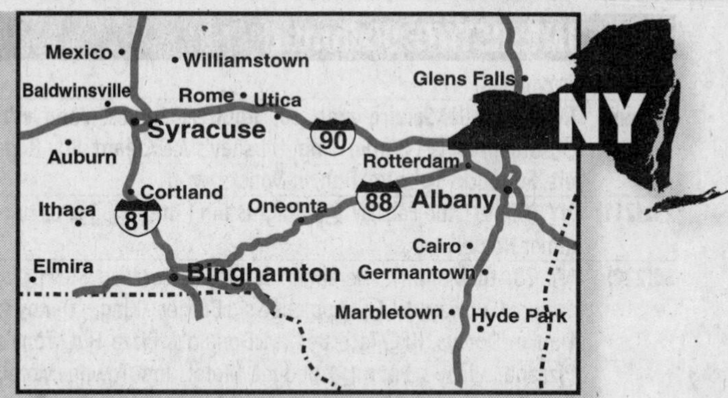

ALBANY

Exit#	Services
5a(4)	Corporate Woods Blvd
5(3.5)	Everett Rd, to NY 5, Central Ave, **S on NY 5** ShopRite, Speedway/dsl Dunkin Donuts, Gateway Diner, Hokkaido Asian, Little Caesar's, McDonald's, Popeye's, Subway, Taco Bell Motel 6, Ramada H, $Tree, Aamco, Advance Parts, AutoZone, Chevrolet, Chrysler/Dodge/Jeep, CVS Drug, Fiat, Ford, Hannaford's Foods, Home Depot, Hyundai, Kia, Mavis Tire, Mazda, Monro, Nissan, PepBoys, PriceChopper Foods, Rite Aid, ShopRite Foods, Verizon
4(3)	NY 85 S, to Slingerlands
3(2.5)	**S** State Offices
2(2)	Fuller Rd, Washington Ave, **S on Washington** Sunoco/Subway Dunkin Donuts Courtyard, CrestHill Suites, Extended Stay America, Fairfield Inn, Hilton Garden, Red Carpet Inn, TownePlace Suites same as 1S
1N(1)	I-87 N, to Montreal, to Albany Airport
1S(1)	US 20, Western Ave, **S** Mobil Black&Blue Rest., Blaze Pizza, Burger King, Capital City Diner, Chipotle Mexican, Coldstone, Creo Rest., Dave&Buster's, Dunkin Donuts, Five Guys, Hana Grill, Ichiban Japanese, McDonald's, Moe's SW Grill, Panera Bread, Peaches Cafe, Provence Rest., Starbucks, TGIFriday's, Uno Grill Hampton Inn, Residence Inn AT&T, Best Buy, CVS Drug, Dick's, Home Depot, JC Penney, Macy's, Michael's, Old Navy, PetsMart, PriceChopper Foods, USPO, Verizon, Walmart
24(149)	I-87 N to Albany, Montreal, S to NYC
153mm	**Guilderland Service Area eb,** Mobil/dsl McDonald's
25(154)	I-890, NY 7, NY 146, to Schenectady
25a(159)	I-88 S, NY 7, to Binghamton, **S** Pilot/Dunkin Donuts/Subway/dsl/scales/24hr
26(162)	I-890, NY 5 S, Schenectady
168mm	**Pattersonville Service Area wb,** Mobil/dsl Hershey's, Roy Rogers, Starbucks atm, NY Mkt, wi-fi
172mm	**Mohawk Service Area eb,** Mobil/dsl McDonald's
27(174)	NY 30, Amsterdam, **1 mi N** Mobil/dsl, Valero/Dunkin Donuts/dsl Best Value Inn, Super 8, Valleyview Motel Alpin Haus RV Ctr (3mi)
28(182)	NY 30A, Fonda, **N** Citgo/rest/dsl/motel/24hr, Sunoco/dsl, TA/Country Pride/dsl/motel/scales/24hr/@ Dunkin Donuts, McDonald's Holiday Inn (7mi), Microtel (4mi), Riverside Motel, Super 8 (8mi) H, st police, truck repair
184mm	**parking area/truck insp area both lanes, litter barrels,**
187mm	**wb, full facilities, living history site**
29(194)	NY 10, Canajoharie, **N** Cumberland, Stewart's/dsl McDonald's, Subway $General, Ace Hardware, BigLots, Rite Aid, Riverfront Park, USPO, **S** Beavers/dsl, Citgo/dsl, Sunoco Mercato Pizza, Village Rest. NAPACare, USPO

INTERSTATE 90 Cont'd

Exit#	Services
210mm	**Indian Castle Service area eb, Iroquois Service Area wb,** Mobil/dsl Burger King, Hershey's Ice Cream, Roy Rogers, Starbucks atm, Dunkin Donuts, wi-fi
29a(211)	NY 169, to Little Falls, N Knights Inn (3mi) H, to Herkimer Home
30(220)	NY 28, to Mohawk, Herkimer, N FasTrac/dsl, Stewart's, Sunoco/Subway/dsl Applebee's, Burger King, Denny's, Dunkin Donuts, KFC/Taco Bell, McDonald's, Pizza Hut, Tony's Pizzaria, Vinny's Pizza Budget Motel, Inn Towne Motel, Red Roof Inn $General, $Tree, Advance Parts, AutoZone, Mavis Tire/auto, Rite Aid, Verizon, vet, Walmart, S FasTrac Little Caesar's, Red Apple Chinese Red Carpet Inn (2mi) Family$, to Cooperstown (Baseball Hall of Fame)
227mm	**Schuyler Service Area wb,** Mobil/dsl Breyer's, McDonald's atm, st police
31(233)	I-790, NY 8, NY 12, to Utica, N Citgo/dsl, Fastrac, Sunoco Applebee's, Burger King, Charlie's Pizza, Franco's Pizza, Good Friend Chinese $Tree, Bass Pro Shop, BigLots, BJ's Whse/gas, Lowe's, PriceChopper Foods, Rite Aid, Walmart/McDonald's, S Speedway/dsl Babe's Grill, Delmonico's Steaks, Denny's, Dunkin Donuts, McDonald's, Moe's SW, Subway, Taco Bell, Wendy's Best Western, Days Inn, Fairfield Inn, Hampton Inn, Happy Journey Motel, Holiday Inn Epress, Knights Inn, Red Roof Inn, Rest Inn AT&T
236mm	I-790 (from eb), to Utica
237.5mm	Erie Canal
238mm	Mohawk River
32(243)	NY 232, Westmoreland, **4-8 mi N** EconoLodge, Quality Inn, Red Carpet Inn, Scottish Inn, **5 mi S** Stewart's Hampton Inn
244mm	**Oneida Service Area eb,** Sunoco/dsl Burger King, Sbarro's, Starbucks atm, gifts
250mm	**parking area eb, litter barrels,**
33(253)	NY 365, to Vernon Downs, Verona, N SavOn Gas/Dunkin Donuts/dsl Inn at Turning Stone, S SavOn Gas/LP/repair Dunkin Donuts, Recovery Grill Fairfield Inn, La Quinta H, Turning Stone Casino
256mm	**parking area wb, litter barrel,**
34(262)	NY 13, to Canastota, N Verona Beach SP Camping, S SavOn/dsl, Sunoco Dunkin Donuts, McDonald's Days Inn, Graziano Motel/rest. Boxing Hall of Fame
266mm	**Chittenango Service Area wb,** Sunoco/dsl Sbarro's, Starbucks atm, wi-fi
34a(277)	I-481, to Syracuse, Chittenango
35(279)	NY 298, The Circle, Syracuse, S Valero/dsl Burger King, Denny's, Dunkin Donuts, East Wok, Grimaldi's, Jimmy John's, Joey's Italian, Jreck Subs, Justin's Grill, Mafia Pizza, McDonald's, Ruby Tuesday Baymont Inn, Best Value Inn, Candlewood Suites, Comfort Inn, Courtyard, Cresthill Suites, Days Inn, Doubletree Inn, Embassy Suites, Extended Stay America, Hampton Inn, Hilton Garden, Homewood Suites, Motel 6, Quality Inn, Ramada Ltd, Red Roof Inn, Residence Inn, Rodeway Inn, Sira Inn, SpringHill Suites, Super 8 Goodyear/auto
280mm	**Dewitt Service Area eb,** Sunoco/dsl Edy's Ice Cream, McDonald's
36(283)	I-81, N to Watertown, S to Binghamton
37(284)	7th St, Electronics Pkwy, to Liverpool, N Best Western, S Speedway/Dunkin Donuts/Godfather's KFC/Taco Bell Holiday Inn, Homewood Suites, Knights Inn, Staybridge Suites Kinney Drug
38(286)	NY 57, to Liverpool, Syracuse, N Fastrac/dsl, KwikFill, Speedway Bangkok Thai, Dunkin Donuts, Pier 57 Diner, Pizza Hut, Salsarita's Grill Hampton Inn (7mi), Super 8 $Tree, Aldi Foods, Midas, NAPA, Rite Aid
39(290)	I-690, NY 690, Syracuse, N Comfort Inn/rest. Camping World RV Ctr, S Holiday Inn Express
292mm	**Warners Service Area wb,** Mobil/dsl Boston Pizza, Edy's Ice Cream, McDonald's
40(304)	NY 34, to Owasco Lake, Weedsport, N Riverforest RV Park, S Fastrac, KwikFill, Sunoco/dsl Arby's, Arnold's Rest., Cj's Rest., DB's Drive-In, Dunkin Donuts, NY Pizzaria, Old Erie Diner, Peters Pizzaria Best Western, Days Inn, Holiday Inn (12mi) $General, Ace Hardware, Bass Pro Shops (12mi), Kinney Drug, NAPA, USPO, Weedsport Foods
310mm	**Port Byron Service Area eb,** Mobil/dsl Boston Pizza, Edy's Ice Cream, McDonald's
318mm	**parking area wb, litter barrels,**
41(320)	NY 414, to Cayuga Lake, Waterloo, S Nice'n Easy/dsl Petro/Iron Skillet/dsl/scales/24hr/@ MaGee Country Diner Hampton Inn (4mi), Holiday Inn (4mi), Microtel (4mi) Cayuga Lake SP/camping, Waterloo Outlets/famous brands (3mi)
324mm	**Junius Ponds Service Area wb,** Sunoco/dsl Dunkin Donuts, Roy Rogers atm, wi-fi
42(327)	NY 14, to Geneva, Lyons, N RV camping, S Mobil/7-11 dsl/scales Belherst (6mi), Best Value Inn (6mi), Days Inn (6mi), Hampton Inn (6mi), Ramada Inn (6mi), Red Carpet Inn Junius Ponds RV Camping, Waterloo Outlets/famous brands (3mi)
337mm	**Clifton Springs Service Area eb,** Sunoco/dsl Roy Rogers, Starbucks atm, gifts
43(340)	NY 21, to Palmyra, Manchester, N Hill Cumorah LDS H (2mi), S Sunoco/dsl Grandpa Joe's Diner, McDonald's Manchester Inn KOA (6mi)
44(347)	NY 332, Victor, S 7-11/dsl, Arrowmart/Subway, Speedway, Sunoco/dsl Dunkin Donuts, KFC, McDonald's, Park Place Rest. Best Value Inn, Budget Inn, Comfort Inn, Travelodge $General, Aldi Foods, AutoZone, casino, CVS Drug, Family$, KOA (4mi), st police, Wade's Foods
350mm	**Seneca Service Area wb,** Mobil/dsl Checker's, Tim Hortons, Villa Pizza atm, wi-fi
45(351)	I-490, NY 96, to Rochester, N Mobil/dsl Biaggi's Rest, BoneFish Grill, Champp's Grill, Distillery Rest., Five Guys, Longhorn Steaks, McDonald's, Moe's SW Grill, Olive Garden, Panera Bread, PF Chang's, Starbucks, Subway, TGIFriday's, Uno Grill Hampton Inn, Springdale Farm B&B $Tree, AT&T, Best Buy, BJ's Whse/gas, Dick's, GNC, Home Depot, JC Penney, Kohl's, Lord&Taylor, Macy's, Michael's, Old Navy, Petsmart, Rite Aid, Staples, Target, Verizon, Von Maur, Walmart, S KwikFill/dsl Burger King, Chili's, Denny's, Taco Bell, Wendy's Best Western, Holiday Inn Express, Homewood Suites, Microtel, Royal Inn Ballantyne RV Ctr
353mm	**parking area eb, litter barrels,**
46(362)	I-390, to Rochester, **N on NY 253 W** Gulf/dsl, Speedway dsl, Sunoco/dsl McDonald's, Peppermint's Rest., Tim Hortons, Wendy's Country Inn&Suites, Days Inn, Fairfield Inn, Microtel, Red Roof Inn, Super 8 Buick/GMC
366mm	**Scottsville Service Area eb,** Mobil/dsl Arby's, Tim Horton atm, info, wi-fi
376mm	**Ontario Service Area wb,** Sunoco/dsl Boston Pizza, Edy's Ice Cream, McDonald's atm, wi-fi
47(379)	I-490, NY 19, to Rochester, N Timberline Camping

SYRACUSE

ROCHESTER

INTERSTATE 90 Cont'd

BATAVIA

Exit#	Services
48(390)	NY 98, to Batavia, N Comfort Inn, Hampton Inn, Holiday Inn Express, S Citgo Applebee's, Bob Evans, Subway, Taco Bell, Tim Horton's, Yume Asian Bistro Best Western, Budget Inn, Clarion, Days Inn, La Quinta, Red Roof Inn, Super 8, Super 8 AT&T, AutoZone, BJ's Whse, Dick's, Home Depot, Kohl's, Marshall's, Michael's, PetCo, Rite Aid, Target, Tops Foods, Verizon, Walmart/Subway
397mm	**Pembroke Service Area eb,** Sunoco/dsl Checker's, Tim Hortons atm, gifts, wi-fi
48a(402)	NY 77, Pembroke, S FLYING J/Denny's/Subway/dsl/LP/scales/24hr, TA/Valero/Country Pride/dsl/scales/24hr/@ Subway Darien Lake Lodge/camping, EconoLodge Sleepy Hollow Camping (8mi)
412mm	**Clarence Service Area wb,** Sunoco/dsl Arby's, Tim Hortons atm, full facilities, info, wi-fi
49(417)	NY 78, Depew, **0-3 mi** N Delta Sonic, Mobil/dsl, Sunoco, Sunoco Applebee's, Arby's, Burger King, Carmine's Rest., Chili's, Chipotle, Coldstone, Cracker Barrel, Dave&Buster's, Dibella's Subs, DQ, Duff's Wings, Dunkin Donuts, Firehouse Subs, Five Guys, Friendly's, Garden Buffet, Jimmy John's, KFC, La Tolteca, McDonald's, Mighty Taco, Moe's SW Grill, Old Country Buffet, Olive Garden, Panera Bread, Picasso's Pizza, Pita Gourmet, Pizza Hut, Pizza Plant, Pomegranate, Protocol Rest., Quaker Steak&Lube, Red Lobster, Russel's Steaks, Salsarita's, Santora's Pizza, Shogun, Starbucks, Starbucks, Subway, Taco Bell, Ted's HotDogs, TGIFriday's, Tim Horton, Tully's Rest., Wendy's Clarion, Econolodge, Microtel, Motel 6, Salvatore's Hotel, Springhill Suites, Staybridge Suites, Super 8 $Tree, Acura, Advance Parts, Aldi Foods, AT&T, AutoZone, Barnes&Noble, Best Buy, BigLots, BJ's Whse/gas, BonTon, Buick/GMC, Chevrolet, Chrysler/Dodge/Jeep, Dick's, Dunn Tire, Firestone/auto, Ford, Goodyear/auto, Hobby Lobby, Home Depot, Honda, Hyundai, JC Penney, Jo-Ann Fabrics, Kohl's, Lowe's, Marshall's, Mavis Tire, Michael's, Office Depot, PetCo, PetsMart, Rite Aid, SteinMart, Target, TJ Maxx, Top's Food/deli, Tuesday Morning, Verizon, vet, Walgreens, Walmart/Subway, Wegman's Foods, S Kwikfill, Mobil/dsl Bob Evans, China 1, Dunkin Donuts, Italian Village, John&Mary's Cafe, McDonald's, Salvatore's Italian, Subway, Tim Horton Garden Place Hotel, Hospitality Inn, La Quinta, Red Roof Inn $Tree, 7-11, Aamco, CarQuest, Top's Foods/gas
419mm	**toll booth**
50(420)	I-290 to Niagara Falls
50a(421)	Cleveland Dr (from eb)
51(422)	NY 33 E, Buffalo, S , st police
52(423)	Walden Ave, to Buffalo, N Applebees, Burger King, Chipotle, Famous Dave's BBQ, IHOP, McDonald's, Ruby Tuesday, Starbucks, Subway, TGIFriday's, Tim Horton Hampton Inn, Holiday Inn Express, Residence Inn $Tree, Aldi Foods, AT&T, AutoZone, Firestone/auto, Ford, Goodyear/auto, Home Depot, Michael's, Office Depot, PetsMart, PriceRite Mkt, Target, Top's Foods, Walmart/Subway, S Delta Sonic, Jim's Trk Plaza/Sunoco/dsl/rest./scales/24hr, KwikFill Alton's Rest., Bar Louie's, Bravo Italiano, Cheesecake Factory, Dunkin Donuts, Gordon Biersch arrest., Jack Astor's Grill, Longhorn Steaks, McDonald's, Melting Pot, Mighty Taco, Milton's Rest., Olive Garden, Panera Bread, PF Chang's, Pizza Hut, Smokey Bones BBQ, Taco Bell, Texas de Brazil Steaks, Tim Horton, Zahng's Buffet Home 2 Suites, Millenium Hotel, Oak Tree Inn Best Buy, Burlington Coats, Cabela's, Dick's, Dunn Tire, JC Penney, Lord&Taylor, Macy's, Marshall's, Mavis Tire, Niagara Hobby, Sam's Club, Verizon

DEPEW

BUFFALO

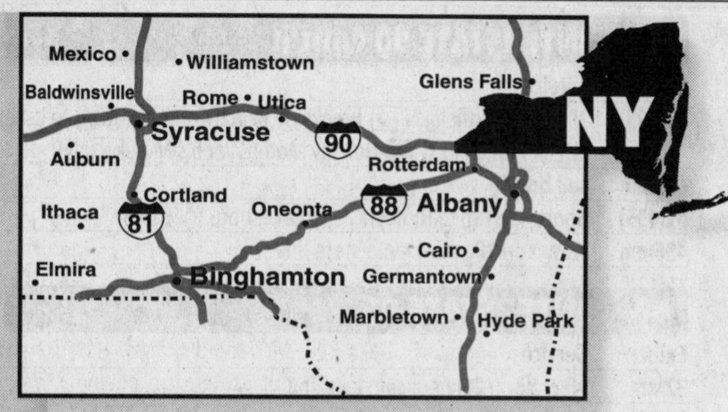

HAMBURG

Exit#	Services
52a(424)	William St
53(425)	I-190, to Buffalo, Niagara Falls, N Best Western
54(428)	NY 400, NY 16, to W Seneca, E Aurora
55(430)	US 219, Ridge Rd, Orchard Park, S Delta Sonic, Sunoco Denny's, Ferro's NY Puzza, Mighty Taco, Subway, Tim Horton, Wendy's Country Inn&Suites, Hampton Inn, Staybridge Suites $General, Aldi Foods, AT&T, BigLots, Goodyear/auto, Home Depot, Mr Tire, Pepboys, Petco, Tops Foods/gas, Verizon, Wegman's Foods
431mm	**toll booth**
56(432)	NY 179, Mile Strip Rd, N Gulf/dsl, Sunoco, Valero Blasdell Pizza, China King, DiPallo's Rest., Odyssey Rest., Whse Rest. EconoLodge $General, CarQuest, CVS Drug, repair, Rite Aid, SaveALot Foods, USPO, S Applebee's, Boston Mkt, Buffalo Wild Wings, Chipotle, ChuckeCheese, El Canelo Mexican, Firehouse Subs, Five Guys, Friendly's, McDonald's, Mongolian Buffet, Olive Garden, Outback Steaks, Panera Bread, Pizza Hut, Red Lobster, Ruby Tuesday, Starbucks, Subway, TGIFriday's, Wendy's $Tree, Aldi Foods, Barnes&Noble, Best Buy, BJ's Whse, BonTon, Firestone/auto, Hobby Lobby, Home Depot, JC Penney, Jo-Ann Etc, Old Navy, PepBoys, TJ Maxx, Wegman's Foods
57(436)	NY 75, to Hamburg, N Mobil/Dunkin Donuts/dsl Arby's, Blasdell Pizza, Buffalo Grill, Denny's, McDonald's, Tim Horton, Uncle Joe's Diner, Waterstone Grill, Wendy's Comfort Inn, Holiday Inn Express, Motel 6, Red Roof Inn Ballentyne's RV Ctr, Chevrolet, Chrysler/Dodge/Jeep, Ford, Lowe's, repair, transmissions, Walmart, S Go Gas, Kwikfill/dsl, Mad J's Burger King, Hideaways Rest., Pizza Hut, Savory Cafe, Subway, Tim Horton Quality Inn, Super 8 $General, Advance Parts, AutoZone, Camping World, Carquest, Goodyear/auto, USPO, vet, Hampton Inn
442mm	**parking area both lanes, litter barrels,**
57a(445)	to Eden, Angola, **2 mi** N Sunoco/dsl
447mm	**Angola Service Area both lanes,** Sunoco/dsl McDonald's, Moe's SW Grill, Subway atm, gifts, wi-fi
58(456)	US 20, NY 5, to Silver Creek, Irving, N Kwikfill, Seneca Hawk Trkstp/dsl Burger King, Colony Rest., Dunkin Donuts, McDonald's, Millie's Rest., Primo's Rest., Subway, Sunset Bay, Sunset Grill, Tim Hortons, Tom's Rest. Lighthouse Inn H, auto repair, to Evangola SP, USPO
59(468)	NY 60, Fredonia, Dunkirk, N Clarion (2mi), Dunkirk Motel (4mi) Lake Erie SP/camping (7mi), S Country Fair/dsl, Kwikfill/dsl Applebee's, Arby's, Azteca Cantina, Bob Evans, Burger King, Denny's, Dunkin Donuts, KFC/Taco Bell, Little Caesar's, McDonald's, Pizza Hut, Subway, Tim Hortons, Wendy's, Wing City Grille Best Western, Comfort Inn, Days Inn $General, $Tree, Advance Parts, Aldi Foods, AT&T, AutoZone, BigLots, Ford/Lincoln, GMC, GNC, Home Depot, Midas, Monro, Rite Aid, TJ Maxx, Tops Foods/gas, Verizon, Walmart/Subway

NY

= gas = food = lodging = other = rest stop

INTERSTATE 90 Cont'd

Exit#	Services
60(485)	NY 394, Westfield, N Brookside Beach Camping, KOA, to Lake Erie SP/camping, S Holiday Motel, Webb's Motel H
494mm	**toll booth**
61(495)	Shortman Rd, to Ripley, N Lakeshore RV Park
496mm	New York/Pennsylvania state line

INTERSTATE 95

Exit#	Services
32mm	New York/Connecticut state line
22(30)	Midland Ave (from nb), Port Chester, Rye, W H, Home Depot, Staples
21(29)	I-287 W, US 1 N, to White Plains, Port Chester, Tappan Zee
20(28)	US 1 S (from nb), Port Chester, E Shell CVS Drug, Ford, Subaru, USPO
19(27)	Playland Pkwy, Rye, Harrison
18b(25)	Mamaroneck Ave, to White Plains, E Shell, Speedway Domino's A&P Foods, Mavis Tire
18a(24)	Fenimore Rd (from nb), Mamaroneck, E Citgo, Gulf
17(20)	Chatsworth Ave (from nb, no return), Larchmont
19.5mm	**toll plaza**
16(19)	North Ave, Cedar St, New Rochelle, E Applebee's, Buffalo Wild Wings, TX Roadhouse Radisson, Residence Inn ShopRite, Toyota, USPO, W H
15(16)	US 1, New Rochelle, The Pelhams, E GasTrack/dsl, Super-Gas AutoZone, Costco/gas, CVS Drug, Harley-Davidson, Home Depot, Walgreens, W repair
14(15)	Hutchinson Pkwy (from sb), to Whitestone Br
13(16)	Conner St, to Mt Vernon, E Gulf/dsl Ramada Inn, W McDonald's Holiday Motel H, Goodyear/auto, Pepboys
12(15.5)	Baychester Ave (exits left from nb)
11(15)	Bartow Ave, Co-op City Blvd, E Applebee's, Bartow Pizza, Burger King, Checker's, Dallas BBQ, Genarro's Pizza, McDonald's, Panera Bread, Popeye's, Red Lobster, Zinhi Chinese $Tree, AT&T, Barnes&Noble, JC Penney, Marshall's, Old Navy, PathMark Foods, Staples, Verizon, W BP/Dunkin Donuts, Sunoco/dsl, Wave/dsl ChuckeCheese, Dunkin Donuts, Pizza Hut, TGIFriday's Aldi Foods, Home Depot
10(14.5)	Gun Hill Rd (exits left from nb), W Pelham Bay Hotel/diner
9(14)	Hutchinson Pkwy
8c(13.5)	Pelham Pkwy W
8b(13)	Orchard Beach, City Island
8a(12.5)	Westchester Ave (from sb)
7c(12)	Pelham Bay Park (from nb), Country Club Rd
7b(11.5)	E Tremont (from sb), W Super FoodTown
7a(11)	I-695 (from sb), to I-295 S, Throgs Neck Br
6b(10.5)	I-278 W (from sb), I-295 S (from nb)
6a(10)	I-678 S, Whitestone Bridge
5b(9)	Castle Hill Ave, W Sunoco McDonald's
5a(8.5)	Westchester Ave, White Plains Rd
4b(8)	Bronx River Pkwy, Rosedale Ave, E BP/Dunkin Donuts
4a(7)	I-895 S, Sheridan Expsy
3(6)	3rd Ave, W H
2b(5)	Webster Ave, W H
2a(4)	Jerome Ave, to I-87
1c(3)	I-87, Deegan Expswy, to Upstate
1b(2)	Harlem River Dr
1a(1)	US 9, NY 9A, H Hudson Pkwy, 178th St, downtown
0mm	New York/New Jersey state line, Hudson River, Geo Washington Br

NYC AREA

NY

INTERSTATE 190 (Buffalo)

Exit#	Services
25.5mm	US/Canada Border, US Customs
25b a	R Moses Pkwy, NY 104, NY 265, Lewiston, E H
24	NY 31, Witmer Rd, E H, st police
23	NY 182, Porter Rd, Packard Rd, E Sunoco/dsl Applebees, Buffalo Wild Wings, Burger King, Chili's, Chipotle DQ, Five Guys, Longhorn Steaks, Mighty Taco, Olive Garden Subway, Tim Horton $Tree, Big Lots, CarQuest, Chrysler/Dodge/Jeep, Fashion Outlets/famous brands, Firestone/auto Goodyear/Auto, Hobby Lobby, Jo-Ann Fabrics, Marshall's, Mavis Tire, Mr Tire, NAPA, Petco, Sam's Club/gas, U-Haul, Verizon Walmart/Subway, Wegman's, W Wendy's Aldi Foods
22	US 62, Niagara Falls Blvd, E Sunoco Arby's, Bob Evans Burger King, Denny's, Dunkin Donuts, Honey's Eatery, KFC McDonald's, My Thai, Pizza Hut, Popeye's, Starbucks, Subway Taco Bell, Wendy's Beat Value Inn, Budget Host, Carava Motel, Hampton Inn, Pelican Motel, Quality Inn, Red Carpe Inn, Super 8, Swiss Cottage Inn $Tree, Advance Parts, AT&T Dunn Tire, Ford, Rite Aid, Target, TJ Maxx, Top's Foods/gas Walgreens, W Econolodge, La Quinta Home Depot
21a	La Salle Expswy
21	NY 384, Buffalo Ave, R Moses Pkwy, E Ashram Hotel, Sheraton, W Gulf American Falls, casino, to NF SP
20.5mm	Niagara River East, **toll booth sb**
20b a	Long Rd, E Budget Motel Kelly's Country Store
19	Whitehaven Rd, E Gulf/dsl, Noco Gas McDonald's Chateu Motel (2mi), Holiday Inn (4mi) $Tree, funpark, KOA (1mi), Top's Foods/gas, W Chevrolet, Hyundai, Toyota, vet
18b a	NY 324 W, Grand Island Blvd, E Gulf/dsl, NOCO/dsl, Sunoco/dsl Burger King, McDonald's, Tim Horton, Wendy's Chateu Motel, Grand Suites $Tree, Advance Parts Tops/gas, W Beaver Island SP
17.5mm	Niagara River East, Niagara River East, **toll booth**
17	NY 266, last free exit nb
16	I-290 E, to I-90, Albany
15	NY 324, Kenmore Ave, E 7-11 city park, W U-Hau
14	Ontario St, E KwikFill McDonald's, Tim Horton Advance Parts, Family$
13	(from nb), same as 14
12	Amherst St, (from nb), downtown
11	NY 198, Buffalo, E First Line
9	Porter Ave, to Peace Bridge, Ft Erie
8	NY 266, Niagara St, E Adams Mark Hotel, W Courtyard, downtown
7	NY 5 W, Church St, Buffalo, downtown
6	Elm St, E H, downtown, W Arena
5	Louisiana St, Buffalo, downtown
4	Smith St, Fillmore Ave, Buffalo, downtown
3	NY 16, Seneca St, from sb, W CarQuest
2	US 62, NY 354, Bailey Ave, Clinton St
1	Ogden St, E Sunoco Wendy's Best Western, Comfort Inn Big Lots, CVS Drug, Family$
.5mm	**toll plaza nb**
0mm	**I-90. I-190 begins/ends on I-90, exit 53.**

NIAGARA FALLS

BUFFALO

INTERSTATE 287 (New York City)

Exit#	Services
12	I-95, N to New Haven, S to NYC. **I-287 begins/ends on I-95, exit 2**
11	US 1, Port Chester, Rye, N BP, Mobil, Sunoco Burger King, Domino's, Dunkin Donuts, McDonald's, Popeye's, Po

NYC AREA

INTERSTATE 287 (New York City) Cont'd

11	Continued Chester Diner, Subway, Taco Bell [lodging] Courtyard [other] [H], Goodyear/auto, Home Depot, Kohl's, Mavis Discount Tire, Nissan, Staples, Verizon, Whole Foods Mkt
10	Bowman Ave, Webb Ave
9N S	Hutchinson Pkwy, Merritt Pkwy, to Whitestone Br
9a	I-684, Brewster
8	Westchester Ave, to White Plains, **S** [gas] BP, Mobil [food] Buffalo Wild Wings, Cheesecake Factory, Chipotle, Five Guys, Morton's Steaks, Panera Bread, PF Chang's, Westchester Burger Co [lodging] Crowne Plaza [other] Chrysler/Dodge/Jeep, [H], Neiman Marcus, Nordstrom, Stop&Shop Foods, Walmart, Westchester Mall Place, Whole Foods Mkt
7	Taconic Pkwy (from wb), to N White Plains
6	NY 22, White Plains
5	NY 100, Hillside Ave, **S** [gas] Gulf, Lukoil [food] Applebee's, Chipotle, Dunkin Donuts, Planet Pizza, Smashburger, Subway [other] Aamco, AutoZone, GNC, Lexus, Mazda, vet
4	NY 100A, Hartsdale, **N** [gas] Shell [other] [H], **S** [gas] Mobil [food] Bamboo Garden Chinese, Burger King [other] BMW/Mini, Jaguar, Mazda/Subaru, Staples
3	Sprain Pkwy, to Taconic Pkwy, NYC
2	NY 9A, Elmsford, **N** [gas] BP, Citgo, Gulf, Mobil, Sunoco [food] Dunkin Donuts, Subway, Taco Bell [other] Mavis Discount Tire, NAPA, Sam's Club, **S** [gas] Shell [food] Wendy's
1	NY 119, Tarrytown, **N** [gas] Shell/dsl, Tesla EVC [food] Cooper's Mill, Qdoba, Ruth's Chris Steaks [lodging] Marriott, Sheraton, **S** [gas] BP/dsl [food] El Dorado Diner [lodging] Extended Stay America, Hampton Inn
0	**I-287 runs with I-87 N.**

BUFFALO

INTERSTATE 290 (Buffalo)

Exit#	Services
8	I-90, NY Thruway, **I-290 begins/ends on I-90, exit 50.**
7b a	NY 5, Main St, **N** [gas] Mobil/dsl, Sunoco [food] Coldstone, Dunkin Donuts, La Nova Pizza/Wings, McDonald's, Panera Bread, Subway, Tim Horton, Wendy's [lodging] Hampton Inn, Wyndham Garden [other] Tops Foods, Walgreens, **S** [gas] Valero [lodging] Hyatt Place
6	NY 324, NY 240, **N** [gas] Gulf/dsl [lodging] Courtyard [other] Cadillac, **S** [gas] Gas Stop [food] China Star, ChuckeCheese, Domino's, McDonald'd, Sheridan Rest., Subway [other] 7-11, Aamco, CVS Drug, Fiat, Hyundai/Subaru, KIA/Mazda, Lexus, Nissan, URGNT CARE, Walgreens
5b a	NY 263, to Millersport, **N** [gas] Gulf [food] Santora's Pizza, Zetti's Pizza [lodging] Candlewood Suites, Comfort Inn, DoubleTree, Marriott, Red Roof Inn, **S** [gas] Mobil [lodging] Homewood Suites [other] Scion/Toyota, VW, Walgreens
4	I-990, to St U
3b a	US 62, to Niagara Falls Blvd, **N** [gas] Mobil/7-11, Sunoco, Valero [food] Anderson's Rest., Blvd Grill, Bob Evans, Dunkin Donuts, Just Pizza, Pancake House, Roadhouse Grill, Ted's Hot Dogs [lodging] Econolodge, Extended Stay America, Holiday Inn, Knight's Inn, Red Carpet Inn, Rodeway Inn, Sleep Inn [other] Chrysler/Dodge/Jeep, Home Depot, Honda, John&Mary's Rest., NAPA, Rite Aid, URGENT CARE, vet, **S** [gas] Delta Sonic, Sunoco/dsl [food] Applebee's, Arby's, BoneFish Grill, Buffalo Wild Wings, Burger King, Carrabba's, Chili's, Chipotle, Corner Bakery Cafe, Denny's, Dibella's Subs, John's Pizza, McDonald's, Moe's SW Grill, Olive Garden, Outback Steaks, Panera Bread, Papa John's, PI Pizza, Starbucks, Subway, TGIFriday, Tim Horton, Tulley's

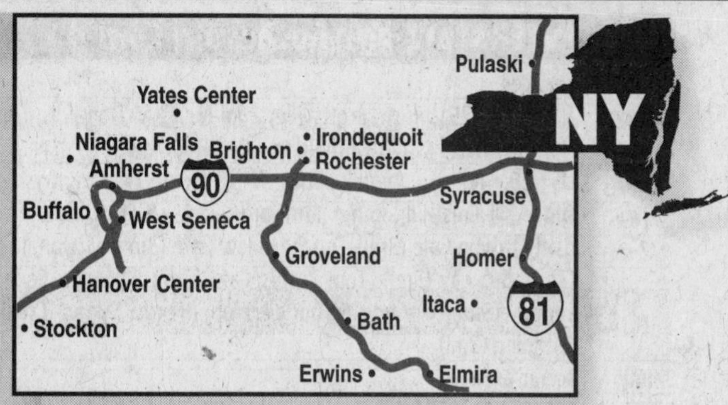

3b a	Continued [lodging] Days Inn, Royal Inn [other] $Tree, AT&T, Barnes&Noble, Best Buy, BJ's/gas, Christmas Tree Shop, Firestone/auto, GNC, Goodyear/auto, JC Penney, Jo-Ann Fabrics, Lowes Whse, Macy's, Michael's, Old Navy, Pepboys, PetCo, PetsMart, Target, TJ Maxx, Trader Joe's
2	NY 425, Colvin Blvd, **N** [food] Athena's Rest., KFC, McDonald's, Subway, Texas Roadhouse, Tim Horton, Wendy's [other] [H], Big Lots, Family$, Top's Foods/gas, **S** [gas] KwikFill [food] Dunkin Donuts [other] Pepboys
1b a	Elmwood Ave, NY 384, NY 265, **N** [gas] KwikFill [food] Franco's Pizza, John's Pizza/Subs, Subway, Touch of Italy [lodging] Center Way Motel [other] [H], $Tree, auto repair, Rite Aid, **S** [gas] Sunoco/dsl [food] Arby's
0mm	I-190. **I-290 begins/ends on I-190 in Buffalo.**

ROCHESTER

INTERSTATE 390 (Rochester)

Exit#	Services
20b a	I-490. **I-390 begins/ends on I-490 in Rochester.**
19(75)	NY 33a, Chili Ave, **N** [other] AutoZone, URGENT CARE, **S** [gas] Sunoco [food] Burger King, KFC, Little Caesar's, Pizza Hut, Subway [lodging] Motel 6, Quality Inn [other] $General
18b a	NY 204, Brooks Ave, **N** [lodging] Ramada Inn, **S** [lodging] Fairfield Inn [other] [airport]
17(73)	NY 383, Scottsville Rd, **S** [gas] 7-11/dsl, Fastrac/dsl
16(71)	NY 15a, to E Henryetta, **N** [other] [H], Costco/gas, **S** [food] Delmonico's Rest., TGI Friday's [lodging] Country Inn&Suites, Courtyard, Hampton Inn, Holiday Inn Express [other] Rite Aid
15(70)	I-590, Rochester
14(68)	NY 15a, NY 252, **E** [food] Dunkin Donuts, Gray's Cafe, Jeremiah's, Outback Steaks, Tully's Rest. [lodging] Extended Stay America, Residence Inn [other] $Tree, Top's Foods/gas, **W** [gas] Mobil/dsl [food] Bar Louie, Boston Mkt, Buffalo Wild Wings, Burger King, Dunkin Donuts, Five Guys, Jimmy John's, Moe's SW, Sonic, Starbucks, Subway, Taco Bell [lodging] Best Western, DoubleTree Inn, Hampton Inn, Holiday Inn, Home 2 Suites [other] Big Lots, Staples, Verizon
13(67)	Hylan Dr, **E** [gas] Fastrac/dsl [food] Cracker Barrel [lodging] Comfort Suites, Homewood Suites, **W** [gas] Mobil/dsl [food] Chili's, Chipotle, ChuckECheese, IHOP, Joe's Crabshack, Longhorn Steaks, McDonald's, Olive Garden, Panera Bread, Qdoba, Red Robin, Smashburger, Starbucks, Subway, Tim Hortons, TX Roadhouse, Uno Grill, Wendy's [other] Aldi Foods, Best Buy, BJ's Whse, Dick's, JC Penney, Lowe's, Marshall's, Michael's, Old Navy, PepBoys, PetCo, Target, Walmart, Wegman's Foods
12(66)	I-90. NY Thruway, NY 253, **W** [gas] Gulf/dsl/scales, Mobil/dsl, Speedway [food] Lehigh Rest., McDonald's, Peppermint's Rest., Tim Hortons, Wendy's [lodging] Country Inn&Suites, Days Inn, Fairfield Inn, Microtel, Red Carpet Inn, Red Roof Inn, Super 8 [other] Buick/GMC

INTERSTATE 390 (Rochester) Cont'd

Exit#	Services
11(62)	NY 15, NY 251, Rush, Scottsville, **2 mi N** McDonald's, Tim Hortons, Wendy's Fairfield Inn, Red Roof Inn
10(55)	US 20, NY 5, Avon, Lima, **N** Exxon Countryside Diner CrestHill Inn, Stratford Inn, **S** Quicklee's/dsl Avon Cafe (3mi), Dutch Hollow Cafe (3mi), McDonald's (3mi), Subway (3mi), Tom Wahls Cafe (3mi) Avon Cedar Lodge (3mi) Chrysler/Dodge/Jeep, Ford, Sugar Creek Camping (3mi)
9mm	scenic area wb
9(52)	NY 15, **N** Mobil/Dunkin Donuts/dsl Fratelli's Rest., Lakeville Rest., McDonald's, Tee&Gee Cafe Rodeway Inn Chevrolet
8(48)	US 20a, Geneseo, **N** Conesus Lake Camping, **2 mi S** Mobil/Dunkin Donuts Applebee's, Denny's, KFC/Taco Bell, McDonald's, Subway, Tim Hortons, Wendy's Hampton Inn, Quality Inn $Tree, Aldi Foods, AT&T, AutoZone, GNC, Petsmart, Verizon, Walmart, Wegman's
7(39)	NY 63, NY 408, Geneseo, **N** st police, **S** Doughboys/dsl, KwikFill, Valero/dsl Dunkin Donuts, McDonald's Alligence B&B, Country Inn&Suites, Geneseo River Hotel/Rest., Greenway Motel Bonadonna Auto, Family$, Letchworth SP, Ridge Camping, Rite Aid, Save-A-Lot Foods
38mm	**both lanes, full facilities, litter barrels, petwalk, vending**
6(33)	NY 36, Mt Morris, Sonyea
5(26)	NY 36, Dansville, **N** KwikFill/dsl, Mobil/7-11/dsl Arby's, Burger King, Dunkin Donuts, McDonald's, Pizza Hut, Subway, Taco Bell $Tree, Advance Parts, BigLots, Chevrolet, Chrysler/Dodge/Jeep, CVS Drug, Rite Aid, Save-A-Lot Foods, Top's Foods/gas, Verizon, **S** TA/Valero/Country Pride/dsl/scales/24hr/@
4(23)	NY 36, Dansville, **N** Sunoco/dsl Logan's Inn H, **S** Skybrook Camping, Stonybrook Park Camping, Sugar Creek Camping, Sunvalley Camping
3(17)	NY 15, NY 21, Wayland, **N** CarQuest (1mi), Holiday Hill Campground (7mi), st patrol
2(11)	NY 415, Cohocton, Naples, **N** Mobil (2mi) Tumble Hill Camping (3mi)
1(2)	NY 415, Avoca, **S** Arrowmart Caboose Motel (3mi) $General, USPO (2mi)

I-390 begins/ends on I-86, exit 36.

INTERSTATE 495 (Long Island)

RIVERHEAD

Exit#	Services
I-495 begins/ends on NY 25.	
73	rd 58, Old Country Road, to Greenport, Orient, **0-2 mi S** BP, Citgo, Mobil/dsl, Speedway/dsl Applebee's, Buffalo Wild Wings, Chipotle, Panera Bread, Starbucks, Taco Bell, TGIFriday's, Wendy's Hilton Garden, Holiday Inn Express Aldi Foods, AT&T, Best Buy, Buick/GMC, Chevrolet, Chrysler/Jeep, Costco/gas, CVS Drug, Dick's, Ford/Lincoln, Harley-Davidson, Home Depot, Honda, Kia/Mazda, Lowe's, Michael's, Nissan/Hyundai, PetCo, Stop&Shop, Subaru/VW, Tanger/famous brands, Target, Toyota, Volvo, Walgreens, Walmart/Subway
72	NY 25, (no ez eb return), Riverhead, Calverton (no EZ eb return), **N** funpark, **S** Speedway Hotel Indigo Tanger/famous brands/foodcourt
71	NY 24, to Hampton Bays (no ez eb return), Calverton, **N** Exxon/dsl
70	NY 111, to Eastport, Manorville, **S** 7-11, EVC, Mobil/dsl McDonald's, Papa Joseph's, Starbucks, Subway CVS Drug, King Kullen Food/drug
69	Wading River Rd, Center Moriches, **S** golf
68	NY 46, to Shirley, Wading River, **S** Mobil Carlo's Pizzaria 7-11
67	Yaphank Ave, **N** USPO
66	NY 101, Sills Rd, Yaphank, **N** Shell/dsl
65.5mm	**parking area both lanes**
65	Horse Block Rd, **N** Baskin-Robbins/Dunkin Donuts $Tree

MEDFORD

Exit#	Services
64	NY 112, to Coram, Medford, **N** Speedway DQ, Subway 7-11, Family$, Lowe's, Michael's, Sam's Club, Staples, Target, Verizon, Walgreens, **S** BP (2), BP/Dunkin Donuts, US/dsl J&R Steaks, Starbucks, Starbucks Comfort Inn, Fairfield Inn 7-11, AutoZone
63	NY 83, N Ocean Ave, **N** Speedway/dsl, Stop'n Shop Applebee's, Burger King, McDonald's, Taco Bell, TGIFriday's 7-11, CVS Drug, Hampton Inn, **S** BP/dsl, Gulf/dsl JR Steaks Ramada Plaza
62	Nicolls Rd, rd 97, to Blue Point, Stony Brook, **N** BP, **S** Charlie Brown's Steaks, Chili's, La Capannina Italian, On the Border, Subway, Wendy's Residence Inn
61	rd 19, to Patchogue, Holbrook, **N** Mobil, **S** Gulf/dsl, Speedway/dsl China 4, Greek Islands Rest., Joe's Pizza/Pasta, Outback Steaks, Subway 7-11, Advance Parts, CVS Drug
60	Ronkonkoma Ave, **N** USPO, **S** Mobil Red Lobster, Smokey Bones BBQ Courtyard
59	Ocean Ave, to Oakdale, Ronkonkoma, **S** BP/Dunkin Donuts, Sunoco Hilton Garden (2mi) 7-11
58	Old Nichols Rd, Nesconset, **N** Gulf/Dunkin Donuts Starbucks Marriott BJ's Whse
57	NY 454, Vets Hwy, to Hauppauge, **N** Gulf/dsl TGIFriday's, **S** BP, Mobil, Shell, Sunoco Dave&Buster's, Subway Hampton Inn 7-11, Mavis Tire, Stop&Shop Foods TJ Maxx, Walgreens, Walmart
56	NY 111, Smithtown, Islip, Smithtown, Islip, **N** BP/Dunkin Donuts/Subway Tropical Smoothie, **S** Sunoco/dsl Cassano Ristorante Holiday Inn Express
55	rd 67, Motor Pkwy, Central Islip, Central Islip, **N** Mobil Chipotle, IHOP, Madison Steaks, Subway GNC **S** Shell/dsl
54	Wicks Rd
53	Sagkitos Pkwy, Bay Shore, Kings Park, Bayshore, **N** BP/7-11 Applebee's Radisson, **S** Mobil
52	rd 4, Commack Rd, N Babylon, Commack, **N** Cumberland Farms, Quik Mart/dsl, Shell/dsl Ara Greek Kitchen, Chick-fil-A, Premier Diner, Starbucks, Starbucks (2) Hampton Inn Costco, Home Depot, Kohl's, Lowe's, Marshall's ShopRite Mkt, Target, Walmart

HICKSVILLE

Exit#	Services
51.5mm	**LI Welcome Ctr eb, parking area wb/ full facilities, litter barrel**
51	NY 231, to Northport, Babylon
50	Bagatelle Rd, to Wyandanch
49N	NY 110 N, to Huntington, **N** Marriott, **S** Jewel Rest.
49S	NY 110 S, to Amityville
48	Round Swamp Rd, Old Bethpage, **S** Cumberland Farms dsl Hilton Garden, Homewood Suites, Sheraton USPO
46	Sunnyside Blvd, Plainview, **N** Holiday Inn, **S** 7-11
45	Manetto Hill Rd, Plainview, Woodbury
44	NY 135, to Seaford, Syosset
43	S Oyster Bay Rd, to Syosset, Bethpage, **N** Cumberland Farm
42	Northern Pkwy, rd N, Hauppauge

INTERSTATE 495 (Long Island) Cont'd

Exit#	Services
41	NY 106, NY 107, Hicksville, Oyster Bay, N Starbucks, Whole Foods Mkt CVS Drug, Marshall's, USPO, S BP, Mobil, Sunoco Arby's, Boston Mkt, Boulder Creek Steaks, Broadway Diner, Chick-fil-A, Chipotle, Dunkin Donuts, Five Guys, McDonald's, On the Border AT&T, Goodyear/auto, Verizon
40	NY 25, Mineola, Syosset, S BP, Speedway/dsl Burger King, Dunkin Donuts, KFC, Kobe Hibachi, McDonald's, Wendy's Hampton Inn, Jericho Inn 7-11, Chrysler/Dodge/Jeep, Home Depot, Kohl's, Staples
39	Glen Cove Rd, N Mobil
38	(from eb) Northern Pkwy E, Meadowbrook Pkwy, to Jones Beach
37	Willis Ave, to Roslyn, Mineola, N BP, Shell Dunkin Donuts, Green Cactus Mexican, Skinny Pizza, S Mobil/dsl Lou Joe Rest.
36	Searingtown Rd, to Port Washington, N H
35	Shelter Rock Rd, Manhasset, S H
34	New Hyde Park Rd
33	Lakeville Rd, to Great Neck, N H
32	Little Neck Pkwy, N Shell Centre Pizza, Chipotle, Five Guys, Panera Bread, Starbucks Petco, Verizon
31	Douglaston Pkwy, S BP/service Burger King, Grimaldi's Pizza, Pinecourt Chinese Fairway Mkt, USPO, vet
30	E Hampton Blvd, Cross Island Pkwy
29	Springfield Blvd, S Gulf/Dunkin Donuts Starbucks GNC
27	I-295, Clearview Expswy, Throgs Neck, N Barney's Blue Bay Diner 7-11, EVC
26	Francis Lewis Blvd
25	Utopia Pkwy, 188th St, N Citgo, Mobil Courtyard, Fairfield Inn, S Gas Sale/dsl, Gulf, Mobil, Shell Applebee's, Arby's, Dunkin Donuts, Five Guys, Hooters, Qdoba, Subway Wyndham Garden Michael's, USPO
24	Kissena Blvd, N BP/dsl Dunkin Donuts, Subway, S Mobil
23	Main St, N New Lake Pavilion
22	Grand Central Pkwy, to I-678, College Pt Blvd, N Holiday Inn Express
21	108th St, N BP/7-11, Mobil Holiday Inn Express
19	NY 25, Queens Blvd, Woodhaven Blvd, to Rockaways, N Cheesecake Factory, Chipotle, Dunkin Donuts, Longhorn Steaks, McDonald's, Olive Garden, Popeye's JC Penney, Macy's, USPO, S Mobil Applebee's, Burger King, Dallas BBQ, Starbucks, Subway Aldi Foods, Costco, CVS, Kohl's, Marshall's, Old Navy, TJ Maxx
18.5	69th Ave, Grand Ave (from wb)
18	Maurice St, N Exxon/Dunkin Donuts/dsl dsl repair, S Maspeth Pizza, McDonald's Holiday Inn Express
17	48th St, to I-278, N Mobil Best Western
16	**I-495 begins/ends in NYC.**

NORTH CAROLINA

INTERSTATE 26

Exit#	Services
71mm	North Carolina/South Carolina state line
69mm	N Pacolet River
67.5mm	**Welcome Ctr wb, full facilities, litter barrels,**
67	US 74 E, to NC 108, Columbus, Tryon, N Shell//dsl, Vgo/dsl Cocula Mexican, Joy Wok, Larkin's Carolina Grill, McDonald's, Subway, Waffle House, Wendy's Advance Parts, CVS Drug, Family$, Food Lion, S Exxon/dsl KFC/Taco Bell, Mtn View Deli Days Inn H, $General, Bi-Lo
59	Saluda, N Saluda Mtn Lodge, S BP/dsl, Marathon/Subway/dsl Crust&Kettle Cafe, Saluda Rest. Orchard Inn B&B (2mi) $General, AppleMill Outlet, Atkins Fruit, camping, repair, vet
56mm	Green River
54	US 25 (from eb), to Greenville, E Flat Rock, to Carl Sandburg Home
53.5mm	2130 ft, Eastern Continental Divide
53	Upward Rd, Hendersonville, N Marathon/Dunkin Donuts/dsl Waffle House, Zaxby's Fairfield Inn, Mtn Inn&Suites Bloomfields Giftshop, Lakewood RV Park, Wildflower RV Park, S Exxon/McDonald's, Shell/pizza Cracker Barrel, Poplar Leaf Cafe, Subway Holiday Inn Express, Quality Inn repair, to Carl Sandburg Home
49b a	US 64, Hendersonville, N Marathon/dsl, Shell/dsl, Sunoco/dsl Chick-fil-A, Golden Corral, Jack-in-the-Box, Moose Cafe, O'Charley's, Sonic, Starbucks, Waffle House, Zaxby's Best Western, Hampton Inn, Quality Inn, Ramada Inn $Tree, Advance Parts, Ingles/gas, PetCo, Sam's Club/gas, Staples, Walmart, World of Clothing, S Exxon/dsl/LP, Shell/dsl Applebee's, Arby's, Binion's Roadhouse, Bojangles, Burger
49b a	Continued King, China Buffet, Denny's, Fatz Café, Hardee's, Harry's Rest., HoneyBaked Ham, KFC, Krispy Kreme, LJ Silver, Lon Sen Chinese, McDonald's, Outback Steaks, Pizza Hut, Subway, Taco Bell, Tequila's Grill, Wendy's Days Inn, EconoLodge, Red Roof Inn H, Aldi Foods, Belk, BigLots, Bi-Lo Foods, Chrysler/Dodge/Jeep, Clark Tire/auto, CVS Drug, Family$, Home Depot, Jo-Ann, Lowe's, NAPA, TJ Maxx, Tuesday Morning, Verizon
46mm	**weigh sta both lanes,**
44	US 25, Fletcher, N Exxon/dsl Hardee's, Subway flea mkt/campground, vet, S Citgo/dsl, Shell/DQ/dsl/scales/24hr, Sonny's/dsl Bojangles, Burger King, McDonald's, Valentina's Mexican Mountain Inn&Suites H, Camping World RV Ctr, USPO
41mm	**both lanes, full facilities, litter barrels, , vending**
40	NC 280, Arden, N Fastop/dsl, Shell/Arby's Bojangles, Carrabba's, Casa Torres, Chili's, Cracker Barrel, Firehouse Subs, IHOP, Jersey Mike's, Little Caesar's, Lonestar Steaks, McDonald's, Moe's SW Grill, Olive Garden, Ruby Tuesday, Sonic, Tamarind Thai, Tokyo Express Budget Motel, Clarion, Comfort Inn, Courtyard, EconoLodge, Hampton Inn, Knight's Inn Acura/Honda, Aldi Foods, Best Buy, BigLots, Dick's, Lowe's, Marshalls, Michael's, Old Navy, Petsmart, Ross, Rutledge Lake RV Park, Target, World Mkt, S Citgo/dsl Circle B Ranch BBQ, J&S Cafeteria Fairfield Inn Asheville Airport, BMW
37	NC 146, Skyland, N Arby's, Brixx Pizza, Broken Egg Cafe, Coldstone, Hickory Tavern, McDonald's, Neo Burrito, PF Chang's, Starbucks, Waffle House, Which Wich? Hilton, Quality Inn Barnes&Noble, CVS Drug, Ingles/gas, REI, S Chevrolet

HENDERSONVILLE

ARDEN

NY NC

ASHEVILLE

INTERSTATE 26 Cont'd

Exit#	Services
34mm	French Broad River
33	NC 191, Brevard Rd, 2 mi N Asheville Farmers Mkt, Bear Creek RV Camp, Toyota, S Citgo, HotSpot/dsl Apollo Flame, Harbor Inn Seafood, LJ Silver, McDonald's, Papa's Mexican, Ryan's, Shogun Buffet, Stoneridge Grill, Subway, Taco Bell, Waffle House Comfort Suites, Country Inn&Suites, Fairfield Inn, Hampton Inn, Hilton Garden, Holiday Inn Express, Rodeway Inn $Tree, Asheville Outlets, Belk, Dillards, Field&Stream, Ingles Foods/dsl, Kia, PetCo, to Blue Ridge Pkwy, Verizon
31b a	I-40, E to Statesville, W to Knoxville
27mm	I-240 E, Patton Ave
I-26 and I-240 run together 3 mi. See NC I-240 exits 1-4.	
25	rd 251, N to UNCA
24	Elk Mtn Rd, Woodfin
23	Merrimon Ave, N Asheville, N Gulf/dsl, HotSpot Bellagio Bistro, Frank's Pizza, Moe's BBQ Days Inn camping, vet
21	New Stock Rd, N Citgo/dsl, Shell Domino's, Granny's Kitchen, Pizza Hut $General, Campfire Lodge RV Park, CVS, Ingles/gas
19b a	N US 25, W US 70, Marshall, N Shell/dsl Arby's, Bojangles, Burger King, Chapala Mexican, IHOP, KFC, La Carreta Mexican, Little Caesars, McDonald's, Peking East, Subway, TCBY, Waffle House, Zaxby's Ace Hardware, Advance Parts, Aldi Foods, AutoZone, BigLots, Ingles/dsl, Roses, URGENT CARE, Verizon, S Shell/DQ/dsl Steak'n Shake $Tree, CVS, Lowe's, Walmart/Subway
18	Weaverville (no EZ return from eb)
17	to Flat Creek
15	rd 197, to Jupiter, Barnardsville
13	Forks of Ivy, N Mkt Ctr/dsl, S Exxon/dsl
11	rd 213, to Mars Hill, Marshall, N tires, S Exxon//Hardee's/dsl, TriCo Bojangles, Osaka Japanese, Subway, Waffle House, Wagon Wheel Rest. Comfort Inn $General, CVS, Ingles/dsl, NAPA
9	Burnsville, Spruce Pine, N to Mt Mitchell SP
7mm	**runaway truck ramp eb, scenic overlook wb**
6mm	**Welcome Ctr/ eb, full facilities**
5.5mm	**runaway truck ramp eb**
5mm	Buckner Gap, elev. 3370
3	to US 23 A, Wolf Laurel, N Exxon/dsl Little Creek Cafe to ski areas
2.5mm	**eb runaway truck ramp**
.5mm	**eb brake insp sta**
0mm	North Carolina/Tennessee state line

NC

WILMINGTON

INTERSTATE 40

Exit#	Services
420mm	**I-40 begins/ends at Wilmington, Services N on US 17** Buffalo Wild Wings Hampton Inn CarQuest, Home Depot, Hyundai, Kia, Kohl's, Land Rover, Mazda, Nissan, Subaru, Toyota, Volvo, **Services S on US 17** BP, Exxon/dsl, Hugo's, Murphy USA/dsl Arby's, Bojangles, Bonefish Grill, Carrabba's, Chick-fil-A, ChopStix, Church's, Cracker Barrel, Dunkin Donuts, Elizabeth's Pizza, Hardee's, Hooters, IHOP, Jason's Deli, McDonald's, Olive Garden, Sonic, Subway, Waffle House Best Western, Budgetel, Comfort Suites, Days Inn, EconoLodge, Extended Stay America, Holiday Inn, MainStay Suites, Quality Inn, Ramada Inn, Red Roof Inn, Sleep Inn, Travel Inn, Wingate Inn Advance Parts, AutoZone, Batteries+, Black's Tires/auto, Cadillac, Costco/gas, Marshall's, Petsmart, Rite Aid, Target, Walgreens, Walmart,
420mm	**Continued** **Services 2-4 mi S on US 117/NC 132** BP/dsl, Exxon/dsl Applebee's, Bojangles, Burger King, Carolina Ale House, Chili's, CiCi's Pizza, College Diner, Cookout, Golden Corral, Hardee's, Hieronymus Seafood, HoneyBaked Ham, Jersey Mike's, Jimmy John's, Kickback Jack's, Little Caesar's, McAlister's Deli, McDonald's, Mission BBQ, Okami Japanese, Outback Steaks, Starbucks, Taco Bell, Wendy's Baymont Inn, Comfort Inn, Country Inn Suites, Courtyard, Holiday Inn Express, Jameson Inn, Staybridge Suites $Tree, Acura/Honda, AT&T, Best Buy, Buick/GMC, Chevrolet, Chrysler/Dodge/Jeep, Dick's, Fiat, Harris-Teeter, Jo-Ann, Lowe's Foods, Lowe's Whse, Mercedes, Old Navy, PetCo, Ross, Sam's Club/gas, Staples, TJ Maxx, to UNCW, URGENT CARE, Verizon, VW
420b a	Gordon Rd, NC 132 N, 2 mi N Kangaroo/dsl, Speedway/dsl Andy's, Domino's, Hardee's, KFC, McDonald's, Waffle House, Zaxby's CVS Drug, KOA (4mi), Rite Aid, vet, Walgreens, S BP/dsl, Go Gas/dsl, Kangaroo/dsl Carolina BBQ, China Wok, McDonald's, Subway $General, Family$, Lowe's Foods, Rite Aid
416b a	I-140, US 17, to Topsail Island, New Bern, Myrtle Beach
414	Holly Shelter Rd, to Brunswick Co beaches, Castle Hayne, S BP, GoGas/dsl, Kangaroo/dsl Carolina Cafe, Domino's, Hardee's, Subway $General, Bo's Foods, CVS Drug, USPO
413mm	NE Cape Fear River
408	NC 210, N Mack/Volvo/Isuzu, S Phoenix TC/Exxon/Subway/dsl/scales, Pilot/Wendy's/dsl/cafe/scales/24hr, Shell/Noble Roman's/dsl Hardee's, McDonald's Advance Parts, Family$, Food Lion, to Moore's Creek Nat Bfd/camping, USPO
398	NC 53, Burgaw, 2 mi S Carolina Petro Hardee's, KFC, McDonald's, Subway Burgaw Motel H, Advance Parts, camping, Family$, Food Lion
390	to US 117, Wallace
385	NC 41, Wallace, N Exxon/Village Subs Bojangles, Mad Boar Rest. Holiday Inn Express Lake Leamon Camping, **1.5 mi S** Hess/dsl, Murphy USA/dsl Burger King, Domino's, McDonald's, Subway, Taco Bell, Zaxby's $General, $Tree, Food Lion, O'Reilly Parts, Verizon, Walgreens, Walmart/Subway
384	NC 11, Wallace
380	Rose Hill, S BP/Subway/dsl (1mi), Marathon (1mi), Pure Duplin Winery
373	NC 24 E, NC 903, Magnolia, N BP/dsl, Exxon/dsl/e-85 H, Cowan Museum
369	US 117, Warsaw
364	NC 24, to NC 50, Clinton, N Pilot/Arby's/Dunkin Donuts/dsl/24hr, S **both lanes, full facilities, litter barrels, petwalk, , , vending,** BP/dsl, Kangaroo/dsl, Marathon, Sunoco/Bojangles KFC, McDonald's, Smithfield's BBQ, Subway, Waffle House, Wendy's Days Inn, Quality Inn,
355	NC 403, to US 117, Goldsboro, Faison, 3 mi N Exxon
348	Suttontown Rd
343	US 701, Newton Grove, 1 mi N Exxon/dsl, to Bentonville Bfd
341	NC 50, NC 55, to US 13, Newton Grove, 1.5 mi N Exxon/dsl Hardee's Food Lion, S BP/McDonald's, Shell/Subway/dsl Smithfield BBQ Family Auto/tire
334	NC 96, Meadow, S Short Stop/dsl
328b a	I-95, N to Smithfield, S to Benson
325	NC 242, to US 301, to Benson, S Marathon/dsl
324mm	**both lanes, full facilities, litter barrels, no overnight parking, petwalk, , , vending**

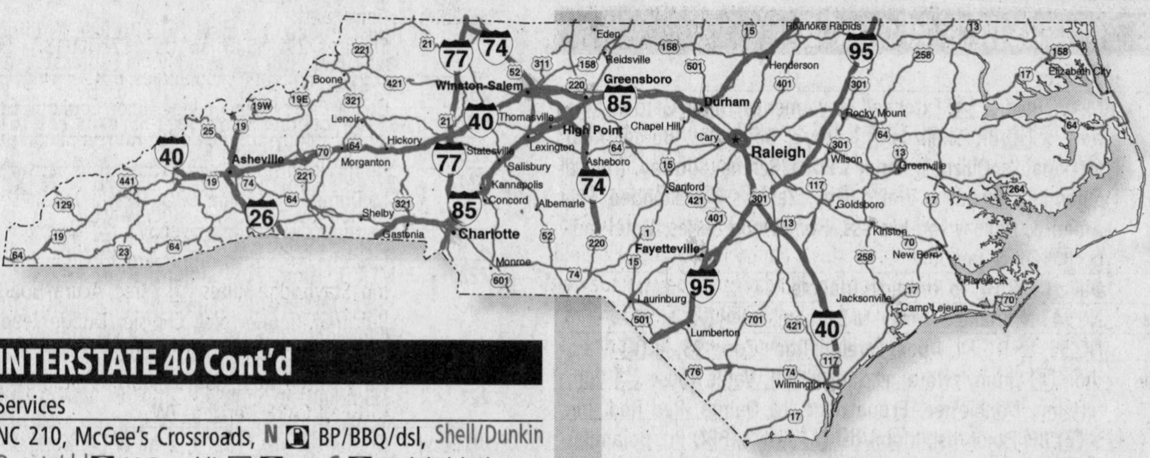

INTERSTATE 40 Cont'd

Exit#	Services
319	NC 210, McGee's Crossroads, N BP/BBQ/dsl, Shell/Dunkin Donuts/dsl McDonald's H, vet, S Mobil/dsl, Sheetz/dsl Bojangle's, China Star, Domino's, Italian Pizza/Pasta, KFC/Taco Bell, Subway, Wendy's $General, AutoZone, CVS Drug, Food Lion
312	NC 42, to Clayton, Fuquay-Varina, N Murphy Express/dsl, Speedway/Dunkin Donuts/dsl/24hr, Speedway/Wendy's/dsl Applebee's, China King, Cookout, Cracker Barrel, Divano's Pizza, Fiesta Mexicana, Hibachi&Co, Hwy 55 Burger, Jersey Mike's Subs, King Chinese, Pizza Inn, Ruby Tuesday, Smithfield BBQ, Wendy's Comfort Inn, Holiday Inn Express, Super 8, Woodspring Suites $Tree, JustTires, Lowe's, URGENT CARE, Verizon, Walmart/McDonald's, S BP/Subway/dsl, Exxon/Burger King, Marathon/dsl, Shell/dsl Bojangle's, Domino's, DQ, Jumbo China, KFC/Taco Bell, Little Caesar's, McDonald's, Snoopy's Hotdogs, Waffle House, Yummi Japan Hampton Inn, Sleep Inn AutoZone, CVS Drug, Food Lion, vet, Walgreens
309	US 70 E, Goldsboro, Smithfield
306b a	US 70 E bus, to Smithfield, Garner, Goldsboro, 1 mi N Citgo/dsl, Kangaroo/Subway/dsl Chrysler/Dodge/Jeep, S Sheetz/dsl Blaze Pizza, Buffalo Bros Pizza, Buffalo Wild Wings, Carolina Alehouse, Char-Grill, Chick-fil-A, Chili's, Chipotle, City BBQ, Coldstone, Five Guys, Kaze Japanese, La Cocina Mexican, Logan's Roadhouse, Longhorn Steaks, McDonald's, Moe's SW Grill, New Japan Express, Panera Bread, Prima Vera Pizza, Red Robin, Starbucks, Subway, TGIFriday's, Wendy's, Zaxby's $Tree, AT&T, Best Buy, BJ's Whse/gas, Burlington, Cabela's, Dick's, GNC, Kohl's, Michael's, Petsmart, Ross, Staples, Target, TJ Maxx
303	Jones Sausage Rd, N Speedway/Dunkin Donuts/dsl Bojangle's, Burger King, Smithfield BBQ, Subway, S Speedway/Dunkin Donuts/dsl
301	I-440 E, US 64/70 E, to Wilson
300b a	Rock Quarry Rd, N SaveALot, S Exxon, Valero/dsl Burger King, Little Caesar's, Subway, Wang's Kitchen Family$, Food Lion, Rite Aid
299	Person St, Hammond Rd, Raleigh (no EZ return eb), 1 mi N Shell/dsl to Shaw U
298b a	US 401 S, US 70 E, NC 50, N Shell/dsl Red Roof Inn, S BP/Circle K, Citgo, Exxon, Exxon/dsl, Mobil, Speedway/dsl Baskin-Robbins/Dunkin Donuts, Bojangle's, Burger King, Cook-Out, Domino's, Golden Corral, Mi Rancho Mexican, Taco Bell, Waffle House Claremont Inn, Comfort Inn, Super 8 AutoZone, Carquest, Family$, Meineke, O'Reilly Parts, Sam's Club/gas
297	Lake Wheeler Rd, N Exxon Subway Farmer's Mkt, S Marathon
295	Gorman St, 1 mi N Exxon/dsl Hardee's, Little Caesar's, Subway Holiday Inn Express Family$, to NCSU, Walgreens, S Kangaroo
293	to I-440, US 1, US 64 W, Raleigh, S Exxon, Shell BJ's Rest., Bob Evans, Chick-fil-A, China King, Chipotle, Coldstone, Cook-Out, Dickey's BBQ, East Garden, Egg&I, HoneyBaked Ham, Jasmin, Jason's Deli, Jersey Mike's Subs, McDonald's, Moe's SW Grill, Noodles&Co, Olive Garden, Panera Bread, Red Lobster, Red Robin, Remington Grill, Ruby Tuesday, Starbucks, Subway, Sweet Tomatoes, Taco Bell, Waffle House, Wild Wing Cafe Best Western, DoubleTree, Fairfield Inn, Hilton Garden, Holiday Inn, Red Roof Inn, SpringHill Suites Best Buy, BJ's Whse, Dick's, Ford, GNC, Home Depot, Jo-Ann Fabrics, Kohl's, Lincoln, Lowe's, Marshalls, Mazda, Michael's, NTB, Office Depot, Old Navy, PetCo, Petsmart, REI, Ross, SteinMart, Target, Verizon, World Mkt
291	Cary Towne Blvd, Cary, 1 mi S Circle K Dave&Buster's, DQ, Five Guys, Jersey Mike's, La Madeleine, Macaroni Grill, McDonald's, On-the-Border, Pei Wei, Penn Sta Subs, Primo Pizza, Starbucks AT&T, Barnes&Noble, Belk, Dillard's, Firestone, Harris Teeter, JC Penney, vet
290	NC 54, Cary, N Sheetz/dsl McDonald's Hyatt Place, Wingate Inn, S Shell/dsl Hampton Inn
289	to I-440, Wade Ave, to Raleigh, N H, Carter-Finley Stadium, museum, to fairgrounds
287	Harrison Ave, Cary, N to Wm B Umstead SP, S BP/Circle/dsl An Cuisine, Bonefish Grill, Burger King, BurgerFi, Carolina Cafe, Chick-fil-A, Jersey Mike's, McDonald's, Moe's SW Grill, NY Pizza, Ruth's Chris Steaks, Starbucks, Subway, Thai Cuisine, Wendy's Embassy Suites, Extended Stay America, TownePlace Suites, Umstead Hotel Bass Pro Shops, Mr Tire
285	Aviation Pkwy, to Morrisville, N Sheetz/dsl Hilton Garden Raleigh/Durham Airport
284	Airport Blvd, N Capital City Chophouse Cambria Suites, Country Inn&Suites, Hyatt Place to RDU Airport, S BP/Circle/dsl, Mobil Bojangles, Carmen's, Cracker Barrel, Hooters, KFC/Taco Bell, Los Tres Magueyes, Peng's Asian, TX Steaks, Waffle House, Wendy's Courtyard, Days Inn, Extended Stay America, Fairfield Inn, Hampton Inn, Holiday Inn, Holiday Inn Express, La Quinta, Microtel, Residence Inn, Sheraton, Staybridge Suites Morrisville Outlets/famous brands/food court
283	I-540 E, **toll I-540 W**, to US 70, Aviation Pkwy
282	Page Rd, S Arby's, Bojangles, Jimmy John's, McDonald's, Mez Cafe, Page Road Grill, Starbucks Comfort Suites, DoubleTree, Sheraton, Sleep Inn, Wingate Inn Office Depot

RALEIGH

CARY

INTERSTATE 40 Cont'd

Exit#	Services
281	Miami Blvd, N Extended Stay America, Hilton Garden, Marriott, S BP, Shell/dsl Arby's, Bojangles, Burger King, McDonald's, Quiznos, Randy's Pizza, Serena, Subway, Tropical Smoothie, Wendy's, Wok'n Grill, Zaxby's Extended Stay America, Holiday Inn Express, Homewood Suites, Hotel Indigo Office Depot
280	Davis Dr, N to Research Triangle
279b a	NC 147 N, Triangle Expwy, to Durham, N H
278	NC 55, to NC 54, Apex, Foreign Trade Zone 93, N Marathon Jimmy's Hotdogs, Sansui Grill, Waffle House Comfort Inn, DoubleTree, EconoLodge, La Quinta, Red Roof Inn, S BP, Exxon/dsl, Mobil/dsl Arby's, BBQ Pit, Bojangles, Brigs Rest., Capt D's, Chick-fil-A, Cinco de Mayo, CookOut, El Dorado Mexican, Golden Corral, Hardee's, Little Caesar's, McDonald's, Papa John's, Pizza Hut, Starbucks, Subway, Taco Bell, Thai 55, Wendy's, William's Kitchen Candlewood Suites, Courtyard, Crossland Suites, Extended Stay America, Residence Inn $Tree, Aamco, Advance Parts, AutoZone, BigLots, Colonial Tire, CVS Drug, Firestone/auto, Food Lion, Jiffy Lube, Just Tires, Meineke, NAPA, O'Reilly Parts, Precision Tune, Walgreens
276	Fayetteville Rd, N Circle K/dsl, Exxon/Circle K/dsl China Cafe, City BBQ, McDonald's, Melting Pot, Orient Garden, Ruby Tuesday, Waffle House, Wendy's GNC, Kroger/dsl, Roses, to NC Central U, Walgreens, S Bufflo Wild Wings, CA Pizza Kitchen, Champp's Rest, Cheesecake Factory, Chili's, Chipotle, Firebird's, Fork-in-the-Road Cafe, Jersey Mike's, Los Tres Mexican, Maggiano's, McAlister's Deli, Melting Pot, Moe's SW Grill, Panera Bread, PF Chang's, Ruth's Chris Steaks, Starbucks, Ted's MT Grill Hilton Garden AT&T, Barnes&Noble, Belk, Best Buy, Buick/Cadillac/GMC, Chevrolet, JC Penney, Macy's, Mercedes, Nordstrom, Old Navy, Porsche, REI, World Mkt
274	NC 751, to Jordan Lake, N BP, Marathon Asian Kitchen, Burger King, Char Grill, Denny's, Dunkin Donuts, Jimmy John's, KFC, Marco's Pizza, Taco Bell, Which Wich?, Wing Stop Advance Parts, CVS Drug, Harris Teeter, Honda, Lexus, Rite Aid, Sheetz/dsl, URGENT CARE, Walgreens, S Bonefish Grill, Bruster's, Chick-fil-A, Penn Sta Subs, Subway, Town Hall Burger Fairfield Inn, Hyatt Aldi Foods, Michael's, PetCo, Target
273	NC 54, to Durham, UNC-Chapel Hill, N BP/dsl, S BP, Shell/dsl Amante Pizza, Hardee's, Jersey Mike's, Nantucket Grill, New China Courtyard (2mi), Hampton Inn, Holiday Inn Express
270	US 15, US 501, Chapel Hill, Durham, N Applebee's, Bob Evans, Carrabba's, Chipotle, Dickey's BBQ, Firehouse Subs, Five Guys, Freddy's, Jason's Deli, Jimmy John's, McAlister's, Moe's SW Grill, NY Pizza, Outback Steaks, Panera Bread, Papa John's, PDQ, Philly Steaks, Red Robin, Starbucks, Xank's Japanese Comfort Inn, Home 2 Suites, Homewood Suites, SpringHill Suites, Staybridge Suites $Tree, AT&T, Barnes&Noble, Best Buy, Dick's, Home Depot, HS, Kohl's, Kroger/dsl, Marshalls, Michael's, Old Navy, Petsmart, to Duke U, Verizon, Walmart/Subway, S Petco Hardee's, La Hacienda, McDonald's, Starbucks, Subway, Wendy's Quality Inn, Red Roof Inn, Residence Inn, Sheraton, University Inn Acura, Advance Parts, AutoZone, BMW, CVS Drug, Food Lion, Lowe's, Mr Tire, Subaru, Trader Joe's
266	NC 86, to Chapel Hill, **2 mi** S BP, Exxon, Speedway/dsl Jersey Mike's, Subway
263	New Hope Church Rd
261	Hillsborough, **1.5 mi** N BP/Circle K, Citgo/dsl McDonald's, Pizza Hut Holiday Inn Express
259	I-85 N, to Durham

I-40 and I-85 run together 30 mi. See I-85, exits 131-161.

Exit#	Services
226	McConnell Rd, S Exxon
224	E Lee St, to US 29 N, to US 220 N, N BP/dsl, Shell/dsl Holiday Inn Express, Rodeway Inn
223	to N US 29, E US 70, N US 20, Reidsville
222	MLK Jr (from eb), Sanford, S Arby's, Biscuitville, Burger King, McDonald's, Subway, Taco Bell Domino's, Ocean Blue Seafood Rest., Wendy's Advance Parts, CVS Drug, Food Lion, Hall Tire Co, Walmart Mkt
221	S Elm-Eugene St, N Citgo/dsl, Valero AutoZone, Family$, Food Lion, O'Reilly Parts, S BP, Shell/dsl EconoLodge, Super 8 Home Depot
220	Randleman Rd, US 220 S, to Greensboro, Ashboro, N Marathon/dsl, Valero Biscuitville, Church's, KFC, McDonald's, Pizza Hut, Sub Sta 2, Subway Greensboro Tire, Harley-Davidson, Rite Aid, Save-A-Lot, S BP, Kangaroo Cook-Out, Mayflower Seafood, Waffle House, Wendy's
219	US 29 S, W US 70, Highpoint (exits left from wb), Charlotte
218	US 220, Freeman Mill Rd, Ashboro
217	Highpoint Rd, Koury Blvd (from wb), N Exxon, Shell/dsl Biscuitville, Burger King, Chili's, Ham's Rest, Hooters, Ichiban Grill, J Butler's Grille, Little Caesar's, Olive Garden, Sakura Japanese, Santa Fe Mexican, Subway, Taco Bell DoubleTree Hotel, Hampton Inn, Holiday Inn, Quality Inn, Red Roof Inn, Super 8 $General, $Tree, Office Depot, S Shell Bonefish Grill, Carrabba's, Darryl's Grill, Jimmy John's, Krispy Kreme, McDonald's, Popeye's, Smokey Bones BBQ, Waffle House, Wendy's, Zaxby's Baymont Inn, Best Western, Comfort Suites, Drury Inn, Howard Johnson, Ramada Inn, Sheraton, Studio 6 Dillard's, Discount Tire, JC Penney, O'Reilly Parts, Walmart Mkt
216	(from eb), Greensboro, N coliseum
214	Wendover Ave, N Sheetz/dsl Burger King, China Buffet, Coldstone, Jake's Diner, Mario's Pizza, Moe's SW Grill, New Orleans Rest., Noodles&Co, Panera Bread, Penn Sta Subs, Ruby Tuesday, Waffle House Extended Stay, Fairfield Inn, Hilton Garden, Holiday Inn Express, Microtel Audi, Costco/gas, CVS Drug, Ford, Nissan, PetCo, Staples, TJ Maxx, Verizon, VW, S Applebee's, Arby's, Biscuitville, Bojangles, Chick-fil-A, Chipotle Mexican, CookOut, Cracker Barrel, Elizabeth's Pizza, Golden Corral, Golden Wok, IHOP, Jimmy John's, Kabuto Japanese, La Hacienda Mexican, Logan's Roadhouse, Longhorn Steaks, McDonald's, O'Charley's, Panda Express, Papa John's, Red Lobster, Steak'n Shake, Subway, Taco Bell, TGIFriday's, Tripp's Rest., Villarosa Italian Comfort Inn, Comfort Inn, Courtyard, Extended Stay America, Hyatt Place, InTown Suites, La Quinta, SpringHill Suites, Suburban Inn, Wingate Inn $Tree, AT&T, Best Buy, Buick/GMC, Chevrolet, Dick's, Field&Stream, GNC, Goodyear, Hobby Lobby, Home Depot, Kohl's, Land River/Jaguar, Lowe's, Mazda, Meineke, Michael's, Old Navy, Petsmart, Ross, Sam's Club/gas, Target, Walmart
213	Guilford College Rd, N BP/dsl Wyndham Garden, S same as 214, Sheetz vet
212b a	I-73, US 241 S, to I-85, to Bryan Blvd, Ashboro, N to
211	Gallimore Dairy Rd, N Freightliner
210	NC 68, to High Point, Piedmont Triad, N Shell Arby's, Carolina's Diner Days Inn, Embassy Suites, Fairview Inn, Holiday Inn, Homewood Suites, Sleep Inn Ford Trucks, Kenworth, to , S Exxon/dsl Bojangles, Dunkin Donuts,

CHAPEL HILL

GREENSBORO

NC

INTERSTATE 40 Cont'd

WINSTON • SALEM

210 Continued
Fatz Cafe, McDonald's, Pizza Hut/Taco Bell, Pollo Pizza/Pasta, Ruby Tuesday, Shoney's, Subway, Wendy's Best Western, Comfort Suites, Courtyard, Extended Stay America, Fairfield Inn, Hampton Inn, Hawthorn Suites, Hilton Garden, Holiday Inn Express, Home 2 Suites, Motel 6, Quality Inn, Red Roof Inn, Residence Inn, SpringHill Suites

208 Sandy Ridge Rd, N Exxon/Subway/dsl, Sheetz/dsl, Speedway/dsl Camping World RV Ctr, S Shell/Circle K/dsl Out Of Doors Mart

206 Lp 40 (from wb), to Kernersville, Winston-Salem, downtown

203 NC 66, to Kernersville, N QM/Subway/dsl, Sheetz/dsl, Speedway/dsl Capt Tom's Seafood, Clark's BBQ, Dairi-O, McDonald's, Wendy's Hampton Inn, Sleep Inn H, Ford, NTB, S Shell/dsl Holiday Inn Express

201 Union Cross Rd, N BP/dsl Blue Naples Pizza, Burger King, China Café, Subway CVS Drug, Food Lion, Walmart Mkt, S Sheetz/dsl Bojangle's

196 I-74, US 311 S, to High Point

195 US 311 N, NC 109, to Thomasville, S Citgo, Speedway/dsl Family$

193b a US 52, NC 8, to Lexington, S Shell, Speedway/dsl Hardee's

193c Silas Creek Pkwy (from eb), same as 192

192 NC 150, to Peters Creek Pkwy, N Shell, Speedway Bojangles, Burger King, Hero House Rest, Hong Kong Buffet, IHOP, KFC, Little Caesar's, Monterrey Mexican, Mr BBQ, Subway, Taco Bell, Tokyo Japanese University Inn $General, $Tree, Acura/Subaru, Audi, AutoZone, BigLots, Ford, Hamrick's, Hyundai, Infiniti, Mazda, Office Depot, Rite Aid, VW, S BP, QM Arby's, Baskin-Robbins/Dunkin Donuts, Cook-Out, Dairi-O, K&W Cafeteria, McDonald's, Papa John's, Pizza Hut, Waffle House, Wendy's, Zaxby's Holiday Inn Express Advance Parts, Aldi Foods, BMW/Mini, CVS Drug, Family$, Food Lion, Honda, Mock Tire, Toyota

190 Hanes Mall Blvd (from wb, no re-entry), N Carolina Alehouse, Chipotle Mexican, Coldstone, Elizabeth's Pizza, Genghis Grill, Jimmy John's, McDonald's, Ruby Tuesday, TGIFriday's, Tripp's Rest. Best Western H, Belk, Dick's, Dillard's, Firestone/auto, JC Penney, Macy's, Marshalls, same as 189, S Bad Daddy's Burger, Burger King, ChuckECheese, Outback Steaks, Pan Asian, Starbucks, Subway Comfort Suites, Microtel

189 US 158, Stratford Rd, Hanes Mall Blvd, N BJ's Rest., Bojangles, Chili's, Golden Corral, Honeybaked Ham, Olive Garden, Red Lobster, Red Robin, Taco Bell, TX Roadhouse Courtyard, Fairfield Inn H, Belk, Buick/GMC, Cadillac, Chevrolet, Dillard's, JC Penney, Macy's, Walgreens, S Shell Applebee's, Bleu Rest., Brixx Pizza, Buffalo Wild Wings, Cheddar's, Chick-fil-A, Firebirds Grill, Five Guys, Hooters, Jason's Deli, Jersey Mike's, KFC/LJ Silver, Longhorn Steaks, Mario's Pizza, Moe's SW Grill, Panera Bread, Qdoba, Subway, Tin Tin Asian, Twin Peaks, Village Tavern, Which Wich?, Zaxby's Extended Stay America, Hampton Inn, Hilton Garden, La Quinta, Residence Inn, Sleep Inn, SpringHill Suites $Tree, AT&T, Barnes&Noble, Best Buy, Costco/gas, CVS Drug, Discount Tire, Hobby Lobby, Home Depot, Kohl's, Lowe's, Michael's, NTB, Petsmart, Ross, Sam's Club/gas, Target, Verizon

188 US 421, to Yadkinville, to WFU (no EZ wb return), Winston-Salem, **1/2 mi N off US 421** BP, Exxon, Kangaroo, Shell Arby's, Burger King, Cook-Out, Dickey's BBQ, McDonald's, Starbucks, Waffle House, Wendy's CarMax, Lexus, Mercedes, Verizon, vet, Walmart/Subway

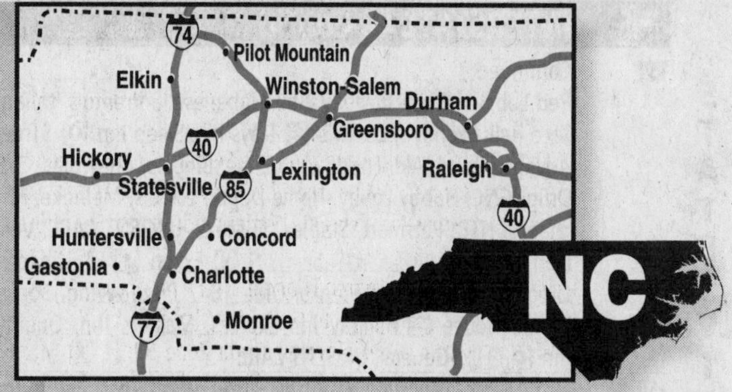

CLEMMONS

184 to US 421, Clemmons, N Mobil/7-11, Shell Applebee's, Dairi-O, Dunkin Donuts, IHOP, K&W Cafe, KFC, Milner Bros Rest., Panera Bread, Steak Escape Quality Inn, S BP/dsl, Circle K, Speedway/dsl Arby's, Biscuitville, Brick Oven Pizza, Burger King, Cracker Barrel, Domino's, Kimono Japanese, Krispy Kreme, Little Richard's BBQ, McDonald's, Mi Pueblo Mexican, Mtn Fried Chicken, Pizza Hut, Ruby Tuesday, Sonic, Starbucks, Subway, Taco Bell, Time to Eat Cafe, Waffle House, Wendy's Super 8, Village Inn $Tree, Advance Parts, AutoZone, BigLots, CVS Drug, GNC, Lowe's Foods, Meineke, NTB, O'Reilly Parts, Staples, USPO, Verizon, vet, Walgreens, Walmart Mkt

182 Bermuda Run, Tanglewood, S Chang Thai, Jersey Mike's, Lee's Chinese, Monte De Rey Mexican, Papa John's, Subway Harris-Teeter, Tanglewood Camping

182mm Yadkin River

180 NC 801, Tanglewood, N Sheetz/dsl Capt's Galley Seafood, Domino's, La Carreta Mexican, Subway Hampton Inn H, Lowe's Foods/dsl, Rite Aid, S BP/McDonald's/dsl, Speedway/dsl Asian View, Bojangles, Jade Garden, Miyabi Japanese, Venezia Italian, Wendy's, Zaxby's $General, Ace Hardware, CVS Drug, Food Lion, Walgreens

177mm **both lanes, full facilities, litter barrels, petwalk, , , vending**

174 Farmington Rd, N Shell/dsl, S vineyards

MOCKSVILLE

170 US 601, Mocksville, N Citgo/dsl, Murphy USA/dsl, TA/Shell/Country Pride/Popeye's/dsl/scales/24hr JinJin Chinese, La Carreta Mexican $Tree, Campers Inn RV Ctr, GNC, Verizon, Walmart/Subway, S BP, Sheetz/dsl, Speedway/Taco Bell Arby's, Bojangles, Burger King, China Grill, Domingo's Mexican, Dunkin Donuts, Dynasty Chinese, East Coast Grill, KFC, Marco's Pizza, McDonald's, Papa John's, Pizza Hut, Sagebrush Steaks, Shiki Japanese, Subway, Waffle House, Wendy's Comfort Inn, Days Inn, HighWay Inn, Scottish Inn H, $General, Advance Parts, Lowe's, O'Reilly Parts, USPO, vet, Walgreens

168 US 64, to Mocksville, N Exxon/dsl Lake Myers RV Resort (3mi), S BP/dsl H

162 US 64, Cool Springs, N Lake Myers RV Resort (5mi), S Shell/dsl Midway Camping

161mm S Yadkin River

154 to US 64, Old Mocksville Rd, N H, S Citgo/dsl Jaybee's Hotdogs repair/tires

153 US 64 (from eb), **1/2 mi S** Citgo/dsl Jaybee's Hotdogs repair/tires

152b a I-77, S to Charlotte, N to Elkin

151 US 21, E Statesville, N Marathon/DQ/dsl, Speedway/dsl Applebee's, Baskin-Robbins/Dunkin Donuts, Bojangles, Chick-fil-A, Chili's, Cook-Out, Cracker Barrel, K&W Cafeteria, KFC, Logan's Roadhouse, McDonald's, Mi Pueblo Café,

NC

= gas = food = lodging = other = rest stop

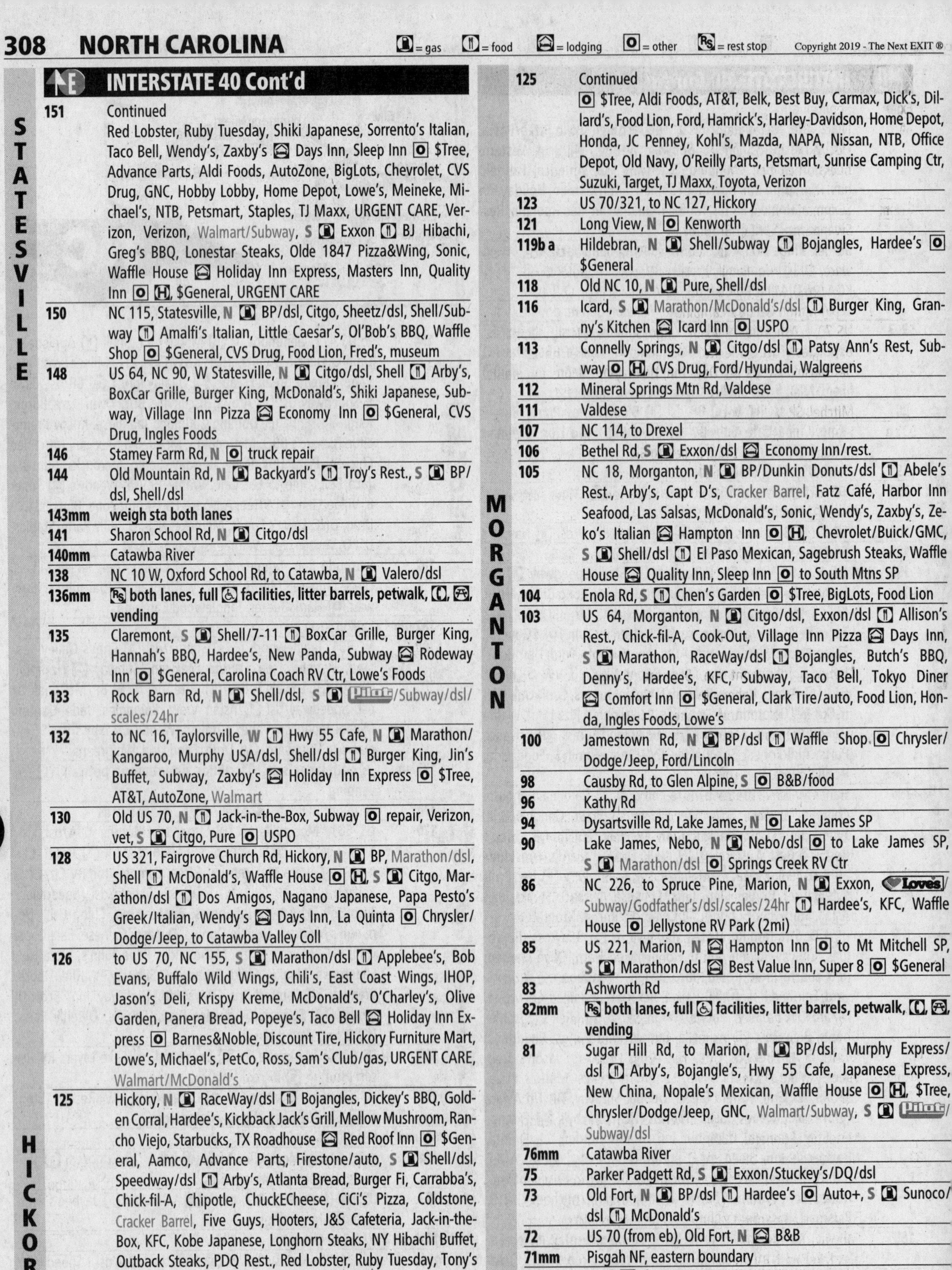

INTERSTATE 40 Cont'd

STATESVILLE

151 Continued
Red Lobster, Ruby Tuesday, Shiki Japanese, Sorrento's Italian, Taco Bell, Wendy's, Zaxby's Days Inn, Sleep Inn $Tree, Advance Parts, Aldi Foods, AutoZone, BigLots, Chevrolet, CVS Drug, GNC, Hobby Lobby, Home Depot, Lowe's, Meineke, Michael's, NTB, Petsmart, Staples, TJ Maxx, URGENT CARE, Verizon, Verizon, Walmart/Subway, S Exxon BJ Hibachi, Greg's BBQ, Lonestar Steaks, Olde 1847 Pizza&Wing, Sonic, Waffle House Holiday Inn Express, Masters Inn, Quality Inn H, $General, URGENT CARE

150 NC 115, Statesville, N BP/dsl, Citgo, Sheetz/dsl, Shell/Subway Amalfi's Italian, Little Caesar's, Ol'Bob's BBQ, Waffle Shop $General, CVS Drug, Food Lion, Fred's, museum

148 US 64, NC 90, W Statesville, N Citgo/dsl, Shell Arby's, BoxCar Grille, Burger King, McDonald's, Shiki Japanese, Subway, Village Inn Pizza Economy Inn $General, CVS Drug, Ingles Foods

146 Stamey Farm Rd, N truck repair

144 Old Mountain Rd, N Backyard's Troy's Rest., S BP/dsl, Shell/dsl

143mm **weigh sta both lanes**

141 Sharon School Rd, N Citgo/dsl

140mm Catawba River

138 NC 10 W, Oxford School Rd, to Catawba, N Valero/dsl

136mm **both lanes, full facilities, litter barrels, petwalk, vending**

135 Claremont, S Shell/7-11 BoxCar Grille, Burger King, Hannah's BBQ, Hardee's, New Panda, Subway Rodeway Inn $General, Carolina Coach RV Ctr, Lowe's Foods

133 Rock Barn Rd, N Shell/dsl, S Pilot/Subway/dsl/scales/24hr

132 to NC 16, Taylorsville, W Hwy 55 Cafe, N Marathon/Kangaroo, Murphy USA/dsl, Shell/dsl Burger King, Jin's Buffet, Subway, Zaxby's Holiday Inn Express $Tree, AT&T, AutoZone, Walmart

130 Old US 70, N Jack-in-the-Box, Subway repair, Verizon, vet, S Citgo, Pure USPO

128 US 321, Fairgrove Church Rd, Hickory, N BP, Marathon/dsl, Shell McDonald's, Waffle House H, S Citgo, Marathon/dsl Dos Amigos, Nagano Japanese, Papa Pesto's Greek/Italian, Wendy's Days Inn, La Quinta Chrysler/Dodge/Jeep, to Catawba Valley Coll

126 to US 70, NC 155, S Marathon/dsl Applebee's, Bob Evans, Buffalo Wild Wings, Chili's, East Coast Wings, IHOP, Jason's Deli, Krispy Kreme, McDonald's, O'Charley's, Olive Garden, Panera Bread, Popeye's, Taco Bell Holiday Inn Express Barnes&Noble, Discount Tire, Hickory Furniture Mart, Lowe's, Michael's, PetCo, Ross, Sam's Club/gas, URGENT CARE, Walmart/McDonald's

HICKORY

125 Hickory, N RaceWay/dsl Bojangles, Dickey's BBQ, Golden Corral, Hardee's, Kickback Jack's Grill, Mellow Mushroom, Rancho Viejo, Starbucks, TX Roadhouse Red Roof Inn $General, Aamco, Advance Parts, Firestone/auto, S Shell/dsl, Speedway/dsl Arby's, Atlanta Bread, Burger Fi, Carrabba's, Chick-fil-A, Chipotle, ChuckECheese, CiCi's Pizza, Coldstone, Cracker Barrel, Five Guys, Hooters, J&S Cafeteria, Jack-in-the-Box, KFC, Kobe Japanese, Longhorn Steaks, NY Hibachi Buffet, Outback Steaks, PDQ Rest., Red Lobster, Ruby Tuesday, Tony's Pizza, Waffle House, Wendy's, Which Wich?, Wild Wok, Zaxby's Baymont Inn, Best Western, Courtyard, Crowne Plaza, Fairfield Inn, Hampton Inn, Hilton Garden, Quality Inn, Sleep Inn

NC

125 Continued
$Tree, Aldi Foods, AT&T, Belk, Best Buy, Carmax, Dick's, Dillard's, Food Lion, Ford, Hamrick's, Harley-Davidson, Home Depot, Honda, JC Penney, Kohl's, Mazda, NAPA, Nissan, NTB, Office Depot, Old Navy, O'Reilly Parts, Petsmart, Sunrise Camping Ctr, Suzuki, Target, TJ Maxx, Toyota, Verizon

123 US 70/321, to NC 127, Hickory

121 Long View, N Kenworth

119b a Hildebran, N Shell/Subway Bojangles, Hardee's $General

118 Old NC 10, N Pure, Shell/dsl

116 Icard, S Marathon/McDonald's/dsl Burger King, Granny's Kitchen Icard Inn USPO

113 Connelly Springs, N Citgo/dsl Patsy Ann's Rest, Subway H, CVS Drug, Ford/Hyundai, Walgreens

112 Mineral Springs Mtn Rd, Valdese

111 Valdese

107 NC 114, to Drexel

106 Bethel Rd, S Exxon/dsl Economy Inn/rest.

MORGANTON

105 NC 18, Morganton, N BP/Dunkin Donuts/dsl Abele's Rest., Arby's, Capt D's, Cracker Barrel, Fatz Café, Harbor Inn Seafood, Las Salsas, McDonald's, Sonic, Wendy's, Zaxby's, Zeko's Italian Hampton Inn H, Chevrolet/Buick/GMC, S Shell/dsl El Paso Mexican, Sagebrush Steaks, Waffle House Quality Inn, Sleep Inn to South Mtns SP

104 Enola Rd, S Chen's Garden $Tree, BigLots, Food Lion

103 US 64, Morganton, N Citgo/dsl, Exxon/dsl Allison's Rest., Chick-fil-A, Cook-Out, Village Inn Pizza Days Inn, S Marathon, RaceWay/dsl Bojangles, Butch's BBQ, Denny's, Hardee's, KFC, Subway, Taco Bell, Tokyo Diner Comfort Inn $General, Clark Tire/auto, Food Lion, Honda, Ingles Foods, Lowe's

100 Jamestown Rd, N BP/dsl Waffle Shop Chrysler/Dodge/Jeep, Ford/Lincoln

98 Causby Rd, to Glen Alpine, S B&B/food

96 Kathy Rd

94 Dysartsville Rd, Lake James, N Lake James SP

90 Lake James, Nebo, N Nebo/dsl to Lake James SP, S Marathon/dsl Springs Creek RV Ctr

86 NC 226, to Spruce Pine, Marion, N Exxon, Loves/Subway/Godfather's/dsl/scales/24hr Hardee's, KFC, Waffle House Jellystone RV Park (2mi)

85 US 221, Marion, N Hampton Inn to Mt Mitchell SP, S Marathon/dsl Best Value Inn, Super 8 $General

83 Ashworth Rd

82mm **both lanes, full facilities, litter barrels, petwalk, vending**

81 Sugar Hill Rd, to Marion, N BP/dsl, Murphy Express/dsl Arby's, Bojangle's, Hwy 55 Cafe, Japanese Express, New China, Nopale's Mexican, Waffle House H, $Tree, Chrysler/Dodge/Jeep, GNC, Walmart/Subway, S Pilot/Subway/dsl

76mm Catawba River

75 Parker Padgett Rd, S Exxon/Stuckey's/DQ/dsl

73 Old Fort, N BP/dsl Hardee's Auto+, S Sunoco/dsl McDonald's

72 US 70 (from eb), Old Fort, N B&B

71mm Pisgah NF, eastern boundary

67.5mm **truck eb**

66 Ridgecrest, N B&B

65 (from wb), to Black Mountain, Black Mtn Ctr

INTERSTATE 40 Cont'd

ASHEVILLE

Exit#	Services
64	NC 9, Black Mountain, N Exxon, Shell/Subway Pizza Hut, S BP/dsl Denny's, McDonald's, Phil's BBQ, Starbucks, Taco Bell, Wendy's Quality Inn Ingles Foods/gas, Rite Aid
63mm	Swannanoa River
59	Swannanoa, N BP/Subway, Shell/dsl Athens Pizza, Burger King, Don Chon Chinese, Papa John's Ace Hardware, CVS Drug, Family$, Harley-Davidson, Ingles Foods/gas, KOA (2mi), Miles RV Ctr/Park, to Warren Wilson Coll, USPO, vet, S Mama Gertie's Camping
55	US 70, E Asheville, N BP, Citgo/Subway, Mobil Arby's, Bojangles, Cocula Mexican, Domino's, Gondolier Italian, Waffle House, Zaxby's Days Inn, Holiday Inn, Motel 6, Quality Inn Family$, Folk Art Ctr, Go Groceries, Tap's RV park, to Mt Mitchell SP, VA, vet
53b a	I-240 W, US 74 a, to Asheville, Bat Cave, S Shell/dsl Sonic, Subway CVS Drug, Ingles, to Blue Ridge Pkwy, N on Fairview Rd Ay Carumba Mexican, China Buffet, J&S Cafeteria, KFC, Little Caesars, McDonald's, Papa John's, Pizza Hut, Subway Ramada Inn $General, Advance Parts, Citgo/dsl, CVS Drug, Hamrick's, Home Depot, Meineke
51	US 25A, Sweeten Creek Rd, S Subway Brookstone Lodge
50	US 25, Asheville, N Market Ctr, Shell, Shell/dsl Arby's, Asaka Japanese, Chapala Mexican, Hardee's, Jimmy John's, LJ Silver, McDonald's, Moe's SW Grill, Ruth's Chris Steaks, Starbucks, Subway, TGIFriday's, TX Roadhouse, Wendy's, Zoe's Kitchen Baymont Inn, Biltmore Village Lodge, Doubletree Inn, Grand Bohemian Hotel, Guesthouse Inn, Residence Inn, to Biltmore House, URGENT CARE, S Speedway/dsl Apollo Flame Rest., Atl Bread Co, Bojangles, Huddle House, Juicy Lucy's Advance Parts, Ingles/deli
47mm	French Broad River
47	NC 191, W Asheville, N Bear Creek RV Camping, S BP/Subway Moose Cafe Comfort Suites, Country Inn&Suites, Fairfield Inn, Hampton Inn, Holiday Inn Express, Rodeway Inn Audi/Porsche/VW, Farmer's Mkt, Ford, Nissan
46b a	I-26 & I-240 E, **2 mi** N multiple services from I-240
44	US 19, US 23, W Asheville, N BP, Shell/DQ/dsl, Speedway/dsl Applebee's, Arby's, Bojangle's, Burger King, Cracker Barrel, Dunkin Donuts, El Chapala Mexican, Fatz Cafe, Hardee's, IHOP, Subway, Waffle House, Wendy's, Yao Grill Comfort Inn, Country Inn&Suites, Ramada Inn, Red Roof Inn, Rodeway Inn, Sleep Inn, Whispering Pines Motel Chevrolet, Chrysler/Dodge/Jeep, Lowe's, Mazda/Mercedes, S McDonald's, Zaxby's Asheville Inn, Holiday Inn, Woodspring Suites Bi-Lo Foods, CVS Drug, Home Depot
41mm	**weigh sta both lanes**
37	Candler, N Sunoco, TA/Country Pride/dsl/scales/24hr/@ Goodyear/truck tires, S Exxon/dsl Days Inn, Plantation Motel $General, KOA
33	Newfound Rd, to US 74, S Exxon
31	Rd 215, Canton, N Sagebrush Steaks Best Value Inn URGENT CARE, S BP/dsl, Marathon/DQ, Shell/dsl Arby's, Bojangles, Burger King, McDonald's, Starbucks, Subway, Taco Bell, Waffle House Quality Inn Ford, Ingles Foods/dsl, RV/truck repair
27	US 19/23, to Waynesville, Great Smokey Mtn Expswy, **3 mi** S Burger King, Coffee Cup Cafe, Subway Super 8, $Tree, Food Lion, GNC, Lowe's, to WCU (25mi)

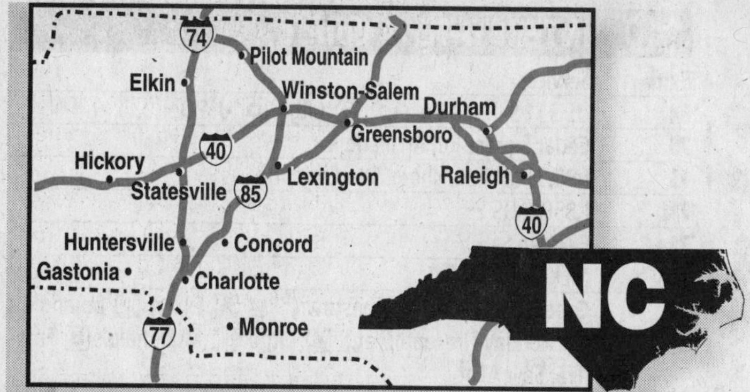

Exit#	Services
24	NC 209, to Lake Junaluska, N /Subway/dsl/scales/24hr/@ Midway Motel, S Shell/cafe/dsl/24hr
20	US 276, to Maggie Valley, Lake Junaluska, S BP/dsl, Exxon/dsl, Marathon (2mi) Creekwood RV Park, Pride RV Resort, Winngray RV Park
16mm	Pigeon River
15	Fines Creek
13mm	Pisgah NF eastern boundary
10mm	**both lanes, full facilities, litter barrels, petwalk, , , vending**
7	Harmon Den
4mm	**tunnel both lanes**
0mm	North Carolina/Tennessee state line

INTERSTATE 74

ASHEBORO

Exit#	Services
23	US 220 S, **I-70/73 begins/ends.**
25	US 220 N, Ellerbe
28	to NC 73 W, Millstone Rd
30	Haywood Parker Rd
33	NC 73
35	Norman
39	Tabernacle Church Rd
41	US 220 S, US 220 A N, Candor
44	NC 211, Candor, Pinehurst, N Exxon/dsl, /Dunkin Donuts/Wendy's/dsl/scales/24hr, S Citgo/dsl $General
49	NC 24, 27, Troy, Carthage, S Citgo Bojangle's, Hardee's, Waffle House Day Inn $General
52	Star, Robbins
56	US 220 A, Ether, Steeds
58	Black Ankle Rd
60	**/visitor ctr both lanes, full facilities**
61	NC 705, Seagrove, Robbins, N Citgo/Hardee's/dsl
66	New Hope Church Rd
68	US 220, NC 134, Ulah, Troy
71	McDowell Rd, N Tank$Tommy, S K&W Cafeteria
72b a	US 64, NC 49, To Lexington, N BP, Speedway/dsl Arby's, Bamboo Garden, Biscuitville, Bojangle's, Burger King, Dunkin Donuts, Huddle House, McDonald's, Taco Bell, Wendy's Comfort Inn Lowe's Foods, S Citgo/dsl Subway Randolph Inn Food Lion
74	(exits left)Salisbury St, Sunset Ave
75	W Presnell St
76	Vision Dr
77	Spero Rd
79	Pineview St
86	(80 from wb) I-73 N (exits left from eb, runs with I-74)

INTERSTATE 74 Cont'd

Exit#	Services
84	US 311 S, Randleman, S [gas] Citgo [other] USPO
79	Cedar Square Rd, Archdale
75	I-85, N to Greensboro, S to Charlotte
71b	I-85BR, US 29
71a	E Green St
70	MLK Dr, S [other] [H]
69	Greensboro Rd, Jamestown, N [gas] Exxon [food] Bojangle's [other] Holiday Tire/auto, vet, S [gas] Citgo [food] McDonald's [other] Family$, SaveALot
67	NC 68, Eastchester Dr, to I-40, S [gas] Marathon/dsl [food] Barbarito's, Honeybaked Ham [other] URGENT CARE
66	Johnson St
65	US 311, N Main St, High Point, S [gas] Sheetz/dsl [food] McDonald's [other] Aldi Foods
63	NC 66, Kernersville
60	High Point Rd
59	Union Cross Rd
56	Ridgewood Rd
I-74 begins/ends on I-40, exit 196.	
Future I-74 connects via US 52 to US 311 around Winston Salem.	
122	Moore-RJR Dr, N [other] Hanging Rock SP
123	King, Tobaccoville, N [gas] Exxon/7-11 [food] Bojangle's, Burger King, KFC, Little Caesar's, Little Italy, McDonald's, Papa John's, Pizza Hut, Stratford BBQ, Subway, Taco Bell, Waffle House, Wendy's [lodging] Bestway Inn [other] $General, $Tree, Advance Parts, CVS Drug, Family$, Food Lion, Lowe's Foods, O'Reilly Parts, Rite Aid, USPO, vet, Walmart
127mm	scenic overlook wb
129	Pinnacle, N [gas] BP/dsl, S [gas] Marathon
131	Pilot Mtn SP
134	NC 268, Pilot Mtn, Elkin, N [gas] Exxon/dsl [food] McDonald's, Mtn View Rest. [lodging] Econolodge [other] Advance Parts, S [gas] Shell/Circle K/dsl, Speedway/Dunkin Donuts/dsl [food] Wendy's
135	Pilot Mtn
136	Cook School Rd, N [gas] Blue Mtn/dsl, Gas&Go [other] Ford
17	US 52 N, to Mt Airy
13	Park Dr
11	US 601, to Mt Airy, Dobson, N [gas] Sheetz/dsl
8	Red Brush Rd, N [gas] Shell/Circle K/dsl
6	NC 89, to Mt Airy, S [gas] FLYING J/Brintle's Rest./dsl/scales/24hr/@, Marathon/Subway/dsl, Shell/Circle K/dsl [food] Copper Pot Rest. [lodging] Best Western
5	(101 from eb) I-77, N to Wytheville, S to Statesville
0mm	**I-74 begins/ends at NC state line, runs with I-77**

KING · PILOT MTN · NC

INTERSTATE 77

Exit#	Services
105mm	North Carolina/Virginia state line
105mm	**Welcome Ctr sb, full [handicapped] facilities, info, litter barrels, petwalk, [phone], [picnic], vending**
103mm	**weigh sta both lanes**
101	I-74 E, to Mt Airy, Winston-Salem, Greensboro, E [other] [H] (12mi)
100	NC 89, to Mt Airy, E [gas] FLYING J/Brintle's Rest./dsl/scales/24hr/@, Marathon/Subway/dsl, Shell/Circle K/dsl [food] Copper Pot Rest. [lodging] Best Western [other] dsl repair, [H] (12mi)
93	to Dobson, Surry, E [gas] BP/DQ/dsl, Exxon/Circle K/dsl [food] Diner, Harvest Grill (2mi), Putters Grill [lodging] Hampton Inn, Surry Inn
85	NC 118, CC Camp Rd, to Elkin, 1-3 mi W [gas] Exxon/7-11/dsl, Murphy Express/dsl, Sheetz/dsl, Speedway/dsl [food] Burger King,
85	Continued KFC, Mazzini's Italian, McDonald's, Sonic, Taco Bell, Zaxby's [lodging] Fairfield Inn [other] [H], $Tree, AT&T, BigLots, Food Lion, Lowe's, Rite Aid, Walmart/Subway
83	US 21 byp, to Sparta (from nb)
82.5mm	Yadkin River
82	NC 67, Elkin, E [gas] BP/Subway/dsl, Citgo/Case Outlet/dsl, Exxon/dsl [food] Arby's, Cracker Barrel, Sixty Seven Pizza [lodging] Best Western [other] Holly Ridge Camping (8mi), W [gas] Speedway/Dunkin Donuts/dsl [food] Bojangles, Breakfastime, McDonald's, Valentino's Pizza, Waffle House, Wendy's [lodging] Days Inn, Hampton Inn, Quality Inn [other] $General, D-Rex Drug, Food Lion, URGENT CARE, vet
79	US 21 S, to Arlington, E [gas] Citgo/Subway/dsl [lodging] Royal Inn, W [gas] BP/dsl [food] Glenn's BBQ [lodging] Best Value Inn
73b a	US 421, to Winston-Salem, 1 mi E [gas] Exxon/Subway/7-11/dsl
72mm	**[RS] nb, full [handicapped] facilities, litter barrels, petwalk, [phone], [picnic], vending**
65	NC 901, to Union Grove, Harmony, E [other] Van Hoy Farms Camping, W [gas] BP/dsl, Exxon/Subway/7-11/dsl [food] Burger Barn [other] $General, Ace Hardware, Fiddler's Grove Camping (2mi)
63mm	**[RS] sb, full [handicapped] facilities, litter barrels, petwalk, [phone], [picnic], vending**
59	Tomlin Mill Rd, W [gas] Valero/dsl
58	**[RS] both lanes, full [handicapped] facilities**
56.5mm	S Yadkin River
54	US 21, to Turnersburg, E [gas] Citgo, W [gas] Exxon/7-11/dsl [food] Arby's, Baskin-Robbins/Dunkin Donuts, Chick-fil-A, Cook-Out, Golden Corral, Zaxby's
51b a	I-40, E to Winston-Salem, W to Hickory
50	E Broad St, Statesville, E [gas] Citgo, Exxon/Kangaroo/dsl, Shell [food] Arby's, Bojangles, Burger King, Domino's, Dunkin Donuts/Hungry Howie's, East Coast Grill, IHOP, Little Caesar's, Los Compadres Mexican, McDonald's, Papa John's, Papa Murphy's Pizza Hut, Shanghai Buffet, Starbucks, Subway, Taco Bell, Wendy's [lodging] Brookwood Inn, Red Roof Inn [other] $General, $Tree AT&T, Belk, Bi-Lo, Food Lion, Rite Aid, URGENT CARE
49b a	US 70, G Bagnal Blvd, to Statesville, E [gas] BP, Citgo/dsl, Citgo/dsl, Marathon/dsl, Shell, Solo [food] KFC, Outback Steaks, Rice Fun Chinese, Subway, Village Inn Pizza, Waffle House [lodging] Best Value Inn, Best Western, Comfort Inn, Courtyard, Hampton Inn, Motel 6, Ramada Inn [other] auto repair, Camping World RV Ctr, Ford/Lincoln, Harley-Davidson, Honda, Nissan, Toyota, W [gas] Citgo/dsl, Exxon/dsl [lodging] Hilton Garden, Microtel [other] Buick/GMC, Carquest, Chrysler/Dodge/Jeep
45	to Troutman, Barium Springs, E [other] KOA, RV Repair
42	US 21, NC 115, to Troutman, Oswalt, E [gas] Pilot/Subway/Dunkin Donuts/dsl/scales/24hr, Sheetz/dsl [food] Bojangles, McDonald's, Taco Bell, Wendy's [other] AutoZone, Lowe's, W [gas] CNG Exxon/dsl [food] Arby's [other] to Lake Norman SP
39mm	**[RS] both lanes, full [handicapped] facilities, litter barrels, petwalk, [phone], [picnic] vending**
36	NC 150, Mooresville, E [gas] Circle K/dsl, Exxon, QT/dsl, Shell dsl [food] Applebee's, CookOut, Denny's, Domino's, Fat Boy Rest., Hong Mei Buffet, Pizza Hut, Pomodoro's, Popeyes, Sonny's BBQ, Taco Bell, Waffle House, Wendy's, Zaxby's [lodging] Days Inn, Fairfield Inn, Holiday Inn Express, Quality Inn [other] $Tree Belk, Big Lots, Cadillac/Chevrolet, GNC, Jo-Ann Fabrics, Kia Kohl's, Subaru, Tuesday Morning, URGENT CARE, Walmart Subway, W [gas] Circle K/dsl, Qt/dsl, Shell/dsl, Speedway dsl [food] Baskin-Robbins/Dunkin Donuts, Bojangles, Buffalo Wild Wings, Charanda Mexican, Chick-fil-A, Chili's, Chipotle Chopstix, Cracker Barrel, Duckworth's Grill, Firehouse Subs, Five Guys, Golden Corral, Hardee's, Hickory Tavern Grill, Hooters

ELKIN · STATESVILLE · MOORESVILLE

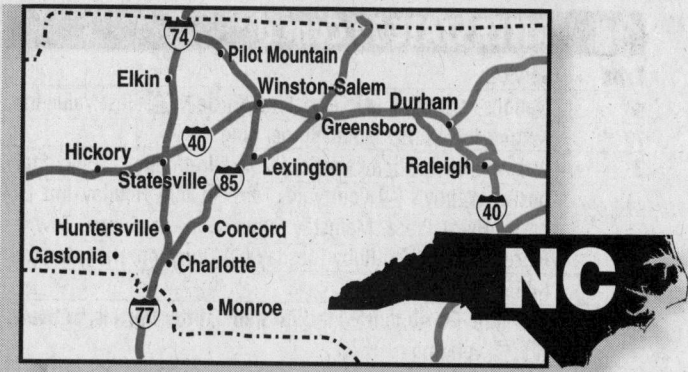

INTERSTATE 77 Cont'd

36 Continued
IHOP, Iron Thunder Grill, LoneStar Steaks, McAlister's Deli, McDonald's, Moe's SW Cafe, Noodles&Co, O'Charley's, Panera Bread, Papa Murphy's, Red Robin, Rita's Custard, Sagebrush Steaks, Showmar's, Smoothie King, Sonic, Starbucks, Steak'n Shake, Subway [lodging] Carolina Inn, Hampton Inn, Sleep Inn, Wingate Inn [other] Advance Parts, AT&T, AutoZone, Best Buy, BJ's Whse/gas, CVS Drug, Dick's, Discount Tire, Food Lion, Hobby Lobby, Lowe's, Michael's, NTB, Old Navy, PetCo, Petsmart, Ross, Sam's Club/dsl, Staples, Target, TJ Maxx, Tuffy Auto, Verizon, vet, Walgreens, World Mkt

35 Brawley School Rd

33 US 21 N, E [gas] Shell [food] Brusco's Pizza, China Express, DQ, Iron Grill Japanese, Jeffrey's Rest, Jets Pizza, McDonald's, Starbucks, Subway [lodging] Candlewood Suites, Hilton Garden, SpringHill Suites, TownePlace Suites [other] [H], W [gas] Citgo/dsl, Marathon/dsl [food] Arby's, Baskin-Robbins/Dunkin Donuts, Sauza's Mexican [other] Food Lion, vet

31 Langtree Rd, W [gas] Shell/dsl

30 Davidson, E [gas] BP, Exxon/dsl [food] Char-Grill, Ming's Chinese, Subway [lodging] Homewood Suites [other] Harris-Teeter, to Davidson College, Woodie's Auto Service, W [food] North Harbor Rest

28 US 21 S, NC 73, Cornelius, Lake Norman, E [gas] Cashion/dsl, Citgo [food] Acropolis Cafe [lodging] Days Inn, Hampton Inn [other] NAPA, vet, W [gas] Marathon/Circle K [food] Asiana, Bojangles, Chicago Dog, Choplin's Rest., Domino's, Dragon Buffet, Fresh Chef Cafe, Honeybaked Ham, Jersey Mike's, Jimmy John's, KFC, Little Caesar's, Mac's BBQ, McAlister's Deli, McDonald's, Pizza Hut, Starbucks, Subway, Taco Bell, Waffle House, Wendy's [lodging] Clarion, Comfort Inn, EconoLodge, Microtel [other] $Tree, Chrysler/Dodge/Jeep, Fresh Mkt, Goodyear/auto, Hyundai, Infiniti, SteinMart, USPO, Walgreens

25 NC 73, Concord, Lake Norman, E [gas] Exxon/7-11/dsl [food] Burger King, Chick-fil-A, Chili's, Duckworth's Grill, IHOP, Longhorn Steaks, McDonald's, Melting Pot, Moe's SW Grill, Panda Express, Panera Bread, Papa John's, Showmar's Rest., Starbucks, Subway, Zaxby's [lodging] Country Inn&Suites, Holiday Inn Express, Quality Inn [other] [H], AAA, Advance Parts, AT&T, GNC, Harris-Teeter, Home Depot, Kohl's, Lowe's, Marshall's, PetCo, Staples, Target, Tuffy Auto, Verizon, vet, W [gas] Shell/Circle K/dsl [food] Bob Evans, Bojangles, Bonefish Grill, Carrabba's, Chipotle, Hickory Tavern Grill, House of Taipei, Jason's Deli, Jimmy John's, Kabuto Japanese, Outback Steaks, Qdoba, Red Rock's Cafe, Starbucks, Subway, Taco Mac, Viva Chicken, Which Wich?, Zoe's Kitchen [lodging] Candlewood Suites, Courtyard, Sleep Inn [other] Barnes&Noble, Dick's, Office Depot, to Energy Explorium, Walgreens, Whole Foods Mkt

CONCORD

23 Gilead Rd, to US 21, Huntersville, E [gas] BP, Pittstop, Shell [food] Baskin-Robbins/Dunkin Dounuts, Bojangles, Chico's Mexican, CookOut, Hardee's, Huntersville Rest., Jersey Mike's, Little Caesar's, Rocky's Pizza, Romanello's Subs, Subway, Taco Bell, Waffle House, Wendy's [lodging] Best Western, Comfort Suites, Hampton Inn, Super 8 [other] AutoZone, Buick/GMC, Food Lion, Ford, Goodyear/auto, Honda, Mazda, O'Reilly Parts, Rite Aid, Toyota, Tuesday Morning, USPO, vet, VW, W [gas] Shell/7-11/dsl [food] Domino's, Firehouse Subs, Five Guys, Fusion Asian, Groucho's Deli, Hawthorne's Pizza, Killington's Rest., McDonald's, Papa Murphy's, Pizza Hut, Starbucks [other] [H], Batteries+, CVS Drug, Earth Fare, GNC, Harris-Teeter, Publix, URGENT CARE, Walgreens

19b a S I-485 Outer, Rd 115, to Spartanburg

Pilot Mountain
Elkin
Winston-Salem
Durham
Greensboro
Hickory
Lexington
Raleigh
Statesville
Huntersville
Concord
Gastonia
Charlotte
Monroe
74
40
85
77
NC

18 Harris Blvd, Reames Rd, E [gas] BP/Arby's, Shell/7-11/dsl [food] Azteca Mexican, Bob Evans, Hickory Tavern, Jack-in-the-Box, Jimmy John's, Subway, Waffle House [lodging] Comfort Suites, Courtyard, Fairfield Inn, Hilton Garden, Holiday Inn Express, Suburban Lodge [other] [H], Advance Parts, Staples, to UNCC, Univ Research Park, URGENT CARE, W [food] Bravo Italian, Buffalo Wild Wings, Chick-fil-A, Chili's, East Coast Grill, Edomae Grill, Firebirds Grill, Firehouse Subs, Five Guys, Fox&Hound, Jersey Mike's, Mimi's Cafe, Moe's SW Grill, Olive Garden, On-the-Border, Panera bread, PF Chang's, Red Robin, Shane's Rib Shack, TGI Friday's, Wendy's [lodging] Drury Inn [other] $Tree, AT&T, Belk, Best Buy, Dick's, Dillard's, Discount Tire, Lowe's, Macy's, Old Navy, Petsmart, REI, Target, Verizon

16b a US 21, Sunset Rd, E [gas] Circle K, QT/dsl, Shell/7-11/dsl [food] Capt D's, Hardee's, KFC, McDonald's, Papa John's, Subway, Taco Bell, Wendy's [lodging] Days Inn, Super 8 [other] $General, AutoZone, Just$ave Foods, NAPA, O'Reilly Parts, W [gas] Circle K/dsl, Citgo/dsl, Shell/dsl/scales/24hr [food] Baskin-Robbins/Dunkin Donuts, Bojangles, Bubba's BBQ, CookOut, Denny's, Domino's, Jack-in-the-Box, Little Caesar's, Subway, Waffle House [lodging] Microtel, Sleep Inn [other] Advance Parts, Aldi Foods, CVS Drug, Family$, Food Lion, Meineke, Walgreens

13b a I-85, S to Spartanburg, N to Greensboro

12 La Salle St, W [gas] Marathon/dsl, Shell/dsl

11b a I-277, Brookshire Fwy, NC 16

10b Trade St, 5th St, E [other] to Discovery Place, W [gas] Circle K [food] Bojangles, Church's [other] Family$

10a US 21 (from sb), Moorhead St, downtown

9 I-277, US 74, to US 29, John Belk Fwy, downtown, E [other] [H], stadium

8 Remount Rd (from nb, no re-entry)

7 Clanton Rd, E [gas] QT/dsl, Shell/dsl [lodging] Quality Inn, Super 8 [other] Family$, W [gas] 7-11/dsl, BP

6b a US 521, Billy Graham Pkwy, E [gas] Citgo, Exxon/dsl, Exxon/dsl (2), QT/dsl [food] Arby's, Azteca Mexican, Bojangles, Burger King, Capt D's, Carolina Prime Steaks, Domino's, Dragon House, Firehouse Subs, HoneyBaked Ham, IHOP, KFC, Papa John's, Tres Pesos Grill, Waffle House [lodging] Baymont Inn, Best Western, Clarion, Days Inn, Ramada, Sheraton [other] CVS Drug, Family$, Home Depot, TJ Maxx, to Queens Coll, Walgreens, W [gas] Circle K [lodging] Courtyard, Embassy Suites, Extended Stay America, Hyatt House, InTowne Suites, La Quinta, Sleep Inn [other] [airport]

5 Tyvola Rd, E [gas] Circle K, Exxon/7-11/dsl, Shell [food] Chili's, Kabuto, McDonald's, Sonny's BBQ, Subway [lodging] Cloverleaf Suites, Comfort Inn, Crowne Plaza, Extended Stay America, Hawthorn Suites, Hilton, Wyndham Garden [other] Aldi Foods, Costco/gas, Maserati, Meineke, Verizon, W [lodging] Extended Stay America, Home 2 Suites, Wingate Inn

CHARLOTTE

NC

INTERSTATE 77 Cont'd

Exit#	Services
4	Nations Ford Rd, E Citgo, Shell/Circle K Best Value Inn, Knights Inn, W Mobil/Burger King
3	Arrowood Rd, E Cafe South, Jack-in-the-Box, Sonic, Starbucks, Wendy's Courtyard, Fairfield Inn, Holiday Inn Express, Hyatt Place, Mainstay Suites, Sonesta Suites, TownePlace Suites, W Ruby Tuesday Drury Inn, Hampton Inn
2	I-485
1.5mm	**Welcome Ctr nb, full facilities, info, litter barrels, petwalk, , vending**
1	Westinghouse Blvd, to I-485 (from nb), E BP/dsl Jack-in-the-Box, Subway, Waffle House Super 8, W Mobil/7-11/dsl
0mm	North Carolina/South Carolina state line

INTERSTATE 85

Exit#	Services
234mm	North Carolina/Virginia state line
233	US 1, to Wise
231mm	**Welcome Ctr sb, full facilities, litter barrels, petwalk, ,**
229	Oine Rd, to Norlina, E BP, W SRA
226	Ridgeway Rd, W to Kerr Lake, to SRA
223	Manson Rd, E USPO, W to Kerr Dam
220	US 1, US 158, Flemingtown Rd, to Middleburg, E Mobil/dsl, W Exxon/dsl/scales/truck wash Chex Trkstp/motel/rest.
218	US 1 S (from sb exits left), to Raleigh
217	Nutbush Bridge, E auto repair, W Kerr Lake RA
215	US 158 BYP E, Henderson (no EZ return from nb), E Citgo, Shell, Speedway/dsl Burger King, Forsyth's BBQ, Golden China, Subway Budget Host, EconoLodge, Scottish Inn $General, Food Lion, repair/tires, Roses, services on US 158
214	NC 39, Henderson, E BP, W Mobil/dsl, Shell to Kerr Lake RA
213	US 158, Dabney Dr, to Henderson, E Marathon, Valero Bamboo Garden, Big Cheese Pizza, Bojangles, Denny's, Domino's, Ichibar Chinese, KFC, McDonald's, Papa John's, Pino's Italian, Subway, Wendy's Family$, Food Lion, Roses, vet, W Shell Chick-fil-A, Golden Corral, Mayflower Seafood, Pizza Hut, Ruby Tuesday, Smithfields BBQ, Taco Bell Red Roof Inn Advance Parts, Buick/Chevrolet/GMC, Chrysler/Dodge/Jeep, Ford/Lincoln, Lowe's, Rite Aid, Staples, Verizon
212	Ruin Creek Rd, E Shell/dsl Cracker Barrel, Mazatlan Mexican, Ribeye's, Waffle House Toyota, W Exxon/Burger King, Sheetz/dsl Baymont Inn, Hampton Inn, Sleep Inn H, $Tree, Belk, JC Penney, Walmart
209	Poplar Creek Rd, W Vance-Granville Comm Coll
206	US 158, Oxford, E Citgo, W BP/dsl
204	NC 96, Oxford, E BP/dsl Comfort Inn, King's Inn Buick/Chevrolet/GMC, Ford, Honda, W Shell, Speedway/dsl, Valero/Popeye's Burger King, China Wok, Cook-Out, Domino's, KFC/Taco Bell, McDonald's, Pizza Hut, Subway, Wendy's Clarion H, GNC
202	US 15, Oxford, W Murphy Express/dsl Bojangles, Hwy 55 Cafe Crown Motel (2mi) $Tree, Verizon, Walmart
199mm	**both lanes, full facilities, litter barrels, petwalk, ,**
198mm	Tar River
191	NC 56, Butner, E BP/dsl, Speedway/dsl Arby's, Bob's BBQ, Bojangles, Diner 56, Domino's, El Rio Mexican, KFC/Taco Bell, McDonald's, Pizza Hut, Pizza Mia, Sonic, Subway,
191	Continued Taste of China, Wendy's Inn at Creedmoor $General, $Tree, Advance Parts, AutoZone, Food Lion, M&H Tires, O'Reilly Parts, Rite Aid, to Falls Lake RA, Verizon, vet, W Exxon, Shell/dsl Hardee's, Old South Rest. Best Western, EconoLodge, Quality Inn auto repair
189	Butner, 1 mi W BP/dsl, Exxon/dsl, Valero BBQ Barn, Subway repair, 1 mi N $General
186b a	US 15, to Creedmoor, E Variety Mart/dsl
185mm	Falls Lake
183	Redwood Rd
182	Red Mill Rd, E Exxon/dsl Kenworth/Isuzu Trucks
180	Glenn School Rd, E Citgo/dsl Hwy 55 Cafe $Tree, AT&T, Verizon, Walmart/Subway
179	E Club Blvd, E Exxon
178	US 70 E, to Raleigh, Falls Lake RA, Research Triangle, E RDU Airport
177	Avondale Dr, NC 55, W BP, Shell American Hero, Arby's, Guanajuato, McDonald's, Subway, Waffle House Advance Parts, AutoZone, Family$
176b a	Gregson St, US 501 N, E Mobil Burger King, Kickback Jack's, PanPan Diner, Randy's Pizza, Ruby Tuesday Hampton Inn W H, Museum of Life&Science
175	Guess Rd, E Citgo Hog Heaven BBQ, Pad Thai Holiday Inn Express, Super 8 Rite Aid, W BP/dsl, Exxon/dsl Pure/dsl Bojangles, IHOP, Jimmy's Hotdogs, McDonald's Popeye's, TX Roadhouse Red Roof Inn $Tree, Costco gas, Family$, GNC, Home Depot, PetsMart, Ross, Verizon, vet
174a	Hillandale Rd, W Bleu Olive, China King, El Corral, Pomodoro Italian Comfort Inn, Courtyard URGENT CARE Walgreens
174b	US 15 S, US 501 S
173	US 15, US 501, US 70, Colemill Rd, W Durham, E BP, Exxon dsl, Mobil, Sheetz/dsl Arby's, Biscuitville, Bojangles, Chick-fil-A, Cookout, Cracker Barrel, DogHouse Rest., Domino's, Japan Express, KFC/Taco Bell, Krispy Kreme, McDonald's, Shanghai Chinese, Subway, Waffle House, Wendy's, Zaxby's Days Inn, Hilton, Motel 6, Quality Inn H, $General, Advance Parts, AutoZone, CVS Drug, Mr Tire, O'Reilly Parts, Rite Aid
172	NC 147 S, to US 15 S, US 501 S (from nb), Durham
170	to NC 751, to Duke U (no EZ return from nb), E Durham Skyland Inn, Scottish Inn, W to Eno River SP
165	NC 86, to Chapel Hill, E Eagles/Burger King/dsl, Sheetz dsl China Fuji, Hwy 55, Papa John's, Subway $Tree, Advance Parts, Home Depot, vet, Walmart, W BP/dsl auto repair
164	Hillsborough, E BP, Citgo/dsl McDonald's Holiday Inn Express, W Shell Bojangles, Colorado Burrito Domino's, Hardee's, Jimmy's Hotdogs, KFC/Taco Bell, Pueblo Viejo Mexican, Subway, Waffle House, Wendy's Microtel $General, $Tree, AutoZone, Food Lion, Ford, Goodyear/auto
163	I-40 E, to Raleigh.
	I-85 S and I-40 W run together 38 mi.
161	to US 70 E, NC 86 N
160	to NC 86 N, Efland, W Exxon/dsl Missy's Grill Andrew's Repair
158mm	**weigh sta both lanes**
157	Buckhorn Rd, E BP/dsl, Petro/Marathon/Dunkin Donuts/Iron Skillet/dsl/scales/24hr/@, W Citgo
154	Mebane-Oaks Rd, E Murphy USA/dsl, Sheetz/dsl China Garden, Ciao Pizza, Hwy 55 Cafe, Starbucks, Subway, Taco Bell, Wendy's, Zaxby's $Tree, AT&T, GNC, Walmart/Subway

HENDERSON

OXFORD

BUTNER

DURHAM

NC

INTERSTATE 85 Cont'd

MEBANE

154 Continued
W BP, Shell/dsl, Speedway/dsl Biscuitville, Blue Ribbon Diner, Bojangles, La Fiesta Mexican, McDonald's, Roma Pizza, Sake Japanese, Waffle House Budget Inn Advance Parts, AutoZone, CVS Drug, Lowe's Foods, Tanger Outlets/famous brands, URGENT CARE, Verizon, vet, Walgreens

153 NC 119, Mebane, E BP/KFC/Pizza Hut/Taco Bell Anna Maria's Pizza, Cracker Barrel, Hibachi, Hursey's BBQ, Jersey Mike's, La Cocina Mexican, Moe's SW Grill, Ruby Tuesday, Sakura Japanese, Smithfield's BBQ Fairfield Inn, Hampton Inn, Holiday Inn Express $General, Lowe's, O'Reilly Parts, vet, W Exxon/Burger King Asian Harbor, Catrina's, Domino's, Papa John's, Subway Food Lion

152 Trollingwood Rd, E Pilot/McDonald's/dsl/scales/24hr, W Loves/Hardee's/dsl/scales/24hr

150 to Roxboro, Haw River, W FLYING J/Denny's/dsl/LP/scales/24hr, Pilot/DQ/Wendy's/dsl/scales/24hr, SpeedCo Days Inn Blue Beacon

148 NC 54, Graham, E BP/dsl, Exxon/Circle K, Shell/dsl Waffle House Quality Inn, W AmMex 2 Cafe

147 NC 87, to Pittsboro, Graham, E Sheetz/dsl AnnaMaria's Pizzeria, Arby's, Bojangles, Great Wall Chinese, Guerrero Mexican, Pizza Hut, Popeye's, Subway, Wendy's Advance Parts, AutoZone, Champion Tire/Repair, Family$, Food Lion, Ford, Just Save, O'Reilly Parts, Rite Aid, W Citgo/dsl, Exxon/dsl, Shell/dsl Biscuitville, Cook-Out, Golden China, La Fiesta Mexican, McDonald's, Taco Bell, Zaxby's $General, CVS Drug, Verizon, Walgreens

BURLINGTON

145 NC 49, Burlington, E BP/dsl, Sheetz/dsl, Shell/dsl Capt D's EconoLodge, Microtel, Motel 6 Harley-Davidson, W BP/dsl Biscuitville, Bojangles, Burger King, China Inn, Hardee's, KFC, Subway Red Carpet Inn, Red Roof Inn, Royal Inn $General, Chrysler/Dodge/Jeep, Family$, Food Lion, Rite Aid

143 NC 62, Burlington, E Sav-Way Hardee's, Waffle House, Wendy's JR Outlet, to Alamance Bfd, W Marathon, Sheetz/dsl Biscuitville, Cutting Board Rest., K&W Cafeteria Ramada Inn $General, auto repair, Cadillac, Chevrolet, Food Lion, Ford, Home Depot, Mazda, vet

141 Huffman Mill Rd, Burlington, E BP, Circle K IHOP, Mayflower Seafood, Outback Steaks Hampton Inn, Holiday Inn Express H, Nissan, W Applebee's, Arby's, Biscuitville, Bojangles, Cancun Mexican, Chick-fil-A, China Gate, Cook-Out, Cracker Barrel, East Coast Cafe, Fire Pit, Golden Corral, Grill 584, Hibachi Buffet, HoneyBaked Ham, Hooters, KFC, Krispy Kreme, La Cocina Mexican, Longhorn Steaks, McDonald's, Mellow Mushroom, O'Charley's, Panera Bread, Sal's Italian, Starbucks, Steak'n Shake, Subway, Taco Bell, Village Grill Best Western+, Country Inn&Suites, Courtyard, Super 8 $Tree, Harris Teeter/dsl, Hyundai, Lowe's, Subaru/Volvo/VW, to Elon Coll, URGENT CARE, Verizon, Walgreens, Walmart/McDonald's

140 University Ave, E H, Toyota, W Brixx Pizza, Buffalo Wing Wings, Burger King, Chick-fil-A, Chili's, Coldstone, Freddy's, Jimmy John's, Little Italy, McDonald's, Moe's SW Grill, Olive Garden, Peking House, Red Bowl Asian, Red Lobster, Red Robin, San Marcos Mexican, Smithfield's BBQ, Starbucks, TX Roadhouse Drury Inn AT&T, Barnes&Noble, Belk, Best Buy, BJ's Whse/gas, Dick's, Dillard's, Discount Tire, GNC, Hobby Lobby, JC Penney, Kohl's, Michael's, Petsmart, Ross, Target, TJ Maxx, Verizon

139mm both lanes, full facilities, litter barrels, vending

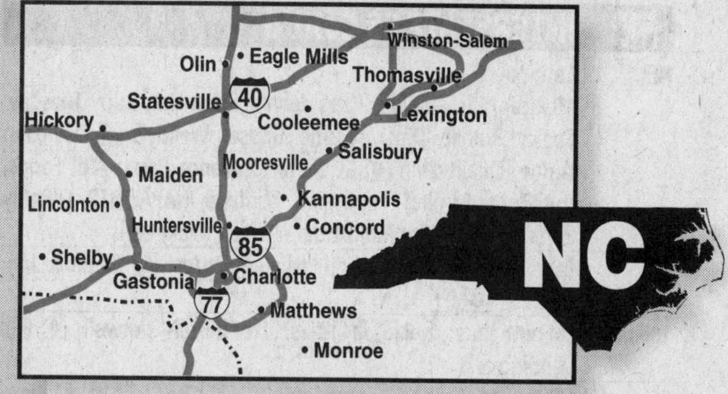

GREENSBORO

138 NC 61, Gibsonville, W TA/BP/Burger King/Popeye's/dsl/scales/24hr/@ truckwash

135 Rock Creek Dairy Rd, W Circle K, Citgo Bojangles, China 1, Ciao Italian, Domino's, Guacamole Mexican, Jersey Mike's Subs, McDonald's, Osaka Japanese, Pizza Hut/Taco Bell, Subway, Zaxby's Comfort Suites $General, CVS Drug, Food Lion, Verizon

132 Mt Hope Church Rd, E Shell/Subway/dsl McDonald's, Pascali's Pizza, W Liberty/dsl, Pilot/Wendy's/dsl/24hr Hampton Inn

131 to I-85 S, to I-73 N, to US 421, Highpoint, Charlotte

129 Youngsmill Rd, W KOA (4mi)

128 Alamance Church Rd, E Citgo/Subway/dsl

126b a US 421, to Sanford, E Hagan Stone Park Camping, W Circle K/dsl, Exxon/Circle K/dsl

124 S Elm, Eugene St, E Murphy Express/dsl Waffle House, W Bamboo Grill, Bojangles, Cracker Barrel, Hwy 55 Cafe, McDonald's, Pizza Hut, Smithfield's BBQ, Starbucks, Subway, Taco Bell, Wendy's, Zaxby's AT&T, Lowe's, Verizon, Walmart/McDonald's

122c b a US 220, to Greensboro, Asheboro (from sb)

121 I-40 W, I-73 N, to Winston-Salem

120 N US 29, E US 70, to I-40 W

119 Groometown Rd, from nb, W Citgo/dsl

118 US 29 S, US 70 W, to High Point, Jamestown, W Grandover Resort H

115mm Deep River

THOMASVILLE

113c I-74, US 311, Ashboro, to Winston-Salem

113a NC 62, Archdale, E Citgo/dsl, W BP/dsl Quality Inn

111 US 311, to High Point, Archdale, E Sheetz/dsl Bamboo Garden, Bojangles, Carolina's Diner, Hardee's, Pizza Hut, Subway, Taco Bell, Wendy's, Zaxby's Days Inn $General, CVS Drug, Food Lion, Lowe's Foods, Walmart Mkt, W Citgo, McDonald's, Mobil/dsl, Shell/Circle K/dsl, Valero/dsl Biscuitville, Cabo Grill, Rancho Rest., Waffle House Comfort Inn, Country Inn&Suites, Fairfield Inn, Hampton Inn, Holiday Inn Express H, O'Reilly Parts, tires, USPO, vet

108 Hopewell Church Rd, Trinity

106 Finch Farm Rd, E BP/dsl, W Sheetz/dsl BBQ Joe's, Subway (1mi)

103 NC 109, to Thomasville, E Exxon/dsl, Mobil/7-11/dsl, Murphy USA/dsl, Sheetz/dsl Arby's, Chen's Kitchen, Cookout Burgers, Elizabeth's Pizza, Subway, Taco Bell, Zaxby's Staylodge $Tree, CVS Drug, Ingles Foods, Lidl Mkt, Walmart/McDonald's, W Exxon/dsl, Fast Fuels/dsl, Shell, Speedway/dsl BBQ Shack, Biscuitville, Bojangles, Burger King, China Garden, Denny's, E Coast Grill, Hardee's, Hunan Chinese, KFC, La Carreta Mexican, Little Caesar's, Mandarin Express, Mazatlan

NC

INTERSTATE 85 Cont'd

103 Continued Mexican, McDonald's, Papa John's, Pizza Hut, Ruby Tuesday, Sonic, Sunrise Diner, Waffle House, Wendy's Davidson Lodge, Quality Inn $General, Advance Parts, Aldi Foods, AutoZone, Family$, Food Lion, Mighty$, NAPA, NTB, O'Reilly Parts, Peebles, Rite Aid, UHaul, Verizon, Walgreens

102 Lake Rd, W Marathon/dsl, Sunoco/dsl Comfort Inn, Microtel H

100mm **both lanes, full facilities, litter barrels, petwalk, vending**

96 US 64, to Asheboro, Lexington, E Citgo/dsl Modern Tire, NC Zoo, W Exxon/dsl, Gulf/dsl Randy's Rest. to Davidson Co Coll

94 Old US 64, E Shell, W Timberlake Gallery

91 NC 8, to Southmont, E BP/dsl, Citgo/dsl, Mobil/7-11 Biscuit King, Bojangle's, Christo Rest., Hunan Express, Kabuki Japanese, KFC, McDonald's, Ocean View Seafood, Subway, Waffle House, Wendy's Days Inn, Red Roof Inn Food Lion, High Rock Lake Camping (7mi), Mock Tire, W Exxon/dsl, Shell/dsl Applebee's, Arby's, Burger King, Cagney's Kitchen, Chick-fil-A, Cracker Barrel, Golden Corral, La Carreta Mexican, Little Caesar's, Mi Pueblo, Pizza Hut (1mi), Subway, Taco Bell, Zaxby's Country Hearth Inn, Quality Inn H, $Tree, Belk, GNC, Lidl Mkt, Lowe's (1mi), Walgreens, Walmart

88 Linwood, W Affordable Suites H

87 US 29, US 70, US 52 (from nb), High Point, W H,

86 Belmont Rd, W Bill's Trkstp/dsl/scales/24hr/@

84 US 29 S, US 70 W, NC 150 (from nb), to Spencer

82 US 29, US 70 (from sb), to Spencer

81.5mm Yadkin River

81 Long Ferry Rd, Spencer, E BP/dsl

79 Spencer Shops SHS, Spencer, E Spencer, **1 mi** W Citgo Bojangles, Subway $General, Food Lion

SALISBURY

76b a US 52, to Albemarle, Salisbury, E BP, Citgo Applebee's, Buffalo Wild Wings, Capriano's, Chipotle, ColdStone, E Coast Grill, IHOP, Pancho Villa, Top China, Which Wich?, Zaxby's Days Inn, Economy Inn, Happy Traveler Inn $Tree, Aldi Foods, AT&T, CVS Drug, Food Lion, GNC, Harley-Davidson, Lowe's, Marshall's, NTB, Old Navy, Petsmart, Rite Aid, Staples, Verizon, vet, Walgreens, W Murphy Express/dsl, Shell/Circle K/dsl, Speedway/dsl Blue Bay Seafood, Bojangles, Burger King, Capt D's, Chick-fil-A, China Buffet, Christo's Rest., Cookout, Cracker Barrel, Hardee's, HoneyBaked Ham, Jersey Mike's, KFC, Marco's Pizza, McDonald's, O'Charley's, Outback Steaks, Panera Bread, Papa John's, Pizza Hut, Starbucks, Taco Bell, Tokyo Express, Wendy's Comfort Suites, Courtyard, Holiday Inn Express H, Advance Parts, AutoZone, BigLots, Family$, Firestone/auto, Goodyear/auto, Office Depot, USPO, Walmart/Subway

75 US 601, Jake Alexander Blvd, E Sheetz/dsl Arby's, Breakfastime Econolodge, Home 2 Suites Hall Automotive, to Dan Nicholas Park, W BP, Citgo, Shell/dsl Casa Grande Mexican, CiCi's Pizza, Ichiban Japanese, Nyoshi Japanese, Waffle House, Wendy's Hampton Inn, Holiday Inn, Quality Inn Buick, Cadillac/Chevrolet, Chrysler/Dodge/Jeep, Ford, GMC, Honda, Kia, Nissan, Toyota

74 Julian Rd, E Honeybaked Ham, Salsarita's Dick's, Hobby Lobby, W Longhorn Steaks, Los Arcos, Olive Garden, Starbucks, Subway $Tree, Belk, Kohl's, Michael's

72 Peach Orchard Rd

71 Peeler Rd, E Loves/Chester's/McDonald's/dsl/scales/24hr, W Pilot/Dunkin Donuts/Subway/dsl/scales/24hr Bojangle's dsl repair

70 Webb Rd, E flea mkt, W Shell/dsl st patrol

68 US 29, US 601, to Rockwell, China Grove, W Bojangle's, Domino's, Gary's BBQ, Hardee's, Jimmie's Rest., Papa John's, Pizza Hut, Subway $General, AutoZone, Family$, Food Lion, Rite Aid

63 Kannapolis, E Pilot/Subway/dsl/scales Waffle House Motel 6, W QT/dsl URGENT CARE

60 Earnhardt Rd, Copperfield Blvd, E Exxon/dsl, Shell/Circle K/dsl Bojangles, Breakfast Time Rest., Copper Grill, Cracker Barrel, Waffle House Country Inn&Suites, Hampton Inn, Sleep Inn H, Discount Tire, URGENT CARE, W Shell/Kangaroo/dsl Casa Grande Mexican, Dragon Wok, Dunkin Donuts, East Coast Wings, Firehouse Subs, Little Caesar's, Logan's Roadhouse, McDonald's, Ruby Tuesday, Steak'n Shake, Subway, Taco Bell, Wendy's Holiday Inn Express AT&T, Hobby Lobby, Kohl's, Lowe's, Petco, Sam's Club/gas, Walmart

59mm **both lanes, full facilities, litter barrels, petwalk, vending**

CONCORD

58 US 29, US 601, Concord, E BP, Marathon/Circle K/dsl, Marathon/dsl, Shell/dsl Applebee's, Capt D's, Chick-fil-A, Chili's, Chipotle, Freddy's, Golden Corral, Jimmy John's, McDonald's, Moe's SW Grill, Mr C's Rest., O'Charley's, Panera Bread, Popeye's, Starbucks, Subway, Wendy's Best Value Inn, Quality Inn, Rodeway Inn H, Belk, Family$, Harris Teeter, JC Penney, Staples, Verizon, Walgreens, W BP, QT/dsl, Speedway/dsl CiCi's, IHOP Comfort Inn, Econolodge, Microtel $General, Ford, Home Depot, st patrol, vet

55 NC 73, to Davidson, Concord, E Shell McDonald's W Shell/Circle K/dsl Days Inn

54 Kannapolis Pkwy, George W Lyles Pkwy, E QT/dsl, SM Subway/dsl Bojangles, China Garden, Marco's Pizza, Off the-Grill Advance Parts, AutoZone, CVS Drug, Firestone auto, Food Lion, Harris Teeter, URGENT CARE, vet, Walgreens W Circle K/dsl Arby's, Asian Cafe, Buffalo Wild Wings Chick-fil-A, Dunkin Donuts, Jersey Mike's, McDonald's, M Pueblo, Showmar's Rest., Starbucks, Zaxby's $Tree, Bes Buy, Dick's, Goodyear/auto, Marshall's, Petsmart, Steinmart Super Target, Verizon

52 Poplar Tent Rd, E Mobil/7-11/dsl R&R BBQ t Lowe's Speedway, W Exxon/7-11/dsl

49 Bruton Smith Blvd, Concord Mills Blvd, E BP/McDonalds Mobil/7-11/dsl Bojangles, Carrabba's, ChuckECheese, Cinco de Mayo Mexican, Cookout, Cracker Barrel, Firehouse Subs Five Guys, Hooters, Hot Shots Grill, Jack-in-the-Box, KFC/Taco Bell, Ruby Tuesday, Sonic, Sonny's BBQ, Starbucks, Subway Taco Bell, TX Land&Cattle Steaks, TX Roadhouse, Waffle House Wendy's, Zaxby's Comfort Suites, Courtyard, Embass Suites, Great Wolf Lodge, Hampton Inn, Hilton Garden, Holida Inn Express, Home Towne Suites, Homewood Suites, Residenc Inn, Sleep Inn, SpringHill Suites, Wingate Inn BJ's Whse gas, Camping World, Camping World Resort (1.5mi), Chrysler Dodge/Jeep, Harley-Davidson, Honda, Kia, to Lowe's Mot Speedway, Toyota, VW, W Circle K/dsl Bonefish Gri Burger King, Carolina Alehouse, Charanda Mexican, Chick-fil-A Chipotle, Dave&Buster's, Denny's, Dunkin Donuts, Foster Grille, Freddy's, Jason's Deli, Jim'n Nick's BBQ, Jimmy John' Mayflower Seafood, McAlisters Deli, Olive Garden, On-th Border, Outback Steaks, Panera Bread, PDQ Cafe, Queen Ci Q, Razzoo's Cafe, Red Lobster, Steak'n Shake, Sticky Finger

NC

INTERSTATE 85 Cont'd

49 Continued
TGI Friday's, Tijuana Flats, Twin Peaks $Tree, AT&T, BassPro Shops, Best Buy, BooksAMillion, Concord Mills Mall, Discount Tire, Firestone/auto, Goodyear/auto, Lowe's, Old Navy, PetCo, Ross, TJ Maxx, URGENT CARE, Verizon, Walmart/Subway

48 I-485, to US 29, to Rock Hill

46 Mallard Creek Church Rd, E Exxon/7-11, Kangaroo, Speedway/dsl China Cafe, Giacomos Pizza, Jack-in-the-Box, Wild Wing Cafe Research Park, vet, W Shell/Circle K Farley's Pizzaria, Hickory Tavern, Rita's, Starbucks, Thai Taste, Toyama Express, Zoe's Kitchen PetCo, Trader Joe's

45b a Harris Blvd, E Applebee's, Bar Louie, Blaze Pizza, Bojangles, Buffalo Wild Wings, Burger King, Cheddar's, Chick-fil-A, Chili's, China Buffet, China Palace, Chipotle, City BBQ, Dunkin Donuts, Five Guys, IHOP, Jersey Mike's Subs, Jimmy John's, Los Arcos, McDonald's, Nakato Steaks, Noodles&Co, Panera Bread, Papa John's, Pei Wei, Picasso's Pizza, Qdoba, Shane's Rib Shack, Shoney's, Showmar's Rest., Starbucks, Taco Bell, Taco Mac Grill, TGIFriday's, Tijuana Flats, Tropical Cafe Country Inn&Suites, Courtyard, Drury Inn, Extended Stay America, Hampton Inn, Hilton, Holiday Inn, Homewood Suites, Microtel, Residence Inn, Sleep Inn H, Food Lion, Kohl's, Michael's, Office Depot, Ross, Sam's Club, to Miz Scarlett's, to UNCC, U Research Park, Verizon, Walgreens, Walmart/McDonald's, **0-2 mi** W Longhorn Steaks, Macaroni Grill, Red Robin, Tony's Pizza SpringHill Suites, TownePlace Suites Harris Teeter, Rite Aid

43 University City Blvd, E Circle K/dsl, Circle K/Subway/dsl Chipotle, Culver's, Golden Corral, Honeybaked Ham, Outback Steaks, Pablo's, Starbucks, Taco Bell, Zaxby's Extended Stay America, Holiday Inn Express, InTowne Suites AT&T, Chevrolet, Discount Tire, Firestone/auto, GNC, Hobby Lobby, IKEA, Marshall's, Old Navy, Petsmart, TJ Maxx, Walmart, World Mkt

42 US 29 (nb only)

41 Sugar Creek Rd, E Shell/dsl, Exxon/7-11/gas Bojangles, McDonald's, Taco Bell, Wendy's Best Value Inn, Brookwood Inn, Continental Inn, Motel 6 Family$, W Shell/Circle K/dsl Chicken Box Rest., Cookout, TX Ranch Steaks Days Inn, Quality Inn, Red Roof Inn, Rodeway Inn, Super 8

40 Graham St, E Exxon/7-11/dsl Budget Inn repair, UPS, Volvo, Western Star, W Marathon/dsl Freightliner

39 Statesville Ave, E Pilot/Subway/dsl/scales/24hr Advance Parts, repair, W Citgo/dsl, Shell/dsl Bojangles Family$

38 I-77, US 21, N to Statesville, S to Columbia

37 Beatties Ford Rd, E 7-11/dsl Burger King, McDonald's, Subway CVS Drug, Family$, Food Lion, USPO, W Citgo

36 NC 16, Brookshire Blvd, E Rodeway Inn repair, W 7-11/dsl, QT/dsl, RaceWay/dsl, XM/dsl Burger King, Jack-in-the-Box, Pier 16 Rest., Subway Family$, Griffin Tire

35 Glenwood Dr, E Exxon Knights Inn, W Shell/dsl

34 NC 27, Freedom Dr, E Citgo/dsl, Shell/Circle K Beauregard's Rest, Bojangles, Capt D's, Cookout, McDonald's, Pizza Hut, Showmar's, Subway, Taco Bell, Wendy's $Tree, Advance Parts, Aldi Foods, AutoZone, Family$, Goodyear, Rite Aid, Save-A-Lot Foods, URGENT CARE, vet, Walgreens, W Charlotte Express JiffyLube

33 US 521, Billy Graham Pkwy, E Shell/dsl Bojangles, KFC/Taco Bell, McDonald's, Wendy's Baymont Inn, Comfort Suites, Royal Inn, Sheraton, SpringHill Suites ,

CHARLOTTE

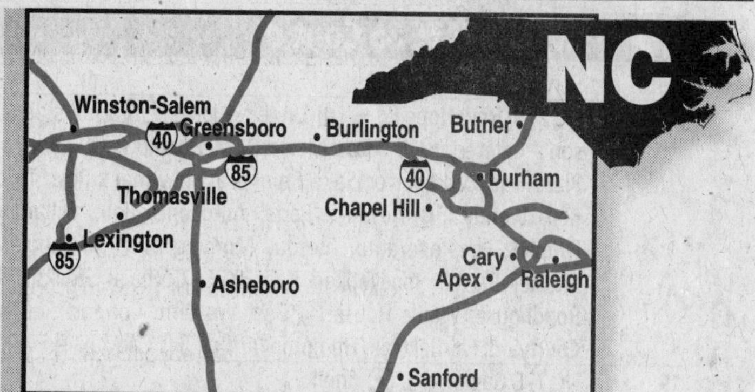

33 Continued
W Exxon/dsl Cracker Barrel, Ichiban, Waffle House EconoLodge, La Quinta, Microtel, Motel 6, Quality Inn, Red Roof Inn, Super 8

32 Little Rock Rd, E Shell/7-11/dsl Airport Inn, Courtyard, Hampton Inn, Holiday Inn, W Citgo/dsl, Shell/7-11 Arby's, Bud's Chicken, Hardee's, Showmar's Rest., Subway Country Inn&Suites, Day's Inn, Wingate Inn Family$, Food Lion, Griffin Tire, Rite Aid

30b a I-485, to 1-77, Pineville

29 Sam Wilson Rd, E BP (1mi) camping, W Loves/Chester's/dsl/scales/24hr, Shell/dsl

28mm **weigh sta both lanes**

27.5mm Catawba River

27 NC 273, Mt Holly, E BP/Dunkin Donuts/dsl, Murphy USA/dsl Arby's, Captain's Cap Seafood, Chick-fil-A, KFC, Pizza Hut, Sake Japanese, Subway, Taco Bell, Waffle House, Wendy's Big Lots, CVS Drug, Family$, Firestone/auto, Lowe's, NAPA, Walgreens, Walmart/Subway, W Citgo/dsl Holiday Inn Express

26 NC 7, E BP/dsl, Marathon/dsl Bojangles, Hardee's, King Buffet, McDonald's, New China, Papa John's Hampton Inn $Tree, Advance Parts, Aldi Foods, AT&T, AutoZone, BiLo, Ford, Verizon, W Belmont Abbey Coll

24mm South Fork River

23 NC 7, McAdenville, W Exxon/dsl, Shell/Subway/dsl Hardee's, Hillbilly's BBQ/Steaks

22 Cramerton, Lowell, E Marathon, Speedway/dsl Applebee's, Chick-fil-A, CiCi's, Jack-in-the-Box, Jersey Mike's Subs, Popeyes, Portofino's, Sakura Japanese, Schlotzsky's, Zaxby's Books-A-Million, Buick/Cadillac/Chevrolet/GMC, Honda, Kia, Kohl's, Lowe's, Old Navy, Petsmart, Sam's Club/gas, U-Haul

21 Cox Rd, E Marathon Akropolis Cafe, Buffalo Wild Wings, Cheddar's, Chili's, Chipotle, ChuckeCheese, Cookout, Dynasty Buffet, Firehouse Subs, Five Guys, Golden Corral, Hibachi Buffet, Krispy Kreme, La Fuente, Logan's Roadhouse, Longhorn Steaks, McAlister's Deli, McDonald's, Olive Garden, On the Border, Panera Bread, Peking Garden, Qdoba, Ruby Tuesday, Starbucks, Steak'n Shake, Subway, Tijuana Flats $Tree, AT&T, Best Buy, Chrysler/Dodge/Jeep, Dick's, Discount Tire, Ford/Subaru, GNC, Hobby Lobby, Home Depot, Lowes Foods, Mary Jo's Cloth, Michael's, Nissan, Office Depot, O'Reilly Parts, PepBoys, Petco, Ross, Target, Tire Kingdom, TJ Maxx, Verizon, vet, Walgreens, Walmart/Subway, W Marathon Arby's, Brixx Pizza, IHOP Super 8 H, $General, Medical Ctr Drug

[gas] = gas [food] = food [lodging] = lodging [other] = other [RS] = rest stop

INTERSTATE 85 Cont'd

GASTONIA

Exit#	Services
20	NC 279, New Hope Rd, E [gas] United, World [food] Capt D's, Jackson's Cafeteria, Los Arcos Mexican, McDonald's, O'Charley's, Pizza Hut, Red Lobster, Sake Japanese, Showmar's Rest, Taco Bell, Wendy's [other] Advance Parts, AutoZone, Belk, Dillard's, Family$, Firestone/auto, Tuesday Morning, W [food] Bojangles, Cracker Barrel, Honeybaked Ham, KFC, Outback Steaks, TX Roadhouse, Waffle House [lodging] Best Western, Comfort Suites, Courtyard, Fairfield Inn, Hampton Inn [other] [H], CarMax
19	NC 7, E Gastonia, E [gas] Shell
17	US 321, Gastonia, E [gas] Citgo/dsl/LP [food] Los Arcos Mexican [lodging] Days Inn, Woodspring Suites [other] Family$, W [gas] Marathon/dsl, QT/dsl [food] Dunkin Donuts, Hardee's, Papa John's [lodging] Holiday Inn Express, Motel 6, Red Carpet Inn
14	NC 274, E Bessemer, E [gas] Citgo/dsl, Murphy USA/dsl [other] Walmart, W [gas] BP/Subway, Citgo/dsl [food] Bojangles, Waffle House [lodging] Express Inn
13	Edgewood Rd, Bessemer City, E [other] to Crowders Mtn SP, W [gas] Exxon
10b a	US 74 W, US 29, Kings Mtn
8	NC 161, to Kings Mtn, E [lodging] Holiday Inn Express [other] camping, W [gas] BP/dsl [food] McDonald's, Mi Pueblito Mexican, Subway, Taco Bell, Waffle House, Wendy's [lodging] Quality Inn, Super 8 [other] [H], $General, Campers Inn RV Ctr
5	Dixon School Rd, E [gas] Citgo/dsl/24hr [other] truck/tire repair
4	US 29 S (from sb)
2.5mm	**Welcome Ctr nb, full [handicapped] facilities, info, litter barrels, petwalk, [phone], [picnic], vending**
2	NC 216, Kings Mtn, E [other] to Kings Mtn Nat Military Park
0mm	North Carolina/South Carolina state line

INTERSTATE 95

ROANOKE RAPIDS / WILSON / KENLY

Exit#	Services
181mm	**Welcome Ctr sb, full [handicapped] facilities, litter barrels, petwalk, [phone], [picnic], vending**, North Carolina/Virginia state line
180	NC 48, to Gaston, to Lake Gaston, Pleasant Hill, W [gas] Pilot/Subway/dsl/scales/24hr
176	NC 46, to Garysburg, W [gas] Shell/dsl [food] Burger King [lodging] Super 8
174mm	Roanoke River
173	US 158, Roanoke Rapids, Weldon, E [gas] BP/dsl, Shell/dsl [food] Frazier's Rest., Ralph's BBQ, Waffle House [lodging] Days Inn, Econolodge, W [gas] BP/dsl, Exxon/DQ/Stuckey's, Murphy USA/dsl, Sheetz/dsl, Shell/dsl [food] Applebee's, Arby's, Bojangles, Burger King, Carolina BBQ, Chick-fil-A, China Lin, Cookout, Cracker Barrel, Hardee's, Ichiban, KFC, Little Caesar's, Logan's Roadhouse, Mayflower Seafood, McDonald's, New China, Papa John's, Pizza Hut, Popeyes, Ruby Tuesday, San Jose Mexican, Starbucks, Subway, Subway, Taco Bell, TX Steaks, Waffle House, Wendy's, Zaxby's [lodging] Baymont Inn, Hampton Inn, Holiday Inn Express, Motel 6, Sleep Inn [other] [H], $General, $Tree, Advance Parts, AutoZone, Belk, BigLots, Firestone/auto, Food Lion, GNC, Harley-Davidson, Honda, Lowe's, O'Reilly Parts, Rite Aid, Save a Lot Foods, Staples, Toyota, URGENT CARE, Verizon, Walgreens, Walmart
171	NC 125, Roanoke Rapids, E [lodging] Hilton Garden [other] Carolina Crossroads RV Resort, Roanoke Rapids Theater, W [gas] Shell/dsl [lodging] Best Western [other] st patrol
168	NC 903, to Halifax, E [gas] Exxon/Subway/dsl, Shell/Burger King/dsl, W [gas] Oasis/Dunkin Donuts/LP/dsl
160	NC 561, to Brinkleyville, E [gas] Exxon, W [gas] Shell/dsl
154	NC 481, to Enfield, 1 mi W [other] KOA
151mm	**weigh sta both lanes**
150	NC 33, to Whitakers, E [other] golf, W [gas] BP/Subway/DQ/Stuckey's/dsl
145	NC 4, to US 301, Battleboro, E [gas] BP/dsl, Exxon/dsl, Marathon/dsl, Shell [food] Carolina BBQ, Denny's, Hardee's, Waffle House [lodging] Ashburn Inn, Best Western, Deluxe Inn, EconoLodge, Economy Inn, Quality Inn, Red Carpet Inn, Travelers Inn
142mm	**[RS] both lanes, full [handicapped] facilities, litter barrels, petwalk, [phone], [picnic], vending**
141	NC 43, Red Oak, E [gas] BP/dsl, Exxon/dsl/LP [other] $General, Smith's Foods
138	US 64, **1 mi E on Winstead** [gas] BP/dsl, Speedway/dsl [food] Bojangles, Cracker Barrel, Gardner's BBQ, Hardee's, Highway Diner, Outback Steaks, TX Steaks, Waffle House [lodging] Candlewood Suites, Comfort Inn, Country Inn&Suites, Courtyard, Doubletree, Hampton Inn, Holiday Inn, Residence Inn [other] [H], Buick/GMC, Harley-Davidson, Honda, Rite Aid, to Cape Hatteras Nat Seashore, URGENT CARE
132	to NC 58, E [gas] Pitstop/dsl, **1 mi W** [gas] BP/dsl
128mm	Tar River
127	NC 97, to Stanhope, E [other] [airport]
121	US 264a, Wilson, **0-4 mi E** [gas] BP, Kangaroo/dsl/LP, Marathon, Murphy USA/dsl, Shell, Speedway/dsl [food] Applebee's, Arby's, Buffalo Wild Wings, Burger King, Chick-fil-A, Chili's, Chopstix, Cookout, Denny's, El Tapatio, Golden Corral, Hardee's, Hibachi Buffet, Jersey Mike's, KFC/LJ Silver, Kobe Express, Mama Mia's Pizzaria, McDonald's, Moe's SW Grill, Olive Garden, Quizno's, Red Chileez Grill, Ruby Tuesday, San Jose Mexican, Sonic, Starbucks, Subway, Teppanyaki, TX Steaks, Waffle House, Wendy's, Zaxby's's [lodging] Candlewood Suites, Hampton Inn, Quality Inn [other] [H], $General, $Tree, Aldi Foods, AT&T, AutoZone, Belk, Best Buy, Big Lots, Chevrolet, Chrysler/Dodge/Jeep, Ford/Lincoln, GNC, Harris-Teeter, Hobby Lobby, Honda, Lowe's, Marshall's, Mr Tire, Nissan, O'Reilly Parts, Petsmart, Ross, Staples, Target, Toyota, URGENT CARE, Verizon, vet, Walmart, White Tires, W [gas] [food] Best-N-Burgers, Bojangles, Burger King, Cracker Barrel, McDonald's, Pino's Pizza [lodging] Comfort Suites, Country Inn&Suites, Fairfield Inn, Hampton Inn, Holiday Inn Express, Jameson Inn, Microtel, Sleep Inn [other] to Country Dr Museum
119b a	I-795 S, US 264, US 117
116	NC 42, to Clayton, Wilson, E [gas] Shell/dsl [other] [H], W [gas] Exxon/dsl [other] Rock Ridge Camping (2mi)
107	US 301, Kenly, E [gas] BP/dsl, Citgo, Exxon/McDonald's/dsl, Fuel Doc, PitStop [food] Andy's Cafe, Golden China, Nik's Pizza, Norman's BBQ, Subway [lodging] Budget Inn, Deluxe Inn, Quality Inn [other] $General, CarQuest, Family$, Food Lion, Ford, O'Reilly Parts, Piggly Wiggly, Tobacco Museum
106	Truck Stop Rd, Kenly, E [gas] FLYING J/Denny's/dsl/LP/scales/24hr, W [gas] Kenly 95/Petro/DQ/Subway/Wendy's/dsl/scales/24hr/@, Pilot/Arby's/dsl/scales/24hr [food] Waffle House [lodging] Days Inn, Motel 6 [other] Blue Beacon, Speedco Lube, Truck-o-Mat
105.5mm	Little River
105	Bagley Rd, Kenly, E [gas] Big Boys/Shell/105 Pizza/dsl/scales/24hr [food] Lowell Mill Rest.
102	Micro, W [gas] Shop'N-Go [food] Backdoor Cafe [other] $General, city park, USPO
101	Pittman Rd
99mm	**[RS] both lanes, full [handicapped] facilities, hist marker, litter barrels, petwalk, [phone], [picnic], vending**
98	to Selma, E [other] RVacation

NC

INTERSTATE 95 Cont'd

Exit#	Services
97	US 70 A, to Pine Level, Selma, E [gas] Mobil/dsl [food] Denny's, Robbins Nest Rest. [lodging] Days Inn [other] J&R Outlet, W [gas] BP/dsl, Exxon/dsl, Shell/dsl [food] Bojangles, Cookout, Don Beto's Tacos, KFC, McDonald's, Shoney's, Waffle House, Wendy's [lodging] EconoLodge, Hampton Inn, Masters Inn, Quality Inn [other] [H]
95	US 70, Smithfield, E [lodging] Best Value Inn, Village Motel, W [gas] Sheetz/dsl, Speedway/dsl, Sunoco/dsl [food] Bob Evans, Burger King, Checker's, CiCi's Pizza, Coldstone, Cracker Barrel, El Sombrero Mexican, Golden Corral, Outback Steaks, Ruby Tuesday, San Marcos Mexican, Subway, TX Steaks, Waffle House, Zaxby's [lodging] Baymont Inn, Best Western, Comfort Inn, Fairfield Inn, Sleep Inn, Super 8 [other] [H], Ava Gardner Museum, Carolina Premium Outlets/famous brands, Harley-Davidson
93	Brogden Rd, Smithfield, W [gas] BP/dsl, Citgo [other] $General
91.5mm	Neuse River
90	US 301, US 701, to Newton Grove, E [gas] BP/dsl, Valero/dsl [lodging] Travelers Inn [other] Happy Trails RV Park, Raleigh Oaks RV Resort, Ronnie's Tires, to Bentonville Bfd (14mi), W [gas] Exxon/dsl [food] Holt Lake BBQ [lodging] Four Oaks Motel/RV Park
87	NC 96, Four Oaks, W [gas] BP/dsl, Speedway/dsl, Walmart Express/dsl [food] McDonald's, Subway [other] $General
81b a	I-40, E to Wilmington, W to Raleigh
79	NC 50, to NC 27, to NC 242, Benson, Newton Grove, E [gas] Citgo/dsl, Short Stop/dsl [food] Char-Grill, Waffle House [lodging] Hampton Inn [other] auto repair, W [gas] Exxon/Burger King/dsl [food] China 8, Domino's, McDonald's, Pizza Hut, Subway, Taco Bell, White Swan BBQ [lodging] Days Inn [other] Advance Parts, auto repair, Family$, Food Lion, Walgreens
78mm	Neuse River
77	Hodges Chapel Rd, E [gas] Loves/Subway/dsl/scales/RV dump/24hr
75	Jonesboro Rd, W [gas] Exxon/Milestone Diner, Pilot/Shell/DQ/Quiznos/dsl/scales/24hr/@
73	US 421, NC 55, to Dunn, Clinton, E [food] Cracker Barrel, Hwy 55 Cafe, McDonald's, Mi Casita Mexican, Panda House Chinese [other] Chevrolet, Chrysler/Dodge/Jeep, Family$, Food Lion, W [gas] Exxon/dsl, Shell, Speedway/dsl [food] Bojangles, Burger King, El Charro Mexican, Fishing Chicken, Hot Dog&Hamburger Heavan, Sagebrush Steaks, Subway, Taco Bell, Triangle Waffle [lodging] Baymont Inn, Days Inn, Hampton Inn, Quality Inn, Super 8 [other] Charlie C's IGA, museum, to Campbell U.
72	Pope Rd, E [lodging] Comfort Inn, Royal Inn, W [gas] BP, Pure/dsl [food] Brass Lantern Steaks [lodging] Fairfield Inn [other] Cadillac/GMC
71	Longbranch Rd, E [gas] Pilot/Circle K/Hardee's/dsl/scales/24hr, W [other] to Averasboro Bfd
70	SR 1811, E [lodging] Relax Inn
65	NC 82, Godwin, E [other] Falcon Children's Home, W [gas] Godwin Mart/dsl
61	to Wade, E [gas] Lucky 7 Trkstp/dsl [other] Fayetteville RV Resort Cottages, W [gas] Exxon/dsl
58	US 13, to Newton Grove, I-295 to Fayetteville, E [gas] Shell/dsl/scales [food] Subway, Waffle House [lodging] Econolodge
56	Lp 95, to US 301 (from sb), Fayetteville, W [gas] Circle K/dsl, Epco/dsl [other] [H], Pope AFB, to Ft Bragg
55	NC 1832, Murphy Rd, W [gas] Circle K/dsl, Epco/dsl
52	NC 24, Fayetteville, W [other] botanical gardens, museum, Pope AFB, to Ft Bragg
49	NC 53, NC 210, Fayetteville, E [gas] BP/dsl, BP/dsl, Exxon/dsl, Marathon [food] Burger King, McDonald's, Pizza Hut, Taco Bell,

SMITHFIELD

DUNN

FAYETTEVILLE

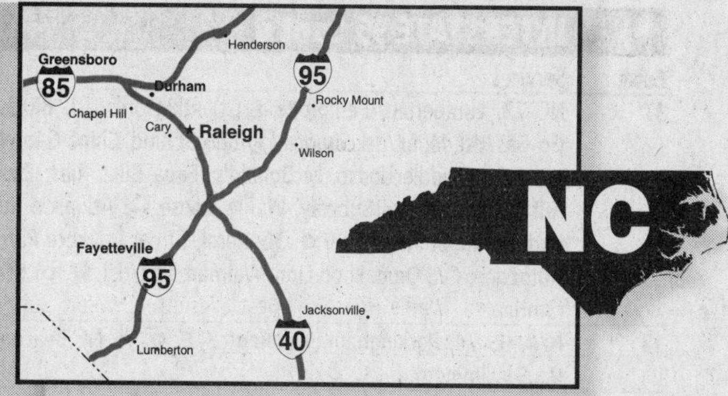

Exit#	Services
49	Continued Waffle House [lodging] Days Inn, Deluxe Inn, Hampton Inn, Motel 6, Tru Hilton [other] $General, W [gas] BP/Subway/dsl, Exxon/dsl, Sunoco/dsl [food] Bojangle's, Cracker Barrel, Ruby Tuesday [lodging] Baymont Inn, Comfort Inn, Doubletree, EconoLodge, Fairfield Inn, Holiday Inn, Holiday Inn Express, Quality Inn, Red Roof Inn, Sleep Inn, Super 8, Sure Stay Inn
48mm	**[RS] both lanes, full [handicapped] facilities, litter barrels, petwalk, [phone], [picnic], vending**
47mm	Cape Fear River
46b a	NC 87, to Fayetteville, Elizabethtown, W [other] [H]
44	Claude Lee Rd, W [other] Lazy Acres Camping, to [airport]
41	NC 59, to Hope Mills, Parkton, E [gas] Circle K/Subway/dsl [food] Bojangles, W [gas] BP/dsl [food] Grandsons Buffet [other] Camping World RV Ctr, Lake Waldo's Camping, Spring Valley RV Park
40	Lp 95, to US 301 (from nb), to Fayetteville, services on US 301 (5-7mi)
33	US 301, St Pauls, E [gas] BP/dsl
31	NC 20, to St Pauls, Raeford, E [gas] BP, Marathon/Huddle House/dsl, Mobil/McDonald's, Valero [food] Burger King, Hardee's [lodging] Days Inn [other] Volvo Trucks, Walgreens, Walmart Mkt, W [gas] BP/dsl, Sunoco [food] Taco Bell [other] Food Lion
25	US 301, E [gas] Sun-Do/dsl
24mm	**weigh sta both lanes**
22	US 301, E [gas] BP, Marathon, Shell/DQ [food] Burger King, Chick-fil-A, China Wok, Denny's, Firehouse Subs, Golden Corral, Hardee's, IHOP, Outback Steaks, Panera Bread, Papa John's, Pizza Hut, Ruby Tuesday, San Jose Mexican, Shogun, Smithfield BBQ, Starbucks, TX Steaks, Waffle House, Wendy's, Zaxby's [lodging] Best Western, Comfort Suites, Hampton Inn, Holiday Inn, Super 8 [other] $Tree, AT&T, Chrysler/Dodge/Jeep, Goodyear/auto, Honda, Lowe's, Lowe's Foods, McDonald's, Toyota, URGENT CARE, Verizon, Walmart/Subway, W [gas] Gulf, Sun-Do/dsl, Sunoco/dsl [food] Bojangles [lodging] Springhill Suites [other] Ford/Lincoln, Kia
20	NC 211, to NC 41, Lumberton, E [gas] BP/dsl, Citgo/dsl, Liberty/dsl [food] Arby's, Arnold's Rest., Bojangles, Burger King, Capt D's, Christopher's, CiCi's Pizza, Cook Out, Dunkin Donuts, Hardee's, Hong Kong Chinese, Hwy 55 Cafe, Kami Japanese, KFC, McDonald's, Shoney's, Sonic, Subway, Taco Bell, Tokyo Express, Village Sta. Rest., Waffle House [lodging] Deluxe Inn, Red Roof Inn [other] [H], Advance Parts, AutoZone, Belk, city park, CVS Drug, Food Lion/deli, JC Penney, Nissan, O'Reilly Parts, Verizon, Walgreens, W [gas] Marathon/dsl, Sun-do/dsl [food] Cracker Barrel, San Jose Mexican [lodging] Comfort Inn, Country Inn&Suites, Days Inn/rest., Fairfield Inn, Knights Inn
19	Carthage Rd, Lumberton, E [gas] [lodging] Rodeway Inn, W [gas] Sunoco [lodging] Motel 6, Royal Inn
18mm	Lumber River

LUMBERTON

NC

INTERSTATE 95 Cont'd

Exit#	Services
17	NC 72, Lumberton, Pembroke, E Atkinson's/dsl, BP/dsl, Go-Gas/dsl, Mobil/dsl, Sunoco Burger King, China Garden, Hardee's, Huddle House, McDonald's, Papa Bill's Ribs, Pizza Hut, Ruby Tuesday, Subway, Waffle House Atkinson Inn, Budget Inn, Southern Inn $General, $Tree, Advance Parts, AutoZone, CVS Drug, Food Lion, Walmart Mkt/dsl, W KOA (3mi)
13	I-74, US 74, Rockingham, Wilmington, E SE NC Beaches, U.S.S Wilmington
10	US 301, to Fairmont
7	to McDonald, Raynham
5mm	**Welcome Ctr nb, full facilities, litter barrels, petwalk, , , vending**
2	NC 130, to NC 904, Rowland
1b a	US 301, US 501, Dillon, E Sunoco, Sunoco (2) Hot Tamale Rest., Peddler Steaks, Pedro's Trkstp Budget Motel, South-of-the-Border Motel Pedro's Campground, W Shell/dsl Waffle House
0mm	North Carolina/South Carolina state line

INTERSTATE 240 (Asheville)

Exit#	Services
9mm	**I-240 begins/ends on I-40, exit 53b a.**
8	Fairview Rd, N Shell/dsl Ay Carumba, Cheddar's, China Buffet, Coldstone, J&S Cafeteria, KFC, Little Caesar's, McDonald's, Papa John's, Subway Ramada Inn $General, Advance Parts, Aldi Foods, Bi-Lo Foods, CVS Drug, Discount Tire, Hamrick's, Kohl's, Petsmart, U-Haul, Walmart/McDonald's, S Citgo Pizza Hut Home Depot
7.5mm	Swannanoa River
7	US 70, N Enmark Best Western Hyundai, Kia, Subaru, S Shell/dsl Applebee's, Bonefish Grill, Buffalo Wild Wings, Burger King, Carrabba's, Chick-fil-A, Chili's, ChuckeCheese, Cici's Pizza, Cook Out, Cornerstone Rest., Cracker Barrel, DQ, Firehouse Subs, IHOP, Jersey Mike's Subs, Longhorn Steaks, McAlister's Deli, McDonald's, McDonald's, Mikado Japanese, O'Charley's, Olive Garden, Outback Steaks, Papa's Mexican, Red Lobster, Starbucks, Subway, Taco Bell, Waffle House, Wild Wok Country Inn&Suites, Courtyard, Days Inn, EconoLodge, Extended Stay America, Hampton Inn, Holiday Inn, Homewood Suites, InTown Motor Inn, Mountaineer Inn, SpringHill Suites, Super 8 $Tree, AT&T, Barnes&Noble, Belk, Best Buy, BigLots, Clark Tire/auto, Dick's, Dillards, Firestone/auto, Ingles Foods/gas, JC Penney, Jo-Ann, Lowe's, Michael's, Midas, Office Depot, Old Navy, Ross, Target, TJ Maxx, Walgreens, Whole Foods Mkt
6	Tunnel Rd (from eb), same as 7
5b	US 70 E, US 74A, Charlotte St, N Exxon, Shell Charlotte St. Grill, Fuddruckers, Starbucks, Two Guys Hogi B&B vet, S Chop House Rest. Renaissance Hotel, Sheraton Civic Ctr
5a	US 25, Merrimon Ave, N Enmark, Exxon/dsl, Shell/dsl Bojangles, Chick-fil-A Green Life Foods, Harris Teeter, Staples, Trader Joe's
4c	Haywood St (no EZ return to eb), Montford, S Carmel's Rest., Isa's Bistro, Roman's Deli B&B, Hotel Indigo downtown
4b	Patton Ave (from eb), downtown
4a	US 19 N, US 23 N, US 70 W, to Weaverville
3b	Westgate, N Green Sage Cafe, Jason's Deli, Oriental Pavilion Country Inn Suites, Crowne Plaza CVS Drug, Earth Fare Foods, Mr Transmission, Sam's Club/gas, Tuesday Mornin
3a	US 19 S, US 23 S, W Asheville, N Shell/dsl A&W/LJ Silver, Bojangles, Burger King, CookOut, Denny's, Dragon China, Que Pasa Mexican, Firehouse Subs, Green Tea Japanese, Jerse Mike's, KFC, Krispy Kreme, Little Caesar's, McDonald's, Neo Burrito, New 1 China, Papa John's, Pizza Hut, Sonic, Subway, Tac Bell, Wendy's, Yoshida Japanese, Zingers Cafe $General, Advance Parts, Aldi Foods, AT&T, AutoZone, Clark Tire/auto, Ingle Foods, Sav-Mor Foods, URGENT CARE, vet, Walgreens
2	US 19, US 23, W Asheville, N Haywood Quickstop/d. Zia Mexican, S B&B Drug
1c	Amboy Rd (from eb)
1b	NC 191, to I-40 E, Brevard Rd, S camping, farmers mkt
1a	I-40 W, to Knoxville
0mm	**I-240 begins/ends on I-40, exit 46b a.**

INTERSTATE 440 (Raleigh)

Exit#	Services
16	I-40. **I-440 begins/ends on I-40.**
15	Poole Rd, E BP, Exxon, W Circle K, Citgo/dsl, Valero dsl Burger King, Family$, Food Lion, KFC/Taco Bell, McDonald's, Subway, Wang's Kitchen
14	I-495, US 64/264, to Wilson, to Rocky Mount
13b a	US 64 bus, New Bern Ave, to Wilson, 0-2 mi E BP/Circle Circle K, Exxon, Exxon/dsl, Murphy USA/dsl, Shell/dsl Bojangles, Burger King, Domino's, McDonald's, Papa John's, Pizz Hut, Popeye's, Ruby Tuesday, Starbucks, Subway, Waffle Hous Wendy's Comfort Suites, Holiday Inn Express, Knights In Microtel, Quality Inn Advance Parts, AutoZone, CVS Dru Firestone/auto, Food Lion, O'Reilly Parts, Plemmons RV C U-Haul, vet, Walgreens, Walmart, W
12	Yonkers Rd, Brentwood Rd
11b a	US 1, US 401, Capital Blvd N, N BP, BP, Exxon, Mobil, Sunoco, Valero/dsl Baskin-Robbins/Dunkin Donuts, Buffa Bros Pizza, Burger King, ChuckeCheese, Cici's, Cookout, Golden Corral, IHOP, Mayflower Seafood, McDonald's, Outba Steaks, Popeye's, Starbucks, Taco Bell, Vallerta Mexican, Waffle House Best Value Inn, Best Western, Extended Stay America, Holiday Inn, La Quinta, Motel 6, Quality Inn $Tree, Advance Parts, AT&T, AutoZone, Food Lion, U-Haul
10	Wake Forest Rd, N Bahama Breeze, Denny's Da Inn, Extended Stay America, Hilton, Hyatt Place, Residen Inn , CVS Drug, S Applebee's, Arby's, Biscuitville, BurgerFi, El Rodeo Mexican, Jersey Mike's, Jimmy John Jumbo China, McDonald's, Melting Pot Rest., Papa John's, Pizza Hut, Qdoba, Subway, Tropical Smoothie Comfort In Courtyard, Extended Stay America Advance Parts, AutoZone, Buick/GMC, Costco/gas, Discount Tire, Hyundai, Maz Ross, Staples, Subaru, Trader Joe's
8b a	6 Forks Rd, North Hills, N Exxon/repair, Tesla EVC Bonefish Grill, Capital Grille, Chick-fil-A, Chuy's, Firebirds Grill, Fi Guys, Fox&Hound Grille, Moe's SW Grill, Panera Bread, Piela Pizza, Pieology, Ruths Chris Steaks, Starbucks, Zoe's Kitchen AC Hotel Marriott, Hyatt House, Renaissance AT& GNC, Harris Teeter, JC Penney, REI, Target
7b a	US 70, NC 50, Glenwood Ave, Crabtree Valley, N BP (2), E dsl Brio Grill, Cheesecake Factory, Fleming's, Kanki Japanese, McDonald's, Panera Bread, PF Chang's Candlewo Suites, Courtyard, Embassy Suites, Fairfield Inn, Hampton I Hilton Garden, Holiday Inn, La Quinta, Marriott, Residence

NC

ASHEVILLE

RALEIGH

INTERSTATE 440 (Raleigh) Cont'd

7b a	Continued Barnes&Noble, Belk, Best Buy, Macy's, McCormick&Shmicks, Old Navy
6	Ridge Rd (from nb), same as 7
5	Lake Boone Tr, W Shell/Circle K Chick-fil-A, McDonald's, Starbucks, Village Deli H, Food Lion, Rite Aid
4b a	to I-40 W, Wade Ave, to RDU
3	NC 54, Hillsboro St, E BP, Exxon Arby's, Bean Sprout Chinese, IHOP, Snoopy's Hotdogs, Waffle House to Meredith Coll, to St Mary's, W to Carter-Finley Stadium
2b a	Western Blvd, E Domino's, Exxon, Shell/Circle K, Speedway/dsl Amedeo's Italian, Bojangles, Cookout, Dunkin Donuts, McDonalds, Popeye's, Subway, Taco Bell, Wendy's Advance Parts, Food Lion, Roses, Shaw U, to NCSU, vet
1d	Melbourne Rd (from sb)
1c	Jones-Franklin Rd
1b a	I-40. **I-440 begins on I-40.**

INTERSTATE 485 (Charlotte)

CHARLOTTE

Exit#	Services
67	I-77, US 21, to Charlotte, Columbia, **I-485 begins/ends.**
65	South Blvd, N Kangaroo Chick-fil-A, Golden Corral, Hooters, McDonald's, Popeyes, Steak'n Shake, Wendy's $Tree, Advance Parts, Big Lots, Chevrolet, Discount Tire, Honda, Jo-Ann, Kohl's, Nissan, Old Navy, Petsmart, Ross, Subaru, Target, Toyota, Verizon, VW, World Mkt, S Arby's Cadillac, CarMax, Mercedes, NAPA, TreadQtrs Auto/tire, vet
64b a	rd 51, N Exxon/dsl, Shell/Circle K/dsl Bojangles, Chili's, CiCi's, CookOut, Firehouse Subs, Jimmy John's, K&W Cafeteria, KFC, McDonald's, Outback Steaks, Pizza Hut, Starbucks, Wendy's Extended Stay America H, Aldi Foods, AutoZone, Bi-Lo, Family$, Firestone/auto, S Kangaroo, Shell/7-11 Applebee's, Buca Italian, Burger King, Capt D's, China Buffet, Harper's Rest., IHOP, Jason's Deli, Longhorn Steaks, McAlister's Deli, Olive Garden, Red Lobster, Sky Asian, Subway, Taco Bell Comfort Suites, Hampton Inn, Hilton Garden, Holiday Inn Express, Quality Inn $General, Barnes&Noble, Belk, Best Buy, Dick's, Dillard's, Food Lion, Home Depot, JC Penney, Macy's, Meineke, Midas, Office Depot, REI, Rite Aid, Sam's Club/gas, SteinMart, Tire Kingdom, TJ Maxx
61b a	US 521 S, Johnston Rd, N Global Rest., Hickory Tavern, Red Robin, Ruby Tuesday, Sticky Fingers, Viva Chicken Homewood Suites, SpringHill Suites Earth Fare Foods, S Kangaroo/dsl 5 Guys Burgers, Duckworth's Grill, Mellow Mushroom Rest., Pei Wei, Starbucks, Stone Mtn Grill, Subway, Tony's Pizza, Vine American Kitchen Ballantyne Hotel, Courtyard, Staybridge Suites CVS Drug
59	Rea Rd, E Exxon/7-11 1511 Cantina, Applebee's, Boneheads Grill, Chick-fil-A, City Tavern, Firebirds Grill, Marble Slab, Noodles Rest., Qdoba, Smashburger, Starbucks, True Pizza, Wendy's Residence Inn GNC, Goodyear/auto, Harris-Teeter, Michaels, Target, vet
57	Providence Rd, rd 16, E Kangaroo/Wendy's Hickory Tavern, Ilios Noche, Papa John's, Penn Sta, The Wok Harris-Teeter, USPO, W Exxon/7-11, Shell BBQ Shack, BT Burgers, Macaroni Grill, On the Border, Red Bowl Rest., Showmars Rest., Starbucks, Subway, Wolfman Pizza CVS Drug, Harris-Teeter, Home Depot, Lowes Whse, Rite Aid, Staples, SteinMart, vet

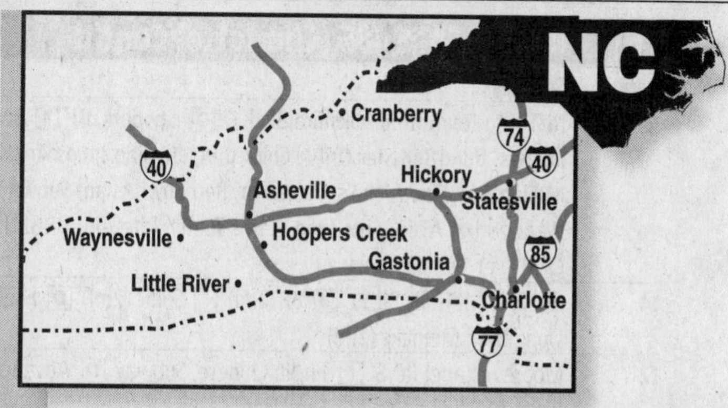

CHARLOTTE

52	E John St, to Matthews
51b a	US 74, to Charlotte, Monroe, E Circle K/dsl, Shell/dsl Country Inn&Suites, InTown Suites, Quality Inn Country Camping RV Ctr, Toyota, W Citgo/dsl, Exxon/7-11, Shell Bojangles, Pizza Hut, TX Roadhouse, Wendy's Courtyard, EconoLodge, Microtel H, Aamco, AutoZone, Best Buy, Costco/gas, Firestone/auto, Goodyear/auto, Goodyear/auto, Lowe's Whse, Sam's Club/gas, Target, Tuesday Morning
49	Idlewild Rd, E Exxon/7-11/dsl Cactus Rose Mexican, China Cafe, Mama's Pizza $Tree, GNC, Harris-Teeter, Meineke, Rite Aid
47	Lawyers Rd, E Gate/dsl Bellacino's Pizza, Best China, Carnita's Mexican, Domino's, McDonald's, Subway CVS Drug, Firestone/auto, Harris-Teeter, vet
44	rd 218, to Mint Hill, W BP/dsl, Shell/7-11 $General, city park, CVS
43	rd 51, to Mint Hill
41	rd 24, rd 27, to Albemarle, E Speedway/dsl Bojangles
39	Harrisburg Rd, W BP/EVC China Garden, Papa John's, Wendy's Food Lion
36	Rocky River Rd, E BP/dsl, Gate/dsl Best China, Bojangles, Capriccio Pizza, Subway CVS Drug, Discount Tire, EMERGENCY, GNC, Harris-Teeter, Tuffy Auto
33	rd 49, to Harrisburg, E Speedway/dsl Cici's Pizza Food Lion, USPO, W BP, Circle K/dsl, Exxon/7-11, Shell/7-11/dsl Arby's, Chopsticks, Domino's, Little Caesar's, Wendy's Family$
32	US 29, N QT/dsl CVS Drug, Walmart Mkt, S Exxon/7-11/dsl, Kangaroo, Speedway/dsl Jack-in-the-Box H, Tire Kingdom
30b a	I-85, N to High Point, S to Charlotte
28	Mallard Creek Rd
26	Benfield Rd, Prosperity Church Rd, Prosperity Ridge Rd, N BP/dsl Bojangle's, IHOP, Jersey Mike's, Papa Murphy's, Starbucks, Subway Aldi Foods, Giffen Bros Automotive, Harris Teeter, Publix, Rite Aid, S Shell/Circle K/dsl
23c	rd 115, to Huntersville, N Shell/7-11/dsl Audi, BMW, Lexus, Mercedes, Walmart
23b a	I-77, to Charlotte, Statesville
21	rd 24, Harris Blvd, S 5 Guys Burgers, Bravo Italian, Buffalo Wild Wings, Chick-fil-A, Chili's, East Coast Grill, Edomae Grill, Firebirds Grill, Firehouse Subs, Fox&Hound, Jersey Mike's, McDonald's, Mimi's Cafe, Moe's SW Grill, Olive Garden, On-the-Border, Panera bread, PF Chang's, Red Robin, Shane's Rib Shack, TGI Friday's, Wendy's Drury Inn $Tree, AT&T, Belk, Best Buy, Dick's, Dillard's, Discount Tire, Lowe's Whse, Macy's, Old Navy, Petsmart, REI, Target, Verizon

NC

INTERSTATE 485 (Charlotte) Cont'd

Exit#	Services
16	rd 16, to Newton, Brookshire Blvd, E city park, W Bojangles, Bull&Barrister Grille, Chick-fil-A, Domino's, Los Arcos, McDonald's, Papa John's, Pizza Hut, Red Bowl Asian, Subway, Wendy's AT&T, AutoZone, Harris-Teeter, Rite Aid, URGENT CARE, vet, Walmart/Subway
14	rd 27, to Mt Holly Rd, W BP (2mi) Sonic (2mi) Food Lion (2mi), Meineke (2mi)
12	Moores Chapel Rd, E Jin Jin Chinese, Subway Advance Parts, CVS Drug, Family$, Food Lion
10b a	I-85, to Spartanburg, Greensboro
9	US 29, US 74, Wilkinson Blvd, S camping
6	West Blvd
4	rd 160, to Fort Mill, N Exxon/7-11/dsl CVS Drug S BP/dsl Bojangles Charlotte Premium Outlets famous brands
3	Arrowood Rd, S Quizno's, Siam Garden
1	S Tryon St, NC 49, N Citgo, Exxon/7-11 Arby's, Bojangles, Chick-fil-A, Chili's, Dragon Buffet, IHOP, Lenny's Subs Luigi's Pizza, McDonald's, O'Charley's, Panera Bread, Qdoba Showmars Rest., Waffle House, Zaxby's Family$, GNC Lowe's Whse, Rite Aid, Walmart, S Kangaroo/dsl, QT dsl Mac's BBQ, Applebee's, Baskin-Robbins/Dunkin Donuts, Burger King, Domino's, Don Pedro Mexican, Firehouse Subs, Fortune Cookie, Hungry Howie's, Joe Momma's Pizza KFC, McAlister's Deli, Pan China, Portofino's, Starbucks, Subway, Taco Bell, Wild Wing Cafe Hilton Garden, Homewood Suites $Tree, AT&T, AutoZone, Discount Tire, Food Lion NAPA, Office Depot, Tire Kingdom, Tuffy Auto, URGENT CARE

NORTH DAKOTA

INTERSTATE 29

Exit#	Services
218mm	US/Canada border, North Dakota state line
217mm	US Customs sb
216mm	historical site nb, tourist info sb
215	ND 59, rd 55, Pembina, E Gastrak/DutyFree Store/dsl, Gastrak/pizza/dsl/scales/24hr Pembina State Museum/info
212	no service
208	rd 1, to Bathgate
203	US 81, ND 5, to Hamilton, Cavalier, W to Icelandic SP (25 mi), **weigh sta both lanes**
200	no service
196	rd 3, Bowesmont
193	no service
191	rd 11, to St Thomas
187	ND 66, to Drayton, E Cenex/pizza/dsl/E-85, Tesoro/dsl Motel 66 city park, USPO
184	to Drayton, **2 mi** E gas/dsl USPO
180	rd 9
179mm	**both lanes (both lanes exit left), full facilities, litter barrels, petwalk, , , vending**
176	ND 17, to Grafton, **10 mi** W gas food lodging
172	65th St NE
168	rd 15, to Minto, Warsaw
164	57th St NE
161	ND 54, rd 19, to Ardoch, Oslo
157	32nd Ave
152	US 81, to Gilby, Manvel, W Manvel/dsl/food
145	US 81 bus, N Washington St, to Grand Forks
141	US 2, Gateway Dr, Grand Forks, E Cenex, Loaf'N Jug/dsl, University Sta/dsl Burger King, Far East Buffet, Little Caesar's, McDonald's, Northside Cafe, Papa Murphy's, Subway, Taco John's Best Value Inn, Budget Inn, EconoLodge, Grand Forks Inn, Ramada Inn, Select Inn, Super 8 H, AT&T, Freightliner, Hugo's Foods, Kia, O'Reilly Parts, Subaru, to U of ND, transmissions, U-Haul, visitors ctr, W Simonson/café/dsl/24hr, StaMart/dsl/RV dump/scales/24hr/@ Hardee's Knights Inn , Budget RV Ctr, dsl repair, Mack/Volvo, NW Tire, to AFB, vet, Walmart/Subway
140	DeMers Ave, E Cenex/dsl, Loaf'N Jug/dsl, Valley Dairy Red Pepper Cafe, Tim Hortons Baymont Inn, Canada Inn,
140	Continued Expressway Suites, Hilton Garden, La Quinta, My Place Suites Sleep Inn, Staybridge Suites H, Alerus Ctr, to U of ND
138	US 81, 32nd Ave S, E Cenex, Holiday/dsl Applebee's Arby's, Buffalo Wild Wings, Burger King, Cherry Berry Yogurt Coldstone, Culver's, Denny's, DQ, Erbert&Gerbert's, Firehouse Subs, Five Guys, Ground Round, HuHot, IHOP, Jimmy John's McDonald's, Noodles&Co, Olive Garden, Panera Bread, Papa Murphy's, Pizza Hut, Pizza Ranch, Qdoba Mexican, Red Lobster, Ruby Tuesday, Sakura Japanese, Starbucks, Subway, T Roadhouse, Wendy's Best Western, C'mon Inn, Country Inn&Suites, Days Inn, Fairfield Inn, Hampton Inn, Holiday Inn Express, Quality Inn, Rodeway Inn, SpringHill Suites $Tree AT&T, Best Buy, Chrysler/Dodge/Jeep, CVS Drug, Ford/Lincoln Gordman's, Hobby Lobby, Hornbacher's Mkt, Hugo's Foods, Penney, Jo-Ann Fabrics, Kohl's, Lowe's, Menards, Michael's, O Navy, PetCo, Sam's Club/gas, Scheel's, Target, Tire 1, Tires+, Maxx, Toyota, Verizon, vet, Walmart/Subway, White Drugcar repair:Natural Grocers, W FLYING J/Subway/dsl/LP/scales RV dump/24hr Grand Forks Camping
130	ND 15, rd 81, Thompson, **1 mi** W gas food
123	to Reynolds, E to Central Valley School
120	**truck insp sb**
118	to Buxton
111	ND 200 W, to Cummings, Mayville, W Big Top Fireworks, Mayville St U
104	Hillsboro, E Casey's, Cenex/Burger King/dsl/LP/24hr Subway Hillsboro Inn H, Hillsboro Camping, USPO
100	ND 200 E, ND 200A, to Blanchard, Halstad
99mm	**both lanes, full facilities, litter barrels, petwalk, , vending**
92	rd 11, Grandin, W Stop&Shop/dsl
86	Gardner
78	Argusville
74.5mm	Sheyenne River
72	rd 17, rd 22, Harwood, E Cenex/pizza/dsl/LP/café/24hr
69	rd 20
67	US 81 bus, 19th Ave N, **1 mi** E Applebee's, Buffalo Wild Wings, Burger King, McDonald's, Pizza Hut, Subway, Taco Bell Candlewood Suites, Days Inn, Homewood Suites CVS Drug, Hector Int Airport, VA H

GRAND FORKS

GRAND FORKS

INTERSTATE 29 Cont'd

Exit#	Services
66	12th Ave N, E [gas] StaMart/dsl/scales/24hr [food] Marlin's Rest. [lodging] Woodspring Suites [other] [H], to ND St U, tuck repair, W [gas] Cenex/dsl [food] Arby's [lodging] Super 8
65	US 10, Main Ave, W Fargo, E [gas] Tesoro/dsl [other] CarQuest, NAPA, OK Tire, vet, W [gas] Cenex/Subway/dsl, Simonson/dsl [food] Hardee's, O'Kelly's Rest., Season Buffet Chinese [lodging] Biltmore on Main Inn [other] CarQuest, Honda, Kia, Lincoln, Mac's Hardware, Mazda, Mercedes, O'Reilly Parts, Recreation RV Ctr, Toyota, VW
64	13th Ave, Fargo, E [gas] Don's, Exxon, Kum&Go/dsl, PetroServe/dsl [food] Acapulco Mexican, Applebee's, Arby's, Buck's Rest, Burger King, ChuckeCheese, DQ, Erbert&Gerbert's Subs, GreenMill Rest., Ground Round, Little Caesar's, Perkins, Sickie's Garage, Subway, Taco John's, Wendy's [lodging] AmericInn, Baymont Inn, Country Inn&Suites, Days Inn, EconoLodge, EconoLodge, Grand Inn, Motel 6, Quality Inn, Quality Suites, Super 8 [other] AT&T, Cash-Wise Foods/drug/gas, CVS Drug, Family$, Goodyear/auto, Meineke, O'Reilly Parts, Tires+/transmissions, Tuesday Morning, Verizon, White Drug, W [gas] All-Stop/dsl, Casey's, Cenex [food] Applebee's, Arby's, Buffalo Wild Wings, Chili's, Culver's, Denny's, Domino's, DQ, Happy Joe's Pizza, KFC, Kobe Japanese, Kroll's Diner, LoneStar Steaks, Longhorn Steaks, McDonald's, Olive Garden, Osaka Japanese, Panchero's Mexican, Panera Bread, Paradiso Mexican, Pizza Hut, Red Lobster, Ruby Tuesday, Santa Lucia Cafe, Schlotzsky's, Spitfire Grill, Subway, Taco Bell, Taco John's, TX Roadhouse [lodging] Econolodge, Fairfield Inn, Fargo Inn, Holiday Inn, Holiday Inn Express, Kelly Inn, Ramada Inn, Red River Lodge [other] $Tree, Audi/VW, Barnes&Noble, Best Buy, BigLots, Cadillac/Chevrolet, Chrysler/Dodge/Jeep, Family Fare Mkt, GNC, Gordman's, Herberger's, Hobby Lobby, Hornbacher's Foods, Hyundai, JC Penney, Jo-Ann, Jo-Ann Fabrics, Kohl's, Lowe's, Macy's, Menards, Michael's, Natural Grocers, Nissan, Old Navy, PetCo, Petsmart, Sam's Club/gas, Target, TJ Maxx, USPO, Walgreens, Walmart/Subway
63b a	I-94, W to Bismarck, E to Minneapolis
62	32nd Ave S, Fargo, E [gas] F&F/dsl, Holiday, Tesoro [food] Arby's, Country Kitchen, Culver's, Jimmy John's, KFC, Little Caesar's, Moe's SW Grill, Noodles&Co, Papa John's, Starbucks, Subway, Taco John's, Village Inn [other] [H], Buick/GMC, Family Fare Mkt, Ford, Freightliner, JiffyLube, Verizon, W [gas] FLYING J/Huddle House/dsl/LP/scales/24hr/@, Loves/McDonald's/Subway/dsl/scales/24hr [lodging] Motel 6 [other] Fargo Tire/repair, Mack/Volvo, Peterbilt
60	52nd Ave S, to Fargo, E [gas] Casey's/dsl/e85 [food] Burger King, W [other] Walmart/Subway
56	to Wild Rice, Horace
54	rd 16, to Oxbow, Davenport
50	rd 18, Hickson
48	ND 46, to Kindred
44	to Christine
42	rd 2, to Walcott
37	rd 4, to Abercrombie, Colfax, E [other] to Ft Abercrombie HS, 3 mi W [gas] gas
31	rd 8, Galchutt
26	to Dwight
24mm	**weigh sta both lanes exit left**
23b a	ND 13, to Wahpeton, Mooreton, **10 mi E** [other] [H], ND St Coll of Science
15	rd 16, to Mantador, Great Bend
8	ND 11, to Hankinson, Fairmount, E [gas] Tesoro/dsl, **3 mi W** [other] camping
3mm	**Welcome Ctr nb, full [handicapped] facilities, litter barrels, petwalk, [phone], [picnic]**
2	rd 22
1	rd 1E, E [other] Dakota Magic Casino/Hotel/rest./gas/dsl
0mm	North Dakota/South Dakota state line

FARGO

INTERSTATE 94

Exit#	Services
352mm	North Dakota/Minnesota state line, Red River
351	US 81, Fargo, N [gas] Casey's, Loaf'n Jug [food] Duane's Pizza, Great Harvest Breads, Great Wall Chinese, Taco Shop [other] [H], Hornbacher's Foods, Medicine Shoppe, vet, S [gas] Tesoro/dsl [food] Burger King, Happy Joe's Pizza, McDonald's, Pepper's Café, Randy's Diner, Subway, Taco Bell [lodging] Rodeway Inn, Vista Inn [other] Hornbacher's/gas, O'Reilly Parts, Verizon
350	25th St, Fargo, N [gas] Casey's, S [gas] Loaf'n Jug/dsl, Phillips/dsl [food] Dolittle's Grill, Ruby Tuesday
349b a	I-29, N to Grand Forks, S to Sioux Falls, **services 1 mi N exit 64**
348	45th St, N **Visitor Ctr/full facilities, litter barrels, [picnic],** [gas] Holiday/dsl, Petro/dsl/Lp/24hrs/@ [food] Carino's, Chipotle, Coldstone, Culver's, Denny's, Dunn Bros Coffee, Granite City, HuHot Mongolian, IHOP, Kroll's Diner, Little Caesar's, Longhorn Steaks, Maddio's Pizza, McDonald's, Noodles&Co, Panda Express, Papa Murphy's, Pizza Hut, Potbelly, Qdoba, Smashburger, Space Aliens Grill, Subway, Wendy's, Wild Bill's [lodging] Best Western, C'Mon Inn, Expressway Suites, Hilton Garden, Holiday Inn Express, Home 2 Suites, MainStay Suites, Ramada Inn, Red Roof Inn, Staybridge Suites, Wingate Inn [other] Blue Beacon, Hobby Lobby, Home Depot, Kohl's, NAPA, Old Navy, Sam's Club, Scheel's Sports, Target, Tuffy Auto, Verizon, Walmart/Subway, S [gas] Casey's/DQ/dsl, Holiday [food] Applebee's, Famous Dave's BBQ, Five Guys, Hardee's, Korean BBQ, Mexican Village, Old Chicago Pizza, Pizza Ranch, Sonic, Taco John's, Taco Shop [lodging] AmericInn, Comfort Suites, Hampton Inn, La Quinta, Residence Inn, Sheraton, Sleep Inn [other] AT&T, Red River Zoo
347	9th St E, Veterans Blvd, N [food] Blarney Stone [lodging] Cambria Inn, Element Hotel, S [gas] Casey's/dsl [food] Firehouse Subs, McDonald's, Papa John's, Subway, Taco Bell [lodging] Microtel, My Place Hotel [other] Cash Wise Foods/dsl, Costco/gas, [H]
346b a	to Horace, W Fargo, S [gas] repair, Tesoro/dsl [other] Harley Davidson

FARGO

ND

INTERSTATE 94 Cont'd

Exit#	Services
343	US 10, Lp 94, W Fargo, N Cenex/dsl Adventure RV Ctr, Pioneer Village, Red River Valley RV Park
342	38th St NE
342mm	**weigh sta wb**
340	to Kindred
338	Mapleton, N Tesoro/dsl
337mm	**truck parking wb, litter barrels**
331	ND 18, to Leonard, Casselton, N Tesoro/Subway/dsl Country Kitchen Days Inn/RV park
328	to Lynchburg
327mm	truck parking eb, litter barrels
324	Wheatland, to Chaffee
322	Absaraka
320	to Embden
317	to Ayr
314	ND 38 N, to Alice, Buffalo, **3 mi** N gas food
310	36th St SE
307	to Tower City, N Cenex/café/dsl/RV Park/24hr, motel
304mm	**both lanes (both lanes exit left), full facilities, info, litter barrels, petwalk, vending**
302	ND 32, to Fingal, Oriska, **1 mi** N city park
298	123rd Ave SE
296	121st Av SE
294	Lp 94, to Kathryn, Valley City, N H, camping
292	Valley City, N PetroServe/Tesoro/café/dsl Sabir's Rest. AmericInn, Grand Stay Hotel, Super 8, Wagon Wheel Inn/rest. H, Ford, to Bald Hill Dam, S Ft Ransom SP (35mi)
291	Sheyenne River
290	Lp 94, Valley City, N Casey's/dsl Burger King, Kenny's Rest., Kirin House Chinese, Pizza Ranch, Subway H, Buick/Chevrolet/GMC, Chrysler/Dodge/Jeep, Family$, Firestone/auto, NAPA, O'Reilly Parts, ShopKo
288	ND 1 S, to Oakes, S Fort Ransom SP (36 mi)
283	ND 1 N, to Rogers
281	to Litchville, Sanborn, **1-2 mi** N gas food lodging
276	Eckelson, S Prairie Haven Camping/gas/dsl
275mm	continental divide, elevation 1490
272	to Urbana
269	Spiritwood
262	Bloom, N
260	Jamestown, N Casey's, Cenex/café/dsl/@ Starlite Motel to St H
259mm	James River
258	US 52 W, US 281, Jamestown, N Exxon/TCBY/dsl, Tesoro/dsl Arby's, DQ, Hardee's, McDonald's, Pizza Ranch, Subway, Taco Bell Comfort Inn, Days Inn, Holiday Inn Express, Jamestown Motel Buffalo Herd/museum, Buick/Chevrolet/GMC, Firestone/auto, NW Tire, O'Reilly Parts, Toyota, S Shell/dsl Applebee's, Burger King, Grizzly's Rest., Hong Kong Buffet, La Carreta Mexican, Paradiso Mexican, Perkins EconoLodge, Fairfield Inn, Hampton Inn, My Place, Quality Inn, Super 8 $Tree, AT&T, Chrysler/Dodge/Jeep, Ford/Lincoln, GNC, Harley-Davidson, Mac's Hardware, Menards, Verizon, Walmart
257	Lp 94 (from eb, exits left), to Jamestown, N dsl repair
256	US 52 W, US 281 N, S H, Jamestown Campground/RV dump (1mi)
254mm	**both lanes, full facilities, litter barrels, petwalk, vending**
251	Eldridge
248	74th Ave SE
245	70th Ave SE
242	Windsor
238	to Gackle, Cleveland
233	58th Ave SE
230	Medina, **1 mi** N Famer's Union/dsl/LP DairyTreat city park, Medina RV Park, USPO
228	ND 30 S, to Streeter
224mm	**wb, full facilities, litter barrels, petwalk, vending**
221	Crystal Springs
221mm	**eb, full facilities, litter barrels, petwalk, vending**
217	Pettibone
214	Tappen, S gas/dsl/food
208	ND 3 S, Dawson, N RV camping, **1/2 mi** S gas food RV camping, to Camp Grassick
205	Robinson
200	ND 3 N, to Tuttle, Steele, S Shell/Subway/Pizza Hut/dsl Cobblestone Inn truckwash
195	20th Ave SE
190	Driscoll, S food
182	US 83 S, ND 14, to Wing, Sterling, S Cenex/dsl Top's Motel (1mi)
176	McKenzie
170	Menoken, S RV Park, to McDowell Dam
168mm	**both lanes, full facilities, litter barrels, petwalk, vending, wifi**
161	Lp 94, Bismarck Expswy, Bismarck, N Cenex/dsl/LP/24hr, Exxon/dsl My Place Peterbilt, Toyota, S Holiday/dsl, Tesoro/Marlin's Rest./dsl/scales/24hr McDonald's Ramada Ltd Capital RV Ctr, Dakota Zoo, dsl repair, Freightliner, Kenworth, OK Tires
159	US 83, Bismarck, N Holiday/dsl, Simonson/dsl Applebee's, Arby's, Buffalo Wings&Rings, China Star, Hong Kong Chinese, KFC, Kroll's Diner, Little Caesar's, Longhorn Steaks, MacKenzie River Pizza, McDonald's, Oahu BBQ, Olive Garden, Papa Murphy's, Paradiso Mexican, Perkins, Pita Pit, Red Lobster, Ruby Tuesday, Space Alien Grill, Taco Bell, Wendy's AmericInn Candlewood Suites, Comfort Inn, Comfort Suites, Country Suites Courtyard, Fairfield Inn, Hampton Inn, Holiday Inn, Holiday Inn Express, Mainstay Suites, Motel 6, Residence Inn, Sleep Inn Staybridge Suites, Super 8, Wingate Inn AT&T, Chevrolet CVS Drug, Dan's Foods/USPO, Dick's, Gordman's, Hancock Fabrics, Hobby Lobby, Honda, Jo-Ann Fabrics, Menards, Michael's Nissan, NW Tire, Ross, UHaul, USPO, VW, Walmart/Subway S Exxon/dsl, PetroServe/dsl, Shell/dsl DQ, East 40 Rest., Hardee's, Pizza Hut, Schlotzsky's, Starbucks, Subway, Taco John's, Woodhouse Rest. Best Value Inn, Days Inn, Kelly Inn La Quinta, Ramada Inn, Super 8 H, O'Reilly Parts
157	Divide Ave, Bismarck, N Shell/dsl Carino's, Coldstone Cracker Barrel, Five Guys, Jimmy John's, Kobe's Japanese, McDonald's, Nardello's Pizza, Pancheros Mexican, Starbucks Subway, Taco John's, TX Roadhouse $Tree, Best Buy GNC, Kohl's, Lowe's, Old Navy, Petsmart, TJ Maxx, Verizon visitor ctr, S Cenex/dsl/E85/LP/RV Dump Stadium Café Hampton Inn Dan's Mkt/USPO
156mm	Missouri River
156	I-194, Bismarck Expswy, Bismarck City Ctr, **1/2 mi** S Dakota Zoo
155	to Lp 94 (exits left from wb), Mandan, City Ctr, same as 153
153	ND 1806, Mandan Dr, Mandan, **1/2 mi** S Cenex/dsl, M&H dsl, PetroServe/dsl, Tesoro Bonanza, Burger King, Dakota Farms Rest., Domino's, DQ, Hardee's, Papa Murphy's, Pizza Hut, Pizza Ranch, Subway, Taco John's North Country Inn

JAMESTOWN

BISMARCK

ND

INTERSTATE 94 Cont'd

MANDAN

153 Continued
Chevrolet, Dacotah Centennial Park, Family$, Ft Lincoln SP (5mi), Goodyear/auto, NAPA, NW Tire, O'Reilly Parts, Subaru, Verizon

152 Sunset Dr, Mandan, **N** Tesoro/dsl Baymont Inn, Comfort Inn Thrifty White Drug, Walmart/Subway, **S** Tesoro/RV dump Fried's Rest.

152mm scenic view eb

147 ND 25, to ND 6, Mandan, **S** FLYING J/Shell/Subway/dsl/scales/24hr

140 to Crown Butte

135mm scenic view wb, litter barrel

134 to Judson, Sweet Briar Lake

127 ND 31 N, to New Salem, **N** Knife River Indian Village (35mi), **S** Cenex/dsl, Tesoro/dsl Sunset Cafe Arrowhead Inn/café DFC/dsl, vet, World's Largest Cow

123 to Almont

120 no service

119mm **both lanes, full facilities, litter barrels, petwalk,**

117 no service

113 no service

HEBRON

110 ND 49, to Glen Ullin

108 to Glen Ullin, Lake Tschida, **3 mi S** gas food lodging camping

102 Hebron, to Glen Ullin, to Lake Tschida, **3 mi S** gas food lodging camping

97 Hebron, **2 mi N** gas food lodging

96.5mm central/mountain time zone

90 no service

84 ND 8, Richardton, **N** Cenex/dsl , Schnell RA, Springfield Mkt, to Assumption Abbey

78 to Taylor

72 to Enchanted Hwy, Gladstone

64 Dickinson, **S** Cenex/Tiger Truckstop/rest./dsl/24hr, Dakota Diner dsl repair, Ford/Lincoln, Honda, NW Tire, Toyota

DICKINSON

61 ND 22, Dickinson, **N** Cenex/dsl/LP, Mobil/Schlotsky's/dsl/scales/24hr, Simonson/dsl Applebee's, Arby's, Burger King, City Brew Coffee, DQ, El Sombrero Mexican, Jimmy John's, Papa Murphy's, Pizza Ranch, Qdoba, Sakura Japanese, Sanford's Rest., Taco Bell, Taco John's, Wendy's AmericInn, Astoria Suites, Best Western, Candlewood Suites, Comfort Inn, Hampton Inn, Holiday Inn Express, Microtel, My Place, Ramada, Red Roof Inn, TownePlace Suites AT&T, Cashwise Foods, Chevrolet/Cadillac, Family Fare Mkt, Goodyear/auto, Herberger's, Midas, O'Reilly Parts, Runnings Hardware, USPO, Verizon, Walmart/Subway, White Drug, **S** Cenex/dsl, Conoco/repair, Holiday/dsl, Tesoro/Domino's/dsl A&W/KFC, Country Kitchen, Don Pedro's Mexican, King Buffet, McDonald's, Perkins, Subway La Quinta, Motel 6, Quality Inn, Relax Inn, Rodeway Inn, Travel Inn , Ace Hardware, museum, visitor info

59 Lp 94, to Dickinson, **N** Buffalo Wild Wings Hawthorn Suites, Woodspring Suites Family Fare/dsl, Menard's, Verizon, **S** camping, , to Patterson Lake RA, services in Dickinson

56 116th Ave

51 South Heart

42 US 85, to Grassy Butte, Belfield,Williston, **N** MVP/dsl T Roosevelt NP (52mi), **S** Cenex/dsl/24hr, Conoco/dsl Trapper's Kettle Rest. Trapper's Inn NAPA

36 Fryburg

32 T Roosevelt NP, **N** **both lanes, full facilities, scenic overlook**

27 Lp 94, **S** Historic Medora (from wb), T Roosevelt NP

24.5mm Little Missouri Scenic River

24 Medora, Historic Medora, **S** Chateau de Mores HS, T Roosevelt NP, visitors ctr

23 West River Rd (from wb)

22mm scenic view eb

18 Buffalo Gap, **N** Buffalo Gap Camping (seasonal)

10 Sentinel Butte, Camel Hump Lake, **S** gas

7 Home on the Range

1 ND 16, **S** **Welcome/Visitor Ctr, full facilities, litter barrels, petwalk,** , FLYING J/Subway/dsl/scales/LP/24hr, Cenex/dsl/LP/24hr Buckboard Inn Beach RV Park

1mm **weigh sta eb, litter barrel**

0mm North Dakota/Montana state line

OHIO

ND OH

INTERSTATE 70

Exit#	Services

225.5mm Ohio/West Virginia state line, Ohio River

225 US 250 W, OH 7, Bridgeport, **N** Marathon, StarFire, Sunoco/dsl DQ, Papa John's, Pizza Hut Advance Parts, AutoZone, Family$, Meineke, NAPA, **S** Clark, Exxon/dsl Domino's

220 US 40, rd 214, **N** Marathon, Sunoco/dsl Comfort Inn, **S** Exxon/dsl Days Inn vet

219 I-470 E, to Bel-Aire, Washington PA, (from eb)

BLAINE

218 Mall Rd, to US 40, to Blaine, **N** BP, Exxon/Subway/dsl, Sheetz/dsl Applebee's, Arby's, Burger King, DeFelice Pizza, Denny's, Eat'n Park, HoneyBaked Ham, King Buffet, Little Caesar's, Outback Steaks, Pizza Hut, Red Lobster, Starbucks, Steak'n Shake, Taco Bell, Tlaquepaque Mexican, Undo's Rest., W Texas Steaks, Wendy's Best Value Inn, Hawthorn Suites, Holiday Inn Express, Knights Inn, Microtel, Red Roof Inn, Super 8, Wingate Inn $General, $Tree, AAA, Advance Parts, Aldi Foods, AT&T, AutoZone, Buick/Cadillac/Chevrolet, CVS Drug, Kroger, Lowe's, Sam's Club, Staples, Stewarts RV Ctr, URGENT CARE, Verizon, Walmart/McDonald's, **S** Bob Evans, Buffalo Wild Wings, Chipotle, Cracker Barrel, Garfield's Rest., KFC/LJ Silver, Longhorn Steaks, McDonald's, Osaka Steaks, Panera Bread, Starbucks, Zhuzi Chinese Candlewood Suites, Fairfield Inn, Residence Inn Boscov's, Chrysler/Dodge/Jeep, Jo-Ann Fabrics, Macy's, Marshall's, NTB

216 OH 9, St Clairsville, **N** BP

215 National Rd, **N** Burger King, Domino's, WenWu Chinese Riesbeck's Foods, USPO

213 OH 331, Flushing, **S** BP, Marathon/Subway/dsl, Sunoco/dsl

211mm **both lanes, full facilities, litter barrels, petwalk, , vending**

208 OH 149,Morristown, **N** Exxon/McDonald's/dsl Schlepp's Rest. Arrowhead Motel (1mi), Days Inn $General, Cannonball Speedway, Ford/Lincoln, **S** Marathon/Quiznos/dsl,

INTERSTATE 70 Cont'd

CAMBRIDGE

208 Continued
Pilot/Subway/dsl/scales/24hr Sleep Inn Barkcamp SP, Harley-Davidson

204 US 40 E (from eb, no return), National Rd

202 OH 800, to Barnesville, S Sunoco/dsl

198 rd 114, Fairview

193 OH 513, Middlebourne, N BP, FuelMart/dsl fireworks

189mm **eb, full facilities, litter barrels, petwalk, , vending**

186 US 40, OH 285, to Old Washington, N Marathon/dsl $General, S GoMart/dsl, Speedway/dsl/scales/24hr

180b a I-77 N, to Cleveland, to Salt Fork SP, I-77 S, to Charleston

178 OH 209, Cambridge, **0-1 mi** N BP/dsl, Sheetz/dsl Bob Evans, Coldstone/Tim Hortons, Cracker Barrel, Denny's, DQ, Forum Rest., KFC, McDonald's, Papa John's, Pizza Hut, Ruby Tuesday, Subway, Wendy's Comfort Inn, Days Inn, Hampton Inn, Holiday Inn Express, Microtel, Quality Inn, Sleep Inn, Southgate Hotel , $General, Advance Parts, AutoZone, BigLots, Cash Saver Foods, Family$, Ford, O'Reilly Parts, Verizon, S Murphy USA/dsl, Pilot/Subway/dsl/scales/24hr Arby's, Buffalo Wild Wings, Burger King, Great Chinese, Little Caesar's, Taco Bell, Tlaquepaque Mexican Baymont Inn $Tree, Aldi Foods, AT&T, Chevrolet, Chrysler/Dodge/Jeep, Spring Valley RV Park (1mi), Verizon, Walmart/Subway

176 US 22, US 40, to Cambridge, N Sunoco/dsl Budget Inn RV camping, st patrol, vet

173mm **weigh sta both lanes**

169 OH 83, to Cumberland, New Concord, N Marathon/dsl Garland Hotel John&Annie Glen Historic Site, RV camping, to Muskingum U

164 US 22, US 40, Norwich, N Baker's Motel, Zane Gray Museum, S antiques, pottery

163mm **wb, full facilities, litter barrels, petwalk, , vending**

ZANESVILLE

160 OH 797, Airport Rd, N Love's/Arby's/dsl/scales/24hr, S BP, Marathon/Subway/dsl Denny's, McDonald's, Wendy's Best Western, Economy Inn, Kautilya Zanesville Hotel , st patrol

157 OH 93, Zanesville, N BP, S Marathon, Shell/dsl st patrol

155 OH 60, OH 146, Underwood St, Zanesville, N Bob Evans, Olive Garden, Oriental Buffet, Red Lobster, Steak'n Shake, Tumbleweed Grill Hampton Inn, Holiday Inn Express, Quality Inn, Wingate Inn , Riesbeck's Mkt, USPO, S Marathon/dsl Cracker Barrel, Subway, Wendy's Baymont Inn, Travel Inn Rite Aid

154 5th St (from eb)

153b Maple Ave (no EZ return from wb), N DQ, Italian Eatery, Papa John's, Tee Jaye's Rest. , CVS Drug, Family$

153a State St, N Speedway/dsl to Dillon SP (8mi), USPO

153mm Licking River

152 US 40, National Rd, N BP/A&W/Subway/dsl, Shell/dsl McDonald's Super 8

142 US 40 (from wb, no EZ return), Gratiot, N RV camping

141 OH 668, US 40 (from eb, no return), to Gratiot, same as 142

132 OH 13, to Thornville, Newark, N Dawes Arboretum (3mi), S BP, Shell Subway (2mi)

131mm **both lanes, full facilities, litter barrels, petwalk, , vending**

129b a OH 79, to Buckeye Lake, Hebron, N Subway Best Western Advance Parts, Kroger/gas, S Donato's Pizza,

OH

129b a Continued
McDonald's, Subway, Taco Bell, Wendy's Motel 6 CarQuest, KOA (2mi)

126 OH 37, to Granville, Lancaster, N Marathon/dsl, Pilot/Chester's/Subway/dsl/scales/24hr, S IA 80 Truckomat/truckwash, TA/BP/Bob Evans/Popeye's/Sbarro's/dsl/scales/24hr/@ Deluxe Inn, Red Roof Inn KOA

122 OH 158, to Baltimore, Kirkersville, N Regal Inn, S Flying J/Denny's/dsl/LP/scales/24hr fireworks

118 OH 310, to Pataskala, N BP/McDonald's, Shell/dsl, Speedway/dsl DQ, S BP/Duke's/Subway/dsl RCD RV Ctr

112c OH 204, to Blecklick Rd (from eb)

112 OH 256, to Pickerington, Reynoldsburg, N BP, Shell/McDonald's Buffalo Wild Wings, Chipotle Mexican, Culver's, Five Guys, IHOP, Logan's Roadhouse, Noodles&Co, O'Charley's, Olive Garden, Panera Bread, Penn Sta, Smokey Bones BBQ, Subway, TGIFriday's Fairfield Inn, Holiday Inn Express AT&T, Best Buy, Jo-Ann Fabrics, Marshall's, NTB, Old Navy, Petco, Petsmart, Sam's Club/gas, Staples, Target, Tire Discounters, Verizon, Walgreens, Walmart/Subway, S Speedway/dsl Arby's, Bob Evans, Cane's, Cold Stone, Cracker Barrel, Donato's Pizza, Firehouse Subs, Iron Chef, Jimmy John's, KFC, La Fogata Mexican, LJ Silver, Longhorn Steaks, Max&Erma's, Omezzo Italian, Red Robin, Skyline Chili, Starbucks, Steak'n Shake, Wendy's Best Western, Comfort Inn, Hampton Inn Advance Parts, Barnes&Noble, Kohl's, Kroger/E85, URGENT CARE, Verizon

COLUMBUS AREA

110 Brice Rd, to Reynoldsburg, N Speedway/dsl, Sunoco Burger King, Donato's, Genji Japanese, Golden China, Popeye's, Subway, TeeJaye's Rest., Tim Horton's, Waffle House Days Inn, Extended Stay America, La Quinta, Red Roof Inn BigLots, Family$, Goodyear/auto, Home Depot, O'Reilly Parts, S BP, Speedway/dsl Applebee's, Arby's, Asian Star, Boston Mkt, Chipotle Mexican, KFC, McDonald's, Starbucks, Subway, Taco Bell, Waffle House Comfort Suites, Motel 6, Rodeway Inn $Tree, Acura, Advance Parts, Aldi Foods, Family$, Fiat, Firestone/auto, Honda, Lowe's, Michael's, Toyota, Walgreens

108b a I-270 N to Cleveland, access to , I-270 S to Cincinnati

107a OH 317, Hamilton Rd, to Whitehall, S Shell/dsl Arby's Burger King, Capt D's, ChuckeCheese, Ichiban Japanese, McDonald's, Papa John's, Pizza Hut, Popeye's, Red Lobster, Steak'n Shake, Taco Bell Hampton Inn, InTown Suites $General, AT&T, PepBoys

105a US 33, to Lancaster, 2 mi N Tat Italian

105b US 33, James Rd, Bexley, N Tat Italian

103b a Livingston Ave, to Capital University, N Exxon, Speedway dsl Mr Hero Subs, Peking Dynasty, Popeye's, Subway Taco Bell, Tim Horton's, Wendy's auto repair, Katz Tires S Marathon, Shell McDonald's, Rally's, White Castle Family$

102 Kelton Ave, Miller Ave

101a I-71 N, to Cleveland

100b US 23, to 4th St, downtown

99c Rich St, Town St (exits left from wb)

99b OH 315 N, downtown

99a I-71 S, to Cincinnati

98b Mound St (from wb, no EZ return), S Speedway Little Caesar's, McDonald's, Rally's Aldi Foods, Family$

98a US 62, OH 3, Central Ave, to Sullivant, same as 98b

97 US 40, W Broad St, N Arby's, Burger King, McDonald's, Subway, Taco Bell, Tim Horton's Knights Inn, Motel 6 Aamco, CVS Drug, U-Haul, USPO

INTERSTATE 70 Cont'd

Exit#	Services
96	I-670 (exits left from eb), to
95	Hague Ave (from wb), S Exxon
94	Wilson Rd, N Marathon/Circle K/Subway/dsl, UDF, S BP, Pilot/Wendy's/dsl/scales/24hr, Shell/dsl, Speedway McDonald's, Waffle House EconoLodge vet
93b a	I-270, N to Cleveland, S to Cincinnati
91b a	to Hilliard, New Rome, N GetGo, Shell, Speedway/dsl Applebee's, Arby's, Buffalo Wild Wings, Burger King, Chick-fil-A, Chipotle, Cracker Barrel, Culver's, Daruma Japanese, Donato's Pizza, El Vaquero Mexican, Fazoli's, Firehouse Subs, Five Guys, Golden Chopsticks, Hot Head Burrito, IHOP, KFC, McDonald's, Olive Garden, Outback Steaks, Panda Express, Panera Bread, Perkins, Red Robin, Rooster's Rest., Skyline Chili, Subway, Supreme Buffet, Taco Bell, Tim Horton's/Coldstone, TX Roadhouse, Wendy's, White Castle, Wild Ginger Asian Best Value Inn, Comfort Suites, Fairfield Inn, Hampton Inn, Hawthorn Inn, Holiday Inn, La Quinta, Motel 6, Red Roof Inn $Tree, Advance Parts, AT&T, Dick's, Discount Tire, Firestone/auto, Ford, GNC, Kohl's, Marshall's, Meijer/dsl, Michael's, Midas, Old Navy, Petsmart, Sam's Club/gas, Target, URGENT CARE, Verizon, Walmart/Subway, S BP/dsl, Marathon/dsl Bob Evans, Handel's Ice Cream, Steak'n Shake Best Western, Country Inn&Suites, Super 8
85	OH 142, to Plain City, W Jefferson, N Prairie Oaks SP, S Battelle Darby SP
80	OH 29, to Mechanicsburg, S hwy patrol
79	US 42, to London, Plain City, N Pilot/Arby's/dsl/scales/24hr Waffle House Camping World RV Ctr, truck/auto repair, S Speedway/Subway/dsl, TA/BP/Pizza Hut/Popeye's/dsl/scales/24hr/@ McDonald's, Taco Bell, Wendy's Holiday Inn Express, Motel 6 H
72	OH 56, to London, Summerford, N Marathon/Subway/dsl, 4 mi S H
71mm	**both lanes, full facilities, litter barrels, petwalk, vending**
66	OH 54, to Catawba, South Vienna, N Fuelmart/dsl/scales, S Speedway/dsl
62	US 40, Springfield, N Harmony Motel H, antiques, auto repair, Harmony Farm Mkt, to Buck Creek SP, S Beaver Valley Camping
59	OH 41, to S Charleston, N H, Harley-Davidson, st patrol, S BP/dsl, Loves/Subway/Wendy's/dsl/scales/24hr antiques
54	OH 72, to Cedarville, Springfield, N BP/dsl, Shell, Speedway/dsl, Sunoco/dsl A&W/LJ Silver, Arby's, Bob Evans, Burger King, Cassano's Pizza/subs, Cracker Barrel, Domino's, Dunkin Donuts, El Toro Mexican, Hardee's, Lee's Chicken, Little Caesar's, McDonald's, Panda Chinese, Popeye's, Rally's, Rudy's Smokehouse, Subway, Taco Bell Baymont Inn, Comfort Suites, Hampton Inn, Holiday Inn Express, Motel 6, Quality Inn, Red Roof Inn, USA Suites H, Advance Parts, BigLots, Family$, Kroger/deli, Rite Aid, Walgreens, S Marathon/dsl
52b a	US 68, to Urbana, Xenia, S to John Bryan SP
48	OH 4 (from wb), to Enon, Donnelsville, N camping, S Speedway
47	OH 4 (from eb), to Springfield, N Enon Beach Camping, S Speedway
44	I-675 S, Spangler Rd, to Cincinnati
43mm	Mad River

SPRINGFIELD

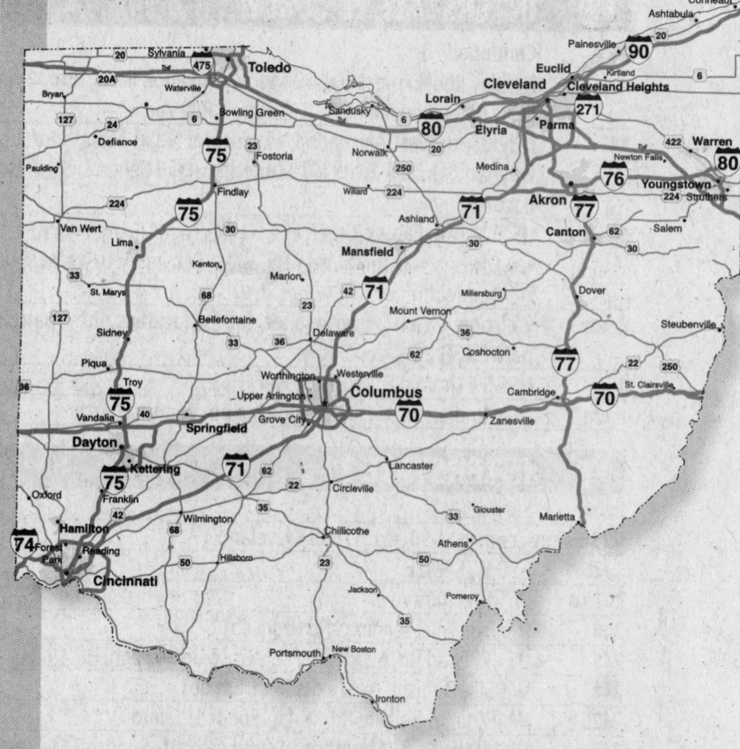

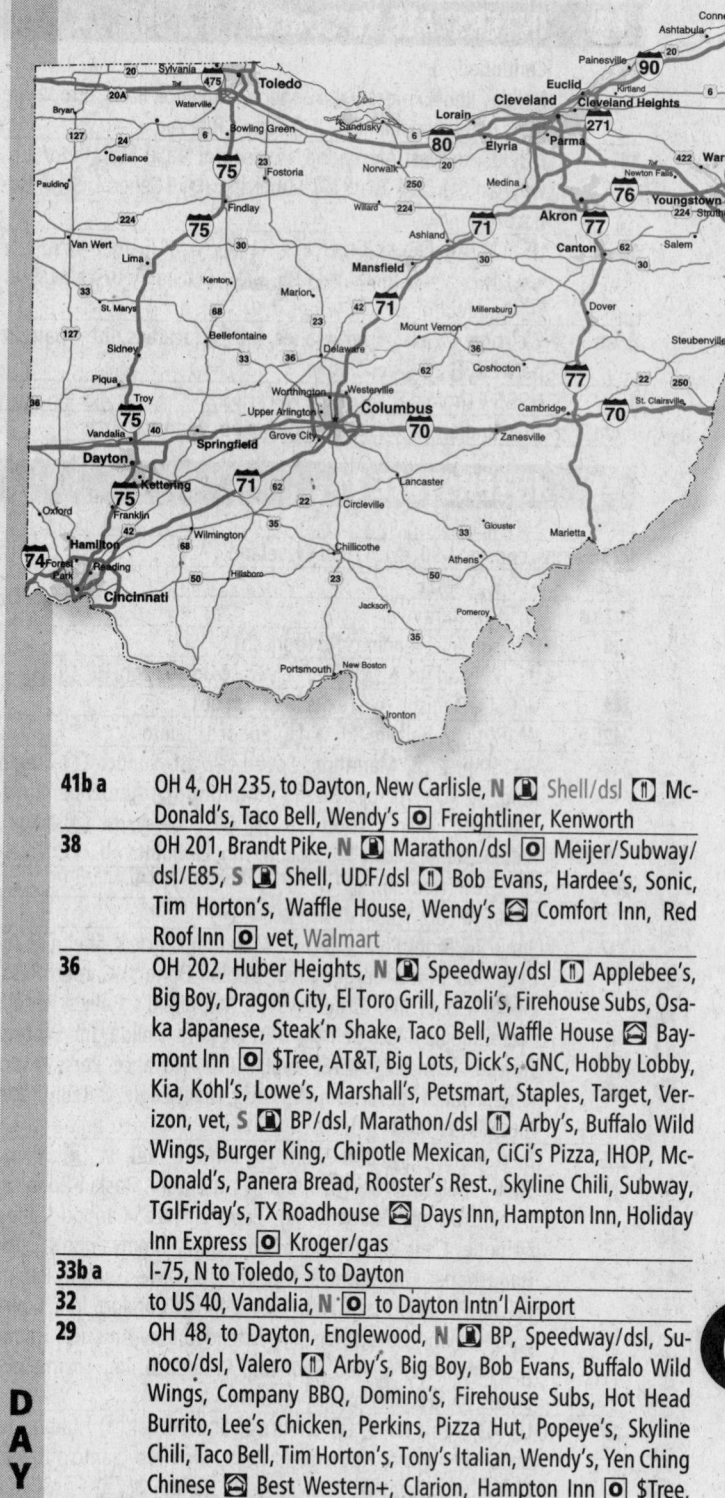

Exit#	Services
41b a	OH 4, OH 235, to Dayton, New Carlisle, N Shell/dsl McDonald's, Taco Bell, Wendy's Freightliner, Kenworth
38	OH 201, Brandt Pike, N Marathon/dsl Meijer/Subway/dsl/E85, S Shell, UDF/dsl Bob Evans, Hardee's, Sonic, Tim Horton's, Waffle House, Wendy's Comfort Inn, Red Roof Inn vet, Walmart
36	OH 202, Huber Heights, N Speedway/dsl Applebee's, Big Boy, Dragon City, El Toro Grill, Fazoli's, Firehouse Subs, Osaka Japanese, Steak'n Shake, Taco Bell, Waffle House Baymont Inn $Tree, AT&T, Big Lots, Dick's, GNC, Hobby Lobby, Kia, Kohl's, Lowe's, Marshall's, Petsmart, Staples, Target, Verizon, vet, S BP/dsl, Marathon/dsl Arby's, Buffalo Wild Wings, Burger King, Chipotle Mexican, CiCi's Pizza, IHOP, McDonald's, Panera Bread, Rooster's Rest., Skyline Chili, Subway, TGIFriday's, TX Roadhouse Days Inn, Hampton Inn, Holiday Inn Express Kroger/gas
33b a	I-75, N to Toledo, S to Dayton
32	to US 40, Vandalia, N to Dayton Intn'l Airport
29	OH 48, to Dayton, Englewood, N BP, Speedway/dsl, Sunoco/dsl, Valero Arby's, Big Boy, Bob Evans, Buffalo Wild Wings, Company BBQ, Domino's, Firehouse Subs, Hot Head Burrito, Lee's Chicken, Perkins, Pizza Hut, Popeye's, Skyline Chili, Taco Bell, Tim Horton's, Tony's Italian, Wendy's, Yen Ching Chinese Best Western+, Clarion, Hampton Inn $Tree, Advance Parts, Aldi Foods, AutoZone, Family$, Grismer/auto, Midas, O'Reilly Parts, Petco, Verizon, vet, S Chipotle, El Toro, McDonald's, MOD Pizza, Panera Bread, Starbucks, Steak'n Shake, Waffle House Comfort Inn, Motel 6 H, AT&T, Meijer/dsl/E85
26	OH 49 S, N Murphy USA/dsl Bob Evans, La Rosa's Pizza, Sonic, Subway URGENT CARE, Verizon, Walmart/Subway, S Shell/dsl Burger King, Wendy's
24	OH 49 N, to Greenville, Clayton, N KOA (seasonal)
21	Arlington Rd, Brookville, N Speedway/Subway/dsl, S Speedway/dsl Arby's, Brookville Grille, Great Wall Chinese, KFC/Taco Bell, K's Rest., Lee's Chicken, McDonald's, Pizza Hut, Rob's Rest., Subway, Waffle House, Wendy's Brookville Inn,

DAYTON

OH

INTERSTATE 70 Cont'd

21	Continued Holiday Inn Express [O] $General, Advance Parts, Brookville Parts, Chevrolet, Family$, IGA Foods, Rite Aid
14	OH 503, to West Alexandria, Lewisburg, N [gas] Marathon/Subway/dsl [food] Dari Twist [lodging] Super Inn [O] $General, S [gas] Sunoco/dsl
10	US 127, to Eaton, Greenville, N [gas] TA/BP/Burger King/Subway/dsl/scales/24hr/@, S [gas] Pilot/Subway/dsl/scales/24hr [lodging] Budget Inn
3mm	**Welcome Ctr eb/[RS] both lanes, full [handicapped] facilities, litter barrels, petwalk, [phone], [picnic], vending**
1	US 35 E (from eb), to Eaton, New Hope
0mm	Ohio/Indiana state line, **weigh sta eb,** Welcome Arch

INTERSTATE 71

Exit#	Services
	I-71 begins/ends on I-90, exit 170 in Cleveland.
247b	I-90 W, I-490 E.
247a	W 14th, Clark Ave
246	Denison Ave, Jennings Rd (from sb)
245	US 42, Pearl Rd, E [gas] BP/7-11, Gas&Go [O] zoo, W [O] [H]
244	W 65th, Denison Ave (exits left from nb)
242b a	W 130th, to Bellaire Rd, W [gas] Sunoco, Valero
240	W 150th, E [gas] Marathon, Speedway/dsl, Sunoco [food] Burger King, Denny's, Happy's Pizza [lodging] Marriott [O] AutoZone, Goodyear/auto, Marc's Foods, W [gas] BP/Subway/dsl [food] Nana's Italian, Somers Rest. [lodging] Holiday Inn, La Quinta
239	OH 237 S (from sb), W [O] to [airport]
238	I-480, Toledo, Youngstown, W [O] [airport]
237	Snow Rd, Brook Park, E [gas] BP, Marathon/Circle K, Shell [food] Arby's, Bob Evans, Burger King, Dunkin Donuts, Garden Rest., Goody's Rest., KFC, Little Caesar's, McDonald's, Rally's, Reddi's Pizza, Subway, Taco Bell [lodging] Best Western, Holiday Inn Express, Howard Johnson [O] $General, $Tree, Advance Parts, AutoZone, Conrad Tire/repair, CVS Drug, Giant Eagle, O'Reilly Parts, Rite Aid, W [O] to [airport]
235	Bagley Rd, E [food] Bob Evans [O] Mr Tire, vet, W [gas] BP/dsl, Shell, Speedway/dsl [food] Aladdin's a Eatery, Baskin-Robbins/Dunkin Donuts, Burger King, Capri a Pizza, Caribou Coffee, Chipotle, Craft Brew Garden, Five Guys, Jimmy John's, Little Hong Kong, Max&Erma's, McDonald's, Olive Garden, Panera Bread, Perkins, Pizza Hut, Taco Bell [lodging] Comfort Inn, Courtyard, Crowne Plaza, Days Inn, Extended Stay America, Hampton Inn, Motel 6, Red Roof Inn, Residence Inn, TownePlace Suites [O] [H], Aldi Foods, Verizon
234	US 42, Pearl Rd, E [gas] Shell/dsl, Sunoco/dsl [food] Hunan Chinese, Jet's Pizza, Katherine's Rest., Mr Hero, Santo's Italian, Three Bros Pizza [O] Audi/Porsche, Honda, W [gas] Gas&Food/dsl, Sheetz/dsl [food] Buffalo Wild Wings, Jennifer's Rest., Mad Cactus Rest., McDonald's [lodging] Kings Inn, La Siesta Motel, Metrick's Motel [O] Home Depot, Lowe's, Walmart/Subway
233	I-80 and Ohio Tpk, to Toledo, Youngstown
231	OH 82, Strongsville, E [gas] Shell [lodging] Holiday Inn, Super 8 [O] Chevrolet, W [gas] BP/7-11/dsl, Marathon/Subway/dsl [food] Applebee's, Buca Italian, Chick-fil-A, Chipotle, DiBella's Subs, Firehouse Subs, Five Guys, Houlihan's, Longhorn Steaks, Macaroni Grill, Panera Bread, Red Lobster, Rockne's Grill, Rosewood Grill, Samurai Japanese, Starbucks, TGIFriday, Zoup! [O] $Tree, AAA, AT&T, Best Buy, Costco/gas, Dick's, Dillard's, Heinen's Mkt, JC Penney, Kohl's, Macy's, Midas, NTB, Old Navy, PetCo, Target, TJ Maxx, Verizon
226	OH 303, Brunswick, E [gas] Shell/dsl [food] Pizza Hut [O] Chrysler/Dodge/Jeep, Hyundai, Subaru, Toyota, vet, VW, W [gas] GetGo, Speedway/dsl, Sunoco/dsl [food] Applebee's, Arby's, Bob Evans, Burger King, Chipotle, Georgio's Pizza, House of Pearl, McDonald's, Muchos Buenos Mexican, Panera Bread, Panini's Grill, Pizza Hut, Sonic, Starbucks, Steak'n Shake, Subway, Taco Bell, Wendy's [lodging] Quality Inn [O] $General, Buehler's Foods, Ford, Giant Eagle Food, GNC, Home Depot, Marc's Mkt, Verizon
225mm	**[RS] nb, full [handicapped] facilities, litter barrels, petwalk, [phone], [picnic]**
224mm	**[RS] sb, full [handicapped] facilities, litter barrels, petwalk, [phone], [picnic]**
222	OH 3, Medina, Hinckley, W [O] st patrol
220	I-271 N, (from nb) to Erie, Pa
218	OH 18, to Akron, Medina, E [gas] BP/dsl, Marathon/dsl, Sunoco/dsl [food] Alexandri's Rest., Baskin-Robbins/Dunkin Donuts, Burger King, DQ, Fresh Food Deli, Master Pizza [lodging] Holiday Inn Express, Quality Inn, Super 8 [O] Kia, Nissan, Verizon, W [gas] Speedway/dsl [food] Arby's, Bob Evans, Brown Derby, Buffalo Wild Wings, Denny's, McDonald's, Pizza Hut, Rocknes Rest., Taco Bell, Waffle House, Wendy's [lodging] Fairfield Inn, Hampton Inn, Motel 6, Red Roof Inn [O] [H], Aldi Foods, Buehler's Foods, Buick/Cadillac/GMC, Chrysler/Dodge/Jeep, Firestone/auto, Harley-Davidson, Honda, Verizon
209	I-76 E, to Akron, US 224, W [gas] Pilot/Subway/dsl/scales/24hr TA/Country Pride/Burger King/Popeye's/dsl/scales/24hr/@ [food] Arby's, McDonald's, Starbucks [lodging] Super 8 [O] Blue Beacon Chippewa Valley Camping (1mi), SpeedCo
204	OH 83, Burbank, E [gas] BP/dsl, Duke/dsl, Loves/Hardee's/dsl/scales/24hr [lodging] Plaza Motel, W [gas] Pilot/Wendy's/dsl/scales/24hr [food] Bob Evans, Burger King, KFC/Taco Bell, McDonald's [O] [H], Lodi Outlets/famous brands
198	OH 539, W Salem
196mm	**[RS] both lanes, full [handicapped] facilities, litter barrels, petwalk, [phone], [picnic] vending**
196	OH 301 (from nb, no re-entry), W Salem
186	US 250, Ashland, E [gas] Marathon [food] Grandpa's Village cheese/gifts, Perkins [O] Hickory, Lakes Camping (7mi) W [gas] Goasis/BP/Pizza Hut/Popeye's/Starbucks/Taco Bell/dsl/24hr, Marathon/Subway/dsl [food] Brian Buffet, Denny's, Dunkin Donuts, Jake's Rest., McDonald's, Wendy's [lodging] Ashland Inn Holiday Inn Express, Quality Inn, Rodeway Inn, Super 8 [O] [H] $Tree, Aldi Foods, AT&T, Buehler's Foods, GNC, Home Depot, st patrol, to Ashland U, URGENT CARE, Verizon, Walmart/Subway
176	US 30, to Mansfield, E [lodging] Heritage Inn [O] fireworks
173	OH 39, to Mansfield
169	OH 13, Mansfield, E [gas] Marathon/7-11/dsl, Murphy USA/dsl [food] Applebee's, Chipotle, Cracker Barrel, Steak'n Shake, Wendy's [lodging] Best Western, La Quinta [O] Mohican SP, Walmart/Subway, W [gas] BP/7-11 [food] Arby's, Bob Evans, Burger King, Charrito Mexican, McDonald's, Subway, Taco Bell [lodging] Hampton Inn, Super 8, Travelodge [O] [H], st patrol
165	OH 97, to Bellville, E [gas] BP, Shell/dsl, Speedway/dsl [food] Buckeye Express Diner, Burger King, Der Dutchman, KC's Rib House McDonald's [lodging] Comfort Inn, Days Inn, Economy Inn, Quality Inn [O] to Mohican SP, W [gas] Loves/Subway/Taco John's/dsl/scales/24hr [food] Wendy's
151	OH 95, to Mt Gilead, E [gas] Duke/BP/deli, Marathon [food] Buckeye Country Diner, McDonald's, Wendy's [lodging] Best Western [O] st patrol, W [gas] Shell/dsl, Sunoco/dsl/E85 [food] Subway [lodging] Knights Inn [O] [H], Mt Gilead SP (6mi)
149mm	**truck parking both lanes**
140	OH 61, Mt Gilead, E [gas] Pilot/Arby's/dsl/scales/24hr W [gas] BP/Taco Bell, Marathon/Subway [food] Farmstead Rest. [O] Cardinal Ctr Camping

AKRON

CLEVELAND

STRONGSVILLE

MANSFIELD

OH

INTERSTATE 71 Cont'd

Exit#	Services
131	US 36, OH 37, to Delaware, E [gas] FLYING J/Denny's/dsl/LP/scales/24hr/@, Pilot/Subway/dsl/scales/24hr [food] Burger King [other] Harley-Davidson, W [gas] BP/dsl, Shell/Tim Hortons [food] Arby's, Bob Evans, Cracker Barrel, KFC/LJ Silver, McDonald's, Panera Bread, Starbucks, Taco Bell, Waffle House, Wendy's, White Castle [lodging] Best Value Inn, Hampton Inn, Holiday Inn Express [other] [H], Alum Cr SP, Cross Creek Camping (6mi)
128mm	[RS] both lanes, full [handicapped] facilities, litter barrels, petwalk, [phone], [picnic], vending
121	Polaris Pkwy, to Gemini Pl, E [gas] BP, Mobil, Shell/dsl [food] Bonefish Grill, Buffalo Wild Wings, Canes, Carfagna's Kitchen, El Alcapulco, Firehouse Subs, Five Guys, McDonald's, Mellow Mushroom Pizza, Pei Wei, Polaris Grill, Skyline Chili, Starbucks, Steak'n Shake, Subway, Tim Horton's [lodging] Fairfield Inn, Four Points Sheraton, Hampton Inn, Holiday Inn Express, Homewood Suites [other] Firestone/auto, Mt Tire, W [gas] BP, Shell/Tim Horton [food] Applebee's, Arby's, Bar Louie, Benihana, BJ's Rest., Brio Grille, Carrabba's, Charley Subs, CheeseCake Factory, Chick-fil-A, Chipotle Mexican, Coldstone, Dave&Buster's, El Vaquero Mexican, Firebird's Grill, Genghis Grill, Honey Baked Ham, Hooters, Jason's Deli, Jersey Mike's, Jimmy John's, Krispy Kreme, Marcella's Italian, Matt the Miller's Tavern, Max&Erma's, McDonald's, Merlot's Rest., Mimi's Cafe, Mitchell Steaks, Molly Woo's, Noodles&Co, O'Charley's, Olive Garden, Panera Bread, Papa John's, Penn Sta Subs, Potbelly's, Qdoba, Quaker Steak, Red Lobster, Red Robin, Rooster's Grill, Smokey Bones BBQ, Sonic, Starbucks, Subway, Taco Bell, Tequilas Mexican, TGIFriday's, TX Roadhouse, Waffle House, Wendy's [lodging] Cambria Suites, Candlewood Suites, Comfort Inn, Extended Stay America, Hilton, Hilton Garden, Residence Inn [other] AT&T, AutoZone, Barnes&Noble, Best Buy, BigLots, Cabela's, Costco/gas, Dick's, Earth Fare Mkt, funpark, GNC, Hobby Lobby, JC Penney, Jo-Ann Etc, Kroger/gas, Lowe's, Macy's, NTB, Old Navy, Petsmart, Target, TireDiscounters, TJ Maxx, Verizon, Von Maur, Walgreens, World Mkt
119b a	I-270, to Indianapolis, Wheeling
117	OH 161, to Worthington, E [gas] BP/dsl, Shell, Speedway/dsl, Sunoco/dsl [food] Burger King, Carfagna's Italian, China Dynasty, Chipotle, Dunkin Donuts/Baskin Robbins, Happy's a Pizza, KFC, LJ Silver, Massey's Pizza, McDonald's, Popeye's, Rally's, Red Lobster, Subway, Super Seafood Buffet, Taco Bell, Wendy's, White Castle [lodging] Comfort Inn, Days Inn, Red Roof Inn [other] $General, auto repair, CVS Drug, Family$, Walgreens, W [gas] GetGo, Shell, Speedway/dsl [food] Asian Kitchen, Bob Evans, China Jade, Domino's, McDonald's, Pizza Hut, Skyline Chili, Subway, Tim Hortons, Waffle House, Wendy's [lodging] Continent Inn, Crowne Plaza, Extended Stay America, Hawthorn Suites, Lexington Inn&Suites, Motel 6, Super 8, Woodspring Suites [other] Advance Parts, AutoZone, Chevrolet, Family$, Giant Eagle Foods, Premier Tire
116	Morse Rd, Sinclair Rd, E [gas] BP, Marathon/dsl, Shell/dsl, Speedway/dsl, Turkey Hill/dsl [food] Chipotle, Jimmy John's, Little Caesars, McDonald's, Papa John's, Subway, Taco Bell, Tim Horton's [lodging] Extend Suites [other] $General, AT&T, Buick/GMC, Chrysler/Dodge/Jeep, CVS Drug, Family$, Firestone/auto, Ford, Kroger, Menard's, Mr Tire, PepBoys, Save-A-Lot Foods, URGENT CARE, W [gas] Sunoco [lodging] Best Value Inn, Motel 6 [other] NTB
115	Cooke Rd
114	N Broadway, W [gas] Sunoco/dsl [food] Broadway Mkt Cafe, Subway
113	Weber Rd, W [gas] Speedway/dsl [other] CarQuest

COLUMBUS AREA

Exit#	Services
112	Hudson St, E [gas] Marathon, Shell/dsl [food] Wendy's [lodging] Holiday Inn Express [other] Family$, W [food] Big Boy [other] Aldi Foods, Lowe's, NTB
111	17th Ave, W [food] McDonald's [lodging] Comfort Suites, Days Inn
110b	11th Ave
110a	5th Ave, E [gas] Sunoco [food] Royal Fish&Chicken, White Castle, W [gas] Valero [food] Buckeye's Express, Church's, KFC, Wendy's [other] AutoZone
109a	I-670
109b	OH 3, Cleveland Ave
109c	Spring St (exits left from sb)
108b	US 40, Broad St, downtown, downtown
108a	Main St
101a[70]	I-70 E, US 23 N, to Wheeling
100b a[70]	US 23 S, Front St, High St, downtown
106a	I-70 W, to Indianapolis
106b	OH 315 N, Dublin St, Town St
105	Greenlawn, E [gas] [food] LJ Silver, White Castle [other] Berliner Park, W [gas] Shamrock
104	OH 104, Frank Rd
101b a	I-270, Wheeling, Indianapolis
100	Stringtown Rd, E [gas] [food] Bob Evans, Charley's Grilled Subs, Chick-fil-A, Chipotle, Coldstone, DQ, El Vaquero Mexican, Five Guys, Fusion Steaks, Jersey Mike's, Longhorn Steaks, O'Charley's, Olive Garden, Panda Express, Panera Bread, Red Robin, Roosters Grill, Smokey Bones BBQ, Sonic, Starbucks, Steak'n Shake, Subway, TX Roadhouse, White Castle [lodging] Best Western, Candlewood Suites, Courtyard, Drury Inn, Hampton Inn, Hilton Garden, Holiday Inn Express, La Quinta, Quality Inn, Red Roof Inn [other] AT&T, Best Buy, Dick's, Discount Tire, Firestone/auto, GNC, Hobby Lobby, Home Depot, Kohl's, Michael's, Petsmart, Staples, Target, TJ Maxx, Verizon, Walmart, W [gas] GetGo, Speedway/dsl, Sunoco/dsl, Turkey Hill/dsl [food] Applebee's, Arby's, Burger King, Cane's Chicken Fingers, China Bell, City BBQ, Cracker Barrel, Donato's Pizza, Fazoli's, Golden Corral, KFC, Mariachi Mexican, McDonald's, Papa John's, Pizza Hut, Rally's, Ruby Tuesday, Starbucks, Subway, Taco Bell, TeeJaye's Rest., Tim Horton, Waffle House, Wendy's [lodging] Comfort Inn, Days Inn, Motel 6, Travelodge [other] Advance Parts, Aldi Foods, AutoZone, BigLots, CVS Drug, Giant Eagle Foods, GNC, Goodyear/auto, Kroger/dsl, PetCo, Tuffy Auto, USPO, Walgreens
97	OH 665, London-Groveport Rd, E [gas] Marathon/Circle K [food] Arby's, Jimmy John's, McDonald's, Subway, Sunny St Cafe, Taco Bell, Tim Horton/Wendy's [other] $Tree, AT&T, Chevrolet, CVS Drug, Kroger/gas/E85, Meijer/E85, TireDiscounters, to Scioto Downs, URGENT CARE, Verizon, vet
94	US 62, OH 3, Orient, W [gas] Sunoco/Subway/dsl [other] Eddie's Repair

INTERSTATE 71 Cont'd

Exit#	Services
84	OH 56, Mt Sterling, E BP/Subway/dsl to Deer Creek SP (9mi)
75	OH 38, Bloomingburg, E fireworks, W Sunoco/dsl
69	OH 41, OH 734, Jeffersonville, E FLYING J/Denny's/dsl/scales/LP/24hr H, W BP, Shell/Subway/dsl Arby's, Wendy's Quality Inn Family$, Walnut Lake Camping
68mm	**both lanes, full facilities, litter barrels, petwalk, vending**
65	US 35, Washington CH, E Shell/dsl, Speedway/dsl, TA/BP/Pizza Hut/Popeye's/dsl/scales/24hr/@ A&W/KFC, Bob Evans, Chipotle Mexican, LJ Silver/Taco Bell, McDonald's, Subway, Waffle House, Wendy's, Werner's BBQ Baymont Inn, Fairfield Inn, Hampton Inn H, Tanger Outlets/famous brands, W Love's/Hardee's/dsl/scales/24hr EconoLodge
58	OH 72, to Sabina
50	US 68, to Wilmington, E H, W BP/dsl, Pilot/Subway/dsl/scales/24hr, Shell/dsl Max&Erma's, McDonald's, Wendy's Budget Inn, Holiday Inn, repair/tires Robert's Centre
49mm	**weigh sta nb**
45	OH 73, to Waynesville, E BP, Shell/dsl 73 Grill H, W Caesar Creek Camping (3mi), Caesar Creek SP (5mi), flea mkt
36	Wilmington Rd, E RV camping, to Ft Ancient St Mem
35mm	Little Miami River
34mm	**both lanes, scenic view, full facilities, litter barrels, petwalk, vending**
32	OH 123, to Lebanon, Morrow, E FLYING J/Wendy's/dsl/scales/24hr, Marathon, Valero Country Kitchen Morgan's Riverside Camping, **3 mi W** Bob Evans, Skyline Chili
28	OH 48, S Lebanon, E Speedway/Speedy's Cafe/dsl Dickey's BBQ, Starbucks, White Castle $Tree, Kohl's, Lowe's, Petsmart, Target, Verizon, W hwy patrol, Lebanon Raceway (6mi)
25	OH 741 N, Kings Mills Rd, E Shell/Popeye's/Dunkin Donuts, Speedway/dsl Buffalo Wings&Rings, Chipotle, DQ, Jimmy John's, McDonald's, Outback Steaks, Ruby Tuesday, Taco Bell, Wendy's Comfort Suites, Great Wolf Lodge, Kings Island Resort Harley-Davidson, Verizon, W Ameristop/Subway, BP Arby's, Big Boy, Burger King, Perkins, Pizza Hut, Skyline Chili, Taste Wok, Waffle House Baymont Inn, Hampton Inn, Microtel, Super 8 CarX, CVS Drug, GNC, Kroger/dsl, vet
24	Western Row, King's Island Dr (from nb), E Sunoco Eli's Grill, Fantastic Wok King's Island Resort
19	US 22, Mason-Montgomery Rd, E Speedway/dsl Arby's, Big Boy, Boston Mkt, Burger King, Cracker Barrel, Dunkin Donuts, Firehouse Subs, Flipdaddy's Burgers, Fricker's, Golden Corral, HoneyBaked Ham, Iron Chef Grill, KFC, Longhorn Steaks, McDonald's, Olive Garden, Pizza Tower, Potbelly, Taco Bell, Wendy's, White Castle Comfort Inn, Red Roof Inn, SpringHill Suites, TownePlace Suites Aldi Foods, AT&T, AutoZone, Barnes&Noble, Best Buy, BigLots, Buick/GMC, Chevrolet, Chrysler/Dodge/Jeep, Costco/gas, Firestone/auto, Ford, GNC, Honda, Infiniti, JC Penney, Kia, Kohl's, Kroger, Lexus, Mazda, Meijer/dsl, Michael's, Nissan, Old Navy, Porsche, Subaru, Target, TireDiscounters, Tires+, Toyota, Tuffy Auto, USPO, Verizon, VW, Walgreens, W BP/dsl, Marathon/dsl, Shell/Dunkin Donuts Abuelo's Mexican, Applebee's, BD Mongolian Grill, Blaze Pizza, Bravo Italian, Burger King, Carrabba's, Chick-fil-A,

CINCINNATI AREA

Exit#	Services
19	Continued Chipotle Mexican, DiBella Subs, Dickey's BBQ, Firebirds Grill, Five Guys, Fox&Hound Grill, Graeter's Cafe, IHOP, Jimmy John's, LoneStar Steaks, McAlister's Deli, Mimi's Cafe, Noodles&Co, Oasis Grill, O'Charley's, Panda Express, Panera Bread, Piada Italian, Qdoba, Red Robin, Remezo Greek, River City Grille, Rusty Bucket, Skyline Chili, Steak'n Shake, Subway, Waffle House, Wendy's, Zoup! Best Western, Hilton Garden, Holiday Inn Express, Homewood Suites, Hyatt Place, La Quinta, Marriott, Mason Inn Dick's, Hobby Lobby, Home Depot, Lowe's, Marshall's, NAPA, Staples, Tuesday Morning, URGENT CARE, vet, Walmart/Subway, Whole Foods Mkt
17b a	I-275, to I-75, OH 32
15	Pfeiffer Rd, E H, W BP, Shell/dsl, Sunoco/dsl Applebee's, Bob Evans, Buffalo Wild Wings, City BBQ, Firehouse Grill, Subway Courtyard, Crowne Plaza, Embassy Suites, Hampton Inn, Holiday Inn Express, Red Roof Inn, Wingate Inn Office Depot
14	OH 126, Reagan Hwy, Blue Ash
12	US 22, OH 3, Montgomery Rd, E BP/dsl, Shell/Dunkin Donuts/Subway, Sunoco Arby's, Bob Evans, Chipotle Mexican, Chuy's, Coopers Hawk, Cucinova, Currito, Ember's, Fusian, Jimmy John's, Outback Steaks, Panera Bread, Penn Sta Subs, Red Lobster, TGIFriday Tuesday Morning, W BP, Marathon Burger King, Cheesecake Factory, Honeybaked Ham, IHOP, Jersey Mike's, Maggiano's, McDonald's, Noodles&Co, Potbelly, Ruby Tuesday, Starbucks, Wendy's Best Western H, AT&T, Barnes&Noble, Dick's, Dillard's, Firestone auto, Fresh Mkt Foods, Macy's, Old Navy, PepBoys, Staples, Taco Bell, TireDiscounters, TJ Maxx, Trader Joe's, Verizon
11	Kenwood Rd, (from nb), W H, same as 12
10	Stewart Rd (from nb), to Silverton, E BMW/Mini, W Marathon/dsl
9	Redbank Rd, to Fairfax, (no ez sb return), E UDF Rally'
8	Kennedy Ave, Ridge Ave W, E Meijer/dsl IHOP Steak&Shake Motel 6 Fresh Thyme Mkt, Kroger/dsl, Petsmart, Target, W Marathon/dsl, Shell/Subway/dsl Gold Star Chili, Hooligan's, Jack-in-the-Box, LJ Silver, McDonald's, Wendy's, White Castle Days Inn $Tree, Aldi Foods, Big Lots, Buick/GMC, Burlington Coats, Family$, Home Depot, Lowes Whse, Office Depot, Remke Mkt, Tire Discounter
7	(from sb) OH 562, Ridge Ave E, Norwood
6	Edwards Rd, E BP, Shell/Popeye's/Dunkin Donuts, Speedway/dsl Boston Mkt, Bravo Italiana, Buca Italian, Buffalo Wild Wings, Capital Grille, Don Pablo's, Donato's, Five Guys, Alexander's Rest., Jason's Deli, Longhorn Steaks, Marco's Pizza, Max&Erma's, PF Chang's, Potbelly, Qdoba, Rusty Bucket, Seasons Grill, Starbucks, The Pub Courtyard AT&T, GNC, Old Navy, REI, SteinMart, TJ Maxx, URGENT CARE, Whole Foods Mkt, W Shell
5	Dana Ave, Montgomery Rd, W Xavier Univ, Zoo
3	Taft Rd (from sb), W U of Cincinnati
2	US 42, Reading Rd, Gilbert ave (from sb), W H, art museum, ballpark stadium arena, downtown
1k j	I-471 S
1d	Main St, downtown
1c b	Pete Rose Way, Fine St, downtown, stadium
1a	I-75 N, US 50, to Dayton
1	**I-71 S and I-75 S run together**
0mm	Ohio/Kentucky state line, Ohio River

OH

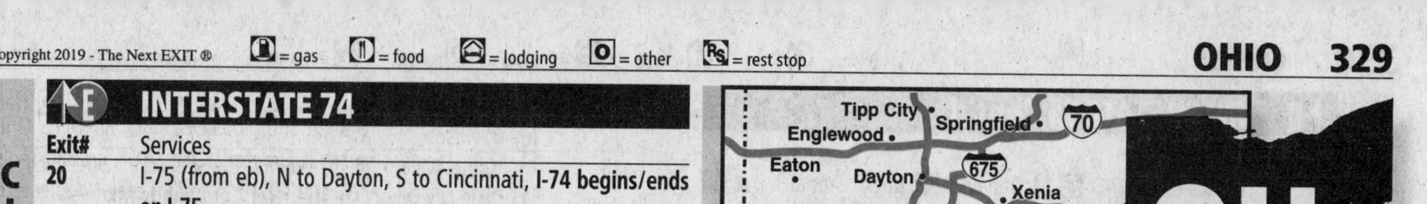

INTERSTATE 74

CINCINNATI

Exit#	Services
20	I-75 (from eb), N to Dayton, S to Cincinnati, **I-74 begins/ends on I-75.**
19	Gilmore St, Spring Grove Ave
18	US 27 N, Colerain Ave
17	Montana Ave (from wb), **N** [gas] BP
14	North Bend Rd, Cheviot, **N** [gas] Shell, Speedway/dsl [food] Big Boy, Dunkin Donuts, Jersey Mike's, Little Caesar's, McDonald's, Papa John's, Pizza Hut, Skyline Chili, Subway, Wendy's, White Castle [other] Family$, Kroger, Petco, Sam's Club/gas, Tire Discounters, Verizon, Walgreens, **S** [gas] Shell [food] Bob Evans [other] vet
11	Rybolt Rd, Harrison Pike, **S** [gas] [food] Chipotle, Longhorn Steaks, Marco's Puzza, McDonald's, Penn Sta Subs, Skyline Chili, Starbucks, Wendy's, White Castle [lodging] Holiday Inn Express [other] AT&T, Kohl's, Meijer/gas, Verizon
9	I-275 N, to I-75, N to Dayton, (exits left from eb)
8mm	Great Miami River
7	OH 128, to Hamilton, Cleves, **N** [gas] BP/dsl, Marathon/dsl [food] Wendy's
5	I-275 S, to Kentucky
3	Dry Fork Rd, **N** [gas] BP/dsl, **S** [gas] Marathon/dsl, Shell/Dunkin Donuts/dsl
2mm	**weigh sta eb**
1	New Haven Rd, to Harrison, **N** [gas] BP/dsl [food] Bob Evans, Buffalo Wild Wings, China Garden, Chipotle Mexican, Cracker Barrel, Dunkin Donuts, GoldStar Chili, Little Caesar's, O'Charley's, Subway [lodging] Best Western+ [other] Ford, Home Depot, Kia, Remke Mkt, Staples, Tires+, URGENT CARE, Verizon, **S** [gas] Shell/Circle K, Speedway/dsl, Sunoco/White Castle, UDF [food] A&W/KFC, Arby's, Big Boy, Burger King, Domino's, DQ, El Mariachi Cantina, Firehouse Subs, Freddy's, Happy Garden, Harrison Rest., Marco's Pizza, McDonald's, Penn Sta Subs, Pizza Hut, Skyline Chili, Taco Bell, Waffle House, Wendy's [lodging] Holiday Inn Express, Super 8 [other] $General, $Tree, Advance Parts, AT&T, AutoZone, BigLots, CVS Drug, Family$, Firestone/auto, GNC, Kroger/dsl, Meineke, NAPA, O'Reilly Parts, Sumerel Tire/auto, Tire Discounters, Walgreens
0mm	Ohio/Indiana state line

HARRISON

INTERSTATE 75

TOLEDO

Exit#	Services
211mm	Ohio/Michigan state line
210	OH 184, Alexis Rd, to Raceway Park, **W** [gas] BP/Circle K/dsl, Pilot/Subway/dsl/scales/24hr [food] Arby's, Bob Evans, Burger King, McDonald's, Taco Bell, Wendy's [lodging] Courtyard, Fairfield Inn, Hampton Inn, Holiday Inn Express [other] Aldi Foods, AutoZone, Meijer/dsl, Menards, URGENT CARE
210mm	Ottawa River
209	Ottawa River Rd (from nb), **E** [gas] BP, Sunoco [food] China King, Little Caesars, Marco's Pizza, River Diner [other] Kroger/E85, Rite Aid, Verizon
208	I-280 S, to I-80/90, to Cleveland
207	Stickney Ave, Lagrange St, **E** [gas] BP, S&G [food] Arby's, McDonald's, Wendy's [other] Family$, Rite Aid, Save-A-Lot Foods
206	to US 24, Phillips Ave, **W** [other] auto repair, transmissions
205b	Berdan Ave, **E** [other] [H], **W** [gas] Valero/dsl [food] Burger King, Subway [other] $General
205a	to Willys Pkwy, to Jeep Pkwy
204	I-475 W, to US 23 (exits left fom nb), to Maumee, Ann Arbor
203b	US 24, to Detroit Ave, **W** [gas] AP, Gas Express/dsl [food] KFC, McDonald's, Rally's, Wendy's [other] Family$, Rite Aid, Save-A-Lot Foods, U-Haul
203a	Bancroft St, downtown
202	Washington St, Collingwood Ave (from sb, no EZ return), **E** [other] [H], $Tree, Art Museum, **W** [food] McDonald's [other] Family$
201b a	OH 25, Collingwood Ave, **W** [other] Toledo Zoo
200	South Ave, Kuhlman Dr
200mm	Maumee River
199	OH 65, Miami St, to Rossford, **E** [lodging] Days Inn
198	Wales Rd, Oregon Rd, to Northwood, **E** [gas] S&G/dsl, Shell/Subway/dsl [food] Arby's, Arturo's Kitchen, China Wok, Coney Island [lodging] Best Value Inn, BridgePointe Inn
197	Buck Rd, to Rossford, **E** [gas] Shell/dsl [food] Tim Horton's, Wendy's, **W** [gas] BP, Sunoco/dsl [food] Denny's, McDonald's, Subway [lodging] American Inn, Knights Inn
195	to I-80/90, OH 795, OH Tpk (**toll**), Perrysburg, **E** [gas] BP/Subway/dsl [lodging] Country Inn&Suites, Courtyard, Hampton Inn, Staybridge Suites [other] Bass Pro Shops, Camping World RV Ctr
193	US 20, US 23 S, Perrysburg, **E** [gas] BP/dsl [food] 1st Wok, Arby's, Big Boy, Bob Evans, Burger King, Chick-fil-A, Chili's, China City, Chipotle, Cocina de Carlos, Cracker Barrel, Five Guys, Fricker's, IHOP, Jimmy John's, KFC, McDonald's, Panera Bread, Penn Sta Subs, Sonic, Starbucks, Subway, Taco Bell, Tim Horton's, Wendy's [lodging] Candlewood Suites, Comfort Suites, EconoLodge, Holiday Inn, Holiday Inn Express, Quality Inn [other] $Tree, Aldi Foods, Belle Tire, Best Buy, Discount Tire, GNC, Hobby Lobby, Home Depot, KOA (7mi), Kohl's, Kroger/gas/E85, Lowe's, Meijer/dsl, Michael's, Petsmart, Target, TJ Maxx, Tuesday Morning, Tuffy, URGENT CARE, Walgreens, Walmart/Subway, **W** [gas] Speedway/dsl [lodging] La Quinta [other] AutoZone, Harley-Davidson
192	I-475, US 23 N (exits left from nb), to Maumee, Ann Arbor
187	OH 582, to Luckey, Haskins
181	OH 64, OH 105, to Pemberville, Bowling Green, **E** [lodging] Holiday Inn Express [other] Meijer/dsl/E85, **W** [gas] BP/dsl, Circle K/Subway/dsl, Speedway/dsl [food] Big Boy, Bob Evans, Buffalo Wild Wings, Burger King, Chipotle Mexican, Coldstone/Tim Horton's, El Zarape Mexican, Fricker's Rest., Hunan Buffet, Jimmy John's, McDonald's, Penn Sta Subs, Starbucks, Waffle House, Wendy's [lodging] Best Western, Days Inn, Hampton Inn, Victory Inn [other] [H], to Bowling Green State U, USPO, Verizon
179	US 6, to Fremont, Napoleon, **W** [other] museum
179mm	[RS] **both lanes, full [handicapped] facilities, litter barrels, petwalk, [phone], [picnic], vending**
175mm	**weigh sta nb**
171	OH 25, Cygnet
168	Eagleville Rd, Quarry Rd, **E** [gas] FuelMart/dsl
167	OH 18, to Fostoria, North Baltimore, **E** [gas] Petro/BP/Iron Skillet/

PERRYSBURG

OH

INTERSTATE 75 Cont'd

FINDLAY

Exit	Services
167	Continued dsl/scales/24hr/@ McDonald's truck repair, W Loves/Arby's/dsl/scales/24hr, Sunoco $General, Great Scot Mkt
165mm	Rocky Ford River
164	OH 613, to McComb, Fostoria, E RV camping, Van Buren SP, W Pilot/Subway/Taco Bell/dsl/scales/24hr
162mm	**weigh sta sb**
161	rd 99, E Shell/Subway/dsl, Speedway/dsl Comfort Suites Ford/Lincoln, hwy patrol, Kia, URGENT CARE, VW, W antiques
159	US 224, OH 15, Findlay, E BP/dsl, Marathon/dsl, Speedway/Speedy's Cafe/dsl Burger King, Culver's, Dakota Grill, Fin's Seafood Grill, Jimmy John's, KFC/LJ Silver, McDonald's, Ming's Great Wall, Pizza Hut, Ralphie's, Spaghetti Shop, Steak'n Shake, Subway, Taco Bell, Wendy's Drury Inn, Motel 6, Red Roof Inn, Rodeway Inn H, Advance Parts, W Murphy USA/dsl, Shell/dsl Bob Evans, Coldstone/Tim Horton's, Cracker Barrel, Denny's, Hokkaido Steaks, Jac&Do's Pizza, Landing Pad, Max&Erma's, Outback Steaks, Tony's Rest., TX Roadhouse, Waffle House Country Inn&Suites, Hampton Inn, Hilton Garden, Holiday Inn Express, Quality Inn AT&T, AutoZone, Best 1 Tires/repair, Chrysler/Dodge/Jeep, Peterbilt, Verizon, Walmart/Subway
158mm	Blanchard River
157	OH 12, Findlay, E Marathon/dsl, W Fricker's Rest. EconoLodge vet
156	US 68, OH 15, to Carey, E H
153mm	**both lanes, full facilities, litter barrels, petwalk, vending**
145	OH 235, to Ada, Mount Cory, E KOA
142	OH 103, to Arlington, Bluffton, E Fairway Inn, W Marathon/Circle K/dsl, Shell Arby's, Burger King, McDonald's/rv parking, Subway, Subway, Taco Bell, Wendy's Comfort Inn $General, auto repair, to Bluffton U, vet
140	Bentley Rd, to Bluffton, W H
135	OH 696, to US 30, to Delphos, Beaverdam, E Speedway/Speedy's Cafe/dsl/24hr, W FLYING J/Denny's/dsl/scales/LP/24hr/@, Pilot/McDonald's/Subway/dsl/24hr/@ $General, Blue Beacon, SpeedCo, tires, truck repair
134	Napolean Rd (no nb re-entry), to Beaverdam
130	Bluelick Rd, E Clark
127b a	OH 81, to Ada, Lima, W Fuelstop/dsl, Valero/dsl Subway, Waffle House Comfort Inn
126mm	Ottawa River
125	OH 309, OH 117, Lima, E Murphy USA/dsl, Speedway/Speedy's Cafe/dsl Applebee's, Bob Evans, Burger King, Capt D's, China Bistro, China Buffet, Cracker Barrel, Hunan Garden, J's Grill, Lock Sixteen Steaks, McDonald's, Olive Garden, Panera Bread, Pizza Hut, Red Lobster, Skyline Chili, Subway, Taco Bell, TX Roadhouse, Wendy's Courtyard, Hampton Inn, Howard Johnson, Motel 6 AT&T, BigLots, Ford/Lincoln, Sam's Club/gas, Verizon, Walgreens, Walmart/McDonald's, W Arby's, Kewpee Hamburger's, Yamato Steaks Country Inn&Suites, Holiday Inn, Travelodge H, $General, Advance Parts, Best 1 Tires/repair, O'Reilly Parts, Rite Aid, Save-A-Lot Foods, Verizon
124	4th St, E Ford/Lincoln, hwy patrol
122	OH 65, Lima, E Speedway/dsl, W Marathon/Subway/dsl Freightliner, GMC, Mack, truck repair, vet, Volvo

LIMA

OH

SIDNEY

Exit	Services
120	Breese Rd, Ft Shawnee, W Shawnee Fuelstop/dsl Harley-Davidson
118	to Cridersville, W Fuelmart/Subway/dsl, Speedway/ds Dixie Ley Diner $General, Community Mkt, vet
114mm	**both lanes, hadicapped facilities, litter barrels, pet walk, vending**
113	OH 67, to Uniopolis, Wapakeneta
111	Bellefontaine St, Wahpakeneta, E TA/Hub Room Rest./dsl scales/@ Country Charm Rest. Knights Inn KOA truck tires, W Clark/dsl, Murphy USA/dsl, Shell Arby's, Bob Evans, Burger King, Capt D's, DQ, El Azteca, Luck Steer Rest., McDonald's, Pizza Hut, Subway, Taco Bell, Waffl House, Wendy's Best Western, Holiday Inn Express, Supe 8 Advance Parts, Aldi Foods, CVS Drug, Lowe's, Neil Armstrong Museum, O'Reilly Parts, st patrol, URGENT CARE, Verizon, Walmart
110	US 33, to St Marys, Bellefontaine, E hwy patrol, KOA
104	OH 219, W Gulf/dsl, Marathon, Shell/Circle K/Subway dsl Budget Host $General
102	OH 274, to Jackson Ctr, New Breman, E bicycle museum W air stream tours
99	OH 119, to Minster, Anna, E 99/dsl, Marathon/ds W Shell, Speedway/Taco Bell/dsl Subway, Wendy' Family$, lube/wash/repair
94	rd 25A, Sidney, E Marathon/deli
93	OH 29, to St Marys, Sidney, W Lake Loramie SP, RV campin
92	OH 47, to Versailles, Sidney, E Speedway/dsl Arby's China Garden, Coldstone, Fuji Steakhouse, Little Caesar's, Subway, Time Horton's, Wendy's H, Advance Parts, AutoZone CVS Drug, NAPA, Save-A-Lot Foods, URGENT CARE, Walgreen W Murphy USA/dsl, Sunoco/dsl Applebee's, Bi Boy, Bob Evans, Buffalo Wild Wings, Burger King, Cazadore Mexican, Culver's, Fricker's, Hong Kong Buffet, KFC, McDonald's, Perkins, Pizza Hut, Smokin Jo's BBQ, Taco Bell, Waffl House Comfort Inn, Country Hearth Inn, Days Inn, Holida Inn Express, Travel Inn $Tree, Aldi Foods, AT&T, Buick Cadillac/Chevrolet/GMC, Chrysler/Dodge/Jeep, Ford/Lincol Kroger/dsl, Lowe's, Menards, Verizon, Walmart/Subway
90	Fair Rd, to Sidney, E Sunoco/dsl, W Loves/Chester's/Godfather's/Hardee's/dsl/scales/24hr, Marathon/DQ dsl Hampton Inn
88mm	Great Miami River
83	rd 25A, Piqua, W Sunoco/MaidRite Cafe/Noble Roman's dsl Chrysler/Dodge/Jeep, Sherry RV Ctr, to Piqua Hist Are
82	US 36, to Urbana, Piqua, E Marathon, Murphy USA/d A&W/LJ Silver, Arby's, China East, China Garden, DQ, Sombrero, KFC, Subway, Taco Bell, Waffle House, Wendy $Tree, Aldi Foods, BigLots, Harley-Davidson, Home Depot, JoAnn Fabrics, st patrol, Verizon, vet, Walmart/Subwa W Speedway Bob Evans, Buffalo Wings&Rings, Cracker Barrel, McDonald's, Red Lobster Budgetel, Comfort Inn, L Quinta Elder Beerman, JC Penney
81mm	**both lanes, full facilities, litter barrels, vending**
78	rd 25A, E H
74	OH 41, to Covington, Troy, E BP/dsl Al's Pizza, Chin Garden, Little Caesars, McDonald's, Pizza Hut, Subway, Tac Bell to Hobart Arena, URGENT CARE, vet, W She Speedway/dsl Applebee's, Big Boy, Bob Evans, Buffalo Wi Wings, Burger King, Chipotle Mexican, Culver's, Fazoli's, Jimm John's, KFC, Logan's Roadhouse, Los Pitayos Mexican, Outbac Steaks, Panera Bread, Penn Sta Subs, Ruby Tuesday, Sak Japanese, Skyline Chili, Steak'n Shake Best Inn, Comfo

TROY

INTERSTATE 75 Cont'd

74 Continued
Suites, Fairfield Inn, Hampton Inn, Holiday Inn Express, Residence Inn [other] $General, $Tree, AT&T, AutoZone, GNC, Grismer Auto Service, Kohl's, Lowe's, Meijer/dsl, Petco, Staples, Tire Discounters, Verizon, Walmart/Subway

73 OH 55, to Ludlow Falls, Troy, E [gas] BP, Shell [food] Boston Stoker Coffee House, Honeybaked Ham, Hot Head Burrito, Lincoln Sq Rest., Papa John's, Subway, Waffle House, Wendy's [lodging] Budget Inn, Motel 6, Royal Inn [other] $General, Kroger/e85, Verizon

69 rd 25A, E [gas] Circle K/dsl, Gulf/dsl [other] Arbogast RV Ctr, Buick/GMC, Chrysler/Dodge/Jeep, Ford

68 OH 571, to West Milton, Tipp City, E [gas] BP/dsl, Shell, Speedway/dsl [food] Burger King, Cassano's Pizza, Domino's, Fox's Pizza, Greenfire Bustro, Hickory River BBQ, Hong Kong Kitchen, Hot Head Burritos, McDonald's, Subway, Taco Bell [other] AT&T, CVS Drug, Family$, FoodTown, Goodyear/auto, Honda, O'Reilly Parts, W [gas] Speedway/dsl [food] Arby's, Big Boy, Bob Evans, Tipp' O the Town Rest., Wendy's [lodging] Holiday Inn Express, La Quinta [other] Main St Parts, Menards, Performance Parts, vet

64 Northwoods Blvd, E [food] El Toro Mexican, Emperial Palace [other] $Tree, Kroger/dsl, W [gas] FLYING J/Subway/dsl/scales/RV dump/24hr

63 US 40, to Donnelsville, Vandalia, E [gas] Speedway/dsl [food] Bunker's Grill, Dragon China, Fricker's [other] AutoZone, repair, W [gas] BP/dsl, Shell, Speedway/dsl [food] Arby's, Burger King, Domino's, Hot Head Burrito, KFC/LJ Silver, McDonald's, Pizza Hut, Rib House, Subway, Taco Bell, Waffle House, Wendy's [lodging] Super 8 [other] Goodyear/auto, Rexall Drug, Rite Aid

61b a I-70, E to Columbus, W to Indianapolis, to Dayton Int Airport

59 Wyse Rd, Benchwood Rd, E [food] El Rancho Grande, Little York Pizza, Shen's [lodging] Hawthorn Suites, Knights Inn, Travelodge [other] BMW/Volvo/VW, Discount Tire, W [gas] Speedway/dsl, Valero/dsl [food] Arby's, Asian Buffet, Big Boy, Bob Evans, Cassano's Pizza, Chick-fil-A, Chipotle Mexican, Coldstone, Cousin Vinny's Puzza, Cracker Barrel, El Toro Mexican, Fazoli's, Fricker's, Golden Corral, Hooters, Longhorn Steaks, Max&Erma's, McAlister's Deli, McDonald's, O'Charley's, Olive Garden, Outback Steaks, Panera Bread, Red Lobster, Ruby Tuesday, Sake Japanese, Skyline Chili, SmashBurger, SmokeyBones BBQ, Steak'n Shake, Subway, Taco Bell, Tim Horton's [lodging] Best Value Inn, Comfort Inn, Courtyard, Days Inn, Drury Inn, Extended Stay America, Fairfield Inn, Hampton Inn, Quality Inn, Red Roof Inn, Residence Inn; Springhill Suites, TownePlace Suites [other] Office Depot, Sam's Club/gas, Verizon, Walmart/Subway

58 Needmore Rd, to Dayton, E [gas] BP/dsl, Shell/McDonald's [food] Hardee's [other] Goodyear/auto, to AF Museum, W [gas] Marathon/dsl, Speedway/dsl, Sunoco/dsl [food] A&W/LJ Silver, Church's, Domino's, Subway, Tim Horton's, Waffle House, Wendy's [other] $General, $Tree, Advance Parts, auto repair, AutoZone, Family$, Kroger/gas, Midas, O'Reilly Parts, USPO, vet, Walgreens

57b Wagner Ford Rd, Siebenthaler Rd, Dayton, E [gas] Marathon [lodging] Ramada Inn

57a Neva Rd

56 Stanley Ave, Dayton, E [gas] Shell, W [gas] Keowee [food] Dragon City Chinese, Gold Star Chili, McDonald's, Pancake House, Taco Bell [lodging] Dayton Motel

55b a Keowee St, Dayton, downtown

54c OH 4 N, Webster St, to Springfield, downtown

54mm Great Miami River

54b OH 48, Main St, Dayton, E [gas] Chevrolet, Honda, W [other] [H], Family$

DAYTON

OH

54a Grand Ave, Dayton, downtown

53b OH 49, 1st St, Salem Ave, Dayton, downtown

53a OH 49, 3rd St, downtown

52b a US 35, E to Dayton, W to Eaton

51 Edwin C Moses Blvd, Nicholas Rd, E [lodging] Courtyard, Marriott [other] [H], to U of Dayton, W [gas] BP/dsl, Loves/Hardee's/dsl/scales/24hr [food] McDonald's, Wendy's [other] SunWatch Indian Village

50b a OH 741, Kettering St, Dryden Rd, E [other] [H], vet, W [gas] Marathon/dsl [food] TJ's Rest. [lodging] Super 8 [other] U-Haul

47 Dixie Dr, W Carrollton, Moraine, E [gas] Shell/dsl [food] Big Boy, Domino's, Waffle House [other] $General, auto repair, transmissions, W [gas] Shell/dsl, Speedway/dsl [food] El Meson, KFC, McDonald's, Pizza Hut, Sonic, Taco Bell, Wendy's [other] $General, USPO

44 OH 725, to Centerville, Miamisburg, E [gas] BP/dsl, Shell, Speedway/dsl [food] Applebee's, Baskin-Robbins, Big Boy, Bonefish Grill, Bravo Italiana, Burger King, ChuckeCheese, Dunkin Donuts, El Toro Mexican, Fazoli's, FirstWatch Cafe, Fricker's, Godfather's, Golden Corral, Hardee's, Jimmy John's, KFC, Logan's Roadhouse, Marion's Puzza, McDonald's, O'Charley's, Olive Garden, Panera Bread, Penn Sta Subs, PF Chang's, Qdoba, Red Lobster, Rooster's Grill, Rusty Bucket Grill, Saka Buffet, Sake Japanese, Skyline Chili, SmashBurger, Starbucks, Steak'n Shake, Subway, Taco Bell, TGIFriday's, Waffle House, Wendy's [lodging] Comfort Suites, Courtyard, Days Inn, DoubleTree Suites, Extended Stay America, Hampton Inn, Hawthorn Suites, Homewood Suites, InTowne Suites, SpringHill Suites, Studio 6, Woodspring Suites [other] [H], $Tree, Advance Parts, Aldi Foods, AT&T, Audi/VW/Porsche/Jaguar, Barnes&Noble, Best Buy, Burlington Coats, Dick's, Discount Tire, Elder Beerman, Grismer Auto Service, Hobby Lobby, Home Depot, Honda/Nissan/Mazda, JC Penney, Jo-Ann Fabrics, Kia, Lowe's, Macy's, Menard's, Michael's, Midas, Monro, NTB, Office Depot, PepBoys, Petsmart, Target, Tire Discounters, Toyota, Verizon, vet, Walmart, W [gas] BP, Marathon, Shell/dsl [food] Bob Evans, LJ Silver, Perkins, Tim Horton's [lodging] Knights Inn, Quality Inn, Red Roof Inn, Super 8 [other] [H], $General, Aamco, CarMax, Chevrolet, Ford, NAPA

43 I-675 N, to Columbus

41 Austin Blvd, E [food] BJ's Rest., Broken Egg Cafe, Chipotle, Chuy's, Coldstone, Dewey's Pizza, Firebirds, Five Guys, Noodles&-Co, Panera Bread, Spicy Olive [lodging] Hilton Garden [other] AT&T, Field&Stream, Kohl's, Kroger/dsl, TJ Maxx

38 OH 73, Springboro, Franklin, E [gas] Shell, Speedway/dsl, Thornton's/dsl [food] Applebee's, Arby's, Bob Evans, Burger King, China Garden, Chipotle Mexican, KFC, LJ Silver, McDonald's, Papa John's, Pizza Hut, Skyline Chili, Subway, Taco Bell, Tim Horton's, Waffle House, Wendy's [lodging] Comfort Inn, Hampton Inn [other] Kroger, O'Reilly Parts, Tire Discounters, USPO, vet, W [gas] Murphy

INTERSTATE 75 Cont'd

MIDDLETOWN

38 Continued
USA/dsl, Shell, Speedway/dsl A&G Pizza, Big Boy, Cazadore's Mexican, Domino's, GoldStar Chili, Lee's Chicken, McDonald's EconoLodge, Holiday Inn Express $General, $Tree, Advance Parts, AutoZone, Brothers Automotive, Kemper Tire, KOI Parts, NAPA, URGENT CARE, USPO, Walgreens, Walmart

36 OH 123, to Lebanon, Franklin, E BP/Mom's Rest./dsl, Pilot/Subway/Pizza Hut/dsl/scales/24hr/@, Shell/Wendy's/dsl McDonald's, Waffle House Motel 6, W Marathon/White Castle/dsl, Sunoco

32 OH 122, Middletown, E McDonald's Days Inn, Red Roof Inn, Super 8 H, CVS Drug, W Applebee's, Arby's, Big Boy, Bob Evans, Cracker Barrel, El Rancho Grande, Golden Corral, GoldStar Chili, Hot Head Burritos, KFC, La Rosa's Pizza, LoneStar Steaks, O'Charley's, Olive Garden, Schlotzsky's, Sonic, Steak'n Shake, Wendy's, White Castle Drury Inn, Fairfield Inn, Hampton Inn, Holiday Inn Express, Quality Inn $General, Aldi Foods, AT&T, AutoZone, BigLots, Elder Beerman, Kohl's, Kroger/dsl, Lowe's, Meijer/dsl, Petco, Staples, Tire Discounters, URGENT CARE, Verizon, Walmart/Subway

29 OH 63, to Hamilton, Monroe, E Shell/Popeye's/dsl, Stony Ridge/dsl Burger King, Chipotle, Culver's, GoldStar Chili, Tim Horton/Wendy's, Waffle House Comfort Inn Premium Outlets/Famous Brands, Tire Discounters, Trader's World, W Speedway/dsl Froggy Blue's, McDonald's, Richard's Pizza, Subway Best Western, Wave Hotel Honda

27.5mm **both lanes, full facilities, info, litter barrels, petwalk, , vending**

24 OH 129 W, to Hamilton, W Dick's

22 Tylersville Rd, to Mason, Hamilton, E Sunoco, Thornton's/dsl Arby's, Bob Evans, BoneFish Grill, Burger King, Cane's, Chick-fil-A, Chipotle, City BBQ, Firehouse Subs, Fricker's, Geisha, Graeter's Grill, Great Wall, IHOP, Jack-in-the-Box, Jimmy John's, KFC, LJ Silver, Longhorn Steaks, McAlister's Deli, McDonald's, Milano's, Noodles&Co, Panda Express, Panera Bread, Perkins, Pizza Hut, Skyline Chili, SmashBurger, Soho Japanese, Starbucks, Subway, Taco Bell, TGIFriday's, Twin Dragon, Waffle House, Wendy's Economy Inn H, AT&T, Big Lots, Firestone/auto, Fresh Mkt, GNC, Goodyear/auto, Home Depot, Kohl's, Kroger, Michael's, Office Depot, Petsmart, Target, Tires+, TJ Maxx, URGENT CARE, Verizon, Walgreens, W Speedway/dsl, Sunoco O'Charley's Wingate Inn Aldi Foods, CarX, Lowe's, Meijer/dsl, Tire Discounters

21 Cin-Day Rd, E Big Boy Holiday Inn Express, W Marathon/dsl, Speedway/dsl, UDF/Subway/dsl Arby's, Domino's, Dunkin Donuts, El Rancho Nuevo, La Rosa's Pizza, Little Caesar's, Papa John's, Sonic, Tikka Grill, Waffle House, Wendy's, White Castle Ace Hardware, AutoZone, Walgreens, Walmart/Subway

19 Union Centre Blvd, to Fairfield, E Bravo Italiana, Champps Rest., Mitchell's Fish Mkt, Original Pancakes, Panera Bread, PF Chang's, Red Robin, Smokey Bones BBQ, Steak'n Shake AT&T, Barnes&Noble, Verizon, W BP/Subway/dsl, Marathon/Circle K, Shell Aladdin's Eatery, Applebee's, Bob Evans, Buffalo Wild Wings, Burger King, Chipotle Mexican, Dingle House, Jag's Steaks, Jimmy John's, McDonald's, Mellow Mushroom, Rancho Nuevo, River City Grille, Skyline Chili, Starbucks, Subway, Tom+Chee, Uno, Wendy's Comfort Inn, Courtyard, Hampton Inn, Hilton Garden, Holiday Inn, Homewood Suites, Marriott, Residence Inn, Staybridge Suites IKEA, Mercedes, Monro, Volvo

16 I-275 to I-71, to I-74

CINCINNATI AREA

15 Sharon Rd, to Sharonville, Glendale, E Sunoco, Thornton's dsl Big Boy, Bob Evans, Cracker Barrel, Jim Dandy BBQ, Rub Tuesday, Skyline Chili, Subway, Waffle House Baymont Inn Drury Inn, Hawthorn Suites, Hilton Garden, Holiday Inn Express, La Quinta, Quality Inn, Red Roof Inn, Travel Inn, on Kemper, W Sunoco Burger King, Cane's, Chick-fil-A, Chili's ChuckeCheese, Five Guys, IHOP, LJ Silver, Macaroni Grill, McDonald's, Panera Bread, Penn Sta Subs, Pizza Hut, Subway, Taco Bell, Tokyo Japanese, Vincenzo's Italian, Wendy's Crosslan Suites, EconoLodge, Extended Stay America, Fairfield Inn, LivIn Suites, Red Lion Hotel, Residence Inn Best Buy, Costco/gas Dick's, Lowe's, Nissan, Sam's Club, Sharonville Conv Ctr, Target

14 OH 126, to Woodlawn, Evendale, E Wingate Inn (3mi GE Plant, W Shell/dsl

13 Shepherd Lane, to Lincoln Heights, E GE Plant, W Taco Bell, Wendy's

12 Wyoming Ave, Cooper Ave, to Lockland, W Marathon/dsl

10a OH 126, Ronald Reagan Hwy

10b Galbraith Rd (exits left from nb), Arlington Heights

9 OH 4, OH 561, Paddock Rd, Seymour Ave, E to Cincinnati Gardens, W fairgrounds

8 Towne St, Elmwood Pl (from nb)

7 OH 562, to I-71, Norwood, Cincinnati Gardens

6 Mitchell Ave, St Bernard, E Mobil, Shell, Sunoco White Castle Quality Inn to Cincinnati Zoo, to Xavier U, Walgreens, W BP/Subway/dsl Gold Star Chili, McDonald's Rally's Advance Parts, Family$, Ford, Honda, Hyundai, Kia Kroger, Tires+

4 I-74 W, US 52, US 27 N, to Indianapolis

3 to US 27 S, US 127 S, Hopple St, E Big Boy, White Castle BudgetHost H, U of Cincinnati, W Shell Isadore's Italian, Wendy's

2b Harrison Ave, W BP/Subway McDonald's Family$ industrial district

2a Western Ave, Liberty St (from sb)

1g Ezzard Charles Dr ((from sb), W Guest Inn

1f US 50W, Freeman Ave (from sb), W Marathon/dsl, Shell Subway Big Boy, Taco Bell, Wendy's, White Castle Guest Inn Ford, NAPA, USPO

1e 7th St (from sb), downtown

1c 5th St, E Hilton, Hyatt, Millennial Hotel to Duke Energy Center, downtown

1a I-71 N, to Cincinnati, downtown, to stadium

0mm Ohio/Kentucky state line, Ohio River

INTERSTATE 76

Exit# Services

65 Ohio/Pennsylvania state line. **See OH TPK, exits 232-234.**

60mm I-76 eb joins Ohio TPK **(toll)**

57 to OH 45, Bailey Rd, to Warren

54 OH 534, to Newton Falls, Lake Milton, N RV camping S Sunoco/dsl camping, to Berlin Lake

52mm Lake Milton

48 OH 225, to Alliance, N camping, to W Branch SP, S Berlin Lake, to Lake Milton SP

45mm **both lanes, full facilities, litter barrels, petwalk, ,**

43 OH 14, to Alliance, Ravenna, N to W Branch SP, S Marathon/Subway/dsl fireworks

38b a OH 5, OH 44, to Ravenna, N BP/dsl, Speedway/dsl Arby's, McDonald's/rv parking, Wendy's, S Marathon/Circle K Subway Cracker Barrel H, $General, auto parts, Giant Eagle Foods, RV camping

OH

INTERSTATE 76 Cont'd

Exit#	Services
33	OH 43, to Hartville, Kent, N BP/dsl, Marathon Salsita's Mexican Comfort Inn, Days Inn, EconoLodge, Hampton Inn, Holiday Inn Express, Super 8 to Kent St U, S Circle K, Speedway/dsl Gionino's Pizza, McDonald's, Pizza Hut, Subway, Wendy's $General, Goodyear Tire/brakes, vet
31	rd 18, Tallmadge, N Murphy USA/dsl #1 Chinese, Applebee's, Beef'O'Brady's, DQ, La Terraza Mexican, Panera Bread $Tree, AT&T, GNC, Kohl's, Lowe's, Marshall's, Petco, Verizon, Walmart/Subway
29	OH 532, Tallmadge, Mogadore
27	OH 91, Canton Rd, Gilchrist Rd, N Bob Evans, S Marathon/Subway/dsl Hardee's Quality Inn
26	OH 18, E Market St, Mogadore Rd, N Marathon/dsl Hamad Tire/repair, S Arby's, McDonald's, Subway, Wendy's $General
25b a	Martha Ave, General St, Brittain, N Circle K/dsl Hilton Garden Mercedes, Toyota, S Goodyear HQ
24	Arlington St, Kelly Ave, S Goodyear HQ
23b	OH 8, Buchtell Ave, to Cuyahoga (exits left from eb), to U of Akron
23a	I-77 S, to Canton
22b	Grant St, Wolf Ledges, Akron, N USPO, S McDonald's Family$, downtown
22a	Main St, Broadway, downtown
21c	OH 59 E, Dart Ave, N H
21b	Lakeshore St, Bowery St (from eb)
21a	East Ave (from wb)
20	I-77 N (from eb), to Cleveland
19	Battles Ave, Kenmore Blvd
18	I-277, US 224 E, to Canton, Barberton
17b	OH 619, Wooster Rd, S Sunoco/dsl H, tires/repair
17a	(from eb, no return) State St, to Barberton, S Papa John's, Papa Roni's Pizza H, Walgreens
16	Barber Rd, S Rocky's/dsl/E85 DQ, Tomaso's Italian Chrysler/Dodge/Jeep, Fiat
14	Cleve-Mass Rd, to Norton, S BP/Blimpie/dsl, Circle K/dsl Arby's, Casa Del Mar Mexican, McDonald's, Pizza Hut, Subway, Wendy's $General, Ace Hardware, Acme Fresh Mkt, Advance Parts, CVS Drug, Family$, Ritzman Drug, USPO, Verizon
13b a	OH 21, N to Cleveland, S to Massillon
11	OH 261, Wadsworth, N Speedway/dsl, S GetGo/E85, Giant Eagle Arabica Cafe, Beef'O'Brady's, Wayback Burger AAA, GNC, Kohl's, Lowe's, MC Sports, PetCo, Target, Verizon
9	OH 94, to N Royalton, Wadsworth, N Marathon/Circle K Applebee's, Arby's, Bob Evans, Burger King, China Express, Chipotle Mexican, Galaxy Rest., Marie's Cafe, McDonald's, Panera Bread, Patron's Mexican, Pizza Hut, Romeo's Pizza, Starbucks, Subway, Taco Bell, Wendy's Comfort Inn, Holiday Inn Express $General, $Tree, BigLots, Buehler's Foods, DrugMart, Goodyear/auto, Home Depot, NTB, Verizon, Walmart/Subway, S Marathon/DQ/dsl, Sunoco Casa Del Rio, Dunkin Donuts, Papa John's Legacy Inn Advance Parts, auto repair, AutoZone, CVS Drug, NAPA, Rite Aid, vet
7	OH 57, to Rittman, Medina, N Marathon/dsl, S H,
6mm	**weigh sta eb**
2	OH 3, to Medina, Seville, N Marathon/Circle K/dsl DQ, Hardee's, Huddle House, Pizzazo's, Subway Comfort Inn, Hawthorn Suites Maple Lakes Camping (seasonal), S Clark, Shell/dsl #1 Chinese, E of Chicago Pizza, El Patron Mexican $General, Ritzman Drug, Verizon

AKRON

Exit#	Services
1	I-76 E, to Akron, US 224on US 224, W Pilot/Subway/dsl/scales/24hr, TA/BP/Burger King/Popeye's/dsl/scales/24hr/@ Arby's, McDonald's, Starbucks Super 8 Blue Beacon, Chippewa Valley Camping (1mi), SpeedCo
0mm	**I-76 begins/ends on I-71, exit 209.**

INTERSTATE 77

Exit#	Services
	I-77 begins/ends on I-90 exit 172, in Cleveland.
163c	I-90, E to Erie, W to Toledo
163b	E 9th St, Tower City
162b	E 22nd St, E 14th St (from nb)
162a	E 30th St, Woodland Ave, Broadway St (from nb), W USPO
161b	I-490 W, to I-71, E 55th, E H
161a	OH 14 (from nb), Broadway St
160	Pershing Ave (from nb), W H
159b	Fleet Ave, E BP/7-11/dsl
159a	Harvard Ave, Newburgh Heights, W BP/Subway/dsl
158	Grant Ave, Cuyahoga Heights
157	OH 21, OH 17 (from sb), Brecksville Rd
156	I-480, to Youngstown, Toledo
155	Rockside Rd, to Independence, E Shell, Sunoco/dsl Aladdin's, Bob Evans, Bonefish Grill, Chipotle, Del Monico's Steaks, Denny's, DiBella's Subs, Jimmy John's, McDonald's, Melt Grill, Outback Steaks, Panera Bread, Potbelly's, Red Robin, Shula's Steaks, Starbucks, Wendy's, Winking Lizard Grill, Zoup Comfort Inn, DoubleTree, Embassy Suites, Holiday Inn, La Quinta, Red Roof Inn AT&T, Drugmart, to Cuyahoga Valley NP, Verizon, Walgreens, W BP/dsl Applebee's, Longhorn Steaks, Wasabi Steaks Courtyard, Crowne Plaza, Hampton Inn, Hyatt Place, Residence Inn
153	Pleasant Valley Rd, to Independence, 7 Hills
151	Wallings Rd
149	OH 82, to Broadview Heights, Brecksville, **1 mi** E BP, Shell/dsl Austin's Grille, Panera Bread, Sakura Japanese, Simon's Rest., Starbucks, Subway CVS Drug, Marc's Foods, vet, Walgreens, W BP, GetGo/dsl Bob Evans, Chipotle Giant Eagle Foods
147	to OH 21, Miller Rd (from sb)
146	I-80/Ohio Tpk, to Youngstown, Toledo
145	OH 21 (from nb), E Pilot/Wendy's/dsl/scales Memories Rest., Subway Days Inn, Hampton Inn, Holiday Inn Express, Motel 6, Super 8
144	I-271 N, to Erie
143	OH 176, to I-271 S, W Shell McDonald's, Panda Chinese, Richfield Cafe, Subway, Teresa's Pizza
141mm	**RS both lanes, full facilities, litter barrels, petwalk, vending**

CLEVELAND

OH

INTERSTATE 77 Cont'd

Exit#	Services
138	Ghent Rd, W [gas] Circle K/dsl [food] Gasoline Ally, Lanning's Rest.
137b a	OH 18, to Fairlawn, Medina, E [gas] BP, GetGo, Shell, Speedway [food] Applebee's, A-Wok, Bob Evans, Boston Mkt, Chick-fil-A, Chili's, Chipotle Mexican, Coldstone, Cracker Barrel, Cucina Italiana, Donato's Pizza, Five Guys, Fleming's Steaks, Gionino's Pizza, HoneyBaked Ham, Hudson's Rest., Hyde Park Grille, Jimmy John's, Macaroni Grill, Max&Erma's, McDonald's, Menchie's, Olive Garden, Pad Thai, Panera Bread, Penn Sta Subs, PF Chang's, Rail Burger Bar, Red Lobster, Robeck's FruitJuice, Starbucks, Steak'n Shake, Subway, Taco Bell, Wendy's, Winking Lizard Grill, Yellow Tail Buffet, Zoup! [lodging] Courtyard, DoubleTree, EconoLodge, Hampton Inn, Hilton, Holiday Inn, Home 2 Suites, Homewood Suites, Motel 6, Quality Inn [other] $Tree, Acme Fresh Mkt, Aldi Foods, AT&T, Barnes&Noble, Best Buy, Dick's, Dillard's, Earth Fare Foods, Ford, Giant Eagle Foods, Goodyear/auto, Hobby Lobby, Home Depot, JC Penney, Jo-Ann Fabrics, Lowe's, Macy's, Michael's, NTB, Old Navy, Petsmart, Sam's Club, Staples, TJ Maxx, Verizon, Walmart, World Mkt, W [gas] Sunoco [food] Burger King, Hooley House Rest., Longhorn Steaks, Outback Steaks, TGIFriday's, Tres Potrillos, Wasabi Grill [lodging] Baymont Inn, Best Western, Extended Stay America, Extended Stay America 2, Hawthorn Suites, Radisson, Residence Inn, Super 8 [other] [H]
136	(exits left from nb) OH 21S, to Massillon
135	Cleveland-Massillon Rd (from nb, no return)
133	Ridgewood Rd, Miller Rd, E [gas] Circle K/dsl, W [food] Old Carolina BBQ, Teresa's Pizza, Tiffany's Bakery [other] Conrad's Automotive
132	White Pond Dr, Mull Ave
131	OH 162, Copley Rd, E [gas] Circle K [food] China Star, Church's, Little Caesar's [other] Save-A-Lot Foods, Walgreens, W [gas] BP/dsl [food] McDonald's, Pizza Hut
130	OH 261, Wooster Ave, E [gas] Circle K, Valero/dsl [food] Ann's Place, Burger King, Church's, McDonald's, New Ming Chinese, Rally's, Subway [other] Advance Parts, AutoZone, Family$, O'Reilly Parts, W [other] Chevrolet, Toyota, U-Haul
129	I-76 W, to I-277, to Kenmore Blvd, Barberton
I-77 S and I-76 E run together. See I-76, exits 21a-22b.	
125b	I-76 E, to Youngstown
125a	OH 8 N, to Cuyahoga Falls, [other] U of Akron
124b	Lover's Lane, Cole Ave
124a	Archwood Ave, Firestone Blvd (from sb), E [gas] BP
123b	OH 764, Wilbeth Rd, E [food] DQ [other] to [airport]
123a	Waterloo Rd (from sb), W [gas] BP, GetGo [food] Burger King, House of Hunan, Hungry Howies, Mi Casa, Papa John's, Paramount Grille, Rally's, Subway, Waterloo Rest. [other] $General, $Tree, American Automotive, Big Lots, Giant Eagle Foods, GNC, Marc's Mkt, Rite Aid, Walgreens
122b a	I-277, US 224 E, to Barberton, Mogadore
120	Arlington Rd, to Green, E [gas] Speedway/dsl [food] Applebee's, Denny's, Golden Corral, IHOP, Jimmy John's, Mr Hero, Shogun, Starbucks, Waffle House [lodging] Comfort Inn, Quality Inn, Red Roof Inn [other] $General, AT&T, AutoZone, Home Depot, Kohl's, Staples, Walmart/Subway, W [gas] [food] Bob Evans, Burger King, Chipotle Mexican, CiCi's Pizza, McDonald's, Panera Bread, Subway, Taco Bell, TGIFriday's, Tommy Li's, Wendy's [lodging] Fairfield Inn, Hampton Inn, Holiday Inn Express, Residence Inn, Woodspring Suites [other] Aamco, Acura, Buick/GMC, Camping World RV Ctr, Chevrolet, GNC, Goodyear/auto, Honda, Hyundai, Infiniti, Lexus, Lowe's, Nissan, Subaru, Target, Verizon
118	OH 241, to OH 619, Massillon, E [gas] Sheetz/dsl, Speedway/dsl [food] Gionino's Pizza, Handel's Ice Cream, Hunan Chinese, Subway, W [gas] Circle K/dsl, GetGo [food] Arby's, DQ, Dunkin Donuts, Hungry Howie's, Jimmy John's, Kasai Japanese, Lucky Star Chinese, McDonald's, Menche's Rest., Quizno's, Starbucks, Subway, Tom Chee Cafe [lodging] Cambria Suites, Super 8 [other] [H], $General, Acme Fresh Mkt, Advance Parts, Conrad Automotive, CVS Dug, Giant Eagle Foods
113	W [lodging] Hilton Garden [other] Akron-Canton Airport, General RV Ctr (2mi)
112	Shuffel St, E [lodging] Embassy Suites
111	Portage St, N Canton, E [gas] Circle K, Marathon/dsl, Sunoco/dsl, TA/Country Pride/dsl/scales/24hr/@ [food] Burger King, Geisen Haus, Jimmy's Rest., KFC, Palombo's Italian, Quaker Steak, Subway, Sylvester's Italian [other] Mr Tire, TrueValue, W [gas] BP/dsl, Speedway/dsl [food] Aladdin's Eatery, Bonefish Grill, Carrabba's, ChuckeCheese, Coldstone, Cracker Barrel, Dunkin Donuts/Baskin-Robbins, Five Guys, IHOP, Longhorn Steaks, McDonald's, Menchie's, Outback Steaks, Panera Bread, Pizza Hut, Red Robin, Rockne's Cafe, Romeo's Pizza, Samantha's Rest., Starbucks, Taco Bell, Wasabi Japanese, Wendy's, Zoup! [lodging] Best Western, Microtel, Motel 6 [other] AAA, At&T, Best Buy, BJ's Whse, Book A Million, Chevrolet, DrugMart, Giant Eagle Foods, Goodyear/auto, Harley-Davidson, Home Depot, Lowe's, Marshall's, Michael's, Old Navy, Sam's Club/gas, Walgreens, Walmart/Subway/auto
109b a	Everhard Rd, Whipple Ave, E [gas] Marathon/Subway/dsl, Speedway/dsl [food] Denny's, Fazoli's, Waffle House [lodging] Comfort Inn, Fairfield Inn, Hampton Inn, Home 2 Suites, Hyatt Place, La Quinta, Residence Inn, Staybridge Suites [other] Buick/GMC, Ford, W [gas] Marathon [food] A1 Japanese Steaks, Angry BBQ, Applebee's, Arby's, Bob Evans, Bravo Italiana, Brown Derby, Buffalo Wild Wings, Buffet Dynasty, Chick-fil-A, Chili's, Chipotle Mexican, CiCi's Pizza, DiBella Subs, Dunkin Donuts, Fox&Hound Grill, Golden Corral, HoneyBaked Ham, Jerzees Grille, Jimmy John's, Katanya Buffet, KFC, Max&Erma's, McDonald's, Mulligan's, Olive Garden, Panera Bread, Papa Bear's, Papa Gyros, Penn Sta Subs, Perkins, Potbelly, Red Lobster, Ruby Tuesday, Sahara Grill, Sakura Japanese, Starbucks, Steak'n Shake, Subway, Taco Bell, TGIFriday's, Tilted Kilt, TX Roadhouse, Wendy's [lodging] Courtyard, Holiday Inn, Knights Inn, Quality Inn, Ramada, Red Roof Inn, Springhill Suites [other] $Tree, Aamco, Aldi Foods, AT&T, Burlington Cots, Dick's, Dillard's, Firestone/auto, Goodyear/auto, Jo-Ann Fabrics, Kohl's, Macy's, Marc's Foods, NTB, Petsmart, Target, TJ Maxx, Tuesday Morning, Verizon, World Mkt
107b a	US 62, OH 687, Fulton Rd, to Alliance, E [gas] Marathon/Circle K, Subway [other] city park, W [gas] Circle K/Dunkin Donuts [other] Pro Football Hall of Fame, URGENT CARE
106	13th St NW, E [other] [H]
105b	OH 172, Tuscarawas St, E [food] McDonald's, W [gas] [food] KFC, Subway [other] AutoZone, CVS
105a	6th St SW (no EZ return from sb), E [gas] Sunoco [food] McDonald's [other] Ford, W [food] Subway [other] [H], AutoZone
104b a	US 30, US 62, to E Liverpool, Massillon
103	OH 800 S, E [gas] Marathon/Subway/dsl, Speedway [food] Arby's, DQ, Italo's Pizza, McDonald's, Peking Chinese, Taco Bell, Waffle House [other] Advance Parts, auto repair, Family$, Goodyear/auto, Rite aid, Save-A-Lot Foods, W [other] Firestone
101	OH 627, to Faircrest St, E [gas] Pilot/Subway/dsl/scales/24hr, Speedway/McDonald's [food] Wendy's [lodging] Fairfield Inn
99	Fohl Rd, to Navarre, W [gas] Sunoco [other] KOA (4mi)
93	OH 212, to Zoar, Bolivar, E [gas] Speedway/dsl [food] Georgio's Grill, McDonald's, Pizza Hut, Wendy's [lodging] Sleep Inn [other] $General

FAIRLAWN

AKRON

CANTON

OH

INTERSTATE 77 Cont'd

93	Continued Giant Eagle Foods, NAPA, to Lake Atwood Region, vet, Zoar Tavern HS (3mi), **W** Marathon/DQ/Subway/dsl KOA
87	US 250W, to Strasburg, **W** Marathon/dsl Hardee's, Manor Rest., McDonald's, Subway Ramada Ltd Family$, Verizon
85	Schneiders Crossing Rd, to Dover, **E** Marathon Arby's, Subway Buehler's Mkt/gas
83	OH 39, OH 211, to Sugarcreek, Dover, **E** BP/dsl, Speedway/dsl Bob Evans, KFC, McDonald's, Shoney's, Wendy's 77 Inn/Grill H, Chrysler/Dodge/Jeep, Flynn's Tires, Ford, Honda, Lincoln, Nissan, **W** Comfort Inn, Country Inn&Suites
81	US 250, to Uhrichsville, OH 39, New Philadelphia, **E** Sheetz/dsl, Speedway Buffalo Wild Wings, Burger King, Denny's, El San Jose Mexican, Hog Heaven BBQ, LJ Silver, McDonald's, Pizza Hut, Taco Bell, TX Roadhouse Best Western, Hampton Inn, Holiday Inn Express, Knights Inn, New Philadelphia Inn, Schoenbrunn Inn $General, $Tree, Advance Parts, Aldi Foods, BigLots, O'Reilly Parts, Walmart/Subway, **W** Auto TP/rest./dsl/scales/24hr Harley-Davidson
73	OH 751, to rd 53, Stone Creek, **W** Marathon/dsl
65	US 36, Port Washington, Newcomerstown, **W** BP, Duke TP/rest./dsl, Speedway/Wendy's McDonald's Hampton Inn, Super 8
64mm	Tuscarawas River
54	OH 541, rd 831, to Plainfield, Kimbolton, **W** Jackie's Rest.
47	US 22, to Cadiz, Cambridge, **E** lodging RV camping, to Salt Fork SP (6mi), **W** BP/repair H, info, to Glass Museum
46b a	US 40, to Old Washington, Cambridge, **W** Marathon/Wendy's/dsl, Speedway/dsl Burger King, Hunan Chinese, Lee's Rest., LJ Silver, McDonald's Family$, Riesbeck's Food
44b a	I-70, E to Wheeling, W to Columbus
41	OH 209, OH 821, Byesville, **W** Circle K, Starfire McDonald's, Subway $General, Family$, museum, to Glenn HS
39mm	**nb, full facilities, litter barrels, petwalk, , , vending**
37	OH 313, Buffalo, **E** Coutos Pizza, Subway to Senecaville Lake, UPSO
36mm	**sb, full facilities, litter barrels, petwalk, , , vending**
28	OH 821, Belle Valley, **E** Sunoco/dsl RV camping, to Wolf Run SP, USPO
25	OH 78, Caldwel, **E** Marathon/dsl, Pilot/Arby's/dsl/scales/24hr, Sunoco/Subway/dsl DQ, Lori's Rest., McDonald's Best Western, Days Inn, Microtel, **W** Comfort Inn
16	OH 821, Macksburg
6	OH 821, to Devola, **E** Exxon/Subway/dsl, **W** Marathon/dsl/LP H, RV camping
3mm	**nb, full facilities, info, litter barrels, petwalk, , , vending**
1	OH 7, to OH 26, Marietta, **E** GoMart/dsl/24hr DQ, Subway Best Western, Comfort Suites, Fairfield Inn, Quality Inn, Red Roof Inn $Tree, Aldi Foods, Buick/GMC, Cadillac/Chevrolet, Chrysler/Dodge/Jeep, Ford/Lincoln, GNC, Lowe's, Toyota, Walmart/McDonald's, **W** BP/dsl, GetGo/dsl, Marathon/dsl, Speedway/dsl Applebee's, Arby's, Bar-B-Cutie, Bob Evans, Burger King, Capt D's, China Fun, E Chicago Pizza, Empire Buffet, KFC, Las Trancas Mexican, Little Caesar's, LJ Silver, McDonald's, Napoli's Pizza, Papa John's, Pizza Hut, Qdoba, Shogun Hibachi, Shoney's, Subway, Taco Bell, Wendy's Hampton Inn, Microtel, Super 8 Advance Parts, AT&T, AutoZone, BigLots, Family$, Food4Less, JoAnn Fabrics, Kroger, Rite Aid, st patrol, TrueValue, Verizon, Walgreens
0mm	Ohio/West Virginia state line, Ohio River

CAMBRIDGE

MARIETTA

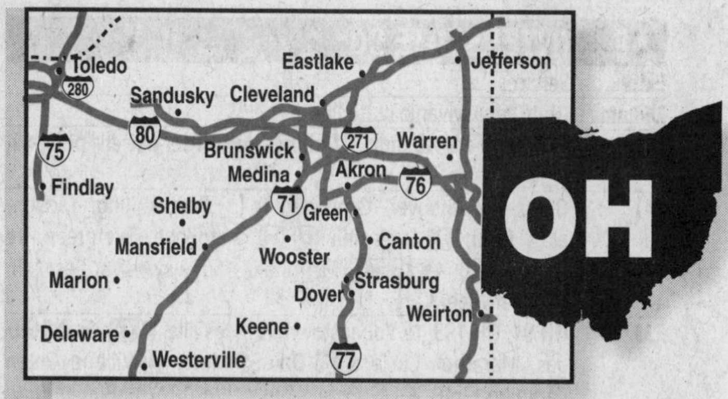

YOUNGSTOWN

INTERSTATE 80

Exit#	Services
237mm	Ohio/Pennsylvania state line
237mm	**Welcome Ctr wb, full facilities, info, litter barrels, petwalk, , , vending**
234b a	US 62, OH 7, Hubbard, to Sharon, PA, Hubbard, **N** FLYING J/Denny's/dsl/LP/scales/24hr, Shell/rest./dsl/scales/motel/24hr/@ Arby's, Burger King, Dunkin Donuts, McDonald's, Waffle House Best Western, Travelodge Blue Beacon, Homestead RV Ctr., tire/dsl repair, **S** Love's/Chester's/Subway/dsl/scales/24hr Chevrolet
232mm	**weigh sta wb**
229	OH 193, Belmont Ave, to Youngstown, **N** GetGo, Speedway/dsl Chad Anthony's Italian, Fortune Garden, Handel's Ice Cream, Sta Square Italian, Subway Hampton Inn, Motel 6, Super 8 Giant Eagle Foods, **S** BP/dsl, Shell Arby's, Bob Evans, Charley's Subs, Denny's, Fiesta Tapatia, Golden Hunan Chinese, Happy Buffet, Ianazones Pizza, Jimmy's Italian, KFC, Little Caesars, LJ Silver, McDonald's, Monteen's Southern Cuisine, Pizza Hut, Señor Jalapeño Mexican, Subway, Taco Bell, Uptown Pizza, Wendy's, Westfork Steaks, Youngstown Crab Co Days Inn, Quality Inn $General, Advance Parts, Aldi Foods, AutoZone, Family$, Firestone/auto, Goodyear/auto, O'Reilly Parts, Rite Aid, SaveALot Foods, vet, Walgreens, Walmart/Subway
228	OH 11, to Warren (exits left from eb), Ashtabula
227	US 422, Girard, Youngstown, **N** Shell/dsl Burger King, DQ, Firegrill BBQ, JibJab Hotdogs, Subway
226	Salt Springs Rd, to I-680 (from wb), **N** BP/Dunkin Donuts/dsl, Sheetz/dsl McDonald's, Waffle House vet, **S** Mr Fuel/Road Rocket Diner/dsl/24hr, Petro/Shell/Iron Skillet/dsl/scales/24hr/@, Pilot/Subway/dsl/scales/24hr Blue Beacon, dsl repair, Frank's Truckwash, SpeedCo
224b	I-680 (from eb), to Youngstown
224a	OH 11 S, to Canfield
223	OH 46, to Niles, **N** Country Fair/dsl, Pilot/McDonald's/dsl/scales/24hr Bob Evans, Dunkin Donuts, IceHouse Rest., Salsita's Mexican Candlewood Suites, Comfort Inn, Holiday Inn Express, Hotel California, **S** BP/dsl, FuelMart/dsl/scales, Sunoco/Subway, TA/Counry Pride/dsl/scales/24hr/@ Arby's, Cracker Barrel, LJ Silver/Taco Bell, Los Gallos Mexican, Perkins, Quaker Steak&Lube, Starbucks, Wendy's Best Western, Country Inn&Suites, EconoLodge, Fairfield Inn, Hampton Inn, Sleep Inn, Super 8 Freightliner/24hr, Harley-Davidson
221mm	Meander Reservoir
219mm	**I-80 wb joins Ohio Tpk (toll)**

For I-80 exits 2-218, see Ohio Turnpike.

INTERSTATE 90

Exit#	Services
244mm	Ohio/Pennsylvania state line
242mm	/weigh sta wb, full facilities, info, litter barrels, petwalk
241	OH 7, to Andover, Conneaut, N Burger King, McDonald's (2mi) Days Inn AutoZone, Evergreen RV Park, S Love's/McDonald's/Subway/dsl/scales/24hr Beef&Beer Café
235	OH 84, OH 193, to Youngstown, N Kingsville, N Grab&Go/gas, Marathon/Circle K Dav-Ed Motel Village Green Camping (2mi), S Circle K/Subway/dsl, TA/BP/Burger King/dsl/scales/24hr/@ Kay's Place Diner Kingsville Motel towing/repair
228	OH 11, to Ashtabula, Youngstown, N (4mi)
223	OH 45, to Ashtabula, N FLYING J/Denny's/Shell/dsl/LP/scales/24hr Mr C's Rest. Best Value Inn, Holiday Inn Express, Ramada, Sleep Inn Buccaneer Camping, S Pilot/Subway/dsl/scales/24hr, SpeedCo Burger King, Clay St Grill, McDonald's, Waffle House Hampton Inn auto repair
218	OH 534, Geneva, N GetGo Best Friend's Grill, Chop's Grille, McDonald's, Pizza Hut, Wendy's Motel 6 Goodyear/repair, to Geneva SP, Willow Lake Camping (4mi), S KwikFill/Subway/dsl/scales/24hr Kenisse's Camping
212	OH 528, to Thompson, Madison, N McDonald's, Pizza Roto Mentor RV Ctr, S Marathon/dsl Heritage Hills Camping (4mi), radiator repair
205	Vrooman Rd, 0-2 mi S BP/dsl, Marathon/dsl Capps Eatery, Subway Indian Point Park, Masons Landing Park
200	OH 44, to Painesville, Chardon, S BP/dsl, Sunoco/dsl McDonald's, Palmer's Bistro, Paninis Grill, Red Hawk Grille, Sunny St Cafe, Teresa's Pizzaria, Waffle House Comfort Inn, Quail Hollow Resort hwy patrol, Reider's Foods, URGENT CARE
198mm	both lanes, full facilities, litter barrels, petwalk, vending
195	OH 615, Center St, Kirtland Hills, Mentor, 1-2 mi N Best Western
193	OH 306, to Mentor, Kirtland, 0-2 mi N BP/7-11/dsl, Shell McDonald's Best Value Inn S Speedway/dsl Burger King Days Inn, Red Roof Inn Kirtland Temple LDS Historic Site
190	Express Lane to I-271 (from wb)
189	OH 91, to Willoughby, Willoughby Hills, N BP/7-11/dsl, Shell/dsl Applebee's, Big Cheese Pizza, Bob Evans, Café Europa, Cracker Barrel, Eat'n Park, Peking Chef, Subway, TX Roadhouse, Wendy's Courtyard, Motel 6, Travelodge CVS Drug, Walgreens, S BMW/Mini, Lexus
188	I-271 S, to Akron
187	OH 84, Bishop Rd, to Wickliffe, Willoughby, S BP/7-11/dsl, Shell Golden Mtn Chinese, McDonald's, Subway, Tony's Pizza Ramada Inn $Tree, Chevrolet, CVS Drug, Giant Eagle Foods, Marc's Foods, Mazda/VW, NTB, O'Reilly Parts
186	US 20, Euclid Ave, N Sunoco McDonald's Quality Inn Ford, radiators/transmissions, Subaru, S Shell Arby's, KFC, Popeye's, R-Ribs, Sidewalk Cafe, Taco Bell $General, Advance Parts, Family$, Firestone/auto, Save-a-Lot Foods
185	OH 2 E (exits left from eb), to Painesville
184b	OH 175, E 260th St, N Shell USPO, S auto/tire repair
184a	Babbitt Rd, N Buick/GMC
183	E 222nd St, N repair, Sunoco/dsl, S BP, Sunoco/dsl vet
182b a	185 St, 200 St, N BP/7-11/dsl Subway Home Depot, Honda, Hyundai, S Marathon/dsl, Shell/dsl, Speedway/dsl
181b a	E 156th St, S BP
180b a	E 140th St, E 152nd St
179	OH 283 E, to Lake Shore Blvd
178	Eddy Rd, to Bratenahl
177	University Circle, MLK Dr, N Cleveland Lake SP, S Rockefeller Park
176	E 72nd St
175	E 55th St, Marginal Rds
174b	OH 2 W, to Lakewood, downtown, N Browns Stadium, Rock&Roll Hall of Fame
174a	Lakeside Ave
173c	Superior Ave, St Clair Ave, N BP, downtown
173b	Chester Ave, S BP
173a	Prospect Ave (from wb), downtown
172d	Carnegie Ave, S Shell/dsl Burger King, KFC, McDonald's Cadillac, downtown
172c b	E 9th St, S to Cleveland St U
172a	I-77 S, to Akron
171b a	US 422, OH 14, Broadway St, Ontario St, N Hilton Garden
171	Abbey Ave, downtown
170c b	I-71 S, to I-490
170a	US 42, W 25th St, S Royal
169	W 44th St, W 41st St, N
167b a	OH 10, West Blvd, 98th St, to Lorain Ave, N S BP/dsl CVS Drug
166	W 117th St, N BP/dsl, GetGo/dsl, Shell Penn Sta Subs Advance Parts, AutoZone, Giant Eagle Foods, Home Depot, Staples, Target, S Gas USA Monro
165	W 140th St, Bunts Rd, Warren Rd, S
164	McKinley Ave, to Lakewood
162	Hilliard Blvd (from wb), to Westway Blvd, Rocky River, S BP, Shell Joe's Rest. USPO, vet
161	OH 2, OH 254 (from eb, no EZ return), Detroit Rd, Rocky River
160	Clague Rd (from wb), S same as 159
159	OH 252, Columbia Rd, N Carrabba's, Damon's Grill, Dave&Busters, Hooley House Grille, Outback Steaks Courtyard Super 8, TownePlace Suites BMW, S BP/7-11 Houlihan's, Jets Pizza, KFC, McDonald's, Taco Bell, Urban Grill Chevrolet, NTB
156	Crocker Rd, Bassett Rd, Westlake, Bay Village, N BP, Shell DoublrTree, Extended Stay America, Holiday Inn Express, Red Roof Inn, Residence Inn, S BP/7-11, Speedway Aladdin's Eatery, Bar Louie, Bob Evans, Brio, Cheesecake Factory, Chipotle Mexican, Don Ramon Mexican, Five Guys, Jersey Mike's, Jimmy John's, Max&Erma's, McDonald's Pizza by Robert, Starbucks, Subway, TGIFriday's, Vieng's Asian Wendy's, Yardhouse a Grille, Zoup! Hampton Inn Aldi Foods, CVS Drug, Dick's, Giant Eagle, GNC, Marc's Foods Trader Joes, Verizon
155	Nagel Rd, Avon Lake, N GetGo/dsl Residence Inn S Drugmart
153	OH 83, Avon Lake, N GetGo/dsl, Marathon/Circle K/Dunkin Donuts/dsl Arby's, Buffalo Wild Wings (2mi), Fujiyama, Istanbul Grill, King Yuan, Perkins, Rush Inn Grille, Wendy's Advance Parts, Ali Foods, AutoZone, Best Buy, Cabela's, Discount Tire, Firestone/auto, JC Penney, Lowe's, PetCo, Walmart S Antonio's Pizza, Applebee's, Bob Evans, Burger King Chipotle, CiCi's Pizza, Coldstone, Five Guys, IHOP, Jimmy John's

INTERSTATE 90 Cont'd

153 Continued
Mandarin House, Moe's SW Grill, Panera Bread, Red Robin, Starbucks, Subway, Winking Lizard Tavern, Zeppe's Pizza, Zoup! AT&T, Costco/gas, CVS Drug, GNC, Heinen's Mkt, Home Depot, Kohl's, Marc's Foods, Marshall's, Michael's, Old Navy, Target, USPO, Verizon, World Mkt

151 OH 611, Avon, **N** BP/7-11/dsl, Pilot/Subway/dsl/24hr McDonald's Fairfield Inn, Woodspring Suites Buick/GMC, Chevrolet, Goodyear/repair, Harley-Davidson, vet, **S** BJ's Whse/gas Mulligan's Grille

148 OH 254, Sheffield, Avon, **N** Quaker Steak&Lube Homewood Suites Ford, Kia, Mazda, Nissan, **S** BP, GetGo, Sheetz/dsl, Speedway/dsl Arby's, Burger King, China Star, Cracker Barrel, KFC, Marco's Pizza, McDonald's, Panera Bread, Pizza Hut, Ruby Tuesday, Sorrento Pizzaria, Steak'n Shake, Subway, Sugarcreek Rest., Taco Bell, Wendy's $General, $Tree, Aldi Foods, Drug Mart, Giant Eagle Mkt, Sam's Club/gas, Verizon

AVON

147mm Black River

145 OH 57, to Lorain, I-80/Ohio Tpk E, Elyria, **N** Burger King, George's Rest. Country Inn&Suites $General, Save-a-Lot, U-Haul, vet, **S** Speedway/dsl Applebee's, Bob Evans, Buffalo Wild Wings, Burger King, Chipotle Mexican, Denny's, Golden Corral, Harry Buffalo, Honeybaked Ham, IHOP, McDonald's, Midway Diner, Olive Garden, Red Lobster, Subway, TX Roadhouse, Wasabi Grill, Wendy's Best Western, Hampton Inn, Quality Inn, Ramada Inn, Red Roof Inn $General, $Tree, AT&T, Best Buy, Conrad's Automotive, Dick's, Firestone/auto, Giant Eagle Mkt, Home Depot, Honda, Hyundai, JC Penney, Jo-Ann Fabrics, Lowe's, Marc's Foods, Petsmart, Staples, Target, Tuffy Repair, Verizon

144 OH 2 W (from wb, no return), to Sandusky

I-90 wb joins Ohio Tpk. WB exits to Ohio/Indiana state line are on Ohio Turnpike, exits 142-0.

INTERSTATE 270 (Columbus)

Exit# Services

55 I-71, to Columbus, Cincinnati

52b a US 23, High St, Circleville, **N** Marathon/Circle K, Speedway/dsl, Turkey Hill/dsl Arby's, Bob Evans, Burger King, China City, KFC, Little Caesar's, LJ Silver, Los Mariachis, McDonald's, Pizza Hut, Ponderosa, Skyline Chili, Subway, Taco Bell, Tim Horton's, Waffle House, Wendy's, White Castle Kozy Inn $General, $Tree, Advance Parts, Aldi Foods, AutoZone, CVS Drug, Family$, Firestone/auto, Kroger/gas, Lowe's, NAPA, O'Reilly Parts, Walgreens, Walmart, **S** BP/dsl Kioto Downs

49 Alum Creek Dr, **N** BP/dsl, Shell/dsl, Thornton's/dsl Donato's Pizza, KFC/LJ Silver, Subway $General, Family$, **S** BP/dsl Arby's, McDonald's, Taco Bell, Wendy's Comfort Inn, Quality Inn

46b a US 33, Bexley, Lancaster

43b a I-70, E to Cambridge, W to Columbus

41b a US 40, **E** Shell, Speedway Bob Evans, City BBQ, Honeybaked Ham, McDonald's, Outback Steaks, Rally's, Steak'n Shake, Taco Bell, Texas Roadhouse auto repair, AutoZone, Family$, NAPA, TJ Maxx, Verizon, Walgreens, **W** Shell/dsl, Speedway, UDF Golden Corral, Hunan Chinese, McDonald's, Mi Mexico, Poblanos Mexican, Subway $General, Family$

39 OH 16, Broad St, **E** GetGo, Speedway/dsl Arby's, Cane's, Chick-fil-A, Chipotle, Donato's Pizza, Dunkin Dontd, Five Guys, Hot Head Burrito, Jets Pizza, Jimmy John's, McDonald's, Noodles&Co, Panera Bread, Penn Sta Subs, Potbelly's, Sonic,

39 Continued
Starbucks, Subway, Sunny St Cafe, Taco Bell, Tim Horton's, Waffle House, Wendy's, White Castle Comfort Suites Giant Eagle Mkt, Goodyear/auto, Grismer Auto Service, Kroger, Menard's, URGENT CARE, Verizon, Walgreens, **W** Shell, Speedway/dsl Chevrolet

37 OH 317, Hamilton Rd, **E** BP/dsl, Speedway/dsl Arby's, Big Boy, Bob Evans, Burger King, Chinese Express, Chipotle, Dunkin Donuts, Firehouse Subs, Jersey Mike's, McDonald's, Panera Bread, Penn Sta Subs, Rusty Bucket, Starbucks, Taco Bell, Tim Horton's Holiday Inn Express Firestone/auto, GNC, Kroger/dsl, **W** Fairfield Inn, Hampton Inn, Hilton Garden Buick/GMC, Subaru/Jaguar/Porsche, Volvo, VW/Audi

35b a I-670W, US 62, **E** Speedway/dsl City BBQ, Little Caesar's, McDonald's, Tim Horton's Advance Parts, AutoZone, CVS Drug, Family$, **W** I-670

33 Easton Way

32 Morse Rd, **E** Marathon/DM, Speedway/dsl, UDF CVS Drug, Mazda, Nissan, Toyota, **W** BP, Shell/Subway, UDF/dsl Abuelo's, Applebee's, BJ's Rest., Champp's Grill, Donato's Pizza, HomeTown Buffet, J Akexander's, Kobe Japanese, Logan's Roadhouse, McDonald's, On-the-Border, Papa John's, Pei Wei, Red Robin, Sakura Steaks, Smokey Bones, Steak'n Shake, Taco Bell, Wendy's Courtyard, Extended Stay America, Hampton Inn, Holiday Inn Express, Residence Inn, ValuePlace AT&T, Best Buy, Cadillac, Carmax, Costco/gas, Dick's, Discount Tire, Field&Stream, Infiniti, Jo-Ann Fabrics, Lexus, Lowe's Whse, Macy's, Mercedes, Michael's, Nordstrom's, NTB, Old Navy, Petsmart, REI, Sam's Club, Staples, Target, TJ Maxx, Trader Joe's, Verizon, Walmart/McDonald's, Whole Foods Mkt, World Mkt

30 OH 161 E to New Albany, W to Worthington

29 OH 3, Westerville, **N** BP/dsl, Shell Arby's, Bob Evans, Chipotle Mexican, City BBQ, Fazoli's, McDonald's, Pizza Hut, Tim Horton's, Wendy's Red Roof Inn Advance Parts, AT&T, Big Lots, CarQuest, Firestone/auto, Kohl's, Kroger, Marc's Mkt, vet, Walmart, **S** Clark/dsl, Speedway/dsl Carsoni's Italian, China House, Domino's, Subway Aldi Foods, Family$, Grismer Tire/auto, Midas, Monro, USPO

OH

27 OH 710, Cleveland Ave, **N** Speedway/dsl Subway, Wendy's Ramada Inn $General, CVS Drug, NAPA Autocare, Tuffy, **S** Turkey Hill/dsl El Rancho Allegre, McDonald's, O'Charley's Embassy Suites Home Depot

26 I-71, S to Columbus, N to Cleveland

23 US 23, Worthington, **N** Bob Evans, Chipotle Mexican, Columbus Fish Mkt, Cucina Italiana, El Acapulco, Hyde Park Steaks, J Alexander's, J Gilbert's Steaks, Lotus Grill, Ruth's Chris Steaks, Starbucks, Subway, Sushiko Japanese, Winking Lizard Courtyard, DoubleTree, Extended Stay America, Homewood Suites, Hyatt Place, Motel 6, Quality Inn, Red Roof Inn, Residence Inn,

INTERSTATE 270 (Columbus) Cont'd

COLUMBUS

23 Continued
Sheraton, TownePlace Suites, ValuePlace, S [food] Aladdin's Eatery, Buca Italian, Cosi Grill, Jimmy John's, McDonald's, Panera Bread, Piada Italian, Starbucks [lodging] Econolodge, Holiday Inn [other] Kroger

22 OH 315, N [gas] BP/dsl, Marathon/dsl [food] Subway

20 Sawmill Rd, N [gas] BP, Marathon/dsl [food] Burger King, IHOP, Logan's Roadhouse, Max&Erma's, McDonald's, Olive Garden, Papa John's, Subway, Taco Bell, Wendy's [lodging] Fairfield Inn [other] Buick/GMC, CVS Drug, Ford, Hyundai, Kroger/gas, Lincoln, Mazda, NTB, Subaru, vet, S [gas] Shell, Speedway [food] Applebee's, Arby's, bd Mogolian, Blue Ginger Asian, Bob Evans, Bonchon, Burger King, Cane's, Charlie's Subs, Chick-fil-A, Chili's, Chipotle Mexican, ChuckeCheese, El Vaquero Mexican, Firehouse Subs, Genji Japanese, Golden Corral, HoneyBaked Cafe, Jimmy John's, Joe's Crabshack, KFC, Krispy Kreme, McDonald's, Mellow Mushroom, Panera Bread, Pizza Hut, Red Lobster, Ruby Tuesday, Starbucks, Steak'n Shake, Subway, Ted's MT Grill, Vicenzos Italian [lodging] Cloverleaf Suites, Hampton Inn, Quality Inn [other] $Tree, Advance Parts, AT&T, AutoZone, Barnes&Noble, Big Lots, Cadillac/Honda, CarMax, Dick's, Discount Tire, Firestone/auto, GNC, Hobby Lobby, Home Depot, Infiniti, Jo-Ann Fabrics, Kohl's, Lexus, Lowe's Whse, Meijer, Meineke, Michael's, Mr Tire, Old Navy, PetCo, Petsmart, Sam's Club/gas, Staples, SteinMart, Target, Toyota, Trader Joe's, Verizon, vet, Whole Foods Mkt

17b a US 33, Dublin-Granville Rd, E [gas] Marathon, Sunoco [food] Bob Evans, Hyde Park Steaks, Jason's Deli, Max&Erma's, McDonald's, Pizza Hut, Subway [lodging] Courtyard, Crowne Plaza, Embassy Suites, Extended Stay America, Hilton Garden, Red Roof Inn, Residence Inn [other] CVS Drug, Fiat, Kroger, Mr Tire, USPO

15 Tuttle Crossing Blvd, E [gas] BP, UDF [food] BJ's Rest., Bob Evans, Boston Mkt, Chipotle Mexican, DiBella's Subs, House of Japan, Longhorn Steaks, Macaroni Grill, McDonald's, Noodles&Co, Panera Bread, PF Chang's, River City Grill, Taco Bell, Wendy's [lodging] Drury Inn, Homewood Suites, Hyatt Place, La Quinta, Marriott [other] JC Penney, W [gas] Shell, Turkey Hill/Subway/dsl [food] Steak'n Shake, Uno Pizzaria [lodging] Staybridge Suites [other] Best Buy, NTB, vet, Walmart/Subway, World Mkt

13 Cemetery Rd, Fishinger Rd, E [gas] Exxon/Subway, Shell, Speedway [food] Burger King, Carrabba's, Chipotle Mexican, Damon's, Dave&Buster's, Donato's Pizza, KFC, Lunada Mexican, Panera Bread, Skyline Chili, Spageddie's, Starbucks, Steak&Shake, Tim Horton's [lodging] Comfort Suites, Homewood Suites [other] $Tree, CVS Drug, Discount Tire, GNC, Home Depot, Lowe's Whse, NTB, Staples, Tire Dicounters, Tuesday Morning, W [gas] GetGo/dsl, Speedway [food] Bob Evans, Marie's Scrambler, Max&Erma's, McDonald's, Rusty Bucket Rest., Tim Horton's, Wendy's [lodging] Hampton Inn, Knights Inn [other] Giant Eagle Mkt, Nissan

10 Roberts Rd, E [gas] Marathon, Thornton's/dsl [food] Subway, Tim Horton's, Wendy's [lodging] ValuePlace, W [gas] Speedway/dsl [food] Tim Horton's, Waffle House [lodging] Courtyard, Quality Inn, Royal Inn [other] CVS Drug, Family$, O'Reilly Parts

8 I-70, E to Columbus, W to Indianapolis

7 US 40, Broad St, E [gas] BP, Speedway/dsl [food] Bob Evans, Boston Mkt, Burger King, ChuckeCheese, McDonald's, Peacock West, Popeye's, TeeJay's, White Castle [other] Advance Parts, Big Lots, Buick/GMC, Chevrolet, GNC, Target, W [gas] GetGo, Speedway/dsl, Thornton's [food] A&W/LJ Silver, Arby's, Canes, KFC, McDonald's, Papa John's, Tim Horton's, Waffle House [lodging] Red Roof Inn [other] [H], CVS Drug, Family$, Giant Eagle Foods, Goodyear/auto, Home Depot, Jo-Ann Fabrics, O'Reilly Parts, Walgreens

5 Georgesville, E [gas] Shell/dsl, Sunoco/dsl, UDF/dsl [food] Jimmy John's, Starbucks [other] Verizon, Walmart, W [food] Applebee's, Arby's, Bob Evans, Buffalo Wild Wings, Chipotle Mexican, DQ, Fiesta Mariachi, KFC/LJ Silver, McDonald's, O'Charley's, Red Lobster, Steak'n Shake, Subway, Taco Bell, Wendy's, White Castle [other] Advance Parts, AT&T, Chrysler/Dodge/Jeep, GNC, Honda, Hyundai/Subaru, Kia, Kroger/gas, Lowe's Whse, NTB, TireDiscounters, Toyota, VW

2 US 62, OH 3, Grove City, N [gas] Turkey Hill/dsl [lodging] ValuePlace, S [gas] Marathon, Shell, Speedway/dsl [food] Big Boy, Burger King, Domino's, Donato's Pizza, Little Caesar's, McDonald's, Subway, Tim Horton/Wendy's, Waffle House, Wedgewood Pizza [other] CVS Drug, Verizon

0mm I-71

INTERSTATE 271 (Cleveland)

CLEVELAND

Exit#	Services
39mm	**I-271 begins/ends on I-90, exit 188.**

36 Wilson Mills Rd, Highland Hts, Mayfield, E [gas] Shell [food] Aladdin's a Eatery, Austin's Steaks, Jersey Mike's, Yours Truly Rest. [lodging] Hilton Garden, Holiday Inn [other] Chrysler/Dodge/Jeep, CVS Drug, Heinen's Mkt, vet, W [gas] Marathon/dsl [food] Burgers 2 Beer, Denny's, Hibachi Steaks, Panera Bread, Qdoba [other] Dick's, DrugMart, Home Depot, Kohl's, Tuesday Morning, Verizon

34 US 322, Mayfield Rd, E [gas] BP/7-11, Circle K [food] Chipotle, DiBella's Subs, Five Guys, Fox&Hound Grille, Georgio's Pizza, Jimmy John's, Marie's Scrambler, Piccolo Italian, Potbelly, Starbucks, Subway, Wendy's [other] [H], CVS Drug, Marc's Foods, Michael's, Mr Tire, Old Navy, Rite Aid, Target, Tire Pros, Walmart, W [gas] Marathon, Shell, Speedway [food] Arby's, Bob Evans, Burger King, ChuckECheese, Dunkin Donuts, Firehouse Subs, Gaetano's Italian, McDonald's, Otani Japanese, Panera Bread, Panini's Grill, Penn Sta Subs, Sonic, Subway, TGI Friday's, Two Bucks Cafe [other] $Tree, AT&T, AutoZone, Best Buy, Conrad's Tire/auto, Costco/gas, CVS Drug, Ford/Lincoln, Giant Eagle Foods, GNC, JoAnn Fabrics, Marshalls, Midas, Nissan, NTB, O'Reilly Parts, Petsmart, Staples, Verizon, World Mkt

32 Brainerd Rd, E [food] Burntwood Tavern, J Alexander's [other] [H], USPO

29 US 422 W, OH 87, Chagrin Blvd, Harvard Rd, E [gas] Mooney, Shell, Speedway [food] Bahama Breeze, Bob Evans, Bravo Italian, Corky&Lenny's Rest., Firehouse Subs, Flemings, McDonald's, Mitchell's Fish Mkt, Paladar Latin Kitchen, Pancake a House, Red Lobster, Starbucks, Stone Oven, Wasabi Japanese, Wendy's [lodging] Courtyard, Extended Stay America, Extended Stay America, Fairfield Inn, Hampton Inn, Super 8 [other] AT&T, Barnes&Noble, CVS Drug, Rite Aid, TJ Maxx, Trader Joe's, Verizon, Whole Foods Mkt, W [gas] BP/Subway, Shell/dsl [food] Giovanni's Ristorante, Hyde Park Steaks, PF Chang's, Winking Lizard Tavern [lodging] Clarion, DoubleTree, Embassy Suites, Homewood Suites, Hotel Indigo, Residence Inn [other] [H], Buick/GMC, Cadillac, Infiniti, NTB, Porsche

28b Harvard Rd, E [food] Red Robin, W [food] Abuelo's, Buffalo Wild Wings, Chick-fil-A, Chipotle, DiBella's Subs, Five Guys, Olive Garden, Panera Bread, Piada Italian, River City Grille, Robeks Cafe, Zoup! [lodging] Aloft, Marriott [other] [H], Verizon

28a OH 175, Richmond Rd, Emery Rd, E [gas] BP, GetGo/dsl, Marathon/Circle K/Subway/dsl [food] Baskin-Robbins/Dunkin Donuts, Don Ramon Mexican, Jimmy John's, McDonald's, Quiznos [other] vet, W [food] BJ's Whse

27b I-480 W

27a US 422 E, E [other] CarMax, Lowe's

INTERSTATE 271 (Cleveland) Cont'd

MACEDONIA

Exit#	Services
26	Rockside Rd, E [gas] Speedway/dsl, Sunoco/dsl [food] Burger King, Subway [other] Family$
23	OH 14 W, Forbes Rd, Broadway Ave, E [gas] Sunoco [food] B&M BBQ, McDonald's, Wendy's [lodging] Holiday Inn Express [other] Sam's Club/dsl, W [gas] Marathon/Circle K/dsl
21	I-480 E, OH 14 E (from sb), to Youngstown
19	OH 82, Macedonia, E [gas] Speedway/dsl/E85 [food] Papa John's, Penn Sta Subs, W [food] Antonio's Pizza, Applebee's, Arby's, Chick-fil-A, Chili's, Chipotle, Coldstone, Fuji Japanese, Golden Corral, Jersey Mike's, McDonald's, Outback Steaks, Panera Bread, Pizza Hut, Popeye's, Steak'n Shake, Taco Bell, Wendy's [other] Aldi a Foods, AT&T, Best Buy, Chevrolet, Discount Tire, Giant Eagle Foods, GNC, Hobby Lobby, Home Depot, Kohl's, Lowe's, NTB, O'Reilly Parts, PetCo, Petsmart, Target, Verizon, Verizon, Walgreens, Walmart/Subway
18b a	OH 8, Boston Hts, to Akron, (exits left from sb), E [gas] BP/7-11/dsl, GetGo, Speedway/dsl [food] Bob Evans, Pacific Chinese [lodging] Country Inn&Suites, Knights Inn, La Quinta, Motel 6, W same as 19
12	OH 303, Richfield, Peninsula
10	I-77, to I-80, OH Tpk (from nb), to Akron, Cleveland
9	I-77 S, OH 176 (from nb), to Richfield
8mm	**[RS] both lanes, full [handicapped] facilities, litter barrels, petwalk, [phone], [picnic]**
3	OH 94, to I-71 N, Wadsworth, N Royalton, W [gas] PetroUSA/dsl
0mm	**I-271 begins/ends on I-71, exit 220.**

INTERSTATE 275 (Cincinnati)

See Kentucky Interstate 275

INTERSTATE 280 (Toledo)

Exit#	Services
13	**I-280 begins/ends on I-75, exit 208.**
12	Manhattan Blvd, E [gas] Sunoco, W [gas] Sunoco/dsl
11	OH 25 S, Eerie St, W [other] Huntington Ctr
10mm	Maumee River
9	OH 65, Front St, E [gas] Sunoco [food] Subway, Tony Packo's Cafe, W [gas] Sunoco/dsl
8	Starr Ave, (from sb only)
7	OH 2, Oregon, E [gas] Sunoco [food] Arby's, Big Boy, Bob Evans, Burger King, Coldstone/Tim Horton's, Empire Chinese, McDonald's, Sonic, Taco Bell, Wendy's [lodging] Comfort Inn, Hampton Inn [other] [H], Ford, to Maumee Bay SP, Walgreens
6	OH 51, Woodville Rd, Curtice Rd, E [gas] BP/dsl, Marathon [food] Bob Evans, Burger King [other] Menards, W [gas] Speedway/dsl [food] Applebee's, Arby's, Big Boy, Gino's Pizza, KFC, LJ Silver, McDonald's, Subway, Taco Bell [lodging] Sleep Inn [other] [H], $General, $Tree, Advance Parts, Meijer/dsl, O'Reilly Parts, Tires+
4	Walbridge
2	OH 795, Perrysburg, W [gas] Sunoco/Subway/dsl
1b	Bahnsen Rd, E [gas] FLYING J/Denny's/dsl/LP/scales/24hr [lodging] Crown Inn, Regency Inn, W [gas] Love's/Arby's/dsl/scales/24hr, Petro/BP/Iron Skillet/dsl/scales/24hr/@ [lodging] Budget Inn [other] Blue Beacon, SpeedCo, Super 8
1a	**I-280 begins/ends on I 80/90, OH Tpk, exit 71.** S [gas] FuelMart/Subway/dsl/scales, Pilot/McDonald's/dsl/scales/24hr, TA/BP/Burger King/Taco Bell/dsl/scales/24hr/@ [other] KOA

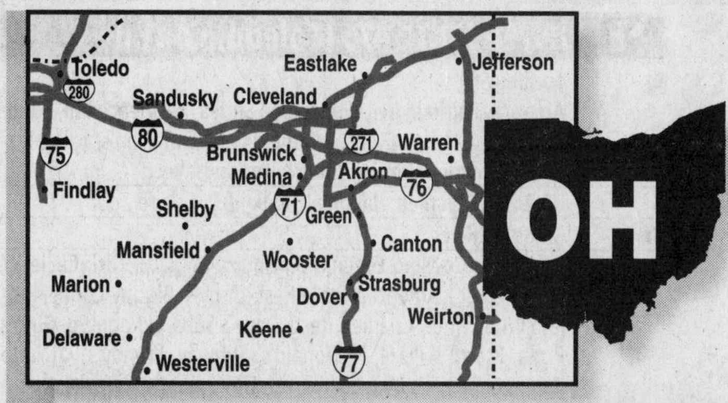

INTERSTATE 475 (Toledo)

TOLEDO

Exit#	Services
20	I-75. **I-475 begins/ends on I-75, exit 204.**
19	ProMedica Pky, Central Ave, S [food] Burger King, Gino's Pizza, Subway [other] [H]
18b	Douglas Rd (from wb)
18a	OH 51 W, Monroe St
17	Secor Rd, N [gas] Clark, Shell/dsl, Sunoco, Valero [food] Applebee's, Bambino's Pizza, Bob Evans, Boston Mkt, Burger King, Famous Dave's BBQ, Hooters, KFC, Monroe St Diner, Penn Sta Subs, Red Robin, Rudy's Hot Dogs, Tim Horton's [other] [H], $Tree, AT&T, Barnes&Noble, Best Buy, Jo-AnnFabrics, Kohl's, Kroger/dsl, O'Reilly Parts, Walgreens, S [gas] [food] Big Boy, Chipotle Mexican, Del Taco, El Vaquero, Five Guys, Jamba Juice, Marie's Scrambler, McDonald's, Original Pancakes, Piada Italian, Pizza Hut, Popeye's, Sonic, Starbucks, Subway, Taco Bell, Uncle John's Pancakes [lodging] Hampton Inn, Holiday Inn Express, Quality Inn, Ramada Inn, Red Roof Inn [other] Batteries+Bulbs, Costco/gas, Fresh Mkt, Home Depot, Rite Aid, Steinmart, U of Toledo
16	Talmadge Rd (from wb, no return), N [gas] BP/dsl, Speedway/dsl [food] Aladdin's Eatery, Bar Louie, bd Mongolian BBQ, Bravo Italiana, Chick-fil-A, Chipotle, Coldstone, IHOP, J Alexander's, Jimmy John's, Longhorn Steaks, Panera Bread, Potbelly, Starbucks [other] Dick's, JC Penney, Kohl's, Macy's, Old Navy
15	Corey Rd (from eb, no return)
14	US 23 N, to Ann Arbor
13	US 20, OH 120, Central Ave, E [gas] Speedway/dsl [food] Bob Evans, Burger King, Magic Wok, McDonald's, Rally's, Subway, Wendy's [other] BMW, Buick/GMC, Chrysler/Dodge/Jeep, Fiat, Ford, Honda, Hyundai, Kia, Nissan, Subaru, Toyota, Walmart, W [gas] BP, Shell, Speedway [food] Buffalo Wild Wings, Jimmy John's, KFC, Tim Horton's [other] Lowe's, Verizon, Walgreens
8b a	OH 2, E [gas] BP/dsl [food] Don Pablo's, Penn Sta Subs, TGIFriday's, TX Roadhouse [lodging] Extended Stay America, Hawthorn Suites, Knights Inn, Red Roof Inn [other] [H], Home Depot, Kohl's, Old Navy, to OH Med Coll, W [gas] BP, Shell/dsl, Speedway/dsl [food] Arby's, Bob Evans, Boston Mkt, Burger King, Chick-fil-A, Chili's, Chinese Cuisine, Chipotle Mexican, IHOP, KFC, Little Caesar's, Mancino's Pizza, Marco's Pizza, McDonald's, Panera Bread, Starbucks, Subway, Taco Bell, Tim Horton's, Waffle House, Wendy's [lodging] Courtyard, Quality Inn [other] $Tree, Aldi Foods, Best Buy, BigLots, Dick's, Firestone/auto, GNC, Kroger/dsl, Menard's, Petsmart, Sam's Club/gas, Target, TJ Maxx, Verizon, Walmart/Subway
6	Dussel Dr, Salisbury Rd, to I-80-90/tpk, E [gas] [food] Amaya's Mexican Grill, Applebee's, Arby's, Bankok Kitchen, Bluewater Grille, Buffalo Wild Wings, Coldstone, Cracker Barrel, Don Juan's, Gino's Pizza, Jimmy John's, Longhorn Steaks, Marie's Scrambler, Max&Erma's, McDonald's, Outback Steaks, Panera Bread, Sam's Diner, Smokey Bones BBQ, Subway, Wendy's, Yoko Japanese [lodging] Country Inn&Suites, Courtyard, Extended Stay

INTERSTATE 475 (Toledo) Cont'd

6 Continued
America, Fairfield Inn, Homewood Suites, Residence Inn, Super 8, **W** [gas] [food] Bob Evans, Briarfield Café, Carrabba's, JoJo's Pizza [lodging] Baymont Inn [other] Churchill's Foods, vet

4 US 24, to Maumee, Napolean, **N** [other] [H], Toledo Zoo

3mm Maumee River

2 OH 25, to Bowling Green, Perrysburg, **N** [gas] BP/dsl, Circle K/dsl, Shell [food] American Table Rest., Arby's, Biggby Coffee, Buffalo Wild Wings, Charlie's Rest., Dave's Subs, El Vaquero, Gino's Pizza, Marco's Pizza, McDonald's, Subway, Wendy's [other] Auto Value, Churchill's Mkt, Costco/dsl, GMC, Goodyear/auto, Hyundai, URGENT CARE, Volvo, VW, **S** [gas] Marathon, Speedway/dsl [food] Bar Louie's, Biaggi's, Blue Pacific Grill, Bob Evans, Marie's Scrambler, Max&Erma's, Nagoya Japanese, Starbucks, Tea Tree Asian, Waffle House [lodging] Economy Inn, Economy Inn, Hilton Garden [other] AT&T, Books-A-Million, GNC, Mytee Automotive, Tireman/auto, URGENT CARE, Verizon, vet

0mm **I-475 begins/ends on I-75, exit 192.**

INTERSTATE 480 (Cleveland)

Exit# Services

42 I-80, PA Tpk, **I-480 begins/ends, 0-2 mi S** [gas] BP, GetGo, Marathon/Circle K, Marathon/Circle K, Sheetz/24hr, Shell [food] Applebees, Baskin Robbins/Dunkin Dounts, Bob Evans, Brown Derby Roadhouse, Buffalo Wild Wings, Burger King, China Chef, Chipotle, Denny's, DQ, El Campesino, Fun Buffet, Happy Moose Grill, Honeybaked Ham, Jimmy John's, KFC, Little Caesar's, McDonald's, Mr Hero, New Peking Chinese, Quizno's, Rockne's Grill, Ruby Tuesday, Sonic, Starbucks, Steak'n Shake, Subway, Taco Bell [lodging] Best Value Inn, Comfort Inn, Econolodge, Fairfield Inn, Hampton Inn, Holiday Inn Express, Microtel, TownePlace Suites, Wingate Inn [other] [H], $General, $Tree, Aldi Foods, All Seasons RV Ctr, AT&T, AutoZone, Defer Tire/auto, Giant Eagle Mkt, GNC, Home Depot, Honda, Hyundai, Kia, Lowes Whse, Midas, NAPA, Nissan, NTB, Save-a-Lot Foods, Staples, Target, to Kent St U, U-Haul, USPO, Van's Tires, Verizon, vet, VW, Walgreens, Walmart

41 Frost Rd, Hudson-Aurora

37 OH 91, Solon, Twinsburg, **N** [food] Arby's, Brewster's, Chipotle, DQ, Mandarin Buffet, Panera Bread, Panini's Grill, Pizza Hut, Taco Bell [other] Comfort Suites, Giant Eagle Mkt, GNC, **S** [gas] BP/7-11

36 OH 82, Aurora, Twinsburg, **N** [gas] BP, McDonald's, Sheetz/dsl [food] Burger King [lodging] Super 8, **S** [gas] Bob Evans, Cracker Barrel, Get'n Go, Wendy's [food] Blue Canyon Rest. [lodging] Hilton Garden

26 I-271, to Erie, PA

25a b c OH 8, OH 43, Northfield Rd, Bedford, **S** [gas] Marathon, Shell, Sunoco [other] Giant Eagle Mkt

24 Lee Rd (from wb)

23 OH 14, Broadway Ave, **N** [gas] Marathon [lodging] Eldorado Motel [other] [H], **S** [other] Freightliner

22 OH 17, Garanger, Maple Hts, Garfield Hts

21 Transportation Blvd, to E 98th St, **N** [other] [H], **S** [gas] GetGo [food] Applebee's, Chipotle, Penn Sta Subs, Starbucks, Steak'n Shake [other] AT&T, Giant Eagle Foods, Verizon

20b a I-77, Cleveland

17 OH 176, OH 17, Cleveland

16 OH 94, to OH 17 S, State Rd, **N** [other] auto repair, Convenient Mart, transmissions, **S** [gas] BP/7-11, Sunoco/dsl [other] Kia

15 US 42, Ridge Rd, **N** [food] Applebee's, Baskin-Robbins/Dunkin Donuts, Boston Mkt, CiCi's Pizza, Coldstone Creamery, El Tolteca Nexican, Hong Kong Buffet, McDonald's, Mr Hero, Penn Sta Subs, Pizza Hut, Rockne's Rest., Skyline a Chili, Starbucks,

15 Continued
TX Roadhouse [other] $General, Giant Eagle Mkt, GNC, Lowe's, Marc's Foods, Michael's, TJMaxx, URGENT CARE, USPO, Verizon, **S** [gas] GetGo, Speedway/Speedy's Cafe/dsl [food] Arby's, Colonial Eatery, Denny's, DQ, Taco Bell, Wendy's [other] $Tree, Advance Parts, AT&T, Best Buy, Buick/GMC, Hyundai, Meineke, Staples, Walgreens

13 Teideman Rd, Brooklyn, **S** [gas] BP/dsl, Sheetz/dsl, Speedway/dsl [food] Buffalo Wild Wings, Burger King, Carrabba's, Chipotle Mexican, Cracker Barrel, Golden Corral, Hooley House Grill, Ice House Grill, IHOP, LJ Silver, McDonald's, Panera Bread, Perkins, Steak 'n Shake, Subway, TGIFriday's, Wild Ginger China Bistro [lodging] Extended Stay America, Hampton Inn [other] Aldi Foods, Home Depot, Jaguar, LandRover, Mazda, Sam's Club/gas, Volvo, Walmart

12b W 150th, W130th, Brookpark, **N** [gas] Marathon [other] Family$, **S** [gas] Marathon/dsl, Shell/dsl [food] Big Boy, Bob Evans, Subway [lodging] Best Value Inn [other] Acura, Chevrolet, Chrysler/Dodge/Jeep, Infiniti, Lexus, Mini, Nissan, Toyota

11 I-71, Cleveland, Columbus

10 S Rd 237, Airport Blvd (wb only)

9 OH 17, Brookpark Rd, **N** [food] Subway [lodging] Hilton Garden, ValuePlace [other] [H], **S** [food] 100th Bomb Group Rest. [lodging] Sheraton [other] [airport]

7 (wb only) Clague Rd, to WestLake

6 OH 252, Great Northern Blvd, to N Olmsted, **N** [gas] BP, Shell, Speedway/dsl [food] Applebee's, Arby's, Bamboo Garden, Bob Evans, Boston Mkt, Brown Bag Burgers, Burger King, Chick-fil-A, Chili's, ChuckeCheese, Daishin Japanese, Denny's, Famous Dave's, Five Guys, Fox's Pizza, Frankie's Italian, Great Wall Buffet, Harry Buffalo, Jersey Mike's, Jimmy John's, Little Caesar's, Lonestar Steaks, Macaroni Grill, Marie's Scrambler, Moe's SW Grill, Olive Garden, Panera Bread, Penn Sta Subs, Popeye's, Rail Burger Bar, Red Lobster, Red Robin, Ruby Tuesday, Smokey Bones BBQ, Wendy's, Wild Mango Rest. [lodging] Candlewood Suites, Courtyard, Extended Stay America, Extended Stay America, La Quinta, Radisson [other] $Tree, Aldi Foods, AT&T, Best Buy, Big Lots, Buick/GMC/Cadillac, Chipotle Mexican, Conrad's Tire/auto, Dick's, Dillard's, Firestone/auto, Home Depot, Honda, Hyundai/VW, JC Penney, Jo-Ann Etc, Macy's, Marc's Foods, Mr Tire, NAPA, NTB, Petsmart, Subaru, Target, Toyota, Walmart, World Mkt

3 Stearns Rd, **N** [other] [H], **S** [food] Razzle's Cafe [other] CVS Drug

2 OH 10, Lorain Rd, to OH Tpk, **S** [gas] BP, Sheetz/dsl, Speedway/dsl [food] Ace's Grille, Chipotle, Gourme Rest., Lone Tree Tavern, McDonald's, Panera Bread, Pizza Pan, Taco Bell [lodging] Motel 6, Super 8

1 OH 10 W, to US 20 (from wb), Oberlin

0mm OH 10, to Cleveland, **I-480 begins/ends on exit 151, OH Tpk**

INTERSTATE 680 (Youngstown)

Exit# Services

14 OH 164, to Western Reserve Rd, **I-680 begins/ends on OH Tpk, exit 234, S** [gas] Shell/Subway/dsl [food] Cafe 422, Carmella's Cafe, Dunkin Donuts, McDonald's, Pizza Hut, Wendy's [other] [H]

11b a US 224, **S** [gas] BP, GetGo, Shell/dsl [food] Applebee's, Burger King, Carabba's, Chick-fil-A, Chipotle, Dunkin Donuts, Honeybaked Ham, IHOP, KFC, LJ Silver, Longhorn Steaks, McDonald's, Nicolinni's Italian, O'Charley's, Olive Garden, Outback Steaks, Papa John's, Perkins, Red Lobster, Smokey Bones, Springfield Grill, Starbucks, Subway, Taco Bell, TGIFriday's, TX Roadhouse [lodging] Best Western, Days Inn, Fairfield Inn, Hampton Inn, Holiday Inn, Red Roof Inn, Residence Inn [other] [H],

OH

INTERSTATE 680 (Youngstown) Cont'd

11b a	Continued $Tree, Aldi Foods, AT&T, Best Buy, Big Lots, Giant Eagle, GNC, Lowe's, Marc's Foods, NTB, Petsmart, Sam's Club/gas, Staples, URGENT CARE, Walmart/Subway
9b a	OH 170, Midlothian Blvd, Struthers, **S** Shell/dsl, Speedway/dsl McDonald's, Subway $General, Rite Aid, Walgreens
8	Shirley Rd, downtown
7	US 62, OH 7, South Ave, downtown
6b a	US 62, OH 7, Mkt St, downtown
5	Glenwood Ave, Mahoning Ave, downtown
4b a	OH 193, to US 422, Salt Springs Rd, **N** H, museum
3c b	Belle Vista Ave, Connecticut Ave
3a	OH 711 E, to I-80 E
2	Meridian Rd, **S** Ford/Peterbilt Trucks
1	OH 11

OHIO TURNPIKE

Exit#	Services
241mm	Ohio/Pennsylvania state line
239mm	**toll plaza,**
237mm	**Mahoning Valley Travel Plaza eb, Glacier Hills Travel Plaza wb,** Sunoco/dsl/24hr McDonald's gifts,
234	I-680 (from wb), to Youngstown
232	OH 7, to Boardman, Youngstown, **N** Sheetz, Valero/dsl DQ, Los Gallos Mexican, Rita's Custard, Steamer's Stonewall Tavern Best Value Inn, Budget Inn, Holiday Inn Express, Super 8 $General, antiques, **S** Pilot/McDonald's/dsl/scales/24hr Davis Motel, Liberty Inn
218	I-80 E, to Youngstown. **OH Tpk runs with I-76 eb, I-80 wb. Services S on Mahoning.**
216	Lordstown (from wb), **N** GM Plant
215	Lordstown (from eb), **N** GM Plant
210mm	Mahoning River
209	OH 5, to Warren, **N** Budget Lodge, **S** Marathon/dsl EconoLodge, Holiday Inn Express
197mm	**Portage Service Plaza wb, Bradys Leap Service Plaza eb,** Sunoco/dsl/24hr McDonald's, Sbarro's, Starbucks gifts,
193	OH 44, to Ravenna
192mm	Cuyahoga River
187	OH 14 S, I-480, to Streetsboro, **0-2mi S** BP, GetGo, Marathon/Circle K, Marathon/Circle K, Sheetz, Shell Applebee's, Baskin Robbins/Dunkin Dounts, Bob Evans, Brown Derby Roadhouse, Buffalo Wild Wings, Burger King, China Chef, Chipotle, Denny's, DQ, El Campesino, Fun Buffet, Happy Moose Grill, Honeybaked Ham, Jimmy John's, KFC, Little Caesar's, McDonald's, Mr Hero, New Peking Chinese, Quiznos, Rockne's Grill, Ruby Tuesday, Sonic, Starbucks, Steak'n Shake, Subway, Taco Bell Best Value Inn, Comfort Inn, EconoLodge, Fairfield Inn, Hampton Inn, Holiday Inn Express, Microtel, TownePlace Suites, Wingate Inn H, $General, $Tree, Aldi Foods, All Seasons RV Ctr, AT&T, AutoZone, Defer Tire/auto, Giant Eagle Mkt, GNC, Home Depot, Honda, Hyundai, Kia, Lowe's, Midas, NAPA, Nissan, NTB, Save-a-Lot Foods, Staples, Target, to Kent St U, U-Haul, USPO, Van's Tires, Verizon, vet, VW, Walgreens, Walmart
180	OH 8, to I-90 E, **N** Baymont Inn, Clarion, **S** BP/dsl to Cuyahoga Valley NRA

STREETSBORO

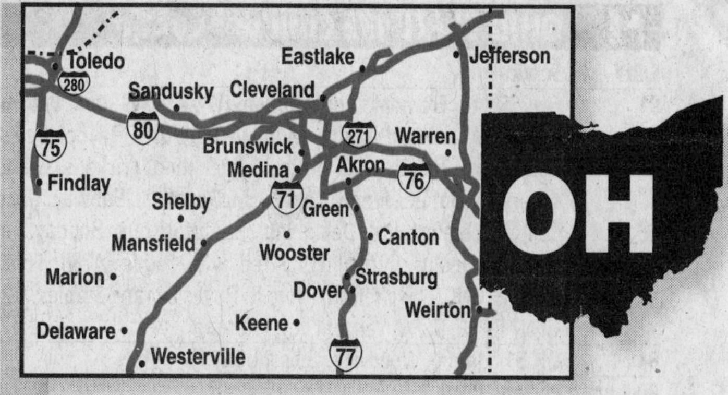

177mm	Cuyahoga River
173	OH 21, to I-77, **N** Pilot/Wendy's/dsl/scales Holiday Inn Express, Motel 6, **S** Memories Rest., Subway Days Inn, Hampton Inn, Super 8
170mm	**Towpath Service Plaza eb, Great Lakes Service Plaza wb,** Sunoco/dsl/24hr Burger King, FoodCourt, Panera Bread, Pizza Hut, Starbucks gifts,
161	US 42, to I-71, Strongsville, **N on US 42** Mobil/dsl, Sheetz/dsl Buffalo Wild Wings, Jennifer's Rest., Mad Cactus Mexican, McDonald's Kings Inn, La Siesta Motel, Metrick's Motel Home Depot, Lowe's, vet, Walmart/Subway, **S on US 42** Elmhaven Motel Burger King, DQ, Fiat, J-Bella Rest., KFC, Marco's Pizza, Mr Hero, Olympia's Cafe, Staples, Tuesday Morning, vet
152	OH 10, to Oberlin, I-480, Cleveland, **N** BP, Sheetz/dsl, Speedway/dsl Ace's Grille, Chipotle, Gourme Rest., Lone Tree Tavern, McDonald's, Panera Bread, Pizza Pan, Taco Bell Motel 6, Super 8, Burger King
151	I-480 E (from eb), to Cleveland,
146mm	Black River
145	OH 57, to Lorain, to I-90, Elyria, **N** Speedway/dsl Applebee's, Bob Evans, Buffalo Wild Wings, Burger King, Chipotle Mexican, Denny's, Giant Eagle Mkt, Golden Corral, Harry Buffalo, Honeybaked Ham, IHOP, McDonald's, Midway Diner, Olive Garden, Red Lobster, Subway, TX Roadhouse, Wasabi Grill, Wendy's Best Western, Country Inn&Suites, Hampton Inn, Quality Inn, Ramada, Red Roof Inn $General, $Tree, AT&T, Best Buy, Conrad's Automotive, Dick's, Firestone/auto, Home Depot, Honda, Hyundai, JC Penney, Jo-Ann Fabrics, Lowe's, Macy's, Marc's Foods, Petsmart, Staples, Target, Tuffy, Verizon, **S** Shell, Speedway/dsl Super 8
142	I-90 (from eb, exits left), OH 2, to W Cleveland
140	OH 58, Amherst, **N** Sunoco/Subway DQ, Moosehead Grill $General, Chrysler/Dodge/Jeep, **S** Ford
139mm	**Service Plaza both lanes,** Sunoco/dsl/24hr Burger King, Great Steak&Potato, Hershey's, Panera Bread, Popeye's, Starbucks gifts, , RV parking
135	rd 51, Baumhart Rd, to Vermilion
132mm	Vermilion River
118	US 250, to Norwalk, Sandusky, **N** Circle K/dsl, Marathon/dsl McDonald's, Subway Country Inn Suites, Days Inn, Hampton Inn, Motel 6, Quality Inn, Red Roof Inn, Super 8 Milan RV Park, to Edison's Birthplace, **S** Colonial Inn
110	OH 4, to Bellevue
100mm	**Service Plaza both lanes,** Sunoco/dsl/24hr Burger King, Sbarro's, Starbucks
93mm	Sandusky River

LORAIN

OHIO TURNPIKE Cont'd

TOLEDO

Exit#	Services
91	OH 53, to Fremont, Port Clinton, N Days Inn, **0-2 mi S** BP/Subway/dsl/24hr, Murphy USA/dsl Applebee's, Bob Evans, Buffalo Wild Wings, Burger King, Fricker's, Grand American Buffet, Jimmy John's, McDonald's, Subway, Taco Bell Comfort Inn, Delux Inn, Hampton Inn, Holiday Inn Express, Quality Inn H, $Tree, Aldi Foods, AT&T, Ford/Lincoln, GNC, Lowe's, Rutherford B. Hayes Library, Staples, URGENT CARE, USPO, Verizon, vet, Walmart
81	OH 51, Elmore, Woodville, Gibsonburg
80.5mm	Portage River
77mm	**Service Plaza both lanes,** Sunoco/dsl/24hr Hardee's, Mancino's, Red Burrito
71	I-280, OH 420, to Stony Ridge, Toledo, N FLYING J/Denny's/dsl/scales/LP/24hr, Loves/Arby's/dsl/scales/24hr, Petro/BP/Iron Skillet/dsl/scales/24hr/@ Budget Inn, Crown Inn, Regency Inn, Super 8 Blue Beacon, SpeedCo, S FuelMart/Subway/dsl/scales, Pilot/McDonald's/dsl/scales/24hr, TA/BP/Burger King/Taco Bell/dsl/scales/24hr/@ KOA
64	I-75 N, to Toledo, Perrysburg, S BP/Subway/dsl Country Inn&Suites, Courtyard, Hampton Inn, Staybridge Suites Bass Pro Shops, Camping World RV Ctr
63mm	Maumee River
59	US 20, to I-475, Maumee, Toledo, N Shell/dsl, Speedway/dsl Bob Evans, East of Chicago Pizza, Golden Lily, McDonald's, Nick's Cafe, Olive Garden, Steak'n Shake, Subway, Waffle House Motel 6 $Tree, Family$, Goodyear/auto, Jo-Ann
59	Continued Fabrics, NAPA, O'Reilly Parts, Rite Aid, Savers, to Toledo Stadium, Walgreens, S Shell/dsl, Speedway/dsl Big Boy, Chipotle Mexican, Deet's BBQ, Five Guys, Fricker's, Jed's BBQ, La Fiesta Mexican, Pizza Hut, Red Lobster, Schlotzsky's, Steak Escape, Taco Bell, Tim Horton's Best Value Inn, Budget Inn, Comfort Inn, Comfort Inn, Days Inn, Hampton Inn, Holiday Inn, Red Roof Inn antiques, AT&T, Ford, Honda, Kroger/dsl, Meijer/dsl, Toyota, Verizon, vet
52	OH 2, to Toledo, N Loma Linda Mexican, S Days Inn , RV/truck repair

WAUSEON

Exit#	Services
39	OH 109, S Country Corral/Winchester's Rest./dsl/scales/24hr
34	OH 108, to Wauseon, S Shell/Subway/dsl/24hr Days Inn, Holiday Inn Express, Rodeway Inn H, **2 mi S on US 20A** Circle K, Murphy USA/dsl Burger King, DQ, Kamwa Chinese, McDonald's, Pizza Hut, Subway, Taco Bell, Wendy's Ace Hardware, AutoZone, Rite Aid, Walmart
25	OH 66, Burlington, N Harrison Lake SP, **3 mi S** Sauder Village Museum/Inn
24.5mm	Tiffen River
20	**Indian Meadow wb/Tiffen River eb Service Plaza,** Sunoco/dsl Burger King, Sbarro's, Starbucks
13	OH 15, to Bryan, Montpelier, S Marathon/dsl, Sunoco Four Seasons Rest., Wynn's Rest. EconoLodge, Holiday Inn Express, Quality Inn, Rainbow Motel Hutch's Dsl Repair
11.5mm	St Joseph River
3mm	**toll plaza,**
2	OH 49, to US 20, N Subway truck repair, truck tires
0mm	Ohio/Indiana state line

OKLAHOMA

INTERSTATE 35

Exit#	Services
236mm	Oklahoma/Kansas state line
235	**weigh sta sb**
231	US 177, Braman, E Conoco/deli/dsl casino
230	Braman Rd
229mm	Chikaskia River
225mm	**Welcome Ctr sb, full facilities, litter barrels, petwalk, , , vending**
222	OK 11, to Blackwell, Medford, Alva, Newkirk, E Conoco/dsl, Shell/dsl Braum's, Cobb's Rest., KFC/Taco Bell, Los Potros Mexican, McDonald's, Subway Best Way Inn, Best Western, Econolodge, Holiday Inn Express, Sleep Inn H
218	Hubbard Rd
217mm	**weigh sta both lanes**
214	US 60, to Tonkawa, Lamont, Ponka City, N OK Coll, E RV Park, W Casey's/dsl, Pilot/Taco Bell/dsl/scales/24hr, Shell/dsl New Western Inn casino
213mm	Salt Fork of Arkansas River
211	Fountain Rd, E Loves/Chester's/Subway/dsl/scales/24hr/RV Dump
209mm	**parking area, litter barrels**
203	OK 15, to Marland, Billings, E Phillips 66/DQ/Subway/dsl/CNG/scales/24hr
199mm	Red Rock Creek
195mm	**parking area both lanes, litter barrels**
194b a	US 412, US 64 W, Cimarron Tpk, to Cimarron, Enid, W Phillips U
193	Airport Rd (from nb, no return)
191mm	Black Bear Creek
186	US 64 E, to Fir St, Perry, E Mobil/Subway/dsl Braum's, McDonald's Super 8 H, museum, W Exxon/dsl Comfort Suites, Holiday Inn Express, Microtel, Regency Inn Chevrolet/Buick/GMC
185	US 77, to Covington, Perry, E American Inn, W Phillips 66/rest/motel/dsl/24hr
180	Orlando Rd

GUTHRIE

Exit#	Services
174	OK 51, to Stillwater, Hennessee, E Phillips 66/dsl Smokey Pokey Cafe Fairfield Inn (12mi), Hampton Inn (12mi), La Quinta (12mi), Residence Inn (12mi) Lake Carl Blackwell RV Park, to OSU
173mm	**parking area sb, parking only, litter barrels**
171mm	**parking area nb, parking only, litter barrels**
170	Mulhall Rd
166mm	Cimarron River
157	OK 33, to Cushing, Guthrie, E Loves/Carl's Jr/dsl/scales/24hr, Valero/Golden Chick/dsl Langston U, W Loves/Subway/dsl, Road Star, Shell/dsl, Valero Arby's, Braum's, El Rodeo Mexican, Pizza Hut, Sonic, The Ribshack Best Value Inn, Hampton Inn, Holiday Inn Express Interstate Motel, La Quinta, Sleep Inn H, OK Terr Museum RV camping
153	US 77 N (exits left from nb), Guthrie, W McDonald's (3mi) Taco Bell (3mi) Buick/Cadillac/GMC, Chevrolet, Chrysler/Dodge/Jeep, Ford
151	Seward Rd, E Shell/cafe/dsl Lazy E Arena (4mi), Pioneer RV park
146	Waterloo Rd, E Phillips 66/dsl, Shell/Subway/dsl

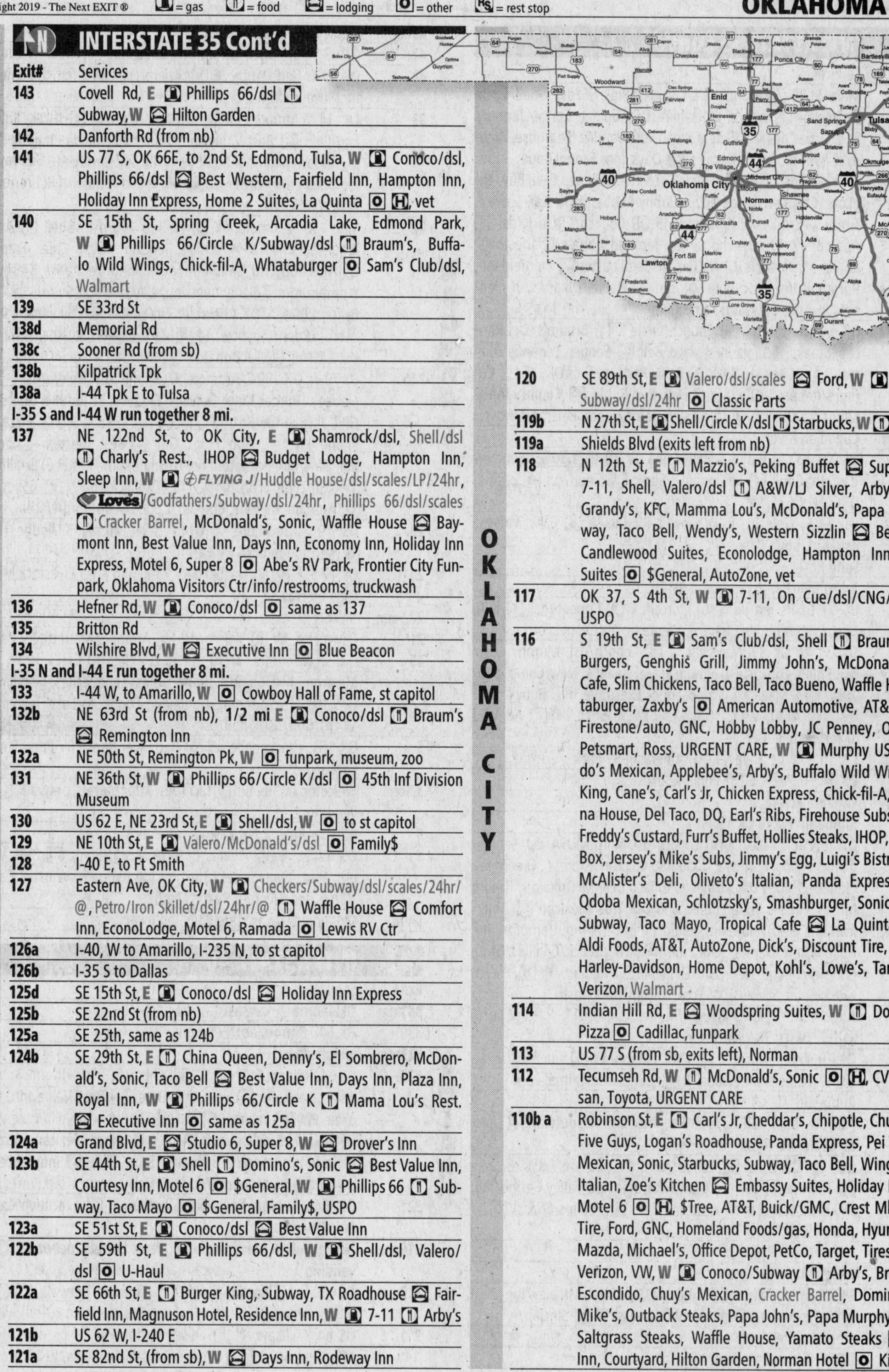

INTERSTATE 35 Cont'd

Exit#	Services
143	Covell Rd, E Phillips 66/dsl Subway, W Hilton Garden
142	Danforth Rd (from nb)
141	US 77 S, OK 66E, to 2nd St, Edmond, Tulsa, W Conoco/dsl, Phillips 66/dsl Best Western, Fairfield Inn, Hampton Inn, Holiday Inn Express, Home 2 Suites, La Quinta H, vet
140	SE 15th St, Spring Creek, Arcadia Lake, Edmond Park, W Phillips 66/Circle K/Subway/dsl Braum's, Buffalo Wild Wings, Chick-fil-A, Whataburger Sam's Club/dsl, Walmart
139	SE 33rd St
138d	Memorial Rd
138c	Sooner Rd (from sb)
138b	Kilpatrick Tpk
138a	I-44 Tpk E to Tulsa
I-35 S and I-44 W run together 8 mi.	
137	NE 122nd St, to OK City, E Shamrock/dsl, Shell/dsl Charly's Rest., IHOP Budget Lodge, Hampton Inn, Sleep Inn, W FLYING J/Huddle House/dsl/scales/LP/24hr, Loves/Godfathers/Subway/dsl/24hr, Phillips 66/dsl/scales Cracker Barrel, McDonald's, Sonic, Waffle House Baymont Inn, Best Value Inn, Days Inn, Economy Inn, Holiday Inn Express, Motel 6, Super 8 Abe's RV Park, Frontier City Funpark, Oklahoma Visitors Ctr/info/restrooms, truckwash
136	Hefner Rd, W Conoco/dsl same as 137
135	Britton Rd
134	Wilshire Blvd, W Executive Inn Blue Beacon
I-35 N and I-44 E run together 8 mi.	
133	I-44 W, to Amarillo, W Cowboy Hall of Fame, st capitol
132b	NE 63rd St (from nb), 1/2 mi E Conoco/dsl Braum's Remington Inn
132a	NE 50th St, Remington Pk, W funpark, museum, zoo
131	NE 36th St, W Phillips 66/Circle K/dsl 45th Inf Division Museum
130	US 62 E, NE 23rd St, E Shell/dsl, W to st capitol
129	NE 10th St, E Valero/McDonald's/dsl Family$
128	I-40 E, to Ft Smith
127	Eastern Ave, OK City, W Checkers/Subway/dsl/scales/24hr/@, Petro/Iron Skillet/dsl/24hr/@ Waffle House Comfort Inn, EconoLodge, Motel 6, Ramada Lewis RV Ctr
126a	I-40, W to Amarillo, I-235 N, to st capitol
126b	I-35 S to Dallas
125d	SE 15th St, E Conoco/dsl Holiday Inn Express
125b	SE 22nd St (from nb)
125a	SE 25th, same as 124b
124b	SE 29th St, E China Queen, Denny's, El Sombrero, McDonald's, Sonic, Taco Bell Best Value Inn, Days Inn, Plaza Inn, Royal Inn, W Phillips 66/Circle K Mama Lou's Rest. Executive Inn same as 125a
124a	Grand Blvd, E Studio 6, Super 8, W Drover's Inn
123b	SE 44th St, E Shell Domino's, Sonic Best Value Inn, Courtesy Inn, Motel 6 $General, W Phillips 66 Subway, Taco Mayo $General, Family$, USPO
123a	SE 51st St, E Conoco/dsl Best Value Inn
122b	SE 59th St, E Phillips 66/dsl, W Shell/dsl, Valero/dsl U-Haul
122a	SE 66th St, E Burger King, Subway, TX Roadhouse Fairfield Inn, Magnuson Hotel, Residence Inn, W 7-11 Arby's
121b	US 62 W, I-240 E
121a	SE 82nd St, (from sb), W Days Inn, Rodeway Inn

OKLAHOMA CITY

Exit#	Services
120	SE 89th St, E Valero/dsl/scales Ford, W Loves/Subway/dsl/24hr Classic Parts
119b	N 27th St, E Shell/Circle K/dsl Starbucks, W Pickles Rest.
119a	Shields Blvd (exits left from nb)
118	N 12th St, E Mazzio's, Peking Buffet Super 8, W 7-11, Shell, Valero/dsl A&W/LJ Silver, Arby's, Braum's, Grandy's, KFC, Mamma Lou's, McDonald's, Papa John's, Subway, Taco Bell, Wendy's, Western Sizzlin Best Western, Candlewood Suites, Econolodge, Hampton Inn, SpringHill Suites $General, AutoZone, vet
117	OK 37, S 4th St, W 7-11, On Cue/dsl/CNG/e10 H, USPO
116	S 19th St, E Sam's Club/dsl, Shell Braum's, Garage Burgers, Genghis Grill, Jimmy John's, McDonald's, Ricky's Cafe, Slim Chickens, Taco Bell, Taco Bueno, Waffle House, Whataburger, Zaxby's American Automotive, AT&T, Best Buy, Firestone/auto, GNC, Hobby Lobby, JC Penney, Office Depot, Petsmart, Ross, URGENT CARE, W Murphy USA Alfredo's Mexican, Applebee's, Arby's, Buffalo Wild Wings, Burger King, Cane's, Carl's Jr, Chicken Express, Chick-fil-A, Chili's, China House, Del Taco, DQ, Earl's Ribs, Firehouse Subs, Five Guys, Freddy's Custard, Furr's Buffet, Hollies Steaks, IHOP, Jack-in-the-Box, Jersey's Mike's Subs, Jimmy's Egg, Luigi's Bistro, Mazzio's, McAlister's Deli, Oliveto's Italian, Panda Express, Pei Wei, Qdoba Mexican, Schlotzsky's, Smashburger, Sonic, Starbucks, Subway, Taco Mayo, Tropical Cafe La Quinta $Tree, Aldi Foods, AT&T, AutoZone, Dick's, Discount Tire, Gordman's, Harley-Davidson, Home Depot, Kohl's, Lowe's, Target, Tires+, Verizon, Walmart
114	Indian Hill Rd, E Woodspring Suites, W Double Dave's Pizza Cadillac, funpark
113	US 77 S (from sb, exits left), Norman
112	Tecumseh Rd, W McDonald's, Sonic H, CVS Drug, Nissan, Toyota, URGENT CARE
110b a	Robinson St, E Carl's Jr, Cheddar's, Chipotle, ChuckECheese, Five Guys, Logan's Roadhouse, Panda Express, Pei Wei, Qdoba Mexican, Sonic, Starbucks, Subway, Taco Bell, Wing Stop, Zio's Italian, Zoe's Kitchen Embassy Suites, Holiday Inn Express, Motel 6 H, $Tree, AT&T, Buick/GMC, Crest Mkt, Discount Tire, Ford, GNC, Homeland Foods/gas, Honda, Hyundai, Kohl's, Mazda, Michael's, Office Depot, PetCo, Target, Tires+, TJ Maxx, Verizon, VW, W Conoco/Subway Arby's, Braum's, Cafe Escondido, Chuy's Mexican, Cracker Barrel, Domino's, Jersey Mike's, Outback Steaks, Papa John's, Papa Murphy's, Rib Crib, Saltgrass Steaks, Waffle House, Yamato Steaks Comfort Inn, Courtyard, Hilton Garden, Norman Hotel Kia

OK

INTERSTATE 35 Cont'd

NORMAN

Exit#	Services
109	Main St, E Murphy USA/dsl, Phillips 66/dsl, Shell/Circle K, Sinclair Arby's, Chick-fil-A, DQ, Golden Corral, Jimmy's Egg, Little Caesar's, Panera Bread, Subway, Waffle House, Wendy's, Whataburger, Zaxby's Days Inn, EconoLodge, Super 8, Travelodge Aldi Foods, AT&T, AutoZone, Best Buy, BigLots, Chrysler/Dodge/Jeep, Hobby Lobby, Kwik Kar, Lowe's, Tires+, Walmart/McDonald's, W Conoco/Circle K/dsl Applebee's, BJ's Brewhouse, Burger King, Cane's, Charleston's, Chili's, McDonald's, Olive Garden, Red Lobster Fairfield Inn, Hampton Inn, La Quinta Barnes&Noble, Dillard's, JC Penney, Jo-Ann, Old Navy, Sam's Club
108b a	OK 9 E, Norman, E Conoco/Circle K Braum's, Del Rancho Steaks, Schlotzsky's, Taco Bell Sooner Legends Inn/rest. $General, NAPA, O'Reilly Parts, to U of OK, W Carino's Italian, IHOP, Jason's Deli, Red Robin Country Inn&Suites, La Quinta Chevrolet, Home Depot, Petsmart, Ross
107mm	Canadian River
106	OK 9 W, to Chickasha, E Casino, W Loves/Subway/dsl/24hr, Shell McDonald's, Sonic Sleep Inn casino, URGENT CARE, vet
104	OK 74 S, Goldsby, E Floyd's RV Ctr, W CNG, Valero/dsl Libby's Cafe
101	Ladd Rd
98	Johnson Rd, E Funtown RV Ctr
95	US 77 (exits left from sb), Purcell, E Conoco/dsl KFC, Mazzio's, Van's BBQ H, $General, AutoZone, Ford
91	OK 74, to OK 39, Maysville, E Conoco/dsl, Murphy USA/dsl, Phillips 66/dsl Braum's, McDonald's, New China, Subway, Taco Mayo EconoLodge, Executive Inn, Ruby's Inn/rest. AT&T, Walmart/Subway, W Shell/dsl A&W/LJ Silver, Taco Bell

PAULS VALLEY

Exit#	Services
86	OK 59, Wayne, Payne, E American RV Park
79	OK 145 E, Paoli, E Phillips 66/dsl
76mm	Washita River
74	Kimberlin Rd, to OK 19
72	OK 19, Pauls Valley, E Conoco/dsl, Murphy USA/dsl, Sunoco/dsl/rest/24hr Arby's, Braum's, Chicken Express, Green Tea Chinese, Happy Days Diner, KFC/Taco Bell, McDonald's, Riviera Maya, Snider's Buffet, Sonic, Subway, Tio's Mexican American Inn, Best Value Inn, Comfort Inn, Days Inn, Hampton Inn, Holiday Inn Express, Relax Inn AT&T, Buick/Cadillac/GMC, Chrysler/Dodge/Jeep, URGENT CARE, Walmart, W Phillips 66/dsl/24hr, Shell/dsl Ford/Lincoln, truckwash
70	Airport Rd, E Loves/Burger King/dsl/LP/scales/24hr/@ H, W T&R RV Resort
66	OK 29, Wynnewood, E Kent's Motel, W Shell/dsl
64	OK 17A E, to Wynnewood, E GW Exotic Animal Park
60	Ruppe Rd
59mm	**both lanes, full facilities, litter barrels, petwalk, , picnic table, RV dump**
55	OK 7, Davis, E Conoco/dsl, Phillips 66/A&W/dsl/24hr The Inn to Chickasaw NRA, Treasure Valley Casino/Inn, W **Chickasaw Nation Welcome Ctr,** Phillips 66/dsl to Arbuckle Ski Area
54.5mm	Honey Creek Pass
53mm	**weigh sta both lanes**
51	US 77, Turner Falls, E Arbuckle Mtn Motel, Mtnview Inn (3mi) RV camping, to Arbuckle Wilderness, W Sinclair/rv park
49mm	scenic turnout both lanes
47	US 77, Turner Falls Area
46mm	scenic turnout both lanes
42	OK 53 W, Springer, Comanche, W Exxon/Subway/dsl
40	OK 53 E, Gene Autry, E Valero/dsl/café/24hr Gene Autry Museum (8mi)

ARDMORE

Exit#	Services
33	OK 142, Ardmore, E Shell, Valero/dsl IHOP, Jimmy's Egg Cafe Best Value Inn, Courtyard, Holiday Inn, La Quinta, Nissan, Red Roof Inn, SpringHill Suites, Super 8 Honda, regional park, tires, W FLYING J/Huddle House/dsl/LP/scales/24hr
32	12th St, Ardmore, E Phillips 66/dsl, Shell Arby's, Braum's, Chick-fil-A, Chili's, Cotton Patch Cafe, Freddy's, Quiznos, Rib Crib, Sakura Hibachi, Santa Fe Steaks, Starbucks, Whataburger Baymont Inn, Candlewood Suites, La Quinta $Tree, AT&T, Chevrolet, Hilton Garden, Hyundai, Lowe's, PetCo, Ross, Toyota, W Loves/Godfather's/Subway/dsl/24hr/@ McDonald's Microtel
31b a	US 70 W, OK 199 E, Ardmore, E Shell/dsl, Valero/dsl Applebee's, Burger King, Denny's, El Chico, El Tapatio, Interurban Grill, Jack-in-the-Box, KFC, McDonald's, Papa John's, Pizza Hut, Prairie Kitchen, Two Frogs Grill Best Western+, Comfort Inn, Days Inn, Hampton Inn, Lexington Inn, Motel 6, Quality Inn AutoZone, Econolodge, Kia, O'Reilly Parts, W Conoco/ds Ardmore RV Park, Chrysler/Dodge/Jeep, Ford/Lincoln, vet
29	US 70 E, Ardmore, E to Lake Murray SP/lodge (8mi), W Hidden Lake RV Park
24	OK 77 S, E By the Lake RV Park, Red River Livestock Mkt, to Lake Murray SP
22.5mm	Hickory Creek
21	Oswalt Rd, W Valero/dsl Ardmore Marietta RV Park
15	OK 32, Marietta, E Valero/dsl/24hr Carl's Jr, La Roca Mexican, McDonald's, Robertson's Sandwiches, Sonic, Subway H, $General, Homeland Foods, to Lake Texoma SP, W Gulf/dsl, Shell/dsl
5	OK 153, Thackerville, W Red River Ranch RV Park, Shorty's Foods/gas
3.5mm	**Welcome Ctr nb, full facilities, litter barrels, petwalk, , , vending**
3	Winstar Blvd, E casino, same as 1
1	US 77 N, E Phillips 66/dsl/CNG Sonic Best Western, Red River Suites, The Inn RV park, Winstar Casino, W Red River RV Resort (3mi)
0mm	Oklahoma/Texas state line, Red River

INTERSTATE 40

ROLAND

Exit#	Services
331mm	Oklahoma/Arkansas state line
330	OK 64D S (from eb), Ft Smith
329mm	**weigh sta wb**
325	US 64, Roland, Ft Smith, N Cherokee Trkstp/Valero/Subway/dsl/scales/24hr Four Star Diner Best Value Inn, Cherokee Inn casino, S Pilot/Wendy's/dsl/scales/24hr, QS/dsl, Shell/dsl/scales Arby's, El Celaya Mexican, Mazzio's, McDonald's, Sonic, Subway, Taco Bell Interstate Inn $General, Marvin's Foods, O'Reilly Parts
321	OK 64b N, Muldrow, S Arena/dsl Executive Inn auto/dsl repair
316mm	**eb, full facilities, info, litter barrels, petwalk, , , vending**
313mm	**wb, full facilities, info, litter barrels, petwalk, , , RV dump, vending**
311	US 64, Sallisaw, N Ed's Truckstop/Phillips 66/diner/dsl, Mr Jiff, Sunoco/dsl El Toro Mexican, Hardee's, KFC/Taco Bell,

OK

INTERSTATE 40 Cont'd

SALLISAW

Exit	Services
311	Continued Pizza Hut, Simple Simon's Pizza Motel 6, Sallisaw Inn H, $General, AutoZone, Brushy Lake SP (10mi), O'Reilly Parts, Sequoya's Home (12mi)
308	US 59, Sallisaw, N Murphy USA/dsl, Sunoco/dsl A&W/LJ Silver, Arby's, Asian Star, Braum's, Cazadore Mexican, China Harbor, Mazzio's, McDonald's, Roma's Italian, Sonic, Subway, Taco Bueno Days Inn, Economy Inn, Golden Spur Motel, Super 8 H, $General, $Tree, AT&T, casino, Verizon, Walmart/Subway, S Valero/dsl Chen's Garden Buick/Chevrolet/GMC, Chrysler/Dodge/Jeep, Ford, KOA, to Kerr Lake, truck/tire repair
303	Dwight Mission Rd
297	OK 82 N, Vian, N FL/dsl Simple Simon, Subway Cherokee Landing SP (24 mi), IGA Foods, to Tenkiller Lake RA (12 mi), USPO, S Sequoia NWR
291	OK 10 N, to Gore, N Greenleaf SP (10mi), Tenkiller SP (21mi)
290mm	Arkansas River
287	OK 100 N, to Webbers Falls, N Loves/Burger King/Subway/dsl/24hr Cox's Buffet Greenleaf SP, parts/tires/repair, Tenkiller SP
286	Muskogee Tpk, to Muskogee
284	Ross Rd
283mm	**parking area both lanes, litter barrels**
278	US 266, OK 2, Warner, N Conoco, Sinclair/dsl (2), Sinclair/McDonald's/dsl El Jaracho Mexican, Sonic, Subway Ambassadors Inn & RV $General
270	Texanna Rd, to Porum Landing, S Campbell's/BBQ
265	US 69 bus, Checotah, N Kwik'n Easy Pizza Hut, Sonic, S Phillips 66/dsl Budget Inn Chevrolet/Chrysler/Dodge/Jeep
264b a	US 69, to Eufaula, 1 mi N FLYING J/Denny's/dsl/LP/scales/24hr, Casey's/dsl, Phillips 66/dsl/24hr Charlie's Chicken, McDonald's, Simple Simon's Pizza, Taco Bell Best Value Inn $General, AT&T, O'Reilly Parts, repair, TrueValue, Walmart/Subway
262	to US 266, Lotawatah Rd, N Sunshine
261mm	Lake Eufaula
259	OK 150, to Fountainhead Rd, S Shell/dsl Lake Eufaula Inn to Lake Eufaula SP
255	Pierce Rd, N KOA
251mm	**both lanes**
247	Tiger Mtn Rd, S Quilt Barn/antiques
240b a	US 62 E, US 75 N, Henryetta, N Conoco/dsl, Loves/dsl, Phillips 66, Shell Arby's, Braum's, Classic Diner, El Charro Mexican, KFC, Mazzio's, McDonald's, Shoney's, Sonic, Subway, Taco Bell, Taco Bueno Days Inn, Economy Inn, Relax Inn Chevrolet, Chrysler/Dodge/Jeep, Ford, O'Reilly Parts, tires/repair, Walmart, S Indian Nation Tpk
237	US 62, US 75, Henryetta, N Shell/dsl Cowboy Corner Rest. Green Country Inn H, Henryetta RV Park (2mi), S Super 8
231	US 75 S, to Weleetka, N Sinclair/dsl Cowpoke's Cafe
227	Clearview Rd, S casino
221	US 62, OK 27, Okemah, N $General/dsl, Express/Subway/dsl/24hr, Phillips 66/McDonald's Mazzio's, Pepino's Mexican, Simple Simon's, Sonic Days Inn $General, Chevrolet, Homeland Foods, NAPA, TrueValue, S Loves/Chester Fried/dsl/24hr casino, H, truck repair
217	OK 48, to Bristow, Bearden, S gas/dsl

HENRYETTA

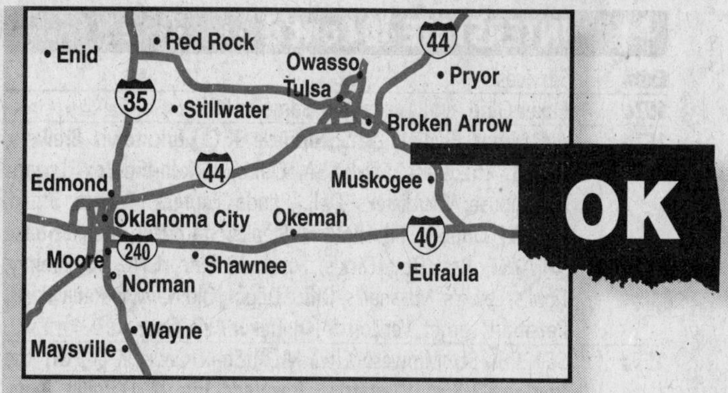

SHAWNEE

Exit	Services
216mm	N Canadian River
212	OK 56, to Cromwell, Wewoka, N auto/tire repair, S Valero/Chester's/Subway/dsl to Seminole Nation Museum (16mi)
208mm	Gar Creek
202mm	Turkey Creek
200	US 377, OK 99, to Little, Prague, N Bar H Bar TC/Shell/dsl/RV park RoadHouse Diner, S Conoco/dsl, Loves/Subway/dsl/24hr, Sinclair/dsl Robertson's Ham Sandwiches, Roundup Rest/RV Park H
197mm	**both lanes, full facilities, litter barrels, petwalk,**
192	OK 9A, Earlsboro, S Valero/Godfather's/Cafe/dsl
189mm	N Canadian River
186	OK 18, to Shawnee, N Phillips 66, Sinclair Denny's American Inn, Comfort Inn, Days Inn, La Quinta, Quality Inn, Super 8, S Shell/Domino's/dsl, Sinclair/dsl Carl's Jr, Cazadorez, Golden Corral, Sonic, Subway, Van's BBQ Colonial Inn Chrysler/Dodge/Jeep, Homeland Foods
185	OK 3E, Shawnee Mall Dr, to Shawnee, N Murphy USA/dsl Buffalo Wild Wings, Chili's, Garage Burgers, KFC, Panda Express, Red Lobster, Santa Fe Steaks, Taco Bueno, Wendy's Holiday Inn Express $Tree, AT&T, Chevrolet, Dillard's, Ford, JC Penney, Jo-Ann, Kohl's, Ross, Walgreens, Walmart/McDonald's, S Phillips 66/Circle K/Quiznos/dsl Braum's, Burger King, Chick-fil-A, Cracker Barrel, Delta Cafe, Freddy's, IHOP, Mazzio's, McAlister's Deli, McDonald's, Popeye's, Qdoba, Rib Crib BBQ, Schlotzky's, Sonic, Starbucks, Subway, Taco Bell, Whataburger Hampton Inn Aldi Foods, CVS Drug, Discount Tire, Hobby Lobby, Kwik Kar, Lowe's, O'Reilly Parts, Petsmart, Staples, TJ Maxx, Verizon
181	US 177, US 270, to Tecumseh, S Shell/dsl Rosa's Mexican dsl repair, Prestige RV Ctr
180mm	N Canadian River
178	OK 102 S, Dale, N Grand TC/Subway/hotel/casino/dsl
176	OK 102 N, McLoud Rd, S Loves/Subway/dsl/24hr, Sinclair/dsl Curtis Watson Rest.
172	Newalla Rd, to Harrah
169	Peebly Rd
166	Choctaw Rd, to Woods, N Loves/McDonald's/Subway/dsl/scales/24hr KOA, S Pilot/Wendy's/dsl/scales/24hr Sonic to Lake Thunderbird SP (11mi)
165	I-240 W (from wb), to Dallas
162	Anderson Rd, N Leisure Time RV Ctr, LP
159b	Douglas Blvd, N OnCue/dsl, Shell/Circle K/dsl A&W/LJ Silver, Denny's, Freddy's, Jimmy John's, KFC, McDonald's, Pizza Hut, Sonic, Subway, Taco Bell, Whataburger Eastland Hills RV Park, S H, Tinker AFB
159a	Hruskocy Gate, N Chrysler/Dodge/Jeep, same as 157, U-Haul, S Tinker AFB, Gate 7

INTERSTATE 40 Cont'd

OKLAHOMA CITY

Exit#	Services
157c	Eaker Gate, Tinker AFB, same as 159
157b	Air Depot Blvd, N Shell/Circle K Bricktown Brewery, Cane's, Cheddar's, Chick-fil-A, Chili's, Jack-in-the-Box, Logans Roadhouse, McAlister's Deli, Panda Express, Panera Bread, Pei Wei, Qdoba Grill, Santa Fe Steaks, Starbucks, Steak&Shake AT&T, Best Buy, Dick's, Firestone/auto, GNC, JC Penney, Kohl's, Lowe's, Marshall's, Office Depot, Old Navy, O'Reilly Parts, Petsmart, Target, Verizon, S Tinker AFB, Gate 1
157a	SE 29th St, Midwest City, N Shell/Circle K On the Border Best Western+, Traveler's Inn O'Reilly Parts, S Ford, Sam's Club/gas
156b a	Sooner Rd, N Conoco/Circle K, Gulf Black Bear Diner, Waffle House Hampton Inn, Hawthorn Suites, Holiday Inn Express, Home 2 Suites, La Quinta, Motel 6, Sheraton, Studio 6 Hobby Lobby, Home Depot, Walmart/Subway, S Best China, Buffalo Wild Wings, Carl's Jr, Garage Grill, Hungry Howie's, Ted's Mexican Candlewood Suites, SpringHill Suites, Super 8 AT&T, Chevrolet/GMC, Discount Tire, Tires+, Toyota, Verizon
155b	SE 15th St, Del City, N Valero/dsl Peter Piper Pizza Family$, Nissan
155a	Sunny Lane Rd, Del City, N Conoco/Subway/dsl Hyundai, U-Haul, S Braum's, Church's, Dunkin Donuts, Sonic $ Tree, $General, Save ALot Foods
154	Reno Ave, Scott St, N Woodspring Suites vet, S 7-11
152	(153 from wb) I-35 N, to Wichita
127	Eastern Ave (from eb), Okla City, N Checkers/Subway/dsl/scales/24hr, Petro/Iron Skillet/dsl/scales/@ Waffle House Comfort Inn, Econolodge, Motel 6 Lewis RV Ctr
151b c	I-35, S to Dallas, I-235 N, to downtown, st capitol
151a	Lincoln Blvd, N Conoco/Subway/Circle K/dsl Earl's Rib Palace, McDonald's, Sonic Hampton Inn, Homewood Suites, Residence Inn Bass Pro Shop, Bricktown Stadium
150c	Robinson Ave (from wb), OK City, N Spaghetti Whse, Zio's Italian Courtyard, Hilton Garden, Residence Inn U-Haul, SpringHill, Staybridge Suites
150b	Harvey Ave (from eb), N Courtyard, Hilton Garden, Renaissance Hotel, Sheraton, downtown
150a	Shields Blvd (from eb), N to downtown
149b	Classen Blvd (from wb), same as 149a, to downtown
149a	Western Ave, Reno Ave, N Conoco/dsl, Shell/dsl, VP/Subway/dsl McDonald's, Sonic, Sweis Gyros, Taco Bell
148c	Virginia Ave (from wb), to downtown
148b	Penn Ave (from eb), N Valero/dsl
148a	Agnew Ave, Villa Ave, N VP/dsl
147c	May Ave
147b a	I-44, E to Tulsa, W to Lawton
146	Portland Ave (from eb, no return), N Phillips 66/Subway/dsl
145	Meridian Ave, OK City, N Conoco/Circle K/dsl, Shell/Circle K/dsl Denny's, Earl's Ribs, Louie's Grill, McDonald's, On the Border, Portofinos Italian, Trapper's Rest. Best Western, Biltmore Hotel, Days Inn, Extended Stay America, Howard Johnson, Red Roof Inn, Sonesta Suites, Studio 6, Super 8, S Phillips 66/Circle K/dsl Arby's, Billy Sims BBQ, Burger King, Charleston Rest., Chili's, Cracker Barrel, Five Star Grill, Frosted Mug Grill, Golden Palace Chinese, IHOP, Mackie's Steaks, San Marcos Mexican, Shorty Smalls Ribs, Sonic, Subway, Taco Bell, Taco Bueno, Waffle House, Whataburger, Zapata's, Zio's Italian AmericInn, Baymont Inn, Best Value Inn, Cambria Suites, Candlewood Suites, Clarion, Comfort Suites, Comfort Suites (2),

YUKON

Exit#	Services
145	Continued Country Inn&Suites, Courtyard, Embassy Suites, Fairfield Inn, Governors Suites, Hampton Inn, Hilton Garden, Holiday Inn, Holiday Inn Express, Home 2 Suites, Hyatt Place, La Quinta, Meridian Inn, Motel 6, Oak Tree Inn, Quality Inn, Ramada, Residence Inn, Sheraton, Sleep Inn, Staybridge Suites, TownePlace Suites, Tru, Wingate Inn, Woodspring Suites, Wyndham Garden Boot Barn
144	MacArthur Blvd, N Phillips 66/dsl, Shell/Circle K/dsl Applebee's, Arby's, Chick-fil-A, China One, Coldstone, Del Taco, Firehouse Subs, Five Guys, Golden Corral, Jack-in-the-Box, Jimmy John's, KFC, McDonald's, Olive Garden, Panda Express, Panera Bread, Qdoba, Sonic, Starbucks, Steak'n Shake, Taco Bueno, Twin Peaks, TX Roadhouse, Zaxby's SpringHill Suites $Tree, AT&T, GNC, Hobby Lobby, Office Depot, Petsmart, Ross, Target, Verizon, Walmart/McDonald's, S Comfort Inn, Green Carpet Inn, Microtel, Travelers Inn Sam's Club/gas
143	Rockwell Ave, N 7-11/dsl, Shell/dsl Buffalo Wild Wings, Burger Joint, Jersey Mike's, Pizza Inn, Taco Bell Homewood Suites, Rodeway Inn Best Buy, Dick's, Discount Tire, Harley Davidson, Home Depot, McClain's RV Ctr, Tires+, S Sands Motel/RV Park/LP Rockwell RV Park
142	Council Rd, N On Cue/dsl/CNG, Tesla EVC BJ's Rest., Braum's, Garage Burgers, Jimmy's Egg, McDonald's, Subway, Taco Mayo, Ted's Mexican, Whataburger Super 40 Inn dsl repair, S TA/Country Pride/dsl/scales/24hr/@ Econo Inn Council Rd RV Park, Ford/Peterbilt, truckwash
140	Morgan Rd, N Pilot/McDonald's/dsl/24hr/@, TA/Popeye's/Fazoli's/dsl/24hr/@ Blue Beacon, S FLYING J/Huddle House/dsl /LP/scales/24hr, LNG, Loves/Subway/dsl/scales/24hr Ricky's Cafe, Sonic Speedco
139	Kilpatrick Tpk
138	OK 4, to Yukon, Mustang, N Catfish Cove Best Value Inn, Comfort Suites, Motel 6 Chrysler/Dodge/Jeep, vet, S Conoco/Circle K/dsl Braum's, Burger King, Golden Chick, IHOP, Interurban Grill, Mama Mo's Pizza, McDonald's, Sonic, Subway, Taco Bell Best Western+, Home 2 Suites, Hyatt Place, La Quinta Aamco, CVS Drug, Homeland Food/drug, Mustang Run RV Park, URGENT CARE
137	Cornwell Dr, Czech Hall Rd, N On Cue/dsl Homeland Food/drug, URGENT CARE
136	OK 92, Garth Brooks Blvd, Yukon, N Murphy USA/dsl, Shell/Circle K A&W/LJ Silver, Billy Sims BBQ, Braum's, Cane's, Chelino's Mexican, CiCi's Pizza, KFC, McDonald's, Popeye's, Primo's Italian, Subway, Taco Mayo, Waffle House, Wendy's, Wendy's Yukon Buffet Hampton Inn $Tree, AutoZone, Big O Tire GNC, NAPA, repair, Sprouts Mkt, Tuesday Morning, USPO, Verizon, Walgreens, Walmart, S Shell/dsl Alfredo's Mexican Arby's, Buffalo Wild Wings, Buffalo Wild Wings, Carino's Italian Cheddar's, Chicken Express, Chick-fil-A, Chili's, Del Taco, DQ Freddy's, Hideaway Pizza, Hooters, Jersey Mike's, Jimmy's Egg Café, Johnnie's Broiler, Logan's Roadhouse, Louie's Grill, McAlister's Deli, Panda Express, Pizza Hut, Rib Crib, Sonic, Starbucks Taco Bueno, Tokyo Moon, Zaxby's Fairfield Inn, Holiday Inn Express, Sleep Inn H, Aldi, AT&T, Big Lots, Discount Tire Ford, GNC, Hobby Lobby, Kohl's, Kwik Kar, Lowe's, Marshall's Petco, PetsMart, Ross, Staples, Target, Tires+
132	Cimarron Rd, S
130	Banner Rd, N Shell/dsl/rest.
129mm	**weigh st both lanes**
127	S Radio Rd, S Loves/Carl's Jr/dsl/scales/24hr

OK

INTERSTATE 40 Cont'd

Exit#	Services	
125	US 81, to El Reno, N Love's/Subway/dsl, Phillips 66/dsl, Shell/dsl Chelino's Mexican, China King, Swadley's BBQ, Taco Mayo Best Value Inn, Economy Express, Ranger Motel $General, Buick/GMC, Chevrolet, Chrysler/Dodge/Jeep, Ford/Lincoln	EL RENO
123	Country Club Rd, to El Reno, N Murphy USA/dsl, Phillips 66, Shell/dsl, Valero/dsl Arby's, Braum's, Burger King, Great-wall Chinese, KFC, Little Caesar's, McDonald's, Pizza Express, Pizza Hut, Subway, Taco Bell, Taco Bueno Fairfield Inn, Hampton Inn, Home 2 Suites, Motel 6 H, AT&T, AutoZone, Walgreens, Walmart, S Denny's, MT Mikes Steaks Baymont Inn, Best Western/RV Park, Days Inn, Holiday Inn Express, Regency Motel	
119	Lp 40, to El Reno	
115	US 270, to Calumet	
111mm	**picnic area eb, litter barrels**	
108	US 281, to Geary, N Shell/Subway/dsl/24hr KOA/Indian Trading Post, to Roman Nose SP, S Phillips 66/Pizza Inn/dsl	
105mm	S Canadian River	
104	Methodist Rd	
101	US 281, OK 8, Hinton, N to Roman Nose SP, S Love's/Chester's/Godfather's/Sonic/dsl/scales Subway Hinton Travel Inn casino, Chevrolet, picnic area, to Red Rock Canyon SP	
95	Bethel Rd	
88	OK 58, to Hydro, Carnegie	
84	Airport Rd, N Phillips 66/dsl/CNG/scales/24hr Lucille's Roadhouse Holiday Inn Express, Travel Inn H, Buick/Cadillac/Chevrolet/GMC, Stafford Aerospace Museum, S La Quinta Chrysler/Dodge/Jeep, Ford/Lincoln	WEATHERFORD
82	E Main St, Weatherford, N Conoco/dsl, Phillips 66/dsl, Shell/dsl Arby's, BBQ Shed, Braum's, Carl's Jr, Chicken Express, Hibachi Buffet, Jerry's Rest., KFC, Little Caesar's, McDonald's, Pizza Hut, Qdoba, Sonic, Subway, Taco Mayo Best Western+, Comfort Inn, Fairfield Inn, Scottish Inn H, $General, Ace Hardware, AT&T, GNC, NAPA, O'Reilly Parts, Savealot Foods, to SW OSU, United Mkt, Walgreens, S Walmart/Subway	
80a	(from eb), N Phillips/dsl Casa Soto Mexican	
81	E Main St (from eb), same as 82	
80	W Main St, Mountainview, Thomas, N Best Value Inn NAPAcare	
71	Custer City Rd, N Love's/Subway/dsl/24hr Cherokee Trading Post/rest.	
69	Lp 40 (from wb, no return), to Clinton	
67.5mm	Washita River	
66	US 183, Clinton, S Shell/dsl Ford	
65a	10th St, Neptune Dr, Clinton, N Branding Iron Rest., China King, Picante Grille Days Inn, Relax Inn, Super 8 United Foods, S Phillips 66/dsl EconoLodge, Holiday Inn Express Hargus RV Park	
65	Gary Blvd, Clinton, N Hutch/dsl Braum's, Italian Villa, KFC/Taco Bell, LJ Silver, Mazzio's, McDonald's, MT Mike's, Palacios Mexican, Pizza Hut, Subway, Taco Mayo Hampton Inn, Motel 6, Ramada Inn, Tradewinds Inn H, $General, $Tree, Rte 66 Museum, Rte 66 Museum, S Holiday Inn Express, La Quinta	CLINTON
62	Parkersburg Rd, S Hargus RV Ctr	
61	Haggard Rd	
57	Stafford Rd	
53	OK 44, Foss, N to Foss SP, S Cenex/dsl	

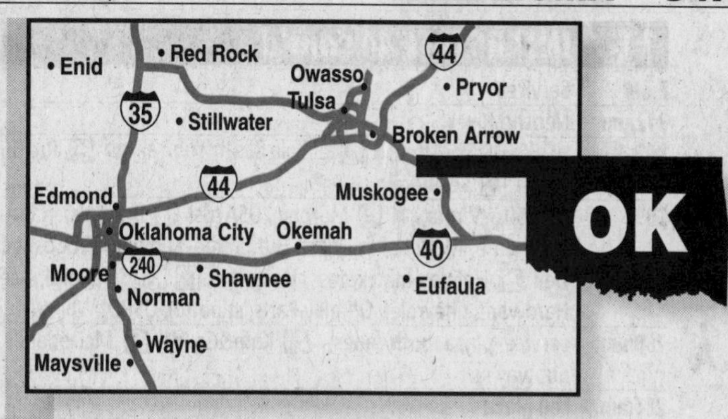

Exit#	Services	
50	Clinton Lake Rd, N KOA/LP/dsl	
47	Canute, S Shell/dsl	
41	OK 34 (exits left from eb), Elk City, N Hutch's/dsl, Love's/Subway/dsl Home Cooking Rest. Elk City Motel, HomeTowne Inn, La Quinta, Motel 6, Sleep Inn, Super 8, Travel Inn H, Elk Run RV Park	ELK CITY
40	E 7th St, Elk City, N Holiday Inn Express Chrysler/Dodge/Jeep, S Hutch's/dsl/CNG Huddle House, Rib Crib Hampton Inn Hobby Lobby, same as 41, Walmart/McDonald's, Wendy's	
38	OK 6, Elk City, N Conoco/dsl, Phillips 66/dsl Arby's, Billy Sims BBQ, Boomtown Grill, China Super Buffet, LJ Silver, McDonald's, Western Sizzlin Bedford Inn, Days Inn Ace Hardware, Elk Creek RV Park, tires, S Phillips 66/dsl Best Western+, Clarion Inn, Comfort Inn Elk City RV Ctr, to Quartz Mtn SP	
34	Merritt Rd	
32	OK 34 S (exits left from eb), Elk City	
26	Cemetery Rd, N Shell/dsl dsl repair, S TA/Taco Bell/Subway/dsl/scales/24hr/@	
25	Lp 40, Sayre, 1 mi N Hutch's/dsl/CNG Western Motel, Windgate Hotel H, Bobcat Creek RV Park, Chevrolet/GMC, Ford	SAYRE
23	OK 152, Sayre, S Cenex/dsl	
22.5mm	N Fork Red River	
20	US 283, Sayre, N FLYING J/Denny's/dsl/LP/RV dump/scales/24hr McDonald's AmericInn to Washita Bfd Site (25mi), Truck lube, truckwash	
14	Hext Rd	
13.5mm	**check sta both lanes, litter barrels**	
11	Lp 40, to Erick, Hext	
10mm	**Welcome Ctr/RS both lanes, full facilities, litter barrels, petwalk, RV dump**	
7	OK 30, Erick, N Motel 6, S Love's/Subway/dsl/scales Simple Simon's Pizza Days Inn	
5	Lp 40, Honeyfarm Rd	
1	**weigh sta eb**	
1	Texola, S RV camping	
0mm	Oklahoma/Texas state line	

INTERSTATE 44

Exit#	Services
329mm	Oklahoma/Missouri state line
321mm	Spring River
314mm	**Oklahoma Welcome Ctr wb, full facilities, info, restrooms**
313	OK 10, Miami, N Conoco, Love's/dsl, Phillips 66/dsl Donut Palace, Subway Best Value Inn, Deluxe Inn, EconoLodge, Hampton Inn, Holiday Inn Express, Legacy Inn, Microtel H, auto repair, casino, Miami RV Park, to NE OK A&M Coll, S Chrysler/Dodge/Jeep

OK

INTERSTATE 44 Cont'd

VINITA

Exit#	Services
312mm	Neosho River
302	US 59, US 69, Afton, S Buffalo Ranch/Subway/dsl Rte 66 Motel $General
289	US 60, Vinita, N Murphy USA/dsl Braum's, Clanton's Cafe, McDonald's, Pizza Hut, Sonic, Subway, Woodshed Deli Holiday Inn Express, Vinita Inn H, $General, Ace Hardware, Chevrolet, O'Reilly Parts, st patrol, USPO, Walmart
288mm	**service plaza both lanes,** Kum&Go/dsl McDonald's, Subway
286mm	**toll plaza**
283	US 69, Big Cabin, N Big Cabin/Subway/dsl/scales/24hr/@ Super 8 Cabin RV Park, trk repair
269	OK 28 (from eb, no re-entry), to Adair, Chelsea
255	OK 20, to Pryor, Claremore, **0-2 mi** N Kum&Go/dsl/e-85, Murphy USA/dsl, QT/dsl Carl's Jr Hampton Inn, Holiday Inn Express, Super 8, Travel Inn, Will Rogers Inn H, $General, museum, to Rogers U, Walgreens, Walmart, Will Rogers Memorial
248	to OK 266, Port of Catoosa, N QT/dsl Comfort Inn (4mi), Hampton Inn (4mi), Microtel (2mi), Will Rogers Inn (4mi) Dave's RV Ctr
244mm	Kerr-McClellan Navigation System
241mm	**Will Rogers Tpk begins eb, ends wb,**
241	OK 66 E, to Catoosa
240b	US 412 E, Choteau
240a	OK 167 N, 193rd E Ave, N IHOP, KFC/Taco Bell, McDonald's, Panda Express, Taco Bueno, Waffle House, Wendy's Cherokee Inn/Casino, Hampton Inn, Hardrock Hotel/Casino, La Quinta AT&T, Petco, Ross, Walgreens, Walmart, S Mazzio's, Port City Diner, Sonic, Subway Holiday Inn Express $General, O'Reilly Parts, tires/repair
238	161st E Ave, N **Cherokee Nation Welcome Ctr,** Sinclair/rest./dsl/scales/24hr truckwash, S QT/dsl/scales/24hr Arby's, Burger King Microtel truckwash
236b	I-244 W, to downtown Tulsa, N
236a	129th E Ave, N FLYING J/Denny's/dsl/LP/24hr Southern Tire Mart, S McDonald's

TULSA

Exit#	Services
235	E 11th St, Tulsa, N Mazzio's, Sonic, Subway Economy Inn, Executive Inn, Knights Inn, Super 8 $General, O'Reilly Parts, Walgreens, S Braum's, Taco Bueno Oak Tree Inn Whse Mkt
234b	same as 235
234a	US 169, N to Owasso, S to Broken Arrow, to
233	E 21st St, N Golden Corral Family$, S El Chico Comfort Suites Dean's RV Ctr
231	US 64, OK 51, to Muskogee, E 31st St, Memorial Dr, N QT/dsl Sonic, Speedy Gonzales Mexican, Subway Delux Inn, Motel 6, Ramada Inn, Tulsa Inn Walgreens, S Shell/Subway Cracker Barrel, IHOP, Jimmy's Egg, McDonald's, Pizza Hut, Ruby Tuesday, Village Inn Best Value Inn, Best Western, Comfort Suites, Country Inn Suites, Courtyard, EconoLodge, Embassy Suites, Extended Stay America, Fairfield Inn, Hampton Inn, Holiday Inn Express, Quality Inn, Sleep Inn, Super 8 Cavender's Boots, Chevrolet, Harley-Davidson, Nissan
230	E 41st St, Sheridan Rd, N Shell Carl's Jr, Chick-fil-A, Chipotle, Desi Wok, Flame Broiler, Jimmy John's, On-the-Border, Panera Bread, Schlotzsky's, Starbucks, Subway, TGIFriday's, Top That! Pizza, Whataburger AT&T, Barnes&Noble, Cartec Automotive, Dillard's, JC Penney, Jo-Ann Fabrics, Michael's, Old Navy,
230	Continued Petco, Petsmart, Reasor's Foods, Ross, Verizon, S Buffalo Wild Wings, Carino's Italian La Quinta Batteries+Bulbs, Best Buy, Home Depot
229	Yale Ave, Tulsa, N Shell El Chico, McDonald's, Subway Firestone/auto, JC Penney, PetCo, S Kum&Go/dsl/e85, Phillips 66/dsl, QT Andy's Custard, Applebee's, Arby's, Braum's, Bravo's Grill, Cane's, Delta Cafe, Jack-in-the-Box, Outback Steaks, Qdoba, Red Lobster, Smoothie King, Sonic, Taco Bell, Village Inn Baymont Inn, Hilton Garden, Holiday Inn Express, Knights Inn, Red Roof Inn H, Kia, vet
228	Harvard Ave, Tulsa, N QT/dsl El Tequila Mexican, McDonald's, NYC Pizza Tradewinds Motel, S Express A&W/LJ Silver, Chili's, Freckle's Frozen Custard, Jamil's Rest, Mario's Pizza, Papa John's, Starbucks, Subway Wingate Inn $Tree, Hobby Lobby, Reasor's Mkt, SteinMart
227	Lewis Ave, Tulsa, S Goldie's Grill Walgreens
226b	Peoria Ave, Tulsa, N Kum&Go/dsl, QT/dsl Arby's, Burger St., Charleston's Rest., China Wok, CiCi's, Egg Roll Express, Jimmy's Egg, KFC, Little Caesars, Mazzio's, Pizza Hut, Ron's Burgers/Chili, Sonic, Subway, Super Buffet, Taco Bell, Taco Bueno Peoria Inn Harley-Davidson, O'Reilly Parts, Reasor's Mkt, Robertson Tire, Walmart Mkt, Whole Foods Mkt, S Braum's, Corner Cafe, Golden Palace, Golden Palace $General, AutoZone, Family$, Walgreens
226a	Riverside Dr
225mm	Arkansas River
225	Elwood Ave, N Chevrolet, Ford, S Budget Inn
224b a	US 75, to Okmulgee, Bartlesville, N QT/dsl Arnold's Burgers, KFC, Mazzio's, Sonic $General, vet, Whse Mkt, S Royal Inn Hurley RV Ctr
223c	33rd W Ave, Tulsa, N Braum's, Domino's, S Conoco Rib Crib BBQ
223b	51st St (from wb)
223a	I-244 E, to Tulsa, downtown
222c	(from wb), S Value Inn
222b	55th Place, N Capri Motel, Crystal Motel, S Best Value Inn, Economy Inn
222a	49th W Ave, Tulsa, N Carl's Jr, Kelly's Country Cooking Monterey Mexican, Subway Gateway Motel, Interstate Inn, Motel 6 $General, BigLots, Mack Trucks, S QT Kitchens/dsl/scales/24hr Arby's, McDonald's, Taco Bueno, Waffle House Comfort Inn, Super 8 Buick/GMC Freightliner, Kenworth
221a	57th W Ave, (from wb), S Buick/GMC
221mm	**Turner Tkp begins wb, ends eb.**
218	Creek Tpk E (from eb)
215	OK 97, to Sand Sprgs, Sapulpa, S Kum&Go/dsl/e85 Freddie's Rest., Subway, Three Amigos Super 8 H, Hunter RV Ctr, Route 66 RV Park
211	OK 33, to Kellyville, Drumright, S Heyburn Lake SP
207mm	**service plaza wb,** Phillips 66/dsl
196	OK 48, Bristow, S Kenny's/dsl, Phillips 66/dsl Mazzio's McDonald's, Pizza Hut, Sonic, Steak'nEgg Rest, Taco Mayo Carolyn Inn $General, $Tree, Ford, O'Reilly Parts Walmart
182mm	**toll plaza**
179	OK 99, to Drumright, Stroud, N Best Western/rest S Kids/dsl, Phillips 66/Subway/dsl 5Star BBQ, Cozumel Mexican, Mazzio's, McDonald's, Sonic Skyliner Motel Sooner Motel H, auto/tire repair, USPO

OK

INTERSTATE 44 Cont'd

Exit#	Services
178mm	**Hoback Plaza both lanes (exits left),** Phillips 66/dsl McDonald's
167mm	**service plaza (from eb), S** Phillips 66/dsl
166	OK 18, to Cushing, Chandler, **S** Phillips 66/dsl B's Rest., Sonic EconoLodge, Lincoln Motel Chandler Tire, Chevrolet/GMC, Ford
158	OK 66, to Wellston, **N** Kum&Go/Subway/dsl/24hr $General
146	Luther-Jones (from eb, no return)
138d	to Memorial Rd, to Enterprise Square
138a	I-35, I-44 E to Tulsa, Turner Tpk
I-44 and I-35 run together 8 mi. See I-35, exits 137-134.	
135mm	**Turner Tpk begins eb, ends wb.**
130	I-35 S, to Dallas, access to services on I-35 S
129	MLK Ave, Remington Park, **N** Park Hill Inn Cowboy Museum, **S** McDonald's, Sonic, Subway Family$
128b	Kelley Ave, OK City, **N** Conoco, VP/Subway/dsl Gabriella's Italian
128a	Lincoln Blvd, **S** Lincoln Mart/dsl Lincoln Inn Express, Oxford Inn st capitol
127	I-235 S, US 77, City Ctr, Broadway St **N on 63rd St** Conoco/Circle K, Shell/Circle K Best Western, Wyndham Garden URGENT CARE
126	Western Ave, **S** Sleep Inn
125c	NW Expressway (exits left from sb)
125	Classen Blvd, (exits left from wb), OK City, **N** Cheesecake Factory, Chili's, Freebirds Burrito, Jamba Juice, Milagro Mexican, Olive Garden, Pei Wei, Smashburger, Subway, Whiskey Cake Kitchen AT&T, Dillard's, JC Penney, Macy's, Old Navy, Ross, Verizon, Walmart/McDonald's, **S** IHOP, McDonald's Courtyard, Hyatt Place, Travelodge
125a	OK 3A, Penn Ave, to NW Expswy, **N** VP Express, **S** Shell/Circle K Braum's Habana Inn auto/tire repair, Family$
124	N May, **N** Shell/Circle K/Subway San Marco's Mexican Days Inn, Motel 6, Super 8 O'Reilly Parts, Sam's Club/dsl, **S** Valero Dunkin Donuts, Jersey Mike's, Starbucks, Wendy's Aamco, Advance Parts, Family$, Ford, Lowe's
123b	OK 66 W, NW 39th, to Warr Acres, **N** 7-11, Shell, Valero/McDonald's/dsl Braum's, Carl's Jr, Jimmy's Egg, Sonic Carlyle Motel, Hospitality Inn Family$, U-Haul
123a	NW 36th St, **S** Woodspring Suites
122	NW 23rd St, **N** 7-11, Conoco/dsl Church's, EggRoll King Tires+, **S** Conoco Arby's, Sonic Family$
121b a	NW 10th St, **N** Shell, **S** 7-11, Sinclair Subway $General, antiques, fairgrounds, Family$, Whittaker's Foods
120b a	I-40, W to Amarillo, E to Ft Smith
119	SW 15th St
118	OK 152 W, SW 29th St, OK City, **E** 7-11, Shamrock A&W/LJ Silver, Burger King, China Panda, CiCi's Pizza, KFC/Taco Bell, McDonald's, Pizza Hut, Sonic, Subway, Taco Bueno $General, $Tree, Advance Parts, AT&T, AutoZone, Buy-4-Less Foods, city park, O'Reilly Parts, Walgreens, **W** Alon/dsl city park, transmissions, U-Haul/LP
117	SW 44th St, **W** auto repair
116b	Airport Rd (exits left from nb), **W**
116a	SW 59th St, **E** Conoco/Circle K Pizza Inn, Subway, Taco Mayo Family$, **W** Will Rogers Airport
115	I-240 E, US 62 E, to Ft Smith
114	SW 74th St, OK City, **E** Nova, Valero/dsl Braum's, Burger King, Perry's Rest. Cambridge Inn, Knights Inn $General

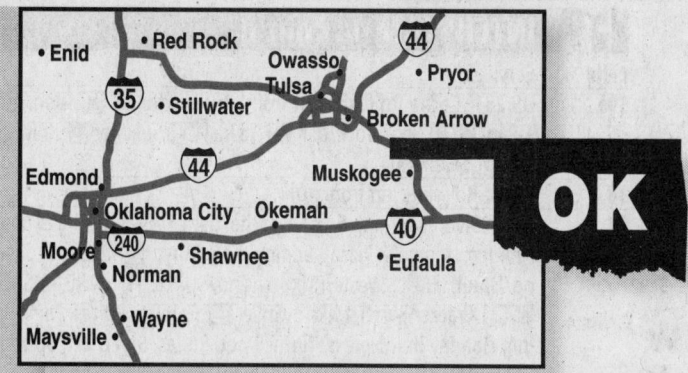

OKLAHOMA CITY

Enid
Red Rock
Owasso
Pryor
Tulsa
Stillwater
Broken Arrow
Edmond
Muskogee
Oklahoma City
Okemah
Moore
Shawnee
Eufaula
Norman
Wayne
Maysville
44
35
240
40
OK

Exit#	Services
113	SW 89th St, **E** 7-11, Loves/Subway/dsl, OG, Valero/dsl Sonic H, CVS Drug
112	SW 104th St, **E** Valero
111	SW 119th St, **E** Little Caesar's, Sonic
110	OK 37 E, to Moore, **E** H
109	SW 149th St, **E** JR's Grill
108mm	S Canadian River
108	OK 37 W, to Tuttle, **W** Conoco/dsl, Phillips 66/dsl Arby's, Braum's, Carlito's Mexican, Jimmy's Egg, KFC/Taco Bell, Little Caesars, Mazzio's, McDonald's, New China, Sonic $General, AT&T, AutoZone, O'Reilly Parts, URGENT CARE, Verizon, Walgreens, Walmart/Subway
107	US 62 S (no wb return), to Newcastle, **E** Comfort Inn, Newcastle Motel casino, Newcastle RV, **S** Loves/Subway/Dunkin Donuts/dsl/scales/24hr
99	H E Bailey Spur, rd 4, to Blanchard, Tuttle, Norman
97mm	**toll booth,**
85.5mm	**service plaza, both lanes exit left,** Phillips 66/dsl McDonald's
83	US 62, Chickasha, **W** Jay's/dsl, Valero/dsl Southern Plains Indian Museum
80	US 81, Chickasha, **E** Phillips 66/Circle K/dsl, Shell/dsl Eduardo's Mexican, Jake's Rib, La Fiesta Mexican, Western Sizzlin Best Value Inn, Hampton Inn, Holiday Inn Express, Maverick Inn, Super 8 Buick/GMC, Cadillac/Chevrolet, Chrysler/Dodge/Jeep, vet, **W** Loves/dsl, Murphy USA/dsl, Valero Arby's, Braum's, Chicken Express, China Dream, China Moon, Domino's, KFC, LJ Silver, Mazzio's Pizza, McDonald's, Napoli's Rest., New China, Pizza Hut, Sakura Japanese, Sonic, Subway, Taco Bell, Taco Mayo Quality Inn, Ranch House Motel H, $General, Ace Hardware, AT&T, AutoZone, Chickasha RV Park, CVS Drug, Ford, Griffith's Repair, O'Reilly Parts, Ralph&Son's Tires/repair, Save-A-Lot Foods, Staples, Verizon, Walgreens, Walmart/Subway
78mm	**toll plaza,**
62	to Cyril (from wb)
53	US 277, Elgin, Lake Ellsworth, **E** Shamrock, Valero/McDonald's/dsl Billy Sim's BBQ, China Garden, Sonic, Subway $General, Family$, tires
46	US 62 E, US 277, US 281, to Elgin, Apache, Comanche Tribe, **last free exit eb**
45	OK 49, to Medicine Park, **W** Loves/Subway/dsl/24hr Burger King, Sonic $General, Wichita NWR
41	to Ft Sill, Key Gate, **W** Ft Sill Museum
40c	Gate 2, to Ft Sill
40a	to Cache
39	US 62 W, to Cache, **E** Alon/dsl, **W** Knights Inn
39b	US 281 (from sb), same as 39a

CHICKASHA

OK

LAWTON

INTERSTATE 44 Cont'd

Exit#	Services
39a	US 281, Cache Rd (exits left from nb), Lawton, **E** Alon/dsl, **1-3 mi W** Shamrock/dsl, Valero/dsl Subway Knights Inn $General
38	Cache Rd (exits left from nb)
37	Gore Blvd, Lawton, **E** Apache/dsl Braum's, Los Tres Amigos, Marco's Pizza, Sonic, Taco Mayo Apache Casino/Hotel, Best Western casino, URGENT CARE, USPO, **W** Cracker Barrel, Mike's Grille Comfort Suites, Fairfield Inn, Holiday Inn Express, Homewood Suites, Sleep Inn, SpringHill Suites Chrysler/Dodge/Jeep, Harley-Davidson
36a	OK 7, Lee Blvd, Lawton, **E** Phillips 66/dsl, **W** Alon/dsl/repair, Barefoot/dsl, Shamrock/dsl, WMS/dsl Big Chef Rest., Braum's, Burger King, KFC/Taco Bell, Leo&Ken's Rest., McDonald's, Salas Mexican, Sonic Motel 6 H, $General, Advance Parts, CVS Drug, vet, Walgreens
33	US 281, 11th St, Lawton, **W**
30	OK 36 (last free exit sb), Geronimo
20.5mm	**Elmer Graham Plaza (both lanes exit left),** Phillips 66/dsl McDonald's info
20	OK 5, to Walters
19.5mm	**toll plaza**
5	US 277 N, US 281, Randlett, last free exit nb
1	OK 36, to Grandfield, **E** Comanche Nation TP/dsl, **W** casino
0mm	Oklahoma/Texas state line, Red River

OKLAHOMA CITY

INTERSTATE 240 (Oklahoma City)

Exit#	Services
16mm	**I-240 begins/ends on I-40.**
14	Anderson Rd, **S** Conoco/dsl
11b a	Douglas Blvd, **N** Tinker AFB
9	Air Depot Blvd
8	OK 77, Sooner Rd, **N** Phillips 66/dsl/CNG/e85 Sonic URGENT CARE, **S** Phillips 66/Popeye's/dsl, Valero/McDonald's/dsl H
7	Sunnylane Ave, **S** Valero/Subway/dsl Woodspring Suites
6	Bryant Ave
5	S Eastern Ave
4c	Pole Rd, **N** Burger King, Subway, TX Roadhouse Fairfield Inn, Magnuson Hotel, Residence Inn
4b a	I-35, N to OK City, S to Dallas, US 77 S, US 62/77 N
3b	S Shields, **N** Valero/dsl Braum's Chrysler/Dodge/Jeep, Home Depot, **S** Discount Tire, Nissan, Subaru
3a	S Santa Fe, **N** Kia, **S** Murphy USA/dsl Chili's, IHOP, Jersey Mike's, Panda Express Lowe's, Staples, Walmart/McDonald's
2b	S Walker Ave, **N** 7-11, Shell/Circle K Johnnie's Broiler, Rib Crib, **S** Burger Joint, Carino's, ChuckeCheese, City Bites, Jimmy's Egg Grill, On-the-Border Holiday Inn Express PepBoys
2a	S Western Ave, **N** 7-11, Conoco Braum's, Burger King, CiCi's Pizza, House of Szechwan, Taste of China $General, Advance Parts, Hyundai, Tires+, vet, **S** 7-11, Valero/dsl A&W/LJ Silver, Chick-fil-A, Garage Burgers, Grandy's, Hibachi Buffet, Jimmy John's, KFC, McDonald's, Popeye's, Red Lobster Best Western, Comfort Inn, Hampton Inn, Home 2 Suites, Quality Inn Chevrolet, Honda, Office Depot
1c	S Penn Ave, **N** Conoco/dsl Cane's, Carl's Jr, Charleston's Rest., Denny's, Golden Corral, Hooters, Old Chicago Pizza, Olive Garden, Outback Steaks, Pioneer Pies, SaltGrass Steaks, Schlotsky's AT&T, Best Buy, BigLots, GNC, Green Acres Mkt, Hobby Lobby, Marshall's, Michaels, Old Navy, Petsmart, Ross, Verizon, **S** Shell/Circle K Hunan Buffet, Joe's Crabshack, Mazzio's, Papa John's, Starbucks, Subway, Taco Bueno, Western Sizzlin $Tree, URGENT CARE
1b	S May Ave, **N** 7-11/gas Abel's Mexican, Jack-in-the-Box, New Mandarin, Taco Bell, Waffle House O'Reilly Parts, **S** Nova, Valero/dsl Braum's, Burger King, Perry's Rest. Cambridge Inn, Knights Inn $General
1a	I-44, US 62, **I-240 begins ends on I-44.**

OREGON

PORTLAND

INTERSTATE 5

Exit#	Services
308.5mm	Oregon/Washington state line, Columbia River
308	Jansen Beach Dr, **E** Chevron/dsl Burger King, Hooters, Starbucks, Taco Bell Oxford Suites, Red Lion Safeway, **W** BJ's Rest., Bradley's Grill, CJ's Deli, Denny's, Jersey Mike's, Jimmy John's, McDonald's, Panera Bread, Stanford's Rest., Starbucks, Subway Best Buy, Burlington Coats, GNC, Home Depot, Jansen Beach RV Park, Michael's, Old Navy, PetCo, Ross, Staples, Target, TJ Maxx, Verizon
307	OR 99E S, MLK Blvd, Union Ave, Marine Dr (sb only), **E** 76/dsl, Jubitz Trvl Ctr/rest/dsl/@ Pizza Mia, Portland Cascade Grill, Subway Courtyard, Fairfield Inn, Portlander Inn, Residence Inn Blue Beacon, truck repair, **W** Expo Ctr
306b	Interstate Ave, Delta Park, **E** Arco Burger King, Burrito House, Elmer's, Mars Meadows Chinese, Shari's Best Western, Days Inn, Motel 6 $Tree, Baxter Parts, Dick's, Lowe's, Portland Meadows, vet, Walmart
306a	Columbia (from nb), same as 306b
305b a	US 30, Lombard St (from nb, no return), **E** Little Caesar's **W** Astro/dsl, Shell/dsl Panda Express, Subway, Wendy's Fred Meyer
304	Rosa Parks Way, **W** 76/dsl, Arco Nite Hawk Cafe Viking Motel U of Portland
303	Alberta St, Swan Island, **E** H, **W** Subway, Taco Bell Monticello Motel, Westerner Motel CarQuest
302b	I-405, US 30 W, **W** to ocean beaches
302a	Rose Qtr, City Ctr, **E** 76/Circle K/dsl, Shell/dsl Bellagio's Pizza, Burger King, Chipotle Mexican, Jersey Mike's, McDonald's, Muchas Gracias, Qdoba Mexican, Starbucks, Wendy's Courtyard, Crowne Plaza, Shiloh Inn H, 7-11, Kia, Schwab Tire, Toyota, Verizon, Walgreens, **W** coliseum
301	I-84 E, US 30 E, **services E off I-84 exits**
300	US 26 E (from sb), Milwaukie Ave, **W** Hilton, Marriott
299b	I-405, US 26 W, to city ctr
299a	US 26 E, OR 43 (from nb), City Ctr, to Lake Oswego
298	Corbett Ave
297	Terwilliger Blvd, **W** Baja Fresh, KFC, La Costita, Starbucks H, Fred Meyer, to Lewis and Clark Coll.

OK OR

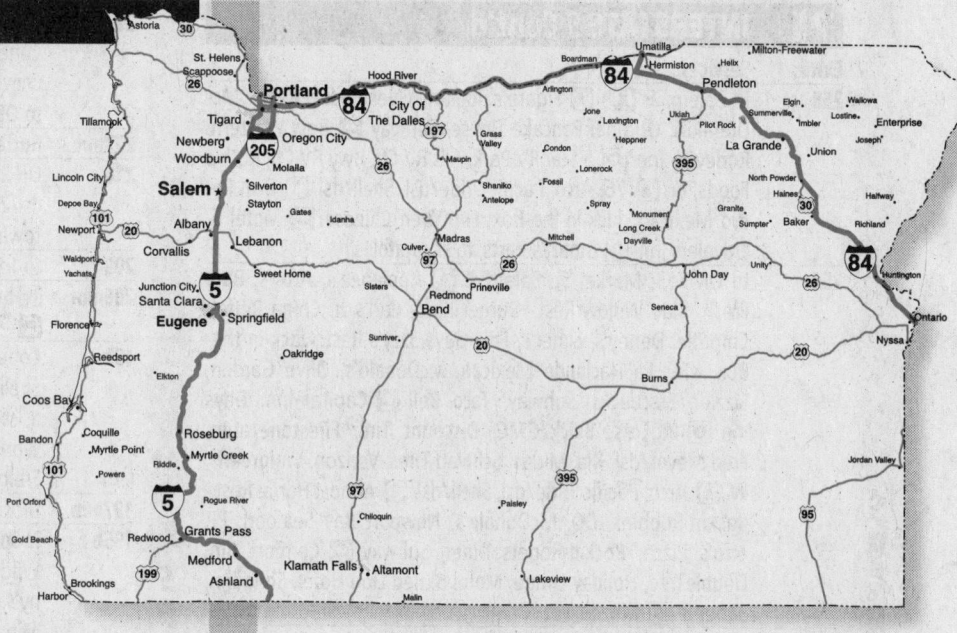

INTERSTATE 5 Cont'd

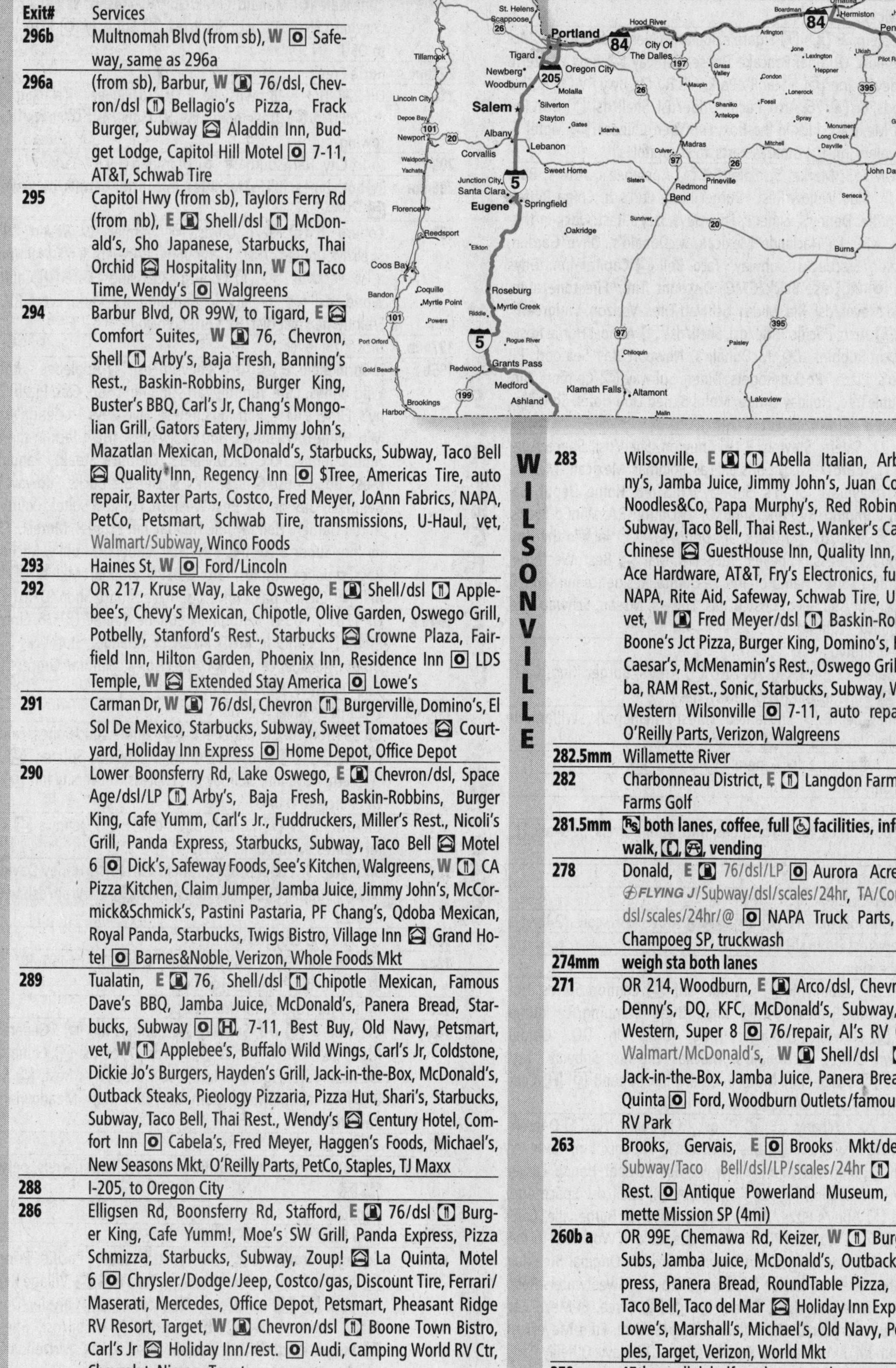

Exit#	Services
296b	Multnomah Blvd (from sb), W Safeway, same as 296a
296a	(from sb), Barbur, W 76/dsl, Chevron/dsl Bellagio's Pizza, Frack Burger, Subway Aladdin Inn, Budget Lodge, Capitol Hill Motel 7-11, AT&T, Schwab Tire
295	Capitol Hwy (from sb), Taylors Ferry Rd (from nb), E Shell/dsl McDonald's, Sho Japanese, Starbucks, Thai Orchid Hospitality Inn, W Taco Time, Wendy's Walgreens
294	Barbur Blvd, OR 99W, to Tigard, E Comfort Suites, W 76, Chevron, Shell Arby's, Baja Fresh, Banning's Rest., Baskin-Robbins, Burger King, Buster's BBQ, Carl's Jr, Chang's Mongolian Grill, Gators Eatery, Jimmy John's, Mazatlan Mexican, McDonald's, Starbucks, Subway, Taco Bell Quality Inn, Regency Inn $Tree, Americas Tire, auto repair, Baxter Parts, Costco, Fred Meyer, JoAnn Fabrics, NAPA, PetCo, Petsmart, Schwab Tire, transmissions, U-Haul, vet, Walmart/Subway, Winco Foods
293	Haines St, W Ford/Lincoln
292	OR 217, Kruse Way, Lake Oswego, E Shell/dsl Applebee's, Chevy's Mexican, Chipotle, Olive Garden, Oswego Grill, Potbelly, Stanford's Rest., Starbucks Crowne Plaza, Fairfield Inn, Hilton Garden, Phoenix Inn, Residence Inn LDS Temple, W Extended Stay America Lowe's
291	Carman Dr, W 76/dsl, Chevron Burgerville, Domino's, El Sol De Mexico, Starbucks, Subway, Sweet Tomatoes Courtyard, Holiday Inn Express Home Depot, Office Depot
290	Lower Boonsferry Rd, Lake Oswego, E Chevron/dsl, Space Age/dsl/LP Arby's, Baja Fresh, Baskin-Robbins, Burger King, Cafe Yumm, Carl's Jr., Fuddruckers, Miller's Rest., Nicoli's Grill, Panda Express, Starbucks, Subway, Taco Bell Motel 6 Dick's, Safeway Foods, See's Kitchen, Walgreens, W CA Pizza Kitchen, Claim Jumper, Jamba Juice, Jimmy John's, McCormick&Schmick's, Pastini Pastaria, PF Chang's, Qdoba Mexican, Royal Panda, Starbucks, Twigs Bistro, Village Inn Grand Hotel Barnes&Noble, Verizon, Whole Foods Mkt
289	Tualatin, E 76, Shell/dsl Chipotle Mexican, Famous Dave's BBQ, Jamba Juice, McDonald's, Panera Bread, Starbucks, Subway H, 7-11, Best Buy, Old Navy, Petsmart, vet, W Applebee's, Buffalo Wild Wings, Carl's Jr, Coldstone, Dickie Jo's Burgers, Hayden's Grill, Jack-in-the-Box, McDonald's, Outback Steaks, Pieology Pizzaria, Pizza Hut, Shari's, Starbucks, Subway, Taco Bell, Thai Rest., Wendy's Century Hotel, Comfort Inn Cabela's, Fred Meyer, Haggen's Foods, Michael's, New Seasons Mkt, O'Reilly Parts, PetCo, Staples, TJ Maxx
288	I-205, to Oregon City
286	Elligsen Rd, Boonsferry Rd, Stafford, E 76/dsl Burger King, Cafe Yumm!, Moe's SW Grill, Panda Express, Pizza Schmizza, Starbucks, Subway, Zoup! La Quinta, Motel 6 Chrysler/Dodge/Jeep, Costco/gas, Discount Tire, Ferrari/Maserati, Mercedes, Office Depot, Petsmart, Pheasant Ridge RV Resort, Target, W Chevron/dsl Boone Town Bistro, Carl's Jr Holiday Inn/rest. Audi, Camping World RV Ctr, Chevrolet, Nissan, Toyota

WILSONVILLE

Exit#	Services
283	Wilsonville, E Abella Italian, Arby's, Chipotle, Denny's, Jamba Juice, Jimmy John's, Juan Colorado, McDonald's, Noodles&Co, Papa Murphy's, Red Robin, Shari's, Starbucks, Subway, Taco Bell, Thai Rest., Wanker's Café, Wendy's, Wong's Chinese GuestHouse Inn, Quality Inn, SnoozInn $Tree, Ace Hardware, AT&T, Fry's Electronics, funpark, GNC, Honda, NAPA, Rite Aid, Safeway, Schwab Tire, URGENT CARE, USPO, vet, W Fred Meyer/dsl Baskin-Robbins, Biscuits Cafe, Boone's Jct Pizza, Burger King, Domino's, Hunan Kitchen, Little Caesar's, McMenamin's Rest., Oswego Grill, Perfect Pizza, Qdoba, RAM Rest., Sonic, Starbucks, Subway, Wow Burger Best Western Wilsonville 7-11, auto repair, Fred Meyer/dsl, O'Reilly Parts, Verizon, Walgreens
282.5mm	Willamette River
282	Charbonneau District, E Langdon Farms Rest. Langdon Farms Golf
281.5mm	**both lanes, coffee, full facilities, info, litter barrels, petwalk, , , vending**
278	Donald, E 76/dsl/LP Aurora Acres RV Park, W FLYING J/Subway/dsl/scales/24hr, TA/Country Pride/Popeye's/dsl/scales/24hr/@ NAPA Truck Parts, SpeedCo Lube, to Champoeg SP, truckwash
274mm	**weigh sta both lanes**
271	OR 214, Woodburn, E Arco/dsl, Chevron Burger King, Denny's, DQ, KFC, McDonald's, Subway, Taco Bell Best Western, Super 8 76/repair, Al's RV Ctr, vet, Walgreens, Walmart/McDonald's, W Shell/dsl Arby's, Elmer's, Jack-in-the-Box, Jamba Juice, Panera Bread, Starbucks La Quinta Ford, Woodburn Outlets/famous brands, Woodburn RV Park
263	Brooks, Gervais, E Brooks Mkt/deli, W Pilot/Subway/Taco Bell/dsl/LP/scales/24hr Carl's Jr., Chalet Rest. Antique Powerland Museum, Freightliner, Willamette Mission SP (4mi)
260b a	OR 99E, Chemawa Rd, Keizer, W Burger King, Firehouse Subs, Jamba Juice, McDonald's, Outback Steaks, Panda Express, Panera Bread, RoundTable Pizza, Starbucks, Subway, Taco Bell, Taco del Mar Holiday Inn Express AT&T, GNC, Lowe's, Marshall's, Michael's, Old Navy, PetCo, REI, Ross, Staples, Target, Verizon, World Mkt
259mm	45th parallel, halfway between the equator and N Pole

OR

INTERSTATE 5 Cont'd

Exit#	Services
258	N Salem, E Figaro's Italian, Guesthouse Rest., McDonald's, Original Pancake House, Subway Best Western, Rodeway Inn 5 Star RV Park, Al's RV Ctr, Hwy RV Ctr, Roth's Foods, W 76, Arco, Pacific Pride/dsl, Shell/dsl Don Pedro Mexican, Jack-in-the-Box, LumYuen Chinese Motel 6, Travelers Inn Stuart's Parts, to st capitol
256	to OR 213, Market St, Salem, E Applebee's, Arby's, Baja Fresh, Blue Willow Rest., Burger King, Carl's Jr, China Buffet, Chipotle, Denny's, Elmer's, Five Guys, Izzy's Rest., Jack-in-the-Box, KFC, La Hacienda Mexican, McDonald's, Olive Garden, Sizzler, Starbucks, Subway, Taco Bell Capital Inn, Days Inn BigLots, Buick/GMC, Discount Tire, Firestone/auto, Fred Meyer/dsl, Kia, Midas, Schwab Tires, Verizon, Walgreens, W Arco, Pacific Pride/dsl, Shell/dsl Almost Home Rest., Baskin-Robbins, DQ, McDonald's, Newport Bay Seafood, Pietro's Pizza, Rockin-Rogers Diner, Subway Comfort Inn, DoubleTree, Holiday Lodge, Motel 6, Red Lion Hotel, Shilo Inn, Super 8 Mazda, vet
253	OR 22, Salem, Stayton, E Chevron, Shell/dsl, Space Age/dsl Burger King, Carls Jr, Las Polomas Mexican, McDonalds/playplace, Shari's, Subway $Tree, Home Depot, Salem Camping/RV Park, ShopKO, to Detroit RA, WinCo Foods, W Shell/dsl Carl's Jr, Denny's, DQ, Jack-in-the-Box, Panda Express, Popeyes, Taco Del Mar Best Western+, Comfort Suites, Hampton Inn, La Quinta, Residence Inn H, AAA, Chrysler/Jeep, Costco/gas, Lowe's, Nissan, Schwab Tire, st police, Walmart
252	Kuebler Blvd
249	to Salem, 2 mi W 76, Arco Arby's, Burger King, Carl's Jr Phoenix Inn Safeway/gas
248	Sunnyside, E Enchanted Forest Themepark, Willamette Valley Vineyards, W Pacific Pride/dsl
244	to N Jefferson, E Emerald Valley RV Park
243	Ankeny Hill
242	Talbot Rd
241mm	**both lanes, full facilities, info, litter barrels, petwalk,**
240.5mm	Santiam River
239	Dever-Conner
238	S Jefferson, Scio, W Loves/Arby's/dsl/scales/24hr
237	Viewcrest (from sb)
235	Millersburg
234	OR 99E, Albany, E Cascade Grill Comfort Suites, Holiday Inn Express , Knox Butte Camping/RV dump, W Chevron Burger King, Carl's Jr, DQ, Golden Town Buffet, McDonald's, Muchas Gracias, Subway, Taco Bell Budget Inn, Motel 6, Quality Inn, Super 8 H, Costco/gas, Kohl's, NAPA, to Albany Hist Dist
233	US 20, Albany, E 76/dsl, Chevron/dsl/LP Denny's, LumYuen Chinese Best Western+, Phoenix Inn, Rodeway Inn Blue Ox RV Park, Chevrolet, Home Depot, Honda, Lassen RV Ctr, st police, Toyota, Walmart, W Shell/dsl, Space Age/dsl Abby's Pizza, Arby's, Baskin-Robbins, Burgerville, Carl's Jr, El Trio Loco, Elmer's, Fox Den Pizza, Golden Wok, Jack-in-the-Box, Los Dos Amigos, Los Tequilos Mexican, Original Breakfast Cafe, Pizza Hut, Sizzler, Skipper's, Starbucks, Sweetwaters Rest., Taco Time, Wendy's Valu Inn H, $Tree, Bi-Mart, CarQuest, Chrysler/Dodge/Hyundai/Jeep/Subaru, Fred Meyer/dsl, Hyundai, JoAnn Fabrics, Knechts's Parts, Old Navy, O'Reilly Parts, Rite Aid, Ross, Schwab Tires, Staples, Target, Walgreens
228	OR 34, to Lebanon, Corvallis, E 76/dsl, Leather's/dsl Pine Cone Cafe Mallard Creek Golf/RV Resort, W Arco/dsl, Chevron/CFN/A&W/dsl, Shell/dsl Subway KOA (5mi), to OSU
222mm	Butte Creek
216	OR 228, Halsey, Brownsville, E 76/Pioneer Villa TrkStp/deli/dsl/24hr/@ Travelodge, W Mobil/dsl parts/repair/towing
209	to Jct City, Harrisburg, W Diamond Hill RV Park
206mm	**both lanes, full facilities, info, litter barrels, petwalk,**
199	Coburg, E Fuel'n Go/dsl Premier RV Resort, W Shell/McDonald's/dsl, TA/Country Pride/Truck'n'Travel Motel/dsl/scales/24hr/@ Coburg Crossing Cafe Camping World, dsl repair, Eugene Kamping RV Park, Evert RV Ctr, Freightliner, hist dist, RV Corral, Volvo
197mm	McKenzie River
195b a	N Springfield, E Arco, Chevron/dsl Applebee's, Buffalo Wild Wings, Cafe Yummi, Carl's Jr, China Sun, Ciao Pizza, Denny's, Elmer's Rest., FarMan Chinese, Five Guys, Hacienda Amigo Mio, HomeTown Buffet, Hop Valley Rest., IHOP, Jack-in-the-Box, Jimmy John's, KFC, McDonald's, Outback Steaks, Panda Express, Roadhouse Grill, Shari's, Sizzler, Starbucks, Subway, Taco Bell, Taco Grande Best Western, Comfort Suites, Courtyard, Hilton Garden, Holiday Inn, Holiday Inn Express, Motel 6, Quality Inn, Super 8 H, Best Buy, Cabela's, Kohl's, Michael's, Ross, st police, Staples, Target, USPO, Walmart Mkt, W Taco Bell Costco/gas, Office Depot, Petsmart, ShopKO, to
194b a	OR 126 E, I-105 W, Springfield, Eugene, **1 mi** W 76, Chevron, Mobil Carl's Jr, MOD Pizza, PF Chang's, Starbucks La Quinta, Residence Inn Albertson's, Natural Grocers, Nissan, Old Navy, Subaru, U Of O
193mm	Willamette River
192	OR 99 (from nb), to Eugene, E Candlewood Suites, Fairfield Inn, W House Of Chen, Starbucks, Subway Best Western, Days Inn, Holiday Inn Express, University Inn Mkt Of Choice, to U of O
191	Glenwood, W 76/dsl, Shell/dsl/LP Denny's Comfort Suites, Motel 6
189	30th Ave S, Eugene, E Shell/dsl/LP Harley-Davidson, NW RV Supply, Shamrock RV Park, W Chevron/dsl, SeQuntial/dsl
188b	OR 99 S (nb only), Goshen
188a	OR 58, OR 99 S to Oakridge, E Deerwood RV Park, W Pacific Pride/dsl tires
186	Dillard Rd, to Goshen (from nb)
182	Creswell, E DQ, Subway Comfort Inn $General, Bi-Mart, golf, OR RV Ctr, W 76/dsl, Arco/dsl China Wok, Creswell Cafe, Figaro's Pizza, Joe's Diner, TJ's Rest. Super 8 $Tree, Creswell Automotive, Dari Mart, Meadowlark RV Park, NAPA
180mm	Coast Fork of Willamette River
178mm	**both lanes, full facilities, coffee, litter barrels, petwalk,**
176	Saginaw
175mm	Row River
174	Cottage Grove, E Chevron/dsl/repair, Pacific Pride/dsl Arby's, Chalerm Thai, Subway, Taco Bell Village Resort/RV park H, AutoZone, Chevrolet/GMC, Chrysler/Dodge/Jeep, Walmart, W Chevron/dsl/LP, Mobil/dsl, Shell/dsl Burger King, Carl's Jr, Jack-in-the-Box, KFC, McDonald's/RV parking, Papa Murphy's, Pinocchio's Pizza, Taco Time, Torero's

SALEM

ALBANY

SPRINGFIELD

EUGENE

INTERSTATE 5 Cont'd

Exit	Services
174	Continued Mexican, Vintage Rest. Best Western, Quality Inn, Relax Inn $Tree, Bi-Mart Foods, Grocery Outlet, O'Reilly Parts, Safeway/dsl, Walgreens
172	6th St (from sb), Cottage Grove Lake (from sb), **2 mi** W Cottage Grove RV Village
170	to OR 99, London Rd (nb only), Cottage Grove Lake, **6 mi** W Cottage Grove RV Village
163	Curtin, E Stardust Motel antiques, W Pass Creek Park/camping
162	OR 38, OR 99, to Drain, Elkton
161	Anlauf (from nb)
160	Salt Springs Rd
159	Elk Creek, Cox Rd
154	Yoncalla, Elkhead
150	OR 99, to OR 38, Yoncalla, Red Hill, W Eagle Valley RV Park
148	Rice Hill, E Arco/LP, FLYING J/Denny's/Subway/dsl/scales/24hr, Pacific Pride/dsl Ranch Rest. Ranch Motel, Rodeway Inn Rice Hill RV Park, towing/dsl repair, W K-R Drive-In
146	Rice Valley
144mm	**sb, full facilities, litter barrels, petwalk,**
143mm	**nb, full facilities, litter barrels, petwalk,**
142	Metz Hill
140	OR 99 (from sb), Oakland, E Tolly's Rest. Oakland Hist Dist
138	OR 99 (from nb), Oakland, E Tolly's Rest. Oakland Hist Dist
136	OR 138W, Sutherlin, E Chevron/dsl, Mobil/dsl Abby's Pizza, Apple Peddler Rest., Burger King, Domino's, McDonald's, Papa Murphy's, Pedotti's Italian, Sol de Sutherlin, Yummy House Best Western+, Motel 6, Relax Inn $Tree, Autocare, AutoZone, I-5 RV Ctr, NAPA, W Shell/dsl Dakota St Pizza, DQ, Si Casa Flores, Starbucks, Subway, Taco Bell Hi-Way Haven RV Camp, Umpqua RV Park
135	Wilbur, Sutherlin, E CFN/dsl, Shell/dsl/LP vet
129	OR 99, Winchester, E Del Ray Cafe Kamper Korner RV Ctr (1mi), Rivers Edge RV Park, st police
129mm	N Umpqua River, N Umpqua River
127	Stewart Pkwy, Edenbower Rd, N Roseburg, E Shell/dsl Shari's Rest., Subway Motel 6, Super 8 Costco/gas, Home Depot, Honda, Lowe's, Mt Nebo RV Park, Verizon, W Mobil, Valero/dsl Applebee's, Del Taco, McDonald's/playplace, Red Robin, Subway, Yummy Chinese Sleep Inn H, Albertson's, Big O Tire, Macy's, Sherm's Foods, vet, Walmart
125	Garden Valley Blvd, Roseburg, E Abby's Pizza, China Buffet, Elmer's, Gilberto's Mexican, Jack-in-the-Box, KFC, Los Dos Amigo's Mexican, McDonald's, Smokin' Friday BBQ, Sonic, Subway, Taco Bell Comfort Inn, Hampton Inn, Quality Inn AT&T, AutoZone, BigLots, Buick/Chevrolet/GMC, Ford/Lincoln, Honda, NAPA, Safeway/dsl, Toyota, U-Haul, Verizon, vet, Walgreens, W Shell/LP/repair Burger King, Carl's Jr, Fox Den Pizza, Panda Express, Pita Pit, Rodeo Steaks, RoundTable Pizza, Si Casa Flores Mexican, Sizzler, Starbucks, Wendy's Best Western, Days Inn H, $Tree, Bi-Mart Foods, Fred Meyer/dsl, JC Penney, JoAnn Fabrics, Marshall's, Michael's, O'Reilly Parts, PetCo, Rite Aid, Ross, Staples, Walgreens
124	OR 138, Roseburg, City Ctr, E Chevron/dsl, Texaco/dsl Denny's Baymont Inn, Holiday Inn Express, Rodeway Inn, Travelodge Rite Aid, W 76/dsl, Mobil/dsl Charley's BBQ, Domino's, KFC/LJ Silver, Pete's Drive-In, Subway, Taco Time Grocery Outlet, Harvard Ave Drug

SUTHERLIN

ROSEBURG

Exit	Services
123	Roseburg, E camping, museum, to Umpqua Park
121	McLain Ave
120.5mm	S Umpqua River
120	OR 99 N (no EZ nb return), Green District, Roseburg, E Rodeway Inn, Shady Oaks Motel, W auto repair
119	OR 99 S, OR 42 W, Winston, E Ingram Dist., W Chevron/A&W/dsl, Loves/Arby's/dsl/scales/LP/24hr, Shell/dsl McDonald's, Papa Murphy's, Subway, Taco Bell $General, Ray's Foods, Rising River RV Park, Western Star RV Park
113	Clarks Branch Rd, Round Prairie, W Quikstop Motel On the River RV Park (2mi)
112.5mm	S Umpqua River, S Umpqua River
112	OR 99, OR 42, Dillard, E Rivers West RV Park
111mm	**weigh sta both directions**
110	Boomer Hill Rd
108	Myrtle Creek, E Chevron Armando's Mexican, Golf Course Cafe, Subway, Tommy's Cafe city park, Myrtle Creek RV Park, Ray's Foods
106	Weaver Rd
103	Tri City, Myrtle Creek, E Tri-City RV Park, W Chevron/A&W/dsl, Pacific Pride McDonald's
102	Gazley Rd, E Surprise Valley RV Park (1mi)
101.5mm	S Umpqua River
101	Riddle, Stanton Park, W camping
99	Canyonville, E Penny Pincher Burger King, El Paraiso 7 Feathers Hotel/casino, Riverside Motel Canyon Mkt, city park, W 7 Feathers Trkstp/café/dsl/scales/24hr/@ Creekside Rest. Holiday Inn Express 7 Feathers RV Resort,
98	OR 99, Canyonville, Days Creek, E Arco/dsl, Mobil/dsl Ken's Cafe, Papa Morgan's Rest., Subway Leisure Inn $General, auto repair, Canyonville Hardware, NAPA, Ray's Foods, USPO, vet, W museum
95	Canyon Creek
90mm	Canyon Creek Pass, elevation 2020
88	Azalea
86	Barton Rd, Quine's Creek, E Quines Creek/dsl Heaven on Earth Rest./rest., Meadow Wood RV Park (3mi)
83	Barton Rd (from nb), E Meadow Wood RV Park/camping
80	Glendale, W Cow Creek/Lp/Rest.
79.5mm	Stage Road Pass, elevation 1830
78	Speaker Rd (from sb)
76	Wolf Creek, W 76/deli/dsl, Pacific Pride/dsl, Shell/dsl Wolf Creek Inn Rest. Creekside RV park, USPO
74mm	Smith Hill Summit, elevation 1730
71	Sunny Valley, E Covered Bridge Store/gas, W Sunny Valley RV Park/motel
69mm	Sexton Mtn Pass, elevation 1960

INTERSTATE 5 Cont'd

GRANTS PASS

Exit#	Services
66	Hugo, E KOA, W Pottsville Museum (3mi)
63mm	**both lanes, full facilities, info, litter barrels, petwalk, vending**
61	Merlin, W Valero/dsl $General, Almeda RV Park, Beaver Creek RV Resort (2mi), OR RV Ctr, Ray's Foods, repair
58	OR 99, to US 199, Grants Pass, W 76/Circle K/dsl, CFN/dsl, Chevron, Mobil/dsl, Shell/dsl/repair, TownePump Gas Black Bear Diner, Burger King, Carl's Jr, China Hut, Denny's, DQ, In-N-Out, Jack-in-the-Box, McDonald's, Muchas Gracias Mexican, Nano's Mexican, Papa Murphy's, Sizzler, Subway, Taco Bell, Uptown Grill, Wendy's Best Way Inn, Buona Sera Inn, Hampton Inn, Hawks Inn, La Quinta, Motel 6, Quality Inn, Red Lion Inn, Redwood Motel, Sunset Inn, Super 8, SweetBreeze Inn, Travelodge H, $Tree, AutoZone, Chevrolet/Honda, Chrysler/Dodge/Jeep, Jack's RV Resort, Nissan, repair, Rouge Valley RV Park, Schwab Tire, st police, towing
55	US 199, Redwood Hwy, E Grants Pass, W Arco/dsl, Mobil/dsl Abby's Pizza, Applebee's, Arby's, Carl's Jr, Elmer's, Jersey Mike's, KFC, Kobe Buffet, La Burrita, McDonald's, MOD Pizza, Panda Express, Pizza Hut, Shari's, Si Casa Flores Mexican, Starbucks, Subway, Taco Bell Best Western, Holiday Inn Express H, $Tree, Albertson's, AT&T, BigLots, Fred Meyer/dsl, Grocery Outlet, Home Depot, Jo-Ann, Moon Mtn RV Park (2mi), O'Reilly Parts, Petco, Rite Aid, RiverPark RV Park (4mi), Ross, Siskiyou RV Ctr, Staples, Verizon, Walmart, Winco Foods
48	Rogue River, E 76/dsl, Chevron/Circle K/dsl Abby's Pizza, Cottage Cafe, Homestead Rest., Subway $General, Ace Hardware, auto repair, Rogue River RA, vet, W La Guayacama, Mkt Basket Deli Bella Rosa Inn, Best Western Bridgeview RV Park, Chinook Winds RV Park, visitors ctr/info, Whispering Pines RV Park
45b	**W Valley of the Rogue SP/ both lanes, camping, full facilities, litter barrels, petwalk,**
45mm	Rogue River
45a	OR 99, Savage Rapids Dam, E Cypress Grove RV Park
43	OR 99, OR 234, to Crater Lake, Gold Hill, E RoadRiver B&B, Rock Point RV Park
40	OR 99, OR 234, Gold Hill, E Figaro's Pizza $General, KOA, Lazy Acres Motel/RV Park, Running Salmon RV Park, W Dardanelle's/gas Dardanelle's Trailer Park
35	OR 99, Blackwell Rd, Central Point, **2-4 mi** W gas food lodging Jacksonville Nat Hist Landmark, st police
33	Central Point, E Chevron, LNG, Pilot/Subway/Taco Bell/dsl/scales/24hr Burger King, KFC, Shari's Rest., Sonic Candlewood Suites (2mi), Courtyard (2mi), Holiday Inn Express, La Quinta, Super 8 Costco/dsl, funpark, W 76/Circle K/dsl, Shell/dsl Abby's Pizza, Little Caesar's, Mazatlan Mexican, McDonald's Albertson's, AT&T, USPO
30	OR 62, to Crater Lake, Medford, E Arco, Chevron/dsl, Witham Trkstp/rest./dsl/24hr/@ Abby's Pizza, Applebee's, Asian Grill, Baskin Robbins, Buffalo Wild Wings, Burger King, Carl's Jr, Del Taco, Denny's, DQ, Elmer's, McDonald's, Olive Garden, Outback Steaks, Panda Express, Papa John's, Papa Murphy's, Pita Pit, Pizza Hut, Red Robin, RoundTable Pizza, Sizzler, Sonic, Starbucks, Subway, Taco Bell, Taco Delite, Thai Bistro, TX Roadhouse, Wayback Burger, Wendy's Comfort Inn, Hampton Inn, Motel 6, Quality Inn, Ramada, Rogue Regency Hotel, Shilo Inn H, $Tree, AT&T, AutoZone, Barnes&Noble, Best Buy, BigLots, Bi-Mart, Chevrolet/Buick/GMC, Discount Tire, Food4Less, Ford/Lincoln, Fred Meyer/dsl, Hobby Lobby, JoAnn,

MEDFORD

Exit#	Services
30	Continued Lowe's, Mazda, Mercedes, Michael's, NAPA, Office Depot, Old Navy, O'Reilly Parts, Petsmart, Ross, Safeway, Schwab Tire, st police, Subaru, TJ Maxx, USPO, Verizon, vet, Walmart/Subway, W 76/dsl, Spirit/dsl Chipotle, In-n-Out, Jack-in-the-Box, Kaleidoscope Pizza, KFC, MOD Pizza, Red Lobster, Subway, Wendy's CarQuest, JC Penney, Kohl's, Macy's, Natural Grocers, Petco, REI, Target, Toyota, Trader Joe's, Verizon
27	Barnett Rd, Medford, E Black Bear Diner, DQ Best Western, Days Inn/rest., Hilton Garden, Homewood Suites, Motel 6, Travelers Inn H, W 76/Circle K/dsl, Chevron/dsl Abby's Pizza, Arby's, Burger King, Carl's Jr, Domino's, El Arriero Mexican, HomeTown Buffet, Jack-in-the-Box, KFC, McDonald's, McGrath's FishHouse, Panda Express, Pizza Hut, Rooster's Rest., Shari's, Starbucks, Subway, Taco Bell, Wendy's Comfort Inn, Holiday Inn Express, Medford Inn, Royal Crest Motel, Sovana Inn, SpringHill Suites, TownePlace Suites $Tree, AT&T, Fred Meyer/dsl, GNC, Grocery Outlet, Harry&David's, O'Reilly Parts, Staples, Verizon, Walgreens, Walmart/McDonald's, WinCo Foods
24	Phoenix, E Petro/Iron Skillet/dsl/scales/RV dump/24hr/@, Shell/dsl Best Value/PearTree RV park Home Depot, Peterbilt, W Chevron/Circle K/dsl Amigos Mexican, Angelo's Pizza, Jack-in-the-Box, McDonald's auto repair, Harley Davidson, Holiday RV Park, Ray's Foods, Rite Aid

ASHLAND

Exit#	Services
22mm	**sb, full facilities, litter barrels, petwalk, vending**
21	Talent, W 76/dsl, Chevron/dsl Subway GoodNight Inn $General, Ashland Talent RV Resort, vet
19	Valley View Rd, Ashland, W 76/dsl, Pacific Pride/dsl, Shell/dsl/LP Burger King, El Tapatio Mexican Comfort Inn, EconoLodge/RV Park Acura, Chevrolet, Ford
18mm	**weigh sta both lanes**
14	OR 66, to Klamath Falls, Ashland, E Chevron/dsl, Mobil/dsl/LP, Valero/dsl El Paraiso Mexican, OakTree Rest. Ashland Hills Inn & Suites, Best Western, Holiday Inn Express, Relax Inn Emigrant Lake Camping (3mi), Glenyan RV Park (3mi), W Arco, Shell Señor Sam's Mexican, Subway, Taco Bell, Wendy's, Wild Goose Cafe Rodeway Inn, Super 8 H, $Tree, Albertson's, AT&T, Bi-Mart, CarQuest, Rite Aid, Schwab Tire, Shop'n Kart, U-Haul, vet
12	**nb, full facilities**
11	OR 99, Siskiyou Blvd (nb only, no return)
6	to Mt Ashland, E Callahan's Siskiyou Lodge/rest. ski area
4mm	Siskiyou Summit, elevation 4310, brake check both lanes
1	to Siskiyou Summit (from nb, no return)
0mm	Oregon/California state line

INTERSTATE 84

ONTARIO

Exit#	Services
378mm	Oregon/Idaho state line, Snake River
377.5mm	**Welcome Ctr wb, full facilities, info, litter barrels, petwalk vending**
376b a	US 30, to US 20/26, Ontario, Payette, N Chevron/dsl A&W/KFC, Burger King, Carl's Jr, China Buffet, Country Kitchen, Denny's, Domino's, DQ, Dutch Bros Coffee, Little Caesar's, McDonald's, Panda Express, Papa Murphy's, Starbucks, Subway, Taco Time, Wingers Best Western, Clarion Motel 6, Quality Inn, Red Lion Inn, Sleep Inn $Tree, AT&T GNC, Home Depot, st police, Staples, Toyota, Verizon, Walgreens, Walmart/Subway, Waremart, S Pilot/Arby's dsl/scales/24hr, Sinclair/dsl East Side Cafe, Gandolfo's Deli

INTERSTATE 84 Cont'd

376b a	Continued Ogawa's Japanese, Sweet Caroline's, Taco Bell Holiday Inn Express, OR Trail Motel, Stockman's Motel, Super 8, Commercial Tire, Les Schwab Tire, NAPA
374	US 30, OR 201, to Ontario, N to Ontario SP, S Loves /Chester's/Subway/dsl/scales/24hr/@, Pacific Pride Budget Inn
373.5mm	Malheur River
371	Stanton Blvd, **2 mi** S to correctional institution
362	Moores Hollow Rd
356	OR 201, to Weiser, ID, **3 mi** N Catfish Junction RV Park, Oasis RV Park
354.5mm	**weigh sta eb**
353	US 30, to Huntington, N info, RV camping, to Farewell Bend SP, **weigh sta wb**
351mm	Pacific/Mountain time zone
345	US 30, Lime, Huntington, **1 mi** N gas food lodging to Snake River Area, Van Ornum BFD
342	Lime (from eb)
340	Rye Valley
338	Lookout Mountain
337mm	Burnt River
335	to Weatherby, N **both lanes, full facilities, litter barrels, Oregon Trail Info, petwalk, , vending**
330	Plano Rd, to Cement Plant Rd, S cement plant
329mm	**pulloff eb**
327	Durkee, N Co-op/dsl/LP/café
325mm	Pritchard Creek
321mm	Alder Creek
317	to Pleasant Valley (from wb)
315	to Pleasant Valley (from wb)
313	to Pleasant Valley (from eb)
306	US 30, Baker, **2-3 mi** S Chevron/dsl Baker City Motel, Bridge Street Hotel, OR Trail Motel/rest., Les Schwab Tire, same as 304, to st police
304	OR 7, Baker, N Chevron/dsl/24hr Super 8, Welcome Inn Grocery Outlet, S Maverik/dsl, Shell/dsl, Sinclair/dsl/rest./scales/24hr, USA/dsl Big Chief's BBQ, Golden Crown, McDonald's, Papa Murphy's, Pizza Hut, Rising Sun Chinese, Starbucks, Subway, Sumpter Jct Rest., Taco Time Eldorado Inn, Geiser Grand Motel, Rodeway Inn, Sunridge Inn, $Tree, Albertson's, Bi-Mart, Carquest, CarQuest, city park, Mtn View RV Park/LP (3mi), museum, O'Reilly Parts, Paul's Transmissions/repair, Rite Aid, Safeway Foods, to hist dist, Verizon
302	OR 86 E to Richland, S , A Frame RV Park/LP, st police
298	OR 203, to Medical Springs
297mm	Baldock Slough
295mm	**both lanes, full facilities, info, litter barrels, petwalk, , vending**
289mm	Powder River
287.5mm	45th parallel, halfway between the equator and north pole
286mm	N Powder River
285	US 30, OR 237, North Powder, N North Powder Motel/cafe, S ski area, to Anthony Lakes
284mm	Wolf Creek
283	Wolf Creek Lane
278	Clover Creek
273	Frontage Rd
270	Ladd Creek Rd (from eb, no return)
269mm	**both lanes, full facilities, info, litter barrels, petwalk, , vending**

BAKER

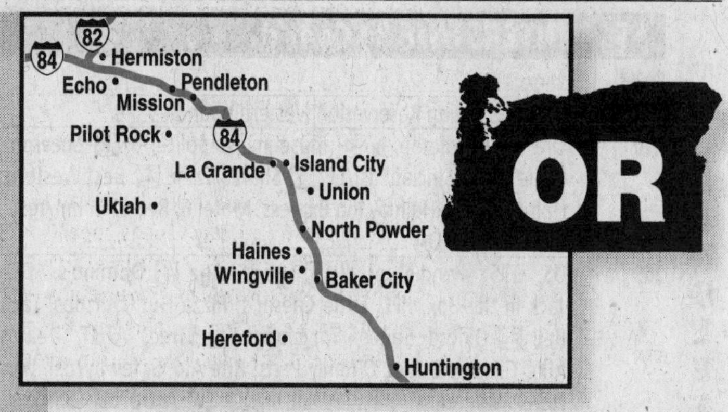

LA GRANDE

268	Foothill Rd
265	OR 203, LaGrande, N , Eagles Hot Lake RV Park, S FLYING J/rest./dsl/scales/24hr SmokeHouse Rest. (2mi) Freightliner
261	OR 82, LaGrande, N Chevron/dsl, Shell/dsl Denny's, Little Caesar's, Pizza Hut, Primo's Pizza, Starbucks, Taco Bell LaGrande Inn AT&T, Chrysler/Dodge/Jeep, Ford, Grocery Outlet, Thunder RV Ctr, Verizon, vet, Walmart/Subway, S 76/Baskin-Robbins/Subway/dsl, Chevron/dsl, Texaco/dsl Chen's Chinese, Domino's, DQ, Dutch Bro's Coffee, KFC, La Fiesta Mexican, Local Harvest Eatery, McDonald's, Moy's Dynasty, Nell's Steakburger, Papa Murphy's, Taco Time, Wendy's Best Western+, Royal Motel, Sandman Inn/Best Value, Super 8, $General, $Tree, Ace Hardware, E OR U, O'Reilly Parts, Rite Aid, Safeway/dsl, Schwab Tire, Wallowa Lake
260mm	Grande Ronde River
259	US 30 E (from eb), to La Grande, **1-2 mi** S Chevron/dsl, Mobil/dsl Burger King Greenwell Motel/rest., Rodeway Inn, Royal Motel, same as 261
257	Perry (from wb)
256.5mm	**weigh sta eb**
256	Perry (from eb)
255mm	Grande Ronde River
254mm	scenic wayside
252	OR 244, to Starkey, Lehman Springs, S camping, chainup area, Hilgard SP
251mm	Wallowa-Whitman NF, eastern boundary
248	Spring Creek Rd, to Kamela, **3 mi** N Oregon Trail Visitors Park
246mm	Wallowa-Whitman NF, western boundary
243	Summit Rd, Mt Emily Rd, to Kamela, **2 mi** N Emily Summit SP, Oregon Trail info
241mm	Summit of the Blue Mtns, elevation 4193
238	Meacham
234	Meacham, S Emigrant Sprs SP
231.5mm	Umatilla Indian Reservation, eastern boundary
228mm	Deadman Pass, **both lanes, full facilities, litter barrel, Oregon Trail info, petwalk, (wb), picnic table, RV Dump (wb), vending**
227mm	**weigh sta wb, brake check area**
224	Poverty Flats Rd, Old Emigrant Hill Rd, to Emigrant Springs SP
223mm	wb viewpoint, no restrooms
221.5mm	eb viewpoint, no restrooms
220mm	**wb runaway truck ramp**
216	Mission, McKay Creek, N Arrowhead Trkstp/Pacific Pride/McDonald's/dsl/24hr DQ, Subway Wildhorse Casino/RV Park
213	US 30 (from wb), Pendleton, **3-5 mi** N Chevron/dsl Travelers Inn Pendleton NHD

INTERSTATE 84 Cont'd

PENDLETON

Exit#	Services
212mm	Umatilla Indian Reservation western boundary
210	OR 11, Pendleton, N museum, st police, S Chevron/Circle K/dsl, Sinclair/dsl/LP Shari's/24hr Best Western, Hampton Inn, Holiday Inn Express, Motel 6, Red Lion Inn/rest., Super 8 KOA
209	US 395, Pendleton, N Space Age Domino's, DQ, Jack-in-the-Box, KFC, Little Caesar's, Pizza Hut, Quiznos, Taco Bell Oxford Suites, Travelodge $Tree, AT&T, Dean's Mkt, Grocery Outlet, O'Reilly Parts, Rite Aid, Safeway/dsl, Verizon, Walgreens, Walmart/Subway, S Astro/dsl, Sinclair/dsl Abby's Pizza, Burger King, Denny's, Dickey's BBQ, McDonald's, Rooster's Rest, Starbucks, Subway, Wendy's Motel 6 H, Les Schwab, Thompson RV Ctr
208mm	Umatilla River
207	US 30, W Pendleton, N Sinclair/dsl/LP Lookout RV Park, truck repair
202	Barnhart Rd, to Stage Gulch, N Woodpecker Truck Repair
199	Stage Coach Rd, Yoakum Rd
198	Lorenzen Rd, McClintock Rd, N trailer/reefer repair
193	Echo Rd, to Echo, Oregon Trail Site
188	US 395 N, Hermiston, N Chevron/dsl (5mi), Pilot/Subway/McDonald's/dsl/24hr/RV park Denny's/24hr (5mi), Jack-in-the-Box (5mi), McDonald's (5mi), Shari's/24hr (5mi) Best Western (5mi), Holiday Inn Express, Motel 6, Oxford Suites (5mi) H (5mi), S Echo HS, Henrietta RV Park (1mi)
187mm	**both lanes, full facilities, info, litter barrels, petwalk,**
182	OR 207, to Hermiston, N Space Age/A&W/dsl/LP/24hr Comfort Inn
180	Westland Rd, to Hermiston, McNary Dam, N trailer repair, S Western Express/dsl Freightliner
179	I-82 W, to Umatilla, Kennewick, WA

BOARDMAN

Exit#	Services
177	Umatilla Army Depot
171	Paterson Ferry Rd, to Paterson
168	US 730, to Irrigon, **8 mi** N Green Acres RV Park, Oasis RV Park, Oregon Trail info
165	Port of Morrow, S Pacific Pride/dsl
164	Boardman, N Chevron/Circle K/dsl, Sinclair/dsl C&D Drive-In, Smiley's Cafe, Sunrise Cafe, Village Rest. Knights Inn, Riverview Motel Boardman RV/Marina Park, city park, USPO, S Shell/dsl Subway Boardman Tire, NAPA, Oregon Trail Library, Rodeway Inn Harvest Town Mkt
161mm	**both lanes, full facilities, litter barrels, petwalk, , vending**
159	Tower Rd, S Loves/Carl's Jr/dsl/scales/24hr
151	Threemile Canyon
147	OR 74, to Ione, Blue Mtn Scenic Byway, Heppner, Oregon Trail Site
137	OR 19, Arlington, S Shell/Circle K/dsl Happy Canyon Cafe, Pheasant Grill, Rivers Edge Deli Rodeway Inn Arlington Hardware, Arlington RV Park/dump, city park, Thrifty Foods
136.5mm	viewpoint wb, , litter barrels
131	Woelpern Rd (from eb, no return)
129	Blalock Canyon, Lewis&Clark Trail
123	Philippi Canyon, Lewis&Clark Trail
114.5mm	John Day River
114	S LePage Park
112	**parking area both lanes**, litter barrels, N John Day Dam

THE DALLES

Exit#	Services
109	Pendleton, N John Day Visitor Ctr, S Sinclair/dsl Bob's T-Bone, Bull Dog Diner Hillview Motel, Tyee Motel Ed's RV Park, Family Mkt/deli, Rufus RV Park
104	US 97, Biggs, N Des Chutes Park Bridge, Maryhill Museum, S 76/Circle K/Noble Roman's/dsl/24hr, Pilot/McDonald's/dsl/scales/24hr, Shell/Subway/dsl Linda's Rest. Dinty's Motel, Three Rivers Inn Dinty's Mkt, dsl/tire repair
100mm	Columbia River Gorge Scenic Area, Deschutes River
97	OR 206, Celilo, N Celilo SP, restrooms, S Deschutes SP, Indian Village
92mm	**pulloff eb**
88	N to The Dalles Dam
87	US 30, US 197, to Dufur, N 76/dsl/24hr, Chevron/dsl McDonald's, Portage Grill Comfort Inn, Shilo Inn Columbia Hills RV Park, Lone Pine RV Park, st police, S Big Jim's Drive-In Celilo Inn
85	The Dalles, N **Riverfront Park, litter barrels, , , playground, restrooms,** marina, S 76/dsl, Chevron, Sinclair Burgerville, Canton Wok, Clock Tower Rest., Domino's, River Tap Rest. Dalles Inn, Oregon Motel H, AJ's Radiators, Dalles Parts, to Nat Hist Dist, TrueValue, USPO
83	(84 from wb)W The Dalles, N Casa El Mirador Legends Hotel/Casino S-Point Automotive, S Astro/dsl, Chevron/dsl, Fred Meyer/dsl Burger King, Denny's, DQ, Dutch Bro's Coffee, Ixtapa Mexican, Jack-in-the-Box, KFC, McDonald's, Papa Murphy's, Pizza Hut, Shari's Rest., Starbucks, Subway, Taco Bell, Taco Time, The BBQ Cousin's Inn/rest., Fairfield Inn, Motel 6, Super 8 H, $Tree, AT&T, AutoZone, Buick/Chevrolet/GMC, Chrysler/Dodge/Jeep, Ford, Fred Meyer, Grocery Outlet, Honda, Jo-Ann Fabrics, Nissan, O'Reilly Parts, PetCo, Rite Aid, Safeway/dsl, Staples, Subaru, Toyota, Verizon, Walgreens
82	Chenowith Area, S 76/dsl Spooky's Café Bi-Mart Foods, Columbia Discovery Ctr, Home Depot, museum, same as 83
76	Rowena, N Lewis & Clark info, Mayer SP, Memaloose SP, windsurfing
73mm	**both lanes, full facilities, litter barrels, petwalk, , , RV dump,** camping, Memaloose SP
69	US 30, Mosier, S USPO
66mm	N **wb, full facilities, litter barrels, picnic table** Koberg Beach SP

HOOD RIVER

Exit#	Services
64	US 30, OR 35, to White Salmon, Hood River, N Chevron/dsl, Shell McDonald's, Riverside Grill, Starbucks Best Western marina, museum, st police, visitors info
63	Hood River, City Ctr, N Valero/dsl Hampton Inn, S Astro 3 River's Grill, Andrew's Pizza, Big Horse Rest., Hood River Rest., Pietro's Pizza Hood River Hotel, Oakstreet Hotel H, USPO
62	US 30, Westcliff Dr, W Hood River, N Charburger, White Buffalo Rest. Columbia Gorge Hotel, Vagabond Lodge, S 76/dsl, Chevron/dsl/LP Domino's, DQ, Egg River Cafe, HoHo Chinese, McDonald's, Pelinti Cafe, Red Carpet Cafe, Starbucks, Subway, Taco Bell Holiday Inn Express, Prater's Motel, Riverview Lodge H, AT&T, Les Schwab Tire, Rite Aid, Safeway, Verizon, Walmart
61mm	**pulloff wb**
60	service rd wb (no return)
58	Mitchell Point Overlook (from eb)
56	N RV camping, Viento SP
55	Starvation Peak Tr Head (from eb), restrooms
54mm	**weigh sta wb**
51	Wyeth, S camping

OR

INTERSTATE 84 Cont'd

Exit#	Services
49mm	**pulloff eb**
47	Forest Lane, Hermon Creek (from wb), O camping
45mm	**weigh sta eb**
44	US 30, to Cascade Locks, N Chevron/dsl, Shell/dsl Bridgeside Rest., Cascade Inn Rest., Eastwind Drive-In, Waterfront Cafe Best Western+, Bridge of the Gods Motel, Cascade Motel, Columbia Gorge Inn O Columbia Mkt, KOA, Stern Wheeler RV Park, to Bridge of the Gods, USPO
41	O Eagle Creek RA (from eb), to fish hatchery
40	N O Bonneville Dam NHS, info, to fish hatchery
37	Warrendale (from wb)
35	Historic Hwy, Multnomah (exits left from both lanes), S O Ainsworth SP, Fishery RV Park, scenic loop highway, waterfall area
31	Multnomah Falls (exits left from both lanes), S Multnomah Falls Lodge/Rest. (hist site) O camping
30	S O Benson SRA (from eb)
29	Dalton Point (from wb)
28	to Bridal Veil (7 mi return from eb), S O USPO
25	N O Rooster Rock SP
23mm	O hist marker, viewpoint wb
22	Corbett, 2 mi S Corbett Mkt View Point Rest. O Crown Point RV Camping
19mm	O Columbia River Gorge scenic area
18	Lewis&Clark SP, to Oxbow SP
17.5mm	Sandy River
17	Marine Dr, Troutdale, N DQ Comfort Inn, S Chevron/dsl, Loves/Chester's/dsl/LP/scales/24hr, TA/Shell/Country Pride/Popeye's/Subway/dsl/scales/24hr/@ Arby's, McDonald's, Shari's/24hr, Subway, Taco Bell Holiday Inn Express, Motel 6 O Premium Outlets/famous brands, Sandy Riverfront RV Resort
16	238th Dr, Fairview, N Arco/dsl/24hr Bronx Eatery, Burger King, Jack-in-the-Box Travelodge O Camping World, Walmart/Subway, S O H
14	207th Ave, Fairview, N Shell/dsl Parkway Grill O auto repair, Portland RV Park, Rolling Hills RV Park
13	181st Ave, Gresham, N Chevron/dsl Hampton Inn, S 76, Arco, Shell Burger King, Canton Pearl, Carl's Jr, Elmer's, McDonald's, Pizza Hut, Shari's, Subway, Wendy's Bridgeway Inn, Days Inn, Extended Stay America, Portland Suites, Sheraton O $Tree, 7-11, U-Haul, vet
10	122nd Ave (from eb)
9	I-205, S to Salem, N to Seattle, to airport, (to 102nd Ave from eb)
8	I-205 N (from eb), N O to airport
7	Halsey St (from eb), Gateway Dist
6	I-205 S (from eb)
5	OR 213, to 82nd Ave (eb only), N Days Inn, S Eastern Cathay Comfort Inn
4	68th Ave (from eb), to Halsey Ave
3	58th Ave (from eb), S 76, Shell/dsl O H, Fred Meyer
2	43rd Ave, 39th Ave, Halsey St, N Burger King, Panera Bread, Starbucks Banfield Motel O Rite Aid, Trader Joe's, S O H, same as 1
1	33rd Ave, Lloyd Blvd (eb only), downtown, N Shell/dsl Burger King, Starbucks O AT&T, S Wendy's O Schwab Tire, same as 2
1	to downtown (wb only), N Applebee's Doubletree, Residence Inn O $Tree, Macy's, Marshall's, Nordstrom, Safeway, S O Cadillac
0mm	**I-84 begins/ends on I-5, exit 301.**

TROUTDALE

PORTLAND

PORTLAND AREA

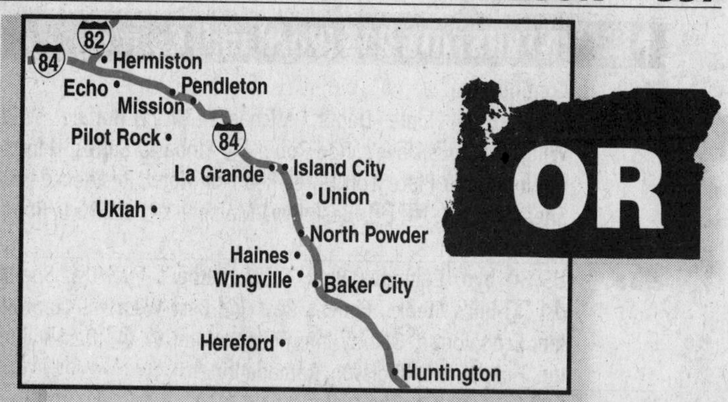

INTERSTATE 205 (Portland)

Exit#	Services
37mm	**I-205 begins/ends on I-5. Exits 36-27 are in Washington.**
36	NE 134th St (from nb), E Chevron/dsl Holiday Inn Express O H, W 7-11, Arco, Mobil, Shell Applebee's, Baskin-Robbins, Billygan's Roadhouse, Burger King, Burgerville, El Tapatio, Jack-in-the-Box, McDonald's, Muchas Gracias, Panda Express, Papa Murphy's, PizzaSchmitzza, Round Table Pizza, Starbucks, Subway, Taco Bell La Quinta, Shilo Inn, Vancouver Inn O 99 RV Park, Albertson's, Fred Meyer, Safeway/dsl, Verizon, Walgreens
32	NE 83rd St, Andreson Rd, Battle Ground, W Shell/dsl/24hr Burger King, Emporor Chinese, Krispy Kreme, Panda Express, Starbucks, Subway, Taco Bell, Taste of China, Weinerschnitzel, Wendy's O Costco/gas, Home Depot, vet
30c b a	WA 500, Orchards, Vancouver, E 76, Shell, Shell, USA ABC Buffet, Applebee's, Burger King, Burgerville, DQ, Imperial Palace, KFC, McDonald's, Papa Murphy's, Subway, Wendy's O 7-11, GNC, Jo-Ann Crafts, Midas, Office Depot, PetCo, repair, Sportsman's Whse, Toyota, Walgreens, W 7-11/dsl, Chevron/dsl, Shell/dsl Burgerville, ChuckeCheese, Golden Tent BBQ, Great Taste Chinese, Hometown Buffet, IHOP, Jack-in-the-Box, Jamba Juice, LaCosta Mexican, Muchas Gracias, Olive Garden, Outback Steaks, Popeyes, Red Lobster, Red Robin, RoundTable Pizza, Shari's, Starbucks, Subway, Taco Bell Best Western, Comfort Suites, Day's Inn, Heathman Lodge, Holiday Inn Express, Howard Johnson's, Residence Inn, Staybridge Inn O $Tree, Americas Tire, auto repair, Barnes&Noble, GNC, JC Penney, Macy's, Old Navy, Petsmart, Ross, Target, TJ Maxx, URGENT CARE, Verizon, Walmart Mkt
28	Mill Plain Rd, E 76, Chevron Applebee's, Baskin-Robbins, Breakfast At Valerie's, Burger King, Burgerville, DQ, Elmer's Rest., Irishtown Grill, Jimmy John's, Kings Buffet, McDonald's, McGrath's Fish House, Muchas Gracias Mexican, Pizza Hut, Shari's, Starbucks, Starbucks, Sweet Tomatoes, Taco Bell, Yummy Mongolian Best Western, DoubleTree Hotel, Extended Stay America, The Guesthouse Motel O $Tree, 7-11, Fred Meyer/dsl, O'Reilly Parts, PetCo, Schwab Tire, Trader Joe's, W 7-11, 76 Arby's, Jack-in-the-Box, Little Caesar's, Subway O H, auto/tire repair, Walgreens, Walmart/McDonald's
27	WA 14, Vancouver, Camas, Columbia River Gorge
25mm	Oregon/Washington state line. Columbia River, **exits 27-36 are in Washington.**
24	122nd Ave, Airport Way, E 7-11/dsl Burger King, China Wok, Dutch Bros Coffee, Jack-in-the-Box, McDonald's, Panera Bread, Shari's, Subway Candlewood Suites, Clarion, Comfort Suites, Courtyard, Fairfield Inn, Hilton Garden, Holiday Inn Express, La Quinta, Shilo Inn/rest., SpringHill Suites, Staybridge Suites,

INTERSTATE 205 (Portland) Cont'd

PORTLAND AREA

24 Continued
Super 8 [other] Home Depot, Michael's, **W** [food] Buffalo Wild Wings, Famous Dave's, Red Robin [lodging] Embassy Suites, Hampton Inn, Hyatt Place, Loft Hotel, Red Lion Hotel, Residence Inn, Sheraton/rest. [other] [airport], Best Buy, Marshall's, PetsMart, Ross, Staples

23b a US 30 byp, Columbia Blvd, **E** [gas] Leather's Fuel/dsl, Shell/dsl [food] Bill's Steaks, Elmer's Rest. [lodging] Best Western, Comfort Inn, Econolodge, Quality Inn, Rodeway Inn, **W** [lodging] Best Value Inn, Holiday Inn, Radisson, Ramada Inn

22 I-84 E, US 30 E, to The Dalles

21b I-84 W, US 30 W, to Portland

21a Glisan St, **E on NE 102nd St** [gas] 76, Arco [food] Applebee's, Carl's Jr, Izzy's Pizza, Jamba Juice, Starbucks, Subway [other] Fred Meyer, Kohl's, Office Depot, Ross, WinCo Foods

20 Stark St, Washington St, **E** [gas] 76/7-11, Chevron/dsl [food] Arby's, Baja Fresh, Burger King, Denny's, Elmer's Rest., Hometown Buffet, Jack-in-the-Box, McMenamin's Rest., Old Chicago Pizza, Olive Garden, Panda Express, Portland Seafood Co, Red Robin, Saylor's, Starbucks, Subway, Village Inn [lodging] Chestnut Tree Inn, Ramada [other] $Tree, Big Lots, Home Depot, Target, Tuesday Morning, Verizon, **W** [food] Stark St Pizza, Taco Bell [lodging] Motel 6 [other] 7-11

19 US 26, Division St, **E** [gas] Space Age/dsl [other] [H], **W** [gas] Shell [food] Burgerville, ChuckeCheese, McDonald's

17 Foster Rd

16 Johnson Creek Blvd, **W** [gas] 76, Arco [food] Applebee's, Bajio, Burger King, Carl's Jr, Five Guys, Hog Wild BBQ, Jack-in-the-Box, Jimmy John's, Krispy Kreme, McDonald's, McDonald's, Outback Steaks, Panda Express, RoundTable Pizza, Starbucks, Taco Bell [other] 7-11, Best Buy, Dick's, Firestone/auto, Fred Meyer/dsl, Home Depot, Knecht's Parts, O'Reilly Parts, PetsMart, RV Ctrs, Trader Joe's, Walgreens, Walmart/Subway

14 Sunnyside Rd, **E** [gas] 76/dsl [food] A&W/KFC, Baja Fresh, Domino's, Gustav's Grill, Jersey Mike's, McMenamin's, Papa John's, Starbucks [lodging] Clarion, Sunnyside Inn [other] [H], Office Depot,

14 Continued
W [gas] Chevron/dsl [food] Burger King, CA Pizza Kitchen, Cheesecake Factory, Chick-fil-A, Chipotle, Claim Jumper, Dave&Buster's, Denny's, DQ, Jimmy John's, McDonald's, Muchas Gracias, Noodles&Co, Old Spaghetti Factory, Olive Garden, Panera Bread, Pieology Pizzaria, Pizza Hut, RAM Rest., Red Robin, Stanford's Rest., Wendy's [lodging] Courtyard, Monarch Hotel/rest. [other] Barnes&Noble, Discount Tire, Hobby Lobby, JC Penney, Kohl's, Macy's, Nordstroms, Old Navy, PetCo, REI, Target, U-Haul, Verizon, World Mkt

13 OR 224, to Milwaukie, **W** [other] CarMax, Lowe's

12 OR 213, to Milwaukie, **E** [gas] Chevron/dsl, Pacific Pride, Shell [food] Denny's, Elmer's, KFC, McDonald's, New Cathay Chinese, Pronto Pizza, Subway, Taco Bell, Wendy's [lodging] Clackamas Inn, Hampton Inn [other] $Tree, 7-11, Fred Meyer, USPO, **W** [lodging] Comfort Suites

11 82nd Dr, Gladstone, **W** [gas] Arco, Chevron [food] High Rocks Rest., McDonald's, Starbucks, Subway [lodging] Holiday Inn Express [other] Harley-Davidson, Safeway

10 OR 213, Park Place, **E** [gas] Chevron/dsl [other] [H], Home Depot, to Oregon Trail Ctr

9 OR 99E, Oregon City, **E** [gas] 76, Chevron/dsl [food] KFC [other] [H], repair, Subaru, **W** [food] La Hacienda Mexican, McDonald's, Shari's, Starbucks, Subway, Thai Rest. [lodging] Best Western+ [other] $Tree, AT&T, Firestone/auto, Michael's, Rite Aid, Ross, URGENT CARE

8.5mm Willamette River

8 OR 43, W Linn, Lake Oswego, **E** [gas] [other] museum, **W** [gas] Chevron/dsl, Shell/dsl [food] Starbucks [other] Mkt of Choice, USPO, Verizon, vet

7mm viewpoint nb, hist marker

6 10th St, W Linn St, **E** [gas] Chevron/LP [food] Five Guys, Ixtapa Mexican, McDonald's, McMenamin's Rest., Papa Murphy's Willamette Coffee House [other] Ace Hardware, Les Schwab **W** [food] Biscuit's Cafe, Subway

4mm Tualatin River

3 Stafford Rd, Lake Oswego, **W** [food] Wanker's Country Store [other] [H]

0mm **I-205 begins/ends on I-5, exit 288.**

PENNSYLVANIA

INTERSTATE 70

NEW STANTON

Exit#	Services
171mm	Pennsylvania/Maryland state line, **Welcome Ctr wb, full [handicapped] facilities, info, litter barrels, petwalk, [phone], [picnic], vending**
168	US 522 N, Warfordsburg, **N** [gas] Fuel/dsl, **S** [other] fireworks
163	PA 731 S, Amaranth
156	PA 643, Town Hill
153mm	**[RS] eb, full [handicapped] facilities, litter barrels, petwalk, [phone], [picnic], vending**
151	PA 915, Crystal Spring, **N** [other] auto repair, **S** [other] Country Store/USPO
149	US 30 W, to Everett, S Breezewood (no immediate wb return), 3 mi **S** [food] McDonald's [lodging] Wildwood Motel
147	US 30, Breezewood, **Services on US 30** [gas] Exxon/dsl, FLYING J/Perkins/dsl/scales/24hr, Sheetz/dsl, Shell, Shell/Dunkin Donuts/Subway/dsl, Sunoco/dsl, TA/Valero/Gateway Rest./Subway/dsl/scales/24hr/@ [food] Bob Evans, Classic American Diner, Hardee's, McDonald's, Pizza Hut, Starbucks, Subplicity, Taco Bell [lodging] Best Western, EconoLodge, Holiday Inn Express, Quality Inn, Wiltshire Motel [other] Blue Beacon

I-70 and I-76/PA Tpk run together 71 mi. See I-76 PA/Tpk exits 148mm-75

77 I-70 E runs with I-76/PA Turnpike eb

58 PA Tpk. I-70 E and I-76/PA Turnpike E run together.

57b a I-70 W, US 119, PA 66 (toll), New Stanton, **N** [gas] Exxon, Sheetz dsl [food] BBG Grill, Bob Evans, Eat'n Park, McDonald's, Pagano' Rest., Pizza Hut, Subway, Szechuan Wok, Wendy's [lodging] Budge Inn, Comfort Inn, Days Inn, EconoLodge, Fairfield Inn, Garde Inn, Hampton Inn, Motel 6, Super 8, **S** [gas] Marathon/dsl, Su noco/dsl [food] Cracker Barrel, La Tavola Ristorante [other] $Genera USPO

54 Madison, **N** [other] KOA, **S** [other] truck repair

53 Yukon

51b a PA 31, West Newton, **S** [other] Volvo/Mack

49 Smithton, **N** [gas] Citgo/rest./dsl/scales/@, FLYING J/Denny's dsl/LP/scales/24hr/@

46b a PA 51, Pittsburgh, **N** [gas] Sunoco/dsl [food] Burger King [lodging] Comfort Inn [other] Buick/Cadillac/Chevrolet, Ford/Kia, Honda, **S** [gas] GetGo/dsl, PP/dsl [food] Clubhouse Grille [lodging] Budget Inn, Clario [other] golf

44 Arnold City

OR PA

INTERSTATE 70 Cont'd

FAYETTE CITY

Exit#	Services
43b a	(43 from eb) PA 201, to PA 837, Fayette City, S Exxon/dsl A&W/LJ Silver, Burger King, Denny's, Domino's, Eat'n Park, Hibachi Buffet, Hoss' Rest., KFC, Little Bamboo, McDonald's, Old Mexico, Pizza Hut, Rita's Custard, Sonny's Grille, Starbucks, Subway, Taco Bell, Wendy's Candlewood Suites, Fairfield Inn, Hampton Inn, Holiday Inn Express $General, $Tree, Advance Parts, Aldi Foods, AT&T, BigLots, CVS Drug, Giant Eagle Foods, GNC, Jo-Ann Fabrics, Lowe's, NAPA, Staples, URGENT CARE, Verizon, Walmart
42a	Monessen
42	N Belle Vernon, S BP/McDonald's/7-11, Sunoco/dsl DQ
41	PA 906, Belle Vernon
40mm	Monongahela River
40	PA 88, Charleroi, N Gulf, Sunoco McDonald's, My Girl's Rest., Subway/TCBY H, Rite Aid, Valley Tire
39	Speers, S Exxon/dsl
37b a	PA 43 (**toll**), N to Pittsburgh, S to CA
36	Lover (from wb, no re-entry)
35	PA 481, Centerville
32b a	PA 917, Bentleyville, S BP/dsl, Pilot/DQ/Subway/dsl/scales/24hr Burger King, King's Rest., McDonald's, Pizza Hut Best Western, Holiday Inn Express $General, Advance Parts, AutoZone, Blue Beacon, Giant Eagle Foods, Rite Aid
31	to PA 136, Kammerer, N Carlton Motel
27	Dunningsville, S Avalon Motel
25	PA 519, to Eighty Four, S BP/7-11 Diner/dsl/24hr, Sunoco/dsl
21	I-79 S, to Waynesburg.

I-70 W and I-79 N run together 3.5 mi.

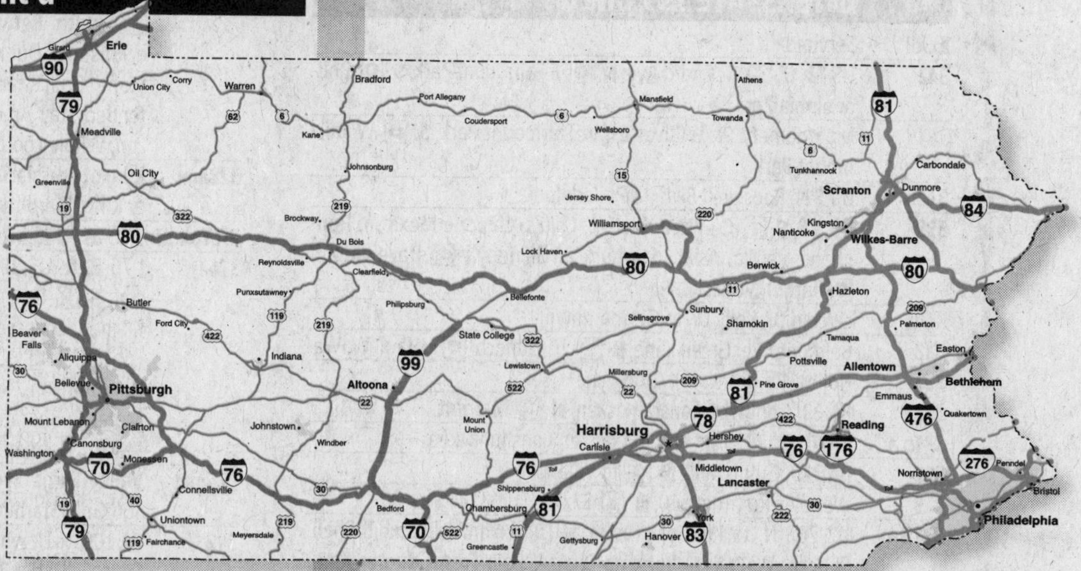

WASHINGTON

Exit#	Services
20	PA 136, Beau St, S to Washington&Jefferson Coll
19b a	US 19, Murtland Ave, N BP/dsl, GetGo Applebee's, Arby's, Asahi Buffet, Buffalo Wild Wings, Chick-fil-A, Cracker Barrel, Five Guys, Fusion Steaks, Ichiban Steaks, Jimmy John's, Krispy Kreme, Longhorn Steaks, Max&Erma's, McDonald's, Moe's SW Grill, Noodles&Co, Olive Garden, Outback Steaks, Panera Bread, Penn Sta Subs, Plaza Azteca, Red Lobster, Red Robin, Rita's Custard, Starbucks, Subway, Taco Bell, TGIFriday's, TX Roadhouse, Wong's Wok, Zoup! SpringHill Suites $Tree, Aldi Foods, AT&T, Dick's, Field&Stream, Ford, Giant Eagle Foods, GNC, Hobby Lobby, Honda, Hyundai, Kohl's, Lowe's, Mercedes, Michael's, Nissan, PetCo, Petsmart, Sam's Club/gas, Save-A-Lot Foods, Target, Toyota, URGENT CARE, Verizon, Walmart/McDonald's, S BP/dsl, Exxon/dsl, Sunoco, Sunoco/dsl A&W/LJ Silver, Bob Evans, Donut Connection, Dunkin Donuts, Eat'n Park, Grand China, KFC, Old Mexico, Papa John's, Pizza Hut, Waffle House Hampton Inn, Motel 6 H, BigLots, Buick/GMC, Chevrolet, Firestone/auto, Home Depot, Jo-Ann Fabrics, Mazda, Pepboys, Staples, Subaru
18	I-79 N, to Pittsburgh.

I-70 E and I-79 S run together 3.5 mi.

Exit#	Services
17	PA 18, Jefferson Ave, Washington, N GetGo/dsl DQ, McDonald's Family$, Rite Aid, S Sunoco/dsl 4Star Pizza, Burger King, China Express, Little Caesar's, Subway $General, Advance Parts, Advance Parts (2), AutoZone, CVS Drug, O'Reilly Parts, Shop'n Save Foods, USPO, Walgreens
16	Jessop Place, N Dean's Suburban Lodge, S auto/truck repair
15	US 40, Chesnut St, Washington, N Food Land, S BP/7-11, Exxon/dsl, Marathon, Sunoco/dsl Bob Evans, Denny's, Dunkin Donuts, Garfield's Rest., McDonald's, Taco Bell, Wendy's Best Value Inn, Comfort Suites, Days Inn, Ramada Inn, Red Roof Inn Jo-Ann, Marshalls, Rite Aid, Ross
11	PA 221, Taylorstown, N BP/dsl, S repair
6	PA 231, to US 40, Claysville, N BP/dsl
5mm	**Welcome Ctr eb, full facilities, , litter barrels, petwalk, vending**
1	W Alexander
0mm	Pennsylvania/Ohio state line

INTERSTATE 76

PHILADELPHIA

Exit#	Services
354mm	Pennsylvania/New Jersey state line, Delaware River, Walt Whitman Br
351	Front St, I-95 (from wb), N to Trenton, S to Chester
350	Packer Ave, 7th St, to I-95 (from eb), S Holiday Inn to sports complex
349	to I-95, PA 611, Broad St, N Citgo Talk of the Town
348	PA 291, W to Chester (exits left from wb)
347a	to I-95 S (exits left from wb)
347b	Passyunk Ave, Oregon Ave, N Burger King, KFC, Little Caesar's, McDonald's, Pizza Hut BJ's Whse, Home Depot, Ross, ShopRite, S FDR Park
346c	28th St, Vare Ave, Mifflin St (from wb)
346b	Grays Ferry Ave, University Ave, N Fresh Grocer, Little Caesar's, McDonald's H, USPO, S 76, Speedway/dsl Dunkin Donuts
346a	South St (exits left from wb)
345	30th St, Market St, downtown
344	I-676 E, US 30 E, to Philadelphia (no return from eb), N LDS Temple
343	Spring Garden St, Haverford

PHILADELPHIA

INTERSTATE 76 Cont'd

Exit#	Services
342	US 13, US 30 W, Girard Ave, N E Fairmount Park, S Philadelphia Zoo
341	Montgomery Dr, W River Dr, W Fairmount Park, S W Fairmount Park
340b	US 1 N, Roosevelt Blvd, to Philadelphia
339	US 1 S, S CA Pizza Kitchen, Chili's, Chipotle Mexican, Houlihans, PeiWei Asian, Starbucks, TGIFriday's Dave's Hotel Target, Verizon
340a	Lincoln Dr, Kelly Dr, to Germantown
338	Belmont Ave, Green Lane, S 76, Sunoco UHaul, WaWa
337	Hollow Rd (from wb), Gladwyne
332	PA 23 (from wb), Conshohocken, N Marriott
331b a	I-476, PA 28 (from eb), to Chester, Conshohocken
330	PA 320, Gulph Mills, S to Villanova U
329	Weadley Rd (from wb), N Exxon
328b a	US 202 N, to King of Prussia, N Exxon/dsl, Lukoil, Shell, Sunoco, WaWa Bahama Breeze, Baja Fresh, Burger King, CA Pizza Kitchen, Capital Grille, Champp's, Cheesecake Factory, Chili's, Fox&Hound, Hooters, Joe's Crabshack, Maggiano's, Morton's Steaks, Panera Bread, Red Lobster, Ruby's Diner, Ruth's Chris Steaks, Sullivan's Steaks Best Western, Doubletree, Fairfield Inn, Hampton Inn, Holiday Inn Express, Hyatt, Inn of King of Prussia, Motel 6, Sheraton Best Buy, Bloomingdale's, Costco, Dick's, Home Depot, Lord&Taylor, Macy's, Neiman Marcus, Nordstrom, Old Navy, S Crowne Plaza
327	US 202 S, to US 420 W, Goddard Blvd, Valley Forge Park, E Valley Forge Park
326	I-76 wb becomes I-76/PA Tpk to Ohio

For I-76 westbound to Ohio, see I-76/PA Turnpike.

INTERSTATE 76 (Turnpike)

Exit#	Services
	PA Tpk runs wb as I-276/I-95, eb ends on NJ Tpk.
6a(I-95)	US 130 exit is in NJ, to Bordentown, N $Tree, Rite Aid, S Conoco/dsl, WaWa/dsl Burger King, Dunkin Donuts
355mm	**PA Tpk/I-276 merges with I-95 N**
352.5mm	**toll plaza**
352	PA 132, Street Rd, EZ tag only, from eb
351	US 1, to I-95, to Philadelphia, N Bar Louie, Bertucci's, Chick-fil-A, Chipotle, Cracker Barrel, Jimmy John's, Longhorn Steaks, McDonald's, On The Border, Panda Express, Red Robin, Starbucks, Uno, Wendy's Crowne Plaza Barnes&Noble, Buick/GMC, CVS Drug, Home Depot, Lowes Whse, Target, Walmart, S 7-11/dsl, Classic/wash, Sunoco/dsl Dunkin Donuts Best Western, Comfort Inn, Courtyard, Hampton Inn, Knights Inn, Neshaminy Inn, Quality Inn, Radisson, Red Roof Inn Indian Motorcycles, Toyota
343	PA 611, Willow Grove, N BP/dsl, Shell/dsl, Speedway/dsl, Sunoco Carrabba's, Dunkin Donuts, Sonic Courtyard, Fairfield Inn, SpringHill Suites 7-11, Home Depot, Lexus, NTB, S Bonefish Grill, China Garden, Domino's, Dunkin Donuts, Ooka Japanese, Tony Roni's Pizza Hampton Inn 7-11, Audi/Infiniti, Best Buy, PepBoys, repair, Staples, transmissions
340	to VA Dr, EZ tag only, from wb, no trucks, WaWa/dsl, EZ tagholder only
339	PA 309, Ft Washington, N LukOil/dsl Friendly's, Subway Best Western, Hilton Garden, Holiday Inn Express BMW, Mercedes, Volvo, WaWa
334	PA Tpk NE Extension, I-476, S to Philadelphia, N to Allentown
333	Germantown Pike, to Norristown, N Lukoil, Sunocc Azteca, Bertucci's, California Pizza Kitchen, Chipotle, Dave&Buster's, Dunkin Donuts, Elevation Burger, PF Chang's, Rec Stone Grill, Starbucks, Zoup! Courtyard, DoubleTree, Extended Stay America, SpringHill Suites Boscov's, Verizon, Whole Foods, S LukOil
328mm	**King of Prussia Service Plaza wb,** Sunoco/dsl/24hr Burger King, Starbucks
	PA Tpk runs eb as I-276, wb as I-76.
326	I-76 E, to US 202, I-476, Valley Forge, N Shell Radisson, S Exxon, LukOil, Shell, Sunoco, WaWa CA Pizza Kitchen, Cheesecake Factory, Chili's, Hooters, Maggiano's, Red Lobster, Ruth's Chris Steaks, Sullivan Steaks Best Western, Hampton Inn, Holiday Inn Express, Hyatt, Inn of King of Prussia, Motel 6, Sheraton Best Buy, Costco, Dick's, Home Depot, Macy's, Neiman Marcus, Nordstrom, Walmart, Wegman's
325mm	**Valley Forge Service Plaza eb,** Sunoco/dsl/24hr Larson Grill, Starbucks
312	PA 100, to Downingtown, Pottstown, N WaWa/dsl Car Sense, Harley-Davidson, S Sunoco/dsl, WaWa Applebee's, Chick-fil-A, Isaac's Deli, Red Robin, Starbucks, Un Grill, Wendy's Clarion, Comfort Suites, Extended Sta America, Fairfield Inn, Hampton Inn, Hilton Garden, Residenc Inn Giant Foods, Target, Walgreens
305mm	**Camiel Service Paza wb,** Sunoco/dsl/24hr Roy Rogers, Starbucks
298	I-176, PA 10, to Reading, Morgantown, N Arby's, DC Dunkin Donuts, Sonic, Subway USA Inn $Tree, AutoZone, Lowe's, Mavis Tire, Verizon, Walmart, S Exxon, Sheetz/dsl McDonald's, Rita's Custard Holida Inn Chevrolet, Rite Aid, USPO
290mm	**Bowmansville Service Plaza eb,** Sunoco/dsl/24hr Burger King, Hershey's, Starbucks
286	US 322, PA 272, to Reading, Ephrata, N Citgo/d Baskin-Robbins/Dunkin Donuts, Park Place Diner, Subway Zia Maria's Eatery Black Horse Inn/rest., S Turkey Hi Comfort Inn, Econolodge, Hampton Inn (11mi), Red Carpe Inn, Red Roof Inn
266	PA 72, to Lebanon, Lancaster, N Speedway/dsl, Sunoco Chester's Comfort Inn Holiday Inn Express (17 m auto repair, Harley-Davidson, NAPA, S Hampto Inn Mt Hope Winery, Pinch Pond Camping
259mm	**Lawn Service Plaza wb,** Sunoco/dsl/24hr Burger King Starbucks RV dump
250mm	**Highspire Service Plaza eb,** Sunoco/dsl/24hr Starbucks, Steak'n Shake
247	I-283, PA 283, to Harrisburg, Harrisburg East, Hershe N Exxon/dsl, Sheetz/dsl, Sunoco Bob Evans, Capit Diner, Chick-fil-A, Chili's, Five Guys, Friendly's, Gilligan's Steak McDonald's, Moe's SW, Subway, Taco Bell, Wendy's Best Western, Courtyard, Harrisburg Hotel, Holiday Inn, La Quinta Red Lion, Red Roof Inn, Sheraton, Sleep Inn, Super 8 GN Harrisburg East Camping, JC Penney, Kia, Petco, Target, Verizo
246mm	Susquehannah River
242	I-83, Harrisburg West, N Shell/dsl, Speedway, Sunoc Bob Evans, John's Diner, McDonald's, Pizza Hut Best Western, Budget Inn, Clarion Inn, Fairfield Inn, Holiday In Express, La Quinta, Motel 6, Quality Inn, Scottish Inn ve S Rutter's/dsl Days Inn, Red Carpet Inn
236	US 15, to Gettysburg, Gettysburg Pike, Harrisburg, N Exxon, Gulf/dsl Isaac's Rest, Marzoni's, McDonald's, Pa John's, Peppermill Rest, Subway, Subway (2) Comfort In

HARRISBURG

PA

INTERSTATE 76 (Turnpike) Cont'd

236 Continued
Country Inn&Suites, Courtyard, EconoLodge, Hampton Inn, Homewood Suites, TownePlace Suites H, U-Haul, vet, **S** Sheetz Arby's, Bros Pizza, Burger King, Cracker Barrel, Subway, Wendy's Motel 6, Wingate Inn $Tree, Giant Food/gas, GNC, Rite Aid

226 US 11, to I-81, to Harrisburg, Carlisle, **N** FLYING J/Denny's/dsl/LP/scales/24hr/@, Gulf/dsl, Loves/Wendy's/dsl/scales/24hr, Petro/Iron Skillet/dsl/scales/24hr/@, Pioneer/dsl, Sunoco/Subway/dsl Arby's, Bob Evans, Carelli's Subs, Dunkin Donuts, Embers Steaks, McDonald's, Middlesex Diner, Rte 11 Diner, Waffle House Best Value Inn, Days Inn, EconoLodge, Hampton Inn, Hotel Carlisle, Knights Inn, Quality Inn, Red Roof Inn, Residence Inn, Rodeway Inn, Super 8, Travelodge Blue Beacon, **S** Rutter's/dsl Hoss' Rest. Best Western, Holiday Inn Express, Motel 6 H, U-Haul, vet

219mm **Plainfield Service Plaza eb,** Sunoco/dsl/24hr Hershey's Ice Cream, Roy Rogers, Starbucks

203mm **Blue Mtn Service Plaza wb,** Sunoco/dsl/24hr Hershy's Ice Cream, Pizza Hut, Roy Rogers, Starbucks

201 PA 997, to Shippensburg, Blue Mountain, **S** Kenmar Motel auto/truck repair

199mm Blue Mountain Tunnel

197mm Kittatinny Tunnel

189 PA 75, Willow Hill, **S** Double Dip Drive-In, Pizza Star Willow Hill Motel/rest.

187mm Tuscarora Tunnel

180 US 522, Mt Union, Ft Littleton, **N** Cutchall's/dsl, Noname/dsl The Family Rest. Downes Motel

172mm **Sideling Service Plaza both lanes,** Sunoco/dsl/24hr Burger King, Famiglia Pizza, Hershey's, Popeye's, Starbucks

161 US 30, Breezewood, **Services on US 30** **N** Exxon/dsl, FLYING J/Perkins/dsl/scales/24hr, Sheetz/dsl, Shell, Shell/Dunkin Donuts/Subway/dsl, Sunoco/dsl, TA/Valero/Gateway Rest./Subway/dsl/scales/24hr/@ Bob Evans, Classic American Diner, Hardee's, McDonald's, Pizza Hut, Starbucks, Subplicity, Taco Bell Best Western, EconoLodge, Holiday Inn Express, Quality Inn, Wiltshire Motel Blue Beacon

161mm **I-70 W and I-76/PA Turnpike W run together.**

148mm **Midway Service Plaza both lanes,** Sunoco/dsl/24hr Sbarro's, Starbucks, Steak'n Shake

146 I-99, US 220, Bedford, **N** GetGo/McDonald's/dsl, PP/dsl, Sheetz/dsl/24hr, Shell/Subway/dsl Bedford Diner, Clara's Place, Denny's, Ed's Steaks, Hoss' Rest., LJ Silver, Pizza Hut, Salsa's Mexican, Wendy's Best Value Inn, Budget Host, Fairfield Inn, Quality Inn, Rodeway Inn, Travelodge Blue Knob SP (15mi), to Shawnee SP (10mi), **S** Hampton Inn

123mm Allegheny Tunnel

112mm **Somerset Service Plaza both lanes,** Sunoco/dsl/24hr Burger King, Pizza Hut, Popeye's, Starbucks

110 PA 601, to US 219, Somerset, **N** KwikFill/dsl, Sheetz Hoss' Rest., King's Rest., Pizza Hut $Inn, Economy Inn Advance Parts, Ford, tires, **S** Somerset TravelCtr/dsl/@, Tesla EVC, Turkey Hill Arby's, Bruster's Ice Cream, DQ, Eat'n Park, KFC, LJ Silver, McDonald's, Pine Grill, Ruby Tuesday, Starbucks, Subway, Summit Diner, Wendy's Budget Host, Budget Inn, Comfort Inn, Days Inn, Econolodge, Hampton Inn, Holiday Inn Express, Quality Inn, Super 8 Harley-Davidson

91 PA 711, PA 31, to Ligonier, Donegal, **N** Tall Cedars Rest., **S** BP/McDonald's, Sunoco/dsl DQ, Subway Days Inn, Holiday Inn Express camping, golf

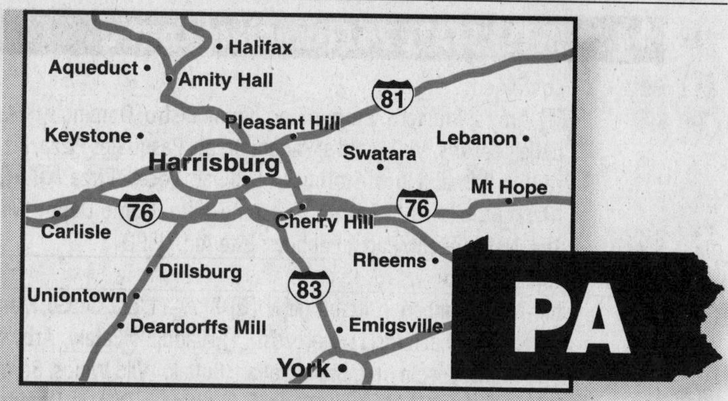

78mm **New Stanton Service Plaza wb,** Sunoco/dsl/24hr Burger King, Hershey's Ice Cream, Quiznos, Starbucks

I-70 E runs with I-76/PA Turnpike eb.

75 I-70 W, US 119, PA 66 (**toll**), New Stanton, **S** BP/7-11/dsl, Exxon, Sheetz, Sunoco BBG Grill, Bob Evans, Campy's Pizza, Cracker Barrel, Eat'n Park, La Tavola Risorante, McDonald's, Pagano's Rest., Pizza Hut, Subway, Szechuan Wok, TJ's Rest., Wendy's Budget Inn, Comfort Inn, Days Inn, EconoLodge, Express Inn, Fairfield Inn, Garden Inn, Super 8 USPO

67 US 30, to Greensburg, Irwin, **N** BP/7-11/dsl, Sheetz/dsl Domino's, DQ H, Ford, Mr Tire, **S** GetGo, Marathon/7-11/dsl, Sheetz/dsl, Sunoco/24hr Applebee's, Arby's, Atria's, Bob Evans, Burger King, Denny's, Double Wide Grill, Dunkin Donuts, Eat'n Park, Fire Pit Grill, Five Guys, KFC, Little Caesar's, McDonald's, Panera Bread, Pizza Hut, Starbucks, Subway, Taco Bell, Wendy's Hampton Inn, Holiday Inn Express $Tree, Advance Parts, Aldi Foods, AT&T, Giant Eagle Foods/24hr, GNC, Kohl's, Rite Aid, Target, Verizon, Walgreens, Walmart

61mm **parking area eb**

57 I-376, US 22, to Pittsburgh, Monroeville, **S** Marathon, Sheetz, Sunoco Arby's, Blaze Pizza, Chick-fil-A, China Palace, Chipotle, Denny's, El Campesino, Five Guys, Golden Corral, Max&Erma's, McDonald's, Outback Steaks, Panda Express, Panera Bread, Penn Sta Subs, Primanti Bros, Red Lobster, Starbucks, Subway, Taco Bell, Wendy's Comfort Suites, Courtyard, Day's Inn, Extended Stay America, Hampton Inn, Holiday Inn Express, Red Roof Inn H, AT&T, Big Lots, CVS Drug, GNC, Honda, Lowes Whse, Marshall's, NTB, Old Navy, Pet Land, PetCo, Rite Aid, to Heinz Field, URGENT CARE

49mm **Oakmont Service Plaza eb,** Sunoco/dsl/e85/24hr Burger King, Starbucks litter barrels,

48.5mm Allegheny River

48 PA 28, to Pittsburgh, Allegheny Valley, New Kensington, **N** Exxon, Sunoco Rite Aid, **S** GetGo, Marathon/dsl, Sheetz/dsl Bob Evans, Burger King, Denny's, Dunkin Donuts, Gino Bro's Pizza, KFC, McDonald's, Pizza Hut, Primanti Bros, Subway, Wendy's Day's Inn, Hampton Inn, Holiday Inn Express, Quality Inn, TownePlace Suites, Valley Motel Advance Parts, AutoZone, Ford, Target

41mm **parking area/call box eb**

39 PA 8, to Pittsburgh, Butler Valley, **0-1 mi** **N** Exxon, GetGo, Sheetz/dsl, Sunoco Applebee's, Atria's Rest., Bruno's Pizza, Buffalo Wild Wings, Eat'n Park, King's Rest., McDonald's, Starbucks, Taco Bell, Wendy's Quality Inn $Tree, Advance Parts, Chrysler/Dodge/Jeep, Dunkin Donuts, Giant Eagle Foods, GNC, Kohl's, Lowes Whse, Petco, Shop'n Save Foods, Target, TJ Maxx, USPO, Walmart/Subway, **S** BP, Sunoco/dsl

= gas = food = lodging = other = rest stop Copyright 2019 - The Next EXIT

INTERSTATE 76 (Turnpike) Cont'd

CRANBERRY

39 Continued
Arby's, Bruster's, Burger King, China Bistro, Domino's, KFC, Little Caesar's, McDonald's, Panera Bread, Pasquales Pizza, Pizza Hut, Primanti Bros, Starbucks, Subway, Vocelli Pizza H, AT&T, AutoZone, CVS Drug, Firestone/auto, Home Depot, Mr. Tire, NTB, O'Reilly Parts, Pepboys, Rite Aid, USPO

31mm **Toll Plaza wb**

28 to I-79, to Cranberry, Pittsburgh, **N** BP/7-11/dsl, GetGo, Marathon/dsl, Sheetz/dsl, Sunoco/dsl Aladdin's Eatery, Arby's, Bob Evans, Boston Mkt, Bravo Italian, Buffalo Wild Wings, Burger King, Chipotle Mexican, Denny's, Domino's, Dunkin Donuts, Dynasty, Eat'n Park, Emiliano's, Firehouse Subs, Five Guys, HotDog Shoppe, Houlihan's, Ichiban Steakhouse, Jason's Deli, Jersey Mike's, Jimmy John's, Mad Mex, Max&Erma's, McDonald's, Monte Cello's Grill, Panda Express, Panera Bread, Perkins, Pizza Hut, Pizza Roma, Primanti Bros, Saga Steaks, Subway, Vocelli Pizza, Wendy's Candlewood Suites, Clarion, Comfort Inn, Doubletree, Hampton Inn, Hyatt Place, Motel 6, Quality Inn, Red Roof Inn, Residence Inn, Super 8, Woodspring Suites $Tree, Aldi Foods, AT&T, AutoZone, Barnes&Noble, Best Buy, Costco/gas, Field&Stream, Firestone/auto, Giant Eagle Foods, GNC, Home Depot, Jo-Ann Fabrics, Marshall's, Michael's, NAPA, PepBoys, Petco, Rite Aid, Toyota, Tuesday Morning, USPO, Verizon, Walgreens, Walmart

23.5mm **pulloff eb**

17mm **parking area eb**

13.4mm **parking area eb**

13mm Beaver River

13 PA 8, to Ellwood City, Beaver Valley, **N** Al's Corner Subway Beaver Falls Motel, Lark Motel, Park Inn H, **S** Super 8

10 PA 60 (toll), to New Castle, Pittsburgh, **S** to

6mm **pulloff eb**

2mm **pulloff eb**

1mm **toll plaza eb, toll plaza eb**

0mm Pennsylvania/Ohio state line

INTERSTATE 78

ALLENTOWN

Exit# Services

77mm Pennsylvania/New Jersey state line, Delaware River

76mm **Welcome Ctr wb, full facilities, litter barrels, petwalk, , vending, toll booth wb**

75 to PA 611, Easton, **N** TurkeyHill/dsl Dunkin Donuts, McDonald's (1mi), Subway Quality Inn Crayola Factory, CVS Drug, **S** Exxon/dsl

71 PA 33, to Stroudsburg, **1 mi N on Freemansburg Ave** CJT Asian, Frank's Pizza, Panera Bread, Ruby Tuesday, TGIFriday's, TX Roadhouse, Wayback Burgers Courtyard Barnes&Noble, Best Buy, Dick's, H, Lowe's, Michael's, Pet Supplies+, ShopRite Mkt, Staples

67 PA 412, Hellertown, **N** TurkeyHill/gas Wendy's Comfort Suites (3mi) H, Chevrolet, **S** Citgo/dsl, Exxon/dsl, Sunoco Bella's Ristorante, Dunkin Donuts, Papa John's, Rocco's Pizza, Roma Pizza, Vassi's Drive-In, Waffle House Holiday Inn Express 7-11, CVS Drug, repair

60b a PA 145 N, PA 309 S, South Fort St, Quakertown

59 to PA 145 (from eb), Summit Lawn

58 Emaus St (from wb), **S** Gulf $General

57 Lehigh St, **N** Sunoco/dsl, WaWa/dsl China House, IHOP, Palumbo Pizza, Queen City Diner, Subway, Willy Joe's Rest.

57 Continued
Best Value Inn $Tree, AAA, BigLots, CVS Drug, Family$, Ford/Lincoln, Home Depot, Infiniti, Kia, Redner's Whse, STS Tires/repair, Toyota, VW, **S** Sunoco, TurkeyHill, Valero A1 Japanese, Bangkok, Brass Rail Rest., Domino's, Dunkin Donuts, McDonald's, Papa John's, Perkins, Pizza Hut, Taco Bell, Rodizio Grill, Rossi's Pizza, Starbucks, Subway, Tilted Kilt Eatery, Wendy's Acura, AT&T, Audi/Mercedes/Porsche, BonTon, Bottom$ Mkt, Buick/GMC, Cadillac/Chevrolet, Chrysler/Dodge/Jeep, Honda, Hyundai, Kost Tire, Mazda, Midas, Ross, Staples, SteinMart, Verizon, Volvo, Williams Tire/auto

55 PA 29, Cedar Crest Blvd, **N** Shell, **S** H

54b a US 222, Hamilton Blvd, **N** Speedway Bamboo Asian, Baskin-Robbins/Dunkin Donuts, Boston Mkt, Carrabba's, Friendly's, Gourmet Buffet, Ice Cream World, McDonald's, Menchie's, Perkins, Pistachio Cafe, Pizza Hut, Subway, Teppan Steaks, TGIFriday's, Wendy's Comfort Suites/rest., Holiday Inn Express, Howard Johnson Bottom$ Mkt, Dorney Funpark, Dorneyville Drug, Office Depot, Rite Aid, Weis Foods, **S** WaWa Dunkin Donuts, Hunan Springs Wingate Inn Queen City Tire, repair, Subaru

53 PA 309 (wb only)

51 to I-476, US 22 E, PA 33 N (eb only), Whitehall

49b a PA 100, Fogelsville, **N** Arby's, Cracker Barrel, Joe's Pizza, Silver, Panda&Fish Chinese, Pizza Hut, Winger Deli Comfort Inn, Hawthorn Inn KOA (7mi), Rite Aid, STS Tire/repair, **S** Shell/Dunkin Donuts, Sunoco, WaWa/dsl Boston Grill, Burger King, Florence Italian, Starlite Diner, Taco Bell, Yocco's Hotdogs Hampton Inn, Hilton Garden, Holiday Inn, Sleep Inn, Staybridge Suites Clover Hill Winery, st police, Toyota

45 PA 863, to Lynnport, **N** Exxon/Subway/dsl, Sunoco/Ne Smithville Diner/dsl truck service, **S** Super 8

40 PA 737, Krumsville, **N** Pine Hill Campground, Robin Hill Park (4mi)

35 PA 143, Lenhartsville, **3 mi S** Robin Hill Park

30 Hamburg, **S** Hamburg Mkt

29b a PA 61, to Reading, Pottsville, **N** Shell//Subway/dsl, WaWa/dsl Baskin-Robbins/Dunkin Donuts, Burger King, Cracker Barrel, Five Guys, JA Buffet, LJ Silver/Taco Bell, Logan's Roadhouse, McDonald's, Pappy T's, Pizza Hut, Red Robin, Wendy's Microtel $Tree, Advance Parts, AT&T, Boat'n Ctr RV, Cabela's Outdoor, GNC, Harley-Davidson (8mi), Hyundai, Lowe's, Pet Supplies+, Russell Stover, Toyota, Verizon, Walmart/Subway

23 Shartlesville, **N** Chromeshop/dsl, Loves/McDonald's/Subway/dsl/scales/24hr Dunkin' Donuts Dutch Mo Appalachian Campsites, **S** Blue Mtn Family Rest. Scottish Inn antiques, camping, Dutch Haus/gifts, USPO

19 PA 183, Strausstown, **N** Lukoil Sheepskin Mot **S** Power/dsl

17 PA 419, Rehrersburg, **N** Best truck/tire repair

16 Midway, **N** Exxon/dsl, Sunoco/dsl J&S Pizza, Midway Diner Comfort Inn, **S** auto/truck repair

15 Grimes

13 PA 501, Bethel, **N** Valero/dsl, **S** Bethel/dsl dsl rep

10 PA 645, Frystown, **S** FLYING J/Huddle House/Subway/dsl/scales/24hr/@ Travel Inn

6 (8 from wb, US 22)PA 343, Fredricksburg, **1 mi S** PP/ Redner's Whse/mkt Esther's Rest. KOA (5mi)

I-81. I-78 begins/ends on I-81, exit 89.

PA

INTERSTATE 79

Exit#	Services
183b a	PA 5, 12th St, Erie, E H, Valley Tire, W Country Fair/dsl, GetGo, Sunoco/dsl Applebee's, Bob Evans, Bruster's, Dunkin Donuts, Eat'n Park, El Canelo Mexican, Five Guys, Hibachi Japanese, KFC, McDonald's, Moe's SW Grill, Panera Bread, Pizza Hut, Serafini's, Taco Bell, Tim Hortons, Wendy's Comfort Inn (2mi) $General, $Tree, Advance Parts, Aldi Foods, BigLots, CVS Drug, Dunn Tire, Family$, Giant Eagle Foods, GNC, Save-a-Lot Foods, Tires-4-Less, to Presque Isle SP, Tuesday Morning, U-Haul, Verizon, vet
182	US 20, 26th St, E Country Fair/dsl, KwikFill Subway H, CVS Drug, Family$, Tops Foods/gas/24hr, W Country Fair/dsl, GetGo/dsl Arby's, Burger King, DQ, Hong Kong Chinese, Hoss's Steaks, Hungry Howie's, Little Caesar's, LJ Silver, McDonald's, Subway, Tim Hortons Glass House Inn $General, AT&T, AutoZone, Ford, Giant Eagle Foods, Monro, O'Reilly Parts, TrueValue, URGENT CARE, USPO, vet, Volvo
180	US 19, to Kearsarge, E Aoyama Japanese, Arby's, Buffalo Wild Wings, Cheddars, Coldstone, Firebirds Grill, Fox&Hound, KFC, Mad Mex, Max&Erma's, McDonald's, Moe's SW Grill, O'Charley's, Olive Garden, Outback Steaks, Primanti Bros, Red Lobster, Smokey Bones BBQ, Starbucks, Wendy's Candlewood Suites, Fairfield Inn, Homewood Suites, SpringHill Suites, TownePlace Suites H, Audi/Cadillac, Barnes&Noble, Bon-Ton, Chrysler/Dodge/Jeep, Dick's, Field & Stream, Firestone/auto, JC Penney, Macy's, Michael's, Petco, PetCo, Rite Aid, Ross, TJ Maxx, Toyota, Verizon, W Country Fair/dsl camping
178b a	I-90, E to Buffalo, W to Cleveland
174	to McKean, E access to gas/dsl, W KOA
166	US 6N, to Edinboro, E Country Fair/dsl, Sheetz McDonald's (3mi), Subway, TacoBell (2mi), Wendy's Comfort Suites Advance Parts, vet, Walmart/Subway
163mm	**both lanes, full facilities, litter barrels, petwalk, vending**
154	PA 198, to Saegertown, Conneautville, E Erie NWR (17mi)
147b a	US 6, US 19, US 322, to Meadville, E All American Gas/wash, Country Fair, GetGo, Sheetz/dsl Applebee's, Arby's, Chovy's Italian, Cracker Barrel, DQ, Five Guys, Hoss's Rest., KFC, Perkins, Pizza Hut, Subway, Super Buffet, Taco Bell Days Inn/rest., EconoLodge, Holiday Inn Express H, URGENT CARE, Advance Parts, AT&T, Family$, Giant Eagle Foods, Home Depot, Jo-Ann Fabrics, Save-a-Lot Foods, W Sheetz/dsl Burger King, Compadres Mexican, King's Rest., McDonald's, Red Lobster, Subway, Tim Hortons, Yuen's Garden Hampton Inn, Quality Inn $Tree, AutoZone, Buick/GMC, Chevrolet, GNC, Staples, to Pymatuning SP, Toyota, URGENT CARE, Verizon, Walmart/Subway
141	PA 285, to Geneva, E to Erie NWR (20mi), W Aunt Bee's Rest./dsl, Citgo/dsl
135mm	**/weigh sta both lanes, full facilities, litter barrels, petwalk, vending**
130	PA 358, to Sandy Lake, W H (13mi), to Goddard SP
121	US 62, to Mercer, E Valley Tire, W Sunoco/dsl st police
116b a	I-80, E to Clarion, W to Sharon
113	PA 208, PA 258, to Grove City, E Country Fair/dsl, Marathon/dsl Compadres Mexican H, W KwikFill/Subway, Sheetz/dsl Eat'n Park, Elephant&Castle Rest., Hoss' Rest., King's Rest., McDonald's, My Bro's Place, Primanti Bros,

E R I E

M E A D V I L L E

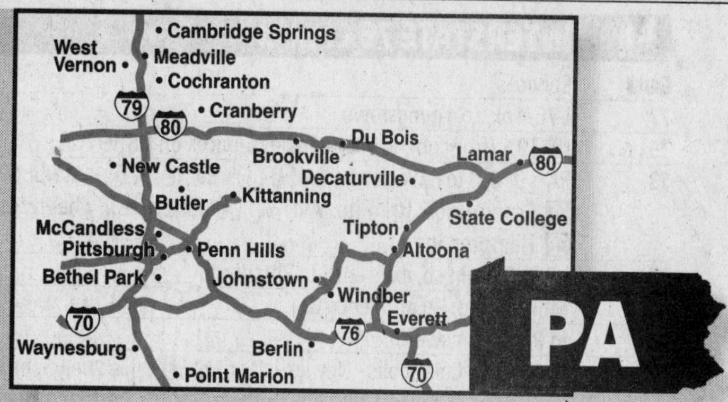

Exit#	Services
113	Continued Taco Bell, Timber Creek Rest., Wendy's Best Western, Candlewood Suites, Comfort Inn, Hampton Inn, Holiday Inn Express, Microtel, Super 8, TownePlace Suites KOA (3mi), Premium Outlets/famous brands
110mm	**/weigh sta sb, full facilities, litter barrels, petwalk, vending**
107mm	**/weigh sta nb, full facilities, litter barrels, petwalk, vending**
105	PA 108, to Slippery Rock, E DQ Evening Star Motel Slippery Rock Camping, to Slippery Rock U
99	US 422, to New Castle, E to Moraine SP, W Pilot/McDonald's/Subway/dsl/scales/24hr Coopers Lake Camping, to Rose Point Camping
96	PA 488, Portersville, E Bear Run Camping, Moraine SP, W Marathon/dsl Brown's Country Kitchen McConnell's Mill SP (3mi)
88	(87 from nb) US 19, PA 68, Zelienople, W Exxon/dsl Burger King, Fox's Pizza, Log Cabin Inn Rest., Pizza Hut
85	(83 from nb), PA 528 (no quick return), to Evans City, W Buick/GMC
83	PA 528, Evans City
80mm	**weigh sta both lanes**
78	(76 from nb, exits left from nb), US 19, PA 228, to Mars, access to I-76, PA TPK, E GetGo/dsl, Gulf/7-11/dsl Anthony's Pizza, Applebee's, Chick-fil-A, Cracker Barrel, DiBella's Subs, Firebirds, Jimmy Wan's Chinese, Juniper Grill, Longhorn Steaks, McDonald's, Moe's SW Grill, Noodles&Co, Olive Garden, Patron Mexican, Red Robin, River City Grille, Smokey Bones BBQ, Starbucks, Subway Best Western+, Courtyard, Hilton Garden, Home 2 Suites, Marriott, TownePlace Suites Dick's, GNC, Kohl's, Lowe's, Petsmart, Staples, Target, TJ Maxx, Verizon, W on US 19 Aladdin's Eatery, Arby's, Bob Evans, Boston Mkt, Bravo Italian, Buffalo Wild Wings, Burger King, Chipotle Mexican, Denny's, Domino's, Dunkin Donuts, Dynasty, Eat'n Park, Emiliano's Mexican, Firehouse Subs, Five Guys, HotDog Shoppe, Houlihan's, Ichiban Steakhouse, Jason's Deli, Jersey Mike's, Jimmy John's, Mad Mex, Max&Erma's, McDonald's, Monte Cello's Grill, Panda Express, Panera Bread, Perkins, Pizza Hut, Pizza Roma, Primanti Bros, Saga Steaks, Subway, Vocelli Pizza, Wendy's Candlewood Suites, Clarion, Comfort Inn, Doubletree, Hampton Inn, Hyatt Place, Motel 6, Quality Inn, Red Roof Inn, Residence Inn, Super 8, Woodspring Suites H, $Tree, Aldi Foods, AT&T, AutoZone, Barnes&Noble, Best Buy, BP/7-11/dsl, Costco/gas, Field&Stream, Firestone/auto, GetGo, Giant Eagle Foods, GNC, Home Depot, Jo-Ann Fabrics, Marathon/dsl, Marshall's, Michael's, NAPA, PepBoys, PetCo, Rite Aid, Sheetz/dsl, Sunoco/dsl, Toyota, Tuesday Morning, USPO, Verizon, Walgreens, Walmart

C R A N B E R R Y

PITTSBURGH

INTERSTATE 79 Cont'd

Exit#	Services
77	I-76/Tpk, to Youngstown
75	US 19 S (from nb), to Warrendale, services on US 19
73	PA 910, to Wexford, E Eat'n Park, Starbucks EconoLodge Rite Aid, W Exxon/dsl, Sheetz/dsl Hampton Inn
72	I-279 S (from sb, exits left), to Pittsburgh
68	Mt Nebo Rd, E Sheetz/dsl
66	to PA 65, Emsworth
65	to PA 51, Coraopolis, Neville Island, E Speedway/Speedway Cafe Kings Grille Fairfield Inn Penske Trucks, W Subway
64.5mm	Ohio River
64	PA 51 (from nb), to Coraopolis, McKees Rocks
60	PA 60, Crafton, E GetGo/dsl Primanti Bros Comfort Inn, EconoLodge, Hilltop Motel, Motel 6 H, W Juliano's Rest. Meineke
59b	I-376 W, US 22 W, US 30 (from nb), W
59a	I-376 E, to Pittsburgh
57	to Carnegie
55	PA 50, to Heidelberg, E on PA 50 Advance Parts, Marathon/dsl, Sunoco Arby's, Bob Evans, ChuckeCheese, Eat'n Park, Jersey Mike's, LJ Silver, McDonald's, Moe's SW, Panera Bread, Pizza Hut, Sonic, Starbucks, Subway, Taco Bell, TX Roadhouse, Walnut Grill, Wendy's $Tree, BigLots, Firestone/auto, Ford, Giant Eagle Foods, GNC, Home Depot, Jo-Ann Fabrics, Lowe's, Mr Tire, Pepboys, Rite Aid, Shop'n Save, TJ Maxx, Tuesday Morning, Walgreens, Walmart
54	PA 50, to Bridgeville, E BP/dsl, GetGo Chipotle, Jimmy John's, McDonald's, Starbucks Holiday Inn Express H, Aldi Foods, Chevrolet, Midas, Monro, NAPA, Rite Aid, USPO, W Sunoco/dsl Five Guys Hampton Inn
50mm	**[RS]/weigh sta both lanes, full facilities, litter barrels, petwalk, [phone], [picnic], vending**
48	South Pointe, W Jackson's Rest. Holiday Inn Express, Hilton Garden, Homewood Suites
45	to PA 980, Canonsburg, E Sheetz Toyota, W Citgo Dunkin Donuts, Hogfathers BBQ, KFC/Taco Bell, Little Caesar's, McDonald's, Papa John's, Pizza Hut, Starbucks, Subway, WaiWai Grill, Wendy's Super 8 $General, Advance Parts, auto/transmission repair, AutoZone, Walgreens
43	PA 519, Houston, E BP/dsl, W Sunoco Freightliner
41	Race Track Rd, E Marathon/dsl Burger King, Dunkin Donuts, McDonald's, Waffle House, Wendy's Cambria Suites, Candlewood Suites, Comfort Inn, Country Inn&Suites, Courtyard, Doubletree, Hampton Inn, Holiday Inn Express, Hyatt Place Audi, Old Navy, racetrack, Tanger Outlets/famous brands, W BP/dsl Microtel Trolley Museum
40	Meadow Lands, W golf, racetrack, Trolley Museum (3mi)
38	I-70 W, to Wheeling

I-79 and I-70 run together 3.5 mi. See I-70, exits 19b-20.

WAYNESBURG

Exit#	Services
34	I-70 E, to Greensburg
33	US 40, to Laboratory, W KOA
31mm	**weigh sta sb**
30	US 19, to Amity, W Exxon/Subway/dsl
23	to Marianna, Prosperity
19	US 19, to PA 221, Ruff Creek, W BP/dsl
14	PA 21, to Waynesburg, E Bob Evans Comfort Inn, Microtel Walmart/Subway, W BP/7-11/dsl, Exxon/dsl, GetGo, Marathon, Sheetz, Sunoco Burger King, DQ, Golden Wok, Hardee's, KFC, Little Caesar's, McDonald's, Pizza Hut,
14	Continued Subway, Taco Bell, Wendy's EconoLodge, Hampton Inn, Super 8 H, $General, $Tree, Advance Parts, Aldi Foods, AT&T, AutoZone, BigLots, Cadillac/Chevrolet/Subaru, Chrysler/Dodge/Jeep, CVS Drug, Giant Eagle Foods, Rite Aid, st police, Subaru, Verizon
7	to Kirby
6mm	**Welcome Ctr/weigh sta nb, full facilities, litter barrels, petwalk, [phone], [picnic], vending**
1	Mount Morris, E Sunoco/Huddle House/dsl/scales/24h Honda/Mazda, W Marathon/dsl
0mm	Pennsylvania/West Virginia state line

STROUDSBURG

INTERSTATE 80

Exit#	Services
311mm	Pennsylvania/New Jersey state line, Delaware River
310.5	**toll booth wb, [phone]**
310	PA 611, Delaware Water Gap, S Fuel On, Gulf Apple Pie Bakery, Doughboys Pizza, Water Gap Diner, **...Welcome Ctr/[RS], full services, info**
309	US 209 N, PA 447, to Marshalls Creek, N Gulf Blue Tequila Mexican, DQ, Dunkin Donuts, Landmark Cafe, Wendy's (2mi) Days Inn, Staybridge Suites H
308	East Stroudsburg, N Exxon/Subs Now H, vet, WaWa, 1 mi S Arby's, Burger King, CiCi's, Friendly's, Holy Guacamole, Ichiban Asian, KFC, McDonald's, Roasted Tomato Grill Budget Motel, Super 8 ShopRite Foods, Walmart/McDonald's
307	PA 191, Broad St, N Hampton Inn H, S Sunoco Compton's Rest. EconoLodge
306	Dreher Ave (from wb, no EZ return), N WaWa
305	US 209, Main St, N Gulf/dsl, Shell Perkins Quality Inn, S Exxon/dsl Holiday Inn Express
304	US 209, to PA 33, 9th St (from wb)
303	9th St, (from eb), N 5 Guys Burgers, Burger King, Dunkin Donuts, Fume Asin, Garfield's Rest., McDonald's, Olive Garden, Panera Bread, Popeye's, Ruby Tuesday, TX Roadhouse, Wendy's $Tree, Best Buy, BJ's/Subway/gas, Bon Ton, Buick/GMC, Chevrolet, CVS Drug, Home Depot, Hyundai, JC Penney, Kia, Michaels, Midas, Old Navy, Petsmart, Staples, Target, Target, TJ Maxx, URGENT CARE, Walgreens, Weis Foods/gas
302	PA 611, to Bartonsville, N Exxon/dsl Big Daddy's BBQ, Chili's, Dickey's BBQ, Dunkin Donuts, East Gourmet Buffet, Frank's Pizza, Ichiban Steaks, Longhorn Steaks, Moe's SW Grill, Red Lobster, Red Robin, Sonic, Studebaker's, Subway Comfort Inn, Hampton Inn, Howard Johnson $Tree, Advance Parts, AT&T, Dick's, Giant Foods/gas, Kohl's, Lowe's, URGENT CARE, Verizon
299	PA 715, Tannersville, N Citgo/dsl, Mobil/Burger King/dsl, Turkey Hill DQ, Dunkin Donuts, FoodCout, Friendly's, Pocono Diner Ramada Ltd, Scotrun Motel $General, CVS Drug, The Crossing Factory Outlet/famous brands, Weis Foods, S Sunoco/dsl Tannersville Diner Days Inn, Summit Resort to Big Pocono SP, to Camelback Ski Area
298	PA 611 (from wb), to Scotrun, N Sunoco/dsl Brick Oven Pizza Great Wolf Lodge, Scotrun Diner/motel to Mt Pocono
295mm	**[RS] eb, full facilities, litter barrels, petwalk, [phone], [picnic], vending**
293	I-380 N, to Scranton, (exits left from eb)
284	PA 115, to Wilkes-Barre, Blakeslee, N WaWa/dsl Best Western, Blakeslee Inn (2mi) Fern Ridge Camping, st police, S Exxon/dsl Ray's Tuscan Villa to Pocono Raceway

PA

E INTERSTATE 80 Cont'd

Exit#	Services
277	PA 940, to PA Tpk (I-476), to Pocono, Lake Harmony, Allentown, N WaWa A&W/LJ Silver, Arby's, McDonald's, Subway Comfort Inn, EconoLodge, Holiday Inn Express, Mtn Laurel Resort, Pocono Inn/Resort, Quality Inn, Split Rock Resort
274	PA 534, N Hickory Run/Valero/rest./dsl/scales/24hr, Sunoco/Subs Now/dsl/24hr towing/repair, S to Hickory Run SP (6mi)
273mm	Lehigh River
273	PA 940, PA 437, to Freeland, White Haven, N Exxon, Fuel One, S Forks Rest., Powerhouse Eatery
270mm	**eb, full facilities, info, litter barrels, petwalk, , , vending**
262	PA 309, to Hazleton, Mountain Top, N Citgo Mary's Rest., Wendy's EconoLodge auto/truck repair, S Valero/dsl Holiday Inn Express Nescopeck SP (5mi)
260b a	I-81, N to Wilkes-Barre, S to Harrisburg
256	PA 93, to Nescopeck, Conyngham, N Citgo/repair, Pilot/Subway/dsl/scales/24hr, S Tom's Kitchen (2mi) Hampton Inn (4mi), Motel 6 H, towing/truck repair
251mm	Nescopeck River
246mm	**/weigh sta both lanes, full facilities, litter barrels, petwalk, , , vending, weather info**
242	PA 339, to Mainville, Mifflinville, N Loves/Arby's/dsl/scales/24hr, Sunoco/Burger King/Subway/dsl McDonald's Super 8, S Exxon/dsl Comfort Inn
241mm	Susquehanna River
241b a	US 11, to Berwick, Lime Ridge, Bloomsburg, N Red Maple Inn (2mi) H, 2-5 mi S Sheetz/dsl, Sunoco/Subs Now/dsl Applebee's, Arby's, Burger King, Domino's, Dunkin Donuts, Kemlar's Rest., Marley's Grill, McDonald's, Morris Rest., Oliran Japanese, Pizza Hut, Rita's Custard, Subway, Taco Bell, Taste of Italy, Wendy's Budget Host, Relax Inn AAA, Ace Hardware, Advance Parts, BigLots, Buick/GMC, Cadillac/Chevrolet, CVS Drug, Ford/Honda, Giant Foods/gas, Kost Tire, Rite Aid, Staples, U-Haul, Weis Foods/gas
236	PA 487, to Bloomsburg, Lightstreet, S Sunoco Denny's Hampton Inn, Relax Inn (2mi), Turkey Hill Inn H, to Bloomsburg U
232	PA 42, Buckhorn, N Exxon/Subs Now, TA/Country Pride/Subway/dsl/scales/24hr/@ Burger King, Cracker Barrel, KFC, Perkins, Quaker Steak&Lube, Ruby Tuesday, Wendy's EconoLodge, Holiday Inn Express AT&T, BonTon, Home Depot, S Carini's Italian, Gourmet Buffet, Olive Garden, Panera Bread Comfort Suites $Tree, Indian Head Camping (3mi), Lowe's, Marshall's, PetCo, Verizon, Walmart/McDonald's
224	PA 54, to Danville, N Exxon/Subway/dsl Quality Inn, S Mobil/dsl Friendly's, McDonald's Best Western, Hampton Inn, Red Roof Inn, Super 8 H
219mm	**both lanes, full facilities, info, litter barrels, petwalk, , , vending**
215	PA 254, Limestonevill, S FLYING J/Penn 80 Rest./Subway/dsl/scales/24hr/@ Eagle Truckwash
212b a	I-180 W, PA 147 S, to Muncy, Williamsport, S Sunoco (1mi)
210.5mm	Susquehanna River
210b a	US 15, to Williamsport, Lewisburg, S Sunoco/dsl Bonanza Holiday Inn Express, Quality Inn H, KOA (5mi)
199	Mile Run
194mm	**/weigh sta both lanes, full facilities, litter barrels, petwalk, , , vending**

HAZLETON

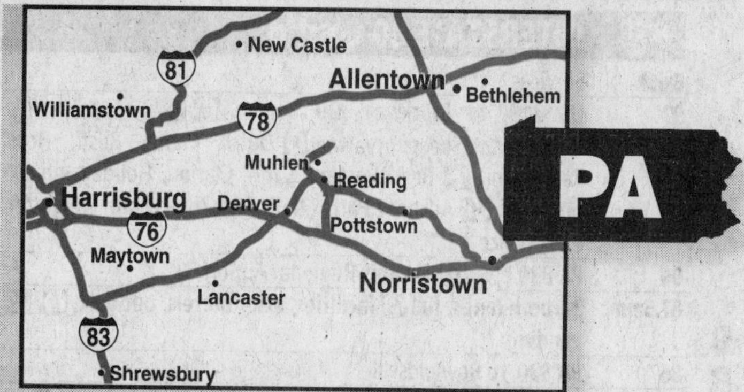

Exit#	Services
192	PA 880, to Jersey Shore, N Sunoco/dsl H, S Valero/dsl towing/truck repair
185	PA 477, Loganton, N Valero Dar's Diner, S Twilight Diner RB Winter SP (12mi)
178	US 220, Lock Haven, 5 mi N KwikFill/dsl, Sheetz/dsl Little Caesar's, Pizza Hut, Ruby Tuesday H, $General, $Tree, Advance Parts, Lowe's, Walmart/Subway, Weis Foods
173	PA 64, Lamar, N Pilot/Subway/dsl/scales/24hr Cottage Rest., McDonald's Hampton Inn, Quality Inn/rest. repair, S FLYING J/Denny's/dsl/LP/scales/24hr/, TA/Country Pride/dsl/scales/24hr/@, Valero
161	I-99, US 220 S, PA 26, to Bellafonte, N Bellefonte Camping, KOA (2mi), S to PSU
158	US 220 S, PA 150, to Altoona, Milesburg, N Bestway/rest./dsl/motel/24hr/@, Shell/Subway, TA/Country Pride/dsl/scales/24hr/@, Valero/dsl McDonald's Quality Inn, S st police
147	PA 144, to Snow Shoe, N Exxon/dsl/repair/24hr, Sunoco/dsl/24hr Snow Shoe Rest., Snow Shoe Sandwich Shop, Subway Hall's Foods, USPO
146mm	**both lanes, full facilities, litter barrels, petwalk, , , vending**
138mm	Moshannon River
133	PA 53, to Philipsburg, Kylertown, N KwikFill/motel/dsl/scales Roadhouse Rest. dsl repair, Mtn View Mkt, USPO, S H, Black Moshannon SP (9mi)
123	PA 970, to Shawville, Woodland, N Woodland Camping, S Gio's BBQ/dsl (2mi), PP/dsl st police, USPO
120mm	Susquehanna River, W Branch
120	PA 879, Shawville, Clearfield, N Sapp Bros/rest./dsl/scales/24hr/@ Days Inn Peterbilt, S BP/dsl, Sheetz, Snappy's Arby's, Burger King, Chinese Buffet, Dunkin Donuts, Dutch Pantry, KFC/Taco Bell, McDonald's Best Western+, Comfort Inn, Hampton Inn, Holiday Inn Express, Red Roof Inn, Super 8 H, Lowe's, Walmart/Subway
111mm	highest point on I-80 east of Mississippi River, 2250 ft
111	PA 153, to Penfield, N to Parker Dam, to SB Elliot SP, S H
101	PA 255, Du Bois, N Snappy's/Quiznos/dsl camping, 1-2 mi S Sheetz/dsl A&W/LJ Silver, Arby's, Burger King, Dubois Buffet, Eat'n Park, Italian Oven, Japan One, McDonald's, Napoli Pizzeria, Perkins, Pizza Hut, Ponderosa, Red Lobster, Ruby Tuesday, Station 101 Grill, Subway, Taco Bell, Valley Dairy Rest., Wendy's Fairfield Inn, Hampton Inn, Homewood Suites H, $General, $Tree, Aldi Foods, BigLots, BonTon, CVS Drug, JC Penney, Jo-Ann Fabrics, Lowe's, Old Navy, PetCo, Rite Aid, Ross, Shop'n Save Foods, st police, Staples, TJ Maxx, URGENT CARE, Verizon, Walmart/Subway

LAMAR

DU BOIS

= gas = food = lodging = other = rest stop

INTERSTATE 80 Cont'd

Exit#	Services
97	US 219, to Brockway, Du Bois, S Pilot/Arby's/dsl/scales/24hr, Sheetz/dsl/24hr Dutch Pantry Rest., Hoss' Rest. (2mi) Best Western (2mi), Clarion, Holiday Inn Express H, Advance Parts (2mi), AutoZone (2mi), Freightliner, st police
90	PA 830 E, N Du Bois Regional Airport
87.5mm	**both lanes, full facilities, litter barrels, petwalk, vending**
86	PA 830, to Reynoldsville
81	PA 28, to Brookville, Hazen, S Brookville, hist dist (2mi)
78	PA 36, to Sigel, Brookville, N FLYING J/Denny's/dsl/LP/scales/24hr, TA/BP/Taco Bell/dsl/scales/Howard Johnson/24hr/@ DQ, McDonald's, Pizza Hut Super 8 NAPA, to Cook Forest SP, S GetGo/dsl, Oring CNG, Sheetz Arby's, Burger King, China Wok, Plyler's Buffet, Subway Gold Eagle Inn, Quality Inn Chrysler/Dodge/Jeep, Family$, truckwash
73	PA 949, Corsica, N to Clear Creek SP, S USPO
70	US 322, to Strattanville
64	PA 66 S, to New Bethlehem, Clarion, N to Clarion U
62	PA 68, to Clarion, N BP, KwikFill/dsl Applebee's, Arby's, Burger King, Eat'n Park, Hunan King, McDonald's, Perkins, Pizza Hut, RRR Roadhouse, Sakura Buffet, Subway, Taco Bell Comfort Inn, Hampton Inn, Holiday Inn Express, Microtel, Motel 6, Park Inn, Quality Inn, Super 8 H, $Tree, Advance Parts, Aldi Foods, AT&T, AutoZone, JC Penney, Verizon, Walmart/Subway
61mm	Clarion River
60	PA 66 N, to Shippenville, N Jiffy/dsl camping, to Cook Forest SP
56mm	**weigh sta both lanes**
53	to PA 338, to Knox, N Satterlee Gas/dsl (cardlock) BJ's Eatery Countryside Crafts/Quilts, Wolf's Camping Resort, S Good Tire Service
45	PA 478, to St Petersburg, Emlenton, 4 mi S Golf Hall of Fame
44.5mm	Allegheny River
42	PA 38, to Emlenton, N Exxon/Subway/dsl, Shell/Trkstp/rest./dsl/scales/24hr Emlenton Motel Gaslight RV Park, truck/RV repair
35	PA 308, to Clintonville
30.5mm	**both lanes, full facilities, litter barrels, petwalk, vending**
29	PA 8, to Franklin, Barkeyville, N Speedway/Speedway Cafe/dsl Arby's, Burger King, King's Rest. Motel 6, Quality Inn Freightliner, S Heath/dsl, KwikFill/dsl/scales/motel/24hr, TA/BP/Subway/dsl/scales/24hr/@ to Slippery Rock U, truckwash
24	PA 173, to Grove City, Sandy Lake, S H, Grove City Coll
19b a	I-79, N to Erie, S to Pittsburgh
15	US 19, to Mercer, N PP/dsl, Shell Burger King, Margarita King Mexican, McDonald's/rv parking Comfort Inn st police, 2 mi S Iron Bridge Rest., Springfield Grill KOA (4mi)
4b a	I-376, PA 60, to PA 18, to Sharon-Hermitage, New Castle, N Sheetz/dsl, Sunoco/Subway/dsl EconoLodge, Hampton Inn, Holiday Inn Express, Park Inn, Quality Inn, Red Roof Inn, Super 8, S DQ, MiddleSex Diner $General
2.5mm	Shenango River
1mm	**Welcome Ctr eb, full facilities, litter barrels, petwalk, vending**
0mm	Pennsylvania/Ohio state line

BROOKVILLE

CLARION

INTERSTATE 81

Exit#	Services
233mm	Pennsylvania/New York state line
232mm	**Welcome Ctr/weigh sta sb, full facilities, litter barrels, petwalk,**
230	PA 171, Great Bend, E Valero Lakeside Camping (5mi), W Exxon/Tim Hortons/dsl, Sunoco/dsl Burger King, Dobb's Country Kitchen, Dunkin Donuts, McDonald's, Subway Colonial Brick Motel Family$, Reddon's Drugs, Rob's Foods
223	PA 492, New Milford, E East Lake Camping/RV Park (3mi), W Gulf/dsl, Sunoco, Valero Green Gables Rest. Blue Ridge Motel, Lynn Lee B&B (1.5mi)
219	PA 848, to Gibson, E Sunoco/Burger King/dsl, W FLYING J/Denny's/dsl/scales/24hr, Exxon/McDonald's/dsl/24hr Holiday Inn Express, st police
217	PA 547, Harford, E Exxon/Subway/dsl/24hr, Mobil/dsl/24hr
211	PA 92, Lenox, E Elk Mtn Ski Area, Shady Rest Camping (3mi), W Pump-N-Pantry/dsl, Shell/dsl Bingham's Rest., Lenox Rest. Lenox Drug
209mm	**sb, full facilities, litter barrel, petwalk, vending**
206	PA 374, to Glenwood, Lenoxville, E Sunoco/dsl to Elk Mountain Ski Resort
203mm	**nb, full facilities, litter barrels, petwalk, vending**
202	PA 107, to Fleetville, Tompkinsville
201	PA 438, East Benton, W Duchniks/dsl/repair B&B Rest
199	PA 524, Scott, E Mobil/dsl, W Exxon/Subway Motel 81 to Lackawanna SP
197	PA 632, Waverly, E Rite Aid, Weis Foods, W Sunoco Doc's Deli Camelot Inn/rest
194	US 6, US 11, to I-476/PA Tpk, Clarks Summit, W Exxon/dsl Sheetz/dsl, Sunoco/dsl, Valero Burger King, Damon's, Dino&Francesco's, Domino's, Dunkin Donuts, Krispy Kreme, Kyoto Japanese, La Tonalteca, McDonald's, Moe's SW Grill, New Century Chinese, Starbucks, Subway, Sunny Chinese, Taco Bell Waffle House, Wendy's Comfort Inn, EconoLodge, Hampton Inn, Nichols Village Inn, Ramada Inn Ace Hardware Advance Parts, Kost Tire, Monro, Rite Aid, Verizon, Weis Foods
191b a	US 6, US 11, to Carbondale, E Sheetz/dsl, Sunoco A&W LJ Silver, Applebee's, Buffalo Wild Wings, Burger King, China Palace, Chipotle, ChuckECheese, Denny's, Dunkin Donuts Five Guys, HoneyBaked Ham, Kobe Japanese, La Tonalateca McDonald's, Olive Garden, Panera Bread, Perkins, Quaker Steak&Lube, Red Lobster, Red Robin, Rita's Custard, Roma Pizza, Royal Buffet, Ruby Tuesday, Starbucks, Subway, TCBY, TGI Friday's, TX Roadhouse, Uno Grill, Viewmont Diner Days Inn, Holiday Inn Express $Tree, Aldi Foods, AT&T, Books-A-Million, Dick's, Field&Stream, Firestone/auto, Harley-Davidson Hobby Lobby, Home Depot, Hyundai, JC Penney, Jo-Ann Crafts Kohl's, Macy's, Marshall's, Michael's, Old Navy, PepBoys Petsmart, Target, TJ Maxx, Verizon, Walmart, William's Tire W to Anthracite Museum
190	Main Ave, Dickson City, E Teppanyaki Buffet, Wendy's Fairfield Inn, Microtel, Residence Inn auto repair, Best Buy, Ford, Lowe's, Sam's Club/gas, Staples, ve W Schiff's Foods, Toyota
188	PA 347, Throop, E Sheetz/dsl, Sunoco/dsl McDonald' Wendy's Dunmore Inn, Quality Inn, Scottish Inn, Slee Inn Advance Parts, BigLots, Monro, Mr Tire, Nissan, Pric Chopper Foods, st police, URGENT CARE, W Exxon/Subway/dsl Burger King, Dunkin Donuts, Friendly's
187	to I-84, I-380, US 6 (no return from nb)

PA

INTERSTATE 81 Cont'd

SCRANTON

Exit#	Services
186	PA 435, Drinker St (from nb), E Valero/dsl, W Exxon/dsl
185	Central Scranton Expwy (exits left from nb), W H
184	to PA 307, River St, W Exxon/Subway/dsl, Valero, Vamco Asian Taste, Dunkin Donuts Sheraton H, $Tree, CVS Drug, Gerrity Foods
182	Davis St, Montage Mtn Rd, E Exxon/Coldstone/Subway/dsl Doc's Oyster House, Gourmet Slice Pizza, Johnny Rockets Cafe, Longhorn Steaks, Nonno's Pizza, Panchero's Mexican, Panera Bread, Quiznos, Ruby Tuesday, Starbucks Comfort Suites, Courtyard, Hampton Inn, Springhill Suites, TownePlace Suites AT&T, GNC, Verizon, W Sunoco Dunkin Donuts, Waffle House, Wendy's EconoLodge CVS Drug, USPO
180	to US 11, PA 502, to Moosic, (exits left from nb), W on US 11 Exxon/dsl, Sunoco Subway
178b a	to US 11, Avoca, E Holiday Inn Express, W Petro/Valero/Iron Skillet/dsl/scales/24hr/@
175b a	PA 315 S, to I-476, Dupont, E Exxon/Subway/dsl, Sunoco/dsl Arby's, McDonald's, Perkins Knights Inn Volvo, W Pilot/Wendy's/dsl/scales/24hr Burger King, Star Asia Buffet, Uncle Joe's Pizza Comfort Inn truck repair, Verizon, Walmart/Subway

WILKES BARRE

Exit#	Services
170b a	PA 115, PA 309, Wilkes-Barre, E Exxon/Subway/dsl, Sunoco/dsl Holiday Inn to Pocono Downs, W Citgo, Sunoco/dsl Buffalo Wild Wings, Burger King, Denny's, Dunkin Donuts, Friendly's, Grotto Pizza, Jersey Mike's, LJ Silver, Longhorn Steaks, McDonald's, Moe's SW Grill, Red Lobster, Sonic, Taco Bell, TGIFriday's, Wendy's Days Inn, Extended Stay America, Fairfield Inn, Holiday Inn Express, Host Inn, Quality Inn, Red Roof Inn H, $General, BonTon, Chevrolet, Goodyear, Harley-Davidson, JC Penney, Macy's
168	Highland Park Blvd, Wilkes-Barre, W Sheetz/dsl, Sunoco, TurkeyHill Applebee's, Bob Evans, Chili's, Chipotle, ChuckeCheese, Cracker Barrel, Five Guys, King's Buffet, La Tolteca Mexican, Logan's Roadhouse, Lucky's SportHouse, Mizu Steaks, Nello's Pizza, Olive Garden, Outback Steaks, Panera Bread, Popeye's, Red Robin, Smokey Bones BBQ, Starbucks, Subway, Wendy's Courtyard, Hampton Inn, Hilton Garden, Motel 6 AT&T, Barnes&Noble, Best Buy, Dick's, Firestone/auto, Home Depot, Kohl's, Lowe's, Marshall's, Michael's, Mr Tire, Nissan, Old Navy, PepBoys, PetCo, Petsmart, PriceChopper, Ross, Sam's Club/gas, Staples, Target, TJ Maxx, U-Haul, URGENT CARE, Verizon, Walgreens, Walmart/Subway, Wegman's Foods
165b a	PA 309 S, (exits left from nb), Wilkes-Barre, W Citgo/dsl, Gulf Dunkin Donuts, McDonald's, Perkins, Taco Bell Comfort Inn, EconoLodge $Tree, Advance Parts, Rite Aid
164	PA 29, to Nanticoke, Ashley
159	Nuangola, W Valero/Subs Now/dsl camping (10mi)
157mm	**/weigh sta sb, full facilities, litter barrels, petwalk, , , vending**
156mm	**/weigh sta nb, full facilities, litter barrels, petwalk, , , vending**
155	to Dorrance, E Sunoco/dsl EconoLodge (2mi), W Blue Ridge Plaza/dsl
151b a	I-80, E to Mountaintop, W to Bloomsburg
145	PA 93, W Hazleton, E Sunoco/dsl, TurkeyHill/dsl Applebee's, Arby's, Bonanza, Damon's, Denny's, Five Stars Chinese, Friendly's, LJ Silver, McDonald's, Perkins, Pizza Hut, Taco Bell, Wendy's Best Western (2mi), Comfort Inn, Fairfield Inn,

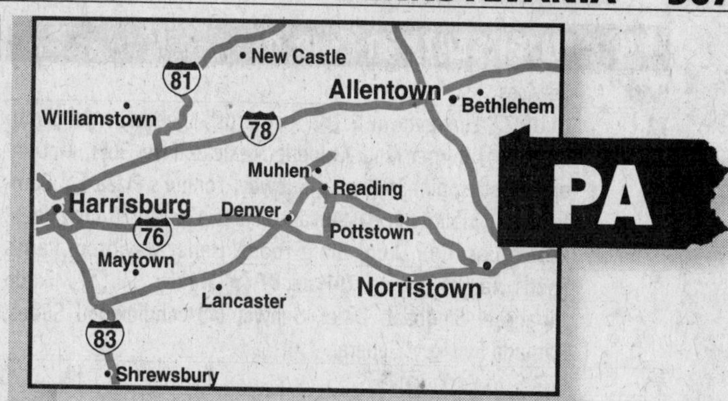

HAZLETON

Exit#	Services
145	Continued Forest Hill Inn, Ramada Inn (2mi) H, $Tree, Advance Parts, Aldi Foods, AT&T, Big Lots, Boscov's, Buick/Cadillac/GMC, Chrysler/Dodge/Jeep, JC Penney, Lowe's, Mazda, Michael's, Old Navy, Petsmart, st police, Staples, Weis Foods, W Shell, Top of the 80's Candlewood Suites, Hampton Inn
143	PA 924, to Hazleton, W Fuelon/Subs Now/dsl/scales, Sunoco/Subway, TurkeyHill/dsl Burger King, Sonic Residence Inn
141	PA 424, S Hazleton Beltway, E Mt Laurel Motel
138	PA 309, to McAdoo, 2 mi E Pines Motel
134	to Delano
132mm	**parking area/weigh sta both lanes**
131b a	PA 54, Mahanoy City, E to Tuscarora/Locust Lake SP, W Shell/dsl, Sunoco/dsl Mainstay Suites
124b a	PA 61, to Frackville, E Cracker Barrel, McDonald's Holiday Inn Express BigLots, BonTon, W Exxon, Gulf/dsl, Speedway Anthony's Pizza, Dutch Kitchen, Subway EconoLodge, Granny's Motel, Rodeway Inn H, Goodyear/auto, Rite Aid, st police
119	High Ridge Park Rd, to Gordon, E Country Inn&Suites
116	PA 901, to Minersville, E 901 Rest.
112	PA 25, to Hegins, W camping
107	US 209, to Tremont
104	PA 125, Ravine, E Exxon/Burger King/dsl/scales/24hr Echo Valley Campground

LEBANON

Exit#	Services
100	PA 443, to Pine Grove, E Exxon/dsl Arby's, McDonald's Comfort Inn, EconoLodge $General, W Pilot/DQ/Subway/dsl/scales/24hr Gooseberry Farms Diner Hampton Inn KOA (5mi), truckwash
90	PA 72, to Lebanon, E Exxon/Subway, Loves/McDonald's/dsl/scales/24hr, Speedway/Blimpie/Dunkin Donuts/dsl DQ, Wendy's Best Western, Days Inn KOA, repair, st police, W Comfort Inn
89	I-78 E, to Allentown
85b a	PA 934, to Annville, 2 mi W Exxon/dsl Funck's Rest. to IndianTown Gap Nat Cem
80	PA 743, Grantville, E Shell/dsl Days Inn, Hampton Inn, W Exxon/dsl Italian Delight Comfort Suites, Holiday Inn camping, racetrack
79mm	**/weigh sta both lanes, full facilities, litter barrels, petwalk, , , vending**
77	PA 39, to Hershey, E Exxon/dsl, Pilot/Pizza Hut/dsl/scales/24hr, Valero/dsl Hershey Rd Rest. Country Inn&Suites, EconoLodge, La Quinta, Motel 6, Scottish Inn st police, to Hershey Attractions, W Exit 77 TP/Subway/dsl, FLYING J/Perkins/dsl/24hr/@, TA/Country Pride/dsl/scales/24hr/@ McDonald's Holiday Inn Express Goodyear, SpeedCo, truck repair

PA

INTERSTATE 81 Cont'd

Exit#	Services
72	to US 22, Linglestown, E Sheetz/dsl, Speedway/dsl, Sunoco/dsl Burger King, Chipotle Mexican, Five Guys, McDonald's, Red Robin, Starbucks, Subway, Tonino's Pizza Comfort Inn, Quality Inn Advance Parts, Chrysler/Dodge/Jeep, Costco/gas, CVS Drug, Giant Foods, Harley-Davidson, Karn's Foods, Target, Toyota, U-Haul, W Turkey Hill Mikado Japanese, Sindbaad Diner, Subway Candlewood Suites, Ramada Inn $General
70	I-83 S, to York,
69	Progress Ave, E Cracker Barrel, Dunkin Donuts, Harvest Grill, Macaroni Grill, Starbucks, Tonino's Grill AT&T, CVS Drug, st police, Susquehanna Shoppes, W Turkey Hill/dsl Arby's, YP Rest. Clarion, Hampton Inn, Red Roof Inn, SpringHill Suites
67b a	US 22, US 322 W, PA 230, Cameron St, to Lewistown
66	Front St, E H, W Exxon, Sunoco Bro's Pizza, Front St Diner, McDonald's, Pizza Hut, Simply Turkey, Taco Bell, Wendy's Best Value, Days Inn
65	US 11/15, to Enola, **1 mi** E Sunoco/dsl, Tom's Al's Pizza, China Taste, DQ, Dunkin Donuts, McDonald's, Subway, Summerdale Diner, Wendy's Quality Inn $Tree, Advance Parts, Fischer Parts, Rite Aid, Sure Fine Foods
61	PA 944, to Wertzville, E Holiday Inn Express H, Giant/dsl, Weiss Mkt, W Turkey Hill/dsl Microtel
59	PA 581, to US 11, to I-83, Harrisburg, **3 mi E on Carlisle Pk** Sheetz/dsl, Sunoco Applebee's, Bob Evans, Burger King, Carrabba's, Denny's, Dunkin Donuts, McDonald's, Outback Steaks, Quaker Steak, TGIFriday's, Wayback Burger, Wendy's Park Inn AutoZone, Buick/GMC, Dick's, GNC, Home Depot, Hyundai, Lowe's, Nissan, NTB, Pepboys, Petsmart, Staples, TJ Maxx
57	PA 114, to Mechanicsburg, **2 mi** E Sheetz/dsl Alfredo's Pizza, Arby's, Dickey's BBQ, Great Wall Chinese, Isaac's Rest., KFC/LJ Silver, McDonald's, Olive Garden, Pizza Hut, Red Robin, Silver Spring Diner, Subway, Taco Bell Baymont Inn CarMax, Giant Foods/gas, Marshall's, Sam's Club/gas, Verizon, Walmart
52b a	US 11, to I-76/PA Tpk, Middlesex, E FLYING J/Denny's/dsl/scales/24hr/@, Pioneer/dsl Bob Evans, Dunkin Donuts, Ember's Steaks, Middlesex Diner Best Value Inn, Days Inn, Hotel Carlisle, Red Roof Inn, Super 8 H, W Gulf, Love's/Wendy's/dsl/24hr, Petro/Iron Skillet/dsl/24hr/@, Sunoco/Subway/dsl Arby's, Carelli's Subs, McDonald's, Rte 11 Diner, Waffle House Best Western, EconoLodge, Hampton Inn, Holiday Inn Express, Knights Inn, Motel 6, Quality Inn, Quality Inn, Residence Inn, Rodeway Inn, Travelodge H, Blue Beacon
49	PA 74 (no EZ sb return), E Sheetz/dsl same as 48, W Trindle Grill AAA
48	PA 74, York Rd (no EZ nb return), E Gulf/dsl Asian Cafe, Red Robin, Starbucks, Subway $Tree, Aldi Foods, Kohl's, Michael's, Petsmart, Rite Aid, Target, Verizon, W Speedway Burger King, Little Caesars, McDonald's, Pizza Hut, Taco Bell BonTon, CVS Drug, Dunkin Donuts, Ford, Lowe's, Midas, Weis Foods
47	PA 34, Hanover St, E Chili's, Cracker Barrel Sleep Inn Home Depot, W Al's Pizza, Applebee's, Bruster's/Nathan's, DQ, Palace China, Panera Bread, Papa John's, Rita's
47	Continued Custard, Subway, Super Buffet, Vinny's Rest, Wendy's AT&T CVS Drug, Rite Aid, Staples, TJ Maxx, Walmart/McDonald's
45	College St, E Gulf/dsl Alfredo Pizza, Arby's, Great Wall Buffet, McDonald's, Subway, Walnut Bottom Diner Days Inn, Super 8 H, Nell's Foods, Tire Pros, Verizon
44	PA 465, Allen Rd, to Plainfield, E Country Inn&Suites, Fairfield Inn H, st police, W Sheetz/dsl Subway
38.5mm	**both lanes, full facilities, litter barrels, petwalk,**
37	PA 233, to Newville, E Pine Grove Furnace SP, W Colonel Denning SP
29	PA 174, King St, E Sunoco/dsl Rodeway Inn, W Gulf, Rutter's/dsl Bros Pizza, Burger King, Domino's, KFC, Little Caesar's, Subway, Taco Bell, Wendy's Best Western, Holiday Inn Express, Theo's Motel $General, Advance Parts, Aldi Foods, AT&T, Cadillac/Chevrolet, CVS Drug, Ford, Verizon, vet, Walmart
24	PA 696, Fayette St, W Pacific Pride/dsl
20	PA 997, Scotland, E Bonanza, McDonald's Comfort Inn, Super 8 BonTon, JC Penney, W Sunoco Sleep Inn
17	Walker Rd, W Sheetz/dsl Aki Steaks, Bruster's/Nathan's, Cafe del Sol, Chipotle Mexican, Fuddrucker's, Longhorn Steaks, Olive Garden, Panera Bread, Red Robin, Sonic, Subway, TGIFriday's, TX Roadhouse Candlewood Suites, Country Inn&Suites AT&T, BJ's/dsl, Buick/Chevrolet/GMC, Ford, Giant Foods/gas, Kohl's, Michael's, Mr Tire, Petsmart, Staples, Target, URGENT CARE, Verizon
16	US 30, to Chambersburg, E Fuel Ctr, Sheetz Arby's, Broadway Deli, Bro's Pizza, Burger King, Dunkin Donuts, Hoss's Rest., KFC, Little Caesars, Perkins, Popeye's, Rita's Custard, Rte 30 Rest., Ryan's, Supreme Buffet, Waffle House, Wendy's Days Inn $Tree, AAA, Aldi Foods, Dick's, Harley-Davidson, Hobby Lobby, Jo-Ann Fabrics, Lowe's, Midas, NAPA, Nissan/Toyota, Petco, TJ Maxx, U-Haul, Verizon, vet, Walmart/Subway, W Speedway/dsl Big Oak Cafe, Burger King, Chambersburg Diner, Copper Kettle, LJ Silver, McDonald's, Pizza Hut, Ruby Tuesday, Starbucks, Subway, Taco Bell Best Western, Clarion, La Quinta H, Advance Parts, AutoZone, Lincoln, URGENT CARE, Walgreens
14	PA 316, Wayne Ave, E Sheetz/dsl Bob Evans, Cracker Barrel Fairfield Inn, Hampton Inn, Red Carpet Inn, W KwikFill, Shell Applebee's, Arby's, China Buffet, China Wok, Denny's, Mario's Italian, Montezuma Mexican, Papa John's, Red Lobster, Stoney's Rest., Subway, Twin Dragon Chinese, Volcano Japanese, Wendy's Holiday Inn Express, Quality Inn, Red Roof Inn $Tree, CVS Drug, Giant Foods/gas, GNC, Mr Tire, Save-a-Lot Foods, Verizon, Weis Foods
12mm	**weigh sta sb**
10	PA 914, Marion
7mm	**weigh sta nb**
5	PA 16, Greencastle, E Shell/dsl, Sunoco/grill/dsl, TA/Country Pride/dsl/scales/24hr/@ McDonald's, Subway, Taco Bell Super 8 Truckwash, Whitetail Ski Resort, W Exxon/dsl Castle Green Motel/rest AutoZone
3	US 11, E Sunoco/dsl Bro's Pizza Comfort Inn, W Sheetz/dsl
2mm	**Welcome Ctr nb, full facilities, litter barrels, petwalk, vending**
1	PA 163, Mason-Dixon Rd, W Stateline Inn, Stateline Motel Keystone RV Ctr
0mm	Pennsylvania/Maryland state line, Mason-Dixon Line

HARRISBURG

CARLISLE

CHAMBERSBURG

PA

INTERSTATE 83

HARRISBURG

Exit#	Services
51b a	**I-83 begins/ends on I-81, exit 70.**
50b a	US 22, Jonestown Rd, Harrisburg, E Speedway/dsl, Sunoco/dsl, USA Applebee's, Arby's, Buffalo Wild Wings, Chipotle Mexican, Cold Stone, Colonial Park Diner, Domino's, El Rodeo Mexican, Five Guys, Gilligan's Grill, Hibachi Grill, LJ Silver, Longhorn Steaks, McDonald's, Old Country Buffet, Olive Garden, Panera Bread, Pizza Hut, Red Lobster, Red Robin, Shogun Asian, Starbucks, Subway, Taco Bell, Tonino's Pizza, Wendy's Aamco, Advance Parts, AutoZone, Best Buy, Bon-Ton, Boscov's, Coscto/gas, Dick's, Ford, Giant Foods, Goodyear/auto, Home Depot, Jo-Ann, Kohl's, Marshall's, Meineke, Michael's, NTB, Old Navy, PepBoys, PetCo, Ross, Shannon Tire/auto, Target, Tires+, U-Haul, Verizon, vet, Weis Foods, William's Tires/repair, W Sunoco/dsl DQ, Dunkin Donuts, Friendly's, Gabriella's Italian, KFC, Roberto's Pizza Rite Aid
48	Union Deposit Rd, E Sunoco Arby's, Burger King, Infinito's Buffet, Panera Bread Best Western, Hampton Inn H, $Tree, Giant Foods/gas, Rite Aid, Staples, URGENT CARE, W Gulf/dsl, Sheetz/dsl ChuckeCheese, Empire Asian Bistro, Great Wall Chinese, Jimmy John's, JoJo's Pizza, McDonald's, Naples Pizza, New China, Outback Steaks, Rita's Ice Cream, Starbucks, Subway, TGIFriday's, TX Roadhouse, Waffle House, Wendy's Country Inn&Suites, EconoLodge, Fairfield Inn, Holiday Inn Express $Tree, BigLots, Family$, Lowe's, PriceRite Foods, Tuesday Morning, Weis Foods
47	(46b from nb), US 322 E, to Hershey, Derry St, E Speedway Papa John's, Pizza Hut Home Depot, Petsmart
46b a	I-283 S, to I-76/PA Tpk, W Taco Bell, Wendy's Days Inn, **services E off I-283 S** Exxon/dsl, Sunoco/dsl Bob Evans, Capitol Diner, Chili's, Five Guys, Friendly's, Lancaster Brewing Rest., Leeds Rest., McDonald's, Moe's SW Grill, Subway Courtyard, EconoLodge, Holiday Inn, Howard Johnson, La Quinta, Red Roof Inn, Sheraton, Sleep Inn, Super 8, Wyndham Garden $General, GNC, JC Penney, Kia, Target, Verizon
45	Paxton St, E Sheetz/dsl Applebees, Burger King, Cafe Fresco, Fiesta Mexico, Hibachi Buffet, Isaac's Rest., McDonald's, Melting Pot, Papa Joe's Pizza, Pizza Hut, Qdoba, Ruby Tuesday, Starbucks, Tomato Pie Cafe Hilton Garden, Homewood Suites, Towneplace Suites Advance Parts, Bass Pro Shops, Macy's, Mazda/Subaru, Meineke, Nissan, Toyota
44b	17th St, 19th St, E Sunoco, Turkey Hill Benihana Japanese, Dunkin Donuts, Hardee's Advance Parts, AutoZone, Buick/GMC, Firestone/auto, Honda, Hyundai, Midas
44a	PA 230, 13th St, Harrisburg, E Family$, W Chevrolet, VW, downtown
43	2nd St, Harrisburg, W Crowne Plaza, Hilton H, st capitol, downtown
42.5mm	Susquehanna River
42	Lemoyne
41b	Highland Park, E Turkey Hill Burger King, KFC, W Sunoco Papa Joe's Ace Hardware, Weis Foods
41a	US 15, PA 581 W, to Gettysburg
40b	New Cumberland, W Gulf/dsl Cedar Cliff Pizza, McDonald's, New China, Subway $General, CVS Drug
40a	Limekiln Rd, to Lewisberry, E Shell/dsl, Sunoco Bob Evans, John's Diner, McDonald's, Pizza Hut Budget Inn, Clarion, Fairfield Inn, Holiday Inn Express, La Quinta, Quality Inn, W Speedway Best Western, Motel 6, Scottish Inn vet
39b	I-76/PA Tpk

New Castle
Williamstown
Allentown
Bethlehem
Muhlen
Reading
Harrisburg
Denver
Pottstown
Maytown
Lancaster
Norristown
Shrewsbury
81 78 76 83
PA

LEWISBERRY

Exit#	Services
39a	PA 114, Lewisberry Rd, E Rutter's/dsl Days Inn, Highland Inn, Red Carpet Inn
38	Reesers Summit
36	PA 262, Fishing Creek, E Speedway/Dunkin Donuts Bruster's, Mamma's Pizza CVS Drug
35	PA 177, Lewisberry, E 601 Pizzaria, W Exxon Francescos, Summit Rest. Alpine Inn
34mm	**parking area/weigh sta sb**
34	Valley Green (from nb), same as 33
33	PA 392, Yocumtown, E Rutter's, Speedway/Dunkin Donuts/dsl Brothers Pizzaria, Burger King, Golden Plate Diner, Hong Kong Buffet, KFC/Taco Bell, Maple Donuts, McDonald's, New China Buffet, Subway Super 8 $Tree, Advance Parts, Darrenkamp's Mkt, GNC, Rite Aid, Verizon, Walmart/Subway
33mm	**parking area/weigh sta nb**
32	PA 382, Newberrytown, E Rutter's/deli/dsl/24hr, Sunoco/dsl, W Exxon/dsl
28	PA 295, Strinestown, W Rutter's/24hr 83 Diner, Wendy's
24	PA 238, Emigsville, W Sunoco/dsl 4 Bros Rest.
22	PA 181, N George St, E Rutter's Comfort Inn, Homewood Suites, W same as 21b

YORK

Exit#	Services
21b a	US 30, Arsenal Rd, to York, E Sheetz/dsl Cheddar's, Clock Diner, Qdoba, San Carlo's Rest., Starbucks Days Inn, EconoLodge, Motel 6, Sheraton AT&T, Buick/GMC, W Royal Farms/dsl, Rutter's/dsl, Sheetz/dsl 5 Guys Burgers, Arby's, Bob Evans, Burger King, Chick-fil-A, Chili's, China Buffet, CiCi's, Denny's, Domino's, DQ, Dunkin Donuts, El Rodeo Mexican, Friendly's, Great Wall, Hardee's, Hoss's, Jimmy John's, KFC, Little Caesars, LJ Silver, Logan's Roadhouse, Lyndon Diner, Maple Donuts, McDonald's, Mission BBQ, Old Country Buffet, Olive Garden, Panera Bread, Pizza Hut, Quaker Steak, Rita's Custard, Ruby Tuesday, Smokey Bones BBQ, Subway, Taco Bell, Wendy's Best Western, Motel 6, Super 8, Wingate Inn $General, $Tree, Acura, Advance Parts, Aldi Foods, AutoZone, BJ's Whse/gas, BMW, Cadillac/Chevrolet, Chrysler/Dodge/Jeep, CVS Drug, Dick's, Giant Foods/gas, Harley-Davidson, Honda, Kia, Kohl's, Lowe's, Macy's, NTB, Old Navy, PepBoys, PetCo, Petsmart, Ross, Staples, Subaru, Target, TJ Maxx, URGENT CARE, Verizon, Walmart/McDonald's, Weis Foods/gas
19	PA 462, Market St, E Rutter's/dsl Applebee's, Arby's, Aroma Buffet, Buffalo Wild Wings, Chick-fil-A, ChuckECheese's, DQ, Fiesta Mexico, Fuddruckers, Jimmy John's, KFC, Outback Steaks, Panera Bread, Papa John's, Perkins, Red Lobster, Rita's Custard, Starbucks, Taco Bell, Tokyo Diner, Wendy's Quality Inn $General, $Tree, Aamco, Advance Parts, Aldi Foods, Burlington Coats, Firestone/auto, Giant Foods/gas, Goodyear/auto, Home Depot, Lowe's, Nissan, NTB, Petco, Sam's Club/gas, Volvo, Walgreens, Walmart, Weis Foods, W H

PA

 = gas = food = lodging = other = rest stop

INTERSTATE 83 Cont'd

Exit#	Services
18	PA 124, Mt Rose Ave, Prospect St, E Pacific Pride/dsl, Rutters Arooga's Grille, Burger King, Five Guys, Nino's Pizza, Parma Pizza Grill, Pizza Hut, Subway, Sweet House Chinese Amelia's Groceries, Nello Tire
16b a	PA 74, Queen St, E Sunoco Baskin-Robbins/Dunkin Donuts, Cracker Barrel, Imperial Gourmet, Isaac's Rest., John's Pizza Shop, Maple Donuts, Ruby Tuesday, Starbucks, Stone Grill Country Inn&Suites, Hampton Inn Giant Foods/gas, W Sheetz/dsl Chipotle, Infinito's Pizza, Jimmy John's, Little Caesar's, McDonald's, Pizza Hut/Taco Bell, S Yorke Diner, Subway, Wendy's $General, $Tree, AT&T, BonTon, CVS Drug, Jo-Ann Fabrics, Price Rite Foods, Tuesday Morning, vet, Walgreens, Weis Mkt
15	S George St, I-83 spur into York, W H
14	PA 182, Leader Heights, E Arby's, Domino's, First Wok, Subway vet, W Rutter's McDonald's Holiday Inn Express Rite Aid
10	PA 214, Loganville, W Rutter's/dsl Mamma's Pizza Midway Motel st police, TrueValue
8	PA 216, Glen Rock, W Shrewsbury Mkt (2mi)
4	PA 851, Shrewsbury, E Tom's/dsl/24hr Bill Bateman's Grill, Cracker Barrel, Papa John's, Ruby Tuesday Hampton Inn Home Depot, TrueValue, W Exxon/dsl Arby's, Chick-fil-A, Coachlight Rest., Emerald Garden Chinese, Ginza Japanese, KFC/Taco Bell, McDonald's, Rita's Custard, Sons of Italy Pizzaria, Starbucks, Subway, Wendy's $Tree, AAA, Advance Parts, Giant Foods, GNC, Mr Tire, Saubel's Foods, Verizon, Walmart
2mm	**Welcome Ctr nb, full facilities, litter barrels, petwalk, , , vending**
0mm	Pennsylvania/Maryland state line

SHREWSBURY

INTERSTATE 84

Exit#	Services
54mm	Pennsylvania/New York state line, Delaware River
53	US 6, PA 209, Matamoras, N **Welcome Ctr/both lanes, full facilities, litter barrels, petwalk, , , vending,** Go24, Shell, TurkeyHill/dsl Polar Bear Rest., The Grill, Two Rivers Grille Appl Inn AutoZone, fireworks, PriceChopper, S Sunoco/dsl Dunkin Donuts, Goodfella's Italian, McDonald's, Peking Garden, Perkins, Subway, Taco Bell, Village Diner, Wayback Burger, Wendy's Best Western, Hampton Inn, Scottish Inn $Tree, Advance Parts, Home Depot, Lowe's, Mavis Tire/auto, Staples, Tristate RV Park, Verizon, Walmart/Subway
46	US 6, to Milford, N Sunoco/dsl, **0-2 mi** S Exxon/dsl, Gulf, TurkeyHill, Xtra Apple Valley Rest., Chang Mao Chinese, China Buffet, Dimmick Inn Steaks, Grotto Italian Rodeway Inn Key Food Mkt, NAPA, Rite Aid, USPO
34	PA 739, to Lords Valley, Dingmans Ferry, S Sunoco/Dunkin Donuts/dsl, Xtra/dsl Bruno Pizza, Carini Pizza, McDonald's, Panda Chinese, Subway Family$, Rite Aid, USPO, Weis Foods
30	PA 402, to Blooming Grove, N st police, to Lake Wallenpaupack
26	PA 390, to Tafton, N Exxon/dsl Tanglewood Ski Area (4mi), to Lake Wallenpaupack, S to Promised Land SP
26mm	**/weigh sta both lanes, full facilities, litter barrels, petwalk, , , vending**
20	PA 507, Greentown, N Exxon/dsl, Sunoco/Subway John's Italian Animal Park (5mi)
17	PA 191, to Newfoundland, Hamlin, N Howe's/Exxon/dsl/scales/24hr Twin Rocks Diner Comfort Inn dsl repair
8	PA 247, PA 348, Mt Cobb, N Gulf/dsl, Sunoco/Burger King/Tim Hortons/dsl, S Exxon/Subway/dsl
4	I-380 S, to Mount Pocono
2	PA 435 S, to Elmhurst
1	Tigue St, S Valero/dsl

I-84 begins/ends on I-81, exit 54.

INTERSTATE 90

Exit#	Services
46mm	Pennsylvania/New York state line, **Welcome Ctr/weigh sta wb, full facilities, litter barrels, petwalk, , , vending**
45	US 20, to State Line, N KwikFill/dsl/scales McDonald's, S Shell/Subway/dsl Red Carpet Inn fireworks, Niagara Falls Info
41	PA 89, North East, N Shell/repair New Harvest Rest. Holiday Inn Express, Vineyard B&B, S Family Affair Camping (4mi), winery
37	I-86 E, to Jamestown
35	PA 531, to Harborcreek, N TA/Country Pride/Pizza Hut/Subway/dsl/scales/24hr/@ Blue Beacon, dsl repair
32	PA 430, PA 290, to Wesleyville, N Country Fair, GetGo/dsl st police
29	PA 8, to Hammett, N Country Fair Wendy's H S Best Value dsl repair, Peterbilt
27	PA 97, State St, Waterford, N Country Fair/dsl, Kwikfill Arby's, Barbato's Italian, Doc Holiday's Grill, McDonald's Days Inn, La Quinta, Red Roof Inn, Tallyho Inn H, S Pilot Subway/dsl/scales/24hr, Sheetz/dsl, Shell/Tim Hortons/dsl Taco Bell Baymont Inn, Quality Inn, Super 8 casino
24	US 19, Peach St, to Waterford, N Country Fair/dsl, Delta Sonic/Subway, GetGo/dsl, KwikFill Applebee's, Burger King, Chick-fil-A, Chipotle Mexican, ChuckeCheese, Cracker Barrel, Dunkin Donuts, Eat'n Park, Famous Dave's BBQ, Five Guys, Golden Corral, KFC, Krispy Kreme, Longhorn Steaks, McDonald's, Old Country Buffet, Olive Garden, Panera Bread, Quaker Steak&Lube, S&S Buffet, Starbucks, Steak'n Shake, Taco Bell, TGIFriday's, Tim Hortons, Torero's Mexican, TX Roadhouse Courtyard, Hilton Garden H, $Tree, Advance Parts, Aldi Foods, AT&T, Best Buy, Giant Eagle Foods, Hobby Lobby, Home Depot, Jo-Ann Fabric, Kohl's, Lowe's, Marshall's, Old Navy, Petsmart, Sam's Club/gas, Staples, Target, URGENT CARE, Verizon, Walmart/Subway, Wegman's Foods, S Country Fair, Shell/Subway Blotto's Grill, Bob Evans Comfort Inn, EconoLodge, Hampton Inn, Holiday Inn Express, Home 2 Suites, Microtel, Residence Inn, Solstice Inn, Wingate Inn waterpark, Best Western+
22b a	I-79, N to Erie, S to Pittsburgh, **3-5 mi** N services in Erie
18	PA 832, Sterrettania, N Marathon/dsl Burger King Presque Passage RV Park, to Presque Isle SP, Waldameer Park (8mi), S Beechwood Rest. Quality Inn go KOA, West Haven RV Park/camping
16	PA 98, to Franklin Center, Fairview, S Follys Camping (2mi), Mar-Da-Jo-Dy Camping (5mi)
9	PA 18, to Girard, Platea, N Fiesler's Service/repair/tire, Langer's Automotive, st police, S Green Roof Inn (2mi)
6	PA 215, to Albion, East Springfield, N lodging
3	US 6N, to Cherry Hill, West Springfield, N lodging on US 20, S State Line/deli/dsl/scales/24hr
2.5mm	**/weigh sta eb, full facilities, info, litter barrels, petwalk, , , vending**
0mm	Pennsylvania/Ohio state line.

ERIE

PA

INTERSTATE 95

Exit#	Services
	Pennsylvania/New Jersey state line, Delaware River. **I-95/I-276 runs eb to NJ TPK.**
42(I-95)	US 13, Delaware Valley, **N** Dallas Diner, McDonald's Ramada Inn 7-11, auto repair, U-Haul, **S** G Fuel, LukOil/dsl, Sunoco/dsl, Valero/dsl, WaWa/dsl Burger King, Dunkin Donuts, Golden Eagle Diner, Italian Family Pizza, Porfirio's Pizza Best Value Inn, Villager Lodge $General, Meineke
40	(from nb) I-295 N, to NJ. **I-95 N merges with PA Tpk/276 to NJ Tpk**
39	PA 413, I-276, to Bristol Bridge, Burlington
37	PA 132, to Street Rd, **W** BP/dsl, Sunoco/dsl Burger King, China Sun Buffet, Dunkin Donuts, Golden Corral, Krispy Kreme, Little Caesar's, McDonald's, Popeye's, Sonic, TX Roadhouse, Wendy's $General, Aldi Foods, GNC, Goodyear/auto, PepBoys, U-Haul, Walgreens, WaWa
35	PA 63, to US 13, Woodhaven Rd, Bristol Park, **W** BP, Liberty, LukOil, Sunoco/dsl Arby's, Bob Evans, Boston Mkt, Burger King, Dunkin Donuts, Dynasty Rest., Grand China Buffet, KFC, McDonald's, Old Haven Pizza, Pizza Hut, Rita's Custard, Taco Bell, Wendy's Holiday Inn Express $Tree, Acme Foods, Dick's, Home Depot, Marshall's, NTB, Verizon, Verizon, Walmart, WaWa
32	Academy Rd, **W**
30	PA 73, Cottman Ave, **W** Sunoco
27	Bridge St, **W** 7-11, Citgo/dsl, Exxon, Lukoil Dunkin Donuts Rite Aid
26	to NJ 90, Betsy Ross Brdg, **W** BP/Dunkin Donuts, Speedway, Sunoco/dsl, WaWa/dsl Applebee's, Burger King, Chick-fil-A, KFC, McDonald's, Sonic, Wendy's $Tree, Advance Parts, Home Depot, Lowe's, SavaLot, ShopRite Foods, Target, Walmart
25	Allegheny Ave, **W** Sunoco/dsl WaWa
23	Lehigh Ave, Girard Ave, **E** casino, **W** Exxon Applebee's, Arby's, Coldstone, Dunkin Donuts, Pizza Hut, Rita's Custard $Tree, AutoZone, CVS Drug, Family$, GNC, PepBoys, Rite Aid, WaWa/dsl
22	I-676, US 30, to Central Philadelphia, Independence Hall
20	Columbus Blvd, Penns Landing, **1-2 mi E on Columbus** BP, Liberty/WaWa/dsl Burger King, Chick-fil-A, ChuckECheese, Dunkin Donuts, Famous Dave's BBQ, IHOP, Longhorn Steaks, McDonald's, Ruby Buffet, Wendy's Holiday Inn Express, Sheraton $Tree, AT&T, Best Buy, GNC, Home Depot, IKEA, Lowe's, Marshall's, Old Navy, PepBoys, ShopRite Foods, Staples, Target, Verizon, Walmart
19	I-76 E, to Walt Whitman Bridge, **W** BP, Liberty, Sunoco/dsl Burger King, Dunkin Donuts, KFC, Little Caesar's, McDonald's, Pizza Hut, Popeye's Holiday Inn $General, Aldi Foods, to stadiums
17	PA 611, to Broad St, Pattison Ave, **W** to Naval Shipyard, to stadium
15mm	Schuykill River
15	Enterprise Ave, Island Ave (from sb)
14	Bartram Ave, Essington Ave (from sb)
13	PA 291, to I-76 W (from nb), to Central Philadelphia, **E** Aloft, Doubletree, Hawthorn Suites, Marriott, Renaissance Inn, Sheraton Four Points, Sheraton Suites, **W** Residence Inn
12	Philadelphia Intl Airport, **E** services same as 10

PHILADELPHIA AREA

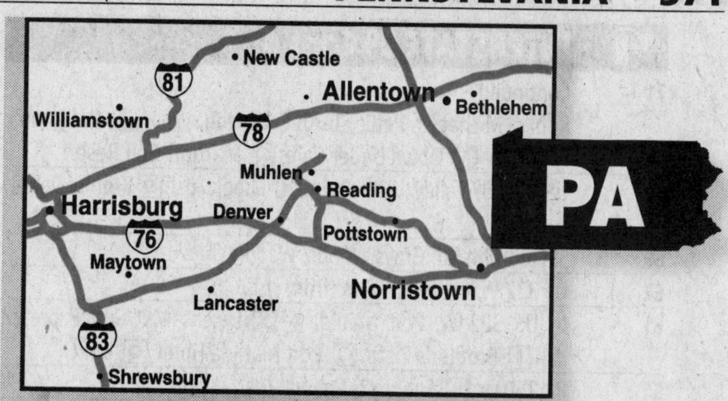

Exit#	Services
10	PA 291, Bartrom Ave, (from nb), Cargo City, **E** Marriott, Renaissance Hotel, **W** WaWa/dsl Ruby Tuesday Courtyard, Embassy Suites, Extended Stay America, Extended Stay America, Fairfield Inn, Hampton Inn, Microtel Heinz NWR
9b a	PA 420, to Essington, Prospect Park, **E** Sunoco/dsl, Valero/dsl Denny's, Lehmans Rest., Mel's Diner, Philly Diner Clarion, Comfort Inn, La Quinta, Motel 6, Red Roof Inn, SpringHill Suites, Wyndham Garden USPO, WaWa
8	to Chester Waterfront, Ridley Park, **E** Royal Farms Wendy's Microtel, SpringHill Suites, **W on US 13** Stargate Diner
7	I-476 N, to Plymouth, Meeting
6	PA 352, PA 320, to Edgmont Ave, **E** McDonald's, Popeye's $General, AT&T, AutoZone, Shoprite, Walmart/Subway, **W** Days Inn
5	Kerlin St (from nb), **E** Sunoco
4	US 322 E, to NJ, to Barry Bridge, **W** Highland Motel
3	(from nb, no EZ return)US 322 W, Highland Ave, **E** Sunoco/dsl $General, Ford, Goodyear
2	PA 452, to US 322, Market St, **W** Exxon/dsl, Royal Farms/dsl, Sunoco/dsl Dunkin Donuts, McDonald's, Subway
1	Chichester Ave, **E** Sunoco fireworks, **W** transmissions, WaWa
0mm	Pennsylvania/Delaware state line, **Welcome Ctr/weigh sta nb, full facilities, litter barrels, petwalk,**

INTERSTATE 99

Exit#	Services
85	**I-99 begins/ends on I-80, exit 161.**
83	PA 350, Bellefonte **E** Weis Foods/gas, **W** Lyken's Mkt Bonfatto's Rest., Burger King, Pizza Hut Rite Aid, TrueValue
81	PA 26 S, to PA 64, to Pleasant Gap
80	Harrison Rd (from nb, no re-entry)
78b a	PA 150, to Bellafonte **W** Sheetz/dsl Bro's Pizza, Colts Rest. EconoLodge auto repair, Ford
76	Shiloh Rd **E** Sheetz/dsl Garfields, McDonald's, Perkins, Quaker Steak, Rey Azteca Best Western $Tree, AAA, Advance Parts, Barnes&Noble, BigLots, BonTon, Chevrolet, JC Penney, Jo-Ann Fabrics, Macy's, Office Depot, Ross, Sam's Club, Subaru, Walmart/Subway
74	Innovation Park, , Beaver Stadium, Penn State U
73	US 322 E, Lewiston, State College
71	Woodycrest, Tofftrees **E** Applebee's, Chick-fil-A, Cracker Barrel, Eat'n park, McDonald's, Olive Garden, Outback Steaks, Red Lobster, Starbucks, TX Roadhouse Hampton Inn, Holiday Inn Express, SpringHill Suites $Tree, Best Buy, Dick's,

ST COLLEGE

PA

INTERSTATE 99 Cont'd

71 Continued
Kohl's, Michael's, PetCo, Target, Verizon, Walmart, Wegman's Foods, W [food] Down Under Cafe [lodging] Marriott Golf Resort

69 US 322 E, Valley Vista Dr E [gas] Sheetz/dsl [other] Home Depot, Lowe's

68 Skytop Mtn Rd, Grays Woods, Waddle

62 US 322 W, to Phillipsburg (from sb)

61 to US 322 W, Port Matilda E [gas] Lykens Mkt/Sub Express/dsl [food] Brother's Pizza [lodging] Port Matilda Hotel [other] USPO

52 PA 350 W [gas] Snappy's/Subway/dsl

48 PA 453, Tyrone W [gas] Sheetz/dsl [food] Burger King, Nino's Pizza, Subway [other] H, a USPO, Rite Aid

45 Tipton, Grazierville W [gas] Rossi's [food] Aunt Nettie's Cafe [other] H, DelGrosso's Funpark, Ford

41 PA 865 N, Bellwood E [other] Ft Roberdeau HS (6mi), W [gas] Martin Gen Store/dsl, Sheetz/dsl [other] DelGrosso's Funpark (3 mi)

39 PA 764 S, Pinecroft W [food] La Scalia Rest. [lodging] Comfort Inn, Days Inn [other] Martin's Foods, Oak Spring Winery

ALTOONA

33 17th St, Altoona E same as 32, W [gas] Sheetz/dsl [other] Aldi Foods, Lowe's, Railroader Museum, U-Haul

32 PA 36, Frankstown Rd, Altoona E [gas] GetGo, Sheetz/dsl [food] Chili's, Chipotle, DQ, Millie's Pizza, Panera Bread, Subway, TX Roadhouse [other] Barnes&Noble, Best Buy, Boscov's, Canoe Cr SP, Dick's, Giant Eagle Foods, GNC, Home Depot, Kohl's, Michael's, PetCo, Ross, Staples, Verizon, W [gas] Sheet/dsl [food] ChuckeCheese, Dunkin Donuts, El Campesino Mexican, Five Guys, Honeybaked Ham, HongKong Buffet, McDonald's, Olive Garden, Papa John's, Perkins, Pizza Hut, Red Lobster, Subway, Wendy's [lodging] EconoLodge, Holiday Inn Express, Super 8 [other] H, $Tree, AT&T, AutoZone, Chrysler/Dodge/Jeep, CVS Drug, Jo-Ann Fabrics, Nissan, Rite Aid, Save-A-Lot, URGENT CARE, USPO, Walgreens

31 Plank Rd, Altoona E [food] Friendly's, Jethro's Rest., King's Rest., Montezuma Mexican, Outback Steaks, TGIFriday's [lodging] Altoona Grand Hotel [other] Field&Stream, Firestone/auto, Sam's Club/gas, st police, Target, TJ Maxx, Walmart/McDonald's, W [gas] GetGo [food] Applebee's, Arby's, Bob Evans, Burger King, Casa Valadez, Champs Grill, Coldstone, Cracker Barrel, Denny's, Eat'n Park, Gourmet Buffet, KFC, Little Caesar's, LJ Silver, Longhorn Steaks, Taco Bell [lodging] Hampton Inn, Motel 6 [other] Advance Parts, BigLots, Buick/GMC, Hobby Lobby, JC Penney, Macy's, Martin's/gas, Petco, Verizon, Weis Foods

28 US 22, to Ebensburg, Holidaysburg

23 PA 36, PA 164, Roaring Spring, Portage E [gas] GetGo/dsl, Sheetz/24hr, Turkey Hill [food] Backyard Burger [other] H, truck repair, Walmart/Subway

15 Claysburg, King, Claysburg, King W [gas] Sheetz/dsl [food] Subway [other] $General

10 to Imler W [food] Slick's Ivy Stone Rest. (2mi), Blue Knob SP (8mi)

7 PA 869, Osterburg, St Clairsville W [food] Slick's Ivy Stone Rest. (2mi), Blue Knob SP

3 PA 56, Johnstown, Cessna E [other] st police, truck parts

1 I-70/76 E [gas] GetGo/McDonald's/dsl, Pacific Pride/dsl, Sheetz/dsl, Shell/Subway/dsl [food] Bedford Diner, Clara's Place, Denny's, Ed's Steaks, Hoss' Rest, LJ Silver, Pizza Hut, Salsa's Mexican, Wendy's [lodging] Best Value, Budget Host, Fairfield Inn, Hampton Inn, Quality Inn, Rodeway Inn, Travelodge

I-99 begins/ends on US 220.

INTERSTATE 295

Exit#	Services
10mm	Pennsylvania/New Jersey state line, Delaware River
10	PA 32, to New Hope, W [other] Washington Crossing Hist Park
9mm	**Welcome Ctr sb, full [handicap] facilities, litter barrels, petwalk, [phone], [picnic], vending**
8	PA 332, to Yardley, Newtown, W [food] Dunkin Donuts [lodging] Hampton Inn [other] H, to Tyler SP
5b a	US 1, W to I-276/PA TPK, Langhorne, Oxford Valley, W [other] H
3	US 1 bus, to PA 413, Penndel, Levittown, E [gas] Shell/7-11/dsl [food] Arrano Hibachi Steaks, ChuckECheese's, Dunkin Donuts, Friendly's, Great American Diner, Hong Kong Pearl, Ming's Asian, Olive Garden, Panera Bread, Red Lobster, Ruby Tuesday, Subway, Wendy's [other] $Tree, Acura, Chevrolet, Chrysler/Dodge/Jeep, Firestone/auto, Ford, GNC, Goodyear/auto, Harley-Davidson, Honda, Hyundai, Jaguar, Kia, Lowe's, Marshall's, Redner's Whse Mkt, Sam's Club, Staples, Subaru, Subaru, Target, VW/Volvo, W [gas] LukOil/dsl [food] Denny's, McDonald's [other] H, Toyota, U-Haul

I-295 begins/ends on I-276/I-95/PA Tpk.

INTERSTATE 476

Exit#	Services
131	US 11, US 6. **I-476 begins/ends on I-81. Services same as I-81 exit 194.**
122	Keyser Ave, Old Forge, Taylor
121mm	**toll plaza**
115	I-81, PA 315, Wyoming Valley, Pittston W [gas] Exxon/Subway/dsl, Pilot/Wendy's/dsl/scales/24hr, Sunoco/dsl [food] Arby's, Burger King, McDonald's, Perkins [lodging] Comfort Inn, Knight' Inn [other] Volvo, Walmart/Subway
112mm	**toll plaza**
105	PA 115, Wilkes-Barre, Bear Creek E [gas] Exxon, Mobil [food] Dunki Donuts
95	I-80, PA 940, Pocono, Hazleton W [gas] WaWa [food] A&W/LJ Silver, Arby's, McDonald's, Subway [lodging] Comfort Inn, EconoLodge Holiday Inn Express, Mtn Laurel Resort, Pocono Inn/Resor Quality Inn, Split Rock Resort
87	PA 903, Jim Thorpe (tag holder only)
86mm	**Hickory Run Service Plaza both lanes,** [gas] Sunoco/d [food] Burger King, Jamba Juice, Quizno's, Starbucks
74	US 209, Mahoning Valley, Lehighton, Stroudsburg W [gas] Citgo Shell/Subway/dsl [food] Trainer's Inn Rest. [lodging] Country Inn& Suites, Hampton Inn
71mm	Lehigh Tunnel
56	I-78, US 22, PA 309, Lehigh Valley E [food] China Hous Dunkin Donuts, Dunkin Donuts, Jamba Juice, Moe's SW Pazzo's Pizza, Red Robin, Subway, Trivet Diner, Wendy [lodging] Econolodge [other] BMW/Mini, Lexus, Maserati, Petc Staples, Tuesday Morning, on US 22 W [gas] Exxon, Sunoc [food] Chris Rest., Potsy Pizza [lodging] Holiday Inn Express, Motel [other] CVS Drug, Dan's Auto Repair, Jaguar, Land Rover
56mm	**Allentown Service Plaza both lanes,** [gas] Sunoco/dsl [food] Famglia Pizza, Hershey's Ice Cream, Roy Rogers, Starbucks
44	PA 663, Quakertown, Pottstown E [gas] BP, Exxon/Subway/d Wawa/dsl [food] Caitlyn&Cody's Diner, Dunkin Donuts, Faraco Pizza [lodging] Hampton Inn, Holiday Inn Express, Quality Inn, SpringHill Suites [other] H
31	PA 63, Lansdale E [gas] Gulf, Lukoil [food] Margaritas Mexica Osaka Japanese [lodging] Courtyard, Holiday Inn [other] H, USP Walgreens, WaWa

INTERSTATE 476 Cont'd

Exit#	Services
20	Germantown Pike W, to I-276 W, PA Tpk W
19	Germantown Pike E
18b a	(18 from sb), Conshohocken, Norristown E Lukoil, Sunoco Andy's Diner, Burger King, Cracker Barrel, Domino's, Dunkin Donuts, Five Guys, Illiano's Pizza, McDonald's, Outback Steaks, Panera Bread, Qdoba, Rita's Ice Cream, Ruby Tuesday, Salad Works, Starbucks, Subway Hampton Inn AT&T, Barnes&Noble, Best Buy, Dick's, Giant Foods, Lowe's, Marshall's, Old Navy, Petsmart, REI, Rite Aid, Ross, Target, Toyota, Verizon, Weis Mkt, W Papa John's, Uno, Wendy's Audi/Porsche, BJ's Whse, Ford, Home Depot, Honda, Hyundai, IKEA, Kia, Mazda, Michael's, Nissan
16b a	(16 from sb), I-76, PA 23, to Philadelpia, Valley Forge
13	US 30 E Shell Campus Pizza, First Watch Cafe, Nova Grill, Starbucks, Winger's H, Staples, to Villanova U, USPO
9	PA 3, Broomall, Upper Darby E Barnaby's Rest. H, URGENT CARE
5	US 1, Lima, Springfield E Chipotle, Dragon Garden, Hibachi Japanese, Moe's SW, Smashburger, Subway AT&T, Giant Foods, Giant Foods, Jo-Ann Fabrics, Marshall's, Old Navy, Petsmart, Staples, Verizon, Walmart
3	Baltimore Pike, Media, Swarthmore E Mobil/dsl Carrabba's, Ruby Tuesday H, Macy's, Swarthmore Coll, Target
1	McDade Blvd E Exxon Dunkin Donuts, McDonald's $Tree, CVS Drug
0mm	**I-476 begins/ends on I-95, exit 7.**

NOTES

RHODE ISLAND

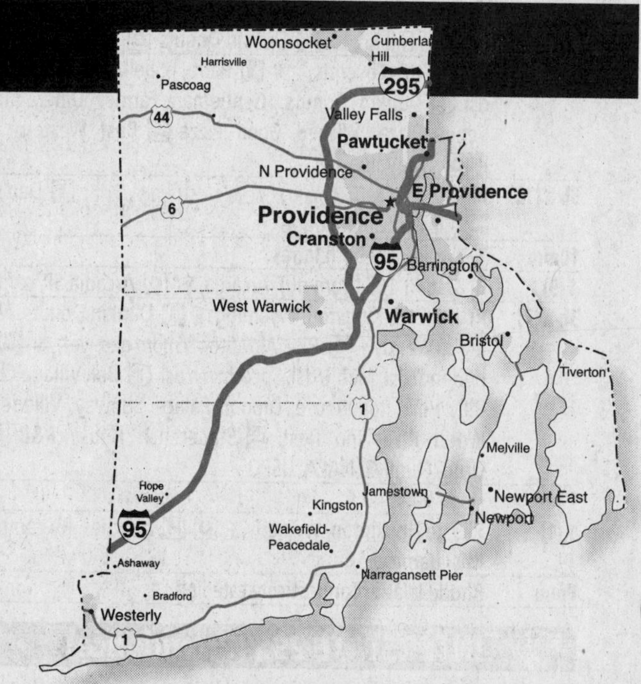

INTERSTATE 95

Exit#	Services
43mm	Rhode Island/Massachusetts state line
30 (42)	East St, to Central Falls, E Dunkin Donuts, Subway
29 (41)	US 1, Cottage St, W d'Angelo
28 (40)	RI 114, School St, E Sunoco H, to hist dist, Yarn Outlet
27 (39)	US 1, RI 15, Pawtucket, W Shell/repair/dsl, Sunoco/dsl/24hr Burger King, Dunkin Donuts, Murphy's Law Hampton Inn
26 (38)	RI 122, Lonsdale Ave (from nb), E U-Haul
25 (37)	US 1, RI 126, N Main St, Providence, E Shell/dsl, Speedway/dsl Chili's, Dunkin Donuts, Gregg's Rest., Subway H, $Tree, Firestone/auto, PepBoys, Walgreens, W NE Express, Speedway Burger King, Chelo's Rest. Aamco
24 (36.5)	Branch Ave, Providence, W Mobil Wendy's Home Depot, Stop&Shop, URGENT CARE, Walmart/Subway, downtown
23 (36)	RI 146, RI 7, Providence, E Mobil/dsl Marriott H, W USPO
22 (35.5)	US 6, RI 10, Providence, E Cheesecake Factory, Dave&Buster's, Fleming's Steaks CVS Drug, Macy's, mall, Nordstrom's
21 (35)	Broadway St, Providence, E Hilton
20 (34.5)	I-195, to E Providence, Cape Cod
19 (34)	Eddy St, Allens Ave, to US 1, W Dunkin Donuts, Wendy's H
18 (33.5)	US 1A, Thurbers Ave, W Shell/dsl Burger King H
17 (33)	US 1 (from sb), Elmwood Ave, W Cadillac, Tires Whse
16 (32.5)	RI 10, Cranston, E Williams Zoo/park
15 (32)	Jefferson Blvd, E Mobil Dunkin Donuts, Shogun Steaks Courtyard, La Quinta, Motel 6, W Ryder Trucks

PA RI

INTERSTATE 95 Cont'd

E GREENWICH

Exit#	Services
14 (31)	RI 37, Post Rd, to US 1, W [gas] CNG, gas/dsl, Shell/dsl [food] Burger King [other] Aldi, CVS Drug, Ford/Lincoln, Mazda, Volvo
13 (30)	1 mi E [gas] Shell, Sunoco/Dunkin Donuts [food] Chelo's Grill, HoneyDew Donuts, Legal Seafood, Subway, Wendy's [lodging] Best Western, Comfort Inn, Extended Stay America, Hampton Inn, Hilton Garden, Holiday Inn Express, Homewood Suites, Radisson, Residence Inn [other] TF Green Airport
12b (29)	RI 2, I-295 N (from sb)
12a	RI 113 E, to Warwick, E [gas] Shell/Dunkin Donuts/dsl [lodging] Crowne Plaza Hotel [other] Lowe's, Stop&Shop, W [gas] Sunoco [food] ChuckeCheese, Wendy's [other] Kohl's, mall, Walmart/Subway
11 (29)	I-295 N (exits left from nb), to Woonsocket
10b a (28)	RI 117, to Warwick, W [other] [H]
9 (25)	RI 4 S, E Greenwich
8b a (24)	RI 2, E Greenwich, E [gas] Shell/dsl [food] Dunkin Donuts, McDonald's, Outback Steaks, Panera Bread, PieZone Pizza, Ruby Tuesday, TX Roadhouse [lodging] Extended Stay America [other] AT&T, CVS Drug, Dave's Mkt, 0-2 mi W [gas] Sunoco/dsl [food] Agave's Mexican, Applebee's, Carrabba's, Chick-fil-A, Chili's, Corner Bakery Cafe, Denny's, Five Guys, KFC, Moe's SW, Olive Garden, PapaGino's Pizza, Smokey Bones BBQ, TGIFriday's, Wendy's [lodging] SpringHill Suites [other] Acura, Aldi Foods, Arlington RV Ctr, Audi/Bentley/BMW/Inifinti/Lexus/Mini/Porsche/Smart, Barnes&Noble, Best Buy, Cadillac, Dick's, Home Depot, Honda, Hyundai, Jaguar, Jo-Ann Fabrics, Land Rover, Lowe's, Mercedes, Michael's, Nissan, PepBoys, Petco, Petsmart, Staples, Stop&Shop, Subaru, Target, VW
7 (21)	to Coventry, E [gas] Mobil/dsl, W [gas] Cumberland [food] Applebee's, Cilantro Mexican, Cracker Barrel, Denny's, Dunkin Donuts, McDonald's, Wendy's [lodging] Hampton Inn, La Quinta, Residence Inn [other] BJ's Whse/gas, CVS Drug, GNC, Home Depot, Verizon, Walmart/Subway
6a (20)	Hopkins Hill Rd, W [food] Dunkin Donuts [other] park&ride
6 (18)	RI 3, to Coventry, W [gas] Petro, Shell/dsl/24hr, Sunoco/dsl [food] Dunkin Donuts, Gentleman Farmer Diner, Subway, Venus Pizza, Wicked Good Pizza [lodging] Best Western, Super 8 [other] TrueValue, vet
5b a (15)	RI 102, W [gas] TA/Shell/Popeye's/dsl/scales/24hr [food] Dan's Rest. [lodging] Classic Motor Lodge
10mm	[RS]/weigh sta both lanes
4 (9)	RI 3, to RI 165 (from nb), Arcadia, W [other] Arcadia SP, camping
3b a (7)	RI 138 E, to Kingston, Wyoming, E [food] Dunkin Donuts, McDonald's, Wendy's [other] Rite Aid, Stop&Shop/gas, vet, W [gas] Cumberland/dsl, Mobil/dsl, Speedway/dsl [food] Bali Village Chinese, Billy Hill's Roadhouse, Dragon Palace, Subway, Village Pizza, Wood River Inn Rest. [lodging] Stagecoach House B&B [other] CVS Drug, Family$, NAPA, USPO
2 (4)	Hope Valley
1 (1)	RI 3, to Hopkinton, Westerly, E [other] [H], beaches, RV camping, to Misquamicut SP
0mm	Rhode Island/Connecticut state line

INTERSTATE 295 (Providence)

PROVIDENCE

Exit#	Services
2b a (4)	I-95, N to Boston, S to Providence. **I-295 begins/ends on I-95, exit 4 in MA. Exits 2-1 are in MA.**
1b a (2)	US 1, E [gas] Mobil/Dunkin Donuts/dsl [food] 99 Rest., Chicago Grill, ChuckeCheese, d'Angelo, Friendly's, Longhorn Steaks, Panera Bread, PapaGino's Italian, Ruby Tuesday, TGIFriday's [other] $Tree, Best Buy, BJ's Whse, Buick/Chevrolet/GMC, CVS Drug, Dick's, Firestone/auto, JC Penney, Jo-Anne Fabrics, Lowe's, Macy's, Marshall's, Michael's, Old Navy, Petco, Petsmart, Staples, Stop&Shop, Target, TJMaxx, Verizon, Walmart, W [gas] Gulf, Shell/dsl [food] Applebee's, Dunkin Donuts [lodging] Holiday Inn Express, Knights Inn, Pineapple Inn [other] CarMax, CVS Drug, Nissan, Subaru, Toyota
0mm	Rhode Island/Massachusetts state line. **Exits 1-2 are in MA.**
11 (24)	RI 114, to Cumberland, E [gas] Shell/dsl, Sunoco [food] Dunkin Donuts, HoneyDew Donuts [other] CVS Drug, Dave's Foods, USPO, W [food] J's Deli, Saki's Pizza/subs [other] Diamond Hill SP
10 (21)	RI 122, E [gas] Gulf [food] Burger King, Dunkin Donuts, Jacky's Rest., McDonald's [other] Verizon, W [food] Casa Vallarta Mexican, Fortune House Chinese, HoneyDew Donuts, Pamfilios Deli, Subway [other] AAA, Ace Hardware, CVS Drug, Rite Aid, Seabra Foods, URGENT CARE
20mm	Blackstone River
19.5mm	[RS] (full facilities)/weigh sta nb, [food] Baskin-Robbins/Dunkin Donuts
9b a (19)	RI 146, Woonsocket, Lincoln, E [gas] Sunoco/dsl [food] Asian Grill, Chili's, Five Guys, McDonald's, Starbucks [lodging] Courtyard [other] $Tree, AT&T, Marshall's, Stop&Shop/gas, Target
8b a (16)	RI 7, N Smithfield, E [food] Terrazza Ristorante, W [gas] 7-11, dsl [food] B's Cafe, Dunkin Donuts, Parentes Rest. [lodging] Hampton Inn, Holiday Inn Express [other] Smith-Appleby House
7b a (13)	US 44, Centerdale, E [gas] Speedway, Valero [food] Cancun Mexican, La Cucina Italian [other] [H], NAPA, repair, W [gas] Exxon/dsl, Mobil, Shell/dsl [food] Applebee's, Burger King, Chelo's Grill, Chicago Grill, Chili's, Chipotle, D'angelo, Dominos, Dunkin Donuts, KFC/Taco Bell, McDonald's, Panera Bread, Papa Gino's, PapaGino's, Sonic, Starbucks, Subway, TinTsin Chinese, Yamato Steaks [other] $Tree, AT&T, Barnes&Noble, CVS Drug, Dave's Foods, Dick's, Home Depot, Kohl's, Michael's, Old Navy, Rite Aid, Staples, Stop&Shop, Target, TJ Maxx, to Powder Mill Ledges WR, URGENT CARE, Verizon
6b c (10)	US 6, to Providence, E [gas] 7-11, Shell [food] Atwood Grill, Burger King, D'Angelo, Denny's, Dunkin Donuts, Jacky's Rest., KFC, Popeye's, Ruby Tuesday, Subway [other] AT&T, AutoZone, BJ's Gas, Buick/GMC, Chevrolet, Chrysler/Dodge/Jeep, CVS Drug, Fiat, Honda, Kia, PetsMart, Rite Aid, Stop&Shop/gas, Town Fair Tire, USPO
6a (9)	US 6 E Expswy, E [food] Chipotle, McDonald's, Ruby Tuesday, Taco Bell [other] $Tree, BJ's Whse, Home Depot, Petsmart, Verizon
5 (8)	[other] RI Resource Recovery Industrial Park
4 (7)	RI 14, Plainfield Pk, E [gas] Speedway/dsl [food] McDonald's [other] $Tree, Walmart/Subway, W [gas] Gulf, Mobil/dsl/24hr [food] Dunkin Donuts, Palmieri Pizza, Subway [other] CVS Drug, repair
3b a (4)	rd 37, Phenix Ave, E [other] TF Green Airport
2 (2)	RI 2 S, to Warwick, E [food] Chicago Grill, Longhorn Steaks, Red Robin [lodging] Extended Stay America [other] JC Penney, Macy's, mall, Marshalls, Old Navy, Verizon, Walgreens, W [gas] Mobil, Sunoco/Subway [food] Burger King, Chili's, Chipotle Mexican, ChuckeCheese, Corner Bakery Cafe, Dunkin Donuts, McDonald's/playplace, Olive Garden, On-the-Border, Panera Bread, Smashburger, Smokey Bones, Starbucks, Subway, Taco Bell, Wendy's [other] AT&T, AutoZone, Barnes&Noble, Best Buy, Chrysler/Dodge/Keep/Kia, Dick's, Hobby Lobby, Home Depot, Jaguar, Kia, Kohl's, Petco, PetsMart, Price Rite Foods, Rite Aid, Staples, Target, TJMaxx, TownFair Tire, Trader Joe's, Verizon, Walmart/Subway
1 (1)	RI 113 W, to W Warwick, same as 2
0mm	**I-295 begins/ends on I-95, exit 11.**

SOUTH CAROLINA

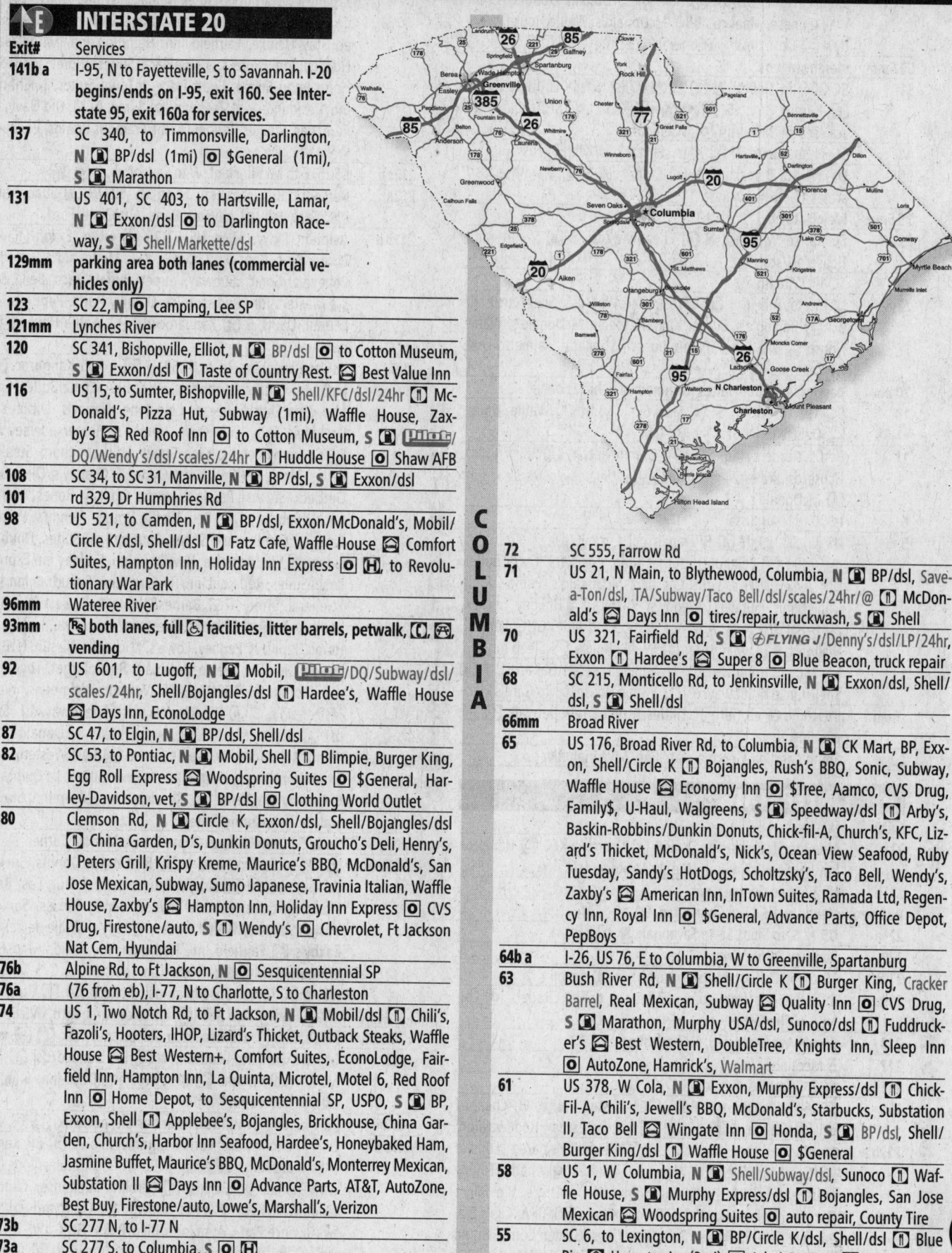

INTERSTATE 20

Exit#	Services
141b a	I-95, N to Fayetteville, S to Savannah. **I-20 begins/ends on I-95, exit 160. See Interstate 95, exit 160a for services.**
137	SC 340, to Timmonsville, Darlington, N [gas] BP/dsl (1mi) [other] $General (1mi), S [gas] Marathon
131	US 401, SC 403, to Hartsville, Lamar, N [gas] Exxon/dsl [other] to Darlington Raceway, S [gas] Shell/Markette/dsl
129mm	**parking area both lanes (commercial vehicles only)**
123	SC 22, N [other] camping, Lee SP
121mm	Lynches River
120	SC 341, Bishopville, Elliot, N [gas] BP/dsl [other] to Cotton Museum, S [gas] Exxon/dsl [food] Taste of Country Rest. [lodging] Best Value Inn
116	US 15, to Sumter, Bishopville, N [gas] Shell/KFC/dsl/24hr [food] McDonald's, Pizza Hut, Subway (1mi), Waffle House, Zaxby's [lodging] Red Roof Inn [other] to Cotton Museum, S [gas] Pilot/DQ/Wendy's/dsl/scales/24hr [food] Huddle House [other] Shaw AFB
108	SC 34, to SC 31, Manville, N [gas] BP/dsl, S [gas] Exxon/dsl
101	rd 329, Dr Humphries Rd
98	US 521, to Camden, N [gas] BP/dsl, Exxon/McDonald's, Mobil/Circle K/dsl, Shell/dsl [food] Fatz Cafe, Waffle House [lodging] Comfort Suites, Hampton Inn, Holiday Inn Express [other] [H], to Revolutionary War Park
96mm	Wateree River
93mm	**[RS] both lanes, full [handicapped] facilities, litter barrels, petwalk, [phone], [picnic], vending**
92	US 601, to Lugoff, N [gas] Mobil, Pilot/DQ/Subway/dsl/scales/24hr, Shell/Bojangles/dsl [food] Hardee's, Waffle House [lodging] Days Inn, EconoLodge
87	SC 47, to Elgin, N [gas] BP/dsl, Shell/dsl
82	SC 53, to Pontiac, N [gas] Mobil, Shell [food] Blimpie, Burger King, Egg Roll Express [lodging] Woodspring Suites [other] $General, Harley-Davidson, vet, S [gas] BP/dsl [other] Clothing World Outlet
80	Clemson Rd, N [gas] Circle K, Exxon/dsl, Shell/Bojangles/dsl [food] China Garden, D's, Dunkin Donuts, Groucho's Deli, Henry's, J Peters Grill, Krispy Kreme, Maurice's BBQ, McDonald's, San Jose Mexican, Subway, Sumo Japanese, Travinia Italian, Waffle House, Zaxby's [lodging] Hampton Inn, Holiday Inn Express [other] CVS Drug, Firestone/auto, S [food] Wendy's [other] Chevrolet, Ft Jackson Nat Cem, Hyundai
76b	Alpine Rd, to Ft Jackson, N [other] Sesquicentennial SP
76a	(76 from eb), I-77, N to Charlotte, S to Charleston
74	US 1, Two Notch Rd, to Ft Jackson, N [gas] Mobil/dsl [food] Chili's, Fazoli's, Hooters, IHOP, Lizard's Thicket, Outback Steaks, Waffle House [lodging] Best Western+, Comfort Suites, EconoLodge, Fairfield Inn, Hampton Inn, La Quinta, Microtel, Motel 6, Red Roof Inn [other] Home Depot, to Sesquicentennial SP, USPO, S [gas] BP, Exxon, Shell [food] Applebee's, Bojangles, Brickhouse, China Garden, Church's, Harbor Inn Seafood, Hardee's, Honeybaked Ham, Jasmine Buffet, Maurice's BBQ, McDonald's, Monterrey Mexican, Substation II [lodging] Days Inn [other] Advance Parts, AT&T, AutoZone, Best Buy, Firestone/auto, Lowe's, Marshall's, Verizon
73b	SC 277 N, to I-77 N
73a	SC 277 S, to Columbia, S [other] [H]

COLUMBIA

Exit#	Services
72	SC 555, Farrow Rd
71	US 21, N Main, to Blythewood, Columbia, N [gas] BP/dsl, Save-a-Ton/dsl, TA/Subway/Taco Bell/dsl/scales/24hr/@ [food] McDonald's [lodging] Days Inn [other] tires/repair, truckwash, S [gas] Shell
70	US 321, Fairfield Rd, S [gas] Flying J/Denny's/dsl/LP/24hr, Exxon [food] Hardee's [lodging] Super 8 [other] Blue Beacon, truck repair
68	SC 215, Monticello Rd, to Jenkinsville, N [gas] Exxon/dsl, Shell/dsl, S [gas] Shell/dsl
66mm	Broad River
65	US 176, Broad River Rd, to Columbia, N [gas] CK Mart, BP, Exxon, Shell/Circle K [food] Bojangles, Rush's BBQ, Sonic, Subway, Waffle House [lodging] Economy Inn [other] $Tree, Aamco, CVS Drug, Family$, U-Haul, Walgreens, S [gas] Speedway/dsl [food] Arby's, Baskin-Robbins/Dunkin Donuts, Chick-fil-A, Church's, KFC, Lizard's Thicket, McDonald's, Nick's, Ocean View Seafood, Ruby Tuesday, Sandy's HotDogs, Scholtzsky's, Taco Bell, Wendy's, Zaxby's [lodging] American Inn, InTown Suites, Ramada Ltd, Regency Inn, Royal Inn [other] $General, Advance Parts, Office Depot, PepBoys
64b a	I-26, US 76, E to Columbia, W to Greenville, Spartanburg
63	Bush River Rd, N [gas] Shell/Circle K [food] Burger King, Cracker Barrel, Real Mexican, Subway [lodging] Quality Inn [other] CVS Drug, S [gas] Marathon, Murphy USA/dsl, Sunoco/dsl [food] Fuddrucker's [lodging] Best Western, DoubleTree, Knights Inn, Sleep Inn [other] AutoZone, Hamrick's, Walmart
61	US 378, W Cola, N [gas] Exxon, Murphy Express/dsl [food] Chick-Fil-A, Chili's, Jewell's BBQ, McDonald's, Starbucks, Substation II, Taco Bell [lodging] Wingate Inn [other] Honda, S [gas] BP/dsl, Shell/Burger King/dsl [food] Waffle House [other] $General
58	US 1, W Columbia, N [gas] Shell/Subway/dsl, Sunoco [food] Waffle House, S [gas] Murphy Express/dsl [food] Bojangles, San Jose Mexican [lodging] Woodspring Suites [other] auto repair, County Tire
55	SC 6, to Lexington, N [gas] BP/Circle K/dsl, Shell/dsl [food] Blue Pig [lodging] Hampton Inn (2mi) [other] John's RV Ctr, S [gas] BP/dsl, Pops,

INTERSTATE 20 Cont'd

55 Continued
Shell/Circle K/DQ/dsl Bojangles, Dunkin Donuts, Great Wall Chinese, Maurice's BBQ, McDonald's, Waffle House, Wendy's Days Inn $General, CVS Drug

52.5mm **weigh sta wb**

51 SC 204, to Gilbert, N Circle K/dsl, Shell/Subway/dsl/24hr Burger King, S Loves/Chester's/McDonald's/dsl/scales/24hr, Mobil/dsl $General

44 SC 34, to Gilbert, N 44Trkstp/rest./dsl/24hr, BP/dsl

39 US 178, to Batesburg, N Exxon/dsl, S Marathon/dsl/scales Hillview Rest.

35.5mm **weigh sta eb**

33 SC 39, to Wagener, N Cheapway/dsl, S Shell/Huddle House/dsl/scales

29 SC 49, Wire Rd

22 US 1, to Aiken, S BP/dsl, RaceWay/dsl, Shell/Circle K/dsl Bojangle's, Burger King, Hardee's, McDonald's, Waffle House Days Inn, Quality Inn $General, Palmetto Lake RV Camping, to USC Aiken

20mm **parking area both lanes (commercial vehicles only)**

18 SC 19, to Aiken, S Shell/Subway/dsl Waffle House Deluxe Inn, Guest Inn H

11 Bettis Academy Rd, SC 144, Graniteville, N Shell/Huddle House/dsl/scales/24hr, S Pilot/Subway/dsl/scales/24hr McDonald's

6 I-520 to N Augusta

5 US 25, SC 121, N BP/repair/dsl, Circle K/dsl, Shell/Circle K/dsl/scales Bojangles, Burger King, Checkers, Crazy Buffet, DQ, Jersey Mike's, Little Caesar's, McDonald's, Pablo's Mexican, Sonic, Subway, Wendy's, Zaxby's Holiday Inn Express $General, Advance Parts, Food Lion, GNC, Verizon, Walmart, S Marathon Waffle House Sleep Inn

1 SC 230, Martintown Rd, N Augusta, N Gas+/dsl, S Shell/Circle K/Subway/dsl Waffle House to Garn's Place

.5mm **Welcome Ctr eb, full facilities, litter barrels, petwalk, , , vending**

0mm South Carolina/Georgia state line, Savannah River

INTERSTATE 26

Exit# Services

221 Meeting St, Charleston, 2 mi E Church's, KFC Hampton Inn Family$, Piggly Wiggly, Visitors Ctr

221b US 17 N, to Georgetown

I-26 begins/ends on US 17 in Charleston, SC.

221a US 17 S, to Kings St, to Savannah, N H

220 Romney St (from wb)

219b Morrison Dr, East Bay St (from eb), N Exxon

219a Rutledge Ave (from eb, no EZ return), to The Citadel, College of Charleston

218 Spruill Ave (from wb), N Charleston

217 N Meeting St (from eb)

216b a SC 7, Cosgrove Ave, to US 17 S

215 SC 642, Dorchester Rd, N Charleston, N El Cheapo/dsl Clarion, S BP/dsl Alex's Rest Rodeway Inn

213b a Montague Ave, Mall Dr, N Piccadilly's, Red Lobster Courtyard, Sheraton, Woodspring Suites Charles Towne Square, S BP/dsl, Mobil, Spinx/dsl Arby's, Big Billy's Burgers, Bufflo Wild Wings, Burger King, Chick-fil-A, CiCi's Pizza, Fatz Cafe, Firehouse Subs, Five Guys, Golden Corral, Grand Buffet, Gringos, Hardee's, IHOP, Jimmy John's, Jim'N Nick's BBQ,

CHARLESTON

213b a Continued
Kamille's Cafe, La Hacienda, McAlister's Deli, McDonald's, Panda Express, Panera Bread, Qdoba, Rita's Custard, Sake Japanese, Starbucks, Steak'n Shake, Waffle House ALoft, Crowne Plaza, Days Inn, EconoLodge, Embassy Suites, Extended Stay Deluxe, Fairfield Inn, Hampton Inn, Hilton Garden, Holiday Inn Express, HomePlace Suites, Homestead Suites, Homewood Suites, Hyatt Place, InTown Suites, N Charleston Inn, Residence Inn, Sleep Inn $Tree, AT&T, Old Navy, Sam's Club/gas, Staples, Tanger Outlet/Framous Brands, Verizon, vet, Walmart/Subway

212c b I-526, E to Mt Pleasant, W to Savannah, S

212a Remount Rd, Hanahan, N **on US 52/78** Sunoco/dsl KFC, Taco Bell Advance Parts, AutoZone, Ford

211b a Aviation Pkwy, N **on US 52/78** Citgo, Exxon Arby's, Burger King, Capt D's, Church's, KFC, McDonald's, Papa John's, Popeye's, Sonic, Subway, Super Buffet, Taco Bell, Zaxby's Masters Inn, Radisson O'Reilly Parts, PepBoys, PetCo, U-Haul, USPO, S Kangaroo/dsl Waffle House Budget Inn

209 Ashley Phosphate Rd, to US 52, N Exxon, Kangaroo Applebee's, Cane's, Carrabba's, Chick-fil-A, China Buffet, Chipotle Mexican, ChuckECheese, Coldstone, Denny's, Dickey's BBQ, Firehouse Subs, Five Guys, Hardee's, Hooters, Jersey Mike's Subs, Jimmy John's, King Street Grill, Longhorn Steaks, Los Reyes, Moe's SW Grill, Noisy Oyster, O'Charley's, Olive Garden, Outback Steaks, Panda Express, Smokey Bones BBQ, Starbucks, Subway, Taco Bell, Waffle House, Wendy's, Wild Wing Cafe Candlewood Suites, Country Inn&Suites, DoubleTree, Extended Stay America, Hawthorn Inn, Holiday Inn Express, InTown Suites, Red Roof Inn, Rodeway Inn, Suburban Inn H, $General, $Tree, AT&T, Barnes&Noble, Belk, Best Buy, BigLots, Books-A-Million, Dillard's, Firestone/auto, GNC, Hobby Lobby, Home Depot, JC Penney, Lowe's, Michael's, Nissan, NTB, Office Depot, Old Navy, Petco, Petsmart, Ross, Target, Toyota, Tuesday Morning, URGENT CARE, Verizon, Walgreens, Walmart/McDonald's, S BP, RaceWay/dsl, Speedway/dsl, Sunoco/dsl Bojangles, Cracker Barrel, IHOP, McDonald's, Osaka Asian, Ruby Tuesday, Waffle House Best Western, Fairfield Inn, Hampton Inn, Hyatt Place, InTown Suites, La Quinta, Motel 6, Quality Inn, Relax Inn, Residence Inn, Sleep Inn, Staybridge Suites, Woodspring Suites

209a to US 52 (from wb), to Goose Creek, Moncks Corner

205b a US 78, to Summerville, N BP/Dunkin Donuts, Speedway/dsl, Sunoco/dsl Arby's, Bruster's, Cook-Out, East Bay Deli, Firehouse Subs, Fortune Garden, Jersey Mike's, Sonic, Starbucks, Subway, Waffle House, Wendy's, Willie Jewell's BBQ, Zaxby's Fairfield Inn, Hampton Inn, Holiday Inn Express, Wingate Inn H, Charleston Southern U, CVS Drug, Family$, S Citgo, Speedway/dsl, Sunoco/dsl Burger King, KFC, Subway, Taco Bell Advance Parts, BiLo, CVS Drug, KO

204mm **eb, full facilities, litter barrels, petwalk, , , vending**

203 College Park Rd, Ladson, N BP, Sunoco/dsl McDonald's, Waffle House Best Western, Days Inn, S Spinx/dsl KOA (2mi)

202mm **wb, full facilities, litter barrels, petwalk, , , vending**

199b a US 17 A, to Moncks Corner, Summerville, N BP, Kangaroo/dsl, Marathon, Pilot/McDonald's/dsl/scales/24hr, Speedway/Dunkin Donuts/dsl Carolina Alehouse, China Chef, China Wok, KFC, Pizza Hut, Subway Courtyard $General, Advance Parts, AutoZone, BiLo, Buick/GMC, CVS Drug, Family$, O'Reilly Parts, vet, S Shell/Circle K Applebee

NORTH CHARLESTON

INTERSTATE 26 Cont'd

SUMMERVILLE

199b a Continued
Atlanta Bread, Bojangles, Box Car Betty's, Burger King, Chick-fil-A, China Token, Cracker Barrel, Domino's, Dunkin Donuts, Five Guys, Hardee's, IHOP, Jersey Mike's Subs, La Hacienda, Logan's Roadhouse, Marble Slab, McAlisters Deli, Mellow Mushroom, Moe's SW Grill, Newk's Eatery, O'Charleys, Panera Bread, Papa John's, Ruby Tuesday, Ryan's, Shoney's, Smashburger, Starbucks, Sticky Fingers, Waffle House, Which Wich?, Zaxby's [lodging] Comfort Inn, Comfort Suites, Country Inn&Suites, EconoLodge, Economy Inn, Hampton Inn, Holiday Inn Express, Quality Inn, Sleep Inn [other] AT&T, Belk, Best Buy, Chrysler/Dodge/Jeep, Dick's, Earthfare Mkt, GNC, Home Depot, Jo-Ann, Kohl's, Lowe's, NTB, Petco, Petsmart, Ross, Staples, Target, TJ Maxx, Verizon, Walgreens, Walmart/McDonald's, World Mkt

194 SC 16, to Jedburg, E [other] access to Foreign Trade Zone 21, W [gas] FLYING J/PJ Fresh/Wendy's/dsl/scales/24hr

187 SC 27, to Ridgeville, St George, N [gas] Shell, S [gas] BP/dsl [other] Francis Beidler Forest (10mi)

177 SC 453, to Holly Hill, Harleyville, S [gas] Shell/dsl [lodging] Ashley Lodge/RV park

174mm **weigh sta both lanes**

172b a US 15, to Santee, St George, S [gas] Horizon/Domino's/Subway/dsl/e-85/scales/24hr

169b a I-95, N to Florence, S to Savannah

165 SC 210, to Bowman, N [gas] Exxon/dsl, S [gas] BP/dsl

159 SC 36, to Bowman, N [gas] Pilot/McDonald's/dsl/scales/24hr/@, S [gas] Exxon

154b a US 301, to Santee, Orangeburg, N [lodging] Days Inn, S [gas] Exxon, Loves/Chesters/Subway/dsl/scales/24hr, Shell/dsl [food] Waffle House

152mm **[rest stop] wb, full [handicapped] facilities, litter barrels, petwalk, [phone], [picnic], vending**

150mm **[rest stop] eb, full [handicapped] facilities, litter barrels, petwalk, [phone], [picnic], vending**

ORANGEBURG

149 SC 33, to Cameron, to SC State Coll, Orangeburg, [other] Claflin Coll

145b a US 601, to Orangeburg, St Matthews, S [gas] BP/dsl, Exxon, Shell, Sunoco/dsl, United/dsl [food] Burger King, Chick-fil-A, Cracker Barrel, Fatz Café, Hardee's, McDonald's, Ruby Tuesday, Seafood Academy, Subway, Waffle House, Wendy's, Zaxby's [lodging] Carolina Lodge, Comfort Inn, Country Inn&Suites, Days Inn, Fairfield Inn, Hampton Inn, Holiday Inn Express, Howard Johnson, Quality Inn, Sleep Inn, Southern Lodge [other] [H], $General, Cadillac/Chevrolet, Chrysler/Dodge/Jeep, Ford, Nissan, Toyota

139 SC 22, to St Matthews, S [gas] Horizon/e-85, Mobil, Pilot/Dunkin Donuts/Arby's/dsl/scales/24hr [other] Sweetwater Lake Camping (2.5mi)

136 SC 6, to North, Swansea, N [gas] Exxon/dsl

129 US 21, N [gas] Shell/dsl

125 SC 31, to Gaston, N [other] Wolfe's Truck/trailer repair

123mm **[rest stop] both lanes, full [handicapped] facilities, litter barrels, petwalk, [phone], [picnic], vending**

119 US 176, US 21, to Dixiana, S [gas] BP/Subway/dsl, Exxon/dsl

116 I-77 N, to Charlotte, US 76, US 378, to Ft Jackson

CAYCE

115 US 176, US 21, US 321, to Cayce, N [gas] BP, Gulf, RaceWay, Shell/dsl [food] Pizza Hut, Waffle House [other] $General, $Tree, Advance Parts, Bi-Lo, CVS Drug, Family$, Reid's Foods, S [gas] Pilot/DQ/Wendy's/dsl/scales/24hr, Shell/dsl [food] Bojangles, Carolina Wings, Great China, Hardee's, McDonald's, Sonic, Subway [lodging] Country Hearth Inn [other] Firestone, Piggly Wiggly

113 SC 302, Cayce, N [gas] Marathon, Mobil/Burger King, Sunoco/dsl [food] Waffle House [lodging] Airport Inn, Knights Inn, Masters Inn [other] $General, AutoZone, O'Reilly Parts, Rite Aid, Save-A-Lot, Toyota, Walgreens, S [gas] BP/dsl, RaceWay, Shell/Circle K

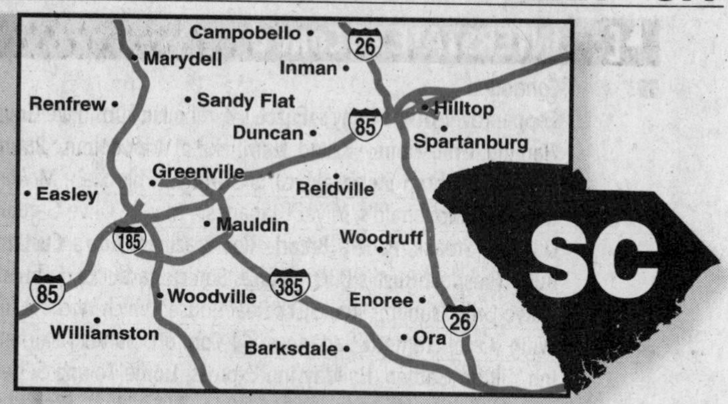

COLUMBIA

113 Continued
[food] Lizard's Thicket, Shoney's, Subway, Waffle House [lodging] Carolina Lodge, Country Inn&Suites, Days Inn, Sleep Inn, Travelers Inn [other] [tire], NAPA

111b a US 1, to W Columbia, N [gas] Murphy USA/dsl, RaceWay, Shell/Circle K/dsl [food] Chick-fil-A, Domino's, Dragon City Chinese, Hardee's, Little Caesar's, Maurice's BBQ, Moe's SW Grill, Ruby Tuesday, San Jose, Sonic, Subway, Tokyo Grill, Waffle House, Zaxby's [lodging] Clarion, Delta Motel, Quality Inn [other] $General, $Tree, AT&T, Bi-Lo, GNC, Hobby Lobby, Pet Supplies+, to USC, Walgreens, Walmart, S [gas] Speedway/dsl [food] Applebee's, China Chef, Fat Boy Greek, Popeye's, Wendy's [other] Aldi Foods, BigLots, Family$, Lowe's, U-Haul

110 US 378, to W Columbia, Lexington, N [food] Grecian Gardens, Happy China, Lizard's Thicket, McDonald's, Rush's Rest., Subway, Waffle House [lodging] America's Inn, Hampton Inn, Holiday Inn [other] CVS Drug, Family$, Food Lion, Toyota, S [gas] Mobil/dsl, Shell/Circle K [food] Atlanta Bread, Bojangles, China Dragon, Firehouse Subs, La Fogata, Pizza Hut [lodging] Executive Inn [other] [H], URGENT CARE

108b a I-126 to Columbia, Bush River Rd, N [gas] BP, Exxon/dsl, Shell/dsl [food] Capt D's, Chick-fil-A, Hardee's, Ruby Tuesday, Schlotzsky's, Waffle House, Wendy's, Zaxby's [lodging] Comfort Inn, Embassy Suites, Extended Stay America, Homewood Suites [other] $General, Advance Parts, Chrysler/Jeep/Dodge, Dodge/Ram, Firestone/auto, Ford/Lincoln, Hyundai, Kia, Mazda, Midas, Office Depot, Riverbanks Zoo, Verizon, S [gas] City Gas, Murphy USA/dsl, Sunoco/dsl [food] Bamboo House, Fuddrucker's, Pizza Hut, Tokyo Grill [lodging] Baymont Inn, Best Western, DoubleTree, Hawthorn Suites, Knights Inn, Sleep Inn [other] AutoZone, GNC, Hamrick's, Walmart

107b a I-20, E to Florence, W to Augusta

106b a St Andrews Rd, N [gas] Exxon/dsl [food] ChuckECheese, IHOP, Papa John's, Sonic, Top China Buffet [lodging] Motel 6 [other] $Tree, Bi-Lo, Camping World RV Ctr, CVS Drug, Infiniti, Jaguar, Nissan, Walgreens, S [gas] BP/dsl, Shell, Speedway/Dunkin Donuts/dsl [food] Domino's, King Buffet, Maurice's BBQ, McDonald's, Nick's Grill, Pizza Hut, Sandy's Hot Dogs, Substation II, Waffle House, WG's Wings, Zaxby's [lodging] EconoLodge, Red Roof Inn [other] $General, KJ's IGA, Tire Kingdom, vet

104 Piney Grove Rd, N [gas] Sunoco/dsl [food] Hardee's, San Jose Mexican, Waffle House [lodging] Quality Inn [other] Costco/gas, Sportsmans Whse, vet, S [gas] Exxon, Shell/dsl [lodging] Country Inn&Suites, Microtel [other] Carmax, Land Rover

103 Harbison Blvd, N [food] Applebee's, Hooters, Wendy's [lodging] Hampton Inn [other] Chevrolet, funpark, Home Depot, Lowe's, S [gas] Shell/Circle K, Speedway/Dunkin Donuts/dsl [food] Bojangles, BoneFish Grill, Buffalo Wild Wings, Carolina Alehouse, Carrabba's, Casa Linda, Chick-fil-A, Chili's, Chipotle Mexican, Coldstone,

IRMO

INTERSTATE 26 Cont'd

Exit	Services
103	Continued Copper River Grill, Denny's, Fazoli's, Firehouse Subs, Five Guys, Flaming Grill, Honey Baked Ham, Huhot Mongolian, Jimmy John's, Longhorn Steaks, Macaroni Grill, Marble Slab, McAlister's Deli, McDonald's, Miyabi Japanese, Miyo's, Olive Garden, Outback Steaks, Panera Bread, Rioz Brazilian, Rita's Custard, Ruby Tuesday, Rush's BBQ, Ryan's, Sonic, Starbucks, Subway, Tokyo Grill, Tsunami Steaks, TX Roadhouse, Which Wich?, Wild Wing Cafe, Yamato Japanese [lodging] Comfort Suites, Fairfield Inn, Hilton Garden, Holiday Inn Express, Home Towne Suites, InTown Suites, Wingate Inn [other] $Tree, AT&T, Belk, Best Buy, Buick/GMC, Dick's, Dillard's, Firestone/auto, Goodyear/auto, JC Penney, Kohl's, Marshalls, Michael's, Midas, NTB, Old Navy, Petsmart, Publix, Ross, Sam's Club/dsl, Staples, SteinMart, Target, TJ Maxx, Verizon, Walmart
102	SC 60, Ballentine, Irmo, **N** [food] Cracker Barrel [lodging] Extended Stay Deluxe, Hyatt Place [other] [H], **S** [gas] JP/dsl, Shell [food] Arby's, Bellacino's Pizza, Dunkin Donuts, Groucho's Deli, Marco's Pizza, Maurice's BBQ, Moe's SW Grill, Papa John's, Smashburger, Taco Bell, Zaxby's, Zoe's Kitchen [lodging] Residence Inn [other] AAA, CVS Drug, Jiffy Lube, same as 103
101b a	US 76, US 176, to N Columbia, **1/2 mi N** [gas] Exxon/Subway/dsl [food] Bojangles, China House, Fatz Café, Fuji Cafe, HotDog Heaven, Jersey Mike's Subs, Zorba's [other] $General, AutoZone, Food Lion, Harley-Davidson, Publix, Rite Aid, Walgreens, **S** [gas] BP, Hickory Point/dsl, Mobil, Shell/dsl [food] Burger King, Lucky's BurgerShack, Waffle House [other] $General, Toyota
97	US 176, to Ballentine, Peak, **N** [food] China 1, Subway [other] Food Lion, **S** [gas] Exxon/dsl
94mm	**weigh sta wb**
91	SC 48, to Chapin, **S** [gas] BP/dsl, Exxon/Taco Bell/dsl, Shell/dsl [food] Bojangles, Farm Boys BBQ, McDonald's, Waffle House [other] to Dreher Island SP, URGENT CARE
85	SC 202, Little Mountain, Pomaria, **S** [other] to Dreher Island SP
82	SC 773, to Prosperity, Pomaria, **N** [gas] Exxon/Circle K/Subway/dsl/24hr, Pilot/Wendy's/dsl/scales/24hr [food] Waffle House
81mm	**weigh sta eb**
76	SC 219, to Pomaria, Newberry, **N** [gas] Loves/McDonald's/Chester's/dsl/scales/24hr, **0-2 mi S** [gas] BP, Murphy USA [food] Burger King, Wendy's [lodging] Hampton Inn (4mi), Holiday Inn Express [other] to Newberry Opera House, Walmart
74	SC 34, to Newberry, **N** [gas] BP/dsl, Shell/dsl [food] Bill&Fran's Café, **2-4 mi S** [gas] Citgo/dsl [food] Arby's, Capt D's, Hardee's, McDonald's, Waffle House [lodging] Days Inn, Days Inn, Economy Inn [other] [H], to NinetySix HS
72	SC 121, to Newberry, **S** [gas] Citgo/dsl [other] [H], to Newberry Coll
66	SC 32, to Jalapa
63.5mm	**[RS] both lanes, full [handicapped] facilities, litter barrels, petwalk, [phone], [picnic], vending**
60	SC 66, to Joanna, **S** [gas] BP/dsl [other] Magnolia RV Park
54	SC 72, to Clinton, **N** [gas] BP/dsl, **S** [gas] Citgo/dsl [food] Fatz Cafe, Zaxby's [lodging] Hampton Inn [other] [H], to Presbyterian Coll
52	SC 56, to Clinton, **N** [gas] Pilot/Subway/dsl/scales/24hr [food] Blue Ocean Rest., McDonald's [lodging] Comfort Suites, Quality Inn, **S** [gas] Citgo/dsl [food] Hardee's, Waffle House, Wendy's [lodging] Days Inn [other] [H]
51	I-385, to Greenville (from wb)
45.5mm	Enoree River
44	SC 49, to Cross Anchor, Union
41	SC 92, to Enoree, **N** [gas] Valero

SPARTANBURG

Exit	Services
38	SC 146, to Woodruff, **N** [gas] HotSpot/Shell/Hardee's/dsl/scales/ 24hr
35	SC 50, Walnut Grove Rd, to Woodruff, **S** [gas] BP/dsl
33mm	S Tyger River
32mm	N Tyger River
28	US 221, to Spartanburg, **N** [gas] Circle K/dsl/24hr, Shell/Subway/dsl [food] Bojangles, Burger King, Italian Pizza, Waffle House [other] [H], Pine Ridge Camping (3mi), to Walnut Grove Plantation
22	SC 296, Reidville Rd, to Spartanburg, **N** [gas] Exxon/dsl, Marathon/Kangaroo/dsl, Spinx/dsl [food] Arby's, Blue Bay Rest. Bruster's, Chief's Rest., Fatz Cafe, Fuddrucker's (1mi), Little Caesars, McDonald's, Outback Steaks, Substation II, Waffle House Wasabi Japanese, Wayback Burger, Zaxby's [other] $General, Advance Parts, to Croft SP, USPO, vet, **S** [gas] 7-11/dsl, QT/dsl, Sunoco/dsl [food] Clock Rest., Denny's, Domino's, Dunkin Donuts, El Limon Mexican, Hardee's, Hong Kong Express, Hunan K, Panda Garden, Papa John's, Subway [lodging] Sleep Inn, Southern Suites Super 8 [other] $General, Abbott Farms, Bi-Lo, CVS Drug, Hyundai Midas, Rite Aid, Toyota, vet, VW, Walgreens
21b a	US 29, to Spartanburg, **N** [gas] Marathon/Circle K, Spinx/dsl [food] A&W/LJ Silver, Bojangles, Brasilia Steaks, Buffalo Wild Wings, Burger King, Chick-fil-A, Chipotle Mexican, ChuckE Cheese, CiCi's, City Range Steaks, Corona Mexican, DQ, Firehouse Subs, FoodCourt, Golden Corral, Jack-in-the-Box, Jason's Deli, Jin Jin Buffet, Kanpai Tokyo, KFC, La Taverna Italian, Longhorn Steaks, McAlister's Deli, Moe's SW Grill, O'Charley's, Olive Garden, Panera Bread, Pizza Hut, Red Bowl Asian, Red Lobster Ruby Tuesday, Ryan's, Starbucks, Subway, Wendy's [lodging] Comfort Suites, Hampton Inn, Hilton Garden, Holiday Inn Express Residence Inn [other] AT&T, Barnes&Noble, Belk, Best Buy, Costco gas, Dick's, Dillard's, Discount Tire, Firestone/auto, Hamrick's Home Depot, JC Penney, Jo-Ann Fabrics, Lowe's, Meineke, Michael's, Office Depot, Old Navy, Petsmart, Rite Aid, Ross, TJ Maxx, Tuesday Morning, USPO, Verizon, Walmart/McDonald's **S** [gas] Marathon/dsl, Shell/dsl [food] Apollo's Pizza, Applebee's Compadre's TexMex, IHOP, McDonald's, Shogun Japanese Starbucks, Taco Bell, Waffle House [other] $Tree, Advance Parts CarQuest, Hobby Lobby, Ingles Foods/gas, Kohl's, Sam's Club gas, Target, TrueValue
19b a	Lp I-85, Spartanburg, **N** [gas] BP/dsl, Valero [food] Cracker Barrel Subway [lodging] Residence Inn, **S** [gas] Valero [lodging] Brookwood Inn
18b a	I-85, N to Charlotte, S to Greenville
17	New Cut Rd, **S** [gas] BP/dsl, Exxon/dsl [food] Burger King, Fat Café, McDonald's, Waffle House [lodging] Days Inn, Howard Johnson, Red Roof Inn, Rodeway Inn
16	John Dodd Rd, to Wellford, **N** [gas] Exxon/Circle K/Aunt M's dsl [other] Camping World RV Ctr
15	US 176, to Inman, **N** [gas] Breakers, Shell/Circle K/dsl/scal [food] Waffle House [other] [H], **S** [gas] QT/dsl [other] Simply RV Ctr
10	SC 292, to Inman, **N** [gas] Shell/Hot Spot/Subway/dsl scales/24hr
7.5mm	Lake William C. Bowman
5	SC 11, Foothills Scenic Dr, Chesnee, Campobello, **N** [gas] Kangaroo/Pilot/Subway/dsl/scales/24hr, **S** [gas] Marathon/L Cricket/dsl
3mm	**Welcome Ctr eb, full [handicapped] facilities, info, litter barrels, petwa [phone], [picnic], vending, wi-fi**
1	SC 14, to Landrum, **S** [gas] Shell/Burger King/dsl [food] Bojangles, China Cafe, Papa John's, Pizza Hut (1mi), Starbucks, Subway [other] $General, Bi-Lo Foods, Ingles/café/gas, Verizon, vet
0mm	South Carolina/North Carolina state line

INTERSTATE 77

Exit#	Services
91mm	South Carolina/North Carolina state line
90	US 21, Carowinds Blvd, E Mobil/Circle K/dsl, QT/dsl Bojangles, Burger King, McDonald's, Zaxby's fireworks, W Circle K/Subway, Exxon/7-11, QT/dsl, Shell/Circle K/Wendy's/dsl Cracker Barrel, Culver's, Famous Dave's, KFC, Moe's SW, Panchito's Mexican Best Western, Clarion, Comfort Inn, Country Inn Suites, Motel 6, Quality Inn Cabela's, Carowinds Camping, Carowinds Funpark
89.5mm	**Welcome Ctr sb, full facilities, info, litter barrels, petwalk, vending, weigh sta nb**
88	Gold Hill Rd, to Pineville, E URGENT CARE, W QT/dsl, Shell/dsl, Valero/dsl Dunkin Donuts, Hardee's, Marco's Pizza WingBonz Cantina Chrysler/Dodge/Jeep, Fiat, Ford, Hyundai, KOA, Publix, vet
85	SC 160, Ft Mill, Tega Cay, E Exxon Brixx Pizza, Carolina Alehouse, Panera Bread, Smashburger, Starbucks Courtyard Ft Mill Drug, W BP/dsl, QT/dsl, Shell/Circle K/dsl Akahana Asian, Big Wok, Burger King, Charanda Mexican, Chick-fil-A, Empire Pizza, Fratelli's Italian, Jimmy John's, Killington's Rest., McAlister's Deli, Moe's SW Grill, Papa John's, Pizza Hut, Starbucks, Wendy's, Zaxby's Hampton Inn, Holiday Inn Express CVS Drug, Firestone/auto, Goodyear/auto, Harris-Teeter, Lowe's, Meineke, vet, Walgreens
84.5mm	**weigh sta sb**
83	SC 49, Sutton Rd, W Loves/Chester/Subway/dsl/scales/24hr
82.5mm	Catawba River
82c	US 21, SC 161, Rock Hill, Ft Mill, E Exxon Freddy's, IHOP, Sonny's BBQ, Steak'n Shake, Zaxby's Comfort Inn Home Depot, Lidl, Petsmart, W Mobil/dsl, QT/dsl, Shell/Circle K, Shell/dsl, Valero Big Wok, Chinese Bistro Deli, Empire Pizza, Hooters, Krispy Kreme, McDonald's, Outback Steaks, Sonic, Starbucks Courtyard H, $General, Food Lion, TreadQtrs Auto, Walgreens
82b a	E Exxon Comfort Inn, Ramada Inn, W Shell/Circle K/dsl Arby's, Bojangles, Burger King, Chick-fil-A, China Kitchen, CiCi's Pizza, Cookout, Fuji Japan, Golden Corral, HoneyBaked Ham, HongKong Chinese, Little Caesar's, Luigi& Sons Italian, Mario's Pizza, McDonald's, Nick's Gyros, Penn Sta. Subs, Pizza Hut, Popeye's, Rock Hill Diner, Sakura Japanese, Subway, Taco Bell, Waffle House, Wendy's Baymont Inn, Best Way, Best Western, Country Inn&Suites, Days Inn, EconoLodge, Economy Express Inn, Howard Johnson, Microtel, Motel 6, Quality Inn, Red Roof Inn $General, $Tree, Advance Parts, Aldi Foods, AutoZone, BigLots, Cadillac/Chevrolet, city park, Family$, Firestone/auto, Midas, NAPA, Office Depot, O'Reilly Parts, PepBoys, Publix, Verizon, York Co Museum
79	SC 122, Dave Lyle Blvd, to Rock Hill, E BP/dsl, Murphy USA/dsl Amber Buffet, Applebee's, Buffalo Wild Wings, Charanda Mexican, Chick-fil-A, Cracker Barrel, Five Guys, Hardee's, Jersey Mike's, Longhorn Steaks, Newk's Eatery, O'Charley's, Ruby Tuesday, TX Roadhouse Comfort Suites, Fairfield Inn, Hampton Inn, Holiday Inn, Home 2 Suites, La Quinta, Staybridge Suites, TownePlace Suites, Tru, Wingate Inn $Tree, AT&T, Belk, Buick/GMC, Discount Tire, Food Lion, Harley Davidson, Hobby Lobby, Honda, JC Penney, Kohl's, Lowe's, Meineke, Nissan, NTB, Sam's Club/dsl, Staples, Toyota, Verizon, Walmart, W Circle K/dsl Baskin Robins/Dunkin Donuts, Bob Evans, Chili's, DQ, Firehouse Subs, Jack-in-the-Box,

ROCK HILL

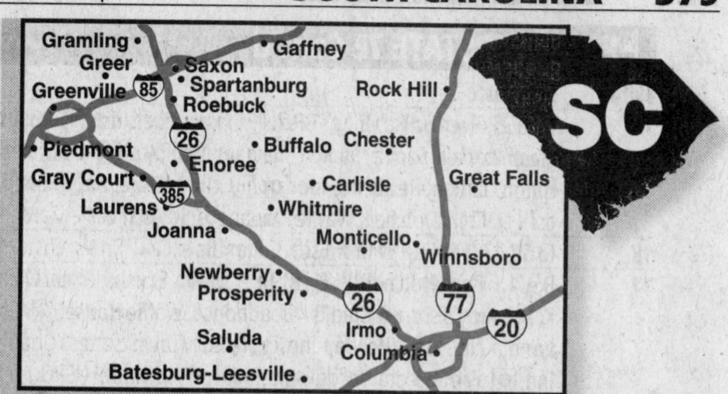

Exit#	Services
79	Continued McAlister's Deli, McDonald's, Mellow Mushroom Pizza, Moe's SW Grill, Olive Garden, Panera Bread, Subway, Taco Bell, Wendy's Extended Stay America, Hilton Garden Best Buy, Books-A-Million, Dick's, Ford, Michael's, Ross, Target, TJ Maxx, URGENT CARE
77	US 21, SC 5, to Rock Hill, E BP/Subway/dsl, Pilot/dsl, QT/dsl to Andrew Jackson SP (12mi), W Valero/dsl Waffle House to Winthrop Coll
75	Porter Rd, E Crown fireworks
73	SC 901, to Rock Hill, York, E FLYING J/Denny's/dsl/scales/LP/24hr, Exxon/dsl, W H
66mm	**both lanes, full facilities, litter barrels, petwalk, vending**
65	SC 9, to Chester, Lancaster, E BP/dsl, Citgo/dsl, QT/dsl, Shell/Subway/dsl Bojangles, China Wok, Waffle House Days Inn, EconoLodge $General, IGA Foods/gas, W Exxon/dsl Burger King, Country Omelet, Front Porch Rest., KFC/Taco Bell, McDonald's, Zaxby's Motel 6, Quality Inn, Super 8 H, vet
62	SC 56, to Fort Lawn, Richburg
55	SC 97, to Chester, Great Falls, E Exxon/dsl, W H, to Chester SP
48	SC 200, to Great Falls, E Shell/Grand Central Rest./dsl/@, W Pilot/Wendy's/DQ/dsl/scales/24hr/
46	SC 20, to White Oak
41	SC 41, to Winnsboro, E to Lake Wateree SP
34	SC 34, to Winnsboro, Ridgeway, E Am Pm/dsl Ridgeway Motel (1mi) Bryan's Auto/tire, Ridgeway Camping (1mi), W Exxon/dsl Waffle House Ramada Ltd
32	Peach Rd, Ridgeway, Little Cedar Creek Camping (2mi)
27	Blythewood Rd, E BP/Dunkin Donuts, Exxon/Bojangles/dsl/24hr Carolina Wings, China King, Hardee's, KFC/Pizza Hut, McDonald's, San Jose Mexican, Subway, Valentina's Greek, Waffle House, Wendy's Comfort Inn, Days Inn, Holiday Inn Express $General, IGA Foods, repair/tires, USPO, vet, W Lizard's Thicket Food Lion, Groucho's Deli
24	US 21, to Wilson Blvd., E BP/dsl, Shell/Subway/dsl auto repair, W Exxon/dsl
22	Killian Rd, E Mobil/Burger King/dsl, Murphy Express/dsl Applebee's, Bojangles, Chick-fil-A, Firehouse Subs, Freddy's, Hardee's, McDonald's, Panda Express, Popeye's, Salsarita's, Steak'n Shake, Subway, Taco Bell, Tropical Cafe, Zaxby's Hampton Inn Acura, Aldi Foods, AutoZone, BMW, CVS Drug, Discount Tire, Firestone, Honda, Kia, Kroger/dsl, Lowe's, Mazda, Rite Aid, Subaru, Toyota, VW, Walgreens, W China Dragon, Monterrey's Mexican Lexus/Buick/GMC/Cadillac, Verizon, Walmart/McDonald's

INTERSTATE 77 Cont'd

COLUMBIA

Exit#	Services
19	SC 555, Farrow Rd, E BP/dsl, Exxon, Shell/dsl Bojangles, Cracker Barrel, Sonic, Subway, Wendy's Courtyard, Hilton Garden, Residence Inn Longs Drug, W Shell/dsl China Kitchen, Waffle House SC Archives
18	to SC 277, to I-20 W (from sb), Columbia
17	US 1, Two Notch Rd, E BP, Citgo, Exxon, Shell/Circle K Arby's, Burger King, TX Roadhouse, Waffle House Columbia NE Hotel, Holiday Inn Express, InTown Suites, Quality Inn Family$, to Sesquicentennial SP, U-Haul, USPO, vet, Walgreens, W Mobil Chili's, Fazoli's, Hooters, IHOP, Lizard's Thicket, Outback Steaks, Waffle House Best Western+, Comfort Suites, EconoLodge, Fairfield Inn, Hampton Inn, La Quinta, Microtel, Red Roof Inn Home Depot
16b a	I-20, W to Augusta, E to Florence, Alpine Rd
15b a	SC 12, to Percival Rd, W Shell
13	Decker Blvd (from nb), W El Cheapo, Spinx/dsl
12	Forest Blvd, Thurmond Blvd, E to Ft Jackson, W BP/dsl, Shell/dsl/24hr Chick-fil-A, Cookout, Domino's, Eastern Buffet, Fatz Café, Golden Corral, McDonald's, Pancho's, Sonic, Subway, Wendy's Extended Stay America, Super 8 $Tree, AT&T, Hobby Lobby, museum, Sam's Club/gas, Tuesday Morning, Verizon, vet, Walmart
10	SC 760, Jackson Blvd, E to Ft Jackson, 2 mi W Shell Applebee's, Bojangles, Buffalo Wild Wings, Maurices BBQ, Moe's SW, Ruby Tuesday, Smashburger, Subway EconoLodge Bilo, Staples, Walgreens, Whole Foods Mkt
9b a	US 76, US 378, to Sumter, Columbia, 0-2 mi E BP, Citgo, Murphy USA/dsl, Shell, Shell/Burger King, Sunoco/dsl Arby's, Bojangles, Capt D's, Chick-fil-A, Domino's, Ichiban, KFC, McDonald's, Pizza Hut, Popeye's, Ruby Tuesday, Rush's Rest., Shoney's, Subway, Taco Bell, Waffle House, Waffle House, Wendy's, Zaxby's Baymont Inn, Candlewood Suites, Comfort Inn, Country Inn&Suites, Days Inn, Hampton Inn, Hampton Inn, Holiday Inn Express, La Quinta, Microtel, Quality Inn, Sleep Inn, TownePlace Suites $Tree, Advance Parts, Aldi Foods, AutoZone, CVS Drug, Family$, Firestone/auto, Ford, Interstate Batteries, Lowe's, NTB, O'Reilly Parts, URGENT CARE, USPO, Verizon, Walgreens, Walmart, W Circle K, Shell CiCi's Pizza, Eric's Mexican, Hardee's, Jimmy John's, Krispy Kreme, Panera Bread, Sonic, Starbucks, Sub Station, Wendy's Best Value Inn $General, BigLots, GNC, Goodyear/auto, Rite Aid, Sav-A-Lot Foods, Target
6b a	Shop Rd, W fairgrounds, to USC Coliseum
5	SC 48, Bluff Rd, W Loves/McDonald's/Subway/dsl/scales/24hr, Shell/Burger King/dsl Bojangles (2mi) $General, Petro/Starbucks/dsl/scales/24hr
3mm	Congaree River
2	SC 35, to Cayce, W Columbia
1	US 21, US 176, US 321 (from sb), Cayce, W accesses same as SC I-26, exit 115.

I-77 begins/ends on I-26, exit 116.

INTERSTATE 85

GAFFNEY

SPARTANBURG

Exit#	Services
106.5mm	South Carolina/North Carolina state line
106	US 29, to Grover, E BP/dsl, W Exxon/dsl, Hickory Point/gas, Mobil/dsl/fireworks, Pilot/Wendy's/dsl/scales/24hr
104	SC 99, Tribal Rd, E Loves/McDonald's/Subway/dsl/scales/24hr, W fireworks
103mm	Welcome Ctr sb, full facilities, info, litter barrels, petwalk, vending
102	SC 198, to Earl, E BP/dsl, Exxon Hardee's, W FLYING J/Denny's/dsl/scales/LP/24hr, Citgo/dsl McDonald's, Waffle House
100mm	Buffalo Creek
100	SC 5, to Blacksburg, Shelby, W Citgo, Exxon/dsl/scales/24h
98	Frontage Rd (from nb)
97mm	Broad River
96	SC 18, E Circle K/Krystal/dsl
95	SC 18, to Gaffney, E Exxon/Circle K/dsl, PetroMax/ds Italian Grill/Pizzaria, Mr Waffle Gaffney Inn, Shamroc Inn to Limestone Coll
92	SC 11, to Gaffney, E Circle K/Subway/dsl, Fast Point/ds Murphy USA/dsl Aegean Pizza, Applebee's, Bojangles Burger King, Chick-fil-A, China Express, CookOut, Daddy Joe BBQ, Domino's, Firehouse Subs, KFC, Little Caesars, McDonald's, Olive Garden, Papa John's, Pete's, Pizza Hut, Popeye's Sagebrush Steaks, Sonic, Taco Bell, Waffle House, Wendy's, Zaxby's Baymont Inn, Super 8 $General, $Tree, Advanc Parts, Aldi Foods, Belk, BigLots, BiLo, Ingles Foods, Lowe's O'Reilly Parts, Rite Aid, to Limestone Coll, USPO, Verizon, Walgreens, Walmart, W Fatz Cafe Homestead Lodg Quality Inn Chevrolet, Foothills Scenic Hwy, to The Peach
90	SC 105, SC 42, to Gaffney, E Pilot/Arby's/dsl/scales/24h QT/dsl Bojangles, Bronco Mexican, Clock Rest., Starbuck Subway, Waffle House Red Roof Inn, Sleep Inn, W Citgo/dsl, Exxon/Burger King Cracker Barrel, Food Court, Outback Steaks Hampton Inn fruit stand, Hamrick's, Prim Outlets/famous brands
87	SC 39, E KOA
83	SC 110, E fruit stand, W Westar/dsl/scales/24hr fruit stand, to Cowpens Bfd
82	Frontage Rd (from nb)
80.5mm	Pacolet River
80	SC 57, to Gossett, E Hot Spot/Shell/dsl
78	US 221, Chesnee, E Citgo/dsl Hardee's Motel 6, QT/dsl, RaceWay/dsl, Sunoco/Burger King/dsl Arby' Bojangles, McDonald's, Southern BBQ, Subway, Waffle Hous Wendy's Hampton Inn, Holiday Inn Express $Genera Advance Parts, Harley-Davidson, Ingles Foods/cafe/dsl
77	Lp 85, Spartanburg, services along Lp 85 exits E
75	SC 9, Spartanburg, E Denny's Best Value Inn, W Marathon/Burger King/dsl, Pure, QT/dsl, RaceWay/d Bruster's, Capri's Italian, CookOut, Copper River Grill, Fa Café, Grapevine Rest, Jade House Asian, La Paz Mexican, McDonald's, Pizza Hut, Waffle House, Zaxby's Comfort In Days Inn CVS Drug, Ingles/cafe/gas, Parr 3 Automotiv USPO
72	US 176, to I-585, E to USCS, Wofford/Converse Co W Kangaroo/dsl, RaceWay/dsl China Fun, El Lim Mexican, Subway, Waffle House $General, Ingles Food cafe/gas
70b a	I-26, E to Columbia, W to Asheville
69	Lp 85, SC 41 (from nb), to Fairforest
68	SC 129, to Greer
67mm	N Tyger River
66	US 29, to Lyman, Wellford, E Exxon/Subway/dsl Waf House
63	SC 290, to Duncan, E Circle K/dsl, Citgo/dsl, QT/dsl, Spin Dunkin Donuts/dsl Chick-Fil-A, Clock Rest., Cracker Barrel, Primo Mexican, Firehouse Subs, KFC, Paisanos Italian, Pizza Ir

INTERSTATE 85 Cont'd

63 Continued
Sake Japanese, Taco Bell, Thai Garden, Waffle House, Zaxby's Baymont Inn, Hampton Inn, Microtel, **W** BP, Marathon/dsl, Pilot/Wendy's/dsl/scales/24hr, TA/BP/DQ/rest./dsl/scales/24hr/@ Bojangles, Demetre's Grill, El Molcajete Mexican, Hardee's, McDonald's Day's Inn, Holiday Inn Express, Quality Inn, Woodspring Suites Blue Beacon, Sonny's RV Ctr, Speedco

62.5mm S Tyger River

60 SC 101, to Greer, **E** Citgo/dsl, Marathon, Sunoco/dsl Landmark Diner, Subway, Theo's Rest, **W** Spinx/Burger King/dsl Bojangles, Waffle House Super 8 BMW Visitor Ctr

58 Brockman-McClimon Rd

57 **W** Greenville-Spartanburg Airport

56 SC 14, to Greer, **E** Citgo/dsl H, **W** QT/dsl, Spinx/dsl Goodyear Truck Tires, Ledford's Adventure RV Ctr

55mm Enoree River

54 Pelham Rd, **E** Marathon/Kangaroo, Stop-A-Minute/dsl Burger King, Corona Mexican, Skin's Hotdogs, Waffle House Best Western, **W** BP/dsl Acapulcos Mexican, Atlanta Bread Co, Bellacino's, Bertolos Pizza, Bojangles, California Dreaming Rest., Chick-fil-A, China Kitchen, Chophouse 47, Dunkin Donuts, Firehouse Subs, Five Guys, Frankie's Pizza, Hardee's, Joe's Crabshack, Joy of Tokyo, Logan's Roadhouse, Macaroni Grill, McDonald's, Moe's SW Grill, On the Border, Palmetto Alehouse, Papa Murphy's, PDQ Rest., Ruby Tuesday, Schlotzsky's, Starbucks, Subway Courtyard, EconoLodge, Extended Stay America, Fairfield Inn, Hampton Inn, Holiday Inn Express, Home2 Suites, MainStay Suites, Marriott, Quality Inn, Residence Inn, Wingate Inn Advance Parts, Bi-Lo, CVS Drug, EarthFare Foods, Goodyear/auto, Verizon, Walgreens, Walmart

51 I-385, SC 146, Woodruff Rd, **E** Brixx Pizza, Buffalo Wild Wings, Chipotle Mexican, Coldstone, Cracker Barrel, Fuddrucker's, IHOP, Lieu's Bistro, Longhorn Steaks, Monterrey Mexican, Oriental House, Panera Bread, PF Chang's, Red Robin, Sticky Fingers Drury Inn, Hampton Inn, Hilton Garden, Homewood Suites, Staybridge Suites Barnes&Noble, Best Buy, Dick's, Goodyear/auto, Hamrick's Outlet, Lowe's, Marshalls, PetCo, Petsmart, Ross, Verizon, vet, Whole Foods Mkt, **W** QT/dsl, RaceWay/dsl Bad Daddy's Burger, Carolina Alehouse, Carrabba's, Cheddars, Chuy's Mexican, Dave&Busters's, Firebirds, HuHot Mongolian, Krystal, Krystal, McDonald's, MidTown Deli, Ruby Tuesday, Ruth's Chris Steaks, Starbucks, Subway, TGIFriday's, Tucanos Brazilian Grill, Twin Peaks Rest, Waffle House, Yardhouse Rest., Zoe's Kitchen Candlewood Suites, Comfort Inn, Crowne Plaza, Days Inn, Embassy Suites, Holiday Inn Express, La Quinta, Micotel AT&T, Cabela's, Costco/gas, Firestone/auto, Home Depot, Old Navy, Target, Trader Joe's

48b a US 276, Greenville, **E** BP/dsl Waffle House Red Roof Inn BMW/Mini, CarMax, to ICAR, **W** Exxon/dsl Arby's, Bojangles, Burger King, Happy China, Hooters, McDonald's, Olive Garden, Pizza Hut/Taco Bell, Ryan's, Subway Comfort Inn, Embassy Suites $Tree, Acura, Audi/Porsche/VW, Bi-Lo, Buick/GMC, Chevrolet/Cadillac, Chrysler/Dodge/Jeep, CVS Drug, Ford/Lincoln, GNC, Honda, Infiniti, Jaguar, Kia, Lexus, Mazda, Meineke, Mercedes, Michael's, Nissan, Office Depot, Old Time Pottery, PepBoys, Petsmart, SteinMart, Subaru, Toyota, Volvo

GREENVILLE

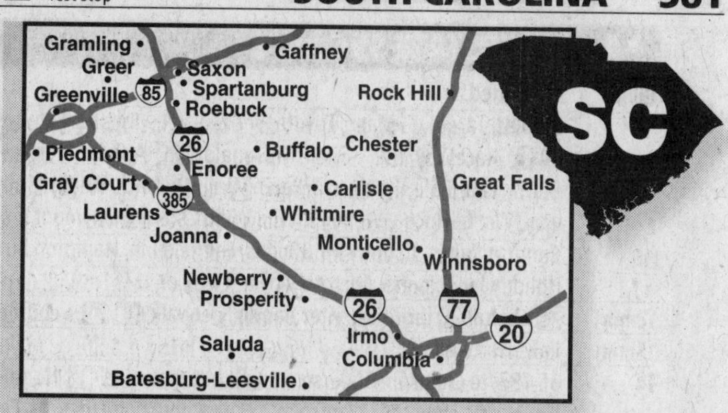

46c rd 291, Pleasantburg Rd, Mauldin Rd, **W** Citgo/dsl Jack-in-the-Box, Papa John's, Subway InTown Suites, Quality Inn, Super Lodge, ValuePlace Aamco, Advance Parts, Bi-Lo/gas, CVS Drug, Home Depot, same as 46ba, Tire Kingdom

46b a US 25 bus, Augusta Rd, **E** Mike&Jack/dsl, QT/dsl, Spinx/dsl, Vgo Burger King, Waffle House Country Hearth Inn, Southern Suites, **W** Economy Inn, Traveler's Inn Home Depot, same as 46c

44 US 25, White Horse Rd, **E** Spinx/Subway/dsl, **W** Citgo/McDonald's, RaceWay/dsl Waffle House H, Freightliner

44a SC 20 (from sb), to Piedmont

42 I-185, to Greenville, I-185 S (toll), Columbia, **W** H

40 SC 153, to Easley, **E** BP/dsl Waffle House, **W** 7-11/dsl, Citgo/dsl, QT/dsl, RaceWay/dsl, Spinx/dsl Arby's, Bojangles, Burger King, Chick-Fil-A, Cracker Barrel, El Sureno Mexican, Firehouse Subs, Huddle House, KFC, Little Caesars, Los Amigos, McDonald's, Papa John's, Pizza House, Pizza Hut/Taco Bell, Sonny's BBQ, Subway, Zaxby's Best Western+, Executive Inn, Hampton Inn (4mi), Super 8 $General, Advance Parts, Bi-Lo, CVS Drug, GNC, Rite Aid, Verizon, Walgreens, Walmart

39 SC 143, to Piedmont, **E** Vgo/dsl, **W** Shell/dsl

35 SC 86, to Easley, Piedmont, **E** BP/Subway (1.5mi), Pilot/McDonald's/dsl/scales/24hr Cancun Mexican, Hardee's (1.5mi), Millhouse Rest., Tony' Pizza O'Reilly Parts, repair/tires, Rite Aid, **W** QT/dsl, Spinx/Pete's Grill/dsl Bojangles

34 US 29 (from sb), to Williamston

32 SC 8, to Pelzer, Easley, **E** 7-11/dsl, Shell/dsl

27 SC 81, to Anderson, **E** BP/dsl, Exxon/dsl Arby's, Fiesta Rodeo Mexican, McDonald's, Waffle House Hampton Inn, Holiday Inn Express H

23mm **RS sb, full facilities, litter barrels, petwalk, vending**

21 US 178, to Anderson, 2 mi **E** BP/dsl, QT/dsl Applebee's, Chick-fil-A, Chili's, Longhorn Steaks, O'Charley's, Waffle House Publix/deli

19b a US 76, SC 28, to Anderson, 2 mi **E** Exxon/dsl, QT/dsl, Shell/dsl, Stop A Minit/dsl Applebee's, Barbarito's, Bojangles, Carson Steaks, Chick-fil-A, Chili's, Chipotle, CookOut, Denny's, Five Guys, Fuddruckers, Golden Corral, Golden Corral, Grand China, Hardee's, Hardee's, Hibachi Grill, Jack-in-the-Box, Logan's Roadhouse, Longhorn Steaks, O'Charley's, Olive Garden, Panera Bread, Red Lobster, Sake Japanese, Starbucks, Tucker's Rest., TX Roadhouse, Zaxby's Best Value Inn, Days Inn, Hilton Garden, Holiday Inn, Rodeway Inn, Super 8 $General, $Tree, Advance Parts, Aldi Foods, AT&T, Best Buy, Chrysler/Dodge/Jeep, Dick's, Ford/Mazda, GNC, Goodyear, Harley-Davidson, Hobby Lobby, Home Depot, Honda, Kohl's, Lowe's, Meineke, Michael's, Nissan, Office Depot, Old Navy, O'Reilly Parts, Petsmart, Publix/deli, Ross, Russell Stover, Sam's Club,

ANDERSON

INTERSTATE 85 Cont'd

19b a Continued
Staples, Target, TJ Maxx, Toyota, Verizon, vet, Walmart/Subway, W RaceWay/dsl, Shell/McDonald's Arby's, Cracker Barrel, Fatz Cafe, Hooters, J Peters Grill, Outback Steaks, Subway, Waffle House, Wendy's, Wild Wing Cafe Baymont Inn, Comfort Suites, Country Inn&Suites, Fairfield Inn, Hampton Inn, Holiday Inn Express, Microtel to Clemson U (11mi)

18mm **nb, full facilities, litter barrels, petwalk, , , vending**

15mm Lake Hartwell

14 SC 187, to Clemson, Anderson, E Marathon/dsl Huddle House camping (1mi), W Hickory Point/dsl Famous Pizza Grill Budget Inn to Clem Research Pk

12mm Seneca River, Lake Hartwell

11 SC 24, SC 243, to Townville, E Exxon/dsl Subway to Savannah River Scenic Hwy, W Shell/dsl Townville Cafe RV camping

9mm **weigh sta nb**

4 SC 243, to SC 24, Fair Play, E Loves/Arby's/dsl/scales/24hr

2 SC 59, to Fair Play, W fireworks

1 SC 11, to Walhalla, W Gazebo Rest. fireworks, to Lake Hartwell SP

.5mm **Welcome Ctr nb, full facilities, info, litter barrels, petwalk, , , vending**

0mm South Carolina/Georgia state line, Lake Hartwell, Tugaloo River

INTERSTATE 95

Exit# Services

198mm South Carolina/North Carolina state line

196mm **Welcome Ctr sb, full facilities, info, litter barrels, petwalk, , , vending**

195mm Little Pee Dee River

DILLON

193 SC 9, SC 57, to N Myrtle Beach, Dillon, E Exxon/dsl, Mobil/dsl, Murphy Express/dsl, Sunoco/dsl B&C Steak/BBQ, Burger King, CookOut, Huddle House, Little Caesar's, Pizza Hut, Popeye's, Subway, Tokyo Cafe, Waffle House, Wendy's, Zaxby's Best Value Inn, Days Inn, Quality Inn, Red Roof Inn, Taco Bell H, $General, $Tree, Advance Parts, AutoZone, CVS Drug, fireworks, Food Lion, O'Reilly Parts, SaveALot Foods, Walgreens, Walmart, W Eastern Cafe Chines Economy Inn Bass Lake RV Camp/LP

190 SC 34, to Dillon, W Loves/Arby's/dsl/scales/24hr

181 SC 38, Oak Grove, E FLYING J/dsl/LP/scales/24hr, BP/Subway/dsl/24hr, Shell/McDonald's/dsl/24hr Shuler's BBQ (5mi) fireworks, W Pilot/DQ/Wendy's/dsl/scales/24hr Best Western

175mm Pee Dee River

170 SC 327, E BP, Pilot/Wendy's/dsl/scales/24hr McDonald's, Subway, Waffle House, Zaxby's Holiday Inn Express Harley Davidson, Missile Museum, to Myrtle Beach

169 TV Rd, to Florence, E dsl repair, Florence RV Park, W BP, Petro/Shell/Iron Skillet/dsl/scales/24hr/@ Best Value Inn Blue Beacon, dsl repair, Peterbilt

FLORENCE

164 US 52, to Darlington, Florence, E Exxon/dsl, RaceWay, Shell/dsl Cracker Barrel, McDonald's, Quincy's, Ruby Tuesday, Waffle House, Wendy's Baymont Inn, Best Western, EconoLodge, Rodeway Inn, Suburban Lodge, Super 8 H, Chrysler/Dodge/Jeep, W Mobil, Pilot/Subway/Taco Bell/dsl, TA/BP/Popeye's/dsl/scales/@ Arby's, Dickey's BBQ, Dunkin Donuts, Fatz Café, Hardee's, Krispy Kreme, Shoney's, Young's Pecans, Zaxby's ComfortSuites, Country Inn&Suites,

164 Continued
Days Inn, Hampton Inn, La Quinta, Microtel, Motel 6, Sleep Inn, Travel House Inn, Tru Hilton to Darlington Raceway, transmissions

160b I-20 W, to Columbia

160a Lp 20, to Florence, E Exxon/dsl, Murphy USA/dsl, Tesla EVC Arby's, Bruster's Ice Cream, Buffalo Wild Wings, Burger King, Chick-fil-A, Chili's, Chipotle, ChuckeCheese, Firehouse Subs, Golden Corral, Hibachi Grill, Hwy 55 Cafe, IHOP, La Bamba Mexican, Longhorn Steaks, Mellow Mushroom, Olive Garden, Outback Steaks, Panera Bread, Percy&Willie's, Red Bowl Asian, Red Lobster, Ruby Tuesday, San Jose's, Subway, Taco Bell, Waffle House, Western Sizzlin, Which Wich? Courtyard, Days Inn, Fairfield Inn, Hampton Inn, Hilton Garden, Holiday Inn Express, Home 2 Hilton, Homewood Suites, Quality Inn, Red Roof Inn, Residence Inn, SpringHill Suites, Staybridge Suites, TownePlace Suites $Tree, Aldi Foods, AT&T, Barnes&Noble, Belk, Best Buy, Big Lots, Dick's, Discount Tire, Hamrick's, Hobby Lobby, Home Depot, JC Penney, Kohl's, Lowes Whse, Petsmart, Sam's Club/dsl, Target, Verizon, Walmart

157 US 76, Timmonsville, Florence, E Citgo/dsl, Kangaroo/dsl, Marathon/dsl, Shell/McDonald's Peking Asian, Waffle House Florence Inn, Travelodge Abbott Farms Peaches, W Bull/dsl Ramada/rest., Swamp Fox Camping (1mi), Tree Top Inn auto repair

153 Honda Way, W Exxon/dsl Honda Plant

150 SC 403, to Sardis, E BP/dsl/scales Hotplate Cafe Budget Inn, W Exxon/dsl

147mm Lynches River

146 SC 341, to Lynchburg, Olanta, E Relax Inn

141 SC 53, SC 58, to Shiloh, E Exxon DonMar RV Ctr, to Woods Bay SP, W Shell

139mm **both lanes, full facilities, litter barrels, petwalk, , , vending**

135 US 378, to Sumter, Turbeville, E BP/dsl, Citgo/dsl/24hr Compass Rest. Day's Inn, W Exxon/Subway/dsl

132 SC 527, to Sardinia, Kingstree

130mm Black River

122 US 521, to Alcolu, Manning, W Exxon/dsl

MANNING

119 SC 261, to Paxville, Manning, **0-1 mi** E Mobil, Murphy USA dsl, Shell/dsl, TA/BP/Pizza Hut/Popeye's/dsl/scales/24hr/@ Bojangles, CookOut, Golden Chick, Huddle House, Mariachi's Mexican, McDonald's, Shoney's, Sonic, Subway, Taco Bell, Waffle House, Wendy's, Yucatan Mexican, Zaxby's Baymont Inn, Days Inn, Hampton Inn, Quality Inn, SureStay H, $General, AutoZone, Chrysler/Dodge/Jeep, CVS Drug, Ford, O'Reilly Parts, truckwash, Verizon, Walmart, W Horizon dsl/e-85, Marathon Super 8 auto repair

115 US 301, to Summerton, Manning, W Shell/dsl Georgio's Rest Knights Inn

108 rd 102, Summerton, E BP/DQ, Travel Depot/dsl Taw Caw Camping (6m), W Days Inn, Deluxe Inn

102 US 15, US 301 N, to N Santee, E Marathon/dsl Santee Resort/Motel Bigwater RV Camping, Santee Lakes Camping, W Horizon/dsl/e-85 to Santee NWR

100mm Lake Marion

99mm **both lanes, full facilities, info, litter barrels, petwalk, , , vending**

98 SC 6, to Eutawville, Santee, E BP/Bojangles, Citgo, Exxon, Mobil Coaster's Seafood, Huddle House, Pizza Hut, Shoney's, Subway Best Value Inn, Best Western, Econolodge, Hampton Inn, Rodeway Inn, Super 8, Whitten In

SANTEE

INTERSTATE 95 Cont'd

98 Continued
$General, IGA Foods, **W** Horizon/dsl/e-85, Marathon/dsl, Shell Burger King, Cracker Barrel, Domino's, Maurice's BBQ, McDonald's, Waffle House, Wendy's Clark Inn/rest., Comfort Inn, Holiday Inn, Howard Johnson, Lake Marion Inn, Quality Inn CarQuest, CVS Drug, Family$, Food Lion, Rivers Country Store, to Santee SP (3mi), USPO

97 US 301 S (from sb, no return), to Orangeburg

93 US 15, to Santee, Holly Hill

90 US 176, to Cameron, Holly Hill, **W** Exxon/dsl

86b a I-26, W to Columbia, E to Charleston

82 US 178, to Bowman, Harleyville, **E** Horizon/Subway, Pilot/Wendy's/DQ/dsl/scales/24hr Peachtree Inn, **W** Shell/dsl tires/truck repair

77 US 78, to Bamberg, St George, **E** FLYING J/Denny's/dsl/scales/24hr, Horizon/Subway/dsl/e-85, Monoco, Sunoco Georgio's Rest., Hardee's, KFC, McDonald's, Pizza Hut, Skynyrd's Grill, Waffle House Best Value Inn, Comfort Inn/RV Park, EconoLodge, Quality Inn $General, Ace Hardware, BiLo, Chevrolet/GMC, CVS Drug, Family$, Ford, USPO, **W** BP, Shell/Taco Bell/dsl Country Hearth Inn, Knights Inn

74mm **parking area (commercial vehicles only sb), weigh sta nb**

68 SC 61, Canadys, **E** BP, Crosco Express, Shell/Subway/dsl to Colleton SP (3mi), truck lube/repair

62 McLeod Rd

WALTERBORO

57 SC 64, Lodge, Walterboro, **E** Citgo/dsl, Horizon/e85, Shell/DQ, Sunoco/dsl Arby's, Bojangles, Burger King, Capt D's, Dimitrio's Rest., Domino's, Dunkin Donuts, Hardee's, Huddle House, KFC, McDonald's, Olde House Café, Subway, Taco Bell, Waffle House, Wendy's Carolina Lodge, Sleep Inn, Southern Inn H, $General, Ace Hardware, Advance Parts, AutoZone, Belk, Family$, Ford, GNC, O'Reilly Parts, Rite Aid, **W** Murphy USA/dsl China Buffet, Zaxby's Super 8 $Tree, AT&T, PetCo, Verizon, Walmart

53 SC 63, to Varnville, Walterboro, Hampton, **E** BP/McDonald's, El Cheapo, Exxon, Petro Express/dsl, Shell/DQ Ruby Tuesday, Shoney's, Waffle House Best Western, Comfort Inn, EconoLodge, Palms Inn, Quality Inn, Ramada Inn, Red Roof Inn, Rice Planter's Inn fireworks, **W** Horizon/dsl Cracker Barrel Country Hearth Inn, Days Inn, Hampton Inn, Holiday Inn Express, Microtel Green Acres Camping

47mm **RS both lanes, full facilities, litter barrels, petwalk, vending**

42 US 21, to Yemassee, Beaufort

40mm Combahee River

38 SC 68, to Hampton, Yemassee, **E** Horizon/dsl/e-85 Family$, **W** BP/Subway/TCBY, Exxon/dsl, Love's/Hardee's/dsl/scales/24hr, Shell/dsl

33 US 17 N, to Beaufort, **E** BP/dsl, Exxon/McDonald's, Marathon/Subway/TCBY, Shell Denny's, Waffle House, Wendy's Best Western, Hampton Inn, Motel 6, Red Roof Inn Confederate Railroad Museum, KOA, The Oaks RV Camping

30.5mm Tullifinny River

29mm Coosawhatchie River

28 SC 462, to Coosawhatchie, Hilton Head, Bluffton, **W** El Cheapo, Tiger Express/dsl

22 US 17, Ridgeland, **W** Sunoco H

21 SC 336, to Hilton Head, Ridgeland, **E** Citgo/dsl, Marathon/dsl McDonald's, Wendy's Boat'n RV Whse, **W** BP/DQ/dsl, Exxon, Gulf/dsl, Shell BBQ Buffet, Bella Pizza, Burger King, Hong Kong Chinese, KFC, Subway, Waffle

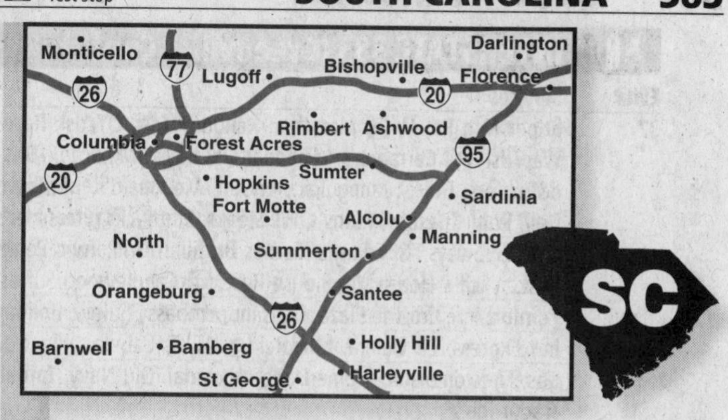

HARDEEVILLE

21 Continued
House Carolina Lodge, EconoLodge, Quality Inn, Travelodge H, $General, Harvey's Foods, Rite Aid

18 SC 13, to US 17, US 278, to Switzerland, Granville, Ridgeland

17mm **parking area both lanes (commercial vehicles only)**

8 US 278, to Bluffton, Hardeeville, **E** BP/Burrito/dsl/scales, Exxon, Kangaroo/McDonald's Waffle House H, Hilton Head info, **W** Horizon/Subway/dsl, Shell/dsl Holiday Inn Express, Motel 6

5 US 17, US 321, to Savannah, Hardeeville, **E** Citgo/dsl, Exxon/Blimpie, Pilot/Subway/dsl/scales/24hr, Shell Mi Tierrita Mexican, Waffle House Days Inn, Economy Inn, Sleep Inn fireworks, to Savannah NWR, **W** Butlers/dsl/repair, Octane/dsl, Speedway/dsl, Sunoco/dsl Burger King, Wendy's Best Western+, Deluxe Inn, Knights Inn, Magnolia Motel, Quality Suites, Red Roof Inn, Rodeway Inn, Stay Express Inn, Super 8 $General, Advance Parts, Family$, fireworks, NAPA

4.5mm **Welcome Ctr nb, full facilities, info, litter barrels, petwalk, vending, wi-fi**

4mm **weigh sta both lanes**

0mm South Carolina/Georgia state line, Savannah River

INTERSTATE 385 (Greenville)

GREENVILLE

Exit#	Services
42	US 276, Stone Ave, to Travelers Rest, **I-385 begins/ends on US 276.**, **E** CarQuest, vet, **1-2 mi W** Spinx/dsl multiple services on US 276, to Greenville Zoo
40b a	SC 291, Pleasantburg Dr, **E** Sunoco Jack-in-the-Box, Little Caesar's, Olive Tree, S&S Cafeteria, Sonic, Starbucks, Subway, Taco Casa, Wendy's $Tree, CVS Drug, Family$, Furman U, to BJU, Walgreens, **W** Citgo/dsl, QT/dsl Domino's, Krispy Kreme Phoenix Inn/Rest., Sleep Inn Cottman Transmissions, Midas
39	Haywood Rd, **E** Spinx Noodleville, Outback Steaks, Portofino's, Tony's Pizzeria Clarion, Courtyard, Hawthorn Inn, Hilton, Hyatt Place, La Quinta Firestone/auto, USPO, **W** Spinx/dsl Applebee's, Backyard Burger, Burger King, Chick-fil-A, Chili's, Chipotle, ChuckeCheese, CiCi's Pizza, CityRange Steaks, Clock Rest., Copper River Grill, Don Pablo, Firehouse Subs, Five Guys, Fried Green Tomatoes, Grille 33, Habiba Mediterranean, Halton Country Buffet, Harbor Inn Seafood, Jason's Deli, Jimmy John's, Kanpai Tokyo, McAlister's Deli, Miyabi Japanese, Moe's SW Grill, Monterrey Mexican, Panera Bread, Papa's&Beer, Rafferdi's, Saskatoon Rest, Starbucks, Stax Grill, Steak'n Shake, Waffle House Baymont Inn, Extended Stay America, Hampton Inn AT&T, Barnes&Noble, Belk, Dillard's, Discount Tire, JC Penney, Jo-Ann, Macy's, TJ Maxx, Verizon, vet

INTERSTATE 385 (Greenville) Cont'd

GREENVILLE

Exit#	Services
37	Roper Mtn Rd, W Marathon/Kangaroo/dsl, QT/dsl, RaceWay/dsl Carrabba's, Cheddar's, Chuy's Mexican, Dave&Busters, HuHot Mongolian, Krystal, McDonald's, MidTown Deli, Ruby Tuesday, Ruths Chris Steaks, Starbucks, Strossner's Cafe, Subway, TGI Friday's, Tucnos Brazilian Grill, Twin Peaks Rest., Waffle House, Yardhouse Rest. Candlewood Suites, Comfort Inn, Crowne Plaza, Days Inn, Embassy Suites, Holiday Inn Express, La Quinta, Microtel AT&T, Cabela's, Costco/gas, Firestone/auto, Home Depot, Hyundai, Old Navy, Target, Trader Joe's
36b a	I-85, N to Charlotte, S to Atlanta
35	SC 146, Woodruff Rd, **0-2 mi** E Marathon, QT/dsl, Spinx Applebee's, Bojangles, Bone Fish Grill, Boston Pizzeria, Bruster's, Chick-fil-A, Chili's, China Buffet, CookOut, Culver's, Dunkin Donuts, Epic Curean Rest., Firehouse Subs, Great Harvest Bread, Green Tomato Buffet, Hardee's, Hibachi Grill, Jersey Mike's, JP's 4 Corners SW Rest., KFC, Krispy Kreme, Little Caesar's, McAlister's Deli, McDonald's, Mimi's Japanese Steaks, Moe's SW Grill, Pizza Inn, Sonic, Starbucks, Stevi B's, Subway, Taco Bell, Topper's Rest., Travinia Italian, Waffle House, Wendy's, Your Pizza Pie, Zaxby's $Tree, AAAAZ, Ace Hardware, Aldi Foods, BigLots, Bi-Lo Foods, Discount Tire, GNC, Hobby Lobby, Kohl's, O'Reilly Parts, Publix, Rite Aid, Sam's Club/gas, Save-a-Lot Foods, Staples, Tire Kingdom, URGENT CARE, USPO, Walmart, W Red Robin Brixx Pizza, Buffalo Wild Wings, Chipotle Mexican, Coldstone, Cracker Barrel, Fuddrucker's, Genghis Grill, IHOP, La Parrilla Mexican, Lieu's Bistro, Longhorn Steaks, Monterrey Mexican, Oriental House, Panera Bread, PF Chang's, Red Robin, Salsarita's, Sticky Fingers, Which Wich? Drury Inn, Hampton Inn, Hilton Garden, Homewood Suites, Staybridge Suites Barnes&Noble, Best Buy, Dick's, Goodyear/auto, Hamrick's Outlet, Lowe's, Marshall's, Petco, Petsmart, REI, Ross, Verizon, vet, Whole Foods Mkt, World Mkt
34	Butler Rd, Mauldin, E Spinx/dsl Arby's, W Bojangles, Dino's Rest., Moretti's Pizzeria, Sub Sta. 2 $General
33	Bridges Rd, Mauldin
31	I-185 **toll**, SC 417, to Laurens Rd, E Marathon, Shell/dsl Hardee's, McDonald's, Subway BiLo, SaveALot Foods, W Spinx/dsl
30	I-185 **toll**, US 276, Standing Springs Rd
29	Georgia Rd, to Simpsonville, W Woodspring Suites
27	Fairview Rd, to Simpsonville, E Shell Carolina Rest., CoachHouse Rest., JB's BBQ, Little Caesar's, McDonald's, Milano Pizzeria, Subway Palmetto Inn H, $General, Advance Parts, AutoZone, Big Lots, CVS Drug, O'Reilly Parts, W Exxon, Murphy USA, Spinx/dsl Anthony's Pizza, Applebee's, Arby's, AZ Steaks, Baskin-Robbins, Bellacino's, Bruster's, Burger King, Chick-fil-A, Cracker Barrel, Epic Buffet, Firehouse Subs, Five Guys, Hibachi House, Hungry Howie's, IHOP, Jack-in-the-Box, Jersey Mike's, KFC, La Fogata Mexican, Mad Cuban, McDonald's, Mei Mei House, Moe's SW Grill, O'Charley's, Panera Bread, Pizza Hut, Ruby Tuesday, Sonic, Starbucks, Subway, Taco Bell, Tequila's Mexican, Waffle House, Wendy's, Zaxby's Comfort Suites, Days Inn, Hampton Inn, Holiday Inn Express, Motel 6, Quality Inn $Tree, AT&T, Belk, Bi-Lo, CVS Drug, GNC, Goodyear/auto, Home Depot, Ingles Foods, Kohl's, Lowe's, Publix, Ross, Target, Tire Kingdom, TJ Maxx, URGENT CARE, USPO, Verizon, Walgreens, Walmart
26	Harrison Bridge Rd, W 7-11/dsl, QT/dsl, same as 27
24	Fairview St, E Marathon Hardee's, Waffle House
23	SC 418, to Fountain Inn, Fork Shoals, E Exxon/pizza/subs/dsl Bojangles, Zaxby's $General, O'Reilly Parts, USPO, W Sunoco/dsl
22	SC 14 W, Old Laurens Rd, to Fountain Inn
19	SC 14 E, to Gray Court, Owings
16	SC 101, to Woodruff, Gray Court
10	rd 23, Barksdale, Ora
9	US 221, to Laurens, Enoree, E S&H Trkstp/dsl Waffle House Budget Lodge, W Walmart Dist Ctr
6mm	**both lanes (both lanes exit left), full facilities, litter barrels, petwalk, , vending**
5	SC 49, to Laurens, Union
2	SC 308, to Clinton, Ora, W H, to Presbyterian Coll in Clinton
0mm	I-26 S to Columbia, **I-385 begins/ends on I-26 at 52mm.**

SIMPSONVILLE

INTERSTATE 526 (Charleston)

CHARLESTON

Exit#	Services
33mm	**I-526 begins/ends.**
32	US 17, **0-1 mi** N Shell, Speedway/dsl Atl Bread, Bojangles, Burger King, Burton's Grill, Cane's, Five Guys, Grimaldi's Brick Oven, IHOP, PF Chang's, Qdoba, Sonic, Taco Bell, TGIFriday, Zoe's Kitchen Courtyard, Hampton Inn Advance Parts, AT&T, Barnes&Noble, Belk, BiLo, Chevrolet, CVS Drug, GNC, Lowes Whse, Midas, Old Navy, Rite Aid, Tire Kingdom, TrueValue, Verizon, Walgreens, **0-1 mi** S Shell/Circle K, Sunoco/dsl Applebees, Arby's, Chick-fil-A, Cici's, Firehouse Subs, Hardee's, Huddle House, Jimmy John's, La Hacienda Mexicana, Liberty Rest., McDonald's, Melvin's Ribs& Cue, Moe's SW Grill, Momma Goldberg's Deli, Outback Steaks, Sticky Fingers, Subway, Wendy's, Zeus Grill Best Western, Clarion, Day' Inn, Extended Stay America, Hampton Inn, Hilton Garden, Holiday Inn, Holiday Inn Express, Mainstay Suites, Quality Inn, Red Roof Inn, Sleep Inn $Tree, Bi-Lo, CVS Drug, Firestone/auto, Harris Teeter, Jiffy Lube, Marshall's, Michaels, NAPA, Office Depot, O'Reilly Parts, Petco, Publix, Staples, TJ Maxx, Trader Joe's, USPO, Verizon, vet, VW, Walmart, Whole Foods Mkt
28	Long Point Rd, N BP, Exxon Bamboo Garden, Beef' Brady's, McAlister's, Moe's SW Grill, Sonic, Starbucks, Subway, Waffle House, Wendy's Charles Pinckney NHS, CVS Drug, Food Lion, Harris Teeter Foods, PetsMart, Ross, Steinmart
26mm	Wando River
24	Daniel Island, S Texaco Dragon Palace, Lana's Mexican, Queen Anne's Steaks/seafood, Subway Hampton Inn Publix
23b a	Clements Ferry Rd
21mm	Cooper River
20	Virginia Ave (from eb), S Speedway Depot
19	N Rhett Ave, N Kangaroo/Subway/dsl, Speedway Hardee's Family$, Food Lion, Rite Aid, S BP
18b a	US 52, US 78, Rivers Ave, N BP/dsl, Kangaroo/dsl, Speedway KFC, Peking Gourmet, Pizza Hut/Taco Bell auto repair, AutoZone, Dodge, Family$, Ford, H&L Foods, S Exxon
17b a	I-26, E to Charleston, W to Columbia
16	Montague Ave, Airport Rd, S Bonefish Grill, Chili's, Denny's, Jersey Mike's, La Hacienda, Panera Bread, Starbucks, Wendy's Embassy Suites, Hilton Garden, Holiday Inn, Homewood Suites, Residence Inn Sam's Club/gas, Staples, Tanger Outlet/famous brands, Walmart/Subway
15	SC 642, Dorchester Rd, Paramount Dr, N Shell/Circle K auto service, Family$, S Citgo/dsl, Sunoco Burger King, Checker's, Domino's, East Bay Deli, Huddle House, Little Caesar's, Pizza Hut, Subway Airport Inn Advance Parts

SD

INTERSTATE 526 (Charleston) Cont'd

15	Continued Bi-Lo Foods, CVS Drug, Family$, Food Lion, Harley-Davidson, U-Haul
14	Leeds Ave, **S** Woodspring Suites boat marina
13mm	Ashley River
11b a	SC 61, Ashley River Rd, **N** Baron's Pizza, Chick-fil-A, McDonald's, O'Charley's H, Food Lion, Home Depot, Jo-Ann, Kohl's, Lowes Whse, Marshall's
10	US 17, SC 7 **E services from US 17** Bessinger's BBQ, Capt D's, Chick-fil-A, CookOut, Dunkin Donuts, Five Guys, Hopsing's Asian, IHOP, King St Grille, Krispy Kreme, La Fontana Italian, McDonald's, Panera Bread, Red Lobster, Ruby Tuesday,
10	Continued Taco Bell Best Western, Evergreen Motel, Holiday Inn Express, Motel 6, Sleep Inn, Town & Country Suites AutoZone, Belk, BiLo, BMW/Mini, Buick/GMC/Cadillac, Chevrolet, Chrysler/Dodge/Jeep, Dick's, Dillard's, Ford/Lincoln, Honda, Hyundai, Hyundai, Infiniti, Jaguar/Range Rover/Porsche, JC Penney, Maserati, Mercedes, Nissan, Pepboys, Petsmart, Ross, Smart, Target, Tire Kingdom, vet, Volvo, **W services from US 17** AMFlag, Shell/Circle K, Speedway/dsl China Fun, Hardees, Inyabi Japanese, Subway, Waffle House Comfort Suites, Econolodge, Hampton Inn, Hawthorn Suites, InTown Suites Acura, Advance Parts, Audi, Carmax, Costco/gas, CVS Drug, DriveTime, Family$, Food Lion, Kia, Lexus, Toyota
9	**I-526 begins/ends on US 17.**

SOUTH DAKOTA

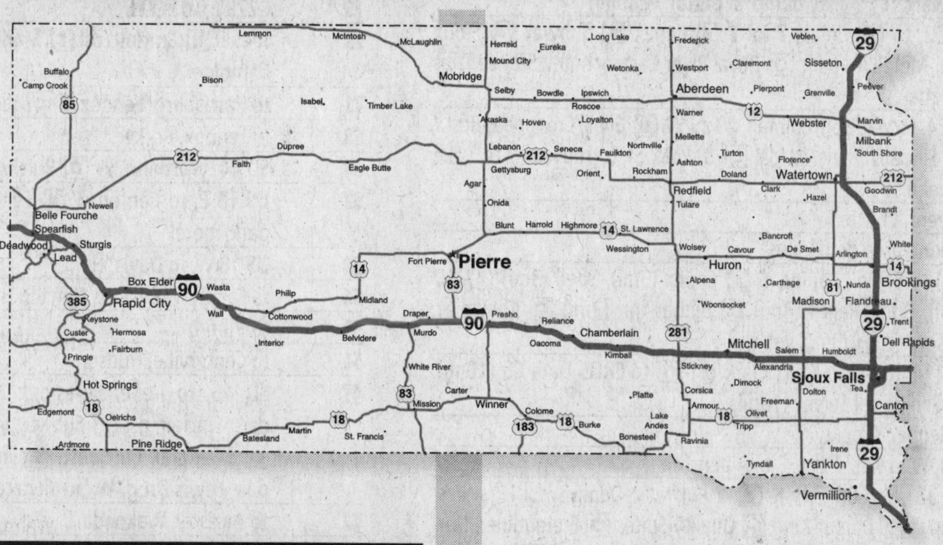

INTERSTATE 29

SISSETON

Exit#	Services
253mm	South Dakota/North Dakota state line
251mm	**Welcome Ctr sb, full facilities, info, litter barrels, petwalk, picnic table, RV dump s**
246	SD 127, to Rosholt, New Effington, **3 mi W** gas food RV camping, Sica Hollow SP (24mi)
242	110th St
235mm	**weigh sta sb**
232	SD 10, Sisseton, **E** Dakota Connection/dsl/casino/24hr Crossroads Cafe, **1-3 mi W** Amstar/dsl, FuelMax/dsl, Sinclair/dsl/e85, Tesoro Cottage Rest, DQ, Pizza Hut, Subway, Taco John's Holiday Motel, I-29 Motel, Super 8 H, Camp Dakotah, Family$, Ft Sisseton SP (35mi), NAPA, ShopKO, Teals Mkt, to Roy Lake SP (25mi)
224	Peever, Sioux Tribal Hqtrs, **E** I-29 Food'n Fill/dsl, **W** Pickerel Lake (16mi)
213	SD 15, to Wilmot, **E both lanes, full facilities, litter barrels, petwalk, , , RV dump, st patrol** to Hartford Beach SP (17mi)
207	US 12, Summit, **E** Cenex/Pizza Hut/Subway/dsl/24hr County Line Camping (1mi), **W** Blue Dog Fish Hatchery (15mi), Waubay NWR (19mi)
201	to Twin Brooks
193	SD 20, to South Shore, Stockholm

WATERTOWN

185	to Waverly, **W** Dakota Sioux Casino/Cenex/rest. (4mi)
180	US 81 S, to Watertown, **5 mi W** Sinclair , Bramble Park Zoo
177	US 212, Watertown, **E** Tesoro/Grainery Cafe/dsl/24hr Holiday Inn Express fireworks, truck repair, truck wash, WW Tires, **0-2 mi W** Cenex/Subway/dsl, Cenex/Subway/dsl (2), Freedom/dsl, Sinclair/dsl, Tesoro/dsl Applebee's, Arby's, Buffalo Wild Wings, Burger King, China Buffet, Culver's, Domino's, DQ, Firehouse Subs, Four Seasons Buffet, Godfather's, Guadalajara Mexican, Hardee's, IHOP, Jimmy John's, KFC, Little Caesar's, Marco's Pizza, McDonald's, Papa Murphy's, Perkins, Pizza Hut, Qdoba, Senor Max's Mexican, Starbucks, Subway, Taco Bell, Taco John's Country Inn Suites, Days Inn, Econolodge, Hampton Inn, Quality Inn $Tree, Advance Parts, AT&T, Chrysler/Dodge/Jeep, Ford/Lincoln, Goodyear/auto, Harley-Davidson, Herberger's, Hobby Lobby, H, Hy-Vee Foods, Menards, NAPA, O'Reilly Parts, ShopKO, Target, Tires+, to Sandy Shore RA (10mi), Verizon, Walgreens, Walmart/Subway
164	SD 22, to Castlewood, Clear Lake, **9 mi E** Cenex/dsl H
161mm	**both lanes, full facilities, litter barrels, petwalk, , , vending**
157	to Brandt
150	SD 28, SD 15 N, to Toronto, **7 mi W** gas food lodging Lake Poinsett RA (24 mi), SD Amateur Baseball Hall of Fame (24 mi)
140	SD 30, to White, Bruce, **W** Oakwood Lakes SP (12mi)

SC

SD

INTERSTATE 29 Cont'd

BROOKINGS

Exit#	Services
133	US 14 byp, Brookings, E WW Tires, W Laura Ingalls Wilder Home (43 mi), museums, to SD St U
132	US 14, Lp 29, Brookings, E Cenex/dsl Applebee's, Whiskey Creek Grill Fairfield Inn, Hampton Inn, Holiday Inn Express, My Place Hotel, Super 8, W Arby's, Backyard BBQ, Buffalo Wild Wings, Burger King, Culver's, DQ, Ground Round, Guadalajara Mexican, Hardee's, Jimmy John's, KFC, King's Wok, McDonald's, Papa John's, Papa Murphy's, Perkins, Pizza Ranch, Qdoba Mexican, Subway, Taco Bell Comfort Suites, Days Inn, Econolodge, Quality Inn H, Advance Parts, AT&T, Buick/Chevrolet/GMC, CarQuest, city park, Lowe's, Verizon, Walmart/Subway
127	SD 324, to Elkton, Sinai
124mm	Big Sioux River
121	to Nunda, Ward, E **both lanes, full facilities, litter barrels, petwalk, , , RV dump, st patrol, vending**
114	SD 32, to Flandreau, **7 mi** E Cenex Subway Sioux River Motel/RV park Royal River Casino/hotel, Santee Tribal Hqtrs
109	SD 34, to Madison, Colman, **20 mi** W Shell/Crossroads Rest./dsl, Sinclair/Prairie Jct/dsl Dakota St U, museum, to Lake Herman SP
104	to Trent, Chester
103mm	**parking area both lanes**
98	SD 115 S, Dell Rapids, E Cenex (3mi), Shell (3mi) DQ (3mi), Pizza Ranch (3mi) Bilmar Inn (3mi) Chevrolet, dsl service, H (3mi), vet
94	SD 114, to Baltic, E Clark/dsl to EROS Data Ctr (10mi), US Geological Survey (10mi)
86	to Renner, Crooks
84b a	I-90, W to Rapid City, E to Albert Lea
83	SD 38 W, 60th St, E FLYING J/Denny's/dsl/LP/scales/24hr/@ Burger King Quality Suites Freightliner, Harley-Davidson, Indian Motorcycles, Truckwash, W fireworks, hwy patrol, Walmart/Subway
82	Benson Rd, E BeefOBrady's Fairfield Inn
81	SD 38 E, Russell St, Sioux Falls, E BP, Food'n Fuel/Quiznos Roll'n Pin Rest. Arena Motel, Best Western+, Dakotah Lodge, Guesthouse Inn, Motel 6, Ramada Inn, Sheraton, Sioux Falls Inn, Sleep Inn, Super 8 golf, Schaap's RV Ctr, W Subway
80	Madison St, E Sinclair/dsl to fairgrounds
79	SD 42, 12th St, E BP, Freedom Burger King, Burger Time, Fry'n Pan, Golden Harvest Chinese, KFC, McDonald's, Pizza Hut, Sneaky's Chicken, Subway, Taco Bell, Taco John's, Tomacelli's Pizza, Wendy's Ramada, Woodspring Suites H, $General, Ace Hardware, BMW/Cadillac/Mercedes, Chevrolet, city park, Lewis Drug, NAPA, Nissan, to Great Plains Zoo/museum, Toyota, USPO, Walgreens, W BP/dsl, Cenex/Chester's/dsl, Food'n Fuel Hardee's Meineke, Tower RV Park
78	26th St, Empire St, E BP/dsl/e85 Buffalo Wild Wings, Carino's Italian, Carnaval Brazillian Grill, Chevy's Mexican, ChuckeCheese, Coldstone, Cracker Barrel, Culver's, Domino's, Granite City Rest, Outback Steaks, Puerto Vallarta, Ruby Tuesday, Sonic ClubHouse Suites, Hampton Inn, Holiday Inn Express, StayBridge Suites BigLots, Home Depot, Michael's, Petsmart, Sam's Club/gas, USPO, World Mkt, W DQ, Papa John's, Starbucks TownePlace Suites Hy-Vee Foods/gas, Lowe's, Tuffy Auto, Verizon

SIOUX FALLS

Exit#	Services
77	41st St, Sioux Falls, E BP, SA/dsl, Shell, Sinclair/dsl Applebee's, Arby's, Burger King, Chili's, Firehouse Subs, Fry'n Pa Rest., Fuddrucker's, HuHot Mongolian, KFC, Lonestar Steaks McDonald's, Old Chicago Pizza, Olive Garden, Pancake House Panda Express, Papa Murphy's, Perkins, Pizza Hut, Pizza Ranch Qdoba Mexican, Red Lobster, Starbucks, Subway, Szechwa Chinese, Taco Bell, Taco John's, TX Roadhouse, Valentino's Wendy's Best Western, Comfort Suites, Courtyard, Fairfield Inn, Microtel, MyPlace Hotel, Red Rock Inn, Residence Inn SpringHill Suites, Super 8 Advance Parts, Barnes&Noble Best Buy, Dick's, Ford/Lincoln, Goodyear/auto, Gordman's Hyundai, Hy-Vee Foods/dsl, JC Penney, Kohl's, Macy's, Mazda Menards, Old Navy, PetCo, ShopKO, Target, Tires+, TJ Max Verizon, Walgreens, Walmart/Subway, Younkers, W Holiday/dsl Burger King, Godfather's, IHOP, Little Caesar's, Perkins, Subway AmericInn, Baymont Inn, Days Inn, La Quinta Red Roof Inn Lewis Drug, USPO
75	I-229 E, to I-90 E
73	Tea, E Sinclair/dsl Marlin's Rest, **1.5mi** W Red Bar Camping
71	to Harrisburg, Lennox, E repair, W RV camping
68	to Lennox, Parker
64	SD 44, Worthing, W Buick/Chevrolet, New Prairie RV Ctr
62	US 18 E, to Canton, E Cenex/pizza/dsl Countryside R park/motel
59	US 18 W, to Davis, Hurley
56	to Fairview, E to Newton Hills SP (12mi)
53	to Viborg
50	to Centerville, Hudson
47	SD 46, to Irene, Beresford, E BP/Burger King, Casey's dsl, Sinclair/dsl Subway Crossroads Motel, Super $General, CarQuest, Chevrolet, Fiesta Foods, Jet Auto Repair, Lewis Drug, W Conoco/Dutch Rest./dsl/scales/24hr
42	to Alcester, Wakonda
41mm	truck check (from sb)
38	to Volin, E to Union Co SP (3mi)
31	SD 48, to Akron, Spink
26	SD 50, to Vermillion, E **Welcome Ctr/ both lanes, full facilities, info, litter barrels, petwalk, , ,** W BP/Subway Pizza Hut/dsl Burger King (6mi), Godfather's Pizza (6mi Jimmy John's (6mi), Red Steakhouse (6mi), Subway (6mi), Tac John's (6mi) Best Western (6mi), Comfort Inn (6mi), Holiday Inn Express (6mi), Prairie Inn (6mi), Super 8 (6mi) (6mi), Hy-Vee Foods (6mi), to Lewis & Clark RA (6mi), to U of S (6mi), Walmart (6mi)
18	Lp 29, to Burbank, Elk Point, E A-1/dsl, Casey's Home Towne Inn
15	to Elk Point, E Kum&Go/Subway/dsl, W fireworks
13mm	**weigh sta nb, parking area sb**
9	SD 105, Jefferson, E Conoco/Choice Cut Rest.
4	North Shore Dr, McCook, **1 mi** W Adams Homestead/nature preserve, KOA (seasonal)
2	SD 105, N Sioux City, E Goode/casino/dsl/E10/20/30 McDonald's, Subway, Taco John's fireworks, USPO, W Casey's, Clark Days Inn, Hampton Inn, Red Carpet Inn, Super 8 KOA
1	Dakota Dunes Blvd, W Cenex/dsl Graham's Grill Country Inn&Suites Dakota Dunes Golf Resort
0mm	South Dakota/Iowa state line, Big Sioux River

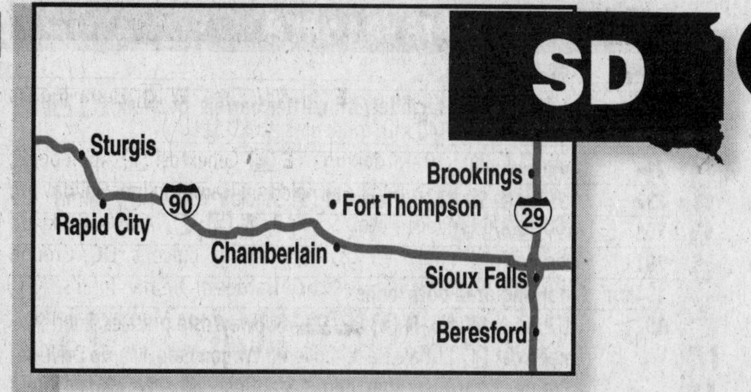

SD

INTERSTATE 90

SIOUX FALLS

Exit#	Services
412.5mm	South Dakota/Minnesota state line
412mm	**Welcome Ctr wb/ [RS] eb, full [handicapped] facilities, info, litter barrels, petwalk, [phone], [picnic], RV dump (wb), weigh sta (wb)**
410	Valley Springs, N [other] Palisades SP (7mi), S [gas] gas [food] food [other] Beaver Creek Nature Area
406	SD 11, Brandon, Corson, N [other] Palisades SP (10mi), S [gas] BP/dsl, Holiday/McDonald's/dsl, Local [food] Brandon Steaks, DQ, Great Wall, Papa Murphy's, Pizza Hut, Pizza Ranch, Subway, Taco John's, Tailgator's Grill [lodging] Holiday Inn Express, Quality Inn [other] Ace Hardware, Lewis Drug, Sturdevant's Parts, Sunshine Foods, to Big Sioux RA (4mi), Verizon
402	EROS Data Ctr, N [other] Jellystone RV Park, tires
400	I-229 S
399	SD 115, Cliff Ave, Sioux Falls, N [other] KOA, Spader RV Ctr, S [gas] BP/Get'n Go/dsl, Conoco, Holiday/dsl/e85, Loves/Grandma Max's/Subway/dsl/scales/24hr/@, Sinclair/dsl [food] Arby's, Burger King, McDonald's/truck parking, Perkins, Taco Bell, Taco John's [lodging] Cloud Nine Motel, Days Inn, EconoLodge, Super 8 [other] [H], Graham Tire, Kenworth, Peterbilt, Volvo
398mm	Big Sioux River
396b a	I-29, N to Brookings, S to Sioux City
395	Marion Rd, Marion, S [other] Walmart/Subway
390	SD 38, Hartford, N [food] Pizza Ranch (3mi) [other] Goos RV Ctr, S [gas] Cowboy Town/dsl
387	rd 17, Hartford, N [gas] BP/dsl [food] Midway Grill, Pizza Ranch (1.6mi) [lodging] AmericInn
379	SD 19, Humboldt, N [gas] Clark/dsl [other] USPO
375mm	E Vermillion River
374	to SD 38, Montrose, **5 mi** S [other] Battle Creek Res., Lake Vermillion RA, RV camping
368	Canistota, **5 mi** S [lodging] Best Western, Canistota Depot Inn, Ortman Hotel
364	US 81, to Yankton, Salem, **1 mi** N [gas] Cenex [lodging] Home Motel [other] Camp America
363.5mm	W Vermillion River
363mm	**[RS] both lanes, full [handicapped] facilities, litter barrels, petwalk, [phone], [picnic], RV dump, st patrol, vending**
357	to Bridgewater, Canova
353	Spencer, Emery, S [gas] FuelMart/Subway/dsl/casino/24hr
352mm	Wolf Creek
350	SD 25, Emery, Farmer, N [other] to DeSmet, Home of Laura Ingalls Wilder
344	SD 262, to Fulton, Alexandria, S [gas] Sinclair/dsl
337mm	**parking area both lanes**
335	Riverside Rd, N [other] KOA (1mi)
334.5mm	[other] James River
332	SD 37 S, to Parkston, Mitchell, N [gas] Cenex/Chester's/dsl, Clark, I-90/Holiday/Marlin's Rest./Subway/dsl/scales/24hr, Mobil/Jimmy John's, Sinclair [food] Arby's, Cattleman's Club Steaks, Chef Louie Steaks, Corona Village Mexican, McDonald's, Perkins, Pizza Hut, Pizza Ranch, Twin Dragon Chinese [lodging] AmericInn, Corn Palace Inn, Days Inn, Quality Inn, Super 8/truck parking, Thunderbird Motel [other] [H], Advance Parts, AutoZone, Chrysler/Dodge/Jeep, Museum of Pioneer Life, O'Reilly Parts, Rondee's Campground, to Corn Palace, transmissions, URGENT CARE, Verizon, Walgreens, S [gas] Shell/Godfather's/Taco Bell/dsl/24hr [food] Culver's, Hardee's, Quiznos, Ruby Tuesday, Whiskey Creek Grill [lodging] Comfort Inn, Hampton Inn, Holiday Inn Express, Kelly Inn [other] $Tree, AT&T, Cabela's, Menards, Verizon, Walmart/Subway

MITCHELL

Exit#	Services
330	SD 37 N, Mitchell, N [gas] Cenex/Chester's/dsl, Shell/dsl, Sinclair/dsl [food] DQ [lodging] Budget Inn, Motel 6, Ramada Inn, Siesta Motel, Travelodge [other] [H], County Fair Foods, Jack's Campers/RV Ctr, Lewis Drug, Mr. Tire, museum, to Corn Palace, weigh sta, S [other] Dakota RV Park
325	Betts Rd, S [other] Famil-e-Fun Camping
319	Mt Vernon, **1 mi** N [gas] Sinclair/dsl, Westey's One Stop/dsl
310	US 281, to Stickney, S [gas] Sinclair/Deli Depot/dsl/24hr [other] to Ft Randall Dam
308	Lp 90, to Plankinton, N [gas] Sinclair/Al's Cafe/dsl [lodging] Cabin Fever Motel/RV Park, Smart Choice Inn [other] Gordy's Camping, Hills RV Park, repair, USPO
301.5mm	**[RS] both lanes, full [handicapped] facilities, litter barrels, [phone], [picnic], RV dump**
296	White Lake, **1 mi** N [gas] Hillman's/dsl [lodging] A-Z Motel [other] USPO, S [other] Siding 36 Motel/RV Park
294mm	Platte Creek
289	SD 45 S, to Platte, S [other] to Snake Cr/Platte Cr RA (25mi)
284	SD 45 N, Kimball, N [gas] Clark, Conoco/Ditty's/Diner/dsl [food] Frosty King [lodging] Dakota Winds Motel, Westwood Inn [other] Parkway Campground, repair/tires, S [other] tractor museum
272	SD 50, Pukwana, 2 mi N [gas] gas [food] food [lodging] lodging, S [other] Snake/Platte Creek Rec Areas (25mi)
265	SD 50, Chamberlain, N [gas] Cenex/DQ/dsl [lodging] AmericInn [other] [H], ShopKO, St Joseph Akta Lakota Museum (4mi), vet, S [gas] SA/dsl [other] Happy Camper Campground
264mm	**[RS] both lanes, full [handicapped] facilities, info, litter barrels, [phone], [picnic], scenic view**
263	Chamberlain, N [gas] Sinclair/dsl [food] McDonald's, Pizza Hut, Subway (1mi), Taco John's [lodging] Bel Aire Motel (1mi), Best Western (1mi), Super 8 [other] Crow Creek Sioux Tribal Hqtrs, SD Hall of Fame
262mm	Missouri River
260	SD 50, Oacoma, N [gas] Clark/dsl, Phillips 66/Arby's/dsl, Shell/dsl [lodging] Al's Oasis/Motel/Camping/cafe/mkt, Baymont Inn, Cedar Shore Motel/Camping (3mi), Econolodge, Howard Johnson, Quality Inn [other] antiques, Buick/Chevrolet, Dakota Camping, Oasis Camping, Old West Trading Post
251	SD 47, to Winner, Gregory
248	SD 47, Reliance, N [gas] Cenex (1mi), Farmer's Union/dsl (1mi) [other] Sioux Tribal Hqtrs, to Big Bend RA
241	to Lyman
235	SD 273, Kennebec, N [gas] Clark/dsl [food] Hot Rods Steaks [lodging] Budget Host, Kings Inn [other] auto repair, KOA, USPO
226	US 183 S, Presho, N [gas] Cenex/dsl, Sinclair/dsl [lodging] Hutch's Motel/café [other] New Frontier RV Park, pioneer museum, repair, vet
225	lp 90, Presho, same as 226
221mm	**[RS] wb, full [handicapped] facilities, info, litter barrels, petwalk, [phone], [picnic], RV dump**
220	no service

CHAMBERLAIN

INTERSTATE 90 Cont'd

Exit#	Services
218mm	eb, full facilities, info, litter barrels, petwalk, , , RV dump
214	Vivian
212	US 83 N, SD 53, to Pierre, N Sinclair/dsl (34mi)
208	no service
201	Draper
194mm	parking area both lanes
192	US 83 S, Murdo, N Pilot/Subway/dsl/Lp/scales/24hr, Pioneer/dsl Buffalo Rest., Covered Wagon Cafe, Murdo Drive-In, Prairie Pizza, Rusty Spur Steaks, Star Rest. American Inn, Best Western, Iversen Inn, Range Country Lodge, Sioux Motel, Super 8 American RV Park/camping, auto museum, city park, Ford, Murdo Foods, USPO, S Country Inn to Rosebud
191	Murdo, N same as 192
188mm	parking area both lanes
183	Okaton, S Ghost Town
177	no service
175mm	central/mountain timezone
172	to Cedar Butte
170	SD 63 N, to Midland, N Conoco/dsl 1880's Town, KOA
167mm	wb, full facilities, litter barrels, petwalk, , , RV dump
165mm	eb, full facilities, litter barrels, petwalk, , , RV dump
163	SD 63, Belvidere, S Belvidere Store/dsl JR's Grill
152	Lp 90, Kadoka, N Conoco/rest./dsl/24hr, S Badlands Petrified Gardens
150	SD 73 S, Kadoka, N Dakota Inn/rest., S Conoco/dsl, Sinclair/pizza/dsl Subway, Sunset Grill Best Value Inn, Budget Host, El Centro Motel/rest., Ponderosa Motel/RV Park, Wagon Wheel Motel, West Motel Kadoka Kampground, repair, to Buffalo Nat Grasslands
143	SD 73 N, to Philip, 15 mi N
138mm	scenic overlook wb
131	SD 240, N Minuteman Missle NHS, S Conoco Badlands Inn (9mi), Cedar Pass Lodge/rest. (9mi) Circle 10 Camping, KOA (11mi), Prairie Home NHS, to Badlands NP
129.5mm	scenic overlook eb
127	no service
121	Bigfoot Rd
116	239th St
112	US 14 E, to Philip
110	SD 240, Wall, N Conoco/dsl, Exxon, Phillips 66/Subway Cactus Cafe, DQ, Red Rock Rest., Roadtrip Cafe, Wall Drug Rest. Ann's Motel, Best Value Inn, Best Western, Days Inn, EconoLodge, Fountain Hotel, Sunshine Inn, Super 8, The Wall Motel, Travelodge, Welsh Motel Ace Hardware, Arrow Campground, Harley Davidson, National Grasslands Visitor Ctr, Pronto Parts, Sleepy Hollow RV Park/Camping, Wall Drug, Wall Foods, Wounded Knee Museum, S Frontier Cabins Motel RV camping, to Badlands NP
109	W 4th Ave, Wall, 1-2 mi N access to same as 110
107	Cedar Butte Rd
101	Jensen Rd, to Schell Ranch
100mm	both lanes, full facilities, info, litter barrels, petwalk, , , RV dump, vending
99.5mm	Cheyenne River
98	Wasta, N Mobil/dsl 24 Express RV Camping, USPO
90	173rd Ave, to Owanka
88	171st Ave (from eb, no re-entry)
84	167th Ave, N Olde Glory Fireworks
78	161st Ave, New Underwood, S Sinclair/dsl, Steve's General Store/dsl/motel/rest. Harry's Hideaway Rest, BJ's Motel Boondocks Camping
69mm	parking area both lanes
67	to Box Elder, N Love's/Hardee'sdsl/scales/24hr Air&Space Museum, Ellsworth AFB
63	(eb only) to Box Elder, S Phillips 66/dsl, Ellsworth AFB
61	Elk Vale Rd, N FLYING J/Conoco/CountryMkt/dsl/e-85/LP/RV dump/scales/24hr/@ Quaker Steak Cambrian Suites, MainStay Suites, My Place Black Hills Visitor Ctr, Cabela's, Dakota RV Ctr, S Conoco/dsl, Sinclair/dsl/e85 Arby's, Dakotah Steakhouse, Marco's Pizza, McDonald's, Perkins, Taco Bell Baymont Inn, Comfort Suites, Fairfield Inn, Home 2 Suites, La Quinta, Residence Inn, Sleep Inn KOA (2mi seasonal)
60	Lp 90, to Mt Rushmore, Rapid City, N Buick/GMC, Chevrolet, Ford/Lincoln, Great Western Tire, Kenworth/Volvo, Nissan, Toyota, S Holiday/dsl Blaze Pizza, Culver's, Famous Dave's, Five Guys, Fuji Japanese Steaks, HuHot Mongolian, Longhorn Steaks, MacKenzie River, Native Grill, Noodles&-Co, On the Border, Panera Bread, Pizza Ranch, Popeyes, Qdoba Mexican, Smiling Moose Deli, Starbucks Staybridge Suites , $Tree, Aamco, AT&T, Gordman's, Menards, Michael's, Nat Coll of Mines/Geology, PetCo, Ross, Sam's Club/dsl, Scheel's Sports, Target, TJ Maxx, Verizon
59	La Crosse St, Rapid City, N Mobil/dsl, Phillips 66 Boston's Rest., Burger King, Denny's, Fuddrucker's, Minerva's Rest., Outback Steaks, Starbucks, TGIFriday's, TX Roadhouse Best Western, Country Inn&Suites, EconoLodge, Hilton Garden, Holiday Inn Express, Super 8 Herberger's, Hobby Lobby, st patrol, S Exxon/24hr, Sinclair Arnold's Diner, China Wok, Golden Corral, Little Caesar's, MillStone Rest., Mongolian Grill, Pacific Rim Cafe, Perkins, Philly Ted's, Subway AmericInn, Days Inn, Fair Value Inn, Foothills Inn, Grand Gateway Hotel, Hampton Inn, Microtel, Motel 6, Quality Inn, Ramada, Rodeway Inn AT&T, URGENT CARE, Walgreens, Walmart/McDonald's
58	Haines Ave, Rapid City, N Fresh Start/dsl Applebee's, Chili's, Hardee's, IHOP, Olive Garden, Red Lobster Best Value Inn, Grand Stay Motel BAM!, Best Buy, Herbergers, JC Penney, Jo-Ann, Kohl's, Lowe's, Petsmart, Tires+, to Rushmore Mall, S Loaf'n Jug, Maverik/dsl ChuckECheese, Dickey's BBQ, Jimmy John's, Papa John's, Pizza Hut, Taco John's, Wendy's , Family$, ShopKO, URGENT CARE
57	I-190, US 16, to Rapid City, Mt Rushmore, 1 mi S on North St Exxon Panchero's Mexican Holiday Inn, Howard Johnson, The Rushmore Hotel Family Thrift Foods, Knecht Home Ctr, Office Depot
55	Deadwood Ave, N Dakota RV Ctr, Harley-Davidson/cafe, S Pilot/Subway/dsl/scales/24hr/@ Marlin's Rest dsl repair
52	Peaceful Pines Rd, Black Hawk, N Lazy JD RV Park (4mi), Three Flags Camping (1mi), S BJ's/dsl, Godfather's Pizza, Longhorn Rest. Family$, USPO
48	Stagebarn Canyon Rd, S Conoco/Haggar's Mkt/food, PitStop/dsl Pizza Hut Ramada $General, Camping World RV Ctr
46	Piedmont Rd, Elk Creek Rd, N Elk Creek Steakhouse Elk Creek RV Park, to Petrified Forest, S Mobil/Country Corner Cafe/Papa John's/dsl Sacora Sta Rest. Sacora Sta Camping
44	Bethlehem Rd, S Jack's RV Ctr (2mi)
42mm	parking area both lanes

MURDO

KADOKA

WALL

RAPID CITY

INTERSTATE 90 Cont'd

Exit#	Services
40	Tilford, S RV Park
39mm	**weigh sta eb**
37	Pleasant Valley Rd, N Kickstands Camp, S Bulldog Camping, Rush-No-More Camping
34	S Black Hills Nat Cemetary, No Name City RV Park
32	SD 79, Jct Ave, Sturgis, N Conoco/dsl, Exxon/dsl Sturgis Grill, Taco John's Best Western H, Ford, Grocery Mart, NAPA, to Bear Butte SP, vet, S Mobil/Arby's/Papa John's/dsl Ford
30	US 14A W, SD 34E, to Deadwood, Sturgis, N Cenex/dsl, Phillips 66/dsl McDonald's, Pizza Hut, Shanghai Chinese, Sturgis Coffee Co $General, CarQuest, Day's End Camping, Family$, Indian Motorcycles, Mr Tire, O'Reilly Parts, ShopKO, USPO, S Conoco/dsl, RanchMart Burger King, DQ, Kang San Asian, Pizza Ranch, Subway Days Inn, Holiday Inn Express, Super 8 BMW Motorcycles, Chevrolet, Verizon
23	SD 34 W, to Belle Fourche, Whitewood, N Northern Hills RV Ctr, S Howdy's/dsl, Mobil/Sonset Sta/dsl Hideaway Diner Tony's Motel USPO
17	US 85 S, to Deadwood, S Cenex/Dickey's BBQ/dsl Deadwood NLH (17mi), Elkhorn Ridge RV Resort, KOA (9mi)
14	US 14A, Spearfish Canyon, N FreshStart/dsl Applebee's, Culver's, Subway Fairfield Inn, Hampton Inn, Holiday Inn/rest., Quality Inn $Tree, AutoZone, Verizon, Walmart, S Phillips 66/dsl KFC/LJ Silver, Perkins, Pizza Ranch, Roma's Rest. Baymont Inn, Super 8, Travelodge Ace Hardware, Bomgaars, Ford/Lincoln, transmissions
12	Jackson Blvd, Spearfish, S Conoco/dsl, Exxon, Loaf'n Jug, Phillips 66/dsl Arby's, Barbacoa's, Domino's, Jade Palace Chinese, McDonald's, Millstone Rest., Papa Murphy's, Pizza Hut, Taco John's Best Western H, Black Hills St U, CarQuest, Chrysler/Dodge/Jeep, historic fish hatchery, same as 10
10	US 85 N, to Belle Fourche, S Burger King, Cedar House Rest., City Brew, Golden Dragon Chinese, Little Caesar's, McDonald's, Philly Ted's, Qdoba, Subway, Taco Bell Days Inn H, Buick/Chevrolet, Cadillac/GMC, KOA, Safeway/dsl, same as 12, USPO, Walgreens
8	McGuigan Rd, W Spearfish, S Phillips 66/dsl KOA (1mi)
2	**1 mi N** McNenny St Fish Hatchery
1mm	**Welcome Ctr eb, full facilities, info, litter barrels, petwalk,** RV dump
0mm	South Dakota/Wyoming state line

STURGIS · SPEARFISH · SIOUX FALLS

INTERSTATE 229 (Sioux Falls)

Exit#	Services
10b a	I-90 E and W. **I-229 begins/ends on I-90, exit 400.**
9	Benson Rd, W Sinclair/pizza/dsl DQ, Jimmy John's, Marlin's Rest. Ford Trucks, Western Star
7.5mm	Big Sioux River
7	Rice St, E winter sports, W to stockyards
6	SD 38, 10th St, E Sinclair A&W, Applebee's, Arby's, Denny's, Domino's, DQ, Fryn' Pan Rest., Jimmy John's, KFC, Pizza Hut, Pizza Ranch, Taco Bell, Tokyo Hibachi, Tomacelli's Italian Super 8 AT&T, AutoZone, Family$, Hy-Vee Foods, O'Reilly Parts, ShopKO, Sturdevant's Parts, USPO, Valvoline, vet, W BP/dsl, Casey's/dsl, Shell Burger King, BurgerTime, Hardee's, Little Caesar's, McDonald's, Pita Pit, Pizza Inn, Pizza Man, Puerto Vallarta, Qdoba Mexican, Subway, Taco John's Rushmore Motel Lewis Drug, vet

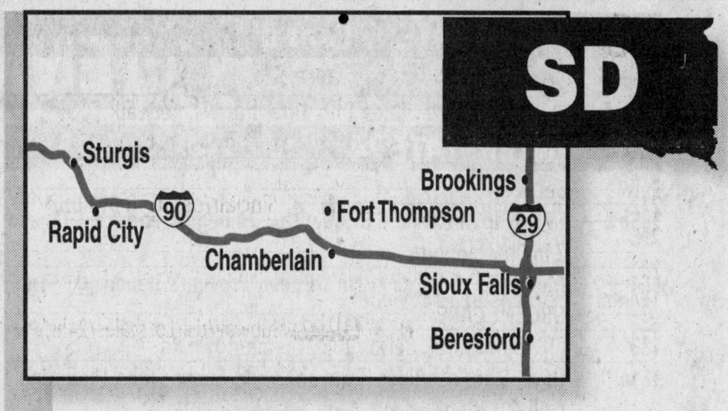

SIOUX FALLS

Exit#	Services
5.5mm	Big Sioux River
5	26th St, E Holiday/dsl Burger King, Cherry Creek Grill, Dario's Pizza, McDonald's, Saigon Panda city park, W H
4	Cliff Ave, E BP
3	SD 115, Lp 229, Minnesota Ave, E city park, W BP/dsl, Sinclair Arby's, Burger King, Camilles Cafe, Culver's, DQ, Famous Dave's BBQ, Golden Bowl Chinese, Hardee's, Little Caesar's/TCBY, McDonald's, Subway $Tree, Ace Hardware, Acura, Buick/GMC, Costco/gas, Hy-Vee Foods/dsl, Kia, Lewis Drug, Staples, tires, USPO, vet
2	Western Ave, E Holiday/dsl Bracco Cafe, DQ, Scooters Coffee, Starbucks, W Cenex/dsl, Holiday Buck's Roadhouse, Burger King, China Buffet, Huhot Mongolian, Lone Star Steaks, Papa Murphy's, PepperJax Grill, Perkins, Qdoba Mexican, Redrossa Pizza, Scheel's, Valentino's H, Advance Parts, AutoZone, Best Buy, Goodyear/auto, Hancock Fabrics, Tuesday Morning
1.5mm	Big Sioux River
1c	Louise Ave, E Holiday/dsl Comfort Suites, Hampton Inn, Holiday Inn Express, Homewood Suites H, Chrysler/Dodge/Jeep, Fiat, Lewis Drug, W Burger King, Five Guys, Jimmy John's, Marco's Pizza, McDonald's, Noodles&Co, Panera Bread, Qdoba Mexican, Royal Palace, Spezia's Rest, Taco John's, Wendy's Hilton Garden Inn Barnes&Noble, Dick's, Honda, Hy-Vee Foods/dsl, JC Penney, Jo-Ann Fabrics, Kohl's, Target, Verizon, Walgreens
1b a	I-29 N and S. **I-229 begins/ends on I-29, exit 75.**

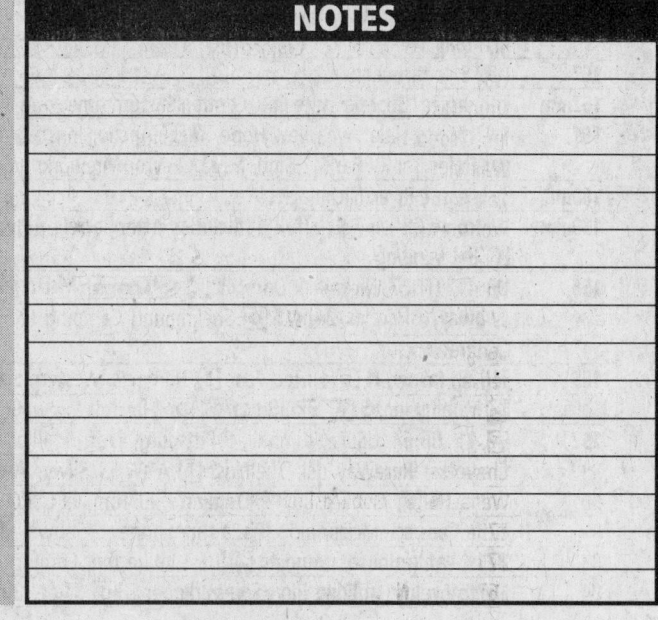

NOTES

TN

TENNESSEE

INTERSTATE 24

CHATTANOOGA

Exit#	Services
185b a	I-75, N to Knoxville, S to Atlanta. **I-24 begins/ends on I-75, exit 2 in Chattanooga.**
184	Moore Rd, **S** Chef Lin's Buffet, Provino's Italian $Tree, URGENT CARE
183	(183a from wb), Belvoir Ave, Germantown Rd
181a	US 41 S, to East Ridge (from eb), **S** Sugar's Ribs, Underdog's Grill King's Lodge
181	Fourth Ave, to TN Temple U, Chattanooga, **N** Citgo/dsl, Exxon/dsl, Hi-Tech Fuel, Stop'n Save Bojangles, Burger King, Capt D's, Hardee's, Krystal, Subway, Waffle House Chatt Inn $General, BiLo, Family$, Mack/Volvo Trucks, NAPA, O'Reilly Parts, repair, vet, **S** Mystik
180b a	US 27 S, TN 8, Rossville Blvd, **N** Best One Tires/service, to UT Chatt, **S** Mapco/dsl, RaceWay/dsl Hamilton Inn auto repair, Family$, NTB, to Chickamauga Battlefield
178	US 27 N, Market St, to Lookout Mtn, Chattanooga, **N** BP/dsl, Citgo Country Hearth Inn, La Quinta, Marriott, Staybridge Suites Chevrolet, Ford/Lincoln, Midas, Nissan, to aquarium, to Chattanooga ChooChoo, U-Haul, **S** RaceWay/dsl KFC Comfort Suites, Motel 6, Red Roof Inn
175	Browns Ferry Rd, to Lookout Mtn, **N** BP, Spirit/dsl China Gourmet, El Rey Mexican Best Value Inn, La Quinta CVS Drug, vet, **S** Mapco/dsl Hardee's, McDonald's Comfort Inn, EconoLodge, Quality Inn $General
174	US 11, US 41, US 64, Lookout Valley, **N** Waffle House Days Inn Racoon Mtn Camping (1mi), st patrol, **S** BP/dsl, Exxon/Circle K/dsl, Murphy USA/dsl Cracker Barrel, Diamond Pizza, Jack's Rest., Logan's Roadhouse, Los 3 Amigos, New China, Taco Bell, Waffle House, Wendy's Best Western, Budget Motel, Clarion, Country Inn&Suites, Fairfield Inn, Hampton Inn, Holiday Inn Express, Knights Inn, Quality Inn, Red Roof Inn, Super 8 $Tree, Ace Hardware, AT&T, URGENT CARE, Verizon, Walmart/Subway
172mm	**eb, full facilities, litter barrels, petwalk, , , vending**
171mm	Tennessee/Georgia state line
169	GA 299, to US 11, **N** Mapco/dsl, **S** BP/Krispy Chicken/dsl/24hr, Citgo, Pilot/Subway/dsl/scales/24hr $General, repair
167	I-59 S, to Birmingham
167mm	Tennessee/Georgia state line, Central/Eastern time zone
161	TN 156, to Haletown, New Hope, **N** Anchor Inn/dsl (1mi) Hales Bar RV Park (2.5mi), **S** Chevron/fireworks
160mm	Tennessee River/Nickajack Lake
159mm	**Welcome Ctr wb/ eb, full facilities, litter barrels, petwalk, , , vending**
158	US 41, TN 27, Nickajack Dam, **N** Loves/McDonald's/Subway/dsl/scales/24hr, **S** Shellmound Camping (2.5mi), fireworks
155	TN 28, Jasper, **N** Hi-Tech/dsl Hardee's, Western Sizzlin Quality Inn, **S** BP/Mapco/dsl H
152	US 41, US 64, US 72, Kimball, S Pittsburg, **N** Phillips 66/fireworks, RaceWay/dsl, Shell/dsl A&W/LJ Silver, Arby's, China Buffet, Cracker Barrel, Domino's, El Toril, KFC, Krystal, Little Caesar's, McDonald's, Pizza Hut, Shoney's, Subway, Taco Bell, Waffle House, Wendy's Best Value Inn, Comfort Inn, Hampton Inn, Holiday Inn Express, Super 8 $Tree, Buick/

MONTEAGLE

MANCHESTER

Exit#	Services
152	Continued Chevrolet/GMC, GNC, Lowe's, Walmart, **3 mi S** Lodge Cast Iron, to Russell Cave NM
143	Martin Springs Rd, **N** Citgo/dsl
135	US 41 N, Monteagle, **N** Marathon/dsl, Pilot/Wendy's/dsl/scales/24hr High Point Rest., Rocky Top Rest., Shan Chinese Family$, Monteagle Parts, USPO, **S** Motel 6
134	US 64, US 41A, to Sewanee, Monteagle, **N** BP/Mapco/McDonald's/dsl Sonic American Eagle Inn CVS Drug, to S Cumberland SP, **S** Exxon/dsl, Marathon/Kangaroo Hardee's, Pizza Hut, Smokehouse BBQ, Subway, Waffle House Best Western, Mountain Inn, Super 8 $General Auto/tire repair, Fred's, Piggly Wiggly, to U of The South
133mm	**both lanes, full facilities, litter barrels, petwalk, , , vending**
128mm	Elk River
127	US 64, TN 50, to Winchester, Pelham, **N** Citgo, Marathon/dsl, **S** Gulf/dsl to Tims Ford SP/RV camping
119mm	**trucks only parking area both lanes**
117	to Tullahoma, USAF Arnold Ctr, UT Space Institute
116mm	**weigh sta both lanes**
114	US 41, Manchester, **N** Exxon/24 Truckers/scales/dsl, Marathon/dsl, Murphy USA/dsl, Shell/dsl Great Wall Chinese, Logan's Roadhouse, O'Charley's, Potrillos Mexican, Starbucks Comfort Suites, Holiday Inn Express, Motel 6, Quality Inn, Scottish Inn, Sleep Inn, Truckers Inn $Tree, AT&T Home Depot, KOA, Nissan, tire/truck repair, Toyota, Verizon Walmart/Subway, **S** Mobil/Circle K, RaceWay/dsl Arby's, Baskin-Robbins, Bojangles, Burger King, Capt D's, Hong Kong Buffet, KFC, Krystal, McDonald's/playplace, Papa John's, Pizza Hut, Rafael's Italian, Subway, Taco Bell, Waffle House Wendy's Days Inn, Microtel, Red Roof Inn, Regency Inn Royal Inn Advance Parts, AutoZone, Family$, Ford/Lincoln, O'Reilly Parts, Russell Stover, USPO, vet
111	TN 55, Manchester, **N** Co-op/dsl, Marathon/dsl, Mobil/Circle K H, to Rock Island SP, vet, **S** Hardee's, J&G Pizza/Steaks, Sonic $General, Gateway Auto, Old Stone Fort SP Rite Aid, to Jack Daniels Dist HS, Walgreens
110	TN 53, Manchester, **N** Exxon, Mobil/Circle K/dsl, Petro/dsl Cracker Barrel, Emma's Rest., Las Fajitas Mexican, Oak Rest. Ambassador Inn, Econolodge, Economy Inn, Hampton Inn H, **S** Shell/dsl Los 3 Amigos, Prater's BBQ Waffle House repair
110mm	Duck River
105	US 41, **N** Exxon/dsl, Marathon/dsl, **S** Dickel HS, tire repair, to Normandy Dam, Whispering Oaks Camping (1.5mi)
97	TN 64, to Shelbyville, Beechgrove, **S** Marathon/dsl
89	Buchanan Rd, **N** Loves/McDonald's/dsl/scales/24hr Subway, **S** Shell/dsl $General, A&L RV Ctr
84	Joe B. Jackson Pkwy, **N** Subway
81	US 231, Murfreesboro, **N** Exxon, Gulf/dsl, Mapco, Shel Cathay Asian, Cracker Barrel, Krystal, Parthenon Grille Shoney's, Sports Seasons Grill, Wendy's Best Value Inn Knights Inn, Quality Inn, Ramada Ltd, Regal Inn H, Chrysler/Dodge/Jeep, Honda, **S** Kangaroo, Mapco/dsl, Mobil Pilot/Arby's/scales/dsl/24hr Bojangles, Burger King, La Siesta Mexican, McDonald's/playplace, Pizza Hut, Rick's BBQ Sonic, Starbucks, Subway, Taco Bell, Waffle House, Whitt's BBQ Zaxby's Select Inn, Vista Suites $General, Advanc

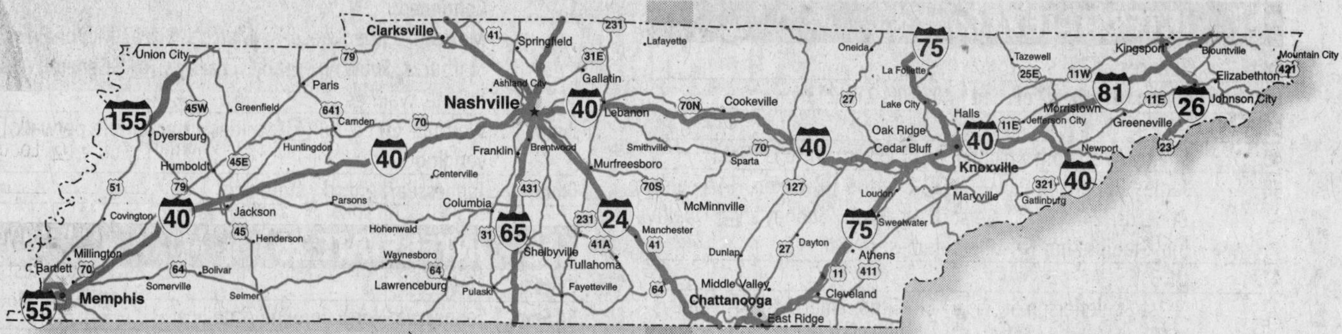

INTERSTATE 24 Cont'd

MURFREESBORO

81 Continued

Parts, AutoZone, Discount Tire, Gateway Auto, Kroger/dsl, O'Reilly Parts, Rite Aid, Toyota, vet

80 New Salem Hwy, rd 99, S [gas] Speedway/Speedy's Cafe/dsl [food] Domino's, Marco's Pizza, Subway

78 TN 96, to Franklin, Murfreesboro, N [gas] Marathon, Murphy USA/dsl, Phillips 66/Church's/White Castle/dsl, Shell/Jack-in-the-Box [food] Arby's, Baskin-Robbins, Bonefish Grill, Buffalo Wild Wings, Carrabba's, Cheddar's, Chick-fil-A, Chipotle, Chophouse, ChuckECheese, Coconut Bay Cafe, Cracker Barrel, Egg&I Cafe, Fazoli's, Firehouse Subs, Five Guys, IHOP, Jason's Deli, Jimmy John's, Jim'n Nick's BBQ, KFC, McDonald's, Mi Patria, Moe's SW Grill, Old Chicago, Olive Garden, Outback Steaks, Panda Express, Panera Bread, Red Lobster, Red Robin, Sam's Grill, Samurai's Cuisine, Sandwich Factory, SmashBurger, Starbucks, Steak'n Shake, Subway, TGIFriday's, Waffle House, Wendy's, Zaxby's [lodging] Baymont Inn, Best Western, Candlewood Suites, Clarion, Comfort Suites, Country Inn&Suites, Days Inn, DoubleTree, EconoLodge, Fairfield Inn, Hampton Inn, Holiday Inn Express, Microtel, Motel 6, Red Roof Inn, Sleep Inn, Super 8 [other] $Tree, Aldi Foods, AT&T, Books-A-Million, Dillard's, Discount Tire, Firestone, Hobby Lobby, Home Depot, JC Penney, Jo-Ann Fabrics, Lowe's, Marshalls, NTB, Petsmart, Ross, Staples, SteinMart, Target, TJ Maxx, to Stones River Bfd, Verizon, vet, Walgreens, Walmart, S [gas] Kangaroo/dsl, Mapco, Marathon/dsl, Shell/dsl [food] Camino Real Mexican, Capt D's, China Garden, Dos Rancheros, DQ, Hardee's, Jersey Mike's Subs, McDonald's, O'Charley's, Papa Murphy's, Pizza Garden, Pizza Hut, Sonic, Subway, Taco Bell, Waffle House, Wasabi Japanese [lodging] Woodspring Suites [other] $General, auto repair, AutoZone, Kohl's, Kroger/dsl, Old Time Pottery, O'Reilly Parts, Rite Aid, Sam's Club/gas, vet, Walgreens

76 Fortress Blvd, Manson Pike, Medical Center Pkwy, N [gas] Thornton's/dsl [food] Bar Louie, Chili's, Culver's, Genghis Grill, Longhorn Steaks, Macaroni Grill, Mimi's Cafe, Newk's Eatery, Peter D's, Starbucks, Subway, Which Wich? [lodging] Embassy Suites, Hilton Garden, Holiday Inn, Residence Inn [other] [H], Barnes&Noble, Belk, Best Buy, Dick's, GNC, Michael's, Old Navy, Petco, Tire Discounters, to Stones River Nat. Bfd, World Mkt, S [gas] Exxon/dsl [food] Sonic [other] Chevrolet/Cadillac/GMC/Buick, Toyota

74b a TN 840, to Lebanon, Franklin

70 TN 102, Lee Victory Pkwy, Almaville Rd, to Smyrna, N [gas] Speedway/Speedy Cafe/dsl/scales [food] Asian Cafe, Bojangles, Mi Tierro Mexican, Naked Fish [other] Publix, S [gas] Kangaroo/Little Caesar's/dsl, Mapco, Shell/dsl [food] Legends Steaks, McDonald's, Sonic, Subway [lodging] Deerfield Inn [other] $General

66 TN 266, Sam Ridley Pkwy, to Smyrna, N [gas] Shell/dsl [food] A&W/LJ Silver, Arby's, Asuka Hibachi, Blue Coast Burrito, Buffalo Wild

NASHVILLE

66 Continued

Wings, Cheddar's, Chick-fil-A, Chili's, CiCi's Pizza, DQ, Famous Dave's BBQ, Firehouse Subs, Five Guys, Hickory Falls Cafe, IHOP, Jersey Mike's Subs, Jim'n Nick's BBQ, Krispy Kreme, La Siesta Mexican, Logan's Roadhouse, Longhorn Steaks, Panda Express, Panera Bread, Papa Murphy's, Pollo Tropical, Razz Grill, Smoothie King, Sonic, Starbucks, Subway, Waffle House, Wendy's, Zaxby's [other] [H], $General, $Tree, AT&T, CVS Drug, Discount Tire, Firestone/auto, GNC, Home Depot/gas, Kohl's, Kroger/dsl, Lowe's, Nashville I-24 Camping (3mi), Petsmart, Publix, Ross, Staples, Target, Tire Discounters, URGENT CARE, Verizon, Walgreens, S [food] Cracker Barrel, O'Charley's, Ruby Tuesday [lodging] Candlewood Suites, Comfort Suites, Fairfield Inn, Hampton Inn, Hilton Garden, Holiday Inn Express, Home 2 Suites, La Quinta, Sleep Inn, TownePlace Suites

64 Waldron Rd, to La Vergne, N [gas] Kangaroo, Kwik Sak, Pilot/Subway/dsl/scales/24hr [food] Arby's, Hardee's, Krystal, McDonald's, Waffle House [lodging] Comfort Inn, Quality Inn, Ramada Inn, S [gas] Mapco/dsl [other] $General

62 TN 171, Old Hickory Blvd, N [gas] Citgo/Subway/dsl, Shell/dsl, TA/BP/Burger King/Popeye's/dsl/scales/24hr/@ [food] Acapulco Burrito [lodging] Rodeway Inn

60 Hickory Hollow Pkwy, N [gas] Exxon/dsl, Mapco, Thornton's/dsl [food] 360 Burger, Burger King, ChuckECheese, KFC/LJ Silver, Logan's Roadhouse, McDonald's/Playplace, New Century Buffet, O'Charley's, Red Lobster, Starbucks, Subway, Taco Bell, Wendy's, Zaxby's [lodging] Country Inn&Suites, Hampton Inn, Holiday Inn Express [other] Chevrolet, Chrysler/Dodge/Jeep, Family$, Firestone/auto, Kroger/gas, Mazda, Office Depot, S [gas] BP/Quiznos/dsl, Shell/Dunkin Donuts [food] Camino Real Mexican, Casa Fiesta Mexican, IHOP, Olive Garden, Shoney's, Steak'n Shake [lodging] Antioch Qtrs, Knights Inn, Super 8 [other] Home Depot, Kia, vet

59 TN 254, Bell Rd, same as 60

57 Haywood Lane, N [gas] Kwik Sak/dsl [food] Hardee's, Whitt's BBQ [other] $General, Walgreens, S [gas] Kangaroo, Shell

56 TN 255, Harding Place, N [gas] Delta/dsl, Exxon, Shell/dsl [food] Applebee's, Bar-B-Cutie, Chicago Gyros, Dunkin Donuts, KFC, McDonald's, Mikado Japanese, Pizza Hut/Taco Bell, Subway, Waffle House, Wendy's [lodging] Executive Inn, M Motel, Stay Lodge, Thrifty Inn [other] $Tree, Sam's Club/gas, S [gas] Delta/dsl, Shell/dsl [food] Burger King, Hooters, Jack-in-the-Box, La Fiesta [lodging] Best Value Inn, Travelodge [other] [H]

54b a TN 155, Briley Pkwy, [other] to Opryland

53 I-440 W, to Memphis

52 US 41, Murfreesboro Rd, N [gas] Phillips 66/dsl, Shell [food] Waffle House [lodging] Best Western, Days Inn, Holiday Inn Express, Rodeway Inn, Super 8, S [gas] Mapco/dsl, SpeedCo/dsl/e85 [food] BP/dsl [other] NAPA

52b a I-40, E to Knoxville, W to Memphis

TN

INTERSTATE 24 Cont'd

NASHVILLE

Exit#	Services
I-24 and I-40 run together 2 mi. See I-40, exits 212-213.	
50b	I-40 W
49	Shelby Ave, (from wb only), S Exxon to LP Field
48	James Robertson Pkwy, N Citgo, S Exxon, TA/Country Pride/dsl/24hr/@ Gerst Haus Rest., Shoney's Quality Inn, Stadium Inn LP Stadium, st capitol
47a	US 31E
47	N 1st St, Jefferson St, N BP, Citgo, Zmart/dsl Family$, S Mystic Gas Clarion, Knights Inn U-Haul
I-24 and I-65 run together. See I-65, exit 87 b a.	
44b a	I-65, N to Louisville, S to Nashville
43	TN 155, Briley Pkwy, Brick Church Pike
40	TN 45, Old Hickory Blvd, N Marathon/Subway/dsl, Phillips 66/dsl, Shell/dsl El Rey Azteca Super 8
35	US 431, to Joelton, Springfield, N H, S BP/Heritage TC/DQ/Subway/dsl, Shell/dsl Family Rest., Mazatlan Mexican, McDonald's Days Inn $General, auto repair, Family$, OK Camping
31	TN 249, New Hope Rd, N Shell/Taco Tico/dsl, S Marathon/dsl, Shell/dsl
24	TN 49, to Springfield, Ashland City, N Mapco/dsl, Marathon/Pizza Hut/dsl Quality Inn H, S Shell/dsl, SS/Dunkin Donuts/Wendy's/dsl Dragon Buffet, KFC/Taco Bell, Sonic, Subway $General Mkt, city park, Hill Foods, USPO, vet
19	TN 256, Maxey Rd, to Adams, N Phillips 66/dsl, S Shell/dsl $General
11	TN 76, to Adams, Clarksville, N Shell/dsl, S Citgo, Exxon/dsl McDonald's, Pancho Villa Grille, Subway, Waffle House Baymont Inn, Comfort Inn, Days Inn, Super 8 H, $General, vet
9mm	Red River
8	TN 237, Rossview Rd, S Dunbar Cave SP
4	US 79, to Clarksville, Ft Campbell, N Exxon/dsl, Shell/dsl Cracker Barrel Best Western, Hilton Garden Sam's Club/gas, Spring Creek Camping (2mi), S BP/dsl, Murphy USA/dsl, Shell/Subway/dsl Applebee's, Arby's, Baskin-Robbins, Buffalo Wild Wings, Burger King, Canela Mexican, Capt D's, Cheddar's, Chick-Fil-A, Chili's, China King, Chipotle, ChuckeCheese, Church's/White Castle, DQ, Fazoli's, Firehouse Subs, Golden Corral, Harbor Cafe, IHOP, Jersey Mike's, KFC, Krispy Kreme, Krystal, LJ Silver, Logan's Roadhouse, Longhorn Steaks, McDonald's, Moe's SW Grill, Noodles&Co, O'Charley's, Old Chicago Pizza, Olive Garden, Outback Steaks, Panera Bread, Rafferty's, Red Lobster, Shogun Japanese, Shoney's, Starbucks, Steak'n Shake, Subway, Taco Bell, Tilted Kilt, TX Roadhouse, Waffle House, Wendy's, Zaxby's Baymont Inn, Best Inn, Best Value Inn, Candlewood Suites, Country Inn&Suites, Courtyard, Days Inn, EconoLodge, Fairfield Inn, Gateway Inn, Guesthouse Inn, Hampton Inn, Hometowne Suites, La Quinta, Mainstay Suites, Microtel, Quality Inn, Ramada Ltd, Red Roof Inn, Rodeway Inn, Super 8, Woodspring Suites H, $Tree, AT&T, Belk, Best Buy, Books-A-Million, Buick/GMC, Dick's, Firestone/auto, Goodyear/auto, Hobby Lobby, Home Depot, Hyundai, JC Penney, Kohl's, Kroger/dsl, Lowe's, Mazda, Office Depot, Petco, Petsmart, Ross, Subaru, Target, TJ Maxx, to Austin Peay St U, to Land Between the Lakes, Toyota, U-Haul, Verizon, Walmart/McDonald's
1	TN 48, to Clarksville, Trenton, N Exxon/dsl, Shell/dsl Clarksville RV Camping, S Exxon/dsl, Shell/dsl Bojangles, Burger King, Coldstone, Dunkin Donuts, El Bracero Mexican, Little Caesar's, Marco's Pizza, McDonald's, Sonic, Starbucks, Subway, Wendy's, Zaxby's $General, AT&T, AutoZone, Walgreens
.5mm	**Welcome Ctr eb, full facilities, litter barrels, petwalk, vending**
0mm	Tennessee/Kentucky state line

CLARKSVILLE

INTERSTATE 26

ERWIN

Exit#	Services
54.5mm	Tennessee/North Carolina state line
54mm	**runaway truck ramp wb**
52mm	**runaway truck ramp wb, scenic overlook eb (no trucks)**
50	Flag Pond Rd
47.5mm	scenic overlook wb (no trucks)
46mm	**N Welcome Ctr/RS both lanes, full facilities, litter barrels, petwalk,**
44mm	Higgins Creek
43	US 19 W, rd 352, Temple Hill Rd
42mm	S Indian Creek
40	Jackson-Love Hwy, Erwin, Jonesborough, N Valero/dsl Mtn Inn H, Nolichucky Gorge Camping (2mi)
37	TN 81, rd 107, Erwin, Jonesborough, N Shell Bojangles, Huddle House, McDonald's, Pal's Drive-Thru, Taco Bell H, USPO, Walgreens, S Super 8 A. Johnson NHS (31mi), River Park Camping (5mi)
36	Main St, Erwin, N BP/dsl, Exxon/dsl/e-85 Azteca Mexican, Hardee's, KFC, Little Caesars, Pizza Hut, Subway, Wendy's $General, Advance Parts, AutoZone, Firestone, Rite Aid
34	Tinker Rd, N Murphy USA/dsl Los Jalapenos, Primo's Pizza Walmart
32	rd 173, Unicoi Rd, to Cherokee NF, N Jerry's Mkt Clarence's Drive-In, Whistle Stop Deli $General, Grandview Ranch Camping (7mi), USPO, S Woodsmoke Camping
27	rd 359 N, Okolona Rd, N Budget Inn (3mi) truck repair
24	US 321, TN 67, Elizabethton, N Shell/Dunkin Donuts/dsl Roan Mtn SP, S BP/dsl Arby's, Burger King, Fox's Pizza, Little Caesar's, LJ Silver, Subway Comfort Inn H, Advance Parts, CVS, Food City/gas, Price Less Foods, to ETSU, Walgreens
23	rd 91, Market St, N DQ, McDonald's, S museum
22	rd 400, Unaka Ave, Watauga Ave
20b a	US 11 E, US 19 N, to Roan St, N Shell/dsl, Sunoco/dsl Arby's, Cootie Brown's Rest., Harbor House Seafood, Hardee's, Little Caesar's, LJ Silver, Mellow Mushroom Pizza, Moto Japanese, Peerless Rest., Perkins, Popeye's, Sonic Best Western, Holiday Inn, Ramada Ltd, Super 8 Acura, Advance Parts, AT&T, AutoZone, BigLots, Ford, Fred's, Honda, Hyundai, Mazda, NAPA Repair, O'Reilly Parts, Subaru, Tuesday Morning, UHaul, VW, S Applebees, Babylon Grill, Bojangles, Bonefish Grill, Brusco's Pizza, Fazoli's, Five Guys, Greg's Pizza, Hana Steaks, Hibachi Grill, Hooters, Jack's City Grill, KFC, Longhorn Steaks, McAlister's Deli, McDonald's, O'Charley's, Olive Garden, Papa Murphy's, Red Lobster, Shoney's, Smokey Bones BBQ, Starbucks, Subway, Taco Bell, TX Roadhouse, Zaxby's Doubletree, Motel 6, Red Roof Inn $General, $Tree, Belk, Books-A-Million, CVS, Dick's, FreeService Tire/auto, JC Penney, Kroger, Office Depot, Target, TJ Maxx, Verizon, Walgreens
19	TN 381, to St of Franklin Rd, to Bristol, N Murphy USA/dsl, Valero/McDonald's Golden Corral, Honeybaked Ham, Logan's Roadhouse, Outback Steaks, Subway Comfort Suite

JOHNSON CITY

INTERSTATE 26 Cont'd

KINGSPORT

19 Continued
Walmart, 0-2 mi S Amigo Mexican, Barberito's Grille, Buffalo Wild Wings, Carrabba's, Cheddar's, Chick-fil-A, Chili's, ChuckECheese's, East Coast Wings, Fuddruckers, IHOP, Jason's Deli, Mad Greek, Ming's Asian, Panera Bread, Rita's Custard, Wendy's, Which Wich? Courtyard, Hampton Inn, Sleep Inn H, AT&T, Barnes&Noble, Best Buy, Home Depot, Kohl's, Lowe's, Michael's, Natural Foods Mkt, Old Navy, PetsMart, Ross, Sam's Club/gas, Steinmart, USPO, Verizon, vet

17 Boone St, N BP, QP/dsl Beef'o Brady's, Bob Evans, Giovanni's Italian, Hardee's, McDonald's, Pal's Drive-in, Pizza+ $General, Ingles Foods/dsl, S Exxon/e-85, Shell/Subway/dsl Cracker Barrel, Domino's, Poblano's Mexican, Waffle House, Wendy's Holiday Inn Express, Quality Inn, Woodspring Suites

13 rd 75, Bobby Hicks Hwy, N BP, Shell Burger King, China Luck, DQ, La Carreta, McDonald's, Pal's Drive-Thru, Papa John's, Pizza Hut, Sicily Italian, Subway, Taco Bell, Yong Asian $General, Advance Parts, Food City/gas, O'Reilly Parts, USPO, Walgreens, S Exxon/dsl

10 Eastern Star Rd, N Phil's Dream Pit BBQ

8b a I-81, to Bristol, Knoxville

6 rd 347, Rock Springs Rd, S Rite Quik/dsl

5mm **Welcome Ctr/, full facilities both lanes, , litter barrels, petwalk**

4 TN 93, Wilcox Dr, N BP/Subway, Mobil/McDonald's/dsl Burger King, Hardee's, La Carreta Mexican, Pizza Hut, Wendy's Comfort Suites, Hampton Inn, Holiday Inn Express, Quality Inn $General, Cave's Drug, Price Less Foods, S Exxon, Mobil/Arby's/dsl/e-85 Pizza+

3 Meadowview Pkwy, N Marriott

1 US 11 W, West Stone Dr, N Shell Little Caesar's, Molcajete's Mexican Super 8 H, Walgreens, S Exxon, Murphy USA/dsl Bojangles, China Star, Fatz Cafe, Sonic, Subway $Tree, Lowe's, Walmart

I-26 begins/ends on US 23.

INTERSTATE 40

Exit#	Services
451mm	Tennessee/North Carolina state line
451	Waterville Rd
447	Hartford Rd, N Citgo/dsl, S BP/dsl Bean Tree Cafe, Pigeon River Smokehouse Foxfire Camping, Shauan's Riverside RV Park, USPO, whitewater rafting
446mm	**Welcome Ctr wb, full facilities, litter barrels, NO TRUCKS, petwalk, , , vending**
443	Foothills Pkwy, to Gatlinburg, Great Smoky Mtns NP
443mm	Pigeon River
440	US 321, to Wilton Spgs Rd, Gatlinburg, N 76/440 Trkstp/cafe/dsl, S Marathon Broasted Chicken Arrow Creek Camping (14mi), CrazyHorse Camping (14mi)
439mm	Pigeon River
435	US 321, to Gatlinburg, Newport, N Exxon/Biodsl/e-85, JSK Express, Marathon, Rite Quik/dsl, Weigel/dsl Arby's, Burger King, Hardee's, KFC, Lois' Country Kitchen, McDonald's, Pizza Hut, SageBrush Steaks, Subway, Taco Bell Motel 6 H, CVS Drug, O'Reilly Parts, Town&Country Drug, USPO, Walgreens, S Mobil/dsl, Murphy USA/dsl Bojangle's, Brooklyn Pizza, Cracker Barrel, Monterrey Mexican, New China, Papa John's, Papa Murphy's, Portabella's, Ruby Tuesday, Waffle House, Wendy's

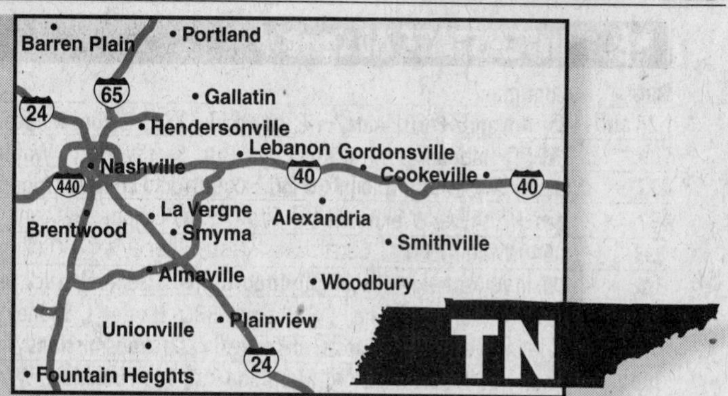

NEWPORT

Exit#	Services
435	Continued Best Western, Family Inn, Hampton Inn, Holiday Inn Express, Knights Inn, Quality Inn $General, $Tree, AT&T, Lowe's, Save-A-Lot Foods, Verizon, Walmart/Subway
432b a	US 70, US 411, US 25W, to Newport, N Exxon/dsl, Marathon/dsl, TimeOut TC/BP/Huddle House/dsl/scales Comfort Inn, Relax Inn Buick/Chevrolet, Chrysler/Dodge/Jeep, KOA (2mi), Tana-See RV Park, truck service, Westgate Tire, S Citgo/dsl, Marathon/dsl, Shell/dsl Family Inn/rest. $General
426mm	**wb, full facilities, litter barrels, petwalk, , , vending**
425mm	French Broad River
424	TN 113, Dandridge, N Marathon/dsl
421	I-81 N, to Bristol
420mm	**eb, full facilities, litter barrels, petwalk, , , vending**
417	TN 92, Dandridge, N Marathon/dsl, Pilot/Subway/dsl/scales/24hr/@ Capt's Galley, Hardee's, McDonald's, Perkins, Ruby Tuesday, Taste of Dandridge Rodeway Inn, S Exxon/Wendy's/dsl, Marathon/dsl, Weigel's/dsl Arby's, Bojangles, LJ Silver/Taco Bell, Shoney's, Waffle House Hampton Inn, Holiday Inn Express, Jefferson Inn, Quality Inn, Super 8 Advance Parts
415	US 25W, US 70, to Dandridge, S Marathon/dsl Sonic (3mi)
412	Deep Sprgs Rd, to Douglas Dam, N Love's/Chester's/Subway/dsl/scales/24hr, Speedway/Speedy's Cafe/dsl
407	TN 66, to Sevierville, Pigeon Forge, Gatlinburg, N Shell/Subway/dsl Chophouse, Cracker Barrel, McDonald's, Uncle Buck's Grill Best Value Inn, Fairfield Inn, Hampton Inn, Holiday Inn Express Bass Pro Shops, Harley Davidson, RV Camping, Smoky Mtn Visitor's Ctr, S BP/Subway/dsl, Exxon/dsl, Mobil/Dunkin Donuts/dsl, Shell/Krystal/dsl Burger King, FlapJack's, Wendy's Best Western, Comfort Suites, Days Inn, Quality Inn Chrysler/Dodge/Jeep, flea mkt, Russell Stover, RV Camping, TN Tourist Info, USPO, multiple services/outlets
402	Midway Rd
398	Strawberry Plains Pk, Strawberry Plains Pk, N BP/dsl, Citgo/dsl, Exxon/dsl, Shell/dsl Aubrey's Rest., McDonald's, Outback Steaks, Waffle House, Wendy's EconoLodge, Hampton Inn, Holiday Inn Express, Knight's Inn, Quality Inn, Red Roof Inn, Rodeway Inn, Super 8 TN RV Ctr, S Pilot/Subway/dsl/scales/24hr, Weigel's Arby's, Burger King, Cracker Barrel, Golden Wok Chinese, KFC, Krystal, Puleo's Grille, Taco Bell Best Western, Comfort Suites, Fairfield Inn, La Quinta, Motel 6
395mm	Holston River
394	US 70, US 11E, US 25W, Asheville Hwy, N BP, Pilot/dsl, Shell/dsl Papa John's, Subway, Wendy's Gateway Inn

DANDRIDGE

TN

INTERSTATE 40 Cont'd

KNOXVILLE

394 Continued
Advance Parts, AutoZone, city park, **S** Exxon, Mapco/dsl Habaneros Mexican, Pizza Hut, Scott's Place, Waffle House Days Inn $General, CVS Drug, Family$, Kroger/gas, NAPA, vet, Walgreens

393 I-640 W, to I-75 N

392 US 11W, Rutledge Pike, **N** Citgo/dsl $General, truck repair, U-Haul, **S** Shell Buddy's BBQ, Hardee's, Shoney's NAPA, Sav-A-Lot Foods, to Knoxville Zoo, transmissions

390 Cherry St, Knoxville, **N** Marathon/dsl, Top Fuel Mart, Weigel's/Subway Happy Garden Chinese Knoxville Inn tires, **S** Exxon Arby's, Little Caesar's, LJ Silver, McDonald's Regency Inn Advance Parts, Family$, O'Reilly Parts, vet, Walgreens

389 US 441 N, Broadway, 5th Ave, **N** Pilot/dsl, Shell/dsl, Star Burger King, KFC, Krystal, McDonald's, Sonic, Subway, Taco Bell, Wendy's $General, Ace Hardware, Belew Drug, CVS Drug, Family$, Firestone/auto, Kroger/dsl, Save-A-Lot Foods, USPO, Walgreens/24hr

388 US 441 S (exits left from wb), **S** Crowne Plaza, Hilton, Holiday Inn downtown, to Smokey Mtns, to U of TN

387a I-275 N, to Lexington

387 TN 62, 17th St, **N** Gas'N Go, Pilot/dsl Hamilton Inn, Royal Inn $General, Food City, vet

386b a US 129, University Ave, to UT

385 I-75 N, I-640 E

I-40 W and I-75 S run together 17 mi.

383 Papermill Rd, **N** Red Roof Inn, **S** Exxon/dsl, Pilot/dsl Barberitos, Buddy's BBQ, Burger King, Five Guys, Krispy Kreme, Sonic, Twin Peaks, Waffle House Courtyard, Hampton Inn, Holiday Inn Express, Travelodge Food City, same as 380, Walgreens

380 US 11, US 70, West Hills, **S** Delta Express, Mapco/dsl Arby's, Brazeiro's Brazilian Steaks, Brixx Pizza, Burro Flojo Mexican, Cheesecake Factory, Chick-fil-A, Chili's, Cookout, Doc's Grille, Dunkin Donuts, Firehouse Subs, Hardee's, Honeybaked Ham, Hooters, IHOP, Jets Pizza, Jimmy John's, Longhorn Steaks, McAlister's Deli, McDonald's, Mooyah Burger, Mr Gatti's, O'Charley's, Olive Garden, Papa John's, Penn Sta Subs, Petro's Chili, PF Chang's, Pizza Hut, PlumTree Chinese, Qdoba Mexican, Red Lobster, Salsarita's Cantina, Starbucks, Subway, Taco Bell, Tropical Smoothie Cafe, TX Roadhouse, Zaxby's Extended Stay America, Ramada Inn $Tree, AT&T, Barnes&Noble, Belk, Dillards, Food City, JC Penney, Kohl's, Office Depot, Old Navy, O'Reilly Parts, Petsmart, REI, Ross, Steinmart, Target, TJ Maxx, Trader Joe's, U-Haul, Walgreens, Whole Foods Mkt

379 Bridgewater Rd, **N** Exxon/Subway/dsl, Pilot/McDonald's/dsl Taco Bell Sam's Club/gas, Walmart/Subway, **S** Conoco/dsl, Marathon/dsl Asia Kitchen, Buddy's BBQ, Burger King, Cheddar's, ChuckeCheese, CiCi's Pizza, Makino Japanese, Misaki Japanese, Shoney's, Sonic, Wendy's InTown Suites Aamco, Advance Parts, AutoZone, Books-A-Million, Buick/GMC, Chrysler/Dodge/Jeep, Firestone/auto, Ford/Lincoln, Hyundai/Subaru, Mazda, Nissan, NTB, Tire Barn, Transmission World

378 Cedar Bluff Rd, **N** Pilot/Taco Bell/dsl, Shell, Weigel's/dsl Arby's, Burger King, Cracker Barrel, Dunkin Donuts, KFC, Little Caesar's, McDonald's, Old Mill Bread Co., Papa John's, Starbucks, Subway, Waffle House, Wendy's Country Inn&Suites, Days Inn, Hampton Inn, Holiday Inn, Quality Inn H, $General, **S** Exxon Applebee's, Blaze Pizza, Cancun Mexican,

378 Continued
Capt D's, Carrabba's, Chipotle, Chuy's Mexican, Famous Dave's BBQ, Firehouse Subs, Fuddrucker's, Hardee's, Jason's Deli, Koko Japanese, Krystal, La Rosa's, Lenny's Subs, Newk's Cafe, Outback Steaks, Panera Bread, Parkside Grill, Peerless Grill, Penn Sta. Subs, Pizza Hut, Puleo's Grill, Rafferty's, Salsarita's, Starbucks, Which Wich?, Zaxby's Baymont Inn, Best Western, Comfort Inn, Courtyard, Embassy Suites, Extended Stay America, Hilton Garden, Home 2 Suites, Microtel, Motel 6, Red Roof Inn, Residence Inn, Towne Place Suites $Tree, Aldi Foods, AT&T, Best Buy, Cadillac, Chevrolet, CVS Drug, Dick's, Fiat, Ford/Lincoln, GNC, Home Depot, Jo-Ann Fabrics, Kia, Kroger/dsl, Lowe's, Pepboys, Staples, Tuesday Morning, Volvo, Walgreens

376 I-140 E, TN 162 N, to Maryville, **N** to Oak Ridge Museum

374 TN 131, Lovell Rd, **N** Shell/dsl, Speedway/Speedy Cafe/dsl/scales/24hr, TA/Country Pride/dsl/scales/24hr/@ Bojangles, Subway, Waffle House Econolodge Harley-Davidson, **S** Pilot/Wendy's/dsl/24hr Abuelo's Mexican, Arby's, Baskin-Robbins, Bonefish Grill, Brixx Pizza, Buffalo Wild Wings, Calhoun's Rest., Chick-fil-A, Chipotle, Connor's Rest., Egg&I Cafe, Flemings, Hurricane Grill, IHOP, Jimmy John's, Kabuki Japanese, Krystal, Lenny's Subs, McAlister's Deli, McDonald's, Mimi's Cafe, Moe's SW Grill, Noodles&Co, O'Charley's, Olive Garden, Panera Bread, Pei Wei, Red Robin, Salsarita's Cantina, Smokey Mtn Brewery, Sonic, Starbucks, Steak'n Shake, Taco Bell, TX Roadhouse, Wasabi Japanese, Zoe's Kitchen Budget Inn, Candlewood Suites, Homewood Suites, SpringHill Suites H, $Tree, Advance Parts, AutoZone, Belk, Best Buy, BMW/Mini, CarMax, Costco/gas, EarthFare Foods, GNC, Hobby Lobby, Honda, Land Rover, Lexus, Marshall's, Mercedes, Old Navy, Petsmart, Ross, Target, Toyota, Walgreens, Walmart/Subway, World Mkt

373 Campbell Sta Rd, **N** Marathon/dsl, Shell/dsl Comfort Suites, Country Inn&Suites, Fairfield Inn, Holiday Inn Express, Super 8 Buddy Gregg RV Ctr, **S** Exxon/dsl, Pilot/dsl, Weigel's Bad Daddy's Burger, Cracker Barrel, Dunkin Donuts, Hardee's, La Parrilla, Longhorn Steaks, Mellow Mushroom, Newk's Grill, Panda Express, Potbelly, Seasons Grille, Taco Boy, Wild Wing Cafe, Zaxby's Clarion, Hampton Inn, Staybridge Suites AT&T, JC Penney, Publix, Verizon, Walgreens

372mm **weigh sta both lanes**

369 Watt Rd, **N** FLYING J/Denny's/dsl/LP/scales/RV dump/24hr, Speedco Blue Beacon, **S** Petro/Iron Skillet/dsl/scales/24hr/@, TA/Marathon/Burger King/Pizza Hut/Popeye's/Subway/dsl/24hr/@ Knoxville Coach & RV

I-40 E and I-75 N run together 17 mi.

368 I-75 and I-40

364 US 321, TN 95, Lenoir City, Oak Ridge, **N** Crosseyed Cricket Camping (2mi), 4-5 mi **S** Loves/McDonald's/Subway/dsl/24hr Ruby Tuesday Days Inn, EconoLodge, Hampton Inn, Holiday Inn Express

362 Industrial Park Rd

360 Buttermilk Rd, **N** Soaring Eagle RV Park

356 TN 58 N, Gallaher Rd, to Oak Ridge, **N** Marathon/dsl, Weigels/dsl Motel 6 $General, 4 Seasons Camping

355 Lawnville Rd, **N** Pilot/Subway/dsl

352 TN 58 S, Kingston, **N** Lakeview Inn, **S** Exxon/dsl, Mobil/dsl, RaceWay Buddy's BBQ, Hardee's, Little Caesar's, McDonald's, Sonic, Subway, Taco Bell Super 8 $General, Cash Saver Foods, Family$, Marina RV Park, to Watts Bar Lake, USPO

TN

INTERSTATE 40 Cont'd

HARRIMAN

Exit#	Services
351mm	Clinch River
350	US 70, Midtown, **S** Weigel's/dsl Bojangles, Gondolier Italian, Subway, Zaxby's H, AT&T, Caney Creek Camping (3mi), Kroger, Lowe's, Walgreens
347	US 27, Harriman, **N** Phillips 66/dsl Hardee's, KFC, LJ Silver, Los Primos Mexican, McDonald's, Pizza Hut, Ruby Tuesday, Subway, Taco Bell, Wendy's Days Inn Big S Fork NRA, to Frozen Head SP, Verizon, **2-3 mi S** Murphy USA/dsl, Shell/Krystal/dsl/24hr, Sunoco/dsl Cancun Mexican, Capt D's, China King, Cracker Barrel, Domino's, McDonald's, Shoney's, Sonic Comfort Inn, Holiday Inn Express, Quality Inn, Rodeway Inn H, Ace Hardware, BigLots, vet, Walmart
340	TN 299 N, Airport Rd
339.5mm	eastern/central time zone line
338	TN 299 S, Westel Rd, **S** Exxon/dsl, Sunoco/dsl Boat-N-RV Ctr/Park
336mm	**parking area/weigh sta eb, litter barrel**
329	US 70, Crab Orchard, **N** Citgo/dsl, Marathon/dsl KOA (4mi), **S** Cumberland Trails SP, Wilson SP
327mm	**wb, full facilities, litter barrels, petwalk, , , vending**
324mm	**eb, full facilities, litter barrels, petwalk, , , vending**
322	TN 101, Peavine Rd, Crossville, **N** Exxon/Subway/dsl, Volunteer/dsl Hardee's, McDonald's Holiday Inn Express Deer Run RV Resort, KOA Camping, Roam-Roost RV Campground, to Fairfield Glade Resort, **S** Shell/dsl Cancun Mexican, Taco Bell Comfort Suites, Hampton Inn, Super 8 H, Chestnut Hill Winery, Cumberland Mtn SP
320	TN 298, Crossville, **N** Pilot/Wendy's/dsl/scales/24hr Butcher's Block Rest., Lefty's BBQ antiques, winery, **S** Shell/DQ/dsl, Speedway/dsl Log Cabin Rest. H, auto repair/tires, Crossville Outlet/famous brands, Save-A-Lot Foods
318mm	Obed River
317	US 127, Crossville, **N** Exxon/dsl, Shell/Circle K/dsl Shoney's, Subway Baymont Inn, Motel 6, Quality Inn repair, to Big South Fork RA, to York SP, **0-2 mi S** Jiffy, Marathon/dsl, Murphy USA/dsl, Shell Arby's, Bojangles, Burger King, Cancun Mexican, Cracker Barrel, La Costa Mexican, McDonalds, Papa John's, Romo's Mexican, Ruby Tuesday, Ryan's, Sonic, Subway, Taco Bell, Tokyo Steaks, Vegas Steaks, Waffle House, Zaxby's Economy Inn, Red Roof Inn H, $General, $Tree, Buick/Cadillac/Chevrolet/GMC, Chrysler/Dodge/Jeep, Ford, GNC, Lowe's, Rite Aid, Shadden Tires, Staples, to Cumberland Mtn SP, Verizon, Walgreens, Walmart
311	Plateau Rd, **S** BP/dsl, Exxon/Hunt Bros Pizza
307mm	**parking area/weigh sta wb, litter barrels**
301	US 70 N, TN 84, Monterey, **N** Shell Burger King, DQ, Rocky Pops BBQ/Catfish, Subway Bethel Inn
300	US 70, Monterey, **N** Citgo/dsl DQ, Hardee's
291mm	Falling Water River
290	US 70, Cookeville, **S** Super/dsl Fiesta Cancun Alpine Suites
288	TN 111, to Livingston, Cookeville, Sparta, **N** Hull SP, **S** Sunoco/dsl, Super Truck&TravelCtr/dsl/24hr Subway Fall Creek Inn
287	TN 136, Cookeville, **N** Marathon/dsl, Murphy USA/dsl, Shell/dsl Applebee's, Arby's, Baskin-Robbins, Blue Coast Burrito, Buffalo Wild Wings, Bully's Rest., Burger King, Capt D's, Cheddars, Chick-fil-A, Chili's, Cookout, Cracker Barrel, Dunkin Donuts, Fazoli's, Firehouse Subs, Fuji Japanese, Golden Corral, Hibachi Buffet, IHOP, Krystal, LJ Silver, Logan's Roadhouse, Longhorn

CROSSVILLE

COOKEVILLE

Exit#	Services
287	Continued Steaks, Marco's Pizza, McDonald's, Nick's Rest., O'Charley's, Olive Garden, Outback Steaks, Papa Murphy's, Pizza Hut, Red Lobster, Ruby Tuesday, Shoney's, Sonic, Starbucks, Steak'n Shake, Subway, Taco Bell, Wendy's Best Value Inn, Best Western, Clarion, Comfort Inn, Comfort Suites, Days Inn, Hampton Inn, Red Roof Inn Aldi Foods, BigLots, Firestone/auto, Harley-Davidson, JC Penney, Kroger/gas, Lowe's, Nissan, st patrol, transmissions, Verizon, Walmart, **S** Marathon/Godfather's/dsl, Pilot/dsl Gondola, KFC, Waffle House Country Inn&Suites, Fairfield Inn, Holiday Inn Express, La Quinta, Motel 6, TownePlace Suites Sam's Club/gas, URGENT CARE
286	TN 135, Burgess Falls Rd, **N** Exxon, Gulf, RaceWay/dsl, Shell/dsl Arby's, Hardee's, Waffle House H, Chrysler/Dodge/Jeep, Ford/Lincoln, Goodyear/auto, Hyundai, Kia, to TTU, Toyota, USPO, **S** Sunoco/dsl Star Motor Inn Burgess Falls SP (8mi)
280	TN 56 N, Baxter, **N** Loves/McDonalds/Subway/dsl/scales/24hr, Speedway/dsl/24hr Huddle House Camp Discovery (2mi), Twin Lakes RV Park (2mi)
276	Old Baxter Rd
273	TN 56 S, to Smithville, **S** Shell Rose Garden Rest. USPO
268	TN 96, Buffalo Valley Rd, **N** Grandville Marina Camping (11mi), **S** to Edgar Evins SP/RV camping
267mm	Caney Fork River
267mm	**both lanes, full facilities, info, litter barrels, petwalk, , , vending**
266mm	Caney Fork River
263mm	Caney Fork River
258	TN 53, Gordonsville, **N** Exxon/KFC/Taco Bell, Shell/dsl McDonald's, Subway, Timberloft Café, Waffle House Comfort Inn to Cordell Hull Dam, **S** Mobil/dsl, Pilot/Wendy's/dsl/scales/24hr Arby's, Cornerstone Cafe, El Corral Mexican, KFC/Taco Bell $General
254	TN 141, to Alexandria
252mm	**parking area/truck sta both lanes, , litter barrels**
245	Linwood Rd
239	US 70, Lebanon, **N** RaceWay/dsl, Shell $General, **S** Phillips 66/Uncle Pete's/dsl/scales Jalisco Mexican
238	US 231, Lebanon, **N** Exxon, Mapco/dsl, Murphy Expess/dsl, Shell/dsl Applebee's, Arby's, Chick-fil-A, Cici's Pizza, Cracker Barrel, Demo's Steaks, El Molino Mexican, Hardee's, Jack-in-the-Box, KFC, Logan's Roadhouse, Los Compadres, McDonald's, Panda Express, Pizza Hut, Ryan's, Shoney's, Starbucks, Subway, Sunset Rest., Taco Bell, Waffle House, Wendy's, White Castle, Whitt's BBQ, Zaxby's Days Inn, EconoLodge, Executive Inn, Holiday Inn Express, Quality Inn, Ramada H, $Tree, Aldi Foods, AT&T, Discount Tire, Lowe's, to Bledsoe SP (23mi),

LEBANON

TN

INTERSTATE 40 Cont'd

238 Continued
Verizon, Walgreens, Walmart/Subway, S Citgo/Pizza Inn/Quiznos/dsl, LNG, Pilot/Subway/DQ/dsl/scales/24hr, Shell/dsl, Speedway/dsl/e85 O'Charley's, Sonic Comfort Suites, Knights Inn, La Quinta, Travel Inn Family RV Ctr, Lebanon Outlets/famous brands, Shady Acres Camping, Timberline Campground, to Cedars of Lebanon SP

236 S Hartmann Dr, N Mapco/dsl, Shell/dsl Chili's, Outback Steaks, Subway Fairfield Inn, Hampton Inn H, Buick/Chevrolet/GMC, Home Depot, Rose Tire

235 TN 840 W, to Murfreesboro

232 TN 109, to Gallatin, N Mapco/Quiznos/dsl, Shell/McDonald's/dsl/24hr, Speedway/dsl, Thornton's/dsl Bellacino's Pizza, Coach's Grill, Sonic, Subway, Waffle House, Wendy's Sleep Inn, Woodspring Suites, S KOA (3mi)

228mm truck sta, wb only

226mm truck sta

229b a Beckwith Rd

226 TN 171, Mt Juliet Rd, N BP/McDonald's/dsl, Exxon/dsl, Murphy Express/dsl, Shell/dsl Arby's, Capt D's, Cheddars, Don Pancho Mexican, Far East Buffet, Five Guys, Longhorn Steaks, Subway Comfort Suites $Tree, Aldi Foods, Firestone/auto, Lowe's, NTB, URGENT CARE, Walmart, S Mapco/Quiznos/dsl Blue Coast Burrito, Bonfire Japanese Steaks, Buffalo Wild Wings, Chick-fil-A, ChuckECheese, Cori's Dog House, Cracker Barrel, Firehouse Subs, Fulin's Asian, Jonathan's, Logan's Roadhouse, Marble Slab, Martin's BBQ, McDonald's, Mi Casa Mexican, NY Pizza, O'Charley's, Olive Garden, Panera Bread, Penn Sta Subs, Pizza Hut, Red Lobster, Red Robin, Salsarita's Cantina, Sonic, Steak'n Shake, Taco Bell, Taziki's Cafe, Waffle House, Wasabi Steaks, Wendy's, Which Wich?, Zaxby's Hampton Inn, Holiday Inn Express, Quality Inn AT&T, Belk, Best Buy, Books-A-Million, Dick's, Discount Tire, Ford, GNC, JC Penney, JoAnn Fabrics, Kroger/dsl, Old Navy, Petsmart, Publix, Ross, Staples, Target, Tire Discounters, TJ Maxx, to Long Hunter SP, Verizon, vet, Walgreens

NASHVILLE

221 TN 45 N, Old Hickory Blvd, to The Hermitage, **0-2 mi** N BP, Delta/dsl, Exxon, RaceWay/dsl Applebee's, Baskin-Robbins/Dunkin Donuts, Buffalo Wild Wings, Burger King, Chick-fil-A, Chili's, Cinco de Mayo, Domino's, DQ, Famous Dave's, Fazoli's, Firehouse Subs, Golden Corral, Hardee's, IHOP, Jack-in-the-Box, Jets Pizza, Las Palmas Mexican, O'Charley's, Outback Steaks, Panera Bread, Penn Sta Subs, Pizza Hut, Qdoba Mexican, Starbucks, Steak'n Shake, Subway, Taziki's Cafe, Waffle House Best Value Inn, Suburban Lodge, Super 8, Vista Inn H, Home Depot, Kroger, Lowe's, PetCo, Staples, Verizon, Walgreens, S Kwik Sak/dsl, Marathon/dsl, Phillips 66/White Castle, Shell/McDonald's

219 Stewart's Ferry Pike, N Mapco/dsl, S Mapco/Subway/dsl, Shell/dsl, Thornton's/dsl China King, Cracker Barrel, La Hacienda Mexican, Sal's Pizza, Subway, Waffle House Comfort Suites, Country Inn&Suites, Days Inn, EconoLodge, Family Inn, Motel 6, Sleep Inn $General, Food Lion, Fred's, vet

216 (216 c from eb)TN 255, Donaldson Pk, N BP/dsl, Mapco, RaceWay/dsl, Shell/dsl Arby's, Backyard Burger, Bar-B-Cutie, Darfon's, Jalisco Mexican, KFC, McDonald's, Panera Bread, Ruby Tuesday, Shoney's, Sonic, Subway, Taco Bell, Waffle House, Wendy's BNA Inn, Country Inn&Suites, Drury Inn, Hampton Inn, Holiday Inn Express, Hyatt Place, La Quinta, Radisson, Red Roof Inn, Sheraton, SpringHill Suites, Super 8 Advance Parts, USPO, Walgreens, S

216b a (from eb), S Nashville Intn'l Airport

215b a TN 155, Briley Pkwy, to Opryland, N **on Elm Hill** Citgo, Mapco Jack-in-the-Box, Waffle House Alexis Inn, Baymont Inn, Club Hotel, Comfort Suites, Courtyard, Doubletree, Extended Stay, Hilton Garden, Holiday Inn, Homewood Suites, La Quinta, Marriott, Nashville Inn, Quality Inn, Residence Inn, TownePlace Suites URGENT CARE, S Phillips 66/dsl Dunkin Donuts, Mazatlan Mexican, Panda House, Subway Hamilton Inn, Hotel Preston

213 US 41 (from wb no return), to Spence Lane, N CNG Kenworth, S Phillips 66/dsl, Shell Waffle House Best Western, Days Inn, Holiday Inn Express, Rodeway Inn, Super 8 same as 212

213b I-24 W

213a I-24 E/I-440, E to Chattanooga

212 Fessler's Lane (from eb, no return), N Freightliner, Harley-Davidson, S BP/dsl, Mapco/dsl, Shell/Dunkin Donuts, SpeedCo/dsl/e85 Burger King, McDonald's, Sonic, Wendy's Scottish Inn Chevrolet, NAPA, same as 213

211mm Cumberland River

211b I-24 W

211a I-24E, I-40 W

210c US 31 S, US 41A, 2nd Ave, 4th Ave, N Hilton, Renaissance Hotel, Sheraton, S museum

210b a I-65 S, to Birmingham

209b a US 70 S, Charlotte Ave, Nashville, N Exxon McDonald's Sheraton Conv Ctr, Country Music Hall of Fame, Firestone, Mazda, S Exxon Burger King, Jack Cawthon's BBQ, Krystal, Sonic, Subway, White Castle Comfort Inn, Hilton Garden Buick/GMC, Hyundai, Toyota, URGENT CARE, Walgreens

208b a I-65, N to Louisville

207 28th Ave, Jefferson St, Nashville, N Subway, Wendy's Family$, to TN St U, S H

206 I-440 E, to Knoxville

205 46th Ave, W Nashville, S Shell/dsl M L Rose Burgers, McDonald's USPO

204 TN 155, Briley Pkwy, S BP/dsl Burger King, China Buffet, Church's/White Castle, Cinco De Mayo, Domino's, Hattie B's Chicken, Jack-in-the-Box, KFC, Las Palmas, Papa John's, Shoney's, Subway, Waffle House, Wendell Smith's Rest., White Castle, Whitt's BBQ Best Western, Comfort Inn, Days Inn, Holiday Inn Express CVS Drug, Family$, Firestone/auto, Kroger/gas, O'Reilly Parts, PepBoys, Sav-a-lot Foods, Walgreens

201b a US 70, Charlotte Pike, N Exxon, Shell/dsl, Thornton's/dsl Bojangles, Cracker Barrel, El Sombrero, Jim 'N Nick's BBQ, Krystal, Little Caesar's, Waffle House, Wayback Burger, Wendy's Super 8 GNC, Kwik Kar, Lowe's Whse, vet, Walmart/Subway, S BP, Delta Express/dsl Arby's, Blue Coast Burrito, Buffalo Wild Wings, Chick-fil-A, Firehouse Subs, IHOP, Logan's Roadhouse, McDonald's, Pizza Hut, Red Robin, Taco Bell $Tree, AT&T, Best Buy, Big Lots, Books-A-Million, Costco/gas, Dick's, Firestone/auto, GNC, Marshall's, Old Navy, PetsMart, Publix, Ross, Target, Uhaul, URGENT CARE, Verizon, World Mkt

199 rd 251, Old Hickory Blvd, N Shell/dsl $General, S BP, Mapco/dsl Sonic, Subway

196 US 70, to Bellevue, Newsom Sta, N Mapco/dsl Shoney's, S BP, Mapco/dsl, Shell/dsl Arby's, Asihi Asian, Baskin Robbins, El Agavero, Jonathan's Grill, O'Charley's, Pizza Hut, Sir Pizza, Sonic, Subway, Taco Bell, Waffle House, Wendy's

TN

INTERSTATE 40 Cont'd

Exit	Services
196	Continued Hampton Inn, Microtel $Tree, AutoZone, Firestone/auto, Home Depot, Michael's, PetCo, Publix, Staples, USPO, Verizon, Walgreens
195mm	Harpeth River
192	McCrory Lane, to Pegram, N Eddie's Mkt (1mi), 4 mi S Loveless Cafe Natchez Trace Pkwy
190mm	Harpeth River
188mm	Harpeth River
188	rd 249, Kingston Springs, N BP, Mapco/Quiznos/dsl, Shell/Arby's/dsl El Jardin Mexican, McDonald's/playplace, Sonic, Subway Best Western, Mid-Town Inn, Relax Inn USPO, S Petro/BP/Quick Skillet/dsl/scales/showers/24hr/@ vet
182	TN 96, to Dickson, Fairview, N BP/dsl Fairview Inn M Bell SP (16mi), S FLYING J/Denny's/dsl/LP/scales/24hr, Citgo/Backyard Burger/Dunkin Donuts/dsl Deerfield Inn
176	I-840
172	TN 46, to Dickson, N Marathon/dsl, Pilot/Wendy's/dsl/scales/24hr, Shell/Dunkin Donuts/Taco Bell/dsl Arby's, Bojangle's, Camino Real, Cracker Barrel, Hardee's, Logan's Roadhouse, McDonald's, Ruby Tuesday, Waffle House Best Western, Comfort Inn, EconoLodge, Fairfield Inn, Hampton Inn, Motel 6, Rodeway Inn, South-Aire Inn, Super 8 H, $General, auto repair, Chappell's Foods, Chevrolet/Buick/GMC, Dickson RV Park, Ford, Nissan, to M Bell SP, truck repair, S Marathon/dsl, Shell/dsl Colton's Steaks, O'Charley's, Sonic Days Inn, Holiday Inn Express, Quality Inn
170	**both lanes, full facilities, litter barrels, petwalk, vending**
166mm	Piney River
163	rd 48, to Dickson, N Loves/McDonald's/Subway/dsl/scales/24hr, Phillips 66/dsl tire repair, S Shell Pinewood Camping (7mi), Tanbark Camping
152	rd 230, Bucksnort, N Sunoco/dsl Rodeway Inn
149mm	Duck River
148	rd 50, Barren Hollow Rd, to Turney Center
143	TN 13, to Linden, Waverly, N Pilot/Arby's/dsl/scales/24hr, Shell Jen's Rest, Log Cabin Rest., Loretta Lynn's Kitchen, McDonald's, Rochelle's BBQ Days Inn, Holiday Inn Express, Knights Inn, Quality Inn KOA/LP, S Speedway/dsl Scottish Inn
141mm	Buffalo River
137	Cuba Landing, N TN River RV Park, S Cuba Landing Rest./gas
133mm	Tennessee River
133	rd 191, Birdsong Rd, 9 mi N Good Sam RV Park, Songbird RV Resort/marina
131mm	**both lanes, full facilities, litter barrels, petwalk, vending**
126	US 641, TN 69, to Camden, N Marathon/Subway/dsl, Shell/North 40/dsl Burger Barn $ General, Paris Landing SP, tire/truck repair, to NB Forrest SP, truck wash, S Marathon/dsl, Shell/dsl Days Inn H, Mouse-tail Landing SP (24mi)
116	rd 114, S RV camping, to Natchez Trace SP
110mm	Big Sandy River
108	TN 22, to Lexington, Parkers Crossroads, N Marathon /dsl/24hr, Phillips 66/dsl, Shell/McDonald's/dsl DQ, Smarter's Rest, Subway Knights Inn city park, USPO, S Exxon Becky's Kitchen, Patty's Rest. Best Value Inn H, $ General, Parkers Crossroads Bfd Visitors Ctr, to Shiloh NMP (51mi)

DICKSON

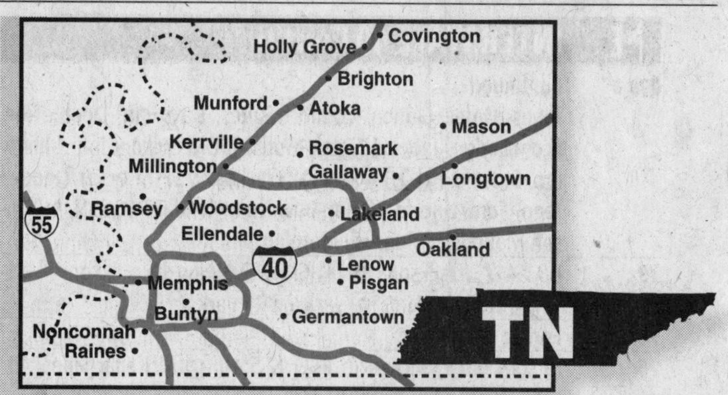

Exit	Services
103mm	**parking area/truck sta eb, litter barrels**
102mm	**parking area/truck sta wb, litter barrels**
101	rd 104, N 101 TP/Real Food/dsl/tires/24hr golf (3mi)
93	rd 152, Law Rd, N Phillips 66/deli/dsl/24hr, S Shell/dsl
87	US 70, US 412, Jackson, N Gulf/dsl, Mapco/Deli/dsl/e85, S Loves/Hardee's/dsl/scales/24hr, Skyline Express/dsl, Speedway/dsl/e85
85	Christmasville Rd, to Jackson, N Exxon/dsl, Pilot/Denny's/dsl/scales/24hr, Speedway/dsl Comfort Inn $General, S Shell/Pizza Pro/dsl Burger King, Jack's, Jet's Pizza, Jiang Jun Chinese, Lenny's Subs, Los Portales, McDonald's, Reggi's BBQ, Sonic, Sparky's, Subway, Taco Bell, Waffle House Holiday Inn Express $Tree, Food Giant
83	Campbell st, N Shell/Old Madina Mkt/dsl Residence Inn, S Courtyard, Hampton Inn
82b a	US 45, Jackson, N Dodge's/dsl, Marathon/dsl Cracker Barrel Best Value Inn, Knights Inn Batteries+Bulbs, Smallwoods RV Ctr (4mi), S Exxon, Hucks/dsl Baskin-Robbins, Burger King, Catfish Galley, ChuckeCheese, DQ, KFC, Krystal, Little Caesar's, LJ Silver, Los Portales Mexican, McDonald's/playplace, Papa John's, Pizza Hut, Popeye's, Sakura Japanese, Sonic, Starbucks, Subway, Taco Bell, Tulum Mexican, Waffle House, Wendy's Executive Inn, La Quinta, Ramada Ltd, Scottish Inn, Travellers Motel $General, $Tree, Advance Parts, AT&T, AutoZone, Belk, BigLots, Firestone/auto, Fred's, Goodyear/auto, JC Penney, Kroger/dsl, Macy's, O'Reilly Parts, Office Depot, vet
80b a	US 45 Byp, Jackson, 0-2 mi N Exxon, Shell/dsl Arby's, Asahi Japanese, Backyard Burger, Baskin-Robbins, Buffalo Wild Wings, Casa Adobe, Cheddar's, Chick-fil-A, Chili's, Cook-Out, Don Pancho, DQ, Dunkin Donuts, Fazoli's, Firehouse Subs, Five Guys, Flat Iron Grill, Fujiyama Japanese, Genghis Grill, HoneyBaked Ham, IHOP, Jason's Deli, Jersey Mike's, Jimmy John's, Lenny's Subs, Longhorn Steaks, Maggie Moo's, Marco's Pizza, McAlisters Deli, Moe's SW Grill, Olive Garden, Outback Steaks, Panda Express, Panera Bread, Perkins, Popeye's, Red Lobster, Red Robin, Snappy Tomato, Sonic, Starbucks, Steak'n Shake, Subway, TGIFriday's, Wendy's, Zaxby's Baymont Inn, Fairfield Inn, Hilton Garden, Howard Johnson $Tree, Aldi Foods, AT&T, AutoZone, Best Buy, Books-A-Million, Buick/Cadillac/Chevrolet/GMC, CarMax, Dick's, Firestone/auto, Gateway Tires/repair, Hobby Lobby, Home Depot, JoAnn Fabrics, Kia, Kohl's, Lowe's, Marshall's, Nissan, Old Navy, Petsmart, Ross, Sam's Club/gas, SteinMart, Target, TJ Maxx, Toyota, Verizon, Walmart/gas, S BP, G/dsl, Mobil/dsl, Shell/dsl Arby's, Asia Garden, Baudo's Rest., Burger King, Checkers, Heavenly Ham, Logan's Roadhouse, McDonald's, O'Charley's, Old Hickory Steakhouse, Old Town Spaghetti, Pizza Hut, Red Bones Grill, Subway, Taco Bell, Waffle House Best Western, Casey

JACKSON

TN

INTERSTATE 40 Cont'd

80b a Continued
Jones Motel, Clarion, Comfort Suites, Days Inn, DoubleTree, EconoLodge, Jackson Hotel, Motel 6, Old Hickory Inn, Quality Inn, Super 8 [other] [H], $General, Chickasaw SP, Chrysler/Dodge/Jeep, Ford/Lincoln, Harley-Davidson, Honda, Hyundai, to Pinson Mounds SP, Tuesday Morning

79 US 412, Jackson, **S** [gas] Citgo/Subway/dsl, Exxon, Valero [lodging] Rodeway Inn [other] Jackson RV Park

78mm Forked Deer River

76 rd 223, **S** [food] McKenzie BBQ (2.5mi) [other] McKellar-Sipes Airport, Whispering Pines RV Park

74 Lower Brownsville Rd

73mm **[Rs] both lanes, full [handicapped] facilities, info, litter barrels, petwalk, [phone], [picnic], vending**

68 rd 138, Providence Rd, **N** [gas] Marathon/dsl [lodging] Rodeway Inn, **S** [gas] Citgo/dsl, TA/Shell/Subway/dsl/scales/24hr/@ [other] Joy-O RV Park

66 US 70, to Brownsville, **N** [other] Ft Pillow SHP (51mi), **S** [gas] Exxon/dsl [lodging] Motel 6

60 rd 19, Mercer Rd

56 TN 76, to Brownsville, **N** [gas] Delta/dsl, Marathon [food] DQ, KFC, McDonald's/playplace, Pizza Hut, Taco Bell [lodging] Comfort Inn, Days Inn, Econolodge, Rodeway Inn, **S** [gas] Exxon/Breakfast Cove/dsl, Valero

55mm Hatchie River

52 TN 76, rd 179, Koko Rd, to Whiteville, **S** [gas] Koko Mkt

50mm **weigh sta both lanes**

47 TN 179, to Stanton, Dancyville

42 TN 222, to Stanton, **S** [gas] Exxon/dsl, [Pilot]/Chester's/Subway/dsl/scales/24hr [lodging] Deerfield Inn

35 TN 59, to Somerville, **S** [gas] Shelldsl/scales [food] Longtown Rest.

29.5mm Loosahatchie River

29 TN 196, Hickory Withe Rd

25 TN 205, Airline Rd, to Arlington, **N** [gas] Shell/dsl, **S** [gas] Exxon/Taco bell/dsl [other] vistor ctr

24 I-269, TN 385, rd 204, to Arlington, Millington, Collierville

20 Canada Rd, Lakeland, **N** [gas] Mobil/dsl, Shell/dsl [food] Cracker Barrel, Waffle House [lodging] Motel 6, Relax Inn, Super 8, **S** [gas] Exxon/Subway/dsl [other] fireworks, Memphis East Camping

18 US 64, to Bartlett, **N** [gas] Shell/Burger King [food] Abuelo's, Buffalo Wild Wings, El Porton Mexican, Firebird's Grill, Hooters, Longhorn Steaks, McAlister's Deli, O'Charley's, Olive Garden, Panera Bread, Steak'n Shake, TGI Friday's, TX Roadhouse [lodging] Best Western, Fairfield Inn, Holiday Inn, Home 2 Suites, La Quinta, SpringHill Suites [other] Buick/GMC, Firestone/auto, Lowe's, Pepboys, same as 16, Sam's Club/gas, Verizon, Walmart, **S** [gas] Circle K/dsl, Citgo, Marathon [food] Backyard Burger, Dunkin Donuts, KFC, Lenny's Subs, Papa John's, Papa Murphy's, Pizza Hut, Subway [other] AT&T, Family$, Kroger/dsl, Sprouts Mkt, Walgreens, Zaxby's

16b a TN 177, to Germantown, **N** [gas] BP/Circle K, Shell/Circle K [food] Abuelo's, Arby's, Bahama Breeze, Baskin Robbins, Buffalo Wild Wings, Burger King, Casa Mexicana, Cheesecake Factory, Chick-fil-A, Chili's, Colton's Steaks, Cook Out, Dave & Buster's, IHOP, J. Alexander's, Joe's Crabshack, Logan's Roadhouse, McDonald's/playplace, On-the-Border, Red Lobster, Red Sun Buffet, Redlands Grill, Starbucks, Subway, Taco Bell, TCBY, Tellini's Italian, Waffle House, Wendy's [lodging] Extended Stay America, Hampton Inn, Hyatt Place [other] [H], $Tree, Barnes&Noble, Best Buy, BigLots, CarMax, Chevrolet, Chrysler/Dodge/Jeep, Dillard's, Ford, Hobby Lobby, Home Depot, Honda, Hyundai,

MEMPHIS

16b a Continued
JC Penney, Macy's, Michael's, Nissan, Office Depot, Old Navy, Petsmart, Target, TJ Maxx, Walgreens, **0-2 mi S** [gas] BP/Circle K, Shell/Circle K [food] Abbay's Rest., Arby's, Backyard Burger, Burger King, Cheddar's, ChuckeCheese, Corky's BBQ, Genghis Grill, Honeybaked Ham, Howard's Donuts, Jason's Deli, Jimmy John's, Jim'n Nick's BBQ, La Hacienda, Lenny's Subs, Little Caesar's, Margarita's Mexican, McDonald's, Newk's Cafe, Osaka, Pei Wei Chinese, Pyros Pizza, Shogun Japanese, Subway, Waffle House, Wendy's [lodging] Comfort Suites, Country Inn & Suites, Hilton Garden, Microtel, Quality Suites [other] Aldi Foods, AT&T, AutoZone, Costco/gas, Dick's, GNC, Gordman's, Kohl's, Kroger/gas, Marshall's, Rite Aid, Ross, Steinmart, Toyota, Tuesday Morning, URGENT CARE, Verizon, vet

15b a Appling Rd, **N** [gas] BP/Circle K/dsl, Shell/dsl [other] [H], **S** [gas] Marathon/dsl [food] Subway [other] Family $

14 Whitten Rd, **N** [gas] Mapco, Shell/Burger King, Valero/dsl, Walmart/dsl [food] Hardee's, McDonald's, Sidecar Café, Taco Bell [other] Firestone/auto, Harley-Davidson, Walmart, **S** [gas] BP/Circle K, Shell/Backyard Burger/dsl [food] Dunkin Donuts, Subway, Supreme Hot Wings [lodging] Candlewood Suites [other] Family$, Walgreens

12 Sycamore View Rd, **N** [gas] Citgo/dsl, Murphy Express/dsl, Shell/dsl [food] Capt D's, Church's, Cracker Barrel, IHOP, Krystal, McDonald's, Ruby Tuesday, Shoney's, Sonic, Starbucks, Taco Bell, Waffle House [lodging] Baymont Inn, Best Value Inn, Comfort Inn, Extended Stay America, GardenTree Hotel, Motel 6, Red Roof Inn [other] $General, AutoZone, Family$, Walgreens, **S** [gas] BP/Circle K/dsl, Exxon, Mapco [food] Beijing Chinese, Burger King, Dos Amigos, Pizza Hut, Popeye's, Subway, Tops BBQ, Wendy's [lodging] Knights Inn, Budgetel, Days Inn, Econolodge, Fairfield Inn, La Quinta, Memphis Inn, Quality Inn, Rodeway Inn [other] Bass Pro Shops

10.5mm Wolf River

10b a (from wb)I-240 W around Memphis, I-40 E to Nashville

12c (from eb)I-240 W, to Jackson, I-40 E to Nashville

12b Sam Cooper Blvd (from eb)

12a US 64/70/79, Summer Ave, **N** [gas] Mapco/dsl, Marathon/dsl [food] Asian Palace, Waffle House [lodging] Welcome Inn [other] U-Haul, **S** [gas] Exxon [food] McDonald's, Subway [other] $Tree, Firestone/auto, Fred's

10 TN 204, Covington Pike, **N** [gas] BP/Circle K [food] McDonald's, Wendy's [other] Audi/VW, Buick/GMC, Chevrolet, Chrysler/Dodge/Jeep/Fiat, Honda, Hyundai, Kia, Mazda, Nissan, Sam's Club, Subaru, SuperLo Food

8b a TN 14, Jackson Ave, **N** [gas] Citgo/dsl [lodging] Motel 6, Sleep Inn [other] Raleigh Tire, **S** [gas] Citgo/dsl, Valero [other] AutoZone, Family$, O'Reilly Parts, repair

6 Warford Rd

5 Hollywood St, **N** [gas] Marathon, Valero/dsl [food] Burger King, Popeye's [other] Family$, **S** [other] Memphis Zoo

3 Watkins St, **N** [gas] Highway/dsl, Jubilee/dsl, Marathon [other] Family$, U-Haul

2a rd 300, to US 51 N, Millington, **N** [other] Meeman-Shelby SP

2 Smith Ave, Chelsea Ave, **S** [gas] Valero

1e I-240 E

1d c b US 51, Danny Thomas Blvd, **N** [other] Ronald McDonald House, St Jude Research Ctr

1a 2nd St (from wb), downtown, **S** [lodging] Crowne Plaza, Holiday Inn, Sheraton [other] Conv Ctr

1 Riverside Dr, Front St (from eb), Memphis, **S** [lodging] Comfort Inn, Courtyard, Sleep Inn [other] Conv Ctr, Riverfront, Visitors Ctr

0mm Tennessee/Arkansas state line, Mississippi River

TN

INTERSTATE 55

MEMPHIS

Exit#	Services
13mm	Tennessee/Arkansas state line, Mississippi River
12c	Delaware St, Memphis, W Super 8
12b	Riverside Dr, E TN Welcome Ctr, downtown Memphis
12a	E Crump Blvd (from nb), E Exxon Capt D's, KFC, LJ Silver, Taco Bell Family$
11	McLemore Ave, Presidents Island, industrial area
10	S Parkway, 1/2 mi E Marathon/dsl
9	Mallory Ave, industrial area
8	Horn Lake Rd (from sb)
7	US 61, 3rd St, E Exxon, Shell Church's, Interstate BBQ, McDonald's $Tree, AutoZone, Family$, Kroger, NAPA, Roses, Save-A-Lot Foods, Walgreens, W MapCo, Marathon/Chester's/dsl KFC, McDonald's, Subway Rest Inn Fuller SP, Indian Museum
6b a	I-240
5b	US 51 S, Elvis Presley Blvd, to Graceland, **0-2 mi W on US 51** Citgo/dsl, Dodge's/dsl, Exxon, Marathon, Shell/dsl Baskin-Robbins, BJ's Wings, Burger King, Checker's, Exline Pizza, KFC, Krispy Kreme, Little Caesar's, McDonald's, Piccadilly's, Subway, Taco Bell American Inn, Days Inn, Guesthouse at Graceland, Heartbreak Hotel/RV Park, Memory Lane Inn H, $General, $Tree, Advance Parts, Aldi Foods, CVS, D&N RV Ctr, Family$, Memphis Visitors Ctr, Presley RV Park, to Graceland, Walgreens, Walgreens
5a	Brooks Rd, E BP, Exxon, Mapco/dsl Burger King, Papa John's, Popeye's Airport Inn, Best Value Inn, Kings Hotel, Motel 6 Freightliner, Peterbilt
2b a	TN 175, Shelby Dr, Whitehaven, E Citgo/Subway/dsl, Exxon, Phillips 66/dsl, Qmart/dsl Colonial Inn, W Exxon/dsl, Shell/dsl, Valero/dsl Burger King, Dixie Queen Burgers, IHOP, McDonald's, Popeye's $General, Family$, Kroger/gas, Save-a-Lot Foods, Toyota, U-Haul, Walgreens
0mm	Tennessee/Mississippi state line

INTERSTATE 65

Exit#	Services
121.5mm	Tennessee/Kentucky state line
121mm	**Welcome Ctr sb, full facilities, litter barrels, petwalk, vending**
120	**Highland Rd**
119mm	weigh/insp sta both lanes
117	TN 52, Portland, E Exxon/Godfather's/Quiznos/dsl, Shell/dsl/fireworks Comfort Suites H, Bledsoe Cr SP (20mi), W Shell/dsl Budget Host fireworks
116mm	Red River
113mm	Red River
112	TN 25, Cross Plains, E Shell/dsl/fireworks $General, antiques, Bledsoe Cr SP (20mi), W Mapco/Subway/dsl
108	TN 76, White House, E Murphy USA/dsl, Nervous Charlie's/dsl, Shell, Speedway/dsl A&W/KFC, Arby's, Bojangles, China Spring, Cracker Barrel, DQ, Dunkin Donuts, Hardee's, Little Caesar's, Los Agaves, McDonald's, Mr Wok, Papa Murphy's, Sonic, Subway, Taco Bell, Waffle House, Wendy's, Zaxby's Hampton Inn, Holiday Inn Express, Motel 6, Quality Inn Ace Hardware, AT&T, city park/playground, Kroger/gas, O'Reilly Parts, Rite Aid, USPO, Walgreens, Walmart/Subway, W Loves/IHOP/dsl/scales/24hr, Shell/dsl Days Inn
104	rd 257, Bethel Rd, W Shell/dsl Owl's Roost Camping

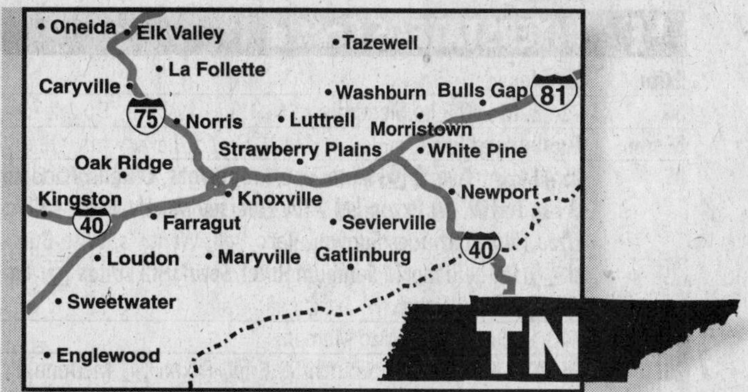

NASHVILLE

Exit#	Services
98	US 31 W, Millersville, E Shell/dsl Subway, Waffle House $General, auto repair, Grand Ol' RV Resort, W Marathon Economy Inn fireworks
97	rd 174, Long Hollow Pike, E BP/dsl, Exxon, Mapco Arby's, Capt D's, Cracker Barrel, Domino's, Happy Asian, Kabuto Japanese, KFC, McDonald's, Papa Murphy's, Quiznos, Shoney's, Subway, Taco Bell, Waffle House, Wendy's Baymont Inn, Courtyard, Days Inn, Hampton Inn, Quality Inn, Red Roof Inn, Somotel, TownePlace Suites Kroger/dsl, USPO, Walgreens, W Shell/dsl Buck's BBQ, DQ, Hardee's, Krystal, Poncho Villa Grill, Sonic La Quinta, Motel 6 Rite Aid, Walgreens
96	Rivergate Pky, E Phillips 66/dsl, Shell/dsl Checkers, Chicago Gyros, El Chico, Fuji Steaks, HoneyBaked Ham, Hooters, Las Palmas Mexican, McDonald's, O'Charley's, Pizza Hut, Subway, Wendy's Best Value Inn, Comfort Suites, Country Inn Suites, Magnuson Hotel, Rodeway Inn H, Dillard's, JC Penney, Macy's, W Marathon, Volunteer, E on Gallatin Arby's, Bar-B-Cutie, Burger King, Chick-fil-A, Chili's, ChuckeCheese, CiCi's, Cookout, Domino's, Fazoli's, IHOP, Jersey Mike's, Jets Pizza, Jimmy John's, Krispy Kreme, Las Fiestas, Logan's Roadhouse, Longhorn Steaks, Olive Garden, Outback Steaks, Panda Express, Panera Bread, Pollo Tropical, Popeye's, Rafferty's, Red Lobster, Ryan's, Sonic, Starbucks, Steak'n Shake, Taco Bell, TGI Friday's, Zaxby's $General, $Tree, $Tree, AT&T, Best Buy, Big Lots, Books-A-Million, Buick/GMC, CarMax, Chevrolet, Chrysler/Dodge/Jeep, CVS Drug, Dick's, Discount Tire, Firestone/auto, Goodyear/auto, Harley-Davidson, Hobby Lobby, Home Depot, Honda, Jo-Ann's Etc, Kia, Lowe's, Nissan, Office Depot, Old Navy, O'Reilly Parts, PepBoys, Petsmart, Target, TJ Maxx, Toyota, URGENT CARE, Verizon, VW, Walgreens, Walmart/Subway/gas
95	TN 386, Vietnam Veterans Blvd (from nb)
92	rd 45, Old Hickory Blvd, E to Old Hickory Dam, W H
90b	TN 155 E, Briley Pkwy, E to Opryland
90a	US 31W, US 41, Dickerson Pike, E Citgo/dsl, Delta/dsl, Exxon/dsl Arby's, Capt D's, Chicago Gyros, China King, Church's, Domino's, Jay's Rest., KFC, Little Caesar's, McDonald's, Pizza Hut, Subway, Taco Bell, Waffle House, Wendy's Days Inn, EconoLodge, Sleep Inn, Super 8 $General, Advance Parts, AutoZone, Family$, O'Reilly Parts, Walgreens, W Murphy USA/dsl $Tree, Lowe's, Walmart
88b a	I-24, W to Clarksville, E to Nashville
87b a	US 431, Trinity Lane, E BP, Loves/Subway/dsl/scales/24hr Church's/White Castle, Krystal, Sonic Cumberland Inn, Delux Inn Piggly Wiggly, W BP, Exxon, Shell/dsl, Victory/dsl Fat Mo's, Jack-in-the-Box, Jack's BBQ, McDonald's, Subway, Taco Bell, Waffle House Best Value Inn, Days Inn, EconoLodge, Halmark Inn, Howard Johnson, King's Inn, Magnuson Hotel, Ravin Hotel, Red Roof Inn, Regency Inn, Rodeway Inn $General, Family$

TN

INTERSTATE 65 Cont'd

Exits	Services
86	I-24 E, to I-40 E, to Memphis
86mm	Cumberland River
85	US 41A, 8th Ave, E [other] AutoZone, Kroger/gas, O'Reilly Parts, to st capitol, W [gas] Exxon [food] Arby's, Jersey Mike's, McDonald's, Pizza Hut, Starbucks, Subway, Taco Bell, Wendy's, Wise Burger [lodging] Fairfield Inn, Millennium Hotel, SpringHill Suites [other] Cadillac, Honda, Lexus
84b a	I-40, E to Knoxville, W to Memphis
209[I-40]	US 70, Charlotte Ave, Church St, E [gas] Exxon [food] McDonald's [lodging] Sheraton [other] Firestone, W [gas] Exxon, Shell/dsl [food] Burger King, Jack Cawthon's BBQ, Krystal, Sonic, Subway, White Castle [lodging] Comfort Inn, Hilton Garden [other] Hyundai, URGENT CARE, Walgreens
82b a	I-40, W to Memphis, E to Nashville
81	Wedgewood Ave, W [gas] BP, Exxon, Shell/dsl [food] Burger King, Subway [other] $General, U-Haul
80	I-440, to Memphis, Knoxville
79	Armory Dr, E on Powell [gas] Shell [food] Applebee's, Firehouse Subs, Jersey Mike's, Logan's Roadhouse, Panda Express, Panera Bread, Pizza Hut, Rafferty's, Subway, Taco Bell, Wendy's [other] BMW, CarMax, Home Depot, Michael's, Petsmart, Ross, Staples, TJ Maxx, Walmart
78b a	rd 255, Harding Place, E [gas] Mapco, Pure, Shell [food] Beijing Chinese, Cracker Barrel, Sub House, Waffle House [lodging] La Quinta, Red Roof Inn [other] CVS Drug, URGENT CARE
74	TN 254, Old Hickory Blvd, to Brentwood, E [food] Coldstone, Fulin's Asian, Longhorn Steaks, Panera Bread, Qdoba Mexican, Waffle House [lodging] Best Western, Holiday Inn Express, Hyatt Place, Sheraton [other] GNC, Target, W [gas] BP, Gulf, Shell/dsl, Twice Daily/dsl [food] Backyard Burger, Blaze Pizza, BurgerFi, Chick-fil-A, Chili's, Chipotle Mexican, Corky's BBQ, Dunkin' Donuts, FirstWatch, Five Guys, Jimmy John's, McAlister's Deli, McDonald's, Moe's SW Grill, Newk's Eatery, O'Charley's, Papa John's, Papa Murphy's, Pei Wei, Pizza Hut, Ruby Tuesday, Starbucks, Subway, Taco Bell, Taziki 's Cafe, Wendy's, Which Wich?, Zoe's [lodging] Baymont, Courtyard, Extended Stay (2), Extended Stay America, Hampton Inn, Hilton Garden, Hilton Suites, Mainstay Suites [other] Cadillac, CVS Drug, Firestone/auto, Fresh Mkt Foods, Kroger, Land Rover, Office Depot, PetCo, Publix, REI, TJ Maxx, Walgreens
71	TN 253, Concord Rd, to Brentwood
69	rd 441, Moores Lane, Galleria Blvd, E [gas] MapCo/dsl, Shell, Tesla EVC [food] Amerigo's Grill, Baskin-Robbins, Cheddar's, Dicky's BBQ, Dunkin Donuts, Fuji Japanese, Hungry Howie's, Mexicali Grill, Outback Steaks, Papa Murphy's, Shogun Japanese, Sonic, Sportsman's Grille, Starbucks [lodging] Hilton Garden, Holiday Inn, Holiday Inn Express, Hyatt Place [other] Acura/Lexus, Advance Parts, Christian Bros. Auto, CVS Drug, Home Depot/dsl, Michael's, Petsmart, Publix, vet, Walgreens, W [gas] BP, Shell/dsl [food] Backyard Burger, Buca Italian, Burger King, Capt D's, Cheesecake Factory, Chili's, Cracker Barrel, Famous Dave's, HoneyBaked Ham, Honeysuckle Grill, J Alexander's Rest., Krispy Kreme, Logan's Roadhouse, Macaroni Grill, McDonald's, Peking Palace, Pizza Hut/Taco Bell, Red Lobster, Schlotzsky's, Stoney River Steaks, Subway, Twin Peaks [lodging] Sleep Inn [other] $Tree, Barnes&Noble, Belk, Best Buy, Costco/gas, Dillard's, Discount Tire, Firestone/auto, JC Penney, Macy's, NTB, Old Navy, Ross, Target, UHaul
68b a	Cool Springs Blvd, E [food] Jersey Mike's, Noodles&Co, Swankys Tacos, Tupelo Honey Cafe [lodging] Courtyard, Embassy Suites, Marriott,

BRENTWOOD

Exits	Services
68b a	Continued Residence Inn, W [gas] Exxon, Shell [food] BoneFish Grill, Burger Up, Canton Buffet, Carrabba's, Chick-fil-A, Chipotle, Chucke-Cheese, Chuy's Mexican, Five Guys, Genghis Grill, Greek Cafe, J Christopher's, Jack-in-the-Box, Jason's Deli, Jersey Mike's, Jim 'N Nicks BBQ, Jimmy John's, Jonathan's Grille, Las Palmas, McAlister's Deli, McDonald's, Moe's SW Grill, Newk's Eatery, Old Chicago, Panda Express, Panera Bread, Papa John's, PF Chang's, Pie Five Pizza, Pizza Hut, Pollo Tropical, Saladworks, Sperry's, Starbucks, Subway, TGIFriday's, Wendy's, Which Wich, Wild Wing Cafe, Zoe's Kitchen [lodging] ALoft, Country Inn&Suites, Hampton Inn, TownePlace Suites [other] Acura, AT&T, Dick's, GNC, Harley-Davidson, Jo-Ann Fabrics, Kroger, Lowe's, Marshall's, Mazda, Office Depot, Sam's Club/gas, Staples, TJ Maxx, to Galleria Mall, Verizon, vet, Walgreens
67	McEwen Dr, E [lodging] Homewood Suites, W [food] Blue Coast Burrito, Brick Top's, Buffalo Wild Wings, Culver's, Firehouse Subs, Granite City, Jamba Juice, Little Caesar's, Marco's Pizza, Pei Wei, Sonic, Subway, Tazikis Mediterranean Cafe [lodging] Drury Inn [other] CarMax, CVS, Kohl's, Petco, Toyota, Walmart, Whole Food Mkt
65	TN 96, to Murfreesboro, Franklin, E [gas] Mapco, Shell/Krystal [food] Cracker Barrel, Sonic, Steak'n Shake [lodging] Best Value Inn, Comfort Inn, Days Inn, La Quinta, Ramada Inn [other] auto repair, Baymont Inn, Buick/GMC, Chevrolet, Honda, Kia, O'Reilly Parts, Subaru, URGENT CARE, Volvo, Walgreens, W [gas] BP/dsl, Shell, Shell/dsl [food] Arby's, Backyard Burger, Bar-B-Cutie, Bleachers Sports Grill, El Agave Mexican, Franklin Chophouse, Franklin Chophouse, Guacamole Mexican, Hardee's, IHOP, Jersey Mike's, KFC, La Terraza Mexican, McDonald's, Nashville Pizza, O'Charley's, Pancho's Mexican, Papa John's, Shoney's, Starbucks, Subway, Taco Bell, Waffle House, Wendy's, Whitts BBQ, Zaxby's [lodging] Best Western, Best Western, Quality Inn [other] $General, $Tree, Aldi Foods, AT&T, BigLots, Chrysler/Dodge/Jeep, Discount Tire, Fiat, Ford/Lincoln, Hobby Lobby, Home Depot, Kroger/dsl, Publix/gas, Rite Aid, Sprouts Mkt, SteinMart, to Confederate Cem at Franklin, Tuesday Morning, Verizon, vet, Walgreens
64mm	Harpeth River
61	TN 248, Peytonsville Rd, to Spring Hill, E [gas] TA/BP/Country Pride/dsl/scales/24hr/@, W [gas] Mapco, Shell/dsl [lodging] Goose Creek Inn
59b a	I-840, Memphis, Knoxville
58mm	W Harpeth River
53	TN 396, Saturn Pkwy, Spring Hill, to TN Scenic Pkwy, Columbia
48mm	**truck insp/weigh sta nb**
46	US 412, TN 99, to Columbia, Chapel Hill, E [gas] Loves/Arbys/dsl/scales/24hr, Marathon/dsl [lodging] Sleep Inn [other] Harley-Davidson, Henry Horton SP, W [gas] Citgo/Subway/dsl, Exxon, Shell, Stan's/Country Store [food] Burger King, Cracker Barrel, McDonald's, Waffle House [lodging] Best Value Inn, Comfort Inn, Comfort Suites, Fairfield Inn, Hampton Inn, Holiday Inn Express, Super 8 [other] [H]
40.5mm	Duck River
37	TN 50, to Columbia, Lewisburg, E [other] [H], TN Walking Horse HQ, W [gas] BP/dsl [other] to Polk Home
32	rd 373, to Lewisburg, Mooresville, E [gas] BP/dsl
27	rd 129, to Lynnville, Cornersville, E [other] Texas T Camping
25mm	**parking area sb**
24mm	**parking area nb**
22	US 31A, to Pulaski, E [gas] Tennesseean Trkstp/Exxon/Pop's BBQ/dsl/scales/24hr/@ [food] McDonald's, Subway [lodging] EconoLodge, W [gas] Pilot/dsl/scales/24hr, Shell/dsl

FRANKLIN

INTERSTATE 65 Cont'd

Exits	Services
14	US 64, to Pulaski, E [gas] Exxon/dsl, Shell/dsl [food] Sarge's Shack Rest. [lodging] Motel 6 [other] to Jack Daniels Distillery (30mi)
6	rd 273, Bryson, E [gas] Shell/rest./dsl/repair [lodging] Best Value Inn [other] dsl repair, W [gas] Marathon/dsl (2mi)
5mm	**weigh sta nb**
4mm	Elk River
3mm	**Welcome Ctr nb, full [handicapped] facilities, info, litter barrels, petwalk, [phone], [picnic]**
1	US 31, rd 7, Ardmore, E [gas] Chevron/dsl, Shell, Victory/Huddle House/dsl [food] $General, Burger King, El Olmeca Mexican, Hardee's, KFC/Taco Bell, McDonald's, Sonic, Subway, Whitts BBQ [other] $General Mkt, $Tree, Daly Tire, O'Reilly Parts
0mm	Tennessee/Alabama state line

INTERSTATE 75

Exit#	Services
161.5mm	Tennessee/Kentucky state line
161mm	**Welcome Ctr sb, full [handicapped] facilities, litter barrels, petwalk, [phone], [picnic], vending**
160	US 25W, Jellico, E [gas] Sunoco/dsl, VP/dsl, W [gas] Exxon/Wendy's/dsl, Shell/Arby's/dsl [food] Hardee's, Heritage Pizza, McDonald's, Subway [lodging] Days Inn, Parkway Inn [other] [H], fireworks, to Indian Mtn SP
156	Rarity Mtn Rd
144	Stinking Creek Rd, 4 mi E [other] Ride Royal Blue Camping
141	TN 63, to Royal Blue, Huntsville, E [gas] Shell/dsl [food] El Rey Azteca, W [gas] Pilot/Subway/dsl/scales/24hr, TA/Shell/Popeye's/dsl [food] Hardee's [lodging] Comfort Inn [other] fireworks, repair/truckwash, to Big South Fork NRA
134	US 25W, TN 63, Caryville, E [gas] Shell [food] Takumi Japanese, Waffle House [lodging] Hampton Inn, Holiday Inn Express, Red Roof Inn, Super 8 [other] [H], $General, Cumberland Gap NHP, to Cove Lake SP, W [gas] Exxon/dsl [food] Scotty's Hamburgers, Shoney's [lodging] Budget Host [other] USPO
129	US 25W S, Lake City, W [gas] BP/dsl, Marathon/Sonic/dsl, Pilot/dsl, Shell/dsl [food] Cracker Barrel, Domino's, Glenn's Pizza, KFC/Taco Bell, La Fiesta Mexican, McDonald's, Subway [lodging] Blue Haven Motel, Econolodge, Lamb's Inn/rest., Scottish Inn [other] $General, Family$, fireworks, same as 128
128	US 441, to Lake City, E [gas] Sunoco [other] Mtn Lake Marina Camping (4mi), W [gas] BP/dsl, Marathon, Weigel's/dsl [lodging] Blue Haven Motel [other] $General, Advance Parts, antique cars, Family$, same as 129, to Norris Dam SP
126mm	Clinch River
122	TN 61, Bethel, Norris, E [gas] Mobil/dsl, Wiegel's/dsl [food] Shoney's [other] antiques, KOA, Museum of Appalachia, Toyota, W [gas] BP/dsl, Exxon/Burger King/Subway/dsl, Git'n Go/dsl, Phillips 66/dsl, Shell/Baskin-Robbins [food] Arby's, Bojangles, Firehouse Subs, Golden Girls Rest., Gondolier Italian, Hardee's, Harrison's Grill, Krystal, LJ Silver, McDonald's, Petro's Chili, Waffle House, Wendy's, Zaxby's [lodging] Baymont Inn, Hampton Inn, Holiday Inn Express, Quality Inn, Red Roof Inn, Super 8 [other] AT&T, Big Pine Ridge SP, Ford, Verizon, Walgreens, Walmart/McDonald's
117	rd 170, Racoon Valley Rd, E [gas] BP/dsl/scales/24hr, W [lodging] Valley Inn [other] Racoon Valley RV Park, Volunteer RV Park
112	rd 131, Emory Rd, to Powell, E [gas] Pilot/DQ/Taco Bell/dsl, Shell/Buddy's BBQ/dsl [food] Arby's, Bruster's, Chick-fil-A, Cook-Out, Firehouse Subs, Five Guys, Jets Pizza, Krystal, McDonald's/

BETHEL

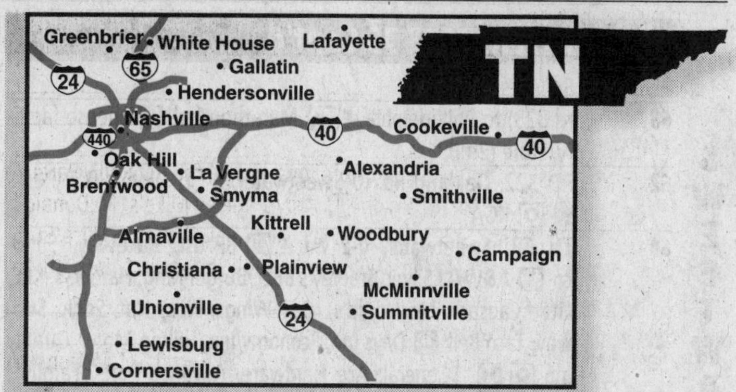

KNOXVILLE

Exit#	Services
112	Continued playplace, Petro's Cafe, Ruby Tuesday, Starbucks, Steak'n Shake, Subway, Taco Bell, Wendy's, Zaxby's [lodging] Comfort Inn, Holiday Inn Express, La Quinta [other] [H], CVS Drug, Ingles/gas, O'Reilly Parts, Rigg's Drug, Verizon, W [gas] Exxon/dsl, Shell/dsl, Weigel's/dsl [food] Aubrey's Rest., Hardee's, Shoney's, Waffle House [lodging] Super 8 [other] Kroger/dsl
110	Callahan Dr, E [gas] Weigel's/dsl [food] Archer's BBQ, Asian Cafe [lodging] Baymont Inn, Express Inn [other] Honda, W [lodging] Scottish Inn [other] Kia, Mack/Volvo
108	Merchants Dr, E [gas] Delta/dsl, Marathon/dsl, Mobil/dsl, Pilot/dsl [food] Applebee's, Cracker Barrel, El Chico, Hooters, Monterrey Mexican, O'Charley's, Pizza Hut, Puelo's Grill, Starbucks, Waffle House [lodging] Best Western, Clarion, Comfort Suites, Hampton Inn, Mainstay Suites, Quality Inn, Red Roof Inn, Sleep Inn [other] Ingles, Valvoline, W [gas] Exxon/dsl, Pilot/Domino's/dsl [food] Austin's Steaks, Burger King, Capt D's, Dunkin Donuts, IHOP, Mandarin House, McDonald's, Nixon's Deli, Outback Steaks, Red Lobster, Subway, Taco Bell [lodging] Best Value Inn, EconoLodge, Motel 6, Select Inn, Super 8 [other] CVS Drug, Walgreens
107	I-640 & I-75
3b[I-640]	US 25W, (from nb), W [other] Chevrolet, Ford, Nissan
1[I-640]	rd 62, Western Ave, E [food] Hardee's, Krystal [other] Advance Parts, Family$, O'Reilly Parts, W [gas] Exxon/dsl, Marathon/dsl, RaceWay/dsl [food] Central Park, Firehouse Subs, KFC, Little Caesars, LJ Silver, McDonald's, Panda Chinese, Shoney's, Subway, Taco Bell, Wendy's [other] CVS Drug, Kroger/dsl, Walgreens
I-75 and I-40 run together 17 mi. See I-40, exits 369 through 385.	
84[368]	I-40, W to Nashville, E to Knoxville
81	US 321, TN 95, to Lenoir City, E [gas] BP/Buddy's BBQ/TCBY/dsl, Exxon/Subway/dsl, Marathon/dsl, Mobil, Murphy USA/dsl, Shell/dsl, Weigel's/dsl [food] Arby's, Aubrey's Rest., Bojangles, Burger King, Capt D's, Chick-fil-A, Chili's, China Buffet, Cinco Amigos Mexican, Cracker Barrel, Domino's, Dunkin Donuts, Firehouse Subs, Gondolier Italian, Hardee's, KFC, McDonald's, Papa John's, Pizza Hut, Shoney's, Taco Bell, Tako Yaki Steaks, Waffle House, Wendy's, Zaxby's [lodging] Days Inn, Hampton Inn, Holiday Inn Express, King's Inn/rest. [other] [H], $General Mkt, $Tree, Advance Parts, AT&T, AutoZone, Big Lots, CVS Drug, Food City/gas, Ford, Ft Loudon Dam, GNC, Great Smokies NP, Home Depot, Ingles, Lazy Acres RV Park (7mi), O'Reilly Parts, Verizon, Walgreens, Walmart/Subway, W [gas] Citgo/dsl [food] Krystal, Ruby Tuesday [lodging] Comfort Inn, EconoLodge, Knights Inn [other] Crosseyed Cricket Camping (6mi), Matlock Tires/Repair
76	rd 324, Sugar Limb Rd, W [other] to TN Valley Winery
74mm	Tennessee River
72	TN 72, to Loudon, E [gas] BP/McDonald's, Exxon/Wendy's/dsl, Weigel's/dsl [food] Bojangles, Cabin Rest., KFC, Taco Bell [lodging] Country Inn&Suites, Inn of Loudon [other] to Ft Loudon SP, W [gas] Marathon [lodging] Best Value Inn [other] Express RV Park

TN

INTERSTATE 75 Cont'd

Exits	Services
68	rd 323, to Philadelphia, E Marathon/dsl cheese factory/store (2mi)
62	RD 322, Oakland Rd, to Sweetwater, E Dinner Bell Rest., W KOA
60	TN 68, Sweetwater, **0-2 mi** E BP/dsl, RaceWay, Sunoco A&W/LJ Silver, Bradley's BBQ, Burger King, Hardee's, KFC, Little Caesar's, McDonald's, Mexi Wings, Pizza Hut, Sonic, Subway, Taco Bell Days Inn, Economy Inn, Hilltop Motel, Quality Inn H, $General, Ace Hardware, Advance Parts, Family$, Ford/Lincoln, O'Reilly Parts, to Lost Sea Underground Lake, Verizon, Walgreens, W Kangaroo/dsl, Marathon Holiday Inn Express, Super 8 flea mkt, to Watts Bar Dam
56	rd 309, Niota, E Pilot/Wendy's/dsl/scales/24hr TN Country Camping, W repair
52	rd 305, Mt Verd Rd, to Athens, E Marathon/dsl (2mi) Subway (2mi) Overniter RV Park, W Athens Lodge
49	TN 30, to Athens, E Exxon, Kangaroo, Marathon, Mobil/dsl, Murphy USA/dsl Applebee's, Arby's, Buddy's BBQ, Burger King, Capt D's, China Wok, Dunkin Donuts, Firehouse Subs, Hardee's, KFC, Krystal, Little Caesar's, McDonald's, Mexi Wing, Ming Dynasty, Papa John's, Pizza Hut, Ruby Tuesday, Shoney's, Sonic, Subway, Subway, Taco Bell, Waffle House, Wendy's, Western Sizzlin, Zaxby's Days Inn, Hampton Inn, Holiday Inn Express, Homestead Inn, Motel 6, Scottish Inn, Super 8 H, $General, $Tree, Advance Parts, Athens I-75 Camping, Belk, BigLots, GNC, Russell Stover, Staples, to TN Wesleyan Coll, URGENT CARE, Verizon, Walgreens, Walmart/Subway, W Mobil/dsl, Speedway/dsl Cracker Barrel Best Value Inn, Comfort Inn
45mm	**both lanes, full facilities, litter barrels, petwalk, vending**
42	rd 39, Riceville Rd, E Citgo/dsl Relax Inn, Rice Inn (2mi)
36	rd 163, to Calhoun, E Hardee's (3mi) Hiwassee/Ocoee River SP
35mm	Hiwassee River
33	rd 308, to Charleston, E Marathon/dsl Hardee's, W Love's/McDonald's/Subway/dsl/scales/24hr
27	Paul Huff Pkwy, **1 mi** E Murphy USA, Shell/dsl Applebee's, Buffalo Wild Wings, Capt D's, Chili's, CiCi's, DQ, Fazoli's, Firehouse Subs, Five Guys, Golden Corral, IHOP, Little Caesar's, Longhorn Steaks, McDonald's, O'Charley's, Olive Garden, Outback Steaks, Panera Bread, Papa Murphy's, Pita Pit, Pizza Hut, Royal Buffet, Santa Fe Steaks, Six Happiness, Sonic, Starbucks, Steak'n Shake, Subway, Taco Bell Baymont Inn, Holiday Inn Express $Tree, Aldi Foods, auto repair/tires, AutoZone, Belk, Buick/Cadillac/GMC, CVS Drug, Discount Tire, Food Lion, Hobby Lobby, Home Depot, JC Penney, Lowe's, PetCo, Publix, Rite Aid, Staples, TJ Maxx, Verizon, Walgreens, Walmart, W Exxon/dsl, Orbit/dsl, Shell/Subway Denny's, Fulin's Asian, Hardee's, Honeybaked Ham, Shane's Ribshack, Stevi B's Pizza, Waffle House, Wendy's Clarion, Classic Suites, Hampton Inn, Quality Inn, Royal Inn, Super 8, Travelodge AT&T, Books-A-Million, Kohl's, Michael's, Ross, Target
25	TN 60, Cleveland, E Chevron/dsl, RaceWay/dsl, Shell/dsl, Sunoco/dsl Bojangles, Burger King, Checkers, Cracker Barrel, Dunkin Donuts, Hardee's, Las Margaritas, McDonald's, Old Fort Rest., Sonic, Waffle House, Wendy's, Zaxby's Colonial Inn, Days Inn, Douglas Inn, EconoLodge, Economy Inn, Fairfield
25	Continued Inn, Howard Johnson, Knights Inn, Travel Inn H, $General, Ace Hardware, BigLots, Cherokee Drug, NAPA, Rite Aid, to Lee Coll, Tuesday Morning, W Comfort Inn, La Quinta, Mtn View Inn, Wingate Inn
23mm	**truck/weigh sta nb**
20	US 64 byp, to Cleveland, **1-4 mi** E FuelMart Ford, Honda, Kia, W Exxon/dsl, Pilot/McDonald's/Subway/dsl/scales/24hr fireworks, KOA (1mi), Toyota
16mm	scenic view sb
13mm	**truck/weigh sta, litter barrels sb**
11	US 11 N, US 64 E, Ooltewah, E BP, Mapco, Murphy USA/dsl, RaceWay/dsl Arby's, Bojangles, Burger King, China Rose, Cracker Barrel, El Matador Mexican, Hardee's, Little Caesars, McDonald's, Pizza Hut, Sonic, Subway, Taco Bell, Wendy's, Western Sizzlin, Zaxby's Hampton Inn, Holiday Inn Express $General, Ace Hardware, BiLo, GNC, O'Reilly Parts, Verizon, Walgreens, Walmart/Subway, W BP/dsl, Shell/dsl Beef'o Brady's, Krystal, Waffle House Super 8 Publix, to Harrison Bay SP
9	TN 317, Apison Pk, Volkswagen Dr, E Shell
7b a	US 11, US 64, Lee Hwy, E Shell/dsl, W BP, Speedway/dsl City Cafe, Waffle House Airport Inn, Best Inn, Best Value Inn, Best Western, EconoLodge, Motel 6, Rodeway Inn, Woodspring Suites Denton's Repair, Harley-Davidson, Jaguar/Land Rover/Porsche/Infiniti
5	Shallowford Rd, E Arby's, CiCi's, Famous Dave's, Forbidden City Chinese, Imperial Garden, J. Alexanders, Jersey Mike's, Krystal, Logan's Roadhouse, Macaroni Grill, McAlister's Deli, McDonald's, Mellow Mushroom Pizza, Melting Pot, Outback Steaks, Panda Express, Ruth's Chris Steaks, Smokey Bones BBQ, Souper Salad, Starbucks, Steak'n Shake, Taco Bell, Zaxby's Courtyard, Embassy Suites, Quality Inn, Wingate Inn Best Buy, Firestone/auto, FreshMkt Foods, Hobby Lobby, Home Depot, Lowe's, Office Depot, Old Navy, Petco, Petsmart, SteinMart, Target, Walgreens, Walmart/Subway, World Mkt, W BP, Citgo/dsl, Exxon/dsl, Shell, Speedway/dsl Applebee's, Cracker Barrel, Fazoli's, Firebox Grill, Fuji Steaks, O'Charley's, Papa John's, Shoney's, Sonic, Subway, TX Roadhouse, Waffle House, Wendy's Comfort Inn, Country Inn&Suites, Days Inn, Fairfield Inn, Guesthouse Inn, Hampton Inn, Hilton Garden, Holiday Inn, Homewood Suites, Knights Inn, La Quinta, MainStay Suites, Red Roof Inn, Residence Inn, Sleep Inn, Staybridge Suites, Super 8, Travelodge H, Bi-Lo, CarMax, CVS Drug, Family$, Goodyear/auto, same as 4a, SaveALot, U of TN/Chatt
4a	(from nb) Hamilton Place Blvd, E Shell Abuelo's, Acropolis, Bar Louie Grill, Big River Grille, BoneFish Grill, Capt D's, Carrabba's, Cheddar's, Chick-fil-A, Chili's, Chop House, DQ, El Meson Mexican, Firebird's, Firehouse Subs, Five Guys, Fox&Hound Grille, Golden Corral, Honeybaked Ham, Jason's Deli, Kanpai of Tokyo, McDonald's, Moe's SW Grill, Olive Garden, Outback Steaks, Panera Bread, PF Chang's, Red Lobster, Red Robin, Salsarita's Mexican, Shogun Japanese, Starbucks, Sticky Fingers BBQ, Taziki's Cafe Hampton Inn, InTown Suites $Tree, AAA, AT&T, Barnes&Noble, Belk, Big Lots, Dick's, Dillard's, Earthfare, Firestone/auto, JC Penney, Jo-Ann, Kohl's, Marshall's, Michael's, Pepboys, Ross, same as 5, Staples, Target, TJ Maxx, Verizon, World Mkt
4	TN 153, Chickamauga Dam Rd,
3b a	TN 320, Brainerd Rd, E Baskin-Robbins, Subway, W BMW

SWEETWATER · ATHENS · CLEVELAND · CHATTANOOGA

INTERSTATE 75 Cont'd

Exits	Services
2	I-24 W, to I-59, to Chattanooga, Lookout Mtn
1.5mm	**Welcome Ctr nb, full [handicapped] facilities, litter barrels, petwalk, [phone], [picnic], vending**
1b a	US 41, Ringgold Rd, to Chattanooga, **E** [gas] BP, Texaco/dsl [food] Wendy's [lodging] Best Value Inn, Best Western, Comfort Inn, Motel 6 [other] Bass Pro Shops, Bi-Lo, Camping World RV Ctr/park, Family$, **W** [gas] Conoco/dsl, Mapco/Quiznos/dsl, Valero/dsl [food] A&W/LJ Silver, Arby's, Baskin-Robbins, Burger King, Cracker Barrel, Hardee's, Krystal, McDonald's, Popeyes, Porto-Fino Italian, Sonic, Subway, Taco Bell, Teriyaki House, Waffle House, Wally's Rest. [lodging] Fairfield Inn, Holiday Inn Express, Super 8, Superior Creek Lodge, Waverly Motel [other] $General, Advance Parts, AutoZone, Family$, O'Reilly Parts, Rite Aid, U-Haul, Walgreens
0mm	Tennessee/Georgia state line

INTERSTATE 81

KINGSPORT

Exit#	Services
75mm	Tennessee/Virginia state line, **Welcome Ctr sb, full [handicapped] facilities, info, litter barrels, petwalk, [phone], [picnic], vending**
74b a	US 11W, to Bristol, Kingsport, **E** [lodging] Fairfield Inn, Hampton Inn [other] [H], **W** [gas] Tesla EVC, Valero/dsl [food] Aubrey's Rest., Bojangle's, Brusco's Pizza, Chick-fil-A, Drake's Rest., Jersey Mike's, La Carreta, McDonald's, Moe's SW, Outback Steaks, Pal's Drive-Thru, Panda Express, Starbucks, Steak'n Shake, Zaxby's [other] Bass Pro Shops, Belk, CarMax, Dick's, GNC, Marshall's, Michael's, Old Navy, Verizon
69	TN 394, to Blountville, **E** [gas] BP/Subway/dsl [food] Arby's, Domino's [other] Advance Parts, Bristol Int Speedway, Lakeview RV Park (8mi), Shadrack Camping
66	rd 126, to Kingsport, Blountville, **W** [gas] Shell/dsl [food] McDonald's
63	rd 357, **E** [gas] BP/Krystal/dsl, Shell/Subway/dsl [food] Cracker Barrel, Wendy's [lodging] La Quinta, Sleep Inn [other] Hamricks, Tri-Cities Airport, **W** [gas] Citgo/dsl [lodging] Econolodge [other] dsl repair, KOA, Rocky Top Camping
60mm	Holston River
59	rd 36, to Johnson City, Kingsport, **E** [gas] Marathon/dsl [lodging] Super 8, **W** [gas] Exxon/dsl, Marathon, Shell/dsl, Sunoco [food] Arby's, Fisherman's Dock Rest., Hardee's, HotDog Hut, Jersey Mike's Subs, La Carreta Mexican, Little Caesar's, Little Caesar's, McDonald's, Moto Japanese, Pal's Drive-Thru, Perkins, Pizza Hut, Plum Tree Rest., Raffaele's Pizza, Sonic, Subway, Taco Bell, The Shack BBQ, Zachary's Steaks [lodging] Comfort Inn, Motel 6 [other] $General, Advance Parts, CVS Drug, Ingles/deli, Murphy's Automotive, O'Reilly Parts, to Warrior's Path SP, URGENT CARE, USPO, Verizon, Walgreens
57b a	I-26
56	Tri-Cities Crossing
50	TN 93, Fall Branch, **W** [other] auto auction, st patrol
44	Jearoldstown Rd, **E** [gas] Marathon
41mm	**[RS] sb, full [handicapped] facilities, litter barrels, petwalk, [phone], [picnic], vending**
38mm	**[RS] nb, full [handicapped] facilities, litter barrels, petwalk, [phone], [picnic], vending**
36	rd 172, to Baileyton, **E** [gas] Pilot/Subway/dsl/scales/24hr, **W** [gas] Marathon/dsl, Shell/Subway/dsl/24hr, TA/Country Pride/dsl/scales/24hr/@ [food] Pizza+ [lodging] 36 Motel [other] $General, Around Pond RV Park, Family$, KOA (2mi)
30	TN 70, to Greeneville, **E** [gas] Marathon/DQ/Stuckey's/dsl
23	US 11E, to Greeneville, **E** [gas] Marathon/Wendy's, Mobil/Subway/dsl [other] Crockett SP, to Andrew Johnson HS, Tri-Am RV Ctr,

Lancing
Clinton
75
Blaine
Oak Ridge
Dandridge
Knoxville
40
Rockwood
Midway
Loudon
Marysville
Ten Mile
Sweetwater
Decatur
Niota
75
Riceville
Cleveland
TN

23	Continued **W** [gas] Exxon/DQ/dsl, Phillips 66/dsl/rest./scales [food] McDonald's, Pizza+, Taco Bell [lodging] Quality Inn, Super 8 [other] Tony's Repair
21mm	**weigh sta sb**
15	rd 340, Fish Hatchery Rd
12	TN 160, to Morristown, **E** [gas] Phillips 66/dsl, **W** [gas] Gulf/dsl [lodging] Days Inn (6mi), Hampton Inn (12mi), Holiday Inn Express (5mi), Super 8 (5mi) [other] to Crockett Tavern HS
8	US 25E, to Morristown, **E** [food] Sonic (2mi), **W** [gas] Weigel's/dsl [food] Bojangle's, Cracker Barrel, Fastop/Subway/dsl, Hardee's, McDonald's [lodging] Best Western+, Hampton Inn, Parkway Inn, Super 8 [other] to Cumberland Gap NHP
4	rd 341, White Pine, **E** [gas] Pilot/McDonald's/dsl/scales/24hr [food] Subway, **W** [gas] Pilot/Dunkin Donuts/Wendy's/dsl/scales/24hr [food] Taco Bell [lodging] Econolodge [other] to Panther Cr SP
2.5mm	**[RS] sb, full [handicapped] facilities, litter barrels, petwalk, [phone], [picnic], vending**
1b a	I-40, E to Asheville, W to Knoxville. **I-81 begins/ends on I-40, exit 421.**

INTERSTATE 640 (Knoxville)

KNOXVILLE

Exit#	Services
9mm	**I-640 begins/ends on I-40, exit 393.**
8	Millertown Pike, Mall Rd N, **N** [gas] Exxon/DQ, Shell [food] Applebee's, Burger King, China Wok, Honeybaked Ham, KFC, Krystal, Mandarin Palace, McDonald's, Pizza Hut, Taco Bell, TX Roadhouse, Wendy's [other] $Tree, AT&T, Belk, Food City/dsl, Jo-Ann, Kohl's, Marshall's, Old Navy, Ross, Sam's Club/dsl, Target, Walmart, **S** [gas] Shell/dsl [food] Amigo's, Cracker Barrel, Little Caesar's, O'Charley's, Sonic [other] Home Depot, Lowe's Whse, PepBoys
6	US 441, to Broadway, **N** [gas] Citgo/dsl, Pilot/dsl [food] Arby's, Cancun Mexican, Chick-fil-A, Chop House, CiCi's, Firehouse Subs, Hardee's, Krispy Kreme, Lenny's Subs, LJ Silver, McDonald's, Panera Bread, Papa John's, Papa Murphy's, Penn Sta Subs, Ruby Tuesday, Sonic, Subway, Taco Bell [other] $General, Advance Parts, AutoZone, BigLots, CVS Drug, Firestone, Food City/gas, Kroger, O'Reilly Parts, repair/tires, Verizon, Walgreens, **S** [food] Bojangle's, Buddy's BBQ, Little Caesar's, Shoney's [other] $General, $Tree, Food City, Office Depot
3a	I-75 N to Lexington, I-275 S to Knoxville
3b	US 25W, Clinton Hwy, **N** [other] Chevrolet, Ford, Nissan, services on frontage rds
1	TN 62, Western Ave, **N** [gas] Exxon/dsl, Marathon/dsl, Raceway/dsl [food] Central Park, Firehouse Subs, KFC, Little Caesars, LJ Silver, McDonald's, Panda Chinese, Shoney's, Subway, Taco Bell, Wendy's [other] CVS Drug, Kroger/dsl, Walgreens, **S** [food] Hardee's, Krystal [other] Advance Parts, Family$, O'Reilly Parts

I-640 begins/ends on I-40, exit 385.

TN

TX

TEXAS

INTERSTATE 10

Exit# Services

ORANGE

880.5mm Texas/Louisiana state line, Sabine River

880 Sabine River Turnaround, N RV camping

879mm **Welcome Ctr wb, full facilities, litter barrels, petwalk, , vending**

878 US 90, Orange, N Gulf/dsl airboat rides, RV Park, S Western Store

877 TX 87, 16th St, Orange, N Exxon/dsl, Shamrock/dsl Little Caesar's, Pizza Hut, Subway Hampton Inn Ace Hardware, Market Basket/deli, S Get'n Go/dsl, Kwik Stop/dsl, Shell/dsl, Valero/dsl 2 Amigo's Mexican, Casa Ole, Church's, DQ, General Wok, Jack-in-the-Box, McDonald's, Popeye's, Sonic, Taco Bell $General, CVS Drug, Family$, Goodyear/auto, HEB Foods, Kroger/dsl, Modica Tires, O'Reilly Parts, Verizon, Walgreens

876 Adams Bayou, frontage rd, N Gary's Café, Señor Toro's Mexican, Taste of Orange Rest., Waffle House Best Price Motel, Best Texan Inn, Days Inn, EconoLodge, Executive Inn, Knights Inn, Motel 6 Toyota, S Chevron/dsl Holiday Inn Express same as 877

875 FM 3247, MLK Dr, N Exxon/dsl, S H, Chrysler/Dodge/Jeep

874 US 90, Womack Rd, to Orange, S H

873 TX 62, TX 73, to Bridge City, N FLYING J/Denny's/dsl/LP/scales/24hr, Exxon/dsl/24hr Studio 6 Blue Beacon, Oak Leaf RV Park, S Pilot/Subway/Wendy's/dsl/scales/24hr, Shell/Church's/dsl, Valero/dsl McDonald's, Sonic, Waffle House, Whataburger Best Western, Comfort Inn, La Quinta

872 N Mimosa Ln, Jackson Dr, from wb

870 FM 1136

869 FM 1442, to Bridge City, S Exxon/dsl

867 frontage rd (from eb)

865 Doty Rd (from wb), frontage rd

864 FM 1132, FM 1135, N Budget Inn TX Star RV Park

862 Lakeside St, Timberlane Dr, N Conoco

VIDOR

861 FM 105, Vidor, N Chevron/dsl, Citgo/dsl, Conoco/dsl, Valero/dsl Casa Ole, Domino's, DQ, Jack-in-the-Box, Little Caesars, McDonald's/playplace, Ming's Buffet, Novrosky's Burgers, Popeye's, Waffle House AutoZone, CVS, Mktbasket Foods, Modica Bros Tires, O'Reilly Parts, Verizon, Walgreens, Walmart, S Citgo/dsl, Exxon/dsl Burger King, Pizza Hut, Sonic, Subway, Taco Bell, Whataburger Best Western, Holiday Inn Express auto repair, Family$

860 Dewitt Rd, frontage rd, W Vidor, S Citgo, Exxon, Mobil/dsl Burger King, Pizza Hut, Sonic, Subway, Taco Bell, Whataburger Best Western, Holiday Inn Express Family$, repair

859 Bonner Turnaround (from eb), Asher Turnaround (from wb), N Boomtown RV Park, S Chevron/Spindletop/dsl/24hr

858 Rose City

856 Old Hwy 90 (from eb), Rose City

855b Magnolia St (from wb)

855a US 90 bus, to downtown, Port of Beaumont

BEAUMONT

854 ML King Pkwy, Beaumont, N Chevron/dsl, Valero/dsl Jack-in-the-Box, S Exxon/dsl, Shamrock/dsl McDonald's

853b 11th St, N Valero/dsl Cafe Del Rio, Red Lobster, Starving Marvin Grill, Waffle House Beaumont Lodge, Days Inn, Red Carpet Inn, Sleep Inn, Studio 6, Travel Inn MktBasket, S Chevron/dsl, Shamrock Checker's, Chula Vista

853b Continued
Mexican, Dunkin Donuts, Jack-in-the-Box, Luby's Oaks Lodge, Rodeway Inn H

853a US 69 N, to Lufkin

852 Harrison Ave, Calder Ave, Beaumont, N Shell/dsl, Valero/dsl Casa Ole Mexican, Casa Tapatia Mexican, Chili's, Frankie's Italian, Olive Garden, Saltgrass Steaks, Tony's BBQ, S Church's, McDonald's La Quinta, Scottish Inn H

851 US 90, College St, N Chevron/dsl, Exxon/dsl, Raceway/dsl Carrabba's, Chicken Express, Floyd's Cajun Cafe, Golden Corral, Hooters, Lupe Tortilla, Outback Steaks, Sartin's Seafood, Tokyo Japanese, Waffle House Howard Johnson, Quality Inn, Ramada, Red Roof Inn Advance Parts, AutoZone, Harley-Davidson, Indian Motorcycles, O'Reilly Parts, URGENT CARE, Verizon, Volvo Trucks, S Exxon/dsl, Mobil, Shell/dsl Catfish Seafood, China Hut, DQ, IHOP, Pizza Hut, Sonic, Taco Bell, Wendy's, Whataburger Best Value, Courtyard, Elegante Motel, Fairfield Inn, Regency Inn, Woodspring Suites H, $Tree, BMW, Chrysler/Dodge/Jeep, CVS Drug, Discount Tire, Firestone/auto, HEB Foods, Honda, Mercedes, Nissan, NTB, Office Depot, Sam's Club/gas, U-Haul, VW, Walgreens

850 same as 851, wb only

849 US 69 S, Washington Blvd, to Port Arthur,

848 Walden Rd, N Shell/dsl Pappadeaux Seafood, Sonic, Subway Comfort Suites, Holiday Inn/rest., La Quinta USPO, S Chevron/dsl, Petro/Iron Skillet/dsl/scales/24hr/@, Shell/dsl Carino's Italian, Cheddar's, Cracker Barrel, Jack-in-the-Box, Joe's Crabshack, Waffle House Candlewood Suites, Hampton Inn, Hilton Garden, Homewood Suites, Knights Inn, Residence Inn, Super 8 Blue Beacon

847 Brooks Rd (from wb), (845 from eb), S Gulf Coast RV Resort, Hidden Lake RV Park

845 TX 364

843 Smith Rd, N Loves/Arby's/Chester's/Godfather's/dsl/scales/24hr

838 FM 365, Fannett, N Alligator Park/Rest., Shell/Bar-H BBQ/gas T&T RV Park

837.5mm no services

833 Hamshire Rd

WINNIE

829 FM 1663, Winnie, N Exxon/dsl, Shell/dsl/24hr, Texaco/Burger King/dsl McDonald's, Taco Bell, Whataburger/24hr Days Inn RV Park, S Chevron/Chester's/dsl, Gulf/Subway/Pizza Hut/dsl/scales/24hr, Texaco/dsl Al-T's Seafood, Exxon/dsl, Hart's Chicken, Jack-in-the-Box, Joe's Italian, Waffle House Best Value Inn, Comfort Inn, Hampton Inn, Holiday Inn Express, La Quinta, Motel 6, Winnie Inn/RV Park H, Chrysler/Jeep/Dodge

828 TX 73, TX 124 (from eb), to Winnie, S H, same as 829

827 FM 1406

822 FM 1410

821 **insp sta wb**

819 Jenkins Rd, W Chevron/Dunkin Donuts/dsl, S Exxon/Stuckey's/Chester's/dsl

817 FM 1724

814 frontage rd, from eb, **both lanes, full facilities, , litter barrels**

813 TX 61 (from wb), Hankamer, N Shell/dsl TX Country Inn, S Exxon/DJ's Diner/dsl McDonald's same as 812

812 TX 61, Hankamer

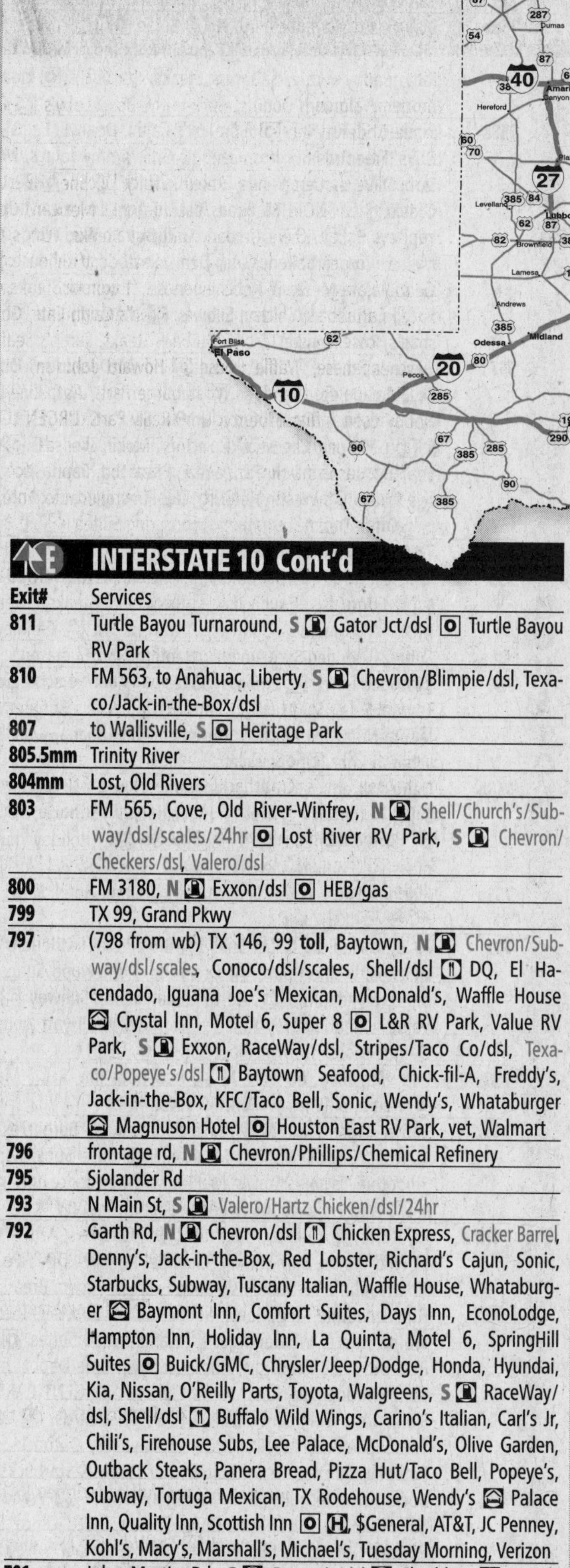

INTERSTATE 10 Cont'd

Exit#	Services
811	Turtle Bayou Turnaround, S Gator Jct/dsl Turtle Bayou RV Park
810	FM 563, to Anahuac, Liberty, S Chevron/Blimpie/dsl, Texaco/Jack-in-the-Box/dsl
807	to Wallisville, S Heritage Park
805.5mm	Trinity River
804mm	Lost, Old Rivers
803	FM 565, Cove, Old River-Winfrey, N Shell/Church's/Subway/dsl/scales/24hr Lost River RV Park, S Chevron/Checkers/dsl, Valero/dsl
800	FM 3180, N Exxon/dsl HEB/gas
799	TX 99, Grand Pkwy
797	(798 from wb) TX 146, 99 toll, Baytown, N Chevron/Subway/dsl/scales, Conoco/dsl/scales, Shell/dsl DQ, El Hacendado, Iguana Joe's Mexican, McDonald's, Waffle House Crystal Inn, Motel 6, Super 8 L&R RV Park, Value RV Park, S Exxon, RaceWay/dsl, Stripes/Taco Co/dsl, Texaco/Popeye's/dsl Baytown Seafood, Chick-fil-A, Freddy's, Jack-in-the-Box, KFC/Taco Bell, Sonic, Wendy's, Whataburger Magnuson Hotel Houston East RV Park, vet, Walmart
796	frontage rd, N Chevron/Phillips/Chemical Refinery
795	Sjolander Rd
793	N Main St, S Valero/Hartz Chicken/dsl/24hr
792	Garth Rd, N Chevron/dsl Chicken Express, Cracker Barrel, Denny's, Jack-in-the-Box, Red Lobster, Richard's Cajun, Sonic, Starbucks, Subway, Tuscany Italian, Waffle House, Whataburger Baymont Inn, Comfort Suites, Days Inn, EconoLodge, Hampton Inn, Holiday Inn, La Quinta, Motel 6, SpringHill Suites Buick/GMC, Chrysler/Jeep/Dodge, Honda, Hyundai, Kia, Nissan, O'Reilly Parts, Toyota, Walgreens, S RaceWay/dsl, Shell/dsl Buffalo Wild Wings, Carino's Italian, Carl's Jr, Chili's, Firehouse Subs, Lee Palace, McDonald's, Olive Garden, Outback Steaks, Panera Bread, Pizza Hut/Taco Bell, Popeye's, Subway, Tortuga Mexican, TX Rodehouse, Wendy's Palace Inn, Quality Inn, Scottish Inn H, $General, AT&T, JC Penney, Kohl's, Macy's, Marshall's, Michael's, Tuesday Morning, Verizon
791	John Martin Rd, S Buc-ee's/dsl Cheddars Woodspring Suites Cadillac/Chevrolet, Ford
790	Ellis School Rd, N Super 8
789	Thompson Rd, N Loves /McDonald's/dsl/scales/24hr@, S FLYING J/Denny's/dsl/scales/24hr/@, TA/Country Pride/dsl/scales/24hr@ Blue Beacon, Truck Lube
788.5mm	eb, full facilities, litter barrels, petwalk
788	sp 330 (from eb), to Baytown
787	sp 330, Crosby-Lynchburg Rd, to Highlands, N Exxon/Domino's/dsl RV Camping (1mi), S Phillips 66/dsl Four Corners BBQ to San Jacinto SP
786.5mm	San Jacinto River
786	Monmouth Dr
785	Magnolia Ave, to Channelview, N Shell/dsl/scales, S Exxon/dsl truckwash
784	Cedar Lane, Bayou Dr, N Valero/dsl Budget Lodge, TX Inn
783	Sheldon Rd, N Chevron/dsl/24hr, Shell/dsl, Valero/dsl Burger King, Church's, Jack-in-the-Box, Pizza Hut, Pizza Inn, Popeye's, Subway, Taco Bell, Whataburger Days Inn, Grand Inn, Holiday Inn, Leisure Inn, Palace Inn, Parkway Inn, Travelers Inn AutoZone, Discount Tire, Family$, FoodFair, USPO, S Chevron/dsl, Texaco/dsl McDonald's, Wendy's Deluxe Inn, Fairfield Inn, Scottish Inn auto repair
782	Dell-Dale Ave, N Exxon/dsl Dell-Dale Motel, Luxury Inn H, S Channelview RV Ctr
781b	Market St, N Clarion H
781a	TX 8, Sam Houston Pkwy, S Gulf/dsl
780	(779a from wb) Uvalde Rd, Freeport St, N Chevron/dsl, Texaco/dsl Capt Tom's Seafood, China Dragon, IHOP, Panda Express, Shipley Donuts, Sonic, Subway, Taco Cabana H, $Tree, Aamco, Ace Hardware, Office Depot, S Baytown Seafood,

B A Y T O W N

TX

INTERSTATE 10 Cont'd

HOUSTON

780 Continued
Golden Corral, Whataburger [other] Firestone/auto, Home Depot, Sam's Club/gas, U-Haul, Verizon, Walmart/McDonald's

779b N [gas] Gulf, Valero/dsl [food] China Dragon, IHOP, Panda Express, Shipley's Donuts, Sonic, Subway, Taco Cabana [lodging] Interstate Motel [other] $Tree, Aamco, Ace Hardware, Office Depot

778b Normandy St, N [gas] Shell/Jack-in-the-Box, Texaco/dsl [lodging] La Quinta, S [gas] Citgo/dsl [food] Cafe Ko, Church's [lodging] Normandy Inn

778a FM 526, Federal Rd, Pasadena, N [food] Burger King, Casa Ole Mexican, KFC/Taco Bell, Pizza Hut, Popeye's, Subway, S [gas] Shell/dsl [food] James Coney Island, Pappadeaux Seafood Kitchen, Pappas BBQ, Pappa's Seafood, Peking Bo Chinese, Saltgrass Steaks, Sonic, Swamp Shack Rest. [lodging] Lamplight Inn, Super 8 [other] AutoZone, Discount Tire, O'Reilly Parts, Scottish Inn

776b John Ralston Rd, Holland Ave, N [gas] Chevron/dsl, Exxon, Texaco [food] Chulas Mexican, Denny's, Fuddruckers, Luby's, Mambo Seafood, Pappasito's Cantina, Subway [lodging] Candlewood Suites, Comfort Inn, Day Inn, Palace Inn, Regency Inn [other] Family$, Fiesta Foods, NTB, URGENT CARE, S same as 778

776a Mercury Dr, N [food] Arandas Mexican, Burger King, McDonald's, Tepatillan Mexican, TX Grill [lodging] Best Western, Hampton Inn, Motel 6, Premier Inn, Quality Inn [other] Volvo Trucks, S [gas] Shell/dsl, Valero/dsl [food] Chili's, Cici's Pizza, Murphy's Deli [lodging] Holiday Inn Express [other] CVS Drug, URGENT CARE

775b a I-610

774 Gellhorn (from eb) Blvd, S [other] Anheuser-Busch Brewery

773b McCarty St, N [gas] Chevron/dsl, Shell

773a US 90A, N Wayside Dr, N [gas] Speedy/dsl [food] Jack-in-the-Box, Whataburger, S [gas] Chevron/dsl, Shell/dsl, Valero [food] Church's, Subway

772 Kress St, Lathrop St, N [gas] Conoco, Exxon [food] Popeye's, S [food] 7 Mares Seafood, Burger King

771b Lockwood Dr, N [gas] Chevron/Subway/dsl [food] McDonald's [other] Family$, Walgreens, S [gas] Shell/dsl [lodging] Palace Inn

771a Waco St

770c US 59 N

770b Jenson St, Meadow St, Gregg St

770a US 59 S, to Victoria

769c McKee St, Hardy St, Nance St, downtown

769a Smith St (from wb), to downtown

768b a I-45, N to Dallas, S to Galveston

767b Taylor St

767a Studemont Dr, Yale St, Heights Blvd, S [gas] Shell/dsl [food] Chick-fil-A, Chili's, Dickey's BBQ, KFC/Taco Bell, Panda Express, Subway [other] AT&T, Petsmart, Staples, Target

766 (from wb), Heights Blvd, Yale St

765b N Durham Dr, N Shepherd Dr, N [gas] Shell/dsl [food] Wendy's [lodging] Howard Johnson [other] vet, S [gas] Valero/dsl [food] Saltgrass Steaks

765a TC Jester Blvd, S [gas] Exxon/dsl, Texaco/dsl [food] Golden Hunan, Starbucks [other] vet

764 Westcott St, Washington Ave, Katy Rd, N [food] Denny's [lodging] Hampton Inn, S [gas] Chevron [food] IHOP, McDonald's [lodging] Scottish Inn

763 I-610

762 Silber Rd, Post Oak Rd, N [food] Chick-fil-A, Dave&Buster's, Jimmy John's, Panda Express, Red Robin, SteaKountry [other] Chrysler/Dodge/Jeep, Fiat, Firestone/auto, IKEA, Walmart, S [food] Jack-in-the-Box, Shipley Donuts [lodging] Crowne Plaza, Holiday Inn Express

761b Antoine Rd, S [gas] Exxon/dsl [other] CVS Drug

761a Wirt Rd, Chimney Rock Rd, S [gas] Exxon/dsl [other] CVS Drug

760 Bingle Rd, Voss Rd, N [food] Burger Shack, Hunan Chef, Pueblo Viejo, Starbucks, Subway [other] AT&T, Home Depot, S [gas] Shell/dsl [food] Sweet Tomatoes

759 Campbell Rd (from wb), N [other] Ranch Mkt, same as 758b

758b Blalock Rd, Campbell Rd, N [food] Sonic [other] [H], Lowe's, S [gas] Chevron/McDonald's/dsl [food] Baskin-Robbins, Goode Co TX BBQ, Pappy's Cafe, Saltgrass Steaks, Starbucks [other] cleaners, Kroger, Walgreens

758a Bunker Hill Rd, N [food] Boudreaux's Cajun, Dennys, Egg&I, Five Guys, Freebirds Burritos, Genghis Grill, Jimmy John's, Marble Slab, Olive Garden, Panda Express, Which Wich? [other] Best Buy, Costco/gas, GNC, HEB Foods/dsl, Jo-Ann, Lowe's, Michael's, PepBoys, S [food] American Island Grill, Buffalo Wild Wings, Ciro's Italian, Corner Bakery Cafe, Denis Seafood, Firehouse Subs, Guadalajara Mexican, Kobe Japanese, Longhorn Steaks, Lupe Tortilla, Russo's NY Pizza, Subway [lodging] Memorial Inn [other] Marshall's, Ross, Verizon

757 Gessner Rd, N [food] Chili's, Chulas Grill, McDonald's, Murphy's Deli, Taco Bell, Wendy's, Whataburger [other] AT&T, CVS Drug, Hobby Lobby, Home Depot, Honda, Sam's Club/gas, U-Haul, S [food] 59 Diner, Cheesecake Factory, Fuddrucker's, Goode Co Seafood, Jason's Deli, Pappadeaux Seafood, Pappasito's, Perry's Steaks [lodging] Westin Hotel [other] [H], Firestone/auto, Ford, Macy's, Office Depot, Target

756 TX 8, Sam Houston Tollway

755 Willcrest Rd, N [other] Discount Tire, Lincoln, Mazda, NTB, U-Haul, S [gas] Citgo/dsl, Exxon/dsl [food] Brenner's Steaks, Denny's, IHOP, McDonald's, Subway, Taste of TX [lodging] Candlewood Suites, Extended Stay America, Hampton Inn, Sheraton

754 Kirkwood Rd, N [lodging] Embassy Suites [other] Audi/Porsche, Lincoln, Toyota, S [gas] Shell/dsl [food] Carrabba's, Prince's Burgers, Shipley Do-Nuts, Spicy Pickle, Starbucks, Taco Cabana, Twin Peaks, Whataburger [other] Chevrolet

753b Dairy-Ashford Rd, N [other] Infiniti, Lexus, Nissan, Volvo, S [gas] Exxon/dsl [food] Chili's, Hibachi Grill, Subway, TX Cattle Steaks [lodging] Courtyard, Hilton Garden, Holiday Inn Express [other] Cadillac, URGENT CARE

753a Eldridge Pkwy, N [gas] Conoco/dsl [lodging] Omni Hotel, S [gas] Valero/dsl [other] Kwik Kar

751 TX 6, to Addicks, N [gas] Shell [food] Bros Pizza, Cattlegard Rest, Quiznos, Waffle House [lodging] Drury Inn, Homewood Suites, Studio 6, Wyndham, S [food] North China, Salata, Subway [lodging] Bea[...] Value, Extended Stay America, Fairfield Inn, Hyatt House, La Quinta, Motel 6, TownePlace Suites [other] USPO

750 Park Ten Blvd, eb only, N [lodging] Red Roof Inn, S [lodging] Marriott [other] Acura, BMW, Buick/GMC, Hoover RV Ctr

748 Barker-Cypress Rd, N [gas] Exxon/Subway [food] BurgerTex Grill, Coaches Grill, El Rancho Mexican, Firehouse Subs, Popeyes, Smoothie Factory, Tony's Mexican [lodging] Residence Inn [other] [H], S [food] Cracker Barrel [other] Hyundai, Subaru, vet, VW

747b a Fry Rd, N [gas] Gulf/dsl, Shell/dsl [food] Applebee's, Arby's, Buffalo Wild Wings, Burger King, Chipotle, Denny's, DQ, Five Guys, Jimmy John's, McDonald's, Panda Express, Panera Bread, Pizza Hut, Smoothie King, Sonic, Souper Salad, Subway, Taco Bell, Waffle House, Whataburger [lodging] Candlewood Suites [other] AAA, Best Buy, HEB Food/gas, Hobby Lobby, Home Depot, Jo-Ann, Kohl's, Kroger/dsl, Ross, Sam's Club/gas, URGENT CARE, Verizon, vet, Walgreens, Walmart, S [gas] Shell/dsl [food] Captain Tom's Seafood, Fazoli's, IHOP, McDonald's, Outback Steaks, Potbelly, Quiznos, Smashburger, Star Chinese, Starbucks, Starbucks, TX Mesquite Grill, Wendy's, Willie's [lodging] Woodspring Suites [other] [H], A&T, Katy Drug, Lowe's, NTB, Office Depot, Petsmart, Randall's Mkt, Target, TJ Maxx, U-Haul

746 W Green Blvd, N [gas] RaceWay/dsl [food] BJ's Rest., Chang Chinese, Cheddar's, Chuy's Mexican, Firehouse Subs, Kubla[...]

INTERSTATE 10 Cont'd

746 Continued
Khan Stirfry, Longhorn Steaks, Nagoya Japanese, Olive Garden, Orleans Seafood Kitchen, Springcreek BBQ, Stadia Grill, Steak'n Shake, TX Roadhouse, Wild Wings Cafe Holiday Inn Express, Palace Inn, S Carl's Jr, Jimmy Changas TexMex Home2 Christian Bros Automotive, CVS Drug, Ford, Honda

745 Mason Rd, N CarMax, S Shell/dsl, Valero/dsl Babin's Seafood, Blackeyed Pea, Burger King, Carino's Italian, Chick-fil-A, Chili's, CjCi's, Dickey's BBQ, DQ, El Patron Mexican, Freebirds Burrito, Hooters, Jack-in-the-Box, Jason's Deli, KFC, Landry's Seafood, Luby's, McDonald's, Panda Express, Papa John's, Pizza Hut, Popeye's, Rudy's BBQ/gas, SaltGrass Steaks, Schlotzsky's, Subway, Taco Bell, Taco Cabana, Whataburger, Which Wich? Comfort Inn&Suites, Hampton Inn, La Quinta, Motel 6, Super 8 $Tree, 99c Store, AutoZone, Chevrolet, Chrysler/Dodge/Jeep, Discount Tire, Fiesta Foods, Firestone/auto, Goodyear/auto, HEB Food/gas, Kia, Toyota, transmissions, Walgreens

743 TX 99, Grand Pkwy, Peek Rd, N La Madeleine, Red Robin H, JC Penney, S Freddy's Steakburgers, Subway Costco/gas, URGENT CARE

741 (742 from wb) Katy-Fort Bend County Rd, Pin Oak Rd, S Murphy USA/dsl, Shell/dsl, Texaco/dsl Alegra Brazilian, Alicia's Mexican, Antonia's Rest, Chick-fil-A, ChuckECheese, CiCi's Pizza, Denny's, Fuddruckers, Jack-in-the-Box, Jimmy John's, JoJo's Mongolian Grill, KFC, LJ Silver/Taco Bell, Los Cucos, Pizza Hut, Popeyes, Rainforest Cafe, Red Lobster, Smashburger, Starbucks, Subway, Subway, TGIFriday's, Whataburger Best Western, Comfort Suites, Country Inn & Suites, Courtyard, Hilton Garden, Holiday Inn, Homewood Suites, Residence Inn, SpringHill Suites H, $Tree, AT&T, BassPro Shops, BooksAMillion, Discount Tire, HEB/dsl, Katy Mills Outlet/famous brands, Marshall's, Nissan, Ross, URGENT CARE, Verizon, Walgreens, Walmart/McDonald's

740 FM 1463, N Exxon/dsl, S Shell/McDonald's/dsl Starbucks

737 Pederson Rd, N Buc-ee's/dsl, Loves/Arby's/dsl/scales/24hr, S Camping World RV Super Ctr, Holiday World RV Ctr

735 Igloo Rd

734 Woods Rd

732 FM 359, to Brookshire, N FLYING J/Denny's/dsl/LP/scales/24hr/@, Exxon/Chester's/dsl, Shell Church's, Orlando's Pizza, Subway Executive Inn RV camping, S Chevron/dsl, Shell/McDonald's/dsl Burger King, Jack-in-the-Box, Popeye's, Taco Bell Holiday Inn, Super 8 truck lube, truckwash

731 FM 1489, to Koomey Rd, N Exxon/dsl Ernesto's Mexican Brooke Hotel RV Park, S Texaco/Dickey's BBQ/dsl La Quinta

729 Peach Ridge Rd, Donigan Rd (730 from wb), S Kathy's/dsl/rest./24hr

726 Chew Rd (from eb), S golf

725 Mlcak Rd (from wb), S Kathy's Korner/dsl

723 FM 1458, to San Felipe, N Exxon/Subway/dsl/scales/24hr Peterbilt, to Stephen F Austin SP (3mi), S Riverside Tire

721 (from wb) US 90, N Shell/Chester's/dsl Chrysler/Dodge/Jeep, Ford

720a Outlet Ctr Dr, N Shell/Chester's/dsl

720 TX 36, to Sealy, N Shell/dsl China Buffet, DQ, Hartz Chicken, McDonald's, Sonic, Tony's Rest. $General, Jones RV Ctr, O'Reilly Parts, Walgreens, S Chevron/Burger King/dsl, Murphy USA/dsl, Shell/dsl, Texaco/dsl Cazadore's Mexican,

SEALY

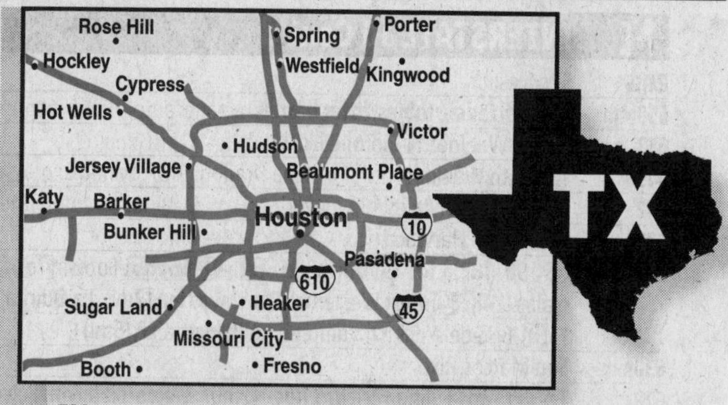

720 Continued
Hinze's BBQ, Jack-in-the-Box, Jin's Asian, Maribelli Italian, Pizza Hut, Subway, Whataburger Best Value Inn, Countryside Inn, Holiday Inn Express, Super 8 $Tree, Verizon, Walmart/Subway

718 US 90 (from eb), to Sealy, N Valero/Huddle House/Subway/dsl, S Exxon/Prasek's Smokehouse/dsl

716 Pyka Rd, N Sunoco/dsl/rest./showers/24hr/@

713 Beckendorff Rd

709 FM 2761, Bernardo Rd, N TA/Carl's Jr/Subway/Dunkin Donuts/dsl/scales/24hr

704 FM 949, N Happy Oaks RV Park (3mi)

699 FM 102, to Eagle Lake, N Happy Oaks RV Park, S Eagle Lake SP (14mi)

698 Alleyton Rd, N Mikeska's BBQ, S Shell/Taco Bell/BBQ/dsl, Valero/Subway/dsl Chrysler/Dodge/Jeep, Ford

697mm Little Colorado River

696 TX 71, Columbus, N Exxon/Burger King/dsl, Shell/dsl #1 Buffet, Blake St. Grill, El Rey Mexican, Jack-in-the-Box, Pizza Hut, Schobel's Rest., Whataburger Columbus Inn, Holiday Inn Express H, AT&T, AutoZone, HEB Foods, Walmart, S Conoco/Church's/Subway/dsl, Phillips 66/dsl, Valero/dsl Los Cabos Mexican, McDonald's, Nancy's Steaks, Sonic Best Value, Comfort Inn, LaQuinta Columbus RV Park

COLUMBUS

695 TX 71 (from wb), to La Grange

693 FM 2434, to Glidden

692mm **both lanes, full facilities, litter barrels, petwalk, RV dump, vending**

689 US 90, to Hattermann Lane, N Whispering Oaks RV Park

682 FM 155, to Wiemar, N Shell/dsl, Valero/dsl DQ, McDonald's, Subway/Texas Burger Motel 6 H, $General, Lowe's Mkt, Tire Pros, S 76/Church's/dsl/24hr, Loves/Chester's/Wendy's/dsl/scales/24hr Buick/Chevrolet/GMC

678mm E Navidad River

677 US 90

674 US 77, Schulenburg, N Pilot/Taco Bell/PJ Fresh/dsl/scales/24hr, Sunoco/Stripes/Taco Co Oak Ridge Smokehouse Best Value Inn, Executive Inn Ford, Potter Country Store, S Shell/dsl, Valero/Subway DQ, Frank's Rest., Guadalajara Mexican, Lucy's Grill, Whataburger Best Western+, Holiday Inn Express $General, Family$, O'Reilly Parts, Schulenberg RV Park

672mm W Navidad River

668 FM 2238, to Engle

661 TX 95, FM 609, to Flatonia, N Citgo/dsl, Valero/dsl Jesito's Mexican, Joel's BBQ, Robert's Steaks Flatonia RV Ranch (1mi), S Exxon/dsl, Shell/McDonald's/Grumpy's Rest./motel/dsl, Valero DQ, Subway Best Western+, Carefree Inn $General, NAPA

TX

INTERSTATE 10 Cont'd

Exit#	Services
658mm	both lanes, tables, litter barrels
653	US 90, Waelder, N Shell/dsl
649	TX 97, to Waelder
642	TX 304, to Gonzales
637	FM 794, to Harwood
632	US 90/183, to Gonzales, N Loves/Subway/dsl/scales/24hr Best Western+, Coachway Inn (2mi), La Quinta, S Buc-ee's/dsl camping, to Palmetto SP (5mi)
630mm	San Marcos River
628	TX 80, to Luling, N Citgo (2mi), Valero/pizza/dsl/24hr H, Riverbend RV Park
625	Darst Field Rd
624.5mm	Smith Creek
621mm	weigh sta both lanes
620	FM 1104
618mm	both lanes, full facitlities, petwalk
617	FM 2438, to Kingsbury
614	toll 130 N, to Austin, Waco
612	US 90
611mm	Geronimo Creek
610	TX 123, to San Marcos, N Exxon/Circle K/dsl, Shell/Subway/dsl Bella Sera Italian, Chili's, IHOP, Los Cucos Mexican Comfort Inn, Days Inn, Hampton Inn, Holiday Inn Express, TownePlace Suites Carters Tires, S Valero/dsl Taco Cabana H
609	TX 123, Austin St, S Phillips 66/dsl, Sunoco/dsl Chevrolet, Home Depot
607	TX 46, FM 78, to New Braunfels, N Valero/Jack-in-the-Box/dsl Motel 6 Ford, S Exxon/dsl, Shell/Circle K/dsl Bill Miller BBQ, Dixie Grille, Garcia's Mexican, McDonald's, Subway, Whataburger Best Value, La Quinta Chrysler/Dodge/Jeep
605	FM 464, N Twin Palms RV Park
605mm	Guadalupe River
604	FM 725, to Lake McQueeney, N Loves/Arby's/dsl/scales/24hr Twin Palms RV Park
603	US 90 E, US 90A, to Seguin, N D&A RV Park, Seguin RV Ctr, S Explore USA RV Ctr
601	FM 775, to New Berlin, N Chevron/Subway/dsl/scales/24hr
600	Schwab Rd
599	FM 465, to Marion
599mm	Santa Clara Creek
597	Santa Clara Rd, N auto racetrack
595	Zuehl Rd
594mm	Cibolo Creek
593	FM 2538, Trainer Hale Rd, N Texaco/dsl tires, S Exxon/Lucille's Rest./dsl/24hr
593mm	Woman Hollering Creek
591	FM 1518, to Schertz, N Alamo Trvl Ctr/Shell/dsl repair, S Valero/dsl/e85
589	Pfeil Rd, Graytown Rd
589mm	Salatrillo Creek
587	LP 1604, Randolph AFB, to Universal City, N EVC/CNG, S Shell/McDonald's/dsl Whataburger
585.5mm	Escondido Creek
585	FM 1516, to Converse, N Chevron/Church's/dsl/scales/24hr Best Western+, S Kenworth, Peterbilt/GMC/Freightliner
585mm	Martinez Creek
583	Foster Rd, N FLYING J/Denny's/dsl/LP/scales/24hr/@, Valero/Subway/dsl/24hr Jack-in-the-Box Comfort Inn,

KIRBY

Exit#	Services
583	Continued La Quinta Blue Beacon, Speedco Lube, Tire Mart, S TA/Chevron/Burger King/Pizza Hut/Popeye's/dsl/24hr/@
582.5mm	Rosillo Creek
582	Ackerman Rd, Kirby, N Pilot/Subway/dsl/scales/24hr, S Petro/Iron Skillet/dsl/scales/24hr/@ El Rodeo Mexican Knights Inn Blue Beacon, Petrolube
581	I-410
580	LP 13, WW White Rd, N Chevron/dsl El Jacalito, La Playa Seafood, Wendy's Motel 6, Red Roof Inn, Rodeway Inn tires, S Exxon/7-11, Valero Bill Miller BBQ El Rodeo Mexican, Lazaritas Mexican, McDonald's, Pizza Hut, Popeye's, Sonic, Subway Best Value, Motel 6, Super 8 $General, Ford/Volvo Trucks, tires/repair
579	Houston St, N Valero/dsl Quality Inn Penske S Chevron, Stripes/Valero/dsl Days Inn, Knights Inn Passport Inn
578	Pecan Valley Dr, ML King Dr, S Shell/Subway/dsl
577	US 87 S, to Roland Ave, S Whataburger Super 8
576	New Braunfels Ave, Gevers St, S Valero McDonald's
575	Pine St, Hackberry St, S Little Red Barn Steaks
574	I-37, US 281
573	Probandt St, N Jack-in-the-Box, Miller's BBQ, S Valero tires/repair, to SA Missions HS

SAN ANTONIO

I-10 and I-35 run together 3 miles. See I-35, exits 156-154a.

Exit#	Services
569c	Santa Rosa St, to Our Lady of the Lake U, downtown
568	spur 421, Culebra Ave, Bandera Ave, S to St Marys U
567	Lp 345, Fredericksburg Rd (from eb upper level accesses I-35 S, I-10 E, US 87 S, lower level accesses I-35 N)
566b	Fresno Dr, S Exxon/dsl Galaxy Inn
566a	West Ave, N Exxon/7-11 DQ, Subway, Whataburger CarCare
565c	(from wb), access to same as 565 a b, S Shell Jimador Mexican, Starbucks La Quinta
565b	Vance Jackson Rd, N Murphy USA/dsl Bill Miller BBQ, IHOP Comfort Inn, Days Inn, EconoLodge Walmart S Shell/dsl Holiday Inn Express
565a	Crossroads Blvd, Balcone's Heights, N Shell/dsl Howard Johnson vet, S Valero/dsl Crossroads BBQ, Dave&Buster's, Denny's, El Pollo Loco, McDonald's, Whataburger SpringHill Suites Firestone/auto, Hobby Lobby, Mazda, Office Depot, Target
564b a	I-410, services off of I-410 W, Fredericksburg Rd
563	Callaghan Rd, N Valero Las Palapas Mexican, Subway Embassy Suites, Marriott $General, Ford, Sprouts Mkt, Toyota, S Exxon/7-11 Mamacita's Rest. Lowe's
561	Wurzbach Rd, N Texaco/dsl Bolo's Grille, Broadway 5050 Grill, County Line BBQ, Egg&I, Firehouse Subs, Fuddruckers, Honeybaked Ham, Jason's Deli, Pappasito's Cantina, Popeye's, Sea Island Shrimphouse, Taste Of China, TX Land& Cattle, Wasabi Grill Extended Stay America, Homewood Suites, Hyatt Place, Motel 6, Staybridge Suites AutoZone, BigLots, HEB Food/gas, Office Depot, Porsche, Tuesday Morning, S Shell/dsl 210 Ceviche Seafood, Alamo Café, Arby's, Chester's Burgers, China Sea, Church's, Denny's, El Taco Tote, Jack-in-the-Box, Mamma Margie's Mexican, McDonald's, Pizza Hut, Ruby Tuesday, Sumo Japanese, Taco Bell, Wendy's Baymont Inn, Best Western, Candlewood Suites, Drury Inn, Hawthorn Suites, La Quinta, Motel 6, Sleep Inn H CarMax
560b	frontage rd (from eb), same as 561

INTERSTATE 10 Cont'd

SAN ANTONIO

Exit#	Services
560a	Huebner Rd, N CA Pizza Kitchen, Chipotle, Fare Wok, Genghis Grill, La Madeleine, Macaroni Grill, Panera Bread, Pericos Mexican, Salata, SaltGrass Steaks Cadillac, Chrysler/Jeep/Dodge, Fiat, Nissan, Old Navy, Ross, S Chevron, Exxon, Shell/Jack-in-the-Box/dsl Cracker Barrel, Jim's Rest., Miller's BBQ Days Inn, Quality Inn, TownePlace Suites
559	Lp 335, US 87, Fredericksburg Rd, N Pearl Inn Holiday Inn Express Acura, S Krispy Kreme, Shell/Jack-in-the-Box/dsl Comfort Suites, Days Inn, HomeGate Studios, Rodeway Inn, SpringHill Suites Infiniti
558	De Zavala Rd, N Chevron, Shell/Subway Bill Miller BBQ, Burger King, Carrabba's, Chick-fil-A, Chili's, Five Guys, Fox&Hound, Joe's Crabshack, KFC/Taco Bell, Logan's Roadhouse, McDonald's, Outback Steaks, Sonic, Starbucks, Taco Cabana, The Earl of Sandwich, Wendy's HEB Foods, Home Depot, Marshall's, PetCo, Petsmart, Steinmart, Target, S IHOP, Popeyes, Schlotzsky's Days Inn, SpringHill Suites, Studio6 Discount Tire, Sam's Club/gas, Verizon, Walmart
557	Spur 53, N Exxon/7-11/dsl Cheddar's, Chuy's Mexican Best Western, EconoLodge, Howard Johnson, Super 8 Audi, Chevrolet, Hyundai, Jaguar/Mazerati/Ferrari, S Valero/Subway/dsl A&W/LJ Silver, Cici's Pizza, Huhot Chinese, IHOP, Matamoro's Cantina, Quiznos, Twin Peaks, Whataburger, Zio's Italian Holiday Inn Costco/gas, Land Rover, Sams Club/gas, Univ of TX at San Antonio, Walmart
556b	frontage rd
556a	to Anderson Lp, S to Seaworld, Six Flags
555	La Quintera Pkwy, N 54th St Rest., BJ's Rest., Bob's Chophouse, Chick-fil-A, Coldstone, Freddy's Steakburger, Hofbrau at the Rim, Islamorada Rest., Maggiano's Little Italy, McDonald's/playplace, Mimi's Cafe, Popeyes, Red Robin, Starbucks, TGIFriday's, Tiago's, Whataburger Courtyard, Hilton Garden, Residence Inn $Tree, AT&T, Bass Pro Shops, Best Buy, Dick's, GNC, JC Penney, Lowe's, Michaels, Old Navy, Ross, Staples, Target, TJ Maxx, World Mkt, S Applebee's, Longhorn Steaks, Olive Garden, Red Lobster Drury Inn, La Quinta, Motel 6 Honda, to La Cantera Pkwy
554	Camp Bullis Rd, N Texaco/dsl Russell CP, S Shell/dsl Rodeway Inn
551	Boerne Stage Rd (from wb), to Leon Springs, N Shamrock/dsl Rudy's BBQ, Sonic, S Bourbon St Seafood, Las Palapas Mexican, Longhorns Rest., Papa Nacho's, Starbucks, Subway CarX, GNC, HEB Foods/dsl, Tesla
550	FM 3351, Ralph Fair Rd, N Exxon/McDonald's/dsl, Valero/dsl Willie's Cafe La Quinta, S Shell/Domino's/dsl Bill Miller's BBQ, Laguna Madre, Rudy's BBQ/gas, Schlotsky's, Taco Cabana Walgreens, Walmart
546	Fair Oaks Pkwy, Tarpon Dr, N Papa John's American Dream RV Ctr, CVS Drug, Harley-Davidson, vet, S Chevron/dsl/café, Exxon/dsl/café Fair Oaks Automotive, Goodyear/auto, Hoover RV Ctr
543	Boerne Stage Rd, to Scenic LP Rd, N Valero/Subway/dsl Fairfield Inn Ancira RV Ctr, Buick/GMC, Chevrolet, Chrysler/Dodge/Jeep, Ford, NAPA, tires/repair, to Cascade Caverns/camping (3mi), S Explore USA RV Ctr, Mercedes, Nissan, Toyota
542	(from wb), N Shamrock Domino's, Pizza Hut, Subway, Wendy's $Tree, Alamo Fiesta RV Park, O'Reilly Parts, same as 540, Verizon

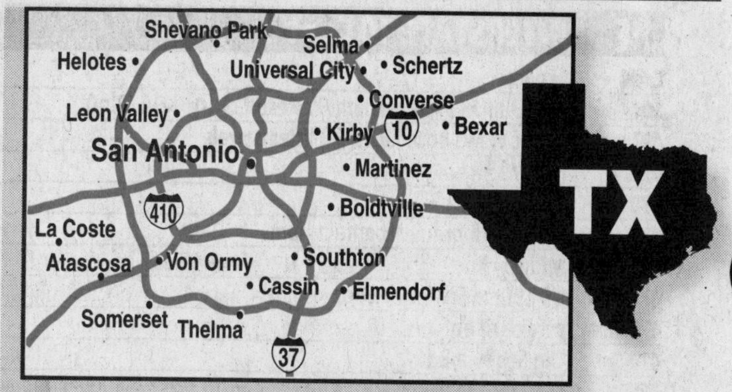

TX

KERRVILLE

Exit#	Services
540	TX 46, to New Braunfels, N Exxon/Taco Bell/dsl, Murphy USA/dsl, Shell/dsl Burger King, Centinela Mexican, Church's, Denny's, DQ, Guadalajara Mexican, Little Caesars, Papa Murphy's, Pizza Hut, Shanghai Chinese, Sonic, Subway, Taco Cabana, Wendy's Comfort Inn, Days Inn, Motel 6 AutoZone, Discount Tire, HEB Food/dsl, Verizon, vet, Walgreens, Walmart, S Chili's, Starbucks, Whataburger Hampton Inn H, Home Depot
539	Johns Rd, N Best Western, S Valero/dsl/LP
538mm	Cibolo Creek
538	Ranger Creek Rd
537	US 87, to Boerne
533	FM 289, Welfare, N PoPo Family Rest. Top of the Hill RV Park (1mi)
532mm	Little Joshua Creek
531mm	**wb, litter barrels**
530mm	Big Joshua Creek
529.5mm	**eb, litter barrels**
527	FM 1621 (from wb), to Waring
526.5mm	Holiday Creek
524	TX 27, FM 1621, to Waring, N vet, **1mi** S Chevron, Shell/dsl
523.5mm	Guadalupe River
523	US 87 N, to Comfort, N Chevron/Chicken Express/dsl, Loves/McDonald's/Subway/dsl/scales/24hr, S Exxon/dsl DQ Executive Inn $General, RV Park/LP
521.5mm	Comfort Creek
520	FM 1341, to Cypress Creek Rd
515mm	Cypress Creek
514mm	**both lanes, full facilities, litter barrels, petwalk, playground, RV dump, vending, wireless internet**
508	TX 16, Kerrville, N Exxon/dsl Buick/Cadillac/Chevrolet, **0-2 mi** S Exxon, Shell/McDonald's/dsl/24hr, Stripes/Taco Co, Valero/dsl/e-85 Bamboo Asian, Bella Sera Italian, Burger King, Chicken Express, Cracker Barrel, DQ, IHOP, Jack-in-the-Box, Little Caesar's, McDonald's, Schlotzsky's, Sonic, Taco Bell, Taco Casa, Valentino's Italian Best Value Inn, Best Western, Days Inn, Econolodge, Hampton Inn, Holiday Inn Express, La Quinta, Motel 6, Quality Inn, Super 8, Yo Ranch Hotel H, $Tree, Advance Parts, BigLots, Home Depot, Kerrville RV Ctr, Lowe's, O'Reilly Parts, vet, Walgreens
505	FM 783, to Kerrville, S Exxon/dsl, **3 mi** S **on TX 27** Exxon/dsl, Phillips 66/dsl, Stripes/Taco Co/dsl Billy Gene's Rest., Chick-fil-A, Chili's, CiCi's, Culver's, Del Norte Rest., Dickey's BBQ, DQ, Fuddruckers, Mamacita's, McDonald's, Pizza Hut, Popeye's, Sonic, Starbucks, Subway, Taco Casa, Wendy's, Whataburger Inn of the Hills $General, AT&T, AutoZone, Chrysler/Dodge/Jeep, CVS Drug, Discount Tire, HEB Foods/gas, Take It Easy RV Resort, Tuesday Morning, Walmart/McDonald's
503.5mm	**scenic views both lanes, litter barrels**

= gas = food = lodging = other = rest stop

TX

INTERSTATE 10 Cont'd

JUNCTION

SONORA

Exit#	Services
501	FM 1338, N Buckhorn RV Resort, S KOA (2mi)
497mm	**scenic views both lanes, litter barrels**
492	FM 479
490	TX 41
488	TX 27, to Ingram, Mountain Home
484	Midway Rd
477	US 290, to Fredericksburg
476.5mm	service rd eb
472	Old Segovia Rd
465	FM 2169, to Segovia, S Phillips 66/rest./dsl River Valley Inn/RV park
464.5mm	Johnson Fork Creek
462	US 83 S, to Uvalde
461mm	**eb, litter barrels**
460	(from wb), to Junction
459mm	**wb, litter barrels**
457	FM 2169, to Junction, N Shell/dsl, S Econolodge RV camping, S. Llano River SP
456.5mm	Llano River
456	US 83/377, Junction, N Alon/dsl, Chevron/dsl, Shell/McDonald's/dsl/24hr Cooper's BBQ, Tia Nena's Mexican Motel 6, S Big Star/dsl, Conoco/dsl, Exxon/Church's/dsl, Pilot/Subway/PJ Fresh/dsl/scales/24hr DQ, Isaack Rest., La Familia Mexican, Lum's BBQ, Sonic Best Western, Lazy T Motel, Legends Inn, Rodeway Inn, Sun Valley Motel, The Hills Motel H, $General, Best Hardware, CarQuest, Family$, Lowe's Mkt, Plumley's Store, S Llano RV Park, to S Llano River SP
452.5mm	Bear Creek
451	RM 2291, to Cleo Rd
448mm	North Creek
445	RM 1674, S camping
444.5mm	Stark Creek
442mm	Copperas Creek
442	RM 1674, to Ft McKavett, N to Ft McKavett SHS
439mm	N Llano River
438	Lp 291 (from wb), to Roosevelt, same as 437
437	Lp 291 (from eb, no EZ return), to Roosevelt, **1 mi** N Simon Bros Mercantile/dsl USPO
429	RM 3130, to Harrell
423mm	**parking area both lanes, litter barrels**
420	RM 3130, to Baker Rd
412	Allison Rd, RM 3130
404	RM 3130, RM 864, N to Ft McKavett St HS, **3 mi** S Love's/Chester's/dsl/scales/24hr, Stripes/Taco Co Holiday Host Motel H
400	US 277, Sonora, N Road Ranger/Church's/desk Sutton Co Steaks Motel 6, S Alon/7-11/dsl, Sunoco/dsl, Sunoco/Stripes/dsl DQ, La Mexicana Rest., Pizza Hut, Sonic, Taco Grill Best Western, Comfort Inn, Economy Inn Family$, USPO
399	(from eb) LP 467, Sonora, N Motel 6, S Sunoco/dsl, Sunoco/Stripes/Taco Co DQ H, RV camping
394mm	**both lanes, full facilities, litter barrel, petwalk, RV dump**
392	RM 1989, Caverns of Sonora Rd, **8 mi** S Caverns of Sonora Camping
388	RM 1312 (from wb)
381	RM 1312 (from eb)
372	Taylor Box Rd, N Exxon/rest./dsl/scales/24hr Super 8 auto museum, Circle Bar RV Park

OZONA

FT STOCKTON

Exit#	Services
368	LP 466, N same as 365 & 363
365	TX 163, Ozona, N Stripes/Godfather's/Taco Co/dsl, Sunoco/dsl, Valero/dsl Cafe Next Door, DQ, Sonic, Subway Best Value Inn, Economy Inn/RV Park, Hampton Inn, Hillcrest Inn, Holiday Inn Express, Quality Inn H, $General, dsl/auto repair, NAPA, to David Crockett Mon, S Pilot/dsl, Sunoco/Stripes El Chato's city park
363	Lp 466, to Ozona
361	RM 2083, Pandale Rd
357mm	Eureka Draw
351mm	Howard Draw
350	FM 2398, to Howard Draw
349mm	**parking area wb, litter barrels**
346mm	**parking area eb, litter barrels**
343	TX 290 W, S Ft. Lancaster Historic Site
337	Live Oak Rd
336.5mm	Live Oak Creek
328	River Rd, Sheffield
327.5mm	Pecos River
325	TX 290, TX 349, to Iraan, Sheffield, N H
320	frontage rd
314	frontage rd
309mm	**both lanes, full facilities, litter barrels, petwalk, wireless internet**
307	US 190, FM 305, to Iraan, N H
298	RM 2886
294	FM 11, Bakersfield, S Chevron/café/dsl
288	Ligon Rd, N many windmills
285	McKenzie Rd, S Domaine Cordier Ste Genevieve Winery
279mm	**eb, litter barrels**
277	FM 2023
273	US 67/385, to McCamey, **wb, litter barrels**
272	University Rd
264	Warnock Rd, N Fort Stockton RV Park/Roadrunner Cafe
261	US 290 W, US 385 S, N Exxon/dsl, S Love's/Carl's Jr/dsl/scales/24hr, Shell/dsl, Stripes/dsl DQ, Pizza Hut, Sonic, Subway All Inn, Budget Inn, Deluxe Inn, Executive Inn H, RV camping, to Big Bend NP
259b a	(259 from eb) TX 18, FM 1053, Ft Stockton, N Shell/Burger King/dsl Guadalajara Mexican I-10 RV Park, tires S FLYING J/Subway/dsl/scales/24hr H
257	US 285, to Pecos, Ft Stockton, N Stripes/Sunoco/Taco Co dsl/scales24hr golf, S Alon/dsl, Chevron/dsl, Exxon dsl, Shell/dsl DQ, KFC/Taco Bell, McDonald's, Pecos Roadhouse, Pizza Hut, Pizza Pro, Sonic, Steak House, Subway Atrium Inn, Best Western+, Candlewood Suites, Days Inn, Fairfield Inn, Hampton Inn, La Quinta, Quality Inn, Texas Inn $General, Ace Hardware, AutoZone, Buick/Chevrolet CarQuest, Comanche Land RV Park, Family$, Firestone/auto Lowe's Foods, McKissak Tires, O'Reilly Parts
256	to US 385 S, Ft Stockton, N HillTop RV, **1 mi** S Shell dsl Dragon Buffet, Howard's Drive-In, K-Bob's Steaks, Subway Comfort Suites, Holiday Inn Express, Motel 6, Sleep Inn, Super 8 auto/RV repair, Big Bend NP, Ford, to Ft Stockton Hist Dist, vet, Walmart
253	FM 2037, to Belding
248	US 67, FM 1776, to Alpine, S to Big Bend NP
246	Firestone
241	Kennedy Rd
235	Mendel Rd
233mm	**both lanes, full facilities, litter barrels, petwalk,**
229	Hovey Rd

E INTERSTATE 10 Cont'd

Exit#	Services
222	Hoefs Rd
214	(from wb), FM 2448
212	TX 17, FM 2448, to Pecos, N , **litter barrels**, S Saddleback RV Camping, Valero/I-10 Fuel/café/dsl
209	TX 17, S Ft Davis NHS, to Balmorhea SP, to Davis Mtn SP
206	FM 2903, to Balmorhea, Toyah, **2 mi** S GasCard Uncles Rest. to Balmorhea SP, USPO
192	FM 3078, to Toyahvale, S to Balmorhea SP
188	Giffin Rd
187	I-20, to Ft Worth, Dallas
186	I-10, E to San Antonio (from wb)
185mm	**both lanes, litter barrels**
184	Springhills
181	Cherry Creek Rd, S Chevron/dsl
176	TX 118, FM 2424, to Kent, S Davis Mtn SP, Ft Davis, to McDonald Observatory
173	Hurd's Draw Rd
166	Boracho Sta
159	Plateau, N Exxon/rest./dsl/24hr
153	Michigan Flat
146	Wild Horse Rd, Wild Horse Rd
146mm	**weigh sta wb**
145mm	**both lanes, full facilities, litter barrels, petwalk, , wireless internet**
140b	Ross Dr, Van Horn, N Loves/Subway/dsl/scales/24hr, Valero/dsl Days Inn, Desert Inn, Sands Motel/rest. Desert Willow RV Park, repair, S Mountain View RV Park/dump
140a	US 90, TX 54, Van Horn Dr, N Hotel El Capitan H, NAPA, S Pilot/Wendy's/dsl/scales/24hr, Valero/dsl Papa's Pantry dsl/tire repair, KOA, RV Dump
138	Lp 10, to Van Horn, N Chuy's Rest. Budget Inn, EconoLodge, King's Inn, Knights Inn, Motel 6, Red Roof Inn, Value Inn, Whitten Inn $General, auto/dsl repair, city park, Eagles Nest RV Park, Oasis RV Park, Porter Foods, UPSO, visitor info, S Chevron/dsl/24hr McDonald's Hampton Inn, Holiday Inn Express, Quality Inn, Super 8 tires/repair
137mm	**weigh sta eb**
136mm	**scenic overlook wb, , litter barrels**
135mm	Mountain/Central time zone
133	(from wb) frontage rd
129	to Hot Wells, Allamore
108	to Sierra Blanca (from wb), same as 107
107	FM 1111, Sierra Blanca Ave, N Exxon/Subway/dsl/24hr Delfina's Mexican to Hueco Tanks SP, truck/tire repair, USPO, S Chevron/dsl Americana Inn Stagecoach Trading Post
105	(106 from wb) Lp 10, Sierra Blanca, same as 107
102.5mm	**insp sta eb**
99	Lasca Rd, N **both lanes, litter barrels, no restrooms**
98mm	**eb, litter barrels, no restrooms**
95	frontage rd (from eb)
87	FM 34, S DriversMart/dsl
85	Esperanza Rd
81	FM 2217
78	TX 20 W, to McNary
77mm	**truck parking area wb**
72	spur 148, to Ft Hancock, S Shell/dsl Angie's Rest. Ft Hancock Motel Family$, USPO
68	Acala Rd
55	Tornillo

VAN HORN

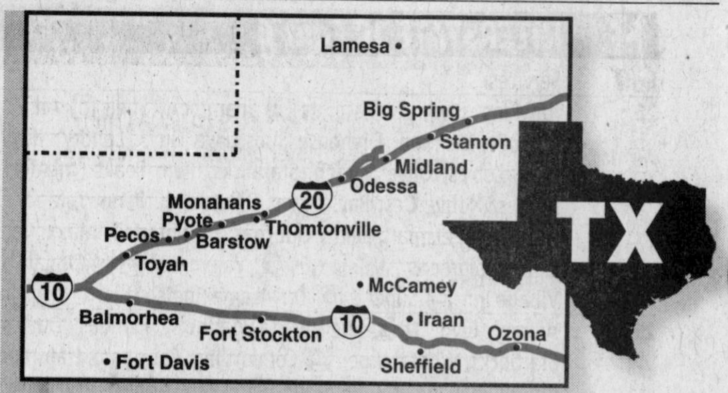

TX

Exit#	Services
51mm	**both lanes, full facilities, litter tables, petwalk,**
49	FM 793, Fabens, S Shell/dsl Church's, Little Caesar's, McDonald's, Subway Fabens Inn/Cafe Family$, San Eli Foods
42	FM 1110, to Clint, S Express/dsl Cotton Eyed Joe's, Mamacita's Rest. Adobe Inn, Best Western, Cotton Valley Motel/RV Park/rest./dump
37	FM 1281, Horizon Blvd, N FLYING J/Denny's/dsl/scales/24hr/@, Loves/Chester's/Subway/dsl/scales/24hr/@ Americana Inn Freightliner, RV Camping, Speedco Lube, S Petro/Valero/Iron Skillet/Subway/dsl/scales/24hr/@ McDonald's Deluxe Inn Blue Beacon
35	Eastlake Blvd.
34	TX 375, Americas Ave, N Chevron/dsl, Valero/Subway/dsl Motel 6, Woodspring Suites Mission RV Camping, Peterbilt, U-Haul, S El Paso Museum of Hist
32	FM 659, Zaragosa Rd, N Alon/7-11 Applebee's, Barrigos Mexican, BJ's Rest., Cheddar's, Chico's Tacos, Chipotle Mexican, Corner Bakery Cafe, Famous Dave's, Five Guys, Furr's Buffet, Genghis Grill, Great American Steaks, IHOP, Jaci-in-the-Box, Jason's Deli, Krispy Kreme, La Malinche Mexican, Logan's Roadhouse, Macaroni Grill, Mama Fu's Asian, McDonald's, Outback Steaks, Pei Wei, Peter Piper Pizza, Potbelly, Sonic, Starbucks, Taco Bell, Village Inn, Whataburger Courtyard, Hampton Inn, Holiday Inn Express AT&T, Chevrolet, Discount Tire, GNC, Kohl's, Lowe's, Michaels, Nissan, Office Depot, Ross, Walgreens, Which Wich, World Mkt, S Valero/dsl Gallego's Mexican city park, vet, Volvo/Mack
30	Lee Trevino Dr, N Exxon Denny's, Los Canarios Mexican, Whataburger La Quinta, Motel 6, Red Roof Inn, Studio 6 Discount Tire, Firestone/auto, Ford, Home Depot, Kenworth/Ford Trucks, Lexus, Mazda, Toyota, S Chrysler/Dodge/Jeep
29	Lomaland Dr, S Alon/7-11 Ramada Harley-Davidson
28b	Yarbrough Dr, El Paso, N Murphy USA, Shell/Coldstone/dsl, Texaco Buffalo Wild Wings, Burger King, ChuckECheese, Corner Bakery, Dunkin Donuts, Grandy's, Hayashi Japanese, Hong Kong Buffet, LJ Silver, McDonald's, Peter Piper Pizza, Sonic, Subway, TX Roadhouse, Wendy's, Whataburger, Wienerschnitzel Days Inn H, AT&T, Big Lots, Office Depot, Ranch Mkt, Ross, Walmart, S Rudy's BBQ, Valero/dsl Applebee's, Fuddrucker's, Julio's Cafe, La Malinche Mexican, Lin's Buffet, Pizza Hut, Rudy's BBQ/gas, Shangri-La, Villa Del Mar Comfort Inn, InTown Suites, La Quinta H
28a	FM 2316, McRae Blvd, N Texaco/dsl, Valero Pizza Hut La Quinta H, Jo-Ann Fabrics, Murphy USA/dsl, S Circle K/dsl Fuddruckers, Gabriel's Mexican, Pizza Hut La Quinta, Quality Inn NAPA, vet
27	Hunter Dr, Viscount Blvd, N Alon/7-11, Valero/dsl Grand China Buffet, Taco Bell La Quinta $General, $Tree, Jo-Ann, S Alon/7-11, Exxon/dsl Whataburger Family$, Food City

EL PASO

[gas] = gas [food] = food [lodging] = lodging [other] = other [rest stop] = rest stop

TX

EL PASO

INTERSTATE 10 Cont'd

Exit#	Services
26	Hawkins Blvd, El Paso, N [gas] Shamrock, Shell [food] Arby's, Chipotle Mexican, Firehouse Subs, Five Guys, Landry's Seafood, Luby's, Olive Garden, Starbucks, Twin Peaks [other] AT&T, Barnes&Noble, Best Buy, Dick's, Dillard's, JC Penney, Macy's, Old Navy, Petsmart, Sam's Club/gas, Steinmart, TJ Maxx, Verizon, Walgreens, Walmart, S [gas] Valero/dsl [food] McDonald's, Village Inn [lodging] Super 8 [other] Tony Lama Boots
25	Airway Blvd, N [gas] Shell/dsl [food] Carino's, Famous Dave's, Starbucks, Whataburger [lodging] Comfort Inn, Courtyard, Hampton Inn, Holiday Inn, Residence Inn [other] El Paso Airport, VW/Volvo/Mercedes, S [gas] Chevron/Subway/dsl/24hr [lodging] Holiday Inn Express, Staybridge Suites
24b	Geronimo Dr, N [food] El Taco Tote, Taco Cabana [lodging] Wingate Inn [other] $Tree, Costco/gas, Kohl's, Marshall's, Office Depot, Ross, Target, Walgreens, S [gas] Alon/7-11/dsl, Circle K [food] Denny's, IHOP [lodging] Embassy Suites, Hilton Garden, Homewood Suites, Hyatt Place, La Quinta [other] URGENT CARE
24a	Trowbridge Dr, N [food] Luby's, McDonald's, Whataburger [other] Ford, Nissan, Walgreens
23b	US 62/180, to Paisano Dr, N [food] Jack-in-the-Box, McDonald's, Whataburger [lodging] Budget Inn, Soluna Inn [other] Ford, to Carlsbad, U-Haul
23a	Raynolds St, S [food] Arby's [lodging] Best Value Inn, Motel 6 [other] [H]
22b	US 54, Patriot Fwy
22a	Copia St, El Paso, N [gas] Alon/7-11, Shamrock [food] KFC
21	Piedras St, El Paso, N [food] Burger King, McDonald's [other] Family$
20	Dallas St, Cotton St, N [gas] Valero [food] Church's, Subway
19	TX 20, El Paso, downtown, N [gas] Chevron, S [lodging] Camino Real Hotel, DoubleTree Inn, Holiday Inn Express
18b	Franklin Ave, Porfirio Diaz St
18a	Schuster Ave, N [other] Sun Bowl, S [other] to UTEP
16	Executive Ctr Blvd, N [gas] Valero [lodging] Best Value Inn
13b a	US 85, Paisano Dr, to Sunland Park Dr, N [gas] Valero [food] Barrigo's Café, Buffalo Wild Wings, Carino's Italian, ChuckECheese, Corner Bakery Cafe, Five Guys, Grand China, IHOP, Olive Garden, PF Chang's, Red Lobster, Sonic, Whataburger [other] $Tree, AT&T, Barnes&Noble, Best Buy, Dillard's, JC Penney, Marshall's, Michael's, Office Depot, Old Navy, Petsmart, Ross, Sprouts Mkt, Target, URGENT CARE, Verizon, vet, S [gas] Shamrock/dsl, Shell [food] State Line BBQ, Bob-O's Funpark, La Malinche Mexican, Little Caesars, McDonald's, Sonic, Subway [lodging] Best Western, Comfort Suites, Country Inn Suites, Extended Stay America, Sleep Inn [other] Buick/GMC, Chrysler/Dodge/Jeep, Family$, Vista Mkt
12	Resler Dr (from wb)
11	TX 20, to Mesa St, Sunland Park, N [gas] Chevron/dsl, Circle K, Mobil/dsl, Valero/dsl [food] AJ's Diner, Chick-fil-A, Chili's, CiCi's, Coldstone, Cracker Barrel, El Taco Tote, Famous Dave's BBQ, Golden Corral, Krispy Kreme, Leo's Mexican, PacoWong's Chinese, Panda Express, Pei Wei, Popeye's, Schlotsky's, Souper Salad, Subway, Taco Bell, TX Roadhouse, Wendy's, Wienerschnitzel [lodging] Comfort Suites, EconoLodge, Fairfield Inn, La Quinta (2), LaQuinta, Red Roof Inn, SpringHill Suites [other] $General, Albertson's, BigLots, Family$, Firestone/auto, GNC, Home Depot, PepBoys, SteinMart, TirePros, USPO, Verizon, Walmart/McDonald's, S [gas] Chevron/dsl, Valero/dsl [food] Ay Caramba Mexican, Burger King, Church's, Golden Buddha, Jack-in-the-Box, KFC, McDonald's, Pizza Hut, Starbucks, Subway, Taco Cabana, Village Inn [lodging] Days Inn, Motel 6, Travelodge [other] $General, $Tree, AutoZone, Big 8 Foods, Hobby Lobby, Martin Tires, Sam's Club/gas, Walgreens

ANTHONY

Exit#	Services
9	Redd Rd, N [gas] Valero [food] Applebee's, Burger King, Double Dave's Pizza, Peter Piper Pizza, Starbucks, Subway [other] Albertson's, Ford, Kohl's, Lowe's, O'Reilly Parts, S [gas] Circle K/dsl, Valero [other] Chevrolet, Honda, Mazda, URGENT CARE, VW, Walmart Mkt
8	Artcraft Rd, S [gas] Shell/dsl [food] Carl's Jr, Church's, Rudy's BBQ/dsl, Subway [lodging] Hampton Inn, Holiday Inn Express, Quality Inn [other] $Tree, Nissan
6	Lp 375, to Canutillo, N [gas] Shell/DQ/dsl [other] Franklin Mtns SP, to Trans Mountain Rd, S [gas] Chevron/McDonald's [food] IHOP, Pizza Hut, Sonic, Starbucks, Whataburger [other] Discount Tire, El Paso Shops/Famous Brands, GNC, Martin Tire
5mm	**truck check sta eb**
2	Westway, Vinton, N [gas] Petro/Valero/Subway/dsl/scales/24hr/@ [other] American RV Park, Camping World (1mi), PetroLube/tires, S [other] truck repair/tires
1	S [food] Great American Steaks [other] Anthony RV Ctr, funpark **Welcome Ctr eb, full [handicap] facilities, info, litter barrels, petwalk, [phone], [picnic], weigh sta wb**
0	FM 1905, Anthony, N [gas] FLYING J/Denny's/dsl/LP/RV dump/24hr, Love's/Chester's/McDonald's/dsl/scales/24hr [food] Carl's Jr [lodging] Best Value Inn, S [gas] Alon/7-11/dsl, Pilot/Subway/Wendy's/dsl/24hr/@ [food] Burger King, KFC/Taco Bell [lodging] Best Western [other] $General, $Tree, Anthony RV Ctr, Big 8 Foods, funpark, tires, truckwash, Walgreens
0mm	Texas/New Mexico state line

INTERSTATE 20

MARSHALL

Exit#	Services
636mm	Texas/Louisiana state line
635.5mm	**Welcome Ctr/[rest stop] wb, full [handicap] facilities, litter barrels, petwalk, [phone], [picnic]**
635	TX 9, TX 156, to Waskom, N [gas] Chevron/Burger King/dsl, Exxon/McDonald's/dsl [food] DQ, Jim's BBQ [other] Family$, USPO
633	US 80, FM 9, FM 134, to Waskom, N [gas] Shell [food] Catfish Village Rest., S [other] Miss Ellie's RV Park
628	to US 80, to frontage rd
624	FM 2199, to Scottsville
620	FM 31, to Elysian Fields, N [other] Timberline RV Park (3mi)
617	US 59, Marshall, **0-2 mi** N [gas] Exxon/dsl, Shell [food] Applebee's, Burger King, Cafe Italia, Catfish Express, Golden Chick, Golden Corral, IHOP, In Japan Steaks, Jalapeño Tree, KFC, Little Caesars, LJ Silver, McDonald's, Pizza Hut, Porky's Smokehouse, Sonic, Subway, Taco Bell, Waffle House, Wendy's, Whataburger [lodging] Baymont Inn, Best Western, Best Western, Comfort Suites, Days Inn, Fairfield Inn, Hampton Inn, Quality Inn [other] $General, Chevrolet, Chrysler/Dodge/Jeep, Ford/Lincoln, NAPA, Save-A-Lot Foods, Toyota, S [gas] Chevron/dsl, Coco/Pony Express/dsl/scales/@, Rudy's/dsl, Valero/dsl [food] JW Diner [lodging] Best Value Inn, EconoLodge, Holiday Inn Express, La Quinta, Motel 6, Super 8 [other] Holiday Springs RV Park (2mi)
614	TX 43, to Marshall, S [other] to Martin Creek Lake SP
610	FM 3251
604	FM 450, Hallsville, N [gas] Valero/dsl [other] 450 Hitchin' Post RV Park, to Lake O' the Pines
600mm	Mason Creek
599	FM 968, Longview, N [other] Kenworth, S [gas] Exxon/Sonic/dsl, Valero Travel Plaza/@ [other] Cowboy RV Park (5mi), Goodyear Truck Tire, truck repair, truck/rv wash
596	US 259 N, TX 149, to Lake O' Pines, N [gas] Exxon/Grandy's/dsl, Shell/Sonic/TX Smokehouse/dsl [food] Burger King, Denny's, Whataburger [lodging] Centerstone Suites, Microtel, Super

INTERSTATE 20 Cont'd

Exit	Services
596	Continued H, S Valero/dsl Cracker Barrel Holiday Inn Express to Martin Lake SP
595b a	TX 322, Estes Pkwy, N Exxon/dsl, EZ Mart Hajalmer's Rest., Jack-in-the-Box, McDonald's, Waffle House Best Value Inn, Best Western, Express Inn, Guest Inn, Knight's Inn, La Quinta Family$, S Alon/dsl, Murphy USA/dsl KFC/Taco Bell Baymont Inn, Days Inn, Motel 6 auto repair, Walmart/Subway
593mm	Sabine River
591	FM 2087, FM 2011, S Fernbrook RV Park (2mi)
589b a	US 259, TX 31, Kilgore (exits left from wb), 1-3 mi S Chevron/dsl, Exxon/dsl Chili's, Kilgore Café, Mazzio's, McDonald's, Taco Bueno Best Value Inn, Comfort Suites, Hampton Inn, Holiday Inn Express AutoZone, Chevrolet, E Texas Oil Museum, Ford, O'Reilly Parts
587	TX 42, Kilgore, N Exxon/dsl Bodacious BBQ, S Shell/Wendy's/dsl Denny's Days Inn Big Rig Lube, E TX Oil Museum, Walmart (3mi)
583	TX 135, to Kilgore, Overton, N EZmart/dsl Liberty City RV Park, Shallow Creek RV Resort
582	FM 3053, Liberty City, N Mobil/Subway/dsl, Shell/Whataburger/dsl Bob's BBQ, DQ, Los Enchiladas, Pizza Boy, Sonic
579	Joy-Wright Mtn Rd
575	Barber Rd
574mm	**both lanes, accessible, litter barrels**
571b	FM 757, Omen Rd, to Starrville
571a	US 271, to Gladewater, Tyler, S Shell/Sonic/Texas Smokehouse/dsl/scales/24hr
567	TX 155, Winona, N Valero/dsl/24hr, S DQ (2mi) Best Value Inn H, Freightliner
565	FM 2015, to Driskill-Lake Rd
562	FM 14, N Bodacious BBQ to Tyler SP, S Pilot/McDonald's/dsl/scales/24hr Northgate RV Park (4mi)
560	Lavender Rd, S 5 Star RV Park (2 mi)
557	Jim Hogg Rd, N Shell/dsl TX Rose RV Park
556	US 69, to Tyler, N Gulf/dsl, Murphy USA/dsl, RaceWay/dsl Burger King, Chicken Express, Chili's, Cole's Grill, Domino's, Eastern Buffet, IHOP, KFC\LJ Silver, McDonald's, Pizza Hut, Pizza Inn, Posado's Cafe, Sonic, Subway, Taco Bell Best Western, Comfort Suites, Hampton Inn, La Quinta, Motel 6 $General, Family$, Fred's, Kwik Kar, Lowe's, Verizon, Walmart/Subway, S Chevron/DQ, Exxon/dsl Cracker Barrel, Wendy's Best Value Inn
554	Harvey Rd
553	TX 49 S (toll), CR 411
552	FM 849, N Valero/dsl Collin St Bakery, Subway vet
548	TX 110, to Grand Saline, N Exxon/dsl, S Valero/dsl
546mm	**cmv insp sta both lanes**
544	Willow Branch Rd, N Willow Branch RV Park
540	FM 314, to Van, N Loves/Carl's Jr/dsl/scales/24hr Bush's Chicken, DQ, Farmhouse Rest, Sonic, Soul Mans BBQ, Subway Fairfield Inn, Van Inn
538mm	**both lanes, full facilities, litter barrels, petwalk, , vending**
537	FM 773, FM 16
536	Tank Farm Rd
533	Oakland Rd, to Colfax, N Shell/Pilot/A&W/LJ Silver/dsl
530	FM 1255, Canton
528	FM 17, to Grand Saline, N Chrysler/Dodge/Jeep

TYLER

CANTON

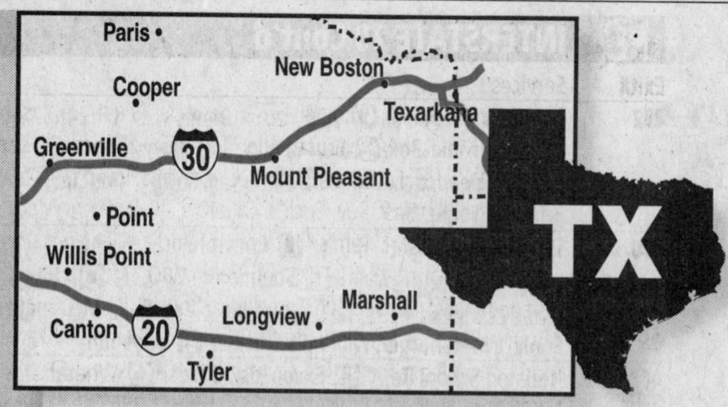

TX

Exit	Services
527	TX 19, N Exxon/dsl Bunker Rest., Chicken Express, Denny's, Jalapeño Tree, Whataburger Motel 6, Quality Inn, Super 8, S Circle K/dsl/24hr, Mobil/dsl, Shell/dsl Dairy Palace, DJ's BBQ, DQ, King's Fish House, McDonald's, Subway, Taco Bell Best Western, Days Inn Ford, Mill Creek Ranch RV Resort, to First Monday SP
526	FM 859, to Edgewood, N water park
523	TX 64, Wills Point, N Shell/dsl/24hr Duke's Rest., Taco Casa Bluebird RV Park, repair
521	Myrtle Springs Rd, S Explore USA RV Ctr, repair, RV camp/dump
519	Turner-Hayden Rd, S Canton RV Park
516	FM 47, to Wills Point, N Fourwinds Steaks, to Lake Tawakoni, S Texaco/dsl Robertson's Café/gas Interstate Motel
512	FM 2965, Hiram-Wills Point Rd
512mm	**cmv inspection sta both lanes**
509	Hiram Rd, S Shell/dsl/cafe/24hr
506	FM 429, FM 2728, College Mound Rd, N Blue Bonnet Ridge RV Park
503	Wilson Rd, S TA/Shell/Country Pride/Pizza Hut/Subway/dsl/LP/24hr/@
501	TX 34, to Terrell, N Exxon/dsl, QT/dsl/scales/24hr, Shell/Subway/dsl Church's, Italrican Cafe, Schlotzsky's, Sonic, Starbucks, Steak&Grill, Waffle House Baymont Inn, Days Inn, Gateway Inn, La Quinta, Motel 6, Quality Inn H, Home Depot, S Circle K/dsl, Valero/dsl/24hr Applebee's, Carmona's Cantina, IHOP, McDonald's, Wendy's Holiday Inn Express, Super 8 Old Navy, Tanger Outlet/famous brands
499b	Rose Hill Rd, to Terrell
499a	to US 80, W to Dallas, same as 498
498	FM 148, to Terrell, N Buc-ee's/dsl, Exxon/Denny's/Subway/dsl, Shell/dsl DQ, Panda Express, Soulman's BBQ, Starbucks, Taco Bueno, Whataburger Discount Tire, S Terrell RV Park
493	FM 1641, S Exxon/Pizza Inn/Taco Mayo/dsl Sonic
491	FM 2932, Helms Tr, to Forney, N Shell/Subway/dsl
490	FM 741, to Forney, N $General
487	FM 740, to Forney, S Forney RV park
483	Lawson Rd, Lasater Rd
482	Belt Line Rd, to Lasater, N Exxon/dsl Smokehouse BBQ, Sonic, S Shell/KFC/Pizza Hut/Subway RV park
481	Seagoville Rd, N Shell/Church's/Dickey's BBQ, Valero/dsl Motel 6, S Lindy's Rest.
480	I-635, N to Mesquite
479b a	US 175, S Marlow/dsl
477	St Augustine Rd, N Family$, S Shell/dsl Sonic
476	Dowdy Ferry Rd
474	TX 310 N, Central Expsy
473b a	JJ Lemmon Rd, I-45 N to Dallas, S to Houston

TERRELL

DALLAS

TX

INTERSTATE 20 Cont'd

Exit#	Services
472	Bonnie View Rd, N FLYING J/Denny's/dsl/LP/24hr, Shell Jack-in-the-Box EconoLodge Blue Beacon, Kenworth, Speedco Lube, S TA/Exxon/Burger King/Taco Bell/dsl/scales/24hr/@
470	TX 342, Lancaster Rd, N Chevron/dsl, Exxon/Popeye's/Subway/dsl/scales/24hr Soulman's BBQ, S Pilot/Wendy's/dsl/scales/24hr LJ Silver/Taco Bell, McDonald's, Sonic, Whataburger, William's Chicken Days Inn
468	Houston School Rd, S Exxon/dsl, QT/dsl Whataburger
467b a	I-35E, N to Dallas, S to Waco, 1 mi N off of I-35E Chevron, Shell McDonald's
466	S Polk St, N Exxon/dsl, Texaco/dsl DQ, Sonic, Subway Family$, S Love's/Carl's Jr/dsl/scales/24hr
465	Wheatland/S Hampton Rds, N Shell/Subway Chick-fil-A, Chili's, Furr's Cafeteria $Tree, Aldi Foods, CVS Drug, GNC, Office Depot, Petsmart, Ross, Target, S Chevron/McDonald's, Murphy USA/dsl, QT/dsl, RaceWay/dsl Arby's, Burger King, Cheddar's, Jack-in-the-Box, Panda Express, Popeye's, Sonic, Spring Creek BBQ, Taco Bell, Wendy's Super 8 H, Home Depot, Honda, Hyundai, Kia, Lowe's, Nissan, Sam's Club/gas, Toyota, Walmart
464b a	US 67, Love Fwy
463	Camp Wisdom Rd, N Chevron/7-11, Exxon Catfish King Rest., Denny's, Taco Bell/LJ Silver, Taco Cabana Best Value Inn, Quality Inn, Royal Inn, Super 7 $Tree, Chrysler/Dodge/Jeep, S Shamrock Burger King, Chubby's Rest., Dave's BBQ, Olive Garden, Red Lobster, Subway, Tortilla Factory
462b a	Duncanville Rd (no EZ wb return), S QT, Shell/dsl Church's, Jack-in-the-Box, Los Lupes Mexican, Popeye's, Whataburger Hilton Garden, Motel 6 Firestone/auto, Kroger
461	Cedar Ridge Rd, S RaceWay/dsl
460	TX 408
458	Mt Creek Pkwy
457	FM 1382, to Grand Prairie, N Shell/7-11/dsl, Valero/dsl Waffle House, S RaceTrac/dsl Jack-in-the-Box to Joe Pool Lake
456	Carrier Pkwy, to Corn Valley Rd, N Chick-fil-A, Dickey's BBQ, Domino's, Don Pablo, Popeyes, Sonic, Starbucks, Taco Cabana, Whataburger AutoZone, Home Depot, Kohl's, Target, S Shell Baskin-Robbins, Boston Mkt, Chapp's Cafe, Cheddar's, Chili's, Chipotle, Denny's, IHOP, Little Caesar's, McDonald's, Spring Creek BBQ, Subway Holiday Inn Express Albertsons/gas, CVS Drug, GNC, Tom Thumb Foods/gas, Verizon, Walgreens
455	TX 151, S QT/dsl
454	Great Southwest Pkwy, N Exxon/dsl, Mobil/7-11/dsl Beto's, Carino's Italian, China Dragon, ChuckeCheese, DQ, Golden Corral, KFC, McDonald's, Taco Bell, Taco Bueno, TX Roadhouse, Waffle House, Wendy's, Wienerschnitzel Comfort Suites, Heritage Inn, Quality Inn H, Firestone/auto, Harley-Davidson, U-Haul, S 7-11, QT/dsl, Shell/Subway/dsl, Valero/dsl Applebee's, Arby's, Buffalo Wild Wings, Burger King, Schlotzsky's, Sonic La Quinta, Super 8 $Tree, AT&T, Discount Tire, Kroger, Office Depot, Petsmart, RaceTrac/dsl, Sam's Club, to Joe Pool Lake, Walgreens, Walmart/McDonald's
453b a	TX 360
452	frontage rd
451	Collins St, New York Ave, N Exxon/dsl, RaceTrac/dsl, Rudy's Store/BBQ/dsl Cotton Patch Cafe, Golden Corral, Jack-in-the-Box, Whataburger Chrysler/Dodge/Jeep, Kia/Mazda/VW, URGENT CARE, S QT, Shell, Valero/dsl Chicken Express, KFC/Taco Bell, McDonald's, Sonic, Subway, Taco Bueno Hampton Inn Buick/GMC, Nissan
450	Matlock Rd, N Abuelo's Mexican, Bar Louie, BJ's Rest., Black-eyed Pea, Bone Daddy's, Boomer Jack's Grill, Chuy's Mexican, Coldstone, Dave&Buster's, Genghis Grill, Houlihan's, India Grill, Jason's Deli, Kincaide's Burgers, McAlister's Deli, Melting Pot, Mercado Juarez, Mimi's Cafe, PF Changs, Plucker's's Wings, Potbelly, Red Robin, Starbucks, Sweet Tomatoes, The Keg Steaks, Wendy's, Which Wich Courtyard, Quality Inn, Residence Inn H, AT&T, Costco/gas, Jo-Ann Fabrics, Lowe's, Old Navy, Petsmart, Staples, World Mkt, S 7-11, RaceWay/dsl, Shell/7-11 Joe's Pizza, Pizza Patron, Starbucks Fry's Electronics, O'Reilly Parts
449	FM 157, Cooper St, N Shell/dsl Cane's, Cheesecake Factory, Chili's, Corner Bakery, Grandy's, Honeybaked Ham IHOP, In-N-Out, McDonald's, Nagoya Japanese, On-the-Border Outback Steaks, Pei Wei, Razzoo's Cajun Café, Red Lobster Rockfish Seafood, Salt Grass Steaks, Souper Salad, Spaghetti Whse, Spring Creek BBQ, Whataburger Best Western Days Inn, Holiday Inn Express, La Quinta, Studio 6, Super 8 Barnes&Noble, Best Buy, Dick's, Dillard's, Discount Tire JC Penney, Macy's, Michael's, Office Depot, Target, TJ Maxx Verizon, S Shell Applebee's, Arby's, Boston Mkt, Burger St, Carl's Jr, Chick-fil-A, Chipotle, Denny's, El Arroyo, El Fenix Mexican, Lin's Buffet, LJ Silver, Macaroni Grill, McDonald's, Olive Garden, Panda Express, Peter Piper Pizza, Schlotsky's, Starbucks, Subway, Taco Bueno, Taco Cabana, TGIFriday In Town Suites, Microtel $Tree, AAA, Acura, Chevrolet, Ford Hobby Lobby, Home Depot, Honda, Hyundai, NTB, Ross, Suzuki Toyota, Walmart/McDonald's
448	Bowen Rd, N QT, RaceTrac/dsl Cracker Barrel, Sonic S Shell
447	Kelly-Elliott Rd, Park Springs Blvd, N 7-11, Valero S Exxon/Subway city park
445	Green Oaks Blvd, N Conoco/dsl, Shell/7-11/dsl Arby's Boston Mkt, Braum's, Burger St, Cafe Acapulco, Chapp's Cafe Chick-fil-A, Church's, CiCi's, Colter's BBQ, Fuzzy's Tacos, Hooters, Jack-in-the-Box, Jay Jay Rest., Joe's Pizza, Mijo's Cafe, Quizno's, Schlotzsky's, Starbucks, Taco Bell, Taco Cabana, Taco Casa, Tai-Pan, Wendy's, Whataburger $Tree, Ace Hardware, Albertsons, AT&T, CVS Drug, Firestone, Kroger/dsl, Meineke, Office Depot, Verizon, Walgreens, S 7-11, Murphy Express/dsl QT/dsl, Valero/dsl Cheddar's, Corky's Pizza, Golden Buffet IHOP, McDonald's, Pancho's Mexican, Panda Express, Sonic Subway, Taco Bueno, Waffle House $General, AutoZone BigLots, Discount Tire, O'Reilly Parts, Tuesday Morning, vet Walmart/Subway
444	US 287 S, to Waxahatchie, from eb, same as 445
443	Bowman Springs Rd (from wb)
442b a	I-820 to Ft Worth, US 287 bus, N Valero Great Western Inn, Knights Inn, S QT/dsl
441	Anglin Dr, Hartman Lane, N Woodspring Suites, S Conoco/dsl
440b	Forest Hill Dr, S Shell/7-11/dsl Braum's, Capt D's, CiCi Pizza, Jack-in-the-Box, Luby's, Sonic, Starbucks, Subway, Taco Bell La Quinta $General, $Tree, AutoZone, CVS Drug Discount Tire, O'Reilly Parts, Super 1 Foods, Walgreens

FT WORTH

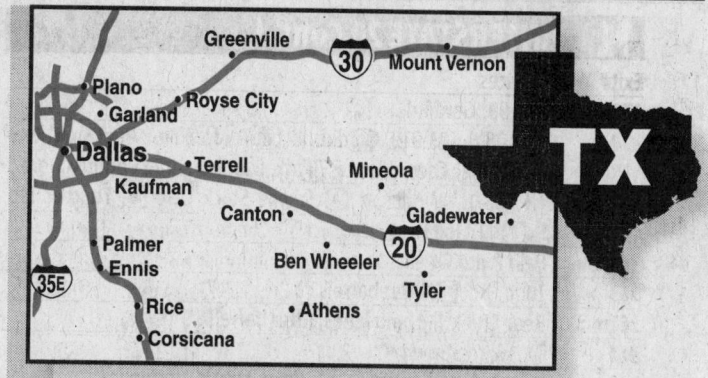

INTERSTATE 20 Cont'd

Exit#	Services
440a	Wichita St, N Chevron/dsl, QT/dsl #1 Chinese, Starbucks, Taco Casa, Wendy's, S Texaco/dsl, Valero Chicken Express, Denny's, Domino's, McDonald's, Pizza Hut, Schlotzsky's, Taco Bueno, Whataburger Best Western, Comfort Inn, Hampton Inn
439	Campus Dr, N Chrysler/Dodge/Jeep, Ford, S Sam's Club/gas
438	Oak Grove Rd, S Valero
437	I-35W, N to Ft Worth, S to Waco
436b	Hemphill St, N Shell/dsl, S Chevrolet
436a	FM 731 (from eb), to Crowley Ave, N Conoco/dsl, Valero/dsl China Express $General, Sav-a-Lot Foods, S BurgerBox, Pizza Hut/Taco Bell, Subway transmissions
435	McCart St, N Shamrock, Shell/dsl, S Mobil/dsl
434b	Trail Lakes Dr, S Shell Sonic, Starbucks, Subway, Wendy's CVS Drug, Family$
434a	Granbury Rd
433	Hulen St, N Shell/dsl Chef Chen, ChuckECheese, Honeybaked Ham, Hooters, Olive Garden, Papa Murphy's, Souper Salad, Subway, TX Roadhouse TownePlace Suites Albertsons, Home Depot, NTB, Petsmart, Sprouts Mkt, TJ Maxx, S Abuelo's Mexican, BJ's Rest., Denny's, Five Guys, In-N-Out, Jack-in-the-Box, Kincaide's Burgers, McDonald's, Panera Bread, Pizza Inn, Potbelly, Red Lobster, Red Robin Hampton Inn Barnes&Noble, Dillard's, Hobby Lobby, Macy's, Michael's, Office Depot, Old Navy, Ross, Sears/auto
431	(432 from wb), TX 183, Bryant-Irvin Rd, N Chevron Chipotle Mexican, Genghis Grill, Keg Steaks, Mimi's Café, On-the-Border, Taste of Asia Best Buy, Cavender's Boots, Kohl's, Lowe's, Petsmart, Sam's Club/gas, S Chevron, Shell/dsl Blackeyed Pea, Chicken Express, Chick-fil-A, Cousin's BBQ, Fox & Hound, Fuddruckers, IHOP, Jimmy John's, Lonestar Oysters, Outback Steaks, Pei Wei, Pizza Hut, Razzoo's Cajun, Rio Mambo, SaltGrass Steaks, Schlotzsky's, Sonic, Starbucks, Subway, Szechuan Courtyard, Extended Stay America, Holiday Inn Express, Homewood Suites, Hyatt Place, La Quinta H, AT&T, Costco/gas, Firestone/auto, Ford, Goodyear/auto, Infiniti, Kwik Kar, Lexus, Mazda, PetCo, Staples, Target, Verizon, Walgreens
430mm	Clear Fork Trinity River
429b	Winscott Rd, N Circle K/dsl Cracker Barrel Best Western, Comfort Suites
429a	US 377, to Granbury, S QT/dsl, RaceTrac/dsl, Shell/dsl, Valero 7-11/dsl, Arby's, Braum's, Burger King, Chicken Express, Chick-fil-A, Domino's, Golden Chick, Jack-in-the-Box, KFC/Taco Bell, McDonald's, NY Pizza, Panda Express, Pizza Hut, Ricky's BBQ, Sonic, Starbucks, Subway, Taco Casa, Taco Villa, Waffle House, Waffle House, Whataburger Motel 6 $General, AutoZone, CVS Drug, O'Reilly Parts, USPO, Walgreens, Walmart
428	I-820, N around Ft Worth
426	RM 2871, Chapin School Rd
425	Markum Ranch Rd
421	I-30 E (from eb), to Ft Worth
420	FM 1187, Aledo, Farmer, parking & ride
419mm	weigh sta eb
418	Ranch House Rd, Willow Park, Willow Park, N Exxon/Taco Casa, Shell/dsl Pizza Hut, Sonic, Subway, Whataburger, S Chevron/dsl Chicken Express, Domino's, McDonald's, Milano's Italian, Mr Jim's Pizza, Railhead BBQ Knights Inn $General, Ace RV Ctr., Brookshire Foods, Cowtown RV Park

Greenville, 30, Mount Vernon, Plano, Garland, Royse City, Dallas, Terrell, Mineola, Kaufman, Canton, Gladewater, Palmer, Ennis, Ben Wheeler, 20, Tyler, 35E, Rice, Athens, Corsicana, TX

WEATHERFORD

Exit#	Services
417mm	no services
415	FM 5, Mikus Rd, Annetta, S Shell/dsl, Signature/dsl 415 RV Ctr
413	(414 from wb), US 180 W, Lake Shore Dr, N Murphy USA/dsl, RaceTrac/dsl, Shell/dsl DQ, Golden Chick, McDonald's, Paleo's Pizza, Sonic, Subway, Taco Bell, Waffle House Buick/Cadillac/Chevrolet/GMC, Ford, Hyundai, Lincoln, Nissan, Suzuki, Toyota, Walgreens, Walmart/Subway, S Valero/dsl
411	Service Rd (from wb), same as 413
410	Bankhead Hwy, S Loves/Subway/dsl/24hr
409	FM 2552 N, Clear Lake Rd, N Petro/Valero/Iron Skillet/dsl/24hr/@ Antonio's Mexican, Granny's Kitchen, Jack-in-the-Box, Little Panda Chinese, Popeyes Heritage Inn, SleepGo Motel H, Blue Beacon, S Shell/dsl
408	TX 171, FM 1884, FM 51, Tin Top Rd, Weatherford, N Exxon, Mobil, Murphy USA/dsl Applebee's, Baker's Ribs, Braum's, Buffalo Wild Wings, Cane's, Chicken Express, China Harbor, CiCi's Pizza, Cotton Patch Cafe, IHOP, Kincade's Burgers, LJ Silver, Logan's Roadhouse, McAlister's Deli, McDonald's, MT Rest., Olive Garden, Panda Express, Rosa's Cafe, Schlotzsky's, Starbucks, Subway, Taco Bell, Taco Bueno, Taco Cabana, Whataburger, Wild Mushroom Steaks La Quinta, Sleep Inn, Super 8 $Tree, AT&T, AutoZone, Belk, Christian Bros Auto, Discount Tire, Firestone/auto, JC Penney, Just Brakes, Michael's, TJ Maxx, Verizon, Walgreens, Walmart/Subway, S Exxon/Subway/dsl, Shell/Burger King/dsl Chick-fil-A, Chili's, Chipotle, Cracker Barrel, Honey Bee Ham, On-the-Border, Tokyo Japanese Steaks, Waffle House, Whataburger Best Western, Candlewood Suites, Comfort Suites, Fairfield Inn, Hampton Inn, Holiday Inn Express, Motel 6, Quality Inn, Super Value Inn Best Buy, GNC, Kohl's, Lowe's, NTB, Petsmart, Ross, Target, URGENT CARE
407	Tin Top Rd (from eb), N Home Depot, S KOA, same as 408
406	Old Dennis Rd, N QT/dsl/scales/24hr, Truck'n Travel Chuck Wagon Rest. Quest Inn, S Pilot/Wendy's/dsl/scales/24hr EconoLodge, Quality 1 Motel Boss Shop Repair
404	Williams Memorial Dr
402	(403 from wb), TX 312, to Weatherford
397	FM 1189, to Brock, N Valero/dsl Oak Creek RV Park
394	FM 113, to Millsap
393mm	Brazos River
391	Gilbert Pit Rd
390mm	**both lanes, full facilities, litter barrels, petwalk, vending**
386	US 281, to Mineral Wells, Stephenville, N Shell/Subway/dsl Gilbert Pecans, S Chevron/Maverick TC/Taco Casa/dsl, Sunoco/Stripes/Taco Co/dsl DQ
380	FM 4, Santo, S RV Park
376	Blue Flat Rd, Panama Rd

TX

= gas = food = lodging = other = rest stop

INTERSTATE 20 Cont'd

Exit#	Services
373	TX 193, Gordon
370	TX 108 S, FM 919, Gordon, N Texaco/Bar-B/dsl, S Exxon/dsl Cactus Rose RV Park, Longhorn Inn/Country Store
367	TX 108 N, Mingus, N Smoke Stack Café Thurber Sta, S NY Hill Rest.
364mm	Palo Pinto Creek
363	Tudor Rd, **litter barrels**
362mm	Bear Creek, **both lanes, litter barrels**
361	TX 16, to Strawn
359mm	**wb, full facilities, litter barrels, petwalk**
358	(from wb), frontage rd
356mm	Russell Creek
354	Lp 254, Ranger
353	**eb, full facilities, litter barrels, vending**
351	(352 from wb), College Blvd
349	FM 2461, Ranger, N Loves/Godfather's/Subway/dsl/scales/24hr DQ Sunset Inn RL RV Park, S Phillips 66/dsl repair
347	FM 3363(from wb), Olden, S TX Steakhouse
345	FM 3363(from eb), Olden, S TX Steakhouse
343	TX 112, FM 570, Eastland, Lake Leon, N Alon/7-11/Subway, Murphy USA/dsl, Shell/dsl Chicken Express, DQ, Golden Chick, McDonald's, Pizza Heaven, Sonic, Taco Bell Holiday Inn Express, La Quinta, Super 8/RV park $General, AT&T, AutoZone, Buick/Cadillac/Chevrolet/GMC, Chrysler/Dodge/Jeep, Ford, O'Reilly Parts, TrueValue, Walmart, S Exxon/dsl Pulido's Mexican Budget Host, Days Inn
340	TX 6, Eastland, N Valero/dsl H, S Shell/dsl
337	spur 490, N The Wild Country RV Park
332	US 183, Cisco, N Alon/Allsups/dsl, Cow Pokes/dsl Chicken Express, DQ, Pizza Heaven, Sonic, Subway Cisco Inn, Executive Inn/RV Park $General, Family$, Hilton Mon (1mi), NAPA
330	TX 206, Cisco, N Sunoco/Stripes/Tacos/dsl/scales/24hr Best Value Inn H, S FLYING J/Denny's/dsl/scales/24hr
329mm	**wb, accessible, litter barrels**
327mm	**eb, accessible, litter barrels**
324	Scranton Rd
322	Cooper Creek Rd
320	FM 880 N, FM 2945 N, to Moran
319	FM 880 S, Putnam, N Fillin Sta/café USPO
316	Brushy Creek Rd
313	FM 2228
310	Finley Rd
308	Lp 20, Baird
307	US 283, Clyde, N Loves/Chester's/Subway/dsl/scales/24hr DQ Baird Motel/RV park/dump, S Alon/Allsups/7-11, Conoco/dsl Robertson's Café
306	FM 2047, Baird, N Chevrolet/GMC, Hanner RV Ctr
303	Union Hill R
301	FM 604, Cherry Lane, N Exxon/dsl McDonald's, Sonic, Whataburger NAPA, S Alon/7-11, Alon/7-11/dsl Chicken Express, Pizza House, Subway Family$, United Mkt, USPO
300	FM 604 N, Clyde, N Chrysler/Dodge/Jeep, S Conoco/dsl White's RV Park/dump
299	FM 1707, Hays Rd
297	FM 603, Eula Rd
296.5mm	**both lanes, full facilities, litter barrels, petwalk, wireless internet**

ABILENE

Exit#	Services
294	Buck Creek Rd, N Big Coun[r]y RV Ctr/park, Buck Creek RV Park/dump, S Abilene RV Park
292b	Elmdale Rd
292a	Lp 20 (exits left from wb)
290	TX 36, Lp 322, S zoo
288	TX 351, N Alon/7-11/dsl, Murphy USA/dsl Buffal[o] Wild Wings, Chick-fil-A, Chili's, Cracker Barrel, DQ, Golden Chick, Jason's Deli, Oscar's Mexican, Panda Express, Subway, Tac[o] Casa, Wendy's Comfort Suites, Courtyard, Days Inn, Executive Inn, Holiday Inn Express, Knights Inn, Quality Inn, Residence Inn, TownePlace Suites, Whitten Inn $Tree, AT&[T], Lowe's, Walmart/Subway, S Super 8 H
286c	FM 600, Abilene, N Alon/7-11/dsl, Alon/Allsups/ds[l] Denny's Best Western, Hampton Inn, Holiday Inn, L[a] Quinta, S Alon/7-11/dsl Sleep Inn
286	US 83, Pine St, Abilene, S Alon/Allsups Frontier In[n] H
285	Old Anson Rd, S Alon/Allsups/dsl Best Value Inn
283b	N US 277, U83, Anson
283a	US 277 S, US 83(exits left from wb)
282	FM 3438, Shirley Rd, S Motel 6 KOA
281	Fulwiler Rd, to Dyess AFB, S to Dyess AFB
279	US 84 E, to Abilene, **1-3 mi S** access to facilities
278	Lp 20, N Conoco/dsl/24hr dsl repair, S Westgo TC Phillips 66/Huddle House/dsl/scales/24hr/@ Mack Trucks Volvo
277	FM 707, Tye, N FLYING J/Denny's/dsl/LP/24hr Peterbilt, truck lube, Tye RV Park, S Alon/7-11/dsl Southe[rn] Tire Mart, USPO
274	Wells Lane
272	Wimberly Rd
270	FM 1235, Merkel, N Alon/dsl/24hr, Conoco/dsl
269	FM 126, N Sonic, Subway Scottish Inn, S Alon/[7-]11/dsl, Phillips 66/dsl DQ, Skeet's BBQ CarQue[st], Family$
267	Lp 20, Merkel, **1mi S** access to gas, food, lodging
266	Derstine Rd
264	Noodle Dome Rd
263	Lp 20, Trent, N RV Park
262	FM 1085, S Alon/7-11/dsl
261	Lp 20, Trent
259	Sylvester Rd
258	White Flat Rd, oil wells
257mm	**both lanes, full facilities, litter barrels, petwalk, vending**
256	Stink Creek Rd
255	Adrian Rd
251	Eskota Rd
249	FM 1856, N Lonestar RV Park
247	TX 70 N, Sweetwater
246	Alabama Ave, Sweetwater
245	Arizona Ave(from wb), same as 244
244	TX 70 S, Sweetwater, N Alon/7-11/dsl/24hr, Chevro[n] Subway/dsl, Murphy USA/dsl Dickey's BBQ, Dominc[o's] DQ, Golden Chick, McDonald's, Subway, Wendy's B[est] Western, Budget Inn, La Quinta, Motel 6 H, AT&T, A[u]toZone, Medicine Place Drug, Verizon, Walmart, S She[ll/] dsl Big Boy's BBQ, Buck's BBQ, Great Wall Buffet, Schl[o]zsky's, Skeet's Grill, Taco Bell Country Hearth Inn, Hampt[on] Inn, Holiday Inn Express, Ranch House Motel/rest., Stay Expr[ess] Inn Chaparral RV Park, Ford, Rainbolt RV Park
243	Hillsdale Rd, Robert Lee St, N Family RV Ctr

SWEETWATER

TX

INTERSTATE 20 Cont'd

Exit#	Services
242	Hopkins Rd, N Loves/Arby's/dsl/scales/24hr Microtel, S TA/Alon/Pizza Hut/Popeye's/dsl/scales/24hr/@ Rolling Plains RV Park, truck wash, truck/tire repair
241	Lp 20, Sweetwater, N gas food lodging, S RV camping
240	Lp 170, N , camping
239	May Rd
238b a	US 84 W, Blackland Rd
237	Cemetery Rd
236	FM 608, Roscoe, N Alon/dsl, Sunoco/Stripes/Taco Co/dsl NAPA, S Retta Mae's Rest
235	to US 84, Roscoe
230	FM 1230, many wind turbines
229mm	wb, litter barrels, accessible
228mm	eb, litter barrels, accessible
227	Narrell Rd
226b	Lp 20(from wb), Loraine
226a	FM 644 N, Wimberly Rd
225	FM 644 S, 1 mi S access to gas food
224	Lp 20, to Loraine, 1 mi S gas food
223	Lucas Rd, S 223 RV Park
221	Lasky Rd
220	FM 1899
219	Lp 20, Country Club Rd, Colorado City
217	TX 208 S, N Sunoco/Stripes/Taco Co/DSL/scales/24hr La Quinta
216	TX 208 N, N Chevron/Subway/dsl DQ Sleep Inn, S Sunoco/Stripes/Taco Co/dsl Golden Chick, Pizza Hut, Sonic American Inn, Hotel Texas, Motel 6, Super 8 (H), $General, City RV Park, Parts+
215	FM 3525, Rogers Rd, N Motel 6 Extended, 2 mi S access to gas food (H)
214.5mm	Colorado River
213	Lp 20, Enderly Rd, Colorado City
212	FM 1229
211mm	Morgan Creek
210	FM 2836, S camping, , to Lake Colorado City SP
209	Dorn Rd
207	Lp 20, Westbrook
206	FM 670, to Westbrook
204mm	N wb, full facilities, litter barrels, petwalk, ,
200	Conaway Rd
199	Iatan Rd
195	frontage rd (from eb)
194a	E Howard Field Rd
192	FM 821, many oil wells
191mm	eb, full facilities, litter barrels, petwalk, ,
190	Snyder Field Rd
189	McGregor Rd
188	FM 820, Coahoma, N Sunoco/Stripes/Taco Co/dsl DQ Coahoma Inn Coahoma RV Park, USPO
186	Salem Rd, Sand Springs
184	Moss Lake Rd, Sand Springs, N Alon/dsl $General, S RV camping
182	Midway Rd
181b	Refinery Rd, N Alon Refinery
181a	FM 700, N , RV camping, 2 mi S (H)
179	US 80, Big Spring, S Alon/7-11 Denny's Camlot Inn, Quality Inn, Super 8 $General, Buick/Cadillac/Chevrolet
178	TX 350, Big Spring, N Shell/dsl tire/truck service, S Pilot/McDonald's/dsl/scales/24hr

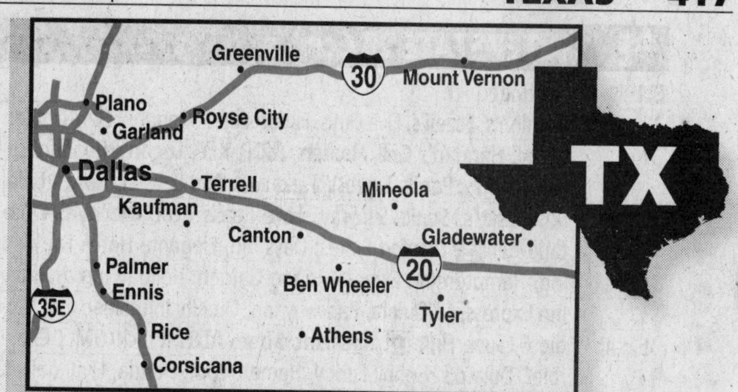

BIG SPRING

Exit#	Services
177	US 87, Big Spring, N Exxon/dsl, TA/Subway/Popeye's/dsl/scales/24hr/@ Texas Cajan Cafe Advantage Inn, La Quinta, Motel 6, Plaza Inn, S Alon/dsl, Sunoco/Stripes/dsl Casa Blanca Mexican, DQ, McAlister's Deli Baymont Inn, Best Western, Hampton Inn, Holiday Inn Express, TownePlace Suites Chrysler/Dodge/Jeep
176	TX 176, Andrews
174	Lp 20 E, Big Springs, S Shell/dsl (H), , Big Spring SP
172	Cauble Rd
171	Moore Field Rd
169	FM 2599
168mm	both lanes, , litter barrels
165	FM 818
158	Lp 20 W, to Stanton, N RV camping
156	TX 137, Lamesa, S Phillips 66/Stripes/Subway/dsl/24hr Sonic Cobblestone Inn, Comfort Inn, Super 8
154	US 80, Stanton, 2 mi S access to gas food lodging
151	FM 829 (from wb)
144	Loop 250, 2-3 mi N services in Midland
143mm	frontage rd (from eb)
142mm	both lanes, ,litter barrels, hits marker
140	FM 307 (from eb)
138	TX 158, FM 715, Greenwood, N Pilot/dsl, Valero/dsl KD's BBQ, Whataburger, S FLYING J/Moe's/dsl/scales/24hr, Sunoco/Stripes/Subway/dsl, Sunoco/Stripes/Taco Co/dsl Baymont Inn
137	Old Lamesa Rd, N Mainstay Suites
136	TX 349, Midland, N Murphy USA/dsl, Sunoco/Stripes/Taco Co/dsl Cici's Pizza, Domino's, IHOP, Jack-in-the-Box, Little Caesar's, McAlister's Deli, McDonald's, Sonic, Starbucks Best Western, Candlewood Suites, Comfort Inn, Country Inn&Suites, Holiday Inn Express, Microtel, Quality Inn, Super 8, West Texas Inn $General, $Tree, Advance Parts, AutoZone, Chavez Tires, Discount Tire, Family$, Petroleum Museum, Verizon, Walmart/Subway, S Daves Gas/NAPA/dsl, Exxon/Burger King/dsl, Pilot/dsl, Stripes/Taco Co/dsl
135	Cotton Flat Rd, S (H)
134	Midkiff Rd, 0-1 mi (Wall St) N Alon/7-11, Exxon/dsl, Shell, Sunoco/Stripes/Subway/dsl Denny's, DQ Best Value Inn, Bradford Inn, Days Inn, Executive Inn, La Quinta, Studio 6, Super 8 (H), Chevrolet, Chrysler/Dodge/Jeep, Ford/ Lincoln, Honda, Midland RV Park, Subaru
131	TX 158, Midland, N Motel 6 Midland RV Park, S Loves/Chester's/Subway/dsl/scales/24hr Suburban Inn
126	FM 1788, N Pilot/McDonald's/dsl/scales/24hr, Sunoco/Stripes/Taco Co/dsl Steak'n Shake, Subway , Carquest, Main Street Mkt/Subway/dsl, museum, Western Auto
121	Lp 338, Odessa, 0-3 mi (TX 191) N Alon/7-11, Stripes/Taco Co/dsl Carino's, Casa Ole, Cheddar's, Chili's, Dickey's BBQ,

MIDLAND

TX

INTERSTATE 20 Cont'd

ODESSA

121	Continued Domino's, Fazoli's, Five Guys, Fuddruckers, Genghis Grill, Golden Corral, Harigan's Grill, Hooters, IHOP, KFC, Logan's Roadhouse, McDonald's, Panda Express, Pizza Hut, Red Lobster, Rosa's Cafe, Schlotzsky's, Sonic, Subway, Twin Peaks Rest, Wendy's, Whataburger Comfort Suites, Days Inn, Elegante Hotel, Fairfield Inn, Hampton Inn Express, Hilton Garden, Holiday Inn, Holiday Inn Express, La Quinta, Parkway Inn, Quality Inn, Sleep Inn, Studio 6, Super Inn $General, $Tree, AT&T, Buick/GMC, Chevrolet, Dillard's, Hobby Lobby, Home Depot, Honda, Hyundai, JC Penney, Lowe's, Mazda, Mkt Street, Nissan, Sam's Club/gas, Staples, Target, Toyota, U of TX Permian Basin, USPO, Walmart/Subway, S FLYING J/McDonald's/dsl/scales/24hr
120	JBS Pkwy, N Candlewood Suites, Comfort Inn, Staybridge Suites, Super 8 Mack/Volvo
118	FM 3503, Grandview Ave, N Alon/dsl Freightliner/Peterbilt
116	US 385, Odessa, N Chevron/dsl, Stripes/Taco Co/dsl DQ, La Margarita Delux Inn, Ramada, Villa West Inn H, $General, city park, Family$, S Alon/dsl, Valero/dsl MainStay Suites, Motel 6
115	FM 1882, N Sunoco/Stripes/Taco Co/dsl, S Loves/McDonald's/Subway/dsl/scales/24hr Blue Beacon
113	TX 302, Odessa
112	FM 1936, Odessa, N Red X Trkstp/dsl
108	Moss Ave, Meteor Crater, Meteor Crater, N Road Ranger/Church's/Subway/dsl/scales/24hr
104	FM 866, Meteor Crater Rd, Goldsmith, N RV park
103.5mm	**weigh sta both directions**
101	FM 1601, to Fenwell, Penwell
93	FM 1053, to Ft Stockton
86	TX 41, N camping, Monahans Sandhills SP
83	US 80, Monahans, 2 mi N H, RV camping
80	TX 18, Monahans, N Chevron/dsl Bar-H Steaks, DQ, Great Wall Buffet, McDonald's, Pappy's BBQ, Pizza Hut, Sonic Candlewood Suites, Holiday Inn Express H, $General, Alco, Family$, Lowe's Foods, O'Reilly Parts, repair/tires, Verizon, S Alon/dsl, Sunoco/Stripes/Subway/dsl, Texaco/Huddle House/dsl/24hr Huddle House Best Value Inn, Best Western, Comfort Inn, Texan Inn Buick/Chevrolet/GMC, Chrysler/Dodge/Jeep, RV Park, vet
79	Lp 464, Monahans, S La Quinta
76	US 80, Monahans, 2 mi N RV camping, to Million Barrel Museum
73	FM 1219, Wickett, N Alon/Allsup's/dsl, S Main St/Subway/dsl
70	TX 65
69.5mm	**both lanes, full facilities, litter barrels, petwalk, wi-fi**
66	TX 115, FM 1927, to Pyote, N Alon/dsl
58	frontage rd, multiple oil wells
52	Lp 20 W, to Barstow
49	FM 516, to Barstow
48mm	Pecos River
44	Collie Rd
42	US 285, Pecos, N FLYING J/Denny's/dsl/scales/24hr, Alon, Sunoco/Stripes/dsl/e85 Alfredo's Mexican, DQ, El Rodeo Mexican, Golden Palace Chinese, Pizza Hut Holiday Inn Express, Motel 6, OakTree Inn, Quality Inn AutoZone, museum, tire repair, Walmart, S Loves/McDonald's/Subway/Chester's/dsl/scales/24hr@ Microtel
40	Country Club Dr, N Cobblestone Inn, Comfort Suites, Fairfield Inn st patrol, S Stripes/Subway Alpine Lodge Rest. Best Western/rest., La Quinta municipal park, Pecos Park/Zoo, RV camping
39	TX 17, Pecos, N Pilot/Dunkin Donuts/PJ Fresh/dsl/scales/24hr H, S Sunoco/Stripes/Subway/dsl/24hr Hampton Inn, La Bonita Inn Buick/Chevrolet/GMC, Pecos Tire, Trapark RV Park
37	Lp 20 E
33	FM 869
29	Shaw Rd, S to TX AM Ag Sta
25mm	**both lanes, accessible, litter barrels, tables**
22	FM 2903, to Toyah, N Valero/dsl
13	McAlpine Rd
7	Johnson Rd
3	Stocks Rd

I-20 begins/ends on I-10, 187mm.

MONAHANS

PECOS

INTERSTATE 27

AMARILLO

Exit#	Services
I-27 begins/ends on I-40, exit 70 in Amarillo.	
123b	I-40, W to Albuquerque, E to OK City
123a	26th Ave, E Discount Gas
122c	from sb only
122a	34th Ave, Tyler St, E Valero Sonic $General
122b	FM 1541, Washington St, Parker St, Moss Lane, W Hungry Howie's, Taco Bell, Thai Express
121a	Hawthorne Dr, Austin St, E Amarillo Motel, W Scottie' Transmissions
121b	Georgia St, E Murphy USA/dsl Buick/GMC, Honda Mazda, Subaru, Walmart/McDonald's
120b	45th Ave, E Waffle House O'Reilly Parts, repair W Toot'n Totum, Valero Abuelo's Mexican, Burger King, Donut Stop, Gatti's Pizza, Grandma's Cocina, McDonald's Whataburger $General, Advance Parts, BMW, Chrysler Dodge/Jeep, Drug Emporium, vet, Walgreens
120a	Republic Ave
119b a	(from sb) Western St, 58th Ave, E Phillips 66/dsl Sonic Subway $General, W Valero/dsl Arby's, Braum's LJ Silver, Pizza Hut, Thai Palace, Wendy's Aamco, U-Hau USPO, Walgreens
119a	(from nb) W Hillside
117	Bell St, Arden Rd, W Valero/dsl Popeye's, Soni $General
116	Lp 335, Hollywood Rd, E Loves/Subway/dsl scales/24hr, Phillips 66/dsl McDonald's, Waffle House Whataburger Comfort Suites, Motel 6, W Holiday In Express H (8mi)
115	Sundown Lane
113	McCormick Rd, E $General, Ford, W Family Campin Ctr
112	FM 2219, E Stater's RV Ctr
111	Rockwell Rd, W Buick/GMC
110	US 87 S, US 60 W, Canyon
109	Buffalo Stadium Rd, W stadium
108	FM 3331, Hunsley Rd
106	TX 217, to Palo Duro Cyn SP, Canyon, E Palo Duro Canyc SP (10mi), Palo Duro RV Park, 3 mi W McDonald's Be Western, Holiday Inn Express Plains Museum, to W A&M
103	FM 1541 N, Cemetery Rd
99	Hungate Rd

INTERSTATE 27 Cont'd

Exit#	Services
98mm	**parking area both lanes, litter barrels**
96	Dowlen Rd
94	FM 285, to Wayside
92	Haley Rd
90	FM 1075, Happy, W gas/dsl
88b a	US 87 N, FM 1881, Happy, same as 90
83	FM 2698
82	FM 214
77	US 87, Tulia
75	NW 6th St, Tulia, 1 mi E Phillips 66/dsl, Shell/dsl Pizza Hut, Sonic Lasso Motel, W same as 74
74	TX 86, Tulia, E Lasso Motel H, W Pilot/Valero/Subway/dsl/scales/24hr Executive Inn
70mm	**litter barrels, parking area both lanes**
68	FM 928
63	FM 145, Kress, 1 mi E gas/dsl food
61	US 87, County Rd
56	FM 788
54	FM 3183, to Plainview
53	Lp 27, Plainview, E H, access to gas, camping, food, lodging
51	Quincy St
50	TX 194, Plainview, E Valero/dsl H, to Wayland Bapt U, W Reddy Hotel
49	US 70, Plainview, E AllStar/dsl, Alon/dsl, Cefco/dsl, Conoco, Stripes/dsl A&W/LJ Silver, Carlito's Mexican, China Dragon, Cotton Patch Café, Domino's, Furr's Café, Leal's Mexican, Pizza Hut, Tokyo Japanese, Woodfire Grill Comfort Suites, Days Inn, Quality Inn $Tree, AutoZone, Beall's, Ford/Lincoln, GNC, NAPA, O'Reilly Parts, Toyota, United Foods, W Murphy USA/dsl, Phillips 66/dsl, Valero/dsl Burger King, Chicken Express, Chili's, Empire Buffet, IHOP, Little Mexico, McDonald's, Mia's Italian, Sonic, Subway, Taco Bell Holiday Inn Express, Plainview Inn, Super 8 Verizon, Walmart/McDonald's
48	FM 3466, Plainview (from nb), E Chevrolet
45	Lp 27, to Plainview
43	FM 2337
41	County Rd
38	Main St
37	FM 1914, Cleveland St, W Conoco/dsl city park, Family$, Lowe's Foods
36	FM 1424, Hale Center
32	FM 37 W
31	FM 37 E
29mm	**RS both lanes, full facilities, litter barrels, petwalk, tornado shelter, vending**
27	County Rd
24	FM 54, W RV park/dump
22	Lp 369, Abernathy
21	FM 597, Main St, Abernathy, W Conoco/dsl DQ $General, USPO
20	FM 597, Abernathy (from nb)
17	CR 53
15	Lp 461, to New Deal, same as 14
14	FM 1729, E Alon/rest./dsl/scales/24hr
13	Lp 461, to New Deal
12	access rd (from nb)
11	FM 1294, Shallowater
10	Keuka St, E Fed Ex
9	Airport Rd, E , W Lubbock RV Park/LP/dump
8	FM 2641, Regis St, E , W Loves/Subway/Chester's/dsl/scales/24hr
7	Yucca Lane, E Pharr RV Ctr
6b a	Lp 289, Ave Q, Lubbock, E Pharr RV
5	B. Holly Ave, Municipal Dr, E Mackenzie SP, W Civic Ctr
4	US 82, US 87, 4th St, to Crosbyton, E funpark, W FLYING J/Subway/dsl/LP/scales/24hr to TTU
3	US 62, TX 114, 19th St, Floydada
2	34th St, E Phillips 66/dsl Pete's Drive Inn, W Valero Josie's #5, Phillips 66, Subway AutoZone, Raff&Hall Drug, U-Haul
1c	50th St, E Buddy's El Charro Family$, W Alon/7-11, Bolton Fuel/dsl, Valero/dsl A&W/LJ Silver, Bryan's Steaks, Burger King, China Star, Church's, Domino's, KFC, McDonald's, McDonald's, Pizza Hut/Taco Bell, Subway, Taco Villa, Tech Cafe, Whataburger, Wienerschnitzel Howard Johnson $General, O'Reilly Parts, United Food/gas, USPO, Walgreens
1b	US 84, E Best Value Inn, Days Inn, W Best Western, Comfort Inn, Country Inn Suites, Holiday Inn Express, Motel 6, Quality Inn, Red Roof Inn, Super 8, Woodspring Suites
1a	Lp 289
1	82nd St. W Phillips 66/dsl, **I-27 begins/ends on US 87 at 82nd St in S Lubbock.**

PLAINVIEW

LUBBOCK

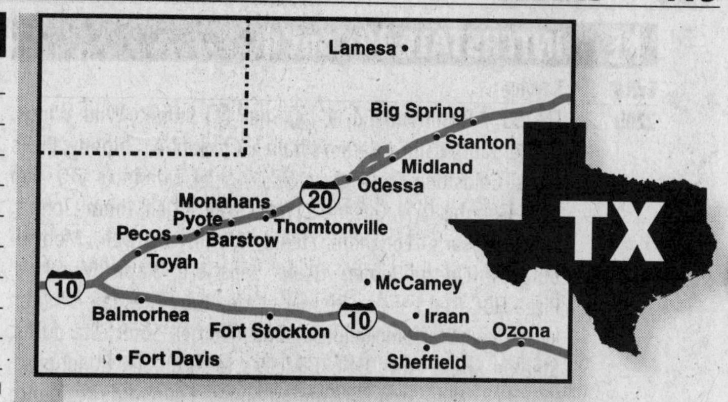

TX

INTERSTATE 30

Exit#	Services
223mm	Texas/Arkansas state line
223b a	US 59, US 71, State Line Ave, Texarkana, N Exxon/dsl, EZ Mart, Shell/dsl Denny's, IHOP, Los Agaves, Naaman's BBQ, Pizza Inn, Waffle House Best Western, Clarion, Holiday Inn Express, Howard Johnson, La Quinta, Quality Inn, Ramada Inn, Regency Inn, Super 8, Texarkana Inn, Wyndham Garden Cooper Tire, KOA, S Chevron/dsl, Exxon, Murphy USA/dsl, RaceWay/dsl, Shell Burger King, Cattleman's Steaks, China Inn, China King, El Chico, Fuzzy's Tacos, Hooters, KFC, Little Caesar's, LJ Silver, Marble Slab, McDonald's, Papa John's, Popeye's, Schlotzsky's, Slim Chickens, Sonic, Starbucks, Subway, Taco Bell, Wendy's, Whataburger Ambassador Inn, Best Value Inn, Days Inn, EconoLodge, Executive Inn, La Quinta, Motel 6, Rodeway Inn $General, $Tree, Albertson's/Sav-On, AutoZone, CVS Drug, O'Reilly Parts, VW, Walgreens, Walmart/Subway
223mm	**Welcome Ctr wb, full facilities, info, litter barrels, petwalk, vending**
222	TX 93, FM 1397, Summerhill Rd, N Shell, Valero/Subway/dsl Applebee's, McDonald's, The One Buffet, Waffle House Motel 6 AT&T, Goodyear Truck Tire, Hyundai, URGENT CARE, S Shell/dsl Bryce's Rest., Catfish King, Sonic Ford, Gateway Tires, Nissan, Walmart Mkt/dsl

TEXARKANA

[gas] = gas [food] = food [lodging] = lodging [other] = other [Rs] = rest stop

TX

INTERSTATE 30 Cont'd

Exit#	Services
220b	FM 559, Richmond Rd, N Shell Buffalo Wild Wings, Burger King, Cane's, Carino's Italian, Chick-fil-A, Chipotle, CiCi's Pizza, Coldstone Creamery, Cracker Barrel, Domino's, DQ, Fuji Grill, Genghis Grill, Gusano's Pizza, Jason's Deli, Jimmy John's, Little Caesar's, Longhorn Steaks, McAlister's Deli, Mooyah Burgers, On-the-Border, Osaka Japanese, Papa Murphy's, Pizza Hut, Red Lobster, Reggie's Cafe, Ruby Tuesday, Schlotzky's, Silver Star Smokehouse, Smashburger, Sonic, Starbucks, Steak'n Shake, Taco Bell, TaMolly's Mexican, TX Roadhouse, Wendy's, Wing Stop Comfort Suites, Courtyard, Residence Inn, TownePlace Suites $General, $Tree, AT&T, Best Buy, Chevrolet, Discount Tire, Home Depot, Honda, Kohl's, Kwik Kar, Meineke, Office Depot, Old Navy, Petsmart, Sam's Club/gas, Super 1 Food/gas, Target, TJ Maxx, Verizon, Walmart Mkt/dsl, S Valero/dsl Arby's, Chili's, ChuckeCheese, Firehouse Subs, Golden Chick, Golden Corral, Grandy's, Lee's China, McDonald's, Olive Garden, Outback Steaks, Subway, Taco Bueno Candlewood Suites, Hampton Inn, Hilton Garden/Conv Ctr, Holiday Inn Express Albertson's/Sav-On, AT&T, Books-A-Million, Cavender's Boots, CVS Drug, Dillard's, Hobby Lobby, JC Penney, Michael's, Ross, Tuesday Morning, Walgreens
220a	US 59 S, Texarkana
219	Pecan St, University Ave, S Exxon, Murphy USA Subway, Wendy's Country Inn&Suites, Fairfield Inn Buick/GMC, Cadillac, Chrysler/Dodge/Jeep, Harley-Davidson, Kia, Lowe's, Mazda, Mercedes, vet, Walmart
218	FM 989, Nash, N Road Runner/dsl Dixie Diner, Papa Poblano's, S Exxon/Burger King/dsl Sonic GMC/Peterbilt, to Lake Patman, Toyota, USPO
213	FM 2253, Leary, S Love's/McDonald's/Subway/dsl/scales/24hr
212	spur 74, S Shell/dsl Lone Star Army Ammo Plant
208	FM 560, Hooks, S Truckstp/dsl/scales/24hr DQ, Sonic $General, Family$, Hooks Tire
207	no services
206	TX 86, S Red River Army Depot
201	TX 8, New Boston, N Shell/dsl, Valero/dsl Pitt Grill Tex Inn Chevrolet, Chrysler/Dodge/Jeep, S Murphy USA/dsl, Shell/dsl Amigo Juan, Catfish King, Church's, Domino's, DQ, KFC/Taco Bell, McDonald's, Pizza Hut, Randy's BBQ, Sonic Best Value Inn, Bostonian Inn, Holiday Inn Express Brookshire's Foods/gas, Ford, O'Reilly Parts, Walmart/Subway
199	US 82, New Boston, 1/2 mi N VP/dsl
198	TX 98, 1/2 mi N VP/dsl
193mm	Anderson Creek
192	FM 990, N Culpeppers Rest.
186	FM 561
181mm	Sulphur River
178	US 259, to DeKalb, Omaha
174mm	White Oak Creek
170	FM 1993
165	FM 1001
162b a	US 271, FM 1402, FM 2152, Mt Pleasant, N Exxon/dsl Applebee's, Blalock BBQ Holiday Inn Express, Super 8 $General, KOA, S Shell/dsl, Valero/Subway/dsl Burger King, McDonald's, Sonic Best Western H, $General, Cadillac/Chevrolet, Chrysler/Dodge/Jeep, Family$, Ford, vet
160	US 271, FM 1734, Mt Pleasant, N Texaco/dsl Senorita's Mexican La Quinta Buick/GMC (1mi), Lowe's, Ramblin Fever RV Park (2mi), Toyota, S Exxon/dsl, Shell/dsl El Chico, IHOP Days Inn, Hampton Inn, Motel 6, Quality Inn Sandlin SP
158mm	**weigh sta both lanes**
156	frontage rd
153	spur 185, to Winfield, Miller's Cove, N Crazy 8, Winfield/dsl, S Shamrock/dsl
150	Ripley Rd, N Lowe's Distribution
147	spur 423, N Love's/Chester's/Subway/dsl/scales/24hr American Inn, Economy Inn tires/repair
146	TX 37, Mt Vernon, N Sonic H, $General, auto repair, Brookshire Foods/gas, O'Reilly Parts, S Cefco/Huddle House/dsl/24hr, Exxon/dsl Burger King, DQ, McDonald's, Mi Casita Super 8 auto/dsl repair, to Lake Bob Sandlin SP
143	**Rs both lanes, full facilities, litter barrels, petwalk, vending**
142	County Line Rd (from eb)
141	FM 900, Saltillo Rd
136	FM 269, Weaver Rd
135	US 67 N
131	FM 69
127	US 67, Lp 301, N Days Inn, Ferrari Inn, Home Spring Suites Motel 6 H, S Shell Home Plate Rest. Best Western
126	FM 1870, College St, S Shell Best Western Firestone/auto, same as 127
125	Bill Bradford Rd, same as 124
124	TX 11, TX 154, Sulphur Springs, N Exxon/dsl Bodacious BBQ, Broadway Buffet, Chicken Express, Don Ialo's Mexican, IHOP, Juan Pablo's Mexican, Metro Diner, Pizza Hut Subway, Wendy's Hampton Inn, Holiday Inn Express, Royal Inn H, $General, AutoZone, Brookshire's Foods/gas CVS Drug, Family$, Ford/Lincoln, FSA Outlet/famous brands O'Reilly Parts, USPO, VF Outlet/famous brands, Walgreens S Exxon/dsl, Murphy USA/dsl, Shell/dsl Braum's Burger King, Chili's, Domino's, Furr's Rest., Jack-in-the-Box McDonald's, Panda Express, Pizza Inn, Sonic, Taco Bell/LJ Silver, Whataburger AT&T, Cody Drug, Discount Wheel&Tire Lowe's, Verizon, Walmart/Subway
123	FM 2297, League St, N Shamrock/dsl, Shell
122	TX 19, to Emory, N Valero/dsl H, Chrysler/Dodge Jeep, to Cooper Lake SP, Travel Time RV Ctr, S CNC Love's/Carl's Jr/dsl/scales/24hr, Pilot/Arby's/dsl/scales/24hr, Valero/Zinga's/dsl dsl repair
120	US 67 bus
116	FM 2653, Brashear Rd, S USPO
112	FM 499 (from wb)
110	FM 275, Cumby, N Phillips 66/dsl, S Shell
104	FM 513, FM 2649, Campbell, S to Lake Tawakoni
101	TX 24, TX 50, FM 1737, to Commerce, N Valero/dsl TX A&M-Commerce, S TX Beach Club Grill
97	Lamar St, N Exxon/dsl Budget Inn, S vet
96	Lp 302
95	Division St, S H
94b	US 69, US 380, Greenville, N Valero/dsl Collin St Bakery, Golden Chick, Senorita's Mexican Days Inn, Royal Inn H, S Exxon, QT/dsl Arby's, McDonald's, Rancho Viejo Economy Inn, Express Inn, Guest Inn, Motel 6, Super
94a	US 69, US 380, Greenville, S QT/dsl, Valero/Subway/dsl Chrysler/Dodge/Jeep

NEW BOSTON · MT PLEASANT · SULPHUR SPGS · GREENVILLE

INTERSTATE 30 Cont'd

Exit#	Services
93b a	US 67, TX 34 N, N [gas] Chevron/Taco Casa/dsl, Exxon/dsl, Shell/dsl, Texaco [food] Applebee's, Braum's, Chicken Express, Chick-fil-A, CiCi's, Cotton Patch Cafe, DQ, Grandy's, IHOP, Jack-in-the-Box, KFC, Little Caesar's, Pizza Hut, Schlotzsky's, Sonic, Starbucks, Subway, Taco Bell, Taco Bueno, Tony's Italian, Wendy's, Whataburger [lodging] Hampton Inn [other] [H], Aldi Foods, AT&T, Beall's, Belk, BigLots, Brookshire's Foods, Cavender's Outfitter, Dick's, Discount Tire, Kwik Kar, Lowe's, Marshall's, O'Reilly Parts, Petco, Staples, transmissions, USPO, Verizon, Walgreens, S [gas] Exxon/dsl, Murphy USA/dsl, Shell/dsl [food] Burger King, Chili's, Cracker Barrel, Molina's Mexican, Papa John's, Red Lobster, Shogun Hibachi, Soulman's BBQ, Subway, TaMolly's Mexican [lodging] Best Western, Comfort Suites, Holiday Inn Express [other] $Tree, Buick/GMC, Ford/Lincoln, Home Depot, Hyundai, Nissan, NTB, Walmart
92	Stratton Pkwy, S [other] Chevrolet/Cadillac
90mm	Farber Creek
89	FM 1570, S [lodging] Luxury Inn
89mm	E Caddo Creek
87	FM 1903, N [gas] Shell/dsl [other] fireworks, S [gas] Pilot/McDonald's/dsl/scales/24hr, Texaco/Huddle House/dsl [food] Baker's Ribs [other] tire repair
87mm	Elm Creek
85	FM 36, Caddo Mills, N [other] KOA
85mm	W Caddo Creek
83	FM 1565 N, N [gas] Exxon/Pizza Inn/dsl
79	FM 2642, N [other] Budget RV Ctr, S [other] vet
77b	FM 35, Royse City, N [gas] Texaco/Subway/dsl/scales/24hr [food] Soulman's BBQ [other] Family$
77a	TX 548, Royse City, N [gas] Shell/dsl [food] Jack-in-the-Box, McDonald's [lodging] American Inn [other] AutoZone, tires, S [gas] Exxon [food] Denny's, Pizza Hut, Rice Express, Sonic, Taco Bell [lodging] Holiday Inn Express
76	Campbell Blvd, N [other] CVS Drug, Walmart
73	FM 551, Fate
70	FM 549, N [other] Happy Trails RV Ctr, McLains RV Ctr, S [gas] Loves/Carl's Jr./dsl/scales/24hr [other] Kia
69	(from wb), frontage rd, N [lodging] Super 8, S [other] Honda, Hyundai, Nissan, Nissan, Toyota
68	TX 205, to Rock Wall, N [gas] 7-11/dsl, Murphy USA/dsl, QT/dsl, Shell [food] Braum's, Chicken Express, Domino's, Joe Willy's Grill, Luigi's Italian, Starbucks, Subway, Taco Casa, Whataburger [lodging] Best Western, Super 8, Woodspring Suites [other] Buick/GMC, Chevrolet, Chrysler/Dodge/Jeep, Ford, Hobby Lobby, vet, Walmart/Subway, S [gas] RaceTrac/dsl, TA/Burger King/Starbucks/dsl/24hr/scales/@ [food] Cane's, Firehouse Subs, Freebird Burritos, In-N-Out, Luby's, Rosa's Cafe, Soulman's BBQ [other] Belk, Costco/gas, Jo-Ann Fabrics, Toyota
67b	FM 740, Ridge Rd, N [gas] Chevron, Murphy USA/dsl [food] Buffet City, Culver's, Denny's, Edohana Hibachi, Grandy's, IHOP, LJ Silver, Logan's Roadhouse, McDonald's, Mellow Mushroom Pizza, Popeye's, Schlotzsky's, Steak'n Shake, Taco Bueno, Taco Cabana, Waffle House, Wendy's [lodging] Hampton Inn [other] Firestone/auto, Goodyear/auto, S [gas] Exxon, Kroger/dsl, Shell [food] Applebee's, Bahama Buck's Ice Cream, Blackeyed Pea, Buffalo Wild Wings, Carino's Italian, Chick-fil-A, Chili's, Chipotle Mexican, ChuckeCheese, CiCi's, Cotton Patch Cafe, Dickey's BBQ, El Chico, Firehouse Subs, Five Guys, Freebirds Burrito, Jack-in-the-Box, Jimmy John's, La Madelein, Mi Cocina, Mooyah Burgers, Olive Garden, On-the-Border, Panda Express, Pizza Hut, Sonic, Soulman's BBQ,

ROCK WALL

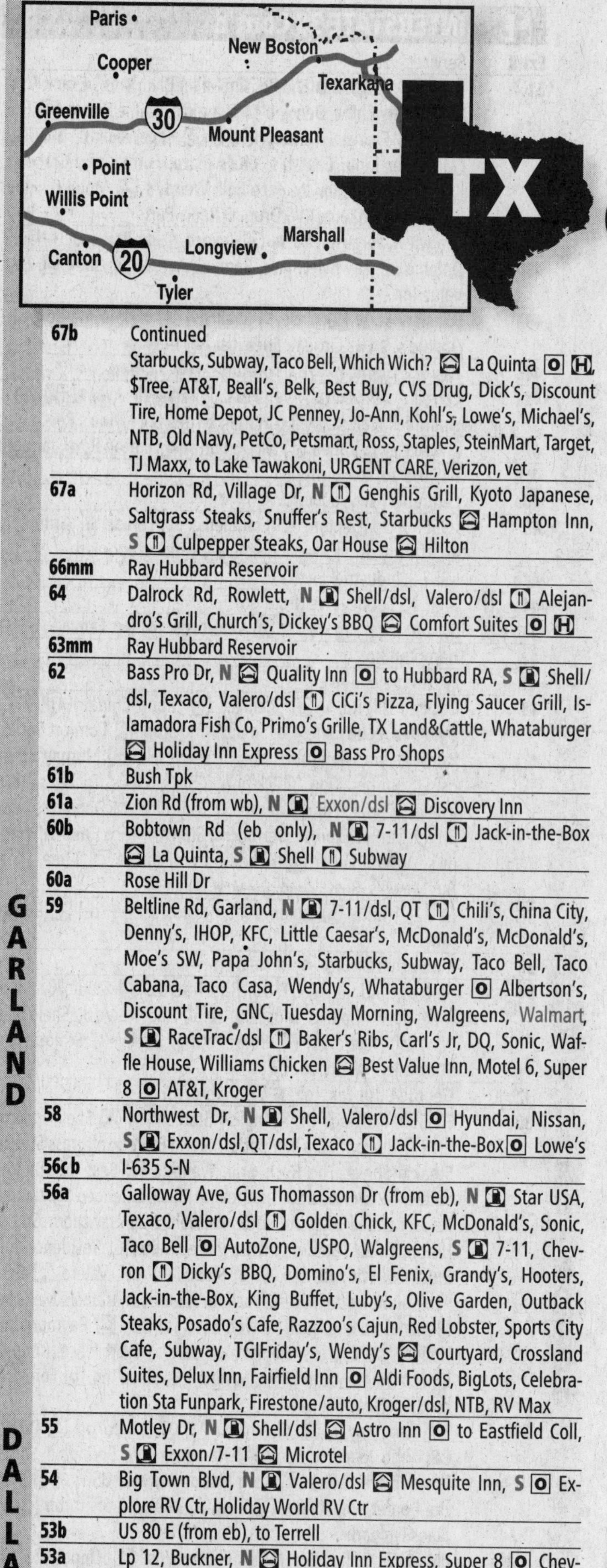

Exit#	Services
67b	Continued Starbucks, Subway, Taco Bell, Which Wich? [lodging] La Quinta [other] [H], $Tree, AT&T, Beall's, Belk, Best Buy, CVS Drug, Dick's, Discount Tire, Home Depot, JC Penney, Jo-Ann, Kohl's, Lowe's, Michael's, NTB, Old Navy, PetCo, Petsmart, Ross, Staples, SteinMart, Target, TJ Maxx, to Lake Tawakoni, URGENT CARE, Verizon, vet
67a	Horizon Rd, Village Dr, N [food] Genghis Grill, Kyoto Japanese, Saltgrass Steaks, Snuffer's Rest, Starbucks [lodging] Hampton Inn, S [food] Culpepper Steaks, Oar House [lodging] Hilton
66mm	Ray Hubbard Reservoir
64	Dalrock Rd, Rowlett, N [gas] Shell/dsl, Valero/dsl [food] Alejandro's Grill, Church's, Dickey's BBQ [lodging] Comfort Suites [other] [H]
63mm	Ray Hubbard Reservoir
62	Bass Pro Dr, N [lodging] Quality Inn [other] to Hubbard RA, S [gas] Shell/dsl, Texaco, Valero/dsl [food] CiCi's Pizza, Flying Saucer Grill, Islamadora Fish Co, Primo's Grille, TX Land&Cattle, Whataburger [lodging] Holiday Inn Express [other] Bass Pro Shops
61b	Bush Tpk
61a	Zion Rd (from wb), N [gas] Exxon/dsl [lodging] Discovery Inn
60b	Bobtown Rd (eb only), N [gas] 7-11/dsl [food] Jack-in-the-Box [lodging] La Quinta, S [gas] Shell [food] Subway
60a	Rose Hill Dr
59	Beltline Rd, Garland, N [gas] 7-11/dsl, QT [food] Chili's, China City, Denny's, IHOP, KFC, Little Caesar's, McDonald's, McDonald's, Moe's SW, Papa John's, Starbucks, Subway, Taco Bell, Taco Cabana, Taco Casa, Wendy's, Whataburger [other] Albertson's, Discount Tire, GNC, Tuesday Morning, Walgreens, Walmart, S [gas] RaceTrac/dsl [food] Baker's Ribs, Carl's Jr, DQ, Sonic, Waffle House, Williams Chicken [lodging] Best Value Inn, Motel 6, Super 8 [other] AT&T, Kroger
58	Northwest Dr, N [gas] Shell, Valero/dsl [other] Hyundai, Nissan, S [gas] Exxon/dsl, QT/dsl, Texaco [food] Jack-in-the-Box [other] Lowe's
56c b	I-635 S-N
56a	Galloway Ave, Gus Thomasson Dr (from eb), N [gas] Star USA, Texaco, Valero/dsl [food] Golden Chick, KFC, McDonald's, Sonic, Taco Bell [other] AutoZone, USPO, Walgreens, S [gas] 7-11, Chevron [food] Dicky's BBQ, Domino's, El Fenix, Grandy's, Hooters, Jack-in-the-Box, King Buffet, Luby's, Olive Garden, Outback Steaks, Posado's Cafe, Razzoo's Cajun, Red Lobster, Sports City Cafe, Subway, TGIFriday's, Wendy's [lodging] Courtyard, Crossland Suites, Delux Inn, Fairfield Inn [other] Aldi Foods, BigLots, Celebration Sta Funpark, Firestone/auto, Kroger/dsl, NTB, RV Max
55	Motley Dr, N [gas] Shell/dsl [lodging] Astro Inn [other] to Eastfield Coll, S [gas] Exxon/7-11 [lodging] Microtel
54	Big Town Blvd, N [gas] Valero/dsl [lodging] Mesquite Inn, S [other] Explore RV Ctr, Holiday World RV Ctr
53b	US 80 E (from eb), to Terrell
53a	Lp 12, Buckner, N [lodging] Holiday Inn Express, Super 8 [other] Chevrolet, Toyota, S [food] Panda Express, Taco Cabana, Whataburger [other] $Tree, Sam's Club/gas, Staples, Walmart

GARLAND

DALLAS

TX

TX

INTERSTATE 30 Cont'd

Exit#	Services
51	(52 a from wb), Highland Rd, Jim Miller Blvd, N [gas] Exxon/7-11 [food] Country China, Denny's, McDonald's, Waffle House [lodging] Holiday Inn Express, Quality Inn, S [gas] RaceWay/dsl, Shell/dsl [food] Burger King, Capt D's, CiCi's Pizza, Furr's Cafe, Grandy's, KFC, Popeye's, Subway, Taco Bell, Wendy's [lodging] Motel 6, Super 7 Inn [other] AutoZone, CVS Drug, O'Reilly Parts
50b a	Longview, Ferguson Rd, N [gas] Texaco, S [other] Brake-O, U-Haul
49b	Dolphin Rd, Lawnview Ave, Samuell Ave, N [gas] Shell [lodging] Best Value Inn
49a	Winslow St, N [gas] Circle K, Shell/dsl [food] Jack-in-the-Box, McDonald's, S [gas] Circle K, Shell/dsl [other] tires
48b	TX 78, E Grand, N [other] arboretum, S [other] fairpark
48a	Carroll Ave, Central Ave, Peak St, Haskell Ave, N [gas] 7-11, Shamrock, Valero [other] [H], Hamm's Tires, S [food] Joe's Rest
47	2nd Ave, S [gas] Shell [food] McDonald's [other] Cotton Bowl, fairpark
46b	I-45, US 75, to Houston
46a	Central Expswy, downtown
45	I-35E, N to Denton, to Commerce St, Lamar St, Griffin St, S [gas] Gulf/dsl [food] McDonald's [lodging] Ambassador Inn
44b	I-35E S, Industrial Blvd
44a	I-35E N, Beckley Ave (from eb)
43b a	Sylvan Ave (from wb), N [gas] Valero/dsl [other] [H], Family$, USPO
42	Hampton Rd
41	Westmoreland Ave
39	Cockrell Hill Rd, N [gas] Shell/dsl [food] Grand China, IHOP, KFC/Taco Bell, Pollo Campero, Sonic, Wing Stop [lodging] Comfort Suites, Fairfield Inn, Hampton Inn [other] Staples, S [gas] Murphy USA/dsl [food] Burger King, Chick-fil-A, Chili's, CiCi's, Dickey's BBQ, Golden Corral, Little Caesar's, Lucky Rice, McDonald's, New Buffet, Panda Express, Starbucks, Subway, Taco Cabana, Wendy's, Whataburger [lodging] Holiday Inn Express [other] $Tree, Best Buy, Lowe's, Ross, Walmart/McDonald's
38	Lp 12, 1 mi N [gas] Exxon/7-11, Texaco/dsl, VP/dsl [food] Burger King
36	MacArthur Blvd, S [other] U-Haul
34	Belt Line Rd, N [gas] QT/dsl, RaceTrac/dsl [lodging] Studio 6, Super 8 [other] Ford, Ripley's Museum, S [gas] RaceTrac/dsl, Shell/Subway/dsl, Valero/dsl [food] Burger King, Popeye's, Schlotzsky's, Starbucks [other] city park, vet
32b a	George Bush Tpk, **toll**, N [gas] Valero/dsl
30	TX 360, Six Flags Dr, Arlington Stadium, N [gas] Shell, Valero/dsl [food] Boston's, Cracker Barrel, Grand Buffet, Saltgrass Steaks, Steak'n Shake, The Rock Grill, Wendy's [lodging] Best Inn, Budget Suites, Candlewood Suites, Crowne Plaza, Extended Stay America, Extended Stay America, Fairfield Inn, Hawthorn Suites, Hilton, Hilton Garden, Hyatt Place, Motel 6, Residence Inn, Studio 6, Wingate Inn, S [gas] Shell/7-11/dsl, Valero [food] Denny's, Humperdink's Rest., Jack-in-the-Box, Mariano's Mexican, McDonald's, Red Neck Heaven Rest, Subway [lodging] Baymont Inn, Holiday Inn Express, Homewood Suites, Hyatt Place, Knight's Inn, La Quinta, Quality Inn, Ranger Inn, Sleep Inn [other] Ford/Lincoln, Six Flags Funpark
29	Ball Park Way, N [gas] Chevron/7-11, QT, Valero/dsl [food] Dicky's BBQ, Rio Mambo, Sonic [lodging] Hampton Inn, Springhill Suites, Towneplace Suites [other] Auto Nation/Toyota, USPO, S [food] On-the-Border, Vila Brazil [lodging] Howard Johnson, Sheraton [other] Six Flags Funpark
28b a	FM 157, Collins St, N [gas] Chevron/dsl [food] Chipotle, IHOP, Mooyah Burgers, Pei Wei, Potbelly, Starbucks, Waffle House [lodging] EconoLodge, HolidayInn [other] BMW, Cadillac, Chrysler/Dodge/

ARLINGTON

Exit#	Services
28b a	Continued Jeep, Mini, Walmart, Whole Foods Mkt, S [food] Arby's, Asian Buffet, Blackeyed Pea, Blue Mesa Grill, Buffalo Wild Wings, Cane's, Chili's, El Chico, Gino's East Pizzaria, Hooters, Jason's Deli, Joe's Crab Shack, Lupe's Grill, Olive Garden, Panda Express, Panera Bread, Pappadeaux, Pappasito's Cantina, Popeye's, Sherlock's Grill, Subway, Taco Bell, Taco Bueno, TGIFriday's, TX Land&Cattle, Wendy's, Which Wich? [lodging] Comfort Suites, Courtyard, Day Inn [other] $Tree, GNC, Home Depot, Michael's, Office Depot, Pep Boys, Petsmart, Ross, SteinMart, TX Stadium, Walgreens
27	Lamar Blvd, Cooper St, N [gas] Gulf [food] Jack-in-the-Box, Subway [other] BigLots, Family$, Kroger/dsl, vet, S [gas] 7-11, QT/dsl, Shell/dsl [food] Burger King, Pappasito's Cantina, Tom's Burgers [lodging] Comfort Suites
26	Fielder Rd, S [other] to Six Flags (from eb)
25mm	Village Creek
24	Eastchase Pkwy, N [food] Jack-in-the-Box, Panda Express [lodging] La Quinta [other] CarMax, Lowe's, Sam's Club/gas, Verizon, Walmart/McDonald's, S [gas] Chevron/7-11/dsl, RaceTrac/dsl, Shell/7-11/dsl [food] Burger King, Chicken Express, CiCi's Pizza, IHOP, McDonald's, No Frills Grill, Pizza Hut, Schlotzsky's, Subway, Taco Bell, Wendy's, Whataburger [other] $Tree, Aldi Foods, AT&T, GNC, Marshall's, Office Depot, Ross, Target
23	Cooks Lane, S [gas] Shell/dsl
21c b	I-820
21a	Bridgewood Dr, N [gas] Chevron/dsl [food] Braum's, Dickey's BBQ, Jack-in-the-Box, KFC, Luby's, Subway, Taco Casa, Wendy's [other] $General, Albertson's, Discount Tire, Firestone auto, Home Depot, U-Haul, S [gas] Conoco, Phillips 66/dsl, QT [food] Taco Bueno, Whataburger/24hr
19	Brentwood Stair Rd (from eb), N [gas] Shell, S [gas] Shamrock, Texaco [other] Family$
18	Oakland Blvd, N [gas] Circle K, Shell/dsl [food] Taco Bell, Waffle House [lodging] Motel 6
16c	Beach St, S [gas] 7-11 [lodging] Motel 6, Stay Express Hotel
16b a	Riverside Dr (from wb), S [lodging] Great Western Inn
15b a	I-35W N to Denton, S to Waco
14b	Jones St, Commerce St, Ft Worth, downtown
14a	TX 199, Henderson St, Ft Worth, downtown
13b	TX 199, Henderson St, N [lodging] Holiday Inn Express, Omni, Sheraton
13a	8th Ave, N [lodging] Holiday Inn Express
12b	Forest Park Blvd, N [food] Pappadeaux Café, Pappa's Burger, Pappasito's, S [other] [H], URGENT CARE
12a	University Dr, City Parks, S [lodging] SpringHill Suites
11	Montgomery St, S [gas] Shell/7-11/dsl [food] Railhead BBQ, Taco Bell, Whataburger
10	Hulen St, Ft Worth, S [food] Buttons Rest., Chick-fil-A, McDonald's, Mi Cocina, Potbelly, Smoothie King, Starbucks [other] Central Mkt, WorldMkt
9b	US 377, Camp Bowie Blvd, Horne St, N [food] Uncle Julio's Mexican, S [gas] 7-11, Exxon/7-11, Texaco/dsl [food] Campisi's Italian, Chipotle, Jack-in-the-Box, Jason's Deli, Jersey Mike's, Jimmy John's, McDonald's, Mexican Inn Cafe, Schlotzsky's, Smashburger, Sonic, Starbucks, Subway, Taco Bueno, Wendy's [other] AT&T, Batteries+Bulbs, URGENT CARE, Walgreens
9a	Bryant-Irvin Rd, S [gas] Shell [other] same as 9b
8b	Ridgmar, Ridglea
8a	TX 183, Green Oaks Rd, N [food] Applebee's, Arby's, Asia Bowl, Cane's, Chick-fil-A, Chipotle, Cowtown BBQ, Del Taco, Don Pablo's, Firehouse Subs, Grand Buffet, Jack-in-the-Box, McDonald's, Olive Garden, Panda Express, Papa Murphy's, Sonic, Subway, Taco Bueno, Whataburger, Woody Creek BBQ

FT WORTH

INTERSTATE 30 Cont'd

8a Continued
Courtyard $Tree, Albertson's, Aldi Foods, AT&T, Best Buy, BigLots, Dillard's, Firestone/auto, JC Penney, Jo-Ann Fabrics, Lowe's, Neiman Marcus, NTB, Office Depot, Old Navy, PetCo, Petsmart, Ross, Sam's Club/gas, Target, U-Haul, Verizon, Walmart/Subway, **S** Fairfield Inn, Hampton Inn

7b a Cherry Lane, TX 183, spur 341, to Green Oaks Rd, **N** Shell/7-11, Texaco/dsl, Valero/dsl ChuckECheese, IHOP, Popeye's, Subway, Wendy's Comfort Inn, Motel 6, Scottish Inn O'Reilly Parts, same as 8a, U-Haul, **S** QT/dsl Holiday Inn, Holiday Inn Express, La Quinta, Quality Inn, Super 8

6 Las Vegas Trail, **N** Chevron/McDonald's/dsl, Conoco/dsl Jack-in-the-Box, Waffle House Days Inn Hyundai, Lincoln, **S** Shell/7-11/dsl, Texaco, Valero/dsl Best Value Inn, Knights Inn, Relax Inn AutoZone, Kia, vet

5b c I-820 N and S

5a Alemeda St (from eb, no EZ return)

3 RM 2871, Chapel Creek Blvd, **S** Exxon/Church's/Subway/dsl Sonic

2 spur 580 E

1b Linkcrest Dr, **S** Gulf/dsl

0mm **I-20 W. I-30 begins/ends on I-20, exit 421.**

INTERSTATE 35

Exit# Services

504mm Texas/Oklahoma state line, Red River

504 frontage rd, access to Texas Welcome Ctr

503mm **parking area both lanes**

502mm **Welcome Ctr sb, full facilities, litter barrels, phone, picnic, TX Tourist Bureau/info, wireless internet**

501 FM 1202, Prime Outlets Blvd, **E** Chrysler/Dodge/Jeep, Ford, **W** Conoco/café/dsl Applebee's, Cracker Barrel Hampton Inn, La Quinta Prime Outlets/famous brands, RV camping, Western Outfitter

500 FM 372, Gainesville, **W** Hitchin' Post/Shell/dsl

498b a US 82, to Wichita Falls, Gainesville, Sherman, **E** Chevron/dsl/24hr, Shell/dsl, Valero/dsl Luigi's Italian Budget Host, Super 8 H, AT&T, URGENT CARE, **W** Exxon/dsl Comfort Suites, Days Inn, Rodeway Inn

497 frontage rd, **W** Valero/dsl

496b TX 51, FM 51, California St, Gainesville, **E** Chevron Arby's, Braum's, Fera's Mexican, IHOP, McDonald's, Sonic, Starbucks, Starbucks, Taco Bell, Taco Casa, Wendy's Holiday Inn Express, Quality Inn Kwik Kar/auto, Lowe's Mkt, **W** Valero Chili's N Central TX Coll

496a to Weaver St

496mm Elm Fork of the Trinity River

495 frontage rd

494 FM 1306

492mm **sb, litter barrels**

491 Spring Creek Rd

490mm **nb, litter barrels**

489 FM 1307, to Hockley Creek Rd

487 FM 922, Valley View, **W** Shell/Subway/Taco Tico/dsl, Valero/dsl DQ USPO

486 Fm 1307, **W** Texaco/dsl Texas Inn $General

485 frontage rd (from sb)

483 FM 3002, Lone Oak Rd, **E** Shell/Church's/Subway/dsl Roberts Lake SP, RV Guys

GAINESVILLE

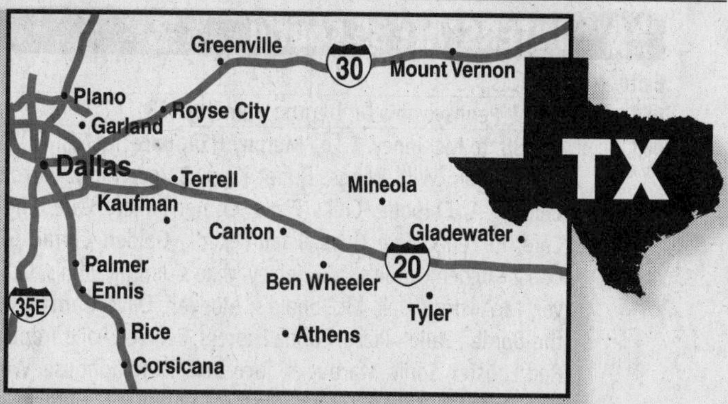

482 Chisam Rd

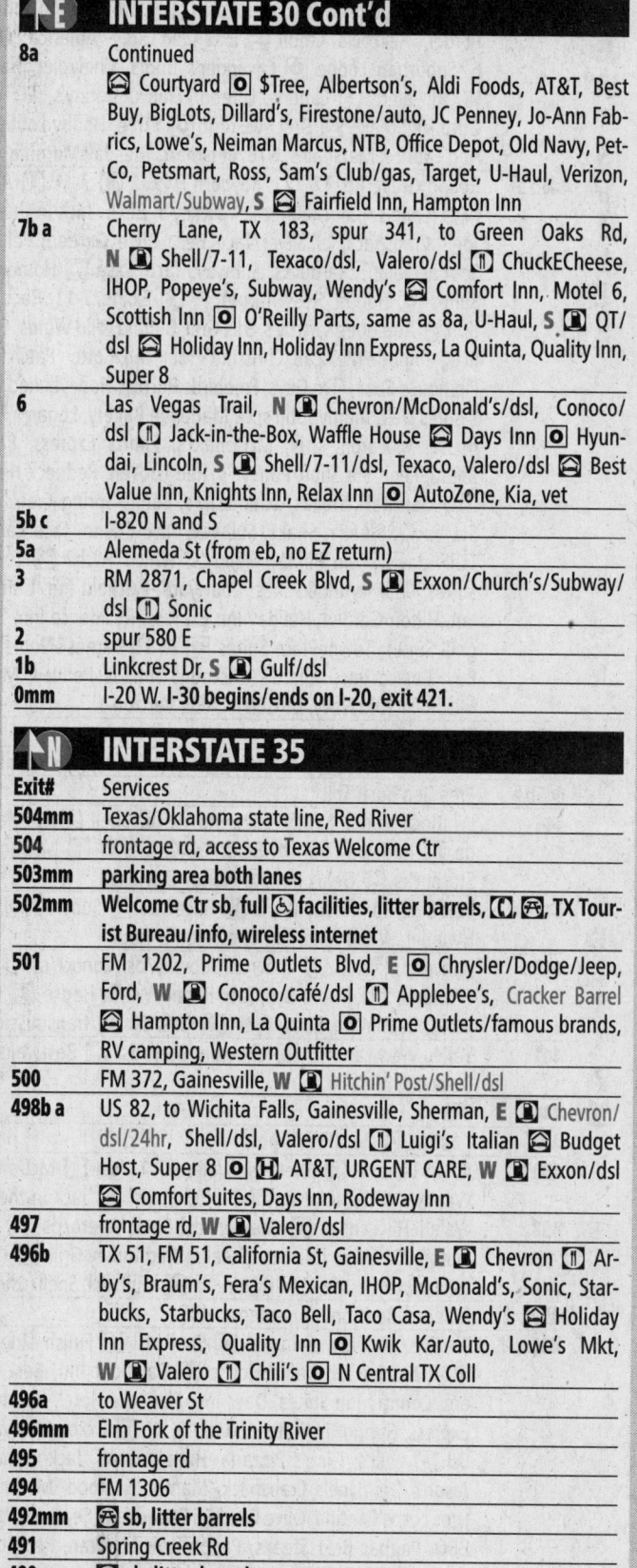

481 View Rd, **W** McClain's RV Ctr

480 Lois Rd, **E** Walmart Dist Ctr

479 Belz Rd, Sanger, same as 478

478 FM 455, to Pilot Pt, Bolivar, **E** QuickTrack, Shell/dsl DQ, Fuzzy's Tacos, Miguelito's, Pizza Hut, Sonic, Subway, Taco Bell Sanger Inn RV park, USPO, **W** Chevron/dsl, Conoco/Chicken Express/dsl Domino's, Jack-in-the-Box, McDonald's Chevrolet, Family$, Kwik Kar Lube, O'Reilly Parts, Ray Roberts Lake and SP, Super Save Foods, Verizon

477 Keaton Rd, **E** Exxon/dsl

475b Rector Rd

475a FM 156, to Krum (from sb)

474 Cowling rd (from nb)

473 FM 3163, Milam Rd, **E** Loves/Subway/dsl/scales/24hr

472 Ganzer Rd, **W** Crandell RV Ctr

471 US 77, FM 1173, Lp 282, to Denton, Krum, **E** TA/Pizza Hut/Taco Bell/dsl/scales/24hr/@ H, **W** Loves/Godfather's/Subway/Wendy's/dsl/scales/24hr Foster's Western Shop, to Camping World RV Supply

470 Lp 288, same services as 469 from sb

469 US 380, University Dr, to Decatur, McKinney, **E** 7-11/dsl, Chevron/Subway, RaceTrac/dsl Braum's, Cane's, Chick-fil-A, Chili's, ChinaTown Café, Cowboy Chicken, Cracker Barrel, Dickey's BBQ, Freebird's Burrito, Luigi's Pizza, McDonald's, Mooyah, Panda Express, Panera Bread, Starbucks, Taco Cabana, Taco Casa, Villa Grande, Whataburger, WhichWich?, Wing Stop Best Western, Fairfield Inn Albertson's/Sav-On, AT&T, GNC, Jo-Ann Fabrics, Kohl's, Kwik Kar, PetCo, Ross, Sam's Club/gas, to TX Woman's U, URGENT CARE, Walmart/McDonald's, Winco Foods, **W** Exxon/dsl, QT/dsl Brisket Burger, Denny's, DQ, Shell/dsl, Waffle House Comfort Inn, Days Inn, Holiday Inn Express, Howard Johnson, La Quinta, Motel 6, Woodspring Suites H, Camping World RV Supply, I-35 RV Ctr

468 FM 1515, Airport Rd, W Oak St, **E** H

467 I-35W, S to Ft Worth

I-35 divides into E and W sb, converges into I-35 nb. See Texas I-35 W.

466b Ave D, **E** Central Grill, Chicken Express, IHOP, Pancho's Mexican $General, to NTSU

466a McCormick St, **E** EKon, Shell/7-11/dsl Pancho's Mexican $General

465b US 377, Ft Worth Dr, **E** RaceTrac/dsl, Valero Layalina Mediterranean, Taco Bell, Whataburger Motel 6, **W** 7-11/dsl Outback Steaks, Sonic Knights Inn

465a FM 2181, Teasley Ln, **E** 7-11 Applebee's, Braum's, Carino's, ChuckeCheese, Domino's, Hooters, KFC, Little Caesar's, Pizza Hut, Subway Hampton Inn, Quality Inn Brookshires Foods, U-Haul, **W** Exxon, Shell/dsl La Milpa Mexican, Rudy's BBQ/gas Best Value Inn, Super 8 vet

DENTON

TX

TX

INTERSTATE 35 Cont'd

LEWISVILLE

Exit#	Services
464	US 77, Pennsylvania Dr, Denton, same as 463
463	Lp 288, to McKinney, E Murphy USA, RaceTrac/dsl Arby's, Buffalo Wild Wings, Buffet King, Burger King, Carl's Jr, Chick-fil-A, Chipotle, CiCi's Pizza, Corner Bakery Cafe, Egg&I Cafe, El Fenix, Five Guys, Fuddrucker's, Golden Corral, Gulf Coast Kitchen, Jason's Deli, Jersey Mike's, Jimmy John's, LJ Silver, McAlister's Deli, McDonald's, Mooyah, Olive Garden, On-the-Border, Palio's Pizza, Panda Express, Pei Wei, Pollo Tropical, Red Lobster, Sonic, Starbucks, Taco Bell, TX Roadhouse, Wendy's, Whataburger Best Western, Courtyard, Hilton Garden $General, $Tree, AT&T, Barnes&Noble, Best Buy, BigLots, Burlington Coats, Dillard's, Discount Tire, Firestone/auto, Goodyear/auto, Hobby Lobby, Home Depot, JC Penney, Kroger/dsl, Kwik Kar, Lowe's, Macy's, Michael's, NTB, Office Depot, Old Navy, PetCo, Petsmart, Ross, Staples, Target, TJ Maxx, Verizon, Walgreens, Walmart, W Chevron/dsl BJ's Rest., Bone Daddy's, Chili's, Chuy's Mexican, Fuzzy's Tacos, Jack-in-the-Box, Papa John's, Schlotzsky's, Wing Stop Homewood Suites EMERGENCY CARE, same as 464, vet
462	State School Rd, Mayhill Rd, E Dickey's BBQ, Subway Residence Inn H, URGENT CARE, W Exxon Shogun Japanese, Sonic Buick/GMC, Cadillac, Chevrolet, Chrysler/Dodge/Jeep, Honda, Toyota
461	Sandy Shores Rd, Post Oak Dr, E Explore USA RV Ctr, Ford, Hyundai, vet, W Christian Bros Auto, Chrysler/Dodge/Jeep, Kia, Mazda, Nissan, Subaru
460	Corinth Pkwy, E McClains RV Ctr, W Harley-Davidson
459	frontage rd, W Destiny RV Resort
458	FM 2181, Swisher Rd, E Circle K, QT/dsl Best Western, Comfort Inn O'Reilly Parts, W Chevron/McDonald's, Exxon/7-11, Murphy USA/dsl Chicken Express, Chick-fil-A, Denny's, IHOP, Jack-in-the-Box, KFC/Taco Bell, Los Cabos, Pizza Hut, Sonic, Starbucks, Subway, Wendy's, Whataburger Albertson's, Aldi Foods, AT&T, AutoZone, Discount Tire, Firestone/auto, GNC, Kwik Kar, URGENT CARE, Verizon, Walgreens, Walmart
457b	Denton Rd, Hundley Dr, Lake Dallas
457a	Hundley Dr (from nb), Lake Dallas
456	Highland Village
456mm	Lewisville Lake
454b	Garden Ridge Blvd
454a	FM 407, Justin, E Valero Old House BBQ, W QT/dsl McDonald's, Subway
453	Valley Ridge Blvd, E Ford, May's RV, W Chevron/dsl Burger King, Fat Cow BBQ, Subway Home Depot, Kohl's, Lowe's, Staples
452	FM 1171, to Flower Mound, E IHOP, Taco Bueno Select Inn H, W Shell Buffet Palace, Burger King, Cane's, Chick-fil-A, Chipotle Mexican, CiCi's Pizza, Grandy's, Korner Cafe, McDonald's, Panda Express, Pizza Hut, Regal Buffet, Smashburger, Sonic, Taco Bell, Taco Cabana, Whataburger $Tree, Albertson's, CVS, DQ, Midas, PetCo, same as 451, Sam's Club/gas, transmissions, U-Haul, URGENT CARE, Walmart
451	Fox Ave, E Shell/dsl Braum's, W Chevron/dsl Cracker Barrel, Starbucks Baymont Inn, EconoLodge VW
450	TX 121, Grapevine, E 7-11, Exxon/dsl Texan Inn Chrysler/Dodge/Jeep, W Chevron, Conoco/dsl Burger King, Church's, Subway, Taco Bell, Waffle House Firestone/auto, Kwik Kar, Nissan, Toyota
449	Corporate Drive, E Valero/dsl Hooters, Kyoto, On-the-Border, Razzoo's Cajun Extended Stay America, Motel 6, Suburban Lodge Cavender's Boots, Chevrolet, Honda, W Valero Cantina Loredo, Chili's, Denny's, El Fenix, Outback Steaks Best Western $Tree, Hobby Lobby, Jo-Ann Fabrics, Marshall's, NTB, Petsmart, Tuesday Morning
448b a	Round Grove Rd, TX 121, Rayburn Fwy, E 7-11 A&W/KFC, Cane's, ChuckeCheese, Dickey's BBQ, Jack-in-the-Box, Joe's Crabshack, LJ Silver/Taco Bell, Olive Garden, Pei Wei, Souper Salad, Starbucks, Subway, Taco Casa Homewood Suites Honda, Ross, Target, W Exxon/7-11, RaceTrac/dsl Applebee's, Arby's, BJ's Grill, Buffalo Wild Wings, Chick-fil-A, Chipotle Mexican, Christina's Mexican, Cotton Patch Rest., Firehouse Subs, Five Guys, Freebirds Burrito, Honeybaked Ham, Jason's Deli, Jimmy John's, La Madeline Bakery, Logan's Roadhouse, Macaroni Grill, McDonald's, Panda Express, Panera Bread, Penn Sta Subs, Popeye's, Red Lobster, Redneck Heaven BBQ, Saltgrass Steaks, Schlotzsky's, Sonic, Spring Creek BBQ, Starbucks, Steak'n Shake, Subway, Taco Bueno, Taco Cabana, TGIFriday's, Twin Peaks, Wendy's, Which Wich? Comfort Suites, Country Inn&Suites, Courtyard, Fairfield Inn, Hampton Inn, Hilton Garden, Holiday Inn Express, Residence Inn, Springhill Suites, TownePlace Suites AT&T, Barnes&Noble, Best Buy, Costco/gas, Dillard's, Discount Tire, JC Penney, Macy's, Michael's, Old Navy, URGENT CARE, Verizon
447a	TX 121, Rayburn Fwy
446	Frankford Rd, E RaceTrac La Hacienda Ranch Grill
445b a	Pres Geo Bush Tpk
444	Whitlock Lane, Sandy Lake Rd, E Shell La Hacienda Rodeway Inn Buick/GMC, Kia, W McDonald's Starbucks Delux Inn Harley-Davidson

DALLAS

Exit#	Services
443	Belt Line Rd, Crosby Rd, E RaceTrac Subway Ford Hyundai, W Shell Chevrolet, U-Haul
442	Valwood Pkwy, E Chevron/Subway/dsl, Conoci/dsl DQ Grandy's, Jack-in-the-Box, Taco Bueno, Waffle House Gues Inn, LoneStar Inn, Super 8, W Gas/dsl transmissions
441	Valley View Lane, W Chevron, Shell/dsl Best Value Inn Days Inn, Motel 6
440b	I-635 E
440c	I-635 W, to DFW Airport
439	Royal Lane, E Shell/dsl, Valero/7-11/dsl McDonald's Wendy's, W Chevron/7-11, Exxon/dsl Jack-in-the-Box
438	Walnut Hill Lane, E Chevron/dsl, Shell, Valero/dsl Burger King, Denny's, Trail Dust Steaks, Wild Turkey Grill Hampton Inn, La Quinta, Quality Inn, W Gulf/dsl, Shell/dsl
437	Manana Rd (from nb), same as 438
436	TX 348, to DFW, Irving, E Shell/dsl Finish Line Grill IHOP, Starbucks, Waffle House Baymont Inn, Best Western, Country Inn Suites, Days Inn, Elegante Hotel, Holiday Inn Express, SpringHill Suites, Studio 6, W Exxon/dsl, Valero/dsl Chili's, Gino's Pizzaria, Humperdinks, Jack-in-the-Box Jason's Deli, Joe's Crabshack, Mambo Seafood, McDonald's Ojos Locos Cantina, Olive Garden, Papadeaux Seafood, Pappa's BBQ, Pappas Bros Steaks, Pappasito's Mexican, Red Lobster Taco Bell, TX L&C, Wendy's Budget Suites, Century Inn
435	Harry Hines Blvd (from nb)
434b	Regal Row, E Chevron/Grandy's/dsl Sam's Grill, Whataburger Motel 6, W Ramada Inn
434a	Empire, Central, E Shell/McDonald's Kay's Rest, Sonic Budget Suites, Candlewood Suites, InTown Suites, Wingate Inn Office Depot, W Exxon/dsl Bombshell Rest., Burger King, Schlotzsky's, Taco Bell

INTERSTATE 35 Cont'd

DALLAS

Exit#	Services
433b	Mockingbird Lane, E Shell/dsl Jack-in-the-Box Budget Suites, Comfort Inn, Crowne Plaza, Hawthorn Suites, Love Field Hotel, Residence Inn Love Field Airport, W Starbucks
433a	(432b from sb) TX 356, Commonwealth Dr
432a	Inwood Rd, E Exxon/7-11 H, Chevrolet, URGENT CARE, W Shell, Texaco/Subway/dsl Taco Cabana, Whataburger Embassy Suites, Extended Stay America, Hampton Inn, Holiday Inn Express, Homewood Suites
431	Motor St, E Chevron Denny's H, W Shell/7-11 Alamo Rest Marriott Suites
430c	Wycliff Ave, E Holiday Inn, Renaissance Hotel, W Hilton Anatole, Hilton Garden
430b	Mkt Ctr Blvd, E World Trade Ctr, W Shell Denny's Best Western, Courtyard, Days Inn, DoubleTree, Fairfield Inn, Sheraton Suites
430a	Oak Lawn Ave, E Holiday Inn, W Shell/dsl Denny's, Medieval Times Rest. to Merchandise Mart
429c	HiLine Ave (from nb)
429b	Continental Ave, Commerce St W, E Hooters, W Exxon, Shell McDonald's, Popeye's, downtown
429a	to I-45, US 75, to Houston
428e	Commerce St E, Reunion Blvd, Dallas, downtown
428d	I-30 W, to Ft Worth
428a	I-30 E, to I-45 S
428b	Industrial Blvd, E Exxon, W Fuel City/dsl, Shamrock
427b	I-30 E
427a	Colorado Blvd, E H
426c	Jefferson Ave, E Shell/dsl
426b	TX 180 W, 8th St, E Shell/dsl
426a	Ewing Ave, E McDonald's, Popeye's
425c	Marsalis Ave, W Chevron, GME Mart Jack-in-the-Box
425b	Beckley Ave, 12th St, sb only, W QT, Shell Wendy's
425a	Zang Blvd, same as 425b
424	Illinois Ave, E Chevron William's Chicken, W Exxon/7-11 Burger King, Church's, Jack-in-the-Box, Little Caesar's, Pancake House, Popeye's, Sonic, Subway, Taco Bell Oak Tree Inn Kroger, Ross, Walgreens
423b	Saner Ave
423a	(422b from nb) US 67 S, Kiest Blvd, W Shell/repair Golden Chick, McDonald's, Subway
421b	Ann Arbor St, W Exxon/dsl
421a	Lp 12E W, E RaceWay/dsl Motel 6, W QT/dsl IHOP, Subway $Tree, Walmart
420	Laureland, E 7-11/dsl Plaza Inn, W Exxon/dsl, Texaco Linfield Inn
419	Camp Wisdom Rd, E Exxon Jack-in-the-Box Oak Cliff Inn, W Chevron, Shell McDonald's Grand Inn U-Haul
418c	Danieldale Rd (from sb)
418b	I-635/I-20 E, to Shreveport
418a	I-20 W, to Ft Worth
417	Wheatland Rd (from nb)
416	Wintergreen Rd, W 7-11 Cracker Barrel, Waffle House Clarion, Days Inn, Hampton Inn, Holiday Inn Express
415	Pleasant Run Rd, E Shell/dsl, Valero/Church's/dsl Bienvenidos Mexican, Chicken Express, Chili's, CiCi's Pizza, Grandy's, IHOP, In-N-Out, Logan's Roadhouse, Sonic, Subway, Taco Cabana, Waffle House Great Western Inn, Hwy Express Inn, Motel 6, Spanish Trails Motel Family$, Home Depot, NAPA,

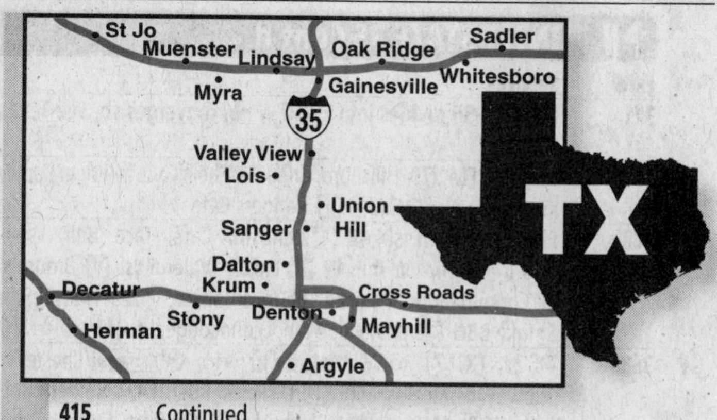

TX

WAXAHATCHIE

Exit#	Services
415	Continued W Burger King, Dicky's BBQ, El Chico, KFC, LJ Silver, Luby's, McDonald's, On the Border, Outback Steaks, Pollo Tropical, Starbucks, Taco Bueno, Wendy's Best Value Inn, La Quinta AT&T, Chevrolet, Discount Tire, Firestone/auto, Ford, Kroger, Office Depot, Ross
414	FM 1382, Desoto Rd, Belt Line Rd, E Murphy USA/dsl Taco Bell, Whataburger Verizon, Walmart/McDonald's, W QT/dsl $Tree
413	Parkerville Rd, W Exxon/Subway/dsl U-Haul
412	Bear Creek Rd, W Shell/dsl Jack-in-the-Box transmissions
411	FM 664, Ovilla Rd, E Exxon/dsl, Murphy USA/dsl, RaceTrac Burger King, Denny's, Dickey's BBQ, DQ, LJ Silver/Taco Bell, McDonald's, Panda Express, Whataburger Comfort Inn Brookshire's Foods, CVS Drug, USPO, Walgreens, Walmart, W Exxon/Subway, Valero
410	Red Oak Rd, E Shell/Pizza Inn/Subway/dsl, Valero/dsl Motel 6, W Hilltop Travel Trailers
408	US 77, TX 342, to Red Oak, E golf
406	Sterrett Rd, E fireworks
405	FM 387, E Phillips 66/dsl, QT/dsl
404	Lofland Rd, industrial area
403	US 287, to Ft Worth, E Murphy USA/dsl, RaceTrac/dsl, Shell/dsl, Valero A&W/LJ Silver, Carino's, Chick-fil-A, Chili's, Chipotle, Domino's, DQ, El Fenix, IHOP, Jack-in-the-Box, KFC, Logan's Roadhouse, McDonald's, Olive Garden, Panda Express, Pizza Hut, Starbuck's, Taco Bueno, Taco Cabana, Waffle House, Wendy's Comfort Suites, Fairfield Inn, Hampton Inn, Holiday Inn Express, LaQuinta H, Belk, Best Buy, Buick/GMC/Chevrolet, Discount Tire, Hobby Lobby, Home Depot, JC Penney, Lowe's, Office Depot, Petsmart, Ross, Target, Walmart, W Chrysler/Dodge/Jeep, Ford
401b	US 287 bus, Waxahatchie, E Motel 6, Super 8
401a	Brookside Rd, E Dallas Suites, Executive Inn
399b	FM 1446
399a	FM 66, FM 876, Maypearl, E Texas Inn, W Exxon/dsl, Shell/Sonic/dsl
397	to US 77, to Waxahachie
391	FM 329, Forreston Rd
386	TX 34, Italy, E Loves/Carl's Jr/dsl/scales/24hr, Shell/Smokehouse BBQ/dsl Sonic $General, W Exxon/Grandy's/McDonald's/dsl/scales Pizza Inn, Subway, Taco Bell Italy Inn truckwash
384	Derrs Chapel Rd
381	FM 566, Milford Rd
377	FM 934
374	FM 2959, Carl's Corner, W Petro/Exxon/Dunkin Donuts/Iron Skillet/dsl/scales/24hr/@
373	I-35E

TX

INTERSTATE 35 Cont'd

HILLSBORO

Exit#	Services
371	I-35 W. **I-35 divides into E and W nb, converges sb, See Texas I-35 W.**
370	US 77 N, FM 579, Hillsboro, E TA/Shell/Country Pride/Burger King/dsl/scales/24hr/@ Rangers Cafe
368b	FM 286 (from sb), E LoneStar Café, Taco Bell, Wendy's Hampton Inn, W Exxon, Valero/dsl Braum's, El Conquistador Mexican, El Taco Jalisco, Pizza Hut, Up In Smoke BBQ Best Value Inn, EconoLodge, La Quinta H
368a	TX 22, TX 171, to Whitney, E 7-11, Loves/Chester's/Subway/dsl/scales/24hr Dickey's BBQ, DQ, Golden Buffet, IHOP, McDonald's, Starbucks Comfort Suites, Days Inn, Motel 6, Quality Inn, Super 8 Hillsboro Outlets/Famous Brands, W 7-11, Chevron/dsl, Mobil, Murphy USA/dsl $Tree, Chicken Express, Jack-in-the-Box, Schlotzsky's, Sonic, Whataburger Thunderbird Motel/rest. AT&T, Chrysler/Dodge/Jeep, Ford, Walmart/Subway
367	Old Bynum Rd (from nb), same as 368
364b	TX 81 N, to Hillsboro (from nb, exits left)
364a	FM 310 (from sb)
363	CR 3111
362mm	**full facilities, litter barrels, petwalk, both directions**
359	FM 1304, W Gulf/dsl/24hr truckwash
358	FM 1242 E, Abbott, E Still Smokin' BBQ
356	Co Rd 3102
355	County Line Rd, E Waco North RV Park
354	Marable St, E Waco North RV Park
353	FM 2114, West, E Chevron/dsl, Shell/Czech Bakery Bush's Chicken, Sonic, Subway Ford, W Exxon/Slovacek's/dsl Best Western Czech Inn Chevrolet, Vintage Automotive
351	FM 1858, E tires/repair
349	Wiggins Rd
347	FM 3149, Tours Rd
346	Ross Rd, W Exxon/Church's/dsl/24hr antiques, I-35 RV Park/LP
345	Old Dallas Rd, W I-35 RV Park/LP
345a	frontage rd, same as 345
343	FM 308, Elm Mott, E Exxon/DQ, Shell/Jct Cafe/dsl/scales/24hr, W $General
342b	US 77 bus, W North Crest RV Park
342a	FM 2417, Crest Dr, W Valero/dsl Bush's Chicken, DQ Motel 6 auto repair, Family$
341	Craven Ave, Lacy Lakeview, E Freightliner, W Chevron, Shell
340	Myers Lane (from nb)
339	to TX 6 S, FM 3051, Lake Waco, E Murphy USA, Valero/dsl Casa Ole, Cici's Pizza, Domino's, El Conquistador, Jack-in-the-Box, Luby's, Pizza Hut, Popeye's, Sonic, Subway, Wendy's, Whataburger, WingStop Holiday Inn $General, $Tree, Advance Parts, Discount Tire, Home Depot, NAPA, to [RV], Walmart, W 7-11/dsl, Chevron, Shell, Valero/dsl Burger King, Cracker Barrel, Heitmiller Steaks, KFC, McDonald's, Starbucks, Taco Bell Fairfield Inn, Hampton Inn AT&T, URGENT CARE
338b	Behrens Circle (from nb), same as 339, E Jack-in-the-Box, Little Caesar's, Sonic GNC, W Shell/dsl/LP Cracker Barrel Best Western, Comfort Suites, Days Inn, Delta Inn, Hampton Inn, Knights Inn, Motel 6, Quality Inn
338a	US 84, to TX 31, Waco Dr, E Chopstix, Collin St Bakery, Denny's, Subway Woodspring Suites AutoZone, Family$,

WACO

Exit#	Services
338a	Continued HEB Food/gas, O'Reilly Parts, Sam's Club/gas, Tesla EVC W Comfort Suites H
337	US 77 business
335c	Lake Brazos Dr, MLK Blvd, E Baylor Stadium, W Buzzard Billy's Red Roof Inn, Scottish Inn H
335mm	Brazos River
335b	FM 434, University Parks Dr, E Starbucks Baylor U, TX Ranger Museum, W 7-11/dsl In-N-Out, Jack-in-the Box Residence Inn
335a	4th St, 5th St, E Exxon/Subway/dsl IHOP La Quinta Baylor U, W Valero/dsl Cane's, Chick-fil-A, Fazoli's, Freddy's, LJ Silver, McAlister's Deli, McDonald's, Panera Bread, Papa John's, Sonic, Taco Bell, Taco Cabana, Wendy's Whataburger CVS Drug
334b	US 77 S, 17th St, 18th St, E Shell/dsl, Valero/dsl Burger King, Fuego Grill, Jimmy John's, Pizza Hut, Popeye's, Schlotzsky's, Vitek's BBQ Budget Inn, Deluxe Inn, La Quinta, Super 8, W Shell Taquerias Mexican H
333a	Lp 396, Valley Mills Dr, E 7-11/dsl El Chico, Elite Café Rudy's BBQ/gas, Trujillo's Mexican, TX Roadhouse Comfort Suites, Motel 6 Kia, Mazda, W RaceWay/dsl, Valero/dsl Bubba's Rest., Bush's Chicken, Catfish King, Chili's Church's, George's Rest., Jack-in-the-Box, Little Caesar's, Pizza Patron, Potbelly, Sonic, Starbucks, Subway, Zoe's Kitchen Home 2 Suites Aamco, Advance Parts, AutoZone CVS Drug, Family$, HEB Foods/dsl, Lincoln, Walgreens
331	New Rd, E Phillips 66/dsl Candlewood Suites, New Road Inn, Relax Inn, Rodeway Inn, W FLYING J/Denny's/dsl/scales/24hr Burger King, Carl's Jr, Hooters, IHOP Quality Inn Harley Davidson
330	Lp 340, TX 6, W Chevron/dsl Buffalo Wild Wings Bush's Chicken, Chuy's Mexican, Don Carlo's Mexican, Heitmiller Steaks, Logan's Roadhouse, Newk's Eatery, Panda Express, Panera Bread, Saltgrass Steaks, Sonic, Starbucks, Subway Hampton Inn, Holiday Inn Express, Homewood Suites TownePlace Suites H, $Tree, AT&T, Belk, Best Buy, Cabela's, Cavender's Boots, Fiat/Alpha Romeo, Ford, Honda, Hyundai, Jo-Ann, Kohl's, Marshall's, Nissan, Office Depot, Old Navy Petco, Ross, Toyota, URGENT CARE, World Mkt
328	FM 2063, FM 2113, Moody, E Pilot/Subway/Wendy's dsl/scales/24hr/@ McDonald's Robinson Inn Kenworth, W Shell/dsl, Valero/dsl DQ Ramada Inn Sleep Inn
325	FM 3148, Moonlight Dr, W Valero/dsl FunTown RV C
323	FM 2837 (from sb), Lorena, W Brookshire Bros/Conoco dsl Pizza House, Sonic
322	Lorena, E Phillips 66/dsl, W Bush's Chicken, Pizza House $General
321	Callan Ranch Rd
319	Woodlawn Rd
318b a	Bruceville
315	TX 7, FM 107, Eddy, E Bruceville-Eddy RV Park, W Family$, to Mother Neff SP
314	Old Blevins Rd
311	Big Elm Rd, E fireworks
308	FM 935, Troy, E Loves/Subway/McDonald's/dsl scales/24hr, Shell/dsl, Valero/dsl, W $General, dsl repair
306	FM 1237, Pendleton, W Goodyear Truck Tires
305	Berger Rd, W Lucky's RV Park, repair
304	Lp 363, Dodgen Loop, E Buc-ee's/dsl, W Shell/Wendy's/dsl Freightliner

TEMPLE

INTERSTATE 35 Cont'd

Exit#	Services
303	spur 290, N 3rd St, Temple, E S-2 Gas Texas Inn
302	Nugent Ave, E Exxon/dsl Baymont Inn, Best Value Inn, EconoLodge, Motel 6, W TX Roadhouse Best Western, Days Inn, Knights Inn, Motel 6
301	TX 53, FM 2305, Adams Ave, E Exxon/dsl, Valero Arby's, Chick-fil-A, KFC, Little Caesar's, LJ Silver, McDonald's, Pizza Hut, Starbucks, Subway, Taco Bell, Whataburger La Quinta H, Advance Parts, HEB Foods/dsl, O'Reilly Parts, URGENT CARE, W TX Roadhouse Best Western
300	Ave H, 49th –57th Sts, E Clem Mikeskas BBQ
299	US 190 E, TX 36, E Shell/dsl Cracker Barrel, Jack-in-the-Box, Luby's, Olive Garden, Sol de Jalisco Budget Inn, Residence Inn, Travelodge H, AT&T, Chrysler/Dodge/Jeep, Natural Grocers, Tires To You, URGENT CARE, Verizon, W BJ's Rest., Chili's, Chipotle Mexican, Five Guys, IHOP, McDonald's, Subway, Taco Cabana Hampton Inn Best Buy, Firestone/auto, GNC, Home Depot, Michael's, Petsmart, Target
298	nb only, to frontage rd, E Longhorn Steaks Residence Inn
297	FM 817, Midway Dr, E Phillips 66/dsl Golden Corral Holiday Inn, Super 8/rest. Buick/GMC/Cadillac, Nissan, W Valero/dsl Goodyear/auto, VW
294b	FM 93, 6th Ave, E Shell/dsl McDonald's Chevrolet, Ford/Lincoln, Toyota, W Subway River Forest Inn Harley-Davidson, U of Mary Hardin Baylor
294a	Central Ave, E Taco Bell, W Shell/dsl Burger King, El Mexicano Grill, Jimmy John's, Pizza Hut, Schlotzsky's, Schoepf's BBQ, Sonic, Starbucks, Whataburger Knights Inn AutoZone, city park, O'Reilly Parts, Parts+, USPO
293b	TX 317, FM 436, Main St
293a	US 190 W, to Killeen, Ft Hood
292	Lp 121 (same as 293a), E Valero/dsl/24hr Budget Host, W 7-11/dsl, Exxon/dsl Oxbow Steaks La Quinta Belton RV Park, Sunbelt RV Ctr
290	Shanklin Rd
289	Tahuaya Rd
287	Amity Rd
286	FM 2484, E Days Inn, Holiday Inn Express, W to Stillhouse Hollow Lake, Tranquil RV Park (2mi)
285	FM 2268, Salado, E Conoco/dsl Subway Holiday Inn Express Brookshire Foods/gas, W Cefco/dsl, Gulf Bush's Chicken, Robertson's Rest., Sonic
284	Stagecoach Rd, E Stagecoach Inn, W Johnny's Steaks
283	FM 2268, FM 2843, to Holland, Salado, E Stagecoach Inn
282	FM 2115, E Valero/dsl
281mm	**both lanes, full facilities, litter barrels, petwalk, RV dump, vending**
280	Grainger Rd, Hackberry Rd, Prairie Dell
279	Hill Rd
277	Rd 305
275	FM 487, to Florence, Jarrell, E Exxon/dsl $General, W Shell/dsl (2), Shell/Krispy Kreme/Pizza Inn/dsl USPO
274	Rd 312, E Exxon/Subway/dsl, FLYING J/Burger King/Denny's/dsl/scales McDonald's
271	Ronald Reagan Blvd, W Shell/Subway/dsl/24hr
268	fm 972, Walburg, E Crestview RV Ctr
266	TX 195, E Phillips 66/dsl, Shell TC/dsl/scales/24hr, W Shell/dsl
265	TX 130 Toll S, to Austin

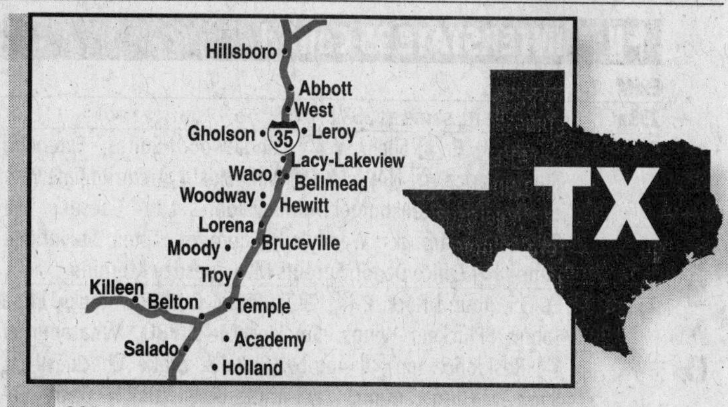

GEORGETOWN

Exit#	Services
264	Lp 35, Georgetown
262	RM 2338, Lake Georgetown, E Valero Chipotle Mexican, KFC, McDonald's, Papa John's, Pizza Hut, Sonic, Starbucks, Subway, Verts Grill $Tree, CVS Drug, Parts+, URGENT CARE, W DQ, Frankie's Pizza, Plaka Greek, Whataburger Candlewood Suites, Georgetown Inn, Holiday Inn Express, La Quinta
261	TX 29, Georgetown, E Shell/dsl Applebee's, Burger King, Chili's, Domino's, Jack-in-the-Box, Jimmy John's, KFC, La Playa, McDonald's, Schlotzsky's, Taco Bell Best Western, Comfort Suites, Hampton Inn HEB Foods, Hobby Lobby, Midas, O'Reilly Parts, same as 262, Tuesday Morning, W Murphy USA/dsl Cane's, Carl's Jr, Casa Ole, Chick-fil-A, CiCi's, Cotton Patch Cafe, Five Guys, George's Rest., IHOP, Longhorn Steaks, Mama Fu's, McAlister's Deli, Panda Express, Panera Bread, Pie Five, Popeye's, Salsa's Mexican, Souper Salad, Starbucks, Taco Cabana, Wendy's AT&T, Beall's, Best Buy, Discount Tire, Home Depot, Kohl's, Michael's, Natural Grocers, Office Depot, Old Navy, Petsmart, Ross, Target, TJ Maxx, Verizon, Walgreens, Walmart/McDonald's
260	RM 2243, Leander, E H, USPO, W Chevron/dsl, Exxon/dsl, Texaco Jack-in-the-Box Econolodge
259	Lp 35, W RV Outlet Ctr, to Interspace Caverns
257	Westinghouse Rd, E Buick/Chevrolet, Chrysler/Dodge/Jeep, Ford/Lincoln, Mazda, Mercedes, Subaru/Volvo, VW
256	RM 1431, Chandler Rd, E BJ Rest., Chili's, Chipotle, Firehouse Subs, Freebirds Burrito, In-N-Out, Jamba Juice, Jimmy John's, La Madeleine, Mimi's Cafe, Mooyah Burger, Panda Express, Papa John's, Pei Wei, Razzoo's Cajun, Starbucks, Steak'n Shake, TGI Friday's, Which Wich?, Zoe's Kitchen Bass Pro Shops, GNC, HEB/dsl, IKEA, JC Penney, Jo-Ann Fabrics, Mazda, Petsmart, REI, Ross, Round Rock Outlet/famous brands, Volvo, Walgreens
254	FM 3406, Round Rock, E Chevron/dsl Gatti's Pizza, Kerby Lane Cafe, La Tapatia, McDonald's, Saucy Rooster Best Western $General, Firestone/auto, Harley-Davidson, Honda, Hyundai, Kia, Toyota, W EVC, Shell/dsl Chuy's Mexican, Cover 3 Rest., Cracker Barrel, Denny's, Double Dave's Pizza, Jack Allen's Kitchen, Mellow Mushroom, Rudy's BBQ/gas, Salt Traders Rest., SaltGrass Steaks Courtyard, Hilton Garden, Holiday Inn, Holiday Inn Express, La Quinta, Red Roof Inn, SpringHill Suites, Woodspring Suites CVS Drug, GMC, Nissan
253b	US 79, to Taylor, E Chevron/dsl/24hr, Texaco/dsl Baskin-Robbins, Casa Garcia's, DQ, Fuddrucker's, KFC, La Tapatia, LJ Silver, Pizza Hut, Short Stop Dogs, Sirloin Stockade Best Western, Wingate Inn $General, Advance Parts, AutoZone, Beall's, Cottman Transmissions, Just Brakes, W Shell/dsl Gatti's Pizza, Hunan Lion, IHOP, La Margarita, Poke Joe's BBQ, Popeye's, Starbucks, Thundercloud Subs Country Inn&Suites, La Quinta, Motel 6, Red Roof Inn, Woodspring Suites $Tree, USPO

ROUND ROCK

TX

INTERSTATE 35 Cont'd

ROUND ROCK

Exit#	Services
253a	frontage rd, same as 253 b
252b a	RM 620, E Shell/dsl Candlewood Suites, Extended Stay America NAPA, W Mobil/dsl Corner Cafe Bakery, Freddy's Steakburgers, Jimmy John's, Little Caesar's, McDonald's, Starbucks, Wendy's Comfort Suites, Staybridge Suites Office Depot, Sprouts Mkt, Tuesday Morning
251	Lp 35, Round Rock, E CiCi's Pizza, Outback Steaks, Papa John's, Pluckers Wings, Smokey Mo's BBQ, Whataburger Residence Inn Aamco, BigLots, Brake Check, W Shell Burger King, Jack-in-the-Box, Luby's, Taco Cabana Days Inn, Marriott, Sleep Inn Austin's Automotive, GNC, NTB, transmissions, Walgreens
250	TX 45, Lp 1, E Chick-fil-A, Chili's, El Taquito, Firehouse Subs, Five Guys, Green Mesquite BBQ, Jason's Deli, Joe's Crabshack, Macaroni Grill, McDonald's, Panda Express, Subway, Twin Peaks Rest. Hampton Inn, Homewood Suites, Residence Inn $Tree, AT&T, Best Buy, Discount Tire, Home Depot, Michael's, Petsmart, Ross, Steinmart, Target, URGENT CARE, Walmart/Subway, W Applebee's, Chipotle, Egg&I Cafe, Hooters, Jimmy John's, Logan's Roadhouse, Longhorn Steaks, Olive Garden, Red Lobster, Schlotzsky's, Tokyo Steaks Extended Stay America, La Quinta Barnes&Noble, Hobby Lobby, Kohl's, Lowe's, Marshall's, Old Navy, PetCo, Sam's Club, World Mkt
248	Grand Ave Pkwy, E 7-11/Subway/dsl, Citgo, Shell/dsl Chucho's Mexican, Gatti's Pizza, Thundercloud Subs, TX Roadhouse Comfort Suites URGENT CARE, W Exxon/McDonald's/dsl
247	FM 1825, Pflugerville, E Exxon/7-11/dsl Bombshells Rest., Burger King, Cheddar's, Domino's, FD's Grillhouse, Jack-in-the-Box, Subway, Taco Cabana, Wendy's Comfort Suites Firestone/auto, GNC, HEB Foods/gas, W Exxon/7-11, Shell/Church's KFC, Miller's BBQ, Sonic Country Inn Suites Goodyear, McSpadden Automotive, Tires-4Less
246	Howard Lane, E Citgo, Exxon/7-11/dsl Arby's, Baby Acapulco, McDonald's, Subway, Wings'n More Home Depot, Kohl's, NTB, W Valero/dsl IHOP, Whataburger Sleep Inn CarMax
245	FM 734, Parmer Lane, to Yager Lane (244 from nb), E Carino's, Chick-fil-A, Chili's, Freebirds Burrito, In-N-Out, Jersey Mike's, Jimmy John's, Kublai Khan, Little Caesar's, Masala Wok, MOD Pizza, My Fit Grill, Panda Express, Pei Wei, Schlotzsky's, Souper Salad, Subway, Verts Grill, Zed's Rest Homewood Suites $Tree, HEB Food/E-85, Hobby Lobby, JC Penney, Kohl's, PetCo, Petsmart, Ross, Sears Grand, Verizon, W Conoco/dsl, Exxon/7-11/dsl, Murphy USA/dsl Buffalo Wild Wings, Golden Corral, Hoho Chinese, Red Robin Courtyard, Fairfield Inn, Hilton Garden, Residence Inn, SpringHill Suites, Staybridge Suites AT&T, CarMax, Discount Tire, Lowe's, Walmart/McDonald's
244	Tech Ridge Blvd, Yager Lane, (from nb, same as 245)
243	Braker Lane, E Valero/dsl Whataburger U-Haul, W Citgo, Shell/dsl Austin Motel, Woodspring Suites $General
241	Rundberg Lane, E Exxon/7-11 Grand China Buffet, Jack-in-the-Box Extended Stay America, Orangewood Inn $General, Chevrolet, U-Haul, W Chevron, Shell Austin Suites, Budget Inn, Budget Lodge, Economy Inn, Holiday Inn Express, Motel 6, Motel 6 (2), Red Roof Inn, Super 8
240a	US 183, Lockhart, E Exxon Jack-in-the-Box Days Inn, Orangewood Inn, W Chevron/dsl Motel 6, Red Roof Inn, Super 8
239	St John's Ave, E Shell Burger King, Chili's, Japon Japanese, Pappadeaux, Pappasito's Mexican Crowne Plaza, Days Inn, DoubleTree, Drury Inn, Econolodge, Hampton Inn, Studio 6 USPO, W Exxon/7-11, Mobil/dsl, Valero/dsl Applebee's, Buffalo Wild Wings, Carrabba's, Denny's, IHOP, Ojos Locos, Panda Express, Wendy's Best Value Inn, Comfort Inn, Country Inn&Suites, Courtyard, Holiday Inn, Hyatt Place, La Quinta, Motel 6, Ramada Inn Ford, Office Depot
238b	US 290 E, RM 222, frontage rds connect several exits, same as 238a
238a	51st St, E Buffet King, Chipotle, Church's, CiCi's, Jamba Juice, La Madeleine, McDonald's, Papa John's, Pieology, SmashBurger, Subway, Tino's Greek, TX Steaks, Which Wich? DoubleTree Hotel, Drury Inn, EconoLodge, Embassy Suites $Tree, Advance Parts, AutoZone, Best Buy, Home Depot, Marshall's, Old Navy, Petsmart, Ross, Staples, Target, Walgreens, W Shell Baby Acapulco, Capt Benny's Seafood Capital Inn, Courtyard, Fairfield Inn, Motel 6, Super 8
237b	51st St, same as 238a
237a	Airport Blvd, W In-N-Out, Jack-in-the-Box, Wendy's GNC, Goodyear, HEB Foods, PetCo, Sears/auto
236.7	lower level accesses downtown, upper level is I-35 thru
236b	39th St, E Chevron/dsl Short Stop Burgers, Subway Fiesta Foods, O'Reilly Parts, U-Haul, W Shell/dsl to U of TX
236a	26th-32nd Sts, E Los Altos Mexican, Subway Days Inn, W Rodeway Inn H
235b	Manor Rd, E Denny's DoubleTree, W Rodeway Inn st capitol, U of TX, same as 236a
235a	MLK, 15th St, W H
234.9	lower level accesses downtown, upper level is I-35 thru
234c	11th St, 12th St, E Chevron/dsl, Shell/dsl Denny's, Wendy's DoubleTree Hotel, Super 8 CVS Drug, W Gulf/dsl, Shell Hilton, Hilton Garden, La Quinta, Marriott, Omni Motel, Radisson, Sheraton H, museum, st capitol, downtown
234b	8th-3rd St, W IHOP
234a	Cesar Chavez St, Holly St, E Shell/dsl, W Chevron/dsl Holiday Inn, downtown
233mm	Little Colorado River
233	Riverside Dr, Town Lake, E Gulf, Shell/dsl Chipotle, Church's, MOD Pizza, Starbucks AT&T, Walgreens
232b	Woodland Ave
232a	Oltorf St, E Chevron/dsl, Gulf, Shell/dsl Donn's BBQ, Luby's, Sonic Best Value, Howard Johnson, La Quinta, Motel 6, Parkwest Inn, W Conoco/dsl, Exxon/7-11 Denny's, Starbucks Best Western, Simco Plaza
231	Woodward St, E same as 232, Wyndham Garden, W Home Depot, Walmart
230b a	US 290 W, TX 71, Ben White Blvd, St Elmo Rd, E Shell/Circle K/dsl Baymont Inn, Courtyard, Fairfield Inn, Hampton Inn, Homewood Suites, Marriott, Omni Hotel, Quality Inn, Red Roof Inn, Residence Inn, SpringHill Suites Acura, W Burger King Candlewood Suites, Days Inn, La Quinta H, Audi, CarMax, Chrysler/Dodge/Jeep, Ford, Hyundai, Kia, Mazda, Nissan, NTB, Toyota
229	Stassney Lane, W Buffalo Wild Wings, Chili's, Chipotle, Jimmy John's, Krispy Kreme, Logan's Roadhouse, Macaroni Grill, Pizza Hut, Trudy's Grill, Twin Peaks Rest., TX Cattle Co Steak

AUSTIN

INTERSTATE 35 Cont'd

229 Continued
Holiday Inn Express, Staybridge Suites Fiesta Foods/gas, Lowe's

228 Wm Cannon Drive, E Exxon, Valero Applebee's, McDonald's, Subway, Taco Bell Brake Check, Discount Tire, HEB Foods, Nissan, W Shell/dsl Burger King, China Harbor, Gatti's Pizza, Golden Corral, KFC, LJ Silver, Taco Cabana, Wendy's, Whataburger Advance Parts, AT&T, BigLots, Chevrolet, Firestone

227 Slaughter Lane, Lp 275, S Congress, E Shell/dsl ChuckE-Cheese, Don Dario's, IHOP Home Depot, Lone Star RV Resort, U-Haul, W Murphy USA/dsl, Valero, Valero/dsl Carino's, Chick-fil-A, Chili's, Chipotle Mexican, Fuddrucker's, Gatti Town, Jack-in-the-Box, Jason's Deli, Longhorn Steaks, Luby's, Mama Fu's, Miller BBQ, Panda Express, Serrano's TexMex, Smashburger, Sonic, Starbucks, Steak'n Shake, Subway, Taco Bell, TGIFriday's, TX Roadhouse, Wendy's, Whataburger $Tree, AT&T, Best Buy, Firestone/auto, GNC, Hobby Lobby, JC Penney, Jo-Ann, Marshall's, Petsmart, Ross, Sam's Club/dsl, Target, URGENT CARE, Verizon, VW, Walgreens, Walmart

226 Slaughter Creek Overpass

225 FM 1626, Onion Creek Pkwy, E Texaco, Valero Subway Harley-Davidson

224 frontage rd (from nb)

223 FM 1327, rd 45 **toll**

221 Lp 4, Buda, E Chevron/McDonald's Starbucks Best Value Inn, Candlewood Suites, Comfort Suites, Holiday Inn Express Ford, Kenworth, W Murphy USA/dsl, Shell/dsl Arby's, Chili's, Cracker Barrel, Dan's Burgers, Domino's, Jack-in-the-Box, KFC/LJ Silver, Little Caesar's, Logan's Roadhouse, Miller BBQ, Papa John's, Pizza Hut, Sonic, Subway, Taco Bell, Whataburger, Zaxby's Hampton Inn, Microtel AT&T, AutoZone, Cabela's, HEB Food/dsl/E-85, O'Reilly Parts, USPO, Verizon, Walgreens, Walmart

220 FM 2001, Niederwald, E Shell Burger King Camper Clinic RV Ctr, Marshall's RV Park, W Crestview RV Ctr/Park, Peterbilt

217 Lp 4, Buda, E Exxon/dsl La Quinta Mack/Volvo, W Valero/dsl Burger King Quality Inn Christian Bros Auto, Home Depot

215 Bunton Overpass, E Exxon/KFC/LJ Silver, Walmart/dsl Carl's Jr, Dickey's BBQ, Dunkin Donuts/Baskin Robbins, Firehouse Subs, Pollo Tropical, Popeye's, Taco Bell, Taco Cabana, Wendy's Hampton Inn H, AT&T, Discount Tire, Firestone/auto, Lowe's, Walgreens, Walmart, W Conoco/dsl, Sunoco/Schlotzky's/dsl Applebee's, Casa Garcia's, Chicken Express, Chick-fil-A, Five Guys, IHOP, Jack-in-the-Box, Jersey Mike's, Little Caesar's, Mama Fu's, McDonald's, MOD Pizza, Panda Express, Papa Murphy's, Starbucks, Subway, Whataburger Comfort Suites $Tree, Explore USA RV Ctr, GNC, HEB Foods/dsl/e85, Kohl's, PetCo, Ross, Target, URGENT CARE, Verizon

213 FM 150, Kyle, E 7-11/dsl, Valero/dsl DQ AutoZone, O'Reilly Parts, W Conoco/dsl Casa Maria Mexican Advance Parts, CVS Drug, repair

210 Yarrington Rd, E Hyundai, W Buick/Chevrolet/GMC, Ford, Plum Creek RV Park

209 weight sta (sb only)

208mm Blanco River

208 frontage rd, Blanco River Rd, W Hilton Garden Buick/Chevrolet/GMC

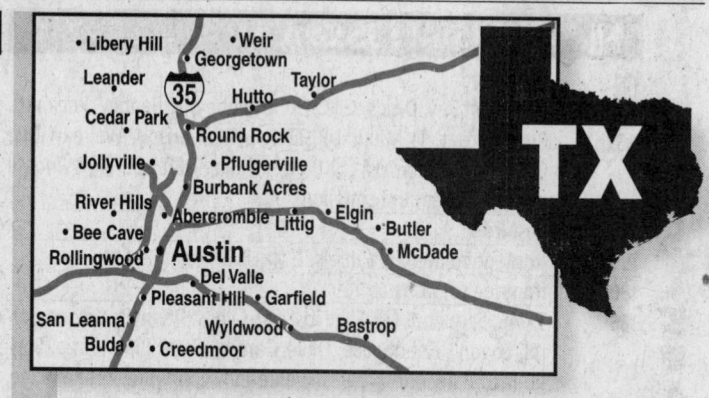

Liberty Hill, Weir, Georgetown, Leander, 35, Taylor, Hutto, Cedar Park, Round Rock, Jollyville, Pflugerville, Burbank Acres, River Hills, Abercrombie, Littig, Elgin, Butler, Bee Cave, McDade, Rollingwood, Austin, Del Valle, Pleasant Hill, Garfield, San Leanna, Wyldwood, Bastrop, Buda, Creedmoor, TX

SAN MARCOS

206 Lp 82, Aquarena Springs Rd, E Conoco, Valero/dsl San Marcos RV Park, W Exxon/dsl, Shell, Shell/dsl Inn-N-Out, Pancake House, Pollo Tropical, Popeye's, Sonic Best Value Inn, Howard Johnson, La Quinta, Motel 6, Quality Inn, Ramada Ltd, Rodeway Inn, Summit Inn, Super 8 to SW TX U

205 TX 80, TX 142, Bastrop, E 7-11/dsl, Exxon, RaceWay/dsl, Shell/dsl, Valero/dsl Cane's, China Palace, Fazoli's, Freebirds Burrito, Jason's Deli, Little Caesar's, Pizza Hut, Subway, Wing Stop Executive Inn, Fairfield Inn $General, AutoZone, CVS Drug, Hobby Lobby, Verizon, Walmart, W Valero A&W/LJ Silver, Burger King, Church's, Chuy's, Five Guys, IHOP, Kobe Japanese, Logan's Roadhouse, McDonald's, Taco Cabana, Wendy's Best Western, Budget Inn, Days Inn, Gateway Inn, Knights Inn, Red Roof Inn, Rodeway Inn Brake Check, city park, HEB/gas, Office Depot, Walgreens

204mm San Marcos River

204b CM Allen Pkwy, W Shell/dsl, Spirit/dsl Casa Maria, DQ, Krispy Kreme, La Fonda Rest., Mazatlan, Plucker's Grill, Sonic Best Western, EconoLodge AutoZone, O'Reilly Parts, transmissions

204a Lp 82, TX 123, to Seguin, E Conoco, Exxon/dsl 54th St Grill, Burger King, Bush's Chicken, Carino's, Chicken Express, Chili's, Freddy's, Luby's, McDonald's, Newk's Eatery, Red Lobster, Starbucks, Whataburger Comfort Suites, Hampton Inn, Wingate Inn H, Aamco

202 FM 3407, Wonder World Dr, E Exxon/dsl, Shell/dsl Carl's Jr, Chick-fil-A, Fuschaks BBQ, Jack-in-the-Box, Panera Bread, Taste of China, Wienerschnitzel Comfort Inn H, $Tree, Best Buy, Discount Tire, Lowe's, Marshall's, Petsmart, Ross, Sams Club/gas, W Valero/dsl TX Roadhouse Candlewood Suites, Country Inn&Suites, Holiday Inn Express repair

201 McCarty Lane, E Embassy Suites, W Firehouse Subs, Panda Express, Sonic AT&T, Beall's, Chrysler/Dodge/Jeep, Firestone/auto, JC Penney, Nissan, Target, URGENT CARE

200 Centerpoint Rd, E Chipotle, Cracker Barrel, Outback Steaks, Subway, Taco Bell, Wendy's GNC, Old Navy, San Marcos Outlets/famous brands, Tanger Outlet/famous brands, W Sunoco/dsl McDonald's, Starbucks, Subway, Whataburger, Zaxby's Baymont Inn, Courtyard Honda

199 Posey Rd, E same as 200, Tanger Outlets/famous brands, Toyota

196 FM 1106, York Creek Rd, W Canyon Trail RV Park

195 Watson Lane, Old Bastrop Rd

193 Conrads Rd, Kohlenberg Rd, W TA/Shell/Country Fare/Popeye's/Subway/dsl/scales/24hr/@ Camping World RV Ctr

191 FM 306, FM 483, Canyon Lake, E Buc-ee's BJ's Rest, Las Palapas, Longhorn Steaks, Newk's Eatery, Panda Express, Panera Bread, Sea Island Shrimphouse, Shogun Japanese, Subway, Whataburger, Which Wich?, Willie's Grill AT&T,

TX

INTERSTATE 35 Cont'd

NEW BRAUNFELS

191 Continued
Belk, Best Buy, Dick's, GNC, Hobby Lobby, JC Penney, Petsmart, Ross, Target, TJ Maxx, URGENT CARE, Verizon, Walmart Dist Ctr, W Exxon/dsl Burger King, HEB/e85 Wingate Inn Nissan, transmissions

190c Post Rd

190b frontage rd, New Braunfels, E Evergreen RV Ctr

190a frontage rd, same as 189

189 TX 46, Seguin, E Shell/dsl Chili's, Denny's, Golden Corral, Logan's Roadhouse, Olive Garden, Peter Piper Pizza, Sonic, Taco Palenque Best Value Inn, Courtyard, EconoLodge, Hampton Inn, La Quinta, Super 8, Travelodge Discount Tire, Home Depot, Kohl's, Office Depot, vet, W Texaco, Valero Applebee's, Bush's Chicken, Chipotle Mexican, IHOP, Mama Fu's, McDonald's, Miller's BBQ, Pizza Hut, Subway, Taco Bell, Taco Cabana, TJ's Burgers, Wendy's Baymont, Best Western, Candlewood Suites, Comfort Suites, Country Inn Suites, Days Inn, Edelweiss Inn, Fairfield Inn, Hilton Garden, Holiday Inn Express, Howard Johnson, Microtel, Motel 6, Quality Inn, Ramada Inn, Rodeway Inn, Sleep Inn H, Walgreens

188 frontage rd, W Garden Buffet, Mamacita's Rest. River Ranch Resort Hyundai, Tuesday Morning

188mm Guadalupe River

187 FM 725, Lake McQueeny Rd, E A&W/LJ Silver, Arby's, Burger King, CiCi's, River Hofbrau, Whataburger $Tree, Aamco, BigLots, Chevrolet, Ford/Lincoln, Jeep, Meineke, vet, W Adobe Café, DQ, Jack-in-the-Box, Jason's Deli Budget Inn H, CVS Drug, River Ranch RV Resort

186 Walnut Ave, E Exxon/Subway, Murphy USA/dsl, Valero/dsl Carl's Jr, Chick-fil-A, Firehouse Subs, McDonald's, Popeye's, Schlotzsky's, Taco Bell Red Roof Inn Jo-Ann, Lowe's, Verizon, Walmart, W Shell/dsl Baskin-Robbins, Bonzai Japanese, Chicken Express, Panda Express, Papa John's, Papa Murphy's, Pollo Tropical, Starbucks $Tree, AutoZone, GNC, HEB Foods/gas, U-Haul, Walgreens

185 FM 1044

184 FM 482, Lp 337, Rueckle Rd, E Shell/dsl Hill Country RV Park, Kia, Mazda, W Pilot/McDonald's/Subway/dsl/scales Jack-in-the-Box

183 Solms Rd, W Exxon/Circle K/dsl

182 Engel Rd

180 Schwab Rd

178 FM 1103, Cibolo Rd, Hubertus Rd, E Exxon/7-11/dsl McDonald's Walgreens, W Valero/Subway/dsl

177 FM 482, FM 2252, W Stone Creek RV Park

176 Weiderstein Rd, same as 175

175 FM 3009, Natural Bridge, E Valero/dsl Chili's, IHOP, Mama Margie's Mexican, McDonald's, Miller's BBQ, Schlotzsky's, Sonic, Taco Cabana Fairfield Inn, Hampton Inn HEB Food/dsl/E-85, Lowe's, Verizon, vet, W Murphy USA/dsl, Shell/dsl, Valero/Subway/dsl Abel's Diner, Arby's, Cane's, Chick-fil-A, Denny's, Domino's, Jack-in-the-Box, Jimmy John's, KFC/Pizza Hut/Taco Bell, Panda Express, Pollo Tropical, Starbucks, Wendy's, Whataburger, Wing Stop Best Western, La Quinta $Tree, URGENT CARE, Walmart/McDonald's

174b Schertz Pkwy, E Shell Chevrolet, W Crestview RV Ctr

174a FM 1518, Selma, E Phillips 66/dsl Rudy's BBQ Audi, Buick/GMC, Honda, Subaru, W Comfort Inn Crestview RV Ctr

SAN ANTONIO

173 Old Austin Rd, Olympia Pkwy, E Baskin Robbins, Charley's Subs, Cheddar's, Chick-fil-A, Chili's, Chipotle Mexican, CiCi's, Firehouse Subs, Five Guys, Freddy's, Genghis Grill, Hooters, IHOP, Las Palapas, Macaroni Grill, Outback Steaks, Panda Express, Panera Bread, Papouli's Greek, Peter Piper Pizza, Red Robin, Sea Island Srimp, Starbucks, Subway, Wendy's Holiday Inn Express AT&T, Beall's, Best Buy, Costco/gas, Discount Tire, GNC, Hobby Lobby, Home Depot, Kohl's, Michael's, NTB, Old Navy, Petsmart, Ross, Target, TJ Maxx, URGENT CARE, Verizon, WorldMkt, W ChuckeCheese, Chuy's Mexican, Freebirds Burritos, Houlihan's Hampton Inn

172 TX 218, Anderson Lp, P Booker Rd, E Buffalo Wild Wings, Coldstone, Gino's East Pizza, IHOP, Jimmy John's, TX Roadhouse, Zio's Hilton Garden, Woodspring Suites Nissan, to Randolph AFB, W Comfort Inn, to SeaWorld

171 Topperwein Rd, same as 170

170 Judson Rd, to Converse, E Carl's Jr, Denny's, Whataburger Great Value Inn, La Quinta H, Ford, Hyundai, Nissan, Toyota, W Exxon/7-11 Best Western Kia, Mazda, Sam's Club/gas

169 O'Conner Rd, Wurzbach Pkwy, E Exxon/7-11/dsl McDonald's, Quiznos, Subway, Taco Cabana Comfort Suites CarMax, Chrysler/Dodge/Jeep, Lowe's, Walgreens, W Shell/dsl, Valero/dsl Jack-in-the-Box, Jim's Rest., Sonic Mi Casa Inn Kia, Mazda

168 Weidner Rd, E Citgo/dsl Comfort Suites, Days Inn, W Chevron Econolodge, Super 8 Harley-Davidson, Volvo Trucks

167b Thousand Oaks Dr, Starlight Terrace, E Valero/dsl

167a Randolph Blvd, E Valero/dsl, W Days Inn, Delta Inn, Midtowne Suites, Motel 6

166 I-410 W, Lp 368 S, W to Sea World

165 FM 1976, Walzem Rd, E Shell, Valero/dsl Applebee's, Baskin Robbins/Dunkin Donuts, Benny's, Buffalo Wild Wings, Burger King, Bush's Chicken, China Harbor, Church's, Domino's, IHOP, In-n-Out, Jack-in-the-Box, KFC/Taco Bell, Las Palapas Mexican, Little Caesar's, LJ Silver, Luby's, McDonald's, Miller's BBQ, Olive Garden, Pizza Hut, Red Lobster, Shoney's, Starbucks, Subway, Taco Cabana, Whataburger Drury Inn $Tree, 99c Store, AutoZone, Cavender's Boots, CVS Drug, Discount Tire, Firestone/auto, HEB/dsl, Home Depot, Office Depot, PepBoys, Petsmart, Ross, Walgreens, Walmart/Subway/dsl W Sonic NTB

164b Eisenhauer Rd, E Exxon/7-11 Hampton Inn, La Quinta Mainstay Suites, Super 8, Woodspring Suites $General

164a Rittiman Rd, E Exxon/7-11, Shell/dsl, Valero/dsl Burger King, Church's, Cracker Barrel, Denny's, Hacienda Tapatia Jack-in-the-Box, McDonald's, Taco Bell, Taco Cabana, Whataburger Best Western, Comfort Suites, Hallmark Inn Hampton Inn, La Quinta, Mainstay Suites, Motel 6, Motel 6 (2), Rittiman Inn, Super 8, Travel Inn, Woodspring Suites W Valero Bill Miller BBQ, Popeye's, Sonic, Subway

163 I-410 S (162 from nb, exits left from sb)

161 Binz-Engleman Rd (from nb), same as 160

160 Splashtown Dr, E Valero/Subway/dsl/24hr Motel 6 W Grady's BBQ Best Value Inn, Budget Lodge, Days Inn, Howard Johnson, Microtel, Motel 6, Travelodge

159b Walters St, E McDonald's, W EconoLodge to Ft Sam Houston

159a New Braunfels Ave, E Shell/dsl, Texaco/Burger King auto/dsl repair, W Chevron/dsl, Valero/dsl Miller BBQ, Sonic Antonian Suites to Ft Sam Houston

INTERSTATE 35 Cont'd

SAN ANTONIO

Exit#	Services
158c	N Alamo St, Broadway
158b	I-37 S, US 281 S, to Corpus Christi, to Alamo
158a	US 281 N (from sb), to Johnson City
157b a	Brooklyn Ave, Lexington Ave, N Flores, E Super 8, W Luby's H, downtown
156	I-10 W, US 87, to El Paso
155b	Durango Blvd, E Best Western, Courtyard, Fairfield Inn, Holiday Inn, La Quinta, Residence Inn H, W McDonald's Candlewood Suites, Doubletree, Motel 6, downtown
155a	South Alamo St, E Exxon, Shell/dsl Church's, Huevos Nuevos, McDonald's, Wendy's Best Western, Days Inn, Holiday Inn, La Quinta, Residence Inn, Travelodge Advance Parts, USPO, W Knights Inn
154b	S Laredo St, Ceballos St, same as 155b
154a	Nogalitos St
153	I-10 E, US 90 W, US 87, Lackland AFB, to Kelly AFB
152b	Malone Ave, Theo Ave, E Taco Cabana, W Shell
152a	Division Ave, E Chevron Bill Miller BBQ, Las Cazuelas Mexican, Whataburger/24hr Econolodge, W Sonic transmissions
151	Southcross Blvd, E Exxon/7-11/dsl, Shell, W Shell/dsl Mazatlan Mexican
150b	Lp 13, Military Dr, E Valero Applebee's, Carl's Jr, Denny's, Don Pedro Mexican, Papa John's, Starbucks, Subway, Taco Cabana La Quinta AutoZone, Discount Tire, Meineke, U-Haul, W Exxon Buffalo Wild Wings, Burger King, Chick-fil-A, Chili's, CiCi's, Freddy's Custard, Hungry Farmer Rest, IHOP, Jack-in-the-Box, KFC, Lin's Buffet, Little Caesar's, LJ Silver, Longhorn Steaks, Mama Margie's Mexican, McDonald's, Olive Garden, Panda Express, Popeye's, Red Lobster, Sea Island Shrimp House, Wendy's, Whataburger $Tree, AT&T, Dick's, Firestone/auto, HEB Foods, Home Depot, JC Penney, Lowe's, Macy's, Office Depot, Old Navy, Ross, Target, Verizon, Walgreens
150a	Zarzamora St (149 fom sb), same as 150b
149	Hutchins Blvd (from sb), E Valero/dsl Motel 6, Woodspring Suites, W H, Chevrolet, Ford, Honda, Hyundai, Kia
148b	Palo Alto Rd
148a	TX 16 S, spur 422 (from nb), Poteet, E Chevron/dsl, Murphy USA/dsl Golden Chick Days Inn CVS Drug, Walmart/Subway, W $General
147	Somerset Rd, E Shell/dsl Ford, W Chrysler/Dodge/Jeep
146	Cassin Rd (from nb)
145b	Lp 353 N
145a	I-410, TX 16
144	Fischer Rd, E Valero/7-11/Subway/dsl/scales/24hr D&D Motel, W Love's/Carl's Jr/dsl/scales/24hr/@ Toyota
142	Medina River Turnaround (from nb)
141	Benton City Rd, Von Ormy, E USPO, W Shell/Parador Café/dsl
140	Anderson Lp, 1604, E Exxon/dsl/24hr Burger King, W Pilot/Subway/dsl/scales/24hr Alamo River RV Resort, to Sea World
139	Kinney Rd
137	Shepherd Rd, E truck repair, W Exxon/Choke Canyon BBQ/dsl/24hr dsl repair
135	Luckey Rd
133	TX 132 S (from sb), Lytle, same as 131
131	FM 3175, FM 2790, Benton City Rd, E Best Western, W HEB/dsl/24hr Bill Miller BBQ, Little Caesar's, McDonald's,

PEARSALL

Exit#	Services
131	Continued Sonic, Subway, Whataburger Days Inn/cafe $General, AutoZone, CVS Drug, Family$, HEB Food/dsl, USPO
129mm	**both lanes, full facilities, litter barrels, petwalk, vending**
127	FM 471, Natalia, W Love's/Subway/Wendy's/dsl/scales/24hr/@
125	FM 770
124	FM 463, Bigfoot Rd, E Ford
122	TX 173, Divine, E Exxon/dsl Chevrolet, Chrysler/Dodge/Jeep, W Chevron/McDonald's/Subway/dsl, Exxon, Shell/dsl CCC Steaks, Church's, Pizza Hut, Sonic, Viva Zapatas Mexican Country Corner Inn O'Reilly Parts, Walmart/Subway
121	TX 132 N, Devine
118.5mm	**weigh sta both lanes**
114	FM 462, Yancey, Bigfoot, E Lucky/dsl, W Shell/dsl USPO
111	US 57, to Eagle Pass, W Road Ranger/Valero/Subway/Chester's/dsl/scales/24hr
104	Lp 35
101	FM 140, Pearsall, E Chevron/dsl Cowpokes BBQ, Jalisco's Mexican Baymont Inn, Garden Inn, Hampton Inn, Pearsall Inn, Royal Inn HEB Foods/dsl, W Exxon/Subway/Church's/dsl/24hr, Petro/Valero/Iron Skillet/dsl/scales/24hr Hungry Hunter Grill Days Inn, Holiday Inn Express, La Quinta, Rio Frio Motel, Southern Inn H
99	FM 1581, to Divot, Pearsall
93mm	**parking/ both lanes, accessible, litter barrels**
91	FM 1583, Derby
90mm	Frio River
86	Lp 35, Dilley
85	FM 117, E Garcia Café Best Western, Days Inn, Relax Inn, Super 8, W Exxon/dsl, Phillips 66/Church's/dsl/CNG/24hr DQ Budget Inn, Sona Inn RV park
84	TX 85, Dilley, E Mobil/Burger King/dsl H, Chevrolet, Lowe's Mkt/dsl, W Shell/Pollo Grande/dsl/24hr, Valero/Subway/dsl/24hr Best Value Inn, Executive Inn NAPA
82	County Line Rd, to Dilley, Dilley
77	FM 469, Millett
74	Gardendale
69	(68 from nb), Lp 35, Cotulla, E Phillips 66/dsl Family$, Lowe's Mkt, W FLYING J/Subway/PJ Fresh/dsl/scales/24hr, Stripes/Taco Co/dsl/scales/24hr McDonald's, Sonic Days Inn, Fairfield Inn, Mainstay Suites, Microtel
65	Lp 35, Cotulla
67	FM 468, to Big Wells, E Exxon/Wendy's/dsl/24hr, JJ's/dsl, Valero/deli/dsl/24hr DQ, El Charro Mexican, Golden Chick, Pizza Hut, Subway, Taco Palenque Baymont Inn, Candlewood Suites, Comfort Suites, Executive Inn, Hampton Inn, Holiday Inn Express, La Quinta, Quality Inn, Super 8, Village Inn

TX

INTERSTATE 35 Cont'd

67	Continued truck repair, W Chevron/dsl/scales/24hr LaSalle Steakhouse Best Western, Hotel Cotulla, Residency Suites Mack/Volvo
63	Elm Creek Interchange
59mm	**both lanes, full facilities, litter barrels, petwalk, , vending**
56	FM 133, Artesia Wells
48	Caiman Creek Interchange
39	TX 44, Encinal, E Love's/Chester Fried/Subway/dsl/scales/24hr, Road Ranger/Church's/dsl/scales/24hr, W Chevron/dsl
38	TX 44 (from nb), Encinal
32	San Roman Interchange
29mm	**inspection sta nb**
27	Callaghan Interchange
24	255 **toll**, Camino Colombia **toll** rd, to Monterrey
22	Webb Interchange
18	US 83 N, to Carrizo Springs, E **TX Travel Info Ctr (8am-5pm)/, full facilities, litter barrels, petwalk, , wireless internet,** W RV Camping
14mm	**parking area sb**
12b	(13 from sb) Uniroyal Interchange, E Pilot/McDonald's/Subway/dsl/scales/24hr Blue Beacon, Southern Tire Mart, W Flying J/Denny's/dsl/scales/24hr, TA/Burger King/Subway/Taco Bell/dsl/scales/24hr/@
12a	Port Loredo
10	Port Laredo Carriers Dr (from nb)
9	Industrial Blvd, to Bob Bullock Lp (from sb only)
8b	Lp 20 W, to Solidarity Bridge
8a	Lp 20 W, to to World Trade Bridge, Milo
5	San Isidro Pkwy
4b	Las Cruces Dr, E Valero/dsl El Pescador
4a	FM 1472
4	FM 1472, Del Mar Blvd, E Exxon/Burger King/dsl Applebee's, Carino's Italian, CiCi's, IHOP, Jack-in-the-Box, McDonald's, Quiznos, Whataburger Extended Stay America, Hampton Inn Best Buy, BigLots, HEB Foods/gas, Marshall's, Old Navy, Target, W La Noria/dsl Days Inn Harley-Davidson
3b	Mann Rd, E Buffalo Wild Wings, Krispy Kreme, Lin's Chinese Residence Inn Ford/Lincoln, Honda, Kia, Lowe's, Mazda, URGENT CARE, W Chili's, Golden Corral, Kettle Pancake House, Subway, Taco Palenque, TX Roadhouse, Whataburger Best Value, Family Garden Inn, Gateway Inn, La Hacienda Motel, Monterey Inn, Motel 6, Red Roof Inn, SpringHill Suites $Tree, AT&T, Home Depot, Kohl's, Michael's, Office Depot, PetCo, Ross, Verizon, Walmart/McDonald's
3a	San Bernardo Ave, E Chick-fil-A, ChuckeCheese, El Taco Tote, Emperor Garden, Fuddrucker's, LJ Silver, Logan's Roadhouse, Luby's, Luby's, Olive Garden, Peter Piper Pizza, Red Lobster, Sirloin Stockade, Tony Roma's Fairfield Inn $General, Advance Parts, HEB Foods/gas, Macy's, NAPA, PepBoys, SteinMart, W Valero Burger King, Danny's Rest., DQ, McDonald's, Pizza Hut, Popeye's, Taco Bell, Taco Palenque, Wendy's Family$, O'Reilly Parts, Sam's Club/gas
2	US 59, Saunders Rd, E Conoco, Shell Jack-in-the-Box , W Exxon/Burger King/dsl, Shell/dsl Church's, Denny's, Subway Best Western, Courtyard, La Quinta, Ramada Plaza, Super8 Advance Parts, AutoZone, AutoZone, Mexico Insurance
1b	Park St, to Sanchez St, W Conoco/dsl La Mexicana Rest., Pizza Hut, Popeye's
1a	Victoria St, Scott St, Washington St (from sb), E Valero, W Chevron, Valero/dsl Dos Marias, McDonald's, Wendy's Firestone/auto

I-35 begins/ends in Laredo at Victoria St, access to multiple services.

LAREDO

INTERSTATE 35 (West)

Exit#	Services
I-35W begins/ends on I-35, exit 467.	
85b	W Oak St, E
85a	I-35E S
84	FM 1515, Bonnie Brae St, E
82	FM 2449, to Ponder
79	Crawford Rd
76	FM 407, to Justin, Argyle, W Exxon/dsl Paradise Mkt
76mm	**both lanes, tables, litter barrels**
74	FM 1171, to Lewisville
72	Dale Earnhardt Way, W Marriott TX Motor Speedway
70	TX 114, to Dallas, Bridgeport, E QT/dsl, Shell/Subway/dsl, Valero/dsl/e85 Holiday Inn Express, Motel 6, Sleep Inn North Lake RV Park, to DFW Airport, W Buc-ee's Marriott TX Motor Speedway
68	Eagle Pkwy, W
67	Alliance Blvd, W FedEx, to Alliance Airport
66	to Westport Pkwy, Keller-Haslet Rd, E Hampton Inn, Hilton Garden, Residence Inn, W 7-11/Wendy's/dsl Bryan's BBQ, Schlotzsky's, Snooty Pig, Subway, Taco Bueno USPO
65	TX 170 E, E Pilot/McDonald's/dsl/scales/24hr IHOP Cabela's/cafe
64	Golden Triangle Blvd, to Keller-Hicks Blvd, E QT/dsl, RaceTrac/dsl/e85 Chrysler/Dodge/Jeep, Kia
63	Heritage Trace, Park Glen, E 7-11 BJ's Rest., Cheddar's, Chick-fil-A, Chipotle, Chuy's, Coldstone, Costa Vida, Cousins BBQ, Free Birds Burritos, Houlihan's, Jason's Deli, McAlister's Deli, McDonald's, Mi Cocina, Panera Bread, Pei Wei, Pie Five, Razzoo's Cajun, Smoothie King, Starbucks, Subway, The Rock Kitchen, Which Wich?, Zoe's Kitchen Courtyard Belk, Best Buy, Dick's, GNC, JC Penney, Kroger/dsl, Petsmart, Verizon, W 7-11/dsl
62	North Tarrant Pkwy, E 54th St Grill, Chili's, Firehouse Subs, Five Guys, Fuzzy's Tacos, HaNaBi Hibachi, Olive Garden, Pizza Inn, Pluckers, Thai Fusion , W Cane's, Chick-fil-A, ChuckECheese, El Pollo Loco, In-N-Out, Jimmy John's, La Madeleine, Old Chicago, Pollo Tropical, Potbelly, Starbucks, Taco Cabana, Tom+Chee, Uncle Julio's, Wendy's $Tree, AT&T, Costco/gas, Hobby Lobby, Old Navy, Petco, Ross, Target, TJ Maxx, Tuesday Morning, URGENT CARE, Winco
60	US 287 N, US 81 N, to Decatur
59	Basswood (sb only), E Chevron/Jack-in-the-Box/dsl Chicken Express, DQ, Sonic, Subway, Taco Bell Home Depot, NTB
58	Western Ctr Blvd, E 7-11/dsl, Shell/Church's Boomer-Jack's, Braum's, Brick House, Chili's, Denny's, Dublin Square Rest., Flips Grill, Genghis Grill, Jake's Burgers, Jimmy John's, On-the-Border, Posados Cafe, Rudy's BBQ, SaltGrass Steaks Shady Oak Grill, Twin Peaks, Wendy's, Which Wich?, Wing Stop Magnuson Hotel, Residence Inn AT&T, W Boston's, Firehouse Subs, Joe's Crabshack, McDonald's, Popeye's Rosa's Cafe, Smoothie King, Starbucks, Subway, Waffle House Whataburger Comfort Inn, Holiday Inn Express, Staybridge Suites repair, URGENT CARE

INTERSTATE 35 (West) Cont'd

FT WORTH

Exit#	Services
57b a	I-820 E&W
56b	Melody Hills Dr
56a	Meacham Blvd, E Shell/7-11 Hilton Garden, Knights Inn, La Quinta, W Texaco/dsl Cracker Barrel, McDonald's, Subway Holiday Inn, Quality Inn, Radisson, Super 8 USPO
55	Pleasantdale Ave (from nb)
54c	33rd St, Long Ave (from nb), W Drivers TC/Subway/dsl/scales Motel 6
54b a	TX 183, NE 28th St, E Lisa's Chicken/dsl, W QT/dsl Stockyards Motel 6 Inn
53	North Side Dr, Yucca Dr, E Shell/7-11/dsl, W Mercado Juarez Café Country Inn&Suites
53mm	Trinity River
52e	Carver St (from nb)
52d	Pharr St (exits left from nb)
52b	US 377N, Belknap
52a	US 377 N, TX 121, to DFW
51a	I-30 E, to Avalene (from nb), downtown Ft Worth
50c a	I-30 W, E to Dallas
50b	TX 180 E (from nb)
49b	Rosedale St, E 7-11/dsl Jack-in-the-Box, W H
49a	Allen Ave, E Valero/dsl, W H
48b	Morningside Ave (from sb), same as 48a
48a	Berry St, E Chevron/McDonald's AutoZone, El Rio Grande Foods, Family$, W RaceTrac/dsl U-Haul, zoo
47	Ripy St, E transmissions
46b	Seminary Dr, E RaceWay Grandy's, Jack-in-the-Box, Taco Cabana, Whataburger Days Inn, Delux Inn, Motel 6, Super 7 Inn NAPA, W Shell, Valero Chalio Mexican, ChuckECheese, Denny's, Sonic, Wendy's Firestone/auto, Pepboys, Ross
46a	Felix St, E Valero Dalworth Inn, W Cesar's Tacos, McDonald's Family$
45b a	I-20, E to Dallas, W to Abilene
44	Altamesa, E Radisson, W Conoco/dsl Rig Steaks, Waffle House Baymont Inn, Comfort Suites, Motel 6, South Lp Inn, Super 8
43	Sycamore School Rd, W Exxon/7-11/dsl Chicken Express, Jack-in-the-Box, Jimmy John's, Sonic, Subway, Whataburger Scottish Inn $General, Home Depot
42	Everman Pkwy, E McDonald's, Starbucks, W QT/dsl/scales, Shell/dsl
41	Risinger Rd, E Chrysler/Dodge/Jeep, W Camping World RV Service/Supplies, McClain's RV Ctr
40	Garden Acres Dr, E Loves/Subway/dsl/scales/24hr Motel 6 H, W 7-11/dsl Chicken Express, Taco Bell
39	FM 1187, McAlister Rd, E QT/dsl H, W Shell/dsl, Valero/dsl Buffalo Wild Wings, Charley's Subs, Firehouse Subs, Logan's Roadhouse, McAlister's Deli, Mooyah Burger, Olive Garden, Panda Express, Red Lobster, Subway, TGIFriday's, Waffle House Magnuson AT&T, Best Buy, Kohl's, Michael's, Old Navy, Petsmart, Ross, Staples, TJ Maxx, URGENT CARE, Verizon
38	Alsbury Blvd, E Mobil/dsl Chili's, Cracker Barrel, Hibachi Japanese, IHOP, McDonald's, Mexican Inn Cafe, On-the-Border, Our Place Grill, Outback Steaks, Spring Creek BBQ Fairfield Inn, Hampton Inn, Holiday Inn Express, La Quinta, Super 8 Discount Tire, Ford, Lowe's Whse, W 7-11/dsl,

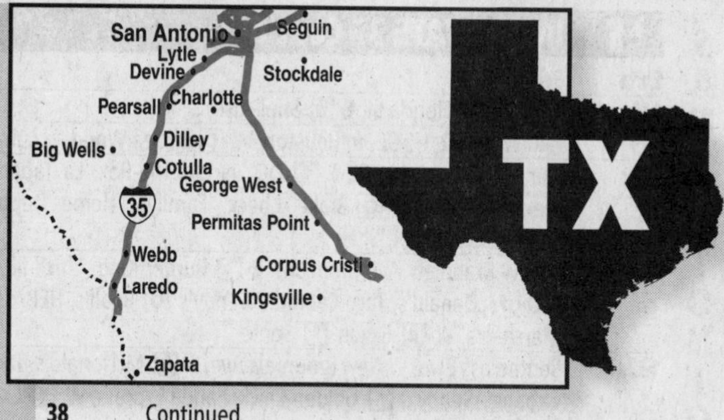

Exit#	Services
38	Continued RaceTrac/dsl Applebee's, Arby's, Burger King, Chick-fil-A, Cotton Patch Cafe, Denny's, El Fenix, Sonic, Taco Cabana, Wendy's Albertson's, Chevrolet, GNC, JC Penney, Michael's, PetsMart, Ross, URGENT CARE, vet
37	TX 174, Wilshire Blvd, to Cleburne, (from sb)
36	FM 3391, TX 174S, Burleson, E 7-11/dsl, Mobil Miranda's Cantina, Sonic, Waffle House Best Western, Days Inn, Quality Inn Harley Davidson, Honda, Hyundai, Nissan, Sam's Club/dsl, W $General, transmissions
35	Briaroaks Rd (from sb), E same as 36, W Mockingbird Hill RV Park (2mi)
32	Bethesda Rd, E Valero Five Star Inn RV Ranch Park, W Mockingbird Hill RV Park
30	FM 917, Mansfield, E Shell/Sonic/dsl $General, W Shell/dsl
27	Rd 604, Rd 707
26b a	US 67, Cleburne, E Chevron/dsl, Exxon/dsl, Texaco/dsl Chicken Express, Domino's, DQ, Lin's Chinese, Little Caesar's, McDonald's, Pizza Hut, Sonic, Subway, Taco Bell, Waffle House, Whataburger Comfort Inn, Holiday Inn Express, La Quinta, Motel 6, Super 8 $General, AutoZone, Brookshire Foods, Family$, Motor Home Specialists, Parts+, RV Tech Ctr, W QT/dsl Burger King CVS Drug
24	FM 3136, FM 1706, Alvarado, E Shell/LJ Silver/dsl/scales/24hr
21	Rd 107, to Greenfield
17	FM 2258
16	TX 81 S, Rd 201, Grandview
15	FM 916, Maypearl, W Mobil/dsl, Shell/Burger King/dsl Subway USPO
12	FM 67
8	FM 66, Itasca, W $General, Ford, litter barrels
7	FM 934, E litter barrels, W Exxon/dsl Golden Chick Cafe
3	FM 2959, E to Hillsboro Airport

I-35W begins/ends on I-35, 371mm.

INTERSTATE 37

Exit#	Services
142b a	I-35 S to Laredo, N to Austin. **I-37 begins/ends on I-35 in San Antonio.**
141c	Brooklyn Ave, Nolan St (from sb), downtown
141b	Houston St, E Comfort Suites, Red Roof Inn Theo's Tires, W Denny's Crockett Hotel, Days Inn, Fairfield Inn, Hampton Inn, Hyatt Hotel, La Quinta, Marriott, Residence Inn, SpringHill Suites Macy's, to The Alamo
141a	Commerce St, E Best Western, Staybridge Suites, W Denny's Hyatt, La Quinta, Marriott Macy's
140b	Durango Blvd, E Bill Miller BBQ to Alamo Dome, downtown

SAN ANTONIO

TX

INTERSTATE 37 Cont'd

Exit#	Services
140a	Carolina St, Florida St, E Shell/dsl
139	I-10 W, US 87, US 90, to Houston, W to Sea World
138c	Fair Ave, Hackberry St, E DQ, Jack-in-the-Box, La Tapatia Mexian, Popeye's Brake Check, Family$, Home Depot, W Exxon/7-11, Shell
138b	E New Braunfels Ave (from sb), E Burger King, Chick-fil-A, IHOP, McDonald's, Taco Cabana, Wendy's Beall's, HEB/dsl, Marshall's, W Exxon Sonic
138a	Southcross Blvd, W New Braunfels Ave, E McDonald's, Taco Cabana, Wendy's Golden Chick, Panda Express, W Exxon Burger King, Sonic
137	Hot Wells Blvd, E Chevron/dsl, W IHOP Motel 6, Super 8
136	Pecan Valley Dr, E Citgo/dsl Church's, KFC/Taco Bell, Pizza Hut Pecan Valley Inn AutoZone, O'Reilly Parts, W H
135	Military Dr, Lp 13, E Shell/dsl, Valero Jack-in-the-Box, Rancho Grande Quality Inn CVS Drug, Mission Trail RV park, W Valero/Subway/dsl A&W/LJ Silver, Buffalo Wild Wings, Buffet Seafood, Burger King, Carino's Italian, Chaba Thai, Chick-fil-A, Chili's, Cracker Barrel, IHOP, Little Caesar's, Longhorn Cafe, Panda Express, Papa John's, Peter Piper Pizza, Sonic, Starbucks, Subway, Whataburger Hampton Inn, Holiday Inn Express, La Quinta H, $Tree, Advance Parts, AT&T, AutoZone, Best Buy, BigLots, Discount Tire, HEB Food/gas, Home Depot, Lowe's, Office Depot, PetCo, Ross, Sam's Club/dsl, Target, to Brooks AFB, Walgreens, Walmart/McDonald's
133	I-410, US 281 S
132	US 181 S, to Floresville, E Shell/7-11/dsl $General
130	Donop Rd, Southton Rd, E Valero/7-11/dsl Tom's Burgers Days Inn Braunig Lake RV Resort, W Shell/dsl car/truckwash
127	San Antonio River Turnaround (from nb), Braunig Lake
127mm	San Antonio River
125	FM 1604, Anderson Lp, E Mobil/dsl/24hr Burger King fireworks, W Exxon/dsl, Pilot/Subway/dsl/scales/24hr, Shell/dsl Miller's BBQ, Sonic, Whataburger fireworks, tires
122	Priest Rd, Mathis Rd, E Valero/dsl $General
120	Hardy Rd
117	FM 536
113	FM 3006
112mm	**both lanes, tables, litter barrels**
109	TX 97, to Floresville, E Chevron/dsl, Exxon/dsl Portrillo's Mexican Chrysler/Dodge/Jeep
106	Coughran Rd
104	spur 199, Leal Rd, to Pleasanton (no immediate sb return), same as 103
103	US 281 N, Leal Rd, to Pleasanton, E Valero/dsl DQ, K&K Cafe Kuntry Inn
98	TX 541, McCoy
92	US 281A, Campbellton
88	FM 1099, to FM 791, Campbellton
83	FM 99, Whitsett, Peggy, E Shell/cafe/dsl, W C Fuels/dsl, Exxon/dsl Choke Canyon BBQ
82mm	**sb, full facilities, litter barrels,**
78mm	**nb, full facilities, litter barrels,**
76	US 281A, FM 2049, Whitsett
75mm	**truck weigh sta sb**
74mm	**truck weigh sta nb**
72	US 281 S, Three Rivers, W Loves/McDonald's/Subway/dsl/scales/24hr/@ Sonic, Van's BBQ Motel 6 to Rio Grande Valley
69	TX 72, Three Rivers, W Valero/Subway/dsl/24hr Reba'n Rose RV Park, to Choke Cyn SP
65	FM 1358, Oakville, E Van's BBQ
59	FM 799
56	US 59, George West, E FLYING J/McDonald's/dsl/scales/24hr, Stripes/Taco Co/dsl/24hr, W Shell/BBQ/dsl/24hr, Valero/Burger King/dsl/24hr
51	Hailey Ranch Rd
47	FM 3024, FM 534, Swinney Switch Rd, W Swinney Switch Cafe Mike's Mkt/gas, Mustang Hollow Camping (4mi)
44mm	**parking area sb**
42mm	**parking area nb**
40	FM 888
36	TX 359, to Skidmore, Mathis, W Road Ranger/Subway/dsl/scales, Shell/McDonald's/dsl, Valero/dsl (1mi) Pizza Hut, Smolik's Smokehouse La Quinta Lake Corpus Christi SRA
34	TX 359 W, E Adventure TX RV Ctr/LP, W Shell, Valero/dsl Church's, Sonic DQ, Pizza Hut $General, O'Reilly Parts, to Lake Corpus Christi SP
31	TX 188, to Sinton, Rockport
22	TX 234, FM 796, to Odem, Edroy
20b	Cooper Rd
19.5mm	**both lanes, accessible, litter barrels**
17	US 77 N, to Victoria
16	LaBonte Park, W **, info, litter barrels,**
15	Sharpsburg Rd (from sb), Redbird Ln
14	I-69, US 77 S, Redbird Ln, to Kingsville, Robstown, **1 mi W** on FM 624 RaceWay/dsl, Shell/dsl, Valero/Burger King/dsl Chili's, CiCi's, Denny's, El Tapatio Mexican, Good'n Crisp Chicken, Miller's BBQ, Papa John's, Pizza Hut, Popeye's, Sonic, Subway, Whataburger, Wienerschnitzel Comfort Inn, Holiday Inn Express H, $General, $Tree, AT&T, AutoZone, Beall's, CVS Drug, Discount Tire, Firestone/auto, GNC, Hobby Lobby, Home Depot, O'Reilly Parts, Petco, Ross, Verizon, Walmart/McDonald's
13b	Sharpsburg Rd (from nb)
13a	FM 1694, Callicoatte Rd, Leopard St
11b	FM 24, Violet Rd, Hart Rd, E Shell/Subway/dsl Chicken Shack, W Exxon/dsl, Valero/dsl Domino's, DQ, Fliz Amancer Mexican, KFC/LJ Silver, Little Caesar's, McDonald's, Pizza Hut, Schlotzsky's, Sonic, Subway, Taco Bell, Whataburger Hampton Inn, Super 8 Advance Parts, AutoZone, Family$, HEB Food/gas, O'Reilly Parts, Walgreens
11a	McKinzie Rd, E Shell Jack-in-the-Box La Quinta, W Valero/dsl
10	Carbon Plant Rd
9	FM 2292, Up River Rd, Rand Morgan Rd, W Valero/dsl Whataburger
7	Suntide Rd, Tuloso Rd, Clarkwood Rd, W CC RV Ctr, Freightliner
6	Southern Minerals Rd, E refinery
5	Corn Products Rd, Valero Way, E Kenworth/Mack, W Gascard/dsl Jalisco II Rest. Best Value, Howard Johnson, ValStay
4b	Lantana St, McBride Lane (from sb), W Airport Inn, Motel 6
4a	TX 358, to Padre Island, W Holiday Inn, Plaza Inn Walmart (4mi)
3b	McBride Lane (from nb), W Gulf Coast Racing

INTERSTATE 37 Cont'd

CORPUS CHRISTI

Exit#	Services
3a	Navigation Blvd, E Valero/dsl Rodeway Inn, W Exxon/7-11/dsl Denny's, La Milpas, Miller BBQ Hampton Inn, Holiday Inn Express, Knights Inn, La Quinta, Super 8 CarQuest
2	Up River Rd, E refinery, W Mr G's BBQ
1e	Lawrence Dr, Nueces Bay Blvd, E refinery, W Valero Church's Red Roof Inn Aamco, AutoZone, Firestone, HEB Foods, USPO
1d	Port Ave (from sb), W Coastal, Shell Vick's Burgers EconoLodge Port of Corpus Christi
1c	US 181, TX 286, Shoreline Blvd, Corpus Christi, W H
1b	Brownlee St (from nb)
1a	Buffalo St (from sb), **0-1 mi W on Shoreline** Sunoco/dsl Burger King, Joe's Crabshack, Landry's Seafood, Subway, Waterstreet Seafood, Whataburger Bayfront Inn, Best Western, Holiday Inn, Omni Hotel, Super 8 U-Haul, USPO, **I-37 begins/ends on US 181 in Corpus Christi.**

INTERSTATE 40

SHAMROCK

Exit#	Services
177mm	Texas/Oklahoma state line
176	spur 30 (from eb), to Texola
169	FM 1802, Carbon Black Rd
167	FM 2168, Daberry Rd
165mm	**check sta wb**
164	Lp 40 (from wb), to Shamrock, **1 mi S** EconoLodge H, check sta eb, museum
163	US 83, to Wheeler, Shamrock, N Chevron/Taco Bell/dsl Best Western+, Motel 6 Ace Hardware, S Conoco/dsl, Tesla EVC, Valero/Subway/dsl McDonald's EconoLodge, Holiday Inn Express, Sleep Inn, Western Motel Family$
161	Lp 40, Rte 66 (from eb), to Shamrock
157	FM 1547, Lela, **1 mi S** West 40 RV Camping
152	FM 453, Pakan Rd
148	FM 1443, Kellerville Rd
146	County Line Rd
143	Lp 40 (from wb), to McLean, N to Rte 66/dsl
142	TX 273, FM 3143, to McLean, N Conoco/dsl Red River Steaks Cactus Inn RV Camping/dump, USPO
141	Rte 66 (from eb), McLean, same as 142
135	FM 291, Rte 66, Alanreed, S Conoco/motel/café/RV park/dump USPO
132	Johnson Ranch Rd, ranch access
131mm	**wb, full facilities, litter barrels, petwalk,**
129mm	**eb, full facilities, littler barrels, petwalk, playground**
128	FM 2477, to Lake McClellan, N Lake McClellan RA/RV Dump
124	TX 70 S, to Clarendon, S RV camping/dump (11mi)
121	TX 70 N, to Pampa
114	Lp 40, Groom, N dsl repair
113	FM 2300, Groom, S Phillips 66/dsl DQ Chalet Inn
112	FM 295, Groom, S gas Biggest Cross
110	Lp 40, Rte 66
109	FM 294
105	FM 2880, grain silo
98	TX 207 S (from wb), to Claude
96	TX 207 N, to Panhandle, N Loves/Subway/dsl/24hr, S Conway Inn/cafe, Executive Inn
89	FM 2161, to Rte 66

AMARILLO

Exit#	Services
87	FM 2373
87mm	**both lanes, litter barrels**
85	Amarillo Blvd, Durrett Rd, access to camping
81	FM 1912, N Valero/dsl
80	FM 228, N AOK RV Park
78	US 287 S (from eb), FM 1258, Pullman Rd, same as 77
77	FM 1258, Pullman Rd
76	spur 468, N FLYING J/Denny's/dsl/LP/RV dump/scales/24hr, Phillips/dsl Buffalo Wild Wings Fairfield Inn, Holiday Inn Express, La Quinta Mack/Volvo Trucks, S Speedco Custom RV Ctr, TX info
75	Lp 335, Lakeside Rd, N Pilot/Subway/McDonald's/dsl/scales/24hr/ Hampton Inn, Holiday Inn, Knights Inn, Super 8 KOA (2mi), Overnite RV Park, S Petro/dsl/rest./scales/@, Valero/dsl Blue Beacon
74	Whitaker Rd, N Big Texan Inn RV camping, S Loves/Subway/dsl/scales/@, TA/Exxon/FoodCourt/dsl/scales/24hr/@ Blue Beacon, Eagle Truckwash, Peterbilt
73	Eastern St, Bolton Ave, Amarillo, N TT/dsl Express Inn, Motel 6, Wood Spring Suites, S Valero/dsl Best Western
72b	Grand St, Amarillo, N Valero/dsl Henk's BBQ Value Inn O'Reilly Parts, S Murphy USA/dsl, Phillips 66, Valero Braum's, Chicken Express, McDonald's, Pizza Hut, Sonic, Starbucks, Subway, Taco Villa, Whataburger Best Value Inn $Tree, Advance Parts, Amigo's Foods, AutoZone, BigLots, GNC a, Meineke, same as 73, URGENT CARE, Walmart
72a	Nelson St, N Cracker Barrel Ashmore Inn, Comfort Inn, La Kiva Hotel, Luxury Inn, Sleep Inn, Super 8 Qtrhorse Museum, S Valero/dsl Domino's Camelot Suites transmissions
71	Ross St, Osage St, Amarillo, N Chevron/dsl, Valero A&W/LJ Silver, Burger King, IHOP, KFC, McDonald's, Schlotsky's, Subway, Wienerschnitzel Clarion, Comfort Inn, Days Inn, Microtel, Quality Inn Discount Tire, S Arby's, Denny's, Fiesta Grande Mexican, Sonic, Taco Bell, Wendy's Baymont Inn, La Quinta, Red Roof Inn Chevrolet, Ford, Hyundai, Sam's Club/gas, USPO
70	I-27 S, US 60 W, US 87, US 287, to Canyon, Lubbock, to downtown Amarillo
69b	Washington St, Amarillo, S TT/dsl DQ CVS Drug, Subway
69a	Crockett St, access to same as 68b
68b	Georgia St, N TT/dsl Dyer's BBQ, Schlotzky's, Sharky's Burrito Co, S Valero Burger King, Church's Chicken, Coldstone, Denny's, Firehouse Subs, Jersey Mike's, Pizza Hut, Sonic, Starbucks, TX Roadhouse, Whataburger Holiday Inn Express Home Depot, Office Depot, Walgreens

INTERSTATE 40 Cont'd

AMARILLO

Exit#	Services
68a	Julian Blvd, Paramount Blvd, N Chili's, Rosa's Cafe same as 67, S Valero Burger King, Chick-Fil-A, Chipotle, Panda Express, Popeyes, Red Lobster, Ruby Tequila's Mexican, TX Roadhouse Holiday Inn Express, Motel 6, Super 8, Travelodge Home Depot, Office Depot, Bubba's BBQ, El Patron, Five Guys
67	Western St, Amarillo, N Phillips 66 Braum's, Burger King, McAlister's Deli, McDonald's, Papa Murphy's, Sonic, Subway, Taco Bell, Wendy's, Aspen Creek Grill, S Murphy Express/dsl, Rudy's/BBQ/dsl, Valero Blue Sky Rest., Cheddar's, IHOP, Jimmy John's, Olive Garden, Waffle House, Wienerschnitzel Baymont Inn, Candlewood Suites, Comfort Suites, Staybridge Suites Discount Tire, Firestone/auto, Michael's, O'Reilly Parts, Petco, same 68
66	Bell St, Amarillo, N Cefco/dsl Fairfield Inn, Red Roof Inn, Relax Inn, Residence Inn Harley-Davidson, S Donut Stop, Taco Bueno CashSaver
65	Coulter Dr, Amarillo, N Phillips 66/dsl Arby's, Golden Corral, Subway, Taco Bell, Waffle House Days Inn, Executive Inn, Holiday Inn, Holiday Inn Express, La Quinta H, Cadillac/Chevrolet, Chrysler/Dodge/Jeep, Firestone/auto, S Chevron/Chicken Express/dsl ChinaStar, CiCi's, Hoffbrau Steaks, Outback Steaks, Pizza Hut, Whataburger 5th Season Inn, Hampton Inn, Sleep Inn AT&T, Goodyear/auto, Verizon
64	Soncy Rd, to Pal Duro Cyn, N Fuddrucker's, Furr's Buffet, Jimmy John's, Lin's Chinese, Plaza Rest., Red Robin Comfort Inn, Country Inn&Suites, Drury Inn, Hilton Garden, Holiday Inn, Homewood Suites USPO, Cavender's Boots, Courtyard, Discount Tire, Extended Stay America, Kabuki, Logan's Roadhouse, Longhorn Steaks, My Place, Saltgrass Steaks, SpringHill Suites, Tru, S Valero/dsl/24hr Applebee's, ChuckeCheese, DQ, Fazoli's, Hooters, Marble Slab Creamery, McAlisters Deli, McDonald's, On-the-Border, Pei Wei, Starbucks, Subway $Tree, Barnes&Noble, Best Buy, Dillard's, Ford, Home Depot, JC Penney, Jo-Ann Fabrics, Kohl's, Lincoln, Old Navy, PetsMart, Ross, Sam's Club/dsl, Target, Verizon, World Mkt
62b	Lp 40, Amarillo Blvd, N Gander Outdoors, S Sundown RV Resort
62a	Hope Rd, Helium Rd, S Cadillac RV camping
60	Arnot Rd, S Love's/Subway/dsl Oasis RV Resort/dump
57	RM 2381, Bushland, N Falcon Stop/dsl grain silos, S Phillips 66/dsl Bushland Burger, Joe's Pizza USPO, vet
55mm	**parking area wb, litter barrels**
54	Adkisson Rd
53.5mm	**parking area eb, litter barrels**
49	FM 809, Wildorado, S Crist Fuel/dsl/LP
42	Everett Rd
37	Lp 40 W, to Vega, **1 mi** N Bonanza Motel same as 36, Walnut RV Park
36	US 385, Vega, N Alon/dsl, Shamrock, Valero/Allsup's/dsl/scales/24hr DQ, Subway Days Inn RV Park, $ General, S Pilot/PJ Fresh/dsl/scales/24hr, Vega Trk Stop/cafe/dsl
35	to Rte 66, to Vega, N Best Value Inn, Bonanza Motel (1mi) same as 36, Walnut RV Park (1mi)
32mm	**both lanes, litter barrels**
28	to Rte 66, Landergin
23	to Adrian, Vega, same as 22
22	TX 214, Adrian, N Midpoint Cafe auto repair, USPO, S Valero/dsl
18	FM 2858, Gruhlkey Rd
15	Ivy Rd
13mm	**both lanes, , litter barrels**
0	Lp 40, to Glenrio
0mm	Texas/New Mexico state line, Central/Mountain time zone

VEGA

INTERSTATE 44

WICHITA FALLS

Exit#	Services
15mm	Texas/Oklahoma state line, Red River
14	Lp 267, E 3rd St, W historical marker, KOA
13	Glendale St, W Subway Beall's
12	Burkburnett, E Valero/dsl Red River Inn, W Alon/7-11/dsl Braum's, Chicken Express, Feedlot Rest., Lite Pan Asian, McDonald's, Whataburger Chevrolet, Ford
11	FM 3429, Daniels Rd
9mm	**both lanes, litter barrels, petwalk**
7	East Rd
6	Bacon Switch Rd
5a	FM 3492, Missile Rd, E El Mejicano Rest., Hunan Chinese, Marco's Pizza st patrol, W Exxon/dsl
5	Access Rd
4	City Loop St
3c	FM 890, W Murphy USA/dsl Cracker Barrel, Jack-in-the-Box, KFC/Taco Bell, Parkway Grill, Subway Walmart/Subway
3b	sp 325, Sheppard AFB
3a	US 287 N, to Amarillo, W Shell/dsl Carl's Jr Howard Johnson
2	Maurine St, E Alon/7-11/dsl, Shell/dsl Best Value Inn, Executive Inn, Motel 6, Quality Inn Chevrolet, Mazda/VW, W Alon/7-11 Denny's, El Chico, LJ Silver, Whataburger Candlewood Suites, Comfort Inn, La Quinta, Red Roof Inn, Super 8
1d	US 287 bus, Lp 370, W FuelStop/dsl Travelodge
1c	Texas Travel Info Ctr, E $Saver
1b	Scotland Park (from nb)
1a	US 277 S, to Abilene, W Arby's EconoLodge
1	Holliday St, W Valero/dsl Arby's, Burger King, Carl's Jr, IHOP, McDonald's, Subway EconoLodge, Motel 6 H, Family$, Walgreens
0mm	Witchita Falls, **I-44 begins/ends on US 287.**

INTERSTATE 45

Exit#	Services
286	to I-35 E, to Denton. **I-45 begins/ends in Dallas.**
285	Bryan St E, US 75 N
284b a	I-30, W to Ft Worth, E to Texarkana, E access to H
283b	Pennsylvania Ave, to MLK Blvd, E Kwikstop
283a	Lamar St
281	Overton St (from sb), W Chevron
280	Illinois Ave, Linfield St, E Star Motel, W Exxon, Shell/dsl
279b a	Lp 12
277	Simpson Stuart Rd, W to Paul Quinn Coll
276b a	I-20, W to Ft Worth, E to Shreveport
275	TX 310 N (from nb, no re-entry)
274	Dowdy Ferry Rd, Hutchins, E Exxon/Subway/dsl, Shell/McDonald's/dsl Gold Inn, La Quinta, Motel 6 auto repair, W Top Fuel/dsl DQ, Jack-in-the-Box, Whataburger

DALLAS

INTERSTATE 45 Cont'd

Exit#	Services
273	Wintergreen Rd, W QT/dsl/scales/24hr
272	Fulghum Rd, E Loves/Carl's Jr/dsl/scales/24hr, W weigh sta both lanes
271	Pleasant Run Rd
270	Belt Line Rd, to Wilmer, E Chevron/Pizza Inn/dsl, W Exxon/Sonic/dsl, Shell/Church's/Subway/dsl Denny's $General, Family$, USPO
269	Mars Rd
268	Malloy Bridge Rd
267	frontage rd
266	FM 660, E Jack-in-the-Box, W Valero/dsl DQ, Pizza Hut
265	Lp 45, Ferris, nb only
263a b	Lp 561
262	frontage rd
260	Lp 45, E Traylor RV Park, W Shell/Sonic/dsl
259	FM 813, FM 878, Jefferson St
258	Lp 45, Palmer, E Chevron/Subway/dsl/scales/24hr golf
255	FM 879, Garrett, E Exxon/dsl, W Chevron/dsl
253	Lp 45, W Shell/Subway/dsl
251b	TX 34, Ennis, E Alon/dsl, QT/dsl Bubba's BBQ, Cotton Patch Cafe, McDonald's Baymont Inn, Comfort Suites, Days Inn, Holiday Inn Express, La Quinta Ford, URGENT CARE, W Chevron/dsl, Exxon/dsl/24hr, Murphy USA/dsl, Valero Braum's, Burger King, Chili's, Chipotle, Denny's, Domino's, DQ, Golden Chick, Grand Buffet, Hilda's Kitchen, IHOP, Jack-in-the-Box, Little Caesar's, Papa John's, Sonic, Starbucks, Subway, Taco Bell, Taco Cabana, Tokyo Grill, Waffle House, Wall Chinese, Wendy's, Whataburger Quality Inn H, $Tree, AT&T, AutoZone, Beall's, Chevrolet, Chrysler/Dodge/Jeep, RV camping, Walmart/McDonald's
251a	Creechville Rd, FM 1181, Ennis, W H
249	FM 85, Ennis, E Budget Inn, W Exxon/Subway/dsl Blue Beacon, repair
247	US 287 N, to Waxahatchie
246	FM 1183, Alma, E Loves/Subway/dsl/scales/24hr, W Chevron/dsl
244	FM 1182
243	frontage rd
242	Calhoun St, Rice, W Shell/Sonic/dsl Family$
239	FM 1126, W Conoco/dsl Rendell RV Ctr
238	FM 1603, E Exxon/rest./dsl/24hr Casita RV Trailers
237	frontage rd
235b	Lp I-45 (from sb), to Corsicana
235a	frontage rd
232	Roane Rd, E 5th Ave
231	TX 31, Corsicana, E Mobil/Taco Casa/dsl, Valero/dsl Jack-in-the-Box Best Western, La Quinta, Super 8 Buick/Cadillac/Chevrolet/GMC, W Exxon/dsl, Shell/Subway/dsl Bill's Fried Chicken, McDonald's Comfort Inn H, Chrysler/Dodge/Jeep, Ford/Lincoln, to Navarro Coll
229	US 287, Palestine, E Exxon/Wendy's/dsl, Shell/dsl Applebee's, Chili's, Collin St Bakery, Denny's, DQ, Panda Express, Schlotsky's, Sonic, Subway, Taco Bell, Whataburger Hampton Inn, Holiday Inn Express Corsicana Outlets, Home Depot, Office Depot, Russell Stover Candies, W Waffle House Days Inn, Motel 6, Traveler's Inn
228b	Lp 45 (exits left from nb), Corsicana, **2 mi W** services in Corsicana
228a	15th St, Corsicana, W Toyota
225	FM 739, Angus, E Conoco/dsl RV park, to Chambers Reservoir

ENNIS

CORSICANA

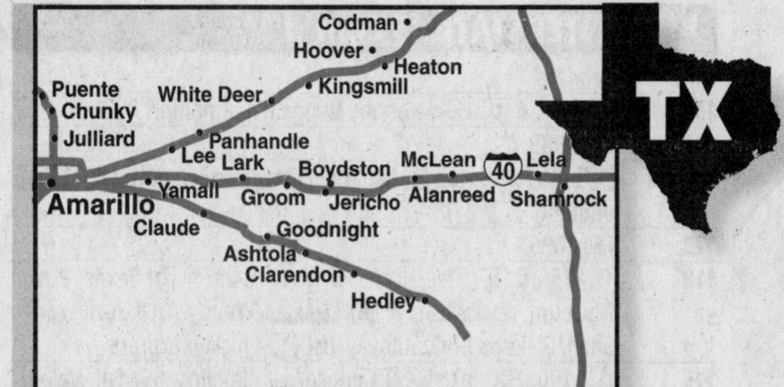

TX

FAIRFIELD

Exit#	Services
221	frontage rd
220	frontage rd
219b	frontage rd
219a	TX 14 (from sb), to Mexia, Richland, W Shell
218	FM 1394 (from nb), Richland, W Shell
217mm	**both lanes, full facilities, litter barrels, petwalk, vending**
213	TX 75 S, FM 246, to Wortham, W Exxon/dsl, Valero/dsl
211	FM 80, to Streetman, Kirvin
206	FM 833, W I-45 RV Park (3mi)
198	FM 27, to Wortham, E Shell/Cole's BBQ Gilberto's Mexican La Quinta H, W Cooper Farms/dsl, Loves/Burger King/dsl/scales/24hr Budget Inn I-45 RV Park (4mi)
197	US 84, Fairfield, E Chevron/dsl, Exxon/dsl, Shell/dsl Bush's Chicken, DQ, Jack-in-the-Box, McDonald's, Sam's Rest., Something Different Rest, Sonic, Subway/TX Burger Days Inn, Holiday Inn Express, Super 8 Brookshire Foods/gas, Chevrolet, Chrysler/Dodge/Jeep, Fred's Store, W Exxon/dsl, Shell/dsl I-45 Rest., KFC/Taco Bell, Mesquite Grill, Pizza Hut, Ponte's Diner Budgetel, Regency Inn Ace Hardware, Ford
189	TX 179, to Teague, E Exxon/Dinner Bell Rest/dsl, W Valero/Chester's/Huddle House/dsl
180	TX 164, to Groesbeck
178	US 79, Buffalo, E Chevron/dsl, Conoco/dsl, Mobil/dsl, Shell/dsl Pizza Hut, Subway/TX Burger $General, Brookshire Foods/gas, Family$, W Exxon/Church's/Subway/Pizza Inn/dsl/scales, Pilot/PJ Fresh/Taco Bell/dsl/scales/24hr, Texaco/dsl Anthony's Rest., Dickey's BBQ, DQ, McDonald's, Rancho Viejo, Sonic Best Value Inn, Hampton Inn, Quality Inn, Super 8
175mm	Bliss Creek
166mm	**weigh sta sb**
164	TX 7, Centerville, E Chevron, Shell/Woody's BBQ/dsl Broken Star Cafe, Country Cousins BBQ, Subway/TX Burger Days Inn, W CNG, Exxon/dsl, Shell/Woody's BBQ/dsl DQ, Jack-in-the-Box, Roble's Mexican
160mm	**sb, tables, litter barrels**
159mm	Boggy Creek
156	FM 977, to Leona, W Exxon/dsl
155mm	**nb, litter barrels**
152	TX OSR, to Normangee, W Shell/Arby's/dsl Yellow Rose RV Park
146	TX 75
142	US 190, TX 21, Madisonville, E Buc-ees/dsl, Exxon/dsl Dickey's BBQ, Shipley's Donuts, Subway Best Western, Madisonville Inn URGENT CARE, W Exxon, Mobil/Church's/dsl, Shell/Subway Jack-in-the-Box, Lakeside Rest, McDonald's, Pizza Hut, Sonic, Taco Bell, TX Burger Budget Motel, Days Inn, Motel 6 H, Ford, Toyota

TX

INTERSTATE 45 Cont'd

HUNTSVILLE

Exit#	Services
136	spur 67, E Home on the Range RV camping/LP (3mi)
132	FM 2989
124mm	**both lanes, full facilities, litter barrels, petwalk, vending**
123	FM 1696
118	TX 75, E Shell/Hitchin Post/dsl/24hr/@ Texas Prison Museum, truckwash, W Pilot/Wendy's/dsl/scales/24hr, Shell/Dickey's BBQ/Subway/dsl Chicken Express
116	US 190, TX 30, E Conoco/dsl, Phillips 66/dsl, Valero/dsl Arby's, Bandera Grill, Church's, Golden Corral, Los Panchitos, Mama Juanita's, McDonald's, Popeye's, Schlotzsky's, Sonic, Whataburger Days Inn, EconoLodge, Holiday Inn Express, La Quinta, Motel 6 AutoZone, Brookshire Foods/gas, Buick/Cadillac/Chevrolet/GMC, Cavander's Boots, Chrysler/Dodge/Jeep, CVS Drug, Family$, Firestone/auto, O'Reilly Parts, vet, Walgreens, W Chevron/dsl, Exxon/dsl, Murphy USA/dsl, Shell Bob Luby's Seafood, Buffalo Wild Wings, Burger King, Cane's, Chili's, Chipotle, Denny's, Five Guys, Grand Buffet, Hartz Chicken, IHOP, Jack-in-the-Box, Little Caesar's, Moe's SW, Olive Garden, Panda Express, Pizza Hut, Rodeo Mexican, Starbucks, Subway, Taco Bell, Wing Stop, Yummy Mongolian Best Western, Hampton Inn H, $Tree, AT&T, Discount Tire, GNC, Hobby Lobby, Home Depot, JC Penney, Kroger/dsl, Marshall's, Office Depot, Petco, Ross, Target, USPO, Verizon, Walmart
114	FM 1374, E Exxon/dsl, Shell DQ, Margaritas Rest. Red Roof Inn, Super 8, W Texaco/dsl, Valero/dsl Country Inn Steaks Best Value Inn, Quality Suites H, Ford, Hyundai
113	TX 19 (from sb), Huntsville, W Ford, Hyundai
112	TX 75, E Big E's Houston Statue, museum, to Sam Houston St U
109	Park 40, W to Huntsville SP
103	FM 1374/1375 (from sb), to New Waverly, W Chevron/Burger King/dsl
102	FM 1374/1375, TX 150 (from nb), to New Waverly, E Valero/dsl (1mi) Waverly Rest., W Chevron/Burger King/dsl (1mi)
101mm	**weigh sta nb**
98	TX 75, Danville Rd, Shepard Hill Rd, E Convenience RV Ctr/repair
97	Calvary Rd
95	Longstreet Rd, Calvary Rd, Willis, E Holiday World, W Loves/Subway/Wendy's/dsl/scales/24hr
94	FM 1097, Longstreet Rd, to Willis, E Kwik Stop/dsl Jack-in-the-Box, Sonic, Taco Bell $General, AutoZone, W Chevron/Popeye's, Shell/dsl Burger King, Chick-fil-A, Cilantros Mexican, Little Caesar's, McDonald's, Papa John's, Pizza Hut, Scholtzsky's, Shipley's Donuts, Subway, Whataburger, WingStop, Yummy Mongolian Best Western GNC, Kroger/dsl, Verizon, Walgreens
92	FM 830, Seven Coves Dr, W Omega Farms RV Park (2mi), RV Park on the Lake (3mi), Thousand Trails Resort (2mi)
90	League Line Rd, E Mobil/McDonald's, Shell/dsl Mama Juanita's Mexican, Waffle House, Wendy's Comfort Inn, Days Inn, La Quinta Conroe Outlets/famous brands, W Chevron/Jack-in-the-Box Cracker Barrel
89	FM 3083, Teas Nursery Rd, Montgomery Co Park, E Exxon/dsl Applebee's, Buffalo Wild Wings, Popeye's, Red Lobster, Smokey Mo's BBQ Fairfield Inn, Homewood Suites

CONROE

Exit#	Services
89	Continued AT&T, Kohl's, Old Navy, Petsmart, Ross, TJ Maxx, W Firehouse Subs, Olive Garden, Wengs Wok, Wild Ginger Japanese Woodspring Suites Cavender's Boots, JC Penney, Verizon
88	Lp 336, to Cleveland, Navasota, E Valero/dsl Arby's, Burger King, Carl's Jr, Chili's, China Delight, Denny's, Domino's, Dunkin Donuts/Baskin Robbins, Los Cucos Mexican, Marble Slab Creamery, Margarita's Mexican, McDonald's, Papa John's, Pizza Hut, Potbelly, Sonic, Subway, Supreme Buffet, TX Roadhouse, Whataburger, Wing Stop Hampton Inn, Holiday Inn Express $Tree, Advance Parts, CVS Drug, Discount Tire, Discount Tire, GNC, HEB Foods/gas, Hobby Lobby, Kroger/gas, Michael's, vet, Walgreens, W Chevron/24hr Casa Ole Mexican, Culver's, Dickey's BBQ, Hunan Village, Jack-in-the-Box, KFC, Ryan's, Starbucks 99c Store, Big Lots, Lowe's, PetCo, Sam's Club/gas, Tuesday Morning, Walmart
87	TX 105, Conroe, E Burger King, CiCi's, El Charrito, Freebirds Burrito, Golden Corral, La Mariposa, McDonald's, Outback Steaks, Popeye's, Saltgrass Steaks Super 8 $General, CVS Drug, Firestone/auto, NTB, W Exxon Cane's, Chick-fil-A, Chipotle, El Bosque Mexican, Five Guys, Luby's, Panda Express, Panera Bread, Papa Murphy's, Schlotzsky's, Shogun Japanese, Smoothie King, Starbucks, Subway, Vero Italian, Whataburger H, Best Buy, Buick/GMC, GNC, Home Depot, Hyundai, Office Depot, Target, Verizon
85	FM 2854, Gladstell St, E Shell/dsl Ford, Honda, Kia, Nissan, UHaul, W Valero Best Value Inn, Motel 6 H, Chevrolet, Chrysler/Dodge/Jeep, DeMontrond RV Ctr, Mazda, Toyota
84	TX 75 N, Frazier St, E Chevron/dsl Corporate Inn, Econolodge, W Shell/dsl China Buffet, IHOP, Incredible Pizza, Pizza Hut, Subway, Taco Cabana, Waffle House Baymont Inn H, Discount Tire, Kroger/dsl, Verizon
83	Crighton Rd, Camp Strake Rd
82	River Plantation Dr
82mm	San Jacinto River
81	FM 1488, to Hempstead, Magnolia, E Citgo/dsl, W Valero/Subway/dsl CamperLand RV Ctr
80	Needham Rd (from sb)
79	TX 242, Needham, E Shell/McDonald's Mama Juanita's Mexican Best Western Costco/dsl, Mercedes, Mini, VW, W Exxon, Murphy USA/dsl Arby's, Burger King, ChuckeCheese, Domino's, Dunkun Donuts, LJ Silver/Taco Bell, Outback Steaks, Panera Bread, Popeye's, Sonic, Starbucks, Subway, Taco Cabana, Twin Peaks, Wendy's, Whataburger, Willie's Grill, Wings'N More Fairfield Inn, Springhill Suites, TownPlace Suites H, BMW/Mini, Firestone/auto, Kohl's, Lowe's Whse, Walgreens, Walmart
78	Needham Rd (from sb), Tamina Rd, access to same as 77
77	Woodlands Pkwy, Robinson, Chateau Woods, E Chevron Babin's Seafood, BJ's Rest., Buca Italian, Buffalo Wild Wings, Chuy's, El Bosque Mexican, Hooters, Lupe Tortilla, Mi Rancho Mexican, Pappadeaux, PeiWei, Red Robin, Saltgrass Steaks, Spring Creek BBQ, Subway Best Value Inn, Courtyard, Holiday Inn Discount Tire, GNC, Home Depot, Michael's, NTB, Old Navy, Petsmart, Sam's Club/gas, SteinMart, vet, Walgreens, W Shell/dsl, Texaco, Valero/dsl, Valero/dsl Blackeyed Pea, Brazilian Steaks, Cane's, Chick-fil-A, Chili's, Chipotle Mexican, Culver's, Denny's, Freebirds Burrito, Guadalajara Mexican, Jack-in-the-Box, Jason's Deli, Jimmy John's, Kirby's Steaks, Luby's, Olive Garden, Red Lobster, Sweet

INTERSTATE 45 Cont'd

HOUSTON

77 Continued
Tomatoes, TGIFriday's, Zoe's Kitchen Clarion, Days Inn, Drury Inn, Hampton Inn, Homewood Suites, La Quinta, Marriott H, Best Buy, Dillard's, HEB Foods, Macy's, Marshall's, Ross, Target, World Mkt

76 Research Forest Dr, Tamina Rd, E Pappas BBQ Firestone/auto, Office Depot, PepBoys, URGENT CARE, W Shell/dsl Bonefish Grill, Carrabba's, Firehouse Subs, Fukuda Japanese, IHOP, Landry's Seafood, Longhorn Steaks, Macaroni Grill, Noodles&Co, Olive Garden, Starbucks, Sweet Tomatoes, TGIFriday's Courtyard, Residence Inn JC Penney, Woodlands Mall

73 Rayford Rd, Sawdust Rd, E Shell/dsl, Valero Cane's, Hartz Chicken, Jack-in-the-Box, McDonald's, Popeye's, Sonic, Starbucks, Thomas BBQ Holiday Inn Express, La Quinta Aamco, AutoZone, O'Reilly Parts, Walgreens, W Shell/dsl Carrabba's, Gino's Pizza, IHOP, Pizza Hut Extended Stay America, Super 8 Brake Check, Discount Tire, GNC, Harley-Davidson, HEB Foods, Jo-Ann

72a Spring Crossing Dr, W Texaco/dsl Fairfield Inn

72b to Hardy Toll Rd from sb

70b Spring-Stuebner Rd, E Hampton Inn Vaughn RV Ctr

70a FM 2920, to Tomball, E Exxon/dsl, Rudy's BBQ/dsl, Shell/dsl Arby's, Chick-fil-A, El Palenque Mexican, Golden Jade Chinese, Hartz Chicken, McDonald's, Subway, Taco Cabana, Wendy's, Whataburger, Zaxby's Best Western, Comfort Suites $Tree, Hyundai, Kohl's, Michael's, O'Reilly Parts, Ross, Toyota, Vaughn's RV Ctr, Verizon, Walmart, W RaceWay Palace Inn U-Haul, vet

68 Holzwarth Rd, Cypress Wood Dr, E Golden Corral, Burger King, Freddy's, Gringo's TexMex, McAlister's Deli, Pizza Hut/Taco Bell, Sonic, Starbucks AT&T, Pepboys, W Exxon/dsl, Murphy Express/dsl, Smashburger Bombshells Rest., Cheddar's, Chipotle, Denny's, Dickey's BBQ, Firehouse Subs, Jack-in-the-Box, Lenny's Subs, Panera Bread, Pizza Hut, Popeye's, Razzoo's Cajun, Schlotsky's, Starbucks EconoLodge, Motel 6, Scottish Inn Advance Parts, Best Buy, Chrysler/Dodge/Jeep, Firestone/auto, Ford/Lincoln, Home Depot, Lowe's Whse, Office Depot, PetCo, Staples, Target, Walgreens

66 FM 1960, to Addicks, E Chevron/dsl Subway, TX Roadhouse Acura, AT&T, BMW, Chevrolet, Honda, Mercedes, Petsmart, Subaru, W Exxon, Valero Chick-fil-A, Cilantros Mexican, Hooters, James Coney Island, McDonald's, Outback Steaks, Panda Express, Pollo Campero, Red Lobster Baymont Inn, Fairfield Inn, Hampton Inn, Hilton Garden, Palace Inn, Quality Inn, Studio 6 H, $Tree, Audi, Infiniti, Jaguar/LandRover, Kroger/dsl, Lexus, NTB, Porsche, U-Haul

64 Richey Rd, E Buffalo Wild Wings, Olive Garden, Taco Bell Best Value Inn, Downtowner Inn, Super 8 CarMax, Discount Tire, Sam's Club/dsl, W FLYING J/Denny's/dsl/scales/24hr Chula's Cantina, El Toro Loco, Joe's Crabshack, Lupe Tortilla, Mamacita's Mexican, Michoacan Rest, SaltGrass Steaks, Subway, Wings'n More SpringHill Suites

63 Airtex Dr, E Exxon/dsl, Sunoco/dsl, Valero/Church's China Bear, Pappasito's Cantina Comfort Suites, Woodspring Suites Cadillac, LoneStar RV Ctr, Nissan, W Exxon/dsl Cracker Barrel, Jack-in-the-Box, Popeye's, Whataburger Best Western, Holiday Inn Express, Sleep Inn

62 Rankin Rd, Kuykendahl, E Best Classic Inn, Scottish Inn, W Chevron/McDonald's, RaceWay/dsl, Shell Shiply Donuts, Sonic Extended Stay Amerca, Palace Inn, SunSuites

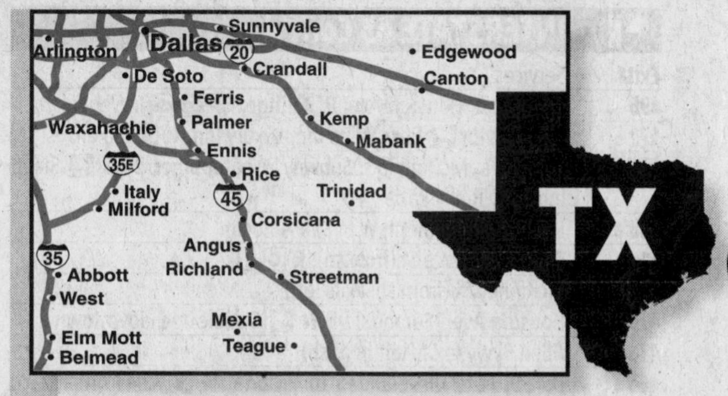

62 Continued
Buick/GMC, DeMontrond RV Ctr, Kia, Lamborghini, Volvo, VW, Walgreens

61 Greens Rd, E Exxon Brown Sugar's BBQ, IHOP, Luna's Mexican Knights Inn Dillard's, W Luby's, Panda Chinese, Subway Comfort Inn 99c Store, Burlington Coats

60c Beltway E

60 (b a from nb) TX 525, W Pappas Seafood U-Haul

59 FM 525, West Rd, E Shell/dsl, Shell/dsl/repair A&W/LJ Silver, Burger King, China Border, CiCi's, Denny's, Domino's, Hanz Diner, Mambo Seafood, McDonald's, Michoacan Rest., Pizza Hut Holiday Inn Express AutoZone, Chrysler/Dodge/Jeep, Family$, Firestone/auto, W Exxon/dsl, Shell/dsl Chili's, Jalisco's Mexican, Panda Express, Papa John's Pizza, Starbucks, Subway, Taco Bell, Taco Cabana, Wendy's, Whataburger, Wing Stop Best Value Inn $Tree, AT&T, Best Buy, Discount Tire, Fry's Electronics, Home Depot, Office Depot, PepBoys, Ross, Verizon, Walmart

HOUSTON

57 (b a from nb) TX 249, Gulf Bank Rd, Tomball, E Chevron, Gulf/dsl, Texaco/Church's Subway, W Shell Sonic, Tampico Seafood Days Inn, Quality Inn CVS Drug, Family$, Giant$

56 Canino Rd, E Taj Inn Suites, W Texaco Denny's, Luby's Deluxe Inn, Gulfwind Motel Ford, Isuzu, Walgreens

55 (b a from nb) Little York Rd, Parker Rd, E Chevron/dsl, Exxon/dsl, Texaco Burger King, China One, McDonald's, Ranchero King Buffet, Subway, Whataburger Advance Parts, Family$, FoodTown, W KFC, La Chicken, Popeye's Walgreens

54 Tidwell Rd, E Exxon/dsl Aunt Bea's Rest, Burger King, Chacho's Mexican, China Border, Pancho's Mexican, Thomas BBQ 99c Store, CVS Drug, W Chevron, Shell Hartz Chicken, McDonald's Guest Motel, Southwind Motel, Symphony Inn, Town Inn Family$, U-Haul

53 Airline Dr, E Discount Tire, Fiesta Foods/drug, W Citgo, Shell/dsl Little Mexico, Whataburger Best Value Inn, Luxury Inn, Palace Inn

52 (b a from nb) Crosstimbers Rd, E Murphy Express/dsl Baskin-Robbins, Burger King, Chick-fil-A, China Star, ChuckeCheese, Cici's, IHOP, Jack-in-the-Box, James Coney Island, KFC, McDonald's, Ojos Locos Cantina, Panda Express, Pappas BBQ, Pizza Hut, Sonic, Subway, Taco Bell $Tree, AT&T, CVS Drug, GNC, Marshall's, Ross, Verizon, Walmart, W Texan Inn

51 I-610

50 (b a from nb) Patton St, Calvacade St, Link Rd, E Citgo, Exxon, Loves/Wendy's/dsl/scales/24hr, Shell Best Value Inn, Luxury Inn, W Astro Inn AutoZone, Family$, NAPA, USPO

TX

HOUSTON

INTERSTATE 45 Cont'd

Exit#	Services
49b	N Main St, Houston Ave, E Citgo, Loves/Wendy's/dsl/scales/24hr Best Value Inn, Luxury Inn, W Exxon/dsl Domino's, McDonald's, Subway, Whataburger/24hr Sleep Inn O'Reilly Parts
48b a	I-10, E to Beaumont, W to San Antonio
47d	Dallas St, Pierce St (from sb), E H
47c	McKinney St (from sb, exits left)
47b	Houston Ave, Memorial Dr, W DoubleTree, downtown
47a	Allen Pkwy (exits left from sb)
46b a	US 59, N to Cleveland, S to Victoria, W Chevron, Texaco McDonald's BMW
45b a	South St, Scott St, Houston, E Phillips 66/Church's/dsl, Shell Scott Inn, W to TSU
44	Cullen Blvd, Houston, W to U of Houston
43b	Tele(Rd, Houston, E Valero/dsl
43a	Tellepsen St, E Luby's, W U of Houston
41b	US 90A, Broad St, S Wayside Dr, E Houston Inn, Palace Inn Walmart/McDonald's, W Chevron/dsl, Exxon Burger King, Chick-fil-A, Jack-in-the-Box, Little Caesar's, McDonald's, Taco Cabana AT&T
41a	Woodridge Dr, E Shell Chinese Buffet, Church's, Denny's, James Coney Island, McDonald's, Pappa's Seafood House, Pizza Hut, Schlotsky's King$, W Bonebrake BBQ, Boudreaux Cajun, China Star, ChuckeCheese, CiCi's, Doneraki Mexican, IHOP, KFC/Taco Bell, Panda Express, Pappas BBQ, Sonic, Starbucks, Subway, Taco Palenque, Wendy's, Whataburger Best Buy, HEB Food/gas, Home Depot, Lowe's, Marshall's, Office Depot, Old Navy, Ross, Verizon
40c	I-610 W
40b	I-610 E, to Pasadena
40a	frontage rd (from nb)
39	Park Place Blvd, Broadway Blvd, E Shell/dsl, W Pemex/dsl, Shell/dsl Kelley's Rest., Papa John's, Subway Chrysler/Dodge/Jeep, Family$
38b	Howard Dr, Bellfort Dr (from sb), E Shell Jack-in-the-Box, Wendy's, W Shell/dsl, Texaco/dsl Chilo's Seafood, VStar Seafood Buffet Camelot Inn, Moonlight Inn, Mustang Inn, Palace Inn
38	TX 3, Monroe Rd, E Shell/dsl, Sunoco/Stripes/dsl, Valero/dsl DQ, Jack-in-the-Box, Ninfa's Mexican, Starbucks, Wendy's Palace Inn AutoZone, Family$, URGENT CARE, W Chevron/dsl, Texaco/dsl Mannie's Seafood, Pappa's BBQ, Subway Holiday Inn Express, Sheraton Firestone/auto, U-Haul
36	College Ave, Airport Blvd, E Valero Aranda's Bakery, Burger House, Church's, DQ, Jack-in-the-Box, Shipley Donuts, Subway, Waffle House Holiday Inn Express O'Reilly Parts, W Gulf/dsl, Shell/dsl, Valero/dsl Denny's, Denny's, Taco Cabana Best Western, Comfort Suites, Courtyard, Days Inn, Drury Inn, Hampton Inn, Holiday Inn, La Quinta, Marriott, Motel 6, SpringHill Suites Discount Tire
35	Edgebrook Dr, E Chevron, RaceWay/dsl, Shell/dsl Arranda's Mexican, Burger King, Chilo's Rest., Jack-in-the-Box, KFC, Popeye's, Subway, Taco Bell Family$, Fiesta Foods, Firestone/auto, Office Depot, vet, W Citgo/dsl James Coney Island, Mambo Seafood, McDonald's, Pizza Hut, Whataburger $General, Cavender's Boots, O'Reilly Parts, Verizon
34	S Shaver Rd, E Conoco McDonald's Island Suites Ford, Kia, Nissan, Toyota, W MurphyUSA/dsl Arby's, China Star Buffet, Chopstix, Ojos Locos, Pancho's Mexican,

LEAGUE CITY

Exit#	Services
34	Continued Pizza Patron, Starbucks, Subway, Wendy's $Tree, 99c Store, AT&T, Discount Tire, Firestone/auto, GNC, Honda, Macy's, Marshall's, NTB, PetsMart, Ross, Staples, Walmart/McDonald's
33	Fuqua St, E Chili's, Denny's, Fuddrucker's, Las Haciendas, Luby's, Olive Garden, Schlotzky's, TGIFriday's Studio 6, Sun Suites Lincoln, Volvo, W Bayou City Wings, Blackeyed Pea, Bombshells Grill, Boudreaux's, Casa Ole, Cici's Pizza, Fox&Hound, Golden Corral, Gringo's Mexican, IHOP, Joe's Crabshack, McDonald's, Outback Steaks, Subway, Taco Bell, Taco Cabana, TX Land&Cattle Steaks, Whataburger Buick/GMC, CarMax, Chevrolet, Home Depot, Sam's Club/gas
32	Sam Houston Tollway
31	FM 2553, Scarsdale Blvd, W Chevrolet
30	FM 1959, Dixie Farm Rd, Ellington Field, E Shell/dsl El Nopalito, Subway Motel 6 H, Chrysler/Dodge/Jeep, Fiat, Infiniti, Subaru, W Exxon/dsl, RaceWay, Shell/dsl McDonald's, Popeye's Palace Inn Lonestar RV, VW
29	FM 2351, Clear Lake City Blvd, to Clear Lake RA, Friendswood, W Hyundai
27	El Dorado Blvd, E Exxon/dsl Carl's Jr, Chick-fil-A, Panera Bread, Starbucks, Taco Bell Firestone/auto, Home Depot, W Bar Louie, Kona Grill, Maggiano's, Perry's Steakhouse, Sonic, Subway, TX Roadhouse, Whataburger, Yardhouse Grill Cadillac, Kohl's, Lexus, Sam's Club/gas, Walmart/McDonald's
26	Bay Area Blvd, E Chevron Bonefish Grill, Buffalo Wild Wings, Chick-fil-A, La Madeleine, Longhorn Steaks, Lupe Tortilla, Noodles&Co, Pei Wei, Potbelly, Red Lobster, Taco Cabana, TGIFriday's, Zio's Kitchen Best Western, Hampton Inn, Hilton Garden, La Quinta H, Barnes&Noble, Best Buy, Lowe's, Michael's, Staples, to Houston Space Ctr, World Mkt, W Valero/dsl Burger King, Cheesecake Factory, Chick-fil-A, ChuckeCheese, Dave&Buster's, Denny's, Five Guys, Los Cucos, McDonald's, Olive Garden, Panda Express, PF Chang's, Starbucks, Subway, Zoe's Kitchen Holiday Inn Express AT&T, Dillard's, Fresh Mkt, JC Penney, Jo-Ann Fabrics, Macy's, Marshall's, Office Depot, Old Navy, Petsmart, Ross, Target, Verizon, vet
25	FM 528, NASA rd 1, E Chevron/dsl, Valero/dsl Bone Daddy's, Cheddar's, Chili's, Chuy's Mexican, Fuddrucker's, Las Hacienda Mexican, Luby's, Marble Slab, McAlister's Deli, Michiru Asian, Pappa's Seafood, Pappasito's Cantina, Rudy's BBQ/dsl, Saltgrass Steaks, Steak'n Shake, Twin Peaks Rest., Waffle House Motel 6, Springhill Suites H, BigLots, Cavendar's Boots, Fry's Electronics, Hobby Lobby, Honda, Mazda, W Floyd's Cajun, Hooters, James Coney Island, Pappa's Cafe, Subway Tuesday Morning
23	FM 518, League City, E RaceWay/dsl, Shell/dsl Center Buffet, La Brisa, Sonic, Subway $Tree, Kroger, W Chevron/dsl, Valero Cracker Barrel, McDonald's, Taco Bell, Waffle House, Wendy's Super 8 Discount Tire, Space Ctr RV Park, U-Haul
22	Calder Dr, Brittany Bay Blvd, E BMW/Mini, Mercedes, Nissan, Toyota, W Acura, Holiday World RV Ctr
20	FM 646, Santa Fe, Bacliff, E MurphyUSA/dsl Chick-fil-A, Cici's Pizza, Denny's, Five Guys, Freebirds Burrito, Jack-in-the-Box, Jimmy Changas, Logan's Roadhouse, Marble Slab, McDonald's, NY Pizzaria, Panda Express, Panera Bread, Pollo Tropical, Quaker Steak, Schlotzky's, Spring Creek BBQ, Subway, Whataburger, Which Wich? Candlewood Suites, Hampton Inn $Tree, AT&T, Best Buy, Firestone/auto, GNC, Hobby Lobby,

INTERSTATE 45 Cont'd

Exit	Services
20	Continued Home Depot, JC Penney, Lowe's, Michael's, NTB, PetsMart, Ross, Staples, Target, TJ Maxx, URGENT CARE, Walmart/McDonald's, W [gas] Chevron/dsl [food] 888 Chinese Rest., Chili's, Subway, Taco Cabana [other] Cabela's, HEB Foods/gas, Kohl's, PetCo, Verizon, Walgreens
19	FM 517, Dickinson Rd, Hughes Rd, E [food] Jack-in-the-Box, Little Mexico [other] Buick/GMC, CVS Drug, Family$, Kia, W [gas] Conoco/dsl, Shell/dsl [food] KFC, McDonald's, Pizza Hut, Sonic, Starbucks, Subway, Taco Bell, Wendy's, Whataburger/24hr [lodging] Days Inn [other] Chrysler/Dodge/Jeep, Ford, Kroger
17	Holland Rd, W [gas] Buc-ee's/dsl [other] Tanger Outlets/Famous Brands, to Gulf Greyhound Park
16	FM 1764 E (from sb), Texas City, same as 15
15	FM 2004, FM 1764, Hitchcock, E [food] Beyond Burger, Gringo's Cafe, Jack-in-the-Box, Olive Garden, Ryan's [lodging] Best Western, Fairfield Inn, Holiday Inn Express, Woodspring Suites [other] [H], Chevrolet/Toyota, DeMontrond RV Ctr, W [gas] Gulf/Subway, MurphyUSA/dsl, Shell [food] Best Wok, IHOP, Little Caesar's, Pizza Hut, Rose Garden Chinese, Sonic, Waffle House, Wendy's, Whataburger, WingStop [other] AT&T, Gulf Greyhound Park, Sam's Club/gas, URGENT CARE, Verizon, Walmart/McDonald's
13	Century Blvd, Delany Rd, W [food] Barcema's Mexican [lodging] Best Value Inn, Super 8 [other] Lazy Days RV Park, VF Factory Outlet/famous brands
12	FM 1765, La Marque, E [gas] Chevron/dsl [food] Domino's, Jack-in-the-Box, Kelley's Rest., Sonic [other] $General, CVS Drug, Family$, W [gas] Texaco/dsl [other] Little Thicket RV Park, UHaul
11	Vauthier Rd
10	E [gas] Exxon, Valero [food] KFC, McDonald's, PitStop BBQ, Subway, W [gas] Shell/dsl [other] Hoover RV Ctr, Oasis RV Park
9	frontage rd (from sb, no return/turnaround)
8	frontage rd (from nb)
7c	frontage rd
7b	TX 146, TX 6 (exits left from nb), Texas City
7a	TX 146, TX 3
6	frontage rd (from sb)
5	frontage rd
4	frontage rd, Village of Tiki Island, W [gas] Valero/dsl [other] **Welcome Ctr**, public boat ramp
4mm	West Galveston Bay
1c	TX 275, FM 188 (from nb), Port Ind Blvd, Teichman Rd, Port of Galveston, E [gas] Citgo, Exxon/dsl, Valero/dsl [lodging] Howard Johnson, Motel 6 [other] Buick/Chevrolet/GMC, Ford, Toyota
1b	71st St (from sb), E [lodging] Best Value Inn [other] same as 1c
1a	TX 342, 61st St, to W Beach, E [gas] RaceWay [food] Subway, WingStop [lodging] Candlewood Suites [other] Big Lots, Family$, GNC, Home Depot, NTB, PetsMart, Target, 0-2 mi W [gas] Chevron/dsl, Citgo, Exxon, Murphy USA/dsl, Shell/Burger King/dsl, Texaco/dsl, Valero [food] Cici's Pizza, Domino's, Golden Corral, Happy Buddah, Healthy Chinese, Jack-in-the-Box, Jimmy John's, KFC, Little Caesar's, Marble Slab, Mario's, McAlister's Deli, McDonald's, Papa John's, Popeye's, Schlotsky's, Sonic, Starbucks, Subway, Taco Bell, Taco Cabana, Waffle House, Whataburger, Yamato Japanese [lodging] Baymont Inn, Comfort Inn, Hilton, Quality Inn, Red Roof Inn, Rodeway Inn, Springhill Suites, Super 8 [other] $Tree, AT&T, AutoZone, CVS Drug, Family$, Firestone/auto, Kroger/dsl, KwikCar, Marshall's, Office Depot, O'Reilly Parts, Randall's Food/gas, Ross, Tuesday Morning, URGENT CARE, USPO, Verizon, Walgreens, Walmart

I-45 begins/ends on TX 87 in Galveston.

GALVESTON

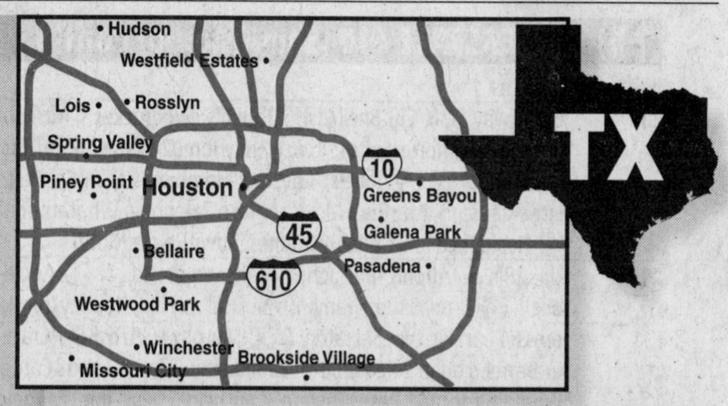

TX

INTERSTATE 410 (San Antonio)

Exit#	Services
53	I-35, S to Laredo, N to San Antonio
51	FM 2790, Somerset Rd
49	TX 16 S, spur 422, N [gas] Chevron, Texaco/dsl [food] Church's, Domino's, Sonic, Subway, Whataburger [lodging] Days Inn [other] [H], to Palo Alto Coll, S [gas] Valero/dsl [food] Jack-in-the-Box [lodging] Best Western
48	Zarzamora St, S [gas] Valero/dsl
47	Turnaround (from eb)
46	Moursund Blvd
44	US 281 S, spur 536, Roosevelt Ave, N [gas] Shell/McDonald's/dsl, Valero/dsl [food] Subway, S [food] Jack-in-the-Box [lodging] Holiday Inn Express
43	Espada Rd (from eb)
42	spur 122, S Presa Rd, N [other] to San Antonio Missions Hist Park, S [gas] Valero/dsl
41	I-37, US 281 N
39	spur 117, WW White Rd
37	Southcross Blvd, Sinclair Rd, Sulphur Sprs Rd, N [gas] Shell/dsl, Valero [other] [H], Family$
35	US 87, Rigsby Ave, E [gas] Exxon/7-11, Murphy USA/dsl, Valero/dsl [food] Denny's, El Rodeo Mexican, Jack-in-the-Box, KFC/Taco Bell, McDonald's [other] $Tree, AT&T, Walmart/McDonald's, W [gas] Chevron/dsl [food] Bill Miller BBQ, Burger King, Domino's, El Tapico Mexican, Habachi Buffet, Laguna Madre, Sonic, Taco Cabana, Whataburger [lodging] Days Inn, Holiday Inn Express [other] Aamco, Advance Parts, Gascard/dsl, U-Haul, vet, Walgreens
34	FM 1346, E Houston St, W [gas] Valero/dsl [other] USPO
33	I-10 E, US 90 E, to Houston, I-10 W, US 90 W, to San Antonio
32	Dietrich Rd (from sb), FM 78 (from nb), to Kirby
31b	Lp 13, WW White Rd
31a	FM 78, Kirby
30	Binz-Engleman, Space Center Dr (from nb)

I-410 and I-35 run together 7 mi. See I-35, exits 161 thru 165.

Exit#	Services
27	I-35, N to Austin, S to San Antonio
26	Lp 368 S, Alamo Heights
25b	FM 2252, Perrin-Beitel Rd, N [gas] Chevron/dsl, Valero/dsl [food] Carl's Jr, KFC/Taco Bell, Schlotsky's, Subway, Tastee-Freez/Wienerschnitzel [lodging] Budget Lodge [other] Brake Check, Family$, S [food] Jim's Rest.
25a	Starcrest Dr, N [gas] Valero [food] Jack-in-the-Box [lodging] Travelodge [other] [H]
24	Harry Wurzbach Hwy, N [food] Taco Cabana, S [food] BBQ Sta. [other] VW
23	Nacogdoches Rd, N [gas] Shell/dsl [food] Bill Miller BBQ, Church's, Formosa Chinese, IHOP, Jimmy John's, Luby's, Pizza Hut, Sonic [lodging] Crowne Plaza, S [gas] Chevron/7-11 [other] Volvo

SAN ANTONIO

TX

INTERSTATE 410 (San Antonio) Cont'd

Exit#	Services
22	Broadway St, N [gas] Shell/dsl [food] Chili's, Fuddrucker's, McDonald's [lodging] Cambria Suites, Courtyard, Home2 Suites, S [gas] Citgo, Valero/dsl [food] Cane's, Chesters Hamburgers, Jim's Rest., Little Caesar's, Martha's Mexican, Taco Palenque, Whataburger [lodging] Residence Inn, Springhill Suites, TownHouse Motel
21	US 281 S, Airport Rd, Jones Maltsberger Rd, N [food] Applebee's [lodging] Drury Suites, Hampton Inn, Holiday Inn, Holiday Inn Express, PearTree Inn, Sheraton, S [gas] Murphy USA/dsl [food] Cracker Barrel, Logan's Roadhouse, Pappadeaux, Texas Land&Cattle, Whataburger [lodging] Best Western, Courtyard, Days Inn, Fairfield Inn, Home2 Suites, La Quinta, Staybridge Suites, TownePlace Suites [other] Nissan, TJ Maxx, Walmart/McDonald's/24hr
20	TX 537, N [gas] Valero [food] Arby's, Chick-fil-A, Jack-in-the-Box, Jason's Deli, Rosario's Mexican, Subway, TGIFriday's, Wendy's [lodging] DoubleTree Hotel, Hilton [other] Barnes&Noble, Best Buy, Brake Check, Cavender's Boots, Chevrolet, Honda, Jo-Ann Fabrics, Lexus, Lincoln, Mazda, Mercedes, Office Depot, PetCo, Ross, Subaru, S [food] Cheesecake Factory, Chipotle, Dickey's BBQ, Earth Burger, Egg&I, El Pollo Loco, Freddy's, Jimmy John's, La Madeleine, Longhorn Steaks, Luby's, Panda Express, Starbucks, Taco Cabana, Twin Peaks [lodging] Aloft [other] AT&T, Chrysler/Dodge/Jeep, CVS Drug, Dillard's, JC Penney, Macy's, Saks 5th, Target, Verizon
19b	FM 1535, FM 2696, Military Hwy, N [food] Guajillos Mexican, Souper Salad, S [food] Denny's, Jim's Rest.
19a	Honeysuckle Lane, Castle Hills
17b	(18 from wb), S [gas] Shell [food] Bill Miller BBQ, Burger King, Pollo Tropical, Subway [other] HEB Foods/gas, NAPA, vet
17	Vance Jackson Rd, N [gas] Valero/dsl [food] Jack-in-the-Box, McDonald's, Sonic, Starbucks, Taco Cabana, Whataburger [lodging] Embassy Suites, Marriott [other] Aamco, AT&T, Discount Tire, S [gas] Petronic, Shell [food] Church's, Subway [other] U-Haul
16b a	I-10 E, US 87 S, to San Antonio, I-10 W, to El Paso, US 87 N
15	Lp 345, Fredericksburg Rd, E [gas] Citgo, EVC [food] Church's, Dave&Buster's, Denny's, El Pollo Loco, El Rodeo, Jack-in-the-Box, Jim's Rest., Luby's, McDonald's, Peter Piper Pizza, Taco Cabana, Wendy's, Whataburger [lodging] Best Value Inn, SpringHill Suites [other] Family$, Firestone/auto, Hobby Lobby, SteinMart, Target, W [gas] Chevron/7-11/dsl [other] CVS Drug
14	(c b a from sb) Callaghan Rd, Babcock Ln, E [gas] Chevron/dsl, Valero/dsl [food] Marie Callender's, Popeye's, Red Lobster, Whataburger [lodging] Best Western, Quality Inn [other] Hyundai, W [gas] Exxon, Shell, Valero [food] Burger King, Chili's, ChopSticks Chinese, DingHow Chinese, Golden Corral, Henry's Tacos, IHOP, Jack-in-the-Box, Jim's Rest, Joe's Crabshack, Las Palapas Mexican, Louie Italian, McDonald's, Nicha's Mexican, Pizza Hut, Quizno's, Subway, Taco Cabana, Wendy's [other] [H], Cavander's Boots, Chevrolet, Home Depot, NTB, Petsmart, Sam's Club/gas, Walmart/Subway/24hr
13	(b a from sb) TX 16 N, Bandera Rd, Evers Rd, Leon Valley, E [food] Outback Steaks, Panda Express [other] Audi, HEB Foods/dsl, Office Depot, Toyota, UHaul, W [food] Bill Miller BBQ, Henry's Tacos, Jim's Rest., Schlotzsky's, Sonic, Taco Cabana [other] Chevrolet
12	(from sb), W [food] Fortune Cookie Chinese, Jason's Deli, Ojos Locos, Olive Garden, Sea Island Shrimp House, Starbucks [other] $Tree, AT&T, Barnes&Noble, Best Buy, Marshall's, Michael's, Old Navy, Petco, Ross
11	Ingram Rd, E [gas] Shell/dsl [food] KFC/Taco Bell, Los Roberto's, Saltgrass Steaks, TX Roadhouse, Vallarta Mexican [lodging] Comfort Suites, Courtyard, Days Inn, Holiday Inn Express, Red Roof Inn,

SAN ANTONIO

Exit#	Services
11	Continued Residence Inn [other] Aamco, Chrysler/Dodge/Jeep, Mazda, Nissan, W [food] Chick-fil-A, ChuckeCheese, Denny's, Fuddrucker's, Jack-in-the-Box, Whataburger [lodging] Best Western [other] Dillard's, Firestone/auto, JC Penney, Macy's, Sears/auto
10	FM 3487, Culebra Rd, E [food] Denny's, J Anthony's Seafood, McDonald's, Wendy's [lodging] La Quinta, Ramada Ltd [other] Harley-Davidson, to St Mary's U, W [gas] Phillips 66 [other] Ford
9	(b a from sb) TX 151, E [food] Subway, W [gas] Murphy USA/dsl [food] 54th St Grill, Buffalo Wild Wings, Carino's Italian, Cheddar's, Chili's, Chipotle Mexican, Cracker Barrel, Dickey's BBQ, Firehouse Subs, IHOP, McAlister's Deli, Panda Express, Schlotsky's, Starbucks, TGIFriday's, Twin Peaks, Whataburger [lodging] Homewood Suites, Quality Inn, Sleep Inn, Springhill Suites [other] $Tree, AT&T, GNC, Home Depot, Lowe's Whse, Office Depot, Petsmart, Ross, Target, to Sea World, URGENT CARE, Verizon, Walmart/McDonald's
7	(8 from sb) Marbach Dr, E [gas] Exxon/7-11 [food] Church's, Golden Wok, IHOP [other] PepBoys, W [gas] Chevron/dsl, Shell/dsl [food] Burger King, Chick-fil-A, Jack-in-the-Box, Jimmy John's, Jim's Rest., KFC, LJ Silver, McDonald's, Peter Piper Pizza, Pizza Hut, Popeye's, Red Lobster, Sonic, Subway, Taco Bell, Taco Cabana, Whataburger/24hr [lodging] Knights Inn, Motel 6 [other] $Tree, Advance Parts, BigLots, BrakeCheck, Discount Tire, Firestone/auto, HEB Foods/gas
6	US 90, E [lodging] Country Inn Motel [other] to Lackland AFB, W [gas] Shell/dsl, Valero/dsl [lodging] Best Western [other] Explore USA RV Ctr
4	Valley Hi Dr, to Del Rio, San Antonio, E [gas] Valero/dsl [food] Burger King, Church's, Little Caesar's, McDonald's, Panda Express, Pizza Hut, Sonic, Subway [other] AutoZone, Family$, HEB Food/gas, O'Reilly Parts, W [gas] Valero [food] Jack-in-the-Box [other] to Lackland AFB, Walgreens
3	(b a from sb) Ray Ellison Dr, Medina Base, E [gas] Chevron/dsl, W [gas] Exxon/dsl, Valero/Subway/dsl [other] Walmart/Subway
2	FM 2536, Old Pearsall Rd, E [gas] Shell/dsl, Valero/dsl [food] Bill Miller BBQ, Church's, Domino's, Little Caesar's, McDonald's, Mexico Taqueria, Sonic, Subway [other] AutoZone, CVS Drug, O'Reilly Parts
1	frontage rd, W [other] Toyota

INTERSTATE 610 (Houston)

Exit#	Services
38c a	TX 288 N, access to zoo, downtown
37	Scott St, N [gas] Citgo, Exxon [other] Family$
36	FM 865, Cullen Blvd, N [lodging] Crystal Inn, S [gas] Chevron/McDonald's, Shell [lodging] Cullen Inn
35	Calais Rd, Crestmont St, MLK Blvd, S [gas] Shell [food] Subway
34	S Wayside Dr, Long Dr, N [gas] Citgo, Shell/dsl, Sunoco/Stripes/dsl [food] Church's, S [gas] Shell, Valero/dsl [food] Jack-in-the-Box [other] NAPA
33	Woodridge Dr, Telephone Rd, N [gas] Shell/dsl [food] ChuckeCheese, Cici's Pizza, Doneraki Mexican, IHOP, KFC/Taco Bell, McDonald's, Panda Express, Pappas BBQ, Starbucks, Taco Palenque, Wendy's [other] Advance Parts, Best Buy, Brake Check, Harley Davidson, HEB Foods/gas, Lowe's, Marshall's, Old Navy, Ross, Verizon, S [gas] Citgo/dsl [food] Spanky's Pizza
32b a	I-45, S to Galveston, N to Houston, [other] to [airport]
31	Broadway Blvd, S [gas] Phillips 66/dsl, Valero/dsl
30c b	TX 225, to Pasadena, San Jacinto Mon
29	Port of Houston Main Entrance
28	Clinton Dr, W [gas] Shell/Burger King/dsl, to Galina Park
27	Turning Basin Dr, industrial area

HOUSTON

INTERSTATE 610 (Houston) Cont'd

Exit#	Services
26b	Market St
26a	I-10 E, to Beaumont, I-10 W, to downtown
24	(b a from sb) US 90 E, Wallisville Rd, E [gas] Citgo/dsl, Gulf/dsl, Loves/Arby's/dsl/scales/24hr, Pilot/McDonald's/dsl/scales, Valero/dsl, Valero/Hartz Chicken/dsl/scales/24hr [food] Chevron/dsl [other] Blue Beacon, W [gas] Citgo/dsl
23b	N Wayside, N [gas] Valero
23a	Kirkpatrick Blvd
22	Homestead Rd, Kelley St, N [gas] Shell/dsl [food] Whataburger [lodging] Super 8, S [gas] Chevron/Subway/dsl/scales
21	Lockwood Dr, W [gas] Texaco/Subway/dsl, N [gas] Chevron/McDonald's, Shell/dsl [food] Church's, Timmy Chan Chinese [other] [H], Family$, Fiesta Foods
20a b	US 59, to downtown
19b	Hardy Toll Rd
19a	Hardy St, Jensen Dr (from eb)
18	Irvington Blvd, Fulton St, N [gas] Chevron, S [gas] Shell/dsl
17b c	I-45, N to Dallas, S to Houston
17a	(eb only) Airline Dr, S [gas] Shell/dsl [food] Jack-in-the-Box [lodging] Western Inn
16	(b a from eb) Yale St, N Main St, Shamrock, N [gas] Exxon/dsl [other] Harley-Davidson, S [gas] Texaco [food] Burger King, KFC/Taco Bell, Starbucks
15	TX 261, N Shepherd Dr, N [food] Five Guys, Gabby's BBQ, Sonic, Starbucks, Taco Cabana, S [gas] Chevron/dsl, Shell [food] Chick-fil-A, Wendy's, Whataburger [other] Home Depot, PepBoys
14	Ella Blvd, N [gas] Exxon [food] Cane's, Carl's Jr, El Pollo Loco, KFC, McDonald's, Popeye's, Taco Bell, S [gas] Murphy USA/dsl, Shell [food] Chipotle, Thomas BBQ [other] [H], BrakeCheck, CVS Drug, Lowe's Whse, Office Depot
13c	TC Jester Blvd, N [gas] Shell [food] Antone's Po' Boys, Denny's, Juanita's Mexican [lodging] Courtyard, SpringHill Suites, S [gas] Phillips 66/dsl
13b a	US 290 (exits left from nb)
12	W 18th St, E [food] Applebee's, Whataburger, W [gas] Shell [food] Burger King [lodging] Sheraton
11	I-10, W to San Antonio, E to downtown Houston
10	Woodway Dr, Memorial Dr, W [gas] Chevron/Pizza Inn/dsl, Shell/dsl [other] Goodyear
9b	Post Oak Blvd, E [lodging] Drury Inn, Hampton Inn, La Quinta, W [food] Champp's Rest., McCormick&Schmick's Café, Starbucks
9a	San Felipe Rd, Westheimer Rd, FM 1093, E [gas] Chevron/dsl, Shell [food] Grotto Rest., Jack-in-the-Box, Le Peep Cafe, Starbucks, Sullivan Steaks [lodging] Extended Stay America, Hampton Inn, La Quinta [other] CVS Drug, NTB, Target, W [gas] Shell [food] CA Pizza Kitchen, Five Guys, Jamba Juice, Panera Bread, Yia Yia Mary's [lodging] Courtyard, Extended Stay America, Marriott, Sheraton [other] AT&T, Best Buy, Dillard's, Nieman-Marcus, Whole Foods Mkt
8a	US 59, Richmond Ave, E [lodging] Extended Stay America [other] CVS Drug, W [gas] Shell [lodging] Holiday Inn [other] Dillards
7	Bissonet St, West Park Dr, Fournace Place, E [food] Beudreax's Kitchen [lodging] Candlewood Suites [other] Home Depot, Petsmart, W [gas] Shell/dsl/repair
6	Bellaire Blvd
5b	Evergreen St
5a	Beechnut St, E [gas] Chevron [food] Boston Mkt, IHOP, Lowe's, McDonald's, Outback Steaks, Panda Express, Subway [other] Hobby Lobby, Verizon, W [gas] Phillips 66, Shell [food] Becks Prime, Chick-fil-A, Escalante Mexican Grill, Fadi's Grill, James Coney Island, La Madeleine, Los Tios Mexican, Saltgrass Steaks, Smoothie King, Starbucks [other] AT&T, Best Buy, GNC, JC Penney, Marshall's, Old Navy, Ross, SteinMart, Target
4a	S Post Oak Rd, Brasswood, E [food] Outback Steaks, W [other] Target, Walmart
3	Stella Link Rd, N [gas] Mobil [food] Domino's [other] 99c Store, Discount Tire, O'Reilly Parts, S [gas] Valero/dsl [other] Brake Check, vet
2	US 90A, N [gas] Exxon/dsl, Mobil, Texaco, Valero [food] Burger King, Chacho's Cantina, Denny's/24hr, KFC, McDonald's, Popeye's, Starbucks, Subway, Wendy's [lodging] Holiday Inn Express [other] CVS Drug, Discount Tire, Family$, Ford, Honda, Mazda, Walgreens, S [gas] Chevron/dsl [food] Golden Corral, Taco Bell, Whataburger/24hr [lodging] Candlewood Suites, CareFree Inn, Motel 6, Motel 6 (2), RainTree Inn [other] Nissan, to Buffalo Speedway
1c	Kirby Dr (from eb), N [lodging] Crowne Plaza, Quality Inn, Sterling Inn, S [food] Joe's Crabshack, Pappadeaux Seafood, Pappasito's Cantina [other] Cavender's Boots, Chevrolet, Hyundai, NTB, Toyota
1b a	FM 521, Almeda St, Fannin St, N [gas] Chevron/dsl, Shell [food] Burger King [other] NRG Arena, S [gas] Shell/dsl [food] McDonald's [other] Aamco, Chrysler/Dodge/Jeep, to Six Flags

HOUSTON

TX

NOTES

= gas = food = lodging = other = rest stop

UT

UTAH

INTERSTATE 15

Exit#	Services
400.5mm	Utah/Idaho state line
398	Portage
392	UT 13 S, Plymouth, E United/A&W/dsl
385	UT 30 E, to Riverside, Fielding, 1 mi E Sinclair/Riverside Grill/dsl
381	Tremonton, Garland, 2 mi E, food, gas, lodging
379	I-84 W, to Boise
376	UT 13, to Tremonton, 2-3 mi E Texaco/Arby's/dsl/scales/24hr JC'S Diner, Subway, Taco Time Marble Motel, N Sandman Motel (3mi)
372	UT 240, to UT 13, to rec area, Honeyville, E Crystal Hot Springs Camping
370mm	**sb, full facilities, info, litter barrels, petwalk, vending**
365	UT 13, Brigham City, W to Golden Spike NHS
363	Forest St, Brigham City, E Loves/Carl's Jr/Subway/dsl/scales/24hr Holiday Inn Express, W Bear River Bird Refuge
362	US 91, to US 89, Brigham City, Logan, E Chevron/dsl, Exxon, Phillips 66/dsl, USA Arby's, Burger King, China Hua Guan, Domino's, Floriberto's Mexican, Hunan Chinese, J&D's Rest., KFC/Taco Bell, McDonald's, Old Grist Mill Bread, Pizza +, Pizza Hut, Sonic, Subway, Taco Time, Wendy's, Wingers Crystal Inn, Howard Johnson Express, Verizon, $General, $Tree, 7-11, AT&T, AutoZone, Buick/Cadillac/Chevrolet, Family$, Golden Spike RV Park, John Watson, Chiropractor (5mi), KOA (4mi), O'Reilly Parts, Schwab Tires, ShopKO, to Yellowstone NP via US 89, Walmart/Subway, W LW/Chevron/DQ/dsl/scales/24hr Days Inn
361mm	**nb, full facilities, litter barrels, petwalk, vending**
359	Port of Entry both lanes
357	UT 315, to Willard, Perry, E FLYING J/Subway/dsl/LP/scales/24hr KOA (2mi), Willard Peak Camping
351	UT 126, to US 89, to Utah's Fruit Way, Willard Bay, W Smith & Edwards Hardware
349	UT 134, N Ogden, Farr West, E 7-11, Maverik/dsl, Phillips 66/Wendy's/dsl Arby's, Bella's Mexican, Burger King, Del Taco, Domino's, Jumbo Burger, McDonald's, Subway, Taco Bell Comfort Inn Jiffylube, W Chevron/dsl Wasatch View RV park
346	to Harrisville, W Chevron/Subway/dsl, dsl repair, Maverik/dsl GriDeli's, Taco Time, Zhang's Chinese Cal Store
344	UT 39, 12th St, Ogden, E 7-11/dsl, Chevron/dsl, Old Frontier Best Western+ to Ogden Canyon RA, W Pilot/Subway/Taco Bell/dsl/24hr Uncle Lee's Cafe Sleep Inn Sierra RV Ctr
343	UT 104, 21st St, Ogden, E FLYING J/Denny's/dsl/LP/24hr, Phillips 66/dsl Big Z Rest, Cactus Red's SW Grill, McDonalds Comfort Suites, Holiday Inn Express, Motel 6, Woodspring Suites RV Repair, W Shell/Blimpie/dsl Super 8 Bideaux RV Ctr, Century RV Park
342	(from nb, no return) UT 53, 24th St, Ogden
341b a	UT 79 W, 31st St, Ogden, W, 1-2 mi E on Wall St Longhorn Steaks, Big O Tires, Chevrolet, Costco/gas, Dillard's, Firestone/auto, Ford, Hyundai, to Weber St U
340	I-84 E (from sb), to Cheyenne, Wyo
339	UT 26 (from nb), to I-84 E, Riverdale Rd, E Exxon/dsl, Sinclair/dsl Applebee's, Arby's, Bajio Grill, Buffalo Wild Wings, Carl's Jr, Chili's, Honeybaked Ham, IHOP, Jamba Juice, Lucky Buffet, McDonald's, Starbucks, Subway, Wendy's Motel 6 $Tree, Best Buy, Buick/GMC, Cadillac, Chrysler/Dodge/Jeep, Good Earth Natural Foods, Gordman's, Harley-Davidson, Home Depot, Honda, Jo-Ann Fabrics, Maverik/dsl, Mazda, Nissan, Petsmart, Sam's Club/gas, Schwab Tire, Target, Toyota, Verizon, Walmart
338	UT 97, Roy, Sunset, E Air Force Museum, W 7-11, Exxon/dsl, Maverik/dsl, Sinclair/dsl A&W/KFC, Arby's, Beez Cafe, Blimpie, Chinese Gourmet, Five Star Chinese, Greek Island Broiler, Japanese Wasabi, La Frontera Mexican, McDonald's, Panda Express, Papa Murphy's, Rancherito's Mexican, Subway, Taco Bell, Village Inn Rest., Warren's Drive-In, Wendy's AutoZone, Citte RV Ctr, CVS Drug, Discount Tire, Family$, Firestone/auto, Harmon's Mkt, Midas, O'Reilly Parts, RiteAid, Sacco's Fresh Mkt, Schwab Tires, Smith's/dsl, transmissions, vet, vet, Walgeens
335	UT 103, Clearfield, E Starbucks Hill AFB, W Conoco, Maverik/dsl, Phillips 66/dsl, Tesoro/dsl Carl's Jr, KFC, McDonald's, Subway, Taco Bell, Winger's Days Inn, EconoLodge C&M Tires
334	UT 193, Clearfield, E Chevron/dsl, Maverik to Hill AFB, W 7-11, Maverik/dsl Domino's AutoZone
332	UT 108, Syracuse, E Applebee's, Bandidos Border Grill, Boston's Rest., Brick Oven, Cafe Rio, Carl's Jr., Chick-fil-A, Chili's, Cracker Barrel, Famous Dave's, Five Guys, Golden Corral, Jimmy John's, Koi Asian, MacCool's Grill, Marie Callender's, Mimi's Cafe, Noodles&Co, Outback Steaks, Panda Express, Papa Murphy's, Red Robin, Rumbi Island Grill, Sonic, Tepanyaki, Zupas Cafe Courtyard, Fairfield Inn, Hampton Inn, Hilton Garden, Holiday Inn Express, Home2Home, La Quinta, TownePlace Suites Barnes&Noble, Big O Tires, Lowe's Whse, Michaels, Office Depot, Petco, Ross, Target, URGENT CARE, Walgreens, W Conoco/dsl Arby's, Burger King, Crown Burger, McDonald's, 7-11, Ford, to Antelope Island
331	UT 232, UT 126, Layton, E Buffalo Wild Wings, Costa Vida, Denny's, Garcia's, McDonald's, Olive Garden, Red Lobster, Sizzler, Training Table Rest., TX Roadhouse, Wendy's Best Western, Comfort Inn $Tree, Dick's, JC Penney, to Hill AFB S Gate, Tuesday Morning, W Exxon/dsl Asian Buffet, Bajio Mexican, Burger King, Cantina SW Grill, ChuckeCheese, Coldstone, Del Taco, IHOP, KFC, Krispy Kreme, La Puente Mexican, Maid Rite Diner, Moon Dog Cafe, Pace's Rest., Rancheritos Mexican, Starbucks, Taco Bell AT&T, Batteries+Bulbs, Big Lots, Buick/GMC, Chevrolet, Chrysler/Dodge/Jeep, Discount Tire, Hancock Fabrics, Hobby Lobby, Home Depot, Kia, Petsmart, Sam's Club/gas, ShopKO, Staples, Verizon, Walmart/McDonald's
330	Layton Pkwy, to UT 126, Layton, E Little Orient Chinese Tire Pros, W Cafe Sabor Camping World RV Ctr
328	UT 273, Kaysville, E 7-11/dsl, Chevron/McDonald's Arby's, Big Daddy's Pizza, Domino's, Dylan's Drive-In, Granny Annie's Rest., Pizza Hut, Subway, Taco Time, Wendy's, Winger's AutoZone, Big O Tire, Fresh Mkt Foods, O'Reilly Parts, Schwab Tire, USPO, Walgreens, W Camping World, Mazda
325mm	**parking area both lanes**
325	UT 225, Lagoon Dr, Farmington, E Subway camping, funpark, W Costa Vida, Dickey's BBQ, Habit Burger, Panda Express, Starbucks, Subway, Zupas Cabela's, Gordmans, Harmon's Mkt, Marshalls, Old Navy, Petco, Ross

BRIGHAM CITY

OGDEN

ROY

LAYTON

KAYSVILLE

UT

INTERSTATE 15 Cont'd

Exit#	Services
324	US 89 N, UT 225, Legacy Pkwy (from sb), 1 mi E Maverik/dsl, Smith's Foods/dsl Burger King, Chevron/dsl, Chopstix Chinese, Javier's Mexican, Papa John's, Subway Hampton Inn Aunt Pam's, Burt Bros/Goodyear/auto, RV Park, to I-84
322	UT 227 (from nb), Lagoon Dr, to Farmington, E Subway Lagoon Funpark/RV Park
319	UT 105, Parrish Lane, Centerville, E 7-11/dsl, Chevron/dsl, Phillips 66/dsl Arby's, Carl's Jr, Chick-fil-A, Chili's, Costa Vida, DQ, Iggy's Grill, IHOP, In-N-Out, La Puente Mexican, Little Caesar's, McDonald's, Papa Murphy's, Ruby River Steaks, Starbucks, Subway, Taco Bell, TacoMaker, Wendy's $Tree, Ace Hardware, Big O Tire, Dave's Auto Repair, Dick's Mkt, GNC, Home Depot, Jo-Ann, Kohl's, Land Rover, O'Reilly Parts, Petsmart, Schwab Tire, Target, Walmart
317	US 89 S (exits left from sb), UT 131, 500W, S Bountiful, E Chevron/dsl, Exxon/dsl, Sinclair/7-11/dsl Starbucks Country Inn Suites Chrysler/Dodge/Jeep, Costco/gas, Office Depot, Parts+, PetCo
316	UT 68, 500 S, W Bountiful, Woods Cross, E Shell Applebee's, Barbacoa Mexican, Cafe Rio, Carl's Jr, Chipotle, ChuckaRama, Coldstone, Del Taco, Five Guys, Jimmy John's, KFC, McDonald's, Mikado Japanese, Panda Express, Pei Wei, Pizza Factory, Pizza Hut, Sizzler, Starbucks, Subway, Taco Bell, TX Roadhouse, Wendy's H, $Tree, AT&T, AutoZone, Barnes&Noble, Costco/gas, Firestone/auto, GNC, Lowe's, Michael's, Midas, Office Depot, O'Reilly Parts, Petco, Ross, ShopKO, Tire Pros, TJ Maxx, Walgreens, W Phillips 66/A&W/dsl InTown Suites vet
315	26th S, N Salt Lake, E Chevron/dsl, Tesoro, Texaco Arby's, Best Burger, Empire Chinese, Kneaders Bakery Cafe, McDonald's, Nielsen's Frozen Custard, Pappa's Steaks, Subway, Taco Time, Village Inn, Wendy's Best Western, Comfort Inn Buick/GMC, Burt Bros Tires, Chevrolet, Discount Tire, Ford/Lincoln, Honda, Mazda, Nissan, Schwab Tire, Smith's Foods, Southfork Hardware, Toyota, Tunex, U-Haul, Walgreens, W IHOP, Lorena's Mexican Hampton Inn, Motel 6
314	Center St, Cudahy Lane (from sb), N Salt Lake, E gas
313	I-215 W (from sb), to
312	US 89 S, to Beck St, N Salt Lake
311	2300 N
310	900 W (from sb), W Salt City Motel
309	600 N, E H, downtown, LDS Temple, to UT State FairPark
308	I-80 W, to Reno,
307	400 S, downtown
306	600 S, SLC City Ctr, 1 mi E Chevron, Phillips 66/dsl, Sinclair Alberto's Mexican, Denny's, McDonald's, Starbucks, Subway, Wendy's Chrystal Inn, Comfort Inn, DoubleTree, Grand America, Hampton Inn, Hilton Garden, Little America, Motel 6, Red Lion Inn, Rodeway Inn, Sheraton, SpringHill Suites Hyundai, LDS Church Offices, to Temple Square, Toyota
305c-a	1300 S, 2100 S UT 201 W, SLC, downtown, E Chevron/Subway/dsl, Shell Carl's Jr, ChuckECheese, Dickey's BBQ, IHOP, Jimmy John's, McDonald's, Starbucks, Tepanyaki Japanese $Tree, Best Buy, Costco/gas, Home Depot, Office Depot, PetsMart, Sams Club/dsl, U-Haul, Walmart, W FLYING J/Denny's/dsl/LP/24hr El Pasa Mexican Blue Beacon, Kia
304	I-80 E, to Denver, Cheyenne
303	UT 171, 3300 S, S Salt Lake, E 7-11, Maverik/dsl, Sinclair/dsl Apollo Burgers, Burger King, Crown Burger, Jimmy John's, McDonald's, Starbucks, Taco Bell Day's Inn, InTowne Suites, W Maverik Buick/GMC

N SALT LAKE

SALT LAKE

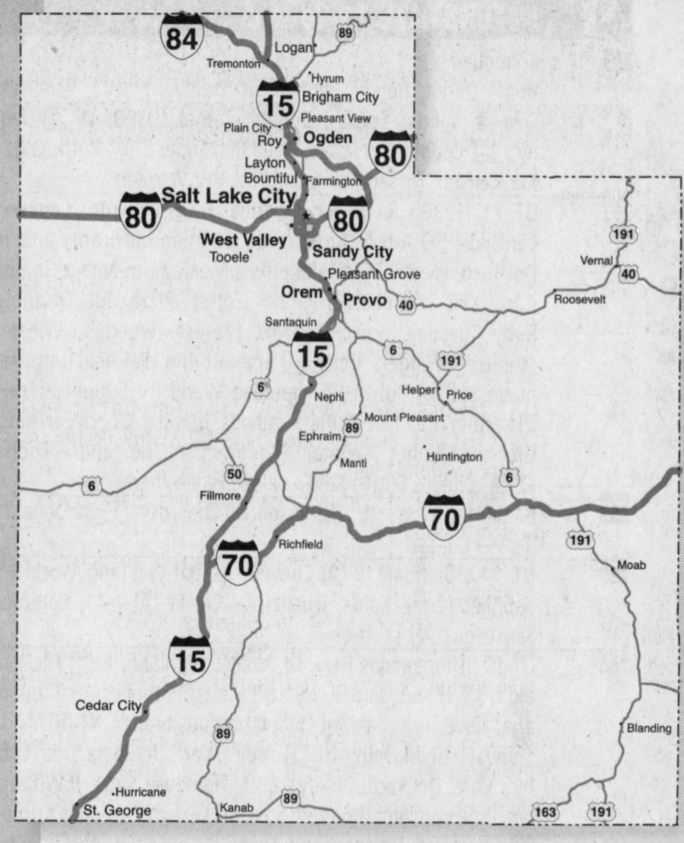

Exit#	Services
301	UT 266, 4500 S, Murray, Kearns, E McDonald's, Subway, Super Grinders Discount Tire, W Chevron/Burger King/dsl, Conoco/dsl, Texaco/dsl Denny's, Subway, Wendy's Baymont Inn, Fairfield Inn, Hampton Inn Lowe's Whse
300	UT 173, 5300 S, Murray, Kearns, E H, W Chevron/dsl, Conoco/dsl, Sinclair/dsl Papa Murphy's, Subway, Taco Time Pavilion Inn Smith's Foods
298	I-215 E and W
297	UT 48, 7200 S, Midvale, E Chevron, Phillips 66/dsl Arctic Circle, Cafe Silvestre, Denny's, Hooters, McDonald's, Mezquite Mexican, Midvale Mining Cafe, Sweet Ginger Chinese, Taco Bell Best Western, Day's Inn, Discovery Inn, InTowne Suites, La Quinta, Motel 6 Family$, Schwab Tire, Solitude Ski Areas, to Brighton, vet, Walgreens, W Sinclair/dsl Culver's, Dunkin Donuts, Jimmy John's, Subway, WinCo Foods Staybridge Suites GNC
295	UT 209, 9000 S, Sandy, E Chevron/dsl, Sinclair/dsl Arby's, Burger King, Ichiban Asian, Schlotzky's, Sconecutter's Rest., Sizzler, Subway Comfort Inn Alta Ski Areas, Discount Tire, Firestone/auto, Ford/Lincoln, NAPA, Rio Rinto Stadium, to Snowbird, W Maverik H, Aamco, BMW Motorcycles, Harley-Davidson, URGENT CARE
293	106th S, Sandy, S Jordan, E Conoco, Shell//dsl A&W/KFC, Buffalo Wild Wings, Carl's Jr., Carver's Steak & Seafood, Chick-fil-A, Chili's, Chipotle Mexican, ChukECheese, Costa Vida, Firehouse Subs, Five Guys, Habit Burger, Iggy's Grill, IHOP, Jim's Rest., La Frontera, Los Cucos Mexican, McDonald's, McGrath's Fishhouse, Mimi's Cafe, Olive Garden, Pei Wei, Rumbi Island Grill, Sampan Chinese, Starbucks, Subway, Sweet Tomatoes, Taco Bell, TGIFriday, Training Table, TX Roadhouse, Village Inn, Wendy's Best Western, Courtyard, Extended Stay America, Hampton Inn, Hilton Garden, Holiday Inn Express, Hyatt House, Marriott, Residence Inn, TownePlace Suites Best Buy, Chevrolet, Chrysler/Dodge/Jeep, Costco/gas, Dillard's, Goodyear/auto,

SANDY

UT

INTERSTATE 15 Cont'd

DRAPER

293 Continued
Home Depot, Honda, Hyundai, JC Penney, Macy's, Petsmart, Scheels Sports, Staples, Subaru, Target, USPO, **W** Denny's Country Inn Suites, Sleep Inn, Super 8 Buick/GMC/Kia, CarMax, Nissan, Sam's Club/dsl, VW, Walmart

291 UT 71, 12300 S, Draper, Riverton, **E** Chevron, Common Cents/dsl Arby's, Arctic Circle, Café Rio Mexican, Carl's Jr, Del Taco, Fazoli's, Guadalahonky's Mexican, In-N-Out, Jamba Juice, KFC, McDonald's, Panda Express, Pizza Hut, Quizno's, Ruby Tuesday, Sonic, Teriyaki Express, Wendy's, Wienerschnitzel, Wingers Diner Comfort Inn, Fairfield Inn, Ramada Ltd Brown RV, Camping World RV Supplies (1mi), Discount Tire, FSA Outlets/famous brands, Goodyear/auto, Greenbax, Kohl's, Mountain Shadows Camping, Smith's Foods, **W** Phillips 66 Sam's Club/gas, Walmart

289 Bangerter Hwy, **W** Exxon/Quiznos/dsl McDonald's 7-11, IKEA

288 UT 140, Bluffdale, **E** Chevron/dsl Camping World RV Supplies (2mi), Kohl's, Quality RV Ctr, **W** 7-11, Common Sense/gas st prison

284 UT 92, Timpanogas Hwy, to Alpine, Highland, **E** McDonald's Hilton Garden, Hyatt Place Cabela's, to Timpanogas Cave, Traverse Mtn Outlets/famous brands, **W** 7-11/Subway/dsl, Maverik/dsl Arby's, Carl's Jr, Costa Vida, Cubby's Cafe, Del Taco, Dickey's BBQ, Firehouse Subs, JCW Burgers, Popeye's, Smashburger, Starbucks, Zaxby's, Zupas Kitcken Courtyard, Hampton Inn, Home 2 Suites, SpringHill Suites Lone Peak RV Ctr, Thanksgiving Point/café

LEHI

282 US 89 S, 12th W, to UT 73, Lehi, **W** Tesoro/dsl

279 UT 73, to Lehi, **E** Texaco/dsl Buffalo Wild Wings, Cafe Rio, Chili's, ChuckARama, Culver's, Del Taco, Denny's, El Pollo Loco, Hibachi House, Jimmy John's, One Man Band Diner, Panda Express, TX Roadhouse, Which Wich?, Wienerschnitzel Motel 6 Costco/gas, Home Depot, Lowe's Whse, Petsmart, Schwab Tire, Verizon, Walgreens, Walmart/Burger King, **W** Chevron/dsl, CNG, Phillips 66/Wendy's Arctic Circle, KFC/Pizza Hut, McDonald's, Moochie's, Papa Murphy's, Subway, Tepanyki Japanese Best Western, Day's Inn, Super 8 7-11, Big O Tire, Dave's Chiropractic, GNC, Macey's, O'Reilly Parts, USPO, vet

278 Main St, American Fork, **E** Phillips 66/dsl, Texaco Chili's, Cobblestone Pizza, Del Taco, In-N-Out, Ottavio's Italian, Pier 49, Sonic, Wendy's H, $Tree, Chevrolet, Chrysler/Dodge/Jeep, Home Depot, Kohl's, Office Depot, Old Navy, Smith's Foods, Subaru, Target, Walmart, **W** Woodspring Suites

276 5th E, Pleasant Grove, **1-2 mi E** Circle K, Conoco/Blimpie, Phillips 66, Texaco Arby's, Carl's Jr, Del Taco, Denny's, Golden Corral, Hardee's, KFC, McDonald's, Subway, Taco Bell, Wendy's Quality Inn H, American Camping, Chevrolet, Stewart's RV Ctr, **W** Buick/GMC, Ford, Land Rover

275 Pleasant Grove, **E** Bajio Grill, Panda Express, Sonic, Wienerschnitzel BMW, Macey's Foods

OREM

273 Orem, Lindon, **E** Exxon/dsl, Holiday Costa Vida Mexican, Del Taco Discount Tire, Home Depot, Lexus, Mercedes, Schwab Tire, **W** Harley-Davidson

272 UT 52, to US 189, 8th N, Orem, **1 mi E** Maverik, Phillips 66 Arby's, Cafe Rio, Denny's, DQ, Sonic La Quinta to Sundance RA

271 Center St, Orem, **E** 7-11, Chevron Burger King, ChuckECheese, McDonald's, Panda Express, Taco Bell, Wendy's, Zaxby's H, Target, USPO, **W** Maverik/dsl DQ

PROVO

269 UT 265, 12th St S, University Pkwy, **1-3 mi E** Chevron, Sinclair, Texaco/Wendy's/dsl Applebee's, Arby's, Carrabba's, Chili's, Fuddrucker's, Golden Corral, HoneyBaked Ham, IHOP, Krispy Kreme, McDonald's, Noodles & Co., Outback Steaks, Pizza Hut, Sakura Japanese, Sizzler, Starbucks, Subway, Thai Evergreen, Village Inn Best Western, Comfort Inn, Courtyard, Hampton Inn, La Quinta Barnes&Noble, Best Buy, Ford, Honda, JC Penney, JiffyLube, Jo-Ann Fabrics, Lowe's Whse, many services on US 89, Mazda, Mazda, Michael's, Nissan, Office Depot, Old Navy, Petsmart, Ross, Subaru, TJ Maxx, to BYU, Toyota, VW, Walmart, **W** Chevron, Chevron/dsl, CNG Domino's, Subway Holiday Inn Express

265b a UT 114, Center St, Provo, **E** 7-11, Conoco, Phillips 66/Wendy's, Shell, Sinclair/dsl Marriott, Travelers Inn, Travelodge H, Albertson's, auto repair, Checker Parts, Firestone/auto, **W** Chevron, Shell/dsl Great Steak Rest., Subway Econolodge KOA, Lakeside RV, to Utah Lake SP

263 US 189 N, University Ave, Provo, **E** Exxon/dsl, Maverik/dsl, Phillips 66/dsl, Shell/dsl A&W/KFC, Arby's, Burger King, ChuckaRama, Kyoto, McDonald's, Papa Murphy's, Ruby River Steaks, Sizzler, Subway, Taco Bell, Village Inn Rest., Wendy's Fairfield Inn, Hampton Inn, Ramada, Residence Inn, Sleep Inn $Tree, Dillard's, Discount Tire, GoodEarth Foods, Home Depot, JC Penney, Les Schwab, Sam's Club/gas, Staples, to BYU, transmissions

SPRINGVILLE

261 UT 75, Springville, **E** FLYING J/Denny's/dsl/scales/24hr, Maverik McDonald's (1mi) Best Western, Holiday Inn Express KOA, RestStop

260 UT 77, Springville, Mapleton, **E** Phillips 66/7-11/dsl Del Taco, IHOP, Mongolian Grill, Papa John's, Pizza Hut, Wendy's Big O Tire, JiffyLube, Walmart/Subway, **W** Chevron/Subway/dsl, Loves/Chester's/McDonald's/dsl/scales/24hr Cracker Barrel Days Inn, Microtel Quality RV Ctr

257b a US 6 E, UT 156, Spanish Fork, **E** Chevron/dsl, Sinclair, Tesoro/dsl, Texaco/dsl/LP Amber Rest., Arby's, Burger King, Cafe Rio, Carl's Jr, China Wok, Costa Vida, Cubby's Cafe, Culver's, Five Guys, Italian Place, Jimmy John's, KFC, Kneaders, Little Caesar's, McDonald's, One Man Band Diner, Papa Murphy's, Pizza Factory, Rita's, Sonic, Starbucks, Subway, Taco Bell, Taco Time, Wendy's, Zupas Kitchen $Tree, AT&T, AutoZone, Big O Tire, Cal Store, Costco/gas, Fresh Mkt/gas, GNC, Good Earth Mkt, Jo-Ann Fabrics, Macey's Foods, O'Reilly Parts, ShopKO, Verizon, Walmart/Subway, **W** Chevrolet

253 UT 164, to Spanish Fork

250 UT 115, Payson, **E** Chevron/dsl McDonald's, Subway Quality Inn H, Mt Nebo Loop, O'Reilly Parts, Payson Foods, RiteAid

248 Payson, Salem, **E** Chevron/dsl, Exxon/Arby's/Subway/dsl Costa Vida, Hunan City, Papa John's, Papa Murphy's, Pizza Hut, Taco Bell, Tsing Tao Asian $Tree, AT&T, AutoZone, Big O Tire, Verizon, Walmart/Subway, **W** Phillips 66/Wendy's/7-11/dsl

244 US 6 W, Santaquin, **E** Maverik/dsl Cubby's Diner, DQ Tire Trax Auto, TrueValue, **W** Chevron/dsl, Sinclair/dsl Brumby's Cafe, Family Tree Rest., Hot Rod Diner, Main St Pizza, Subway, Taco Time auto/tire care, Family$, Ford, Main St Mkt, Nat Hist Area, USPO

242 to S Santaquin, **W** Chevron/dsl

233 UT 54, Mona, **W** Shell/Subway/dsl

228 UT 28, to Nephi, **2-4 mi W** services

225 UT 132, Nephi, **E** Exxon/dsl/LP Main St Pizza, One Man Band Diner, Taco Time, **W** Chevron/Arby's/dsl, Phillips 66/7-11/Wendy's/dsl Economy Inn H, Big O Tire

INTERSTATE 15 Cont'd

NEPHI

Exit#	Services
222	UT 28, to I-70, Nephi, E Chevron/dsl, Exxon/scales/dsl/24hr, Texaco/dsl Burger King, Mickelson's Rest., Subway Motel 6, National 9 Inn, Super 8 dsl repair, W FLYING J/Denny's/dsl/LP/scales/24hr Lisa's Country Kitchen Best Western, Safari Motel H, dsl repair, High Country RV Park
207	to US 89, Mills
202	Yuba Lake, access to boating, camping, (C), rec services
188	US 50 E, to I-70, Scipio, E Chevron/Subway/dsl, Texaco/dsl Scipio Hotel, W FLYING J/DQ/dsl/rest stop/24hr
184	ranch exit
178	US 50, to Delta, W to Great Basin NP
174	to US 50, Holden, W to Great Basin NP

FILLMORE

Exit#	Services
167	Lp 15, Fillmore, E Chevron/dsl, Sinclair/dsl 5 Buck Pizza Best Western/rest. H, CarQuest, city park, golf, Goodyear, KOA (3mi), WagonsWest RV Park, W Chevron/Subway/rest stop/dsl, Texaco/dsl Carl's Jr tires/repair
163	Lp 15, to UT 100, Fillmore, E Conoco/Burger King/Costa Vida/dsl, Maverik/dsl Hong Kong Chinese, Larry's Drive-In Comfort Inn H, KOA, W Chevron/dsl/24hr Travel & Rest Inn
158	UT 133, Meadow, E Conoco/dsl, Shell/dsl
153mm	view area sb
151mm	view area nb
146	Kanosh, 2 mi E gas chainup area
138	ranch exit
135	Cove Fort Hist Site, E Chevron/Subway/rest stop/dsl repair/tires
132	I-70 E, to Denver, E Capitol Reef NP, Fremont Indian SP
129	Sulphurdale, chainup area
125	ranch exit
120	Manderfield, chainup area nb

BEAVER

Exit#	Services
112	to UT 21, Beaver, Manderfield, E Chevron/dsl, Conoco/dsl, Sinclair/dsl Arshel's Café, Carl's Jr, Crazy Cow Cafe, Hunan Chinese, McDonald's, Subway Beaver Lodge, Best Western, Country Inn, De Lano Motel/RV Park, Motel 6 H, auto/RV/dsl repair, Family$, Hometown Mkt, KOA (1mi), W FLYING J/cafe/dsl/scales/24hr Denny's, Wendy's Days Inn, Super 8 to Great Basin NP
109	to UT 21, Beaver, E Phillips 66/dsl, Shell/Burger King/dsl/RV dump, Spirit/dsl Best Western, Comfort Inn H, auto repair, Cache Valley Cheese, Mike's Foodtown, NAPA, United Camping, W Blu LNG, Chevron/DQ/dsl KanKun Mexican, Timberline Rest. Quality Inn to Great Basin NP, truck wash
100	ranch exit
95	UT 20, to US 89, to Panguitch, E Bryce Canyon NP
88mm	**RS both lanes, full (handicapped) facilities, hist site, litter barrel, petwalk, (C), picnic table**
82	UT 271, Paragonah
78	UT 141, 1 mi E Chevron/dsl, Maverik Days Inn NAPA, ski areas, W TA/Subway/Taco Bell/LP/dsl/scales/24hr/@
75	UT 143, 2 mi E Chevron, Maverik, Phillips 66/dsl Days Inn Parowan Mkt, to Brian Head/Cedar Breaks Ski Resorts
71	Summit
62	UT 130, Cedar City, E Loves/Carl's Jr/Subway/dsl/scales/24hr, Phillips 66/dsl Allberto's Mexican H, Country Aire RV Park, KOA (2mi), st patrol, W Maverik/dsl, Shell/dsl/24hr/dsl repair/@ Travelodge
59	UT 56, Cedar City, 0-2 mi E Chevron/DQ/dsl, Conoco/dsl, Maverik, Phillips 66/dsl/LP, She'll/dsl A&W/KFC, Arby's,

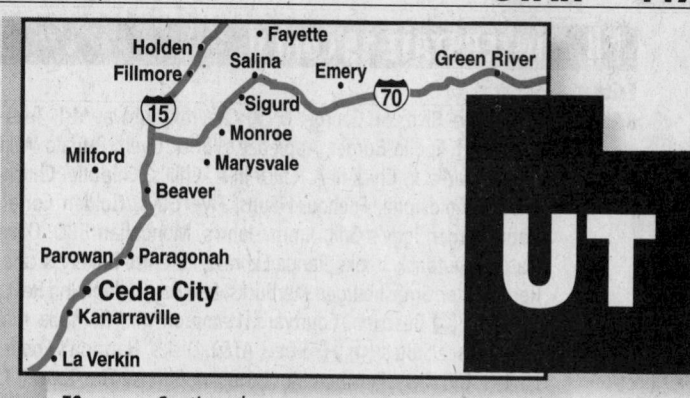

Holden, Fayette, Fillmore, Salina, Emery, Green River, 15, 70, Sigurd, Monroe, Milford, Marysvale, Beaver, Parowan, Paragonah, Cedar City, Kanarraville, La Verkin, UT

CEDAR CITY

Exit#	Services
59	Continued Burger King, China Kitchen, Denny's, Depot Grill, Firehouse Subs, Great Harvest Bread Co., Hermie's Drive-In, Hong Kong Buffet, IHOP, Jimmy John's, Little Caesar's, McDonald's/playplace, Papa Murphy's, Pizza Factory, Sizzler, Sonny Boy's BBQ, Subway, Taco Bell, Valerie's Tacos, Wendy's, Zaxby's Abbey Inn, Best Value Inn, Best Western, Quality Inn, Stratford Hotel Buick/Chevrolet, Goodyear/auto, Lin's Mkt, Mr Tire, NAPA, Tire Pros, USPO, Verizon, W Maverik/dsl, Sinclair/dsl Subway Motel 6, Ramada, Super 8
57	Lp 15, to UT 14, Cedar City, 0-2 mi E Chevron/repair/24hr, Phillips 66/dsl, Shell, Sinclair/dsl DQ, Subway, Taco Time Clarion, Comfort Inn, Courtyard, Holiday Inn Express, La Quinta, SpringHill Suites H, $Tree, AutoZone, Big O Tire, Bryce Cyn, CAL Ranch, Duck Crk, Jo-Ann Fabrics, NAPACare, Navajo Lake, O'Reilly Parts, Smith's Food/dsl, Staples, TJ Maxx, to Cedar Breaks, Verizon, W Chevron/dsl, USA Applebee's, Cafe Rio, Chili's, Costa Vida, Del Taco, Dickey's BBQ, Five Buck Pizza, Jack-in-the-Box, Lupita's Mexican, Ninja Japanese, Panda Express, Papa John's, Starbucks, Subway, Winger's Hampton Inn GNC, Home Depot, Tunex, Verizon, Walgreens, Walmart/McDonald's
51	Kanarraville, Hamilton Ft
44mm	**RS both lanes, full (handicapped) facilities, hist site, litter barrels, petwalk, (C), (picnic)**
42	New Harmony, Kanarraville, W Shell/dsl
40	to Kolob Canyon, E scenic drive, tourist info/(C), Zion's NP
36	Black Ridge
33	Snowfield
31	Pintura
30	Browse
27	UT 17, Toquerville, E Grand Canyon, Lake Powell, to Zion NP
23	Leeds, Silver Reef (from sb), 3 mi E hist site, Leed's RV Park/gas, museum
22	Leeds, Silver Reef (from nb), same as 23
16	UT 9, to Hurricane, E Texaco/dsl Holiday Inn Express Harley-Davidson, Walmart Dist Ctr
13	Washington Pkwy, E Maverik/dsl Black Bear Diner
10	Middleton Dr, Washington, E Phillips 66/dsl, Sinclair/dsl, USA Alvero's Mexican, Arby's, Arctic Circle, Benja's Thai, Bishop's Cafe, Buca Italian, Burger King, Costa Vida, Del Taco, Dickey's BBQ, Don Pedro's Mexican, El Pollo Loco, Freddy's, Hungry Howie's, IHOP, In-N-Out, Jack-in-the-Box, Jimmy John's, Little Caesar's, Mad Pita, McDonald's, Peppers Cantina, Pizza Factory, Pizza Hut, Qdoba, Red Robin, Royal Thai, Sonic, Subway, TX Roadhouse, Wendy's Country Inn&Suites, Quality Inn AAA, Albertsons/Sav-On, AutoZone, Barnes&Noble, Best Buy, Costco/gas, Dillard's, Discount Tire, Home Depot, JC Penney, Jo-Ann Fabrics, Kohl's, Natural Grocers, O'Reilly Parts, PetCo, Tunex, Verizon, vet, Walmart/Subway, W Chevron/dsl/LP, Texaco/dsl auto repair, St George RV Park/camping

INTERSTATE 15 Cont'd

ST GEORGE

Exit#	Services
8	St George Blvd, St George, E Chevron/Subway/dsl, Texaco/dsl Apollo Burger, Applebee's, Brick Oven, Buffalo Wild Wings, Carl's Jr, Chick-fil-A, Chick-fil-A, Chili's, Chipotle, Chuck-aRama, Coldstone, Firehouse Subs, Five Guys, Golden Corral, Habit Burger, Iggy's Grill, Jimmy John's, Mongolian BBQ, Olive Garden, Outback Steaks, Panda Express, Paradise Bakery & cafe, Red Lobster, Smashburger, Starbucks, Subway, Village Inn Rest., Winger's Best Inn, Courtyard, Hampton Inn, Ramada Inn, TownePlace Suites H, $Tree, AT&T, Dick's, Harmon's Foods, Lowe's, Old Navy, Petsmart, Ross, Staples, Sunrise Tire, Target, TJ Maxx, Tuesday Morning, Verizon, Zion Outlets/famous brands, W Conoco/dsl, Maverik, Shell/dsl, Sinclair/dsl, Texaco/dsl A&W/KFC, Burger King, Cafe Rio, Denny's, Iceberg Drive-In, Larsen's Drive-In, McDonald's, Ocean Buffet, Panda Garden, Papa John's, Port of Subs, Red Ginger Asian, Sakura Japanese, Taco Bell, Taco Time, Tropical Smoothie, Wendy's Best Western, Chalet Motel, Coronada Inn, Days Inn, EconoLodge, Economy Inn, Knights Inn, Motel 6, Rodeway Inn, Sands Motel, SunTime Inn, Super 8 Auto Tech/tires, Big O Tire, Desert Coach RV Ctr, NAPA, O'Reilly Parts, Rite Aid, to LDS Temple, vet
6	UT 18, Bluff St, St George, E Chevron/dsl/24hr, Sinclair/dsl, Texaco/dsl Cracker Barrel, Culver's, Jack-in-the-Box, Player's Grill, Rib Chop House, Subway Ambassador Inn, Comfort Inn, Fairfield Inn, Hilton Garden Buick/GMC, Hyundai, Kia, museum, Subaru, VW, W Shell, Texaco Arby's, Beijing Buffet, Black Bear Diner, Burger King, Denny's, Domino's, DQ, Jimmy John's, McDonald's, Pizza Hut, Ricardo's Rest., SF Pizza Best Value Inn, Best Western, Claridge Inn, Clarion Suites, Crystal Inn, Howard Johnson, Lexington Hotel, Quality Inn, St George Inn H, auto/truck repair, AutoZone, Big O Tire, Cadillac/Chevrolet, Camping World RV Ctr, Chrysler/Dodge/Jeep, Ford/Lincoln, funpark, Goodyear/auto, Honda, Mazda, Nissan, TempleView RV Park, Toyota, U-Haul
5	Dixie Dr
4	Brigham Rd, Bloomington, E Pilot/Burger King/dsl/scales/24hr La Quinta, W Chevron/Subway/Taco Time/dsl, USA/dsl Dickey's BBQ, Hungry Howie's, Peppers Cantina, Wendy's Wingate Inn Walmart/Subway
2	UT 7 E, Southern Pkwy, E , W Terrible Herbst/dsl Hampton Inn
1	Port of Entry/**weigh sta both lanes**
0mm	Utah/Arizona state line

INTERSTATE 70

GREEN RIVER

Exit#	Services
232mm	Utah/Colorado state line
227	Westwater
221	ranch exit
214	to Cisco
204	UT 128, to Cisco
193	Yellowcat Ranch Exit
190mm	**Welcome Ctr wb, full facilities, info, litter barrels, vending**
187	Thompson, N Exxon/7-11/dsl Ballard RV Park
185mm	**parking area eb**
182	US 191 S, Crescent Jct, to Moab, N Papa Joe's, S to Arches/Canyonlands NP
181mm	**eb, full facilities, litter barrels, scenic view**
175	ranch exit
164	UT 19, Green River, 1-3 mi N Phillips 66/Burger King/dsl, Pilot/Westwinds/rest/dsl/scales/24hr, Silver Eagle/Blimpie/dsl, Tesla EVC Tamarisk Rest. Best Value Inn, Comfort Inn, Continued Holiday Inn Express, Knights Inn, Motel 6, River Terrace Inn, Super 8 KOA, Powell River Museum, same as 160, tires/repair
160	UT 19, Green River, 0-2 mi N Chevron/Subway/dsl, Conoco/Arby's/dsl Cathy's Pizza, Chowhound, La Veracruzana, Ray's Rest. Budget Inn, Robbers Roost, Sleepy Hollow Motel Ace Hardware, city park, Green River SP, NAPA/repair, same as 164, Shady Acres RV Park, USPO
157	US 6 W, US 191 N, to Price, Salt Lake
149	UT 24 W, to Hanksville, to Capitol Reef, Lake Powell, Goblin Valley SP
146	restrooms wb, view area
144mm	**runaway truck ramp eb**
143mm	restrooms, view area both lanes
142mm	**runaway truck ramp eb**
138mm	**brake test area, restrooms eb**
131	Temple Mt Rd
122mm	Ghost Rock View Area both lanes, restrooms
116	to Moore, N view area both lanes
115	N view area eb
108	ranch exit
105mm	Salt Wash View Area both lanes
99	ranch exit
91	UT 10 N, UT 72, to Emery, Price, 12 mi N gas, S to Capitol Reef NP
86mm	**S both lanes, full facilities, litter barrels, petwalk**
73	ranch exit
63	Gooseberry Rd
56	US 89 N, to Salina, US 50 W, to Delta, NEXT SERVICES 109 MI EB, 0-1 mi N Conoco/dsl, Maverik/dsl, Phillips 66/Carl's Jr/dsl, Sinclair/Burger King/dsl Denny's, El Mexicano Mexican, Losta Motsa Pizza, Mom's Cafe, Subway EconoLodge, Rodeway Inn, Super 8 Barretts Foods, Butch Cassidy RV Camp, Family$, NAPA, Peterbilt, truck/RV/auto repair, S Loves/Arby's/dsl/scales/24hr
48	UT 24, to US 50, Sigurd, Aurora, 1-2 mi S gas food Capitol Reef NP, to Fishlake NF
40	Lp 70, Richfield, 0-2 mi S FLYING J/Pepperoni's/dsl/LP/rest./24hr, Chevron/dsl, Maverik/dsl, Texaco/dsl Arby's, Frontier Village Rest., Papa Murphy's, Subway, Taco Time Best Western, Budget Host, Days Inn/rest., Holiday Inn Express, Super 8 H, Big O Tire, Buick/Cadillac/Chevrolet/GMC, Chrysler/Dodge/Jeep, city park, Fresh Mkt, IFA Store, NAPA, RV/truck repair, USPO
37	Lp 70, Richfield, 1-2 mi S Phillips 66/Wendy's/dsl, Silver Eagle/Burger King/dsl Dickey's BBQ, KFC/Taco Bell, Little Caesar's, Lotsa Motsa Pizza, McDonald's, Pizza Hut, Steve's Steaks, Wingers Comfort Inn, Fairfield Inn, Hampton Inn, Motel 6, New West Motel, Quality Inn, Royal Inn $Tree, Ace Hardware, AutoZone, Ford, golf, Home Depot, KOA, O'Reilly Parts, Pearson Tire, st patrol, to Fish Lake/Capitol Reef Parks Verizon, Walmart/Subway
31	Elsinore, Monroe, S Silver Eagle/DQ/dsl
25	UT 118, Joseph, Monroe, S Flying U Country Store/dsl/RV park
23	US 89 S, to Panguitch, Bryce Canyon
17	N camping, chain-up area (WB), Fremont Indian SP, info museum,
13mm	**brake test area eb**
7	Ranch Exit
3mm	Western Boundary Fishlake NF
1	N Chevron/Subway/rest stop (2mi) Historic Cove Fort
0mm	I-15, N to SLC, S to St George.

I-70 begins/ends on I-15, exit 132.

INTERSTATE 80

Exit#	Services
197mm	Utah/Wyoming state line, Utah/Wyoming state line
191	Wahsatch
187	ranch exit
185	Castle Rock
182mm	Port of Entry/**weigh sta wb**
178	Emery (from wb)
170	**Welcome Ctr wb/ eb, full facilities, litter barrels, petwalk, , , RV dump, vending**
169	Echo
168	I-84 W, to Ogden, I-80 E, to Cheyenne
166	litter barrels, view area both lanes
162	Coalville, **N** Phillips 66/dsl/mart Best Western CamperWorld RV Park, Holiday Hills RV Camp/LP, **S** Chevron/dsl, Sinclair/dsl Polar King, Subway Griffith's Foods, NAPA, to Echo Res RA, USPO
155	UT 32 S, Wanship, **S** Sinclair/dsl to Rockport SP
150	**toll gate promontory**
146b a	US 40 E, to Heber, Provo, **N** Sinclair/Blimpie/Pizza Hut/dsl, **S** Phillips 66/7-11/dsl Burt Bros Tires, Home Depot
146	view area/**chain up wb**
145	UT 224, Kimball Jct, to Park City, **N** Chevrolet, Ford, Park City RV Park, vet, **S** Chevron/dsl Arby's, Cafe Rio, Coldstone, Del Taco, Five Guys, Freebirds Burrito, Ghidottis Italian, Great Harvest Bread Co, Jimmy John's, Loco Lizard Cantina, McDonald's, Panda Express, Papa John's, Pizza Hut, Red Rock Cafe, Ruby Tuesday, Starbucks, Subway, Szechwan Chinese, Taco Bell, Wendy's, Whole Foods Mkt Best Western, Hampton Inn, Holiday Inn Express Best Buy, Best Buy, GNC, Michaels, Outlet Mall/famous brands, Petco, RV camping, Smith's Foods/dsl, Staples, TJ Maxx, to ski areas, USPO, visitors info, Walmart
144mm	view area eb
141	ranch exit, **N** Phillips 66/Subway/dsl Burt Bros Tires, to Jeremy Ranch, **S** Billy Blanco Mexican camping, Fresh Mkt, ski area
140	Parley's Summit, Parley's Summit, **S** Sinclair/dsl No Worries Café
137	Lamb's Canyon
134	UT 65, Emigration Canyon, East Canyon, Mountaindale RA
133	utility exit (from eb)
132	ranch exit
131	(from eb) Quarry
130	I-215 S (from wb)
129	UT 186 W, Foothill Dr, Parley's Way, **N** H
128	I-215 S (from eb)
127	UT 195, 23rd E St, to Holladay
126	UT 181, 13th E St, to Sugar House, **N** Chevron A&W/KFC, Carl's Jr, Chick-fil-A, Olive Garden, Red Lobster, Sizzler, Taco Bell, Training Table, Wendy's Extended Stay America ShopKO, Verizon
125	UT 71, 7th E St, **N** Dee's Rest., Jimmy John's, Little Caesar's, Olympian Rest., Starbucks AT&T, Firestone, Pepboys
124	US 89, S State St, **N** 7-11 Astro Burgers, Burger King, Starbucks, Subway, Taco Bell Access RV Ctr, Chrysler/Dodge/Jeep, Discount Tire, vet, **S** A&W/KFC Ramada Inn
123mm	I-15, N to Ogden, S to Provo

KIMBALL JCT

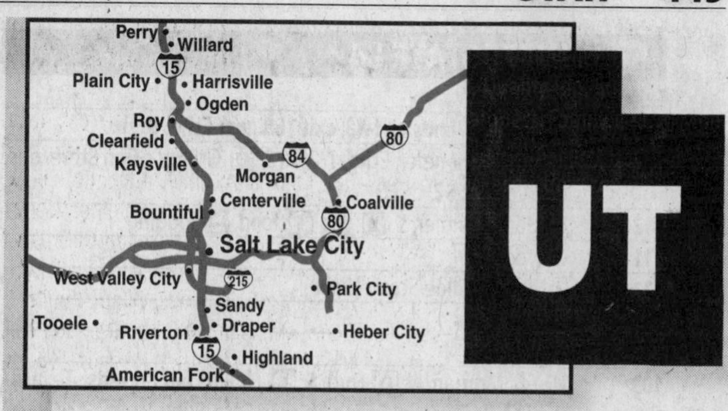

UT

I-80 and I-15 run together approx 4 mi. See I-15, exits 305-307.

Exit#	Services
121	600 S, to City Ctr
120	I-15 N, to Ogden
118	UT 68, Redwood Rd, to N Temple, **0-1 mi N on N Temple** Chevron/Subway/dsl, Loves/Arby's/dsl/scales/24hr, Shell/dsl A&W/KFC, Apollo Burger, Burger King, Carls Jr, Denny's, Taco Bell, Wendy's Airport Inn, Baymont Inn, Candlewood Suites, Comfort Suites, Holiday Inn Express, Motel 6, Radisson, Salt Lake Inn, **S** Maverik/dsl H
117	I-215, N to Ogden, S to Provo
115b a	Bangerter Hwy, **N** to Salt Lake Airport
114	Wright Bros Dr (from wb), **N** same as 113
113	5600 W (from eb), **N** Phillips 66/dsl Perkins, Port of Subs, Subway Comfort Inn, Courtyard, DoubleTree, Fairfield Inn, Hampton Inn, Hilton Garden, Holiday Inn, Homewood Suites, Hyatt Place, La Quinta, Microtel, Quality Inn, Ramada Inn, Residence Inn, SpringHill Suites, Super 8, Tru
111	7200 W
104	UT 202, Saltair Dr, to Magna, **N** beaches, Great Salt Lake SP
102	UT 201 (from eb), to Magna
101mm	view area wb
99	UT 36, to Tooele, **S** FLYING J/Denny's/dsl/scales/LP/24hr, Chevron/Subway/dsl, TA/Burger King/Taco Bell/dsl/scales/24hr/@, Texaco/dsl Del Taco, McDonald's Comfort Inn/Suites, Oquirrh Motel/RV Park H, SpeedCo
88	to Grantsville
84	UT 138, to Grantsville, Tooele
77	UT 196, to Rowley, Dugway
70	to Delle, **S** Delle/Tesoro/café/dsl
62	to Lakeside, Eagle Range, military area
56	to Aragonite
55mm	**both lanes, full facilities, litter barrels, petwalk, , , vending**
49	to Clive
41	Knolls
26mm	architectural point of interest
10mm	**both lanes, full facilities, litter barrels, observation area, petwalk, , , vending**
4	Bonneville Speedway, **N** Sinclair/dsl/café/24hr
3mm	Port of Entry, **weigh sta both lanes**
2	UT 58 (no EZ wb return), Wendover, **S** Shell/dsl, Sinclair/dsl Subway Best Western+, Bonneville Inn, Knights Inn, Motel 6, Nugget Hotel/casino, Quality Inn, Super 8, Western Ridge Motel auto repair, Carquest, Family$, KOA, Montego Bay Hotel/Casino, USPO
0mm	Utah/Nevada state line, Mountain/Pacific time zone

SALT LAKE CITY

UT

INTERSTATE 84

RIVERDALE

Exit#	Services
120	**I-84 begins/ends on I-80, exit 168 near Echo, Utah.**
115	Ut 65 S, to Henefer, Echo, **1/2 mi S** Grump's Gen Store/gas, to E Canyon SP, USPO
112	UT 86 E, Henefer, **S** gas food lodging
111	Croydon
111mm	Devil's Slide Scenic View
108	Taggart
106	ranch exit
103	UT 66, Morgan, **N** Ford, **S** Phillips 66/7-11/dsl, Texaco/dsl J's Drive-in, Spring Chicken Café, Subway Ace Hardware, city park, E Canyon SP, Family$, Ridley's Mkt, URGENT CARE, USPO
96	Peterson, **N** Sinclair/dsl (3mi) Nordic Valley Ski Areas, Powder Mtn, to Snow Basin, **S** Phillips 66/dsl
94mm	**wb, full facilities, litter barrels, petwalk,**
92	UT 167 (from eb), to Huntsville, **N** Sinclair/dsl (2mi) city park (2mi), to ski areas
91mm	**S eb, full facilities, litter barrels, petwalk,**
87b a	US 89, to Ogden, Layton, Ogden, **N** McDonald's (2mi), Wendy's (2mi) Best Western Cheese Outlet, Goodyear/auto, **S** to Hill AFB
85	S Weber, Uintah
81	to I-15 S, UT 26, Riverdale Rd, **N** Exxon/dsl, Sinclair/dsl Applebee's, Arby's, Bajio Grill, Buffalo Wild Wings, Carl's Jr, Chili's, Honeybaked Ham, IHOP, Jamba Juice, Lucky Buffet, McDonald's, Starbucks, Subway, Wendy's $Tree, Best Buy, Buick/GMC, Cadillac, Good Earth Foods, Gordman's, Harley-Davidson, Home Depot, Honda, Jo-Ann, Kia, Lowe's Whse, Mazda, Nissan, PepBoys, Petsmart, Sam's Club/gas, Schwab Tire, Target, Toyota, Verizon, Walmart/McDonald's, **S** Motel 6 Chrysler/Dodge/Jeep

I-84 and I-15 run together. See I-15 , exits 344 through 379.

Exit#	Services
41	I-15 N to Pocatello
40	UT 102, Tremonton, Bothwell, **N** Chevron/Poblano's/dsl/wash/24hr, Maverik/dsl, Sinclair/Burger King/dsl/scales/@, Tesla EVC Denny's, McDonald's, Wendy's Hampton Inn, Western Inn C&R Rv Ctr, H (4mi), O'Reilly Parts, RV/truck/tire repair, **S** to Golden Spike NHS
39	to Garland, Bothwell, **N** H
32	ranch exit
26	UT 83 S, to Howell, **S** to Golden Spike NHS
24	to Valley
20	to Blue Creek
17	ranch exit
16	to Hansel Valley (from wb)
12	ranch exit
7	Snowville, **N** FLYING J/Pepperoni's/dsl/LP/24hr, Sinclair/A&W/dsl Mollie's Café, Ranch House Diner Outsiders Inn city park, Lotti-Dell RV camping, USPO
5	UT 30, to Park Valley
0mm	Utah/Idaho state line

INTERSTATE 215

SALT LAKE CITY

Exit#	Services
29	**I-215 begins/ends on I-15.**
28	UT 68, Redwood Rd, **E** Pony Express RV Park, **W** FLYING J/Pepperoni's/dsl/LP/24hr/@, Maverik/dsl Lotus Chinese
26	Legacy Pkwy
25	22nd N
23	7th N, **E** Exxon/dsl, Loves/Arbys/dsl/scales/24hr (1.5 mi), Maverik Denny's, KFC, McDonald's, Papa Murphy's, Subway, Taco Bell, Wendy's Motel 6 $Tree, Family$, Super Saver Mkt, **W** Airport Inn, Baymont Inn, Candlewood Suites, Comfort Suites, Holiday Inn Express, Radisson
22b a	I-80, W to Wendover, E to Cheyenne
21	California Ave, **E** Sapp Bros/Sinclair/Burger King/dsl/@, Tesoro/7-11/dsl RV/Truckwash, **W** Chevron/dsl Port of Subs
20b a	UT 201, W to Magna, 21st S, **W** Maverik/dsl Del Taco Goodyear, Kenworth
18	UT 171, 3500 S, W Valley, **E** 7-11 Applebee's, Chili's, Costa Vida Mexican, Cracker Barrel, Greek Souvlaki, IHOP, Kowloon Cafe Baymont Inn, Country Inn Suites, Crystal Inn, Extended Stay America, Holiday Inn Express, La Quinta, Sleep Inn, Staybridge Suites H, PepBoys, **W** Cafe Rio, In-N-Out, Jimmy John's, Olive Garden, Pizza Hut, Red Robin, Smashburger, TGIFriday's, Wendy's, Winger's, Zupas Embassy Suites AT&T, Big O Tire, Costco/gas, CVS Drug, JC Penney, Office Depot, Petco, Ross, Staples, Verizon
15	UT 266, 47th S, **E** 7-11, Conoco/dsl Dee's Rest., KFC, Mad Greek, Pizza Hut, Taco Time, Village Inn, Wendy's Fresh Mkt, Goodyear/auto, Rite Aid, Walgreens, **W** Chevron/dsl Arby's, Arctic Circle, Tammie's Diner vet, Sinclair/dsl
13	UT 68, Redwood Rd, **E** Chevron, Shell/dsl Apollo Burger, Applebee's, Arby's, Burger King, Carl's Jr, City Buffet, Dickey's BBQ, Domino's, Francesco's Rest., Freebirds Burrito, Honey Baked Ham, McDonald's/playplace, Panda Express, Starbucks, Subway, TX Roadhouse Extended Stay America $Tree, AT&T, Harmon's Mkt, Jo-Ann Fabrics, PetsMart, Ross, ShopKO, Verizon, Walmart/McDonald's
12	I-15, N to SLC, S to Provo
11	same as 10 (from eb)
10	UT 280 E, **E** Tesoro Papa John's AutoZone, Sam's Club/gas, **W** A&W/KFC, Applebee's, Arby's, Braza Grill, Brio Grill, CA Pizza, Cheesecake Factory, ChuckARama, Corner Bakery Cafe, Jason's Deli, Macaroni Grill, McDonald's, Olive Garden, Panda Express, Red Lobster, Red Robin, RedRock Cafe, Starbucks, Subway, Taco Bell, Village Inn H, Dillard's, Firestone/auto, Honda, Marshalls, Midas, Nordstrom, Pepboys, ShopKO, Sprouts Mkt, Verizon
9	Union Park Ave, **E** Applebee's, Bucca Italian, Buffalo Wild Wings, Cafe Rio, Carl's Jr, Chick-fil-A, Chili's, Chipotle, Denny's, Dickey's BBQ, Famous Dave's BBQ, Firehouse Subs, Five Guys, Longhorn Steaks, Noodles&Co, Panda Express, Pei Wei, Smashburger, Subway, Wendy's Hawthorn Suites, Super 8 $Tree, Barnes&Noble, Dick's, GNC, Gordman's, Home Depot, Michaels, Old Navy, Petco, Ross, Smith's Foods, Target, T.Maxx, Verizon, Walmart/Subway, **W** Shell Crystal Inn Motel 6 Extended Firestone/auto, Office Depot
8	UT 152, 2000 E, **E** Chevron KFC, McDonald's, Sonic Taco Bell Whole Foods Mkt, **W** Phillips 66/dsl Subway, Wendy's Discount Tire
6	6200 S, **E** Jimmy John's, Luna Blanca, Pie Five, Starbucks Trio Cafe, Zupas Hyatt Place, Residence Inn Alta, Brighton, Snowbird, Solitude/ski areas
5	UT 266, 45th S (from sb), Holladay, **W** Sinclair
4	39th S, **E** Chevron/dsl, Sinclair/dsl Barbacoa Grill, Rock Mtn Pizza, Subway Ace Hardware, Dan's Mkt, **W** H
3	33rd S, Wasatch, **W** Smith's/dsl Cafe Rio, Five Guys, KFC Taco Bell, McDonald's, Shivers Burgers, Wendy's Petsmart REI, Smith's Mkt
2	I-80 W
0	**I-215 begins/ends on I-80, exit 130.**

VERMONT

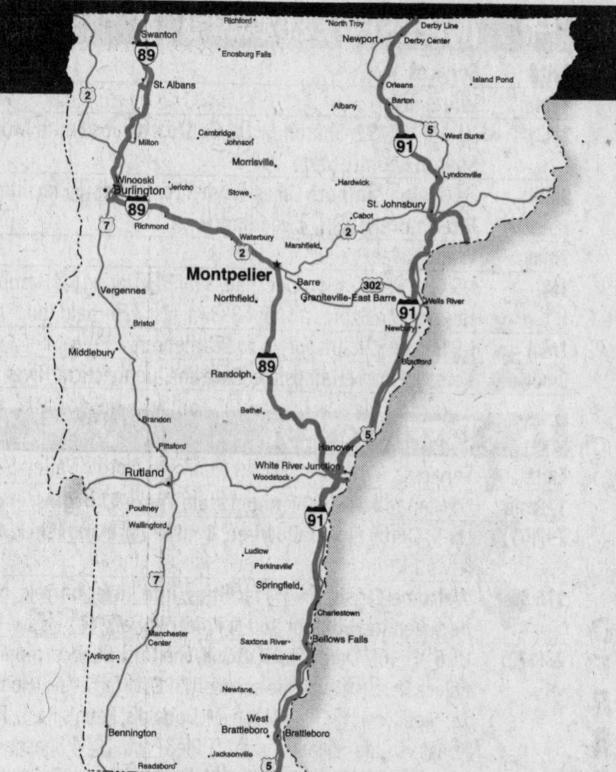

[N] INTERSTATE 89

ST ALBANS

Exit#	Services
130mm	US/Canada Border, Vermont state line, **I-89 begins/ends.**
22(129)	US 7 S, Highgate Springs, **E** [gas] Irving/dsl [other] DutyFree
129mm	Latitude 45 N, midway between N Pole and Equator
128mm	Rock River
21(123)	US 7, VT 78, Swanton, **E** [gas] Shell/dsl, **W** [gas] Mobil/Subway/dsl, Shell, Sunoco/dsl [food] Dunkin Donuts, McDonald's, Pam's Pizza, Shaggy's Snack Bar [other] Aubuchon Hardware, Hannaford Foods, NAPA
20(118)	US 7, VT 207, St Albans, **E** [other] Chevrolet, Toyota, **W** [gas] Mobil/Subway/dsl, Sunoco [food] Burger King, Dunkin Donuts, Hibachi Buffet, KFC/Taco Bell, McDonald's, Oriental Kitchen, Pizza Hut [other] [H], Advance Parts, AT&T, Aubuchon Hardware, Buick/GMC/Cadillac, Ford, Hannaford Foods, Jo-Ann Fabrics, Kinney Drug, PriceChopper Foods, Staples, TJ Maxx, Verizon, Walmart/Subway
19(114)	US 7, VT 36, VT 104, St Albans, **W** [gas] Mobil/dsl, Shell/dsl [food] Dunkin Donuts, Subway [lodging] La Quinta [other] [H], st police, vet
111mm	**[RS] both lanes, full [handicapped] facilities, info, litter barrels, petwalk, [phone], [picnic], vending, wifi**
18(107)	US 7, VT 104A, Georgia Ctr, **E** [gas] Mobil/dsl, Shell [food] GA Farmhouse Rest. [other] GA Auto Parts, Homestead RV Park, repair, USPO
17(98)	US 2, US 7, **E** [gas] Mobil, Shell/dsl [other] camping (4mi), **W** [other] camping (6mi), to NY Ferry, Lake Champlain Islands
96mm	**weigh sta both lanes**

BURLINGTON

Exit#	Services
16(92)	US 7, US 2, Winooski, **E** [gas] Mobil [food] Lighthouse Rest. [lodging] Hampton Inn [other] Costco, CVS Drug, Osco Drug, Shaw's Foods, **W** [gas] Citgo, Irving, Shell/dsl [food] Athens Diner, Burger King, Jr's Italian, McDonald's, Subway [lodging] Motel 6, Quality Inn
15(91)	VT 15 (from nb no return), Winooski, **E** [lodging] Days Inn, Handys Extended Stay Suites [other] to St Michael's Coll., **W** [gas] Mobil/dsl, Shell [other] USPO
90mm	Winooski River
14(89)	US 2, Burlington, **E** [gas] Gulf, Mobil, Shell/dsl, Sunoco, Valero [food] Al's Cafe, Applebee's, Chicken Charlie's, Dunkin Donuts, Hana Japanese, Leonardo's Pizza, McDonald's, Moe's SW Grill, Outback Steaks, Pulcinella's, Quiznos, Rotisserie, Starbucks, Subway, Trader Dukes, Wind Jammer Rest., Zachary's Pizza [lodging] Anchorage Inn, Best Western, Comfort Inn, DoubleTree Hotel, Holiday Inn, Homewood Suites, La Quinta [other] Aubuchon Hardware, Barnes&Noble, BonTon, Hannaford Foods, Healthy Living Mkt, JC Penney, Jo-Ann Fabrics, Kohl's, Midas, PriceChopper, Rite Aid, Trader Joe's, USPO, **W** [gas] Mobil/dsl, Shell [lodging] Sheraton [other] [H], Advance Parts, Michael's, PetCo, Staples, to UVT, Verizon
13(87)	I-189, to US 7, Burlington, **N** [gas] Citgo/dsl, Sunoco/dsl [food] Buffalo Wild Wings, China Express, Five Guys, Starbucks, Subway [other] $Tree, GNC, Hyundai/Subaru, Kinney Drug, PriceChopper Foods, Shaw's Foods, TJ Maxx, USPO, Walgreens, **2 mi W on US 7 S** [gas] Gulf, Irving, Mobil/dsl, Shell/dsl, Sunoco [food] Burger King, Chicago Grill, Denny's, Koto Japanese, Lakeview House Rest., McDonald's, Olive Garden, Panera Bread, Pauline's Cafe, Subway, Zen Garden [lodging] Comfort Suites, Ho-Hum Hotel, Holiday Inn Express, Maple Leaf Motel, North Star Motel, Travelodge [other] Acura/Audi/VW, Advance Parts, Buick/Cadillac/GMC, Chevrolet, Chrysler/Dodge, Ford, Hannaford Foods, Jeep, Lowe's, Nissan, Tire Whse, Toyota/Scion, URGENT CARE, Verizon, VW
12(84)	VT 2A, to US 2, to Essex Jct, Williston, **E** [gas] Mobil, Sunoco/Dunkin Donuts/dsl [food] 99 Rest., Chili's, Friendly's, Longhorn Steaks, Moe's SW Grill, Panera Bread, Starbucks, TX Roadhouse, VT Taphouse [lodging] Fairfield, TownePlace Suites [other] Best Buy, CVS Drug, Dick's, Hannaford Foods, Home Depot, Marshall's, Natural Provisions Mkt, Old Navy, Petsmart, Shaws Foods/Osco, st police, Staples, Verizon, Walmart, **W** [lodging] Courtyard, Residence Inn
82mm	**[RS] both lanes (7am-11pm), full [handicapped] facilities, litter barrels, petwalk, [phone], [picnic], vending, WiFi**
11(79)	US 2, to VT 117, Richmond, **W** [gas] Mobil/dsl
67mm	**parking area/weigh sta sb**
66mm	**weigh sta nb**

MONTPELIER

Exit#	Services
10(64)	VT 100, to US 2, Waterbury, **E** [gas] Mobil/dsl, Shell/dsl [food] Pizza Shoppe [lodging] Best Western/rest [other] Shaws Foods/Osco Drug, True-Value, **W** [gas] Citgo/dsl [food] Maxi's Rest., Zachary's Pizza [other] USPO
9(59)	US 2, to VT 100B, Middlesex, **W** [food] Red Hen Baking Co [other] museum, st police
8(53)	US 2, Montpelier, **1 mi E** [gas] Citgo, Gulf/dsl, Mobil, Shell/dsl, Shell/dsl [food] China Star, Dunkin Donuts, Julio's, Sarducci's Rest., Simply Subs, Village Pizza [lodging] Capitol Plaza Hotel [other] Aubuchon Hardware, Bond Parts, camping (6mi), Rite Aid, Shaw's Foods, Sunoco/repair, to VT Coll
7(50)	VT 62, to US 302, Barre, **E** [gas] Irving/dsl [food] Applebee's [lodging] Comfort Suites, Hilltop Inn [other] [H], camping (7mi), Honda, JC Penney, Shaw's Foods, Subaru, Toyota/Scion, Walmart
6(47)	VT 63, to VT 14, S Barre, **4 mi E** camping, food, gas, info, lodging
5(43)	VT 64, to VT 12, VT 14, Williamstown, **6 mi E** camping, food, gas/dsl, lodging, **W** to Norwich U
41mm	1752 ft, highest elevation on I-89
34.5mm	**weigh sta both lanes**
4(31)	VT 66, Randolph, **E** [other] RV camping (seasonal 1mi), **W** [gas] Mobil/dsl [food] lodging (3mi), McDonald's [other] [H], RV camping (5mi)
30mm	**parking area sb**
3(22)	VT 107, Bethel, **E** [gas] Mobil/dsl [food] Eaton's Rest., Village Pizza [other] to Jos Smith Mon (8mi), **1 mi W** [gas] Irving/dsl/LP [other] Rite Aid, st police, vet

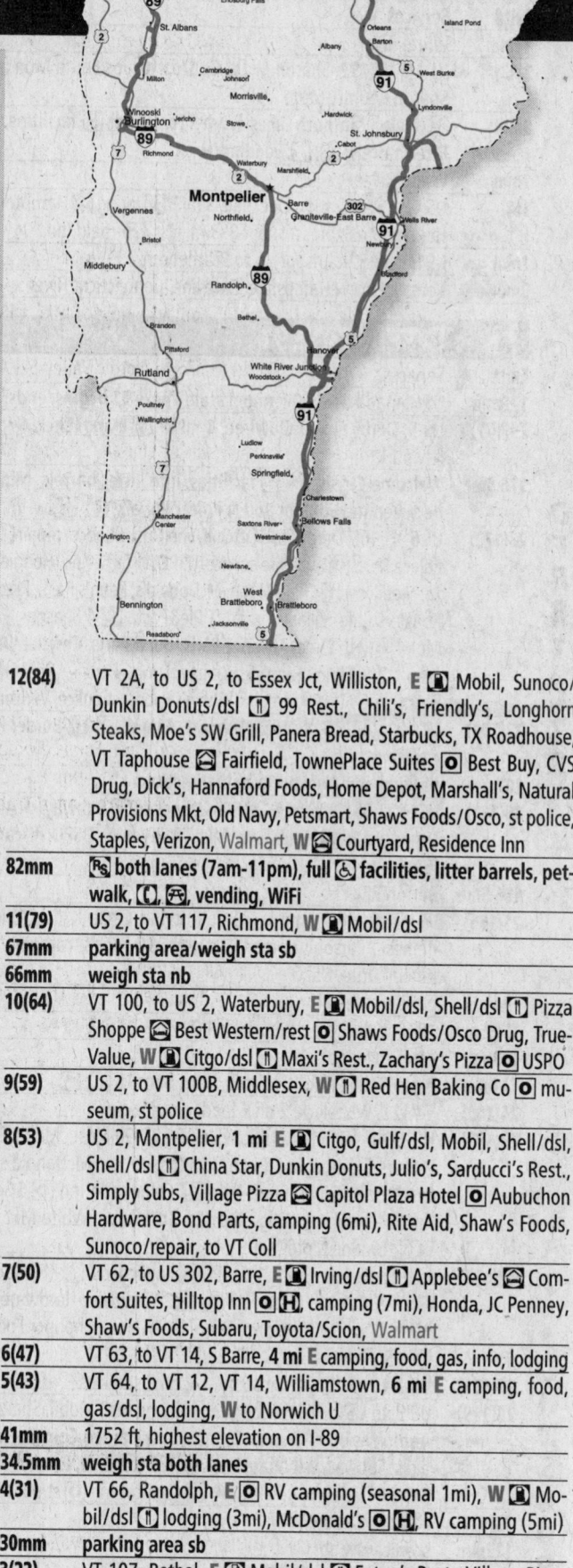

VT

= gas = food = lodging = other = rest stop

INTERSTATE 89 Cont'd

Exit#	Services
14mm	White River
2(13)	VT 14, VT 132, Sharon, W Gulf/dsl Jos Smith Mon (6mi), Sharon Country Store, USPO
9mm	**/weigh sta both lanes (7am-11pm), full facilities, info, litter barrels, , , vending, wi-fi**
7mm	White River
1(4)	US 4, to Woodstock, Quechee, **3 mi E** Irving Hampton Inn, Holiday Inn Express, Super 8, **3 mi N** Fairfield Inn
1mm	I-91, N to St Johnsbury, S to Brattleboro
0mm	Vermont/New Hampshire state line, Connecticut River

VT

INTERSTATE 91

DERBY CTR

Exit#	Services
178mm	US/Canada Border, Vermont state line, **I-91 begins/ends.**
29(177)	US 5, Derby Line, E Dutyfree, **1 mi W** Irving/Circle K/dsl city park
176.5mm	**Welcome Ctr sb, full facilities, info, litter barrels, Midpoint between the Equator and N Pole, petwalk, , , wi-fi**
28(172)	US 5, VT 105, Derby Ctr, E Gulf, Shell/dsl, Sunoco/repair Cow Palace Rest. auto/tire service, USPO, W Irving/Hoagie's Pizza, Mobil/dsl China Moon, McDonald's, Penn's Rest., Pizza Hut, Roasters Cafe, Village Pizza, VT Pie&Pasta 4 Seasons, Pepin's Motel H, $Tree, Advance Parts, Bond Parts, Chrysler/Dodge/Jeep, CVS Drug, Family$, Kinney Drug, Parts+, PriceChopper Foods, Rite Aid, RV camping, Shaw's Foods, st police, Verizon
27(170)	VT 191, to US 5, VT 105, Newport, **3 mi W** H, Border Patrol, camping, info
167mm	**parking area/weigh sta both directions**
26(161)	US 5, VT 58, Orleans, E Irving, Sunoco Subway Austin's Drugs, Family$, Thibaults Mkt, TrueValue, USPO, Wcamping (5mi)
156.5mm	Barton River
25(156)	VT 16, Barton, **1 mi E** Gulf, Irving/Circle K/dsl Ming's Chinese, Parson's Corner Rest. C&C Foods, camping (2mi), Kinney Drug, USPO
154mm	**parking area nb**
150.5mm	1856 ft, highest elevation on I-91
143mm	scenic overlook nb
141mm	**sb, full facilities, info, litter barrels, , **
24(140)	VT 122, Wheelock, **2 mi E** food, gas, lodging
23(137)	US 5, to VT 114, Lyndonville, E Gulf/dsl, Mobil/Dunkin Donuts Hoagie's Pizza, Lyndon Buffet, McDonald's, Miss Lyndonville Diner, Pizza Man Colonnade Inn $General, CarQuest, Kinney Drug, Rite Aid, TrueValue, White Mkt Foods, W Lyndon Motel
22(132)	to US 5, St Johnsbury, **1-2 mi E** Sunoco/dsl KFC/Taco Bell, Kham's Cuisine, Pizza Hut H, Aubuchon Hardware, Bond Parts, Buick/GMC, Kinney Drug, NAPA, PriceChopper Foods, repair, Subaru
21(131)	US 2, to VT 15, St Johnsbury, **1-2 mi E** services
20(129)	US 5, to US 2, St Johnsbury, E Irving/dsl, Mobil, Shell/dsl Anthony's Diner, Dunkin Donuts, East Garden Chinese, McDonald's, Subway, Winegate Rest. **welcome ctr,** Family$, Kevin's Repair, museum, Rite Aid, W Comfort Inn st police
19(128)	I-93 S to Littleton NH
122mm	scenic view nb
18(121)	to US 5, Barnet, E camping (5mi), W camping (5mi)
115mm	**parking area sb**
113mm	**parking area nb**
17(110)	US 302, to US 5, Wells River, NH, W P&H Trkstp/rest./dsl/scales/24hr camping (9mi), H (5mi)
100mm	**nb , full facilities, info, litter barrels, petwalk, , , sb parking area**
16(98)	VT 25, to US 5, Bradford, E Mobil/dsl/LP/café Hungry Bear Grill, Oasis Grill Bradford Motel Bond Parts, Family$, Hannafords Foods, Kinney Drug, NAPA, Pierson Farm Mkt, W st police
15(92)	Fairlee, E Gulf, Irving/dsl, Sunoco/dsl Fairlee Diner, Subway camping, USPO, Wings Mkt/deli, W golf
14(84)	VT 113, to US 5, Thetford, **1 mi E** camping, W camping
13(75)	US 5, VT 10a, Hanover, NH, E H, to Dartmouth, W Citgo Norwich Inn Rest. Subaru, USPO
12(72)	US 5, White River Jct, Wilder, E Gulf/dsl, Mobil
11(71)	US 5, White River Jct, E Mobil/dsl, Shell/Subway/dsl China Moon, Crossroads Country Café, McDonald's Comfort Inn Ford/Lincoln, Hyundai, Toyota, USPO, W Citgo, Irving/Dunkin Donuts, Sunoco/dsl Fairfield Inn, Hampton Inn, Holiday Inn Express, Super 8, White River Inn H
10N(70)	I-89 N, to Montpelier
10S	I-89 S, to NH,
68mm	**weigh sta both lanes**
9(60)	US 5, VT 12, Hartland, E H, W Mobil (1mi) Hartland Diner info
8(51)	US 5, VT 12, VT 131, Ascutney, E Citgo/dsl, Gulf/dsl, Irving/Circle K, Sunoco/Dunkin Donuts/dsl Ascutney House Rest., Mr G's Rest. Yankee Village Motel H, Getaway Camping (2mi), USPO, W auto repair/tires
7(42)	US 5, VT 106, VT 11, Springfield, W Irving/Circle K/Subway/dsl/scales/24hr Holiday Inn Express camping, H (5mi)
39mm	**weigh sta sb**
6(34)	US 5, VT 103, to Bellows Falls, Rockingham, E Shell/dsl Leslie's Rest. Rodeway Inn, W Sunoco/dsl st police (6mi)
5(29)	VT 121, to US 5, to Bellows Falls, Westminster, **3 mi E** food, gas, lodging,
24mm	**parking area both lanes**
22mm	**weigh sta sb**
20mm	**parking area nb**
4(18)	US 5, Putney, W Rod's/repair, Sunoco/dsl/LP/24hr Katy's Cafe, Putney Diner, Putney Food Coop/deli, Putney Village Pizza camping (3mi), Putney Gen Store/deli, USPO
3(11)	US 5, VT 9 E, Brattleboro, E Agway/dsl, Citgo/dsl, Mobil/dsl, Sunoco 99 Rest., China Buffet, Dunkin Donuts, Fast Eddy Cafe, House of Pizza, KFC, McDonald's, Panda North, Taco Bell, Thin Crust Pizzaria, Village Pizza, Wendy's Best Inn, Colonial Motel, Hampton Inn, Holiday Inn Express, Motel 6, Quality Inn, Super 8 Advance Parts, Aldi Foods, AT&T, Bond Parts, Buick/Chevrolet/GMC, Chrysler/Dodge/Jeep, Family$, Ford, GNC, Hannaford Foods, Rite Aid, Staples, Subaru, TrueValue, USPO, Verizon
2(9)	VT 9 W, to rd 30, Brattleboro, W VT Country Deli st police to Marlboro Coll
1(7)	US 5, Brattleboro, E Gulf/dsl, Irving/Circle K/dsl, Mobil, Dunkin Donuts, Shell/Subway/dsl Burger King, FC Chinese, Georgio's Pizza, VT Inn Pizza EconoLodge H, PriceChopper Foods, Rite Aid, to Ft Dummer SP, vet, Walgreens
6mm	**Welcome Ctr nb, full facilities, info, litter barrels, petwalk, , , playground, vending, wi-fi**
0mm	Vermont/Massachusetts state line

ST JOHNSBURY

BRATTLEBORO

INTERSTATE 93

See New Hampshire Interstate 93

VIRGINIA

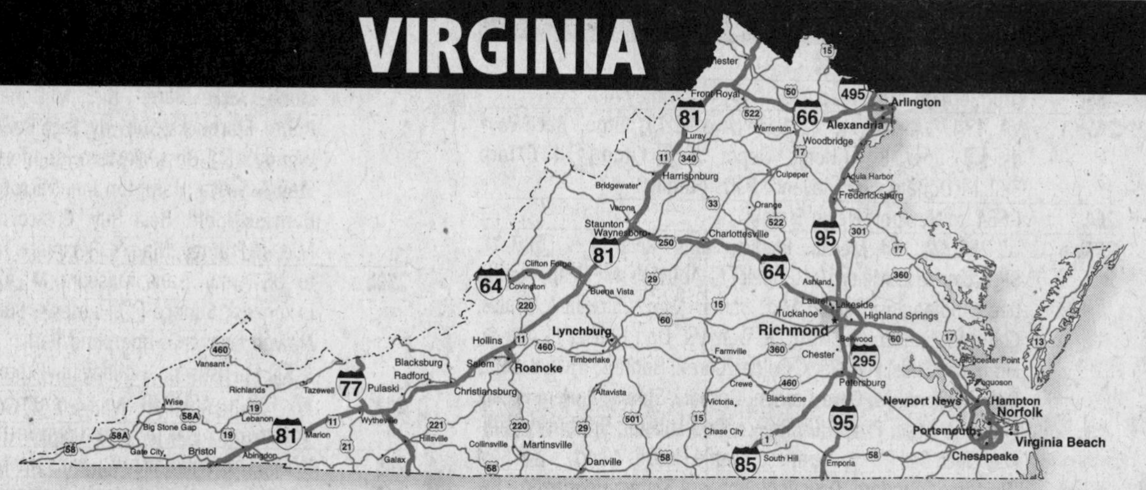

VA

NORFOLK

INTERSTATE 64

Exit#	Services
299b a	I-264 E, to Portsmouth. **I-64 begins/ends on I-264.**
297	US 13, US 460, Military Hwy, N 7-11, Exxon McDonald's, Papa John's
296b a	US 17, to Portsmouth, N 7-11 Hardee's, McDonald's, Papa John's, Pizza Hut, Subway, Zino's Cafe Comfort Inn $General, Food Lion, USPO, vet
294mm	S Br Elizabeth River
292	VA 190, to VA 104 (from eb, no EZ return), Dominion Blvd, S 7-11 #1 China, Burger King, Royal China, Subway Family$, Food Lion
291b a	I-464 N, VA 104 S, to Elizabeth City, Outer Banks, same services as 292
290b a	VA 168, Battlefield Blvd, to Nag's Head, Manteo, N Burger King Woodspring Suites $General, BigLots, Kroger, Merchant's Auto Ctr, NAPA, S 7-11, BP/DQ, Shell Applebee's, Baskin-Robbins, Burger King, Carrabba's, Chick-fil-A, ChuckECheese's, CookOut, Denny's, Dunkin Donuts, Five Guys, Golden Corral, Grand China Buffet, Hardee's, Hunan Wok, Jade Garden, Little Caesar's, Panda Express, Sonic, Starbucks, Taco Bell, TGIFriday's, Tropical Smoothie Café, TX Roadhouse, Waffle House, Wendy's, Wildwing Café Hampton Inn, InTown Suites, Quality Inn, Studios For Less H, $Tree, AT&T, Goodyear/auto, Home Depot, Kohl's, Lowe's, Nissan, Rite Aid, Sam's Club/gas, USPO, vet, Walgreens, Walmart
289b a	Greenbrier Pkwy, N 7-11, Citgo/dsl, WaWa/dsl Burger King, McDonald's, Subway, Taco Bell, Wendy's Extended Stay America, Hampton Inn, Holiday Inn Express, Marriott, Red Roof Inn, Staybridge Suites, Wingate Inn Acura, auto repair, Chevrolet, Chrysler/Jeep, Dodge, Ford, GMC, Hyundai, JoAnn Fabrics, Kia, Lincoln, Mazda, Toyota, U-Haul, vet, VW, S 7-11 Abuelo's Mexican, Baker's Crust, Boston Mkt, Buffalo Wild Wings, Chipotle, Coldstone, Cracker Barrel, Fazoli's, Firehouse Subs, Hooters, Jason's Deli, Jersey Mike's Subs, Jimmy John's, Joe's Crabshack, Kyoto Japanese, Los Burritos, McDonald's, Moe's SW, Olive Garden, Panera Bread, Pizza Hut, Pop's Diner, Qdoba, Red Robin, Ruby Tuesday, Smokey Bones BBQ, Starbucks, Subway, Tropical Smoothie, Zero's Subs, Zoe's Kitchen Aloft Hotel, Comfort Suites, Courtyard, Extended Stay, Fairfield Inn, Hilton Garden, Homewood Suites, Residence Inn, SpringHill Suites, Sun Suites AT&T, Barnes&Noble, Best Buy, Dillard's, Food Lion, Harris Teeter, Macy's, Marshall's, Michael's, Office Depot, Old Navy, Petsmart, Ross, Steinmart, Target, TJ Maxx, Verizon, Walgreens
286b a	Indian River Rd, N BP/dsl, Gulf, SkyMart/dsl, Speedway/dsl Dunkin Donuts, Golden China, Hardee's CVS, S Exxon/dsl CookOut, Ellen's BBQ, Oriental Cuisine, Oriental Cuisine, Waffle House 7-11
285mm	E Branch Elizabeth River
284a	I-264, to Norfolk, to VA Beach (exits left from eb)
284b	Newtown Rd
282	US 13, Northampton Blvd, N Citgo/dsl Krispy Kreme, McDonald's, Starbucks, Taco Bell, Wendy's Quality Inn, Sleep Inn to Chesapeake Bay Br Tunnel
281	VA 165, Military Hwy (no EZ eb return), N Shell/dsl EconoLodge Aamco, Chysler/Dodge/Jeep, Fiat, S 7-11, Citgo Burger King, Chick-fil-A, CookOut, Firehouse Subs, Hooters, IHOP, Jersey Mike's Subs, Jimmy John's, KFC, Little Caesar's, Logan's Roadhouse, Max&Erma's, Panera Bread, Qdoba, Ruby Tuesday, Sonic, Starbucks, Taco Bell, Wendy's Candlewood Suites, Days Inn, Doubletree, Hampton Inn, Holiday Inn, Holiday Inn Express, InTown Suites, La Quinta, Residence Inn BJ's Whse/dsl, FarmFresh Foods, Food Lion, GNC, Home Depot, Lowe's, Nissan, Pep Boys, Petco, Petsmart, Target, TJ Maxx, Verizon, Walgreens, Walmart/Subway
279	Norview Ave, N WaWa/dsl China House, Franco's Italian, Golden Corral, Pizza Hut, Wendy's $General, $Tree, 7-11/dsl, Food Lion, Tire City, to & botanical garden
278	VA 194 S (no EZ return)
277b a	VA 168, to Tidewater Dr, N 7-11, Shell Bojangles, Domino's, Fuddrucker's, Hardee's, Ruby Tuesday Advance Parts, Food Lion, Walmart/Subway, S Honda
276c	to US 460 W, VA 165, Little Creek Rd, (from wb only), N Race Coast/dsl, S BP, Shell Firehouse Subs, KFC, McDonald's, Moe's SW, Papa John's, Starbucks, Taco Bell, Wendy's AutoZone, FarmFresh Foods, GNC, Harris Teeter, Kroger, Rite Aid, USPO, Walgreens
276b a	I-564 to Naval Base (exits left from wb)
274	Bay Ave (from wb), S to Naval Air Sta
273	US 60, 4th View St, Oceanview, N 7-11/dsl Economy Inn, Motel 6 Oceanview Pier
272	W Ocean View Ave, N Willoughby Seafood, S Sunset Grill
270mm	Chesapeake Bay Tunnel
269mm	**weigh sta eb**
268	VA 169 E, to Buckroe Beach, Ft Monroe, N Citgo Hardee's, McDonald's, S to VA Air&Space Ctr
267	US 60, to VA 143, Settlers Ldg Rd, S Golden City Chinese, Subway, Tropical Smoothie H, to Hampton U

INTERSTATE 64 Cont'd

HAMPTON

Exit#	Services
265c	(from eb), to Armistead Ave, N to Langley AFB
265b a	VA 134, VA 167, to La Salle Ave, N Citgo, RaceWay/dsl Super 8 Home Depot, S Citgo KFC/Taco Bell, McDonald's Advance Parts, Family$
264	I-664, to Newport News, Suffolk
263b a	US 258, VA 134, Mercury Blvd, to James River Br, N 7-11, BP, Exxon/dsl, Miller's/dsl, Shell Abuelo's Mexican, Applebee's, Bojangles, Boston Mkt, Burger King, Chick-fil-A, Chili's, China Wok, Chipotle Mexican, Denny's, Dog House, El Azteca, Firehouse Subs, Five Guys, Golden Corral, Hooters, IHOP, Jason's Deli, McDonald's, Olive Garden, Outback Steaks, Panera Bread, Parklane Rest., Pizza Hut, Rally's, Red Lobster, Starbucks, Subway, Taco Bell, Tokyo Japanese, Waffle House, Wendy's Best Western, Courtyard, Days Inn, Embassy Suites, Holiday Inn Express, Quality Inn, Red Roof Inn $Tree, AT&T, Barnes&Noble, Chevrolet/Mazda, FarmFresh Foods, Food Lion, Ford, GNC, Goodyear/auto, JC Penney, Jo-Ann Fabrics, Marshall's, Michael's, NAPA, Nissan, Office Depot, PetCo, Ross, Target, U-Haul, USPO, Verizon, Volvo, Walgreens, Walmart, S Citgo/dsl, Miller's/dsl, WaWa/dsl Burritos Mexican, Chick-fil-A, CiCi's Pizza, Coldstone, Cracker Barrel, Domino's, Dunkin Donuts, Joe's Crabshack, La Parrilla, Little Caesar's, Longhorn Steaks, Pizza Hut, Rita's, Sonic, Steak'n Shake, Waffle House, Zaxby's Ambassador Inn Suites, Hilton Garden, InTown Suites, Relax Inn, SpringHill Suites 7-11, Aamco, Advance Parts, BassPro Shop, BigLots, BJ's Whse/Subway/gas, CVS Drug, Dollar General, Firestone/auto, Lowe's, Office Depot, PepBoys, Toyota, Walmart Mkt
262	VA 134, Magruder Blvd (from wb, no EZ return), N 7-11, Exxon Country Inn&Suites, Suburban Lodge Audi, Hyundai, Mercedes
261b a	Center Pkwy, to Hampton Roads, N Candlewood Suites, Hampton Inn (2mi), S 7-11, Shell Anna's Italian, ChuckECheese's, Fortune Garden Chinese, Gus's NY Pizza, McDonald's, Peking Chinese, Pizza Hut/Taco Bell, Plaza Azteca, Ruby Tuesday, Subway $Tree, FarmFresh Foods, Food Lion, GNC, Rite Aid, TJMaxx
258b a	US 17, J Clyde Morris Blvd, N BP, Shell/dsl Domino's, New China, Waffle House BudgetLodge, Country Inn&Suites, Holiday Inn Express, Host Inn, PointPlaza Hotel, Quality Inn 7-11, Advance Parts, Family$, Food Lion, S Kangaroo, WaWa/dsl Angelo's Steaks, Burger King, DQ, KFC/Taco Bell, McDonald's, Papa John's, Starbucks, Subway, Vinny's Pizza, Wendy's Motel 6 H, museum, Rite Aid, Subaru, VW
256b a	Victory Blvd, Oyster Point Rd, N Kangaroo/dsl, Murphy USA/dsl Arby's, Burger King, Chick-fil-A, China Ocean, Hardee's, McDonald's, Panda Express, Pizza Hut, Ruby Tuesday, Saisaki Asian, Sonic, Starbucks, Subway, Three Amigos Mexican, TX Roadhouse, Uno Grill CandleWood Suites, Courtyard, Hampton Inn, Hilton Garden, Staybridge Suites, TownePlace Suites $Tree, FarmFresh Foods, GNC, Goodyear/auto, Kroger, Walgreens, Walmart, S Crestwood Suites, Jameson Inn
255b a	VA 143, to Jefferson Ave, N Exxon/dsl, Shell/dsl Chili's, CookOut, Donato's Pizza, Firehouse Subs, Five Guys, Golden Corral, HoneyBaked Ham, Hooters, Jason's Deli, Longhorn Steaks, McDonald's, Moe's SW Grill, Olive Garden, Panera Bread, Papa John's, Red City Buffet, Red Lobster, Smokey Bones BBQ, Sonic, Starbucks Comfort Suites H, Acura, Buick/Cadillac/GMC, Chrysler/Dodge/Jeep, FarmFresh Foods/deli, Fiat, GNC, Home Depot, Kohl's, Lowe's, Michael's, PetCo, Ross, Sam's Club/gas, TJ Maxx, Trader Joe's, Tuesday Morning,

WILLIAMSBURG

Exit#	Services
255b a	Continued Walgreens, Walmart, S Applebee's, Buffalo Wild Wings, Carrabba's, Cheddar's, Chick-fil-A, Chipotle Mexican, Coldstone, Cracker Barrel, KFC, McDonald's, Outback Steaks, Red Robin, Starbucks, Subway, Taco Bell, TGIFriday's, Waffle House, Wendy's Best Western, Comfort Inn, Courtyard, Extended Stay America, Hampton Inn, Microtel, Residence Inn 7-11, Barnes&Noble, Best Buy, Costco/dsl, Dick's, Dillard's, Fresh Mkt, JC Penney, Macy's, Petsmart, Target, Verizon, World Mkt
250b a	to US Army Trans Museum, N 7-11/gas, Dodge's Store, Exxon/dsl, Sunoco Hardee's, Subway B&L Auto Repair, Newport News Campground/Park (1mi), to Yorktown Victory Ctr, S Ft Eustis Inn, Holiday Inn Express, Mulberry Inn 7-11
247	VA 143, to VA 238 (no EZ return wb), N 7-11/gas to Yorktown, S to Jamestown Settlement
243	VA 143, to Williamsburg, exits left from wb, S same as 242a
242b a	VA 199, to US 60, to Williamsburg, N Wyndham Garden Best Buy, Dick's, Kohl's, Target, to Yorktown NHS, water funpark, 1 mi S 7-11/gas, Sunoco, WaWa/dsl China's Cuisine, Doraldo's Italian, KFC, McDonald's, Sportsmans Grille, Starbucks, Subway, Taco Bell, Wendy's, Whaling Co Rest. Country Inn&Suites, Courtyard, Quality Inn Busch Gardens, to Jamestown NHS, to William&Mary Coll
238	VA 143, to Colonial Williamsburg, Camp Peary, **2-3 mi** S **on US 60** Exxon/7-11, Shell Aberdeen Barn Rest., Applebee's, Arby's, Chili's, Chipotle Mexican, Cracker Barrel, DQ Firehouse Subs, Five Guys, Golden Corral, Hooters, IHOP, Jefferson Steaks, KFC, Kyoto, McDonald's, Outback Steaks, Pancake House, Pizza Hut, Plaza Azteca, Red Hot&Blue, Sal's Rest. Seafare Rest., Smokehouse Grill, Subway, Taco Bell, Uno Grille Wendy's Best Inn, Best Western, Comfort Inn, Country Inn&Suites, Days Inn, EconoLodge, Embassy Suites, Fairfield Inn Hampton Inn, Hampton Inn, Hilton Garden, Holiday Inn Express Holiday Inn/rest., Homewood Suites, La Quinta, Quality Inn Residence Inn, Sleep Inn, SpringHill Suites, Travelodge H Anvil Camping (4mi), CVS Drug, Goodyear/auto
234	VA 646, to Lightfoot, **1-2 mi** N KOA, **2-3 mi** S Exxon dsl, Shell/dsl Burger King, Chick-fil-A, China Wok, Hardee's, IHOP, McDonald's, Sonic, Starbucks, Subway Great Wolf Lodge, Holiday Inn Express, Super 8 H, $Tree, Ford Home Depot, Lowe's, PetCo, Ross, Toyota, USPO, Walmart, Williamsburg Campark
231b a	VA 607, to Norge, Croaker, N 7-11/gas to York River SP, **1-3 mi S on US 60** Shell/dsl Candle Light Kitchen, China Star, Daddy-O's Pizza, Jimmy's Grill, Pizza Hut EconoLodge American Heritage RV Park, CVS Drug, FarmFresh Deli/gas, Food Lion, Honda, Hyundai, USPO
227	VA 30, to US 60, to West Point, Toano, S Shell/dsl, Sta Subway/dsl McDonald's
220	VA 33 E, to West Point, N Mobil/dsl
214	VA 155, to New Kent, Providence Forge, S Exxon/DC dsl Antonio's Pizza, Tops China
213mm	**both lanes, full facilities, litter barrels, petwalk,** vending
211	VA 106, to Talleysville, to James River Plantations, S Loves/Arby's/dsl/scales/24hr, Pilot/Subway/dsl/scales 24hr Burger King
205	VA 33, VA 249, to US 60, Bottoms Bridge, Quinton, N Exxon/dsl, Star Express, Valero Julio's Mexican, Maria's Italian, Panda Garden, Pizza Hut, Subway, Wendy's Food Lion, Verizon, S FasMart, Shell/dsl Bojangle's, McDonald's Food Lion, Rite Aid

INTERSTATE 64 Cont'd

Exit#	Services
204mm	Chickahominy River
203mm	**weigh sta both lanes**
200	I-295, N to Washington, S to Rocky Mount, to US 60
197b a	VA 156, Airport Dr, to Highland Springs, **N** [gas] Shell/dsl, Valero [food] Antonio's Pizza, Domino's, Hardee's, Subway, Tops China [other] $General, 7-11, Advance Parts, CVS Drug, Farmers Foods, **S** [gas] BP, Chubby's/dsl, Shell/7-11, WaWa [food] Arby's, Burger King, Mexico Rest., Pizza Hut, Roberto's Italian, The Patron, Waffle House [lodging] All Day Inn, Best Value Inn, Courtyard, EconoLodge, Hampton Inn, Hilton Garden, Holiday Inn, Holiday Inn Express, Homewood Suites, Microtel, Motel 6, Quality Inn, Red Roof Inn, Super 8 [other] to [airport]
195	Laburnum Ave, **N** [other] auto repair, **S** [gas] 7-11, Exxon, WaWa/dsl [food] Applebee's, Capt D's, Chick-fil-A, China King, CiCi's Pizza, CookOut, Cracker Barrel, Firehouse Subs, Five Guys, Hardee's, IHOP, KFC, Little Caesar's, Longhorn Steaks, McDonald's, Olive Garden, Panera Bread, Papa John's, Popeye's, Qdoba Mexican, Red Lobster, Steak'n Shake, Subway, Taco Bell, TGIFriday's, Wendy's [lodging] Hyatt Place, Sheraton [other] $General, $Tree, AT&T, CarQuest, CVS Drug, GNC, JC Penney, Kroger, Lowe's, Michael's, Petsmart, Publix, Target, Walgreens
193b a	VA 33, Nine Mile Rd, **N** [gas] Exxon/Subway/dsl, Sunoco/dsl [other] PepBoys, **S** [other] [hospital]
192	US 360, to Mechanicsville, **N** [gas] Exxon/dsl, Shell [food] McDonald's [other] Tuffy Repair, **S** [gas] Shell, Valero
190	I-95 S, to Petersburg, 5th St. **S** [lodging] Hilton, Marriott [other] coliseum, st capitol
I-64 and I-95 run together, see VA I-95 exits 76-78.	
187	I-95 N (exits left from eb), to Washington.
186	I-195, to Powhite Pkwy, from wb, Richmond
185b a	US 33, Staples Mill Rd, Dickens Rd
183c	from wb, US 250 W, Broad St, Glenside Dr N, same as exit 183
183b a	US 250, Broad St E, Glenside Dr S., **N** [gas] Sheetz/dsl [food] McDonald's, Mission BBQ, Nanking, Olive Garden, Subway, Taco Bell, TGIFriday's, Waffle House [lodging] Best Western, Econolodge/Rodeway, Embassy Suites, Hampton Inn, Knights Inn, Residence Inn, Super 8, Woodspring Suites [other] AutoZone, Honda, vet, Volvo, **S** [food] Chipotle, Denny's, Jersey Mike's, O'Charley's, Plaza Azteca, Starbucks [lodging] Candlewood Suites, Courtyard, Westin [other] [hospital], Aldi Foods, Home Depot, Target, to U of Richmond, vet, Walmart
181b a	Parham Rd, **N** [gas] Citgo, Exxon [other] Chrysler/Dodge/Jeep
180	Gaskins Rd, **N** [gas] BP, Shell/dsl [food] Applebee's, Coldstone, Cracker Barrel, Dickey's BBQ, Golden Corral, IHOP, Kickback Jack's Rest., McDonald's, O'Charley's, Pizza Hut, Starbucks, Subway, Taco Bell [lodging] 7-11, Exxon, Fairfield Inn, Holiday Inn Express, Mapco, SpringHill Suites [other] $Tree, Advance Parts, AutoZone, Costco/gas, Goodyear/auto, Kroger/gas, Lowe's, Martin's Foods, Mazda, Michael's, Sam's Club/gas, Tesla
178b a	US 250, Broad St, Short Pump, **N** [gas] 7-11, Exxon, Wawa/dsl [food] Blaze Pizza, BurgerWorks, Capital Alehouse, Chipotle Mexican, Corner Bakery Cafe, DQ, Dunkin Donuts, Firehouse Subs, Five Guys, Hondo's Rest., Joey's Hotdogs, Leonardo's Pizza, Moe's SW Grill, Noodles, Panera Bread, Potbelly, Silver Diner, Starbucks, Taziki's [lodging] Comfort Suites, Courtyard, Extended Stay America, Hampton Inn, Hilton Garden, Homestead Suites, Hyatt Place, Residence Inn [other] CarMax, CVS Drug, Firestone/auto, Ford, Marshall's, Ross, Verizon, **S** [gas] 7-11, Shell [food] Arby's, Bertucci's, BJ's Rest., Bonefish Grill, Buffalo Wild Wings, Burger King, Capt D's, Carolina Alehouse, Carrabba's, Cheesecake Factory,

RICHMOND

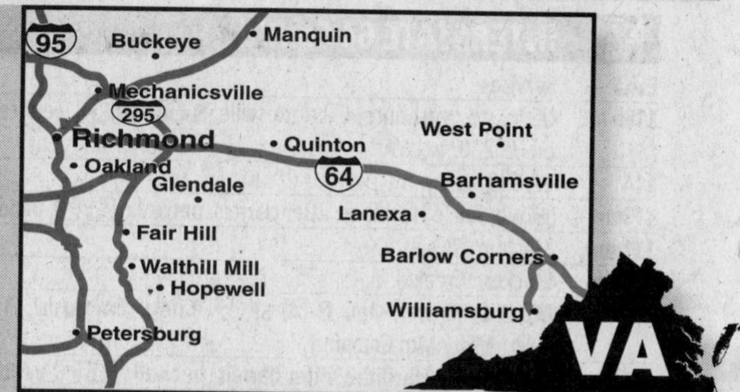

Exit#	Services
178b a	Continued Chick-fil-A, Chili's, Chipotle Mexican, Chuy's Mexican, Dave&Buster's, Domino's, Genghis Grill, HoneyBaked Ham, Jason's Deli, Jersey Mike's Subs, Jimmy John's, Kanpai, KFC, Kona Grill, LJSilver, Longhorn Steaks, Maggiano's Italian, McDonald's, Olive Garden, Panda Express, Panera Bread, Plaza Azteca, Qdoba, Shula's Steaks, Sonic, Starbucks, Taco Bell, TGIFriday's, Wendy's [lodging] Candlewood Suites, Hilton, Hyatt House, Wingate Inn [other] $Tree, AT&T, Barnes&Noble, Best Buy, Buick/Chevrolet/GMC, CarQuest, Dick's, Dillard's, GNC, Hobby Lobby, Home Depot, Kohl's, Kroger, Lowe's, Macy's, Martin's Foods, Nissan, Nordstrom, NTB, Petco, Petsmart, REI, Staples, Steinmart, Target, Tom Leonard's Mkt, Trader Joe's, Verizon, Walmart, Whole Foods Mkt, World Mkt
177	I-295, to I-95 N to Washington, to Norfolk, VA Beach, Williamsburg
175	VA 288, Chesterfield
173	VA 623, to Rockville, Manakin, **0-2 mi S** [gas] Exxon/dsl, Shell/dsl, Valero/Subway/dsl [food] McDonald's, Sunset Grill, Taco Bell [other] $General, Food Lion, vet
169mm	**[rest stop] both lanes, full [handicapped] facilities, litter barrels, petwalk, [phone], [picnic], vending**
167	VA 617, to Goochland, Oilville, **N** [gas] Exxon/dsl, **S** [gas] BP/dsl
159	US 522, to Goochland, Gum Spring, **N** [gas] Exxon/dsl, **S** [gas] BP/DQ/dsl, Citgo
152	VA 629, Hadensville, **1 mi S** [gas] BP, Liberty
148	VA 605, Shannon Hill
143	VA 208, to Louisa, Ferncliff, **N** [other] Small Country Camping (7mi), **S** [gas] Citgo/dsl, Exxon/dsl
136	US 15, to Gordonsville, Zion Crossroads, **N** [gas] Sheetz/dsl [food] Arby's, Dunkin Donuts, IHOP, Lelo's Pizza, Popeye's, Subway, Taco Bell, Wendy's [lodging] Best Western+ [other] Advance Parts, Lowe's, Verizon, Walmart, **S** [gas] BP/McDonald's/dsl/24hr, Exxon/Burger King/dsl, Shell/dsl/scales [food] Crescent Rest.
129	VA 616, Keswick, Boyd Tavern
124	US 250, to Shadwell, **2 mi N** [gas] BP, Exxon, Mobil/dsl, Shell, Speedway [food] Applebee's, Bojangle's, Burger King, Chick-fil-A, Chipotle, Dunkin Donuts, Guadalajara Mexican, Hardee's, Jersey Mike's, Jimmy John's, McDonald's, Shadwell's Rest., Starbucks, Taco Bell, TipTop Rest., Wendy's [lodging] Hilton Garden [other] [hospital], Audi/VW, BMW, CarMax, Ford, Giant Foods, Kia, Mercedes, Porsche, Rite Aid, Toyota, **S** [lodging] Comfort Inn
123mm	Rivanna River
121	VA 20, to Charlottesville, Scottsville, **N** [gas] BP/dsl, **S** [other] KOA (10mi), to Monticello
120	VA 631, 5th St, to Charlottesville, **N** [gas] Exxon/dsl, Sunoco/dsl [food] Burger King, Domino's, Hardee's, Subway, Taco Bell, Waffle House [lodging] Holiday Inn, Sleep Inn [other] CVS Drug, Family$, Food Lion

RICHMOND

CHARLOTTESVILLE

VA

VA

WAYNESBORO

LEXINGTON

COVINGTON

INTERSTATE 64 Cont'd

Exit#	Services
118b a	US 29, to Lynchburg, Charlottesville, N H, services N on US 220, to UVA
114	VA 637, to Ivy
113mm	**wb, full facilities, litter barrels, petwalk, vending**
111mm	Mechum River
108mm	Stockton Creek
107	US 250, Crozet, **1mi** N BP/dsl, Citgo, Exxon/dsl, **1 mi** S Misty Mtn Camping
105mm	**eb, full facilities, litter barrels, petwalk, vending**
104mm	scenic area eb, litter barrels, no truck or buses
100mm	scenic area eb, hist marker, litter barrels, no truck or buses
99	US 250, to Waynesboro, Afton, N Colony Motel Skyline Drive, to Blue Ridge Pkwy, to Shenandoah NP, S Afton Inn
96	VA 622, to Lyndhurst, Waynesboro, **3 mi** N Shell, Speedway Quality Inn Waynesboro Camping
95mm	South River
94	US 340, to Stuarts Draft, Waynesboro, N 7-11/dsl, Exxon/dsl Applebee's, Buffalo Wild Wings, Cracker Barrel, Five Guys, Golden Corral, KFC, Outback Steaks, Panera Bread, Pizza Hut, Plaza Azteca, Ruby Tuesday, Silk Road Rest., Sonic, Starbucks, Waffle House, Wendy's Best Western+, Comfort Inn, Days Inn, Holiday Inn Express, Residence Inn, Super 8 H, Home Depot, Lowe's, Martin's Food/gas, Verizon, vet, Walmart, Waynesboro N 340 Camping (9mi), S Mobil/dsl Chick-fil-A, McAlister's Deli, McDonald's Aldi Foods, AT&T, Books-A-Million, GNC, Kohl's, Michael's, Petsmart, Ross, Target
91	Va 608, to Stuarts Draft, Fishersville, N Citgo/Subway (1mi), Shell/dsl Hampton Inn H, Eaver's Tires, S Sheetz/dsl McDonald's, Wendy's Shenadoah Acres Camping (8mi), Walnut Hills Camping (9mi)
89mm	Christians Creek
87	I-81, N to Harrisonburg, S to Roanoke
	I-64 and I-81 run together 20 miles. See I-81, exits 195-220.
55	US 11, to VA 39, N Exxon Burger King, Crystal Chinese, Naples Pizza, Ruby Tuesday, Waffle House Best Western+, Sleep Inn, Super 8, Wingate Inn $Tree, Ford, Lowe's, Stonewall Jackson Museum, Verizon, Walmart, S Marathon/7-11/Subway, Mobil/DQ/dsl Applebee's, Country Cookin Best Western, Comfort Inn, Country Inn&Suites, Holiday Inn Express, Motel 6
50	US 60, rd 623, to Kerrs Creek, Lexington
43	rd 780, to Goshen
35	VA 269, rd 850, Longdale Furnace
33mm	**truck eb**
29	VA 269, VA 42 E, S Sunoco/dsl
27	US 60 W, US 220 S, VA 629, Clifton Forge, N to Douthat SP, S BP/dsl, Exxon Bella Pizza, Pizza Hut (2mi) CVS Drug, Family$, Kroger
24	US 60, US 220, Clifton Forge, **1 mi** S Shell/dsl DQ, Hardee's auto repair
21	to rd 696, Low Moor, N Loves/McDonald's/Subway/dsl/scales/24hr, S Exxon Penny's Diner Travelodge H
16	US 60 W, US 220 N, to Hot Springs, Covington, N BP/Subway/dsl, Exxon/dsl, Shell Burger King, Cucci's, San Juan Mexican, Western Sizzlin Best Value Inn, Hampton Inn, Magnuson Hotel, Pinehurst Hotel to ski area, S McDonald's Compare Inn, Taco Bell
14	VA 154, to Hot Springs, Covington, N Citgo, Exxon/Arby's KFC, LJ Silver, Subway, Wendy's $General, Advance Parts,
14	Continued AutoZone, CVS Drug, Family$, Food Lion, URGENT CARE, Verizon, S Applebee's, China House, Trani's Grille $Tree, Chevrolet, Walmart
10	US 60 E, VA 159 S, Callaghan, S Marathon/dsl/LP
7	rd 661
2.5mm	**Welcome Ctr eb, full facilities, litter barrels, no trucks, petwalk,**
1	Jerry's Run Trail, N to Allegheny Trail
0mm	Virginia/West Virginia state line

DC AREA

INTERSTATE 66

Exit#	Services
77mm	Constitution Ave, to Lincoln Mem. **I-66 begins/ends in Washington, DC.**
76mm	Potomac River, T Roosevelt Memorial Bridge
75	US 50 W (from eb), to Arlington Blvd, G Wash Pkwy, I-395, US 1 S Iwo Jima Mon
73	US 29, Lee Hwy, Key Bridge, to Rosslyn, N Marriott S Holiday Inn
72	to US 29, Lee Hwy, Spout Run Pkwy (from eb, no EZ return) N Shell Virginia Inn, S Starbucks, Tarbouch Gri CVS Drug, Giant Foods, Walgreens
71	VA 120, Glebe Rd (no EZ return from wb), N H S Sunoco Booeymonger Grill, IHOP, Melting Pot, P Chang's Comfort Inn, Holiday Inn
69	US 29, Sycamore St, Falls Church, N Exxon/7-11, S EconoLodge vet
68	Westmoreland St (from eb), same as 69
67	to I-495 N (from wb), to Baltimore, Dulles Airport
66b a	VA 7, Leesburg Pike, to Tysons Corner, Falls Church, N Exxon, Sunoco China King, Jason's Deli, Ledo Pizza, Noodles& Co, Starbucks, Subway, Tara Thai 7-11, Trader Joe's, Verizon, Whole Foods Mkt, S Citgo Baja Fresh, Domino's Jimmy John's, McDonald's, Starbucks, Subway CVS Drug Giant Foods, GNC, Kia, Staples, vet, Volvo
64b a	I-495 S, to Richmond
62	VA 243, Nutley St, to Vienna, S Citgo Baja Fresh, Domino's, McDonald's, Starbucks, Subway CVS Drug, Michael' Safeway Foods/gas, Walgreens
60	VA 123, to Fairfax, S Exxon, Shell, Sunoco 29 Dine Denny's, Freddy's Steakburgers, Fuddruckers, Hooters, McDonald's, Outback Steaks, Panera Bread, Papa John's, Red Lobste Smashburger, Subway Best Western, Hampton Inn, Holiday Inn Express, Residence Inn Chevrolet, CVS Drug, Ki Mazda, Rite Aid, Subaru, to George Mason U, Toyota
57b a	US 50, to Dulles Airport, N Brio Tuscan, Cheesecake Factory Extended Stay America, Marriott access to same 55, JC Penney, Lord&Taylor, Macy's, S BP, Shell/dsl Ch potle, Chuy's, Jimmy John's, McDonald's, Wendy's Comfo Inn/rest., Courtyard, SpringHill Suites AT&T, Ford, Gia Foods, Honda, Nissan, NRA Museum, VW/Volvo, Walmart
55	Fairfax Co Pkwy, to US 29, N Exxon, Sunoco Applebe Blue Iguana Café, Burger King, Cantina Italiana, Chick-fil-A, C potle, Dunkin Donuts, Guapo's, Jason's Deli, Jersey Mike's, Jo Crabshack, Logan's Roadhouse, McDonald's, Noodles&Co, O ive Garden, Pizza Hut, Red Robin, Starbucks, Subway, Taco B Wendy's Hyatt Regency, Residence Inn H, Best B BJ's Whse/gas, Dick's, Fair Oaks Mall, GNC, Kohl's, Michae Petsmart, Target, Verizon, Walmart, Whole Foods Mkt, World M
53b a	VA 28, to Centreville, S same as 52, Dulles Airport, Manass Museum

INTERSTATE 66 Cont'd

Exit#	Services
52	US 29, to Bull Run Park, Centreville, N Sunoco/dsl Bull Run Park/RV Dump, Goodyear/auto, S Exxon, Sunoco/dsl Charlie Chang's, Dickey's BBQ, Five Guys, IHOP, My Thai, Pancho Villa, Panda Express, Pizza Hut, Starbucks, Subway $Tree, Advance Parts, AT&T, Giant Foods, SpringHill Suites, Trader Joe's, USPO, vet, Walgreens
49mm	**both lanes, full (facilities) facilities, litter barrels, petwalk,**
47b a	VA 234, to Manassas, N Shell/dsl Cracker Barrel, Golden Corral, Jerry's Subs, Uno, Wendy's Courtyard, Holiday Inn Express, La Quinta, Wyndham Garden Duluth Trading Co, Kohl's, Manassas Nat Bfd, Old Navy, S 7-11, BP, Exxon, RaceWay/dsl, Shell/repair, Sunoco Arby's, Baja Fresh, Bob Evans, Burger King, Cafe Rio, Checker's, Chick-fil-A, Chili's, China Palace, Chipotle Mexican, ChuckECheese's, CiCi's, City Grille, Coldstone, Denny's, Domino's, DQ, Dunkin Donuts, Firehouse Subs, Food Lion, Great American Buffet, Hibachi Buffet, Hooters, IHOP, Jersey Mike's, Jimmy John's, KFC, Logan's Roadhouse, McDonald's, Olive Garden, Panda Express, Panera Bread, Papa John's, Pizza Hut, Pollo Campero, Popeye's, Potbelly's, Red Hot&Blue BBQ, Red Lobster, Starbucks, Subway, Subway, Taco Bell, TGIFriday's, Wendy's Best Western, Comfort Suites, Days Inn, Hampton Inn, Holiday Inn, Quality Inn, Red Roof Inn, Residence Inn, Woodspring Suites $Tree, Advance Parts, Aldi Foods, AT&T, AutoZone, Barnes&Noble, Best Buy, Buick/GMC, Burlington Coats, Chevrolet, Costco/gas, CVS Drug, Dick's, Family$, Giant Foods, GNC, Home Depot, Honda, Lowe's, Macy's, Marshall's, Merchant Auto Ctr, Michael's, Mr Tire, NTB, Office Depot, PepBoys, Petsmart, Reines RV Ctr, Ross, Shopper's Foods, Staples, Toyota, Tuesday Morning, URGENT CARE, Verizon, vet, Walgreens, Walmart
44	VA 234 S, Manassas, S to Bristoe Sta Bfd SP
43b a	US 29, to Warrenton, Gainesville, S 7-11, BJ's/gas, Sunoco/dsl, WaWa BJ's Rest, Burger King, Chick-fil-A, Chili's, Chipotle, Coldstone, Domino's, Famous Dave's, Firebirds Grill, Five Guys, Grafton St Rest., IHOP, Joe's Pizza/Subs, KFC, McDonald's, MOD Pizza, Out of the Blue Seafood, Panera Bread, PeiWei, Potbelly, Qdoba, Smashburger, Starbucks, Subway, Taco Bell, Uncle Julio's Hampton Inn, SpringHill Suites, Woodspring Suites Advance Parts, Best Buy, Cabela's, CVS Drug, Giant Food/drug, GNC, Lowe's, Petsmart, Piedmont Tire/auto, Target, Verizon, Walgreens
40	US 15, Haymarket, N Greenville Farms Camping (5mi), H, S Sheetz/dsl Burapa Cafe, Chick-fil-A, Foster's Grill, Giuseppe's Italian, Little Caesar's, McDonald's, Papa John's, Penn Sta Subs, Starbucks, Subway, Young Chow Cafe CVS Drug, Food Lion, Kohl's, Verizon, Walmart
31	VA 245, to Old Tavern, **1 mi** N Sunoco/dsl USPO
28	US 17 S, Marshall, N BP/McDonald's/dsl Anthony's Pizza, Foster's Grille, Great Wall Chinese, Old Salem Cafe, Subway Food Lion, vet
27	VA 55 E, Rd 647, Marshall, **1 mi** N Citgo/dsl, Exxon/dsl/LP Marshall Diner
23	US 17 N, VA 55, Delaplane (no re-entry from eb)
20mm	Goose Creek
18	VA 688, Markham
13	VA 79, to VA 55, Linden, Front Royal, S 7-11/dsl, Exxon/dsl Applehouse Rest./BBQ/gifts Skyline Drive, to Shenandoah NP
11mm	Manassas Run
7mm	Shenandoah River
6	US 340, US 522, to Winchester, Front Royal, N 7-11, Mobil/7-11/dsl Applebee's, Checkers, China City Buffet, Cracker Barrel, IHOP, Ledo Pizza, Los Potrillos, McAlister's Deli, Mikado, Panda Express, Roy Rogers, Starbucks, TGIFriday's, Tropical Cafe TownePlace Suites $Tree, Aldi Foods, AT&T, Buick/GMC, Ford, GNC, Lowe's, PetCo, Staples, Target, URGENT CARE, Walmart, S 7-11, Exxon/Dunkin Donuts/Subway, Shell McDonald's Hampton Inn Poe's Southfork Camping (2mi)
1b a	I-81, N to Winchester, S to Roanoke
0mm	**I-66 begins/ends on I-81, exit 300.**

INTERSTATE 77

Exit#	Services
67mm	Virginia/West Virginia state line, East River Mtn
66	VA 598, to East River Mtn
64	US 52, VA 61, to Rocky Gap
62	VA 606, to South Gap
62mm	**Welcome Ctr sb, full facilities, info, litter barrels, petwalk, , , vending**
59mm	**nb, full facilities, litter barrels, petwalk, , , vending**
58	US 52, to Bastian, E BP/Front Porch Cafe/dsl, W Exxon/Circle K, Loves/Arby's/dsl/scales/24hr
56mm	**runaway ramp nb**
52	US 52, VA 42, Bland, E Sunoco Subway $General, W Circle K/DQ/dsl Big Walker Motel
51.5mm	**weigh sta both lanes**
48mm	Big Walker Mtn
47	VA 717, **6 mi** W to Deer Trail Park/NF Camping
41	VA 610, Peppers Ferry, Wytheville, E Sagebrush Steaks Best Western, Sleep Inn, Super 8, W Exxon/dsl/scales/24hr, TA/BP/Country Pride/Popeye's/Subway/Taco Bell/dsl/scales/24hr/@ Southern Diner Comfort Suites, Country Inn&Suites, Fairfield Inn, Hampton Inn, Ramada Inn, Tru Hilton
40	I-81 S, to Bristol, US 52 N
	I-77 and I-81 run together 9 mi. See I-81, exits 73-80.
32	I-81 N, to Roanoke
26mm	New River
24	VA 69, to Poplar Camp, E New River Trail Info Ctr, to Shot Tower HP, W Circle K/Subway/dsl
19	VA 620, W
14	US 58, US 221, to Hillsville, Galax, E Mobil/Subway Peking Palace Red Carpet Inn H, LakeRidge RV Resort (14mi), W BP, Exxon/dsl, Gulf/dsl/24hr McDonald's, Pizza Inn, Shoney's, TCBY, Wendy's Comfort Inn, Hampton Inn, Holiday Inn Express, Motel 6, Quality Inn, Super 8 Carrollwood Camping, Chevrolet

INTERSTATE 77 Cont'd

Exit#	Services
8	VA 148, VA 775, to Fancy Gap, E Gulf Fancy Gap Cafe (2mi) Lakeview Motel/rest., Mountain Top Motel $General, Chance's Creek RV Ctr, KOA (2mi), to Blue Ridge Pkwy, USPO, W BP/dsl, Exxon/Circle K/dsl Countryview Inn, Scottish Inn
6.5mm	runaway truck ramp sb
4.5mm	runaway truck ramp sb
3mm	runaway truck ramp sb
1	VA 620, E Loves/McDonald's/Subway/dsl/scales/24hr
.5mm	Welcome Ctr nb, full facilities, info, litter barrels, petwalk,
0mm	Virginia/North Carolina state line

INTERSTATE 81

Exit#	Services
324mm	Virginia/West Virginia state line
323	rd 669, to US 11, Whitehall, E Exxon, W FLYING J/Denny's/Subway/dsl/LP/scales/24hr
321	rd 672, Clearbrook, E Citgo/Old Stone Cafe/dsl Woolen Mills Grill
320mm	Welcome Ctr sb, full facilities, litter barrels, petwalk, vending
317	US 11, Stephenson, E Chick-fil-A, Guan's Garden, Las Trancas, McDonald's, Subway, Tropical Smoothie Café, TX Roadhouse AT&T, Lowe's, Petsmart, Target, Verizon, W Exxon/Dunkin Donuts/dsl, Sheetz, Shell/7-11/Burger King, Sunoco/dsl Denny's, Pizza Hut/Taco Bell Comfort Inn, EconoLodge, Holiday Inn Express (3mi) H, Candy Hill Camping
315	VA 7, Winchester, E Exxon, Sheetz/dsl Bamboo Garden, Ledo's Pizza, Little Caesars, Sonic, Starbucks, Waffle House TownePlace Suites $Tree, Chrysler/Dodge/Jeep, GNC, Goodyear/auto, Martin's Foods/gas, PetCo, URGENT CARE, Walgreens, W Exxon/Dunkin Donuts/Subway, Liberty/dsl, Shell/dsl 5 Guys Burgers, Apple Blossom Diner, Arby's, Camino Real Mexican, KFC, McDonald's, NIK Italian, Pizza Hut, Wendy's Hampton Inn, Winchester Inn AutoZone, CVS Drug, Family$, Food Lion, Food Maxx, Sharp Shopper Mkt, TrueValue
314mm	Abrams Creek
313	US 17/50/522, Winchester, E Exxon/Baskin-Robbins/Dunkin Donuts/Subway, Liberty/dsl, Mobil/7-11/dsl, Shell/dsl Apple Valley Diner, Chinatown, Cracker Barrel, Golden Corral, Hibachi Grill, IHOP, Los Tolteco's Mexican, TX Steaks, Umberto's Pizza Aloft Hotel, Candlewood Suites, Fairfield Inn, Holiday Inn, Red Roof Inn, Sleep Inn, Super 8, Travelodge BigLots, Costco/gas, Food Lion, Jo-Ann Fabrics, Nissan, vet, W Sheetz/dsl Bob Evans, Buca Italian, Chili's, China Jade, China Wok, Chipotle Mexican, ChuckECheese's, CiCi's, Coldstone, Dickey's BBQ, Five Guys, Glory Days Grill, Ichiban Japanese, Jimmy John's, KFC, Longhorn Steaks, McDonald's, Okinawa Steaks, Olive Garden, Panera Bread, Perkins, Rancho Mexican, Red Lobster, Roy Rogers, Ruby Tuesday, Subway, Taco Bell, TGIFriday's, Waffle House, Wendy's Best Western, Hampton Inn, Hilton Garden, Wingate Inn $Tree, AT&T, Belk, Best Buy, Books-A-Million, Dick's, Hobby Lobby, Home Depot, JC Penney, Kohl's, Lowe's, Martin's Foods, Merchants Tire, Michael's, Old Navy, PepBoys, Petsmart, Ross, Staples, Target, TJ Maxx, to Shenandoah U, URGENT CARE, Verizon, Walgreens, Walmart

WINCHESTER

Exit#	Services
310	VA 37, to US 50W, W Citgo/dsl, Shell/7-11/dsl Carrabba's, McDonald's, Outback Steaks, Subway Country Inn&Suites H, Aldi Foods, Camping World, Candy Hill Camping (6mi), CarQuest, Honda, Volvo, VW
307	VA 277, Stephens City, E Liberty/dsl, Shell/Burger King/dsl, Shell/Subway/dsl Arby's, China House, Del Rio Mexican, Domino's, Ginger Asian, KFC/Taco Bell, McDonald's, Pizza Hut, Roma Italian, Waffle House, Wendy's Comfort Inn, Holiday Inn Express $General, 7-11, Advance Parts, AutoZone Food Lion, Martin's Foods/gas, Rite Aid, Verizon, W Exxon/Dunkin Donuts, Sheetz/dsl
304mm	weigh sta both lanes
302	rd 627, Middletown, E Exxon/dsl, W 7-11, Liberty/dsl McDonald's Econolodge $General, to Wayside Theatre
300	I-66 E, to Washington, Shenandoah NP, Skyline Dr
298	US 11, Strausburg, E Exxon/McDonald's/dsl/LP, Shell/7-11 dsl Anthony's Pizza, Arby's, Burger King, Castiglia Italian Ciro's Pizza, Denny's, Golden China, Great Wall Buffet Fairfield Inn, Ramada Inn Advance Parts, Family$, Food Lion Verizon, W Battle of Cedar Grove Camping, to Belle Grove Plantation
296	US 48, VA 55, Strausburg, E museums
291	rd 651, Toms Brook, E Budget Inn (3mi), W Loves/Arby's/dsl/scales/24hr, Pilot/DQ/Subway/dsl scales/24hr truckwash/repair
283	VA 42, Woodstock, E Liberty/7-11, Sheetz, Shell/Dunkin Donuts Arby's, Burger King, China Wok, KFC, Las Trancas, McDonald's, Pizza Hut, Taco Bell, Tony's Pizza, Wendy's Comfort Inn, Hampton Inn, Holiday Inn Express H CVS Drug, Family$, Food Lion, Rite Aid, to Massanutten Military Academy, W Exxon/dsl, Sunoco China Wok, Cracker Barrel, Domino's, Paisano's Pizza, Subway $Tree, Ford Lowe's, NAPA Care, Walmart
279	VA 185, rd 675, Edinburg, E Exxon/dsl, Shell/dsl Sal Italian Bistro auto repair, Creekside Camping (2mi), USPO
277	rd 614, Bowmans Crossing
273	VA 292, RD 703, Mt Jackson, E 7-11, Exxon/dsl, Liberty/dsl/scales/24hr, Sheetz/dsl/scales/24hr Burger King, Chi King, Denny's, Italian Touch, Subway Motel 6 $General, Food Lion, to Mt Jackson Hist Dist, USPO
269	rd 730, to US 11, Shenandoah Caverns, E Shell/dsl W Shenandoah Valley Camping
269mm	N Fork Shenandoah River
264	US 211, New Market, E Exxon/Subway/dsl, Liberty/dsl Mobil/dsl, Shell/dsl Appleseed's Rest., Burger King, Italian Job, McDonald's Quality Inn Endless Caverns Camping Skyline Dr, to Shenandoah NP, W 7-11 Days Inn New Market Bfd SHP
262mm	[RS] both lanes, full facilities, litter barrels, petwalk, vending
257	US 11, VA 259, to Broadway, 3-5 mi E Liberty/7-11/Burger King/dsl Endless Caverns Camping, KOA
251	US 11, Harrisonburg, W Exxon/dsl, Pilot/Subway/dsl scales/24hr Economy Inn
247b a	US 33, Harrisonburg, E Citgo/dsl, Exxon/dsl, Royal/dsl Sheetz/dsl, Shell/dsl, Walmart Applebee's, Aroma Buffet Bob Evans, Bravo Italian, Bruster's, Buffalo Wild Wings, Burger King, Chick-fil-A, Chili's, Chipotle, CiCi's Pizza, Cook Out, Domino's, Dunkin Donuts, El Charro Mexican, Firehouse Subs, Five Guys, Franco's Pizza, Golden Corral, Great Wok, IHOP, Jess' Lunch, Jimmy John's, McAlister's Deli, McDonald's, O'Charley's

WOODSTOCK

VA

HARRISONBURG

INTERSTATE 81 Cont'd

247b a Continued
O'Neill's Grill, Outback Steaks, Panera Bread, Qdoba, Quaker Steak&Lube, Red Lobster, Ruby Tuesday, South Fork BBQ, Subway, Taco Bell, Tilted Kilt, TX Roadhouse, Waffle House, Wendy's, Which Wich?, Wood Grill Buffet Best Western, Candlewood Suites, Comfort Inn, Courtyard, Doubletree, EconoLodge, Fairfield Inn, Hampton Inn, Motel 6, Quality Inn, Residence Inn, Sleep Inn $Tree, AT&T, Barnes&Noble, Belk, Best Buy, Books-A-Million, Cadillac/Chevrolet, Costco/gas, Dick's, Firestone/auto, Home Depot, JC Penney, Kohl's, Kroger, Lowe's, Martin's Foods/gas, Michael's, Nissan, Old Navy, PetCo, Petsmart, Ross, Staples, Target, TJ Maxx, to Shenandoah NP, to Skyline Dr, Tuesday Morning, URGENT CARE, Verizon, Walmart/McDonald's, **W** Exxon/dsl, Liberty/dsl, Royal/dsl, Sheetz/dsl Arby's, Ciro's Pizza, DQ, Dragon Palace, Golden China, Hardee's, KFC, Kyoto, L'Italia, Little Caesars, McDonald's, Papa John's, Sam's Hotdogs, Subway Advance Parts, BigLots, CVS Drug, Family$, Food Lion, URGENT CARE

245 VA 659, Port Republic Rd, **E** Campus Corner, Exxon/dsl, Liberty/dsl, Royal/dsl China Express, Corgan's Publick House, El Charro, McDonald's, Subway, Tropical Smoothie, Vito's Italian Days Inn H, CVS Drug, Food Lion, **W** Asian City, Jimmy John's, Starbucks to James Madison U

243 US 11, to Harrisonburg, 0-2 mi **W** Exxon/dsl, Harrisonburg Travel Ctr/diner/dsl/scales, Liberty, Sheetz/dsl, Shell/7-11/dsl Burger King, Cracker Barrel, Griddle&Grill, McDonald's, Pano's Rest., Pizza Hut, Subway, Taco Bell Country Inn Suites, Hampton Inn, Holiday Inn Express, Microtel, Motel 6, Ramada Inn, Super 8 $General, Advance Parts, AutoZone, CarMax, Family$, Ford, Honda, Hyundai, Kia, Lincoln, Subaru, Toyota, USPO

240 VA 257, rd 682, Mount Crawford, **E** Shell/7-11/dsl McDonald's, **W** Exxon/Burger King/dsl (1mi)

235 VA 256, Weyers Cave, **E** Shell/dsl, **W** BP/Subway/dsl, Exxon/dsl Freightliner, to Grand Caverns

232mm **both lanes, full facilities, litter barrels, petwalk, , vending**

227 rd 612, Verona, **E** BP/Subway/dsl Waffle Inn, **W** 7-11/Wendy's, Exxon, Shell/dsl Burger King, Ciro's Pizza, Hardee's, McDonald's Knights Inn $General, antiques, Food Lion, Good Sam RV Park (3mi), Rite Aid

225 VA 262, Woodrow Wilson Pkwy, **E** Motel 6, **W** Days Inn, Holiday Inn/rest.

STAUNTON

222 US 250, Staunton, **E** BP, Royal/dsl Cracker Barrel, Hometown Grill, McDonald's, Mrs Rowe's Rest., TX Steaks Best Western, Red Roof Inn, Sleep Inn, **W** Sheetz, Speedway/dsl Baskin-Robbins/Dunkin Donuts, Burger King, Chili's, Country Cookin, Firehouse Subs, KFC, Massaki Japanese, Pizza Hut, Starbucks, Waffle House Comfort Inn, EconoLodge American Frontier Culture Museum, AT&T, auto repair, AutoZone, Lowe's, Martin's Foods/gas, Toyota, URGENT CARE, Walmart/Subway

221 I-64 E, to Charlottesville, Skyline Dr, Shenandoah NP

220 VA 262, to US 11, Staunton, 1 mi **W** Citgo, Exxon, Shell A&W/LJ Silver, Applebee's, Arby's, Burger King, CiCi's Pizza, El Puerto, Jimmy John's, Kathy's Rest., Kline's Dairy Bar, Maria's Italian, McDonald's, Papa John's, Red Lobster, Sam's HotDogs, Sauced Grill, Subway, Taco Bell, Wendy's Budget Inn, Hampton Inn $General, $Tree, Advance Parts, Belk, Buick/GMC, Cadillac/Chevrolet, Chrysler/Dodge/Jeep, CVS Drug, Food Lion, Ford/Lincoln, Harley-Davidson, Honda, Hyundai,

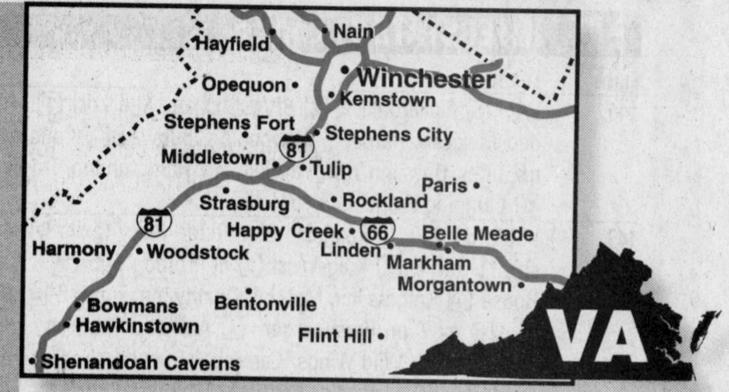

220 Continued
JC Penney, Kia/Mazda, Kroger/dsl, Nissan, NTB, Obaugh RV Ctr, Petco, Staples, Subaru, TJ Maxx, Verizon, vet, VW

217 Rd 654, to Mint Spring, Stuarts Draft, **E** GB/dsl Days Inn, **W** Exxon/Circle K/dsl/24hr, Liberty/LP Relax Inn KOA

213b a US 11, US 340, Greenville, **E** BP/Subway, Loves/McDonalds/dsl/scales/24hr, Pilot/Arby's/scales/dsl/24hr, Shell Edelweiss Rest. Hometowne Inn KOA (3mi)

205 Rd 606, Raphine, **E** BP/dsl, Exxon/Burger King/dsl, Fuel City/Smiley's BBQ/dsl/24hr, Petro/Iron Skillet/Papa John's/Popeye's/Subway/dsl/scales/24hr/@ Blue Beacon, **W** Pilot/Wendy's/dsl/scales/24hr Comfort Inn/rest. Peterbilt

200 RD 710, Fairfield, **E** BP/McDonald's/dsl, Pure Frank's Pizza, **W** Exxon/Subway/dsl, Shell/dsl

199mm **sb, full facilities, litter barrels, petwalk, , , vending**

LEXINGTON

195 US 11, Lee Hwy, **E** Maple Hall Country Inn, **W** Exxon/dsl, TA/Shell/IHOP/dsl/scales/24hr/@ Days Inn, Howard Johnson, Quality Inn Lee-Hi Camping, repair

191 I-64 W (exits left from nb), US 60, to Charleston

188b a US 60, to Lexington, Buena Vista, 3-5 mi **E** BP, Exxon Burger King, Hardee's Buena Vista Inn $General, Family$, Food Lion, to Blue Ridge Pkwy, to Glen Maury Park, to Stonewall Jackson Home, **W** Exxon/dsl, Exxon/McDonald's/dsl Hardee's, Pizza Hut, Taco Bell Hampton Inn H, Food Lion, Marshall Museum, to Washington&Lee U, VMI

180 US 11, Natural Bridge, (180a exits left from sb), **E** Relax Inn Cave Mtn NF, Jellystone Camping, **W** Shell/dsl Pink Cadillac Diner Budget Inn KOA

175 US 11 N, to Glasgow, Natural Bridge, **E** Exxon Natural Bridge Hotel/rest. (2mi) Jellystone Camping (6.5mi), to James River RA

168 VA 614, US 11, Blue Ridge Pkwy, Arcadia, **E** Shell/dsl Mtn View Rest. Wattstull Inn Middle Creek Camping (6mi), 2 mi **W** Exxon Burger King

167 US 11 (from sb), Buchanan

162 US 11, Buchanan, **E** Exxon/dsl to BR Pkwy, **W** Citgo/Subway

158mm **sb, full facilities, litter barrels, petwalk, , , vending**

156 RD 640, to US 11, **E** Exxon/Brugh's Mill/dsl

150 US 11/220, to Fincastle, **E** Circle K/dsl/24hr, Dodge's/dsl, Pilot/Subway/dsl/24hr Angelle's Diner, Bella Pizza, Country Cookin, Cracker Barrel, Hardee's, McDonald's, Shoney's, Taco Bell Comfort Inn, Holiday Inn Express, Motel 6, Quality Inn, Red Roof Inn $General Mkt, Berglund RV Ctr, truckwash, **W** BP/dsl, Exxon/dsl, GB Bojangle's, Little Caesar's, Pancho's Mexican, Pizza Hut, Three Lil' Pigs BBQ, Wendy's Howard Johnson, Super 8 Kroger/dsl, Verizon, vet

149mm **weigh sta both lanes**

VA

INTERSTATE 81 Cont'd

Exit#	Services
146	VA 115, Cloverdale, E BP/dsl, Exxon, Shell/dsl El Rodeo Mexican, Hardee's, McDonald's, Subway Country Inn&Suites, Days Inn/rest., Fairfield Inn, Hampton Inn, Tru Hilton Camping World, CVS, to Hollins U
143	I-581, US 220, to Roanoke, Blue Ridge Pkwy (exits left from sb), **1 mi** E Kroger/dsl El Toreo, Subway, Waffle House Knights Inn, Motel 6, Quality Inn, Super 8 Honda, **2-3 mi E on Hershberger** Abuelo's Mexican, Applebee's, Buffalo Wild Wings, Carrabba's, Cheddar's, Chick-fil-A, Hardee's, IHOP, Logan's Roadhouse, Longhorn Steaks, O'Charley's, Olive Garden, Panera Bread, Red Palace Chinese, Red Robin, Rodio Grande, Shaker's, Smokey Bones BBQ, Starbucks, TGIFriday's, Zaxby's Best Western+, Comfort Inn, Courtyard, Extended Stay America, Hampton Inn, Holiday Inn, Home 2 Suites, Hyatt Place, MainStay Suites, Residence Inn, Sheraton $Tree, AT&T, Barnes&Noble, Belk, Best Buy, BigLots, Dick's, Exxon, Home Depot, Macy's, Michael's, Murphy USA/dsl, NTB, Old Navy, Petsmart, Shell, Staples, Target, U-Haul, Verizon, Walmart
141	VA 419, Salem, E Liberty/7-11/dsl, Marathon/Burger King Hardee's, IHOP, McDonald's, Starbucks Baymont Inn, Days Inn, Fairfield Inn, Holiday Inn Express, La Quinta H, Chevrolet, GNC, Kroger/gas, **1 mi W** BP/Subway/dsl, Citgo Billy's Barn Rest.
140	VA 311, Salem, **1 mi E** Mac&Bob's Cafe, **1 mi W** BP/Subway/dsl, Citgo Billy's Barn Rest., Hanging Rock Grill/golf
137	VA 112, VA 619, Salem, E BP, Exxon/dsl, Go-Mart, Marathon, Sheetz/dsl Angelle's Diner, Anthony's Cafe, Applebee's, Arby's, Bojangle's, Burger King, Chick-fil-A, Denny's, DQ, Dunkin Donuts, Dynasty Buffet, El Rodeo Mexican, Firehouse Subs, Hardee's, Jimmy John's, K&W Cafeteria, KFC, Mamma Maria Italian, McDonald's, Omelette Shoppe, Pizza Hut, Starbucks, Subway, Taco Bell, Tokyo Express, Waffle House, Wendy's, Zaxby's Comfort Suites, Motel 6, Quality Inn, Super 8 $General, $Tree, Aamco, Advance Parts, AutoZone, BigLots, Food Lion, Goodyear, Kroger/dsl, Lowe's, NTB, O'Reilly Parts, Verizon, Walgreens, Walmart/Subway, W Hampton Inn, Howard Johnson
132	VA 647, to Dixie Caverns, E Citgo/dsl Blue Jay Motel Dixie Caverns Camping
129mm	**nb, full facilities, litter barrels, petwalk, , , vending**
128	US 11, VA 603, Ironto, E Shell, W Exxon/Dixie's/Subway/dsl/24hr
118c b a	US 11/460, Christiansburg, E Shell/dsl Cracker Barrel, Denny's Days Inn, Fairfield Inn, Holiday Inn Express, Homewood Suites, Quality Inn, Super 8, Wyndham, W Exxon/Subway/dsl, Liberty/7-11/dsl, Shell Country Cookin, Hardee's, LJ Silver, McDonald's, Pizza Hut, Ruby Tuesday, Wendy's EconoLodge, Shayona Inn H, $General, Advance Parts, Chevrolet, Chrysler/Dodge/Jeep, Food Lion, Ford, Honda, Hyundai, Kia, Subaru, to VA Tech, Toyota
114	VA 8, Christiansburg, E to Blue Ridge Pkwy, **0-1 mi W** Citgo/dsl Burger King, Pizza Inn, Subway Budget Inn $General Mkt, USPO
109	VA 177, VA 600, E H, **0-2 mi W** Exxon/dsl, Marathon Best Western, Comfort Inn, La Quinta, Super 8 (2mi) Buick/Cadillac/Chevrolet
107mm	**both lanes, full facilities, litter barrels, petwalk, , , vending**
105	VA 232, RD 605, to Radford, **2-4 mi W** Citgo, Exxon, dsl Sal's Italian Executive Motel museum
101	RD 660, to Claytor Lake SP, E Claytor Lake Inn, Sleep Inn repair, W Exxon/DQ/dsl, Shell/Omelette Shoppe/Taco Bell/dsl/scales/@
98	VA 100 N, to Dublin, E Exxon/Subway/dsl, Marathon Bojangles, Shoney's Hampton Inn, Holiday Inn Express, Quality Inn to Wilderness Rd Museum, W Liberty/dsl, Marathon/dsl, Shell/Papa John's/dsl Arby's, Burger King, Domino's, El Ranchero Mexican, Fatz Cafe, McDonald's, Waffle House, Wendy's Super 8 $General, NAPA, O'Reilly Parts, Verizon, Walmart/Subway
94b a	VA 99 N, to Pulaski, **0-3 mi W** BP, Exxon/dsl, Speedway/dsl China Wall, Compadre's Mexican, Domino's, Hardee's, KFC, Kimono Japanese, Little Caesar's, McDonald's, Sonic, Subway, Taco Bell, Wendy's H, $General, Advance Parts, CVS, Family$, Food Lion, O'Reilly Parts
92	Rd 658, to Draper, E to New River Trail SP
89b a	US 11 N, VA 100, to Pulaski, E auto/truck repair
86	Rd 618, Service Rd, W Sunoco/Appletree Rest./dsl repair
84	Rd 619, to Grahams Forge, W Exxon/Circle K/DQ/dsl/24hr, Loves/Chester's/Subway/dsl/scales/24hr Fox Mt Inn, Trail Motel
I-81 S and I-77 N run together 9 mi.	
81	I-77 S, to Charlotte, Galax, to Blue Ridge Pkwy
80	US 52 S, VA 121 N, to Ft Chiswell, E FLYING J/Denny's/dsl/scales/24hr/@, Exxon/Burger King/dsl Wendy's Hampton Inn, Super 8 Blue Beacon, Ft Chiswell RV Park, NAPA, W Circle K/dsl, Citgo McDonald's Comfort Inn Speedco
77	Service Rd, E FLYING J/Denny's/dsl/scales/LP/RV Dump/24hr, Circle K/Subway/dsl/24hr, Speedway/Dunkin Donuts/dsl Burger King KOA, W Exxon/dsl, Pilot/Arby's/DQ/dsl/scales/24hr st police
73	US 11 S, Wytheville, E Exxon/dsl, Go-Mart Applebee's, Bob Evans, Cracker Barrel, Dawghouse, El Puerto Mexican, Hardee's, Papa John's, Peking Chinese, Shoney's, Sonic, Waffle House, Wendy's Budget Host, Days Inn, EconoLodge, Holiday Inn Express, La Quinta, Motel 6, Quality Inn, Red Roof Inn, Rodeway Inn, Travelodge H, $General, AutoZone, Buick, Chevrolet/GMC, CVS Drug, Food Lion, Ford, Goodyear/auto, Harley-Davidson, Nissan, Rite Aid, Rural King
I-81 N and I-77 S run together 9 mi	
72	I-77 N, to Bluefield, **1 mi N on I-77 exit 41** E Sagebrush Steaks Best Western, Sleep Inn, Super 8, **1 mi N on I-77 exit 41** W Exxon/Circle K/dsl/24hr, TA/Country Pride/Popeye's/Subway/Taco Bell/dsl/scales/24hr/@ Southern Diner Comfort Suites, Country Inn&Suites, Fairfield Inn, Hampton Inn, Ramada/rest., Tru Hilton
70	US 21/52, Wytheville, E BP/dsl, Sheetz/dsl Bojangles, China Wok, El Patio Mexican, KFC/Taco Bell, Little Caesar's, McDonald's, Ruby Tuesday, Starbucks, Subway, Tokyo Japanese, Wendy's H, $Tree, Food Lion, GNC, Lowe's, O'Reilly Parts, PetCo, Verizon, Walmart/Subway, W Kangaroo Comfort Inn
67	US 11 (from nb, no re-entry), to Wytheville
61mm	**nb, full facilities, litter barrels, NO TRUCKS, petwalk, , , vending**
60	VA 90, Rural Retreat, E Shell/dsl Dutch Pantry, McDonald's $General, camping, to Rural Retreat Lake
54	rd 683, to Groseclose, E Exxon, Sunoco/dsl The Barn Rest. Relax Inn Settler's Museum

ROANOKE · SALEM · CHRISTIANSBURG · WYTHEVILLE · VA

INTERSTATE 81 Cont'd

MARION

Exit#	Services
53.5mm	**sb, full facilities, litter barrels, petwalk, , , vending**
50	US 11, Atkins, W Circle K/Subway/dsl/24hr, Exxon Comfort Inn NAPA Care
47	US 11, to Marion, W Citgo/Subway, Gas'N Go, Shell/dsl Arby's, Bojangle's, Burger King, Charley's Philly Steaks, China House, KFC/Taco Bell, Little Caesar's, McDonald's, Mi Puerto Mexican, Pizza Hut, Sonic, Wendy's Best Value Inn, EconoLodge, Travel Inn H, $General, $Tree, Advance Parts, AutoZone, Buick/Chevrolet/GMC, CVS Drug, Food City, Food Lion, Ford, Ingles, Marion Drug, O'Reilly Parts, to Hungry Mother SP (4mi), Verizon, Walgreens, Walmart
45	VA 16, Marion, E Valero/dsl Mt Rogers NRA, to Grayson Highlands SP, W Sunoco Hardee's NAPA, USPO
44	US 11, Marion, W $General, Vet
39	US 11, rd 645, Seven Mile Ford, W Interstate Camping
35	VA 107, Chilhowie, E Chilhowie Pizza, Hardee's Knights Inn, W Exxon/dsl, Gas'N Go, Mobil/Main St Mkt, Shell/dsl McDonald's, Riverfront Rest., Subway, Taco Bell $General, Food City, Greever's Drugs, USPO
32	US 11, to Chilhowie
29	VA 91, to Damascus, Glade Spring, E Marathon/Subway/dsl, Petro/Iron Skillet/dsl/24hr/@, Valero/Wendy's Giardino's Italian, Pizza+ EconoLodge, Knights Inn $General, Peterbilt, W Exxon, Shell/dsl, Spirit El Burrito Loco vet
26	rd 737, Emory, W Macado's (1mi) to Emory&Henry Coll, USPO (1mi)
24	VA 80, Meadowview Rd, E Loves/McDonald's/Subway/dsl/scales/24hr, W Harvest Table
22	rd 704, Enterprise Rd, E Marathon/dsl H
19	US 11/58, to Abingdon, E Shell/Subway/Dunkin Donuts/dsl, Walmart/dsl Bojangle's, DQ, McDonald's, Pizza+ $Tree, Lowe's, to Mt Rogers NRA, URGENT CARE, vet, Walmart, W BP/dsl, Exxon/dsl, Marathon/Huddle House Bella's Pizza, Burger King, Cracker Barrel, Harbor House Seafood, Papa Tom's Cantina, Pita's Country Inn Suites, Fairfield Inn, Quality Inn, Red Roof Inn $General
17	US 58A, VA 75, Abingdon, E Mobil/dsl Domino's, LJ Silver Hampton Inn, W Exxon, Gas'n Go Arby's, Capt D's, Charley's Philly Steaks, China Wok, Fuji Express, Hardee's, Little Caesar's, Los Arcos, McDonald's, Papa John's, Shoney's, Subway, Taco Bell, Wendy's Super 8 Advance Parts, Food City, GNC, Kroger/dsl
14	US 19, VA 140, Abingdon, W BP/dsl, Exxon, Shell/dsl McDonald's, Milano's Italian, Moon Dog Cafe, Subway Comfort Inn, Comfort Suites Chevrolet, Ford/Lincoln, Riverside Camping (10mi)
13.5mm	**TRUCKERS ONLY nb, full facilities, litter barrels, , , vending**
13	VA 611, to Lee Hwy, W Shell/dsl Kenworth, Mack, Volvo
10	US 11/19, Lee Hwy, W Exxon, Marathon/dsl, Shell/dsl Deluxe Inn, Economy Inn, Evergreen Inn, Red Carpet Inn
7	Old Airport Rd, E Shell/dsl Bojangles, Cheddar's, Cracker Barrel, Sonic Days Inn, Hilton Garden, W Marathon, Sunoco/Wendy's, Valero/dsl Chick-fil-A, Chili's, Cook-Out, Domino's, El Patio Mexican, Five Guys, Golden Corral, IHOP, Jersey Mike's Subs, Kobe Japanese, Logan's Roadhouse, Los Arcos, Mellow Mushroom, O'Charley's, Olive Garden, Pal's Drive-In, Perkins, Red Lobster, Starbucks, Subway, Taco Bell Courtyard, Holiday Inn, Motel 6, Quality Inn $General, $Tree,

ABINGDON

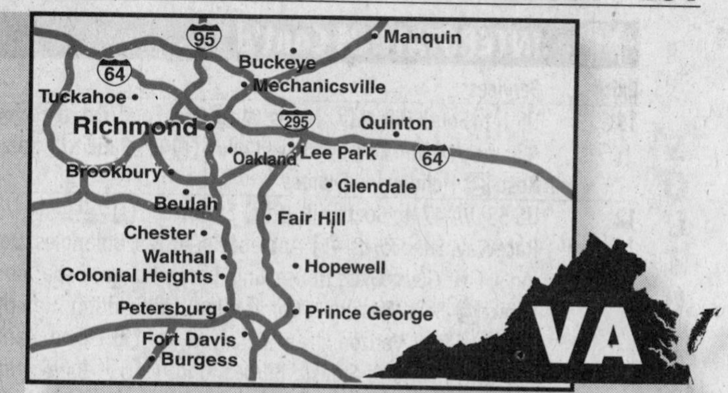

BRISTOL

Exit#	Services
7	Continued Advance Parts, AT&T, AutoZone, Best Buy, Books-A-Million, Food City/gas, Home Depot, Office Depot, Petsmart, Ross, Sam's Club/gas, Sugar Hollow Camping, Target, TJ Maxx, Verizon, Walmart
5	US 11/19, Lee Hwy, E Shell Arby's, Burger King, Hardee's, KFC, LJ Silver, McDonald's, Shoney's Budget Inn, Red Roof Inn Harley-Davidson, O'Reilly Parts, Price Less Foods, USPO, W Exxon/dsl, Sheetz/dsl Buffalo Wild Wings, Zaxby's Comfort Inn Aldi Foods, Buick/GMC, Cabela's, Hobby Lobby, Kings Tire, Lowe's
3	I-381 S, to Bristol, 1 mi E Gas'n Go/dsl, Mobil/dsl, Shell/dsl Krystal, Subway EconoLodge Food City, vet
1b a	US 58/421, Bristol, 1 mi E 5 Mart/dsl, Exxon/dsl, Shell Burger King, Capt D's, KFC, McDonald's, Sonic, Subway, Taco Bell, Wendy's Rodeway Inn H, $Tree, Chrysler/Dodge/Jeep, CVS Drug, Kroger/dsl, Toyota, UHaul, Verizon, vet, Walgreens
0mm	Virginia/Tennessee state line, **Welcome Ctr nb, full facilities, info, litter barrels, NO TRUCKS, petwalk, , , vending**

VA

INTERSTATE 85

PETERSBURG

Exit#	Services
I-85 begins/ends on I-95.	
69	US 301, I-95 N, Wythe St, Washington St, Petersburg
68	I-95 S, US 460 E, to Norfolk, Crater Rd
65	Squirrel Level Rd, E to Richard Bland Coll, W BP
63b a	US 1, to Petersburg, E Chubby's/dsl, Exxon/KFC/dsl, Shell/Burger King/dsl Hardee's, Taco Bell, Waffle House Holiday Inn Express $General, W McDonald's
61	US 460, to Blackstone, E Mapco/Subway/dsl Joe's Rest., W , auto repair
55mm	**both lanes, full facilities, litter barrels, petwalk, , , vending**
53	VA 703, Dinwiddie, W Exxon/dsl to 5 Forks Nat Bfd
52mm	Stony Creek
48	VA 650, DeWitt
42	VA 40, McKenney, W BP, Citgo, Exxon
40mm	Nottoway River
39	VA 712, to Rawlings, W Davis TC/Exxon/Dunkin Donuts/Subway/dsl/scales/24hr, Race-In/Nottoway Rest.
34	VA 630, Warfield, W Exxon/dsl
32mm	**both lanes, full facilities, litter barrels, petwalk, , , vending**
28	US 1, Alberta, W Exxon Family Dollar
27	VA 46, to Lawrenceville, E to St Paul's Coll
24	VA 644, to Meredithville
22mm	**weigh sta both lanes**
20mm	Meherrin River

SOUTH HILL

INTERSTATE 85 Cont'd

Exit#	Services
15	US 1, to South Hill, E [gas] Hines, W [gas] Hot Food/dsl, Loves /Subway/McDonald's/dsl/scales/24hr [food] El Saucito, Kahill's Rest. [lodging] Holiday Inn Express
12	US 58, VA 47, to South Hill, E [gas] Exxon/dsl, Pilot/Shell/dsl, RaceWay, Sunoco/dsl [food] Applebee's, Arby's, Bojangles, Domino's, Five Guys, Glass House Grill, Luca's Italian, Papa John's, Sonic [lodging] Best Western+, Comfort Inn, Fairfield Inn, Hampton Inn [other] $Tree, Verizon, Walmart/Subway, W [gas] Exxon, Kangaroo/dsl [food] Brian's Steaks, Burger King, Cracker Barrel, Hardee's, KFC/Taco Bell, McDonald's, New China, Pizza Hut, Subway, Wendy's [lodging] Best Value Inn, Days Inn, Quality Inn [other] [H], $General, AutoZone, CVS Drug, Family$, Food Lion, Home Depot, O'Reilly Parts, Roses
4	VA 903, to Bracey, Lake Gaston, E [gas] Exxon/Simmon's/dsl/scales/24hr/@, Sunoco/Subway/Papa John's/dsl [food] Huddle House, Top This Pizza [other] $General, Americamps Camping (5mi), W [gas] Shell/Pizza Hut/Quizno's [lodging] Lake Gaston Inn
3mm	Lake Gaston
1mm	**Welcome Ctr nb, full [handicapped] facilities, litter barrels, petwalk, [phone], [phone], [picnic], vending**
0mm	Virginia/North Carolina state line

DC AREA

INTERSTATE 95

Exit#	Services
178mm	Virginia/Maryland state line, Potomac River, W Wilson Br
177c b a	US 1, to Alexandria, Ft Belvoir, E [food] Great American Steaks [lodging] Budget Host, Hampton Inn, Red Roof Inn, Relax Inn [other] Chevrolet, Chrysler/Dodge/Jeep, W [gas] Liberty/repair, Speedway
176b a	VA 241, Telegraph Rd, E [gas] BP, Speedway/dsl, W [food] Ted's MT Grill [lodging] Courtyard, Extended Stay America, Holiday Inn, SpringHill Suites
174	Eisenhower Ave Connector, to Alexandria
173	rd 613, Van Dorn St, to Franconia, E [lodging] Comfort Inn, 1 mi W [gas] Exxon, Shell [food] Dunkin Donuts, Jerry's Subs, McDonald's, Red Lobster [other] Aamco, Giant Foods, NTB
170a	I-495 N, **I-495 & I-95 N run together to MD, to Rockville**
170b	I-395 N, to Washington
169b a	rd 644, Springfield, Franconia, E [food] Bertucci's, Dunkin Donuts, Houlihan's, Silver Diner, Starbucks, Subway, TGIFriday's [lodging] Best Western, Comfort Inn, Courtyard, Extended Stay America, Hampton Inn, Hilton [other] [H], AT&T, Barnes&Noble, Best Buy, Dick's, Firestone/auto, Ford, Home Depot, JC Penney, Macy's, Michael's, Nissan, Old Navy, Petsmart, Staples, Subaru, Target, W [gas] BP, Shell, Sunoco [food] Blue Pearl Buffet, Chick-fil-A, Chipotle Mexican, Deliah's Grill, Domino's, Dunkin Donuts, Five Guys, Hard Times Cafe, KFC, McDonald's, Noodles&Co, Outback Steaks, Panda Express, Popeye's, Starbucks, Subway [lodging] Holiday Inn Express, Homewood Suites, Motel 6, Residence Inn, TownePlace Suites [other] 7-11, Advance Parts, CarQuest, Chrysler/Dodge/Jeep, CVS Drug, Giant Foods, GNC, Goodyear/auto, Mr Tire, Toyota, Trader Joe's, USPO, Verizon, vet, VW
167	VA 617, Backlick Rd (from sb), W [gas] InterFuel/dsl
166b a	VA 7100, Newington, to Ft Belvoir, E [gas] Pkwy Express [food] Wendy's [lodging] Embassy Suites [other] NTB, Toyota, U-Haul, W [gas] Exxon/7-11/dsl [food] McDonald's [other] Costco
163	VA 642, Lorton, E [gas] Shell/repair, Sunoco/dsl [other] auto repair, W [gas] Shell/dsl [food] Antoneli's Pizza, Burger King, Gunston Wok, Kabob Factory Rest.
161	US 1 S (exits left from sb, no reentry nb), to Ft Belvoir, Mt Vernon, Woodlawn Plantation, Gunston Hall
160.5mm	Occoquan River
160b a	VA 123 N, Woodbridge, Occoquan, E [gas] Sunoco [food] Taco Bell [lodging] Hampton Inn, Quality Inn [other] Aldi Foods, Food Lion, Mr Transmissions, W [gas] Exxon/repair/dsl, Fast Fuels, Shell/dsl [food] KFC, Madigan's Waterfront Rest., McDonald's, VA Grill, Wendy's [other] 7-11, same as 161
158b a	VA 294, Prince William Pkwy, Woodbridge, W [gas] 7-11, Exxon, Shell, Sunoco/dsl [food] Bonefish Grill, Boston Mkt, Bungalow Alehouse, Chick-fil-A, Chipotle Mexican, ChuckeCheese, Coldstone, Famous Dave's BBQ, Firehouse Subs, Hooters, IHOP, Macaroni Grill, McDonald's, Noodles&Co, Old Country Buffet, On-the-Border, Panda Express, Panera Bread, Qdoba, Red Lobster, Red Robin, Smokey Bones BBQ, Starbucks, Taco Bell, TGIFriday's, Wendy's [lodging] Country Inn&Suites, Courtyard, Fairfield Inn, Holiday Inn Express, Residence Inn, SpringHill Suites [other] $Tree, Advance Parts, Best Buy, CarMax, Dick's, GNC, JC Penney, Lowe's, Michael's, Office Depot, Petsmart, Sam's Club/gas, Shopper's Foods, Target, Verizon, Walmart/Subway
156	VA 784, Potomac Mills, E [food] Brixx Woodfired Grill, Firebird Grill, PF Chang's, Potbelly, Starbucks, Travinia Italian, Uncle Julio's Grill, Zoe's Kitchen [lodging] Hilton Garden, Homewood Suites [other] [H], AT&T, Old Navy, REI, to Leesylvania SP, Wegman's Mkt, W [gas] Mobil/dsl, Shell/dsl, Sunoco/dsl [food] Bahama Breeze, Bob Evans, Bobby's Burger, Buffalo Wild Wings, Burger King, Char Broil Grill, Cheesecake Factory, Chili's, China King Buffet, Denny's, Domino's, DQ, Guapo's, Hard Times Cafe, Los Amigos, McDonald's, Olive Garden, Outback Steaks, Paisano's, Popeye's, Sakura Japanese, Silver Diner, Subway, Wendy's [lodging] Best Western, Wytestone Suites [other] Costco/gas, Family$, Firestone/auto, IKEA, Jo-Ann Fabrics, Marshalls, Nordstrom Rack, NTB, Potomac Mills Outlets/Famous Brands, Staples, Tuesday Morning, U-Haul, vet
154mm	**[RS]/weigh sta both lanes**
152	VA 234, Dumfries, to Manassas, E [gas] BP/dsl, Express, Exxon/dsl, Shell/dsl, Valero/Subway [food] Applebee's, China One, KFC, McDonald's, Ruby Tuesday, Taco Bell [lodging] Sleep Inn, Super 8 [other] 7-11, Food Lion, Meineke, NAPA Autocare, Walmart, Weems-Botts Museum, W [gas] 7-11, Exxon [food] Asian Pa[...] Chick-fil-A, Cracker Barrel, Five Guys, IHOP, Jerry's Subs, Mor[...] Clair Rest., Panera Bread, Starbucks, Subway, Tiziano Italia[n], Waffle House [lodging] Comfort Inn, Days Inn, EconoLodge, Hampton Inn, Holiday Inn [other] AT&T, Prince William Camping, Rite Aid, Shoppers Foods, Target, URGENT CARE
150	VA 619, Quantico, to Triangle, E [food] Dunkin Donuts, McDonald's [lodging] Ramada Inn [other] 7-11, to Marine Corps Base, W Prince William Forest Park
148	to Quantico (2mi) E [gas] Gulf/dsl [food] Subway [lodging] Courtya[rd] [other] to Marine Corps Base
143b a	to US 1, VA 610, Aquia, E [gas] 7-11, Exxon/Circle K/dsl, Valero [food] Carlos O'Kelly's, El Gran Charro, KFC, McDonald's, Mick[...] Rest., Papa John's, Pizza Hut, Ruby Tuesday, Subway [lodging] Best Western, Fairfield Inn, Hampton Inn, Staybridge Suites, Suburban Extended Stay, Towne Place Suites [other] Aquia Pines Camping, Nissan, Rite Aid, Tires+, W [gas] 7-11, Exxon/dsl, Kangaroo, WaWa [food] 5 Guys Burgers, Applebee's, Baskin-Robbins/Dunkin Donuts, Bob Evans, Buffalo Wild Wings, Burger King, Chick-fil-A, Chili's, China Wok, CiCi's, Firehouse Subs, Hardee's, Hibachi Buffet, IHOP, Jersey Mike's, Jimmy the Greek, Kobe Japanese, Little Caesar's, McDonald's, Moe's SW Grill, Outback Stea[ks]

DUMFRIES

VA

INTERSTATE 95 Cont'd

143b a Continued
Pancho Villa, Panera Bread, Popeye's, Starbucks, Taco Bell, Umi Japanese, Wendy's Comfort Inn, Country Inn&Suites, Quality Inn, Super 8, Wingate Inn $General, $Tree, Aldi Foods, AutoZone, Best Buy, CVS Drug, Giant Foods, GNC, Home Depot, Kohl's, Lowe's, Merchant's Tire, Michael's, PetCo, Petsmart, Ross, Shopper's Foods, Staples, Target, TJ Maxx, Toyota, URGENT CARE, Verizon, Walmart/McDonald's

140 VA 630, Stafford, E 7-11, Sunoco/dsl, Valero McDonald's H, W Exxon/dsl, Shell/dsl

137mm Potomac Creek

136 rd 8900, Centreport, 2 mi E Valero/dsl, W

133b a US 17 N, to Warrenton, E Exxon/dsl Arby's Knights Inn, Motel 6 7-11, auto/truck repair, CarQuest, W EastCoast/Subway/dsl, Shell/dsl, WaWa/dsl Aladin Grill, Burger King, Dunkin Donuts, Hardee's, McDonald's, Pancho Villa Mexican, Panera Bread, Perkins, Ponderosa, Popeye's, Sam's Pizza&Subs, Subway, Taco Bell, Waffle House, Wendy's Best Value Inn, Clarion, Comfort Suites, Country Inn&Suites, Days Inn, Holiday Inn Express, Quality Inn, Sleep Inn, Super 8, Super Value Inn, Wingate Inn Advance Parts, AutoZone, Blue Beacon, Food Lion, Honda, Petsmart, Target, Verizon

132.5mm Rappahannock River

132mm **sb, full facilities, litter barrels, petwalk, vending**

130b a VA 3, to Fredericksburg, E BP/dsl, Gulf/dsl, Shell/dsl, Wawa Aladin Cafe, Arby's, Bob Evans, Dixie Bones BBQ, Dunkin Donuts, Friendly's, Honeybaked Ham, KFC, Lonestar Steaks, McDonald's, Pizza King, Popeye's, Shoney's, Starbucks, Subway, Teppanyaki Buffet, Wendy's Best Western, Quality Inn H, AutoZone, Batteries+Bulbs, BigLots, Home Depot, PepBoys, Staples, Tuesday Morning, U-Haul, Verizon, W Exxon/dsl, Murphy USA, Sheetz/dsl, Valero, WaWa 5 Guys Burgers, A&W/LJ Silver, Applebee's, BoneFish Grill, Bravo!, Buffalo Wild Wings, Burger King, Cancun Mexican, Carrabba's, Checker's, Cheeburger Cheeburger, Chick-fil-A, Chili's, Chipotle Mexican, ChuckeCheese, CiCi's Pizza, Cracker Barrel, Dunkin Donuts, Firebirds Grill, Firehouse Subs, Hibachi Buffet, IHOP, Jimmy John's, Joe's Crabshack, Krispy Kreme, Logan's Roadhouse, McDonald's, Melting Pot, Noodles&Co, O'Charley's, Olive Garden, Outback Steaks, Pancho Villa, Panda Express, Panera Bread, Park Lane Grill, Peter Chang, Potbelly, Qdoba, Quaker Steak, Red Lobster, Ruby Tuesday, Ryan's, Sam's Pizza, Santa Fe Grill, Shane's Ribshack, Smokey Bones BBQ, Starbucks, Subway, Taco Bell, TGIFriday's, Tito's Diner, TX Roadhouse Best Western, Hampton Inn, Hilton Garden, Homewood Suites, Hospitality House, Residence Inn, Super 8, WoodSpring Inn $General, $Tree, AAA, Aldi Foods, AT&T, AutoZone, Barnes&Noble, Belk, Best Buy, BJ's Whse, Books A Million, Costco/gas, CVS Drug, Dick's, Food Lion, GNC, Hobby Lobby, JC Penney, Kohl's, Lowe's, Macy's, Meineke, Mercedes, Merchants Tire, Michael's, NTB, Office Depot, Old Navy, Petsmart, Target, Verizon, vet, Volvo, Walmart, Wegman's Foods, Yankee Candle

126 US 1, US 17 S, to Fredericksburg, E 7-11/dsl, BP/dsl, Exxon/Circle K, Gulf/dsl, Shell/dsl, Wawa Arby's, Denny's, DQ, Friendly's, Golden Corral, Hardee's, Hooters, McDonald's, Pizza Hut, Poncho Villa Mexican, Ruby Tuesday, Subway, Taco Bell, Vita Felice Italian, Waffle House Best Value Inn, Country Inn&Suites, Days Inn/rest., EconoLodge, Fairfield Inn, Hampton Inn, Howard Johnson, Knights Inn, Motel 6, Royal Inn, TownePlace Suites H, $General, $Tree, Advance Parts, Aldi Foods,

FREDERICKSBURG

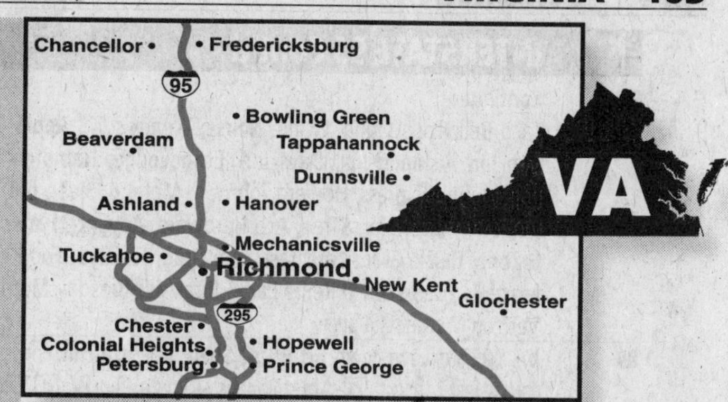

126 Continued
AutoZone, BMW Cycles, Buick/GMC, Chrysler/Dodge/Jeep, CVS Drug, Family$, Fiat, Food Lion, Hyundai, Kia, Little Tires, Mazda, Midas, Nissan, Rite Aid, Subaru, Tires+, VW, W 7-11, 95 Fuel Stop/dsl, Exxon/Circle K, WaWa/dsl 5 Guys Burgers, Applebee's, Arby's, Asian Diner, Bob Evans, Buffalo Wild Wings, Burger King, Chick-fil-A, Chili's, China King, Chipotle Mexican, Coldstone Creamery, Cracker Barrel, Dickey's BBQ, El Charro Mexican, Famous Dave's BBQ, Firehouse Subs, Golden China, KFC, Kobe Japanese, Legends Grill, Longhorn Steaks, Mad Crab Grill, McDonald's, Mexico Rest., Mimi's Cafe, Panera Bread, Papa John's, Red Robin, Salsarita's Cantina, Sonic, Starbucks, Steak'n Shake, Subway, Taco Bell, Wendy's Candlewood Suites, Holiday Inn Express, Sleep Inn, WyteStone Suites AT&T, Carmax, CVS Drug, Dick's, Firestone/auto, GNC, Jo-Ann Fabrics, Kohl's, Lowe's, Marshalls, Merchant Tire/auto, Petsmart, Rite Aid, Ross, Staples, Target, URGENT CARE, USPO, Verizon, vet, Walmart/Subway, World Mkt

118 VA 606, to Thornburg, E Shell/dsl Camping World, to Stonewall Jackson Shrine, W 7-11, Citgo/dsl, Exxon, Shell/DQ/dsl, Valero Angela's Italian, Domino's, McDonald's, Subway, Taco Bell Best Western+, Holiday Inn Express, Quality Inn $General, Family$, Food Lion, KOA (7mi), to Lake Anna SP, USPO

110 VA 639, to Ladysmith, E Shell/dsl, W Citgo/dsl, Exxon/dsl Domino's, Guiseppe's Rest., Lin's Gourmet, McDonald's, Subway, Timbers Rest. $General, Family$, Food Lion, Lady Smith Drug, Lady Smith Tire/repair, Verizon

108mm **both lanes, full facilities, litter barrels, pet walk, vending**

104 VA 207, to US 301, Bowling Green, E Exxon/dsl, FLYING J/Golden Corral/dsl/Lp/scales/24hr/@, Gulf/7-11/dsl, Loves/DQ/Subway/dsl/scales/24hr, Mr Fuel/dsl, Valero/dsl Arby's, McDonald's, Wendy's Knights Inn, Super 8 Blue Beacon, SpeedCo, to Ft AP Hill, W FLYING J/Denny's/dsl/scales/RV dump/24hr, Exxon/dsl Waffle House City Studio, Comfort Inn, Days Inn/rest., EconoLodge CarQuest, USPO

98 VA 30, Doswell, E 7-11, Doswell TP/motel/dsl/scales/24hr/@, Exxon Burger King, Denny's Best Western, Country Inn&Suites, Days Inn, La Quinta Camp Wilderness, King's Dominion Camping, to King's Dominion Funpark, truckwash/service

92 VA 54, Ashland, E Sunoco, W 7-11/dsl, EC/Krispy Kreme/dsl, Exxon/Subway, Kangeroo/dsl, Shell/dsl, Sunoco/Circle K/dsl, TA/Valero/Country Pride/dsl/scales/24hr/@ Anthony's Pizza, Applebee's, Arby's, Brickoven Rest., Burger King, Capt D's, Chick-fil-A, China Wok, Cracker Barrel, DQ, El Azteca, GNC, Hardee's, Jersey Mike's Subs, KFC/LJ Silver, McDonald's, New China Buffet, Pizza Hut, Ponderosa, Ruby Tuesday, Starbucks,

VA

FREDERICKSBURG

INTERSTATE 95 Cont'd

92 Continued
Taco Bell, Tops China, Waffle House, Wendy's [lodging] Apple Garden Inn, Ashland Inn, Days Inn, EconoLodge, Hampton Inn, Holiday Inn Express, Howard Johnson, Motel 6, Sleep Inn, Super 8 [other] $General, $Tree, Ace Hardware, Advance Parts, AutoZone, Buick/GMC, CarQuest, CVS Drug, Family$, Food Lion, Martin's Foods/dsl, O'Reilly Parts, Rite Aid, Tuesday Morning, Verizon, Walmart/Subway

89 VA 802, to Lewistown Rd, E [gas] Shell, TA/Pizza Hut/Popeye's/dsl/scales/24hr/@ [other] Americamps RV Camp, W [food] Bojangles, Dunkin Donuts, Subway, Wendy's [lodging] Country Inn Suites [other] Bass Pro Shops, Harley Davidson, Kosmo Village Camping, McGeorge's RV Ctr

86b a VA 656, Elmont, to Atlee, E [gas] Sheetz/dsl, Valero/dsl [food] Burger King, Mario's Italian, McDonald's, Pizza Hut, Subway [other] CVS Drug, Food Lion, tire/auto repair, vet, W [gas] Wawa/dsl [food] Applebee's, Arby's, BBQ, Buffalo Wild Wings, Chick-fil-A, Chili's, Chipotle Mexican, CiCi's Pizza, Coldstone Creamery, Famous Dave's BBQ, Firehouse Subs, Halligan BBQ, Jade Chinese, Jersey Mike's Subs, McDonald's, O'Charley's, O'Dragon Buffet, Panera Bread, Papa John's, Pizzaro, Plaza Azteca Mexican, Red Robin, Roda Japanese, Shoney's, Sonic, Starbucks, Subway, TX Roadhouse, Wendy's [lodging] Candlewood Suites, Comfort Suites, Courtyard, Hampton Inn, SpringHill Suites [other] $Tree, 7-11, AT&T, Barnes&Noble, Best Buy, Burlington, Dick's, Firestone/auto, GNC, Goodyear/auto, Home Depot, JC Penney, Martin's Foods, Merchant's Tire, Michael's, Petsmart, Ross, Shell/dsl, Target, Tire America, Walgreens

ELMONT

84b a I-295 W, to I-64, to Norfolk

83b a VA 73, Parham Rd, W [gas] 7-11, Exxon/DQ, Shell/dsl, Wawa [food] Aunt Sarah's, Burger King, Firehouse Subs, Frida's Cafe, Hardee's, Hawks BBQ, KFC/Taco Bell, McDonald's, Popeyes, River City Diner, Starbucks, Subway, Waffle House, Wendy's [lodging] Best Value Inn, Best Western, Cavalier Motel, Days Inn, EconoLodge, Knights Inn, Quality Inn, Sleep Inn [other] $Tree, BigLots, Food Lion, Lowe's, Verizon, Walmart

82 US 301, Chamberlayne Ave, E [gas] BP/dsl, Sunoco/dsl, Valero/dsl, Wawa [food] KFC, McDonald's, Pizza Hut/Taco Bell, Subway [lodging] Super 8 [other] $Tree, Family$, Food Lion, USPO, W [gas] Exxon/Circle K

81 US 1, Chamberlayne Ave (from nb), same as 82

80 Hermitage Rd, Lakeside Ave (from nb, no return), W [gas] Citgo/Subway [other] Ginter Botanical Gardens, Goodyear/auto

79 I-64 W, to Charlottesville, I-195 S, to U of Richmond

78 Boulevard (no EZ nb return), E [gas] [lodging] Clarion, W [other] [H], stadium, to VA HS

76 Chamberlayne Ave, Belvidere, E [other] [H], VA Union U

75 I-64 E, VA Beach, to Norfolk, [airport]

74c US 33, US 250 W, to Broad St, W [other] [H], Museum of the Confederacy, st capitol

74b Franklin St, E [other] Richmond Nat Bfd Park

74a I-195 N, to Powhite Expswy, downtown

73.5mm James River

73 Maury St, to US 60, US 360, industrial area

69 VA 161, Bells Rd, E Port of Richmond, W [gas] Exxon/dsl, Shell/dsl [food] McDonald's, Subway [lodging] Candlewood Suites, Hampton Inn, Holiday Inn, Red Roof Inn

67b a VA 895 (toll E), VA 150, to Chippenham Pkwy, Falling Creek, W [gas] BP/dsl, RaceWay/dsl, Shell/dsl [food] Burger King, Hardee's [other] Food Lion, U-Haul

RICHMOND

64 VA 613, to Willis Rd, E [gas] BP, Exxon/Circle K/dsl [food] Waffle House [lodging] Best Value Inn, Knights Inn, W [gas] 7-11, Citgo/dsl, Shell/dsl, Sunoco [food] Burger King, Maury's BBQ, McDonald's, Subway [lodging] Country Inn&Suites, La Quinta, Sleep Inn, VIP Inn [other] Drewry's Bluff Bfd, flea mkt

62 VA 288 N, to Chesterfield, Powhite Pkwy, W [other] to [airport]

61b a VA 10, Chester, E [gas] RaceWay/dsl [food] Don Pepe Mexican, Hardee's [lodging] Comfort Inn, Courtyard, Hampton Inn, Holiday Inn Express, Homewood Suites, Quality Inn [other] [H], City Point NHS, Petersburg NBF, to James River Plantations, W [gas] Exxon/Circle K/dsl, Gulf/dsl, Mobil/Circle K/dsl, Shell/dsl, Sunoco/dsl [food] Applebee's, Bojangles, Brass Monkey Grill, Buffalo Wild Wings, Burger King, Capt D's, Chili's, Chipotle, CiCi's Pizza, Cracker Barrel, Denny's, Don Papa Mexican, Friendly's, Hardee's, Hooters, IHOP, KFC, Logan's Roadhouse, McDonald's, O'Charley's, Panera Bread, Peking Chinese, Pizza Hut, Shoney's, Sonic, Starbucks, Subway, Taco Bell, The Patron Cantina, Wendy's [lodging] Country Inn&Suites, Days Inn, Fairfield Inn, InTown Suites, Suburban Lodge, Super 8 [other] $General, $Tree, Aamco, AT&T, Big Lots, Chevrolet, CVS Drug, Food Lion, GNC, Home Depot, Kohl's, Kroger/gas, Lowe's, Martin's Foods, NAPA, PetCo, Rite Aid, Target, to Pocahontas SP, Verizon

CHESTER

58 VA 746, to Ruffinmill Rd, E [gas] Pilot/Wendy's/dsl/scales/24hr [other] Honda, Hyundai, Kia, Nissan, Subaru, Toyota, VW, W [gas] 7-11, Exxon/Subway/dsl, Wawa/dsl [food] McDonald's [lodging] Candlewood Suites, Comfort Inn, EconoLodge [other] Family$

54 VA 144, Temple Ave, Hopewell, to Ft Lee, E [gas] Exxon/Burger King, Sheetz/dsl, Shell, Sunoco/Circle K/dsl, Wawa/dsl [food] Applebee's, Arby's, Buffalo Wild Wings, Chick-fil-A, China Buffet, Chipotle, CiCi's Pizza, Denny's, Firehouse Subs, Five Guys, Golden Corral, Great China, IHOP, Jimmy John's, Longhorn Steaks, McDonald's, Olive Garden, Outback Steaks, Panera Bread, Pizza Hut, Red Lobster, Ruby Tuesday, Sonic, Starbucks, Subway, Taco Bell, TX Roadhouse, Wendy's [lodging] Comfort Suites, Hampton Inn, Hilton Garden, Holiday Inn, Woodspring Suites [other] $Tree, AAA, AT&T, Best Buy, BooksAMillion, Dick's, Discount Tire, Home Depot, JC Penney, Jo-Ann Fabrics, Macy's, Marshall's, Michael's, NTB, Old Navy, Petsmart, Sam's Club/gas, Staples, Target, Verizon, Walmart/Subway, W [gas] Circle K/dsl [food] DQ, Hardee's, Waffle House [other] to VSU, U-Haul

53 S Park Blvd, E same as 54

52.5mm Appomattox River

52 Washington St, Wythe St, E [gas] Marathon/dsl, Valero/dsl [food] Jade Garden [lodging] Knights Inn, Royal Inn [other] Petersburg Nat Bfd, W [gas] Liberty [other] [H]

51 I-85 S, to South Hill, US 460 W

50d Wythe St, (from nb), same as 52

50b c E [gas] 7-11 [lodging] Flagship Inn

50a US 301, US 460 E, to Crater Rd, County Dr, E [gas] BP, RaceWay/dsl, Star Express [food] Hardee's [lodging] American Inn, Budget Inn, California Inn, EconoLodge [other] [H]

48b a Wagner Rdon Crater Rd, W [gas] Gulf/dsl, Wawa [food] Arby's, Bojangles, Burger King, Capt D's, KFC, King's BBQ, Little Caesar's, Pizza Hut, Plaza Mexico, Subway, Taco Bell, Taste of China [lodging] Country Inn&Suites, Super 8 [other] $General, $Tree, Advance Parts, [H], Martin's Foods, O'Reilly Parts, PepBoys, USPO, Verizon, Walgreens, Walmart

47 VA 629, to Rives Rd, W [gas] Citgo, Shell/dsl [food] Bojangles, KFC, Outlaw's Rest. [lodging] Heritage Motel [other] Ace Hardware, same as 48 on US 301, Softball Hall of Fame Museum, Walmart

46 I-295 N (exits left from sb), to Washington

PETERSBURG

VA

INTERSTATE 95 Cont'd

Exit#	Services
45	US 301, E Shell/dsl, W Exxon/Circle K Lighthouse Rest., Nanny's Rest., Steven Kent Rest. Comfort Inn, Days Inn, Hampton Inn, Holiday Inn Express, Howard Johnson, Quality Inn
41	US 301, VA 35, VA 156, E Exxon/dsl/scales/24hr Nino's N Italian Rest. EconoLodge South 40 camp resort, W Travelers Inn
40mm	**weigh sta both lanes**
37	US 301, Carson, W BP/dsl, Shell/dsl
36mm	**nb, full facilities, litter barrel, petwalk, , , vending**
33	VA 602, W Davis/Exxon/Subway/Starbucks/dsl/scales/24hr, Moble/Wendys/dsl Denny's, Little Italy, Popeye's Hampton Inn, Sleep Inn
31	VA 40, Stony Creek, to Waverly, W Citgo/dsl, Shell/dsl Tastee Hut Family$
24	VA 645
20	VA 631, Jarratt, W Exxon/Blimpie/Pizza Hut/dsl/24hr, Sunoco/dsl $General, Ford
17	US 301,1 mi E Knights Inn, Reste Motel Jellystone Park Camping
13	VA 614, to Emporia, E Exxon/Chester's/dsl, Shell/dsl
12	US 301 (from nb)
11b a	US 58, Emporia, to South Hill, E Citgo/Burger King, Exxon/Blimpie/LJ Silver, Shell/dsl Applebee's, Arby's, Carolina BBQ, Cracker Barrel, Domino's, Hardee's, KFC, McDonald's, Pizza Hut, Taco Bell, Wendy's, Wong's Garden Country Inn&Suites, Fairfield Inn, Rodeway Inn H, Advance Parts, Buick/Chevrolet/GMC, CVS Drug, Family$, Food Lion, NAPA, O'Reilly Parts, Rite Aid, Verizon, Walmart, W Exxon, Pilot/Sadler/5 Guys Burgers/dsl/scales/24hr/@, Race-In/Quiznos/dsl Bojangles, Pino's Pizza, Shoney's Best Western, Days Inn, Hampton Inn, Holiday Inn Express, Quality Inn, Sleep Inn
8	US 301, E Citgo, Simmons/Exxon/Huddle House/dsl/scales/24hr Motel 6, Red Carpet Inn truck repair
4	VA 629, to Skippers, E Loves/McDonald's/dsl/scales/24hr, Pilot/Dunkin Donuts/Subway/dsl/scales/24hr, Shell/IHOP, W AmericanInn
3.5mm	Fountain's Creek
.5mm	**Welcome Ctr nb, full facilities, litter barrels, petwalk, , , vending**
0mm	Virginia/North Carolina state line

EMPORIA

INTERSTATE 264 (Norfolk)

Exit#	Services
23mm	I-264 begins/ends. BP, Shell convention ctr
22	Birdneck Rd, N Pizza Hut museum, vet, S Shell/dsl Dunkin Donuts, Max&Erma's, McDonald's/playplace, Subway DoubleTree Family$, Food Lion, O'Reilly Parts
21	VA Beach Blvd, First Colonial Rd, N BP, Shell Applebee's, Arby's, Burger King, Chick-fil-A, China Wok, Chipotle, DQ, Five Guys, IHOP, KFC, McDonald's, Moe's SW Grill, Otani Japanese, Outback Steaks, Panera Bread, Pizza Hut, Plaza Azteca, Schlotzsky's, Shogun Japanese, Sonic, Starbucks, Subway, Taco Bell, Virginian Steaks, Wendy's, Zero's Subs Advance Parts, CVS, GNC, JoAnn Fabrics, Kroger/dsl, Michael's, Office Depot, Petsmart, Rite Aid, SteinMart, Target, Toyota, Trader Joe's, USPO, Verizon, vet, Walgreens, Whole Foods Mkt, S Shell, Wawa/dsl 7-11, CarQuest, Firestone/auto, NAPA

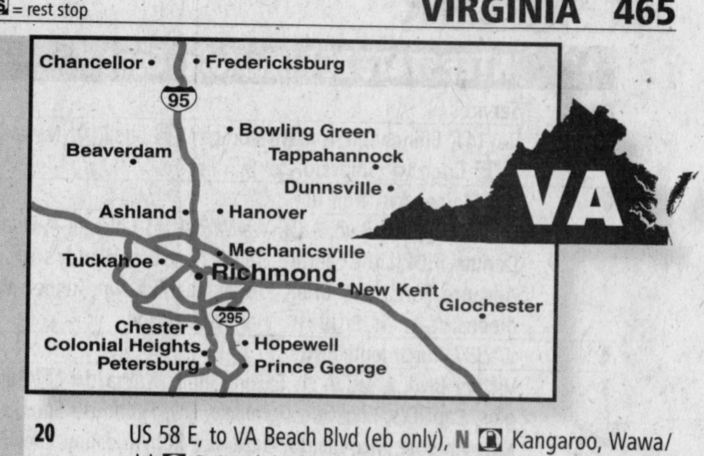

Exit#	Services
20	US 58 E, to VA Beach Blvd (eb only), N Kangaroo, Wawa/dsl Bojangle's, Capt. George's Seafood, China Moon, Hardee's, Ruby Tuesday, Starbucks, Subway 7-11, Family$, Food Lion, Kia/Lincoln, Lowe's, PepBoys, TJ Maxx, Tuesday Morning, vet
19	Lynnhaven Pkwy, N 7-11, Wawa Ensenada Mexican, Iggle's, Lucky Express, Subway Audi, Chevrolet, Ford, Hobby Lobby, Hyundai, Jaguar, Porsche, Subaru, VW, Walmart Mkt, S Five Guys, McDonald's, Olive Garden, Starbucks, Taco Bell Walmart
18	Rosemont, N Exxon Bonefish Grill, Burger King, Denny's, Hardee's, Jade Garden, KFC, LJ Silver, McDonald's, Mi Casita Mexican, Papa John's, Pizza Hut, Starbucks, Taco Bell, Wendy's, Zero's Subs EconoLodge $Tree, Acura, AutoZone, BJ's Whse/gas, CarMax, Chrysler/Dodge/Jeep, Food Lion, Home Depot, Honda, Kroger, Nissan, Petsmart, NTB, Rite Aid, Sam's Club/gas, Walgreens, S Speedway/dsl, Wawa/dsl Four Seasons Chinese $General, CVS
17.5mm	**inspection sta wb only**
17a b	Independance Blvd, N Exxon Bahama Breeze, Cheesecake Factory, Chipotle, IHOP, Jason's Deli, Macaroni Grill, Max&Erma's, McDonald's, Mission BBQ, Panera Bread, PF Chang's, Ruby Tuesday, Smokey Bones BBQ, Starbucks, Taco Bell, Village Inn, Wendy's Candlewood Suites, Crowne Plaza, Days Inn, Extended Stay, Hilton Garden, Motel 6, Westin Barnes&Noble, Best Buy, Dick's, Kohl's, Michael's, Old Navy, Steinmart, Target, Walgreens, S 7-11, Exxon/dsl, Wawa/dsl Arby's, Azteca Mexican, Domino's, Firehouse Subs, Golden Corral, Hardee's, KFC, Panda China, Quiznos, Starbucks, Subway, Taco Bell, TX Roadhouse, Zero Subs InTown Suites $General, auto repair, Food Lion, Mazda, Rite Aid, vet
16	Witchduck Rd
15a b	Newtown Rd, N Capt D's, Domino's, McDonald's, Taco Bell, Wendy's Homewood Suites, TownePlace Suites 7-11, AutoZone, S BP, Shell Denny's Courtyard, Hampton Inn, Holiday Inn, La Quinta, Red Roof Inn, SpringHill Suites 7-11, Rite Aid
14b a	I-64, US 13, to Military Hwy
13	US 13, Military Hwy, N Shell Arby's, Boston Mkt, Lonestar Steaks, Mongolian BBQ, Norfolk Garden Korean, Piccadilly, Schlotzsky's Days Inn, EconoLodge, Motel 6, Ramada Ltd Costco/gas, CVS, Firestone/auto, Ross
12	Ballentine Blvd, N H, Norfolk SU
11b a	US 460, VA 166/168, Brambleton Ave, Campostello Rd, N 7-11 Chick-fil-A
10	Tidewater Dr, City Hall Ave, exits left from eb, N Shell McDonald's, Popeye's
9	St Paul's Blvd, Waterside Dr, S to Harbor Park Stadium
8	I-464 S, to Chesapeake
7.5mm	tunnel

VA

INTERSTATE 264 (Norfolk) Cont'd

Exit#	Services
7b a	VA 141, Effingham St, Crawford St, N Shell Naval H, S Citgo Shipyard
6	Des Moines Ave (from eb)
5	US 17, Frederick Blvd, N WaWa/dsl Chick-fil-A, Dunkin Donuts, IHOP, Little Caesar's, Rally's, Taco Bell, Wendy's H, Advance Parts, CVS Drug, Kroger, to Midtown Tunnel, Walgreens, Walmart, S Harley-Davidson
4	VA 337, Portsmouth Blvd
3	Victory Blvd, N 7-11, Exxon, Shell, WaWa/dsl Bojangles, Capt D's, CookOut, Domino's, DQ, Firehouse Subs, KFC, Krispy Kreme, McDonald's, Pizza Hut, Ruby Tuesday, Taco Bell, Tops China, Wendy's $Tree, Advance Parts, AutoZone, BigLots, Lowe's, PepBoys, S Royal Farms/dsl, Valero/dsl
2b a	Greenwood Dr
0mm	**I-264 begins/ends on I-64, exit 299.**

VA

INTERSTATE 295 (Richmond)

MECHANICSVILLE

Exit#	Services
53b a	I-64, W to Charlottesville, E to Richmond, to US 250, **I-295 begins/ends.**
51b a	Nuckols Rd, **1 mi** N Miller's/dsl, Valero Cheeburger, Chen's Chinese, Home Team Grill, McDonald's, Nonna's Pizzaria, Pizza Hut, Rico's Mexican, Samurai Japanese, Starbucks, Subway, Tropical Smoothie Cafe CVS Drug, Food Lion, Walgreens, S Exxon/Mkt Cafe USPO
49b a	US 33, Richmond, S JJ's Grille, Little Angela's, Little Caesar's, Little Szechuan, Nuevo Mexico $ General, 7-11, CVS
45b a	Woodman Rd1-2mi S 7-11 Little Caesar's $General, CVS Drug, Meadow Farm Museum
43	I-95, US 1, N to Washington, S to Richmond (exits left from nb), **N on US 1** Shell/dsl Applebee's, Arby's, BBQ, Buffalo Wild Wings, Chick-fil-A, Chili's, Chipotle Mexican, Coldstone, Famous Dave's BBQ, Firehouse Subs, McDonald's, O'Charley's, O'Dragon buffet, Panera Bread, Papa John's, Pizzaro, Plaza Azteca Mexican, Red Robin, Roda Japanese, Shoney's, Starbucks, Subway, TX Roadhouse, Wendy's Candlewood Suites, Comfort Suites, Courtyard, Hampton Inn, SpringHill Suites $Tree, AT&T, Barnes&Noble, Best Buy, Burlington, Dick's, Firestone/auto, GNC, Goodyear/auto, Home Depot, JC Penney, Macy's, Martin's Foods, Merchant's Tire, Michael's, Petsmart, Ross, Target, Tire America, Walgreens, **1-2 mi** S 7-11, Shell, WaWa Aunt Sarah's, Burger King, Frida's Mexican, Hardee's, KFC/Taco Bell, McDonald's, Ming's Dynasty, Starbucks, Subway, Waffle House, Wendy's Best Value Inn, Cavalier Motel, Days Inn, EconoLodge, Knights Inn, Sleep Inn $Tree, Food Lion, Lowe's, Walmart
41b a	US 301, VA 2, E BP/dsl, Valero/dsl, WaWa/dsl Bojangles, Burger King, China Kitchen, Dunkin Donuts, Marty's Grill, McDonald's, Popeye's, Stevi B's, Subway, Tropical Smoothie Cafe, Wendy's, Zheng Chinese $General, AT&T, AutoZone, Kroger/gas, URGENT CARE, Verizon, vet, Walgreens, **0-4 mi** W Exxon/dsl Friendly's Holiday Inn, Super 8, Travelodge
38b a	VA 627, Pole Green Rd, **0-1 mi** E 7-11, Exxon/dsl, Sunoco/dsl Antonio's Pizza, Bell Cafe, Bruster's, Chen's Rest., Mimmo's Rest., Patron Mexican, Subway Food Lion, vet, W 7-11, Valero Pasta House CVS, H
37b a	US 360, E BP, Shell/dsl, Valero Applebee's, Arby's, Buffalo Wild Wings, Burger King, Chick-fil-A, Cookout, Cracker Barrel, DQ, Franco's, Gus' Italian, IHOP, Jersey Mike's, KFC,
37b a	Continued McDonald's, Mexico Rest., Moe's SW Grill, Noodles&Co, Outback Steaks, Panera Bread, Papa John's, Peking Chinese, Pizza Hut, Roma Italian, Ruby Tuesday, Shoney's, Starbucks, Subway, Taco Bell, Waffle House, Wendy's Hampton Inn, Holiday Inn Express $Tree, Advance Parts, Aldi Foods, AT&T Best Buy, BJ's Whse/gas, CVS, Food Lion, GNC, Home Depot Kohl's, Marshall's, Old Navy, Petsmart, Target, Verizon, Walgreens, Walmart/Burger King, W 7-11, Sunoco/dsl, Valero/dsl $General, to Mechanicsville
34b a	VA 615, Creighton Rd, E 7-11, Valero
31b a	VA 156, E Exxon/dsl to Cold Harbor Bfd, W Shell (4mi), Valero Hardee's (4mi) Courtyard (4mi), EconoLodge (4mi), Holiday Inn Express (4mi), Motel 6 (4mi)
28	I-64, to US 60, W museum
25	Rd 895 W (**toll**), to Richmond
22b a	VA 5, Charles City, E Exxon/dsl DQ Shirley Plantation, W Valero/Subway/dsl China Taste, Portabella' Cafe Food Lion, Richmond Nat Bfd, Rite Aid
18mm	James River
16	Rivers Bend Blvd
15b a	VA 10, Hopewell, E BP/dsl Burger King H, James River Plantations, W EC/Subway/dsl, Exxon/McDonald's dsl, Sheetz, WaWa/dsl Cesare's Ristorante, Chen's Rest Jalapeno's, Rivers Bend Grill, Taco Bell, Wendy's, Wing's Pizza Hyatt Place, Residence Inn CVS Drug, Food Lion
13mm	Appomattox River
9b a	VA 36, Hopewell, E Citgo, Gulf, WaWa/dsl Bojangles, El Nopal, Hardee's, KFC, Little Caesar's, McDonald's, Rosa's Italian Best Western, EconoLodge, Fairfield Inn, StayOver Suites $General, Advance Parts, AutoZone, Family$, O'Reilly Parts Verizon, vet, Walgreens, W BP/dsl, Exxon, Shell/dsl, Sunoco dsl Burger King, Denny's, DQ, Dragon Express, Dunkin Donuts, Kanpai Japanese, McDonald's, Papa John's, Pizza Hut, Ruby Tuesday, Shoney's, Starbucks, Subway, Taco Bell, Top's China Waffle House, Wendy's Baymont Inn, Candlewood Suites Hampton Inn, Quality Inn $Tree, Chevrolet, Family$, Food Lion, Rite Aid, to Petersburg Nat Bfd, U-Haul, US Army Museum
5.5mm	Blackwater Swamp
3b a	US 460, Petersburg, to Norfolk, E EC/Subway/dsl, Pilot Wendy's/dsl/scales/24hr Prince George BBQ, **1-2 mi** W BP/dsl McDonald's
1	I-95, N to Petersburg, S to Emporium, **I-295 begins/ends.**

HOPEWELL

INTERSTATE 495 (DC)

Exit#	Services
57	I-95 S, I-395 N, I-95 N. **I-495 & I-95 N run together. See MD I-95 exits 25b a-2b a.**
54b a	VA 620, Braddock Rd, S Shell/dsl Hong Kong Express 7-11, Ctr for the Arts, Geo Mason U, NTB, Rite Aid Safeway Foods, USPO
52b a	VA 236, Little River Tpk, Fairfax, E Liberty/dsl, Sunoco repair Chicken Loco, KFC/Taco Bell, Little Caesar's, McDonald's, Wendy's $Tree, 7-11, Advance Parts, GNC, Petco Safeway Foods
51	VA 657, Gallows Rd, W Exxon H, 7-11
50b a	US 50, Arlington Blvd, Fairfax, Arlington, E Marriott W Shell, Sunoco/dsl 5 Guys Burgers, Chevy's Mexican Grevey's Rest, Jasmine Garden, McDonald's, Panda Express Panera Bread, Papa John's, Starbucks, Sweetwater Tavern, Uno Grill, Wendy's Residence Inn H, CVS Drug, Midas, Staples, Target, URGENT CARE, vet

INTERSTATE 495 (DC) Cont'd

WASHINGTON AREA

Exit#	Services
49c b a	I-66 (exits left from both lanes), to Manassas, Front Royal
47b a	VA 7, Leesburg Pike, Tysons Corner, Falls Church, E Westin, W BP/dsl, Exxon, Shell/dsl BJ's Rest., Chili's, Jimmy John's, McDonald's, Olive Garden, On-the-Border, Panera Bread, Silver Diner, Starbucks, Subway, Wendy's Embassy Suites, Hilton Garden AT&T, Best Buy, Bloomingdale's, Buick/Chevrolet/GMC, Chrysler/Dodge/Jeep, CVS Drug, Marshall's, Mr Tire, PetCo, Petsmart, Staples, Subaru/VW, TJ Maxx
46b a	VA 123, Chain Bridge Rd, W Gulf/dsl, Sunoco/dsl Cheesecake Factory, Maggiano's, PF Chang's Courtyard, Crowne Plaza Macy's
45b a	VA 267 W (toll), to I-66 E, to Dulles Airport
44	VA 193, Langley
43	G Washington Mem Pkwy, no trucks
42mm	Virginia/Maryland state line, Potomac River. **Exits 41-27 are in Maryland.**
41	Clara Barton Pkwy, Carderock, Great Falls, no trucks
40	Cabin John Pkwy, Glen Echo (from sb), no trucks
39	MD 190, River Rd, Washington, Potomac
38	I-270, to Frederick
36	MD 187, Old Georgetown Rd, S H
35	(from wb), I-270
34	MD 355, Wisconsin Ave, Bethesda
33	MD 185, Connecticut Ave, N LDS Temple, S Citgo/repair, Giant/dsl, Liberty Chevy Chase Mkt, Starbucks
31b a	MD 97, Georgia Ave, Silver Spring, N H, S BP/dsl, Exxon/dsl, Shell, W Express/dsl Armand's Pizza, Domino's, Mayflower Chinese CVS Drug, Snider's Foods, Staples, vet
30b a	US 29, Colesville, N BP/dsl, Citgo, Shell Chipotle, McDonald's, Papa John's, Red Maple Asian, Starbucks, Subway 7-11/Jerry's Subs, CVS Drug, Safeway Foods
29b a	MD 193, University Blvd
28b a	MD 650, New Hampshire Ave, N BP, Exxon/dsl, Shell/repair Domino's, Quizno's, Starbucks, Urban BBQ 7-11, CVS Drug, Safeway Foods
27	I-95, N to Baltimore, S to Richmond.

I-495 & I-95 S run together. See MD I-95, exits 25b a-2b a.

INTERSTATE 664 (Norfolk)

PORTSMOUTH

Exit#	Services
15b a	I-64 to Chesapeake, I-264 E to Portsmouth & Norfolk. **I-664 begins/ends on I-64, exit 299.**
13b a	US 13, US 58, US 460, Military Hwy, E Shell/Frank's/dsl Bowers Hill Inn
12	VA 663, Dock Landing Rd
11b a	VA 337, Portsmouth Blvd, E 7-11, Citgo, Shell/dsl, Speedway Applebee's, Arby's, Buffet City, Burger King, Chick-fil-A, Chili's, ChuckECheese, DQ, Dunkin Donuts, Five Guys, Golden Corral, IHOP, McDonald's, Olive Garden, Outback Steaks, Piccadilly, Pizza Hut, Pizza Hut, Red Lobster, Red Robin,

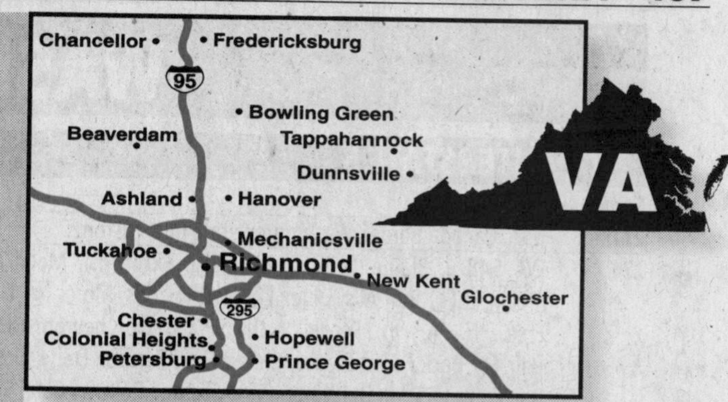

Exit#	Services
11b a	Continued Starbucks, Subway, Taco Bell, Wendy's Extended Stay 4 Less, Hampton Inn, Holiday Inn Express $Tree, AutoZone, Best Buy, Big Lots, BJ's Whse/gas, Buick, Firestone/auto, Food Lion, Ford, Home Depot, Merchant's Auto Ctr, Michael's, Old Navy, Petsmart, Ross, Sam's Club/gas, Target, Tuesday Morning, Walmart, W 7-11 Burger King, Cracker Barrel, Old Bay Seafood, Subway, Waffle House Candlewood Suites, Fairfield Inn Lowe's
10	VA 659, Pughsville Rd, E 7-11, Citgo, Shell La Tolteca Food Lion, Rite Aid, vet
9b a	US 17, US 164, E 7-11, Speedway/dsl, Wawa Burger King, Capt D's, Domino's, DQ, Dunkin Donuts, Great Wall Chinese, KFC, McDonald's, Papa John's, Pizza Hut, Sonic, Taco Bell, Waffle House, Wendy's Budget Lodge, Extended Stay America, Sleep Inn, Studios & Suites for Less, Super 8 $Tree, Advance Parts, Chevrolet, Honda, Hyundai, Kia, NAPA, Nissan, O'Reilly Parts, tires, Toyota, W Buffalo Wild Wings, Subway Comfort Suites, Hilton Garden H, Harris Teeter, to James River Br
8b a	VA 135, College Dr, E 7-11, Murphy USA/dsl Applebee's, Arby's, Chick-fil-A, Chipotle, Firehouse Subs, IHOP, McDonald's, Panda Express, Panera Bread, Ruby Tuesday, Subway, Taco Bell, TX Roadhouse, Wendy's, Zaxby's Dick's, Discount Tire, Food Lion, GNC, Kohl's, Petsmart, Rite Aid, TJ Maxx, Walmart, W Riverstone Chophouse Courtyard, TownePlace Suites
11.5mm	insp sta nb
9mm	James River
8mm	tunnel
7	Terminal Ave
6	25th St, 26th St, E 7-11 McDonald's, W Subway
5	US 60 W, 35th St, Jefferson Ave, E Fast&Easy #1 Chinese, Church's, King's Pizza Hornsby Tire
4	Chesnut Ave, Roanoke Ave
3	Aberdeen Rd, W 7-11 Hardee's, McDonald's, Wendy's
2	Powhatan Pkwy, E 7-11, 1-2 mi W Coldstone, Joe's Crabshack, Longhorn Steaks Hilton Garden, SpringHill Suites Bass Pro Shop, BJ's Whse/gas, Lowe's
1b a	I-64, W to Richmond, E to Norfolk. **I-664 begins/ends on I-64.**

VA

NOTES

WASHINGTON

INTERSTATE 5

WA

Exit#	Services
277mm	USA/Canada Border, Washington state line, customs
276	WA 548 S, Blaine, E Chevron/dsl, Exxon/dsl, Mobil/dsl, Shell/dsl Big Al's Diner Northwoods Motel Duty Free, NAPA, to Peace Arch SP, W Chevron/dsl/repair Back Forest Steaks, Chada Thai, Edaleen Dairy, Ocean Bay Chinese, Pasa Del Norte, Pizza Factory, Railway Cafe, Starbucks, Tony's Cafe Anchor Inn, Bay Side Motel, Cottage by the Bay B&B, International Motel, Sunset Inn **Welcome Ctr,** Blaine Marine Park, USPO
275	WA 543 N (from nb, no return), E Chevron/dsl, Mkt/dsl, Shell/dsl Burger King, Subway $Tree, Border Tire, Cost-Cutter Foods, Rite Aid, truck customs
274	Peace Portal Drive (from nb, no return), Blaine, W Shell/dsl Lizzie's Cafe Semi-ah-moo Resort
270	Birch Bay, Lynden, W Shell/Domino's/Subway/dsl Bob's Burgers, Jack-in-the-Box, Subway Semi-ah-moo Resort Birch Bay Mkt, Thousand Trails Camping, vet
269mm	**Welcome Ctr sb, full facilities, info, litter barrels, petwalk, , , vending**
267mm	**nb, full facilities, info, litter barrels, petwalk, , , vending**
266	WA 548 N, Grandview Rd, Custer, W Arco Birch Bay SP
263	Portal Way, E Pacific Pride/dsl, Shell/dsl El Nopal Mexican AA RV Park, Cedars RV Park
263mm	Nooksack River
262	Main St, Ferndale, E Chevron/dsl, Pilot/Subway/dsl/scales/24hr McDonald's Super 8 GCR Tires, vet, W Gull/dsl, Shell/dsl Bob's Burgers, Domino's, DQ, Jack-in-the-Box, Papa Murphy's, Sonic, Starbucks, Taco Time Motel 6 $Tree, Grocery Outlet, Haggen's Foods, NAPA, O'Reilly Parts, Schwab Tire, Verizon, vet, Walgreens
260	Slater Rd, Lummi Island, E Arco/dsl antiques, El Monte RV Ctr, 4 mi W Silver Reef Hotel/Casino Lummi Ind Res
258	Bakerview Rd, E Asian Fusion, Five Guys, IHOP, Jack-in-the-Box, Papa Murphy's, Port of Subs, Starbucks, Subway, Taco Time La Quinta Costco/dsl, Fred Meyer/dsl, Verizon, W 76/7-11, Arco, Mkt/dsl Mykono's Greek Rest. Holiday Inn Express, Hotel Bellingham, Shamrock Motel , Bellingham RV Park, st patrol
257	Northwest Ave, E Jack-in-the-Box, Starbucks Home 2 Hilton, La Quinta, SpringHill Suites, TownePlace Suites Cadillac/Chevrolet
256b	Bellis Fair Mall Pkwy (from nb), E JC Penney, Target
256a	WA 539 N, Meridian St, E Shell/dsl, Super Gas/dsl Arby's, Asian 1, Boston's Rest., Buffalo Wild Wings, Burger King, China Palace, Chipotle, Denny's, Domino's, DQ, Jimmy John's, Lilia's Mexican, McDonald's, Mi Mexico, Olive Garden, Red Robin, Shari's, Starbucks, Subway, Taco Bell, Taco Time, Thai House Rest., Wendy's, Wonderful Buffet Baymont Inn, Best Western, Comfort Inn, Holiday Inn Express, Oxford Suites, Quality Inn $Tree, AT&T, Barnes&Noble, Best Buy, Dick's, Hobby Lobby, Home Depot, JC Penney, Kohl's, Macy's, Marshall's, Michael's, Midas, O'Reilly Parts, Office Depot, O'Reilly Parts, PetCo, Petsmart, Rite Aid, Ross, Schwab Tire, Sierra Trading Post, Target, TJ Maxx, U-Haul, Verizon, Walgreens, Walmart/McDonald's, WinCo Foods, W Slo Pitch Grill EconoLodge, Rodeway Inn
255	WA 542 E, Sunset Dr, Bellingham, E 76, Chevron/dsl, Shell/dsl A&W/KFC, Applebee's, El Gitano Mexican, Hawaii BBQ, Jack-in-the-Box, Panda Express, Panda Palace, RoundTable Pizza, Starbucks, Taco Bell Jo-Ann Fabrics, Lowe's, Rite Aid, Safeway/dsl, to Mt Baker, Tuesday Morning, USPO, Verizon, Walgreens, W
254	Iowa St, State St, Bellingham, E 76, Mobil/dsl Audi/VW, Chrysler/Dodge/Jeep, Honda, Hyundai, Kia, Mercedes, Nissan, Subaru, Toyota, Volvo, W Chevron/dsl, Shell DQ, McDonald's, Starbucks, Subway AutoZone, Ford, Midas, NAPA, O'Reilly Parts
253	Lakeway Dr, Bellingham, E Little Caesar's, Papa John's, Papa Murphy's, Port of Subs, Rhodes Cafe, Sol de Mexico, Subway, Woods Coffee Guesthouse Inn, Sheraton Fou[r] Points 7-11, Discount Tire, Fred Meyer/dsl, URGENT CARE, Whole Foods Mkt, W same as 252
252	Samish Way, Bellingham, E same as 253, W 76, Chevron, dsl, SuperGas/dsl Boomers Drive-In, Busara Thai Cuisine, Domino's, El Agave, El Albanil Mexican, Five Columns Greek, Kyoto Steaks, McDonald's, Pizza Hut, Sehome Diner, Starbucks, Subway, Taco Time, Wendy's Bay City Motel, Bellinghan[m] Lodge, Cascade Inn, Coachman Inn, Days Inn, Motel 6, Vill[a] Inn $Tree, Ace Hardware, AT&T, Haggen Foods, REI, Rit[e] Aid, URGENT CARE, vet, Walgreens
250	WA 11 S, Chuckanut Dr, Bellingham, Fairhaven Hist Dis[t] W Arco, Shell/repair Starbucks, Subway to Alask[a] Ferry, to Larrabee SP
246	N Lake Samish, E Lake Padden RA, W Shell/dsl
242	Nulle Rd, S Lake Samish
240	Alger, E Shell/dsl/LP/RV dump Alger Grille Whi[s]pering Firs Motel/RV Parking
238mm	**both lanes, full facilities, litter barrels, petwalk, , , vending**
236	Bow Hill Rd, E Skagit Hotel Casino/rest./dsl/LP
235mm	**weigh sta sb**
234mm	Samish River
232	Cook Rd, Sedro-Woolley, E Chevron/dsl, Shell/dsl, Tesla EV Bob's Burgers, Jack-in-the-Box, Starbucks, Subway Fai[r]field Inn , KOA (3mi)
231	WA 11 N, Chuckanut Dr, E Camping World RV Ctr, Halte[r]man's RV Ctr, Kia, vet, W st patrol, to Larrabee SP (14mi)
230	WA 20, Burlington, E Chevron, Shell/dsl Applebee['s], Carino's Italian, Jack-in-the-Box, Mi Mexico, MOD Pizza, O[ut]back Steaks, Papa Murphy's, Pizza Factory, Pizza Hut/Taco Be[ll], Popeye's, Red Robin, Starbucks Cocusa Motel, Sterli[ng] Motel , $Tree, 7-11, AutoZone, Fred Meyer/dsl, Hagg[en] Foods, JC Penney, Macy's, Schwab Tire, Skagit Transmissio[n], Target, to N Cascades NP, Walgreens, W Pacific Prid[e]/dsl McDonald's Holiday Inn Express Harley-Davi[d]son, Hyundai, to San Juan Ferry
229	George Hopper Rd, E Arco, Mobil/dsl Carl's Jr, Chipo[tle] Mexican, Five Guys, Jamba Juice, Jimmy John's, McDonal[d's], Olive Garden, Panera Bread, Sakura Japanese, Shari's, St[ar]bucks, Subway, Taco Del Mar, Wendy's Candlewood Suit[es], Hampton Inn AT&T, Best Buy, Costco/gas, Dick's, Disco[unt] Tire, Home Depot, Kohl's, Michael's, Old Navy, Outlet Sho[ps]/famous brands, Petsmart, Ross, See's Candies, Verizon, W Chrysler/Jeep/Dodge, Ford/Lincoln, Honda, Mazda, N[is]san, Subaru, Toyota, VW

BLAINE

BELLINGHAM

BURLINGTON

 = gas = food = lodging = other = rest stop

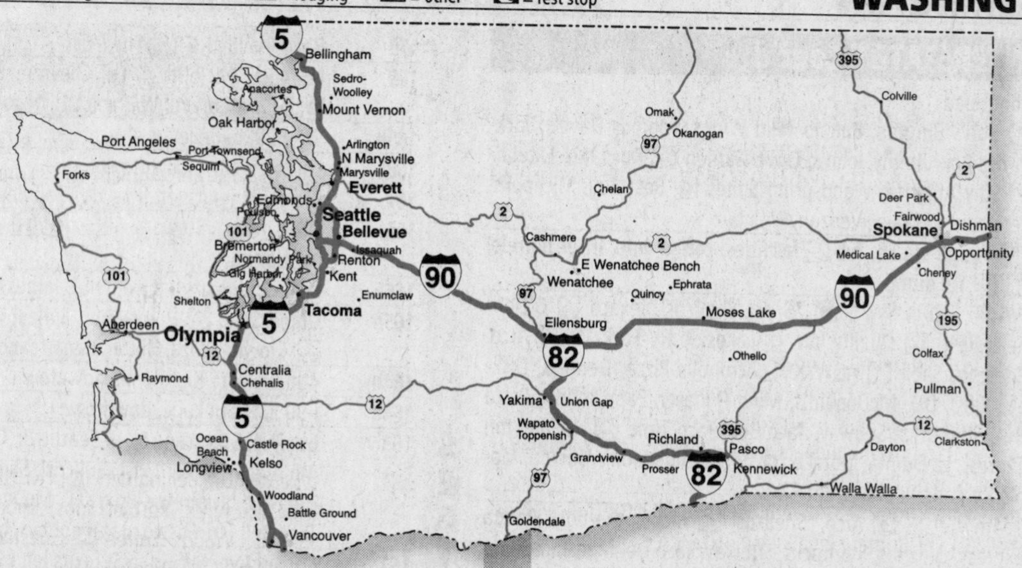

MT VERNON

WA

INTERSTATE 5 Cont'd

Exit#	Services
228mm	Skagit River
227	WA 538 E, College Way, Mt Vernon, E A&W, Big Scoop Rest., Denny's, Dragon Inn, El Gitano, Firehouse Subs, Hong Kong Rest., Jack-in-the Box, Jersey Mike's, KFC, Max Dale's Steak Chops, Moreno's Mexican, Papa Murphy's, Pizza Hut, Riverside Cafe, RoundTable Pizza, Starbucks, Subway, Taco Bell, Taco Time Days Inn, West Winds Motel $Tree, Ace Hardware, AutoZone, Grocery Outlet, Hobby Lobby, Jo-Ann Fabrics, Motorworks, Office Depot, O'Reilly Parts, PepBoys, PetCo, Rite Aid, Safeway/dsl, Tire Factory, Verizon, W APP/dsl, Shell/dsl Arby's, Burger King, Burgermaster, DQ, Fortune Chinese, IHOP, Los Compadres, Panda Express, Royal Star Buffet Best Western, Quality Inn, Tulip Inn Blade RV Ctr, Chevrolet, Lowe's, Riverbend RV Park, URGENT CARE, Walmart/Subway
226	WA 536 W, Kincaid St, E H, W Old Towne Grainery Rest., Skagit River Brewing Co City Ctr, NAPA, Red Apple Mkt, visitor info
225	Anderson Rd, E 76/dsl CarQuest, Country Motorhomes, W Chevron Evert's RV Ctr, Freightliner, Poulsbo RV Ctr
224	WA 99 S (from nb, no return), S Mt Vernon, E food, gas/dsl
221	WA 534 E, Conway, Lake McMurray, E 76/dsl farmers mkt, W 76/dsl, Chevron/dsl/LP Conway Deli Channel Lodge/Rest. (11mi) Blake's RV Park/marina (6mi), USPO
218	Starbird Rd
215	300th NW, W Interstate/dsl
214mm	**weigh sta nb**
212	WA 532 W, Stanwood, Bryant, W 76/dsl, Shell/Burger Stop/dsl Camano Island SP (19mi)
210	236th NE, E Angel Winds Casino, River Rock/dsl
209mm	Stillaguamish River
208	WA 530, Silvana, Arlington, E 76, A1/dsl, Arco/dsl, Chevron/dsl, Pilot/PJ Fresh/dsl/scales/24hr Denny's, Subway Arlington Motel Chevrolet, to N Cascades Hwy, W Mobil/dsl
207mm	**both lanes, full facilities, coffee, litter barrels, petwalk, RV dump, vending**
206	WA 531, Lakewood, E 7-11, 76/dsl, Arco, Shell Alfy's Pizza, Buzz Inn Steaks, Domino's, Jack-in-the-Box, Jersey Mike's, Jimmy John's, KFC, Little Caesar's, McDonald's, Moose Creek BBQ, Olympia Pizza, Panda Express, Papa Murphy's, Peking Palace, Starbucks, Subway, Taco Time, Wendy's Best Western+,
206	Continued Quality Inn, Wyndham Garden $Tree, AT&T, Chrysler/Dodge/Jeep, Ford, Harley-Davidson, Honda, Jo-Ann Fabrics, Lowe's, O'Reilly Parts, Rite Aid, Safeway/dsl, Schwab Tire, vet, Walmart/Subway, W Bonefish Grill, Boston's, Buffalo Wild Wings, Burger King, Chipotle, Coldstone, Firehouse Subs, Five Guys, Hop Jack's, IHOP, Jamba Juice, MOD Pizza, Outback Steaks, Pizza Hut, Popeye's, Qdoba, Red Robin, Starbucks, Taco Bell, Taco Bell AT&T, Best Buy, Costco/gas, Dick's, Discount Tire, Firestone/auto, Hobby Lobby, Marshall's, Michael's, Office Depot, PetCo, Target, to Wenburg SP, Tuesday Morning, Verizon
202	116th NE, E Shell/dsl Arby's, Blazing Onion Burger, Carl's Jr, DQ, Papa John's, Popeye's, Sonic, Starbucks, Subway, Taco Bell Home 2 Suites $Tree, Kohl's, Petsmart, Rite Aid, Ross, URGENT CARE, Verizon, WinCo Foods, W Chevron/dsl, Donna's Trkstp/Gull/dsl/scales/24hr/@ McDonald's, Olive Garden, RAM Rest. Seattle Outlets/famous brands, st patrol, Tulalip Resort/Casino
200	88th St NE, Quil Ceda Way, E 7-11, Shell/dsl/LP Applebee's, Jersey Mike's, Mkt St Cafe, Starbucks Holiday Inn Express Haggen's Foods, W USA Bob's Burgers, Panera Bread, Port of Subs Cabela's, casino, Home Depot, Walmart/McDonald's
199	WA 528 E, Marysville, Tulalip, E 76, Arco, Chevron/dsl, Shell/dsl Burger King, Don's Rest./24hr, DQ, Jack-in-the-Box, Jimmy John's, Las Margaritas Mexican, MOD Pizza, Subway Village Motel/Rest. Albertson's, AT&T, Big Lots, JC Penney, Petco, Rite Aid, Staples, Verizon, Walgreens, W 76, Chevron/dsl McDonald's, Taco Time, Wendy's Quality Inn casino, Chevrolet, Robinson RV Ctr, Subaru, to Tulalip Indian Res
198	Port of Everett (from sb), Steamboat Slough, st patrol
195mm	Snohomish River
195	Port of Everett (from nb), Marine View Dr
194	US 2 E, Everett Ave, W Shell/dsl City Ctr, Schwab Tire
193	WA 529, Pacific Ave (from nb), W Denny's, Hunan Palace Best Western, Delta Hotel, Travelodge H, Lowe's
192	Broadway, to 41st St, W 76/dsl, Chevron, Shell Buzz Inn Steaks, IHOP, Little Caesar's, Quiznos, Starbucks, Subway Travelodge City Ctr, Verizon
189	WA 526 W, WA 527, Everett Mall Way, Everett, E Arco, Chevron, Shell/dsl Alfy's Pizza, Burger King, Buzz Inn Steaks, Subway, Wendy's EconoLodge, Extended Stay America Costco/gas, vet, WinCo Foods, W Shell/dsl

INTERSTATE 5 Cont'd

189 Continued
Bob's Burgers, Buffalo Wild Wings, Famous Dave's, Jack-in-the-Box, Jimmy John's, Olive Garden Days Inn, Extended Stay America, Woodspring Suites Best Buy, Michael's, Petsmart, TJ Maxx, Verizon, Walmart

188mm **/weigh sta sb, full facilities, coffee, info, litter barrels, , , RV dump**

186 WA 96, 128th SW, E 76/dsl, Shell/dsl, Texaco O'Donnells Rest. Quality Inn Lakeside RV Park, W Arco, Chevron, Shell A&W/KFC, Acropolis Pizza, Denny's, Dickey's BBQ, DQ, McDonald's, Ming Dynasty, Papa John's, Pizza Hut, Starbucks, Subway, Taco Bell, Taco Time Holiday Inn Express, La Quinta, Motel 6 $Tree, Albertson's/Sav-on, Maple RV Park, PepBoys, vet

183 164th SW, E Arco, Shell/dsl Jack-in-the-Box, Panda Express, Quiznos, Starbucks, Subway, Taco Del Mar, Taco Time Walgreens, Walmart, W Chevron/dsl Five Guys, MOD Pizza, Subway Fred Meyer/dsl, vet

182 WA 525, Alderwood Mall Blvd, to Alderwood Mall, E I-405 S, to Bellevue, W Arco Anthony's SeafoodGrill, Azteca Mexican, Buffalo Wild Wings, Cafe Rio, Claim Jumper, Fatburger, Jersey Mike's, Keg Steaks, Macaroni Grill, Panera Bread, PF Chang's, Qdoba Mexican, Red Robin, TCBY Homewood Suites, Residence Inn JC Penney, Kohl's, Macy's, Nordstrom, REI, Rite Aid, Ross, See's Candies, Target, vet, World Mkt

181 44th Ave W, to WA 524, Lynnwood, E 76/dsl, Arco, Shell Chick-fil-A, Jimmy John's, Little Caesar's, McDonald's/playplace, Old Spaghetti Factory, Starbucks Embassy Suites, Extended Stay America, Hampton Inn, Holiday Inn Express Albertson's, Barnes&Noble, Best Buy, Jaguar, Land Rover, Lowe's, Old Navy, O'Reilly Parts, PetCo, Staples, Verizon, vet, Whole Foods Mkt, W 76/dsl, Arco, Shell/repair Applebee's, Arby's, Buca Italian, Chipotle Mexican, ChuckeCheese, Denny's, Ezell's Chicken, Harbour Buffet, IHOP, Jack-in-the-Box, KFC, McDonald's, Olive Garden, Panda Express, Red Lobster, Rock Woodfire Pizza, Starbucks, Subway, Taco Bell, Taco del Mar, Taco Time, Todo Mexico, Wendy's, Zeeks Pizza Best Value Inn, Best Western, Courtyard, La Quinta 7-11, Fred Meyer/dsl, Goodyear/auto, Grocery Outlet, Schwab Tire, URGENT CARE, USPO, vet

179 220th SW, Mountlake Terrace, Mountlake Terrace, W Shell/dsl Azteca Mexican, Port of Subs, Subway , vet

178 236th St SW (from nb), Mountlake Terrace

177 WA 104, Edmonds, E Chevron/dsl, Shell/dsl Domino's, Gabriel's Fire BBQ, Mazatlan Mexican, McDonald's/playplace, Pagliacchi Pizza, Starbucks, Subway, Time Out Burger, Todo Mexico Motel 6 O'Reilly Parts, RiteAid, Thriftway Foods, URGENT CARE

176 NE 175th St, Aurora Ave N, to Shoreline, E Safeway/dsl

175 WA 523, NE 145th, 5th Ave NE

174 NE 130th, Roosevelt Way

173 1st Ave NE, Northgate Way, E EVgo EVC Azteca Mexican, BlueFin Grill, CA Pizza Kitchen, Chipotle Mexican, Domino's, Five Guys, Gate Buffet, Jimmy John's, Mama Stortini's, Ram Rest., Red Robin, Stanford's Rest. Barnes&Noble, Best Buy, Dick's, Discount Tire, JC Penney, Macy's, Nordstrom, Old Navy, Petco, Ross, Target, Verizon, W 76, Chevron, Shell/dsl McDonald's, Saffron Grill, Starbucks Hotel Nexus 7-11

172 N 85th, Aurora Ave

171 WA 522, Lake City Way, Bothell

SEATTLE

170 Ravenna Blvd, E Shell/dsl

169 NE 45th, NE 50th, E Chevron, Shell Qdoba, Subway , PetCo, U of WA, vet, W to Seattle Pacific U, zoo

168b WA 520, to Bellevue

168a Lakeview Blvd, downtown

167 Mercer St (exits left from nb), Fairview Ave, Seattle Ctr

166 Olive Way, Stewart St, E , W SpringHill Suites Honda

165a Seneca St (exits left from nb), James St, E

165b Union St, E Homewood Suites, W Ruth's Chris Steak Crowne Plaza, Hilton, Renaissance Inn, Sheraton

164b 4th Ave S, to Kingdome, downtown

164a I-90 E, to Spokane, downtown

163 6th Ave, S Spokane St, W Seattle Br, Columbian Way, **1 mi W on 4th Ave S** Arco/dsl, Gull/dsl, Shell Arby's, Burger King, Denny's, Jack-in-the-Box, KFC, McDonald's, Starbucks, Subway, Taco Bell Costco/gas, Pepboys, USPO

162 Corson Ave, Michigan St (exits left from nb), same as 161

161 Swift Ave, Albro Place, W 76/dsl, Shell/dsl Starbuck Georgetown Inn Verizon

158 Pacific Hwy S, E Marginal Way, W Chevron/dsl NAPA

157 ML King Way

156 WA 539 N, Interurban Ave (no EZ return to sb), Tukwil E Pacific Pride/dsl Billy Baroos Rest., W 76/ds Shell/dsl Jack-in-the-Box, Quiznos, Starbucks, Sunny Teriyaki Days Inn

154b WA 518, Burien, W Extended Stay America

154a I-405, N to Bellevue

153 S Center Pkwy, (from nb), E Chevron/dsl Applebee Azteca Mexican, Bahama Breeze, BJ's Rest., Buffalo Wild Wing Burger King, CA Pizza Kitchen, Cheesecake Factory, Chipot Mexican, ClaimJumper, Coldstone, Duke's ChowderHouse, Famous Dave's, Five Guys, Grazie Ristorante, IHOP, Jamba Juic Mayflower of China, McDonald's, Mizuki Buffet, Mizuki Japane Steaks, Mongolian Grill, Old Spaghetti Factory, Olive Garde Outback Steaks, Panda Express, Panera Bread, Qdoba Mexica Red Robin, Simply Thai, Sizzler, Stanford's Rest., Starbucks, Subway, Thai Cuisine, Zoopa DoubleTree Inn, Holiday Inn Express, Hotel Interurban $Tree, Acura, AT&T, Barnes&Nob Best Buy, Big Lots, Firestone/auto, JC Penney, Jo-Ann Fabri Kohl's, Lowe's, Macy's, Michael's, Nordstrom, Nordstrom Ra Office Depot, Old Navy, PetCo, Petsmart, REI, Ross, See's Candi Target, Tuesday Morning, Verizon, World Mkt

152 S 188th, Orillia Rd, W 76/dsl Dave's Diner, Denny Jack-in-the-Box, Taco Bell DoubleTree Hotel, Hampton I La Quinta, Motel 6 city park, to

151 S 200th, Military Rd, E 76/Subway/dsl Motel W 7-11, 76, Chevron IHOP Best Value Inn, B Western, Comfort Inn, Country Inn Suites, Days Inn, Fairfi Inn, Hampton Inn, Holiday Inn Express, Residence Inn, Sle Inn AutoZone, city park, O'Reilly Parts, U-Haul

149 WA 516, to Kent, Des Moines, E Century Motel Po bo RV Ctr, W Arco, Chevron/dsl, Shell/dsl Churc Los Cabos Mexican, McDonald's, Pizza Hut, Starbucks, S way Garden Suites, Kings Arms Motel $Tree, Low Meineke, to Saltwater SP, Walgreens

147 S 272nd, E Chevron/dsl, **W on Pacific Hwy** Arco, Sh dsl Jack-in-the-Box, Little Caesar's, McDonald's, P Murphy's, Starbucks, Subway, Taco Bell AutoZone, Ba Drug, Safeway

143 S 320th, Federal Way, W 76/dsl, Arco Applebee's, teca Mexican, Black Angus, Black Bear Diner, Buffalo Wild Wi

SEATTLE

WA

INTERSTATE 5 Cont'd

143 Continued
Cafe Rio, Chick-fil-A, Chipotle Mexican, Church's, Coldstone, Denny's, Domino's, Grand Peking, Ivar's Seafood, Jasmine Mongolian, Jimmy John's, McDonald's, Mika Japanese Buffet, Old Country Buffet, Panda Express, Panera Bread, Papa Murphy's, Qdoba Mexican, Ram Rest., Red Lobster, Red Robin, Starbucks, Subway, Taco Time, Tokyo Japanese Steaks, Village Inn, Wendy's [lodging] Best Western+, Clarion, Comfort Inn, Courtyard, Extended Stay America, Hampton Inn [other] AT&T, Barnes&Noble, Best Buy, Campeon Mkt, Dick's, Jo-Ann Fabrics, Kohl's, Macy's, Marlene's Natural Mkt, Michael's, O'Reilly Parts, PetCo, Petsmart, Rite Aid, Ross, Safeway/dsl, Target, TJ Maxx, to Dash Point SP, Trader Joe's, Tuesday Morning, Verizon, Walmart/McDonald's

142b a WA 18 E, S 348th, Enchanted Pkwy, **E** [other] funpark, **W** [gas] Chevron, Shell/dsl [food] Arby's, Biscuits Cafe, Burger King, Del Taco, Denny's, Jack-in-the-Box, Jamba Juice, Jimmy Mac's Roadhouse, KFC, McDonald's, Olive Garden, Panda Express, Popeye's, Puerta Vallarta, Quiznos, RoundTable Pizza, Shari's, Starbucks, Subway, Taco Bell, Taco Del Mar, Taco Time, Thai Bistro, The Rock Pizza, Time Out Grill [lodging] Day's Inn, Quality Inn, Red Lion Inn [other] [H], AT&T, Chevrolet, Costco/gas, Discount Tire, Hobby Lobby, Home Depot, Lowe's, Office Depot, O'Reilly Parts, Pepboys, Schwab Tire, UHaul, Verizon, Walmart/Subway

140mm **[RS] both lanes, full facilities, litter barrels, petwalk, RV dump, weigh sta nb**

137 WA 99, Fife, Milton, **E** [gas] 76/dsl, Chevron/dsl, Shell [food] DQ, Johnny's Rest., Warthog BBQ [lodging] Motel 6 [other] Acura, Cadillac, RV Country, visitor info, **W** [gas] 76/dsl, 76/dsl [food] Arby's, Denny's, Fife Thai Rest., Jersey Mike's, KFC, McDonald's, Pick Quick Burgers, Pizza Hut, Poodle Dog, Sapporo Japanese, Starbucks, Subway, Taco Bell, Taco Time, Wendy's [lodging] Days Inn, EQC Motel/casino, Quality Inn [other] 7-11, Audi/Porsche, Mercedes, O'Reilly Parts, Schwab Tire, Tacoma RV Ctr, Verizon

136b a Port of Tacoma, **E** [gas] CFN/dsl [other] Baydos RV Ctr, BMW, Costco, Honda, I-5 Motors, Mini, Peterbilt, **W** [gas] 76/dsl, Gull/dsl, Loves/Chester's/Subway/dsl/scales/LP/RV dump/24hr, Shell/dsl [food] Jack-in-the-Box [lodging] Extended Stay America, Guesthouse Inn, Port of Tacoma Inn, Rodeway Inn, Sunshine Motel, Travelodge [other] Fife RV Ctr, Goodyear/biodsl, Harley-Davidson, Johnson RV Ctr, Land Rover/Jaguar/Lexus, Meineke, NAPA, Poulsbo RV Ctr, truck repair, Volvo

TACOMA

135 Bay St, Puyallup, **E** [gas] 76/Tahoma Express [other] Majestic RV Park (4mi), **W** [food] Subway [lodging] La Quinta [other] to Tacoma Dome

134 Portland Ave (from nb), same as 135

133 WA 7, I-705, **W** [lodging] Best Western, Courtyard, Holiday Inn Express [other] City Ctr, museum, Tacoma Dome

132 WA 16 W, S 38th, Gig Harbor, to Bremerton, **W** [food] Adriatic Grill, BJ's Rest., Buffalo Wild Wings, Chipotle, Five Guys, Jamba Juice, Jimmy John's, Krispy Kreme, Panera Bread, Red Robin, Wendy's [other] $Tree, Best Buy, Costco/gas, Firestone/auto, Ford/Toyota, Goodyear/auto, JC Penney, JoAnn Fabrics, Macy's, Nordstrom, Old Navy, PetCo, REI, to Pt Defiance Pk/Zoo, Verizon, World Mkt

130 S 56th, Tacoma Mall Blvd, **W** [gas] Shell/dsl [food] Axteca Mexican, ChuckeCheese, Jack-in-the-Box [lodging] Extended Stay America

129 S 72nd, S 84th, **E** [gas] Chevron, Valero [food] Applebee's, Burger King, DQ, Elmer's, Famous Dave's, IHOP, Jack-in-the-Box, Jimmy John's, Mongolian Grill, Olive Garden, Popeye's, Red Lobster, RoundTable Pizza, Shari's, Starbucks, Subway [lodging] Hampton Inn, Motel 6, Shilo Inn [other] Bass Pro Shops, WinCo Foods, **W** [food] Hooters [lodging] Clarion [other] Home Depot, to Steilacoom Lake

128 S 84th St (from nb)same as 129, **E** [gas] 76, Shell/dsl [food] Denny's, Ginger Palace, Greatwall Chinese, Subway [lodging] American Lodge, Comfort Inn, Crossland Suites, Econolodge, Hampton Inn, Holiday Inn Express, Howard Johnson, Red Lion Hotel, Rothem Inn, Travelodge, **W** [gas] Shell/dsl [other] $Tree, Discount Tire

127 WA 512, S Tacoma Way, Puyallup, Mt Ranier, **W** [gas] 7-11, 76/7-11, Arco/dsl [food] AAA Buffet, DQ, Ivar's Seafood, Mazatlan Mexican, McDonald's, Sizzler, Starbucks, Taco Time, Wendy's [lodging] Candlewood Suites, Western Inn [other] Advance Parts, Grocery Outlet, O'Reilly Parts

WA

125 to McChord AFB, Lakewood, **W** [gas] 76/Circle K/dsl, Chevron, Mobil, Shell/dsl [food] A&W/KFC, Carr's Rest., Church's, Denny's, Greek Cafe, Jack-in-the-Box, Pizza Hut, Subway, Wendy's [lodging] Holiday Inn Express, Home Motel, TownePlace Suites [other] [H], 7-11, Aamco, Ford, NAPA, O'Reilly Parts, tires/repair, U-Haul

124 Gravelly Lake Dr, **W** [gas] 76/Circle K, Arco/repair [food] El Toro Mexican, Pizza Casa, same as 125

123 Thorne Lane, Tillicum Lane

122 Berkeley St, Camp Murray, **W** [gas] Chevron/repair [food] Gertie's Grill, Jack-in-the-Box, KFC, McDonald's, Papa John's, Popeye's, Starbucks, Subway, Taco Bell [other] 7-11, AutoZone

120 Ft Lewis, **E** [other] Ft Lewis Military Museum

119 Du Pont Rd, Steilacoom, **E** to Ft Lewis, **W** [gas] [food] Happy Teriyaki, Starbucks, Subway [lodging] Hampton Inn, Home 2 Suites

118 Center Dr, **W** [gas] Chevron/dsl [food] Farrelli's Pizza, Fortune Cookie Chinese, Jack-in-the-Box, Koko's Wok, McDonald's, McNamara's Eatery, Pizza Hut, Quiznos, Starbucks, Subway, Super Buffet, Viva Mexico [lodging] Best Western, Fairbridge Inn, Fairfield Inn

117mm **weigh sta nb**

116 Mounts Rd, Old Nisqually, **E** [other] golf, **W** [food] Eagles Pride Grill

115mm Nisqually River

114 Nisqually, **E** [gas] Arco/dsl, Chevron/repair/Lp [food] Medicine Creek Cafe, Nisqually Grill [other] Nisqually Auto Repair, Nisqually RV Park, River Bend RV Park (3mi), WLYH RV Park (2mi)

111 WA 510 E, Marvin Rd, to Yelm, **E** [gas] 76/Circle K, Chevron/dsl, Shell/dsl [food] Burger King, Chipotle, Coldstone, Domino's, Firehouse Subs, Hawk's Prairie Rest./casino, Jack-in-the-Box, Jamba Juice, Jersey Mike's, KFC/LJ Silver, Lemon Grass Rest., McDonald's, Panda Express, Panera Bread, Papa Murphy's, Popeye's, Puerto Vallarta, RAM Rest., Red Robin, Starbucks, Subway, Super Buffet, Taco Del Mar, Taco Time, Vinny's NY Pizza [lodging] Best Western+, Day's Inn [other] $Tree, AT&T, Best Buy, BigLots, Costco/gas, Grocery Outlet, Harley Davidson, Home Depot, O'Reilly Parts, Petco, Rite Aid, Safeway/gas, Schwab Tire, Verizon, Walgreens, Walmart/Subway, WLYH RV Park (2mi), **W** [gas] 7-11/dsl [food] Mayan Mexican, Meconi's Subs [other] Cabela's, Tolmie SP (5mi)

= gas = food = lodging = other = rest stop

WA

INTERSTATE 5 Cont'd

OLYMPIA

Exit#	Services
109	Martin Way, Sleator-Kenny Rd, E Main Chinese Buffet, Taco Bell, The Rock Pizza Discount Tire, ShopKO, W 76/dsl, Shell/dsl Brewery City Pizza, Burger King, Casa Mia, Denny's, Domino's, El Serape Mexican, Jimmy John's, Red Lobster, Shari's, Subway Comfort Inn, La Quinta, Quality Inn, Ramada Inn, Super 8 H, Point S Tire
108	Sleater-Kinney Rd, E Shell/dsl Applebee's, Arby's, Carl's Jr, McDonald's/playplace, Pizza Hut/Taco Bell, Starbucks, Wendy's Candlewood Suites, Holiday Inn Express $Tree, Firestone/auto, Fred Meyer/dsl, GNC, Kohl's, Marshall's, Michael's, Office Depot, Petsmart, Rite Aid, Target, Tuesday Morning, Verizon, W Arco/dsl, Shell Casa Mia, Dirty Dave's, El Sarape Mexican, Jack-in-the-Box, Panda Express, Starbucks, Subway Hampton Inn, Ramada Inn H, AT&T, Lowe's, Point S Tires, Safeway/gas, same as 109
107	Pacific Ave, E Shell/dsl/E-85 DQ, Fajita Grill, Izzy's Pizza, Shari's, Subway, Taco Time Albertson's, Home Depot, Ross, vet, W H, Coumbs RV Ctr
105	St Capitol, W 76/Subway/dsl, Chevron/dsl Quality Inn to St Capitol
104	US 101 N, W Olympia, to Aberdeen, W 7-11, Arco, Chevron/dsl, Shell/Oly Burger/dsl Jack-in-the-Box Extended Stay America, Red Lion Hotel Buick/GMC, Chevrolet/Cadillac, Ford, Honda, Hyundai, Kia, Lincoln/Mazda, Nissan, Subaru, VW
103	2nd Ave, Deschutes Ave, to hist dist
102	Trosper Rd, Black Lake, E Shell Brewery City Pizza, Burger King, DQ, El Sarape Mexican, Jack-in-the-Box, KFC, McDonald's, Starbucks, Subway, Taco Bell, Taco Time Best Western, Motel 6, Tumwater Inn O'Reilly Parts, Schwab Tire, Tumwater Auto Repair, Verizon, W Chevron, Mobil Best Buffet, Little Caesar's, Panda Express, Papa Murphy's, Pizza Hut, Starbucks, Subway, Taco Del Mar, The Brick Rest. Albertson's, Alderbrook RV Park, AutoZone, Costco/gas, Fred Meyer/dsl, GNC, Home Depot, URGENT CARE, Walgreens, Walmart
101	Tumwater Blvd, E Chevron, Shell/dsl DQ (1mi), Inferno's Pizza, Meconi's Pizza, Red Wagon Burgers Comfort Inn, GuestHouse Inn, Olympia Camping 7-11, USPO
99	WA 121 S, 93rd Ave, Scott Lake, E Pilot/McDonald's/Subway/dsl/scales/24hr Ace Hardware, American Heritage Camping, Olympia Camping
95	WA 121, Littlerock, 3 mi E Millersylvania SP, RV camping, W Chevron/dsl (3mi) Farmboy Drive-In Freightliner
93.5mm	**sb, full facilities, coffee, info, litter barrels, petwalk, , vending**
91mm	**nb, full facilities, coffee, info, litter barrels, petwalk, , vending**
88	US 12, Rochester, E Blair's I-5 RV Ctr, I-5 Truckwash, W Arco, CFN/dsl, Chehalis/Burger King/dsl, Chevron/dsl, Shell DQ, Figaro's Pizza, Jack-in-the-Box, Jack-in-the-Box, Mariachi Mexican, McDonald's, Quiznos, Starbucks Fairfield Inn, Great Wolf Lodge auto repair, Outback RV Park (2mi)
82	Harrison Ave, Factory Outlet Way, Centralia, E Arco Burger King, Burgerville, Casa Ramos Mexican, DQ, Jimmy John's, Panda Chinese, Papa Pete's Pizza, Peking House Chinese, Pizza Hut, Quiznos, Thai Dish, Wendy's Centralia Inn, King Oscar Motel, Motel 6, Quality Inn AutoZone, VF/famous brands, W Chevron/dsl, Mobil/dsl, Texaco Arby's, Bill&Bea's, Country Cousin Rest., Denny's, Domino's, Jack-in-the-Box,

CENTRALIA

Exit#	Services
82	Continued McDonald's, Papa Murphy's, Starbucks, Subway, Taco Bell Motel 6 AT&T, Centralia Outlets/famous brands, city park, Midway RV Park, O'Reilly Parts, Rite Aid, Safeway dsl, Schwab Tire, Verizon
82mm	Skookumchuck River
81	WA 507, Mellen St, E Chevron/dsl, Shell/dsl Subwa Empress Inn, Lakeview Inn, Pepper Tree Motel/RV Park dump, W H
79	Chamber Way, E Mobil/dsl Jalisco Mexican Chrysler/Dodge/Jeep/Fiat, museum, Tires, Inc., vet, visitor inf W Chevron/dsl/LP/e85 Applebee's, Burger King, McDonald's, Sonic, Starbucks, Subway, Taco Bell, Taco Del Ma Wendy's $Tree, GNC, Grocery Outlet, Home Depot, Mchael's, O'Reilly Parts, st patrol, Toyota, Verizon, Walgreen Walmart/McDonald's
77	WA 6 W, Chehalis, E 76/dsl, Cenex/dsl/LP Dairy Bar, Jeremy's Cafe Holiday Inn Express NAPA, Schwab Tire, USPO W Rainbow Falls SP (16mi), truck parts, veterans museum
76	13th St, E Arco, Chevron/dsl Denny's, Jack-in-the-Bo Kit Carson Rest., Subway Best Western+, Econolodge, R lax Inn Awesome I-5 RV Ctr/RV dump, Baydo's RV Ctr, For W RV park/dump
74	Labree Rd
72	Rush Rd, Napavine, E Shell/dsl/scales Burger Kin McDonald's, RibEye Rest., Subway Country Canopy R Ctr/repair, W Loves/Carl's Jr/dsl/scales/24hr, Shel dsl Arby's, Starbucks, Taco Bell
72mm	Newaukum River
71	WA 508 E, Onalaska, Napavine, E 76/dsl KC Truck Par
68	US 12 E, Morton, E Arco/dsl, Texaco/dsl Spiffy's Re Mt Ranier NP, to Lewis&Clark SP, W 76/rest./dsl
63	WA 505, Winlock, W Shell/Chesters/dsl/LP
60	Toledo Vader Rd, Toledo
59	WA 506 W, Vader, E Shell/dsl Beesley's Cafe Park, W Chevron/Subway/dsl Country House Rest.
59mm	Cowlitz River
57	Jackson Hwy, Barnes Dr, E R&R Tires, W Texaco/Ge Cee's/café/dsl/scales/24hr/@ repair, RV camping
55mm	**both lanes, full facilities, litter barrels, petwalk, , vending**
52	Barnes Dr, Toutle Park Rd, E Paradise Cove RV Park/general store, W Toutle River RV Resort
50mm	Toutle River
49	WA 504 E, Castle Rock, E Chevron/dsl/LP, Shell/dsl 49 Diner, Burger King, C&L Burgers, El Compadre Mexican, Pa Pete's Pizza, Subway 7 West Motel, Mt St Helens M tel, Timberland Inn Seaquest SP (5mi), W McDonald's visitor info
48	Castle Rock, E Cedars RV Park/dump, W city park
46	Pleasant Hill Rd, Headquarters Rd, E Cedars RV Park/du
44mm	**weigh sta sb, weigh sta sb**
42	Bridge Dr, Lexington, W Chevron/dsl Subway a repair
40	to WA 4, Kelso-Longview, W Texaco Econolodge
39	WA 4, Kelso, to Longview, E Arco, Shell Denny Jack-in-the-Box, McDonald's, Shari's, Starbucks, Subway, Ta Time Motel 6, Red Lion Hotel, Super 8 $Tree, Br Hollow RV Park, city park, Rite Aid, Verizon, W Burger Ki DQ, Fiesta Bonita Mexican, Izzy's Pizza, Panera Bread, Red L ster, Taco Bell Comfort Inn, GuestHouse Inn JC Penn museum, Safeway/dsl, Target

KELSO

INTERSTATE 5 Cont'd

KALAMA

Exit#	Services
36	WA 432 W, to WA 4, to US 30, Kelso, E U-Neek RV Ctr, W RV Camping, Toyota
32	Kalama River Rd, E Fireside Café Camp Kalama RV Park/camping/gifts
31mm	Kalama River
30	Kalama, E Chevron/dsl Burger Bar, Columbia Rest., Lucky Dragon Chinese, Playa Azul Mexican, Poker Pete's Pizza, Subway Motel 6 antiques, Godfrey's Drug, USPO, W Spirit/dsl McMenamin's Kalamazoo Inn RV camping
27	Todd Rd, Port of Kalama, E Rebel/Shell/café/dsl/24hr
22	Dike Access Rd, W Taco Bell Columbia Riverfront RV Park, O'Reilly Parts, Schwab Tire, Verizon, Walmart/Subway
21	WA 503 E, Woodland, E Arco/dsl, Chevron, Pacific Pride/dsl, Shell/LP/dsl America's Diner, Burgerville, Casa Tapatia, DQ, Fat Moose Grill, Grocery Outlet, Guilliano's Pizza, Mali Thai, OakTree Rest., Rosie's Rest. Best Western, Lewis River Inn, Rodeway Inn Ace Hardware, Hi-School Drug, Woodland Shores RV Park, W Astro Antony's Pizzaria, Carl's Jr, Guadalajara Mexican, Los Pepes Mexican, McDonald's, Papa Murphy's, Starbucks, Subway $Tree, NAPA, repair/tires, Safeway/dsl
20mm	N Fork Lewis River
18mm	E Fork Lewis River
16	NW La Center Rd, La Center, E Shell/dsl Twin Dragons Rest. (2mi) Paradise Point SP, Tri-Mountain Golf/rest., W Ilani Casino/Hotel
15mm	**weigh sta nb**
14	WA 501 S, Pioneer St, Ridgefield, E Arco Country Café, Papa Pete's Pizza, Subway, Teriyaki Thai Big Fir RV Park (4mi), Ridgefield WR, to Battleground Lake SP (14mi), Tri-Mountain RV Park, vet, W Chevron/dsl
13mm	**sb, full facilities, info, litter barrels, petwalk, , , RV dump, vending**
11	WA 502, Battleground, **nb, full facilities, info, litter barrels, petwalk, , RV dump, vending**
9	NE 179th St, W Chevron/dsl RV Park
7	I-205 S (from sb), to I-84, WA 14, NE 134th St, E 7-11, Arco, Mobil Applebee's, Billygan's Roadhouse, Burger King, Burgerville, Jack-in-the-Box, McDonald's, Muchas Gracias, Panda Express, Round Table Pizza, Starbucks, Subway, Taco Bell Holiday Inn Express, Quality Inn, Shilo Inn H, 99 RV Park, Albertson's, Safeway/dsl, Verizon, Walgreens, W Shell Baskin-Robbins, Bruchi's, El Tapatio, Garlic Jim's Pizza, Papa Murphy's, PizzaSchmitzza, Planet Thai, Starbucks, Subway La Quinta AT&T, Fred Meyer, URGENT CARE
5	NE 99th St, E Burgerville, Carl's Jr, Del Taco, Domino's, Fat Dave's Rest., Popeyes, Quiznos 7-11, AutoZone, Harley-Davidson, Walgreens, Walmart/Subway, Winco Foods/gas, W Arco/dsl, Chevron/dsl Applebee's, Bortolami's Pizza, McDonald's, Subway, Taco Del Mar $Tree, Grocery Outlet, Kohl's, Office Depot, PetCo, Target, Verizon
4	NE 78th St, Hazel Dell, E 7-11, 76 Baja Fresh, Baskin Robbins, Burger King, Canton Chinese, Don Pedro Mexican, Dragon Buffet, Izzy's Grill, KFC, McDonald's, Muchas Gracias Mexican, PeachTree Rest., Pizza Hut, Skipper's, Starbucks, Subway, Taco Bell Quality Inn Aamco, AT&T, CarQuest, CostLess Parts, Firestone, Fred Meyer, Jo-Ann, O'Reilly Parts, Tire Factory, U-Haul, W Shell/dsl/LP Buffalo Wild Wings, Chipotle Mexican, Five Guys, Jack-in-the-Box, Jazzy John's BBQ,

VANCOUVER

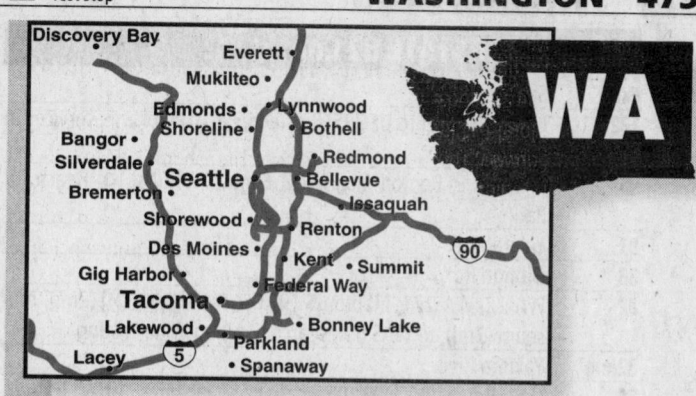

Discovery Bay, Everett, Mukilteo, Edmonds, Lynnwood, Shoreline, Bothell, Bangor, Redmond, Silverdale, Seattle, Bellevue, Bremerton, Issaquah, Shorewood, Renton, 90, Des Moines, Kent, Summit, Gig Harbor, Federal Way, Tacoma, Lakewood, Bonney Lake, Parkland, Lacey, 5, Spanaway

WA

Exit#	Services
4	Continued Jimmy John's, Little Caesar's, Panda Express, Pita Pit, RoundTable Pizza, Starbucks, Wendy's GNC, Hancock Fabrics, Natural Grocers, Petsmart, Ross, Safeway, Tuesday Morning
3	NE Hwy 99, Main St, Hazel Dell, E 7-11 Muchas Gracias Mexican, Pizza Hut, Skippers, W Arco/dsl, Chevron/dsl Papa Murphy's Safeway, transmissions
2	WA 500 E, 39th St, to Orchards
1d	E 4th, Plain Blvd W, to WA 501, Port of Vancouver
1c	Mill Plain Blvd, City Ctr, E Clark Coll, W Chevron Black Angus Comfort Inn st patrol
1b	6th St, E Joe's Crabshack, Who Song & Larry's Mexican, W EconoLodge, Hilton, Red Lion Hotel
1a	WA 14 E, to Camus, E H, W EconoLodge, Hilton
0mm	Washington/Oregon state line, Columbia River

INTERSTATE 82

Exit#	Services
11mm	**I-82 Oregon begins/ends on I-84, exit 179.**
10	Westland Rd, E to Umatilla Army Depot
5	Power Line Rd
1.5mm	Umatilla River
1	US 395/730, Umatilla, E Jack-in-the-Box (5mi) Best Western (8mi), Motel 6 (8mi), Oxford Inn (5mi), Quality Inn/rest. (2mi) Hatrock Camping (8mi), to McNary Dam, W **Welcome Ctr, weigh sta** Chevron/dsl, Mobil/Subway/dsl, Shell/Crossroads Trkstp/dsl/rest./24hr Tillicum Motel, Umatilla Inn Harvest Foods, st police, Umatilla Marina/RV Park, USPO
132mm	Washington/Oregon state line, Columbia River
131	WA 14 W, to McNary Dam, Plymouth, N RV camping
130mm	**weigh sta wb**
122	Coffin Rd
114	Locust Grove Rd
113	US 395 N, to I-182, Kennewick, Pasco, st patrol, **2-4 mi N** Exxon/Circle K/dsl, Metro/dsl, USA/dsl A&W/KFC, Azteca Mexican, Bob's Burgers, Burger King, Carl's Jr, Costa Vida, Denny's, Dickey's BBQ, DQ, Jack-in-the-Box, Little Caesar's, McDonald's, Original Pancake House, Osaka Asian, Panda Express, Papa John's, Starbucks, Subway, Taco Bell, Taco Bell Baymont Inn, Best Western+, Comfort Suites, Hampton Inn, La Quinta, Motel 6 H, AT&T, Blue Dog RV Ctr, Fred Meyer/dsl, GNC, Harley-Davidson, Home Depot, PetCo, Rite Aid, Safeway/dsl, st patrol, Traveland RV Ctr, Verizon, vet, Walgreens, Walmart/Subway
109	Badger Rd, W Kennewick, N Exxon/Subway/dsl, Sunmart/dsl Silo Grill Quality Inn (3mi), Red Lion Hotel (3mi), Super 8 (3mi), S Columbia Sun RV Park
104	Dallas Rd, 3 mi N Conoco/dsl

KENNEWICK

INTERSTATE 82 Cont'd

WA

Exit#	Services
102	I-182, US 12 E, to US 395, Richland, Pasco, Spokane, services in Richland
96	WA 224 E, Benton City, **N** [gas] Conoco/cafe/dsl [other] Beach RV Park
93	Yakitat Rd
88	Gibbon Rd
82	WA 22, WA 221, Mabton **S** [gas] Conoco/dsl [other] [H] (2mi), museum (2mi), to WAS U Research (2mi), to Wine Tasting
82mm	Yakima River
80	Gap Rd, **S** [RS] **both lanes, full [handicap] facilities, litter barrels, [phone], [picnic], rv dump,** [gas] Chevron/dsl, Loves/Carl's Jr/dsl/scales/24hr, Pacific Pride/dsl, Shell/dsl/scales [food] Barn Rest., Burger King, Domino's, Dutch Bros Coffee, El Rancho Alegre, Golden Horse Chinese, KFC/Taco Bell, McDonald's, Starbucks, Subway [lodging] Best Western+, Holiday Inn Express, Vintners Inn [other] [H], Ford, Schwab Tire, ShopKO, URGENT CARE, Verizon, Wine Country RV Park
76mm	**weigh sta eb**
75	County Line Rd, Grandview **S** [gas] Cenex/Deli/dsl, Safeway/dsl [food] Papa Murphy's [other] O'Reilly Parts, same as 73
73	Stover Rd, Wine Country Rd, Grandview **S** [gas] Chevron/Subway/dsl, Conoco/dsl [food] 10-4 Café, DQ, Eli&Kathy's Rest., Garcia's Mexican, New Hong Kong [lodging] Apple Valley Motel, Grandview Motel [other] Chrysler/Dodge/Jeep, IGA Mercado, RV park/dump, Safeway/dsl, Schwab Tire
69	WA 241, to Sunnyside, **N** [gas] Arco/dsl, Shell/dsl/scales/24hr [food] A&W, Burger King, Carl's Jr, China Buffet, El Charrito Mexican, Green Olive Cafe, KFC, Little Caesar's, McDonald's, Mongolian BBQ, Panda Garden, Papa Murphy's, Pizza Hut, Popeye's, Subway, Taco Bell [lodging] Best Western+, Quality Inn [other] $Tree, AT&T, auto repair, AutoZone, Buick/Chevrolet, Fiesta Foods, GNC, Grocery Outlet, JC Penney, Nissan, O'Reilly Parts, Rite Aid, Ross, Walmart/Subway
67	Sunnyside, Port of Sunnyside, **N** [gas] Chevron/CFN/dsl, Conoco/dsl/e85 [food] Jack-in-the-Box [other] [H], BiMart Foods, **S** [other] Dari-Gold Cheese
63	Outlook, Sunnyside, **3 mi N** [food] Snipe's Rest. [lodging] Rodeway Inn, Sunnyside Inn [other] Sunnyside RV Park
58	WA 223 S, to Granger **S** [gas] Arco/dsl/tacos, Conoco/dsl
54	Division Rd, Yakima Valley Hwy, to Zillah **S** [other] Teapot Dome NHS
52	Zillah, Toppenish, **N** [gas] 76/dsl, Chevron/Circle K/dsl, Shell/Circle K/dsl [food] El Porton Mexican, McDonald's, Pizza Hut, Subway [lodging] Best Western+
50	WA 22 E, to US 97 S, Toppenish, **3-4 mi S** [food] Legends Buffet/casino, McDonald's [lodging] Quality Inn [other] [H], Murals Museum, RV Park, to Yakima Nation Cultural Ctr
44	Wapato, **N** [gas] Donald Store/dsl
40	Thorp Rd, Parker Rd, Yakima Valley Hwy
39mm	Yakima River
38	Union Gap (from wb), **1 mi S** [other] gas, lodging, museum
37	US 97 (from eb) **S** [gas] Conoco/dsl
36	Valley Mall Blvd, Yakima **S** [gas] Arco/dsl, Cenex/dsl, Chevron/Gearjammer/Subway/dsl/scales/24hr/@ [food] A&W/KFC, Applebee's, Buffalo Wild Wings, Burger King, Carl's Jr, Denny's, El Porton Mexican, Famous Dave's, Jack-in-the-Box, Krispy Kreme, McDonald's, Miner's Drive-In, Old Country Buffet, Old Town Sta Rest., Outback Steaks, Panda Express, Panera Bread, SeaGalley Rest., Shari's, Starbucks, Subway, Taco Bell [lodging] Best Western+, Quality Inn, Super 8 [other] AT&T, Best Buy, Cabela's, Canopy RV Ctr,
36	Continued Costco/gas, Dick's, Frank's Tire, Gap Autoparts, Hobby Lobby, Home Depot, JC Penney, Kohl's, Lowe's, Macy's, Marshall's, Michael's, Office Depot, Old Navy, PetCo, Petsmart, Rite Aid, Ross, ShopKO, st patrol, TJ Maxx, Toyota, URGENT CARE, Verizon, WinCo Foods
34	WA 24 E, Nob Hill Blvd, Yakima, **N** [other] dsl/repair, Sportsma SP, **S** [gas] 76/dsl, Arco/dsl, CFN/dsl, Nob Hill/dsl [other] [H], 19t Hole RV Park, Circle K, Fiesta Foods, Freightliner, Kenwort O'Reilly Parts, Peterbilt, Volvo
33	Yakima Ave, Yakima, **E** [lodging] Baymont Inn, My Place, **N** [gas] Chev ron/dsl, Shell/dsl [food] Burger King, El Mirador Mexican [lodging] Ox ford Inn&Suites [other] Chevrolet, Honda, Walmart/McDonald' **S** [gas] 7-11, Arco [food] Bob's Burgers, Domino's, DQ, Pizza Hu Taco Bell [lodging] Fairfield Inn, Hilton Garden, Holiday Inn, Howa Johnson, Ledgestone Hotel, Motel 6, Red Lion Hotel, Red Ro Inn [other] $Tree, BigLots, Schwab Tire, Target
31b a	US 12 W, N 1st St, to Naches **S** [gas] Arco/dsl, Conoco/ds Shell [food] Golden Moon Chinese, Jack-in-the-Box, Mel's Dine NY Teryaki, Red Lobster, Subway, Tammy's Mexican, Waffle Cafe [lodging] Best Western+, Budget Inn, Days Inn, Econolodg Economy Inn, Fairbridge Inn, Red Apple Motel, Sun Country In Sunshine Motel, Yakima Inn [other] Harley-Davidson, Trailer In RV Park
30	WA 823 N, Rest Haven Rd, to Selah
29	E Selah Rd, **N** [other] fruits/antiques
26	WA 821 N, to WA 823, Canyon Rd, **N** [gas] Chevron/Noble R mans/Subway/dsl
24mm	**[RS] eb, full [handicap] facilities, litter barrels, [picnic], RV dump**
23mm	Selah Creek
22mm	**[RS] wb, full [handicap] facilities, litter barrels, [picnic], RV dump**
21mm	S Umptanum Ridge, elevation 2265
19mm	Burbank Creek
17mm	N Umptanum Ridge, elevation 2315
15mm	Lmuma Creek
11	Military Area, Military Area
8mm	Manastash Ridge, elevation 2672, view point both lanes
3	WA 821 S, Thrall Rd
0mm	I-90, E to Spokane, W to Seattle. **I-82 begins/ends on I-90, e 110.**

SUNNYSIDE

YAKIMA

INTERSTATE 90

Exit#	Services
300mm	Washington/Idaho state line, Spokane River
299	State Line, Port of Entry, **N** [food] Panda Express [other] Cabela Walmart/Subway
297	**weigh sta wb**
296	Otis Orchards, Liberty Lakes, **N** [gas] 76/dsl [food] Legend's G [lodging] Best Western+ [other] Buick/GMC, Kia, Mercedes, Porsc **S** [gas] Cenex/dsl, Chevron/LP [food] Barlow's Rest., Carl's Jr, D How Asian, Domino's, Field House Pizza, Jimmy John's, McD ald's, Papa Murphy's, Pizza Hut, Starbucks, Subway, Taco B Taco Time [lodging] Quality Inn [other] Safeway, Home Depot, O'Re Parts, Peterbilt, RnR RV Ctr, TireRama, URGENT CARE, vet, W greens, Yoke's Mkt
294	Country Vista Dr, Appleway Ave
293	Barker Rd, Greenacres, **N** [gas] Chevron/Trkstp/dsl/scales, C oco/dsl [food] Wendy's [other] Camping World RV Ctr, Freed RV Ctr, Harley-Davidson, **S** [gas] Exxon/Subway/dsl, Mobil/ [other] NW RV Ctr, repair, USPO
291b	Sullivan Rd, Veradale, **N** [food] Arby's, Hong Kong Buffet, Kri Kreme, Outback Steaks, Panera Bread [lodging] Hampton Inn, My Pla

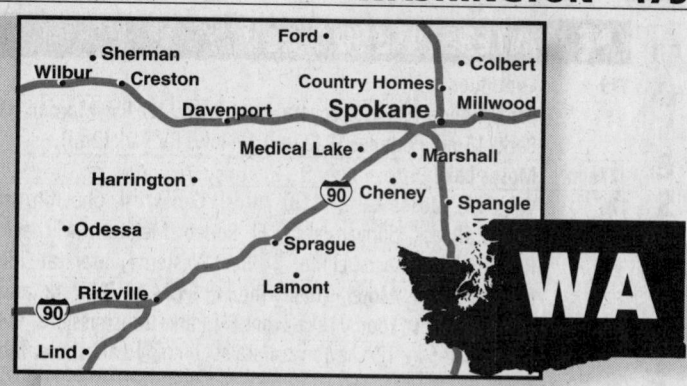

INTERSTATE 90 Cont'd

VERADALE

291b Continued
Oxford Suites, Residence Inn AT&T, Barnes&Noble, Best Buy, Jo-Ann Fabrics, Verizon, S Chevron/dsl, Conoco/dsl DQ, Five Guys, Jack-in-the Box, Jimmy John's, KFC, Little Caesar's, Max Rest., McDonald's, Mongolian BBQ, Noodle Express, Panda Express, Pizza Hut, Pizza Pipeline, RoundTable Pizza, Schlotzsky's, Shari's, Starbucks, Subway, Taco Bell, Wendy's, Zelia's Cafe Mirabeau Park Hotel, Ramada Inn $Tree, Ace Hardware, Fred Meyer/dsl, GNC, Hancock Fabrics, Kohl's, Lowe's, Michael's, NAPA, PetCo, Petsmart, Ross, Schwab Tire, USPO, Walgreens, Walmart/McDonald's

291a Evergreen Rd, N Azteca Mexican, Black Angus, Boston's Rest, Buffalo Wild Wings, Cafe Rio, Honeybaked Ham, IHOP, Red Robin, Twigs Bistro Dick's, Hobby Lobby, JC Penney, Macy's, Old Navy, Staples, TJ Maxx, S Exxon/dsl, Maverik/dsl

289 WA 27 S, Pines Rd, Opportunity, N Sam's/dsl Black Pearl Rest., Subway 7-11, S Cenex, Conoco/dsl, Holiday/dsl Applebee's, DQ, Jack-in-the-Box, Jimmy John's, Qdoba Mexican Comfort Inn H, NW Auto, repair, Walgreens

287 Argonne Rd, Millwood, N Holiday/dsl Burger King, Caruso's Sandwiches, Denny's, Domino's, DQ, Jack-in-the-Box, Longhorn BBQ, McDonald's, Panda Express, Papa Murphy's, Pizza Hut, Starbucks, Subway, Taco Time, Timber Creek Grill, Wendy's Baymont Inn, Motel 6, Super 8 $Tree, Albertson's, O'Reilly Parts, Savon, URGENT CARE, Verizon, vet, Walgreens, Yoke's Foods, S Cenex/dsl, Conoco Casa de Oro Mexican, Jimmy John's, Little Caesar's, Starbucks Fairfield Inn, Holiday Inn Express Ace Hardware, Rite Aid, Safeway

SPOKANE

286 Broadway Ave, N FLYING J/Conoco/rest./dsl/LP/scales/24hr/@, Chevron/dsl Goodyear, Smacky's Cafe, Zip's Burgers Rodeway Inn International Trucks, Kenworth, Schwab Tire, S 7-11

285 Sprague Ave, N Dragon Garden Chinese, IHOP, Jack-in-the-Box, McDonald's, Panda Express, Starbucks, Subway, Wendy's ParkLane Motel/RV Park $Tree, Advance Parts, AutoZone, Costco/gas, Home Depot, Lowe's, O'Reilly Parts, Verizon, Volvo Trucks, Walmart, S Conoco Burger Express, Cottage Cafe, Puerta Vallarta Mexican, Starbucks, Taco Time Acura, CarMax, Chevrolet, Chrysler/Dodge, Ford, Honda, Hyundai, Mazda, Nissan, Toyota, transmissions, vet

284 Havana St (from eb, no EZ return), N Mobil/dsl, S Conoco/dsl Fred Meyer/dsl

283b Freya St, Thor St, N Chevron/dsl, Mobil/dsl, S Conoco/dsl Fred Meyer/dsl

283a Altamont St

282b 2nd Ave, N Conoco/dsl Ramada Inn Office Depot

282a WA 290 E, Trent Ave, Hamilton St, N Conoco/dsl Comfort Inn Office Depot

281 US 2, US 395, to Colville, N 7-11, Conoco, Exxon, Mobil/dsl Arby's, Dick's Hamburgers, Frankie Doodles Rest., Starbucks, Taco Time Days Inn, FairBridge Inn Firestone/auto, Schwab Tire, U-Haul, S Quality Inn H, URGENT CARE

280b Lincoln St, N 76/dsl, Chevron Atilano's Mexican, Carl's Jr, Domino's, Jack-in-the-Box, McDonald's, Molly's Rest., Taco Bell, Thai Cuisine, Zip's Burgers Honda, Lexus, Subaru, Toyota, Troy's Tire, S H

280a Spokane, downtown, N 76/dsl, Chevron/McDonald's/dsl, Conoco Frank's Diner, Jenny's Diner, Pizza Hut, Subway Grocery Outlet

CHENEY

279 US 195 S, Pullman, to Colfax

277b a US 2 W (no ez wb return), to Grand Coulee Dam, N Blvd Motel, EconoLodge, Hampton Inn, Motel 6, Quality Inn Fairchild AFB

276 Geiger Blvd, N FLYING J/dsl/LP/24hr Denny's, Subway Airway Express Inn, Best Western+ st patrol, USPO, S Conoco/dsl

272 WA 902, Medical Lake, N Mobil/dsl Overland Sta/RV Park, S Exxon/Subway/dsl, Petro/Iron Skillet/Subway/dsl/scales/24hr/@ McDonald's Super 8 Freightliner, Ponderosa Falls RV Resort, Speedco, truck repair

270 WA 904, Cheney, Four Lakes S Holiday Inn Express (4mi), Willow Springs Motel (6mi) E WA U, Peaceful Pines RV Park (7mi)

264 WA 902, Salnave Rd, to Cheney, Medical Lake, **2 mi N camping**

257 WA 904, Tyler, to Cheney S Peaceful Pines RV Park (10mi), to Columbia Plateau Trail SP, Tyler RV Park

254 Fishtrap S Fishtrap RV camping/tents

245 WA 23, Sprague S Chevron/dsl Viking Drive-In Sprague Motel/RV park 4 Seasons RV Park (6mi), Sprague Lake Resort/RV Park

242mm **both lanes, full facilities, litter barrels, petwalk, , RV dump (eb), tourist/weather info**

231 Tokio, N **weigh sta both lanes**, S Templin's Café/CFN/dsl RV Park

226 Schoessler Rd

221 WA 261 S, Ritzville, City Ctr, N Chevron/McDonald's, Conoco/dsl, Exxon/Circle K/Subway/dsl Cow Creek Cafe/gifts, Ritz Roadhouse, Starbucks, Taco Del Mar, Zip's Rest. Best Western, Days Inn/RV park, Empire Motel, Top Hat Motel H, hist dist, S Loves/Carl's Jr/dsl/scales/24hr

220 to US 395 S, Ritzville, N Bronco/dsl, Texaco/dsl Jake's Cafe Top Hat Motel Days Inn/RV Park, Harvest Foods, NAPA, Schwab Tire, st patrol

215 Paha, Packard

206 WA 21, Odessa, to Lind

199mm **both lanes, full facilities, litter barrels, petwalk, , RV dump, vending**

196 Deal Rd, to Schrag

188 U Rd, to Warden, Ruff

184 Q Rd

182 O Rd, to Wheeler

179 WA 17, Moses Lake, N Chevron/dsl, Conoco/Subway/dsl, Ernie's Trkstp/76/café/dsl/24hr, Sunval/dsl, Texaco/dsl Arby's, Bob's Cafe, Burger King, Carl's Jr., Denny's, DQ, Dragon Express, McDonald's, Shari's, Starbucks, Subway, Taco Bell, Wendy's Comfort Suites, El Rancho Motel, Fairfield Inn, Holiday Inn Express, Moses Lake Inn, Ramada Inn, Sure Stay Inn+, Wingate Inn H, $Tree, Chevrolet, Chrysler/Dodge/Jeep,

WA

MOSES LAKE

INTERSTATE 90 Cont'd

179 Continued
Ford, Honda, Lowe's, Toyota, vet, S I-90 RV, Mardon RV Park (15mi), Potholes SP (22mi), Willows RV Park (2mi)

177mm Moses Lake

176 WA 171, Moses Lake, N 76/dsl, Cenex/dsl, Chevron/dsl, Shell, SP/dsl, Sunval/dsl El Rodeo Mexican, Michael's Rest., Subway, Taco Del Mar Best Western+, Interstate Inn, Motel 6, Oasis Motel, Quality Inn H, AAA RV Park, auto repair, Harvest Foods, Lake Front RV Park, transmissions, vet, S Half-Sun TP/Chevron/dsl/scales/24hr Lakeshore Motel

175 Westshore Dr (from wb), to Mae Valley, N Blue Heron SP, S st patrol

174 Mae Valley, N Suncrest Resort/RV, S Chevron/dsl Pier 4 RV Park, st patrol

169 Hiawatha Rd

164 Dodson Rd, N Sunbasin RV park/camp (1mi)

162mm wb, full facilities, litter barrels, petwalk, RV dump

161mm eb, full facilities, litter barrels, petwalk, RV dump

WA

154 Adams Rd

151 WA 281 N, to Quincy, N Shell/pizza/subs/dsl H (12mi), Shady Grove RV park, to Grand Coulee Dam

149 WA 281 S, George, N H (12mi), S BW&M/Chester's/dsl, Shree's Trkstp/Subway/dsl/scales/24hr

143 Silica Rd, N to The Gorge Ampitheatre

139mm N Wild Horses Mon, scenic view both lanes

137 WA 26 E, to WA 243, Othello, Richland

137mm Columbia River

136 Huntzinger Rd, Vantage, N Chevron/dsl/24hr Blustery's Burger Drive-in, Golden Harvest Rest. Riverstone Vantage Resort/RV Park, to Ginkgo SP, Vantage Gen. Store, S to Wanapum SP (3mi)

126mm Ryegrass, elevation 2535, both lanes, full facilities, litter barrels, petwalk,

115 Kittitas, N Shell/dsl/LP Main Stop Rest. Olmstead Place SP, UHaul

ELLENSBURG

110 I-82 E, US 97 S, to Yakima

109 Canyon Rd, Ellensburg, N 76, Astro/dsl, Chevron, Exxon/Circle K Arby's, Burger King, Carl's Jr, Fiesta Mexican, Jimmy John's, Los Cabos Mexican, McDonald's, Oyama Japanese, Papa Murphy's, RanchHouse Rest., Roadhouse Grill, Rodeo City BBQ, Starbucks, Subway, Taco Bell, Taco Del Mar, Teriyaki Wok, Wendy's, Westside Pizza Best Western+, Comfort Inn, Holiday Inn Express, Red Lion Inn, Super 8 H, Advance Parts, AutoZone, Chevrolet, NAPA, O'Reilly Parts, Rite Aid, Schwab Tire, Super 1 Foods, TrueValue, S Conoco/Sak's/dsl/scales/LP/24hr Buzz Inn Steaks Days Inn/RV park

106 US 97 N, to Wenatchie, N 76/dsl, Chevron/dsl, Conoco/dsl, Loves /Subway/dsl/scales/24hr DQ, IHOP, Perkins Econolodge, Hampton Inn Buick/Cadillac/GMC, Canopy Country RV Ctr, Chrysler/Dodge/Jeep, truck repair, Truck/RV Wash, S KOA, st patrol

101 Thorp Hwy, N Arco/dsl antiques/fruits/vegetables

93 Elk Heights Rd, Taneum Creek

92.5mm Elk Heights, elev 2359

89mm Indian John Hill, elevation 2141, both lanes, full facilities, litter barrels, petwalk, RV dump, vending

85 WA 970, WA 903, to Wenatchie, N 76/dsl, Gas Save/dsl, Shell/dsl Cottage Café, Giant Burger, Homestead BBQ Aster Inn, Chalet Motel, Cle Elum Traveler's Inn, EconoLodge Trailer Corral RV Park, vet

CLE ELUM

84 Cle Elum (from eb, return at 85), N Chevron/dsl, Short Stop/Subway/dsl, Warrior's/dsl Best Thai, Burger King, Caboose Grill, DQ, El Caporal Mexican, Los Cabos Mexican, MaMa Vallones, McDonald's, Sunset Café, Taco Bell Best Western Snowcap, Stewart Lodge, Timber Lodge Inn $Tree, Cle Elum Hardware, museum, Safeway/dsl, URGENT CARE, USPO

81mm Cle Elum River

80 Roslyn, Salmon la Sac, N Suncadia Resort/rest. (4mi)

80mm weigh sta both lanes

78 Golf Course Rd S Sun Country Golf/RV Park

74 W Nelson Siding Rd

71 Easton S Easton Store/dsl/LP Easton Motel Iron Horse SP, John Wayne Tr, USPO

71mm Yakima River

70 Sparks Rd, Easton, Lake Easton SP, N Shell/RV Town/dsl/café Backwoods Cafe, Mtn High Burger repair, Silver Ridge Ranch RV Park, S Lake Easton RV Camping, Lake Easton SP

63 Cabin Creek Rd

62 Stampede Pass, elev 3750, to Lake Kachess, N Lake Kachess Lodge

54 Hyak, Gold Creek S Ski Area

53 Snoqualmie Pass, elev 3022 S Chevron Summit Pancake House Summit Lodge info, Lee's Summit Mkt, to rec areas

52 W Summit (from eb), same as 53

47 Tinkham Rd, Denny Creek, Asahel Curtis, N chain area, S RV camping/dump

45 USFS Rd 9030, N to Lookout Point Rd

42 Tinkham Rd

38 N fire training ctr

35mm S Fork Snoqualmie River

34 468th Ave SE, Edgewick Rd, N Gull/dsl/deli, Shell/dsl, TA Country Pride/Popeyes/dsl only/24hr/@ Warriors/dsl Edgewick Inn Norwest RV Park

32 436th Ave SE, 1 mi N Snoqualmie Ranger Sta, gas, lodging S Riverbend Cafe Iron Horse SP (3mi)

31 WA 202 W, North Bend, Snoqualmie, N Chevron/dsl Shell/dsl Arby's, Blimpie, Burger King, Los Cabos, McDonald's, Mongolian Grill, Papa Murphy's, Starbucks, Subway Taco Time North Bend Motel, Sallish Lodge, Sunset Motel H, NorthBend Outlets/famous brands, O'Reilly Parts Safeway/dsl

27 North Bend, Snoqualmie (from eb), N Woodman's Steaks H

25 WA 18 W, Snoqualmie Pkwy, Tacoma, to Auburn, N Shell dsl/e85 (1.5mi) weigh sta

22 Preston, N Shell/dsl Rhodes BBQ, Subway LP USPO, S Blue Sky RV Park

20 High Point Way

18 E Sunset Way, Issaquah S Shell (1mi) Flying Pie Pizza Las Margaritas, Mandarin Garden, Stan's BBQ, Sunset Alehouse $Tree

17 E Sammamish Rd, Front St, Issaquah, N Coho Cafe Coldstone, Fatburger, Ivan's Rest., Jamba Juice, Krispy Kreme McDonald's, Panda Express, Papa John's, Qdoba Mexican, Starbucks, Subway AT&T, Bartell Drug, Best Buy, Fred Meyer Home Depot, URGENT CARE, Walgreens, S Arco/dsl, Cenex/dsl, Chevron/dsl, Shell/dsl Boehms Chocolates, Domino's, Stan's BBQ, Subway, XXX Rootbeer Big O Tire

15 WA 900, Issaquah, Renton, N Arco/dsl, Chevron IHOP O'Char Thai, Red Robin, Taco Time, Tully's Coffee Holiday Inn

INTERSTATE 90 Cont'd

ISSAQUAH

Exit#	Services
15	Continued Motel 6 Barnes&Noble, Big Lots, Costco/gas, Lowe's, Michael's, Office Depot, PCC Natural Mkt, Petsmart, to Lk Sammamish SP, S Shell/dsl 12th Ave Cafe, Baskin-Robbins, Burger King, Cafe Rio, Chipotle Mexican, Corner Cafe Bakery, Dickey's BBQ, Five Guys, Frankie's Pizza, Issaquah Cafe, Jack-in-the-Box, Jamba Juice, Jersey Mike's, KFC/Taco Bell, La Venadita, McDonald's, Panera Bread, Papa Murphy's, Potbelly, Starbucks, Starbucks, Subway, Taco Time, The Egg&Us Rest., Tuttabella Pizza, WildFin Grill Hilton Garden, Homewood Suites Chevrolet, Firestone/auto, Ford, GNC, Hobby Lobby, O'Reilly Parts, PetCo, QFC Foods, REI, Rite Aid, Ross, Safeway, See's Candies, Target, Trader Joe's, USPO, Verizon
13	SE Newport Way, W Lake Sammamish S 76/dsl Starbucks, Subway Matthew's Thriftway Mkt, vet
11	SE 150th, 156th, 161st, Bellevue, N Shell Cypress Coffee, DQ, Jack-in-the-Box, Lil' Jon Rest., McDonald's, Shibuya Grill, Starbucks, Subway Embassy Suites, Hyatt House, Quality Inn, Silver Cloud Inn 7-11, LDS Temple, Nissan, Subaru/VW, Toyota, vet, S 76, Chevron, Shell/dsl, Standard/dsl Domino's, Outback Steaks, Pizza Hut, Starbucks Larkspur Landing Suites Honda, O'Reilly Parts, Rite Aid, Safeway, Trailer Inn RV Park
10	I-405, N to Bellevue, S to Renton, services located off I-405 S, exit 10

SEATTLE

Exit#	Services
9	Bellevue Way
8	E Mercer Way, Mercer Island
7c	80th Ave SE (exits left from wb)
7b a	SE 76th Ave, 77th Ave, Island Crest Way, Mercer Island S Chevron/dsl, Shell/dsl McDonald's, Qdoba, Starbucks, Subway, Thai Rest. New Seasons Mkt, QFC Mkt, Walgreens
6	W Mercer Way (from eb), same as 7
5mm	Lake Washington
3b a	Ranier Ave, Seattle, downtown, N Shell/dsl
2c b	I-5, N to Vancouver, S to Tacoma
2a	4th Ave S, to stadiums
0	**I-90 begins/ends on I-5, exit 164.**

INTERSTATE 182 (Richland)

RICHLAND

Exit#	Services
14.5	I-182 begins/ends on US 395 N.
14b a	US 395 N, WA 397 S, OR Ave, N FLYING J/dsl/scales/24hr, King City/Shell/rest/dsl/@ Burger King, Subway Arrowhead RV Park, Freightliner, Peterbilt, S Knights Inn
13	N 4th Ave, Cty Ctr, N CFN/dsl Airport Motel, Starlite Motel, S 76/dsl, Chevron/dsl H, Green Tree RV park, Tire Pros, vet
12b	N 20th Ave, N Best Western+, Red Lion Hotel
12a	US 395 S, Court St, **S on Court St** Chevron, Circle K/dsl, Conoco, Exxon/Jack-in-the-Box, Petro, Shell/dsl, USA A&W/KFC, Andy's Rest., Baskin-Robbins, Burger King, Domino's, El Mirador Mexican, Little Caesar's, McDonald's, Oriental Express, Papa Murphy's, Pizza Hut, RoundTable Pizza, Subway, Taco Bell, Wendy's $Tree, Albertson's, AutoZone, Blue Dog RV Ctr, Cadillac/Chevrolet, Dean RV Ctr, Ford, Hyundai, Mazda, Nissan, Rite Aid, U-Haul, USPO, Walgreens
9	rd 68, Trac, N Exxon/Circle K/dsl, Maverik/dsl, Porter's/dsl Antonio'sPizza, Applebee's, Arby's, Bruchi's, Cousin'sRest., Dickey's BBQ, Domino's, DQ, Fiesta Mexican, Hacienda del Sol,

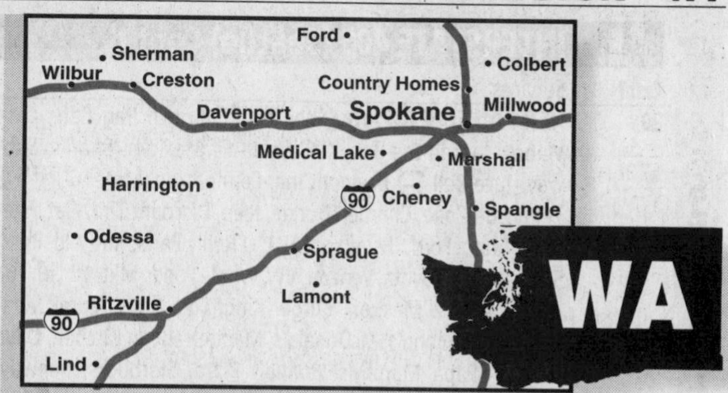

Exit#	Services
9	Continued IHOP, Jack-in-the-Box, Little Caesar's, McDonald's, Panda Express, Pier 39 Seafood, Pita Pit, Pizza Hut, Shakey's Pizza, Sonic, Starbucks, Subway, Taco Bell Hampton Inn, Holiday Inn Express, MyPlace $Tree, AT&T, Discount Tire, Firestone/auto, Franklin County RV Park, Grocery Outlet, Lowe's, O'Reilly Parts, Schwab Tire, URGENT CARE, Verizon, Walgreens, Walmart/Subway, Yokes Foods, S Maverik/dsl
7	Broadmoor Blvd, N Sleep Inn Camping World, GNC, Subaru, vet, S Exxon/Circle K/dsl Broadmoor RV Ctr, KOA
6.5mm	Columbia River
5b a	WA 240 E, Geo Washington Way, to Kennewick, N Conoco/dsl Anthony's Rest., Applebee's, Jack-in-the-Box, Starbucks Courtyard, Economy Inn, Hampton Inn, Red Lion Hotel, Shilo Inn, TownePlace Suites $Tree, AT&T, Winco Foods
4	WA 240 W, N Shell/dsl El Porton Mexican, McDonald's, Starbucks BMW, Fred Meyer/dsl
3.5mm	Yakima River
3	Keene Rd, Queensgate, N Exxon/Circle K, Maverik/dsl, USA/dsl A&W/KFC, Bob's Burgers, Burger King, Costa Vida, Dickey's BBQ, Fiesta Mexican, Five Guys, Krispy Kreme, LJ Silver, McDonald's, Panda Express, Panera Bread, Qdoba, Starbucks, Sterling's Rest., Stick+Stone Pizza, Subway, Taco Bell AT&T, GNC, Home Depot, Marshall's, PetCo, Ross, Schwab Tire, Target, Tire Factory, Verizon, Walmart/Subway, S Chevron/dsl MOD Pizza tires/repair
0mm	**I-182 begins/ends on I-82, exit 102.**

WA

INTERSTATE 405 (Seattle)

Exit#	Services
30	I-5, N to Canada, S to Seattle, **I-405 begins/ends on I-5, exit 182.**
26	WA 527, Bothell, Mill Creek, E McDonald's, Rama House Thai, Starbucks Extended Stay America, W Shell/dsl Applebee's, Arby's, Bamboo House, Bangkok Cafe, Baskin-Robbins, Bonefish Grill, Chick-fil-A, Crystal Creek Cafe, Five Guys, Grazie Ristorante, Imperial Wok, Jack-in-the-Box, Jimmy John's, Little Caesar's, MOD Pizza, Outback Steaks, Papa Murphy's, Qdoba Mexican, Starbucks, Subway, Taco Bell, Taco Time, Wendy's, Zeek's Pizza Comfort Inn, Extended Stay America, Hilton Garden, Holiday Inn Express 7-11, Bartell Drug, Goodyear/auto, Lake Pleasant RV Park, QFC Foods, Rite Aid, URGENT CARE, vet
24	NE 195th St, Beardslee Blvd, E Chevron/dsl Subway, Teryaki Etc. Country Inn&Suites, Red Lion Inn, Residence Inn Exotic vet
23b	WA 522 W, Bothell
23a	WA 522 E, to WA 202, Woodinville, Monroe
22	NE 160th St, E Chevron, Shell/dsl Top Mkt/deli

SEATTLE

WA

INTERSTATE 405 (Seattle) Cont'd

Exit#	Services
20	NE 124th St, **E** [gas] Arco, Shell/dsl [food] Brown Bag Cafe, Cafe Veloce, Jack-in-the-Box, KFC, Santa Fe Mexican, Shari's, Subway, Taco Bell [lodging] Baymont Inn, Comfort Inn, Motel 6 [other] [H], 7-11, AutoZone, Chrysler/Dodge/Jeep, Discount Tire, Fiat, Firestone/auto, Ford, Hyundai, NAPA, O'Reilly Parts, Rite Aid, Ross, Schwab Tire, Toyota, Verizon, VW, Whole Foods Mkt, **W** [gas] 76/dsl [food] Azteca Mexican, Burger King, Five Guys, Izumi Japanese, Jimmy John's, McDonald's, Mediterranean Kitchen, Olive Garden, Papa Murphy's, Romio's Pizza, Starbucks, Subway, Taco Del Mar, Taco Time, Wendy's [lodging] Courtyard [other] AT&T, Buick/GMC, Fred Meyer/dsl, GNC, QFC Foods
18	WA 908, Kirkland, Redmond, **E** [gas] 76/Circle K/dsl, Chevron, Texaco/dsl [food] Baskin-Robbins, Little Caesar's, McDonald's, Starbucks, Subway, Taco Time, Tres Hermanos [other] Chevrolet, Costco, Honda, Kia, Mazda, PepBoys, PetCo, Safeway, Tuesday Morning, U-Haul, URGENT CARE, vet, Walgreens, **W** [gas] Shell/dsl [food] Acropolis Pizza, Papa John's, Starbucks, Subway, Wendy's [other] QFC Foods, Tire Pros
17	NE 70th Pl
14b a	WA 520, Seattle, Redmond
13b	NE 8th St, **E** [gas] Arco, Chevron/dsl, Shell/dsl [food] Burger King, Chick-fil-A, Taco del Mar [lodging] Hotel 116 [other] [H], Bartell Drugs, Best Buy, Cadillac, Chevrolet, Ford, Home Depot, Infiniti, Mercedes, Porsche, Volvo, Whole Foods Mkt, **W** [food] Starbucks, Subway [lodging] Courtyard, Hyatt
13a	NE 4th St, **E** [lodging] Extended Stay America, Hampton Inn [other] Chrysler/Dodge/Jeep, Lexus, **W** [food] Azteca Mexican, Subway [lodging] Hilton, Hotel Bellevue, Marriott, Red Lion/Bellevue Inn, Residence Inn, Sheraton
12	SE 8th St, **W** [lodging] Residence Inn
11	I-90, E to Spokane, W to Seattle
10	Cold Creek Pkwy, Factoria, **E on Factoria Blvd** [gas] 76, Chevron [food] Applebee's, Burger King, Chipotle, Coldstone, Domino's, El Tapatio Mexican, Goldberg's Rest., Great Harvest Bread, Jamba Juice, Jimmy John's, KFC, McDonald's, MOD Pizza,
10	Continued Novilhos Brazilian Steaks, Panda Express, Panera Bread, Ricardo's Mexican, Romio's Pizza, Shanghai Cafe, Starbucks, Subway, Taco Bell, Taco Time, Thai Ginger, Tokyo Japanese [other] 7-11, AT&T, Bartell Drug, Midas, Old Navy, O'Reilly Parts, PetCo, QFC Foods, Rite Aid, Safeway, Target, TJ Maxx, Verizon, Walmart
9	112th Ave SE, Newcastle, [C]
7	NE 44th St, **E** [food] Denny's, McDonald's, Starbucks, Subway, Taco Del Mar, Teriyaki Wok [lodging] EconoLodge
6	NE 30th St, **E** [gas] Arco, **W** [gas] Chevron/dsl, Shell/dsl [other] 7-11
5	WA 900 E, Park Ave N, Sunset Blvd NE, **W** [food] Five Guys, Jimmy John's, Panda Express, Panera Bread, Potbelly, Red Robin, Torero's Mexican [lodging] Hampton Inn, Hyatt House, Residence Inn [other] AT&T, Dick's, Fry's Electronics, GNC, Lowe's, Marshall's, Petsmart, Ross, Staples, Target, Verizon, World Mkt
4	WA 169 S, Wa 900 W, Renton, **E** [food] Shari's [lodging] Quality Inn [other] Aqua Barn Ranch Camping, **W** [food] Burger King, Pizza Dudes, Subway [lodging] Renton Inn [other] $Tree, 7-11
2	WA 167, Rainier Ave, to Auburn, **E** [lodging] Hilton Garden, Larkspur Landing, SpringHill Suites, TownePlace Suites [other] [H], **W** [gas] Arco/dsl, Chevron, Chevron, Mobil/dsl [food] A&W/KFC, Applebee's, Baskin-Robbins, Chipotle, Domino's, IHOP, Jack-in-the-Box, Jimmy John's, Jimmy Mac's Roadhouse, King Buffet, Little Caesar's, Mazatlan Mexican, McDonald's, Papa Murphy's, Pizza Hut, Popeye's, Sonic, Starbucks, Subway, Taco Bell, Taco Time, Wendy's, Yankee Grill [lodging] Red Lion Hotel [other] AutoZone Buick/Cadillac/GMC, Chevrolet, Chrysler/Dodge/Jeep, Discount Tire, Firestone/auto, Ford, Fred Meyer/dsl, Hyundai, Kia Mazda, Midas, O'Reilly Parts, Safeway/gas, Schwab Tire, Subaru, Toyota, vet, Walgreens, Walmart
1	WA 181 S, Tukwila, **E** [gas] Chevron/dsl [food] Jack-in-the-Box Taco Bell, Wendy's [lodging] Courtyard, Embassy Suites, Extended Stay America, Hampton Inn, Ramada, Residence Inn Woodspring Suites [other] 7-11, **W** [gas] [food] Subway, Taco Del Mar [lodging] Comfort Suites, Homewood Suites [other] fun center
0mm	I-5, N to Seattle, S to Tacoma, WA 518 W. **I-405 begins/ends on I-5, exit 154.**

WEST VIRGINIA

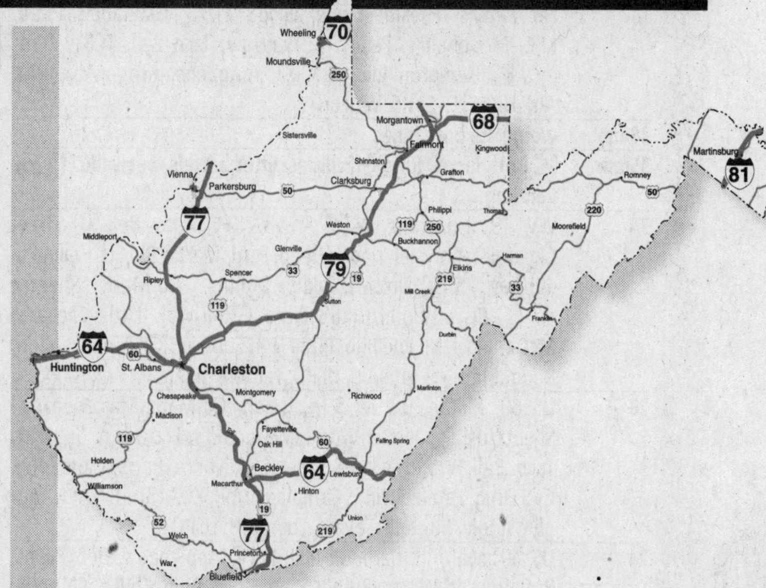

INTERSTATE 64

LEWISBURG

Exit#	Services
184mm	West Virginia/Virginia state line
183	VA 311, (from eb, no reentry), Crows (from eb)
181	US 60, WV 92 (no ez wb return), White Sulphur Springs, **0-2 mi** **N** GoMart/dsl, Marathon/Godfather's, Shell April's Pizzaria, Hardee's Budget Inn, Greenbrier Resort, Old White Motel autocare, Family$, Food Lion, Rite Aid, ski area, to Midland Trail, USPO
179mm	**Welcome Ctr wb, full facilities, info, litter barrels, petwalk,**
175	US 60, WV 92, Caldwell, **N** Exxon, Shell/Subway/dsl, Sunoco/Mountaineer Mart/dsl Cook's Country Kitchen, McDonald's, Wendy's $General, **S** Greenbrier SF
173mm	Greenbrier River
169	US 219, Lewisburg, Hist Dist, **N** Shell Biscuit World Relax Inn Federated Parts, **S** Exxon/dsl, Gomart, Shell, Walmart/dsl Applebee's, Arby's, Bellacino's, Bob Evans, China Palace, Dickey's BBQ, Hardee's, Papa John's, Ruby Tuesday, Shoney's, Subway, Taco Bell Fairfield Inn, Hampton Inn, Holiday Inn Express, Quality Inn, Super 8 H, $Tree, AT&T, AutoZone, Buick/Chevrolet, Ford, Lowe's, URGENT CARE, Verizon, Walmart
161	WV 12, Alta, **S** Citgo/dsl Alta Sta/cafe Greenbrier River Camping (14mi)
156	US 60, Midland Trail, Sam Black Church, **N** Exxon/Arby's/dsl, Shell/dsl
150	rd 29, rd 4, Dawson, **S** Exxon Cheddar's Cafe Dawson Inn RV camping
147mm	**runaway truck ramp wb**
143	WV 20, Green Sulphur Springs, **N** Liberty/dsl
139	WV 20, Sandstone, Hinton, **S** Citgo/dsl Blue Stone SP (16mi), Richmonds Store/USPO, to Pipestem Resort Park (25 mi)
138mm	New River
136mm	**runaway truck ramp eb**
133.1mm	Sandstone Mtn, elev 2765
133	WV 27, Pluto Rd, Bragg, **S** RV camping, mandatory truck stop eb
129	WV 9, Shady Spring, **N** to Grandview SP, **S** Exxon/dsl, Shell/dsl Subway Little Beaver SP
125b a	WV 307, Airport Rd, Beaver, **N** Shell/dsl Biscuit World Sleep Inn, **1 mi S** GoMart/gas, Marathon/dsl, Sheetz/dsl Arby's, Dickey's BBQ, DQ, El Mariachi, Hardee's, KFC, Little Caesar's, LJ Silver, McDonald's, Subway, Wendy's Advance Parts, CVS Drug, Family$, Kroger, USPO, Walgreens
124	US 19, Eisenhower Dr, E Beckley, **1-2 mi N** GoMart/gas Capt D's, Raleigh Diner Green Bank Motel, Microtel H, $General, last exit before **toll** rd wb
121	I-77 S, to Bluefield

I-64 and I-77 run together 61 mi. See I-77, exits 42 through 100.

CHARLESTON

Exit#	Services
59	I-77 N (from eb), to I-79
58c	US 60, Washington St, **N** BP, Exxon, GoMart/dsl Family$, **S** 5th Quarter Steaks, Capt D's, Panera Bread, Shoney's, Wendy's Courtyard, Embassy Suites, Hampton Inn, Holiday Inn Express, Marriott H, civic ctr, Goodyear/auto, Macy's
58b	US 119 N (from eb), Charleston, downtown, same as 58c
58a	US 119 S, WV 61, MacCorkle Ave
56	Montrose Dr, **N** Exxon/dsl, Marathon/dsl, Speedway/dsl Hardee's, Los Agaves Mexican Holiday Inn, Microtel,
56	Continued Wingate Inn $General, Acura, Advance Parts, Chevrolet, Dodge, Hyundai, Kia, NAPA, Rite Aid, VW
55	Kanawha Tpk (from wb)
54	US 60, MacCorkle Ave, **N** Burger King, Casa Garcia, Graziano's Pizza, Krispy Kreme, Subway $Tree, AT&T, Kroger/dsl, TJ Maxx, **S** Bob Evans, Husson's Pizza, KFC, LJ Silver, McDonald's, Pizza Hut, Schlotzsky's, Taco Bell, Wendy's H, Aamco, Family$, Harley-Davidson, Honda, Mazda, URGENT CARE
53	Roxalana Rd, to Dunbar, **S** GoMart/dsl BiscuitWorld, Capt D's, Gino's Pizza, Graziano's Pizza, Los Agaves, McDonald's, Subway, Wendy's Dunbar Plaza Motel, Super 8 $General, Advance Parts, Aldi Foods, CVS Drug, Family$, Jo-Ann Fabrics, Kroger/dsl, NTB, Rite Aid
50	WV 25, Institute, **S** GoMart/dsl
47b a	WV 622, Goff Mtn Rd, **N** Exxon/dsl, GoMart, Speedway/dsl BiscuitWorld, Bob Evans, Capt D's, Domino's, Gino's Pizza, Little Caesar's, McDonald's, Papa John's, Pizza Hut, Subway, Taco Bell, Wendy's Motel 6 Advance Parts, AT&T, Autozone, Family$, Kroger/gas, Rite Aid, Save-a-Lot, URGENT CARE, Walgreens, **S** Arby's, Asian Buffet, Barnyard BBQ, Buffalo Wild Wings, Burger King, Cracker Barrel, Golden Corral, HoneyBaked Ham, La Roca Mexican, Sakura Japanese, TGIFriday's Comfort Inn, Holiday Inn Express, Sleep Inn $Tree, Lowe's, Staples, Walmart
45	WV 25, Nitro, **N** Pilot/Arby's/dsl/scales/24hr Chevrolet, **S** Exxon/dsl, GoMart, Speedway/dsl BiscuitWorld, Checker's, DQ, Gino's Pizza, McDonald's, Subway, Wendy's $General
44.3mm	Kanawha River
44	US 35, St Albans, **S** Shell/7-11/dsl
40	US 35 N, Winfield, Pt Pleasant, **S** Sheetz/dsl, Speedway/dsl DQ
39	WV 34, Winfield, **N** BP/Arby's, GoMart/dsl Applebee's, Bob Evans, Rio Grande Mexican, Taste of Asia Holiday Inn Express, Red Roof Inn $General, $Tree, Advance Parts, Aldi Foods, BigLots, Elder-Beerman, GNC, Home Depot, USPO, **S** GoMart, TA/Country Pride/dsl/scales/24hr/@ Biscuit World, Burger King, Capt D's, China Chef, El Rancho Grande,

WV

INTERSTATE 64 Cont'd

39	Continued Fat Patty's, Fireside Grille, Gino's Pizza, Graziano's Pizza, KFC, McDonald's, Penn Sta., Subway, Taco Bell, TCBY, Wendy's [lodging] Hampton Inn [other] AT&T, AutoZone, Kroger/dsl, Rite Aid, URGENT CARE, Verizon
38mm	**weigh sta both lanes**
35mm	**[RS] both lanes, full [handicap] facilities, litter barrels, petwalk, [phone], [picnic], vending**
34	WV 19, Hurricane, **N** [food] Arby's, KFC, Taco Bell [other] $Tree, Chevrolet, Chrysler/Dodge/Jeep, Ford, Martin RV Ctr, Walmart/Subway, **S** [gas] Exxon/Dunkin Donuts, Go-Mart, Sheetz/dsl [food] BiscuitWorld/Gino's Pizza, China Wok, Little Caesar's, McDonald's, Mi Pueblito, Pizza Hut, Subway [lodging] American Inn, Budget Inn [other] Rite Aid, USPO, vet, Walgreens
28	US 60, Milton, **0-2 mi S** [gas] Exxon, Go-Mart, Marathon/dsl, Sheetz/dsl [food] Biscuit World, McDonald's, Pizza Hut, Subway, Taco Bell, Wendy's [other] $General, Advance Parts, AutoZone, CVS Drug, Family$, Jim's Camping (2mi), KOA (3mi), NAPA, Piggly Wiggly, Rite Aid, Save-A-Lot foods, USPO
20	US 60, Mall Rd, Barboursville, **N** [food] Applebee's, Bob Evans, Buffalo Wild Wings, Burger King, Chick-fil-A, Chili's, Chipotle, IHOP, Logan's Roadhouse, McDonald's, Olive Garden, Panera Bread, Qdoba Mexican, Ruby Tuesday, Super China, Wendy's [lodging] Comfort Inn [other] BAM!, Best Buy, Dick's, Drug Emporium, Elder-Beerman, Firestone/auto, Hobby Lobby, JC Penney, Jo-Ann Fabrics, Kohl's, Lowe's, Macy's, Michael's, NTB, Old Navy, Walmart/Subway, **S** [gas] BP/dsl, Sheetz/dsl [food] Cracker Barrel, Fat Patty's, Outback Steaks, Shogun Japanese, Sonic, Steak&Shake, Subway, Taco Bell [lodging] Best Western, Hampton Inn, Holiday Inn [other] Toyota
18	US 60, to WV 2, Barboursville, **N** [food] Bellacino's, O'Charley's, Starbucks [other] $Tree, Home Depot, Marshall's, Office Depot, Petco, Target, **S** [gas] Shell/7-11 [food] Biscuit World, Gino's, Giovanni's Pizza, Hardee's, Papa John's [other] Food Fair, Kia, Kroger/gas, NAPA, Rite Aid, Walgreens
15	US 60, 29th St E, **N** [gas] GoMart/dsl, Shell/dsl, Speedway/dsl [food] #1 Kitchen, Arby's, Biscuit World, Burger King, Honeybaked Ham, Subway, Waffle House, Wendy's [lodging] Huntington Motel, Quality Inn [other] [H], $General, AT&T, BigLots, NAPA, Save-a-Lot Foods, st police, Verizon, Walmart/McDonald's, **S** [gas] Exxon [food] Fazoli's, Golden Corral, KFC, Little Caesar's, Marco's Pizza, McDonald's, Penn Sta., Taco Bell [lodging] Days Inn, Red Roof Inn [other] Buick/Cadillac/GMC, CVS Drug, Honda, Nissan, Subaru, VW
11	WV 10, Hal Greer Blvd, **0-2 mi N** [gas] Marathon/Subway [food] Arby's, Baskin-Robbins, Biscuit World, Bob Evans, El Ranchito Mexican, Frostop Drive-In, McDonald's, Papa John's, Ritzy's Cafe, Wendy's [lodging] Fairfield Inn, Hampton Inn, Ramada Ltd, Super 8, TownePlace Suites [other] [H], AutoZone, Chrysler/Dodge/Jeep, Rite Aid, **S** [other] Beech Fork SP (8mi)
10mm	**Welcome Ctr eb, full [handicap] facilities, litter barrels, petwalk, [phone], [picnic], vending**
8	WV 152 S, WV 527 N, **N** [other] URGENT CARE, vet, **S** [gas] GoMart/dsl, Speedway/dsl
6	US 52 N, W Huntington, Chesapeake, **N** [gas] Sheetz/dsl, Speedway/dsl [food] Pizza Hut, Shoney's, Wendys [other] [H], $General, AutoZone, BigLots, Family$, Save-A-Lot Foods
1	US 52 S, Kenova, **0-1 mi N** [gas] Exxon, Shell/dsl [food] Burger King, Evaroni's Pizza, Gino's Pizza, Hermanos Nunez Mexican, McDonald's, Stewart's Hotdogs, Taco Bell [lodging] Hollywood Motel [other] $General, Advance Parts, CVS Drug, NAPA, Save-A-Lot, USPO
0mm	West Virginia/Kentucky state line, Big Sandy River

HUNTINGTON

WV

MORGANTOWN

INTERSTATE 68

Exit#	Services
32mm	West Virginia/Maryland state line
31mm	**Welcome Ctr wb, full [handicap] facilities, litter barrels, petwalk, [phone], [picnic], vending**
29	rd 5, Hazelton Rd, **N** [gas] Sunoco/dsl [lodging] Microtel (1mi), **S** [other] Big Bear Camping (3mi), Pine Hill RV Camp (4mi)
23	WV 26, Bruceton Mills, **N** [gas] BFS/Subway/dsl/24hr, Sunoco/Little Sandy's Rest./dsl/24hr [food] Mill Stone Rest. [lodging] Maple Leaf Motel [other] antiques, Auto+ Parts, Family$, USPO
18mm	Laurel Run
17mm	**runaway truck ramp eb**
16mm	**weigh sta wb**
15	WV 73, WV 12, Coopers Rock, **N** [other] Chestnut Ridge SF, Sand Springs Camping (2mi)
12mm	**runaway truck ramp wb**
10	WV 43 N, to rd 857, Fairchance Rd, Cheat Lake, **N** [gas] BFS/DQ/Little Caesar's/dsl, Exxon/dsl [food] Angelo's Pizza, Dragon Cafe [other] USPO, vet, **S** [food] Burger King [lodging] Lakeview Resort
9mm	Cheat Lake
7	rd 705, Pierpont Rd, **N** [gas] BFS/Little Caesar's/Subway/TCBY, Exxon/Taco Bell/dsl [food] Fox's Pizza Den, Fujiyama Steaks, Honeybaked Ham, IHOP, McDonald's, Outback Steaks, Ruby Tuesday, Wendy's [lodging] Holiday Inn Express, Super 8 [other] [H], Books-A-Million, Family$, GNC, Lowe's, Michael's, Shop'n Save Foods, to WVU Stadium, **S** [gas] Sunoco/dsl [food] Apple Annie's, Don Patron Mexican, Rita's Custard [other] Chrysler/Dodge
4	rd 7, to Sabraton, **N** [gas] BFS/Subway/dsl, Sheetz/dsl [food] Arby's, Burger King, Dunkin Donuts, Hardee's, KFC, LJ Silver, McDonald's, Popeye's, Shoney's, Wendy's [lodging] SpringHill Suites, Suburban Lodge [other] $General, $Tree, Advance Parts, AutoZone, CVS Drug, Family$, Kroger/dsl, NAPA, Save-A-Lot Foods, USPO, **S** [gas] Marathon/Circle K, Sunoco/dsl [food] China City
3mm	Decker's Creek
1	US 119, Morgantown, **N** [gas] Go-Mart/dsl [lodging] Morgantown Inn/rest., Quality Inn [other] tires, **S** [gas] Sheetz/dsl, Tesla EVC [food] Denny's, Mariachi Loco [other] $Tree, to Tygart L SP, Walmart/Subway
0mm	I-79, N to Pittsburgh, S to Clarksburg. **I-68 begins/ends on I-79, exit 148.**

INTERSTATE 70

Exit#	Services
14mm	West Virginia/Pennsylvania state line
13.5mm	**Welcome Ctr wb, full [handicap] facilities, litter barrels, petwalk, [phone], [picnic], vending**
11	WV 41, Dallas Pike, **N** [gas] TA/Country Pride/dsl/scales/24hr/@ [lodging] Comfort Inn, **S** [gas] Exxon, Marathon/DQ/dsl [lodging] EconoLodge [other] RV camping
10	rd 65, to Cabela Dr, **N** [gas] Sheetz/dsl [food] Applebee's, Bob Evans, Cheddar's, Coldstone, Eat'n Park, El Paso Mexican, Five Guys, Fusion Steaks, Jimmy John's, Logan's Roadhouse, McDonald's, Olive Garden, Panera Bread, Primanti Bros, Quaker Steak, TX Roadhouse, Wendy's [lodging] Fairfield Inn, Hampton Inn, Hawthorn Suites, Microtel [other] AT&T, Best Buy, Books-A-Million, Cabela's, GNC, JC Penney, Kohl's, Old Navy, PetCo, Russell Stover Candies, Target, TJ Maxx, Verizon, Walmart/Subway, **S** [gas] Sheetz/dsl [lodging] Holiday Inn Express, Suburban Lodge [other] Buick/GMC, Chevrolet, Ford/Lincoln, Honda, Hyundai, Nissan, Toyota
5	US 40, WV 88 S, Tridelphia, **N** [gas] Marathon/dsl [food] Pizza Hut, Subway, Wendy's [lodging] Super 8 [other] Chrysler/Dodge/Jeep,

INTERSTATE 70 Cont'd

WHEELING

Exit	Services
5	Continued Family$, Riesbeck's Foods, Subaru/VW, URGENT CARE, vet, **S** Marathon/dsl Arby's, DQ, McDonald's, Undo's Rest. Advance Parts, AT&T, AutoZone, museum, Rite Aid
5a	I-470 W, to Columbus
4	WV 88 N (from eb), Elm Grove, same as 5
3.5mm	**weigh sta eb**
2b	Washington Ave, **N** $General, **S** Figaretti's Italian H
2a	rd 88 N, to Oglebay Park, **N** Marathon/dsl, Sheetz AC Buffet, Bob Evans, DeFelice Bros Pizza, Hardee's, Little Caesar's, Papa John's, Perkins, Subway, Tim Hortons Hampton Inn, SpringHill Suites Advance Parts, CVS Drug, Kroger/gas, NTB, URGENT CARE, Verizon
1b	US 250 S, WV 2 S, S Wheeling
1mm	**tunnel**
1a	US 40 E, WV 2 N, Main St, downtown, **S** Knights Inn
0	(from wb)US 40 W, Zane St, Wheeling Island, **N** Exxon/dsl Burger King, KFC
0mm	West Virginia/Ohio state line, Ohio River

INTERSTATE 77

PARKERSBURG

Exit#	Services
186mm	West Virginia/Ohio state line, Ohio River
185	WV 14, WV 31, Williamstown, **W WV Welcome Ctr/ full facilities, info, litter barrels,** Clark, GoMart/dsl, Shell (1mi) Dutch Pantry Econolodge/Rodeway Inn , Glass Factory Tours
179	WV 2 N, WV 68 S, to Waverly, **E** Exxon/dsl , **W** BP/dsl Burger King, Hardee's (3mi) Red Carpet Inn, Sleep Inn H
176	US 50, 7th St, Parkersburg, **E** to North Bend SP, **W** BP/7-11, GoMart Domino's, DQ, Hardee's, Little Caesar's, McDonald's, Mountaineer Rest./24hr, Omelette Shoppe, Wendy's Economy Inn, Travelodge Advance Parts, AutoZone, Chrysler/Dodge/Jeep, CVS Drug, Family$, Ford/Lincoln, Honda, Hyundai, Kroger/dsl, Mercedes, NAPA, Rite Aid, to Blennerhassett Hist Park, Toyota
174	WV 47, Staunton Ave, **1 mi E** GoMart/Sub Express/dsl $General
174mm	Little Kanawha River
173	WV 95, Camden Ave, **E** Marathon/dsl, **1-4 mi W** Hardee's Blennerhassett Hotel H
170	WV 14, Mineral Wells, **E** BP/dsl/repair, GoMart/Taco Bell/dsl, Liberty Trkstp/dsl/24hr McDonald's, Wendy's Comfort Suites, Hampton Inn, **W** Cracker Barrel, Napoli's Pizza Holiday Inn Express, Microtel, Mineral Wells Inn
169mm	**, weigh sta both lanes**
166mm	**both lanes, full facilities, litter barrels, petwalk, , , RV dump, vending**
161	WV 21, Rockport, **W** Marathon/dsl
154	WV 1, Medina Rd
146	WV 2 S, Silverton, Ravenswood, **E** Ruby Lake Camping (4mi), **W** Exxon/DQ, Marathon/dsl McDonald's (3mi), Subway (4mi), Wendy's (3mi) Scottish Inn
138	US 33, Ripley, **E** BP/dsl, Marathon/dsl, Murphy USA/dsl, Sheetz/dsl Arby's, KFC, Las Trancas Mexican, LJ Silver, McDonald's, Pizza Hut, Taco Bell, Wendy's Holiday Inn Express, Super 8 $Tree, AutoZone, Family$, Kroger/dsl, NAPA, Rite Aid, Sav-A-Lot Foods, Verizon, Walmart/Subway, **W** Exxon/dsl Bob Evans, Ponderosa, Shoney's, Subway Quality Inn H

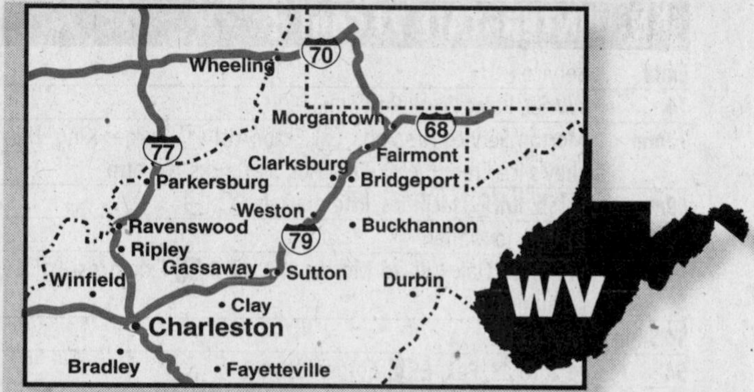

CHARLESTON

Exit	Services
132	WV 21, Fairplain, **E** BP/7-11/dsl, GoMart/dsl, Speedway/dsl/24hr Burger King, Fratello's Italian $General, Ford, Statts Mills RV Park (6mi), **W** Loves/Chester's/McDonald's/dsl/scales/24hr
124	WV 34, Kenna, **E** Exxon Your Family Rest.
119	WV 21, Goldtown, same as 116
116	WV 21, Haines Branch Rd, Sissonville, **4 mi E** Rippling Waters Camping
114	WV 622, Pocatalico Rd, **E** BP/dsl $General
111	WV 29, Tuppers Creek Rd, **W** BP/Subway/dsl Gino's (2mi), McDonald's (2mi), Tudor's Biscuit World, Wendy's (2mi)
106	WV 27, Edens Fork Rd, **W** Marathon/dsl/country store Sunset Motel (3mi)
104	I-79 N, to Clarksburg
102	US 119 N, Westmoreland Rd, **E** BP/7-11, GoMart Hardee's Foodland/gas
101	I-64, E to Beckley, W to Huntington
100	Broad St, Capitol St, **W** Subway Best Western, Charleston Capitol Hotel, Marriott H, Cadillac/GMC, Firestone, Rite Aid, USPO
99	WV 114, Capitol St, **E** , **W** BP/7-11, Exxon/Noble Roman's Domino's, McDonald's, Wendy's st capitol, to museum
98	35th St Bridge (from sb), **W** Shell/7-11/dsl Husson's Pizza, KFC, McDonald's, Steak Escape, Subway, Taco Bell, Wendy's H, Rite Aid, to U of Charleston
97	US 60 W (from nb), Kanawha Blvd
96	US 60 E, Midland Trail, Belle, **W** Anchor Pizza, Biscuit World, Gino's Budget Host
96mm	**W Va Turnpike begins/ends**
95.5mm	Kanawha River
95	WV 61, to MacCorkle Ave, **E** GoMart/dsl/24hr, Marathon/Subway/dsl Bob Evans, IHOP, McDonald's, TX Steaks Country Inn&Suites, Days Inn, Holiday Inn Express, Knights Inn, Motel 6, Red Roof Inn Advance Parts, AutoZone, **W** Exxon/dsl, GoMart, Shell/7-11/dsl Applebee's, Arby's, Bojangle's, Burger King, Capt D's, China Buffet, Cracker Barrel, Firehouse Subs, Fujiyama Japanese, Hooters, La Carreta, Little Caesar's, Pizza Hut, Taco Bell $Tree, AT&T, Drug Emporium, GNC, GNC, Kings Tire, Kroger/dsl, Lowe's, Piggly Wiggly, URGENT CARE, Verizon, vet
89	WV 61, WV 94, to Marmet, **E** Exxon/Subway/dsl/24hr, GoMart/dsl, Sunoco/dsl BiscuitWorld, Gino's Pizza, Hardee's, LJ Silver, Wendy's $General, Family$, Family$, Ford, Kroger/dsl, NAPA, Rite Aid, USPO
85	US 60, WV 61, East Bank, **E** Marathon/dsl, Shell/Arby's/dsl Gino's Pizza, McDonald's, Shoney's $General, Chevrolet, Rite Aid
82.5mm	**toll booth**
79	Cabin Creek Rd, Sharon

WV

INTERSTATE 77 Cont'd

Exit#	Services
74	WV 83, Paint Creek Rd
72mm	Morton Service Area nb, Exxon/dsl Burger King, Hershey's Ice Cream, KFC, Pizza Hut, Starbucks atm
69mm	**sb, full facilities, litter barrels, ,**
66	WV 15, to Mahan
60	WV 612, Oak Hill, to Mossy, **1/2 mi** E Exxon/dsl RV camping
56.5mm	**toll plaza**
54	rd 2, rd 23, Pax, E Corner/dsl
48	US 19, N Beckley, **1-4 mi E on US 19/WV 16** Exxon/Subway, Sheetz/dsl Bob Evans, Buffalo Wild Wings, Burger King, Cheddar's, Chick-fil-A, Chili's, Dickey's BBQ, Five Guys, Honeybaked Ham, LJ Silver, Logan's Roadhouse, McDonald's, Olive Garden, Panera Bread, Peking Buffet, Qdoba, Rally's, Ryan's, Starbucks, Subway, Taco Bell, Wendy's Days Inn $General, $Tree, Advance Parts, AT&T, AutoZone, Belk, BigLots, Buick/GMC, Chevrolet, Chrysler/Dodge/Jeep, CVS Drug, Dick's, Food Lion, Goodyear/auto, Hobby Lobby, Honda, Hyundai, JC Penney, Jo-Ann Fabrics, Kia/Subaru, Kohl's, Kroger/gas, Lowe's, NAPA, Nissan, Petsmart, Rite Aid, RV Ctr, Sam's Club/gas, Staples, TJ Maxx, Toyota, U-Haul, Walgreens, Walmart
45mm	**Tamarack Service Area both lanes,** W Exxon/dsl Burger King, Hershey's Ice Cream, Quiznos, Sbarro's, Starbucks gifts
44	WV 3, Beckley, E Exxon/dsl, Marathon/dsl, Shell/Dickey's BBQ Applebee's, Bojangle's, Burger King, Campestre Mexican, DQ, Fujiyama Japanese, Hooters, IHOP, McDonald's, Omelet Shoppe, Outback Steaks, Pizza Hut Courtyard, EconoLodge, Fairfield Inn, Howard Johnson, Quality Inn/rest., Super 8, Travelodge H, Advance Parts, CVS Drug, Kroger/gas, Rite Aid, Tires, URGENT CARE, W BP/Subway/dsl, Go-Mart/dsl Bob Evans, Cracker Barrel, Pasquale Italian, Ruby Tuesday, Sam's Hotdogs, TX Steaks, Wendy's Baymont Inn, Comfort Inn, Country Inn&Suites, Hampton Inn, Holiday Inn, Microtel
42	WV 16, WV 97, to Mabscott, **2 mi** E H, W BP/dsl, Go-Mart Arby's, Gino's Pizza/Biscuit World, Subway AutoValue Repair, O'Reilly Parts, USPO, Walmart/Subway
40	I-64 E, to Lewisburg
30mm	**toll booth**
28	WV 48, to Ghent, E Exxon/dsl, Marathon/dsl Subway Appalachian Resort Inn (12mi), Glade Springs Resort (1mi) to ski area, W Knight's Inn
26.5mm	elevation 3252, Flat Top Mtn
20	US 19, to Camp Creek, E Exxon/dsl, W Camp Creek SP/RV camping
18.5mm	Bluestone River, scenic overlook/parking area/**weigh sta sb**
17mm	**Bluestone Service Area/weigh sta nb, full facilities, picnic area, scenic view** Exxon/dsl Blimpie, Hershey's Ice Cream, Starbucks, Uno Pizza atm/fax
14	WV 20, Athens Rd, E Pipestem Resort SP, to Concord U
9mm	**WV Turnpike begins/ends**
9	US 460, Princeton, E **Welcome Ctr/Rest Area both lanes, full facilities, , litter barrels, petwalk** Walmart/dsl Campestre Mexican, Kimono Japanese, Outback Steaks, Ryan's Country Inn&Suites, Fairfield Inn , $Tree, AT&T, URGENT CARE, Verizon, Walmart/Subway, W BP/dsl, Exxon, Sheetz/dsl, Shell/Subway Applebee's, Arby's, Bob Evans, Bojangles, Capt D's, Chick-fil-A, Chili's, Cracker Barrel, Dolly's Diner, DQ, Hardee's, McDonald's, Shoney's, Starbucks, Taco Bell, TX Steaks, Wendy's Days Inn, Eden Rock Motel, Hampton Inn,
9	Continued Holiday Inn Express, Microtel, Quality Inn, Sleep Inn, Turnpike Motel H, Hyundai, Lowe's
7	WV 27, Twelve Mile Rd
5	WV 112 (from sb, no re-entry), to Ingleside
3mm	East River
1	US 52 N, to Bluefield, **4 mi** W KFC/LJ Silver, Wendy's EconoLodge, Quality Inn H, to Bluefield St Coll
0mm	West Virginia/Virginia state line, East River Mtn

BECKLEY

PRINCETON

WV

INTERSTATE 79

Exit#	Services
160mm	West Virginia/Pennsylvania state line
159	**Welcome Ctr sb, full facilities, info, litter barrels, petwalk, , , vending**
155	US 19, WV 7, **0-3 mi** E GetGo, Sheetz/dsl Cheddar's, Chili's, Chipotle, CiCi's Pizza, Cracker Barrel, Evergreen Buffet, Golden Corral, Longhorn Steaks, McDonald's, Olive Garden, Red Lobster, Starbucks, TX Roadhouse Best Western, EconoLodge, Fairfield Inn H, $Tree, Barnes&Noble, Best Buy, Buick/Chevrolet/GMC, CVS Drug, Dick's, Giant Eagle Foods, GNC, Old Navy, PetCo, Sam's Club/dsl, Target, TJ Maxx, to WVU, Walmart/Subway, W BFS/dsl Burger King, DQ, Firehouse Subs, Little Caesar's, Tim Hortons Candlewood Suites, La Quinta Harley-Davidson, Hobby Lobby
153	University Towne Ctr, E Buffalo Wild Wings, Fusion Japanese, Wendy's Courtyard, Hampton Inn Kia
152	US 19, to Morgantown, E BFS/dsl, Exxon Arby's, China Wok, McDonald's, Pizza Hut, Subway, Taco Bell EconoLodge Advance Parts, BigLots, URGENT CARE, W Bob Evans, Burger King, Garfield's Rest. Microtel Belk, Elder-Beerman, JC Penney, Lowe's
150mm	Monongahela River
148	I-68 E, to Cumberland, MD, **1 mi** E Go-Mart/dsl, Sheetz/dsl, Tesla EVC Denny's, Mariachi Loco, Subway Morgantown Motel, Quality Inn, Ramada Inn $Tree, tires, to Tygart Lake SP, Walmart
146	WV 77, to Goshen Rd, W Pilot/deli/dsl/scales/24hr (RV accessible dsl only)
141mm	**weigh sta both lanes**
139	WV 33, E Fairmont, E Sunoco, W Exxon, K&T/dsl/scales repair, RV camping, to Prickett's Ft SP
137	WV 310, to Fairmont, E Exxon/dsl, Sunoco Clarion to Valley Falls SP, vet, W Shell/dsl Domino's, KFC, McDonald's, Subway, Wendy's H, $General, Advance Parts, Family$, Shop'n Save Foods
136	rd 273, Fairmont
135	WV 64, Pleasant Valley Rd
133	Kingmont Rd, E Exxon/Fazoli's/dsl, Marathon/Subway/dsl Cracker Barrel Hampton Inn, Holiday Inn Express, Super 8, W Shell/Quiznos/dsl DJ's Diner Quality Inn
132	US 250, S Fairmont, E BFS/DQ/dsl, Walmart/dsl Applebee's, Arby's, Bob Evans, Colasessano's Italian, Dutchman's Daughter, El Rey Mexican, Firehouse Subs, Grand China, Hardee's, Little Caesar's, McDonald's, Mi Pueblo, Subway, Taco Bell Days Inn, Fairfield Inn, Microtel, Red Roof Inn $General, Ace Hardware, Advance Parts, Chrysler/Dodge/Jeep, GNC, NAPA, Sav-A-Lot Foods, Shop'n Save, to Tygart Lake SP, Walmart/Subway, W Exxon/dsl, GoMart/dsl, Sunoco/dsl Burger King, Steak Escape H, AT&T, Buick/GMC, Ford/Lincoln, Toyota, Trailer City RV Ctr

MORGANTOWN

INTERSTATE 79 Cont'd

CLARKSBURG

Exit#	Services
125	WV 131, Saltwell Rd, to Shinnston, E [food] Oliverio's Rest. (4mi) [other] Kia, W [gas] BFS/Burger King/dsl, Exxon/dsl
124	rd 279, Jerry Dove Dr, E [gas] BFS, Exxon/Dunkin Donuts/dsl [food] Buffalo Wild Wings, DQ, Firehouse Subs, Little Caesar's, Mi Margherita [lodging] Microtel, Wingate Inn, W [gas] Sheetz/dsl [food] IHOP, Subway, TGIFriday [lodging] Comfort Suites, Courtyard, Hawthorn Suites, Holiday Inn Express [other] [H]
123mm	**[RS] both lanes, full [handicapped] facilities, info, litter barrels, petwalk, [phone], [picnic], RV dump, vending**
121	WV 24, Meadowbrook Rd, E [gas] GoMart, Sheetz/dsl [food] Biscuit World, Bob Evans, Gino's Pizza [lodging] Hampton Inn [other] Hyundai/Subaru, W [gas] Exxon/dsl [food] Burger King, Garfield's Rest., Outback Steaks [lodging] Super 8 [other] Dick's, Honda, JC Penney, Jo-Ann Fabrics, Marshall's, NTB, Old Navy, Target
119	US 50, to Clarksburg, E [food] A&W/LJ Silver, Brickside Grille, Chick-fil-A, Denny's, Eat'n Park, Grand China, KFC, Las Trancas, Little Caesar's, McDonald's, McDonald's (2), Panera Bread, Pizza Hut, Primanti Bros, Starbucks, Taco Bell, TX Roadhouse, Wendy's [lodging] Best Western+, Days Inn, Sleep Inn, SpringHill Suites, Sutton Inn, Townplace Suites [other] $Tree, Advance Parts, Autozone, BigLots, Family$, GNC, Home Depot, Kohl's, Kroger/dsl, Lowe's, Monro, Sam's Club/gas, URGENT CARE, USPO, Verizon, Walgreens
117	WV 58, to Anmoore, E [gas] BFS/dsl [food] Applebee's, Arby's, Burger King, Honeybaked Ham, Ruby Tuesday, Ryan's, Subway [lodging] Hilton Garden [other] Aldi Foods, AT&T, El Rey Mexican, Staples, Walmart/Subway
115	WV 20, Nutter Fort, to Stonewood, E [gas] BP/7-11/dsl, Exxon/dsl [other] $General, Stonewood Bulk Foods, W [lodging] Greenbrier Motel (5mi)
110	Lost Creek, E [gas] General Store/dsl [other] USPO
105	WV 7, to Jane Lew, E [gas] Jane Lew Trkstp/dsl/rest., Valero/dsl/rest. [lodging] Days Inn, W [gas] GoMart [other] $General, Kenworth/Mack/Volvo
99	US 33, US 119, to Weston, E [gas] GoMart/dsl, Marathon/DQ/Little Caesars/dsl, Sheetz/dsl [food] Burger King, Gino's Pizza, McDonald's, Patron Mexican, Peking Buffet, Steer Steakhouse, Subway [lodging] Hampton Inn (9mi), Holiday Inn Express, Quality Inn/rest., Super 8 [other] $Tree, Advance Parts, Blackwater Falls, GNC, to Canaan Valley Resort, Walmart/dsl, **0-2 mi W** [gas] Exxon/Arby's/dsl, Go-Mart [food] Domino's, Giovanni's, Hardee's, KFC, LJ Silver, Pizza Hut, Subway, Wendy's [other] [H], $General, Chrysler/Dodge/Fiat, CVS Drug, Ford, NAPA, NAPACare, Rite Aid, Save-a-Lot
96	WV 30, to S Weston, E [other] Broken Wheel Camping, to S Jackson Lake SP
91	US 19, to Roanoke, E [gas] Marathon/dsl [food] Stillwaters Rest. [other] camping, to S Jackson Lake SP
85mm	**[RS] both lanes, full [handicapped] facilities, info, litter barrels, petwalk, [phone], [picnic], RV dump, vending**
79.5mm	Little Kanawha River
79	WV 5, Burnsville, E [gas] Exxon [lodging] 79er Motel/rest. [other] Burnville Dam RA, W [gas] GoMart [other] Cedar Cr SP
76mm	Saltlick Creek
67	WV 4, to Flatwoods, E [gas] BP/Arby's/dsl, Go-Mart/dsl, Shell/dsl [food] Custard Stand, KFC/Taco Bell, McDonald's, Subway [lodging] Day's Hotel [other] antiques, Buick/Chevrolet, KOA, to Sutton Lake RA, W [gas] Exxon/dsl, Pilot/Moe's SW Grill/dsl/scales/24hr [food] China Buffet, Shoney's, Starbucks, Wendy's [other] Bulk Foods, Flatwood Factory Stores, Walmart

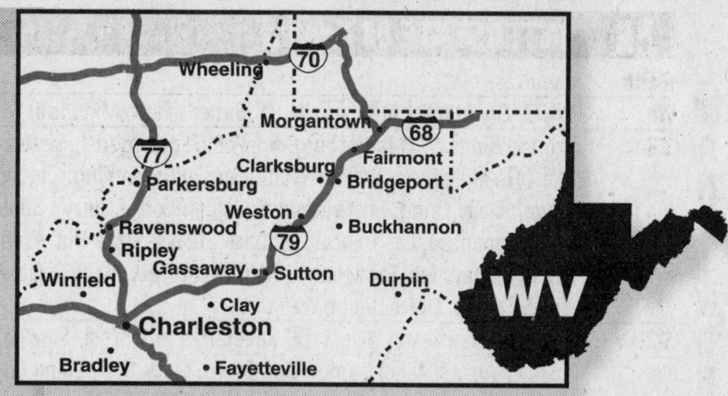

CHARLESTON

Exit#	Services
62	WV 4, Gassaway, to Sutton, E [lodging] Elk Motel [other] Sutton Lake Camping, W [gas] GoMart [food] LJ Silver, Pizza Hut [lodging] Microtel [other] [H], AutoZone, CVS Drug, Ford, Kroger/deli
57	US 19 S, to Beckley
52mm	Elk River
51	WV 4, to Frametown, E antiques, food
49mm	**[RS] both lanes, full [handicapped] facilities, litter barrels, petwalk, [phone], [picnic], RV dump, vending**
46	WV 11, Servia Rd
40	WV 16, to Big Otter, E [gas] GoMart/dsl, W [gas] Exxon/dsl
34	WV 36, to Wallback, **10 mi E** [food] BiscuitWorld, Gino's Diner, Subway
25	WV 29, to Amma, E [gas] Exxon/dsl
19	US 119, VW 53, to Clendenin, E [gas] BP/7-11/dsl [other] Rite Aid (3mi), Speedway/dsl (3mi)
9	WV 43, to Elkview, E [gas] GoMart/dsl [food] Burger King, Penn Sta Subs [other] AutoZone, W [gas] Exxon/Arby's/dsl, Speedway/dsl [food] La Carreta, Little Caesar's, McDonald's, Picanha Steaks, Subway [lodging] La Quinta [other] $Tree, Advance Parts, AT&T, CVS Drug, Kroger/dsl
5	WV 114, to Big Chimney, **1 mi E** [gas] Exxon [food] Hardee's [other] Rite Aid, Smith's Foods
1	US 119, Mink Shoals, E [food] Harding's Family Rest. [lodging] Sleep Inn
0	I-77, S to Charleston, N to Parkersburg. **I-79 begins/ends on I-77, exit 104.**

INTERSTATE 81

Exit#	Services
26mm	West Virginia/Maryland state line, Potomac River
25mm	**Welcome Ctr sb, full [handicapped] facilities, info, litter barrels, petwalk, [phone], [picnic]**
23	US 11, Marlowe, Falling Waters, E [gas] Exxon/AC&T/Subway/dsl [food] Kings Rest., Red Lantern Chinese [other] $General, Falling Waters Camping (1mi), Food Lion, W [gas] BP/dsl [other] 7-11, Outdoor Express RV Ctr
20	WV 901, Spring Mills Rd, E [gas] Sheetz/dsl [food] China Spring, Cinco de Mayo, Little Caesar's, McDonald's, Pizza Montese, Popeye's, Tokyo Cafe [lodging] Motel 6 [other] $Tree, Advance Parts, Walmart/Subway, W [gas] Shell/dsl [food] Burger King, Domino's [lodging] Quality Inn
16	WV 9, N Queen St, Berkeley Springs, E [gas] Crown/dsl, Exxon/Subway/dsl, Sheetz [food] Arby's, China King, Domino's, Dunkin Donuts, Hoss's, KFC, La Trattoria, LJ Silver, McDonald's, Meridian Cafe, Mrs McCracken's Diner, Pizza Hut, Popeye's, Rita's Custard, Subway, Taco Bell, Waffle House [lodging] Care Free Inn, Comfort Inn, Knights Inn, Super 8 [other] Advance Parts, Aldi Foods, AutoZone, BigLots, Carquest, CVS Drug, Family$, Food Lion, URGENT CARE, USPO, Walgreens, W [gas] Shell/Subway/dsl

INTERSTATE 81 Cont'd

MARTINSBURG

Exit#	Services
14	rd 13, Dry Run Rd, E [other] [H], W [other] Butler's Farm Mkt (1mi)
13	rd 15, Kings St, Martinsburg, E [gas] BP/Subway/dsl, Sheetz/dsl [food] Applebee's, Buffalo Wild Wings, Burger King, Cracker Barrel, Daily Grind, Fiesta Tapatia, Golden Corral, Jerry's Subs, Kobe Japanese, Las Trancas, Outback Steaks, Pizza Hut, Wendy's [lodging] Days Inn, Fairfield Inn, Holiday Inn/rest. [other] [H], Chevrolet/Toyota, Office Depot, Walmart
12	WV 45, Winchester Ave, E [gas] Sheetz/dsl, Shell/dsl, Sunoco/dsl [food] Arby's, Asian Garden, Bob Evans, Chick-fil-A, China City Buffet, Chipotle, Five Guys, McDonald's, Olive Garden, Panda Express, Panera Bread, Papa John's, Ruby Tuesday, Ryan's, Taco Bell, Waffle House [lodging] Hampton Inn [other] Advance Parts, AutoZone, BonTon, Food Lion, Lowe's, Martin's Foods/gas, Nahkeeta
12	Continued Camping, W [food] Ledo Pizza, Logan's Roadhouse, Subway, Tropical Smoothie [lodging] Hilton Garden [other] $Tree, AT&T, Best Buy, Books-A-Million, Dick's, GNC, Michael's, Petsmart, Target, TJ Maxx, URGENT CARE
8	rd 32, Tablers Sta Rd, E [gas] Sheetz/dsl
5	WV 51, Inwood, to Charles Town, E [gas] 7-11, BP, Liberty, Sheetz/dsl, Shell/dsl [food] Arby's, Burger King, Domino's, DQ, McDonald's, Pizza Hut, Pizza Oven, Subway, Waffle House [lodging] Hampton Inn [other] Advance Parts, CVS Drug, Family$, Food Lion, NAPA, Rite Aid, URGENT CARE, USPO, W [other] Lazy-A Camping (9mi)
2mm	**Welcome Ctr/weigh sta nb, full [handicapped] facilities, info, litter barrels, petwalk, [phone], [picnic], vending**
0mm	West Virginia/Virginia state line

WISCONSIN

INTERSTATE 39

WASSAU

Exit#	Services
211	US 51, rd K, Merrill, 2 mi W [gas] Cenex [food] Chip's Burgers, Hardee's, Pine Ridge Rest., Pizza Hut [other] [airport]
208	WI 64, WI 17, Merrill, E [food] KFC, Taco Bell, W [gas] KwikTrip/dsl, Mobil/Arby's/dsl [food] 3's Company Rest., Culver's, Los Mezcales, Mama De Luca's Pizza, McDonald's, Subway [lodging] Americinn, Badger Hotel, EconoLodge [other] [H], $Tree, Chrysler/Dodge/Jeep, O'Reilly Parts, Piggly Wiggly, to Council Grounds SP, Verizon, Walmart
206mm	Wisconsin River
205	US 51, rd Q, Merrill, E [gas] BP/Hwy 51/rest./dsl/24hr [other] Buick/Cadillac/Chevrolet, fireworks
197	rd WW, to Brokaw, W [gas] Mobil/dsl
194	US 51, rd U, rd K, Wausau, E [gas] F&F/dsl, KwikTrip/dsl [food] McDonald's, Subway, Taco Bell, W [food] BP/Arby's/dsl [other] Ford, Kia, Nissan, Subaru, Toyota
193	Bridge St, E [other] CVS Drug, W [other] [H]
192	WI 29 W, WI 52 E, Wausau, to Chippewa Falls, same as 191 b
191b	Sherman St, E [gas] BP, Holiday/dsl [food] Applebee's, Buffalo Wild Wings, Dickey's BBQ, Great Dane Rest., Jimmy John's, King Buffet, Little Caesar's, McDonald's, Milwaukee Burger Co, Noodles&Co, Panera Bread, Papa Murphy's, Qdoba, Starbucks, Subway, Toppers Pizza [lodging] Courtyard, Hampton Inn, La Quinta, Motel 6, Plaza Hotel, Super 8 [other] County Mkt/USPO, ShopKo, Trig's Foods, Walgreens, W [gas] KwikTrip/dsl [food] 2510 Deli, Hardee's [other] [H], Cadillac, Home Depot, Honda, Menards
191a	WI 29, Chippewa Falls
190mm	Rib River
190	rd NN, E [gas] Mobil/Burger King [food] El Tequila Salsa, IHOP [lodging] Hilton Garden, W [gas] The Store/Subway/dsl [lodging] Quality Inn [other] Granite Mtn Ski Area, Rib Mtn Ski Area, st patrol
188	rd N, E [gas] KwikTrip/dsl, Phillips 66/dsl [food] Dunkin Donuts, Fazoli's, HuHot, McDonald's, Olive Garden, Panda Express, Red Robin, Rococo Pizza, Ropa Pizza, Starbucks, TX Roadhouse [lodging] Days Inn [other] $Tree, Aldi Foods, Audi/VW, Barnes&Noble, Best Buy, Chevrolet, Dick's, GNC, Gordman's, Hobby Lobby, Hyundai, JoAnn Fabrics, King's RV Ctr, Kohl's, Michael's, Old Navy, PetCo, Petsmart, Sam's Club/gas/dsl, Tires+, TJ Maxx, Walmart/Subway, W [other] Rib Mtn SP
187mm	**I-39 begins/ends. Freeway continues N as US 51.**

STEVENS PT

Exit#	Services
187	WI 29 E, to Green Bay
186mm	Wisconsin River
185	US 51, Rothschild, Kronenwetter, E [gas] BP/dsl [food] Achiban, Arby's, Culver's, Denny's, Green Mill Rest., Subway [lodging] Best Western, Cedar Creek Lodge, EconoLodge, Holiday Inn, Motel 6, Stoney Creek Inn [other] Harley-Davidson, Pick'n Save Foods
181	Maple Ridge Rd, Kronenwetter, Mosinee, E [other] Peterbilt, vet, Volvo, W [other] Kenworth
179	WI 153, Mosinee, W [gas] Cenex/Subway/dsl, KwikTrip/dsl, Shell/dsl [food] McDonald's, StageStop Rest. [lodging] Quality Inn [other] vet
175	WI 34, Knowlton, to WI Rapids, 1 mi W [other] Mullins Cheese Factory
171	rd DB, Knowlton, W [gas] gas [food] food [lodging] lodging [other] Rivers Edge Camping
165	US 10 W, to Marshfield (no nb re-entry)
163	Casimir Rd
161	US 51, Stevens Point, W [gas] BP, Kwik Trip/dsl, The Store [food] China Wok, Coldstone, Cousins Subs, Culver's, Dosirak Korean, Hardee's, Jimmy John's, KFC, McDonald's, Michele's Rest., Noodles&Co, Perkins, Pizza Hut, Rococo's Pizza, Starbucks, Subway, Taco Bell, Topper's Pizza [lodging] Baymont Inn, Comfort Suites, Country Inn&Suites, Days Inn [other] $Tree, Trig's Foods, Verizon
159	WI 66, Stevens Point, W [gas] KwikTrip/dsl [other] [H], Ford, Honda, Hyundai, Nissan, VW
158	US 10, Stevens Point, E [gas] F&F/dsl, KwikFill/dsl/e85, Mobil/dsl, The Store/Subway/dsl [food] Amber Grille, Applebee's, Arby's, Buffalo Wild Wings, Culver's, DQ, El Mezcal Mexican, Fazoli's, Grazie's Grill, Hibachi Buffet, McDonald's, Taco Bell [lodging] Fairfield Inn, Holiday Inn Express [other] Aldi Foods, AT&T Chrysler/Dodge/Jeep, Target, W [gas] BP/dsl [food] Hilltop Grill Tommy's Grill [lodging] EconoLodge, La Quinta
156	rd HH, Whiting, E [gas] The Store/Subway/dsl [food] Charcoal Grill Chili's, Golden Corral, McDonald's, Panda Express, Panera Bread, Starbucks [other] $Tree, Best Buy, GNC, JoAnn Fabrics, Kohl's Lowe's, Michael's, PetCo, Staples, TJ Maxx, Walmart/Subway
153	rd B, Plover, W [gas] Cenex, Kwik Trip/dsl, Mobil/Dunkin Donuts/dsl [food] Arby's, Bamboo House, Burger King, Culver's, Happy Wok, IHOP, KFC, McDonald's, Papa Murphy's, Subway, Taco Bell, Tempura House Asian [lodging] AmericInn, Comfort Inn, Hampton Inn [other] city park, Copp's Foods, dsl repair, Menards, NAPA ShopKo, Toyota, Verizon, vet, Younkers

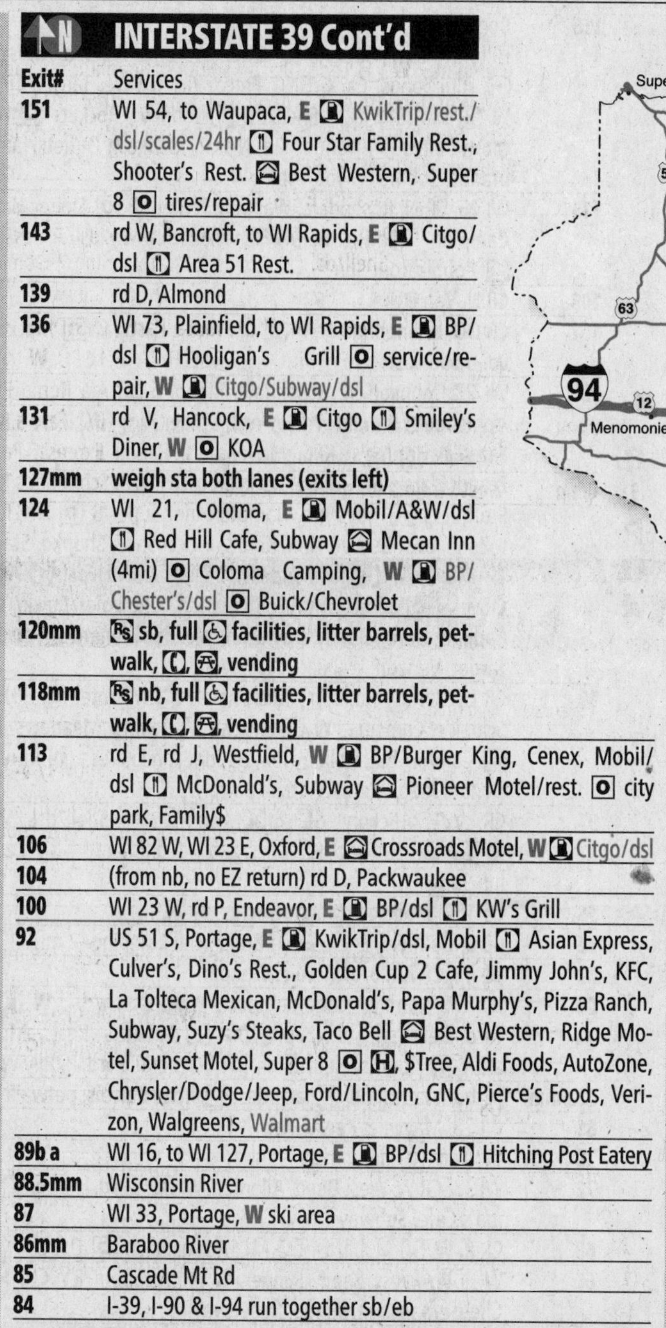

INTERSTATE 39 Cont'd

Exit#	Services
151	WI 54, to Waupaca, E KwikTrip/rest./dsl/scales/24hr Four Star Family Rest., Shooter's Rest. Best Western, Super 8 tires/repair
143	rd W, Bancroft, to WI Rapids, E Citgo/dsl Area 51 Rest.
139	rd D, Almond
136	WI 73, Plainfield, to WI Rapids, E BP/dsl Hooligan's Grill service/repair, W Citgo/Subway/dsl
131	rd V, Hancock, E Citgo Smiley's Diner, W KOA
127mm	**weigh sta both lanes (exits left)**
124	WI 21, Coloma, E Mobil/A&W/dsl Red Hill Cafe, Subway Mecan Inn (4mi) Coloma Camping, W BP/Chester's/dsl Buick/Chevrolet
120mm	**sb, full facilities, litter barrels, petwalk, , vending**
118mm	**nb, full facilities, litter barrels, petwalk, , vending**
113	rd E, rd J, Westfield, W BP/Burger King, Cenex, Mobil/dsl McDonald's, Subway Pioneer Motel/rest. city park, Family$
106	WI 82 W, WI 23 E, Oxford, E Crossroads Motel, W Citgo/dsl
104	(from nb, no EZ return) rd D, Packwaukee
100	WI 23 W, rd P, Endeavor, E BP/dsl KW's Grill
92	US 51 S, Portage, E KwikTrip/dsl, Mobil Asian Express, Culver's, Dino's Rest., Golden Cup 2 Cafe, Jimmy John's, KFC, La Tolteca Mexican, McDonald's, Papa Murphy's, Pizza Ranch, Subway, Suzy's Steaks, Taco Bell Best Western, Ridge Motel, Sunset Motel, Super 8 H, $Tree, Aldi Foods, AutoZone, Chrysler/Dodge/Jeep, Ford/Lincoln, GNC, Pierce's Foods, Verizon, Walgreens, Walmart
89b a	WI 16, to WI 127, Portage, E BP/dsl Hitching Post Eatery
88.5mm	Wisconsin River
87	WI 33, Portage, W ski area
86mm	Baraboo River
85	Cascade Mt Rd
84	I-39, I-90 & I-94 run together sb/eb

PORTAGE

INTERSTATE 41

Exit#	Services
171	I-43 S, to Milwaukee, US 41/141 N, to Marinette
170	US 141 S, Velp Ave, E Mobil Burger King, Taco Bell, W BP/A&W/dsl, Shell/dsl Gilligan's Rest., Julie's Rest., McDonald's, River St Grill, Subway, Watering Hole Rest. AmericInn Bumper Parts, CVS Drug, Family$, Harley Davidson
168c b	WI 29, WI 32, Shawano Ave, Dousman St, E Comfort Suites Buick/Cadillac/GMC
168	WI 32, WI 54, Mason St, E Burger House, Pizza Hut Home Depot, W Mobil, Shell/Papa John's/dsl Bon Orient Buffet, Chili's, Fazoli's, Hardee's, Little Caesar's, Los Banditos, McDonald's, Schlotsky's Festival Foods, GNC, O'Reilly Parts, Sam's Club, Walmart/Subway
167	CR VK, Lombardi Ave, Hazelwood Ln, E Shell Chucke-Cheese, Margaritas, Red Lobster Cabela's, Copp's Foods, Lambeau Field

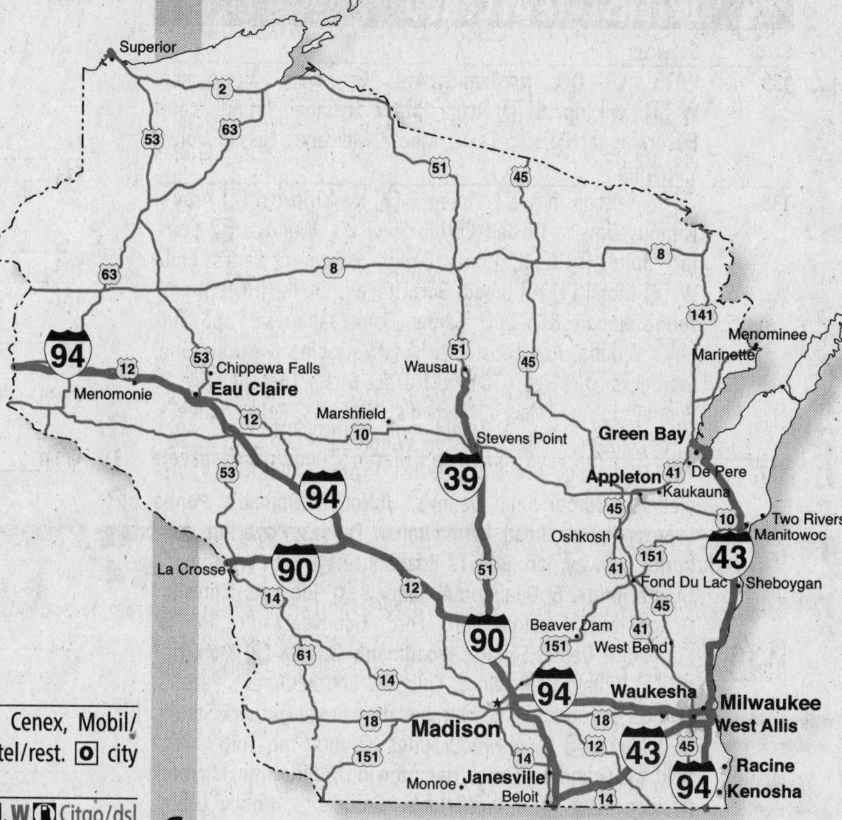

GREEN BAY

Exit#	Services
165	WI 172, to I-43
164	CR AAA, Oneida St, Waube Ln, E KwikTrip/dsl, Shell/dsl Applebee's, Cousins Subs, Culver's, Denny's, Five Guys, Grazie's Italian, Hardee's, Olive Garden, Perkins, Starbucks, Subway, Wendy's Baymont Inn, Comfort Inn, EconoLodge, Fairfield Inn, Hampton Inn, Holiday Inn Express, Motel 6, Ramada, Super 8 $Tree, Honda, Jo-Ann, W BP/dsl Los Magueyes Country Inn Suites, Microtel
163b	WI 32 N, Green Bay
163a	CR G, Main Ave, E Mobil/dsl, Shell/dsl Burger King, Dunkin Donuts, Jimmy John's, McDonald's, Papa John's, Papa Murphy's, Starbucks, Subway $General, AutoZone, CVS Drug, Festival Foods, Peterbilt, USPO, Walgreens, W BP/A&W/Taco Bell/dsl/scales
161	CR F, Scheuring Rd, De Pete, E Mobil/Arby's/dsl, Shell/dsl Culver's, DQ, Plank Road Rest. Sleep Inn $Tree, Menard's, Verizon, Walmart/Subway
157	CR S, Freedom, W BP/Chester's/Godfather's/dsl
154	CR U, Wrightstown
153	**weigh sta nb**
150	CR J, Kaukauna, E Chrysler/Dodge/Jeep, W BP/dsl Freightliner
148	WI 55, Seymour, Kaukauna, E KwikTrip/dsl, Shell/Arby's/dsl Days Inn, W Chevrolet/Buick/GMC
146	CR N, Little Chute, Kimberly, E Mobil/McDonald's/Subway/dsl, Shell/dsl, Sunoco Burger King, Culver's, Tom's Drive In Country Inn Suites, W Simon's Cheese Store
145	WI 441 S
144	CR E, Ballard Rd, E Shell/dsl Baskin Robbins, Hardee's, McDonald's H, W AmericInn, Cambria Suites
142	WI 47, Richmond St, Black Creek, E Mobil Fazoli's, Jimmy John's, Little Caesar's, McDonald's, Starbucks, Taco Bell Snug In Motel Kohl's, Walgreens, W KwikTrip/dsl, Arby's

WI

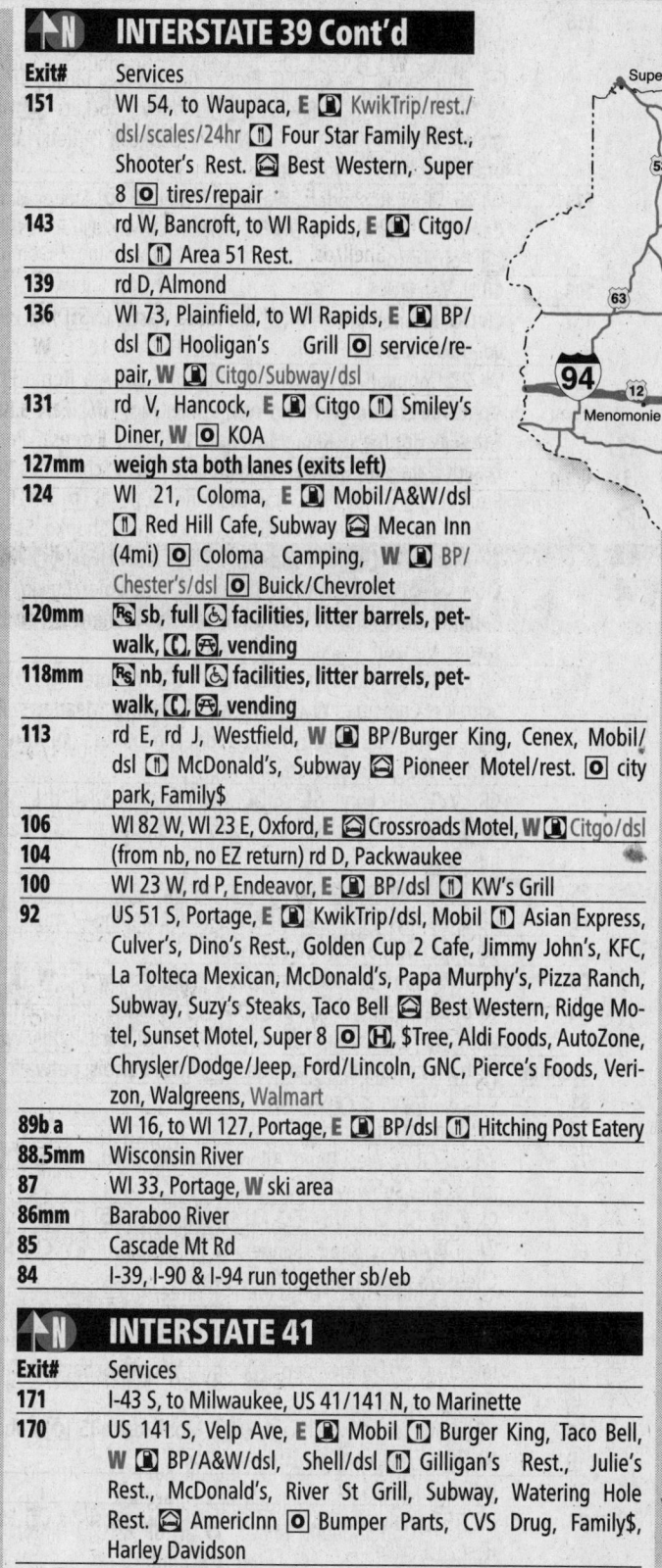

INTERSTATE 41 Cont'd

Exit#	Services
139	WI15, CR OO, Northland Ave, Greenville, Hortonville, W KwikTrip/dsl Acura, BMW, Hyundai, Infiniti, Land Rover/Jaguar/Porsche, Lexus, Mazda, Mercedes, Nissan, Volvo, VW/Audi
138	WI 96, Wisconsin Ave, Fremont, E KwikTrip/dsl Arby's, Famous Dave's, Golden Corral, Stevi B's, Wendy's Comfort Suites CarX, Home Depot, Petsmart, Sam's Club, W Mobil Atl Bread, Buca Italian, Chili's, IHOP, Jimmy John's, Noodles&Co, Olive Garden, Osaka Japanese, Papa Murphy's, Qdoba, Red Lobster, Schlotsky's, Solea Mexican Grill, Starbucks $Tree, AT&T, Costco/dsl, Dick's, Discount Tire, JC Penney, Jo-Ann, Macy's, Menard's, Michael's, Petco, Scheel's, Target, Tires+, TJ Maxx, Verizon, Walgreens, Walmart/Subway
137	WI 125, College Ave, E BP/dsl, Express, KwikTrip Applebee's, Burger King, Denny's, HuHot, McDonald's, Panda Express, Panera Bread, Parma Italian, Perkins, Pizza Hut, Starbucks, Subway, Taco Bell, TX Roadhouse Best Western, La Quinta, Motel 6, Quality Inn, Super 8 Big Lots, Chrysler/Dodge/Jeep, Firestone/auto, Ford, Goodyear/auto, Honda, Kia, Office Depot, Subaru, Woodman's Gas, W KwikTrip/dsl Buffalo Wild Wings, Chipotle, ChuckECheese, Fazoli's, Five Guys, Fuddrucker's, Machine Shed Rest., Outback Steaks, TGIFriday's Candlewood Suites, Country Inn Suites, Fairfield Inn, GrandStay Suites, Hampton Inn, Holiday Inn, Microtel, Residence Inn Barnes&Noble, Gordman's, Hobby Lobby, Old Navy, USPO
136	CR BB, Prospect Ave, W BP, Mobil/Subway Van Zealand Autocare
134	US 10 E, WI 441 N
133	CR II, Winchester Rd
132	Main St, Oak Ridge Rd (no return nb or sb), E BP/dsl, Citgo/dsl Bradke's Rest. Chevrolet/Buick/Cadillac
131	WI 114, CR JJ, Winneconne Ave, Hilbert, Sherwood, E Citgo/dsl, Express, KwikTrip/dsl Burger King, Ground Round, Hardee's, KFC, Little Caesar's, McDonald's, Papa Murphy's, Pizza Hut, Starbucks, Subway Best Western, Days Inn $Tree, Advance Parts, CVS Drug, Festival Foods, Firestone/auto, Ford/Lincoln, GNC, Pick'n Save, Shopko, W A&W, Applebee's, Arby's, Culver's, Jimmy John's, Perkins, Qdoba, Taco Bell Kohl's, Verizon, Walgreens, Walmart/Subway
129	Bell St, Breezewood Ln, W Mobil Solea Mexican
124	WI 76, Jackson St, E Mobil, W KwikTrip/dsl/CNG, Sunoco truck repair
120	US 45, US 10 W, New London
119	WI 21, Omro Rd, Oshkosh, E DQ La Quinta, W KwikTrip/dsl, Shell/McDonald's Cousins Subs, Culver's, Panera Bread, Papa Murphy's, Rocky Rococo Pizza, Subway, Wendy's Holiday Inn Express Chevrolet/Buick/GMC/Cadillac, Dick's, Festival Foods, H, Lowe's, Menard's, Verizon
117	9th Ave, E KwikTrip/dsl Benvenuto's Italian, Buffalo Wild Wings, China King, Cousins Subs, Golden Corral, IHOP, Jimmy John's, Little Caesar's, McDonald's, Olive Garden, Pizza Hut, Qdoba, Red Robin, Starbucks, Subway, Taco Bell Comfort Suites AT&T, Best Buy, CVS Drug, Duluth Trading, Hobby Lobby, Jo-Ann, Ross, Shopko, Staples, TJ Maxx, Verizon, Walgreens, W Burger King, Domino's, Perkins, Pizza Ranch NAPA, Walmart/Subway
116	WI 44, WI 91, S Park Ave, Ripon Rd, E BP/dsl, Mobil/dsl Applebee's, Arby's, Charcoal Pit, Fazoli's, Friar Tuck's Rest., Hardee's, Noodles&Co, Subway AmericInn, Fairfield Inn,
116	Continued Hilton Garden, Super 8 $Tree, Advance Parts, air museum, Aldi Foods, CarX, GNC, Petco, Pick'n Save, Target, Tires+, W KwikTrip/dsl, Shell/dsl Johnny Rockets Hawthorn Suites Honda, Kia, Nissan, Oshkosh Outlets/famous brands, Subaru, Toyota, vet, VW
113	WI 26, CR N, Rosendale, Waupun, Pickett, E Sleepy Hollow Camping (2mi), W Planeview/Subway/dsl/scales/24hr Cobblestone Inn
106	CR N, Van Dyne
101	CR OO, Winnebago St, E BP/Rest./dsl/scales Mack/Volvo, truck wash
99	WI 23, Johnson St, Rosendale, Ripon, E Ala Roma Pizza, Applebee's, Buffalo Wild Wings, Burger King, DQ, Faro's Rest., Fazoli's, Hardee's, KFC, McDonald's, Panda Express, Panera Bread, Pizza Hut, Qdoba, Rocky Rococo Pizza, Schriener's Rest., Starbucks Days Inn, Hampton Inn, Super 8 AT&T, AutoZone, Best Buy, Jo-Ann, Kohl's, Pick'n Save, Shopko, Staples, TJ Maxx, W KwikTrip/dsl, Shell/Subway/dsl Arby's, Culver's $Tree, Aldi Foods, CarX, Chevrolet/Buick/GMC/Cadillac, Ford, Harley Davidson, Mazda, Menard's, Petsmart, Target, Verizon, Walmart/Subway
98	CR D, Military Rd, E McDonald's Microtel F&F/dsl, Schiek's Camoers, W BP/dsl Rolling Meadows Rest. Comfort Inn, Holiday Inn, Holiday Inn Express Chrysler/Dodge/Jeep, Merz RV Ctr, st patrol
97	CR VVV, Hickory St, E KwikTrip/dsl, Shell/dsl, W Loves/Subway/dsl/scales/24hr, Marathon/dsl Country Inn Suites
95	US 152, Madison, Manitowoc, E H
92	CR B, Oakfield, Eden, E Breezy Hill Camping (2 mi)
87	WI 49, CR KK, Brownsville, Waupun
85	WI 67, Lomira, Campbellsport, E Exxon/dsl, W BP/Taco Bell/dsl, Shell/Subway/dsl Bublitz's Rest., McDonald's Country Hearth Inn $General, Ford, Piggly Wiggly
82.5mm	**both lanes, full facilities, litter barrels, petwalk**
81	WI 28, Mayville, Kewaskum
76	CR D, W fireworks
72	WI 33, CR W, West Bend, Allenton, W BP/dsl, Mobil Alma's Cafe, Subway
68	CR K, W Mobil/dsl MJ Stevens Rest. USPO
66	WI 144, West Bend, Slinger, W Freedom RV Ctr, Held's Cheese/sausage, Slinger Speedway
64	WI 60, to Jackson, Slinger, Hartford, E Scenic RV Ctr, W BP/dsl, Citgo, KwikTrip/dsl Burger King Chevrolet, Chrysler/Dodge/Jeep, H, Piggly Wiggly, Schaefer's Service Ctr
60	CR FD, to WI 145, Richfield, E Mobil/dsl/e85 Cabela's, W BP/McDonald's/dsl/scales/24hr
59	(from nb) US 45 W
57	WI 167, Holy Hill Rd, E Mobil/Subway/dsl, W Exxon/Rest./dsl/scales
54	WI 167, CR Y, Lannon Rd, Germantown, E KwikTrip/dsl Best Western, Country Inn Suites
52	CR Q, County Line Rd, E Briscoe Co Wood Grill, W Mobil/dsl, Speedway/dsl Applebee's, Arby's, Buffalo Wild Wings, Burger King, Cracker Barrel, Jimmy John's, KFC, McDonald's, Panda Express, Pizza Hut/Taco Bell, Starbucks, Wendy's Holiday Inn Express, Super 8 AT&T, Best Buy, Costco/dsl, Kohl's, Target
51b a	Pilgrim Rd, W KwikTrip Kramerz Burgers, Topper AutoZone, Walmart Mkt

APPLETON OSHKOSH RIPON WI

INTERSTATE 41 Cont'd

MILWAUKEE

Exit#	Services
50b a	WI 74 W, WI 100 E, Menomonee Falls, E [other] Buick/GMC, Fordcar repair:VW, W [gas] Mobil [lodging] De Martinis Pizza, Radisson [other] Monro
48	WI 145, E [other] Sam's Club/gas, Woodman's Mkt/gas
47b	CR PP, Good Hope Rd, E [food] Point Burger Bar, Ruby Tuesday [lodging] Comfort Suites, Hilton Garden [other] CarMax, Chevrolet, Mazda, Nissan, Toyota
47	WI 175, Appleton Ave
46	CR E, Silver Spring Dr, E [gas] Marathon/dsl, Mobil/dsl [food] Arby's, Athens Rest., Cousins Subs, KFC, McDonald's, Subway, Taco Bell, Wendy's [lodging] Hampton Inn, La Quinta [other] Goodyear/auto, Harley Davidson, Petro Mart, W [gas] Speedway/dsl
45	CR EE, Hampton Ave, E [gas] Citgo, W [gas] BP/dsl
44	WI 190, Capitol Dr, E [food] Subway [other] Walgreens, W [gas][food] Arby's, Burger King, Chick-fil-A, Chipotle, Culver's, Jimmy John's, McDonald's, Noodles&Co, Potbelly's, Qdoba, Starbucks [other] Advance Parts, GNC, Home Depot, Petco, Pick'n Save, Ross, Target, Walmart Mkt
43	Burleigh St, E [food] Corner Bakery Cafe, Osgood's Rest., Pizza Man [other] Dick's, [H], Meijer, Old Navy, TJ Maxx, W [food] Dickey's BBQ, Wendy's [lodging] Cousins Subs [other] Aldi Foods, Firestone/auto, Lowe's
42b	North Ave W, E [gas] [food] Applebee's, Buffalo Wild Wings, Cheesecake Factory, Dave&Buster's, Denny's, Five Guys, Maggiano's, McCormick&Schmick, Panera Bread, PF Chang's [lodging] Extended Stay America, Holiday Inn Express, Radisson [other] Barnes&Noble, Best Buy, Macy's, Nordstrom's, Walgreens
42a	WI 100, Mayfair Rd, North Ave E (from nb), E [food] Dave&Buster's, W [food] Firehouse Subs [lodging] Crowne Plaza [other] Kia, Pick'n Save, USPO
40	Watertown Plank Rd, Swan Blvd, E [other] [H], W [lodging] Crowne Plaza
39	US 18, Wisconsin Ave, Bluemound Rd, E [other] [H]
1b a	I-94
1d	WI 53, Greenfield Ave, E [food] Subway [other] CVS Drug, Family$, W [gas] BP/dsl, Speedway/dsl [food] Griddlers Cafe, Las Fajitas, McDonald's, Starbucks [other] O'Reilly Parts, Walgreens
1e	(from sb) Lincoln Ave, E [other] same as 2 E
2a	(from sb) National Rd (wb)
2b	(from sb) Oklahoma Ave, E [gas] Citgo [other] auto repair, [H]
3	Beloit Rd
4	**I-41 S runs with I-43 N/I-894 E, then I-94 E. See I-43 exits 5-9 and I-94 exits 316-347.**
0mm	Wisconsin/Illinois state line

INTERSTATE 43

GREEN BAY

Exit#	Services
192mm	**I-43 begins/ends at Green Bay on US 41.**
192b	US 41 S, US 141 S, to Appleton, **1 mi S services on Velp Ave** [gas] BP/A&W/dsl, Express/dsl, Mobil, Shell/dsl [food] Burger King, Gilligan's Rest., Julie's Cafe, McDonald's, Riverstreet Grill, Subway, Taco Bell, Watering Hole Rest [lodging] AmericInn [other] Bay Parts, Bumper Parts, CVS Drug, Family$, Harley-Davidson, Trans Motive Auto
192a	US 41 N, US 141 N
189	Atkinson Dr, to Velp Ave, Port of Green Bay, W [gas] Shell/dsl
188mm	Fox River
187	East Shore Dr, Webster Ave, W [gas] Shell/dsl/24hr [food] McDonald's, Subway, Wendy's [lodging] Hampton Inn, Hyatt [other] [H]
185	WI 54, WI 57, University Ave, to Algoma, E [other] U of WI GB, W [gas] Mobil, Shell/A&W [food] Green Bay Pizza, Subway, Taco Bell [other] Family$, University Foods, Walgreens
183	Mason St, rd V, E [food] Culver's, Mackinaw's Grill [lodging] Country Inn&Suites, Super 8 [other] [H], URGENT CARE, **1 mi** W [gas] BP, Mobil/dsl, Shell [food] Applebee's, Arby's, Burger King, China Buffet, Fazoli's, KFC, Little Caesar's, McDonald's, Noodles&Co, Papa John's, Papa Murphy's, Perkins, Pizza Hut, Pizza Ranch, Qdoba, Sonic, Starbucks, Taco Bell [other] $General, Advance Parts, Aldi Foods, AutoZone, Batteries+Bulbs, Chevrolet, Chrysler/Dodge/Jeep, Copps Foods, Family$, Hobby Lobby, Kohl's, Mazda, Nissan, O'Reilly Parts, PetCo, ShopKO, Subaru, Tires+, Walgreens, Walmart/Subway
181	Eaton Rd, rd JJ, E [gas] BP/McDonald's/dsl [food] Hardee's, Jimmy John's, Luigi's, Sgambati's Pizza, Taco John's [other] Ford/Kia, Home Depot, W [gas] Mobil/Subway/dsl, Shell [food] A&W, Ravine Grill [lodging] AmericInn [other] Farm&Fleet/gas, Festival Foods, Menards
180	WI 172 W, to US 411 exit, W [gas] BP/Taco Bell/24hr, Citgo/Country Express/dsl/scales/24hr, KwikTrip/dsl, Shell/Subway/dsl [food] Burger King, McDonald's, Tuscon's Rest. [lodging] Holiday Inn Express [other] [H], AT&T, Copps Foods, Costco/gas, GNC, Target, to stadium, Verizon, Walgreens, multiple services
178	US 141, to WI 29, rd MM, Bellevue, E [gas] Shell/Arby's/dsl, W [other] repair
171	WI 96, rd KB, Denmark, E [gas] BP/dsl [food] deGrande Rest, McDonald's, Steve's Cheese, Subway [other] Shady Acres Camping
168mm	[RS] **both lanes, full [handicapped] facilities, litter barrels, petwalk, [phone], [picnic], vending**
166mm	Devils River
164	WI 147, rd Z, Maribel, W [gas] BP/dsl
160	rd K, Kellnersville
157	rd V, Hillcrest Rd, Francis Creek, E [gas] Citgo/Subway/dsl, Marathon/diner/dsl
154	US 10 W, WI 310, Two Rivers, to Appleton, E [other] [H]

MANITOWOC

Exit#	Services
153mm	Manitowoc River
152	US 10 E, WI 42 N, rd JJ, Manitowoc, E [food] TimeOut Grill [other] [H], antiques, maritime museum
149	US 151, WI 42 S, Manitowoc, E [gas] BP, Citgo/dsl, KwikTrip/dsl, Mobil, Shell/dsl [food] A&W, Applebee's, Arby's, Buffalo Wild Wings, Burger King, Charcoal Grill, China Buffet, Culver's, DQ, Fork&Knife Rest, Four Seasons Rest., Frier Tuck's Sandwiches, Hardee's, Jimmy John's, KFC, Little Caesar's, McDonald's, Panda Express, Papa Murphy's, Perkins, Pizza Ranch, Qdoba, Starbucks, Taco Bell, Wendy's [lodging] Birch Creek Inn, Harbor Town Inn, Holiday Inn, Quality Inn [other] [H], $Tree, Advance Parts, Aldi Foods, AutoZone, Buick/Cadillac/Chevrolet/GMC, Chrysler/Dodge/Jeep, Copps Foods, Family$, Festival Foods, GNC, Goodyear/auto, Hobby Lobby, Kohl's, Lowe's, O'Reilly Parts, PetCo, ShopKO, Tires+, USPO, Verizon, vet, Walgreens, Walmart/Subway,

Hixton
Stevens Point
Amherst
De Pere
Green Bay
Denmark
Millston
Plainfield
Appleton
Sparta
Tomah
Richford
Oshkosh
New Lisbon
90
Fond du Lac
Plymouth
La Valle
Baraboo
Dekorra
39
West Bend
Watertown
Menomonee Falls
Madison
94
Milwaukee
New Berlin
Edgerton
Caledonia
Janesville
Dubuque
Beloit
43
WI

INTERSTATE 43 Cont'd

149 Continued
W Shell/McDonald's Subway AmericInn Harley-Davidson, Menards

144 rd C, Newton, E Mobil/dsl antiques

142mm weigh sta sb

137 rd XX, Cleveland, E Citgo/Subway/dsl Wildflower Cafe Kessler's Old World Guesthouse Wagner's RV Ctr

128 WI 42, Howards Grove, E BP/dsl/24hr, KwikTrip/dsl Culver's, Hardee's, Harry's Diner, Shuff's Rest., TX Roadhouse Quality Inn Pomp's Tire, W Mobil/dsl/scales Menards, Walmart/Subway

126 WI 23, Sheboygan, E BP, KwikTrip/dsl, Tesla EVC Applebee's, Cousins Subs, Culver's, McDonald's, New China, Noodles&Co, Pizza Hut/Taco Bell, Pizza Ranch La Quinta, Super 8 H, Aldi Foods, Batteries+Bulbs, BigLots, Festival Foods, Firestone/auto, Ford/Kia, Goodyear/auto, Hobby Lobby, Honda/Mazda, Hyundai/Mazda, Kohl's, NAPA, ShopKO, Subaru, Toyota

123 WI 28, rd A, Sheboygan, E Citgo/dsl/24hr, Mobil/McDonald's/dsl Coldstone, Cruisers Cafe, Jimmy John's, Perkins, Qdoba, Starbucks, Subway, Wendy's AmericInn, Holiday Inn Express CarX, Harley-Davidson/Cruisers Burgers, Walmart/Subway, W Arby's, Buffalo Wild Wings, Chili's $Tree, AT&T, Best Buy, Boston's Store, GNC, Home Depot, Jo-Ann Fabrics, Petsmart, Target, TJ Maxx

120 rds OK, V, Sheboygan, E Citgo/dsl, Loves/Hardee's/Subway/dsl/scales/24hr Hwy Ridge Rest. Sleep Inn camping, Nissan, to Kohler-Andrae SP, VW, 1 mi W Horn's RV Ctr

116 rd AA, Foster Rd, Oostburg, 1 mi W Judi's Place Rest., Pizza Ranch, Subway Piggly Wiggly/gas

113 WI 32 N, rd LL, Cedar Grove, W Citgo/dsl/repair, Mobil/dsl, Sunoco/Fueling Depot Country Grove Rest. (1mi), Cousins Subs Lakeview Motel

107 rd D, Belgium, E Lake Church Inn/grill Harrington Beach SP, W BP/McDonald's/dsl/24hr, How-Dea Trkstp/Hobo's Korner Kitchen/dsl/scales, Mobil/dsl/24hr Bic's Place, Say Cheese Outlet, Subway Rodeway Inn repair, USPO

100 WI 32 S, WI 84 W, Port Washington, E Citgo/dsl, Mobil Arby's, McDonald's, Pizza Hut, Subway Country Inn&Suites, Holiday Inn (2mi) Allen-Edmonds Shoes, Goodyear/auto, Sentry Foods, ShopKO Express, True Value, vet, W Nisleit's Country Rest.

97 (from nb, exits left), WI 57, Fredonia

96 WI 33, to Saukville, E Citgo Culver's (1mi), KFC/LJ Silver Best Hardware, Buick/Cadillac/Chevrolet, Camping World RV Ctr, Chrysler/Dodge/Jeep, Ford, O'Reilly Parts, Piggly Wiggly, Walgreens, Walmart, W Exxon/McDonald's, KwikTrip/dsl Domino's, DQ, La Chimenea Mexican, Lam's Chinese, Lam's Chinese, Papa Murphy's, Subway, Taco Bell Motel 6 repair/tires

MILWAUKEE

93 WI 32 N, WI 57 S, Grafton, 2 mi E George Webb Rest. vet, W Flannery's Cafe (2mi)

92 WI 60, rd Q, Grafton, E BP/dsl GhostTown Rest., Water St Rest. Hampton Inn, W Citgo/DQ/dsl Charcoal Grill, Noodles&Co, Qdoba, Quiznos, Starbucks, Subway Comfort Inn H, Aldi Foods, AT&T, Best Buy, Costco/gas, Dick's, Home Depot, Kohl's, Meijer, Michael's, Petsmart, Target, Verizon

89 rd C, Cedarburg, W Mobil/dsl Cedar Crk Settlement Café (6mi) StageCoach Inn (3mi), Washington House Inn (3mi) H

85 WI 57 S, WI 167 W, Mequon Rd, W BP, Mobil, QStop/dsl, Shell Caribou Coffee, Chancery Rest., Cousins Subs, Culver's, DQ, First Watch Cafr, Jimmy John's, Leonardo's Pizza, McDonald's, Noodles&Co, Panera Bread, Papa Murphy's, Pizza Hut, Starbucks, Subway, Taco Bell Chalet Motel H, Ace Harware, AT&T, Marshall's, Metro Mkt, Sendik's Foods, Verizon, vet, Walgreens

83 rd W, Port Washington Rd (from nb only)

82b a WI 32 S, WI 100, Brown Deer Rd, E BP, Sendik's/dsl Baskin-Robbins, Benji's Deli, Jimmy John's, Jose's Blue Sombrero, Maxfield's Pancakes, McDonald's, Noodles&Co, Peking Chef, Qdoba, Starbucks, Subway, Toppers Pizza Best Buy, CVS Drug, Fresh Mkt, GNC, Land's Inlet, Walgreens

80 Good Hope Rd, E Dr Dawg, Jimmy John's, King's Wok, Samurai Japanese North Shore Suites, Radisson Pick'n Save Foods, to Cardinal Stritch U

78 Silver Spring Dr, E BP, Citgo Applebee's, Bar Louie, BD Mongolian, Boston Mkt, Bravo Italian, Buffalo Wild Wings, Burger King, CA Pizza Kitchen, Cheesecake Factory, Cousins Subs, Devon Steaks, Fiddleheads Coffee, Five Guys, Food Court, McDonald's, Panera Bread, Papa Murphy's, Perkins, Pizza Hut, Qdoba, Sprecher's Rest., Subway, Taco Bell La Quinta, La Quinta, Motel 6 AT&T, Barnes&Noble, Batteries+Bulbs, Goodyear/auto, Kohl's, Nissan, Trader Joe's, USPO, Verizon, Walgreens, W H

77b a (from nb), E Anchorage Rest., Solly's Grille Holiday Inn

76b a WI 57, WI 190, Green Bay Ave, E Home Depot, W BP/dsl Burger King

75 Atkinson Ave, Keefe Ave, E Mobil, W BP

74 Locust St

73c North Ave (rom sb), E Wendy's, W McDonald's

73b North Ave (from nb), downtown

73a WI 145 E, 4th St (exits left from sb), Broadway, downtown

72c Wells St, E Hilton H, Civic Ctr, museum

72b (from sb), I-94 W, to madison

72a (310c from nb, exits left from sb), I-794 E, I-94 W to Madison, to Lakefront, downtown

311 WI 59, National Ave, 6th St, downtown

312a Lapham Blvd, Mitchell St, W BP, Citgo

312b (from nb), Becher St, Lincoln Ave

314a Holt Ave, E SP Mart/dsl Applebee's, Arby's, China King, Jimmy John's, Little Caesar's, Starbucks, Subway, Taco Bell, Wendy's $General, Family$, Home Depot, Pick'n Save Foods, Piggly Wiggly, Target, vet, W H, to Alverno Coll

314b Howard Ave

10b I-94 S to Chicago, E

9b a WI 241, 27th St, E Clark, Supreme/dsl Arby's, Benny's Cafe, Burger King, Famous Dave's, Pizza Hut, Sonic, Subway Suburban Motel AutoZone, Subaru, Target, USPO, Walgreens, W Boston Mkt, Buffalo Wild Wings, Chipotle Mexican, Denny's, Jimmy John's, McDonald's, New China, Omega Rest., Panda Express, Papa John's, Rich's Cakes, Starbucks, Taco Bell, Wong's Wok, Zebb's Rest Quality Inn, Rodeway Inn H, $Tree, AAA, Advance Parts, Chevrolet, CVS Drug, Firestone/auto, Ford, Goodyear/auto, Kohl's, Marshall's, Michael's, Pick'n Save Foods, Save-A-Lot Foods, Walgreens, Walmart

8a WI 36, Loomis Rd, E BP/dsl, Paul's Gas Los Mariachi's Aldi Foods, Walgreens, W Griddler's Cafe to Alverno Coll

7 60th St, E Speedway/dsl Subway, Wendt's Grille Harley-Davidson, W Speedway/dsl URGENT CARE

WI

INTERSTATE 43 Cont'd

Exit#	Services
5b	76th St (from sb, no EZ return), E Applebee's, Bakers Square, Buca Italian, Burger King, Carrabba's Italian, Chick-fil-A, Cousins Subs, El Beso, Griddler's Cafe, Hooters, Jersey Mike's, Jimmy John's, Kopp's Burgers, Kyoto Japanese, Longhorn Steaks, McDonald's, Noodles&Co, Old Country Buffet, Olive Garden, Outback Steaks, Panera Bread, Qdoba, Red Lobster, Red Robin, Ruby Tuesday, Starbucks, TGIFriday's, Topper's Pizza, Traditional Pancake House, Wendy's $Tree, AT&T, Barnes&Noble, Best Buy, Firestone/auto, Goodyear, JC Penney, Jo-Ann Fabrics, Kohl's, Macy's, Midas, PetCo, Petsmart, Sendik's Food Mkt, Tuesday Morning, Verizon, Walmart, W Arby's, Pizza Hut, Subway Advance Parts, Family$, Pick'n Save Foods, TJ Maxx, USPO, Walgreens, Panda Express
5a	WI 24 W, Forest Home Ave, E Citgo/dsl Boerner Botanical Gardens, Welk's Auto
61	(4 from sb), I-894/US 45 N, I-43/US 45 S
60	US 45 S, WI 100, 108th St (exits left from sb), E BP, Hometown, Kwik Pantry, Marathon A&W, Amore Italian, Ann's Italian, Chipotle Mexican, Confucious Chinese, Cousins Subs, Culver's, DQ, Dunkin Donuts, Fortune Chinese, George Webb Rest., McDonald's, McGuire's Grill, Noodles&Co, Open Flame Grill, Papa Murphy's, Pizza Hut, Starbucks, Subway, Taco Bell $Tree, AutoZone, Chevrolet, O'Reilly Parts, Pick'n Save, USPO, vet, Walgreens, W Andy's/dsl Forum Rest., McDonald's, Organ Piper Pizza, Subway Aldi Foods, Badger Transmissions, Goodyear, NAPA, Nissan, vet, Walgreens, Walmart/Subway
59	WI 100, Layton Ave (from nb, exits left), Hales Corner, W BP/Cousins Subs same as 60
57	Moorland Rd, E KwikTrip/dsl Applebee's, Stonefire Pizza Co, TX Roadhouse, Zaffiro's Pizza La Quinta Costco/dsl, W Speedway/dsl Arby's, Buffalo Wild Wings, Cusina Real, Panera Bread, Pap John's, Quaker Steak&Lube, Subway Holiday Inn Express Firestone/auto, GNC, Michael's, Target
54	rd Y, Racine Ave, 1-2 mi E BP/dsl, KwikTrip Cousins Subs, Culver's, McDonald's, Piggly Wiggly, Walgreens
50	WI 164, Big Bend, W KwikTrip/dsl/e85 McDonald's
44mm	Fox River
43	WI 83, Mukwonago, E BP/dsl Aldi Foods, Chevrolet, Chrysler/Dodge/Jeep, Home Depot, H, Walmart, W Citgo Boneyard Grille, Chen's Kitchen, Domino's, DQ, Taco Bell Rodeway Inn
38	WI 20, East Troy, W BP/dsl, Pilot/Road Ranger/Subway/dsl/24hr, Shell/McDonald's Burger King, Cousins Subs, Dos Amigos, Genoa Pizza, Grist Mill Rest., LD's BBQ $General, Carquest, Chrysler/Dodge/Jeep
36	WI 120, East Troy, E Alpine Valley Resort, W Quality Inn Suites
33	Bowers Rd, E to Alpine Valley Music Theatre
32mm	**both lanes, full facilities, litter barrels, petwalk, vending**
29	WI 11, Elkhorn, W fairgrounds
27b a	US 12, to Lake Geneva, E H
25	WI 67, Elkhorn, E Mobil/dsl AmericInn Buick/Chevrolet/GMC, Chrysler/Dodge/Jeep, vet, W Speedway/dsl/24hr Burger King, Subway Hampton Inn (2mi) Dehaan Auto/RV Ctr
21	WI 50, Delavan, E Brodie's Beef, Chili's, China 1, Culver's, Domino's, Jimmy John's, Panera Bread, Papa Murphy's, Starbucks,

DELAVAN

BELOIT

BELOIT

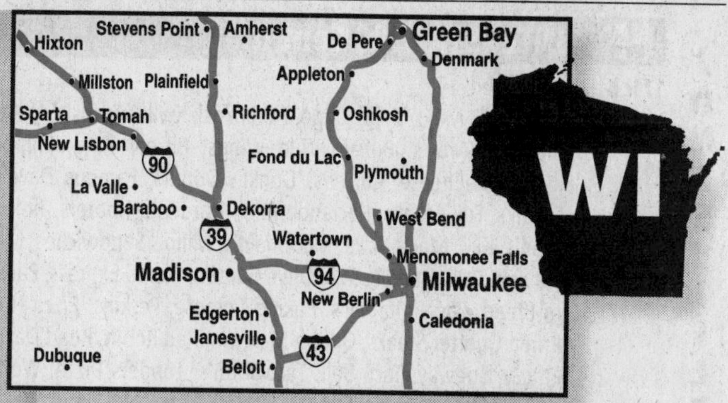

Exit#	Services
21	Continued Subway, Yoshi Japanese Aldi Foods, AT&T, F&F Tires, golf, Kohl's, Lowe's, Petsmart, Staples, Verizon, Walmart, W Mobil/Dunkin Donuts/dsl KFC, McDonald's, Perkins, Pizza Hut, Taco Bell, Wendy's Comfort Suites, Super 8 $Tree, AutoZone, Cadillac/Chevrolet, Ford/Lincoln, GNC, NAPA, Piggly Wiggly, ShopKO, Walgreens
17	rd X, Delavan, Darien, W BP/dsl
15	US 14, Darien, E Mobil/dsl West Wind Diner
6	WI 140, Clinton, E Citgo/Subway/TCBY/dsl $General, Ford
2	rd X, Hart Rd, E Butterfly Fine Dining
1b a	I-90, E to Chicago, W to Madison, S Mobil/McDonald's, Pilot/Taco Bell/dsl/scales/24hr, Shell, Speedway/dsl Applebee's, Arby's, Asia Buffet, Buffalo Wild Wings, Culver's, Doc's Rest., Jimmy John's, Little Caesar's, Little Mexico, Noodles&Co, Papa Murphy's, Qdoba, Road Dawg Rest., Starbucks, Subway, Wendy's Baymont Inn, Fairfield Inn, Hampton Inn, Quality Inn, Rodeway Inn, Super 8 $Tree, Aldi Foods, AT&T, Buick/GMC, Cadillac/Chevrolet, GNC, Menards, NTB, O'Reilly Parts, Staples, Walmart

I-43 begins/ends on I-90, exit 185 in Beloit.

INTERSTATE 90

Exit#	Services
187mm	**Wisconsin/Illinois state line, I-90 & I-39 run together nb.**
187mm	**Welcome Ctr wb, full facilities, info, litter barrels, petwalk, vending**
185b	I-43 N, to Milwaukee
185a	WI 81, Beloit, S Mobil/McDonald's/dsl, Pilot/Taco Bell/dsl/scales/24hr, Shell, Speedway/dsl Applebee's, Arby's, Asia Buffet, Buffalo Wild Wings, Culver's, Doc's Rest., Jimmy John's, Little Caesar's, Little Mexico, Noodles&Co, Papa Murphy's, Qdoba, Road Dawg Rest., Starbucks, Subway, Wendy's Baymont Inn, Fairfield Inn, Hampton Inn, Quality Inn, Rodeway Inn, Super 8 $Tree, Aldi Foods, AT&T, Buick/GMC, Cadillac/Chevrolet, GNC, Menards, NTB, O'Reilly Parts, Staples, Walmart
183	Shopiere Rd, rd S, to Shopiere, S BP/Rollette/dsl/24hr H, repair
181mm	**weigh sta wb**
177	WI 11 W, Janesville, 2 mi S KwikTrip/dsl S WI Airport, to Blackhawk Tec Coll
175b a	WI 11 E, Janesville, to Delavan, N BP/Subway/dsl Baymont Inn H, vet, S Lannon Stone Motel city park
171c b	US 14, WI 26, Janesville, N TA/Mobil/Wendy's/dsl/scales/24hr/@ Coldstone, Cozumel Mexican, Fuddruckers, HomeTown Buffet, IHOP, Quaker Steak, Starbucks, Subway, TX Roadhouse Holiday Inn Express, Microtel Aldi Foods, Best Buy, GNC, Home Depot, Michael's, NTB, Old Navy, PetCo,

WI

JANESVILLE

INTERSTATE 90 Cont'd

171c b Continued
Staples, TJ Maxx, S Citgo, Exxon/dsl, Kwik Trip/dsl Applebee's, Arby's, Buffalo Wild Wings, Burger King, Chipotle, ChuckeCheese, Culver's, Dunkin Donuts, Famous Dave's, Fazoli's, Fuji Steaks, Hacienda Real, Hardee's, Hooters, Jimmy John's, KFC, Mac's Pizza, McDonald's, Milio's Sandwiches, Milwaukee Grill, Noodles&Co, Olive Garden, Panda Express, Panera Bread, Papa Murphy's, Peking Chinese, Perkins, Pizza Hut, Prime Quarter Steaks, Qdoba Mexican, Red Robin, Road Dawg Eatery, Subway, Taco Bell, Taco John's, Toppers Pizza, World Buffet Quality Inn, Super 8 H, $Tree, Aldi Foods, AT&T, AutoZone, Big Lots, CarQuest, CVS Drug, F&F, Festival Foods, Ford/Lincoln, Harley-Davidson, Hobby Lobby, Hyundai, JC Penney, Kohl's, Mazda, Menards, Nissan/Kia/Subaru, O'Reilly Parts, ShopKO, Target, Toyota, USPO, Verizon, Walgreens

171a WI 26, N BP/dsl Cracker Barrel Hampton Inn, Motel 6, Ramada/rest. Chrysler/Dodge/Jeep, Sam's Club, URGENT CARE, VW, Walgreens, Walmart, S same as 171c b

168mm **eb, full facilities, litter barrels, petwalk, vending**

163.5mm Rock River

163 WI 59, Edgerton, to Milton, N Mobil/Subway/dsl, Shell/Dunkin Donuts/Taco John's/dsl Blue Gilly's Rest., Culver's, McDonald's, WI Cheese Store Quality Inn marina

160 US 51S, WI 73, WI 106, Oaklawn Academy, to Deerfield, S BP/dsl/scales/24hr/@ H, Creek View Camping (2mi)

156 US 51N, to Stoughton, S Coachman's Inn/rest. H

147 rd N, Cottage Grove, to Stoughton, S BP/Arby's/dsl, Road Ranger/Pilot/Subway/dsl/scales Lake Kegonsa SP

146mm **weigh sta eb**

MADISON

142b a (142a exits left from wb) US 12, US 18, Madison, to Cambridge, N BP/dsl Roadhouse Rest. Best Value Inn, Magnuson Grand Hotel casino, Harley-Davidson, S Citgo/dsl, Phillips 66/Arby's/dsl, Shell/dsl Denny's Days Inn, Sleep Inn H, Menards, UWI

138a I-94, E to Milwaukee, W to La Crosse (exits left from eb)

I-90 W and I-94 W run together for 93 miles.

138b WI 30, Madison, S

135c b US 151, Madison, N BP/dsl Erin's Cafe, Happy Wok, Milio's Sandwiches, Uno Grill Cambria Suites, Courtyard, Fairfield Inn, GrandStay Suites, Holiday Inn, Staybridge Suites Buick/GMC, Chrysler/Dodge/Jeep, Ford, Honda, Hyundai, Kia, Mazda, Nissan, Subaru, Toyota

135a US 151, Madison, S BP, Citgo, Mobil, Shell Applebee's, Arby's, Buffalo Wild Wings, Chili's, Chipotle Mexican, Cracker Barrel, Culver's, Denny's, Dickey's BBQ, DoLittle's Woodfire Grill, Fazoli's, Hardee's, Hometown Buffet, Hooters, IHOP, Imperial Garden, Jimmy John's, KFC, McDonald's, Milio's, Noodles&Co, Olive Garden, Outback Steaks, Panera Bread, Perkins, Pizza Hut, Potbelly, Qdoba, Red Lobster, Red Robin, Rocky's Pizza, Starbucks, Taco Bell, Takumi Japanese, TGIFriday's, Toppers's Pizza, TX Roadhouse, Wendy's Best Western, Comfort Inn, Crowne Plaza Hotel/rest., EconoLodge, Hampton Inn, Howard Johnson, Microtel, Motel 6, Red Roof Inn, Residence Inn, Rodeway Inn, Super 8 $Tree, Aldi Foods, AT&T, Barnes&Noble, Best Buy, Burlington Coats, city park, Dick's, Firestone/auto, Goodyear/auto, Gordman's, Hobby Lobby, Home Depot, Hy-Vee Foods, JC Penney, JoAnn Fabrics, Kohl's, Marshalls, Menards, Michaels, Office Depot, Old Navy, Petsmart, Savers, ShopKO, st patrol, Target, Verizon

132 US 51, Madison, De Forest, N Shell/Pinecone Rest/dsl/24hr Camping World RV Ctr, S TA/BP/Subway/Popeye's/dsl/

132 Continued
scales/24hr/@ Freightliner/GMC/Volvo/White, Goodyear, Peterbilt, WI RV World

131 WI 19, Waunakee, N Kwik Trip/dsl, Mobil/dsl, Speedway/dsl A&W, McDonald's, Rodeside Grill Days Inn, Super 8 fireworks, Kenworth, Mousehouse Cheesehaus, truckwash

126 rd V, De Forest, to Dane, N BP/A&W/Rococo's/dsl, Phillips 66/Arby's/dsl Burger King, Culver's, McDonald's, Subway, Taco Bell Holiday Inn Express Cheese Chalet, KOA, S Exxon, Shell Comfort Inn dsl repair

119 WI 60, Arlington, to Lodi, S Mobil/A&W/Cousins Subs/dsl A&W, Rococo's Pizza Quality Inn dsl/tire repair

115 rd CS, Poynette, to Lake Wisconsin, N BP/dsl McDonald's, Subway auto repair, dsl truck/trailer repair, Smokey Hollow Camping, S Love's/Hardee's/dsl/scales/24hr

113mm **both lanes, full facilities, litter barrels, petwalk, vending**

111mm Wisconsin River

108b a I-39 N, WI 78, to US 51 N, to Wis Dells, Portage, N H, S BP, Mobil, Petro/Iron Skillet/DQ/Subway/dsl/24hr/@ Comfort Suites, Days Inn Blue Beacon

106mm Baraboo River

WISCONSIN DELLS

106 WI 33, Portage, N H, S   Circus World Museum, Devil's Lake SP, SkyHigh Camping, to Cascade Mtn Ski Area, Wayside Park

92 US 12, to Baraboo, N BP/dsl, Citgo/Subway/dsl, Exxon, Mobil/Dunkin Donuts/dsl/24hr Buffalo Phil's Grille, Burger King, Cheese Factory Rest, Cracker Barrel, Culver's, Denny's, Domino's, Famous Dave's BBQ, Field's Steaks, Green Owl Pizza, Marley's Rest., McDonald's, Milio's, Monk's Grill, Noodles&Co, Pizza Ranch, Ponderosa, R Place Italian, Sarento's Italian, Starbucks, Taco Bell, Uno Grill, Wintergreen Grill Alakai Hotel, Country Squire Motel, Dell Creek Motel, Glacier Canyon Lodge, Grand Marquis Inn, Great Wolf Lodge, Holiday Inn Express, Kalahari Resort, Ramada, Wilderness Hotel, Wintergreen Hotel Mkt Square Cheese, Tanger Outlets Famous Brands, URGENT CARE, Verizon, S Motel 6 H, Jellystone Camping, Mirror Lake SP, Red Oak Camping, Scenic Traveler RV Ctr

89 WI 23, Lake Delton, N Phillips 66, Shell/dsl Brathouse Grill, Denny's Diner, Howie's Rest., KFC, Moosejaw Pizza Hilton Garden, Kings Inn, Malibu Inn, Olympia Motel, Travelodge Crystal Grand Music Theatre, Jellystone Camping, USPO, S McDonald's $Tree, Country Roads RV Park, Home Depot, Jo-Ann, Kohl's, Springbrook Camping, Walmart/Subway

87 WI 13, Wisconsin Dells, N Citgo/dsl, Mobil/Arby's/dsl, Shell/Dunkin Donuts Applebee's, Bunyan's Rest., Burger King, Coldstone, Culver's, Denny's, IHOP, Jimmy John's, McDonald's, Mexicali Rose Rest., Perkins, Starbucks, Taco Bell, Wei's Chinese Ambers Resort, AmericInn, Baymont Inn, Best Western, Econolodge, Polynesian Hotel, Quality Inn, Super 8 golf, info, KOA, Sherwood Forest Camping, Walgreens, waterpark

85 US 12, WI 16, Wisconsin Dells, N Fairway Motel KOA, Sherwood Forest Camping, Standing Rock Camping, to Rocky Arbor SP, S   Piccadilly's Arrowhead Camping, Days End Motel, Edge-O-the-Dell RV Camping, Summer Breeze Resort

79 rd HH, Lyndon Sta, S BP/Subway/dsl/24hr

76mm **wb, full facilities, litter barrels, petwalk, vending**

74mm **eb, full facilities, litter barrels, petwalk, vending**

WI

INTERSTATE 90 Cont'd

Exit#	Services
69	WI 82, Mauston, N Mauston TP/BP/Taco Bell/24hr, Pilot/Wendy's/dsl/scales/24hr, Shell/24hr China Buffet, Family Rest. Best Western Oasis, Quality Inn, Super 8 Carr Valley Cheese, to Buckhorn SP, S KwikTrip/Hearty Platter Rest/dsl/scales/24hr, Mobil Culver's, Hardee's, Log Cabin Deli, McDonald's, Pizza Hut, Roman Castle Rest., Subway Alaskan Inn H, $General, Buick/Chevrolet, Family$, Festival Foods, O'Reilly Parts, ShopKO, Verizon, vet, Walgreens
61	WI 80, New Lisbon, to Necedah, N Mobil/A&W/Subway/dsl/scales/24hr, Shell/McDonald's/dsl Edge O' the Woods Motel, Travelers Inn Buckhorn SP, Chrysler/Dodge/Jeep, fireworks, Ford, S KwikTrip/24hr city park, Elroy-Sparta ST Tr, USPO
55	rd C, Camp Douglas, N to Camp Williams, Volk Field, wayside, S BP/dsl, Mobil/Home Front Cafe/dsl K&K Motel to Mill Bluff SP
48	rd PP, Oakdale, N Road Ranger/Pilot/Subway/dsl/scales/24hr antiques, KOA, truck/car wash, S Loves/Hardee's/dsl/scales/24hr Mill Bluff SP, repair
45	I-94 W, to St Paul

I-90 E and I-94 E run together for 93 miles.

TOMAH

Exit#	Services
43	US 12, WI 16, Tomah, N BP/dsl, KwikTrip/dsl/24hr Burnstadt's Café, DQ Daybreak Inn, Rest Well Motel H, Burnstadt's Mkt, vet
41	WI 131, Tomah, to Wilton, N KwikTrip/dsl/24hr, Mobil/dsl Burnstadts Cafe Daybreak Inn vet
28	WI 16, Sparta, Ft McCoy, N BP/diner/dsl/scales Best Western H
25	WI 27, Sparta, to Melvina, N Cenex/Arby's/dsl, KwikTrip/dsl, Mobil/Taco Bell, Shell/dsl Burger King, Culver's, DQ, KFC, McDonald's, Pizza Hut, Sparta Rest., Subway Country Inn, Super 8 H, $General, $Tree, Buick/Chevrolet, Family$, Ford, Hansens IGA, O'Reilly Parts, Walgreens, Walmart/Subway
22mm	**RS wb, full facilities, litter barrels, petwalk, vending**
20mm	**RS eb, full facilities, litter barrels, petwalk, vending**
15	WI 162, Bangor, to Coon Valley, N gas
12	rd C, W Salem, N Cenex/cafe/dsl/24hr Coulee Region RV Ctr, NAPA, Neshonoc Camping, S BP/Subway/dsl AmericInn Peterbilt
10mm	**weigh sta eb**

LA CROSSE

Exit#	Services
5	WI 16, La Crosse, N Arby's, BA Burrito, Buffalo Wild Wings, Ciatti's Italian, Coldstone, Manny's Mexican, Outback Steaks Baymont Inn, Hampton Inn, Microtel $Tree, Aldi Foods, Freightliner, Home Depot, Walmart/Subway, Woodman's Foods/gas/lube, S Kwik Trip/dsl/24hr Bamboo House, Burracho's Mexican Grill, Carlos O'Kelly's, Chucke-Cheese, Culver's, Fazoli's, HuHot Grill, Jimmy John's, McDonald's, Olive Garden, Perkins, Starbucks, TGIFriday's, TX Roadhouse Holiday Inn Express H, Barnes&Noble, Best Buy, Chevrolet, Dick's, F&F, Ford/Lincoln, Hobby Lobby, JC Penney, Kohl's, Michael's, ShopKO, Target, Walgreens
4	US 53 N, WI 16, to WI 157, La Crosse, N Harley-Davidson, S Kwik Trip, TO Applebee's, Burger King, Caribou Coffee, China Inn, Cousins Subs, Famous Dave's BBQ, Grizzly's Rest., Ground Round, Panera Bread, Papa Murphy's, Red Lobster, Rococo's Pizza, Shogun Hibachi, Subway, Taco Bell, Wendy's Comfort Inn H, Festival Food/24hr, GNC, Goodyear/auto, La Crosse River St Trail, Office Depot, Old Navy, PetCo, Petsmart, Sam's Club, Tires+, TJ Maxx, Verizon

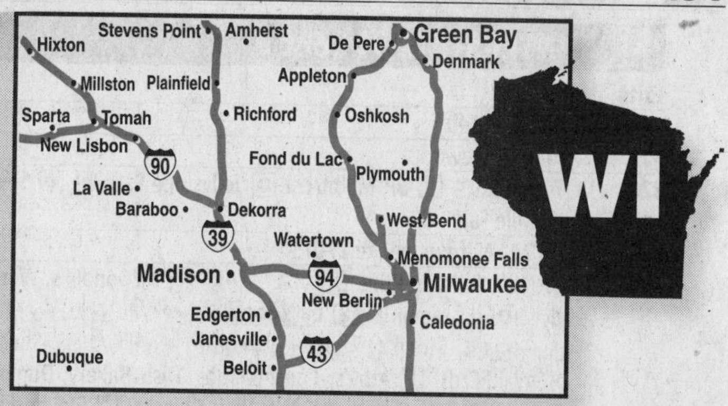

Exit#	Services
3	US 53 S, WI 35, to La Crosse, S Clark/dsl, Kwik Trip Hardee's, KFC, La Crosse Rest., McDonald's, North Country Steaks, Perkins, Pizza Hut, Subway Best Value Inn, Best Western, Econolodge, Motel 6, Quality Inn, Settle Inn, Super 8 ShopKO, to Great River St Trail, U-Haul, Viterbo Coll, Walgreens
2.5mm	Black River
2	rd B, French Island, N S BP/dsl Days Inn/rest. Quillin's Mkt
1mm	**Welcome Ctr eb, full facilities, info, litter barrels, petwalk, vending**
0mm	Wisconsin/Minnesota state line, Mississippi River

INTERSTATE 94

KENOSHA

Exit#	Services
349mm	Wisconsin/Illinois state line, **weigh sta nb**
348.5mm	**weigh sta wb**
347	WI 165, rd Q, Lakeview Pkwy, E **Welcome Ctr nb, full facilities, litter barrels, petwalk,** BP/dsl Chancery Rest., Culver's, McDonald's Radisson Old Navy, Premium Outlets/famous brands
345	rd C, E Holiday Inn Express (1mi)
345mm	Des Plaines River
344	WI 50, Lake Geneva, to Kenosha, 1 mi E Buffalo Wild Wings, Cheddar's, Cousins Subs, Dickey's BBQ, Famous Dave's, Mobil/dsl, Noodles&Co, Olive Garden, Panda Express, Perkins, Pizza Hut, Shell/Dunkin Donuts/dsl, Sparti's Gyros, Starbucks, Subway, Tuscany Bistro, TX Roadhouse, White Castle, Woodman's/gas Candlewood Suites, Holiday Inn Express, La Quinta, Super 8 H, AT&T, Best Buy, Chevrolet, Dick's, GNC, JC Penney, Petsmart, Target, Verizon, Walgreens, W BP/dsl, Speedway/dsl Arby's, Birchwood Grill, Cracker Barrel, KFC, McDonald's, Phoenix Rest., Wendy's Best Western, Comfort Inn, Country Inn&Suites, Hampton Inn, Value Inn BratStop Cheese Store, CarMax, Honda, Nissan, Subaru, Toyota
342	WI 158, to Kenosha, E Harley-Davidson, W antiques
340	WI 142, rd S, to Kenosha, E Kenosha TP/BP/Subway/dsl/E85/LP/scales/24hr H, W Mars Cheese Castle Rest. Oasis Inn Fun Time RV Ctr, to Bong RA
339	rd E
337	rd KR, to Mt Pleasant, W Apple Holler Rest./orchard
335	WI 11, to Mt Pleasant, Burlington, to Racine
333	WI 20, Waterford, to Racine, E KwikTrip/dsl/24hr, Shell/Cousins Subs/dsl Burger King, McDonald's Days Inn, Excel Inn, Holiday Inn Express H, Toyota, W Citgo/Wendy's/dsl/24hr, Petro/Mobil/Iron Skillet/dsl/scales/24hr/@ Chicken'n Waffles, Culver's, Route 20 Outhouse Grill, Subway Quality Inn Burlington RV Ctr, visitor info
329	rd K, Thompsonville, to Racine, E Pilot/Arby's/Subway/dsl/scales/24hr A&W dsl repair

WI

INTERSTATE 94 Cont'd

Exit#	Services
328mm	weigh sta eb
327	rd G, W fireworks
326	7 Mile Rd, E BP, Mobil/dsl Jellystone Park, W Seven Mile Fair
325	WI 241 N (from wb), to 27th St
322	WI 100, to Ryan Rd, E KwikTrip/dsl McDonald's, Wendy's dsl repair, W Loves/Denny's/dsl/LP/scales/RV dump/24hr, Mobil, Pilot/Subway/dsl/LP/scales/24hr, Shell/A&W/KFC/dsl Arby's, Cousins Subs, Dish Bakery, Dunkin Donuts, Perkins, Starbucks, Yen Hwa Chinese Staybridge Suites, Value Inn AutoZone, Blue Beacon, Freightliner/repair, H, Pick'n Save, vet, Walgreens
321	Drexel Ave
320	rd BB, Rawson Ave, E BP/7-11/dsl, Mobil Applebee's, Burger King La Quinta
319	rd ZZ, College Ave, E Shell/Subway, Speedway/dsl Branded Steer Rest., McDonald's Candlewood Suites, Comfort Suites, Country Inn&Suites, Crowne Plaza, Days Inn, EconoLodge, Fairfield Inn, Hampton Inn, Holiday Inn Express, MainStay Suites, Motel 6, Red Roof Inn Burlington Coats, W Royal
318	WI 119, E
317	I-43, I-894 (from wb)
316	I-43 S, I-894 W (I-94 exits left from eb), to Beloit, E Clark/dsl Martino's Hotdogs
314b	Howard Ave, to Milwaukee, W to Alverno Coll
314a	Holt Ave, E SP Mart/dsl Applebee's, Arby's, China King, Little Caesar's, Starbucks, Subway, Wendy's $General, Family$, Home Depot, Pick'n Save Foods, Sentry Foods, Target, vet, W H, to Alverno Coll
312b a	Becher St, Mitchell St, Lapham Blvd, W BP, Citgo
311	WI 59, National Ave, 6th St, downtown
310a	13th St (from eb), E H
310b	I-43 N, to Green Bay
310c	I-794 E, E Hilton Lake Michigan Port of Entry, to downtown
309b	26th St, 22nd St, Clybourn St, St Paul Ave, N H, to Marquette U
309a	35th St, N URGENT CARE
308c b	US 41
308a	VA Ctr, S Miller Park
307b	68th-70th St, Hawley Rd
307a	68th-70th St
306	WI 181, to 84th St, N H, S Olympic Training Facility
305b	I-41 N, US 45 N, to Fond du Lac, N H
305a	I-894 S, I-41 S, US 45 S, to Chicago, S to
304b a	WI 100, N 7-11, Amstar/dsl, BP, Shell/dsl Cousins Subs, Domino's, Ghengis Khan BBQ, Habanero's Mexican, HoneyBaked Cafe, Jimmy John's, Mo's Irish Grill, Peony Chinese, Qdoba, Rococo's, Starbucks, Subway, Taco Bell Crowne Plaza, Forty Winks Inn H, zoo, S Amstar, BP/dsl, Speedway/dsl Culver's, DQ, Fazoli's, McDonald's, Pallas Rest., Starbucks, Toppers Pizza, Wendy's Days Inn Aldi Foods, Midas, O'Reilly Parts, Sam's Club, U-Haul, Walgreens
301b a	Moorland Rd, N **on US 18** BP/dsl, Mobil Bakers Square, Bravo Italiano, Buffalo Wild Wings, Chipotle, CiCi's, Cooper's Hawk, Culver's, Five Guys, Fleming's Rest., Food Court, Fuddrucker's, Hooters, Jamba Juice, Jersey Mike's, Marty's Pizza/subs, McDonald's, Mitchell's Fish Mkt, Noodles&Co, Original Pancake House, Qdoba, Red Robin, Starbucks, Stir Crazy,
301b a	Continued Subway, TGIFriday's Courtyard, Sheraton, TownePlace Suites AT&T, Barnes&Noble, CVS Drug, F&F Tire, Firestone/auto, Fresh Mkt Foods, Goodyear/auto, JC Penney, Jo-Ann Fabrics, Metro Mkt, Michael's, Office Depot, PetCo, Petsmart, SteinMart, TJ Maxx, Verizon, vet, Walgreens, World Mkt, S Champp's Grill, Outback Steaks, Panera Bread, Starbucks Best Western Midway, Brookfield Suites, Country Inn&Suites, Residence Inn golf, Pick'n Save Foods, Walgreens, Walmart
297	WI 164 S, US 18, rd JJ, Blue Mound Rd, Barker Rd, **0-2 mi** N BP, Clark Applebee's, BoneFish Grill, Boston Mkt, Brookfield Rest., Bullwinkle's Rest., Carrabba's, Chili's, ChuckE-Cheese's, Cousins Subs, Emperors Kitchen, George Webb Rest., Hom Woodfired Grill, Jimmy John's, Jose's Mexican, KFC, Kopp's Custard, Laredo's Mexican, Mama Mia's, McDonald's, Melting Pot, Olive Garden, Perkins, Potbelly, Starbucks, Subway DoubleTree, Extended Stay America, Hampton Inn, La Quinta, Motel 6, Quality Inn H, $Tree, Acura, Advance Parts, Aldi Foods, Best Buy, GNC, Hobby Lobby, Lexus/Mazda/VW, Meineke, Metro Mkt, S Clark, PDQ Arby's, Burger King, Chancery Rest., Cousin's Subs, Culver's, Famous Dave's BBQ, La Fuente Mexican, McDonald's, Meiji Chinese, New China, Oscar's Burgers, Papa Murphy's, Sonic, Starbucks, Subway, Taco Bell, Topper's Pizza, TX Roadhouse, Wendy's Baymont Inn, Extended Stay America, Super 8 AT&T, Buick/GMC, Cadillac, CarMax, Chevrolet, Farm&Fleet, Firestone/auto, Ford, Home Depot, Honda, Hyundai, Infiniti/Maserati/Mercedes/Porsche, Jaguar/Land Rover/Volvo, Kia, Kohl's, Menards, Midas, Nissan, Sam's Club, st patrol, Subaru, Target, Tires+, Walgreens, Woodman's/gas
295	rd F, to WI 74, Waukesha, N KwikTrip/dsl Jimmy John's Marriott, S H, to Carroll U
294	WI 164, rd J S, to Waukesha, N Mobil/Subway/dsl Machine Shed Rest., Thunder Bay Grille Holiday Inn, Wildwood Lodge, S Expo Ctr, Peterbilt
293c	WI 16 W, Pewaukee (from wb), N GE Plant
293b a	rd T, Wausheka, Pewaukee, S KwikTrip/dsl, Mobil Arby's, Asian Fusion, Canyon City Wood Grill, Cousins Subs, Culver's, Denny's, Dunkin Donuts, Feng's Kitchen, Jimmy John's, McDonald's, Mr. Wok, Papa Murphy's, Qdoba, Rococo's Pizza, Spring City Rest., Subway, Taco Amigo, Topper's Pizza, Weissgerber's Gasthaus Rest., Wendy's Best Western $Tree, AutoZone, CVS Drug, Firestone/auto, GNC, Goodharvest Mkt, Jo-Ann Fabrics, Office Depot, Pick'n Save Foods, Verizon, Walgreens
291	rd G, rd TT, N Country Springs Inn
290	rd SS, Pewaukee
287	WI 83, Hartland, to Wales, N Applebee's, Five Guys, Hardee's, McDonald's, Noodles&Co, Panera Bread, Perkins, Qdoba, Starbucks, Water St Brewery/rest. Country Pride Inn, Holiday Inn Express Albrecht's Mkt, Best Buy, GNC, Kohl's, Marshalls, Verizon, Walgreens, S BP, PDQ/dsl/24hr Burger King, Coldstone, DQ, Jimmy John's, Marty's Pizza, Pacific Asia Bistro, Pizza Hut, Rocky Rococo Pizza, StoneCreek Coffee, Subway La Quinta $Tree, Ace Hardware, Home Depot, PetCo, Target, Tires+, vet, Walmart/Subway
285	rd C, Delafield, N BP/dsl, Mobil/deli Delafield Hotel to St John's Military Academy, S to Kettle Moraine SF
283	rd P, to Sawyer Rd

WI

MILWAUKEE

WAUKESHA

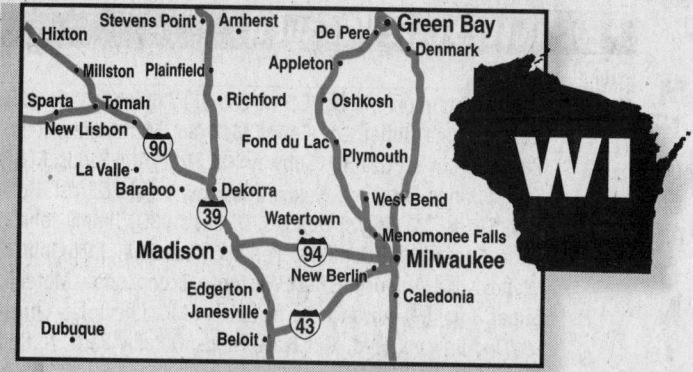

INTERSTATE 94 Cont'd

Exit#	Services
282	WI 67, Dousman, to Oconomowoc, 0-2 mi N KwikTrip/dsl, Mobil Chili's, Cousins Subs, Culver's, Eat Smart Cafe, Feng's Kitchen, Jimmy John's, Pizza Hut, Qdoba, Quiznos, Rococo's Pizza, Rosati's Pizza, Starbucks, Stone Creek Coffee, Subway Hilton Garden, Olympia Resort Ace Hardware, Aldi Foods, AT&T, Brennan's Mkt, Ford, GNC, Pick'n Save, vet, Walgreens, S Staybridge Suites H, Harley-Davidson, Old World WI HS (13mi), to Kettle Morraine SF (8mi)
277	Willow Glen Rd (from eb, no return)
275	rd F, Ixonia, to Sullivan, N Mobil/dsl Concord Gen Store, S camping
267	WI 26, Johnson Creek, to Watertown, N BP/McDonald's/dsl, Shell/dsl/rest./scales/24hr Arby's, Hwy Harry's Cafe Comfort Suites, Days Inn Goodyear/auto, Johnson Creek Outlet Ctr/famous brands, Old Navy, S KwikTrip/dsl Culver's, Qdoba, Starbucks, Subway, Taco Bell H, Kohl's, Menards, to Aztalan SP
266mm	Rock River
264mm	**wb, full facilities, litter barrels, petwalk, , , vending**
263mm	Crawfish River
261mm	**eb, full facilities, litter barrels, petwalk, , , vending**
259	WI 89, Lake Mills, to Waterloo, N Mobil/rest/dsl/24hr Best Value Inn truck repair, S BP/dsl/E85, KwikTrip/dsl Jimmy John's, McDonald's, Pizza Pit, Subway Pyramid Motel/RV park Ace Hardware, Buick/Chevrolet, Country Campers, to Aztalan SP, URGENT CARE, vet, Walgreens
250	WI 73, Deerfield, to Marshall
244	rd n, Sun Prairie, Cottage Grove, N BP/dsl Subway, S BP/dsl, KwikTrip Arby's
240	I-90 E.

I-94 and I-90 run together 93 miles. See I-90, exits 48-138

TOMAH

Exit#	Services
147	I-90 W, to La Crosse
143	US 12, WI 21, Tomah, N Shell/dsl A&W/LJ Silver, Perkins AmericInn, Best Western, Microtel, Super 8 Humbird Cheese/gifts, U-Haul, S BP, KwikTrip/Denny's/dsl/scales/24hr Arby's, China Buffet, Culver's, Dunkin Donuts, Ground Round, Ground Round, KFC, McDonald's, Papa Murphy's, Pizza Hut, Starbucks, Subway, Taco Bell Cranberry Lodge, EconoLodge, Hampton Inn, Quality Inn H, $Tree, Ace Hardware, Advance Parts, Aldi Foods, Burger King, Chrysler/Dodge/Jeep, Ford, GMC, NAPA, O'Reilly Parts, to Ft McCoy (9mi), Verizon, Walmart/Subway
135	rd EW, Warrens, N Cenex/dsl 3 Bears Resort Jellystone Camping, S Bog Rest.
128	rd O, Millston, N Black River SF, camping, S Cenex/dsl USPO
123mm	**/scenic view both lanes, full facilities, litter barrels, petwalk, , , vending**
116	WI 54, N Cenex/Subway/Taco Johns/dsl/LP Perkins AmericInn, Best Western Arrowhead/rest., Comfort Inn Black River RA, Parkland Camp, S FLYING J/Denny's/dsl/24hr/@, KwikTrip/dsl Arby's, Burger King, Culver's, McDonald's, Oriental Kitchen, Pizza Hut Days Inn $General, Buick/Chevrolet/GMC, Walmart/Subway
115mm	Black River
115	US 12, WI 27, Black River Falls, to Merrillan, S Holiday/dsl Hardee's, KFC, Subway, Sunrise Rest. H, Ace Hardware, Gordy's Mkt, Harley-Davidson
105	to WI 95, Hixton, to Alma Center, N Motel 95/camping KOA (3mi), S Cenex/dsl, Clark/dsl/24hr Timber Valley Rest. city park, USPO

Hixton
Stevens Point
Amherst
De Pere
Green Bay
Denmark
Millston
Plainfield
Appleton
Sparta
Tomah
Richford
Oshkosh
New Lisbon
90
Fond du Lac
Plymouth
La Valle
Baraboo
Dekorra
West Bend
39
Watertown
Madison
94
Menomonee Falls
Milwaukee
New Berlin
Edgerton
Caledonia
Janesville
Dubuque
43
Beloit
WI

EAU CLAIRE

Exit#	Services
98	WI 121, Northfield, Pigeon Falls, to Alma Center, S Cenex/dsl auto/truck repair
88	US 10, Osseo, to Fairchild, N BP/DQ, Exxon/Webb Rest./dsl/scales/24hr, Mobil/dsl Hardee's, Moe's Diner 10-7 Inn, Super 8 Chevrolet, Ford, Stoney Cr RV Park, S SA/dsl McDonald's, Subway, Taco John's Osseo Inn H, Family$
81	rd HH, rd KK, Foster, S Cenex/dsl/LP Foster Cheesehaus
70	US 53, Eau Claire, S Gander Outdoors, st police, N off Golf Rd Holiday/dsl Applebee's, Asia Palace, Buffalo Wild Wings, Caribou Coffee, Chipotle, Coldstone, Culver's, Fazoli's, Fired Up Pizza, Firehouse Subs, Fuji Steaks, Grizzly's Grill, HuHot Chinese, Jade Garden, Jimmy John's, Johnny's Italian Steaks, Mancino's, Manny's Grill, McDonald's, Noodles&Co, Olive Garden, Panera Bread, Papa Murphy's, TGIFriday's, TX Roadhouse Baymont Inn, Country Inn&Suites, Grandstay, Holiday Inn $Tree, Aldi Foods, AT&T, Bam!, Best Buy, JC Penney, Jo-Ann Fabrics, Kohl's, Menards, Michael's, PetCo, Petsmart, Ross, Sam's Club, Scheel's Sports, Target, TJ Maxx, Tuesday Morning, Verizon, Walmart/Subway, Younkers
68	WI 93, to Eleva, N Holiday, KwikTrip/dsl Burger King, Cousins Subs, DQ, Famous Dave's BBQ, Great Harvest Bread Co, Hardee's, Red Robin EconoLodge BigLots, Chrysler/Dodge/Jeep, Festival Foods, Firestone/auto, Goodyear/auto, Gordy's Mkt, Kia, NAPA, Nissan, Subaru, transmissions, vet, S Holiday/dsl Metropolis Resort Audi/VW, Ford/Lincoln, Honda, Hyundai
65	WI 37, WI 85, Eau Claire, to Mondovi, N Holiday/dsl, KwikTrip/dsl Arby's, China Buffet, Godfather's Pizza, Green Mill Rest., Hardee's, Jimmy John's, Mancino's, McDonald's, Pizza Hut, Randy's Rest., Red Lobster, Starbucks, Subway, Taco Bell, Wendy's Best Value Inn, Best Western, Clarion, Hampton Inn, Motel 6, Plaza Hotel, Quality Inn, Scottish Inn, Super 8 H, Adams Automotive, Gordy's Mkt, ShopKo, Verizon, Walgreens, S tires
64mm	Chippewa River
59	to US 12, rd EE, to Eau Claire, N Holiday/Burger King/dsl/24hr, Holiday/Subway/dsl/24hr Dana's Grill, McDonald's, North Crossing Rest. AmericInn, Days Inn, Knights Inn H, Freightliner, Mack/Volvo Trucks, Peterbilt, S dsl repair
52	US 12, WI 29, WI 40, Elk Mound, to Chippewa Falls, S U-Fuel/e85
49mm	**weigh sta wb**
45	rd B, Menomonie, N Cenex/Subway/dsl/scales/24hr, Loves/Hardee's/dsl/scales/24hr, S KwikTrip/dsl/scales/24hr Quality Inn H, dsl repair, Kenworth, truckwash, Walmart Dist Ctr
44mm	Red Cedar River
43mm	**s both lanes, full facilities, litter barrels, petwalk, , , vending, weather info**

WI

INTERSTATE 94 Cont'd

MENOMONIE

Exit#	Services
41	WI 25, Menomonie, N Cenex/E85 Applebee's, Caribou Coffee, China Buffet, Los Cabos Mexican, Menominee Rest., Papa Murphy's, Pizza Hut, Subway $Tree, Aldi Foods, AT&T, Twin Springs Camping, Walmart/Subway, S F&F/dsl, Holiday, SA/dsl Arby's, Denny's, Dickey's BBQ, Jimmy John's, Little Caesar's, McDonald's, Perkins, Taco Bell, Taco John's, Wendy's AmericInn, Best Western+, EconoLodge, Motel 6, Super 8 H, Advance Parts, Buick/GMC, Chevrolet, Chrysler/Dodge/Jeep, Ford, Mkt Place Foods, O'Reilly Parts, to Red Cedar St Tr, Verizon, Walgreens
32	rd Q, to Knapp
28	WI 128, Wilson, Elmwood, to Glenwood City, N KwikTrip/Denny's/dsl/24hr, S camping, dsl repair, Eau Galle RA
24	rd B, to Baldwin, N Woodville Motel, S camping, Eau Galle RA
19	US 63, Baldwin, to Ellsworth, N Freedom/dsl, KwikTrip/Subway/dsl A&W, Culver's, DQ, Hardee's, McDonald's AmericInn H, S Super 8 fireworks
16	rd T, Hammond
10	WI 65, Roberts, to New Richmon, N BP/dsl (2mi), FLYING J/McDonald's/dsl/scales/24hr Barnboard Rest. (2mi), S Freightliner

HUDSON

Exit#	Services
8mm	weigh sta eb
4	US 12, rd U, Somerset, N BP/dsl, TA/Country Pride/dsl/scales/24hr/@ Regency Inn to Willow River SP, vet
3	WI 35 S, to River Falls, S U of WI River Falls
2	rd F, Carmichael Rd, Hudson, N BP/repair, Freedom/dsl, Holiday Applebee's, Caribou Coffee, Culver's, Domino's, Fiesta Loca, Jimmy John's, KFC, Papa Murphy's, Taco John's Royal Inn $Tree, Family Fresh Foods, GNC, repair, Target, Verizon, Walgreens, S F&F/dsl, Holiday/dsl, KwikTrip/dsl, Shell Arby's, Buffalo Wild Wings, Burger King, Caribou Coffee, Chipotle Mexican, Coldstone, Denny's, Green Mill Rest., Jersey Mike's, Kingdom Buffet, Kirin Ichiban, Leeann Chin, Little Caesar's, McDonald's, Noodles&Co, Panda Express, Perkins, Pita Pit, Pizza Hut, Sapporo Japanese, Smashburger, Starbucks, Subway, Taco Bell, Wendy's Comfort Suites, Fairfield Inn, Hampton Inn, Holiday Inn Express, Hudson House Hotel, Quality Inn, Super 8 H, Aldi Foods, AT&T, AutoZone, Chevrolet/GMC, Chrysler/Dodge/Jeep, County Mkt Foods, Ford, Home Depot, Menards, NAPA, O'Reilly Parts, Tire-Pros, Tires+, to Kinnickinnic SP, USPO, Verizon, Walmart
1	WI 35 N, Hudson, 1 mi N Freedom/dsl, Holiday Carbones Pizzeria, DQ
0mm	Wisconsin/Minnesota state line, St Croix River

WI WY

WYOMING

INTERSTATE 25

BUFFALO

Exit#	Services
300	I-90, E to Gillette, W to Billings. **I-25 begins/ends on I-90, exit 56.**
299	US 16, Buffalo, E Cenex/dsl, Exxon/dsl, Maverik/dsl Winchester Steaks Buffalo Inn, Comfort Inn, Hampton Inn, Holiday Inn Express Bighorn Tire, Deer Park Camping, KOA, vet, W Cenex/dsl/24hr Bozeman Tr Steaks, Dash Inn Rest., Hardee's, McDonald's, Pizza Hut, Sub Shop, Subway, Taco John's Days Inn, Quality Inn, Rodeway WYO Motel, Super 8 H, Ace Hardware, Family$, Indian RV Camp, O'Reilly Parts, to Yellowstone, Domino's
298	US 87, Buffalo, W Nat Hist Dist Info
291	Trabing Rd
280	Middle Fork Rd
274mm	**parking area both lanes, litter barrels**
265	Reno Rd
254	Kaycee, E Exxon/dsl Country Inn Diner, Invasion Rest. Cassidy Inn Motel, Siesta Motel Kaycee Gen. Store, museum, NAPA Repair, Powder River RV Park, USPO, W **both lanes, full facilities, litter barrels, petwalk,** Sinclair/pizza/subs/dsl/LP/motel KC RV Park
249	TTT Rd
246	Powder River Rd
235	Tisdale Mtn Rd
227	WY 387 N, Midwest, Edgerton, Oil Field Museum
223	no service
219mm	**parking area both lanes, litter barrels**
216	Ranch Rd
210	Horse Ranch Creek Rd, Midwest, Edgerton
197	Ormsby Rd
191	Wardwell Rd, to Bar Nunn, W Loaf'N Jug/dsl KOA
189	US 20, US 26 W, to Shoshone, W Port of Entry

CASPER

Exit#	Services
188b	WY 220, Poplar St, E McDonald's, The Fort Eatery Best Western, Hampton Inn, Hilton Garden, La Quinta, Motel 6, Quality Inn, W Exxon Burger King, Casper's Rest., DQ Harley-Davidson, to Ft Casper HS
188a	Center St, Casper, E Conoco/dsl, Shell/dsl Poor Boys Steaks, Taco John's National 9 Inn, Ramada, Showboat Motel, W La Cocina, Starbucks, Subway Days Inn, Parkway Plaza Motel/cafe USPO
187	McKinley St, Casper, E Loaf'N Jug/dsl Ranch House Motel
186	US 20, US 26, US 87, Yellowstone St, E city park, dsl repair transmissions/repair, W Exxon H, auto repair, Chevrolet/Subaru, Kia, O'Reilly Parts
185	WY 258, Wyoming Blvd, E Casper, E Kum&Go/dsl, Loaf'n Jug/dsl Applebee's, Hacienda Mexican, IHOP, Outback Steaks, Southern BBQ HQ, TX Roadhouse Baymont Inn C'mon Inn, Comfort Inn, Hotel bet, Murdoch's Ranch Store, Smith RV Ctr, W FLYING J/Conoco/Subway/dsl LP/scales/24hr, Exxon/dsl, Loaf'n Jug Arby's, Buffalo Wild Wings, Burger King, Denny's, DQ, Five Guys, Golden Corral Hamburger Stand, Hardee's, KFC/LJ Silver, McDonald's, Mongolian Grill, Old Chicago Grill, Olive Garden, On The Border Perkins, Pizza Hut, Pizza Ranch, Qdoba, Red Lobster, Sanford's Cafe, Starbucks, Taco Bell, Taco John's, Village Inn, Wendy's 1st Interstate Motel, Candlewood Suites, Courtyard Holiday Inn Express AutoZone, Best Buy, Dick's, Home Depot, JC Penney, Macy's, Natural Grocers, Nissan, PetCo, Plains Tire, Ross, Safeway Foods/dsl, Sam's Club/gas, Staples, Target to Oregon Tr, Verizon, Walgreens, Walmart
182	WY 253, Brooks Rd, Hat Six Rd, E Sinclair/Lou's Rest/d Sonic Sleep Inn Rivers Edge Camping, to Wilkins SP, W Famous Dave's BBQ, FireRock Rest., Keg&Cork Rest

INTERSTATE 25 Cont'd

DOUGLAS

182	Continued Subway Best Western, Holiday Inn, Mainstay Suites Buick/Cadillac/GMC, Chrysler/Dodge/Jeep, Kohl's, Marshall's, Menards, Toyota, VW
171mm	**parking area both lanes, litter barrels**
165	Glenrock, E dinosaur museum, same as 160
160	US 87, US 20, US 26, E Glenrock, E G-Rock's, Paisley Shawl All American Inn, Hotel Higgins B&B Deer Creek Village Camping, to Johnston Power Plant
156	Bixby Rd
154	Barber Rd
153mm	**parking area both lanes, litter barrels**
151	Natural Bridge
150	Inez Rd
146	La Prele Rd
140	WY 59, Douglas, E Conoco/Subway/dsl, Maverik/dsl, Shell/dsl Arby's, La Costa Mexican, McDonald's, Taco John's Douglas Inn, Holiday Inn Express, La Quinta, Sleep Inn, Super 8 Chrysler/Dodge/Jeep, city park, Ford, KOA, Lone Tree Village RV Park, Pioneer Museum, vet, WY St Fair
135	US 20, US 26, US 87, Douglas, E Loaf'n Jug/dsl, Sinclair/dsl, Sinclair/rest./dsl/24hr 4 Seasons Chinese, Pizza Hut, Plains Trading Post Rest., Village Inn 1st Interstate Inn, 4 Winds Motel, Budget Inn Express, Plains Motel auto repair, Douglas Hardware, Family$, O'Reilly Parts, Safeway Foods/dsl, Shopko, Verizon
129mm	**parking area both lanes**
126	US 18, US 20 E, Orin, E **Orin Jct Rest Area both lanes, full facilities, litter barrels, petwalk, RV dump,** Sinclair/Orin Jct Trkstp/dsl/café
125mm	N Platte River
111	Glendo, E Sinclair/dsl Glendo Marina Café Glendo Lakeside RV camping, to Glendo SP, USPO
104	to Middle Bear
100	Cassa Rd
94	El Rancho Rd
92	US 26 E, Dwyer, E **both lanes, full facilities, litter barrel, petwalk, RV dump,** Ft Laramie NHS, to Guernsey SP

WHEATLAND

87	Johnson Rd
84	Laramie River Rd
84mm	Laramie River
80	US 87, Laramie Power Sta, Wheatland, Laramie Power Sta, E Sinclair/A&W/Chester's/dsl Pizza Hut Best Western, Super 8 Arrowhead RV Park, Buick/Cadillac/Chevrolet, CarQuest, Chrysler/Dodge/Jeep, Family$, Ford, museum, Safeway Foods, same as 78, ShopKo
78	US 87, Wheatland, E Cenex/dsl, Maverik/dsl, Shell/dsl Arby's, Burger King, Subway, Taco John's, Western Sky's Diner All American Motel, Motel 6, West Winds Motel, WY Motel visitors ctr, Wheatland Country Store, W Exxon/dsl, Pitstop/dsl Mtn View RV Park
73	WY 34 W, to Laramie
70	Bordeaux Rd
68	Antelope Rd
66	Hunton Rd

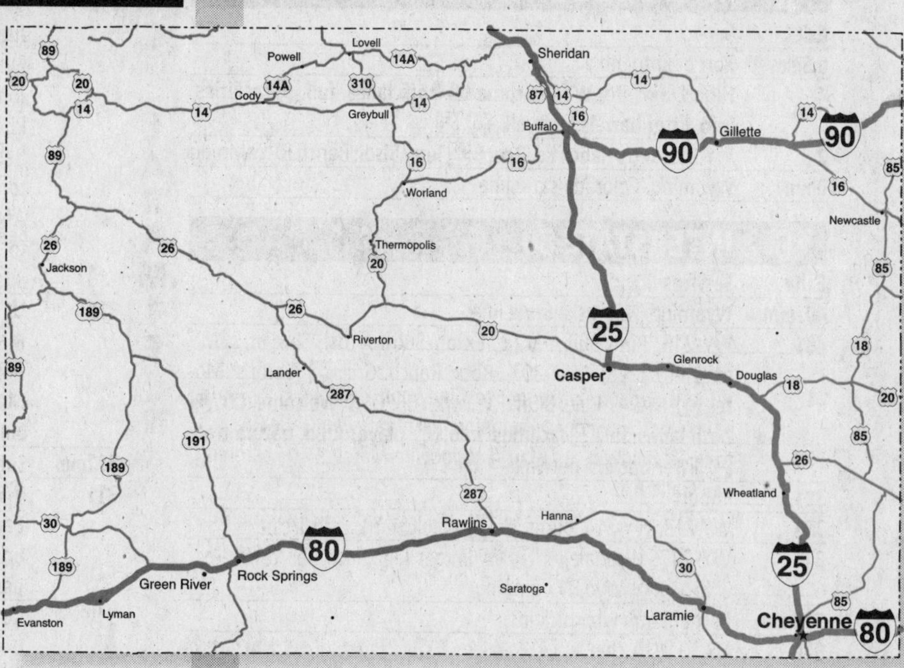

CHEYENNE

65.5mm	**parking area both lanes, litter barrels**
65	Slater Rd
64mm	Richeau Creek
57	TY Basin Rd, Chugwater
54	Lp 25, Chugwater, E **both lanes, full facilities, litter barrels, petwalk, RV dump,** Buffalo Lodge/Grill RV camping
47	Bear Creek Rd
39	Little Bear Community
36mm	Little Bear Creek
34	Nimmo Rd
33mm	Horse Creek
29	Whitaker Rd
25	ranch exit
21	Ridley Rd
17	US 85 N, to Torrington, W Little Bear Rest. (2mi)
16	WY 211, Horse Creek Rd
13	Vandehei Ave, E Loaf'n Jug/Subway, Maverik/dsl Mr Gem's Pizza, Silvermine Subs, W Shamrock/dsl
12	Central Ave, Cheyenne, E **on Yellowstone Rd** Exxon/dsl, Loaf'n Jug Arby's, Godfather's, Godfather's, Great Harvest Bread, McDonald's, Pizza Hut, Starbucks, Subway, Taco John's Rodeway Inn Albertsons, Big O Tire, Frontier Days Park, Peerless Tire
11b	Warren AFB, Gate 1, Randall Ave, E museum, to WY St Capitol
10b d	Warren AFB, Gate 2, Missile Dr, WY 210, HappyJack Rd, W to Curt Gowdy SP
9	US 30, W Lincolnway, Cheyenne, E Exxon/Downhome Diner/dsl Outback Steaks, Village Inn Best Value Inn, Candlewood Suites, Days Inn, Hampton Inn, Holiday Inn Express, La Quinta, Luxury Inn, Motel 6, My Place, Super 8, Towne Place Suites Buick/Cadillac/GMC, Chevrolet, Ford/Lincoln, Home Depot, Honda, Hyundai, Mazda, Nissan, Subaru, Toyota, W Little America/Sinclair/dsl/rest./motel/@
8d b	I-80, E to Omaha, W to Laramie
7	WY 212, College Dr, E Loves/Wendy's/dsl/scales/24hr/@, Sinclair/Subway/dsl/24hr Arby's A-B RV Park (2mi), W FLYING J/Denny's/dsl/LP/scales/24hr/@ McDonald's Quality Inn

WY

[gas] = gas [food] = food [lodging] = lodging [other] = other [rest stop] = rest stop

INTERSTATE 25 Cont'd

Exit#	Services
6.5mm	Port of Entry nb
4	High Plains Rd, **WY Welcome Ctr both lanes, full facilities, info, litter barrels, petwalk,**
2	WY 223, Terry Ranch Rd, **2 mi** **E** Terry Bison Ranch RV camping
0mm	Wyoming/Colorado state line

INTERSTATE 80

Exit#	Services
402mm	Wyoming/Nebraska State line
401	WY 215, Pine Bluffs, **N** Exxon/Subway/dsl, Sinclair/A&W/dsl/24hr/@ Cafe 307, Rock Ranch Grill Gator's Motel NAPA, Pine Bluff RV Park, USPO, **S Welcome Ctr/ both lanes, full facilities, info, , playground, nature trail, , litter barrels, petwalk**
391	Egbert
386	WY 213, WY 214, Burns, **N** Antelope Trkstp/dsl/cafe
377	WY 217, Hillsdale, **N** TA/Burger King/Taco Bell/dsl/scales/24hr/@ Wyo RV Camping
372mm	Port of Entry wb, truck insp
370	US 30 W, Archer, **N** Sapp Bros/T-Joe's Rest./dsl/scales/24hr/@ Rodeway Inn fireworks, repair, RV park
367	Campstool Rd, **N** Pilot/Subway/dsl/scales/24hr Best Western+ KOA (seasonal), Volvo Trucks, **S** to Wyoming Hereford Ranch
364	WY 212, to E Lincolnway, Cheyenne, **N** Walmart/dsl, **S** AB Camping (4mi), Peterbilt, **1-2 mi N on Lincoln way** Exxon/dsl, Kum&Go/dsl, Loaf'n Jug/Subway Burger King, KFC, McDonald's, Shari's Rest., Subway, Taco Bell, Wendy's H, $Tree, AutoZone, Big O Tire, BigLots, Family$, Harley-Davidson, Hobby Lobby, Murdoch's Ranch Store, O'Reilly Parts, Sierra Trading Post, Walgreens
362	US 85, I-180, to Central Ave, Cheyenne, Greeley, **1 mi N** Kum&Go/dsl Arby's, Carls' Jr, Hacienda Mexican, Jimmy John's, Papa John's, Village Inn H, CarQuest, Family$, museum, st capitol, Verizon, **S** Exxon/dsl, Loaf'n Jug/dsl, Sinclair/dsl Burger King, Little Caesar's, Pizza Hut, Sonic, Subway, Taco John's Comfort Inn, Holiday Inn, Roundup Motel, SpringHill Suites AutoZone, Family$, Hideaway RV Village, Safeway Foods/gas, transmissions
359c a	I-25, US 87, N to Casper, S to Denver
358	US 30, W Lincolnway, Cheyenne, **N** Exxon/dsl/24hr, Little America/Sinclair/dsl/motel/@ Outback Steaks Best Value Inn, Candlewood Suites, Days Inn, Fairfield Inn, Hampton Inn, Holiday Inn Express, La Quinta, Luxury Inn, Motel 6, My Place Inn, Super 8, TownPlace Suites H, Buick/GMC/Cadillac, Chevrolet, Ford/Lincoln, Home Depot, Honda, Hyundai, Mazda, Nissan, Subaru, Toyota
357	Wy 222, Roundtop Rd
348	Otto Rd
345	Warren Rd, **N truck parking**
342	Harriman Rd
339	Remount Rd
335	Buford, **S** Phin Deli/dsl
333mm	**parking area both lanes,** point of interest
329	Vedeauwoo Rd, **N** camping, **S** Nat Forest RA, to Ames Monument
323	WY 210, Happy Jack Rd, **N** **both lanes, full facilities, litter barrels, petwalk, , ,** elev. 8640, Lincoln Monument, to Curt Gowdy SP
322mm	**chain up area both lanes**
316	US 30 W, Grand Ave, Laramie, **0-2 mi N** Exxon/dsl, Loaf'N Jug, USA Gas Almanza's Mexican, Applebee's, Arby's, Burger King, Chili's, Dickey's BBQ, Hong Kong Buffet, Jimmy John's, Luciano's Italian, McAlister's Deli, McDonald's, Mr Jim's Pizza, Papa Murphy's, Perkins, Sonic, Starbucks, Subway, Taco Bell, Taco John's, Village Inn, Wendy's AmericInn, Hampton Inn, Hilton Garden, Holiday Inn, Quality Inn H, $Tree, AT&T, Buick/Chevrolet/GMC, Ford/Lincoln, GNC, Ridley's Mkt, to UW, Toyota, URGENT CARE, Verizon, Walgreens, Walmart/Subway
313	US 287, to 3rd St, Laramie, Port of Entry, **N** Exxon, Gasa-Mat, Loaf'N Jug, Phillips 66/dsl, Shell/dsl Chuck Wagon Rest., Corona Village Mexican, Qdoba Laramie Valley Inn, Motel 8, Sunset Inn H, Honda, Laramie Plains Museum, NAPA, Nissan, **S** Motel 6, Ramada Inn USPO
312mm	Laramie River
311	WY 130, WY 230, Snowy Range Rd, Laramie, **N** WY Terr Park, **S** Conoco/dsl, Exxon/Chester's/Papa John's/dsl, Phillips 66/dsl McDonald's, Subway Best Value Inn repair/tires, to Snowy Range Ski Area
310	Curtis St, Laramie, **N** Loves/Carl's Jr/Subway/dsl/scales24hr@, Pilot/Wendy's/dsl/scales/24hr/@ Best Western, Days Inn, EconoLodge, Super 8 H, KOA, repair, **S** Blue Beacon, Petro/Iron Skillet/dsl/scales/24hr/@ Comfort Inn, Fairfield Inn Chrysler/Dodge/Jeep
307mm	**parking area both lanes**
297	WY 12, Herrick Lane
290	Quealy Dome Rd, **S** Exxon/A&C Truckstop/dsl
279	Cooper Cove Rd
272mm	Rock Creek
272	WY 13, to Arlington, **N** gas, RV camping
267	**S** **both lanes, full facilities**
262mm	**parking area both lanes**
260	CR 402
259mm	E Fork Medicine Bow River
257mm	Medicine Bow River
255	WY 72, Elk Mtn, to Hanna, **N** Conoco/dsl, **S** Elk Mtn Hotel/rest
238	Peterson Rd
235	WY 130, S US 30/87, **N** Shell/dsl
229mm	N Platte River
228	**both lanes, , litter barrels, petwalk**
221	E Sinclair, **N** Sinclair/rest/dsl/24hr camping, to Seminoe SP
219	W Sinclair, **N** camping, to Seminoe SP
215	Cedar St, Rawlins, **N** Conoco/dsl, Shell/KFC/Taco Bell/dsl, Sinclair/dsl Asian Bistro, Burger King, McDonald's, Penny's Diner, Pizza Hut, Subway, Taco John's 1st Choice Inn, Comfort Inn, Days Inn, Econolodge, Fairfield Inn, Hampton Inn, Holiday Inn Express, OakTree Inn, Rawlings Western Lodge $Tree, Bomgaars, Buick/Chevrolet/GMC, CarQuest, Chrysler/Dodge/Jeep, City Mkt/dsl, Do-It Hardware, Frontier Prison NHS, museum, O'Reilly Parts, to Yellowstone/Teton NP, Walmart/dsl
214	Higley Blvd, Rawlins, **N** Microtel KOA, **S** TA/Shell/Subway/dsl/scales/24hr/@ Best Value Inn
211	WY 789, to US 287 N, Spruce St, Rawlins, **N** Conoco/dsl, Exxon/dsl, Loaf'n Jug, Sinclair/dsl Cappy's Rest., Four Season Rest. Best Western, Express Inn, La Bella, Motel 7, Rodeway Inn, Super 8, Travelodge H, Family$, Red Desert Rose Camping, V1/LP, Verizon

CHEYENNE LARAMIE RAWLINS WY

INTERSTATE 80 Cont'd

Exit#	Services
209	Johnson Rd, N FLYING J/Denny's/dsl/LP/scales/24hr
206	Hadsell Rd (no return)
205.5mm	continental divide, elev 7000
204	Knobs Rd
201	Daley Rd
196	Riner Rd
190mm	**parking area wb, litter barrels**
189mm	**parking area eb, litter barrels**
187	WY 789, Creston, Baggs Rd
184	Continental Divide Rd
173	Wamsutter, N Loves/Chester's/Subway/dsl/24hr/@, S Conoco/dsl/repair/café/24hr Broadway Café, Southern Comfort Cafe Wamsutter Motel
165	Red Desert
158	Tipton Rd, continental divide, elev 6930
156	GL Rd
154	BLM Rd
152	Bar X Rd
150	Table Rock Rd
146	Patrick Draw Rd
144mm	**both lanes, full facilities, litter barrels, petwalk,**
143mm	**parking area both lanes, litter barrels**
142	Bitter Creek Rd
139	Red Hill Rd
136	Black Butte Rd
133mm	**parking area both lanes**
130	Point of Rocks, N Conoco/dsl RV Park
122	WY 371, to Superior
111	Airport Rd, Baxter Rd, S
107	Pilot Butte Ave, Rock Springs, S Kum&Go/dsl/e85, Sinclair/dsl Pizza Hut Sands Inn/cafe, Springs Motel
104	US 191 N, Elk St, Rock Springs, N FLYING J/Denny's/dsl/LP/24hr, Chevron/dsl, Conoco/dsl, Exxon, Kum&Go/dsl/e-85, Mobil/dsl McDonald's, Pasta Veloce, Renegade Rest., Santa Fe SW Grill, Subway, Taco Time Best Western, EconoLodge/rest. Buick/GMC, to Teton/Yellowstone Nat Parks via US 191, truck repair, S Exxon/dsl Days Inn
103	College Dr, Rock Springs, S Loaf'n Jug/dsl Domino's H, W WY Coll
102	WY 430, Dewar Dr, Rock Springs, N Exxon, Loaf'N Jug/dsl, Sinclair/dsl, Tesla EVC Applebee's, KFC/LJ Silver, Sapporo Japanese, Taco Time Baymont Inn, Clarion, Comfort Inn, Motel 6 $Tree, Cadillac/Chevrolet, Chrysler/Dodge, Herberger's, Home Depot, JC Penney, Jo-Ann, Murdoch's, Petco, Ross, Smith's Foods, TJ Maxx, S Dickey's BBQ, Kum&Go/dsl, Loaf'N Jug/dsl, Sinclair/dsl Arby's, Bonsai Chinese, Burger King, Cafe Rio, Chopstix Chinese, Dickey's BBQ, Golden Corral, IHOP, Jimmy John's, Little Caesar's, McDonald's, Papa Murphy's, Pizza Hut, Quizno's, Sonic, Starbucks, Subway, Taco Bell, Village Inn, Wendy's, Winger's, Wonderful House Chinese Hampton Inn, Holiday Inn, Holiday Inn Express, Homewood Suites, Motel 8, My Place, Quality Inn, Super 8, Western Inn H, Albertsons/Sav-on, AutoZone, Big O Tire, Family$, Ford/Lincoln, NAPA, Nissan, O'Reilly Parts, Staples, Verizon, Walgreens, Walmart/Subway
99	US 191 S, E Flaming Gorge Rd, N KOA (1mi), S Shell/Cruel Jack's/dsl/rest./24hr/@ Log Inn Rest., Ted's Rest. fireworks, truck repair
94mm	Kissing Rock

ROCK SPGS

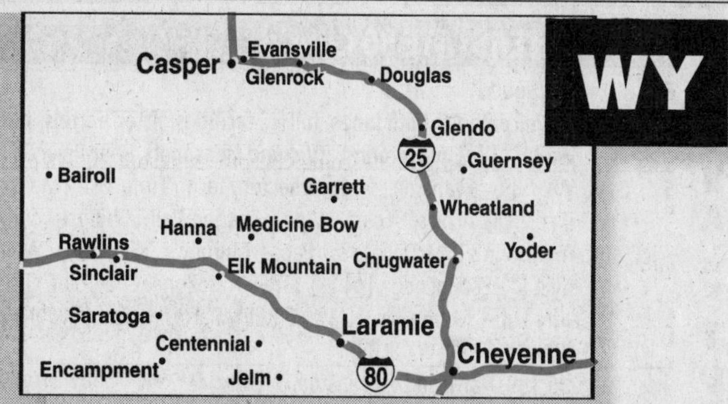

GREEN RIVER

Exit#	Services
91	US 30, to WY 530, Green River, 2 mi S Loaf'N Jug/dsl, Maverik/dsl Arctic Circle, McDonald's, Pizza Hut, Subway, Taco Time Coachman Inn, Mustang Inn, Super 8 Expedition NHS, Family$, same as 89, to Flaming Gorge NRA
89	US 30, Green River, S Exxon/dsl Penny's Diner, Pizza Hut, Staci Ann's Cafe Hampton Inn, OakTree Inn, Super 8, Western Inn Adam's RV Service, The Travel Camp, to Flaming Gorge NRA
87.5mm	Green River
85	Covered Wagon Rd, S Adams RV parts/service, The Travel Camp
83	WY 372, La Barge Rd, N to Fontenelle Dam
78	(from wb)
77mm	Blacks Fork River
72	Westvaco Rd
71mm	**parking area both lanes**
68	Little America, N Sinclair/Little America Hotel/rest./dsl/24hr/@ RV camping
66	US 30 W, to Teton, Yellowstone, Fossil Butte NM, Kemmerer
61	Cedar Mt Rd, to Granger
60mm	**parking area both lanes**
53	Church Butte Rd
49mm	**parking area wb**
48	Lp 80, Lyman, Ft Bridger, Hist Ft Bridger
45mm	Blacks Fork River
41	WY 413, Lyman, N Gas'n Go/cafe/dsl, S **both lanes, full facilities, litter barrels, petwalk,** Taco Time Gateway Inn (2mi), KOA (1mi)
39	WY 412, WY 414, to Carter, Mountain View
34	Lp 80, to Ft Bridger, S Wagon Wheel Motel Ft Bridger NHS, Ft Bridger RV Camp, to Flaming Gorge NRA
33.5mm	**parking area eb**
33	Union Rd
30	Bigelow Rd, N TA/Shell/Burger King/Taco Bell/Fork In the Road/dsl/scales/24hr/@, S fireworks
28	French Rd
28mm	French Rd, **parking area both lanes**
24	Leroy Rd
23	Bar Hat Rd
21	Coal Rd
18	US 189 N, to Kemmerer, to Nat Parks, Fossil Butte NM
15	Guild Rd (from eb)
14mm	**parking area both lanes**
13	Divide Rd
10	Painter Rd, to Eagle Rock Ski Area, to Eagle Rock Ski Area
6	US 189, Bear River Dr, Evanston, N Pilot/Subway/dsl/scales/24hr Don Pedro's Mexican, Jody's Diner Econolodge, Motel6, PrairieInn, VagabondMotel Phillips RV Park, repair/tires, truck wash, Wyo Downs Racetrack (10mi),

INTERSTATE 80 Cont'd

EVANSTON

6	Continued S **Welcome Ctr both lanes, full facilities, litter barrels, petwalk, , , playground, RV dump (seasonal),** Bear River SP
5	WY 89, Evanston, N Chevron/Taco Time/dsl, Maverik/dsl Arby's, Costa Vida, DragonWall Chinese, Jimmy John's, McDonald's, Papa Murphy's, Subway, Wendy's EconoLodge H, $Tree, AutoZone, Chevrolet, GNC, Jiffy Lube, Murdoch's, NAPA, O'Reilly Parts, Verizon, Walmart/Subway, S WY St H
3	US 189, Harrison Dr, Evanston, N FLYING J/Subway/dsl/scales/24hr, Chevron/dsl, Shell, Sinclair, Tesla EVC JB's, Lotty's Rest., TC's Rest., Wally's Burgers Best Western/rest., Comfort Inn, Days Inn, Hampton Inn, HillCrest Motel, Holiday Inn Express, Howard Johnson, Quality Inn, Super 8 Chrysler/Dodge/Jeep, USPO, S KFC/Taco Bell H, fireworks
.5mm	**Port of Entry eb, weigh sta wb**
0mm	Wyoming/Utah state line

INTERSTATE 90

SUNDANCE

Exit#	Services
207mm	Wyoming/South Dakota state line
205	Beulah, N Sinclair/dsl/LP Buffalo Jump Rest. Beulah Campground, Sand Creek Trading Post/gas/cafe, USPO, S Ranch A NHP (5mi)
204.5mm	Sand Creek
199	WY 111, to Aladdin, N **Welcome ctr/ (both directions), full facilities, , litter barrels, , petwalk,** to Devil's Tower NM, to Vore Buffalo Jump NHP (2mi)
191	Moskee Rd
189	US 14 W, Sundance, N Conoco/dsl/24hr Best Western H, Mt View Camping, museum, to Devil's Tower NM, S **both lanes, full facilities, info, litter barrels, petwalk, , , playground,** port of entry/weigh sta, RV dump
187	WY 585, Sundance, N Fresh Start/dsl, Sinclair/dsl Aro Rest., Higbee's Cafe, Subway Bear Lodge, Best Western, Budget Host Arrowhead, Rodeway Inn H, auto repair, Decker's Foods, museum, NAPA, to Devil's Tower
185	to WY 116, to Sundance, S Conoco/dsl, same as 187
178	Coal Divide Rd
177mm	**parking area both lanes**
172	Inyan Kara Rd
171mm	**parking area both lanes, litter barrels**
165	Pine Ridge Rd, to Pine Haven, N Cedar Ridge RV Park (10mi), to Keyhole SP
163mm	**parking area both lanes**
160	Wind Creek Rd
154	US 14, US 16, S Sinclair/dsl Donna's Diner, Subway Cozy Motel, Moorcourt Motel, Rangeland Motel/RV Park, Wyo Motel city park, Diehl's Foods/gas, museum, USPO
153	US 16 E, US 14, W Moorcroft, N **both lanes, full facilities, litter barrels, petwalk, , ,** S same as 154
152mm	Belle Fourche River
141	Rozet, S All Seasons RV Park (3.5mi)
138mm	**parking area both lanes**
132	Wyodak Rd
129	Garner Lake Rd, S Arbuckle Lodge auto repair, Crazy Woman Camping (3mi), Harley-Davidson, High Plains Camping
128	US 14, US 16, Gillette, N Kum&Go, Maverik/dsl, MG Oil/dsl, Sinclair/Papa John's/dsl Mona's American/Mexican, Taco John's, Village Inn Howard Johnson, Mustang Motel,

GILLETTE

128	Continued National 9 Inn, Quality Inn Crazy Woman Camping (2mi), East Side RV Ctr., Port of Entry, S Arbuckle Lodge High Plains Camping
126	WY 59, Gillette, N Cenex/dsl, Loaf'N Jug, Sinclair/Papa John's/dsl China King Buffet, Hardee's, Little Caesar's, McDonald's, Pizza Carrello, Pokey's BBQ, Prime Rib Rest., Starbucks, Subway Best Value Inn city park, Family$, Smith's Foods, Tire Factory, Verizon, S FLYING J/dsl/24hr, Exxon, Loaf'N Jug/dsl A&W/LJ Silver, Adriano's Italian, Applebee's, Arby's, Armando's Taco, Buffalo Wild Wings, Burger King, DQ, Goodtimes Grill/Taco John's, Great Wall Chinese, Jimmy John's, KFC, Las Margarita's Mexican, Old Chicago Grill, Papa Murphy's, Perkins, Pizza Hut, Qdoba Mexican, Quiznos, Ruby Tuesday, Smiling Moose Deli, Subway, Taco Bell, Wendy's, Wyo Rib Chophouse Candlewood Suites, Country Inn&Suites, Days Inn, Fairfield Inn, Holiday Inn Express, Home 2 Suites, La Quinta, Oak Tree Inn, Ramada Plaza, Wingate Inn $Tree, Albertson's, AT&T, AutoZone, Big O Tire, city park, GNC, Goodyear Truck Tire, Home Depot, Jo-Ann, Menards, Midas, Office Depot, O'Reilly Parts, Osco Drug, Petco, Plains Tire, Tire-O-Rama, Verizon, vet, Walgreens, Walmart/Subway
124	WY 50, Gillette, N Kum&Go/dsl, Shell/Burger King/dsl, Sinclair/Papa John's/dsl Hong Kong Rest., Los Compadres Mexican, Pizza Hut, Rooster's Rest., Subway Best Western/rest., Budget Inn, Comfort Inn, Hampton Inn, Motel 6, Super 8, TownePlace Suites H, Crazy Woman Camping, Don's Foods, Ford, S Kum&Go/dsl McDonald's Bighorn Tire, Buick/Chevrolet/GMC, Chrysler/Dodge/Jeep
116	Force Rd
113	Wild Horse Creek Rd
106	Kingsbury Rd
102	Barber Creek Rd
91	Dead Horse Creek Rd
89mm	Powder River
88	Powder River Rd, N **both lanes, full facilities, litter barrels, petwalk, , ,** RV Park
82	Indian Creek Rd
77	Schoonover Rd
73.5mm	Crazy Woman Creek
73	Crazy Woman Creek Rd
69	Dry Creek Rd
68.5mm	**parking area wb**
65	Red Hills Rd, Tipperary Rd
60mm	**parking area both lanes, litter barrels**

BUFFALO

58	US 16, to Ucross, Buffalo, **0-3 mi** S Cenex/dsl/24hr, Exxon dsl, Maverik/dsl Bozeman Tr Steaks, Dash Inn Rest., Hardee's, McDonald's, Pizza Hut, Sub Shop, Subway, Taco John's Winchester Steaks Buffalo Inn, Comfort Inn, Days Inn Hampton Inn, Holiday Inn Express, Quality Inn, Rodeway WYO Motel, Super 8 H, Ace Hardware, Bighorn Tire, Deer Park Camping, Family$, Indian RV Camp, KOA, Nat Hist Dist, O'Reilly Parts, Verizon, vet
56b	I-25 S, US 87 S, to Buffalo
56a	25 Bus, 90 Bus, to Buffalo, **services 2mi S (from eb)**
53	Rock Creek Rd
51	Lake DeSmet, **1 mi** N Lake Stop gas/motel/cafe Lake De Smet RV park
47	Shell Creek Rd
44	US 87 N, Piney Creek Rd, to Story, Banner, N Ft Phil Kearney, museum, **5 mi** S Wagon Box Cabins/Rest.
39mm	scenic turnout wb

WY

INTERSTATE 90 Cont'd

SHERIDAN

Exit#	Services
37	Prairie Dog Creek Rd, to Story
33	Meade Creek Rd, to Big Horn
31mm	**parking area eb**
25	US 14 E, Sheridan, N Quality Inn Dalton's RV Ctr, S Cenex/dsl, Exxon/dsl, Holiday/dsl, Maverik/dsl Arby's, Burger King, Goodtimes/Taco John's, Jimmy John's, Little Caesar's, Los Agaves, McDonald's, Ole's Pizza, Papa John's, Papa Murphy's, Perkins, Qdoba, Starbucks, Subway, Taco Bell, Wendy's Candlewood Suites, Days Inn, Fairfield Inn, Holiday Inn, Holiday Lodge, Mill Inn $Tree, Ace Hardware, Albertson's/Osco Drug, AT&T, AutoZone, Buick/GMC, Chrysler/Dodge/Jeep, Firestone/auto, Ford/Lincoln, GNC, Goodyear/auto, Home Depot, Midas, NAPA, O'Reilly Parts, Petco, Sheridan Coll, Tire-Rama, to Hist Dist, Toyota, Verizon, vet, Walgreens, Walmart/Subway
23	WY 336, 5th St, Sheridan, N **both lanes, full facilities, litter barrels, petwalk, RV dump,** Rock Stop/Subway/dsl Comfort Inn, **1-2 mi** S Cenex, Holiday/dsl DQ, Powder River Pizza Alamo Motel, Best Value Inn, Best Western, Hampton Inn, Motel 6 city park, Honda, Peter D's RV Park, radiators, Sheridan Cty Museum
20	to Main St, Sheridan, W Common Cents/dsl, N KOA, S Cenex/dsl, Exxon/dsl/scales/24hr, Gasamat/dsl, Maverik/dsl

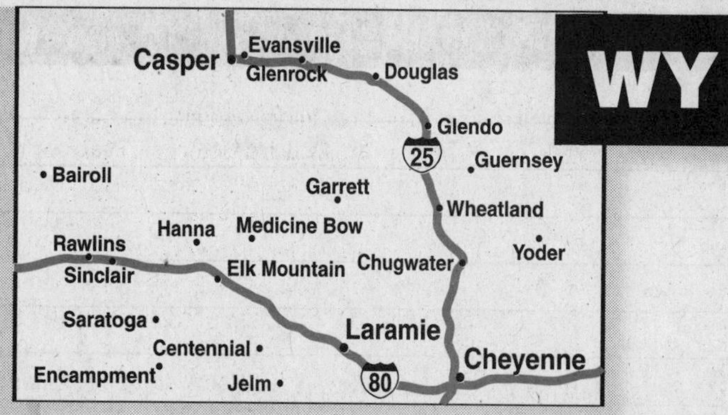

Exit#	Services
20	Continued Domino's, Kim's Rest., McDonald's, Pizza Hut Bramble Motel, Budget Inn, Rodeway Inn, Stage Stop Motel, Super 8, Super Saver Motel, Trails End Motel/rest. H, Peerless Tires, Verizon
16	to Decker, Montana, **port of entry**
15mm	Tongue River
14	WY 345, Acme Rd
9	US 14 W, Ranchester, **1 mi** S Conoco/dsl Conner Bfd NHS, Foothills Campground, Lazy R Campground, to Yellowstone/Teton NPs, Western Motel
1	Parkman
0mm	Wyoming/Montana state line

NOTES

WY

NOTES

Assist A Fellow Traveler with...

Published annually, the Next EXIT® provides the best USA Interstate Highway Information available. Use this form to order another copy of the Next EXIT® for yourself or for someone special.

The 2019 edition of the Next EXIT® is $19.95 plus shipping.

Please send ______ copies of the Next Exit® to the address below.

I've enclosed my check or money order for:

☐ $19.95 plus $7.00 US Shipping ($26.95) per copy.

☐ $19.95 plus $11.00 Canadian Shipping ($30.95) per copy.

Name:____

Address:____________________________ Apt./Suite #____________

City: __________________________ State: ______ Zip:____________

THREE EASY ORDER OPTIONS:

1. MAIL ORDER FORM TO: the Next EXIT®, Inc.
PO Box 888
Garden City, Utah 84028

2. ORDER ON THE WEB AT: www.theNextExit.com

3. GIVE US A CALL & USE YOUR CHARGE CARD: 1-800-NEX-EXIT or 1-800-639-3948

More digital options are available at www.theNextExit.com